Eastern Europe

Tom Masters, Lisa Dunford, Mark Elliott, Patrick Horton, Cathryn Kemp,
Steve Kokker, Vesna Maric, Jeanne Oliver, Robert Reid, Wendy Taylor,
Matt Warren, Richard Watkins, Neil Wilson

Contents

Highlights	6	Romania	573
Getting Started	9	Russia	645
Itineraries	15	Serbia & Montenegro	699
The Authors	21	Slovakia	743
Snapshot	25	Slovenia	785
Albania	27	Ukraine	823
Belarus	61	Regional Directory	869
Bosnia & Hercegovina	83	Transport in Eastern Europe	886
Bulgaria	115	Health	904
Croatia	173	World Time Zones	908
Czech Republic	233	Language	909
Estonia	295	Behind the Scenes	931
Hungary	331	Index	934
Latvia	395		
Lithuania	419		
Macedonia	449		
Moldova	471		
Poland	495		

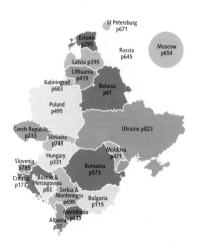

Destination Eastern Europe

Changing in a hundred different and exciting ways, the vast region known in travellers' short-hand as Eastern Europe offers pretty much everything. The EU expansion may have made half the region's countries even more user-friendly than they were, but the 11 non-EU members still draw the adventurous, and many places in both camps remain tantalisingly undiscovered.

First there are the stunning cities; Prague, Budapest, Kraków and St Petersburg are no secret, but all have so much more to discover than most people see. Less well-known draws such as charming Ljubljana, medieval Tallinn, sunny Dubrovnik, elegant Lviv, Art Nouveau Rīga and cosmopolitan Bratislava remain delightfully free of mass tourism. And have you even heard of rising stars Veliko Târnovo, Český Krumlov or Hrodna?

Then there's the nature: Bulgaria's Rila Mountains, the High Tatra in Poland and Slovakia, wonderful Lake Ohrid in Macedonia and Albania, the fabled Curonian Spit in Lithuania and Russia, Latvia's Gauja Valley and Slovenia's unique Škocjan Caves… what else could you want? But don't forget the beaches (Eastern Europe has nice beaches? Oh yes). There's the shimmering Black Sea, Croatia's Dalmatian Coast, the surprisingly lovely Baltic coastline, and the current Holy Grail of the independent traveller – the virgin white beaches of Albania.

If that's not enough, come to see the remains of the communist century in Moscow, the dark relics of Nazism in Poland, some of the world's greatest art and whitest nights in St Petersburg, mythic Transylvania, the cliffs of the Crimea, post-Milošević Serbia, and the intriguing unknowns of Moldova and Montenegro, Bosnia and Hercegovina, and Belarus. Why are you still reading the introduction? You've made the right decision, now get planning.

ST PETERSBURG (p671)
Russia's former imperial capital –
an unrivalled architectural
ensemble on water – is pure magic

RĪGA (p399)
Art-Nouveau heaven,
Latvia's exciting capital is an
increasingly popular destination

WESTERN LITHUANIA AND
THE CURONIAN SPIT (p440)
One of the most magical
slices of the Baltics

VYSOKÉ TATRY (p763)
Enjoy the views, walks,
valleys and clear lakes
of Slovakia's mountains

LVIV (p839)
Western Ukraine's graceful survivor,
Lviv has centuries of architecture
and culture to discover

KRAKÓW (p515)
One of few Polish cities to
survive WWII unscathed,
Kraków's Old Town is magnificent

PRAGUE (p241)
One of Europe's most fascinating cities,
with myriad spires, graceful bridges
and a magnificent castle

300 km
180 miles

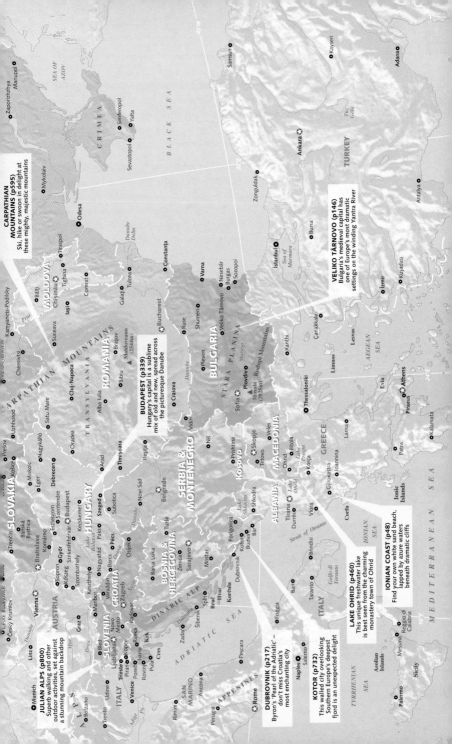

CARPATHIAN MOUNTAINS (p595)
Ski, hike or swoon in delight at these mighty, majestic mountains

VELIKO TÁRNOVO (p146)
Bulgaria's medieval capital has one of Europe's most dramatic settings on the winding Yantra River

BUDAPEST (p339)
Hungary's capital is a sublime mix of old and new, spread across the picturesque Danube

JULIAN ALPS (p800)
Superb walking and other outdoor activities, set against a stunning mountain backdrop

DUBROVNIK (p217)
Byron's 'Pearl of the Adriatic' – don't miss Croatia's most enchanting city

KOTOR (p732)
This walled city overlooking Southern Europe's deepest fjord is an unexpected delight

LAKE OHRID (p460)
This unique freshwater lake is best seen from the charming monastery town of Ohrid

IONIAN COAST (p48)
Find your own white sand beach, lapped by azure waters beneath dramatic cliffs

Eastern Europe is chock-full of delights, many of which refuse to fall into line with the region's stereotypes. There are of course the cities, many already metropolises in medieval times, which have survived the ravages of history to be the amazing ensembles they are today. As well as taking in the ones you've heard of, visit some of the lesser known cities or towns in this book.

The entire region is wrapped in sandy beaches and criss-crossed by stunning mountain ranges. These make for some magnificent exploration opportunities, whether it be extreme sports, or rest and relaxation at the popular resorts on the Black Sea coast. Don't forget the Baltic, which is very warm in the summer months. Poland and the Baltic countries all have some great beaches and wonderful landscapes untouched by mass tourism.

JONATHAN SMITH

Be seduced by dynamic Budapest (p339), a city steeped in history and pulsating with modern life

Treasure what was so nearly lost; sunny Dubrovnik (p217), Croatia

JAN STROMME

Explore Albania's dramatic Ionian coast (p48), where clear azure waters lap white beaches

BILDAGENTUR-ONLINE.COM/TH-FOTO / ALAMY

GRANT DIXON

Venture into Slovenia's Julian Alps (p800), dotted with fairytale castles and ancient churches

Take a spin around Kraków's magnificent Rynek Główny (Old Market Square; p519)

KRZYSZTOF DYDYNSKI

RICHARD NEBESKY

Uncover the reality beneath the hype; yes, Prague (p241) really is all that and more

Come in from the cold and explore St Petersburg's astonishing Hermitage (p675), in the Winter Palace

STEVE KOKKER

PAUL GREENWAY

Cross over to another world in Bulgaria's medieval capital, Veliko Târnovo (p146)

RICHARD NEBESKY

Ski, climb, hike... the options are endless in the Vysoké Tatry (p763), Slovakia

Sip a strong, black coffee and marvel at the view over Kotor fjord (p732), Serbia and Montenegro

PATRICK HORT

JEFF GREENBERG

Indulge in lavish opera and décor at frugal prices; Ivano-Franko Opera and Ballet Theatre in Lviv (p839), Ukraine

Getting Started

Travelling through Eastern Europe can be both staggeringly carefree and frustratingly difficult, largely depending on where you decide to go and how you decide to travel.

Without exception the easiest countries to visit are the new EU-members (the Czech Republic, Estonia, Hungary, Latvia, Lithuania, Poland, Slovakia and Slovenia) and Croatia. These are generally the destinations with the most progressive authorities, fewest restrictions and most tourist facilities. That said, they can also be more expensive than the rest of the region and certainly attract more visitors.

The other Balkan countries (Albania, Bosnia and Hercegovina, Bulgaria, Macedonia, Moldova, Romania, and Serbia and Montenegro) are still fairly easy to get around and have tourist infrastructures ranging from the excellent (Bulgaria) to the virtually nonexistent (Albania). Russia, Belarus and Ukraine, however, haven't moved on much since the Cold War. Believe it or not, two decades after *perestroika* you still need to get an official invitation to visit Russia, Belarus or Ukraine before you'll be granted a visa!

WHEN TO GO

Eastern Europe has a surprisingly consistent weather pattern for a region its size. High season runs from May until September; in July and August you'll find Prague, Budapest, Kraków and anywhere beachy teeming with backpackers and coach tours. The best time to visit is either side of the summer peak – May, June and September stand out, as it's not too hot, too crowded or overbooked anywhere.

Travelling out of season can result in some real bargains in accommodation, although many places where tourism is the main industry all but close down during the low season. Also, bear in mind that Russia, the Baltics, Belarus and Ukraine have very cold winters, with -20°C not being unusual anywhere between November and February, although average temperatures are far less extreme. Winter is cold everywhere, although the further south you get the milder it is – Albania's average winter temperature is an extremely mild 9°C.

See Climate Charts (p874) for more information

COSTS AND MONEY

Despite steadily rising prices in the region's more popular cities and resorts, it's still true to say that Eastern Europe remains far cheaper than Western Europe. However, don't come expecting to live like royalty on

---

DON'T LEAVE HOME WITHOUT...

It's relatively easy to find almost anything you need in Eastern Europe and, since you'll probably buy things as you go along, it's better to start with too little rather than too much.

Backpacks are still the most popular method of carrying gear, as they're convenient, especially for walking. Travel packs (combined backpack/shoulder bags) are particularly popular; the straps zip away inside the pack when they're not needed, so you almost have the best of both worlds. Backpacks or travel packs can be made reasonably theft-proof with small padlocks. Another alternative is a large, soft zip bag fitted with a wide shoulder strap so it can be carried with relative ease. Forget suitcases unless you're travelling in style; if you do take one, make sure it has wheels allowing you to drag it along behind you. Watch out on those cobblestone streets.

a few dollars a day – even the least touristy niches of the region such as Belarus or Albania are well aware of travellers' spending power and price things accordingly.

Trying to give daily budgets for such a huge region is hard indeed: backpackers staying in hostels and eating cheaply can expect to spend around €30 to €40 per day, probably more in cities such as Moscow, Prague and Budapest. Those wanting to have a more comfortable trip (staying in mid-range accommodation and eating in decent restaurants most of the time) will need to look for between €60 and €70. These are very much ballpark figures; in the countryside you'll be able to get by on far less, while if you're in bigger cities during high season and visiting lots of museums and sights, you'll find you need more than that.

Unthinkable as it would have been just five years ago, these days as long as you have an ATM card, you need not worry about money in any major Eastern European city.

All major credit and debit cards are accepted by ATMs, including those on the Cirrus/Maestro platform. However, always have a back-up plan, so if an ATM is not working you won't be stranded. Most major banks will do cash advances on credit cards (you'll need to bring your passport) and, of course, exchange travellers cheques.

Travellers cheques are the safest way to carry large sums of money – they can be replaced if lost or stolen, and when stolen, cannot be cashed by the thief. However, they are a pain sometimes, and should never be relied upon outside major towns.

Cash is the easiest way to carry money, but once it's gone, it's gone. The euro and US dollars are the currencies most easily exchanged. In many places you can even pay for hotel accommodation in euros, although never assume this to be the case. The days of currency controls in Eastern Europe are gone, so there's no need to fear converting your 'hard' currency and being unable to re-exchange it before leaving the country. However, many countries' currencies are difficult to exchange elsewhere. In most cases it's best to change any currency into either euros, dollars or the currency of your next destination before leaving, even if this means getting bad exchange rates at the border.

READING UP
Books

There's a huge number of books about the region and while the most pertinent titles for each country are listed in the individual country directories, the following books provide an interesting introduction to the complexities and idiosyncrasies of Eastern Europe as a region.

A must for understanding the Balkan mind is is Rebecca West's classic *Black Lamb & Grey Falcon*, a huge unclassifiable look at the Balkans on the eve of WWII through the eyes of a lone British female, as she makes her way through Bosnia, Serbia, Kosovo, Albania and Croatia in 1937. Her pro-Serbian sentiment has made the book unfashionable since the area's recent ethnic cleansing, although her dark assertion that 'the whole world is a vast Kosovo, an abominable blood-logged plain' seems to have rung true some fifty years after she wrote it. This is a magnificent, poetic and fascinating account.

A road trip like none other is described in hilarious, poignant detail in Allen Noren's excellent *Storm: A Motorcycle Journey of Love, Endurance and Transformation*. Against the odds, Noren undertakes a motorbike journey that takes in Russia, Estonia, Latvia, Lithuania and Poland, among other places, accompanied by his long-suffering girlfriend Suzanne,

An unconventional travel guide and Lonely Planet send-up, *Molvania: A Land Untouched by Modern Dentistry* (Santo Cilauro et al) creates a fictitious land in Eastern Europe that's the 'next big thing'. A good laugh for anyone travelling in the region and sick of guidebooks!

who is less than impressed with the record-breaking cold and general climatic nastiness.

Stealing From a Deep Place details Brian Hall's two-year bicycle journey across communist Central Europe in the late 1980s, during which he manages to meet the Budapest intelligentsia. This charming book provides a human portrait of the region at a time when change was on the cards, but was still something few dared to take seriously.

Websites

There's a huge amount of up-to-date information on the Web and, whether you're planning a weekend in Prague or a two-month odyssey through the entire region, you'll find the Web an invaluable tool.

Hostels.com (www.hostels.com/en/easterneurope.html) This site has a list of most hostels and budget accommodation in Eastern Europe, organised by country. There are plenty of photos so you get an idea of what you are letting yourself for!

In Your Pocket (www.inyourpocket.com) This Vilnius-based desktop publishing company has enjoyed incredible success. The formula is simple: they produce frequently updated booklets about scores of destinations within Eastern Europe, which are financially supported by advertising. You can download a huge amount of information in PDF form from the website – all for free!

Rail Europe (www.raileurope.com) Gives lots of information on timetables, routes and prices for most of the region (but not the former Soviet Union). Instead, check out www.poezda.net for detailed information about the entire former Soviet Union.

Thorn Tree (http://thorntree.lonelyplanet.com) Lonely Planet interactive travellers' message board. There's a dedicated section for posts relating to Eastern Europe and a huge number of travellers able to give up-to-the-minute advice.

XE (www.xe.com)
An up-to-the-second online currency exchange calculator. Find out the current rates for all Eastern European currencies, and see exactly how much your trip is going to cost you.

TOP FIVE MUST-READS

Eastern Europe's creative wealth is immense, nowhere more so than in its ever-challenging, ever-innovative literary production. The list below barely scrapes the surface, but these titles are warmly recommended by the authors of this book and will make great companions on any trip.

- *The Joke* (Milan Kundera) An insight into Czechoslovak society during the communist era. In a moment of anger, Ludvik sends his girlfriend a postcard with the message 'Optimism is the opium of the people! A healthy atmosphere stinks of stupidity! Long live Trotsky!' It's a joke, meant to shock her, but instead, she reports him to the party, and a downward spiral of persecution and paranoia begins.

- *Death and the Penguin* (Andrei Kurkov) A charming novel about life and loneliness in post-Soviet Ukraine. Unsuccessful writer Viktor adopts Misha the penguin from Kyiv Zoo when it runs out of money to buy the animals food. Together they have many curious adventures in the magical Ukrainian capital, although they soon become embroiled in something far darker than they had ever imagined.

- *The Notebook* (Agota Kristof) The first book in a trilogy about war-torn Hungary, this coldly narrated, simple novel follows inseparable twins sent to live with their evil grandmother during WWII. The brutalising effects of the war, their grandmother's hatred and a lack of love turn them into true monsters before the reader's eyes. Watch out for the shock ending!

- *The Concert* (Ismail Kadare) History dissected by Albania's greatest living writer. Set during the break between President Enver Hoxha and China in the 1970s, this book follows the lives of the party elite and those who seek to join their ranks. A fascinating account of a hidden time.

- *Sarajevo Marlboro* (Miljenko Jergovic) This collection of short stories from Bosnian journalist Jergovic has established itself as a classic in just a few years. Within its pages, life rather than death is extolled, and while the dark events of the war in Bosnia are always present, the warmth and humanity of the stories are the overwhelming impression left with the reader.

EASTERN EUROPE WORLD HERITAGE LIST

This list of sights deemed 'world heritage' by Unesco includes some – but not all – of the most remarkable attractions of the region. Presently only Moldova and Bosnia and Hercegovina have yet to feature on this prestigious register of all that is culturally and historically significant in Eastern Europe. For more information see whc.unesco.org.

Albania
Ancient ruins of Butrint

Belarus
Belavezhskaja Pushcha National Park
Mir Castle complex

Bulgaria
Boyana Church
Ivanovo rock-hewn churches
Kazanlâk's Thracian tomb
Madara horseman relief
Nesebâr's Old Town
Pirin National Park
Rila Monastery
Srebârna Nature Reserve
Thracian Tomb of Sveshtari

Croatia
Dubrovnik's Old Town
Plitvice Lakes National Park
Poreč's Euphrasian Basilica
Šibenik's Cathedral of St James
Split's historic centre with the Diocletian's Palace
Trogir's Old Town

Czech Republic
Český Krumlov's historic centre
Holašovice historical village
Holy Trinity Column in Olomouc
Jewish Quarter and St Procopius' Basilica in Trebíc
Komeríz Castle and gardens
Kutná Hora medieval silver town & Church of St Barbara
Lednice-Valtice Cultural Landscape
Litomyšyl Castle
Pilgrimage Church of St John Nepomuk at Zelena Hora
Prague's historic centre
Telč's Old Town
Vila Tugendhat in Brno

Estonia
Tallinn's Old Town

Hungary
Budapest's Castle District, the banks of the Danube and Andrássy Avenue
Fertö/Neusiedlersee Cultural Landscape
Hollókö (traditional village)
Hortobágy National Park
Karst caves at Aggtelek (shared with Slovakia)

MUST-SEE MODERN MOVIES

There's no better way to whet your appetite for travel than by seeing films about the region. Mention Eastern European film to most people and they'll think of slow-paced psychological dramas in black and white, a stereotype that couldn't be less true these days. Against all odds, Eastern Europe has a small but creatively dynamic film industry, as well as a long history of classic (erm, slow-paced, black and white) films.

- *Black Cat White Cat* Light and generous comedy from Serbian master Emir Kusturica. When the unlucky Matko gets in debt to a powerful gangster, he agrees to marry his son to the gangster's daughter. The young couple, however, have other plans. A wonderful film sending up almost everyone on the Balkan Peninsula.
- *Brother* Cult post-*perestroika* gangster movie starring ill-fated heart-throb Sergei Bodrov as a renegade fighting the mafia for social justice in St Petersburg. The tragic death of the star has sealed the film's fate as a Russian *Rebel Without a Cause*. Just don't watch the terrible sequel!
- *Divided We Fall* Excellent comedy-drama. In Nazi-occupied Czechoslovakia, a childless couple agree to hide a Jewish friend at great personal risk, punishable by execution. With dark Czech humour, the film highlights the divisions in Czech society caused by the war.

Pannonhalma Benedictine Abbey
Pécs' early Christian cemetery
Tokaj wine-growing region

Latvia
Rīga's historic centre

Lithuania
Curonian Spit (shared with Kaliningrad, Russia)
Kernave Archaeological Site
Vilnius' historic centre

Macedonia
Ohrid and its lake

Moscow & St Petersburg
Church of the Ascension, Kolomenskoye
Kremlin and Red Square in Moscow
Monuments of Vladimir and Suzdal
St Petersburg's historic centre
Trinity Monastery of St Sergius in Sergiev Posad

Poland
Auschwitz concentration camp
Białowieża Forest
Castle of the Teutonic Order in Malbork
Churches of Peace in Jawor and Swidnica
Kraków's historic centre
Mannerist architecture of Kalwaria Zebrzydowska pilgrimage site
Medieval town of Toruń
Muzakowski
Warsaw's Old Town

Wieliczka Salt Mine near Kraków
Wooden Churches of Southern Małopolska
Zamość's Old Town

Romania
Biertan fortified church near Sighişoara
Bucovina painted churches
Dacian fortresses in the Orastie Mountains
Danube Delta
Horezu Monastery near Curtea de Argeş
Maramureş,' wooden churches
Sighişoara's historic centre

Serbia & Montenegro
Decani Monastery
Durmitor National Park
Kotor and its gulf
Stari Ras and Sopoćani Monastery
Studenica Monastery

Slovakia
Banská Štiavnica medieval mining centre
Bardejov Town Conservation Reserve
Slovakian Karst and Aggtelek Caves (shared with Hungary)
Spišský hrad
Vlkolinec folk village near Ružomberok

Slovenia
Škocjan Caves

Ukraine
St Sophia Cathedral and Caves Monastery in Kyiv
Historic centre of Lviv

■ *Before the Rain* Stylish and beautiful, this unusual Macedonian masterpiece brings together three very different faces of modern Macedonia with generosity and understanding. Underlining the senselessness of war, *Before the Rain* sums up the Balkan tragedy of the 1990s.

■ *Slogans* This ponderous and poignant film about 1980s Stalinist Albania depicts life in a small village as seen through the eyes of a young teacher arriving to take up his first post. A love story interwoven with the denouncement of a social misfit, *Slogans* is a touching and lovely film.

TOP FIVE FESTIVALS

Eastern European towns and cities come alive during festivals, making them a great time to visit. See each country chapter for detailed dates and information about local festivals. Some of our favourites are below.

■ **Prague Spring, Czech Republic** (12 May–3 June) One of Europe's biggest festivals of classical music, inspired by Czech composer Smetana, kicks off the summer. The festival begins with a parade from his grave at Vyšehrad to the Smetana Hall, where his *Má vlast* is performed.

■ **White Nights, St Petersburg** (late June) For the ultimate in 24-hour partying, join the hedonistic crowds who celebrate the longest days of the year in Russia's northern capital – for two weeks the sky never gets fully dark.

Encumbered with plaudits such as 'greatest film of all time,' Eisenstein's masterpiece *Battleship Potemkin* has influenced most film directors since. The famous scene of the massacre on the Odesa steps with a baby's pram tumbling to destruction should be familiar to all.

Eastern Europe's cities get intolerably crowded in peak season. Traffic congestion on the roads is a major problem, and visitors will do themselves and residents a favour if they forgo driving and use public transport.

- **Jaanipäev, Estonia** (23 June) The biggest occasion of the year in Estonia is the night of 23 June, St John's Eve (or Jaanipäev), a celebration of the pagan Midsummer's Night, best experienced out in the countryside where huge bonfires are lit for all-night parties.
- **EXIT Festival, Novi Sad, Serbia** (July) Come July, Novi Sad's citadel hosts this excellent festival with five or more stages shaking to the best in rock, hip-hop and techno. The event is hugely popular and attracts people from all over the region.
- **Sziget Festival, Budapest, Hungary** (late July to early August) A week-long world-music bash on Óbudai Island, where people come out from all over Europe to camp and party. There are more than 1000 acts with bands from around the world and more than 60 venues. Visit www.sziget .hu/festival_english for more information.

RESPONSIBLE TRAVEL

In Eastern Europe's nature reserves and national parks, be sure to follow the local code of ethics and common decency and pack up your litter. Minimise the waste you must carry out by taking minimal packaging and no more food than you will need. Don't use detergents or tooth-paste (even if they are biodegradable) in or near natural water sources. When camping in the wild (checking first to see that it's allowed), bury human waste in holes at least 15cm deep and at least 100m from any nearby water.

Itineraries

CLASSIC ROUTES

THE BIG FIVE   Three Weeks

Begin your trip in magical **Prague** (p241), spending several days absorbing the city and some nearby towns, such as beer-lovers' mecca **Plzeň** (p271) and beautiful **Kutná Hora** (p263). Head into Poland to stunning **Kraków** (p515) with its gobsmacking Old Town. This is a great base for visiting the beautiful **Tatra Mountains** (p529) and the harrowing but essential trip to **Auschwitz** (p524). From Poland travel to Slovakia, where you can enjoy magnificent scenery in the **Vysoké Tatry (High Tatra)** (p763) before pursuing more urban activities in lovely **Bratislava** (p749). Next to stunning **Budapest** (p339); from here visit the lovely Hungarian countryside – try the baroque city of **Eger** (p382) with it's ancient castle and many wine cellars. Now take the plunge into non-EU Romania and explore the mythic valleys of **Transylvania** (p591). Use **Cluj-Napoca** (p606) as your base for visiting the medieval region of **Maramureş** (p616) and stunning **Braşov** (p595) before heading on to **Bucharest** (p580), where you can drink in the monolithic architecture and enjoy the city's relaxed pace.

This is a great trip for any first-time visitor to Eastern Europe, taking in five of the most popular and accessible countries in the region. It begins in the Czech Republic and wends its way through Poland, Slovakia, Hungary and Romania, providing a fantastic introduction to a region in transition.

THE BALKAN SHUFFLE

Four Weeks

Begin in lively little Slovenia with a cheap flight to charming **Ljubljana** (p790). Enjoy superb scenery and adrenaline-rush mountain sports in the magnificent **Julian Alps** (p800) before heading south to the Croatian coast and working your way through **Dalmatia** (p202) and its gorgeous beaches to delightful **Dubrovnik** (p217). Enjoy the stunning Old Town and explore the lovely surrounding islands. Take the opportunity to see Bosnia from Dubrovnik – perhaps a day trip to **Mostar** (p99) to see the newly reconstructed bridge or a night or two in dynamic, bustling **Sarajevo** (p90) – before continuing south into lovely Montenegro. Stay the night in historic **Kotor** (p732) and see its charming walled city before heading over into once-mysterious Albania. From the northern city of **Shkodra** (p51) take a bus straight on to **Tirana** (p36), a mountain-shrouded, ramshackle capital quickly on the rise. Enjoy a day or two here and make an excursion to **Kruja** (p44) before taking a bus through the stunning mountains into little-explored Macedonia, ending up in lovely **Ohrid** (p460). Spend at least two days here – enjoy its multitude of sights and swimming in the beautiful eponymous lake. Make your way to **Skopje** (p454), Macedonia's fun capital, from where you can head overland through Serbia to the booming post-Milošević metropolis of **Belgrade** (p705) and then back on to Croatia and its lovely capital of **Zagreb** (p181). From here you can come full circle to Ljubljana, or carry on and explore elsewhere in Croatia.

This wonderful trip – unthinkable a decade ago – takes you through some of Europe's youngest countries and down the spectacular coastline of the former Yugoslav states and Albania. Beginning in Ljubljana the route snakes through six more Balkan states to bring you back to where you started.

EAST OF EAST TOUR

Three to Four Weeks

Begin in bustling **Warsaw** (p502) where you can see the reconstructed Old Town and learn about the town's dark history. From here, head by train to **Lviv** (p839), Ukraine's most lovely city, and spend a few days here before crossing the country to graceful **Kyiv** (p830), the Jerusalem of East Slavonic culture. You'll need a couple of days in the capital to enjoy its sights before taking the sleeper train to monolithic **Moscow** (p654), Europe's biggest city and a place of the most striking extremes. A visit to the **Golden Ring** (p668) is also highly recommended, to get a sense of Russian life outside big cities. **St Petersburg** (p671) is next on the agenda – staggeringly beautiful and full of cultural life, you can easily spend three or four days in the city itself, although there are abundant sights outside the city, such as the tsarist palaces at **Petrodvorets**, **Pushkin** and **Pavlovsk** (p682). Exiting Russia to Estonia, you'll love charming medieval **Tallinn** (p302) and can visit the **Lahemaa National Park** (p314) for some rural delights. Next up is **Riga** (p399), an exceptional city with a huge wealth of Art-Nouveau architecture that is generally considered Europe's finest. Make sure you don't ignore Latvia's other highlights such as the medieval castles and caves of **Sigulda** (p410) and the lovely **coastline** (p412). Unsung Baltic gem Lithuania is next. Enjoy charming **Vilnius** (p424) and the amazing **Curonian Spit** (p443) on the Baltic Sea before re-entering Poland and heading back to Warsaw.

The nitty-gritty of Eastern Europe – this trip is fascinating, but involves careful visa planning. It takes you in a circle from Poland, through Ukraine and Russia to the lovely and largely undiscovered Baltic countries.

ROADS LESS TRAVELLED

THE IONIAN TO THE BALTIC
Three to Four Weeks

Arriving in Albania at **Saranda** (p48), stay the night before travelling either up the beautiful **coastline** (p48) or via historic **Gjirokastra** (p50) to **Tirana** (p36), where you can spend a day or two before taking the bus to **Prishtina** (p725) in Kosovo. Then on into Romania, via Macedonia and the lively Serbian capital **Belgrade** (p705). Stop in **Timişoara** (p613) to admire the town centre and surrounding areas before pressing on into Ukraine. Make a beeline for lovely **Lviv** (p839) and its exceptional architecture before taking the train to deeply Soviet Belarus. **Minsk** (p66) is a fascinating place for anyone with an interest in communist monumentalism, while **Brest Fortress** (p74) and charming little **Hrodna** (p76) are more accessible – but equally unbackpackery – destinations. On leaving Belarus, you'll be struck by the progressiveness of Lithuania. Take the easy trip over to **Vilnius** (p424) where you can enjoy the nightlife, and then take in studenty **Kaunas** (p435) before entering one of Russia's least-explored regions, **Kaliningrad** (p683). Here you'll find remnants of Prussian Königsburg in the **regional capital** (p685) and be able to make a trip out to the **Curonian Spit** (p691), spending a night in nature amid the sand dunes. From here, take a bus to **Gdańsk** (p550) or **Gdynia** (p556) – two of Poland's more characterful and charming Baltic ports, near some great Baltic beaches too.

A paradoxical way to begin perhaps – get a cheap flight to the mother of all package tourist destinations, Corfu, and take the daily ferry just 27km into a different world. Beginning on Albania's magnificent and as yet totally undeveloped coastline, weave your way north through the continent to Poland's equally neglected Baltic coast.

BLACK SEA ADVENTURE

Three to Four Weeks

Start with a cheap flight from Western Europe to **Burgas** (p154) on Bulgaria's Black Sea coast; enjoy the beaches here as well as visiting gorgeous **Sozopol** (p156) and **Nesebâr** (p159) before making your way to the graceful medieval capital of Bulgaria at **Veliko Târnovo** (p146). After a day or two, head on to strikingly modern **Bucharest** (p580) where you can make plenty of side trips to typical Romanian towns such as **Snagov** (p589) or the lovely Black Sea coast at **Constanţa** (p629). Cross into the Romanian province of **Moldavia** (p620) and visit the lovely one-time national capital at **Iaşi** (p620). From here make your way into neighbouring Moldova, a country as mysterious and unknown to the outside world as any in Europe. You can spend a few days in the green and charming capital **Chişinău** (p476) as well as exploring nearby towns such as wine-lover heaven **Cricova** (p483) and fascinating **Tiraspol** (p486), capital of the uniquely backward republic of **Transdniestr** (p485). Head across the border to (comparatively) progressive Ukraine and the charming, cosmopolitan melting pot that is **Odesa** (p851). Here you can soak up the exciting town, enjoying the Black Sea before heading for the **Crimea** (p855), the largely Russian-populated peninsula that stretches lazily out into the Black Sea and has been a favourite summer spot for two centuries. Start in **Yalta** (p858) for your Soviet summer holiday experience, before moving along the coast to **Sevastopol** (p861) and back through **Bakhchysaray** (p858) to see the remarkable Khan's Palace. From here, head on to **Kyiv** (p830) and end the trip in the fascinating Ukrainian capital.

Black Sea resorts are enormously popular with package tourists, but few people travel along its interesting coastline or inland to see the fascinating variety of landscapes, the historic towns and busy capitals. This route, beginning in Burgas and ending in Kyiv, takes in some of the region's highlights such as wonderful Bulgarian mountain towns, mysterious Moldova and the dramatic Crimea.

TAILORED TRIPS

WORLD HERITAGE LISTED SIGHTS

One Month

Begin this most cultured of trips in Moscow to see the **Kremlin** (p659) and **Red Square** (p659) with day trips to Sergiev Posad for the **Trinity Monastery of St Sergius** (p670), and **Suzdal** (p669) and **Vladimir** (p670). Head west through Belarus, stopping at **Mir Castle** (p73) and the fabulous **Belavezhskaja Pushcha National Park** (p65) before entering Poland. Stop in medieval **Zamość** (p536) before heading to **Kraków** (p515) where you can

see **Auschwitz** (p524) in a day trip before carrying on to see the historic centres of **Prague** (p241), **Kutná Hora** (p263), **Český Krumlov** (p276), **Telč** (p285) and the Vila Tugendhat in **Brno** (p280). Cross into Slovakia and stop at **Spišský hrad** (p775), then on to **Bardejov** (p775). Press on into Hungary and stop off to explore the wine-producing region of **Tokaj-Hegyalja** (p385) before steaming on to sumptuous Budapest with its **Castle District** (p346). Head south via **Pécs** (p372) for the early Christian cemetery before crossing into Croatia. Stunning sights here include the **Plitvice Lakes National Park** (p205), **Split's old centre** (p205), that of **Trogir** (p212) and finally, the jewel in Croatia's glittering crown, sublime **Dubrovnik** (p217).

JEWISH HERITAGE TRIP

Two to Three Weeks

Begin in Rīga and learn about the deportation of Latvia's Jewish population at the **Jews in Latvia Museum** (p404), then visit the haunting memorial to the **Salaspils Concentration Camp** (p409) before going south to Lithuania. Vilnius has plenty of interest including the **Holocaust Museum** (p429) and the **Vilna Gaon Jewish State Museum of Lithuania** (p429). Nearby there's **Trakai** (p433), still home to some 360 Karaite Jews. Stop in Kaunas for a visit to the chilling **Ninth Fort** (p438) and the **Sugihara House & Foundation** (p438), home to Japanese consul and sometime Schindler of Lithuania, Chiune Sugihara. Next to Poland; head straight for **Warsaw** (p502), taking in the wealth of museums, memorials and other sights associated with the

ghetto and the holocaust. Stopping first at **Lublin** (p532) where you can walk the Jewish heritage trail, head for **Kraków** (p515) where there are a number of fascinating sights, including the 15th-century Old Synagogue, remarkable for having survived WWII. Make the harrowing trip to **Auschwitz** (p524) and **Birkenau** (p525) for a shocking first-hand glimpse of human evil. From here carry on to Prague's **Staré Město** (p251) to visit Josefov, the Prague Jewish Museum, and the Old-New Synagogue – the continent's oldest Jewish house of worship. End in **Budapest** (p339) where you'll find a flourishing Jewish population of 80,000 and some 25 active synagogues, including Europe's largest, the 1859 Great Synagogue.

The Authors

TOM MASTERS
Coordinating Author & Russia

First visiting Eastern Europe aged 14 when he went to stay with family friends in Bulgaria, Tom has had a love affair with the once-obscure region since he can remember. Aged 15 he travelled around the area by train with his intrepid mother (an experience not unlike a Graham Greene novel), and at 18 finally got to see Russia, his true passion. Since graduating from the University of London with a degree in Russian, Tom has returned more times that he can remember, living in St Petersburg and working throughout the region. Despite living in London (having never adapted to the Russian winter), he finds himself back in Russia all the time and has also written Lonely Planet's *St Petersburg*.

My Favourite Trip

I'd have to start in Sofia (p121), where warm memories and good friends make for a great start to an overland train journey. After a couple of days I'd move on to Bulgaria's centre – Plovdiv (p134) is a favourite, as is Veliko Târnovo (p146), which must have the most unforgettable setting of any city in Eastern Europe. Going north to Bucharest (p580) I'd enjoy seeing how much it's changed since I first went there a year after the revolution. I'd carry on to wonderful Kyiv (p830), then Moscow (p654) for some hedonistic nights out, and finally aim to end up in St Petersburg (p671) some time during the White Nights, a perfect opportunity to relax, relive my student days and lose all track of time in the balmy summer nights.

LISA DUNFORD
Hungary

Lisa has dreamed of Hungary since she learnt that that's where her grandpa was born. While completing her BA in International Affairs from George Washington University, she was a part of one of the first study-abroad programmes in newly opened Hungary. She loved living in Budapest and after college moved to nearby Bratislava, from where she travelled frequently to her former home and took Hungarian classes. She continues to travel to Hungary every year to visit cousins and explore a land she loves. Lisa is also the author of the Hungary chapter in Lonely Planet's *Europe on a Shoestring*.

MARK ELLIOTT
Slovenia

Mark, a Belgium-based Brit, is best known as a tourism specialist on Azerbaijan and the Caucasus. Mark has visited Eastern and Central Europe repeatedly since childhood. In 1989, as the Berlin Wall began to wobble, he abandoned glittering prospects as a vacuum cleaner salesman to join Czechoslovakia's Velvet Revolution in Prague. He stayed on in the region, working as an English teacher while the Iron Curtain melted. His early visits to Slovenia included once arriving in Ljubljana by mistake when his Athens–London bus was hijacked by Metaxa smugglers. Mark has worked on many other travel guides including Lonely Planet's *Russia & Belarus*.

PATRICK HORTON
Bosnia & Hercegovina, Serbia & Montenegro

Born with restless feet his journeys have lead him to the more arcane areas of the world such as North Korea and Cuba. Donning his author disguise of sunnies, fedora and trench coat, Patrick prowled around the Balkans to unearth the traveller hotspots in Serbia and Montenegro and Bosnia and Hercegovina. Patrick has had many photographs published in Lonely Planet guides and has contributed as an author to many Lonely Planet books including *Russia & Belarus*.

CATHRYN KEMP
Latvia, Lithuania, Moldova & Romania

Cathryn started travelling in 1990 when she studied art at the Moscow Institute of Architecture. Several trips through Russia and Ukraine later, and a passion for travel was born. Cathryn has worked on a number of Lonely Planet guides, including *Romania & Moldova* and *Europe on a Shoestring*.

STEVE KOKKER
Estonia & Russia

Steve is a die-hard Eastern European lover, having spent most of his time since 1996 living away from his native Montreal, basing himself in his father's homeland of Tallinn, Estonia, and trekking through the Baltic region, Russia and beyond. He's been writing and photographing for Lonely Planet since 1998, and was responsible for the Estonia chapter and the Kaliningrad section of the Russia chapter for this book.

VESNA MARIC
Albania & Macedonia

Vesna Maric was born in Mostar, Bosnia and Hercegovina in 1976 and moved to Britain at the age of 16. She studied Czech Literature in London and lived in Prague for a year, before working for the BBC World Service for three and a half years. She has written magazine articles, produced radio features, worked on short films and likes to photograph insignificant things. Her latest, and as she claims most exciting, project was travelling to Albania and Macedonia for this book.

JEANNE OLIVER   Croatia

Jeanne is a freelance journalist, born in New Jersey and living in the south of France. She has been visiting and writing about Croatia since 1996, shortly after the new country was 'born'. Travelling the country by bus, boat, train and car, she's swum in its waters, hiked its trails and stuffed her backpack full of local cheese, homemade brandy and a handful of recipes to keep her going until the next trip. She's looking forward to eventually visiting every one of Croatia's islands, especially now that she's finally figured out how to read the Jadrolinija schedule.

ROBERT REID   Bulgaria

Prompted by gut, whim or a sense of rebellion in the American 'Heartland,' little Robert delved into old issues of Soviet Life as a wayward teen to unveil the world of Eastern Europe. He minored in Russian at the University of Oklahoma, and – at last – studied in St Petersburg and talked about the Rolling Stones on Echo Moscow radio station in Moscow, before traipsing throughout Eastern Europe for several months. Bulgaria – with its Black Sea shores, its Cyrillic pride, its clunky communist-era hotels, its light(er) food – has always been a favourite. He lives in Brooklyn, New York.

WENDY TAYLOR   Belarus & Ukraine

Wendy Taylor has been a Slavophile since reading Crime and Punishment in Mrs Piedmonte's English class. The more she learned about the mysteries of Russia and the USSR, the more intrigued she became – but by the time she was studying Slavic Languages and Literatures at UC Berkeley and Moscow State University, the Soviet Union was no more. After graduating, she worked as an editor and writer in Moscow at the Moscow Times and other publications, and worked for two years as an editor for Lonely Planet. Wendy also contributed to Russia & Belarus and Europe on a Shoestring.

MATT WARREN   Slovakia

Matt made his first foray into Eastern Europe as a fresh-faced schoolboy. The Iron Curtain was slowly parting and after living for four months in Budapest, he hitched his way from north to south, taking in Poland, the Czech Republic, Slovakia, Romania, Bulgaria and Turkey. As a UK-based journalist, he has subsequently worked in Eastern European destinations as diverse as Kaliningrad, Kosovo and Lithuania, and last year passed through again on his motorbike en route between Edinburgh and Istanbul. He has previously worked on many Lonely Planet titles including Czech & Slovak Republics.

RICHARD WATKINS   Poland
Born in Wales and a graduate of Oxford University, Richard's first paid job after leaving the academic world was teaching conversational English to college students in Bulgaria. Since then the travel bug has well and truly caught hold, and Richard has wandered around the globe as a backpacker, English teacher and more recently, as a travel guidebook writer. Richard has written for several other Lonely Planet titles, including *Poland* and *Best of Prague*.

NEIL WILSON   Czech Republic
Neil first swung a rucksack on his back when he was 15, tramping the hills of Scotland, his home country, and developing a taste for venturing off the beaten track. After working as a geologist for several years, he gave up the rock business for the more precarious life of a freelance writer and photographer. Since 1988 he has travelled in five continents and written around 40 travel and walking guides for various publishers. His first trip to the Czech Republic was in 1995, and he has been back many times, working in recent years on Lonely Planet's *Czech & Slovak Republics* and the *Prague* city guide.

Snapshots

The dynamic and fast-changing world of Eastern Europe was comprehensively divided in two when in May 2004 eight of the region's countries joined the EU. To say that this has changed the regional dynamic would be a massive understatement – to put it into historical perspective, just a decade and a half ago most of these countries were members of Comecon (the communist version of the EU), grey and undemocratic Moscow satellites with little or no self-determination. Now, for better or for worse (and you'll be given a massive breadth of opinion by locals on your travels) they are part of a huge European superstate where the market economy is king, trade barriers and borders no longer exist, and democracy and human rights are enshrined as sacrosanct.

The eagerness with which the EU has embraced its new members has been viewed with great suspicion by Russia, which feels its traditional 'sphere of influence' has been breached and is gently fuming at its impotence to do anything about it. The EU accession countries, however, all clearly see their destiny as being part of Europe and view the idea that they are somehow in Russia's sphere of influence as a vaguely humorous hangover from the days of Stalin, the man who, with Churchill and Roosevelt, famously divided up postwar Europe on the back of a dinner napkin in Yalta in 1945.

Indeed, some states – particularly the Baltic countries, which have been independent of Soviet power since only 1991 – see EU membership as the sole way of guaranteeing that they'll never be subjugated by their massive eastern neighbour again. Little Kaliningrad, the Russian enclave between Poland and Lithuania, was particularly irate about EU expansion – it now finds itself surrounded by only EU states.

The EU expansion has also caused internal dissent – Poland, the largest of the new EU states, saw the ongoing national debate about abortion reopen as the devout Catholic majority demanded guarantees that Brussels would not interfere with its strict antiabortion laws, while other countries have struggled to bring their economic practices in line with thousands of Brussels-created directives.

Meanwhile the people of plucky little Slovenia, a net contributor to the EU (ie putting in more money than it receives), even questioned the point of entering the union at all, although in the end their European idealism triumphed over potential economic loss.

Outside the union reaction ranged from shrugging in the coffee houses of Albania, where comments are often made about how little chance they have of *ever* joining the EU, to jokes in Bulgaria: 'We were little brother to the Ottoman Empire for 500 years, they collapsed. Then the Nazis and Soviets, and they collapsed. NATO, USA and EU, watch out!'

In fact, Bulgaria along with Balkan neighbours Romania and Croatia are waiting in the wings, and if all goes to plan, will join the EU in 2007. Not so for the rest of the former Yugoslavia, still licking its very real wounds from a decade of war and ethnic cleansing. Luckily the whole region is currently peaceful (although a freak outbreak of violence in Kosovo in 2004 sent shockwaves throughout Europe) and efforts are now focused on nation-building and encouraging peaceful coexistence. Since Slobodan Milošević's removal from power in 2000 and his on-going trial at the Hague for war crimes began, the entire region has gone some way to breaking with the brutal 1990s, although some key alleged war

A gem of Czech new wave cinema, the comedy drama *Closely Observed Trains* follows a young recruit to the railway services under the Nazi occupation. His thoughts are concentrated on losing his virginity, but sooner or later the graver implications of the occupation set in.

A brilliant and not particularly short film by Polish master Krzysztof Kieslowski, *A Short Film About Love* follows teenage Tomek's voyeuristic obsession with his sexually liberated neighbour Magda. When they finally meet, love is replaced by sex and the tables are quickly turned.

The daring film *When Father was Away on Business* addresses the brutal reality of Tito's Yugoslavia, and is enormously touching. It's told from the perspective of young Malik, who believes his father is away on business, though the truth is somewhat darker...

criminals such as Radovan Karadžić and Ratko Mladić remain at large. Wounds across the region will not truly begin to heal until these men are brought to justice. Moreover, many uncomfortable situations remain, particularly the status of Kosovo within Serbia and that of the Republika Srpska within Bosnia and Hercegovina. The next decade will be vital to the process of the renewal of interethnic trust and tolerance, although signs such as the highly symbolic rebuilding of the Old Bridge between the Muslim and Croat quarters of Mostar are cautiously positive.

Russia and its remarkably Soviet neighbours Ukraine, Belarus and Moldova are still incredibly backward looking and remain very cautious about any kind of reform. Despite the relative liberalism (not to mention vast criminality and corruption) of the Yeltsin years when Russia made some real steps to becoming a modern European nation under Yeltsin's heir, Putin, the clock appears to have been put back and the Kremlin has once again clamped down on the media, human rights and, most notoriously, Chechnya. Ukraine, Belarus and Moldova never really made any attempt to progress towards the western democratic model anyway, particularly Belarus, which still regularly makes the press for being the 'last dictatorship in Europe'.

While the region changes fast, oscillating unpredictably between democracy and autocracy, corruption and Brussels-approved transparency, much of course remains the same. If you look beyond superficial concessions to modernity you'll see rural life and folk traditions continuing pretty much everywhere as they have done for centuries. This is what is so enduringly fascinating about the region – the ravages of first fascism, then communism and now capitalism have done little to dent the deeply felt sense of individuality and nationhood in the Eastern European peoples. Travelling across just two or three countries can reveal such stark contrasts that the myth of regional similarities between the many cultures, languages, histories and religions that Eastern Europe boasts will be swiftly exploded. Even the name of the region can be controversial for some. The inhabitants of Slovenia, Hungary and the Czech Republic look genuinely perplexed when told that they are in Eastern Europe; they have long believed themselves to be an integral part of Mitteleuropa and have for a long time looked west rather than east for inspiration. The Baltics now look more to Scandinavia that to the former Soviet Union, while of course the colossus Russia laughs off any suggestion that its vast expanses could be confined by anything as cramped as one continent...

A Bulgarian cinematic classic (no, really) *The Goat Horn* is set during the Turkish occupation. A young girl avenges her mother's rape and murder by tracking down three of the four culprits and killing them with a goat's horn. Before she kills the fourth, (more) tragedy strikes.

Albania

CONTENTS

Highlights   28
Itineraries   28
Climate & When to Go   30
History   30
People   32
Religion   33
Arts   33
Environment   34
Food & Drink   35
Tirana   **36**
History   36
Orientation   36
Information   36
Dangers & Annoyances   38
Sights   38
Sleeping   39
Eating & Drinking   40
Entertainment   41
Shopping   41
Getting There & Away   41
Getting Around   42
Around Tirana   42
Southern Albania   **46**
Vlora   47
Ionian Coast   48
Saranda   48
Gjirokastra   50
Korça   50
Northern Albania   **51**
Shkodra   51
Lezha   53
Albania Directory   **53**
Accommodation   53
Activities   53
Books   54
Business Hours   54
Courses   54
Dangers & Annoyances   54
Disabled Travellers   54
Embassies & Consulates   55
Gay & Lesbian Travellers   55
Holidays   55
Language   55
Maps   55
Media   55
Money   56
Post   56
Telephone & Fax   57

Tourist Information   57
Visas   57
Women Travellers   57
Transport in Albania   **57**
Getting There & Away   57
Getting Around   59

Sandy and pebbly beaches stretch all the way down the Adriatic and Ionian coasts and traditional villages perch on the majestic misty mountains. In Berat, families still inhabit the hill-top castle guarding the sun-bleached houses in the town below; labyrinthine streets snake through Gjirokastra, its gloomy castle brooding above the town. Apollonia and Butrint fascinate with classical ruins in rural settings that you won't want to leave. Yet visiting Albania remains something only for the 'adventurous' and many people associate it with former isolation, peppered with stories of crime and poverty. In reality, the visitor will find a warm and sincerely hospitable country with a fantastic nature, breathtaking mountain landscapes and long sandy white beaches by the clear blue sea.

FAST FACTS

- **Area** 28,748 sq km
- **Capital** Tirana
- **Currency** lekë; €1 = 126 lekë; US$1= 101 lekë; UK£1 = 182 lekë; A$1 = 74 lekë; ¥100 = 93 lekë; NZ$1 = 69 lekë
- **Famous for** Ismail Kadare, beautiful beaches
- **Key Phrases** *Përshëndetje* (hello), *mirupafshim* (goodbye)
- **Official Language** Albanian
- **Population** 3.5 million
- **Telephone Codes** country code ☎ 355; international access code ☎ 00
- **Visas** no visa needed for citizens of the EU, Australia, New Zealand, the US, and Canada; see p57 for details

HIGHLIGHTS

- The bustling, dusty streets and café culture of the capital **Tirana** (p36)
- The winding mountain road to **Kruja** (p44); views that stretch for miles down the hazy plains, and imposing grey rock mountains
- The sunny 'museum city' of **Berat** (p46) and its amazing, still-inhabited Citadel
- The clear blue Ionian Sea at the gorgeous beaches at **Dhërmi** (p48)
- The magic of **Gjirokastra**'s (p50) steep cobbled streets and ancient stone houses

ITINERARIES

- **Three days** Treat yourself to a day in Tirana and hop on a *furgon* (minibus) the next morning for a day in stunning Kruja and some rare antique and souvenir shopping. Day three is for exploring Berat.
- **One week** Go south, crossing the stunning Llogaraja Pass towards the azure sea at Dhërmi for a day at the beach. Catch a cab from nearby Saranda to the fascinating archaeological site at Butrint. The final treat is Gjirokastra's old town and its ancient houses and streets.

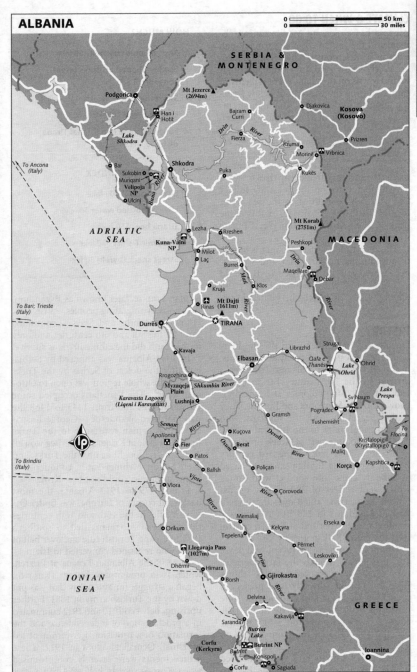

ALBANIA

0 — 50 km
0 — 30 miles

SERBIA & MONTENEGRO

Podgorica

Mt Jezerce (2694m)

Han i Hotit

Bajram Curri

Djakovica

Kosova (Kosovo)

Fierza

Kruma

Prizren

Drin River

Morinë
Vrbnica

Lake Shkodra

To Ancona (Italy)

Shkodra

Puka

Kukës

Bar
Sukobin
Muriqani
Velipoja NP
Ulcinj

Buna River

Lezha

Rreshen

Mt Korab (2751m)

MACEDONIA

ADRIATIC SEA

Kuna-Vaini NP

Milot
Laç

Peshkopi

Burrel

Drin River

Maqellare
Debar

To Bari; Trieste (Italy)

Kruja

Klos

Rinas

Mat River

Mt Dajti (1611m)

TIRANA

Durrës

Kavaja

Librazhd

Struga

Elbasan

Qafa e Thanës

Lake Ohrid

Ohrid

Rrogozhina

Shkumbin River

Myzaqeja Plain

Lake Prespa

Karavasta Lagoon (Liqeni i Karavastas)

Lushnja

Gramsh

Pogradec

Sv Naum

Seman River

Devoll River

Tushemisht

To Florina

Apollonia

Kuçova

Berat

Kristalopigi (Krystallopigi)

Fier

Patos

Osum

Poliçan

Maliq

Korça

Kapshtica

To Brindisi (Italy)

Ballsh

Vjose River

Çorovoda

River

Vlora

Memaliaj

Kelçyra

Erseka

Orikum

Tepelena

Përmet

Leskoviku

Llogaraja Pass (1027m)

Drino River

Dhërmi
Himara

IONIAN SEA

Borsh

Gjirokastra

Delvina

GREECE

Saranda

Butrint Lake

Kakavija

Corfu (Kerkyra)

Butrint NP

Butrint

Ioannina

Konispoli

Corfu

Sagiada

CLIMATE & WHEN TO GO

Albania has a pleasant Mediterranean climate and the Ionian coast is warm enough even in winter months when temperatures are rarely below zero. In Tirana and other inland towns on the plains there is plenty of rainfall during the winter, but below freezing temperatures are rare. The high mountains often experience heavy snow between November and March.

In the summer Tirana is sweltering, especially in July when temperatures reach the high 30°Cs, and even in the mountain towns the mercury frequently rises to 40°C. The temperatures on the coast are milder and you can cool down in the sea water together with the Albanians, as this is the peak of their tourist season. See Climate Charts p874.

The best time to visit Albania is spring or autumn, particularly May and September, when you can sightsee in the mild sunshine, enjoy the blossoming cherry and almond trees, or watch the golden leaves fill the streets.

HISTORY

During the 2nd millennium BC the Illyrians, the ancestors of today's Albanians, occupied the western Balkans. The Greeks arrived in the 7th century BC to establish self-governing colonies at Epidamnos (now Durrës), Apollonia and Butrint. They traded peacefully with the Illyrians, who formed tribal states in the 4th century BC. The south became part of Greek Epirus.

In the second half of the 3rd century BC, an expanding Illyrian kingdom based at Shkodra came into conflict with Rome, which sent a fleet of 200 vessels against Queen Teuta (who ruled over the Illyrian Ardian kingdom) in 228 BC. A long war resulted in the extension of Roman control over the entire Balkan area by 167 BC.

Under the Romans, Illyria enjoyed peace and prosperity, though the large agricultural estates were worked by slave labour. Like the Greeks, the Illyrians preserved their own language and traditions despite centuries of Roman rule. The main trade route between Rome and Constantinople, the Via Egnatia, ran from Durrës to Thessaloniki.

When the Roman Empire was divided in AD 395, Illyria fell within the Eastern

---

HOW MUCH?

- **Shot of mulberry raki** 100 lekë
- **Bunker-shaped ashtrays (great souvenirs!)** 500 lekë
- **Short taxi ride** 300 lekë
- **Loaf of bread** 50 lekë
- **Fërgesë Tiranë (traditional Tirana dish)** 300 lekë

LONELY PLANET INDEX

- **Litre of petrol** 100 lekë
- **Litre of bottled water** 50 lekë
- **Tirana beer** 150 lekë
- **Souvenir T-shirt** 800 lekë
- **Street snack (byrek)** 30 lekë

Roman Empire, later known as Byzantium. Invasions by migrating peoples – Visigoths, Huns, Ostrogoths and Slavs – continued through the 5th and 6th centuries and only in the south did the ethnic Illyrians survive.

In 1344 Albania was annexed by Serbia, but after the defeat of Serbia by the Turks in 1389 the whole region was open to Ottoman attack. The Venetians occupied some coastal towns, and from 1443 to 1468 the national hero Skanderbeg (George Kastrioti) led Albanian resistance to the Turks from his castle at Kruja. Skanderbeg won all 25 battles he fought against the Turks, and even Sultan Mehmet-Fatih, conqueror of Constantinople, could not take Kruja.

From 1479 to 1912 Albania, the most backward corner of Europe, was under Ottoman rule. In the 15th and 16th centuries thousands of Albanians fled to southern Italy to escape Turkish rule and over half of those who remained converted to Islam.

In 1878 the Albanian League at Prizren, which is in present-day Kosova (Kosovo), began a struggle for autonomy that was put down by the Turkish army in 1881. Further uprisings between 1910 and 1912 culminated in a proclamation of independence and the formation of a provisional government led by Ismail Qemali at Vlora in 1912. These achievements were severely compromised when Kosovo, nearly half of Albania, was ceded to Serbia in 1913. With the outbreak of WWI, Albania was occupied in succession by the armies of Greece, Serbia, France, Italy and Austria-Hungary.

In 1920 the capital city was moved from Durrës to less-vulnerable Tirana. Thousands of Albanian volunteers converged on Vlora, forcing the occupying Italians to withdraw. Ahmet Zogu became the ruler of Albania and declared himself King Zogu I in 1928, but his close collaboration with Italy backfired in April 1939 when Mussolini ordered an invasion of Albania. Zogu fled to Britain and used gold looted from the Albanian treasury to rent a floor at London's Ritz Hotel.

On 8 November 1941 the Albanian Communist Party was founded with Enver Hoxha (Hodja) as first secretary, a position he held until his death in April 1985. The communists led the resistance against the Italians and, after 1943, against the Germans, ultimately tying down 15 combined German-Italian divisions.

The Rise of Communism

After the fighting had died down, the communists consolidated power. In January 1946 the People's Republic of Albania was proclaimed, with Hoxha as president.

In September 1948 Albania broke off relations with Yugoslavia, which had hoped to incorporate the country into the Yugoslav Federation. Instead, Albania allied itself with Stalin's USSR and put into effect a series of Soviet-style economic plans.

Albania collaborated closely with the USSR until 1960, when a heavy-handed Khrushchev demanded that a submarine base be set up at Vlora. Breaking off diplomatic relations with the USSR in 1961, the country reoriented itself towards the People's Republic of China.

From 1966 to 1967 Albania experienced a Chinese-style cultural revolution. Administrative workers were suddenly transferred to remote areas and younger cadres were placed in leading positions. The collectivisation of agriculture was completed and organised religion banned.

Following the Soviet invasion of Czechoslovakia in 1968, Albania left the Warsaw Pact and embarked on a self-reliant defence policy. Some 700,000 igloo-shaped concrete bunkers (see below), conceived of by Hoxha, serve as a reminder of this policy.

With the death of Mao Zedong in 1976 and the changes that followed in China after 1978, Albania's unique relationship with China also came to an end, and the country was left isolated and without allies.

Post-Hoxha

Hoxha died in April 1985 and his longtime associate Ramiz Alia took over the leadership. Keenly aware of the economic decay caused by Albania's isolationist path, Alia began a liberalisation programme in 1986 and also broadened Albania's ties with foreign countries. Travellers arriving in Albania at this time no longer had their guidebooks confiscated or their beards and

---

BUNKER LOVE

On the hillsides, beaches and generally most surfaces in Albania, you will notice small concrete domes looking down on you through their rectangular slits. Sometimes their presence will surprise you for they sprout in areas you least expect them to be. Meet the bunkers: Enver Hoxha's paranoid concrete legacy, built over 35 years from 1950 to 1985.

Made out of concrete and iron, these hard little mushroom-like creations are almost impossible to destroy, since they were built to repel the threat of foreign invasion and can resist full tank assault.

Mr Hoxha hired a chief engineer to design a super-resistant bunker who then had to vouch for his creation's strength by standing inside it while it was bombarded by a tank. The shell-shocked engineer emerged unscathed and the bunkers were built; the estimated number of these concrete look-out posts is 700,000.

Today, apart from being an indestructible reminder of a cruel past regime, they serve no real purpose, and as they are impossible to move, the locals try to make them 'blend in' by painting them, putting potted plants on them, or sometimes simply using them as their little love pads.

long hair clipped by border barbers, and short skirts were allowed.

In June 1990, inspired by the changes that were occurring elsewhere in Eastern Europe, some 4500 Albanians took refuge in Western embassies in Tirana. After a brief confrontation with the police and the Sigurimi (secret police) these people were allowed to board ships for Brindisi in Italy, where they were granted political asylum.

After student demonstrations in December 1990, the government agreed to allow opposition parties. The Democratic Party, led by heart surgeon Sali Berisha, was formed. Further demonstrations produced new concessions, including the promise of free elections and independent trade unions. The government announced a reform programme and party hardliners were purged.

In early March 1991, as the election date approached, some 20,000 Albanians fled the country's crumbling economy and nonexistent infrastructure, seeking a 'better life' abroad. They set out from Vlora to Brindisi by ship, creating a crisis for the Italian government, which had begun to view them as economic refugees. Most were eventually allowed to stay.

The March 1992 elections ended 47 years of communist rule. After the resignation of Alia, parliament elected Sali Berisha president in April. In September 1992 former president Alia was placed under house arrest after he wrote articles critical of the Democratic government. In August 1993 the leader of the Socialist Party, Fatos Nano, was also arrested on corruption charges.

A severe crisis developed in late 1996, when private pyramid investment schemes – widely thought to have been supported by the government – collapsed spectacularly. Around 70% of Albanians lost their savings, in total over US$1 billion, resulting in nationwide disturbances and riots. New elections were called, and the victorious Socialist Party under Nano – who had been freed from prison by the rampaging mob – was able to restore some degree of security and investor confidence.

Albania shuddered again during November 1998 when Azem Hajdari (a very popular Democratic Party deputy) was assassinated, but the riots following his death were eventually contained.

In spring 1999 Albania faced a crisis of a different sort. This time it was the influx of 465,000 refugees from neighbouring Kosovo during the NATO bombing and the Serbian ethnic-cleansing campaign. While this put a tremendous strain on resources, the net effect has in fact been positive. Substantial amounts of international aid money have poured in, the service sector has grown and inflation has declined to single digits.

Since 2002 the country has found itself in a kind of miniboom with much money being poured into construction projects and infrastructure renewal.

The country has been developing steadily since 2002, with construction projects and infrastructure renewal being the priority issues. Albanian politics and the economy have been consistently stable, but work still has to be done to ensure that there is an end to electricity shortages and other infrastructure deficiencies that plague the country.

PEOPLE

In July 2003 the population was estimated to be 3,582,205, of which approximately 95% is Albanian, 3% Greek and 2% 'other' – comprising Vlachs, Roma, Serbians and Bulgarians. The Vlach are an old ethnic group in the Balkans, whose name is supposed to originate from the Greek word *vlach* which means 'shepherd'. They are historically a trading community, who are by now well integrated into all of the Balkan societies.

One of the best things about Albania is its people, who are kind and warm and unquestioningly generous. Most speak more than one foreign language: Italian is almost a second language in the north and centre, as well as the coast of the country, and Greek is widespread in the southern regions where the Greek minority is concentrated along the Drino River. You can rely on the majority of young people to speak English, but learning a few words of the very difficult Albanian language will delight your hosts. Note that Albanians shake their heads sideways to say yes *(po)* and usually nod and 'tsk' to say no *(jo)*. This can be rather confusing until you get used to it, but it'll keep you on your toes!

The Shkumbin River forms a boundary between the Gheg cultural region of the north and the Tosk region in the south. The people in these regions still vary in dialect, musical culture and traditional dress.

RELIGION

Albanians are 70% Muslim, 20% Christian Orthodox and 10% Catholic, but in most cases this is merely nominal. Religion was banned during communism and Albania was the world's only officially atheist state from 1967 to 1990. Despite the fact that the people are now free to practise their faith, Albania remains a very secular society and it is difficult to assess how many followers each faith can claim since the 2001 census didn't include a question on religion.

The Muslim faith has a branch called 'Bektashism', similar to Sufism, and its world headquarters have been in Albania since 1925, when the order was expelled from Turkey. Rather than mosques the Bektashi followers go to *teqe* – temple-like buildings without a minaret, often built specifically for their purpose, but sometimes housed in former churches. *Teqes* are usually found in mountain towns or on hill tops in towns where they were built to escape persecution, and you will no doubt come across at least one of them.

ARTS
Visual Arts

The art scene in Albania is slowly on the rise. One of the first 'signs of art' that will strike you are the multicoloured buildings of Tirana, a project organised by the capital's mayor Edi Rama, himself a painter. One of his paintings can be found at the National Art Gallery in Tirana (see p39) at the permanent Portraits exhibition.

There are still some remnants of socialist realism, with paintings and sculptures adorning the walls and gardens of galleries and museums, although many were destroyed after the fall of the communist government as a reflex against the old regime. Some of these are absolutely beautiful, but unfortunately none are for sale.

An up-and-coming artist is Norway-based Anri Sala, whose video installations are a modern account of Albanian life.

One of the most delicious Albanian art treats is to be found in Berat's Onufri Museum (see p46). Onufri was the most outstanding Albanian icon painter of the 16th and 17th centuries and his work is noted for its unique intensity of colour, using natural dyes that are as fresh now as the day he painted them.

Music

Polyphony, the blending of several independent vocal or instrumental parts, is a southern Albanian tradition dating from ancient Illyrian times. Peasant choirs perform in a variety of styles, and the songs, usually with an epic-lyrical or historical theme, may be dramatic to the point of yodelling, or slow and sober, with alternate male and female voices combining in harmony. Instrumental polyphonic *kabas* (a sedate style, led by a clarinet or violin alongside accordions and lutes) are played by small Roma ensembles. Musical improvisation is accompanied by dancing at colourful village weddings. One well-known group, which often tours outside Albania, is the Lela Family of Përmet.

An outstanding recording of traditional Albanian music is the CD *Albania, Vocal and Instrumental Polyphony* in the series 'Le Chant du Monde' (Musée de l'Homme, Paris).

Literature

There is no substantial body of Albanian literature before the 19th century as the Ottomans banned the teaching of Albanian in schools, fearing the spread of anti-Turkish propaganda. The adoption of a standardised orthography in 1908, when the literary movement rose together with the Albanian national movement, led to Albanian independence in 1912. A group of romantic patriotic writers at Shkodra, such as Migjeni (1911–1938) and Martin Çamaj (1925–1992), wrote epics and historical novels.

Perhaps the most interesting writer of the interwar period was Fan Noli (1880–1965). Educated as a priest in the USA, Noli became premier of Albania's Democratic government until it was overthrown in 1924, when he returned to head the Albanian Orthodox Church in America. Although many of his books are based on religion, the introductions he wrote to his own translations of Cervantes, Ibsen, Omar Khayyám and Shakespeare established him as Albania's foremost literary critic.

The only Albanian writer who is widely read outside Albania is the contemporary Ismail Kadare (1936–). His books are not only enriching literary works, but are also a great source of information on Albanian traditions, history and social events. They exquisitely capture the atmosphere of the country's towns, such as the lyrical descriptions of Kadare's birthplace Gjirokastra in *Chronicle in Stone* (1971) where wartime experiences are seen through the eyes of a boy. *Broken April* (1990), set in the northern highlands before the 1939 Italian invasion, describes the life of a village boy who is next in line in the desperate cycle of blood vendettas (see boxed text this page).

Cinema

With its turbulent historical events, Albania has provided the backdrop for some interesting celluloid moments. Filmgoers in the West have had the opportunity to see Gjergj Xhuvani's comedy *Slogans* (2001), based on the autobiographical short story by Ylljet Alicka, *Slogans of Stone* (well known in Albania), a satirical account of life during communist times.

Another film worth seeing is *Lamerica* (1995), a brilliant and stark look at Albanian postcommunist culture. Woven loosely around a plot about a couple of Italian scam artists, and Albanians seeking to escape to Bari, Italy, the essence of the film is the unshakeable dignity of the ordinary Albanian in the face of adversity.

The renowned Brazilian director Walter Salles *(Central Station)* adapted Ismail Kadare's novel *Broken April* and, having kept the novel's main theme, moved the action to Brazil in *Behind the Sun* (2001).

ENVIRONMENT
The Land

More than three-quarters of Albania is made up of mountains and hills. There are three zones: a coastal plain, a mountainous region and an interior plain. The coastal plain extends approximately 200km from north to south and up to 50km inland. The 2000m-high forested mountain spine, which stretches the entire length of Albania, culminates at Mt Jezerce (2694m) in the north, near the Serbian border. The country's highest peak is Mt Korab (2751m), which is located on the border with Macedonia to the east. The interior plain is alluvial, with seasonal precipitation. It is poorly drained and therefore alternately arid or flooded and is often as inhospitable as the mountains.

Albania has suffered some devastating earthquakes, including the one that struck in 1979, leaving at least 100,000 people homeless.

THE KANUN

The *Kanun* (Code) consists of 1262 articles covering every aspect of daily life: work, marriage, family organisation, property questions, hospitality, economy etc. Many people in northern Albania still live by its strict laws.

The most important things in life, according to the *Kanun,* are honour (personal and family) and hospitality. If these two are disrespected by any individual, the family of the person responsible can become involved in the dreadful cycle of killing known as the blood feud. 'An offence to honour is not paid for with property, but by the spilling of blood or by a magnanimous pardon (through the mediation of good friends)' states the *Kanun* (*Kanuni I Lekë Dukagjinit: The Code of Lekë Dukagjini* by Lekë Dukagjini, Shtjefen Gjecov and Leonard Fox). Only men are involved in blood feuds, and it is their duty to avenge the life and honour of their clan by 'taking blood' (murdering) a member of the clan who originally committed murder against their family. Cycles of killings of families 'in blood' can go on for generations, and entire families are often left without male members as a result.

In some cases, reconciliation is possible through mediation between the families in conflict. Usually, the mediators are respected village elders, and after an agreement has been reached to end the feud (usually through a financial payment or land sharing, or by taking a *besa* – 'a sacred oath') the families seal their peace by eating a 'Meal of Blood' prepared by the murderer's family.

Hospitality is so important in these parts of Albania that the guest 'takes on a god-like status' according to the anthropologist Kauhiko Yamamoto. There are 38 articles giving instructions on how to treat a guest – an abundance of food, drink and comfort is at his or her disposal, and it is also the host's duty to avenge the murder of his guest, should this happen during their visit.

The most popular version of the *Kanun* is that of Lekë Dukagjin, the chief of the most powerful clan in 15th-century Albania, although many claim that the Code is in fact much older.

The longest river in Albania is the Drin (285km), which drains into Lake Ohrid. In the north the Drin flows into the Buna River, which connects Lake Shkodra to the sea. The Ionian littoral, especially the 'Riviera of Flowers' stretching from Vlora to Saranda, offers magnificent scenery from the highest peak in this region, the Llogaraja Pass (over 1000m). Forests cover 40% of the land, and the many olive trees, citrus plantations and vineyards give Albania a Mediterranean air.

Wildlife

Albania's territory is rich in flora with beech trees and oak, and patches of rare Macedonian pine *(pinus peuce)* in the lower regions. Birch, pine and fir cover the mountain sides until they reach 2000m, after which all is barren.

There are several wetland sites at the mouths of the Buna, Drin and Mati Rivers in the north and at the Karavasta Lagoon south of Durrës, with many interesting and rare birds (white pelicans, and white-headed ducks, among others) to spot for those with a keen pair of binoculars.

There is an abundance of medicinal plants, and herbal medicine is big in both urban and rural areas.

Most of Albania's national parks, although theoretically protected areas, are not really protected by anything but their remoteness, and tree cutting and hunting still take place. There are no hiking maps of the national parks, nor are there generally any hotels or camping grounds. The only place that does have accommodation is the Llogaraja Mountain (p48), where you can also go for shorter hikes. Independent camping is not advisable because the mountains are almost completely uninhabited and have no mobile phone coverage; help in case of an injury would be impossible to find.

Environmental Issues

With the collapse of communism, during which there were around 2000 cars in the country, the number of roaring automobiles has risen drastically to something around 300,000, many of which are old Mercedes allegedly stolen from Western Europe. In March 2004 reports claimed that Tirana was now considered to be the most polluted capital in Europe. In response to this serious problem, the country's environ-ment department and the transport ministry have set up an emergency group to draft laws that would help control cars and the fumes they exude.

Albania's current environment minister Et'hem Ruka has made Tirana's pollution a priority and has already clamped down on the factories in the central town of Elbasan, where the huge petrochemical factory belched enormous amounts of toxic fumes over the valley for years, making the soil so contaminated that in some places planting food crops is forbidden.

There is also a saddening amount of rubbish in the cities (with the mysterious exception of Korça) and the countryside, disfiguring the landscape and destroying wildlife. Albanians are, however, doing their bit to improve these conditions and there is considerable Western investment in aiding this process.

FOOD & DRINK

Albanian cuisine is mainly dominated by delicious roast lamb in the mountains and fresh fish and seafood dishes near the coast. Innards, veal escalopes, *biftek* (beef loin), *qebaps* (kebabs) and *qoftë* (meat balls) are also very popular. *Fërgesë Tiranë* is a traditional Tirana dish of innards, eggs and tomatoes cooked in an earthenware pot. If you are a vegetarian and despairing as you read this, worry not – there are some delicious Turkish-style vegetable dishes to be had too, such as roast peppers and aubergines, cauliflower moussaka and plenty of *kos* (yogurt) is served in restaurants to accompany any dish.

You will find *byrek* stands all over the place, the Balkan alternative to fast food and a delicious budget option at that. *Byrek* comes in many forms: filled with cheese, tomato, meat, or spinach and layered with thin slices of filo pastry.

Albanians do not eat desserts after their meal, but they do drink a shot of *raki* before they tuck into their food, as an aperitif. This is very popular and there are three different types of *raki* to be had in Albania: grape *raki* (the most common one), *mani raki* (mulberry, an Albanian type), and *šljivovica* (plum, a Slav type). Ask for home-made if possible *(raki ë bërë në shtëpi)*. If *raki* is not your cup of tea, try *Rilindja* wine (Merlot) which is very good.

TIRANA

☎ 042 / pop 553,435

Tirana is a city of dusty streets, shady boulevards with elegant Italian 30s architecture, street markets, trendy bars, parks, beautiful mosques, rows of moneychangers, remnants of socialist-realist art and fun nightlife. It's surprising to see how different one street is from the next and to discover a small lake and a lush park at the city's edge. There's plenty to see and explore on foot, and you'll be happy to know that the city won't bleed your finances dry as other capitals might.

Tirana lies close to midway between Rome and Istanbul. Mt Dajti (1612m) rises to the east.

HISTORY

Founded by a Turkish *pasha* (military governor) in 1614, Tirana developed into a craft centre with a lively bazaar. In 1920 the city was made the capital of Albania as the powers-that-be decided it was better to rule the country from its centre rather than from Durrës, the more vulnerable capital on the coast.

ORIENTATION

Tirana revolves around the busy central Sheshi Skënderbeg (Skanderbeg Sq) from where various streets and boulevards radiate out like spokes of a wheel. Running south is the shady Bulevardi Dëshmorët e Kombit, great for strolling and looking at the communist relics and near the trendy part of Blloku. Running north, Bulevardi Zogu I leads to the busy train and bus station where bus conductors shout out their destinations like market sellers. Most sights and services are within a few minutes' walk of Sheshi Skënderbeg.

All the incoming buses will drop you off at the bus and train station at the end of Bulevardi Zogu I, a five-minute walk north from the city centre.

INFORMATION

Bookshops

Adrion International Bookshop (☎ 235 242; ☽ 9am-9pm) In the Palace of Culture on the right-hand side, it has a selection of Penguin literary classics, maps of Tirana and Albania, and an excellent selection of books about Albania.

TIRANA IN TWO DAYS

Start your day with croissants in **Pasticeri Francaise** (p40) and stroll up to **Sheshi Skënderbeg** (p38) to explore the National Museum of History. Look around Et'hem Bey Mosque and march down to the National Art Gallery. Admire the stunning views of Tirana at sunset as you wine and dine at the **Sky Restaurant** (p40). Drink and party in the trendy **Blloku** (p39).

On day two visit **Kruja** (p44), where the castle walls hide the Skanderbeg Museum, a fascinating Ethnographic Museum and the Dollma *teqe* (Bektashi temple), full of history. Don't forget to do some shopping at the lovely bazaar and have a traditional Albanian lunch in one of its small restaurants. Back in Tirana, dinner at **Villa Ambassador** (p41) is obligatory for a diverse, mouthwatering menu.

Internet Access

All charge from 150 to 200 lekë per hour.

F@stech (☎ 251 947; Rruga Brigada e VIII; ☽ 8.30am-11pm) A 1st-floor joint, with high stools bringing you up to your walled-in screen.

Interalb Internet (☎ 251 747; Rruga Dëshmorët e 4 Shkurtit Pall 25/1; ☽ 8am-10pm) Just plain not-so-old computers.

Tir@na-Online (☎ 068-280 7679; Rruga Qemal Stafa Pall 218; ☽ 8am-10pm)

Medical Services

ABC Clinic (☎ 234 105; 360 Rruga Qemal Stafa; ☽ 8am-4pm Mon-Fri) Opposite the New School, with English-speaking doctors, ABC offers a range of services including regular (US$60) and emergency (US$90) consultations.

All-night Pharmacy (☎ 222 241; Bulevardi Zogu I) Just off Sheshi Skënderbeg.

Money

While there are plenty of banks in Tirana, there were few international ATMs at the time of writing. Most of the ATMs you see are only attached to the local banks and do not take Visa or MasterCard, so bring either cash or travellers cheques with you.

The unavoidable independent money exchangers operate directly in front of the main post office and on Sheshi Skënderbeg and offer the same rates as the banks. Changing money here is not illegal or

TIRANA

| 0 | 500 m |
| 0 | 0.3 miles |

A **B** **C** **D**

INFORMATION
ABS Clinic.................................... 1 D3
Adrion International Bookshop....(see 33)
Albania Travel & Tours................... 2 B4
All-night pharmacy........................ 3 C4
American Bank of Albania............ 4 C6
American Embassy........................ 5 D6
British Embassy............................. 6 B4
Bulgarian Embassy....................... 7 B4
DHL.. 8 C4
DHL.. 9 C5
F@stech..................................... 10 C5
German Embassy......................... 11 B4
Greek Embassy........................... 12 B4
Interalb Internet......................... 13 C6
Macedonian Embassy................. 14 B4
Main Post Office......................... 15 C4
National Bank............................. 16 C4
National Savings Bank Branch....(see 44)
Post Office Sub Branch............... 17 C4
Post Office Sub Branch............... 18 B6
Serbia & Montenegro Embassy.... 19 B4
Telephone Centre....................... 20 C4
Telephone Centre....................(see 15)
Tir@na-Online............................ 21 D4
Turkish Embassy......................... 22 B4
Unioni Financiar Tiranë Exchange.23 C5
World Travel............................(see 1)

SIGHTS & ACTIVITIES   (pp38–9)
Archaeological Museum.............. 24 C6
Clock Tower.............................(see 27)
Congress Building....................... 25 C6
Equestrian Statue of Skënderbeg.26 C4

Et'hem Bey Mosque...................... 27 C4
Former Enver Hoxha Museum....... 28 C5
Former Residence of Enver Hoxha.29 C6
Former Sigurimi HQ.................(see 30)
Government Buildings................. 30 C5
National Art Gallery.................... 31 C5
National Library.......................(see 33)
National Museum of History........ 32 C4
Palace of Culture........................ 33 C4
Prime Minister's Residence......... 34 C6
Pyramid.................................(see 28)
Selman Stërmasi (Dinam) Stadium...35 B6

SLEEPING   (pp39–40)
Guva e Qetë............................... 36 C5
Hotel California.......................... 37 B4
Hotel Dajti................................. 38 C5
Hotel Endri................................. 39 C6
Hotel Lugano.............................. 40 B4
Hotel Miniri................................ 41 C4
Kalaja.. 42 C5
Qëndra Stefan............................ 43 D4
Rogner Hotel Europapark Tirana.. 44 C6
Tirana International Hotel............ 45 C4

EATING   (pp40–1)
Food Market............................... 46 D4
Food Market............................... 47 C5
La Voglia.................................... 48 C5
Pasticeri Francaise...................... 49 C5
Serenata.................................... 50 B4
Sky Restaurant........................... 51 C5
Villa Ambassador....................... 52 D6

DRINKING   (pp40–1)
Buda Bar................................... 53 B6
Q.. 54 B5

ENTERTAINMENT   (p41)
Academy of Arts......................... 55 C6
Boom Boom Room....................... 56 B6
Kinema Millenium 2.................... 57 C5
Kinema Millennium..................... 58 C4
Qemal Stafa Stadium.................. 59 C6
Rozafa club................................ 60 C6
Theatre of Opera & Ballet........... 61 C4

SHOPPING   (p41)
Public Market............................. 62 D4

TRANSPORT   (pp41–2)
Albanian Interlines..................... 63 C4
Albtransport.............................. 64 B4
Alitalia..................................(see 32)
Austrian Airlines.....................(see 44)
Bus & Minibus Station to
  Durrës & North........................ 65 C3
Bus Departure Point for Prishtina.. 66 C4
Bus/Minibus Terminal................. 67 A5
Europcar.................................... 68 C4
Hertz.. 69 C4

TRANSPORT (continued)   (pp41–2)
Minibuses to Elbasan, Pogradec &
  Korça..................................... 70 C6
Olympic Airways......................... 71 C4
Southern Bus Station.................. 72 B6
Swiss International Airlines.......(see 44)
Turkish Airlines......................(see 45)
Zogu i Zi terminal....................... 73 A3

OTHER
Tirana University........................ 74 C6

Train Station
65

To Airport (26km);
Kruja (32km);
Durrës (38km)
73

Rruga Mine Peza
Bulevardi Zogu I
Rruga e Barrikadave
Rruga Qemal Stafa
Rruga Hoxha Tasim

Rruga Durrësit
Rruga Mine Peza
Rruga Ded Gjo Luli
Rruga Mihal Duri

Rruga Muhamet Gjollesha
Rruga Skënderbeg
Rruga Naim Frashëri

Rruga e Kavajës
To Durrës (38km);
Berat (122km)

Sheshi Skënderbeg

Sheshi Avni Rustemi roundabout

Lana River

Rruga Ismail Qemali
Rruga Myslym Shyri

Rruga Murat Toptani

Bulevardi Gjergj Fishta/Bulevardi Zhan D'Ark
Bulevardi Bajram Curri

Blloku

Rruga Sami Frashëri
Rruga Ismail Qemali
Rruga Dëshmorët e 4 Shkurtit
Rruga Dëshmorët e Kombit

Rruga Lidhja e Durrësit
Rruga Themistokli Germenji

Rruga Elbasanit

Parku Kombëtar

To Martyrs' Cemetery
& Former Palace of King
Zogu (1km); Elbasan
(54km); Pogradec (140km);
Korça (181km)

To Tirana
(Tirana Zoo)

Rruga Margarita Tutulani

dangerous, but do count the money you receive before handing yours over.

American Bank of Albania (Rruga Ismail Qemali 27; ☺ 9.30am-3.30pm Mon-Fri) A reliable, secure place to cash your travellers cheques (2% commission). The Amex representative.

National Savings Bank Branch (☎ 235 035; Bulevardi Dëshmorët e Kombit; ☺ 10.30am-5pm Mon-Fri) Located in the Rogner Hotel Europapark Tirana, it offers MasterCard advances, cashes US dollar, euro and sterling travellers cheques for 1% commission and exchanges cash.

Unioni Financiar Tiranë Exchange (☎ 234 979; Rruga Dëshmorët e 4 Shkurtit) Just south of the Main post office, it offers Western Union wire transfer services.

World Travel (☎ 227 998; Mine Peza 2) Cashes travellers cheques for 2% commission.

Post

DHL Rruga Dëshmorët e 4 Shkurtit (☎ 232 816; fax 257 294; DHLAlbania@tia-co.al.dhl.com; Rruga Dëshmorët e 4 Shkurtit 7/1); Rruga Ded Gjo Luli (☎ 227 667; fax 233 934; Rruga Ded Gjo Luli 6) The international courier service has two offices in Tirana.

Main post office & telephone centre (☎ 228 262; Sheshi Çameria; ☺ 8am-8pm Mon-Fri) Adjacent on a street jutting west from Sheshi Skënderbeg. Another telephone centre is on Bulevardi Zogu I, about 400m past Sheshi Skënderbeg on the right-hand side. There are additional sub-branch post offices on Bulevardi Zogu I and on Rruga Mohamet Gjollesha.

Tourist Information

Tirana does not have an official tourist office, but travel agencies can help (see below for details). *Tirana in Your Pocket* (www .inyourpocket.com) tells you what's hot, and is available at bookshops and some of the larger kiosks for 300 lekë.

Another useful reference is *Tirana: The Practical Guide and map of Tirana* with telephone numbers and addresses for everything from hospitals to banks to embassies, though some of the entries are only in Albanian. This is also available at the main hotels and bookshops for 200 lekë.

Travel Agencies

Travel agencies and airlines of all descriptions and destinations abound on Rruga Mine Peza, but not all operators speak English.

Albania Travel & Tours (☎ 329 83; fax 339 81; Rruga Durrësit 102; ☺ 8am-8pm Mon-Fri, 8am-2pm Sat & Sun) A good place to arrange ferry tickets from Durrës (see p58), and/or book private rooms, or possibly tours around the country.

DANGERS & ANNOYANCES

Beware the potholes! Tirana's streets are badly lit during the night so arm yourself with a pocket torch to light your way around but watch out for the potholes during the day too. Some of these monsters are over a metre deep so you could incur serious injury. There are occasional power cuts in the city so the pocket torch idea stretches further.

Crossing the street is not for the fainthearted and you need to adopt a love for adrenaline-fuelled high-risk activities before you attempt this.

SIGHTS

Sheshi Skënderbeg is the best place to start witnessing the daily goings-on around you as kids in their orange plastic cars whizz past your ankles and real cars kick up the dust at the **equestrian statue of Skanderbeg** himself on the southern side of the square. If you stop to examine his emblematic goat's head helmet, the minaret of the **Et'hem Bey Mosque** (1789–1823) will catch the corner of your eye on the left. The small and elegant mosque is one of the oldest buildings left in the city, spared from destruction during the atheism campaign of the late '60s because of its status as a cultural monument. Take your shoes off and go inside to take a look at the beautifully painted dome. Behind it is the tall **clock tower** (☎ 243 292; admission free; ☺ 9am-1pm & 4-6pm Mon, Wed & Sat) which you can climb and watch the square and its colourful Ferris wheel entertain the tiny Tiranans.

On the northern side of the square, beside the 15-storey Tirana International Hotel, is the **National Museum of History** (admission 300 lekë; ☺ 8am-1pm Mon-Sat), the largest museum in Albania, which holds most of the country's archaeological treasures. Do take a guide (there are English-, French- and Italian-speaking guides) around the museum, as most of the information is in Albanian; it's common to tip the guide 100 lekë or 200 lekë. The fantastic **mosaic mural** entitled *Albania* adorning the museum's façade shows Albanians victorious from Illyrian times through to WWII.

If you are an archaeological glutton, there is more to be seen in the **Archaeological Museum** (admission 200 lekë; ☺ 10.30am-2.30pm Mon-Fri) on Mother Teresa Sq close to the main **university building**.

To the east of Sheshi Skënderbeg is the white stone **Palace of Culture**, which has a theatre, shops and art galleries. Construction of the palace began as a gift from the Soviet people in 1960 and was completed in 1966, after the 1961 Soviet-Albanian split. The entrance to the **National Library** is on the south side of the building.

One of the most impressive buildings on the west of the square is the large Italian red-brick **National Bank building** whose shady entrance rests on three heavy square pillars.

Stroll down the spacious tree-lined Bulevardi Dëshmorët e Kombit to Tirana's **National Art Gallery** (admission 100 lekë; ☉ 9am-1pm & 5-8pm Tue-Sun) where the garden is adorned with statues of proud partisans. See the astonishing exhibition of icons inside by Onufti, the renowned 16th-century master of colour (see p39). There is also a room adjacent to the gallery space where you can see busts of Mother Teresa and Enver Hoxha, among others. Temporary exhibitions are on the ground floor.

Take a break next door in **Hotel Dajti** for a whiff of Italian-30s-meet-communism and feel transported to a different time in this tranquil building with soft armchairs and low chandeliers as the sunlight peeks through the ochre drapes.

If you fancy a break from the city buzz, carry on down the boulevard into the lush **Parku Kombëtar** (National Park), with a *Teatri Veror* (open-air theatre) and an artificial lake, where Tiranans get fit, breathe some fresh air, or spend a romantic moment or two.

WALKING TOUR: COMMUNIST TIRANA

Built for the flamboyant fascist parades, the pine- and palm-tree lined Bulevardi Dëshmorët e Kombit was also the stomping ground of Albania's communist nomenklatura (political elite).

From the main square, start your walk down Bulevardi Dëshmorët e Kombit, and spot the now brightly painted **government buildings**, recognisable by their very serious military guards. Just behind the last building on the left-hand side were the headquarters of the once much-feared Sigurimi, communist Albania's answer to the KGB.

Further down on the left, after crossing the bridge over the tiny Lana River, you'll see the sloping white-marble and glass walls of the **Pyramid**, aka the **former Enver Hoxha Museum** (1988), designed by Hoxha's daughter and son-in-law. Now used as a disco and conference centre, the building never really took off as a museum, but does very well as a slide for children. Another creation of the dictator's daughter and son-in-law is the square **Congress Building**, just a little down the boulevard. Opposite is the **Prime Minister's Residence** where Enver Hoxha and cronies would stand and view military parades from the 2nd-floor balcony.

Follow Rruga Ismail Qemali, the street on the southern side of the Congress Building, and enter the once totally forbidden but now totally trendy **Blloku**, the former exclusive Communist Party elite hang-out. When the area was first opened to the general public in 1991, Albanians flocked to see the style in which their 'proletarian' leaders lived. If we are to judge by the **former residence of Enver Hoxha**, the three-storey pastel-coloured house on the corner of Rruga Dëshmorët e 4 Shkurtit and Rruga Ismail Qemali, their style was not so grand. Now housing some government offices, an English-language school, and a nice bar popular with students, the only thing left of its former glory are a couple of dishevelled-looking palm trees.

About 1km southeast on Rruga Elbasanit is the **Martyrs' Cemetery** (Varrezat e Dëshmorëve), where some 900 partisans who died in WWII are buried. Enver Hoxha was buried there after his death in 1985. His coffin was dug up in 1992 and reburied in an ordinary graveyard on the other side of town, though his tombstone remains.

Some still come here to pay their respects to the former dictator (especially on his birthday on 16th October), and you can still see fresh flowers on his brown tombstone, next to the white figure of **Mother Albania** (1972) clutching her laurel and a star and watching the city lights. Nearby, on the other side of the highway, is the **former palace of King Zogu**, now a government guesthouse.

SLEEPING

Tirana's accommodation is improving and there are a few good budget options as well as some quality mid-range and more pricey top-end places to lay your head.

ALBANIA

Budget

Albania Travel & Tours (☎ 329 83; fax 339 81; Rruga Durrësit 102; ☺ 8am-8pm Mon-Fri, 8am-2pm Sat & Sun) The best money-saving option is renting a private room here for around 2600 lekë per person. Other travel agencies may also be able to find you a private room.

Hotel Endri (☎ 244 168, 229 334; Pall 27, fl 3 apt 30, Rruga Vaso Pasha 27; r US$20) Good value and located where all the action is, in Blloku. The 'hotel' is basically two sparkling clean rooms in a run-down building next to the owner Petrit Alikaj's apartment. Sturdy wooden doors, nice bathrooms, excellent showers.

Kalaja (☎ 250 000; Rruga Murat Toptani; s & d per person 1500 lekë, with shared bathroom 1000 lekë) This kitsch hotel has clean rooms with tiled floors, technicolour linen and TVs. Some have balconies.

Guva e Qetë (☎ 235 491/440; fax 222 228; Rruga Myslym Shyri 25; s/d US$30/40) Hunter's lodge-style, wooden walls, photos of tigers, owls and other wild beasts on the walls, spacious rooms with TVs and brand-new bathrooms.

Qëndra Stefan (Stephen Center; ☎ /fax 253 924; stephenc@icc.al.eu.org; Rruga Hoxha Tasim 1; s/d US$30/50 incl breakfast) Airy, light en suite rooms with pressed white linen and a great roof-terrace. It's also metres away from a nice fruit and vegetable market (p41). This place is run by US evangelists, so smoking and drinking is not allowed on the premises.

Mid-Range

Hotel California (☎ /fax 253 191/2; Rruga Mihal Duri 2/1; s/d US$50/70) Lyrically named and thankfully nothing like the song, the rooms are clean with comfy beds, TVs, telephones and sparkling bathrooms.

Hotel Lugano (☎ /fax 222 023; Rruga Mihal Duri 34; s/d US$50/70) The newly renovated rooms have heavy red drapes on the windows, good beds, and some, though not all, have kitsch marble-copy bathrooms that may give you a shock in the morning. It's opposite Hotel California.

Hotel Dajti (☎ 251 031; fax 251 036; Bulevardi Dëshmorët e Kombit 6; s/d US$50/80) The grandiose décor in the reception area is not so apparent in the rooms upstairs. Clean and comfortable enough with large beds, and massive terraces, the rooms experience severe water and electricity shortages. The small terrace in the front is a great place for a break in the shade, though.

Hotel Miniri (☎ 230 930; fax 233 096; Rruga e Dibres 3; s/d US$60/96) Just off Sheshi Skënderbeg, this place is bland, but the rooms are adequate with phone and TV and the location is undoubtedly premium.

Top End

Tirana International Hotel (☎ 234 185; http://hotel tirana.albnet.net; Sheshi Skënderbeg; s/d US$140/190; P ⊠ ⌨) Tall, glass and imposing, this is one of the buildings that dominate the city's skyline. The rooms are sleek and luxurious, and have great views of the busy square. The hotel accepts MasterCard, Amex and Diners Club.

Rogner Hotel Europapark Tirana (☎ 235 035; www.rogner.com; Bulevardi Dëshmorët e Kombit; s/d US$210/250; P ⊠ ⌨ ⌚) This is where most of the internationals sleep, drink, eat and swim in the open-air pool. The rooms are spacious and very comfortable, and the restaurant has tasty international cuisine. Drink into the night on the cool terrace. Amex, Visa and MasterCard accepted.

EATING & DRINKING

If you thought that cuisine in Tirana's restaurants might be monotonous or that eating out would be a down-market experience, you were wrong. Rruga Dëshmorët e 4 Shkurtit, the buzzing central street of Blloku area, is the top spot for cafés, bars and restaurants.

Pasticeri Francaise (☎ 251 336; Rruga Deshmoret e 4 Shkurtit 1; breakfast 150 lekë; ☺ 8am-10pm) One of the few breakfast spots in Tirana, this French-owned place has red walls and high ceilings, and the small lamps light individual tables giving it an ooh-la-la feeling!

Qëndra Stefan (☎ 253 924; Rruga Hoxha Tasim 1; mains 300-400 lekë; ☺ 8am-10pm Mon-Sat; ⌧) A friendly place for breakfast or Chinese and Mexican lunch if you want something different; located in the hotel of the same name.

La Voglia (☎ 228 678; Rruga Dëshmorët e 4 Shkurtit; mains 350-400 lekë; ☺ 8am-11pm) This place is in the small busy square off the street; enjoy some delicious bruschettas and pizzas alfresco with one of their great cappuccinos.

Sky Restaurant (Sky Tower, Rruga Dëshmorët e 4 Shkurtit; mains 500 lekë; ☺ 9am-midnight) Spectacular city views from the revolving restaurant and the breezy terrace on top of one of the highest buildings in town. Watch the sunset with good pasta, rice or couscous dishes.

Villa Ambassador (☎ 038-202 4293; Rruga Themistokli Gërmenji; mains 500 lekë; ☒ noon-11.30pm) A homely atmosphere, fantastic service and tasty Albanian dishes for carnivores and vegetarians alike. This former embassy is among Tirana's best food choices.

There are two great food markets, one off Rruga Abdyl Frasheri and the other one on Rruga Hohxa Tasim, with certified organic fruit and vegetables and dairy products.

Serenata (☎ 273 088; Rruga Mihal Duri 7; mains 500-1000 lekë; ☒ 9am-midnight) Specialising in Korçan food, which consists of meat dishes like oven-baked liver, veal and wild boar, and vegetarian delicacies such as the Korça spinach and ricotta pancake-thin *byrek* served on a wooden board, or roasted peppers and aubergines in vinegar. This place is traditionally decorated and has gentle Korçan music *(serenata)* tinkling from the speakers.

Living Room Bar (☎ 242 481; Bulevardi Zhan d'Ark, Pall Italiane 1; ☒ 24hr) One of the hippest places to drink and dance in Tirana, with an eclectic DJ on weekends and a good crowd. Cool lampshades, '70s armchairs and sofas for you to lounge on when you're danced (or drunk) off your feet.

Buda Bar (☎ 068-205 8825; Rruga Ismail Qemali; ☒ 9am-late) All about a relaxed atmosphere with subdued lighting, incense burning, chaise longues and armchairs abounding with cushions.

ENTERTAINMENT

There is a good choice of entertainment options in Tirana, in the form of bars, clubs, cinema, performances and exhibitions. For the low-down on events and exhibitions check out the monthly leaflet *ARTirana* (a free supplement to *Gazeta Shqiptare*), which contains English, French, Italian and Albanian summaries of the cultural events currently showing in town.

Cinemas

Kinema Millennium (☎ 248 647; Rruga e Kavajës; admission 200-400 lekë) The best cinema in Tirana, it shows recent box-office hits (earlier shows are cheaper).

Kinema Millenium 2 (☎ 253 654; Rruga Murat Toptani; admission 200-500 lekë) A second location nearby shows art-house productions and boasts a lovely garden bar. All films are shown in the original language with Albanian subtitles.

Live Music

Next to the university, Qemal Stafa Stadium often hosts pop concerts and other musical events. Look out for street banners bearing details of upcoming events. Football matches are held here every Saturday and Sunday afternoon.

Boom Boom Room (☎ 243 702; Gjin Bue Shpata; ☒ 7pm-2am) A smoky jazz crowd with live performances most evenings and a lively atmosphere.

Theatre of Opera and Ballet (TOB; Sheshi Skënderbeg; performances from 7pm, winter from 6pm) Check the listings and posters outside for performances. You can usually buy tickets half an hour before the show for 200 lekë.

Academy of Arts (☎ 257 237; Sheshi Nene Teresa) Classical music performances take place throughout the year in this building opposite the Archaeological Museum. Prices vary according to the programme.

Nightclubs

Rozafa Club (Rruga Ismail Qemali; ☒ 8pm-late) Next door to the Buda Bar, this is the place to dance till dawn. House, hard house and techno dominate the DJ repertoire.

SHOPPING

Tirana's eclectic public market, north of the Sheshi Avni Rustemi roundabout several blocks east of the clock tower, is largest on Thursday and Sunday. Some stalls sell folk objects such as carved wooden trays, small boxes, wall hangings and bone necklaces, but many just sell cheap house supplies for the locals.

There are a few good souvenir shops around Sheshi Skënderbeg, on Rruga Durrësit and Bulevardi Zogu I. Most of them sell the same things: Albanian flags, carved wooden plates, and traditional textiles.

GETTING THERE & AWAY
Air

Many of the airline offices are on Rruga Durrësit, just off Sheshi Skënderbeg. **Alitalia** (☎ 230 023; Sheshi Skënderbeg) has an office behind the National Museum of History, and **Swiss International Air Lines** (☎ /fax 232 011; Bulevardi Dëshmorët e Kombit) and **Austrian Airlines** (☎ /fax 374 355; Bulevardi Dëshmorët e Kombit) are at Rogner Hotel Europapark Tirana. **Olympic Airways** (☎ 228 960; Ve-Ve Business Centre, Bulevardi Zogu I) is north of the Tirana International

Hotel, and **Turkish Airlines** (☎ 234 185) is in the Tirana International Hotel.

Bus

The *furgon* (minibus) system can seem pretty confusing at first, so pay attention now: all *furgons* going north (Kruja, Lezha, Shkodra) leave and drop you off at the Zogu i Zi terminal just off Rruga Durrësit. If you are going south, your bus/*furgon* will leave from Rruga e Kavajës, west of Sheshi Skënderbeg.

The following table will give you an idea of distances and average costs involved for departures from Tirana. *Furgons* are usually 40% to 50% more expensive than buses.

Destination	Cost	Duration	Distance
Berat	250 lekë	3½hr	122km
Durrës	100 lekë	1hr	38km
Elbasan	300 lekë	1½hr	54km
Fier	260 lekë	3hr	113km
Gjirokastra	700 lekë	7hr	232km
Korça	700 lekë	4hr	181km
Kruja	150 lekë	¾hr	32km
Kukës	1000 lekë	8hr	208km
Pogradec	600 lekë	3½hr	150km
Saranda	800 lekë	8hr	284km
Shkodra	300 lekë	2½hr	116km
Vlora	300 lekë	4hr	147km

Note that both buses and *furgons* normally leave when full. Pay the driver or conductor on the bus.

Car & Motorcycle

For car rental, **Hertz** (☎ 255 028; Rruga Ded Gjo Lulli) has vehicles starting from €70 per day for an Opel Corsa and takes Visa payments. **Europcar** (☎ 246 192; Rruga e Durrësit, L.61) offers similar services. Driving in Albania is only for those with nerves of steel as roads are often bad and kamikaze local drivers try to overtake on even the bendiest of bends and is therefore not recommended.

Train

The run-down train station is at the northern end of Bulevardi Zogu I. Eight trains daily go to Durrës (55 lekë, one hour, 36km). Trains also depart for Elbasan (160 lekë, four hours, three daily), for Pogradec (245 lekë, seven hours, twice daily), for Shkodra (150 lekë, 3½ hours, twice daily) and for Vlora (210 lekë, 5½ hours, twice daily).

GETTING AROUND
To/From the Airport

Mother Teresa Airport is 26km northwest of Tirana. There is no public transport to the airport so you'll have to taxi it to and fro (which should cost about €30).

Car & Motorcycle

Some of the major hotels offer guarded parking; others have parking available out front.

Taxi

Taxi stands dot the city and charge 400 lekë for a ride inside Tirana (600 lekë at night). Make sure you reach an agreement with the driver before setting off. **Radio Taxi** (☎ 377 777), with 24-hour service, is particularly reliable.

AROUND TIRANA
Durrës

☎ 052 / pop 85,000

An ancient city and Albania's old capital, Durrës has a 10km-long built-up beach stretching south where families play football and people stroll and cool down in the shallow waters of the Adriatic. Unfortunately, cars also drive on the beach which can make sunbathing something of a risky activity. Ancient remains, an interesting museum and good bus and train connections make Durrës a great base for archaeological exploration of places such as Apollonia, and a quieter alternative to the capital.

ORIENTATION

The town centre is easily covered on foot, although you might do well to get a taxi to any of the far ends of the beach. In the centre, the Xhamia e Madhe Durrës mosque can serve as a point of orientation: the archaeological attractions are immediately around it, and the train and bus stations plus the harbour are to the east. The palace of King Ahmet Zogu and the lighthouse are west, on the hill-top.

INFORMATION

The **post office** and **telephone centre** (Rruga Aldo Moro) are located one block west of the train and bus stations. Several Internet cafés operate in the town. All charge around 200 lekë per hour.

Galaxy Internet Café (☎ 068-213 5637; Rruga Taulantia)
Interalb Internet (Rruga N Frashëri)

Patrik Internet (Rruga Aleksandër Goga)
Savings Bank of Albania (☽ 8am-2pm Mon-Fri)
Across the bus parking lot from the train station, it changes
travellers cheques and offers MasterCard advances for a
1% commission.

SIGHTS

The newly built **Archaeological Museum** (admission 200 lekë; ☽ 8am-4pm Wed-Sun) on the waterfront is well lit and has artefacts from the Greek, Hellenistic and Roman periods on the ground floor. The Byzantine collection is expected to open soon.

Beyond the museum are the 6th-century **Byzantine city walls**, built after the Visigoth invasion of AD 481 and supplemented by round Venetian towers in the 14th century.

The impressive but neglected **Roman amphitheatre** was built on the hillside just inside the city walls between the 1st and 2nd centuries AD; in its prime it had the capacity to seat 15,000 spectators. Roam the vaults where the gladiators entered the arena and smell the memory of the bloodthirsty lions.

On the hill top west of the amphitheatre stands the **former palace of King Ahmet Zogu**,

which is not open to the public as it is a military area. It's a 1.5km walk to the top of the hill, but the views of the bay make it well worth the climb. A **lighthouse** stands on the next hill from where you can enjoy the royal views and check out the bunker constellation (see boxed text p31).

In the town centre you can find the small **Roman baths** directly behind Aleksandër Moisiu Theatre, on the central square. The large and not-so-graceful **Xhamia e Madhe Durrës** mosque on the square was erected with Egyptian aid in 1993, after the original one was destroyed in the earthquake of 1979.

SLEEPING

Durrës has a variety of accommodation in the city itself and many, many hotels line the long beaches of Kavaja and Golemi i Mali Robit.

In Town
Albania Travel & Tours (☎ 24 276; fax 25 450; Rruga Durrah; ☽ 8am-8pm) Near the port, they may be able to help arrange a private room given advance notice.

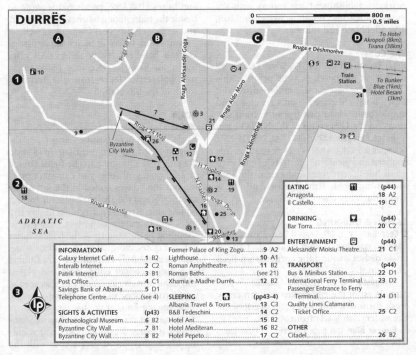

DURRËS

INFORMATION		
Galaxy Internet Café.................1	B2	
Interalb Internet.......................2	C2	
Patrik Internet.........................3	B1	
Post Office...............................4	C1	
Savings Bank of Albania............5	D1	
Telephone Centre...............(see 4)		
SIGHTS & ACTIVITIES	(p43)	
Archaeological Museum............6	B2	
Byzantine City Wall..................7	B1	
Byzantine City Wall..................8	B2	

Former Palace of King Zogu........9	A2	
Lighthouse.............................10	A1	
Roman Amphitheatre...............11	B2	
Roman Baths......................(see 21)		
Xhamia e Madhe Durrës...........12	B2	
SLEEPING	(pp43-4)	
Albania Travel & Tours.............13	C3	
B&B Tedeschini.......................14	C2	
Hotel Ani...............................15	B2	
Hotel Mediteran.....................16	B2	
Hotel Pepeto.........................17	C2	

EATING		(p44)
Arragosta...............................18	A2	
Il Castello...............................19	C2	
DRINKING		(p44)
Bar Torra...............................20	C2	
ENTERTAINMENT		(p44)
Aleksandër Moisiu Theatre.........21	C1	
TRANSPORT		(p44)
Bus & Minibus Station..............22	D1	
International Ferry Terminal.......23	D2	
Passenger Entrance to Ferry		
Terminal................................24	D1	
Quality Lines Catamaran		
Ticket Office...........................25	C2	
OTHER		
Citadel..................................26	B2	

B&B Tedeschini (☎ 24 343, 068-224 6303; ipmcrsp@icc .al.eu.org; Dom Nikoll Kaçorri 5; per person US$15) This gracious, 19th-century former Italian consulate has airy rooms with antique furniture, watched over by portraits of former consuls. From the square fronting the mosque, walk towards Il Castello. Take the first right, a quick left, then a quick right.

Hotel Mediteran (☎ 24 319; fax 27 074; Rruga Kolonel Thomson; per person €20) Perched on the corner of the city walls, behind Bar Torra, this friendly family-run place has great views of monuments and the sea from some of its balconies.

Hotel Pepeto (☎ 24 190; fax 26 346; Rruga H Troplini; s/d US$40/60; ✖) Hardly any views but there is laundry service at the hotel just off the square fronting the mosque. The rooms are decent, clean, quiet, with good showers, TV and air-con. For deluxe pleasure, the attic suite upstairs at US$60 per night is laden with sheepskin rugs on floors, beds and chairs alike – oh yes, and an exercise bike.

Hotel Ani (☎ 24 288; fax 30 478; Lagja 1, Rruga Taulantia; s/d US$60/90; ✖) On the waterfront opposite the museum, this relatively upmarket establishment has rooms with sea views (and some building work), air-con, TV, telephone and minibar.

The Coast

Hotel Besani (☎ 068-203 5781; Skëmbi i Kavajës; s/d US$20/40) If the beach is your priority, this is one of the best choices among dozens of beach hotels. Sea-view rooms are clean and comfortable. Head east from the train station and it's 1km south of the NATO base.

Hotel Akropoli (☎ 0579-22 142, 068-214 0070; Golem; s/d US$30/40) Another 5km south is this modern and pleasant resort-style hotel with an in-house restaurant and a small outdoor swimming pool. Ring beforehand for a complimentary chauffeur service.

EATING & DRINKING

Il Castello (☎ 26 887; Rruga H Troplini 3; mains 400 lekë; ☎ 9am-11pm) Good seafood, fish or pasta dishes, around the corner from B&B Tedeschini.

Arragosta (☎ 26 477, Rruga Taulantia; ☽ 9am-11pm) West of the city centre you can enjoy fresh shrimp or fish on a patio overlooking the water. Fish starts from 900 lekë per kg.

Bunker Blue (per plate 350 lekë; ☽ 11am-10pm) The best food option in Durrës. Not actually a bunker, although it is blue, this taverna right on the beach 1km south of the harbour has fresh and cheap fish and seafood.

Bar Torra (Rruga Kolonel Thomson; ☽ 8am-midnight) Housed in a fortified tower, there are inside tables where cannon used to fire. There's a roof terrace for cheap alfresco eating (order a panini for 100 lekë) or drinking coffee, cocktails or beer under the stars.

ENTERTAINMENT

You could pay a visit to the **Aleksandër Moisiu Theatre** (Rruga Aldo Moro). Its frequent theatrical productions are performed only in Albanian, however.

GETTING THERE & AWAY

Albania's 720km railway network centres on Durrës. There are eight trains a day to Tirana (55 lekë, one hour), two to Shkodra (150 lekë, 3½ hours) via Lezha, three to Pogradec (245 lekë, 6¾ hours) via Elbasan, and two to Vlora (210 lekë, five hours) via Fier. The train station is beside the Tirana highway, conveniently close to central Durrës.

Furgons to Tirana (150 lekë, one hour) and buses (100 lekë, one hour) leave from beside the train station whenever they're full, and service elsewhere is frequent as well.

Numerous travel agencies along Rruga Durrah handle ferry bookings. All offer much the same service (see p58). International ferries leave from the terminal south of the bus station.

Kruja
☎ 053 / pop 17,400

Kruja's impressive beauty starts from the journey itself, up the winding road, into the grey rocky mountain. The fields stretch around you, and soon you can start making out the houses seated in the lap of the mountain, and the ancient castle jutting out on one side. Kruja is a magnificent day trip from Tirana and the best place for souvenir shopping in the country – the bazaar hides antique gems and quality traditional ware, such as beautifully embroidered traditional tablecloths, copper coffee pots and plates, and hand-woven rugs. You can also see the wonderful process of women hand-weaving these rugs (*qilims*) at the bazaar.

As you get off the bus a statue of Skanderbeg (George Kastrioti, 1405–68) wielding his mighty sword greets you, with the

ALBANIA

sharp mountain edges as his backdrop. In fact, this hill-top town attained its greatest fame between 1443 and 1468 when national hero Skanderbeg made Kruja his seat of government. At a young age, Kastrioti, son of an Albanian prince, was handed over as a hostage to the Turks, who converted him to Islam and gave him a military education at Edirne. There he became known as Iskander (after Alexander the Great) and Sultan Murat II promoted him to the rank of *bey* (governor), thus the name Skanderbeg (Skënderbeg).

In 1443 the Turks suffered a defeat at the hands of the Hungarians at Niš in present-day Serbia and Montenegro, which gave the nationally minded Skanderbeg the opportunity he had been waiting for to abandon the Ottoman army and Islam and rally his fellow Albanians against the Turks. Among the 13 Turkish invasions he subsequently repulsed was that led by his former commander Murat II in 1450. Pope Calixtus III named Skanderbeg the 'captain general of the Holy See' and Venice formed an alliance with him. The Turks besieged Kruja four times. Though beaten back in 1450, 1466 and 1467, they took control of Kruja in 1478 (after Skanderbeg's death) and Albanian resistance was suppressed.

The main sight in Kruja is the splendid **castle** and its rather retro-modernistic **Skanderbeg Museum** (admission 200 lekë; ☉ 8am-1pm & 3-8pm). Designed by Enver Hoxha's daughter and son-in-law, it mainly displays replicas of armour and paintings depicting Skanderbeg's struggle against the Ottomans.

The **Ethnographic Museum** (☎ 22 225; admission 200 lekë; ☉ 8am-1pm & 3-8pm) is certainly one of the most interesting experiences in Kruja. Set in an original 19th-century house opposite the Skanderbeg Museum that used to belong to an affluent Albanian family, you can see the level of luxury and self-sufficiency maintained in the household with the production of food, drink, leather, weapons etc, including their very own steam bath. The English-speaking guide will explain everything in detail; it's polite to give the guide a tip of 100 or 200 lekë.

Dollma teqe is a small place of worship for the Bektashi branch of Islam (see p33), maintained by successive generations of the Dollma family since 1789. It was resurrected after the fall of the communist

regime and is now functioning again. The views from the terrace of the plains below are breathtaking.

Kruja is 6.5km off the main road to Tirana. A cab to Kruja from Tirana will cost around 3000 lekë while a *furgon* will cost 150 lekë.

Mt Dajti National Park

Mt Dajti (1610m) is a national park visible from Tirana 25km to the east. It is the most accessible mountain in the country and many Tiranans go there on the weekends to escape the city rush and have a spit-roast lamb lunch. Put your sturdy shoes on for a gentle hike in the lovely, shady beech and pine forests and have a coffee and enjoy the spectacular views from the wide terrace of Restaurant Panorama, the most popular spot on Dajti.

The only downside is that there is no public transport to the mountain, so unless you have private transport you will have to get a taxi from the city; the ride takes about 45 minutes, whereupon you can arrange to phone the driver to pick you up when you want to go back. The taxi ride shouldn't set you back more than 600 lekë to 700 lekë each way.

If you are driving, the road to Dajti starts on Rruga Qemal Stafa past the Chateau Linza Hotel.

Apollonia

The ruined city of ancient **Apollonia** (Pojan; admission 700 lekë; ☉ 9am-5pm) is 12km west of Fier, itself 89km south of Durrës. Set on rolling hills among olive groves, the views expand for miles around the plains below.

Look at the picturesque 3rd-century BC **House of Mosaics**, and examine the elegant pillars on the façade of the city's 2nd-century AD administrative centre. The Byzantine church of St Mary is a jewel with fascinating gargoyles on the outside pillars. In the church garden you can see artefacts displayed, although marked only in Albanian.

Apollonia was founded by Corinthian Greeks in 588 BC and quickly grew into an important city-state, minting its own currency. Under the Romans the city became a great cultural centre with a famous school of philosophy. Julius Caesar rewarded Apollonia with the title 'free city' for supporting him against Pompey the Great during the civil war in the 1st century BC, and sent his nephew Octavius, the future Emperor Augustus, to complete his studies there. After a series of military disasters, the population moved southward into present-day Vlora, and by the 5th century only a small village with its own bishop remained at Apollonia.

Apollonia is best visited on day trips from Tirana or Durrës. The lack of public transport to Apollonia means that you will have to get a bus/*furgon*/train to the nearest town, Fier. The bus from Durrës will cost 200 lekë (1½ hours), and it's 300 lekë from Tirana (two hours). Once in Fier, you will have to get a taxi – you should expect to be charged around 2500 lekë for a return journey (30 minutes each way) and an hour's waiting-time.

Berat
☎ 062 / pop 47,700

Berat is one of Albania's most beautiful towns and thanks to being the second 'museum city' in the country, its churches and mosques were spared destruction during the atheist campaign. Divided by the Osum River, one part of the town is perched on the hill top and overlooks the houses resting at the foot of the hill on the opposite riverbank. Sometimes called the 'city of a thousand windows', Berat features white houses stacked on top of each other and their many panes reflect and multiply the sun.

In the 3rd century BC an Illyrian fortress called Antipatria was built here on the site of an earlier settlement. The Byzantines strengthened the hill-top fortifications in the 5th and 6th centuries, as did the Bulgarians 400 years later. The Serbs, who occupied the citadel in 1345, renamed it Beligrad, or 'White City', and there is speculation that this is where the town's name comes from. In 1450 the Ottoman Turks took Berat. After a period of decline the town began to thrive in the 18th and 19th centuries as a Turkish crafts centre specialising in woodcarving. For a brief time in 1944 Berat was the capital of liberated Albania.

SIGHTS
There is plenty to see in this small town and the best place to start is the impressive

14th-century **citadel** (admission 50 lekë; ⊗ 24hr) along a ridge high above the gorge. The citadel is still inhabited and the houses below the castle form the traditionally Muslim quarter called **Mangalem**. Inside the citadel walls is the **Onufri Museum** (admission 100 lekë; ⊗ 9am-2pm Mon-Fri), in the church of St Mary, displaying some of the most spectacular colour work in iconographic art by master Onufri (see p33).

Two mosques, both near the city centre by the river, are worth seeing: the slim minaret of the 16th-century **Leaden Mosque** (Xhamiëe Plumbit) piercing the sky, and the 19th-century **Bachelors' Mosque** (Xhamië e Beqarëvet) with enchanting paintings on the external walls.

A seven-arched stone bridge (1780) leads to **Gorica**, the Christian quarter, where you can visit the old **Monastery of St Spyridon** and see the lovely citadel and its houses stretching before you.

SLEEPING & EATING
Tomori Hotel (☎ 34 462; fax 34 602; s/d €30/40) A tower-block hotel with nice, clean rooms overlooking either the citadel or the mountains. There's a good restaurant and lively terrace bar downstairs. It's located on the main square by the bus station.

Nova Restaurant (mains 500 lekë; ⊗ 10am-11pm) Succulent shish kebabs with generous salad portions on a sunny terrace overlooking the citadel. It's east of the citadel entrance.

GETTING THERE & AWAY
Buses and *furgons* go frequently between Tirana and Berat. From Tirana, they leave from Rruga e Kavajës, and go every hour on the hour until 5pm. From Durrës, they depart from outside the railway station. The journey takes 2½ to three hours and costs 250 lekë. In Berat, all buses depart and arrive at the bus station, next to the Leaden Mosque.

SOUTHERN ALBANIA

Stunning views of sharp, snowcapped mountain peaks, wide green valleys zigzagged by rivers, and inviting white beach crescents touching the gentle blue sea make southern Albania the most visually exciting part of the country.

VLORA
☎ 033

One of Albania's major cities, the Mediterranean port of Vlora (the ancient Avlon) is where the Adriatic and Ionian Seas meet and form a blue line across the clear waters. This is a bustling little city with a long palm-tree lined avenue stretching across the centre of town towards the seafront and the beaches, with plenty to explore for a day or two. Vlora's main claim to fame is that it was the place where Albanian independence was proclaimed in 1912.

Information

Everything you'll need in Vlora is on the avenue of Sadik Zotaj which runs across the centre of the city. A small room with half a dozen computers passes for an **Internet café** (per hr 200 lekë; ⓨ 9am-noon) halfway up the long avenue. On the lower end is the **Savings Bank of Albania** (ⓨ 8am-2pm) and the main post office with its three branches and telephone centres dotted along the avenue.

Sights

If you walk from the top of Zotaj towards the harbour, you will first see the **Independence** or **Flag Sq**. The dark **Independence Monument** stands proud against the sky, representing the key figures in the movement for Albania's sovereignty as the flag bearer hoists the double-headed eagle into the blue.

Walk down towards the **Muradi Mosque**, a small elegant structure in red and white stone with a modest minaret, whose exquisite design is attributed to one of the greatest Ottoman architects, Sinan Pasha, himself Albanian-born. On the other side of the avenue is the **Historical Museum** (admission 100 lekë; ⓨ 9am-2pm & 7-9pm Tue-Sun), housed in what was originally the town hall, with artefacts showing the history of the Vlora area up until recent times. Opposite, behind an inconspicuous grey metal gate, is the **Ethnographic Museum** (admission 100 lekë; ⓨ 9am-2pm Tue-Sun). This house saw the establishment of the Labëria Patriotic Club, which played a major part in Albania's movement for independence. Further down and by the harbour is the **Museum of Independence** (admission 100 lekë; ⓨ 9am-noon & 5-8pm) with plenty of old ministerial ornaments, photographs and maps, all recording Albania's road to sovereignty.

Vlora's **main beaches** stretch south from the harbour and the further you go, the better they get. Skela is the harbour beach area with many hotels and restaurants, continuing down to Plazhi i Ri, the long sandy space which can get quite crowded. A good 2km walk, tranquil Uji i Ftohtë is the best beach by far with its clear waters.

Sleeping

Palma (☎ 29 320; Uji i Ftohtë beach; per person €8) Seated on top of a hill with views of the Bay of Vlora to die for, this magnificent former workers' camp still gives off a whiff of socialist idealism. An explosion of light, colour and large 70s patterns, encircled by gorgeous gardens, this is the best budget choice. There are basic double and triple rooms with run-down bathrooms.

Tozo (☎ 23 819; Lagja Isa Boletini; per person €15) Just off Zotaj, behind a small park, this friendly and comfortable little hotel has luxurious beds in large rooms, good bathrooms, air-conditioning and TVs.

Amantia (☎ 24 853; Skela Beach; r €30) A wooden hut-style hotel with a communal porch on the 1st floor where you can imagine someone playing the blues. Small rooms overlook the harbour and have air-conditioning, good bathrooms and TVs.

Eating

Kobolira (☎ 068-220 4430; Skela Beach; mains 340-400 lekë; ⓨ 9am-11pm) For traditional Vloran baked fish (tavë peshku), this is your place.

Riciola (☎ 069-255 3469; Skela Beach; mains 400 lekë, fresh fish around 1000 lekë; ⓨ 9am-11pm) Good fish dishes and seafood pasta in a convivial local atmosphere.

Getting There & Away

Getting to Vlora from Tirana and Durrës is easy, with buses and *furgons* whizzing back and forth in the morning hours. The bus fare is 300 lekë (400 lekë for the *furgon*) and the journey lasts around three hours. Buses from Vlora to Saranda (six hours) and on to Gjirokastra (700 lekë, 5½ hours) leave at 6 and 7am. In Vlora, the bus terminus is easily spotted by the Muradi Mosque.

There's a daily ferry to Brindisi during the summer leaving each side at 10pm and docking at 7am. You can book through **Skenderbeg Lines** (in Brindisi ☎ 0831-52 54 48; fax 0831-56 26 62; Corso Garibaldi 100; per person €36).

IONIAN COAST
Llogaraja Pass (National Park)

The road going south from Vlora climbs up to the Llogaraja Pass, over 1000m high, for some of Albania's most spectacular scenery and delicious spit-roast lamb. If you are going to Dhërmi or Himara, this is the road you will take and you will see clouds descending onto the mountain, steep hillsides crashing into the sea below, shepherds on the plains guiding their herds, and thick forests where deer, wild boar and wolves roam. Despite the lame name the **Tourist Village** (Fshati Turistik; ☎ 068-212 8640; per chalet 8000 lekë) is the best place to stay if you decide to breathe the fresh air in Llogaraja. Wooden chalets with modern amenities, fresh food and pure spring water house up to four people.

Dhërmi & Drymades Beaches

Going down the coast road from Llogaraja Pass, the immaculate white crescent beaches and the azure waters will lure you from below. Dhërmi has several comfortable hotels, a beautiful long beach and is a popular summer destination among the locals and the expats. **Dhërmi Hotel** (☎ 068-224 6805; s/d 3000/5000 lekë), right on the beach, has decent rooms that all look onto the sea. The bathrooms are sparkling clean and the hotel restaurant serves excellent fresh fish mains for 500 lekë.

A half-hour walk through some olive groves brings you to Drymades, a quieter option, with a white virgin beach stretching before you. You can stay in a bungalow, camp or simply sleep under the stars on the beach. To get to Drymades, turn off the asphalted road going down into Dhërmi, at the sign indicating 1200m to Drymades Beach. **Drymades Hotel** (☎ 068-228 5637; per bungalow 4000 lekë) is a constellation of bungalows under the shade of pine trees, a step away from the blue sea. Each can house two to three people, although the interiors are a little shabby. There's a bar and restaurant in the shade, plus a beach bar with a straw roof.

Himara
☎ 0393

This sleepy, dusty small town has a lovely beach that comes alive in the summer months with holiday-makers strolling down the promenade. The waters are clear and

warm, the beach sandy and the fresh fish in the restaurants delicious. Himara, although small, is the largest town between Vlora and Saranda. **Likoka** (☎ 2745, 068-226 3608; per person €20) is a white, circular hotel halfway down the beach with spacious rooms and light balconies for alfresco breakfasts overlooking the sea. Eat fish, pizza or pasta on the veranda of the hotel restaurant for 450 lekë.

Getting There & Away

Buses go regularly between Vlora and Saranda via Himara and stop at the Llogaraja Pass and Dhërmi on the way. Ask the conductor when you get on to let you off at your destination. At Llogaraja, the best place to be dropped off is at the Tourist Village, 1km from the summit. In Dhërmi, the bus stop is in the village on the mountain road and you have to make your own way down to the beach, which is an easy 10-minute walk downhill (not so easy on the way back though).

Buses run from 7am between Saranda, Himara and Vlora, and *furgons* go from Himara itself, from the seafront at the end of the promenade.

Possibly the best and certainly the most comfortable way to see everything is by hydrofoil linking Corfu with Saranda, Himara and Vlora and back. This operates only in the summer months, on Wednesdays and Saturdays, but daily in August. Contact **Colombo Agency** (☎ 033-23 578/27 659) in Vlora for details.

SARANDA
pop 12,000

Horseshoe-shaped Saranda is a stone's throw from the Greek island of Corfu (27km) and a good point to cross into Albania from Greece and vice versa. Its houses descend from the hillsides, small boats bob on the blue sea, people stroll up and down the relaxing promenade and the town boasts around 290 sunny days a year. An early Christian monastery dedicated to 40 saints (Santi Quaranta) gave Saranda its name.

Most of Saranda's attractions are a little outside of the town itself. Nearby is the mesmerising ancient archaeological site of Butrint, the hypnotic Blue Eye Spring, and some lovely beaches at Ksamili village where you can dip and refresh after a day of exploring.

Information

Change money at **Exchange Mario** (☎ 0852-23 61; Rruga Vangeli Gramoza) or with the crowds of moneychangers near the central square. Receive money at the Western Union office in the modern **post office** (☎ 0852-23 45; Vangjel Pango) nearby. Cardphones abound while mobile-phone users can pick up Greek transmitters as well as Albanian ones. Email and print from the coffee-less **Internet Café** (Rruga 1 Maji; per hr 250 lekë).

Sights

The ancient ruins of **Butrint** (☎ 0732-46 00; admission 700 lekë; ⊗ 8am-7.30pm), 18km south of Saranda, are renowned for their size and beauty. In a fantastic natural setting, part of a 29-sq-km national park, you will need at least three hours to lose yourself and thoroughly explore this fascinating place. Bring water and snacks with you, as there are no eating and drinking facilities at the site.

The poet Virgil (70–19 BC) claimed that the Trojans founded Buthrotum (Butrint), but no evidence of this has been found. Although the site had been inhabited long before, Greeks from Corfu settled on the hill in Butrint in the 6th century BC. Within a century Butrint had become a fortified trading city with an acropolis. The lower town began to develop in the 3rd century BC and many large stone buildings had already been built by the time the Romans took over in 167 BC. Butrint's prosperity continued throughout the Roman period and the Byzantines made it an ecclesiastical centre. The city subsequently went into decline, and it was almost abandoned by 1927 when Italian archaeologists arrived and began carting off any relics of value to Italy. WWII interrupted their work and some of these relics, such as the 'Goddess of Butrint' have since been returned to Tirana's National Museum of History.

As you enter the site the path leads to the right, to Butrint's 3rd-century BC **Greek theatre**, secluded in the forest below the acropolis. Also in use during the Roman period, the theatre could seat about 2500 people. Close by are the small **public baths**, with geometric mosaics, which are unfortunately buried under the sand and cannot be seen. You are allowed to make a small hole to peek at the mosaics, but don't touch them, and do cover it up again.

Deeper in the forest is a wall covered with crisp Greek inscriptions, and a 6th-century palaeo-Christian **baptistry** decorated with colourful mosaics of animals and birds, again under the sand. Beyond are the impressive arches of the 6th-century **basilica** built over many years. A massive **Cyclopean wall** dating back to the 4th century BC is further on. Over one gate is a splendid relief of a lion killing a bull, symbolic of a protective force vanquishing assailants.

The top of the hill is where the **acropolis** once was; there's now a castle here, which is closed, but you can have a look around the courtyard. The view of the city from above gives you a good idea of its layout. You can enjoy the views of Lake Butrint from the courtyard and see the Vivari Channel which connects it to the Straits of Corfu.

There are no buses. A cab to Butrint from Saranda will cost around 2000 lekë and you can usually negotiate to get there and back and see the Blue Eye Spring for 4000 lekë.

The **Syri i Kalter** (Blue Eye Spring), about 15km east of Saranda, is a hypnotic spring of deep-blue water surrounded by electric-blue edges like the iris of an eye. It feeds the Bistrica River and its depth is still unknown. This is the perfect picnic spot, under the shade of the oak trees.

A better bathing alternative to Saranda's beaches is the sandy **Ksamili Beach** 17km south, with four small dreamy islands within swimming distance.

There is no public transport to Syri i Kalter or Ksamili Beach, so unless you are driving, you will have to get a taxi. A return journey to Syri i Kalter will cost you around 1000 lekë with half an hour's waiting-time, and around 500 lekë to Ksamili Beach. Since you will probably want to spend a longer time at Ksamili Beach, you can take the phone number of your taxi driver so you can arrange pick-up.

Sleeping & Eating

Kaonia (☎ 0852-26 00/26 08; Rruga 1 Maji; s/d 2000/3000 lekë) A lovely small hotel on the seafront with great beds, power showers, TVs and sea views.

Pizzeri Evangjelos (☎ 0852-54 29; ne Shetitore; pizzas 350-600 lekë; ⊗ 11am-11pm) Superb wood-oven pizzas are served up in the garden.

Getting There & Away

A daily ferry and hydrofoil service plies between Saranda and Corfu (US$17 one way). Call **Petrakis Lines** (☎ 0030-661-31649/38690/25155; http://corfu2.250free.com/petrakis/1.htm El Venizeleou New Port 491 00, Corfu, Greece) in Corfu for schedules from Corfu. The hydrofoil normally leaves Saranda at 10am.

Buses to Tirana (1000 lekë, eight hours) and Gjirokastra (300 lekë, 1½ hours) leave from Saranda's bus station four times daily, while there are two to three services a week to Korça (1000 lekë, eight hours).

A taxi to the Greek border at Kakavija will cost 3500 lekë while a cab to the border near Konispoli will cost around 3000 lekë.

GJIROKASTRA

☎ 084 / pop 24,500

Ancient Gjirokastra watches over the magnificent valley beneath it from its rocky perch, and visitors climbing its steep cobbled streets will be enchanted by the magic of the place. Spend the day absorbing the life of its labyrinthine streets, where the pace is slow and suspended in the past, and for an architectural feast, check out the unique houses and the dark castle overlooking the town.

Gjirokastra means 'silver castle' in Greek (Argyrokastro) and the town was well established and prosperous by the 13th century, but declined after the arrival of the Turks in 1417. The 17th century brought about improvement and the town became a major trading centre with a flourishing bazaar where embroidery, felt, silk and the still-famous white cheese were traded. One of the Ottoman Empire's most prominent individuals, Ali Pasha Tepelena, seized the town in the early 19th century and strengthened the citadel.

Gjirokastra was the birthplace of former dictator Enver Hoxha who awarded it the status of 'museum city' and thus special care was taken to retain its traditional architecture.

Sights

Gjirokastra's **19th-century houses** are a rare experience, and are reason enough to visit this small town. Their grey slate roofs blend into each other when seen from the front of the **castle** (admission 500 lekë; ☽ 8am-8pm), the city's most dominant feature.

Built from the 6th century AD onwards, this brooding giant was used as a prison by King Zogu, the Nazis and the communists until 1971, when it became a museum. You can see the torture rooms if you are that way inclined. There is also a weapons display in one of the dreary rooms inside the castle. A 1957 **US military spy plane** displayed on the ramparts is a bizarre addition to the scene.

Sleeping & Eating

Guest House Haxhi Kotoni (☎ 35 26; Lagja Palorto 8, Rruga Bashkim Kokona; s/d incl breakfast 1500/2000 lekë) A cheaper option, with small but clean and comfy double rooms with TV and heating.

Kalemi (☎/fax 467 260; Lagja Palorto; r incl breakfast 4000 lekë) A cross between a hotel and a museum, this is the most authentic experience of old Albania, with original carved wood ceilings and stone fireplaces in the 1st floor rooms. The breakfast is delicious.

Argjiro (off Sheshi Çerçiz Topulli; mains 300-400 lekë; ☽ 11am-midnight) This small homely restaurant offers tasty traditional dishes.

Riçiola restaurant (☎ 069-255 3469; Lagja Palorto; mains 450 lekë; ☽ 11am-midnight) If you want spectacular views of the castle and town with your dinner, walk uphill or use the complimentary pick-up and drop-off service.

Getting There & Away

Buses to and from Gjirokastra stop on the main highway, 1.5km from the old town. Taxis can take you into town for about 200 lekë. Buses to Tirana (1000 lekë, eight hours) are fairly frequent. There are four a day to Saranda (300 lekë, 1½ hours) and one to Korça (700 lekë, six hours). You'll need to take a taxi to get to the Greek border at Kakavija (1500 lekë, 30 minutes).

KORÇA

☎ 082 / pop 62,200

Korça's wide, tree-lined streets are dotted with grandiose warm-coloured French-style houses and the town prides itself as being one of the most 'civilised' places in Albania, with no mud or rubbish in the streets. It is a good place to spend a day and relax with a stroll in the evening looking at the houses and the many domes of the Orthodox cathedral in the main town square. There is a busy market by the bus station where goats get sold and carried off like handbags, and where you can buy everything, from fruit and vegetables to pumping music and livestock.

Sleeping & Eating

Hotel Gold (☎ 46 894; Rruga Kiço Golniku 5; s/d 1888/2830 lekë) The best budget option in town with clean rooms, TVs and heating, and en suite bathrooms. Follow the signs for 800m from the avenue leading from the bus stop to the main square.

Hotel Grand (☎ 43 168; fax 42 677; Central Sq; s/d 2950/4720 lekë) Around the corner from the bus station, this is a comfortable hotel with a rather grandiose and gilded reception area and large plants. The rooms are spacious, the beds good and bathrooms have shower curtains – a rarity in Albania.

Restaurant Alfa (☎ 44 385; Bulevardi Shën Gjergji; mains 400-500 lekë; ☷ 9am-midnight Mon-Sat) Off the main square with a tasty Greek menu and a good atmosphere.

Vasport (☎ 50 388; Rruga Naim Frashëri; mains around 500-600 lekë; ☷ 9am-midnight) Opposite the cathedral with a popular bar on the ground and 1st floors, the restaurant has a rustic feel, decent meat and good wine.

Getting There & Away

Buses and *furgons* all congregate at the official bus station, north of the main square. Arriving *furgons* will normally drop their passengers off on the main square also. *Furgons* to Tirana (700 lekë, four hours) depart when full.

For Greece there are three buses daily to Thessaloniki (€19, seven hours) and four a week to Athens (€30, 16 hours) at noon on Sunday, Monday, Thursday and Friday. Go to the ticket office in the street behind the Grand Hotel to book your seat.

Note: you can take a *furgon* to the border at Kapshtia for around 300 to 400 lekë, but a Greek taxi from the Albanian–Greek border to Florina or Kastoria alone will cost you a minimum of €30. There are only two to three inconveniently timed local buses daily linking the Greek border village of Krystallopigi with Florina, and none to Kastoria. The direct international bus from Korça is by far the best option; the trip takes around two hours.

NORTHERN ALBANIA

The northern Albanian landscape is a mixture of rich wildlife, swamps and lagoons around Shkodra and Lezha and high, unforgiving mountains in the northeast (named the Accursed Mountains, Bjeshkët e Namuna, in Albanian). Visits to northern Albania still involve some element of risk due to continuing instability in the neighbouring region. The main road corridor from Tirana to the border with Serbia and Montenegro (the area where Shkodra and Lezha are located) is generally fine.

SHKODRA

☎ 0224 / pop 91,300

Shkodra (also Shkodër), the traditional centre of the Gheg cultural region, is one of the oldest cities in Europe. Rozafa fortress is beautiful and the Marubi permanent photography exhibition is fascinating. Despite being slightly run down, the city makes a good half-day introduction to Albania for those entering from Serbia and Montenegro.

By 500 BC an Illyrian fortress already guarded the strategic crossing just west of the city where the Buna and Drin Rivers meet, through which all traffic moving up the coast from Greece to Montenegro must pass.

Queen Teuta's Illyrian kingdom was based here in the 3rd century BC. Despite wars with Rome in 228 and 219 BC, Shkodra was not taken by the Romans until 168 BC. Later the region passed to Byzantium before becoming the capital of the feudal realm of the Balshas in 1350. In 1396 the Venetians occupied Shkodra's Rozafa Fortress, which they held against Suleiman Pasha in 1473 but lost to Mehmet Pasha in 1479. The Turks lost 14,000 men in the first siege and 30,000 in the second.

As the Ottoman Empire declined in the late 18th century, Shkodra became the centre of a semi-independent *pashalik* (a region governed by a *pasha*, an Ottoman high official), which led to a blossoming of commerce and crafts. In 1913 Montenegro attempted to annex Shkodra (it succeeded in taking Ulcinj), a move not approved of by the international community, and the town changed hands often during WWI. Badly damaged by the 1979 earthquake,

Shkodra was subsequently repaired and now is Albania's fourth-largest town.

The route inland to Kosovo also begins in Shkodra. North of Shkodra, line after line of cement bunkers point the way to the Han i Hotit border crossing into Serbia and Montenegro (33km). Tirana is 116km south.

Sights

Two kilometres southwest of Shkodra, near the southern end of Lake Shkodra, is **Rozafa Fortress**, founded by the Illyrians in antiquity and rebuilt much later by the Venetians and Turks. The fortress derives its name from a woman named Rozafa, who was allegedly walled into the ramparts as an offering to the gods so that the construction would stand. The story goes that Rozafa asked that two holes be left in the stonework so that she could continue to suckle her baby. Nursing women still come to the fortress to smear their breasts with milky water taken from a spring here. There are marvellous views from the highest point.

WHEN A WOMAN BECOMES A MAN

The unusual phenomenon of the 'sworn virgin' – when a woman 'becomes' a man – still persists in rare instances in northern Albania (and some other parts of the Balkans), and is particular mainly to mountain villages, where local communities still live according to the traditional social code the *Kanun* (see p34).

According to the *Kanun* 'a woman is known as a sack made to endure as long as she lives in her husband's house'. It also states clearly that only sons who are over 15 can inherit the family's wealth. Since a woman can never own any of the family property (as she herself is considered only a part of that property), the family's wealth is at risk if there are no sons and all the male family members are deceased. A woman can then effectively become a man (a 'sworn virgin') in order to preserve her family's wealth and honour. Another reason (although this happens rarely) for becoming a 'sworn virgin' is if a woman refuses to enter into an arranged marriage. A woman can become a 'sworn virgin', either through her own choice or by the choice of her parents, any time before marriage.

Family duties normally fulfilled by sons or other male members, such as keeping the memory of the deceased alive, organising the household, inheriting the property, going to war, defending the family or taking part in blood feuds (see p34), are all effectively performed by the 'sworn virgin'. When she becomes a man, a 'sworn virgin' crops her hair, wears man's clothes, smokes, drinks and generally takes part in social activities limited to men. She takes a vow of celibacy (hence the 'sworn virgin') and may never get married. She usually adopts a masculine equivalent of her name and is henceforth known to the village by that name. Most of these women also become masculine in their behaviour, and it is often very hard to tell they are not actually men.

Most people in the village know that the 'sworn virgin' is in fact a woman, but she is nevertheless always treated as a man and respected as such by all the other men in the village. She is, however, referred to as 'aunt' or 'sister' by her relatives. The majority of the 'sworn virgins' are happy with their chosen lives as men, despite their renunciation of sexuality, marriage and childbirth. Leading a man's life is a great source of prestige in their society, whereas the role of women is to work and bear children. Women cannot take part in any social gatherings, except to serve food and drink to guests, and have no power to make decisions about their own lives or those of their children.

Many Albanians are unaware of the phenomenon of the 'sworn virgin', and it is not considered to be a subject of much interest. For those who live in rural areas and know of this tradition, it is part of normal life. Furthermore, 'sworn virgins' are not of interest to the feminist movement in Albania, as they reinforce the very patriarchal values they are fighting against. Similarly, 'sworn virgins' have no interest in any women's movement, since their values are the same as those held by men.

Some predict that this phenomenon will disappear with the erosion of close-knit extended families, arranged marriages and male-only inheritance rules, and in any case, as Albania becomes more accessible, the tradition will certainly have to adapt to the rules of the modern world.

(For more information on this subject, see *Women who Become Men – Albanian Sworn Virgins* by Antonia Young, Berg 2000).

Hidden inside a building that looks like a block of flats, the **Marubi Permanent Photo Exhibition** (Muhamet Gjollesha; admission free; ☉ 9am-1pm) boasts fantastic photography by the Marubi 'dynasty', Albania's first and foremost photographers. The first-ever photograph taken in Albania is here, taken by Pjetër Marubi in 1858. The exhibition shows fascinating portraits, places and events, including that of a young Enver Hoxha giving a speech while he was still in local government in Gjirokastra. Not only is this a rare insight into what things looked like in old Albania, it is also a collection of mighty fine photographs. To get there, go northeast of the clock tower into Çlirimi street, and Muhamet Gjollesha street darts off to the right. As the building is unmarked, you may have to ask for directions.

Good accommodation has been slow to emerge, so it's best to visit Shkodra as a day trip. There are frequent *furgons* from Tirana to Shkodra and back (300 lekë, 2½ hours), leaving Tirana from the Zogu i Zi terminal and dropping you off at the Shkodra bus station, on the outskirts of town, near Rozafa Castle.

LEZHA
☎ 0215

This quiet little town was home to one of Albania's most significant historic moments: it is the place where Gjergj Kastriot, Skanderbeg (see p44), brought the Albanian clan heads to unite against their common enemy, the Ottomans. He was also buried here in 1468, in Lezha's cathedral. The Ottomans ravaged his tomb some years later, and turned the cathedral into a mosque.

You can see **Skanderbeg's memorial tomb**, with the double-headed eagle flag stretched behind his bronze bust, in the remains of the cathedral. The double-headed eagle, now the emblem on Albania's flag, was originally Skanderbeg's family emblem.

Perhaps the most interesting reason for coming to Lezha is outside the town itself: **Hotel i Gjuetisë** (☎ 069-217 0898; Ishulli i Lezhës; r 2000 lekë, mains 500 lekë), Mussolini's former hunting lodge. Built in the 1930s by Mussolini's son-in-law, this gorgeous stone building with a fantastic restaurant (with open fireplaces) has recently reopened. It is set in a quiet wetland park rich with flora and rare birds, where you can stroll around while your food is being prepared, unless you choose to stay the night and do some proper exploring, of course. *Furgons* from Tirana to Shkodra stop at Lezha. The journey takes 1½ hours and costs 200 lekë. To get to Hotel i Gjuetisë you will have to take a taxi, which shouldn't set you back more than 500 lekë.

For bird enthusiasts, Velipoja and Kuna-Vaini National Parks are both nearby.

ALBANIA DIRECTORY

ACCOMMODATION

The accommodation reviews in this chapter are listed in order of price, from cheapest to most expensive. Albania's budget accommodation (from US$20 to US$30 for singles and US$30 to US$50 for doubles) is usually decent and clean; breakfast is often included in the price. Mid-range hotels are a notch up, with telephones and a touch of glamour to the rooms. They range from US$50 to US$60 for singles and US$70 to US$100 for doubles. Top-end hotels are on a par with modern European hotels in terms of comfort and facilities. Most top-end places offer satellite TV, Internet access, and some have swimming pools. Room prices start at US$140 to US$210 for a single, and US$190 to US$250 double.

Accommodation has undergone a rapid transformation in Albania, with the opening of new, custom-built, private hotels to replace the run-down state ones. Priced at about US$35 to US$50 and upwards per person per night (usually including breakfast), they are modern and clean, with good facilities and comfortable beds. Another positive development for visitors is the conversion of homes or villas into so-called private hotels. For budget travellers, these are without doubt the best way to go.

You can often find unofficial accommodation in private homes by asking around. Camping is possible in the southern area and sometimes on the deserted beaches.

ACTIVITIES

Swimming is great all along the Adriatic and Ionian coasts (see Southern Albania p46). You can go bird-watching around

ALBANIA

Lezha (see p53) and hiking in Mt Dajti National Park (p45).

BOOKS

For a helpful list of Albanian words and phrases check out the *Mediterranean Europe phrasebook* from Lonely Planet, while *Colloquial Albanian* (1994), by Isa Zymberi, is a good teach-yourself language course, accompanied by a cassette.

Albania (1983) by Philip Ward is great for rare insights into the communist period and a historic overview.

The Albanians – A Modern History (1999), by Miranda Vickers, is a comprehensive and very readable history of Albania from the time of Ottoman rule to the restoration of democracy after 1990.

Biografi (1993), by New Zealander Lloyd Jones, is a rather arresting story set in post-1990 Albania and is a semi-factual account of the writer's quest for the alleged double of former communist dictator Enver Hoxha.

The Accursed Mountains: Journeys in Albania (1999), is a negative account of journalist Robert Carver's credibility-stretching journey through postcommunist Albania in 1996.

The Best of Albanian Cooking (1999), by Klementina Hysa and R John Hysa, is one of scant few books on the subject of Albanian cuisine and contains a wide range of family recipes.

High Albania (published in 1909 and reprinted in 2000), written by Albania's 'honorary citizen', Edith Durham, recounts her travels in northern Albania in the early 20th century.

James Pettifer's *Albania and Kosovo Blue Guide* (2001) is a thoroughly informed source for answering any questions on Albanian history and a good guide of things to see.

An excellent source of rare and out-of-print books on Albania is **Harfield Books of London** (☎ 020-8871 0880; www.harfieldbooks.com; 81 Replingham Rd, Southfields, London SW18 5LU). Also try **Oxus Books** (☎ /fax 020-8870 3854; 121 Astonville St, London SW18 5AQ), which has a catalogue you can request.

BUSINESS HOURS

Most businesses open at 8.30am, and some close for a siesta from noon to 4pm, opening again from 4pm to 7pm. Banking hours are shorter (generally 8.30am to 2pm). Restaurants are normally open from 8.30am to 11pm, and bars from 8.30am to midnight or later.

COURSES

The **University of Tirana** (☎ 22 8402; http://pages .albaniaonline.net/ut/unitirana_en/default_en.htm; Mother Teresa Sq) runs a summer-school programme in Albanian language and culture from mid-August to mid-September. The registration fee is US$100.

DANGERS & ANNOYANCES

Many prejudices surround Albania, but the country is now safe for travel. There are no gun-toting maniacs and, in fact, you will probably be more readily helped here than in any other European country.

You are advised to avoid travelling in the far north of the country around Bajram Curri because of the continuing instability in the neighbouring region. There may still be land mines near the northern border with Kosovo around Bajram Curri.

Don't flash money around. If accosted by Roma women and children begging, the best thing to do is to ignore them.

As Albania was closed for so long, black travellers may encounter some curious stares; in fact most visitors to Albania can expect to encounter such stares!

Corrupt police may attempt to extort money from you by claiming that something is wrong with your documentation, or they might try another pretext. Strongly resist paying them anything without an official receipt. If stopped, stay calm and smile. Allow the police to shoulder the onus of communication. They will probably give up if they can't make you understand. Always keep at least a copy of your passport with you.

You should also be aware of abysmal roads and chaotic driving conditions. Drive defensively and never at night.

Do not drink the tap water; plenty of bottled water is available.

Beware the potholes!

DISABLED TRAVELLERS

There are few special facilities for travellers in wheelchairs. However, there are toilets that cater for disabled people in the **Tirana International Hotel** (Sheshi Skënderbeg) and the

Rogner Hotel Europapark Tirana (Bulevardi Dësh-morët e Kombit).

EMBASSIES & CONSULATES
Albanian Embassies & Consulates
Below are some of the main addresses for Albanian embassies.

Canada (☎ 613-236 4114; fax 613-236 0804130; Albert St, Suite 302, ON K1P 5G4, Ottawa)

France (☎ 01 45 53 51 32; 13 rue de la Pompe, Paris 75016)

Germany (☎ 228 351 044/046/047; fax 228 351 048; Durrenstrasse 35-37, 53 173 Bonn)

Greece (☎ 21 0723 4412; fax 21 0723 1972; Karahristou 1, GR-114 21 Athens)

Italy (☎ 6 8621 4475/8214; fax 6 8621 6005; Via Asmara 5, 00 199 Rome)

Netherlands (☎ 70 427 2101; fax 70 427 2083; Anna Paulownastraat 09b, 2518 BD, The Hague)

UK (☎ 020-7730 5709; fax 020-7828 8869; 24 Buckingham Gate, 2nd Floor, London SW1 E6LB)

USA (☎ 202-223 4942; fax 202-628 7342; 2100 S St NW, Washington DC 20008)

Embassies & Consulates in Albania
The following embassies are in Tirana (area code ☎ 042):

Bulgaria (☎ 233 155; fax 232 272; Rruga Skënderberg 12)

France (☎ 234 250; fax 234 442; Rruga Skënderberg 14)

Germany (☎ 232 048; fax 233 497; Rruga Skënderberg 8)

Greece (☎ 223 959; fax 234 443; Rruga Frederik Shiroka 3)

Macedonia (☎ 233 036; fax 232 514; Rruga Lekë Dukagjini 2)

Netherlands (☎ 240 826/828/839/841; fax 232 723; tir@minbuza.nl; Rruga Asim Zeneli 10)

Serbia and Montenegro (☎ 232 089; fax 223 042; Rruga Durrësit 192/196)

Turkey (☎ 233 399; fax 232 719; Rruga E Kavajës 31)

UK (☎ 234 973; fax 247 697; Rruga Skënderberg 12)

USA (☎ 247 285; fax 232 222; Rruga Elbasanit 103)

GAY & LESBIAN TRAVELLERS
Homosexuality became legal in Albania early in 1995, but as in all Balkan countries, attitudes are highly conservative.

HOLIDAYS
Ramadan and Bajram, variable Muslim holidays, are also celebrated.

New Year's Day 1 January
Easter Monday March/April
Labour Day 1 May
Independence Day 28 November
Liberation Day 29 November
Christmas Day 25 December

LANGUAGE
Albanian (Shqip) is an Indo-European language, a dialect of ancient Illyrian, with a number of Turkish, Latin, Slavonic and (modern) Greek words, although it constitutes a linguistic branch of its own. It has 36 characters and shares certain grammatical features with Romanian, although there is debate as to where and when the languages diverged. The grammar is similar to any other Indo-European language, but Albanian is quite difficult and many of the words do not sound familiar at first.

Most Albanian place names have two forms as the definite article is a suffix. An example of this is *bulevardi* (the boulevard), as opposed to *bulevard* (a boulevard), or the capital city's name Tirana, which is the definite form of the name, meaning 'the Tirana', as opposed to Tiranë, in its indefinite form. In this chapter we use the definite form, the one most commonly used in English.

The two main dialects of Albanian, Tosk and Gheg, have diverged over the past 1000 years. In 1909 a standardised form of the Gheg dialect of Elbasan was adopted as the official language, but since WWII a modified version of the Tosk dialect of southern Albania has been used. A unified Tosk and Gheg written form of Albanian was established in 1972 at the Congress of Orthography in Tirana and this form is now universally accepted.

Outside the country, Albanians resident in Kosovo and other parts of former Yugoslavia speak Gheg, whereas those in Greece speak Tosk, and in Italy they speak yet another dialect called Arberesh.

See the Language chapter on p909 for pronunciation guidelines and useful words and phrases.

MAPS
The 1:450,000 *Albania World Travel Map* published by Bartholomew is also very detailed. The best map of the country is the 1:300,000 *Albania* map published by Euro Map, but unfortunately it is out of print. Buy a map before you arrive in Albania as they may be hard to find in the country.

MEDIA
The public broadcaster, Albanian Radio and TV (RTSh), operates national radio

and TV networks. Competition looms from private stations, which mushroomed in the late 1990s. Some 75 private TV channels and 30 radio stations were on the air by 2001, but not all have the licence to broadcast all over the country. Radio stations are mainly commercial music stations and are not vital in news distribution. Newspapers are often directly owned by political parties and trade unions and sensationalism is often the norm in the print media. Dependence on external funding tends to limit their objectivity.

Newspapers

A diverse range of newspapers is printed in Tirana and the independent daily *Koha Jonë* is the paper with the widest readership.

The *Albanian Daily News* is a fairly dry English-language publication that has useful information on happenings around Albania. It's generally available from major hotels for 300 lekë, or you can read it online at www.AlbanianNews.com.

Foreign newspapers and magazines, including the *Times,* the *International Herald Tribune* and the *Economist,* are sold at most major hotels and at some central street kiosks, though they tend to be a few days old.

Radio

The BBC World Service can be picked up in and around Tirana on 103.9FM, while the Voice of America's mainly music programme is on 107.4FM. Some of the most popular Albanian radio stations are: Albanian Radio and TV (RTSh), a public broadcaster; Radio Tirana, an external service run by RTSh, with programmes in eight languages including English; and the private stations Top Albania Radio and Radio Koha.

TV

There are many TV channels available in Albania including the state TV service TVSH, the private station TVA and, among others, Eurosport, several Italian channels and even a couple of French ones.

MONEY
Credit Cards

Credit cards are accepted only in the larger hotels and travel agencies. A few places in

Tirana and Durrës will offer credit-card advances (usually for MasterCard, not Visa). Many of the ATMs that you see around are only attached to the local banks and do not take Visa or MasterCard, so bring either cash or travellers cheques with you.

Currency

Albanian banknotes come in denominations of 100, 200, 500 and 1000 lekë. There are five, 10, 20 and 50 lekë coins. Since 1997, all notes issued are smaller and contain a sophisticated watermark to prevent forgery. In 1964 the currency was revalued 10 times; prices on occasion may still be quoted at the old rate (3000 lekë instead of 300).

Everything in Albania can be paid for with lekë but most of the hotel prices are quoted in US dollars or euros, both of which are readily accepted as alternative currencies for the lekë.

Moneychangers

Some banks will change US-dollar travellers cheques into US cash without commission. Travellers cheques (euro and US dollar) may be used at major hotels, but cash is preferred everywhere. You can change sterling travellers cheques at **Rogner Hotel Europapark Tirana** (Bulevardi Dëshmorët e Kombit).

Every town has its free currency market, which usually operates on the street in front of the Main post office or state bank. Such transactions are not dangerous or illegal and it all takes place quite openly, but do make sure you count the money twice before tendering yours. The advantages are that you get a good rate and avoid the 1% bank commission.

In Albania US dollars and euros are the favourite foreign currency. You will not be able to exchange Albanian currency outside of the country.

POST

Outside of main towns there are few public mail boxes in Albania, but there is an increasing number of modern post offices springing up around the country where you can hand in your mail directly.

Letters to the USA and Canada cost 90 lekë and postcards 50 lekë. Letters to Australia, Africa and Asia cost 60 lekë and postcards 40 lekë. Within Europe letters cost 50 lekë and postcards 30 lekë, while to neighbouring countries the rates are 30 lekë and 20 lekë respectively. Within Albania the rates are 20 lekë and 15 lekë.

TELEPHONE & FAX

Long-distance telephone calls made from main post offices are cheap, costing about 90 lekë a minute to Italy. Calls to the USA cost 230 lekë per minute. Faxing can be done from the Main post office in Tirana for the same cost as phone calls, or from major hotels, though they will charge more. There are two mobile phone providers (Vodafone and AMC) and most areas of the country are now adequately covered. Check that a roaming agreement exists with your home service provider. Mobile numbers begin with ☎ 068 or ☎ 069. Albania's country phone code is ☎ 355. For domestic directory enquiries call ☎ 124; international directory assistance is ☎ 122. Phonecards are available from the post office in versions of 50 units (560 lekë), 100 units (980 lekë) and 200 units (1800 lekë).

EMERGENCY NUMBERS

- Police ☎ 129
- Ambulance ☎ 127
- Fire Brigade ☎ 128

TOURIST INFORMATION

There are no tourist information offices in Albania, but hotel receptionists or travel agencies will help you with directions. You can buy city maps of Tirana in bookshops and larger kiosks in the capital, but in most of the other towns they're unobtainable. In addition, many streets lack signs and the buildings have no numbers marked on them! Some streets don't seem to have any name at all. However, you will find that most of the towns are small enough for you to get around without them.

VISAS

No visa is required by citizens of EU countries or nationals of Australia, Canada, New Zealand, South Africa or the USA. Travellers from other countries should check with an Albanian embassy (see p55) for appropriate visa requirements. Citizens of all countries – even those entering visa-

free – will be required to pay an 'entry tax' at the border. The entry tax for all visitors is €10. Israeli citizens pay US$30.

Upon arrival you will fill in an arrival and departure card. Keep the departure card, which will be stamped, with your passport and present it when you leave.

WOMEN TRAVELLERS

Albania is quite a safe country for women travellers, but it is important to be aware of the fact that outside Tirana it is mainly men who go out and sit in bars and cafés in the evenings, whereas the women generally stay at home. While they are not threatening, it may feel strange to be the only woman in a bar, so it is advisable to travel in pairs if possible, and dress conservatively.

TRANSPORT IN ALBANIA

GETTING THERE & AWAY
Air

Mother Teresa Airport is 26km northwest of Tirana. There is no exchange office at the airport and no public telephones, so try to arrange a pick-up in advance through your hotel. Taxis ply the route to Tirana and will charge you €20. Major airlines that serve Mother Teresa airport and their contact number in Tirana (area code ☎ 042) include:

Ada Air (code ZY; ☎ 56 111; www.adaair.com)
Adria Airways (code JP; ☎ 28 483; www.adria.si)
Albanian Airlines (code LV; ☎ 35 162/33 494; www.flyalbanian.com)
Austrian Airlines (code OS; ☎ 23 938; www.aua.com)
Lufthansa (code LH; ☎ 350 54/8; www.lufthansa.com)
Malév Hungarian Airlines (code MA; ☎ 34 163; www.malev.hu)
Olympic Airways (code OA; ☎ 28 961/35 053; www.olympicairlines.com)
Turkish Airlines (code TK; ☎ 34 185; www.turkishairlines.com)

Land
BORDER CROSSINGS
Greece

There are border crossings between Korça and Florina at Kapshtica/Krystallopigi, and between Ioannina and Gjirokastra at Kakavija/Kakavia. A new border crossing north of the Greek port of Igoumenitsa at Konispoli/Sagiada has been opened.

ALBANIA

Kosovo

The only really viable crossing for travellers is at Morinë/Vrbnica between Kukës and Prizren. However, bear in mind that this whole area is not a good place to travel solo or independently as there is still instability in the region. Travellers on the through-buses to Prishtina should have no problems.

Macedonia

The best two crossings are those on Lake Ohrid. The southern crossing is at Tushëmisht (near Sveti Naum, 29km south of Ohrid), and the northern crossing is at Qafa e Thanës (between Struga and Pogradec). If you are taking a bus to/from Macedonia (Tirana–Struga–Tetovo), you will use the northern crossing. You may spend around half an hour at the border while regularities are checked, but it is generally a smooth procedure.

The southern crossing is most commonly crossed on foot, as taxis from Pogradec will drop you off just before the Macedonian border. You can then wait for the hourly bus to Ohrid on the Macedonian side of the border.

Serbia & Montenegro

The only border crossing is at Han i Hotit (between Shkodra and Podgorica), though a new crossing has been planned for some time at Muriqan/Sukobin, which would link Ulcinj, in Montenegro, and Shkodra much more conveniently.

BUS

Buses to Thessaloniki (€35, 10 hours) leave at 6am each morning from in front of **Albanian Interlines** (☎ 222 272; Bulevardi Zogu I) in Tirana. Buses to Athens (€50, 24 hours) also leave from here three times a week.

Buses to Prishtina, the capital of Kosovo, depart daily from beside the Tirana International Hotel on Sheshi Skënderbeg at 6pm (€30, 12 hours). If you're bound for Macedonia, you will need to take the daily bus to Tetovo, Macedonia (also from here) and from Tetovo, you can take a frequent local bus to Skopje.

Buses for Istanbul and Sofia leave from **Albtransport** (☎ 223 026; Rruga Mine Peza, Tirana; ☽ 8am-4pm Mon-Fri). The Sofia bus (€35, 15 hours) leaves at 10am on Wednesday. Two buses depart for Istanbul (€55, 24 hours) at 10am and 1pm on Monday, and go via Sofia.

CAR & MOTORCYCLE

Bringing a car or motorcycle to Albania is still a risky business as bad roads can be a problem. Additionally, your insurance Green Card may not cover Albania. But it is feasible to transit the country from, say, Serbia and Montenegro to Macedonia or Greece in two days, if you are determined. You'll need to park the car in a secure park overnight in Tirana and continue the next day.

Roads are slowly being improved and there are dual carriage ways between Tirana and Durrës and on the approaches to the main land borders, as well as a new road into and through Llogaraja Pass. The road leading from the Qafa e Thanës border crossing between Macedonia and Albania is good at first and the latter part of the road leading to Elbasani and then Tirana is slowly being repaired.

The local petrol, Ballshi, is allegedly impure and can do some damage to your engine but there are plenty of petrol stations around the country with unleaded petrol. Repair garages abound, but do beware that most of the spare parts are aimed at Mercedes cars, as they comprise a 99% majority in the country.

Drivers will need to be extra careful of the kamikaze driving techniques and be aware that traffic police regularly stop cars in an effort to extract fines for so-called infringements. For information on how to deal with this, see p54. For more information on driving conditions see p59.

Sea

The Italian company of Adriatica di Navigazione operates ferry services to Durrës from Bari (€60, 8½ hours) daily and from Ancona (€85, 19 hours) four times a week, leaving both Italy and Albania at 10pm and docking at the other end at 7am. Cars cost €90/100 in low/high season. Bicycles are carried free. In Bari you are able to buy ferry tickets from **Agestea** (☎ 080-553 1555; agestea.bari02@interbusiness.it; Via Liside 4). In Ancona it's **Maritime Agency Srl** (☎ 071-204 915; tickets.adn@maritime.it; Via XXIX Settembre 10). In Albania tickets are sold by any number of the travel agencies in Durrës or Tirana.

ALBANIA

DEPARTURE TAX

Airport departure tax is €10, payable in euros or lekë. A €4 tariff is imposed on people leaving Albania by ferry, and there's a €1 daily tariff on vehicles, payable upon crossing the border out of the country.

The fastest ferry connection between Bari and Durrës is via the passenger catamarans operated by Quality Lines (€60, 3½ hours). These high-speed vessels leave Durrës daily at 10am and 4.30pm. The Durrës agent can be contacted on ☎ 052-24 571.

The car ferry *Expresso (Grecia)* runs each Tuesday and Saturday at 1pm to Durrës from Trieste (and returns on Wednesday and Sunday at 7pm). The trip on deck costs US$40/50 in low/high season. In Durrës contact **KAD Shipping** (☎ 052-25 154; fax 052-20 341) or any travel agency. In Trieste contact **Agemar** (☎ 39-040-222/737/688; www.agemar.it) or any travel agency selling ferry tickets.

See p50 for information on travel between Corfu and the small southern Albanian port of Saranda.

GETTING AROUND
Bicycle
Although many Albanians cycle short distances, cycling through the country is not recommended, especially if you are not familiar with the abysmal driving on Albanian roads. Furthermore, many roads are not paved and there are no cycling paths anywhere in the country.

Bus
Most Albanians travel around their country in private *furgons* or larger buses. These run fairly frequently throughout the day between Tirana and Durrës (38km) and other towns north and south. Buses to Tirana depart from towns all around Albania at the crack of dawn. Pay the conductor on board; the fares are low (eg Tirana–Durrës is 100 lekë). Tickets are rarely issued.

City buses operate in Tirana, Durrës and Shkodra (pay the conductor). Watch your possessions on crowded city buses.

Car & Motorcycle
Albania has only acquired an official road traffic code in recent years and most motor-ists have only learned to drive in the last five or six years. The road infrastructure is poor and the roads badly maintained, but the number of cars on the road is growing daily. There are plenty of petrol stations in the cities and increasing numbers in the country. If you are driving to Albania, a 4WD is advisable.

Hazards include pedestrians who tend to use the roads as an extension of the footpaths; animals being herded along country roads; gaping potholes; a lack of road warnings and signs; and reckless drivers. Park your vehicle in a secure location, such as hotel grounds.

It is not advisable to drive at night in any part of Albania because of poor visibility on the roads and bad driving conditions.

Unleaded fuel is generally widely available along all major highways, but fill up before driving into the mountainous regions. A litre of unleaded petrol costs 100 lekë, while diesel costs close to 70 lekë.

Hitching
With buses so cheap, hitching will probably only be an emergency means of transport. You can afford to be selective about the rides you accept as everyone will take you if they possibly can. You can get an indication of where a car might be going from the letters on the licence plate: Berat (BR), Durrës (DR), Elbasan (EL), Fier (FR), Gjirokastra (GJ), Korça (KO), Kruja (KR), Lezha (LE), Pogradec (PG), Saranda (SR), Shkodra (SH), Tirana (TR) and Vlora (VL).

However, hitching is never totally safe and Lonely Planet doesn't recommend it as a form of transport.

Local Transport
Most Albanians travel around in private *furgons* (minibuses) or larger buses. Bus/*furgon* activity starts at the crack of dawn and usually ceases by 2pm. Fares are low and tickets are rarely issued. Shared *furgons* leave when they are full or almost full. They usually cost more than the bus, but they're still cheap. Pay the driver or assistant when you get out.

Train
Prior to 1948 Albania had no railways, but the communists built up a limited north–south rail network based at Durrës. Today, however, nobody who can afford

other types of transport takes the train, even though train fares are about a third cheaper than bus fares. The reason will be obvious once you board – the decrepit carriages typically have broken windows and no toilets and are agonisingly slow.

Daily passenger trains leave Tirana for Shkodra (3½ hours, 98km), Fier (4¼ hours), Ballsh (five hours), Vlora (5½ hours) and Pogradec (seven hours). Seven trains a day also make the 1½-hour trip between Tirana and Durrës (500 lekë).

Belarus
Беларусь

CONTENTS

Highlights 62
Itineraries 62
Climate & When to Go 62
History 63
People 64
Religion 65
Arts 65
Environment 65
Food & Drink 66
Minsk **66**
History 66
Orientation 66
Information 66
Sights 67
Sleeping 69
Eating 70
Drinking 71
Entertainment 71
Shopping 71
Getting There & Away 72
Getting Around 72
Around Minsk 73
Elsewhere in Belarus **74**
Brest 74

Hrodna 76
Belarus Directory **78**
Accommodation 78
Business Hours 78
Embassies & Consulates 78
Festivals & Events 79
Holidays 79
Insurance 79
Language 79
Money 79
Post 80
Telephone & Fax 80
Visas 80
Transport in Belarus **81**
Getting There & Away 81
Getting Around 82

BELARUS

FAST FACTS

- **Area** 207,600 sq km
- **Capital** Minsk
- **Currency** Belarusian rouble (BR); €1 = BR2688; US$1 = BR2170; UK£1 = BR3,900; A$1 = BR1584; ¥100 = BR1982; NZ$1 = BR1481
- **Famous for** gymnast Olga Korbut, bearing the brunt of Chernobyl, the dictatorial President Lukashenko
- **Key Phrases** Dobree dzhen (hello), kalee laska (please), dzyahkooee (thanks)
- **Official Languages** Belarusian and Russian
- **Population** 10 million
- **Telephone Codes** country code ☎ 375; international access code ☎ 8+ 10
- **Visa** invitations (US$75), visas (US$100 to US$200) and proof of medical insurance required of most visitors, see p80

Typically, visitors to Belarus fall into three categories: people retracing their roots, human-rights workers and Slavophiles. But even if you don't fit into one of those categories, there's nothing stopping you from venturing into this country, which has been unfairly shrouded in mystery and hearsay.

Architecturally, the capital city of Minsk is a testament to Soviet ideology, but it is also surprisingly Westernised (and is even beginning to show a bit of a flashy side). And if you're going to see one Soviet WWII memorial in your life, make it the epic Brest Fortress, only a five-hour train ride from Minsk.

Don't make the common mistake of confusing the country's inscrutability for inaccessibility. Getting a visa isn't difficult (just do it in advance), and tourists will be untouched by the current government's repressive ways. Belarusians are delighted and flattered by foreign visitors, and fully deserve their reputation of being warm, interesting, cultured and eloquent people.

HIGHLIGHTS

- Check out the grandiose Stalinist architecture, eclectic restaurants and cosy cafés of **Minsk** (p66)
- Visit the mellow pedestrian streets, colourful wooden homes and epic WWII memorial of **Brest** (p74)
- Look at the endless pastoral scenes and hobnob with natives on the **train** (p82) from Minsk to Brest

ITINERARIES

Belarusian cities and towns are not packed with tourist attractions, so you can count on each of these itineraries feeling rather leisurely.

- **Three Days** Give Minsk two days and a then take a day trip to Dudutki, Mir, Njasvizh or Khatyn.
- **One Week** Follow the three-day itinerary, then add one or two days in Brest (at least one for the fortress) and a day in Hrodna or a visit to Belavezhskaja Pushcha National Park before you return to the capital.

CLIMATE & WHEN TO GO

Belarus has a continental climate, which becomes marginally less temperate as you move from southwest to northeast. Average January temperatures are between -4 and -8°C, with frosts experienced for five to six months

HOW MUCH?

- **Belavezhskaja (herbal firewater)** BR5980
- **Belarus Sineokaja vodka** BR12,950
- **Straw doll** BR4000 to BR10,000
- **Plate of draniki (potato pancakes)** BR3000 to BR6000
- **Milavitsa brassiere** BR15,000

LONELY PLANET INDEX

- **Litre of petrol** BR1700
- **Litre of bottled water** BR550
- **Half-litre of bottled Krynitsa beer** BR1000
- **Souvenir Lukashenko poster (size A1)** BR790
- **Street snack (hot dog)** BR1500

of the year. The warmest month is July, when temperatures can reach up to 30°C, but the average temperature is 18°C. June and August are the wettest months.

Since Belarus is not visited by many tourists, you won't have to worry about when to go to beat the crowds. See p79 if you'd like to make your trip coincide with local festivities.

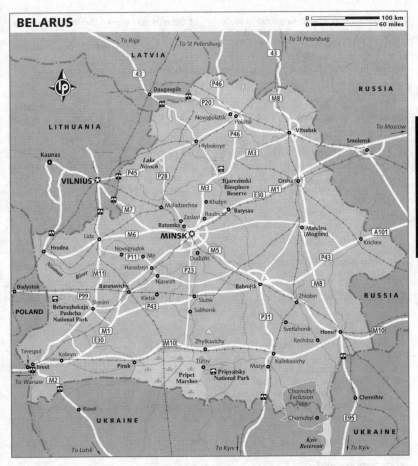

HISTORY

Evidence of human occupation in Belarus goes back to the early Stone Age. Eastern Slav tribes were here by the 6th to 8th centuries AD. The area fell under the control of Kyivan Rus (the most powerful state in Europe), but in the 14th century Belarus was gradually taken over by Lithuania and became part of the Polish-Lithuanian Grand Duchy. It was to be 400 years before Belarus came under Russian control, a period in which Belarusians became linguistically and culturally differentiated from the Russians to their east and the Ukrainians to their south.

At this time, trade was controlled by Poles and Jews and most Belarusians remained peasants, poor and illiterate. After the Partitions of Poland (1772, 1793 and 1795–96), Belarus was absorbed into Russia and faced intense Russification policies. Due to their cultural stagnation, their absence from positions of influence and their historical domination by the Poles and Russians, any sense among speakers of Belarusian that they were a distinct nationality was slow to emerge.

During the 19th century Belarus was part of the Pale of Settlement, the area where Jews in the Russian Empire were required to settle, and Jews formed the majority in many cities and towns before WWII.

In March 1918, under German occupation during WWI, a short-lived independent

Belarusian Democratic Republic was declared, but the land was soon under the control of the Red Army. The 1921 Treaty of Rīga allotted roughly the western half of modern Belarus to Poland, which launched a programme of Polonisation that provoked armed resistance by Belarusians.

The area under Bolshevik control, the Belarusian Soviet Socialist Republic (BSSR), was a founding member of the USSR in 1922.

The Soviet regime in the 1920s encouraged Belarusian literature and culture but in the 1930s under Stalin, nationalism and the Belarusian language were discouraged and their proponents ruthlessly persecuted.

The 1930s also saw industrialisation, agricultural collectivisation, and purges in which hundreds of thousands were executed – most in the Kurapaty Forest outside Minsk.

In September 1939 western Belarus was seized from Poland by the Red Army. When Nazi Germany invaded Russia in 1941, Belarus was on the front line and suffered greatly.

German occupation was savage and partisan resistance widespread until the Red Army drove the Germans out in 1944, with massive destruction on both sides. Hundreds of villages were decimated, and barely a stone was left standing in Minsk. At least 25% of the Belarusian population (over two million people) died between 1939 and 1945. Many of them, Jews and others, died in 200-plus concentration camps; the third-largest Nazi concentration camp was set up at Maly Trostenets, outside Minsk, where over 200,000 people were executed.

Western Belarus remained in Soviet hands at the end of the war, with Minsk developing into the industrial hub of the western USSR and Belarus becoming one of the Soviet Union's most prosperous republics.

The 1986 Chornobyl (spelt Chernobyl in Russian) disaster left about a quarter of the country seriously contaminated, and its effects are still felt today, particularly in the southeastern regions of the country.

On 27 July 1990, in response to the growth of nationalist feeling, the republic issued a declaration of sovereignty within the USSR. On 25 August 1991 a declaration of full national independence was issued. With no history whatsoever as a politically or economically independent entity, the country of Belarus was one of the oddest products of the disintegration of the USSR.

Since July 1994 Belarus has been governed by Aleksandr Lukashenko, a former collective-farm director (a common derogatory nickname for him is *kolkhoznik,* from *kolkhoz,* collective farm). His presidential style has been autocratic and authoritarian and, in 1996, in a bid to increase his powers he held what the West still regards as an illegitimate referendum. This effectively stripped the authority of the parliament (now appointed by Lukashenko) and made the entire government subservient to him. It also extended his term for two years.

Since then the opposition has been reduced to just a few (often mutually-opposed) groups, which hold rallies in Minsk but have been unable to unify popular support. Numerous outspoken critics of the Lukashenko regime have been arrested, imprisoned or have simply disappeared.

In 1997 Lukashenko and Russian president Boris Yeltsin signed a treaty to work toward the political and economic unification of their two countries. However, Lukashenko's loose-cannon character has caused Russia to shy away from the idea, and progress towards the union's goals has been halting at best.

Lukashenko again won a majority in 2001 and is now scheduled to stay in power until (at least) 2006. He has been ambitious about forming closer political and economic ties with Russia, but Putin has remained somewhat aloof on the matter. The country has become, politically, an isolated island in the centre of Europe.

PEOPLE

There are approximately 10 million people in Belarus, of which 81.2% are Belarusian, 11.4% Russian, 4% Polish and 2.4% Ukrainian, with the remaining 1% consisting of other groups. This results in a rather homogeneous population, with many sharing characteristic physical attributes like fair hair and piercing blue eyes.

Throughout history the Belarusian people have been the underclass in their own country, with little distinct culture or history of their own. As such, Belarusians are quiet, somewhat reserved people. Less demonstrative and approachable than Russians, they are just as friendly and generous, if not more so, once introductions are made.

RELIGION

Belarus, like Ukraine, has always been a crossing point between Latin and Eastern Orthodox Christianity, with Polish Catholics to the west and Orthodox Russians to the east. Some 80% of the populace is Eastern Orthodox.

About 20% of the population (about two million people) is Roman Catholic, of whom 15% are ethnic Poles.

During the early 1990s the Uniate Church (an Orthodox sect that looks to Rome, not Moscow) was re-established and now it has a following of over 100,000 members. There's also a small Protestant minority, the remnant of a once-large German population. Also see the boxed text 'Orthodoxy & Visiting Churches' (p828).

Prior to WWII 10% of the national population was Jewish, and in cities like Minsk, Hrodna and Brest, Jews made up between one-third and three-quarters of the population. They now make up about 0.3% of the country's population.

ARTS

The hero of early Belarusian literary achievement was Francysk Skaryna (after which the main drag in Minsk is named). Born in Polatsk but educated in Poland and Italy, the scientist, doctor, writer and humanist became the first person to translate the Bible into the Belarusian language. In the late 16th century the philosopher and humanist Symon Budny printed a number of works in Belarusian. The 19th century saw the beginning of modern Belarusian literature with works by writers and poets such as Maxim Haradsky, Maxim Bohdanovich, Janka Kupala and most notably Jakub Kolas.

Belarusian folk music is well known and no visitor to the country should miss a performance. Modern folk music originated from ritualistic ceremonies: either based on peasant seasonal feasts or, more commonly, on the traditions of church music (hymns and psalms) which became highly developed in Belarus from the 16th century onwards. The band Pesnyary have been extremely popular since the 1960s for having put a modern twist on traditional Belarusian folk music.

The Belarusian ballet is one of the most talented in all of Eastern Europe. See p71 for information on seeing a performance.

ENVIRONMENT

Belarus has an area of 207,600 sq km. It's a flat country, consisting of low ridges dividing broad, often marshy lowlands with more than 11,000 small lakes. In the south are the Pripet Marshes, Europe's largest marsh area. The marshland area known as Polesye in the south of the country is dubbed locally the 'lungs of Europe', because air currents passing over it are re-oxygenated and purified by the swamps.

Because of the vast expanses of primeval forests and marshes, Belarusian fauna abounds. The most celebrated animal is the *zoobr* (European bison), the continent's largest land mammal. They were hunted almost to extinction by 1919, but were fortunately bred back into existence from 52 animals that had survived in zoos. Now several hundred exist, mainly in the Belavezhskaja Pushcha National Park.

Around 6% of Belarusian land is protected. There are a number of national parks in the country, including Berezinsky Biosphere Nature Reserve. Narchanski National Park, Braslav Lakes National Park, Pripyatsky National Park, as well as Belavezhskaja Pushcha National Park.

Trips to Belarusian national parks and biosphere reserves, including arranged activities and camping or hotel stays, are possible; contact a tourist agency in Minsk for all but the Belavezhskaja, which is best arranged with Brest agencies. Going independently is either not allowed or rather impractical. To arrange trips, try www.belarus .ecotour.ru or www.belintourist.by.

Belavezhskaja Pushcha National Park (☎ 01631-56 370), a Unesco World Heritage Site, is the oldest wildlife refuge in Europe, the pride of Belarus and the most famous national park in the country. The reserve went from obscurity to the front page in late 1991 as the presidents of Belarus, Russia and Ukraine signed the death certificate of the USSR – a document creating the Commonwealth of Independent States (CIS) – at the Viskuli dacha here.

The 1986 disaster at Chornobyl has been the defining event for the Belarusian environment. The dangers of exposure to radiation for the casual tourist, particularly to the areas covered in this guide, are negligible. For more about Chornobyl, see p829.

BELARUS

FOOD & DRINK

Belarusian cuisine rarely differs from Russian cuisine (see p653), although there are a few uniquely Belarusian dishes. *Draniki* are potato pancakes, *kolduni* are delicious, thick potato dumplings stuffed with meat, and *kletsky* are dumplings stuffed with mushrooms, cheese or potato. *Manchanka* are pancakes served with a thick gravy.

Belavezhskaja is a bitter herbal alcoholic drink. Of the Belarusian vodkas, Charodej is probably the most esteemed (but can be hard to find); it was the official vodka of the '99 Oscars and was allegedly served at the millennium party of the prince of Monaco. Other popular souvenir-quality vodkas are Belarus Sineokaja and Minskaja.

Although the cuisine is largely meat based, and although the concept of vegetarianism (let alone veganism) is not exactly widespread, it is possible to find some dishes without meat, although eating vegan will be considerably more difficult. Here's how to say 'I am a vegetarian (male/female)': 'ya vyeh-gyeh-tah-ree-AHN-yets/-ka'.

MINSK МИНСК

☎ 017 / pop 1.68 million

Minsk is an odd city. It's a place where you can walk past the door to the KGB headquarters, and then cross the street and walk down to the sushi place at the end of the block. It straddles two worlds, managing to be a heavily trafficked bridge to the ghost of Soviet past while maintaining a forward-looking eye towards the benefits of capitalism. It's communism with a cappuccino.

HISTORY

There's a palpable pride about Minsk, the pride of a survivor. It has come back from the dead several times in its almost millennium of existence. Its greatest suffering came in WWII, when barely a stone was left standing, and half the city's people perished, including almost the entire population of 50,000 Jews. Stalin had the city rebuilt from scratch, and to this day the architecture reflects his grandiose aesthetic.

ORIENTATION

Minsk's (say that 10 times fast) hectic, huge main thoroughfare, praspekt Francyska Skaryny, is a six-lane monster extending over 11km from the train station to the outer city limits. The most interesting section is between the stubbornly austere and huge Ploshcha Nezalezhnastsi (Independence Square; Ploshchad Nezavisimosti in Russian) and Ploshcha Peramohi. To cross large busy streets, there are often underground passageways, called *perekhodi*.

Here and in other cities, local maps are found in bookshops and in most kiosks.

INFORMATION

Belintourist (☎ 226 98 40; www.belintourist.by; praspekt Masherava 19A; ☽ 8am-1pm & 2-8pm Mon-Sat, 9am-5pm Sun & holidays) City tours or trips to Mir, Dudutki, Njasvizh and Belavezhskaja Pushcha National Park can be arranged. Hotels booked through Belintourist are discounted.

MINDING YOUR MANNERS

If you have the honour of being invited into a home for a meal you should bring a gift. A bottle of wine (Georgian is a favourite), a cake or a bouquet of flowers (odd numbers only) are fine offerings. If children will be present, you may want to bring them a small gift as well.

Shoes aren't worn in homes – *tapochki* (slippers) will be provided for you once you remove your shoes. Casual dress is expected and alcohol is almost certain to be present. Also, guests are expected to give at least one toast – if no English is spoken, a toast to friendship will do nicely (za *droozh*-boo).

Superstitions are too numerous to list in their entirety, but here are a few you may encounter while visiting a home:

■ women should not sit at the corner of a table (she won't get married)

■ never light a cigarette off of a candle (a sailor will die)

■ never shake hands across a threshold (bad luck)

■ never place an empty bottle on a table (it will cause a fight – on the floor is OK)

MINSK IN TWO DAYS

Start with a walk down **praspekt Francyska Skaryny** (right), have lunch at **Express Krynitsa** (p70) then visit the **Museum of the Great Patriotic War** (p69). Have dinner at **Strawnya Talaka** (p70) then check out nearby **Rakovsky Brovar** (p71) for some killer home brews. Also pay a visit to the Minsk's **Island of Tears** monument and the **Traetskae Pradmestse** (below) and have some pancakes at **Blinnaya Strana** (p70).

The next day, take a day trip to either **Dudutki** (p73) for its open-air museum and a traditional meal, **Mir** (p73) with its castle and archaeological museum, **Njasvizh** (p73) and its fortifications, or the memorial town of **Khatyn** (p74).

Beltelekom (☎ 217 11 05; vulitsa Enhelsa 14; ☽ 24hr) Reservations often required to use the Internet.
Central post office (☎ 227 84 92; praspekt Francyska Skaryny 10; ☽ 8am-8pm Mon-Fri, 10am-5pm Sat & Sun) In addition to the regular postal service there's Express Mail for domestic and international post.
EcoMedservices (☎ 220 45 81; vulitsa Tolstoho 4; ☽ 24hr) The closest thing to a reliable, Western-style clinic.
Soyuz Online (☎ 226 02 79; vulitsa Krasnaarmejskaja 3; ☽ 24hr) In the DomOfitserov; enter the door on the right.
Tsentralnaja Kniharnya (☎ 227 49 18; praspekt Francyska Skaryny 19; ☽ 10am-8pm Mon-Fri, 10am-6pm Sat) Bookshop where you can get your very own poster of Aleksandr Lukashenko. Maps are here too.

SIGHTS

The ravages of WWII absolutely levelled Minsk, meaning very few buildings older than about 60 years remain. However, after the war, the city was promptly rebuilt with a victorious, fiercely proud, Soviet flair, and this is what is most visually interesting about Minsk. Make sure to take a slow walk down praspekt Francyska Skaryny (see the Walking Tour of Soviet Ideology, right) to get the full effect.

Across from Traetskae Pradmestse, at the end of a little footbridge, is the evocative Afghan war memorial **Island of Tears**. Standing on a small island connected by a walking bridge, it's built in the form of a tiny church, with four entrances, and is surrounded by towering gaunt statues of sorrowful mothers and sisters of Belarusian soldiers who perished in the war between Russia and Afghanistan (1979–89). Look for the small statue of the crying angel, off to the side – it is the guardian angel of Belarus.

In addition to what's here, the faux Old Town, called **Traetskae Pradmestse**, is worth strolling through for its little cafés, restaurants and shops.

Walking Tour of Soviet Ideology

After it was obliterated in WWII, Minsk was rebuilt from the ground up, under the direction of Stalin. A walk down praspekt Francyska Skaryny is a testament to the grandiose monumentalism the Soviets were so famous for.

Ploshcha Nezalezhnastsi is dominated by the **Belarusian Government Building** (behind the Lenin statue) on its northern side, and the equally proletarian **Belarusian State University** on the south side.

Many of Minsk's main shops and cafés are northeast of the main square, ploshcha Nezalezhnastsi, including Soviet **GUM** (which stands for 'government all-purpose store'); it's a bit more Western now. An entire block at No 17 is occupied by a yellow neoclassical building with an ominous, temple-like Corinthian portal – the **KGB headquarters**. On the other side of the street is a long narrow park with a **bust of Felix Dzerzhynsky**, the founder of the KGB's predecessor (the Cheka) and a native of Belarus.

Between vulitsa Enhelsa and vulitsa Janki Kupaly is a square that is still referred to by its Russian name, Oktyabrskaya ploshchad. Here you'll find the impressive, severe **Palats Respubliki** (Palace of the Republic), a concert hall. Also on this square is the classical, multi-columned **Trade Unions' Culture Palace**, and next to this, the recommended **Museum of the Great Patriotic War** (p69).

Across the street is Tsentralny Skver (Central Square), a small park on the site of a 19th-century marketplace. The dark-grey building is **Dom Ofitserov** (Officer's Building), which has a tank memorial in front, devoted to the soldiers who freed Minsk from the Nazis. Behind this is the lifeless-looking, seriously guarded **Presidential Administrative Building**, where Lukashenko resides, works and practices his bully routine.

Ploshcha Peramohi (Victory Square; Ploshchad Pobedy in Russian) is marked by a giant **Victory Obelisk** and its eternal flame.

BELARUS

MINSK

0 _____ 1 km
0 _____ 0.5 miles

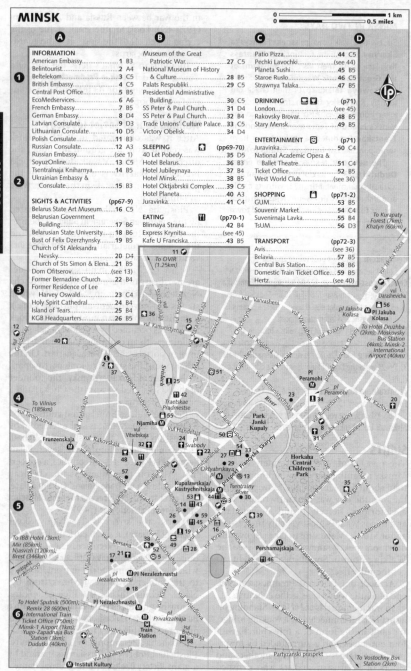

INFORMATION
American Embassy....................1 B3
Belintourist............................2 A4
Beltelekom...........................3 C5
British Embassy......................4 C5
Central Post Office..................5 B5
EcoMedservices......................6 A6
French Embassy.....................7 B5
German Embassy.....................8 D4
Latvian Consulate...................9 D3
Lithuanian Consulate..............10 D5
Polish Consulate.....................11 B3
Russian Consulate..................12 A3
Russian Embassy..................(see 1)
SoyuzOnline..........................13 C5
Tsentralnaja Kniharnya...........14 B5
Ukrainian Embassy &
   Consulate..........................15 B3

SIGHTS & ACTIVITIES   (pp67-9)
Belarus State Art Museum........16 C5
Belarusian Government
   Building.............................17 B6
Belarusian State University.......18 B6
Bust of Felix Dzerzhinsky.........19 B5
Church of St Aleksandra
   Nevsky..............................20 D4
Church of Sts Simon & Elena....21 B5
Dom Ofitserov....................(see 13)
Former Bernadine Church........22 B4
Former Residence of Lee
   Harvey Oswald....................23 C4
Holy Spirit Cathedral..............24 B4
Island of Tears.......................25 B4
KGB Headquarters..................26 B5

Museum of the Great
   Patriotic War........................27 C5
National Museum of History
   & Culture............................28 B5
Palats Respubliki......................29 C5
Presidential Administrative
   Building..............................30 C5
SS Peter & Paul Church.............31 D4
SS Peter & Paul Church.............32 B4
Trade Unions' Culture Palace......33 C5
Victory Obelisk.......................34 D4

SLEEPING   (pp69-70)
40 Let Pobedy........................35 D5
Hotel Belarus.........................36 B3
Hotel Jubileynaya.....................37 B3
Hotel Minsk...........................38 B5
Hotel Oktjabrskii Complex........39 C5
Hotel Planeta...........................40 A3
Juravinka..............................41 C4

EATING   (pp70-1)
Blinnaya Strana.......................42 B4
Express Krynitsa...................(see 45)
Kafe U Franciska.....................43 B5

Patio Pizza...........................44 C5
Pechki Lavochki...................(see 44)
Planeta Sushi.........................45 B5
Staroe Ruslo..........................46 C5
Strawnya Talaka.....................47 B5

DRINKING   (p71)
London.............................(see 45)
Rakovsky Brovar......................48 B5
Stary Mensk...........................49 B5

ENTERTAINMENT   (p71)
Juravinka..............................50 C4
National Academic Opera &
   Ballet Theatre......................51 C4
Ticket Office...........................52 B5
West World Club..................(see 36)

SHOPPING   (pp71-2)
GUM...................................53 B5
Souvenir Market......................54 C4
Suvenirnaja Lavka....................55 B5
TsUM...................................56 D3

TRANSPORT   (pp72-3)
Avis................................(see 36)
Belavia.................................57 B5
Central Bus Station..................58 B6
Domestic Train Ticket Office......59 B5
Hertz...............................(see 40)

Museums

There are several interesting museums in Minsk. Nothing is in English, but the exhibits are often self-explanatory.

Don't leave town without visiting the **Museum of the Great Patriotic War** (☎ 277 56 11; praspekt Francyska Skaryny 25A; admission BR3000; ☿ 10am-6pm Tue-Sun), where Belarus' horrors and heroism during WWII are exhibited in photographs, huge dioramas and other media. Particularly harrowing are the photographs of partisans being executed in recognisable central Minsk locations. The big sign above the building (ПОДВИГУ НАРОДА ЖИТЬ В ВЕКАХ) means 'The Feats of Mankind Will Live on for Centuries.'

At the **Belarusian State Art Museum** (☎ 227 71 63; vulitsa Lenina 20; admission BR5000; ☿ 11am-7pm Wed-Sun). you'll find the country's largest collection of Belarusian art as well as some minor European paintings and ceramics.

The **National Museum of History & Culture** (☎ 227 36 65; vulitsa Karla Marxa 12; admission BR7000; ☿ 11am-7pm Thu-Tue) takes you on a journey through the turbulent history of the nation.

Churches

Breaking the theme of Soviet classicism that dominates ploshcha Svabody is the red-brick catholic **Church of Sts Simon & Elena** (praspekt Savetskaja 15; services ☿ 9am & 7pm Mon-Fri; 10am, noon & 7pm Sat; 9am, 11am, 1pm & 7pm Sun), built in 1910. Its tall, gabled bell tower and attractive detailing are reminiscent of many brick churches in the former Teutonic north of Poland.

The baroque, twin-towered orthodox **Holy Spirit Cathedral** (pl Svabody; services ☿ 6pm Tue-Sun), built in 1642, stands confidently on a small hill. It was once part of a Polish Bernardine convent, along with the former Bernardine Church next door, which now houses city archives.

Across the vulitsa Lenina overpass is the attractively restored 17th-century **Sts Peter & Paul Church** (vulitsa Rakovskaja 4; services ☿ 6pm), the city's oldest church (built in 1613, looted by Cossacks in 1707 and restored in 1871). Now it is awkwardly dwarfed by the surrounding morose concrete structures.

Another red-brick one is the **Church of St Aleksandr Nevsky** (vulitsa Kazlova 11; services ☿ 6-8pm). Built in 1898, it was closed by the Bolsheviks, opened by the Nazis, closed by the Soviets and now it's open again. It's said that during WWII, a bomb crashed through the roof and landed plum in front of the altar, but never detonated.

SLEEPING

If you're staying more than a few days, it could be a good idea to consider renting an apartment. There are various online agencies that can help you; one option is **Belarus Rent** (www.belarusrent.com). Rates range from about €15 to €50. Stay in a hotel at least one night for visa-registration purposes.

Budget

Hotel Sputnik (☎ 229 36 19; vulitsa Brilevskaja 2; s US$26-40, d US$50-60) Sputnik is one of those rare hotels that is both the cheapest *and* the best value. Yes, the lobby is on the grim side, but the rooms are unusually spacious (although of standard quality) and you can't beat the price. Plus there's an onsite Indian restaurant, the Taj (p71). Bus No 100, which runs along praspekt Francyska Skaryny, stops across the street.

A couple of inappropriately named alternatives include:

40 Let Pobedy (☎ 236 79 63; fax 236 73 13; vulitsa Azgura 3; s BR81,440, d 58,330-150,000; Ⓟ) The name means '40 Years of Victory', but the dingy rooms are nothing to celebrate.

Hotel Druzhba (☎ 226 24 81; vulitsa Tolbukhina 3; s & d US$40-50; Ⓟ) The name means 'Friendship' but reception doesn't know the first thing about the word. It's by metro Park Chaljuskintsau 2km northeast of town.

Mid-Range

Hotel Belarus (☎ 209 75 37; www.belarus-hotel.com; vulitsa Starazhouskaja 15; s US$47-80, d US$60-90; Ⓟ)

QUIRKY MINSK

Just across the bridge over the Svislach River, on the west bank, is the **former residence of Lee Harvey Oswald** (vulitsa Kamunistychnaja 4); it's the bottom left apartment. The alleged assassin of former US president John F Kennedy lived here for a couple of years in his early 20s. He arrived in Minsk in January 1960 after leaving the US Marines and defecting to the USSR. Once here, he truly went native: he got a job in a radio factory, married a Minsk woman, had a child – and even changed his name to Alek. But soon he returned to the United States and…you know the rest.

BELARUS

This towering 23-storey giant has several renovated floors, but aside from the best city views (ask for a room facing the centre), there is nothing noteworthy about it. The buffet breakfast is mediocre but is served on the top floor, with panoramas.

Hotel Jubileynaya (☎ 226 90 24; fax 226 91 71; praspekt Masherava 19; s US$50-65, d US$64-84; **P** **🕱**) There is not quite enough of a difference in room quality to justify the significant difference in price between Jubileynaya and Planeta (below). The lobby area is hardly distinguishable and the rooms here only have slightly less appeal.

Hotel Oktjabrskii Complex (☎ 222 64 93; fax 227 33 14; vulitsa Enhelsa 13; s/d US$58/78, ste US$102-134; **P**) This 'complex' is right next to the Presidential Administration Building. It's a classic old-school Soviet-style hotel, but perhaps because it has historically dealt with regional politicos, staff know something about service. The whole place has a sort of stillness that could be intriguing or creepy.

Hotel Planeta (☎ 226 78 55; fax 226 77 80; praspekt Masherava 31; s/d US$89/110, ste US$140-160; **P** **🕱**) Some rooms at the Planeta have been renovated and some not, which gives you a bit of a selection with regards to price vs non drabness. The suites have air-conditioning.

IBB Hotel (☎ 270 39 94; www.ibb.com.by; praspekt Gazety Pravda 11; s/d €65/90) This oasis/complex is a German–Belarusian joint venture. It has all Western standards and is therefore a really smart deal, although its location (just off the praspekt Dzerzhinskovo highway to Brest) might be a drawback.

Top End

Hotel Minsk (☎ 209 90 74; www.hotelminsk.by; vulitsa Francyska Skaryny 11; s US$120-160, d US$170-220, ste US$210-800; **P** **🕱** **🖳**) It's new, it's central, it's European, it's successful and it's where the diplomats stay. Rooms are on the wee side for the price, but all have air-conditioning, a hairdryer, bidet and satellite TV. Access to the gym, Jacuzzi, saunas, and business centre, as well as a buffet breakfast and secure parking, are included in the price. A fancy underground mall is due to open next door.

Juravinka (☎ 206 39 96; fax 227 55 42; vulitsa Janki Kupaly 25; s/d/ste US$130/190/800; **P** **🕱** **🖳** **🕮**) Frequented by the country's fancy folk (politicians etc), this complex includes a bowling alley, pool, fitness centre and an elegant restaurant. The suite is locally famous for its opulence. There are only about a dozen rooms, so book ahead.

EATING

The selection of restaurants is perhaps one of the highlights of Minsk. As the city reinvents itself more and more as a cosmopolitan outpost, the quantity and quality of restaurants (regional and foreign) rise. Belarusian restaurants tend to strive towards a common theme, going for either the underground-cellar look or the country-home setting, but almost always with staff in traditional folk costume.

Regional

Blinnaya Strana (vulitsa Maxima Bahdanovicha; mains BR1600-3000; 🕑 9am-11pm) Welcome to Pancake Country. This fast-food joint is perfect for a quick snack of fresh hot *blini* (crepes) in either savoury or sweet forms.

Express Krynitsa (☎ 226 17 08; praspekt Francyska Skaryny 18; mains BR2000-10,000; 🕑 11am-11pm) Now this is real Soviet cafeteria-style eating – although quite a bit better and more modern than the old-school kind. Plus there are huge windows to sit by for people-watching.

Staroe Ruslo (☎ 217 84 70; vulitsa Uljanauskaja; mains BR2000-18,000; 🕑 noon-11pm) Don't be fooled by the lacklustre exterior, inside is some of the best food in town. There are several soups to choose from, and lots of cheesy or mushroomy dishes.

Strawnya Talaka (☎ 223 27 94; vulitsa Rakovskaja 18; mains BR5000-26,000; 🕑 10am-late) An intimate, delectable dinner amid sophisticated Slavic décor.

Kafe U Francyska (☎ 222 48 02; praspekt Francyska Skaryny 19; mains BR10,000-40,000; 🕑 11am-11pm) Possibly the only place in Belarus that has 'tourist trap' written all over it. But there's an effigy of Francysk Skaryna (p65) himself to greet you (or scare you) at the bottom of the entry's stairs. Besides, where else can you get a metre of sausage? Or a metre of vodka shots, for that matter?

Pechki Lavochki (☎ 227 78 79; praspekt Francyska Skaryny 22; 🕑 8am-midnight Mon-Sun; meals US$6-15) Settle down with a Russian beer ($2) and a selection of Belarusian cuisine, or sample one of the seasonally changing 'festivals' of other cuisines: past festivals have included Hungarian, Georgian, Armenian, and even 'Soviet.'

Foreign

On Francyska Skaryny there's a trio of mutually owned chain restaurants: Patio Pizza, Ispansky Kutok and Pechki Lavochki.

Patio Pizza (☎ 227 17 91; praspekt Francyska Skaryny 22; ☽ noon-midnight Mon-Sun; pizzas $6-12) Come here for possibly the best pizza in the country. There's a salad bar with lettuce and veggies (in addition to Slavic-style mayonnaise concoctions).

Taj (☎ 229 35 92; vulitsa Brilevskaja 2; mains BR5000-16,000; ☽ 11am-midnight) Thank Krishna for Indian expats. Here, in the lobby of Hotel Sputnik, you'll find a big menu with lots of vegetarian choices, and there's live Indian music and dancing at 8pm. Service and décor are a little uptight, but that doesn't mean you have to be.

Planeta Sushi (☎ 210 56 45; praspekt Francyska Skaryny 18; sushi & mains BR600-104,000; ☽ noon-1am) It's a million miles away from being Belarusian, but if you've been travelling for a while and are sick of meat-and-potato meals, don't miss this place. The sushi is surprisingly fresh for such a landlocked locale.

DRINKING

Be careful about drinking alcohol in public. You'll see other people doing it, (teens hanging out and playing guitar) but it's technically illegal and therefore you could be asking for trouble.

Rakovsky Brovar (☎ 206 64 04; vulitsa Vitsebskaja 10; ☽ noon-midnight). This two-storey brewery/beer hall is the place to drink, although better and cheaper food can be had elsewhere. There are four house brews ranging from 11% to 13% alcohol, and one nonalcoholic selection.

Good cafés include **Stary Mensk** (☎ 289 14 00; praspekt Francyska Skaryny 14; ☽ 10am-11pm) and **London** (☎ 289 15 29; praspekt Francyska Skaryny 18; ☽ 10am-11pm). They are under the same ownership and therefore very similar.

ENTERTAINMENT
Performing Arts

If you like the performing arts, you're in for a treat. Some of the best ballet in Eastern Europe takes place in Minsk, and for peanuts. Opera costs between BR2500 and BR6000 and performances are held at 7pm on Thursday, Saturday and Sunday. Ballet costs from BR2000 to BR12,000 and performances are at 7pm on Tuesday, Wednesday, Friday and Sunday.

National Academic Opera & Ballet Theatre (☎ 234 06 52; ploshcha Parizhskoy Kamunni 1) Some think the ballet here is better than at the Bolshoi in Moscow. The opera ain't bad either.

Theatre, especially youth theatre, is very popular. To buy advance tickets or to find out what's on, head to the **ticket office** (☎ 288 22 63; praspekt Francyska Skaryny 13; ☽ noon-5pm Sun & Mon, 9am-9pm Tue-Sat); there are more places for tickets in the underground crosswalks in the centre. Same-day tickets are usually available only from the venues.

Nightclubs

Between the stir-crazy expat community and the large young population in Minsk, demand for quality nightlife is high, and supply is beginning to meet the demand.

Don't show up at a club before midnight or you'll look like a ninny. Also nightclubs often exercise what they call 'face control' – if they don't like the looks of you, you're not getting in. This has to do with security more than with fashion and beauty, but don't wear trainers unless you want to dance out on the pavement. There are numerous little flash-in-the-pan clubs. The best thing to do if you're looking for the local hot new thing is to ask a local hot young thing. The following clubs have been around for a while and probably won't be folding anytime soon.

West World Club (☎ 239 17 98; vulitsa Starazhouskaja 15; cover BR6000-12,000; ☽ 8pm-6am) Because of its circular shape, locals call this place 'Shaiba' (hockey puck). It's quite a scene, with the city's dubiously nouveau riche and prostitutes aplenty, as well as visiting Turks, Azeris and Georgians.

Remix 28 (☎ 777 14 24; vulitsa Chkalava 12; cover BR14,000; ☽ 8pm-2am Mon-Fri, 11pm-late Sat) Much more humble in scope than West World, this small, futuristic place plays electronica. It's walkable from Hotel Sputnik and right by a No 100 bus stop.

Games

Juravinka (☎ 206 69 09; vulitsa Janki Kupaly 25; game BR25,000-39,000; ☽ 2pm-5am Mon-Fri, 11am-6am Sat & Sun) It's not just a hotel, it's a bowling alley. Friday night is expat night.

SHOPPING

Folk art is the main source of souvenirs, which include carved wooden trinkets,

BELARUS

ceramics and woven textiles. Unique to Belarus are wooden boxes intricately ornamented with geometric patterns composed of multicoloured pieces of straw. These are easily found in city department stores and in some museum kiosks.

Souvenirs are often sold in hotel lobbies and department stores. ost days, a small outdoor souvenir market operates in the small space between the Trade Unions' House of Culture and the Museum of the Great Patriotic War. Just walk past the cheesy paintings and you'll find crafts in the back.

Suvenirnaya Lavka (☎ 234 54 51; vulitsa Maxima Bahdanovicha 9; ☺ 10am-7pm Mon-Fri, 10am-6pm Sat) Excellent quality and helpful and patient service here; staff speak some English. You'll find straw crafts, wooden boxes, lots of beautifully embroidered linens, and Belarusian vodka – as well as Belavezhskaja.

Oddly enough, Belarus is a good place to buy good-quality, inexpensive lingerie. The Belarusian company **Milavitsa** (www.mila vitsa.com.by) makes pretty, stylish bras and underwear, and they sell for a fraction of what Westerners pay. Check the department stores, such as **TsUM** (☎ 284 81 64; praspekt Francyska Skaryny 54; ☺ 9am-9pm Mon-Sun) for Milavitsa products – but know that there are no dressing rooms.

GETTING THERE & AWAY
Air
International flights entering and departing Belarus do so at the **Minsk-2 international airport** (☎ 017-279 10 32), about 40km east of Minsk. Some domestic flights as well as those to Kyiv, Kaliningrad and Moscow depart from the smaller **Minsk-1 airport** (☎ 017-222 54 18), only a few kilometres from the city centre.

Bus
You can buy tickets at the Central station for any destination, but find out which of the four stations you're departing from (ask: ka-*koi* av-toh-vak-*zal*?).
Central (☎ 227 04 73; vulitsa Bobruiskaja 6) By the train station.
Moskovsky (☎ 219 36 27; vulitsa Filimonava 61) Near Maskouskaja metro station.
Vostochny (☎ 248 58 21; vulitsa Vaneeva 34) To get here from the train station, take bus No 8 or trolley No 20 or 30; get off at 'Avtovokzal Vostochny'.

Yugo-Zapadnaja (☎ 226 31 88; vulitsa Zheleznodorozhnaja 41) To get here, take bus No 1, 32 or 41 from vulitsa Druzhnaja at the central bus station. Get off at 'Yugo-Zapadnaja Stantsija'.

See p82 for price and schedule information on buses departing Minsk for Hrodna and Brest, and p81 for other Eastern European destinations.

Train
The Minsk train station is relatively new and modern, and has received architecture awards. Food and left-luggage services are available here. Nothing is in English yet, but there are picture-signs.

You can buy tickets at the train station, but its staff are often more courteous at the train ticket offices. If you do buy your ticket at the station, consider first going to one of the computers by the ATMs to get all the information you need for ticket purchase (the computer will give you departure/arrival, train number and cost) The ATMs here offer US dollars or Belarusian roubles.

Minsk train station (☎ 005 or 596 54 10) Domestic/CIS and international tickets are sold here, but you may have to try a few different windows before you get the right one.
Domestic train ticket office (☎ 225 61 24; praspekt Francyska Skaryny 18; ☺ 9am-8pm Mon-Fri, 9am-7pm Sat & Sun) Advance tickets for domestic and CIS destinations.
International train ticket office (☎ 225 30 67; vulitsa Voronyanskoho 6) Advance tickets for non-CIS destinations.

See p82 for price and schedule information on trains departing Minsk for Hrodna and Brest, and p81 for other Eastern European destinations.

GETTING AROUND
From Minsk-2 airport, a 40-minute taxi ride into town should cost US$25, but you'll be lucky to get it for under US$40, as taxi drivers will drive a hard bargain if you're not Belarusian. There are buses (BR2800, 90 minutes, hourly) that bring you to the central bus station. There are also regular minibuses that make the trip in under an hour and cost BR5000. If you arrive by train, you're already in town.

City transport maps are for sale at kiosks by bus stops.

Buses, trams, trolleybuses and the metro cost BR250 per ride and operate from 5.30am to 1am, serving all of the city. Peak hours are 8am to 10am and 4pm to 7pm – expect to be crammed in at these times.

Bus No 100 and the metro are going to be your best friends in Minsk. Bus No 100 comes every 5 to 15 minutes and plies praspekt Francyska Skaryny as far as you need to go. You can buy a bus ticket from the person on board wearing a bright vest. Once you get the ticket, punch it at one of the red buttons placed at eyelevel on poles. Metro stations are marked by a green 'M' but are sometimes not very eye-catching.

Taxis can be hailed from the street by making a gesture as if you're dribbling a basketball (private cars will often stop, which is fine, unless they already have a passenger) or you can call a cab (☎ 061 or ☎ 007). State your destination and negotiate a price before getting in. The better your Russian, the better the price – even if you call, so have a local do it for you if you can.

AROUND MINSK

Trips to any of these places can be challenging to make independently if you don't speak Russian, but are easily arranged through Belintourist (p66) or other travel agencies. If you do decide to get to these places using public transport, keep in mind that Sunday evenings are often booked in advance for the return trip to Minsk, as people are returning from their country homes.

Dudutki Дудуткі
☎ 01713
Near the sleepy, dusty village of Dudutki, which is 40km south of Minsk (15km east after a turn-off from the P23 highway) is an open-air **museum** (☎ 7 25 25; admission BR50,000; ☼ 10am-8pm Tue-Sun) where 19th-century Belarusian country life is re-created. Best of all, though, is the sumptuous traditional meal you can order, prepared on the premises (BR38,000).

There is no regular bus or *electrichka* (electric train) connection with Dudutki. A taxi will cost US$50 (there and back), or Belintourist can arrange for a four-hour minibus excursion for US$60.

Mir Мір
☎ 01596 / pop 2500
About 85km southwest of Minsk and 8km north off the Minsk–Brest road is the small town of Mir, where the 16th-century **Mir Castle** sits overlooking a pond. It was once owned by the powerful Radziwill princes and has been under Unesco protection since 1994. Today the castle is under restoration, but one tower is already open as an **archaeological museum** (☎ 2 36 10, 2 30 35; admission BR5000, guided tour in Russian for 1-10 people BR20,000; ☼ 10am-5pm Wed-Sun).

From Minsk's central bus station, buses to Navahrudak (Novogrudok in Russian) stop in Mir (BR6600, 2½ hours). During the week, there are eight buses to Navahrudak and 12 buses back each day, and at weekends there are 14 buses there and 17 buses back.

If you want to try to hit both Mir and Njasvizh (below) in one day, there are two buses (BR2165, at 1.58pm and 4.59pm) that leave from Mir and arrive at Njasvizh one hour later.

Njasvizh Нясвіж
☎ 01770 / pop 15,000
Njasvizh, 120km southwest of Minsk, is one of the oldest sites in the country, dating from the 13th century. It reached its zenith in the mid-16th century while owned by the mighty Radziwill magnates, who had the town redesigned and rebuilt with the most advanced system of fortification known at the time.

The impressive and sombre **Farny Polish Roman Catholic Church** was built between 1584 and 1593 in early baroque style and features a splendidly proportioned façade. Just beyond the church is the red-brick arcaded **Castle Gate Tower**. Built in the 16th century, the tower was part of a wall and gateway controlling the passage between the palace and the town. Here there's an **excursion bureau** (☎ 5 41 45; vulitsa Leninskaja 19; ☼ 8am-5pm Mon-Fri) where you pay to enter the fortress grounds (BR5000). **Guided tours** (☎ 5 31 32; vulitsa Geysika; BR40,000; ☼ 8am-5pm) for 1 to 25 people last 1½ hours and are available daily for BR40,000. They're in Russian or Belarusian only – and worth taking only if you understand the language.

Further on is a causeway leading to the **Radziwill Palace Fortress** (1583) designed by the Italian architect Bernardoni (who was also responsible for the Farny Church). In Soviet times it was turned into a sanatorium and now it's abandoned.

From the Vostochny bus station in Minsk, there are four buses to Njasvizh (BR10,000,

BELARUS

2½ hours) Sunday to Thursday and six buses Friday and Saturday.

See the previous section on Mir for information about seeing both Mir and Njasvizh in one day.

Khatyn Хатынь
☎ 01774

The hamlet of Khatyn, which is 60km north of Minsk, was burned to the ground by Nazis on 22 March 1943. All but one of its 149 inhabitants (including 85 children) perished in the fire. The site is now a sobering memorial centred on a sculpture modelled on the only survivor, Yuzif Kaminsky.

There's no reliable public transport to Khatyn, but a taxi will cost around US$50 for the return journey from Minsk. Organised trips are available through Belintourist (US$70 for one to two people, US$90 for three to nine people).

ELSEWHERE IN BELARUS

There remains much to entice the traveller off the beaten path. In cities such as Hrodna historic vestiges remain, and many of the small villages are still lost somewhere in the 18th century. The countryside is serene with great swathes of forest, clusters of lakes, streams and rivers.

BREST БРЭСТ
☎ 0162 / pop 300,000

Brest was where the Treaty of Brest Litovsk was negotiated in March 1918. On the border with Poland, the city has always had a more Western feel than elsewhere in the country. Aside from its laid-back pace and charming side streets, Brest is home to a true wonder of the Soviet era – the Brest Fortress, an astounding WWII memorial.

Information

The website www.brestonline.com has good local information and some pictures.

Belpromstroi Bank (ploshcha Lenina; ⏲ 8.30am-7.30pm Mon-Fri, 8.30am-6.30pm Sat, 8.30am-5.30pm Sun) Has a currency exchange, Western Union and a nearby ATM. Another branch, with shorter hours, is across from the train station.

Beltelekom (☎ 22 13 15; praspekt Masherava 21; per hr BR1800; ⏲ 24hr) Internet access; long-distance calls can be made from here as well.

Brest Intourist (☎ 22 19 00; praspekt Masherava 15; ⏲ 9am-6pm Mon-Fri) Inside Hotel Intourist; super-friendly and can organise city tours and trips to national parks.

Sights
BREST FORTRESS

If you are going to see only one Soviet WWII memorial in your life, make it **Brest Fortress** (Brestskaja krepost; ☎ 20 41 09; praspekt Masherava; admission free). It's at the western end of praspekt Masherava, about a 20-minute walk (3km) from the centre; the hourly bus No 17 travels between here and Hotel Intourist.

The fortress was built between 1838 and 1842, but by WWII it was used mainly for housing soldiers. Nevertheless, two regiments bunking here at the time of the sudden German invasion in 1941 defended the aged fort for an astounding month.

The **Brest Fortress main entrance** has a sombre sound presentation, and as you leave a short tunnel, on the left, you'll see some **tanks** and the stone *Thirst* **statue**. After you cross a small bridge, to your right are the brick **ruins of the White Palace**, where the 1918 Treaty of Brest-Litovsk – which marked Russia's exit from WWI – was signed. Farther to the right is the **Defence of Brest Fortress Museum** (☎ 20 03 65; admission BR3000; ⏲ 9.30am-5pm Tue-Sun). Its extensive and dramatic exhibits demonstrate the plight of the defenders. Near this museum is Kafe Tsitadel (p76).

On the other side of the fortress, you'll see a collection of **cannons**, which kids like to climb on (makes for cute pictures). Behind this area is the entrance to the new **Brest Art Museum** (☎ 20 08 26; admission BR2100; ⏲ 10am-6pm Wed-Sun), which holds art done by Brest citizens and some local crafts.

Heading to the **main monuments** – a stone soldier's head projecting from a massive rock, entitled *Valour*, and a sky-scraping obelisk – you'll see an eternal flame and stones bearing the names of those who died (several are marked 'unknown'). Sombre orchestral music is pumped into the area, and there are often men and women in period military uniforms marching to the music.

Behind the *Valour* rock is the attractive, recently renovated Byzantine **Nikalaivsky Church**, the oldest church in the city, which dates from when the town centre occupied the fortress site. It holds regular services.

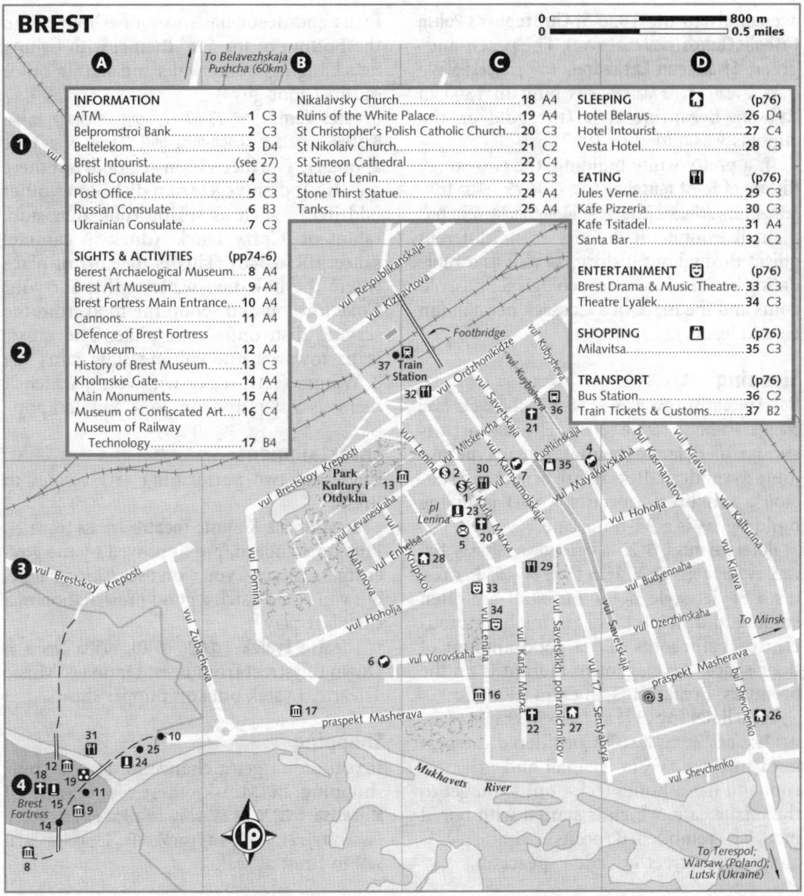
BREST
0 800 m
0 0.5 miles
To Belavezhskaja Pushcha (60km)
A
B
C
D
1
2
3
4
INFORMATION
ATM ... 1 C3
Belpromstroi Bank ... 2 C3
Beltelekom ... 3 D4
Brest Intourist ... (see 27)
Polish Consulate ... 4 C3
Post Office ... 5 C3
Russian Consulate ... 6 B3
Ukrainian Consulate ... 7 C3
SIGHTS & ACTIVITIES (pp74-6)
Berest Archaelogical Museum ... 8 A4
Brest Art Museum ... 9 A4
Brest Fortress Main Entrance ... 10 A4
Cannons ... 11 A4
Defence of Brest Fortress Museum ... 12 A4
History of Brest Museum ... 13 C3
Kholmskie Gate ... 14 A4
Main Monuments ... 15 A4
Museum of Confiscated Art ... 16 C4
Museum of Railway Technology ... 17 B4
Nikalaivsky Church ... 18 A4
Ruins of the White Palace ... 19 A4
St Christopher's Polish Catholic Church ... 20 C3
St Nikolaiv Church ... 21 C2
St Simeon Cathedral ... 22 C4
Statue of Lenin ... 23 C3
Stone Thirst Statue ... 24 A4
Tanks ... 25 A4
SLEEPING (p76)
Hotel Belarus ... 26 D4
Hotel Intourist ... 27 C4
Vesta Hotel ... 28 C3
EATING (p76)
Jules Verne ... 29 C3
Kafe Pizzeria ... 30 C3
Kafe Tsitadel ... 31 A4
Santa Bar ... 32 C2
ENTERTAINMENT (p76)
Brest Drama & Music Theatre ... 33 C3
Theatre Lyalek ... 34 C3
SHOPPING (p76)
Milavitsa ... 35 C3
TRANSPORT (p76)
Bus Station ... 36 C2
Train Tickets & Customs ... 37 B2
vul Respublikanskaja
vul Kizhavtova
Footbridge
Train Station
vul Ordzhonikidze
vul Kubysheva
vul Kuybisheva
vul Savetskaja
vul Mitskevicha
vul Lenina
vul Brestskoy Kreposti
Park Kultury i Otdykha
pl Lenina
vul Karla Marxa
vul Kamsamolskaja
Pushkinskaja
vul Mayakavskaha
bul Kasmanatov
vul Kirava
vul Kalturina
vul Hoholja
vul Levaneiskaha
vul Enhelsa
vul Krupskoi
vul Nahanova
vul Fomina
vul Zubacheva
vul Budyennaha
vul Dzerzhinskaha
To Minsk
vul Vorovskaha
vul Savetskikh pohranichnikov
vul 17 Sentyabrya
praspekt Masherava
bul Shevchenko
vul Shevchenko
Mukhavets River
Brest Fortress
To Terespol; Warsaw (Poland); Lutsk (Ukraine)

To the south is **Kholmskie Gate**; its bricks are decorated with crenulated turrets and its outer face is riddled with hundreds of bullet and shrapnel holes. Beyond the Kholmskie G ate is the **Bereste archaeological museum** (☎ 20 55 54; admission BR3000; 9.30am-6pm Tue-Sun), which has several old log cabins found on nearby land.

OTHER SIGHTS

Arguably the most interesting museum in town is the **Museum of Confiscated Art** (☎ 20 41 95; vulitsa Lenina 39; admission BR2100; 10am-5pm Tue-Sun). The collection of once-stolen icons and other precious items is unlike anything else you'll see in the country – the smugglers definitely went for the cream of the crop.

New on the scene is the **Museum of Railway Technology** (☎ 27 47 64; praspekt Masherava 2; group of 1-20 people BR20,000; 9am-5pm Wed-Sun). Tours are only in Russian, and it is pricey, but train buffs will love it even if they don't understand the guide. If that fails, just walking by and seeing the trains through the cast-iron fence is interesting enough (if you walk to Brest Fortress, you'll pass it).

With its gold cupolas and yellow-and-blue façades shining gaily in the sunlight, the breathtakingly detailed 200-year-old Orthodox **St Nikolaiv Church** (cnr vulitsa Savetskaja & vulitsa Mitskevicha) is one of many lovely churches in Brest. On ploshcha Lenina, a **statue of Lenin** points east towards Moscow, but it appears more to be pointing across the street accusingly to the 1856 **St Christopher's Polish Catholic Church** (ploshcha Lenina). The peach-and-green **St Simeon Cathedral**, (cnr praspekt Masherava & vulitsa Karla Marxa) was built in 1865 in Russian-Byzantine style (the gold on the cupolas was added in 1997).

In a pretty white building, the two-storey **History of Brest Museum** (☎ 23 16 25; vulitsa Levaneiskaha 3; admission BR2100; ☷ 10am-5pm Tue-Sun) has a small exhibit on the city in its different guises throughout history, as well as a Bible dating back to 1563, archaeological finds, old coins and the mace of a Cossack hetman (an elected leader).

Sleeping

Hotel Intourist (☎ 20 20 82; www.brest-intourist.com; praspekt Masherava 15; s/d €21/36) The Intourist is similar to Belarus (below), but maybe not quite as modern. Rooms are bright and spacious, and Brest Intourist (p74) is in the building, as is a 24-hour café.

Hotel Belarus (☎ 22 16 48; bresttourist@tut.by; bulvar Shevchenko 6; s €22-26, d €36-41, ste €49-60; ℗) Yes, it's a Soviet-style hotel, but staff are often smiling and helpful. All rooms have modernised bathrooms and a good amount of floor space. An elegant restaurant is on the premises. Breakfast is an extra BR6000.

Vesta Hotel (☎ 23 71 69; fax 23 78 39; vulitsa Krupskoi 16; s/d BR60,000/80,000) Considered the best joint in town, Vesta is small and privately run, and has a homy feel – until you get to the onsite café, which is staffed with bored men. The remodelled rooms are quite pleasant and the street outside is peaceful.

Eating

Kafe Tsitadel (Brest Fortress; mains BR800-6000; ☷ 10am-10pm, closed 2nd Tue of month) If you're starving and stuck at the fortress, Kafe Tsitadel is your only hope. Surly staff toss *pelmeni* (dumplings) and chicken Kiev in your general direction, but it would be better to stick to the Snickers or chips sold behind the bar.

Kafe Pizzeria (☎ 23 51 27; vulitsa Pushkinskaja 5; mains BR2000-6000; ☷ 11am-11pm) It's not what you might think. This relatively subdued, slightly classy restaurant is popular with locals. There are about six pizzas on the menu; the rest is Russian food. It's good value.

Santa Bar (☎ 26 36 05; vulitsa Ordzhonikidze 7; mains BR5000-20,000; ☷ 11am-4pm & 5-11pm) Under the same ownership as Jules Verne (below). The Santa Bar menu has more of a seafood focus and décor has more of a 'Journey to the Bottom of the Sea' theme, with fishing nets hanging on the walls and staff in sailor outfits (poor guys).

Jules Verne (☎ 23 67 17; vulitsa Hoholja; mains BR5000-30,000; ☷ noon-midnight) This is a true anomaly. The focus is on seafood, but there are also Indian vegetarian dishes and other odd items, such as spring rolls, dim sum, rabbit or 'Crazy Duck' (duck in caramel sauce, BR10,440). This is the sort of place where the bow-tied waiter will pour your Coke for you and scoop the food from the serving dish onto your plate. The music leans towards low-volume slow jams (eg 'I Wanna Get Freaky wit' You'), which it seems is a step up from loud Russian pop.

Entertainment

There are two performing arts venues in Brest.

Brest Drama & Music Theatre (vulitsa Lenina 21) Puts on standard, pre-approved by the government pieces – you won't see *Chicago* here, but you could catch a good presentation of a Chekhov play.

Theatre Lyalek (☎ 26 60 03; vulitsa Lenina 6) Down the street from Brest Drama & Music Theatre, Lyalek puts on puppet shows.

Shopping

If you didn't get a chance to do your bra-shopping in Minsk, there's a branch of **Milavitsa** (☎ 26 64 69; www.milavitsa.com.by; vulitsa Pushkinskaja 21; ☷ 10am-7pm Mon-Fri, 10am-4pm Sat & Sun) in Brest as well.

Getting There & Away

For schedules and prices to other Belarus destinations, see p82; for other Eastern Europe destinations, see p81.

The **train station** (☎ 005) has onsite customs. There's an interesting mosaic in the customs hall. The **bus station** (☎ 004 or 23 81 42) is in the centre of town.

HRODNA ГРОДНА
☎ 0152 / pop 300,000

By the looks of it, you'd never know that Hrodna (Grodno in Russian) is one of the bigger Belarusian cities. The quiet streets and modest homes give the impression that you're in a large village. In fact, like a large village, there's not tons for travellers to do in Hrodna. But if you're visiting the country from Poland or Lithuania, and it's on your way, it's worth a stop – if only to stroll through the parks and witness everyday life in an average Belarusian city. Because of its proximity to both Lithuania (42km away) and Poland (24km away), Hrodna once had a very multiethnic population – including a large Jewish contingency, which after WWII was wiped out.

The city centre is about 2km southwest of the train station and occupies an elevated portion of land overlooking a shallow bend in the Nioman River to the south.

Information

Belpromstroi Bank (vulitsa Telegrafnaya 8) Inside is a currency exchange; outside is a 24-hour ATM.

Beltelekom (☎ 73 00 61; vulitsa Telegrafnaya 24; per hr BR1700; ☼ 24hr) Phones and two-dozen new computers; peak hours are 5pm to 7pm.

Main post office (☎ 44 17 92; vulitsa Karla Marxa 29; ☼ 9am-5pm Mon-Fri, 9am-2pm Sat) Next door is a bank with a currency exchange.

Vedy (☎ 44 82 44; vulitsa Azeshka 38; ☼ 10am-7pm Mon-Thu, 10am-6pm Fri, 10am-4pm Sat) Inside you'll find a town map for sale, although kiosks also sell them.

Sights

At the northeastern corner of Ploshcha Savetskaja is the proud and pointy baroque **Farny Cathedral**, perhaps the most impressive church in Belarus. Built during Polish rule in the 18th century and still Catholic, it boasts a row of ornate altars leading to a huge main altarpiece constructed of multiple columns interspersed with sculpted saints.

The **Bernadine Church & Seminary** (vulitsa Parizhskoy Kamuni 1) was originally built in the 16th century but has architecture reflecting the next two centuries as well (Gothic, Renaissance, baroque).

About 250m northeast is a haunted-looking **19th-century synagogue** (Vjalikaja Traetskaja vulitsa), now the largest in Belarus. Just beyond, turn left down a shaded lane and over a wooden bridge through a pretty park to a white obelisk, which is a **monument to the city's 850th anniversary**. From there head south (left) and you'll find on the river banks the **Church of SS Boris & Hlib** (☎ 72 86 39), a small, unassuming church on a hillside. Upon closer inspection, you'll quickly note that half of the structure is wooden,

BELARUS

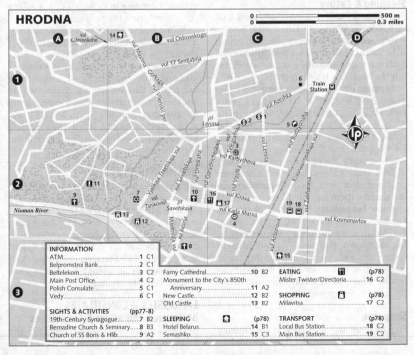

HRODNA

0 — 500 m
0 — 0.3 miles

Nioman River

INFORMATION			
ATM	1 C1		
Belpromstroi Bank	2 C1		
Beltelekom	3 C2	EATING	(p78)
Main Post Office	4 C2	Mister Twister/Directoria	16 C2
Polish Consulate	5 C1		
Vedy	6 C1	SHOPPING	(p78)
		Milavitsa	17 C2
SIGHTS & ACTIVITIES	(pp77-8)		
19th-Century Synagogue	7 B2	SLEEPING	(p78)
Bernadine Church & Seminary	8 B3	Hotel Belarus	14 B1
Church of SS Boris & Hlib	9 A2	Semashko	15 C3

SIGHTS		TRANSPORT	(p78)
Farny Cathedral	10 B2	Local Bus Station	18 C2
Monument to the City's 850th		Main Bus Station	19 C2
Anniversary	11 A2		
New Castle	12 B2		
Old Castle	13 B2		

BELARUS

and half is brick, embedded with colourful stone crosses. The stone parts date from the 12th century. It's currently a candidate for the Unesco World Heritage List.

There are actually two castles in town, but don't get your hopes up. Neither are very impressive to look at. **Novy Zamak** (New Castle; ☎ 44 72 69; admission BR3000; ☺ 10am-6pm Tue-Sun) dates from the 18th century. After the original opulent rococo building was destroyed by fire in 1944, it was rebuilt (notice the Soviet emblem above the columns) and now only the entrance gates are original. Just a smidge to the northwest is **Stari Zamak** (Old Castle; ☎ 44 60 56; BR3500; ☺ 10am-6pm Tue-Sun), which is hard to believe is a castle at all – especially from the inside, which has a cheap linoleum floor and stinks of rotten cabbage. Apparently, an original section of wall to the left as you enter still remains from the 14th-century building.

Locals are proud that Hrodna has the only zoo in Belarus. You may notice it, right next to the train station, but steer clear unless you want to be haunted for the rest of your life by images of very sad animals.

Sleeping & Eating
Hotel Belarus (☎ 44 16 74; vulitsa Kalinovskoho 1; s/d incl breakfast BR58,000/85,000) This typical Soviet-style place is somewhat popular with young Belarusians, which makes it a little noisy. Staff are friendly and the rooms are clean, but the breakfast is unforgettably dismal.

Semashko (☎ 75 02 99; vulitsa Antonova 10; s/d incl breakfast BR90,000/100,000; P) Housed in a pretty yellow building, this small, privately run place is new on the scene and is actually really good value. You simply won't find nicer rooms for the price, and the doubles are a steal if you're splitting the cost. Rooms have plenty of floor space and sunshine, and bathrooms are new and modern. Seriously consider calling ahead – there are only 12 rooms.

Mister Twister/Directoria (☎ 77 09 89; vulitsa Karla Marxa 10; mains BR6000-13,000; ☺ noon-midnight) Perhaps to make up for the few eateries to be found in town, this place has two different restaurants with the same ownership, same menu and same kitchen. Only the décor differs, so take your pick between funky eclectic modern design and a maritime theme.

Shopping
Step right up and get your very own quality Belarusian-made over the shoulder boulder holder at **Milavitsa** (☎ 73 02 22; vulitsa Karla Marxa 12; ☺ 10am-7pm Mon-Fri, 10am-4pm Sat & Sun). See p72 for more on Milavitsa.

Getting There & Away
For schedules and prices to other Belarus destinations, see p82; for other Eastern Europe destinations, see p81.

Hrodna's **train station** (☎ 44 85 56) is walkable from the centre. The small, rundown **main bus station** (☎ 44 71 80) sits about 100m behind the local bus station, which is larger. **Express minibuses** (☎ 72 02 30) leave from the main bus station. The ticket counter is outside the main building, facing the platforms.

BELARUS DIRECTORY

ACCOMMODATION
Farmers and villagers are generally generous about allowing campers to pitch a tent on their lot for an evening. Outside national parks you may camp in forests and the like, provided you don't make too much of a ruckus. Camping in or near a city is asking for trouble from the police.

While budget and mid-range accommodation standards in Belarus tend to be lower than in the West, they are still generally acceptable and often better than in Russia or Ukraine. Top-end places, of which there are few in Belarus, are for the most part equitable to what you would expect from a top-end place in the West. In this book, accommodations are listed in a general budget order, and within that breakdown, they are listed by preference.

BUSINESS HOURS
Lunch is usually for an hour and anytime between noon and 2pm. Offices are generally open 9am to 6pm during the work week, with banks closing at 5pm. Shops are open from about 9am or 10am to about 9pm Monday to Saturday, closing on Sunday around 6pm if they're open at all that day. Restaurants and bars usually open around 10am and close around 10pm to midnight.

EMBASSIES & CONSULATES
Belarusian Embassies & Consulates
Belarusian embassies abroad include the following (if your country doesn't have a

Belrusian mission, contact the nearest one to you).

Canada (☎ 613-233 9994; belamb@igs.net; 600-130 Albert St, Ottawa, Ontario)

France (☎ 01 44 14 69 79; fax 01 44 14 69 70; 38 blvd Suchet, 75016 Paris)

Germany (☎ 030-5 36 35 934; fax 030-5 36 35 924; Am Treptower Park 32, 12435 Berlin)

Latvia (☎ 732 3411; fax 732 28 91; Jezus baznicas iela 12, Riga 1050)

Lithuania (☎ 225 1666; fax 225 1662; Mimdaugo gatvõ 13, Vilnius)

Poland (☎ 022-617 23 91; fax 022-617 84 41; Ul Atenska 67, 03-978 Warsaw)

Russia (☎ 095-924 7031; fax 095-928 6633; Maroseyka ul 17/6, 101000 Moscow)

UK (☎ 020-7937 3288; fax 020-7361 0005; 6 Kensington Court, London W8 5DL)

Ukraine (☎ 044-290 0201; fax 044-290 34 13; vulitsa Sichnevoho Povstannya 6, 252010 Kyiv)

USA (☎ 202-986 1604; fax 202-986 1805 1619; New Hampshire Ave NW, Washington, DC 20009)

Embassies & Consulates in Belarus

France (☎ 017-210 28 68; fax 017-210 25 48; ploshcha Svabody 11)

Germany (☎ 017-288 17 52; fax 284 85 52; vulitsa Zakharava 26)

Latvia (☎ /fax 017-284 74 75; vulitsa Darashevicha 6a)

Lithuania (☎ 017-285 24 49; fax 017-234 72 00; vulitsa Zakharava 68)

Poland Minsk (☎ 017-283 23 10; fax 017-236 49 92; vulitsa Krapotkina 91a); Brest (☎ 0162-22 20 71; fax 017 210 32 38; vulitsa Kubysheva 34); Hrodna (☎ 0152-96 74 69; fax 0152-75 15 87; vulitsa Budzyonaha 48a)

Russia Minsk (☎ 017-222 49 85; fax 017-250 36 64; vulitsa Gvardeiskaja 5a); Brest (☎ 0162-25 56 70; fax 0162-22 24 73; vulitsa Vorovskaha 19)

UK (☎ 017-210 59 20; britinfo@nsys.by; vulitsa Karla Marxa 37)

Ukraine Minsk (☎ /fax 017-283 19 58; vulitsa Staravilenskaja 51); Brest (☎ 0162-23 75 26; vulitsa Pushkinskaja 16-1)

USA (☎ 017-210 12 83; consularminsk@usembassy .minsk.by; vulitsa Staravilenskaja 46)

FESTIVALS & EVENTS

The night of 6 July is a celebration with pagan roots called Kupalye, when young girls gather flowers and throw them into a river as a method of fortune-telling, and everyone else sits by lake or riverside fires drinking beer. In Minsk the Belarusian Musical Autumn, in the last 10 days of November, is a festival of folk and classical music and dance.

HOLIDAYS

New Year's Day 1 January
Orthodox Christmas 7 January
International Women's Day 8 March
Constitution Day 15 March
Catholic & Orthodox Easter March/April
Labour Day (May Day) 1 May
Victory Day 9 May
Independence Day 3 July
Catholic Christmas 25 December

Note that Independence Day is the date Minsk was liberated from the Nazis, not the date of independence from the USSR, which is uncelebrated.

INSURANCE

Visitors are required to possess medical insurance from an approved company covering their entire stay. It's probably unlikely you'll ever be asked for it. If your coverage is not accepted, insurance is also sold at entry points and is relatively cheap; see www.bela rusconsul.org for costs and details. Note that medical coverage is not required for holders of transit visas (see p80).

LANGUAGE

Belarusian is closely related to both Russian and Ukrainian. Today Russian dominates in nearly all aspects of social life and has been the second official language since 1995. There is little state support for keeping Belarusian alive and flourishing and many citizens are quite apathetic, if slightly embarrassed, about the subject. While much of the signage is in Belarusian (street signs, inside train and bus stations), usage is indiscriminate. There is a small but strong and growing group of student nationalists who are working to support the use of Belarusian.

MONEY

Belarusian roubles are commonly known as *zaichiki* ('rabbits': named for the one-rouble note first issued in 1992 that featured a leaping rabbit). It's overwhelming at first, the number of denominations: the bunny money comes in bills of 5, 10, 20, 50, 100, 500, 1000, 5000, 10,000, 20,000 and 50,000. Thank God there are no coins. There is serious talk of changing the currency back to Russian roubles, but developments on that have stalled.

ATMs and currency-exchange offices are not hard to find in any city. Major credit cards are accepted at many nonbudget places in Minsk. Travellers cheques are for the most part too difficult to cash, but Western credit/debit cards are widely accepted. Some businesses quote prices in euros or US dollars; prices in this chapter conform to quotes of individual businesses.

POST

The word for post office is *pashtamt*. Posting a 20g letter within Belarus costs BR65 and to any other country BR585. The best way to mail important, time-sensitive items is with the Express Mail Service (EMS), offered at most main post offices.

TELEPHONE & FAX

Avoid using payphones in Belarus; they require special phonecards and are a hassle. It's better to find your local Beltelekom, a state-run company, often open 24 hours. You can access the Internet, place international and domestic calls, and send and receive faxes at these offices. Domestic calls cost less than US$0.01 per minute within a city, and around US$0.03 per minute to elsewhere in the country. International calls are much cheaper after 9pm. Calls after 9pm to the UK cost around US$0.22 per minute; to the US US$0.33; to Canada US$0.39.

To dial within Belarus, dial ☎ 8, wait for the new tone, then city code (including the first zero) and the number. To dial abroad, dial ☎ 8+ 10, country code, city code and the number. To phone Belarus from abroad, dial ☎ 375 followed by the city code (without the first zero) and number.

For operator inquiries in English (9am to 5pm), call the Minsk number ☎ 017-221 84 48.

Getting a pre-paid SIM card for your mobile phone in Belarus involves jumping through several expensive hoops. The start-up fee is BR87,00, and then you need to pay a monthly rental fee of BR17,200 and another BR60,000, which is considered 'advance payment' on calls. If you haven't completely

---

EMERGENCY NUMBERS

- Ambulance ☎ 02
- Fire ☎ 01
- Police ☎ 03

---

given up yet, your phone needs to be tested, which will cost you another BR40,000. Contact **Velcom** (☎ 217 84 93; www.velcom.by; Melnikayte 14; ☺ 9am-8.30pm Mon-Fri, 9.30am-2.30pm Sat).

VISAS

Visa regulations change frequently; check www.belarusembassy.org for details and updates. Most foreigners need a visa. Arranging one before you arrive in the country is essential: although you can get a visa at Minsk-2 airport, you will need to show an invitation or proof of hotel reservation – and still, it's iffy, and not recommended.

There are four types of visas: transit, good for three days; visitor, if your invitation comes from an individual, for a home stay; tourist, issued if you have a hotel reservation; and business, if your invitation is from a business.

Transit visas are not available at the border; they can be obtained at any Belarusian consulate upon presentation of tickets showing the final destination as outside of Belarus. (Note: the possession of a valid Russian visa is *not* enough to serve as a transit visa for Belarus). Tourist and visitor visas are issued for 30 days, while business visas are valid for 90 days and can be multientry.

By far the simplest (but most expensive) way to get a visa is to apply through a travel agency. Alternatively, you can take a faxed confirmation from your hotel to the nearest Belarusian embassy and apply yourself.

Although it's rarely asked for, foreigners must possess medical insurance (see p79) from a pre-approved company, except if you're on a transit visa.

Once you enter Belarus, your visa must be registered; hotels will do this. Keep the small bits of registration papers to show customs upon departure. In theory, you'll be fined if you don't have them. In practice, these are rarely asked for. Visitor visas must be registered within three days at **OVIR** (Minsk ☎ 017-288 71 02; vulitsa Orlovskaja 58; ☺ 2-7pm Tue & Fri, 10am-1pm Wed, 9am-1pm Sat; Brest ☎ 0162-20 54 47; vulitsa Ostrovskaya 12; ☺ 9am-1pm & 2-6pm Mon-Fri), a ministry that is notoriously difficult; consider getting a tourist visa instead of a visitor visa, and register it at a hotel. Theoretically you can also extend your visa at OVIR, but staff don't seem to know this, so it may be difficult – it could be easier to leave the country and get a new visa.

These companies offer invitations (tourist and business) and visa advice:
www.belarusrent.com
www.belarustravel.by
www.visatorussia.com.

TRANSPORT IN BELARUS

GETTING THERE & AWAY
Air
See p72 for Minsk airport information. Departure tax is included in the cost of all flights whether the ticket is bought inside or outside the country. In Eastern Europe, Belarus' national airline **Belavia** (code B2; ☎ 227 67 89; www.belavia.by; vulitsa Njamiha 14) has direct flights to Moscow (US$170, 1½ hours, twice daily), Kyiv (US$160, thrice weekly, 1.5 hours) and Rīga (US$205, 75 minutes, five weekly).

The following are the main international airlines with offices in Minsk (area code ☎ 017).

Austrian Airlines (code OS; ☎ 289 19 70; www .austrianair.com)
El Al (code LY; ☎ 211 26 05; www.elal.co.il)
Lithuanian Airlines (code TE; ☎ 220 74 12; www.lal.lt)
LOT Polish Airlines (code LO; ☎ 226 66 28; www.lot.com)
Lufthansa (code LH; ☎ 284 71 30; www.lufthansa.com)
Swiss International Air Lines (code LX; ☎ 289 19 70; www.swiss.com)
Transaero (code UN; ☎ 289 14 53; www.transaero.ru)

Land
BUS
Train travel is a much more comfortable way to get around.

From Minsk there are daily buses to Moscow (BR34,000, 14 hours) and St Petersburg (BR41,200, 17 hours) and twice-daily buses to Rīga (BR40,000, 10 hours). Buses to Vilnius (BR18,000, four hours) leave four or five times a day.

From Brest there are about five buses daily to Warsaw (BR20,000, five hours) and at least one daily to Lviv in Ukraine (BR14,000, nine hours). Through-buses go on to Prague (BR160,000, 15 hours) once a week on Tuesdays.

From Hrodna there are express minibuses departing for Kaunas in Lithuania (BR15,000, four hours, daily), as well as to Rīga (BR28,300, eight hours, twice weekly), Vilnius (BR10,000, five hours, once daily

Friday to Sunday) and Warsaw (BR25,000, six hours, five weekly).

CAR & MOTORCYCLE
According to **Belintourist** (www.belintourist.by), the national travel agency, all foreign drivers must buy insurance at the border (it's quite cheap: about €5 for 15 days, paid in euros, US dollars or Russian roubles). The agency also offers some sort of priority border service, which involves paying for a confirmation number that purportedly speeds you through the checkpoints – but we haven't tested it.

Drivers should enter Belarus via one of the 10 main border crossings, as indicated on Map p93. International driving permits are recognised in Belarus. Roads in Belarus are predictably bad, but the main highways are decent. Fuel is available on the outskirts of most major cities but may be difficult to find elsewhere.

See also p82.

TRAIN
See the boxed text (p82) for tips on train-riding etiquette.

Prices (in Belarusian roubles) are listed as *kupeyny/platskartny*. Second *(kupeyny)* class will get you a place in a four-person car. *Platskartny* compartments, while cheaper, have open bunk accommodations and are not great for those who value privacy.

In addition to the following, there are two *kupeyny* trains daily to Warsaw (BR60,000, seven hours).

The following is for trains departing Minsk.

Destination	Cost (k/p)	Duration	Frequency
Kaliningrad	BR56,000/36,000	12hr	1 daily
Kyiv	BR45,000/27,000	12hr	1 daily
Lviv	BR43,000/27,000	13½hr	3-4 weekly
Moscow	BR70,000/45,000	11hr	dozens daily
Prague	BR230,000/–	11½hr	1 daily
Rīga	BR100,000/70,000	7½hr	3-4 weekly
St Petersburg	BR78,000/47,000	16hr	2-3 daily
Vilnius*	BR12,000*	4½hr	1 daily
Warsaw	BR90,000/–	11hr	3 daily

*sitting only

For Brest trains leaving for Poland you have to go through customs at the station, so get there early. In summer there are Brest trains to Simferopol in Ukraine (12½ hours) every other day. Note that the Brest–Lviv train arrives at 3am.

From Brest:

Destination	Cost (k/p)	Duration	Frequency
Chernivtsi	BR40,000/25,500	19hr	odd dates
Kyiv	BR42,500/27,500	15½hr	odd dates
Lviv	BR31,000/20,000	12hr	2 daily
Moscow	BR70,000/45,000	12-15hr	4 daily
Prague	BR191,210/–	17½hr	1 daily
St Petersburg	BR75,000/47,500	20hr	1 daily
Warsaw	BR53,000/–	3-5hr	2 daily

GETTING AROUND

Trains between major cities are moderately frequent and cheap – and the views are lovely. Buses are cheaper and more frequent.

Rentals cost US$60 to US$120 a day. For car-rental companies in Minsk, see right.

Hitching is never entirely safe in any country in the world, and Lonely Planet doesn't recommend it.

There are no regular domestic flights.

Train

Most of the train stations for towns covered in this chapter have an ATM, currency exchange and left-luggage (BR500 to BR900). Trains between Minsk and Brest (BR23,000/17,000, six hours) leave at least once daily. Between Minsk and Hrodna (BR20,000/15,000, six hours), trains leave two or three times a day. *Platskartny* trains between Brest and Hrodna (BR18,000, eight to 10 hours) leave daily and take so

---

TRAIN-RIDING ETIQUETTE

One of the best ways to meet locals is to take a train. Know that passengers may want to share their food with you – turning it down could be awkward and difficult. Common train food is fruit, sausage, cheese and bread (junk food is sort of frowned upon). Do offer to share your snacks and cigarettes with other passengers (they may refuse but you should be somewhat insistent – it's all part of the process).

---

long because they take a roundabout route, through Baranavichy, to get there without entering Poland.

Make sure your train doesn't go through Poland, or you'll need an extra entry on your Belarus visa.

Bus

There is at least one daily bus between Minsk and Brest (BR16,000 to BR19,000, five hours) and dozens daily between Minsk and Hrodna (BR13,000 to BR20,000, 5½ hours). Between Hrodna and Brest there are dozens of daily buses or minibuses (BR18,000, four to six hours).

Car & Motorcycle

The Brest–Minsk highway (Brestskoye shosse; E30/M1) is an excellent two-laner, but have a supply of new US$1 bills for the frequent tollbooths (they only charge cars with foreign licence plates).

With spare parts rare, road conditions rugged and getting lost inevitable, driving or riding in Belarus is undeniably problematic, but is always an adventure and the best way to really see the country. Know that signs are almost always in Cyrillic.

Drivers from the US or EU can use their own country's driving licence for six months. Cars drive in the right-hand lane, children 12 and under must sit in a back seat, and your blood-alcohol should be no higher than *zero* percent. Fuel is usually not hard to find, but try to keep your tank full, and it would even be wise to keep some spare fuel as well.

You will be instructed by signs to slow down when approaching GAI (road police) stations, and not doing so is a sure-fire way to get a substantial fine. You may see GAI signs in Russian (ГАИ) or in Belarusian (ДАЙ).

Car rental (with or without a driver) is pricey (US$60 to US$120 a day) but could be worth it if you're splitting the cost with a small group and want to get out of town a bit.

Avis (☎ 017-234 79 90; belideal@avis.solo.by; vulitsa Staravilenskaja 15, Minsk) At Hotel Belarus; English spoken.
Hertz (☎ /fax 017-226 7383; rent-car@mail.ru; vulitsa Masherava 15, Minsk) At Hotel Planeta; English spoken.

Bosnia & Hercegovina

CONTENTS

Highlights 84
Itineraries 85
Climate & When to Go 85
History 85
People 88
Religion 88
Arts 88
Environment 89
Food & Drink 89
Sarajevo 90
History 90
Orientation 90
Information 91
Sights 93
Tours 94
Festivals & Events 95
Sleeping 95
Eating 95
Drinking 97
Entertainment 97
Shopping 97
Getting There & Away 97
Getting Around 98
Around Sarajevo 98
Southern Bosnia
& Hercegovina 99
Mostar 99
Međugorje 103
Central & Northern Bosnia
& Hercegovina 105
Travnik 105
Banja Luka 106
Bihać 108
Bosnia & Hercegovina
Directory 110
Accommodation 110
Activities 110
Books 110
Business Hours 110
Customs 111
Dangers & Annoyances 111
Disabled Travellers 111
Embassies & Consulates 111
Gay & Lesbian Travellers 111
Holidays 111
Internet Resources 111
Language 112
Maps 112

Money 112
Photography & Video 112
Post 112
Telephone & Fax 112
Tourist Information 112
Visas 112
Transport in Bosnia
& Hercegovina 113
Getting There & Away 113
Getting Around 114

Stunning mountain scenery with swirling green rivers and a meld of Eastern and Western cultures characterise this country. It's been a crossroads between Byzantine and Catholic Europe, between Turkish and Austro-Hungarian empires, between the spheres of influence of Serbia and Croatia. Such a mix in the past produced a tolerant culture rich in diversity.

The wars of the 1990s almost destroyed the country but Bosnia and Hercegovina is on a slow road to recovery. Croatia and Muslim Bosnia come together in Mostar, where the old bridge, now rebuilt, will hopefully be symbolic of a reunion. Unfortunately access to much of the glorious mountain scenery is limited due to mines and unexploded ordnance. Once the long process of clearance is achieved then pristine countryside will be out there ready to explore. Already the former Olympic Games ski areas are open to an increasing number of visitors who can also raft and kayak on the rivers.

There's vibrancy about Bosnia and Hercegovina; a cultural depth and warmth for visitors, and Sarajevo is becoming a world-class tourist capital.

FAST FACTS

- **Area** 51,129 sq km
- **Capital** Sarajevo
- **Currency** convertible mark (KM); €1 = 1.96KM; US$1= 1.57KM; UK£1 = 2.82KM; A$1 = 1.14KM; ¥100 = 1.43KM; NZ$1 = 1.07KM
- **Famous for** 1984 Winter Olympics, the bridge at Mostar
- **Key Phrases** *Zdravo* (hello), *hvala* (thanks), *molim* (please), *dovidjenja* (goodbye)
- **Official Language** Bosniak, Croatian and Serbian
- **Population** 3.99 million (estimate)
- **Telephone Codes** country code ☎ 387; international access code ☎ 00
- **Visas** not required for most visitors; see p112

HIGHLIGHTS

- Explore the revitalised and dynamic city of **Sarajevo** (p90), and its old Turkish quarter, Baščaršija, with ancient mosques, craft shops and cafés serving traditional Bosnian coffee
- Cross the elegant, ancient bridge of **Mostar** (p99), destroyed in the recent war and now rebuilt as a symbol of hope
- Flock with Catholic pilgrims to **Medugorje** (p103) site of Virgin Mary apparitions
- Catch the **train** (p102) from Mostar to Sarajevo and window-gaze as it chugs alongside the emerald Neretva River before climbing the mountains via tunnels, viaducts and switchbacks
- Raft the rolling Una River through gorges near **Bihać** (p108)

> **WARNING: LAND MINES**
>
> Hundreds of thousands of mines and unexploded ordnance make for danger, not only in the country but also around suburbs and in war-damaged buildings.
>
> Sarajevo's **Mine Action Centre** (Map p85; ☎ 033-209 762; www.bhmac.org; ☙ 8am-4pm Mon-Fri) has valuable mine-awareness information.
>
> Outside city centres the golden rule is to stick to asphalt and concrete surfaces. Don't enter war-damaged buildings, avoid areas that look abandoned and regard every centimetre of ground as suspicious.

ITINERARIES

- **One week to 10 days** Arrive in Mostar from coastal Croatia and take a day trip to Medjugorje before wandering north to Sarajevo. Visitors easily get stuck in Sarajevo, which might just push this itinerary to 10 days. If you arrive from Zagreb, then start at Sarajevo.
- **Two weeks** Adding to the above, visitors will fit in more time in Medjugorje, do an organised tour out of Sarajevo and visit Travnik and Bihać (maybe some rafting), and possibly journey on to Serbia and Montenegro via Banja Luka.

CLIMATE & WHEN TO GO

Bosnia and Hercegovina has a mix of Mediterranean and central European climates (see Climate Charts p873); it gets hot in summer but quite chilly in winter, especially at elevations where snowfall can last until April.

The best time to visit is spring or summer; skiers will come between December and February. Don't worry about a seasonal crush of tourists just yet.

HISTORY

The region's ancient inhabitants were Illyrians, who were followed by the Romans, who settled around the mineral springs at Ilidža near Sarajevo. When the Roman Empire was divided in AD 395, the Drina River, today the border between Bosnia and Hercegovina, and Serbia and Montenegro, became the line that divided the Western Roman Empire from Byzantium.

The Slav groups arrived in the late 6th and early 7th centuries. In 960 the region became independent of Serbia, only to pass through the hands of other conquerors: Croatia, Byzantium, Duklja (modern-day Montenegro) and Hungary. The first Turkish raids came in 1383 and by 1463 Bosnia was a Turkish province with Sarajevo as its capital. Hercegovina is named after Herceg (Duke) Stjepan Vukčić, who ruled the southern part of the present republic from his mountain-top castle at Blagaj near Mostar until the Turkish conquest in 1482. The ruins of this castle can still be seen today above the mountain cliff from which issues the Buna River.

Bosnia and Hercegovina was assimilated into the Ottoman Empire during the 400 years of Turkish rule, forming the boundary between the Islamic and Christian worlds. Wars against Venice and Austria were frequent; Venice at one time attacked Mostar.

As the influence of the Ottoman Empire declined in the 16th and 17th centuries, the Turks strengthened their hold on Bosnia and Hercegovina to become a bulwark against attack. During the mid-19th century, national revival movements led to a reawakening among the South Slavs, and in 1875–76 peasants rose against the Turkish occupiers in Bosnia and Hercegovina and Bulgaria.

In 1878 Russia inflicted a crushing defeat on Turkey in a war over Bulgaria, and it was

BOSNIA & HERCEGOVINA

> **HOW MUCH?**
>
> - **Short taxi ride** 5KM
> - **Internet access** 3KM per hour
> - **Coffee** 1KM
> - **Slug of šlivovica** 1.50KM
> - **Movie ticket** 3KM
>
> **LONELY PLANET INDEX**
>
> - **Litre of petrol** 1.56KM
> - **Litre of water** 2KM
> - **Half-litre of beer** 2KM
> - **Souvenir Bosnian coffee set** from25KM
> - **Street snack (burek)** 2KM

decided at the Congress of Berlin in the same year that Austria-Hungary would occupy Bosnia and Hercegovina. The population naturally wanted autonomy and had to be coerced into the Habsburg Empire. Bosnia and Hercegovina was also kicked into the modern age with industrialisation and the building of railways and infrastructure. Ivo Andrić's *Bridge over the Drina* succinctly describes these changes in the town of Višegrad.

Resentment against foreign occupation intensified in 1908 when Austria annexed Bosnia and Hercegovina outright. The assassination of the Habsburg heir Archduke Franz Ferdinand by a Bosnian Serb in Sarajevo on 28 June 1914 led Austria to declare war on Serbia. Russia and France supported Serbia, and Germany backed Austria, and soon the world was at war. The British Empire was dragged in and later the Americans. These alliances still resonate today, with the Russians and French being seen as pro-Serb and Austrians and Germans pro-Croat.

Following WWI Bosnia and Hercegovina was taken into the Serb-dominated Kingdom of the Serbs, Croats and Slovenes (renamed Yugoslavia in 1929). During 1941 the Axis powers annexed Bosnia and Hercegovina to the fascist Croatian state, but the area's mountains quickly became a wartime partisan stronghold. After the war Bosnia and Hercegovina was granted republic status within Yugoslavia, which was ruled until 1980 by Josip Broz Tito.

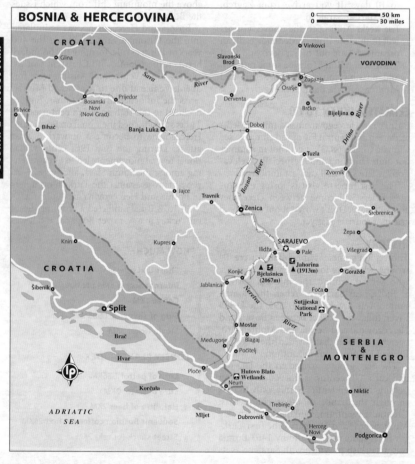

In the republic's first free elections in November 1990, the communists were defeated easily by nationalist Serb and Croat parties and a predominantly Muslim party favouring a multiethnic Bosnia and Hercegovina. The Croat and Muslim parties united their efforts against Serb nationalists, and independence from Yugoslavia was declared on 15 October 1991. Serb parliamentarians withdrew and set up their own government at Pale, 20km east of Sarajevo. Bosnia and Hercegovina was recognised internationally and admitted to the UN, but talks between the parties broke down.

The War

War broke out in April 1992. The Serbs began seizing territory aided by their inheritance of most of the Yugoslav National Army's (JNA) arms. Sarajevo came under siege by Serb irregulars on 5 April 1992. Bosnian Serbian forces began a campaign of brutal 'ethnic cleansing', expelling Muslims from northern and eastern Bosnia and Hercegovina to create a 300km corridor joining Serb ethnic areas in the west of Bosnia and Hercegovina with Serbia proper.

In 1992 the UN authorised the use of force to ensure the delivery of humanitarian aid, and 7500 UN troops were sent to Bosnia and Hercegovina. However, this UN Protection Force (Unprofor) was notoriously impotent.

Ethnic partition seemed increasingly probable. The Croats wanted their own share and in early 1993 fighting erupted between the Muslims and Croats; the latter instigated a deadly siege of the Muslim quarter of Mostar, culminating in the destruction of Mostar's historic bridge in 1993.

Even as fighting between Muslims and Croats intensified, NATO finally began to take action against the Bosnian Serbs. A Serbian mortar attack on a Sarajevo market in February 1994 left 68 dead, and US fighters belatedly began enforcing the no-fly zone over Bosnia and Hercegovina by shooting down four Serb aircraft.

Meanwhile the USA pressured the Bosnian government to join the Bosnian Croats in a federation. Soon after, Croatia took the offensive against the Serbs, overrunning Croatian Serb positions and towns in Croatia, in 1995. With Croatia now heavily involved, a pan-Balkan war seemed closer than ever.

Again, Bosnian Serb tanks and artillery attacked Sarajevo. When NATO air strikes to protect Bosnian 'safe areas' were finally authorised, the Serbs captured 300 Unprofor peacekeepers and chained them to potential targets to keep the planes away.

In July 1995 Unprofor's futility was highlighted when Bosnian Serbs attacked the safe area of Srebrenica, slaughtering an estimated 7500 Muslim men as they fled through the forest. This horrendous massacre has only been publicly acknowledged by Bosnian Serbs as an actuality in 2004.

The end of Bosnian Serb military dominance was near as European leaders loudly called for action. Croatia renewed its own internal offensive, expelling Serbs from the Krajina region of Croatia.

With Bosnian Serbs battered by two weeks of NATO air strikes in September 1995, US President Bill Clinton's proposal for a peace conference in Dayton, Ohio, USA was accepted.

The Dayton Agreement

The Dayton Agreement stipulated that the country would retain its prewar external boundaries, but would be composed of two parts, or 'entities'. The Federation of Bosnia and Hercegovina (the Muslim and Croat portion) would administer 51% of the country, which included Sarajevo, and the Serb Republic, Republika Srpska (RS), 49%.

The agreement emphasised the rights of refugees (1.2 million in other countries,

THE TWO ENTITIES OF BOSNIA & HERCEGOVINA

and one million displaced within Bosnia and Hercegovina itself) to return to their prewar homes. A NATO-led peace implementation force became the Stabilisation Force (SFOR), whose current mandate has no definite time limit.

After Dayton

Threatened sanctions forced Radovan Karadžić to step down from the RS presidency in July 1996 and Biljana Plavsić, his successor, split from the hardline Karadžić. Banja Luka, Plavsić's power base, took over from Pale as the RS capital in January 1998.

A new, relatively liberal Bosnian Serb prime minister Milorad Dodik pushed several Dayton-compliant measures through the RS parliament, including common passports, a common licence plate and a new common currency called the convertible mark. Dodik lasted until November 2000, when he failed to be re-elected; despite his efforts, reforms continue to stall.

Bosnia and Hercegovina today remains divided along ethnic lines, but tensions have ebbed. More people are now crossing between the RS and the Federation and more refugees are returning home.

The Dayton Agreement also emphasised the powers of the Hague-based International Court of Justice and authorised NATO to arrest indicted war criminals. Minor players have been arrested but the two most-wanted war criminals – Bosnian Serb leader Radovan Karadžić and his military henchman Ratko Mladić – remain at large. Several SFOR hunts for them have ended in embarrassing failure.

PEOPLE

According to the 1991 census Bosnia and Hercegovina's prewar population was around 4.5 million. Today it is estimated at just fewer than 4 million. No subsequent census has been taken but massive population shifts have changed the size of many cities. The population of Banja Luka grew by over 100,000, absorbing many Croatian Serb refugees, and initially Sarajevo and Mostar shrank, although the former has been growing again.

Serbs, Croats and Bosnian Muslims are all Southern Slavs of the same ethnic stock. Physically they are indistinguishable. The prewar population was incredibly mixed

with intermarriage common, but ethnic cleansing has concentrated Croats in Hercegovina (to the south and west), Muslims in Sarajevo and central Bosnia and Hercegovina, and Serbs in the north and east.

Inhabitants are known as Bosnian Serbs, Bosnian Croats or Bosniaks (Muslims).

RELIGION

The division of Europe between Catholicism and Orthodoxy placed a fracture line straight through Bosnia and Hercegovina. The west fell under the aegis of Rome and became Roman Catholic while the east looked to Constantinople and the Orthodox Church.

Orthodoxy and Catholicism aside, a Christian cult developed in the early Middle Ages, known as the Bogumils, who formed their own Bosnian Church. When the Ottoman Turks invaded, many of these adherents converted to Islam, most probably in a trade-off to retain civil privileges.

At the end of the 15th century Spain and Portugal evicted its Jews, who were offered a home by the Turks in Bosnia and Hercegovina, adding a fourth religion.

Today, about 40% of the population is Muslim, 31% is Orthodox, 15% Roman Catholic, 4% Protestant and 10% other religions. Most Bosnian Serbs are Orthodox and most Bosnian Croats are Catholic.

Across Bosnia and Hercegovina churches and mosques are being built (or rebuilt) at lightning speed. This is more symptomatic of strong nationalism than religion, since most people are fairly secular.

ARTS

Sarajevo, in the old Yugoslavia, was the cultural capital of the federation, but the 1990s wars put an end to that with participants fleeing back to their home republics or emigrating. Consequently, the arts scene in the country has taken a massive blow from which it has yet to recover.

Bosnia's best-known writer is Ivo Andrić (1892–1975), winner of the 1961 Nobel Prize for Literature. His novels *The Travnik Chronicles* and *Bridge over the Drina*, both written during WWII, are fictional histories dealing with the intermingling of Islamic and Orthodox societies in the small Bosnian towns of Travnik and Višegrad.

Bosnia and Hercegovina has done well with film. Danis Tanović won an Oscar in

2002 for his film *No Man's Land*. The film portrays the relationship between a Serb soldier and a Muslim soldier caught alone in the same trench while Sarajevo was under siege. Another well-respected Bosnian film about the siege is *The Perfect Circle* (1997), whose protagonist is a poet.

Sarajevo and Mostar have many galleries and Sarajevo has a first-class regional public gallery. Many artists stayed on during the war and their work has obviously been influenced by such dramatic events.

The craft industry is well developed with artisans fashioning ornamental or practical items from copper and brass, and jewellery in gold and silver. All these items can be found in the lanes of Kujundžiluk (p100) in Mostar and Baščaršija (p92) in Sarajevo.

ENVIRONMENT

Bosnia and Hercegovina is a mountainous country of 51,129 sq km in the central Balkans. Only 8% of the land is below 150m and 30 mountain peaks rise between 1700m and 2386m. Just a toe of land connects it to the sea through Croatia.

The dry and arid south gives way to a central mountainous core descending again to the green rolling hills of the north and the northeast flatlands that form the southern tip of the Hungarian plain.

Limestone forms much of the uplands creating distinctive scenery with light-grey craggy hills and caves. The rivers shine green and possess a clarity to them that's unusual elsewhere in Europe; they are also part of the country's wealth given their potential for electricity generation. Most of them flow north into the Sava; only the Neretva cuts south from Jablanica through the Dinaric Alps to Ploče on the Adriatic Sea.

There are two main national parks. Sutjeska still has remnants of a Unesco-protected primeval forest going back 20,000 years, while the Hutovo Blato wetlands are a prime sanctuary for migratory birds. About half of the country, mostly the north, is covered in forest, beech at lower altitude giving way to fir trees. Wildlife lives mainly in these forests and includes rabbits, foxes, weasels, otters, wild sheep, ibex, deer, lynxes, eagles, hawks and vultures. At higher altitudes there are bears and wolves.

Mines and unexploded ordnance puts much of the country around the former battle zones out of reach, but with local guides visits are quite feasible. These leftovers from war, the infrastructure damage, air pollution from metallurgical plants and rubbish disposal are significant environmental problems for Bosnia and Hercegovina.

FOOD & DRINK
Staples & Specialities

Bosnia's Turkish heritage is savoured in grilled meats such as *ćevapčići* (minced lamb or beef), *šnicla* (steak) or *kotleti* (rack of veal). Often accompanying these is a half-loaf of spongy *somun* bread.

Stews are popular, often cooked slowly over an open fire, with favourites such as *bosanski lonac* (Bosnian stew of cabbage and meat) or *dinstana teletina sa povrćem* (veal and vegetable stew).

Burek sold in *pekara* (bakery shops) is a substitute for a missed breakfast and come either filled with *sir* (cheese), *meso* (meat) or *krompiruša* (potato). Snacks for vegetarians are *sirnica* (cheese pie) or *zeljanica* (spinach pie) and for full-blown meals there are stewed bean dishes and stuffed peppers or courgette dishes.

The ubiquitous pizza and pasta props up the national cuisine and fish is also readily available, especially trout from various fish farms on the nation's rivers.

For sugar-soaked desserts, try baklava or *tufahije* (an apple cake topped with walnuts and whipped cream). Many cities make good cheese; feta-like Travnik cheese is especially well known.

Fine wines from Hercegovina include Žilavka (white) and Blatina (red). These are best sampled in regional wineries; Međugorje has some fine offerings. A meal can always be washed down with a shot of *šljivovica* (plum brandy) or *loza* (grape brandy).

Where to Eat & Drink

In the larger towns and cities there are plenty of small cafés and restaurants offering mostly traditional Bosnian food. In Mostar's old town and Sarajevo's Baščaršija every other establishment seems to be a place offering *ćevapčići*; you just have to follow your nose to find the nearest. Similar snack places can also be found around bus stations.

There are fewer restaurants in the ski resorts as the hotels capture their clients with half- and full-board accommodation.

BOSNIA & HERCEGOVINA

Alcohol is readily available even in Muslim areas and there are enough bars to make a good pub crawl in Mostar, Banja Luka and Sarajevo.

Coffee is however the main social lubricant; people, mostly men, meet to sip their Bosnian coffee, smoke, play cards or just talk the world into some sort of order. The coffee is served in a long-handled small brass pot from which the precious black liquid is carefully decanted into thimble-sized cups. Two lumps of sugar are usually added or the lump is held in the mouth and the coffee sipped through it. A piece of Turkish delight and a glass of water may also be taken.

Vegetarians & Vegans

The emphasis on meat in the diet means that vegetarians and vegans are hard done by. Vegetarian restaurants are a rarity: only one restaurant in Sarajevo, the Karuzo (p96), offers a meatless menu. However, many traditional and top-end restaurants will have several vegetarian dishes, although a pure vegan would have great trouble in following a strict diet when eating out.

SARAJEVO

☎ 033 / pop 602,500

Sarajevo is a small city with a global reputation and is now starting to attract tourists for more than its warring past. Those who arrive here will discover a multicultural city where East and West merge and that multiplicity is reflected in the monuments and variety of buildings in the city centre.

Sarajevo's size makes it very personable; visitors feel comfortable from the outset and gain a sense of belonging that is elusive in larger cities. This may be the reason why people intending to visit for a couple of days get stuck here for a week or more.

You don't need to invest much energy in appreciating Sarajevo. It's an easily walkable capital with good public transport and as it's a very open city there's a lot to watch. Sitting down at a café in Baščaršija gives you a ringside seat on a theatre of life.

Sarajevo bustles with energy. Rattly trams run around the city centre, innumerable cafés spread over the streets and locals spend leisurely evenings strolling down the main pedestrian street, Ferhadija. The energy poured into Bosnia and Hercegovina's recovery has rendered Sarajevo one of the fastest-changing cities in Europe.

HISTORY

While the region had its attractions for those who populated prehistory, it wasn't until the Romans arrived that Sarajevo gained a significant mention on the pages of history. Their legions, always on the lookout for a new bathhouse for some 'R and R', founded the settlement Aquae Sulphurae around the sulphur springs at Ilidža.

Sarajevo then slipped back into obscurity until the Turks arrived in the mid-15th century and their governors set up house and stayed until 1878. The city became an important market and stopping place on the east–west trading routes. It was during this time that the city gained its name, originating from the Turkish *saraj* (palace).

The 'on the go' Austro-Hungarians replaced the fading Ottoman Empire, bringing railways that connected Sarajevo and its outlook to the West. Sarajevo had street lighting before Vienna, as there were doubts about the safety of electricity and it was deemed wiser to try it out in the colonies first of all. Austro-Hungarian rule was effectively given notice on the Latin Bridge by the fatal pistol shot that killed Archduke Franz Ferdinand.

Seventy years later, in 1984, Sarajevo again attracted world attention by hosting the 14th Winter Olympic Games. Then from 1992 to 1995 the infamous siege of the city grabbed the headlines and horrified the world. Ratko Mladić, the Bosnian Serb commander, is reported as saying, 'Shoot at slow intervals until I order you to stop. Shell them until they can't sleep, don't stop until they are on the edge of madness.'

Sarajevo's heritage of six centuries was pounded into rubble and Sarajevo's only access to the outside world was via a 1km tunnel under the airport. Over 10,500 Sarajevans died and 50,000 were wounded by Bosnian Serb sniper fire and shelling. The endless new graveyards near Koševo stadium are a silent record of those terrible years.

ORIENTATION

Sarajevo is nestled in a wide valley created by the Miljacka River. The distant mountains of Jahorina and Bjelašnica, host to the 1984 Olympics, flank the city to the south.

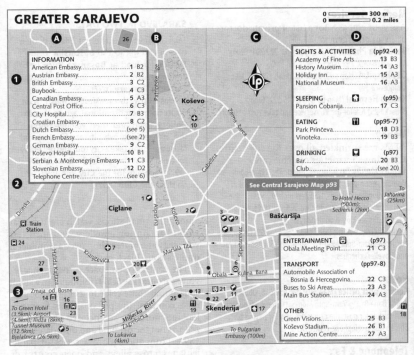

GREATER SARAJEVO

0 — 300 m
0 — 0.2 miles

INFORMATION	
American Embassy	1 B2
Austrian Embassy	2 B2
British Embassy	3 C2
Buybook	4 C3
Canadian Embassy	5 A3
Central Post Office	6 C3
City Hospital	7 B3
Croatian Embassy	8 C2
Dutch Embassy	(see 5)
French Embassy	(see 2)
German Embassy	9 C2
Koševo Hospital	10 B1
Serbian & Montenegrjn Embassy	11 C3
Slovenian Embassy	12 D2
Telephone Centre	(see 6)

SIGHTS & ACTIVITIES	(pp92-4)
Academy of Fine Arts	13 B3
History Museum	14 A3
Holiday Inn	15 A3
National Museum	16 A3
SLEEPING	(p95)
Pansion Čobanija	17 C3
EATING	(pp95-7)
Park Prinčeva	18 D3
Vinoteka	19 B3
DRINKING	(p97)
Bar	20 B3
Club	(see 20)

ENTERTAINMENT	(p97)
Obala Meeting Point	21 C3
TRANSPORT	(pp97-8)
Automobile Association of Bosnia & Hercegovina	22 C3
Buses to Ski Areas	23 A3
Main Bus Station	24 A3
OTHER	
Green Visions	25 B3
Koševo Stadium	26 B1
Mine Action Centre	27 A3

See Central Sarajevo Map p93

From the airport 6.5km to the southwest, the main road runs up to the suburb of Ilidža, then swings east through Novo Sarajevo. In doing so it passes the yellow Holiday Inn, home to journalists during the war, and becomes the section of road that gained notoriety as 'sniper alley'. The bus and train stations are to the north. Near the town centre the road runs alongside the Miljacka River, before leaving it at Baščaršija, which occupies the east end of town.

If you take a taxi up to Sedrenik on the northeastern side you get a fine view of the city and mountains behind.

STREET ADDRESSES

At the end of a number of addresses in this chapter, you'll notice the letters 'bb' instead of a street number. This shorthand, which stands for *bez broja* (without a number) is used by businesses or other nonresidential institutions, indicating that it's an official place without a street number.

INFORMATION
Bookshops

BuyBook (☎ 716 450; www.buybook.com.ba) Radićeva (Map p91; Radićeva 4; ☺ 9am-10pm Mon-Sat, 10am-6pm Sun); Zelenih Beretki (Map p93; ☎ 712 000; Zelenih Beretki 8; ☺ 9am-10pm Mon-Sat) The Radićeva branch has books on the Balkans and an in-house café. The Zelenih Beretki branch has art book specialists, English newspapers and magazines, and CDs at the Karabit Café (p97).

Šahinpašić (Map p93; ☎ 220 111; www.btc sahinpasic.com; Mula Mustafe Bašeskije 1; ☺ 9am-8pm Mon-Sat, 10am-2pm Sun) English-language newspapers, magazines, cheap English classics, maps and a stack of Lonely Planets.

Internet Access

Albatros (Map p93; ☎ 555 483; Sagrdžije 27; per hr 3KM; ☺ 9am-midnight)
Click (Map p93; ☎ 236 914; Kundurdžiluk 1; per hr 3KM; ☺ 9am-11pm)

Left Luggage

Main bus station (Map p91; Put Života 8; for 3hr 1.50KM, each subsequent hr 0.50KM) Useful while you go into town to look for accommodation.

Medical Services

Ask your embassy for a list of private doctors or in an emergency:

Baščaršija Pharmacy (Map p93; ☎ 272 301; Obala Kulina Bana 40; ☒ 24hr)

City Hospital (Map p91; State Hospital; ☎ 291 100; Kranjčevića 12)

Koševo Hospital (Map p91; ☎ 445 522; Gradska Bolnička 25) Ask for the VIP service and take your passport.

Money

ATMs are sprinkled all over the city centre, accepting all varieties of debit cards.

Airport Money Exchange (airport; ☒ 11am-6pm Mon-Sat, noon-7pm Sun) The bureau has an all-card ATM, cashes travellers cheques, transfers money and will give cash advances on your credit card. A financial lifesaver when banks are closed on Sundays.

Turkish Ziraat Bank (Map p93; ☎ 720 209; Ferhadija 10; ☒ 8.30am-8pm Mon-Fri, 9am-noon Sat) All-card ATM and travellers cheques.

Post

Central post office (Map p91; ☎ 650 618; Obala Kulina Bana 8; ☒ 7am-8pm Mon-Sat) Queue at counter 17, which is for post; the others are only for paying bills. There's also a telephone centre here.

Telephone & Fax

Telephone centre (Map p91; ☎ 650 618; Obala Kulina Bana 8; ☒ 7am-8pm) At the central post office.

Tourist Information

Tourist Information Centre (Map p93; ☎ 220 724, 532 606; www.sarajevo-tourism.com; Zelenih Beretki 22a; ☒ 9am-8pm Mon-Fri, 9am-4pm Sat, 10am-2pm Sun) A most helpful place with books, maps, brochures and ready answers for those awkward tourist questions. It can also provide information on the rest of the country.

Travel Agencies

Centrotrans (Map p93; ☎ 205 481; ferhadija16@hotmail .com; Ferhadija 16; ☒ 8am-8pm Mon-Fri, 8am-2pm Sat) Books international bus tickets and is part of the Eurolines trans-Europe bus network.

Relax Tours (Map p93; ☎ /fax 263 190; www.relaxtours .com; Zelenih Beretki 22; ☒ 9am-8pm Mon-Fri, 9am-5pm Sat) Books airline and ferry tickets.

SIGHTS
Baščaršija & Around   Map p93

A labyrinth of polished-cobble laneways makes up Baščaršija, the bustling old Turkish Quarter, where, behind the tourist panache, Sarajevo keeps its soul. Lose yourself

SARAJEVO IN TWO DAYS

Take a tram trip just to get oriented, then dive in and get lost in **Baščaršija** (below). Surface for food at **Bosanska Kuća** (p96) and walk over the river to check out the **Sarajevo Brewery** (p97).

Wake up with breakfast at **Mash** (p96). Appreciate some national art at the **Art Gallery** (p94) and then wander through the archaeology exhibits at the **National Museum** (p94). Take a city tour and get ready for a night out starting at the **Zlatna Ribica** (p97), then aim for the **City Pub** (p97) and finish at the **Club** (p97).

among the small shops, watch craftsmen at work, bargain for jewellery, and then rest your legs at a coffee shop over a thimbleful of the strong black stuff.

The central open space of Baščaršija revolves around the **Sebilj** (fountain) in a small square that some refer to as Pigeon Square on account of the pigeons. This fountain, looking more like an enclosed Oriental gazebo, is not the original and only dates from 1891. From the square a series of parallel lanes, cross alleys and open courtyards strike off in all directions to a boundary of the National Library in the east and Gazi-Husrevbey Mosque in the west.

The stylish Austro-Hungarian **National Library**, with Moorish touches, was targeted by the Serbs as a repository of Bosnian books and manuscripts, and therefore a people's culture. An incendiary shell on 25 August 1992, 100 years after construction began, wiped out a heritage. Restoration work is slow and many books may be irreplaceable. The library now has a glass and steel dome provided by the Austrian government.

Austrian Archduke Franz Ferdinand and his wife Sophie paused at the National Library (then the town hall) on that fateful 28 June 1914 and then rode west along the riverside in an open car to the **Latin Bridge** (where Zelenih Beretki meets the river). It was here that Gavrilo Princip stepped forward to fire his pistol, killing both and sparking off a war by the Austro-Hungarians against Serbia, which in turn, through a series of European alliances, led to WWI.

The elegant stone Latin Bridge is being repaired and the plaque bearing the foot-

CENTRAL SARAJEVO

INFORMATION	
Albatros................................	1 C3
Baršaršija Pharmacy...............	2 D4
BuyBook...............................	3 B4
Centrotrans..........................	4 B4
Click....................................	5 C4
Japanese Embassy..................	6 A4
Tourist Information Centre......	7 B4
Turkish Ziraat Bank................	8 B4
Šahinpašić............................	9 A3

SIGHTS & ACTIVITIES	(pp92–4)
Art Gallery............................	10 B4
Bosniak Institute...................	11 B3
Catholic Church....................	12 B3
Eternal Flame.......................	13 A4
Gazi-Husrevbey Mosque.........	14 C3
Jewish Synagogue.................	15 C3
Latin Bridge.........................	16 C4
Morića Han..........................	17 C3
National Library....................	18 D3
Novi Hram Gallery.................	19 B3
Orthodox Cathedral..............	20 B4
Orthodox Church..................	21 C3
Sebilj..................................	22 C3
Svrzo House.........................	23 C2

SLEEPING	(p95)
Guest House Halvat...............	24 D2
Hotel Europa Garni................	25 C4
Kod Keme............................	26 C4

Relax Tours...........................	27 B4
Sartour................................	28 C3
Turistička Agencija Ljubičica...	29 C3
Unis Tours............................	30 A4
Villa Orient..........................	31 D3

EATING	(pp95–7)
Bosanska Kuća......................	32 C3
Butik-Badem........................	33 C4
Dveri..................................	34 C3
Inat Kuća............................	35 D4
Indoor Market.......................	36 A4
Karuzo................................	37 B3
Mash..................................	38 A4
Outdoor Market....................	39 A3
Pekara Edin.......................(see 29)
Restaurant Jež......................	40 B4
To Be or Not to Be................	41 C4

DRINKING	(p97)
City Pub...............................	42 B4
Karabit Café.....................(see 3)
Sarajevo Brewery..................	43 D4
Zlatna Ribica........................	44 A3

ENTERTAINMENT	(p97)
National Theatre...................	45 A4

SHOPPING	(p97)
Bosnian Handicrafts..............	46 C3
Craft Shops..........................	47 D3

TRANSPORT	(pp97–8)
Bus Stop for Lukavica............	48 C4

prints of the assassin will be replaced, along with the bust of the archduke. The footprints plaque was ripped out of the pavement during the recent war because Princip was a Bosnian Serb. There are plans to open a museum at the north side of the bridge.

Look for **Sarajevo roses** on the pavements. These are skeletal hand-like indentations where a shell has exploded. Some of these are symbolically filled in with red cement. Often you will see a series of brass plaques giving the names of those killed by that shell.

Morića Han (near Saraći 73) was once a tavern when Sarajevo was a stopover on the ancient crossroads between east and west. Wickerwork chairs for coffee drinkers have

replaced benches for weary travellers and a carpet shop with waist-high stacks of rugs fills the former stables. Several times this *han* has been burnt down and this reincarnation dates from the 1970s.

Nearby is evidence of Sarajevo's multicultural past with places of worship for four religions. Sarajevans are proud to point out their close vicinity as a measure of their society. These places include the neo-Gothic 1889 **Catholic church** (Ferhadija bb) and the **Jewish synagogue** (Mula Mustafe Bašeskije). The **Novi Hram Gallery** (Mula Mustafe Bašeskije 38), next door to the synagogue, has displays of historical documents relating to Bosnia and Hercegovina's Jews. There's also the old **Orthodox Church** (☎ 534 783; Mula Mustafe Bašeskije 59), which predates the yellow-and-brown Orthodox cathedral. Don't miss the **museum** (free admission) inside the church, which showcases Russian, Greek and local icons, as well as tapestries and old manuscripts. The nearby **Gazi-Husrevbey Mosque** (☎ 532 144; Veliki Mudželeti 21; www.vakuf-gazi.ba; ☼ 9am–noon, 2.30-4pm & 5.30-7pm) was built by masons from Dubrovnik in 1531. There's a guide available free between 2.30pm and 4pm.

Just north of Baščaršija, **Svrzo House** (☎ 535 264; Glodžina 8; admission 2KM; ☼ 10am–5pm Tue-Sat, 10am-1pm Sun) shows the lifestyle of a well-to-do, 18th-century Muslim family. The owners lived in the house until 1952 when it was passed over to the city. Turkish homemakers were a tidy lot and everything not in use was put away, including the bedding. That's why the rooms may seem a little bare. There's a useful brochure in English.

Opposite the Catholic church, bibliophiles might enjoy the **Bosniak Institute** (☎ 279 800; www.bosnjackiinstitut.org; Mula Mustafe Bašeskije 21; ☼ 10am-2pm Sat), which has a collection of old Bosnian and Turkish books; groups can request a free English-language tour.

If you're ever so slightly interested in art then visit the **Art Gallery** (☎ 266 550; Zelenih Beretki 8; admission 2KM; ☼ noon-2pm Tue-Sat), with its comprehensive range of the region's modern and contemporary art.

At the western end of the city centre is the **eternal flame** that commemorates the sacrifices of WWII.

Skenderija   Map p91
The **central post office** (Obala Kulina Bana 8; ☼ 7am-8pm Mon-Sat) should be visited for its splendid imperial interior and the big hanging brass clock. Almost opposite across the river is the stunningly graceful **Academy of Fine Arts**, now an art school.

Novo Sarajevo   Map p91
The three-year siege made Sarajevo a war zone. The road into the city from the airport (now Zmaja od Bosne) was dubbed 'sniper alley' because Serb snipers in surrounding hills picked off civilians crossing the road. The bright yellow **Holiday Inn** was the home to international journalists, as it was the city's only functioning hotel. The side facing Sniper's Alley was heavily damaged, but the hotel has since been given a facelift.

Across from the Holiday Inn is the **National Museum** (☎ 668 026; www.zemaljskimuzej.ba; Zmaja od Bosne 3; adult/concession 5/1KM; ☼ 10am-2pm Tue-Sun, to 7pm Wed in summer), which makes a good stab at presenting the early history of the country. Parts of the museum are still closed but galleries with engaging ethnology and archaeology collections are open. The gardens behind contain a botanical collection.

The adjacent **History Museum** (☎ 210 418; Zmaja od Bosne 5; admission 5KM; ☼ 9am-2pm Mon-Fri, 9am-1pm Sat & Sun) adds the more recent history, displaying old photographs of Bosnia and Hercegovina. The outstanding exhibit is a room of harrowing exhibits from the 1990s war; many are personal belongings that bear some imprint of the siege.

Airport
The tunnel that saved Sarajevo! Most of the 800m stretch under the airport has collapsed, but the **Tunnel Museum** (☎ 628 591; Tuneli 1; admission 5KM; ☼ 9am-5pm winter, 9am-7pm summer), on the far (southwestern) side of the airport, shows visitors have just a glimpse of what it must have been like. The house that provided the tunnel's cover has a small museum of digging equipment and photos.

Goat Bridge
For a break from city life an old road leads alongside the Miljacka River eastwards from the National Library to an old Turkish bridge (the Goat Bridge), some eight kilometres upstream. It's pleasant for a walk or a cycle.

TOURS
Green Visions (Map p91; ☎ 717 290; Radnićka bb; www.greenvisions.ba; ☼ 9am-5pm Mon-Fri) is an active ecotourism organisation that works in promoting and preserving the country's pristine upland environment. It runs hiking treks, mountain biking and rafting events as well as visits to traditional Bosnian villages. It takes zero risks with mines and operates in places that were never areas of conflict.

The Tourist Information Centre has a list of city tour guides; **Sartour** (Map p93; ☎ 238 680, 061 800 263; www.sartour-hostel-sarajevo.ba; Mula Mustafe Bašeskije 63; ☼ 9am-7pm Nov-Apr, 7am-8pm May-Oct) and **Turisticka Agencija Ljubicica** (Map p93; ☎ 232 109, 066 131 813; www.hostelljubicica.com; Mula Mustafe Bašeskije 65; ☼ 8am-10pm winter, 7am-11pm summer) also run city tours.

FESTIVALS & EVENTS

The Tourist Information Centre has a monthly Programme of Cultural Events; check www.sarajevoarts.ba as well.

Baščaršija Noči (Nights of Baščaršija) Basically an excuse to put on and enjoy a whole range of international events in July covering dance, music and street theatre.

Sarajevo Film Festival (www.sff.ba) Presents not only new commercial releases but also art house movies at a globally acclaimed festival in August.

Futura Has been an annual festival of electronic music held in October; check with the Tourist Information Centre for future dates.

International Theatre Festival (MESS; Oct)

International Jazz Festival (www.jazzfest.ba; Nov)

SLEEPING

There are a number of accommodation agencies in Sarajevo, and there's probably more to come as the backpacker market develops. They have access to private homes whose owners rent out rooms or apartments of varying sizes and quality. These agencies may also have their own hostels. Always look before you 'buy', make sure the agency gives you a receipt and registers you with the police.

Budget

Turistička Agencija Ljubičica (Map p93; ☎ 232 109, 066 131 813; www.hostelljubicica.com; Mula Mustafe Bašeskije 65; hostel r from €8-16, private r €6-20; 🕑 8am-10pm winter, 7am-11pm summer) This helpful and hospitable 'would you like a coffee?' agency has a nearby hostel or can arrange private rooms. By arrangement it collects from the airport or stations.

Sartour (Map p93; ☎ 238 680, 061 800 263; www.sartour-hostel-sarajevo.ba; Mula Mustafe Bašeskije 63; beds €15; 🕑 9am-7pm Nov-Apr, 7am-8pm May-Oct) This amiable agency has a renovated hostel about a kilometre from Baščaršija with a mix of doubles and dorms plus another hostel near the Holiday Inn. Collection from airport or stations is free.

Kod Keme (Map p93; ☎ 531 140; Ćirčiluk Mala 15; s/d from 35/40KM) A private house with seven spick-and-span rooms in a quiet back street just south of the Gazi-Husrevbey Mosque.

Green Hotel (☎ 639 701; www.green.co.ba; Ustanička bb, Ilidža; s/d/tr 45/70.2/105KM) For those who work out, this tidy cheapie comes with a free fully equipped gym and sauna. The tram terminus is a 150m jog away with a 20-minute ride into Baščaršija or you could run all the way.

Other recommendations:

Relax Tours (Map p93; ☎ /fax 263 190; www.relaxtours.com; Zelenih Beretki 22; r 50KM; 🕑 9am-8pm Mon-Fri, 9am-5pm Sat) Books hotel rooms including ski hotels.

Unis Tours (Map p93; ☎ 667 229; www.unis-tours.ba, in Bosnian; Ferhadija 16; s/d 42/74KM; 🕑 9am-8pm Mon-Fri, 9am-5pm Sat) Books central rooms and accepts Visa and MasterCard.

Mid-Range

Pansion Čobanija (Map p91; ☎ 441 749; fax 203 937; Čobanija 29; s/d 80/120KM) With a big open lounge and leather chairs it feels as if you're staying with mates. All rooms are different, with the upstairs ones better; consider 202 with its neo–Art Deco mirrored furniture.

Guest House Halvat (Map p93; ☎ /fax 237 714; www.halvat.com.ba; Kasima Dobrače 5; s/d 89/119KM; 🖳 🖵) A suitable choice for a family visiting Sarajevo as children are welcome and those under 13 stay free. There are four doubles and one single, so families should book in advance. Downstairs there's cosy lounge and breakfast area.

Hotel Hecco (☎ 273 730; Medresa 1; s/d/tr 70/100/140KM; 🖵 P) A new hotel designed by an architect who felt that an atrium needs a water feature and that cream marble everywhere is a good idea. It works, making the place feel positively cheerful. Of course that's helped by the staff's friendly attitude.

Top End

Villa Orient (Map p93; ☎ 232 754; orient@bih.net.ba; Oprkanj 6; s/d 150/200KM; 🖵) Architecturally it's a Turkish delight with a traditional Balkan exterior and burgundy-and-cream theme colours inside. The Villa is a boutique hotel with most angles covered; there's a free fitness centre, Internet (3KM per hour) and a coffee bar open until midnight.

Hotel Europa Garni (Map p93; ☎ 232 855; www.europa-garni.ba; Vladislava Skarića 3; s/d 183/286KM; P) Built postwar with quite a few modern adoptions including wheelchair access, this hotel is slap-bang in the centre of Baščaršija. The private parking is useful and may well tip the balance in this hotel's favour.

EATING

The eating out scene is well established in Sarajevo. At the snack or quick-lunch level there are the ćevabdžinicas (places selling ćevapčići); some of the fancy expensive ones are no better than the hole-in-the-wall

BOSNIA & HERCEGOVINA

variety. A bit more upmarket, and aimed at the tourist, are a string of restaurants offering Bosnian cuisine with a little more variety. The top-notch restaurants attract the international clients (there's lots of them) with international cuisines. The majority of eateries are in the centre, in Baščaršija, and up from the river on the south side.

Restaurants

To Be or Not to Be (Map p93; ☎ 233 205; Čizmedžiluk 5; mains 4-8KM; ☼ 11am-11pm) Somewhat similar in style to the Dveri, To Be or Not to Be offers grills, generous salads and tangy seafood dishes.

Dveri (Map p93; ☎ 537 020; Prote Baković bb; mains 5-12KM; ☼ 11am-4pm & 7-11pm; ⚑) A small, small restaurant-in-hiding which could just pass as someone's kitchen laid out to expect family guests. You sit on a bench and watch the cook prepare your meal in surroundings hung with strings of garlic, chillies and corn cobs. The speciality is Macedonia Polenta, a wedge of polenta flavoured with garlic and cream and speckled with ham.

Park Prinčeva (Map p91; ☎ 222 708; mains 7-15KM; Iza Hidra 7; ☼ 9am-late) The restaurant for a romantic liaison: tables overlook the twinkling lights of Sarajevo way down below, velvet music tinkles from the keys of the white piano, and there's Bey's soup (a Bosnian aphrodisiac) on the menu. During the day the restaurant has the best views ever of the town from its terrace.

Karuzo (Map p93; ☎ 444 467; Mehmeda Spahe bb; mains 6-18KM; ☼ noon-3pm & 6-11pm Mon-Fri, 6-11pm Sat) Currently Sarajevo's only sushi and meatless-menu restaurant. Mirrored walls expand the shoebox dimensions but space is limited and only seats 18. The upshot is come early or book, as it's a popular joint. The owner takes a personal interest in your food order and cooks it himself.

Vinoteka (Map p91; ☎ 214 996; Skenderija 12; mains 14-20KM; ☼ 11am-3pm & 7-11pm, bar to 1am) A two-floor restaurant and wine bar that gathers together various European cooking schools into something that has the expat French and Italian customers asking for more. The menu changes weekly, uses only fresh ingredients and although up-market is not too expensive for an occasional splurge.

Restaurant Jež (Map p93; ☎ 650 312; Zelenih Beretki 14; mains 16-20KM; ☼ 5pm-late) The name means 'hedgehog', which doesn't feature on

the menu of this swish underground restaurant. The entrance is down an alley opposite the Orthodox cathedral. Past the old BMW motorcycle, down the stairs, through the antiques arcade, and you're there. The cuisine is typical Bosnian tinged with international extras and the warm seafood salad is worth a try. While you're waiting count the grandmother clocks on the wall.

Cafés
Map p93

Mash (☎ 308 616; Branilaca Sarajeva; mains 3-14KM; ☼ 7.30am-1am Mon-Thu, 7.30am-3am Fri, 9am-3am Sat, 10am-midnight Sun) Sometimes another *burek* brekkie might be too much to face, in which case Mash does offer a Western-style alternative. There are sandwiches, snacks and a few veggie dishes (eg veg fajitas) for those who come to graze or who just want to be quiet and recover from some late-night activity.

Bosanska Kuća (☎ 237 320; Bravadžiluk 3; mains 6-9KM; ☼ 24hr) 'Come eat,' says the waiter in national costume, inviting you into a restaurant promoting Bosnian tradition in food and setting. This snappy joint makes choosing easier with its colour-picture menu, maybe a kebab, some grilled fish, or stuffed peppers or aubergines for vegetarians.

Inat Kuća (Spite House; ☎ 447 867; Velika Alifakovac 1; mains 7-10KM; ☼ 8am-11pm) The restaurant was once over the river but when the authorities wanted to demolish it during construction of the town hall, the owner insisted it be reconstructed here – hence the name. No spite in the offerings, however, which range from snacks, maybe the *kselo mlijelo* (drinking yogurt) to balance a sticky baklava, a bowl of chips and beer or a full-blown grill. In warm weather the riverside terrace is the spot for a bit of afternoon relaxation and reading.

Quick Eats
Map p93

Bakeries for *burek* and pizza slices dot all the roads in the centre. For the ubiquitous *čevapčići*, follow your nose.

Pekara Edin (Mula Mustafe Bašeskije 69; ☼ 24hr) An always-open bakery selling pizza slices, pastries and *burek*. The *krompiruša* (spicy potato *burek*) provides just the wake-up call for a sleepy palette.

Butik-Badem (☎ 533 135; Abadžiluk 12; ☼ 8am-11pm) This health food shop, just downhill from the cobbled square in Baščaršija, has alternative snacks, from yummy chocolate-coated pistachios to fruit bars and nuts.

BOSNIA & HERCEGOVINA

Self-Catering
Map p93

The **outdoor market** (Mula Mustafe Bašeskije; 7am-5pm), behind the cathedral, overflows with fruit and vegetables. Its counterpart, the remarkable neo-classical **indoor market** (Mula Mustafe Bašeskije 4a; 7am-5pm Mon-Sat, 7am-2pm Sun) deals with dairy products and meats.

DRINKING

Drinking places and bars turn over rapidly in this city: go away for a few months and there'll be somewhere new and the favourite of last month will have closed.

Club (Map p91; 550 550; Maršala Tita 7; 10am-late) Bit difficult to find: take the first door on the left after the entrance and then go down the stairs. There's no sign as the management prefer recommendations by word of mouth. This sassy basement joint grooves to DJ music or local bands on weekends. Different rooms cater for drinking, dancing or for just chatting up others under the seductive lighting; out back a restaurant cooks up sizzling pizzas (12KM to 25KM).

Bar (Map p91; Maršala Tita 7; 7am-3am) A laidback club with white deck chairs and bolsters under the trees; listen to the music and hang out.

Zlatna Ribica (Map p93; 215 369; Kaptol 5; 9am-late) A collision of aesthetics such as baroque, *fin-de-siècle* Paris and Vienna, and Art Deco crash together in this warmly lit bar. Nature abhors a vacuum and so does the owner, filling every nook and cranny with period knick-knacks; it's a visual feast. Drinks come with a side plate of complimentary nuts and dried figs and the *rakija* (brandy) glass has a little glass cap.

City Pub (Map p93; 299 916; Despićeva bb; mains 6-9KM; 8am-late) A daytime café bar, with Lebanese and Mexican taste ticklers. At night it's a big music and drinking venue with local bands playing blues, jazz or rock most nights. This pub swings, even the bouncers smile.

Karabit Café (Map p93; 712 000; Zelenih Beretki 8; 9am-10pm Mon-Sat, 10am-6pm Sun) Often the place to go when others are closed, you've had enough of them or you're out of ideas. Buy a book, read a magazine, think heavy thoughts and let the coffee or booze edge you back into life.

Sarajevo Brewery (Map p93; 445 430; Trg Heroja 35; mains 8-18KM; noon-late) Above the river on the south bank stands a large red-and-cream edifice with copper drainpipes that is Sarajevo's famous brewery. Now part of it has been converted into a cavernous bar, all dark stained wood and brass railings. It serves standard Sarajevo beer plus a pleasant dark beer with a caramel aftertaste. When you've had just too much (liquid), ride the brass-doored lifts downstairs to the loo.

ENTERTAINMENT

The Tourist Information Centre is always well up on what's on in town.

Cinemas

Many cinemas show American films with subtitles; for extra comfort, try the **Obala Meeting Point** (Map p91; 668 186; Hamdije Kreševljakovića 13; admission from 3KM) cinema in Skenderija.

Check the daily cinema listings under the 'Kina' column in Sarajevo's daily paper, *Oslobođenđje*.

Theatre

The **National Theatre** (Map p93; 663 647; Obala Kulina Bana 9) often holds concerts, ballets and plays.

SHOPPING
Map p93

Baščaršija is the shopping magnet with small craft shops specialising in enamelled and sculptured copper and brassware, jewellery, clothes and carpets. Be adventurous and bargain.

Don't miss the *Survival Map* (15KM), a cartoon-like map of wartime Sarajevo, available in bookshops.

Bosnian Handicrafts (in Tuzla 035-282 554; www.bosnianhandicrafts.com; Culhan 1; 8am-8pm Mon-Fri, 9am-7pm Sat, 10am-4pm Sun) in Baščaršija is a nonprofit organisation working with refugees who produce colourful woven items.

GETTING THERE & AWAY
Air

For information on connections via Sarajevo airport see p113.

Bus

Courtesy of the country's political division, Sarajevo is blessed with two bus stations. Buses to Banja Luka go from both.

In winter buses for the ski fields leave from near the National Museum at 9am, and return from the ski fields at 3.30pm (fare from 7KM).

Bus schedules do change but the Tourist Information Centre always has a current schedule.

MAIN BUS STATION

Services from this **station** (Map p91; ☎ 213 100; Put Života 8) serve all places outside the RS as well as Banja Luka. Frequent buses go to Mostar (9KM one-way, 2½ hours), three to Bihać (27KM, 6½ hours) and two to Banja Luka (21KM, 5 hours).

For Croatia, three buses run to Zagreb (€30, eight hours), four to Split (€30, eight hours) and one to Dubrovnik (€30, seven hours, 7.15am).

LUKAVICA BUS STATION

This **station** (☎ 057-677 377; Lukavica village) has six buses to Belgrade (20KM, eight hours), four to Podgorica (€10, eight hours) and hourly buses to Banja Luka (18.50KM, five hours).

For the Lukavica terminus take trolleybus No 103 from Austrijski Trg to the last stop and walk 150m, or take a taxi.

Train

Services from the **train station** (Map p91; ☎ 655 330; Put Života 2) run to Mostar (9KM, three hours, departs 6.20am and 7pm) and Banja Luka (21KM, five hours, departs 10.30am) with international services to Zagreb and Budapest (see p113).

GETTING AROUND
To/From the Airport

A taxi (15KM) is the only way to get into town from the **airport** (☎ 234 841, 289 200; Kurta Schorka 34). A cheaper alternative is to take the taxi to Ilidža (5KM) and transfer to tram No 3 (1.20KM) for Baščaršija.

Car & Motorcycle

Much of Baščaršija is pedestrianised and the rest is narrow, making parking either illegal or impossible. The best option is to park to the west and use the tram.

Rental agencies at the airport include **Budget** (☎ 427 670), **Hertz** (☎ 235 050), **Avis** (☎ 463 598), **Europcar** (☎ 289 273) and **National** (☎ 893 500). Prices start from about €40 a day.

Public Transport

An efficient tram network runs east–west between Baščaršija and Ilidža. Tram No 4 from Baščaršija peels off at the main bus station; tram No 1 goes between the main bus station and Ilidža. Buy tickets at kiosks near tram stations (1.20KM, or 1.50KM from the driver). Punch your ticket on board; there are inspectors about. Bus and trolleybus tickets work the same way.

Taxi

All of Sarajevo's taxis have meters that begin at 2KM and cost about 1KM per kilometre. Call **Radio Taxi** (☎ 1515) or **Yellow Taxi Cab** (☎ 1516).

AROUND SARAJEVO

Jahorina and Bjelašnica hosted most of the 1984 Winter Olympics and offer some of Europe's best-value skiing. In winter hotels and *pansions* (pensions) only accept guests staying for a whole week with the change-over day on Saturday. All accommodation offers a choice of B&B, half- or full-board; due to this plus the effects of the war, restaurants are limited although in season there'll be the ubiquitous *čevapčići* stands.

Jahorina
☎ 057

In the RS 25km southeast of Sarajevo lie the nearly deserted slopes of Mt Jahorina with 20km of runs for alpine and Nordic skiing. Due to the absence of large-scale development, the resort has a quaint, frozen-in-time feel. The winter season is mid-December to the end of March.

Pansion Sport (☎ 270 333; granzov@paleol.net; r per person 25-55KM; **P**) is a pleasant Swiss chalet–style guesthouse at the base of the ski runs. Rates are dependent on the season and in summer the place is only open on Saturdays and Sundays. Ski equipment rental is a possibility in the winter.

Hotel Košuta (☎ 270 401; fax 270 400; per person half-board 33-75KM Dec-Feb, per person B&B/half-board/full-board 30/33/38KM Mar-Nov; **P**) is a big, made-for-the-Olympics hotel just 50m from the ski lift. Some rooms have balconies and those at the back have the best views.

Pansion Budva (☎ 270 481; fax 270 480; s/d/tr 70/90/105KM, breakfast/half-board/full-board extra 5/ 10/20KM;

WARNING

Stay on the groomed ski runs as there are mines in the vicinity of both resorts.

P) is a brand-new exercise in light wood and blue furnishings that's open all year. Very cosy and friendly and a complete contrast to the large impersonal hotels.

Hotel Kristal (☎ 270 430; www.kristal-jahorina .com; winter s/d B&B 75/130, half-board 65/150, full-board 95/170KM; P 💻) is fully open in summer when you bargain those winter prices down. It can be booked out for winter by August.

Bjelašnica
☎ 033

A more compact area than Jahorina and within the Federation of Bosnia and Hercegovina. There's only one hotel, but fortunately it's only a few minutes from all the skiing action.

Hotel Maršal (☎ 279 100; www.hotel-marsal.ba; summer B&B/half-board/full-board 42/52/62KM, winter 72/82/92KM; P 💻) is a well-equipped hotel of several storeys with commanding views over the nearby ski slops. It will take guests for less than seven days in winter but slaps on a surcharge. Added attractions include a disco with bands in the winter season, excursions out to old Bosnian villages and transport to Igoman, a small nearby skiing field with a lift and ski jump.

SOUTHERN BOSNIA & HERCEGOVINA

MOSTAR
☎ 036 / 94,000

Mostar, a beautiful and ancient town, derives its name from the 16th-century gracefully arched bridge that spans the emerald Neretva River. Mostar means 'keeper of the bridge'.

The bridge, now 21st century rather than 16th, was destroyed by Croat shelling in November 1993. Rebuilt, it is hoped again to be a symbol of intercommunity unity. On 22 July 2004 the bridge was reopened with fine words of hope for the future and reconciliation between Muslims and Croats.

Once divided only by the Neretva River, war cut Mostar into Muslim and Croat sectors. Beautiful buildings from the Turkish and Austro-Hungarian periods were shelled into skeletons of stone. Many remain along the former front line but the

old Turkish-era centre is being rebuilt and patched up.

Once again visitors wander along cobbled streets, visit 16th-century mosques and houses, browse through artisans shops, munch through a plate of *čevapčići* or sip coffee with the locals on pavement cafés.

Orientation
Mostar is a divided city. Though there are no physical barriers, Croats live on the western side of the Neretva River and Muslims on the east (though Muslims also control a small strip on the river's west bank). People are now starting to cross and for travellers there's absolutely no fuss.

You'll find maps for sale at kiosks and tourist agencies.

Information
INTERNET ACCESS
Cob Net (☎ 555 301; back of Maršala Tita bb; per hr 1KM; 🕑 8am-10pm)
Hotel Bristol (☎ 500 100; Mostarskog Bataljona bb; per hr 5KM; 🕑 24hr) One Internet computer in the foyer that's free to guests.

LEFT LUGGAGE
Luggage storage is available in the bus station for 2KM per item per day.

MONEY
Raiffeisen Bank (☎ 398 398; Kralja Tvrtka; 🕑 8am-4.30pm Mon-Fri, 8am-1pm Sat) Cashes travellers cheques and has an ATM that takes all cards.
Zagrebačka Bank (☎ 312 120; Kardinala Stepinca 18; 🕑 8am-2.30pm Mon-Fri, 8am-noon Sat) Does Western Union transfers, cashes travellers cheques and has an ATM that takes all cards.

POST
Post office (☎ 327 915; Dr Ante Starčevića bb; 🕑 7am-7pm Mon-Fri, 7am-6pm Sat) Poste-restante mail from window 12 and a bureau de change.

TELEPHONE & FAX
Telephone Centre (☎ 327 915; Dr Ante Starčevića bb; 🕑 7am-8pm Mon-Fri, 7am-7pm Sat, 8am-noon Sun)

TOURIST INFORMATION
Tourist Information Centre (☎ 397 350; www .hercegovina.ba; Oneščukova bb; 🕑 9am-9pm) A useful one-stop shop. Sells maps, guidebooks and postcards, and books accommodation, buses, planes and trains.

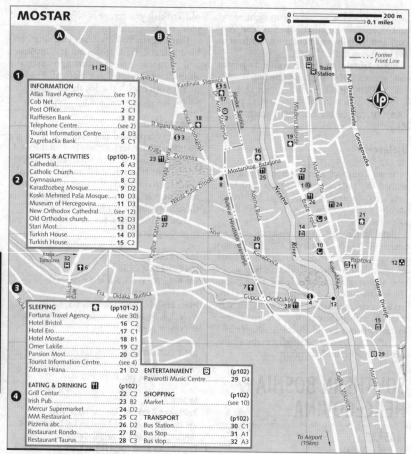

MOSTAR

INFORMATION
Atlas Travel Agency..................(see 17)
Cob Net.................................**1** C2
Post Office............................**2** C1
Raiffeisen Bank.....................**3** B2
Telephone Centre.................(see 2)
Tourist Information Centre....**4** D3
Zagrebačka Bank...................**5** C1

SIGHTS & ACTIVITIES (pp100-1)
Cathedral.............................**6** A3
Catholic Church....................**7** C3
Gymnasium...........................**8** C2
Karadžozbeg Mosque.............**9** D2
Koski Mehmed Paša Mosque..**10** D3
Museum of Hercegovina........**11** D3
New Orthodox Cathedral.....(see 12)
Old Orthodox church............**12** D3
Stari Most.............................**13** D3
Turkish House.......................**14** D3
Turkish House.......................**15** C2

SLEEPING (pp101-2)
Fortuna Travel Agency...........(see 30)
Hotel Bristol........................**16** C2
Hotel Ero.............................**17** C2
Hotel Mostar.......................**18** B1
Omer Lakiše.........................**19** C2
Pansion Most.......................**20** C3
Tourist Information Centre.....(see 4)
Zdrava Hrana.......................**21** D2

EATING & DRINKING (p102)
Grill Centar..........................**22** C2
Irish Pub..............................**23** B2
Mercur Supermarket............**24** D2
MM Restaurant....................**25** C2
Pizzeria abc.........................**26** D2
Restaurant Rondo................**27** B2
Restaurant Taurus...............**28** C3

ENTERTAINMENT (p102)
Pavarotti Music Centre.........**29** D4

SHOPPING (p102)
Market................................(see 10)

TRANSPORT (p102)
Bus Station..........................**30** C1
Bus Stop..............................**31** A1
Bus stop..............................**32** A3

TRAVEL AGENCIES

Atlas Travel Agency (☎ 326 631; fax 318 771; Kardinala Stepinca bb; ⏲ 9am-4pm Mon-Fri, 9am-noon Sat) Books hotels, flights, ferries and arranges car rental; maps available.

Fortuna Travel Agency (☎ 552 197; www.fortuna.ba; Trg Ivana Krndelja 1; ⏲ 8am-4.30pm Mon-Fri, 9am-1pm Sat) Sells maps and booklets, books accommodation, and arranges plane and ferry tickets and car hire.

Sights

Stari Most (Old Bridge), built in 1556 to replace a nearby wooden bridge, was named the Petrified Moon on account of its slender and elegant beauty. The towers of Tara and Helebija stand as architectural anchors to the bridge and as guardians of the crossing. Semicircular Tara, on the west bank, served as a gunpowder and ammunition store; Helebija, on the east bank, housed a dungeon on its lower floors and a guardhouse above. Herceguša, a third tower, stands behind the Tara.

Before the war there used to be an annual competition for young men to jump off the bridge into the river 21m below. The certificates that were awarded were brandished to impress friends and had a certain pulling power among the girls of the town.

A good photo spot is a small terrace garden amid some art galleries next to 158 Maršala Tita on the eastern bank.

The cobbled old town, called **Kujundžiluk**, stretches down both sides of Stari Most and is filled with small shops selling Turkish-style souvenirs. It gains its name from the craft of *kujunžije* (copper smithing) that is carried out here.

Along the eastern side, the most famous mosque in Mostar is the **Karadžozbeg Mosque** (1557). The top of its minaret was blown off in the hostilities and the mosque is being reconstructed. Nearby, the slightly younger 1618 **Koski Mehmed Paša Mosque** (9am-6pm) is an adequate substitute for a visit.

Between the two mosques, the 350-year-old **Turkish House** (☎ 550 677; Bišoevića 13; admission €1; 9am-3pm Nov-Feb, 8am-8pm Mar-Oct) is furnished for the life of a Bosnian somebody.

The symbolism of the courtyard is intriguing: the ground is decorated with circles of pebbles divided into five sectors denoting the number of times a good Muslim must pray each day. The fountain has 12 spouts for the months, filling four watering pots that refer to the seasons. Surrounding the fountain are three stone globes, one for the day we were born, the second facing Mecca for the life we lead and the third for death.

Upstairs the rooms are divided into men's and women's quarters. Muslim men had more than one wife and a white cloth draped over a closed door was a signal that that wife was ready to receive her husband.

The back room of the house directly overhangs the river.

There is an even older **Turkish house** (☎ 550 913; Gaše Ilića 21; admission 2KM; 8am-8pm), older than the bridge, with a fascinating interior, behind the Pavarotti Music Centre.

The dramatic **former front line**, which now essentially divides the town between Muslims and Croats, runs along the street behind Hotel Ero, then one street west to the main boulevard. Gutted buildings still stand, their empty windows gaping like skeletal eye sockets.

A once-stately building is the now damaged 1896 **Gymnasium** (school; cnr Nikole Šubic Zrinoki & Bulevar Hrvatskih Branitelja), a solid piece of Austro-Hungarian architecture softened up by Moorish flourishes. In the background stands the **Catholic Church** with an out of proportion campanile (bell tower). The original was extended after the war and smacks of a 'my campanile is higher than your minaret' one-upmanship. Poor workmanship has meant that it's acquired a lean. Higher up

on the hillside above is a large white cross that's also a recent addition.

The **Museum of Hercegovina** (☎ 551 602; Bajatova 4; admission 1.5KM; 9am-2pm Mon-Fri, 10am-noon Sat) is the former house of Džemal Bijedić, ex-head of the Yugoslav government who died in mysterious circumstances in 1978. Now a small museum dedicated more to Mostar than him, it has as its prize exhibit a 10-minute film on how Mostar used to be before 1990, the bridge jumping competition and the actual destruction of the bridge.

At the bottom of the hill is a telling graveyard where all headstones share the same date of death. Further up Bajatova, after the road passes under Udame Divizije, is a large mound of rubble. This was the New Orthodox church, hit by Croat shelling in 1993. Behind this rubble, and protected by being in a depression, is the Old Orthodox church, which survives but cannot be entered.

Sleeping

Both **Fortuna Travel Agency** (☎ 552 197; www .fortuna.ba; Trg Ivana Krndelja 1; per person 20-50KM; 8am-4.30pm Mon-Fri, 9am-1pm Sat) and the **Tourist Information Centre** (☎ 397 350; www.herce govina.ba; Onešćukova bb; 9am-9pm) book private accommodation.

Omer Lakiše (☎ 551 627; Mladena Balorde 21a; B&B with shared bathroom 20KM) Omer is a kindly retired professor with a smattering of English who lets out rooms in his private house. There are eight beds in two rooms and homeliness compensates for the shared bathroom and full rooms.

Zdrava Hrana (☎ /fax 550 969; Trg 1 Maja 20; per person s/d/apt from 25-55KM) A leg-stretch uphill on the east side will take you to this place which is suitable for small groups. This *pansion* has some apartments with a basic kitchen but no cooking facilities. So a DIY breakfast is possible or ordered breakfasts cost 5KM.

Hotel Mostar (☎ 322 679; fax 315 693; Kneza Domagoja bb; s/d 52/84KM) This standard hotel offers the best value of the town's major hotels.

Pansion Most (☎ 552 528; fax 552 660; Adema Buća 100; s/d 58/101KM;) An eight-room *pansion* on the western edge of the old town that's a cheery place, spick and span, with a receptionist who speaks excellent English. A small café fronts the *pansion* and other services include currency exchange, maps and brochures and a laundry room.

Hotel Bristol (☎ 500 100; www.bristol.co.ba; Mostarskog Bataljona bb; s/d 72/111KM; 🗙 🖵) Opened in 1904 as a fine Austro-Hungarian building it's been much modified in the interim by town planners and artillery. All the rooms have balconies making those facing the river a better option. The restaurant is reminiscent of a noisy canteen. There's one Internet computer in the foyer that's free to guests.

Hotel Ero (☎ 386 777; www.ero.ba; Dr Ante Starčevića; s/d 79/136KM; 🅿 🗙 🖵) This former state hotel, now in private hands, has been greatly brightened up, with surfaces of light-coloured wood, cream paint and white marble. All rooms have balconies and this hotel has disabled access. The fading Croat emblem on the wall outside reflects on a nationalist past.

Eating & Drinking

Ćevapčići spots are everywhere, and restaurants with divine views of the river cluster along the western river bank near Stari Most; enjoy a *šopska salata* (consisting of chopped tomato, cucumber and onion, topped with grated soft white cheese) and a fresh trout.

Grill Centar (☎ 061 198 111; Braće Fejića 13; grills 3-4KM; 🕑 7am-10.30pm) Restaurant's too grand a word for this little noshing place equipped with wooden benches and tables and a quick turnover of happy customers. The local recommendation is *ćevapčići* with *kajmak* (a salted cream turned to cheese) and a round lump of *lepinon* (bread).

Pizzeria abc (☎ 194 656; Braće Fejića 45; mains 5-9KM; 🕑 8am-11pm Mon-Sat, noon-11pm Sun) Top notch for all the varieties of pasta as well as for 25 varieties of pizza with a host of ingredients: broccoli, sardines, Gorgonzola, veal, shrimp etc. But maybe not all together. You can sit by the big windows, gaze out onto the lower town and just wonder how long that fig tree growing out of the minaret opposite will survive.

MM Restaurant (☎ 580 192; Mostarskog Bataljona bb; meals 6-12KM; 🕑 8am-10pm Mon-Sat) Buffet presentation makes this a visitor-friendly feeding station. The food's lip-smacking good with some veg options or a ham and eggs breakfast for 3KM.

Restaurant Rondo (☎ 322 100; cnr Kraljice Katerine & Save Kovačevića; mains 7-14KM; 🕑 7am-midnight; 🗙) Slap-bang on the roundabout, hence the name of this restaurant. The Rondo

is a suitable example of how you can eat cheaply in a seemingly expensive joint: the *zelzanica stagana* (spinach pie) for 3KM, the *gibanica* (cheese pie) for 4KM or choice of nine soups 2.50KM.

Restaurant Taurus (☎ 212 617; off Onešćukova; mains 8-15KM; 🕑 8am-late) This old mill is down by one of the medley of small streams that flow into the Neretva below Onešćukova. Within is a barn-like restaurant with a large fireplace for sitting by under ancient smoke-stained beams. The Buddha on the fireplace has a smoked-out look too. A roofed terrace looks out onto the river.

Mercur Supermarket (Maršala Tita bb; 🕑 7am-10pm) Has plenty of different food goodies for the self-caterers.

Irish Pub (☎ 315 338; www.irishpub-mo.com, in Bosnian; Kralja Zvonimira 15b; 🕑 8am-11pm Sun-Thu, 8am-1am Fri & Sat) A try-hard Irish pub; a few reproduction knick-knacks don't make for the genuine thing, but it serves Guinness and Kilkenny Bitter, so things aren't that bad.

There's a cluster of café bars on Kralja Tomislava that attract younger people with drinks, fast food and games rooms.

Entertainment

Pavarotti Music Centre (☎ 550 750; www.pavarottimusiccentre.com; Maršala Tita 179; 🕑 9am-10pm) This is the hub of Mostar's cultural activities for young people with a variety of exhibitions and concerts.

Getting There & Away

Mostar lies on the route between Sarajevo and the coast. Frequent buses from the **bus station** (☎ 552 025; Trg Ivana Krndelja) run to Sarajevo, Split, Dubrovnik and Zagreb.

Buses to Međugorje (4KM, 40 minutes) go from the bus stop at the junction of Biskupa Čule and Ilića.

The **train station** (☎ 552 198) is upstairs from the bus station. Twice daily trains travel to the coast at Ploče and two onto Sarajevo; one train each day starts or terminates in Zagreb. See (p113) for departure and arrival times.

The airport is for charter flights only.

Around Mostar

About 15km southeast of Mostar is the village of **Blagaj** on the green Buna River. To the side of where the river gushes out of a gaping cave at the base of a cliff is a 16th-century **Tekija** (Dervish monastery; ☎ 573 221; admission 2KM;

BOSNIA & HERCEGOVINA

THE ADVANTAGES OF TRAINS

Travellers going to Sarajevo from Mostar should consider the twice-daily train that originates at Ploče on the coast. The best train, involving an early start, leaves the neglected station in Mostar at 7.20am.

Don't expect a big train, maybe a loco and two carriages; you'll probably get a compartment to yourself. There is a buffet service, of sorts, including a range of spirits (which at that early hour might be just a tad too early) and coffee.

This is a formidable journey (for the train that is). The first part of the journey involves running alongside the pea-green Neretva River, which, nicely situated in a gorge, has been dammed for electricity. If you ate trout in Mostar likely as not it came from one of the fish farms here. Leaving the gorge the train executes a massive U-turn and goes through a series of loops, switchbacks, tunnels and viaducts as it climbs slowly over the Bjelašnica Mountains to Sarajevo.

Another useful train where poor patronage works to the traveller's advantage is the overnight Banja Luka to Belgrade service. While the service is marginally cheaper than the bus it takes longer. But which would you have? Arrive in Belgrade in the early hours in a cramped bus seat or by train in your own compartment and seating that allows you to stretch right out?

(🕑 8am-9pm). Dervishes meet here every May. Two wooden tombs in an upper room house the bodies of two Tajik dervishes who arrived with the Turks at the end of the 15th century. Downstairs, among the souvenirs, you might find a fez in your size.

MEĐUGORJE

☎ 036 / pop 4,300

Međugorje is a remarkable place, a religious tourist resort attracting Catholics worldwide: Germans, French, Koreans, Italians and English mingle here with Irish. And when the Irish are in town there's plenty of craic (and Guinness) to be had as well. Either be a pilgrim or observe the efforts of religious endeavour.

On 24 June 1981 six teenagers in this once dirt-poor mountain village claimed they'd seen a miraculous apparition of the Virgin Mary, and Međugorje's instant economic boom began. Now Međugorje is awash with pilgrims, tour buses, souvenir shops, travel agencies and *pansions*.

The Catholic Church has not officially acknowledged the apparitions (the first in Europe since Lourdes, France, in 1858 and Fatima, Portugal, in 1917). Three of the original six still claim to see the vision daily, while the Virgin Mary only appears for the other three on special days.

Međugorje largely escaped the war – some locals attribute this to divine protection but a more likely explanation is that it's an exclusively Croatian area. The killing fields came as close as 35km away.

The crowds swell around Easter, the Walk of Peace celebrating the anniversary of the first Virgin Mary appearance in 1981, the Assumption of the Virgin (15 August) and the Nativity of the Virgin (first Sunday after 8 September).

If the accommodation is sold out or you don't want to stay overnight then Mostar is less than hour away by bus.

Orientation

A town without street names or numbers! The road from Mostar enters town and turns southwest at the post office from where it's only 500 metres to St James' Church. Most of the shops, restaurants, banks and travel agencies are on this strip. There are also some *pansions* but most are spread alongside lanes reaching out into the fields and vineyards. Southwest behind the church is Mt Križevac, while Apparition Hill is to the south.

Any of the travel agents can provide a topographical map.

Information

The euro is the favoured foreign currency and is used in most pricing.

Globtour (☎ /fax 651 393, 651 593) Books ferries and runs buses to Split, Dubrovnik and Sarajevo.

Paddy Travel (☎ /fax 651482; paddy@tel.net.ba; 🕑 9am-3pm Mon-Sat Nov-Mar, 9am-6pm Mon-Sat Apr-Oct) Books accommodation, changes travellers cheques and organises day trips.

Post Office (☎ 651 510; 🕑 7am-9pm Mon-Sat, 10am-5pm Sun) Internet (4KM per hr), telephone, postal services and cash advances on credit cards.

Ured Informacija (☎ 651 988; www.medjugorje.hr; 🕑 9am-6pm) Information office for church schedules and the Virgin Mary monthly message.

Vox Tours (☎ /fax 650 771; 🕑 9am-5.30pm Mon-Fri, 9am-2pm Sat) Books airline and ferry tickets and arranges car rental.

Zagrebačka Bank (☎ 650 862; 🕑 8am-2.30pm Mon-Fri, 8am-noon Sat) Cashes travellers cheques and has an ATM that accepts all cards.

Sights & Activities

Completed in 1969, **St James' Church** is a hub of daily religious activity with services in many languages.

Behind and some 200m beyond the church is the **Resurrected Saviour**, also known as the Weeping Knee statue, so called because this gaunt metallic figure of Christ on the Cross oozes liquid at the knee. Pilgrims bring their rosaries, medallions and small bottles and hold them up to capture the supposedly holy fluid. Indeed a water-like substance does ooze from a faint crack but whether this is a matter of a miracle or some internal plumbing is for the devout or sceptic to decide.

Apparition Hill, where the Virgin was first seen on 24 June 1981, is near Podbrdo hamlet, southwest of town. A rocky, well-worn path leads uphill, the rocks shine like marble polished by many passing feet, some barefoot in acts of penitence. On the way are 10 Stations of the Cross where pilgrims stop to pray. A statue of the Virgin part way up the hill marks the place where she was supposedly seen, with a cross in the background, conveying a message of peace. To reach Apparition Hill, take the road curving left (east) from the centre of town, and follow the signs to Podbrdo (1.5km away).

Mt Križevac (Cross Mountain) lies about 2.5km southwest of town. The 45-minute hike to the top leads to a white cross, planted there in 1934 to commemorate the 1900th anniversary of Christ's death. The devout prostrate themselves to pray the rosary at the 14 Stations of the Cross along the route. Wear sturdy shoes as the path is precipitously rocky - unless you're doing it the hard way, in bare feet. No candles please as there's a fire danger.

Remedial cold beers are available at one of the several café-bars at the bottom of the hike.

If trudging up rocky hillsides is not enough activity, then the **Cirdle International** (☎ 651 401; Tromeđa bb; admission from €2.50; 🕑 9am-9pm) sports complex about 2km away on the Mostar road can offer swimming, tennis, football and a

fitness centre. On the other hand, for a bit of mollycoddling there's massage, a Jacuzzi, sauna and solarium so pilgrims can return home spiritually and physically refreshed.

Sleeping

With 17,000 rooms, Međugorje probably has more accommodation than the rest of Bosnia and Hercegovina combined. Likely as not you'll be sleeping under a cross or image of the Virgin Mary nailed to the wall.

Beds are fairly easy to find, except around major holidays. *Pansions* and hotels can fill with tour groups, so book in advance. Most *pansion* rooms look the same, though they are most expensive around the church. Proprietors will usually offer the choice of B&B, half-board or full-board. Homemade meals are usually complemented with a bottle of *domaći vino* (homemade wine).

The town's few hotels are blander and more expensive than the *pansions*, and the rooms are not much better.

Pansion Zemo (☎ /fax 651 878; www.medjugorje travel.com/zemo; Kozine district; camp site per person & tent/B&B/half-board €3/9/14) Away from the town bustle, this camping ground/*pansion* lies about 1km southeast of the church in village fields. Some rooms have bathrooms, others share.

Pansion Ivo (☎ 651 973; s/d €12/24) A small private house that's been able to benefit from the local boom and now extra floors are being built on. There are several smallish, modern rooms that are plainly equipped but are absolutely fine for a couple of days' stay. The Ivo is just about opposite the Diskont store.

Pansion Park (☎ 651 155; fax 651 494; per r B&B/half-board/full-board €15/22/28) Fronted by a big garden with plenty of seating these two large Swiss chalet–style houses are set back from the main street. Rooms are big and roomy and downstairs is a large restaurant to cater for those who have half- or full-board.

Pansion Stanko Vasilj (☎ 651 042; per person B&B/half-board/full-board €15/20/25) This pansion nicely mixes the two local earners, religion and wine, as it is also a vineyard with a rambling ivy-woven tavern and a bar stacked with full wine barrels - it could be the 1900s. It's 200m southeast of the bottom of the Mt Križevac trail.

Paddy Travel (☎ /fax 651482; paddy@tel.net.ba; r from €15; 🕑 9am-3pm Mon-Sat Nov-Mar, 9am-6pm Mon-Sat Apr-Oct) You'd better believe it, fluent Croatian spoken in an Irish brogue by the owners. They're extremely friendly, helpful and have access to 15 of the town's *pansions*.

Vox Tours (☎ /fax 650 771; per person half-board/full-board from €20/26; 🕑 9am-5.30pm Mon-Fri, 9am-2pm Sat) Over the road from Paddy Travel, Vox Tours deals with most of the *pansions* in town.

Eating

Many people will opt for half- or full-board at their hotels and *pansions*. Nevertheless there are several good restaurants not only for nosh but for a knees-up too.

Galija (☎ 651 535; mains €4-5; 🕑 10am-11pm) Revels in Italian cooking and the *risotto alle verdue* (risotto with vegetables and herbs), one of several vegetarian dishes, is a treat. A good risotto can be hard to find, more often they're just sludgy rice but not here.

Dubrovnik (☎ 651 472; mains €3-6; 🕑 7am-late) Similar in menu and price to the Galija but it scores on desserts: try the walnut pancake. It also serves Guinness and it's not unknown for an impromptu accordion band to strike up a few jigs and have the Irish dancing.

Pizzeria Colombo (pizzas €5-7; 🕑 8am-midnight) Obviously catering to the many Irish pilgrims who flock to Međugorje, this popular place between the post office and the church has pizza and, Hail Mary!, Guinness. The font on the bar dispensing this nectar is protected with a rosary to ensure a continual flow of this restorative elixir.

Diskont (☎ 650 780; 🕑 7am-10pm) is a biggish supermarket, for a small town, about 100m from the post office on the road towards Mostar.

Shopping

There are several specialist shops selling kitsch religious knick-knacks, mostly of cheap value and construction. Crosses, medallions, candles, rosaries, jigsaws of the Virgin Mary, statues, Christs in snow domes, and vestments can be bought in these supermarkets of reliquaries. One hundred euro will buy you the vestments to hold your own mass or €2500 a 1.5-metre statue of the Virgin Mary.

These aside a few stalls sell exquisitely sewn lacework or big chunky woollen sweaters. As there is no specific commandment against copyright piracy, there are a number of shops selling very cheap CDs.

Getting There & Around

Most visitors come to Međugorje from Croatia with **Globtour** (☎ /fax 651 393, 651 593), running buses from Split (18KM, 3½ hours) and Dubrovnik, via Mostar (18KM, three hours). Frequent local buses run to Mostar (4KM, 40 minutes): ask at the post office when the next one will be.

Taxis overcharge a flat fee of €5 to anywhere in the town.

CENTRAL & NORTHERN BOSNIA & HERCEGOVINA

TRAVNIK

☎ 030 / 27,500

With its lovely medieval castle and pristine natural springs, the town of Travnik is well worth a day trip from Sarajevo or a stop on the way to Banja Luka.

Tucked into a narrow valley only 90km northwest of Sarajevo, Travnik served as a seat of Turkish viziers who ruled Bosnia and Hercegovina from 1699 to 1851. The town became an international crossroads with France and Austria opening embassies in the town, and their diplomatic lives formed the basis for *The Travnik Chronicles* written by Travnik-born Ivo Andrić.

Although wartime fighting between Muslims and Croats went on in the surrounding hills, the town itself was mostly spared.

Orientation & Information

Travnik's main street, Bosanska, runs east–west. The **bus station** (☎ 792 761) is off Bosanska on the western end of town, within sight of the **post office** (☎ 547 102; Prnjavor), which can issue MasterCard advances. **Telecent@r** (☎ 518 850; Bosanska 120; 🕑 7am-11pm Mon-Sat, 9am-11pm Sun) has Internet access for 1KM per hour.

Sights

The **medieval castle** (☎ 518 140; admission 2KM; 🕑 10am-6pm Apr-Nov) was built in the 15th century to hold the Turks at bay. It never proved itself as the Bosnian state was already collapsing and the defenders surrendered. The Turks strengthened the fortifications and it remains largely intact today. Turn left on Bosanska before the Many-Coloured Mosque, go through the underpass and then straight up the hill. Cross the high arched bridge over the river and enter via an iron gate.

If it's winter and you're desperate to visit, ask at the anthropological and archaeological **museum** (☎ 518 140; off Bosanska; adult/concession 1.5/1KM; ☼ 9am-3pm Mon-Fri, 10am-2pm Sat & Sun). The museum, on two floors, presents an eclectic variety of fossils, minerals, stuffed fauna and artefacts from the Turkish period.

This museum also has the key, if needed, to the **Ivo Andrić museum** (☎ 518 140; Mustafa Kundić; admission 1.50KM; ☼ 9am-3pm Mon-Fri, 10am-2pm Sat & Sun), upstairs from Restaurant Divan, the 'birthplace' of the famed Bosnian author of *Bridge over the Drina* and *The Travnik Chronicles*. On display you will find Andrić's texts in many languages, photos of the 1961 Nobel Prize ceremonies and, in case you never go, a photograph of the actual bridge over the Drina at Višegrad. Don't be fooled, though: the museum was reconstructed in 1974 and is not the original birth house, which did stand in the vicinity.

Given Andrić's fame it's most surprising that there's no street or building named after him here. Town council please note!

At the eastern end of Bosanska is the famous **Many-Coloured Mosque**, which allegedly contains hairs from the prophet Mohammed's beard. Built in 1851 on the site of a burnt-down 1757 original, it has an eastern rather than a western minaret and the exterior has some rather fine decoration hence the name. Underneath the mosque is a small shopping mall.

Just east of the mosque is **Plava Voda** (Blue Water), where a rushing mountain stream is crossed by small wooden bridges. This is a favourite summer spot for idling. A number of stalls sell touristy knick-knacks and there are a few restaurants.

Viziers' turbes (tombs) in the town reflect the importance of Travnik as the capital of Bosnia in the 18th and 19th centuries. There are a couple on Bosanska near the Hotel Lipa. Some corporate entity has thoughtfully provided explanatory boards, in English, providing historical background to the town.

Sleeping & Eating
Pansion Oniks (☎ 512 182; Žitarnica bb; s/d 35/70KM) Behind the café of the same name near the Many-Coloured Mosque, Pansion Oniks has reasonable rooms but might be noisy being near the town bypass.

Hotel Lipa (☎ 511 604; Lažajeva 116; s/d 70/140KM) Renovated and renamed this is the top hotel in a town where several others have met the fate of closure. Everybody's friendly although not too much English is spoken. The rooms have cable TV and there's an interesting choice for the broadminded.

Restaurant Divan (☎ 818 141, 061 372 365; Mustafa Kundić; mains 8-10KM) Directly below the Ivo Andrić museum, Restaurant Divan might have the best food in town. Nothing adventurous but there's solid Bosnian cuisine and a chance to try *Travnički sir*, the famed local cheese made from sheep's milk.

Plava Voda (☎ 618 322; Šumeće 14; mains 4-7.5KM) A small streamside restaurant specialising in trout, which can be taken with a cool beer and salad on the terrace.

Getting There & Away
Buses go to Sarajevo (9KM, two hours, almost hourly), Banja Luka (13KM, three hours, four daily) and Bihać (21KM, six hours, six daily).

BANJA LUKA
☎ 051 / pop 200,000
The Republika Srpska capital is a suitable place for a breather and a look at RS life. Banja Luka was never much of a tourist centre. A 1969 earthquake destroyed about 80% of the town and in 1993 local Serbs updated the damage by blowing up all 16 of the city's mosques. The 1580 Ferhadija, a famous mosque originally built with the ransom money for an Austrian count, is due to be rebuilt but its site is still an empty plot.

Down by the emerald Vrbas River the large 16th-century castle is about the oldest thing around and is host to a summer festival of music, dance and theatre.

Orientation
The main street is Kralja Petra 1 Karadordevića (Kralja Petra), named after the great Serbian hero who led the first insurrection against the Turks in Serbia, and it runs northeast to southwest. The Vrbas River takes much the same route but in a lazy winding way. Parallel to Kralja Petra on the east side is Veselina Maslaše, a strip of cafés and bars plus stalls selling CDs, videos and the like. The castle is just south of the city centre.

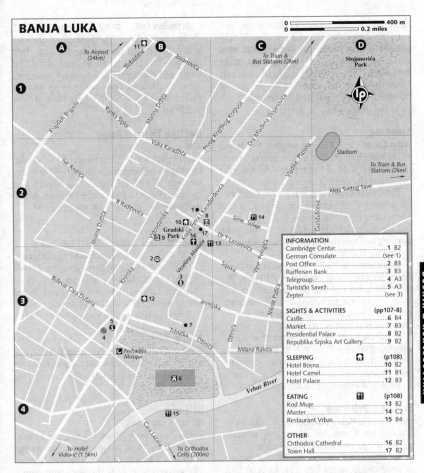

BANJA LUKA

INFORMATION	
Cambridge Centar	1 B2
German Consulate	(see 1)
Post Office	2 B3
Raiffeisen Bank	3 B3
Telegroup	4 A3
Turistički Savež	5 A3
Zepter	(see 3)

SIGHTS & ACTIVITIES	(pp107-8)
Castle	6 B4
Market	7 B3
Presidential Palace	8 B2
Republika Srpska Art Gallery	9 B2

SLEEPING	(p108)
Hotel Bosna	10 B2
Hotel Camel	11 B1
Hotel Palace	12 B3

EATING	(p108)
Kod Muje	13 B2
Master	14 C2
Restaurant Vrbas	15 B4

OTHER	
Orthodox Cathedral	16 B2
Town Hall	17 B2

BOSNIA & HERCEGOVINA

The bus station and nearby train station are about 3km northeast of the centre and the airport is some 25km north.

Information

Only RS-issued phonecards work in Banja Luka so it's better to phone from the post office. There are plenty of ATMs, including one outside the post office.

Cambridge Centar (☎ 221 730; Kralja Petra 103; ☼ 9am-9pm Mon-Fri, 9am-5pm Sat) For English-language magazines and classic literature.

Post office (☎ 211 336; Kralja Petra 93; ☼ 7am-8pm Mon-Fri, 7am-6pm Sat) Telephones and MasterCard advances.

Raiffeisen Bank (☎ 222 224; Jevrejska bb; ☼ 8.30am-7.30pm Mon-Fri, 8am-2pm Sat) Has an all-cards ATM and cashes travellers cheques.

Telegroup (☎ 213 388; Braće Mažar bb; per hr 2.50Km; ☼ 8am-11pm Mon-Sat, 10am-10pm Sun) Internet access.

Turistički Savez (☎ 212 323; tursavbl@teol.net; Kralja Petra 75; ☼ 8am-5pm Mon-Sat) This small office is somewhat difficult to find. It's down a side alley off Kralja Petra. It has maps and brochures and some staff speak a little English.

Zepter (☎ 211 100; Jevrejska bb; ☼ 8am-7pm Mon-Fri, 8am-1pm Sat) Will change KM to dinars for Serbia.

Sights

The large 16th-century **castle** of Roman origin, on the banks of the Vrbas River, is worth a wander around. The benches of the amphitheatre, overgrown with plants, were burned for fuel during the war. A path leads down beside the castle and along the Vrbas bank for a distance. Apart from that there's little else to see besides some decent buildings along Kralja Petra, including the **presidential palace**, the **Orthodox cathedral** (under restoration) and the **Republika Srpska Art Gallery.** Chess maniacs might like to challenge the locals to a game on one of the big pavement boards painted in Gradski Park near the post office.

Sleeping

Hotel Camel (☎ 319 922; cnr Slobodene & Jovanovića 41; s/d/tr 68/81/94; P 🛏) A mid-market hotel on the west side of town that'd be a useful backup if the central ones are full.

Hotel Vidović (☎ 217 217; fax 211 100; Kozarska 85; s/d 70/81KM; P 🛏) Down a leafy road a few kilometres from the centre, this quiet hotel has clean, fresh rooms. The secure off-road parking makes this an attractive stop for motoring visitors.

Hotel Bosna (☎ 215775; info@hotelbosna.com; Kralja Petra 97; old s/d 67/104KM, renovated s/d 102/144KM; P) A grand hotel right in the heart of matters with some perfectly adequate and cheap unrenovated rooms. A big restaurant, bar and shops augment this city hotel.

Hotel Palace (☎ 218 723; Kralja Petra 60; www.inecco.net/palas-sm; s/d/tr from €41/66.70/76.90; P 🛏) A long strip of a hotel fronted by pavement cafés. Inside, in addition to 'home from home' rooms, a sauna and fitness centre are available.

Eating & Drinking

Veselina Maslaše, parallel to Kralja Petra but one block east, has a long strip of cafés, pastry shops and ice-cream vendors.

Kod Muje (☎ 358 492; snacks 2-5KM; 🕐 7am-11pm) A good cheap eatery but a bit hard to find. From Kralja Petra strike southeast. With the town hall on your left, cross Veselina Maslaše and wander down an opposite laneway. This big wooden cabin-like restaurant with plastic tablecloths is a big fave with SFOR troops.

Restaurant Vrbas (☎ 464 608; Braće Potkornjaka 1; mains 6-11KM; 🕐 7am-11pm; P) Come here for the setting, a terrace under leafy plane trees nestling over the river's edge. The service allows you time to dawdle and tackling the big portions means that you're not moving from here in a rush.

Master (☎ 317 444; Sime Solaje 7; mains 8-12KM; 🕐 10am-midnight) Jaded by all that grilled meat? Then try Mexican; the locals have certainly warmed to enchiladas, fajitas and a Corona beer or two.

Orthodox Celts (☎ 467 700; Stevana Bulajića 12; 🕐 9am-1am) Take a few posters of Ireland, pull pints of Guinness, Kilkenny and Harp and you've got yourself an Irish pub. This lively and often packed bar hides beneath a suburban house. Live music happens several times a week but it's only rock 'n' roll, not Irish.

Getting There & Away
AIR

The airport, some 25km north of Banja Luka, has flights to Belgrade with JAT. At the time of research the RS airline Air Srpska was grounded due to financial problems. A taxi to the airport should cost about 30KM.

BUS

From the **bus station** (☎ 315 865; Prote N. Kostića 38) there are hourly buses to Belgrade (23KM, seven hours), three daily to Zagreb (23KM, seven hours), and seven daily to Sarajevo (23KM, five hours). Four buses run to Bihać (11KM, three hours).

A taxi to the station should cost 5KM.

TRAIN

The **train station** (☎ 300 752; Srpskih Boraca 17) has some useful international connections to Belgrade, coastal Croatia and Zagreb (see p113).

BIHAĆ
☎ 037 / pop 65,000

Tucked up in northwest Bosnia and Hercegovina, Bihać is earning a reputation as one of Bosnia's more outdoors-oriented towns. The attraction here is the wide and gently rolling Una River, bursting into action now and again with tumbling rapids. This makes it an ideal place for kayaking and rafting. The Una Regatta in the last week of July is three days of messing about in boats.

Orientation

The usual approach is from Novi Grad on the Croatian border following the Una southwest through an impressive limestone gorge. The Una River cleaves the town into a western side with the town centre and an eastern side with some expensive riverside hotels and restaurants. On that side Bihaćkih Branilaca leads out of town northwards to Novi Grad and south, past the bus station on Put V Korpusa, to Sarajevo.

Information

Centar (Put V Korpusa 5; per hr 2KM) Internet access.

Post office (☎ 332 332; Bosanska bb; ☼ 7am-9pm Mon-Sat, 9am-noon Sun) Poste-restante facilities, MasterCard cash advances.

Raiffeisen Bank (☎ 329 000; Dana Državnosti 5; ☼ 8am-6pm Mon-Fri, 8am-2pm Sat) Cashes travellers cheques and has an ATM that accepts all cards.

Telephone office (☎ 310 055; Bosanska 3; ☼ 7am-9pm Mon-Sat, 9am-noon Sun) Opposite the post office.

Tourist office (☎ 222 777; Dr Irfana Ljubijankića 13; ☼ 8am-4pm Mon-Fri) A clued-up organisation with its finger on river activities and accommodation possibilities.

Sights

The lofty, stone **captain's tower** on the western side of the river dates from the early 16th century. It was a prison from 1878 to 1959 but now holds a nifty multilevel **museum** (☎ 223 214; admission 1KM; ☼ 9am-4pm Mon-Fri, 9am-2pm Sat) featuring sarcophagi from the Bihać area and the history of the town.

Behind the tower are the remains of the Church of St Anthony, destroyed in WWII. The original St Anthony is now the Fethya Mosque at the other end of the town and was converted by the Turks took in the 1530s. At the end of the 17th century the Croats ousted the Turks and built a new St Anthony's. It was never completely finished and war damage has left just a bell tower.

Adjacent is a Muslim turbe containing the bodies of two martyrs.

Activities

The rafting season usually runs from March to October and there are two main outfits who can provide for water thrill-seekers. Both need a minimum of about six but it's always possible to join up with another group. Prices depend upon the length and complexity of the trip. They can cater for both nervous first-timers and hard cases.

Both owners will collect by arrangement from the bus station.

Una Kiro Rafting (☎ /fax 223 760, 061 192 338; www.una-kiro-rafting.com; Muse Ćazima Ćatića 1) Based at Golubic, 6km from Bihać, this outfit also offers kayak lessons, equipment and accommodation. Camping is available from €5 per person and there's a free kayak available for just messing around in.

Una Rafting (Sport Bjeli; ☎ 223 502, 061 138 853; www.unarafting.com; Klokot, Pecikovići bb; rafting 40-80KM) Based about 12km away from Bihać, this outfit offers rafting, kayaking and mountain biking plus accommodation.

For information on fishing, ask the tourist office.

Sleeping

There's a range of accommodation with the rafting outfits providing camping or basic accommodation, some good *pansions* and some expensive hotels down on the river which are not worth a look. If these are full ask the tourist office for some alternatives.

Hut Aduna (☎ 310 487; Put V Korpusa bb; per person 5KM; **P**) An under-the-trees camping ground, about 5km out of town between the Una River and the Sunce Hotel. Sites are powered and there's a toilet and shower block.

MB Lipovaća (☎ 351 620; Dr Irfana Ljubijankića 91; s 32-45KM, d/tr 80/120KM; **P**) About 2km out of town, this decent hotel has all the usual mod cons although the cheaper singles are without TV. Catch up on all that holiday reading.

Hotel Park (☎ 332 553; fax 331 883; Put V Korpusa bb; unrestored s/d 44/88KM, restored s/d 54/98KM; **P**) The town's big hotel and probably the best bet for value, especially if you go for the unrestored rooms, which are perfectly adequate.

Villa Una (☎ /fax 311 393; Bihaćkih Branilaca 20; s/d 50/70KM; **P**) Centrally placed near the river and good value for a sparkling-clean private home with well-equipped rooms.

Eating

Express (☎ 332 380; Bosanska 5; mains 3-5KM; ☼ 7am-10pm) Express by name, express by nature. Choose, point and eat well at this cafeteria near the post office. Choices are hot meals, salads, cakes and drinks.

Meno (☎ 311 511; Bihaćkih Branilaca 35; pizzas 5-10KM; ☼ 8am-11pm) The top place in town for pizza with a wide range and sizes. It's a takeaway place as well.

Sunce (☎ 310 487; Put V Korpusa bb; mains 8-15KM; ☼ 8am-11pm) A big fancy restaurant built jutting out over the Una River some 5km south of town. Big plate-glass windows look out onto the river with its weir, islets and old mill. The house speciality is Plata Una, 30KM for two, which is an antipasto

BOSNIA & HERCEGOVINA

dish with nearly everything on it. Of course trout features on the menu.

River Una (☎ 310 014; Džemala Bijedića 12; mains 10-15KM; ☼ 7am-11pm) This restaurant offers a central serene riverside setting, with the water lapping at your feet, in which to enjoy some well-garlicked squid and fine trout.

Samoposluga (☎ 55312 601; Bihaćkih Branilaca bb; ☼ 7.30am-10pm Mon-Sat, 8am-3pm Sun) A sizeable supermarket next to Villa Una that should cater to your feed-yourself requirements.

Tasun (Bihaćkih Branilaca bb; ☼ 24hr) A jumping all-night bar that's the hangout of those in Bihać with time and money to party.

Getting There & Away

Bihać is best reached via Banja Luka. Services from the **bus station** (☎ 350 676; Put V Korpusa bb) are somewhat limited with two buses daily to Banja Luka (11KM, three hours), three to Sarajevo (28KM, six hours) and five daily to Zagreb (21KM, 2½ hours)

Trains are still very infrequent and only local, as much repair work still needs to be done to the infrastructure.

BOSNIA & HERCEGOVINA DIRECTORY

ACCOMMODATION

Prices quoted for summer are for July to September. Winter prices relate to the ski season, generally December to February. Prices in this chapter are listed in budget order (from cheapest to most expensive).

Private accommodation is easy to arrange in Sarajevo and is also possible in Mostar. Elsewhere, ask the local people at markets or shops.

Staying in a home is not only cheaper, but also usually very pleasant. Likely as not, your hosts will ply you with coffee, pull out old pictures of Tito (depending on their politics), and regale you with many tales of old Yugoslavia's glorious past.

Sarajevo is well blessed for budget accommodation and as more visitors go to Mostar cheaper accommodation will become more available.

Most towns will have *pansions* (pensions, guesthouses) that are generally slightly humbler and more personable than the hotels. Hotels are everywhere. Some have

not changed since the days of their state ownership while some have been privatised and modernised.

Unless otherwise mentioned breakfast is not included with private accommodation but is for *pansions* and hotels. Also unless stated all rooms have private bathrooms. Most hotels and all but the cheapest *pansions* have cable TV. There are no laundrettes, but *pansions* and hotels will usually do laundry if asked. Prices vary; expect about 10KM to 20KM a load. Sarajevo has dry-cleaning facilities.

ACTIVITIES

Outdoor activities such as hiking and camping are severely compromised by the presence of mines. However, Jahorina and Bjelašnica, Bosnia and Hercegovina's ski resorts (see p98), are again open.

The rafting season runs from March to October. The Una River near Bihać (p108) is particularly popular for this.

Green Visions (Map p91; ☎ /fax 033-207 169; www .greenvisions.ba; Terezija bb) is a Sarajevo ecotourism agency popular with expat workers that runs outdoors trips. See (p94).

BOOKS

Zoë Brân's *After Yugoslavia*, part of the Lonely Planet Journeys series, follows the author's travels through the former Yugoslavia in the aftermath of the collapse, reflecting on her earlier journey to the region in 1978.

While Rebecca West's mammoth *Black Lamb & Grey Falcon* (published 1941) remains a classic piece of travel writing, its 1937 ending is of no use for understanding what happened next. Noel Malcolm's *Bosnia: A Short History* is a good country-specific complement that brings history more up to date.

Misha Glenny's *The Balkans, Nationalism, War, and the Great Powers, 1804–1999*, has some telling pages on the background to the recent war. *Balkan Babel* by Sabrina Ramet is an engaging look at Yugoslavia from Tito to Milošević.

BUSINESS HOURS

Official hours are 8am to 4pm Monday to Friday; banks open Saturday mornings. Shops are open longer hours and many open on Sunday.

CUSTOMS

Removing your shoes is usual in Muslim households; the host will provide slippers. When greeting acquaintances in Sarajevo or elsewhere in the Federation, it is customary to plant one kiss on each cheek. In the RS, three kisses (one-one-one) is the norm.

DANGERS & ANNOYANCES

Bosnia and Herzegovina's greatest danger is that some areas are heavily mined; see the boxed text on p85. Nationalism runs strong in some parts of the country (notably the RS and Croat areas to the south and west), but this should not affect international travellers, who can expect a warm welcome almost everywhere.

DISABLED TRAVELLERS

There has been much effort to make things easier for travellers with disabilities, especially those with wheelchairs. This is partly in response to those who have been disabled through war and also through rebuilding to Western standards. Smaller hotels won't have lifts and disabled toilets are still rare.

EMBASSIES & CONSULATES
Bosnian Embassies & Consulates

Bosnia and Herzegovina has embassies and/ or consulates in the following countries; www.mvp.gov.ba has further listings.

Australia (☎ 02-6232 4646; fax 02-6232 5554; 6 Beale Crescent, Deakin, ACT 2600)

Canada (☎ 613-236 0028; fax 613-236 1139; 130 Albert St, Suite 805, Ottawa, Ontario K1P 5G4)

Croatia (☎ 01-48 19 420; fax 01-48 19 418; Pavla Hatza 3, PP27, 10001 Zagreb)

France (☎ 01 42 67 34 22; fax 01 40 53 85 22; 174 Rue de Courcelles, 75017 Paris)

Germany Berlin (☎ 030-814 712 33/4/5; fax 030-814 712 31 Ibsenstrasse 14, D-10439); Bonn (☎ 0228-35 00 60; fax 0228-35 00 698 Friedrich-Wilhelm strasse 2, 53113); Munich (☎ 089-982 80 64/5; fax 089-982 80 79 Montsalvat strasse 19, 80804 Munich)

Netherlands (☎ 70-358 85 05; fax 70-358 43 67; Bezuidenhoutseweg 223, 2594 AL Den Haag)

Slovenia (☎ 01-432 40 42; fax 01-432 22 30; Kolarjeva 26, 1000 Ljubljana)

UK (☎ 020-7373 0867; 5-7 Lexham Gardens, London W1R 3BF)

USA Washington DC (☎ 202-337 1500; fax 202-337 1502; 2109 E St NW, Washington, DC 20037); New York (☎ 212-593 1042; fax 212-751 9019; 866 UN Plaza, Suite 580, New York, NY 10017)

Embassies & Consulates in Bosnia & Hercegovina

The nearest embassies for Australia, Ireland and New Zealand are found in Belgrade, Ljubljana and Rome respectively. These countries have representation in Sarajevo:

Austria (Map p91; ☎ 033-279 400; fax 033-668 339; Džidžikovac 7)

Bulgaria (☎ 033-668 191; fax 033-668 182; possar@bih .net.ba; Soukbunar 5)

Canada (Map p91; ☎ 033-222 033; 033-fax 222 004; Grbavička 4/2)

Croatia (Map p91; ☎ 033-444 331; fax 033-472 434; Mehmeda Spahe 16)

France (Map p91; ☎ 033-668 151; fax 033-212 186; Mehmed-bega K. Lj 18)

Germany Sarajevo (Map p91; ☎ 033-275 000; fax 033-652 978; Mejtaš Buka 11-13); Banja Luka (☎ 051-277 949; fax 051-217 113; Kralja Petra 103, Banja Luka)

Japan (Map p93; ☎ 033-209 580; fax 033-209 583; M.M.Bašeskije 2)

Netherlands (Map p91; ☎ 033-223 404; fax 033-223 413; Grbavička 4/1)

Serbia and Montenegro (Map p91; ☎ 033-260 080; fax 033-221 469; Obala Maka Dizdara 3a)

Slovenia (Map p91; ☎ 033-271 260; fax 033-271 270; Bentbaša 7)

UK (Map p91; ☎ 033-444 429; fax 033-666 131; britemb@bih.net.ba; Tina Ujevića 8)

USA (Map p91; ☎ 033-445 700; fax 033-659 722; opabih@pd.state.gov; Alipašina 43)

GAY & LESBIAN TRAVELLERS

Homosexuality is not at all well regarded in Bosnia and Herzegovina, although Sarajevo is more tolerant. Homosexuality is legal and the age of consent is 16. There are no public organisations for contact.

HOLIDAYS

Bajram, a twice-yearly Muslim holiday (February and November or December), is observed in parts of the Federation. Easter and Christmas are observed but Orthodox and Catholic dates may not coincide.

New Year's Day 1 January
Independence Day 1 March
May Day 1 May
National Statehood Day 25 November

INTERNET RESOURCES

Bosnia and Herzegovina's natural and cultural wonders are talked up at www.bhtourism.ba, which is administered by the Office of the High Representative, itself a good source of news, see www.ohr.int. The website www.insidebosnia.com has news on events and other interesting links. The government website www.mvp.gov.ba gives details on embassies and visas.

LANGUAGE

Notwithstanding different dialects, the people of Bosnia and Hercegovina basically speak the same language. However, that language is referred to as 'Bosniak' in the Muslim parts of the Federation, 'Croatian' in Croat-controlled parts and 'Serbian' in the RS.

The Federation uses the Latin alphabet; the RS uses Cyrillic. See the Croatian and Serbian section of the Language chapter (p909).

MAPS

Freytag & Berndt produces a good 1:250,000 road map of Bosnia and Hercegovina. Maps of Mostar, Sarajevo and Banja Luka are readily available from bookshops, kiosks or tourist information centres.

MONEY

ATMs

ATMs are all over the place with MasterCard, Visa and their offshoots being accepted.

Credit Cards

Visa, MasterCard and Diners Club are readily accepted by larger establishments all over the country.

Currency

The euro is the shadow currency. The convertible mark (KM), Bosnia's currency, is tied to the euro at a rate of 1KM to €0.51129. Many establishments (especially hotels) accept euros (notes only) and sometimes also list their prices in euros.

When changing money, it's best to ask for small bills as shops often are hard-pressed for change.

Travellers Cheques

Travellers cheques can be readily changed at Raiffeisen and Zagrebačka banks, one or both of which have branches in the places mentioned in this chapter.

PHOTOGRAPHY & VIDEO

Photographing military installations (including airports, bridges, checkpoints, troops

and bases) and embassies is forbidden. If in doubt, ask before taking photographs.

POST

Post and telephone offices are usually combined. Poste-restante service is available at all cities included in this book; letters should be addressed to: (Name), Poste Restante, (postcode), Bosnia and Hercegovina.

Postcodes are: Travnik 72270, Banja Luka 78101, Bihać 77000, Medugorje 88266, Mostar (Zapadni) 88000. A fee is usually charged when the mail is picked up.

TELEPHONE & FAX

Phonecards, for local or short international calls at public phones, can be bought at post offices or street kiosks for 2KM or 5KM.

There's a button labelled 'language' to give you instructions in English. Unfortunately, cards issued in the Serbian, Croatian or Bosnian parts of the country are not interchangeable.

It's cheaper to use the telephone section of post offices for longer calls. Calls to Australia/Britain/North America cost 2.09/1.05/1.05KM. One page of fax to the same destinations costs the same.

Dial ☎ 1201 for the international operator and ☎ 1188 if you need local directory information.

Telephone numbers starting with 061 in this chapter are for mobile phones.

EMERGENCY SERVICES

- Fire ☎ 123
- Medical emergency ☎ 124
- Police ☎ 122
- Roadside emergency ☎ 1282/1288

TOURIST INFORMATION

Larger cities, including Sarajevo, Banja Luka, Mostar, Bihać and Medugorje, have tourist offices. The underemployed staff are generally delighted to see travellers and will dispense maps, brochures and advice.

VISAS

Citizens of the EU and the following countries do not require a visa: Andorra, Australia, Brunei, Canada, Croatia, Japan, Kuwait, Liechtenstein, Macedonia, Malaysia,

Monaco, New Zealand, Norway, Qatar, Russia, San Marino, Serbia and Montenegro, Switzerland, the Vatican, Turkey and the USA.

Citizens of all other countries must apply for a visa; forms can be obtained from Bosnia and Hercegovina consular offices. An application for a private visit visa must be accompanied by a letter of invitation from a citizen of the country while a tourist visa application must be accompanied by a voucher from the tourist agency organising the visit.

The cost of a single entry visa is €31, a multiple-entry visa for up to 90 days €57 and a multiple-entry visa for over 90 days €72. One photograph needs to accompany the application. For a full list and application requirements check the government website www.mvp.gov.ba.

TRANSPORT IN BOSNIA & HERCEGOVINA

GETTING THERE & AWAY
Air
Bosnia and Hercegovina's main airport is at Sarajevo; Mostar has an airport but only receives charter flights. The country's other airport is that of Banja Luka in the RS. The airline Air Srpska was not flying at the time of research due to financial reasons.

Bosnia and Hercegovina is served by a few European airlines such as Austrian Airlines, Lufthansa and Adria Airways, which pick up at intercontinental hubs like London, Frankfurt and Vienna. No discount airlines fly into Bosnia and Hercegovina but cheap flights to Dubrovnik in Croatia and a bus trip into the country would be worth investigating.

The following airlines (Sarajevo phone numbers) serve **Sarajevo airport** (☎ 289 100; www.sarajevo-airport.ba):

Adria Airways (code JP; ☎ 232 125; www.adria-airways.com)
Austrian Airlines (code OS; ☎ 202 059; www.aua.com)
Croatia Airlines (code OU; ☎ 666 123; www.croatiaairlines.hr)
JAT (code JU; ☎ 259 750; www.jat.com)
Lufthansa (code LH; ☎ 278 590; www.lufthansa.com)
Malév Hungarian Airlines (code MA; ☎ 473 200; www.malev.hu)

Scandjet (code FLY; ☎ 266 430; www.scandjet.se)
Swiss International Air Lines (code LX; ☎ 208 971; www.swiss.com)
Turkish Airlines (code TK; ☎ 666 092; www.turkishairlines.com)

JAT serves **Banja Luka airport** (☎ 051-835 210).

Land
A return ticket is cheaper than two single tickets.

BORDER CROSSINGS
There are no problems in crossing any of the borders that Bosnia and Hercegovina has with Croatia, and Serbia and Montenegro.

BUS
Well-established bus routes link Bosnia and Hercegovina with its neighbours and Western Europe.

Međugorje, Mostar, Sarajevo and Bihać have bus connections with Split and Dubrovnik on the coast and Zagreb in Croatia.

Sarajevo and Banja Luka have services to Belgrade and Podgorica in Serbia and Montenegro.

Sample routes to Western Europe from Sarajevo are Munich (€54, 16 hours, daily), Amsterdam (€125, 32 hours, Tuesday, Thursday and Saturday) and Brussels (€105, 27 hours, Tuesday and Saturday).

CAR & MOTORCYCLE
Drivers need to ensure that they have Green Card insurance for their vehicle and an International Driving Permit. Fuel is readily available in towns but it's sensible not to get too low, especially at night when stations may be closed. Spares for European-made cars should be readily available and there'll be mechanics in all largish towns.

TRAIN
A daily service connects Ploče (on the Croatian coast) and Zagreb (Croatia) via Mostar, Sarajevo and Banja Luka; another connects Ploče and Sarajevo via Mostar.

Ploče	Mostar	Sarajevo	Banja Luka	Zagreb
5.47am	7.10am	9.34am	3.36pm	7.46pm
10.18am	8.56am	6.41am		
3.50pm	5.20pm	7.39pm		
11.02pm	9.40pm	7.21pm	1.04pm	8.57am

An overnight train runs from Sarajevo to Budapest (€45/65 in 1st/2nd class, 11 hours, 10.25pm). Another overnight train runs from Banja Luka to Belgrade (22.5KM, nine hours, 9.15pm).

GETTING AROUND
Air
Air Srpska and Air Bosna were the only domestic airlines, but due to financial problems they no longer operate. There may be future efforts to resuscitate them.

Bicycle
Only adventurous foreigners cycle out into the countryside, where the roads can be very hilly. Do not venture off established concrete or asphalt surfaces because of the risk of mines. There is a core of cyclists in Sarajevo but, again, they tend to be foreigners.

Bus
Bosnia and Hercegovina's bus network is comprehensive and reliable although some buses verge on the decrepit. Some services between distant towns may be limited. As in other matters the Federation and RS run separate services. Stowing luggage usually costs up to 2KM per item, depending on the route. Buses usually run on time, although they are slow due to winding roads and occasional stops for drivers and passengers to eat and smoke.

COSTS
Sample fares are 11KM Mostar to Sarajevo, 9KM Sarajevo to Travnik and 11KM from Banja Luka to Bihać.

RESERVATIONS
Generally, reservations aren't really necessary except on international buses or on infrequent long-distance services during holiday times.

Car & Motorcycle
Narrow roads, hills and bends, although through beautiful countryside, make for slow progress by car but for some challenging motorcycling. Some drivers believe they're immortal and drive like maniacs, passing even on sharp curves.

AUTOMOBILE ASSOCIATIONS
Automobile Association of Bosnia and Hercegovina (Map p91; ☎ 033-212 771; www.bihamk.ba; Skenderija 23, 71000 Sarajevo) offers road assistance and towing services for members. A membership costs 35KM per year.

HIRE
Many car-rental places have sprung up, particularly in Sarajevo. Car rental is also available in Banja Luka, Mostar and Medugorje. Prices usually start at €43/240 for one day/week with unlimited mileage.

Car hire firms in the Federation do not operate in Republika Srpska and vice versa.

A deposit, usually in the form of a credit card slip, your International Driving Permit and a show of your passport (they'll take a photocopy) are all that's needed.

Check the car in the presence of the renter for existing damage and nonfunctioning items.

ROAD RULES
Driving is on the right, seat belts must be worn and the tolerated level of alcohol in the blood is .05. Speed limits are 60km/h for urban roads and 80km/h for rural roads.

Local Transport
TAXI
Taxis are readily available and cheap, though outside Sarajevo and Banja Luka they may not have (or turn on) meters. If there is no meter, agree on the price before you set off.

Train
There are far fewer trains than buses and they don't necessarily connect with where visitors might go. However, they're more comfortable, there's more to see from them and they can be used as an alternative to the bus for transport between Banja Luka, Sarajevo and Mostar. About 10 daily trains chug out of Sarajevo to minor destinations. Trains from Banja Luka travel locally within the RS.

Bulgaria
България

CONTENTS

Highlights	117
Itineraries	117
Climate & When to Go	117
History	117
People	119
Religion	119
Arts	120
Environment	120
Food & Drink	120
Sofia	**121**
History	121
Orientation	121
Information	123
Sights	124
Courses	125
Sleeping	125
Eating	126
Drinking	127
Entertainment	127
Shopping	127
Getting There & Away	127
Getting Around	129
Around Sofia	129
Rila & Pirin Mountains	**130**
Rila Monastery	130
Blagoevgrad	131
Sandanski	131
Melnik	132
Borovets	132
Bansko	133
Plovdiv & Rodopi Mountains	**134**
Plovdiv	134
Bachkovo Monastery	140
Pamporovo	140
Smolyan	140
Shiroka Lâka	141
Trigrad	141
Central Balkans	**141**
Koprivshtitsa	142
Karlovo	143
Kazanlâk	144
Sliven	144
Kotel	145
Pleven	145
Troyan & Around	146
Veliko Târnovo	146
Around Veliko Târnovo	150
Shumen	151

Ruse	152
Rusenski Lom Nature Park	154
Black Sea Coast	**154**
Burgas	154
Sozopol	156
South of Sozopol	158
Nesebâr	159
Sunny Beach	160
Varna	160
North of Varna	164
Northwest Bulgaria	**165**
Vidin	165
Belogradchik	165
Bulgaria Directory	**166**
Accommodation	166
Activities	167
Books	167
Business Hours	167
Courses	167
Dangers & Annoyances	168
Discount Cards	168
Embassies & Consulates	168
Festivals & Events	168
Gay & Lesbian Travellers	169
Holidays	169
Internet Resources	169
Language	169
Money	169
Post	170
Telephone	170
Tourist Information	170
Tours	170
Visas	170
Transport in Bulgaria	**170**
Getting There & Away	170
Getting Around	171

BULGARIA

Eastern Europe's last stop to the south, Bulgaria wins hearts with its surprising beauty and cultural oddities. Some highlights are obvious: gold-sand beaches (and resorts) on the Black Sea, enormous Alp-like mountains with cheaper ski slopes than in Western Europe, medieval monasteries and forts carved from mountains, and cute whitewashed revival-era buildings and taverns smacking of a *Prequel to Hansel & Gretel* film set. Others unveil for those who linger longer: outrageously heroic mountain-top communist-era monuments, morning chats at queues for hot cheese-filled *banitsa* pastries, old guys whispering to baby goats in plastic bags to keep them quiet on trains, and 'hangover-free' red wine sipped from plastic jugs at picnics where everyone sings unabashedly.

Bulgaria hasn't burst forth as a 'new democracy' with the same gusto as some of Eastern Europe. Although its system changed in 1989, Bulgaria clings to a clunky dual-pricing scheme from the communist days, has waffled a bit between capitalism and socialism, and its economy has dropped low enough that many old fogeys say they preferred the days in red. Some people can seem a little hands-up, heads-down at times, but if you ask your way, you're likely to have a chuckling companion lead you.

After checking the NATO box in 2004, and licking its chops over the prospect of joining the EU by 2007, Bulgaria is on the cusp of change. So it's a good time to go.

FAST FACTS

- **Area** 110,910 sq km
- **Capital** Sofia
- **Currency** leva (lv); €1 = 1.96lv; US$1 = 1.55lv; UK£1 = 2.84lv; A$1 = 1.45; ¥100 = 1.44; NZ$1 = 1.08
- **Key Phrases** *zdrasti* (hello), *blagodarya* (thank you), *imati li?* (do you have?), *kolko struva?* (how much?), *oshte bira molya* (another beer please)
- **Famous for** Black Sea beaches, monasteries, yogurt
- **Official Language** Bulgarian
- **Population** 8 million
- **Telephone Codes** country code ☎ 359; international access code ☎ 00
- **Visa** no visa required for citizens of Australia, Canada, EU, New Zealand, USA and several other nations; see p170 for details

HOW MUCH?

- **Night in Sofia hostel** 20lv
- **Sofia–Plovdiv bus ticket** 8lv
- **Museum admission** 3 to 5lv
- **Varna city map** 3lv
- **Day rental car** 25 to 50lv

LONELY PLANET INDEX

- **Litre of petrol** 1.60lv
- **Litre of bottled water** 0.50lv
- **Kamenitza beer** 0.80lv
- **Souvenir T-shirt** 3lv to 5lv
- **Street snack – banitsa** 0.50lv

HIGHLIGHTS

- Off the Bucharest–Istanbul tracks, the hilly former-capital **Veliko Târnovo** (p146) leans over a sharp curving river with rock climbing, biking and medieval hill towns nearby
- With a cobbled old town and ancient Roman ruins (everywhere!), **Plovdiv** (p134) is Bulgaria's most relaxing city
- The Black Sea's southern beaches, from **Sozopol** (p156) to **Sinemorets** (p158) is where Bulgarians go to avoid the resorts
- Bulgaria's mountainous southwest – with the **Rila and Pirin** (p130) and **Rodopi** (p134) ranges – have rough and easy hikes, and wee villages to take in wine or local festivals
- The capital **Sofia** (p121) has a pet mountain and the nation's most cosmopolitan scene for drinking, eating and meeting artsy locals

ITINERARIES

- **One Week** Stop off at Veliko Târnovo for a couple days, then bus to Plovdiv for Roman ruins and up to Koprivshtitsa to see a cool revival-era town. Finish with chic dining and a wander around the centre in bustling Sofia.
- **Two Weeks** Start in Sofia for a couple days, then head south to Rila Monastery for a night, and another in Melnik for the country's best wine. Go, via Sofia, into Plovdiv for two days, and east to Sozopol for two or three days of beach hopping.

Bus up to Varna for a night, then to off-the-beaten-track Shumen to see nearby Madara horseman. Finish with two or three days in Veliko Târnovo.

CLIMATE & WHEN TO GO

Bulgaria has a temperate climate with cold, damp winters and hot, dry summers. See Climate Charts, p873, for more. From mid-July to August, Bulgaria swarms with tourists, particularly at Black Sea resorts. For beaches in the hot sun, a better time is September; off-season is too quiet, as almost everything's closed from October to March. The ski slopes fill from mid-December to March or mid-April, while much of the country's attractions trim hours.

If you're not beach-bumming or skiing, spring or autumn are great times (particularly May), as there are very few tourists, and theatres and other cultural venues awake from hibernation.

HISTORY
Becoming Bulgaria

Thracians moved into the area in the 4th millennium BC, and by 100 AD Romans controlled the lands. The first Slavs migrated from the north here in the 5th century, and the First Bulgarian State was formed in 681.

By the time the Byzantine Empire conquered Bulgaria in 1014 (after blinding 15,000 Bulgarian troops in one bloody poke-fest), the first state had created a language, the Cyrillic alphabet, a church, and – spurned on by enforced conversion to Christianity – a people (a mix of Slavs, Proto-Bulgarians and a few Thracians).

Bulgaria's second kingdom, based in Veliko Târnovo, began in 1185 and saw much warfare with Serbs, Hungarians and the Ottoman army, who took control in 1396.

Life with the Ottomans

The next 500 years were spent living 'under the yoke' of Ottoman rule. The Orthodox church persevered by quietly holing up in monasteries (some built in mountain sides). Higher taxes for Christians saw many convert to Islam.

During the 18th and 19th centuries, many butt-kicking 'awakeners' are credited with reviving Bulgarian culture. A monk named Paiisi wrote a book about Bulgarian history to inspire pride amongst

BULGARIA

BULGARIA

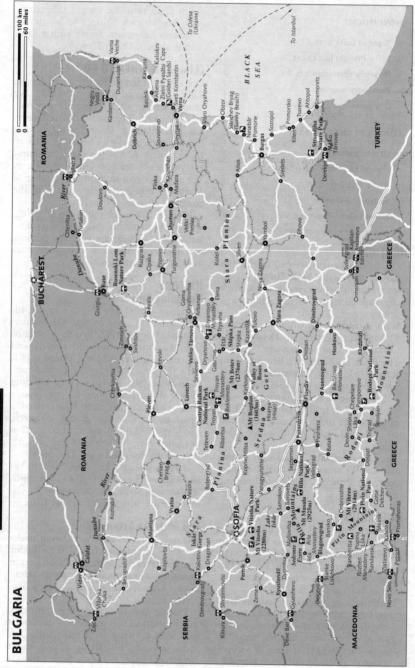

Bulgarians and encourage them not to feel inferior to Greeks. By the 1860s several revolutionaries (including Georgi Rakovski, Vasil Levski and Hristo Botev) organised *cheti* (rebels) bands for the (failed) April Uprising of 1870. With Russia stepping in, the Ottoman army was defeated in 1878, and Bulgaria became independent again.

Nazis & Soviets

With eyes on lost Macedonia, and following a series of topsy-turvy painful Balkan wars including WWI, Bulgaria surprisingly aligned with Nazi Germany in WWII – Germany only just won out over the USSR for Bulgaria's allegiance – with hopes to expand its borders. Famously, Tsar Boris III said 'no' to Hitler, refusing to send Bulgaria's Jewish population to concentration camps, sparing up to 50,000 lives.

As the war waned to a close, Bulgaria did a final flip-flop over to the Soviet side, but it did little to smooth relations with the West or the USSR following WWII. Bulgaria embraced communism wholeheartedly (even proposing in 1973 to join the Soviet republics).

Modern Bulgaria

Since Bulgaria entered democracy in 1989, average monthly salaries have reportedly dipped to around US$150 (meaning a daily *banitsa*, public-toilet tinkle, two coffees and two bus rides take up about 35% of a salary!). Many believe only joining the EU can ignite a rebound. In 1994, the Bulgarian Socialist Party (BSP) won elections over the Union of Democratic Forces (UDF).

Former Tsar, Simeon II, was elected Prime Minister in 2001.

Of all things a Bulgarian spy was arrested in Vienna in 2003.

A current joke in Bulgaria: 'We were little brother to the Ottoman Empire for 500 years, they collapsed. Then the Nazis and Soviets, and they collapsed. NATO, USA and EU, watch out!'

PEOPLE

The official population of Bulgaria is 7.97 million, with Bulgarians and Slavs constituting 83.5%. The largest minorities are Turks (9.5%) and Roma (4.6%); and there are also smaller populations of Russians, Jews and Greeks.

Dyed hair is a big thing these days, with – at one count – 56% of the women in a Rodopi village sporting gold, bronze, red, purple or some sort of dyed hair.

A few famous Bulgarians include Christo, an environmental artist famous for wrapping Berlin's Reichstag in silver fabric in 1995; John Vincent Atanassof, actually a Bulgarian-American, who invented the computer in the late 1930s; and Hristo Stoichkov, the country's favourite footballer, who won the Golden Boot in the 1994 World Cup.

RELIGION

During the communist era Bulgaria was officially atheist. These days, about 84% of the population are Orthodox and 12% are Muslims (almost all are Sunni).

Orthodox monasteries thrived quietly during the period of Ottoman rule. They not only played an important part for the Orthodox religion, but also national independence; many 'awakeners' in the 19th-century organised revolts from monasteries. Today roughly 160 monasteries (of 400 total) are active.

BULGARIA

ARTS
Architecture
Bulgaria's 19th-century revival saw many town make overs with quaint, traditionally styled *kâshta* buildings (whitewashed walls, wood shutters, wood-carved ceilings, hand-woven carpets) built close alongside (sometimes over) cobbled streets. This massive source of Bulgarian pride is evident in many towns, such as Koprivshtitsa (p142), Kotel (p145), Tryavna (p150) and Plovdiv's Old Town (p135).

Art
Bulgaria's most treasured art is on the walls of medieval monasteries and churches, like Boyana Church near Sofia (p129), Arbanasi's Nativity Church (p150) and the paintings by Zahari Zograf (1810–53) at the big-time monasteries at Rila (p130), Troyan (p146) and Bachkovo (p140).

Not to be overlooked are the ever-heroic communist-era monuments standing on hilltop vantage points; the one in Shumen (p151) is best.

Literature
Aleko Konstantinov wrote the enduring *Do Chicago y Nazat* (To Chicago and Back) following his trip to the World's Fair in 1893, and it has made the city (in Bulgaria cutely pronounced like 'che-ka-go' rather than 'shi-ka-go') one of Bulgaria's favourite cities. No English translation is available.

Music
The currently popular 'wedding music,' aka *chalga* (or 'truck driver music'), is a Turkish-sounding synth-pop with dumb lyrics. Essentially no one in the country admits to liking Azis, a seriously flamboyant, sexually ambiguous *chalga* performer, who sells more CDs than nearly any Bulgarian artist.

Traditional music – played with *gaida* (bagpipes), *tambura* (four-stringed lute) and *tâppan* (drum) – is widespread too. Click on a TV and see it on several channels nightly or watch for it at concerts or special events. There are schools where you can learn how to play it at Shiroka Lâka (p141) and Kotel (p145).

In recent years, Bulgarian folk singing – of dissonant, tonal harmonies – has made a splash internationally, with several CDS including the series, *Le Mystére des Voix Bulgares* (The Mystery of the Bulgarian Voice).

Bulgarian opera is world famous. Sofia holds the best opera concerts, but many halls in the country have terrific ensembles, Varna (p160) and Stara Zagora included.

ENVIRONMENT
The Land
Bulgaria (110,910 sq km) lies in the heart of the Balkan Peninsula, stretching 502km from the Serbian border to the Black Sea.

Bulgaria is one-third mountains. The Stara Planina (meaning 'Old Mountain', also known as the Balkan Mountains) stretch across central Bulgaria, nearly reaching the sea. In the southwest are three higher ranges – Rila Mountains, south of Sofia (home to the country's highest point, Mt Musala, 2925m), and just south the Pirin Mountains, reaching Greece; to the east are the Rodopi Mountains.

Wildlife
Although Bulgaria has some 56,000 kinds of living creatures – including one of Europe's largest bear populations – most visitors see little wildlife, unless venturing deeper into the thickets and mountains. Rusenski Lom Nature Park (p154) is an excellent place to view critters, with two-thirds of Bulgaria's mammal species (eg bears, deer, wild goats) present and many birds (eg Egyptian vultures, great eagle owls, pelicans, ducks).

Bulgaria's Valley of Roses, around Kazanlâk (p144), still produces most of the world's rose oil. About 35% of the country is covered by forests, of which 60% are original.

Offshore seals and dolphins are on the nation's endangered list, and bears are becoming rarer due to illegal poaching.

National Parks
Bulgaria has four national parks (Rila, Pirin, Rodopi, Central Balkans) and ten nature parks, all of which offer some protection to the environment (and tourist potential).

FOOD & DRINK
Staples & Specialities
There are two kinds of Bulgarian food: Bulgarian food and pizza. The former is comprised of many lighter dishes, with Turkish or Greek influence. Salads – like the everywhere-you-look *shopska* (tomatoes, onions,

cucumbers and cheese) – start most meals. Main dishes are mostly grilled beef, pork, lamb and chicken – such as the *kebabche* (spicy meat sausages) – or heavier stews such as *kavarma*. Sides (like boiled potatoes or cheese-covered chips) are ordered separately.

Vegetarians are not at a loss. Aside from salads, most restaurants have yogurt- or vegetable-based soups and several egg dishes. There are some skewered vegetables alongside the meats. Most Chinese restaurants (look for red lanterns hanging out front) have veggie dishes.

Well-made pizza, served by slice or as pie, is everywhere. A popular street snack is 'American popcorn'.

Breakfast for most Bulgarians is espresso, cigarettes (plural intended) and a hot cheese-filled *banitsa* pastry, available at small bakeries (often named *zakuska*, 'breakfast').

Wine is super in Bulgaria, particularly Melnik's red; says one local, 'our wine is as good as France's, and their worst is worse than our worst.' *Rakiya* is a local (potent) brandy with strong regional specialities everywhere.

Where to Eat & Drink

Evocative Bulgarian *kâshta* restaurants, it must be said, don't differ from one another much (only in soundtrack: local folk music, *chalga*, Elton John). Bansko's *mehana* eating scene (p133) is the most atmospheric; Sofia's the most edgy (p126). A 10% tip is expected at sit-down restaurants, though sometimes it's included with the *smetka* (bill).

Essentially every main street in Bulgaria sells pizza slices or doner kebabs for 1lv or less. Cafés also act as de facto bars, serving local beer, wine and brandies. Many towns you'll come across have more standard beer houses (*birarias*).

SOFIA СОФИЯ

☎ 02 / pop 1,114,000

OK, in comparison with Eastern European capitals to the north, Sofia is something of a Novosibirsk, an urban smear without any serious standout attractions, or even a clear central square or street. But that's just the first impression. The whole Bulgarian

world twirls around Sofia and its shady gold-brick streets and parks give it energy and confidence that lures some travellers into its artier nooks for (no joke) weeks. Also, Sofia has a huge pet mountain in Mt Vitosha, about 10km south, with skiing and hiking options waiting all year. Take that Budapest!

HISTORY

Settled perhaps 7000 years ago by a Thracian tribe, and later named Serdica by Romans, Sofia is – despite the years – young. It was an outpost of 1200 residents when it became the nation's unlikely fourth capital in 1879 for its geographical location (ie proximity to ever-sought Macedonia). In the decades thereafter much thought-out or aesthetic development was curbed by war and communism.

The name (changed from Serdica in the 15th century) comes from the Greek word for wisdom, not from an Italian.

ORIENTATION

Sofia's main bus and train station are across bul Maria Luisa from each other, about 500m north of the start of the centre, which is reached by bul Maria Luisa. This street ends at pl Sveta Nedelya. Extending south is ritzy bul Vitosha.

East of pl Sveta Nedelya, along ul Tsar Osvoboditel, are many government buildings, then a block north, pl Aleksander Nevski. Cupping the centre to the east is busy

---

SOFIA IN TWO DAYS

Visit the huge **Aleksander Nevski Church** (p124), then see the **Ethnographical Museum** (p124) and make your own 'Ministry of Silly Walks' jokes at the **changing of the guards** (p124). Lunch at **Motto** (p126) and stroll posh bul Vitosha to monolith **NDK** (p125) for deck views of Sofia. Tram back to see **Sveta Nedelya Cathedral** (p125) and the **Ladies Market** (p127). Eat dinner at **Divaka** (p126) and ponder anti-fascism over wine at **Hambara** (p127).

Spend day two hiking (or skiing) on **Mt Vitosha** (p129), possibly making your way down to **Boyana** (p129) or **Studentski Grad** (p125) for beers at sunset.

BULGARIA

BULGARIA

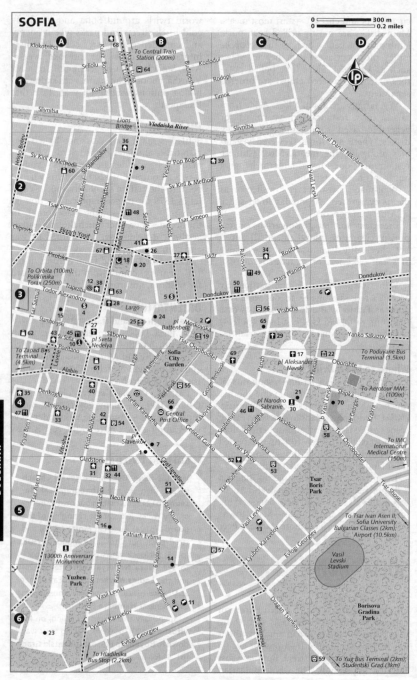

SOFIA

0 — 300 m
0 — 0.2 miles

A B C D

1

2

3

4

5

6

Klokotnitsa

Seliolu

Kozlodui

Slivnitsa

Kulaz Boris

68

To Central Train
Station (200m)

64

Budapeshta

Kozlodui

Rodopi

Timok

Slivnitsa

General Danail Nikolaev

Hristo Botev

Sv Kiril & Metodii

Slivnitsa

Lions
Bridge

Vladaiska River

36

9

Veslets

Pop Bogomil

39

Sv Kiril & Metodii

b Vasil Levski

Knyaz Boris I

George Washington

Tsar Simeon

Stamboliyski

Chiprovtsi

Ekzarh Yosif

48

Serdika

Tsar Simeon

Veslets

Berkovski

Maria Luisa

Pirotska

67

41

26

18

20

37

Iskar

Rakovski

34

Rostza

49

Stara Planina

Dondukov

To Orbita (100m);
Poliklinika
Torax (250m)

Todor Aleksandrov

Trapezitsa

12 38

63

28

4

Largo

15

27

25

24

5

50

Dondukov

56

Vrabcha

6

Tsar Samuil

Stamboliyski

62

43

45

10

Sv Sofia

Pozitano

Lavele

Alabin

61

40

pl Sveta
Nedelya

Saborna

Lege

Al Battenberg

pl
Battenberg

2

Moskovska

65

29

Yanko Sakazov

To Poduyane Bus
Terminal (1.5km)

Tsar Osvoboditel

19

Sofia City
Garden

Vasil Levski

George Benkovski

69

17

pl Aleksander
Nevski

22

Oborishte

To Aerotour MM
(100m)

Shipka

Hr Georgiev

Kaluja

55

66

Central
Post Office

3

Stefan Karadzha

Rakovski

6 Septemvri

46

21

pl Narodno
Sabranie

30

Dobrudha

Aksakov

Parip

9 Fevruari

b Vasil Levski

Tsar Osvoboditel

70

58

To IMC
International
Medical Centre
(150m)

To Zapad Bus
Terminal
(4.5km)

35

47

Denkoglu

Kaniigradska

33

Hristo Belchev

42

54

Pl
Slaveikov

7

1

Gladstone

31

32 44

General Gurko

Ivan Vazov

Slavenska

52

53

Tsar Shishman

Tsar Boris
Park

To Tsar Ivan Asen II;
Sofia University;
Bulgarian Classes (2km);
Airport (10.5km)

Knyaz Boris I

Tsar Asen I

Vitosha

Angel Kanchev

16

Neofit Rilski

Han Krum

51

Patriarh Evtimii

Vasil Levski

13

Vasil Levski

Lyuben Karavelov

Evlog Georgiev

Vasil
Levski
Stadium

Fritjof Nansen

1300th Anniversary
Monument

Yuzhen
Park

Rakovski

6 Septemvri

14

57

8 11

Borisova
Gradina
Park

23

Lyuben Karavelov

Evlogi Georgiev

Hr Smirnenski

Dragan Tsankov

59

To Yug Bus Terminal (2km);
Studentski Grad (3km)

To Hladilnika
Bus Stop (2.2km)

INFORMATION		
Book Market	1	B4
British Embassy	2	B3
BTC	3	B4
Bulbank	4	A3
Central Cooperative Bank	5	B3
Danish Embassy	6	D3
Dom na Knigata	7	B4
Hungarian Embassy	8	B6
Immigration Office	9	B2
National Tourism Information & Advertising Centre	10	A3
Polish Embassy	11	B6
Quest	12	A3
Turkish Embassy	13	C5
Usit Colours	14	B5
Zig Zag	15	A3
Zip Limited	16	A5

SIGHTS & ACTIVITIES	(pp124-5)	
Aleksander Nevski Church	17	C4
Aleksander Nevski Crypt	(see 17)	
Banya Bashi Mosque	18	B3
Ethnographical Museum	19	B3
Mineral Baths	20	B5
National Art Gallery	(see 19)	
National Assembly	21	C4
National Gallery for Foreign Art	22	D4
NDK (National Palace of Culture)	23	A6
Party House	24	B3
President's Building	25	B3

Spring Wells	26	B3
Sveta Nedelya Cathedral	27	A3
Sveta Petka Samardjiiska Church	28	A3
Sveta Sofia Church	29	C3
Tsar Osvoboditel Statue	30	C4

SLEEPING	🛏	(pp125-6)
Art'Otel	31	A5
Art Hostel	32	A5
Baldjieva Hotel	33	A4
Hostel Kervan	34	C3
Hostel Mostel	35	A4
Hotel Enny	36	B2
Hotel Iskår	37	B3
Hotel Maya	38	A3
Hotel Pop Bogomil	39	C2
Internet Hostel	40	A4
Markela Accommodation Agency	41	B3
Red Star Hostel	42	A4
Sofia Hostel	43	A3

EATING	🍴	(pp126-7)
Divaka	44	B3
Dream House	(see 40)	
Happy Bar & Grill	45	A3
Motto	46	C4
Oazis Supermarket	(see 63)	
Pri Yafata	47	A4
Trops Kåshta	48	B2
TskC	49	C3
Zakuska	50	C3

DRINKING	🍸	(p127)
Babbles	(see 52)	
Hambara	51	B5
Poison's	52	C5

ENTERTAINMENT	🎭	(p127)
Blaze Club	53	C5
Escape	54	B4
Ivan Vazov National Theatre	55	B4
Multiplex	(see 23)	
National Opera House	56	C3
Odeon	57	C5
Spartacus	58	D4
Swingin' Hall	59	D6

SHOPPING	🛍	(p127)
Ladies Market	60	A2
Orion Ski Shop	61	A4
Pavement Vendors	(see 17)	
Souvenir Shop	(see 19)	
Stenata	62	A3
TsUM	63	B3

TRANSPORT		(pp127-9)
MTT	64	B1
Penguin Travel	65	C3
Rila Bureau Centre Office	66	B4

OTHER		
Central Hali Shopping Centre	67	A3
Princess Hotel	68	B1
St Nikolai Russian Church	69	C4
Sofia University	70	D4

bul Vasil Levski, which meets bul Vitosha by the blob that is NDK (National Palace of Culture).

An updated city map (widely available) with transport routes is crucial for extended stays or a self-guided trip to Mt Vitosha.

INFORMATION
Bookshops
Book market (pl Slaveikov) This daily open-air market sells some English second-hand novels and is open during daylight hours.

Dom na Knigata (☎ 981 7897; ⏰ 8am-8pm Mon-Sat, 9am-6pm Sun) Book nuts' best haven in Bulgaria is found on ul Graf Ignatieve, across from pl Slaveikov. Messy racks of paperbacks in English, French, German and Spanish, including long-out-of-print titles from Sofia Press.

Emergency
For police matters between 8am and 6pm, you (allegedly) can reach an English-speaking operator at ☎ 988 5239, French-speaking ☎ 982 3028. Otherwise, call ☎ 166.

Internet Access
BTC (ul General Gurko; per hr 2lv; ⏰ 24hr) 11 Internet computers.

Quest (ul Trapezitsa 4; per hr 1.20lv; ⏰ 24hr) Net and games.

Left Luggage
Train Station (per bag daily 0.80lv; ⏰ 6am-10pm) This basement office serves train and bus travellers.

Media
Sofia Echo is an English-language paper, with entertainment listings, that comes out Friday (2.40lv – ouch!).

A few freebie publications list restaurants and bars: the quarterly *Sofia Inside & Out*, the monthly *Sofia City* (www.sofiacityguide.com) and the weekly *Programata* (in Bulgarian only; its website www.programata.bg has an English version).

Medical Services
Two of Sofia's better private medical clinics include:

Poliklinika Torax (☎ 988 5259, 980 5791; bul Stamboliyski 57; ⏰ 24hr)

IMC International Medical Centre (☎ 944 9326, 0888 778 060; ul Gogol 28; ⏰ 24hr)

Money
Most foreign exchange booths along bul Vitosha, bul Maria Luisa and bul Stamboliyski run non stop.

Bulbank (ul Lavele & ul Todor Alexandrov; ⏰ 8.30am-4.30pm Mon-Fri) Changes travellers checks for €1 per transaction (booths 1 or 3); sometimes, enigmatically, they require 'bank documentation'.

BULGARIA

Central Cooperative Bank (☎ 930 6912; ul Dondukov 7B; ◔ 8.15am-4.45pm Mon-Fri) Charges 1.2% fee on travellers checks.

Telephone

Most Internet cafés have net phone calls overseas for as little as 0.20lv per minute. **BTC** (ul General Gurko; ◔ 24hr) Snazzy phone booths and Internet computers.

Tourist Information
National Tourism Information & Advertising

Centre (☎ 987 9778; www.bulgariatravel.org; ul Sveta Sofia; ◔ 9am-5.30pm Mon-Fri) Has national brochures. English-speaking staff don't have much other information at hand, but will try to find it.

Travel Agencies

Aerotour MM (☎ 943 4900; www.aerotourmm.com; ul Shipka 34; ◔ 9am-7pm Mon-Fri) Arranges visas in four or five days for Russia, Ukraine, Belarus, Moldova and Georgia.

Orbita (☎ 987 9128; orbita@ttm.bg; bul Hristo Botev 48; ◔ 9am-5pm Mon-Fri) Issues student cards for 10lv.

Usit Colours (☎ 937 3175; ul Vasil Levski 35; ◔ 9.30am-6.30pm Mon-Fri) Student discounted fares.

Zig Zag (☎ 980 5102; www.zigzag.dir.bg; bul Stamboliyski 20V, enter from ul Lavele; ◔ 9am-6.30pm Mon-Fri) Super-helpful English-language staff charge a 5lv consultation fee to book rooms, give advice on hikes and activities around the country. Zig Zag works with Odysseia-In, a national agency.

Zip Limited (☎ 986 9260; ul Patriah Evtimii 44; ◔ 9am-6pm Mon-Fri, 10.30am-2.30pm Sat) STA affiliate offering student discounts on air fares.

Visas

Immigration Office (☎ 982 3316; bul Maria Luisa 48; ◔ 9am-12.30pm, 1.30-5pm Mon-Fri) This hectic office (in an unmarked entrance of the 'MBP' building) can extend visas by three months for 200lv.

SIGHTS

In addition to the central area, good walking grounds include the huge Borisova Gradina Park, the residential ul Tsar Ivan Asen II (just north of the park) and Studentski Grad (p125). For some more ideas, see Around Sofia (p129).

Ploshad Aleksander Nevksi

Gold-domed and massive, Sofia's premier focal point – and the one Sofia site you have to see – is **Aleksander Nevski Church** (pl Aleksander Nevski; admission free; ◔ 7am-7pm), built

between 1892 and 1912. It's named after a Swedish-born Russian warrior in honour of the Russian liberators (including the 200,000 who died fighting the Ottomans). This and the Russian **Tsar Osvoboditel statue**, two blocks south, sandwich the Bulgarian **National Assembly**.

On the church's northwestern corner, a door leads down to the **Aleksander Nevski Crypt** (☎ 981 5775; adult/student 3/1.50lv; ◔ 10.30am-6.30pm Tue-Sun) containing many national icons from centuries stretching back to the 5th century.

Northeast is the large **National Gallery for Foreign Art** (ul 19 Fevruari; adult 1.5lv, free Sun; ◔ 11am-6.30pm Wed-Mon) with diverse international works, including a Rodin bust and some Monet (mistakenly credited to 'More').

To the west (with an eternal flame burning outside), **Sveta Sofia Church** (admission free; ◔ 7am-7pm summer, 7am-6pm winter) dates from the 5th century and inspired the name of the city. You can see earthquake-battered mosaics under the stone floor.

Around Sofia City Garden

This fountain-filled park – a couple of blocks southwest of pl Aleksander Nevski – is lined with cafés in good weather and surrounded by a gold-brick road.

To the north is the former Royal Palace, now home to two museums. The better of the two is the **Ethnographical Museum** (☎ 988 1974; ul Tsar Osvoboditel; adult 3lv; ◔ 10am-5.30pm Tue-Sun Apr-Nov, 11am-3.30pm Dec-Mar). With a dozen rooms and loads of English signs, this museum gives a greater regional context to the whys and whats of traditional Bulgarian architecture, costumes and customs than most such museums in the country. Though such folk talk is slightly at odds with its palatial setting.

Also in the palace, the **National Art Gallery** (☎ 980 0093; ul Tsar Osvoboditel; adult/student 3/1.50lv; ◔ 10.30am-6.30pm Tue-Sun summer, 10.30am-6.30pm Tue-Sat winter) is a squeaky-floored 10-hall museum, with often changing exhibits dedicated to Bulgarian art.

Across from the giant white **Party House** (closed to public), is the **President's Building** (also closed to the public), the site of the Ministry of Silly Walks, um, that is the **changing of the guards**, where three feather-capped guys slap boot soles on the pavement (on the hour during daylight hours).

Around Ploshad Sveta Nedelya

In the heart of pl Sveta Nedelya (a big block west of the President's Building) is well-lit, ornate **Sveta Nedelya Cathedral** (admission free; ☉ 7am-7pm), built between 1856 and 1863. Just north, accessed via an underpass, the **Sveta Petka Samardjiska Church** (adult 5lv; ☉ 10am-7pm Mon-Sat, 10am-2pm Sun) is a (rather overpriced) small church that pokes up its 14th-century steeple from the underpass amidst a sea of traffic. The shop sells 'Holly Water' (sic) for 2lv.

North on bul Maria Luisa are the ornate **mineral baths** (long-time under restoration) and (past ul Ekzarh Yosif) **spring wells**, where locals fill bottles. Nearby is the unmistakable **Banya Bashi Mosque** (admission free; ☉ dawn-dusk).

To the south, bul Vitosha faces its far-off namesake, Mt Vitosha. One kilometre south of pl Sveta Nedelya is **Yuzhen Park**, home to a falling-apart monument and the gigantic 'viva-1981!' **NDK** complex, with cafés, shops, cinema and some events. On most days, its viewing deck is open.

Studentski Grad

A few kilometres closer to Mt Vitosha (south of the centre), Student Town is literally that, an enclave of college students living in a spread-out neighbourhood of drab communist-era apartment blocks with Sofia's hippest new cafés and bars at their base – a fascinating mix.

Bowl big and beyond limits at **Mega Xtreme Bowling** (☎ 969 2600; ul Stefanov; per game 3-5lv; ☉ 10am-4am), about 500m north of the minibus terminus. There's also a bar and live music.

Get out here by minibus No 7 from bul Maria Luisa or No 8 along ul Rakovski (1lv one way). City bus No 94 comes here from ul Tsarigradsko Shose, across from Sofia University.

COURSES

A department of **Sofia University** (☎ 710 069; www.deo.uni-sofia.bg; ul Kosta Loulchev 27) offers Bulgarian-language courses (the three-week class costs €220) as well as song and dance classes.

SLEEPING

Sofia has super hostels although its hotels are pricier than what you'll find in most of Bulgaria. The train station has an iffily run accommodation bureau with iffily kept hours. The EBP Tours office in the train station (p128) finds nearby private rooms for 20lv. Most hostels lower the price if you stay a few days. Prices here include breakfast and are for summer; most drop by €1 or €2 in winter. Some of the cheaper hostels can be a little noisy at night.

Budget

Art Hostel (☎ 987 0545; www.art-hostel.com; ul Angel Kânchev 21a; dm €10) This laid-back, nook-and-cranny hostel gets its subtitle, which is 'Usually we spend in our time in the garden', for its leafy courtyard out back. Past guests have helped transform small spaces – like the wee kitchen and cool hang-out area inside – into a cosy scene where travellers mix with arty locals, who sometimes stage exhibitions. You're not likely to get to sleep early here.

Hostel Mostel (☎ 0889 223 296; www.hostelmostel.com; ul Denkoglu 2; dm €10; s/d with shared bathroom €12/15) Lovingly run by a Bulgarian couple, who speak English and give rides back from the train station, this appealing new hostel has eight- and six-bed dorms, plus a private room. There's lots of light, free Internet, lockers, cheap international calls and loads of travel tips. The kitchen has a washing machine (€2 per load). Managers occasionally take interested guests on walks through Gypsy neighbourhoods.

Markela Accommodation Agency (☎ 980 4925; www.markela.hit.bg; ul Ekzarh Yosif 35, rm 103; ☉ 8.30am-7.30pm Mon-Fri, 9.30am-4.30pm Sat & Sun) Run by a few friendly ladies (a couple speak some English) who can hook you up with single/double rooms for 20/30lv, 2lv more for TV. Apartments start at 30lv, but most are 50lv to 65lv.

Internet Hostel (☎ 989 9419; ul Alabin 50A, 2nd fl; dm €8-10) This small hostel – unsigned at research time – has four rooms (16 beds) facing a small sitting area and a kitchen and laundry (3lv). The great veggie restaurant Dream House (p126) is downstairs.

Sofia Hostel (☎ 989 8582; ul Pozitano 16; dm €10) Bulgaria's first hostel has family decorations giving the small place a kindergarten feel (in a good way). No English, but Bulgarians lessons are free.

Hostel Kervan (☎ 983 9428; www.kervanhostel.com; ul Rositza 3; dm €10) Clean, stylish and new (with antique radios and old maps in the entry), the Kervan has 15 beds, one shower and a kitchen. Kervan rent bikes too (€10 per day).

Red Star Hostel (☎ 986 3341; ul Angel Kânchev 6, 3rd fl; dm €10, r €13-15) At research time the same folks from the Internet Hostel had nearly opened the promising, superbly named Red Star Hostel, with kitchen, laundry, and bikes for rent.

Mid-Range

Hotel Central (☎ 931 1724; d 40lv) Located at the train station, Hotel Central is there for the desperate.

Hotel Maya (☎ 989 4611; ul Trapezitsa 4; s/d 45/70lv) Clean and homey, this central guesthouse has rooms on either side of a rooftop courtyard overlooking TsUM shopping centre. Unfortunately the private bathrooms are tiny and side-by-side down the hall. No English is spoken, but staff don't let the language barrier stop a conversation.

Hotel Enny (☎ 983 1649; ul Pop Bogomil 46; s 20 & 30lv, d 40lv without bathroom, s/d 50/60lv without toilet, s/d 60/80lv with bathroom) Quieter rooms with private bath are in the building behind. A café/bar courtyard is open in summer. The lone 20lv single is super small and fills quickly. All other rooms have TV.

Hotel Iskâr (☎ 986 6750; ul Iskâr 11; r €25 & 37) This hotel is in a good location, set back slightly from the street, with small but well-kept rooms. The cheaper ones don't have TV and the private bathroom is across the hall. There's a small bar downstairs.

Hotel Pop Bogomil (☎ 983 7065; ul Pop Bogomil 5; r €32-39) Run by the family from the Hotel Iskâr the less central Hotel Pop Bogomil has a bit more space in its rooms and a nice new café.

Top End

Baldjieva Hotel (☎ 987 2914; ul Tzar Asen 23; incl breakfast s €48-57, d €58-69) The more expensive rooms are worth the extra euro (with a balcony facing a brick courtyard and more space). Some rooms are a little worn, but it's a fine mid-range deal.

Art'Otel (☎ 980 6000; ul Gladston 44; r incl breakfast €90-105) Owned by the Barcelona football team manager, and bursting with more character than you'll likely find at bigger business hotels, this new shady-lane hotel has 22 colour-themed rooms (some with Mt Vitosha views) in a stylish, art-adorned space. There's a small fitness centre and a restaurant good enough to attract non-guests.

EATING

Sofia has the country's most dynamic and stylin' dining. Appealing new places are popping up constantly – try between bul Vitosha and ul Rakovski. Cheap pizza slices and kebabs are hard to miss.

Oazis Supermarket (bul Maria Luisa; ☺ 8.30am-8.30pm) On north side of TsUM shopping centre.

Zakuska (ul Dondukov 25; banitsas 0.40lv; ☺ 7am-8.30pm Mon-Sat, 8am-6pm Sun) If a hot cheese-filled *banitsa* breakfast eludes you, this small bakery keeps busy all day.

Trops Kâshta (ul Maria Luisa 26; salads 1lv, mains 2-3lv; ☺ 8am-9pm) For cheap, fast, point-and-eat cafeteria-style food, Trops is your new comrade. This is one of several serving Bulgarian stews and veggie dishes, and it's half off after 8pm.

Dream House (ul Alabin 50A; mains 2-2.50lv; ☺ 11.30am-10pm) A dream for meatless dining, this cool-mint restaurant, up a flight from the ul Alabin trams, serves heaps of tasty soups and meals, including a lovely potato steak with bamboo and mushrooms.

Divaka (ul Gladston 54; grills 1.10-3.90lv, mains 2-3.80lv; ☺ 24hr) This sprawling modern four-room restaurant gets filled daily with happy Bulgarians chomping on low-cost traditional fare – grilled meats, fish fillets, cheese-covered chips. The back courtyard is half open-air, half glassed-in. You may have to wait for a seat at night; they don't take reservations.

Happy Bar & Grill (pl Sveta Nedelya; grills 3-5.19lv; ☺ 24hr) This chain institution is Bulgaria's 'American grill', which fills with locals looking for mostly Bulgarian grilled meals served by mini-skirted waitresses. There's a full breakfast menu from 8 to 11am.

TsKC (☎ 926 6722; ul Rakovski 99; mains 3-7.5lv; ☺ 11.30am-11pm) One of a few eateries dating from the communist era, this Bulgarian restaurant still hosts live shows (supposedly nightly) in its very 1982 décor. Fewer diners than in the good ol' days.

Motto (☎ 987 2723; ul Aksakov 18; pasta 5lv, mains 4.20-9lv; ☺ 9am-1am) Snazzy Sofians lounge after work, way after work, in this relaxing electronica-fueled chic eatery with teak seats, or out back in the leafy courtyard. The jumbo burger (4lv) is as advertised. There are several veggie and fish options and it's OK to come for just cocktails. DJs spin on weekend nights.

Pri Yafata (☎ 980 1727; ul Colinska 28; grills 2.50-12lv, mains 5-12.50lv; ⏰ 10am-midnight) An excellent introduction to Bulgarian cuisine (and traditional costumes), this chain restaurant (forgivably trite) packs in locals and tourists for its grilled meats (rabbit with veggies is 7.50lv) and live folk music after 8pm. It's best to reserve ahead for dinner.

DRINKING

Look for *Programata*'s free annual *Club Guide* for listings in English. Studentski Grad (p125) has many good bars too.

Hambara (ul 6 Sevtemvri 22; ⏰ 8pm-late) Located in a century-old grain storage building, where a WWII anti-fascist (thus illegal) press was based, this low-key place is unsigned, and down a dark path (watch for fanged gnomes). There's jazzy music and some Latin rhythms. Most of Sofia doesn't know about it, but it's Bulgaria's best bar.

Poison's (ul Tsar Shushman 22; ⏰ 10am-2am) This place has a nice leafy outdoor space and pavement standing spots, which fill with 20-something locals. Behind it is **Babbles**, a bright cube-shaped bar that makes you feel like you're getting drunk inside an M&M.

ENTERTAINMENT
Cinemas

Odeon (☎ 989 2469; ul Patriarh Evtimii 1; tickets 1-3lv) Sofia's premier art-house cinema, screening new and old foreign-language films (sometimes with English subtitles).

The latest films are shown in many cinemas, including **Multiplex** (☎ 951-5101; NDK; tickets 4-5lv).

Nightclubs

Escape (☎ 088 746 8064; ul Angel Kânchev 1; cover 2-3lv; ⏰ 8.30pm-late) Sofia's big kids' favourite disco.

Blaze Club (ul Slavenska 36; ⏰ 10am-3am) DJs a-spin, disco ball a-turns at this tiny hipster-hanging club with tri-level sitting areas.

Spartacus (☎ 088 955 1279; ⏰ 6.30pm-late Tue-Thu, 11pm-late Fri & Sat) At the underpass near Sofia University, this is Bulgaria's oldest gay disco (and recently renovated).

Live Music

National Opera House (☎ 987 1366; ul Vrabcha 1) Opera is taken seriously in this country and this place features Sofia's best.

Swingin' Hall (☎ 963 0696; bul Dragan Tsankov 8) More contemporary music (rock, jazz) staged most nights.

Theatre

Ivan Vazov National Theatre (☎ 986 2252; cnr uls Dyakon Ignatii & Vasil Levski) Facing the Sofia City Garden, this red-and-white theatre stages plays – great if you know Bulgarian or enjoy being confused.

SHOPPING

Pavement vendors (pl Aleksander Nevski) Sell antiques from the communist-era, icons and traditional crafts. There's a good selection of nifty Soviet cameras, some for as little as 10lv; the fake Leicas are more.

Souvenir shop (ul Tsar Osvoboditel; ⏰ 9.30am-6pm) At the Ethnographical Museum, this shop is your quick-need-Bulgarian-gift-for-relative-back-home saviour. There are all sorts of woodcarvings, traditional costumes and other knick-knacks for sale.

Stenata (☎ 980 5491; ul Tsar Samuil 63; ⏰ 9.30am-7pm Mon-Fri, 10am-5.30pm Sat) Outfits folks with hiking and rock-climbing gear, including tents, sleeping bags and maps. They do not offer rentals.

Orion Ski Shop (☎ 986 4157; ul Pozitano; ⏰ 10am-7.30pm Mon-Fri, 10am-4pm Sat) Sells all sorts of ski gear, including some second-hand stuff.

TsUM (ul Maria Luisa; ⏰ 10am-8pm Mon-Sat, 11am-5.30pm Sun) The former communist-era mall, TsUM's five floors are now filled with Reebok, Swiss Army, Nike and Miss Sixty.

Ladies Market (ul St Stambolov; ⏰ dawn-dusk) A lively, messy market (mostly food), a couple of blocks west of bul Maria Luisa.

GETTING THERE & AWAY
Air

Hemus Air flies to Varna Monday to Saturday (€58 one way plus €8 departure tax), with extra flights in summer, when there are also flights to Burgas (about €40 one way). Travel agents book flights (see p124).

The departures terminal has an information booth (☎ 937 2211) and there's an ATM outside, across from the arrivals hall.

See p170 for more information on contacting airlines.

BULGARIA

Bus

DOMESTIC BUSES

Sofia's Central Bus Terminal – sprawled in a parking lot just before the Princess Hotel, about 1km north of central pl Sveta Nedelya – is the nation's most unorganised, with dozens of private bus companies hawking tickets and a lone public stand. At research time, the bus station was bracing to move next to the train station (across bul Maria Luisa); hopefully that will bring more order.

Generally it's possible to show up between the hours of 8am and 5 or 6pm and get a bus to the following destinations within an hour:

Blagoevgrad 5lv, two hours
Burgas 15lv, 5½ hours
Pleven 8-10lv, 2½ hours
Plovdiv 8lv, two hours
Ruse 10-12lv, 4½ hours
Shumen 15lv, five hours
Sliven 12lv, four hours
Stara Zagora 10lv, three hours
Varna 19lv, six hours
Veliko Târnovo 10lv, 3½ hours
Vidin 10lv, 4½ hours

The following destinations may require more pre-planning:

Bansko 7lv, three hours, one daily (frequent from Zapad station)
Belogradchik 7lv, four hours, one daily
Kazanlâk 7lv, 2½ hours, three daily
Koprivshtitsa 5.50lv, 2½ hours, one daily
Kotel 16lv, five hours, two daily
Nesebâr 17lv, 6½ hours, five daily
Pamporovo 12.20lv, four hours, seven daily
Smolyan 13lv, 4½ hours, seven daily
Sozopol 17lv, six hours, two daily
Troyan 7lv, four hours, two daily

Those heading to Borovets must transfer in Samokov. Minibuses leave for Samokov (3lv, 1½ hours) from Sofia's **Yug Bus Terminal** (☎ 722 345) half-hourly between 7am and 8pm. To get there, take tram 18 from centre; it's below an underpass.

From the **Zapad Bus Terminal** (Ovcha Kupel; ☎ 955 5362; bul Tsar Boris III), there are nearly hourly buses to Bansko (5lv) from about 7am to 5pm, and a lone daily bus to Rila town. Reach the station by bus No 260 from pl Ruski Pametnik or tram No 5 from pl Makedonia, west of centre on ul Alabin.

The **Poduyane Bus Terminal** (☎ 477 262; bul V1 Vazov), northeast of the centre, has additional services to Troyan and Gabrovo.

INTERNATIONAL BUSES

Many bus companies sell tickets to bordering countries and beyond. Ticket prices can vary, so ask around. Sample fares include:
Athens 85lv, 12 to 13 hours, one or two daily (Tuesday to Sunday)
Belgrade 32-58lv, nine hours, two daily
Bucharest 46-50lv, 10 hours, three weekly (Tuesday, Thursday, Sunday)
Istanbul 20lv, eight to 10 hours, nine daily
Thessaloniki 28-37lv, six to seven hours, two to six daily

MTT (☎ 983 2665; www.SKGT-BG.com; bul Maria Luisa 84; ⏰ 7.30am-8pm or later) works with several bus lines. Downstairs in the train station is friendly **EBP Tours** (☎ 931-1500; ⏰ 6am-7pm Mon-Fri, 6am-4pm Sat & Sun).

Train

Sofia's **Central Train Station** (bul Maria Luisa) is a bit confusing, though departures and arrivals are listed in English on a large computer screen on the main floor, where there's an information booth (usually no English). You buy same-day tickets for Vidin, Ruse and Varna on the main floor, all other domestic destinations downstairs. Advance tickets are available at another office downstairs. Finding the right platform isn't always a breeze; ask a few people. There's an ATM on the main floor.

International tickets can be purchased at the often frightfully rude **Rila Bureau** (☎ 932 3346; ⏰ 7am-11.30pm) in the northern part of the main floor, or at its pleasantly helpful **centre office** (☎ 987 0777; ul General Gurko 5; ⏰ 7am-6.30pm Mon-Sat).

Train fare examples are contained in the following.
Athens 63lv, 16½ hours, one daily
Belgrade 26lv, 8½ hours, one daily
Blagoevgrad 4.30lv, 2½ to three hours, six daily
Bucharest 35.50lv, 11½ hours, two daily
Burgas 11.10lv, 6½ to 7½ hours, four daily
Gorna Oryahovitsa (near Veliko Târnovo) 7.90lv, 4½ hours, 10 daily
Karlovo 4.80lv, 2½ to 3½ hours, five daily
Koprivshtitsa 3.60lv, two to 2½ hours, four daily
Istanbul 36.50lv, 14½ hours, one daily
Plovdiv 5lv, 2½ hours, 12 daily
Ruse 10.30lv, seven hours, four daily

Shumen 10.70lv, 6½ to seven hours, five daily
Sliven 7.90lv, 4½ to 5½ hours, three daily
Varna 13.50lv, 7½ to 8½ hours, six daily
Vidin 8.30lv, 5½ hours, three daily

Trams 1, 7 and 14 connect the station with pl Sveta Nedelya.

GETTING AROUND
To/From the Airport
An OK Taxi booth in the arrivals hall arranges metered cabs to the centre (about 7lv or 8lv). Outside is a bus stop, where bus No 84 leaves for a stop along bul Vasil Levski, near Sofia University. Also, minibus No 30 travels between bul Maria Luisa and the airport.

Car & Motorcycle
Parking is a problem in Sofia, but signed parking garages are available (1lv per hour, or 6lv to 7lv overnight).

Most travel agents rent cars. **Penguin Travel** (☎ 988 2163; penguin@einet.bg; ul Moskovska 29, bldg 2; 🕑 9.30am-6pm Mon-Fri, plus Sat in summer) rents cars from €16 daily in summer. You could also check out **AutoJet** (www.rentacar.bg).

Public Transport
Sofia's trams, buses and metro line work on the same ticket system. A single ride is 0.50lv, a day pass is 2.10lv. Ticket booths are near most stops, and many newsstands sell tickets too. Single-ride tickets must be validated once you board; disguised officials charge a 5lv fine if you're caught without one (they frequent the trams between the centre and the train station).

Minibuses ply many useful city routes at 1lv per ride.

Sofia's relatively new metro line reaches western suburbs but is little use to travellers. A new line, going southeast, was under construction at research time.

Taxi
Sofia's taxis have a reputation for overcharging foreigners. Chances are less likely if you call for a cab; **OK Taxi** (☎ 973-2121) is a good choice.

AROUND SOFIA
Boyana Бояна
Once a separate village (now officially a part of Sofia), hillside Boyana has a couple

of prime-time attractions (at prime-time prices), reached by public transport from the city centre. (Or by hiking down trails from Mt Vitosha.)

The capital's best museum, the **National Historical Museum** (☎ 955 7604; bul Okolovrusten Pat; adult/student 10/5lv, guide 10lv; 🕑 9.30am-6pm Apr-Oct, 9am-5.30pm Nov-Mar) boasts some of the nation's most treasured pieces – the world's oldest gold (4th millennium BC), remarkable Thracian horse decorations – housed in the very 1970s former presidential residence. The catches are that it's expensive and far removed from its previous grand locale on bul Vitosha. The huge building is behind a row of trees.

Built between the 11th and 19th centuries, the inside walls of the **Boyana Church** (☎ 959-0939; adult/student 10/5lv, guide 5lv; 🕑 9.30am-5.30pm Apr-Dec, 9am-5pm Jan-Mar), 1.5km south of the museum, feature some 90 medieval frescoes, most dating from 1259 and are certainly among Bulgaria's finest. Only 10 visitors can enter at a time, so it sometimes gets backed up. The church is 200m from the bus stop – up and to the left.

One way to get there is by hailing minibus No 21 going southwest along bul Vasil Levski, which passes the museum, then by the church. The 45-minute walk between may not be the most appealing, but taxis are around.

Vitosha Витоша
The feather in Sofia's cap is this 23km by 13km mountain range (part of Vitosha Nature Park), just south of the city. At summer weekends, many Sofians come to hike, picnic and berry-pick.

Several *hizhas* (mountain huts), of varying condition, and hotels can be found atop the mountains.

It's worth paying 5lv for the Cyrillic trail map *Vitosha Turisticheska Karta* (1:50,000), available in Sofia.

CHAIRLIFTS
A popular way to get high up quick is from a couple of lift stations at the mountain base. When operating, both lifts run from about 9am to 5pm. In some months lifts run only Thursday to Sunday, or just weekends; at some spells they may be closed for a couple weeks. There's no clear schedule for this; ask in town.

BULGARIA

The cheaper of the two, **Dragalevtsi** (☎ 967 2511) is 2km up from the Dragalevtsi village bus stop (walk up the road next to the creek). From there it's a 1lv to ride to Bai Krâstyo, then it's a 1lv to ride a second lift to Goli Vrâh (1837m).

Simeonovo sends six-person gondolas to the peaks. It's 5lv to Aleko, a popular base for hikes and more ski lifts.

It's a 30-minute hike between the top of the two lifts.

HIKES

Dozens of well-marked trails await your boot tread. Popular ones include the steep 90-minute trip up Mt Cherni Vrâh (2290m) from Aleko; a three-hour trek east of Mt Sredets (1969m) from Aleko past Goli Vrâh to Zlatni Mostove; and a three-hour hike from Boyana Church past a waterfall to Zlatni Mostove.

SKIING

Cheaper than other Bulgarian slopes (lift ticket is just €7), Vitosha's ski season runs from mid-December to April; don't go on cloudy days in Sofia. There are 29km of ski runs (including one 5km stretch) ranging from easy to very difficult. Rental equipment can be had at Aleko Ski Centre at the top of the chairlift. Drop by Sofia's Orion Ski Shop (p127) for advice.

GETTING THERE & AWAY

About 2km south of NDK in Sofia, the useful **Hladilnika bus stop** (ul Srebârna), just east of bul Cherni Vrâh, has several Vitosha-bound buses. No 122 leads directly to the Simeonovo chairlift. No 64 goes to Dragalevtsi centre and on to Boyana. Get to Hladilnika by minibus No 25 from ul Rakovski or tram No 9 just east of NDK.

From Sofia's **Zapad bus terminal**, bus No 61 goes up to Zlatni Mostove.

RILA & PIRIN MOUNTAINS

These two Alp-like mountain chains (also national parks), between Sofia and the Greek border, are made of serious rocky-topped peaks brimming with rewarding and strenuous hiking paths, and clear streams rushing past monasteries and some appealing towns. Easy access points are west of the range, at Dupnitsa and Blagoevgrad (near the Rila mountains) and Sandanski (near the Pirin mountains).

Hiking

All paths are well signed. For Rila hikes, the monastery is a possible starting point, with four trails meeting others higher up. Day hikes are certainly possible. For longer ones, it's best to start up at Maliovitsa (northeast of Rila, reached by bus from Samokov), where you can reach the monastery (mostly downhill) on a one- or two-night trip via Sedemte Ezera (Seven Lakes).

Pirin hikes are generally tougher and sparser than Rila, with less day-hike potential. A popular starting point is at Popina Lûka, near Sandanski, with many lakes and waterfalls to visit.

Drop by Zig Zag in Sofia (p124) for tour information or tips. Be sure to get the *Rila* and/or *Pirin* maps (1:55,000) by Kartografia if you're venturing out (each are 5lv). *Hizhas* are indicated on maps, though some have fallen into disrepair; get more information on these at www.rilanationalpark.org and www.pirin-np.com.

RILA MONASTERY РИЛСКИ МАНАСТИР
☎ 07054

Bulgaria's most famous **monastery** (admission free; ☉ 6am-9pm or 10pm), set in a towering forested valley 120km south of Sofia, is a frequent destination for day-trippers on tours from around the region. It's gorgeous, drips with history and is near excellent hikes, but for many travellers an hour is enough.

Day trips to Rila from Sofia (widely available around the country) range from about €30 to €50 or more. Seeing Rila by public transport is not worth it in a day (though possible), as there are no direct buses. Consider staying overnight there, and try to avoid crowded summer weekends.

First built in 927, and heavily restored in 1469, the monastery helped keep Bulgarian culture and language alive during Ottoman rule. A fire engulfed most buildings in 1833, but it was rebuilt shortly thereafter. It's been on the Unesco World Heritage list since 1983.

The entrance to the monastery is from the west (where buses drop people off) at

Dupnitsa Gate, and around the east side at Samokov Gate.

Sights
The 300 monk cells fill four levels of colourful balconies, overlooking the large misshapen courtyard. The **Nativity Church**, built in the 1830s, contains 1200 magnificent murals – the ones outside more easily viewed. Just east, the 23m stone **Hrelyu Tower** is all that remains from the 14th century.

Nearby, the two-storey **Ethnographic Museum** (adult/student 5/3lv; 8.30am-4.30pm) houses many ornate woodwork pieces (it's a cross frenzy); museum pride soars over its double-sided Rila Cross, with 140 biblical scenes (tiny guys) done over a 12-year period in the late 1800s.

Sleeping & Eating
There are a couple of hotels and restaurants outside Samokov Gate, but it's best to stay in the monastery's simple **rooms** (2208; r with shared bathroom US$15). It can get cold, and there aren't many extra blankets, so bringing a sleeping bag is advised (and essential in winter).

Getting There & Away
At the time of research there were no direct buses connecting Sofia and the monastery or Rila town, 22km west. However, there are frequent buses from Sofia to Blagoevgrad (below) and from Blagoevgrad to Rila town. Rila is also accessible from Dupnitsa (65km south of Sofia). At research time four daily buses left Rila village for the monastery (1.2lv, 40 minutes) at 7.40am, 12.40pm, 3.15pm, 3.50pm, and five returned at 8.10am, 9am, 2.10pm, 5pm and 5.10pm. These times may change. Rila town has an ATM and a hotel but no taxis – if you arrive after the last bus to the monastery, you're likely seeing a night's worth of it.

BLAGOEVGRAD БЛАГОЕВГРАД
073 / pop 77,900
Primarily a transit town, just east of the Rila Mountains and 100km south of Sofia, cosmopolitan Blagoevgrad (home of American University) nevertheless booms with its student base's hey-let's-mingle energy.

The train station and neighbouring two bus stations are about 1km west of the centre. Start yourself – by city bus or taxi (about

1.5lv) – at pl Makedonia. South, across the stream, is the Varosha old quarter. Extending north (to the university and post office) and south (on ul Todor Aleksandrov) are active pedestrian malls.

Several foreign-exchange offices, banks and Internet cafés are in the centre.

Sights
The rather unexciting Varosha has a nice black-red-and-white striped church and, nearby, the expansive **History Museum** (885 372; bul Aleksandâr Samboliyski; admission 3lv; 9am-noon, 1-6pm Mon-Fri), though sadly its exhibits are in Bulgarian only.

Up the hill to the south is the vast **Forest Park**, 700m from the museum.

Sleeping
Alfatour Travel Agency (885 049; ul Krali Marko 4; 8am-6pm Mon-Fri, 9am-2pm Sat) Claims to find private rooms for 9.50lv per person. It's 600m southwest of pl Makedonia along ul Todor Aleksandrov (look for a small park to the right).

Voenen Klub Hotel (885 128; pl Makedonia; s/d 30/32lv;) Has 12 recently remodelled rooms on the east side of the square.

Eating & Entertainment
Food (mostly pizza) is easy to find around the centre. **Club Extreme** (off ul Todor Aleksandrov; cover 2lv; 10.30pm-4am Tue-Sun) is a new spacey disco, just west of pl Makedonia.

Getting There & Away
The main bus station is 100m south of the train station, outside of which some buses arrive/depart. Hourly buses leave from the main station from 6am to 6pm for Sofia (5lv, 1¾ hours) and Sandanski (3.20lv, 80 minutes) and from 7am to 8pm to Rila town (1.3lv, 45 minutes). Several buses go to Bansko (3lv, 65 minutes) and two to Melnik (4lv, two hours).

Six trains per day connect Blagoevgrad with Sofia (4.30lv, 2½ to three hours).

SANDANSKI САНДАНСКИ
Spartacus' birthplace, Sandanski is a pleasant town useful for its (sometimes confusing) connections to Melnik (1.3lv, 40 minutes, four daily) and Sofia (7.20lv, hourly) via Blagoevgrad (3.20lv). Some Sofia-bound buses leave from the main bus

station, which is 200m south of pedestrian mall ul Makedonia (with banks and Internet nearby); other buses leave from a private bus stop, on ul Stefan Karchev, a block north of the pedestrian mall. Super-value **Hotel Aneli** (☎ 0746-31-844; ul Gotse Delchev 1; r 28lv) is within view of the stop.

MELNIK МЕЛНИК
☎ 07437 / pop 275

Amidst the jutting, 'sand pyramid' part of the Pirins only 15km from Greece, little Melnik is home to unique white-washed, stone-built revival buildings and, frankly, the country's best wine, which is widely sold in plastic jugs and served by tap from giant wooden barrels. Best yet, many locals swear the wine here is 'hangover free'. Selfless research methods back up the claim.

From the bus stop, unnamed roads run on either side of a (mostly dry) creek run into town. Halfway, on the northern side, is a post office and pay phone. Melnik has no bank, foreign exchange, ATM or Internet (stock up in Sandanski or Blagoevgrad).

Sights

Mitko Manolev Winery (Shestaka; ☼ morning to dusk) overlooks Melnik from atop a hill on the town's east side; follow the road (and signs) about 350m east of the post office. This 250-year-old winery – carved out from a hill – serves its wines at 0.50lv per glass at cool cellar temperature.

Located to the south on the hill is **Kordopulov House** (admission 2lv; ☼ 8am-8pm), a giant revival-period home (actually first built in 1754) with high-ceiling rooms decked in traditional style. Past the winery to the north are the battered remains of the 10th-century **Bolyaskata Kâshta**, offering nice vantage points.

Church ruins are everywhere. Head up 300m to the big hill to the south (accessed from a path 80m east of the post office) to see some atop the ridge overlooking town.

ROZHEN MONASTERY РОЖЕНСКИ МАНАСТИР
This hilltop **monastery** (suggested donation 2lv; ☼ 7am-9pm), 7km east by road, was originally built in 1217, but most of what remains was redone in the mid-18th century. It's an atmospheric place, with woodcarvings and a mural-filled church, but probably most rewarding is the hiking trail that leads 3km

between Melnik and the site; it takes about an hour downhill from the monastery.

The best option is to bus up to Rozhen village from Melnik (0.50lv, 20 minutes, three daily), walk 800m up to the hilltop site, then walk to Melnik (signs point west, going behind the monastery). Some parts can be slippery; wear good shoes and don't chance it during rain.

Sleeping & Eating

Most of the traditional-style private homes let out simple rooms with shared bathroom for as little as 8lv per person. Try the homes on the hillsides. *Mehanas* generally have rooms too.

Mehana Megdana (☎ 088 866 6047; r per person with shared bathroom 8-10lv) Just before the post office, Mehana Megdana's rooms are plain but clean.

Lumparova Kâshta (☎ 218; r with shared bathroom 30 or 40lv) A tall home with triple and quadruple rooms (one with balcony) up the hill to the north. Reach it from the small path just past the pillared building (next to the post office).

Hotel Despot Slav (☎ 248, fax 271; s/d incl breakfast 50/60lv) On the main strip leading towards the winery, Hotel Despot Slav has Melnik's comfiest rooms with wood floors and TV.

Loznitsite Tavern (mains 2-9lv; ☼ 11.30am-midnight) Loznitsite Tavern, across from the post office, has vine-covered decks and a big Bulgarian menu, including several veggie options.

Getting There & Away

Four daily buses leave for Sandanski (1.7lv, 40 minutes). To head further into the mountains (eg Gotse Delchev) you'll need to catch transport in Sandanski.

BOROVETS БОРОВЕЦ

The ski slopes of Bulgaria's first ski resort, in the central-north Rila mountains about 70km southeast of Sofia, boom between December and April, particularly so at weekends (things are quieter in summer, though the gondola leads to high-up hikes). Its 23 ski runs include Bulgaria's longest. Ski equipment is on hand (about 40lv daily); a day lift pass is 44lv. Package trips often offer savings.

Other than resorts, there's an unnamed **motel** (r 15lv) with plain rooms, on the road to Hotel Rila; **Hotel Deniv** (☎ 052-605 033; d incl breakfast €20) is near the slopes. It's generally cheaper to stay in Samokov, 9km north; **Hotel Koala** (☎ 099-350 783; ul Hristo Zografov 25; d summer/winter 22/30lv) has comfy rooms (though the halls are freezing).

Half-hourly minibuses go to Samokov, where just as frequent minibuses go to Sofia (3lv, 1½ hours).

BANSKO БАНСКО
☎ 07443 / pop 9740

Far more than the ski town it's known to be, friendly Bansko – at the base of Mt Vihren (2914m) and the Pirin mountains – probably has the country's best *mehanas*, with rollicking folk bands playing many nights all year. Many souvenir stands hoist *suveniri* signs in Bulgarian (rather than English or German), geared to the many Bulgarian tourists. In summer, lifts or buses can be taken up to mountain hikes and *hizhas*.

Orientation
Buses and trains stop about 300m north of the central pl Nikola Vaptsarov, reached along ul Todor Aleksandrov. From the square ul Pirin goes south to pl Vûzhrazhdane and on to the ski lifts and, 2km further, the national park entrance. West of pl Nikola Vaptsarov is the short pedestrian mall ul Tsar Simeon. *Where in Bansko?* (2lv) is a useful ad-filled map.

Information
Bansko has surprisingly few Internet cafés; the cramped **Club Ultimate** (ul Balev; 90 min 1lv; ☿ 9am-midnight), a block north of pl Nikola Vaptsarov, has pokey connections and features Bruce Dickinson–era Iron Maiden.

Aside from the many foreign-exchange offices, try **DSK Bank** (ul Tsar Simeon; ☿ 8am-noon, 1.30-4.30pm Mon-Fri), with an ATM. The post office is west on ul Tsar Simeon.

In absence of a tourist information centre, **Oasis-A** (☎ 8076; ul Tsar Simeon; ☿ 9am-7pm Mon-Fri, 10am-7pm Sat, 10am-2pm Sun) is a new agency that offers information and sells slightly discounted lift passes. Four-hour Rila Monastery trips are 35lv.

Sights
The **Kâshta-Museum of Nikola Vaptsarov** (☎ 8304; pl Nikola Vaptsarov; admission 2lv; ☿ 9am-noon & 2-5.45pm) is dedicated to an appealing local

poet who lived here at a time when words could get you shot. (And did.) Arrested for anti-fascist poems written during WWII, Vaptsarov was executed in 1942 at the same age as Jesus, a fact not lost on the curators here. Ask to hear the tape in English, French or German.

The **Sveta Troitsa Church** (pl Vûzhrazhdane; ☿ 7.30am-6pm) is particularly striking for its wood-carved interior and gloomy, faded murals. At last pass a stork lived atop the clock tower; a kid named him Stefano.

Kâshta-Museum of Neofit Rilski (☎ 8272; ul Pirin 17; admission 2lv; ☿ 9am-noon & 2-5pm), behind the church, has five revival-style rooms where a pioneer of secular education lived; the tape in English is hard to hear.

Activities
HIKING
Pirin paths are accessed just south. In summer minibuses go to Banderitsa (3lv, three daily) to access trails to lakes and *hizhas*.

SKIING
The ski season in Bansko lasts from mid-December to April. There are two major mountains – the lower Chalin Valog, and the bigger Shiligarnika, higher up. An all-day lift pass for all four lifts is a whopping 48lv; rentals are available at the mountain.

The **Ski Board Centre** (☎ 603 988; ul Pirin 19; hr vary) has ski equipment for sale and rents bikes in summer.

Festivals & Events
The Pirin Sings Folk Festival is staged nearby in August, as is the International Jazz Festival.

Sleeping
Look for signs advertising private rooms. Unofficial camping is possible in the national park.

Turisticheski Dom Edelvais (☎ 8277; pl Vûzhrazhdane; r per person 10.30lv) Plain old rooms with thin mattresses on worn wood floors and shared bathroom, but it's central and Bansko's cheapest.

Alpin Hotel (☎ 8075; ul Neofit Rilski 6; s/d incl breakfast 25/39lv) Seventeen older, but clean, rooms on an atmospheric lane behind the Rilski house. The sauna is 4lv.

Duata Smarcha (☎ 2632; ul Velyan Ognev 2; s/d incl breakfast 28/56lv) One of many *mehanas* that offer rooms, this is 50m southeast of pl Vûzhrazhdane and has a gorgeous garden sitting area.

Hotel Mir (☎ 2500; ul Neofit Rilski 28; s/d/apt incl breakfast 35/50/75lv summer, 45/70/105lv winter) Run like a big home, this super hotel – with inviting alpine-style wood rooms – is in a residential pocket, east of Sveta Troitsa Church. The top-floor apartment has a mountain-facing balcony and fits four. The jumbo egg-and-pancake breakfast is served in the downstairs hang-out restaurant. There's also a laundry service and a sauna (5lv) as well as Ping-Pong in summer.

Eating

Bansko has dozens of appealing *mehanas* focusing on eating hearty Bulgarian fare and having fun doing it.

Baryakova Mehana (ul Velyan Ognev 3; mains 3-12lv; Ⓨ 11.30am-midnight) This homely tavern (east of pl Vûzhrazhdane) with whitewashed walls and a roaring fireplace serves grilled meats and local specialities sizzling over a flame, as vested musicians pump out traditional tunes. Full glasses of Melnik red wine come from the barrel.

Momini Dvori (pl Nikola Vaptsarov; pizzas 4.20-6.90lv; Ⓨ 11.30am-midnight) Twigs on the wall and a fire a-roarin', this dark, rustic pizzeria/BBQ cooks up Bansko's best egg-on-top pizzas.

Getting There & Away

From the **bus station** (ul Patriarh Evtimii), buses go to Sofia (7lv, three hours, at least six daily), Blagoevgrad (3lv, one hour, nine daily), Plovdiv (7lv, 3½ hours, two daily) and Gotse Delchev (3lv, one hour, nine daily).

Bansko is on the wonderful narrow-gauge railway through mountains to Septemvri (on the Sofia–Plovdiv line). The train station is on ul Akad Yordan Ivanov. The train (3.30lv, five hours, three daily) goes slowly, but offers great glimpses of local life both out the window and in the train carriage. If bored, count tunnels and stops (at last tally, tunnels beat stops 31–18).

PLOVDIV & RODOPI MOUNTAINS

Bulgaria's second city, Plovdiv, lies just within the cusp of the Thracian plain, with the deeply forested Rodopi Mountains (with culturally rich villages) looming to the south. Plovdiv is the easiest gateway to Smolyan (the key Rodopi hub) and Pamporovo ski resort, but less frequent buses (with changes) do connect the Pirin mountains to the west.

Hiking

Shiroka Lâka, 24km northwest of Smolyan, is a good base for hikes. A popular one is the five-hour hike south to Golyam Perelik (where there's a *hizha*), or there's a two-day hike from Shiroka to Trigrad via Mugla (a mountain town with accommodation). A shorter hike connects Trigrad with Yagodina Cave in less than three hours.

Trail maps split the Rodopis into the western and eastern ranges (5lv each). All coverage in this section focuses on the western portion.

Ask at one of the Smolyan tourist offices for hiking tips, or drop by Zig Zag in Sofia (p124).

PLOVDIV ПЛОВДИВ

☎ 032 / pop 340,640

Super Plovdiv! Bulgaria's most appealing city, Plovdiv displays its Roman guts with crumbled walls and theatre steps spilling out into the open at every turn in its laid-back and compact centre and hilly Old Town. Any Bulgarian site in the hunt for 'country's best' must reckon with Plovdiv, and the whole country seems to know it.

Plovdiv – known as Philippopolis to the Romans in the 3rd century AD, but settled thousands of years before by Thracians – has several plump hills, mounds really, that look like burps from the mountains southwest.

Orientation

Plovdiv's train station and (main) Yug Bus Terminal are about 600m southwest of the central pl Tsentralen. From the square, the main pedestrian mall, ul Knyaz Aleksandâr stretches 500m north to pl Dzhumaya. East from pl Dzhumaya, via ul Sâborna, is the cobbled and revered Old Town, all easily explored by foot. The centre's northern border is the reed-filled Maritsa River.

It's worth pointing out how massive the Roman town was. Below pl Dzhumaya are the (visible) rows of a Roman stadium, which extended all the way south to the present post office.

Information

Plovdiv lacks a tourist information centre, but you'll find scores of travel agents. A good Internet resource is www.plovdivcity guide.com. Foreign-exchange offices (and ATMs) abound on the pedestrian mall (ul Knyaz Aleksandâr) and on ul Ivan Vazov.

Bank BDK (ul Rayko Daskalov; 🕑 8.30am-4.30pm Mon-Fri)

Bulbank (ul Ivan Vazov 4; 🕑 8.30am-4.30pm Mon-Fri)

Call Centre (ul Balkan; international calls per min 0.20lv; 🕑 10am-11pm)

Inter Jet Tours (☎ 653 001; www.interjet-bg.com; ul Knyaz Aleksandâr 35; 🕑 9am-5pm winter, 9am-6pm summer) Arranges treks and rent cars (from €16 daily during summer).

Litera (pl Dzhumaya; 🕑 8.30am-8.30pm Mon-Fri, 10am-7pm Sat) Has English-language novels and regional maps.

R-Net (ul Aleksandâr Ekzarh 43; per hr from 0.50lv; 🕑 24hr) Internet access.

Speed (ul Kynaz Aleksandâr; per hr 1lv; 🕑 24hr) Internet access.

St Vrach Medical Centre (☎ 609 859; ul Hristo Botev 81; 🕑 8am-6pm)

Train station (☎ 622-732; bul Hristo Botev) Has 24 hour luggage storage (0.80lv daily). All bus stations have left luggage at select hours. Yug Bus Station (🕑 5:30am-9pm) charges 0.50lv daily.

Sights
OLD TOWN

Revival-era wood-shuttered homes lean over wee cobbled lanes (and antique shops) in this hilly neighbourhood, east of the pedestrian mall.

Seeing the 22 rooms inside the Old Town's most striking building (built in 1847) is an added bonus to the country's finest **Ethnographical Museum** (☎ 625 654; ul Dr Chomakov 2; admission 4lv; 🕑 9am-noon & 2-5.30pm summer, 9am-noon & 2-5pm winter) – with many traditional outfits upstairs, including the masked *kukeri* costumes from the Rodopi region with pointed noses and bell-belts, various tools and a Plovdiv scene painting behind an old piano you can play.

The country's most impressive Roman ruin, the **Theatre of Ancient Philippopolis** (admission 3lv; 🕑 9am-5.30 summer, Wed-Sun winter) – an amphitheatre – is easily seen (for free) outside the gates, but entry lets you tread on worn steps approaching their 2000th birthday. Resist the temptation to scrawl 'Deep Purple' on the walls; someone's beaten you to it anyway. The theatre holds various events from June to October.

Tucked behind walls, with a bell tower at its apex, the **Church of St Constantine & Elena** (ul Sâborna 24; admission free; 🕑 dawn-dusk) dates from the 4th century AD, though much of what you see was rebuilt in 1832.

The **Ruins of Eumolpias** (ul Dr Chomakov; admission free; 🕑 24hr), scattered upon Nebet Tepe hilltop, date from a Thracian settlement from about 5000 BC. Look for a green-and-white smokestack to the southeast. It rises above the Kamenitza brewery, where Plovdiv's beer is made. Some of it gets drunk up here too.

BULGARIA

QUIRKY PLOVDIV

Hug the 'Great Gossiper'
The statue in the central steps honours Milyu, the great gossiper of Plovdiv in the 1980s and '90s, who won fans for his unsubtle listening-in to passers-by. No-one claims hugging the **Milyu statue** brings luck, but it damn well might.

A nod to the 'Seventh'
Proudly a seven-hill town (like Rome), Plovdiv lost one during the communist era, when it was broken down to provide stone steps in the Old Town. Honour it – with a tear in a beer, or over a *banitsa* – at the gaping-hole **seventh hill site**, 100m south of the Hill of the Liberators.

Bring your own robe
The unique group Byalo Bratstvo (White Brothers) – named the colour of their robed attire – has greeted the sun atop the **Hill of the Liberators** at sunrise daily for decades (and mystified many joggers in the process). Witness it if you can wake in time. (But don't sing 'Here Comes the Sun'. They've heard that one before.)

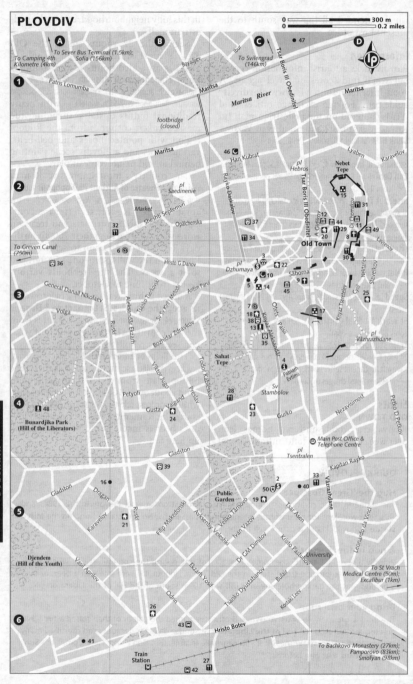

PLOVDIV

0 .... 300 m
0 .... 0.2 miles

To Sever Bus Terminal (1.5km);
To Camping 4th   Sofia (156km)
Kilometre (4km)

To Svilengrad
(146km)

To Greven Canal
(750m)

Maritsa River

footbridge
(closed)

Maritsa

Maritsa

Han Kubrat

pl
Hebros

Nebet
Tepe

Old Town

pl
Saedinenie

Market

Sheshti Septemvri

Opâlchenska

Hristo G Danov

pl
Dzhumaya

Sáborna

pl
Vâzrazhdane

General Danail Nikolaev

Volga

Sahat
Tepe

Sv
Stambolov

Bunardjika Park
(Hill of the Liberators)

pl
Tsentralen

Main Post Office &
Telephone Centre

Public
Garden

Djendem
(Hill of the Youth)

University

To St Vrach
Medical Centre (50m);
Excalibur (1km)

Train
Station

Hristo Botev

To Bachkovo Monastery (27km);
Pamporovo (83km);
Smolyan (98km)

Something in a slightly more modern vein is the enormous 19th-century **Church of Sveta Bogoroditsa** (ul Sâborna; admission free; ⏲ 7am-midnight). This is Plovdiv's centre for religious ceremonies, including those at Easter.

Be sure to note the interesting murals near the enterance that depict scenes of Ottoman soldiers threatening Orthodox Bulgarians.

OTHER SIGHTS

Overlooking the ruins of a Roman stadium below the square, the **Dzhumaya Mosque** (Friday mosque; pl Dzhumaya; admission free; ⏲ dawn-dusk) originally dates from 1368 – the first in Balkan Europe – but was renovated after a 1928 earthquake (note the cracks inside). A few hundred worshippers show up for prayers at 1.30pm Friday.

If travellers' ennui begins to congeal, bowl it to dust at **Excalibur** (☎ 631 852; ul Sankt Peterburg; game 4-5lv; ⏲ 9am-6am), a popular new castle-themed bar (1.5km east of the train station). And there's a fricking go-cart raceway out back (from 1.20lv per lap). Take Bus No 9, 22 or 44 from the centre.

The nation's biggest canal, the impressive 2.5km river-fed **Greven Canal**, is 1km west of the centre. The last communist-built project features sculler rallies and is surrounded with jogging paths and shady Loven Park. Take bus No 10 west as far as it goes on ul Sheshti Septemvri, then walk 200m northwest.

Sleeping
BUDGET

Camping 4th Km (☎ 951 360; bul Bulgaria; camp site 3lv, bungalows 30 & 40lv) If you should insist, camp sites are available, 4km west of the centre. There are plenty of trees to block views of civilisation, plus a 24 hour restaurant. The bungalows are a bit sad. It's near the end of the line for several buses: bus No 22 goes there from bul Tsar Boris III Obedinitel, bus No 4, 18 and 44 from bul Bulgaria (head north up bul Tsar Boris III Obedinitel to catch this bus), or No 222 from outside the train station.

Tourist's House (Turisticheska Kâshta; ☎ /fax 635 115; ul Slaveikov 5; dm 20lv, s/d with shared bathroom 28/48lv) By far Plovdiv's best budget deal, this 19th-century three-storey 'hostel,' just east (and down) from the Old Town hill, offers cheap beds in a traditional building. A former school, the hotel has six rooms (including two dorm rooms) and an occasionally used top-floor room. High wood-carved ceilings loom over rooms and there's a TV lounge and traditional rugs. The downstairs bar rocks sometimes, as does the summer garden bar (serving free breakfast May to October).

Queen Mary (☎ 629 306; ul Gustav Vaigand 7; r per person incl breakfast 15lv; ✳) Putting a splash in

INFORMATION	
Bank BDK	**1** C3
Bulbank	**2** C5
Call Centre	**3** C3
Inter Jet Tours	**4** C4
Litera	**5** C3
R-Net	**6** B3
Speed	**7** C3

SIGHTS & ACTIVITIES	(pp135-7)
Church of St Constantine & Elena	**8** D2
Church of Sveta Bogoroditsa	**9** C3
Dzhumaya Mosque	**10** C3
Ethnographical Museum	**11** D2
Hindliyan Kâshta	**12** D2
Milyu Statue	**13** C3
Roman Stadium Ruins	**14** C3
Ruins of Eumolpias	**15** D2
Seventh Hill Site	**16** A5
Theatre of Ancient Philippopolis	**17** D3

SLEEPING 🛏	(pp137-8)
Accommodation Agency	**18** C3
Esperansa	**19** C5
Hotel Hebros	**20** D2
Hotel Leipzig	**21** B5
Hotel-Bar Central	**22** C3
PBI Hostel	**23** C4
Queen Mary	**24** B4
Tourist's House	**25** D3
Trakiya Hotel	**26** B6

EATING 🍴	(pp138-9)
Billa	**27** B6
Chevermeto	**28** C4
Hebros House	(see 20)
Janet	**29** D2
King's Stable	**30** D3
Orientalska Cladkarnitsa Dzhumayata	(see 10)
Raha Tepe	**31** D2
Ristorante da Lino	**32** B2
Trimontium Princess Hotel Restaurant	**33** D5
Zakuska	**34** C2

ENTERTAINMENT 🎭	(p139)
Caligula	**35** C3
Flamingo Cinema	**36** A3
Infinity Club	**37** C2
Nikolai Masalitinov Dramatic Theatre	**38** C3
Speis	**39** B5

TRANSPORT	(pp139-40)
MTT	**40** C5
Rila Bureau	**41** A6
Rodopi Bus Terminal	**42** B6
Yug Bus Terminal	**43** B6

OTHER	
Balabanov Kâshta	**44** D2
Danov House	**45** C3
Historical Museum	(see 49)
Imaret Mosque	**46** C2
International Plovdiv Fairgrounds	**47** C1
Monument to the Soviet Army	**48** A4
Nedkovich House	**49** D2
Police	**50** C5
Zlatyo Boyadjiev House	(see 30)

BULGARIA

a quiet residential street with an unmissable portrait of a different British queen (Elizabeth II), this B&B has several clean rooms run by an English-speaking doctor.

PBI Hostel (☎ 638 467; ul Naiden Gerov 13; dm €10, r per person €15) Relatively new hostel debut for the Thracian plain, PBI pales to the communal glory of Sofia's better hostels despite its super location. Three dorm rooms have maps on walls, but are rather bare. A plastic curtain separates three showers from the tiny kitchen. The lone 'VIP' room has private bathroom.

In summer cuddly touts offering unofficial rooms (likely 20lv or less per person) will approach you at the stations. Agencies around town offer rooms too. A couple, loosely keeping daily hours in summer (from 9am to 6pm or later), can be reached by phone all year: **Esperansa** (☎ 260 653; 265 127 24hr; ul Ivan Vazov 14), a nine-minute walk from the main stations, arranges rooms in the centre (single/double 25/40lv) and outside it (single/double 20/35lv); and the unnamed **accommodation agency** (☎ 272 778, 632 428 24hr; ul Knyaz Aleksandâr 28) on the main pedestrian mall (watch for black sign) offers rooms at €10 per person.

MID-RANGE

Hotel Leipzig (☎ 632 252; bul Ruski 70; s/d 45/66lv) West of the centre and standing a dozen stories in its peach-salmon and blue colour scheme, this old hotel could use a little touch-up, but most rooms have choice views.

Trakiya Hotel (☎ 624 101; ul Ivan Vazov 84; s/d 45/75lv) This cheerful place is across from the train station. Double-paned windows and thick curtains keep out noise and light from after-hours activity nearby. The comfy rooms have fans, and at least one has a German football blanket.

Hotel-Bar Central (☎ 622 348; ul K Stoilov 7; s/d €35/50) This new hotel – the bar is no biggie – has five swankish, inviting rooms in an atmospheric spot just east of the Dzhumaya Mosque. Reserve ahead in summer.

TOP END

Hotel Hebros (☎ 260 180; www.hebros-hotel.com; ul Stoilov 51; r incl breakfast €90) Those looking for a classic Old-Town sleep should spring for this inviting hotel, with back courtyard, Jacuzzi and sauna. Each of the six rooms is

done up in lush 19th-century design, with varying looks. There's a restaurant on the premises, see p138.

Eating

Most of the pedestrian mall spots are drinks-oriented, and many stands sell pizza slices or kebabs for 1lv.

RESTAURANTS

Chevermeto (☎ 628 605; ul Dondukov; mains 2.60-8lv; 9am-2am Mon-Sat) Sure the Old Town has the charm, but Chevermeto delivers its own goods with its communist-era bomb shelter location under Sahat Tepe hill. Its menu (ask for the lone English menu, and some help) focuses on Balkan specialities (including Turkish, Greek, Serbian, even Armenian dishes). Serbian rissoles (4.20lv) are spicy bite-sized sausages. Vegetarians can opt for several veggie skewers. Outside seating is best during the day. After 9pm, live music blares past the mammoth doors in the shelter.

Janet (☎ 626 044; ul 4th Yanuari 3; mains 5-14lv; 11am-11.30pm) Old Town restaurant in a traditional 1863 home, with four inside halls and an outdoor deck. Specialises in Bulgarian dishes and does a tasty rabbit cacciatore (with mushrooms and sausage) for 9lv. Menu in English.

Ristorante da Lino (☎ 631 751; ul Sheshti Septemvri 125; pastas from 5lv, mains 6-19lv; noon-3pm & 7pm-midnight Mon-Sat) Set in a small converted monastery, this good break-from-Bulgaria eatery serves classy Italian food. Beef fillet is 10lv, prawns in Catalan sauce are 19lv. Good thing they take credit cards.

Hebros Hotel (☎ 260 180; ul Stoilov 51; mains 12-21lv; lunch & dinner) A cosy basement Old Town restaurant with live music, a changing menu and superbly prepared nouveaux Bulgarian meals. There's always a fish dish or two. Staples like the wild mushrooms and tomato soup break the norm.

The Trimontium Princess Hotel **restaurant** (pl Tsentralen) has a daily breakfast buffet (8lv).

CAFÉS

Orientalska Cladkarnitsa Dzhumayata (ul Balkan 44; baklava 1.50lv; 7.30am-9pm Mon-Sat, 7.30am-8pm Sun) On the northern side of the mosque, this is Plovdiv's best place for one of several types of flaky, fresh baklava.

QUICK EATS

Zakuska (ul Rayko Daskalov; snacks 0.50-0.80lv; ☺ breakfast & lunch) Get your hot *banitsas* (some fruit filled) and other breads at this buzzing stand. Locals often two-fist 'em.

SELF-CATERING

Billa (ul Makedonia; ☺ 8am-9pm Mon-Sat, 9am-8pm Sun) Self-caterers can visit huge Billa, a grocery store next to the Rodopi bus station.

Drinking

Rahap Tepe (ul Dr Chomakov; snacks 1.10-4lv; ☺ 10am-midnight Apr-Oct) Near the top of Old Town's Nebet Tepe hill, this outside spot has good views to the west, enjoyed by many a midday beer sipper.

King's Stable (ul Sâborna; cocktails 3.40lv, sandwiches 1.80lv; ☺ 8.30am-2am Apr-Oct) This leafy, decked bar (hidden behind Zlatyo Boyadjiev House) serves Plovdiv's cool kids (and a few tourists) drinks and coffees.

Entertainment

A couple of free colour weeklies list event times and locations (in Bulgarian only). *Plovdiv Info* is the best.

Flamingo Cinema (☎ 644 004; ul Sheshti Septemvri 128; tickets 3lv) Foreign films (with Bulgarian subtitles) are shown at several venues citywide, including this four-screen, modern theatre.

Speis (☎ 626 765; ul Gladston 15; tickets 2lv) Another theatre where you can see foreign films; this place is slightly older.

Nikolai Masalitinov Dramatic Theatre (☎ 632 348; ul Knyaz Aleksandâr 38) If your Bulgarian is confident, you might enjoy the plays this theatre runs most nights.

Infinity Club (☎ 0888 281 431; ul Bratya Pulievi 4; ☺ 10pm-late) Discos regularly open (and close); this club is one of the most popular in town.

Caligula (☎ 626 867; ul Kynaz Aleksandâr 30; ☺ 10am-8am) Plovdiv's biggest gay club, sitting proudly smack in the middle of the pedestrian mall.

Getting There & Away

BUS

Plovdiv has three bus stations. The main **Yug Bus Terminal** (☎ 626 937; bul Hristo Botev) is 100m east of the train station.

About 200m south the **Rodopi Bus Terminal** (☎ 777 607), accessible from the overpass east of Yug or by underpass from the train station, sends buses south and to Karlovo. Over a kilometre north of the river, **Sever Bus Terminal** (☎ 553 705) has buses to Koprivshtitsa, Troyan and Veliko Târnovo; get there by minibus No 4 from ul Tsar Boris III Obedinitel, or taxi (about 1.50lv).

Sample fares follow; buses leave/arrive at Yug unless otherwise noted.

Athens (via Sofia) 90lv, 15 hours, one to three daily
Bansko 6lv, four hours, one daily (at 3pm)
Blagoevgrad 7 to10lv, four hours, three daily
Burgas 15lv, four hours, two daily
Hisarya 1.80lv, one hour, 12 daily
Istanbul 30lv, six hours, six daily
Karlovo 2.80lv, 1½ hours, hourly 6am-8pm
Kazanlâk 3.50 to 5lv, two hours, two daily (Rodopi), two daily (Sever)
Koprivshtitsa 5.50lv, two hours, one daily (Sever)
Pamporovo 7lv, two hours, hourly 6am to 7pm except noon (Rodopi)
Ruse 13lv, seven hours, one daily (Sever)
Sliven 6lv, 2½ hours, nine daily
Smolyan 7.50lv, 2½ hours, hourly 6am to 7pm except noon (Rodopi)
Sofia 8lv, two hours, half-hourly 6am-12.30pm & hourly 2-8pm
Troyan 6.50lv, 3½ hours, one daily (Sever)
Varna 15lv, seven hours, two daily
Veliko Târnovo 10lv, 4½ hours, three daily & two daily (Sever)
Velingrad 5.50lv, two hours, one daily (Sever)

MTT (☎ 624 274; pl Tsentralen; ☺ 7:30am-8pm or later), next to the Trimontium Hotel, sells international tickets.

TRAIN

Direct trains from Plovdiv's fine old **train station** (☎ 622 732; bul Hristo Botev) include the following:

Burgas 7.90lv, five hours, three to six daily
Istanbul 33 to 49lv, 11 hours, one daily
Karlovo 2.40lv, 1½ hours, six daily
Septemvri 1.90lv, 45 minutes, 14 to 15 per day (all but one to/from Sofia stop here)
Sofia 5lv, 2½ hours, 13 or 14 per day, every hour or two from 3am to 7.30pm
Stara Zagora 2.80lv, two to 2½ hours, 10 to 12 daily
Varna 7lv, six hours, three daily
Veliko Târnovo 4.80lv, five hours, two daily

No direct trains go to Ruse (9lv, 8½ to ten hours). It's easiest to make connections in Stara Zagora or Gorna Oryahovitsa.

For international tickets, go to **Rila Bureau** (☎ 643 120; bul Hristo Botev 31a; ☺ 8am-6pm Mon-Fri, 8am-2pm Sat).

BACHKOVO MONASTERY
БАЧКОВОСКИ МАНАСТИР

Bulgaria's second-biggest **monastery** (admission free; ☺ 6am-10pm), 27km south of Plovdiv, is worth popping into on the way to Rodopi.

Founded in 1083, and restored in the 17th century, Bachkovo's central courtyard is filled with a 12th-century **Archangel Church** and a larger 17th-century **Church of the Assumption of Our Lady** with candle-smoke-stained walls and remarkably shiny altar; the churches are attached by a walk-through archway. A small museum is nearby, and (through a gate) the early 17th-century St Nicholas Chapel. Ask about nearby **hikes** into the forested hills.

You can stay in the basic **rooms** (r per person with shared bathroom 10lv).

Buses bound for Smolyan will let you off here, at the southern end of the village. Parking is 0.50lv.

PAMPOROVO ПАМПОРОВО
☎ 3021

This popular ski resort, 83km south of Plovdiv, has eight ski runs and 25km of cross-country trails in a thick-pine mountain-top location. Rental equipment is about 30lv, a lift ticket 45lv. A bus connects the centre – near the T-junction of the roads to Smolyan, Plovdiv and Shiroka Lâka/Devin, where the bus stop is – to the lifts. It's quiet off-season.

About 900m up from the bus stop, the huge **Hotel Perelik** (☎ 8405; d incl breakfast 110-170lv; P) caters to package tourists. Visit www.pmk-bg.com for links to several other options, including **Hotel Snezhanka** (☎ 8316; d incl breakfast 80-140lv; P), which is nice, and a little less expensive. Cheaper accommodation is 15km south in Smolyan.

Buses between Plovdiv and Smolyan stop here.

SMOLYAN СМОЛЯН
☎ 0301 / pop 34,300

By setting – in a sweeping valley between sky-scraping Rodopi peaks of mixed greens – Smolyan could be Bulgaria's most beautiful city, but on the streets – spread-out, 'lacking harmony with nature' as one local

complains – it feels a bit lacklustre. That said, the location (near Pamporovo's ski runs) wins out and Smolyan swings its own swagger with remarkably good attractions.

Orientation & Information

Buses arrive near the west end of long bul Bulgaria (at the 'old centre'). About 250m east it becomes a pedestrian mall, where you'll find a **tourist office** (☎ 63 885; bul Bulgaria 80; ☺ 9am-1pm & 2-6pm Mon-Fri), **Access Internet Club** (per hr 1lv; ☺ 24hr) and, 750m east (after it rejoins vehicular traffic), a **Bulbank** (☺ 8.30am-4.30pm Mon-Fri) with 24-hour ATM.

Another 1km east on bul Bulgaria, near the 'new centre' and museums, is another (more helpful) **tourist office** (☎ 62 530; bul Bulgaria 5; ☺ 9am-noon & 12.30-5.30pm), with handouts on area hikes and accommodation.

Sights

The **Historical Museum** (☎ 62 727; pl Bulgaria 3; adult/student 5/3lv; ☺ 9am-noon & 1-5pm Tue-Sun), a five-minute walk up steps (just east of the tourist office in the new centre), is one of the nation's best, with numerous English signs on three floors outlining Bulgaria's ethnographical past. Highlights include an artful display of hanging bells, a cool Thracian helmet from the 5th century BC and full-bodied *kukeri* costumes (think *Star Wars* bar scene plus chicken feet).

The **Art Gallery** (☎ 62 328; adult/student 5/1lv; ☺ 9am-noon & 1-5pm Tue-Sun), across from the Historical Museum, has seven halls of modern art (mostly Bulgarian); much of it rather derivative. Zdravko Palazov's *Posledniyat Den na Mira* (Last Day of the World) – of two preoccupied men not noticing a nude woman – is intriguing.

The **Planetarium** (☎ 23 074; admission 5lv, minimum 3 visitors; ☺ English shows 2pm Mon-Sat, 11am Sun), open since 1975, features a domed-ceiling show of outer space (about 40 minutes, also in French and German) that conjures a cosmonautic, past despite its updated soundtrack. The best part is watching the stars for real via the mega-telescope on clear Wednesday evenings (admission 2lv).

Sleeping

Info centres have a partial list of private accommodation available.

Three Fir-Tree House (☎ 38 228; dreltannen@mbox .digsys.bg; ul Srednogorec 1; s/d incl breakfast 24/36lv) The owner of this lovely hotel is as proud of the namesake trees out front as the nicely furnished rooms (hair dryer, iron, free water, sheepskin blankets, balconies). The breakfast is huge. The hotel provides a 1lv shuttle service to Pamporovo in winter. It's 250m from the bus station, down the steps at the start of the bul Bulgaria pedestrian mall.

Babylon Hotel (☎ 63 268; d/apt 24/30lv) Uphill from the pedestrian mall, about 200m past the visitors centre, Babylon is a distant second to Fir-Tree for central hotels. Rooms are simple and clean; try to get one facing away from the traffic.

Getting There & Away

Hourly buses leave Smolyan's **bus station** (☎ 34 251) north to Plovdiv, stopping in Pamporovo and at Bachkovo Monastery (if you ask). Smolyan has important, but infrequent, links into the mountains. At research time six daily buses left for Devin (4lv, 1½ hours) via Shiroka Làka (2lv, 40 minutes).

SHIROKA LÀKA ШИРОКА ЛЪКА
☎ 03030 / pop 1501

Ridiculously cute Shiroka Làka, 24km west of Smolyan, is a stream-side town of Roman bridges and 19th-century whitewashed villas, which give a very other-era vibe (maybe it's the dung heaps). Its clickety-clackety name makes even some Bulgarians chuckle. The best time to visit is early March, when locals adorn hilarious full-bodied animal-like costumes during the *kukeri* festival (p168).

Most visitors rush in for an hour on a tour bus, perhaps see the **Ethnographic Museum** (at the town's east end; very iffy hours). But it's a good potential base for Pamporovo, and many hiking trails loom in the hills above. There's a small tourist centre with erratic opening hours.

It's possible to study traditional music (or sit in on a recital) at the revered **Folk Music and Instruments High School** (☎ 333; smu_shirokalukka@abv.bg), across the water; it's closed July to mid-September.

The small family-run **Hotel Kalina** (☎ 675; r incl breakfast summer/winter 15/20lv) is by the centre, where the *kukeri* festival is held in early March, with clean modern rooms. Near the music school is the bigger **Hotel Shiroka Làka** (☎ 341; r 20lv).

Six daily buses between Devin and Smolyan stop here; from Smolyan to Shiroka costs 2lv and takes 45 minutes, from Smolyan to Devin is 4lv, 1½ hours.

TRIGRAD ТРИГРАД
☎ 3040

This modest town, 23km south of Devin, is reached by (as some locals dub it) a 'special road' (dirt, rocks, holes). It bumps its way to town past the dramatic Devil's Throat Gorge, cut open by a rushing stream way below.

The town's not much (no bank or ATM), but the area provides an outdoorsy mecca for activities such as horse riding, rafting, rock climbing and caving.

The stream runs (mostly out of sight) through the dark, deep **Devil's Throat Cave** (☎ 220; admission 2.5lv, minimum 5 people), 2km north of town. More adventurous trips are at **Haidouk Cave** (☎ 200, 889 245 071; per person 30lv), a guided four-hour trip, where you're lowered a long way down into the cave. From Trigrad, it's possible to hike to **Yagodina Cave** (2½ hours), where there are hourly tours.

There are a couple of guesthouses with rooms for about 16lv to 20lv per person.

One daily bus connects Trigrad with Devin.

CENTRAL BALKANS

This broad swipe of lovely and surprisingly high mountains – called the Stara Planina (Old Mountain) locally – occupies much of Bulgaria's belly. The area is dotted with towns in 19th-century revival style (Veliko Târnovo, Koprivshtitsa, Tryavna and Kotel are standouts). Some of the many hiking paths through the broad Central Balkans National Park can also be cross-country skied or biked. Other wind-swept hubs are more off-the-beaten track (Karlovo, Kazanlàk, Sliven and Shumen).

Check www.staraplanina.org for more information.

Some travellers find themselves changing trains or buses in the Stara Planina's outer reaches at the big hubs of Stara Zagora, where there's a nice central garden, a Roman tile floor in the post office and little else to see.

KOPRIVSHTITSA КОПРИВШТИЦА

☎ 07184 / pop 2645

Bulgaria's capital of revival architecture (113km east of Sofia) has some 400 19th-century buildings – with unparalleled ease of a combination visit to open ones – that can excite even the most cynical or worn-out traveller. The forested hikes in the surrounding Sredna Gora hills add to the appeal.

It can be a bit tricky getting there, and you won't be alone, particularly in summer when heat-escaping city folk from Sofia and Plovdiv pour into this higher-up town to cool off.

Koprivshtitsa was the setting for a key early revolt against the Turks, the 20 April 1876 Uprising. Its re-enactment (held 1 or 2 May actually) along with the Folklore Days Festival (mid-August) are popular annual events; check with the tourist information centre (p142) for details.

Orientation

The town spreads north–south for 1km along a small creek and is walkable. The bus stop is about 100m south of the centre, which is at pl 20 April. The train station (Gara Koprivshtitsa) is 9km north of town.

Information

The **tourist information centre** (☎ 2191; pl 20 April; ☾ 9am-6pm) has helpful English-speaking staff that can arrange private stays, rent bikes (9lv for four hours) and sell town maps with hiking info (2lv).

The **DSK Bank** (☾ 8am-4pm Mon-Fri), next to the bus station, has a 24 hour ATM and exchanges money. The gold **post office** (Lyuben Karavelov; ☾ 7.30am-noon & 1-4.30pm Mon-Fri) has telephone services.

Across the creek from pl 20 April, **Heroes Internet Agency** (ul Hadzhi Nencho Palaveev 49; per hr 1.2lv; ☾ 9am-midnight) has a rather pokey connection.

Sights

If you visit a traditional home only once in Bulgaria, make it here. Six of Koprivshtitsa's traditional homes are now 'house museums,' and a super-value combo ticket (5lv) is available to see all; otherwise it's 3lv

KOPRIVSHTITSA

0 — 200 m
0 — 0.1 miles

INFORMATION
DSK Bank..1 B2
Heroes Internet Agency...................2 B1
Post Office...3 B3
Telephone Centre.......................(see 3)
Tourist Information Centre............4 B1

SIGHTS & ACTIVITIES (pp142-3)
Benkovski House.................................5 D3
Debelyanov House.............................6 A1
Equestrian Statue...............................7 D3
Kableshkov House..............................8 A2
Karavelov House.................................9 B1
Lyutov House....................................10 B3
Market..11 B3
Oslekov House..................................12 A1

SLEEPING (p143)
Emi-98...13 B1
Hotel Kalina......................................14 B1
Hotel Trayanova Kâshta..................15 A2
Voivodenets Hostel..........................16 B1

EATING (p143)
Pizzeria..17 B1
Starata Kâshta..................................18 B2

TRANSPORT (p143)
Bus Stop..19 B1

OTHER
April Uprising Mausoleum...............20 B2
Hadzhi Nencho Palaveev
  Cultural Centre..............................21 B3

To Train Station (9km);
Sofia (113km)

To Plovdiv
(106km)

To Hotel Panorama
(150m)

BULGARIA

each. All have signs in English and keep the same hours (☼ 9am-5.30pm summer, 9am-5pm winter) but alternate Monday or Tuesday off (see listings). The six pack is:

■ **Benkovski House** (ul Georgi Benkovski 5; ☼ closed Tue) Exhibits on the cavalier who continued the 1876 uprising in surrounding areas. Near an impressive equestrian statue 400m southeast of the centre.

■ **Debelyanov House** (ul Dimcho Debelyanov 6; ☼ closed Mon) Home of the 'tender poet' killed in WWI; he was not as short as the ceiling suggests (the floors were raised for renovation).

■ **Kableshkov House** (ul Todor Kableshkov 8; ☼ closed Mon) The home of the intriguing chairman of the revolutionary committee, this house has a wavy tri-façade and must-see old photos of blokes with remarkable moustaches.

■ **Karavelov House** (ul Hadzhi Nencho Palaveev 39; ☼ closed Tue) Three-section home where the brothers Karavelov grew up; Lyuto ran a revolutionary press (see it here) and Petko was an early post-independence politician.

■ **Lyutov House** (Topalov House; ul Nikola Belovezhdov 2; ☼ closed Tue) Most colourful of the homes, with vibrant walls and ceilings.

■ **Oskelov House** (ul Gereniloto 4; ☼ closed Mon) Detailed home of one of the town's 19th-century tax collectors.

Sleeping

The tourist office can help arrange private rooms from 20lv per person (most are 30lv and up); one cheapie is **Emi-98** (☎ 2245; ul Vekilova 9; r 20lv per person).

Voivodenets Hostel (☎ 2145; ul Vekilova 5; dm 8lv) Old home with nice sitting area downstairs but mostly cramped rooms with two to 10 beds in each. Not much room to store the pack. When it's full, the owners run another hostel in town too.

Hotel Panorama (☎ 2035; www.panoramata.com; ul Georgi Benkovski 40; s/d incl breakfast €18/24) Super-friendly English-speaking family runs this hotel with nice views of the southern part of town (worth the 300m walk from the bus stop). Panorama were building eight new rooms with balconies at research time.

Hotel Kalina (☎ 2032; ul Hadzhi Nencho Palaveev 35; s/d incl breakfast 36/50lv) Next to the Karavelov House, and facing a nice yard, Kalina has six traditional rooms with altering themes.

Hotel Trayanova Kâshta (☎ 3057; ul Gereniloto 5; r/apt 40/80lv) Off a cobbled lane, this home often fills its huge traditionally decked-out rooms early.

Eating

Pizzeria (ul Hadzhi Nencho Palaveev; sandwiches & slices 1lv; ☼ 8am-7pm) Those looking for quick and cheap food can go to this place, north of pl 20 April.

Traditional *kâshtas* are found on side streets, some keeping seasonal hours. One good one is **Starata Kâshta** (☎ 0887 733 430; ul Hadzhi Nencho Palaveev; mains 2.70-5.10lv; ☼ 8.30am-midnight), next to the bus stop, with a particularly delicious *kavarma*.

Getting There & Away

The bus service is sadly infrequent. At research time, one mid-afternoon bus from Sofia (5.50lv, 2½ hours) and one from Plovdiv (5.50lv, 2½ hours) arrived here (after the information centre closed). The return trips were made in the wee hours Monday to Saturday, and Sunday afternoon.

Four trains connect Koprivshtitsa and Sofia (3.10lv, 1¾ to 2½ hours) and there's one to Burgas (8.30lv, five hours); taxis and buses meet trains (though some readers have reported that buses may wait an hour or more for a subsequent train to arrive).

KARLOVO КАРЛОВО

☎ 0335 / pop 28,000

Famous for its mountainous backdrop and revolutionary hero Vasil Levski, quiet Karlovo can offer an interesting stopoff (a few hours, maybe a day). It also has bus services to the leafy spa town of **Hisarya** (17km southwest), big with Bulgarians.

On the town's southern side, the train station is 200m southeast from the rather elusive bus station. Past the park from the train station is ul Vasil Levski, which snakes 1km north through old lanes to the centre, at pl 20 Yuli, where there's a bank, ATM, Internet and grub.

Sights

Levski's name is all over the country, and the **Museum Vasil Levski** (☎ 93 489; ul Gen Kortzov 57; admission 2lv; ☼ 8.30am-1pm & 2-5.30pm), about 100m west of the centre, is very much *the* place to learn a bit more about Mr V. It includes period-styled rooms in his birthplace home (restored in 1933), a chapel housing a lock of hair he cut when he de-monked to join the revolution in 1864, and a small museum with 13 paintings and some old belongings. A tape tells the tale in English, French, German and Spanish.

Sleeping

Hotel Fani (no ☎; ul Levski 73; r per person 10lv) A couple of basic family hotels are about 150m north of the train station, including this one, which has two rooms (with shared bathroom).

In the centre are possibly the nation's worst-value rooms at the **Hotel Sherev** (☎ 93 380; pl 20 Yuli; s/d incl breakfast 48/60lv). No TV or AC at this price, and at least one room has a chunk of wall panelling missing, but the English-speaking staff are chipper.

Getting There & Away

The bus station's daily service includes one morning bus to Sofia (7lv, two hours), hourly buses from 6am to 8pm to Plovdiv (2.80lv, 1¼ hours), six to Hisarya (1.20lv, 40 minutes), three to Troyan (3.50lv, 1½ hours) and two to Kazanlâk (4.40lv, one hour).

The train station sends five daily trains to Sofia (4lv to 4.80lv, 2½ hours), six to Plovdiv (4lv, 1½ hours), and seven to Kazanlâk (2.80lv, one hour) with the three fast ones continuing on to Burgas (9lv, four hours).

KAZANLÂK КАЗАНЛЪК
☎ 0431 / pop 62,750

Just below Shipka Pass and in the heart of the Valley of Roses, sleepy Kazanlâk comes alive for its annual rose festival in early June. At other times, there's not too much to lure passing travellers' attention.

The central pl Sevtopolis is about 400m north of the train and bus stations (via ul Rozova Dolina), with a money exchange, banks and plenty of eating places.

Sights

A small 4th-century **Thracian tomb** (admission 20lv; 9am-6pm May-Oct), in Tyulbe Park about 300m northeast of the centre, has remarkably well-preserved ceiling paintings (and a nice echo) and is a Unesco World Heritage site. Far cheaper is the carefully re-created **tomb copy** (admission 2lv), which is often open in summer, and sometimes open off-season too.

Nearby is the **Kulata Ethnological Complex** (☎ 21 733; ul Knyaz Mirski; admission incl rose liquor tasting 3lv or 4lv; 8am-noon & 1-6pm). Inside the grounds you'll find a replica of a one-storey peasant's home and wooden sheds with agricultural implements and carts. A courtyard leads to the two-storey House of Hadzhi Eno, built by a wealthy rose merchant in the style typical of the Bulgarian national revival period.

A couple of blocks north of the centre, the **Iskra Museum & Art Gallery** (☎ 63 762; ul Sv Kiril i Metodii; adult/student 2/1lv; 9am-5.30pm Mon-Fri) has plenty of Bulgarian art and Neolithic, Thracian and Roman pieces (with some English signs).

Sleeping

Hadzhi Eminova Kâshta (☎ 62-595; bul Nikola Petkov 22; r 20lv, apt 40 & 50lv) Next to the Kulata complex, this place has four terrific-value traditional rooms.

Hotel Voenen Klub (☎ 64 754; bul Rozova Dolina 8; s/d 41/62lv) Halfway between the stations and the centre, the Hotel Voenen Klub offers plain, clean rooms.

Getting There & Away

Daily bus services include four buses to Plovdiv (3.20lv to5.15lv, 2½ hours), four to Veliko Târnovo (5lv to 6lv, three hours), six to Sofia (7lv, three hours) and two to Burgas (8lv, three hours).

Three trains head to Sofia daily (6.50lv, 3½ hours) and two to Burgas (6.50lv, three hours).

SLIVEN СЛИВЕН
☎ 044 / pop 100,690

Where plains meet 1000m craggy peaks, Sliven – known as Bulgaria's 'windy city' – is often overlooked (its skanky sounding name probably doesn't help), but it can hold its own for a half-day or longer.

Central pl Hadzhi Dimitâr is reached by the same-named street from the train and bus stations, 500m and 750m south respectively. Extending southeast from the centre, the long pedestrian mall ul Tsar Osvoboditel marks the crest of Sliven action.

Several banks sporting ATMs are on ul Hadzhi Dimitâr and ul Tsar Osvoboditel. The hidden **Internet Club** (ul Tsar Osvoboditel; 90min 1lv; 9am-10pm) is downstairs at the Voenen Klub.

Sights

Sliven's top attraction is the **'blue rocks'** (*sinite skali*), facing town from the northeast, which are accessible by the **chairlift** (one way 5lv; ☉ 8.30am-4.30pm Mon-Fri, 12.30-4.30pm Sat). At the top are hiking trails and a hotel (closed for renovation at research time). To get there, take bus No 116 from the market (facing pl Hadzhi Dimitâr) to the end of the line, where it's a 20-minute walk (the lift is visible). Or ask a taxi to take you to the 'lift' (3lv to 4lv).

In town, the **Hadzhi Dimitâr Museum** (☎ 622 496; ul Asenova 2; admission 2lv; ☉ 9am-noon & 2-5pm Mon-Fri), across the river from the market, is dedicated to a local 19th-century revolutionary.

Sleeping & Eating

Hotel Sliven (☎ 27 065; pl Hadzhi Dimitâr; s/d incl breakfast 40/60lv) This is a classic old communist-era high-rise hotel with iffy plumbing, 1980s décor and friendly staff (who keep updated transport schedules handy and do laundry).

Restaurant Maki (ul Tsar Osvoboditel; pizzas & mains 2-4.55lv; ☉ 7am-1am) Maki has a photo menu, lots of smokers, and a needlessly adopted McDonald's 'M' sign out front.

Getting There & Away

The small bus terminal has frequent bus services to Burgas (6lv, two hours) and Kotel (3lv, 1½ hours), as well as Veliko Târnovo, Plovdiv and Sofia. Most trains on the Sofia–Burgas line stop in Sliven.

KOTEL КОТЕЛ

☎ 0453 / pop 7000

Remote Kotel (*Ko*-tel) is a long-time carpet-making centre in the hills about 50km northeast of Sliven. Not yet a big-time draw, it has enough lovely revival-era homes to rival Koprivshtitsa's 19th-century vibe.

Locals artisans' contracts to outfit the Ottoman army in the mid 1800s spared the town from many woes of the era (including taxes), though Kotel was home for 126 'enlighteners' during the hotbed of revolutionary activity from 1877–78.

From the bus station walk up a few blocks to the centre, where you'll find an ATM (and a pink city hall). Extending west, ul Izvorska (home to Monday and Thursday markets) leads to Galata old town past an **information**

centre (☎ 2334; ul Izvorska 14; ☉ 9am-7pm), which has info on hikes to nearby Zherevna, plus Internet access.

Sights

Kotel has several museums. The best is the dramatic **History Museum** (National Revival Kotel Enlighteners; ☎ 2549; admission 3lv; ☉ 8am-noon & 1-5pm), on the central square, showing loads of revolutionary doodads and Georgi Rakovski's mammoth mausoleum. The enthusiastic manager knows English and likes to use it.

About 500m west of the centre is **Izvorite Park**, where you can see the source of the town's 'crazy river'.

Courses

You can learn to play the *gaida* and other traditional Bulgarian music and dance at the **Philip Kotev School** (☎ 2215; smu_k_l@mail .bg; ul Geori Zahariev 2, 8970), which sometimes holds recitals.

Sleeping & Eating

Kotel Hotel (☎ 2885; r 20lv) This rather dreary hotel is towards the park.

Starata Vodenitsa (☎ 2360; r 30lv) Reached from the old town along ul Krum Petrov, this place has seven dark-wood, traditionally styled rooms, each with fireplace and locally made rugs – the rooms are among the best value in the country, and its restaurant is Kotel's best.

Getting There & Away

A regular bus service connects Kotel with Sliven, Shumen and Burgas.

PLEVEN ПЛЕВЕН

☎ 064 / pop 122,150

Poor grey Pleven. This Danubian plains city's historical importance – as the setting of key battles against the Turks in 1877 – seems a little worn out these days, like an old general in an outgrown, war-torn uniform. Some travellers make their way here (just northwest of the Central Balkans) to catch a ride south to Troyan or guzzle the city's tasty eponymous beer.

The bus and train stations are 800m north (via ul Popov) from the active centre (from pl Sveti Nikolai to pl Svoboda), where you can find banks, exchange offices and Internet access. Stretching northwest from the centre is the leafy, café-lined pedestrian mall of ul Vasil Levski.

Pleven plays up its past with a few (rather overpriced) attractions. Probably the best (with a 360-degree painting made in the early 1980s) is the **Military-Historical Museum** (Panorama; ☎ 22 919; Skobelev Park; admission 5lv; ☻ 9am-noon & 1-5pm Tue-Sat), a walkable 1.5km from the centre in a canon-filled hilly park (go south till the pedestrian mall ends and veer right, up steps past a breaking-the-chains heroic statue).

Back in the centre is the surprisingly worthwhile **Svetlin Rusev Art Gallery** (☎ 888 342; ul Doiran 75; admission free; ☻ 10.30am-6.30pm Tue-Sat), housed in a red-and-white former spa. It has four floors of modern art, including Picasso and Goya on the top floor. Pavel Koichev's *The Table* is an unfinished sculpture of misshapen world figures.

Next to the bus and train stations, the woeful and outdated **Hotel Pleven** (☎ 830 181; pl Republika; r US$25) has 150 get-you-through-the-night beds.

Pleven bus station sends 15 daily buses to Sofia (8lv, 2½ hours), four to Ruse (4lv, 2½ hours) and one or two to Troyan (5lv, 1¼ hours). Several trains stop here en route to Sofia (5.90lv, 3½ hours) and Varna (9lv, 5½ hours).

TROYAN & AROUND ТРОЯН

Hilly Troyan's biggest claims to fame are its proximity to the Central Balkans National Park (with hiking paths and downhill skiing at Beklemeto) and the Troyan Monastery, 10km southeast of town. Several spa towns are in the mountains to the west, including Ribaritsa (with villas for rent).

About 1km south of Troyan's bus and train stations is a **tourist information centre** (☎ 0670-35 674; ul Vasil Levski 133; ☻ 10am-6pm Mon-Fri, plus Sat in summer). Banks and Internet are found along ul Vasil Levski.

There are a couple of hotels, including the hilltop **Park Hotel Panorama** (Kâpina Hotel; ☎ 0670-22 930; r 20, 45 & 75lv), 800m south of the bus station (and just up to the right). It was up for renovation at research time and could lose the cheap rooms.

One of Bulgaria's most popular monasteries, the nearby **Troyan Monastery** (admission free; ☻ 6am-10pm) was established in the 1500s and is famed for Zahari Zograf's apocalyptic murals (painted in the 1840s) inside

and outside the Church of the Holy Virgin. The small **museum** (admission 3lv; ☻ 8am-7pm) dedicated to Vasil Levski, who spent time during the rebellion here, is for fanatics only. Simple **rooms** (☎ 06952-2866; r per person €10), with shared bathroom, are available.

Troyan is reached by bus from Sofia, Pleven and Karlovo. The Troyan bus station serves much of the region, including buses to Beklemeto. Eleven daily buses bounce between town and the monastery weekdays, five a day at weekends (0.80lv, 20 minutes).

VELIKO TÂRNOVO ВЕЛИКО ТЪРНОВО
☎ 062 / pop 75,000

In the running for Eastern Europe's Next Big Thing, this medieval capital has of-the-era homes perched above a sharp S-shaped gorge split open by a snaking river, and the best damn ruined citadel in the country. Veliko is not only good to look at and easily accessible (right on the Bucharest–Istanbul tracks), but is near hill towns that make excellent day-trip fodder. Some visiting foreigners stay for good; you'll see real estate agencies posting property ads in English around town.

Veliko was capital of the Second Bulgarian Kingdom (1185–1393).

Orientation

Sloping ul Hristo Botev leads north from the Yug Bus Terminal to pl Maika Bulgaria, where ul Vasil Levski heads west, and the main crawl ul Nezavisimost heads east for a kilometre. This street looms way over the gorge, with (slightly confusing) side streets and stairways weaving down to the water.

Note that signs pointing to attractions in town are often turned to point in the wrong direction.

Information

The main streets winding through town have many foreign-exchange offices.

Bezanata (ul Hristo Botev; per hr 0.50-0.90lv; ☻ 24hr) Nearly 80 computers in a massive submarine-style café.

Internet Club (ul Nezavisimost 3; per hr 1lv; ☻ 24hr) Has 90 computers.

Ladybird (ul Hadzhi Dimitâr 25; per load 3.5lv; ☻ 10am-6pm Mon-Sat, 10am-5pm Sun) An actual Bulgarian drop-off laundry service.

United Bulgarian Bank (ul Hristo Botev; ☻ 8.30am-4.30pm Mon-Fri) Charges just 0.20lv to cash travellers cheques. Its ATM is inside.

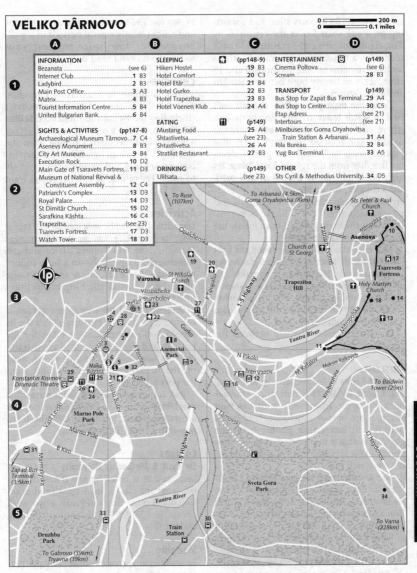

VELIKO TÂRNOVO

0 — 200 m
0 — 0.1 miles

INFORMATION
Bezanata..................................(see 6)
Internet Club...............................1 B3
Ladybird....................................2 B3
Main Post Office.........................3 A3
Matrix.......................................4 B3
Tourist Information Centre...........5 B4
United Bulgarian Bank.................6 B4

SIGHTS & ACTIVITIES   (pp147-8)
Archaeological Museum Târnovo...7 C4
Asenevs Monument......................8 B3
City Art Museum...........................9 B4
Execution Rock.........................10 D2
Main Gate of Tsaravets Fortress...11 D3
Museum of National Revival &
  Constituent Assembly.............12 C4
Patriarch's Complex...................13 D3
Royal Palace.............................14 D3
St Dimitâr Church......................15 D2
Sarafkina Kâshta.......................16 C4
Trapezitsa.............................(see 23)
Tsarevets Fortress.....................17 D3
Watch Tower............................18 D3

SLEEPING   (pp148-9)
Hikers Hostel.............................19 B3
Hotel Comfort...........................20 C3
Hotel Etâr................................21 B4
Hotel Gurko..............................22 B3
Hotel Trapezitsa........................23 B3
Hotel Voenen Klub.....................24 A4

EATING   (p149)
Mustang Food...........................25 A4
Shtastivetsa.........................(see 23)
Shtastlivetsa............................26 A4
Stratilat Restaurant...................27 B3

DRINKING   (p149)
Ulitsata...............................(see 23)

ENTERTAINMENT   (p149)
Cinema Poltova.......................(see 6)
Scream....................................28 B3

TRANSPORT   (p149)
Bus Stop for Zapat Bus Terminal...29 A4
Bus Stop to Centre....................30 C5
Etap Adress.........................(see 21)
Intertours...........................(see 21)
Minibuses for Gorna Oryahovitsa
  Train Station & Arbanasi..........31 A4
Rila Bureau..............................32 B4
Yug Bus Terminal......................33 A5

OTHER
Sts Cyril & Methodius University...34 D5

BULGARIA

Main post office (ul Nezavisimost) There is also a telephone centre here.

Matrix (ul Nezavisimost; international calls per min 0.25lv; ☽ 24hr) Telephone services cheaper than the post office.

Tourist Information Centre (☎ 22 148; tic_vt@ mobikom.com; ul Hristo Botev; ☽ 9am-6pm Mon-Sat Apr-Sep, closed Sat Oct-Mar) Remarkably helpful centre

with English-speaking staff who can arrange private accommodation, book rental cars for 25lv daily, sell regional maps (4lv) and offer tips on seeing the region.

Sights
TSAREVETS FORTRESS
About a kilometre from the centre, this mammoth **fortress** (admission 5lv; ☽ 8am-7pm

Apr-Sep, 9am-5pm Oct-Mar) sits stoic and sprawling on a site shared over the centuries by Thracians, Romans and Byzantines. What's seen now, a triangular high-walled fortress with the remains of over 400 houses and 18 churches, was largely built between the 5th and 12th centuries.

From the **main gate**, follow the left wall past a **watch tower** to the northern end where you can see **execution rock** where the naughty (or accused naughty) were once pushed from. Back south, the giant Bulgarian flag flies from the ruined **Royal Palace**. Its high-up neighbour is the renovated **patriarch's complex**. Inside are surprisingly modern, nearly colourless, historic murals and a suspended altar (1985; Teofan Sokervo). Back near the main gate, you can follow the south wall to **Baldwin Tower**.

The after-dark 40-minute **sound and light show** (☎ 636 828; admission 12lv) takes place over the scene when 30 tourists have paid. Ask at the gate or at bigger hotels, if a show's on. Or, as one local said, 'when the tourists come and pay for the show, the whole town watches from outside for free.'

Bus No 20 makes the trip between the centre and the site.

MUSEUMS

Sarafkina Kâshta (ul Gurko 88; admission 4lv; ☒ 9am-noon & 1-6pm Mon-Fri) is a two-storey former banker's home from 1861 with a set-up sitting room upstairs, including traditional objects and interesting photos from the glory days that a matter-of-fact guide may point out ('it is rich women, it is 1910 scene, it is very rich man...').

The **Archaeological Museum Târnovo** (☎ 601 528; ul Ivan Vazov; admission 4lv; ☒ 8am-noon & 1-6pm Tue-Sun Apr-Oct, 9am-5pm Tue-Sun Nov-Mar) features Roman ruins laying amok outside its marbled stone walls. In 2003 it added the tomb of King Kaloyan inside, which was recently found at Veliko's Holy Martyrs Church.

The **City Art Museum** (☎ 638 941; admission 3lv; ☒ 10am-6pm Tue-Sun, free Thu), facing town from behind the huge Asenevs Monument, hangs typical Veliko scenes downstairs, and less predictable, mostly communist-era paintings upstairs. Dimitâr Hinkov's 1988 rendering of a traditional donkey-cart scene is curiously called *Far-Off Romance*.

The **Museum of National Revival & Constituent Assembly** (ul Ivan Vazov; adult/student 4/2lv; ☒ 9am-6pm Wed-Mon) is packed with photos and relics (mostly revival period) in a well-arranged two-storey space, but most is lost to those who can't read Bulgarian.

CHURCHES

Veliko is home to numerous churches, particularly in the old Asenova quarter (including the Byzantine-influenced **St Dimitâr Church**, Veliko's oldest), reached across a wood-plank pedestrian bridge from the fortress. Many churches, however, keep inconsistent hours and some charge about 4lv to enter. Try calling ☎ 638 841 if you want to get into one.

Activities

Trapezitsa (☎ 635 823; www.trapezitca1902.com; ul Stefan Stambolov 79; ☒ 9am-6pm Mon-Fri) arranges rock-climbing trips, offers advice and can sometimes set up climbs on a huge indoor wall at the Palace of Culture and Sport, site of an international climbing competition in 2003.

Gorgona (☎ 601 400; www.gorgona-shop.com, in Bulgarian; ul Zelenka 2; ☒ 10am-1pm & 2-7pm Mon-Fri, 10am-2pm Sat) rents mountain bikes for 8lv per day and can point you to good trails. Helmets available. To find Gorgona, head up the steps cross ul Nezavisimost from the post office.

Ask at the tourist centre about **horse riding** and **hiking** in the area. Down along the river are **waterside trails**; head south 30 minutes to pop into a small Turkish village.

Courses

Sts Cyril & Methodius University (☎ 639 869; issblc@uni-vt.bg; ul Teodosi Tarnovski 2) has Bulgarian language classes in August (and occasionally at other times of year); a two-week course is €380/190 with/without lodging and meals.

Sleeping

Touts offering private rooms (15lv per person) usually await buses and trains at the stations. There's no (legal) camping around town. Someone, please open a hostel!

Hotel Trapezitsa (☎ 622-061; ul Stefan Stambolov 79; s/d 31/46lv) This central and cheap hotel has 30 rooms that attract youthful guests. No TV. The price (with a 3lv discount for students), not to mention gorge views from the backside rooms, makes it Veliko's best deal.

Hotel Etâr (☎ 621 890; ul Ivailo 2; s/d 30/60lv, with shared bathroom 24/48lv) This old commie-era tower hotel has clean but stuffy rooms (about 80 in all); higher-up ones have fortress views.

Hotel Voenen Klub (☎ 601 521; ul Marno Pole; r 40-60lv) This new hotel, made from an old red-and-white military club, has 15 uninspired but comfy rooms.

Hotel Comfort (☎ 628 728; ul P Tipografov 5; r incl breakfast €25-40; 🐾) Past the crafts-lined square, many of the Comfort's dozen rooms have full-frontal views of the fortress and the light show – a few with balconies. The enthusiastic owners help out with area tours and pay for the taxi fare if you're coming from Veliko station. Some private bathrooms are across the hall.

Hotel Gurko (☎ 627 838; ul Gurko 33; s/d incl breakfast 70/90lv) For that revival feel, this traditional *mehana*, just down from the centre, has red-vested staff and features comfy wood-floor rooms with balconies facing the river.

Hikers Hostel (☎ 0889 691 661; www.hikers-hostel .org; ul Rezervoarska 91; dm/d incl breakfast €10/20) This clean and exceptionally friendly new hostel is a 5-minute uphill walk from the old town. It's a tiny place (two dorms and a double room) so book ahead in summer. They'll pick you up free, wherever you arrive, if you call ahead (including from the Gorna Oryahovitsa train station if they're in a good mood).

Eating & Drinking

Kebabs and pizza slices are easily found on ul Nezavisimost.

Mustang Food (ul Maika Bulgaria; mains 1.75-4.50lv; 🕙 24hr) For a lapse into the West, this Americanised diner serves a full breakfast of eggs, bacon, hash browns and toast (2.75lv) all day.

Stratilat Restaurant (ul Rakovski 11; sandwiches & pizzas from 2lv; 🕙 24hr) A popular café – the focus is drink and super desserts – has outdoor seating that fills quickly.

Shtastlivetsa (mains 3.30-7.50lv; 🕙 10am-11pm; ul Marno Pole ☎ 603 054; ul Marno Pole 7; ul Stefan Stambulov ☎ 600 656; ul Stefan Stambulov 79) A traditional Bulgarian eatery that feels less contrived than some. Its two floors often fill early. The highlights on the big menu include Yugoslavian meat fingers, breaded squid and several egg dishes.

Ulitsata (ul Stambolov 79; draft beer 0.70lv; 🕙 7am-3am) is the local *biraria* of choice, with a few choice balcony seats facing the gorge, and local brew on tap.

Entertainment

Scream (ul Nezavisimost; admission 1-2lv; 🕙 9pm-late) This disco appeals to the rather scantily clad student base.

Cinema Poltava (☎ 620 542; tickets 2-4lv; ul Nezavisimost 3) Plays foreign movies with Bulgarian subtitles.

Getting There & Away

BUS

Private buses leave from the **Yug Bus Terminal** (ul Hristo Botev), a 15-minute walk downhill from the centre. Hourly (if not more frequent) buses en route to Sofia (10lv, three hours) and Varna (10lv, three hours) stop here. There are also roughly six daily buses to Ruse (5lv, two hours), two to Plovdiv (10lv, four hours), and service to Gabrovo (40 minutes). One bus company, Etap Adress (domestic) and Intertours (international) has offices at the Hotel Etâr.

The quiet public **Zapad Bus Terminal**, 4km west of the centre, sends buses to Troyan (4lv, two hours) and hourly buses to Gabrovo (3lv, 40 minutes). Bus No 10, among others, heads west to the terminal from ul Vasil Levski.

CAR

The tourist information centre (p146) can arrange rental cars for just 25lv.

TRAIN

Veliko's small train station sends about six daily trains to Ruse (4.30lv, 2½ to 3½ hours) and Tryavna (1.20lv, 1½ hours). A much busier station is just 8.5km north at Gorna Oryahovitsa, a stop on the Sofia–Varna line. Minibuses along ul Vasil Levski, or bus No 10 east from the centre, head there frequently.

There's a walkway from the train platform (away from station) that connects to an underpass leading to ul Hristo Botev, near the bus station. Catch bus No 4, 5, 13, 30 or 70 heading south from outside the station to reach the centre.

Buy international tickets at the **Rila Bureau** (☎ 622 1330; ul Tsar Kolyan; 🕙 8am-noon, 1-4.30pm Mon-Fri).

BULGARIA

AROUND VELIKO TÂRNOVO

Much of the following can be seen in a day if you have (motorised) wheels. Tryavna's tourist centre can rent camping gear if you're keen to stay in the sticks.

Arbanasi Арбанаси

☎ 062 / pop 1500

Five kilometres from Veliko Târnovo, high-on-a-hill Arbanasi is less a town than a fine collection of spread-out old walled churches and villas, some of which serve as classy *mehanas* or hotels. Many a blissful beer-soaked afternoon has been spent watching Veliko turn gold, pink or purple in the setting sun from up here.

One of the country's most interesting churches, the 16th-century **Nativity Church** (☎ 604 323; admission 4lv, guide 8lv; ☯ 9am-6pm Apr-Oct, 9am-5pm Nov-Mar), 200m west of the bus stop, is a shock to enter. It was built ho-hum and low to trick the Ottomans from thinking it a place for (Orthodox) worship. Inside, it bursts with ceiling-to-floor colourful murals depicting 2000 scenes, including the evocative 'wheel of life' and a man-headed serpent in the Garden of Eden.

About 200m west of the town bus stop, the creaking-floored, 17th-century **Konstantsalieva Kâshta** (admission 4lv; ☯ 9am-6pm Apr-Oct, 9am-5pm Nov-Mar) has several interesting rooms decked out old-style for you to browse through.

Panorama (☎ 623 421; d 30 & 40lv; P ⓧ) is a simple hillside hotel – about 400m west of the bus stop (towards end of road) – and has three rooms and a pool, all at a super-value price. Its English-speaking staff also run a basic eatery. Other outdoor cafés are nearby.

Just west of the bus stop, **Boyarska Kâshta & Restaurant** (☎ 620 484; d incl breakfast €40) – with wide-open garden seating – has comfortable, if overpriced, rooms.

It's about 3 or 4lv to reach Arbanasi by taxi from Veliko. Some Gorna Oryahovitsa–bound minibuses from ul Vasil Levski in Veliko stop in Arbanasi (all come within a 700m walk of the centre). A bus makes the trip less frequently.

Dryanovo Monastery Дряновски Манастир

Top-heavy cliffs stoop over this charming stream-side **monastery** (admission free; ☯ 7am-10pm), 24km south of Veliko. Following its get-go in the 12th century, the monastery's been destroyed a time or two, and was last rebuilt in the early 18th century. Some monks here are quite chatty.

From the bridge nearby, a 300m path leads past a waterfall to the 1200m-long **Bacho Kiro cave** (admission about 3lv; ☯ 8.30am-6pm Apr-Oct, 10am-4pm Nov-Mar), with two tours for groups available. A hiking path starts here too.

It's possible to stay in the simple **monastery rooms** (per person 10lv) with shared bathroom or – better yet – in the neighbouring **Komplex Vodopadi** (☎ 0676-2314; d €13), where some rooms sport huge balconies. About 500m towards the highway are basic bungalows for 6lv per person.

Gabrovo-bound buses will stop at the turn-off (if requested), about 5km south of the town Dryanovo, where it's a 1.5km walk to the monastery. Those with cars pay 1lv to park.

Etâr Етър

Played up by travel agents and organised tours, the **Etâr Ethnographic Village Museum** (☎ 066-801 838; adult/student 6/4lv; ☯ 9am-6pm May-Oct, 9am-4.30pm Nov-Apr) is an open-air museum with set-up shops and workshops recreating Bulgaria's revival period of the 19th century. A nice 3km-walk uphill is the pleasant **Sokolski Monastery**.

Hotel Perla (☎ 066-801 984; d/apt 38/44lv) – just before the Etâr gate – has six huge, very inviting rooms and is run by a super friendly father-son team who would likely accept your invitation to slurp beers at the tavern on the facing hill.

To get here by public transport, take a bus to the large town of Gabrovo, 8km north, and take blue-and-white city bus No 8 to the gate, or No 1 or 7 to near Hotel Perla; buses run every half hour. A taxi to Gabrovo is about 5lv.

Tryavna Трявна

☎ 0677 / pop 12,200

As Bulgaria's woodcarving capital – with an old town centre and revival-era storefronts – Tryavna is an Arbanasi without the tourists, an Etâr without the ticket price.

ORIENTATION & INFORMATION

Tryavna is 39km south of Veliko, 13km east of Gabrovo. Its bus and train stations are opposite each other on the north side of town. Follow ul Angel Kânchev (just east of the stations), or the road along the tracks, 400m south (over the creek) to the cobbled centre.

The **tourist office** (☎ 2247; www.tryavna.bg; ul Angel Kânchev 22; ♥ 9am-noon & 2-5pm Mon-Fri) is next to the post office. The English-speaking staff can suggest local hikes or bike rides, and – wow – rent camping equipment for Stara Planina overnighters. There's an ATM next door.

SIGHTS

Tryavna has about a dozen museums and churches. All museums are allegedly open 9am to 6pm daily April to October, 8am to 5pm other times; entrance is 2/1lv for adults/students.

West of the tourist centre is **Shkolo** (☎ 2517), a school-turned-art museum with 500 regional artists' works.

Over the arched bridge to ul Slaveikov, you will pass several workshops. Around 150m further is the **Daskalov House** (1808; ul Slaveikov 27), Bulgaria's lone woodcarving museum, with historic locally made items (particularly impressive are the mounted wood portraits and figures).

SLEEPING & EATING

The tourist office arranges private rooms for 8-15lv per person.

Zograf (☎ 4970; ul Slaveikov 1; s/d €24/40) Has new rooms next to the old bridge, with a huge courtyard *mehana*.

Kompleks Brâshlyan (☎ 3019; bungalows 36lv, d 40-60lv) The best sleeping is up here, overlooking town from a shady spot north of the centre; its bigger rooms have huge leather sofas (Bulgarian cowboy style!) and balconies. There's a restaurant and outdoor deck for afternoon cocktails. Cross the tracks past the old bridge, and head up and to the right.

Starata Loza (ul Slaveikov 44; mains 2.80-7.50lv; ♥ 8am-midnight) Across from the Daskalov House, Starata Loza serves of tasty Bulgarian fare.

GETTING THERE & AWAY

Tryavna has half-hourly bus connections with Gabrovo, but nowhere else. Nine daily trains go to/from Veliko Târnovo (2.50lv, 50 minutes).

Shipka Pass Шипченски проход

The scene of an important Russian-Turkish battle in 1877, Shipka Pass (about 60km south of Veliko) is accented by the bare-top 1326m Mt Stoletov and the six-storey **Freedom Monument** (admission 2lv; ♥ 9am-5pm) with displays on the battles and, up top, 360-degree views of the Stara Planina and Valley of the Roses below (hey kids, it's Kazanlâk!).

It's a Shipka tradition to finish off with **buffalo yoghurt** (cup 1.3lv) at the stands below.

Hourly buses between Kazanlâk and Gabrovo will drop you off at the pass, where you can hail the next. Shipka town is 13km south.

SHUMEN ШУМЕН

☎ 054 / pop 89,050

Set along a long sweeping mountain, halfway between Varna and Ruse, Shumen lacks the quaint cobbled-lane punch of some historical towns, but its neighbours (forts, monuments, ancient capitals), notably friendly folks (some cab drivers round *down* fares) and Shumensko beer make it an interesting place to linger a day or two. Its historic core is tied with Bulgaria's beginnings in the sweet 7th century.

Orientation & Information

The main square, pl Osvobozhdenie, is about 1km west (and slightly uphill) from the neighbouring bus and train stations. About halfway is a **Bulbank** (♥ 8.45am-4.30pm Mon-Fri) with an ATM. In the centre is the **International Call Centre** (♥ 7am-11pm) with Internet access and calls abroad for 0.40lv per minute.

Sights

From afar just an enigmatic slab of grey overlooking town, up close the super **Creators of the Bulgarian State Monument** (admission free; ♥ 24hr) welcomes those who climb 1300m up the obvious steps from the centre with incredible cubist-style horseback figures peering down from between crevices like stone Don Quixotes. The monument was built in 1981 to commemorate Bulgaria's 1300th birthday. It's possible to taxi to the top.

On a hilltop 6km west of the centre, the **Shumen Fortress** (adult/student 3/1.5lv; ♥ 8am-5pm loosely) is a spread-out site dating from the early Iron Age. Thracians, Romans and

Byzantines have left their mark as well. A taxi is about 2.50lv from the centre. It's possible to walk between the fort and the monument, but paths are not always clear.

Everything in the impressive 18th-century (and still active) **Tombul Mosque** (ul Doiran; admission 2lv; ☉ 9am-5pm), 500m southwest of pl Osvobozhdenie, is original – much of the paint atmospherically lost to the ages.

Sleeping & Eating

Orbita Hotel (☎ 52 398; Pripoden Park; s/d 40/50lv) On the way to the fortress (just past the brewery) and next to a small zoo, this hotel has clean rooms in a hunting-lodge type building (*The Shining* minus the 'redrum') set in a thicket of woods.

Hotel Madara (☎ 57 451; pl Osvobozhdenie; s/d 66/92lv) Tall-boy Hotel Madara is overpriced, has a floor devoted to local businesses, but is clean and near the 'action'.

A few old-school *mehanas* are on ul Tsar Osvoboditel, about 200m west of Hotel Madara.

Pekin Chinese Restaurant (mains 3.50-6lv; ☉ 11.30am-midnight) Half a block north of bul Slavyanski – take the street with the stop light – this Chinese restaurant serves heaping portions of noodle and rice dishes.

Getting There & Away

Numerous buses en route to Sofia (15lv, six hours) and Varna (5lv, 1½ hours) stop at Shumen's bus station. Daily services also include a handful to Ruse (5lv, 2½ hours) and Veliko Târnovo (7lv, two hours), five to Madara (1lv, 20 minutes) and three to Veliki Preslav (1lv to 1.3lv, 30 to 60 minutes).

Nine daily direct trains leave for Varna (3.90lv, two hours), five for Sofia (10.70lv, seven hours), one to Ruse (5.30lv, three hours) and one to Plovdiv (9.50lv, six hours). A couple of trains stop at Madara.

Call ☎ 800 184 to get a taxi.

Note that group taxis *returning* to Shumen from Madara or Veliki Preslav can often be taken from outside the bus stops for 1lv or 2lv.

Around Shumen

MADARA МАДАРА

Know that cute horseman on the *stotinki* coins you carry? The original bas-relief, carved in a viva-Bulgaria fever onto the side of a 100m cliff in the 8th century, is at the superb **Madara National Historical & Archaeological Reserve** (☎ 05313-55 487; admission 3lv; ☉ 8am-6.30pm summer, 8am-5pm winter), a 2km uphill walk from the Madara town bus stop (the sign reads 'Madara Konnik'). The trip is made more worth it for the lovely area, home to an intriguing rock chapel, an open-air cave wall, and a mountain-top fort with views of Shumen.

About 100m before the entrance are some cosy cabins and a sign pointing to a camping/bungalow area. The cosy cabins are at **Motel Magarski** (☎ 0531-32063; motel _madarskikonnik@abv.bg; bungalows €15-30), near the rider in relief, and come with bathrooms, plus views of Shumen from the outside sitting area. For cheaper sleeping, follow nearby signs about 300m to **'Camping'** (☎ 098 724888 mobile phone; camp sites per person 3lv, bungalows 5lv). This camping ground is a bit unkempt, but in a nice setting; the bungalows here are pretty shoddy.

VELIKI PRESLAV ВЕЛИКИ ПРЕСЛАВ

The background to Bulgaria's important second capital – active from 893 to 972 – is laid out 18km southwest of Shumen. Preslav's glory days are explained at the well-organised **National History-Archaeological Museum** (☎ 0538-2630; www.museum-preslav.com; adult/student 3/1.5lv; ☉ 8am-6pm summer, 9am-5pm winter), with exhibits including the pieced-together icon of St Theodore (a famed symbol seen nationwide). The museum is about 2km from the centre – a couple of signs point the way, but you may have to ask.

Just east, and below, are the capital **ruins**, free to explore.

RUSE РУСЕ

☎ 082 / pop 162,130

Booming during the week and often dead quiet at weekends, Ruse (aka Rousse) is busy for its train links with Romania across the Danube River. Frankly, it doesn't always make the greatest first (or last) impression of Bulgaria for travellers. Most of the town's focus has turned inward, away from its Danube location, and several museums sit still behind closed doors. But its central square is lively and the nearby Rusenski Lom Nature Park provides terrific rural adventures.

Ruse's March Days Music Festival is held in the last two weeks of March.

Orientation

From the bus and train station, ul Borisova leads 2km north to the central pl Svoboda, from where the busy pedestrian mall ul Aleksandrovska extends northwest. The Danube is a few blocks farther north from pl Svoboda.

Information

Bulbank (pl Sveta Troitsa; ☷ 8.30am-4.30pm) Just southwest of pl Svoboda; 24-hour ATM.

Central post office (pl Svoboda)

Cyberia (ul Ravonska; per hr 1lv; ☷ 9am-10pm) Internet access in a building courtyard a block north of pl Svoboda.

Elit Travel (☎ 825 070; ul Olimni Panov 199; ☷ 9am-12.30pm & 1-6pm Mon-Fri) Stocks brochures.

Rusenski Lom Nature Park Office (☎ 272 397; ul Gen Skobelev 7; ☷ 9am-5pm Mon-Fri) Helpful staff can point out camp sites, where to hike along the river, and arrange visits of the Ivanovo Rock Monastery in the nearby park. Look for the official sign and walk in (enter from ul Tinka Dzhein).

Telenet (ul Ravonska; international calls per min 0.26-0.69lv; ☷ 8am-11pm) A block north of pl Svoboda.

Sights

Ruse has several museums in town, which in recent years have closed their doors; ask at Elit Travel for the latest (though they haven't always known in the past) or at the administration office of the **History Museum** (☎ 825-008; museum@ru-se.com; pl Knyaz Al Battenberg; ☷ 9am-noon & 2-5pm), west of the centre. Confusingly, this place isn't really a museum, just a source of information.

Rousse Art Gallery (☎ 221-494; ul Borisova 39; admission 0.50lv; ☷ 9am-1pm & 2-6pm Tue-Sun) is a scruffy modern space with edgier exhibits than in most Bulgarian art museums, and – hey – it's open at weekends.

Shut down at research time, the **Museum of the Urban Lifestyle in Ruse** (ul Tsar Ferdinand 39; admission 3lv; ☷ 9am-noon & 2-5pm Mon-Fri) is likely to reopen its doors. It's housed in a mustard-and-brown traditional home, facing the river and the towering Riga Hotel. Exhibits include hundred-year-old furnishings, crockery and costumes.

At Revivalists Park, east of pl Svoboda on ul Petkov, have a peek inside the gold-domed **Pantheon of the National Revival** (admission free; ☷ 9am-noon & 1-5pm Mon-Fri), honouring 19th-century soldiers.

It's worth having a poke around the neighbourhood streets west of pl Svoboda (near the Danube), which are home to some fine old houses.

Sleeping

Dunav Tours (☎ 825 048; dtbktu@dunavtours.bg; ul Olimpi Panov; s 28lv, d 40-44lv; ☷ 9am-5.30pm Mon-Fri) This office, two blocks southwest of pl Svoboda, can book private rooms.

Hotel Ruse (☎ 823 255; ul Borisova 69; s/d 41/52lv) This well-signed new hotel has 10 slightly garish rooms with TV; most have sparkling-clean private bathroom. It's midway between the train station and the centre, a 10-minute walk.

Anna Palace (☎ 825 005; www.annapalace.com; ul Kniajeska 4; s/d incl breakfast 90/120lv; ☷ ☷) This new splurge hotel occupies a grand gold-and-white 19th-century palace near the river in an appealing residential area, several blocks west of the centre. Rooms are finely decorated, though some people may think they're a bit on the small side.

Eating & Drinking

Gradski Hali (ul 93 Aleksandrovska; ☷ 8am-10pm) Around pl Svoboda and the pedestrian mall ul Aleksandrovska you can find cheap kebabs and snacks, and this supermarket.

Terassa (☎ 824 460; ul Pridunavski 6A; mains 3.50-6lv; ☷ 10am-2am) OK, it's an Irish pub, but a riverside one with Bulgarian food and wide-open windows with views of the Danube (and Romania!). And Murphy's on tap of course.

Getting There & Away

Ruse's **Yug Bus Terminal** (ul Pristanishtna) has frequent daily buses heading to Sofia (10lv, five hours), Veliko Târnovo (5lv, two hours) and Burgas (11lv, 4½ hours). No buses link Ruse with Bucharest. A few daily buses to towns in Rusenski Lom Nature Park leave from Iztok Bus Terminal, 4.5km east of the centre. City bus Nos 2 and 13 go there from ul Skobelev, near the roundabout four blocks east of ul Borisova.

The train station, next to Yug, has four daily trains to Sofia (14.70lv, seven hours), four to Veliko Târnovo (6lv, 2½ to 3½ hours), two to Varna (9.75lv, four hours), and three to Bucharest (15lv, three hours), which spends half its duration stopped for border checks. In the station, **Rila Bureau** (☎ 228 016; ☷ 9-noon & 1-5.30pm Mon-Fri) sells international train tickets.

RUSENSKI LOM NATURE PARK
ПРИРОДЕН ПАРК РУСЕНСКИ ЛОМ

Starting just southwest of Ruse, this 32.6-sq km park is home to winding rivers, other-era villages wedged between cliffs, hiking paths, rock-climbing sites, and cave and rock monasteries. In summer nearly 200 bird species flock here.

The western part of the park – with the town of Ivanovo and the more appealing Koshov and Cherven – is the best way to access the park. Another, Nisovo, is further east. Before setting out, drop by the nature park office in Ruse (see p153) for advice.

The **Ivanovo Rock Monastery** (admission 3lv; ☽ 9am-noon & 1-6pm Wed-Sun) is 4km east of the town: a centuries-old sanctuary cut into cliffs with remarkably well-preserved colourful murals from the 14th century.

In Cherven, spread-out remains of the 6th-century **citadel** (admission 3lv when attendant is present, free otherwise) sit atop a cliff at a sharp bend in the river.

Rooms in traditional homes are available in Cherven and Koshov for about 35lv including meals; ask around in the towns.

Buses from Ruse's Iztok Bus Terminal go a few times a day to Cherven, via Ivanovo and Koshov. Nisovo is reached on the Opaka-bound bus. It's feasible to enter at one town and hike to the next – ask at the Ruse park office (p153).

BLACK SEA COAST

For the majority of travellers to Bulgaria, the blue-green water and golden beaches along the Black Sea coast *are* Bulgaria. Gateway towns Varna and Burgas, and resortburgs Sunny Beach, Golden Sands and Albena sizzle with bodies in summer. Also popular are Sozopol and Nesebâr: inviting seaside towns with long histories. The southern half of the coast is revered, even by folk up north, as home to the best beaches.

Most hotels raise their rates in June, again in July and August, then back a bit in September. At many other times of year, as one local said, 'it's just you and the dogs'.

Before taking a splash, take a moment to reflect on this body of water: landlocked and a long-time treasure for a grab bag of the non-Western world (Muslims, Roma, communists).

BURGAS БУРГАС
☎ 056 / pop 193,320

Many a first glimpse of Bulgaria or the Black Sea comes courtesy of this port town and transport hub. Its beach is so-so, but open-air plastic-seat cafés on two big-time pedestrian malls lined with a mishmash of architectural styles give it a relaxed air, making Burgas (bur-*gas*) a reasonable back-up to Sozopol or elsewhere as a beach-hopping base.

Orientation

One of the nation's longest pedestrian malls, ul Aleksandrovska runs north from the train station and Yug Bus Terminal. At pl Svoboda (300m north) it meets another pedestrian mall, ul Bogoridi – the busier of the two – which extends east to the Maritime Park and the water.

Information

Bulbank (ul Aleksandrovska; ☽ 8.30am-4pm Mon-Fri)
Helikon Bookshop (☎ 800 231; pl Troikata 4; ☽ 9am-8pm Mon-Sat, 10am-8pm Sun) Great selection of maps.
Seanet (ul Morska 40; per hr 1-1.60lv; ☽ 24hr) Internet – and it's OK to bring beer in from the corner stand.

Sights

Burgas' **beach** has a 2km-long strip and its long concrete pier does see a lot of strolling (not to mention to-and-fro barges offshore). Running alongside is the pleasant, if decaying, Maritime Park.

The museums in town aren't knockouts, but probably the best is the **Ethnographical Museum** (☎ 842 587; ul Slavyanska 69; adult/student

---

TOP FIVE BEACHES

- **Sinemorets** – where Bulgarians go when they don't want to be at a resort
- **Sunny Beach** – the Black Sea Coast's top resort has cause for its fame
- **Sozopol** – best overall base, with historical town and two beaches
- **Primorsko** – resort town with wide calm beach
- **Varna** – beats Burgas for best urban spot for a splash

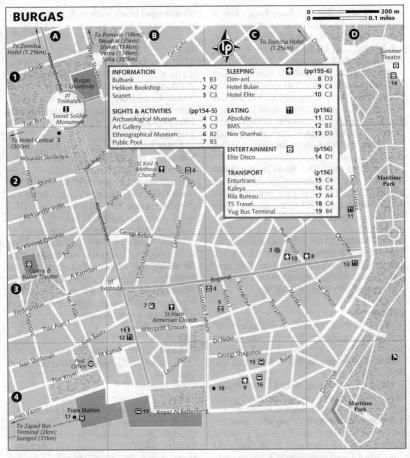

BURGAS

0 .... 200 m
0 .... 0.1 miles

INFORMATION	
Bulbank.....................................**1** B3	
Helikon Bookshop......................**2** A2	
Seanet......................................**3** C3	

SIGHTS & ACTIVITIES	(pp154–5)
Archaeological Museum............**4** C3	
Art Gallery................................**5** C3	
Ethnographical Museum.............**6** B2	
Public Pool...............................**7** B3	

SLEEPING	(pp155–6)
Dim-ant.....................................**8** D3	
Hotel Bulair...............................**9** C4	
Hotel Elite.................................**10** C3	

EATING	(p156)
Absolute....................................**11** D2	
BMS..**12** B3	
Nov Shanhai.............................**13** D3	

ENTERTAINMENT	(p156)
Elite Disco................................**14** D1	

TRANSPORT	(p156)
Enturtrans..................................**15** C4	
Kaleya......................................**16** C4	
Rila Bureau...............................**17** A4	
TS Travel...................................**18** C4	
Yug Bus Terminal.......................**19** B4	

2/1lv; 8am-noon & 1-5pm Mon-Fri), with two floors of hundred-year-old traditional clothing. On some summer Saturdays it opens its doors. A combo ticket (4lv) lets you take in three museums.

On the main mall, the pink **Archaeological Museum** (843 541; ul Bogoridi 21; admission 2lv; 9am-noon & 1-5pm Mon-Sat Jun-Sep, 9am-noon & 1-5pm Mon-Fri Oct-May) has old Thracian and Roman pieces.

Housed in a former synagogue south of ul Bogoridi, the **Art Gallery** (842 169; ul Mitropolit Simeon 24; admission 2lv; 9am-noon & 2-6pm Mon-Fri) has three floors of icons and Bulgarian art.

The towering Hotel Bulgaria at pl Svoboda – the rooms are not recommended –

now houses a basement **public pool** (admission 5lv; 9am-10pm).

Sleeping

Several accommodation agencies around offer deals in private rooms for fewer leva than you'll find in hotels. **Dim-ant** (840 779; dimant91@abv.bg; ul Tsar Simeon 15; 8.30am-8pm summer, closed Sun winter) arranges rooms in Burgas and along the coast. Rooms are about 10lv per person, an apartment for four is 40 to 50lv. **TS Travel** (see p156) also books rooms (about €10).

Zornitsa Hotel (816 266; bloque 45, Zornitsa; tr 30lv) Sleep with socialism in this out-of-the-way 1960s high-rise dorm, in the Zornitsa neighbourhood 2km north of the train station. Each room has three beds (10lv a pop), with a shared bathroom for every two rooms. Get there by bus 12A from the centre. It's just east of the giant grey hospital, past the football stadium.

Hotel Central (☎ 815 488; ul Ivailo 60; s/d/apt 44/50/60lv) Dated, remote but clean, the Central has the cheapest rooms within a short walk to the centre. Apartments have AC. From the Soviet monument (750m north of the train station on ul Aleksandrovska), head west for 400m, turning right midway through a park.

Hotel Elite (☎ 845 779; ul Morska 35; s/d incl breakfast 50/56lv; 🗷) In a pleasant location off ul Bogodini, the Elite has nice new rooms – some with balcony, all with phone. All in all, Burgas' best. But avoid the cramped attic room.

Hotel Bulair (☎ 844 389; www.bulair.bulhosting .com; ul Bulair 7; r incl breakfast 70lv; 🗷) A few steps from the bus and train stations, this new hotel has 14 modern, quite comfy rooms in a done-up historic-style building.

Eating

Walk up busy ul Bogoridi to find the snack that suits you. Along the water are several beach cafés, open in summer.

Absolut (ul Demokratsiya 22; 🕑 24hr) Small but well-stocked grocery.

BMS (ul Aleksandrovska; mains 3-3.50lv; 🕑 8am-10pm) Fluorescently lit, peppy pick-and-point cafeteria with good Bulgarian victuals.

Nov Shanhai (☎ 843 105; ul Bogoridi 61; mains 2.5-6lv; 🕑 noon-midnight) One of several popular choices at the eastern end of ul Bogoridi, this Chinese restaurant serves heaping platters including many veggie options.

Entertainment

Bogoridi and Aleksandrovska's cafés are de-facto bars, with outside drinking buzzing most hours. Burgas' hottest dance spot is the L-shaped and slightly worn **Elite Disco** (Maritime Park; cover 2lv; 🕑 10.30pm-3am), near the beach.

Getting There & Away

For information on transport to nearby beach towns, see the boxed text.

AIR

The airport, north of town, sees many charter flights in summer. Bus No 15 (0.40lv,

15 minutes) heads to/from Yug Bus Terminal every half hour from 6am to 11pm.

BUS

Most buses and microbuses leave from and arrive at the convenient **Yug Bus Terminal** (near ul Aleksandrovska & ul Bulair). However, Varna-bound buses from central Bulgaria usually drop off Burgas passengers at the **Zapad Bus Terminal**, 2km north of centre. City bus No 4 connects the two.

Buses from Yug connect Burgas with Sofia (13lv to 15lv, six hours, 10 daily) and Plovdiv (10lv, four hours, two daily). There are also several buses daily to Veliko Târnovo (10lv, four hours), Varna (6lv to 7lv, 2½ hours, every 30 or 40 minutes) as well as spots along the coast (see below). One bus goes to Kotel from Zapad station daily.

Travel agencies along ul Bulair sell reserved seats for buses too. **Enturtrans** (☎ 844 708; ul Bulair 22; 🕑 6.30am-1am) handles domestic trips only. Across the street, **Kaleya** (☎ 844 208; ul Bulair 11; 🕑 8am-6.30pm) can get you on Istanbul-bound buses (35lv, seven hours), which leave a few times daily.

CAR

TS Travel (☎ 845 060; www.TStravel.net; ul Bulair 1; 🕑 9am-6pm Mon-Sat) rents cars starting from €44 daily.

TRAIN

The nicely renovated train station sells domestic train tickets behind old-school ticket booths. Off-season daily direct train links include: Sofia (11.10lv, seven to eight hours, seven daily), Plovdiv (7.90lv, four to five hours, three daily), Sliven (4.10lv, 1¾ hours, three daily), Kazanlâk (6.50lv, three hours, two daily) and Karlovo (7.60lv, 4¾ hours, two daily). Usually one or two more trains make the routes in summer.

A train to Bucharest runs in summer only; buy tickets at **Rila Bureau** (☎ 845 242; 🕑 8am-5pm Mon-Fri) in the station.

SOZOPOL СОЗОПОЛ
☎ 0550 / pop 5001

All things said, Sozopol – with two sandy beaches, a pretty island offshore, a stone-step historic centre on a jutting peninsula, cheaper prices than Nesebâr or Sunny Beach, and more beaches to the south – is Bulgaria's Black Sea base of choice for those

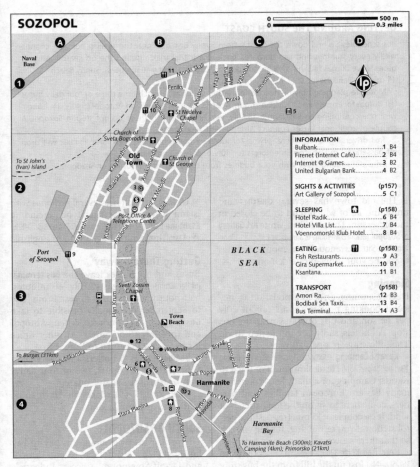

SOZOPOL

INFORMATION	
Bulbank	1 B4
Firenet (Internet Cafe)	2 B4
Internet @ Games	3 B2
United Bulgarian Bank	4 B2

SIGHTS & ACTIVITIES	(p157)
Art Gallery of Sozopol	5 C1

SLEEPING	(p158)
Hotel Radik	6 B4
Hotel Villa List	7 B4
Voennomorski Klub Hotel	8 B4

EATING	(p158)
Fish Restaurants	9 A3
Gira Supermarket	10 B1
Ksantana	11 B1

TRANSPORT	(p158)
Amon Ra	12 B3
Bodibali Sea Taxis	13 B4
Bus Terminal	14 A3

not on package trips. This is not a revelation, however, and elbow room can be scarce under the summer sun.

Orientation & Information

The town, 31km southeast of Burgas, has two parts: the peninsular old and inland new (Harmanite). The bus terminal is roughly between the two.

In the old town, you'll find several foreign-exchange offices (including one that says 'the best change you can ever made') and a couple of banks including **United Bulgarian Bank** (ul Apolonia 11A; 8.30am-4.30pm Mon-Fri) with an ATM. The small **Internet @ Games** (ul Apolonia 23; per hr 1-1.5lv; 9am-4am) has quick connections.

In the new town's centre there's a **Bulbank** (ul Republikanska; 8.30am-4.30pm Mon-Fri) and an Internet café, **Firenet** (ul Republikanska; 9am-1am), too.

Sights

Sozopol has two good **beaches**. The slightly nicer town beach, about 500m long, has umbrellas to rent. The much longer Harmanite Beach is lined with beach cafés.

Just offshore is the 6.6 sq km **St John's (Ivan) Island**. A 19th-century lighthouse watches over some 13th-century monastery ruins and, at times, 70 species of birds. Sea taxis make the 30-minute trip (20lv return for up to five people) from near the naval base in Sozopol between June and September.

BULGARIA

GETTING AROUND THE SOUTH COAST

Bus schedules up and down the coast – from Sunny Beach to near the Turkish border – change wildly every summer and can be pared back to a (daily) trickle during the off season. All year buses leave Burgas half-hourly 6am to 8pm for Sozopol (2.10lv, 40 minutes), Sunny Beach (2.50lv, 45 minutes) and Nesebâr (2.40lv, 50 minutes).

More pre-planning may be needed for further spots; at research time three or four daily buses left Burgas for Primorsko (3.50lv, one hour), Kiten (3.80lv, 1¼ hours) and Ahtopol (5.40lv, 1¾ hours), with one continuing to Sinemorets (5.80lv, two hours); usually these do *not* stop in Sozopol. A couple of additional buses connect Ahtopol and Sinemorets.

Taxi drivers are everywhere, prying for lucrative beach-hopping trips. Burgas taxis will drop off passengers in last-stop Sinemorets for 40lv or 50lv in summer.

Consider renting a car with your buddies from travel agents in Burgas or Sozopol.

The old town has several **churches** and museums, all of which tend to be closed in the off season. The pink-and-white **Art Gallery of Sozopol** (ul Kiril & Metodii 70; admission 1.5lv; ☾ 10am-7pm Mon-Sat) has enough sea-motif paintings to soothe your inner-pirate demons.

Sleeping

During summer, an accommodation agency stand booking private rooms (about 20lv per person and up) operates near the bus stop. All hotels, sadly, are in the new town. The following are open all year.

Kavatsi Camping (☎ 22 261; camp sites per person 10lv; bungalows 45lv) Head 4km south of town to Kavatsi Camping for a shady Slavic paradise; many Eastern European families, and partiers, come here to sit on the long stretch of sand. It's a couple of kilometres past the petrol station if you're walking. It's big enough so that there's always a space for a tent.

Hotel Radik (☎ 3706; ul Republikanska 4; r per person 15-25lv; ✷) Just up the hill from the bus stop, a friendly elderly couple (no English) run this bright place with spotless rooms that have balcony and refrigerator. It's a great deal, plus there's a terrace bar in summer.

Hotel Villa List (☎ /fax 22 235; ul Cherno More 5; s incl breakfast 28-57lv, d incl breakfast 40-94lv; ✷) Has 80 excellent rooms overlooking the town beach, but gets lots of summer tour groups.

Eating

A good place to sample fresh cuts of Black Sea fish is at the open-air fish restaurants along the port (open summer only).

Gira supermarket (ul Kraybrezhna; ☾ 8.30am-8.30pm) Across from the sea taxis, this small unsigned place (named for the manager's grandma) has wine and sandwich stuff.

Ul Morksi Skali has several *mehanas* with island views and terrific food, including **Ksantana** (☎ 122 454; ul Morski Skali 7; mains 3.20-12lv; ☾ 11am-11pm) with a huge menu in English.

Getting There & Away

Buses and minibuses leave the **bus terminal** (ul Han Krum) for Burgas (2.10lv, 40 minutes, half-hourly 6am to 9pm) all year. From June to September it's usually possible to take buses south to Primorsko, Kiten, Ahtopol and (possibly) Sinemorets. At other times it's necessary to return to Burgas first.

Bodibali (☎ 23 460) offers a bus service to Sofia (17lv, eight hours, two or four daily) from Harmanite's main square.

Amon Ra (ul Republikanska), in Harmanite, rents cars in summer only.

SOUTH OF SOZOPOL

The principal towns along this bay-to-bay linked stretch – Primorsko, Kiten, Ahtopol and far-off Sinemorets – access Bulgaria's best beaches, though the towns lack the historical charm of Sozopol or Nesebâr. It's possible, with patience and planning, to hop around by public bus; see p156.

The bustling resort town of **Primorsko** aspires to be Sunny Beach's little bro, and many Eastern European package trippers do come here for the 3km-long sheltered beach, ideal for swimming and boating. Private rooms are available on scene. The pale-yellow **Liliya 2** (☎ 0550 32 326; lilia_prim@abv.bg; ul 3 Mart 1) is a new hotel with nice rooms.

Southbound buses also stop at **Kiten**, 5km south, with hotels and two beaches.

About 35km south of Primorsko, and after the road gets bumpy, is the larger town of **Ahtopol**, with a pretty good long beach and plenty of accommodation. **Hotel Valdi** (☎ 0550 62 230; ul Chervem More; r 40-50lv summer; 🄇) has dated but clean rooms, some with balconies. At least three daily buses head south to Sinemorets.

Bulgaria ends its Black Sea turf with a bang in **Sinemorets**, 11km north of the (closed) Turkish border. The town is just new villas scattered along bumpy dirt roads on a wide bare bluff that bows down toward a bay cupped with lovely golden sand – and another, better one just beyond. Visitors are often stopped by border patrol outside town; bring your passport. This area – and inland west – comprises the wildlife-lush **Strandjha Nature Park**, though access to its trails from Sinemorets weren't open at last pass.

In town, **Horizon** (☎ 0550 66 026; r 40lv) has six rooms about 400m beyond the bus stop.

NESEBÂR НЕСЕБЪР
☎ 0554 / pop 9500

About 35km north of Burgas, historic and touristy Nesebâr sits out on a small rocky isthmus on the south end of the wide (just about perfect) bay that's home to Sunny Beach (Slânchev Bryag) a couple kilometres away. A Unesco World Heritage site, Nese-bâr – if anything a tad nicer than Sozopol – flaunts its centuries, back to 3000 BC when Thracians settled Mesembria here.

Biochim Commercial Bank (ul Mesembria; 🄈 8.30am-12.15pm & 1-5.30pm Mon-Fri) cashes travellers checks and has an ATM. Internet is available in summer at the **White House Hotel** (ul Tsar Simeon 2), and in Nesebâr's new town (about 1km west) all year.

Sights
CHURCHES

Even the churched-out should stroll by Nesebâr's Byzantine-influenced beauties (or ruins of their former shining selves), all built between the 6th and 14th centuries AD and once numbering about 80. Most are free; some close off season.

Now in ruins, the towering frame of the 6th-century **Basilica** (ul Mitropolitska) juts over the town's historic centre; local kids often use the wide-open interior as a football pitch, balls bouncing off the ancient walls.

One of the best preserved is **Pantrokrator Church** (ul Mesembria), a 14th-century church with bell tower that now houses an art gal-

lery. You can see, for a small fee, medieval murals in **St Stefan Church** (ul Ribarska) and **St Spa's Church** (ul Aheloi). Most churches are jealous of the water-facing lookout spot of earthquake-battered (and busted) **St John Aliturgetos Church** (ul Mena).

OTHER SIGHTS

There's a couple of museums in town, including the **Archaeological Museum** (☎ 26 018; ul Mesembria 2; admission 2.50lv; 🄈 9am-noon & 1-5pm Mon-Sat), next to the old town gate, which sees a daily tide of quick-look visitors in summer for its Thracian tombs and Roman tablets. Hours are loose in the off season.

Sleeping

Unlike Sozopol, you can stay in the old town here (as well as the new town). Most lodgings are part of the package trip loop.

Summertime travel agencies book private rooms. **Ekotour-BG** (☎ 43-200; ul Priboina), in the new town, arranges rooms for around 10lv per person. If all's full, try the town Ravda, 5km south.

The following hotels are open all year. The website www.nesebar.com lists others.

Hotel Toni (☎ 42 403; ul Kraybrezhna; r summer/off-season 55/30-35lv; 🄇) This friendly family hotel (just past the St Georgi) is unsigned. It has 12 quite cosy rooms, some with seriously great balconies overlooking Sunny Beach. Rates include breakfast in summer.

St Georgi Hotel (☎ 44 045; www.gsk.5u.com; ul Sadala 10; d incl breakfast summer/off-season 80/40lv) Stylish St Georgil, facing Sunny Beach, has a dozen rooms, often full of package tourists.

Hotel Rony (☎ 44 002; ul Chaika 1; r incl breakfast summer/off-season 75/45lv; 🄇) For back up, check out these uninspired, but tidy and passable, rooms near the old town gate.

Eating

Vega Restaurant (off ul Mesembria; mains 4-12lv; 🄈 9am-midnight) Run by a friendly family that often end nights pouring the *rakiya* at a nearby table, Vega Restaurant has four terraces overlooking the water and big-portion Bulgarian meals.

Tangra Mehana (ul Neptun; mains 4.50-16lv; 🄈 11am-10pm) One of several more upscale fish restaurants at the end of the main drag. The vine-covered outside seats fill quickly. Go for the grilled bluefish snagged offshore (16lv) or English breakfast (5lv).

BULGARIA

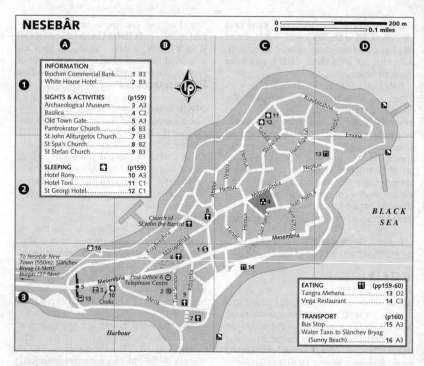

NESEBÂR

INFORMATION
Biochim Commercial Bank........1 B3
White House Hotel.................2 B3

SIGHTS & ACTIVITIES   (p159)
Archaeological Museum..........3 A3
Basilica.............................4 C2
Old Town Gate....................5 A3
Pantrokrator Church..............6 B3
St John Aliturgetos Church.......7 B3
St Spa's Church...................8 B2
St Stefan Church..................9 B3

SLEEPING   (p159)
Hotel Rony........................10 A3
Hotel Toni........................11 C1
St Georgi Hotel...................12 C1

EATING   (pp159-60)
Tangra Mehana....................13 D2
Vega Restaurant...................14 C3

TRANSPORT   (p160)
Bus Stop..........................15 A3
Water Taxis to Slânchev Bryag
  (Sunny Beach)....................16 A3

BLACK SEA

Church of St John the Baptist

To Nesebâr New Town (550m); Slânchev Bryag (3.5km); Burgas (37.5km)

Post Office & Telephone Centre

Harbour

Getting There & Away
Not all Varna–Burgas buses along the coast leave the main highway, 2km west. Nesebâr-bound buses stop in the new town, 1km west, and at the old town gate. From the bus stop at the old gate, up to half a dozen daily buses (more in summer) head north to Varna (6lv, two hours) and more often to Burgas (2.10lv, 40 minutes). Buses and water taxis go to Sunny Beach every 15 or 30 minutes, or it's a 30-minute walk.

SUNNY BEACH СЛЪНЧЕВ БРЯГ
Built for tourism, Nesebâr's famous neighbour Sunny Beach (Slânchev Bryag) is a long strip of fine beach speckled with hotels marking (clearly) the eras they came from. The centre is near the fading Hotel Kuban, with ATMs and Internet cafés and lots of places to eat lining the 300m walkway to the water.

There are about 150 hotels to choose from; essentially all are locked into the package trip frenzy and open during summer only. Two that occasionally post reasonable rates include giant pink **Hotel Globus** (☎ 0554 22 018), by the sea, and new **Hotel Koral** (☎ 0554 23 108) on the highway.

See Burgas, Nesebâr and Varna sections on p156, left and p163 respectively for bus details.

VARNA ВАРНА
☎ 052 / pop 314,540
Even without the Black Sea at its lip, Varna would be a Bulgarian highlight. Big it is, but with one of the country's most rewarding museums, heaps of exposed Roman-wall ruins, and of course the water. From Varna, there are easy pops north and south to beaches, and not bad ones in town. Thracians lived in the area from 4000 BC, and Greek sailors – that means more navy outfits – re-founded it as Odessos in the sixth century BC.

Information
Bulbank (ul Slivnitsa; ⏰ 8.30am-4pm Mon-Fri)
Frag (pl Nezavisimost; per hr 0.50-1lv; ⏰ 24hr) Internet access below the Dramatic Theatre building; beer's for sale!
Peralnya (ul Voden; per load 2.5-4.3lv; ⏰ 9am-7pm Mon-Fri, 9am-6pm Sat) Drop-off laundry service.

Pinginivite (ul 27 Juli 13; 7am-7pm Mon-Fri, 10am-6pm Sat & Sun) This bookshop stocks plenty of maps and some English-language titles.

SG Expressbank (ul Devnya & Preslav; 8.30am-4.30pm Mon-Fri) One of several banks with ATMs near the train station.

Top Tel (ul Filaret 9; international calls per min 0.35lv; 9am-9pm)

Tourist Information Centre (602 907; www .tourexpo.bg; bul Tsar Osvoboditel 36; 9am-7pm Mon-Fri, 9am-1pm Sat) Brand-spanking new centre has regional brochures and can arrange rooms or rent cars (from €28).

Sights

ARCHAEOLOGICAL MUSEUM

Housed in a grand old two-storey building (a former girl's school), this large **museum** (ul Maria Luisa 41; adult/student 4/2lv; 10am-5pm Tue-Sun Apr-Sep, 10am-5pm Tue-Sat Oct-Mar) is up for Bulgaria's best. It's filled with over 100,000 pieces from some 6000 years of area history, all remarkably well explained in English. No place better helps contextualise the waves of change this fine land has faced.

In the first room, a wall display posts finds of chronological periods (Stone Age, Bronze Age, Roman, Ottoman etc) to show how art evolved. Don't miss the sculpted goatee on the 3rd-millenium BC Thracian tomb. More serious highlights are the gold and copper pieces from the Varna Eneolithic Necropolis, dating from 4500 BC.

PRIMORSKI PARK & THE BEACH

Stretching for 8km, Primorski Park claims to be Europe's largest seaside park, and is a popular strolling ground for locals, freckled with museums, a kiddie ride park, heroic statues and numerous popcorn vendors.

At its south end, the outside ships, planes and canyons of the **National Navy Museum** (bul Primorski 2; adult/student 2/1lv; 10am-5pm Mon-Fri) can be easily viewed over the gate. To the north, a 1km shaded promenade leads to the **Liberators Monument**.

To the south of the park are pockets of fairly good **beaches**, as there are up north (just east of the Liberators Monument), plus many discos and bars (in summer).

OTHER SIGHTS

Wedged impossibly between the St Anastasios Orthodox Church and more modern apartment buildings, the leftovers of the 2nd-century AD **Roman Thermae** (ul Khan Krum & San Stefano; adult/student 3/2lv; 10am-5pm May-Oct, Tue-Sat Nov-Apr) comprise the largest ruins in Bulgaria. Frankly there's not much to see inside that you can't from outside.

The greatest of Varna's churches, the mammoth onion-domed **Cathedral of the Assumption of the Virgin** (pl Mitropolitska Simeon; admission free; 7.30am-5.30pm Mon-Fri, 7.30am-6.30pm Sat & Sun) is filled with colourful murals and a dark-wood altar.

Varna's second-best museum, housed in an 1860 revival building, is the **Ethnographic Museum** (ul Panagyurishte 22; adult/student 4/2lv; 10am-5pm Tue-Sun Apr-Sep, 10am-5pm Tue-Sat Oct-Mar) with exhibits of local dress nicely arranged by region and healthy servings of old tools (look for the giant scissors).

Festivals & Events

You're likely to witness something of the renowned Varna Summer International Festival, which features all sorts of music between May and October; try the Tourist Information Centre (p160) for details.

Sleeping

The bus and train stations have accommodation bureaus (with sketchy winter hours).

Victorina (603 541; Tsar Simeon 36; 7am-9pm Jun-Sep, 10am-6pm Mon-Fri Oct-May) Across from the train station, Victorina arranges rooms north of ul Maria Luisa for 20lv to 24lv in summer (14lv to 16lv off-season); central locations are around 60lv in summer.

Flag Hostel (648 877; flagvarna@yahoo.com; ul Opalchenska 25, 1st fl; dm 20lv) Bulgaria's first Black Sea hostel opened in 2004. The Australian-run hostel ('a nine-minute walk from the beach') has three six-bed rooms in a modern building, with laundry, kitchen, a terrace and flags plastering the walls.

Hotel Relax (361 586; www.hotelrelax2.com; ul Stephan Karadja 22; r 35-50lv;) In a 19th-century home, this laid-back 14-room hotel has odds-and-ends furnishings, like the hilarious addition of a 100-year-old piano in one room. There's a garden bar in summer.

Voennomorski Club (213 0237; ul Vladislav Varenchik 2; d 30lv; s/d 40/44lv;) Filling the top two floors of the bright blue building opposite the onion domes, 'BNK' has rather musty rooms (honestly, a bit stinky at last pass) with renovated bathrooms (shared suite style), which are set around a retro-loungey TV hall.

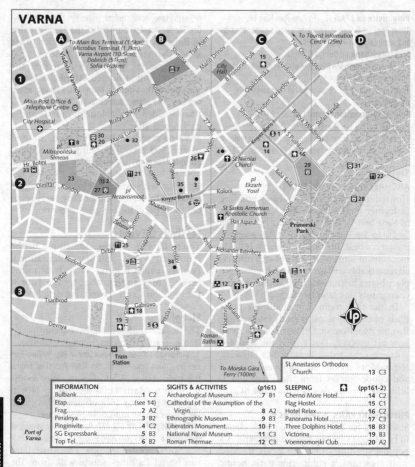

VARNA

Map legend

INFORMATION
Bulbank	1 C2
Etap	(see 14)
Frag	2 A2
Peralnya	3 B2
Pinginivite	4 C2
SG Expressbank	5 B3
Top Tel	6 B2

SIGHTS & ACTIVITIES (p161)
Archaeological Museum	7 B1
Cathedral of the Assumption of the Virgin	8 A2
Ethnographic Museum	9 B3
Liberators Monument	10 F1
National Naval Museum	11 C3
Roman Thermae	12 C3

SLEEPING (pp161-2)
Cherno More Hotel	14 C2
Flag Hostel	15 C1
Hotel Relax	16 C2
Panorama Hotel	17 C3
Three Dolphins Hotel	18 B3
Victoria	19 B3
Voennomorski Club	20 A2

St Anastasios Orthodox Church............13 C3

Cherno More Hotel (☎ 612 243; ul Slivnitsa 33; r incl breakfast US$25-50; ℗ ✖) Most rooms at this former Balkantourist beaut and still very-central high-rise wear decades-old scars (and still have those cute commie radios in), but the location and sea views from each room's balconies can't be beat. Do not use the laughably over-priced laundry service.

Panorama Hotel (☎ 687 300; www.panoramabg .com; bul Primorski 31; s/d incl breakfast 100/140lv; ✖) For the swank set and splurgers: this new hotel across from the sea has Varna's most comfy and modern rooms. Rates include breakfast and use of the fitness centre.

Three Dolphins Hotel (☎ 600 911; ul Gabrovo 27; s/d incl breakfast 50/60lv) One of a couple of small

hotels on this street, the Dolphins' rooms are a bit musty and old, but it is handily near the train station.

Eating & Drinking

In and off Knyaz Boris I and Slivnitsa pedestrian malls are many outdoor cafés, bars and restaurants. Just west of the Dramatic Theatre building, on ul Dimitâr Kondov, is an open-air market.

Pavatonka (ul Tsar Simeon & Debâr; banitsas 0.50lv; ⏱ 6am-6pm Mon-Fri, 7am-1pm Sat & Sun) Some of the country's best *banitsas*, served hot out of the oven most of the day. Go for fruit-filled.

Chuchura (ul Dragoman 11; lunches 2.28-3lv, meats 2.5-6lv; ⏱ 11.30am-11.30pm) Just off the pedestrian mall (behind McDonald's, alas), this

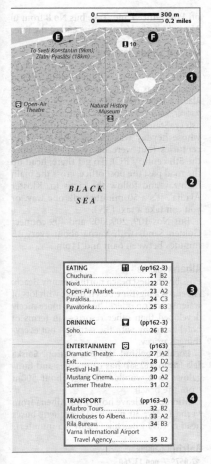

EATING	🍴	(pp162-3)
Chuchura	21	B2
Nord	22	D2
Open-Air Market	23	A2
Paraklisa	24	C3
Pavatonka	25	B3

DRINKING	🍷	(pp162-3)
Soho	26	B2

ENTERTAINMENT	🎭	(p163)
Dramatic Theatre	27	A2
Exit	28	D2
Festival Hall	29	C2
Mustang Cinema	30	A2
Summer Theatre	31	D2

TRANSPORT		(pp163-4)
Marbro Tours	32	B2
Microbuses to Albena	33	A2
Rila Bureau	34	B3
Varna International Airport Travel Agency	35	B2

19th-century tavern whips up excellent Bulgarian meals. Anything grilled in the brick oven up front is super – that pork chop is incredibly lean. There are a few veggie options, including rice-filled vine leaves covered in yoghurt and dill.

Nord (beach; fish 3-9lv; 🕑 7am-4am) One of the few beach-side eateries open all year, Nord packs in local young things for cold mugs of beer and plates of calamari and sprat.

Paraklisa (🕾 223 495; bul Primorski 47; mains 6-20lv; 🕑 11am-11pm Mon-Sat) Housed in a former church/hospital from the 1860s, Paraklisa fills seats with its finely prepared regional dishes (pork fillet with couscous is a winner; there's also a full menu page of veggie options). Classical music is balanced by

wilfully graffitied walls inside. The courtyard seating is best, but catches traffic noise.

Soho (ul 27 Juli; 🕑 9am-midnight) Away from the main pedestrian-mall crawl, Soho is a small but stylish corner bar good for coffee or cocktails.

Entertainment

Posters advertise DJs, concerts and discos around town. In summer, most action is at the beach bars that open up for all-day (and much of the night) beer-soaked fun; one is the disco **Exit** (Primorski Park) – follow the white footsteps. **Dramatic Theatre** (Opera House; 🕾 223 388; www.operavarna.bg; pl Nezavisimost) hosts theatre or music frequently. The **Summer Theatre** (🕾 228 385; Primorski Park), with fake Roman columns, stages summer events.

For films, **Mustang Cinema** (bul Vladislav Varenchik; 3lv) and **Festival Hall** (ul Slivnitsa) play English-language films with Bulgarian subtitles.

Getting There & Away
AIR
The **Varna airport** (🕾 650 835), west of town, booms with charter flight action from mid April to October; at other times there's a lone daily flight to/from Sofia. Bus No 409 waddles out there, past the bus station, from the centre. Tickets are available in town at the **Varna International Airport agency** (🕾 612 588; ul Knyaz Boris I 15; 🕑 8am-7pm).

BUS
The **main bus terminal** (bul Vladislav Varenchik) is 2km northwest of the city centre. Bus Nos 409 and 148 stop near the main cathedral and at Slivinitska and Knyaz Boris I. Tickets for private buses can be bought at agencies in town, such as **Etap** (🕾 604 674; ul Slivnitsa 33; 🕑 9am-8pm) at the Hotel Cherno More, which is helpful for confirming bus times All services leave from the main terminal.

Direct buses include the following:

Athens 95lv, 26 hours, one daily
Balchik 2.50lv, 50 minutes, five daily
Burgas 7lv, two hours, every 30 or 40 minutes
Istanbul 40lv, 10 hours, two daily
Plovdiv 15lv, six hours, two daily
Ruse 8.40lv, four hours, two daily
Shumen 5lv, 1½ hours, three daily, plus Sofia buses
Sliven 10lv, three hours, one daily
Sofia 19lv, seven to eight hours, every 45 minutes
(via Shumen and Veliko Târnovo)
Veliko Târnovo 8lv, four hours, every 45 minutes

BULGARIA

FERRY
London Sky Travel (☎ 601 330; inflot@tea.bg; Morska Gara) has restarted its ferry service to Odesa, Ukraine for US$100 to US$120, one way.

MICROBUS
The **microbus terminal** (Avtogara Mladost; ☎ 800 038; ul Knyaz Cherkazki), 200m west of the bus station, sends little buses to Burgas hourly 7am to 5pm, and to Albena and Balchik hourly 6.30am to 7.30pm. Less frequent services go to Nesebâr (via Sunny Beach) and Shumen.

Microbuses also leave for Albena (2.5lv, 30 minutes) nearly every hour 8am to 5pm from a convenient stop off at ul Maria Luisa, about 150m west of the main cathedral.

TRAIN
Direct train services from the **main train station** (bul Primorski) link Varna to Sofia (12.50lv, 8½ hours, six daily), Plovdiv (9.90lv, 6½ hours, three daily), Ruse (6.90lv, four hours, two daily), Shumen (3.90lv, 1½ hours, eight daily) and other towns.

Direct trains to Bucharest are available in summer only. At other times transfers are required. All international tickets must be purchased at **Rila Bureau** (☎ 632 348; ul Preslav 13; ⏱ 8am-5.30pm Mon-Fri, 8am-3.30pm Sat), a few minutes' walk from the station.

Getting Around
Local bus routes are listed on the Domino city map; it's 0.50lv per ride. Some taxi drivers get giddy as giddy geese by overcharging foreign travellers – make sure posted rates aren't inflated and the meter is on.

Most travel agencies rent cars more cheaply than airport offices of Hertz or Avis. **Marbro Tours** (☎ 600 735; ul Maria Luisa 8; ⏱ 8.30am-6.30pm Mon-Fri) can fix you up with wheels from €20 daily.

NORTH OF VARNA
Just up from Varna are several upmarket beach resorts that cater to rich foreigners on package tours. All can be visited on day trips from Varna or Balchik.

Sveti Konstantin Свети Константин
Just 9km north of Varna, this small resort has several hotels along a pretty beach. The tiny, **Sv Konstantin & Sv Elena Monastery** (admission free; ⏱ dawn to dusk, except Sun morning) is just

off Post Office Lane. Take bus No 8 from ul Maria Luisa in Varna to the end of the line.

Golden Sands Златни Пясъци
Bulgaria's second-largest resort, 18km northeast of Varna, Golden Sands (Zlatni Pyasâtsi) has a 4km stretch of beach. The **Aladzha Monastery** (admission 2lv; ⏱ closed Mon summer, Sun & Mon winter) is a bizarre rock monastery. Stairs lead to and around the caves, whose heyday was in the 13th and 14th centuries (but were likely inhabited since the 5th century BC). To get there, head up the road past the post office, cross the main highway and follow the signs to 'Kloster Aladja'. It's a 50-minute walk one way, or you can take a taxi (3lv).

Bus Nos 109, 209, 309 and 409 connect Golden Sands with Varna about every 15 minutes between 6am and 11pm.

Albena Албена
Possibly the best beach north of Sunny Beach, Albena is a big-time beach resort with lots of water sports on offer. The area is more nicely developed than other resorts – in terms of hotel harmony with the setting – but everything is pricey.

Located behind the bus station, **Gorska Feia** (☎ 0579 62 961) has camp sites and bungalows in a wooded setting, about 500m from the beach.

Microbuses leave hourly for Albena from Varna (2.5lv, 30 minutes). Frequent buses head north to Balchik (1.20lv, 15 minutes).

Balchik Балчик
☎ 0579 / pop 13,760
Wedged between a rocky shoreline and white chalk bluffs, Balchik – a 'real' town, after the commercialised resorts – is a good alternative base for northern beaches.

The bus stop is 1km above the historic centre, by the water. Near the centre is a **DCK Bank** (⏱ 8.30am-4.30pm Mon-Fri) with an ATM.

In the 1920s, when the region was part of Romania, King Ferdinand built the **Summer Palace Queen Marie & Botanical Gardens** (Dvoretsa; admission 2lv; ⏱ 8am-8pm summer, 8am-7pm winter) for his wife because she wanted something 'small and romantic' (as a guide tells it). The palace, indeed, is small (and mixes Islamic and Bulgarian revival styles); it's set near the water below lush gardens, a waterfall and several villas (all that's the romantic bit).

It's an easy 2km walk from the centre along the restaurant-lined seaside promenade.

Several accommodation agencies are opposite the port area and can find private rooms from 10lv per person. One agent is **Sea Foods Ltd** (☎ 72 531; seafoods@hotmail.com; ⏰ 8.30am-8pm summer only).

Esparansa (☎ 75 148; ul Cherno More 16; r with shared bathroom US$16-20), about 150m up from the port, is a four-room hotel open seasonally. It's a step into another (past) world, with lace tablecloths and overflowing bookcases dressing up four very eclectic rooms.

Balchik Hotel (☎ 72 809; r incl breakfast summer/winter 50/25lv) faces quiet pl Nezavisimost, 400m up from the port, and has 30 clean rooms and friendly English-speaking staff.

In summer buses wind down the coast hourly to Varna (2.50lv, one hour) stopping at beach resorts, less frequently in the off season. Six daily buses go north to Kavarna (2lv, 30 minutes).

Kaliakra Cape Нос Калуакра

This 2km-long headland – its name meaning 'beautiful' – pokes out into the Black Sea about 30km northeast of Balchik. It's a big-time boat and/or bus day trip for resort folk to the south, but is worth the effort. Most of the cape is part of the **Kaliakra Nature Reserve** (admission 3lv; ⏰ 24hr), where you can witness the ruins of an 8th-century citadel being defecated on by 300 species of birds.

The catch is that no public transport gets here. From Balchik, bus to Kavarna and take a taxi. A return taxi from Balchik is about 40 or 45lv in summer.

NORTHWEST BULGARIA

Neglected, even mocked, Bulgaria's little pinkie – wedged between Romania and Serbia – sees few foreign travellers. Vidin is a gateway to Romania by river or to Serbia via bus, and is nearby to Belogradchik's fortress. The train from Sofia goes past impressive Iskâr Gorge, south of Mezdra.

VIDIN ВИДИН

☎ 094 / pop 64,900

If rivers could rank cities, Vidin would score for its locals' misty-eyed devotion to the Danube. But rivers don't. While its newly developed riverside park (with a metal-plank pavement that doubles as a wall in case of flooding) offers Bulgaria's finest spot to hang with the mighty Dan, Vidin is most useful as a link to Belogradchik.

The main square (pl Bdintsi), two blocks north of the bus and train stations, is home to the **Bulgarian Post Bank** (⏰ 8.30am-4.30pm Mon-Fri) and an ATM. The pedestrian mall ul Tsar Simeon Veliki extends northwest (with foreign-exchange offices), and leafy ul Bada Vida follows the river north.

Sights

About 1km north of the centre is the interesting **Baba Vida Museum-Fortress** (☎ 601 705; admission 2lv; ⏰ 8.30am-5pm Mon-Fri, 10am-4.30pm Sat & Sun), dating from a 1st-century Roman citadel, though much of what remains was rebuilt by Turks in the 1600s. Nearby is a narrow **beach**. A bit north is an island locals swim to in summer. Freighter ships deter some from taking the plunge.

Sleeping

Voennomorski Klub Hotel (☎ 601 428; ul Baba Vida 15; r per person 15lv) Housed on the top floor of an 1860s red-and-gold building facing the park, the seven rooms with shared bathroom are slightly rundown, but the owner will sketch fish at the slightest prod.

On the central square, **Hotel Bononia** (☎ 606-031; pl Bdintsi; s/d 35/60lv) is by far Vidin's comfiest stay.

Getting There & Away

Fourteen daily buses connect Vidin with Sofia (10lv, four hours), six buses with Belogradchik (2.5lv, 1¼ hours). Allegedly two daily buses head for Nagoutin, Serbia, from in front of the station.

The train station, across from the bus station, sees four daily trains en route to/from Sofia (7.30lv, 5¼ hours).

Talk about a bridge to Romania is still talk. You can cross by ferry to Calafat, Romania, twice a day (8lv) from a dock near the centre. A more expensive car ferry is north of town.

BELOGRADCHIK БЕЛОГРАДЧИК

☎ 0936 / pop 7600

A sprawling village along a rising mountain, remote Belogradchik draws many Bulgarian travellers to see its phenomenal fortress and stirring craggy red-rock peaks so lifelike they're named for people. (Some say travellers who litter were turned to stone here... no, not really, but who knows?)

The town has a bank with an 24-hour ATM on the main road, which starts a block up from the bus station.

Sights

Propped upon and between jagged peaks, the huge **Kaleto Fortress** (admission 2.5lv; ⏰ 8am-8pm Apr-Oct, 8am-4.30pm Nov-Mar), a kilometre walk up from the main square (follow the signs, veer left at the old mosque), is probably Bulgaria's most interesting fort. Its Turk-built outer walls surround a nearly hidden garrison gate; above are smooth spots to sit and listen to sheep bells clang from far-off fields. Romans first built here in the 1st century AD, and the site was later used to fight off Hungarian troops (unsuccessfully) in the 14th. Ask at the information stand about visits to nearby **caves**.

It's possible to loop back on trails behind the fort to town, via the **Belogradchiski Skali** rock formations (aka 'Bulgaria's Grand Canyon'), which are accessible from town, starting about 100m from behind (and down from) the main square.

Sleeping & Eating

Hotel Rai (☎ 3735; r 30lv, with shared bathroom 20lv) Facing the bus station, the friendly Hotel Rai has recently renovated rooms, one with a balcony.

Madona (☎ 5546; www.hotelmadona.hit.bg, in Bulgarian; ul Hristo Botev 26; s/d 30/40lv, with shared bathroom 25/35lv) This B&B has very small, but nice, traditional rooms in a home that feels gingerbread housey. It's 600m up from the main square (follow signs to 'hotel').

About 100m further along is good eating at **Restaurant Elit** (mains 3-5lv).

Getting There & Away

Six daily buses go to/from Vidin (2.5lv, 1¼ hours) and four are scheduled to meet trains en route to Sofia at Oroshets station (0.50lv, 20 minutes), 15km east.

BULGARIA DIRECTORY

ACCOMMODATION

Bulgaria's accommodation options are a grab bag. On the Black Sea, stylish new hotels rise

every year, while in towns like Karlovo a lone decades-old hotel quietly decomposes on the central square with a floor rented out as local office space.

Accommodation listings in this guide have been ordered by pricing from cheapest to most expensive (ie budget to top end).

In addition to the following, most active monasteries have barebone rooms for as little as 10lv per night (just no drinking binges kids).

Camping

Camping is not on the rise in Bulgaria. Generally 'camping' here refers to rather lifeless areas where bungalows sit side by side in a small thicket of woods. Camp sites can be cheap though (3lv or 5lv). Discreet camping outside the camping ground is, as one local says, 'no problem – just don't have a loud party – and say you have permission if anyone asks.' In other words, it's not technically legal.

Hizhas dot the mountainous areas and range in quality. Many are now privately run; some more remote ones are free. Most Bulgaria maps show these.

The Tryavna information centre (p150) rents camping gear.

Private Rooms

Shoestringers should rent private rooms (*stai pod naem*), often offered from agencies, signed homes or from English-speaking touts at stations. Rates start at 10lv or 15lv per person in smaller towns, 20lv in places like Sofia, Plovdiv and Varna. Often private rooms mean shared bathroom in a shared flat with a family; sometimes grandma sleeps in the kitchen.

Hostels

Sofia's good hostel scene numbers over half a dozen, but you'll find only a couple of others elsewhere (including Plovdiv and Varna). It's generally 20lv for a bed; queues for a lone shower aren't uncommon.

Hotels

Generally hotels have private bathrooms (or a private bathroom down the hall), in-room TV, heat and a fan if not AC, and a free breakfast half the time. All entries in this chapter have private bathrooms and TV unless otherwise noted. Most double rooms have two twin beds. Average rates for a cheapie are around 30lv for a single, 40lv for a double. In some tourist locations, at off-season, that rate can drop by 10lv. Higher-end hotels – recently built, in more modern style (and with thicker walls) – generally start at 45lv to 60lv for a single.

Many old communist-era Balkan tourist high-rises still plod ahead in these new times. These are often ridiculed, but it's worth staying at one once (Varna and Sliven are good choices): they often have good locations, and seeing their interiors (unworking mint-and-beige phones, grey-and-brown 1970s drapes and chunky AM radios) feels like stepping into the Cold War era. Won't be there forever.

ACTIVITIES

Hiking options in the four principal mountain ranges abound (over 37,000km in all), see these sections for hiking tips: Rila (p130), Pirin (p130), Rodopi (p134) and Central Balkans/Stara Planina (p141). Kartografia publish excellent trail maps, available in Sofia and elsewhere. Zig Zag in Sofia (p124) runs guided tours and gives well-informed tips. *The Mountains of Bulgaria* by Julian Perry Cordee lists many multi-day hikes to *hizhas* around the country, but is out of date (1995).

Some trails are open to mountain bikes, or can be cross-country skied in winter.

Bulgaria's gaining fame as a cheap downhill ski (and snowboarding) destination. However, its three main resorts – Borovets (p132), Bansko (p133) and Pamporovo (p140) – aren't necessarily dirt cheap; a one-day lift ticket is €20 to 24, with an extra 20 to 40lv to rent equipment. Mt Vitosha (p129) is cheaper. The ski season runs mid-December to mid-April. You'll save money doing package deals, available in Sofia. Check www.bulgariaski.com for loads of information plus package deals. Also, **Exploring Ltd** (☎ 088 851 9476; www.exploring-bg.com) runs super ski trips, some out to liftless areas otherwise not accessible, for €30 to €40 per day.

Rock climbing is on the rise, with good options all over, including outside Veliko Târnovo; visit Trapezitsa (p148) there for information on tours.

Caving tours are another draw, such as ones near Belogradchik (p165) and thrilling tours at Trigrad (p141).

REGISTRATION AT HOTELS

Technically you have register your passport details with police every night during your stay in Bulgaria, and show customs officials the documents upon leaving the country. Nearly all hotels and private accommodation agencies, even camp sites, will do this automatically for you upon check-in.

Some travellers have reported about very grumpy border officials when even a couple days are missing from passports (and grumbles could mean a fine, or getting turned back), but most of the time you'll exit without having to show any.

BOOKS

Lonely Planet's *Bulgaria* offers more comprehensive coverage of the country. For history, RJ Crampton's *A Concise History of Bulgaria* gives a quick (if a little dull) overview from pre-Thracians era to post-communism. Bill Bryson pokes a little fun at Sofia in his 1992 book *Neither Here Nor There: Travels in Europe*.

BUSINESS HOURS

Banks and most public offices are open Monday to Friday, roughly 8.30am to 4.30pm, sometimes with an hour off for lunch. Many shops, and certainly foreign-exchange booths, are open daily; most Internet cafés are open 'nonstop' (24 hour). Many post offices are open daily.

Many Bulgarian museums and stores post opening hours straight-faced, but adherence is rarely set in stone or even expected. It can depend on the season (in winter, some museums may close for a few weeks unexpectedly, while summer sees longer hours) or the whim of the guy with the keys ('oh sorry, Hristo is meeting a cousin in Pleven, come back tomorrow'). Hours in this chapter run the official line, but brace yourself for the occasional burp.

'Summer' and 'winter' refer to either side of daylight savings.

COURSES

It's possible to study Bulgarian language in Sofia (p125) and Veliko Târnovo (p148). You can also learn traditional Bulgarian music or dance at heralded schools in Kotel (p145) and Shiroka Lâka (p141).

BULGARIA

DANGERS & ANNOYANCES

Don't leave bags unattended at train or bus stations, or wear an unzipped backpack, and you're likely to have no problems in Bulgaria. Cars can be common targets for crime, however; put valuables out of sight, and consider parking it where there's a 'nonstop' attendant to watch it.

You will be warned that Roma will rob you, which becomes more of an annoyance to hear than anything. Bulgaria has many stray dogs, often well fed by locals.

Smoke is a huge annoyance unless you like teary red eyes. Most hotels do not have smoke-free rooms.

DISCOUNT CARDS

Students can save 50% on ticket admission at most museums, and on airfares at some travel agents. In Sofia, Orbita (p124) can issue student cards.

EMBASSIES & CONSULATES
Bulgarian Embassies & Consulates

Australia (☎ 02-9327 7592; fax 02-9327 8067; 14 Carlotta Rd, Double Bay, NSW 2028)

Canada (☎ 1-613-789 3215; fax 1-613-789 3524; 325 Steward St, Ottawa, ON N1K6K5)

France (☎ 01 45 51 85 90; www.bulgaria.com/embassy /france; 1 Ave Rapp, 75007 Paris)

Germany (☎ 030-201 09 22; bbotscaft@myokay.net; Mauerstrasse 11, Berlin 10117)

Greece Athens (☎ 30-1-647 8105; fax 30-1-647 8130; 33 Stratigou allari St, 15452 Athens); Thessaloniki (☎ 031-829 210; Edmundo Abot 1, Thessaloniki)

Ireland (☎ 01-660 3229; fax 01-660 3915; 22 Burlington Rd, Dublin)

Israel (☎ 972-3-524 1798; fax 972-3-524 1798; 124 Rehov ibn Gavirol, 62308 Tel Aviv)

Macedonia (☎ 91-229 444; fax 91-11 61 39; 3 Zlatko Shnaider St, Skopje)

Netherlands (☎ 070-350 30 51; www.embassy -bulgaria.nl; Duinroosweg 9, 2597 KJ The Hague)

Romania (☎ 01-230 21 50; fax 01-230 76 54; Str Rabat 5, sec 1, Bucharest)

Serbia (☎ 11-64 62 22; fax 11-64 10 80; 26 Birchaninova St, Belgrade)

Turkey Ankara (☎ 0312-426 7455; Atatürk Bulvari 124, Kavaklidere, Ankara); Istanbul (☎ 0212-269 0478; fax 0212-264 1011; Adnan Saygun Caddesi 44, Ulus, Mahallesi, Istanbul)

UK (☎ 020-7584 9400; www.bulgarianembassy.org.uk; 186-88 Queen's Gate, London SW7 5HL)

USA (☎ 1-202-387 0174; www.bulgaria-embassy.org; 1621 22nd St NW, Washington DC 2008)

Embassies & Consulates in Bulgaria

Designated visiting hours for citizens or those seeking visas are listed. New Zealanders can turn to the UK Embassy for assistance.

Australia (☎ 02-946 1334; ul Trakia 37) Main office in Athens, call for hours.

Canada (☎ 02-943 3704; ul Assen Zlatarov 11)

Denmark (☎ 02-980 0830; bul Dondukov 54; ☽ 9am-4pm Mon-Fri)

France (☎ 02-946 1040; www.ambafrance-bg.org, in French; ul Oborishte 21A; ☽ 9am-noon, 3-6pm Mon-Fri)

Germany (☎ 02-918-38-116; ul Frederic Joliot-Curie 25; ☽ 8am-5pm Mon-Thu, 8am-1.30pm Fri)

Greece (☎ 02-946 1750; ul Evlogi Georgiev 103; ☽ 8.30am-4pm Mon-Fri)

Hungary (☎ 02-963 1135; ul 6 Sevtembri 57; visas ☽ 9am-11am Mon, Wed & Fri)

Ireland (☎ 02-981 2094; bul Stamboliiski 55, fl 4)

Macedonia (☎ 02-701 560; ul Frederic Joliot-Curie 17)

Netherlands (☎ 02-816 0300; www.netherlands embassy.bg; ul Oborishte 15; ☽ 10am-noon Mon-Fri)

Poland (☎ 02-987 2610, visa info ☎ 02-981 8545; ul Han Krum 46; visas ☽ 9am-1pm Mon-Wed & Fri)

Romania (☎ 02-973 3510; bul M Eminesku 1; visas ☽ 3-5pm Tue, 10am-noon Wed & Thu)

Russia (☎ 02-963 0914; www.bulgaria.mid.ru, in Russian; bul Dragan Tskankov 28)

Turkey (☎ 02-935 5500; bul Vasil Levski 80; ☽ 9.30am-1pm Mon-Fri)

UK (☎ 02-933 9222; www.british-embassy.bg; ul Moskovksa 9; ☽ 8am-5pm Mon-Fri)

USA (☎ 02-963 1391; www.usembassy.bg; ul Kapitan Andreev 1; ☽ 2-4pm Mon-Fri)

FESTIVALS & EVENTS

Bulgaria hosts many fascinating shindigs. City-run music and cultural events run from spring to autumn. Koprivshtitsa's folk festival is a big one (see p142) and Varna's music festival (p161) spans nearly half a year; others are listed throughout this chapter.

As part of the national custom of Martenitsa in March, most Bulgarians wear red-and-white yarned figures till they see a stork, when they tie the figure to a tree.

Also in March, the *kukeri* festival – famous in Shiroka Lâka (p141) – is held on the first Sunday before Lent, when oddly masked dancers ward off evil spirits.

On May 21 some towns hold a pagan event for Sts Constantine and Elena Day, by walking barefoot over hot coals.

GAY & LESBIAN TRAVELLERS

Consensual homosexual sex is legal in Bulgaria. One of the nation's biggest stars, male singer Azis, is purposely sexually ambiguous, but Bulgaria is not yet gay friendly.

The best source for discos, bars, even a nude gay beach, is available at www.bulgay ria.com. **Bulgarian Gay Organization Gemini** (www.bgogemini.org) is a largely political organisation in Sofia, but can help point out places to go.

HOLIDAYS

Official public holidays are:
New Year's Day 1 January
Liberation Day aka National Day; 3 March
Orthodox Easter Sunday & Monday March/April; one week after Catholic/Protestant Easter
St George's Day 6 May
Cyrillic Alphabet Day 24 May
Unification aka National Day; 6 September
Bulgarian Independence Day 22 September
National Revival Day 1 November
Christmas 25 & 26 December

INTERNET RESOURCES

In addition to the following, specialised websites are also listed in relevant sections throughout this chapter.
www.bdz.bg/eng/index_eng.htm Train schedule and fares; bookmark this one
www.bulgariatravel.org Official tourist site, with detailed background and photos
www.onlinebg.com News, shopping, links
www.sofiacityguide.com Monthly publication's website, with loads of national information
www.sofiaecho.com English-language paper that has national coverage, travel tips and extensive archives

LANGUAGE

Almost everything is written in Cyrillic (even 'kseroks' for Xerox). Most Bulgarians in their late 20s and older know a fair bit of Russian. English is the vogue second-language of choice these days, though many people speak German.

The English term 'bugger' allegedly comes from a derogatory term for Bulgarian.

See p910 for a list of useful Bulgarian words and phrases.

MONEY

In touristy places and up-market hotels, many prices are quoted in euros, or sometimes US dollars. Prices in this chapter conform to quotes of individual businesses.

ATMs

ATMs (cash points) are ubiquitous and compatible with foreign cards (ask your banks). Even towns like Rila and Belogradchik have 24 hour ATMs. Smaller mountain and beach towns are exceptions (eg Melnik and Sinemorets).

Cash

The local currency, the lovely leva (lv), comprise 100 *stotinki*. It's been pegged to the euro (roughly 2:1) since January 2002. In touristy places and up-market hotels, many prices are quoted in euro, sometimes US dollars. Banknotes come in denominations of one, two, five, 10, 20 and 50 *leva* and coins in one, two, five, 10, 20 and 50 *stotinki*. (Bus game: whoever makes the best poem with 'stotinki' wins.)

Exchanging Money

It's not a problem changing money – foreign-exchange offices (many working nonstop) are in every town. You'll get receipts from these, and at banks, but there's no reason to hold onto it. US dollars, UK pounds and euro are the best currencies to carry. Occasionally you may be approached by folks on the street changing money – rip-offs are not unknown.

Foreigner Prices

Brace yourself for an official dual-pricing scheme, where foreigners pay double (or more) the local price at museums and hotels. Its sting is most poignantly felt when a museum is 500% the cost and exhibits are in Bulgarian only. Many Bulgarians oppose this state policy that pads entrepreneur pockets only; some hoteliers bypass it (not many). Prices should be the same as for locals at shops, restaurants and for transport.

Travellers Cheques

American Express and Thomas Cook cheques can be cashed at nearly all banks. Bulbank, the country's official bank, often charges the lowest commission rate – officially €1 per transaction (not per cheque), though some branches may need to be reminded of this.

POST

Sending a postcard to anywhere outside Bulgaria costs 0.32lv; letters to 20g cost 0.83lv to Europe, 0.87lv outside Europe. Many post offices in bigger cities are open daily.

TELEPHONE

In most cities and towns, you'll find a Bulgarian Telecommunications Centre (BTC) inside, or next to, the main post office, from where you can make local or international calls (it's about 0.55lv per minute during the day to call the UK, 0.44lv after 9pm). But when possible, use Net cards (accessed by toll-free numbers from bigger cities) or make international Net calls from Internet cafés. Rates are as little as 0.20lv per minute to call the UK, US or Australia.

Nearly all Mobika and BulFon telephone booths use phone cards (*fonkarta*) for local or international calls. Cards are available from newsstands for 5 to 25lv. By the way, orange BulFon booths double as free clocks – pick up the receiver to see the time.

The mobile phone craze has certainly reached Bulgaria. M-tel and Globul are the two operators. Numbers have different codes (eg ☎087 and 088) and are usually indicated by 'GSM' or 'mob' on signs. Costs are much more expensive than land lines.

Phone numbers in Bulgaria have a penchant for change.

EMERGENCY NUMBERS

- Ambulance ☎ 150
- Fire ☎ 160
- Police ☎ 166

Phone Codes

To ring Bulgaria from abroad, dial the international access code then ☎ 359, followed by the area code (minus the first zero) then the number.

To call direct out of Bulgaria, dial ☎ 00 followed by the country code.

TOURIST INFORMATION

Bigger centres in Bulgaria – Sofia, Plovdiv, Varna – lack real city-oriented tourist information centres, while smaller places like Smolyan have two offices with English-speaking staff and tons of brochures. For information, you can always resort to the many travel agents or hotels. In some places, small ad-filled brochures (the like that are free in many countries) are sold for a whopping 2lv or 3lv.

TOURS

The idea of independent travel is a foreign concept for many Bulgarians, and many travel agents offer (and push) city, regional or thematic tours. Some are worthy, such as hiking tours into the rugged mountains, rock-climbing tours to areas that are hard to find, or the trips to difficult-to-reach Rila Monastery (p130). Also see Travel Agencies sections in the text, and the Activities section above (p167).

From abroad, try **Sunquest** (www.sunquestholidays.co.uk) or **Balkan Holidays** (www.balkanholidays.co.uk) for package trips to the Black Sea coast or mountains.

VISAS

At the time of research, citizens of the following countries don't require a visa, and are instead issued a free 30-day entry stamp at any Bulgarian border, international airport or seaport: Australia, Canada, Ireland, Israel, Japan, New Zealand, Poland, UK and USA; citizens of other EU countries will receive 90-day tourist visas. Visitors on business will have to apply for a visa before entry.

The easiest way to get an extension on your stay is by leaving the country and returning the same day or next. It is also possible to pay 200lv for an extension at the passport offices in Sofia and Plovdiv.

See the boxed text (p167) for documents you may need upon leaving the country.

TRANSPORT IN BULGARIA

GETTING THERE & AWAY

Air

Bulgaria's two most active airports are in Sofia (☎ 02-937 2211) and Varna (☎ 052-650 835), with summer charter flights making daily appearances in Burgas too. The three, plus Plovdiv, are jockeying to be Bulgaria's first budget-airline destination, but no set plans have been made.

No additional departure tax is levied outside the price of your ticket.

Airlines flying to/from Bulgaria include:

Aeroflot (code SU; www.aeroflot.com; ☎ 02-937 3191)

Air France (code AF; www.airfrance.com; ☎ 02-945 9277, 02-980 6150)

Air Malta (code KM; www.airmalta.com; ☎ 02-933 1033)

Alitalia (code AZ; www.alitalia.it; ☎ 02-981 6702)

Austrian Airlines (code OS; www.aua.com; ☎ 02-980 2323)

British Airways (code BA; www.britishairways.com; ☎ 02-945-9227, 02-937-3111)

Bulgaria Air (code FB; www.air.bg; ☎ 02-937 3243, 02-865 9557)

ČSA (Czech Airlines; code OK; www.csa.cz/en; ☎ 02-937 3175)

Hemus Air (code DU; www.hemusair.bg; ☎ 02-981 8330)

LOT Polish Airlines (code LO; www.lot.com; ☎ 02-937 3161, 02-987 4562)

Lufthansa (code LH; www.lufthansa.com; ☎ 02-937 3141, 02-980 4141)

KLM (code KLM; www.klm.com; ☎ 02-981 9910)

Malév (Hungarian Airlines; code MA; www.malev.com; ☎ 02-981 5091)

Turkish Airlines (code TK; www.turkishairlines.com; 02-945 9145, 02-988 3596)

Land

BORDER CROSSINGS

The most popular entry/exit into Bulgaria and the region is at the Ruse–Giurgiu border with Romania (en route to/from Bucharest); few buses cross the Danube here, so most travellers go by train, enduring a 90-minute border check on both sides.

Macedonia-bound buses and trains leave from Sofia (via the Gyueshevo–Deve Bair crossing) and Blagoevgrad (via the Stanke Lischkovo–Delçevo crossing); Belgrade-bound buses and trains from Sofia cross at Kalotina–Dimitrovgrad, Serbia (some travellers have preferred the train on this route). It's also possible to get to Serbia by bus from Vidin, via the Vrâshka Chuka–Zajc crossing.

See the Transport chapter for information on getting to Turkey and Istanbul by train, bus or sea.

BUS

International tickets to the region (and beyond) are available at practically any bus station in the country. There's not one set price, so it's worth checking a couple of companies to find the cheapest fare.

CAR & MOTORCYCLE

Drivers bringing cars in are asked to pay a 'road fee' at the border, based on where you're going. One option is to say you're heading to the nearest big city (eg if crossing from Greece, say 'going to Sofia' and pay €10, rather than €50 for Varna). Allegedly you won't have to show the receipt upon leaving. Drivers must also pay a €3 'disinfection fee'. There is talk of implementing tolls on Bulgarian highways by 2005 – at time of writing all were toll-free.

TRAIN

Tickets for international trains can be bought at any Rila Bureau (www.bdz-rila .com/index-en.htm; most open weekdays only) or at some stations' dedicated ticket offices (most open daily) at larger stations with international connections.

The daily Trans-Balkan Express (between Budapest and Thessaloniki, Greece) stops at Ruse, Gorna Oryahovitsa (near Veliko Târnovo), Sofia and Sandanski.

A daily train connects Sofia with Belgrade (and good connections to Western and Central Europe) and Istanbul.

The Bulgaria Express (between Sofia and Moscow) stops in Ruse and Pleven once weekly, three times in summer. From mid-June to September, trains leave from Varna and Burgas en route to Bucharest, Budapest, Bratislava and Prague. Also, another summer train connects Bucharest with Sofia, via Ruse and Gorna Oryahovitsa.

River

You can ferry across the Danube River from Vidin (p165) or cross by train from Ruse (p153).

GETTING AROUND

Travelling around Bulgaria is cheap. Prices are the same for foreigners as locals.

Air

Hemus Air flies between Sofia and Varna daily (€58 one way, plus €8 domestic departure tax), with extra flights in summer, when there are also flights to Burgas (about €40 one way). See p170 for airline contact information.

BULGARIA

Bicycle

Traffic is relatively light outside the cities, but winding curves in the mountains and/or potholes everywhere can be obstacles.

Bulgaria has few bike-rental options; you can rent wheels at Zig Zag (p124) or Hotel Kervan (p125) in Sofia, in Veliko Târnovo (p148) or the tourist information centre in Koprivshtitsa (p142). Most towns have bike shops that can make repairs or sell some spare parts. You may need to pay an extra fee to take a bike on a train or bus; ask.

Boat

Sadly there's no regular boat service down the Danube River.

Bus

Buses (public and private) and minibuses connect all cities and major towns. Private buses – some quite modern with TV and bathrooms – surprisingly cost little more than the more ramshackle public ones. For shorter trips, either is fine.

Unfortunately centralised information for schedules doesn't exist, and schedules change frequently. This chapter lists prices, duration for trips and number of buses daily – *use as a gauge only.*

Bigger bus stations have a confusing array of private bus booths advertising overlapping destinations with other private booths. The public bus stops generally have a list of timetables outside. In most cases, buses leave from around 7am to 6pm or so. Most bus stations have a left-luggage service.

Car & Motorcycle

Renting a car from a local agent – not an international company, who may charge four or five times the rate – is a great way to beach-hop or visit mountain villages.

A car can be found in bigger cities for €15 to €30 per day, usually with unlimited kilometres and insurance thrown in. Some companies, such as Penguin in Sofia (p129) allow free drop-offs in select cities in Bulgaria. See individual entries for listings.

To rent you normally need to be 21 and have a driver's licence from your own

---

WHEN'S THE TRAIN LEAVE?

For updated daily schedules and fares for domestic routes, click on 'Services & Prices' at www.bdz.bg/eng/index_eng.htm. For international trains, check www.bdz-rila.com/index-en.htm. (The former is the winner of the 'LP Eastern Europe/Bulgaria Most Useful Website Award.' It's an obscure honour, but has many cult fans.)

country. Most road conditions are pretty good, and traffic reasonably light. Most roads are well signed in Cyrillic and English. On smaller roads (like the road to Trigrad), you may have to negotiate big bumps. If oncoming traffic flicks their lights, it's likely a police speed trap is around the corner. Speed limits are well signed; usually 120km/h on main highways, or 90km/h on smaller ones.

Train

Bulgarian trains are fun, as carriage seats expose a bit more local life than you'll get on buses (though that can mean cigarette smoke). Trains – all run by the Bulgarian State Railways (BDZh) – are generally cheaper too. Some have better views than a bus (including the pretty Bansko–Septemvri route). *Ekspresen* (express) and *bârz* (fast) trains zip along similar to a bus' pace, while slow *pâtnicheski* (passenger) trains tinker on the tracks.

Most Europe-wide rail passes can be purchased in Bulgaria, but will not be good value for getting around Bulgaria.

For the trip, bring what food or water you'll need. Most train stations are signposted in Cyrillic, and no announcements are made on board.

Essentially all train stations have a left-luggage service (about 0.80lv for 24 hour per bag).

Listings in this chapter are for second-class seats and off-season schedules. An extra daily train or two runs some routes in summer, particularly serving the Black Sea coast.

Croatia

CONTENTS

Highlights	174
Itineraries	174
Climate & When to Go	175
History	175
People	178
Religion	179
Arts	179
Environment	179
Food & Drink	180
Zagreb	**181**
History	181
Orientation	184
Information	184
Sights	185
Tours	186
Festivals & Events	186
Sleeping	186
Eating	187
Drinking	188
Entertainment	188
Shopping	189
Getting There & Away	189
Getting Around	190
Istria	**190**
Poreč	191
Rovinj	192
Pula	195
Gulf of Kvarner	**197**
Rijeka	198
Opatija	200
Krk Island	201
Dalmatia	**202**
Zadar	202
Split	205
Solin (Salona)	210
Trogir	212
Hvar Island	212
Korčula Island	214
Orebić	216
Mljet Island	216
Dubrovnik	217
Croatia Directory	**223**
Accommodation	223
Activities	224
Books	224
Business Hours	225
Customs	225
Disabled Travellers	225

Embassies & Consulates	225
Festivals & Events	226
Holidays	226
Internet Access	226
Internet Resources	226
Media	226
Money	226
Post	227
Telephone	227
Tourist Information	227
Tours	227
Visas	228
Transport in Croatia	**228**
Getting There & Away	228
Getting Around	230

CROATIA

Croatia is Eastern Europe's best-kept secret. Its lush islands, unspoiled fishing villages, beaches, lakes, waterfalls and walled cities were the star attraction of the former Yugoslavia before it split apart in 1991. The essential fabulousness of the country was forgotten as the region descended into war, but travellers are once again discovering its many treasures.

With almost 6000km of coastline winding around innumerable bays and some 1100 islands offshore, there's a dream spot for every taste. The magnificent walled city of Dubrovnik, on the country's southern tip, is Croatia's crown jewel, with lovely Hvar and Korčula islands within easy reach. Istria, on the north coast, is famous for its delicious food, rocky beaches and relaxed, Italian-influenced lifestyle. Austrian influence is most pronounced in Croatia's capital, Zagreb, a calm and gracious city. Yet, wherever you go in Croatia, you'll find easy-going, tolerant people, accustomed to welcoming visitors and proud of the country they fought so hard to establish.

FAST FACTS

- **Area** 56,538 sq km
- **Capital** Zagreb
- **Currency** kuna (KN); €1=7.45KN; US$1=5.97KN; UK£1=10.73KN; A$1=4.33KN; ¥100=5.46KN; NZ$1=4.87KN
- **Famous for** neckties, war, Tito
- **Key Phrases** *bog* (hello), *doviđenja* (goodbye), *hvala* (thanks), *pardon* (sorry)
- **Official Language** Croatian
- **Population** 4.5 million
- **Telephone codes** country code ☎ 385; international access code ☎ 00
- **Visas** unnecessary for citizens of the EU, USA, Australia and Canada; see p228

HIGHLIGHTS

- The luminous marble streets, finely ornamented buildings and heavy stone walls of **Dubrovnik** (p217)
- The nightlife that throbs within the old palaces of **Hvar town** (p212) while the pine-covered island sleeps
- The excitement of a *moreška* sword dance in **Korčula** (p214)
- The untamed natural beauty of **Mljet** (p216) and its lakes, coves and island monastery
- The cobbled streets and unspoiled fishing port of **Rovinj** (p192)

ITINERARIES

- **One week** After a lovely day in Zagreb head down to Split. Spend a day exploring Diocletian's Palace and Solin before taking ferries to Hvar and Korčula. End with three days in Dubrovnik, taking a day trip to Mljet.
- **Two weeks** After two days in Zagreb, head to Pula for a three-day stay, taking day

CROATIA

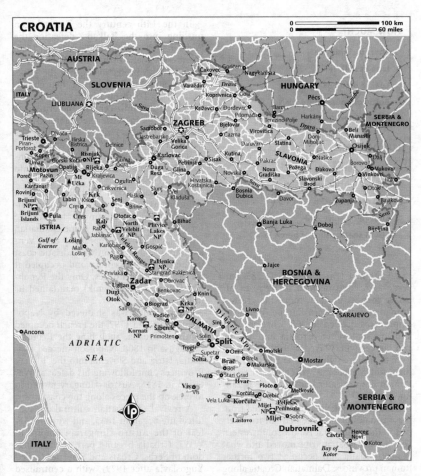

CROATIA

trips to Rovinj and Poreč. Head south to Zadar for a night and then go on to Split for a two-night stay. Take ferries to Hvar and Korčula before ending with three days in Dubrovnik and a day trip to Mljet.

CLIMATE & WHEN TO GO

The climate varies from Mediterranean along the Adriatic coast, with hot, dry summers and mild, rainy winters, to continental inland, with cold winters and warm summers. You can swim in the sea from mid-June until late September. Coastal temperatures are slightly warmer south of Split. The peak tourist season runs from mid-July to the end of August. Prices are

highest and accommodation scarcest during this period. See the Climate Charts on p874 for more.

The best time to be in Croatia is June. The weather is beautiful, the boats and excursions are running often and it's not yet too crowded. The end of May and the beginning of September are also good, especially if you're interested in hiking.

HISTORY

In 229 BC the Romans began their conquest of the indigenous Illyrians by establishing a colony at Solin (Salona), close to Split in Dalmatia. Emperor Augustus then extended the empire and created the provinces of Illyricum (Dalmatia and Bosnia)

CROATIA

HOW MUCH?

- **Short taxi ride** 35KN
- **Litre of milk** 7KN
- **Loaf of bread** 3KN
- **Bottle of house white** 20KN
- **Newspaper** 5KN

LONELY PLANET INDEX

- **Litre of petrol** 8KN
- **Litre of bottled water** 5KN
- **33cl of Karlovačko Beer** 10KN
- **Souvenir T-shirt** 75KN
- **Street snack – slice of burek** 7KN

and Pannonia (Croatia). In AD 285 Emperor Diocletian decided to retire to his palace fortress in Split, today the greatest Roman ruin in Eastern Europe. When the empire was divided in 395, what are now known as Slovenia, Croatia and Bosnia and Hercegovina stayed with the Western Roman Empire, while present Serbia, Kosovo and Macedonia went to the Eastern Roman Empire, later known as the Byzantine Empire.

Around 625, Slavic tribes migrated from present-day Poland. The Serbian tribe settled in the region that is now southwestern Serbia. The Croatian tribe moved into what is now Croatia and occupied two former Roman provinces: Dalmatian Croatia along the Adriatic, and Pannonian Croatia to the north.

By the early part of the 9th century both settlements had accepted Christianity but the northern Croats fell under Frankish domination while Dalmatian Croats came under the nominal control of the Byzantine Empire. The Dalmatian duke Tomislav united the two groups in 925 in a single kingdom that prospered for nearly 200 years.

Late in the 11th century the throne fell vacant and a series of power struggles weakened central authority and split the kingdom. The northern Croats, unable to agree upon a ruler, united with Hungary in 1102 for protection against the Orthodox Byzantine Empire.

In the 14th century the Turks began pushing into the Balkans, defeating the Serbs in 1389 and the Hungarians in 1526. Northern Croatia turned to the Habsburgs of Austria for protection against the Turks in 1527 and remained part of their empire until 1918. To form a buffer against the Turks, in the 16th century the Austrians invited Serbs to settle the Vojna Krajina (Military Frontier) north of Zadar. The Serbs in the borderlands had an autonomous administration under Austrian control; these areas were reincorporated into Croatia in 1881.

The Adriatic coast fell under Venetian influence as early as the 12th century, although Hungary continued to struggle for control of the region. Some Dalmatian cities changed hands repeatedly until Venice imposed its rule on the Adriatic coast in the early 15th century and occupied it for nearly four centuries. Only the Republic of Ragusa (Dubrovnik) maintained its independence.

After Venice was shattered by Napoleonic France in 1797, the French occupied southern Croatia, abolishing the Republic of Ragusa in 1808. Napoleon merged Dalmatia, Istria and Slovenia into the 'Illyrian Provinces', but following his defeat at Waterloo in 1815, Austria-Hungary moved in to pick up the pieces along the coast.

A revival of Croatian cultural and political life began in 1835, and with the defeat of the Austro-Hungarian empire in WWI, Croatia became part of the Kingdom of Serbs, Croats and Slovenes (called Yugoslavia after 1929), with a centralised government in Belgrade. Italy had been promised control of the Adriatic coast as an incentive to join the war against Austria-Hungary in 1915 and it held much of northern Dalmatia from 1918 to 1943, which explains the strong Italian influence along the coast.

After the German invasion of Yugoslavia in March 1941, a puppet government dominated by the fascist Ustaša movement was set up in Croatia and Bosnia and Hercegovina under Ante Pavelić (who fled to Argentina after WWII). At first the Ustaša tried to expel all Serbs from Croatia to Serbia. But when the Germans stopped this because of the problems it was causing the Ustaša launched an extermination campaign that rivalled the Nazis in its brutality. Although there is much controversy over the number of victims, estimates indicate that from 60,000 to 600,000 ethnic Serbs, Jews and Roma were murdered.

Not all Croats supported these policies, however. Josip Broz, known as Maršal Tito, was himself of Croat-Slovene parentage and tens of thousands of Croats fought bravely with his partisans. Massacres of Croats conducted by Serbian Četniks in southern Croatia and Bosnia forced almost all antifascist Croats into the communist ranks, where they joined the numerous Serbs trying to defend themselves from the Ustaša. In all, about a million people died violently in a war that was fought mostly in Croatia and Bosnia and Hercegovina.

Recent History

After the war, Maršal Tito became the prime minister of the new Yugoslav Federation and divided it into five republics: Croatia, Serbia, Slovenia, Bosnia and Hercegovina and Macedonia. Even with a Stalin-style system of state planning, Croatia and Slovenia moved far ahead of the southern republics economically, leading to demands by reformers, intellectuals and students for greater autonomy. The 'Croatian Spring' of 1971 caused a backlash and purge of the reformers, who were jailed or expelled from the Communist Party.

Tito's habit of borrowing from abroad to flood the country with cheap consumer goods produced an economic crisis after his death in 1980. The sinking economy provoked greater tension among Yugoslavia's ethnic groups, which came to a head when Serbian politician Slobodan Milošević whipped Serbs into a nationalist frenzy over the aspirations of the Albanian majority in the province of Kosovo.

Fearing a renewal of Serbian hegemony, many Croats felt the time had come to end more than four decades of communist rule and attain complete autonomy into the bargain. In the free elections of April 1990 Franjo Tudjman's Hrvatska Demokratska Zajednica (HDZ; Croatian Democratic Union) easily defeated the old Communist Party. On 22 December 1990 a new Croatian constitution was promulgated, changing the status of Serbs in Croatia to a national minority.

The constitution's failure to guarantee minority rights, and mass dismissals of Serbs from the public service, led the 600,000-strong ethnic Serb community to demand autonomy. When Croatia declared independence from Yugoslavia on 25 June 1991, the Serbian enclave of Krajina proclaimed its independence from Croatia.

Heavy fighting broke out in Krajina (the area around Knin, north of Split), Baranja (the area north of the Drava River opposite Osijek) and Slavonia (the region west of the Danube). The 180,000-member, 2000-tank Yugoslav People's Army, dominated by Serbian communists, began to intervene on its own authority in support of Serbian irregulars, under the pretext of halting ethnic violence.

In the three months following 25 June, a quarter of Croatia fell to Serbian militias and the federal army. In September the Croatian government ordered a blockade of 32 federal military installations in the republic, gaining much-needed military equipment. In response, the Yugoslav navy blockaded the Adriatic coast and laid siege to the strategic town of Vukovar on the Danube.

In early October 1991 the federal army and Montenegrin militia moved against Dubrovnik to protest against the ongoing blockade of their garrisons in Croatia. On 7 October the presidential palace in Zagreb was hit by rockets from Yugoslav air-force jets in an unsuccessful assassination attempt on President Tudjman. Heroic Vukovar finally fell on 19 November when the Yugoslav army ended a bloody three-month siege by concentrating 600 tanks and 30,000 soldiers there. During the six months of fighting in Croatia 10,000 people died, hundreds of thousands fled and tens of thousands of homes were deliberately destroyed.

Independence

After the Croatian parliament amended its constitution to protect minority and human rights the European Community (EC), succumbing to strong pressure from Germany, recognised Croatia in January 1992. This was followed three months later by US recognition and in May 1992 Croatia was admitted to the UN.

In January 1993 the Croatian army suddenly launched an offensive in southern

Krajina, pushing the Serbs back as much as 24km in some areas and recapturing strategic points. The Krajina Serbs vowed never to accept rule from Zagreb; in June 1993 they voted overwhelmingly to join the Bosnian Serbs (and eventually Greater Serbia).

The self-proclaimed 'Republic of Serbian Krajina' held elections in December 1993, which no international body recognised as legitimate or fair. Continued 'ethnic cleansing' left only about 900 Croats in Krajina out of an original population of 44,000.

On 1 May 1995 the Croatian army and police entered and occupied western Slavonia, east of Zagreb, causing some 15,000 Serbs to flee the region. At dawn on 4 August 1995 the military launched a massive assault on the rebel Serb capital of Knin. Outnumbered by two to one, the Serb army fled to northern Bosnia, along with about 150,000 civilians whose roots in the Krajina stretched back centuries. The military operation lasted just days, but was followed by months of terror. Widespread looting and burning of Serb villages, as well as attacks on the few remaining elderly Serbs, seemed designed to ensure the permanence of this massive population shift.

The Dayton Agreement, signed in Paris in December 1995, recognised Croatia's traditional borders and provided for the return of eastern Slavonia, a transition that was finally completed in January 1998.

Croatia's first president, Franjo Tudjman, died in 1999 after presiding over a regime notable for corruption, cronyism and suppression of dissent. The centre-left coalition that took power in 2000 swiftly made known their desire to enter the European mainstream but failed to make a dent in Croatia's serious economic problems. The road to privatisation has been bumpy, unemployment remains at a stubbornly high 22%, inflation is at 5.4% and the average monthly salary is only 5411KN (about €730). In the elections of 2003 Tudjman's reformed HDZ party was returned to power on a promise to reduce the detested Value Added Tax (VAT) from 22% to 20%. Ivo Sanader, called 'the grey man', was named prime minister but the HDZ parliamentary majority remains weak.

In April 2004 the European Commission recommended that negotiations be opened with a view to admitting Croatia to the EU. A major sticking point remains the return of Serbs who fled during the war. In many cases their homes have been reoccupied by Croats and no legal mechanism is in place to give back or provide new housing for the returning refugees. Croatia is also expected to comply with the International Criminal Tribunal for the former Yugoslavia (ICTY) by handing over accused war criminals.

PEOPLE

Croatia has a population of roughly 4.5 million people. Before the war Croatia had a population of nearly five million, of which 78% were Croats and 12% were Serbs. Bosnians, Hungarians, Italians, Czechs, Roma and Albanians made up the remaining 10%. Today Croats constitute 89% of the population, as there was a large influx of Croats from other parts of the former Yugoslavia after the war. Now, slightly less than 5% of the populations are Serb, followed by 0.5% Bosnians and about 0.4% each of Hungarians and Italians. Small communities of Czechs, Roma and Albanians complete the mosaic. Most Serbs live in eastern Croatia (Slavonia) where ethnic tensions between the Serbs and Croats run highest. The largest cities in Croatia are Zagreb (780,000), Split (188,700), Rijeka (144,000), Osijek (114,600) and Zadar (72,700).

Croats are united by a common religion, Catholicism, and a common sense of themselves as European. If you ask a Croat what distinguishes Croatian culture from Bosnian or Serbian culture, the answer is likely to be a variant of 'We are Western and they are Eastern'. Even Croats who bear no particular ill will towards other ethnicities will nonetheless note that their former compatriots in Bosnia and Hercegovina, Macedonia and Serbia and Montenegro eat different food, listen to different music, have different customs and, of course, go to different churches.

Although the shelling of Dubrovnik and the atrocities committed in eastern Slavonia and the Krajina have left a bitter taste in those regions, many Croatians are increasingly open to questioning the conduct of the 'Homeland War'. Self-examining books and articles are a staple of the country's intellectual life but the extradition to the Hague of Croatian generals accused of war crimes remains highly controversial.

RELIGION

Croats are overwhelmingly Roman Catholic, while virtually all Serbs belong to the Eastern Orthodox Church. In addition to doctrinal differences, Orthodox Christians venerate icons, allow priests to marry and do not accept the authority of the Roman Catholic pope. Long suppressed under communism, Catholicism is undergoing a strong resurgence in Croatia and churches have good attendance on Sunday. The Pope has visited Croatia several times and religious holidays are scrupulously observed. Muslims make up 1.2% of the population and Protestants 0.4%, with a tiny Jewish population in Zagreb.

ARTS

The exhibition pavilion (p185) in Zagreb is a good place to keep up with the latest developments in Croatian art.

Painting

Vlaho Bukovac (1855–1922) was the most notable Croatian painter in the late 19th century. Important early-20th-century painters include Miroslav Kraljević (1885–1913) and Josip Račić (1885–1908). Post-WWII artists experimented with abstract expressionism but this period is best remembered for the naive art that was typified by Ivan Generalić (1914–92). Recent trends have included minimalism, conceptual art and pop art. Contemporary artists that are attracting notice include Jasna Barišić of Zadar, Andrea Musa of Split, and Višeslav Aralica and Ivana Ožetski of Zagreb.

Sculpture

The work of sculptor Ivan Meštrović (1883–1962) is seen in town squares throughout Croatia. Besides creating public monuments, Meštrović designed imposing buildings, such as the circular Croatian History Museum (p185) in Zagreb. Both his sculptures and architecture display the powerful classical restraint he learnt from Auguste Rodin. Meštrović's studio in Zagreb (p185) and his retirement home at Split (p208) have been made into galleries of his work.

Music & Dance

Croatian folk music has many influences. The *kolo*, a lively Slavic round dance where men and women alternate in the circle, is accompanied by Roma-style violinists or players of the *tambura*, a three- or five-string mandolin popular throughout the country. The measured guitar-playing and rhythmic accordions of Dalmatia have a gentle Italian air.

A recommended recording available locally on CD is *Narodne Pjesme i Plesovi Sjeverne Hrvatske* (Northern Croatian Folk Songs and Dances) by the Croatian folkloric ensemble Lado. The 22 tracks on this album represent nine regions, with everything from haunting Balkan voices reminiscent of Bulgaria to lively Mediterranean dance rhythms. Traditional Croatian music has influenced other musicians, most notable the Croatian-American jazz singer Helen Merrill who recorded Croatian melodies on her album, *Jelena Ana Milcetic a.k.a. Helen Merrill*.

On the radio, you're likely to hear a lot of 'turbofolk', charged up folk music that is widely popular throughout former Yugoslavia. Split-born Severina Vuckovic enjoys tremendous popularity, probably enhanced by a compromising video circulating on the Internet. Also popular are Doris Dragović and Mirakul Gibonni.

ENVIRONMENT
The Land

Croatia is half the size of present-day Serbia and Montenegro in area and population. The republic swings around like a boomerang from the Pannonian plains of Slavonia between the Sava, Drava and Danube Rivers, across hilly central Croatia to the Istrian Peninsula, then south through Dalmatia along the rugged Adriatic coast.

The narrow Croatian coastal belt at the foot of the Dinaric Alps is only about 600km long as the crow flies, but it's so indented that the actual length is 1778km. If the 4012km of coastline around the offshore islands is added to the total, the length becomes 5790km. Most of the 'beaches' along this jagged coast consist of slabs of rock sprinkled with naturists. Don't come expecting to find sand, but the waters are sparkling clean, even around large towns.

Croatia's offshore islands are every bit as beautiful as those off the coast of Greece. There are 1185 islands and islets along the tectonically submerged Adriatic coastline, 66 inhabited. The largest are Cres, Krk,

Lošinj, Pag and Rab in the north; Dugi Otok in the middle; and Brač, Hvar, Korčula, Mljet and Vis in the south. Most are barren and elongated from northwest to southeast, with high mountains that drop right into the sea.

National Parks

When the Yugoslav Federation collapsed, eight of its finest national parks ended up in Croatia, occupying nearly 10% of the country. Brijuni near Pula is the most carefully cultivated park, with well-preserved Mediterranean holm oak forests. The mountainous Risnjak National Park near Delnice, east of Rijeka, is named after one of its inhabitants – the *ris* (lynx).

Dense forests of beech and black pine in the Paklenica National Park near Zadar are home to a number of endemic insects, reptiles and birds. The abundant plant and animal life, including bears, wolves and deer, in the Plitvice Lakes National Park between Zagreb and Zadar has warranted its inclusion on Unesco's list of World Natural Heritage Sites. Both Plitvice Lakes and Krka National Parks (near Šibenik) feature a dramatic series of cascades and incredible turquoise lakes.

The 101 stark and rocky islands of the Kornati Archipelago and National Park make it the largest in the Mediterranean. The island of Mljet near Korčula also contains a forested national park, and the North Velebit National Park includes Croatia's longest mountain range.

Environmental Issues

The lack of heavy industry in Croatia has left the country largely free of industrial pollution, but its forests are under threat from acid rain from neighbouring countries. The dry summers and brisk *maestral*

winds pose substantial fire hazards along the coast. The sea along the Adriatic coast is among the world's cleanest especially throughout Istria and the southern Adriatic. Waste disposal is a pressing problem in Croatia, with insufficient and poorly regulated disposal sites.

FOOD & DRINK

A restaurant (*restauracija*) or pub may also be called a *gostionica* and a café is known as a *kavana*. Self-service cafeterias are quick, easy and inexpensive, though the quality of the food tends to vary quite a lot. Better restaurants aren't that much more expensive if you choose carefully. The cheapest dishes are pasta and risotto, which can be filling meals. Fish dishes are often charged by weight (from 280KN to 320KN per kilogram), which makes it difficult to know how much a certain dish will cost but an average portion is about 250g. Some restaurants tack on a 10% cover charge, which is *supposed* to be mentioned on the menu.

Breakfast is included in the price of the hotels mentioned in this chapter and usually includes a juice drink, bread, cheese, yogurt, cereal and cold cuts, as well as coffee and tea. No restaurants serve breakfast.

A load of fruit and vegetables from the local market can make a healthy, cheap picnic lunch. There are plenty of supermarkets in Croatia; cheese, cold cuts, bread, wine and milk are readily available and fairly cheap. The person behind the meat counter at supermarkets will make a big cheese or bologna sandwich for you upon request and you only pay the price of the ingredients.

Staples & Specialities

Croatian meals often start with a dish of locally smoked ham or Pag cheese with olives. A Zagreb speciality is *štrukli* (boiled

---

MYSTERIOUS FLAVOURS

No Croatian cook could do without it yet it is almost unknown outside former Yugoslavia. It's the secret ingredient in nearly every fish, vegetable or meat dish yet it's hard to describe what it actually contains. What is it ? It's 'Vegeta', sold by the kilo in nearly every grocery store. We know that there's salt, sugar, corn starch and various dehydrated vegetables plus 'flavour enhancers' that end in –ate in there. There are also 'spices' of indeterminate composition. We don't know how it works its magic in Croatian dishes, but even the simplest sauces are imbued with subtle flavours. Pick up a package and add a tablespoon or so to your favourite tomato sauce. *Dobar tek!* (Bon appetit!)

cheesecake), served either plain as a starter or sugared as a dessert. In the north you also might begin with a hearty *Zagorska juha od krumpira* (potato soup Zagorje style) or *manistra od bobića* (beans and fresh maize soup), while coastal folk follow the Italian habit of beginning with a serving of spaghetti or risotto. *Risotto neri* (black risotto) made from squid in its own ink is a particular delicacy.

For a main meal, the Adriatic coast excels in seafood, including scampi (look for *scampi bouzzara*), *prstaci* (shellfish), *lignje* (calamari) and Dalmatian *brodet* (fish stew served with polenta). Istria is known for its *tartufe* (truffles), which frequently appear in risotto or pasta dishes or flavouring meat. The season is from October to January; any other time the chef is using preserved truffles. In Zagreb and in the north you'll find exquisite spit-roasted goose, duck and lamb. Turkey with *mlinci* (baked noodles) is another Zagrebian wonder.

For fast food you can usually snack on *čevapčići* (spicy beef or pork meatballs), *ražnjići* (shish kebab), *burek* (a greasy layered pie made with meat) or *sira* (cheese), which is cut on a huge metal tray.

It's customary to have a small glass of brandy before a meal and to accompany the food with one of Croatia's fine wines – there are about 700 to choose from! Croatians often mix their wine with water, calling it *bevanda*. Croatia is also famous for its *šljivovica* (plum brandies), *travarica* (herbal brandies), *vinjak* (cognacs) and liqueurs, such as maraschino (a cherry liqueur made in Zadar) or herbal *pelinkovac*. Italian-style espresso is popular in Croatia.

Zagreb's Ožujsko *pivo* (beer) is very good but Karlovačko *pivo* from Karlovac is even better. You'll probably want to practise saying *živjeli!* (cheers!).

Vegetarians & Vegans

Outside of Zagreb, vegetarian restaurants are few and far between but Croatia's vegetables are usually locally grown and quite tasty. *Blitva* (swiss chard) is a nutritious side dish often served with potatoes. Pasta, risotto and pizza are often made from scratch and lacto-ovo vegetarians will appreciate Croatia's wide variety of cheese. Look for the sharp lamb's-milk cheese from the island of Pag.

ZAGREB

☎ 01 / pop 780,000

Zagreb is finally coming into its own as an intriguing combination of Eastern and Western Europe. The sober Austro-Hungarian architecture in the town centre houses newly opened boutiques with the latest fashions from France and Italy. Bohemian cafés and sleek cocktail bars enliven the medieval streets of the old Kaptol and Gradec neighbourhoods. The Croatian appreciation of food is divided between its traditional hearty meat and potatoes restaurants and a new smattering of more worldly flavours.

Spreading up from the Sava River, Zagreb sits on the southern slopes of Mt Medvednica and throbs with the energy you would expect from a capital city, but the bustle of business life is interrupted by the long, refreshing stretch of park that bisects the town centre. With simmering nightlife and a wealth of outdoor cafés, packed from the first hint of mild weather, there's no shortage of diversions. Plus, there's an assortment of museums and galleries to explore and a regular concert schedule for the culturally minded.

HISTORY

Medieval Zagreb developed from the 11th to the 13th centuries in the twin villages

---

ZAGREB IN TWO DAYS

From Trg Jelačića, take a stroll through Kaptol and Gradec, stopping to admire the **Cathedral** (p185), the **Archiepiscopal Palace** (p185), the **Dolac vegetable market** (p185), the **Stone Gate** (p185), **St Mark's Church** (p185) and the **Banski Dvori Palace** (p185) for the changing of the guard. Visit the **Museum of the City of Zagreb** (p185) and the **Meštrović Studio** (p185). Have a drink at **Indy's** (p188) and dine at **Baltazar** (p188) or **Kaptolska Klet** (p187). On day two, explore the lower town. Visit the **Museum Mimara** (p186), the **Strossmayer Gallery of Old Masters** (p185) and the **Archaeological Museum** (p186). Take a break in the park along Zrinjskog. Head to **Boban** (p187) for lunch and **Konoba Čiho** (p188) for dinner.

ZAGREB

A **B** **C** **D**

1

16

53

75

38

To Australian Embassy (100m);
Romanian Embassy (500m);
Mirogoj (2km)

Kaptol

Miklousiceva

Zvonimirova

Ribnjak

Park
Ribnjak

72

28

35

Demetrova

Bazaricetova

Opaticka

Basaricekova

13

23 42

Markovicev 40
trg

Gradec

26 65 27

Dverce
preichova

Kamenita

Kuslanova

43

70

Opatovina

Kaptol

58

25

2

To Bosnian Embassy (400m);
Hungarian Embassy(500m);
Serbia & Montenegro
Embassy (1km); Bulgarian
Embassy (1km)

Britanski
trg

Aleksandrove
stube

Strossajera

Dezmanova

Vranicanijeva

Strossmayerovo

Jezuitski
trg

33

34 41

setaliste
stube Ivana Zajca

Zakmardija

Pod
zidom

Skalinska

29

Vlaska

Basaniceva

Cesarceva

56

60

Ilica

32

47

62 52

76

Ilica

77 57 78

Trg
Jelacica

10

1

Jurisiceva

Amruseva

14

To ADP Gloria (50m);
Hotel Ilica (250m)

55

Frankopanska

Gundelicceva

Varsavska

66

Trg Petra
Preradovica

Oktagon

63

49

2

Bogoviceva

Petrinjska

Dalmatinska

Medulicceva

Prilaz Gjure Dezelica

18 5

11

Masarykova

Preradoviceva

Berislaviceva

Teslina

19

54

22

67

Trg Nicole
Subica
Zrinskog
(Zrinjevac)

81

20

4

4

Klaiceva

Roosveltov
trg

37

30

73

8

Trg
Mazuranicev

64

68

Donji Grad

Andrije Hebranga

Kovaciceva

3

Katanciceva

36

44

15

Strossmajerov
trg

Krsnjavoga

79

82

Trg brace
Mazuranicev

Vukotinoviceva

Marulicev
trg

39

21

Svaciicev
trg

Kumiciceva

Haulikova

Baruna Trenka

71

Tomiceva

31

12

Trg kralja
Tomislava

51

5

Jukiceva

Vodnikova

Runjaninova

Mihanoviceva

24

Botanic Gardens

Starcevicev
trg

Grgurova

50

46

Train Station

Tmjanska

6

7

Savska

Koturaska

Ulica

Bednjanska

Zelmiska

Miramarska

Miramarska

Paromlinska

Padicev
trg

P

83

74

To New Zealand Consulate
(500m); Motel Plitvice; Jarun Lake;
Studenski dom Stjepan Radic;
Studenthotel Cvjetno Naselje;
Brazil (1km); Aquarius (1.5km);
Plitvice (140km)

To German Embassy (150m);
Hotel Fala (1km);
Di Prom (3km)

To US Embassy (10km);
Airport (17km)

0 — 200 m
0 — 0.1 miles

INFORMATION
Albanian Embassy	1	D3
Algoritam	2	C3
Art Net Club	3	C4
Atlas Travel Agency	4	D4
Canadian Embassy	5	A3
Croatian National Tourist Board	6	E2
Czech Embassy	7	A6
Dali Travel	(see 47)	
Dental Emergency	8	B4
Long-Distance Telephone Centre	(see 9)	
Main Post Office	9	E5
Main Tourist Office	10	D3
Marko Polo	11	B3
National Parks Information Office	12	D5
Petecin	13	D1
Pharmacy	14	A3
Police Station	15	D4
Polish Embassy	16	B1
Predom	17	E4
Slovakian Embassy	18	A3
Slovenian Embassy	(see 7)	
Sublink	19	C3
Tourist Office Annex	20	D4
Zagreb County Tourist Association	21	C4

SIGHTS & ACTIVITIES (pp185-6)
Archaeological Museum	22	D3
Archiepiscopal Palace	(see 25)	
Banski Dvori Palace	23	C1
Botanic Gardens	24	B5
Cathedral of the Assumption of the Blessed Virgin Mary	25	D2
Croatian History Museum	26	B2
Croatian Naive Art Museum	27	C2
Croatian Natural History Museum	28	B1
Dolac Vegetable Market	29	D2
Ethnographic Museum	30	B4
Exhibition Pavilion	31	D4
Funicular Railway	32	C2
Galerija Klovićevi Dvori	33	C2
Lotršćak Tower	34	C2
Meštrović Studio	35	C1
Modern Gallery	36	D4
Museum Mimara	37	A4
Museum of the City of Zagreb	38	C1
National Library	39	B5
Sabor	40	C2
St Catherine's Church	41	C2
St Mark's Church	42	C1
Stone Gate	43	C2
Strossmayer Gallery of Old Masters	44	D4

SLEEPING (pp186-7)
Arcotel Allegra	45	E5
Central Hotel	46	D5
Croatian YHA	47	B2
Evistas	48	E5
Hotel Dubrovnik	49	C3
Hotel Esplanade	50	C5
Omladinski Hotel	51	D5
Pansion Jägerhorn	52	C3

EATING (pp187-8)
Baltazar	53	D1
Boban	54	C3
Frankopan	55	B3
Fruit & Vegetable Market	56	A3
Gavrilović	57	C3
Kaptolska Klet	58	D2
Konoba Čiho	59	E4
Makrovona	60	A3
Mimice	61	E3
Murano 2000	(see 50)	
Vincek	62	C2

DRINKING (p188)
Bulldog	63	C3
Indy's	(see 65)	
Kazališna Kavana	64	B4
Tolkien's House	65	C2

ENTERTAINMENT (pp188-9)
Academy of Music	66	B3
BP Club	67	C3
Croatian National Theatre	68	B4
Glob@l	69	E4
Kazalište Komedija	(see 76)	
Komedija Theatre	70	D2
Puppet Theatre	71	D4
Purgeraj	72	D1
Sokol klub	73	B4
Vatroslav Lisinski Concert Hall	74	D6

SHOPPING (p189)
Bornstein	75	D1
Kroata Cravata	76	C3
Rokotvorine	77	C3
Vartek's department store	78	D3

TRANSPORT (p189)
Avis Autotehna	79	A4
Budget Rent-a-Car	80	E4
Croatia Airlines	81	D3
Hertz	82	A4

OTHER
City Hall	83	C6

Šalata

Langov trg

To KBC Rebro (1km);
Ravnice Hostel (2km);
Maksimir Stadium;
Zoo (3km)

Vlaška

Iblerov trg

Trg hrvatskih velikana

Martićeva

To HAK Information Centre (50m)

Đorđićeva

Trg Žrtava Fašizma

Boškovićeva

Križanićeva

Trg kralja Petra Krešimira IV

P Hatza

Kneza Borne

Augusta Šenoe

To Bus Station (100m);
UK Embassy (1.6km)

Branimirova

Strojarska c

Tmjanska

CROATIA

of Kaptol and Gradec, which make up the city's hilly Old Town. Kaptol grew around St Stephen's Cathedral (now renamed the Cathedral of the Assumption of the Blessed Virgin Mary) and Gradec centred on St Mark's Church. The two hill-top administrations were bitter and often warring rivals until a common threat in the form of Turkish invaders emerged in the 15th century. The two communities merged and became Zagreb, capital of the small portion of Croatia that hadn't fallen to the Turks in the 16th century. As the Turkish threat receded in the 18th century, the town expanded and the population grew. It was the centre of intellectual and political life under the Austro-Hungarian empire and became capital of the Independent State of Croatia in 1941 after the German invasion. The 'independent state' was in fact a Nazi puppet regime in the hands of Ante Pavelić and the Ustaša movement, even though most Zagrebians supported Tito's partisans.

In postwar Yugoslavia Zagreb took second place to Belgrade but continued expanding. The area south of the Sava River developed into a new district, Novi Zagreb, replete with the glum residential blocks that were a hallmark of postwar Eastern European architecture. Zagreb has been capital of Croatia since 1991 when the country became independent.

ORIENTATION

The city is divided into Lower Zagreb, where most shops, restaurants and businesses are located, and Upper Zagreb, defined by the two hills of Kaptol and Gradec. As you come out of the train station, you'll see a series of parks and pavilions directly in front of you and the twin neo-Gothic towers of the cathedral in Kaptol in the distance. Trg Jelačića, beyond the northern end of the parks, is the main city square of Lower Zagreb. The bus station is 1km east of the train station. Tram Nos 2 and 6 run from the bus station to the train station, with No 6 continuing to Trg Jelačića.

INFORMATION

Bookshops

Algoritam (Gajeva; Hotel Dubrovnik) Off Trg Jelačića, Algoritam has a wide selection of books and magazines to choose from in English, French, German, Italian and Croatian.

Emergency

Police station (☎ 45 63 311; Petrinjska 30) Assists foreigners with visa problems.

Internet Access

Art Net Club (☎ 45 58 471; Preradovićeva 25; per hr 20KN; ☯ 9am-11pm) Zagreb's flashiest Internet café, it frequently hosts concerts and performances.
Sublink (☎ 48 11 329; Teslina 12; per hr 20KN; ☯ 9am-10pm Mon-Sat, 3-10pm Sun) It was here first and has a comfortable set up.

Laundry

If you're staying in private accommodation you can usually arrange with the owner to do your laundry, which would be cheaper than the two options listed below. Five kilograms of laundry will cost about 60KN.
Petecin (Kaptol 11; ☯ 8am-8pm Mon-Fri)
Predom (Draškovićeva 31; ☯ 7am-7pm Mon-Fri)

Left Luggage

Garderoba (per day 10KN; ☯ 24hr) In the train station.
Garderoba (per hr 1.20KN; ☯ 5am-10pm Mon-Sat, 6am-10pm Sun) In the bus station.

Medical Services

Dental Emergency (☎ 48 28 488; Perkovčeva 3; ☯ 24hr)
KBC Rebro (☎ 23 88 888; Kišpatićeva 12; ☯ 24hr) East of the city, it provides emergency aid.
Pharmacy (☎ 48 48 450; Ilica 43; ☯ 24hr)

Money

There are ATMs at the bus and train stations and the airport as well as numerous locations around town. Exchange offices at the bus and train stations change money at the bank rate with 1.5% commission. Both the banks in the train station (open 7am to 9pm) and the bus station (open 6am to 8pm) accept travellers cheques.
Atlas travel agency (☎ 48 13 933; Zrinjevac 17) The Amex representative in Zagreb.

Post

Main Post Office (Branimirova 4; ☯ 24hr Mon-Sat, 1pm-midnight Sun) Holds poste-restante mail. This post office is also the best place to make long-distance telephone calls and send packages.

Tourist Information

Main tourist office (☎ 48 14 051; www.zagreb -touristinfo.hr; Trg Jelačića 11; ☯ 8.30am-8pm Mon-Fri, 9am-5pm Sat, 10am-4pm Sun) Distributes city maps and free leaflets. It also sells the Zagreb Card, which costs 60KN and includes 72 hours of free transport and a 50% discount on museums.

Marko Polo (☎ 48 15 216; Masarykova 24) Handles information and ticketing for Jadrolinija's coastal ferries.

National Park Information Office (☎ 46 13 586; Trg Tomislava 19; ☷ 8am-4pm Mon-Fri) Has details on Croatia's national parks.

Tourist office annex (☎ 49 21 645; Trg Nikole Šubića Zrinjskog 14; ☷ 9am-6pm Mon-Fri) Same services as the main tourist office, but stocks fewer publications.

Zagreb County Tourist Association (☎ 48 73 665; www.tzzz.hr; Preradovićeva 42; ☷ 8am-4pm Mon-Fri) Has information about attractions in the region outside Zagreb.

Travel Agencies

Dali Travel (☎ 48 47 472; hfhs-cms@zg.htnet.hr; Dežmanova 9; ☷ 9am-5pm Mon-Fri) The travel branch of the Croatian YHA. Can provide information on HI hostels throughout Croatia and make advance bookings.

SIGHTS
Kaptol

Zagreb's colourful **Dolac vegetable market** (☷ 7am-2pm) is just up the steps from Trg Jelačića and continues north along Opatovina. The twin neo-Gothic spires of the 1899 **Cathedral of the Assumption of the Blessed Virgin Mary** (formerly known as St Stephen's Cathedral) are nearby. Elements of the medieval cathedral on this site, destroyed by an earthquake in 1880, can be seen inside, including 13th-century frescoes, Renaissance pews, marble altars and a baroque pulpit. The baroque **Archiepiscopal Palace** surrounds the cathedral, as do 16th-century fortifications constructed when Zagreb was threatened by the Turks.

Gradec

From ul Radićeva 5, off Trg Jelačića, a pedestrian walkway called stube Ivana Zakmardija leads to the **Lotršćak Tower** (☎ 48 51 768; admission 5KN; ☷ 11am-7pm Tue-Sun) and a **funicular railway** (one way 3KN; ☷ 6.30am-9pm) built in 1888, which connects the lower and upper towns. The tower has a sweeping 360-degree view of the city. To the east is the baroque **St Catherine's Church**, with Jezuitski trg beyond. The **Galerija Klovićevi Dvori** (☎ 48 51 926; Jezuitski trg 4; adult/student 20/10KN; ☷ 11am-7pm Tue-Sun) is Zagreb's premier exhibition hall where superb art shows are staged. Further north and to the east is the 13th-century

Stone Gate, with a painting of the Virgin, which escaped the devastating fire of 1731.

Gothic **St Mark's Church** (☎ 48 51 611; Markovićev trg; ☷ 11am-4pm & 5.30-7pm) marks the centre of Gradec. Inside are works by Ivan Meštrović, Croatia's most famous modern sculptor. On the eastern side of St Mark's is the **Sabor** (1908), Croatia's National Assembly.

West of the church is the 18th-century **Banski Dvori Palace**, the presidential palace, with guards at the door in red ceremonial uniform. Between April and September there is a changing of the guard ceremony at noon at the weekend.

Not far from the palace is the former **Meštrović Studio** (☎ 48 51 123; Mletačka 8; adult/concession 20/10KN; ☷ 10am-6pm Tue-Fri, 10am-2pm Sat), now housing an excellent collection of some 100 sculptures, drawings, lithographs and furniture created by the artist. Other museums nearby include the less-than-gripping **Croatian History Museum** (☎ 48 51 900; Matoševa 9; temporary exhibitions adult/concession 10/5KN; ☷ 10am-5pm Mon-Fri, 10am-1pm Sat & Sun); the lively and colourful **Croatian Naive Art Museum** (☎ 48 51 911; Ćirilometodska 3; adult/concession 10/5KN; ☷ 10am-6pm Tue-Fri, 10am-1pm Sat & Sun); and also the **Croatian Natural History Museum** (☎ 48 51 700; Demetrova 1; adult/concession 15/7KN; ☷ 10am-5pm Tue-Fri, 10am-1pm Sat & Sun) which has a collection of prehistoric tools and bones plus exhibits on the evolution of plant and animal life in Croatia. The best is the **Museum of the City of Zagreb** (☎ 48 51 364; Opatička 20; adult/concession 20/10KN; ☷ 10am-6pm Tue-Fri, 10am-1pm Sat & Sun), with a scale model of old Gradec, atmospheric background music, and interactive exhibits that fascinate kids. Summaries in English and German are in each room of the museum, which is in the former Convent of St Claire (1650).

Lower Town

Zagreb really is a city of museums. There are four in the parks between the train station and Trg Jelačića. The yellow **exhibition pavilion** (1897) across the park from the station presents changing contemporary art exhibitions. The second building north, also in the park, houses the **Strossmayer Gallery of Old Masters** (☎ 48 95 115; adult/concession 20/15KN; ☷ 10am-1pm & 5-7pm Tue, 10am-1pm Wed-Sun). When it's closed you can still enter the interior courtyard to see the Baška

CROATIA

Slab (1102) from the island of Krk, one of the oldest inscriptions in the Croatian language.

The fascinating **Archaeological Museum** (☎ 48 73 101; Trg Nikole Šubića Zrinjskog 19; adult/concession 20/10KN; ⏰ 10am-5pm Tue-Fri, 10am-1pm Sat & Sun) has a wide-ranging display of artefacts from prehistoric times through to the medieval period. The ambient sounds and light put you in a contemplative mood. Behind the museum is a garden of Roman sculpture that is turned into a pleasant open-air café in the summer.

West of the Centre

The **Museum Mimara** (☎ 48 28 100; Rooseveltov trg 5; adult/concession 20/15KN; ⏰ 10am-5pm Tue, Wed, Fri & Sat, 10am-7pm Thu, 10am-2pm Sun) houses a diverse collection amassed by Ante Topić Mimara and donated to Croatia. Housed in a neo-Renaissance palace, the collection includes icons, glassware, sculpture, Oriental art and works by renowned painters such as Rembrandt, Velázquez, Raphael and Degas. The **Modern Gallery** (☎ 49 22 368; A Hebrangova 1) presents temporary exhibitions that offer an excellent chance to catch up with the latest in Croatian painting.

The neobaroque **Croatian National Theatre** (Trg Maršala Tita 15) dates from 1895 and has Ivan Meštrović's sculpture *Fountain of Life* (1905) in front. The **Ethnographic Museum** (☎ 48 26 220; Trg Mažuranićev 14; adult/concession 15/10KN; ⏰ 10am-6pm Tue-Thu, 10am-1pm Fri-Sun) has a large collection of Croatian folk costumes, accompanied by English captions. To the south is the Art-Nouveau **National Library** (1907). The **Botanical Gardens** (Mihanovićeva; admission free; ⏰ 9am-7pm Tue-Sun) is attractive for its plants and landscaping, as well as its restful corners, perfect for a family picnic.

Out of town

A 20-minute ride north of the city centre on bus No 106 from the cathedral takes you to **Mirogoj** (Medvednica; ⏰ 6am-10pm), one of the most beautiful cemeteries in Europe. The sculptured and artfully designed tombs lie beyond a majestic arcade topped by a string of cupolas. Don't miss the flower-bedecked tomb of Croatia's last president-dictator, Franjo Tudjman. Some Croats were very sad at his death, some were slightly sad, and some wondered if the international community would have paid Croatia as much

for his extradition to the war crimes tribunal at the Hague as they paid Serbia for Milošević.

TOURS

The main tourist office sells tickets for two-hour walking tours (95KN), which operate Monday afternoon and Tuesday and Thursday mornings leaving from in front of the tourist office on Trg Jelačića, as well as three-hour bus tours (150KN) that operate Wednesday and Friday afternoons and weekend mornings. Tours are conducted by noted journalists and novelists.

FESTIVALS & EVENTS

During odd-numbered years in April there's the **Zagreb Biennial of Contemporary Music**, Croatia's most important music event. Zagreb also hosts a **festival of animated films** (www.animafest.hr) during even-numbered years in June and a **film festival** (www.zagreb filmfestival.com) in October. Croatia's largest international fairs are the Zagreb spring (mid-April) and autumn (mid-September) grand trade fairs. In July and August the **Zagreb Summer Festival** presents a cycle of concerts and theatre performances on open stages in the upper town. For a complete listing of Zagreb events, see www.zagreb -convention.hr.

SLEEPING

Budget accommodation is in short supply in Zagreb. An early arrival is recommended, since private room–finding agencies are an attractive alternative and usually refuse telephone bookings. Prices for private rooms run from about 170/220KN per single/double, and apartments cost at least 300KN per night. There's usually a surcharge for staying only one night. **Evistas** (☎ 48 39 554; fax 48 39 543; evistas@zg.htnet.hr; Augusta Šenoe 28; s 172-227KN, d 234-314KN, apt 364-835KN; ⏰ 9am-1.30pm & 3-8pm Mon-Fri, 9.30am-5pm Sat) is closest to the train station. **ADP Gloria** (☎ 48 23 567; www.adp-glorija .com, in Croatian; Britanski trg 5; ⏰ closed Sun), just west of town, is another option for private rooms. **Di Prom** (☎ 65 50 039; fax 65 50 233; Trnsko 25a; ⏰ closed Sun) is south of the town centre with rooms in Novi Zagreb.

Budget

Motel Plitvice (☎ 65 30 444; fax 65 30 445) It's not in Plitvice at all but near the town of Lučko on the Obilaznica Hwy southwest of Zagreb. The motel sometimes runs a minibus from Savski Most. Call to find out if and when the service is operating. Otherwise, take tram No 7 or 14 to Savski Most and then the 125, 165 or 168 bus to Lučko village, from where the motel/camping ground is about a 20-minute walk. There's a lake and sports centre nearby and it's open year-round.

Omladinski Hotel (☎ 48 41 261; fax 48 41 269; Petrinjska 77; per person in 6/3-bed dm 73/83KN, d 211KN) Some say it's a dump. We prefer to call it an auditory and visual challenge with maintenance issues. Checkout is at 9am. At least it's in the centre of town.

Ravnice Hostel (☎/fax 23 32 325; www.ravnice -youth-hostel.hr; Ravnice 38d; dm 99KN; ☐) This is really a delightful option, designed and run by an Australian woman. Comfortable, clean rooms have two, four or 10 beds. Solo female travellers would be most comfortable here. Tram Nos 4, 7, 11 and 12 will take you there.

Studentski dom Stjepan Radić (☎ 36 34 255; Jarunska 3; dm 125KN) This student dorm is near Jarun Lake and its nightlife in the southwest of the city. Take tram No 5 or 17.

Studenthotel Cvjetno Naselje (☎ 61 91 239; dm 210KN; ☽ mid-Jul–Sep) Off Slavonska avenija in the south of the city, this dormitory has good rooms each with a bathroom. Take tram No 4, 5, 14, 16 or 17 southwest on Savska cesta to 'Vjesnik'.

Mid-Range

Hotel Ilica (☎ 37 77 522; www.hotel-ilica.hr; in Croatian; Ilica 102; s/d/tw/apt 349/449/549/749KN; P ☒) For a small hotel, you can't do better than this stylish joint just west of town with comfortable rooms and friendly service. Tram Nos 6, 11 and 12 stop right outside the entrance.

Hotel Fala (☎/fax 61 94 498; www.hotel-fala-zg.hr; Trnjanske ledine 18; s/d 350/470KN; P ☒) The small rooms have no frills but the price is right and you're not too terribly far from the town centre.

Central Hotel (☎ 48 41 122; www.hotel-central.hr; Branimirova 3; s/d 520/680KN; ☒) Entirely renovated with modern, plush rooms, this hotel represents good value for money, especially given its location across from the train station. The service is coldly efficient.

Pansion Jägerhorn (☎ 48 33 877; fax 48 33 573; Ilica 14; s/d/apt 550/750/900KN; ☒) The downstairs

restaurant is known for serving wild game but there's no wildness in the civilised rooms here. Everything is up to date and well maintained.

Hotel Dubrovnik (☎ 48 73 555; www.hotel-dubrov nik.htnet.hr; Gajeva 1; s/d from 650/850KN; ☒) Business travellers love this modern hotel right in the centre of town. Services, rooms and facilities are all first-rate.

Top End

Arcotel Allegra (☎ 46 96 000; www.arcotel.at/allegra; Branimirova 29; r 680-2410KN; P ☒ ☒ ☐) Billing itself as Zagreb's first 'lifestyle hotel', it's clear that the style of life is quite high here. Your lifestyle, should you choose to accept it, will include ultracontemporary Mediterranean-inspired décor, and a fitness centre, plus rooms and accoutrements for your business meetings. The hotel is gay friendly.

Hotel Esplanade (☎ 45 66 666; esplanade@esplanade .hr; Mihanovićeva 1; s/d 1875/2025KN; P ☒ ☒ ☐) This six-storey, 215-room hotel, built in 1924, is an Art-Nouveau masterpiece with marble-panelled halls and stately rooms equipped with every comfort. There's also an in-house restaurant (p188). It was built next to the train station for the Agatha Christie crowd when simply everyone took the Orient Express, darling.

EATING

As befits an up-and-coming international city, Zagreb presents a fairly wide array of culinary styles. Exotic spices are not part of the Croatian gastronomic vocabulary, but you can't go wrong with fish, pizza, pasta and roasted meats.

Mimice (☎ no phone; Jurišićeva 21; mains 12-30KN; ☽ closed Sun) It's a local favourite and deservedly so. The fish is sure to be fresh because turnover is high, especially at noontime when workers in the offices around Trg Jelačića turn out in droves for their lunch.

Boban (☎ 48 11 549; Gajeva 9; mains 30-50KN) This Italian restaurant/bar/café offers sophisticated food at good prices. It has an outdoor terrace and an indoor lounge and terrace that is popular with Zagreb yuppies. Try the gnocchi made from squid ink and topped with salmon sauce.

Kaptolska Klet (☎ 48 14 838; Kaptol 5; mains 55-70KN) This huge and inviting space is comfortable for everyone from solo diners to

---

STREET NAMES

In Zagreb, you may notice a discrepancy between the names used in this book and the names you'll actually see on the street. In Croatian, a street name can be rendered either in the nominative or possessive case. The difference is apparent in the name's ending. Thus, Ulica Ljedevita Gaja (street of Ljudevita Gaja) becomes Gajeva ulica (Gaja's street). The latter version is the one most commonly seen on the street sign and used in everyday conversation. The same principle applies to a square *(trg)* which can be rendered as Trg Petra Preradovića or Preradovićev trg. Some of the more common names are: Trg svetog Marka (Markov trg), Trg Josipa Jurja Strossmayera (Strossmayerov trg), Ulica Andrije Hebranga (Hebrangova), Ulica Pavla Radića (Radićeva), Ulica Augusta Šenoe (Šenoina), Ulica Ivana Tkalčića (Tkalčićeva) and Ulica Nikole Tesle (Teslina). Be aware also that Trg Nikole Šubića Zrinjskog is almost always called Zrinjevac.

Also, at the end of a number of addresses in this chapter, you'll notice the letters 'bb' instead of a street number. This shorthand, which stands for *bez broja* (without a number) is used by businesses or other nonresidential institutions, indicating that it's an official place without a street number.

---

groups of noisy backpackers. Although famous for its Zagreb specialities such as grilled meats, spit-roasted lamb, duck, pork and veal as well as home-made sausages, it turns out a nice platter of grilled vegetables and a vegetable loaf.

Makronova (☎ 48 47 115; Ilica 72; mains 70KN; ☻ closed Sun) All very Zen, purely macrobiotic and more than welcome for those of the vegan persuasion. There's also shiatsu treatment, yoga classes and feng shui courses.

Frankopan (☎ 48 48 547; Frankopanska 8; mains 35-85KN) It's a gilt trip with chubby cherubs frolicking on the ceiling while you munch on relatively adventurous dishes. The prices are good because meals are prepared by a hostelry school.

Konoba Čiho (☎ 48 17 060; Hatza 15; mains from 55KN; ☻ closed Sun) Tucked away downstairs, this cosy restaurant turns out a startling assortment of fish and seafood, grilled, fried and combined in delicious stews.

Baltazar (☎ 46 66 824; Nova Ves 4; mains from 70KN; ☻ closed Sun) Duck, lamb, pork, beef and turkey are cooked to perfection here, served with a good choice of local wines.

Murano 2000 (☎ 456 66 66; Mihanovićeva 1; mains 90-200KN; ☻ closed Sun) Here are the tastiest, most creative dishes in town served with polish in the dining room of the Hotel Esplanade, a world-class hotel.

There's a **fruit and vegetable market** (Britanski trg; ☻ 7am-3pm) and you can pick up yummy fresh produce at Dolac (p185), and local cheese, smoked meat and cold cuts at nearby **Gavrilović** (☻ closed Sun). Slurp up dessert at **Vincek** (☎ 45 50 834; Ilica 18), famous for its ice cream.

DRINKING

The architecture may be sober but the nightlife definitely is not, especially as the weather warms up and Zagrebians take to the streets. Wander along Tkalčićeva in the upper town or around along bar-lined Bogovićeva, just south of Trg Jelačića, which turns into prime meet-and-greet territory each evening. Tkalčićeva attracts a slightly funkier crowd. The places listed below open around noon for café society and turn into bars around dinner time.

Bulldog (☎ 48 17 393; Bogovićeva 6) Belgian beer loosens up a crowd of young execs, sales reps, minor politicos and expats.

Tolkien's House (☎ 48 51 776; Vranicanijeva 8) Decorated in the style of JRR Tolkien's books, it's very Frodo.

Indy's (☎ 48 52 053; Vranicanijeva 4) This friendly bar presents a dazzling assortment of juicy and fruity cocktails on an outdoor terrace.

Brazil (☎ 091 200 24 81; Veslačka bb) Parked on the Sava River, this bar on a boat refreshes a throng of thirsty revellers and offers occasional live music.

Kazališna Kavana (☎ 48 55 851; Trg Maršala Tita) Everyone seems to wind up at this café, known as Kav Kaz, at one time or another, even though it's beyond pretentious.

ENTERTAINMENT

Zagreb is a happening city. Its theatres and concert halls present a great variety of programmes throughout the year. Many (but not all) are listed in the monthly brochure *Zagreb Events & Performances,* which is available from the tourist office. Otherwise, drop in at Art Net Club (p184) and peruse the many flyers announcing breaking developments on the music scene.

Discos & Clubs

The dress code is relaxed in most Zagreb clubs but neatness counts. The cover usually runs to 30KN and the action doesn't heat up until near midnight.

Aquarius (☎ 36 40 231; Ljubeka bb) On Lake Jarun, this is the night temple of choice for Zagrebians of all ages and styles. The design cleverly includes an open-air terrace on the lake and the sound is usually house. Take tram No 17 to the Jarun stop.

Purgeraj (☎ 48 14 734; Park Ribnjak) A funky, relaxed space to listen to live rock, blues, rock-blues, blues-rock, country rock. You get the idea.

Glob@l (☎ 48 76 146; P Hatza 14) Gays and lesbians are more than welcome to take in the friendly, tolerant vibes.

Sokol klub (☎ 48 28 510; Trg Maršala Tita 6) Across the street from the Ethnographic Museum, Sokol is fashionable without being snooty and the dance floor is always packed.

BP Club (☎ 48 14 444; Nikole Tesle 7; ☉ 5pm-1am) Famous for its high-quality musicians and occasional jam sessions, this is one of Zagreb's classic addresses.

Sport

Basketball is popular in Zagreb, and from October to April games take place in a variety of venues around town, usually at the weekend. The tourist office can provide you with the schedule.

Football (soccer) games are held every Sunday afternoon at the **Maksimir Stadium** (Maksimirska 128), on the eastern side of Zagreb; catch tram No 4, 7, 11 or 12 to Bukovačka. If you arrive too early for the game, Zagreb's zoo is just across the street.

Theatre

It's worth making the rounds of the theatres in person to check their programmes. Tickets are usually available for performances, even for the best shows. A small office marked 'Kazalište Komedija' (look out for the posters) also sells theatre tickets; it's

in the Oktogon, a passage connecting Trg Petra Preradovića to Ilica 3.

Croatian National Theatre (☎ 48 28 532; Trg Maršala Tita 15; box office ☉ 10am-1pm & 5-7.30pm Mon-Fri, 10am-1pm Sat, 30 min before performances Sun) This neobaroque theatre was established in 1895. It stages opera and ballet performances.

Komedija Theatre (☎ 48 14 566; Kaptol 9) Near the cathedral, the Komedija Theatre stages operettas and musicals.

Vatroslav Lisinski Concert Hall (ticket office ☎ 61 21 166; Trg Stjepana Radica 4; ☉ 9am-8pm Mon-Fri, 9am-2pm Sat) Just south of the train station, this concert hall is a prestigious venue where symphony concerts are held regularly.

Concerts also take place at the **Academy of Music** (☎ 48 30 822; Gundulićeva 6a) off Ilica. Another entertainment option is the **Puppet Theatre** (Baruna Trenka 3; performances 5pm Sat, noon Sun).

SHOPPING

Ilica is Zagreb's main shopping street.

Vartek's department store (Trg Jelačića) You can get in touch with true Croatian consumerism at this new store.

Kroata Cravata (Oktogon) Croatia is the birthplace of the necktie (cravat). Kroata Cravata has locally made silk neckties at prices that run from 175KN to 380KN.

Rokotvorine (Trg Jelačića 7) This place sells traditional Croatian handicrafts, such as red-and-white embroidered tablecloths, dolls and pottery.

Bornstein (☎ 48 12 361; Kaptol 19) If Croatia's wine and spirits have gone to your head, get your fix at Bornstein, which presents an astonishing collection of brandy, wine and gourmet products.

GETTING THERE & AWAY
Air

For information about the flights to and from Zagreb, see p228 and p230.

Bus

Zagreb's big, modern **bus station** (☎ 61 57 983; www.akz.hr, in Croatian) has a large, enclosed waiting room and a number of shops, including grocery stores. You can buy most international tickets at windows No 17 to 20.

Buses depart from Zagreb for most parts of Croatia, Slovenia and places beyond. Buy an advance ticket at the station if you're planning to travel far.

CROATIA

The following domestic buses depart from Zagreb:

Destination	Cost	Duration	Frequency
Dubrovnik	205-410KN	11hr	7 daily
Korčula	195KN	12hr	1 daily
Krk	136KN	4-5hr	4 daily
Ljubljana	115KN	2½hr	2 daily
Osijek	88KN	4hr	8 daily
Plitvice	50KN	2½hr	19 daily
Poreč	123KN	5hr	6 daily
Pula	114-161KN	4-6hr	13 daily
Rab	144KN	4½-5hr	2 daily
Rijeka	75-129KN	2½-3hr	21 daily
Rovinj	132KN	5-8hr	8 daily
Split	112-143KN	6-9hr	27 daily
Varaždin	51KN	1¾hr	20 daily
Zadar	97-157KN	4-5hr	20 daily

For international bus connections see p228.

Train

The following domestic trains depart from **Zagreb train station** (☎ 060 33 34 44):

Destination	Cost	Duration	Frequency
Osijek	117KN	4½hr	4 daily
Pula	123KN	5½hr	2 daily
Rijeka	102KN	5hr	5 daily
Split	138KN	6½-9hr	6 daily
Varaždin	47KN	3hr	13 daily
Zadar	134KN	8hr	4 daily

All daily trains to Zadar stop at Knin. Reservations are required on fast InterCity (IC) trains and there's a supplement of 5KN to 15KN for fast or express trains.

For international train connections see p229.

GETTING AROUND

Zagreb is a fairly easy city to navigate, whether by car or public transport. Traffic isn't bad, there's sufficient parking, and the efficient tram system should be a model for other polluted, traffic-clogged European capitals.

To/From the Airport

The Croatia Airlines bus to Zagreb airport, 17km southeast of the city, leaves from the bus station every half-hour or hour from about 5.30am to 7.30pm, depending on flights, and returns from the airport on about the same schedule (25KN). A taxi would cost about 250KN.

Car

Of the major car-rental companies, you could try **Budget Rent-a-Car** (☎ 45 54 936) in the Hotel Sheraton, **Avis Autotehna** (☎ 48 36 006) at the Hotel Opera and **Hertz** (☎ 48 46 777; Vukotinovićeva 1). Prices start at 300KN per day. Zagreb is relatively easy to navigate by car but remember that the streets around Trg Jelačića and up through Kaptol and Gradec are pedestrian only. Watch out for trams sneaking up on you.

Croatian Auto Club (HAK) Information Centre (☎ 46 40 800; Derenčinova 20) Helps motorists in need.

Public Transport

Public transport is based on an efficient but overcrowded network of trams, though the city centre is compact enough to make them unnecessary. Tram Nos 3 and 8 don't run at weekends. Buy tickets at newspaper kiosks for 6.50KN or from the driver for 8KN. Each ticket must be stamped when you board. You can use your ticket for transfers within 90 minutes but only in one direction.

A *dnevna karta* (day ticket), valid on all public transport until 4am the next morning, is 18KN at most Vjesnik or Tisak news outlets. (See p184 for details of the Zagreb Card.) Controls are frequent on the tram system with fines for not having the proper ticket starting at €30.

Taxi

Zagreb's taxis ring up 8KN per kilometre after a whopping flag fall of 25KN. On Sunday and from 10pm to 5am there's a 20% surcharge.

ISTRIA

Istria (Istra to Croatians) is the heart-shaped 3600-sq-km peninsula just south of Trieste, Italy, that retains a pronounced Italian influence. Sometimes called the 'new Tuscany', the Istrian interior is a peaceful landscape of green rolling hills, drowned valleys and fertile plains. The rugged and indented coastline is enormously popular with Italian tourists, comfortable with the excellent pasta and seafood on the menus and the fact that Italian is a second language for most Istrians.

Perhaps they dream of the days when the string of Istrian resorts was a part of Italy. Italy seized Istria from Austria-Hungary in 1918, was allowed to keep it in 1920, then had to give it to Yugoslavia in 1947. Tito wanted Trieste (Trst) as part of Yugoslavia too, but in 1954 the Anglo-American occupiers returned the city to Italy so that it wouldn't fall into the hands of the 'communists'. Today the Koper to Piran strip belongs to Slovenia while the rest is held by Croatia. Visit Piran quickly, then move south to Pula, a perfect base from which to explore Poreč and Rovinj.

POREČ

☎ 052 / pop 10,450

Poreč (Parenzo in Italian) sits on a low, narrow peninsula halfway down the western coast of Istria. The town is the centre of a region dotted with sprawling tourist resorts, but vestiges of earlier times and a quiet, small-town atmosphere (at least in the low season) make it well worth a stop. There are the magnificent mosaics in the Euphrasian Basilica, and places to swim off the rocks north of the old town.

History

The Romans called the town Parentium and made it an important administrative base, leaving their mark on the rectangular street plan, which still is evident. After the fall of Rome, Poreč came under the rule of the Byzantines and constructed the famous Euphrasian Basilica, now a World Heritage Site. It was later ruled by Venice, then Austria.

Orientation

The compact old town is squeezed into the peninsula and packed with thousands of shops. The ancient Roman Dekumanus (a Roman longitudinal road) with its polished stones is still the main street, bisected by the latitudinal Cardo. Hotels, travel agencies and excursion boats are on the quay, Obala Maršala Tita, which runs from the small-boat harbour to the tip of the peninsula. The bus station is directly opposite

the small-boat harbour just outside the old town.

Information

INTERNET ACCESS

Internet Centre (☎ 427 075; Grahalića 1; per hr 42KN) A full service Internet and computer centre.

LEFT LUGGAGE

Garderoba (☽ 6am-8pm Mon-Sat, 6am-5pm Sun)

MONEY

You can change money at any of the town's travel agencies.

Istarska Banka (A Negrija 6) Has an ATM.

POST

Main post office (Trg Slobode 14) Has a telephone centre.

TOURIST INFORMATION

Tourist Office (☎ 451 293; www.istra.com/porec; Zagrebačka 11; ☽ 8am-10pm Mon-Sat year-round, 9am-1pm & 6-10pm Sun Jul & Aug)

TRAVEL AGENCIES

Atlas travel agency (☎ 434 983; Eufrazijeva 63) Represents Amex.

Di Tours (☎ 432 100, 452 018; www.di-tours.hr; Prvomajska 2) Finds private accommodation.

Fiore tours (☎ /fax 431 397; fiore@pu.htnet.hr; Mate Vašića 6) Also handles private accommodation.

Istra Line (☎ 451 067; P Setaliste 2) If you follow Nikole Tesle until it becomes Kalčića you'll come to Mate Vašića, where you'll find this agency in a pink building.

Sunny Way agency (☎ 452 021; Negrija 1) Has information about boat connections to Italy.

Sights

The main reason to visit Poreč is to visit the 6th-century **Euphrasian Basilica** (☎ 431 635; admission free; ☽ 7.30am-8pm, to 7pm Oct-Mar), which features some wonderfully preserved Byzantine gold mosaics. The sculpture and architecture of the basilica are remarkable survivors of that distant period. For 10KN you may visit the 4th-century mosaic floor of the adjacent early Christian basilica or visit the baptistry and climb the bell tower for a spectacular view of the region.

The numerous historic sites in the old town include the ruins of two **Roman temples**, between Trg Marafor and the western end of the peninsula. Archaeology and history are featured in the **Regional Museum**

(☎ 431 585; Dekumanus 9; adult/concession 10/5KN; ☺ 10am-1pm & 5-9pm Jul-Aug, 10am-1pm rest of year) in an old baroque palace. The captions are in German and Italian but there's an explanatory leaflet in English.

From May to mid-October there are passenger boats (20KN return) every half-hour to **Sveti Nikola**, the small island opposite Poreč Harbour, for some wonderful swimming. The boats depart from the wharf on Obala Maršala Tita.

Festivals & Events

Annual events in Poreč include the day-long **Folk Festival** (June) and the **Musical Summer** (May to September). Ask about these at the tourist office.

Sleeping

All of the travel agencies listed on p191 find private accommodation. Expect to pay from 165/240KN for a room with shared/private bathroom in the high season, plus a 30% surcharge for stays less than three nights. There are a limited number of rooms available in the old town and it's wise to reserve far in advance for the July to August period.

BUDGET

Camping grounds are large, well-organised little cities with plenty of activities. Take the 'Zelena Laguna' resort tourist train (20KN), which runs half-hourly or hourly from the town centre between April and October, or the boat shuttle. Prices in high season run about 50KN per person and 60KN for a site.

Autocamp Zelena Laguna (☎ 410 541) Well-equipped for sports, this autocamp can house up to 2700.

Autocamp Bijela Uvala (☎ 410 551) Housing up to 6000, the camping ground can be crowded.

MID-RANGE

Hotel Poreč (☎ 451 811; www.hotelporec.com; s/d 445/678KN; ☒) Near the bus station and an easy walk from the old town, you'll find freshly renovated and comfortable rooms in this hotel.

Hotel Neptun (☎ 400 800; fax 431 531; Obala Maršala Tita 15; s/d 436/685KN; P ☒) This is the best hotel in the town centre, which is an advantage if you want to be in the centre

of the action, but it also means being in the centre of a traffic snarl in peak season. The front rooms with harbour view are unbeatable.

Hotel Hostin (☎ 432 112; www.hostin.hr; Rade Končara 4; per person 556KN; P ☒ ☒ ☐ ☒) One of the newer entries on the hotel scene, this sparkling place is in verdant parkland just behind the bus station. An indoor swimming pool, fitness room and sauna are nice little extras plus the hotel is only 70m from a pebble beach. The price includes obligatory half-board.

Eating

Barilla (☎ 452 742; Eufrazijeva 26; mains 50-90KN) This authentic Italian restaurant serves delicious pasta and pizza as well as more sophisticated Italian dishes on two outdoor terraces.

Konoba Ulixes (☎ 451 132; Dekumanus 2; mains 40-100KN) Truffles are one of Istria's most precious products and you can taste them here in pasta, with beef or fresh tuna.

There is a large supermarket and department store next to Hotel Poreč, near the bus station.

Getting There & Away

From the **bus station** (☎ 432 153; Karla Hugesa 2), buses depart for Rovinj (23KN, one hour, seven daily), Zagreb (123KN to 155KN, five hours, six daily) and Rijeka (55KN, 5½ hours, eight daily), and Pula (33KN, 1¼ hours, 12 daily). Between Poreč and Rovinj the bus runs along the Lim Channel, a drowned valley. To see it clearly, sit on the right-hand side if you're southbound, or the left if you're northbound.

The nearest train station is at Pazin, 30km east (five buses daily from Poreč).

For information about bus and boat connections to Italy and Slovenia see p228.

ROVINJ

☎ 052 / pop 14,200

Yes, it is touristy and residents are developing a sharp eye for maximising their profits but Rovinj (Rovigno in Italian) is one of the last of the true Mediterranean fishing ports. Fishermen haul their catch into the harbour in the early morning, followed by a horde of squawking gulls, and mend their nets before lunch. Prayers for a good catch are sent forth at the massive Cathedral of

St Euphemia, whose 60m tower punctuates the peninsula. Wooded hills and low-rise luxury hotels surround a town webbed by steep, cobbled streets. The 13 green, offshore islands of the Rovinj archipelago make for pleasant, varied views and you can swim from the rocks in the sparkling water below Hotel Rovinj.

Orientation & Information

The bus station is in the southeastern corner of the old town and there's an ATM next to the entrance, as well as the Autotrans Travel Agency, which will change money.

INTERNET ACCESS

Planet Tourist Agency (☎ 840 494; Sv Križ 1; per hr 30KN) The most convenient Internet access in Rovinj has a couple of computers.

LAUNDRY

Lavanderie Galax (☎ 814 059; M Benussi; per 5kg 5KN) It may be pricey but at least you can get your clothes washed.

LEFT LUGGAGE

Garderoba (☺ 8am-9pm daily Jun-Sep, 8am-3pm Mon-Fri, 8am-2pm Sat Oct-May) At the bus station.

POST

Main post office (M Benussi 4) Situated across from the bus station, you can make phone calls here.

TOURIST INFORMATION

Tourist office (☎ 811 566; fax 816 007; www.tzgrovinj .hr; Obala Pina Budicina 12; ☺ 8am-9pm Mon-Sat, 9am-1pm Sun Jun-Sep, 8am-3pm Mon-Fri, 8am-noon Sat Oct-May) Just off Trg Maršala Tita, this office is less than a fountain of information; more of a trickle.

TRAVEL AGENCIES

Eurostar Travel (☎ 813 144; Obala Pina Budicina 1) Has schedules and tickets for boats to Italy.

Futura Travel (☎ 817 281; futura-travel@pu.htnet.hr; M Benussi 2)

Marco Polo (☎ 816 616; www.marcopolo.hr; Istarska 2)

Planet Tourist Agency (☎ 840 494; Sv Križ 1)

Sights

The **Cathedral of St Euphemia** (☺ 10am-noon & 2-5pm), which completely dominates the town from its hill-top location, was built in 1736 and is the largest baroque building in Istria. It reflects the period during

the 18th century when Rovinj was the most populous town in Istria, an important fishing centre and the bulwark of the Venetian fleet.

Inside the cathedral, don't miss the tomb of St Euphemia (martyred in AD 304) behind the right-hand altar. The saint's remains were brought from Constantinople in 800. On the anniversary of her martyrdom (16 September) devotees congregate here. A copper statue of her tops the cathedral's mighty tower.

Take a wander along the winding narrow backstreets below the cathedral, such as **ul Grisia**, where local artists sell their work. Each year in August Rovinj's painters stage a big open-air art show in town.

The Rovinj **Regional Museum** (☎ 816 720; Trg Maršala Tita; adult/concession 10/8KN; ☺ 9am-12.30pm & 6-9pm Mon-Sat mid-Jun–mid-Sep, 10am-1pm Tue-Sat rest of year) contains an unexciting collection of paintings and a few Etruscan artefacts that have been found in Istria; it's worth a visit when the weather turns bad. Captions are only in Croatian and Italian.

When you've seen enough of the town, follow the waterfront south past Hotel Park to **Punta Corrente Forest Park**, which was established in 1890 by Baron Hütterodt, an Austrian admiral who kept a villa on Crveni otok (Red Island). Here you can swim off the rocks, climb a cliff or just sit and admire the offshore islands.

Tours

Delfin Agency (☎ 813 383), near the ferry dock for Crveni otok, runs half-day scenic cruises to the Lim Channel for 130KN per person, or you can go with one of the independent operators at the end of Alzo Rismondo that run half-day and full-day boat trips around the region. There's an hourly ferry to the lovely and wooded Crveni otok (20KN return) and a frequent ferry to nearby Katarina Island (10KN return) from the same landing. Get tickets on the boat or at the nearby kiosk. These boats operate only from May to mid-October.

Festivals & Events

The city's annual events include the **Rovinj-Pesaro Regatta** (early May), **Rovinj Summer** concert series (July and August) and the **Grisia Art Market** on the 2nd Sunday of August. The tourist office has full details.

Sleeping

Private rooms with two beds cost 200KN in high season with a small discount for single occupancy. The surcharge for a stay of less than three nights is 50% and guests who stay only one night are punished with a 100% surcharge, but you should be able to bargain the surcharge away outside of July and August. You can book directly from www.inforovinj.com or consult one of the travel agencies listed on p193. There are almost no rooms at all available in the old town however.

Polari Camping (☎ 800 376; per person/camp sites 55/30KN) This spot is about 5km southeast of town and is much larger than Porton Biondi, but it also has more facilities.

Porton Biondi (☎ 813 557; per person/camp sites for 55/35KN) Less than a 1km from the town (on the Monsena bus route).

Hotel Monte Mulin (☎ 811 512; mulin@jadran.tdr .hr; s/d 241/410KN; **P**) On the wooded hillside overlooking the bay just beyond Hotel Park, it's about a 15-minute walk to this hotel, heading south of the bus station. Rooms are bland but perfectly serviceable.

Hotel Rovinj (☎ 811 288; fax 840 757; Sv Križ; s/d from 380/640KN; **✷**) This hotel has a splendid location overlooking the sea and is undergoing renovation which may make it more expensive.

Vila Lili (☎ 840 940; www.cel.hr/vilalili; Mohorovi-cica 16; s/d 410/750KN; **✷**) The comfort level at this small hotel is excellent, and includes satellite TV, a sauna and bright, modern rooms. It's just a short walk out of town past the marina.

Hotel Villa Angelo D'Oro (☎ 840 502; hotel.angelo@ vip.hr; Via Svalba 38-42; s/d 823/1455KN; **✷**) This new luxury hotel in a renovated Venetian building has plush, lavishly decorated rooms with satellite TV, minibar, and a free sauna and Jacuzzi room.

Eating

Most of the fish and spaghetti places along the harbour cater to the more upmarket crowd.

Cantinon (☎ 811 970; Alzo Rismondo 18; fish mains from 40KN) This welcoming restaurant is becoming touristy but locals still come here for the variety of well-prepared fresh fish.

Veli Jože (☎ 816 337; Sv Križ 1; mains 30-140KN) In an interior crammed with knick-knacks or at tables outside, you can feast on a wide assortment of Istrian delicacies.

Picnickers can buy supplies at the supermarket only about 25m downhill from the bus station or in one of the kiosks selling *burek* near the vegetable market.

Getting There & Away

From the **bus station** (☎ 811 453; Trg na Lokvi 6), there's a bus from Rovinj to Pula, which sometimes continues on to Poreč (23KN to 40KN, one hour), eight buses daily to

---

MAGIC MUSHROOMS?

The truffle trade is less like a business than a highly profitable cult. It revolves around an expensive, malodorous fungus endowed with semimagical powers, which is collected by shadowy characters who deal in cash and smuggle their booty across borders. Devotees claim that once you've tasted this small, nut-shaped delicacy, all other flavours seem insipid.

Although France, Spain and Italy are the traditional truffle-producing countries, Istrian truffles are rapidly gaining a foothold in the marketplace. Even at 14KN per gram, the price is significantly cheaper than other European truffles and the taste is said to be at least as good as their more expensive counterparts. In fact, there have been unconfirmed reports that certain nefarious parties are collecting Istrian truffles and packaging them as Italian truffles.

The truffle-hunting season lasts from October to January, during which time at least 3000 people and 9000 to 12,000 dogs are wandering around Istrian forests. The Motovun region is especially rich in truffles, but they are also found on the slopes of Mt Učka and in the Labin region. Truffle hunters are so determined to remain underground (for obvious tax reasons) that they will never admit to truffle hunting, no matter how unmistakable the evidence.

Some people believe truffles are an aphrodisiac, though scientific research has failed to uncover any basis for this claim. Conduct your own experiment: get a truffle and mix a few shavings into scrambled eggs or sprinkle them on top of a risotto. Turn the lights way down low, put on some nice music and see what happens.

Rijeka (73KN, 3½ hours), nine daily to Zagreb (132KN to 146KN, five to eight hours), one daily each to Koper (79KN, three hours) and Split (295KN, 11¼ hours), and one daily each to Dubrovnik (379KN, 17½ hours) and Ljubljana (155KN, 5½ hours, July and August). Prices and durations vary between different companies and routes.

The closest train station is Kanfanar, 19km away on the Pula–Divača line.

PULA

☎ 052 / pop 62,400

Pula (the ancient Polensium) is a large regional centre with a wealth of Roman ruins to explore. Its star attraction is a remarkably well-preserved amphitheatre that dominates the town centre and is often the scene of concerts and shows. Despite its busy commercial life, Pula retains an easygoing small-town appeal. Nearby are some rocky wooded peninsulas overlooking the clear Adriatic waters, which explain the many resort hotels and camping grounds circling the city. Most residents head out to Verudela Peninsula for the nightlife and swimming coves.

Orientation

The bus station is 500m northeast of the town centre. The centre of town is Giardini, while the harbour is west of the bus station. The train station is near the water, about 500m north of town.

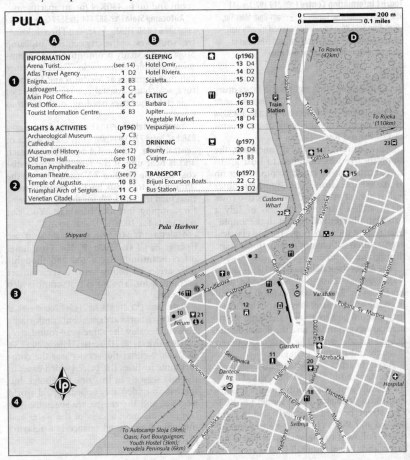

PULA

INFORMATION	
Arena Turist	(see 14)
Atlas Travel Agency	1 D2
Enigma	2 B3
Jadroagent	3 C3
Main Post Office	4 C4
Post Office	5 C3
Tourist Information Centre	6 B3

SIGHTS & ACTIVITIES	(p196)
Archaeological Museum	7 C3
Cathedral	8 C3
Museum of History	(see 12)
Old Town Hall	(see 10)
Roman Amphitheatre	9 D2
Roman Theatre	(see 7)
Temple of Augustus	10 B3
Triumphal Arch of Sergius	11 C4
Venetian Citadel	12 C3

SLEEPING	(p196)
Hotel Omir	13 D4
Hotel Riviera	14 D2
Scaletta	15 D2

EATING	(p197)
Barbara	16 B3
Jupiter	17 C3
Vegetable Market	18 D4
Vespazijan	19 C3

DRINKING	(p197)
Bounty	20 D4
Cvajner	21 B3

TRANSPORT	(p197)
Brijuni Excursion Boats	22 C2
Bus Station	23 D2

Information

You can exchange money in travel agencies or at either of the post offices where there is an ATM.

Arena Turist (☎ 529 400; fax 529 401; www.arenaturist .hr; Splitska 1a) In the Hotel Riviera, Arena Turist finds private accommodation.

Atlas travel agency (☎ 393 040; atlas.pula@atlas .hr; Starih Statuta 1) Finds private accommodation and organises tours.

Enigma (☎ 381 615; Kandlerova 19; per hr 20KN) Internet access.

Jadroagent (☎ 210 431; jadroagent-pula@pu.htnet.hr; Riva 14) Has schedules and tickets for boats connecting Istria with Italy and the islands.

Main post office (Danteov trg 4; ☼ 7am-8pm) You can make long distance calls.

Tourist Information Centre (☎ 219 197; fax 211 955; www.pulainfo.hr; Forum 2; ☼ 9am-8pm Mon-Sat, 10am-6pm Sun) With knowledgeable and friendly staff, this centre provides maps, brochures and schedules of upcoming events in Pula and around Istria.

Sights

Pula's most imposing sight is the 1st-century **Roman amphitheatre** (☎ 219 028; Flavijevska; adult/ concession 16/8KN; ☼ 8am-9pm Jun-Sep, 8.30am-4.30pm Oct-May) overlooking the harbour and northeast of the old town.

Built entirely from local limestone, the amphitheatre was designed to host gladiatorial contests and could accommodate up to 20,000 spectators. The 30m-high outer wall is almost intact and contains two rows of 72 arches. Around the end of July a Croatian film festival is held in the amphitheatre, and there are pop, jazz and classical events, often with major international stars, throughout summer.

The **Archaeological Museum** (☎ 218 603; Cararina 3; adult/concession 12/6KN; ☼ 9am-7pm Mon-Sat, 10am-3pm Sun Jun-Sep, 9am-3pm Mon-Fri Oct-May) is uphill from the town centre. Even if you don't visit the museum be sure to visit the large sculpture garden around it, and the **Roman theatre** behind the museum. The garden is entered through 2nd-century twin gates.

Along Istarska are **Roman walls** that mark the eastern boundary of old Pula. Follow these walls south and continue down Giardini to the **Triumphal Arch of Sergius** (27 BC). The street beyond the arch winds right around old Pula, changing names several times. Follow it to the ancient **Temple of Augustus** and the **old town hall** (1296).

The 17th-century **Venetian Citadel**, on a high hill in the centre of the old town, is worth the climb for the view if not for the meagre exhibits in the tiny **Museum of History** (Kaštel; admission 7KN; ☼ 8am-7pm daily Jun-Sep, 9am-5pm Mon-Fri Oct-May) inside.

Sleeping

The tip of the Verudela Peninsula, about 6km southwest of the city centre, is a vast tourist complex with plenty of sprawling hotels that you can book through Arena Turist (left).

The travel agencies listed left find private accommodation, although there is little available in the town centre itself. Count on paying from 110KN per person for a double room and up to 430KN for an apartment.

Autocamp Stoja (☎ 387 144; fax 387 748; per person/ camp site & car 50/110KN; ☼ Apr-Oct) Three kilometres southwest of the city centre, Autocamp Stoja is on a shady promontory, with swimming possible off the rocks. There are more camping grounds at Medulin and Premantura, which are coastal resorts southeast of Pula (take the buses heading southeast from town).

Youth Hostel (☎ 391 133; pula@hfhs.hr; camp sites/ B&B/half-board 72/110/142KN) Only 3km south of central Pula, this hostel overlooks a beach and is near one of the region's largest discos. Take the No 2 or 7 Verudela bus to the 'Piramida' stop, walk back to the first street, then turn left and look for the sign. The rate for camping includes breakfast. You can rent tents for 10.50KN, year round.

Scaletta (☎ 541 599; www.hotel-scaletta.com; Flavijeska 26; s/d 410/535KN; P ✿) This hotel offers beautifully decorated and thoughtfully arranged rooms with every comfort accounted for. The hotel restaurant is also first-rate.

Hotel Omir (☎ 210 614; fax 213 944; Dobricheva 6; s/ d 424/550KN) Rooms are small but comfortable here. Prices stay the same year-round.

Hotel Riviera (☎ 211 166; fax 211 166; Splitska 1; s/d 437/715KN) Neither the service nor the comfort quite justifies the price (which eases in the low season) in this one-star hotel, but there is an undeniably appealing old-world elegance and the rooms are spacious. The front rooms have a view of the water and the wide shady hotel terrace is a relaxing place for a drink.

CROATIA

Eating

The best local restaurants are out of town but the cheapest places are in the centre and the eating isn't bad. You'll have a number of choices along Kandlerova.

Jupiter (☎ 214 333; Castropola 38; mains from 25KN) This popular place serves up the best pizza in town and the pasta is good too.

Barbara (☎ 219 317; Kandlerova 5; mains from 25KN) It's your basic calamari and čevapčići but well done and in a great people-watching location.

Vespazijan (☎ 210 016; Amfiteatarska 11; mains from 30KN) This unpretentious spot conjures up yummy risottos and a variety of seafood dishes.

Self-caterers can pick up vegetables, cold cuts and local cheese at the morning vegetable market.

Drinking & Entertainment

The streets of Flanatička, Kandlerova and Sergijevaca are lively people-watching spots, and the Forum has several outdoor cafés that fill up in the early evening.

Cvajner (Forum) The trendiest café/gallery in town, with a stunning, art-filled interior.

Bounty (☎ 218 088; Veronska 8) Irish beer and cheer are served up in liberal doses here.

Posters around Pula advertise live performances at the amphitheatre or details of rave parties at two venues in Verudela: Oasis and Fort Bourguignon.

Getting There & Away

BOAT

For information about ferries to Italy, see Getting There & Away (p229).

BUS

The buses that travel to Rijeka (48KN, 2½ hours, 20 daily) are sometimes crowded, especially the eight that continue to Zagreb, so be sure to reserve a seat in advance. Going from Pula to Rijeka, be sure to sit on the right-hand side of the bus for a stunning view of the Gulf of Kvarner.

Other destinations you can reach from the **bus station** (☎ 502 997; Istarske Brigade bb) include: Rovinj (23KN, 40 minutes, 18 daily); Poreč (32KN, one hour, 12 daily); Zagreb (124KN to 147KN, five hours, 11 daily); Zadar (161KN, seven hours, four daily); Split (215KN to 278KN, 10 hours, four daily); and Dubrovnik (366KN, 15 hours, one daily).

TRAIN

There are two daily trains to Ljubljana (115KN, four hours) and two to Zagreb (123KN, 6½ hours), but you must board a bus for part of the trip.

Getting Around

The only city buses of use to visitors are bus No 1, which runs to the camping ground at Stoja, and bus Nos 2 and 7 to Verudela, which pass the youth hostel. Frequency varies from every 15 minutes to every 30 minutes, with service from 5am to 11.30pm daily. Tickets are sold at newsstands for 10KN and are good for two trips.

Around Pula

BRIJUNI ISLANDS

The Brijuni (Brioni in Italian) island group consists of two main pine-covered islands and 12 islets just northwest of Pula. Notable as the summer residence of Maršal Tito, the Brijuni islands are now a highly groomed and scrupulously maintained national park. Some 680 species of plants grow on the islands, including many exotic subtropical species, which were planted at Tito's request. Tito's former private hunting grounds are now a safari park where elephants, zebras and antelope roam.

You may only visit Brijuni National Park with a group. Instead of booking an excursion with one of the travel agencies in Pula, Rovinj or Poreč, which costs 340KN, you could take a public bus from Pula to Fažana (8km), then sign up for a tour (180KN) at the **Brijuni Tourist Service** (☎ 525 883) office near the wharf. It's best to book in advance, especially in summer.

Also check along the Pula waterfront for excursion boats to Brijuni. The five-hour boat trips from Pula to Brijuni (60KN) may not actually visit the islands but only sail around them. Still, it makes a nice day out.

GULF OF KVARNER

The Gulf of Kvarner (Quarnero in Italian) covers 3300 sq km between Rijeka and Pag island in the south. Protected by the Velebit range in the northeast, the Gorski Kotar in the north and the Učka massif in the east, the climate is gentle and the range of vegetation wide.

The largest city is the busy commercial port of Rijeka, only a few kilometres from the aristocratic Opatija riviera. The large islands of Krk, Cres, Lošinj and Rab also have their share of admirers, who come for the luxuriant slopes dipping down to the sea.

RIJEKA
☎ 051 / pop 144,000
As Croatia's largest port, Rijeka (Fiume in Italian) is full of boats, cargo, fumes, cranes and the bustling sense of purpose that characterises most port cities. All of the buses, trains and ferries that form the network connecting Istria and Dalmatia with Zagreb and points beyond seem to pass through Rijeka, making the town almost impossible to avoid. Since Rijeka is hardly one of the 'must-see' destinations, the café-lined boulevard Korzo is refreshingly tourist free, and few visitors make the trek up to Trsat Castle for the views over the gulf. With stately 19th-century buildings, a tree-lined promenade along the harbour and a smattering of museums and restaurants, you won't regret spending a day here.

Orientation
The **bus station** (☎ 060 333 444; Trg Žabica) is south of the Capuchin Church in the centre of town. The **train station** (ul Krešimirova) is a seven-minute walk west of the bus station.

The Jadrolinija ferry wharf (there's no left-luggage section) is just a few minutes east of the bus station. Korzo runs in an easterly direction through the city centre towards the fast-moving Rječina River.

Information
INTERNET ACCESS
Hotel Continental (Andrije Kašića Miočica; per hr 10-15KN) This hotel east of town has a full bank of modern computers.

LAUNDRY
Blitz (Krešimirova 3a; ☺ 7am-8pm Mon-Fri, 7am-1pm Sat) Situated between the bus and train stations, Blitz will do a small load of laundry for 60KN.

LEFT LUGGAGE
Garderoba (per day 10KN; ☺ 5.30am-10.30pm) In the bus station.
Garderoba (per day 10KN; ☺ 24hr) In the train station.

INFORMATION		
Hostelling International	1	B2
Main Post Office	2	B2
Telephone Centre	(see 2)	
Tourist Information Centre	3	B2

SIGHTS & ACTIVITIES		(p199)
Capuchin Church	4	A1
Church of St Jerome	5	B2

Church of St Vito	6	C2
City Tower	7	C2
Modern Art Gallery	8	B2
Natural History Museum	9	C1
Naval and Historical Museum	10	C1

SLEEPING		(p199)
Hotel Bonavia	11	B2

EATING		(p199)
Feral	12	C3
Grocery Stores	(see 14)	
Zlatna Školja	13	B2

TRANSPORT		(pp199-200)
Bus Station	14	A2
ITR Rentacar	15	A2
Jadroagent	16	C2
Jadrolinija	17	A2

MONEY

There's no ATM at the train station, but the exchange offices adjacent to the train and bus stations keep long hours. There are a number of ATMs dotted along Korzo, as well as an exchange counter in the main post office.

POST

Main post office (Korzo) Opposite the old City Tower, the post office also houses a telephone centre.

TOURIST INFORMATION

Hostelling International (☎ 264 176; Korzo 22) Sells HI cards and is a good source of information about Croatian hostels.

Tourist Information Centre (☎ 335 882; www .tz-rijeka.hr; Korzo 33) Distributes *Rijeka Tourist Route*, a walking-tour guide that is so well produced it makes you actually want to stay and look around.

Sights

Rijeka's main orientation point is the **City Tower** (Korzo), which was originally one of the main gates to the city, and is one of the few monuments to have survived the earthquake of 1750.

The **Modern Art Gallery** (☎ 334 280; Dolac 1; adult/concession 10/5KN; ✦ 10am-1pm & 5-9pm Tue-Sun) is in the upstairs scientific library opposite Hotel Bonavia. The **Naval and Historical Museum** (☎ 213 578; Muzejski trg 1; adult/student 10/1KN; ✦ 9am-1pm Tue-Sat) traces the development of sailing, with models and paintings of ships and portraits of the captains. The **Natural History Museum** (☎ 334 988; Lorenzov prolaz 1; adult/student 10/5KN; ✦ 9am-7pm Mon-Fri, 9am-2pm Sat) is devoted to regional geology and botany.

Also worth a visit is the 13th-century **Trsat Castle** (admission 15KN; ✦ 9am-11pm Tue-Sun Apr-Nov, 9am-3pm Tue-Sun Dec-Mar), which is on a high ridge overlooking Rijeka, and the canyon of the Rječina River. If you have some more time to kill, stroll into some of Rijeka's churches, such as **Church of St Vito** (Trg Grivica 11), **Church of St Jerome** (Trg Riječke Rezolucije) or the ornate **Capuchin Church** (Trg Žabica), all open for mass only.

Sleeping

The tourist office can direct you to the few options for private accommodation, most of which are a few kilometres out of town on the road to Opatija. It's just as easy to go on to Opatija, where there are more and better choices for hotels and private accommodation (for details on getting to/from Opatija see p201).

Hotel Continental (☎ 372 008; www.jadran-ho teli.hr, in Croatian; Andrije Kašića Miočića; s/d 376/425KN; P ☑) This old building, northeast of the town centre, has spacious rooms that could use an overhaul. At least you're close to Internet access (opposite).

Hotel Bonavia (☎ 333 744; www.bonavia.hr; Dolac 4; s/d from 830/980KN; P ☒ ☒ ☑ ☒) The four-star Bonavia is the only hotel in the centre of town and it has all of the niceties that businesspeople on generous expense accounts find indispensable.

Eating

If you get hungry on Sunday, you'll have to head to one of the hotel restaurants, since nearly every restaurant in town will be closed.

Feral (☎ 212 274; Matije Gupca 5B; mains from 60KN) The marine theme runs strong here with slightly cheaper seafood than Zlatna Školja, but it's still beautifully prepared.

Zlatna Školja (☎ 213 782; Kružna 12; mains 100KN) The fetching maritime décor puts you in the mood to savour the astonishingly creative seafood dishes here. The wine list is also notable.

There are several 24-hour grocery stores in and around the bus station.

Getting There & Away
CAR

Close to the bus station, **ITR Rent a Car** (☎ 337 544; Riva 20) has rental cars for about 300KN per day.

BOAT

Croatia's national boat carrier, **Jadrolinija** (☎ 211 444; www.jadrolinija.hr; Riva 16), has tickets for the large coastal ferries that run all year between Rijeka and Dubrovnik. For fares, see p230. For information on all boats to Croatia contact **Jadroagent** (☎ 211 276; Trg Ivana Koblera 2).

BUS

There are 13 buses daily between Rijeka and Krk (33KN, 1½ hours), via the huge Krk Bridge. Buses to Krk are overcrowded and a ticket in no way guarantees a seat. Don't worry – the bus from Rijeka to Krk empties fast so you won't be standing for long.

CROATIA

Other buses departing from Rijeka are headed for:

Destination	Cost	Duration	Frequency
Baška (Krk Island)	42KN	2hr	1 daily
Dubrovnik	205-309KN	13hr	2 daily
Poreč	55KN	4½hr	5 daily
Pula	48KN	2½hr	17 daily
Rab	87KN	3½hr	2 daily
Rovinj	73KN	3½hr	10 daily
Split	161-231KN	8½hr	11 daily
Trieste	62KN	2-3hr	3 daily
Zadar	115KN	5hr	12 daily
Zagreb	75-129KN	2½-3hr	21 daily

For international connections see p228.

TRAIN

Four trains run daily to Zagreb (102KN, five hours). There's also a daily direct train to Osijek (162KN, eight hours) and a daily train to Split that changes at Ogulin where you wait for two hours (142KN, 10 hours). Several of the seven daily services to Ljubljana (86KN, three hours) require a change of trains at the Slovenian border and again at Bifka or Bistrica in Slovenia, but there are also two direct trains. Reservations are compulsory on some *poslovni* (express) trains.

OPATIJA
☎ 051 / pop 12,719

Opatija, just a few kilometres due west of Rijeka, was where fashionable 19th-century aristocrats came to 'take the waters'. The Lungomare, a shady waterfront promenade that stretches for 12km along the Gulf of Kvarner, offers genteel exercise and a calming view of the mountainous coast. The nightlife is decidedly uncalming; there's far more going on here than in Rijeka. And to rest your weary head, there's a wide choice of hotels with baroque exteriors and high-ceilinged plush interiors that offer good value for money.

Information

There's no left-luggage facility at **Opatija bus station** (Trg Vladimira Gortana), which is in the town centre, but Autotrans Agency at the station will usually watch luggage.
Atlas travel agency (☎ 271 032; Maršala Tita 116) Accommodation and excursions.

Da Riva (☎ 272 482; www.da-riva.hr; Maršala Tita 162) Finds private accommodation and organises group transfers to regional airports.
GIT travel agency (☎ /fax 271 967; gi-trade@ri.htnet .hr; Maršala Tita 65) Finds private accommodation.
Internet Café (☎ 271 511; Maršala Tita 85; per hr 20KN) Offers Internet access in a comfortable environment.
Main post office (Eugena Kumičića 2; ⏰ 8am-7pm Mon-Sat) Behind the market.
Tourist office (☎ 271 310; www.opatija-tourism.hr; Maršala Tita 101; ⏰ 8am-7pm Mon-Sat & 2-6pm Sun Jun-Sep, 9am-noon & 2-4.30pm Mon-Sat Oct-May) Has some information on local events.

Activities

Opatija is not a museum/gallery kind of place. Come for the swimming in the coves along the Lungomare or just stroll the great seaside promenade. There's also hiking up Mt Učka. Head to the tourist office (p200) for details.

Sleeping & Eating

Private rooms are abundant and reasonably priced. The travel agencies listed above (left) have rooms starting at 150KN to 210KN, depending on the amenities.

The hotel scene is competitive and offers good value for money, especially outside of July and August. Most hotels are handled by **Liburnia Hotels** (☎ 710 300; www.liburnia.hr).

Camping Opatija (☎ 704 387; fax 704 112; Liburnjska 46, Ičići; per person/camp sites 30/50KN; ⏰ May-Sep) Right on the sea and only 5km south of town.

Hotel Residenz (☎ 271 399; residenz@liburnia.hr; Maršala Tita 133; s/d from 325/550KN) This place has stodgy but decent rooms in a classic building. You can use the swimming pool at the neighbouring Hotel Kristol and the Residenz is right on the sea. More expensive rooms with balconies are available.

Hotel Kvarner (☎ 271 233; kvarner@liburnia.hr; s/d from 410/580KN; P ☒) This genteel 19th-century establishment has an indoor and outdoor swimming pool and has easy access to the sea. The hotel oozes elegance and has more expensive rooms that have sea views and balconies.

Maršala Tita is lined with a number of decent restaurants offering pizza, grilled meat and fish. For a special meal, the best choice is **Bevanda** (☎ 712 769; Zert 8; mains from 70KN), located on the port, which has the freshest fish and a good wine list.

Entertainment

An **open air-cinema** (Park Angiolina) screens films and presents occasional concerts nightly at 9.30pm from May to September. There's a boisterous bar scene centred around the harbour, plus the ever-popular Caffé Harbour or Hemingways.

Getting There & Away

Bus No 32 stops in front of the train station in Rijeka (11KN, 30 minutes) and runs right along the Opatija Riviera, west of Rijeka, every 20 minutes until late in the evening. If you're looking for accommodation, it's easiest to get off at the first stop and walk downhill, passing hotels and other agencies on the way to the bus station.

KRK ISLAND

☎ 051 / pop 18,000

The comparatively barren and rocky Krk (Veglia in Italian) is Croatia's largest island, connected to the mainland in 1980 by the enormous Krk Bridge. The northern part of the island is the site of Rijeka airport, which was a boon to the island economy at the cost of rapid overdevelopment. Real estate was quickly snapped up leaving few areas untouched. Still, the main town (also called Krk) is rather picturesque, and the popular resort of Baška at the island's southern end has a 2km-long pebbly beach set below a high ridge.

Krk Town

Tiny Krk town has a compact medieval centre on a scenic port. From the 12th to 15th centuries, Krk town and the surrounding region remained semi-independent under the Frankopan Dukes of Krk, an indigenous Croatian dynasty, at a time when much of the Adriatic was controlled by Venice. This history explains the various medieval sights in Krk town, the ducal seat.

The bus from Baška and Rijeka stops by the harbour, a few minutes' walk from the old town of Krk. There's no left-luggage facility at Krk bus station. The **Turistička Zajednica** (☎ /fax 221 414; www.tz-krk.hr, in Croatian; Velika Placa 1; ☼ 8am-3pm Mon-Fri) is in the city wall's Guard Tower. You can change money at any travel agency and there's an ATM in the shopping centre near the bus station.

The lovely 14th-century **Frankopan Castle** and 12th-century Romanesque **cathedral** are in the lower town near the harbour. In the upper part of Krk town are three old **monastic churches**. The narrow streets of Krk are worth exploring.

SLEEPING & EATING

There is a range of accommodation in and around Krk, but many places only open during summertime. Private rooms can be organised through **Autotrans** (☎ 221 172; www .autotrans.hr) at the bus station. You can expect to pay from about 140/160KN for a single/double.

Autocamp Ježevac (☎ 221 081; per person/camp sites 40/40KN; ☼ mid-Apr–mid-Oct) On the coast, a 10-minute walk southwest of Krk town, is this camping ground with easy sea access and merciful shade.

Veli Jože (☎ /fax 220 212; damir.dugandzija@sb .htnet.hr; Vitezića 32; dm incl breakfast 145KN) This relatively new hostel is located in a spruced-up older building and is open year-round. Rooms have three, four or six beds.

Hotel Marina (☎ 221 128; Obala Hrvatske Mornarice 6; www.hotelikrk.com: s/d 435/625KN) It's really nothing special, but this is the only hotel right in the town centre.

There are a number of restaurants around the harbour, but for something different, try **Konobo Nono** (Krčkih iseljenika 8; mains from 65KN) which offers *šurlice* (homemade noodles topped with goulash), as well as grilled fish and meat dishes.

Baška

At the southern end of Krk Island, Baška is popular for its 2km-long pebbly beach set below a dramatic, barren range of mountains. Although crowded in summer, the old town and harbour make a pleasant stroll and there's always that splendid beach. The bus from Krk stops at the top of a hill on the edge of the old town, between the beach and the harbour.

The main street of Baška is Zvonimirova, which overlooks the harbour, while the beach begins at the western end of the harbour, continuing southwards past a big sprawling hotel complex. The town's **tourist office** (☎ 856 544; www.tz-baska.hr; Zvonimirova 114; ☼ 8am-8pm daily mid-Jun–Sep, 8am-3pm Mon-Fri Oct–mid-Jun) is just down the street from the bus stop. To arrange hotels or camping, contact **Hoteli Bašaka** (☎ 656 801; www .hotelibaska.hr). For private accommodation,

there's **Gulliver** (☎ 586 004; pdm-baska@ri.htnet
.hr; Zvonimirova 98).

GETTING THERE & AWAY
About 14 buses a day travel between Rijeka and Krk town (32KN, 1½ hours), of
which six continue on to Baška (16KN, up
to one hour). One of the Rijeka buses is
to/from Zagreb (90KN, four hours). To go
from Krk to Zadar, take one of the many
buses to Kraljevica and then change to a
southbound bus.

DALMATIA

Roman ruins, spectacular beaches, old
fishing ports, medieval architecture and
unspoilt offshore islands make a trip to
Dalmatia (Dalmacija) unforgettable. Occupying the central 375km of Croatia's
Adriatic coast, Dalmatia offers a matchless
combination of hedonism and historical
discovery. The jagged coast is speckled
with lush offshore islands and dotted with
historic cities.

Split is the largest city in the region and a
hub for bus and boat connections along the
Adriatic, as well as home to the late Roman
Diocletian's Palace. Nearby are the early
Roman ruins in Solin. Zadar has yet more
Roman ruins and a wealth of churches. The
architecture of Hvar and Korčula recalls
the days when these places were outposts of
the Venetian empire. None can rival majestic
Dubrovnik, a cultural and aesthetic jewel.

The dramatic coastal scenery is due to
the rugged Dinaric Alps, which form a
1500m-long barrier that separates Dalmatia
from Bosnia and Hercegovina. After the last
Ice Age part of the coastal mountains were
flooded, creating the sort of long, high islands seen in the Gulf of Kvarner. The deep,
protected passages between these islands
are a paradise for sailors and cruisers.

ZADAR

☎ 023 / pop 72,700
The main city of northern Dalmatia, Zadar
(ancient Zara) is one of Croatia's more un-
derrated destinations. The marble, traffic-
free streets of the old town are replete with
Roman ruins, medieval churches and several
fascinating museums. Massive 16th-century
fortifications still shield the city on the land-
ward side, with high walls running along the
harbour. The tree-lined promenade along
Obala kralja Petra Krešimira IV is perfect
for a lazy stroll or a picnic, and there are
several small beaches east of the old town.
More beaches lie to the northwest at Borik
as well as on the islands of Ugljan and Dugi
Otok, both within easy reach of the town.

History
In the past 2000 years Zadar has escaped
few wars. Its strategic position on the
Adriatic coast made Zadar a target for the
Romans, the Byzantine, Venetian and Austro-Hungarian empires, and Italy. Although
it was damaged by Allied bombing raids in
1943–44 and Yugoslav rockets in 1991, this
resilient city has been rebuilt and restored,
retaining much of its old flavour. Don't forget to sample Zadar's famous maraschino
cherry liqueur.

Orientation
The train station and the **bus station** (☎ 211
035) are adjacent and are 1km southeast
of the harbour and old town. From the
stations, Zrinsko-Frankopanska ul leads
northwest past the main post office to the
harbour. Buses marked 'Poluotok' run from
the bus station to the harbour. Narodni trg
is the heart of Zadar.

Information
INTERNET ACCESS
Multi-net (☎ 302 207; Stomorica 8; per hr 30KN)

LEFT LUGGAGE
Garderoba (per day 10KN; ◷ 24hr) At the train station.
Garderoba (per day 10KN; ◷ 7am-9pm Mon-Fri) At the
bus station.
Garderoba (per day 10KN; ◷ 7am-8pm Mon-Fri,
7am-3pm Sat) At the Jadrolinija dock.

POST
Main post office (Poljana Pape Aleksandra III) You can
make phone calls here.

TOURIST INFORMATION
Tourist office (☎ 316 166; tzg-zadar@zd.htnet.hr;
Mihe Klaića 5; ◷ 8am-8pm Mon-Sat, 8am-1pm Sun
Jun-Sep, 8am-6pm Mon-Sat Oct-May)

TRAVEL AGENCIES
Aquarius Travel Agency (☎ /fax 212 919; juresko@zd
.htnet.hr; Nova Vrata bb) Accommodation and excursions.

ZADAR

0 ————————— 200 m
0 ————————— 0.1 miles

INFORMATION
Aquarius Travel Agency	**1** D2
Garderoba	**2** D2
Main Post Office	**3** C2
Miatours	**4** C2
Multi-net	**5** C3
Tourist Office	**6** D3

SIGHTS & ACTIVITIES (pp203-4)
Archaeological Museum	**7** C2
Art Gallery	**8** D3
Cathedral of St Anastasia	**9** C2
Forum	**10** B2
Franciscan Monastery	**11** B2
Museum of Church Art	**12** C2
National Museum	**13** C2
St Donatus Church	**14** C2
St Šimun Church	**15** D3

SLEEPING (p204)
Jović Guest House	**16** C4

EATING (p204)
Burek Stands	(see 21)
Dva Ribara	**17** C3
Konoba Marival	**18** D3
Restaurant Martinac	**19** B2
Supermarket	**20** D2
Vegetable Market	**21** D2

DRINKING (p204)
Central Kavana	**22** C3
Kult Caffe	**23** C3

TRANSPORT (p205)
Croatia Airlines	**24** C1
Croatia Express	**25** C2
Jadroagent	**26** C1
Jadrolinija	**27** B1
Jodrolinija Stall	**28** C1

OTHER
Medieval Tower	**29** D4
Orthodox Church	**30** B2
Ruins	**31** C4
St Krševan	**32** C2
Town Gate	**33** D4
Town Watchtower	**34** D3

Atlas travel agency (☎ 235 850; atlas@zadar.net; Branimirova Obala 12) Across the footbridge over the harbour, and just northeast of Narodni trg, Atlas finds private accommodation and runs excursions.

Miatours (☎ /fax 212 788; miatrade@zd.htnet.hr; Vrata Sveti Krševana) Accommodation and excursions.

Sights & Activities

Most attractions are near **St Donatus Church** (Šimuna Kožičića Benje; admission 5KN; ✆ 9.30am-2pm & 4-6pm Mar-Oct), a circular 9th-century Byzantine structure built over the Roman forum. Slabs for the ancient forum are visible in the church and there is a pillar from the Roman era on the northwestern side. In summer ask about the musical evenings here (featuring Renaissance and early bar-oque music). The outstanding **Museum of Church Art** (Trg Opatice Čike bb; adult/student 20/10KN; ✆ 10am-12.30pm daily, 6-8pm Mon-Sat), in the Benedictine monastery opposite St Donatus, offers three floors of elaborate gold and silver reliquaries, religious paintings, icons and local lacework.

The 13th-century Romanesque **Cathedral of St Anastasia** (Trg Svete Stošije; ✆ only for Mass) has some fine Venetian carvings in the 15th-century choir stalls. The **Franciscan Monastery** (Zadarscog mira 1358; admission free; ✆ 7.30am-noon & 4.30-6pm) is the oldest Gothic church in Dalmatia (consecrated in 1280), with lovely interior Renaissance features and a large Romanesque cross in the treasury, behind the sacristy.

CROATIA

The most interesting museum is the **Archaeological Museum** (Trg Opatice Čike 1; adult/student 10/5KN; ☺ 9am-1pm & 6-9pm Mon-Fri, 9am-1pm Sat), across from St Donatus, with an extensive collection of artefacts, from the Neolithic period through the Roman occupation to the development of Croatian culture under the Byzantines. Some captions are in English and you are handed a leaflet in English when you buy your ticket.

Less interesting is the **National Museum** (Poljana Pape Aleksandra III; admission 5KN; ☺ 9am-noon & 5-8pm Mon-Fri), just inside the sea gate, featuring photos of Zadar from different periods, and old paintings and engravings of many coastal cities. The same admission ticket will get you into the **art gallery** (Smiljanića; ☺ 9am-noon & 5-8pm Mon-Fri, 9am-1pm Sat). One church worth a visit is **St Šimun Church** (Šime Budinica; ☺ 8am-noon & 6-8pm Jun-Sep), which has a 14th-century gold chest.

There's a swimming area with diving boards, a small park and a café on the coastal promenade off Zvonimira. Bordered by pine trees and parks, the promenade takes you to a beach in front of Hotel Kolovare and then winds on for about a kilometre up the coast.

Tours

Any of the many travel agencies around town can supply information on tourist cruises to the beautiful Kornati Islands, river-rafting and half-day excursions to the Krka waterfalls.

Festivals & Events

Major annual events include the **town fair** (July and August), the **Dalmatian Song Festival** (July and August), the **musical evenings** in St Donatus Church (August) and the **Choral Festival** (October).

Sleeping

Most visitors head out to the 'tourist settlement' at Borik, 3km northwest of Zadar, on the Puntamika bus (6KN, every 20 minutes from the bus station). Here there are hotels, a hostel, a camping ground, big swimming pools, sporting opportunities and numerous 'sobe' (rooms) signs; you can arrange a private room through a travel agency in town (see p202). Expect to pay about 140KN per person for a nice room with a bathroom.

Autocamp Borik (☎ 332 074; per person/camp site 30/60KN) This large camping ground is just steps away from Borik beach.

Borik Youth Hostel (☎ 331 145; zadar@hfhs.hr; Obala Kneza Trpimira 76; B&B/half-board 90/120KN) Friendly and well-kept, this hostel is near the beach at Borik.

Jović Guest House (☎ 214 098, 098 330 958; Šime Ljubića 4a; d 300KN) If you want to stay in town, the best choice is this 12-room guesthouse in the heart of town, with smallish but cool and attractive rooms with bathroom. The price does not include breakfast but there are plenty of cafés around where you can have your morning meal. If you can't reach the owner, the rooms can be reserved through Aquarius Travel Agency (p202).

In Borik, **Hotel Mediteran** (☎ 337 500; www .hotelmediteran-zd.hr; M Gupca 19; s/d 380/495KN; P 🍴 💻) has comfortable rooms and is fairly close to the beach. You can also try the **Hotel President** (☎ 333 464; www.hotel-president .hr; Vladana Desnice 16; rooms 835KN; P 🍴 💻) for the full first-class treatment, also near the beach.

Eating

Dva Ribara (Blaža Jurjeva 1; mains from 40KN) With a wide range of food and an outdoor terrace, Dva Ribara is justifiably popular with the local crowd.

Konoba Marival (☎ 213 239; Don Ive Prodana 3; mains from 45KN) If your mama married a fisherman, she'd probably dream up the kinds of dishes that are served here. The ambience is also homy and intimate.

Restaurant Martinac (Papavije 7; mains from 55KN) The secluded backyard terrace behind this restaurant provides a relaxed atmosphere in which to sample delicious risotto and fish.

There's a **supermarket** (cnr Široka & Sabora) that is open longer hours, and you'll also find a number of *burek* stands around the vegetable market.

Drinking

In summer the many cafés along Varoška and Klaića place their tables on the street; it's great for people-watching.

Central Kavana (Široka) A spacious café and hang-out with live music at the weekend.

Kult Caffe (Stomarica) Draws a young crowd who listen to rap music indoors or relax on the large shady terrace outside.

Getting There & Away

AIR

Zadar's airport, 12km east of the city, receives charter flights and **Croatia Airlines** (☎ 250 101; Poljana Natka Nodila 7) flights from Zagreb daily. A Croatia Airlines bus meets all flights and costs 15KN; a taxi into town costs around 175KN.

BOAT

The Jadrolinija coastal ferry from Rijeka to Dubrovnik calls at Zadar twice weekly (138/168KN low/high season, six hours). It arrives around midnight. The **Jadrolinija** (☎ 254 800; Liburnska obala 7) office is on the harbour and has tickets for all local ferries, or you can buy ferry tickets from the Jadrolinija stall on Liburnska obala.

Jadroagent (☎ 211 447; jadroagent-zadar@zd.htnet .hr; Poljana Natka Nodila 4) is just inside the city walls and has tickets and information for all boats.

For information on boat connections to Italy see p229.

BUS & TRAIN

Zadar is on the coastal route that goes from Rijeka down to Split and Dubrovnik. There are four daily trains to Zagreb (84KN, 9¾ hours) that change at Knin, but the bus to Zagreb is quicker and stops at Plitvice Lakes National Park (32KN, three hours).

Croatia Express (☎ 250 502; croatiae@zd.htnet .hr; Široka) sells bus tickets to many German cities. See p228.

Around Zadar

PLITVICE LAKES

Plitvice Lakes National Park (admission Oct-May/Jun-Sep 75/95KN, students 45/55KN) lies midway between Zagreb and Zadar. The 19.5 hectares of wooded hills enclose 16 turquoise lakes, which are connected by a series of waterfalls and cascades. The mineral-rich waters carve new paths through the rock, depositing tufa (new porous rock) in continually changing formations. Wooden footbridges follow the lakes and streams over, under and across the rumbling water for an exhilaratingly damp 18km. Swimming is not allowed. Your park admission is valid for the entire stay and also includes the boats and buses you need to use to see the lakes. There is accommodation on site, as well as private accommodation nearby. Check the

options with the National Park information office in Zagreb (see p185).

Getting There & Away

All buses from Zadar to Zagreb stop at Plitvice (32KN, three hours). It is possible to visit Plitvice for the day on the way to or from the coast but be aware that if they are full buses will not pick up passengers at Plitvice. Luggage can be left at the **tourist information centre** (☎ 053-751 015; www.np-plitvice .com; ☺ 7am-8pm), located at the first entrance to the park.

SPLIT

☎ 021 / pop 188,700

Split (Spalato in Italian), the largest Croatian city on the Adriatic coast, is a major industrial city ringed with apartment-block housing of stupefying ugliness, but the remarkable Diocletian's Palace (which is now a World Heritage Site) makes a visit to the city worthwhile – and a visit is indispensable if you'll be visiting one of the many islands within reach of Split. In the centre of town, within the ancient walls of Diocletian's Palace, rises the majestic cathedral surrounded by a tangle of marble streets containing shops and businesses. The entire western end of town is a vast, wooded mountain park with beaches below and pathways above. A refurbished harbourside promenade lined with cafés makes for a pleasant stroll, and the high coastal mountains set against the blue Adriatic provide a striking frame, best appreciated as your ferry heads into or out of the port.

History

Split achieved fame when Roman emperor Diocletian (AD 245-313), who was noted for his persecution of the early Christians, had his retirement palace built here from 295 to 305. After his death the great stone palace continued to be used as a retreat by Roman rulers. When the neighbouring colony of Salona was abandoned in the 7th century, many of the Romanised inhabitants fled to Split and barricaded themselves behind the high palace walls, where their descendants continue to live to this day.

The town was hard-hit economically (although not militarily) when the former Yugoslavia split up, and is still struggling to

CROATIA

regains its footing. It's clearly less prosperous than Zagreb or Dubrovnik, which helps explain why so many residents flock to the bus station and port to hawk their extra rooms to disembarking tourists.

Orientation

The bus, train and ferry terminals are adjacent on the eastern side of the harbour, a short walk from the old town. Obala hrvatskog narodnog preporoda, the waterfront promenade, is your best central reference point in Split.

Information

BOOKSHOPS

Algoritam (Map p207; Bajamontijeva 2) A good English-language bookshop.

INTERNET ACCESS

Mriža (Map p207; ☎ 321 320; Kružićeva 3; per hr 20KN)

LEFT LUGGAGE

Garderoba (🕑 6am-10pm) At the bus station.
Garderoba (Obala Kneza Domagoja 6; 🕑 7am-9pm)

The train station's left luggage office is about 50m north of the station.

MONEY

Change money at travel agencies or the post office. You'll find ATMs around the bus and train stations.

POST

Main post office (Map p207; Kralja Tomislava 9) There's also a telephone centre (🕑 7am-9pm Mon-Sat) here.

TOURIST INFORMATION

Internet Games & Books (Map p207; ☎ 338 548; Obala Kneza Domagoja 3) Luggage storage, information for backpackers, used books and an Internet connection for 35KN per hour.

Turist Biro (Map p207; ☎ /fax 342 142; turist-biro -split@st.htnet.hr; Obala hrvatskog narodnog preporoda 12) Arranges private accommodation and sells guidebooks and the Split Card.

Turistička Zajednica (Map p207; ☎ /fax 342 606; www.visitsplit.com; Peristyle; 🕑 9am-8.30pm Mon-Sat, 8am-1pm Sun) Has information on Split; sells the Split Card for 60KN, offering free and discounted admission to Split attractions.

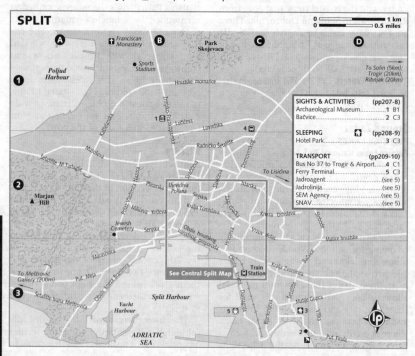

SPLIT

| | 0 ———— 1 km |
| | 0 ———— 0.5 miles |

SIGHTS & ACTIVITIES (pp207-8)
Archaeological Museum...............1 B1
Bačvice.................................2 C3

SLEEPING (pp208-9)
Hotel Park...............................3 C3

TRANSPORT (pp209-10)
Bus No 37 to Trogir & Airport......4 C1
Ferry Terminal..........................5 C3
Jadroagent.............................(see 5)
Jadrolinija.............................(see 5)
SEM Agency...........................(see 5)
SNAV....................................(see 5)

To Solin (5km);
Trogir (20km);
Ribnjak (20km)

Franciscan Monastery
Park Skojevaca
Poljud Harbour
Sports Stadium
Hrvatske mornarice

To Lisičina
To Meštrović Gallery (200m)
Marjan Hill
Jewish Cemetery

See Central Split Map
Train Station

Split Harbour
Yacht Harbour
ADRIATIC SEA

Put Finela

TRAVEL AGENCIES
Atlas travel agency (Map p207; ☎ 343 055; Nepotova 4) The town's Amex representative.
Daluma Travel (Map p207; ☎ /fax 338 484; daluma -st@st.htnet.hr; Obala Kneza Domagoja 1) Finds private accommodation.

Sights
DIOCLETIAN'S PALACE   Map p207
The old town is a vast open-air museum and the new information signs at the important sights explain a great deal of Split's history.
Diocletian's Palace (entrance: Obala hrvatskog narodnog preporoda 22), facing the harbour, is one of the most imposing Roman ruins in existence. It was built as a strong rectangular fortress, with walls measuring 215m from east to west, 181m wide at the southernmost point and reinforced by square corner towers. The imperial residence, mausoleum and temples were south of the main street, now called Krešlmirova, connecting the east and west palace gates.

Enter through the central ground floor of the palace. On the left are the excavated **basement halls** (adult/concession 6/3KN; ☉ 10am-6pm), which are empty but still impressive. Go through the passage to the **peristyle**, a picturesque colonnaded square, with a neo-Romanesque cathedral tower rising above. The **vestibule**, an open dome above the ground-floor passageway at the southern end of the peristyle, is overpowering-ly grand and cavernous. A lane off the

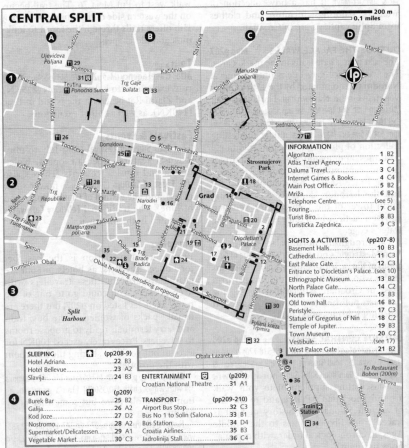

CENTRAL SPLIT

INFORMATION
Algoritam	**1** B2
Atlas Travel Agency	**2** C2
Daluma Travel	**3** C4
Internet Games & Books	**4** C4
Main Post Office	**5** B2
Mriža	**6** B2
Telephone Centre	(see 5)
Touring	**7** C4
Turist Biro	**8** B3
Turistička Zajednica	**9** C4

SIGHTS & ACTIVITIES (pp207-8)
Basement Halls	**10** B3
Cathedral	**11** C3
East Palace Gate	**12** C3
Entrance to Diocletian's Palace	(see 10)
Ethnographic Museum	**13** B2
North Palace Gate	**14** C2
North Tower	**15** B3
Old town hall	**16** B2
Peristyle	**17** C3
Statue of Gregorius of Nin	**18** C2
Temple of Jupiter	**19** B3
Town Museum	**20** C2
Vestibule	(see 17)
West Palace Gate	**21** B2

SLEEPING (pp208-9)
Hotel Adriana	**22** B3
Hotel Bellevue	**23** A2
Slavija	**24** B3

EATING (p209)
Burek Bar	**25** B2
Galija	**26** A2
Kod Joze	**27** D2
Nostromo	**28** A2
Supermarket/Delicatessen	**29** A1
Vegetable Market	**30** C3

ENTERTAINMENT (p209)
Croatian National Theatre	**31** A1

TRANSPORT (pp209-210)
Airport Bus Stop	**32** C3
Bus No 1 to Solin (Salona)	**33** B1
Bus Station	**34** D4
Croatia Airlines	**35** B3
Jadrolinija Stall	**36** C4

CROATIA

peristyle opposite the cathedral leads to the **Temple of Jupiter**, which is now a baptistry.

On the eastern side of the peristyle is the **cathedral**, originally Diocletian's mausoleum. The only reminder of Diocletian in the cathedral is a sculpture of his head in a circular stone wreath, below the dome which is directly above the baroque white-marble altar. The Romanesque wooden doors (1214) and stone pulpit are notable. For a small fee you can climb the tower .

In the Middle Ages the nobility and rich merchants built their residences within the old palace walls; the Papalic Palace is now the **town museum** (☎ 341 240; Papalićeva ul 5; adult/concession 10/5KN; ☉ 9am-noon & 5-8pm Tue-Fri, 10am-noon Sat & Sun Jun-Sep, 10am-5pm Tue-Fri, 10am-noon Sat & Sun Oct-May). It has a tidy collection of artefacts, paintings, furniture and clothes from Split; captions are in Croatian.

OUTSIDE THE PALACE WALLS   Map p207
The east palace gate leads to the market area. The west palace gate opens onto medieval Narodni trg, dominated by the 15th-century Venetian Gothic **old town hall**. The **Ethnographic Museum** (☎ 344 164; Narodni trg; adult/student 10/5KN; ☉ 10am-1pm Tue-Fri Jun-Sep, 10am-4pm Tue-Fri, 10am-1pm Sat & Sun Oct-May) has a mildly interesting collection of photos of old Split, traditional costumes and memorabilia of important citizens; captions are in Croatian.

Trg Braće Radića, between Narodni trg and the harbour, contains the surviving north tower of the 15th-century Venetian garrison castle, which once extended to the water's edge.

Go through the north palace gate to see Ivan Meštrović's powerful 1929 **statue of Gregorius of Nin**, a 10th-century Slavic religious leader who fought for the right to perform Mass in Croatian. Notice that his big toe has been polished to a shine; it's said that touching it brings good luck.

OUTSIDE CENTRAL SPLIT   Map p206
The **archaeological museum** (☎ 318 720; Zrinjsko-Frankopanska 25; adult/student 10/5KN; ☉ 9am-noon & 5-8pm Tue-Fri, 9am-noon Sat & Sun), north of town, is a fascinating supplement to your walk around Diocletian's Palace and to the site of ancient Salona. The history of Split is traced from Illyrian times to the Middle Ages, in chronological order, with explanations in English.

The finest art museum in Split is **Meštrović Gallery** (☎ 358 450; Šetalište Ivana Meštrovića 46; adult/student 15/10KN; ☉ 9am-9pm Tue-Sun Jun-Sep, 9am-4pm Tue-Sat, 10am-3pm Sun Oct-May). You'll see a comprehensive, well-arranged collection of works by Ivan Meštrović, Croatia's premier modern sculptor, who built the gallery as his home in 1931–39. Although Meštrović intended to retire here, he emigrated to the USA soon after WWII. Bus No 12 runs to the gallery from Trg Republike every 40 minutes.

From the Meštrović Gallery it's possible to hike straight up **Marjan Hill**. Go up ul Tonća Petrasova Marovića on the western side of the gallery and continue straight up the stairway to Put Meja ul. Turn left and walk west to Put Meja 76. The trail begins on the western side of this building. Marjan Hill offers trails through the forest to lookouts and old chapels.

Tours
Atlas travel agency (Map p207; ☎ 343 055; Nepotova 4) runs excursions to Krka waterfalls (225KN) and Zlatni Rat beach on the island of Brač (140KN), as well as other excursions.

Festivals & Events
The **Split Summer Festival** (mid-July to mid-August) features open-air opera, ballet, drama and musical concerts. There's also the **Feast of St Dujo** (7 May), a flower show (May) and the **Festival of Popular Music** (end of June). The traditional **February Carnival** is presented in the old town.

Sleeping
Private accommodation is the best bet for budget travellers, as hotels in Split are geared towards business travellers with deep pockets. You could go to one of the travel agencies listed on p207, but there are usually packs of women at the bus, train and ferry terminals ready to propose rooms to travellers. Prices rarely exceed 100KN for a room but you'll be sharing the bathroom with the proprietor.

Slavija (Map p207; ☎ 347 053; fax 344 062; Buvinova 3; r with/without bath 450/350KN) Has a great location in the old town but somewhat noisy rooms.

Hotel Bellevue (Map p207; ☎ 347 499; fax 362 383; www.hotel-bellevue-split.hr; bana Josipa Jelačića 2; s/d 490/682KN) The Bellevue is an old classic that has seen better days. Rooms on the street side can be noisy but the location is good and the rooms are well tended. If you take a taxi from the port get ready for a long, meandering ride as the driver navigates the many one-way streets.

Hotel Adriana (Map p207; ☎ 340 000; info@hotel -adriana.com; Obala hrvatskog narodnog preporoda 9; s/d 550/750KN; ✺) This new entry on the hotel scene has eight fresh new rooms, some of which have a sea view. All are soundproofed. Prices stay the same all year.

Hotel Park (Map p206; ☎ 406 400; www.hotelpark -split.hr; Hatzeov perivoj 3; s/d 795/1015KN; P ✺ 🖳) Close to the centre, this hotel nonetheless provides a resort experience with a large shady terrace and an easy walk to the beach. Rooms are nicely decorated and comfortable, although not large.

Eating

Galija (Map p207; Tončićeva; pizzas from 26KN) Hands down the best pizza in town, this perennial favourite still packs in a young, lively crowd.

Kod Joze (Map p207; ☎ 347 397; Sredmanuška 4; mains from 40KN) A die-hard faction of locals keeps this informal *konoba* (a small, family-owned bistro) alive and kicking. It's Dalmatian all the way – ham, cheese and green tagliatelle with seafood.

Restaurant Boban (Map p207; ☎ 510 142; Hektorovićeva 49; mains from 60KN) The décor may be sober and traditional but this family-owned restaurant devotes considerable effort to keeping its menu up to date. The risotto is perfection and the angler wrapped in bacon, mouth watering.

Nostromo (Map p207; ☎ 091 405 66 66; Kraj Sv Marije 10; mains from 65KN) Marine creatures of all persuasions form a delightful menu in this sweetly decorated spot next to the fish market.

There's a spiffy **Burek Bar** (Map p207; Domaldova 13) near the main post office, and the vast **supermarket/delicatessen** (Map p207; Svačićeva 1) has a wide selection of meat and cheese for sandwiches. The vegetable market has a wide array of fresh local produce.

Entertainment

In summer everyone starts the evening at one of the cafés along Obala hrvatskog narodnog preporoda and then heads towards the Bačvice (Map p206) complex on the beach. These former public baths offer restaurants, cafés, discos and venues for live rock and salsa. During winter, opera and ballet are presented at the **Croatian National Theatre** (Trg Gaje Bulata; best seats about 60KN); tickets for the same night are usually available. Erected in 1891, the theatre was fully restored in 1979 in the original style; it's worth attending a performance for the architecture alone.

Getting There & Away

AIR

The country's national air carrier, **Croatia Airlines** (Map p207; ☎ 362 997; Obala hrvatskog narodnog preporoda 8), operates flights between Zagreb and Split up to four times every day (475KN, one hour). Rates are lower if you book in advance.

BOAT

You can buy tickets for passenger ferries at the **Jadrolinija stall** (Map p207; Obala Kneza Domagoja). There are also several agents in the large ferry terminal opposite the bus station that can assist with boat trips from Split: **Jadroagent** (Map p206; ☎ 338 335) represents Adriatica Navigazione for its connections between Split and Ancona; **Jadrolinija** (Map p206; ☎ 338 333) handles all car ferry services that depart from the docks around the ferry terminal; **SEM agency** (Map p206; ☎ 338 292) handles tickets between Ancona, Split and Hvar; and **SNAV** (Map p206; ☎ 322 252) has a four-hour connection to Ancona and Pescara.

For more details on connections to/from Italy see p229.

BUS

Advance bus tickets with seat reservations are recommended. There are buses from the main **bus station** (Map p207; ☎ 060 327 327; www .ak-split.hr, in Croatian) beside the harbour to:

Destination	Cost	Duration	Frequency
Dubrovnik	72-111KN	4½hr	12 daily
Ljubljana	230KN	10hr	1 daily
Međugorje	54-89KN	3hr	4 daily
Mostar	54-65KN	2-4hr	4 daily
Pula	215-278KN	10hr	3 daily
Rijeka	161-231KN	8hr	14 daily
Sarajevo	93-128KN	7hr	11 daily
Zadar	66-89KN	3hr	26 daily
Zagreb	112-143KN	6-9hr	27 daily

CROATIA

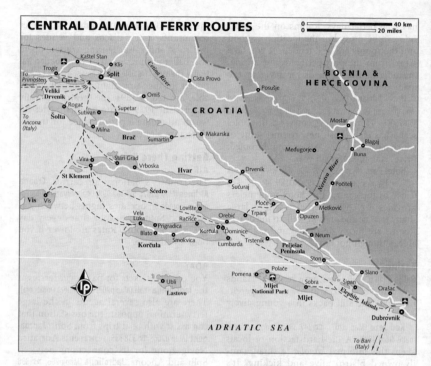

CENTRAL DALMATIA FERRY ROUTES

Touring (Map p207; ☎ 338 503; Obala Kneza Domagojeva 10), near the bus station, represents Deutsche Touring and sells tickets to German cities.

Bus No 37 to Solin, Split airport and Trogir leaves from a local bus station on Domovinskog, 1km northeast of the city centre (see Map p206).

TRAIN

There are four trains daily that run between Split and Zagreb (90KN to 131KN, eight to nine hours depending on the service and the time of day), and Split and Šibenik (33KN, 90 minutes).

Getting Around

There's an airport bus stop on Obala Lazareta 3. The bus (30KN, 30 minutes) leaves about 90 minutes before flight times, or you can take bus No 37 from the bus station on Domovinskog (9.50KN for a two-zone ticket).

A one-zone ticket costs 7KN for one trip in Central Split if you buy it from the driver but 11KN for two trips and 55KN for 10

trips if you buy it from a kiosk. There's a kiosk that also distributes bus maps at the city bus stop.

SOLIN (SALONA)

The ruins of the ancient city of Solin (known as Salona by the Romans), among the vineyards at the foot of mountains 5km northeast of Split, are the most interesting archaeological site in Croatia. Today surrounded by noisy highways and industry, Salona was the capital of the Roman province of Dalmatia from the time Julius Caesar elevated it to the status of colony. Salona held out against the barbarians and was only evacuated in AD 614 when the inhabitants fled to Split and neighbouring islands in the face of Avar and Slav attacks.

Sights

A good place to begin your visit is at the main entrance, near Caffe Bar Salona. There's a small **museum and information centre** (admission 10KN; 🕙 9am-6pm Mon-Sat Jun-Sep, 9am-1pm Mon-Sat Oct-May) at the entrance, which

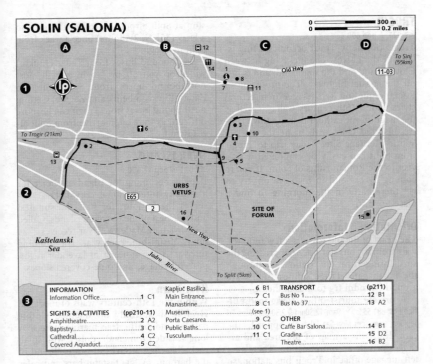

SOLIN (SALONA)

0 ————— 300 m
0 ————— 0.2 miles

To Sinj (55km)

To Trogir (21km)

Old Hwy

11-03

URBS VETUS

E65

2

Kaštelanski Sea

Jadro River

New Hwy

To Split (5km)

SITE OF FORUM

INFORMATION		Kapljuč Basilica	6	B1	TRANSPORT	(p211)
Information Office	1 C1	Main Entrance	7	C1	Bus No 1	12 B1
		Manastirine	8	C1	Bus No 37	13 A2
SIGHTS & ACTIVITIES	(pp210-11)	Museum	(see 1)			
Amphitheatre	2 A2	Porta Caesarea	9	C2	OTHER	
Baptistry	3 C1	Public Baths	10	C1	Caffe Bar Salona	14 B1
Cathedral	4 C2	Tusculum	11	C1	Gradina	15 D2
Covered Aquaduct	5 C2				Theatre	16 B2

also provides a helpful map and some literature about the complex.

Manastirine, the fenced area behind the car park, was a burial place for early Christian martyrs before the legalisation of Christianity. Excavated remains of the cemetery and the 5th-century basilica are highlights, although this area was outside the ancient city itself. Overlooking Manastirine is **Tusculum** with interesting sculptures embedded in the walls and in the garden.

The Manastirine-Tusculum complex is a part of an archaeological reserve which can be freely entered. A path bordered by cypress trees runs south towards the northern **city wall** of Salona. Note the **covered aqueduct** along the inside base of the wall. The ruins in front of you as you stand on the wall were the early Christian cult centre, which include the three-aisled, 5th-century **cathedral** and a small **baptistry** with inner columns. **Public baths** adjoin the cathedral on the eastern side.

Southwest of the cathedral is the 1st-century east city gate, **Porta Caesarea**, later engulfed by the growth of Salona in all directions. Grooves in the stone road left by ancient chariots can still be seen at this gate.

Walk west along the city wall for about 500m to **Kapljuč Basilica** on the right, another martyrs' burial place. At the western end of Salona is the huge 2nd-century **amphitheatre**, destroyed in the 17th century by the Venetians to prevent it from being used as a refuge for Turkish raiders.

Getting There & Away

The ruins are easily accessible on Split city bus No 1 direct to Solin every half-hour from the city bus stop at Trg Gaje Bulata.

From the amphitheatre at Solin it's easy to continue to Trogir by catching a westbound bus No 37 from the nearby stop on the adjacent new highway. If, on the other hand, you want to return to Split, use the underpass to cross the highway and catch an eastbound bus No 37 (buy a four-zone ticket in Split if you plan to do this).

Alternatively, you can catch most Sinj-bound buses (5KN, 10 daily) from Split's main bus station to take you to Solin.

CROATIA

TROGIR
☎ 021 / pop 600

Trogir (formerly Trau) occupies a tiny island in the narrow channel lying between Čiovo Island and the mainland, and is just off the coastal highway. The profusion of Romanesque and Renaissance architectural styles within 15th-century walls, as well as the magnificent cathedral at the town centre, inspired Unesco to name the town a World Heritage Site. A day trip to Trogir from Split can easily be combined with a visit to the Roman ruins of Solin. If you're coming by car and in high season, try to get there early in the morning to find a place to park.

Orientation & Information

The heart of the old town is a few minutes' walk from the bus station. After crossing the small bridge near the station, go through the north gate. Trogir's finest sights are around Narodni trg to the southeast.

A private tourist office, **Čipiko Tourist Office** (☎ 881 554; ⏲ 9am-12.30pm & 2.30-5pm Mon-Fri Sep-Jun, 9am-8pm Mon-Sat Jul-Aug), opposite the cathedral, sells a map of the area and arranges private accommodation. There's no left-luggage office in Trogir bus station, so you may end up toting your bags around town.

Sights

The glory of the three-nave Venetian **Cathedral of St Lovro** (Trg Ivana Pavla II; ⏲ 9.30am-noon year-round & 4.30-7pm daily during summer) is the Romanesque portal of *Adam and Eve* (1240) by Master Radovan, the earliest example of the nude in Dalmatian sculpture. Enter the building via an obscure back door to see the perfect Renaissance Chapel of St Ivan and the choir stalls, pulpit, ciborium (vessel used to hold consecrated wafers) and treasury. You can even climb the cathedral tower, if it's open, for a great view. Also located on the square is the renovated **Church of St John the Baptist** with a magnificent carved portal and an interior showcasing a *Pietá* by Nicola Firentinac.

Getting There & Away

In Split, city bus No 37 leaves from the bus station on Domovinskog. It runs between Trogir and Split every 20 minutes (15KN, one hour) throughout the day, with a short stop at Split airport en route. There's also a ferry (35KN, 2½hours) once a week from Split to Trogir.

Southbound buses from Zadar (130km) will drop you off in Trogir, as will most northbound buses from Split going to Zadar, Rijeka, Šibenik and Zagreb. Getting northbound buses from Trogir can be more difficult, as they often arrive from Split already full.

HVAR ISLAND
☎ 021 / pop 12,600

Rapidly becoming the island of choice for a swanky international crowd, Hvar deserves the honour, for it is the sunniest and greenest of the Croatian islands. Called the 'Croatian Madeira', Hvar receives 2724 hours of sunshine each year. The stunning interior is a panorama of lavender fields, peaceful villages and pine-covered slopes.

Hvar Town

Within the 13th-century walls of medieval Hvar lie beautifully ornamented Gothic palaces and traffic-free marble streets. A long seaside promenade, dotted with small rocky beaches, stretches from each end of the harbour. A few tasteful bars and cafés along the harbour are relaxing spots for people-watching. For more activity, hop on a launch to the Pakleni islands, famous for nude sunbathing.

ORIENTATION

Car ferries from Split deposit you in Stari Grad but local buses meet most ferries in summer for the trip to Hvar town. The town centre is Trg Sv Stjepana, 100m west of the bus station. Passenger ferries tie up on Riva, the eastern quay, in front of Pelegrini Travel.

INFORMATION

Atlas travel agency (☎ 741 670) On the western side of the harbour.

Garderoba (⏲ 7am-midnight) The left luggage office is in the bathroom next to the bus station.

Hotel Slavija (☎ 741 820; fax 741 147; Riva; per hr 20KN) Internet access.

Mengola Travel (☎ /fax 742 099; megola-hvar@st .htnet.hr) Finds private accommodation.

Pelegrini Travel (☎ /fax 742 250; kuzma.novak@st .htnet.hr) Also finds private accommodation.

Post office (Riva) You can make phone calls here.

Tourist office (☎ /fax 742 977; www.hvar.hr; ☼ 8am-1pm & 5-9pm Mon-Sat, 9am-noon Sun Jun-Sep, 8am-2pm Mon-Sat Oct-May) In the arsenal building on the corner of Trg Sv Stjepana.

SIGHTS & ACTIVITIES

The full flavour of medieval Hvar is best savoured on the backstreets of the old town. At each end of Hvar is a monastery with a prominent tower. The Dominican **Church of St Marko** at the head of the bay was largely destroyed by Turks in the 16th century but you can visit the local **archaeological museum** (admission 10KN; ☼ 10am-noon Jun-Sep) in the ruins. If it is closed you'll still get a good view of the ruins from the road just above, which leads up to a stone cross on a hill top offering a picture-postcard view of Hvar.

At the southeastern end of Hvar you'll find the 15th-century Renaissance **Franciscan Monastery** (☼ 10am-noon & 5-7pm Jun-Sep & Christmas week & Holy Week), with a wonderful collection of Venetian paintings in the church and adjacent **museum** (admission 10KN; ☼ 10am-noon & 5-7pm Mon-Sat Jun-Sep), including *The Last Supper* by Matteo Ingoli.

Smack in the middle of Hvar is the imposing Gothic **arsenal**, its great arch visible from afar. The local commune's war galley was once kept here. Upstairs off the arsenal terrace is Hvar's prize; the first **municipal theatre** (admission 10KN; ☼ 10am-noon & 5-7pm) in Europe (1612), rebuilt in the 19th century. Hours can vary and you enter through the adjoining **Gallery of Contemporary Croatian Art** (arsenal; admission 10KN; ☼ 10am-noon & 7-11pm Jun-Sep & Christmas week & Holy Week, 10am-noon low season).

On the hill high above Hvar town is a **Venetian fortress** (1551), and it's worth the climb up to appreciate the sweeping panoramic views. The fort was built to defend Hvar from the Turks, who sacked the town in 1539 and 1571.

There is a small town beach next to the Franciscan Monastery, but the best beach is in front of the Hotel Amphora, around the western corner of the cove. Most people take a launch out to the offshore islands that include the naturist Pakleni islands of Jerolim and Stipanska and lovely Palmižana.

In front of the Hotel Amphora, **Diving Centar Jurgovan** (☎ 742 490) is a large operation that offers a certification course, dives (€40 with equipment) and all sorts of water sports (banana boating, snorkelling, water-skiing), as well as hotel packages.

SLEEPING

Accommodation in Hvar is extremely tight in July and August: a reservation is highly recommended. For private accommodation, try Mengola Travel or Pelegrini (opposite). Expect to pay from 160/280KN per single /double with bathroom in the town centre.

Mala Milna (☎ 745 027; per person/camp sites 40/30KN) This restful camping ground is the closest, only 2km southeast of town.

Jagoda & Ante Bracanović Guesthouse (☎ 741 416; 091 520 37 96; virgilye@yahoo.com; Poviše Škole; s 100-120KN, d 190-220KN) This friendly place is close to the town centre and offers six spacious rooms, each with a bathroom, balcony and kitchen access.

Hotel Slavija (☎ 741 820; fax 741 147; Riva; s/d 533/840KN; ☐) The great thing here is that you step off the passenger boat from Split and into hotel reception. The location on the harbour is the main selling point and the rooms are more than acceptable. Reservations for this and the other large hotels in and around the old town are handled by **Sunčani Hvar** (☎ 741 026; www.suncanihvar.hr).

Hotel Podstine (☎ 741 118; www.podstine.com; s/d 659/1147KN; ☼) Just 2km southwest of the town centre on the secluded Podstine cove lies this beautifully restored and romantic hotel with its own private beach.

EATING

The pizzerias along the harbour offer predictable but inexpensive eating.

Konoba Menego (☎ 742 036; mains 40KN) Located on the stairway over the Benedictine convent, this eatery is a good choice.

Bounty (☎ 742 565; mains from 60KN) Next to Mengola travel agency, this place is a long-time favourite for its succulent fish, pasta and meat dishes at reasonable prices.

Macondo (☎ 741 851; mains from 60KN) Head upstairs from the northern side of Trg Sv Stjepana for mouth-watering seafood.

The **grocery store** (Trg Sv Stjepana) is a viable restaurant alternative and there's a morning market next to the bus station.

DRINKING

Hvar has some of the best nightlife on the Adriatic coast, mostly centred around the harbour.

CROATIA

Carpe Diem (☎ 742 369; Riva) From a groggy breakfast to late-night cocktails, there is no time of day when this swanky place is dull. The music is smooth, the drinks fruity and expensive, and the sofas more than welcoming.

Nautika (Fabrika) Offering cocktails with names like 'Sex on the Beach' and nonstop dance music, from techno to hip-hop, this place is ground zero for Hvar's explosive nightlife. Just up the street is Kiva Bar, where you can chill out and talk between dance numbers.

GETTING THERE & AWAY

The Jadrolinija ferries between Rijeka and Dubrovnik stop in Stari Grad before continuing to Korčula. The **Jadrolinija agency** (☎ 741 132; Riva) sells boat tickets.

Car ferries from Split call at Stari Grad (32KN, one hour) three times daily (five daily in July and August) and there's an afternoon passenger boat from Split to Hvar town (23KN, 50 minutes) that goes on to Vela Luka on Korčula Island (22KN, one hour). See p229 for information on international connections. Buses meet most ferries that dock at Stari Grad in July and August, but if you come in winter it's best to check first with one of the travel agencies to make sure the bus is running. A taxi costs about 100KN.

It's possible to visit Hvar on a (hectic) day trip from Split by catching the morning Jadrolinija ferry to Stari Grad, a bus to Hvar town, then the last ferry from Stari Grad directly back to Split.

KORČULA ISLAND

☎ 020 / pop 16,200

Rich in vineyards and olive trees, the island of Korčula was named Korkyra Melaina (Black Korčula) by the original Greek settlers because of its dense woods and plant life. As the largest island in an archipelago of 48, it provides plenty of opportunities for scenic drives, particularly along the southern coast.

Swimming opportunities abound in the many quiet coves and secluded beaches, while the interior produces some of Croatia's finest wine, especially dessert wines made from the *grk* grape cultivated around Lumbarda. Local olive oil is another product worth seeking out.

Korčula Town

On a hilly peninsula jutting into the Adriatic sits Korčula Town, a striking walled town of round defensive towers and red-roofed houses. Resembling a miniature Dubrovnik, the gated, walled Old Town is crisscrossed by narrow stone streets designed to protect its inhabitants from the winds swirling around the peninsula. Korčula Island was controlled by Venice from the 14th to the 18th centuries, as is evident from the Venetian coats of arms adorning the official buildings. If you don't stop in Korčula, one look at this unique town from the Jadrolinija ferry will make you regret it.

ORIENTATION

The big Jadrolinija car ferry drops you off either in the west harbour next to the Hotel Korčula or the east harbour next to Marko Polo Tours. The Old Town lies between the two harbours. The large hotels and main beach lie south of the east harbour, and the residential neighbourhood Sveti Nikola (with a smaller beach) is southwest of the west harbour. The town bus station is 100m south of the Old Town centre.

INFORMATION

There are ATMs in town at Splitska Banka and Dubrovačka Banka. You can change money there, at the post office, or at any of the travel agencies.

Atlas travel agency (☎ 711 231) Represents Amex, runs excursions and finds private accommodation.

Jadrolinija office (☎ 715 410) About 25m up from the west harbour.

Marko Polo Tours (☎ 715 400; marko-polo-tours@du .htnet.hr; east harbour) Finds private accommodation and organises excursions.

Post office Hidden next to the stairway up to the Old Town, the post office also has telephones.

Tino's Internet (☎ 091 509 11 82; Ul Tri Sulara; per hr 25KN) Tino's other outlet is at the ACI Marina; both are open long hours.

Tourist office (☎ 715 701; www.korcula.net; Obala Franje Tudjmana bb; ☽ 8am-3pm & 5-9pm Mon-Sat, 8am-3pm Sun Jun-Sep, 8am-1pm & 5-9pm Mon-Sat Oct-May) An excellent source of information, located on the west harbour.

SIGHTS

Other than following the circuit of the former city walls or walking along the shore, sightseeing in Korčula centres on Cathedral Square. The Gothic **Cathedral of St Mark** (10am-noon, 5-7pm Jul & Aug, off season Mass only) features two paintings by Tintoretto (*Three Saints* on the altar and *Annunciation* to one side).

The **treasury** (711 049; Trg Sv Marka Statuta; admission 10KN; 9am-7pm Jun-Aug) in the 14th-century Abbey Palace next to the cathedral is worth a look; even better is the **Town Museum** (711 420; Trg Sv Marka Statuta; admission 10KN; 9am-1.30pm Mon-Sat Jun-Aug) in the 15th-century Gabriellis Palace opposite. The exhibits of Greek pottery, Roman ceramics and home furnishings have English captions. It's said that Marco Polo was born in Korčula in 1254; you can climb the **tower** (admission 5KN; 10am-1pm & 5-7pm Mon-Sat Jul & Aug) of what is believed to have been his house.

There's also an **Icon Museum** (Trg Svih Svetih; admission 8KN; 10am-1pm Mon-Sat) in the Old Town. It isn't much of a museum, but visitors are let into the beautiful old **Church of All Saints**.

In the high summer season water taxis at the east harbour collect passengers to visit various points on the island, as well as Badija Island, which features a 15th-century Franciscan monastery (now a dormitory), plus Orebić and the nearby village of Lumbarda, which both have sandy beaches.

TOURS
Both **Atlas travel agency** (711 231) and **Marko Polo Tours** (715 400; fax 715 800; marko-polo -tours@du.htnet.hr) offer a variety of boat tours and island excursions.

SLEEPING
The big hotels in Korčula are overpriced, but there are a wealth of guesthouses that offer clean, attractive rooms and friendly service. Atlas and Marko Polo Tours arrange private rooms, charging from 200KN to 220KN for a room with a bathroom, and with apartments starting at about 400KN. Or, you could try one of the following options.

Autocamp Kalac (711 182; fax 711 146; per person/camp sites 40/50KN) This attractive camping ground is behind Hotel Bon Repos in a dense pine grove near the beach.

Depolo (/fax 711 621; tereza.depolo@du.htnet .hr; d with/without sea view 240/200KN;) In the residential neighbourhood close to the Old Town of Sveti Nikola and 100m west of the bus station, this guesthouse has spiffy and modern rooms.

Tarle (711 712; fax 711 243; Stalište Frana Kršinića; d with/without kitchen 270/210KN) Next to the Hotel Marko Polo, about 500m southeast of the bus station, this place has a pretty enclosed garden and attractive rooms with balconies.

Other guesthouses nearby for about the same price include **Peručić** (/fax 711 458), with great balconies, and the homy **Ojdanić** (/fax 711 708; roko-taxi@du.htnet.hr). Local Ratko Ojdanić also has a water taxi and a lot of experience with fishing trips around the island.

EATING
Planjak (711 015; Plokata 19 Travnja; mains from 50KN) This restaurant-grill, between the supermarket and the Jadrolinija office in town, is popular with a local crowd who appreciate the fresh, Dalmatian dishes as much as the low prices.

Gradski Podrum (Kaparova; mains from 65KN) Serves up local specialities, such as Korčula-style fish boiled with potatoes and topped with tomato sauce.

Adio Mare (711 253; Ulica Sveti Roka; mains 80KN) The charming, maritime décor here puts you in the mood for fish.

There's a supermarket next to Marko Polo Tours.

ENTERTAINMENT
Between May and September there's **moreška sword dancing** (tickets 60KN; 9pm Thu) by the Old Town gate; performances are more frequent during July and August. The clash of swords and the graceful movements of the dancers/fighters make an exciting show. Atlas, the tourist office or Marko Polo Tours sell tickets.

GETTING THERE & AWAY
Transport connections to Korčula are good. There's one bus every day to Dubrovnik (80KN, three hours), one to Zagreb (195KN, 12 hours), and one a week to Sarajevo (152KN, eight hours).

There's a regular afternoon car ferry between Split and Vela Luka (35KN, three hours), on the island's western end, that stops at Hvar most days. Six daily buses link Korčula town to Vela Luka (24KN, one hour), but services from Vela Luka are reduced at the weekend.

From Orebić, look for the passenger launch (15KN, 15 minutes, at least four times daily year-round), which will drop you off near Hotel Korčula right below the Old Town's towers. There's also a car ferry to Dominče (10KN, 15 minutes) which stops near the Hotel Bon Repos, where you can pick up the bus from Lumbarda or take a water taxi to Korčula town (10KN). For international connections see p229.

OREBIĆ

Orebić, on the southern coast of the Pelješac Peninsula between Korčula and Ploče, offers better beaches than those found at Korčula, 2.5km across the water. The easy access by ferry from Korčula makes it the perfect place to go for the day. The best beach in Orebić is Trstenica cove, a 15-minute walk east along the shore from the port.

Getting There & Away

In Orebić the ferry terminal and the bus station are adjacent to each other. Korčula buses to Dubrovnik, Zagreb and Sarajevo stop at Orebić. See the Korčula section (p215) for additional bus and ferry information.

MLJET ISLAND

☎ 020 / pop 1111

Of all the Adriatic islands, Mljet (Meleda in Italian) may be the most seductive. Over 72% of the island is covered by forests and the rest is dotted by fields, vineyards and small villages. Created in 1960, **Mljet National Park** occupies the western third of the island and surrounds two saltwater lakes, Malo Jezero and Veliko Jezero. Most people visit the island on excursions from Korčula or Dubrovnik, but it is now possible to take a passenger boat from Dubrovnik or come on the regular ferry from Dubrovnik and stay a few days for hiking, cycling and boating.

Orientation & Information

Tour boats arrive at Pomena wharf at Mljet's western end. Jadrolinija ferries arrive at Sobra on the eastern end and they are met by a local bus for the 1½-hour ride to Pomena and Polače. The *Nikolina* passenger boat from Dubrovnik docks at Sobra and then the little town of Polače,

about 5km from Pomena. You can enter the National Park from either Pomena or Polače. The **tourist office** (☎ 744 186; np -mljet@np-mljet.hr; ☉ 8am-1pm & 5-8pm Mon-Fri Oct-May, 8am-8pm Mon-Sat & 8am-1pm Sun Jun-Sep) is in Polače, and the only ATM on the island is at the Odisej hotel in Pomena. The admission price for the national park is 65/45KN adult/concession during July and August, 45/30KN from September to June. The price includes a bus and boat transfer to the **Benedictine monastery** and there is no park admission price if you stay overnight on the island.

Sights & Activities

From Pomena it's a 15-minute walk to a jetty on **Veliko Jezero**, the larger of the two lakes. Here you can board a boat to a small lake islet and have lunch at a 12th-century **Benedictine monastery**, which now houses a restaurant.

Those who don't want to spend the rest of the afternoon swimming and sunbathing on the monastery island can catch an early boat back to the main island and spend a couple of hours walking along the shore of the lake before taking the late-afternoon excursion boat back to Korčula or Dubrovnik. There's a small landing on the main island opposite the monastery where the boat operator drops off passengers upon request. It's not possible to walk right around Veliko Jezero because there's no bridge over the channel that connects the lakes to the sea.

Mljet is good for cycling; several restaurants along the dock in Polače and the Odisej hotel in Pomena rent bicycles (90KN per half day). If you plan to cycle between Pomena and Polače be aware that the two towns are separated by a steep mountain. The bike path along Veliko Jezero is an easier pedal but it doesn't link the two towns.

Tours

See p215 and p220 in Korčula and Dubrovnik respectively for agencies offering excursions to Mljet. The tour lasts from 8.30am to 6pm and includes the park entry fee. The boat trip from Korčula to Pomena takes at least two hours, less by hydrofoil; from Dubrovnik it takes longer. Lunch isn't included in the tour price and the opportunities for self-catering are limited.

Sleeping

The Polače **tourist office** (☎ 744 186; np-mljet@np -mljet.hr; ⊗ 8am-1pm & 5-8pm Mon-Fri Oct-May, 8am-8pm Mon-Sat & 8am-1pm Sun Jun-Sep) arranges private accommodation at 200KN per double room in summer but it is essential to make arrangements before arrival in peak season. There are more *sobe* (private rooms) signs around Pomena than Polače, but practically none at all in Sobra.

There's no camping permitted inside the national park but there are two grounds outside it.

Marina (☎ 745 071; per person/camp sites 25/25KN; ⊗ Jun-Sep) This a small camping ground is in Ropa, about 1km from the park.

Camping Mungos (☎ 745 300; Babino Poje; per person/camp sites 47/30KN; ⊗ May-Sep) Not very shady, but well located, this new camping ground is not far from the beach and the lovely grotto of Odysseus.

The only hotel option available on the island is the **Odisej** (☎ 744 022; www.hotelodisej .hr; d from 335KN; ⊠) in Pomena, which has decent enough rooms and offers a range of activities.

Eating

Nine (☎ 744 037; Pomena; mains from 80KN) The Nine, opposite hotel Odisej, is by the sea and, though touristy in high season, turns out succulent seafood.

Getting There & Away

It's possible to make a quick visit to Mljet by a regular morning ferry (32KN, two hours) from Dubrovnik in July and August.

The rest of the year the ferry leaves Dubrovnik in the mid-afternoon Monday to Saturday, or Sunday evening. The ferry docks in Sobra where it is met by a bus. The big Jadrolinija coastal ferries also stop at Mljet twice a week in summer and once a week during the rest of the year.

The *Nikolina* is a small boat that makes a 2¾-hour run to and from Dubrovnik to Polače three times a week, leaving in the morning and returning in late afternoon (45KN).

Tickets are sold in the **Turistička Zajednica** (Map pp218-9; ☎ 417 983; Gruška obala bb) in Gruž, at **Atlantagent** (Map pp218-9; ☎ 419 044; obala Stjepana Radića 26; ⊗ 10am-4pm) in Dubrovnik, or on board, but it's wise to buy in advance as the boat fills up quickly.

DUBROVNIK
☎ 020 / pop 43,770

Whether you call it 'paradise on earth' (George Bernard Shaw) or merely 'the pearl of the Adriatic' (Lord Byron), Dubrovnik is clearly special. Enclosed in a curtain of stone walls, the town centre is radiant with the light reflected from its white marble paving stones. The main pedestrian thoroughfare, Placa, is a melange of cafés and shops with outstanding monuments at either end. Churches, monasteries and museums ornamented with finely carved stone recall an eventful history, and the vibrant artistic tradition is continued with regular concerts and plays. Beyond the walls stretch the crystal-blue waters of the southern Adriatic, sprinkled with tiny islands for the hedonistically inclined.

History

Founded 1300 years ago by refugees from Epidaurus in Greece, medieval Dubrovnik (Ragusa until 1918) shook off Venetian control in the 14th century, becoming an independent republic and one of Venice's more important maritime rivals, trading with Egypt, Syria, Sicily, Spain, France and later Turkey. The double blow of an earthquake in 1667 and the opening of new trade routes to the east sent Ragusa into a slow decline, ending with Napoleon's conquest of the town in 1806.

The deliberate and militarily pointless shelling of Dubrovnik by the Yugoslav army in 1991 sent shockwaves through the international community but, when the smoke cleared in 1992, traumatised residents cleared the rubble and set about repairing the damage. With substantial international aid, the famous monuments were rebuilt and resculpted, the streets sealed and the clay roofs retiled. Reconstruction has been extraordinarily skilful but you will notice different shades of rose-tiled roofs as you walk around the city walls.

After a steep postwar decline in tourism, visitors are once again flocking to Dubrovnik. It has become a main port of call for Mediterranean cruise ships, whose passengers are sometimes elbow-to-elbow in peak season. Come in June or September if you can but whatever the time of year the interlay of light and stone is enchanting. Don't miss it.

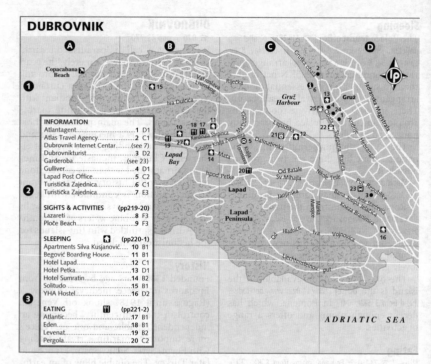

DUBROVNIK

INFORMATION
Atlantagent	1 D1
Atlas Travel Agency	2 C1
Dubrovnik Internet Centar	(see 7)
Dubrovnikturist	3 D2
Garderoba	(see 23)
Gulliver	4 D1
Lapad Post Office	5 C2
Turistička Zajednica	6 C1
Turistička Zajednica	7 E3

SIGHTS & ACTIVITIES (pp219–20)
Lazareti	8 F3
Ploče Beach	9 F3

SLEEPING (pp220–1)
Apartments Silva Kusjanović	10 B1
Begović Boarding House	11 B1
Hotel Lapad	12 C1
Hotel Petka	13 D1
Hotel Sumratin	14 B2
Solitudo	15 B1
YHA Hostel	16 D2

EATING (pp221–2)
Atlantic	17 B1
Eden	18 B1
Levenat	19 B2
Pergola	20 C2

ADRIATIC SEA

Orientation

The Jadrolinija ferry terminal and the bus station are a few hundred metres apart at Gruž, several kilometres northwest of the Old Town, which is closed to cars. The main street in the Old Town is Placa (also called Stradun). Most accommodation is on the leafy Lapad Peninsula, west of the bus station.

Information
BOOKSHOPS

Algoritam (Map p221; Placa) Has a good selection of English-language books, including guidebooks.

INTERNET ACCESS

Dubrovnik Internet Centar (Map p221; ☎ 311 017; Starčevića 7; ☒ 9am-9pm; per hr 20KN)

LEFT LUGGAGE

Garderoba (Map pp218-9; ☒ 5.30am-9pm) At the bus station.

MONEY

You can change money at any travel agency or post office. There are numerous ATMs in town, near the bus station and near the ferry terminal.

POST

Main post office (Map p221; cnr Široka & Od Puča)
Lapad post office (Map pp218-9; Šetalište Kralja Zvonimira 21)

TOURIST INFORMATION

Tourist Information Centar (Map p221; ☎ 323 350; fax 323 351; Placa 1) Across from the Franciscan monastery in the Old Town, it's privately run and moderately helpful.
Turistička Zajednica (www.tzdubrovnik.hr) outside Pile gate (Map pp218-9; ☎ 427 591; Ante Starčevića 7; ☒ 8am-8pm Mon-Sat, 9am-noon Sun Jun-Sep, 9am-7pm Mon-Fri, 9am-1pm Sat Oct-May); Old Town (Map p221; ☎ 321 561; Placa bb); at the harbour (Map pp218-9; ☎ 417 983; Gruška obala bb) Offers maps and the indispensable Dubrovnik Riviera guide. The harbour branch has limited information.

TRAVEL AGENCIES

Atlas travel agency outside Pile gate (Map p221; ☎ 442 574; Sv Đurđa 1); Old Town (Map p221; ☎ 323 609; Lučarica 1); at the harbour (Map pp218-9; ☎ 418 001; Gruška obala) In convenient locations, this agency is

ENTERTAINMENT (p222)
Latino Club Fuego......................(see 7)
Open-air Cinema.........................**21** C1

TRANSPORT (pp222-3)
Boat to Mljet..............................**22** D1
Bus Station................................**23** D2
Jadroagent................................**24** D1
Jadrolinija Ferry Terminal &
 Office....................................**25** D1

OTHER
Fort Lovrjenac...........................**26** E3
Hotel Kompas............................**27** B2

extremely helpful for general information as well as finding private accommodation. All excursions are run by Atlas.
Dubrovnikturist (Map pp218-9; ☎ 356 959; fax 356 885; dubrovnikturist@net.hr; Put Republike 7) The option closest to the bus station for finding private accommodation, renting cars etc.
Gulliver (Map pp218-9; ☎ 313 300; fax 419 119; Obala Stjepana Radića 32) Near the Jadrolinija dock, Gulliver finds private accommodation, changes money and rents cars and scooters.

Sights & Activities
OLD TOWN   Map p221
You will probably begin your visit at the city bus stop outside **Pile Gate**. As you enter the city Dubrovnik's wonderful pedestrian promenade, Placa, extends before you all the way to the **clock tower** at the other end of town.

Just inside Pile Gate is the huge Onofrio Fountain (1438) and **Franciscan monastery** (☼ 9am-5pm) with a splendid cloister and the third-oldest functioning **pharmacy** (☼ 9am-5pm) in Europe; it's been operating since 1391. The **church** (☼ 7am-7pm) has recently undergone a long and expensive

restoration to startling effect. The **monastery museum** (adult/concession 10/5KN; ☼ 9am-5pm) has a collection of liturgical objects, paintings and pharmacy equipment.

In front of the clock tower at the eastern end of Placa, is the **Orlando Column** (1419) – a favourite meeting place. On opposite sides of Orlando are the 16th-century **Sponza Palace** (originally a customs house, then later a bank), which now houses the **State Archives** (☎ 321 032; admission free; ☼ 8am-3pm Mon-Fri, 8am-1pm Sat), and **St Blaise's Church**, a lovely Italian baroque building built in 1715 to replace an earlier church destroyed in the 1667 earthquake. At the end of Pred Dvorom, the wide street beside St Blaise, is the baroque **Cathedral of the Assumption of the Virgin**. Located between the two churches, the 1441 Gothic **Rector's Palace** (adult/concession 15/7KN; ☼ 9am-2pm Mon-Sat Oct-May, 9am-5pm daily Jun-Sep) houses a museum with furnished rooms, baroque paintings and historical exhibits. The elected rector was not permitted to leave the building during his one-month term without the permission of the senate. The narrow street opposite opens onto Gundulićeva Poljana, a bustling morning market. Up the stairs at the southern end of the square is the **Jesuit monastery** (1725).

As you proceed up Placa, make a detour to the **Museum of the Orthodox Church** (adult/concession 10/5KN; ☼ 9am-1pm Mon-Fri) for a look at a fascinating collection of 15th- to 19th-century icons.

By now you'll be ready for a leisurely walk around the **city walls** (adult/concession 30/10KN; ☼ 9am-7pm), which has entrances just inside Pile Gate, across from the Dominican monastery and near Fort St John. Built between the 13th and 16th centuries, these powerful walls are the finest in the world and Dubrovnik's main claim to fame. They enclose the entire city in a protective veil over 2km long and up to 25m high, with two round and 14 square towers, two corner fortifications and a large fortress. The views over the town and sea are great – this walk could be the high point of your visit.

Whichever way you go, you'll notice the 14th-century **Dominican monastery** (adult/concession 10/5KN; ☼ 9am-6pm) in the north-eastern corner of the city, whose forbidding fortress-like exterior shelters a rich trove of paintings from Dubrovnik's finest 15th- and 16th-century artists.

CROATIA

Dubrovnik has many other sights, such as the unmarked **synagogue** (ul Žudioska 5; admission free; ⏲ 10am-1pm Mon-Fri) near the clock tower, which is the second oldest synagogue in Europe. The uppermost streets of the Old Town below the north and south walls are pleasant to wander along.

BEACHES

Ploče (Map pp218-9), the closest beach to the old city, is just beyond the 17th-century **Lazareti** (Map pp218-9; a former quarantine station) outside Ploče Gate. There are also hotel beaches along the **Lapad Peninsula** (Map pp218-9), which you are able to use without a problem. The largest is outside the Hotel Kompas.

An even better option is to take the ferry that shuttles half-hourly in summer to lush **Lokrum Island** (35KN return), a national park with a rocky nudist beach (marked FKK), a botanical garden and the ruins of a medieval Benedictine monastery.

Tours

Atlas travel agency (p218) offers full-day tours to Mostar (240KN), Medugorje (220KN), the Elafiti Islands (240KN) and Mljet (350KN), among other destinations. Its tour to Montenegro (310KN) is a good alternative to taking the morning bus to Montenegro, since the bus schedules make a day trip there impractical.

Festivals & Events

The **Dubrovnik Summer Festival** (mid-July to mid-August) is a major cultural event, with over 100 performances at different venues in the Old Town. The **Feast of St Blaise** (3 February) and **carnival** (February) are also celebrated.

Sleeping

Private accommodation is generally the best option in Dubrovnik, but beware of the scramble of private owners at the bus station or Jadrolinija wharf. Some offer what they say they offer, others are rip-off artists. Be aware that most accommodation in the Old Town involves sharing the flat with the owner's family. Apartments Silva Kusjanović, Begović Boarding House and Apartments van Bloemen (right) are reputable and can often refer you to other places if they are full. All will meet you at

the station if you call in advance. Otherwise head to any of the travel agencies or the Turistička Zajednica. Expect to pay about 200KN to 220KN a room in high season.

OLD TOWN   Map p221
Budget
Apartments van Bloemen (☎ 323 433, 091 33 24 106; www.karmendu.tk; Bandureva 1; apt 750KN; ⌗) This is Dubrovnik's most personal and original accommodation, with a great location in the Old Town. All four apartments are beautifully decorated with original art; three of them sleep three people comfortably.

Top End
Pucić Palace (☎ 324 111; www.thepucicpalace.com; Od Puća 1; s/d 2200/4000KN; P ⌗) Right in the heart of the Old Town, these palatial digs have been designed and decorated to the cutting edge of fashion. Warm and cosy it's not but the countesses and moguls that stay here probably don't care.

OUTSIDE THE OLD TOWN   Map pp218-9
Budget
Solitudo (☎ 448 200; Iva Dulčića 39; per person/camp sites 32/60KN) This pretty and renovated camping ground is within walking distance of the beach.

YHA hostel (☎ 423 241; dubrovnik@hfhs.hr; Vinka Sagrestana 3; B&B/half-board 95/140KN) It's not exactly restful here, but you'll have a lot of fun.

Apartments Silva Kusjanović (☎ 435 071, 098 244 639; antonia_du@hotmail.com; Kardinala Stepinća 62; per person 100KN) Sweet Silva has four large apartments that can hold four to eight beds. All have terraces with gorgeous views and it's possible to barbecue.

Begović Boarding House (☎ 435 191; fax 452 752; Primorska 17; per person 110KN) A long-time favourite with our readers, this friendly place in Lapad has three rooms with shared bathroom and three apartments. There's a terrace out the back with a good view. Breakfast is an additional 30KN.

Mid-Range
Hotel Sumratin (☎ 436 333; hot-sumratin@du.htnet.hr; Šetalište Kralja Zvonimira 31; s/d 355/600KN; P) About 200m from the water, this calm hotel offers good value for money.

Hotel Petka (☎ 410 500; www.hotelpetka.com; Obala Stjepana Radića 38; s/d from 510/690KN; P ⌗) Situated opposite the Jadrolinija ferry landing,

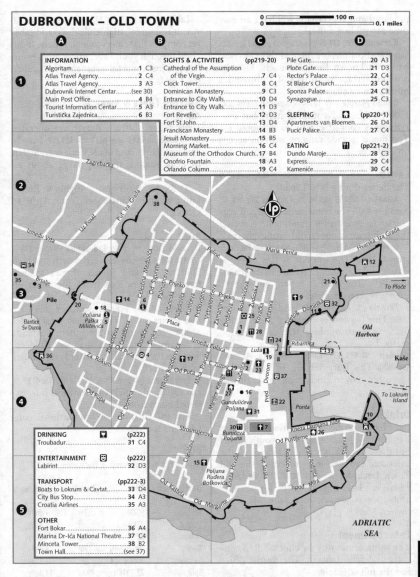

DUBROVNIK – OLD TOWN

| 0 | 100 m |
| 0 | 0.1 miles |

INFORMATION
Algoritam............................1 C3
Atlas Travel Agency................2 C4
Atlas Travel Agency................3 A3
Dubrovnik Internet Centar......(see 30)
Main Post Office....................4 B4
Tourist Information Centar.......5 A3
Turistička Zajednica................6 B3

SIGHTS & ACTIVITIES (pp219-20)
Cathedral of the Assumption
 of the Virgin.......................7 C4
Clock Tower..........................8 C4
Dominican Monastery..............9 C3
Entrance to City Walls............10 D4
Entrance to City Walls............11 D3
Fort Revelin.........................12 D3
Fort St John.........................13 D4
Franciscan Monastery.............14 B3
Jesuit Monastery...................15 B5
Morning Market.....................16 C4
Museum of the Orthodox Church.17 B4
Onofrio Fountain...................18 A3
Orlando Column....................19 C4

Pile Gate.............................20 A3
Ploče Gate...........................21 D3
Rector's Palace.....................22 C4
St Blaise's Church..................23 C4
Sponza Palace.......................24 C3
Synagogue...........................25 C3

SLEEPING (pp220-1)
Apartments van Bloemen.........26 D4
Pucić Palace.........................27 C4

EATING (pp221-2)
Dundo Maroje.......................28 C3
Express...............................29 C4
Kamenice.............................30 C4

DRINKING (p222)
Troubadur............................31 C4

ENTERTAINMENT (p222)
Labirint...............................32 D3

TRANSPORT (pp222-3)
Boats to Lokrum & Cavtat.......33 D4
City Bus Stop........................34 A3
Croatia Airlines.....................35 A3

OTHER
Fort Bokar...........................36 A4
Marina Dr-Ića National Theatre....37 C4
Minceta Tower......................38 B2
Town Hall..........................(see 37)

ADRIATIC
SEA

CROATIA

Hotel Petka won't bowl you over with charm but the location is great for getting back and forth to the ferry.

Hotel Lapad (☎ 432 922; www.hotel-lapad.hr; Lapadska Obala 37; s/d 600/775KN; ✼ ☒) This hotel is a solid, old limestone structure with simple but cheerful rooms and an outdoor swimming pool.

Eating
OLD TOWN
Map p221

There are dozens of places to chow down in the Old Town but there's not a great deal of variety. Pizza, pasta, pasta, pizza. Yawn.

Express (☎ 329 994; Marojice Kaboge 1; mains from 16KN) It's self-service here, but the soups, salads, vegetables and desserts are freshly prepared and vegetarians will have an easy time assembling a meal.

Kamenice (☎ 421 499; Gundulićeva poljana 8; mains from 40KN) Portions are huge at this convivial hang-out known for its mussels. Plus, its outdoor terrace is on one of Dubrovnik's more scenic squares.

Dundo Maroje (☎ 321 445; Kovačka; mains from 55KN) Nothing adventurous here, but everything is cooked exactly as it should be. The menu is wide ranging with an accent on seafood.

LAPAD   Map pp218-9
The better dining is in Lapad.

Atlantic (☎ 098 185 96 25; Kardinala Stepinca 42; mains from 40KN) The homemade pasta and vegetarian lasagne are outstanding here, even if the ambience is not terribly atmospheric.

Levenat (☎ 435 352; Šetalište Nika i Meda Pucića 15; mains 45-120KN) The interior at this eatery is classic and the outdoor terrace has a smashing view. The food is superb and there's even a vegetarian plate.

Pergola (☎ 436 848; Kralja Tomislava 1; mains from 50KN) This is another consistently satisfying place with an outdoor terrace and good seafood.

Eden (☎ 435 133; Kardinala Stepinca 54; mains 55-90KN) The leafy terrace upstairs is an agreeable spot to enjoy meat, pasta or fish dishes.

Drinking
Bars have sprung up like mushrooms on Bana Josipa Jelačića near the youth hostel but these days thirsty young singles fill the cafés and terraces on Bunićeva in the Old Town. **Troubadur** (Map p221; ☎ 412 154; Gundulićeva Poljana) is a long-time favourite for jazz; the ambience is joyous, especially when the owner, Marko, plays.

Entertainment
The summer months are chock-full of concerts and folk dancing. The tourist office has the full schedule.

Latino Club Fuego (Map pp218-9; Starčevića 2) Despite the name, at this disco you'll find a gamut of dance music that includes techno and pop.

Open-air cinema (Map pp218-9; Kumičića) In Lapad, this spot allows you to watch movies, shown in their original language, by starlight.

Labirint (Map p221; ☎ 322 222; Svetog Dominika 2) A vast restaurant, nightclub, disco and cabaret complex that caters to high rollers. It can chew through your wallet pretty quickly unless you just come for a romantic cocktail on the roof terrace.

Getting There & Away
AIR
Daily flights to/from Zagreb are operated by **Croatia Airlines** (Map p221; ☎ 413 777; Brsalje 9). The fare runs about 400KN one way, higher in peak season; the trip takes about an hour.

There are also nonstop flights to Rome, London and Manchester from April to October.

BOAT
In addition to the **Jadrolinija** (Map pp218-9; ☎ 418 000; Gruž) coastal ferry north to Hvar, Split, Zadar and Rijeka, there's a local ferry that leaves Dubrovnik for Sobra on Mljet Island (26KN to 32KN, 2½ hours) throughout the year. In summer there are two ferries a day. There are several ferries a day year-round to the outlying islands of Šipanska, Sugjuraj, Lopud and Koločep. See also the Central Dalmatia Ferry Routes map on p210.

Jadroagent (Map pp218-9; ☎ 419 009; fax 419 029; Radića 32) handles ticketing for most international boats from Croatia.

For information on international connections see p228.

BUS
Buses from Dubrovnik include:

Destination	Cost	Duration	Frequency
Korčula	80KN	3hr	1 daily
Mostar	77KN	3hr	2 daily
Orebić	80KN	2½hr	1 daily
Rijeka	295-309KN	12hr	4 daily
Sarajevo	160KN	5hr	1 daily
Split	72-111KN	4½hr	14 daily
Zadar	160-190KN	8hr	7 daily
Zagreb	205-401KN	11hr	7 daily

There's a daily 11am bus to the Montenegrin border, from where a Montenegro bus takes you to Herceg Novi (60KN, two hours) and on to Kotor (100KN, 2½ hours) and Bar (130KN, three hours). In a busy summer season and at weekends buses out of Dubrovnik can be crowded, so book a ticket well before the scheduled departure time.

Getting Around

Čilipi international airport is 24km southeast of Dubrovnik. The Croatia Airlines airport buses (25KN, 45 minutes) leave from the main **bus station** (Map pp218-9; ☎ 357 088) 1½ hours before flight times. A taxi costs around 200KN).

Dubrovnik's buses run frequently and generally on time. The fare is 10KN if you buy from the driver but only 8KN if you buy a ticket at a kiosk.

Around Dubrovnik

Cavtat is a small town that curves around an attractive harbour bordered by nice beaches. Although it does not have as many interesting sights as Dubrovnik, Cavtat does make a good alternative place to stay if Dubrovnik is fully booked out or the summer crowds become overwhelming. Don't miss the memorial chapel to the Račič family designed by Ivan Meštrović.

A day trip can be made from Dubrovnik to this resort town, just to the southeast. Bus No 10 to Cavtat runs often from Dubrovnik's bus station and there are three daily boats during the summer (40KN).

CROATIA DIRECTORY

ACCOMMODATION

Accommodation listings in this guide have been ordered by pricing from cheapest to most expensive (ie budget to top end).

Along the Croatian coast accommodation is priced according to three seasons, which tend to vary from place to place. Generally October to May are the cheapest months, June and September are mid-priced, but count on paying top price for the peak season, which runs for a six-week period in July and August. Prices quoted in this chapter are for the peak period and do not include 'residence tax', which runs from about 4KN to 7.50KN depending on the location and season. Deduct about 25% if you come in June, the beginning of July and September, about 35% for May and October and about 50% for all other times. Note that prices for rooms in Zagreb are pretty much constant all year and

that many hotels on the coast close in winter. Some places offer half-board which is bed and two meals a day, usually breakfast and one other meal. It can be good value if you're not too fussy about what you eat.

Camping

Nearly 100 camping grounds are scattered along the Croatian coast. Opening times of campgrounds generally run from mid-April to September, give or take a few weeks. The exact times change from year to year so it's wise to call in advance if you're arriving at either end of the season.

Many camping grounds, especially in Istria, are gigantic 'autocamps' with restaurants, shops and row upon row of caravans. Expect to pay up to 100KN for the camp site at some of the larger establishments but half that at most other camping grounds, in addition to 38KN to 48KN per person.

Nudist camping grounds (marked FKK) are among the best because their secluded locations ensure peace and quiet. However, bear in mind that freelance camping is officially prohibited. A good site for camping information and links is www.camping.hr.

Hostels

The **Croatian YHA** (☎ 01-48 47 472; www.hfhs.hr; Dežmanova 9, Zagreb) operates youth hostels in Dubrovnik, Zadar, Zagreb and Pula. Non-members pay an additional 10KN per person daily for a stamp on a welcome card; six stamps entitles you to a membership. Prices in this chapter are for high season during July and August; prices fall the rest of the year. The Croatian YHA can also provide information about private youth hostels in Krk, Zadar, Dubrovnik and Zagreb.

Hotels

Hotels are ranked from one to five stars with the most in the two- and three-star range. Features, such as satellite TV, direct-dial phones, hi-tech bathrooms, minibars and air-con, are standard in four- and five-star hotels and one-star hotels have at least a bathroom in the room. Many two- and three-star hotels offer satellite TV but you'll find better décor in the higher categories. Unfortunately the country is saddled with too many 1970s, concrete-block hotels, built to warehouse package tourists, but there are more and more options for those looking for smaller and more personal establishments. Prices for hotels in this chapter are for the pricey six-week period that begins in mid-July and lasts until the end of August. During this period some hotels may demand a surcharge for stays of less than four nights but this surcharge is usually waived during the rest of the year, when prices drop steeply. In Zagreb prices are the same all year.

Breakfast is included in the prices quoted for hotels in this chapter, unless stated otherwise.

Private Rooms

Private rooms or apartments are the best accommodation in Croatia. Service is excellent and the rooms are usually extremely well kept. You may very well be greeted by offers of *sobe* as you step off your bus and boat but rooms are most often arranged by travel agencies or the local tourist office. Booking through an agency is somewhat more expensive but at least you'll know who to complain to if things go wrong.

The most expensive rooms are three star and have private bathrooms, in establishments resembling small guesthouses. Some of the better ones are listed in this chapter. It's best to call in advance as the owners will often meet you at the bus station or ferry dock. In a two-star room, the bathroom is shared with one other room; in a one-star room, the bathroom is shared with two other rooms or with the owner who is usually an elderly widow. Breakfast is usually not included but can sometimes be arranged for an additional 30KN; be sure to clarify whether the price agreed upon is per person or per room. If you're travelling in a small group it may be worthwhile to get a small apartment with cooking facilities, which are widely available along the coast.

It makes little sense to price-shop from agency to agency since prices are fixed by the local tourist association. Whether you deal with the owner directly or book through an agency, you'll pay a 30% surcharge for stays of less than four nights and sometimes 50% or even 100% more for a one-night stay, although you may be able to get them to waive the surcharge if you arrive in the low season. Prices for private rooms in this chapter are for a four-night stay in peak season.

ACTIVITIES
Diving

The clear waters and varied underwater life of the Adriatic have led to a flourishing dive industry along the coast. Cave diving is the real speciality in Croatia; night diving and wreck diving are also offered and there are coral reefs in some places, but they are in rather deep water. You must get a permit for a boat dive: go to the harbour captain in any port with your passport, certification card and 100KN. Permission is valid for a year. If you dive with a dive centre, they will take care of the paperwork. Most of the coastal resorts mentioned in this chapter have dive shops. See **Diving Croatia** (www.diving-hrs.hr) for contact information.

Hiking

Risnjak National Park at Crni Lug, 12km west of Delnice between Zagreb and Rijeka, is a good hiking area in summer. Hiking is advisable only from late spring to early autumn. The steep gorges and beech forests of Paklenica National Park, 40km northeast of Zadar, also offer excellent hiking.

Kayaking

There are countless possibilities for anyone carrying a folding sea kayak, especially among the Elafiti and Kornati Islands. Lopud makes a good launch point from which to explore the Elafiti Islands – there's a daily ferry from Dubrovnik. Sali on Dugi Otok is close to the Kornati Islands and is connected by daily ferry to Zadar.

BOOKS

Lonely Planet's *Croatia* is a comprehensive guide to the country. There's also Zoë Brân's *After Yugoslavia,* part of the Lonely Planet Journeys series, which recounts the author's return to a troubled region.

As Croatia emerges from the shadow of the former Yugoslavia, several writers of Croatian origin have taken the opportunity to rediscover their roots. *Plum Brandy: Croatian Journeys* by Josip Novakovich is a sensitive exploration of his family's Croatian background. *Croatia: Travels in Undiscovered Country* by Tony Fabijancic recounts the life of rural folks in a new Croatia. For a comprehensive account of the personalities and events surrounding the collapse of the former Yugoslavia it would be hard to go past *Yugoslavia: Death of a Nation* by Laura Silber and Allan Little, based on the 1995 BBC TV series of the same name. Richard Holbrooke's *To End a War* is a riveting look at the people and events surrounding the Dayton Agreement. *Café Europa* is a series of essays by a Croatian journalist, Slavenka Drakulić, which provides an inside look at life in the country since independence. Rebecca West's travel classic, *Black Lamb & Grey Falcon,* contains a long section on Croatia as part of her trip through Yugoslavia in 1937. Marcus Tanner's *Croatia: A Nation Forged in War* provides an excellent overview of Croatia's history.

BUSINESS HOURS

Banking and post office hours are 7.30am to 7pm on weekdays and 8am to noon on Saturday. Many shops are open 8am to 7pm on weekdays and until 2pm on Saturday. Along the coast life is more relaxed; shops and offices frequently close around noon for an afternoon break and reopen around 4pm. Restaurants are open long hours, often noon to midnight, with Sunday closings outside of peak season. Cafés are generally open from 10am to midnight, bars from 9pm to 2am. Internet cafés are also open long hours, usually seven days a week.

CUSTOMS

Travellers can bring their personal effects into the country, along with 1L of liquor, 1L of wine, 500g of coffee, 200 cigarettes and 50mL of perfume. The import or export of kuna is limited to 15,000KN per person.

DISABLED TRAVELLERS

Because of the number of wounded war veterans, more attention is being paid to the needs of disabled travellers. Public toilets at bus stations, train stations, airports

---

DANGERS & ANNOYANCES

Personal security, including theft, is not really a problem in Croatia, but the former confrontation line between Croat and federal Yugoslav forces is still undergoing de-mining operations. The hills behind Dubrovnik still contain some mines so don't go wandering off on your own before checking with a local.

---

and large public venues are usually wheelchair accessible. Large hotels are wheelchair accessible but very little private accommodation is. The bus and train stations in Zagreb, Zadar, Rijeka, Split and Dubrovnik are wheelchair accessible but the local Jadrolinija ferries are not. For further information, get in touch with **Savez Organizacija Invalida Hrvatske** (☎ /fax 01-48 29 394; Savska cesta 3; 10000 Zagreb).

EMBASSIES & CONSULATES
Croatian Embassies & Consulates

Croatian embassies and consulates abroad include:

Australia (☎ 02-6286 6988; 14 Jindalee Cres, O'Malley, ACT 2601)
Canada (☎ 613-562 7820; 229 Chapel St, Ottawa, Ontario K1N 7Y6)
France (☎ 01 5370 0287; 2 rue de Lubeck, Paris)
Germany Berlin (☎ 030-219 15 514; Ahornstrasse 4, Berlin 10787); Bonn (☎ 022-895 29 20; Rolandstrasse 52, Bonn 53179)
Ireland (☎ 1 4767 181; Adelaide Chambers, Peter St, Dublin)
Netherlands (☎ 70 362 36 38; Amaliastraat 16; The Hague)
New Zealand (☎ 09-836 5581; 131 Lincoln Rd, Henderson, Box 83200, Edmonton, Auckland)
South Africa (☎ 012-342 1206; 1160 Church St, 0083 Colbyn, Pretoria)
UK (☎ 020-7387 2022; 21 Conway St, London W1P 5HL)
USA (☎ 202-588 5899; www.croatiaemb.org; 2343 Massachusetts Ave NW, Washington, DC 20008)

Embassies & Consulates in Croatia

The following addresses are in Zagreb (area code ☎ 01):

Albania (☎ 48 10 679; Jurišićeva 2a)
Australia (☎ 48 91 200; www.auembassy.hr; Kaptol Centar, Nova Ves 11)
Bosnia and Hercegovina (☎ 46 83 761; Torbarova 9)
Bulgaria (☎ 48 23 336; Novi Goljak 25)
Canada (☎ 48 81 200; zagreb@dfait-maeci.gc.ca; Prilaz Gjure Deželića 4)
Czech Republic (☎ 61 77 239; Savska 41)
France (48 93 680; consulat@ambafrance.hr; Hebrangova 2)
Germany (☎ 61 58 105; www.deutschebotschaft -zagreb.hr, in German; avenija grada Vukovara 64)
Hungary (☎ 48 22 051; Pantovčak 128/I)
Ireland (☎ 48 77 900; Zrinskog 5)
Netherlands (☎ 46 84 880; nlgovzag@zg.htnet.hr; Medveščak 56)
New Zealand (☎ 65 20 888; avenija Dubrovnik 15)

Poland (☎ 48 99 444; Krležin Gvozd 3)
Romania (☎ 45 77 550; roamb@zg.htnet.hr;
Mlinarska ul 43)
Serbia and Montenegro (☎ 01 45 79 067;
Pantovčak 245)
Slovakia (☎ 48 48 941; Prilaz Gjure Deželića 10)
Slovenia (☎ 63 11 000; Savska 41)
UK (☎ 60 09 100; I Lučića 4)
USA (☎ 66 12 200; www.usembassy.hr; Ul Thomasa
Jeffersona 2)

FESTIVALS & EVENTS

In July and August there are **summer festivals** in Dubrovnik, Split, Pula and Zagreb. Dubrovnik's summer music festival emphasises classical music with concerts in churches around town, while Pula hosts a variety of pop and classical stars in the Roman amphitheatre and also hosts a **film festival**. **Mardi Gras** celebrations have recently been revived in many towns with attendant parades and festivities, but nowhere is it celebrated with more verve than in Rijeka.

HOLIDAYS

New Year's Day 1 January
Epiphany 6 January
Easter Monday March/April
Labour Day 1 May
Corpus Christi 10 June
Day of Antifascist Resistance 22 June; marks the outbreak of resistance in 1941
Statehood Day 25 June
Victory Day and National Thanksgiving Day 5 August
Feast of the Assumption 15 August
Independence Day 8 October
All Saints' Day 1 November
Christmas 25 & 26 December

INTERNET ACCESS

Internet cafés are springing up everywhere. The going rate is about 20KN per hour, and connections are usually good. They can be busy, especially with kids playing online games.

INTERNET RESOURCES

Croatia Homepage (www.hr.hr) Hundreds of links to everything you want to know about Croatia.
Dalmatia Travel Guide (www.dalmacija.net) All about Dalmatia, including reservations for private accommodation.
Find Croatia (www.findcroatia.com) More Croatia links, with an emphasis on tourism and outdoor activities.

Visit Croatia (www.visit-croatia.co.uk) Easy to navigate with updated travel and tourist information.

MEDIA
Newspapers & Magazines

The most respected daily in Croatia is *Vjesnik*, but the most daring paper is the satirical news weekly *Feral Tribune*. Its investigative articles and sly graphics keep Croatian politicians and businesspeople edgy. The English-language *Croatia Monthly* covers optimistic social, political and cultural developments. American, British and French newspapers and magazines are available in most destinations in this chapter.

Radio & TV

The three national TV stations fill a lot of their air time with foreign programming, generally American, and always in the original language. For local news, residents of Zadar, Split, Vinkovci and Osijek turn to their regional stations. Croatian Radio broadcasts news in English four times daily (8am, 10am, 2pm and 11pm) on FM frequencies 88.9, 91.3 and 99.3.

MONEY
Changing Money

Exchange offices may deduct a commission of 1% to change cash or travellers cheques, but some banks do not. Hungarian currency is difficult to change in Croatia and Croatian currency can be difficult to exchange in some neighbouring countries.

Costs

Accommodation takes the largest chunk of a travel budget, and costs vary widely depending on the season. If you travel in March you'll quite easily find a private room for 100KN per person, but prices climb upward to double that in July and August. Count on 30KN for a meal at a self-service restaurant and 35KN to 50KN for an average intercity bus fare.

Credit Cards

Amex, MasterCard, Visa and Diners Club cards are widely accepted in large hotels, stores and many restaurants, but don't count on cards to pay for private accommodation or meals in small restaurants. ATMs accepting MasterCard, Maestro, Cirrus, Plus and Visa are available in most bus and train stations, airports, all major cities and most small towns. Many branches of Privredna Banka have ATMs that allow cash withdrawals on an Amex card.

Currency

The currency is the kuna. Banknotes are in denominations of 500, 200, 100, 50, 20, 10 and 5. Each kuna is divided into 100 lipa in coins of 50, 20 and 10. Many places exchange money, all with similar rates.

Tax

A 22% VAT is usually imposed upon most purchases and services, and is included in the price. If your purchases exceed 500KN in one shop you can claim a refund upon leaving the country. Ask the merchant for the paperwork, but don't be surprised if they don't have it.

Tipping

If you're served well at a restaurant, you should round up the bill, but a service charge is always included. (Don't leave money on the table.) Bar bills and taxi fares can also be rounded up. Tour guides on day excursions expect to be tipped.

POST

Mail sent to Poste Restante, 10000 Zagreb, Croatia, is held at the **main post office** (Branimirova 4; ☒ 24hr Mon-Sat, 1pm-midnight Sun) next to the Zagreb train station. A good coastal address to use is c/o Poste Restante, Main Post Office, 21000 Split, Croatia. If you have an Amex card, most Atlas travel agencies will hold your mail.

TELEPHONE
Mobile Phones

Croatia uses GSM 900/1800 and the two mobile networks are Cronet and VIP. If

---

EMERGENCY NUMBERS

- Police ☎ 92
- Fire Brigade ☎ 93
- Ambulance ☎ 94
- Roadside Assistance ☎ 987
- Tourist Information (Croatian Angels) ☎ 062 999 999 (April to October)

---

your mobile is compatible, SIM cards are widely available and cost about 300KN.

Phone Codes

To call Croatia from abroad, dial your international access code, ☎ 385 (Croatia's country code), the area code (without the initial zero) and the local number. When calling from one region to another within Croatia, use the initial zero. Phone numbers with the prefix 060 are free and numbers that begin with 09 are mobile numbers which are billed at a much higher rate – figure on about 6KN a minute. When in Croatia, dial ☎ 00 to speak to the international operator.

Phonecards

To make a phone call from Croatia, go to the town's main post office. You'll need a phonecard to use public telephones, but calls using a phonecard are about 50% more expensive. Phonecards are sold according to *impulsa* (units), and you can buy packs of 25 (15KN), 50 (30KN), 100 (50KN) and 200 (100KN) units. These can be purchased at any post office and most tobacco shops and newspaper kiosks.

TOURIST INFORMATION

The **Croatian National Tourist Board** (☎ 45 56 455; www.htz.hr; Iblerov trg 10, Importanne Gallerija, 10000 Zagreb) is a good source of information. There are regional tourist offices which supervise tourist development, and municipal tourist offices which have free brochures and good information on local events. Some arrange private accommodation.

Tourist information is also dispensed by commercial travel agencies such as **Atlas** (http://atlas-croatia.com), Croatia Express, Generalturist and Kompas, which also arrange private rooms, sightseeing tours and so on. Ask for the schedule for coastal ferries.

Croatian tourist offices abroad include:

UK (☎ 020-8563 7979; info@cnto.freeserve.co.uk; Croatian National Tourist Office, 2 Lanchesters, 162-64 Fulham Palace Rd, London W6 9ER)

USA (☎ 212-279 8672; cntony@earthlink.net; Croatian National Tourist Office, Suite 4003, 350 Fifth Ave, New York, NY 10118)

TOURS

An interesting option for sailing enthusiasts is **Katarina Line** (☎ 051-272 110; www.katarina-line.hr;

CROATIA

Tita 75, Opatija), which offers week-long cruises from Opatija to Krk, Rab, Dugi Otok, Lošinj and Cres, or cruises from Split to Dubrovnik that pass the Kornati Islands. Prices run from €250 to €480 a week per person depending on the season and cabin class and include half-board. For specific tours in individual regions, see Tours in the destination sections.

VISAS

Visitors from Australia, Canada, New Zealand, the EU and the USA do not require a visa for stays of less than 90 days. For other nationalities, visas are issued free of charge at Croatian consulates. Croatian authorities require all foreigners to register with the local police when they first arrive in a new area of the country, but this is a routine matter that is normally handled by your hotel, hostel or camping ground, or the agency that organises your private accommodation.

TRANSPORT IN CROATIA

GETTING THERE & AWAY
Air

The major airports in the country are as follows:

Dubrovnik (☎ 020-773 377; www.airport
-dubrovnik.hr)
Pula (☎ 052-530 105; www.airport-pula.com)
Rijeka (☎ 051-842 132)
Split (☎ 021-203 506; www.split-airport.hr)
Zadar (☎ 023-313 311; www.zadar-airport.hr)
Zagreb (☎ 01-62 65 222; www.zagreb-airport.hr)

In addition to domestic connections to Zagreb, Rijeka has a direct flight to London (Heathrow), Pula has a direct flight to Manchester, and Split has direct flights to Manchester, London (Gatwick), Prague and Rome (Fiumicino).

Dubrovnik has direct flights to Manchester, London (Gatwick), Glasgow, and Vienna as well as flights to Zagreb and Split.

Zagreb is connected domestically to Dubrovnik, Split, Pula, Rijeka and Zadar and internationally to all European capitals plus Munich, Frankfurt, Istanbul, and Damascus.

Zadar receives domestic flights from Zagreb only.

The following are the major airlines flying into the country:

Adria Airways (code JD; www.adria-airways.com; ☎ 01-48 10 011)
Aeroflot (code SU; www.aeroflot.ru; ☎ 01-48 72 055)
Air Canada (code AC; www.aircanada.ca; ☎ 01-48 22 033)
Air France (code AF; www.airfrance.com; ☎ 01-48 37 100)
Alitalia (code AZ; www.alitalia.it; ☎ 01-48 10 413)
Austrian Airlines (code OS; www.aua.com; ☎ 062 65 900)
British Airways (code BA; www.british-airways.com)
Croatia Airlines (code OU; ☎ 01-48 19 633; www .croatiaairlines.hr; Zrinjevac 17, Zagreb) Croatia's national carrier has recently stepped up its service.
ČSA (code OK; www.csa.cz; ☎ 01-48 73 301)
Delta Airlines (code DL; www.delta.com; ☎ 01-48 78 760)
KLM-Northwest (code KL; www.klm.com; ☎ 01-48 78 601)
LOT Polish Airlines (code LO; www.lot.com; ☎ 01 48 37 500)
Lufthansa (code LH; www.lufthansa.com; ☎ 01-48 73 121)
Malév Hungarian Airlines (code MA; www.malev.hu; ☎ 01-48 36 935)
Turkish Airlines (code TK; www.turkishairlines.com; ☎ 01-49 21 854)

Land
BUS
Austria

Eurolines runs buses from Vienna to Zagreb (€32, six hours, two daily), Rijeka (€47, 8¼ hours), Split (€51, 15 hours) and Zadar (€43, 13 hours).

Bosnia & Hercegovina

There are daily connections from Sarajevo (€22, five hours, daily) and Mostar (€10.65, three hours) to Dubrovnik; from Sarajevo to Split (€14 to €16, seven hours, five daily), which stop at Mostar; and from Sarajevo to Zagreb (€28, eight hours) and Rijeka (€34, 10 hours).

Italy

Trieste is well connected with the Istrian coast. There are around six buses a day to Rijeka (€7.50, two to three hours), plus buses to Rovinj (€10.50, 3½ hours, three daily) Poreč (€8.50, 2¼ hours, three daily) and Pula (€14, 3¾ hours, four daily). There are fewer buses on Sunday. To Dalmatia there's a daily bus that leaves at 5.30pm and stops at Rijeka, Zadar (€32, 7½ hours), Split (€35.60, 10½ hours) and Dubrovnik (€64, 15 hours).

There's also a bus from Venice, Monday to Saturday, that stops in Poreč (€19, 2½ hours), Rovinj (€21, three hours) and Pula (€24, 3¼ hours). For schedules, see www .saf.ud.it. There's also a weekly bus in the summer from Milan to Poreč, Rovinj and Pula (€49, 8½ hours).

Serbia & Montenegro

There's one bus each morning from Zagreb to Belgrade (€25.50, six hours). At Bajakovo on the border, a Serbia and Montenegrin bus takes you on to Belgrade. The border between Serbia and Montenegro and Croatia is open to visitors, allowing Americans, Australians, Canadians and Brits to enter visa-free. There's a daily bus from Kotor to Dubrovnik (100KN, 2½ hours, daily) that starts at Bar and stops at Herceg Novi.

Slovenia

Slovenia is also well connected with the Istrian coast. There is one weekday bus between Rovinj and Koper (€11, three hours) and Poreč and Portorož (€5.50, 1½ hours), as well as a daily bus in summer from Rovinj to Ljubljana (5050SIT, 5½ hours) and Piran (2020SIT, 2½ hours).

There are also buses from Ljubljana to Zagreb (3070SIT, three hours, two daily), Rijeka (2280SIT, 2½ hours, one daily) and Split (6550SIT, 10½ hours, one daily).

CAR & MOTORCYCLE

The main highway entry/exit points between Croatia and Hungary are Goričan (between Nagykanisza and Varaždin), Gola (23km east of Koprivnica), Terezino Polje (opposite Barcs) and Donji Miholjac (7km south of Harkány). There are dozens of crossing points to/from Slovenia, too many to list here. There are 23 border crossings into Bosnia and Hercegovina and 10 into Serbia and Montenegro, including the main Zagreb to Belgrade highway. Major destinations in Bosnia and Hercegovina, like Sarajevo, Mostar and Međugorje, are accessible from Zagreb, Split and Dubrovnik.

Motorists require vehicle registration papers and the green insurance card to enter Croatia. Bear in mind that if you rent a car in Italy, many insurance companies will not insure you for a trip into Croatia. Border officials know this and may refuse you entry unless permission to drive into Croatia is clearly marked on the insurance documents. Most car rental companies in Trieste and Venice are familiar with this requirement and will furnish you with the correct stamp. Otherwise, you must make specific inquiries.

See p231 for road rules and further information.

TRAIN
Austria

The *Ljubljana* express travels daily from Vienna to Rijeka (€65.50, 11½ hours, two daily) through Ljubljana, and the EuroCity *Croatia* travels from Vienna to Zagreb (€60.50, 6½ hours). Both travel via Maribor, Slovenia.

Hungary

The four daily trains from Zagreb to Budapest (€30, 6½ hours) also stop in Nagykanisza, the first main junction inside Hungary (€11, two hours).

Italy

Between Venice and Zagreb (€41, eight hours) there's a daily connection that runs through Ljubljana.

Serbia & Montenegro

There are five daily trains which connect Zagreb with Belgrade (€17.50, six hours).

Slovenia

There are up to eleven trains daily between Zagreb and Ljubljana (€23, 2¼ hours) and four between Rijeka and Ljubljana (€25, three hours).

Sea

Regular boats from several companies connect Croatia with Italy and Slovenia. All of the boat-company offices in Split are located inside the ferry terminal.

Jadrolinija (www.jadrolinija.hr; Rijeka ☎ 051-211 444; Riva 16; Ancona ☎ 071-20 71 465; Bari ☎ 080-52 75 439), Croatia's national boat line, runs car ferries from Ancona to Split (€44, 10 hours) and Zadar (€41, seven hours), and a line from Bari to Dubrovnik (€49, eight hours).

Lošinska Plovidba (Rijeka ☎ 051-352 200; www .losinjska-plovidba.hr) runs boats connecting Koper, Slovenia, with Pula (€9, 4½ hours) and Zadar (€23, 13½ hours).

SEM (www.sem-marina.hr; Split ☎ 021-338 292; Gat Sv Duje; Ancona ☎ 071-20 40 90) connects Ancona with Zadar and Split, continuing on to Stari Grad (Hvar).

SNAV (www.snav.com; Ancona ☎ 071-20 76 116; Naples ☎ 081-76 12 348; Split ☎ 021-322 252) has a fast car ferry that links Pescara and Ancona with Split (€73, 4½ hours) and Pescara with Hvar (€80, 3½ hours), as well as a passenger boat that connects Civitanova and Ancona with Zadar (€70, 3¼ hours).

Adriatica Navigazione (www.adriatica.it, in Italian; Venice ☎ 041-781 611; Ancona ☎ 071-20 74 334) connects Ancona and Split and runs between Trieste and Rovinj (€15.49, 3½ hours).

Venezia Lines (☎ 041-52 22 568; www.venezialines .com; Santa Croce 518/A, Venice 30135) runs passenger boats from Venice to the following destinations once, twice or three times weekly, depending on the season: Pula (€45, three hours), Rovinj, (€45, 3¾ hours) and Poreč (€45 2½ hours) as well as from Trieste to Rovinj (€45, 2¼ hours) and Poreč (€45, 1¼ hours).

Archibugi (Ravena ☎ 0544-422 682; archibugi@tin .it; Via Magazzini anteriori 27, Ravenna; Rijeka 051-325 540; travel.rijeka@transagent.hr; Verdijeva 6 Rijeka) runs a daily ferry from July to mid-September connecting Ravenna to Rijeka (€40, eight hours).

In Croatia, contact **Jadroagent** (☎ 052-210 431; jadroagent-pula@pu.htnet.hr; Riva 14) in Pula and **Istra Line** (☎ 052-451 067; Partizansko 2) in Poreč for information and tickets on boats between Italy and Croatia.

DEPARTURE TAX

There is an embarkment tax of €3 from Italian ports.

GETTING AROUND
Air

Croatia Airlines is the one and only carrier for flights within Croatia. The price of flights depends on the season and you get better deals if you book ahead. Seniors and people aged under 26 get discounts. There are daily flights between Zagreb and Dubrovnik (549KN, one hour), Pula (170KN, 45 minutes), Split (207KN, 45 minutes) and Zadar (341KN, 40 minutes).

Bicycle

Cycling is a great way to see the islands and bikes are fairly easy to rent in most tourist spots. Many tourist offices have helpful maps of cycling routes. Bike lanes are nearly unknown in Croatia, however; you'll need to exercise extreme caution on the many narrow two-lane roads.

Boat

Year-round Jadrolinija car ferries operate along the Bari–Rijeka–Dubrovnik coastal route, stopping at Zadar, Split, and the islands of Hvar, Korčula and Mljet. Services are less frequent in winter. The most scenic section is Split to Dubrovnik, which all Jadrolinija ferries cover during the day. Ferries are a lot more comfortable than buses, though somewhat more expensive. From Rijeka to Dubrovnik the deck fare is €21/25 low/high season with high season running from about the end of June to the end of August; there's a 20% reduction on the return portion of a return ticket. With a through ticket, deck passengers can stop at any port for up to a week, provided they notify the purser beforehand and have their ticket validated. This is much cheaper than buying individual sector tickets but is only good for one stopover. Cabins should be booked a week ahead, but deck space is usually available on all sailings.

Deck passage on Jadrolinija is just that: *poltrone* (reclining seats) are about €4 extra and four-berth cabins (if available) begin at €37/44 low/high season (Rijeka to Dubrovnik). Cabins can be arranged at the reservation counter aboard ship, but advance bookings are recommended if you want to be sure of a place. You must buy tickets in advance at an agency or Jadrolinija office since they are not sold on board. Bringing a car means checking in two hours in advance.

Local ferries connect the bigger offshore islands with each other and the mainland. Some of the ferries operate only a couple of times a day and, once the vehicular capacity is reached, the remaining motorists must wait for the next available service. During summer the lines of waiting cars can be long, so it's important to arrive early.

Foot passengers and cyclists should have no problem getting on but you must buy your tickets at an agency before boarding since they are not sold on board. You should bear in mind that taking a bicycle on these services will incur an extra charge, which depends on the distance.

Bus

Bus services are excellent and relatively inexpensive. There are often a number of different companies handling each route so prices can vary substantially, but the prices in this book should give you an idea of costs (and unless otherwise noted, all bus prices are for one-way fares). Following are some prices for the most popular routes:

Destination	Cost	Duration	Frequency
Zagreb-Dubrovnik	205-401KN	11hr	7 daily
Zagreb-Korčula	195KN	12hr	1 daily
Zagreb-Pula	114-161KN	4-6hr	13 daily
Zagreb-Split	112-143KN	6-9hr	27 daily
Dubrovnik-Rijeka	300-309KN	12hr	4 daily
Dubrovnik-Split	100-111KN	4½hr	14 daily
Dubrovnik-Zadar	160-190KN	8hr	7 daily

It's generally best to call or visit the bus station to get the complete schedule but the following companies are among the largest:

Autotrans (☎ 051-66 03 60; www.autotrans.hr) Based in Rijeka with connections to Istria, Zagreb, Varaždin and Kvarner.

Brioni Pula (☎ 052-502 997; www.brioni.hr, in Croatian) Based in Pula with connections to Istria, Trieste, Padua, Split and Zagreb.

Contus (☎ 023-315 315; www.contus.hr) Based in Zadar with connections to Split and Zagreb.

At large stations bus tickets must be purchased at the office; book ahead to be sure of a seat. Tickets for buses that arrive from somewhere else are usually purchased from the conductor. Buy a one-way ticket only or you'll be locked into one company's schedule for the return. Most intercity buses are air-conditioned and make rest stops every two hours or so. Some of the more expensive companies charge extra for a video system that allows you to watch Croatian soap operas during your trip. If you plan to catch a nap, bring earplugs since there's bound to be music playing. Luggage stowed in the baggage compartment under the bus costs extra (7KN a piece, including insurance).

On schedules, *vozi svaki dan* means 'every day' and *ne vozi nedjeljom ni praznikom* means 'not Sunday and public holidays'. Check www.akz.hr, in Croatian, for information on schedules and fares to and from Zagreb.

Car & Motorcycle

Any valid driving licence is sufficient to legally drive and rent a car; an international driving licence is not necessary. **Hrvatski Autoklub** (HAK; Croatian Auto Club) offers help and advice, plus there's the nationwide **HAK road assistance** (vučna služba; ☎ 987).

Petrol stations are generally open 7am to 7pm and often until 10pm in summer. Petrol is Eurosuper 95, Super 98, normal or diesel. See www.ina.hr for up-to-date fuel prices.

You have to pay tolls on the motorways around Zagreb, to use the Učka tunnel between Rijeka and Istria, the bridge to Krk Island, as well as the road from Rijeka to Delnice. The long-awaited motorway connecting Zagreb and Split is scheduled to open in 2005 and will cut the travel time to the coast to about five hours. For general news on Croatia's motorways and tolls, see www.hac.hr.

ROAD RULES

Unless otherwise posted, the speed limits for cars and motorcycles are 50km/h in the built-up areas, 80km/h on main highways and 130km/h on motorways. On any of Croatia's winding two-lane highways, it's illegal to pass long military convoys or a line of cars caught behind a slow-moving truck. The maximum permitted amount of alcohol in the blood is – none at all! It is also forbidden to use a mobile phone while driving. Drive defensively, as some local drivers lack discipline, to put it mildly.

RENTAL

The large car-rental chains represented in Croatia are Avis, Budget, Europcar and Hertz. Throughout Croatia, Avis is allied with the Autotehna company, while Hertz is often represented by Kompas.

Independent local companies are often much cheaper than the international chains, but Avis, Budget, Europcar and Hertz have the big advantage of offering one-way rentals that allow you to drop the car off at any one of their many stations in Croatia free of charge.

Prices at local companies begin at around 350KN a day with unlimited kilometres. Shop around as deals vary widely and 'special' discounts and weekend rates are often available. Third-party public liability insurance is included by law, but make sure your quoted price includes full collision insurance, called collision damage waiver (CDW). Otherwise your responsibility for damage done to the vehicle is usually determined as a percentage of the car's value. Full CDW begins at 40KN a day extra (compulsory for those aged under 25), theft insurance is 15KN a day and personal accident insurance another 40KN a day.

Sometimes you can get a lower car-rental rate by booking the car from abroad. Tour companies in Western Europe often have fly-drive packages that include a flight to Croatia and a car (two-person minimum).

Hitching

Hitching is never entirely safe, and we don't recommend it. Hitchhiking in Croatia is unreliable. You'll have better luck on the islands, but in the interior cars are small and usually full.

Local Transport

Zagreb has a well-developed tram system as well as local buses, but in the rest of the country you'll only find buses. In major cities such as Rijeka, Split, Zadar and Dubrovnik buses run about every 20 minutes, and less often on Sunday. Small medieval towns along the coast are generally closed to traffic and have infrequent links to outlying suburbs.

Taxis are available in all cities and towns, but they must be called or boarded at a taxi stand. Prices are rather high (meters start at 25KN).

Train

Train travel is about 15% cheaper than bus travel and often more comfortable, although slower. The main lines run from Zagreb to Rijeka, Zadar and Split and east to Osijek. There are no trains along the coast. Local trains usually have only unreserved 2nd-class seats. Reservations may be required on express trains. 'Executive' trains have only 1st-class seats and are 40% more expensive than local trains.

On posted timetables in Croatia, the word for arrivals is *dolazak* and for departures it's *odlazak* or *polazak*. For train information check out **Croatian Railway** (www.hznet.hr, in Croatian).

Czech Republic

CONTENTS

Highlights	234	Embassies & Consulates	289
Itineraries	236	Festivals & Events	289
Climate & When to Go	236	Gay & Lesbian Travellers	289
History	236	Holidays	290
People	239	Internet Resources	290
Religion	239	Money	290
Arts	239	Post	290
Environment	240	Telephone	290
Food & Drink	240	Tourist Information	291
Prague	**241**	Visas	291
Orientation	244	**Transport in the Czech**	
Information	244	**Republic**	**291**
Dangers & Annoyances	248	Getting There & Away	291
Sights	248	Getting Around	292
Tours	253		
Festivals & Events	253		
Sleeping	253		
Eating	255		
Drinking	256		
Entertainment	257		
Shopping	259		
Getting There & Away	260		
Getting Around	260		
Around Prague	262		
Bohemia	**265**		
Terezín	265		
Litoměřice	265		
Bohemian Switzerland			
National Park	267		
Karlovy Vary	267		
Loket	271		
Plzeň	271		
České Budějovice	274		
Hluboká Nad Vltavou	276		
Český Krumlov	276		
Šumava	279		
Adršpach-Teplice Rocks	279		
Moravia	**280**		
Brno	280		
Telč	285		
Moravian Wine Country	287		
Czech Republic Directory	**287**		
Accommodation	287		
Activities	288		
Business Hours	288		
Customs	288		
Dangers & Annoyances	288		
Disabled Travellers	288		

The Czech Republic is a country of fairytale castles, forests and fish ponds, medieval towns and Renaissance chateaux. There's a rich heritage to explore – unravel Czech history and you'll get a deeper understanding of Europe as a whole – with the added bonus of the world's finest beer to lubricate debate. And at the centre of it all lies Prague, one of the most beautiful and cultured cities in the world.

No matter which direction you travel across Europe, you're sure to pass through the Czech Republic at some point. Landlocked deep in the heart of the continent, it has been fought over and occupied by its bigger neighbours for most of its history, and only emerged as a separate country in 1993. When they joined the EU in 2004, Czechs celebrated their return to the centre of a united Europe.

Everyone visits Prague – and you certainly should, too – but it's well worth making the effort to see other parts of the country – the pretty spa town of Karlovy Vary, the enchanting chateau of Český Krumlov and the spectacular scenery of Adršpach-Teplice.

FAST FACTS

- **Area** 78,864 sq km
- **Capital** Prague
- **Currency** Czech crown (Kč); €1 = 31.41Kč; US$1 = 25.22Kč; UK£1 = 45.48Kč; A$1 = 18.43Kč; ¥100 = 21.10Kč; NZ$1 = 17.32Kč
- **Famous for** beer, ice hockey, Kafka, Dvořák
- **Key Phrases** *Dobrý den/ahoj* (hello/informal), *na shledanou* (goodbye), *děkuji* (thank you), *promiňte* (excuse me)
- **Official Language** Czech
- **Population** 10.2 million
- **Telephone codes** country code ☎ 420; international access code ☎ 00; there are no telephone codes in the Czech Republic
- **Visas** Most travellers won't need one (see p291); if you do, arrange in advance.

HIGHLIGHTS

- Tune out the tourist crowds of **Prague** (p241) and soak up a city rooted in art, architecture and existential angst
- Discover **Český Krumlov**'s (p276) fairytale castle and medieval townscape, and relax, messing about on the river
- Imbibe the wisdom of the brewer's art at **Plzeň** (p271), the fountainhead of the world's finest beer
- Explore one of Europe's most bizarre landscapes among the spectacular sandstone pinnacles and ravines of **Adršpach-Teplice Rocks** (p279)

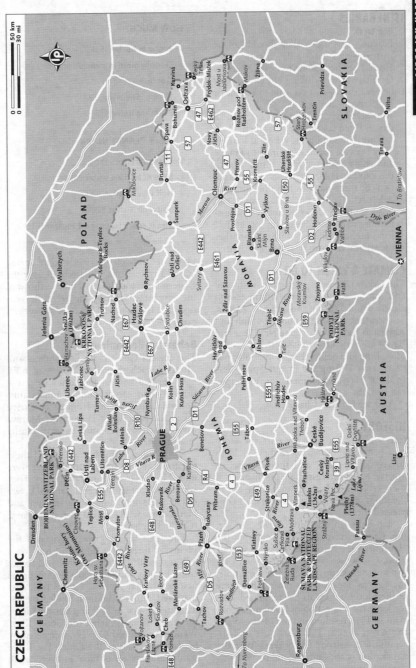

CZECH REPUBLIC

CZECH REPUBLIC

ITINERARIES

■ **One week** Devote at least three days to Prague – it's a city that should not be rushed – and make a day trip to Kutná Hora. Then head south to Český Krumlov for a day or two chilling out by the river before heading east via Brno to Vienna or Bratislava.

■ **Two weeks** Arriving from the west, spend a day in Plzeň tasting the beer, then take a bus north to sample the waters at Karlovy Vary (or vice versa). Continue to Prague and enjoy a relaxed four or five days in the capital. Hiking fans should make a two- or three-day diversion northeast to Adršpach-Teplice Rocks; lazybones can head south to Český Krumlov for sunbathing and more beer. Stop off at Telč for a night on the way to Brno (another night) and the Moravian Wine Country.

HOW MUCH?

■ **Night in hostel** 350Kč

■ **Double room in pension** 900Kč

■ **Goulash** 100Kč

■ **Shot of Slivovice** 35Kč

■ **Postcard home** 9Kč

LONELY PLANET INDEX

■ **Litre of petrol** 25Kč

■ **Litre of bottled water** 30Kč

■ **Half litre of beer** 30Kč

■ **Souvenir T-shirt** 300Kč

■ **Street snack (sausage & mustard)** 10Kč

CLIMATE & WHEN TO GO

The Czech climate is temperate, with cool and humid winters, warm summers and clearly defined spring and autumn seasons. The weather is best in summer, but July and August as well as Christmas-New Year and Easter are very busy, so it's better to visit in May, June and September. Winter also has its charms. During the Prague Spring festival (in May), accommodation in Prague can be tight.

Also see Climate Charts p874.

HISTORY

Czech history is in large part the story of a people doing whatever they could to survive occupation, and they themselves are far more interested in the history of their rebels and heretics than they are of the kings, emperors and dictators who oppressed them.

Slap-bang in the middle of Europe, the Czechs have been invaded by the Habsburgs, the Nazis, the Soviets, and tour groups; some see membership of the EU as just another occupation. At the same time, the Czechs' location has meant that none of their local upheavals has remained local for long: their rejection of Roman Catholicism in 1418 resulted in the Hussite Wars; the revolt against Habsburg rule in 1618 set off the disastrous Thirty Years' War; the annexation of the Sudetenland in 1938 was the first stuttering step towards WWII; the liberal reforms of the 1968 Prague Spring led to a rolling of tanks from all over the Eastern Bloc; and the peaceful overthrow of the government during the Velvet Revolution stands as a model for freedom-seekers everywhere.

Bohemian Beginnings

The ancient Czech lands of Bohemia and Moravia, each ringed by ranges of hills, have formed natural territories since the time of their earliest human inhabitants. Bohemia took its name from a Celtic tribe called the Boii, Moravia from the Morava River, itself a Germanic name meaning 'marsh water'.

Slavic tribes from the east settled these territories, and from 830 to 907 they were united in the Great Moravian Empire. They adopted Christianity after the arrival in 863 of the Thessalonian missionaries Cyril and Methodius, who created the first Slavic (Cyrillic) alphabet.

The first home-grown dynasty, the Přemysls, threw up a couple of huts on a hill in the 9th century in what was to become Prague, and fathered a dysfunctional first family that gave the Czechs their first martyred saints – Ludmila, killed by her daughter-in-law in 874, and her grandson, the pious Prince Václav (or Good 'King' Wenceslas; reigned 921–29), murdered by his brother Boleslav the Cruel. You'll see statues and images of them in churches all over the country.

The rule of the Přemysls ended in 1306 and, in 1310, John of Luxembourg came to the Bohemian throne through marriage and annexed the kingdom to the German Empire. The reign of his son, Charles IV (1346–78), who became Holy Roman Emperor, saw the first of Bohemia's two 'Golden Ages' – Charles founded Prague's St Vitus Cathedral, built Charles Bridge, established Charles University, and discovered the hot springs of Karlovy Vary. The second was the reign of Rudolf II (1576–1612), who made Prague the capital of the Habsburg Empire and drew many great artists, scholars and scientists to his court. Bohemia and Moravia remained under Habsburg dominion for the best part of 400 years.

Under the Habsburg Thumb

In 1415 the Protestant religious reformer Jan Hus, rector of Charles University, was burnt at the stake for heresy. Hus led a movement which espoused – among other things – letting the congregation taste the sacramental wine as well as the host (the Hussites' symbol was the communion chalice). His ideas inspired the religious and nationalist Hussite movement, which plunged Bohemia into civil war between 1419 and 1434.

When the Austrian – and Catholic – Habsburg dynasty ascended the Bohemian throne in 1526, the fury of the Counter-Reformation was unleashed on the Czech Lands. On 23 May 1618 a group of Protestants threw two Habsburg councillors from a Prague Castle window. The squabble escalated into the Catholic–Protestant Thirty Years' War (1618–48), which was to devastate much of central Europe and shatter Bohemia's economy.

The defeat of the Protestant uprising at the Battle of White Mountain in 1620 marked the start of a long period of forced re-Catholicisation, Germanisation and oppression of Czech language and culture. The baroque architectural style, which flourished in the 17th and 18th centuries, was the outward symbol of Catholic victory over the Protestant heretics.

National Reawakening

The Czechs began to rediscover their linguistic and cultural roots at the start of the 19th century during the so-called Národní obrození (National Revival). As overt political activity was banned, the revival was a cultural one; important figures included historian Josef Palacký and composer Bedřich Smetana and a distinctive neo-Renaissance architecture emerged, exemplified in Prague's National Theatre and National Museum.

The drive towards an independent Czech and Slovak state was realised after WWI, when the collapse of the Habsburg Empire saw the creation of the Czechoslovak Republic on 28 October 1918. The first president was Tomáš Garrigue Masaryk. Three-quarters of the Austro-Hungarian empire's industrial power was inherited by Czechoslovakia, as were three million Germans, mostly in the border areas of Bohemia (the pohraniči, known in German as the Sudetenland).

But the Czechs' elation was to be short-lived. Under the infamous Munich Pact of September 1938, Britain and France agreed not to oppose the annexation of the Sudetenland by Nazi Germany, and in March 1939 the Germans went on to occupy the rest of the country (calling it the Protectorate of Bohemia and Moravia).

The rapid occupation meant the country's historic buildings suffered little damage. However, most of the Czech intelligentsia and 80,000 Jews died at the hands of the Nazis. When Czech paratroopers assassinated the Nazi governor Reinhardt Heydrich in 1942, the entire town of Lidice was wiped out in revenge.

Communist Coup

After the war, the Czechoslovak government expelled 2.5 million Sudeten Germans – including antifascists who had fought the Nazis – from the Czech borderlands, confiscating their property. During the forced marches out of Czechoslovakia many were interned in concentration camps; it is estimated that tens of thousands of them died. In 1997 Czech Prime Minister Václav Klaus and German chancellor Helmut Kohl signed a declaration of mutual apology, but many Sudeten Germans are still campaigning for the restitution of lost land and houses.

In 1947 a power struggle developed between the communist and democratic forces, and in early 1948 the Social Democrats withdrew from the postwar coalition. The result was the Soviet-backed coup d'état of 25 February 1948, known as Vítězný únor (Victorious February). The new communist-led government set up the dictatorship of the proletariat and communist leader Klement Gottwald became the country's president.

The whole industrial sector was nationalised and the government's economic policies nearly bankrupted the country. The 1950s were years of harsh repression when thousands of noncommunists fled the country. Many people were imprisoned, and hundreds were executed or died in labour camps, often for little more than a belief in democracy or religion. A series of Stalinist purges was organised by the Communist Party, during which many people, including top members of the party itself, were executed.

Prague Spring & Velvet Revolution

In April 1968 the new first secretary of the Communist Party, Alexander Dubček, introduced liberalising reforms to create 'socialism with a human face' – referred to as the 'Prague Spring'. Censorship ended, political prisoners were released and decentralisation of the economy began. Moscow was not happy, but Dubček refused to bow to pressure to withdraw the reforms. The result was the Soviet invasion of 20 August 1968, when Soviet tanks rumbled through the streets of Prague, and Czechoslovakia was occupied by 200,000 Soviet and Warsaw Pact soldiers.

Renewed dictatorship saw the expulsion of around 14,000 Communist Party functionaries and 500,000 party members lost their jobs. Many educated professionals were made street cleaners and manual labourers. Dissidents were routinely imprisoned.

In 1977 the trial of the rock group The Plastic People of the Universe inspired the formation of the human-rights group Charter 77. (The communists saw the musicians as a threat to the status quo, while others viewed the trial as part of a pervasive assault on human rights.) Made up of a small group of Prague intellectuals, including the playwright/philosopher Václav Havel, Charter 77 functioned as an underground opposition throughout the 1980s.

By 1989 Gorbachev's *perestroika* was sending shock waves through the region and the fall of the Berlin Wall on 9 November raised expectations of change in Czechoslovakia. On 17 November an officially sanctioned student march in Prague was smashed by police; daily demonstrations followed and the protests widened, with a general strike on 27 November. Leading dissidents, with Havel at the forefront, formed the anti-Communist Civic Forum that negotiated the resignation of the Communist government on 3 December.

A 'Government of National Understanding' was formed, and Havel was elected president on 29 December. The days after the 17 November demonstration became known as Sametová revoluce (the 'Velvet Revolution'), because there were no casualties.

Velvet Divorce

With the removal of the strong central authority provided by the communists, old antagonisms between Slovakia and Prague reemerged. The federal parliament tried to stabilise the situation by giving both the Czech and Slovak Republics full federal status within a Czech and Slovak Federated Republic (ČSFR). But these moves failed to satisfy Slovak nationalists. Meanwhile the Civic Forum had split into two factions: the centrist Civic Movement and the Civic Democratic Party (ODS).

The June 1992 elections sealed Czechoslovakia's fate. Václav Klaus' ODS took 48 seats in the 150-seat federal parliament; while 24 went to the Movement for a Democratic Slovakia (HZDS), a left-leaning Slovak nationalist party led by Vladimír Mečiar.

In July, goaded by Mečiar's fiery rhetoric, the Slovak parliament voted to declare sovereignty. Despite numerous efforts the two leaders could not reach a compromise, and they decided that splitting the country was the best solution. On 1 January 1993 Czechoslovakia ceased to exist for the second time. Prague became capital of the new Czech Republic, and Havel was elected its first president.

Thanks to booming tourism and a solid industrial base, the Czech Republic started strongly. Unemployment was negligible, shops were full and many cities were getting face-lifts; by 2003 Prague enjoyed the highest standard of living in Eastern Europe. However, capitalism also meant a shortage of affordable housing, rising crime and a deteriorating health system.

In 2003, following two terms as president, Havel was replaced by former prime minister Klaus – it took three elections for Czechs to settle on a new president, and the uncharismatic Klaus is far from the popular leader Havel was. While Klaus stands for free-market economy and ever-increasing privatisation, the current prime minister, Vladimír Špidla, is much more left-leaning.

The Czech Republic became a member of NATO in 1999, and joined the EU on 1 May 2004. If all goes well, it will take on the euro in 2007.

PEOPLE

The population of the Czech Republic is 10.2 million, and is fairly homogeneous; 95% of the population are Czech and 3% are Slovak. After WWII three million Sudeten Germans were evicted from the country, and today only about 150,000 of this group remain, comprising about 1.5% of the current population. There is a significant Roma population (0.3%), which is subject to widespread hostility and racist attitudes, and suffers from high levels of poverty and unemployment.

RELIGION

Most Czechs are either atheist (39.8%) or nominally Roman Catholic (39.2%), but church attendance is low. There are also small Protestant (4.6%) and Orthodox (3%) congregations, while the Jewish community (1% of the population in 1918) today numbers only a few thousand. Religious tolerance is well established and the Catholic Church makes little attempt to involve itself in politics.

ARTS
Literature

Though he wrote in German, Franz Kafka was one of Bohemia's greatest writers. With a circle of other German-speaking Jewish writers in Prague he played a major role in the literary scene at the beginning of the 20th century.

After WWI Jaroslav Hašek devoted himself to taking the piss out of the Habsburg empire and its minions; his folk masterpiece is *The Good Soldier Švejk*, a hysterically funny, rambling study of one Czech soldier during WWI.

Bohumil Hrabal (1914–97) was one of the finest Czech novelists of the 20th century;

The Little Town Where Time Stood Still is a good-humoured portrayal of the interactions in a small, close-knit community.

Milan Kundera (b 1929) is considered the most widely known Czech writer internationally, with one of his books, *The Unbearable Lightness of Being,* having been made into a film. His first novel, *The Joke,* gives a penetrating insight into the paranoia of the communist era.

One of the most interesting of contemporary Czech writers is poet and rock lyricist Jáchym Topol, whose stream-of-consciousness novel *Sister City Silver* is an exhilarating exploration of postcommunist Prague.

Music

Bedřich Smetana (1824–84), the first great Czech composer and an icon of Czech pride, created a national style by incorporating folk songs and dances into his classical compositions. His best-known pieces are the operas *Prodaná Nevěsta* (The Bartered Bride) and *Dalibor a Libuše* (Dalibor and Libuše, named after the two main characters), and the symphonic-poem cycle *Má vlast* (My Homeland). Prague Spring (p253), the country's biggest festival, is dedicated to Smetana and begins with a parade from the composer's grave at Vyšehrad to the Smetana Hall, where *Má vlast* is then performed.

Antonín Dvořák (1841–1904) is perhaps everyone's favourite Czech composer. His best-known works include his symphony *From the New World* (composed in the USA while lecturing there for four years), his *Slavonic Dances* of 1878 and 1881, the operas *The Devil & Kate* and *Rusalka,* and his religious masterpiece, *Stabat Mater.*

Painting

Think Art Nouveau and you're probably thinking Alfons Mucha (1860–1939).

Though he lived mostly in Paris and is associated with the French Art Nouveau movement, Mucha's heart remained at home in Bohemia and much of his work visits and revisits themes of Slavic suffering, courage and cross-nation brotherhood. The most outstanding of his works is a series of 20 large canvasses called the *Slav Epic*, which are presently in Moravský Krumlov (p285), and his interior decoration in the Municipal House in Prague (see p251), but his design and print work can be seen all over the Czech Republic.

ENVIRONMENT

The Czech Republic is a landlocked country bordered by Germany, Austria, Slovakia and Poland. The land is made up of two river basins: Bohemia in the west, drained by the Labe (Elbe) River flowing north into Germany; and Moravia in the east, drained by the Morava River flowing southeast into the Danube. Each basin is ringed by low, forest-clad hills, notably the Šumava range along the Bavarian–Austrian border in the southwest, the Krušné hory (Ore Mountains) along the northwestern border with Germany, and the Krkonoše mountains along the Polish border east of Liberec. The country's highest peak, Sněžka (1602m), is in the Krkonoše. In between these ranges are rolling plains mixed with forests and farm land. The forests – mainly spruce, oak and beech – still cover one-third of the country.

The South Bohemian landscape is characterised by a network of hundreds of linked fish ponds and artificial lakes. The biggest lake in the republic, the 4870-hectare Lake Lipno (p279), is also in South Bohemia. East Bohemia is home to the striking 'rock towns' of the Adršpach-Teplice Rocks (p279).

National Parks

Though numerous areas are set aside as national parks and protected landscape areas, the emphasis is on visitor use as well as species and landscape protection. National parks and protected areas make up approximately 15% of the Czech Republic, including the Bohemian Switzerland (p267) and Šumava (p279) national parks, and the Adršpach-Teplice Protected Landscape Area (p279).

Environmental Issues

The forests of northern Bohemia and Moravia have been devastated by acid rain created by the burning of poor-quality brown coal at factories and thermal power stations. The most affected region is the eastern Ore Mountains where most of the trees are dead. In recent years sulphur dioxide levels in Prague have declined, while carbon monoxide pollution from cars and trucks has increased. The emissions have been cleared up in recent years.

There is tension between the Czech government and non-nuclear Austria over the Temelín nuclear power station in South Bohemia. Austria threatened to block the Czechs' entry to the EU if they did not close it down, but in 2004 the Czechs announced plans to expand the station.

FOOD & DRINK

On the surface, Czech food seems very similar to German or Polish food: lots of meat served with *knedlíky* (dumplings) and cabbage. The little differences are what make the food here special – eat a forkful of *svíčková* (roast beef served with a sour cream sauce and spices) sopped up with fluffy bread *knedlíky* and you'll be wondering why you haven't heard more about this cuisine.

Staples & Specialities

Traditional Czech cuisine is strong on meat, *knedlíky* and gravy, and weak on fresh vegetables – the classic Bohemian dish is *knedlo-zelo-vepřo* – bread dumplings, sauerkraut and roast pork. Other tasty home-grown delicacies to look out for include *cesneková* (garlic soup), *svíčková na smetaně* (roast beef with sour cream sauce and cranberries) and *kapr na kmíní* (fried or baked carp with caraway seed). *Ovocné knedlíky* (fruit dumplings), with whole fruit, are served as a dessert with cottage cheese or crushed poppy seeds and melted butter.

The Czech Republic is a beer drinker's paradise – where else could you get two or three 500mL glasses of top-quality Pilsner for under a dollar? One of the first words of Czech you'll learn is *pivo* (beer); alcohol-free beer (yuck!) is *nealkoholické pivo*. The Czechs serve their draught beer with a high head of foam.

Bohemian *pivo* is probably the best in the world – the most famous brands are Budvar (p274) and Pilsner Urquell (p271). The South Moravian vineyards (p287) produce reasonable *bílé víno* (white wines).

Special alcoholic treats include Becherovka (see p268) and *slivovice* (plum brandy). *Grog* is rum with hot water and sugar. *Limonáda* often refers to any soft drink, not just lemonade.

Where to Eat & Drink

A *bufet* or *samoobsluha* is a self-service, cafeteria-style place with *chlebíčky* (open sandwiches), salads, *klobásy* (spicy sausages), *špekačky* (mild pork sausages), *párky* (frankfurters), *guláš* (goulash) and of course *knedlíky*. Some of these places are tucked to the side of *potraviny* (food shops). A *bageteria* serves made-to-order sandwiches and baguettes.

A *pivnice* is a pub without food, while a *hospoda* or *hostinec* is a pub or beer hall that serves basic meals. A *vinárna* (wine bar) may have anything from snacks to a full-blown menu. The occasional *kavárna* (café) has a full menu but most serve only snacks and desserts. A *restaurace* is any restaurant.

Restaurants start serving as early as 11am and carry on till midnight; some take a break between lunch and dinner. Main dishes may stop being served well before the advertised closing time, with only snacks and drinks after that.

Vegetarians & Vegans

Outside of Prague, which has a good range of options, vegetarians will have a very hard, and dull, time of it. Vegans will find life next to impossible. There are a few standard *bezmasá jídla* (meatless dishes) served by most restaurants: the most common are *smažený sýr* (fried cheese) and vegetables cooked with cheese sauce. The pizza places that you'll find in almost every town make a good standby.

Habits & Customs

Most beer halls have a system of marking everything you eat or drink on a small piece of paper that is left on your table, then totted up when you pay (say *zaplatím, prosím* – I'd like to pay, please). Waiters in all Czech restaurants, including the expensive ones, often whisk away empty plates

from under your nose before you manage to swallow the last of your *knedlíky*.

In a pub, always ask if a chair is free before sitting down (*Je tu volno?*). The standard toast involves clinking together first the tops, then the bottoms of glasses, then touching the glass to the table; most people say '*Na zdraví* ' (to health).

PRAGUE

pop 1.19 million

Magic, golden, mystical Prague, Queen of Music, City of a Thousand Spires, famed for Kafka, the Velvet Revolution, and the world's finest beers. The locals call her *matička Praha* (Little Mother Prague), the cradle of Czech culture and one of Europe's most fascinating cities.

Tourist brochures go into overload when describing the Czech capital, but the city lives up to the hype. Unlike battle-scarred Warsaw, Budapest and Berlin, Prague escaped WWII almost unscathed – the city centre is a smorgasbord of stunning architecture, from Gothic, Renaissance and baroque to neoclassical, Art Nouveau and cubist. There's a maze of medieval lanes to explore, riverside parks for picnics, lively bars and beer gardens, jazz clubs, rock venues, museums and art galleries galore.

Prague is an unmissable stop on any trip through Eastern Europe. Beware, though – Prague is a city that gets under your skin, and many people stay longer than they mean to. As Kafka once wrote, 'this little mother has claws'.

PRAGUE IN TWO DAYS

Spend half of your first day taking in the sights at **Prague Castle** (p248), then wander down to **Malá Strana** (p250) for a look at St Nicholas Church and a saunter across Charles Bridge. Make time on day two for a tour of the **Municipal House** (p251) and a visit to **Vyšehrad**. Be sure to savour a beer or two somewhere – **U malého Glena** (p257) for a jazz vibe, **U Zlatého Tygra** (p257) for tradition – before eating at a restaurant with a view of the river – the terrace at **Hergetova Cihelna** (p255) can't be beaten.

CZECH REPUBLIC

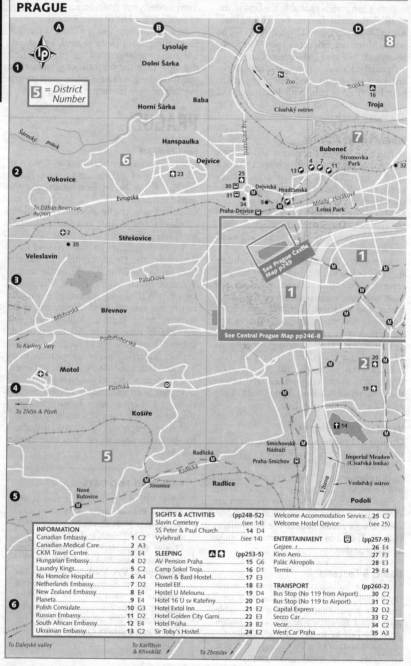

PRAGUE

5 = District Number

INFORMATION
Canadian Embassy	**1** C2
Canadian Medical Care	**2** A3
CKM Travel Centre	**3** E4
Hungarian Embassy	**4** D2
Laundry Kings	**5** C2
Na Homolce Hospital	**6** A4
Netherlands Embassy	**7** D2
New Zealand Embassy	**8** E4
Planeta	**9** E4
Polish Consulate	**10** G3
Russian Embassy	**11** D2
South African Embassy	**12** E4
Ukrainian Embassy	**13** C2

SIGHTS & ACTIVITIES (pp248-52)
Slavín Cemetery	(see 14)
SS Peter & Paul Church	**14** D4
Vyšehrad	(see 14)

SLEEPING (pp253-5)
AV Pension Praha	**15** G6
Camp Sokol Troja	**16** D1
Clown & Bard Hostel	**17** E3
Hostel Elf	**18** E3
Hostel U Melounu	**19** D4
Hotel 16 U sv Kateřiny	**20** D4
Hotel Extol Inn	**21** E2
Hotel Golden City Garni	**22** E3
Hotel Praha	**23** B2
Sir Toby's Hostel	**24** E2

Welcome Accommodation Service... **25** C2
Welcome Hostel Dejvice............(see 25)

ENTERTAINMENT (pp257-9)
Gejzee...r	**26** E4
Kino Aero	**27** F3
Palác Akropolis	**28** E3
Termix	**29** E4

TRANSPORT (pp260-2)
Bus Stop (No 119 from Airport)	**30** C2
Bus Stop (No 119 to Airport)	**31** C2
Capital Express	**32** D2
Secco Car	**33** E2
Vecar	**34** C2
West Car Praha	**35** A3

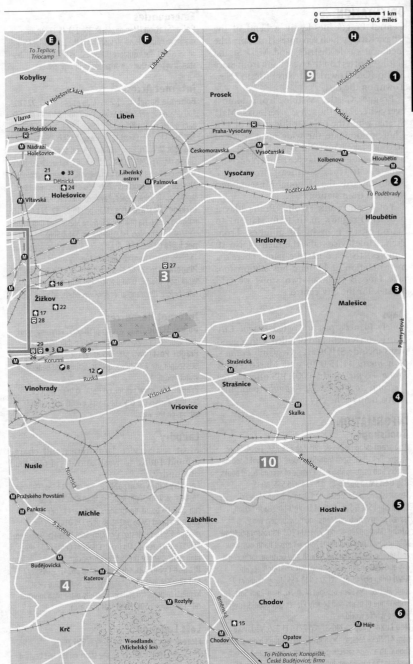

0 | 1 km
0 | 0.5 miles

E **F** **G** **H**

9

1

To Teplice;
Triocamp

Kobylisy

Mladoboleslavská

Liberecká

V Holešovičkách

Prosek

Kbelská

Vltava

Libeň

Praha-Vysočany

Praha-Holešovice

Nádraží
Holešovice

Praha-Vysočany

Českomoravská

Vysočanská

Kolbenova

Hloubětín

2

21 ● 33

Libeňský
ostrov

Palmovka

Vysočany

To Poděbrady

Poděbradská

Dělnická

24

Holešovice

Hloubětín

Vltavská

Hrdlořezy

3

18

27

3

Žižkov

Malešice

22

17

Průmyslová

28

10

29 ● 3

9

26 Korunní

Strašnická

4

8

12

Strašnice

Ruská

Vinohrady

Vršovická

Vršovice

Skalka

Nusle

Nuselka

10

Švehlova

Pražského Povstání

Pankrác

Hostivař

5

Michle

Záběhlice

5. května

Budějovická

Brněnská

Kačerov

Chodov

4

Roztyly

6

Krč

15

Woodlands
(Michelský les)

Chodov

Opatov

Háje

To Průhonice; Konopiště;
České Budějovice; Brno

CZECH REPUBLIC

ORIENTATION

Central Prague nestles in a bend of the Vltava River, which separates Hradčany (the medieval castle district) and Malá Strana (Little Quarter) on the west bank from Staré Město (Old Town) and Nové Město (New Town) on the east.

Prague Castle, visible from almost everywhere in the city, overlooks Malá Strana, while the twin Gothic spires of Týn Church dominate the wide open space of Staroměstské nám (Old Town Square). The broad avenue of Václavské nám (Wenceslas Square) stretches southeast from Staré Město towards the National Museum and the main train station.

You can walk from Praha-hlavní nádraží (Prague's main train station) to Staroměstské nám in 10 minutes. From Praha-Holešovice, take the metro (also 10 minutes) to Staroměstské nám. There's a metro station at Florenc bus station too; take Line B (yellow) two stops west to Můstek for the city centre.

Maps

Lonely Planet's plastic-coated *Prague City Map* is convenient and detailed. Other good maps include SHOCart's GeoClub *Praha – plán města* (1:15,000) and Marco Polo's *Praha – centrum* (1:5,000). PIS offers a free *Welcome to the Czech Republic* pamphlet with a map of the city centre.

INFORMATION
Bookshops

Anagram (Map pp246-8; ☎ 224 895 737; Týn 4, Staré Město; ☽ 10am-8pm Mon-Sat, 10am-6pm Sun) Good on history and culture; also has a range of second-hand books.

Big Ben (Map pp246-8; ☎ 224 826 565; Malá Štupartská 5, Staré Město; ☽ 9am-6.30pm Mon-Fri, 10am-5pm Sat & Sun) Lots of English-language fiction, travel, poetry, history. Mags and newspapers too.

Globe (Map pp246-8; ☎ 224 934 203; Pštrossova 6, Nové Město; ☽ 10am-midnight) Famous expat hang-out; new and second-hand books in English and German, including a gay and lesbian interest section. Bar and Internet café.

Kiwi (Map pp246-8; ☎ 224 948 455; Jungmannova 23, Nové Město; ☽ 9am-6.30pm Mon-Fri, 9am-2pm Sat) Wide range of maps and Lonely Planet guidebooks covering the whole world.

Neo Luxor (Map pp246-8; ☎ 221 111 336; Václavské nám 41, Nové Město; ☽ 8am-8pm) Prague's biggest bookshop with a wide selection of English, German and French books in the basement. Internet access (1Kč per minute).

Emergencies

Police Station (Map pp246-8; ☎ 261 45 17 60; Jungmannovo nám 9, Nové Město) This is the place to go for a crime report (for insurance purposes), as it's the only police station in town that can organise an interpreter.

Internet Access

Bohemia Bagel Staré Město (Map pp246-8; ☎ 224 812 560; Masná 2; per min 1.50Kč; ☽ 7am-midnight Mon-Fri, 8am-midnight Sat & Sun) Malá Strana (Map pp246-8; ☎ 257 310 694; Újezd 16; per min 1.50Kč; ☽ 7am-midnight Mon-Fri, 8am-midnight Sat & Sun) See p255.

Globe (Map pp246-8; ☎ 224 934 203; Pštrossova 6, Nové Město; per min 1.50Kč, no minimum; ☽ 10am-midnight) Also has Ethernet sockets where you can connect your own laptop (same price; cables provided, 50Kč deposit).

Internet Nescafé Live (Map pp246-8; ☎ 221 637 168; Rathova Pasaž, Na příkopě 23, Nové Město; per min 1.70Kč; ☽ 9am-10pm Mon-Fri, 10am-8pm Sat & Sun)

net k@fe (Map pp246-8; Na poříčí 8, Nové Město; per min 1Kč; ☽ 9am-11pm) Cheapest in the city centre.

Planeta (Map pp242-3; ☎ 267 311 182; Vinohradská 102, Vinohrady; per min 0.40-0.80Kč; ☽ 8am-11pm) Cheap rates before 10am and after 8pm weekdays, all weekend.

Internet Resources

Dopravní podnik (www.dp-praha.cz) Everything you ever wanted to know about Prague's public transport.

Prague Post (www.praguepost.cz) Local English-language newspaper site with news, events, listings and general visitor info.

Prague TV (www.prague.tv) Nothing to do with TV, but this site has the city's best arts, events and nightlife listings on the web.

Laundry

Most self-service laundrettes will charge around 140Kč to wash and dry a 6kg load of laundry.

Laundry Kings (Map pp246-8; ☎ 603 713 855; Dejvická 16, Dejvice; 7am-10pm Mon-Fri, from 8am Sat & Sun) Expat-run. Bulletin board, newspapers, Internet (1.50Kč per hour).

Laundryland (Map pp246-8; ☎ 221 014 632; Na příkopě 12, Nové Město; ☽ 9am-8pm Mon-Fri, 9am-7pm Sat, 11am-7pm Sun) On the 1st floor of Černá Růže shopping centre, above the Panská entrance.

Prague Cyber Laundromat (Map pp242-3; ☎ 222 510 180; Korunní 14, Vinohrady; ☽ 8am-8pm) Near Náměstí Míru metro station. Friendly place with Internet café (per hour 1.50Kč) and kids play area.

Left Luggage

Florenc bus station (per bag per day 25Kč; ☽ 5am-11pm) Halfway up the stairs on the left beyond the main ticket hall.

Main train station (per small/large bag per day 15/30Kč; 24hr) On Level 1. There are also lockers (two 5Kč coins).

Medical Services

There are several 24-hour pharmacies in the centre, including **Praha lékárna** (Map pp246-8; ☎ 224 946 982; Palackého 5, Nové Město); for emergency service after hours, ring the bell.

Canadian Medical Care (Map pp242-3; ☎ 235 360 133, after hrs ☎ 724 300 301; Veleslavínská 1, Veleslavín; 8am-6pm Mon, Wed & Fri, 8am-8pm Tue & Thu) Expat centre with English-speaking doctors, 24-hour medical aid, physiotherapist and pharmacy.

Na Homolce Hospital (Map pp242-3; ☎ 257 271 111, after hrs ☎ 257 272 527; 5th fl, Foreign Pavilion, Roentgenova 2, Motol) City's main casualty department.

Polyclinic at Národní (Map pp246-8; ☎ 222 075 120; Národní třída 9, Nové Město) With English-, French- and German-speaking staff.

Money

The major banks – Komerční banka, Živnostenská banka and ČSOB – are the best places for changing cash, but using a debit card in an ATM gives a better rate of exchange. Avoid *směnárna* (private exchange booths), which advertise misleading rates and make exorbitant charges.

Amex (Map pp246-8; ☎ 222 800 237; Václavské nám 56, Nové Město; 9am-7pm)

Česká spořitelna (Map pp246-8; Václavské nám 16, Nové Město; 8am-5pm Mon-Fri)

ČSOB (Map pp246-8; Na příkopě 14, Nové Město; 8am-5pm Mon-Fri)

Komerční banka (Map pp246-8; Václavské nám 42, Nové Město; 8am-5pm Mon-Fri)

Travelex (Map pp246-8; ☎ 221 105 276; Národní třída 28, Nové Město; 9am-1.30pm & 2-6.30pm)

Živnostenská banka (Map pp246-8; Na příkopě 20, Nové Město; 8am-4.30pm Mon-Fri)

Post

To use the **main post office** (Jindřišská 14, Nové Město; 7am-8pm), take a ticket from one of the automated machines just outside the main hall (press button No 1 for stamps and parcels, No 4 for EMS). Wait until your number *(lístek číslo)* comes up on the electronic boards inside; these tell you which window to go to for service *(přepážka)*.

You can pick up poste-restante mail at window No 1 and buy phonecards at window No 28. Parcels weighing up to 2kg, as well as international and Express Mail Service (EMS) parcels are sent from window Nos 7 to 10. (Note that these services close at 1pm on Saturday and all day Sunday.)

Telephone

There's a 24-hour telephone centre to the left of the right-hand post office entrance. Bohemia Bagel (opposite) has phones for making international calls (5Kč per minute).

Tourist Information

Prague Information Service (PIS, Pražská informační služba; Map pp246-8; ☎ 12 444; www.prague-info.cz); Old Town Hall (Staroměstské nám; 9am-7pm Mon-Fri, 9am-6pm Sat & Sun); Nové Město (Na příkopě 20; 9am-7pm Mon-Fri, 9am-5pm Sat & Sun); Malá Strana Bridge Tower (Charles Bridge; 10am-6pm Apr-Oct) English-speaking staff. Maps, brochures, guides, public transport tickets, concert tickets, accommodation desk, currency exchange etc.

Travel Agencies

Čedok (Map pp246-8; ☎ 224 197 777, 800 112 112; www.cedok.cz; Na příkopě 18, Nové Město; 9am-7pm Mon-Fri, 9am-1pm Sat) Tour operator and travel agency. Also offers accommodation bookings, excursions, concert and theatre tickets, car rental and money exchange.

CKM Travel Centre (Map pp242-3; ☎ 222 721 595; www.ckm.cz; Mánesova 77, Vinohrady; 10am-6pm Mon-Thu, 10am-4pm Fri) Books air and bus tickets, with discounts for those aged under 26. Sells youth cards.

Eurolines-Sodeli CZ (Map pp246-8; ☎ 224 239 318; Senovážné nám 6, Nové Město; 8am-6pm Mon-Fri) Agent for Eurolines buses.

GTS International (Map pp246-8; ☎ 222 211 204; www.gtsint.cz; Ve Smečkách 33, Nové Město; 8am-6pm Mon-Fri, 11am-3pm Sat) Youth cards and air, bus and train tickets.

DANGERS & ANNOYANCES

Prague's crime rate is low compared to Western standards, but beware of the pickpockets who regularly work the crowds at the astronomical clock, Prague Castle and Charles Bridge, and on the central metro and tram lines, especially tourists getting on or off crowded tram Nos 9 and 22.

Being ripped off by taxi drivers is another hazard. Most taxi drivers are honest, but a sizable minority who operate from tourist areas greatly overcharge their customers (even Czechs). Try not to take a taxi from Václavské nám, Národní třída and other tourist areas. It's better to phone for a taxi

CZECH REPUBLIC

CENTRAL PRAGUE

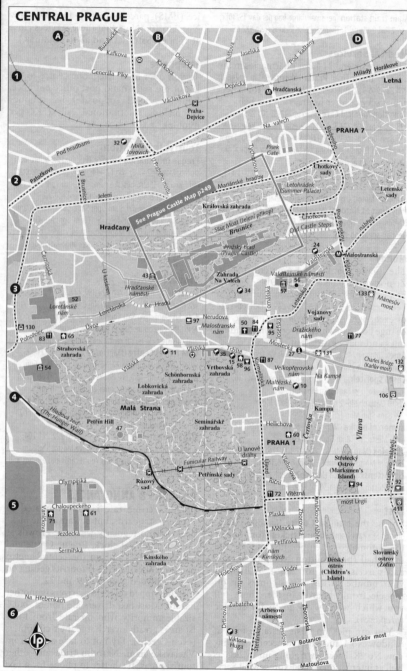

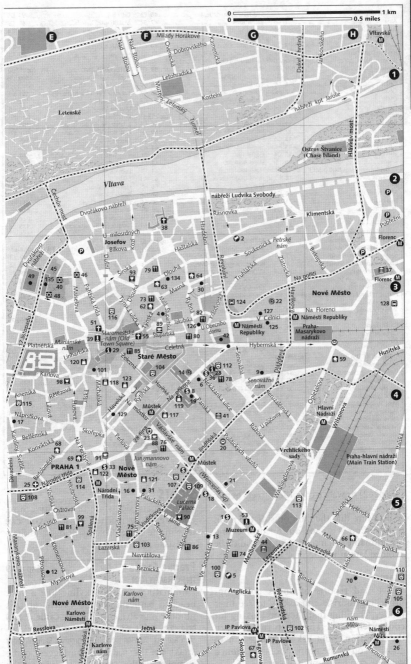

INFORMATION
Amex..1 G5
Anagram.....................................(see 89)
Australian Consulate..................2 G3
Austrian Embassy........................3 C6
Big Ben Bookshop.......................4 F3
Bohemia Bagel..........................(see 72)
Bohemia Bagel..........................(see 73)
Bulgarian Embassy......................5 G6
Čedok...6 F4
Česká Spořitelna..........................7 F5
ČSOB..8 F4
Euroines-Sodeli CZ......................9 G4
French Embassy.........................10 C4
German Embassy.......................11 B4
Globe...12 E6
GTS International.......................13 G5
Internet Nescafe Live................14 F4
Irish Embassy............................15 C4
Kiwi..16 F5
Klub mladých cestovatelů (KMC)..17 E4
Komerční banka.........................18 F5
Laundryland..............................19 F4
Main Post Office........................20 G4
Neo Luxor..................................21 G5
net k@fe....................................22 G3
Police Station............................23 F4
Polish Embassy..........................24 D3
Polyclinic at Národní.................25 E5
Prague Cyber Laundromat.........26 H6
Prague Information Service
  (Malá Strana Bridge Tower).....27 C4
Prague Information Service
  (Nové Město)...........................28 G4
Prague Information Service
  (Old Town Hall).......................29 F4
Prague Wheelchair Users Organisation..30 F3
Praha Lékárna...........................31 F5
Slovak Embassy.........................32 B2
Travelex....................................33 E5
UK Embassy...............................34 C3
US Embassy...............................35 C4
Živnostenská banka...................36 G4

SIGHTS & ACTIVITIES   (pp248-52)
Astronomical Clock..................(see 29)
City of Prague Museum.............37 H3
Convent of St Agnes.................38 F2
Jan Hus Monument....................39 E3
Klaus Synagogue.......................40 E3
Malá Strana Bridge Tower.........(see 27)
Mucha Museum..........................41 G4
Municipal House........................42 G3
National Gallery.........................43 B3
National Museum.......................44 G5
Old Jewish Cemetery.................45 E3
Old Town Hall..........................(see 29)

Old-New Synagogue.................46 E3
Petřín Tower.............................47 B4
Pinkas Synagogue.....................48 E3
Rudolfinum...............................49 E3
St Nicholas Church (Malá Strana)..50 C3
St Nicholas Church (Staré Město)..51 E3
Sanctuary of Our Lady of Loreta..52 A3
Statue of St Wenceslas..............53 G5
Strahov Library.........................54 A4
Týn Church................................55 F3
Wallenstein Gardens.................56 C3
Wallenstein Palace....................57 C3

SLEEPING   (pp253-5)
Aria Hotel.................................58 C4
Hostel Jednota.........................59 H4
Hostel Sokol.............................60 C4
Hostel SPUS Strahov.................61 A5
Hostel Týn................................62 F3
Hotel Antik...............................63 F3
Hotel Josef...............................64 F3
Hotel Questenberk....................65 A3
Mary's......................................66 H5
Pension Březina........................67 G6
Pension Unitas..........................68 E4
Penzión U Medvídků.................69 E5
Stop City..................................70 H6
Welcome Hostel Strahov...........71 A5

EATING   (pp255-6)
Beas Vegetarian Dhaba.............(see 62)
Bohemia Bagel (Malá Strana)....72 C5
Bohemia Bagel (Staré Město)....73 F3
C/Česká hospoda v Krakovské...74 G5
Café FX....................................(see 102)
Country Life.............................75 F5
Country Life.............................(see 118)
Dobrá čajovna..........................76 F4
Hergetova Cihelna....................77 D3
Kogo..78 G4
Orange Moon...........................79 F3
Pivnice Radegast......................80 F3
Pizzeria Kmotra........................81 E5
Red Hot & Blues.......................82 F3
Sate...83 A3
Square.....................................84 C3
Staroměstská restaurace...........85 F4
Titanik Steak House..................86 F5
Vinárna U Maltézských rytířů....87 C4

DRINKING   (pp256-7)
Café Praha................................88 F4
Ebel Coffee House.....................89 F3
Jáma..90 F5
Káva.Káva.Káva........................91 E5
Kavárna Slávia..........................92 D5
Kozička....................................93 F3

Letní bar...................................94 D5
Malostranská beseda.................95 C3
U malého Glena........................96 C4
U zeleného čaje.........................97 B3
U Zlatého Tygra........................98 E4
Velryba....................................99 E5

ENTERTAINMENT   (pp257-9)
AghaRTA jazz centrum.............100 G6
Black Theatre of Jiří Srnec.......(see 114)
Bohemia Ticket International....101 E4
Club Radost FX.......................102 G6
Divadlo Minor.........................103 F5
Dvořák Hall.............................(see 49)
Estates Theatre.......................104 F3
FOK Box Office.......................(see 42)
Gejzee..r.................................105 H6
Karlovy lázně..........................106 D4
Kino Světozor..........................107 F5
Laterna Magika.......................108 E5
Lucerna Music Bar...................109 F5
Maler......................................110 H6
National Theatre.....................111 D5
Palace Cinemas.......................112 G4
Prague State Opera.................113 G5
Reduta Jazz Club.....................114 E5
Smetana Hall...........................(see 42)
Theatre on the Balustrade.......115 E5
Ticketpro................................116 F3

SHOPPING   (pp259-60)
Bontonland.............................117 F4
Manufaktura...........................118 E4
Moser.....................................119 F4
Rott Crystal.............................120 E4
Supraphon..............................121 F5
Tesco Department Store...........122 E5
Tupesy lidová keramika...........123 F4

TRANSPORT   (pp260-2)
Čedaz Minibus Stop.................124 G3
České dráhy............................125 G3
City Bike.................................126 F3
Czech Airlines (ČSA)...............127 G3
Eurolines Bohemia Evroexpress
  International..........................(see 128)
Florenc Bus Station.................128 H3
Kingscourt Express..................129 F4
Pohořelec Tram Stop...............130 A3
Prague Venice Jetty (Čertovka).131 D4
Prague Venice Jetty
  (Charles Bridge)....................132 D4
Prague Venice Jetty (Mánes Bridge)..133 D3
Praha Bike..............................134 F3

OTHER
Museum of Decorative Arts......135 E3

(see p262) or walk a couple of streets before hailing one.

Be aware that the park outside the main train station is a hang-out for drunks and questionable characters and should be avoided late at night.

Scams

We've had reports of bogus police approaching tourists and asking to see their money, claiming that they are looking for counterfeit notes. They then run off with the cash. If in doubt, ask the 'policeman' to go with you to the nearest police station; a genuine cop will happily do so.

SIGHTS

All the main sights are in the city centre, and are easily reached on foot; you can take in the castle, Charles Bridge and Staroměstské nám in a day.

Prague Castle   Map p249
INFORMATION

Dominating Prague's skyline like a vast, beached battleship is the Czech capital's number one attraction, **Prague Castle** (Pražský hrad; ☎ 224 373 368; www.hrad.cz, in Czech; ☉ 9am-5pm Apr-Oct, 9am-4pm Nov-Mar; grounds 5am-midnight Apr-Oct, 6am-11pm Nov-Mar). The biggest castle complex in the world, according to the

Guinness Book of Records, and known to Praguers simply as 'Hrad', it feels more like a small town than a castle. It is still the seat of Czech power, both political and symbolic, housing the president's office as well as the ancient Bohemian crown jewels.

There are ticket options to choose from. **Ticket B** (adult/concession 220/110Kč) is the best value, giving access to St Vitus Cathedral (choir, crypt and tower), Old Royal Palace and Golden Lane; **Ticket A** (350/175Kč) includes all of these plus the Basilica of St George, Powder Tower, and Story of Prague Castle exhibit. You can buy tickets at the **Castle Information Centre** in the Third Courtyard and at the entrance to the main sights. Most of the castle is wheelchair accessible.

SIGHTS
The main entrance is at the western end. There you can watch the **changing of the guard** – their stylish blue uniforms were created by Theodor Pistek, costume designer for the film *Amadeus* – every hour, on the hour. The biggest show is at noon, when a band plays from the windows above the courtyard.

The **Matthias Gate** leads through to the second courtyard and the **Chapel of the Holy Cross** (souvenir shop; concert tickets on sale here). On the north side is the **Prague Castle Gallery** (adult/concession 100/50Kč; ☼ 10am-6pm), with a good collection of European baroque art.

The third courtyard is dominated by **St Vitus Cathedral**, a glorious French Gothic structure begun in 1344 by order of Emperor Charles IV, but not finally completed until 1929. Inside, the nave is flooded with colour from beautiful **stained-glass windows** created by eminent Czech artists of the early 20th century, including one by Alfons Mucha (3rd chapel on the left as you enter the cathedral) illustrating the lives of SS Cyril and Methodius. In the apse is the massive **tomb of St John of Nepomuk** – two tonnes of floridly baroque silver watched over by a squadron of hovering cherubs.

The 14th-century chapel on the cathedral's southern side with the black imperial eagle on the door contains the **tomb of St Wenceslas**, the Czechs' patron saint and the Good King Wenceslas of the Christmas carol. Wenceslas' zeal in spreading

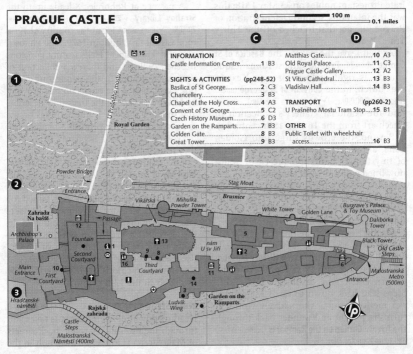

PRAGUE CASTLE

0 _____ 100 m
0 _____ 0.1 miles

INFORMATION		Matthias Gate..................................**10** A3
Castle Information Centre.............**1** B3		Old Royal Palace..............................**11** C3
		Prague Castle Gallery......................**12** A2
SIGHTS & ACTIVITIES (pp248-52)		St Vitus Cathedral...........................**13** B3
Basilica of St George.......................**2** C3		Vladislav Hall..................................**14** B3
Chancellery.......................................**3** B3		
Chapel of the Holy Cross...............**4** A3		TRANSPORT (pp260-2)
Convent of St George......................**5** C2		U Prašného Mostu Tram Stop.....**15** B1
Czech History Museum....................**6** D3		
Garden on the Ramparts.................**7** B3		OTHER
Golden Lane......................................**8** B3		Public Toilet with wheelchair
Great Tower......................................**9** B3		access..**16** B3

Christianity and his submission to the German King Henry I led to his murder by his brother, Boleslav I; legend says that he was stabbed to death while clinging to the Romanesque lion's-head handle that now graces the chapel door. The smaller door on the far side, beside the windows, leads to a chamber where the Bohemian crown jewels are kept (not open to the public).

On the other side of the transept, you can climb the 287 steps of the cathedral's **Great Tower** (9am-4.15pm Apr-Oct) for a great view over the city.

On the southern side of the cathedral's exterior is the **Golden Gate** (Zlatá brána) a triple-arched doorway topped by a 14th-century mosaic of the Last Judgment – to the left, the righteous are raised into heaven, to the right, sinners are cast into hell.

Opposite is the entrance to the **Old Royal Palace** with its huge and elegantly vaulted **Vladislav Hall**, built between 1486 and 1502. A ramp at the far end allowed mounted horsemen to ride into the hall for indoor jousts. Two Catholic councillors were thrown out the window of the adjacent **Chancellery** by irate Protestant nobles on 23 May 1618; this was the infamous Second Defenestration of Prague, the act that touched off the Thirty Years' War.

As you leave the palace, the **Basilica of St George** (1142), Prague's finest Romanesque church, is right in front of you. Next to the church, in the **Convent of St George** (adult/concession 100/50Kč; 10am-6pm Tue-Sun), you'll find the National Gallery's collection of Czech art from the 16th to 18th centuries.

Beyond, the crowds surge into Golden Lane, a 16th-century tradesmen's quarter of tiny houses built into the castle walls; now lined with souvenir shops, it's an overcrowded tourist trap that you can safely miss, though fans might want to know that Franz Kafka lived and wrote in his sister's tiny house at No 22 from 1916 to 1917.

On the right, just before the gate leading out of the castle, is the Lobkowicz Palace, which houses the **Czech History Museum** (adult/concession 40/20Kč; 9am-5pm). From the eastern end of the castle, the Old Castle Steps lead back down towards Malostranská metro station. Alternatively, you can turn sharp right and wander back through the lovely **Garden on the Ramparts** (admission free; 10am-6pm Apr-Oct).

The easiest way to get to the castle without an uphill hike is on tram No 22 or 23 from Národní třída on the southern edge of Staré Město, Malostranské nám in Malá Strana, or Malostranská metro station to the U Prašného mostu stop. If you want to wander through Hradčany (see the following section) first, stay on the tram until the next stop but one, Pohořelec.

Hradčany   Map pp246-8

The lanes and stairways of Hradčany are an ideal place to wander – most of this area extending west from Prague Castle is residential, with just a single strip of shops and restaurants (Loretánská and Pohořelec). Before it became a borough of Prague in 1598, Hradčany was almost levelled by Hussites and fire – in the 17th century palaces were built on the ruins.

The 18th-century Šternberg Palace just outside the castle entrance is home to the main branch of the **National Gallery** (220 514 599; adult/concession 150/70Kč; 10am-6pm Tue-Sun), the country's principal collection of 14th- to 18th-century European art.

A passage at Pohořelec 8 leads up to the **Strahov Library** (220 516 671; adult/concession 70/50Kč; 9am-noon & 1-5pm), the country's largest monastic library, built in 1679. The Philosophy and Theological Halls feature gorgeous frescoed ceilings, and there's a collection of natural curiosities in the connecting corridor. Look out for the books on tree growing bound in the bark of the trees they describe, and the long, brown, leathery things beside the model ship – the prudish attendant will tell you they're tanned elephants' trunks, but they're actually whales' penises.

The exuberantly baroque **Sanctuary of Our Lady of Loreta** (224 510 789; Loretánské nám 7; adult/concession 90/70Kč; 9.15am-12.15pm & 1-4.30pm) is a place of pilgrimage, famed for its fabulous treasury of religious artefacts encrusted in diamonds, pearls and gold. In the cloister is a 17th-century replica of the Santa Casa in the Italian town of Loreta, itself said to be the house of Virgin Mary in Nazareth, miraculously transported to Italy by angels in the 13th century.

Malá Strana   Map pp246-8

Heading downhill from the castle takes you through the beautiful baroque back streets of Malá Strana (Little Quarter), built in the

17th and 18th centuries by victorious Catholic clerics and nobles on the foundations of the Renaissance palaces of their Protestant predecessors. Today it's an upmarket neighbourhood crammed with embassies and government offices.

Close to the café-crowded main square of Malostranské nám is **St Nicholas Church** (admission 50Kč; 9am-6pm Apr-Oct, 9am-4pm Nov-Mar), one of the greatest baroque buildings in the city – if you only visit one church in Prague, make it this one. Take the stairs up to the gallery to see the 17th-century *Passion Cycle* paintings and the scratchings of bored 1820s tourists.

East of the square, along Tomášská, is the impressive **Wallenstein Palace** (Valdštejnský palác; admission free; 10am-5pm Sat & Sun), built in 1630 and now home to the Czech Republic's Senate. Albrecht von Wallenstein, a notorious general in the Thirty Years' War who started out on the Protestant side but defected to the Catholics, built this palace with the expropriated wealth of his former comrades. In 1634 the Habsburg Emperor Ferdinand II learned that Wallenstein was about to switch sides again and had him assassinated. The fresco on the ceiling of the palace's baroque hall shows Wallenstein glorified as a warrior at the reins of a chariot.

You can enter the adjacent **Wallenstein Gardens** (admission free; 10am-6pm Mar-Sep) via the palace or from Letenská, a block to the east. These beautiful gardens boast a giant Renaissance loggia, a fake stalactite grotto full of hidden animals and grotesque faces, fine bronze sculptures by Adrian de Vries (copies; the originals were looted by the Swedish army in 1648 and are still in Stockholm), and a picturesque pond full of giant carp.

Malá Strana is linked to Staré Město by the elegant **Charles Bridge** (Karlův most). Built in 1357, and graced by 30 statues dating from the 18th century, it was the city's only bridge until 1841. Take a leisurely stroll across, but first climb the **Malá Strana bridge tower** (adult/concession 40/30Kč; 10am-6pm Oct-Apr) for a great bird's-eye view of bridge and city. In the middle of the bridge is a bronze statue (1683) of St John of Nepomuk, a priest who was thrown to his death from the bridge in 1393 for refusing to reveal the queen's confessions to King Wenceslas IV. Crammed with tourists and lined with jewellery stalls, portrait artists and the odd jazz band, the bridge is best appreciated at dawn, before the crowds arrive.

On a hot summer afternoon you can escape the tourist throngs by riding the **funicular railway** (for an ordinary 12Kč tram ticket, runs every 10 to 20 minutes from 9.15am to 8.45pm) from Újezd up to the rose gardens on **Petřín Hill**. From here it's a sweaty climb up 299 steps to the top of the iron-framed **Petřín Tower** (adult/concession 50/40Kč; 10am-7pm Apr-Oct, 10am-5pm Sat & Sun Nov-Mar), built in 1891 in imitation of the Eiffel Tower, for one of the best views of Prague. A stairway behind the tower leads down into a series of picturesque lanes that will take you back to Malostranské nám.

Staré Město   Map pp246-8

On the Staré Město (Old Town) side of Charles Bridge narrow and crowded Karlova leads east towards Staroměstské nám, Prague's **Old Town Square**, dominated by the twin Gothic steeples of **Týn Church** (1365), the baroque wedding cake of **St Nicholas Church** (1730s), not to be confused with the more famous St Nicholas Church in Malá Strana (p250), and the clock tower of the **Old Town Hall** (224 228 456; Staroměstské nám 12; adult/concession 40/20Kč; 11am-6pm Mon, 9am-6pm Tue-Sun Apr-Oct, to 5pm Nov-Mar) – you can climb to the top (or take the lift) and look down on the crowds gathered to watch the famous **astronomical clock** (1410) which springs to life on the hour with its parade of apostles and a bell-ringing skeleton. At the centre of the square is the **Jan Hus Monument**, erected in 1915 on the 500th anniversary of the religious reformer's execution at the stake.

The shopping street of Celetná leads east from the square to the gorgeous Art Nouveau **Municipal House** (Obecní dům; nám Republiky 5; guided tours 150Kč; 7.30am-11pm), a cultural centre decorated by the finest Czech artists of the early 20th century. The guided tour takes in the impressive Smetana Concert Hall and a series of beautifully decorated rooms – if the murals in the Lord Mayor's Hall pique your interest in artist Alfons Mucha, you can find out more at the Mucha Museum (see p252).

South of the square is the neoclassical **Estates Theatre** (Stavovské divadlo; 1783), where the premiere of Mozart's *Don Giovanni* was performed on 29 October 1787 with the maestro himself conducting.

Josefov – the area north and northwest of Staroměstské nám – was once the city's Jewish Quarter. It retains a fascinating variety of monuments, all of which are now part of the **Prague Jewish Museum** (☎ 224 819 456; adult/concession 450/300Kč; ☼ 9am-6pm Sun-Fri Apr-Oct, to 4.30pm Nov-Mar). The museum's collection of artefacts has a remarkable origin. In 1942 the Nazis gathered objects from 153 Jewish communities in Bohemia and Moravia for a planned 'museum of an extinct race' to be opened once their extermination programme was completed.

The oldest still-functioning synagogue in Europe, the early Gothic **Old-New Synagogue** (Červená 1), was built in 1270; opposite is the Jewish town hall with its picturesque 16th-century clock tower. The 1694 **Klaus Synagogue** (U Starého hřbitova 1) houses an exhibition on Jewish customs and traditions, while the **Pinkas Synagogue** (Široká 3) is now a holocaust memorial, its interior walls inscribed with the names of 77,297 Czech Jews, including Franz Kafka's three sisters.

The **Old Jewish Cemetery** (entered from the Pinkas Synagogue), with its 12,000 tombstones, is the most evocative corner of Josefov, the oldest grave dated 1439. By 1787 when the cemetery stopped being used, it had become so crowded that burials were carried out one on top of the other, up to 12 layers deep! You can get a free peek at the cemetery through a tiny opening in the wall to the north of the **Museum of Decorative Arts** on 17.listopadu, or from the lobby outside the 1st-floor public toilets in the museum itself.

Tucked away in the northern part of Staré Města's narrow streets is one of Prague's oldest Gothic structures, the magnificent **Convent of St Agnes** (☎ 221 879 111; U Milosrdných 17; adult/concession 100/50Kč; ☼ 10am-6pm Tue-Sun) housing the National Gallery's collection of Bohemian and Central European medieval art, dating from the 13th to the mid-16th centuries.

Nové Město   Map pp246-8

Nové Město (New Town) is new only in relation to Staré Město – it was founded in 1348! Its main focus is the broad, sloping avenue of **Václavské nám** (Wenceslas Square), lined with shops, banks and restaurants and dominated by a **statue of St Wenceslas** on horseback. The square has always been a focus for demonstrations and public gatherings, and beneath the Wenceslas statue there is a shrine to the victims of communism, including students Jan Palach and Jan Zajíc, both of whom burned themselves alive in 1969 in protest at the Soviet invasion.

Looming above the southeastern end of the square is the imposing, neo-Renaissance **National Museum** (☎ 224 497 111; Václavské nám 68; adult/concession 100/50Kč; ☼ 10am-6pm May-Sep, to 5pm Oct-Apr). Despite the ho-hum collections covering prehistory, mineralogy and stuffed animals (captions mostly in Czech only), the grand interior of the 1890 building includes a pantheon of Czech politician, writers, composers, artists and scientists, and is worth a visit in its own right.

Fans of artist Alfons Mucha, best known for his Art Nouveau posters of glowing Slavic maidens garlanded with flowers, can admire a range of his work at the **Mucha Museum** (☎ 221 451 333; Panská 7; adult/concession 120/60Kč; ☼ 10am-6pm), along with an interesting video on his life and art. See also Moravský Krumlov (p285).

The **City of Prague Museum** (☎ 224 227 490; Na Poříčí 52; adult/concession 60/30Kč; ☼ 9am-6pm Tue-Sun), housed in a grand, neo-Renaissance building near Florenc metro station, charts the growth of the city from prehistory to the turn of the 19th century, culminating in a huge scale model of Prague made in 1826–37. Among the many intriguing exhibits are the brown silk funeral cap and slippers worn by astronomer Tycho Brahe when he was interred in the Týn Church in 1601 (they were removed in 1901).

Vyšehrad   Map pp242-3

If you want to escape the tourist crowds, pack a picnic and take the metro to the ancient hilltop fortress **Vyšehrad** (admission free; ☼ 9.30am-6pm Apr-Oct, to 5pm Nov-Mar), perched on a cliff top above the Vltava on the southern edge of Nové Město. It's dominated by the twin towers of **SS Peter & Paul Church**, founded in the 11th century but rebuilt in neo-Gothic style between 1885 and 1903 – take a look at the Art Nouveau murals inside. The **Slavín Cemetery**, beside the church, contains the graves of many distinguished Czechs, including the composers Smetana and Dvořák. The view of the Vltava from the battlements along the southern side of the citadel is superb.

WHAT'S FREE

You can watch the changing of the guard at Prague Castle, wander around the castle courtyards and gardens, and visit the nave of St Vitus Cathedral without buying a ticket. The Wallenstein Palace and Gardens in Malá Strana also have free admission.

Admission to the National Museum is free on the first Monday of each month, and all the galleries run by the City of Prague are free on the first Tuesday of a month. On the first Thursday of the month the City of Prague Museum charges only 1Kč admission.

Staroměstské nám and Charles Bridge are magical (and free) nocturnal attractions, and often have jazz bands busking for pennies.

TOURS

City Walks (☎ 608 200 912, 222 244 531; www.prague walkingtours.com; per person 300-450Kč) Guided walks ranging from 90-minute Prague Intro (begins at the Old Town Hall astronomical clock at 12.30pm) to the four-hour Insider Tour (starts at St Wenceslas statue in Václavské nám at 9.45am).

Prague Walks (☎ 603 271 911; www.praguewalks.com; per person 300-390Kč) Interesting walks with themes ranging from architecture to pubs in Žižkov to the Velvet Revolution.

Prague Venice (☎ 603 819 947; www.prague-venice .cz; adult/child 270/135Kč; ⊙ 10.30am-11pm Jul & Aug, to 8pm Mar-Jun, Sep & Oct) Operates 30-minute cruises in small boats under the hidden arches of Charles Bridge and along the Čertovka mill stream in Kampa. Jetties at the Staré Město end of Charles Bridge, on the Čertovka stream in Malá Strana, and at the west end of Mánes Bridge, near Malostranská metro station.

FESTIVALS & EVENTS

Prague Spring (www.festival.cz; 12 May-3 Jun) One of Europe's biggest festivals of classical music kicks off the summer ...

Prague Autumn (www.pragueautumn.cz; 12 Sep-1 Oct) ... and another one draws it to a close.

Prague International Jazz Festival (www.jazzfestival praha.cz/jazz; late Oct)

Christmas Market (1-24 Dec)

New Year's Eve (31 Dec) Free-flowing beer, mad crowds in Staroměstské nám, and fireworks over the castle.

SLEEPING

If you're visiting at New Year, Christmas or Easter, or during May to September, book accommodation well in advance. Prices quoted here are for high season, generally April to October; however, even these rates can increase by up to 15% on certain dates, notably at Christmas, New Year, Easter, and at weekends in May (during the Prague Spring festival). Some hotels, but not all, have slightly lower rates in July and August; almost all slash their high season rates by 20% to 40% from November to March.

If you're staying for more than a couple of nights, it's worth considering an apartment. There are lots of one- to six-person apartments available for as short a stay as a single night, and many offer excellent value. Check out the listings on the Stop City and Mary's websites listed below.

Accommodation Agencies

AVE (☎ 251 551 011; www.avetravel.cz; Praha-hlavní nádraží, Nové Město; ⊙ 6am-11pm) Convenient offices at the main train station, Praha-Holešovice train station, Ruzyně airport and PIS offices (see p245).

Hostels in Prague (www.hostel.cz) Website database of around 60 hostels, with a secure online booking system.

Mary's (Map pp242-3; ☎ 222 253 510; www. marys.cz; Italská 31, Vinohrady; ⊙ 9am-9pm) Private rooms, hostels, *pensions*, apartments and hotels in all price ranges in Prague and surrounding area.

Stop City (Map pp246-8; ☎ 222 521 233; www .stopcity.com; Vinohradská 24, Vinohrady; ⊙ 10am-9pm Apr-Oct, 11am-8pm Nov-Mar) Specialises in apartments, private rooms and *pensions* in the Vinohrady and Žižkov areas.

Welcome Accommodation Service (Map pp242-3; ☎ 224 320 202; www.bed.cz; Zikova 13, Dejvice) Offers rooms in student dormitories, hostels and hotels.

Budget

Camp Sokol Troja (Map pp242-3; ☎ 233 542 908; www.camp-sokol-troja.cz; Trojská 171a, Troja; camp sites per person/car 105Kč/90Kč; ⊙ year round; P ▣) This convivial riverside camping ground, with kitchen and laundry, is one of half a dozen in the suburb of Troja, 15 minutes north of the centre via tram No 14 or 17.

Clown & Bard Hostel (Map pp242-3; ☎ 222 716 453; www.clownandbard.com; Bořivojova 102, Žižkov; dm/d 250Kč/900Kč; P ▣) Set in the heart of Žižkov's pub district, the bright and buzzing Clown and Bard is a full-on party place – don't come here looking for peace and quiet.

Hostel Elf (Map pp242-3; ☎ 222 540 963; www .hostelelf.com; Husitská 11, Žižkov; dm/s/d 290/700/840Kč) Readers have recommended this convivial hostel, with its little beer-garden terrace, cosy lounge and cheerful dorms. Less than 10 minutes' walk from Florenc bus station.

Sir Toby's Hostel (Map pp242-3; ☎ 283 870 635; www.sirtobys.com; Dělnická 24, Holešovice; dm 290-340Kč, s/d 900/1100Kč; P ⌨) Set in a quiet, nicely refurbished apartment building with a spacious kitchen and common room, and run by friendly, cheerful staff, Sir Toby's is only 10 minutes north of the city centre by tram.

Hostel Sokol (Map pp246-8; ☎ 257 007 397; post@sokol-cos.cz; Tyršův dům, Nostícova 2, Malá Strana; dm 350Kč; ✗) Set in a converted 18th-century mansion, Sokol can get a bit crowded – not to mention swelteringly hot in midsummer (there's no air-con) – but it's cheerful, clean and central.

Hostel Jednota (Map pp246-8; book through Alfa Tourist Service ☎ 224 230 038; www.alfatourist.cz/ejednota .html; Opletalova 38, Nové Město; dm/s/d incl breakfast 350/550/760Kč; ☺ mid-Jul–mid-Sep; ⌨) Don't be put off by the glum Soviet-style lobby – the rooms at Jednota are bright, airy and well laid-out for maximum privacy.

Hostel U Melounu (Map pp242-2; ☎ 224 918 322; www.hostelumelounu.cz; Ke Karlovu 7, Vinohrady; dm/s/d 380/550/900Kč; P ⌨) An attractive hostel in a historic building on a quiet street, U Melounu has the added advantage of a peaceful, sunny garden complete with barbecue.

There's plenty of budget accommodation to be found in the student complex opposite the Strahov football stadium, west of the centre.

Hostel SPUS Strahov (Map pp246-8; ☎ 220 513 419; www.spushostels.cz; Chaloupeckého, Block 4, Strahov; dm/s/d 250/480/760Kč; P) **Welcome Hostel Strahov** (Map pp246-8; ☎ 224 320 202; www.bed.cz; Vaníčkova, Block 3, Strahov; dm/s/d 150/400/600Kč; P) **Welcome Hostel Dejvice** (Map pp242-2; ☎ 224 320 202; www.bed.cz; Zikova 13, Dejvice; s/d 500/700Kč; ⌨)

Mid-Range

Hotel Extol Inn (Map pp242-2; ☎ 220 876 541; www.ex tolinn.cz; Přístavní 2, Holešovice; s/d from 700/1190Kč; P) Recently renovated and excellent value, this bright, modern inn offers hefty discounts on economy rooms for HI members. The more expensive three-star rooms (1290/1990Kč) have private bathroom, TV, minibar and free use of sauna and whirlpool.

Pension Březina (Map pp246-8; ☎ 296 188 888; www.brezina.cz; Legerova 41, Vinohrady; s/d economy 1100/1300Kč, luxury 2000/2200Kč; P) A welcoming *pension* in a converted Art Nouveau apartment block with small garden. Ask for a room at the back; those facing the street can be pretty noisy. It's five minutes south of IP Pavlova metro station.

Hostel Týn (Map pp246-8; ☎ 224 808 333; www .hostel-tyn.web2001.cz; Týnská 19, Staré Město; dm/d/tr 400/1100/1350Kč; ✗) Spotless two- to six-bed rooms, a superb location only 200m from Staroměstské nám, and a sauna, Jacuzzi and vegetarian restaurant in the same courtyard – what more could you ask for?

Pension Unitas (Map pp246-8; ☎ 224 211 802; www. unitas.cz; Bartolomějská 9, Staré Město; dm 270-500Kč, s/d 1100/1400Kč; ✗) This former convent is an interesting place to stay – its cramped rooms were once prison cells (ex-president Havel once did time here), with shared bathrooms and a generous breakfast included. Choice of cramped dorms or more spacious *pension* rooms.

AV Pension Praha (Map pp242-2; ☎ 272 951 726; www.pension-praha.cz; Malebná 75, Chodov; d with/ without bathroom 2000/1500Kč; P ✿) A readers' favourite, this garden villa in the southeastern suburbs offers bright, modern rooms, breakfast on the patio, and even a pool for the kids. It's a five-minute walk east of Chodov metro station.

Hotel Golden City Garni (Map pp242-2; ☎ 222 711 008; www.goldencity.cz; Táboritská 3, Žižkov; s/d/tr 1650/2450/2700Kč; P ✗ ⌨) Golden City is a converted 19th-century apartment block with crisp, clean, no-frills rooms, good buffet breakfasts and friendly, helpful staff. It's just three stops east of the main train station on tram No 5, 9 or 26.

Penzión U Medvídků (Map pp246-8; ☎ 224 211 916; www.umedvidku.cz; Na Perštýně 7, Staré Město; s/d 2150/3300Kč) Cosy and centrally located, 'At the Little Bear' is a traditional pub and restaurant with several attractive rooms upstairs. For a romantic splurge, choose one of the historic attic rooms with exposed wooden beams.

Hotel 16 U sv Kateřiny (Map pp242-2; ☎ 224 920 636; www.hotel16.cz; Kateřinská 16, Nové Město; s/d incl breakfast from 2500/3400Kč; P ✗ ⌨) Near the Botanic Gardens and about five minutes' walk from Karlovo nám metro station, this homely little hotel is quiet, clean and very comfortable. There's a peaceful terraced garden out the back (try to get a back room if you don't mind having twin beds) and a small bar.

Hotel Antik (Map pp246-8; ☎ 222 322 288; www.hotel antik.cz; Dlouhá 22, Staré Město; s/d 3590/3990Kč) A delightful little hotel, the Antik has brand-new fittings in a 15th-century building (no lift). The 12 rooms are cosy (ask for one with a balcony), there's a little garden and the staff are lovely. The attached coffee shop is strewn with more of the eponymous antiques.

Top End

Hotel Josef (Map pp246-8; ☎ 221 700 111; www .hoteljosef.cz; Rybná 20, Staré Město; s/d from €147/167; P ⊗ ⬜) The Josef is a stunning boutique hotel designed by London-based Czech architect Eva Jiřičná. Design highlights include glass-walled en suite bathrooms and the suspended spiral staircase in the lobby. There are two wheelchair-accessible rooms.

Hotel Questenberk (Map pp246-8; ☎ 220 407 600; www.questenberk.cz; Úvoz 5, Hradčany; s/d €168/240; P ⊗ ❄ ⬜) Originally Strahov Monastery's hospital, this brand-new hotel is close to the castle and the Sanctuary of Our Lady of Loreta. Its pleasant, sunny rooms are furnished with antique pine and all the mod cons – every room has an Internet connection for your laptop.

Hotel Praha (Map pp242-3; ☎ 224 341 111; www.htl praha.cz; Sušická 20, Dejvice; s/d US$180/210; P ☎) A luxury complex with stunning views over castle and city, this hotel was built in 1981 to house visiting Communist Party apparatchiks (bureaucrats). Since 1989 a host of celebrities, including Tom Cruise, Bob Dylan and Johnny Depp, have stayed here.

Aria Hotel (Map pp246-8; ☎ 225 334 111; www.aria-hotel.net; Tržiště 9, Malá Strana; d from €195; P ⊗ ⬜) Five-star luxury with a musical theme – each room is dedicated to a composer or musician, and contains a selection of their music. Other facilities include a music and movie library, screening room, fitness centre and steam room.

EATING

Prague has a vast selection of restaurants offering all kinds of cuisines and price ranges. You can take your pick of bargain Czech beer halls dishing up no-nonsense pork-and-*knedlíky* fare, or enjoy a riverside view in a chic French or Italian restaurant with a high-flying clientele and prices to match.

In between, there's everything from Thai to Mexican, and Indian to Japanese.

Places in Prague's main tourist streets and squares tend to be pricey, but you can find considerably cheaper eats just by walking a block or two away from the crowds. Most pubs offer snacks as well as full meals, and there are countless stands in Václavské nám selling traditional street snacks such as *párek* (hot dog) or *bramborák* (potato pancake).

Prague has an ever-increasing number of wholly vegetarian restaurants, and most other eating places now have at least one or two veggie dishes on the menu. Most restaurants are open from 11am to 10 or 11pm.

Hradčany & Malá Strana   Map pp246-8

Bohemia Bagel (☎ 224 812 560; Újezd 18, Malá Strana; mains 50-100Kč; ☒ 7am-midnight Mon-Fri, from 8am Sat & Sun) A great informal place to eat, with fresh bagel sandwiches, home-made soups and free coffee refills; one of the few places offering early morning breakfast. Doubles as an Internet café (see p244). There's another branch at Masná 2 in Staré Město.

Sate (☎ 220 514 552; Pohořelec 3, Hradčany; mains 80-110Kč; ☒ 11am-10pm) A down-to-earth place, just five minutes' walk west of the castle, serving tasty and inexpensive Indonesian and Malaysian dishes such as *nasi goreng* (fried rice with vegies, prawns and egg) and beef *rendang* (coconut-based curry).

Hergetova Cihelna (☎ 257 535 534; Cihelná 2b, Malá Strana; mains 200-550Kč; ☒ 9am-2am) A converted *cihelná* (brickworks) may not sound like a promising spot for a restaurant, but this beautifully restored 18th-century building enjoys one of Prague's hottest locations, with a riverside terrace offering sweeping views of Charles Bridge and Staré Město. The food is of equally high quality, from pizzas and burgers to steaks and seafood.

Other places on this side of the river that are worth a look include the delightfully old-fashioned wine bar **Vinárna U Maltézských rytířů** (☎ 257 533 666; Prokopská 10, Malá Strana; mains 200-400Kč; ☒ 11am-11pm), and the chic, sleek and unashamedly modern **Square** (☎ 257 532 109; Malostranské nám 5, Malá Strana; mains 200-500Kč; ☒ 9am-12.30am).

Staré Město   Map pp246-8

Beas Vegetarian Dhaba (Týnská 19; meals 78-93Kč; ☒ 8.30am-8pm Mon-Fri, 10am-6pm Sat & Sun) This stylish and friendly little place offers a vegetarian curry (changes daily) served with rice, salad, chutneys and raita; an extra 15Kč gets you a drink and dessert.

Pivnice Radegast (☎ 222 328 237; Templová 2; mains 60-120Kč; 11am-12.30am) This is a classic, old-fashioned beer hall set in a Gothic cellar, serving good cheap Czech food; try the tasty *guláš*.

Country Life (☎ 257 044 419; mains 75-150Kč) Staré Město (Melantrichova 15; 8.30am-7pm Mon-Thu, 8.30am-4pm Fri, 11am-6pm Sun) Nové Město (Jungmannova 1; 9.30am-6.30pm Mon-Sat, 10am-4pm Sun) This all-vegan cafeteria offers inexpensive salads, sandwiches, pizzas, *guláš*, soy drinks, sunflower-seed burgers etc.

Orange Moon (☎ 222 325 119; Rámová 5; mains 165-220Kč; 11.30am-11.30pm) An Asian restaurant combining sunny colours upstairs and a red-brick cellar downstairs, Orange Moon features Thai woodcarvings and sleekly modern fittings. The menu is a mouthwatering list of authentic Thai, Burmese and Indian dishes.

Staroměstská restaurace (☎ 224 213 015; Staroměstské nám 19; mains 100-300Kč; 9am-midnight Apr-Oct, from 11am Nov-Mar) The best-value place on Staroměstské nám, with good Czech food and beer; if you're watching the pennies, it's cheaper to eat indoors than at the outside tables.

Red Hot & Blues (☎ 222 314 639; Jakubská 12; mains 140-390Kč; 9am-11pm) An American-owned, New Orleans–style place with a little courtyard, traditional jazz on the sound system, and live jazz or blues nightly. It serves great nachos, burgers, burritos and shrimp creole, plus some wicked desserts.

Nové Město   Map pp246-8
Dobrá čajovna (☎ 224 23 14 80; Václavské nám 14; snacks 50-150Kč; 10am-11pm Mon-Sat, 2-11pm Sun) Along a passage off Václavské nám, away from the heaving crowds on the street, this teahouse is a little haven of oriental rugs and cushions.

Česká hospoda v Krakovské (☎ 222 210 204; Krakovská 20; mains 65-155Kč; 11am-11pm) Fuel up on pork, *knedlíky* and *pivo* at this welcoming and convivial Bohemian pub, whose slightly smoky atmosphere is brightened by polished wood, checked tablecloths and fresh flowers.

Pizzeria Kmotra (☎ 224 934 100; V Jirchářích 12; pizza 70-160Kč; 11am-midnight) One of Prague's oldest and best pizzerias, offering more than two-dozen varieties cooked in a wood-fired oven. Gets busy after 8pm – there are more tables downstairs.

Titanic Steak House (☎ 296 226 282; Štěpánská 22; mains 90-190Kč; 11am-11pm Mon-Sat, 3-11pm Sun) Titanic is a cool and quiet place with terracotta tiles, cane chairs and a laid-back atmosphere, offering a range of salads and steaks with various sauces. And despite the name, there's no sinking feeling when the bill arrives.

Café FX (☎ 224 254 776; Bělehradská 120, Vinohrady; mains 110-230Kč; 8.30am-5am) This hippy-chic café, all draped chiffon and tasselled lampshades, at Club Radost FX (see p258) serves some of the best food in Prague – and it's all vegetarian. Dishes range from Mexican to Indian to Thai.

Kogo (☎ 224 214 543; Na příkopě 22; pizzas 150-250Kč, mains 200-450Kč; 9am-midnight) Chic but child-friendly (highchairs provided), with tables spilling into the leafy courtyard in summer, Kogo is a stylish but laid-back place serving top-notch pizza, pasta, steak and seafood. Good range of wines available by the glass.

DRINKING
Prague is a beer drinker's paradise – where else could you get two half-litre glasses of top-quality Pilsner for under a dollar? Bohemian beer is probably the best in the world – the most famous brands are Budvar and Plzeňský Prazdroj (Pilsner Urquell), and Prague's own Staropramen.

As with eating, you can find cheaper drinks by keeping away from the popular tourist areas; there are plenty of bars selling half-litres for 20Kč or less, compared with 60Kč and up around Malostranské nám and Staroměstské nám. Traditional pubs open from 11am to 11pm daily; more stylish modern bars open from noon to 1am, and often stay open till 3am or 4am on Friday and Saturday.

Before the communist coup Prague had a thriving café scene, and since 1989 it has returned with a vengeance. The summer streets are crammed with outdoor tables, and good-quality tea and coffee are widely available.

Cafés
U zeleného čaje (Map pp246-8; ☎ 257 530 027; Nerudova 19, Malá Strana; 11am-10pm) The non-smoking 'Green Tea', on the way up to the

castle, is a charming little tea house serving speciality teas from all over the world.

Ebel Coffee House (Map pp246–8; ☎ 222 222 018; Týn 2, Staré Město; ☼ 9am-10pm) Superb coffee only a few minutes' walk from Staroměstské nám – if you can't face the watery instant served up with your hotel breakfast, head to Ebel for a jolt of full-fat, 98-octane arabica.

Káva.Káva.Káva (Map pp246–8; ☎ 224 228 862; Národní třída 37, Nové Město; ☼ 7am-10pm) Tucked away in the Platýz courtyard, this is an American-owned café where you can indulge in huge cappuccinos, chocolate brownies, carrot cake and other goodies. There's also Internet access (2Kč per minute) via desktop computers and a wireless hotspot.

Kavárna Slávia (Map pp246–8; ☎ 224 220 957; Národní třída 1, Nové Město; mains 100-250Kč; ☼ 8am-midnight Mon-Fri, 9am-midnight Sat & Sun) The most famous of Prague's old cafés, a cherry wood and onyx shrine to Art Deco elegance.

Pubs

Malostranská beseda (Map pp246–8; ☎ 257 532 092; Malostranské nám 21, Malá Strana; ☼ 5pm-1am) This is a big, bustling bar popular with students where rock, jazz, folk and country can be heard nightly from 8.30pm.

U malého Glena (Map pp246–8; ☎ 290 003 967; Karmelitská 23, Malá Strana; ☼ 10am-2am) A long-established bar and café housed in a vaulted stone cellar where local jazz and blues bands play most nights from 9pm.

Letní bar (Summer Bar; Map pp246–8; Střelecký Ostrov, Malá Strana; ☼ noon-midnight Jun-Sep) Basically a shack serving Budvar in plastic cups (20Kč), this is the place to pick up a beer before hitting the little beach at the northern end of Střelecký Ostrov (Marksmen's Island).

U Zlatého Tygra (Map pp246–8; ☎ 222 221 111; Husova 17, Staré Město; ☼ 3-11pm) One of the few old-town drinking holes that has hung on to its soul – and its low prices. It was novelist Bohumil Hrabal's favourite hostelry – there are photos of him on the walls – and the place that President Havel took Bill Clinton to show him a real Czech pub.

Kozička (Map pp246–8; ☎ 224 818 308; Kozí 1, Staré Město; ☼ noon-4am Mon-Fri, 6pm-4am Sat & Sun) The 'Little Goat' is a permanently buzzing basement bar with taped mainstream music, a young clientele and standing-room only after midnight.

Jáma (Map pp246–8; ☎ 224 222 383; V jámě 7, Nové Město; ☼ 11am-1am) The 'Hollow' is a popular

expat bar with a restaurant, beer garden and reasonable prices. The clientele includes both tourists and young Praguers.

Velryba (Map pp246–8; ☎ 224 912 484; Opatovická 24, Nové Město; ☼ 11am-midnight Sat-Thu, 11am-2am Fri) The 'Whale' is an arty café-bar – quiet enough to have a real conversation – with veg-friendly snacks, a smoky back room and a basement art gallery. Lots of local students hang out here.

ENTERTAINMENT

From clubbing to classical music, puppetry to performance art, there is no shortage of entertainment in Prague. While it has long been one of Europe's centres of classical music and jazz, it is now famed for its rock and post-rock scenes as well. In such a rapidly changing city, it is quite possible that some places listed here will have changed by the time you arrive. For up-to-date listings, check the *Prague Post, Culture in Prague* (available from PIS offices; see p245) and the *Do města – Downtown* free leaflet, and keep an eye out for posters and bulletin boards.

For classical music, opera, ballet, theatre and some rock concerts – even the most 'sold-out' *vyprodáno* (events) – you can often find a ticket or two on sale at the box office 30 minutes or so before the performance starts. In addition, there are plenty of ticket agencies around Prague that will sell the same tickets at a high commission.

Although some expensive tickets are set aside for foreigners, non-Czechs normally pay the same price as Czechs at the box office. Tickets can cost as little as 30Kč for standing-room only to over 900Kč for the best seats in the house; the average price is about 500Kč. Be wary of touts selling concert tickets in the street – they often offer good prices, but you may end up sitting on stacking chairs in a cramped hall listening to amateur musicians, rather than the grand concert hall that was implied.

Ticket Agencies

FOK Box Office (Map pp246–8; ☎ 222 002 336; U obecního domu 2, Staré Město; ☼ 10am-6pm Mon-Fri) For classical concert tickets.

Ticketpro (Map pp246–8; ☎ 296 329 999; www.ticketpro.cz; Salvátorská 10, Staré Město; ☼ 9am-12.30pm & 1-5.15pm Mon-Fri) All kinds of events. Also has branches in PIS offices (see p245) and many other places.

Bohemia Ticket International (Map pp246-8; ☎ 224 227 832; www.ticketsbti.cz; Malé nám 13, Staré Město; ☺ 9am-5pm Mon-Fri, 9am-2pm Sat) All kinds of events.

Classical Music & Performance Arts

Rudolfinum (Map pp246-8; ☎ 227 059 352; nám Jana Palacha, Staré Město; box office 10am-12.30pm & 1.20-6pm Mon-Fri) One of Prague's main concert venues is the Dvořák Hall, housed in the neo-Renaissance Ruldolfinum.

Municipal House (Obecní dům; ☎ 222 002 101; nám Republiky 5, Staré Město; box office ☺ 10am-6pm Mon-Fri) Another one of Prague's main concert venues is Smetana Hall in the city's wonderful Art Nouveau Municipal House. It always hosts the opening concert of the Prague Spring festival.

Prague State Opera (Státní opera Praha; Map pp246-8; ☎ 224 227 266; Legerova 75, Nové Město) Opera, ballet and classical drama (in Czech) are performed at the neo-Renaissance Prague State Opera.

National Theatre (Národní divadlo; Map pp246-8; ☎ 224 913 437; Národní třída 2, Nové Město) Classical drama, opera and ballet are also performed at the National Theatre.

Laterna Magika (Map pp246-8; ☎ 224 914 129; Nová Scéna, Národní třída 4, Nové Město; tickets from 600Kč; box office ☺ 10am-8pm Mon-Sat) Next door to the National Theatre is the modern Laterna Magika, Prague's most famous stage spectacular, a unique multimedia show interweaving dance, opera, music and film.

Estates Theatre (Stavovské divadlo; Map pp246-8; ☎ 224 215 001; Ovocný trh 1, Staré Město) Every night during summer (mid-July to the end of August) this theatre stages performances of *Don Giovanni* by **Opera Mozart** (☎ 271 741 403; www.mozart-praha.cz); anyone who's been to a high school production of *Godspell* will be familiar with the production values.

Lots of organ concerts and recitals for tourists are performed in old churches and in historic buildings, but unfortunately many are of poor quality. You'll see stacks of fliers advertising these in every tourist office and travel agency around Prague. Seat prices begin at around 350Kč, and the programmes change from week to week.

Clubs & Live Music

Karlovy lázně (Map pp246-8; ☎ 222 220 502; Smetanovo nábřeží 198, Staré Město; cover 50-120Kč; ☺ 9pm-5am) Huge club complex near Charles Bridge,

playing anything from 1960s hits to the latest DJ mixes on each of its three floors.

Lucerna Music Bar (Map pp246-8; ☎ 224 217 108; Lucerna pasaž, Vodičkova 36, Nové Město; ☺ 8pm-3am) The long-running and much-loved Lucerna is a grungy basement bar with a crowded, student-union atmosphere and an eclectic programme of live music ranging from rock and blues to classical and even gospel.

Palác Akropolis (Map pp246-8; ☎ 222 712 287; Kubelikova 27, Žižkov; ☺ 24hr) A 'cultural complex' comprising pub, café, club, live music stage and theatre, the Akropolis is Prague's coolest venue – expect anything from hip-hop, house and reggae to jazz, bhangra (Asian pop music) and world music.

Club Radost FX (Map pp246-8; ☎ 224 254 776; Bělehradská 120, Vinohrady; cover 100Kč; ☺ 10pm-5am) Prague's most comfortable, gorgeous and stylish clubbing venue offers lounge, soul, R&B, Buddha nights, house and alternative.

Jazz

Prague has dozens of jazz clubs.

Reduta Jazz Club (Map pp246-8; ☎ 224 912 246; Národní třída 20, Nové Město; cover 200Kč; ☺ 9pm-3am) Founded in 1958 and one of the oldest in Europe.

You can also hear live jazz every night at the unpretentious **AghaRTA jazz centrum** (Map pp246-8; ☎ 222 211 275; Krakovská 5, Nové Město; ☺ 9pm-midnight), and in the cosy basement at U malého Glena (p257).

Theatre

Black Theatre of Jiří Srnec (Map pp246-8; ☎ 257 921 835; Reduta Theatre, Národní 20, Nové Město; tickets from 370Kč) Several venues around town stage the uniquely Czech 'black light theatre' or 'magic theatre' shows that involve imaginative combinations of mime, ballet, animated film and puppetry. The original and best is the Black Theatre of Jiří Srnec.

Theatre on the Balustrade (Divadlo na zábradlí; Map pp246-8; ☎ 222 868 868; Anenské nám 5, Staré Město; box office ☺ 2-7pm Mon-Fri, 2 hr before show Sat & Sun) Plays by former president Václav Havel are often staged (in Czech, of course) at this theatre.

Divadlo Minor (Map pp246-8; ☎ 222 231 351; Vodičkova 6, Nové Město; box office ☺ 9am-1.30pm & 2.30-8pm Mon-Fri, 11am-8pm Sat & Sun) The children's theatre offers a fun mix of puppets and pantomime. There are performances at 9.30am Monday to Friday and at 7.30pm Tuesday and Wednesday, and you can usually get a ticket at the door before the show.

Gay & Lesbian Venues

Termix (Map pp242-3; ☎ 222 710 462; Třebízckého 4A, Vinohrady; admission free; ☺ 8pm-5am) Prague's newest gay bar and club, with an industrial/high-tech vibe (lots of steel, glass and a car sticking out of one wall), cute bar staff, a regular house/techno night (Thursday) and a dark room.

Maler (Map pp246-8; ☎ 222 013 116; Blanická 28, Vinohrady; ☺ 9am-11pm Mon-Thu, 9am-4am Fri & Sat, 1-10pm Sun) A small and intimate café-club with a thriving lesbian scene, Maler pulls in a mixed crowd through the week and stages lesbian discos on Friday and Saturday (cover 50Kč), and the 'Ladies Secret Club' night once a month.

Gejzee..r (Map pp242-3; ☎ 222 516 036; Vinohradská 40, Vinohrady; cover 50-70Kč, free Thu & before 10.30pm Fri & Sat; ☺ 8pm-4am Thu, 9pm-6am Fri & Sat) Prague's biggest G&L club, with two bars, a huge dance floor, video-projection system, dark room and erotic cinema, Gejzee..r pulls in large crowds at weekends and for special 'meet a partner' evenings.

Downtown Café Praha (Map pp246-8; ☎ 724 111 276; Jungmannovo náměstí 21, Nové Město; ☺ 9am-11pm Mon-Thu, to midnight Fri, 10am-midnight Sat, to 11pm Sun) Gay-owned and -operated Downtown – does any other café have a 'wait-staff hair styled by…' credit in its menu? – is a cool little place with cakes and cocktails that are almost as gorgeous as the staff. Grab a seat on the shady terrace and lap up the eye candy.

Cinemas

Most films are screened in their original language with Czech subtitles *(české titulky)*, but Hollywood blockbusters are often dubbed into Czech *(dabing)*; look for the labels 'tit.' or 'dab.' on cinema listings. Tickets generally cost from 90Kč to 170Kč.

Kino Aero (Map pp242-3; ☎ 271 771 349; Biskupcova 31, Žižkov) Prague's best-loved art-house cinema, with themed weeks, retrospectives and unusual films, often with English subtitles.

Kino Světozor (Map pp246-8; ☎ 224 946 824; Vodičkova 41, Nové Město) Your best bet for seeing Czech films with English subtitles, this place is under the same management as Kino Aero but is more central.

Palace Cinemas (Map pp246-8; ☎ 257 181 212; Slovanský dům, Na příkopě 22, Nové Město) Central

Prague's main popcorn palace – a modern 10-screen multiplex showing first-run Hollywood films.

SHOPPING

Prague's main shopping streets are in Nové Město – Václavské nám, Na příkopě, 28.října and Národní třída – but there are plenty more tourist-oriented shops on Celetná, Staroměstské nám, Pařížská and Karlova in Staré Město. Here you should be able to find almost anything you need. Prague's souvenir specialities include Bohemian crystal, ceramics, marionettes and garnet jewellery.

Tesco Department Store (Map pp246-8; ☎ 222 003 111; Národní třída 26, Nové Město; ☺ 8am-9pm Mon-Fri, 9am-8pm Sat, 10am-8pm Sun) has four floors of clothes, electrical and household goods, plus Prague's best-stocked **supermarket** (☺ 7am-10pm Mon-Fri, 8am-8pm Sat, 9am-8pm Sun).

Crystal

Moser (Map pp246-8; ☎ 224 211 293; Na příkopě 12, Nové Město; ☺ 10am-8pm Mon-Fri, 10am-7pm Sat & Sun), Founded in 1857, Moser is the big name for top-quality Bohemian crystal.

Both Moser and **Rott Crystal** (Map pp246-8; ☎ 224 229 529; Malé nám 3, Staré Město; ☺ 10am-7pm), housed in a beautiful neo-Renaissance building, are worth a look even if you're not buying.

Handicrafts, Antiques & Ceramics

Manufaktura (Map pp246-8; ☎ 221 632 480; Melantrichova 17, Staré Město; ☺ 10am-7.30pm) Several branches of Manufaktura around the city centre sell traditional Czech handicrafts, wooden toys and hand-made cosmetics.

There are a handful of good antique and bric-a-brac shops along Týnská and Týnská ulička, near Staroměstské nám.

For a range of ceramics in traditional Moravian folk designs, head for **Tupesy lidová keramika** (Map pp246-8; ☎ 224 210 728; Havelská 21, Staré Město; ☺ 10am-6pm).

Music

Supraphon (Map pp246-8; ☎ 224 948 718; Jungmannova 20, Nové Město; ☺ 9am-7pm Mon-Fri, 9am-1pm Sat) If you fancy taking home a CD of music by Dvořák or Smetana, Supraphon specialises in classical music.

Bontonland (Map pp246-8; ☎ 224 473 080; Václavské nám 1, Nové Město; ☺ 9am-8pm Mon-Sat, 10am-7pm Sun)

A music megastore stocking classical, jazz, folk, rock, metal, Czech pop compilations and a limited selection of vinyl.

GETTING THERE & AWAY
See also p291.

Bus
The main terminal for international and domestic buses is **Florenc Bus Station** (ÚAN Florenc; Map pp246-8; ☎ 900 144 444; Křižíkova 4, Karlín) – ÚAN is short for *Ústřední autobusové nádraží*, or 'central bus station' – 600m northeast of the main train station. Some regional buses depart from stops near metro stations Anděl, Dejvická, Černý Most, Nádraží Holešovice, Smíchovské Nádraží and Želivského. You can find online bus timetables at www.jizdnirady.cz.

At Florenc you can get information at **window No 8** (6am-9pm), or use the touchscreen computer. If you get no joy there, try the friendly **Tourbus** (☎ 224 210 221; www .tourbuspraha.cz; 8am-8pm Mon-Fri, 9am-8pm Sat & Sun) travel agency at the far end of the hall.

Short-haul tickets are sold on the bus. Long-distance domestic tickets are sold at the station from AMS window Nos 1 to 4 in the central hall. Tickets can be purchased from 10 days to 30 minutes prior to departure.

There are usually more departures in the mornings. Buses, especially if full, sometimes leave a few minutes early, so be there at least 10 minutes before departure time; if you have not taken your seat five minutes before departure, you may lose your reservation. Many services don't operate at weekends, so trains can be a better bet then.

There are direct bus services from Florenc bus station to Brno (150Kč, 2½ hours, hourly), České Budějovice (125Kč, 2¾ hours, four daily), Karlovy Vary (130Kč, 2¼ hours, eight daily), Litoměřice (61Kč, 1¼ hours, hourly) and Plzeň (80Kč, 1½ hours, hourly).

Most buses from Prague to České Budějovice (120Kč, 2½ hours, 16 daily) and Český Krumlov (140Kč, three hours, seven daily) depart from Ná Knížecí bus station, at Anděl metro's southern entrance, or from the bus stop at Roztyly metro station.

Train
Prague's main train station is **Praha-hlavní nádraží** (Map pp246-8; ☎ 221 111 122; Wilsonova, Nové Město). International tickets, domestic and international couchettes and seat reservations are sold on level 2 at even-numbered windows from 10 to 24, to the right of the stairs leading up to level 3. Domestic tickets are sold at the odd-numbered windows from 1 to 23 to the left of the stairs. You can check train timetables online at www. vlak.cz.

There are three other major train stations in the city. International trains between Berlin and Budapest often stop at Praha-Holešovice station on the northern side of the city, while some domestic services terminate at Praha-Masarykovo in Nové Město, or Praha-Smíchov south of Malá Strana. This can be confusing, so study the timetables carefully to find out which station your train departs from/arrives at.

You can also buy train tickets and get timetable information from the **ČD Centrum** (6am-7.30pm) at the south end of Level 2 in Praha-hlavní nádraží, and at the **České drahy** (Czech Railways; Map pp246-8; ☎ 224 617 069; www.cd.cz; V Celnici 6, Nové Město; 9am-6pm Mon-Fri, 9am-noon Sat) travel agency.

There are direct trains from Praha-hlavní nádraží to Brno (160Kč, three hours, eight daily), České Budějovice (204Kč, 2½ hours, hourly), Karlovy Vary (274Kč, four hours, three daily), Kutná Hora (62Kč, 55 minutes, seven daily) and Plzeň (140Kč, 1½ hours, eight daily). There are also a few departures daily to Brno and Bratislava from Praha-Holešovice.

GETTING AROUND
To/From the Airport
Prague's Ruzyně airport is 17km west of the city centre. To get into town, buy a ticket from the public transport (DPP) desk in arrivals and take bus No 119 (12Kč, 20 minutes, every 15 minutes) to the end of the line (Dejvická), then continue by metro into the city centre (another 10 minutes; no new ticket needed). Note, you'll need a half-fare (6Kč) ticket for your backpack or suitcase.

Alternatively, take a **Cedaz minibus** (☎ 220 114 296) from just outside arrivals; buy your ticket from the driver (90Kč, 20 minutes, every 30 minutes 5.30am-9.30pm). There are city stops at Dejvická metro and at nám Republiky. You can also get a Cedaz minibus right to the door of your hotel or any other address (360Kč for one to four people, 720Kč for five to eight). You can phone to book a pick-up for the return trip.

Airport Cars (☎ 220 113 892) taxi service, whose prices are regulated by the airport administration, charge 650Kč (20% discount for return trip) into the centre of Prague (a regular taxi fare *from* central Prague should be about 450Kč). Drivers speak some English and accept Visa cards.

Bicycle Rental

Praha Bike (Map pp246-8; ☎ 732 388 880; www.praha bike.cz; Dlouhá 24, Staré Město; ☯ 9am-7pm) Good, new bikes with lock, helmet and map, plus free luggage storage. Two-hour rentals start at 220Kč, or 540Kč for six hours. Also offers student discounts and group bike tours.

City Bike (Map pp246-8; ☎ 776 180 284; Královdvorská 5, Staré Město; ☯ 9am-7pm) Two-hour tours start at 450Kč. Much better value is the four-hour tour plus two-hour unaccompanied ride for 500Kč. Nine hours of riding on your own is 700Kč.

Car & Motorcycle

Driving in Prague is no fun. Trying to find your way around while coping with trams, lunatic drivers and pedestrians, one-way streets and police on the lookout for a little handout, will make you wish you'd left the car at home. Try not to arrive or leave on a Friday or Sunday afternoon or evening, when half the population seems to head to and from their weekend houses.

Central Prague has many pedestrian-only streets, marked with Pěší Zóná (Pedestrian Zone) signs, where only service vehicles and taxis are allowed, and parking can be a nightmare. Meter time limits range from two to 24 hours at around 40Kč per hour. Parking in one-way streets is normally only allowed on the right-hand side. Traffic inspectors are strict, and you may well be towed. There are several car parks at the edges of Staré Město and around the outer city close to metro stations.

Public Transport

All public transport is operated by **Dopravní podnik hl. m. Prahy** (DPP; ☎ 296 191 817; www.dpp .cz) which has information desks at **Ruzyně airport** (☯ 7am-10pm) and in five metro stations – **Muzeum** (☯ 7am to 9pm), **Můstek** (☯ 7am to 6pm), **Anděl** (☯ 7am to 6pm) and **Nádraží**

Holešovice (☯ 7am to 6pm) – where you can get tickets, directions, a multilingual system map, a map of *Noční provoz* (night services) and a detailed English-language guide to the whole system.

You need to by a ticket before you board a bus, tram or metro. Tickets are sold from machines at metro stations and major tram stops, at newsstands, Trafiky snack shops, PNS and other tobacco kiosks, hotels, all metro station ticket offices and DPP information offices.

A *jízdenka* (transfer ticket) valid on tram, metro, bus and the Petřín funicular costs 12Kč (half-price for six- to 15-year-olds); large suitcases and backpacks also need a 6Kč ticket. Kids under six ride free. Validate (punch) your ticket by sticking it in the little yellow machine in the metro station lobby or on the bus or tram the first time you board; this stamps the time and date on it. Once validated, tickets remain valid for 60 minutes from the time of stamping, if validated between 5am and 8pm on weekdays, and for 90 minutes at all other times. Within this time period, you can make unlimited transfers between all types of public transport (you don't need to punch the ticket again).

There's also a short-hop 8Kč ticket, valid for 15 minutes on buses and trams, or for up to four metro stations or two zones. No transfers are allowed with these, and they're not valid on the Petřín funicular nor on night trams or buses. Being caught without a valid ticket entails a 400Kč on-the-spot fine (50Kč for not having a luggage ticket). The inspectors travel incognito, but will show a badge when they ask for your ticket. A few may demand a higher fine from foreigners and pocket the difference, so insist on a *doklad* (receipt) before paying.

You can also buy tickets valid for 24 hours (70Kč) and three/seven/15 days (200/250/280Kč). Again, these must be validated on first use only; if a ticket is stamped twice, it becomes invalid.

On metro trains and newer trams and buses, an electronic display shows the route number and the name of the next stop, and a recorded voice announces each station or stop. As the train, tram or bus pulls away, it says: *Příští stanice* (or *zastávka*)... meaning 'The next station (or stop) is...', perhaps noting that it's a *přestupní stanice* (transfer station). At metro stations, signs point you towards the *výstup* (exit) or to a *přestup* (transfer to another line).

The metro operates from 5am to midnight daily. There are three lines: Line A runs from the northwestern side of the city at Dejvická to the east at Skalka; line B runs from the southwest at Zličín to the northeast at Černý Most; and line C runs from the north at Nádraží Holešovice to the southeast at Háje. Line A intersects line C at Muzeum, line B intersects line C at Florenc and line A intersects line B at Můstek.

After the metro closes, night trams (Nos 51 to 58) and buses (Nos 501 to 512) still rumble across the city about every 40 minutes through the night. If you're planning a late evening, find out if one of these services passes near where you're staying.

Taxi

Prague taxi drivers are notorious for overcharging tourists – if possible, avoid picking up a taxi in busy tourist areas such as Václavské nám. The best way to avoid being ripped off is to telephone a reliable taxi company such as **AAA** (☎ 223 113 311) or **ProfiTaxi** (☎ 261 314 151). If you feel you're being overcharged ask for an *účet* (bill). Most taxi trips within the city centre should cost around 100Kč to 150Kč.

AROUND PRAGUE

The following places are worth a visit, and can easily be visited on day trips from Prague using public transport.

Karlštejn

Fairy-tale **Karlštejn Castle** (☎ 274 008 154; www .hradkarlstejn.cz; Karlštejn; ⏰ 9am-6pm Tue-Sun Jul & Aug, to 5pm May, Jun & Sep, to 4pm Apr & Oct, to 3pm Nov-Mar) perches above the Berounka River, 30km southwest of Prague. Erected by the Emperor Charles IV in the mid-14th century, it crowns a ridge above the village, a 20-minute walk from the train station.

The castle's highlight is the **Chapel of the Holy Rood**, where the Bohemian crown jewels were kept until 1420, with walls covered in 14th-century painted panels and precious stones. The 45-minute guided tours (in English) on Route I cost 200/100Kč for adult/ concession tickets. Route II, which includes the chapel (July to November only), must be prebooked at 300/100Kč adult/concession per person.

Trains from Praha-hlavní nádraží and Praha-Smíchov train stations to Beroun stop at Karlštejn (46Kč, 45 minutes, hourly).

Konopiště

The assassination in 1914 of the heir to the Austro-Hungarian throne, Archduke Franz Ferdinand d'Este, sparked off WWI. For the last twenty years of his life he avoided the intrigues of the Vienna court, hiding away southeast of Prague in what had become his ideal country retreat, **Konopiště Chateau** (☎ 317 721 366; Benešov; ⏰ 9am-5pm Tue-Sun May-Aug; 9am-4pm Tue-Fri, to 5pm Sat & Sun Sep; 9am-3pm Tue-Fri, to 4pm Sat & Sun Apr & Oct; 9am-3pm Sat & Sun Nov, closed 12.30-1pm).

There are three guided tours available. **Tour III** (in English 250Kč, no concession) is the most interesting, visiting the private apartments used by the archduke and his family, which have remained unchanged since the state took over the chateau in 1921. **Tour II** (in English adult/child 145/75Kč) takes in the **Great Armoury**, one of the largest and most impressive collections in Europe.

The castle is a testament to the archduke's twin obsessions – hunting and St George. Having renovated the massive Gothic and Renaissance building in the 1890s, and installed all the latest technology – electricity, central heating, flush toilets, showers and a lift – Franz Ferdinand decorated his home with his hunting trophies. His game books record that he shot around 300,000 creatures during his lifetime, from foxes and deer to elephants and tigers. About 100,000 of them adorn the walls, each marked with the date and place it met its end – the **Trophy Corridor** and antler-clad **Chamois Room** (both on Tour III) are truly bizarre sights.

The archduke's collection of art and artefacts relating to St George is no less impressive, amounting to 3750 items, many of which are on show in the **Muzeum sv Jiří** (adult/child 25/10Kč) beneath the terrace at the front of the castle.

There are frequent direct trains from Prague's hlavní nádraží to Benešov u Prahy (64Kč, 1¼ hours, hourly). There are also buses from Prague's Roztyly metro station to Benešov (36Kč, 40 minutes, twice hourly); their final destination is usually Pelhřimov or Jihlava.

Konopiště is 2.5km west of Benešov. Local bus No 2 (7Kč, six minutes, hourly) runs from a stop on Dukelská, 400m north of the train station (turn left out of the station, then first right on Tyršova and first left) to the castle car park. Otherwise it's a 30-minute walk. Turn left out of the train station, go left across the bridge over the railway, and follow Konopištská street west for 2km.

Kutná Hora

In the 14th century Kutná Hora rivalled Prague as the most important town in Bohemia, growing rich on the veins of silver ore that laced the rocks beneath it. The silver *groschen* that were minted here at that time represented the hard currency of Central Europe. But the good times came to an end as the silver ran out and mining ceased in 1726, leaving the medieval townscape largely unaltered. Today it's an attractive place with several fascinating and unusual historical attractions. In 1996 it was added to Unesco's World Heritage List.

ORIENTATION & INFORMATION

Kutná Hora hlavní nádraží (the main train station), is 3km northeast of the old town centre. The bus station is more conveniently located on the northeastern edge of the old town.

The easiest way to visit Kutná Hora on a day trip is to arrive on a morning train from Prague, then make the 10-minute walk from Kutná Hora hlavní nádraží to Sedlec Ossuary. From there it's another 2km walk or a five-minute bus ride into town.

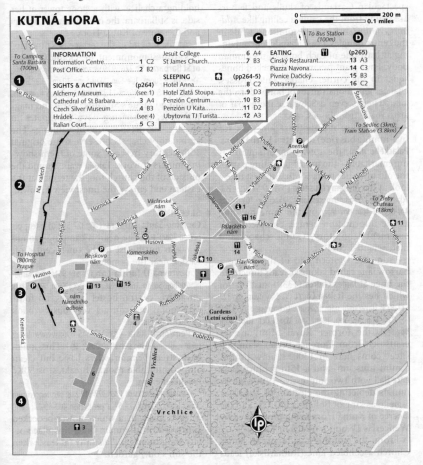

KUTNÁ HORA

INFORMATION	
Information Centre................1 C2	
Post Office.........................2 B2	
SIGHTS & ACTIVITIES (p264)	
Alchemy Museum................(see 1)	
Cathedral of St Barbara........3 A4	
Czech Silver Museum...........4 B3	
Hrádek.............................(see 4)	
Italian Court.....................5 C3	
Jesuit College.....................6 A4	
St James Church.................7 B3	
SLEEPING (pp264-5)	
Hotel Anna........................8 C2	
Hotel Zlatá Stoupa...............9 D3	
Penzión Centrum................10 B3	
Penzión U Kata..................11 D2	
Ubytovna TJ Turista.............12 A3	
EATING (p265)	
Čínský Restaurant...............13 A3	
Piazza Navona...................14 C3	
Pivnice Dačický..................15 B3	
Potraviny.........................16 C2	

The helpful **information centre** (☎ 327 512 378; www.kh.cz; Palackého nám 377; 9am-6pm Apr-Sep, 9am-5pm Mon-Fri, 10am-4pm Sat & Sun Oct-Mar) books accommodation and has Internet access (1Kč per minute, 15Kč minimum).

SIGHTS

A 10-minute walk south from Kutná Hora hlavní nádraží leads to the remarkable **Sedlec Ossuary** (Kostnice; ☎ 327 561 143; adult/concession 45/30Kč; ☯ 8am-6pm Apr-Sep, 9am-noon & 1-5pm Oct, to 4pm Nov-Mar). When the Schwarzenberg family purchased Sedlec monastery in 1870 they allowed a local woodcarver to get creative with the bones which had been piled in the crypt for centuries. The bones belonged to no fewer than 40,000 people, and the result was spectacular. Garlands of skulls and femurs are strung from the vaulted ceiling like *Addams Family* Christmas decorations, while in the centre dangles a vast chandelier containing at least one of each bone in the human body. Four giant pyramids of stacked bones squat in the corner chapels, and crosses, chalices and monstrances of bone adorn the altar. There's even a Schwarzenberg coat of arms made from bones.

From Sedlec it's another 2km walk (or five-minute bus ride) to central Kutná Hora. **Palackého nám**, the town's main square, is unremarkable – the most interesting part of the old town lies to its south. But first take a look at the **Alchemy Museum** (☎ 327 511 259; Palackého nám 377; adult/concession 40/25Kč; ☯ 10am-5pm Apr-Oct, to 4pm Nov-Mar), in the same building as the information centre, complete with basement laboratory, Gothic chapel and mad-scientist curator.

From the western end of the square a narrow lane called Jakubská leads directly to the huge **St James Church** (1330), just east of which lies the **Italian Court** (Vlašský dvůr; ☎ 327 512 873; Havlíčkovo nám 552; adult/concession 70/50Kč; ☯ 9am-6pm Apr-Sep, 10am-5pm Mar & Oct, 10am-4pm Nov-Feb), the former Royal Mint; master craftsmen from Florence began stamping silver coins here in 1300. It now houses a mint museum, and a 15th-century **Audience Hall** with two impressive 19th-century murals depicting the election of Vladislav Jagiello as king of Bohemia in 1471, and the Decree of Kutná Hora being proclaimed by Wenceslas IV and Jan Hus in 1409.

From the southern side of St James Church a cobbled lane (Ruthardská) leads

to the **Hrádek** (Little Castle), a 15th-century palace that houses the **Czech Silver Museum** (České Muzeum Stříbra; ☎ 327 512 159; adult/concession 60/30Kč; ☯ 10am-6pm Jul & Aug, 9am-6pm May, Jun & Sep, 9am-5pm Apr & Oct, closed Mon year-round). The exhibits celebrate the mines that made Kutná Hora wealthy, including a huge wooden device once used to lift up to 1000kg of rock from the 200m-deep shafts. You can even don a miner's helmet and lamp and join a 45-minute tour (110/70Kč) through 500m of **medieval mine shafts** beneath the town.

Just beyond the Hrádek is a 17th-century former **Jesuit college**, fronted by a terrace with a row of 13 baroque sculptures of saints, inspired by those on Prague's Charles Bridge. Check out the second one along – the woman holding a chalice, with a stone tower at her side, is St Barbara, the patron saint of miners and therefore of Kutná Hora.

At the far end of the terrace is Kutná Hora's greatest monument, the Gothic **Cathedral of St Barbara** (☎ 776 393 938; adult/concession 30/15Kč; ☯ 9am-5.30pm Tue-Sun May-Sep, 10am-11.30am & 1-4pm Apr & Oct, 10am-11.30am & 2-3.30pm Nov-Mar). Rivalling Prague's St Vitus in size and magnificence, its soaring nave culminates in elegant, six-petalled ribbed vaulting. The ambulatory chapels preserve some original 15th-century frescoes, some of them showing miners at work. Take a walk around the outside of the church too; the terrace at the eastern end enjoys the finest view in town.

SLEEPING

Camping Santa Barbara (☎ 327 512 051; tent per person 70Kč; Ⓟ) The nearest camping ground is 800m northwest of the town centre off Česká, near the cemetery.

Ubytovna TJ Turista (☎ 327 514 961; nám Národního odboje 56; dm 160Kč; reception ☯ 5-6pm; Ⓟ) This attractive, central hostel has several four-bed rooms but can get very busy – book ahead if possible.

Penzión U Kata (☎ 327 515 096; www.volny.cz /ukata; Uhelná 596; s/d 300/400Kč; Ⓟ) This quiet, back-street *pension* offers basic but clean and comfortable rooms. Breakfast is 50Kč per head extra.

Penzión Centrum (☎ 327 514 218; penzioncentrum .kh@tiscali.cz; Jakubská 57; r per person 400-600Kč; Ⓟ) Tucked away in a quiet, flower-bedecked courtyard off the main drag, this place offers snug rooms and a sunny (at least when the sun's out) garden.

Hotel Anna (☎ 327 516 315; hotel.anna@seznam.cz; Vladislavova 372; s/d 730/1050Kč; **P**)) The Anna offers comfy, modern rooms with shower, TV and breakfast in a lovely old building with an atmospheric stone-vaulted cellar restaurant.

Hotel Zlatá Stoupa (☎ 327 511 540; zlatstoupa@iol.cz; Tylova 426; s/d from 1070/1800Kč; **P**)) If you feel like spoiling yourself, the most luxurious place in town is the elegantly furnished 'Golden Mount'. We like a hotel room whose minibar contains full-size bottles of wine.

EATING

Pivnice Dačický (☎ 327 512 248; Rakova 8; mains 60-100Kč; ☺ 11am-11pm) Get some froth on your moustache at this old-fashioned, wood-panelled Bohemian beer hall, where you can dine on *knedlíky* while envying the folk who phoned ahead for the whole roast piglet.

Piazza Navona (☎ 327 512 588; Palackého nám 90; mains 100-130Kč; ☺ 9am-midnight May-Sep, to 8pm Oct-Apr) Feed up on pizza at this homely Italian café bar, plastered with Ferrari flags and Inter Milan pennants; tables spill onto the main square in summer.

Čínský Restaurant (☎ 327 514 151; nám Národního odboje 48; mains 90-200Kč; ☺ 11am-10pm Tue-Sat) Set in a plush old house with a garden out back, the imaginatively named 'Chinese' is a little heavy on the MSG but still manages a tasty chicken *gung-po*. Makes a change from those *knedlíky*.

There's a convenient **potraviny** (grocery; ☺ 6am-6pm Mon-Fri, 7am-noon Sat) on the eastern side of the main square.

GETTING THERE & AWAY

There are direct trains from Prague's hlavní nádraží to Kutná Hora hlavní nádraží (62Kč, 55 minutes, seven daily).

Buses to Kutná Hora from Prague (68Kč, 1¼ hours, hourly) depart from station No 2 at Florenc bus station; services are less frequent at weekends.

BOHEMIA

The ancient land of Bohemia makes up the western two-thirds of the Czech Republic. The modern term 'bohemian' comes to us via the French, who thought that Roma came from Bohemia; the word *bohémien* was later applied to people living an unconventional lifestyle. The term gained currency in the wake of Puccini's opera *La Bohème* about a community of poverty stricken artists in Paris.

TEREZÍN

The massive red-brick ramparts of the double fortress at Terezín (Theriesenstadt in German) were built by the Habsburgs in the 18th century to repel the might of the Prussian army. But the place is better known for its role as a notorious WWII prison and concentration camp. Around 150,000 men, women and children, mostly Jews, passed through on the way to the extermination camps of Auschwitz-Birkenau; 35,000 of them died here of hunger, disease or suicide; only 4000 survived. From 1945 to 1948 the fortress served as an internment camp for the Sudeten Germans who were expelled from Czechoslovakia after the war.

The **Terezín Memorial** (☎ 416 782 225; www.pamatnik-terezin.cz) consists of two main parts – the Museum of the Ghetto in the Main Fortress, and the Lesser Fortress, a 10-minute walk east across the Ohře River. Admission to one part costs 160/130Kč; a combined ticket for both is 180/140Kč.

The **Museum of the Ghetto** (Muzeum ghetta; ☺ 9am-6pm Apr-Oct, to 5.30pm Nov-Mar) records daily life in the camp during WWII through moving displays of paintings, letters and personal possessions; the Nazi documents recording the departures of trains to 'the east' chillingly illustrate the banality of evil.

Around 32,000 prisoners, many of them Czech partisans, were incarcerated in the **Lesser Fortress** (Malá pevnost; ☺ 8am-6pm Apr-Oct, to 4.30pm Nov-Mar); you can take a grimly fascinating self-guided tour through the prison barracks, isolation cells, workshops, morgues and former mass graves, before arriving at the bleak execution grounds where more than 250 prisoners were shot.

Terezín is northwest of Prague, 3km south of Litoměřice; buses between Prague and Litoměřice stop at both the main square and the Lesser Fortress. There are frequent buses between Litoměřice bus station and Terezín (8Kč, 10 minutes, at least hourly).

LITOMĚŘICE

pop 25,100

The cheerful town of Litoměřice offers some light relief from the horrific history of nearby

Terezín. Founded by German colonists in the 13th century, it prospered in the 18th century as a royal seat and bishopric. Today the old town centre has many picturesque buildings and churches, some of them designed by the baroque architect Ottavio Broggio, who was born here.

The old town lies across the road to the west of the adjacent train and bus stations, guarded by the surviving remnants of the 14th-century town walls. Walk along Dlouhá to the central square, Mírové nám.

The **information centre** (☎ 416 732 440; www .litomerice.cz, in Czech; Mírové nám 15; ☾ 8am-6pm Mon-Fri, to 5.30pm Sat, 9.30am-4pm Sun May-Sep; 8am-5pm Mon & Wed, to 4.15pm Tue & Thu, to 4pm Fri, 8am-11am Sat Oct-Apr) is in the town hall.

Sights

The broad and beautiful main square is lined with Gothic arcades and pastel façades, dominated by the tower of **All Saints Church**, the step-gabled **Old Town Hall**, and the distinctive **House at the Chalice** (Dům U Kalicha) – the green copper artichoke sprouting from the roof is actually a chalice, the traditional symbol of the Hussite church. The thin slice of baroque wedding cake at the uphill end of the square is the **House of Ottavio Broggio**.

Along Michalská on the southwest corner of the square you'll find another house where Broggio left his mark, the excellent **North Bohemia Fine Arts Gallery** (☎ 416 732 382; Michalská 7; adult/concession 32/18Kč; ☾ 9am-noon & 1-6pm Tue-Sun Apr-Sep, to 5pm Oct-Mar) with the priceless Renaissance panels of the Litoměřice Altarpiece.

Turn left at the end of Michalská and follow Domská towards grassy, tree-lined Domské nám on Cathedral Hill, passing pretty **St Wenceslas Church**, a true baroque gem, along a side street to the right. At the top of the hill is the town's oldest church, **St Stephen Cathedral**, dating from the 11th century.

Go through the arch to the left of the cathedral and descend a steep cobbled lane called Máchova. At the foot of the hill turn left then first right, up the zigzag steps to the **old town walls**. You can follow the walls to the right as far as the next street, Jezuitská, where a left turn leads back to the square.

Sleeping & Eating

Autocamp Slavoj (☎ 416 734 481; kemp.litomerice@post .cz; camp sites 70Kč plus per person/car 65/50Kč; ☾ May-Sep; P) On Střelecký ostrov, just south of the train and bus stations; take the footpath under the railway just west of the station.

Pension Prislin (☎ 416 735 833; pension@prislin .cz; Ná Kocandě 12; s/d 700/1100Kč; P) A view across the river and breakfast in the garden are good reasons for choosing the family-friendly Prislin. It's five minutes' walk east of the town square, along the main road.

U Svatého Václava (☎ 416 737 500; usvateho vaclava@hotmail.com; Svatovaclavská 12; s/d 600/1000Kč) Tucked away in the shadow of St Wenceslas Church, this pretty villa houses a tiptop *pension* with sauna, well-equipped rooms and a homely apron-toting owner who whips up a fine breakfast.

Hotel Salva Guarda (☎ 416 732 506; www.salva -guarda.cz; Mírové nám 12; s/d 920/1450Kč; P) The top hotel in town is set in the lovely Renaissance House at the Black Eagle – Emperor Ferdinand III stayed here in 1566 – though the cosy rooms with bathroom and TV are in a modern wing at the back. It also has the best **restaurant** (mains 100-200Kč; ☾ 11am-11pm Sun-Thu, to 1am Fri & Sat) on the square, a vaulted Gothic room with art on the walls (the owner runs a commercial gallery) and a menu ranging from smoked pork to salmon in herb butter.

Music Café Viva (☎ 608 437 783; Mezibraní 5; mains 80-200Kč; ☾ 11am-11pm) Housed in former bastion in the old town walls opposite the train station, this hip, music-oriented eatery has a cocktail bar below, a restaurant above and creaking wood beams galore. The menu includes tasty *bramboráky* (potato pancakes), kebabs and steaks, and there's a set lunch on weekdays for just 69Kč.

Café Espresso (Mírové nám 40; coffee 40Kč; ☾ 8am-9pm Mon-Sat, noon-9pm Sun) In the arcade beneath the Old Town Hall, this pleasant café serves good coffee, ice cream and cakes.

There's a handy **bakery & grocery** (pekárna-potraviny; ☾ 7am-7pm Mon-Fri, 7am-noon Sat, 8am-noon Sun) at the top end of the square.

Getting There & Away

Direct buses from Prague to Litoměřice (61Kč, 1¼ hours, hourly) depart from station No 17 at Florenc bus station (final destination Ustí nad Labem).

BOHEMIAN SWITZERLAND NATIONAL PARK

The main road and rail route between Prague and Dresden follows the powerful, fast-flowing Labe (Elbe) River where it has gouged a sinuous, steep-sided valley through a high sandstone plateau on the border between the Czech Republic and Germany. The scenic landscape of sandstone pinnacles, giddy gorges, dark forests and high meadows that stretches to the east of the river is the **Bohemian Switzerland National Park** (Národní park České Švýcarsko), so named because of two 19th-century Swiss artists who liked the landscape so much they moved here permanently.

Only a few hundred metres south of the German border, **Hřensko** is a cute village of pointy-gabled, half-timbered houses crammed into a narrow sandstone gorge at the point where the Kamenice River flows into the Labe. It's overrun with German day-trippers at summer weekends, when the main street is lined with stalls selling cheap clothing, but it only takes a few minutes to walk upstream to the start of the hiking trails.

A signposted 16km circular hike takes in the main sights; allow five to six hours. From the eastern end of Hřensko a trail leads via ledges, walkways and tunnels through the mossy chasms of the **Kamenice River Gorge**. There are two sections – **Edmundova Soutěska** (Edmund's Gorge; ☼ 9am-6pm daily May-Aug, Sat & Sun only Apr, Sep & Oct) and **Divoká Soutěska** (Savage Gorge; ☼ 9am-5pm daily May-Aug, Sat & Sun only Apr, Sep & Oct) – that have been dammed; here you continue by punt, poled along by a ferryman through a canyon barely five metres wide and 50m to 150m deep. There's a charge for each ferry trip (adult/concession 50/25Kč).

A kilometre beyond the end of the second boat trip, a blue-marked trail leads uphill to the Hotel Mezní Louka; across the road, a red-marked trail continues climbing through the forest to the spectacular rock formation **Pravčická Brána** (adult/concession 50/25Kč; ☼ 10am-6pm Apr-Oct, 10am-4pm Sat & Sun Nov-Mar), the largest natural arch in Europe. Nestled improbably in a rocky nook beneath the arch is the **Falcon's Nest**, an ornate 19th-century chateau that now houses a national park museum and restaurant. From here the red trail descends westward back to Hřensko.

Sleeping & Eating

Pension Lugano (☎ 412 554 146; fax 412 554 156; Hřensko; s/d incl breakfast 540/1080Kč; P) A bright and cheerful place in the centre of Hřensko.

Restaurace U Raka (☎ 412 554 157; Hřensko 28; mains 80-200Kč; ☼ 10am-9.30pm) Near Pension Lugano is a pretty little half-timbered cottage with a sun-trap terrace serving Czech specialities; try the local *pstruh* (trout).

Up in the hills, **Hotel Mezní Louka** (☎ 412 554 220; Mezní Louka 71; s/d 700/1050Kč; P) is a modernised 19th-century hiking lodge with a decent **restaurant** (mains 90-170Kč; ☼ 9am-7pm Mon-Thu, to 9pm Fri & Sat, 8am-6pm Sun). Across the road is **Camp Mezní Louka** (☎ 412 554 084; per tent/bungalow 50Kč/400Kč; P).

If you have a car, there are lots of pretty *pensions* scattered along the minor road to Janov and Ružova, a few kilometres to the southeast of Hřensko.

Getting There & Away

There are frequent local trains from Dresden to Schöna (€4.80, 1¼ hour, every half-hour), on the German (west) bank of the river opposite Hřensko. From the station, a little ferry shuttles back and forth to Hřensko (€0.80 or 10Kč, three minutes) on demand.

From Prague, take a bus (84Kč, 1¾ hours, five daily) to Děčín, then another to Hřensko (14Kč, 20 minutes, four daily). Alternatively, catch a Dresden-bound train and get off at Bad Schandau (184Kč, two hours, eight daily), then a local train back to Schöna (€1.60, 12 minutes, every half-hour).

On weekdays there are three buses a day (year-round) between Hřensko and Mezní Louka (8Kč, 10 minutes), and two a day at weekends (July to September only).

KARLOVY VARY

pop 60,000

Karlovy Vary (Karlsbad in German) is the oldest and biggest of Bohemia's fashionable spa towns. Wealthy hypochondriacs with oversized sunglasses, yappy dogs and heavy golden jewellery flock here from Germany, Austria and Russia to take the waters and sign up for courses of 'lymphatic drainage', 'hydrocolonotherapy' (shudder), and other grimly Teutonic-sounding treatments.

But even if the prospect of being slathered in smelly mud and hosed down by a Rosa Kleb look-alike doesn't appeal, Karlovy Vary offers plenty of more tempting activities, such as strolling along the river banks admiring the elegant colonnades and baroque mansions, sipping beer at riverside cafés, and hiking in the wooded hills above the town.

According to legend, Emperor Charles IV discovered the hot springs in 1350 while hunting a stag (Karlovy Vary means 'Charles' Hot Springs'). During the spa's glory days, which lasted from the early 18th century until WWI, the town was patronised by royalty, including Tsar Peter the Great and Emperor Franz Josef I, and attracted big-name celebrities such as Beethoven, Bismarck, Brahms, Chopin, Goethe, Wagner, Paganini, Liszt, Schiller, Tolstoy, Freud and Karl Marx, who came to take the waters and indulge in the town's seductive cocktail of convalescence and culture – music, entertainment and conversation were always an important part of the spa cure. Busts and plaques commemorating the great and the good grace the promenades all around the town.

Orientation

Karlovy Vary has two train stations – Dolní nádraží (Lower Station), beside the main bus station, and Horní nádraží (Upper Station), across the Ohře River north of the city centre.

Trains from Prague arrive at Horní nádraží. To get into town, take bus No 11, 12 or 13 from the stop across the road to the Tržnice station; No 11 continues to Divadelní nám in the spa district. Alternatively, it's 10 minutes on foot; cross the road outside the station and go right, then first left on a footpath that leads downhill under the highway. At its foot, turn right on U Spořitelny, then left at the far end of the big building and head for the bridge over the river.

The Tržnice bus stop is three blocks east of Dolní nádraží, in the middle of the town's modern commercial district. Pedestrianised TG Masaryka leads east to the Teplá River; from here the old spa district stretches upstream for 2km along a steep-sided valley.

Information

Infocentrum (☎ 353 224 097; www.karlovyvary.cz; Lázeňská 1; ☾ 8am-6pm Mon-Fri, 10am-4pm Sat & Sun) Maps, brochures and general tourist info. Branch office at Dolní nádraží.

Internet Café (☎ 359 002 230; Hotel Thermal, IP Pavlova 11; per hr 80Kč; ☾ 10am-10pm) Go past the hotel reception and turn left.

Main post office (TG Masaryka 1; ☾ 7.30am-7pm Mon-Fri, 7am-1pm Sat, 7am-noon Sun) Includes a telephone centre.

VIR Centrum (☎ 603 360 181; TG Masaryka 12; per hr 80Kč; ☾ 10am-10pm) Internet access.

Sights

At the heart of the old spa district is the neo-classical **Mill Colonnade** (Mlýnská Kolonáda), where crowds stroll and bands play in the summer. There are several other elegant colonnades and imposing 19th-century spa buildings scattered along the Teplá River, though the 1970s concrete monstrosity of the **Hotel Thermal** spoils the effect slightly.

You can pretend to be a spa patient by purchasing a *lázeňské pohár* (spa cup) and a box of *oplátky* (spa wafers) and sampling the various hot springs (free); the Infocentrum has a leaflet describing them all. There are 12 springs in the 'drinking cure', ranging from the **Rock Spring** (Skalní Pramen), which dribbles a measly 1.3L/min, to the lusty **Geyser** (Vřídlo), which spurts 2000L/min in a steaming, 14m-high jet. The latter is housed in the 1970s **Geyser Colonnade** (Vřídelní Kolonáda; admission free; ☾ 6am-7pm), which also sells spa cups and wafers.

The sulphurous spring waters carry a whiff of rotten eggs. **Becherovka**, a locally produced herbal liqueur, is famously known as the '13th spring' – a few shots will take away the taste of the spring waters, and leave you feeling sprightlier than a week's worth of 'hydrocolonotherapy'.

If you want a look inside one of the old spa buildings without having to endure the rigours of 'proktologie' and 'endoskopie', nip into **Spa No 3** (Lázně III) just north of the Mill Colonnade – it has a café upstairs, which gives you an excuse to stick your nose in. The faded entrance hall offers a glimpse of white-tiled institutional corridors stretching off to either side, lined with the doors to sinister-sounding 'treatment rooms' and echoing to the flip-flopped footsteps of muscular, grim-faced nurses. Shiver.

The most splendid of the traditional spa buildings is the beautifully restored **Spa No 1** (Lázně I) at the south end of town, which dates from 1895 and once housed Emperor Franz Josef's private baths. Across the river

KARLOVY VARY

0 _____ 400 m
0 _____ 0.2 miles

INFORMATION
Infocentrum Branch Office............1 A4
Infocentrum.....................................2 C5
Internet Café...............................(see 11)
Main Post Office............................3 B4
VIR Centrum...................................4 B4

SIGHTS & ACTIVITIES (pp268–70)
Castle Spa 5 C5
Church of St Lucas.........................6 C5
Church of SS Peter & Paul.............7 B5
Diana Lookout Tower.....................8 B6
Gegser Colonnade.........................9 C5
Grandhotel Pupp.........................10 C6

Hotel Thermal..............................11 B4
Jan Becher Museum......................12 A4
Karl Marx Monument....................13 B5
Karlovy Vary Museum...................14 C6
Mill Colonnade.............................15 C5
Open-Air Thermal Pool.................16 B4
Spa No 1.......................................17 C6
Spa No 3.......................................18 C4

SLEEPING (pp270–1)
Buena Vista Hostel.......................19 D5
Čedok...20 A4
Hotel Kavalerie.............................21 A4
Pension Villa Basileia....................22 C6

Pension Villa Rosa........................23 C5
W-privat..24 A4

EATING (p271)
Café Elefant..................................25 C5
Parlament.....................................26 A4
Restaurant Bernard.......................27 C4
Restaurant Promenáda..................28 C5
Thailand Restaurant......................29 C5
Vg Vegetarian Restaurant.............30 B4

TRANSPORT (p271)
Main Bus Station...........................31 A4
Tržnice Bus Station.......................32 B3

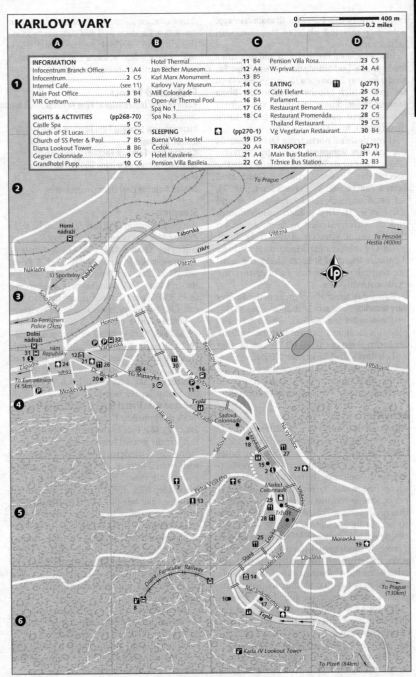

from here is the baroque **Grandhotel Pupp**, a former meeting place of the European aristocracy.

Just north of the hotel, a narrow alley leads to the bottom station of the **Diana Funicular Railway** (single/return 30/50Kč; ☒ every 15min 9am-6pm), which climbs 166m to the **Diana Lookout Tower**. There are great views from the top, and pleasant walks back down through the forest.

If you descend north from Diana towards the **Karl Marx Monument** and Petra Velikého (Peter the Great Street), you can visit the spectacular Russian Orthodox **Church of SS Peter & Paul** (kostel sv Petra a Pavla; 1897), set amid an enclave of elegant villas and spa hotels. Its five golden onion domes and colourful exterior were modelled on the Byzantine Church of the Holy Trinity in Ostankino near Moscow. It and the Anglican **Church of St Lucas** along the road are reminders of the town's once-thriving expat communities.

Rainy day alternatives include the **Karlovy Vary Museum** (Nová Louka 23; adult/concession 30/15Kč; ☒ 9am-noon & 1-5pm Wed-Sun), which has displays on local and natural history, and the **Jan Becher Museum** (☎ 353 170 156; www.janbecher .cz; TG Masaryka 57; adult/concession 100/25Kč; ☒ 9am-5pm), dedicated to the 18th-century inventor of the local liqueur; the website has some interesting ideas for Becherovka cocktails.

Activities

Although the surviving traditional *lázně* (spa) centres are basically medical institutions, many of the town's old spa and hotel buildings have been renovated as modern spa and 'wellness' hotels that cater for more hedonistic tastes, offering thermal pools, saunas, cosmetic treatments, aromatherapy, massage, manicure, pedicure and so on. **Castle Spa** (Zámecké Lázně; ☎ 353 222 649; Zámechý vrch; basic admission €15; ☒ 7.30am-7.30pm) is a recently modernised spa centre, complete with subterranean thermal pool, that retains some old-fashioned atmosphere. Basic admission gets you one hour loafing in the pool; a more expensive four-hour session (€65) adds on a full-body massage and the chance to experiment with traditional spa treatments such as hydro-massage, 'electroaerosol inhalation' and 'gum irrigation'.

If all you want is a straight, no-nonsense swim, head for the large **open-air thermal pool**

(bazén; admission 30Kč per hr; ☒ 8am-8.30pm Mon-Sat, 9am-9.30pm Sun, closed every third Mon) perched on the cliff top overlooking the Hotel Thermal. There's also a **sauna** (☒ 10am-9.30pm), a solarium and a fitness club here.

Festivals & Events

Karlovy Vary International Film Festival (www.kviff .com; early Jul)
International Student Film Festival (www.freshfilms fest.net; late Aug)
Karlovy Vary Folklore Festival (early Sep)
Jazzfest Karlovy Vary (early Sep) International jazz festival.
Dvořák Autumn (Sep) Classical music festival.

Sleeping

Accommodation is pricey, and can be tight during weekends and festivals; book ahead. Agencies **Čedok** (☎ 353 223 335; Dr Bechera 21; ☒ 9am-6pm Mon-Fri, 9am-noon Sat) and **W-Privat** (☎ 353 227 768; nám Republiky 5; ☒ 8.30am-5pm Mon-Fri, 9.30am-1pm Sat) can book private rooms from 350Kč per person. Infocentrum (p268) can find hostel, *pension* and hotel rooms.

Penzión Hestia (☎ 353 225 985; hestiakv@volny .cz; SOU Bldg, Stará Kysibelská 45; r per person 155Kč; Ⓟ) Hestia is a spacious and comfortable student hostel offering two- and four-bed rooms. It's a 20-minute walk east of the centre; or take bus No 6 from Tržnice to the Blahoslavova stop.

Buena Vista Hostel (☎ 353 239 002; www.premium -hotels.com/buenavista; Moravská 44; r per person 230-260Kč; Ⓟ ▣) This is the only place in town that's really geared towards backpackers, offering clean, modern, two- to six-bed rooms with shared kitchen and an outdoor terrace with good views. Breakfast is 80Kč extra. It's a steep hike uphill from the river; alternatively, take bus No 11 or 13 from Horní nádraží or Tržnice to the Ná výhlidce stop.

Europension (☎ 353 332 117; www.pension-euro .cz; Studentská 45; s/d 650/1100Kč; Ⓟ) On the far western edge of town on the road to Plzeň (take bus No 6 from Tržnice to U Zámečku stop), this bright and modern 15-room place offers en suite rooms with TV at bargain rates.

Hotel Kavalerie (☎ 353 229 613; www.kavalerie.cz; TG Masaryka 43; s/d 1150/1400Kč; Ⓟ) Quiet, homely and central, the Kavalerie is probably the best-value hotel in the town centre. It's only five minutes' walk from the lower train and bus stations, and the same from the spa area.

Pension Villa Rosa (☎ 353 239 120; www.villa rosa.cz; Ná výhlidce 22; s/d from 1000/1300Kč; P ☐) Perched high above the river, the Villa Rosa combines bright, comfy rooms with a striking location – go for the more expensive doubles (2000Kč) and suites (2600Kč) which have balconies with stunning views over the town.

Pension Villa Basileia (☎ 353 224 132; www.villa basileia.cz; Mariánskolázeňská 4; s/d 1400/1750Kč; P ☒) A posh *pension* that was once home to a countess, the Basileia has a delightful riverside location, a summer garden with terrace and pool, and luxurious accommodation. Ask for a room overlooking the river.

Eating

Parlament (☎ 353 586 155; Zeyerova 5; mains 70-90Kč; ☽ 9am-10pm Mon-Sat) A good bet for cheap food, serving salads and sandwiches as well as pork, sauerkraut and *knedlíky*, and other classic Czech dishes. Outdoor tables in summer.

Vg Vegetarian Restaurant (☎ 353 229 021; IP Pavlova 25; mains 60-100Kč; ☽ 11am-10pm) This basic cafeteria-style eatery (around the back of the building) offers meat-free soups, salads, sandwiches and hearty hot dishes.

Restaurant Bernard (☎ 353 221 667; Ondřejská 14; mains 90-110Kč; ☽ 11.30am-10pm) A cosy, rustic, wood-panelled cellar with half a dozen convivial booths, the Bernard has a genial, moustached host in waistcoat and apron dishing up tasty Czech pub grub washed down with Pilsner Urquell. Live jazz every second Friday from 8pm.

Café Elefant (☎ 353 223 406; Stará Louka 30; snacks 50-150Kč, coffee 50Kč; ☽ 9am-10pm) Perhaps Karlovy Vary's most popular and elegant café, the Elefant has been a favoured celebrity haunt since 1715. Grab a riverside table and savour some *sachertörte* (Viennese chocolate cake) and *vídenská káva* (Viennese coffee – topped with whipped cream).

Thailand Restaurant (☎ 602 490 538; Tržiště 37; mains 90-170Kč; ☽ 11am-1pm) Despite the name, the menu here is mostly Chinese, as is the décor – all tasselled lanterns, laughing Buddhas and lashings of the lucky colour (red). Their *Tom yam gaeng* (Thai hot and sour soup) is less than authentic, but the Chinese dishes are tasty.

Restaurant Promenáda (☎ 353 225 648; Tržiště 31; mains 200-500Kč; ☽ 11am-2.30pm & 6-10pm) If you're looking for a special meal, this elegant little restaurant (in the hotel of the same name) has crisp linen, professional service, good wine and superb Czech cuisine with a gourmet's touch.

Getting There & Around

Direct buses to Prague (130Kč, 2¼ hours, eight daily) and Plzeň (86Kč, 1½ hours, hourly) depart from the main bus station beside Dolní nádraží train station.

There are direct (but slow) trains from Karlovy Vary to Prague (250Kč, four hours). Heading west from Karlovy Vary to Nuremberg, Germany (920Kč, three hours, two a day), and beyond, you'll have to change at Cheb (Eger in German). A slow but scenic alternative is a trundle north through the hills and forests to Leipzig (850Kč, 4½ hours, 10 daily); there are several routes, involving two or three changes of train – check online timetables at www.vlak.cz or www.bahn.de.

Local buses cost 10Kč; there are ticket machines at the main stops. Bus No 11 runs hourly from Horní nádraží to Tržnice in the commercial district, and on to Divadelni nám. Bus No 2 runs between Tržnice and Grandhotel Pupp (Spa No 1) every half-hour or so from 6am to 11pm daily.

LOKET

Wrapped snugly in a tight bend of the Ohre River, the village of Loket is a pretty little place that has attracted many famous visitors from nearby Karlovy Vary; a plaque on the façade of the Hostinec Bílý Kůň on the chocolate-box town square commemorates Goethe's seven visits. The forbidding **castle** (☎ 352 684 104; Zámecká 67; adult/concession 80/50Kč; ☽ 9am-4.30pm Apr-Oct, to 3.30pm Nov-Mar), perched high above the river, has a museum dedicated to locally produced porcelain, but the village's main attraction is just wandering around admiring the views.

You can walk from Karlovy Vary to Loket along a 17km blue-marked trail, starting at the Diana lookout; allow three hours. Otherwise, buses from Karlovy Vary to Sokolov stop at Loket (21Kč, 30 minutes, hourly).

PLZEŇ

pop 175,000

Plzeň (Pilsen in German) is famed among beer-heads worldwide as the motherlode of all lagers, the fountain of eternal froth – Pilsner lager was invented here in 1842. It's the home

CZECH REPUBLIC

town of Pilsner Urquell (Plzeňský prazdroj), the world's first and finest lager beer. 'Urquell' (in German; *prazdroj* in Czech) means 'original source' or 'fountainhead', and beer drinkers from around the world flock to worship at the Pilsner Urquell brewery.

Plzeň is the capital of West Bohemia, a gritty industrial city with an attractive old town centre ringed with tree-lined gardens. As well as being famous for beer it is home to the Škoda Engineering Works, established by Emil Škoda in 1869. A producer of high-quality armaments, the complex was subjected to heavy bombing at the end of WWII; today it produces heavy machinery and locomotives (Škoda cars are made at a separate plant in Mladá Boleslav, northeast of Prague).

Orientation

The main bus station is west of the centre on Husova, opposite the Škoda Engineering Works. Plzeň-hlavní nádraží, the main train station, is on the eastern side of town, 10 minutes' walk from nám Republiky, the old town square. Tram No 2 goes from the train station to the centre of town and on to the bus station.

There are **left-luggage** offices at both the bus station (per small/large bag 10 Kč/20Kč; 8am-8pm Mon-Fri) and the train station (per small/large bag 10 Kč/20Kč; 24hr).

Information

City Information Centre (378 035 330; www.plzen-city.cz; nám Republiky 41; 10am-6pm Apr-Sep, 10am-5pm Mon-Fri, 10am-3.30pm Sat & Sun Oct-Mar)
Internet Kavárna Aréna (377 220 402; Františkánská 10; per min 0.90Kč; 9am-10pm Mon-Fri, 10am-10pm Sat & Sun) On the first floor; press buzzer for entry.
Main post office (Solní 20; 7am-7pm Mon-Fri, 8am-1pm Sat, 8am-noon Sun) Includes a telephone centre.

Sights

In summer people congregate at the outdoor beer bar in nám Republiky, the broad and sunny old town square, beneath the glowering, Gothic **Church of St Bartholomew** (admission 20Kč; 10am-4pm Wed-Sat, noon-7pm Sun Apr-Dec). Inside the soaring 13th-century structure there's a Gothic Madonna (1390) on the high altar and fine stained-glass windows. On the outside of the church, around the back, is an iron grille – touch the angel and make a wish. You can climb the 102m church **tower** (admission 20Kč; 10am-6pm), the highest in Bohemia, for a great view of the city.

The **Brewery Museum** (377 235 574; Veleslavínova 6; adult/concession 60/30Kč, with guide 100/50Kč; 10am-6pm Apr-Dec, 10am-4pm Jan-Mar) is a block east of the square in an authentic medieval malt house; you can sample the lager in the museum's own bar.

In previous centuries beer was brewed, stored and served in a labyrinth of tunnels beneath the old town. The earliest were probably dug in the 14th century and the latest date from the 19th century; some 500m of passages are now open to the public, and you can take a 30-minute guided tour at the **Plzeň Historical Underground** (377 225 214; Perlová 4; adult/concession 45/25Kč; 9am-5pm Tue-Sun Jun-Sep, Wed-Sun Oct, Nov, Apr & May). The temperature is a constant 10°C, so take a jacket.

The **Great Synagogue** (602 441 943; Sady Pětatřicátníků 11; admission 50Kč; 11am-5pm Sun-Fri), to the west of the old town, is the third largest in the world – only those in Jerusalem and Budapest are bigger – built in the Moorish style in 1892 by the 2000 or so Jews who lived here then. English tours cost 50Kč extra.

True beer aficionados will make the pilgrimage east across the river to the famous **Pilsner Urquell Brewery** (377 062 888; www.beerworld.cz; tour 120Kč; 10am-9pm Mon-Sat, 10am-8pm Sun) to prostrate themselves at the famous twin-arched gate and wail 'We're not worthy! We're not worthy!' One-hour guided tours (with beer tasting) in English or German begin at 12.30pm and 2pm daily; no advance booking needed.

Sleeping

CKM (377 236 393; info@ckmplzen.cz; Dominikánská 1; 9am-6pm Mon-Fri) This travel agency can find you a room in a student hostel in summer (from 150Kč per person).

Ubytovna TJ Lokomotiva (377 448 041; info@tjloko-plzen.cz; Úslavská 75; r per person 150Kč) This clean and comfortable sports centre hostel offers two- to four-bed rooms with shared facilities, just ten minutes' walk south of the train station.

Pension v Solní (377 236 652; www.volny.cz/pensolni; Solní 8; s/d 600/1020Kč) Set in a pleasant little town house close to the main square, this cosy *pension* has only three rooms, so bookings are essential.

Hotel Slovan (377 227 256; http://hotelslovan.pilsen.cz; Smetanovy sady 1; s/d 530/810Kč; P) This is

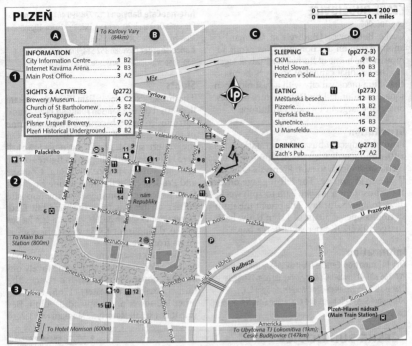

PLZEŇ

0 ———— 200 m
0 ———— 0.1 miles

INFORMATION	
City Information Centre................1	B2
Internet Kavárna Aréna................2	B3
Main Post Office...........................3	A2

SIGHTS & ACTIVITIES	(p272)
Brewery Museum..........................4	C2
Church of St Bartholomew............5	B2
Great Synagogue..........................6	A2
Pilsner Urquell Brewery................7	D2
Plzeň Historical Underground......8	B2

SLEEPING	(pp272-3)
CKM...9	B2
Hotel Slovan...............................10	B3
Penzion v Solní..........................11	B2

EATING	(p273)
Měšťanská beseda......................12	B3
Pizzerie......................................13	B2
Plzeňská bašta............................14	B2
Slunečnice.................................15	B3
U Mansfeldu..............................16	B2

DRINKING	(p273)
Zach's Pub.................................17	A2

a grand old hotel with a magnificent central stairway dating from the 1890s. The cheaper rooms are a bit tired-looking, but you can splurge on posher rooms with bath & TV for 1450/2100Kč.

Hotel Morrison (☎ 377 370 952; www.morrison.cz; Thámova 9; s/d 700/1000Kč; **P**) The Morrison is a small, family-friendly hotel in a renovated town house 1km south of the city centre. All rooms are en suite with TV.

Eating & Drinking
Plzeňská bašta (☎ 377 237 262; Riegrova 5; mains 60-80Kč; ☺ 10.30am-midnight Mon-Sat, 10.30am-10pm Sun) This local institution, supported by a network of ancient wood beams, has oodles of personality, lashings of beer and big plates of meaty, local grub.

U Mansfeldu (☎ 377 333 844; Dřevěna 9; mains 65-185Kč; ☺ 11am-11pm Mon-Sat, 11am-9pm Sun; ☒) A busy modern pub with lots of gleaming copper and young, efficient staff, U Mansfeldu serves up hearty Bohemian fodder washed down with Pilsner Urquell.

Měšťanská beseda (☎ 378 037 922; Kopeckého sady 13; mains 80-150Kč; ☺ 9am-10pm) Enjoy a cof-

fee or a light meal in elegant Art Nouveau surroundings in this renovated cultural centre. There's live classical music from 6pm to 9pm on Tuesdays.

You can get decent pizzas at **Pizzerie** (☎ 377 237 965; Solní 9; pizza 65Kč; ☺ 10am-10pm Mon-Thu, 10am-11pm Fri, 11am-11pm Sat, 11.30am-10pm Sun), and healthy baguettes at **Slunečnice** (☎ 377 236 093; Jungmannova 4; sandwiches 35Kč; ☺ 8am-5pm Mon-Fri, 8am-noon Sat).

You can hear live bands at **Zach's Pub** (☎ 377 223 176; Palackého nám 2; cover 80-150Kč; ☺ 1pm-1am Mon-Thu, 1pm-2am Fri, 5pm-2am Sat, 5pm-midnight Sun), which serves draught Guinness as well as local beers.

Getting There & Away
All international trains from Munich and Nuremberg to Prague stop at Plzeň. There are fast trains from Plzeň to Prague (140Kč, 1½ hours, eight daily) and České Budějovice (162Kč, two hours, five daily).

If you're heading for Karlovy Vary, take a bus (86Kč, 1¾ hours, five daily). There are also express buses to Prague (80Kč, 1½ hours, hourly).

CZECH REPUBLIC

ČESKÉ BUDĚJOVICE

pop 100,000

České Budějovice (Budweis in German) is another stop on the Bohemian beer trail, famous as the home of Budweiser Budvar lager. It's the regional capital of South Bohemia, a charming medieval city with a vast old town square surrounded by 18th-century arcades, one of the largest of its kind in Europe.

Orientation

From the adjacent bus and train stations it's a 10-minute walk west down Lannova třída, then Kanovnická, to nám Přemysla Otakara II, the main square. The left-luggage office at the bus station is open 7am to 7pm weekdays, to 2pm Saturday. The one at the train station is open 2.30am to 11pm daily; both charge 10Kč/20Kč per small/large bag.

Information

City Information Centre (Městské informační centrum; ☎ 386 801 413; infocb@c-budejovice.cz; nám Přemysla Otakara II 1; ✆ 8.30am-6pm Mon-Fri, to 5pm Sat, 10am-4pm Sun) Sells maps and can arrange guides, tickets and accommodation.

Internet Café Babylon (☎ 728 190 461; 5th fl, nám Přemysla Otakara II 30; per min 1Kč; ✆ 10am-10pm Mon-Fri, 1-10pm Sat, 1-9pm Sun)
Kanzelsberger (☎ 386 352 584; Hroznová 17) Bookshop with English-language books upstairs.

Sights

The broad expanse of **Nám Přemysla Otakara II**, centred on the **Samson Fountain** (1727) and surrounded by 18th-century arcades, is one of the largest town squares in Europe. On the western side stands the baroque **town hall** (1731), topped with allegorical figures of the cardinal virtues: Justice, Wisdom, Courage and Prudence. On the hour a tune rings out from its tower. Looming above the opposite corner of the square is the 72m-tall **Black Tower** (adult/concession 20/10Kč; ✆ 10am-6pm Tue-Sun Apr-Oct), dating from 1553, which offers great views from the top.

The streets around the square, especially Česká, are lined with some lovely old burgher houses. West near the river is the former **Dominican monastery** (1265) with another tall tower and a splendid pulpit. Beside it is a small **Motorcycle Museum** (☎ 387 200

ČESKÉ BUDĚJOVICE

0 — 200 m
0 — 0.1 miles

INFORMATION	
City Information Centre	1 A2
Internet Café Babylon	2 B2
Kanzelsberger	3 B2

SIGHTS & ACTIVITIES	(pp274-5)
Black Tower	4 B2
Cathedral of St Nicholas	5 B2
Dominican Monastery	6 A2
Motorcycle Museum	7 A2
Museum of South Bohemia	8 B3
Rabenštejn Tower	9 A1
Samson Fountain	10 B2
Town Hall	(see 1)

SLEEPING ⌂	(p275)
AT Pension	11 B3
CKM	12 D2
Hotel Klika	13 A2
Penzión Centrum	14 B2
Penzión Centrum	15 A2

EATING ⊓	(p275)
Café de Columbia	16 A2
Hong Kong Restaurant	17 B3
Pizzeria U Dvou Domů	18 A2
Restaurace Budvarka	19 B2

DRINKING ⊡⊡	(p275)
Caffè Bar Piccolo	20 B2
Singer Pub	21 A2

TRANSPORT	(pp275-6)
Bus Station	22 D2

849; Piaristické nám; adult/concession 40/20Kč; 9am-5pm Wed-Sun), which has a fine collection of Czech Jawas and a handful of wonderful WWII Harley-Davidsons. The **Museum of South Bohemia** (Jihočeské muzeum; ☎ 387 929 328; adult/concession 45/10Kč; 9am-12.30pm & 1-5.30pm Tue-Sun), with its extensive collection on history, books, coins, weapons and wildlife, is southeast of the centre.

Just as beer from Pilsen (see Plzeň p271) is called Pilsner, so beer from Budweis is called **Budweiser**. Indeed, the founders of US brewer Anheuser-Busch chose the brand name Budweiser in 1876 because it was synonymous with good beer. The name has been used by both breweries since the late 19th century, and a century-long legal tussle over the brand name continues. However, there's no contest as to which beer is superior; one taste of Budvar and you'll be an instant convert. True.

The **Budweiser Budvar Brewery** (☎ 387 705 341; www.budvar.cz; cnr Pražská & K Světlé; tour Mon-Fri 70Kč, Sat & Sun 100Kč; 9am-5pm) is 3km north of the main square. Group tours run throughout the day and the 2pm tour (Monday to Friday only) is open to individual travellers; beer tasting costs 22Kč extra. The brewery's **beer hall** is open 10am to 10pm daily.

Sleeping

The City Information Centre and the youth travel agency **CKM** (☎ 386 351 270; Lannova třída 63; 9am-5pm Mon-Thu, to 3.30pm Fri) can arrange dorm accommodation from 120Kč per person.

Pension U výstaviště (☎ 387 240 148; trpakdl@email.cz; U výstaviště 17; r per person 240Kč; P) The closest thing to a travellers hostel is this student accommodation block. It's 30 minutes from the city centre on bus No 1 from outside the bus station to the fifth stop (U parku); the *pension* is about 100m up the street (Čajkovského) on the right.

Kolej jihočeské univerzity (☎ 387 774 201; Studentská 13-19; d 350Kč; P) Another student block, 2km west of the centre, offering beds from July to September.

Small private *pensions* are a better deal than hotels.

AT Pension (☎ 387 312 529; Dukelská 15; s/d 500/800Kč) It doesn't look like the dowdy pink décor has been updated since 1910 (the date over the door), but this homely *pension* gets high marks for friendliness.

Penzión Centrum (☎ 386 352 030; Na Mlýnské stoce 6; d 850Kč) Just off Kanovnická, Penzión Centrum has been recommended by readers.

Penzión Centrum (☎ 387 311 801; penzion_restaurant@centrum.cz; Biskupská 3; s/d 800/1000Kč) Namesake (but no relation), this Penzión Centrum has also been recommended by readers.

Hotel Klika (☎ 387 318 171; www.hotelklika.cz; Hroznová 25; s/d 1450/1950Kč) This newly refurbished place on the river's edge, with traces of the 14th-century walls still visible in the restaurant, stylishly blends old world charm and modern functionality. The rooms, all sanded wood and bright décor, are light and airy.

Eating & Drinking

Pizzeria U Dvou Domů (☎ 777 696 948; Panská 17; pizzas 75-120Kč; 10am-9pm Mon-Fri, 3-9pm Sat) There's not much more to this little place (it seats about eight) than a wood-fired oven, some sublime smells and a man who really knows his pizza.

Café de Columbia (☎ 387 315 915; Česká 30; mains 100-200Kč; 10am-11pm Mon-Sat, 11am-10pm Sun) Despite the Latin American name, this place has a traditional feel with its ochre walls, dark wood beams and Regency-style tables and chairs. There's a solid menu of the steak, pork chop and fish variety, with some speciality dishes like chilli con carne.

Restaurace Budvarka (☎ 387 705 344; Karla IV 8; mains 135-185Kč; 10am-11pm Mon-Sat, to 9pm Sun) This cheerful Czech beer hall is owned by the Budvar brewery, and occasionally lays on a live brass band to add some oompah to your *knedlíky*. It serves tasty traditional South Bohemian and Moravian dishes such as roast duck and fried carp with caraway seed.

If the brewery tour whetted your appetite for the local beer, you can carry on imbibing at the **Singer Pub** (☎ 386 360 186; Česká 55; 11am-11pm), a top place to kick off an evening.

And if all you're after is a cappuccino, the best coffee in town is served at friendly little **Caffé Bar Piccolo** (Ná Mlýnské stoce 9; 7.30am-7pm Mon-Thu, to 10pm Fri & Sat).

Getting There & Away

There are fast trains from České Budějovice to Prague (204Kč, 2½ hours, hourly) and Plzeň (162Kč, two hours, five daily). Heading for Vienna (740Kč, four hours, two daily) you'll have to change at Gmünd, or take a direct train to Linz (375Kč, 2¼ hours, one daily) and change there.

The bus to Brno (210Kč, 3½ to 4½ hours, four daily) travels via Telč. Twice a week there's a direct Eurolines bus to Linz (400Kč, 2½ hours) and Salzburg (700Kč, 4½ hours) in Austria.

HLUBOKÁ NAD VLTAVOU

A crow pecking the eyes from a severed Turks' head – the grisly emblem of the Schwarzenberg family – may be a recurrent motif in the décor of Hluboká nad Vltavou's neo-Gothic **chateau** (☎ 387 967 045; 9am-6pm Jul & Aug, 9am-6pm Tue-Sun May-Jun, 9am-5.30pm Apr, Sep & Oct), but it is hard to imagine an image more at odds with the building's overtly romantic theme. The castle was rebuilt by the Schwarzenberg family between 1841 and 1871 with a profusion of turrets and crenellations supposedly inspired by England's Windsor Castle; the palace's 144 rooms remained in use right up to WWII. There are four guided tours to choose from; **Tour I** (adult/concession with an English-speaking guide 150/80Kč) takes in the main attractions. The surrounding park is open throughout the year. The **information centre** (☎ 387 966 164; Masarykova 35), opposite the church, can help with accommodation.

Hluboká is 10km north of České Budějovice, and is easily accessible by bus (10Kč, 20 minutes, two hourly).

ČESKÝ KRUMLOV

pop 14,600

Český Krumlov, in Bohemia's deep south, is one of the most picturesque towns in Europe. It's a little like Prague in miniature – it has a stunning castle above the Vltava River, an old town square, Renaissance and baroque architecture, and hordes of tourists milling through the streets, but all on a smaller scale; you can walk from one side of town to the other in 10 minutes. There are plenty of lively bars and riverside picnic spots – in summer it's a popular hang-out for backpackers. It can be a magical place in winter, though, when the crowds are gone and the castle is blanketed in snow.

Český Krumlov's original Gothic border fortress was rebuilt as a huge Renaissance chateau by Italian architects in the 16th century. Second only to Prague Castle in size and splendour, it was the seat of the lords of Rožmberk, who possessed the largest landed estate in Bohemia. The town's appearance has remained almost unchanged since the 18th century; in 1992 it was added to Unesco's World Heritage List.

Orientation

The bus station is east of the town centre, but if you're arriving from České Budějovice get off at the Špičák bus stop (the first in the town centre, just after you pass beneath a road bridge). The train station is 1.5km north of the town centre; bus Nos 1, 2 and 3 go from the station to the Špičák bus stop. From the bridge over the main road beside the bus stop, Latrán leads south into town.

Don't take a car into the centre of the old town; use one of the car parks around the perimeter. The one on Chvalšinská, north of the old town, is the most convenient for the castle.

Information

Infocentrum (☎ 380 704 622; www.ckrumlov.cz; nám Svornosti 2; 9am-8pm Jul & Aug, to 7pm Jun & Sep, to 6pm Apr, May & Oct, to 5pm Nov-Mar) Official tourism, transport and accommodation information, books and maps. Internet access 5Kč per 5 minutes.

Unios Tourist Service (☎ 380 712 219; www.unios.cz; Castle Courtyard; 9am-6pm, Internet café to 9pm) Tourist information, accommodation booking and Internet café (1Kč per minute).

Sights

The old town is almost encircled by a looping bend of the Vltava River, watched over by **Český Krumlov Castle** (☎ 380 704 721; 9am-6pm Tue-Sun Jun-Aug, to 5pm Apr, May, Sep & Oct) sprawling along a ridge above the west bank, its ornately decorated fairytale **Round Tower** (30/20Kč) looking like a space rocket designed by Hans Christian Andersen. There are three different guided tours on offer: **Tour I** (adult/concession 150/80Kč) takes in the over-the-top Renaissance and baroque apartments that the aristocratic Rožmberk and Schwarzenberg families once called home; **Tour II** (adult/concession 140/70Kč) concentrates on the Schwarzenbergs and visits the apartments used by the family in the 19th century; the **Theatre Tour** (adult/concession 180/90Kč) explores the chateau's remarkable rococo theatre, complete with original stage machinery. You can wander through the courtyards and gardens for free.

The path beyond the fourth courtyard leads across **Most ná Pláštia**, a bridge with a spectacular view, and up to the castle gardens. A ramp to the right leads to the **former**

ČESKÝ KRUMLOV

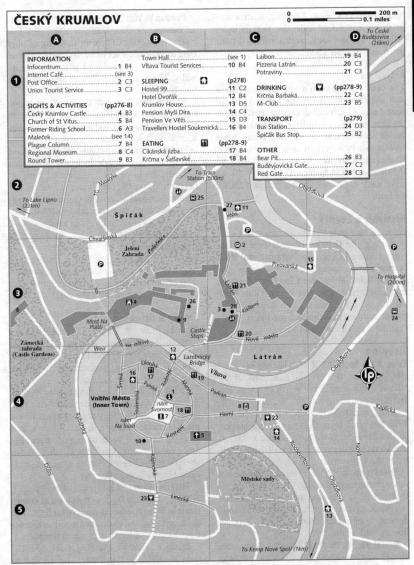

INFORMATION	
Infocentrum	1 B4
Internet Café	(see 3)
Post Office	2 C3
Unios Tourist Service	3 C3

SIGHTS & ACTIVITIES	(pp276-8)
Český Krumlov Castle	4 B3
Church of St Vitus	5 B4
Former Riding School	6 A3
Maleček	(see 14)
Plague Column	7 B4
Regional Museum	8 C4
Round Tower	9 B3

Town Hall	(see 1)
Vltava Tourist Services	10 B4

SLEEPING	(p278)
Hostel 99	11 C2
Hotel Dvořák	12 B4
Krumlov House	13 D5
Pension Myší Díra	14 C4
Pension Ve Věži	15 D3
Travellers Hostel Soukenická	16 B4

EATING	(pp278-9)
Cikánská jizba	17 B4
Krčma v Šatlavské	18 B4

Laibon	19 B4
Pizzeria Latrán	20 C3
Potraviny	21 C3

DRINKING	(pp278-9)
Krčma Barbaká	22 C4
M-Club	23 B5

TRANSPORT	(p279)
Bus Station	24 D3
Špičák Bus Stop	25 B2

OTHER	
Bear Pit	26 B3
Budějovická Gate	27 C2
Red Gate	28 C3

riding school, now a restaurant. The relief above the door shows cherubs offering the head and boots of a vanquished Turk – a reference to Adolf von Schwarzenberg who conquered the Turkish fortress of Raab in the 16th century. From here the Italian-style **Zámecká zahrada** (castle gardens) stretch away towards the **Bellarie summer pavilion**.

Across the river is nám Svornosti, the old town square, ringed by pleasant cafés and overlooked by the Gothic **town hall** and a baroque **plague column** (1716). Above the square is the striking Gothic **Church of St Vitus** (1439), and nearby is the **Regional Museum** (☎ 380 711 674; Horní 152; adult/concession 60/30Kč; ⏰ 10am-5pm May-Sep, to 6pm Jul & Aug, 9am-4pm

Tue-Fri, 1-4pm Sat & Sun Apr & Oct-Dec), with a surprisingly interesting collection that includes folk art, archaeology, and a model of the town as it was in 1800.

Activities

The big attraction on a hot summer day is just messing about on the river. You can rent canoes, rafts and rubber rings from various places, including **Maleček** (☎ 380 712 508; Rooseveltova 28; ☒ 9am-5pm); a half-hour splash in a two-person canoe costs 300Kč. **Vltava Tourist Services** (☎ 380 711 988; Kájovská 62; ☒ 9am-noon & 12.30-5pm) rents bikes (320Kč a day) and organises horse riding (250Kč an hour).

Festivals & Events

Infocentrum sells tickets to major festivals, including the **Chamber Music Festival** in late June and early July, the **International Music Festival** (www.czechmusicfestival.com) during August and **Jazz at Summer's End Festival** at the end of August. The **Five-Petalled Rose Festival** in mid-June features two days of street performances, parades and medieval games (expect a small admission fee).

Sleeping

Kemp Nové Spolí (☎ 380 728 305; tent per person 55Kč; ☒ Jun-Aug; ℗) On the east bank of the Vltava River about 2km south of town. The facilities are basic but the management is friendly and the riverside location idyllic. Take bus No 3 from the train or bus station to the Spolí mat. šk. stop (eight a day on weekdays); otherwise it's a half-hour walk from the old town.

Krumlov House (☎ 380 711 935; www.krumlovhostel .com; Rooseveltova 68; dm/d 250/600Kč) This excellent hostel is situated in a peaceful spot overlooking the river, and offers spacious dorms, cooking facilities, a small English library and a laundry.

Hostel 99 (☎ 380 712 812; hostel99@hotmail.com; Věžní 99; dm/d 300/600Kč; 🖳) Laid-back lodgings set in the city walls, with a sunny outdoor terrace, barbecue, laundry and bike hire.

Travellers Hostel Soukenická (☎ 380 711 345; www.travellers.cz; Soukenická 43; dm/d incl breakfast 270/760Kč) The Travellers is a big, brash party place with a lively bar and occasional live music. There's also a beautiful four-bed, self-catering apartment (2000Kč a night) in the attic.

Pension Ve Věži (☎ 380 711 742; info@reality-kolar .cz; Pivovarská 28; d/tr/q 1200/1500/1800Kč; ℗) For character you can't beat this impossibly cute little *pension* set in a fairy-tale medieval round tower, originally a bastion in the city walls. There are only four rooms, so book well ahead.

Pension Myší Díra (☎ 380 712 853; www.cesky krumlov-info.cz; Rooseveltova 28; s/d incl breakfast 1290/1390Kč; ℗) This welcoming *pension* has a great location overlooking the river, and bright, beautiful rooms with lots of pale wood and quirky hand-made furniture; room No 12, with the huge corner bath and naughty decorations on the bed, is our favourite. Deluxe rooms and weekends (June to August) are 300Kč extra, but rates fall by 40% in winter. Breakfast is served in your room.

Hotel Dvořák (☎ 380 711 020; www.dvorakck .genea2000.cz; Radniční 101; s/d 3000/3700Kč; ℗) If you fancy splashing out for a spot of luxury, the Dvořák has plush carpets, studded leather sofas, marble-clad bathrooms and views across the river to the castle.

Eating & Drinking

Cikánská jizba (☎ 380 717 585; Dlouhá 31; mains 70-110Kč; ☒ 3-11pm Mon-Thu, to midnight Fri & Sat) Enjoy hearty Czech and Roma grub in this crowded, convivial, vaulted pub, with live Gypsy music at weekends.

Laibon (☎ 380 728 456; Parkán 105; mains 70-150Kč; ☒ noon-2pm & 6-10pm) One of the town's rare meat-free zones, this snug veg oasis offers great couscous, curry and pasta dishes, and local specialities such as potato pancakes and *halušky* (tiny potato *knedlíky* with sheep's-milk cheese). Has an attractive outdoor terrace beside the river.

Pizzeria Latrán (☎ 380 712 651; Latrán 37; pizza 75-135Kč; ☒ 11am-midnight) Top-notch pizza comes straight from the wood-fired oven here. The drifting aromas of garlic and wood smoke attract locals and tourists in equal numbers.

Krčma v Šatlavské (☎ 380 713 344; Horní 157; mains 100-200Kč; ☒ 11am-11pm) The flickering candlelight, soot-blackened ceiling and a fireplace that takes up half of one wall make this a truly atmospheric medieval cellar restaurant. Pork and beef are barbecued on the open fire, and your wine is served in rustic earthenware beakers.

Self-caterers will find a handy **potraviny** (Latrán 55; ☒ 7am-6pm Mon-Fri, 7am-noon Sat, 9am-3pm Sun) near the castle entrance.

For outdoor boozing sessions with a view, **Krčma Barbakán** (Horní 26; ☿ noon-11pm, to midnight Fri & Sat) has a superb terrace perched high above the river. **M-Club** (cnr Rybářská & Plešivecké schody; ☿ 4pm-2am) offers pounding rock music and a pool table.

Getting There & Away

There are direct buses from Prague to Český Krumlov (140Kč, three hours, seven daily) via České Budějovice; some buses depart from Prague's Ná Knížecí bus station, near Anděl metro, others from Florenc.

Local buses (26Kč, 50 minutes, seven daily) and trains (46Kč, one hour, eight daily) run to České Budějovice, where you can change for onward travel to Brno, Plzeň or Austria.

ŠUMAVA

The Šumava is a range of thickly forested hills stretching for 125km along the border with Austria and Germany; the highest summit is Plechý (1378m), west of Horní Planá. Before 1989 the range was divided by the Iron Curtain, a line of fences, watchtowers, armed guards and dog patrols between Western Europe and the communist East; many Czechs made a bid for freedom by creeping through the forests here in the dead of night. Today the hills are popular for hiking, cycling and cross-country skiing.

The **Povydří trail** along the Vydra (Otter) River in the northern Šumava is one of the most popular walks in the park. It's an easy 7km hike along a deep, forested river valley between Čeňkova Pila and Antýgl, with the Vydra itself running alongside between huge, rounded, granite boulders. Buses run between Sušice and Modrava, stopping at Čeňkova Pila and Antýgl. Most of these places have plenty of accommodation.

Around the peak of **Boubín** (1362m), the 46-hectare *prales* (virgin forest) is the only part of the Šumava forest that is regarded as completely untouched by human activities. The trailhead is 2km northeast of the zastávka Zátoň train stop (not Zátoň town train station) at Kaplice, where there is a car park and a basic camping ground. From here it's an easy 2.5km to U pralesa Lake on a blue and green marked trail. To reach the top of Boubín peak, remain on the blue trail; it's a further 7.5km to the top. To return,

follow the trail southwest to complete the loop. The complete loop should take about five hours.

If you'd rather lie in the sun than sweat up a hill, then head for **Lake Lipno**, a 30km-long reservoir south of Český Krumlov. Known as 'the Czech Riviera', it's lined with camping grounds, swimming areas and water sports centres, and there's even a yacht marina at Lipno nad Vltavou. You can get full details from the Infocentrum in Český Krumlov (see p276).

Getting There & Away

Up to eight trains a day run from České Budějovice and Český Krumlov to Volary (120Kč, three hours), calling at Horní Planá and Nová Pec on Lake Lipno. From May to September, buses cover a similar route (78Kč, two hours).

From Volary, trains continue north to Strakonice via Zátoň (28Kč, 30 minutes, four daily).

The Povydří trail is best approached from Sušice, which can be reached by direct bus from Prague (110Kč, 2½ hours, two daily). Another bus links Sušice with Čeňkova Pila and Antýgl (44Kč, one hour, two or three daily).

ADRŠPACH-TEPLICE ROCKS

The Czech Republic's most bizarre and beautiful scenery lies near up the Polish border, in a protected landscape region known as the Adršpach-Teplice Rocks (Adršpašsko-Teplické skály). Thick layers of stratified sandstone have been eroded and fissured by water and frost to form giant towers and pinnacles riven by deep, narrow chasms. Discovered by mountaineers in the 19th century, the region is still a favourite with rock climbers and hikers. Sandy trails lead through pine-scented forests, loud with the drumming of woodpeckers, and loop among the pinnacles, assisted here and there by steep ladders and flights of stairs.

There are two main clusters of rock formations – **Adršpach Rock Town** (Adršpašské skalní město) and **Teplice Rock Town** (Teplické skalní město) – hence the mouthful of a name. They now comprise a single state nature reserve, about 15km east of Trutnov. At the entrance to each rock town there's a ticket booth (adult/concession 50/20Kč; ☿ 8am-

6pm Apr-Nov) where you can pick up a useful 1:25,000 trail map. Outside the official opening hours you can enter for free.

There's a small **information office** (☎ 491 586 012; www.skalyadrspach.cz; ☼ 8am-12.30pm & 1-5.30pm) near Adršpach train station. In summer the trails are busy and you may have to book accommodation at least a week ahead; in winter (snow lingers as late as mid-April) you'll have this stunning landscape mostly to yourself, though some of the trails may be closed.

If you're pushed for time, walk the green loop trail at Adršpach (1½ hours). It leads through deep mossy ravines ringed by soaring rock towers to the **Great Lookout** (Velké panorama) – a view over serried ranks of sandstone pinnacles rising above a sea of contorted pines – before threading through the **Mouse Hole** (Myší dírá), a vast vertical fissure whose walls are barely shoulder-width apart.

The blue loop trail at Teplice (2½ hours) passes a metal staircase leading strenuously up to **Střmen**, a rock tower once occupied by an outlaw's timber castle, before continuing through the area's most spectacular pinnacles to the chilly ravine of **Siberia** (Sibiř). An excellent day hike (four to five hours) which takes in all the region's highlights links the head of the Teplice trail, beyond Sibiř, to Adršpach via the **Wolf Gorge** (Vlčí rokle). You can return from Adršpach to Teplice by walking along the road (one hour) or you can catch a train (10 minutes).

Sleeping & Eating

Campers can choose between **Autokemping Bučnice** (☎ 491 581 387; kubikovi.adrspach@tiscali.cz; camp sites 40Kč plus per person/car 40/40Kč; ☼ May-Sep), about 300m northwest of Teplice nad Metují-skály train station, and the more basic **Camp Kamenec** (☎ 604 989 353; www.camp .adrspach.cz; tent plus 2 people 58Kč, car 30Kč; ☼ May-Sep), 500m west of Teplice nad Metují-zastávka train station.

Just outside the entrance to Teplice Rock Town you will find the friendly **Penzión U Skalního potoka** (☎ 491 581 317; www.penzion .adrspach.cz/en; r per person 250-290Kč; Ⓟ), a hikers' favourite, and the attractive, modern **Pension Skály** (☎ 491 581 174; pension.skaly@email .cz; bed per person 550Kč; ✗) with comfortable en suite rooms.

At Adršpach, the cosy little **Hotel Lesní zátiší** (☎ 491 586 202; grofit@mbox.vol.cz; 800/1400/1800Kč; Ⓟ) sits right at the start of the rocks trail.

Getting There & Away

There are direct buses from Prague's Černý Most metro station to Trutnov (125Kč, 2¾ hours, hourly).

Single-car trains toot and rattle their way along the toytown railway line from Trutnov to Adršpach (40Kč, one hour) and Teplice nad Metují (46Kč, 1¼ hours, eight daily). There are three stations with the latter name – get off at the first (Teplice nad Metují-skály) for the rocks and Autokemping Bučnice, the second (Teplice nad Metují-zastávka) for the town and Camp Kamenec.

There are also frequent trains from Teplice nad Metují station to Týniště nad Orlicí (76Kč, 1½ hours, eight daily) where you can pick up the early evening train to Wrocław in Poland (224Kč, 4¼ hours, one daily).

MORAVIA

BRNO
pop 387,200

Buzzing, bustling Brno – capital of Moravia, and the Czech Republic's second city – is a good place to experience Czech city living away from the tourist crowds of Prague. It's a modern place – except for the largely 18th- and 19th-century old town – with a thriving cultural scene, some interesting historical sights and many museums and art galleries.

Orientation

Brno hlavní nádraží (the **main train station**) is at the southern edge of the old town, with a major tram stop outside. Opposite the station is the beginning of Masarykova which leads north to triangular nám Svobody, the city's main square. The **main bus station** (Brno ÚAN Zvonařka) is 800m south of the train station, beyond Tesco. To get there, go through the pedestrian tunnel under the train tracks, then follow the crowd along the elevated walkway.

There are two **left-luggage** (per small/large bag 15/30Kč) offices in the train station – one upstairs (☼ 24hr) opposite the lockers, and another downstairs (☼ 5am to 11pm) by the

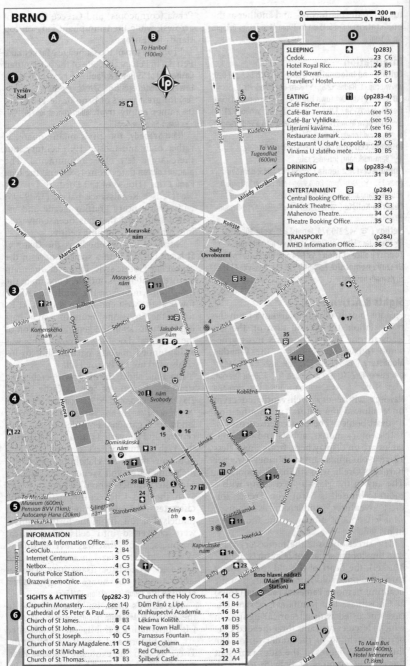

BRNO

0 ——— 200 m
0 ——— 0.1 miles

SLEEPING	(p283)
Čedok..........................23	C6
Hotel Royal Ricc.............24	B5
Hotel Slovan..................25	B1
Travellers' Hostel...........26	C4

EATING	(pp283-4)
Café Fischer..................27	B5
Café-Bar Terraza...........(see 15)	
Café-Bar Vyhlídka.........(see 15)	
Literární kavárna...........(see 16)	
Restaurace Jarmark........28	B5
Restaurant U císaře Leopolda 29	C5
Vinárna U zlatého meče...30	B5

DRINKING	(pp283-4)
Livingstone...................31	B4

ENTERTAINMENT	(p284)
Central Booking Office.....32	B3
Janáček Theatre.............33	C3
Mahenovo Theatre..........34	C4
Theatre Booking Office....35	C3

TRANSPORT	(p284)
MHD Information Office.........36	C5

INFORMATION	
Culture & Information Office.....1	B5
GeoClub.............................2	B4
Internet Centrum..................3	C5
Netbox...............................4	C3
Tourist Police Station............5	C1
Úrazová nemocnice...............6	D3

SIGHTS & ACTIVITIES	(pp282-3)
Capuchin Monastery.............(see 14)	
Cathedral of SS Peter & Paul....7	B6
Church of St James................8	B3
Church of St John.................9	C4
Church of St Joseph..............10	C5
Church of St Mary Magdalene..11	C5
Church of St Michael.............12	B5
Church of St Thomas.............13	B3

Church of the Holy Cross........14	C5
Dům Pánů z Lípé..................15	B4
Knihkupectví Academia..........16	B4
Lékárna Koliště...................17	D3
New Town Hall.....................18	B5
Parnassus Fountain...............19	B5
Plague Column.....................20	B4
Red Church.........................21	A3
Špilberk Castle....................22	A4

To Haribol
(100m)

To Vila
Tugendhat
(600m)

Tyršův
Sad

Moravské
nám

Sady
Osvobození

Moravské
nám

Jakubské
nám

Komenského
nám

nám
Svobody

Dominikánská
nám

To Mendel
Museum (600m);
Pension BVV (1km);
Autocamp Hana (20km)

Zelný
trh

Kapucínské
nám

Brno hlavní nádraží
(Main Train
Station)

To Main Bus
Station (400m);
Hotel Interservis
(1.8km)

tunnel to the platforms – and another at the bus station (⏲ 5.15am to 10pm Mon-Fri, to 6.15pm Sat & Sun).

Information

Culture and Information Office (KIC; ☎ 542 211 090; www.brno.cz; Radnická 8; ⏲ 8am-6pm Mon-Fri, to 5pm Sat & Sun) In the Old Town Hall. Can book accommodation.

GeoClub (☎ 542 129 571; Pasaž KB, nám Svobody 21; ⏲ 9am-6pm Mon-Fri, 9am-noon Sat) Sells a wide range of maps and Lonely Planet guides.

Internet Centrum (Masarykova 22; per hr 40Kč; ⏲ 8am-midnight) Internet café.

Knihupectví Academia (☎ 542 217 945; nám Svobody 13; ⏲ 9am-7pm) Bookshop with fiction in English and German, and pleasant café upstairs.

Lékárna Koliště (☎ 545 424 811; Koliště 47) 24-hour pharmacy.

Netbox (☎ 542 210 174; Jezuitská 3; per hr 50Kč; ⏲ 9am-1am Mon-Sat, 2pm-1am Sun) Internet café.

Tourist police station (☎ 974 626 100; Bartošová 1)

Úrazová nemocnice (☎ 545 538 111; Ponávka 6) The city's main hospital.

Sights & Activities

Heading north along Masarykova from the train station, the second turn on the left leads to one of the country's most gruesome tourist attractions – the **Capuchin Monastery** (☎ 542 213 232; Kapucínské nám 5; adult/concession 40/20Kč; ⏲ 9am-noon & 2-4.30pm Tue-Sat, 11am-11.45am & 2-4.30pm Sun Feb-mid Dec, Mon also May-Sep), whose dry, well-ventilated crypt once allowed the natural mummification of dead bodies. The desiccated corpses of 18th-century monks, abbots and local notables are on display here, from a nameless 12-year-old ministrant to chimney-sweeper Barnabas Orelli, who still has his boots on. The guy in the glass-topped coffin with a room to himself is Baron von Trenck soldier: adventurer, gambler and womaniser, who left pots of money to the monastery in his will.

The street opposite the monastery leads into the sloping square of **Zelný trh** (Cabbage Market), the heart of the old town, where carp were once sold from the waters of the beautiful baroque **Parnassus Fountain** (1695) at Christmas. The fountain is a symbolic cave encrusted with allegorical figures, in which Hercules restrains three-headed Cerberus, watchdog of the underworld. The three female figures at the sides represent the ancient empires of Babylon (crown),

Persia (cornucopia) and Greece (quiver of arrows), while the triumphant lady on top stands for Europe.

From the top of the Cabbage Market take Petrská to Petrov Hill, site of the gargantuan **Cathedral of SS Peter & Paul**. You can climb the **tower** (adult/concession 25/20Kč; ⏲ 10am-5pm Tue-Sun) for great views of Brno or descend into its rather empty **crypt** (adult/concession 15/10Kč; ⏲ 10am-5pm Tue-Sun).

Nám Svobody, the city's main square, is rather drab and mostly 19th century, but there are a few older monuments. The **plague column** dates from 1680, and the **Dům Pánů z Lipé** (House of the Lords of Lipá) at No 17, is a Renaissance palace (1589–96) with 19th-century graffito façade and arcaded courtyard that has been converted into a boutique shopping centre.

North of nám Svobody is the **Church of St James** (1473), with a soaring nave in the purest late Gothic style. However, the main feature of interest is outside. Look up at the first-floor window on the south side of the tower at the west end of the church. At its top is the tiny stone figure of a man baring his buttocks in the general direction of the cathedral. Local legend claims this was a disgruntled mason's parting shot to his rivals working on Petrov Hill.

On a hill above the old town perches the sinister silhouette of **Špilberk Castle** (☎ 542 215 012; www.spilberk.cz; ⏲ 9am-6pm May-Sep, to 5pm Oct-Apr, closed Mon Sep-Jun), surrounded by lovely landscaped gardens. Founded in the 13th century and converted into a citadel during the 17th century, it served until 1855 as a notorious prison for Habsburg opponents, including Baron von Trenck (see Capuchin Monastery earlier) who died here in 1749.

In the late 18th century parts of the **casemates** – the labyrinthine, brick-vaulted tunnels that run within the fortifications – were converted into cells for political prisoners, a role that was revived during WWII when the Nazis incarcerated – and executed – Czech partisans here. The restored tunnels now house a creepy **museum of prison life** (adult/concession 30/15Kč).

The castle's main building is home to the **Brno City Museum** (adult/concession 70/35Kč), with fascinating exhibits on Renaissance art, city history and modern architecture. There is also an exquisite **Baroque Pharmacy** (adult/concession 20/10Kč; ⏲ 9am-6pm Tue-Sun

May-Sep), dating from the mid-18th century and rescued from a former convent hospital, and **lookout tower** (adult/concession 20/10Kč) with a superb view – you can pick out the white limestone crags of Mikulov (p287) on the southern horizon. A combined ticket (adult/concession 90/45Kč) allows admission to casemates, museum and tower.

Gregor Mendel (1822–84), the Augustinian monk whose studies of peas and bees at Brno's Abbey of St Thomas established the modern science of genetics, is commemorated in the excellent **Mendel Museum** (☎ 543 424 043; www.mendel-museum.org; Mendlovo nám 1; adult/concession 80/40Kč; ☪ 10am-6pm, closed Mon & Tue Nov-Apr), housed in the Abbey itself, just west of town. Mendel's achievements are clearly explained, and complemented by works of contemporary art on related themes, including a giant hanging mobile of colourful agate discs showing the hereditary transmission of Huntington's disease. In the garden are the brick foundations of the greenhouse where Mendel tended his pea plants. Brno has many other museums and art galleries – get details from the Culture and Information Office.

Fans of modern architecture will love Brno, which has many examples of cubist, functionalist and internationalist styles. Finest of all is the functionalist **Vila Tugendhat** (☎ 545 212 118; Černopolní 45; tours adult/ concession 80/40Kč; ☪ 10am-6pm Wed-Sun), northeast of town, designed by Mies van der Rohe in 1930. It's best to ring the Vila and book a tour in advance.

Festivals & Events
The big event on Brno's sporting calendar is August's **Motorcycle Grand Prix** (www .motograndprix.com; admission 490Kč), when the city packs out with petrol heads. The race circuit is just off the D1 road to Prague, 10km west of Brno.

Sleeping
Čedok (☎ 542 321 267; Nádražní 10/12; ☪ 9am-5pm Mon-Fri, 9am-noon Sat) Čedok can arrange accommodation in student dormitories during July and August, and private rooms from 550Kč per person per night. Most are far from the centre, but can easily be reached on public transport.

Autocamp Hana (☎ 549 420 331; www.hana .veverskabityska.cz; Veverská bítýška; camp sites 40-60Kč

plus per person/car 80/60Kč; ☪ May-Sep) Attractive camping ground at the northwestern end of Brněnska přehrada Lake, about 20km northwest of the city centre. From the train station take tram No 1 westbound to the Prístaviště stop, then bus 303 to Veverská bítýška. In summer you can also take a boat along the lake from Prístaviště.

Hotel Interservis (☎ 545 234 232; Lomená 48; r per person 225Kč) South of the centre, this HI-listed student hostel rents beds in double rooms. Take tram No 12 eastbound from the train station to the end of the line, go through the underpass and continue south on the main road, then turn left along Pompova.

Travellers' Hostel (☎ 542 213 573; www.travellers .cz; Jánská 22; dm incl breakfast 270Kč; ☪ Jul & Aug) Set in a grand old building in the heart of the old town, this place provides the most central cheap beds in the city.

Pension BVV (☎ 541 159 167; praskova@c-box.cz; Hlinky 28A; s/d incl breakfast 750/980Kč) The extra walk (it's 1.5km west of the centre) is well rewarded at this three-star place, where comfy rooms, perma-smile service and hearty breakfasts come as standard.

Hotel Slovan (☎ 541 321 207; www.hotelslovan.cz; Lidická 23; s/d 1200/1600Kč; Ⓟ) A business hotel offering plain but pleasant-enough rooms with TV and private bathroom, just north of the centre. Rates can double during the Grand Prix and trade fairs.

Hotel Royal Ricc (☎ 542 219 262; www.romantic hotels.cz; Starobrněnská 10; s/d 3200/3500Kč; Ⓟ) Brno's top choice for a romantic getaway, the Ricc is a luxurious Renaissance palace with stone vaults, timber ceilings, and the odd antique scattered here and there. There's also a restaurant, wine bar and summer terrace.

Eating & Drinking
Restaurace Jarmark (☎ 543 237 320; Mečova 2; mains 60Kč; ☪ 8.30am-11pm) On the first floor of the Velký Špalíček shopping centre, this is a cheerful cafeteria-style place serving homemade pastas, fresh salads (both fruit and vegetable), sandwiches, cakes and tarts.

Haribol (☎ 545 215 636; Lužanecká 4; mains 50-90Kč; ☪ 11am-4pm Mon-Fri) A basic, Hare Krishna–run restaurant north of town that dishes up wholesome vegetarian food, often with an Indian flavour.

Vinárna U zlatého meče (☎ 542 211 198; Mečova 3; mains 60-135Kč; ☪ 9am-midnight) 'At The Golden Sword' is a pleasant place to sample a bottle of local wine with some classic Moravian dishes; it has outdoor tables in summer with a view of St Michael's Church.

Restaurant U císaře Leopolda (☎ 542 516 606; Orlí 3; mains 85-165Kč; ☾ 11am-11pm Mon-Thu, 11am-midnight Fri & Sat, noon-10pm Sun) A cosy, brick-vaulted cellar restaurant with crisp table linen, smartly aproned waiters and a menu of hearty Italian dishes.

Livingstone (☎ 542 210 090; Dominikánská nám 5; ☾ noon-1am) Hidden away through an archway, this raucous bar has Irish pub-style décor complemented by a tank of piranhas, a set of Andy Warhol–themed Laughing Cow prints and a glitter globe. It tends to fill up late.

Café-Bar Vyhlídka (☎ 602 739 953; nám Svobody 17; ☾ 10am-2am Mon-Thu, to 4am Fri, 1pm-4am Sat, ·1pm-2am Sun) is a hipper-than-hip style bar on the 5th floor of the renovated Dům Pánů z Lipé, with regular DJ nights. Upstairs on the 6th floor is **Café-Bar Terraza** (☾ 10am-11pm), which has a brilliant roof terrace with views of the castle over the rooftops.

For a quiet coffee while you read the paper, try stylish **Café Fischer** (☎ 542 221 880; Masarykova 8-10; ☾ 8am-10pm Mon-Fri, from 9am Sat, from 10am Sun) or the peaceful **Literární kavárna** (Literary Café; nám Svobody 13; ☾ 9am-7pm) in the Knihupectví Academia (p282).

Entertainment

Brno has an excellent theatre and classical music scene – the tickets aren't cornered by scalpers and profiteers as they are in Prague. However, you are expected to dress up a bit for a concert. You can find entertainment listings (mostly in Czech) in the monthly freesheet *Metropolis* (www.netpolis.cz, in Czech) and in the monthly booklet *Kam v Brne* (Where in Brno; www.kamvbrne.cz, in Czech; 30Kč), both of which are available in bookshops and from the Culture and Information Office.

Theatre Booking Office (předprodej; ☎ 542 321 285; Dvořákova 11; ☾ 8am-5.30pm Mon-Fri, 9am-noon Sat) You can buy theatre tickets at this office behind the Mahenovo Theatre.

Central Booking Office (Centrální předprodej; ☎ 542 210 863; Běhounská 17; ☾ 9am-1pm & 2-6pm Mon-Fri) This office sells tickets to rock, folk and classical concerts at a variety of venues.

Janáček Theatre (Janáčkovo divadlo; Sady Osvobození) Opera and ballet are performed at the modern theatre, named after the composer Leoš Janáček, who spent much of his life in Brno.

Mahenovo Theatre (Mahenovo divadlo; Dvořákovo 11) The neobaroque Mahenovo Theatre, a beautifully decorated old-style theatre in an 1882 building designed by the famous Viennese theatrical architects Fellner and Hellmer, presents classical drama in Czech and operettas.

Getting There & Away

There are frequent buses from Brno to Prague (150Kč, 2½ hours, hourly) and Bratislava (125Kč, 2¼ hours, hourly). Buses to Vienna (350Kč, 2½ hours, two daily) depart from station No 20 at the bus station.

There are trains to Prague (160Kč, three hours) every two hours. Direct Eurocity trains from Brno to Vienna (575Kč, 1¾ hours, five daily) arrive at Vienna's Süd-bahnhof.

Getting Around

You can buy public transport tickets from tram-stop vending machines, hotels, newsstands, and the **MHD Information Office** (Novobranská 18; ☾ 6am-6pm Mon-Fri, 8am-3.30pm Sat). Tickets valid for 40/60 minutes cost 13/19Kč, and allow unlimited transfers; 24-hour tickets are 50Kč. There's also a 10-minute no-transfer ticket (8Kč).

You can order a cab from **City Taxis** (☎ 542 321 321).

Around Brno
SLAVKOV U BRNA

Slavkov u Brna is better known to history by its Austrian name – **Austerlitz**. On 2 December 1805 the notorious Battle of the Three Emperors was fought over the open, rolling countryside between Brno and Slavkov, where Napoleon Bonaparte's Grande Armée defeated the combined forces of Emperor Franz I (Austria) and Tsar Alexander I (Russia). The battle was decided at **Pracký kopec**, a hill 12km west of Slavkov, marked by the monumental **Cairn of Peace** (Mohyla míru; adult/concession 40/20Kč; ☾ 9am-6pm Jul-Aug, to 5pm May, Jun & Sep, 9am-5pm Tue-Sun Apr, 9am-3.30pm Tue-Sun Oct-Mar) and a small museum detailing the horrors of the battlefield, which claimed 20,000 lives.

Reenactments of the battle take place each year, on or around the anniversary, with a huge commemorative event on 2 to 4 December 2005, the 200th anniversary (www.austerlitz2005.com).

Pracký kopec is awkward to reach by public transport. Take a local train from Brno to Ponětovice (28Kč, 25 minutes, 10 daily), and walk 3.5km southeast through Prace.

MORAVIAN KARST

The limestone plateau of the Moravian Karst (Moravský kras), 20km north of Brno, is a speleologist's delight, riddled with caves and canyons carved by the sub-terranean Punkva River. There's a car park at Skalní Mlýn, at the end of the public road from Blansko, with an information desk and ticket office. A 'tourist train' (adult/concession 40/30Kč return) shuttles back and forth along the 1.5km between the car park and the cave entrance, or you can walk there in 20 minutes.

The first part of the tour through the famous **Punkva Caves** (Punkevní jeskyně; ☎ 516 413 575; www.cavemk.cz; adult/concession 100/50Kč; ⏰ 10am-3.50pm Mon, 8.20am-3.50pm Tue-Sun Apr-Sep, to 5pm daily Jul & Aug, 8.40am-2pm Tue-Sun Oct-Mar) involves an amazing 1km walk through caverns draped with stalactites and stalag-mites before you emerge, blinking, at the bottom of the Macocha Abyss. You then board a small, electric-powered boat for a cruise along the underground Punkva River back to the entrance.

At weekends and in July and August tick-ets for cave tours can sell out up to a week in advance, so book well ahead. The tour is wheelchair accessible.

Just beyond the Punkva Caves entrance a cable car (50/40Kč return, 70/50Kč com-bined tourist train and cable-car ticket) will whisk you to the upper rim of the spectacular **Macocha Abyss**, a dizzying 140m-deep sinkhole. Or if that seems too lazy, you can hike to the top on a blue-marked trail (2km).

The comfortable **Hotel Skalní Mlýn** (☎ 516 418 113; www.smk.cz; mains 60-150Kč; s/d 890/1200Kč; Ⓟ) is right beside the car park. Near the top of the Macocha Abyss is **Chata Macocha** (mains 50Kč; dm 230Kč), a basic hikers' hostel and restaurant; book through Hotel Skalní Mlýn.

From Brno there are frequent trains to Blansko (34Kč, 30 minutes, hourly). Buses depart from Blansko bus station (across the bridge from the train station) to Skalní Mlýn (12Kč, 15 minutes, five daily Apr-Sep). Check times at the Brno Culture and Information Office before setting off. You can also hike an 8km trail from Blansko to Skalní Mlýn (two hours).

MORAVSKÝ KRUMLOV

If you have been impressed by the works of Art Nouveau artist Alfons Mucha in Prague's Municipal House (p251) and Mucha Museum (p252), then you might want to visit this obscure little town near Brno where his greatest achievement is on display (Mucha was born in the nearby village of Ivančice). The **Slav Epic** (Slovan-ská epopej; ☎ 515 322 789; adult/concession 50/25Kč; ⏰ 9am-noon & 1-4pm Tue-Sun Apr-Oct, to 5pm Jul & Aug), painted between 1919 and 1926, is housed in a slightly moth-eaten Re-naissance chateau located 300m off the main square, the only venue big enough to accommodate it. Twenty monumental canvases – total area around 0.5 sq km – depict events from Slavic history and mythology. Though different from the Art Nouveau style of the artist's famous Paris posters, these canvases retain the same mythic, romanticised quality, full of wild-eyed priests, medieval pageantry and battlefield carnage, all rendered in sym-bolic shades; in the artist's own words, 'black is the colour of bondage, blue is the past, yellow the joyous present, orange the glorious future'.

Moravský Krumlov lies 40km southwest of Brno. There are frequent local trains from Brno's hlavní nádraží to Moravský Krumlov (46Kč, 50 minutes, 10 daily); it's a 2.5km walk west from the station to the chateau.

TELČ
pop 6000

Telč is a quiet and pretty town, a good place to relax by the waterside with a book and a glass of wine. The old town, ringed by medi-eval fish ponds and unspoilt by modern buildings, is a Unesco World Heritage Site.

The bus and train stations are a few hun-dred metres apart on the eastern side of town. A 10-minute walk along Masarykova takes you to nám Zachariáše z Hradce, the old town square. A left-luggage service is available at the train station 24 hours a day.

CZECH REPUBLIC

The **information office** (☎ 567 243 145; nám Zachariáše z Hradce 10; www.telc-etc.cz; ☺ 8am-5pm Mon-Fri, 11am-4pm Sat & Sun) is in the town hall; you can check email here (1Kč per minute).

Sights

In a country famed for its picturesque old town squares, Telč's sprawling, cobble-stoned **nám Zachariáše z Hradce**, ringed with Gothic arcades and elegant Renaissance façades, out-picturesques the lot. In the evening, when the tour groups have gone, it's a peaceful, magical place.

At the square's northwestern end is the town's greatest monument, the **Water Chateau** (☎ 567 243 821; tours in Czech adult/concession 70/35Kč, in English adult/concession 140/70Kč; ☺ 9am-11.45am & 1-5pm Tue-Sun May-Aug, to 4pm Apr, Sep & Oct), a jewel of Renaissance architecture. Tour A takes you through some of the finest Renaissance halls in the country, including a ballroom (the Golden Room) with a coffered wooden ceiling adorned with 30 gilded reliefs of mythical figures. Tour B visits the private apartments inhabited by the aristocratic owners until 1945.

At the entrance to the castle you can peer into the sparkly **Chapel of All Saints**, where trumpeting angels stand guard over the tombs of Zacharias of Hradec, the castle's founder, and his wife. The local **historical museum** (adult/concession 20/10Kč; ☺ 9am-11.45am & 1-5pm Tue-Sun May-Aug, to 4pm Apr, Sep & Oct), in the courtyard, has a scale model of Telč dated 1895 showing that the townscape hasn't changed one bit since then.

Sleeping & Eating

There's no backpacker hostel in town, but there are several cheap *pensions* around the main square, and the information office can book private rooms (from around 300Kč per person). If you have a sleeping bag, you can crash at the very basic, summer-only sports club **SK Telč** (☎ 567 231 873; krejcib@seznam.cz; Mládkova; r per person 90Kč; ☺ office 4-6pm Jun, 11am-noon & 6-7pm Jul & Aug).

Privat Nika (☎ 567 243 104; nám Zachariáše z Hradce 45; s/d 500/800Kč; Ⓟ) Nika has two bright and modern double rooms tucked behind the Renaissance gable of a little house overlooking the old town square.

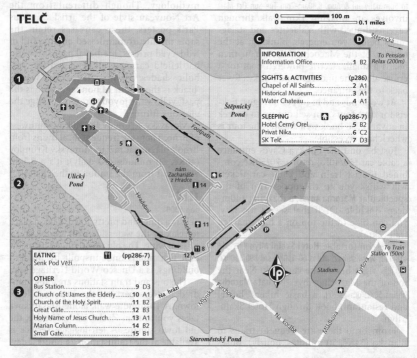

TELČ

0   100 m
0   0.1 miles

INFORMATION	
Information Office	1 B2

SIGHTS & ACTIVITIES	(p286)
Chapel of All Saints	2 A1
Historical Museum	3 A1
Water Chateau	4 A1

SLEEPING	(pp286-7)
Hotel Černý Orel	5 B2
Privat Nika	6 C2
SK Telč	7 D3

EATING	(pp286-7)
Šenk Pod Věží	8 B3

OTHER	
Bus Station	9 D3
Church of St James the Elderly	10 A1
Church of the Holy Spirit	11 B2
Great Gate	12 B3
Holy Name of Jesus Church	13 A1
Marian Column	14 B2
Small Gate	15 B1

To Pension Relax (200m)

Štěpnická

Štěpnický Pond

Footpath

Seminářská

Ulický Pond

nám Zachariáše z Hradce

Hradební

Palackého

Mazarykova

To Train Station (50m)

Stadium

Mlýnská Furchova

Na hrázi

Na Korábě

Mládkova

Tyršova

Staroměstský Pond

Penzión Relax (☎ 567 213 126; penzion.relax@post .cz; Na posvátné 29; s/d 450/900Kč; P) A comfortable and homely place where rooms come with TV and phone, Relax is a few minutes walk north of the old town.

Hotel Černý Orel (☎ 567 243 222; www.cernyorel.cz; nám Zachariáše z Hradce 7; s/d 1150/1650Kč; P) Right in the heart of the old town square, the 'Black Eagle' is the biggest and poshest hotel in town; rooms are comfy but bland. It has one room adapted for wheelchair users.

Šenk pod věží (☎ 567 243 889; Palackého 116; mains 90–140Kč; ♥ 11am-3pm & 6-9pm Mon-Fri, 11am-10pm Sat, 11am-4pm Sun) This is a friendly bar and restaurant with a cosy dining room serving good pizzas and a mean garlic soup (that you'll continue to enjoy for the next few days). Out back is a summer terrace overlooking the town moat.

Getting There & Away

There are five buses per day from Prague to Telč (120Kč, 2½ hours). Buses between České Budějovice and Brno also stop at Telč (90Kč, two hours, two daily).

MORAVIAN WINE COUNTRY

If you're heading south from Brno to Vienna, the Moravian wine country lies directly en route. Bohemian beer is famous worldwide, but until recently the wines of South Moravia were little known outside the Czech Republic.

The standard of Czech wine has soared since the fall of communism in 1989, as small producers have concentrated on the quality end of the market. Although Czech red wines – such as the local speciality, Svatovavřinecké (St Lawrence) – are mostly pretty average, Czech whites can be very good indeed.

There are lots of *vinné sklepy* (wine cellars), *vinoteky* (wine shops) and *vinárny* (wine bars) to explore, as well as some spectacular chateaux. The Culture and Information Office in Brno sells maps and guides covering the wine country.

Mikulov

The picturesque town of **Mikulov** lies at the heart of the Moravia's largest wine-growing region, which specialises in dry, fruity whites like Veltlínské Zelené, Vlašský Ryzlink and Müller-Thurgau.

The **tourist information office** (☎ 519 510 855; www.mikulov.cz; Nám 30; ♥ 8am-6pm Mon-Fri, 9am-

6pm Sat & Sun Jun-Sep, 8.30am-noon & 1-5pm Mon-Fri Oct-May) is on the main square, beneath the impressive Renaissance **chateau** (☎ 519 510 255; adult/concession 40/20Kč; ♥ 9am-5pm Tue-Sun May-Sep, to 4pm Apr & Oct), seat of the Dietrichstein and Liechtenstein families.

There are plenty of buses from Brno to Mikulov (42Kč, one hour, 14 daily), and a less frequent service between Mikulov and Vienna (210Kč, two hours, two daily).

Lednice & Valtice

A few kilometres east of Mikulov is the **Lednice-Valtice Cultural Landscape**, 200 sq km of managed woodland, channelled streams, artificial lakes and tree-lined avenues dotted with baroque, neoclassical and neo-Gothic chateaux. Effectively Europe's biggest landscaped garden, it was created over a period of several centuries by the dukes of Liechtenstein, and has been designated a Unesco World Heritage Site.

The town's main attraction is the massive neo-Gothic pile of **Lednice Chateau** (☎ 519 340 128; tours 60Kč or 100Kč; ♥ 9am-6pm Tue-Sun May-Aug, to 5pm Sep, to 4pm Sat & Sun only Apr & Oct), the Liechtensteins' summer palace. Embellished with battlements, pointy pinnacles and dog-shaped gargoyles, it gazes across a vast, island-dotted artificial lake to a minaret-shaped folly. You can wander through the gorgeous gardens for free.

The huge baroque chateau at Valtice houses the **National Wine Salon** (Národní salon vín; ☎ 519 352 744; www.salonvin.cz; Zámek 1; ♥ 9.30am-5pm Tue-Sat), where you can choose among various wine-tasting sessions costing from 99Kč to 399Kč per person (minimum five people). Next door is the **Zámecké vinoteka** (♥ 10am-6pm), a wine shop where you can get a free tasting before you buy.

There are five buses a day from Mikulov to Lednice (24Kč, 40 minutes), and one a day from Brno (64Kč, 1¾ hours).

CZECH REPUBLIC DIRECTORY

ACCOMMODATION

The accommodation reviews in this chapter are listed in order of price, from cheapest to most expensive. In the Prague section, budget means less than 1000Kč for a double,

CZECH REPUBLIC

Mid-range is 1000Kč to 4000Kč, and top end is more than 4000Kč.

You usually have to show your passport when checking in at accommodation in the Czech Republic; a few old-fashioned places might insist on keeping it for the duration of your stay, but you can demand to get it back as soon as the receptionist has registered your details. If they hang on to it, don't forget to ask for it back before you leave!

There are several hundred camping grounds spread around the Czech Republic; most are open from May to September only and charge around 50Kč to 100Kč per person. Camping on public land is prohibited.

Klub mladých cestovatelů (Map pp246-8; KMC Young Travellers Club; ☎ 222 220 347; www.kmc.cz; Karolíny Světlé 30, Prague 1) is the HI affiliate in Prague, and can book hostel accommodation throughout the country for you. In July and August many student dormitories become temporary hostels, while a number in Prague have been converted into year-round backpacker hostels. Prague and Český Krumlov are the only places in the Czech Republic with a solid choice of backpacker-oriented hostels.

Dorm beds costs around 370Kč to 500Kč in Prague, 250Kč to 350Kč elsewhere; it's best to book ahead. An HI-membership card is not usually needed, although it will often get you a reduced rate. An ISIC, ITIC, IYTC or Euro26 card may also get you a discount.

Another category of hostel accommodation is *turistické ubytovny* (tourist hostels), which provide very basic and cheap (150Kč to 300Kč) dormitory accommodation; rooms can usually be booked through the local tourist information office or KMC branch. You can find private rooms in most tourist towns (look for signs reading *privát* or *Zimmer frei* – like B&Bs without the breakfast), and many tourist information offices can book them for you; expect to pay from 250Kč to 500Kč per person outside Prague. Some have a three-night minimum-stay requirement.

Pensions (penzióny) are a step up: small, homely and often family-run, but offering rooms with private bathroom, and often breakfast too. Rates range from 1000Kč to 1500Kč for a double room (1500Kč to 2500Kč in Prague).

Hotels in central Prague and Brno are expensive, whereas those in smaller towns are usually much cheaper. Two-star hotels usually offer reasonable comfort for about 600Kč to 800Kč for a double, or 800Kč to 1200Kč with private bathroom (about 50% higher in Prague).

ACTIVITIES

There is good **hiking** among the hills of the Šumava (p279) south of Český Krumlov, in the forests around Karlovy Vary (p267), in the Moravian Karst (p285) and in the Adršpach-Teplice Rocks (p279). **Canoeing** and **rafting** are popular on the Vltava River around Český Krumlov (p278), and the whole country is ideal for **cycling** and cycle touring.

BUSINESS HOURS

Outside Prague, almost everything closes on Saturday afternoon and all day Sunday. Most restaurants are open every day; most museums, castles and chateaus are closed on Mondays year round.

Banks 8am to 4.30pm Monday to Friday

Bars 11am to 11pm daily

Post offices 8am to 6pm Monday to Friday, 8am to noon Saturday

Restaurants 11am to 10pm daily

Shops 8.30am to 5pm or 6pm Monday to Friday, 8.30am-noon or 1pm Saturday

CUSTOMS

Customs officers can be strict about antiques and will confiscate goods that are even slightly suspect. There is no limit to the amount of Czech or foreign currency that can be taken into or out of the country, but amounts exceeding 350,000Kč must be declared.

DANGERS & ANNOYANCES

Pickpocketing can be a problem in Prague's tourist zone, and there are still occasional reports of robberies on overnight international trains. There is intense racism directed at the local Roma population, which occasionally results in verbal abuse, and even assault, directed at darker-skinned visitors.

DISABLED TRAVELLERS

Ramps for wheelchair users in the Czech Republic are becoming more common, but cobbled streets, steep hills and stairways often make getting around difficult. Public transport is a major problem as most buses, trains and trams don't have wheelchair access. Major tourist attractions such as Prague Castle do have wheelchair access though – anything described as *bezbarierová* is 'barrier-free'.

Prague Wheelchair Users Organisation (Map pp246-8; Pražská organizace vozíčkářů; ☎ 224 827 210; pov@gts.cz; Benediktská 6, Josefov) publishes a Web guide to Barrier-Free Prague (www.pov.cz/cd-rom/startwww.htm) in English and German.

EMBASSIES & CONSULATES
Czech Embassies & Consulates

Australia Canberra (☎ 02-6290 1386; www.mzv.cz/canberra; 8 Culgoa Circuit, O'Malley, Canberra ACT 2606) Sydney (☎ 02-9371 0860; www.mzv.cz/sydney; 169 Military Rd, Dover Heights, Sydney NSW 2030)

Canada (☎ 613-562 3875; www.mzv.cz/ottawa; 251 Cooper St, Ottawa, Ontario K2P 0G2)

France (☎ 01 72 76 13 00; www.mzv.cz/paris; 75 Bd Hausmann, 75008 Paris)

Germany (☎ 030-22 63 80; www.mzv.cz/berlin; Wilhelmstrasse 44, 10117 Berlin)

Ireland (☎ 031-668 1135; www.mzv.cz/dublin; 57 Northumberland Rd, Ballsbridge, Dublin 4)

Netherlands (☎ 070-346 9712; www.mzv.cz/hague; Paleisstraat 4, 2514 JA The Hague)

New Zealand (☎ 09-353 9766; auckland@honorary.mzv.cz; Level 24, Bank of NZ Towers, 125 Queen St, Auckland) Postal address: PO Box 3798, Auckland.

UK (☎ 020-7243 1115; www.mzv.cz/london; 26 Kensington Palace Gardens, London W8 4QY)

USA (☎ 202-274 9100; www.mzv.cz/washington; 3900 Spring of Freedom St NW, Washington, DC 20008)

Embassies & Consulates in the Czech Republic

Most embassies and consulates are open at least 9am to noon Monday to Friday. See also p291.

Australia (Map pp246-8; ☎ 296 578 350; fax 296 578 352; Klimentská 10, Nové Město) Honorary consulate for emergency assistance only (eg a stolen passport); nearest Australian embassy is in Vienna.

Austria (Map pp246-8; ☎ 257 090 511; www.austria.cz; Viktora Huga 10, Smíchov) Website in Czech and German.

Bulgaria (Map pp246-8; ☎ 222 211 258; bulvelv@mbox.vol.cz; Krakovská 6, Nové Město)

Canada (Map pp242-3; ☎ 272 101 800; www.canada.cz; Muchova 6, Bubeneč)

France (Map pp246-8; ☎ 251 171 711; www.france.cz; Velkopřerovské nám 2, Malá Strana) Website in Czech and French.

Germany (Map pp246-8; ☎ 257 113 111; www.deutschland.cz; Vlašská 19, Malá Strana) Website in Czech and German.

Hungary (Map pp242-3; ☎ 233 324 454; huembprg@vol.cz; Českomalínská 20, Bubeneč)

Ireland (Map pp246-8; ☎ 257 530 061; www.irishembassy.cz; Tržiště 13, Malá Strana)

Netherlands (Map pp242-3; ☎ 224 312 190; www.netherlandsembassy.cz; Gotthardská 6/27, Bubeneč)

New Zealand (☎ 222 514 672; egermayer@nzconsul.cz; Dykova 19, Vinohrady) Honorary consulate providing emergency assistance only (eg stolen passport); the nearest NZ embassy is in Berlin.

Poland Embassy (☎ 257 530 388; www.ambpol.cz; Valdštejnská 8, Malá Strana) Consular Dept (☎ 224 228 722; konspol@mbox.vol.cz; V úžlabině 14, Strašnice) Go to Consular Dept for visas.

Russia (Map pp242-3; ☎ 233 374 100; rusembassy@cdnet.org; Pod Kaštany 1, Bubeneč)

Slovakia (Map pp246-8; ☎ 233 113 051; www.slovakemb.cz, in Slovak; Pod Hradbami 1, Dejvice)

South Africa (Map pp242-3; ☎ 267 311 114; saprague@terminal.cz; Ruská 65, Vršovice)

Ukraine (Map pp242-3; ☎ 233 342 000; emb_cz@mfa.gov.ua; Charlese de Gaulla 29, Bubeneč)

UK (Map pp246-8; ☎ 257 402 111; www.britain.cz; Thunovská 14, Malá Strana)

USA (Map pp246-8; ☎ 257 530 663; www.usembassy.cz; Tržiště 15, Malá Strana)

FESTIVALS & EVENTS
Festival of Sacred Music (www.mhfb.cz; Easter) Brno.

Prague Spring (www.festival.cz; May) International music festival.

Big Beat (www.musicfest.cz; May) Rock festival, Český Krumlov.

Five-Petalled Rose Festival (Jun) Medieval festival, Český Krumlov.

Karlovy Vary International Film Festival (www.kviff.com; Jul)

Český Krumlov International Music Festival (www.auviex.cz; Jul-Aug)

Dvořák Autumn (Sep) Classical music festival, Karlovy Vary.

Moravian Autumn (www.mhfb.cz; Sep) International music festival, Brno.

GAY & LESBIAN TRAVELLERS

The bimonthly magazine **Amigo** (www.amigo.cz) has a few pages in English, and an English-language website. **GayGuide.Net Prague** (www.gayguide.net/Europe/Czech/Prague) is another useful source of information. Homosexuality is legal in the Czech Republic (the age of consent is 15), but Czechs are not yet accustomed to seeing public displays of affection; it's best to be discreet.

HOLIDAYS

New Year's Day 1 January
Easter Monday March/April
Labour Day 1 May
Liberation Day 8 May
SS Cyril and Methodius Day 5 July
Jan Hus Day 6 July
Czech Statehood Day 28 September
Republic Day 28 October
Struggle for Freedom and Democracy Day 17 November
Christmas 24 to 26 December

INTERNET RESOURCES

Czech.cz (www.czech.cz) Government site with lots of useful info on travel, tourism and business, including latest visa requirements.
Czech Tourism (www.visitczechia.com) Official tourist information.
IDOS (www.idos.cz) Train and bus timetables.
Mapy (www.mapy.cz) Online maps.
Radio Prague (www.radio.cz) Excellent site (in English, French, German, Spanish and Russian) dedicated to Czech news, language and culture.

MONEY

Currency

The Czech crown (Koruna česká, or Kč), is divided into 100 hellers or *haléřů* (h). Banknotes come in denominations of 20, 50, 100, 200, 500, 1000, 2000 and 5000Kč; coins are of 10, 20 and 50h and one, two, five, 10, 20 and 50Kč.

Keep small change handy for use in public toilets, telephones and tram-ticket machines, and try to keep some small denomination notes for shops, cafés and restaurants – getting change for the 2000Kč notes that ATMs spit out can be a problem.

Exchanging Money

There is no black market; anyone who offers to change money in the street is a thief.

There's a good network of *bankomaty* (ATMs) throughout the country. The main banks – Komerční banka, ČSOB and Živnostenská banka – are the best places to change cash and travellers cheques or get a cash advance on Visa or MasterCard. American Express and Thomas Cook/Travelex

offices change their own cheques without commission. Credit cards are widely accepted in petrol stations, mid-range and top-end hotels, restaurants and shops.

Beware of *směnárna* (private exchange offices), especially in Prague – they advertise misleading rates, and often charge exorbitant commissions or 'handling fees'.

Costs

Food, transport and admission fees are fairly cheap, but accommodation in Prague can be expensive. Staying in hostels and buying food in supermarkets, you can survive on US$15 a day in summer. Staying in private rooms or *pensions*, eating at cheap restaurants and using public transport, count on US$25 to US$30 a day. Get out of the capital and your costs will drop dramatically. Some businesses quote prices in euros; prices in this chapter conform to quotes of individual businesses.

Tipping

Tipping in restaurants is optional, but increasingly expected in Prague. If there is no service charge you should certainly round up the bill to the next 10 or 20Kč (5% to 10% is normal in Prague). The same applies to tipping taxi drivers.

POST

General delivery mail can be addressed to Poste Restante, Pošta 1, in most major cities. For Prague, the address is Poste Restante, Jindřišská 14, 11000 Praha 1, Czech Republic. An aerogram costs 8Kč; letters up to 20g cost 9Kč to European countries, 14Kč elsewhere.

TELEPHONE

All Czech phone numbers have nine digits – you have to dial all nine for any call, local or long distance. You can make international

---

EMERGENCY NUMBERS

- All emergencies ☎ 112
- Ambulance ☎ 155
- Automobile Emergencies (ABA) ☎ 1240
- Fire ☎ 150
- Municipal Police ☎ 156
- Police ☎ 158

calls at main post offices or directly from card-phone booths. The international access code is ☎ 00. The Czech Republic's country code is ☎ 420.

There are payphones all over the place, some taking coins, some phonecards. You can buy phonecards from post offices, hotels, newsstands and department stores for 175Kč or 320Kč.

Mobile phone coverage (GSM 900) is excellent. Mobile phone numbers in the Czech Republic begin with 60, 72, 73 or 77.

TOURIST INFORMATION

The following Czech Tourism (www.czech tourism.com) offices provide information about tourism, culture and business in the Czech Republic.

Austria (☎ 01-533 2193; Herrengasse 17, 1010 Vienna)

Canada (☎ 416-363 9928; Czech Airlines Office, 401 Bay St, Suite 1510, Toronto, Ontario M5H 2Y4)

France (rue Bonaparte 18, 75006 Paris) No phone enquiries.

Germany (Friedrichstr. 206, 10969 Berlin) No phone enquiries.

Poland (☎ 22-629 29 16; Al. Róż 16, 00-555 Warsaw)

UK (information line ☎ 09063-640641) Office not open to callers.

USA (☎ 212-288 0830; 1109 Madison Ave, New York, NY 10028)

VISAS

Everyone requires a valid passport (or identity card for EU citizens) to enter the Czech Republic. Citizens of EU and EEA countries do not need a visa for any type of visit. Citizens of Australia, Canada, Israel, Japan, New Zealand, Switzerland and the USA can stay for up to 90 days without a visa; other nationalities do need a visa. Visas are not available at border crossings or at Prague's Ruzyně airport; you'll be refused entry if you need one and arrive without one.

Visa regulations change from time to time, so check www.czech.cz, or one of the Czech embassy websites listed on p289.

TRANSPORT IN THE CZECH REPUBLIC

GETTING THERE & AWAY
Air

The Czech Republic's main international airport is **Prague-Ruzyně** (☎ 220 113 314; www

.csl.cz/en). The national carrier, **Czech Airlines** (ČSA; Map pp246-8; ☎ 220 104 310; www.csa.cz; V celnici 5, Nové Město), has direct flights to Prague from many Eastern European cities, including Warsaw, Krakow, Budapest, Moscow and Kyiv. SkyEurope offers low-cost flights (from 2000Kč one way) from Prague to Košice in Slovakia.

The main international airlines serving Prague are:

Aer Lingus (code EI; ☎ 221 667 407; www.aerlingus.ie)

Aeroflot (code SU; ☎ 224 812 682; www.aeroflot.ru)

Air Baltic (code BT; ☎ 257 532 829; www.airbaltic.lv)

Air France (code AF; ☎ 221 662 662; www.airfrance.com)

Alitalia (code AZ; ☎ 221 629 150; www.alitalia.com)

Austrian Airlines (code OS; ☎ 220 116 272; www .austrianairlines.com)

British Airways (code BA; ☎ 222 114 444; www .britishairways.com)

Croatia Airlines (code OU; ☎ 222 222 235; www .croatiaairlines.hr)

ČSA (code OK; ☎ 220 104 310; www.csa.cz)

EasyJet (code EZY; www.easyjet.com)

El Al (code LY; ☎ 224 226 624; www.elal.co.il)

JAT (code JU; ☎ 224 942 654; www.jat.com)

KLM (code KL; ☎ 233 090 933; www.klm.com)

LOT Polish Airlines (code LO; ☎ 222 317 524; www .lot.com)

Lufthansa (code LH; ☎ 220 114 456; www.lufthansa.com)

Malév Hungarian Airlines (code MA; ☎ 224 224 471; www.malev.com)

SAS Scandinavian Airlines (code SK; ☎ 220 116 031; www.scandinavian.net)

SkyEurope Airlines (code NE; www.skyeurope.com)

SN Brussels Airlines (code SN; ☎ 220 114 323; www .flysn.com)

Turkish Airlines (code TK; ☎ 221 518 386; www .turkishairlines.com)

Land
BUS

Prague's main international bus terminal is Florenc Bus Station, 600m north of the main train station. The peak season for bus travel is from mid-June to the end of September, when there are daily buses to major European cities; outside this season, frequency falls to two or three a week.

The main international bus operators serving Prague are:

Capital Express (Map pp242-3; ☎ 220 870 368; www.capitalexpress.cz; U výstaviště 3, Holešovice; ☺ 8am-6pm Mon-Thu, 8am-5pm Fri) Five buses a week (daily in summer) from London to Prague and Brno via Plzeň. ISIC discount.

Eurolines-Bohemia Euroexpress International (Map pp246-8; ☎ 224 218 680; www.bei.cz; Florenc Bus Station, Křižíkova 4-6, Karlín) Buses to destinations all over Europe.

Eurolines-Sodeli CZ (Map pp246-8; ☎ 224 239 318; www.eurolines.cz; Senovážné nám 6, Nové Město; ☻ 8am-6pm Mon-Fri) To France, Spain, Switzerland and Poland.

Kingscourt Express (Map pp246-8; ☎ 224 234 583; www.kce.cz; Havelská ulice 8, Staré Město; ☻ 8am-6pm Mon-Fri, 8am-1pm Sat) Four buses per week (six in summer) from London to Prague and Brno via Plzeň.

Sample one-way fares from Prague include:
Bratislava 320Kč, 4¾ hours
Brno 150Kč, 2½ hours
Budapest 1230Kč, 7¼ hours
Frankfurt 1250Kč, 8½ hours
Salzburg 890Kč, 7½ hours
Vienna 600Kč, five hours
Warsaw 800Kč, 10½ hours
Wrocław 670Kč, 4¾ hours

CAR & MOTORCYCLE

Motorists can enter the country at any of the many border crossings marked on most road maps (see Map p235 for all major 24-hour crossings).

You will need to buy a *nálepka* (motorway tax coupon) – on sale at border crossings, petrol stations and post offices – in order to use Czech motorways (100/200Kč for 10 days/one month).

See also opposite.

TRAIN

International trains arrive at Prague's main train station (Praha-hlavní nádraží, or Praha hl. n.), or the outlying Holešovice (Praha Hol.) and Smíchov (Praha Smv.) stations.

Prague and Brno lie on the main line from Berlin and Dresden to Bratislava and Budapest, and from Hamburg and Berlin to Vienna. Trains from Frankfurt and Munich pass through Nuremberg and Plzeň on the way to Prague. There are also daily express trains between Prague and Warsaw via Wrocław or Katowice.

Sample one-way fares to Prague include:
Berlin €44, five hours
Salzburg €37, eight hours
Frankfurt €61, 7½ hours
Bratislava €18, 4¾ hours
Vienna €29, 4½ hours
Kraków €28, 8½ hours
Warsaw €36, 9½ hours

You can buy tickets in advance from Czech Railways (České dráhy, or ČD) ticket offices and various travel agencies. Seat reservations are compulsory on international trains. International tickets are valid for two months with unlimited stopovers. Inter-Rail (Zone D) passes are valid in the Czech Republic, but Eurail passes are not.

GETTING AROUND

Bicycle

The Czech Republic offers some good opportunities for cycle touring. Cyclists should be careful, though, as minor roads are often very narrow and have potholes, and in the towns cobblestones and tram tracks can be a dangerous combination, especially when it has been raining. Theft is a problem, especially in Prague and other large cities, so a good lock is essential.

It's fairly easy to transport your bike on Czech trains. First purchase your train ticket and then take it with your bicycle to the railway luggage office. There you fill out a card, which will be attached to your bike; on the card you should write your name, address, departure station and destination.

The cost of transporting a bicycle is 40Kč to 60Kč depending on the length of the journey. You can also transport bicycles on most buses if they are not too crowded and if the bus driver is willing.

Bus

Within the Czech Republic buses are often faster, cheaper and more convenient than the train, though not as comfortable. Many bus routes have reduced frequency (or none) at weekends. Buses occasionally leave early, so get to the station at least 15 minutes before the official departure time.

Most services are operated by the national bus company **ČSAD** (information line ☎ 475 200 014; www.csadbus.cz); you can check bus timetables online at www.jizdnirady.cz. Ticketing at main bus stations is computerised, so you can often book a seat ahead and be sure of a comfortable trip. Way stations are rarely computerised and you must line up and pay the driver.

The footnotes on printed timetables may drive you crazy – the following tips may help. Crossed hammers means the bus runs on *pracovní dny* (working days), ie Monday to Friday only; a Christian cross means it runs on Sundays and public holidays; and numbers in circles refer to particular days of the week (1 is Monday, 2 Tuesday etc). *Jede* means 'runs', *nejede* means 'doesn't run', and *jede denne* means 'runs daily'. *V* is 'on', *od* is 'from' and *do* is 'to' or 'until'.

Fares are very reasonable; expect to pay around 80Kč for a 100km trip. Prague to Brno costs 150Kč, Prague to Karlovy Vary is 130Kč.

Car & Motorcycle
DRIVING LICENCE
Foreign driving licences are valid for up to 90 days. Strictly speaking, licences that do not include photo identification need an International Driving Permit as well, although this rule is rarely enforced – ordinary UK licences without a photo are normally accepted without comment.

FUEL
There are plenty of petrol stations, many open 24/7. Leaded petrol is available as *special* (91 octane) and *super* (96 octane), unleaded as *natural* (95 octane) or *natural plus* (98 octane); the Czech for diesel is *nafta* or just *diesel*. *Autoplyn* (LPG gas) is available in every major town but at very few outlets. Natural 95 costs around 25.50Kč per litre, diesel 23.90Kč.

HIRE
The main international car-rental chains all have offices in Prague. Small local companies offer better prices, but are less likely to have fluent, English-speaking staff; it's often easier to book by email than by phone. Typical rates for a Škoda Felicia are around 700Kč a day including unlimited kilometres, collision damage waiver and value-added tax (VAT). Reputable local companies include:

Secco Car (Map pp242-3; ☎ 220 802 361; www.sec-cocar.cz; Přístavní 39, Holešovice)

Vecar (Map pp242-3; ☎ 224 314 361; www.vecar.cz; Svatovítská 7, Dejvice)

West Car Praha (Map pp242-3; ☎ 235 365 307; www.westcarpraha.cz, in Czech; Veleslavínská 17, Veleslavín)

ROAD RULES
Road rules are the same as in the rest of Europe. A vehicle must be equipped with a first-aid kit, a red-and-white warning triangle and a nationality sticker on the rear; the use of seat belts is compulsory. Drinking

and driving is strictly forbidden – the legal blood alcohol level is zero. Police can hit you with on-the-spot fines of up to 2000Kč for speeding and other traffic offences (be sure to insist on a receipt).

Speed limits are 30km/h or 50km/h in built-up areas, 90km/h on open roads and 130km/h on motorways; motorbikes are limited to 80km/h. At level crossings over railway lines the speed limit is 30km/h. Beware of speed traps.

You need a motorway tax coupon (see opposite) to use the motorways; this is included with most rental cars.

Police often mount checkpoints, stopping vehicles for random checks. They are generally looking for locals driving without insurance or overloaded goods vehicles. If you are stopped, present your licence, passport and insurance or rental documents; as soon as the officer realises you're a tourist, you'll probably be waved on.

Local Transport
City buses and trams operate from around 4.30am to midnight daily. Tickets must be purchased in advance – they're sold at bus and train stations, newsstands and vending machines – and must be validated in the time-stamping machines found on buses and trams and at the entrance to metro stations. Tickets are hard to find at night, at weekends and out in residential areas, so carry a good supply.

Taxis have meters – just make sure they're switched on.

Train
Czech Railways provides efficient train services to almost every part of the country. Fares are based on distance; one-way, 2nd-class fares cost around 64/120/224/424Kč for 50/100/200/400km. For travel within the Czech Republic only, the Czech Flexipass is available (from US$48 to US$78 for three to eight days' travel in a 15-day period).

The sales clerks at ticket counters seldom speak English, so try writing down your destination, with the date and time you wish to travel, on a piece of paper and showing it to them. You can check train timetables on www.vlak.cz.

Train categories include:

EC (EuroCity) Fast, comfortable international trains, stopping at main stations only, with 1st- and 2nd-class coaches; supplementary charge of 60Kč, reservations recommended.

Ex (express) As for IC (below), but no supplementary charge.

IC (InterCity) Long-distance and international trains with 1st- and 2nd-class coaches; supplement of 40Kč, reservations recommended.

R *(rychlík)* The main domestic network of fast trains with 1st- and 2nd-class coaches and sleeper services; no supplement except for sleepers; express and *rychlík* trains are usually marked in red on timetables.

Sp *(spěšný)* Slower and cheaper than *rychlík* trains, 2nd class only.

Os *(osobní)* Slow trains using older rolling stock that stop in every one-horse town, 2nd-class only.

If you need to purchase a ticket or pay a supplement on the train for any reason, tell the conductor *before* they ask for your ticket or you'll have to pay a fine. Some Czech train conductors may try to intimidate foreigners by pretending there's something wrong with their ticket. Don't pay any 'fine', 'supplement' or 'reservation fee' unless you first get a *doklad* (written receipt).

Estonia

CONTENTS

Highlights	297
Itineraries	297
Climate & When to Go	297
History	297
People	299
Sport	299
Religion	299
Arts	299
Environment	301
Food & Drink	302
Tallinn	**302**
History	302
Orientation	303
Information	303
Sights	305
Festivals & Events	308
Sleeping	308
Eating	309
Drinking	311
Entertainment	311
Shopping	312
Getting There & Away	312
Getting Around	314
Northeastern Estonia	**314**
Lahemaa National Park	314
Narva & Around	315
Southeastern Estonia	**315**
Tartu	315
Otepää	319
Haanja Nature Park	320
Setumaa	320
Southwestern Estonia & The Islands	**320**
Pärnu	320
Kihnu & Ruhnu Islands	323
Viljandi & Around	323
Hiiumaa	324
Saaremaa	325
Estonia Directory	**326**
Accommodation	326
Activities	326
Business Hours	327
Customs	327
Embassies & Consulates	327
Festivals & Events	327
Gay & Lesbian Travellers	328
Holidays	328
Language	328

Money	328
Post	328
Telephone	328
Visas	328
Transport in Estonia	**329**
Getting There & Away	329
Getting Around	330

ESTONIA

Ten years ago, it didn't help to describe Estonia's location as 'in the Baltics' or even 'near Finland' – the first made people think of a war zone, the second brought images of snow drifts and vodka (well, at least the vodka part was right!). Now that the bite-sized country has joined the EU, word is out that Estonia is the pretty little country that could – and did! Its subtle, quiet charms weave their way into your heart before you're aware of it.

Perhaps due to its history of constant domination, Estonia, since regaining independence from the Soviet Union in 1991, has been anxious to accent what distinguishes it from the rest of Europe – even as it approaches it economically, politically and ideologically. Now it's strutting its stuff and waiting to be admired.

Apart from the obvious charms of the capital Tallinn and its enchanting Unesco-protected Old Town, the country boasts a one-two combination of low population and stretches of fabulous nature. That means that despite Estonia's miniature size, you can enjoy its unspoilt seaside, be alone on an island, and drink in nature, all the while enjoying the comforts of a thoroughly modern e-savvy country.

In Tallinn, brush up on your medieval history while exploring the city's café and bar culture. In Tartu, find out what 'Tartu spirit' means. In Pärnu, tend to your sunburn all night in beachside discos. On the island of Saaremaa, visit vestiges of WWII and an intact castle, and drink in sumptuous coastal views.

FAST FACTS

- **Area** 45, 226 sq km
- **Capital** Tallinn
- **Currency** kroon (EEK); €1=15.65EEK; US$1 = 12.54EEK; UK£1 = 22.62EEK; A$1 = 9.17EEK; ¥100 = 11.48EEK; NZ$1 = 8.61EEK
- **Famous for** Arvo Pärt (composer), Erki Nool (athlete), Carmen Kass (supermodel), Vana Tallinn (a liqueur)
- **Key Phrases** *Tere!* (hi!), *äitah* (thanks), *mis su nimi on?* (what's your name?), *kui palju sa maksab?* (how much does this cost?)
- **Official Language** Estonian
- **Population** 1.35 million
- **Telephone Codes** country code ☎ 372; international access code ☎ 00
- **Visas** EU nationals and citizens of the US, Canada and Australia do not need a visa to enter; see p883 for details

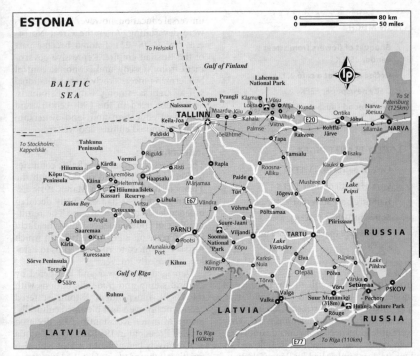

ESTONIA

HIGHLIGHTS

- No trip to Estonia would be complete without several hours of blissful hanging out on Tallinn's **Raekoja plats** (p305) and exploring the historic **Old Town** (p305)
- Get away from city life for a day or two at the **Lahemaa National Park** (p314), where you can look for beavers, go canoeing or discover your own slice of deserted coastland
- Head out to lovely **Saaremaa** (p325) to check out a meteorite crater (p325) with a bottle of local brew in hand
- For an experience you'll be recounting for years, try a floating sauna, sweating it up atop a raft travelling through bog country in **Soomaa National Park** (p324)

ITINERARIES

- **Five Days** Hit Tallinn at a weekend, get your sightseeing, partying and café-bar culture fill, then head out to Lahemaa National Park or west to the islands of Saaremaa and/or Hiiumaa and enjoy nature on an organised tour or on your own. A trip to Pärnu or Tartu will complete the picture.

- **Two Weeks** There will be time to explore Tallinn more deeply and take a trip to an island off its shores. Saaremaa should be on your agenda, as well as Tartu, from where you can head into southern and southeastern Estonia, taking in Suur Munamägi and Setumaa. Or you can opt for fun in the sun in Pärnu, with a venture out to the remote island of Kihnu from there.

CLIMATE & WHEN TO GO

Between May and September is the best time of the year to travel to Estonia as there's better weather and longer days. 'White nights', when the skies darken slightly for only a few hours each night, peak in late June but the sun rarely sets from mid-May to mid-August. June can still be nippy; the warmest temperatures come in July to August (see Climate Charts p874). Winter is temperate, dark and damp but has a special magic. Slushy, drizzly March is the only really depressing month.

HISTORY

It's commonly held that in the mid-3rd millennium BC Finno-Ugric tribes came either

HOW MUCH

▪ **Bouquet of flowers from street vendor** 35EEK

▪ **Coffee & cake at a café** 25EEK

▪ **Daily newspaper** 5EEK

▪ **Kg of blood sausages** 35EEK

▪ **Film and popcorn** 90EEK to 130EEK

LONELY PLANET INDEX

▪ **Litre of petrol (95)** 12EEK

▪ **Litre of bottled water** 14EEK

▪ **Half-litre beer store/bar** 15/28EEK

▪ **Souvenir T-shirt** 150EEK

▪ **Street snack (pack of roasted nuts)** 25EEK

from the east or south to the territory of modern-day Estonia and parts of Latvia, and mixed with the tribes who had been present from the 8th millennium BC. They were little influenced from outside until German traders and missionaries, followed by knights, were unleashed by Pope Celestinus III's 1193 crusade against the 'northern heathens'. In 1202 the Bishop of Rīga established the Knights of the Sword to convert the region by conquest; southern Estonia was soon subjugated, the north fell to Denmark.

After a crushing battle with Alexander Nevsky in 1242 on the border of present-day Estonia and Russia, the Knights of the Sword were subordinated to a second band of German crusaders, the Teutonic Order, which by 1290 ruled the eastern Baltic area as far north as southern Estonia, and most of the Estonian islands. Denmark sold northern Estonia to the knights in 1346, placing Estonians under servitude to a German nobility that lasted till the early 20th century. The Hanseatic League (a mercantile league of medieval German towns bound together by trade) encompassed many towns on the routes between Russia and the west and prospered under the Germans, although many Estonians in rural areas were forced into serfdom.

By 1620 Estonia had fallen under Swedish control. The Swedes consolidated Estonian Protestantism and aimed to introduce universal education, however frequent wars were devastating. After the Great Northern War (1700–21), Estonia became part of the Russian empire. Repressive government from Moscow and economic control by German powers slowly forged a national self-awareness among native Estonians. Serfs were freed in the 19th century and improved education and land-ownership rights promoted culture and welfare.

Independence

The Soviets abandoned the Baltic countries to Germany at the end of WWI with the Treaty of Brest-Litovsk in March 1918. Estonian nationalists had originally declared independence on 24 February. The resulting War of Independence led to the Tartu Peace Treaty on 2 February 1920, in which Russia renounced territorial claims to Estonia, supposedly forever.

Damaged by the war and hampered by a world slump and trade disruptions with the USSR, independent Estonia suffered economically even as it bloomed culturally. Prime Minister Konstantin Päts declared himself President in 1934 and ruled Estonia as a relatively benevolent dictator who also quietly safeguarded the USSR's interests.

Soviet Rule & WWII

The Molotov-Ribbentrop Pact of 23 August 1939, a nonaggression pact between the USSR and Nazi Germany, secretly divided Eastern Europe into Soviet and German spheres of influence. Estonia fell into the Soviet sphere and by August 1940 was under occupation. Estonia was 'accepted' into the USSR after fabricated elections and, within a year, over 10,000 people in Estonia were killed or deported. When Hitler invaded the USSR in 1941, many saw the Germans as liberators, but during their occupation about 5500 people died in concentration camps. Some 40,000 Estonians joined the German army to prevent the Red Army from reconquering Estonia, while nearly twice that number fled abroad.

Between 1945 and 1949, with Stalinism back on course, agriculture was collectivised and industry nationalised, and 60,000 more Estonians were killed or deported. An armed resistance lead by the now-legendary *metsavennad* (forest brothers) fought Soviet rule until 1956.

New Independence

On 23 August 1989, on the 50th anniversary of the Molotov-Ribbentrop Pact, an estimated two million people formed a human chain across Estonia, Latvia and Lithuania, calling for secession from the USSR. In November of that year Moscow granted the three republics economic autonomy. Independence came suddenly, however, in the aftermath of the Moscow putsch against Gorbachev. Estonia's declaration of complete independence on 20 August 1991 was immediately recognised by the West and by the USSR on 6 September.

In October 1992 Estonia held its first democratic elections, which brought to the presidency Lennart Meri, who oversaw the removal of the last Russian troops in 1994. Mart Laar became prime minister, leading a government focused on launching radical reform policies, committed to European integration and NATO membership.

The decade since independence, with its sweeping transformations on all levels of society, saw frequent changes of government and no shortage of scandal and corruption charges; this even as the country came to be seen as the post-Soviet economic miracle. Today Arnold Rüütel is president and Juhan Pats prime minister. In 2004, Estonia officially entered both NATO and the EU. While there are a large number of Euro-sceptics in the country, the majority of the population is happy to return to the European fold. Estonia plans to adopt the euro as its currency by 2007.

PEOPLE

Estonia's population is 68% Estonian, 26% Russian, 2% Ukrainian, 1% Belarusian and 1% Finnish. In 1934 over 90% of the population was native Estonian. Ethnic Russians are concentrated in Tallinn and in the industrial northeast, forming 40% and up to 96% of the respective populations. While much was made of tension between Estonians and Russians in the 1990s (especially in the Russian media), the two communities live together in relative harmony. While the youngest generations now mix freely, in general Estonians and Russians have little to do with each other.

Estonians are closely related to the Finns, and more distantly to the Sami (indigenous Laplanders) and Hungarians, but not to the Latvians and Lithuanians, who are of Indo-European heritage. Estonians are originally a rural people, historically cautious of outsiders and stereotypically most comfortable when left alone. Women are less shy and more approachable than men, though both exude a natural reticence and cool-headed distance in social situations. Of course, much has changed over the last decade, and travellers will find it easy to strike up a conversation and make friends.

SPORT

With over 3700km of coastline, all forms of water sports are popular in Estonia come the summer sun. As Estonia is a flat country, bicycling is hugely popular, though more as a sport than a method of transport within cities. Major bike marathons are held in Tartu (p318) and Otepää, which is also the country's cross-country ski capital. Basketball is the unofficial national sport, and courts small and large are found all over Estonia.

A well-known name in the sports world is Erki Nool, the decathlon gold-medal winner at the 2000 Olympics.

RELIGION

From 1987 to 1990 there was a surge of interest in religion as the state Lutheran Church allied itself to the independence cause. However, that enthusiasm has now waned. While numerous sects and religious organisations have recently set up shop in Estonia, including the Church of Latter Day Saints (whose well-dressed and clean-cut representatives can be seen daily on the streets of Tallinn), Seventh Day Adventists, Jehovah's Witnesses, Hare Krishnas and even the Children of God, these have made inroads primarily with the Russian-speaking population. There are several thousand Muslims in Estonia and some 600 registered Buddhists and 260 Jews.

ARTS

Most travellers are likely to notice paintings and ceramics of bright pastel colours and fanciful animal compositions as emblematic of contemporary Estonian art, especially works by the one-man industry Navitrolla, whose playful world vision adorns postcards, coffee mugs, posters and café walls. The art world in Estonia is much wider than that, however, even though some disciplines

ESTONIA

have hit a level of excellence (jewellery and ceramics, for example) at the expense of others (art photography is almost non existent).

Music

Estonia has a strong and internationally well-respected classical music tradition, most notably its choirs. The Estonian Boys Choir has been acclaimed the world over. Hortus Musicus is Estonia's best-known ensemble, performing Middle Ages and Renaissance music. Composer Arvo Pärt is renowned worldwide for his haunting sonic blend of tension and beauty, with outwardly simple but highly complex musical structures. The three main Estonian composers of the 20th century are Rudolf Tobias, Mart Saar and Eduard Tubin. Veljo Tormis writes striking music based on old runic chants. His best-known works include the difficult-to-perform *Curse Upon Iron*.

In jazz, the duo of saxophonist Villu Veski and piano accordionist Tiit Kalluste incorporate elements of Nordic music and lore into their work.

Hard rock thrives in Estonia with groups like Venaskond, Tuberkuloised and the U2-style Mr Lawrence. The more approachable Ultima Thule and Compromise Blue are two of the country's longest-running and most beloved bands. Jäääär are also at the top, with their album *Tartu-Väike Puust Linn* (Tartu – Small Wooden Town) ranking among the best Estonian albums. Excellent folk bands include Untsakond and Väikeste Lõõtspillide Ühing. Linnu Tee and Echosilence are highlights of the progressive rock scene.

The pop and dance-music scene is strong in Estonia, exemplified by the country's strong performances in that revered indicator of true art, Eurovision (they hosted the contest in 2002). Maarja and Liisi Koikson are popular pop singers, while Hedvig Hanson blends jazz and rock with surprising results.

Literature

Estonian literature began with the poems and diaries of Kristjan Jaak Peterson, who died when he was but 21 years old in the early 19th century. His lines 'Can the language of this land/carried by the song of the wind/not rise up to heaven/and search for its place in eternity?' are engraved in stone in Tartu and his birthday is celebrated as Mother Tongue Day (14 March).

Until the mid-19th century, Estonian culture was preserved only by way of an oral folk tradition among the peasants. Many of these stories were collected around 1861 to form the national epic *Kalevipoeg* (The Son of Kalev), by Friedrich Reinhold Kreutzwald, inspired by Finland's *Kalevala*. The *Kalevipoeg* relates the adventures of the mythical hero, and ends in his death, his land's conquest by foreigners and a promise to restore freedom. The epic played a major role in fostering the national awakening of the 19th century.

Lydia Koidula (1843–86), the face of the 100EEK note, was the poet of Estonia's national awakening and first lady of literature.

Anton Hansen Tammsaare is considered the greatest Estonian novelist for his *Tõde ja Õigus* (Truth and Justice), written between 1926 and 1933. Eduard Vilde (1865–1933) was a controversial turn-of-the-century novelist and playwright who wrote *Tabamata Ime* (Unattainable Wonder). He wrote with sarcasm and irony about parochial mindsets and had a penchant for lengthy descriptions of how 19th-century German landlords whipped their peasants.

Jaan Kross (b 1920) is the best-known Estonian author abroad, and several of his most renowned books, including *The Czar's Madman* and *The Conspiracy and Other Stories*, have been translated into English. Tõnu Õnnepalu's *Piiririik* (Border State; published under the pseudonym Emil Tode) has also been translated and was the best-selling Estonian novel of the 1990s.

Cinema

The first 'moving pictures' were screened in Tallinn in 1896, and the first theatre opened in 1908. Johannes Pääsuke is considered the first Estonian film maker. Estonia's cinematographic output has not been prolific, but there are a number of standouts. Estonian's most beloved film is Arvo Kruusement's *Kevade* (Spring; 1969), an adaptation of Oskar Luts' country saga. Grigori Kromanov's *Viimne reliikvia* (The Last Relic; 1969), was a brave, unabashedly anti-Soviet film which has been screened in some 60 countries.

More recently Sulev Keedus' lyrical *Georgica* (1998), about childhood, war, and life on the western islands, and Jaak Kilmi's *Sigade Revolutsioon* (Pigs' Revolution; 2004), about an anti-Soviet uprising at a teenager's summer camp, have made the rounds at international film festivals.

Architecture

Even in Soviet times Estonian architects were respected for their creative, daring concepts and for their tenacious incorporation of natural elements into their designs. In the 1990s Estonian architects were responsible for the influx of glass, steel and aluminium skyscrapers in Tallinn, whose flagrant modernity counterbalances the Old Town's equally flagrant demonstration of its deeply rooted history.

Of note throughout Estonia are the one-to four-storey wooden buildings from the early 20th century. Efforts were often made to incorporate traditional and rural elements into their designs, a back-to-roots trend which has recurred periodically throughout the 20th century. Striking examples of wooden architecture are in the Kalamaja and Kadriorg (p307) regions of Tallinn.

Visual Arts

The undisputed national treasure here is eclectic graphic artist Eduard Wiiralt. He is considered not only a superb local artist, but a truly international genius based on the wide variety of his themes and styles.

Navitrolla's populist work is instantly recognisable: fanciful landscapes in which humans play no part. Yet his style inherits much from another great artist, Jüri Arrak. Other contemporary artists continuing in the tradition of playful, almost naive art include Priit Pangsepp and Toomas Vint.

Theatre

It is telling of the role theatre has played in Estonia's cultural life that many of the country's theatre houses were built solely from donations collected from private citizens. The Estonia Theatre and the Estonia Drama Theatre in Tallinn, the Vanemuine Theatre in Tartu and others throughout the country were all built on proceeds collected door to door.

Modern theatre is considered to have begun in Tartu. It was there that Lydia Koidula's *The Cousin from Saaremaa* became the first Estonian play performed in public.

Experimental theatre and multimedia performances are becoming more accepted in a previously conservative arena. Fine 5 Dance Theatre and Nordstar Dance Theatre are two of the finest modern dance and performance troupes in the country. Two highly original theatre directors on the current scene include Katri Kaasik-Aaslav and Elmo Nüganen.

ENVIRONMENT

With an area of 45,226 sq km, Estonia is only slightly bigger than Denmark. It is mainly low lying, with extensive bogs and marshes; Suur Munamägi (318m; p320) in the southeast near Võru is the highest point. In Southern Estonia, the regions Võrumaa and Setumaa are characterised by gentle hills. Nearly 50% of the land is forested and 22% is wetlands, with peat bogs 7m deep in places. The 3794km-long coastline is heavily indented. More than 1500 islands make up nearly 10% of Estonian territory and there are over 1400 lakes, the largest of which is Lake Peipsi (3555 sq km).

The Baltic Glint is Estonia's most prominent geological feature. Made up of 60-million-year-old limestone banks that extend 1200km from Sweden to Lake Ladoga in Russia, they form impressive cliffs along Estonia's northern coast, especially in the east – at Ontika the cliffs stand 50m above the coast.

Since independence there have been major 'clean-up' attempts to counter the effects of Soviet-era industrialisation. In 2004 the International Marine Organisation designated the heavily polluted Baltic Sea one of the planet's five particularly sensitive areas (despite Russia's protests), which opens the way for greater protection and stricter standards.

Toxic emissions in the industrialised northeast of Estonia have been reduced sharply and new environmental-impact legislation aims to minimise the effects of future development.

National Parks

Most of the population of Estonia's rare or protected species can be found in one of the several national parks, nature reserves and parks. There are beavers, otters, flying squirrels, lynxes, wolves and brown bears in these areas. White and black storks are common in southern Estonia.

ESTONIA

ESTONIA

Estonia's western islands and areas in national parks boast some of the most unspoilt landscapes in Europe, and air pollution, even in the cities, remains very low by European standards. Almost 20% of Estonia's lands are protected to some degree, more than double the European average. Thus far, the only Unesco World Heritage Site is Tallinn's Old Town. Some of the most popular national parks are Lahemaa (p314), Soomaa (p324) and the Haanja Nature Park (p320).

FOOD & DRINK

The conventional excuse for the heaviness of the local cuisine is the northern climate…but that only goes so far in explaining the proclivity towards fatty and carbohydrate-heavy meals. The Estonian diet relies on *sealiha* (pork), red meat, *kana* (chicken), *vurst* (sausage), *kapsa* (cabbage) and *kartul* (potato). Sour cream is served with everything but coffee, it seems. *Kala* (fish) appears most often as a smoked or salted starter. *Forell* (smoked trout) is one good speciality. *Sült* (jellied meat) will likely be served as well. At Christmas time *verivorst* (blood sausages) are made from fresh blood and wrapped in pig intestine (joy to the world indeed!). Those really in need of a transfusion will find blood sausages, blood bread and blood dumplings available in most traditional Estonian restaurants and some shops year-round.

Though the idea that a meal can actually be spicy or vegetarian has taken root, you'll need to hit one of Tallinn's or Tartu's ethnic restaurants for exotic spices or mains that don't include meat. Veganism is completely unknown, except to the local Hare Krishnas! Places with good vegetarian options are highlighted in the Eating sections for each city. Delicious and inexpensive freshly baked cakes, breads and pastries are available everywhere.

Restoran (restaurants) and *kohvik* (cafés) are plentiful and pubs also serve meals. Most Estonians have their main meal at lunch time, and accordingly most establishments have excellent-value set lunches. Menus are commonly available in English or are readily translated. When invited to someone's house for dinner, a gift is not expected but a bottle of wine is well appreciated.

Õlu (beer) is the favourite alcoholic drink in Estonia and the local product is very much in evidence. The best brands are Saku and A Le Coq, which come in a range of brews. *Viin* (vodka) and *konjak* (brandy) are also popular drinks. Vana Tallinn, the very sweet and very strong (40% to 50% alcohol) liqueur of unknown extraction, is an integral part of any Estonian gift pack. Eesti Kali is the favourite (Estonian) brand of *kvass*, originally made from fermented bread but containing no alcohol.

TALLINN

pop 400,000

Picture a heady mix of medieval church spires, glass-and-chrome skyscrapers, imported DJs spinning tunes in underground clubs, cosy wine cellars inside 15th-century basements, lazy afternoons soaking up sun and beer suds on Raekoja plats, plus bike paths to beaches and forests and yacht rides in a sprawling bay – with a few Soviet monuments thrown in for added spice. That's today's Tallinn.

Back in 1992 travellers were already anxious to pin the now-clichéd label 'the next Prague' onto a Tallinn still reeling from its Soviet days. Now that label is regaining currency, though false comparisons disguise the fact that Tallinn has very much its own vibe. The jewel in Tallinn's crown remains the two-tiered Old Town, a 14th- and 15th-century jumble of turrets, spires and winding cobbled streets. A freshly built city centre core with miniskyscrapers of chrome and glass give a modern sheen to a city which already had a lot going for it. Despite its small size and easy-going rhythm of life, it boasts a vibrant population of Estonians and Russians and loads of opportunities for fun and discovery.

HISTORY

In 1219 the Danes set up a castle and installed a bishop on Toompea ('Tallinn' comes from the Danish *taani linnus*, which means 'Danish castle'). German traders arrived and Tallinn joined the Hanseatic League in 1285, becoming a vital link between east and west. By the mid-14th century, after the Danes had sold northern Estonia to the German knights, Tallinn was a major Hanseatic town. The merchants and artisans in the lower town built a fortified wall to separate themselves from the bishop and knights on Toompea.

Prosperity faded in the 16th century as Swedes, Russians, Poles and Lithuanians all fought over the Baltic region. The city grew in the 19th century and by WWI had a population of 150,000. In 1944 Soviet bombing destroyed several central sectors including a small section on the Old Town's fringes. After WWII, industry developed and Tallinn expanded quickly, with much of its population growth due to immigration from outside Estonia. Politically and economically, Tallinn is the driving force of modern Estonia.

ORIENTATION

Tallinn fronts a bay on the Gulf of Finland and is defined by Toompea (*tom*-pe-ah), the hill over which it has tumbled since the Middle Ages. Toompea, the upper Old Town, has traditionally been the centre of Tallinn and the medieval seat of power. The lower Old Town spreads around the eastern foot of Toompea, still surrounded by much of its 2.5km defensive wall. Its centre is Raekoja plats (Town Hall Sq).

Around the Old Town is a belt of green parks which follows the line of the city's original moat defences, as well as the modern city centre.

INFORMATION
Bookshops

Allecto (☎ 681 8731; Väike-Karja tänav 5; ☼ 10am-7pm Mon-Fri, 10am-5pm Sat) Best bet for foreign-language books.

Apollo (☎ 654 8485; Viru tänav 23; ☼ 10am-8pm Mon-Fri, 10am-6pm Sat & Sun) Lots of Lonely Planet and travel titles, plus a comfy café on the 2nd floor.

Rahva Raamat (☎ 644 3682; Pärnu maantee 10; ☼ 9am-8pm Mon-Fri, 10am-5pm Sat & Sun)

TALLINN IN TWO DAYS

Wander around the **Old Town**, climbing **Oleviste Church** (p305) for a great view, stopping at several cafés and pubs around the Raekoja plats (Town Hall Sq). On the second day, do what most tourists don't – step out of the Old Town, explore the **Kadriorg** (p307) region and walk out to **Pirita** (p307) for a few hours on the beach. Hit a nightclub or go bar-hopping before calling it a day.

Internet Access

There are over 300 wireless Internet (WiFi) areas throughout Estonia, many of them scattered throughout the capital. Many cafés have a few terminals. The central post office also has computer terminals on the 2nd floor, though it charges twice as much as anywhere else to use them.

Matrix Club (☎ 641 9442; Tartu Maantee 31; ☼ 24hr; per hr 15EEK)

Neo Internetcafé (☎ 628 2333; Väike Karja tänav 12; ☼ 24hr; per hr 35EEK) Full printing services.

Medical Services

Aia Apteek (☎ 627 3607; Aia tänav 10; ☼ 8.30am-midnight) One of the many well-stocked pharmacies around town.

East Tallinn Central Hospital (☎ 620 7015; Ravi tänav 18) Full range of services, including a polyclinic and a 24-hour emergency room.

Südalinna Arstide (☎ 660 4072; Kaupmehe tänav 4) This private clinic has ear, nose, and throat specialists and other general practitioners on staff.

Money

Currency exchange is available at all transport terminals, exchange bureaus around the city, the post office and inside all banks and major hotels. ATMs are so numerous, you're likely to trip over one.

Estravel (☎ 626 6266; www.estravel.ee; Suur-Karja tänav 15) A travel agent (see p304) and the official agent for Amex.

Tavid (☎ 627 9900; Aia tänav 5; ☼ 24hr) This exchange bureau has reliably good rates.

Post

Central post office (☎ 625 7300; Narva maantee 1; ☼ 7.30am-8pm Mon-Fri, 8am-6pm Sat) Full postal services, including express mail, faxes and telegrams. You can receive a fax at ☎ 661 6054 (12EEK per page).

Telephone

If you're one of the few not sporting a mobile phone, you can buy 30EEK, 50EEK and 100EEK chip cards from newsstands to use for local and international calls at any one of the blue phone boxes scattered around town.

Tourist Information

1182 (☎ 1182; www.1182.ee) This charged information service is accessible only from mobile phones, but the website is extremely useful.

Infotelefon (☎ 626 1111) This provides free, practical information in English 24 hours a day.

ESTONIA

TALLINN

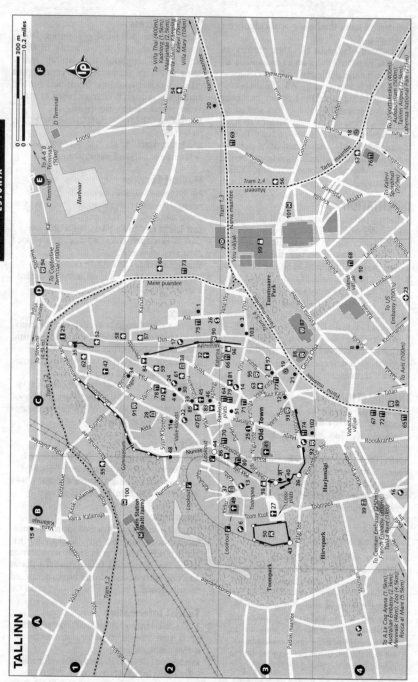

INFORMATION
Aia Apteek..............................1 D2
Allecto...................................2 C3
Apollo...................................3 D3
Baltic Tours...........................4 C2
British Embassy.....................5 A4
Canadian Embassy................6 B3
Central Post Office................7 D3
Division of the Export of Cultural
  Objects..............................8 D4
Dutch Embassy.....................9 C3
Estonian Foreign Ministry....10 D4
Estonian Holidays...............11 C2
Estravel...............................12 C3
Finnish Embassy..................13 B3
Irish Embassy.......................14 C3
Kalma Saun..........................15 B1
Latvian Embassy..................16 B4
Lithuanian Embassy.............17 D2
Matrix Club..........................18 E4
Neo Internetcafé..................19 C3
Raeturist..............................20 F2
Rahva Raamat......................21 C3
Russian Consulate................22 C2
Süadalinna Arstide...............23 D4
Swedish Embassy.................24 C2
Tallinn Tourist Information
  Centre...............................25 C3
Tavid...................................26 D2

SIGHTS & ACTIVITIES   (pp305-8)
Alexander Nevsky Cathedral....27 B3
Applied Art Museum.............28 C2
Broken Line Monument.........29 D1
Brotherhood of Blackheads...30 C2
Chapel of Our Lady..........(see 42)
Danish King's Courtyard........31 B3
Dominican Monastery...........32 C2
Draakon gallery....................33 C2
Former KGB headquarters.....34 C2
Great Coast Gate..................35 D1
Great Guild......................(see 47)
Kiek-in-de-Kök.....................36 B3
Knighthood House.................37 B3
Linnamuuseum.....................38 C2

Maritime Museum.............(see 35)
Museum of Occupation and Fight for
  Freedom.............................39 B4
Neitsitorn............................40 B3
Niguliste Church...................41 C3
Observation deck.............(see 42)
Oleviste Church...............(see 42)
Paks Margareeta................(see 35)
Pikk Herman bastion............43 B3
Pikk Jalg Gate Tower............44 C2
Pühavaimu Kirik...................45 C2
Raeapteek............................46 C2
St Catherine's Catholic Church..(see 32)
St Olaus' Guild..................(see 30)
State History Museum...........47 C3
Tallinn Town Wall.................48 C2
Toomkirik............................49 B3
Toompea Castle....................50 B3
Town Hall.............................51 C3

SLEEPING   (pp308-9)
Beata Hostel.........................52 D1
Cassandra Apartments..........53 E4
Dorell..................................54 F2
Hostel Alur...........................55 B1
Hotel G9..............................56 E3
Old House Guesthouse..........57 D2
Old House.............................58 D1
Olevi Residents....................59 C2
Rasastra Bed & Breakfast......60 D2
Schlösse Hotel.......................61 C2
Three Sisters Hotel................62 C1
Vana Tom.............................63 C3
Villa Hortensia.................(see 81)

EATING   (pp309-11)
Café Anglais.........................64 C3
Café VS................................65 C4
Controvento..........................66 C3
Deli 24................................67 C4
Eesti Maja............................68 D4
Kohvik Narva........................69 B3
Kompressor...........................70 C3
Olde Hansa...........................71 C3
Peetri Pizza..........................72 C4

Peetri Pizza..........................73 D2
Pizza Americano...................74 C3
Rimi.....................................75 D2
Stockmann............................76 E4
Sultan..................................77 C3
Texas Honky Tonk.................78 C2
Toidumailm......................(see 99)
Troika..................................79 C3
Vanaema Juures...................80 B3

DRINKING   📷   (p311)
Café-Chocolaterie.................81 C3
Hell Hunt..............................82 C2
Kehrwieder...........................83 C2
Levist Väljas.........................84 C2
Maiasmokk............................85 C2
Tristan ja Isolde................(see 51)
Von Krahli Teater Baar..........86 C3

ENTERTAINMENT   📷 (pp311-12)
Club Hollywood.................(see 93)
Estonia Theatre & Concert Hall..87 D3
Estonian Drama Theatre.........88 C3
G-punkt...............................89 C4
Kinomaja..............................90 D2
Linnateater...........................91 C2
Pitetilevi.........................(see 99)
Privé...................................92 C3
Sõprus.................................93 C3
Terrarium.............................94 D1
X-Baar.................................95 C3

SHOPPING   📷   (p312)
Domini Canes.......................96 C3
Kodukäsitöö..........................97 C3
Navitrolla Galerii..................98 B3
Viru Keskus..........................99 D3

TRANSPORT   (pp312-14)
Bus Platform.......................100 B2
Bus to Airport.....................101 E3
Estonian Air........................102 C3

OTHER
Viru Gate............................103 D3

ESTONIA

In Your Pocket (www.inyourpocket.com) The king of the region's listings guide has up-to-date information on everything to do with arriving, staying and having fun in Tallinn and other cities in Estonia. Its guides are on sale at bookshops.

Tallinn Tourist Information Centre (☎ 645 7777; www.visitestonia.com; Niguliste tänav 2; ✆ 9am-8pm Mon-Fri, 10am-6pm Sat & Sun May-Aug, 9am-6pm Mon-Fri, 10am-5pm Sat & Sun Sep, 9am-5pm Mon-Fri, 10am-3pm Sat Oct-Apr) Near Raekoja plats, this offers a full range of services. Here you can purchase the Tallinn Card (60EEK to 325EEK), which gives free admission to museums, discounts and rides on public transport.

Travel Agencies
City and country tours, guided trips to provincial Estonia, and accommodation in other towns are all part of most travel agencies' stock in trade. Leading ones:

Baltic Tours (☎ 630 0460; www.bt.ee; Pikk tänav 31)
Estonian Holidays (☎ 627 0500; www.holidays.ee; Lai tänav 5)
Estravel (☎ 626 6266; www.estravel.ee; Suur-Karja tänav 15)

SIGHTS
Old Town
RAEKOJA PLATS & AROUND
Raekoja plats (Town Hall Sq) has been the centre of Tallinn life since markets began here probably in the 11th century (the last was held in 1896). It's dominated by the only surviving Gothic **town hall** (☎ 645 7900; adult/student 25/15EEK; ✆ tower 11am-6pm May-Aug) in northern Europe (early 14th century, reconstruction 1402–04) and faced by pretty, pastel buildings from the 15th–17th centuries. Old Thomas, Tallinn's symbol and guardsman, has been keeping watch from his perch on the weathervane atop Town Hall since 1530. This is Tallinn's pulsing heart: all summer there are outdoor cafés imploring you to take a load off your feet and people-watch; come Christmas time, a huge pine tree is erected in the middle (a tradition some 550 years old) and becomes the city's main meeting point. Whether bathed in sunlight or sprinkled with snow, this is always an inviting spot.

The **Raeapteek** (Town Council Pharmacy), on the northern side of Raekoja plats, is another ancient Tallinn institution; there's been a pharmacy or apothecary's shop here since at least 1422, though the present façade is of the 17th century. Duck through the arch beside it into narrow Saia käik (White Bread Passage), at the far end of which is the lovely 14th-century Gothic **Pühavaimu kirik** (Holy Spirit Church; ☎ 644 1487; ☼ 10am-4pm), used by Lutherans. Its colourful clock on the wall outside is the oldest in Tallinn, the carvings inside date from 1684 and the tower bell was cast in 1433. There are free concerts at 6pm Monday.

A medieval merchant's home houses the **Linnamuuseum** (City Museum; ☎ 644 6553; cnr Pühavaimu & Vene tänav 17; adult/student 25/10EEK; ☼ 10.30am-6pm Wed-Mon Mar-Oct, 10.30am-7pm Nov-Feb), which traces Tallinn's development from its beginnings through to 1940 with some informative displays and curious artefacts. The intricate wooden door alone is worth a look-see.

Also on Vene tänav (Estonian for 'Russian', named for the many Russian merchants who lived in the street), in the courtyard at No 16, is the 1844 **St Catherine's Catholic Church**, whitewashed and looking like it belongs in Spain. A door in the courtyard leads into the **Dominican Monastery** (☎ 644 4606; Vene tänav 16/18; adult/student 25/15EEK; ☼ 9.30am-6pm mid-May–mid-Sep), founded in 1246 as a base for Scandinavian monks. Today the monastery complex houses Estonia's largest collection of **stone carvings**.

The majestic 15th-century **Niguliste Church** (☎ 644 9911; Niguliste tänav 3; adult/student 35/20EEK; ☼ 10am-5pm Wed-Sun), a minute's walk south of Raekoja plats, is now used to stage concerts and serves as a **museum** of medieval church art.

At the foot of the slope below the Niguliste Church is the carefully exposed wreckage of the buildings that stood here before the Soviet bombing of Tallinn on the night of 9 March 1944.

LOWER TOWN

From Pühavaimu kirik, you can stroll along Pikk tänav, which runs north to the **Great Coast Gate** – the medieval exit to Tallinn's port. It's lined with the 15th-century houses of merchants and gentry as well as buildings of several old Tallinn guilds. In the 1440 building of the **Great Guild**, to which

the most important merchants belonged, is the **Ajaloomuuseum** (State History Museum; ☎ 641 1630; Pikk tänav 17; adult/student 10/8EEK; ☼ 11am-6pm Thu-Tue). It features Estonian history up to the 18th century and has ceramics, jewellery and archaeological delights. No 18 is the 1911 **Draakon gallery** (☎ 646 4110; ☼ 10am-6pm Mon-Fri, 10am-5pm Sat & Sun) with its fabulous sculpted façade.

Crane your neck up at Pikk tänav 19 – there's a coy black cat waiting to surprise you. The **Brotherhood of Blackheads** and **St Olaus' Guild** are in adjoining buildings at Pikk tänav 24 and 26. The Blackheads were unmarried, mainly foreign merchants whose patron saint, Mauritius, appears with his head between two lions on the building's façade (dating from 1597).

At the northern end of Pikk tänav stands a chief Tallinn landmark, the **Oleviste Church**. This is a great place to start any Tallinn expedition as there's a superb **observation deck** (☎ 6214421; adult/student 20/10EEK; ☼ 10am-6pm) halfway up its 124m structure offering the city's best views, hands down, of the Old Town (it's a long and narrow climb up, though – bring a hanky to wipe off the sweat).

First built in the early 13th century, it was once the world's tallest building (it used to tower 159m before several fires and reconstructions brought it down to its present size). The church is dedicated to the 11th-century King Olav II of Norway, but linked in local lore with another Olav (Olaf), the church's legendary architect, who fell to his death from the tower. It's said that a toad and a snake then crawled out of his mouth. The incident is recalled in one of the carvings on the east wall of the 16th-century **Chapel of Our Lady**, which adjoins the church. Most of the church was rebuilt after a fire during the 1820s.

Just south of the church is the **former KGB headquarters** (Pikk tänav 46/48), whose basement windows were bricked up to conceal the sounds of interrogations.

The Great Coast Gate is joined to **Paks Margareeta** (Fat Margaret), the rotund 16th-century bastion which protected this entrance to the Old Town. Inside the bastion is the **Meremuuseum** (Maritime Museum; ☎ 641 1408; Pikk tänav 70; adult/student 25/10EEK; ☼ 10am-6pm Wed-Sun). The exhibits are decidedly ho-hum, but there are great views from the rooftop café.

Just beyond the bastion stands the **broken line monument**, a black, curved slab in memory of victims of the Estonia ferry disaster. In September 1994, 852 people died when the ferry sank en route from Tallinn to Stockholm.

While Pikk was the street of traders, **Lai tänav**, running roughly parallel, was the street of artisans, whose traditions are recalled in the **Tarbekunstimuuseum** (Applied Art Museum; ☎ 641 1927; Lai tänav 17; adult/student 20/10EEK; ☺ 11am-6pm Wed-Sun). You'll find an excellent mix of historical and contemporary ceramics, glass, rugs, metal and leatherwork.

Suur-Kloostri tänav leads to the longest-standing stretch of the **Lower Town Wall**, with nine towers along Laboratooriumi. A very worthy detour is to the **Tallinn Town Wall** (☎ 644 9867; Gümnaasiumi tänav 3; adult/student 10/7EEK; ☺ 11am-7pm Mon-Fri, 11am-4pm Sat & Sun). Three empty towers are connected here and visitors can explore their nooks and crannies for themselves. Again, the views from the tower 'windows' are splendid.

TOOMPEA

A regal approach to Toompea is through the red-roofed 1380 **Pikk jalg gate tower** at the western end of Pikk tänav in the lower town, and then along Pikk jalg (Long Leg). The 19th-century Russian Orthodox **Alexander Nevsky Cathedral** dominates Lossi plats at the top of Pikk jalg. It was built as a part of Alexander III's policy of Russification, and sited strategically across from **Toompea Castle**, Estonia's traditional seat of power. The *riigikogu* (parliament) meets in the pink baroque-style building, an 18th-century addition to the castle. Nothing remains of the original 1219 Danish castle. Still standing are three of the four corner towers of its successor, the Knights of the Sword's Castle. Finest of these towers is the 14th-century **Pikk Hermann** (Tall Hermann) at the southwestern corner, from which the state flag is raised every morning at sunrise to the tune of the Estonian anthem.

The Lutheran **Toomkirik** (Dome Church; ☎ 644 4140; Toom-Kooli tänav; ☺ 9am-5pm Tue-Sun) is Estonia's oldest church; on the site of a 1219 Danish church, it dates from the 14th century. Inside the impressive, austere and damp church are finely carved tombs and coats of arms. Across the street, an 18th-century noble's house is now **Rüütelkonna-hoone** (Knighthood House; ☎ 644 9340; Kiriku plats 1;

adult/student 20/5EEK; ☺ 11am-6pm Wed-Sun), the Art Museum of Estonia's main branch, featuring Estonian artists. From Toomkirik, follow Kohtu tänav to the city's favourite lookout over the Lower Town – it's also Photo Opportunity No 1 in Tallinn!

A path leads down from Lossi plats through an opening in the wall to the **Danish King's Courtyard** where, in summer, artists set up their easels. There are excellent views over the lower town – get your cameras out! One of the towers, the **Neitsitorn** (Virgin's Tower), has a **café** (☎ 644 0896; Lühike jalg 9A; ☺ 11am-10pm) inside with good views.

Nearby **Kiek-in-de-Kök** (☎ 644 6686; Komandanti tee 2; adult/student 15/10EEK; ☺ 10.30am-6pm Tue-Sun), a tall tower built in about 1475, is a museum that holds several floors of maps and models of old Tallinn, weapons and a photographic gallery. Its name is Low German for 'Peep into the Kitchen' – from the upper floors of the tower medieval voyeurs could see into the kitchens of the Old Town.

The **Museum of Occupation and Fight for Freedom** (☎ 668 0250; Toompea tänav 8; adult/student 10/5EEK; ☺ 11am-6pm Tue-Sun), just down the hill from Toompea, is a new and worthwhile display of Estonia's history of occupation, focusing on the most recent Soviet one.

Kadriorg

To reach the pleasant, wooded **Kadriorg Park** 2km east of the Old Town along Narva maantee, take tram No 1 or 3 to the last stop. The park and the 1718–36 Kadriorg Palace were designed for Peter the Great for his wife Catherine I. The **Kadriorg Palace & Foreign Art Museum** (☎ 606 6400; Weizenbergi tänav 37; adult/student 35/20EEK; ☺ 10am-5pm Tue-Sun May-Sep, 10am-5pm Wed-Sun Oct-Apr) makes for a dreamy hour or so – the 17th- and 18th-century foreign art is mainly unabashedly romantic. A walk through the streets around Kadriorg, with their charming wooden architecture, is definitely recommended. Between the wars, this was Tallinn's most elite area.

Towards Pirita

Jutting north of Kadriorg alongside the sea coast is Pirita tee, Tallinn's greatest promenade. Summer sunsets around midnight are particularly romantic from here, and it's the city's nicest biking and Rollerblading area. North of Kadriorg you come to the **Lauluväljak**, the Song Festival grounds, an

ESTONIA

impressive amphitheatre which hosts song festivals and big concerts (Jacko played here in 1997). One kilometre north of Kadriorg, **Maarjamäe Palace** (☎ 601 4535; Pirita tee 56; adult/ student 10/8EEK; ☯ 11am-6pm Wed-Sun) contains the part of the Estonian History Museum covering the mid-19th century onwards.

Heading further north, you pass the foreboding **Soviet obelisk** locally dubbed 'the Impotent's Dream'. It's the focal point of a 1960 Soviet war memorial that's now more cracked and crumbling than inspiring. A small German cemetery is behind it. **Pirita Yacht Club**, some 1.5km beyond Maarjamäe Palace, and the **Olympic Yachting Centre** were venues for the 1980 Olympic sailing events. International regattas are still held here. In summer you can rent rowing boats and pedal boats at **Pirita Rowboat Rental** (☎ 621 2105; Kloostri tee 6; per hr from 25EEK; ☯ 10am-10pm mid-May–Sep) beside the bridge over the river. For an unforgettable yacht trip out into Tallinn Bay, contact **Emerald** (☎ 504 3031; www.spinnaker .ee). It offers three- and four-hour cruises from €120 for 12 persons.

North of the bridge are a beach backed by pine woods and the 15th-century Swedish **Convent of St Brigitta** (☎ 605 5044; Merivälja tee 18; adult/student 20/10EEK; ☯ 9am-7pm Jun-Aug, 10am-6pm Sep, Apr & May, noon-4pm Oct-Mar), ruined by war in 1577. The long stretch of clean beaches on the other side of Pirita tee are popular in the summer. Bus Nos 1, 8 and 34 run between the city centre and Pirita.

Zoo & Rocca al Mare

About 4.5km from the Old Town, the **Tallinn Zoo** (☎ 694 3300; Paldiski maantee 145; adult/child 39/23EEK; ☯ 9am-7pm May-Aug, 9am-5pm Mar-Apr & Sep-Oct, 9am-3pm Nov-Feb) boasts one of the world's largest collections of mountain goats and sheep and 334 different species of animals (including hyenas), birds, reptiles and fish. Opposite the zoo is **Tivoli** (☯ 656 0110; www .tivoli.ee, in Estonian; Paldiski Maantee 100; ☯ 11am-8pm) a small amusement park for kids.

A kilometre beyond the zoo, Ran-namõisa tee turns right towards Rocca al Mare and its **Open Air Museum** (☎ 654 9117; Vabaõhumuuseumi tee 12; adult/child 28/12EEK; ☯ buildings 10am-6pm May-Sep, grounds 10am-8pm). Most of Estonia's oldest wooden structures (mainly farmhouses as well as a 1699 chapel and a windmill) are preserved here. On Sunday mornings there are folk song-and-dance

shows. There's also a **tavern** (mains from 75EEK; ☯ 10am-6pm) serving traditional Estonian meals. Kids will love the entire place – and not only for the horse rides!

FESTIVALS & EVENTS

Jazzkaar (mid-Apr) One of Tallinn's hot-ticket events, this brings together jazz greats from around the world in a series of concerts.

Old Town Days (early Jun) Usually lasting four days, this sees the Old Town come alive with market stalls, concerts, dancing and medieval-themed merry-making.

Beer Summer (early Jul) One of the most popular festivals of the year, this beer-guzzling, rock-band-listening extravaganza happens under and around big tents near the Lauluväljak (Song Festival) grounds.

Dance Festival (www.saal.ee; Aug) International modern dance troupes usually stage exciting performances.

SLEEPING

It's not easy to be disappointed in Tallinn's accommodation scene – you'd have to really try. With a wide array of tasteful, clean, often unique and sumptuous hotels and guesthouses to choose from, your lodging is likely to be a highlight of your visit. In the last decade, many superb four- and five-star hotels have opened, many of the best inside carefully refurbished medieval houses. Lower budget options are to be found in the Old Town as well as outside the centre.

Apartment Rental

Rasastra Bed & Breakfast (☎ 661 6291; www.bedbreak fast.ee; Mere puiestee 4) Can set you up with a room in a private home from 260EEK per person.

Cassandra Apartments (☎ 630 9820; www.cassandra -apartments.com; Tartu maantee 18) Several spacious, comfy apartments in a modern chrome-and-glass skyscraper are yours from 1500EEK.

Budget

Kämping Kalevi (☎ 623 9191; Kloostrimetsa tee 56a; camp site/car 80/240EEK, 2-/4-person wood cabin 350/530EEK; ☯ mid-May–mid-Sep) Fresh air, friendly owners and a lovely forested locale make this camping ground a winner. There are shared showers and toilets and an on-site café. Take bus No 34 from the underground bus stop at Viru Keskus to the Motoklubi stop.

Merevaik (☎ 655 3767; 5th fl, Sõpruse puiestee 182; dm/s/d/tr 150/320/370/450EEK) Some 5km from the centre, this place offers basic lodgings with a common room and self-catering kitchens.

There's a discount of up to 10% for ISIC and YHA card-holders. Take trolleybus No 2 or 3 from near Vabaduse väljak at the very beginning of Estonia puiestee and get off at the Linnu tee stop.

Beata Hostel (☎ 641 1171; Uus tänav 35; dm/s/d 250/360/600EEK) A small hostel tucked into an Old Town corner. There is no common space here and little sense of community but it's a great place to crash; the main dorm room (10 beds) is spacious and the separate singles/doubles are very sweet.

Hostel Alur (☎ 631 1531; www.alurhostel.com; Rannamäe tee 3; dm/s/d/tr 250/500/750/990EEK) Not the liveliest of hostels, but it's clean, friendly, (a bit too) quiet and just a stone's throw from the train station and Old Town. There's 10% discount for ISIC and YHA card-holders.

Old House (☎ 641 1464; www.oldhouse.ee; Uus tänav 26; dm incl breakfast 290EEK, 1-/2-/3-/5-/6-person r incl breakfast 390/550/825/900/1080EEK) You won't get a better location than at this recently refurbished hostel in the Old Town. Sure, the walls are paper-thin, but it's cosy, spotless and the breakfast is hearty. There's a 10% discount with ISIC.

Old House Guesthouse (☎ 641 1464; www.old house.ee; Uus tänav 22; s/d/tr incl breakfast 450/650/975EEK) Nearly adjacent to the Old House (above) and run by the same people, the guesthouse has the same pros and cons, though the rooms here are more spacious and private. The sumptuous apartments scattered throughout the Old Town are excellent value (350EEK to 2000EEK) and can fit four persons.

Mid-Range

Hotel G9 (☎ 626 7100; www.hotelg9.ee; Gosiori tänav 9; s/d/tr 500/600/750EEK) A two-minute walk from the modern city centre, this nondescript but modern, cheerful place is a very good deal.

Dorell (☎ 626 1200; www.dorell.ee; Karu tänav 39; s 550-700EEK, d 600-800EEK) One of the best deals in this category if being in the centre is important. What it lacks in aesthetic splendour it makes up for with convenience.

Stroomi (☎ 630 4200; Randla tänav 11; s 500-550EEK, d 700-950EEK) Some 5km from the centre (20 minutes on Bus No 40 from the underground bus stop inside Viru Keskus, or take bus No 3 on Narva Maantee, 150m east of the main post office), this simple though perfectly decent place has some advantages: it's a two-minute walk from a beach, and you get to see a different side of Tallinn life in this residential,

mainly Russian neighbourhood. It also hires out bicycles and Rollerblades; a pair of bikes are rented for 45EEK per hour; two pairs of Rollerblades are 30EEK per hour.

Villa Hortensia (☎ 641 8017, 504 6113; Vene tänav 6; s 600-900EEK, d 800-1200EEK) This is a real treat – nestled into one of the Old Town's most atmospheric courtyards is this small, irresistibly charming hotel. Most rooms are split-level but tiny, with beds in a loft area under skylights opening onto Old Town roofs.

Top End

Olevi Residents (☎ 627 7650; www.olevi.ee; Olevimägi tänav 4; s/d/ste from 1100/1600/3500EEK; ⊠ ⚟) Each room has its own character here in this Old Town oasis, some with antiques, others with arched ceilings and bits of the original medieval building showing through. The suites are worth a splurge here. The rooms on the top floor have a sea view.

Three Sisters Hotel (☎ 630 6300; www.threesisters hotel.com; Pikk tänav 71; s/d/ste from 3900/4200/5650; ⊠ ⚟) Sumptuous luxury in a lovingly refurbished medieval building: original design elements have been preserved alongside high-tech comforts. Cool your wine in a hole in the centuries-old wall, run a bath in an old-fashioned tub and dream away...

Villa Mary (☎ 667 7000; www.grandhotel.ee/villa; Rohuneeme tee 103; ste from 4500EEK) About a 10km drive from the centre in a gorgeous location by the sea, this slice of heaven utilises not medieval elements but nature itself as a main part of its aesthetic. The bright entrance hall is as inviting as the lovely rooms. Owners can organise transport to/from the town.

Schlössle Hotel (☎ 699 7700; www.schlossle-hotels .com; Pühavaimu tänav 13-15; s 4150-5000EEK, d 4800-5500EEK, ste 6850-8500EEK; ⊠ ⚟) These breath-taking rooms in a complex of buildings that have witnessed 600 years of Tallinn life are among the nicest in the country. All needs are catered for under its five stars, and the cellar restaurant is first-rate.

EATING

Many ethnic restaurants can be found serving anything from Turkish meze to Thai Kai Phad – though even on exotic dishes, be prepared for an Estonian touch (the sudden appearance of sour cream or cucumbers for example)! Very reasonable lunch specials abound in the city (30EEK to 50EEK), so it's economical to fill up during daytime.

ESTONIA

AUTHOR'S CHOICE

Café VS (☎ 626 2627; www.cafévs.ee; Pärnu maantee 28; mains 55-125EEK; ☻ 10am-1am Mon-Thu, 10am-3am Fri & Sat, 1pm-1am Sun) A trendsetter on the food and club music scene for years, this fashion-conscious restaurant, bar and, by night, club, takes its industrial décor seriously – and so do its very beautiful-people clientele. The expansive menu specialises in Indian food – it's the city's best, hands down. Many vegetarian options.

Olde Hansa (☎ 627 9020; Vana Turg 1; ☻ 11am-midnight; mains 75-225EEK) If you'll splurge just once in Tallinn, here's where to do it. This medieval-themed restaurant (more authentic than kitsch!) boasts first and foremost the most ebullient and friendly service in the city, plus exotic meats (elk, wild boar) and home-made delights like juniper cheese and honey beer. It's a fun atmosphere inside or out on the terrace, and the food and its creative presentation is always first-rate.

Restaurants

BUDGET

Texas Honky Tonk (☎ 631 1755; Pikk tänav 43; mains from 40EEK; ☻ noon-midnight Sun-Thu, noon-2am Sat & Sun) No one does Americana quite so well in Tallinn. The menu is mostly Tex-Mex (the burritos are superb), and the atmosphere lively and yippee-ayo-ta-yay fun.

Kompressor (☎ 646 4210; Rataskaevu tänav 3; mains from 45EEK; ☻ 11am-1pm Mon-Thu, 11am-2am Fri-Sun) Eat one of the enormous, stuffed pancakes and you'll be full for the rest of the day. The large hall and casual atmosphere make it a great hang-out too.

MID-RANGE

Controvento (☎ 640 0470; Vene tänav 12; pizzas from 50EEK, mains from 110EEK; ☻ noon-11pm) A veteran on the Tallinn dining scene, this local favourite serves up excellent Italian fare in cosy surroundings (especially on the 1st floor). On the meat-heavy menu the pork in marsala sauce is a winner.

Eesti Maja (☎ 645 5252; www.eestimaja.ee; Lauteri tänav 1; buffet 75EEK, mains from 100EEK; ☻ 11am-11pm) Here's a good place to sample some traditional Estonian fare, in a fun, folksy interior. The small weekday lunch buffet is a good deal and lets you try some of the heavy, exotic fare without a full-plate commitment.

Troika (☎ 627 6245; Raekoja plats 15; mains from 115EEK; ☻ noon-11pm) Tallinn's best Russian restaurant is a fully fledged experience in itself, what with the wild hunting-themed murals, live accordion players, and an old-style country tavern upstairs. Both appetisers and main meals are delicious. You can't leave without downing a few vodka shots (but keep an eye on the alcohol prices).

TOP END

Sultan (☎ 644 4400; Väike-Karja 8; mezes 35-125EEK; ☻ 5pm-midnight) Meze is the operational word here – delicious little platters of Turkish dishes (with an Iberian accent thanks to the Spanish-trained cook!). The menu is lamb-heavy, and there are several vegetarian choices. There's Turkish coffee and Turkish traditional dancing and a water-pipe (hookah) salon downstairs.

Vanaema Juures (Grandma's Place; ☎ 626 9080; Rataskaevu tänav 12; mains 140EEK; ☻ noon-10pm Mon-Fri, noon-6pm Sun) One of Tallinn's most stylish restaurants in the 1930s, it still ranks as a top choice for authentic Estonian fare. The atmosphere is on the formal side but not too stodgy – and the food is succulent (much more than blood sausages on offer, have no fear).

Villa Thai (☎ 641 9347; Vilmsi tänav 6; mains 75-195EEK, lunch special 50EEK; ☻ noon-11pm) Delicious Thai and Tandoori specialities followed by a stroll through surrounding Kadriorg – what more can you ask for? This is one of the most sublimely decorated restaurants in town, with exotic imported furniture in Buddhist harmony with all the bamboo and curtains. Food is top-notch.

Cafés

Most places listed under Drinking (opposite) also serve up tasty food, and some cafés and restaurants double as bars or clubs come evening.

Kohvik Narva (☎ 660 1786; Narva maantee 10; mains 35-65EEK; ☻ 10am-8pm Mon-Sat, 10am-6pm Sun) One of the only places left in Tallinn where you can step back into the USSR, this is kitsch without even being aware of it. The décor is decidedly brown and faded red, the service dismissive and the menu full of staples from the times of yore like wieners, Chicken Kiev, *plov* (pilaf with pieces of meat and vegetables) and borscht. Have fun!

Café Anglais (☎ 644 2160; Raekoja plats 14; mains from 55EEK; ☑ 11am-11pm) There's a waft of Vienna and Paris in this airy room overlooking Raekoja plats. A favourite with Tallinn's eccentrics and expats, this elegant café serves up some of the best home-made cakes in town. Try the warm salads too. Ever-changing art exhibits and, come evening, a piano player who looks more like a boxer add the final touches of class.

Quick Eats

There are some fast-food options along Viru tänav and better ones inside the Viru Keskus shopping centre.

Deli 24 (☎ 669 1816; Pärnu maantee 20; mains 25EEK; ☑ 24hr) Cafeteria-style but decent grub charged by weight in very orange surroundings.

Peetri Pizza (delivery ☎ 656 7567; Pärnu maantee 22 & Mere puiestee 6; ☑ 11am-10pm) This chain opened as soon as Estonia broke free from the USSR and so was practically synonymous with freedom. It's survived the throes of capitalism and remains a local favourite, doling out tasty thin-crusted and pan pizzas.

Pizza Americano (☎ 644 8837; Müürivahe tänav 2; ☑ 11.30am-10.30pm; pizzas from 85EEK) Thick, tasty pizzas of every possible permutation and combination are on offer here, including several vegetarian options.

Self-Catering

Don't wait to be served, get it all yourself at the best supermarkets in the centre: **Toidumailm** (Viru väljak 4; ☑ 8am-10pm) inside the Viru Keskus, the grocery section of **Stockmann** (Liivalaia tänav 53; ☑ 9am-10pm Mon-Fri, 9am-9pm Sat & Sun), and **Rimi** (Aia tänav 7; ☑ 9am-10pm).

DRINKING

Tallinn without its café and bar culture is simply inconceivable. Even in Soviet times Tallinn was renowned for its cafés. Due to the charm of the surroundings, the Old Town is the obvious place to head to for cellar bars and absurdly cosy cafés.

Tristan ja Isolde (☎ 644 8749; Town Hall Bldg, Raekoja plats 1; ☑ 8am-11pm) You may be turned off Starbucks forever when you step into this tiny café with intimate medieval surroundings. Essential for lovers of fine coffee.

Café-Chocolaterie (☎ 641 8061; Vene tänav 6; ☑ 10am-11pm) In a city of cosy cafés, this one wears the 'cosy' crown. Inside it's like a hideaway at your grandma's place, and the courtyard terrace among the unfinished buildings is a welcome, raw contrast to some hyperstylised Old Town hang-outs. Heavenly, handmade chocolates are the trump card of this superb café.

Kehrwieder (☎ 644 0818; Saiakäik 1; ☑ 8am-11pm) Another crazily comfy café where you can stretch out on a couch, read by lamplight and bump your head on the arched ceilings. Coffees, teas, ice cream and ambience galore are the things here. Try to catch one of the live DJ jam sessions here some evening.

Maiasmokk (Sweet-Tooth; ☎ 646 4066; Pikk tänav 16; ☑ 8am-7pm Mon-Sat, 10am-6pm Sun) The city's longest-running café (open since 1884) still draws a (slightly older) crowd who appreciate the classic feel, elaborate ceiling mirror, the Old World feel and the pastries (some of which look like they've been there since opening day, but who cares – it's the atmosphere that counts!).

Hell Hunt (☎ 681 8333; Pikk tänav 39; ☑ noon-2am) A trouper on the pub circuit for years, this place boasts an amiable atmosphere and reasonable prices for local-brewed beer and cider (half-litre for 24EEK).

Von Krahli Teater Baar (☎ 626 9096; Rataskaevu tänav 10/12; ☑ noon-1am Sun-Thu, noon-3am Fri & Sat) One of the city's best bars. It has live bands (and sometimes stages fringe plays) and is a good place to meet interesting locals.

Levist Väljas (☎ 507 7372; Olevimägi tänav 12; ☑ 3pm-3am Sun-Thu, 3pm-6am Fri & Sat) In this cellar bar, it's not only telephones which are 'out of range' (what its name translates to) – so are the clientele! The wobbly seats, cheap booze and drafty interior attracts a refreshingly motley crew of punks, has-beens and anyone else who strays from the well-trodden tourist path.

ENTERTAINMENT

It's a small capital as capitals go but there's never a dull moment here, whether in a wild club, laid-back bar or concert hall. Buy tickets for concerts and main events at **Piletilevi** (www.piletilevi.ee) and its central locations, like inside Viru Keskus. Events are posted on city centre walls, advertised on flyers found in shops and cafés, and listed in newspapers as well as in *In Your Pocket*.

ESTONIA

Nightclubs

Club Hollywood (☎ 627 4770; www.club-hollywood
.ee; Vana-Posti tänav 8; ☺ 10pm-5am Wed-Sat) A multilevel emporium of mayhem, this is the
one to draw the largest crowds. The Friday
hip-hop evenings are the most popular.

Terrarium (☎ 661 4721; Sadama tänav 6; ☺ 10pm-
5am Wed-Sat) A more down-to-earth club experience is ensured here; prices are lower
and there's less attitude than in the posher
Old Town clubs. But the DJs still kick out
the disco and the 20-something crowd laps it
up. The outdoor terrace is a big draw – anything can happen in the little pool there!

Privé (☎ 631 0545; Harju tänav 6; ☺ 10pm-6am Wed-
Sat) Tallinn's most elite club (you can tell by
the deep red curtains and oxygen bar) gets
rowdiest on Saturdays. High prices (and good
DJs) attract a beautiful and foreign crowd.

Gay & Lesbian Venues

X-Baar (☎ 692 9266; Sauna tänav 1; ☺ 2pm-1am)
The only place in the Old Town flying the
rainbow flag is Tallinn's premier gay bar,
whose minuscule dance floor comes alive
late at weekends.

G-Punkt (Pärnu maantee 23; ☺ 4pm-midnight Sun-
Tue & Thu, 4pm-2am Wed, Fri & Sat) The fact that
this friendly and cosy club is hidden in an
alley behind Pärnu maantee and has no sign
recalls the secrecy of old Eastern European
gay bars. Wednesday night is its big disco
and drama night.

Theatre

Estonia Theatre & Concert Hall (theatre ☎ 626 0215,
concert hall ☎ 614 7760; Estonia puiestee 4) The city's
biggest concerts and shows are held here.
It's Tallinn's main theatre, and also houses
the Estonian national opera and ballet.

Estonian Drama Theatre (☎ 680 5555; Pärnu
maantee 5) Stages mainly classical plays and
tends to avoid modern or alternative fare.

Linnateater (City Theatre; ☎ 665 0800; www.linna
teater.ee; Lai tänav 23) This theatre always stages
something memorable – watch for its summer plays on an outdoor stage.

Cinemas

Check out what's on at www.superkinod.ee.
No dubbing here (this is a civilised country!);
all films play in their original languages,
subtitled into Estonian and Russian.

Sõprus (☎ 644 1919; www.kino.ee, in Estonian; Vana-
Posti tänav 8) Housed in a magnificent Stalin-

era theatre, this art-house cinema has an
excellent repertoire of European, local and
independent productions.

Another great art-house cinema is **Kinomaja**
(☎ 646 4510; Uus tänav 3).

Sport

A Le Coq Arena (☎ 627 9940; Asula tänav 4c) About
1.5km southwest of town, this sparkling,
newly refurbished arena is home to Tallinn's
football team Flora, which is filled with
Estonia's toughest, meanest players. Watching a match is great fun.

Kalev Sporhidall (☎ 644 5171; Staadioni tänav 8)
Basketball is Estonia's most passionately
watched game, and the best national tournaments are usually held in this stadium just
south of town.

SHOPPING

The Old Town is full of small shops selling Estonian-made handicrafts, costumes,
leather-bound books, ceramics, jewellery,
silverware, stained-glass windows and objects carved out of limestone. These are
traditional Estonian souvenirs – these and
a bottle of Vana Tallinn, of course! They
are also on sale inside the **Viru Keskus** (☎ 610
1400; Viru Väljak 4; ☺ 8am-10pm) and other shopping centres. The Draakon gallery (p306)
sells some lovely handmade glassware.
There are also several antique shops selling Soviet memorabilia and Russian icons;
there are a few lined up along Aia tänav
(on the outside of the western walls) in
the Old Town.

Navitrolla Galerii (☎ 631 3716; Pikk jalg 7;
☺ 10am-6pm Mon-Fri, 10am-4pm Sat & Sun) Find
this artist's fanciful paintings as original
artworks or on T-shirts!

Domini Canes (☎ 644 5286; Katerina käik; ☺ 11am-
6pm) A lovely gallery-workshop where the ancient craft of glassmaking is revived for all to
see. There are lovely stained-glass works.

Kodukäsitöö (☎ 631 4076; Müürivahe 17; ☺ 9am-
5pm) One of the many good places to find
locally made handicrafts.

GETTING THERE & AWAY

Air

For information on flights in and out of
Tallinn see p329. **Tallinn airport** (☎ 605 8888;
www.tallinn-airport.ee) is 3km southeast of the
city centre on Tartu maantee. Schedules are
on its website.

Boat

See p329 for information about the many services available between Tallinn and Helsinki and Stockholm. Tallinn's sea-passenger terminal is at the end of Sadama, about 1km northeast of the Old Town. Tram Nos 1 and 2 and bus Nos 3, 4 and 8 go to the Linnahall stop (by the Statoil petrol station), five minutes' walk from terminals A, B and C. Terminal D is at the end of Lootsi tänav, better accessed from Ahtri tänav. A taxi between the centre and any of the terminals will cost about 40EEK.

Bus

Buses to places within about 40km of Tallinn depart from the platform next to the train station. You can get information and timetables from **Harju Linnid** (☎ 644 1801). For detailed bus information and to buy advance tickets for all other destinations, contact the central bus station **Autobussijaam** (☎ 680 0900; www.bussireisid.ee, in Estonian; Lastekodu tänav 46), which is just southeast of the city centre. Tram No 2 or 4 will take you there.

Car & Motorcycle

There are 24-hour petrol stations at strategic spots within the city and along major roads leading to and from Tallinn. The Pärnu maantee Neste has a car-repair service.

Car rental in Tallinn is spectacularly overpriced. You can rent cars in Tartu or Pärnu instead and save a bundle (contact the tourist information centres in each city).

Some of the major agencies to check out for car rental:

Avis (☎ 605 8222; www.avis.ee; Liivalaia tänav 13/15) Just south of the centre.
Hertz (☎ 605 8923; www.hertz.ee) At the airport.
Tulika Rent (☎ 612 0012; www.tulika.ee; Tihase tänav 34) Southwest of the centre.

Train

Tallinn's **Balti jaam** (Baltic Station; ☎ 615 6851; www.edel.ee) is on the northwestern edge of the Old Town, a short walk from Raekoja plats, or three stops on tram No 1 or 2 north from the tram stop at the southern end of Mere puiestee. There are domestic services to many cities and towns throughout Estonia.

ISLAND ESCAPE

Who says you can't relive your favourite scenes from *The Blue Lagoon* in Nordic Estonia? Sure, it's no Bora Bora, but the country offers its share of lovely shoreline and remote island landscapes to play around in. An excellent getaway from Tallinn is to the nearby islands of Aegna and/or Naissaar.

Tiny **Aegna**, just 3 sq km, has been populated for centuries by local fishermen and, from 1689, postal workers who operated mail boats from there to Sweden via Finland. During Soviet times it was an off-limits military base, but since the 1990s Tallinners have been building summerhouses there or just using it for a quick escape into remote nature. There are some military remnants, an old church and cemetery, remains of a medieval village and long stretches of nearly-always deserted beaches.

Naissaar, much larger at 11km by 4km, has an even livelier history, more tourism possibilities and even a boulder that has a circumference of 26.7m! There's a 19th-century cemetery for English sailors from the Crimean and Russo–Swedish wars, which attests to the island's military history. It was off limits in Soviet times, and there's the remnant of an old army village, bunkers and mine factory to explore. There's a revived, old-fashioned guesthouse, plus a church from 1856 and other attractions, but again, stretches of quiet beach are its largest draws. Just up the hill from the dock is the Nature Park Centre where you can get lots of info, a warming coffee and a meal.

Tallinn's tourist information centre can suggest accommodation on both islands. Otherwise contact the **Aegna Hostel** (☎ 510 3653). To stay at Naissaar's **Männiku küla** (camp site 25EEK, s 100-200EEK, d 200-400EEK) or book tours (100EEK) of Naissaar, contact **Naisaare Reisid** (☎ 639 8000; www.naissaarereisid.ee, in Estonian).

MS Monika (☎ 56 577 021; www.saartereisid.ee, in Estonian; adult/student/bicycle return 200/125/50EEK) runs twice-daily boats from Wednesday to Sunday from Pirita's harbour to Aegna then Naissaar, then back to Pirita. It's possible to stay overnight on either island, or just spend about five hours wandering or biking and return to Tallinn the same day.

GETTING AROUND
To/From the Airport

Bus No 2 runs every 20 to 30 minutes from terminals A and D via Gonsiori tänav in the centre. From the airport, it's just five bus stops to the centre. A taxi to/from the centre should cost about 50EEK.

Public Transport

Tallinn has an excellent network of buses, trolleybuses and trams that usually run from 6am to midnight. *Piletid* (tickets) are sold from street kiosks (adult/student 10/7EEK) or can be purchased from the driver (15EEK). Validate your ticket using the hole punch inside the vehicle. All public transport timetables are posted at www.tallinn.ee.

Taxi

There is a glut of taxis in Tallinn – more per capita than in Helsinki. Save for some jowly drivers at the train station, port and airport, drivers are honest and rides metered, costing from 4.50EEK to 8EEK per kilometre. Try **Iks Takso** (☎ 638 1381) or **Raadiotakso** (☎ 601 1111). Throughout central Tallinn, the ecologically sound **Velotakso** (☎ 508 8810) offers rides on egg-shaped vehicles run by pedal power and enthusiasm, and charges 35EEK anywhere within central Tallinn.

NORTHEASTERN ESTONIA

While the area to the east of Tallinn is an attractive unspoilt national park, as you travel closer to Narva an industrial landscape emerges. Despite some polluted areas, the region has fine cliff-top views out to sea, historic sites and a number of picturesque towns (like Sillamäe, a living museum of Stalin-era architecture). The population of eastern Estonia is predominantly Russian-speaking.

LAHEMAA NATIONAL PARK
☎ 32

A rocky stretch of the north coast – encompassing 251 sq km of marine area plus 474 sq km of hinterland with 14 lakes, eight rivers and many waterfalls – forms the lovely. Roads crisscross the park from the Tallinn – Narva highway, and some places are accessible by bus. This is the perfect getaway for a day or more in nature.

Information

Lahemaa National Park Visitors Centre (☎ 95 555; www.lahemaa.ee; ⊙ 9am-7pm May-Aug, 9am-5pm Sep, 9am-5pm Mon-Fri Oct-Apr) is located in Palmse, 8km north of Viitna (71km east of Tallinn) in the park's southeast, and is superhelpful. It's worth getting in touch with the centre before heading out. For an outstanding personal guide, contact **Anne Kurepalu** (anne@phpalmse.ee).

Sights & Activities

There is an unlimited amount of sightseeing, hiking, biking and boating to be done here; remote islands can also be explored. A highlight would be a canoe trip down one of the rivers which run through the park; the visitors centre can help organise this. The park has several well-signposted nature trails (a popular one is the Beaver Trail) and cycling paths winding through it. The small coastal towns of **Võsu**, **Käsmu** and **Loksa** are popular seaside spots in summer. Käsmu is a particularly enchanting village, one of Estonia's prettiest. The **Meremuuseum** (Sea Museum; ☎ 38 136; adult/student 10/5EEK; ⊙ 24hr) explains the tiny village's rich naval history in a pleasant space by the sea. There are also **prehistoric stone barrows** (tombs) at Kahala, Palmse and Vihula, and a **boulder field** on the Käsmu Peninsula.

Lahemaa also features some historic **manor houses**: Kolga, Vihula, Palmse and Sagadi. Two are open to public. **Palmse Manor** (adult/student 20/7EEK; ⊙ 10am-7pm May-Sep, 10am-1pm Oct-Apr), near the visitors centre, was once a wholly self-contained Baltic-German estate and **Sagadi** was another opulent residence (built in 1749) that now houses the **Forest Museum** (☎ 58 888; museum & manor adult/student 30/10EEK; ⊙ 11am-6pm Tue-Sun 15 May-30 Sep, by arrangement 1 Oct-May 14).

Sleeping & Eating

The visitors centre arranges accommodation to suit every budget and can advise on the best camping spots. In Võsu and Käsmu there are many guesthouses lining the street; it's possible to show up and browse, but in midsummer, they might all be full.

Ojaärse hostel (☎ 34 108; sagadi.hotell@rmk.ee; dm 200EEK) A dream version of a hostel, this is a lushly converted 1855 farmhouse 1.5km southeast of Palmse. Dorms have between two and ten beds.

Viitna Holiday Centre (☎ 93 651; d 350EEK, with shared bathroom 200EEK) Being only a five-minute walk from the Viitna bus stop is convenient, and the tranquil wooded area beside a clean lake is lovely, but the downside is that it's on the park's outskirts. There's an on-site café.

Toomarahva (☎ 52 511; toomarahva@hot.ee; Altja village; camp sites/s/d/2-person barn incl breakfast 25/225/550/500EEK) 'Rustic' is an cliché, but this lovely guest/farmhouse deserves it. A two-minute walk from the sea in the tiny village of Altja (some 10km by road east of Võsu). The split-level little barn is a treat. Other meals beside breakfast can be ordered.

Getting There & Away
There are some 19 buses daily from Tallinn to Rakvere, which stop at Viitna (30EEK, one hour), and one a day from Tallinn to Käsmu and Võsu. From Viitna, you can hike or hitchhike to the visitors centre, or call a **taxi** (☎ 509 2326) from Võsu to pick you up.

NARVA & AROUND
☎ 35 / pop 67,752
Estonia's easternmost town is separated only by the thin Narva River from Ivangorod in Russia and is almost entirely populated by Russians. Narva was a Hanseatic League trading point by 1171. Later it became embroiled in Russia's border disputes with the German knights and Sweden. Ivan III of Muscovy founded Ivangorod in 1492 and its large castle still menacingly faces Narva's castle, providing an unusual and picturesque architectural composition. Narva was almost completely destroyed in WWII.

There is a **tourist information centre** (☎ 60 184; narva@visitestonia.com; Puškini tänav 13) in the city centre. The bus and train stations are located together at Vaksali tänav 2, opposite the Russian Orthodox Voskresensky Cathedral. Walk north up Puškini tänav to the castle (500m) and the centre.

Sights
Restored after WWII, **Narva Castle**, guarding the Friendship Bridge over the river to Russia, dates from Danish rule in the 13th century. The castle houses the **Town Museum** (☎ 99 247; adult/student 30/10EEK; ⏰ 10am-6pm Wed-Sun). The baroque **town hall** (1668–71), on Raekoja väljak north of the bridge, has also been restored. On the square in front of the train station is a **monument** to the Estonians who were loaded into cattle wagons here in 1941 and deported to Siberia.

About 12km north of Narva is the pretty but dilapidated resort of **Narva-Jõesuu**, popular since the 19th century for its long, white, sandy beaches. There are many unique, impressive early-20th-century wooden houses and villas throughout the town.

Sleeping & Eating
The tourist information centre can recommend guesthouses, hotels and restaurants.

Hostel Jusian (☎ 62 656; jusian@hot.ee; Kreenholmi tänav 40; d with shared bathroom 300EEK) On the bare-bones side, but perfectly comfortable.

Hostel Vanalinn (☎ 73 253; Koidula tänav 6; s/d 490/750EEK) Inside this charming 17th-century house just north of the castle are comfortable rooms with bizarre colour schemes.

Hotel King (☎ 72 404; www.hotelking.ee; Lavetstrovi tänav 9; s/d from 590/790EEK) Just two blocks from the border is this very comfortable hotel/restaurant (meaty mains from 60EEK).

German Pub (☎ 91 548; Puškini tänav 10; mains from 45EEK) Cosy pub serving great food (lots of sausages!) in cheerful surroundings.

Getting There & Away
Narva is 210km east of Tallinn on the road to St Petersburg, 140km away. From Tallinn there are over 20 buses (65EEK to 100EEK, three to 3½ hours) and a train daily (50EEK, 3½ hours). There are 10 daily buses from Narva to Tartu and many to nearby cities. Buses and maxitaxis go to the beach resort town of Narva-Jõesuu throughout the day.

SOUTHEASTERN ESTONIA

The focus of southeastern Estonia is the historic university town of Tartu, the country's second largest city. Beyond Tartu is an attractive region of gentle hills, beautiful lakes and the traditional lands of the Setu people.

TARTU
☎ 7 / pop 101,190
Tartu lays claim to being Estonia's spiritual capital. Locals talk about a special Tartu *vaim*, or Tartu spirit, encompassed by the time-stands-still, 19th-century feel of many of its streets, lined with wooden houses, and by the ethereal beauty of its parks and riverfront. Small and provincial, with the quietly flowing Emajõgi River running through it, it's also a university town with students

ESTONIA

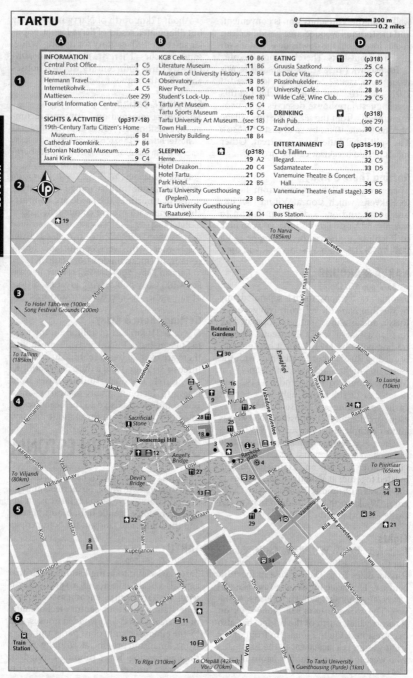

TARTU

0		300 m
0		0.2 miles

INFORMATION
Central Post Office..................1 C5
Estravel.................................2 C5
Hermann Travel.....................3 C4
Internetikohvik......................4 C5
Mattiesen.........................(see 29)
Tourist Information Centre......5 C4

SIGHTS & ACTIVITIES (pp317-18)
19th-Century Tartu Citizen's Home
  Museum.............................6 B4
Cathedral Toomkirik...............7 B4
Estonian National Museum......8 A5
Jaani Kirik.............................9 C4

KGB Cells.............................10 B6
Literature Museum.................11 B6
Museum of University History...12 B4
Observatory..........................13 B5
River Port.............................14 D5
Student's Lock-Up.............(see 18)
Tartu Art Museum.................15 C4
Tartu Sports Museum 16 C4
Tartu University Art Museum...(see 18)
Town Hall............................17 C5
University Building.................18 B4

SLEEPING (p318)
Herne...................................19 A2
Hotel Draakon.......................20 C4
Hotel Tartu...........................21 D5
Park Hotel............................22 B5
Tartu University Guesthousing
  (Pepleri).............................23 B6
Tartu University Guesthousing
  (Raatuse)............................24 D4

EATING (p318)
Gruusia Saatkond..................25 C4
La Dolce Vita........................26 C4
Püssirohukelder.....................27 B5
University Café......................28 B4
Wilde Café, Wine Club...........29 C5

DRINKING (p318)
Irish Pub..........................(see 29)
Zavood................................30 C4

ENTERTAINMENT (pp318-19)
Club Tallinn..........................31 D4
Illegard.................................32 C5
Sadamateater........................33 D5
Vanemuine Theatre & Concert
  Hall...................................34 C5
Vanemuine Theatre (small stage).35 B6

OTHER
Bus Station...........................36 D5

making up nearly one-fifth of the population; this injects a boisterous vitality into the leafy, serene and pleasant surroundings. During the Student Days festival at the end of April, carnival-like mayhem erupts throughout the city.

Around the 6th century, there was an Estonian stronghold on Toomemägi Hill. In 1030, Yaroslav the Wise of Kyiv is said to have founded a settlement here called Yuriev. By the early 13th century the ruling Knights of the Sword had placed a bishop, castle and cathedral on Toomemägi Hill.

The university, founded in 1632, developed into one of the foremost 19th-century seats of learning. The Estonian nationalist revival in the 19th century had its origins here, and Tartu was the location for the first Estonian Song Festival in 1869. Tartu provides visitors with a truer glimpse of the Estonian rhythm of life than Tallinn, boasts great museums and is a convenient gateway to exploring southern Estonia.

Orientation

Toomemägi Hill and the area of older buildings between it and the Emajõgi River are the focus of 'old' Tartu. At its heart is Raekoja plats (Town Hall Sq). Ülikooli tänav and Rüütli tänav are the main shopping streets; ATMs are scattered throughout the centre.

Information

Central post office (Vanemuise tänav 7; ☽ 8am-7pm Mon-Fri, 9am-4pm Sat)

Estravel (☎ 440 300; tartu1@estravel.ee; Vallikraavi tänav 2) Official Amex agent.

Hermann Travel (☎ 301 444; tartu@hermann.ee; Lossi tänav 3) Specialises in nature tours but arranges pretty much anything.

Internetikohvik (☎ 423 443; Küüni 2; ☽ 11am-11pm; per hr 25EEK) Internet access.

Mattiesen (☎ 309 721; Vallikraavi tänav 4; ☽ 9am-7pm Mon-Sat, 10am-6pm Sun) Bookshop that stocks an extensive range of maps.

Tourist information centre (☎ /fax 442 111; http://turism.tartumaa.ee; Raekoja plats 14; ☽ 9am-5pm Mon-Fri, 10am-3pm Sat & Sun) It has an excellent range of local maps, books and brochures, can book accommodation and tour guides and sells the listings guide *Tartu Today* (15EEK).

Sights & Activities

At the town centre on Raekoja plats is the **town hall** (1782–89), topped by a tower and weather vane and fronted by a statue of lovers kissing under an umbrella. Nearby at No 18, the former home of Colonel Barclay de Tolly (1761–1818) is a wonderfully crooked building housing the **Tartu Art Museum** (☎ 441 080; www.tartmus.ee, in Estonian; Raekoja plats 18; adult/student 20/5EEK; ☽ 11am-6pm Wed-Sun).

The main **university building** (☎ 375 100; Ülikooli tänav 18) dates from 1803. It houses the **Tartu University Art Museum** (☎ 375 384; adult/child 8/5EEK; ☽ 11am-5pm Mon-Fri) and **Student's Lock-Up** (adult/child 5/4EEK; ☽ 11am-5pm Mon-Fri), where 19th-century students were held for their misdeeds. Further north, the Gothic brick **Jaani Kirik** (St John's Church), founded in 1330, is still undergoing extensive restoration from Soviet bombing in 1944. It has rare terracotta sculptures surrounding the main portal.

Tartu Sports Museum (☎ 300 750; Rüütli tänav 15; adult/student 30/20EEK; ☽ 11am-6pm Wed-Sun) showcases much more than Estonian Olympic excellence. There's a display of the life of a 19th-century postman, and constantly revolving exhibits. Nearby, the **19th-Century Tartu Citizen's Home Museum** (☎ 361 545; Jaani tänav 16; adult/student 8/5EEK; ☽ 10am-4pm Wed-Sun) is worth a peak; inside you can see how a burgher from the 1830s lived – and have a cup of tea.

Rising to the west of Raekoja plats is the splendid Toomemägi Hill, landscaped in the manner of a 19th-century English park. The 13th-century Gothic **cathedral Toomkirik** at the top was rebuilt in the 15th century, despoiled during the Reformation in 1525, and partly rebuilt in 1804–07 to accommodate the university library, which is now the **Museum of University History** (☎ 375 674; adult/student 20/5EEK; ☽ 11am-5pm Wed-Sun).

Also on Toomemägi Hill are the 1838 **Angel's Bridge** (Inglisild), with a good view of the city; the 1913 **Devil's Bridge** (Kuradisild); and the **observatory** (☎ 376 932). The observatory is not regularly open, but it can be opened and toured by special reservation.

Tartu, as the major repository of Estonia's cultural heritage, has an abundance of first-rate museums. Among them is perhaps the country's best: the **Estonian National Museum** (☎ 421 311; www.erm.ee; Kuperjanovi tänav 9; adult/student 20/14EEK; ☽ 11am-6pm Wed-Sun), which traces the history, life and traditions of the Estonian people. The former KGB headquarters now house the sombre **KGB Cells** (☎ 461 717; Riia maantee 15b; adult/student 5/3EEK; ☽ 11am-6pm Tue-Sat).

ESTONIA

For information about Emajõgi River **cruises** from Tartu's **river port** (Sadam; ☎ 340 026; Soola tänav 5), contact **Laevatöö** (☎ 340 025). Services run twice-weekly to the remote island of Piirissaar.

Festivals & Events

Two of the biggest events in the local calendar are both sporting events. The **Tartu ski marathon**, a 60km cross-country trek from Otepää, involves hundreds of enthusiastic skiers in mid-February. The **Tartu Bicycle Marathon** (www.tartumaraton.ee, in Estonian) is a 136km race held at the end of May, with a shorter, second one held in mid-September.

Sleeping

BUDGET & MID-RANGE

Tartu University Guesthousing (☎ 409 959, 409 955; www.kyla.ee; s 150-250EEK; d 400EEK) Raatuse (Raatuse tänav 22); Pepleri (Pepleri tänav 14); Purde (Purde 27) Three student dorms offer cheap, clean accommodation. The Raatuse locale is brand-new but bathrooms are shared; on Pepleri, also modern and spiffy, each room has a private bathroom; the Purde dorm is out of the way and run-down. Advance reservations are a must!

Hotel Tähtvere (☎ 421 364; Laulupeo tänav 19; s/d from 200/350EEK) A pleasant 1km walk west from the centre, this run-down but perfectly decent place is located by a park, sports complex and concert stadium. It has comfortable, if nondescript rooms.

Herne (☎ 441 959; Herne tänav 59; per person with shared bathroom 200EEK) A 1km walk northwest of the city through a traditionally poor neighbourhood of charismatic wooden houses brings you to this lovely B&B with four rooms and a clean bathroom.

Hotel Tartu (☎ 314 300; Soola 3; dm/s/d 300/695/995EEK) Across from the bus station isn't the most charming location, but this hotel's recently renovated rooms are lovely. The dorm rooms hold only three and are spotless. There's a 15% student discount.

TOP END

Park Hotel (☎ 427 000; www.parkhotell.ee; Vallikraavi tänav 23; s/d 800/1080EEK, ste 1300-1800EEK) The interiors are on the plain side but the hotel's location, nestled in among the trees at the foot of Toomemägi Hill, provides a haven close to the centre. There's a 10% Internet booking discount.

Hotel Draakon (☎ 442 045; www.draakon.ee; Raekoja plats 4; s 975EEK, d 1550-2200EEK, ste 2600-2990EEK) Overlooking Raekoja plats, this elegant hotel has ultrastylish rooms. The doubles with private sauna are well worth the upgrade.

Eating & Drinking

University Café (Ülikooli tänav 20; mains 35EEK; ✆ 9am-5pm Mon-Fri, 11am-5pm Sat) This old-world café with beautiful wooden floors is a must for a light lunch or afternoon tea. It's located in the original part of the university (dating from 1632).

La Dolce Vita (☎ 407 545; Kompanii tänav 10; mains 35-60EEK; ✆ 11.30am-10pm) Excellent pizzas, calzones and other Italian fare are the things that make you purr in this comfy restaurant.

Püssirohukelder (☎ 303 555; Lossi tänav 28; mains 40-100EEK; ✆ noon-2am Sun-Thu, noon-3am Fri & Sat) Set majestically in a cavernous old gunpowder cellar, this place doubles as a boisterous pub and is a great place to dine on tasty meat and fish dishes.

Gruusia Saatkond (☎ 441 386; Rüütli tänav 8; mains from 40EEK; ✆ noon-midnight Sun-Thu, noon-2am Fri & Sat) Yum…spices – a rarity in these parts! Great Georgian soups and meat kebabs are the stars here, not the salads, which have nothing Georgian about them save for their names.

Wilde Café, Wine Club & Irish Pub (☎ 309 764; Vallikraavi tänav 4; mains from 55EEK; ✆ café 9am-7pm Mon-Sat, 10am-6pm Sun; wine club 5pm-midnight Tue-Thu, 5pm-2am Fri & Sat; pub noon-midnight Sun-Thu, noon-3am Fri & Sat) One of the city's most pleasant places to relax, no matter your mood – choose grace and elegance in the café/wine club or something more lively at the upstairs pub (with a killer terrace and great menu) – all this, great ambience and WiFi to boot!

Zavood (☎ 441 321; Lai tänav 30; ✆ 4pm-2am) This low-key bar attracts an alternative, down-to-earth crowd with its inexpensive drinks and lack of attitude. It sometimes features a student band.

Entertainment

Club Tallinn (☎ 403 157; Narva Maantee 27; ✆ 10pm-4am Wed, Fri & Sat) This often gets the vote as the best club in Estonia. Multifloored, with many nooks and crannies, it shines with its top-notch DJs, theme evenings and an eager, enthusiastic and young crowd.

Illegaard (☎ 434 424; Ülikooli tänav 5; ✆ noon-2am Mon-Fri, 7pm-2am Sat) This alternative jazz bar in a cosy vault attracts an artsy crowd. The Friday night live shows and Monday night piano bars are the most popular evenings.

Vanemuine Theatre & Concert Hall (☎ 440 165, 377 530; www.vanemuine.ee, in Estonian, www.concert.ee; Vanemuise tänav 6) The first Estonian-language theatre troupe performed here in 1870 and the venue still regularly hosts an array of classical and alternative theatrical and musical performances. It also stages performances at its **small stage** (☎ 440 160; Vanemuise tänav 45a) and **Sadamateater** (☎ 344 248; Soola tänav 5b).

Getting There & Away
Some 50 buses a day run to/from Tallinn (50EEK to 80EEK, 2½ to 3½ hours). There are also two trains daily (70EEK to 120EEK, 2½ to 3½ hours).

OTEPÄÄ
☎ 76 / pop 2200
The small hilltop town of Otepää, 44km south of Tartu, is the centre of a pretty area beloved by Estonians for its hills and lakes – and thus its endless opportunities for sports. The area is dubbed (tongue-in-cheek) as the 'Estonian Alps' as this is where most of the country's skiing activities are centered. There are also a few bicycle marathons which pass through the area.

Orientation & Information
The centre of town is the triangular main 'square', Lipuväljak, with the bus station just off its eastern corner. There you'll find the **tourist information centre** (☎ 61 200; www .otepaa.ee; Lipuväljak 13; ☻ 9am-6pm Mon-Fri, 10am-5pm Sat & Sun). The post office, bank and main food shop are beside the bus station. Staff at the **Otepää Travel Agency** (☎ 54 060; otepaarb@hot .ee) are efficient and friendly.

Sights & Activities
Otepää's pretty little 17th-century **church** is on a hilltop about 100m northeast of the bus station. It was in this church in 1884 that the Estonian Students' Society consecrated its new blue, black and white flag, which later became the flag of independent Estonia. The former vicar's residence now houses two museums: **Eesti Lipu Muuseum** (Flag Museum; ☎ 55 075) and **Suusamuuseum** (Ski Museum; ☎ 63 670; suusamuuseum@hot.ee). Both can be visited by appointment, or just show up and try your luck.

The tree-covered hill south of the church is the **Linnamägi** (Castle Hill), a major stronghold from the 10th to 12th centuries. There are traces of old fortifications on top, and good views of the surrounding country.

The best views, however, are along the shores of the 3.5km-long **Pühajärv** (Holy Lake) just southwest of town. The lake was blessed by the Dalai Lama and a monument on the eastern shore commemorates his visit in 1992. Every summer in early June the lake is anointed in a different way by thousands of raucous partiers during the **Beach Party Festival** (www.beachparty.ee).

It would be a shame to visit and pass by the lovely countryside surrounding town. To rent bikes, Rollerblades, skis and snowboards, as well as hop onto fun bike and canoe tours, contact **Fan Sport** (☎ 77 537; www .fansport.ee), which has three offices in Otepää including one located inside the **Karupesa Hotel** (☎ 61 500; www.karupesa.ee; Tehvandi tänav 1A). There's also lots to do and see in the nearby **Otepää Nature Park** (☎ 55 876; Kolga tee 28), 232 sq km of lakes, forest and walking trails.

Sleeping & Eating
Edgari (☎ 54 275; Lipuväljak 3; s/d 250/350EEK) One of the cheapest places to stay right in town, this is a guesthouse that feels like a hostel, with thin walls, a shared kitchenette and communal lounge, all in a pleasant but bland atmosphere.

Setanta Irish Pub & Hotel (☎ 68 200; www .setanta.ee, in Estonian; Núpli village; d from 500EEK; mains 70-100EEK) Better known for its Irish Pub, this lively place just 3km southeast of Otepää has some fabulous rooms which boast great views over Lake Pühajärv.

Oti Pubi (☎ 69 840; Lipuväljak 26; mains 55-900EEK; ☻ 10am-midnight Sun-Thu, 10am-2am Sat & Sun) This modern, octagonal, English-style pub turns into a disco by night, and serves up decent though standard fare any time. Look out for live concerts: they tend to be boisterous, memorable events.

Getting There & Away
Daily bus services to/from Otepää include Tartu (25EEK to 30 EEK, 45 minutes to 1½ hours, 15 daily), Tallinn (100EEK, 3½ hours, three daily) and Võru (30EEK, 1¼ hours, one daily).

ESTONIA

HAANJA NATURE PARK

☎ 78

This 17,000-hectare protected area south of the city of Võru includes some of the nicest scenery in the country and is where several of the best tourist farms in the region are located. The nature park's **headquarters** (☎ 29 090) in the village of Haanja can provide detailed information about the area as well as hiking and skiing opportunities.

Suur Munamägi

Suur Munamägi (literally Great Egg Hill!), 17km south of Võru, is the highest hill in the Estonia, Latvia and Lithuania at just over 318m, though it's still easy to miss if you're not on the lookout for it. It's covered in trees, though you can climb to the top and then up the 29m **observation tower** (☎ 78 847; ☯ 10am-8pm May-Aug, 10am-5pm Sep, 10am-8pm Sat & Sun Oct). On a very clear day you can see Russia, Latvia and lots of lush trees. The summit and tower are a 10-minute climb from the Võru–Ruusmäe road, starting about a kilometre south of the otherwise uninspiring village of Haanja.

SETUMAA

☎ 78

Lying in the far southeastern part of Estonia is the (politically unrecognised) area of Setumaa. Unlike the rest of Estonia, this part of the country never came under the control of the Teutonic and German tribes, but fell under Novgorod's and later Pskov's subjugation. The Setu people, originally Finno-Ugric, then became Orthodox, not Lutheran. The whole of Setumaa was contained within independent Estonia between 1920 and 1940, but the greater part of it is now in Russia. Today the Setu culture is tragically in decline. There are approximately 4000 Setu in Estonia (about another 3000 in Russia), half the population of the early 20th century.

Aside from the large, silver breastplate that is worn on the women's national costume, what sets the Setu aside is their singing style, known as *runnoverse*: a phrase is sung by one singer (often the eldest in the community) and then repeated several times by a chorus. There is no musical accompaniment and the effect sounds almost archaic.

Museums worth visiting here include the **Setu House Museum** (adult/student 12/5EEK; ☯ 11am-5pm Tue-Sun May-Oct) in the quaint village of Obinitsa, where there's also a formidable stone statue of the Setu Song Mother lording over a small lake, and the **Setu Farm Museum** (☎ 64 359; adult/student 12/5EEK; ☯ noon-5pm Tue-Sun) in Värska. The **tourist information centre** (☎ 54 190) in Obinitsa is a good source of information and can advise on a number of local places to stay, including working farms which are always fun for the kids.

There are six daily buses between Tartu and Värska (50EEK to 55EEK, 1¾ hours), and one per day between Tartu and Haanja (75EEK, 2½ hours).

SOUTHWESTERN ESTONIA & THE ISLANDS

PÄRNU

☎ 44 / pop 45,000

Pärnu (*pair*-nu), 127km south of Tallinn on the road to Rīga, is Estonia's leading seaside resort and a magnet for party-loving Estonians and mud-cure-seeking Finns. Its name alone is synonymous with fun in the sun. Most of the town, however, is docile, with wide leafy streets and sprawling parks.

In the 13th century the Knights of the Sword built a fort at Pärnu. It became a Hanseatic port in the 14th century and flourished in the 17th century under Swedish rule. From 1838 the town grew as a resort, with mud baths, the beach and good weather (in the Baltic region 'good' is relative!). Many Soviet-era sanatoriums have been revived as hotels and treatment centres, and Pärnu is once again booming.

Information

The town lies on either side of Pärnu River's estuary, which empties into Pärnu Bay.

Central post office (☎ 71 111; Akadeemia tee 7; ☯ 8am-6pm Mon-Fri, 9am-3pm Sat)

Rütli Internetipunkt (☎ 31 552; Rüütli tänav 25; per hr 20EEK; ☯ 10am-9pm Mon-Fri, 10am-6pm Sat & Sun) You can access the Internet here and at the New Art Museum (p322; 30EEK per hour).

Tourist information centre (☎ 73 000; www.parnu .ee; Rütli tänav 16 ☯ 9am-5pm Mon-Fri) On the main commercial street in the heart of the Old Town, around 150m southwest of the bus station. When the information centre is closed, tourist info is given out at the Hotell Pärnu's reception (p322).

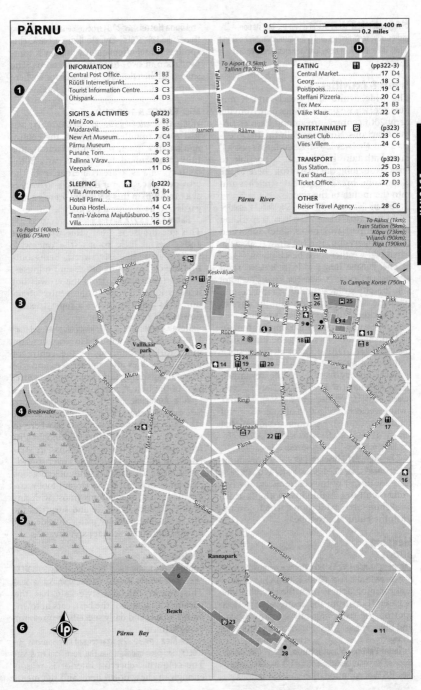

PÄRNU

0 / 400 m
0 / 0.2 miles

INFORMATION
Central Post Office.....................1 B3
Rüütli Internetipunkt..................2 C3
Tourist Information Centre.........3 C3
Ühispank..................................4 D3

SIGHTS & ACTIVITIES (p322)
Mini Zoo...................................5 B3
Mudaravila................................6 B6
New Art Museum.......................7 C4
Pärnu Museum..........................8 D3
Punane Torn..............................9 C3
Tallinna Värav..........................10 B3
Veepark..................................11 D6

SLEEPING (p322)
Villa Ammende........................12 B4
Hotell Pärnu............................13 D3
Lõuna Hostel...........................14 C4
Tanni-Vakoma Majutüsburoo...15 C3
Villa.......................................16 D5

EATING (pp322-3)
Central Market........................17 D4
Georg.....................................18 C3
Poistipoiss...............................19 C4
Steffani Pizzeria.......................20 C4
Tex Mex..................................21 B3
Väike Klaus.............................22 C4

ENTERTAINMENT (p323)
Sunset Club.............................23 C6
Viies Villem.............................24 C4

TRANSPORT (p323)
Bus Station.............................25 D3
Taxi Stand...............................26 D3
Ticket Office............................27 D3

OTHER
Reiser Travel Agency................28 C6

To Aiport (3.5km);
Tallinn (130km)

Pärnu River

To Pootsi (40km);
Virtsu (75km)

To Rähni (1km);
Train Station (5km);
Kõpu (73km);
Viljandi (90km);
Riga (190km)

To Camping Konse (750m)

Breakwater

Rannapark

Beach

Pärnu Bay

ESTONIA

Ühispank (Rüütli tänav 40a) Behind the bus station; cashes travellers cheques and gives cash advances on credit cards. There's an ATM here, but they aren't hard to find in town.

Sights & Activities

The wide, white-sand beach and Ranna puiestee, whose fine buildings date from the early 20th century, are among Pärnu's finest attractions. Note especially the 1927 neo-classical **Mudaravila** (☎ 25 520; Ranna puiestee 1) mud bath cure building. It is possible to walk west along the coast from here to the 2km stone breakwater that stretches out into the mouth of the river.

Veepark (Water park; ☎ 51 166; Side tänav 14; adult 85-125EEK; student 60-85EEK; ☼ 10am-10pm), a sparkling new water park with pools, slides, tubes and other slippery fun, is a big draw, especially when bad weather ruins beach plans.

The **Punane Torn** (Red Tower; Hommiku tänav; adult/student 10/5EEK; ☼ 10am-6pm Mon-Fri, 10am-3pm Sat), the city's oldest building (and despite its name, white), survives from the days of the Knights of the Sword. Parts of the 17th-century Swedish moat and ramparts remain in Vallikäär Park, including the tunnel-like **Tallinna Värav** (Tallinn Gate) at the western end of Kuninga.

Local history features at the revamped **Pärnu Museum** (☎ 33 231; Rüütli tänav 53; adult/student 30/15EEK; ☼ 10am-6pm Wed-Sun). Not far away an eclectic collection of cute, colourful reptiles and passive pythons reside at **Mini Zoo** (☎ 55 16 033; Akadeemia tee 1; adult/child 25/15EEK; ☼ 10am-6pm Mon-Fri, 11am-4pm Sat & Sun).

The **New Art Museum** (☎ 30 772; www.chaplin.ee; Esplanaadi tänav 10; adult/student 15/10EEK; ☼ 9am-9pm), southwest of the centre, is among Estonia's cultural highlights, with its café, bookshop and exhibitions which always push the cultural envelope.

Sleeping
BUDGET
Camping Konse (☎ 53 435 092; www.konse.ee; Suur-Jõe 44a; camp sites/d/tr from 100/500/650EEK) One of several camping options near the city, this one is barely 1km from the centre on a perfect spot on the river, and offers tent, rowboat and bike rentals. Most rooms share bath and shower.

Tanni-Vakoma Majutüsburoo (☎ 31 070; tanni@online.ee; Hommiku tänav 5; per person 130-300EEK) Organises B&B accommodation in local homes.

Lõuna Hostel (☎ 30 943; hostellouna@hot.ee; Lõuna tänav 2; dm 180-250EEK) Overlooking a park, this spotless hostel offers quality budget accommodation in two- to seven-bed rooms. The shared kitchen doubles as social room, where people exchange fun-in-the-sun tales.

MID-RANGE & TOP END
Villa (☎ 45 216; Suur-Posti 22; d/tr 600/700EEK; ✗) Just a few minutes' walk from the central market in a quiet, residential section, this fully modernised two-storey early-20th-century villa is a great alternative to the crowded places nearer the beach. Privacy is at a premium in this B&B, and there's a nice garden to have your morning tea.

Rähni (☎ 36 222; Riia maantee 57; s/d 600/800EEK) This guesthouse is great value with bright and cheerful little rooms (the one with skylight is particularly sweet). Being outside the centre has its pluses and minuses, though (you're away from the crowds but it takes longer to get to the centre of action!). As a bonus, there's a super-friendly downstairs restaurant-bar.

Hotell Pärnu (☎ 78 911; Rüütli tänav 44; s/d from 1290/1490EEK; ✗ ✗) Housed in a nondescript multistoreyed building in the centre of town, but it does offer full services and free use of its sparkling (and tiny) fitness centre. Part of the Best Western fold.

Villa Ammende (☎ 73 888; www.ammende.ee; Mere puiestee 7; s/d 1100/1450EEK, ste 2850-6000EEK; ✗) If money's no object, this is where to spend it. Class and luxury abound in this fabulously refurbished 1905 Russian Art-Nouveau building, which lords over sprawling grounds. This hotel-restaurant's gorgeous exterior is matched by an elegant lobby, individually furnished rooms (most with antiques), top-notch service and surprises for the guests, like a winter picnic outside with bonfire and vodka schnapps. A dream!

Eating
Georg (☎ 31 110; Rüütli tänav 43; mains 20-50EEK; ☼ 7.30am-7.30pm Mon-Fri, 9am-7.30pm Sat & Sun) This smoky cafeteria-style café has the cheapest, though not the best, eats in town. Soups, salads and daily specials are great for a quick fill-up.

Tex Mex (☎ 30 929; Akadeemia tänav 5; mains 50-100EEK; ☼ noon-midnight Sun-Thu, noon-1am Fri & Sat) The colourful, cheerful interior is reason enough to chow down here, and the menu boasts a tempting array of first-rate Mexican fare.

Steffani Pizzeria (☎ 31 170; Nikolai tänav 24; mains from 50EEK; 🕙 11am-midnight Sun-Thu, 11am-2am Fri & Sat) The city's best pizza and pasta are doled out in this homy country-kitchen-style restaurant which also boasts many vegetarian choices.

Väike Klaus (☎ 77 208; Supeluse tänav 3; mains from 60EEK; 🕙 11am-midnight Mon-Fri, 11am-2am Sat & Sun) This German-inspired pub is a great place for a meaty lunch to offset those healthy mud treatments – or for a game of pool upstairs as a break from beach volleyball.

Poistpoiss (☎ 64 862; Vee tänav 12; mains 65-200EEK; 🕙 noon-midnight Sun-Thu, noon-2am Fri & Sat) One of Pärnu's highlights, this converted 17th-century postal house has taken the shape of a traditional Russian tavern and serves up scrumptious, memorable Russian-styled meals. At weekend evenings things can get mighty gleeful after everyone's downed a few vodka shots.

The **central market** (cnr Karja & Suur-Sepa tänav) is southeast of the centre.

Entertainment

Sunset Club (☎ 30 670; Ranna puiestee 3; 🕙 10pm-6am Fri & Sat, 10pm-4am Sun, Wed & Thu) Pärnu's biggest and most famous nightclub, set in a grandiose 1939 seafront building. Imported DJs and bands plus a wild young crowd keep things moving until the early hours.

Viies Villem (☎ 27 999; Kuninga tänav 11; 🕙 11am-midnight Sun-Thu, 11am-2am Fri & Sat) This cellar pub is a fine place for catching local live music and is a guaranteed hit any night of the week.

Getting There & Away

More than 20 buses daily connect Pärnu with Tallinn (50EEK to 75EEK, two hours). Tickets for a multitude of other destinations including Rīga and beyond are available at the Pärnu bus station **ticket office** (☎ 71 002; Ringi tänav; 🕙 5am-8.30pm), across from the bus station. There are also two daily Tallinn-Pärnu trains (40EEK, three hours), though the train station is an uncomfortable 5km away from the centre, down Riia maantee.

KIHNU & RUHNU ISLANDS
☎ 44

Six-kilometre-long Kihnu (population 497), in the Gulf of Rīga 40km southwest of Pärnu, is almost a living museum of Estonian cul-

ture. Many of the island's women still wear traditional colourful striped skirts and the community adheres to Orthodox traditions.

Ruhnu (population 64), smaller than Kihnu, is 100km southwest of Pärnu. For several centuries the island supported a Swedish population of 300, who abandoned it on 6 August 1944 to escape the advancing Red Army. Traces of the community, including a 1644 **wooden church**, poignantly remain.

Kihnurand Travel Agency (☎ 69 924; www.kihnu .ee, in Estonian) on Kihnu is the best agency for arranging full-day or longer excursions there. **Reiser Travel Agency** (☎ 71 480; www.reiser .ee; Kuuse tänav 1) in Pärnu also arranges trips to Ruhnu and Kihnu.

There are regular ferries (adult/student/car 40/20/150EEK, 1½ hours) from the **Munalaiu port** (☎ 96 312) in the village of Pootsi, 40km southwest of Pärnu. **Air Livonia** (☎ 75 007; www .airlivonia.ee) has one or two daily flights from Pärnu to Kihnu (120EEK one way), but only from October to April, and twice weekly flights to Ruhnu (adult/student 300/200EEK one way). To get to the **Pärnu airport** (☎ 75 000), take Bus No 23 from the bus station 20 minutes northwest.

VILJANDI & AROUND
☎ 43 / pop 20,500

One of Estonia's most charming towns, Viljandi, 90km east of Pärnu, is a relaxed place to stop for a day or more or to use as a base for exploring the country's largest floodplain and bog area (no laughing!). The town itself, settled since the 12th century, has a 19th-century flow to it, with many of its small buildings from that time, and it's easy to feel like you've slipped into the past. The **tourist information office** (☎ 30 442; Vabaduse väljak 6; 🕙 9am-6pm Mon-Fri, 10am-3pm Sat & Sun) can help with accommodation and tours and has a computer terminal for free Internet access.

A highlight is visiting **Lossimäed** (Castle Park), which sprawls out from behind the tourist information office. A picturesque green area with spectacular views over Lake Viljandi, here are the ruins of a 13th- to 15th-century castle founded by the Knights of the Sword, open for all to see and muck about in. In town, the excellent **Kondase Keskus** (☎ 33 968; Pikk tänav 8; adult/student 15/5EEK; 🕙 10am-7pm Wed-Sun) is worth a look as it is the country's only art gallery devoted to naïve art.

ESTONIA

Some 40km west of Viljandi is the **Soomaa National Park** (☎ 57 164; www.soomaa.com), a rich land of bogs, marsh, crisscrossing rivers and iron-rich black pools of water, perfect for a quick summer dip. Much more interesting than what the word 'bog' implies, this 37,000-hectare park is full of quirky opportunities: from a walk through the unique landscape of swampland, to a single-trunk canoe trip down one of the rivers, or an unforgettable sauna atop a floating raft.

Sleeping & Eating

The folks at Soomaa National Park can set you up with accommodation on their territory. Viljandi is full of nice pub-restaurants, cafés and B&Bs, which the tourist information office can recommend.

Inkeri (☎ 34414; Pikk tänav 4; s 300EEK, d 400-500EEK) This small guesthouse inside a health centre on one of Viljandi's most charming streets has comfy rooms. The largest room is worthwhile for its balcony and views onto Castle Park.

Sevan (☎ 55 665 295; Posti tänav 6; mains from 45EEK; ⏰ 10am-11pm) The best Armenian cooking in Estonia is found in this unassuming café – the *harcho* (spicy lamb and rice soup) and dolma will have you purring.

Getting There & Away

Viljandi is served by at least 12 daily buses from both Tallinn (70EEK to 85EEK, 2½ to four hours) and Pärnu (50EEK, 1½ hours) and 15 from Tartu (40EEK to 50EEK, one hour). There is no public transport to the Soomaa National Park, but by car, the well-signposted visitors centre is 24km west of the village of Kõpu, itself 17km west of Viljandi. **Unistar Auto** (☎ 55 921; Tehnika tänav 2) has cars for rent from 600EEK a day – a very convenient way to explore the lovely surroundings and Soomaa National Park.

HIIUMAA

☎ 46 / pop 10,350

Hiiumaa, Estonia's second biggest island, is a quiet, sparsely populated haven with some delightful stretches of coast rich in bird life. The commercial centre of the island is Kärdla, where you'll find the useful **tourist information centre** (☎ 22 232; www.hiiumaa.ee; Hiiu tänav 1; ⏰ 9am-6pm Mon-Fri, 10am-3pm Sat & Sun mid-May–mid-Sep, 9am-5pm Mon-Fri mid-Sep–mid-May) and most of the island's services, including a bank, post office and supermarket.

Sights

The Hiiumaa headquarters of the **Biosphere Reserve of the West Estonian Archipelago** (☎ 22 101; www.hiiuloodus.ee, in Estonian; Vabriku väljak 1; ⏰ 9am-6pm Mon-Fri) and the tourist information centre can organise boat trips (200EEK to 600EEK per hour) and advise on other nature tourism opportunities around the Takhuna Peninsula, Käina Bay and Hiiumaa Islets reserve.

Headquartered 3km from Lihula on the mainland, the **Matsalu Nature Reserve** (☎ 47-24 236; www.matsalu.ee), encompassing coastal areas on both the mainland and on Hiiumaa, is a prime migration stopover and an essential destination for birding enthusiasts.

Other attractions on Hiiumaa are its lighthouses; **Kõpu Peninsula** was the site of an ancient 16th-century lighthouse (although the present one dates from 1845). The picturesque **Sääre Tirp** on the southern coast of Kassari will also reward a visit with a memorable walk out to sea along a thinning spit of land and rock.

At **Suuremõisa**, 6km inland from Heltermaa port, you can see the late-baroque **Suuremõisa manor and park** (adult/student 10/5EEK; ⏰ 10am-5pm May-Sep).

Sleeping & Eating

The Kärdla tourist information centre can advise on a range of accommodation options throughout Hiiumaa.

Eesti Posti Puhkekeskus (☎ 91 871; Posti tänav 13; camp sites 35EEK, dm from 125EEK; ✗) Here you'll find well-kept though sparse rooms in a homy building that until recently was Kärdla's post office, and also places to pitch a tent.

Allika Guesthouse (☎ 29 026; Suuremõisa; s/d from 450/900EEK) Part of the Suuremõisa complex, these buildings were meant for the servants. The rooms are beautifully refurnished, most with tasteful antiques.

Adramadrus (☎ 32 082; Vabaduse tänav 15, Kärdla; mains from 45EEK; ⏰ 11am-midnight Sun-Thu, 11am-1am Fri & Sat) This is the perfect place to try out the locally brewed beers: the old-style tavern feel here makes things comfy and cosy, and the menu is varied.

Getting There & Away

Ferries travel between Rohuküla and Heltermaa four to six times daily (adult/student/

car 45/20/95EEK, 1½ hours). Two to three daily buses from Tallinn travel with the ferry directly to Kärdla or Käina (4¾ hours, 140EEK). **Avies Air** (☎ 605 8022; www .avies.ee) flies between Tallinn and Kärdla (adult/student one way 180/200EEK, 35 minutes, twice a day Monday to Friday).

SAAREMAA
☎ 45 / pop 35,580
Saaremaa (literally 'island land') is synonymous to Estonians with space, peace, fresh air, local beer and healthy bread. Tourists would add 'charming, rustic villages, remains of WWII, a meteorite crater and a fairy-tale castle' to the list – plus second the vote for beer! Saaremaa has a long history of beer home-brewing, and even its factory-produced brew has a great reputation. Tullik and X (with a whopping 10% alcohol count) are the most popular (but don't mention that they're now brewed in Tartu!). Tehumardi (still packing a wallop at 8%) is another favourite. You'll see lovely old wooden beer steins on display in many pubs and museums on the island. Estonia's largest island offers lots of ways to escape and relax among the juniper groves.

During the Soviet era, the entire island was off limits (due to an early-radar system and rocket base stationed there), even to 'mainland' Estonians, who needed a permit to visit. This resulted in a minimum of industrial build-up and the unwitting protection of the island's rural charm.

Orientation & Information
To reach Saaremaa you must first cross Muhu, the small island where the ferry from the mainland docks and which is connected to Saaremaa by a 2.5km causeway. Kuressaare, the capital of Saaremaa, on the south coast is a natural base for visitors.

Kuressaare's **tourist information office** (☎ 33 120; www.saaremaa.ee; Tallinna tänav 2; ⏱ 9am-7pm Mon-Fri, 9am-5pm Sat, 9am-3pm Sun May-Sep, 9am-5pm Mon-Fri Oct-Apr) can assist with anything you may require to get oriented on the island. Internet access is available at **Kultuurikeskus** (Tallinna maantee 6; per hr 20EEK; ⏱ 10am-7pm Mon-Fri, 10am-4pm Sat).

You can change money at the bus station or at any of the several banks on Raekoja plats. The **post office** (Torni maantee 1) is north of the town square.

Sights
The yellow **town hall** in the main Raekoja plats (Town Hall Sq) dates from 1654. Opposite stands the baroque **Weighing House** built in 1663.

The island's most distinctive landmark is the fantastic **Bishop's Castle** (1338–80) at the southern end of the town. It looks plucked from a fairy tale, and now houses the **Saaremaa Regional Museum** (☎ 56 307; adult/child 30/15EEK; ⏱ 11am-6pm Wed-Sun).

At Angla, 40km from Kuressaare just off the road to the harbour on the Leisi road, is a photogenic group of five **windmills** by the roadside. Two kilometres away, along the road opposite the windmills, is **Karja church**, a striking 13th- to 14th-century German Gothic church.

At Kaali, 18km from Kuressaare on the road leading to the harbour, is a 100m-wide, water-filled **crater** formed by a meteorite 2700 years ago. In ancient Scandinavian mythology the site was known as 'the sun's grave'. It's Europe's largest and most accessible meteorite crater, but looks mighty tiny up close!

Saaremaa's magic can really be felt along the **Sörve Peninsula**, jutting out south and west of Kuressaare. This sparsely populated strip of land saw some of the heaviest fighting in WWII. Some bases and antitank defence lines still stand. A bike or car trip along the coastline provides some of the most distinctive sights on the island. Several daily buses from Kuressaare bus station head down the coast of the peninsula. Yet a trip anywhere on this island is likely to be memorable – particularly the sparsely populated, wilder northwestern section.

Tours
Arensburg travel agency (☎ 33 360; abr@tt.ee; Tallinna maantee 25, Kuressaare) This agency knows the island like the back of its proverbial hand and offers a number of tours, though it specialises in boat trips to remote islands such as Abruka.
Saaremaa Reisibüroo (☎ 55 079; Lossi tänav 11, Kuressaare) Another group of winners who can help arrange your excursions.

Sleeping
The tourist information office can organise beds in private apartments in Kuressaare and throughout the region. There are also numerous farm stays available across the island.

ESTONIA

Kämping Mändjala (☎ 44 193; www.mandjala.ee, in Estonian; camp site/cabin per person 35/210EEK) Just 10km west of Kuressaare is this pleasant camping ground, which also has cabins. Buses from Kuressaare to Torgu or Sääre (three per day) go to the Mändjala bus stop, about 500m beyond the site. The reception staff can inform you about various water-sporting possibilities.

Saaremaa School Hostel (☎ 54 388, 24 432; www.syg.edu.ee; Hariduse tänav 13, Kuressaare; dm/s/d 145/250/350EEK) A very cool hostel; being attached to a school, there's a small gym and Internet room. A bonus is that dorm rooms hold no more than four persons. The friendly staff can hook you up with a guide and any info you need. There's access to a kitchen too.

Hotell Arensburg (☎ 24 700; www.sivainvest.ee; Lossi tänav 15, Kuressaare; s 420-710EEK, d 590-990EEK, ste 1400-1800EEK; ❄) Located in a lovely building near Kuressaare's main square, this hotel has great service and a lovely terrace out back. Rooms are decent, if a bit formal and heavy on hospital green.

Eating & Drinking

Kohvituba (☎ 55 679 475; Kohtu tänav 3, Kuressaare; ☽ 10am-6pm Mon-Fri, 10am-4pm Sat) So tiny you wouldn't want to stretch your arms out too broadly in it, but this snug café has the island's best selection of coffees and teas to go with the freshly baked cakes and pies, yum…

Pub Vaekoda (☎ 33 020; Tallinna maantee 3, Kuressaare; mains 50-100EEK; ☽ 10am-1am) Right on Raekoja plats, this is an old local favourite. Warm ambience, a good selection of meat and fish dishes and a large bar selection have proven a winning mix.

Mõnus Villem (☎ 31 901; Tallinna maantee 63B, Kuressaare; mains 50-100EEK; ☽ 10am-midnight Sun-Thu, 10am-2am Fri & Sat) A sprawling restaurant-pub just out of the centre has 30EEK lunch specials, a varied menu, a pool table, darts and live music at weekends. The food's not the thing here, the atmosphere is.

Veski (☎ 33 776; Pärna tänav 19, Kuressaare; meals 45-145EEK; ☽ noon-midnight Sun-Thu, noon-2am Fri & Sat) How often can you say you've dined inside a windmill? Without being too touristy, this place keeps both quality and ambience at a premium. There are some vegetarian choices, plus a children's menu. Treat yourself!

Getting There & Around

A vehicle ferry runs throughout the day from Virtsu on the mainland to the island of Muhu, which is joined by a causeway to Saaremaa. At least nine direct buses daily travel each way between Tallinn and Kuressaare (160EEK, 4½ hours) via the ferry. There are also three daily buses to/from Tartu, and two per day to/from Pärnu. **Avies Air** (☎ 605 8022; www.avies.ee) flies from Tallinn to Kuressaare twice per day Monday to Friday and once on Sunday (adult/student one way 255/315EEK, 45 minutes).

ESTONIA DIRECTORY

ACCOMMODATION

Finding a decent place to lay your head in Estonia is generally not a problem; places, even budget ones, are usually clean and very orderly. Tallinn has a glut of amazing top-end hotels with full services and luxuries, and a so-so selection of mid-range choices, however in smaller towns and villages it shouldn't be a problem finding budget accommodation at a B&B or hostel for under 250EEK per person. There are a few *kämpingud* (camping grounds; open from mid-May to September) that allow you to pitch a tent, but most consist mainly of permanent wooden cabins, with communal showers and toilets. Places are listed in our Sleeping sections in order of ascending price.

There are a number of homestay organisations that will rent you a room in a private home, which is an excellent way to experience local life. Farms offer more than a choice of rooms: in many cases meals, sauna and a wide range of activities. Your best bet would be to book via the regional tourist information centres throughout Estonia. There's an excellent search engine at www.visitestonia.com for all types of accommodation throughout the country.

ACTIVITIES

Many travel agencies can arrange a variety of activity-based tours of Estonia. **Raeturist** (☎ 668 8400; www.raeturist.ee; Narva maantee 13A), based in Tallinn, organises excellent cross-country bicycle tours. **Jalgrattakeskus** (☎ 637 6779; Tartu maantee 73), just southeast of Tallinn centre, rents bicycles by the hour with deals for long-term rentals.

Cross-country skiing is extremely popular, head to Otepää (p319) where there are several skiing centres that hire out equipment. See www.otepaa.ee for more information.

Saunas are an Estonian institution and come close to being a religious experience. The most common type is the dry, Finnish style. Most hotels have saunas. If you're looking to convert, the best public sauna is **Kalma Saun** (☎ 627 1811; Vana-Kalamaja tänav 9A, Tallinn; 🕓 10am-11pm). In Tallinn, the most popular beaches are at Pirita and Stroomi.

BUSINESS HOURS

Businesses don't keep general hours; specific opening hours are given throughout the chapter.

CUSTOMS

If arriving from another EU country, the limits for alcohol and tobacco are generous; see www.customs.ee for the latest restrictions. Antique objects made outside Estonia before 1850 or in Estonia before 1945 need special permits to be taken out of the country; these can be obtained from the **Division of the Export of Cultural Objects** (☎ 644 6578; Sakala tänav 14, Tallinn).

EMBASSIES & CONSULATES

For up-to-date contact details of Estonian diplomatic organisations as well as foreign embassies and consulates in Estonia, contact the **Estonian Foreign Ministry** (☎ 631 7600; www.vm.ee; Islandi Väljak 1, Tallinn).

Estonian Embassies & Consulates

Australia (☎ 02-9810 7468; estikon@ozemail.com.au; 86 Louisa Rd, Birchgrove, Sydney NSW 2041)
Canada (☎ 416-461 0764; estconsu@ca.inter.net; 202-958 Broadview Ave, Toronto, Ontario M4K 2R6)
Finland (☎ 9-622 0260; www.estemb.fi; Itäinen Puistotie 10, 00140 Helsinki)
France (☎ 01-56 62 22 00; 46, rue Pierre Charron, 75008 Paris)
Germany Berlin (☎ 30-25 460 600; www.estemb.de; Hildebrandstrasse 5 10785 Berlin); Hamburg (☎ 40-450 40 26; fax 450 40 515; Badestrasse 38, 20143 Hamburg)
Ireland (☎ 1-219 6730; embassy.dublin@mfa.ee; Riversdale House St Ann's, Ailesbury Rd, Dublin)
Latvia (☎ 781 20 20; www.estemb.lv; Skolas iela 13, Rīga)
Lithuania (☎ 5-278 0200; www.estemb.lt; Mickeviciaus gatvė 4a, Vilnius)
Netherlands (☎ 3120-316 54 40; embassy.hague@mfa .ee; Snipweg 101, 1118 DP Amsterdam Schiphol Airport)

Russia Moscow (☎ 095-290 5013; www.estemb.ru; Malo Kislovski 5, 103009 Moscow); St Petersburg (☎ 812-109 0920; fax 109 0927; Bolsaja Monetnaja 14, St Petersburg)
Sweden (☎ 08-5451 2280; www.estemb.se; Tyrgatan 3, Stockholm)
UK (☎ 020-7589 3428; www.estonia.gov.uk; 16 Hyde Park Gate, London SW7 5DG)
USA Washington DC (☎ 202-588 0101; www.estemb.org; 2131 Massachusetts Ave, NW, Washington DC 20008); New York (☎ 212-883 0636; www.nyc.estemb.org; 600 3rd Ave, 26th fl, New York, NY)

Embassies & Consulates in Estonia

Countries with embassies or consulates in Tallinn:
Australia (☎ 650 9308; mati@standard.ee; Marja tänav 9) Southwest of the centre.
Canada (☎ 627 3311; tallinn@canada.ee; Toom-Kooli tänav 13)
Finland (☎ 610 3200; Kohtu tänav 4)
France (☎ 631 1492; www.ambafrance-ee.org, not in English; Toom-Kuninga 20)
Germany (☎ 627 5300; www.germany.ee, in Estonian & German; Toom-Kuninga tänav 11) Southwest of the centre.
Ireland (☎ 681 1888; embassytallinn@eircom.net; Vene tänav 2)
Latvia (☎ 627 7850; Tõnismägi tänav 10)
Lithuania (☎ 641 2014; fax 641 2013; Uus tänav 15)
Netherlands (☎ 631 0580; www.netherlandsembassy .ee; Harju tänav 6)
Russia Tallinn (☎ 646 4146; www.estonia.mid.ru, in Russian; Lai tänav 18); Narva (☎ 35-60 652; fax 60 654; Kiriku tänav 8)
Sweden (☎ 640 5600; www.sweden.ee; Pikk tänav 28)
UK (☎ 667 4700; www.britishembassy.ee; Wismari tänav 6)
USA (☎ 668 8100; www.usemb.ee; Kentmanni tänav 20) Southeast of the centre.

FESTIVALS & EVENTS

Estonia has a busy festival calendar, encompassing all kinds of cultural interests.
All-Estonian Song Festival (www.laulupidu.ee) Convenes every five years and culminates in a 30,000-strong traditional choir, due in Tallinn in 2009.
Baltika International Folk Festival A week of music, dance and displays focusing on Baltic and other folk traditions, this festival is shared between Rīga, Vilnius and Tallinn; the next one will be in Tallinn in June 2007.
Beer Summer (www.ollesummer.ee) A hugely popular festival taking place in Tallinn (at the Song Festival Grounds on the road to Pirita) in early July.
Jaanipäev (St John's Eve; Jun 23) The biggest occasion in Estonia; a celebration of the pagan Midsummer's Night, best experienced out in the country where huge bonfires are lit for all-night parties.

ESTONIA

GAY & LESBIAN TRAVELLERS

While open displays of same-sex affection are discouraged in Estonia, the overall attitude is more of curiosity and openness than antagonism. Most local gays and lesbians live to some degree 'in the closet'. For more information, you can contact the **Estonian Gay League** (☎ 653 4812; gayliit@ hotmail.com).

HOLIDAYS

New Year's Day 1 January
Independence Day 24 February
Good Friday & Easter March/April
Spring Day 1 May
Victory Day (1919; Battle of Võnnu) 23 June
Jaanipäev (St John's Day; Midsummer's Night) 24 June
Day of Restoration of Independence (1991) 20 August
Christmas Day 25 December
Boxing Day 26 December

LANGUAGE

Like Finnish, Estonian belongs to the Finno-Ugric family of languages. It's a fantastically difficult language to learn, with 14 cases and a lack of gender, double infinitives, articles and even a lack of the future tense. Most every Estonian in Tallinn speaks at least some English – many speak it fluently; many elsewhere have some knowledge of English. However, fewer Russians speak English.

A small, yet growing, number of Russians in Estonia speak Estonian, but most Estonians also speak some Russian, even though not all of them will feel comfortable or happy speaking it.

See the Language chapter at the back of the book for pronunciation guidelines and useful words and phrases.

MONEY

Estonia introduced its own currency, the kroon (EEK; pronounced krohn) in June 1992; it's now pegged to the euro. The kroon comes in two, five, 10, 25, 50, 100 and 500EEK notes. One kroon is divided into 100 sents, and there are coins of five, 10, 20 and 50 sents, as well as one- and five-kroon coins.

The best foreign currencies to bring into Estonia are euros and US dollars, although all Western currencies are readily exchangeable.

All major credit cards are widely accepted; Visa is the most common, Amex the least. Most banks (but not stores and restaurants) accept travellers cheques, but their commissions can be high. There are frequent student, pensioner and group discounts on transport, in museums and in some shops upon presentation of accredited ID.

The *käibemaks* consumption tax, levied on most goods and services, is 18%. Tipping has become the norm in the last few years, but generally no more than 10% is expected.

POST

Mail service in and out of Estonia is highly efficient. There is a poste-restante bureau, where mail is kept for up to one month, at Tallinn's **central post office** (Narva maantee 1, Tallinn 10101). To post a letter up to 20g to Scandinavia/Europe/rest of the world costs 6/6.50/8EEK.

TELEPHONE

To call other cities in Estonia, dial the city code and telephone number (for example, to call Tartu, dial ☎ 7 followed by the six-digit number). All Estonian phone numbers, including their city code, add up to seven digits (save for mobile numbers, which begin with ☎ 5 and can be eight digits long). Estonia's country code is ☎ 372. There is no international operator here: the regular operator (no English spoken) is ☎ 165.

EMERGENCY NUMBERS

- 24-hour roadside assistance ☎ 1188
- Fire, ambulance and urgent medical advice ☎ 112
- Police ☎ 110
- Tallinn's First Aid hotline ☎ 697 1145 can advise you in English about the nearest treatment centres

---

VISAS

Ensure your passport will last at least two months more than your travels. Citizens of EU countries, plus Australia, Canada, the USA and many other countries can enter Estonia visa-free for a maximum 90-day stay over a six-month period. Visa regulations are constantly changing, so check

Tiered houses in Berat (p46),
Albania

Beaches around Dubrovnik (p220), Croatia

Medieval Hvar Town (p212), on Hvar Island,
Croatia

Wooden walkways in the Plitvice
Lakes National Park (p205), Croatia

JONATHAN SMITH

WWII Memorial at Brest
Fortress (p74), Belarus

PHILIP GA...

Rila Monastery (p130), set against Bulgaria's Rila
Mountains

The village of Bansko (p133) sits beneath Bulgaria's Pirin Mountains

TOM COCKRE...

with an Estonian consulate or embassy or directly with the **Estonian Foreign Ministry** (☎ 631 7600; www.vm.ee; Islandi Väljak 1, Tallinn). Note that visas cannot be obtained at the border.

TRANSPORT IN ESTONIA

GETTING THERE & AWAY
Air

The national carrier **Estonian Air** (☎ 640 1101; www.estonian-air.ee; Vabaduse väljak 10) links Tallinn with 13 cities in Europe and Russia, and at reasonable prices. A number of other airlines also serve the Tallinn airport.

Air Baltic (code BT; ☎ 605 8633; www.airbaltic.lv)

ČSA (code OK; ☎ 630 9397; www.csa.cz)

Estonian Air (code OV; ☎ 640 1101; www.estonian-air.ee)

Finnair (code AY; ☎ 611 0905; www.finnair.com)

LOT Polish Airlines (code LO; ☎ 646 605; www.lot.com)

Lufthansa (code LH; ☎ 681 4630; www.lufthansa.com)

SAS Scandinavian Airlines (code SK; ☎ 666 3030; www.scandinavian.net)

Copterline (www.copterline.ee) runs pricey helicopter flights between Helsinki and Tallinn's Copterline Terminal near the port hourly from 7am to 9pm (one way 767EEK to 3100EEK, 18 minutes).

Land
BUS

Buses are the cheapest but least comfortable way of reaching the Baltics. **Eurolines** (☎ 680 0909; www.eurolines.ee, in Estonian; Bus Station, Lastekodu tänav 46, Tallinn) runs direct buses daily to Tallinn from several destinations within Germany, with connecting services to cities throughout Western Europe. Direct services connect Tallinn to Rīga (200EEK to 275EEK, five to 5½ hours, eight daily) and Vilnius (370EEK, 10½ hours, two daily).

Buses leave Tallinn for St Petersburg five times daily (280EEK, eight hours). There is also one bus from Tallinn to Kaliningrad daily (300EEK, 15 hours).

CAR & MOTORCYCLE

From Finland, just put your vehicle on a Helsinki–Tallinn ferry. If approaching Estonia from the south from Western Europe, you'll need to cut across Poland,

which few drivers get excited about, and make sure to avoid crossing through Kaliningrad or Belarus – not only will you need hard-to-get visas for these countries, you are likely to face hassles from traffic police and encounter roads in abominable conditions! See also p330.

TRAIN

An overnight train runs every evening between Moscow and Tallinn (690/490EEK in 2nd/3rd class, 15½ hours).

Sea
FINLAND

About 25 ferries and hydrofoils (catamarans) cross between Helsinki and Tallinn daily. Ferries make the crossing in 2½ to 3½ hours, hydrofoils in just over an hour. All companies provide concessions and charge higher prices for weekend travel. Expect to pay around the price of an adult ticket extra to take a car.

Tallink (☎ 640 9808; www.tallink.ee, in Estonian) runs up to 12 ferries and hydrofoils daily. Ferry tickets start from 190EEK and hydrofoil tickets cost from 315EEK. **Lindaline** (☎ 699 9333) makes up to eight hydrofoil crossings each way daily. A one-way trip costs from 345EEK. **Eckerö Line** (☎ 631 8606) operates a daily or twice-daily car-carrying catamaran from Terminal B, making the crossing in 3½ hours, with one-way tickets starting from 220EEK. **Nordic Jet Line** (☎ 613 7000) has several car-carrying catamarans departing Terminal C, making the trip in around 1½ hours, several times a day; one-way tickets cost from 300EEK. **Silja Line** (☎ 611 6661; www.silja.ee, in Estonian) ferries make the crossing between Tallinn and Helsinki in 1½ hours with worthwhile day-trip packages available to Helsinki. Prices start from 340EEK.

SWEDEN

Tallink (☎ 640 9808; www.tallink.ee) runs nightly ferries from Tallinn's Terminal D to Stockholm (from 650EEK, 15 hours), as well as daily ferries from Paldiski, 52km west of Tallinn, to Kappelskär near Stockholm (from 450EEK, 12 hours). There are slight reductions for students and children under 18. Tickets should be booked well in advance in Tallinn or Stockholm's Free Harbour **Frihamnen** (☎ 08-667 0001).

GETTING AROUND
Air
Avies Air (☎ 605 8022; www.avies.ee) operates flights from Tallinn to Kuressaare on Saaremaa once or twice daily from Sunday to Friday. It also has twice-daily flights to Kärdla on Hiiumaa Monday to Friday. **Air Livonia** (☎ 44 75 007; www.airlivonia.ee) has twice-weekly flights to Ruhnu and flights in wintertime to Kihnu from Pärnu (p323).

Bicycle
Estonia is predominantly flat, with good roads and light traffic, and distances between urban centres are relatively small – perfect for this green mode of travel. As few locals cycle within main cities, be wary of inconsiderate motorists. A number of travel agencies offer bicycle tours. There are Tallinn cycling road maps at www.tallinn.ee, listed under public transport timetables.

Bus
Long-distance buses serve all major Estonian towns. Buses are a good option, as they are generally cheaper, more frequent, and faster than trains, and cover many destinations not serviced by the rail network.

Buses to within about 40km of Tallinn leave from the local bus station beside the train station. Information and timetables can be had 24 hours via **Harju Linnid** (☎ 644 1801). For detailed bus information and advance tickets for all other country destinations, contact the central bus station **Autobussijaam** (☎ 680 0900; www.bussireisid.ee, in Estonian; Lastekodu tänav 46).

Car & Motorcycle
An International Driving Permit (IDP) is necessary, as are your vehicle's registration papers and compulsory accident insurance, which can be bought at border crossings. Fuel and service stations are widely available, though spare parts for sports or luxury cars might be hard to find.

Train
Trains are slower and rarer than buses; the most frequent trains service the suburbs of Tallinn. Regional train schedules are listed at www.edel.ee.

Hungary

CONTENTS

Highlights	332
Itineraries	332
Climate & When to Go	333
History	333
People	336
Sport	336
Religion	336
Arts	336
Environment	337
Food & Drink	338
Budapest	**339**
History	339
Orientation	342
Information	342
Dangers & Annoyances	345
Sights & Activities	346
Tours	348
Sleeping	348
Eating	350
Drinking	352
Entertainment	352
Shopping	353
Getting There & Away	354
Getting Around	354
The Danube Bend	**355**
Szentendre	355
Visegrád	357
Esztergom	358
Northwestern Hungary	**360**
Győr	361
Sopron	364
Lake Balaton	**366**
Balatonfüred	367
Tihany	368
Keszthely	369
South Central Hungary	**372**
Pécs	372
Around Pécs	376
Southeastern Hungary	**376**
Kecskemét	376
Kiskunság National Park	379
Szeged	379
Northeastern Hungary	**382**
Eger	382
Szilvásvárad	385
Tokaj	385
Hungary Directory	**387**
Accommodation	387

Activities	387
Books	388
Business Hours	388
Courses	388
Customs	388
Disabled Travellers	388
Discount Cards	388
Embassies & Consulates	389
Festivals & Events	389
Gay & Lesbian Travellers	389
Holidays	389
Language	389
Media	390
Money	390
Post	390
Telephone & Fax	390
Tourist Information	391
Visas	391
Women Travellers	391
Work	391
Transport	**391**
Getting There & Away	391
Getting Around	393

Great wine, thermal spas, Gypsy music and goulash soup – yes. But Hungary is so much more than her stereotypes. In one compact country you can see Roman ruins, ancient castles, Turkish minarets and baroque cities, or you can experience the more rural pleasures of a cowboy riding astride five horses, storks nesting on streetlamps, and a sea of apricot trees in bloom. Cosmopolitan Budapest is a capital to rival any on the continent – with world-class operas, monumental historical buildings, and the Danube River flowing through the middle of it all. It's no wonder that many Magyars consider their nation more central than Eastern European. Prices though remain somewhere in the middle: not nearly as high as Austria or nearly as reasonable as the Ukraine. Having established itself as a state in the year 1000, Hungary has a long history, a rich culture and strong folk traditions that are well worth exploring in more depth. So go ahead, dive in.

FAST FACTS

- **Area** 93,000 sq km
- **Capital** Budapest
- **Currency** Forint (Ft); €1 = 247Ft; US$1 = 194Ft; UK£ = 3585Ft; A$1 = 144Ft; ¥100 = 135Ft; NZ$1 = 182Ft
- **Famous for** paprika, Bull's Blood and czárdás music
- **Key Phrases** *Jo napot kivanok* (good day), *szia* (hi/bye), *köszönöm* (thank you)
- **Official Language** Hungarian (Magyar)
- **Population** 10 million
- **Telephone Codes** country code ☎ 36; international access code ☎ 00; intercity access code ☎ 06
- **Visa** No visa required for most countries if stay is less than 90 days; see p391

HIGHLIGHTS

- The night-time view from atop Buda's **Castle Hill** (p346) is not to be missed. The city awash in lights, the gothic Parliament building glowing like a birthday cake: the Queen of the Danube still reigns.
- An ancient castle, baroque architecture, wooded hills, and loads and loads of wine – all superb reasons to come to **Eger** (p382).
- The Hungarian *puszta* (plain) is the stuff of myth and legend. See the cowboys ride at Bugac in **Kiskunság National Park** (p379).

- Tour an enormous 16th-century mosque-turned-Catholic church and other Turkish sights in the southern town of **Pécs** (p372).
- Get off the beaten track in Budapest at the **Aquincumi Múzeum** (p346), and walk among the excavated ruins of a 2nd-century Roman town.

ITINERARIES

- **One week** Spend at least three days visiting Budapest: see Castle Hill and Heroes' Square, but also take time to explore museums that pique your interest or hang out at a pavement café. Your fourth day might be spent on a day trip to see the open-air museum in Szentendre or the monumental cathedral at Esztergom. For nights five and six choose a provincial town or two to visit. Pécs has the greatest monuments of the Turkish period; Eger is a baroque town set in red-wine country; and lovely squares and nearby horse farms are the attractions in Kecskemét.

■ **Two weeks** With two weeks to travel, you can spare a fourth day in Budapest and still have time to cover a lot of ground. Nothing in this chapter is more than five hours by train from Budapest. After heading south to Pécs, seek out the towns of the Great Plain. Szeged is on the Tisza River and Kecskemét is further north. Finish your trip in Eger. Alternatively, if you are looking for a beach holiday, spend some time exploring the towns around Lake Balaton. Tihany is a rambling hillside village filled with craftsman houses, set on a peninsula that is a protected nature zone. Keszthely is an old town with a great palace in addition to a beach.

CLIMATE & WHEN TO GO

Hungary has a temperate Continental climate. July and August are the warmest months, and when highs hit 27°C it can feel much hotter given that most places don't have air-con. Spring is unpredictable, but usually arrives in April. November is already rainy and chilly; January and February are the coldest, dreariest months, with temperatures dropping below 0°C. September, with loads of sunshine, mild temperatures and grape harvest festivals in the countryside, may be the best time to visit. May, with a profusion of flowers and sunshine, is a close second. See p874 for details.

The busiest tourist season is July and August, Lake Balaton is especially crowded, but hotels quote high season prices from April to October. In provincial and smaller towns, attractions are often closed, or have reduced hours from October to May.

HISTORY
Pre-Hungarian Hungary

Long before Magyar tribes swept in, the plains of the Carpathian Basin were fertile ground for waves of migration from both

---

HOW MUCH?

■ **Lángos (fried dough snack)** 120-220Ft

■ **Hostel bed** 1600-3000Ft

■ **Loaf of bread** 160Ft

■ **Mid-range double room** €30-50

■ **Symphony ticket in Budapest** 1200-2500Ft

LONELY PLANET INDEX

■ **Litre of petrol** 265Ft

■ **Litre of bottle water** 150Ft

■ **Beer (a bottle from grocery store)** 130Ft

■ **Souvenir T-shirt** 900-2500Ft

■ **Street snack (gyro)** 500Ft

---

east and west. The Celts occupied the Carpathian Basin in the 3rd century BC but were conquered by the Romans just before the Christian era. The lands west of the Danube (Transdanubia) in today's Hungary became part of the Roman province of Pannonia with a Roman legion stationed at the town of Aquincum (today Óbuda). The Romans brought writing, planted the first vineyards in Hungary and built baths near some of the region's many thermal water sources.

A new surge of nomadic tribesmen, the Huns, arrived on the scene and by AD 441 leaders Attila and his brother Bleda had put an end to Roman rule in the area. The Hun's short-lived empire did not outlast Attila's death (453) and remaining tribesmen fled back from whence they came. The Huns were followed by the Goths, Longobards and the Avars, a powerful Turkic people who controlled parts of the area from the 5th to the 8th centuries. The Avars were subdued by Charlemagne in 796, leaving space for the Franks and Slavs to move in.

The Conquest

Historians usually set the Magyar (Hungarian) move-in date to around 896, when Árpád led the alliance of seven tribes into the region. The Magyars terrorised much of Europe with raids reaching as far as Spain. They were stopped at the Battle of Augsburg

HUNGARY

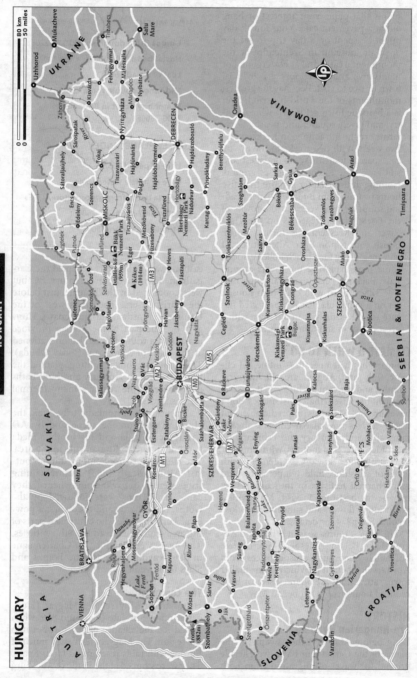

in 955 and subsequently converted to Christianity. Hungary's first king and its patron saint, István (Stephen), was crowned on Christmas Day in 1000, marking the foundation of the Hungarian state.

Medieval Hungary was a powerful kingdom that included Transylvania (now in Romania), Transcarpathia (now in Ukraine), modern-day Slovakia and Croatia. Under King Matthias Corvinus (1458–90), Hungary experienced a brief flowering of Renaissance culture. But the Turks were on the frontier: in 1526 they defeated the Hungarian army at Mohács and by 1541, Buda Castle had been seized and Hungary was sliced in three. The central part, including Buda, was in Ottoman Turk hands while Transdanubia, present-day Slovakia, and parts of Transcarpathia were ruled by Hungarian nobility based in Pozsony (Bratislava) under the auspices of the Austrian House of Habsburg. The principality of Transylvania, east of the Tisza, prospered as a vassal state of the Ottoman Empire.

Habsburg Hegemony & the Wars

After the Turks were evicted from Buda in 1686, Habsburg domination of Hungary began. The 'enlightened absolutism' of the Habsburg monarchs Maria Theresa (r 1740–80) and her son Joseph II (r 1780–90) helped the country leap forward economically and culturally. Rumblings of Hungarian independence surfaced off and on, but it was the unsuccessful 1848 Hungarian revolution that started to shake the Habsburg oligarchy. After Austria was defeated in war by Prussia in 1866 a weakened empire struck a compromise with Hungary in 1867, creating a dual monarchy. The two states would be self-governing in domestic affairs, but act jointly in matters of common interest, such as foreign relations. The Austro-Hungarian Monarchy lasted until WWI.

After WWI and the collapse of the Habsburg Empire in November 1918, Hungary was proclaimed a republic, but she had been on the losing side of the war. The 1920 Treaty of Trianon stripped the country of more than two-thirds of its territory – which today is still a hot topic of conversation.

In 1941 Hungary's attempts to recover lost territories drew the nation into war on the side of Nazi Germany. When leftists tried to negotiate a separate peace in 1944, the Germans occupied Hungary and brought the fascist Arrow Cross Party to power. The Arrow Cross immediately began deporting hundreds of thousands of Jews to Auschwitz. By early April 1945, all of Hungary had been liberated by the Soviet army.

Communism

The communists had assumed complete control of the government by 1947 and began nationalising industry and dividing up large estates among the peasantry. On 23 October 1956 student demonstrators demanding the withdrawal of Soviet troops were fired upon. The next day Imre Nagy, the reformist minister of agriculture, was named prime minister. On 28 October Nagy's government offered amnesty to all those involved in the violence and promised to abolish the hated secret police, the ÁVH (known as ÁVO until 1949). On 4 November Soviet tanks moved into Budapest, crushing the uprising. When the fighting ended on 11 November, some 25,000 people were dead. Then the reprisals began: an estimated 20,000 people were arrested; 2000 were executed, including Nagy; and another 250,000 fled to Austria.

By the 1970s Hungary had abandoned strict central economic control in favour of a limited market system, often referred to as 'Goulash Communism'. In June 1987 Károly Grósz took over as premier and Hungary began moving towards full democracy. The numbers of East Germans able to get around the Wall by leaving through Hungary may have contributed to its crumbling.

The Republic

At their party congress in February 1989 the Hungarian communists agreed to give up their monopoly on power. The Republic of Hungary was proclaimed in October, and democratic elections were scheduled for March 1990. Hungary changed political systems with scarcely a murmur, and the last Soviet troops left the country in June 1991.

The painful transition to a full market economy resulted in declining living standards for most people and recession in the early 1990s, but the end of the 20th and early 21st century have seen astonishing growth. Behind the economic surge are European, Asian and North American companies that have invested more than US$20 billion over the past decade, mainly because wages and operational costs are relatively low. Hungary's workforce is also considered flexible, skilled and highly educated.

Hungary became a fully fledged member of NATO in 1999. The April 2002 elections brought the Hungarian Socialist Party (MSZP), allied with the Alliance of Free Democrats (SZDSZ), to power under Prime Minister Péter Medgyessy, a free-market advocate who had served as finance minister. And in a national referendum during April 2003, the Hungarian people voted to join the European Union (EU). Amid street parties and fireworks, Hungary became one of the newest members of the EU along with nine other countries on May 1 2004. The dissolution of intra-Europe customs controls at airports and borders was immediate, but other changes will take time. Small businesses worry that the cost of complying with increased regulations will force many to close. It's unlikely that border restrictions with neighbouring members Austria, Slovakia and Slovenia will be completely removed any time soon, and the possible use of the euro as national currency is still years away. The ultimate influence of EU membership on Hungary remains to be seen.

PEOPLE

Approximately 10.2 million Magyar (Hungarian) people live within the national borders, and another five million Hungarians and their descendants are abroad. The estimated 1.44 million Hungarians in Transylvania (now Romania) constitute the largest ethnic minority in Europe, and there are another 520,000 in Slovakia, 295,000 in Serbia and Montenegro, 157,000 in Ukraine and 40,600 in Austria.

Ethnic Magyars make up approximately 93% of the population according to 2001 census data. Many minority groups estimate numbers to be significantly higher than official counts. There are 13 recognised minorities in the country, including Germans (0.6%), Slovaks (0.2%), Croatians (0.1%), Romanians (0.07%), Ukrainians (0.04%) and Rusyns (0.01%). The number of Roma is officially put at 1.8% of the population though some sources place it as high as 4%.

SPORT

The Formula One Hungarian Grand Prix, held in mid-August, is the year's biggest sporting event. The **Hungaroring** (www.hungaroring.hu) track is 19km north of Budapest, in Mogyoród, but hotels in the capital fill up and prices skyrocket.

RELIGION

Of those Hungarians declaring religious affiliation, about 52% are Roman Catholic, 16% Reformed (Calvinist) Protestant, 3% Evangelical (Lutheran) Protestant, 2.5% Greek Catholic, 1% Orthodox and 0.1% Jewish (down from a pre-WWII population of nearly 10 times the current size).

ARTS

Hungary in general, and Budapest in particular, is known for its traditional culture with a strong emphasis on the classical – and for good reason. The history of Hungarian arts and letters includes world-renowned composers and writers whose work is well worth seeking out. Opera, symphony and ballet are valued here, and even provincial towns have decent companies. For more contemporary influences, you may have to look a little harder, but they're out there, especially in Budapest: experimental dance companies, galleries and auction houses, avant-garde theatre and world beat musicians. Add to the mix the folk music, art and handicrafts that have grown out of village life or minority culture, and you have an arts scene that, while steeped in the past, is far from staid.

Music

By far the most influential Hungarian musician, composer and pianist is Franz (or Ferenc) Liszt (1811–86), who described himself as 'part Gypsy', and some of his works, notably *Hungarian Rhapsodies,* echo Romani music. Ferenc Erkel (1810–93) is the father of Hungarian opera, and the stirringly nationalist *Bánk Bán* is a standard at the Hungarian State Opera House in Budapest. Béla Bartók (1881–1945) and Zoltán Kodály (1882–1967) made the first systematic study of Hungarian folk music; both integrated some of their findings into their compositions.

Hungarian folk musicians play violins, zithers, hurdy-gurdies, bagpipes and lutes on a five-tone diatonic scale. Gypsy music, as it is known and played in Hungarian restaurants from Budapest to Boston, is urban schmaltz. At least two fiddles, a bass and a cymbalom (a curious table-toplike stringed instrument played with sticks) are *de rigueur*. Real Romani music is harder to find, but worth a listen. Part of the problem is identifying it: although this genre is distinctly different from the schmaltzy variety, both are often translated into English as 'gypsy music' – look for the word 'authentic' before the moniker, or for the group's village origins (Romani groups often come from far eastern Hungary). Romani music may incorporate different wind and string instruments (clarinet, bass, guitar), odd music-makers (such as jars and spoons), or may be sung a cappella. Kalyi Jag (Black Fire) is one of the best modern groups. Parno Graszt (White Horse) is a folk ensemble of musicians and dancers dedicated to preserving Romani musical traditions, who also borrow from other regional folk styles. (One of their songs sounds quite like a Jewish wedding dance.) They have gained an international reputation from performing their range of sad to frenetic songs, in Hungarian and Romani, across Europe.

In addition to hearing classical concerts in Budapest's large, ornate halls, you can attend concerts in churches, and festivals sometimes bring the music outdoors. Rock, jazz, blues, funk – just about any music you're looking for is on tap at Budapest's many night spots.

Literature
Poetry and literature have both echoed and influenced history in Hungary, so it's not surprising that much of the nationally recognised work reflects a sombre mood, sometimes known as *honfibú*, literally 'patriotic sorrow', or a sense of hopeless struggle against oppression.

Sándor Petőfi (1823–?) is Hungary's most celebrated poet. A line from his work *National Song* became the rallying cry for the War of Independence in 1848–49, in which he fought and is commonly thought to have died, though there is some speculation about that. His comrade-in-arms, János Arany (1817–82), wrote epic poetry. The prolific novelist and playwright Mór Jókai (1825–1904), gave expression to heroism and honesty in works such as *The Man with the Golden Touch*. Lyric poet Endre Ady (1877–1919) attacked narrow materialism; poet Attila József (1905–37) expresses the alienation felt by individuals in the modern age; and novelist Zsigmond Móricz (1879–1942) examines the harsh reality of peasant life in Hungary. Corvina Books publishes translations and anthologies of their works.

Three noteworthy contemporary writers in English translation are György Konrád (1933–), Péter Nádas (1942–) and Péter Esterházy (1950–). But it's the 2002 Nobel prizewinner, Imre Kertész, who has attracted the most attention. In works such as his novels *Fateless* and *Kaddish for a Child Not Born,* he writes from a young boy's perspective about life in a Holocaust concentration camp, and its aftereffects, connecting the singular experience to larger worldly themes.

Visual Arts
Favourite painters from the 19th century include realist Mihály Munkácsy (1844–1900), the so-called painter of the plains, and Tivadar Kosztka Csontváry (1853–1919). Győző Vásárhelyi (1908–97), who changed his name to Victor Vasarely when he emigrated to Paris, is considered the 'Father of Op Art'. In the 19th and early 20th century, the Zsolnay family created world-renowned decorative art in porcelain. Ceramic artist Margit Kovac (1902-1977), a Hungarian National Treasure, produced a prolific number of statues and ceramic objects during her career.

Much money was spent on socialist-realist art under the communist system. The transition to a free-market economy in which artists were no longer subsidised was a bumpy one, but today upscale galleries and auction houses host contemporary and innovative artists. The traditional embroidery, weavings and ceramics of the nation's *népművészet* (folk art) also perseveres and there is at least one handicraft store in every town.

ENVIRONMENT
The Land
Hungary occupies the Carpathian Basin to the southeast of the Carpathian Mountains. Water dominates much of the country's geography. The Duna (Danube River) divides the Nagyalföld (Great Plain) in the east from the Dunántúl (Transdanubia) in the west. The Tisza (597km in Hungary) is the country's longest river, and historically has been prone to flooding. The country has hundreds of small lakes and is riddled with thermal springs. Lake Balaton (596 sq

km, 77km long), in the west, is the largest freshwater lake in Europe outside Scandinavia. Hungary's 'mountains' to the north are merely hills, with the country's highest peak being Kékes (1014m) in the Mátra Range.

Wildlife

There are plenty of common European animals (deer, wild hare, boar, otter) as well as some rarer species (wild cat, lake bat, Pannonian lizard), but three-quarters of the country's 450 vertebrates are birds, especially waterfowl. Hungary is a premier European sight for bird-watching. Endangered or vulnerable populations include eastern imperial eagles, saker falcons and the great bustard. An estimated 70,000 cranes pass through every year and a great number of storks arrive in the northern uplands and on the Great Plain every spring.

National Parks

There are 11 national parks throughout Hungary. Bükk National Park, north of Eger, is a mountainous limestone area of forest and caves. Kiskunság National Park (p376, www.knp.hu) and Bugac (p379), near Kecskemét, and Hortobágy National Park (www.hnp.hu) in the Hortobágy Puszta (a World Heritage Site), outside Debrecen, protect the unique grassland environment of the plains.

Environmental Issues

Pollution is a large and costly problem. Harmful emissions from low-grade fuels such as coal and the high numbers of buses and cars, especially in Budapest, affect the air quality. The over-use of nitrate fertilisers in agriculture threatens ground water beneath the plains. However, there has been a marked improvement in air and water quality in recent years as Hungary attempts to conform to EU environmental standards.

FOOD & DRINK
Staples & Specialities

The omnipresent seasoning in Hungarian cooking is paprika, a mild red pepper that appears on restaurant tables as a condiment beside the salt and black pepper, as well as in many recipes. *Pörkölt*, a paprika-infused stew, can be made from different meats, including *borju* (veal), but usually it has no vegetables. *Galuska* (small, gnocchi-like dumplings) are a good accompaniment to soak up the sauce. The well-known *paprikas csirke* (chicken paprikash), is stewed chicken in a tomato-cream-paprika sauce (not as common here as in Hungarian restaurants abroad). *Töltött kaposzta* (cabbage rolls stuffed with meat and rice) is cooked in a roux made with paprika, and topped with sour cream, as is *székelygulyás* (stewed pork and sour cabbage). Another local favourite is *halászlé* (fisherman's soup), a rich mix of several kinds of poached freshwater fish, tomatoes, green peppers and…paprika.

Leves (soup) is the start to any main meal in a Hungarian home; some claim that you will develop stomach disorders if you don't eat a hot, daily helping. *Gulyás* (goulash), although served as a stew outside Hungary, is a soup here, cooked with beef, onions and tomatoes. Traditional cooking methods are far from health-conscious, but they are tasty. Frying is a nationwide obsession and you'll often find fried turkey, pork and veal schnitzels on the menu.

For dessert you might try the cold *gyümölcs leves* (fruit soup) made with sour cherries and other berries, or *palincsinta* (crepes) filled with jam, sweet cheese or chocolate sauce. A good food-stand snack is *lángos*, fried dough that can be topped with cheese and/or *tejföl* (sour cream).

Two Hungarian wines are known internationally: the sweet, dessert wine Tokaji Aszú and the full-bodied red, high in acid and tannin, Egri Bikavér (Eger Bull's Blood). But the country produces a number of other eminently drinkable wines as well. Hungarian beers sold nationally include Dreher and Kőbanyai; Borosodi is a decent amber brew. For the harder stuff, try *pálinka*, a strong, firewater-like brandy distilled from a variety of fruits, but most commonly plums or apricots. Zwack distillery produces Unicum, a bitter aperitif that has been around since 1790; it tastes a bit like the medicine doctors give you to induce vomiting – but it's popular.

Where to Eat & Drink

An *étterem* is a restaurant with a large selection, formal service and formal prices. A *vendéglő* is smaller, more casual and serves homestyle regional dishes. The over-used term *csárda*, which originally meant a rustic country inn with Gypsy music, can now mean anything – including super-touristy. To keep prices down, look for: *étkezde* (a tiny 'eating place' that may have a counter or sit-down service), *önkiszolgáló* (self-service canteen), *kinai gyorsbüfé* (Chinese 'fast' food), *grill* (generally serving gyros or kebabs and other grilled meats from the counter) or a *szendvicsbar* (with open-face sandwiches to go).

There are still a number of stuffy Hungarian restaurants with condescending waiters, formal service and Gypsy music left over from another era. For the most part, avoiding places with tuxedoed waiters is a good bet.

Wine has been produced in Hungary for thousands of years and you'll find it available by the glass or bottle everywhere. There are plenty of pseudo British–Irish–Belgian pubs, smoky *söröző* (a Hungarian pub, often in a cellar, where drinking is taken very seriously), *borozó* (a wine bar, usually a dive) and nightclubs, but the most pleasant place to imbibe a cocktail or coffee may be in a café. A *kávéház* may primarily be an old-world dessert shop, or it may be essentially a bar with an extensive drinks menu; either way they sell alcoholic beverages in addition to coffee. In spring, pavement tables sprout alongside the new flowers.

Vegetarians & Vegans

Traditional Hungarian food is heavy and rich. Meat, sour cream and fat abound and *saláta* generally means a plate of marinated vegetables (cucumbers, cabbage, beets and/or carrots). At least in Budapest, other alternatives are available, especially at Italian or Asian restaurants.

Some not-very-light, but widely available dishes for vegetarians to look for are *rántott sajt* (fried cheese), *gombafejek rántva* (fried mushroom caps), *gomba leves* (mushroom soup) and *túrós* or *káposzta csusza* (short, wide pasta with cheese or cabbage). *Bableves* (bean soup) usually contains meat.

Habits & Customs

The Magyar are a polite people and their language is flowered with courtesies. To toast someone's health before drinking, say *egéségére* (egg-eh-shaig-eh-ray), and to wish them a good appetite before eating, *jo étvágat* (yo ate-vad-yaht). If you're invited to someone's home, always bring a bunch of flowers and/or a bottle of good local wine.

BUDAPEST

☎ 1 / pop 1.8 million

Soak under the stone arches of a centuries-old thermal bath by day and then party at a swank nightclub, rivalling any in Western Europe, by night: Budapest today is a study in contrasts – of new and old, West and East. The commerce-rich, modern city has new business-class train cars with Internet access and a multitude of glass-encased shopping malls and corporation headquarters. But walk the streets and you're just as likely to see ornate 19th-century mansions, some of which have been glowingly restored in bright pastels (especially on Andrássy út), and some of which wait to be discovered under years of grey. Medieval building populate Castle Hill and the Roman ruins in Aquincum represent truly ancient history. Alongside classy restaurants (with Western prices) competing for the young professionals' business, it's still possible to find a tasty, reasonable, homestyle meal at a price more akin to those found in neighbouring countries to the East. Budapest is steeped in history, but she is no museum town; the city is constantly evolving and that's the best thing about it – Budapest pulses with life.

HISTORY

Strictly speaking, the story of Budapest begins only in 1873 with the administrative union of three cities that had grown together: Buda, west of the Danube; Óbuda (the oldest part of Buda) to the north; and Pest on the eastern side of the river. But the area had been occupied for thousands of years before Budapest as we know it existed. The Romans built a settlement at Aquincum (Óbuda) during the first centuries of the Christian Era. In the 1500s, the Turks arrived uninvited and stayed for almost 150 years. The Habsburg Austrians helped kick the invaders out, but then made themselves at home for 200 more years.

At the turn of the 20th century, under the dual Austro-Hungarian monarchy, the population of Budapest exploded and many buildings date from that boom. The city suffered some damage in the two world wars and the 1956 revolution left structures pockmarked with bullet holes. But today many of the old buildings have been restored, and

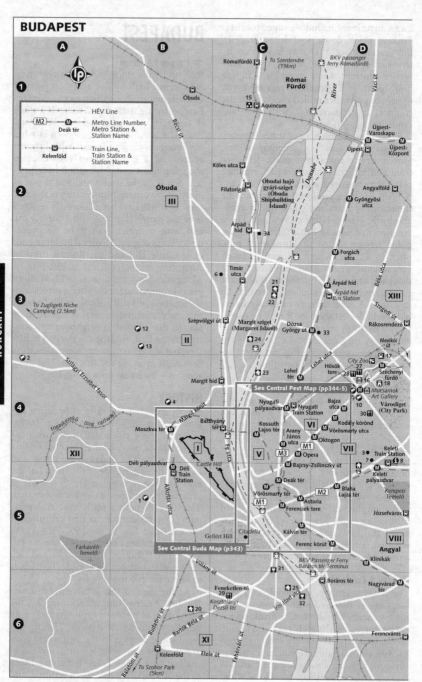

BUDAPEST

HÉV Line

M2 ⓜ Metro Line Number, Metro Station & Station Name
Deák tér

Kelenföld ⓔ Train Line, Train Station & Station Name

Rómaifürdő
To Szentendre (19km)
BKV passenger ferry Rómaifürdő

Római Fürdő

Óbuda

15 Aquincum

Újpest-Városkapu
Újpest Újpest-Központ
Váci út

Köles utca

Óbudai hajó gyári-sziget (Óbuda Shipbuilding Island)

Filatorigát

Óbuda

III

Angyalföld
Gyöngyösi utca

Árpád híd 34

Forgách utca

Timár utca 6

21 22

Árpád híd
Árpád híd Bus Station

XIII

Szegedi út
Szépvölgyi út
Margit sziget (Margaret Island)
Dózsa György út 33
Rákosrendező

To Zugligeti Niche Camping (2.5km)

12

13

II

24

Mexikói út 17

City Zoo 27
Hősök tere 28 16 Széchenyi fürdő 18

Lehel tér

23

Margit híd

Mucsarnok Art Gallery
Városliget (City Park)

See Central Pest Map (pp344-5)

Nyugati pályaudvar Nyugati Train Station

VI

Bajza utca

10

Kodály körönd
Vörösmarty utca

30

Margit körút

4

Battyhány tér

Moszkva tér

Kossuth Lajos tér

Arany János utca
Oktogon
M1

VII

Keleti Train Station
3

Déli pályaudvar

Fő utca

Castle Hill

I

Déli Train Station

V

M3 Opera

Bajcsy-Zsilinszky út

7
19

Keleti pályaudvar

8

XII

fogaskerekű (cog railway)

Deák tér

Blaha Lujza tér

M2 Astoria

Szilágyi Erzsébet fasor

Alkotás utca

Vörösmarty tér
M1

Ferenciek tere

Kálvin tér

Kerepesi Temető

Józsefváros

Farkasréti Temető

Gellért Hill

Citadella

See Central Buda Map (p343)

Ferenc körút

VIII

Angyal

Klinikák

Villány út

31

BKV Passenger Ferry Boráros tér Terminus

Boráros tér

Nagyvárad tér

Feneketlen-tó 29

20

Kosztolányi Dezső tér

25

32

Ferencváros

XI

Budaörsi út

Bartók Béla út

Fehérvári út

Etele út

Balatoni út

Kelenföld

To Szobor Park (5km)

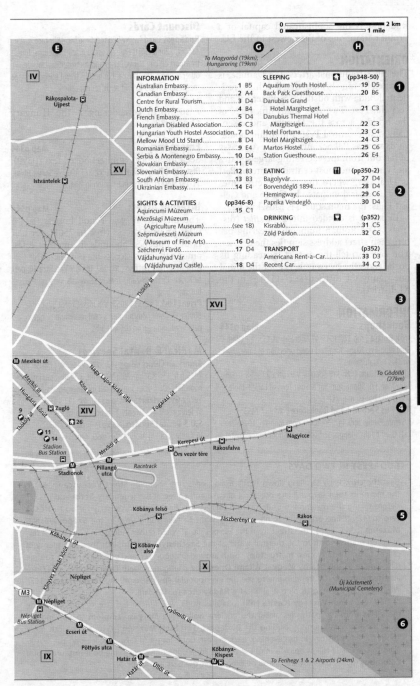

INFORMATION
Australian Embassy...............................1 B5
Canadian Embassy...............................2 A4
Centre for Rural Tourism.....................3 D4
Dutch Embassy...................................4 B4
French Embassy...................................5 D4
Hungarian Disabled Association..........6 C3
Hungarian Youth Hostel Association...7 D4
Mellow Mood Ltd Stand......................8 D4
Romanian Embassy.............................9 E4
Serbia & Montenegro Embassy.........10 D4
Slovakian Embassy............................11 E4
Slovenian Embassy............................12 B3
South African Embassy......................13 B3
Ukrainian Embassy............................14 E4

SIGHTS & ACTIVITIES   (pp346-8)
Aquincumi Múzeum............................15 C1
Mezősági Múzeum
  (Agriculture Museum).................(see 18)
Szépművészeti Múzeum
  (Museum of Fine Arts)..................16 D4
Széchenyi Fürdő................................17 D4
Vájdahunyad Vár
  (Vájdahunyad Castle)...................18 D4

SLEEPING   (pp348-50)
Aquarium Youth Hostel.....................19 D5
Back Pack Guesthouse......................20 B6
Danubius Grand
  Hotel Margitsziget........................21 C3
Danubius Thermal Hotel
  Margitsziget.................................22 C3
Hotel Fortuna...................................23 C4
Hotel Margitsziget...........................24 C3
Martos Hostel...................................25 C6
Station Guesthouse..........................26 E4

EATING   (pp350-2)
Bagolyvár..27 D4
Borvendéglő 1894.............................28 D4
Hemingway.......................................29 C6
Paprika Vendeglő..............................30 D4

DRINKING   (p352)
Kisrabló...31 C5
Zöld Párdon......................................32 C6

TRANSPORT   (p352)
Americana Rent-a-Car.......................33 D3
Recent Car.......................................34 C2

Budapest is the sophisticated capital of a proud nation, one of the newest in the EU.

ORIENTATION

The city's traditional artery, the Danube, is spanned by nine bridges that link hilly, residential Buda with bustling, commercial and very flat Pest. Two ring roads link three of the bridges across the Danube and essentially define central Pest. Important boulevards such as Rákóczi út and leafy Andrássy út fan out from these, creating large squares and circles. The most central square in Pest is Deák tér, where the three metro lines meet. Buda is dominated by Castle and Gellért Hills; the main square is Moszkva tér.

Budapest is divided into 23 *kerület* (districts). The Roman numeral appearing before each street address signifies the district. You can also tell the district by reading its postal code: the two numbers after the initial one signify the district (ie H-1114 is in the XI district).

INFORMATION

Bookshops   Map p344

Irók Boltja (☎ 322 1645; VI Andrássy út 45; ☼ 10am-6pm Mon-Fri, 10am-3pm Sat) Good selection of Hungarian writers in translation.

Libri Stúdium (☎ 318 5680; V Váci utca 22; ☼ 10am-7pm Mon-Fri, 10am-3pm Sat & Sun) Tons of coffee-table and travel books, many LP titles.

Red Bus Second-hand Bookstore (☎ 337 7453; V Semmelweiss utca 14; ☼ 10am-6pm Mon-Fri, 10am-3pm Sat) Used English-language books, next door to the hostel.

Discount Cards

Budapest Card (www.budapestinfo.hu; 48hr card 4350Ft, 72hr 5450Ft) Free access to many museums, free transport on city trams, buses and metros, discounts on other services. Buy the card at hotels, travel agencies, large metro station kiosks and some tourist offices.

Also worth considering is the Hungary Card (p388).

Emergency   Map p344

See Emergency Numbers boxed text (p390).

District V Police Station (☎ 373 1000; V Szalay utca 11-13) Most central police station in Pest.

Internet Access   Map p344

The majority of year-round hostels (p348) offer Internet access (free to 250Ft per half hour). Budapest abounds in Internet cafés, among the most accessible of which are:

Ami Internet Coffee (☎ 267 1644; V Váci utca 40; per hr 700Ft; ☼ 9am-2am) Tons of terminals, very central, but superbusy.

Privat Link (☎ 334 2057; VIII József körút 52; per hr 800Ft; ☼ 24hr) Buy an hour's card minimum to get a password and sign on day or night.

Medical & Dental Services

American Clinics (Map p343; ☎ 224 9090; I Hattyú utca 14, 5th fl; ☼ 8.30am-7pm Mon-Thu, 8.30am-6pm Fri, 8am-noon Sat, 10am-2pm Sun) On call for emergencies 24/7.

Teréz Gyógyszertár (Map p344; ☎ 311 4439; VI Teréz körút 41) Twenty-four hour pharmacy.

S.O.S Dental Service (Map p344; ☎ 322 0602; VI Király utca 14) Around-the-clock dental care.

BUDAPEST IN TWO DAYS

Beat the crowds by strolling down Pest's main pedestrian shopping street **Váci utca** (p347) in the morning, then savour a late breakfast of cake and coffee at the legendary **Gerbeaud** (p352), before taking the millennium underground (M1, yellow line) from Vörösmarty tér up to **Hősök tere** (p347). If fine art's your thing, you may want to take some time in the **Szépmüvészeti Múzeum** (p347) across the street from the Heroes' Sq. If you'd rather indulge in a soak, go a few hundred metres north to the thermal water at the **Széchenyi Fürdő** (p347). There are plenty of places to grab a bite a few metro stops south around Oktogon tér, and you might want to time it so you're at the nearby **Magyar Állami Operaház** (Hungarian State Opera House, p347) for an afternoon tour. Or stand in line to see the ever-popular spy museum, the **Terror Háza** (p347). Wind up your evening sipping it all in at a **Ráday utca** (p350) café.

Day two, climb **Várhegy (Castle Hill)** (p346) in Buda, wander the old streets and appreciate the views from the pathways along the ancient walls. Tour **Mátyás Templom** (p346) and explore the many museums, including the **Budapesti Történeti Múzeum** (p346) to find out more about the city's history. In the evening, back in Pest, don't forget to take a walk along the waterfront to see Castle Hill lit up. You might even stop for a drink or a meal at the boat-restaurant-pub **Columbus** (p352) to enjoy the scene before you hit the bars and clubs.

CENTRAL BUDA

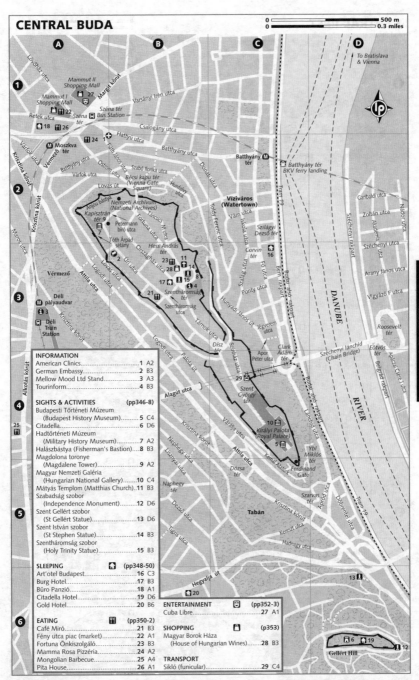

0 — 500 m
0 — 0.3 miles

To Bratislava & Vienna

HUNGARY

DANUBE

RIVER

Gellért Hill

INFORMATION	
American Clinics	1 A2
German Embassy	2 B3
Mellow Mood Ltd Stand	3 A3
Tourinform	4 B3

SIGHTS & ACTIVITIES	(pp346-8)
Budapesti Történeti Múzeum (Budapest History Museum)	5 C4
Citadella	6 D6
Hadtörténeti Múzeum (Military History Museum)	7 A2
Halászbástya (Fisherman's Bastion)	8 B3
Magdolona toronye (Magdalene Tower)	9 A2
Magyar Nemzeti Galéria (Hungarian National Gallery)	10 C4
Mátyás Templom (Matthias Church)	11 B3
Szabadság szobor (Independence Monument)	12 D6
Szent Gellért szobor (St Gellért Statue)	13 D6
Szent István szobor (St Stephen Statue)	14 B3
Szentháromság szobor (Holy Trinity Statue)	15 B3

SLEEPING	(pp348-50)
Art'otel Budapest	16 C3
Burg Hotel	17 B3
Büro Panzió	18 A1
Citadella Hotel	19 D6
Gold Hotel	20 B6

EATING	(pp350-2)
Café Miró	21 B3
Fény utca piac (market)	22 A1
Fortuna Önkiszolgáló	23 B3
Mamma Rosa Pizzéria	24 A2
Mongolian Barbecue	25 A4
Pita House	26 A1

ENTERTAINMENT	(pp352-3)
Cuba Libre	27 A1

SHOPPING	(p353)
Magyar Borok Háza (House of Hungarian Wines)	28 B3

TRANSPORT	
Sikló (funicular)	29 C4

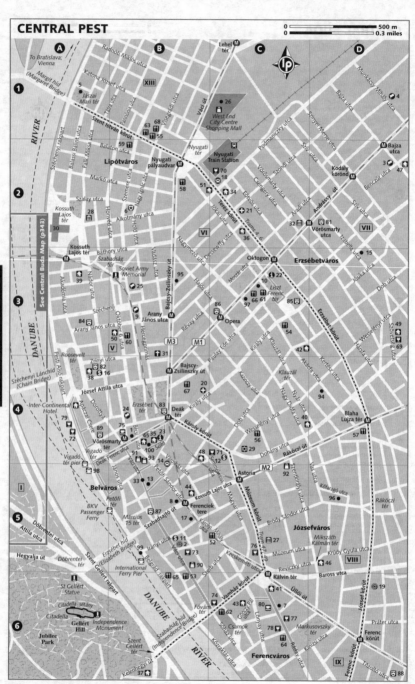

INFORMATION
American Express	1	B4
Ami Internet Coffee	2	B5
Austrian Embassy	3	D2
Croatian Embassy	4	D1
Debrecen Summer University Branch	5	A1
District V Police Station	6	B2
Hungarian Equestrian Tourism Association	7	C6
Ibusz	8	B5
Irish Embassy	9	B3
Irók Boltja	10	C3
K&H Bank	11	B5
K&H Bank	12	C4
Libri Stúdium	13	B5
Main Post Office	14	B4
National Association of Village Tourism	15	D3
OTP Bank	16	A4
Pegazus Tours	17	B5
Post Office	18	C2
Privat Link	19	D6
Red Bus Second-hand Bookstore	(see 48)	
S O S Dental Service	20	B4
Teréz Gyógyszertár	21	C2
Tourinform Liszt Ferenc Square	22	C3
Tourinform Main Office	23	B4
UK Embassy	24	B4
US Embassy	25	B3
Vista Visitor Centre	(see 67)	

SIGHTS & ACTIVITIES (pp346-8)
Budapest Eye	26	C1
Gellért Fürdő	(see 37)	
Magyar Nemzeti Múzeum (Hungarian National Museum)	27	C5
Néprajzi Múzeum (Ethnography Museum)	28	A2
Nagy Zsinagóga (Great Synagogue)	29	C4
Parlament	30	A2
Szent István Bazilika	31	B3

Terror Háza	32	C2
Váci utca	33	B5

SLEEPING (pp348-50)
Best Hostel	34	C2
Best Hotel Service	35	B4
Caterina Hostel	36	C2
Danubius Hotel Gellért	37	B6
Four Seasons Hotel	38	A4
Garibaldi Guesthouse	39	A3
Hostel Marco Polo	40	C4
Hotel Ibis Centrum	41	C6
Hotel Queen Mary	42	C3
Kálvin Ház	43	C6
Leo Panzió	44	B5
Mellow Mood Central Hostel	45	B4
Museum Guest House	46	D5
Radio Inn	47	D2
Red Bus Hostel	48	B4
Red Bus II	49	D3
To-Ma Travel Agency	50	B3
Yellow Submarine Hostel	51	B2

EATING (pp350-2)
Cafe Károlyi	52	C5
Fatál	53	B6
Frici Papa	54	C3
Három Testvér	55	B1
Kék Rózsa	56	C4
Kaiser's	57	D4
Kaiser's	58	B2
Kis Italia	59	B2
Kisharang	60	B3
Menza	61	C3
Nagycsarnok (Great Market)	62	C6
Okay Italia	63	B1
Ráday Étkezde	64	C6
Taverna Dionysos	65	B6
Vörös és Fehér	66	C3
Vista Café	67	B4
Wabisabi	68	B1

DRINKING (p352)
Angyal	69	D3
Bahnhof Music Club	70	C2
Café Eklektika	71	C4
Columbus	72	A4
Fat Mo's	73	B5
For Sale	74	C6
Gerbeaud	75	B4
Irish Cat Pub	76	C5
Paris, Texas	77	C6
Shiraz	78	C6
Spoon	79	A4
Teaház a Vörös Oroszlánhoz	80	C6

ENTERTAINMENT (pp352-3)
Bábszínház (Budapest Puppet Theatre)	81	D2
Duna Palota	82	A4
Gödör Klub	83	B4
Kalamajka Táncház	84	A3
Liszt Ferenc Zeneakadémia	85	C3
Magyar Állami Operaház (Hungarian State Opera House)	86	C3
Music Mix	87	B5
Trafó Bár Tangó	88	D6
Vigadó Jegyiroda	89	A4

SHOPPING (p353)
Folkart Centrum	90	B5
Folkart Kézművesház	91	B4
Magyar Palinka Háza	92	C5
Rózsavölgyi Music Shop	93	B4

TRANSPORT (pp354-5)
BKV Office	94	D4
Hungarian Bicycle Touring Association	95	B3
Kenguru	96	D5
MÁV Ticket Office	97	C3
Mahart PassNave Sightseeing Cruises	98	A5
Mahart PassNave Ticket Office	99	B5
Yellow Zebra Bikes	100	B4

Money
Map p344

ATMs are quite common, especially on the ring roads and main arteries. Most banks have both ATMs and exchange services. Banks have standardised hours nationwide. See p388 for information about opening and closing times.

American Express (☎ 235 4330; V Deák Ferenc utca 10; ⏱ 9am-5.30pm Mon-Fri, 9am-2pm Sat) Will change its own travellers cheques without commission; not the best rates.

K&H Bank (V Váci utca 40) Quite central.

OTP Bank (V Nádor utca 6) Favourable rates.

Post
Map p344

Main post office (V Városház utca 18) Pick up poste restante mail here.

Tourist Information

The Hungarian National Tourist Board, in conjunction with the Budapest Tourism Office, runs Tourinform offices in Budapest.

Tourinform (☎ 06 80 630 800 24hr hotline; www.Budapestinfo.hu); Main Office (Map p344; ☎ 438 8080; V Sütő utca 2; ⏱ 8am-8pm); Liszt Ferenc Square (Map p344; ☎ 322 4098; VI Liszt Ferenc tér 11; ⏱ 10am-6pm Mon-Fri); Castle Hill (Map p343; ☎ 488 0475; I Szentháromság tér; ⏱ 10am-7pm)

Travel Agencies

You can get information, book tours and transport, and arrange accommodation at travel agencies in Budapest. They also sell discount cards.

Ibusz (Map p344; ☎ 485 2716; www.ibusz.hu; V Ferenciek tere 10; ⏱ 9am-5pm Mon-Fri, 9am-1pm Sat Jul-Aug) The main branch of this national agency has an exchange office, books private rooms and pensions, and sells air and train tickets – the works.

Mellow Mood Ltd Stand (Map pp340-1 & p343; ☎ 413 2065; www.mellowmood.hu; Keleti & Déli train stations; ⏱ 7am-8pm) Staff at these two train station stands will help you find hostel and other accommodation, as well provide info. Affiliated with the Hungarian Youth Hostel Association and Hostelling International (HI).

Vista Visitor Centre (Map p344; ☎ 268 0888; www.vista.hu; VI Paulay Ede utca 2; ⏱ 9am-6pm Mon-Fri, 10am-3pm Sat) Book apartments and arrange tours here. Internet access, café onsite.

DANGERS & ANNOYANCES

Overall, Hungary is a very safe country with little violent crime, but scams can be a problem in the capital. Overcharging in taxis is not unknown and we have received reports of unscrupulous waiters stealing credit-card information. Watch out for tricks on the street: the usual pickpocket method is for someone to distract you (by running into you, dropping something etc) while an accomplice makes off with your goods. And guys should avoid drop-dead gorgeous women who approach (especially around Váci utca) and offer to take them to a local nightspot. Disreputable clubs hire these women to lure you in and then charge insane rates for drinks (upwards of €80 a pop) for you and the girls, who order refills adeptly.

There is a small but persistent neo-Nazi presence in Budapest that wants to blame Jews, Roma, Asians or blacks for the ills of the world, but for now their action seems to be limited to rallies and protests.

SIGHTS & ACTIVITIES
Buda   Map p343
High above the Danube, **Várhegy** (Castle Hill) contains most of the medieval buildings left in Budapest. From the red line metro station at Moszkva tér, climb the staircase on your left to street level; continue left up Várfok utca, or cross the street and board the Vár bus (a minibus with a picture of a castle on the sign). Wandering around the old streets and appreciating the city views is part of the attraction, so get off at the first stop after the Vienna Gate and wander around.

To the right, in Kapisztrán tér, the **Magdolona toronye** (Magdalen Tower) is all that's left of a Gothic church destroyed here during WWII. The white neoclassical building facing the square is the **Hadtörténeti Múzeum** (Military History Museum; ☎ 356 9522; I Tóth Árpád sétány 40; adult/student 400/120Ft; ✆ 10am-6pm Tue-Sun Apr-Sep, 10am-4pm Oct-Mar).

Walk south along the ramparts promenade and you are looking out at the mansions of the Buda Hills. Follow the third alleyway to your left and you reach Szentháromság tér and the **Szentháromság szobor** (Holy Trinity Statue) at its centre. Don't miss the neo-Gothic **Mátyás Templom** (Matthias Church; ☎ 489 0717; I Szentháromság tér; adult/student 550/270Ft; ✆ 9am-5pm Mon-Sat, 1-5pm Sun), with a colourful tiled roof and lovely murals inside. Franz Liszt's *Hungarian Coronation Mass* was played here for the first time at the coronation of Franz Joseph and Elizabeth in 1867. Nowadays there are classical music concerts some evenings.

Across the square is the **Magyar Borok Háza** (House of Hungarian Wines; ☎ 212 1031; www.magyar borokhaza.hu; Szentháromság tér 6; wine tasting 3500Ft; ✆ noon-8pm) where you can sample varieties from across the country. To the south is an equestrian **Szent István szobor** (St Stephen Statue), of Hungary's first king (István). Behind the monument, walk along **Halászbástya** (Fishermen's Bastion; Szentháromság tér; adult/student 300/150Ft; ✆ 8.30am-11pm). The fanciful, neo-Gothic arcade built on the fortification wall is prime picture-taking territory with views of the river and the parliament beyond.

Tárnok utca runs southeast to Dísz tér, past which is the entrance for the **Siklo** (Funicular; Szent György tér; uphill/downhill ticket adult 600/500Ft, child 3-14 years 350Ft; ✆ 7.30am-10pm) that can take you down the hill to Clark Ádám tér. The massive **Királyi Palota** (Royal Palace) occupies the far end of Castle Hill; inside are the **Magyar Nemzeti Galéria** (Hungarian National Gallery; ☎ 375 7533; I Szent György tér 6; adult/student 800/400Ft; ✆ 10am-6pm Tue-Sun) and the **Budapesti Történeti Múzeum** (Budapest History Museum; ☎ 375 7533; I Szent György tér 2; adult/student 400/250Ft; ✆ 10am-6pm daily mid-May–mid-Sep, 10am-4pm Wed-Mon mid-May–mid-Sep).

To the south of Castle Hill is Gellért Hill, atop which sits the **Citadella** (☎ 365 6076; 300Ft; ✆ 8am-10pm): built by the Habsburgs after the 1848 revolution to 'defend' the city from further Hungarian insurrection, it was never used as a fortress. There are awesome views, exhibits, a restaurant and a hotel. The **Szabadság szobor** (Independence Monument), the lovely lady with the palm leaf proclaiming freedom throughout the city at the eastern end of the Citadella, was erected as a tribute to the Soviet soldiers who died liberating Hungary in 1945, but both the victims' names in Cyrillic letters on the plinth and the memorial statues of Soviet soldiers were removed a decade ago. Take tram No 19 along the riverfront from Clark Ádám tér and climb the stairs behind the waterfall and **Szent Gellért szobor** (St Gellért Statue), follow the path through the park opposite the entrance to the Danubius Hotel Gellért. Or take bus No 27 which runs almost to the top of the hill from Móricz Zsigmond körtér, southwest of the Gellért Hotel (and accessible using tram Nos 19 and 49).

The city's most famous thermal spa is the **Gellért Fürdő** (Gellért Baths; Map p344; ☎ 466 6166; Gellért Hotel, XI Kelenhegyi út; thermal baths & swimming pool

2700Ft; ☺ 6am-7pm Mon-Fri, 6am-5pm Sat & Sun May-Sep; baths only Oct-Apr) below Gellért Hill. Soaking in this Art Nouveau palace has been likened to taking a bath in a cathedral.

Many of the statues that once commemorated Soviet liberators and socialists are now on display at **Szobor Park** (Statue Park; Map pp340-1; ☎ 227 7446; www.szoborpark.hu; XXII Szabadkai út; admission 600Ft; ☺ 10am-dusk) in southwest Buda. Take tram No 19 from Clark Ádám tér to the XI Etele tér terminus, then catch a yellow Volán bus to Diósd-Érd. A direct bus goes from Deák tér in Pest at 11am daily (2450Ft return, including admission).

Seven kilometres north of Buda's centre, in Óbuda, the **Aquincumi Múzeum** (Map pp340-1; ☎ 430 1563; III Szentendre út 139; adult/student 700/300Ft; ☺ 10am-5pm Tue-Sun Apr-Oct, to 6pm May-Sep, grounds open 9am) contains the heart of the most complete 2nd-century Roman civilian town ruins left in Hungary. Take the HÉV from the Batthyány tér metro stop.

Pest   Map p344

Continental Europe's oldest underground – Budapest's M1 yellow line metro, constructed in the 19th century – runs beneath leafy Andrássy út. Start along the yellow line at **Hősök tere** (Heroes' Square; Map pp340-1), above the metro station of the same name. The monument was constructed to honour the millennial anniversary (1896) of the Magyar conquest of the Carpathian Basin and showcases statues of important tribal leaders, kings and statesmen. Across the street, the **Szépművészeti Múzeum** (Museum of Fine Arts; Map pp340-1; ☎ 469 7100; www.2.szepmuveszeti.hu; XIV Hősök tere; adult/student 900/500Ft; ☺ 10am-5.30pm Tue-Sun) houses a collection of foreign art, including an impressive number of El Grecos.

Adjacent **Városliget** (City Park; Map pp340-1) has boating on a small lake in the summer, ice skating in winter, and duck feeding year round. The park's schizophrenic **Vájdahunyad Vár** (Vájdahunyad Castle; Map pp340-1) is made in varied architectural styles typical of historic Hungary, including baroque, Romanesque, Gothic and Tudor. Originally a millennial celebration exhibit hall, the castle now contains the **Mezősági Múzeum** (Agriculture Museum; ☎ 343 0573; Városliget; adult/student 500/200Ft; ☺ Tue-Fri & Sun 10am-5pm, Sat 10am-6pm), with a decent exhibit on Hungarian viticulture. Look north and you spy the huge cupola that is part of the **Széchenyi Fürdő** (Széchenyi Baths;

Map pp340-1; ☎ 363 3210; XIV Állatkerti út 11; 1700Ft; ☺ 6am-7pm Mon-Fri, 6am-5pm Sat & Sun), built in 1908. Don't be afraid to open doors and explore; in addition to the outdoor pools, there are spas, saunas and steam rooms that vary in temperature hidden throughout the humongous building.

If you walk southwest from Hősök tere on Andrássy út, you'll pass many grand, World Heritage listed 19th-century buildings. Otherwise take the yellow line metro to the **Terror Háza** (Terror House; ☎ 374 2600; www.terror haza.hu, Hungarian only; Andrássy út 60; foreigner 3000Ft; ☺ 10am-6pm Tue-Fri, 10am-7.30pm Sat & Sun), near the Vörösmarty utca stop. This museum of spying and atrocities, in what was once the headquarters of the dreaded ÁVH secret police, always attracts a crowd. It's worth ogling the opulence of the 1884 neo-Renaissance **Magyar Állami Operaház** (Hungarian State Opera House; ☎ 332 8197; www.opera.hu; VI Andrássy út 22; tours 1200Ft; ☺ 3pm & 4pm), a few metro stops further down the road. **Váci utca**, Pest's extensive pedestrian shopping street, begins at the southwest terminus of the yellow line, Vörösmarty tér. It's tourist central, but the line of cafés and shops are worth seeing – at least once. The **Nagycsarnok** (Great Market; IX Vámház körút 1-3; ☺ 6am-5pm Mon, 6am-6pm Tue-Fri, 6am-2pm Sat) is a vast steel and glass structure with produce vendors on the ground floor, souvenirs and snacks on the 1st floor.

Other sights and museums are scattered about Pest. The huge, riverfront **Parlament** (Parliament; ☎ 441 4904; www.mkogy.hu; V Kossuth Lajos tér 1-3; adult/student 1700/800Ft; ☺ 8am-6pm Mon-Fri, 8am-4pm Sat, 8am-2pm Sun for Hungarian-language tours), with all its crazy spires, dominates Kossuth Lajos tér. English-language tours are at 10am and 2pm daily. Across the park is the **Néprajzi Múzeum** (Ethnography Museum; ☎ 473 2400; www.hem.hu; Kossuth Lajos tér 12; adult/student 500/250Ft; ☺ 10am-6pm Tue-Sun), with an extensive collection of national costumes among the permanent displays on folk life and art. Look for the mummified right hand of St Stephen in the chapel of the colossal **Szent István Bazilika** (☎ 311 0839; V Szent István tér; church admission free, treasury adult/student 200/150Ft, dome adult/student 500/400Ft; ☺ 9am-7pm Mon-Sat, 1-4pm Sun) near Bajcsy-Zsilinszky út. Northeast of the Astoria metro stop is what remains of the Jewish quarter. The twin-towered, 1859 **Nagy Zsinagóga** (Great Synagogue; ☎ 342 8949; VII Dohány utca 2; synagogue & museum adult/child 600/200Ft; ☺ 10am-5pm Mon-Thu, 10am-2pm Fri & Sun) has a museum with a

HUNGARY

harrowing exhibit on the Holocaust. A few blocks south along the *kis körút* (little ring road) is the **Magyar Nemzeti Múzeum** (Hungarian National Museum; ☎ 338 2122; www.hnm.hu; VIII Múzeum kis körút 14-16; adult/student 800/400Ft; ☻ 10am-6pm Tue-Sun) and its historic relics – archaeological finds to coronation regalia.

For a different view, rise above it all in the **Budapest Eye** (☎ 238 7623; www.budapesteye .hu; VI Váci út 1-3; adult/child 3000/2000Ft, extra to take photos; ☻ 10am-6pm May-Oct), a hot-air balloon tethered to the West End Shopping Mall.

TOURS

To tour the Danube, **Mahart PassNave sightseeing cruises** (☎ 484 4013; www.mahartpassnave.hu; V Vigadó Tér Pier; ☻ Apr-Oct) runs 1½-hour sightseeing cruises (2400Ft) and lunch and dinner buffet cruises (2800Ft). On Wednesday and Sunday from May to September, folklore evening cruises (9500Ft) include region dishes, Gypsy music and folk dancing. Tickets can be purchased at the pier before departure.

For a fun way to tour the city by bicycle – day or night – **Yellow Zebra Bikes** (☎ 2668777; www .yellowzebrabikes.com; V Sütő utca 2, in courtyard; adult/ student 4500/4000Ft; ☻ 8.30am-8pm May-Sep, 10am 6pm Nov-Feb, 9.30am-7.30pm Mar-Apr & Oct) offers rentals (one day 3000Ft). Their office has Internet access and is quite the English speaker hang-out. The same company runs **Absolute Walking Tours** (☎ 06 30 211 8861; www .absolutetours.com), and both have tours departing from Deák tér. You could take the entertaining 3½-hour town walking tour (adult/student 4000/3500Ft). But why do that when you could opt for one of their theme tours – the Hammer & Sickle or the Pub Crawl (adult/student 5000/4500 Ft)?

SLEEPING

Accommodation prices and standards are still pretty reasonable in Budapest. Many year-round hostels occupy middle floors of old apartment buildings (with or without a lift) in central Pest. Come summer (July to late August), student dormitories at colleges and universities open to all travellers. HI-affiliated **Mellow Mood Ltd** (Map pp340-1 and map p343; p345) runs many summer, and a few year-round, hostels in town and has stands at Keleti and Déli train stations. Tourinform and the Hungarian Youth Hostel Association publish a youth hostel brochure you can pick up, or see online (www.youthhostels.hu).

Private rooms assigned by travel agents are plentiful, but not always central. Costs range from 4000Ft to 7500Ft for a single, 9000Ft to 12,000Ft for a double and 12,000Ft to 14,000Ft for a small apartment, with a supplement if you stay fewer than four nights. **Ibusz** (Map p344; p345) has the most extensive listings in town (some with photos on their website) and **Vista Visitor Centre** (Map p344; p345) is good for apartments.

Two other private room brokers:
Best Hotel Service (Map p344; ☎ 318 4848; www .besthotelservice.hu; V Sütő utca 2; ☻ 8am-8pm)
To-Ma Travel Agency (Map p344; ☎ 353 0819; www .tomatour.hu/beut/; V Október 6 utca 22; ☻ 9am-noon & 1-8pm Mon-Fri, 9am-5pm Sat & Sun)

Buda   Map p343
BUDGET
Zugligeti Niche Camping (Map pp340-1; ☎ 200 8346; www.campingniche.hu; XII Zugligeti út 101; camp site 1/2 people 1900/2800Ft, caravan site 1/2 people 2800/3700Ft; ☻ May-Oct) The location, in the Buda Hills at the bottom station of a chair lift, is great for hiking. Sights have good tree cover but are awfully close together. There's a restaurant nearby. Take bus No 158 from Moszkva tér to the terminus.

Back Pack Guesthouse (Map pp340-1; ☎ 385 8946; www.backpackbudapest.hu; XI Takács Menyhért utca 33; dm/r 2200-2800/6600Ft; ☒ ☐) Zany, laid-back, island-time feel in the suburbs. Escape the city's noise and take a snooze in the back-garden hammock. Dorm rooms have five to 11 beds, and there's one small double. Take bus No 7 (Erzsébet híd or Keleti train station in Pest), tram No 49 from the little ring road in central Pest, or tram No 19 from Batthyány tér in Buda.

Citadella Hotel (☎ 466 5794; www.citadella.hu; XI Citadella sétány, Gellért Hill; dm/r €10/51; ☒) What could be better than sleeping in a historic old fortress? Well, ok, the furniture could be newer, but the place has great views. Solo travellers may prefer somewhere more central, as it's a bit isolated and the disco can get loud. Take bus No 27 from XI Móricz Zsigmond körtér in Buda, then hike.

Martos Hostel (Map pp340-1; ☎ 209 4883; reception@hotel.martos.bme.hu; XI Sztoczek utca 5-7; s/d with shared bathroom €16/20; ☒) Primarily student accommodation, Martos is open year-round to all. Doubles with toilet and shower are available (€32). It's a few minutes' walk from Petőfi Bridge (tram No 4 or 6).

MID-RANGE

Büro Panzió (☎ 212 2929; buro-panzio@axelero.hu; II Dékán utca 3; s/d 6000-8000/10,000-12,000Ft; ✗ 🖳) Fabric colours are your basic '80s black with mint green and pink, but rooms are clean enough. The central Moszkva tér transportation hub – metro stop, tram stations – is barely seconds away.

Gold Hotel (☎ 209 4775; www.goldhotel.hu; I Hegyalja út 14; s/d €64-84/74-94; P ✗ ✗ 🖳) The rooms are bright, cheerful and modern. The golden yellow façade below at Gellért Hill is rather palatial. Rooms in the turret have extra little seating areas. Take bus No 8 from Elizabeth Bridge or bus No 78 from Keleti train station in Pest.

Burg Hotel (☎ 2120269; www.burghotelbudapest.com; I Szentháromság tér 7-8; s/d €79-99/89-109; ✗ ✗ 🖳) Contemporary comfort at the absolute heart of Castle Hill: you can't beat the price-location-value combination. Front desk staff are surprisingly friendly and accommodating, unlike many 'service' professionals in the Castle district. Ask for a room that looks out on Mátyás Templom.

TOP END

Danubius Hotel Gellért (Map p344; ☎ 889 5500; www .danubiusgroup.com/gellert; XI Szent Gellért tér 1; s/d €66-130/150-210; P ✗ 🖳 ⛲) Constructed between 1916 and 1918, this has long been the grand dame of the Danube. Unfortunately the faded elegance is not quite up to today's luxury standards. The real reason to stay here is that big, fluffy bathrobe in the closet you can wear in the guest elevator on your way to free access to the Gellért Baths (p346).

Art'otel Budapest (☎ 487 9487; www.artotel.hu; I Bem rakpart 16-19; r €198-318; P ✗ ✗ 🖳) The interiors of the design-driven Art'otel make a sleek statement. Even the rose-coral carpets with white brush strokes seem like graphic art. This is trendy at its finest – wireless, high-speed Internet access and all. Rooms for the disabled traveller are available.

Pest   Map p344

BUDGET

Caterina Hostel (☎ 269 5990; www.caterinahostel .hu; VI Teréz körút 30, 3rd fl; dm/s/d 2000/5000/8000Ft; ✗ 🖳) Clean, bright and modern: plants complement freshly painted walls. This small place (no lounge) is run by a couple with young children. The clientele is quiet, even if the street noise that seeps in isn't.

Museum Guest House (☎ 318 9508; www.budapest hostel.com; VIII Mikszáth Kálmán tér 4, 1st fl; dm 2600-3000Ft; ✗ 🖳) Wind your way through the maze of rooms. Eclectic décor includes some bunk lofts with blanket curtains and red log bedsteads. No doubles. The building is on a calm square off the main road. The associated **Aquarium Youth Hostel** (Map pp340-1; ☎ 322 0502; www.budapesthostel.com; VII Alsóerdősor utca 12, 2nd fl; dm/s/d 2800/3900/7800Ft; 🖳) has newer, more basic bunk bed rooms, as well as doubles.

Red Bus Hostel (☎ 266 0136; www.redbusbudapest .hu; V Semmelweis utca 14, 1st fl; dm/s/d 2900/6500/7500Ft; ✗ 🖳) Congenial owners are part of the reason that the very central Red Bus has such a faithful following. Spacious, if spartan, rooms with wood floors are another. Next door is an associated English-language used bookstore. There's a **Red Bus II** (☎ 321 7100; VI Szövetség utca 35; dm/s/d 2700/6500/7500Ft; ✗ 🖳) near Keleti train station.

Garibaldi Guesthouse (☎ 302 3457; baldiguest@ hotmail.com; V Garibaldi utca 5; per person €20-45) Numerous apartments on several floors of an old building have been turned into double, triple, quad and five-person guestrooms that have kitchen facilities. A mish-mash of antiques give the place a bohemian feel. Some small rooms with shared bath (€18) are in the inquisitive owners' flat.

Other recommended hostels:

Station Guesthouse (Map pp340-1; ☎ 221 8864; www .stationguesthouse.hu; XIV Mexikói út 36/b; dm/r 1900-2700/6400Ft; ✗ 🖳) Party house: 24-hour bar, pool table, occasional live music. Red bus No 7 from Keleti train station.

Yellow Submarine Hostel (☎ 331 9896; www.yellow submarine hostel.com; VI Teréz körút 56, 3rd fl; dm/s/d 2800/7000/8000Ft; ✗ 🖳) Overlooking busy ring road, near Nyugati.

Best Hostel (☎ 332 4934; www.besthostel.hu; VI Podmaniczky utca 27, 1st fl; dm/s/d 3000/4200/8400Ft; ✗ 🖳) Closest to Nyugati train station, not too, too noisy.

Mellow Mood Central Hostel (Map p344; ☎ 411 1310; www.mellowmoodhostel.com; V Bécsi utca; dm in 4-/6-/8-bed room 3200/3500/4000Ft; r 11,200Ft; ✗ 🖳)

MID-RANGE

Hostel Marco Polo (☎ 413 2555; www.marcopolohostel .com; VII Nyár utca 6; dm/s/d 3800-5800/10,800-12,800/ 14,200-17,000Ft; ✗ 🖳) With telephones and satellite TV in the rooms, and a bar-restaurant in the cellar, this Mellow Mood Ltd hostel is more like a hotel. Bright blues and yellows colour the nifty rooms. The neighbourhood is not the world's most polished, but it's safe.

Hotel Queen Mary (☎ 413 3510; www.hotelqueen mary.hu; Kertész utca 34; s/d €42-62/55-69; ✖ ✖) The 19th-century building has been nicely re-furbished in yellow, with clean-line modern furniture in the rooms. It still has that new hotel smell. If you're travelling in a group, ask about the triples (€70–87) and quads (€84–100).

Radio Inn (☎ 342 8347; www.radioinn.hu; VI Benczúr utca 19; s/d w/o breakfast €45-50/50-70; ✖) Not rooms but apartments – with full kitchens, sitting areas and one or two bedrooms – fill this attractive lodging. Embassies are your neigh-bours on the quiet, tree-lined street near Bajza utca metro stop (M1 yellow line).

Leo Panzió (☎ 266 9041; www.leopanzio.hu; V Kos-suth Lajos utca 2/A, 2nd fl; s/d €45-66/69-82; ✖ ✖) Just steps from Váci utca, the Leo is in the mid-dle of everything. Rooms have an Art Deco-ish flair with cherry-stained beds inset with blonde wood. Some have views of Elizabeth Bridge. The tiny bathrooms sparkle.

Kálvin Ház (☎ 216 4635; www.kalvinhouse.hu; IX Gönczy Pál utca 6; s/d €55-62/65-82; ✖ ▢) One of the few historic pensions in town – the Vic-torian antiques and high ceilings are a stand out. That the place has laundry service and Internet access is a bonus. The restored 19th-century, coral-colour building is near Kálvin tér metro and Ráday utca nightlife.

Also good options:

Hotel Fortuna (Map pp340-1; ☎ 288 8100; www .fortunahajo.hu; Szent István Park, waterfront; s/d/tr with shared bath €16-20/24-30/32-40; **P**) Float on a boat (hotel) in the Danube. Doubles with bathroom and satellite TV cost €60–80.

Hotel Ibis Centrum (☎ 215 8585; www.ibis-centrum .hu; IX Ráday utca 6; s/d without breakfast €59-69/85-106; **P** ✖ ✖ ▢) So, so near the bar and café scene. The style is chain hotel modern and modular.

Hotel Margitsziget (Map pp340-1; ☎ 329 2949; hotelmargitsziget@axelero.hu; XIII Margitsziget; r 14,500Ft; **P** ▢) Good-value, budget resort: tennis courts, swim-ming pool and sauna.

TOP END

The 1873 splendour of the **Danubius Grand Hotel Margitsziget** (Map pp340-1; 889 4700; www.dan ubiusgroup.com/grandhotel; XIII Margitsziget; s/d €131-164/150-184; **P** ✖ ✖ ▣) contrasts with the contemporary nature of its sister, the **Danu-bius Thermal Hotel Margitsziget** (Map pp340-1; ☎ 889 4700; www.danubiusgroup.com/thermalhotel; XIII Margit-sziget; s/d €144-174/164-194; **P** ✖ ✖ ▣). The two are connected via an underground pas-

sageway and guests at both enjoy free use of the upscale baths at the Thermal. The park-covered Margaret Island setting is a green oasis in the city. Budapest's newest five-star hotel, the **Four Seasons Hotel** (☎ 268 6000; www.foursea sons.com; Roosevelt tér 5-6; r €270-700; **P** ✖ ✖ ▣), inhabits the Art Nouveau Gresham Palace. Restored to Dr Seuss-esque elegance with mushroom-shaped windows, whimsical ironwork and glittering gold decorative tiles on the exterior, it provides superb views of the Danube through Roosevelt Park.

EATING

The capital city has both chic restaurants with Western European prices and workers' canteens where you can get a decent meal for very little money. Fast-food restaurants and to-go windows abound on the ring roads and in pedestrian areas. The train and bus stations all have food stands.

Ráday utca and Liszt Ferenc tér are the two most popular traffic-free streets. The moment the weather warms up, pavement tables bloom alongside the tulips. Both areas have tons of cafés, restaurants, snack shops and bars, but Ráday utca is a little more cut-ting edge, and shouldn't be missed.

Buda   Map p343
BUDGET

Fény utca piac (market; II Fény at Retek utca; ☽ 6am-5pm Mon-Fri, 6am-2pm Sat) Next to the Mammut shopping mall I, this market has picnic sup-plies and produce on the ground-level food stands and butcher shops on the first floor.

For a bite to eat near the castle, climb the passageway stairs to **Fortuna Önkiszolgáló** (☎ 375 2401; I Hess András utca 4, 1st fl; ☽ 11.30am-2.30pm Mon-Fri; ✖). The cafeteria serves all the fried favourites. Or if you're in Moszkva tér, try **Pita House** (☎ 315 1479; II Margit körút 105; mains 500-800Ft; ☽ 8am-midnight; ✖) for gyros and falafel pitas. A helping from the salad bar costs 410Ft.

MID-RANGE

Mamma Rosa Pizzéria (☎ 201 3456; I Ostrom utca 31; pizza & pasta 690-1100Ft; ☽ 11am-11pm; ✖) It's hard to resist the smells coming from this cellar Italian restaurant. Relax among murals reminiscent of ancient Rome.

Café Miró (☎ 375 5458; I Úri utca 30; mains 690-2190Ft; ☽ 9am-midnight) Most restaurants on Castle Hill have surly service and are full of tourists. This arty café is no exception, but the soups and Greek salad are good. For dessert there are plenty of cakes to choose from, but the delicious *erdei gyümölcskremleves* (forest berry soup) is topped with a scoop of vanilla ice cream.

TOP END

Hemingway (Map pp340-1; ☎ 381 0522; XI Kosztolányi D tér 2, Feneketlen tó; mains 1850-3100Ft; ☺ noon-midnight; ✗) A bit of panache: dine on a terrace overlooking the Bottomless Lake. Entrées include lamb cutlet with a blue-cheese mint sauce.

Mongolian Barbecue (☎ 353 6363; XII Márvány utca 19/A; before/after 5pm 1990/3690Ft; ☺ noon-midnight; ✗) Choose your meat and watch as it's grilled in front of you. The all-you-can-eat price includes as much house beer and wine as you can sink too.

Pest   Map p344
BUDGET

Frici Papa (☎ 351 0197; Király utca 55; mains 400-700Ft; ☺ 11am-8pm Mon-Sat) Basic, no frills Hungarian food. For the price there's a surprising amount of white-meat chicken in the soup.

Kisharang (☎ 269 3861; V Október 6 utca 17; mains 490-850Ft; ☺ 11am-8pm Mon-Fri, 11.30am-4.30pm Sat & Sun) Lantern-like lamps hang low over chequered tablecloths in a wonderful little *étkezde* (canteen), serving simple dishes that change daily. Expect to wait for a table.

Három Testvér (☎ 342 2377; VII Erzsébet körút 17; mains 750-850Ft; ☺ 24hr) Turkish casseroles are dished up around the clock. Vegetarians rejoice; there are always great looking aubergine and vegetable dishes.

Kis Italia (☎ 269 3145; V Szemere utca 22; pizza & pasta 760-990Ft; ☺ 11am-10pm Mon-Sat; ✗) Descend into this cellar restaurant for interesting pizza combinations – like bacon, onion and pickle – at interesting prices. Just ignore the cheesy synthesizer player in the corner; he's not too loud.

Of the many carry-out windows and self-service places mixed among the cafés and bars on Ráday utca, **Ráday Étkezde** (☎ 219 5451; Ráday utca 29; mains 420-650Ft; ☺ 6am-4pm Mon-Fri) is a reliable choice. The *főzelék*, a sort of creamed vegetable stew, is particularly good. Budapest's main market, the **Nagycsarnok** (Great Market; IX Vámház körút 1-3; ☺ 6am-5pm Mon, 6am-6pm Tue-Fri, 6am-2pm Sat) vends fruit and vegetables, deli items, fish and meat. Food stalls on the upper level sell beer, sausage and tasty *lángos*

among other quick eats. There's also a cafeteria – a bit of a tourist trap – with a Gypsy violinist and mid-range prices. Grocery store chains are everywhere in Pest; Kaiser's has a branch facing Blaha Lujza tér and one opposite Nyugati train station on Nyugati tér.

MID-RANGE

Menza (☎ 413 1482; V Liszt Ferenc tér 2; mains 890-1990Ft; ☺ 11am-11pm; ✗) A parody of Communist colours and styles (a *menza* was a state-run canteen), Menza impels Hungarians to drag their out-of-town guests here to see what much of '70s Budapest looked like – well into the '90s. Traditional Hungarian favourites are done stylishly.

Paprika Vendeglö (Map pp340-1; ☎ 06 70 574 6508; Dózsa György út 72; mains 950-1600Ft; ☺ 11am-11pm) Step inside what looks like a rustic Hungarian farm house on the very urban street bordering City Park (M1 yellow line, Hősök tere). Good game dishes.

Wabisabi (☎ 412 0427; XIII Visegrádi utca; mains 1080-1480Ft; ☺ 11am-11pm Sun-Thu, Fri & Sat 11am-midnight; ✗) Come here for organic, vegan-friendly, Asian-inspired food – a rarity in meat-crazy Hungary.

Cafe Károlyi (☎ 328 0117; V Károlyi Mihály utca 16; mains 1200-2700Ft; ☺ 8.30am-midnight Mon-Fri, 9.30am-midnight Sat & Sun; ✗) A trendy, upscale take on local ingredients: goose liver enveloped in a crepe pocket with plum sauce, anyone? Full breakfasts are also pretty good.

Okay Italia (☎ 349 2991; XIII Szent István körút 20; pizza & pasta 1280-1690Ft; ☺ 11am-11.30pm; ✗ ✗) Faux painting re-creates rustic, marigold-yellow plaster walls and a waterfall trickles down beside the wrought iron staircase. The food at this expat favourite is just as well executed. Vegetarians might opt for gnocchi with spinach in a cream sauce.

Other recommendations:

Kék Rózsa (☎ 342 8981; VII Wesselényi utca 9; mains 850-1600Ft; ☺ 11am-10pm) Three course Hungarian menus 1200Ft-1800Ft.

Taverna Dionysos (☎ 318 1222; V Belgrád rakpart 16; mains 1250-2750Ft; ☺ noon-midnight; ✗) Go for Greek.

Vista Café (☎ 268 0888; VI Paulay Ede utca 7; mains 800-1600Ft; ☺ 9am-11pm Mon-Fri, 10am-11pm Sat & Sun) Hungarian, Mediterranean, Italian – a little of everything, including Internet terminals.

TOP END

Vörös és Fehér (☎ 413 1545; VI Andrássy út 41; mains 1400-3500Ft; ☺ noon-midnight) Swank bistro décor complements the offerings at this up-to-the-minute wine bar. You can savour wines from around the country one decilitre at a time (430–2300Ft). Entrées are upscale international, with weekly specials such as a veal chop with sage leaves and olive polenta.

Fatâl (☎ 266 2607; V Váci utca 67, cnr Pintér utca; mains 1580-2490Ft; ☽ 11.30am-2am) A whimsical menu prefaces the fun at this cellar restaurant with medieval adornment. The homy Hungarian dishes are served in gigantic portions. We've heard comment that waiters can be brusque with foreigners, but that wasn't our experience. Book ahead.

Bagolyvár (Map pp340-1; ☎ 468 3110; XIV Állatkert út 2; mains 1600-3500Ft; ☽ noon-11pm) Gundel's first sibling, the Owl's Castle, is known for Hungarian classics done impeccably. The hidden courtyard tables are a pleasant surprise.

Borvendéglő 1894 (Map pp340-1; ☎ 468 4040; XIV Állatkert út 2; mains 1650-2700Ft; ☽ 6-11pm Tue-Sat) This wine cellar is one of the two sister restaurants to the world-famous (and overpriced) Gundel restaurant around the corner. The best things about the place are the flights of wine for tasting and the traditional Hungarian drinking snacks – goose cracklings, steak tartar and *pogacs* (salty, buttery biscuits).

DRINKING
The outdoor pavement tables all over the city are some of the most pleasant places to drink in nice weather. On warm summer evenings the many tables along pedestrian-only Ráday utca and Liszt Ferenc tér are all full, giving the squares a festive feel. Many pubs are in cellars and have live music or turn into minidiscos midnight at weekends.

Buda
Map pp340-1

Kisrabló (☎ 209 1588; XI Zenta utca 3; ☽ 11am-2am) The eclectic pub décor here resembles a boat's hull, busty masthead and all. Take tram No 19 or 49 one stop past Danubius Hotel Gellért.

Zöld Pardon (Iríní József utca at Petőfi híd; ☽ 9am-6am mid-Apr–mid-Sep) College students on a budget flock to the big, seasonal beer garden-disco near Petőfi Bridge.

Pest
Map p344

For Sale (☎ 267 0267; V Vámház körút 2; ☽ noon-1am) Throwing peanut shells on the floor is a novelty that makes this pub especially popular with Hungarian college-age guys.

Live music starts at 8pm; jazz on Sundays.

Paris, Texas (☎ 281 0570; XI Ráday utca 22; ☽ 10am-2am Mon-Fri, 1pm-2am Sat, 4pm-2am Sun) An old west saloon decorated with turn-of-the-20th-century photos of Budapest; oh well, expats seem to like it.

Shiraz (☎ 218 0881; IX Mátyás utca 22, at Ráday utca; ☽ noon-midnight; ✻) Take me to the kasbah. You can sit on low cushions and smoke a water pipe filled with fruit tobacco or drink apple tea if you don't want anything harder.

Gerbeaud (☎ 429 9000; V Vörösmarty tér 7; ☽ 9am-9pm; ✻ ✻) Cake-and-coffee culture king, Gerbeaud has been serving since 1870.

Teaház a Vörös Oroszlánhoz (☎ 430 570; VI Jókai tér 8; ☽ 11am-11pm Mon-Sat, 3-11pm Sun; ✻ ✻) Exotic scents waft from the Teahouse at the Red Lion, where esoteric books are also sold.

Of the pubs in Pest, **Fat Mo's** (☎ 267 3199; V Nyári Pál utca 11; ☽ noon-2am Mon-Wed, noon-4am Thu-Fri, 6pm-4am Sat, 6pm-2am Sun; ✻ ✻) is one of the best, with live music Sunday through Thursday. **Irish Cat Pub** (☎ 266 4085; V Múzeum körút 41; ☽ 11am-2am) runs a close second.

If you want to enjoy an adult beverage aboard a boat on the Danube, **Spoon** (☎ 411 0933; V Vigadó tér 3; ☽ noon-2am; ✻ ✻) is the swank restaurant-café-lounge option. Next door, so to speak, **Columbus** (☎ 266 9013; Vigadó tér 4; ☽ noon-midnight; ✻) is a more down-to-earth and pub-like boat.

ENTERTAINMENT
Tickets for classical music concerts, jazz sessions, dance performances, folk concerts and operas or operettas are still quite reasonable by Western European standards, and the venues are often stunning. Tourinform (see p345) and ticket offices can help you find out what's playing, or look in the free, bimonthly *Programme Magazine*, available at tourist spots. The free, weekly *Pesti Est* (available at restaurants and clubs) lists live music acts and guest DJs for clubs. The weekly *Budapest Sun* (www.budapestsun.com) has a 10-day event calendar online, and a style and entertainment section in the Thursday newspaper. Budapest Week Online (www.budapestweek .com) has events, music and movie listings, reviews and articles. Unless otherwise noted, entertainment sights are in Pest.

Gay & Lesbian Venues
Map p344

Angyal (☎ 351 6490; VII Szövetség utca 33; ☽ 10pm-5am Fri & Sat) Budapest's flagship gay nightclub has three bars and plays high-energy dance mixes. Men only on Saturday (admission 800Ft).

Café Eklektika (☎ 266 3054; V Semmelweiss utca 21; ☯ noon-midnight Mon-Fri, 5pm-midnight Sat & Sun) The town's only real lesbian venue attracts a mixed, beat generation-type crowd.

Live Music & Theatre

Magyar Állami Operaház (Hungarian State Opera House; ☎ 332 8197; www.opera.hu; VI Andrássy út 22) Given the incredible, gilt interior (1884), every opera performance is an event with a capital E. The ballet company performs here as well.

Liszt Ferenc Zeneakadémia (☎ 342 0179; www .musicacademy.hu; VI Liszt Ferenc tér 8 ☯ 10am-2pm Mon-Fri, 2-8pm Sat & Sun for ticket office) The Art Deco great hall in the 1907 Music Academy hosts impressive classical symphony concerts. Tickets are sold only at the onsite ticket office.

Kalamajka Táncház (☎ 354 3400; www.aranytiz .hu, Hungarian only; V Arany Janos utca 10; ☯ 9pm-2am Sat) The regular jovial Hungarian crowd did not quite make the transition to the new address of this Saturday-night folk music dance. There may be a few oddballs in attendance now, but this is still where you'll hear the most authentic music.

Classical concerts are held regularly in the city's churches, including Mátyás Templom (Map p343; p346) on Castle Hill in Buda. **Hungária Koncert** (☎ 317 2754; www.ticket info.hu) organises slightly kitschy folk and Gypsy music and dance shows at the **Duna Palota** (V Zrínyi utca 5) and the **Bábszínház** (Budapest Puppet Theatre; VI Andrássy út 69) among other venues. You can buy tickets for these, and most other types of performance, at ticket brokers like **Music Mix** (☎ 266 1655; V Váci utca 33; ☯ 10am-6pm Mon-Fri, 10am-3pm Sat) and **Vigadó Jegyiroda** (☎ 327 4322; V Vigadó tér 6; ☯ 10am-8pm Mon-Fri).

Nightclubs

Clubbing in Budapest can mean anything from a floor-thumping, techno dance club to a hip place to hang out and listen to jazz. Cover charges range from 200Ft to 1000Ft.

Gödör Klub (☎ 06 20 943 5463; V Erzsébet tér; ☯ 2pm-2am) A large underground club (with a glass ceiling revealing the square above) provides the venue for truly eclectic live music – from world beat to the Doors to jazz – played to a local audience of all ages, shapes and sizes.

Trafó Bár Tangó (☎ 456 2049; IX Lilliom utca 41; ☯ 6pm-1am) An arty crowd makes the scene beneath the eponymous cultural house and exhibit space. Latin, jazz and disco tunes.

Cuba Libre (Map p343; ☎ 345 8367; Lövőház utca 1-5, Mammut II, 4th fl; ☯ noon-midnight Sun-Wed, noon-5am Thu-Sat) Pretty people pose in black on the top floor of – of all things – a shopping mall in Buda. The large terrace is surprisingly nice. Dance, funk and R&B tunes set the beat inside.

Bahnhof Music Club (☎ 302 4751; VI Teréz körút 55, Nyugati Pályaudvar; ☯ 10pm-4am Thu-Sat) Teeny-boppers shake it on two dance floors in this club above the train station. The queue to get in forms early.

SHOPPING

Foodstuffs, folk arts, wines and spirits, and music are just some of the country-specific things to buy in Budapest. Tons of shops along Váci utca (p347) and stands on the top floor of the Nagycsarnok (p347) sell Hungarian souvenirs such as dolls in folk dress, T-shirts, embroidered table cloths, goose liver pate, Hungarian-made Pick salami, paprika in fancy bags, CDs, etc. The old town centre at Szentendre (p355), just 40 minutes away by commuter rail, has even more souvenir shops and stands.

Folkart Kézmöveshaz (☎ 318 5143; V Régiposta utca 12; ☯ 10am-7pm Mon-Fri, 10am-4pm Sat) Some of the most authentic, handmade folk crafts available in Budapest. You can buy embroidered folk costumes from Kalocsa, leatherwork horsewhips from the plains, and woven items from across the country.

Folkart Centrum (☎ 318 4697; V Váci utca 58; ☯ 10am-7pm daily) This folk art store has a good selection of regional ceramics and porcelain ware.

Rózsavölgyi Music Shop (☎ 318 3500; V Szervita tér 5; ☯ 9.30am-7pm Mon-Fri, 10am-5pm Sat) Both classical and folk music CDs and tapes are on sale here.

There's an excellent selection of Hungarian wines at the **Magyar Borok Háza** (House of Hungarian Wines; Map p343; ☎ 212 1031; www.magyar borokhaza.hu; Szentháromság tér 6; ☯ noon-8pm) in Buda, and of fruit brandies and wine at the **Magyar Palinka Háza** (☎ 235 0488; VIII Rákóczi út 17; ☯ 9am-7pm Mon-Sat) in Pest.

GETTING THERE & AWAY
Air
Main international carriers fly in and out of Budapest's **Ferihegy 2** (☎ 296 9696) airport, 24km southeast of the centre on Highway 4; low-cost airlines use the older **Ferihegy 1** (☎ 296 7000) airport, next door. For carriers flying within Eastern Europe, see p391; for more on getting to Budapest from outside Eastern Europe, see p887.

Boat
In addition to their hydrofoils that travel internationally to Bratislava and Vienna (p393), **Mahart PassNave** (Map p344; ☎ 484 4005; www.mahartpassnave.hu; Vigadó Tér Pier) ferries depart for Szentendre, Visegrád and Esztergom in the Danube Bend daily, April to October.

Bus   Map pp340–1
Volánbusz (☎ 219 8080; www.volanbusz.hu), the national bus line, has an extensive list of destinations from Budapest. All international buses and some buses to/from southern Hungary use **Népliget bus station** (☎ 264 3939; IX Üllői út 131). **Stadion bus station** (☎ 252 4498; XIV Hungária körút 48-52) serves most domestic destinations. Most buses to the northern Danube Bend arrive at and leave from the **Árpád híd bus station** (☎ 329 1450, off XIII Róbert Károly körút). All stations are on metro lines, and all are in Pest. If the ticket office is closed, you can buy your ticket on the bus.

For details of international bus services within Eastern Europe, see p392; for destinations further afield, see p893.

Car & Motorcycle
Car rental is not recommended if you are staying in Budapest. The public transportation network is extensive and cheap, whereas parking is scarce and there are more than enough cars and motor emissions on the congested streets already. If you want to venture into the countryside, travelling by car may be the best way to see it. Daily rates start around €40 per day with kilometres included. If an office is not at the airport, the company will usually provide free pick up and delivery within Budapest or at the airport during office hours. All the major international chains have branches at Ferihegy 2 airport.
Americana Rent-a-Car (☎ 350 2542; www.americana .matav.hu; XIII Dózsa György út 65; 8am-6pm Mon-Fri, 8am-noon Sat) Reliable office in the Ibis Volga hotel.

Recent Car (☎ 453 0003; www.recentcar.hu; III Óbudai hajógyári-sziget 131; ◷ 8am-8pm) One of the cheapest.

Train
The Hungarian State Railways, **MÁV** (☎ 461 5400 domestic information, 461 5500 international information; www.elvira.hu) covers the country well and has its schedule online. The **MÁV Ticket Office** (Map p344; ☎ 461 5400; VI Andrássy út 35; ◷ 9am-6pm Mon-Fri Apr-Sep, 9am-5pm Mon-Fri Oct-Mar) provides information and sells domestic and international train tickets and seat reservations, but you can also buy tickets at the busy stations.

The commuter rail, HÉV, begins at Batthyány tér in Buda and travels north through the suburbs. If you have a *turista* pass, you still need a supplemental ticket to get to Szentendre, the northern terminus, and towns outside the city limits.

Keleti train station (Eastern; Map pp340–1; ☎ 333 6342; VIII Kerepesi út 2-4) handles international trains from Vienna and many other points east, plus domestic trains to/from the north and northeast. For some Romanian, German and Slovak destinations, as well as domestic ones to/from the northwest and the Danube Bend, head for **Nyugati train station** (Western; Map p344; ☎ 349 0115; VI Nyugati tér). For trains bound for Lake Balaton and the south, go to **Déli train station** (Southern; Map p343; ☎ 375 6293; I Krisztina körút 37). All three main train stations are on metro lines.

For details of international trains within Eastern Europe, see p392; for trains travelling to places outside Eastern Europe, see p894.

GETTING AROUND
To/From the Airport
The simplest, most cost-effective way to get to town is to take the **Airport Minibus** (☎ 296 8555; one way/return 2100/3600Ft; ◷ 5am-1am) directly to the place you're staying. Buy tickets at the clearly marked stands in the arrivals halls. The cheapest way is to take the BKV Ferihegy bus (from outside the baggage claim at Ferihegy 2, or on the main road outside Ferihegy 1) to the end of its run, the Kőbánya-Kispest stop, which is at the M2 blue line metro terminus (Map pp340–1). Then ride the metro to your destination. The bus ride takes about 25 minutes, as does the metro ride to the central metro hub (Deák tér). You need a 230Ft ticket, available at newsstands or vending machines, which you can validate on the

bus and in the metro. If you want to switch metro lines, you'll need a second ticket.

Boat

May to August, the **BKV passenger ferry** (☎ 06 20 955 3782; www.ship-bp.hu, Hungarian only) departs from Boráros tér terminus beside Petőfi Bridge, south of the centre, and heads to Pünkösdfürdő terminus north of Aquincum, with many stops along the way. Tickets (adult/child 500/400Ft from end to end) are usually sold on board. The ferry stop closest to the Castle District is Batthyány tér, and Petőfi tér is not far from Vörösmarty tér, a convenient place to pick up the boat on the Pest side.

Public Transport

Public transport is run by **BKV** (☎ 342 2335; www.bkv.hu). The three underground metro lines (M1 yellow, M2 red, M3 blue) meet at Deák tér in Pest. The HÉV above-ground suburban railway runs north from Batthyány tér in Buda. A *turista* transport pass is only good on the HÉV within the city limits (south of the Békásmegyer stop). There's also an extensive network of buses, trams and trolleybuses. Public transport basically operates from 4.30am until 11.30pm, plus 18 night buses (marked with an 'É') run along main roads.

A single ticket for all forms of transport is 140Ft (60 minutes of uninterrupted travel, no metro line changes). A transfer ticket (230Ft) is valid for one trip with one validated transfer within 90 minutes. The three-day *turista* pass (2200Ft) or a seven-day pass (2600Ft) make things easier, both allowing unlimited travel inside the city limits. Keep your ticket or pass handy; the fine for 'riding black' is 2000Ft on the spot, or 5500Ft if you pay later at the **BKV Office** (Map p344; ☎ 461 6544; VII Akácfa utca 22; ⏰ 6am-8pm Mon-Fri, 8am-2pm Sat).

Taxi

Overcharging foreigners (rigged meters, detours…) is common. Never get into a taxi that does not have an official yellow licence plate, the logo of a taxi firm, and a visible table of fares. If you have to take a taxi, it's best to call one; this costs less than if you flag one down. Make sure you know the number of the landline phone you're calling from as that's how the dispatcher can establish your address (though you can call from

a mobile too). Dispatchers usually speak English. **City** (☎ 211 1111), **Fő** (☎ 222 2222) and **Rádió** (☎ 377 7777) are reliable companies.

THE DANUBE BEND

North of Budapest, the Danube breaks through the Pilis and Börzsöny Hills in a sharp bend before continuing into Slovakia. Here medieval kings once ruled Hungary from majestic palaces overlooking the river at Esztergom and Visegrád. East of Visegrád, the river divides, with Szentendre and Vác on different branches. Today the easy access to historic monuments, rolling green scenery – and tons of souvenir craft shops – lure many day-trippers from Budapest.

SZENTENDRE

☎ 26 / pop 22,700

A pretty little town of steep and narrow streets, Szentendre (*sen*-ten-dreh) is just 19km north of Budapest. With its Orthodox churches, charming old centre, plentiful cafés, art and craft galleries and souvenir shops so close to the capital, the place swells with crowds – especially in summer and at weekends. Outside town is the largest openair village museum in the country.

Orientation & Information

From the HÉV and bus stations, walk under the subway and up Kossuth Lajos utca to Fő tér, the centre of the Old Town. The Duna korzó and the river embankment is a block east of this square. The Mahart Ferry Pier is about 1km northeast on Czóbel sétány, off Duna korzó. There are no left-luggage offices at the HÉV or bus stations.

Tourinform (☎ 317 965; Dumtsa Jenő utca 22; ⏰ 9am-6.30pm Mon-Fri, 10am-2pm Sat) has information about the numerous small museums and galleries in town. The **OTP Bank** (Dumtsa Jenő utca 6) is just off Fő tér, and the **main post office** (Kossuth Lajos utca 23-25) is across from the bus and train stations. **Game Planet** (☎ 505 068; Petőfi Sándor utca 1; ⏰ 10am-10pm) is an Internet café with access for 300Ft per hour.

Sights & Activities

Begin your sightseeing at the colourful Fő tér, the town's main square. Here you'll find many buildings from the 18th century, including the **Emlékkereszt** (Memorial

HUNGARY

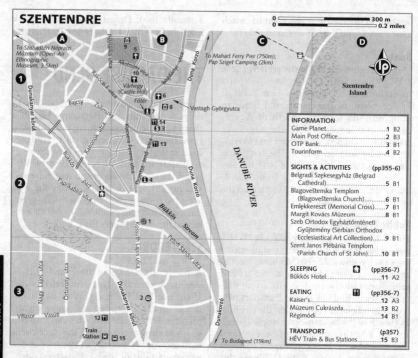

SZENTENDRE

0 — 300 m
0 — 0.2 miles

To Szabadtéri Néprajzi
Múzeum (Open-Air
Ethnographic
Museum, 3.5km)

To Mahart Ferry Pier (750m);
Pap Sziget Camping (2km)

Szentendre
Island

DANUBE RIVER

Bükkös Stream

To Budapest (19km)

INFORMATION	
Game Planet.............................1	B2
Main Post Office.......................2	B3
OTP Bank.................................3	B1
Tourinform..............................4	B2

SIGHTS & ACTIVITIES	(pp355-6)
Belgradi Székesegyház (Belgrad Cathedral)...........................5	B1
Blagoveštenska Templom (Blagoveštenska Church).......6	B1
Emlékkereszt (Memorial Cross)...7	B1
Margit Kovács Múzeum.............8	B1
Szeb Ortodox Egyháztörténeti Gyüjtemény (Serbian Orthodox Ecclesiastical Art Collection)...9	B1
Szent Janos Plébánia Templom (Parish Church of St John).......10	B1

SLEEPING 🏠	(pp356-7)
Bükkös Hotel...........................11	A2

EATING 🍴	(pp356-7)
Kaiser's..................................12	A3
Múzeum Cukrászda...................13	B2
Régimódi................................14	B1

TRANSPORT	(p357)
HÉV Train & Bus Stations..........15	B3

Cross; 1763) and the 1752 Serbian Ortho-dox **Blagoveštenska Templom** (Church; ☎ 310 554; Fő tér; admission 200Ft; ⏰ Tue-Sun 10-5) which is small, but stunning.

All the pedestrian lanes surrounding the square burst with shops, the merchandise spilling out into displays on the streets. Shopkeepers are so used to the tourist hoards they automatically speak to you in English, German or French first. Downhill to the east, off a side street on the way to the Danube, is the **Margit Kovács Múzeum** (☎ 310 244; Vastagh György utca 1; adult/student 600/400Ft; ⏰ 10am-6pm Feb-Oct). Kovács (1902–77) was a ceramicist who combined Hungarian folk, religious and modern themes to create her much beloved figures. Uphill to the northwest, a narrow passageway leads up from between Fő tér 8 and 9 to Castle Hill and the **Parish Church of St John** (Várhegy), rebuilt in 1710, from where you get great views of the town and the Danube. Nearby, the tall red tower of the Serbian **Belgradi Székesegyház** (Belgrade Cathedral; Pátriárka utca), from 1764, casts its tall shadow. You can hear beautiful chanting wafting from the open doors during services. The **Szerb Ortodox**

Egyháztörténeti Gyüjtemény (Serbian Ecclesiastical Art Collection; ☎ 312 399; Pátriárka utca 5; adult/student 200/100Ft; ⏰ 10am-6pm Wed-Sun mid-Mar–Oct, 10am-4pm Fri-Sun Nov–mid-Mar) is in the courtyard.

Don't miss the extensive **Szabadtéri Néprajzi Múzeum** (Open-Air Ethnographic Museum; ☎ 502 500; adult/student 800/400Ft, ⏰ 9am-5pm Tue-Sun Apr-Oct) outside town. Walking through the fully furnished ancient wooden and stone homes, churches and work buildings brought here from around the country, you can see what rural life was – and sometimes still is – like in different regions of Hungary. The five reconstructed villages of this *skansen* (vil-lage museum) are not close to each other, but you can take a wagon ride (500Ft) be-tween them. In the centre of the park stand Roman-era ruins. Frequent weekend festi-vals give you a chance to see folk costumes, music and dance, as well as home crafts. To get here, take the bus marked 'Skansen' from stand No 7 (100Ft, 20 minutes, hourly).

Sleeping & Eating

Seeing Szentendre on a day trip from Buda-pest is probably your best bet. The town can be easily covered in a day, even if you spend a couple of hours at the open-air museum. For private rooms in town, head west of the centre around the Dunakanyar körút ring road, and look for 'Zimmer frei' signs. Szentendre is a tourist town and there are plenty of places around the old town to sit at an outside table and grab a bite to eat.

Pap Sziget Camping (☎ 310 697; www.pap-sziget .hu; camp site per person €6, caravan site €15, 2-bedroom bungalows €32-40, motel room with shared bathroom €22; May–mid-Oct; P) The grounds have large shade trees, a sandy beach and 120 tent and caravan sites. Bungalows are raised on stilts with parking below. Take bus No 1, 2 or 3, the place is 2km from north of town on Szentendre Island.

Bükkös Hotel (☎ 312 021; Bükkös part 16; s/d €40/45; P) A Maria-Theresa yellow exterior and a dark-wood reception hall welcome you to this 16-room hotel in an old building. The location's good, on a stream between the HÉV station and the Old Town.

Régimódi (☎ 311 105; Dumtsa Jenő utca 2; mains 700-1200Ft; 11am-11pm) So near the main square your best bet is to choose a pavement table and enjoy the people parade. Régimódi sells a filling Hungarian set menu for about 1500Ft.

Múzeum Cukrászda (☎ 310 545; Dumtsa Jenő utca 14; cakes 190-280Ft; 10am-7pm) Stop by for their inviting cakes and take away a fanciful forest creature sculpted in marzipan sugar.

A large **Kaiser's** (HÉV Állomás 1) supermarket is next to the HÉV station if you want to give Szentendre's touristy cafés a miss and have a riverside picnic.

Getting There & Away

The most convenient way to get to Szentendre is to take the commuter HÉV train from Buda's Batthyány tér metro station to the end of the line (370Ft, 40 minutes, every 10 to 15 minutes).

From mid-May to mid-September, three Mahart PassNave (p354) ferries travel daily from Budapest's Vigadó tér pier to Szentendre (950Ft, 1½ hours) at 9am, 10.30am and 2pm. Return trips are at 12.20pm, 4pm and 5pm. The 9am boat continues on from Szentendre to Visegrád at 10.40am. In April and October, only the daily 9am departure from Budapest (continuing on to Visegrád only on weekends) and the 4pm return to Budapest from Szentendre run.

VISEGRÁD
☎ 26 / pop 1500

Looking out from the ruins of a citadel high on a hill above a curve in the Danube, it's easy to see how defensible Visegrád (vish-eh-grahd) would be. The first fortress here was built by the Romans as a border defence in the 4th century. Hungarian kings built a mighty citadel on the hill top, and a lower castle near the river, after the 13th-century Mongol invasions. In the 14th century a royal palace was built on the flood plain at the foot of the hills and in 1323 King Charles Robert of Anjou, whose claim to the local throne was being fiercely contested in Buda, moved the royal household here. For nearly two centuries Hungarian royalty alternated between Visegrád and Buda.

The destruction of Visegrád came first at the hands of the occupying Turks and then at the hands of the Habsburgs who destroyed the citadel to prevent Hungarian independence fighters from using it. All trace of the palace was lost until 1934 when archaeologists, by following descriptions in literary sources, uncovered the ruins that you can visit today.

The small town has two distinct areas: one to the north around Mahart ferry pier and another, the main town, about 1km to the south. There's now a Tourinform office, but the town does have a website that discusses much of the history in English (www.visegrad.hu; click on Műemlékek).

Sights & Activities

The partial reconstruction of the **Királyi Palota** (Royal Palace; ☎ 398 026; Fő utca 29; adult/student 400/200Ft; 9am-4.30pm Tue-Sun), 400m south of the Mahart pier, only hints at its former magnificence. Inside, a small museum is devoted to the history of the palace and its excavation and reconstruction.

The palace's original Gothic fountain, along with town history exhibits, is in the museum at **Salamon torony** (Solomon's Tower; ☎ 398 233; adult/child 400/200Ft; 9am-4.30pm Tue-Sun May-Sep), a few hundred metres north of the palace. The tower was part of a lower castle controlling river traffic. From here you can climb the very steep path uphill to the **Visegrád Cittadella** (☎ 398 101; Várhegy; adult/student 750/350Ft; 9.30am-5.30pm) directly above. While the citadel (1259) ruins itself are not as spectacular as its history, the view

HUNGARY

of the Danube Bend from the walls is well worth the climb. From the town centre a trail leads to the citadel from behind the Catholic church on Fő tér; this is less steep than the arduous climb from Solomon's Tower. A local bus runs up to the citadel from the Mahart PassNave ferry pier three times daily (more often in July and August).

Sleeping & Eating

As with the other towns in Danube Bend, Visegrád is an easy day trip from Budapest, so it's not necessary to stay over if you don't want to.

Jurta Camping (☎ 398 217; camp site per person 1450Ft, yurt per person 3050Ft; ☼ May-Sep) On Mogyoróhegy (Hazelnut Hill), about 2km northeast of the citadel, the camp sight is pretty and green. There aren't bungalows, but there are yurt tents for rent with five beds in each. The 'Kisvillám' bus goes to Jurta Camping from the ferry pier at 9.25am, 12.25pm and 3.25pm, June to August.

Visegrád Tours (☎ 398 160; Rév utca 15; ☼ 8am-5pm) This extremely accommodating travel agency in the town centre provides information and books private rooms for between 5500Ft and 6500Ft per person, per night.

Hotel Honti Panzió (☎ 398 120; hotelhon@axelero .hu; Fő utca 66; s/d pension r 8000/11,600Ft, s/d hotel r 10,300/11,900Ft; P) Honti is a friendly pension filled with homy rooms. More expensive, bigger, newer rooms in the adjacent hotel building still have wooden furniture and rose-coloured curtains your aunt might have made.

Reneszánsz (☎ 398 081; Fő utca 11; mains 1200-2400Ft; ☼ noon-10pm). If you go in for men in tights and silly hats, this medieval banquet-style restaurant can be entertaining. A royal feast, with pheasant soup, roast meats and unlimited wine, costs 4000Ft.

Two options in the town centre are the **Grill Udvar** (Rév utca 6; mains 500-1000Ft; ☼ 11am-11pm), for pizzas and grilled meat, and **Gulyás Csárda** (☎ 398 329; Mátyás Király utca; mains 1000-2000Ft; ☼ 11am-10pm), for reliable Hungarian standards and cymbalom music.

Getting There & Away

Buses go often Visegrád from Budapest's Árpád híd bus station (463Ft, 1 hour 15 minutes, at least hourly), the Szentendre HÉV station (405Ft, 45 minutes, every 45 minutes) and Esztergom (405Ft, 45 minutes, hourly).

On weekends in late April and during most of October, a ferry runs from Budapest to Visegrád (1050Ft, 3½ hours) at 9am (via Szentendre), returning to Budapest from Visegrád at 4pm. From May to September that same ferry runs daily. There is an additional departure at 7.30am from late May to August, which continues on to Esztergom at 10.50am. The return departure from Visegrád to Budapest is at 5.30pm. On weekends from June to August there is a also high-speed hydrofoil service from Budapest to Visegrád (2000Ft, one hour), departing from Budapest at 9.30am and Visegrád at 4.45pm.

ESZTERGOM

☎ 33 / pop 28,900

A town full of ecclesiastic wonders, Esztergom (es-ter-gohm) has been the seat of Roman Catholicism in Hungary since the 19th century. The soaring Esztergom Bazilika is home to the Primate of Hungary and surrounding museums contain many Christian treasures.

The significance of this town reaches far back into history. The 2nd-century Roman emperor-to-be Marcus Aurelius wrote his famous *Meditations* while he camped here. In the 10th century, Stephen I, founder of the Hungarian state, was born and crowned at the cathedral. From the late 10th to the mid-13th centuries Esztergom served as the Hungarian royal seat. In 1543 the Turks ravaged the town and much of it was destroyed only to be rebuilt in the 18th and 19th centuries. Many of the old buildings in the centre date from those centuries.

Orientation & Information

The train station is on the southern edge of town, about a 10-minute walk south of the bus station. From the train station, walk north on Baross Gábor út, then along Ady Endre utca to Simor János utca, past the bus station to the town centre. Don't be fooled by the run-down buildings along the walk; the town's true character reveals itself once you get to the hill below the cathedral.

K&H Bank (Rákóczi tér) does foreign exchange transactions. The **post office** (Arany János utca 2) is just off Széchenyi tér. **Gran Tours** (☎ 502 000; Rákóczi tér 25; ☼ 8am-6pm Mon-Fri) is the best source of information in town.

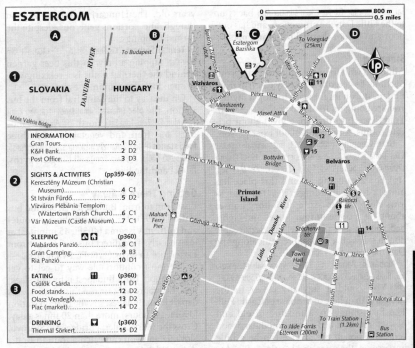

ESZTERGOM

INFORMATION
Gran Tours...................................1 D2
K&H Bank....................................2 D2
Post Office..................................3 D3

SIGHTS & ACTIVITIES (pp359-60)
Keresztény Múzeum (Christian
    Museum)................................4 C1
St István Fürdő............................5 D2
Vízíváros Plébánia Templom
    (Watertown Parish Church)....6 C1
Vár Múzeum (Castle Museum)....7 C1

SLEEPING (p360)
Alabárdos Panzió.........................8 C1
Gran Camping..............................9 B3
Ria Panzió....................................10 D1

EATING (p360)
Csülök Csárda..............................11 D1
Food stands.................................12 D2
Olasz Vendeglő............................13 D2
Piac (market)...............................14 D2

DRINKING (p360)
Thermál Sörkert...........................15 D2

Sights & Activities

The **Esztergom Bazilika** (☎ 411 895; admission free; ☼ 7am-6pm), on a hill above the Danube, is hard to miss – it's the largest church in Hungary. The colossal building is easily seen from the train window en route from Bratislava to Budapest. Reconstructed in the neoclassical style, much of the building dates from the 19th century; the oldest section is the white and red marble **Bakócz Kápolna** (Bakócz Chapel; 1510) that was moved here. You can climb up the winding steps to the top of the cupola for 200Ft. The **kincsház** (treasury; adult/student 400/200Ft; ☼ 9am-4.30pm Mar-Oct, 11am-3.30pm Mon-Fri & 10am-3pm Sat Nov–mid-Mar) contains priceless objects, including ornate vestments and the 13th-century Hungarian coronation cross. Among those buried in the **altemplom** (crypt; 100Ft; ☼ 9am-5pm) under the cathedral is the controversial Cardinal Mindszenty, who was imprisoned by the communists for refusing to allow Hungary's Catholic schools to be secularised.

At the southern end of the hill is the **Vár Múzeum** (Castle Museum; ☎ 415 986; adult/student 460/240Ft; ☼ 10am-6pm Tue-Sun Apr-Oct, 10am-4pm Nov-Mar), inside the reconstructed remnants of the medieval royal palace (1215), which was built upon previous castles. The earliest excavated sections on the hill date from the 2nd to 3rd centuries. Look at archaeological and royal history exhibits as you wander through the labyrinth of rooms.

Southwest of the cathedral along the banks of the Little Danube, narrow streets wind through the Víziváros (Watertown) district, home to the **Víziváros Plébánia Templom** (Watertown Parish Church; 1738) at the start of Berényi Zsigmond utca. The **Keresztény Múzeum** (Christian Museum; ☎ 413 880; Berényi Zsigmond utca 2; adult/student 400/200Ft; ☼ 10am-5.30pm Tue-Sun) is in the adjacent Primate's Palace (1882). The stunning collection of medieval religious art includes a Virgin Mary statue from the 11th century.

Cross the bridge south of Watertown Parish Church and about 100m further south is **Mária Valéria Bridge**. Destroyed during WWII, it once again connects Esztergom with Slovakia and the city of Štúrovo. **St István Fürdő** (☎ 312 249; Bajcsy-Zsilinszky utca 14; adult/child 500/200Ft; ☼ 9am-6pm May-Sep, indoor pool only 6am-6pm Mon &

Sat, 6am-7pm Tue-Fri, 9am-4pm Sun Oct-Apr) backs up to the Little Danube promenade and has outdoor and indoor thermal baths and pool.

Sleeping

Although with frequent transportation connections Esztergom is an easy day trip from Budapest, you might want to stop a night if you are going on to Slovakia. Contact Gran Tours (see Information, above) about private rooms, for around 4000Ft per person.

Gran Camping (☎ 411 953, fortanex@alexero.hu; Nagy-Duna sétány 3; camp site per person 1950Ft, dm/r 1700/6000Ft; bungalows 9000-13,000Ft; ☼ May-Sep; ℗) For a camping ground this place has quite a lot of buildings: elevated bungalows sleep four to six; a dormitory houses about 100 people in four-, five- and eight-bed rooms; and the motel has serviceable doubles. It's all a 10-minute walk along the Danube from the cathedral.

Alabárdos Panzió (☎ 312 640; www.alabardospanzio .hu; Bajcsy-Zsilinszky utca 49; s/d 6500-7500/7500-8500Ft; ℗) You couldn't stay any closer to the cathedral than here at the base of Castle Hill. The furnishings are a mixture of old and new (some iron beds, some modular wood veneer). Though the service can be a little impersonal, the price and location are right.

Ria Panzió (☎ 313 115; www.riapanzio.com; Batthyány Lajos utca 11; s/d €40/48; 🖳 ℗) Doubles are fresh, with newly painted white walls, wood floors and royal blue linen. Relax on the terrace or arrange an adventure through the family-owners – rent a bicycle maybe, or take a water- skiing trip on the Danube in summer.

Eating & Drinking

Jáde Forrás Étterem (☎ 400 949; Hősök tere 11; mains 600-1400Ft; 11am-11pm; ✗) Jáde does a mean Hunan chicken and has a reduced price buffet at lunch. A four-course set menu is 1750Ft.

Olasz Vendeglö (☎ 312 952; Lőrinc utca 5; pizza & pasta 700-1000Ft, mains 1000-1400Ft; ☼ 11am-10pm Sun-Thu, 11am-midnight Fri & Sat; ✗) Pizzas and pastas at the originally named Italian Restaurant are among the few vegetarian options in town. Mains include dishes like fruit-stuffed chicken breasts.

Csülök Csárda (☎ 312 420; Batthyány Lajos utca 9; mains 1390-1890Ft; ☼ noon-midnight; ✗ 🐾) You'll be at no loss to meet other tourists in this supercentral eatery that claims to be 300

years old. The Hungarian cooking is good though, and portions generous, despite the formal trappings.

Térmal Sörkert (Kis-Duna sétány; ☼ 10am-10pm May-Oct) Sipping a brew in this beer garden behind the thermal baths is a relaxing way to spend a balmy summer evening.

On the way to the cathedral from the bus station, the **piac** (market; Símor Janos utca; ☼ 7am-4pm Mon-Fri, 7am-1pm Sat), north of Arany János utca, has fruit and vegetables, and three **food stands** (Bajcsy-Zsilinszky utca, cnr Szent István fürdő; snacks 200-600Ft; ☼ 8am-8pm) sell burgers, gyros, falafel and the like.

Getting There & Away

Buses run to/from Budapest's Árpád híd bus station (579Ft, 1½ hours on shortest route) and to/from Visegrád (405Ft, 45 minutes) at least hourly. Two direct buses a day go from Esztergom to Győr (1160Ft, two hours).

The most comfortable way to get to get to Esztergom from Budapest is by rail; sleek, new, EC-approved cars run this route. Trains depart from Budapest's Nyugati train station (490Ft, 1½ hours) more than 20 times a day. Cross the Mária Váleria Bridge into Štúrovo, Slovakia and you can catch a train to Bratislava, which is an hour and a half away.

Mahart PassNave ferries (p354) depart from Budapest to Esztergom (via Visegrád, 1200Ft, 5½ hours) once a day from late May through August (7.30am). The daily return trip to Budapest departs from Esztergom at 3.20pm. Weekends June to August there is also a high-speed hydrofoil service between Budapest and Esztergom (2300Ft, 2½ hours), via Visegrád, departing from Budapest at 9.30am and from Esztergom at 3.20pm. From June through August, a ferry service between Esztergom and Visegrád (700Ft, two hours) departs Esztergom at 9am and returns from Visegrád at 3.30pm.

NORTHWESTERN HUNGARY

The decidedly Austro-Hungarian Empire feel of towns in northwestern Hungary attests to its proximity to Austria. This region beyond the Bakony Hills is bounded by the Danube in the east and the Alps in the west. Ancient history was good to this corner of

Cafés on Prague's Staroměstské nám (Old Town Square; p251), Czech Republic

Trail through a narrow cleft in the Adršpach-Teplice Rocks (p279), Czech Republic

NEIL WILSON

MARTIN MOOS

Interior of the neo-Renaissance Hungarian State Opera House (p347), Hungary

Outdoor swimming pool at the Széchenyi Fürdo (p347), Budapest

MARTIN MOOS

RICHARD NEBESKY

Rīga's World Heritage–listed Old Town (p402), Latvia

CRAIG PERSHOUSE

A corner tower of Bishop's
Castle (p325), in Kuressaare,
Estonia

JONATHAN SMITH

TOM COCKREM

The baroque Russian Orthodox Holy Spirit
Church (p429) in Vilnius, Lithuania

JONATHAN SMI

Fourteenth-century Trakai Castle (p434), Lithuania

Hungary: it was part of Roman territories in the first centuries of the Christian era, but never fully occupied by the Turks in the 15th to 16th centuries. The old quarters of Sopron and Győr are brimming with what were once the residences of prosperous burghers and clerics. Fertőd, outside Sopron, is a magnificent baroque palace and Pannonhalma, outside Győr, is an early Benedictine monastery still in operation.

GYŐR

☎ 96 / pop 129,500

A sizable pedestrian centre filled with old streets and buildings make riverside Győr (pronounced jyeur) an inviting place for a stroll – even if there isn't one stand-out attraction. Students hang out at the many pavement cafés in this university town.

Midway between Budapest and Vienna, Győr sits at the point where the Mosoni-Danube, Rábca and Rába Rivers meet. This was the site of a Roman town named Arrabona. In the 11th century, Stephen I established a bishopric here and in the 16th century, a fortress was erected to hold back the Turks.

Orientation & Information

The large neobaroque City Hall (1898) rises up to block out all other views across from the train station. Baross Gábor utca, which leads to the old town and the rivers, lies diagonally across from City Hall. Much of central Győr is pedestrianised, making parking difficult.

The **Tourinform** (☎ 311 711; Árpád út 32; ☽ 8am-6pm Mon-Fri, 9am-3pm Sat) is small, but helpful, and offers currency exchange. The **Ibusz** (☎ 311 700; Kazinczy utca 3; ☽ 8.30am-4pm Mon-Fri) travel agency arranges private rooms and area tours, including to Pannonhalma. Oddly enough, the **Polarnet Internet Café** (Czuczor Gergely utca 6; per hour 180Ft; ☽ 9am-8pm) is above a clothing shop, with the entrance around the corner in an alleyway. Other town services:
Main post office (Bajcsy-Zsilinszky út 46)
OTP Bank (Baross Gábor 16)

Sights & Activities

The enchanting **Karmelita Templom** (Carmelite Church; 1725) and many fine baroque palaces line riverfront Bécsí kapu tér. On the northwestern side of the square are the fortifications built in the 16th century to stop the Turks. A short distance east is the building where Bonaparte spent his only night in Hungary in 1809, **Napoleon Háza** (Napoleon House; Király utca 4). Walk around the old streets and stop in at a pavement café or two.

North up Káptalandomb (Chapter Hill), in the oldest part of Győr, is the solid baroque **Egyhaz** (Cathedral; ☽ 10am-noon & 2-5pm daily). Situated on the hill, it was originally Romanesque, but most of what you see inside dates from the 17th and 18th centuries. Don't miss the Gothic Héderváry Chapel on the southern side of the cathedral, which contains a glittering 15th-century bust of King (and St) Ladislas. West of the cathedral, the **Püspőkvár** (Bishop's Castle; ☎ 312 153; adult/student 300/150Ft; ☽ 10am-6pm Tue-Sun) houses the Diocesan Treasury. The architecture represents a variety of styles; the tower was constructed in the 14th century, but the building saw a major overhaul in the 18th century. At the bottom of the hill on Jedlik Ányos utca is the **Ark of the Covenant** statue dating from 1731. From here you can head north to a bridge overlooking the junction of the city's three rivers.

In Széchenyi tér, the heart of Győr, is the fine **Szent Ignác Templom** (St Ignatius Church; 1641) and the Mária Ozlop (Column of the Virgin; 1686) statue. Cross the square to the **Xantus János Múzeum** (☎ 310 588; Széchenyi tér 5; adult/student 500/250Ft; ☽ 10am-6pm Tue-Sun), built in 1743, to see exhibits on the city's history. Next door is the **Patkó Imre Gyűjtemény** (Imre Patkó Collection; ☎ 310 588; Széchenyi tér 4 adult/child 300/150Ft; ☽ 10am-6pm Tue-Sun), a fine small museum contained in a 17th-century house. Collections include 20th-century Asian and African art. Look for the highly decorated baroque ceiling at the **Becés Gyógyszertár Múzeum** (Jesuit Pharmacy Museum; ☎ 320 954; Széchenyi tér 9; admission free; ☽ 7.30am-4pm Mon-Fri).

The water in the pools at thermal bath **Rába Quelle** (☎ 522 646; Fürdő tér 1; adult/student per day 1600/1000Ft; ☽ 8am-10pm) range from 29°C to 38°C. Renovàted, revamped and reopened in 2003, it's almost an entertainment complex. One pool has a huge stoneface waterfall, another a waterslide. There's a restaurant, bar and beauty shop onsite as well as the requisite massage services.

PANNONHALMA ABBEY

Take a half a day and make the short trip to visit this ancient and impressive **Pannonhalmi**

HUNGARY

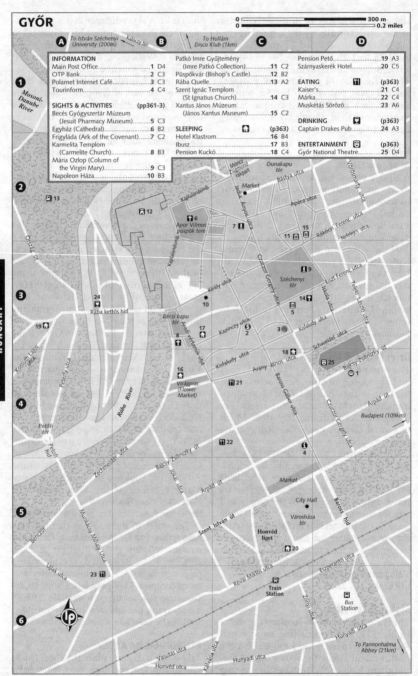

GYŐR

INFORMATION
Main Post Office	**1** D4
OTP Bank	**2** C3
Polarnet Internet Café	**3** C3
Tourinform	**4** C4

SIGHTS & ACTIVITIES (pp361-3)
Becés Gyógyszertár Múzeum (Jesuit Pharmacy Museum)	**5** C3
Egyház (Cathedral)	**6** B2
Frigyláda (Ark of the Covenant)	**7** C2
Karmelita Templom (Carmelite Church)	**8** B3
Mária Oszlop (Column of the Virgin Mary)	**9** C3
Napoleon Háza	**10** B3

Patkó Imre Gyűjtemény (Imre Patkó Collection)	**11** C2
Püspökvár (Bishop's Castle)	**12** B2
Rába Quelle	**13** A2
Szent Ignác Templom (St Ignatius Church)	**14** C3
Xantus János Múzeum (János Xantus Museum)	**15** C2

SLEEPING (p363)
Hotel Klastrom	**16** B4
Ibusz	**17** B3
Pension Kuckó	**18** C4

Pension Pető	**19** A3
Szárnyaskerék Hotel	**20** C5

EATING (p363)
Kaiser's	**21** C4
Márka	**22** C4
Muskétás Söröző	**23** A6

DRINKING (p363)
Captain Drakes Pub	**24** A3

ENTERTAINMENT (p363)
Győr National Theatre	**25** D4

Mosoni-Danube River

Móricz Zsigmond rakpart · Dunakapu tér · Market · Bástya utca · Kapuhalándomb · Anyos utca · Apáca utca · Vörösmarty utca

13

12

Apor Vilmos püspök tere · 6 · 7 · 11 · 15 · Rákóczi Ferenc utca · Nefelejcs utca

Kaptalándomb · 9 · Széchenyi tér · Liszt Ferenc utca · Teleki László utca

Király utca · 10 · 14 · 5 · Kazinczy utca · Kisfaludy utca

Rába kettős híd · 24 · 19 · Bécsi kapu tér · Andrássy utca · 8 · 17 · 2 · 3 · 18 · 25 · Schweidel utca · Baicsy-Zsilinszky út · 1

Rába River · Virágpiac (Flower Market) · 16 · Kisfaludy utca · 21 · Arany János utca · Baross Gábor utca · Árpád út · Budapest (109km)

Kossuth Lajos utca · Petőfi tér · Petőfi híd · 22 · Czuczor Gergely utca

Schmeidel utca · Baicsy-Zsilinszky út · Jókai utca · Árpád út · Market · Munkácsy Mihály utca · Bencér

Szent István út · City Hall · Városháza tér · Honvéd liget · 20 · Baross híd

Újlak utca · 23 · Révai Miklós utca · Train Station · Bus Station · Esperanto utca · Zrínyi utca · Hunyadi utca

Vasútás utca · Kálvária utca · Hunyadi utca · Honvéd utca · To Pannonhalma Abbey (21km)

0 — 300 m
0 — 0.2 miles

Főapátság (Pannonhalma Abbey; ☎ 570191; www.osb.hu, no English; Vár 1; adult/student Hungarian tour 1200/500Ft, adult/student foreign-language tour 1900/1200Ft), now a Unesco World Heritage Site. Most buildings in the complex date from the 13th to the 18th centuries; highlights include the Romanesque basilica (1225), the Gothic cloister (1486) and the impressive collection of ancient texts in the library. Because it's an active monastery, the abbey must be visited with a guide. From mid-March to mid-November, foreign-language tours in English, Italian, German, French and Russian are conducted at 11.20am, 1.20pm and 3.20pm. You can take a Hungarian tour (with foreign-language text available) on the hour 9–11am and 1–4pm from June to September, and 10–11am and 1–3pm from October to March. From October through May the abbey is closed Monday.

Pannonhalma is best reached from Győr by bus as the train station is 2km southwest of the abbey. A direct bus runs daily from the Győr bus station to the abbey (Pannonhalma, vár főkapu stop) at 8am, 10am and noon (289Ft, 40 minutes), returning at 8.50am, 12.50pm and 5.35pm. Buses go from Győr to the town of Pannonhalma hourly. The abbey is a 15-minute, uphill walk from there.

Sleeping

For private rooms ask at the Ibusz travel agency (see Information, above).

István Széchenyi University (☎ 503 447; Héderváry út 3; dm 1600-2000Ft) Dormitory accommodation is available year-round at this huge university north of the town centre.

Pension Kuckó (☎ 316 260, fax 312 195; Arany János utca 33; s/d/apt 5900/7490/9900Ft; ✗) An old town house outfitted with bright modern trimmings. The two apartments, with small kitchens, and the café on the ground floor are especially new. Sister property **Pension Petö** (☎ 313 412; Kossuth Lajos utca 20; s/d 7200/8900Ft; ✗) is not far across the river.

Szárnyaskerék Hotel (☎ 314 629; Révai Miklós utca 5; r with/without bath 7100/4800Ft) You can't be closer to the train and bus station, but there is a certain griminess here. Still, it's cheap and on the first Friday of the month a folk dance party takes place in the basement.

Hotel Klastrom (☎ 516 910; www.hotels.hu/klastrom; Zechmeister utca 1; s/d/tr 12,500/16,800/19,300Ft; P ✗ ▢) Sleep in a Carmelite friary that is more than 250 years old. Vaulted arch ceilings grace many of the public and guest rooms. Dark modern furniture contrasts appropriately with stark white walls. The interior courtyard looks like a formal garden.

Eating & Drinking

Márka (☎ 320 800; Bajcsy-Zsilinszky út 30; mains 450-490Ft; ✆ 11am-3.30pm Mon-Fri) Dine cafeteria-style for lunch. Enter through the pastry shop.

Muskétás Söröző (☎ 317 627; Munkácsy Mihaly utca 10; mains 630-790Ft; ✆ 11am-midnight, bar to 1am) Eminently reasonable, this pub and eatery is especially popular with students from the nearby music college. Dine or drink downstairs in the cellar or continue through to the outdoor tables in the courtyard at the rear. The menu has turkey breasts stuffed with a variety of ingredients.

Captain Drakes Pub (☎ 517 412; Radó sétány 1; mains 800-2000Ft; ✆ 11am-11pm) Tables spill across a terrace on the little island in the Rába River. Inside there's a wooden ship theme going on. In addition to cold beers, that taste especially good al fresco on summer nights, Hungarian staples are served here.

A massive Kaiser's supermarket and department store takes up much of the block at Arany János utca and Aradi vértanúk útja.

Entertainment

In summer there's a month-long festival of music, theatre and dance from late June. In March, Győr hosts many events in conjunction with Budapest's Spring Festival.

Győr National Theatre (☎ 314 800; Czuczor Gergely utca 7) The celebrated Győr Ballet and the city's opera company and philharmonic orchestra all perform at the towns main, modern theatre. Tourinform can help with performance schedules.

Hullám Disco Klub (☎ 315 275; Héderváry utca 22; ✆ 6pm-4am Fri & Sat) House music and guest DJs attracts a 20-something crowd to this disco.

Getting There & Away

Buses travel to Budapest (1160Ft, two hours, hourly), Pannonhalma (289Ft, 40 minutes, hourly), Sopron (1160Ft, two hours, seven daily) Esztergom (1270Ft, two hours, one daily), Balatonfüred (1270Ft, 2½ hours, four daily) and Vienna (3790Ft, two hours, two daily).

Győr is well connected by express train to Budapest's Keleti and Déli train stations

(1632Ft, 1½ hours, 15 daily) and to Sopron (1282Ft, 1½ hours, 14 daily). Six daily trains connect Győr with Vienna's Westbahnhof (4700Ft, two hours).

SOPRON

☎ 99 / pop 55,000

Medieval walls, built on Roman foundations, still enclose much of the old town centre in Sopron (*shop*-ron). The Mongols and Turks never got this far, so unlike many Hungarian cities, numerous medieval buildings remain in use. In Roman times, the town was called Scarbantia. Today, the town sits on the Austrian border, only 69km south of Vienna. In 1921 the town's residents voted in a referendum to remain part of Hungary, while the rest of Bürgenland (the region to which Sopron used to belong) went to Austria. Many day-trippers come here from Austria to shop for cheaper goods and for dental services. The region is known for producing good red wines, such as Kékfrancos, which you can sample in local cafés and restaurants.

Orientation & Information

From the main train station, walk north on Mátyás Király utca, which becomes Várkerület, part of a loop following the line of the former city walls. Előkapu (Front Gate) and Hátsókapu (Back Gate) are the two main entrances in the walls. The bus station is northwest of the old town on Lackner Kristóf utca.

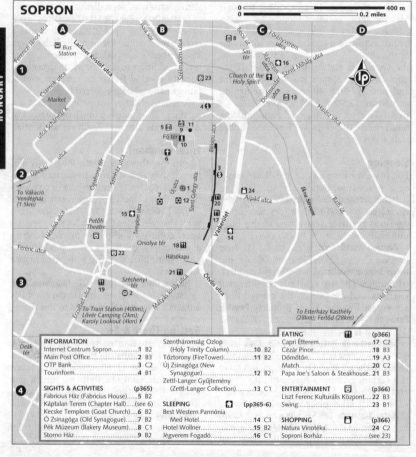

INFORMATION	
Internet Centrum Sopron	1 B2
Main Post Office	2 B3
OTP Bank	3 C2
Tourinform	4 B1

SIGHTS & ACTIVITIES	(p365)
Fabricius Ház (Fabricius House)	5 B2
Káptalan Terem (Chapter Hall)	(see 6)
Kecske Templom (Goat Church)	6 B2
Ó Zsinagóga (Old Synagogue)	7 B2
Pék Múzeum (Bakery Museum)	8 C1
Storno Ház	9 B2
Szentháromság Ozlop (Holy Trinity Column)	10 B2
Tóztorony (FireTower)	11 B2
Új Zsinagóga (New Synagogue)	12 B2
Zettl-Langer Gyűjtemény (Zettl-Langer Collection)	13 C1

SLEEPING	(pp365-6)
Best Western Pannónia Med Hotel	14 C3
Hotel Wollner	15 B2
Jégverem Fogadó	16 C1

EATING	(p366)
Capri Étterem	17 C2
Cézár Pince	18 B3
Dömötöri	19 A3
Match	20 C2
Papa Joe's Saloon & Steakhouse	21 B3

ENTERTAINMENT	(p366)
Liszt Ferenc Kulturális Központ	22 B3
Swing	23 B1

SHOPPING	(p366)
Natura Vinotéka	24 C2
Soproni Borház	(see 23)

Internet Centrum Sopron (☎ 310 252; Új utca 3; per hr 400Ft; ☯ 11am-8pm Mon-Fri, 10am-5pm Sat)
Main post office (Széchenyi tér 7-10)
OTP Bank (Várkerület 96/a)
Tourinform (☎ 338 892; www.sopron.hu; Előkapu 11; ☯ 9am-noon & 1-5pm Mon-Fri, 9am-1pm Sat)

Sights & Activities

Fő tér is the main square in Sopron; there are several museums, monuments and churches scattered around it. Above the old town's northern gate rises the 60m-high **Tűztorony** (Fire Tower; ☎ 311 327; Fő tér; adult/student 500/250Ft; ☯ 10am-6pm Tue-Sun), run by Soproni Múzeum. The building is a true architectural hybrid: The 2m-thick square base, built on a Roman gate, dates from the 12th century, the middle cylindrical and arcaded balcony was built in the 16th century and the baroque spire was added in 1680. You can climb the 154 steps for views of the Alps. In the centre of Fő tér is the **Szentháromság Ozlop** (Holy Trinity Column; 1701). On the north side of the square is **Storno Ház** (☎ 311 327; Fő tér 8; adult/student 800/400Ft; ☯ 10am-6pm Tue-Sun Apr-Aug, 10am-2pm Tue-Sun Sep-Mar), where King Mátyás stayed in 1482 while his armies lay siege to Vienna. Today it houses a local history exhibition. Upstairs at **Fabricius Ház** (☎ 311 327; Fő tér 6; adult/student 1000/500Ft; ☯ 10am-6pm Tue-Sun Apr-Aug, 10am-2pm Tue-Sun Sep-Mar) walk through recreated rooms decorated as you would have seen in 17th- and 18th-century town homes. In the basement, see stone sculptures and other remains from Roman times. The back rooms of the ground floor are dedicated to an archaeology exhibit.

Beyond the square is the 13th-century **Kecske Templom** (Goat Church; Templom utca 1), whose name comes from the heraldic animal of its chief benefactor. Below the church is the **Káptalan Terem** (Chapter Hall; ☎ 338 843; admission free; ☯ 10am-noon & 2-5pm Tue-Sun May-Sep), part of a 14th-century Franciscan monastery with frescoes and stone carvings.

The **Új Zsinagóga** (New Synagogue; Új utca 11), built in the 14th century, is now private housing and offices. The medieval **Ó Zsinagóga** (Old Synagogue; ☎ 311 227; Új utca 22; adult/student 400/200Ft; ☯ 10am-6pm Tue-Sun May-Sep), also built in the 14th century, is in better shape than many scattered around the country and contains a museum of Jewish life.

There are many other small museums in town. Two in the Ikva district, northeast of

centre, are quite interesting: the **Zettl-Langer Gyűjtemény** (Zettl-Langer Collection; ☎ 335 123; Balfi út 11; 300Ft; ☯ 10am-noon Tue-Sun Apr-Oct, Fri-Sun only Nov-Mar) of antiquities, ceramics, paintings and furniture; and the **Pék Múzeum** (Bakery Museum; ☎ 311 327; Bécsí út 5; adult/student 350/150Ft; ☯ 10am-2pm Tue-Sun May-Aug) in a house and shop used by bakers' families from 1686 to 1970.

To visit the hills surrounding Sopron, take bus No 1 or 2 to the Szieszta Hotel and hike up through the forest to the 394m-tall **Károly Lookout** (Lóvérek; adult/student 250/150Ft; ☯ 9am-8pm May-Aug, 9am-4pm Sep-Apr) for the view.

ESTERHÁZY KASTHÉLY

Don't miss **Esterházy Kasthély** (☎ 537 640; Hadyn utca 2, Fertőd; adult/student 1000/600Ft; ☯ 10am-6pm Tue-Sun mid-Mar–Oct, 10am-4pm Fri-Sun Nov–mid-Mar), a magnificent, Versailles-style baroque extravaganza 28km outside town in Fertőd. Built in 1766, this 126-room palace was owned by one of the nation's foremost families. You have to put on felt booties and slip around the marble floors under gilt chandeliers with a Hungarian guide, but information sheets in various languages are on hand. From May to October piano and string quartets perform regularly in the frescoed concert hall where Joseph Haydn worked as court musician to the Esterházys from 1761 to 1790. The Haydn Festival takes place here in early September. The Tourinform in Győr can help you with performance schedules. Fertőd is easily accessible from Sopron by bus (348Ft, 45 minutes, hourly); the town is dominated by the palace and its grounds.

Sleeping

Lővér Camping (☎ 311 715; Kőszegi út; camp site per person 1200Ft; bungalow 3000Ft; ☯ mid-Apr–mid-Oct) Bungalows and camp sites are mostly shaded. The park sometimes puts on concerts. Take bus No 12 from the bus and train station to get to the hill, Pócsi-domb, about 2½km south of the city centre.

Vákació Vendégház (☎ 338 502; www.szallasinfo .hu/vakaciovendeghaz; Ade Endre út 31; per person 2150Ft; ☒) Brand-spankin' new: you can't beat the neatness at this hostel. Many of the guests are Hungarian students. Rooms have two to 12 beds each; there's no kitchen. It's about a 15-minute walk west of the centre.

Jégverem Fogadó (☎ 510 113; www.jegverem .hu; Jégverem utca 1; s/d 5000/8000Ft) Nondescript furniture in five large rooms belies the

HUNGARY

18th-century building this pension occupies. The restaurant's menu has multiple variations on the fried-meat cutlet theme (mains 850Ft to 1890Ft). The reception desk is also a bar.

Hotel Wollner (☎ 524 400; www.wollner.hu; Templom utca 20; s/d/tr €63/75/95; ☒ Ⓟ) The rooms in the 300-plus-year-old palace are simple and elegant, some with sleigh beds. Navigate through the multilevel passageways to a raised garden terrace in the back of the property. The cellar *borozó* (wine bar) has more than 110 varieties on hand.

Best Western Pannónia Med Hotel (☎ 312 180; www.pannoniahotel.com; Várkerület 75; s/d 16,800/18,900-25,900Ft; Ⓟ ☒ ☒) You can't say that this 18th-century hotel isn't nice: opulent lobby, hand-carved antiques in the rooms, indoor swimming pool. Still, it might just be a tad overpriced.

Esterházy Kasthély (☎ 537 640; www.castles.hu /esterhazy; Hadyn utca 2, Fertőd; d 25,000Ft; ☒) June through September you can stay in one of the less ornate rooms in a wing of the Esterházy Palace. When remodelling is complete, rooms will be furnished in period reproductions. A fine courtyard is available for guest use only. Breakfast is not included.

Eating & Drinking

Cézár Pince (☎ 311 337; Hátsókapu 2; mains 480-890Ft; ☉ 11am-11pm) Wooden platters with a variety of wurst and cheese make a good lunch or snack at this cellar restaurant.

Capri Étterem (☎ 311 525; Várkerület 103; mains 550-960Ft; ☉ noon-10pm Mon-Sat; ☒ ☒) Real Italian: the salad bar looks like an antipasto buffet, aubergines and all. After a dish like the *spenótos galuska* (spinach gnocchi) sink into the sumptuous tiramisu.

Papa Joe's Saloon & Steakhouse (☎ 340 933; Várkerület 108; mains 1200-3500Ft; ☉ 11am-midnight Sun-Fri, 11am-2am Sat; ☒) Grilled steaks are the speciality here, clearly. You can watch them being cooked on the open grill in the back. The courtyard is wagon-wheel rustic.

Dömötöri (☎ 506 624; Széchenyi tér 13; cakes 165-265Ft; ☉ 7am-10pm Mon-Thu, 7am-11pm Fri & Sat, 8am-10pm Sun) On sunny afternoons, a long line of people wait for ice-cream-to-go. Inside, the old-world furnishings are quite Victorian; outside white wrought-iron tables on the umbrella-shaded terrace are brighter. Either way, the cakes are great.

If you have a craving for coffee or something stronger, there are several cafés around Fő tér to stop at.

For self-catering head for the **Match** (Várkerület 100) supermarket.

Entertainment

Liszt Ferenc Kulturális Központ (☎ 517 517; Liszt Ferenc tér 1; ☉ 9am-5pm Tue-Fri, 9am-noon Sat for ticket office) A concert hall, a café and exhibition space all rolled into one. The information desk has the latest on classical music and other cultural events in town.

Swing (☎ 06 20 214 8029; Várkerület 15; ☉ 5pm-midnight Sun-Fri, 5pm-2am Sat) Live jazz, country, rock or blues play nightly.

Shopping

Several shops in town sell regional wines. You might try **Natura Vinotéka** (☎ 866 488; Várkerület 59, entrance on Árpád utca; ☉ 9am-5pm Mon-Fri, 9am-1pm Sat), a quaint cellar with attentive owners, or the larger-scale **Soproni Borház** (☎ 510 022; Várkerület 15; ☉ 11am-11pm Tue-Sun), below the Swing nightclub.

Getting There & Away

There are four buses a day to Budapest (2220Ft, four hours), nine to Győr (1160Ft, two hours). Trains to Budapest's Keleti train station (2564Ft, 2½ to 3 hours) depart from Sopron eight times a day, to Győr (802–1282Ft, 1½ hours, 14 daily). To get to Vienna's Südbahnhof the best way is to take the train (€12, 1½ hours, 10 daily). You clear border checks before you get on the train.

LAKE BALATON

At 77km long Lake Balaton is the largest freshwater lake in Europe outside Scandinavia. Take a walk, rent a bike, go for a swim or just relax in a beer garden; this region is all about being outside. Shallow water, sandy beaches and condominiums attract visitors to the southeastern shore where the commercialised towns are pretty characterless. More established towns, trees and rolling hills, deeper water and less sand await on the northwestern shore. Towns on both sides are packed in July and August, and all but deserted December to February. Many facilities such as museums, pensions and restaurants close for the winter.

Balatonfüred is easily accessed from all points; Tihany peninsula is a nature reserve and a village too cute to be true. Keszthely is really the only town that's a town in its own right – apart from year-round lake traffic. Nearby Hévíz is a spa centre with a huge thermal *tó* (lake).

BALATONFÜRED
☎ 87 / pop 13,500
Walking the hillside streets, you catch glimpses of the easy grace that 18th- and 19th-century Balatonfüred (*bal-ah-tahn fuhr-ed*) must have enjoyed. Today many of the old buildings could use a new coat of paint and the renowned curative waters can be taken by prescription only. Stick by the lake, where a tree-filled park leads down to the waterfront, the pier and outdoor cafés. The hotels here are a bit cheaper than those on the neighbouring Tihany peninsula, making this a good base for exploring.

Orientation & Information
The adjacent bus and train stations are on Dobó István utca, 1km from the lake.

The main **Tourinform** (☎ 580 480; www.balaton fured.hu; Petőfi Sándor utca 68; ☉ 9am-8pm Mon-Fri & 9am-6pm Sat & Sun Jun-Sep, 9am-5pm Mon-Fri & 9am-1pm Sat Mar-May & Oct, 9am-5pm Mon-Fri Nov-Feb) is inconveniently located 1km northeast of the centre; a second **Tourinform** branch (☎ 580 480; Széchenyi utca 47; ☉ 9am-5pm Mon-Fri, 9am-1pm Sat May-Sep; 9am-3pm Mon-Fri Oct-Apr) is annoyingly situated about 1.5km to the southwest.
OTP Bank (Petőfi Sándor utca 8)
Post office (Zsigmond utca 14)

Sights & Activities
The park along the central lakeshore, near the ferry pier, is worth a promenade. You can take a one-hour **pleasure cruise** (☎ 342 230; www .balatonihajozas.hu; Mahart ferry pier; adult/child 900/ 600Ft) at 2pm and 4pm daily, May to August. The **disco hajo** (disco boat; ☎ 342 230; www.balaton ihajozas.hu; Mahart ferry pier; 1400Ft), a two-hour cruise with music and drinks available, leaves at 9pm Tuesday through Sunday, June to August. **Kisfaludy Strand** (Aranyhíd sétány; adult/student 260/160Ft; ☉ 9am-10pm mid-Jun–mid-Sep), along the footpath 800m northeast of the pier, is a relatively sandy beach. A good way to explore

HUNGARY

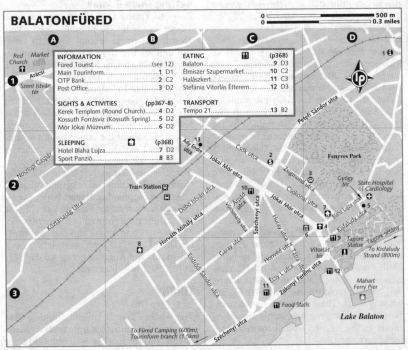

BALATONFÜRED

0 ———— 500 m
0 ———— 0.3 miles

INFORMATION	
Füred Tourist	(see 12)
Main Tourinform	1 D1
OTP Bank	2 C2
Post Office	3 D2

SIGHTS & ACTIVITIES	(pp367-8)
Kerek Templom (Round Church)	4 D2
Kossuth Forrásvíz (Kossuth Spring)	5 D2
Mór Jókai Múzeum	6 D2

SLEEPING	(p368)
Hotel Blaha Lujza	7 D2
Sport Panzió	8 B3

EATING	(p368)
Balaton	9 D3
Élmiszer Szupermarket	10 C2
Halászkert	11 C3
Stefánia Vitorlás Étterem	12 D3

TRANSPORT	
Tempo 21	13 B2

the waterfront is to rent a bike from **Tempo 21** (☎ 480 671; Ady Endre utca 52; per hr/day 350/2400Ft; ⊙ 9am-5pm Mon-Fri, 9am-1pm Sat).

North of the pier, the 1846 **Kerek Templom** (Round Church; cnr Jókai Mór & Honvéd utca) was undergoing renovations at the time of research. **Mór Jókai Múzeum** (☎ 343 426; Honvéd utca 1; adult/child 200/100Ft; ⊙ 10am-6pm Tue-Sun May-Oct) commemorates the life of the acclaimed novelist in what was once his summer house (1871). The heart of the old spa town is Gyógy tér, where **Kossuth Forrásvíz** (Kossuth Spring, 1853) dispenses slightly sulphuric water that people actually drink for health. Don't stray far from a bathroom afterwards.

Sleeping

In peak season (late May to early September) tons of guesthouses and private individuals rent rooms. Tourinform (see Information, above) has a long list of such accommodation on their website, or you might just want to look for signs due south of the train and bus stations on Enrődi Sándor utca.

Ibusz travel agency lists nine pages of private accommodation in the Balaton area on their website (www.ibusz.hu).

Füred Camping (☎ 580 241; Széchenyi utca 24; camp & caravan sites 850-4900Ft, plus per person 625-1350Ft, 2-bedroom bungalows 10,000-25,600Ft; ⊙ Apr–mid-Oct) This sprawling beachfront complex 2½km west of the centre has watersport rentals, swimming pools, tennis courts, a restaurant, a convenience shop and daily programmes. Shall I go on? Not all tent and caravan sites have shade; site price is determined by the size, the month and the number of people.

Sport Panzió (☎ /fax 340720; Horváth Mihály utca 35; s/d 3800/7600Ft; P ⊠) Simple and superior. Request one of the two top-floor rooms for views out onto the lake. Honey-coloured wood is the theme in the bedrooms, restaurant and sauna. One hour on the squash court costs 1900Ft.

Hotel Blaha Lujza (☎ 581 210; www.hotelblaha.hu; Blaha Lujza utca 4; s/d 8100/10,400-11,800Ft; P) Part of this hotel was once the holiday home of the much-loved 19th-century Hungarian actress-singer Blaha Lujza. Her picture, and charming old photos of the lake, grace hallway walls. There's a lot of the contemporary wood and maroon-upholstered furniture in the relatively small rooms, but it looks nice.

Eating

The eastern end of Tagore sétány is a strip of pleasant bars and terraced restaurants. You'll find a plethora of food stalls West along the lake and Zákonyi Ferenc utca.

Halászkert (☎ 343 039; Zákonyi Ferenc utca 3; mains 1000-1500Ft; ⊙ 11am-10pm Apr-Sep; ⊠) Come here for the *korhely halászlé* (drunkard's fish soup) and other freshwater fish dishes.

Balaton (☎ 481 319; Kisfaludy utca 5; mains 1000-2200Ft; ⊙ 11am-11pm; ⊠) In the waterfront park sits a shaded terrace full of rustic tables. This may look like just a beer garden, but Balaton serves a full range of Hungarian specialities. Inside the casual restaurant a dead tree seems to grow out of the floor.

Stéfania Vittorlás Étterem (☎ 343 407; Tagore sétány 1; cakes 110-260Ft; ⊙ 10am-midnight; ⊠) A touristy place with touristy prices but a great lakeside view. Skip the restaurant and enjoy something from the cake and ice-cream shop in the same location instead.

Pack a picnic lunch or dinner with supplies from the **Élmiszer Szupermarket** (Jókai Mór utca 16).

Getting There & Away

Buses to Tihany (174 Ft, 30 minutes) and Veszprém (289Ft, 30 minutes) leave every 15 minutes or so (except at lunch time) throughout the day. For the northwestern lakeshore towns like Keszthely (810Ft, 1½ hours, nine daily) take the bus, since you have to switch in Talpoca with the train.

Budapest-bound buses (1390Ft) depart from Balatonfüred four times daily and take between two and three hours to get there. Trains take about the same amount of time (1282Ft, 12 daily). There are a number of towns on the train line with 'Balaton' or 'Füred' somewhere in their name, so double-check which station you're getting off at.

April to September **Mahart ferries** (☎ 342 230; www.balatonihajozas.hu; Mahart ferry pier) ply the water from Balatonfüred to Tihany (660Ft, 20 minutes) and Siófok (on the southeastern shore; 1200Ft, 55 minutes) eight times a day in July and August, six times a day May to June and in September.

TIHANY

☎ 87 / pop 1200

The whole Tihany peninsula, jutting 5km into Lake Balaton, is a nature reserve. Many people consider this the most beautiful place on the lake, especially in March when the almond trees are in bloom. The unmistakenly quaint village of the same name sits on the eastern side of the peninsula's high plateau. Ceramics, embroidery and other folk-craft stores fill the bucolic village houses. Prices are a bargain compared to Budapest or Szentendre, and everyone knows it. You can easily shake the tourist hordes by going hiking – maybe to the Belső́tó (Inner Lake) or the reedy (and almost dried up) Külső́tó (Outer Lake). Bird-watchers, bring your binoculars: the trails have abundant birdlife.

Orientation & Information

The harbour where ferries to/from Balatonfüred dock is a couple of kilometres downhill from the village of Tihany. Buses pull up in the heart of town, outside the post office on Kossuth Lajos utca.

Tourinform (☎ 448 804; www.tihany.hu; Kossuth Lajos utca 20; ⏰ 9am-7pm Mon-Fri & 9am-6pm Sat & Sun Jun-Aug, 9am-5pm Mon-Fri & 9am-3pm Sat May & Sep, 9am-3pm Mon-Fri Oct-Apr) sells hiking maps and film, as well as providing tourist information.

Sights & Activities

You can spot Tihany's twin-towered **Apátság Templom** (Abbey Church; ☎ 448 405; adult/student 400/200Ft; ⏰ 9am-6pm May-Sep, 10am-5pm Apr & Oct, 10am-3pm Nov-Mar), dating from 1754, from a long way off. Entombed in the church's crypt is the abbey's founder, King Andrew I. The Deed of Foundation for the abbey is the earliest existing document that contains Hungarian words (now stored at the Pannonhalma Abbey archives near Győr; see p361). The admission fee includes entry to the attached **Apátsági Múzeum** (Abbey Museum; ☎ 448 405; ⏰ 9am-6pm May-Sep, 10am-5pm Apr & Oct, 10am-3pm Nov-Mar). The path behind the church leads to outstanding views; it can be quite windy up there.

Follow the pathway along the ridge north from the church in the village and you pass a tiny **szabadtéri néprajzi múzeum** (open-air ethnographical museum; ☎ 714 960; Pisky sétány 10; adult/student 200/100Ft; ⏰ 10am-6pm Tue-Sun May-Sep). It's easy to miss the small cluster of fully outfitted folk houses among all the rest of the old houses that are now shops.

Back at the clearing in front of the church, there's a large hiking map with all the trails marked. Following the green trail northeast of the church for an hour will bring you to an Oroszkút (Russian Well) and the ruins of the Óvár (Old Castle), where the Russian Orthodox monks, brought to Tihany by Andrew I, hollowed out cells in the soft basalt walls.

Sleeping & Eating

This is an easy day trip from Balatonfüred. The place is pretty small, so there's no reason to stay over unless you're hiking. The Tihany Tourinform website, www.tihany .hu, lists almost 50 houses that rent private rooms, or you could look for a *'Zimmer frei'* sign in one of the windows on the small streets north of the church.

Erika Hotel (☎ 448 010; fax 448 646; Batthyány utca 6; r €60; ⏰ May-Sep; P ✕ ⬛) The pink, 16-room inn is right in the centre of the village. The small swimming pool makes for a refreshing surprise; a cocktail from the bar completes the picture.

Stég Pub (☎ 06 70 503 0208; Kossuth Lajos utca 18; mains 750-980Ft; ⏰ 10am-10pm Sun-Thu, 10am-midnight Fri & Sat) Pizzas and salads augment the Hungarian menu at this friendly place. In nice weather, sit in the courtyard.

Of the many touristy eatery options, two have especially good views: the awning-covered back terrace at **Fogas Csárda** (☎ 448 658; Kossuth Lajos utca 9; mains 1450-2400Ft; ⏰ 11am-11pm May-Oct) overlooks the Inner Lake and the peninsula's interior; and the terrace at the **Rege Café** (☎ 448 280; Kossuth Lajos utca 22; cakes 330-520Ft; ⏰ 10am-6pm) where you can peer down on Lake Balaton and the harbour.

Getting There & Away

Buses travel along the 11km of mostly lakefront road between the centre of Tihany village and Balatonfüred's train station (174 Ft, 30 minutes) about 20 times a day. The advantage here is that you don't have to hike up the hill from the harbour, but the bus does stop there too.

Passenger ferries sail between Tihany and Balatonfüred from late April to late October (680Ft, 20 minutes, six to eight daily). The Abbey Church is high above the pier; you can follow a steep path up to the village from there.

KESZTHELY

☎ 83 / pop 21,800

Follow Kossuth Lajos utca, the long pedestrian street in the centre of the old town, and you'll reach the incredible Festetics Palace, built in 1745. Stroll through the beautifully cultivated lakefront park and it's not long before you reach a partying public beach. So whether you're seeking history or sun-worshipping hedonism, Keszthely (*kest*-hay) has at least a little of each. The town lies a little more than 1km northeast of the lake and with the exception of a few guesthouses, almost everything stays open year round.

Orientation & Information

The bus and train stations, side by side at the end of Mártírok útja, are fairly close to the ferry pier. Walk northeast on Kazinczy utca, and you'll see the water off to your right in a few hundred metres. To get to town, turn left and head towards Kossuth Lajos utca.

Tourinform (☎ 314 144; www.keszthely.hu; Kossuth Lajos utca 28; ☺9am-8pm Mon-Fri & 9am-6pm Sat Jul-Aug, 9am-5pm Mon-Fri & 9am-1pm Sat Sep-Jun) doles out information on the whole Lake Balaton area. **Keszthely Tourist** (☎ 312 031; Kossuth Lajos utca 25; ☺9am-5pm Mon-Fri) puts together water-oriented sports and spa packages and represents several private accommodation businesses.

There's a huge OTP Bank facing the park south of the Catholic church on Kossuth Lajos utca and close by is the **main post office** (Kossuth Lajos utca 48).

Sights & Activities

The glimmering white, 100-room **Festetics Kastély** (Festetics Palace; ☎ 312 190; Kastély utca 1; museum adult/student 1200/600Ft; ☺10am-5pm Tue-Sun)

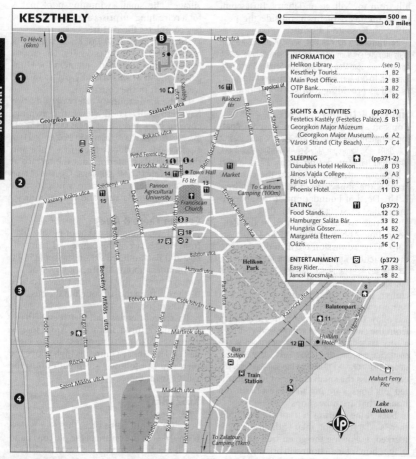

KESZTHELY

0 — 500 m
0 — 0.3 miles

To Hévíz (6km)

Lehel utca

INFORMATION
Helikon Library...............................(see 5)
Keszthely Tourist.................................**1** B2
Main Post Office.................................**2** B3
OTP Bank..**3** B2
Tourinform..**4** B2

SIGHTS & ACTIVITIES (pp370-1)
Festetics Kastély (Festetics Palace)..**5** B1
Georgikon Major Múzeum
    (Georgikon Major Museum)......**6** A2
Városi Strand (City Beach)............**7** C4

SLEEPING (pp371-2)
Danubius Hotel Helikon......................**8** D3
János Vajda College.............................**9** A3
Párizsi Udvar......................................**10** B1
Phoenix Hotel....................................**11** D3

EATING (p372)
Food Stands.......................................**12** C3
Hamburger Saláta Bár.......................**13** B2
Hungária Gösser.................................**14** B2
Margaréta Étterem.............................**15** A2
Oázis..**16** C1

ENTERTAINMENT (p372)
Easy Rider..**17** B3
Jancsi Kocsmája.................................**18** B2

Georgikon utca

Szalasztó utca

Rákóczi tér

Tapolcai út

Bakacs utca

Pethő Ferenc utca

Városház utca

Fő tér

Town Hall

Market

Pannon Agricultural University

Franciscan Church

To Castrum Camping (100m)

Balaton utca

Hunyadi utca

Helikon Park

Eötvös utca

Csók István utca

Balatonpart

Mártírok útja

Hullám Hotel

Bus Station

Train Station

Mahart Ferry Pier

Lake Balaton

To Zalatour Camping (1km)

Georgikon utca

Bercsényi Miklós utca

Vaszary Kolos utca

Deák Ferenc utca

Vak Bottyán utca

Széchenyi utca

Fodor Imre utca

Cifrum utca

Rózsa utca

Szent Miklós utca

Múzeum utca

Kossuth Lajos utca

Festetics út

Római utca

Honvéd utca

Madách utca

Park utca

Kazinczy utca

Erzsébet királyné utca

Bem József utca

Lovassy Sándor utca

Pál utca

Bercsényi Miklós utca

HUNGARY

was first built in 1745; the wings were extended out from the original building 150 years later. About a dozen rooms in the one-time residence have been turned into a museum. Many of the decorative arts in the gilt salons were imported from England in the mid-1800s. If you can, take one of the evening candlelight tours sometimes offered in summer months. The **Helikon Könyvetár** (Helikon Library), in the baroque south wing, is known for its 900,000 volumes and its handcarved furniture, crafted by a local artisan.

In 1797 Count György Festetics, an uncle of the reformer István Széchenyi, founded Europe's first agricultural institute, the Georgikon, here in Keszthely. Part of the original school is now the **Georgikon Major Múzeum** (Georgikon Farm Museum; ☎ 311 563; Bercsényi Miklós utca 67; adult/student 300/150Ft; ⏰ 10am-5pm Tue-Sat, 10am-6pm Sun May-Oct).

The lakefront area centres on the long Mahart pier, which has a small café near the ferry landing at the end. April to September you can take a one-hour **pleasure cruise** (☎ 312 093; www.balatonihajozas.hu; Mahart ferry pier; adult/student 1100/500Ft) on the lake at 1pm and 3pm daily. **Városi Strand** (City Beach; Vásár tér; adult/student 400/270Ft; ⏰ 8.30am-7pm ticket office, gates open to midnight May-Sep) is not far east of the pier, near plenty of beer stands and food booths. There are other beaches you can explore further afield; some hotels have private shore access.

HÉVÍZ

Just 6km northwest of Keszthely is the spa town (pop 4200) of **Hévíz** (www.heviz.hu). People utilised the warm mineral water here for centuries, first for a tannery in the Middle Ages and later for curative purposes (it was developed as a private resort in 1795). One of Europe's largest thermal lakes, the five-hectare **Gyógytó** (Parkerdő; 3 hr/day 900/1600Ft; ⏰ 8.30am-5pm May-Sep, 9am-4pm Oct-Apr), gurgles up in the middle of town. The hot spring is a crater some 40m deep that disgorges up to 80 million litres of warm water a day. The surface temperature here averages 33°C and never drops below 26°C, allowing bathing year-round. Water lilies especially like the temperatures. Cross one of the bridges leading to the pavilion at lake centre to change your clothes. You can rent towels, inner tubes and even swimsuits. Then follow the catwalks and piers that fan out to find the

place where you want to plunge in. Both the water and the bottom mud are slightly radioactive; the minerals are said to alleviate various medical conditions. Don't worry if you feel a pain in your knee after your visit that you didn't have before; that's the impurities leaving your joint.

To get there take the bus from Keszthely station (127Ft, 15 minutes, every 15 to 30 minutes). The lake park is across Deák tér from the Hévíz bus station. Walk right around the park to get to the closest year-round entrance in the east.

Sleeping

Like most summer-oriented tourist destinations, prices vary dramatically depending on the month. Private rooms can cost a bit more here than in the nonresort areas of Hungary (doubles from €35); **Keszthely Tourist** (☎ 312 031; Kossuth Lajos utca 25; ⏰ 9am-5pm Mon-Fri) represents several private lodgings and apartment houses.

Zalatour Camping (☎ 312782; kesztcamo@zalaszam .hu; Ernszt Géza sétány; camp & caravan sites 1450-2400Ft; bungalows 3000-4200Ft, apartments 7900-9300Ft; ⏰ mid-Apr–mid-Oct; Ⓟ ⓡ) About 1km south of town, this waterfront camp has access to a rocky shore and a somewhat reedy beach. The apartments are a bit nicer than the bungalows (both sleep up to four). Don't come here for quiet; facilities include a restaurant, late-night bar, gift shop, sauna and sun beds, and a dog kennel in addition to sports stuff.

János Vajda College (☎ 311361; Gagarin utca 4; dm 1600-3000Ft) This student dorm is open to all from July to August.

Phoenix Hotel (☎ 312 631; Balatonpart 4; s/d 5500-7300/7000-8800Ft; Ⓟ) This is as close as you can get to the water for as little money as you can spend if you're not camping. The low-lying wood building is in a shady grove of trees at the edge of the lakefront park. Bike rental is only 300Ft for an hour and 900Ft for the day.

Danubius Hotel Helikon (☎ 889 600; www.danu biushotels.com/helikon; Balatonpart 5; s/d €25-77/40-106; Ⓟ ⓧ ⓚ ⌨ ⓡ) This full-scale resort looks pretty plain-Jane from the outside, but the rooms have all been redone in sea blues and light wood. Glass doors on the wedge-shape patios manoeuvre so there is nothing but air between you and your lake view. A bridge from the hotel leads to a private little beach island with water-sport rentals.

Párizsi Udvar (☎ 311 202; www.hotels.hu/parizsi
_udvar; Kastély utca 5; d/tr 7900-9900/9600-12,600Ft,
4-bed/5-bed r 13,000-15,000/13,500-15,600Ft) Large
basic rooms share kitchen facilities in what
was once part of the Festetics Kastély complex. The central courtyard adds to the quiet
of the place.

Eating

Open-air, self-service restaurant stands
and bars line the trail between Kazinczky
utca and the waterfront, west of the ferry
pier. You can get a *lángos* snack (deep-fried
dough with assorted toppings) or go for a
full meal of goulash soup and a fried-fish
main. In summer, places open between
8am and 10am and close at 10pm or later.
Off-season hours vary but there's generally something open from 10am to 8pm.
In town, Kossuth Lajos utca has a number
of pavement cafés in the pedestrian area.
There are a number of small grocery shops
just south on the same street.

Hamburger Saláta Bár (Erzsébet királyné utca at
Jókai utca; breakfast 220-290, burgers 330-450Ft; ✆ 7am-
9pm) Marinated salads are also on offer at
this small fast-food joint.

Oázis (☎ 311 023; Rákóczi tér 3; lunches 430-520Ft;
✆ 11am-4pm Mon-Fri; ✗) A rare vegetarian eatery; the small menu changes daily. It's not
gourmet, but there is broccoli – sometimes.

Margaréta Étterem (☎ 314 882; Bercsényi Miklós
út 60; mains 600-1240Ft; ✆ 11am-10pm; ✗) Locals
come for the good Hungarian food and
the casual, convivial vibe. Everyone here
is friendly. The patio with red-chequered
tablecloths is cheery too.

Hungária Gösser (☎ 312 265; Kossuth Lajos utca 35;
1390-1990Ft; ✆ 10am-10pm; ✗ ✗) You might try
the goose liver or order a steak at the slightly
upscale Gösser. The menu includes Germanic and Hungarian specialities. Stained-
glass windows filter the light entering the
lovely old building on the main square.

Entertainment

Numerous cultural performances take place
during the Balatonfest in May, and the Dance
Festival in September. Tourinform has more
info on events throughout the year.

Besides the waterfront bar stands, Kossuth Lajos utca is where to look for pubs;
Jancsi Kocsmája (Kossuth Lajos utca 46; ✆ noon-
midnight Mon-Fri, 6pm-midnight Sat & Sun) is the most
fun – mostly filled with young people, tin

advertising signs hanging on the wall. **Easy
Rider** (☎ 319 842; Kossuth Lajos utca 79; ✆ 10am-10pm
Sun-Thu, 10am-4am Fri & Sat) turns into a disco at
about 10pm on weekends.

Getting There & Away

Buses to Hévíz (127Ft, 15 minutes) leave at
least every 30 minutes during the day. Other
towns served by buses include Badacsony
(347Ft, 30 minutes, six daily), Veszprém
(1040Ft, two hours, 12 daily), Balatonfüred
(810Ft, 1½ hours, seven daily) and Budapest (2780Ft, three hours, six daily).

Keszthely is on a branch rail line linking
the lake's southeastern shore with Budapest
(2324Ft, three hours, eight daily). To reach
towns along Lake Balaton's northern shore
by train, you have to change at Tapolca.

April to September, Mahart ferries link
Keszthely with Badacsonytomaj (1200Ft,
two hours, one to three daily) and other,
smaller lake towns.

SOUTH CENTRAL HUNGARY

Southern Hungary has a distinctly eastern
feel to it, especially compared to areas near
Austria (and Habsburg influence). Croatia
and Serbia and Montenegro (parts of which
were once in Hungary) are close by, and
it's here that the historical remnants of the
150-year Turkish occupation can be most
strongly felt. In the Danube village of Mohács, the Hungarian army under King Lajos
II was routed by a vastly superior Ottoman
force in 1526.

The region is bounded by the Danube River
to the east, the Dráva River to the south and
west, and Lake Balaton to the north. Generally flat, the Mecsek and Villány Hills rise
up in isolation from the plain. The weather
always seems to be a few degrees warmer
here than in other parts of the country: the
sunny clime is great for grape growing and
oak-aged Villány reds are well regarded, if
highly tannic.

PÉCS

☎ 72 / pop 158,900

In Pécs (pronounced paich), near the
southern border of Hungary, the Turks left
their greatest monuments from 150 years

of occupation. These, together with imposing churches, a lovely synagogue, and more than a dozen museums, make Pécs one of the nation's most interesting larger cities. Green parks and great hiking in the Mecsek Hills only add to the appeal. Harkány is a nearby spa town that is an easy day trip.

History has far from ignored Pécs. The Roman settlement of Sopianae on this site was the capital of the province of Lower Pannonia for 400 years. Christianity flourished here in the 4th century and by the 9th century the town was known as Quinque Ecclesiae for its five churches (it's still called Fünfkirchen in German). In 1009 Stephen I made Pécs a bishopric. The first Hungarian university was founded here in the mid-14th century. City walls were erected after the Mongol invasion of 1241, but 1543 marked the start of almost a century and a half of Turkish domination. After the Ottomans were kicked out, the town was almost deserted and it took several centuries to establish a commercial centre once again. In the 19th century the manufacture of Zsolnay porcelain and other goods, such as Pannonia sparkling wine, helped put Pécs back on the map.

Orientation & Information

The train station is a little more than 1km south of the old town centre. Take bus No 30 for two long stops from the station to Kossuth tér to reach the centre, or you can walk up Jókai Mór utca. The bus station is a few blocks closer, next to the market. Follow Bajcsy-Zsilinszky utca north.

Tourinform (☎ 213 315; www.pecs.hu; Széchenyi tér 9; 8am-5.30pm Mon-Fri, 9am-4pm Sat May-Sep, 8am-4pm Mon-Fri Sep-Mar) has **Internet access** (per hr 100Ft) and tons of local info, including a list of museums. The **main post office** (Jókai Mór utca 10) is in a beautiful Art Nouveau building (1904) with a colourful Zsolnay porcelain roof. There are plenty of banks and ATMs scattered around town. **Ibusz** (☎ 212 157; Apáca utca 1; r per person 2540Ft; 8am-5pm Mon-Fri, 8am-2pm Sat) travel agency has a currency exchange booth, rents private rooms and books transportation tickets.

Sights & Activities

The sight of the huge mosque – which dominates the city's central square, Széchenyi tér – is really quite striking. The **Mecset Templom** (Mosque Church; ☎ 321 976; Széchenyi tér; admission free; 10am-4pm Mon-Sat, 11.30am-4pm Sun mid-Apr–mid-Oct, 10am-noon Mon-Sat, 11.30am-2pm Sun mid-Oct–mid-Apr), as it's commonly known, has long since gone Christian, but the Islamic elements inside, such as the *mihrab* (prayer niche) on the southeastern wall, are easy to spot. Constructed in the mid-16th century from the stones of an earlier church, the mosque underwent several appearance changes through the years – including the addition of a steeple and siding. In the late 1930s the building was restored to its medieval form.

East along Ferencesek utca at No 35, you'll pass the ruins of the 16th-century, Turkish **Memi Pasa Fürdője** (Pasa Memi Bath) before you turn south on Rákóczi út to get to the **Hassan Jakovali Mecset** (Mosque; ☎ 313 853; Rákóczi út 2; adult/student 140/80Ft; 10am-1.30pm & 2-6pm Thu-Tue Apr-Sep), c 1540. Though wedged between two modern buildings, this smaller mosque is more intact than the larger and comes complete with a minaret. A small museum of Ottoman history is inside.

North of Széchenyi tér, the minor **Régészeti Múzeum** (Archaeology Museum; ☎ 312 719; Széchenyi tér 12; adult/student 300/150Ft; 10am-4pm Tue-Sun Apr-Oct) contains Roman artefacts found in the area. From here, climb Szepessy Ignéc utca and turn west (left) on Káptalan utca, which is a street lined with museums. **Zsolnay Porcélan Múzeum** (☎ 324 822; Káptalan utca 2; adult/student 700/350Ft; 10am-4pm Apr-Oct Tue-Sun) is on the eastern end of this strip. English translations provide a good history of the artistic and functional ceramics produced from this local factory's illustrious early days in the mid-19th century to the present.

Continue west to Dóm tér and the walled bishopric complex containing the four-towered **Szent Péter Bazilika** (☎ 513 030; Dóm tér; complex ticket adult/student 1000/500Ft; 9am-5pm Mon-Sat, 1-5pm Sun). The oldest part of the building is the 11th-century crypt. The 1770 **Püspöki Palota** (Bishop's Palace; 2-5pm late Jun-Aug) stands in front of the cathedral, and a 15th-century **barbakán** (barbican), is the only stone bastion to survive from the old city walls.

The early Christian cemeteries from the Roman town of Sopianae became part of the Unesco World Heritage List in 2000. An excavated 4th-century **Ókeresztény Mauzóleum** (Christian Mausoleum; ☎ 312 7190; Szent István tér 12; adult/student 350/200Ft; 10am-4pm Tue-Sun Apr-Oct) has striking frescoes of Adam and Eve, and Daniel in the lion's den. The

HUNGARY

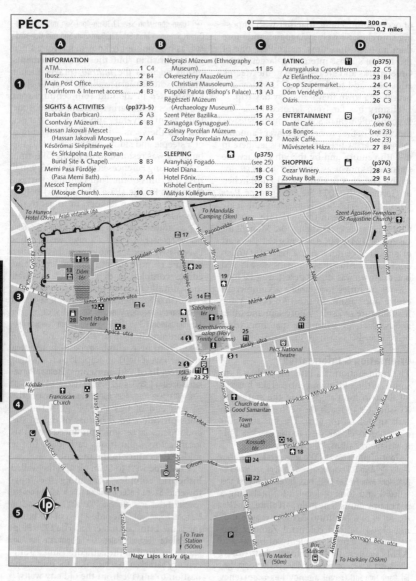

PÉCS

0 — 300 m
0 — 0.2 miles

INFORMATION	
ATM	**1** C4
Ibusz	**2** B4
Main Post Office	**3** B5
Tourinform & Internet access	**4** B3

SIGHTS & ACTIVITIES	(pp373-5)
Barbakán (barbican)	**5** A3
Csontváry Múzeum	**6** B3
Hassan Jakovali Mescet	
(Hassan Jakovali Mosque)	**7** A4
Késörómai Sírépítmények	
és Sírkápolna (Late Roman	
Burial Site & Chapel)	**8** B3
Memi Pasa Fürdöje	
(Pasa Memi Bath)	**9** A4
Mescet Templom	
(Mosque Church)	**10** C3

Néprajzi Múzeum (Ethnography	
Museum)	**11** B5
Ókeresztény Mauzóleum	
(Christian Mausoleum)	**12** A3
Püspöki Palota (Bishop's Palace)	**13** A3
Régészeti Múzeum	
(Archaeology Museum)	**14** B3
Szent Péter Bazilika	**15** A3
Zsinagóga (Synagogue)	**16** C4
Zsolnay Porcélan Múzeum	
(Zsolnay Porcelain Museum)	**17** B2

SLEEPING	(p375)
Aranyhajó Fogadó	(see 25)
Hotel Diana	**18** C4
Hotel Fönix	**19** C3
Kishotel Centrum	**20** B3
Mátyás Kollégium	**21** B3

EATING	(p375)
Aranygaluska Gyorsétterem	**22** C5
Az Elefánthoz	**23** B4
Co-op Szupermarket	**24** C4
Dóm Vendéglö	**25** C3
Oázis	**26** C3

ENTERTAINMENT	(p376)
Dante Café	(see 6)
Los Bongos	(see 23)
Mozik Caffé	(see 23)
Müvészetek Háza	**27** B4

SHOPPING	(p376)
Cezar Winery	**28** A3
Zsolnay Bolt	**29** B4

Késörómai Sírépítmények és Sírkápolna (Late Roman Burial Site & Chapel; Apáca utca 8 & 14 adult/student 350/200Ft; 10am-4pm Tue-Sun Apr-Oct) is also richly decorated.

East of the Christian tombs is the **Csontváry Múzeum** (310 544; Janus Pannonius utca 11; adult/student 600/300Ft; 10am-4pm Tue-Sun Apr-Oct), displaying the work of the incomparable painter

Tivadar Kosztka Csontváry (1853–1919). He is known for his pastoral paintings of life on the *puszta*, but he did some impressive early town scenes as well.

Pécs' beautifully preserved 1869 **zsinagóga** (synagogue; 315 881; Kossuth tér; adult/child 200/100Ft; 10am-5pm Sun-Fri May-Oct) is south of Széchenyi tér.

Not too far from the Hassan Jakovali Mosque, the **Néprajzi Múzeum** (Ethnography Museum; ☎ 315 629; Rákóczi út 15; adult/student 350/200Ft; ⏰ 10am-4pm Tue-Sun Apr-Oct) has a rich collection of folk costumes and old photos from Hungarian and South Slav villages in the area.

Sleeping
BUDGET
Ibusz (☎ 212 157; Apáca utca 1; ⏰ 8am-5pm Mon-Fri, 8am-2pm Sat) arranges private rooms for 2540Ft per person.

Mandulás Camping (☎ 515 655; Ángyán János utca 2; camp sites per person 1200Ft, motel r 3200Ft, hotel r 5800Ft; ⏰ May-Oct) Take bus No 33 or 34 from the centre 3km up into the Mecsek Hills.

Mátyás Kollégium (☎ 312 888; Széchenyi tér 11; dm/d/tr 1400/4000/6000Ft; ☒) In July and August the college opens up its dormitory to travellers.

MID-RANGE
Kishotel Centrum (☎ 311 707; Szepessy Ignác utca 4; s/d/tr 4500/5800/8750Ft) Paintings cover just about every inch of wall space, bric-a-brac decorates shelves and the furniture is mix-and-match: it's just like staying at a Hungarian *nagymama* (grandma's) house. The central hall on the ground floor has a small fridge and a hot plate you can borrow, but there aren't many other facilities.

Hotel Fönix (☎ 311 680; www.fonixhotel.hu; Hunyadi János út 2; s/d 5290/7990-9490Ft) Odd angles and sloping eaves characterise the asymmetrical Hotel Fönix. Rooms show a bit of wear, so this is second choice to the Diana.

Hotel Diana (☎ 328 594; www.dianahotel.hu, Hungarian only; Tímár utca 4A; s/d 7000/10,000Ft; ☒) The small, immaculate hotel near the synagogue has rustic accents like split-wood chair rails in the guest and breakfast rooms. A four-bed room goes for 13,600Ft. Double room No 5 has a great skylight that opens.

TOP END
Aranyhajó Fogadó (☎ 310 263; www.hotels.hu/arany hajo_pecs; Király utca 3; s/d €48/64-85; P ☒ ☐) A fresh coat of salmon-coloured paint really brightens up this 16th-century building on the main pedestrian street. Rooms are traditionally furnished – not exactly antiques, not exactly modern. The friendly young staff at the desk genuinely make you feel like they want you to come back. You can even order room service here.

Eating
Pubs, cafés and fast-food eateries line pedestrian Király utca.

Aranygaluska Gyorsétterem (☎ 310 210; Irgalmasok utca 4; mains 430-640Ft; ⏰ 7.30am-8pm Mon-Fri, 7.30am-5pm Sat & Sun; ☒) Cafeteria meals here are the best deal in town. Office workers know it too; the place is packed at lunch. The Hungarian staples are served up in large portion; *töltöt paprika* (stuffed peppers) alone makes a filling meal.

Oázis (☎ 215 367; Király utca 17; mains 500-1000Ft; ⏰ 10am-11pm) Unlike at most of the kebab stands across Hungary, the owner at this take-away actually hails from the Middle East. You can taste the difference. There's a little counter space if you want to eat inside.

Az Elefánthoz (☎ 216 055; Jókai tér 6; mains 1100-2000Ft; ⏰ 11am-11pm; ☒ ☒) An unatmospheric Italian restaurant serves really good soups, pastas and pizzas. Salads, like the tuna and onions on lettuce, are entrée-sized. The non-smoking section is only three booths.

Dóm Vendéglö (☎ 210 088; Király utca 3; mains 1300-2500Ft; ⏰ noon-11pm; ☒ ☒) If you like meat, Dóm Vendéglö is for you. Beef, venison, pork, turkey and duck – take your pick. The dining room looks like a hollow wooden church or castle and the smoking section is on the upper floor of the church structure. Enter at the rear of the courtyard under the Aranyhajó Fogadó hotel.

The Co-op Szupermarket is at the corner of Irgalmasok and Timár utcas.

Entertainment
Pécs has well-established opera and ballet companies as well as a symphony. **Tourinform** (☎ 213 315; www.pecs.hu; Széchenyi tér 9; ⏰ 8am-5.30pm Mon-Fri, 9am-4pm Sat May-Sep, 8am-4pm Mon-Fri Sep-Mar) has schedule information. The free biweekly *Pécsi Est* lists what's on at nightclubs and at the cinema.

Müvészetek Háza (☎ 315 388; Széchenyi tér 7-8) The Artists' House is a cultural venue that hosts classical musical performances. A schedule is posted outside.

Los Bongos (☎ 06 20 468 9491; Jókai tér 6; 390-550Ft; ⏰ 6pm-2am Mon-Sat) Fridays are a Latin fiesta, but every night sizzles. This nightclub is on the floor above Az Elefánthoz restaurant and Mozik Caffé.

Mozik Caffé (☎ 215 026; Jókai tér 6; ⏰ 9am-midnight) A more relaxed place to imbibe your beverage of choice than the nightclub

HUNGARY

above. Outdoor café tables reach far into the pedestrian square.

Dante Café (☎ 210 361; Janus Pannonius utca 11; ⏰ 10am-1am) An intellectual and student crowd gathers on the ground floor below the Csontváry Museum. Live jazz and other music plays Thursday through Saturday.

Shopping

Cezar Winery (☎ 214 490; Szent István tér 12; ⏰ 9am-5.30pm Mon-Fri) This building is where the family of Janos Pannonius made sparkling wine from 1859 to 1995. You can still buy Pannonia *pezsgő* (champagne), under new owners, in the on-site shop and view the production facilities through glass walls.

A number of *régiség* (antique stores) in town have old Zsolnay porcelain decorative art pieces for sale, and you can buy a set of today's china at the **Zsolnay Bolt** (☎ 310 172; Jókai tér 2; ⏰ 10am-4pm Tue-Sun).

Getting There & Away

Buses for Harkány (347Ft, 40 minutes) leave every 15 minutes throughout the day. At least four buses a day connect Pécs with Budapest (2660Ft, 4½ hours), two with Keszthely (1740Ft, three hours) and eight with Szeged (2310Ft, four hours).

Pécs is on a main rail line with Budapest's Déli train station (2610Ft, 2½ hours, eight daily). One daily train runs from Pécs (8.40pm) to Osijek (1880Ft, two hours) in Horvátország (Croatia).

AROUND PÉCS

Harkány

The hot springs at **Harkány** (www.harkany.hu, no English), 26km south of Pécs, have medicinal waters with the richest sulphuric content in Hungary. The indoor and outdoor baths and pools of the **Gyógyfürdő** (☎ 480 251; www.harkanyfurdo.hu; Kossuth Lajos utca 7; adult/student 1500/850Ft; ⏰ 9am-10pm mid-Jun–Aug, 9am-8pm Sun-Thu & 9am-10pm Fri & Sat Sep–mid-Jun) range in temperature from 26°C to 33°C in summer and from 33°C to 35°C in winter. You might consider booking a spa service, mud bath or massage. The town is basically the thermal bath complex in a 12-hectare park surrounded by holiday hotels and restaurants. Buses between Harkány and Pécs (347Ft, 40 minutes) depart frequently, about every 15 minutes. The Harkány bus station is at the southeast corner of the park.

SOUTHEASTERN HUNGARY

Where the Tisza River drainage basin meets the wide expanse of level *puszta* (prairie or steppe), so begins the Nagyalföld (Great Plain) of myth and legend. For centuries this area, its horsemen and shepherds have represented the Hungarian ethos in poems, songs, paintings and stories. Much of the *alföld* has been turned into farmland for growing apricots and raising geese, but other parts are little more than grassy, saline deserts sprouting juniper trees. Kiskunság National Park, including the Bugac Puszta, protects this unique environment.

KECSKEMÉT

☎ 76 / pop 108,181

Located about halfway between Budapest and Szeged, Kecskemét (*Kech*-kah-mate) is a green, pedestrian-friendly city with interesting Art Nouveau architecture. Claims to fame include the locally produced *barack* (apricot) jam and *pálinka* (potent brandy), *libamaj* (goose liver) dishes, and the nearby Kiskunság National Park and horse farms.

Orientation & Information

Central Kecskemét is made up of squares that run into one another and consequently it's hard to distinguish between. The main bus and train stations are opposite each other in József Katona Park. A 10-minute walk southwest along Nagykőrösi utca brings you to the first of the squares, Szabadság tér.

Tourinform (☎ 481 065; www.kecskemet.hu; Kossuth tér 1; ⏰ 8am-5pm Mon-Fri, 9am-1pm Sat Jul-Aug) is in the northeastern corner of the large Town Hall. They can also help you with information about Kiskunság National Park. The **OTP Bank** (Szabadság tér 1/A) is central, does foreign exchange, and has an ATM. The **main post office** (Kálvin tér 10) is to the southeast. Surf the web at **Piramis Internet Café** (☎ 418 134; Csányi utca 1-3; per hour 540Ft; ⏰ 10am-8pm Mon-Fri, 1-8pm Sat & Sun), upstairs in the courtyard of a small shopping mall.

Sights

Walk around the parklike squares, starting at Szabadság tér and admire the eclectic building styles, including the technicolour

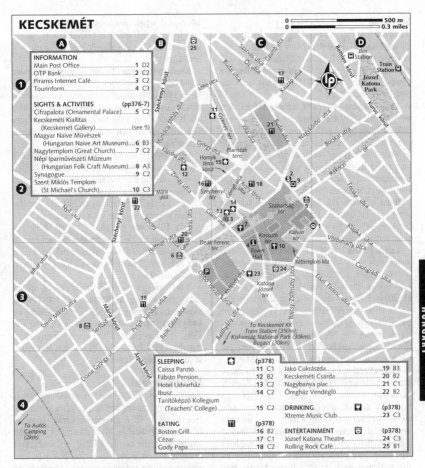

KECSKEMÉT

0   500 m
0   0.3 miles

INFORMATION
Main Post Office...................1 D2
OTP Bank..............................2 C2
Piramis Internet Café..............3 C2
Tourinform............................4 C3

SIGHTS & ACTIVITIES (pp376-7)
Cifrapalota (Ornamental Palace)......5 C2
Kecskeméti Kiallitas
  (Kecskemét Gallery).................(see 5)
Magyar Naive Müvészek
  (Hungarian Naive Art Museum)....6 B3
Nagytemplom (Great Church).........7 C2
Népi Iparmüvészeti Múzeum
  (Hungarian Folk Craft Museum)....8 A3
Synagogue..............................9 C2
Szent Miklós Templom
  (St Michael's Church)..............10 C3

SLEEPING (p378)
Caissa Panzió...........................11 C1
Fábián Pension........................12 B2
Hotel Udvarház.......................13 C2
Ibusz.....................................14 C2
Tanítóképző Kollegium
  (Teachers' College)................15 C2

EATING (p378)
Boston Grill.............................16 B2
Cézar.....................................17 C2
Gody Papa..............................18 C2

Jako Cukrászda........................19 B3
Kecskeméti Csárda...................20 B2
Nagybanya piac.......................21 C1
Öregház Vendéglő....................22 B2

DRINKING (p378)
Xtreme Music Club...................23 C3

ENTERTAINMENT (p378)
József Katona Theatre...............24 C3
Rolling Rock Café.....................25 B1

To Autós
Camping
(2km)

To Kecskemét KK
Train Station (350m);
Kiskunság National Park (30km);
Bugacs (30km)

HUNGARY

Art Nouveau of the **Cifrapalota** (Ornamental Palace; Rákóczi út 1). At the time of research the building was being restored, with the completion date as yet unknown, but check out the impressive interiors by touring the **Kecskeméti Kiallitas** (Kecskemét Gallery; ☎ 480 776) when the building reopens. Across the street, the Moorish building is the former **synagogue** (Rákóczi út 2), now an office building and exhibit hall called the House of Technology.

Kossuth tér is dominated by the massive Art Nouveau **Városháza** (Town Hall, 1897), which is flanked by the baroque **Nagytemplom** (Great Church, 1806) and the earlier **Szent Miklós Templom** (St Michael's Church), dating from the 13th century. Nearby is the magnificent 1896 **József Katona Színház** (Katona

József tér 5), a neobaroque theatre with a statue of the Trinity (1742) in front of it.

The town's museums are scattered around the main squares' periphery. Go first to the **Magyar Naive Müvészek** (Hungarian Naive Art Museum; ☎ 324 767; Gáspár András utca 11; adult/student 150/50Ft; ☯ 10am-5pm Tue-Sun), in the Stork House (1730) northwest off Petőfi Sándor utca. It has an impressive small collection; the folk themes are especially noteworthy. Further to the southwest, the **Népi Iparmüvészeti Múzeum** (Hungarian Folk Craft Museum; ☎ 327 203; Serfőző utca 19a; adult/student 200/100Ft; ☯ 10am-5pm Tue-Sun) has a definitive collection of regional embroidery, weaving and textiles, as well some furniture, woodcarving and agricultural tools. A few handicrafts are for sale at the entrance.

Sleeping

Tourinform (p376) can help you locate the numerous colleges that offer dormitory accommodation in July and August; one good choice is the central **Tanítóképzö Kollégium** (Teachers' College; ☎ 486 977; Piaristák tere 4; dm students/adults 1600Ft/2000Ft).

Autós Camping (☎ 329 398; Csabai Géza körút 5; camp site 1/2 people 1350/2100Ft, caravan site 2200Ft, bungalows 5400Ft; ✆ Apr-Oct) As the name implies, this place is more vehicle- than tent- camping oriented, with big treeless plots. Don't be surprised if it's jammed with caravans and Germanic speakers. Take bus No 1 to get southwest of town.

Ibusz (☎ 486 955; Kossuth tér 3; ✆ 8am-5pm Mon-Fri Sep-Jun, 9am-1pm Sat Jul-Aug) travel agency brokers private rooms from 2000Ft per person, with a four-night minimum.

Caissa Panzió (☎ 481 685; www.caissachessbooks.com; Gyenes tér 18, 4th fl; s 3900-6900Ft, d 4900-8900Ft, tr 8300-10,300Ft, q 9700-11,700Ft) Rooms on several floors in an apartment block provide a slightly cheaper, shabby-chic alternative – some with shared bathrooms. The manager publishes chess manuals and sponsors tournaments in the big lounge on the ground floor. There's no breakfast, but you can ask for a key and share the kitchen facilities.

Fábián Pension (☎ 477 677; www.hotels.hu/fabian; Kápolna utca 14; s/d 6900/7000-8900Ft; ✖ ✖) A truly fabulous, family-run place. Clean rooms have TV and minibar. Homemade jam and sweets are served along with your cold cuts and bread at breakfast. Rooms look out at a flower-full courtyard. Mum and daughter will help you plan an independent trip to the national park or to a horse farm; they also rent bicycles.

Hotel Udvarház (☎ 413 912; Csányi utca 1-3; s/d/tr 11,900/14,500/17,500Ft; Ⓟ ✖) Curvilinear blonde and turquoise wood furnishings define the contemporary style of this hotel on the first floor above a shopping arcade (across from Piramis Internet Café). A few rooms have air-con; ask first if this is important to you.

Eating

Öregház Vendéglö (☎ 496 973; Kölcsey utca 3; mains 600-1000Ft; ✆ 11am-10pm; ✖) For a tasty, meat-oriented Hungarian meal like *cigany pecsenye* (literally 'gypsy's roast'; a mixed grill with tender cutlets of pork and chicken, a piece of bacon and a sausage) join the tables of friends and families gathered here.

Blue-and-white *kékfestö* (indigo dyed) tablecloths and curtains make the place homy and it's completely nonsmoking – a real rarity.

Kecskeméti Csárda (☎ 488 686; Kölcsey utca 7; mains 1290-1990Ft; ✆ 11am-11pm; ✖) This is what a stereotypical Hungarian country inn *(csárda)* restaurant looks like – Gypsy musician and all. It may seem a bit touristy, but it's where residents go to celebrate special occasions. There's courtyard dining.

Cézar (☎ 328 849; Kaszap utca 4; mains 1300-2350Ft; ✆ 12-3pm & 6-11pm Tue-Sun; ✖) A genuine Italian chef cooks at this rustic Italian restaurant, so the tables are always choc full of appreciative locals. Vegetarians might opt for the grilled vegetable plate with aubergines.

Jako Cukrászda (☎ 505 949; Petöfi Sándor utca 7; cakes 110-265Ft; ✆ 7am-7pm Mon-Fri, 9am-7pm Sat & Sun) A multitude of cakes, puddings and strudels tempt from behind a long, modern glass-and-chrome case.

You can get some decent, cheap, quick eats and a beer at **Boston Grill** (☎ 484 444; Kápolna utca 2; burgers 320-550Ft; ✆ 11am-10pm) or **Gody Papa** (☎ 415 515; Arany János utca 3; pizzas 330-550Ft; ✆ 11am-11pm). The open-air market, **Nagybani Piac** (Budai utca; ✆ 7am-1pm Mon-Sat) is south of Erdösi Imre út.

Entertainment

Tourinform has a list of what concerts and performances are on, or check out the free *Kecskeméti Est* (www.est.hu, Hungarian only) available at restaurants around town. Nightlife can be a little dull weekdays outside the summer months, but you can always enjoy a coffee or a glass of wine from one of the cafés on Kossuth tér and watch the people go by.

József Katona Theatre (☎ 483 283; Katona József tér) See operettas and symphony performances in a 19th-century building.

Rolling Rock Café (☎ 506 190; Jókai utca 44; ✆ noon-5am Thu-Sat, noon-midnight Tue-Wed) The coolest place in town for live music and an adult beverage has a big, glowing green Rolling Rock beer bottle at the rear.

Xtreme Music Club (☎ 500 927; Kisfaludy utca 4; ✆ 5pm-2am Tue-Sat) College students from the area go clubbing here at weekends.

Getting There & Away

Frequent buses depart for Budapest (1040Ft, two hours, every 40 minutes) and for Szeged (1040Ft, two hours, hourly). A direct rail line links Budapest's Nyugati station with Kecskemét (1094Ft, 1½ hours, 12 daily) and Kecskemét with Szeged (1844Ft, 1¼ hours, hourly except at lunch time).

KISKUNSÁG NATIONAL PARK

Totalling 76,000 hectares, **Kiskunsági Nemzeti Park** (www.knp.hu) consists of half a dozen 'islands' of protected land. Much of the park's alkaline ponds, dunes and grassy 'deserts' with juniper trees are off limits. **Bugac** (*Boo*-gats) village, about 30km southwest of Kecskemét, is the most accessible part of the park. Here you can see the famous Hungarian cowboys ride at a daily horse show from May to October. The rest of the year, ask at the Kecskemét Tourinform to see if they know of a tour group you might join.

The company that owns **Bugaci Karikás Csárda** (☎ 575-1212; Nagybugac 135; mains 1200-2500Ft; 11am-11pm) restaurant runs the **horse show** (adult/student 1000/500Ft; ☑ 1.15pm May-Oct), which is the main attraction in the village. You can take a **wagon ride** (1000Ft; ☑ 12.15pm May-Oct) to go the few kilometres to the **Pásztor Múzeum** (Shepherd Museum; admission free; ☑ 10am-5pm May-Oct) first or just walk down the sand road to the staging ring. Once the show starts, the horse herders crack their whips, race one another bareback and ride 'five-in-hand', a breathtaking performance in which one *csikós* (cowboy) gallops five horses at full speed while standing on the backs of the rear two. And of course you can always stop for some wine and Gypsy music in the *csárda* afterwards.

The best way to get to Bugac is by bus from Kecskemét (245Ft). The 11am bus from the main terminal gets you to the park entrance around noon. Another option is to take the narrow-gauge train (312Ft) from the Kecskemét KK train station (south of the town centre) to the Móricgát stop (two after the Bugac stop) and walk across the field towards the conical-shaped roof of the Shepherd Museum. Departures are at 8am, 2.10pm and 7.50pm daily. After the show, the first bus back to Kecskemét passes by the park entrance at 5.15pm on weekdays, and 6.35pm on weekends (a change at Jakabszállás is required for the last one). The return train departs from Móricgát at 6.04pm and 11.54pm.

SZEGED

☎ 62 / pop 175,500

Szeged (*seh*-ged), a lively college town on the southern Great Plain, straddles the Tisza River just before Serbia and Montenegro. The Maros River from Romania enters the Tisza just east of the centre. With all that water around, flooding is not uncommon. Much of the old town is architecturally homogeneous, as it was rebuilt after the disastrous 1879 flood destroyed large parts of the city. A highlight is the many ornate and colourful one-time palaces that now contain businesses or house several families. Two worldwide exports are produced locally: Pick salami and Szegedi paprika.

Orientation & Information

The train station is south of the city centre on Indóház tér; tram No 1 rides from it along Boldogasszony sugárút into to the centre of town (five stops to Széchenyi tér). The bus station, on Mars tér, is to the west of the centre and is within easy walking distance via pedestrian Mikszáth Kálmán utca.

The **Tourinform** (☎ 488 690; Dugonics tér 2; ☑ 9am-5pm Mon-Fri) office is hidden in a courtyard. **Matrix Café** (☎ 423 830; Kárász utca 5; per hr 500Ft; ☑ 24hr) has dozens of Internet terminals and just as many for game-addict use only.

Main post office (Széchenyi tér 1)

OTP Bank (Klauzál tér 4)

Sights & Activities

East of Széchenyi tér, the huge, neoclassical **Móra Ferenc Múzeum** (☎ 549 040; Várkert; adult/student 400/200Ft; ☑ 10am-5pm Tue-Sun) peers down on the Tisza River. There are interesting exhibits on the Avar people (5th to 8th centuries) who lived in the area, on the area's folk life and art, as well as a room dedicated to the 1879 flood. North of the museum is a long, waterview park with walking paths and playground equipment.

Another good place to stroll is through the green, parklike Széchenyi tér and south along the main pedestrian boulevard, Kárász utca, where you might stop at a pavement café. To the west, the **Új Zsinagóga** (New Synagogue; ☎ 423 849; Gutenberg utca 13; adult/student 250/100Ft; ☑ 10am-noon & 1-5pm Sun-Fri Apr-Sep, 10am-2pm Sun-Fri Oct-Mar) is the most beautiful Jewish house of worship in Hungary and is still in use. An ornate, blue- and gold-painted interior graces the 1903 Art Nouveau building.

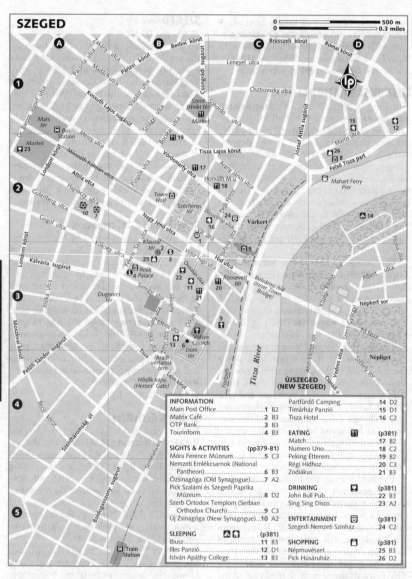

SZEGED

0 _____ 500 m
0 _____ 0.3 miles

INFORMATION	
Main Post Office	1 B2
Matrix Café	2 B3
OTP Bank	3 B3
Tourinform	4 B3

SIGHTS & ACTIVITIES	(pp379-81)
Móra Ferencz Múzeum	5 C3
Nemzeti Emlékcsarnok (National Pantheon)	6 B3
Ózsinagóga (Old Synagogue)	7 A2
Pick Szalámi és Szegedi Paprika Múzeum	8 D2
Szerb Ortodox Templom (Serbian Orthodox Church)	9 C3
Új Zsinagóga (New Synagogue)	10 A2

SLEEPING	(p381)
Ibusz	11 B3
Illes Panzió	12 D1
István Apáthy College	13 B3

Partfürdő Camping	14 D2
Tímárház Panzió	15 D1
Tisza Hotel	16 C2

EATING	(p381)
Match	17 B2
Numero Uno	18 C2
Peking Étterem	19 B2
Régi Hídhoz	20 C3
Zodiákus	21 B3

DRINKING	(p381)
John Bull Pub	22 B3
Sing Sing Disco	23 A2

ENTERTAINMENT	(p381)
Szegedi Nemzeti Színház	24 C2

SHOPPING	(p381)
Népmuvészet	25 B3
Pick Húsáruház	26 D2

Free organ concerts here are common on summer evenings. The nearby **Ózsinagóga** (Old Synagogue; Hajnóczy utca 12) was built in 1843.

The **Szeged Open-Air Festival** is held in Dom tér from mid-July to late August. Running along three sides of the square is the **Nemzeti Emlékcsarnok** (National Pantheon) – statues and reliefs of 80 Hungarian notables. One

block northeast, inside the **Szerb Ortodox Templom** (Serbian Orthodox Church; cnr Béla & Somogyi utca; adult/student 150/100Ft; ☼ 8am-8pm) have a look at the fantastic iconostasis – a central gold 'tree' with 60 icons hanging off its 'branches'.

Just north of the Old Town ring road is the **Pick Szalámi és Szegedi Paprika Múzeum** (☎ 421 814; Felső Tisza Part 10; adult/student 240/180Ft;

3-6pm Tue-Fri & 1-4pm Sat). Two floors of exhibits and old photos show the traditional methods of production. There's a small gift stand in the museum and a butcher shop around the corner in this factory building.

Sleeping

Plenty of student accommodation is open to travellers in July and August, including the central **István Apáthy College** (☎ 545 896; Eötvös utca 4; dm 1600-2500Ft; ✖). Ask Tourinform for more information. **Ibusz** (☎ 471 177; www.ibusz.hu; Oroszlán utca 3; per person 4000-5000Ft; 9am-5pm Mon-Fri, 9am-1pm Sat) travel agency can help with private rooms.

Partfürdő Camping (☎ 430 843; Közép-kikötő sor; camp site per person 1200Ft, bungalows 12,000Ft; mid-May–Sep; P) This green, grassy campsite is across the river in New Szeged. Bungalows sleep up to four people.

Illes Panzió (☎ 315 640; Maros utca 37; s/d 5900/6900Ft; P) A wife-and-husband team are refurbishing a very old building north of the centre, and they've completed most of it. Rooms have a fresh new feel, especially given the cool tile floors and polished wood work. There's no breakfast, TVs or room phones.

Tímárház Panzió (☎ 425 486; Maros utca 26; s/d/tr 8200/10,000/14,800Ft; P) Boxy rooms are sparsely furnished with low-lying modern beds and flat-faced armoires. Once upon a time the centuries-old building was a tannery, but you'd never guess. The wood shudders and carriage doors make it look much less utilitarian than that.

Tisza Hotel (☎ 478 278; www.tiszahotel.hu; Wesselényi utca 1; s/d with bathroom 10,800/13,800Ft; ✖ P) Grand may be an overused adjective to describe old, 1885 hotels, but it applies. For 2000Ft extra you can upgrade to a room with colonial furniture. The best deals are rooms with a shower, but the toilet is in a shared rest room down the hall (single/double 7900Ft/10,900Ft). A hot buffet breakfast is spread in the ornate ground floor restaurant; there's also a café and a bar.

Eating

Numero Uno (☎ 424 745; Széchenyi tér 5; mains 360-730Ft; 11am-11pm Mon-Sat, noon-11pm Sun; ✖) Good pizzas and calzones on the main square. There's a garden out back.

Peking Étterem (☎ 422 884; Bocskai utca 8; mains 600-1200Ft; 11.30am-11pm) Popular and always reliable; come here for good Chinese.

Régi Hídhoz (☎ 420 910; Oskola utca 4; mains 780-1200Ft; noon-11pm Sun-Thu, 11am-midnight Fri & Sat; ✖) While in town you have to try Szegedi *halászlé*, the fish soup the area is known for, and this is a place as good as any to do so. The rustic dining room has faux-treated yellow plaster walls and ceramics hanging as decorations.

Zodiákus (☎ 420 914; Oskola utca 13; mains 890-2100Ft; 11am-midnight Mon-Thu, 11am-1am Sat, 1am-4pm Sun; ✖) Low lighting, barrel ceilings, amber walls and stylised Zodiac sign art make for a sultry, upscale environment. Imaginative entrées include things like beef tenderloin cooked to order and topped with red currants and cheddar cheese. The staff are exceptionally accommodating: no room in nonsmoking? The host will pull a table from a banquet room and squeeze you in.

There's a **Match** (Széchenyi tér 8) supermarket.

Entertainment

Proving that this is a college town is the vast array of bars, clubs and other nightspots, especially around Dugonics tér. Nightclub programmes are listed in the free *Szegedi Est* magazine. Tourinform can help you find out about classical music concerts and other more high-brow entertainment.

Szegedi Nemzeti Színház (☎ 479 279; Deák Ferenc utca 12-14) Since 1886 the Szeged National Theatre has been the centre of cultural life in the city. Opera, ballet and drama performances take the stage.

John Bull Pub (☎ 484 217; Oroszlán utca 6; 10am-midnight Sun-Thu, 10am-1am Sat & Sun) Join the 20-somethings drinking on the small patio or in the cosy pub – if you can find a free table.

Sing Sing Disco (cnr Mars tér & Dr Baross József utca; 10pm-4am Wed-Sat) A pretty typical hyper-party, bounce-around place. Sing Sing sometimes has theme nights. Admission starts at 500Ft, depending on the guest DJ.

Shopping

Népművészet (☎ 423 029; www.folkart.balna.hu, no English; Kárász utca 9; 10am-6pm Mon-Fri, 10am-1pm Sat) This folk art store has a large selection of handwoven textiles, handpainted boxes and miniature replicas of what used to be given as a bridal dowry chest.

Pick Húsáruház (☎ 421 879; Martos utca 21; 3-6pm Mon, 7am-6pm Tue-Fri, 6am-noon Sat) You can buy a stick of Pick salami, as well as other meats, right from the factory store.

HUNGARY

Getting There & Away

Buses run to Budapest (2430Ft, three hours, six daily), Kecskemét (2430Ft, two hours, 10 daily) and Pécs (3010Ft, four hours, eight daily), among other destinations. If you're heading to Serbia and Montenegro, buses make the 1½ hour run to Subotica daily at 10am (800Ft).

Szeged is on the main rail line to Budapest's Nyugati train station (2324Ft, 2½ hours, 11 daily), stopping halfway along in Kecskemét (1844Ft, 1¼ hours, 11 daily). You have to change in Békéscsaba to get to Arad (2946Ft, 3½ hours, three daily) in Romania. Two daily trains (6.35am, 4.25pm) go direct from Szeged to Subotica (1434Ft, two hours) in Serbia and Montenegro.

NORTHEASTERN HUNGARY

The level plains and grasslands give way to a chain of wooded hills as you head north and east. These are the foothills of the Carpathian Mountains (in modern-day Ukraine), which stretch along the Hungarian border with Slovakia. Though you'll definitely notice the rise in elevation, Hungary's highest peak of Kékes-tető is still only a proverbial bump in the road at 1014m. The microclimates in several of the hill groupings are quite conducive to wine production. Eger and Tokaj are known worldwide for their red and sweet dessert wines, respectively. Not far north of Eger is Szilvásvárad: the Hungarian home of the snow-white Lipizzaner horses makes a good day trip.

EGER

☎ 36 / pop 57,000

Wine tasting is what draws most visitors to Eger (*egg*-air), but it is also a lovely, walkable baroque city with a great hilltop castle. It was here in 1522 that Hungarian defenders temporarily stopped the Turkish advance into Western Europe and helped preserve Hungary's identity. Legend has it that István Dobó fortified his badly outnumbered soldiers with red wine while they successfully defended Eger against the siege. When the Turks saw the red-stained beards, rumours circulated that the Hungarians were drinking bull's blood to attain their strength. Thus the name of the region's most famous red wine came to be Egri Bikavér (Eger Bull's Blood). Unfortunately the Turks returned in 1596 and managed to capture Eger Castle. They were finally evicted in 1687.

In the 18th century, Eger played a central role in Ferenc Rákóczi II's attempt to overthrow the Habsburgs, and it was then that a large part of the castle was razed by the Austrians. Credit goes to the bishops of Eger for erecting most of the town you see today. Eger has some of Hungary's finest architecture, especially examples of Copf (Zopf in Hungarian), a transitional style between late baroque and neoclassicism found only in Central Europe. Just a 20-minute walk southwest of the centre, dozens of small wine cellars are to be found carved into the sides of Szépasszony-völgy (Valley of the Beautiful Women).

Orientation & Information

The main train station is a 15-minute walk south of town, on Vasút utca, just east of Deák Ferenc utca. The Egervár train station, which serves Szilvásvárad and other points north, is a five-minute walk north of the castle along Bástya utca on Vécseyvölgy utca. The bus station is west of Széchenyi István utca, Eger's main drag.

The helpful staff at **Tourinform** (☎ 517 715; www.eger.hu; Bajcsy-Zsilinszky utca 9; ☷ 9am-5pm Mon-Fri, 9am-1pm Sat, to 6pm Mon-Fri Jul-Aug) has lots of regional information on hand, including an accommodation guide. Behind the full-service **Egri Est Café** (☎ 411 105; Széchenyi István utca 16; ☷ 11am-midnight Sun-Thu, 11am-4am Fri-Sat) exterior is Internet access for 500Ft per hour.

OTP Bank (Széchenyi István utca 2)

Post office (Széchenyi István utca 22)

Sights & Activities

A 20-minute walk southwest of the centre, **Szépasszony völgy** (Valley of the Beautiful Women; off Király utca) is home to dozens of small wine cellars that truck in, store and sell Bull's Blood and other regional red and white wines. Walk the horseshoe-shaped street through the valley and you'll find doors open between about 10am and 5pm. Stop in front of one that strikes your fancy and ask (*megkosztólhatok?*) to taste their wares (50Ft per decilitre). Some cellars are just a stone cave with a few big casks and a counter, others are decked out with covered tables, mood music

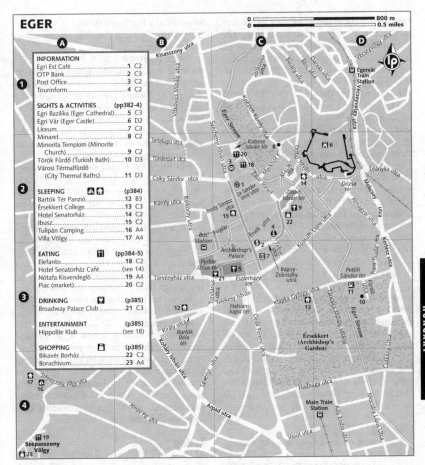

EGER

0 — 800 m
0 — 0.5 miles

INFORMATION
Egri Est Café....................................1 C2
OTP Bank...2 C3
Post Office.......................................3 C2
Tourinform.......................................4 C2

SIGHTS & ACTIVITIES (pp382-4)
Egri Bazilika (Eger Cathedral)........5 C3
Egri Vár (Eger Castle)....................6 D2
Líceum...7 C3
Minaret..8 C2
Minorita Templom (Minorite
   Church)...9 C2
Török Fürdő (Turkish Bath)........10 D3
Városi Termalfürdő
   (City Thermal Baths).................11 D3

SLEEPING (p384)
Bartók Tér Panzió.........................12 B3
Érsekkert College..........................13 C3
Hotel Senatorház.........................14 C2
Ibusz...15 C2
Tulipán Camping...........................16 A4
Villa Völgy.....................................17 A4

EATING (pp384-5)
Elefánto..18 C2
Hotel Senatorház Café.............(see 14)
Nótafa Kisvendeglő......................19 A4
Piac (market)................................20 C2

DRINKING (p385)
Broadway Palace Club..................21 C3

ENTERTAINMENT (p385)
Hippolite Klub..........................(see 18)

SHOPPING (p385)
Bikavér Borház.............................22 C2
Borachivum...................................23 A4

---

and a waiter wearing a bow tie. If you want
wine to go, you can bring an empty plastic
bottle (Coke, water, anything) and have it
filled for about (600Ft per 1½ litres); they'll
also sell you a kitschy little plastic barrel full.
It's easy to drink a lot here – more than one
person has fallen over in the park at the entrance to the valley. Remember that there is a
zero-tolerance policy for driving in Hungary
with any alcohol in your system.

Back in town, the most striking attraction
is **Egri Vár** (Eger Castle; ☎ 312 744; Vár 1; adult/student
combined ticket 800/400Ft; ☼ 8am-8pm Tue-Sun Apr-Aug,
8am-7pm Sep, 8am-6pm Oct & Mar, 8am-5pm Nov-Feb), a
huge walled complex at the top of the hill
off Dósza tér. First fortified after an early
Mongol invasion in the 13th century, the

earliest ruins onsite are the foundations of
St John's Cathedral, built in the 12th century
and destroyed by the Turks. The excellent
István Dobó Múzeum (admission included with castle),
inside the Bishop's Palace (1470), explores
the history and development of the castle
and the town. Other exhibits such as the
Panoptikum (Waxworks; adult/student 300/200Ft) and
the **Éremverde** (Minting Exhibit; adult/student 150/100Ft)
cost extra. Even on days when the museums
are closed, you can walk around the grounds
and battlements and enjoy the views if you
buy a *sétaljegy* (strolling ticket, 300/150Ft).

East of the castle hill is a 40m-high **minaret** (Knézich Károly utca; 200Ft; ☼ 10am-6pm Mar-Oct),
the northernmost monument left from the
Turkish occupation in the 16th century.

Don't try to climb the 97 narrow spiral steps to the top if you're claustrophobic. The **Minorita Templom** (Minorite Church; Dobó István tér), built in 1771, is a glorious baroque building. In the square in front are statues of national hero István Dobó and his comrades -in-arms routing the Turks in 1552.

The first thing you see as you come into town from the bus or train station is the neoclassical **Egri Bazilika** (Eger Cathedral; Pyrker János tér 1), built in 1836. Directly opposite is the Copf-style **Líceum** (Lyceum; ☎ 520 400; Esterházy tér 1; ⊙ 9.30am-3.30pm Tue-Sun Apr-Sep, 9.30am-1pm Sat & Sun Oct-Mar), dating from 1765, with a 20,000-volume frescoed **könyvetár** (library; adult/student 450/300Ft) on the 1st floor and an 18th-century observatory in the **Csillagászati Múzuem** (Astronomy Museum; adult/student 450/300Ft) on the 6th floor. Climb three more floors up to the observation deck for a great view of the city and to try out the camera obscura, the 'eye of Eger', designed in 1776 to entertain the locals.

The Archbishop's Garden was once the private reserve of papal princes, but today the park is open to the public. Inside the park, the **Városi Térmalfürdő** (City Thermal Baths; ☎ 411 699; adult/child 500/350Ft; ⊙ 6am-7.30pm Mon-Fri, 9am-7pm Sat & Sun May-Sep, 9am-6pm daily Oct-Apr) has open-air, as well as covered, pools with different temperatures (40°C being the hottest) and mineral contents. The **Török Fürdő** (Turkish Bath; Fürdő utca 3), built between 1610 and 1617, is open only to those with a doctor's order.

Sleeping

A number of colleges in town offer accommodation in July and August, including the 132-bed **Érsekkert College** (☎ 413 661, fax 520 440; Klapka György utca 12; dm 1400-2000Ft).

Ibusz (☎ 311 451; www.ibusz.hu; Széchenyi István utca 9; ⊙ 8am-4pm Mon-Fri, 9am-1pm Sat Jun-Sep) can help organise private rooms, starting at 3000Ft a night per person.

Tulipán Camping (☎ 410 580; www.home.zonnet .nl/tulipan/; Szépasszony-völgy utca 71; camp site per person 1450Ft, caravan site with electricity per person 1950Ft, hotel r 7680Ft, 4-/5-person bungalows 5500/9900Ft; P ⊡) Tile-covered bathroom facilities look like they should be in a house; OK, so it'd have to be one with lots of children. The five-person bungalow has one bedroom, a living room, a kitchen and a bathroom. The four-person cabin is just a room (no kitchen or bath). The hotel rooms have minifridges and include breakfast. Some of the caravan

sites are in a big, treeless field. It's all stumbling distance from the valley wine cellars and it's open year-round.

Bartók Tér Panzió (☎ 515 556, fax 515 572; Bartók Béla tér 8; s/d/tr 5000/8000/10,000Ft; ☒) A very agreeable place. Basic rooms with skylights and pastel colours are organised around a courtyard in an old town building. A five-bed room costs 14,500Ft. The same people operate St Kristof Panzio, at the end of the square for the same prices. Come to the address given here for information.

Villa Völgy (☎ 321 664; www.hotels.hu/villavolgy; Szépasszony-völgy, Tulipánkert utca 5; s/d 8200/13,600Ft; P ☒) An upscale hotel in the heart of wine-tasting country. Sleeping here does feel like staying at a country manor house or villa, albeit a very stylish one. The interior design is contemporary blonde wood with splashes of bold colour in the curtains and graphic art rugs. You can look out your window at the beer garden and the graceful restaurant building across the lawn, at the hillside vineyards or at the caravan camping ground next door – the only drawback.

Hotel Senatorház (☎ 320 466; www.hotels.hu /senatorhaz; Dobó István tér 11; r €56-70; P ☒) Approaching this 18th-century inn and its restaurant-café at night along the cobblestone square with the lights of Eger Castle glowing above, it's hard to imagine anything more romantic. Traditional wood furnishings decorate the 11 guest rooms that have minibars, satellite TV – the works.

Eating

At the base of Szépasszony-völgy utca there are numerous small terrace *büfé* (snack bars) that resemble food stands but employ a waiter to serve you at your picnic table. They have full Hungarian menus – and beer and wine, of course. There are also numerous restaurants and cafés along pedestrian Széchenyi István utca in town. The area is know for it's *pistrang* (trout) dishes.

Piac (market; Katona István tér; ⊙ 6am-6pm Mon-Fri, 6am-1pm Sat, 6am-10am Sun) Come to the covered market to get fruit, vegetables, meat and bread. Upstairs there are food stands selling sausages, snacks and some full meals that you eat standing at bar-height tables.

Elefanto (☎ 411 031; Katona István tér 2; mains 1350-2500Ft, pizzas 490-900Ft; ⊙ 11am-midnight; ☒) Dine al fresco on the large covered terrace. This is a casual place that sometimes has light music.

Hotel Senatorház Café (☎ 320 466; Dobó István tér 11; mains 1400-3000Ft; 🕙 11am-midnight; 🍴) Sitting in the main square for a meal is delightful. Even better, stop by in the evening for a candlelit dessert. The *palincsinta* (crepes) stuffed with baked apples and cinnamon, served with cream, shouldn't be missed.

The four fully fledged restaurants in Szépasszony-völgy are pretty similar and a little touristy: large garden seating areas, formal waiters, wine and some Gypsy music, but **Nótafa Kisvendeglö** (☎ 311 375; Szépasszony völgy utca 2; mains 650-1200Ft; 🕙 11am-11pm) seems the most low-key, and it has tasty, tender pork dishes. Bring mosquito spray.

Entertainment
The Tourinform office can tell you what concerts and musicals are on at theatres in the area, the Lyceum and at Eger Cathedral. The free *Egri Est* magazine has nightlife listings.

Broadway Palace Club (Pyker János tér 3; 🕙 Wed, Fri & Sat 10am-6am) Shake it to the freshest music. There are also café tables outside.

Hippolite Klub (☎ 411 031; Katona tér 2; 🕙 10am-4am) A mild-mannered restaurant by day, Hippolite turns funky disco with music starting at 9pm.

Shopping
You can buy bottled wine at shops like **Bikavér Borház** (☎ 413 262; Dobó Istvan tér 2; 🕙 10am-5pm), but why do that when you can go to the source at Szépasszony-völgy. Ask a cellar to fill up your plastic jug straight from the cask, or if you insist on having a glass bottle, **Borachivum** (Szépasszony völgy utca; 🕙 10am-6pm), at No 33, sells them.

Getting There & Away
Buses make the trip from Eger to Szilvásvárad (405Ft, 45 minutes, nine daily). Other destinations available include: Budapest (1500Ft, two hours, 15 daily), Kecskemét (2080Ft, 4½ hours, three daily) and also Szeged (2660Ft, 5½ hours, three daily). To get to Tokaj by bus, you have to go past it to Nyíregyháza and switch.

Eight trains a day connect Egervár station with Szilvásvárad (312Ft, one hour). Departing from the main train station, change at Füzesabony to get to Tokaj (1762Ft, two hours, seven daily). Direct trains run from Eger to Budapest's Keleti station (1968Ft, two hours) four times a day.

SZILVÁSVÁRAD
☎ 36 / pop 1850
The Bükk Hills, most of which fall within the 43,000-hectare **Bükk Nezmeti Park**, lies to the north of Eger. A good way to explore the hills is a day trip to the village of Szilvásvárad, 28km north. It's an ideal base for hiking and the centre of Lipizzaner *(Lipcsai)* horse breeding in Hungary, with some 250 prize white horses in local stables. There's no tourist office here, but the Tourinform in Eger (p382) has information and sells hiking maps.

The bus from Eger will drop you off in the centre on Egri út. Park utca is off Egri, north of the bus stop, Szalajka Völgy is to the south. You get off the train at Szilvásvárad-Szalajkavölgy, the first of the town's two stations. Follow Egri út east and then north (left) for about 10 minutes into town. At the turn, if you go right instead you'll get to the valley.

Learn more about the intelligent, ancient Lipizzaner horse breed at the **Lipcsai Múzeum** (☎ 355 135; Park utca 8; adult/student 300/200Ft; 🕙 9am-noon & 1-4pm), with history exhibits and a few live animals in an 18th-century stable. Call a day ahead to arrange a carriage or a horseback ride. At the beginning of Szalajka Völgy there are restaurants, souvenir shops and tracks where Lipizzaner coaches race some summer weekends. You can park here for 100Ft per hour. Hike from here further into the valley, or take a ride on a **keskeny nyomtávú vasút** (narrow-gauge railway; ☎ 355 197; Szalajka-völgy utca 6; adult/student 200-400/100-300Ft; 🕙 May-Sep).

Nine daily buses connect Szilvásvárad and Eger (405Ft, 45 minutes). Trains to the Egervár train station take about an hour (312Ft, eight daily).

TOKAJ
☎ 47 / pop 4650
The region has been on the Unesco World Heritage List since 2002, although grapevines have been grown in the hills surrounding Tokaj village for at least 1000 years. The volcanic soil and unique microclimate promote the growth of *Botrytis cinerea* (noble rot) on the grapes. It's these ugly shrivelled up grapes covered with fungus that produce some world-class dessert wine, Tokaji Aszú. King Louis XIV famously called Tokaj 'the wine of kings and the king of wines'. The sweetness is rated from 3 (least) to 6 (the most). Tokaj

also produces less sweet wines: Szamorodni (like dry sherry), Furmint and Háslevelú (the driest of all). However, all still have a bit of the characteristic apple flavour. The village itself spreads out in a valley at the confluence of the Tisza and the Bodrog Rivers. Look for the nesting storks on telephone poles and chimneys from March through September.

Orientation & Information

Trains arrive 1200m south of the town centre; walk north on Baross Gábor utca, turn left on Bajcsy-Zsilinszky út and it turns into Rákóczi út, the main thoroughfare. The bus station is much more convenient, in town, on Seráz utca. **Tourinform** (☎ 552 070; www.tokaj .hu; Serház utca 1; ◷ 9am-4pm Mon-Fri) is just off Rákóczi út.

Sights & Activities

Start at the **Tokaji Múzeum** (☎ 352 636; Bethlen Gábor utca 13; adult/student 300/200Ft; ◷ 10am-4pm Tue-Sun May-Nov), which leaves nothing unsaid about the history of Tokaj, the region and its wines. After you're thoroughly knowledgeable, head to the 600-year-old cellar **Rákóczi Pince** (☎ 352 408; Kossuth tér 15; ◷ 10am-6pm) for a tasting and a tour. Bottles of wine mature underground in the long cave-like corridors (one measures 28m x 10m). A flight of six Tokaj wines costs 2000Ft. The correct order of sampling Tokaj wines is: Furmint, dry Szamorodni, sweet Szamorodni and then the Aszú wines – from three to six puttony (the sweetest). If you only want to taste the Aszú, a three-decilitre glass costs 216–636Ft, with a minimum of four glasses to taste.

Wine cellars (pincek) that are less formal and still sell tastings are scattered throughout town, on the roads leading into (Tarcali) and out of (Bodorgkeresztúrí) town. Look for signs on Rákóczi út, on Bem út and on Hegyalja utca (southeast of town off Bajcsy-Zsilinszky út). Other town attractions include the **Tokaji Galéria** (☎ 352 003; Bethlen Gábor utca 17; admission free; ◷ 10am-4pm daily May-Oct), in an 18th-century Greek Orthodox church, with works by local artists. The crumbling **Nagy Zsinagóga** (Great Synagogue; Serház utca 55), a short distance to the east is being restored.

Sleeping & Eating

Tourinform lists searchable private accommodation on its website www.tokaj.hu. The newest, nicest pensions are southeast

of town and require at least a 20-minute walk to get to the centre.

Tisza Panzió (☎ 552 008, fax 552 009; Tarcali út 52; s/d 4000/6000Ft; P X) Open only a couple of years, this panzió still feels new. It's simple and modern, and each room has TV and telephone. Tarcal út is about 25 minutes south of town along Bajcsy-Zsilinszky út (southwest of the train station). Here's hoping they start renting out bicycles.

Lux (☎ 352 145; Serház utca 14; d/tr 5400/7500Ft) This friendly six-room pension has obviously been well loved, and well used, but it is central. No breakfast.

Millennium Hotel (☎ 352 242; www.tokajmil lennium.hu; Bajcsy-Zsilinszky út 34; s/d 8800/10,200Ft; P X) Sleek décor and up-to-date amenities, such as unlimited wireless Internet connection in the guest rooms, live up to the new century name. Use of the wellbeing centre fitness room, sauna and Jacuzzi are included, but breakfast is 1100Ft extra. The hotel sits near the confluence of the Bodrog and Tisza Rivers.

Makk Marci (☎ 352 336; Liget köz 1; pizzas 430-920Ft; ◷ 8am-8pm) You can't beat pizza that tastes good and is cheap.

Róna (☎ 352 116; Bethlen Gábor utca 19; mains 1300-1900Ft; ◷ 11am-10pm, to 9pm Nov-Feb) The speciality of the house is fish, drawn from nearby rivers, but there are other Hungarian options here as well, although they are nothing fancy.

Degenfeld (☎ 553 050; Kossuth tér 1; mains 1800-2600Ft; ◷ 11.30am-10pm; X X)Budapest-quality cuisine at provincial prices. Delight your tastebuds with lemon-tarragon venison or orange-ginger duck breast. The Degenfeld palace was built in 1870 and the white tablecloths, fresh flowers and upholstered French imperial chairs in the dining room do it justice. A few rooms upstairs are for rent.

Shopping

You can buy wine at any of the places mentioned for tasting or stop at the **Furmint Vinotéka** (☎ 353 340; Bethlen Gábor utca 12; ◷ 9am-5pm) wineshop for a large local selection.

Getting There & Away

No direct buses connect Tokaj with Budapest or Eger. Two buses a day go to Nyíregyháza (463Ft, 40 minutes) where you can connect to either.

Four express trains a day travel to and from Budapest's Keleti station (2610Ft, two hours 45 minutes) and one local to Budapest's Nyugati (2762Ft, 4½ hours). Change at Füzesabony to get to Eger (1762Ft, two hours, five daily). Up to 18 trains a day connect Tokaj with Nyíregyháza (442Ft, 40 minutes), from where you can take a train to the Hungarian border town of Zahony and into Csop, in the Ukraine.

HUNGARY DIRECTORY

ACCOMMODATION

Clearly the capital, Budapest, has the widest variety of lodging prices, but even in provincial towns you can find camping grounds, hostels and private rooms in the Budget range; *panziók* (pensions), guesthouses and small hotels in the mid-range; and multi-amenity hotels at the top end. Reviews in this chapter are ordered according to price. Hungary's more than 400 camping grounds are listed in Tourinform's *Camping Hungary* map/brochure (www.camping.hu). Facilities are generally open May to October and difficult to reach without a car.

The **Hungarian Youth Hostel Association** (Map pp340-1; Mellow Mood Ltd; ☎ 1-413 2065; www.youth hostels.hu; main office, VII Baross tér 15, 3rd fl, Budapest) keeps a list of year-round hostels throughout Hungary. In general, year-round hostels have a communal kitchen, laundry and Internet service, sometimes a lounge, and a basic bread-and-jam breakfast may be included. Having a HI card is not required, but it may get you a 10% discount. From July to August, students vacate college and university dorms and administration opens them to travellers. Local Tourinform offices can help you locate such places.

Renting a private room in a Hungarian home is another budget option and can be a great opportunity to get up close and personal with the culture: you generally share a bathroom with the family. Prices outside Budapest run from 2200Ft to 5500Ft per person per night.

Mid-range accommodation may or may not have a private bathroom, satellite TV and in-room phone, but all top-end places do. A cold breakfast buffet is usually included in the price at pensions, and there are hot breakfasts included at hotels. A reasonable place might bill itself as a *kishotel* (small hotel) because it has

satellite TV and minibars. Air-conditioning is scarce nationwide, but you're more likely to find it at higher priced establishments. Hotels usually have restaurants or bars, and other amenities like a sauna or a pool. You can sometimes save money by taking a hotel room with a private shower, but toilet down the hall. The definition of 'nonsmoking room' in both mid-range and top-end properties varies: some places say the rooms are nonsmoking, but ash trays and matches are provided in each. Those listed with a nonsmoking icon in this chapter have stricter policies.

An engaging alternative is to stay in a rural village or farm house, but only if you have wheels – most places are truly remote. Contact Tourinform, the **National Association of Village Tourism** (Map p344; FAOS; ☎ 1-268 0592; VII Király utca 93) or the **Centre for Rural Tourism** (Map pp340-1; FTC; ☎ 1-321 4396; www.ftur.hu; VII Dohány utca 86) in Budapest.

ACTIVITIES

Hungary has more than 100 thermal baths open to the public and many are attached to hotels with wellbeing packages. Two thermal baths in Budapest (p346), one at Harkány (p373) and the large thermal lake at Hévíz (p371) are covered in this chapter. Request the Hungarian National Tourist Office (HNTO) brochure *Water Tours in Hungary* from Tourinform; it's a gold mine of information for planning spa itineraries.

There's also a helpful HNTO *Riding in Hungary* booklet on equestrian tourism, or you could contact the **Hungarian Equestrian Tourism Association** (Map p344; MLTSZ; ☎ 1-456 0444; www.equi.hu; IX Ráday utca 8, Budapest). **Pegazus Tours** (Map p344; ☎ 1-317 1644; www.pegazus.hu; V Ferenciek tere 5) organises horse-riding tours, and occasionally bicycle tours as well.

Hiking enthusiasts may enjoy the trails around Tihany at Lake Balaton, the Bükk Hills north of Eger or the plains at Bugac Puszta south of Kecskemét. Hiking maps usually have yellow borders. Bird watchers could explore these same paths or take a tour with **Birding Hungary** (☎ 70-214 0261; www .birdinghungary.com; PF 4, Budapest 1511).

All admission prices in this chapter are listed as they are quoted on signs in Hungary (adult/student). Usually, children and pensioners can get into places for the same discounted price.

HUNGARY

TOP FIVE WAYS TO TAKE A BATH

- Soak in palatial elegance – tiled mosaics, stained-glass skylights – at the **Gellért Fürdő** (p346) inside the hotel of the same name in Buda.

- Bubble up in the jetted central section in one of the expansive outdoor thermal pools at the turn-of-the-century **Széchenyi Fürdő** (p347) in City Park in Pest.

- Float among lilies in the summer and steam in the winter at one of Europe's largest thermal lakes, the **Gyógytó** in Hévíz (p371).

- Go modern at the **Rába Quelle** (p361) thermal spa in Győr: slide down the waterslide, splash under the two-storey waterfall.

- Take a romantic summer evening swim in the outdoor thermal mineral pool of the **Gyógyfürdő** (p376) in Harkány; the high sulphur content might do you good.

BOOKS

Not to be modest, but an excellent overall guidebook is Lonely Planet's *Hungary*, while the *Budapest* guide takes an in-depth look at the capital. For an easy introduction to the nation's past, check out *An Illustrated History of Hungary* by István Lázár. Read László Kontler's *A History of Hungary* for a more in-depth, but easy-to-read, study.

Poetry is a national interest in Hungary; you can read a sample in the bilingual anthology *The Lost Rider* by Corvina Books. The 2002 Nobel prizewinner, Imre Kertész, writes about the Holocaust and its aftereffects in the novels *Fateless* and *Kaddish for a Child Not Born*.

BUSINESS HOURS

With some rare exceptions, opening hours *(nyitvatartás)* are posted on the front door of establishments; *nyitva* means 'open' and *zárva* is 'closed'. Large, chain grocery stores are usually open from 7am to 6pm Monday through Friday, and to 1pm on Saturday. Smaller ones, especially in Budapest, may be open on weekends or holidays as well. Most towns have a 'nonstop' convenience store, and many have hypermarkets, such as Tesco, that are open 24 hours. Main post offices are open 8am to 6pm weekdays, and to noon or 1pm Saturday. Bank hours are from 8am to 4pm Monday to Thursday and 8am to 1pm on Friday.

COURSES

The granddaddy of all the Hungarian language schools, **Debreceni Nyári Egyetem** (Debrecen Summer University; ☎ 52-489 117; www.nyari egyetem.hu; Egyetem tér 1, PO Box 35, Debrecen 4010), in eastern Hungary, is the most well known and the most well respected. It organises intensive two- and four-week courses during July and August and 80-hour, two-week advanced courses during winter. The **Debrecen Summer University Branch** (Map p344; ☎ 1-320 5751; XIII Jászai Mari tér 6) in Budapest puts on regular and intensive courses.

CUSTOMS

You can bring and take out the usual personal effects, 200 cigarettes, 1L of wine or champagne and 1L of spirits. You are not supposed to export valuable antiques without a special permit; this should be available from the place of purchase. You must declare the import/export of any amount of cash exceeding 1,000,000Ft.

DISABLED TRAVELLERS

Most of Hungary has a long way to go before it becomes accessible to the disabled, although audible traffic signals are becoming more common and there are Braille markings on the higher-denominated forint notes. For more information, contact the **Hungarian Disabled Association** (Map pp340-1; MEOSZ; ☎ 1-388 5529; meosz@matavnet.hu; III San Marco utca 76, Budapest).

DISCOUNT CARDS

Those planning extensive travel in Hungary might consider the **Hungary Card** (☎ 1-266 3741; www.hungarycard.hu), which gives: 50% discounts on seven return train fares; three 33%-off one-way train trips; 50% off some bus and boat travel; free entry to some museums and attractions outside Budapest; up to 25% off selected accommodation; and 20% off the price of the Budapest Card (p342). Available at Tourinform and Volánbusz offices, larger train stations, some newsagents and petrol stations throughout Hungary, the card costs 7935Ft and is valid for one year.

EMBASSIES & CONSULATES

To find out more about Hungarian embassies around the world, or foreign representation in Hungary, contact the **Ministry of Foreign Affairs** (☎ 1-458 1000; www.kum.hu).

Hungarian Embassies & Consulates

Hungarian embassies around the world include the following:

Australia (☎ 02-6282 2555; 17 Beale Crescent, Deakin, ACT 2600)
Canada (☎ 613-230 9614; 299 Waverley St, Ottawa, Ontario K2P 0V9)
France (☎ 1-5636 0754; 7-9 Square Vergennes, 75015 Paris)
Germany (☎ 030-203 100; Unter den Linden 76, 10117 Berlin)
Ireland (☎ 01-661 2902; 2 Fitzwilliam Place, Dublin 2)
Netherlands (☎ 70-350 0404; Hogeweg 14, 2585 JD Den Haag)
UK (☎ 020-7235 5218; 35 Eaton Place, London SW1X 8BY)
USA (☎ 202-362 6730; 3910 Shoemaker St NW, Washington, DC)

Embassies & Consulates in Hungary

Embassies in Budapest (phone code ☎ 1) include:

Australia (Map p340-1; ☎ 457 9777; XII Királyhágó tér 8–9; ☺ 9am-5pm Mon-Thu, 9am-2pm Fri)
Austria (Map p344; ☎ 479 7010; VI Benczúr utca 16; ☺ 8am-10am Mon-Fri)
Canada (Map p340-1; ☎ 392 3360; XII Zugligeti út 51-53; ☺ 8am-4pm Mon-Fri)
Croatia (Map p344; ☎ 269 5854; VI Munkácsy Mihály utca 15; ☺ 9am-5pm Mon-Fri)
France (Map pp340-1; ☎ 374 1100; VI Lendvay utca 27; ☺ 9am-noon Mon-Fri)
Germany (Map p343; ☎ 1-488 3500; I Úri utca 64-66; ☺ 9am-noon Mon-Fri)
Ireland (Map p344; ☎ 302 9600; V Szabadság tér 7-9; ☺ 9.30am-1pm & 2 -4pm Mon-Fri)
Netherlands (Map pp340-1; ☎ 336 6300; II Füge utca 5-7; ☺ 10am-noon Mon-Fri)
Romania (Map pp340-1; ☎ 348 0271; XIV Thököly út 72; ☺ 9.30am-noon, closed Wed)
Serbia and Montenegro (Map pp340-1; ☎ 322 9838; VI Dózsa György út 92/b; 10am-1pm Mon-Fri)
Slovakia (Map pp340-1; ☎ 460 9011; IV Stefánia út 22–24; ☺ 9:30am-noon Mon-Fri)
Slovenia (Map pp340-1; ☎ 438 5600; II Cseppkő utca 68; ☺ 9am-noon Mon-Fri)
South Africa (Map pp340-1; ☎ 392 0999; II Gárdonyi Géza út 17; ☺ 9am-12.30pm Mon-Fri)
UK (Map p344; ☎ 266 2888; V Harmincad utca 6; ☺ 10.30am-1.30pm & 2.30-5.30pm Mon-Fri)
Ukraine (Map pp340-1; ☎ 422 4120; XIV Stefánia út 77; ☺ 9am-noon Mon-Wed & Fri by appointment only)
USA (Map p344; ☎ 475 4400; V Szabadság tér 12; ☺ 8.15am-5pm Mon-Fri)

FESTIVALS & EVENTS

The best annual events include the following:
Budapest Spring Festival (Mar)
Balaton Festival (May) Based in Keszthely.
Hungarian Dance Festival (late Jun) In Győr.
Sopron Festival Weeks (late Jun–mid-Jul)
Győr Summer Cultural Festival (late Jun–late Jul)
Hortobágy International Equestrian Days (Jul)
Szeged Open-Air Festival (Jul)
Kőszeg Castle Theatre Festival (mid- to late Jul)
Pepsi Sziget Music Festival (late Jul–early Aug) On Óbudai hajógyári-sziget (Óbuda Shipbuilding Island) in Budapest.
Hungaroring Formula One Grand Prix (mid-Aug) at Mogyoród, 24km northeast of Budapest
Budapest Autumn Festival (mid-Oct–early Nov)

GAY & LESBIAN TRAVELLERS

There is no openly antigay sentiment in Hungary, but neither is there a large openly gay population. The organisations and nightclubs that do exist are generally in Budapest. For up-to-date information on venues, events, groups etc, contact **GayGuide. Net** (☎ 06 30 932 3334; http://budapest.gayguide.net).

HOLIDAYS

Hungary's 10 public holidays are:
New Year's Day 1 January
1848 Revolution Day 15 March
Easter Monday March/April
International Labour Day 1 May
Whit Monday May/June
St Stephen's Day 20 August
1956 Remembrance Day 23 October
All Saints' Day 1 November
Christmas Day 25 December
Boxing Day 26 December

LANGUAGE

Hungarians speak Magyar (Hungarian), and unlike the vast majority of tongues you'll hear in Europe, it is not an Indo-European language. It is traditionally categorised as

HUNGARY

Finno-Ugric, distantly related only to Finnish and Estonian. Many older Hungarians, particularly in the western part of the country, can understand German and many young people, particularly in Budapest, speak some English. Any travel-related business will have at least one staff member who can speak English.

Hungarians always put surnames before given names, in writing and in speech. But don't worry, no one expects foreigners to reverse their names upon introduction.

MEDIA

Budapest has two English-language weeklies: the expat oriented *Budapest Sun,* with a useful 'Style' arts and entertainment supplement, and the *Budapest Business Journal* (550Ft). Some Western English-language newspapers, including the *International Herald Tribune,* are available on the day of publication in Budapest and in other large western Hungary cities. Many more newspapers, mainly British, French and German, are sold a day late. International news magazines are also widely available.

MONEY

The unit of currency is the Hungarian forint (Ft). Coins come in denominations of one, two, five, 10, 20, 50 and 100Ft, and notes are denominated 200, 500, 1000, 2000, 5000, 10,000 and 20,000Ft. ATMs are quite common throughout the country, including train stations, and they accept most credit and cash cards. Banks usually offer exchange services as well as ATMs. Branches can be found around the main square in an Old Town centre, or on the main thoroughfare leading to it. Bank hours are from 8am to 4pm Monday to Thursday and 8am to 1pm on Friday. Visa and MasterCard are the most widely accepted credit cards, but some smaller lodgings still only accept cash. Some businesses quote prices in euros; prices in this chapter conform to quotes of individual businesses.

POST

A postcard costs 50Ft within Hungary, 110Ft within Europe, and 150Ft to the rest of the world. A *légiposta* (airmail) letter costs 190Ft within Europe, 380Ft to the rest of the world for up to 20g. Although you can buy stamps at some youth hostels and hotels, go to a post office to actually send your letter or card. If you put it in a post box on the street, it may languish for weeks. Otherwise, service is pretty speedy – a few days to Europe and about a week to the US.

Mail addressed to poste restante in any town or city will go to the main post office (*főposta*). When collecting poste-restante mail, look for the sign '*postán maradó küldemények*'. If you hold an American Express credit card or are carrying their travellers cheques, you can have your mail sent to **American Express** (Map p344; V Deák Ferenc utca 10, Budapest), where it will be held for one month.

TELEPHONE & FAX

Hungary's country code is ☎ 36. To make an outgoing international call, dial ☎ 00 first. To dial city-to-city (and all mobile phones) within the country, first dial ☎ 06 (dialling in from out of the country, leave off the 06), wait for the second dial tone and then dial the city code and phone number. All localities in Hungary have a two-digit city code, except for Budapest, whose code is ☎ 1. Mobile phone numbers all start with the prefix ☎ 06 but are countrywide numbers (ie they have no city code). Budapest numbers have seven digits, most others six digits.

The best place to make international telephone calls is from a phone box with a phone card, which you can buy at newsstands in 2000Ft and 5000Ft denominations. Some cards, such as Neophone, get you an international call for as little as 19Ft per minute. Buy a Matáv *telefonkártya* at newsstands (800Ft) to make domestic calls at card-operated machines. Some pay phones still take coins. Telephone boxes with a black-and-white arrow and red target on the door and the word '*Visszahívható*' display a telephone number, so you can be phoned back.

EMERGENCY NUMBERS

- General emergency ☎ 112 (English spoken)
- Police ☎ 107
- Fire ☎ 105
- Ambulance ☎ 104
- English-language crime hotline ☎ 1-438 8000
- Car assistance (24 hours) ☎ 188

TOURIST INFORMATION

The HNTO has a chain of 120 **Tourinform** (☎ 30 30 30 600 hotline; www.tourinform.hu, www.hungary.com) information offices across the country and is represented in 19 countries abroad. These are the best places to ask general questions and pick up brochures. The HNTO also operates a Tourinform hotline in Hungarian, English and German.

If your query is about private rooms, flights or international train travel, you may have to ask a commercial travel agency; most towns have at least a couple. The oldest, Ibusz, is arguably the best for private accommodation.

VISAS

To enter Hungary, everyone needs a valid passport, or for citizens of the European Union, a national identification card. Citizens of virtually all European countries, the USA, Canada, Israel, Japan, New Zealand and Australia do not require visas to visit Hungary for stays of up to 90 days within a six-month period. UK citizens do not need a visa for a stay of up to six months. South Africans, however, do require a visa. Check with the **Ministry of Foreign Affairs** (☎ 1-458 1000; www.kum.hu) for an up-to-date list of which country nationals require visas.

Visas are issued at Hungarian consulates or missions, most international highway border crossings, Ferihegy airport and the International Ferry Pier in Budapest. However, visas are never issued on trains and rarely on buses.

WOMEN TRAVELLERS

Hungarian men can be very sexist in their thinking, but they are also big on being polite, so women do not suffer any particular form of harassment.

For assistance and/or information ring the **Women's Line** (Nővonal; ☎ 06 80 505 101) or **Women for Women against Violence** (NANE; ☎ 1-267 4900), which operates from 6pm to 10pm daily.

WORK

Working legally in Hungary always involved a Byzantine paper chase and it looks like it will get harder given EU membership requirements. The government has announced it will crack down on illegal workers. No one thinks they're going to target English teachers, but the work situation for foreigners *is* in a state of flux.

TRANSPORT

GETTING THERE & AWAY

Air

From Budapest's Ferihegy 2 airport you can reach destinations in Eastern and Western Europe, the UK, Russia and connect to places beyond. Malév is the Hungarian national airline. Low-cost airlines fly from Ferihegy 1 to off-market airports in Western Europe, such as London Stansted.

Vienna's Schwechart airport is only about three hours from Budapest by bus, less to western Hungary, and often has less expensive international airfares since it handles more traffic.

Aeroflot (code SU; ☎ 318 5955; www.aeroflot.com) Flights to Russia.

Austrian Airlines (code OS; ☎ 327 9080; www.aua.com) Less than an hour's flight to Vienna.

ČSA (code OK; ☎ 318 3175; www.czech-airlines.com) At least three flights daily to/from Prague.

Lot Polish Airlines (code LO; ☎ 266 4772; www.lot.com) Budapest direct to Warsaw & connecting to other Polish & Russian cities.

Malév Hungarian Airlines (code MA; ☎ 235 3888; www.malev.hu) Flights to Vienna, Kyiv and Odesa in Ukraine, Timişoara in Romania, Split and Dubrovnik in Croatia, Varna and Sofia in Bulgaria, Prague in the Czech Republic, Kraków and Warsaw in Poland, and Moscow in Russia.

Sky Europe (code NE; ☎ 777 7000) A low-cost airline that flies daily to Warsaw, Poland, & three days a week to Split & Dubrovnik, Croatia.

Tarom Romanian Air Transport (code RO; ☎ 235 0809; www.tarom.ro) Direct flights to & from Bucharest.

Land

Hungary has excellent land transport connections with its seven neighbours. Most of the departures listed are from Budapest, though other cities and towns closer to the various borders can also be used as springboards.

BICYCLE & WALKING

Cyclists may have a problem crossing at Hungarian border stations since bicycles are banned on motorways and national highways with single-digit route numbers.

If you're heading north, there are three crossings to and from Slovakia where you should not have any problems. Bridges link Esztergom with Štúrovo and Komárom with Komárno. At Sátoraljaújhely, northeast of Miskolc, there's a highway border

HUNGARY

crossing over the Ronyva River which links the centre of town with Slovenské Nové Mesto. Many border guards frown on walking across borders, particularly in Romania, Serbia and Montenegro and Ukraine; in those places, there are sometimes helpful drivers willing to give you a lift for a small price.

BUS

Most international buses arrive at the Népliget bus station (p354) in Budapest. **Eurolines** (☎ 1-219 8080; www.eurolines.com), in conjunction with its Hungarian affiliate, **Volánbusz** (☎ 1-219 8080; www.volanbusz.hu), is the international bus company of Hungary. There's a 10% youth discount for those under 26. Useful international buses include those from Budapest to: Vienna city centre (5490Ft, 3½ hours, four daily), Bratislava, Slovakia (Pozsony; 4400Ft, four hours, one daily), Subotica in Serbia and Montenegro (Szabatka; 3300Ft, four hours; daily), Rijeka in Croatia (7900Ft, 10 hours, one weekly), Prague in the Czech Republic (9500Ft, eight hours, five weekly), and Sofia in Bulgaria (12,500Ft, 15 hours, four weekly).

Four buses a day (7.30am, 11.15am, 5.15pm and 7.15pm) run from Vienna International Airport in Austria to the Népliget bus station in Budapest (€28). **Mitch's Tours** (☎ 06 70 588 306; www.mitchstours.com; adult/student €32/29) runs a shuttle bus service between Deák tér or several hostels in the Budapest area and the airport or hostels in Vienna (departs Vienna 8.30am, departs Budapest 1.30pm).

CAR & MOTORCYCLE

Border controls between Hungary and her new EU neighbours (as of 1 May, 2004), Slovakia and Austria, were not scheduled to be removed at the time of research, but there will be no more customs checks at these points. Third-party insurance is compulsory for driving in Hungary. If your car is registered in the EU, it's assumed you have it. Other motorists must show a Green Card or buy insurance at the border.

HITCHING

In Hungary, hitchhiking is legal except on motorways. Hitchhiking is never an entirely safe way to travel and we don't recommend it, but if you're willing, **Kenguru** (Map p344; ☎ 1-266 5837; www.kenguru.hu; VIII Kőfaragó

utca 15, Budapest; open 8am-6pm Mon-Fri, 10am-4pm Sat) is an agency that matches riders with drivers. Hitch a ride to Amsterdam (11,000Ft), Munich (5500Ft) or Paris (11,700Ft), among other destinations.

TRAIN

The Hungarian State Railways, **MÁV** (☎ 1-461 5500 international information; www.elvira.hu Hungarian only, www.mav.hu) links up with international rail networks in all directions and its schedule is available online. MÁV sells Inter-Rail passes to European nationals (or residents of at least six months). Hungary is in Zone D along with the Czech Republic, Slovakia, Poland and Croatia. The price for any one zone is €226/158/113 for adult/youth (12–26)/child (four–12). There are big discounts on return fares only between Hungary and former communist countries: up to 65% to Slovakia, Slovenia and Croatia; 70% to Romania; 40% to Serbia and Montenegro; 40% to the Czech Republic and Poland; and 50% to Ukraine, Bulgaria, Belarus and Russia. For tickets to Western Europe you'll pay the same as everywhere else unless you're aged under 26 and qualify for the 30% to 50% BIJ discount. For tickets or more information about passes and discounts, ask at the MÁV Ticket Office (p354) in Budapest.

Eurail passes are valid, but not sold, in Hungary. EuroCity (EC) and Intercity (IC) trains require a seat reservation and payment of a supplement. Most larger train stations in Hungary have left-luggage rooms open at least 9am to 5pm. There are three main train stations in Budapest, so always note the station when checking a schedule online; for more information see p354.

Some direct connections from Budapest to neighbouring countries include: Vienna (6600Ft, 3½ hours, five daily); Bratislava, Slovakia (Pozsony; 5600Ft, 2½ hours, eight daily); Arad (7400Ft, 4½ hours, six daily) and Bucharest, Romania (18,600Ft, 13 to 15 hours, five daily); Csop (7600Ft, 4½ hours, two daily) and Kyiv, Ukraine (18,400Ft, 24 hours, one daily), continuing to Moscow (25,400Ft, 37 hours, one daily); Zagreb, Croatia (9000Ft, five to seven hours, three daily); Belgrade, Serbia and Montenegro (9400Ft, seven hours, two daily); Ljubljana, Slovenia (13,700Ft, 8½ hours, three daily). Other direct train destinations in Eastern Europe include: Prague, Czech Republic

(14,850Ft, nine hours, two daily); Kraków, Poland (13,500Ft, 10½ hours, one daily); Sofia, Bulgaria (18,200Ft, 18–26 hours, two daily). Fares listed are for second-class tickets without seat reservation; first-class tickets are usually 50% more. For information on international destinations outside Eastern Europe, see the main Transport chapter of this book (p894).

River

There's an international Mahart PassNave hydrofoil service on the Danube daily from April to early November between Budapest and Vienna (5½ hours), stopping in Bratislava (3½ hours). Adult one-way/return fares for Vienna are €75/99, for Bratislava €68/93. Students with ISIC cards pay €59/84. Boats leave from the Nemzetközi hajóállomás (International Ferry Pier), next to the **Mahart PassNave Ticket Office** (Map p344; ☎ 484 4013; www.mahartpassnave.hu; Belgrád rakpart). The ticket office in Vienna is **Mahart PassNave Wien** (☎ 01-72 92 161; Handelskai 265).

GETTING AROUND
Air

Hungary does not have any scheduled internal flights.

Bicycle

Hungary now counts 2500km of dedicated bicycle lanes around the country, with more on the way. For information and advice, contact the helpful **Hungarian Bicycle Touring Association** (MKTSZ; Map p344; ☎ 1-311 2467; mktsz@enternet .hu; VI Bajcsy-Zsilinszky út 31) in Budapest.

Boat

In summer there are regular passenger ferries on Lake Balaton and on the Danube from Budapest to Szentendre, Visegrád and Esztergom. Details of the schedules are given in the relevant destination sections.

Bus

Domestic buses, run by **Volánbusz** (☎ 1 219 8080; www.volanbusz.hu) cover an extensive nationwide network. The buses are generally relatively new, and everybody and their grandmother takes them, so they are safe. Bus travel is the best option if you are travelling between cities outside the capital, or on shorter hops, especially around Lake Balaton. Bus fares average 1270Ft per 100km.

Timetables are posted at stations and stops. Some footnotes you could come across include *naponta* (daily), *hétköznap* (weekdays), *munkanapokon* (on work days), *munkaszüneti napok kivételével naponta* (daily except holidays), and *szabad és munkaszüneti napokon* (on Saturday and holidays). A few large bus stations have luggage rooms, or a bathroom attendant who you pay to watch your bags, but these generally close by 6pm.

Car & Motorcycle

Limited access Motorways (M1, M3, M7) require toll passes (10-day, 2000Ft) that can be purchased at petrol stations and at some motorway entrances. Check with your rental company; the car may already have an annual pass.

Many cities and towns require that you 'pay and display' when parking. The cost averages about 100Ft an hour in the countryside, and up to 180Ft on central Budapest streets.

AUTOMOBILE ASSOCIATIONS

The so-called 'Yellow Angels' of the Hungarian Automobile Club do basic breakdown repairs for free if you belong to an affiliated organisation such as AAA in the USA or AA in the UK. You can telephone 24 hours a day on ☎ 188 nationwide.

DRIVING LICENCE

Your normal, home country driving licence is sufficient for driving in Hungary.

FUEL & SPARE PARTS

Unleaded (*ólommentes*) petrol (*benzin*) in 95 and 98 octane is available all over the country and costs 254/265Ft per litre, respectively. Most stations also have diesel fuel (*gázolaj*) costing 225Ft per litre and you can pay by credit card. The Hungarian Automobile Club can assist with repairs.

HIRE

In general, you must be at least 21 years old and have had your licence for at least a year to rent a car. Drivers under 25 often have to pay a surcharge.

INSURANCE

Third-party insurance is compulsory. If your car is registered in the EU, it's assumed

HUNGARY

you have it. Other motorists must show a Green Card or buy insurance at the border. Rental cars come with Green Cards.

ROAD RULES

The most important rule to remember is that there's a 100% ban on alcohol when you are driving, and this rule is *very* strictly enforced. (Police even stalk the parking lots of expensive, outlying restaurants.) Do not think you will get away with one glass of wine at lunch; if caught with 0.001% alcohol in your blood, you will be fined up to 30,000Ft. If your blood alcohol level is high, you will be arrested and your licence taken away.

Other than that, drive on the right side of the road in Hungary. The use of seat belts in the front (and in the back, if fitted) is compulsory, but this is often ignored. Motorcyclists must wear helmets. Using a mobile phone while driving is prohibited in Hungary. *All* vehicles must have their headlights switched on throughout the day outside built-up areas. Motorcyclists must illuminate them at all times.

Speed limits are: 50km/h in built-up areas; 80km/h on secondary and tertiary roads; 100km/h on highways; and 120km/h on motorways. Exceeding the limit can earn you a fine of between 5000Ft and 30,000Ft.

Hitching

Hitching is never entirely safe in any country in the world, and we don't recommend it. Hitchhiking is, however, legal in Hungary except on the motorways.

Local Transport

Public transport is efficient and extensive, with city bus and, in many towns, trolleybus services. Budapest and Szeged also have trams, and there's an extensive metro (underground or subway) and a suburban commuter railway in Budapest. Purchase tickets at newsstands before travelling and validate them once aboard. Inspectors do check tickets, especially on the metros in Budapest.

Train

MÁV (☎ 1 461 5400 domestic information; www.elvira.hu) operates reliable train services on its 8000km of tracks, which branch out from Budapest like spokes on a wheel from a hub. Schedules are available online and computer information kiosks are popping up at rail stations around the country. Second-class domestic train fares are 824Ft per 100km, first-class fares are usually 50% more. IC trains are express trains, the most comfortable and the newest. *Gyorsvonat* (fast trains) take longer and use older cars; *személyvonat* (passenger trains) stop at every village along the way. Seat reservations *(helyjegy)* cost extra and are required on IC and some fast trains; these are indicated on the timetable by an 'R' in a box or a circle. (A plain 'R' means seat reservations are available.)

In all stations a yellow board indicates departures *(indul)* and a white board arrivals *(érkezik)*. Express and fast trains are indicated in red, local trains in black. In some stations, large black-and-white schedules are plastered all over the walls. To locate the timetable you need, first find the posted railway map of the country, which indexes the route numbers at the top of the schedules. Most train stations have left luggage offices that are open at least from 9am to 5pm.

You might consider purchasing a Hungarian Rail Pass before entering the country. The cost is US$76 for five days of 1st-class travel within 15 days and US$95 for 10 days within a month. You would need to use it a lot to get your money's worth.

Latvia

CONTENTS

Highlights	396
Itineraries	396
Climate & When to Go	397
History	397
People	398
Religion	398
Arts	398
Environment	398
Food & Drink	398
Riga	**399**
Orientation	399
Information	399
Dangers & Annoyances	402
Sights	402
Festivals & Events	404
Sleeping	404
Eating	405
Drinking	407
Entertainment	407
Getting There & Away	407
Getting Around	407
Around Riga	408
Eastern Latvia	**409**
Sigulda	410
Cēsis	411
Valmiera	412
Western Latvia	**412**
Kuldīga	412
Ventspils	413
Liepāja	413
Latvia Directory	**413**
Accommodation	413
Activities	414
Books	414
Business Hours	414
Children	414
Customs	414
Disabled Travellers	414
Embassies & Consulates	414
Festivals & Events	415
Gay & Lesbian Travellers	415
Holidays	415
Internet Access	415
Language	415
Maps	415
Media	415
Money	415
Post	416
Telephone	416
Tourist Information	416
Visas	416
Transport in Latvia	**416**
Getting There & Away	416
Getting Around	417

LATVIA

There's no need to sex up this Baltic beauty. Latvia (Latvija) has a magical charm guaranteed to lure any unwary traveller into her clutches.

From the sparkling coastline with ice-blue seas and white sands to the stunning wilderness of Gauja National Park, Latvia has the strange feel of a land on the brink of fame and fortune. Her jewel in the crown is the eclectic, elegant city of Rīga which combines a Unesco World Heritage Old Town with Art Nouveau grandeur and contemporary commerce.

Yet this tiny, vibrant nation grew out of the intense suffering of its people under the occupations of the Soviets and Nazis. You'll never believe it shed its Russian stranglehold less than two decades ago as it has a serenity and charm rarely found elsewhere in Europe.

Traditional life and customs are still apparent yet Latvia has a heady ride into an uncertain future.

FAST FACTS

- **Area** 64, 600 sq km
- **Capital** Rīga
- **Currency** Lats (Ls); €1=0.68Ls; US$1=0.53Ls; UK£1=0.98Ls; A$1=0.39Ls; ¥100=0.50Ls; NZ$1=0.37Ls
- **Famous for** Winning the Eurovision Song Contest 2002
- **Key Phrases** *labdien/sveiki* (hello), *cik?* (how much?), *paldies* (thank you)
- **Official Languages** Latvian
- **Population** 2.3 million
- **Telephone Codes** country code ☎ 371; international access code ☎ 00
- **Visas** None required up to 90 days for EU countries, Australian, New Zealand and US citizens; see p416

HIGHLIGHTS

- The cobbled medieval streets, Art Nouveau flourishes and skyline of spires and turrets in beautiful **Rīga** (p399)
- Breathe in the clean bracing air where the seas meet at solitary **Cape Kolka** (p412)
- Chill out, sunbathe or hike westwards on deserted beaches at **Jūrmala** (p408)
- Bobsleigh, bungee jump off a cable car or take it easy counting castles in magnificent **Sigulda** (p410)
- Go wolf-spotting or bog walking in **Ķemeri National Park** (p408)

ITINERARIES

- **Three days** Spend two days exploring Rīga then visit Sigulda or Jūrmala.
- **One week** Spend two days in Rīga, a day trip to Sigulda and the Gauja National Park, then head up the coast road to Cape Kolka, return to Rīga via Ventspils and on the last day see Rundāle Palace.

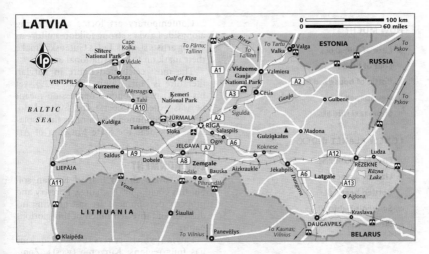

CLIMATE & WHEN TO GO

Latvia's climate is wet, with relatively harsh, long winters and warm, short summers. Take your thermals between December and March when temperatures drop below freezing. Between June and August the thermometer can hit the heady heights of 28°C.

Latvians will tell you any time's a good time to go – and they're right. Snow-scenes and deserted beaches in winter vie with sunbathing and spectacular sunsets in summer.

HISTORY

The history of Latvia is best described as a troubled whirlwind of fierce struggle and downright rebellion.

Latvians descended from tribes which settled on the Baltic coast in 2000 BC. They were pagan until 1190 when the first Christian missionaries tried to convert them – only for the Livs (Latvia's ethnic minority) to jump into available rivers to wash off their baptism.

In 1210 the German Knights of the Sword charged in and conquered Latvia and dominated for several hundred years.

Latvia was then conquered by Poland in 1561 and Catholicism was firmly rooted. Sweden then colonised Latvia (seen by many as a golden age for Latvia) in 1629 until the Great Northern War (1700–21), after which she became part of Russia.

Soviet occupation occurred from 1939 to 1941 with the Molotov-Ribbentrop Pact, heralding a Communist 'election' victory, incorporation into the USSR, nationalisation, mass killings and about 35,000 deportations. Latvia was occupied partly or wholly by Nazi Germany from 1941 to 1945, and its Jewish population was nearly wiped out. An estimated 175,000 Latvians were killed or deported.

The first major public protest of the *glasnost* (openness) era was on 14 June 1987 when 5000 people rallied at Rīga's Freedom Monument to commemorate the 1941 Siberia deportations. On 23 August 1989 about two million Latvians, Lithuanians and Estonians formed a 650km human chain from Vilnius, through Rīga, to Tallinn, to mark the 50th anniversary of the Molotov-Ribbentrop Pact.

The Latvian Popular Front was formed to fight for independence. After its supporters won a big majority in the March 1990 elections, Russia barged back in on 20 January 1991. Soviet troops stormed the Interior Ministry building in Rīga, killing four people.

The August 1991 coup attempt in Moscow turned the tables and Latvia declared full independence on the 21st. It was recognised first by the West then, on 6 September, by the USSR. Latvia's first democratic elections were held in June 1993.

World Heritage status was bestowed upon Latvia's capital in 1997 and Rīga celebrated its 800th birthday in 2001, the same year the Dalai Lama visited the city.

HOW MUCH?

- **Litre of milk** 0.6Ls
- **Loaf of bread** 0.3Ls
- **Bottle of house red** 8Ls
- **Newspaper** 1Ls
- **Short taxi ride** 5Ls

LONELY PLANET INDEX

- **Litre of petrol** 2.5Ls
- **Litre of water** 1Ls
- **Bottled beer** 0.8Ls
- **Souvenir T-shirt** 7Ls
- **Street snack** 0.8Ls

On May 1 2004 the EU opened its doors to 10 new members, including Latvia with huge expectations of better times to come and the securing of its border with Russia. As cheap labour threatens to flood out of Latvia to other EU states, the future remains unclear but imbued with optimism.

PEOPLE

Latvia's 2.3 million inhabitants are very different in temperament from their flamboyant Lithuanian and calm Estonian neighbours. Here you'll find a steely strength hidden beneath a withdrawn people who have to be coaxed into friendship. Hardly surprising considering their history of oppression and the fact that Latvians are still a minority group in each of their main cities.

RELIGION

More than 60% of Latvians are Lutheran, yet that's no barrier to the wealth of denominations in this tolerant nation. Almost 30% of the population is Russian and hence mostly Russian Orthodox, while there's a significant Roman Catholic minority countrywide.

ARTS

The traditional importance of song as Latvia's greatest art form is shown in the 1.4 million *dainas* (folk songs), identified and collected by Krišjānis Barons (1835–1923). In tribute to its rich oral history Latvia has held a song festival in Rīga every five years for the last 125 years.

Contemporary art forms are thriving alongside Latvia's strong folklore culture as young artists such as Tadas Gutauskas make their mark on the international arena.

The most celebrated figure in Latvian literature is Jānis Rainis (1865–1929), yet his criticism of political oppression meant he was exiled to Siberia and Switzerland. There's a monument to him in the Esplanade park near the State Museum of Art in Rīga.

ENVIRONMENT

Forest covers almost half of Latvian soil but this could quickly change. Forestry and property development are fast growing industries and threaten much of this glorious nature.

Latvia (which covers 64,600 sq km) has four regions; Kurzeme (west), Zemgale (south), Vidzeme (east) and Latgale (southeast).

Creatures such as wild boar, wolves and deer roam the woodlands of Latvia along with one of the world's rarest bovine species, the Latvian Blue Cow. Legend has it that a mermaid brought them from the sea.

National Parks

More than a million hectares of land, forest and lakes are protected as national parks: Slītere, Ķemeri, Gauja (www.gnp.lv) and North Vidzeme Biosphere Reserve (www.biosfera.lv). Protecting these lands is vital so only camp in designated areas.

Environmental Issues

Pollution is another threat to Latvia's beauty. Soviet factories and chemical plants have left their mark but the clean-up has begun.

FOOD & DRINK

Traditional Latvian cuisine is not for the faint-hearted (or vegetarians). Pork, pork and even more pork is what these Baltic brothers love – and they'll wash half a side of pig down with *alus* (beer).

Half Russian, half Germanic, Latvian cuisine is hearty food designed to keep the cold out, such as potato-based dishes, *Zupa* (soups), *siļe* (herring), and *lasis* (salmon). One thing that will warm your cockles is Rīga Black Balsam, a treacley alcoholic beverage with potent medicinal qualities – apparently.

Restorans (restaurants) normally open from 10am to 11pm; all have menus outside so you can peruse what's on offer without looking silly inside. For authenticity choose anywhere that doesn't have an English menu and resort to gesticulating wildly before getting a plate of pig's trotters and a balsam by mistake! See p918 for some handy phrases. Dining is an adventure so embrace Latvian food.

Vegetarian options are limited outside of Rīga – even the most harmless of potato pancakes comes smothered in bacon bits so we've highlighted veg options.

Eating is not a drawn-out affair; it's traditionally done to refuel before resuming work, but Rīga now has some top-class restaurants for those who prefer sumptuous, relaxed dining. If you're lucky enough to be invited for a meal with a local, make sure you bring flowers (an odd number only, for superstitious reasons) and don't even think about being vegetarian. Grin and eat until your combats won't fit anymore then waddle home content.

RĪGA

pop 790,000

Intriguing Rīga casts a spell on anyone who visits this enchanting medieval Baltic city.

Unwary travellers are lured into winding cobbled streets flecked with snow or dappled with sunlight; they're transfixed by swirling Art Nouveau architecture and warm bars with candles flickering in the windows. Then just as you can't take the beauty of the Unesco World Heritage Old Town any longer, you look up to find a bewitching skyline of castle turrets and church steeples.

But this fairy-tale city, once dubbed the 'Paris of the East', is also a major metropolis. It's careering through the 21st century with a queue of eager backers pouring much-needed money into its infrastructure. So much so that Unesco has warned Rīga that it may withdraw its special protected status due to the number of glittering glass hotels and business centres springing up like mushrooms after the rain.

Lavish beauty and timeless elegance mark this city as a place you won't want to leave. It's a restless fusion of the old and new

---

RĪGA IN TWO DAYS

Early birds can see the sunrise over the steeples of Rīga atop **Bastejkalns** (Bastion Hill; p403). Then spend the day discovering the Old Town. See the **Dome Cathedral** (p402) and get a bird's-eye view of the city up **St Peter's** steeple (p402). Then finish the day by nourishing your soul with dinner at **Kamāla** (p406).

On day two steel yourself for the horrors of the **Museum of the Occupation of Latvia** (p403) then unwind by finding the Old and New Town **Art Nouveau architecture** (see the boxed text Nouveau Riche, p403). Book tickets for the **opera** (p407) for a musical climax to your trip.

---

which has created a potent charm – you have been warned!

ORIENTATION

The Daugava River arches through Rīga. On the eastern bank is Vecrīga (Old Rīga), the city's historic heart with a skyline dominated by three steeples: St Peter's, Dome Cathedral and St Jacob's.

The train and bus stations are five minutes' walk apart on the southeastern edge of Old Rīga. The ferry terminal is 1.5km north of Akmens Bridge in Old Rīga.

INFORMATION
Bookshops

Globuss (☎ 722 6957; Vaļņu iela 26; ⏰ 8am-10pm) Get your mag fix with international titles downstairs and a small but excellent range of English-language novels upstairs.
Jāņa sēta (☎ 724 0892; Elizabetes iela 83–85; ⏰ 10am-7pm Mon-Fri, 11am-5pm Sat) Superb collection of travel titles and maps including Lonely Planet guides to the region and world!

Internet Access

Dualnet (☎ 781 4440; Peldu iela 17; ⏰ 24hr; per hr 1Ls) Have a beer and settle back to read your emails, day or night.
Internet Kafe (☎ 722 0030; Vaļņu iela 41; ⏰ 24hr; per hr 0.45Ls) Rīga's cheapest option for surf lovers.

Left Luggage

Baggage store (⏰ 5.30am-11pm; per piece 1Ls) In the bus station.
Left-luggage room (⏰ 4.30am-midnight; per piece 1Ls) In the basement of the train station.

CENTRAL RĪGA

INFORMATION
American Embassy	**1** E3
ARS Clinic	**2** F1
Australian Embassy	**3** E2
British Embassy	**4** E1
Canadian Embassy	**5** G1
Central Post Office	**6** F3
Chequepoint Exchange	(see 19)
City of Rīga Information Centre	**7** D5
DS Medical Service	**8** G2
Dualnet	**9** D5
Estonian Embassy	**10** G1
French Embassy	**11** E3
German Embassy	**12** F3
Globuss	**13** E5
Internet Kafe	**14** E5
Jāṇa Sēta	**15** G4
Latvia Tours	**16** D4
Latvia Tours	(see 71)
Latvia Worldwide	**17** D3
Latvian Tourism Development Agency	**18** C4
Parex Banka	**19** E4
Rīga Sightseeing	(see 7)
Russian Embassy	**20** D1
Student & Youth Travel Bureau	**21** H2
Unibanka	**22** C4
Vecpilsētas aptieka	**23** F5

SIGHTS & ACTIVITIES (pp402-4)
Dome Cathedral	**24** C4
Elizabetes iela 10b	**25** E1
Freedom Monument	**26** F3
Great Guild	**27** D4
House of Blackheads	(see 7)
Jews in Latvia Museum	**28** F1
Laima Clock	**29** E4
Memorials to victims of 20 January 1991	**30** D3
Ministry of Culture	**31** D3
Museum of Decorative & Applied Arts	**32** E5
Museum of the History of Rīga & Navigation	(see 24)
Museum of the Occupation of Latvia	**33** D5
Outdoor Ice Rink	**34** D4
Powder Tower	**35** D3
Rīga Castle	**36** C3
Russian Orthodox Cathedral	**37** F2
Saeima	**38** C3
St Jacob's	**39** C4
St Peter's	**40** D5
St Roland Statue	**41** D5
Small Guild	**42** D4
State Museum of Art	**43** E1
Swedish Gate	**44** D3
Three Brothers	**45** C4
Town Hall	**46** D5
War Museum	(see 35)

SLEEPING (pp404-5)
Ainvaras Boutique Hotel	**47** D5
Centra	**48** E5
Forums	**49** F5
Grand Palace Hotel	**50** C4
Hotel Bergs	**51** H4
Hotel Rīga	**52** E4
Konventa Sēta	**53** E5
Laine	**54** F1
Old Town Hostel	**55** F5

Patricia	**56** G4
Posh Backpackers	**57** G6
Radi Un Draugi	**58** E5
Radisson	**59** A6
Valnis	**60** E3
Vecriga Hotel	**61** E4

EATING (pp405-6)
Alus Sēta	**62** D4
Central Market	**63** F6
Fellini	**64** H4
Habibi	**65** D5
John Lemon	**66** D5
Ķiploka Krogs	**67** C4
Kamāla	**68** D4
Pelmeņi XL	**69** D4
Pizza Jazz	**70** F3
Sievasmātes p īrādziņi	**71** E4
Tower	**72** D3
Turku Restorāns	**73** E5

DRINKING (p407)
A.Suns bar	(see 84)
Dickens	**74** D5
Melnais kaķis	**75** D4
Monte Kristo	**76** H1
Orange Bar	**77** E5
Pulkvedim neviens neraksta	**78** D6
Rīgas Balzams	**79** D3
Tim McShane's	**80** D4
XXL	**81** G4

Kronvalda Parks

National Theatre

Pils 🏰 18
Pils laukums
Mazā Pils iela
🏰 50
Pils iela
45 67

Anglikāṇu
St Saviour's Church
22 $

Doma laukums

24

68

85

Old Rīga

46

Rātslaukums
33 7

Strēlnieku laukums
Grēcinieku iela

66
47 66 65
Pērļu iela
78

Boat Tours Landing

Boat Tours Landing

Akmens Bridge

Daugava River

To Ferry Terminal (200m)

To Rīga International Airport (8km); Jūrmala (30km)
Vanšu Bridge

To Lauku Ceļotājs (400m)

LATVIA

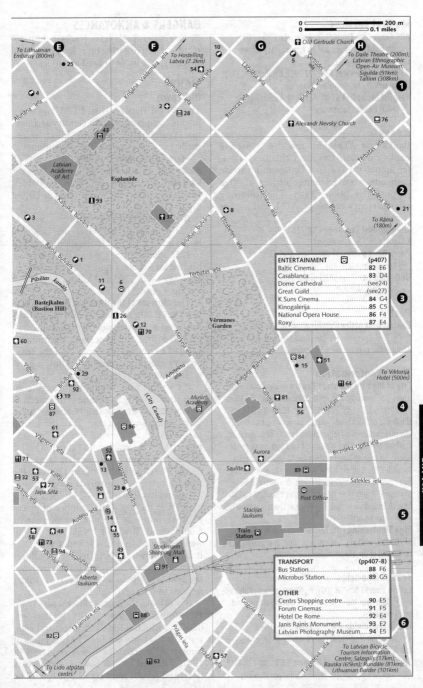

0 [____] 200 m
0 [____] 0.1 miles

E
To Lithuanian
Embassy (800m)
● 25
◆ 4
Alunāna iela

F
To Hostelling
Latvia (7.2km)
54 ⌂
Skolas iela
Dzirnavu iela
2 ✚
▥ 28

10
◆

G
◆ 5
Ģertrūdes iela
Lāčplēša iela
Barnicas iela
Brīvības iela

● Old Gertrude Church

To Daile Theatre (200m);
Latvian Ethnographic
Open-Air Museum;
Sigulda (51km);
Tallinn (308km)

1

● Alexandr Nevsky Church   ▣ 76

Krišjāņa Valdemāra iela

▥ 43

Latvian
Academy
of Art

Esplanāde

⌷ 93

⌂ 37

Kalpaka bulvāris
Brīvības bulvāris
Elizabetes iela

◆ 8

Tērbatas iela
Dzirnavu iela
Blaumaņa iela

Tērbatas iela
Lāčplēša iela

2

● 21

To Rāma
(180m)

◆ 3

Raiņa bulvāris

◆ 1

Pilsētas kanāls

Bastejkalns
(Bastion Hill)

11 ◆   6 ◆

⌷ 26

◆ 12
⌂ 70

Vērmanes
Garden

Tērbatas iela

ENTERTAINMENT	🎭	(p407)
Baltic Cinema		82 E6
Casablanca		83 D4
Dome Cathedral		(see24)
Great Guild		(see27)
K.Suns Cinema		84 G4
Kinogalerija		85 C5
National Opera House		86 F4
Roxy		87 E4

3

⌂ 60

Valņu iela

Brīvības bulvāris

◆ 29
⌷ 92
$ 19
⌂ 87

61
⌂

Vāgnera iela

Merķeļa iela

Arhitektu iela

(City Canal)

Music
Academy

⌷ 86

🎭 84
● 15

⌂ 51

Krišjāņa Barona iela
Kaļķu iela

⌷ 81

⌂ 56

⌂ 51

Marijas iela

🎭 64

To Viktorija
Hotel (500m)

4

⌷ 71

Kaļķu iela

▥ 32   ⌂ 53
⌷ 77
Jaņa Sēta
Skārņu iela

⌂ 58   ⌷ 48
⌷ 73   ▥ 94
Alksnāja iela

Alberta
laukums

13 jūnvāra iela

52
⌂
13

90
⌂
23 ●
14
@

55
⌂

49
⌂

Aspazijas bulvāris
Audēju iela

Vecpilsētas iela

Stockmann
Shopping Mall

🎭 91

Aurora
⌂

Saulite ⌂

89 🚌

Post Office
✉

Stacijas
laukums

Train
Station 🚉

Birznieka-Upīša iela

Satekles iela

5

6

82 🎭

⌂ 88

Prāgas iela

🚌 88

⌷ 63

⌂ 57

Gogoļa iela

Turgeņeva iela

Prāgas iela

TRANSPORT		(pp407-8)
Bus Station		88 F6
Microbus Station		89 G5

OTHER		
Centrs Shopping centre		90 E5
Forum Cinemas		91 F5
Hotel De Rome		92 E4
Janis Rainis Monument		93 E2
Latvian Photography Museum		94 E5

To Lido atpūtas
centrs

To Latvian Bicycle
Tourism Information
Centre; Salaspils (17km);
Bauska (65km); Rundāle (81km);
Lithuanian Border (101km)

H

LATVIA

Medical Services

ARS Clinic (☎ 720 1001/3; Skolas iela 5; ☪ 24hr) English-speaking service and an **emergency home service** (☎ 720 1003).

DS Medical Services (☎ 722 9942; Elisabetes iela 57) Dental services for expats and travellers.

Vecpilsētas aptieka (☎ 721 3340; Audēju iela 20; ☪ 24hr) Excellent pharmacy.

Money

Banks and ATMs dot the city. Most big banks can cash travellers cheques, transfer money via Western Union and provide cash advances. Exchange offices at Rīga Airport give poorer rates. The following offer currency exchange, ATM, and money transfer:

Chequepoint Exchange (☎ 722 1219; Kaļķu iela 28; ☪ 8am-10pm)

Parex Banka (☎ 701 0873; Smilšu iela 3; ☪ 9am-8.30pm Mon-Fri)

Unibanka (☎ 721 5502; Pils iela 23; ☪ 9am-5pm Mon-Fri)

Post

Central post office (☎ 701 8804; Stacijas laukams 1; ☪ 8am-8pm Mon-Fri, 8am-6pm Sat, 8am-4pm Sun) About 400m north of the train station.

Tourist Information

City of Rīga Information Centre (www.rigatourism .com) Old Town (☎ 703 7900; Rātslaukams 6; ☪ 10am-7pm); bus station (☎ 722 0555; ☪ 10am-6pm) Inside the House of Blackheads you can book tours, find free city maps and info on regional tourism. English-speaking staff sell the Rīga Card: a discount card costing 8L for 24 hours, 12Ls for 48 hours or 16Ls for 72 hours; half price for under 16s. You get a free sightseeing tour of the city, free rides on trolleybuses and trams, free entry to some museums, a copy of *In Your Pocket* and discounts on taxi hire, clubs and car rental. The office at the bus station is a small sister branch.

Rīga Sightseeing (☎ 727 1915, 652 0806; adult/child 9/5Ls) Daily walking, bus and boat tours of Rīga which can be booked at the above information centre.

Travel Agencies

Latvia Tours (☎ 708 5001; hq@latviatours.lv; Kaļķu iela 8; ☪ 9am-7pm Mon-Fri) Agent for leading airlines and tour companies.

Latvia Worldwide (☎ 732 6006; Torņa iela 4; ☪ 9am-7pm Mon-Fri) Excellent service and friendly multilingual staff.

Student & Youth Travel Bureau (SJCB; ☎ 728 4818; sjcb@sjcb.lv; Lāčplēsa iela 29; ☪ 9am-5pm Mon-Fri)

DANGERS & ANNOYANCES

Beware of stray potholes or cracks in the pavement – as you're gazing up at Rīga's beautiful skyline you're liable to twist an ankle!

SIGHTS
Old Town

The World Heritage–listed Old Town is a joyous cacophony of 17th century architecture, crumbling streets and church spires, made for Rīga's main activity: strolling.

Start at the **Dome Cathedral** (☎ 721 3498; admission 0.5Ls; ☪ 1-5pm Tue-Fri, 10am-2pm Sat, closed Sun & Mon), the largest church in the Baltics, which also boasts the world's fourth-largest organ (1880).

It's the heart of the city, with concerts held inside its majestic belly (see the cathedral board for details). The foundations were laid in 1211 and the stone tombs it contains were blamed for a cholera epidemic that broke out after a flood in 1709 and killed one-third of the city's residents.

The **Museum of the History of Rīga & Navigation** (☎ 735 6676; admission 1Ls; ☪ 11am-5pm Wed-Sun) is in a cloister next to the cathedral. Children love the gruesome mummified hand of a criminal on display and the 16th-century executioner's sword. Allow a good hour to wander round.

It's a short walk southeast through cobbled streets to Rīga's skyline centrepiece, **St Peter's** (☎ 722 9426; Skārņu iela 19; admission (tower) 1.5Ls; ☪ 10am-5pm, closed Mon). Take the lift up to the excellent viewing tower 72m skyward (the spire reaches 123.25m). The lift guy will lend you his binoculars if you ask nicely. The church was built in 1209 and the wooden tower was destroyed several times.

Legend has it that in 1667 builders threw glass from the top – the number of pieces it broke into was the number of years it would stand. It didn't break after its fall was cushioned by straw – and a year later it burned down. Rebuilt in 1973, builders again threw glass down and it shattered into thousands of pieces so the future of Rīga's famous tower seems safe.

It overlooks the **House of Blackheads** (☎ 704 4300; Rātslaukams 6; admission 1Ls; ☪ 10am-5pm, closed Mon) which is Rīga's architectural gem. Built in 1344 for the Blackheads' guild of unmarried merchants, it was damaged in 1941, flattened by the Soviets seven years later, and rebuilt from scratch in 2000. The town hall opposite was also raised from the ashes in 2002. A statue of Rīga's patron saint, **St Roland** (Rātslaukams), stands in the **Town Hall Square** between the two buildings. He's a replica of the original, erected in 1897, which was moved to St Peter's during WWII to protect him.

The **Great Guild** (Amatu iela 5) and the **Small Guild** (Amatu iela 6), 14th-century buildings once the seat of wealthy German power brokers, now house the Philharmonic Orchestra. Snoop around by asking the attendants nicely (and paying 0.5Ls) as the guilds boast exquisite stained glass windows.

Show off some nifty Torville and Dean moves on the city's **outdoor ice rink** (Līvu laukams; admission 1Ls; ☺ 11am-midnight Mon-Thu, 11am-1am Fri, 10am-1am Sat, 10am-midnight Sun winter), overlooked by the Small Guild.

Meander from here north to the round 14th-century **Powder Tower** (Torņa iela) which has nine Russian cannonballs still embedded in its walls. From here go under the **Swedish Gate** (cnr Torņa & Aldaru iela) which was built into the city walls in 1698 to celebrate Swedish occupation. Legend has it that the sensitive executioner would place a red rose on the window ledge before that day's execution.

Along Mazā Pils iela are Rīga's oldest stone houses, Nos 17, 19 and 21, which have been dubbed the **Three Brothers**. On Jēkaba iela is Latvia's **Saeima** (parliament) at No 11. Medieval **Rīga Castle** (Pils laukams 3), built in 1330, now houses the president and a museum of foreign art.

Dividing the Old and New Towns is the **Freedom Monument** (Map p400; Brīvības bulvāris) topped by a bronze statue of Liberty (affectionately known to locals as Milda) holding three stars, representing the historic regions of Kurzeme, Latgale and Vidzeme. During the Soviet years the Freedom Monument was off limits, and placing flowers at Milda's base was a crime for which people were deported to Siberia.

The **Laima Clock** (illuminated at night) stands nearby – a traditional meeting place for lovers. From here, east of Old Rīga's jumbled streets, the city's old defensive moat – now a canal – snakes through parks between wide 19th-century boulevards.

In **Bastejkalns** (Bastion Hill), west of the monument, five red stone slabs lie as **Memorials to the Victims of 20 January 1991**, who were killed here when Soviet troops stormed the nearby Interior Ministry.

The 19th-century **Russian Orthodox cathedral** on Brīvības bulvāris is worth a visit.

Museums

Both the Soviet and Nazi occupations of Latvia during the last half-century are chronicled in the chilling yet spirited **Museum of the Occupation of Latvia** (☎ 721 2715; Strēlnieku Laukams 1; www.occupationmuseum.lv; admission free; ☺ 11am-5pm, closed Mon). An inscription inside the museum reads: 'They took it all – our native land, our honour and our name. They punished us for being human beings.' Anon.

NOUVEAU RICHE

Lavish decoration became Rīga's signature architectural style at the turn of the 20th century. You'll soon get neck-ache as you wander, awestruck by the arched peacocks, sculpted or twisted faces with flowing hair, delicate flowers and elegant Parisian decorations which elevate this ancient city to a high art form.

Based on the idea that design should embrace the decadent and expressive, Art Nouveau transformed the architecture of Rīga into a hedonist's playground in stone and wood. The movement dedicated to the 'beautiful' arose in Paris, Munich and Vienna but it was Rīga which took the charm to its bosom. The splendour of the Old Town is reflected in its status as a Unesco World Heritage Site.

After 1904 one-third of all buildings were made in this style, each one decorated individually. Local architects were employed to add dazzling façades to the city's structures.

Keep your eyes peeled as you walk the city's cobbled streets. Some of the best examples of richly decorated Art Nouveau are on Alberta iela (Nos 2, 4, 8 and 13, all by Mikhail Eisenstein); Elizabetes iela 33, 10b; famously Paul Mandelstamm's apartment at Kaleju iela 23; jauniela 25/29 by Wilhelm Bockslaff; and many more.

LATVIA

Here you witness the desperate fight for freedom and see a mock-up of a Siberian barracks. The must-see exhibition ends with the sobering facts – during the occupations 550,000 Latvians were lost, more than a third of the population. Allow two hours to absorb the detail.

The **Latvian Ethnographic Open-Air Museum** (☎ 799 4106; Brīvības gatve 440; www.virmus.com; adult/concession 1/0.50Ls; ☒ 11am-5pm mid-May–mid-Oct, closed last day of each month) is another essential sight. It houses over 90 buildings from rural Latvia and has traditional crafts and music to enjoy. Perfect for kids. Take bus No 1 from the corner of Merķeļa iela and Tērbatas iela to the Brīvdabas muzejs stop.

The **State Museum of Art** (☎ 732 4461; K Valdemāra iela 10a; admission 1.70Ls; ☒ 11am-5pm Wed-Mon) has a ground floor hall dedicated to contemporary art, sculpture and photography, while the Latvian masters of old are shown among the Soviet grandeur of ruched net curtains, marble columns and red carpets.

The **War Museum** (Smilšu iela 20; ☎ 722 8147; admission 0.5Ls; ☒ 10am-5pm Wed-Sun) shows the violent history of this tiny nation – through Swedish, Polish German and Soviet occupation – by way of photos and war relics.

The **Museum of Decorative & Applied Arts** (☎ 722 9736; Skārņu iela 10; admission 1Ls; ☒ 11am-5pm, closed Mon) has stern attendants patrolling the eccentric melee of Latvian textiles, china and tapestry. Worth a visit for the bridal plates and amber jewellery.

The **Jews in Latvia Museum** (☎ 728 3484; www.muzeji.lv/guide/pages_e/hebreji.html; Skolas iela 6; admission by donation; ☒ 10am-5pm Mon-Fri) has a captivating exhibit not only of the extermination of the Jews in Latvia during wartime but also of their historical cultural presence in the country. Ask to see the 10-minute introductory video that contains some chilling footage shot by an amateur German soldier.

FESTIVALS & EVENTS

Baltic Ballet Festival (Apr) Dancers and companies from around the Baltics gather in Riga between the 22nd and 24th.

Gadatirgus (Jun) Folklore festival held during the first weekend in June at Rīga's Ethnographic Open-Air Museum.

Summer Singing Fair (25 Jul) Across Riga's squares and marketplaces Latvians do what they love best – sing traditional pieces.

Arsēnals Cinema Forum (Sep) Between the 17th and 19th Rīga hosts an international film festival.

SLEEPING
Budget

Finding cheap rooms in Rīga's Old Town can give you the Baltic blues but there are a few good options. Be prepared to employ any devious means to get a room in high season as there ain't no rooms in this city between May and August. You should try to book in advance.

Patricia (☎ 728 4868; tourism@parks.lv; Elizabetes iela 22; s/d 16/26Ls incl breakfast) Bed down with a local in rooms in private flats across the city.

Posh Backpackers (☎ 721 0917; posh@poshbackpackers.lv; Pūpolu Str 5; dm/d 8/16Ls) A clean and friendly home-from-home, this old warehouse is within the central market precincts so can feel bustling. The 59 beds are in large, airy but old-fashioned dorms just one minute's walk away from the bus and train stations. Lacks kitchen facilities or any 'extras'.

Old Town Hostel (☎ 614 7214; oldtown@hostel.lv; Valnu iela 43; dm 9Ls) Marble floors, chandeliers on all four floors, a spiral staircase, sauna, Internet and 30 comfy beds make this a star find. Tanya the manager speaks good English, Latvian and Russian and will make you feel at home. An excellent price and location in the historic quarter of Rīga.

Viktorija (☎ 701 4111; info@hotel-viktorija.lv; A Čaka iela 55; s/d renovated 30/40Ls, s/d with shared bathroom 15/20Ls) Housed in a lovely Art Nouveau building, this hotel now has renovated – and hence more expensive – rooms. For comfort and cleanliness the new pads are a good choice. Unrenovated cheap rooms with shared bathrooms can still be had for a pittance. Take your earplugs though as this hotel is on the busiest street of Rīga's New Town so there's no need for a morning alarm clock – just let the hustle and bustle do it for you!

Valnis (☎ 721 3785; Vaļņu iela 2; apt 1-/2-person 20/30Ls) At last! The apartments are clean and have en-suite bathrooms and are smackbang in the Old Town but quiet. It's hidden down a dingy courtyard with a small sign at the end so be vigilant in finding it. Not a bad choice.

Coming out of the train station you'll notice the **Saulite** (☎ 722 4546; Merķeļa iela 12; s/d 20/30Ls) hotel which offers the kind of security and comfort of usual seedy station haunts. Avoid if possible, especially if a lone female.

Mid-Range

Treat yourself to a bit of luxury with one of these tasty stays – go on, you're worth it…

Laine (☎ 728 8816; info@laine.lv; Skolas iela 11; s/d from 30/40Ls) A good central find in a courtyard off the main street. Staff here pride themselves on their welcome and friendliness, which gives the whole place a home-from-home feel. The rooms may have overly brash colour schemes but the wooden summer terrace and cosy restaurant make up for it. Good value.

Radi un Draugi (☎ 722 0372; www.draugi.lv; Mārstaļu iela 1; s/d from 33/42Ls) Raved about by many who love the Scandinavian feel of the place – clean rooms with en suite, breakfast and friendly staff. There's a plush, serene bar for guests on the 1st floor and a strange 80s décor café downstairs. This place has gotten popular so book well ahead as it's often full all summer. An Old Town gem with disabled access and lift (once you get off the cobbles!).

Vecriga Hotel (☎ 721 6037; www.vecriga.lv; Gleznotāju iela 12; s/d 65/75Ls) Utterly charming 18th-century town house renovated into Rīga's loveliest little hotel on a cobbled backstreet. The 10 rooms are little wooden nooks with large comfy beds and pristine bathrooms. Despite lurid paintings in the bar/restaurant there's good Latvian food, a small courtyard and a cosy feeling about the place. The Dalai Lama himself stayed here – so if it's good enough for him…(take a look in the leather-bound guest book for his handwritten message).

Konventa Sēta (☎ 708 7501; reservation@konventa .lv; Kalēju iela 9/11; s/d 46/55Ls) Take yourself back in time and unwind in a place loaded with history. This unique and lovely hotel is in the restored courtyards of a 15th-century convent, with 10 medieval buildings each named after their original uses. Rooms are plush and understated and there's disabled access.

Forums (☎ 781 4680; reservation@hotelforums.lv; Valņu iela 45; d 37-48Ls, tr 57Ls) Cosy hotel inside a converted town house with dark wooden furnishings and elegant appeal. It's sandwiched between the Old Town and station and if you can afford it it's worth investing in the top floor suite with private sauna for the ultimate stay.

Centra (☎ 722 6441; hotel@centra.lv; Audēju iela 1; s/d 50/60Ls) Cool minimalist sleep palace with a sleek white interior and sensational location in the heart of the Old Town. You won't want to leave this calming haven. Rooms on the 4th floor have great city views.

Top End

You're spoiled for choice in Rīga if you've got a few hundred euro to fritter away. Stay the night in some of Europe's loveliest, most soulful rooms. Keeps out the riffraff anyway.

Ainavas Boutique Hotel (☎ 781 4316; Peldu iela 23; s/d 60/80Ls) The words enchanting and luxurious and gorgeous were made for this small hotel which makes Rīga's first claim at irresistible boutique status. Each room is decorated differently on the theme of Latvian nature, inspired by a beautiful photo hanging at the bedhead. The soothing rooms have satellite TV and en-suite bathrooms. And if that isn't enough you can sip brandy watching crackling flames in the hotel's 15th-century bar.

Hotel Bergs (☎ 777 0900; www.hotelbergs.com; Elizabetes iela 83/85; apt 90-199Ls) Newly built in a very regal Latvian style, this grand yet strangely homely hotel has style oozing out of every new brick. The rooms are all designed individually and are plush and sleek. Outside it's surrounded by a charming courtyard strung with fairy lights.

Grand Palace Hotel (☎ 704 4000; grandpalace @schlosse-hotels.com; Pils iela 12; d/ste from 130/265Ls) This is the best of the bunch – and the choice of legendary celebrities such as Catherine Deneuve rather than mere mortals. Each of the rooms is a lavish concoction of regal blues and gold and anyone staying here will feel like a queen (if they're not already one). There's a sauna, steam room, acclaimed restaurant and fitness centre to bring out the goddess in anyone.

Among other city choices are two landmark hotels, **Hotel Riga** (☎ 704 4222; info@hotelriga .lv; Aspazijas bulvāris 1–3; s/d 50/65Ls) and the **Radisson** (☎ 706 1111; info.riga@radissonsas.com; Kugu iela 24; s/d 80-225Ls).

EATING

Oh joy – the curse of stodgy, bland Baltic food has vanished in a maelstrom of excellent, cheap restaurants which will transport you from Italy to India in the blink of a blini.

There is plenty to choose from, restaurants also line Kaļķu iela and there are bar/cafés around Doma laukams (Cathedral Square).

Restaurants

INTERNATIONAL

Kamāla (☎ 721 1332; Jauniela 14; mains 3Ls; 🕑 7-10pm) Settle into deep cushions at the carved wooden tables at this wonderful restaurant which was named after the wife of Vishnu and the daughter of the milk ocean. One hundred per cent veg, and mostly Ayurvedic, the dishes on offer such as spinach *paneer*, tofu kebabs, warming veg soup and salads will soothe your soul.

Turku Restorāns (Mārstaļu iela 4; mains 3Ls; 🕑 noon-midnight) An opulently decorated Turkish restaurant with good, cheap dishes to delight diners. Ask for a hookah pipe to puff while choosing between the array of tasty kebabs and steaks.

Habibi (Peldu iela 24; 🕑 noon-midnight) Take it easy here. A laid-back vibe, mouthwatering Arabian dishes and belly dancers take your mind off the rigours of travel. Fruit-flavoured tobacco costs 5Ls a pipe.

Tower (☎ 721 6155; Smilšu iela 7; mains 6Ls; 🕑 11am-1am) The polar opposite to Kamāla in cool minimalist style but no less soothing. This warm Scandinavian restaurant offers an authentic menu of beef, pickled herring and proper hamburgers in a stylish blue and pale wood setting.

Fellini (☎ 728 4801; Marijas iela 13; mains 7Ls; 🕑 noon-midnight) Stop everything! The steak is the best in Europe, nay the planet. And with an excellent wine list, a choice of experimental pasta dishes and salads it's clear that this ain't no ordinary chef at work in Rīga's classiest restaurant. It's not – Chef Erasmo from Naples is cooking up a storm so go try.

LATVIAN

Ķiploka krogs (☎ 721 1451; Jēkaba iela 3; mains 3Ls; 🕑 11am-11pm) We hope you like garlic because this charming little place has a fixation for it. Vampires need not book. If you fancy garlic soup, garlic roasted chicken, garlic salad and garlic ice cream for dessert then you've found paradise. If you're on a first date there's a parsley sprig aperitif!

Alus Sēta (☎ 722 2431; Tirgoņu iela 6; mains 4Ls; 🕑 10am-1am) Dark, brown wood bar/restaurant with good Latvian cooking. Wash down traditional favourites like *shashlik*, salads and potatoes with plenty of home-brewed Lido beer. Has a homely feel rather like a cosy brown bar in Holland.

Cafés

Rāma (K Barona iela 56; mains 1Ls; 🕑 9am-midnight Mon-Sat, 11am-7pm Sun) This Hare Krishna sanctuary dishes up huge veg meals at cost price. An absolute treasure with a set menu changing every day at this seriously karmic venue.

John Lemon (☎ 722 6647; Peldu iela 21; mains 2Ls; 🕑 10am-midnight Mon-Fri; 10am-5am Sat, noon-midnight Sun) So good it should be illegal. Slinky green 60s space-station sofas with orange walls, a pink bar and an excellent cheap menu. Pasta dishes, jacket potatoes and breakfasts make this a funky favourite, especially with women.

Quick Eats

Sievasmātes p īrādziņi (Kaļķu iela 10; 🕑 9am-9pm) Literally called Mother-in-Law's *pīrāgi* (filled pasties or rolls) this is probably the cheapest joint in Rīga. The cute little pasties come stuffed with meat, mushrooms, fruit or cheese for a mere 1Ls.

Pelmeņi XL (☎ 722 2728; Kaļķu iela 7; 🕑 9am-4am) Their speciality is *vareņiki* (dumplings) made with mushrooms or sauerkraut and huge *pelmeņi* (Russian ravioli-like dumpling), stuffed with pork, chicken or vegetables or cheese at 1.50Ls a go.

Lido atpūtas centrs (☎ 728 2187; Krasta iela 76; mains 2Ls; 🕑 10am-11pm) Beloved of Latvian families who flood the vast eating and entertainment complex at weekends. Spend the day here discovering Latvian traditional food and drink at its most kitsch. Take bus No 107 from in front of the train station to the Lido stop.

Pizza Jazz (☎ 721 1237; Raiņa bulvāris 15; mains 3Ls; 🕑 10am-midnight) Excellent position on the boulevard overlooking the Freedom Monument, this is possibly Rīga's finest pizza place. Watch the world go by and enjoy the full Italian magic from one of more than 20 types on offer, along with salads and desserts. So popular it's worth booking on Friday and Saturday nights.

Self-Catering

Rimi (Centra Shopping Mall; 🕑 9am-8pm) A supermarket with a yummy fresh bread and pastries section.

Central market (Prāgas iela; 🕑 7am-4pm) Located in five huge hangars behind the bus station, it has rows of cheeses, sauerkraut, fish, eels, sweets, chocolates and fresh honey.

DRINKING

Rīga has a reputation as a party city. Clubs and bars are spread across the city so there's no distinct nightlife area.

Most places are open from 11am until 1am on weeknights and until dawn breaks on Friday and Saturday nights so swap your slippers and hot chocolate for your dancing shoes and vodka cocktail and show the locals how it's done!

A.Suns (Elizabetes iela 83/85) Round the back of K.Suns cinema, this friendly, open-plan place is an expat favourite. The neon signs around the walls must give off a strange allure because it's always packed at weekends. Bar grub can be had but the emphasis is on sinking beers.

Dickens (Grēcinieku iela 9/1) Enjoy a pint surrounded by Latvians pretending they're in Blighty. Weird but pretty authentic pub which screens English premiership matches.

Tim McShane's (Tirgoņu iela 10) You can't step a foot outside Ireland without falling into an Irish bar. As good as any other for pre-club boozing.

Pulkvedim neviens neraksta (No-one Writes to the Colonel; Peldu iela 26–28) An offbeat dance bar with two floors of alternative music. Very trendy crowd.

Orange Bar (Jāņa sēta 5) Small bar filled to the brim with young locals at weekends. DJs on Friday and Saturday nights playing alternative sounds.

Melnais kaķis (Black Cat; Meistaru iela 10–12) See where the bikers go to play. This is an institution because it's open until 7am for food, drinks and lots of heavy rock.

Rīgas Balzams (Torņa iela 4) Sells what it says on the sign. 'Enjoy' shots of the infamous black poison in this lovely, cosy little downstairs bar.

Monte Kristo (Elizabetes iela 10; 8am-9pm Mon-Sat, 10am-8pm Sun) It's a mecca for coffee-drinkers and tea-lovers. Choose your cuppa from leaf teas and coffee beans stacking the walls. Also serves delicious tarts and cakes.

ENTERTAINMENT

Rīga has independent and mainstream cinemas, a glorious opera house, circus and theatre to keep you amused. Listings for films, ballets and any cultural events are found in city guides *Rīga This Week* and *In Your Pocket* or check www.rigathisweek.lv.

Cinemas

K.Suns (728 5411; Elizabetes iela 83/85; tickets before 5pm 1.50L, thereafter 2.50Ls) Independent cinema with loyal crowd.

Kinogalerija (722 9030; Jauniela 24; www.kino galerija.lv, in Latvian; admission 2Ls) The Nordic film festival often shows movies here in this intimate cinema.

Baltic Cinema (13 Janvāra iela 8) New multiplex showing Hollywood releases. Rates differ for matinee, Monday and weekend shows.

Classical Music

Great Guild (Lielā ģilde; Amatu iela 5) The concert hall of the renowned Latvia National Symphonic Orchestra. Check listings for concert details.

Dome Cathedral (721 3498; Doma Laukams 1; ticket 3-10Ls) Stages weekly concerts; see listings or check the board outside the cathedral.

Clubs

XXL (728 2276; Kalniņa iela 4; 6pm-7am) This gay club *is* Rīga's gay scene – with hard techno DJs and a dark room.

The mainstream clubs in Rīga are dodgy/flash-your-cash **Roxy** (Kaļķu iela 24) and trendy **Casablanca** (Smilšu iela 1–3).

Opera & Theatre

National Opera House (707 3777; www.opera .lv; Aspazijas bulvāris 3; 10am-7pm) Known as 'The White House' by locals, this awesome building is home to the Rīga Ballet, where Mikhail Baryshnikov made his name, and the Latvian National Opera. The Rīga Opera Festival, staged in June, is held here.

Daile Theatre (727 9566; Brīvības iela 75) Stages national and international productions. Check the theatre's box office for ticket prices/productions.

GETTING THERE & AWAY

For information on international flights, buses, trains and ferries, see p416. For national transport information see p417.

Air

There are direct flights from Rīga to/from Estonia and Lithuania. There are no internal flights within Latvia.

GETTING AROUND
To/From the Airport

Rīga International Airport (Lidosta Rīga; 720 7009; www.riga-airport.com) is 8km west of the centre.

Bus No 22 runs from outside the terminal building to the central bus station stop on 13 Janvāra iela every 30 minutes, from 6am to 11.15pm. The fare is 0.20Ls and it takes 30 minutes. A taxi from the Old Town to the airport costs 8Ls.

Car & Motorcycle

For car rental try **National** (☎ 720 7710), **Sixt** (☎ 720 7121) or **Budget** (☎ 720 7327) in the arrivals hall of Rīga Airport. For more information see p417.

Motorists must pay 5Ls per hour to enter the Old Town.

Public Transport

The bus, trolleybus and tram routes are clearly marked on Jāņa sēta's *Rīga City Map*. Tickets (0.20Ls) are sold on board by drivers or conductors. Monthly passes for all three are sold at news kiosks and tram booths and cost 11.70Ls. The Rīga Card gives discounts on transport (see p402). City transport runs from 5.30am to 12.30am daily.

Taxi

Those yellow run-arounds charge 0.3Ls per km by day and 0.4Ls per km by night. Insist the meter is switched on and always haggle for a fixed price before embarking on longer journeys. Either find a cab at the rank outside Hotel De Rome on Brīvibas bulvāris or call **Rigas Taksometru Parks** (☎ 800 1313) or **Rīga Taxi** (☎ 800 1010).

AROUND RĪGA

When city life gets too much there's plenty to escape to within reach of Rīga. Head for the beaches of Jūrmala, enjoy the palaces of the Zemgale region or have a chilling history lesson at Salaspils.

Jūrmala
pop 56,000

Life's definitely a beach on this 32km stretch of white sands, ice-blue seas, bracing air and pale sand dunes.

Jūrmala (seashore) has been a Latvian secret for far too long and it's time they shared this string of 14 townships and heady coastline. Dubbed the 'pearl of Latvia', this is the largest resort in the Baltics and a stunning blend of carved wooden houses, Blue Flag beaches and murmuring pine trees. This is

definitely an up-and-coming seaside resort with Eastern European prices.

The 4km-stretch between Bulduri and Dubulti is where the hotels, guesthouses, bars and shops are, with Majori's Jomas iela the main pedestrian hub.

And within a whisper is Ķemeri National Park, a natural wonder of protected land established in 1997 and stretching across 42 hectares. Bogs, marshland and forest contain rare birds such as the lesser spotted eagle, rare plants, as well as red deer, wolves and wild boar.

INFORMATION
Tourist Information (☎ 776 4676; www.jurmala.lv; Jomas iela 42, Majori; ☼ 9am-6pm Mon-Fri, 10am-4pm Sat –summer only) The centre has maps, leaflets and guide *Jūrmala This Week*.

Ķemeri National Park Visitor Centre (☎ 776 5387; Meža mājа; nacionalparks@kemeri.apollo.lv; ☼ 10am-4pm May–mid-Oct) Gives information on forest trails, flora and fauna and spa resorts.

SIGHTS & ACTIVITIES
See the incredible **wooden architecture** at Bulduri and Dzintari, soak up rays on the best **beaches** of Bulduri, Dubulti and Majori, climb the highest **dunes** at Lielupe, get away from it all by heading westwards onto deserted sands, make a splash in Vaivari at the **Nemo Water Park** (☎ 773 6392; nemo@apollo.lv; Atbalss iela 1) or simply go for a paddle.

SLEEPING & EATING
Kempings Nemo (☎ 773 6392; nemo@apollo.lv; Atbalss iela 1, Vaivari; camp sites 3Ls, chalet bed per person 13Ls) Camp or wake up in a chalet at this popular spot for families at the water park.

Elina Guesthouse (☎ 776 1665; Lienes iela 43; d Jun-Aug 25Ls, Sep-May 15Ls) Beautiful wooden house with elegant, understated rooms.

Majori Hotel (☎ 776 1380; Jomas iela 29, Majori; s/d 6 May-5 Sep 33/48Ls, winter 21/33Ls) Three-star hotel with views of the river and an excellent restaurant serving good Latvian fodder (mains 7Ls).

Jomas iela in Majori is lined with bars and restaurants. Among them try:
Veranda (☎ 776 3127; Jomas iela 58; mains 5Ls; ☼ 11am-11pm) Old-fashioned bar/restaurant with rough edges but good basic Latvian staples such as *shashlik* and salads.
Sue's Asia (Jomas iela 74; mains 5Ls; ☼ noon-11pm) Serves Indian, Thai and Chinese food in a new, plush restaurant on the main pedestrian route.

GETTING THERE & AWAY

Microbuses run from near Rīga train station. Take either the Dubulti or Jaunķemeri bus to Majori (1Ls, 25 minutes). Trains go every 20 minutes to Dubulti on the Tukums, Sloka or Ķemeri services (0.51Ls, 35 minutes). Most go to Majori but not all.

Salaspils

'Behind this gate the earth groans', reads the inscription inside the incredible concrete edifice which marks the ghost of the Salaspils Concentration Camp.

Between 1941 and 1944 an estimated 45,000 Jews from Rīga and approximately 55,000 other people, including Jews from other Nazi-occupied countries and prisoners of war, were murdered here, 15km southeast of Rīga. Yet today the site is a place of peaceful solitude amid whispering pine trees on the Daugava River. A metronome encased inside a black marble wall beats out never-ending time. It is a haunting memorial.

The concrete sculpture on the left on entering reads: 'On this way went crying children, mothers, fathers and grandfathers – all went to die. Who will count those unsaid words? Who will count the lost years which Nazi bullets killed…?'

Four giant sculptures of figures, entitled *The Humiliated, The Mother, The Unbroken* and *Solidarity* look up to the sky and seem to ask 'why?'. The keeper of the site sells brochures for 0.50Ls to this place you won't forget.

GETTING THERE & AWAY

From Rīga take a suburban train (10 daily) on the Ogre–Krustpils line to Dārziņi (not Salaspils) station. A path leads from the station to the *piemineklis* (memorial), a 15-minute walk. Women should be aware that this is a solitary site and there have been reports of robbery on this track.

Zemgale

Central Latvia has a wealth of palaces to explore within day-trip distance of Rīga.

Rundāles pils (Rundāle Palace; ☎ 396 2197; www .rpm.apollo.lv; adult/concession 1.50/1Ls; ☼ 10am-6pm May-Oct, to 5pm Nov-Apr) sits in all its majesty in Pilsrundāle, 77km south of Rīga.

The architect of the Winter Palace in St Petersburg, the flamboyant Bartolomeo Rastrelli from Italy, brought a slice of Russian royalty and baroque splendour to little Latvia with this 18th-century gem.

It was designed and was built for Baron Ernst Johann von Bühren (1690–1772), Duke of Courland. Some 40 of the palace's 138 rooms are open to visitors, as are the extensive landscaped gardens which are breathtakingly beautiful in summer.

Smell the ashes of the cooking fires in the kitchen, see the Baron's ornate floral rooms and imagine life two centuries ago in this rather strangely placed palace.

Rundāle can be combined in a day trip with **Bauska** (population 10,700), a country town just 12km east, on the main Rīga to Vilnius road. The imposing **Bauska Castle** (1443–56) was constructed for the Livonian Knights, blown up in 1706 during the Great Northern War, and rebuilt in the 1970s. Merriment fills the castle grounds during July's Festival of Ancient Music.

Jelgava pils (Jelgava Palace; ☎ 300 5617; Leilā iela 2; adult/child 1/0.5Ls; ☼ 10am-4pm Mon-Fri) is another gem for Rastrelli-lovers, lying 42km west of Rīga in Zemgale region's largest town. The 300-room baroque palace sits 750m east of the centre.

GETTING THERE & AWAY

Without private transport this area is tricky to get to. Buses run to Bauska from Rīga every 30 minutes between 5am and 11pm (1.20Ls, 1¼ hours). Once at **Bauska bus station** (☎ 392 2477; Slimnicas iela 11) take one of only a handful of buses west to Rundāles pils (not Rundāle, which is 2.5km further west).

Buses run every 20 minutes between Rīga and Jelgava and minibuses go every hour (0.8Ls, 1¼ hours). There are hourly local trains (0.74Ls, 55 minutes) and some of the international services to Kaunas and Vilnius stop here.

EASTERN LATVIA

Shake off the city by immersing yourself in Latvia's eastern heart: the Vidzeme region. Its ancient forests, deep ravines and historic castles lure unsuspecting urban travellers into blissful commune with nature.

Be warned – the heady scent of pine forest in the exquisite Gauja National Park, which covers 49,000 hectares of land in the valleys of the Gauja River, could make you dizzy.

The sight of castle turrets peeping through dense woodland curves in Sigulda could seduce you into extending your stay.

The tempestuous medieval history of Cēsis, which is the only town within the Gauja National Park, will pump blood through your veins. And when you've experienced all that, come flying down to earth at Valmiera's ski resort.

SIGULDA

☎ 79 / pop 10,855

Swoon at the 'Switzerland of Latvia' as this gorgeous town is known. This enchanted place lies 53km east of Rīga and boasts a string of medieval castles and legendary caves, and is the gateway to the beautiful Gauja National Park.

It is also a minor health resort and winter sports centre, sporting an Olympic bobsleigh run.

Information

Gauja National Park Visitor Centre (☎ 71 345; www.gnp.gov.lv; Baznīcas iela 3, Sigulda; ☺ 9.30am-7pm Apr-Oct, 10am-4pm Nov-Mar)

Tourism Information Centre (☎ 71 335; info@sigulda.lv; Pils iela 6; ☺ 10am-7pm May-Oct, to 5pm Nov-Apr)

Sights

Sigulda's main attraction is the **Turaidas muzejrezervāts** (Turaida Museum Reserve; www.turaida-muzejs.lv; adult/concession 1/0.5Ls; ☺ 10am-5pm Nov-Apr, 10am-6pm May-Oct), the grounds of which house **Turaidas pils** (Turaida Castle; ☎ 71 402; ☺ 10am-5pm Nov-Apr, 10am-6pm May-Oct). The site was a Liv stronghold and the red-brick archbishop's castle was built in 1214.

There's an interesting museum inside the 15th-century granary charting the region from 1319 to 1561. Children will adore the **Dainu Hill Song Garden**, with 25 beautiful stone sculptures of Latvian folklore characters made by artist Indulis Ranka scattered among the grounds.

Between the tower and road, near the small wooden-spired **Turaida Church**, two lime trees shade the grave of the 'Turaida Rose' (see boxed text below).

There's little left of **Sigulda Castle**, which was built between 1207 and 1226, and its ruins are more a memory of the Knights' stronghold.

On the way to the ruins from town you pass the 1225 **Sigulda Church**, rebuilt in the 18th century, and the 19th-century New Sigulda Castle, the former residence of Prince Kropotkin. To the west of the Sigulda castles is a **cable car**, recently renovated, which runs every 30 minutes between 7.30am and 6.30pm across to Krimulda Castle (0.75/1Ls one way/return).

Activities

Thrill-seekers can fly down Sigulda's **bobsled track** (☎ 73 813; Šveices iela 13; admission per person 2Ls; ☺ Oct-Mar) in groups of five people.

Makars Tourism Bureau (☎ 73 724; www.makars.lv; Peldu iela 2) organises **boat trips** along the Gauja River. In winter it rents equipment for **cross-country** and **downhill skiing**. Skiers and snowboarders can use Latvia's steepest track at **Kaķīšu Trase** (☎ 65 79 939; per run 0.25Ls; ☺ 2-10pm Thu & Fri, noon-10pm Sat, 9am-midnight Sun) or at the more popular **Siguldas Pilsētas Trase** (☎ 94 47 713; per run 0.25Ls; ☺ 2-10pm Mon-Fri, noon-midnight Sat).

THE ROSE OF TURAIDA

An abandoned baby girl was found near Turaida Castle during the Swedish–Polish war. She was rescued, named Maija and grew up to become a beautiful maiden who fell in love with the castle gardener Victor Heil. The lovers met in Gutmaņa Cave.

One summer's day in 1620 Maija got a message apparently from Heil to meet in the cave – she went and her dead body was found there later that day. Heil was suspected of murder, then a Polish army deserter confessed to the local judge that his soldier mate Jakubowsky had fallen in love with Maija and asked her to marry him. When she refused he became angry and swore to get revenge on her by luring her to the cave to rape her so she was no longer a virgin. Jakubowsky sent the false message, Maija arrived and he attacked her. Maija said he could have her magic scarf which protects all men from injury and if he didn't believe her he could strike her with his sword to prove its powers. He did that – and she was slain. Heil was freed and the legend of their tragic love lives on today.

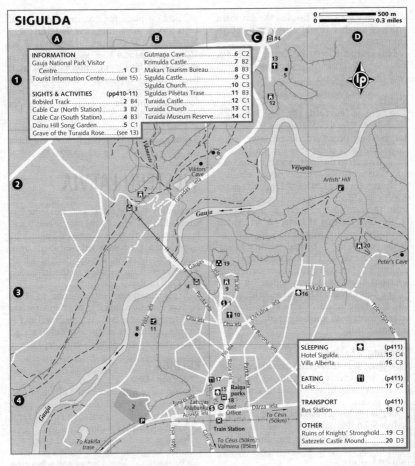

SIGULDA

INFORMATION	
Gauja National Park Visitor Centre................................**1** C3	
Tourist Information Centre........(see 15)	
SIGHTS & ACTIVITIES (pp410-11)	
Bobsled Track................................**2** B4	
Cable Car (North Station)............**3** B2	
Cable Car (South Station)............**4** B3	
Dainu Hill Song Garden..............**5** C1	
Grave of the Turaida Rose.......(see 13)	

Gutmaņa Cave.............................**6** C2
Krimulda Castle............................**7** B2
Makars Tourism Bureau...............**8** B3
Sigulda Castle...............................**9** C3
Sigulda Church............................**10** C3
Siguldas Pilsētas Trase...............**11** B3
Turaida Castle.............................**12** C1
Turaida Church...........................**13** C1
Turaida Museum Reserve............**14** C1

SLEEPING	🛏 (p411)
Hotel Sigulda................................15 C4	
Villa Alberta................................16 C3	

EATING	🍴 (p411)
Laiks...17 C4	

TRANSPORT	(p411)
Bus Station....................................18 C4	

OTHER	
Ruins of Knights' Stronghold......19 C3	
Satezele Castle Mound................20 D3	

From the cable car over the Gauja River you can **bungee jump** (☎ 72 531; Poruka iela 14; 13Ls; ☿ from 6.30pm Sat & Sun May-Sep).

Sleeping & Eating

Hotel Sigulda (☎ 72 263; www.hotelsigulda.lv; Pils iela 6; s/d 24/30Ls) Slick, modern hotel in the centre of Sigulda which boasts a steam room, sauna and pool and a charming restaurant with an excellent Latvian menu.

Villa Alberta (☎ 71 060; villaalberta@apollo.lv; Livkalna iela 10a; s/d 25/55Ls) Sumptuous yet cosy guesthouse near the castle which has tradinal-style rooms made for snuggling up in. No restaurant.

Laiks (☎ 50 104; Pils iela 8; mains 4Ls) Close to Hotel Sigulda, this bar/café/restaurant has

a wide-enough menu to suit most travellers and a traditional Latvian atmosphere with hearty food.

Getting There & Away

Thirteen trains run daily to Sigulda from Rīga (0.71Ls, one hour) and buses run every hour from Rīga, starting at 8.15am until 5.25pm (0.9Ls, one hour).

CĒSIS

☎ 41 / pop 17,588

Proud Cēsis has a rich history and an enviable position inside the stunning Gauja National Park. Locals boast that the 'real' Latvia exists within its medieval streets as Cēsis was the capital of Livonia in the Middle Ages

(1237) and the castle housed the Livonian order of knights. It will celebrate its 800th anniversary in 2006.

Cēsis Tourism Information Centre (☎ 21 815; www.cesis.lv; Pils Laukams 1; ☼ 9am-5pm Mon-Fri) is near the New Castle.

Sights

The ruins of **Cēsis Castle** (☎ 22 615; Pils Laukams 11; adult/child 0.7/0.4Ls; ☼ 10am-5pm Tue-Sun) are Latvia's best preserved. The Master of the Livonian Order chose it as his residence in 1237. It suffered during the wars of the 16th and 17th centuries and was never rebuilt.

Nearby the **New Castle** (☎ 22 615; Pils Laukams 9; adult/child 0.5/0.3Ls; ☼ 10am-5pm Tue-Sun), dating from the late 18th century, is now home to the **Cēsis Museum of History & Art** which chronicles events from prehistoric times to the present day. The Lademacher Tower has amazing views. The **Museum Garden** has a sculpture of Lenin in a coffin, removed from Vienības Laukams (Union Square) in 1990.

The **Baltic Medieval Festival** is held annually each June in Cēsis Castle Park, drawing large crowds with jousting, medieval dancing and music.

Sleeping & Eating

Hotel Cēsis (☎ 20 122; Vienības Laukams 1; s/d 30/42Ls) Large, comfortable hotel with 72 beds, the best restaurant in town and a sauna for weary guests.

Katrina (☎ 07 700; Mazā Katrīnas iela 8; s/d 24/32Ls) Stylish Scandinavian-style rooms in a renovated late-19th century building in the heart of the old town with a decent restaurant and sauna.

Getting There & Away

Four trains run daily from Rīga (1.10Ls, 1½ hours) and buses run every hour between 6.15am and 6.55pm daily (1.4Ls, one hour 40 minutes).

VALMIERA

☎ 42 / pop 28,500

Latvia's outdoor pursuits centre is 30km north of Sigulda. Don't bother entering unless you are prepared to fling yourself off a ski slope or paddle your way up the Gauja River.

Book trips in the national park or activities through the **Tourist Information Centre** (☎ 07 177; Rīgas iela 10; ☼ 9am-5pm Mon-Fri).

The best place for accommodation and trips for the adventurous is **Hostel Eži** (☎ 07 263; www.ezi.lv; Kr Valdemara 1; f Mon-Fri/Sat & Sun 14/16Ls, dm Mon-Fri/Sat & Sun 5/6Ls; ☼ 9am-7pm). A member of Hostelling International, staff here can book canoeing tours on the Gauja River (20Ls per day) or the Salaca River (60Ls for three days), cycle hire (5Ls per day) and cycle tours (25Ls per day).

Four trains run daily on the Rīga–Cēsis–Valmiera line (1.37Ls, two hours) and there are hourly buses (1.5Ls, two hours).

WESTERN LATVIA

Framed by the icy Baltic sea, Kurzeme has some of Latvia's most stunning scenery and least populated havens. Crowned by glorious Cape Kolka, the coast road westwards from Rīga is an unspoilt coastal delight which climaxes with the meeting of the Baltic Sea and Gulf of Rīga.

Experience the settlements of Livs (Latvia's ethnic minority), the dense forests of Slītere National Park, the medieval architecture and charm of ancient Kuldīga, and the port cities of Ventspils and Liepāja.

KULDĪGA

☎ 33 / pop 14,000

The capital of Kurzeme in the Middle Ages, this town 152km west of Rīga boasts Ventas Rumba (the widest waterfall in Europe) and a charming medieval quarter.

Kuldīga was founded in 1242 when the German Order of Knights built a castle on the banks of the Venta River and it became a thriving cultural and trade centre in the 14th century.

The **Tourist Information Centre** (☎ 22 259; www.kuldiga.lv, in Latvian; Baznīcas iela 5; ☼ 9am-5pm Mon-Sat, 10am-2pm Sun May-Oct, 9am-5pm Mon-Fri Nov-Apr) is in the old Town Hall.

Sights

The **oldest wooden building** (Baznīcas iela 7) in Kurzeme, dating from 1670, is found nestled on Rātslaukams (Town Hall Square) near the 17th-century **old Town Hall** (Baznīcas iela 5) which was once the town prison. The new Town Hall in Renaissance style (1860) stands at the southern end of the square.

The **waterfall**, which stretches 249m across the Venta River, is an astonishing sight and close to the **Livonian Order Castle ruins** on the river's west bank.

Sleeping & Eating

Jāņa Nams (☎ 23 456; Liepājas iela 36; s/d 11/20Ls) Kuldīga's best choice of hotel has clean, comfy rooms and a funky restaurant and bar. Friendly staff provide information on the town.

Stender's (☎ 22 703; Liepājas iela 3; ☽ 11am-10pm Sun-Thu, 11am-4am Fri & Sat) Don't get too excited but Kuldīga has a bar with live music at weekends and so-called club nights. You might get lucky with bar snacks.

Getting There & Away

Six buses run daily from Rīga (2.30Ls, two hours 20 minutes).

VENTSPILS

☎ 36 / pop 44,000

One of the largest ports on the Baltic Sea, wealthy Ventspils is the Dallas of Latvia. The city, 60km north of Kuldīga, is a major gateway for oil and chemical exports to Russia; the flourishing bars, restaurants and works of art springing up everywhere are testament to this.

For tourist information contact the **Ventspils Tourist Information Office** (☎ 22 263; www .tourism.ventspils.lv; Tirgus iela 7; ☽ 8am-7pm Mon-Fri, 8am-5pm Sat, 10am-5pm Sun May-Oct, 9am-5pm Mon-Fri, 10am-3pm Sat Nov-Apr).

Sights

Ventspils boasts one of the oldest medieval fortresses in Latvia. The 13th-century **Livonian Order Castle** (☎ 22 031; Jana iela 17; admission 1Ls; ☽ 9am-6pm May-Oct, 10am-5pm Nov-Apr) has a permanent digital exhibition called Living History and the Ghost Cellar which shows art, music and concerts, and makes an afternoon well spent.

Another brilliant display is the **Seaside Open-Air Museum** (☎ 24 467; Riņķa iela 2; admission free; ☽ 10am-6pm May-Oct, 11am-5pm Wed-Sun Nov-Apr) dedicated to Latvia's fishing traditions. There is a narrow-gauge railway and an anchor trail to keep any child amused.

Families in particular will love the clean beach and **Aqua Park** (☎ 65 853; Medņu iela 19; adult/child per day 3/1.5Ls; ☽ 10am-10pm May-Sep). The **city stadium** hosted the national Eurovision Song Contest final in 2002 (which Latvia won).

Sleeping & Eating

Seaside Camping (☎ 27 925; www.camping.vent spils.lv; Vasamīcu iela 56; camp site 1.5Ls, chalet 10-20Ls) Without doubt the best camping ground in the Baltics – if not the world. Gorgeous wooden chalets set against pine forests within a whisper of the beach.

Vilnis (☎ 68 880; Talsu iela 5; s & d 45Ls) Sleek, modern rooms in a shiny, marble-filled hotel with a fine restaurant.

Bugins (Lielā iela 1/3) This funky log cabin remains popular despite being force-fed MTV along with your traditional Latvian fodder.

Getting There & Away

Buses leave Rīga every hour between 7am and 10.30pm (3Ls, two hours 50 minutes).

LIEPĀJA

☎ 34 / pop 90,000

Number three city in Latvia, Liepāja, 11km south on the Baltic coast, has a thriving naval port (built by Russian Tsar Alexander III in 1890 and used as a Soviet military base until the early 1990s), clean stretches of beach and a bustling centre.

The **Tourist Information Office** (☎ 80 808; www.liepaja.lv; Lielā iela 11; ☽ 9am-6pm Mon-Fri, 9am-5pm Sat) is on-hand to help you explore or book accommodation.

In August the city hosts Latvia's largest annual rock festival, **Liepājas Dzintars** (Amber of Liepāja) which is a crowd-pleaser.

Hourly buses run to/from Rīga (3.20Ls, 3½ hours) and there are six buses daily to/from Kuldīga (1.55Ls, 2¼ hours) and Ventspils (2.55Ls, 3¾ hours).

LATVIA DIRECTORY

ACCOMMODATION

Book beds well in advance for Rīga as it's fast becoming a haunt for stag parties and hen trips as well as more civilised tourism. The **Latvian Tourism Development Agency** (www .latviatourism.lv) has an informative website and maps for forward planning.

There are few decent camping grounds in Latvia with the exception of Ventspils, where wooden chalets are available as well as camp sites.

Latvia has 11 hostels – some better than others. Check with **Hostelling Latvia** (☎ 921 8560; www.hostellinglatvia.com; Siguldas Pr 17-2, Rīga) and book accommodation on the Net. Prices range from 5Ls to 15Ls per night.

For country stay holidays, **Lauku Ceļotājs** (☎ 761 7600; www.traveller.lv; Kuģu iela 11, Rīga) arranges B&B accommodation in farmhouses and guesthouses in rural Latvia. Prices range from 11Ls to 20Ls per night including breakfast but there can be a minimum stay/charge per holiday. It publishes an annual catalogue, *Country Holidays*.

Hotels are springing up all over Rīga but be warned they generally cater for the business traveller with an expense account to flash. See the excellent *In Your Pocket* website (www.inyourpocket.com/Latvia/riga) for the full range of budget, mid-range and top-end choices. Expect to pay upwards of 40Ls to 60Ls per double room in the budget/mid-range options and much more for the top-end places.

The cheapest hotels outside Rīga cost between 8Ls to 20Ls for a room in a budget/mid-range place. Many places off the beaten track don't yet have a luxury option. Prices in this chapter are listed in budget order (from cheapest to most expensive).

ACTIVITIES

Latvia's abundance of unspoilt nature lends itself to outdoor pursuits. Whether canoeing or kayaking down the Gauja River (see p412), hiking on nature trails and bird-watching in Ķemeri National Park (p408), or bungee jumping or skiing in Sigulda (p410), there's plenty to keep most fidgets happy.

Most national park offices have hiking maps and some information about the area's activities.

BOOKS

Learn about a culture from its belly. *Latvian National Kitchen* by Nína Masiļūne chronicles the heavy peasant dishes, such as pigs trotters, which have fed the nation.

The Holocaust in Latvia 1941–44 by Andrew Ezergailis is harsh but essential reading to understand the psyche of the nation. It's the first comprehensive study of the Jewish bloodshed by Latvians and Germans.

The Story of Rīga by Andris Kolbergs charts the capital's history and cultural trends.

BUSINESS HOURS

Most shops open between 10am and 6pm in the larger towns/cities on weekdays and

Saturdays. Banks are generally open between 9am and 5pm weekdays and shut at weekends. Bars and restaurants vary but the general rule is they open between 10am and 11am and stay open until 11pm Monday to Thursday nights, 2am Friday nights and 4am Saturday nights.

In the country times vary according to the weather/seasons/personality of the owner!

CHILDREN

Latvians adore children and there's lots for them to do. There's ice-skating in Rīga's historic centre, a wealth of parks and beaches in the towns and coastal villages, hiking trails in the national parks and a smattering of museums to keep them amused. Some places such as the Latvian Ethnographic Open-Air Museum (see p404) have family days with an emphasis on entertainment for kiddies.

CUSTOMS

People over 18 can bring in 2L of alcohol, 5L of beer and 200 cigarettes without paying duty tax. You can bring any amount of hard currency. Customs rules are posted on www.latviatourism.lv or check with the **Ministry of Culture** (☎ 721 4100; Pils iela 22, Rīga; ☯ 8:30am-5pm Mon-Fri).

DISABLED TRAVELLERS

The cobbled streets of Rīga's Old Town are little use to anyone using a wheelchair, though most of the newer hotels have slopes as well as steps at their entrances. It's a hangover from Soviet disinterest that there's little in the way of help for less mobile travellers who must rely on their travel company for information and advice. There are lifts and personal wheelchair assistance at Rīga Airport.

EMBASSIES & CONSULATES
Latvian Embassies & Consulates
Latvian representation abroad includes:
Australia (☎ 02-9744 5981; fax 02-974 760 55; 32 Parnell St, Strathfield, 2135, Sydney)
Canada (☎ 613-238 6014; Latvia-embassy@magma.ca; 208 Albert St, Ste 300, Ottawa, K1P 5G8 Ontario)
Estonia (☎ 646 1313; ilze@latvia.lv; Tõnismägi 10, EE10119 Tallinn)
France (☎ 01 53 64 58 10; ambleton@wanadoo.fr; 6 Villa Said, F-75116 Paris)
Germany (☎ 030-8260 02 22; latembger@mfa.gov.lv; Reinerzstrasse 40–41, D-14193 Berlin)

Ireland (☎ 1 662 16 10; embassy.ireland@mfa.gov.lv; 14 Lower Leeson St, Dublin 2)
Lithuania (☎ 52 131 220; lietuva@latvia.balt.net; Čiurlionio 76, LT-2009 Vilnius)
Netherlands (☎ 70 306 39 34; embassy.netherlands@ mfa.gov.lv; Balistraat 88, 2585 XX's-Gravenhage)
Russia (☎ 095 9252707; latemb@co.ru; Chapligina 3; RUS-103062 Moscow)
UK (☎ 020-7312 0040; embassy@embassyoflatvia.co.uk; 45 Nottingham Place, London W1U 5LR)
USA (☎ 202-726 8213; Latvia@ambergateway.com; 4325 17th St NW, Washington, DC 20011)

Embassies & Consulates in Latvia

The following diplomatic offices are in Rīga:
Australia (☎ 722 2383; Raiņa bulvāris 3)
Canada (☎ 722 6315; Baznīcas iela 20/22)
Estonia (☎ 781 2020; Skolas iela 13)
France (☎ 703 6600; Raiņa bulvāris 9)
Germany (☎ 722 9096; Raiņa bulvāris 13)
Lithuania (☎ 732 1519; Rūpniecības iela 24)
Netherlands (☎ 732 61 47; Torņu iela 4, Jacob's Barracks, bldg 1a, LV 1050)
Russia (☎ 733 2151; Antonijas iela 2)
UK (☎ 777 4700; Alunāna iela 5)
USA (☎ 703 6200; Raiņa bulvāris 7)

FESTIVALS & EVENTS

Latvia is awash with festivals marking seasonal changes or as an excuse to have fun. The key events are the Baltika International Folk Festival, which Latvia hosts every three years, and the All-Latvian Song & Dance Festival, held every five years.

Easter celebrations are held throughout Rīga and the country; check the **Culture Department of Rīga Council** (☎ 704 3651) for details. See p404 for information on festivals and events in Rīga.

GAY & LESBIAN TRAVELLERS

Rīga's gay scene revolves around established club XXL (see p407). Compared to gay scenes across the rest of Europe, Latvia's is a fledgling operation but no less fun. Rejoice in www.gay.lv (in Latvian) which has links with gay and lesbian clubs, groups and information.

HOLIDAYS

Latvia's national holidays include:
New Year's Day 1 January
Good Friday March/April
Labour Day 1 May
Mother's Day 2nd Sunday in May
Ligo (Midsummer Festival) 23 June
Jāni (Summer solstice) 24 June
Day of Proclamation of the 18 November Latvian Republic, 1918 18 November
Christmas Eve & Day 24 & 25 December
Boxing Day 26 December
New Year's Eve 31 December

INTERNET ACCESS

Internet access is largely confined to Rīga, where an hour will set you back 1Ls; most are open 24 hours.

Visitors should acquire the RJ-11 plug to click into Latvia's phone cable network. Then using dial-up software (Apollo is a suggestion), dial 9008080 and surf away. Remember that hotel phone rates vary wildly.

LANGUAGE

That crazy language everyone is speaking is actually an endangered species; it's one of only two surviving Baltic branches of the Indo-European language family. Join in or speak English and French which is spoken by younger Latvians, Russian by older.

MAPS

Good country/area maps are published by **Jāņa sēta** (☎ 731 7540; www.kartes.lv) and are found in good bookshops and some kiosks.

MEDIA

The *Baltic Times* is the only credible English-language weekly while excellent city guide *Rīga In Your Pocket* is as necessary to a stay in these parts as your passport and trousers with elasticized waists (for the beer and pig trotters overload).

Tune into the BBC World Service on 100.5FM or the Latvian equivalent Latvijas Radio I (90.7) and Radio 2 (91.5). The most popular commercial channels in Latvia are Mix FM on 102.7, Radio SWH at 105.2 and European Hit Radio on 104.3FM.

Most hotels have cable TV. Rīga's interactive channel TV5 is linked to TVNET Web portal and is the only Latvian station which can be viewed live on the Internet, broadcasting between 8am and 2am daily.

MONEY

The national currency is the Lat (Ls). One Lat equals 100 santīmi. Latvia may adopt the euro after 2006. Banks, ATMs and exchange

LATVIA

offices will convert currency. Rīga has plenty
of ATMs and most hotels and restaurants
accept the major credit cards. Tattered notes
are still refused at exchange booths so keep
all banknotes pristine.

National bank **Latvijas Bankas** (Latvian Bank;
www.bank.lv) posts daily exchange rates on its
website.

POST

Main post offices open from 9am to 6pm
on weekdays and 9am to 1pm on Saturday
and Sundays.

Mail generally takes between five and
seven days to reach Europe and 10 to 14 days
for America and Australia. It costs 0.20Ls to
send a postcard and 0.30Ls for a standard
letter to Europe, 0.4Ls to the USA.

Telegrams can be sent by phone (☎ 900
2178; ☼ 24hr). The poste-restante desk at the
train station **post office** (☎ 701 8804; Stacijas laukums 1) keeps mail for one month. Address
letters to Poste Restante, Rīga 50, LV-1050,
Latvia.

There's an express mail service at Rīga
Airport; **DHL Freight Express Latvia** (☎ 707 0400).

TELEPHONE

To make an international call to Latvia, dial
371 followed by the city code and number.
Local Rīga numbers have seven digits and
start with a '7' and all countrywide numbers
have seven digits including the area code.

Most public phones use phonecards
which can be bought in denominations of
two, three or 5Ls from kiosks. International
cards are done by **Telenets** (www.telenets.lv) and
lattelekom (www.lattelekom.lv).

EMERGENCY NUMBERS

- Police ☎ 02
- Fire ☎ 01
- Ambulance ☎ 03

TOURIST INFORMATION

The **Latvian Tourism Development Agency** (☎ 722
9945; fax 750 8468; www.latviatourism.lv; Pils laukums 4;
Rīga) has a tourist office in most towns and
cities (see the individual Information sections throughout this chapter).

There are Latvian tourist offices in **Finland**
(☎ 09-2784774; latviatravel@kolumbus.fi; Mariankatu 8B,

SE-00170 Helsinki) and **Germany** (☎ 0251-2150742;
www.gobaltic.de; Salzmannstrasse 152, D-48159 Münster).

VISAS

Holders of EU passports don't need a visa
to enter Latvia; nor do Australian, New
Zealand and US citizens if staying for less
than 90 days. Check with the **Department of
Citizenship & Immigration** (☎ 721 9639; pmlp@pmlp
.gov.lv) for further details.

TRANSPORT IN LATVIA

GETTING THERE & AWAY
Air
Rīga Airport (☎ 720 7009; www.riga-airport.com) is
served by direct flights from Amsterdam,
Berlin, Brussels, Copenhagen, Frankfurt,
Helsinki, Kyiv, London's Heathrow, Moscow, Prague, Stockholm, Tallinn, Vilnius
and Warsaw.

Carriers at the airport include:
Air Baltic (code BT; www.airbaltic.lv; ☎ 720 7777;
☼ 5am-8pm Mon-Thu, 5am-7pm Fri, 5am-6.30pm Sat,
5am-9pm Sun) National carrier which now does cheap
no-frills deals.
British Airways (code BA; ☎ 720 7097; www.britishair
ways.com; ☼ 9am-5pm Mon-Fri, 9am-1pm Sat & Sun)
Lufthansa (code LH; ☎ 750 7711; www.lufthansa.com;
☼ 9am-6pm Mon-Fri, 11am-3pm Sat & Sun).

Land
BUS
Rīga's **Bus Station** (☎ 900 0009; Prāgas iela 1;
☼ 5am-midnight) has international bus companies **Eurolines** (☎ 721 4080; www.eurolines.lv;
☼ 8am-11pm) and **Ecolines** (☎ 721 4512; www.eco
lines.lv; ☼ 7am-9.30pm).

Eurolines has daily services to Vilnius
(7Ls, four daily), Moscow (12Ls), Hamburg
(50Ls), Tallinn (8.50Ls, five daily), St Petersburg (11Ls) and Berlin (44Ls). Ecolines has
daily buses to Kyiv (24Ls), Odesa (31Ls),
France (69Ls), Amsterdam (59Ls), London
(77Ls), and Karlshamn (17Ls), Oslo (25Ls)
and Kristianstad (17Ls) in Sweden.

International buses leave from platforms
1, 1a and 2.

CAR & MOTORCYCLE
Insurance is compulsory and can be bought
at the border points. Latvia and surrounding Baltic countries have an abundance of
garages for fuel, parts and repairs.

See p408 for further information on road rules and car hire.

TRAIN

At Rīga's **Train Station** (Centrālā Stacija; ☎ 583 2134; Stacijas Laukams) go to international ticket booth Nos 1 to 6 for trains to/from Latvia.

International services include two daily to Moscow (*Latvijas Ekspresis*, 24/38/45Ls for seat/couchette/1st class, 17½ hours), and one daily service to St Petersburg (*Baltija*, 21/33/48Ls for seat/couchette/1st class, 14 hours).

Vilnius can only be reached by bus.

Sea

Ferries depart from Rīga's **Ferry Terminal** (☎ 720 5460; Eksporta iela 1), 1.5km downstream of Akmens Bridge. Tickets for Rīga–Stockholm trips can be bought at travel agencies; prices start as low as 20Ls.

GETTING AROUND
Air

There are no internal flights in Latvia.

Bicycle

Cyclists can get advice from the Latvian Bicycle Tourism Information Centre (www.velokurjers. lv; Jēkabpils iela 19a). Cycling is easy as Latvia is flat but roads in rural areas leave much to be desired so take all necessary repair equipment.

Bus

The best way to get around Latvia is by bus: it's quicker and cheaper than the train. Timetables are to the right inside the Rīga's bus station, as is an **Information Centre** (☎ 722 0555; ☻ 10am-6pm).

Destination	Cost	Duration	Distance	Frequency
Bauska	1.20Ls	1½hr	65km	30 min
Cēsis	1.40Ls	2hr	90km	hourly
Daugavpils	3Ls	3½hr	230km	hourly
Kolka	3Ls	5¾hr	160km	1 daily
Kuldīga	2.30Ls	3hr	150km	6 daily
Liepāja	3.20Ls	4hr	220km	hourly
Sigulda	0.90Ls	1hr	50km	hourly
Talsi	1.70Ls	2½hr	115km	9 daily
Valmiera	1.30Ls	2½hr	120km	about 12 daily
Ventspils	2.70Ls	2½-4hr	200km	12 daily

Car & Motorcycle

Driving across Latvia can be a surreal experience; an hour can go by in the furthest reaches with only a horse and cart or dishevelled tractor to pass.

Expect potholes, gravel roads and ancient traffic on rural routes while the A2 Sigulda road, A6 Ogre road A8 Jelgava and A10 Jūrmala routes are Western-standard highways. Your home driving licence is normally acceptable with car hire firms and at the borders.

Driving is on the right-hand side. There's zero tolerance on drinking and driving (and a hefty fine of 450Ls if caught). Keep strictly to speed limits (generally 50km/h within towns and between 70km/h and 110km/h on highways) as police can fine 5Ls to 50Ls on the spot. Headlights must be on at all times while driving. Using a mobile phone when driving is illegal.

Cars can be hired but daily costs are high – as much as 60Ls to 100Ls. Firms based at Rīga airport include:
Baltic Car Lease (☎ 720 7121; ☻ 9am-6pm Mon-Fri)
Budget (☎ 720 7327; ☻ 10am-6pm)
National Car Rental (☎ 720 7710; ☻ 9am-8.30pm Mon-Fri, 11am-6pm Sat, 11am-8.30pm Sun)

Hitching

Hitching is never totally safe, and Lonely Planet doesn't recommend it. Lone women in particular should exercise caution. However, in rural areas hitching may be the only bet due to sporadic public transport – keep to daylight hours and travel in pairs.

Local Transport

Trams, buses and trolleybuses (buses that run by electricity from overhead wires) provide public transport around towns and cities. Most run from about 5.30am to midnight. Tickets cost a flat rate of 0.20Ls and must be punched in a machine on board the tram, bus or trolleybus. Check all this on the website of the **Tram & Trolleybus authority** (www.ttp.lv).

Taxis officially cost 0.30Ls per kilometre in the day and 0.40Ls after 10pm. Expect to have to haggle your fare if you're a tourist as these tariffs are deemed an irrelevance by local cabbies – you're rich right?

Train

Train services are generally slow and cumbersome. The timetables are posted on the

Internet by **Latvian Railways** (www.ldz.lv). Local trains are generally dirty, not known for their safety and basic in the extreme. Women travelling solo may prefer to travel by a different method as making a trip on a train means you will be the centre of attention.

Train tickets are sold in the main departures hall; window Nos 1 to 6 sell tickets for international trains; window Nos 7 to 9 sell tickets for main-line services; and window Nos 10 to 13 sell tickets for slower suburban trains. Main-line services include: Daugavpils (2.32Ls, 3½ hours, 218km, seven daily), Valmiera (1.37Ls, 3½ hours, 168km, four daily), Sigulda (0.71Ls, three hours, 13 daily). Trains run every 20 minutes to Majori at Jūrmala (0.51Ls, 25 minutes).

Lithuania

CONTENTS

Highlights	420
Itineraries	421
Climate & When to Go	421
History	421
People	422
Arts	422
Environment	423
Food & Drink	423
Vilnius	**424**
Orientation	424
Information	424
Sights	425
Festivals & Events	430
Sleeping	430
Eating	431
Drinking	432
Entertainment	432
Shopping	432
Getting There & Away	432
Getting Around	433
Around Vilnius	433
Eastern & Southern Lithuania	**434**
Aukštaitija National Park	434
Druskininkai	435
Central Lithuania	**435**
Kaunas	435
Šiauliai	439
Western Lithuania	**440**
Klaipėda	440
Palanga	443
Neringa	443
Nemunas Delta	444
Lithuania Directory	**444**
Accommodation	444
Activities	445
Business Hours	445
Disabled Travellers	445
Embassies & Consulates	445
Festivals & Events	446
Holidays	446
Money	446
Post	446
Telephone	446
Tourist Information	446
Visas	447
Transport in Lithuania	**447**
Getting There & Away	447
Getting Around	447

LITHUANIA

Possibly the Baltic countries' finest weapon of mass attraction – lovely Lithuania is a treasure-trove of unspoilt natural beauty, magical coastline and cobbled baroque cities. Until now she's been one of Europe's best-kept secrets; hidden away on the edge of Russia in that weird ex-Soviet bit no-one really knew anything about. But since EU ascension in May 2004, the spotlight has fallen on her. And the world is just beginning to like what it sees.

This tiny nation is a bastion of eccentricity and spirit. It threw off the might of the Soviet Union less than two decades ago and is careering into the future with an optimism rarely seen elsewhere. You'll love the sense of the bizarre here – the unofficial breakaway republic of artists in the capital Vilnius, which also boasts the world's only statue of Frank Zappa, set against fairy-tale baroque churches and a skyline of bewitching spires.

There's also the strange Hill of Crosses at Šiauliai, the breathtaking natural wonder of the Curonian Spit, deep ancient forests and the former capital Kaunas to entertain and transfix the visitor.

FAST FACTS

- **Area** 65, 200 sq km

- **Capital** Vilnius

- **Currency** litas; €1= 3.45 litų; US$1= 2.77; litų; UK£1= 4.98 litų; A$1= 2.01 litų; ¥100= 2.53 litų; NZ$1= 1.90 litų

- **Famous for** world's only Frank Zappa statue

- **Key Phrases** *Labas* (hello), *ačiū* (thanks), *prašau* (please), *taip* (yes), *ne* (no), *viso gero* (goodbye)

- **Official Languages** Lithuanian, Russian

- **Population** 3.5 million

- **Telephone Codes** country code ☎ 370; international access code ☎ 00

- **Visa** none required for citizens of the EU, Australia, Canada, New Zealand or the USA; see p447 for details

HIGHLIGHTS

- Enjoy the beautiful cobbled streets, baroque architecture and skyline of church spires in ravishing **Vilnius** (p424)
- Hear the wind breathe between the thousands of crosses at the eerie Hill of Crosses in **Šiauliai** (p439)
- Breathe in pure air and scent of pine forests on the enchanting **Curonian Spit** (p443)
- Party till dawn at Lithuania's answer to package-holiday craziness, **Palanga** (p443)
- Hike, boat or camp in the serene wilderness of **Aukštaitija National Park** (p434)

LITHUANIA

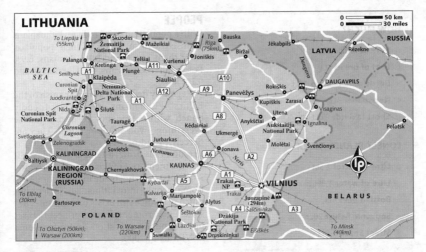

ITINERARIES

■ **One Week** Explore Vilnius for three days, then take a trip to Trakai then Šiauliai and spend a couple of days in Nida (on the Curonian Spit).

■ **Three Weeks** Time to see it all; spend quality time in Vilnius and Trakai, head to Šiauliai then Palanga for some partying. Explore Klaipėda, chill out on the Curonian Spit, then head back east via Kaunas. Camp in Aukštaitija National Park.

CLIMATE & WHEN TO GO

Any time is a good time to go to Lithuania, but remember the thermals in winter (between mid-November and mid-March when temperatures barely rise above freezing) and sunscreen in its beautiful and fleeting summer (from June to August with temperatures of around 20°C – and rain).

Winter lasts about six weeks longer in the inland east of the country than on the coastal west.

HISTORY

It's the classic riches to rags story – Lithuania once had an empire stretching from the Baltic to the Black Sea. It was the mighty Lithuanian leader Gediminas who pushed Lithuania's borders south and east between 1316 and 1341. In 1386 marriage forged an alliance with Poland against the German knights that lasted 400 years. In 1410 the Teutonic Order was decisively defeated at the battle of Grünwald in Poland.

But Lithuania was destined to disappear off the maps of Europe. In the 18th century, the Polish–Lithuanian state was so weakened by division that it was carved up by Russia, Austria and Prussia (successor to the Teutonic Order) in the partitions of Poland (1772, 1793 and 1795–96).

Vilnius was a bastion of Polish culture in the 19th century and a focus of uprisings against Russia. Lithuanian nationalists declared independence on 16 February 1918 with Kaunas as the capital, as Polish troops had annexed Vilnius from the Red Army in 1919.

In 1940, after the Molotov-Ribbentrop Pact, Lithuania was forced into the USSR. Within a year 40,000 Lithuanians were killed or deported. Up to 300,000 more people, mostly Jews, died in concentration camps and ghettos during the 1941–44 Nazi occupation.

The USSR ruled again between 1945 and 1952. An estimated 200,000 people were murdered or deported to Siberia. Armed partisans resisted Soviet rule from the forests but tens of thousands of 'forest brothers' were massacred by 1953.

In the late 1980s Lithuania led the Baltic push for independence. The popular front, Sajūdis, won 30 seats in the March 1989 elections for the USSR Congress of People's Deputies. Lithuania was the first Soviet state to legalise noncommunist parties. In February 1990 Sajūdis was elected to form a majority in Lithuania's new

HOW MUCH?

■ **Litre of milk** 1.8Lt

■ **Loaf of bread** 1Lt

■ **Bottle of house red** 15Lt

■ **Newspaper** 3Lt

■ **Short taxi ride** 10Lt

LONELY PLANET INDEX

■ **Litre of petrol** 2.5Lt

■ **Litre of water** 1.99Lt

■ **Bottled beer** 4Lt

■ **Souvenir T-shirt** 20Lt

■ **Street Snack** 5-8Lt

Supreme Soviet (now the parliament), which on 11 March declared Lithuania independent.

Moscow marched troops into Vilnius and cut off Lithuania's fuel supplies. In January 1991, Soviet troops stormed key buildings in Vilnius. Fourteen people were killed at the TV tower and Lithuanians barricaded Seimas (their parliament). In the wake of heavy condemnation from the West, the Soviets recognised Lithuanian independence on 6 September, bringing about the first of the Baltic republics.

The last Soviet troops left the country on 31 August 1993. Lithuania replaced the rouble with the litas, joined NATO in April 2004 and was accepted as a full member of the EU on 1 May 2004.

But Lithuania's accession into Europe has not been without some controversy. In April 2004 the constitutional court ruled that President Rolandas Paksas violated the country's constitution by arranging citizenship for Yuri Borisov, a businessman with alleged links to organised crime. The president was impeached and ousted days later. Mr Borisov, who denies any wrongdoing, donated 1.2 million litų to Mr Paksas' election campaign in 2003.

Fears of a flood of cheap labour leaving Lithuania to work elsewhere in Europe may yet prove true but the optimism and hope of this nation looks set to propel it into a glowing future.

PEOPLE

With a population of 3.5 million, Lithuanians themselves form 81.8% of their populace. After them, you'll find 8.1% Russians, 6.9% Poles, 1.4% Belarusians, 1% Ukrainians and 0.1% Jews.

Regularly described as the 'Spanish of the Baltics', Lithuanians are a lively, friendly bunch with a tendency to overdramatise everything – you won't be bored. They are fiercely proud of their national identity, as a result of the brutal attempts to eradicate it and the memories of their long-lost empire. Attempts are being made to incorporate the Roma people into Lithuanian society but much prejudice still exists on both sides despite a government-funded project that set up a public-education centre for Roma in Vilnius in 2000.

ARTS

Lithuanian contemporary art is slowly being discovered, with young, ambitious painters/ sculptors such as Tadas Gutauskas exhibiting work on the international stage. Other home-grown artists can be seen at Europas Parkas Sculpture Park at the geographical centre of Europe (19km from Vilnius), and the Užupis district in the capital. Both are part of an art scene growing in stature.

But Lithuania's best-known national artist will always be Mikalojus Konstantinas Čiurlionis (1875–1911), a depressive painter who also composed symphonic poems and piano pieces.

Music is at the heart of the Lithuanian spirit, and Lithuania is the jazz giant of the Baltics with its highlight, the Kaunas Jazz Festival.

Lithuanian fiction began with the late-18th-century poem *Metai* (The Seasons) by Kristijonas Donelaitis. Antanas Baranauskas' 1860 poem *Anykščiai Pine Forest* uses the forest as a symbol of Lithuania. Literature suffered persecution from the tsarist authorities, who banned use of the Latin alphabet. Nineteenth-century nationalists drew their inspiration from Polish writer Adam Mickiewicz who began his great poem *Pan Tadeusz* with 'Lithuania, my fatherland...' (he regarded himself part Lithuanian).

National revival poet Maironis heralded the start of modern Lithuanian poetry with the romantic *Pavasario balsai* (Voices of

Spring). The Lithuanian Diaspora has also produced major cultural figures, including the poet Tomas Venclova and the novelist Antanas Škėma, whose *A White Shroud* has been compared to the work of James Joyce.

ENVIRONMENT
The Land
Lush forests and more than 4000 lakes mark the landscape of Lithuania, a country which is largely flat with a 100km-wide lowland centre. Retreating glaciers left behind higher areas in the northwest (the Žemaičių upland), across the southeast (the Baltic highlands) and in the east (stretches of the Lithuanian–Belarusian uplands including the country's highest hill, 294m Juozapinė). Forest covers a third of the country.

Wildlife
Lithuania's forests contain many creatures such as real-life wild boar, wolves, deer and elk. Aukštaitija National Park (p434) is home to these creatures as well as many rare bird and animal species such as white-tailed and golden eagles.

The dunes and wooded areas of Neringa are also home to 37 different mammal species, 470 types of butterfly and 200 bird species.

National Parks
Lithuania has five national parks, and many more acres of protected land. Its highlight is the Curonian Spit (Kuršių Nerija; www .nerija.lt), 85 sq km of sand in a tongue shape looping out into the Baltic Sea. It was made a Unesco World Heritage landscape in December 2000. The other parks are: Aukštaitija (300 sq km) in eastern Lithuania, Dzūkija (www.dzukijosparkas.lt in Lithuanian; 550 sq km) in southern Lithuania, Trakai (www.trakai.lt) and Žemaitija (www .zemaitijosnp.lt; 200 sq km) in the northwest. The western Nemunas Delta wetlands are 35,000 hectares of waterways, which are rich in birdlife.

Environmental Issues
Pollution is part of the ugly Soviet legacy, and today there is still one of the world's most dangerous nuclear reactors chugging away in the heart of the stunningly beautiful Aukštaitija National Park. Ignalina Nuclear Power Station, similar in design to Chernobyl, lies 120km north of Vilnius and despite the EU spending €236 million in the last decade to improve safety (including €10 million to shut the first of the two reactors by 2004) it faces total closure by 2009 at a cost of €3.2 billion.

Other problems Lithuania faces include the threat of large-scale pollution from a recently discovered arsenal of decomposing chemical weapons. About 40,000 bombs and mines lie on the seabed 70 nautical miles off Klaipėda where Soviet forces sank German ships, and the cargo from these ships could threaten Neringa's fragile coastline.

The Būtingė oil terminal, off the northwestern coast near Latvia, continues to enrage both environmentalists, with a 60-ton oil spill in November 2001, and economists, with its huge losses. The state owns 60% of the terminal and it cost €266 million to build.

FOOD & DRINK
Unbuckle your belts for the gastronomic delights of good, hearty Lithuanian cooking. The food was tailor-made for those peasants out working the fields so it's seriously stodgy comfort eating rather than delicate morsels. Based on potatoes, meat and dairy goods it's not the best place for vegetarians so we've highlighted options for those who shun the pleasures of pigs trotters and the infamous Zeppelin.

The *Cepelinai* (Zeppelin) is an airship-shaped parcel of thick potato dough, filled with cheese, meat or mushrooms – and it's the national dish designed to keep out the Latvian winter cold.

Other artery-clogging staples are *bulvinai blynai*: pancakes of grated potato stuffed with dairy products, including *varške* (curd) and *rūgusis pienas* (sour milk), though meat and other vegetables are standard. Another good stand-by is *koldūninė* (small ravioli-like dumplings that are stuffed with cheese, mushrooms or meat).

The best local brands of *alus* (beer) are Utenos and Kalnapilis. No drink would be complete without a bar snack, *kepta duona* (deep-fried black bread with garlic).

Lithuanians drink *midus* (mead), such as Žalgiris and Suktinis, which are as much as 60% proof, and *gira* (made from fermented grains or fruit and brown rye bread).

LITHUANIA

Restaurants are generally open between 10am and 11pm. Aim for those without an English menu as they're more likely to be cheaper and more authentic. There are no hard and fast rules about dining. Lithuanians eat a hearty breakfast of brown bread and a fried omelette with salad, lunch is a quick bite and dinner is the main meal. You'll probably be offered soup, pork and potatoes then maybe a violently coloured ice-cream dish for desert. It's food you fuel up on not dine on, and it's all good stuff – just don't expect to be wafer-thin by the time you leave!

VILNIUS

☎ 5 / pop 600,000

Strangeness defines this bewitching city. It may be a recognised Unesco World Heritage Site, it may have a beautiful baroque Old Town yet there's a distinctly quirky edge to Vilnius that makes it stand out from most European cities.

Aside from all the beauty, the new Western shops and the bars and clubs, there's a magic here rarely found elsewhere. This magic comes in the form of its oddest residents. Frank Zappa, the psychedelic musician, is forever immortalised here in the world's only statue of him. A community of artists, drunks and dreamers have set themselves up as an unofficial official independent republic complete with borders, a mayor, an annual Independence Day and even passport control. And even the mayor

of Vilnius joins in the madness with his own webcam and interesting municipal schemes.

There's nowhere else in the world like this little place in the southeastern corner of Lithuania. And there's nowhere else you'll rather be once you're sitting in a candle-lit bar in a crumbling courtyard watching Vilnius go by.

ORIENTATION

The heart of Vilnius is Katedros aikšte (Cathedral Sq), with Gediminas Hill rising behind it. Southwards are the streets of the Old Town; Gedimino prospektas, to the west, is the axis of the newer part of the city. The train and bus stations are 1.5km south of Katedros aikšte.

INFORMATION
Bookshops
Littera (☎ 268 7258; Šv Jono gatvė 12; ◷ 9am-6pm Mon-Fri, 10am-3pm Sat) Has a superb selection of foreign-language books and magazines inside the University courtyard.
Vaga (☎ 249 8392; Gedimino prospektas 50; ◷ 10am-7pm Mon-Fri, 11am-4pm Sat) Located just west of the centre.

Cultural Centres
America Centre (☎ 266 0330; www.usembassy.lt; Pranciškonų 3-6; ◷ closed Jul & Aug)
British Council (☎ 264 4890; www.britishcouncil.lt; Jogailos gatvė 4; ◷ 9am-4pm, closed 15 Jul-19 Aug)
French Cultural Centre (☎ 231 2984; Didžioji gatvė 1; www.centrefrancais.lt, in French and Lithuanian; ◷ 9am-5pm Mon-Fri)

Emergency
International Police Commission (☎ 272 6159, 271 6221) Has staff who speak English, French and German and can deal with foreigners who are victims of crime. Ring ☎ 112 in an emergency. See boxed text (p446) for specific emergency numbers.

Internet Access
Collegium (☎ 261 8334; Pilies gatvė 22; per hr 8Lt; ◷ 8am-10pm)
V002 (☎ 279 1866; ianplinka@post.5ci.lt; Ašmenos gatvė 8; ◷ 24hr) Boasts a resident iguana and a coffee bar. Different rates for day/night usage.

Left Luggage
Deposit bags at *bagažinė* (left-luggage rooms) inside the following.

VILNIUS IN TWO DAYS

Make a wish at the secret *Stebuklas* spot in **Katedros aikšte** (p425) then hike up **Gedimino Hill** (p427) for a view of the city. Wander up cobbled **Pilies Gatvė** (p428) on your way to the famous **Gates of Dawn** (p429). Finish the night with cocktails at trendy **G-Lounge** (p431).

On day two head out to **Trakai** (p443) for a morning exploring the castle and homesteads of the Karaites people, a tiny Jewish sect. Back in Vilnius hike up **Three Crosses Hill** (p427) to watch the sunset then dine at **Literatai** (p431) overlooking the cathedral.

Bus station mall (per bag per day 3Lt; 5.30am-9pm Mon-Fri, 7am-9pm Sat)
Train station basement (per bag per day 2Lt; 5.30am-9pm Mon-Fri, 7am-9pm Sat)

Medical Services
24-hour pharmacy (Gedimino Vaistinė; ☎ 261 0135; Gedimino prospektas 27).
Baltic-American Medical and Surgical Clinic
(☎ 234 2020; Antakalnio gatvė 124; 24hr) Professional, Western-standard health care at Vilnius University Antakalnis hospital approximately 1km northeast of town.

Money
Vilnius is littered with ATMs and banks, most offering the usual exchange, money transfer, travellers cheques and cash-advance services. Bankas Snoras kiosks are dotted over town and have ATMs and some banking services.
24-hour currency exchange (Parex Bankas; ☎ 213 5454; Geležinkelio gatvė 6) The best rates can generally be found here. It's on your left as you exit the train station, which also has an ATM.
Hansabank (☎ 212 7861; Vokiečių gatvė 26; 9am-5pm Mon-Fri)
Vilniaus Bankas (☎ 262 7869; Vokiečių gatvė 9; 8am-6pm Mon-Fri) Takes Thomas Cook and Amex travellers cheques and has ATMs.

Post
Central post office (☎ 262 5468; www.post.lt; Gedimino prospektas 7; 7am-7pm Mon-Fri, 9am-4pm Sat) Has the incongruous honour of a pizza bar slap bang inside it. If, instead of a *margherita*, you'd rather post a letter it will cost you 1.7Lt to send anywhere abroad via airmail, or 1.2Lt if it's a postcard.
EMS (☎ 261 6759; Gedimino prospektas 7; 7am-7pm Mon-Fri, 9am-4pm Sat) Express post inside the post office. Packages to London start at 111Lt and New York 96Lt.

Tourist Information
The city now has tourist signs in English and Lithuanian around the Old Town.
City bus tours (☎ 273 8625; 10Lt) Bright yellow buses do city tours from Rotušės aikštė (City Hall Square) up to five times a day (none at all Monday, Tuesday) and last one hour.
Kelvita Tourist Information (☎ 231 0229; Geležinkelio gatvė 16; 8am-6pm Mon-Fri) In the international hall of the train station, these guys sell visas for Belarus, Russia and the Ukraine and they can sort out accommodation and car rental too!
Vilnius Tourist Information Centre (www.vilnius.lt)
Vilniaus gatvė (☎ 262 9660; Vilniaus gatvė 22;

9am-7pm Mon-Fri); Old Town Hall (☎ 262 6470; Didžioji gatvė 31; 9am-7pm Mon-Fri); train station (☎ 269 2091; Geležinkelio iela 16; 9am-6pm Mon-Fri, 10am-4pm Sat & Sun) English-, Polish- and German-speaking staff at these friendly centres have a wealth of glossy brochures and general information. They can also arrange tour guides and hotel bookings. Be warned that there's a room reservation fee of 6Lt.

Travel Agencies
Baltic Travel Service (☎ 212 0220; www.bts.lt, in Lithuanian; Subačiaus gatvė 2; 8am-6pm Mon-Fri, 10am-4pm Sat) All the usual services plus a nice line in countryside holidays.
Lithuanian Student & Youth Travel Bureau
(☎ 239 7397; www.jaunimas.lt, in Lithuanian; Basanavičiaus gatvė 30/13; 9am-6pm Mon-Fri, 10am-2pm Sat) Cheap fares for ISIC cardholders, employment in Europe opportunities and discount flights. It's just west of the centre.

SIGHTS
Katedros aikštė & Around
Start any trip to Vilnius at its heart: **Katedros aikštė** (Cathedral Sq), where everyone from babushkas to teenagers, the devout and a few tourists mixed in hang out and be seen every evening.

Vilnius Cathedral (☎ 261 1127; Katedros aikštė 1), which was reconsecrated in 1989 after being used as a gallery during the Soviet period, dominates the square with its classic, 18th-century white façade and is hence the focus point for the city. Amuse yourself

---

TOP FREE STUFF

- Make a wish once you've found the elusive *Stebuklas* tile in Katedros aikštė (above).

- Perform a miracle by praying to the black virgin Mary at the Gates of Dawn (p429).

- Get lost in the university's maze of courtyards (p428).

- Watch sunset/sunrise over the Three Crosses Hill (p427).

- Go abroad; visit the self-declared republic of Užupio, see the constitution, watch the drunks then see the angel (p428).

LITHUANIA

VILNIUS

0 |———| 200 m
0 |———| 0.1 miles

A   **B**   **C**   **D**

To Russian Embassy (2km)

Upės gatvė

Ukmergės gatvė

To Kalvarijų Market (700m); Akropolis (3km)

Šeimyniškių gatvė

47

Ratnyčių gatvė

Žalgirio Stadium

Juozapavičiaus gatvė

Kalvarijų gatvė

Neris

Goštauto gatvė

Žaliasis Tiltas

34

Tumo Vaižganto gatvė

Vasario 16-Osios gatvė

Jakšto gatvė

Žygimantų gatvė

40

To SS Peter & Paul Church (600m)

Lukiškių aikštė

To Prie Parlamento; Ministerija (200m); Vaga (220m); Seimas (400m); Canadian Embassy (800m); Estonian Embassy (1km); Church of the Saint Virgin's Apparition (1km); Russian Embassy (2.4km)

2
27

65

Vienuolio gatvė

Vilniaus gatvė

Tilto gatvė

Žvejų gatvė

Mindaugo Tiltas

Kosciuškos gatvė

To British Embassy (500m); Baltic-American Medical & Surgical Clinic (1km)

Gedimino prospektas

Savivaldybės aikštė

71
9
8

Arsenalo gatvė

70
28

Kalnų Park

To Ritos Smoklė (500m)

Taurakalnis

Pamėnkalnio gatvė

Jogailos gatvė

54
66

22

Gedimino Hill

37

Vilniuaus gatvė

Tatorių gatvė

35

Three Crosses Hill

Akmenų gatvė

Tauro gatvė

23

5
17

Katedros aikštė

79

Šventaragio

Barboros Radvilaitės gatvė

36
20

Palangos gatvė

Klaipėdos gatvė

Liejyklos gatvė

Vigrigo gatvė

Daukanto aikštė

75
38

32

Šv. Mykolo

60
42
26
5
77
10

Bernardinų gatvė

Maironio gatvė

30

Youth Park (Sereikiškių Parkas)

To Filaretai Hostel (500m)

Kalinausko gatvė

To German Embassy (300m); Latvian Embassy (750m); Vingis parkas (1.2km)

73
1

76
50

Dominikonų gatvė

Universiteto gatvė

55

Švarco gatvė

48
12
52

68
59

43
29

Užupis

61
19

57

To Youth Tourist Centre (400m); Užupio Vieišbutis (1km)

Vilnia

Krivių gatvė

To Lithuanian Student & Youth Travel Bureau (750m); Teacher's University Hostel (800m); Coca-Cola Plaza (800m); TV & Radio Centre (1.1km); TV Tower (7km); Gariūnai Market (10km); Paneriai (10km); Trakai (28km); Kaunas (100km); Druskininkai (112km); Klaipėda (310km)

Basanavičiaus gatvė

64

Traky gatvė

13
53

Žydų gatvė

Vokiečių gatvė

49
15

Savičiaus gatvė

Bokšto gatvė

Maironio gatvė

Aukštaičių gatvė

7

Mindaugo gatvė

Algirdo gatvė

3

Lydos gatvė

Ašmenos gatvė

Naugarduko gatvė

Ligoninės gatvė

Rūdninkų gatvė

18
56
62

Rotušės aikštė

16
72
46

63
31

Šv. Kazimiero gatvė

80
39

25
58

6
24
67
74
33

Subačiaus gatvė

Daukšos gatvė

Aušros Vartų gatvė

21

41

Bazilijonų gatvė

Pylimo gatvė

45

Rasų gatvė

Šopeno gatvė

Sodų gatvė

44

Seinų gatvė

Geležinkelio gatvė

Pelesos gatvė

Lentpjūvio gatvė

69

14

To Airport (3.5km)

1

Train Station

To E-Guest House (700m)

LITHUANIA

INFORMATION		
24-hour Currency Exchange	1	B6
24-hour Pharmacy	2	A2
American Centre	3	B4
American Consulate	4	A3
Australian Consulate	5	B3
Baltic Tourist Service	6	C5
Belarus Embassy	7	A5
British Council	8	B3
Central Post Office	9	B3
City Bus Tours	(see 16)	
Collegium	10	C4
Ems	(see 9)	
Finn Embassy	11	B4
French Cultural Centre	(see 59)	
French Embassy	12	C4
Hansabank	13	B4
Kelvita Tourist Information	14	B6
Littera	(see 38)	
Vilniaus Bankas	15	B4
Vilnius Tourist Information Centre (Old Town Hall)	16	C5
Vilnius Tourist Information Centre (Train Station)	(see 14)	
Vilnius Tourist Information Centre	17	B3
VOO2	18	B5

SIGHTS & ACTIVITIES	(pp425-30)	
Angel of Užupis Statue	19	D4
Frank Zappa Memorial	20	A3
Gates of Dawn	21	C5
Gedimino Tower	22	C3
Higher Castle Museum	(see 22)	
Holocaust Museum	23	A3
Holy Spirit Church	24	C5
Lower Castle Museum	(see 22)	
Map of the Ghetto	25	B5

Mickiewicz Museum	26	C4
Museum of Genocide Victims	27	A2
National Museum	28	C3
Orthodox Assumption Virgin Church	29	C4
St Anne's Church	30	D4
St Casimir's Church	31	C5
St John's Church	32	C4
St Teresa's Church	33	C5
Statues on Žaliasis Tiltas	34	B2
Three Crosses	35	D3
Vilna Gaon Jewish State Museum of Lithuania	36	B3
Vilnius Cathedral	37	C3
Vilnius University	38	C3

SLEEPING 🏠	(pp430-1)	
AAA Guest House Mano Liza	39	B5
Congress	40	B2
Gintaras	41	B6
Litinterp	42	C3
Mabre Residence Hotel	43	C4
Mikotel	44	C6
Old Town Hostel	45	C6
Radisson SAS Astorija	46	C5
Reval Hotel Lietuva	47	A1
Stikliai	48	C4

EATING 🍴	(pp431-2)	
Aukštaičiai	49	B4
Balti Drambliai	50	B4
Da Antonio	51	C4
G-Lounge	52	C4
La Provence	53	B4
Literati	54	C3
PUB	55	C4
Savas Kampas	56	B5
Užupio Picerija	57	D4

DRINKING 🍸	(p432)	
Bix	58	C5
Café de Paris	59	C4
Pilies Menė	60	C3
Sky Bar	(see 47)	
Užupio Kavinė	61	D4

ENTERTAINMENT 🎭	(p432)	
Brodvėjus	62	B5
Helios	63	C5
Lietuva	64	A4
Lithuanian Opera & Ballet Theatre	65	B2
National Drama Theatre	66	B3
National Philharmonic	67	C4

SHOPPING 🛍	(p432)	
Daily Craft Market	68	C4

TRANSPORT	(pp432-3)	
Bus Station	69	B6
Eurolines	(see 69)	

OTHER		
Applied Arts Museum	70	C2
City Hall	71	B3
Contemporary Art Centre	72	C5
House of Teachers	73	B4
Old Town Hall	(see 16)	
Orthodox Church of the Holy Spirit	74	C5
President's Palace	75	C3
St Catherine's Church	76	B4
St Michael's Church	77	C4
St Nicholas' Church	78	B5
Statue of Grand Duke Gediminas	79	C3
Synagogue	80	B5

by hunting for the secret *Stebuklas* (miracle) tile, which, if found can grant a wish if you spin around it three times. It marks the spot where the Tallinn–Vilnius human chain ended in 1989.

On religious days join the throng of people walking in and out of the building – and be amazed that the site was actually once pagan. A centuries-old **ritual stone** was discovered when the foundations were dug. The first wooden cathedral was built here in the 13th century, and rebuilt during the 15th century in Gothic style. The outside was completely redone in today's form between 1783 and 1801. The 5m **bronze statues** of St Helene, St Stanislav and St Casimir on top of the cathedral were levelled in 1956 but resurrected following restoration work. The interior showpiece is the **Chapel of St Casimir**, created from 1623 to 1636, which boasts a bizarre laughing Madonna, a baroque cupola with coloured marble and white stucco sculptures.

Behind the cathedral is **Gedimino Tower**, at the top of the 48m **Gedimino Hill** (Gedimino Kalnas) with the **Higher Castle Museum** (☎ 261 7453; admission 2Lt; ☾ 11am-5pm Tue-Sun Nov-Apr, 10am-7pm Tue-Sun May-Oct), which has models of the castle as it was in the 14th and 18th

centuries, on top. A **funicular** (one way/return 1/2Lt; ☾ 10am-6pm Tue-Sun) now runs from the barracks up to the tower.

The **Lower Castle Museum** (☎ 262 9988; Katedros aikštė 3a; ring ahead for opening times) is the site of the Royal Palace and an important Lithuanian archaeological dig. The Palace was built in the 16th century and was, for 300 years, the home of the grand dukes of Lithuania. A guided tour in English can be had from the team that is working on the site.

Nearby, the **National Museum** (☎ 262 9426; www.lnm.lt, in Lithuanian; Arsenalo gatvė 1; adult/concession 4/2Lt; ☾ 10am-5pm Wed-Sun) has a fantastic collection of ethnographic exhibits ranging from costumes to tools, weapons and jewellery. Kids will love the reconstructed dwellings of ancient Lithuanian peoples. Well worth an afternoon's perusal.

Spot the white **Three Crosses** atop Three Crosses Hill and aim in their direction. At the top of this landmark Vilnius skyline fixture are the three big fellas themselves. They're said to have stood here since the 17th century in memory of three monks who were crucified at this spot. The crosses, erected in 1989, are replicas of three knocked down and buried by the Soviet authorities.

LITHUANIA

East of Katedros aikštė is the magnificent **St Peter & Paul Church** at the far end of Kosciuškos gatvė. It's a treasure trove of sparkling white stucco sculptures of real and mythical people, animals and plants, with touches of gilt, paintings and statues. The decoration was done by Italian sculptors between 1675 and 1704. The tomb of the Lithuanian noble who founded the church, Mykolas Kazimieras Pacas, is on the right of the porch as you enter. Catch trolleybus No 2, 3 or 4 from the Arkikatedra stop near the cathedral.

Old Town

This breathtaking Unesco World Heritage site is a charming mix of pastel-coloured baroque churches and cobbled streets framed by 15th- and 16th-century architecture.

Wander from Katedros aikštė southwards along Pilies gatvė, Didžioji gatvė and Aušros Vartų gatvė and take in the fairy-tale beauty of this idyllic little city.

Vilnius University occupies the block between Pilies gatvė and Universiteto gatvė. The university, founded in 1579, was one of the greatest centres of Polish learning and produced many notable scholars in the 17th and early 19th centuries, before being closed by the Russians in 1832. It reopened in 1919 and now has 14,000 students.

The history faculty of the university hosts the world's first **Centre for Stateless Cultures** (☎ 268 7293; statelesscultures@centras.lt), for those

groups that maintain neither an army nor navy, including the Yiddish, Roma and Karaimic cultures.

The 12 linked courtyards of the university can be entered by several passages and gates. The southern gate on Šv Jono gatvė brings you into the Didysis or Skarga Courtyard, in early 17th-century Mannerist style, and **St John's Church** (Šv Jono bažnyčia), which features an outstanding 18th-century baroque façade. The arch through the 16th-century building opposite St John's leads to a two-domed **observatory** whose late-18th-century façade is adorned with zodiac reliefs. The other main courtyard is the Sarbievijus Courtyard, reached from the north of the Didysis Courtyard.

Nearby is the **Mickiewicz museum** (☎ 261 8836; Bernardinų gatvė 11; ☷ 10am-5pm Tue-Fri, 10am-2pm Sat & Sun). Romantic poet Mickiewicz grew up near Vilnius and studied at its university (1815–19) before he was exiled for anti-Russian activities. His work inspired the 19th-century Polish nationalists and, despite being Polish, he famously wrote the Lithuanian national song *Pan Thaddeus*, which opens 'Lithuania, My Fatherland!'

A stroll away, across Maironio gatvė is the fine 1581 brick façade of **St Anne's Church** (Šv Onos bažnyčia), a Gothic architectural masterpiece that Napoleon wished he could take to Paris in the palm of his hand. The church just behind it was part of a 16th-century Bernardine monastery.

CAPITAL CURIOSITIES

Vilnius is a funny old place – beautiful baroque wonderfulness sits alongside complete craziness – and the locals take it all in their stride.

Take the **Independent Republic of Užupis** for example. When you cross that little Vilnia River (or Užupis seaside by those in the know), you enter an unofficial breakaway republic of artists, squatters and drunks who have declared themselves a separate state from Lithuania. The 41 points of the constitution are inlaid on metal sheets in English and Lithuanian, including 'Everyone has the right to love and take care of the cat, everyone has the right to be happy, everyone has the right to be unhappy…' etc. See the glorious Angel of Užupis statue, unveiled on 1 April 2002.

And there's **Frank Zappa**. No introduction needed – except for the fact that this American rock and roll weirdo legend is now immortalised in brass and stuck in a small grim concrete courtyard on Kalinausko gatvė. It's the only statue of its kind in the world and was made by Dr Konstantinas Bogdanas, the great sculptor of Lenins. It was erected in 1995 by the Lithuanian Frank Zappa fan club!

Finally, there are the incredible **statues on Žaliasis Tiltas** (Green Bridge), which spans the Neris River just north of the centre. Named after a Red Army general, the sculptures at four points on the metal bridge are a blatant reminder of Lithuania's communist past – and yet weren't torn down like the rest of the Lenins and comrades because the locals adore them!

Further down Maironio, at No 12, stands a lovely Russian Orthodox **Church of the Holy Mother of God** (1346), which was damaged in the late 17th century and reconstructed (1865–68).

Southern Didžioji gatvė widens into a plaza, which was the centre of Vilnius life from the 15th century. **St Casimir's Church** (Šv Kazimiero bažnyčia) is Vilnius' oldest baroque church. It was built by Jesuits (1604–15) and under Soviet rule was a museum of atheism.

Aušros Vartų gatvė was once the start of the Moscow road. On the eastern side of the street is the big, pink, domed 17th-century **Holy Spirit Church** (Šv Dvasios bažnyčia), Lithuania's chief Russian Orthodox church. The preserved bodies of three 14th-century martyrs lie in a chamber in front of the altar. The Catholic **St Teresa's Church** (Šv Teresės bažnyčia) is early baroque (1635–50) outside and more elaborate late baroque inside.

At the southern end of Aušros Vartų gatvė are the **Gates of Dawn** (Aušros Vartai), the only one of the town wall's original nine gate towers still intact. A door on the left opens on to a staircase leading to a little 18th-century chapel directly over the gate arch. Here is a 'miracle-working' **icon of the Virgin**, which was souvenired from the Crimea by Grand Duke Algirdas in 1363. The chapel is one of Eastern Europe's leading pilgrimage destinations. In 2003 more than 1500 people marched from Suwalki in Poland to Vilnius to see her and pay homage.

New Town

Vilnius boasts a new European boulevard after its premier street Gedimino prospektas was given a face-lift between 2002 and 2003. It's a grand road with the cathedral at one end and the silver-domed **Church of the Saint Virgin's Apparition** at the other.

Along the boulevard, shopaholics will find the Western stores they crave and it's also lined with bars, restaurants, hotels and squares along its 1.75km length.

A statue of Lenin once towered over **Lukiškių aikštė**, about 500m east of the cathedral along Gedimino prospektas. The building facing the square was the KGB headquarters and prison. It is now the **Museum of Genocide Victims** (Genocido Aukų Muziejus;

JEWISH VILNIUS

By the 18th century Vilnius was referred to as the 'Jerusalem of Lithuania' with a strong teaching tradition and Jewish culture. More than 80,000 Jews were wiped out during Nazi and Soviet occupation in Vilnius alone (250,000 in Lithuania). These are must-see sites:

- **Holocaust Museum** (☎ 262 0730; Pamėnkalnio gatvė 12; ☯ 9am-5pm Mon-Thu, 9am-4pm Fri)

- **Vilna Gaon Jewish State Museum of Lithuania** (☎ 261 7907; www.litjews .org; Pylimo gatvė 4; ☯ 9am-5pm Mon-Thu, 9am-4pm Fri) Also based here is the Jewish Community of Lithuania offering community services.

- A map of the ghetto created to house the city's Jews before they were slaughtered is at Rūdninkų gatvė 18.

☎ 249 6264; admission 4Lt; ☯ 10am-6pm Tue-Sun) and is a must-see of any visit to Vilnius. Names of those who were murdered in the former KGB prison are carved into the stone walls outside. Inside there's a museum guide (Russian-speaking) who was a former inmate in the prison where thousands of Lithuanians were tortured before being sent to Siberia. The showpiece is the execution cell where glass floors reveal remnants of those killed in the chamber. It's a chilling but necessary history lesson in human suffering. Spend a couple of hours taking it in.

North of Gedimino prospektas is the **Seimas** (parliament) building. There lie the remains of barricades erected in January 1991 to halt Soviet tanks.

Just over 1km southwest of the parliament, at the western end of Čiurlionio gatvė, is pleasant **Vingis parkas**, whose huge stage is the setting for the Lithuanian Song Festival.

The 326m **TV tower** (where Soviet tanks and troops killed 14 people and injured many more as they fought through the crowd that encircled it on 13 January 1991) is in the suburb of Karoliniškes, which is across the river from Vingis parkas. Carved wooden crosses stand as memorials to the victims. Trolleybus No 16 from the train station and No 11 from Lukiškių aikštė go to the Televizijos Bokstas stop. The more adventurous could try Europe's highest **bungee jump** from this TV Tower for 250Lt.

More crosses stand outside the **TV & Radio Centre**, which was also stormed by Soviet troops that same night. It's 2.5km west of the city centre.

FESTIVALS & EVENTS

Vilnius Carnival (www.saldogrupe.lt) The first carnival in the Baltics, kicked off between May 28 and June 6 2004.
Vilnius Festival Month-long classical music festival held in June and organised by the Lithuanian National Philharmonic Society.

SLEEPING
Budget

This gorgeous treasure of a city is getting very popular indeed so try to book cheap rooms in advance as you'll be left fighting over the last beds in summer from June to August.

Filaretai Hostel (☎ 215 4627; www.filaretaihostel.lt; Filaretų gatvė 17; per person in 6–8-bed dm 24-29Lt, tr 28-32Lt, d 45Lt, plus 5Lt extra 1st night) Lovely, friendly and quieter hostel just a wee walk out of the Old Town. There's a clean kitchen, washing machine and satellite TV in a cosy shared lounge. We like it a lot. Take bus No 34 from outside the bus and train stations to the seventh stop. It is affiliated to the Lithuanian Hostels Association and can arrange saunas and canoeing trips.

Youth Tourist Centre (Jaunųjų turistų centras; ☎ 261 1547; Polocko gatvė 7; tr or q 24Lt per person) It's cheap, clean, relatively cheerful, not much to shout about but it'll mean you get your head down and is close to Filaretai if it's full.

Old Town Hostel (☎ 262 5357; www.balticbackpackers.com; Aušros Vartų gatvė 20/10; per person 32Lt) Take your earplugs or enjoy this party hostel. It's where you go to meet other travellers, swap tales and get drunk. Not for the faint-hearted but not for the choosy either. It's also a two-minute walk from the train and bus station.

Užupio Viešbutis (Užupis Hotel; ☎ 264 3113; Paupio gatvė 31a; per person 30-170Lt) This is a huge, imposing manor house with entrance around the back, parking for a million cars and a front garden. Inside it's a crumbling but good-value place with friendly young staff and lots of travellers eager to stay in Užupis and soak up the bohemian atmosphere.

Teacher's University Hostel (☎ 213 0509; Vivulskio gatvė 36; s/d/tr 65/28/24Lt) Does what it says on the tin – with cheap basic rooms in an uninspiring building but there's always a room of some crazy description to be had. Enough said.

Litinterp (☎ 212 3850; www.litinterp.lt; Bernardinų gatvė 7-2; s 80-100Lt, d 140-160Lt) Some of the best-value rooms in Vilnius with excellent service. Either stay in the gorgeous, clean guesthouse or be placed with a local family. These guys also offer car rental, tours and B&Bs in Klaipėda, Nida, Palanga and Kaunas. Totally recommended.

When arriving at Vilnius train station you can't miss **Gintaras** (☎ 273 8034; www.hotelgintaras.lt; Sodų gatvė 14; s 80-190Lt, d 110-199Lt, tr 249Lt). Be warned that its position is therefore dubious but the renovated rooms are good value.

Mid-Range

There are a few smart and fairly unusual places to stay if you've got a few more litų to spend. These are worth a try:

E-Guest House (☎ 266 0730; www.e-guesthouse.lt; Ševčenkos gatvė 16; d/apt 180/260Lt) Quirky and central, it's a concept guesthouse with a hi-tech bent for those of you that can't be away from your laptop for a second. Each modern room has a free dial-up Internet connection and if you're missing your wee computer they'll rent you a laptop too. It's about 700m southwest of the centre.

Mikotel (☎ 260 9626; mikotel@takas.lt; Pylimo gatvė 63; s/d/tr 180/240/360Lt) The Mikotel is functional, modern and close to the train station. Not the most atmospheric of places but has its own little quirks such as contemporary artworks on the walls and access to the kitchen to cook your own dinner.

Congress (☎ 269 1919; www.congress.lt; Vilniaus gatvė 2/15; s/d/ste 300/400/560Lt) This sweeping grand hotel actually has a nice, comfy feel to it. The rooms are sleek but cosy with dark wood and low lighting. And if you've got 1000Lt to spare you could book into the star-studded (literally) presidential suite. Go on, you're worth it!

Top End

If you've got hundreds of lovely litų there are some utterly gorgeous places to rest your weary head. These are the pick of the beautiful bunch.

AAA Guest House Mano Liza (☎ 212 2225; hotel@aaa.lt; Ligoninės gatvė 5; s/d/ste 320/340/480Lt) This guesthouse is an elegant, romantic hideaway hidden away from the madding crowds down a cobbled side street. It's a chocolate-on-the-pillow place with impeccable service, beautiful rooms and a serene air. Not one for young kids.

Mabre Residence Hotel (☎ 212 2087; mabre@ mabre.lt; Maironio gatvė 13; s/d/ste 320/430/580Lt; ☒ ☎) An enchanting choice for the *crème de la crème* of visitors. This secluded hotel is in a Russian Orthodox Monastery and lost none of its charm after a renovation. Try to get an attic room as they have air-con. There's also a sauna and hair salon.

Reval Hotel Lietuva (☎ 272 6200; www.reval hotels.com; Konstitucijos gatvė 20; s/d/ste €110/130/230) Once the ugliest hotel in all of Lithuania, this ex-communist monstrosity was transformed into a glittering palace of comfort and luxury; there's a bar on the 22nd floor. Treat yourself.

Stikliai (☎ 264 9595; www.stikliaihotel.lt; Gaono gatvė 7; s/d/ste €150/180/225, apt €255-355Lt) Prepare to be dazzled with one of Lithuania's finest hotels. Inside it's jaw-droppingly gorgeous with chintz to die for, an inside balcony dripping with plants and rooms fit for the prince/princess you really are.

Radisson SAS Astorija (☎ 212 0110; reservations .vilnius@radissonSAS.com; Didžioji gatvė 35/2; s/d €170/185) This yellow classical fancy is in Vilnius' prime spot, overlooking ravishing St Casimir's Church. Inside it's exactly what you'd expect – sheer unadulterated luxury. From the modern, gorgeous rooms to the friendly service, disabled facilities and all the mod cons known to man it's a top choice.

EATING

From curry to *kepta duona*, *cepelinai* to *haute cuisine*, Vilnius is bursting with international eateries and traditional gut-busters. From budget to blowout you'll find a good range to suit all pockets.

Head to Gedimino prospektas for contemporary eats or, for Lithuanian and international haunts, stay in the Old Town around Vokiečių gatvė. Restaurants are generally open 10am to 11pm daily.

Savas Kampas (☎ 212 3203; Vokiečių gatvė 4; lunch 10Lt) Set lunch is an institution – a pot of the day cooked in an open fire – it's excellent value for filling, tasty nourishment.

Užupio Picerija (☎ 215 3666; Paupio gatvė 3; mains 15Lt; ☺ 8am-11pm) The only restaurant in Užupis – and a strange place to sit among plush surroundings, eating pizza while watching the drunks hang out in this crazy republic. The words above the oven read: 'an island in the midst of a river did arise' – never a truer word!

Balti Drambliai (☎ 262 0875; Vilniaus gatvė 41; mains 15Lt) Veg heaven; the menu veers from Indian to Mexican to Italian favourites but there ain't no meat anywhere in sight.

Aukštaičiai (☎ 212 0169; Antokolskio gatvė 13; mains 15Lt; ☺ noon-midnight) Hang onto your Zeppelins as this recently opened treasure has some of the best, and most affordable, Lithuanian food in the city. You can even sample the enormous yards of beer served in a giant test tube – if you're brave enough that is.

PUB (☎ 261 8393; Dominikonų gatvė 9; mains 15-20Lt; ☺ 11am-2am Mon-Thu, 10am-5am Fri & Sat) From shepherd's pie to fish and chips and the occasional platter of pigs trotters, this cosy split-level restaurant/bar is a backpacker favourite. It's not glamorous but the friendly people here will keep you nourished with hearty fodder such as their excellent homemade burgers.

G-Lounge (☎ 260 9430; Didžioji gatvė 11; mains 20Lt) Probably the the trendiest restaurant/bar in Vilnius boasting superb fusion/Asian cooking, divinely stylish white décor and DJs playing tunes while you eat. Totally recommended.

Prie Parlamento (☎ 249 6606; Gedimino prospektas 46; mains 20-25Lt; ☺ 10am-3am Mon-Thu, 10am-5am Fri & Sat, 10am-2am Sun) This is a more upmarket, expat haunt with a menu based on seafood. It's about 200m west of the centre.

Da Antonio (☎ 262 0109; Pilies gatvė 20; mains 25Lt) Expensive for an Italian place but absolutely worth it. This is more of a bistro serving excellent Italian antipasto, salads and fish/meat dishes in an intimate setting. Recommended.

Literatai (☎ 261 1889; Gedimino Prospektas 1; mains 30Lt) Battling for the top Vilnius eatery, the Scandinavian-influenced menu is a delight. The lobster bisque is to die for, the fish dishes are beyond memorable. The service is good, the wine's great – it's a winner.

La Provence (☎ 261 6573; Vokiečių gatvė 24; mains 40Lt; ☺ 11am-midnight) A superb menu – some say the best in the city – with lamb, deer and steak alongside perfect French staples such as snails, and a wide-ranging wine list. Shame about the snooty service.

Fresh milk straight from the cow's udder, honey and smoked eels are just some of the culinary delights to be found at **Kalvarijų market** (7am-noon Tue-Sun), to the north of the city centre.

DRINKING

Pilies Menė (Pilies gatvė 8; 10am-midnight) This place is always a good place to start especially on a Friday night with live jazz.

Bix (Etmonų gatvė 6) A favourite among the city's young, studenty crowd and pulls in backpackers.

Užupio kavinė (Užupio gatvė 2) It's a haven for artists, musicians and various bohemian, long-haired drunk people. This Vilnius institution has a riverside terrace.

Café de Paris (Didžioji gatvė 1) Joined to the French Cultural Centre this is one of the best bars in Vilnius with an eclectic crowd, good tunes and no banging techno.

Sky Bar (Konstitucijos gatvė 20) Twenty-two floors up at the Reval Lietuva Hotel with the best views in the city, the Sky Bar has a requisite number of beautiful people and heavenly (but pricey) cocktails.

ENTERTAINMENT

Vilnius has cinemas, an opera house, theatres and concert halls to delight any cultured visitor. Check listings in the local bible, *Vilnius In Your Pocket*. The tourist information centres (TICs) post up events listings.

Cinemas

Lietuva (262 3422; www.ktlietuva.lt, in Lithuanian; Pylimo gatvė 17) has the largest screen in Lithuania, while **Coca-Cola Plaza** (265 2525; Savanorių gatvė 7) is a multiplex with 12 screens and seats for the disabled.

Vilnius also has a €10 million Akropolis shopping complex with ice-skating rink and multiscreen **cinema** (248 4848; Ozo 25).

Classical Music

The **National Philharmonic** (266 5216; Aušros Vartų gatvė 5; box office 11am-7pm Tue-Sat, 11am-1pm Sun) is a sublime concert hall.

Lithuanian Opera & Ballet Theatre (262 0727; www.opera.lt; Vienuolio gatvė 1; 10am-7pm Mon-Fri, 10am-6pm Sat, 10am-3pm Sun) Classical productions

in a stunning building that should be seen even by nonopera buffs.

Nightclubs

Get a grip of the local music/clubbing scene by checking the party website www.ore.lt, in Lithuanian.

Hanging around Vokiečių gatvė in the summer is a safe bet for nightlife potential. In the warm months temporary bars line the Old Town street and many clubs are within staggering distance.

Clubs worth checking include:

Ministerija (Gedimino prospektas 46) Prie Parlamento's popular downstairs club, which gets very sweaty and jammed with a young fun crowd.

Brodvėjus (Mėsinių 4) Has two bars, local DJs and live music for a relaxed, traveller crowd.

Helios (Didžioji gatvė 28) Serious house music played loud and dirty for a hot young crowd.

Men's Factory (www.gayclub.lt, in Lithuanian) Centre of Vilnius' gay scene, changing its location as we went to press. Check the website for its new address.

Theatre

National Drama Theatre (262 9771; www.teatras.lt; Gedimino Prospektas 4; 10am-6pm Mon-Fri, 11am-6pm Sat & Sun) Stages national and international productions.

SHOPPING

For Western high-street/chain stores head to Gedimino prospektas. For traditional crafts the daily craft market at the triangular meeting point of Didžioji and Pilies gatvės has stalls in abundance selling amber, artworks and carved wooden trinkets.

Vilnius' main markets are Gariūnai, off the road to Kaunas west of the city, and Kalvarijų (p432), north of the city centre, where you can join the scrum of babushkas jostling for bargains.

GETTING THERE & AWAY

For information on international flights, bus, train and ferry services see (p447).

Air

There are direct flights from Vilnius to Rīga and Tallinn, and many Scandinavian, Western European and Eastern European cities. Between 22 May and 11 September there are once-weekly internal flights between Vilnius and Palanga operated by **Lithuanian Airlines** (www.lal.lt).

GETTING AROUND
To/From the Airport

Vilnius airport (☎ 230 6666; www.Vilnius-airport.lt; Rodūnios gatvė 2) sits 5km south of the city.

Take either bus No 1 between the airport and train station or bus No 2 between the airport and Lukiškių aikštė; both cost 1Lt each way. Some minibuses also make the journey to Lukiškių aikštė and cost 2Lt per trip (see p448 for information about catching a microbus). A taxi from the airport to the city centre should cost no more than 20Lt and it's cheaper if you call ahead. See numbers under Taxi see below.

Car & Motorcycle

For car rental try **Eurorenta** (☎ 8-611 16611; ☾ 24hr), **Budget** (☎ 230 6708; www.budget.lt; ☾ 24hr) or **Avis** (☎ 232 9316; www.avis.lt; ☾ 8am-5pm Mon-Fri, 9am-4pm Sat & Sun) in the arrivals hall of the airport.

Remember to drive on the right and look for designated parking areas as they are generally manned (for a small fee) to avoid the worry of car theft, which is rife in Lithuania.

Public Transport

Trolleybuses and buses run daily from 4am to midnight. A single ticket for any mode of public transport costs 0.80Lt if bought from a press kiosk or 1Lt when bought from the driver. Validate your ticket by punching it in a machine on the bus or trolleybus. An unpunched ticket warrants a 20Lt on-the-spot fine.

Minibuses shadow most routes; expect to pay 2Lt per journey. Check the website www.vilniustransport.lt for details and maps of local transport. A monthly pass costs 35Lt.

Taxi

Taxis officially charge 1Lt to 1.30Lt per kilometre but it's cheaper and safer to call ahead. There are ranks outside the train station; in front of the Old Town Hall on Didžioji gatvė and outside the Radisson SAS Astorija hotel.

Recommended numbers for cab companies are (☎ 1445, 1422, 1313, 1818, 1446 or 1411); no code is required.

AROUND VILNIUS

Once you tire of city life there are ways of entertaining yourself: either face Lithuania's brutal past at the former Nazi death camp of Paneriai or take a boat across Trakai lake to see the castle.

Paneriai (Ponar)

Lithuania's brutal history is starkly portrayed at Paneriai, a site of Jewish mass murder, 10km southwest of central Vilnius. Between July 1941 and July 1944, 100,000 people were killed here.

From the entrance a path leads to the small **Paneriai Museum** (☎ 260 2001; Agrastų gatvė 17; ☾ 11am-6pm Wed-Sat; call to check winter opening times).

Paths lead to grassed-over pits where the Nazis burnt the exhumed bodies of their victims to hide the evidence of their crimes.

There are about 20 suburban trains daily (some terminating in Trakai or Kaunas) from Vilnius to Paneriai station (0.90Lt, 20 minutes). From the station, it is a 1km walk southwest straight along Agrastų gatvė to the site.

Trakai

☎ 528 / pop 38,200

The ancient capital of Lithuania is a dreamy day trip away. Two castles sit among five scenic lakes just 28km west of Vilnius.

It was Gediminas who made this charming complex his capital in 1321. The castles were built over the next 100 years to fend off the German knights.

Trakai is also famous for the presence of the Karaites (or Karaimai) people. They're a mixed Judaic and Hebrew sect that originated in Baghdad, who adhere to the Torah (rejecting the rabbinic Talmud). They are named after the term *Kara*, which means 'to study the scriptures' in both Hebrew and Arabic. Some Karaites were brought to Trakai from the Crimea by Vytautas around 1400 to serve as bodyguards. Of the 10,000 Karaites left in the world, 360 live in Lithuania (mostly in Trakai).

INFORMATION

Tourist Information Centre (☎ 51934; trakaitic@is.lt; Vytauto gatvė 69; ☾ 8.30am-4.15pm Mon, 8.30am-5.30pm Tue-Fri, 9am-5pm Sat) Sells maps and books accommodation.

Trakai National Park Information Bureau (☎ 55776; www.trakai.lt; Karaimų 5; ☾ 8am-5pm Mon-Thu, 8am-3.45pm Fri) Arranges guided tours of the park and the surrounding area, and also issues fishing permits.

LITHUANIA

SIGHTS

The highlight of the trip here has got to be **Trakai Castle & Museum** (☎ 58246; Pilies island; admission adult/child 8/4Lt; ✆ 10am-6pm, closed Mon). Dating from the 14th century, the red-brick castle was renovated in 1955 after being destroyed in the 17th and 18th centuries.

The moated main tower has a cavernous central court and a range of galleries, halls and rooms with exhibits tracing the history of the castle.

The **Karaite Ethnographic Exhibition** (☎ 55286; Karaimų gatvė 22; ✆ 10am-6pm Wed-Sun) is an incredible look at a fast-disappearing culture/religion. The little wooden carved building houses photographs, scriptures, weapons, tools and items of jewellery.

Along Karaimų gatvė, No 30 is an early 19th-century **Kenessa** (prayer house) of the Karaites in among the wooden cottages.

The remains of Trakai's **Peninsula Castle** are towards the northern end of town, in a park close to the shore of Lake Luka. The castle is thought to have been built between 1362 and 1382 by Vytautas' father, Kęstutis.

SLEEPING & EATING

Kempingas Slėnyje (☎ 53880; www.camptrakai.lt; Slėnio 1; per person 25-120Lt) This excellent camping complex and hostel is 5km out of Trakai on the northern side of Lake Galvė. You can pitch your tent by the lake or stay in wooden cabins or the hostel, which has a sauna, a diving club, boat rental and hot-air balloon rides.

Galvė (☎ 51345; Karaimų gatvė 41; per person 30Lt) Boasts the best view in Trakai – over the lake and castle – so just remember not to look too closely at your room as it will be basic to say the least.

Trakų Viešbutis (☎ 55505; Ežero gatvė 7; s/d 260/260Lt) That's more like it. Sitting on the edge of Lake Totoriškių this is a rather exclusive haven and is as comfy and lovely as the price suggests.

Apvalaus Stalo Klubas (☎ 55595; Karaimų gatvė 53; mains 10-20Lt) Lovely waterside French restaurant with separate pizzeria and stunning sunset views.

GETTING THERE & AROUND

More than 30 buses daily, between 6.47am and 8.45pm, run between Vilnius bus station and Trakai (3Lt, 45 minutes). There are

eight trains daily (2.80Lt, 40 minutes) plus more at weekends.

From the train station in Trakai, take Vytauto gatvė north to the bus station, then continue north to Karaimų gatvė and the castles.

EASTERN & SOUTHERN LITHUANIA

Escape into the deep, magical wilderness of Lithuania's forested eastern and southern regions. In the east is Aukštaitija National Park, beloved by Lithuanians who treasure its natural wonder and serenity.

In the south is the leafy spa town of Druskininkai and its vaguely controversial neighbour Grūto Parkas.

AUKŠTAITIJA NATIONAL PARK
☎ 386

Lithuania's first national park (founded in 1974) is a 400-sq-km wonderland of rivers, lakes, centuries-old forests and tiny villages still steeped in rural tradition. Around 70% of the park is pine, but there's oak, spruce and deciduous forest to breathe in and explore.

Based in Palūšė Village, the excellent **tourism centre** (☎ 52891; www.paluse.lt, in Lithuanian) is the first port of call in Aukštaitija. The staff organise accommodation, excursions, hikes, boat trips and nature trails. You can also pitch a tent here, hire a wooden chalet or kip down in one of the basic **rooms** (dm 15Lt, room 95Lt). Buy your compulsory park permit (2Lt) here.

Head the 175m up **Ladakalnis** for the park's best view – and some say the most magnificent, heart-stopping view in all Lithuania. Ancient pagans used to make sacrifices to Lada (the ancient goddess who gave birth to the planet) on this peak, which gives it a distinctly eerie feel.

The **Ancient Beekeeping Museum** (Stripeikiai Village; ✆ 10am-7pm May–mid Oct, closed mid-Oct–Apr) is a shrine to this ancient art and explores the spiritual links between bees and the gods of pagan Lithuania and Egypt.

Ginuciai Water Mill (☎ 36419; d/tr 50/70Lt) is the only intact watermill in the region and is supposedly haunted by the devil. Stay a night and find out!

Don't be fooled by the horrible exterior of **Aukštaičių Užeiga** (☎ 47473; mains 10Lt; ◷ 9am-midnight); inside it's friendly, cosy and has a decent menu of Lithuanian favourites. The cooks do a good BBQ too.

There's a **post office** (☎ 64643; d/q 27/47Lt) with guesthouse rooms upstairs.

Without private transport the park is tricky to get to but not impossible. There's a daily train to/from Vilnius and Ignalina. Once in Ignalina get a taxi to Palūšė (8Lt to 10Lt).

DRUSKININKAI
☎ 313 / pop 20,000

Spa town Druskininkai, 130km south of Vilnius, is the most famous health resort in Lithuania. Way back in the 18th century, people started visiting for the reputed healing powers of the waters. Visitors still come for the mud baths and various Soviet-style treatments as well as the serene leafy surroundings.

The **Tourist Information Centre** (☎ 51777; Gardino gatvė 1; ◷ 9am-5pm Mon-Fri) can book accommodation.

Druspolis (☎ 52886; Dineikos gatvė 9; s 20-60Lt; d 40-100Lt) is an imposing wooden hotel with a variety of basic and more comfy rooms for most budgets. Eat at **Nostalgija** (☎ 55947; Čiurlionio gatvė 55; mains 10Lt), a nicely positioned restaurant on the shores of the lake; it serves. Lithuanian staples in a pleasant airy setting.

From mud baths to mud slinging – the semicontroversial **Grūto Parkas** (☎ 55511; hesona@druskininkai.omnitel.net; adult/child 5/2Lt; ◷ 9am-sunset) draws visitors to its strange collection of Lenins and Stalins. Open since 2000, the theme park, which is 7km from Druskininkai, is a Soviet sculpture park filled with those communist monstrosities formerly based in parks and squares across Lithuania.

There are four direct buses daily (14.50Lt, two hours, 125km) between Vilnius and Druskininkai. You can ask to be let off and it's a well signposted 1km walk to the park.

CENTRAL LITHUANIA

Central Lithuania is a flat plain punctured only by small villages and one large city, Kaunas, between tracts of strangely barren landscape. The northern sector of the largely desolate area has Lithuania's most interesting attraction – the eerie Hill of Crosses.

KAUNAS
☎ 37 / pop 378,900

'Kaunas is Kaunas', as the saying goes. The residents of Lithuania's second city, 100km west of Vilnius, seem strangely accepting when they talk about their industrial urban hotbed.

But there's a lot more to Kaunas that meets the eye. Don't be fooled by the endless rows of Soviet-style housing estates and belching factories as you enter the city.

In the past few years the city has undergone a dramatic transformation with an explosion of shops, bars, hotels and restaurants. There's a historic Old Town, a strong cultural and arts scene and a pretty boulevard forming the main artery of the city, which was founded in the 13th century.

Orientation

The most attractive part of Kaunas is its historic heart, Rotušės aikštė (City Hall Sq), between the two rivers at the western end of the city centre. The new town is focused on the pedestrianised Laisvės alėja, which is further east. Here you'll find the major shops, hotels, restaurants, galleries and museums. The long-distance bus station and the train station are about 1km south of the eastern end of Laisvės alėja, down Vytauto prospektas.

Information

Admission to museums usually cost between 2Lt and 5Lt and they are generally closed on Monday.

Bendroji Medicinos Praktika (☎ 313 665; Savanorių prospektas 423; ◷ 9am-7pm Mon-Fri, 9am-2pm Sat) Offers dental, medical and general health services approximately 1km northeast of town.

Hansabank (☎ 322 454; Laisvės alėja 79; ◷ 8am-6pm Mon-Fri, 8am-3pm Sat) Offers full banking services.

Humanitas (☎ 209 581; Vilniaus gatvė 11; ◷ 10am-7pm Mon-Fri, 10am-5pm Sat) Excellent bookshop.

Kaunas Regional Tourist Information Centre (☎ 323 436; www.kaunas.lt; Laisvės alėja 36; ◷ 9am-6pm Mon-Fri, 9am-3pm Sat Apr-Sep, 9am-6pm Mon-Thu, 9am-5pm Fri Oct-Mar) Swanky new information centre can book accommodation and tours and sell you maps and brochures.

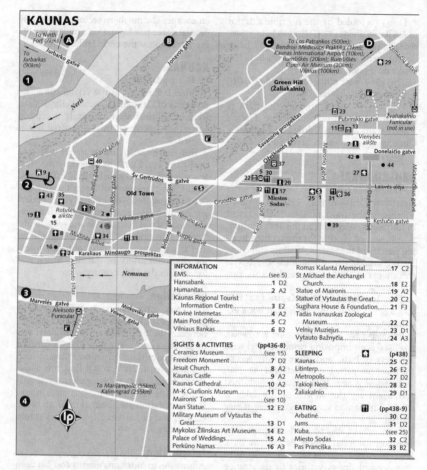

KAUNAS

INFORMATION	
EMS	(see 5)
Hansabank	1 D2
Humanitas	2 A2
Kaunas Regional Tourist Information Centre	3 E2
Kavinė Internetas	4 A2
Main Post Office	5 C2
Vilniaus Bankas	6 B2

SIGHTS & ACTIVITIES	(pp436-8)
Ceramics Museum	(see 15)
Freedom Monument	7 D2
Jesuit Church	8 A2
Kaunas Castle	9 A2
Kaunas Cathedral	10 A2
M-K Čiurlionis Museum	11 D1
Maironis' Tomb	(see 10)
Man Statue	12 E2
Military Museum of Vytautas the Great	13 D1
Mykolas Žilinskas Art Museum	14 E2
Palace of Weddings	15 A2
Perkūno Namas	16 A3

Romas Kalanta Memorial	17 C2
St Michael the Archangel Church	18 E2
Statue of Maironis	19 A2
Statue of Vytautas the Great	20 C2
Sugihara House & Foundation	21 F3
Tadas Ivanauskas Zoological Museum	22 C2
Velnių Muziejus	23 D1
Vytauto Bažnyčia	24 A3

SLEEPING	(p438)
Kaunas	25 E2
Litinterp	26 E2
Metropolis	27 D2
Takioji Neris	28 E2
Žaliakalnio	29 D1

EATING	(pp438-9)
Arbatinė	30 C2
Jums	31 E2
Kuba	(see 25)
Miesto Sodas	32 C2
Pas Pranciška	33 B2

Kavinė Internetas (☎ 225 364; Vilniaus gatvė 26; per hr 7Lt; ☼ 10am-10pm)

Main post office (☎ 401 368; Laisvės alėja 102; ☼ 7.30am-6.30pm Mon-Fri, 7.30am-4.30pm Sat) Has a branch of express post service EMS in the basement.

Vilniaus Bankas (☎ 307 016; Laisvės alėja 82; ☼ 8am-4pm Mon-Thu, 8am-3pm Fri) Offers full banking services.

Sights
ROTUŠĖS AIKŠTĖ

Start any trip to Kaunas wandering through the charming Old Town streets. The central square is surrounded by 15th- and 16th-century German **merchants' houses**. The 18th-century white, baroque former city hall now houses the **Palace of Weddings** and

the **Ceramics Museum** (☎ 203 572; Rotušės aikštė; admission 2Lt; ☼ 11am-5pm Tue-Sun).

A **statue of Maironis**, the priest and poet considered radical by the Soviets, stands in the square.

The southern side of the square is dominated by an 18th-century twin-towered **Jesuit church**.

Just off the southeastern corner of the square is the intriguing 16th-century brick **Perkūno namas** (House of Perkūnas; Aleksoto gatvė 6), built as offices on the site of a temple to Perkūnas, the Lithuanian god of thunder. Backing onto the river is Lithuania's biggest church, **Vytauto bažnyčia** (Vytautas church), which was built in the Gothic style by the great leader himself in 1402.

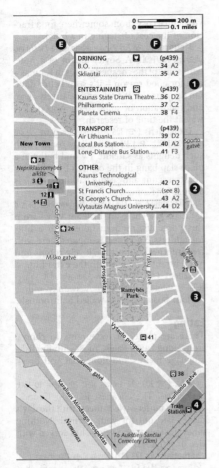

DRINKING 🍷 (p439)
B.O. 34 A2
Skliautai.............................35 A2

ENTERTAINMENT 🎭 (p439)
Kaunas State Drama Theatre....36 D2
Philharmonic.......................37 C2
Planeta Cinema...................38 F4

TRANSPORT (p439)
Air Lithuania.......................39 D2
Local Bus Station...............40 A2
Long-Distance Bus Station......41 F3

OTHER
Kaunas Technological
    University......................42 D2
St Francis Church................(see 8)
St George's Church.............43 A2
Vytautas Magnus University....44 D2

New Town

Sporto gatvė

28
Nepriklausomybės aikštė
3
18
12
14

26

Miško gatvė

Vytauto prospektas

Traku gatvė

21

Ramybės Park

Vytauto prospektas

41

Kaunakiemio gatvė

Karaliaus Mindaugo prospektas

Nemunas

38

Čiurlionio gatvė

Train Station

To Aukštieji Sančiai Cemetery (2km)

Kaunas Cathedral, on the northeastern corner of the square, owes much to baroque reconstruction, but the early 15th-century Gothic shape of its windows remain. **Maironis' tomb** is outside the south wall of the cathedral. A reconstructed tower is all that remains of the 13th-century **Kaunas Castle**.

NEW TOWN

The amazing transformation of Kaunas is resplendent in the form of Laisvès alèja (Freedom Ave), which resembles more a European boulevard than a former communist thoroughfare.

Swanky bars, shops and restaurants line the 2km-long pedestrian route, which is the main artery of Kaunas.

At its western end the **Tadas Ivanauskas Zoological Museum** (☎ 229 675; Laisvės alėja 106; 11am-5pm Tue-Sun) contains 13,000 stuffed animals to amuse and educate children of all ages. It's a musty delight and things in jars get quite gruesome. A must.

Nearby stands a **statue of Vytautas the Great**. In 1972, in the park opposite, student Romas Kalanta burnt himself to death as a protest against Soviet occupation. A **memorial** to him was unveiled here in 2002 in the form of 19 stones representing each one of his tragic years and cast-iron sheets representing the burnt pages of history.

The blue, neo-Byzantine 1893 **St Michael the Archangel Church** dominates the eastern end of Laisvės alėja from its position on the adjacent Nepriklausomybės aikštė (Independence Sq).

Worshippers leaving the church are met with the infamous **Man statue**. You can't miss him – and his nakedness. The work of sculptor Petras Mozūras caused outrage when it was erected (!) in 1991.

He stands in front of the **Mykolas Žilinskas Art Museum** (☎ 222 853; Nepriklausomybės aikštė 12; 🕥 11am-5pm). Inside there's the only Rubens in Lithuania and a wide collection of Lithuanian and international artworks.

Vienybės aikštė (Unity Sq) contains the main buildings of the Kaunas Technical University and the smaller Vytautas Magnus University. The **Freedom Monument**, dated 16 February 1918 (the day Lithuania declared independence), was erected in 1928. It was hidden during the Stalin era, and put back in place on 16 February 1989.

Nearby, the **Military Museum of Vytautas the Great** (☎ 320 939; Donelaičio gatvė 64; 🕥 11am-5.30pm Tue-Sun) recounts Lithuania's history from prehistoric times to the present day. Of particular interest is the wreck of the aircraft in which two of Lithuania's greatest modern heroes, Darius and Girėnas (pictured on the 10Lt note), attempted to fly nonstop from New York to Kaunas in 1933. The heroes are buried in the **Aukštieji Sančiai Cemetery** (Ašmenos gatvė 1) approximately 2km southeast of town.

Next door to the military museum is the **M-K Čiurlionis Museum** (☎ 229 475; Putvinskio gatvė 55; 🕥 11am-5pm, closed Mon), with an extensive collection of the romantic symbolic paintings of Čiurlionis (1875–1911), Lithuania's beloved artist and composer.

LITHUANIA

Prepare yourself to come face to face with Beelzebub in his hundreds at the bizarre and fantastic **Velnių Muziejus** (Devil Museum; ☎ 221 587; Putvinskio gatvė 64; ☉ 11am-5pm, closed Mon). More than 2000 devil statuettes are on show, gathered by landscape-artist Antanas Žmuidzinavičius (1876–1966).

Out of town – 20km out to be precise – is the must-see **Rumšiškės Open Air Museum** (☎ 47392; ☉ 10am-6pm Tue-Sun May-Oct). It's a time-travel adventure back into Lithuania's rural past with an incredible collection of dwellings, farms, schools and mills from each region of the country. Buses leave from Kaunas station or take a Vilnius bus and get off at Rumšiškės stop.

NINTH FORT

Built in the late 19th century, the **Ninth Fort** (☎ 377 750; Žemaičių Plentas 73; admission 4Lt; ☉ 10am-4pm Wed-Sun), 7km from Kaunas, was used by the Russians in WWI to defend their western frontier against Germany. During WWII the Nazis used it as a death camp. An estimated 80,000 people, mostly members of Kaunas' Jewish population, were murdered here. The site of the mass grave is marked by stark, monumental sculptures. Take bus No 35 or 23 from the bus station; they run at least every 30 minutes between 1.50am and 9.15pm.

The **Sugihara House & Foundation** (☎ 332 881; Ožeškienės gatvė 17; ☉ 10am-5pm Mon-Fri May-Sep, noon-4pm Oct-Apr) is the home of Chiune Sugihara, the Japanese consul to Lithuania (1939–40) who saved the lives of thousands of Polish Jews by issuing visas (against orders) to get them out and away from persecution and certain death.

Festivals & Events

The Kaunas Jazz Festival happens in April when an international crowd flocks to the city for a month of jazz events.

Sleeping

Crazy Kaunas is not well-endowed with cheap hotels and there aren't any hostels. Book in advance. The Tourist Information Centre (TIC) can arrange bookings for you free of charge. Out of season knock 10% off the prices given here.

Litinterp (☎ 228 718; kaunas@litinterp.lt; Gedimino gatvė 28; s/d/tr 80/140/180Lt) An excellent B&B choice; these ever-brilliant people will find

you a nice cosy room somewhere for a fraction of the cost of staying in a hotel.

Metropolis (☎ 205 992; Daukanto gatvė 21; s/d incl breakfast 100/140Lt) A Soviet dream of a hotel with some of the cheapest rooms in Kaunas – and for good reason – it's seen better days. On the plus side it's safe and relatively clean and renovation of some rooms was underway at the time of research.

Takioji Neris (☎ 306 100; Donelaičio gatvė 27; s/d from 100/140Lt; **P**) Proper comfy rooms with such delights as satellite TV and baths in a place slap bang in the centre of town. Also boasts a sauna and secure parking, which is a must for Kaunas.

Žaliakalnio (☎ 321 412; Savanorių prospektas 66; s/d 220/260Lt; ▯) There are brilliant views from this gorgeous, modern hotel with a hilltop address. You'll feel pampered here with free Internet connection, lovely rooms and a restaurant terrace worth the extra litų.

Kaunas (☎ 750 850; www.kaunashotel.lt; Laisvės alėja 79; s/d/ste 320/400/500Lt) A swanky pillow parlour boasting glass-walled bathrooms!

Eating

There are plenty of restaurants to choose from along Laisvės alėja, most with English-language menus and none that will break the bank.

Kuba (☎ 209 932; Laisvės alėja 79; mains 10-15Lt; ☉ 9am-7pm) The cheapest joint in Kaunas, Kuba is a buffet-style canteen with the day's dishes laid out for your perusal. Nothing fancy, just meat and veg dishes served with rice or potatoes.

Arbatinė (☎ 323 732; Laisvės alėja 100; mains 15Lt; ☉ 9am-6pm Mon-Fri, 10am-6pm Sat) A café that sets vegan pulses racing with its dairy/meat-free policy. It serves sandwiches, salads and smoothies so is perfect for lunch.

Jums (☎ 203 705; Laisvės alėja 61; mains 15Lt) This is the nicest café/restaurant in Kaunas. Aside from staring at the grass on the ceiling or art on the walls, you can peer at an excellent fusion menu with such wonders as beef teriyaki and chicken in champagne. Recommended.

Pas Pranciška (☎ 203 875; Zamenhofo gatvė 11; mains 15-25Lt) Serves delicious Lithuanian dishes in a traditional setting. It's an institution in Kaunas and serves the finest *cepelinai* in all the land.

Miesto Sodas (☎ 424 424; Laisvės alėja 93; mains 20-30Lt; ☉ 11am-midnight) Very trendy eatery with funky orange décor and excellent international menu. The steaks are the biz and there's live music sometimes too.

Drinking

There are cool hang-outs aplenty in funky Kaunas.

B.O. (Muitinės gatvė 9) is where students and bohemian types hang out. **Skliautai** (Rotušės aikštė 26) has a tiny courtyard filled with local arty types and an older crowd.

Entertainment

Check out what's on in the *Kaunas & Klaipėda In Your Pocket* guide or ask at the TIC. Kaunas has a strong theatre tradition and often has classical concerts.

Los Petrankos (Savanorių prospektas 124), a nightclub just northeast of the centre, has a state-of-the-art sound system for up to 1500 clubbers.

Other options are:

Kaunas State Drama Theatre (☎ 224 064; Laisvės alėja 71; box office ☷ 10am-7pm)

Philharmonic (☎ 222 558; Sapiegos 5; box office ☷ 2-6pm)

Planeta Cinema (☎ 338 330; Vytauto prospektas 6)

Getting There & Away

AIR

Kaunas International Airport (☎ 399 307; Savanorių prospektas) is located 10km north of the Old Town in the suburb of Karmėlava. Minibuses run to the airport from the bottom of Savanorių prospektas (1Lt).

International flights are operated by **Air Lithuania** (☎ 228 176; Kęstučio gatvė 69; ☷ 8am-6pm Mon-Fri, 9am-3pm Sat) to Hamburg, Oslo and Billund via Palanga.

BUS

From Kaunas' **long-distance bus station** (☎ 409 060; Vytauto prospektas 24), **Kautra Bus Lines** (☎ 342 440; www.kautra.lt) runs buses to the European cities of St Petersburg, Kaliningrad, Rīga and Tallinn.

Domestic routes include frequent daily buses to Vilnius (13Lt, two hours, 100km), Klaipėda (30Lt, three hours, 210km), Palanga (28Lt to 32Lt, 3½ hours, 230km) and Šiauliai (20Lt to 23Lt, three hours, 140km).

TRAIN

Using Kaunas **train station** (☎ 372 260; Čiurlionio gatvė 16) 12 daily trains go to/from Vilnius

(9.80Lt, two hours). There are eight daily trains to/from Klaipėda (23.40Lt, six hours), one to/from Rīga (22Lt, five hours) and three to/from Šiauliai (14.10Lt, three hours). Kaunas–Šeštokai trains connect with the Šeštokai–Suwałki train into Poland and there's also one Moscow train.

ŠIAULIAI

☎ 41 / pop 147,000

Lithuania's fourth-largest city is a stone's throw from the legendary Hill of Crosses. The city, which has a history of fire, plague and other troubles, lies 140km north of Kaunas and is the centre of the northwestern region of Žemaitija (or Samogitia).

Orientation & Information

The main north–south street is Tilžės gatvė, with the bus station to the south and SS Peter & Paul's Church northwards. The main east–west axis is Vilniaus gatvė.

The **Tourist Information Centre** (☎ 523 110; www.siauliai.lt; Vilniaus gatvė 213; ☷ 9am-6pm Mon-Fri, 10am-3pm Sat) arranges trips to the Hill of Crosses, and has maps and brochures on the city.

Vilniaus Bankas (Tilžės gatvė) offers currency exchange. The post office is at Aušros alėja 42. **West Express** (☎ 523 333; Vasario 16-osios gatvė 48) sells train and plane tickets.

Hill of Crosses

Lithuania's most incredible, awe-inspiring sight is the legendary **Hill of Crosses** (Kryžių kalnas). It is a two-hump hillock blanketed by thousands of crosses. The sound of the evening breeze tinkling through the crosses that appear to grow on the hillock is indescribable and unmissable. Each and every cross represents the amazing spirit, soulfulness and quietly rebellious nature of these people.

Legend says the tradition of planting crosses began in the 14th century. The crosses were bulldozed by the Soviets, but each night people crept past soldiers and barbed wire to plant yet more, risking their lives or freedom to express their national and spiritual fervour. Kryžių kalnas has now become a place of national pilgrimage.

Some of the crosses are devotional, others are memorials (many for people deported to Siberia) and some are finely carved folk-art masterpieces.

LITHUANIA

This strange place lies 10km north of Šiauliai, 2km east off the road to Joniškis and Rīga. You can get to the hill from Šiauliai by bus, microbus or taxi. Buses run daily from 5am till 11pm from Šiauliai bus station (0.80Lt) or you can pay 1Lt and grab a microbus. Microbuses run from 6am till 11pm and are quicker. Get off at the Domantai stop and walk the 2km track to the hill. Look for the sign 'Kryžių kalnas 2'. A one-way taxi costs about 25Lt to 30Lt.

Sleeping

Youth Hostel (☎ 523 992; romaspp@takas.lt; Rygos gatvė 36; dm 15Lt) Simple, cheap beds and not much else.

Šiauliai (☎ 437 333; Draugystės prospektas 25; s/d from 60/80Lt) You've got to love this spectacularly ugly Soviet masterpiece. Millions of sunny rooms with hardly any mod cons and surly staff – the perfect ex-communist experience!

Getting There & Away

BUS

Daily services from the **bus station** (☎ 525 058; Tilzes gatvė 109) include those to: Vilnius (24Lt to 27Lt, four hours, about 12 buses), Kaunas (17.50Lt, three hours, about 20 buses), Klaipėda, (20Lt, 2½ hours, six buses), Rīga (14.50Lt, three hours, eight buses) and Tallinn (8½ hours, one bus).

TRAIN

From the **train station** (☎ 430 652; Dubijos gatvė 44) each day there are frequent trains to Vilnius (24.10Lt, four hours), Kaunas (14.10Lt, four hours), Klaipėda (14.50Lt, four hours) and Rīga (2½ hours).

WESTERN LITHUANIA

Shhhhhhh! Don't tell anyone else about this magical little part of the planet. Western Lithuania has some of the Baltic region's most beautiful landscape on its luscious coastal stretch, crowned with glittering jewel, the Curonian Spit (Kuršių Nerija).

The sea port of Klaipėda comes alive each year with the Sea Festival, crowds flock to party-mecca Palanga and the rest head to the fishing villages of Nida or Juodkrantė on the spit while the Nemunas Delta remains a tranquil nature zone. There's much

to keep you happy here. Western Lithuania has the lot – sand, sea and soul.

KLAIPĖDA

☎ 46 / pop 194,000

Klaipėda is the oldest city in Lithuania (1252) and gateway to the lush natural beauty of the Curonian Spit. However, Lithuania's third-largest city has some little gems of its own. Most notably it was once the German town of Memel, and some of the Germanic architecture remains including the famous bell tower

Hitler annexed the town in 1939 and towards the end of WWII it was wrecked when the Red Army invaded.

Orientation

The Danės River flows west across the city centre to the Curonian (Kuršių) Lagoon, 4km from the open Baltic Sea. The main street is Manto gatvė, which becomes Tiltų gatvė south of the river. The Old Town is centred on Tiltų gatvė. Most hotels, restaurants, banks and the train and bus stations are north of the river.

Information

Central post office (☎ 315 022; Liepų gatvė 16; ☽ 8am-7pm Mon-Fri, 9am-4pm Sat)

Krantas Travel (☎ 395 111; Teatro aikštė 5; ☽ 9am-5pm Mon-Fri) Offers car rental, shipping information and booking, and tours of the region.

Omnitel (☎ 412 360; Manto gatvė 18; per hr 3Lt; ☽ 9am-7pm Mon-Fri, 9am-5pm) Provides Internet access.

Tourist Information Centre (☎ 412 186; Turgaus gatvė 5; ☽ 8.30am-6.30pm Mon-Fri, 9am-3pm Sat & Sun May-Aug, 8.30am-6.30pm Mon-Fri Sep-Apr) Has moved to swanky larger premises and stocks as much info as you could ever need. Sells maps, brochures and posts lists of what's on daily.

Vilniaus Bankas (☎ 310 925; Turgaus gatvė 15; ☽ 8am-6pm Mon-Thu, 8am-5pm Fri) Offers full banking services.

Sights

South of the river, off Turgaus gatvė, is Teatro aikšte (Theatre Sq). Here there's an important landmark: the 1818 **Klaipėda Theatre** (Teatro aikštė 2; ☽ 11am-2pm & 4-6pm). Hitler stood on the balcony of this theatre in 1939 to announce the incorporation of Memel into Germany. Here too stands Klaipėda's much-loved statue of Ännchen von Tharau,

KLAIPĖDA

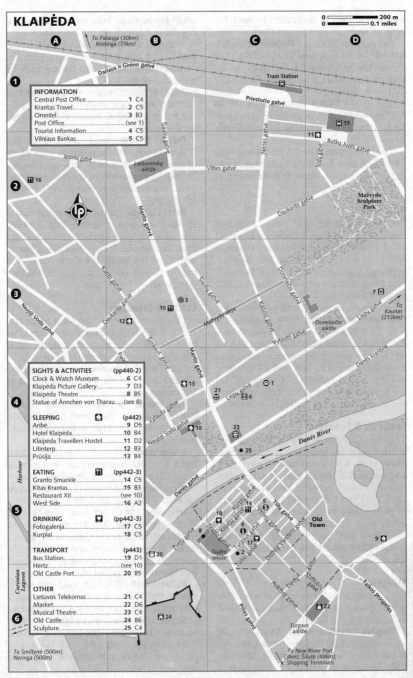

0 _____ 200 m
0 _____ 0.1 miles

To Palanga (30km);
Kretinga (35km)

Dariaus ir Girėno gatvė

Train Station

Priestočio gatvė

INFORMATION
Central Post Office.........................1 C4
Krantas Travel.............................2 C5
Omnitel.....................................3 B3
Post Office...............................(see 1)
Tourist Information........................4 C5
Vilniaus Bankas...........................5 C5

Janonio gatvė

Lietuvninkų aikštė

Vilties gatvė

Šiaulių gatvė

Neries gatvė

Sodų gatvė

Butkų Juzės gatvė

Mažvydo Sculpture Park

Daukanto gatvė

Manto gatvė

Kanto gatvė

Naujoji Uosto gatvė

Daukanto gatvė

Simkaus gatvė

Šiaulių gatvė

Donelaičio gatvė

Mažvydo alėja

Kaluvo gatvė

Kalno gatvė

Liepų gatvė

Donelaičio aikštė

To Kaunas (213km)

Danės krantinė

Vytauto gatvė

SIGHTS & ACTIVITIES   (pp440-2)
Clock & Watch Museum....................6 C4
Klaipėda Picture Gallery..................7 D3
Klaipėda Theatre..........................8 B5
Statue of Ännchen von Tharau....(see 8)

SLEEPING   (p442)
Aribė......................................9 D5
Hotel Klaipėda............................10 B4
Klaipėda Travellers Hostel................11 D2
Litinterp.................................12 B3
Prūsija...................................13 B4

EATING   (pp442-3)
Granto Smucklė...........................14 C5
Kitas Krantas.............................15 B3
Restaurant XII...........................(see 10)
West Side................................16 A2

DRINKING   (pp442-3)
Fotogalerija.............................17 C5
Kurpiai.................................18 C5

TRANSPORT   (p443)
Bus Station..............................19 D1
Hertz..................................(see 10)
Old Castle Port..........................20 B5

OTHER
Lietuvos Telekomas......................21 C4
Market...................................22 D6
Musical Theatre..........................23 C4
Old Castle...............................24 B6
Sculpture................................25 C4

Danės River

Danės gatvė

Danės gatvė

Vytauto gatvė

Naujoji Sodo gatvė

Old Town

Kurpių gatvė

Tiltų gatvė

Vėžeių gatvė

Žvejų gatvė

Teatro gatvė

Kepėjų gatvė

Turgaus gatvė

Tomo gatvė

Teatro aikštė

Didžioji Vandens gatvė

Aukštoji gatvė

Daržų gatvė

Bažnyčių gatvė

Taikos prospektas

Pilies gatvė

Turgaus aikštė

Harbour

Curonian Lagoon

To Smiltynė (500m);
Neringa (500m)

To New River Port
(3km); Šilutė (48km);
Shipping Terminals

LITHUANIA

unveiled in 1989 in dedication to the 17th-century German poet Simon Dach.

North of the river, the **Klaipėda Picture Gallery** (☎ 410 412; Liepų gatvė 33; adult/child 3/1.50Lt; ♥ noon-6pm Tue-Sat, noon-5pm Sun) has a sculpture garden and an impressive collection of 20th-century works.

The quirky **Clock & Watch Museum** (☎ 410 413; Liepų gatvė 12; adult/child 4/2Lt; ♥ 11am-4.30pm Tue-Sat, 11am-3.30pm Sun) has clocks from Gothic to nuclear.

The nearby **post office** (1893) has a unique 48-bell carillon inside its bell tower, making it the largest musical instrument in Lithuania.

SMILTYNĖ

Smiltynė is just across the thin strait that divides Klaipėda from its achingly beautiful coastal sister, Neringa. It has one of nature's best playgrounds to explore with beaches, high dunes and pine forests. The more adventurous can have a traditional sauna (5Lt) on the Baltic coast.

Smiltynė's biggest crowd-pleaser is the **Aquarium & Dolphinarium** (☎ 490 751; adult/student 6/3Lt; ♥ 10.30am-6.30pm Tue-Sun Jun-Aug, 10.30am-5.30pm Wed-Sun May & Sep, 10.30am-4.30pm Sat & Sun Oct-Apr). Sea-lion performances (admission extra 4Lt) are at 11.15am and 1.15pm, and dolphin shows (adult/child extra 10/5Lt) are at noon and 3pm. Free ferries run here every half hour from the Old Castle port.

Festivals & Events

The city celebrates its nautical heritage with a flamboyant **Sea Festival** each summer that draws crowds for a weekend of merriment and nautical extravaganzas. It takes place in late July each year and has been running since 1934 and has around 100 events such as parties, musical concerts, shows and art exhibitions. For ship-lovers the city joins the 'Baltic Sail' event in 2005 and traditional sailing vessels will visit Klaipėda during the festival.

Sleeping

Budget beds are not too much of an endangered species in Klaipėda but call ahead, especially for the hostel.

Klaipėda Travellers Hostel (☎ 211 879; guest place@yahoo.com; Butkų Juzės gatvė 7/4; dm 32Lt) Jurga is the hostess with the mostest at this nice little hostel with spotlessly clean beds, a

small kitchen and bike rental/tours of the region, just 50m from the bus station.

Litinterp (☎ 310 296; klaipeda@litinterp.lt; Šimkaus gatvė 21/4; s/d from 70/100Lt) Arranges B&B accommodation in private homes with or without a host.

Aribė (☎ 490 940; Bangų gatvė 17A; s/d incl breakfast 120/160Lt; P) Clean, modern with car parking but it has small rooms and no night-time restaurant.

Prūsija (☎ 412 081; Šimkaus gatvė 6; s/d 160/180Lt) If you like your accommodation with a hint of strangeness thrown in then head for the 'Prussia'. Crazy swirls of concrete cover the walls, the furniture is interesting but staff are friendly.

Hotel Klaipėda (☎ 404 372; hotel@klaipedahotel .lt; Naujoji Sodo gatvė 1; s/d/ste from 180/260/430Lt) The classiest hotel in the city – if you ignore the outside! It may look like a Soviet nightmare but inside it's plush, has all the mod cons and many extra, and a fabulous skyline bar.

Eating & Drinking

Manto gatvė is the bustling heart of the city and is lined with bars and restaurants so head for there. Restaurants generally open 10am till 11pm, bars may stay open an hour longer. There's a good selection of international places and the old chestnut that is Lithuanian pizza.

Kitas Krantas (☎ 314 687; Manto gatvė 11; mains 15Lt; ♥ 9am-midnight) Tuck into cheap Chinese fodder or sip a cocktail at this perennially trendy place.

Granto Smucklė (☎ 411 683; Kepėjų gatvė 10; mains 20Lt) A good steakhouse serving – you guessed it, sides of beef all named after English towns (?). It turns into a bar and club after 9pm so eat early if banging music isn't your thing.

West Side (☎ 411 585; Kanto gatvė 44; mains 20-25Lt; ♥ noon-2am) An American-themed restaurant/bar/lifestyle choice with superb menu, fantastical décor and all the bright young things you could wish for crammed into this recommended place.

Restaurant XII (☎ 404 371; Naujoji Sodo gatvė 1; mains 20-30Lt) This is a gorgeous restaurant/ bar on the 12th floor of Hotel Klaipėda and is Klaipėda's newest and hottest place to be seen. Choose from the imperial starters, chicken wings, pork ribs – all beautifully presented – while ignoring how snooty the staff are.

Kurpiai (☎ 410 555; Kurpių gatvė 1a) Possibly Lithuania's best bar with live jazz every night and an appreciative raucous crowd.

Fotogalerija (Tomo gatvė 7) Small cosy bar in the heart of the Old Town.

Getting There & Away

Klaipėda **bus station** (☎ 411 547; Butkų Juzės 9) sees daily buses to Vilnius (41Lt, 13 daily), Kaunas (30Lt, 18 daily), Liepaja via Palanga (11.10Lt, two daily), Palanga (3Lt, every 40 minutes) and Kaliningrad via Nida (25Lt, two daily). There are frequent Smiltynė–Nida buses.

There are fewer train services. Three run daily to Vilnius (14.50Lt, 4½ hours) and one to Kaunas (14.50Lt, four hours) from the **train station** (☎ 296 385; Priestoties 5a).

See p447 for ferry services.

PALANGA

☎ 460 / pop 19,550

A pensioners paradise in winter and party mecca in summer, Palanga seaside resort is 25km north of Klaipėda and has a lovely long, white stretch of beach and loads of bars and restaurants.

Vytauto gatvė, the main street, runs parallel to the coast about 1km inland. The Catholic church at Vytauto gatvė 51 marks roughly the middle of town. From here Basanavičiaus gatvė (currently under renovation) runs to the pier.

The **Tourist Information Centre** (☎ 48811; www.palangatic.lt; Kretingos gatvė 1; ☺ 9am-5.30pm Mon-Fri) adjoins the tiny bus station.

The botanical park is at the southern end of Vytauto gatvė, with an excellent amber museum in the former palace of the noble Polish Tyszkiewicz family.

Litinterp in Klaipėda (p442) can arrange B&Bs in Palanga.

Sachmatine (☎ 51655; Basanavičiaus gatvė 45; r 190Lt) Slap bang at the end of the pier this party hotel has a club, garish rooms and a noisy pizzeria. It's like a package holiday all rolled into one.

Palanga (☎ 41414; Birutės gatvė 60; s/d 300/400Lt; ⊠) The cream of the crop, this designer hotel has a swimming pool, swanky Italian restaurant and exquisitely tasteful rooms.

There are plenty of eating options along Basanavičiaus gatvė including **Kavinė 1925 Baras** (☎ 52560; Basanavičiaus gatvė 4; mains 15-20Lt), which serves soups, snacks and pancakes in a wooden cabin.

For details of summer Palanga–Vilnius flights see p447. There are regular daily buses to Vilnius (43Lt, six hours), Kaunas (30Lt, 3½ hours), Klaipėda (3Lt) and Rīga (32Lt).

NERINGA

☎ 469 / pop 2528

Neringa is as close to heaven as you're likely to come. The fresh air and scent of pine are at their headiest on this thin tongue of sand, much of which is a 4km-wide national park.

Waves from the Baltic Sea pound one side, the Curonian Lagoon laps the other. The winds and tree-felling have sculpted the dunes on the fragile Curonian Spit (Kuršių Nerija), which was made a Unesco World Heritage landscape in December 2000. The northern half is Lithuanian, the southern Russian, and a road runs the full 97km length into the Kaliningrad Region.

You'll have to pay a fee to enter the national park if you're arriving by car (15Lt) or motorbike (7Lt).

Go and discover this little treasure before the rest of the world does.

Nida

Neringa's main settlement is **Nida** (Nidden), which sits at the southern end of the Lithuanian section of the spit, 50km from Klaipėda.

In winter it's a charming fishing village that goes about its business while being lashed by storms that dredge up Baltic gold (amber) onto its shores. In summer it's a resort that doubles in population.

INFORMATION

The **Tourist Information Centre** (☎ 52345; Taikos gatvė 4; ☺ 10am-8pm) has a wealth of information from boat trips to booking accommodation. The tiny bus station is opposite the TIC.

You'll find an ATM nearby at the **Hansabank** (Taikos gatvė 5).

SIGHTS & ACTIVITIES

Get a great view of the spit by climbing up designated paths on **Parnidis Dune** (52m) to the sundial. The 'Lithuanian Sahara' is a breathtaking sight.

The **Ethnographic Museum** (☎ 52372; Naglių gatvė 4; admission 2Lt) is an old fisherman's cottage, which has been left as it was in the 19th century and is well worth a peek.

Nobel-prize winning German writer Thomas Mann had a house – now a **museum** (☎ 52260; admission 2Lt; Skruzdynės gatvė 17) – here in the 1930s.

Otherwise hire a bike from the TIC, go on a fishing boat or walk through those whispering pines and go for a paddle.

SLEEPING & EATING

Summer really hots up on the bed front so book in advance. Litinterp in Klaipėda (see p442) can arrange rooms.

Medikas (☎ 52985; Kuverto gatvė 14; dm 25Lt winter only, d/tr 120/130Lt) This place is only for bargain hunters as it's basic with Soviet-era standards of decoration and cleanliness.

Linėja (☎ 52390; Taikos gatvė 18; s/d from 120/150Lt) Has a bowling alley and sauna as well as chintzy rooms that are clean and comfy.

Seklyčia (☎ 52945; Lotmiškio gatvė 1; mains 25-30Lt; ☑ 9am-midnight) It serves *haute cuisine* Nida style and offers lovely views of the dunes of Nida and the best *kepta duona* in Lithuania.

Juodkrantė

Juodkrantė is a nice little village that you'll pass through on the way to Nida. It's worth a stop for its rather strange attractions.

Top of the strange sights list is the **Raganų Kalnas** (Witches' Hill), a spooky sculpture trail through gorgeous forest with large, fairytale Lithuanian wooden carvings. Unmissable. There's also a 2.5km sculpture trail along the lagoon edge.

If you like the calm compared to the busier Nida you may want to stay a night. **Santauta** (☎ 53167; Kalno gatvė 36; s 20-70Lt, d 45-110Lt, tr 70-180Lt) has a full range of budget and more comfy rooms while **Kurena** (☎ 53101; Liudviko Rėzos 10; d from 250Lt) is a new, tasteful haven.

Part of the Neringa experience is to buy and taste the freshly caught and smoked fish from one of the little wooden house on Rėzos gatvė. Otherwise **Pamario Takas** (☎ 53388; Rėzos 42) is at the end of the Witches' Hill trail for much-need refreshment.

Getting There & Away

A passenger ferry departs every half hour from the Old Castle port in Klaipėda for the northern tip of Neringa. Pedestrians are free. Motorists use the vehicle ferry at the **New River port** (Nemuno gatvė 8), 3km south.

From Smiltynė buses and microbuses run throughout the day to/from Nida (7Lt, one hour), stopping at Juodkrantė on the way.

NEMUNAS DELTA

South of Klaipėda and hugging western Lithuania is this beautiful cluster of islands, which has been protected as a national park since 1992.

Bird-watchers should head here as the wetlands are home to many rare birds and acts as an important area for migratory waterfowl. The **Ventės Ragas Ornithological Station** (☎ 441-54480) does research into local birdlife.

Rusnė is the largest village on the island and it's the base for the **information centre** (☎ 441-58154; Pakalnės gatvė 40a; ☑ 8am-5pm Jun-Aug, 8am-5pm Mon-Fri Sep-May), which can arrange farm-stay accommodation.

Private transport or a tour with **Krantas Travel** (www.krantas.lt) are the only ways to explore this incredible area.

LITHUANIA DIRECTORY

ACCOMMODATION

Book beds well in advance if coming to Vilnius as, like the rest of the Baltics, it's fast becoming the number-one choice for stag nights and hen parties, as well as being fashionable on the travelling circuit. The **Lithuanian State Tourism Department** (www.tourism.lt) has a good website for forward planning, listing rural farm stays, health resorts and hotels.

There are no camping grounds to recommend in Lithuania. They are generally basic, dirt cheap (5Lt to 20Lt for a camp site, 15Lt to 30Lt for a wooden cabin) and run down. There are moves by the Lithuanian Tourist Board to spruce up facilities but we're still waiting. The national parks have basic camping grounds and there are private ones dotted around Palanga and Trakai.

The **Lithuanian Hostels Association** (☎ 215 4627; www.filaretaihostel.lt; Filaretų gatvė 17) is based at the largest hostel it runs (Filaretai Hostel in Vilnius). The association runs a second hostel in Vilnius' Old Town, and has an affiliated hostel in Klaipėda. A bed in a shared room costs 24Lt to 32Lt a night.

Budget travellers can also look to **Litinterp** (www.litinterp.lt), which offers B&Bs and self-catering facilities in Vilnius, Klaipėda, Kaunas, Palanga and Nida. In Vilnius prices start at 80Lt for a single, while outside the capital city the rates are from 70Lt.

TICs can book countryside home stays from 100Lt a double, or check the Tourism department website listed earlier.

Hotels are plentiful in Vilnius, most offering decent rates by European standards: between 80Lt to 200Lt for a night, with mid-range coming in at 140Lt and above. Check the excellent *Vilnius In Your Pocket* guide (www.inyourpocket.com) for the whole range of choices. In rural places hotel choice can be limited and the standard poor to say the least with accompanying price reductions. Palanga is fast becoming expensive even out of season so haggle or book in advance for cheaper rates.

Useful websites for booking accommodation or pretrip planning include www .visitlithuania.lt, www.vilniushotels.lt and www.lithuanianhotels.com. Reviews in this chapter are ordered according to price.

ACTIVITIES

The pagan roots of Lithuanians are revealed by their love of nature; ancient oak trees were still being worshipped a mere six centuries ago. Travellers can boat and hike in the wilderness of Aukštaitija National Park (p434), sweat in a traditional sauna at Smiltynė (p442)and enjoy the frozen experiences of ice-fishing or skiing.

Krantas Travel (www.krantas.lt) organises tours of the western Nemunas Delta wetlands (p444), which are rich in birdlife.

As Lithuania is flat, cycling is becoming more popular. Most towns/cities have bike hire either from Litinterp, the TICs or private hotels/guesthouses.

Mushrooming is a relic of Lithuania's traditional way of life and a beloved pastime. There are deadly poisonous varieties so only eat what you know is safe.

BUSINESS HOURS

Most shops open between 10am and 6pm on weekdays and Saturday in the larger towns and cities. Expect rural places to have their own code of conduct. Main post offices open between 7am and 7pm on weekdays and between 9am and 4pm on Saturday. In smaller towns/villages opening times can differ greatly. Banks are open between 8am and 5pm on weekdays only. Restaurants tend to open at 10am and shut at 11pm, but those that are attached to bars/clubs may not shut till dawn!

DISABLED TRAVELLERS

Lithuania is not the most friendly country for disabled travellers; the cobbled streets of Vilnius' Old Town make it difficult for wheelchair users and the visually impaired. Public transport is not easily accessible, although a few hotels and bars do cater for the disabled.

EMBASSIES & CONSULATES
Lithuanian Embassies & Consulates

Lithuania has representatives in the following countries:

Australia (☎ 02-9498 2571; 40B Fiddens Wharf Rd, Killara, Sydney, NSW 2071)

Canada (☎ 613-567 5458; 130 Albert St, Suite 204, Ottawa, Ontario K1P 5G4)

Estonia (☎ 2-631 4030; amb.ee@urm.lt; Uus tn 15, Tallinn)

France (☎ 01 40 54 50 50; 22 Blvd de Courcelles, Paris)

Germany (☎ 030-890 68 10; Charitestrasse 9, 10711 Berlin)

Ireland (☎ 1 6688292; 90 Merrion Rd, Ballsbridge, Dublin 4)

Latvia (☎ 2-732 1519; Rūpniecibas iela 22, 1010 Riga)

Netherlands (☎ 70 385 5418; nl.urm.lt; Koninginnegracht 78, 2514 AH The Hague)

New Zealand (☎ 09-336 7711; 28 Heather St, Parnell, Auckland)

Russia Moscow (☎ 095-785 8605, Borisoglebsky per 10, Moscow 121069);

Kaliningrad (☎ 0112-55 14 44; ul Proletarskaya 133, Kaliningrad)

UK (☎ 020-7486 6401; 84 Gloucester Pl, London W1H 3HN)

USA (☎ 202-234 5860; 2622 16th St NW, Washington, DC 20009)

Embassies & Consulates in Lithuania

The following embassies and consulates are in Vilnius (area code ☎ 5):

Australia (☎ 212 3369; aust.con.vilnius@post.omnitel .net; Vilniaus gatvė 23)

Belarus (☎ 249 0950; www.belarus.lt; Mindaugo gatvė 13)

Canada (☎ 249 0950; vilnius@canada.lt; Gedimino prospektas 64)

Estonia (☎ 278 0200; sekretar@estemb.l; A Mickevičiaus gatvė 4a)

Finland (☎ 212 16 21; sanomat.vil@formin.fi; Klaipėdos gatvė 6)

France (☎ 212 29 79; www.ambafrance-lt.org; Švarco gatvė 1)

Germany (☎ 210 6400; germ.emb@takas.lt; Sierakausko gatvė 24)

Netherlands (☎ 269 00 72; www.netherlandsembassy .lt; Business Centre 2000, Floor 4, Jogailos gatvė 4)

Latvia (☎ 213 1260; lietuva@latvia.balt.net; MK Čiurlionio gatvė 76)

Russia (☎ 272 1763; rusemb@rusemb.lt; Latvių gatvė 53/54)

UK (☎ 212 2070/1; be-vilnius@britain.lt; Antakalnio gatvė 2)

USA (☎ 266 5500; mail@usembassy; Akmenų gatvė 6)

FESTIVALS & EVENTS

Lithuania hosts a great many cultural, spiritual and nonsensical events each year. With the addition of the Vilnius Carnival, they're hoping to rival Rio! Here's a few:

Kaunas Jazz Festival (Apr)

New Baltic Dance (3-9 May) International contemporary dance festival.

St Christopher Summer Festival (Jul) Month-long annual festival of jazz in Vilnius, choir music, orchestra and solo performances.

HOLIDAYS

National holidays include:

New Year's Day 1 January

Independence Day 16 February; anniversary of 1918 independence declaration. The Restoration of Lithuania's 11 March Independence

Easter (Good Friday and Easter Monday) April

Labour Day 1 May

State Holiday 6 July; commemoration of Grand Duke Mindaugas' coronation

All Saints' Day 1 November

Christmas Day 25 December

Boxing Day 26 December

MONEY

Lithuania's currency is the litas (plural: litų; Lt). The litas comes in 10, 20, 50, 100, 200 and 500Lt notes and one, two and five litų coins. One litas is 100 (almost worthless) centų (ct).

Lithuania's main cities and towns have banks and exchange offices that convert currency. Vilnius, Klaipėda, Kaunas and Šiauliai all have major bank chains, which have ATMs and money-transfer facilities,

can cash travellers cheques and give cash advances. The euro is accepted in hotels as legal tender; some prices are only quoted in euros but across the rest of your trip all costs are in litų. Smaller places may have only one bank and/or one ATM so forward planning may prove necessary.

POST

Sending a letter abroad by airmail costs 1.70Lt, a postcard costs 1.20Lt; within Lithuania it costs 1/0.8Lt, respectively.

Mail generally takes up to seven days to reach the rest of Europe and up to 14 days to get to the USA. There's an express mail service, **DHL** (☎ 22345), at Vilnius airport.

TELEPHONE

The Lithuanian telephone network was digitised in 2002 and all the area access codes were changed. If you are in doubt about a code check on the website www.telecom.lt.

To call other cities within Lithuania, dial ☎ 8, wait for the tone, then dial the city code and phone number.

To make an international call dial ☎ 00 before the country code. To call Lithuania from abroad, dial ☎ 370 then the city code, followed by the phone number.

To call a mobile you need nine digits; if in doubt, take the number and count back nine digits from the last number. Then always precede that with an 8. If taking your own mobile to Lithuania it's worth getting a local SIM card. Omnitel or Bitė offer cards in denominations of 20/40/100Lt.

Once you know what city code to dial you can leap into one of the blue booths dotted around the cities. They're card-only. Cards are sold at newsstands and are in units of 50/100/200 costing 9/16/30Lt. Dial ☎ 8191 for the operator.

EMERGENCY NUMBERS

In an emergency, call:

- Fire ☎ 01
- Police ☎ 02
- Ambulance ☎ 03

TOURIST INFORMATION

In Lithuania the tourist information centres (TICs) are dotted around the country.

They are coordinated by the **Lithuanian Tourist Board** (www.tourism.lt).

VISAS

For Lithuania's European neighbours, a valid passport is the only entry requirement for a stay of up to 90 days within a single year. Thankfully, Australian, UK, Canadian, USA and New Zealand nationals are subject to the same requirement. Saying that, though, it's always worth checking visa status before making a trip. Citizens from nations not included in the visa-free gang must apply for a tourist visa. A single-entry visa costs US$20 to US$25 and a visa can't be bought on Lithuania's borders. Contact the **Consular Department of Ministry of Foreign Affairs** (☎ 262 0147; www.urm.lt) for all visa-related information.

TRANSPORT IN LITHUANIA

GETTING THERE & AWAY
Air

Vilnius **airport** (☎ 5-230 6666; www.vilnius-airport .lt; Rodūnios gatvė 2) is served by direct flights from Amsterdam, Berlin, Brussels, Copenhagen, Frankfurt, Helsinki, Kyiv, London, Moscow, Prague, Rīga, Stockholm, Tallinn and Warsaw. Carriers based at the airport (area code ☎ 5) include:

Aeroflot (code SU; ☎ 232 9300; www.aeroflot.com; ☉ 9am-6pm Mon-Fri)

Estonian Air (code OV; ☎ 273 9022; www.estonian-air .com; ☉ 9am-6pm Mon-Fri)

Lufthansa (code LH; ☎ 230 6031; www.lufthansa.com; ☉ 9am-5pm Mon & Fri, 8am-6pm Tue-Thu, 7.20am-3.20pm Sat & Sun)

SAS Scandinavian Airlines (code SK; ☎ 235 6000; www.scandinavian.net; ☉ 9am-5pm Mon-Fri, 11am-5pm Sat & Sun)

Land
BUS

Vilnius **bus station** (☎ 216 2977; Sodų gatvė 22) is served by international buses to Amsterdam (350Lt), Brussels (370Lt), Kaliningrad (48Lt), London (495Lt), Minsk (22Lt), Moscow (96Lt), Prague (160Lt), Rīga (40Lt, five daily), Rome (445Lt), Stockholm (191Lt), Tallinn (90Lt, two daily) and Vienna (300Lt).

Eurolines (☎ 215 1377; www.eurolines.com; ☉ 6am-10pm) and **Toks** (☎ 216 0054; www.toks.lt; ☉ 6am-9pm) are the carriers and both are based inside the bus station. Buses are comfortable and have refreshments and toilets

CAR & MOTORCYCLE

Insurance is compulsory and can be bought at the border crossings. The wait for motorists on the Lithuanian–Polish borders at Kalvarija and Lazdijai can be from two minutes to two days. The Lithuanian–Belarusian border crossings are notoriously slow. Crossing into Latvia is much speedier, expect waits of no longer than an hour. See p448 for road rules and further information.

TRAIN

Vilnius **train station** (☎ 233 0088; www.litrail.lt; Geležinkelio gatvė 16) is served by trains to Moscow (270/139Lt in 1st/2nd class, 13 hours, one daily), St Petersburg (215/129Lt, 14 hours, even-numbered days) and Kaliningrad (165/93Lt, seven hours, one daily). The Warsaw train leaves on even-numbered days to Šeštokai (three hours, 198km, 18.80Lt). See p901 for more on train classes.

Sea

Ferries run from Klaipėda to Karlshamm in Sweden (six times weekly), Kiel (daily) and Sassnitz (daily except Thursday) in Germany, and Frederica (four times weekly) and Copenhagen (four times weekly) in Denmark. Expect to pay a €10 surcharge for harbour fees on top of the ticket price. For ticket costs and booking contact **Krantas Travel** (www.krantas.lt).

GETTING AROUND
Air

Between mid-May and mid-September (the dates vary each year) there is an internal flight between Vilnius and Palanga every Saturday with **Air Lithuania** (☎ 213 1322; www .airlithuania.lt).

Bicycle

Get information, help and advice about cycling in Lithuania from the **Lithuanian Bicycle Information Centre** (www.bicycle.lt). The centre offers organised tours of the region, bicycle rental, specific travel guides and maps.

Lithuania may not be for the serious wheeler as it lacks the hills that make road racing fun but it's perfect for a holiday activity for the same reason! Take emergency repair kits as necessary items may be harder to find than in other parts of Europe.

Bus

The **Vilnius bus station** (☎ 216 2977; Sodų gatvė 22) is south of the Old Town next to the train station. Timetables for local and international buses are displayed on a large board in the main hall. If you're still confused head to the information centre, which has English-speaking staff, in the ticket hall.

Bus timetables change frequently so check www.toks.lt. Daily domestic buses from Vilnius to destinations in Lithuania include Druskininkai (14.5Lt, two hours, 125km, seven daily), Kaunas (13Lt, two hours, 100km, every 20 minutes; also regular microbuses), Klaipėda (41Lt, five to seven hours, 310km, eight daily), Palanga (43Lt, six hours, 340km, seven daily), Šiauliai (27Lt, 4½ hours, 220km, two daily) and Trakai (3.5Lt, 45 minutes, 28km, 30 daily).

Car & Motorcycle

Numerous 24-hour petrol stations selling Western-grade fuel and offering repairs/parts are dotted at strategic points across Vilnius and the main highways. Most Western car manufacturers have representation in Vilnius.

Litinterp (www.litinterp.lt) rents chauffeured or self-drive cars and minibuses in Vilnius, Kaunas and Klaipėda from 210Lt a day. Other hire companies based in Vilnius include **Rimas** (☎ 277 6213; rimas.cars@is.lt), which has the cheapest self-drive cars to rent from about 80Lt to 100Lt a day.

Driving across Lithuania is a pleasure on Western-standard highways A1 to Klaipėda/Kaunas, A2 northwards, A3 to Minsk and A4 to Gardinas.

The speed limit in Lithuania is 50km/hr in cities, 90km/hr to 110km/hr outside the city and on highways. Headlights must be switched on at all times and winter tyres must be fitted between November 1 and March 1.

Local Transport

Microbuses zoom around most cities and offer a quicker and slightly more expensive way of getting from A to B at 1Lt to 2Lt per journey compared with buses. To take a microbus simply stand on the route you require and flag one down.

Train

The train station in Vilnius is next to the bus station. It has undergone a radical reinvention as a sleek modern transport complex and is a joy to hang around in. It's a shame then that the train service is as slow and cumbersome as ever.

Go down the funky escalators to get to the tracks where you'll find daily domestic services to Kaunas (9.80Lt, 1¼ to two hours, nine daily), Klaipėda (30Lt, five hours, three daily), Paneriai (0.90Lt, 15 minutes, 23 daily), Šiauliai (24Lt, four hours, three daily) and Trakai (2.50Lt, 40 minutes, five daily).

Macedonia

CONTENTS

Highlights	450
Itineraries	450
Climate & When to Go	451
History	451
People	453
Religion	453
Arts	453
Environment	454
Food & Drink	454
Skopje	**454**
Orientation	456
Information	456
Sights	456
Sleeping	457
Eating	458
Drinking	458
Entertainment	458
Shopping	458
Getting There & Away	459
Getting Around	459
Lake Matka	459
Southern Macedonia	**460**
Ohrid	460
Around Ohrid	463
Bitola	464
Western Macedonia	**465**
Sv Jovan Bigorski Monastery	465
Macedonia Directory	**465**
Accommodation	465
Activities	466
Books	466
Business Hours	466
Customs	466
Dangers & Annoyances	466
Disabled Travellers	466
Embassies & Consulates	466
Festivals & Events	467
Gay & Lesbian Travellers	467
Holidays	467
Internet Resources	467
Language	467
Maps	467
Media	467
Money	468
Post	468
Responsible Travel	468
Telephone & Fax	468
Visas	468
Women Travellers	468
Transport in Macedonia	**469**
Getting There & Away	469
Getting Around	470

The Former Yugoslav Republic of Macedonia (FYROM) is a real treat for travellers, especially those who like open spaces, majestic mountains, fantastic lakes and soaring waterfalls, spiced up with outdoor activities such as trekking, skiing or swimming, and stirred with a rich helping of culture along the way. There are remote Orthodox monasteries to be discovered, ancient mosques to be seen, and you can roam around rich Oriental bazaars in Skopje and Bitola. The town of Ohrid is an unforgettable discovery, with its magnificent lake and charming churches. In addition, Macedonia's up-and-coming capital Skopje is a kicking little city with a good nightlife and a buzzing youth scene – for crazy nights out if you overdose on the healthy life.

FAST FACTS

- **Area** 25,713 sq km
- **Capital** Skopje
- **Currency** Macedonian Denar (MKD); €1 = 62.58MKD; US$1=50.16MKD; UK£1 = 90.01MKD; A$1 = 36.34MKD; ¥100 = 45.92MKD; NZ$1 = 34.28MKD
- **Phrases** Zdravo (hello), prijatno (goodbye)
- **Famous for** ancient monasteries, Mother Teresa (born in Skopje)
- **Official Languages** Macedonian, Albanian
- **Population** 2 million
- **Telephone Codes** country code ☎ 389; international access code ☎ 99
- **Visas** not needed for EU passport holders; most others do require one, see p468

HIGHLIGHTS

- The smooth mirror of **Lake Ohrid** (p460), where swans glide at dusk and the small streets of the town dart between seven spectacular churches
- Urban vibe meets colourful Turkish bazaar in the up-and-coming capital **Skopje** (p454), featuring an exciting arts and music scene and a great riverside promenade
- A magnificent hike up the mountain to the mystical **Treskavec Monastery** (p464), with bare rock and views to die for
- Amidst ski-piste mountains, inhale the holiness at the **Sv Jovan Bigorski Monastery** (p465) – monks in black, fabulous nature, and the arm of St John

ITINERARIES

- **Three days** Spend a day in Skopje in the old town bazaar and visiting the enchanting Turkish baths-cum-art galleries, mosques and churches. Next day get a bus to Ohrid and spend two days simply exploring, finding your way to the churches then cooling down in the glorious lake.
- **One week** Go forth to the Sv Naum monastery near Ohrid for a day with ancient frescoes, wailing peacocks and boat rides on the lake. Catch the morning sun on your way up to Treskavec monastery, where you will be stunned by the architecture, frescoes and the views. To the west, the Sv Jovan Bigorski monastery offers peace plus nearby hiking and skiing.

CLIMATE & WHEN TO GO

Macedonia's summers are hot and dry. Snow falls on all the mountainous areas from November to April, but in the higher mountains the snow can stay until the end of May, which makes it great for skiing. The temperatures vary widely: summer temperatures can reach 40°C, while in winter it can drop as low as -30°C. The average annual temperatures are above 10°C almost everywhere.

The best time to enjoy Macedonia is between May and September, and the peak tourist season is from mid-July to mid-August, which is also when Macedonians take their holidays.

HISTORY

Historical Macedonia (from whence Alexander the Great set out to conquer the ancient world in the 4th century BC) is mostly contained in present-day Greece, a point Greeks are always quick to make when discussing contemporary Macedonia's use of the name. Romans subjugated the Greeks of ancient Macedonia and the area to the north during the mid-2nd century BC. When the empire was divided in the 4th century AD, this region came under the Eastern Roman Empire ruled from Constantinople. Slavs settled in the area in the 7th century AD.

In the 9th century the region was conquered by Car Simeon (r 893–927) and later, under Car Samoil (r 980–1014), Macedonia was the centre of a powerful Bulgarian state. Samoil's defeat by Byzantium in 1014 ushered in a long period when Macedonia passed back and forth between Byzantium, Bulgaria and Serbia. After the crushing defeat of Serbia by the Ottomans in 1389, the Balkans and therefore Macedonia became a part of the Ottoman Empire.

In 1878 Russia defeated Turkey, and Macedonia was ceded to Bulgaria by the Treaty of San Stefano. The western powers, fearing the creation of a powerful Russian satellite in the heart of the Balkans, forced Bulgaria to return Macedonia to Ottoman rule.

In 1893 Macedonian nationalists formed the Internal Macedonian Revolutionary Organization (IMRO) to fight for independence from Turkey, culminating in the

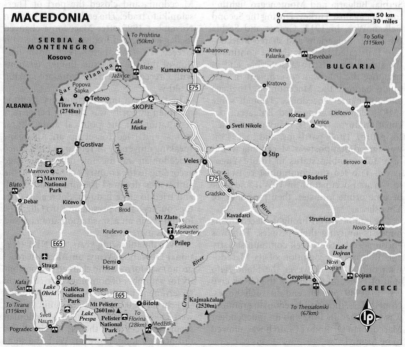

MACEDONIA

Ilinden uprising of August 1903, which was brutally suppressed in October of the same year. Although the nationalist leader Goce Delčev died before the revolt, he has become the symbol of Macedonian nationalism.

The First Balkan War of 1912 saw Greece, Serbia, Bulgaria and Montenegro fighting together against Turkey. During the Second Balkan War, in 1913, Greece and Serbia ousted the Bulgarians and shared Macedonia. Frustrated by this, IMRO continued the struggle against royalist Serbia, and in response the interwar government in Belgrade banned the Macedonian language and the name Macedonia. Though some IMRO elements supported Bulgarian occupation during WWII, many more joined Josip Broz Tito's partisans, and in 1943 it was agreed that postwar Macedonia would have full republic status in future Yugoslavia. Tito led the communist resistance to German occupation in WWII and later became prime minister, then president, of Yugoslavia.

The end of WWII brought Macedonians hopes of unifying their peoples. This was encouraged by the Greek communist party and Bulgaria's recognition of its Macedonian minorities. However the Stalin–Tito split of 1948 and the end of the Greek civil war in 1949 put an end to such hopes. Nonetheless, the first Macedonian grammar was published in 1952 and an independent Macedonian Orthodox Church was allowed to be formed.

Over the subsequent 40 years Yugoslavia as a state prospered in comparison with the other socialist Eastern European states. Citizens were relatively free to move in and out of Yugoslavia, and the country was quite open as a tourist destination.

On 8 September 1991 Macedonians held a referendum on independence. Seventy-four percent voted in favour and in January 1992 the country declared its full independence from the former Yugoslavia. Belgrade cooperated by ordering all federal troops to withdraw and, because the split was peaceful, road and rail links were never broken.

Greece delayed diplomatic recognition of Macedonia by demanding that the country find another name, worried that the term Macedonia implied territorial claims on northern Greece. At the insistence of Greece, Macedonia was forced to use the 'temporary' title FYROM (the Former Yugoslav Republic of Macedonia) in order to be admitted to the UN in April 1993. When the USA (following six EU countries) recognised FYROM in February 1994, Greece declared an economic embargo against Macedonia and closed the port of Thessaloniki to trade. The embargo was lifted in November 1995 after Macedonia changed its flag and agreed to discuss its name with Greece. To date, there's been no resolution of this thorny issue, though relations with Greece on the trade front are looking healthy.

In the meantime, the country's ethnic Albanian minority was seeking better representation on the political and cultural fronts, and tried to set up an Albanian-speaking university in Tetovo in 1995. Since Macedonian was the only official language according to the country's constitution, the authorities declared the university illegal and tried to close it down. Soon after that, the country's then president, Kiro Gligorov, lost an eye in an assassination attempt, and tensions increased.

Over the following years, the NLA (National Liberation Army; an Albanian rebel group) was formed and claimed responsibility for a number of bombings carried out on government institutions. This culminated in February 2001 in armed conflict in the west of the country, between Macedonian security forces and the NLA. Hostilities did not last long, however. With the signing of the Ohrid Framework Agreement in August 2001, the Macedonian government agreed to greater political participation for the Albanian minority, official recognition of the Albanian language, as well as an increase in the number of ethnic Albanian police officers throughout the country (although there is still a way to go before the two groups are fully reconciled).

After the unfortunate death of Macedonian president Boris Trajkovski in a plane accident in Bosnia and Hercegovina in February 2004, the presidency was taken by former prime minister, Branko Crvenkovski, in elections in April the same year.

PEOPLE

According to the 2002 census the republic's 2,0022,547 population is divided as follows: Macedonians of Slav ethnicity (66.6%); Albanians (25%); Turks (4%); Roma (2.7%); Serbs (1.8%); and Vlachs (0.5%). The Macedonians are a hospitable people who are extremely proud of their country. If you can help it, don't discuss politics, and if you can't help it, discuss with caution, as a variety of subjects are sensitive.

Although in the majority of larger towns and cities dress is tight, colourful and revealing amongst women and men, do dress modestly when visiting a church, monastery or mosque or you may not be allowed in. Take care to dress with respect when walking around predominantly Muslim areas, too, no matter how hot it may be!

RELIGION

Most Macedonians belong to the Macedonian Orthodox Church, and most Albanians to Islam. Indeed, you will see plenty of churches and mosques throughout the country. Since 1991 there has been a resurgence of religion within the country, and of the Orthodox Church in particular, with monasteries coming to life once again.

ARTS
Cinema

The most significant Macedonian film to come out in the last decade is *Before the Rain* (1995) directed by Milčo Mančevski. Visually stunning, with a great cast and a haunting soundtrack, the film is a manifold take on the tensions between Macedonians and ethnic Albanians. Filmed partly in Lon-

don and partly in Macedonia, you will be able to spot the Sv Jovan (St John) at Kaneo church in Ohrid, and the Treskavec monastery. Mančevski also released *Dust* in 2001, an interesting account of 20th century Ottoman Macedonia.

Dance

The most famous Macedonian folk dance is probably *Teškoto oro* (the Difficult dance). Music for this beautiful male dance is provided by the *tapan* and *zurla*. Performed in traditional Macedonian costume, it is often included in festivals or concerts.

Other dances include *Komitsko oro,* symbolising the struggle of Macedonian freedom fighters against the Turks, and *Tresenica,* a women's dance from the Mavrovo region.

The *oro* is similar to the *kolo,* a circle dance, danced throughout the Balkans.

Music

The oldest form of Macedonian folk music involves the *gajda* (bagpipes). This instrument is played solo or is accompanied by the *tapan* (two-sided drum), each side of which is played with a different stick to obtain a different tone. These are often augmented by *kaval* (flute) and/or *tambura* (small lute with two pairs of strings). Macedonia has also inherited (from a long period of Turkish influence) the *zurla* (double-reed horn), also accompanied by the *tapan,* and the *Čalgija* music form, involving clarinet, violin, *darabuk* (hour-glass shaped drum) and *doumbuš* (banjo-like instrument).

Bands playing these instruments may be heard and enjoyed at festivals such as the Balkan Festival of Folk Dances & Songs in Ohrid in mid-July (p462) or the Ilinden festival in Bitola in early August. Nearly all Macedonian traditional music is accompanied by dancing.

Macedonia also has some quality modern music, such as the internationally-known DJ Kiril Džajkovski and bands like Anastasia and Mizar, all of whom combine traditional music with electronic sounds. Džajkovski and Anastasia have both composed brilliant soundtracks for the films of Milčo Mančevski (see Cinema, p453). You can hear some of their music at Skopje's summer outdoor clubs (see p458).

Another musical treat in Macedonia are Roma bands, popular at any celebration, who often play traditional Roma songs made famous by the Bosnian band leader Goran Bregović. One of the most popular Roma singers, the velvety-voiced Esma Redžepova, is a Macedonian.

ENVIRONMENT
The Land
Much of Macedonia's 25,713 sq km consists of a plateau between 600m and 900m above sea-level. The Vardar River crosses the middle of the country, passing Skopje on its way to the Aegean Sea near Thessaloniki. Ohrid and Prespa lakes in the southwest drain into the Adriatic Sea via Albania. At a depth of 294m, Lake Ohrid is the deepest lake on the Balkan Peninsula. In the northwest, the Šar Planina marks the border with Kosovo. Titov Vrv (2748m) is the country's highest peak.

Wildlife
Macedonia belongs to the eastern Mediterranean and Euro-Siberian vegetation region and is home to a large number of plant species in a relatively small geographical area. The high mountains are dominated by pines, while on the lower mountains beech and oak dominate. On the mountain slopes of the Šar Planina and on Mt Bistra the poppy grows in abundance, the juice of which is considered the best-quality opium juice in the world.

Macedonia is a boundary area between two different zoological zones – the high mountain region and the low Mediterranean valley region. The fauna of the forests is abundant and includes bears, wild boar, wolves, foxes, squirrels, chamois and deer. The lynx is found, although very rarely, in the mountains of western Macedonia, particularly on Šar Planina, while deer inhabit the region of Demir Kapija. Forest birds include the blackcap, the grouse, the black grouse, the imperial eagle and the forest owl.

The Yugoslav shepherd dog, šarplaninec, from the Šar Planina, is known worldwide. It stands some 60cm tall and is a brave, fierce fighter in guarding and defending flocks from bears or wolf packs.

Lakes Ohrid, Prespa and Dojran are separate fauna zones, a result of territorial and temporal isolation. Lake Ohrid's fauna is a relic of an earlier era. The lake is known for letnica trout, lake whitefish, gudgeon and roach, as well as certain species of snails

of a genus older than 30 million years. It is also home to the mysterious European eel, which comes to Lake Ohrid from the distant Sargasso Sea to live for up to 10 years. It makes the trip back to the Sargasso Sea to breed, dies and its offspring start the cycle anew.

National Parks
Macedonia's three national parks are Pelister (near Bitola), Galičica (between Lakes Ohrid and Prespa) and Mavrovo (between Ohrid and Tetovo). The road towards Lake Prespa offers fantastic views of Lake Ohrid on one side and Prespa on the other.

FOOD & DRINK
Turkish-style grilled mincemeat is available almost everywhere and there are self-service cafeterias in most towns for the less adventurous. Balkan *burek* (cheese, spinach, potato or meat in filo pastry) and yogurt make for a cheap and delicious breakfast. Try it in a *burekdžinica* (*burek* shop). Taste the Macedonian *tavče gravče* (beans cooked in a skillet). You may see Ohrid Lake trout on the menu, but be aware that it's on the verge of extinction (see p468).

Other dishes to try are *teleška čorba* (veal soup), *riblja čorba* (fish soup), *kebapci* (kebabs), *mešana salata* (mixed salad) and the *šopska salata* (mixed salad with grated white cheese).

Skopsko Pivo is the local beer. It's strong and quite cheap. DAB is a German brew now made locally under licence. Big-brand European beers are also available. There are a good number of commercially produced wines of average to better quality and the national firewater is *rakija,* a strong distilled spirit made from grapes. *Mastika,* an ouzo-like spirit, is also popular.

SKOPJE СКОПЈЕ

☎ 02 / pop 600,000

The up-and-coming city of Skopje is a buzzing capital with plenty of bars, restaurants, and outdoor clubs with a fun, young crowd. During the day you can climb up to Tvrdina Kale (the city fort) overlooking the town from a hilltop, wander around the old bazaar and eat delicious *kebapci* (barbecued meat rolls). Check out the small shops full of animal skins, copper coffee pots and jewellery, and step into the beautiful old Turkish baths, now the city's art galleries, where the domed ceilings let in natural light through carved star-shaped holes that make the ceiling look like the night sky. Skopje has a number of beautiful old mosques and churches you can spend a quiet moment in.

The city is divided into the old and new towns by the Vardar river and connected by the beautiful 15th-century Kamen Most (Stone Bridge). A leafy riverside promenade has been built in the last year and you can take an afternoon stroll in Skopje's lovely city park (which, conveniently, is where outdoor summer nightclubs are).

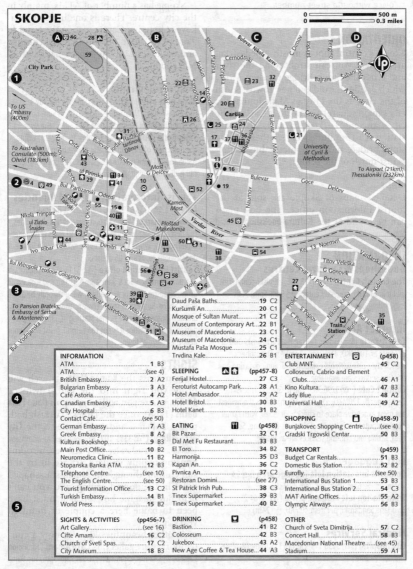

SKOPJE

Daud Paša Baths	19 C2
Kuršumli An	20 C1
Mosque of Sultan Murat	21 C2
Museum of Contemporary Art	22 B1
Museum of Macedonia	23 C1
Museum of Macedonia	24 C1
Mustafa Paša Mosque	25 C1
Trvdina Kale	26 B1

INFORMATION
ATM	1 B3
ATM	(see 4)
British Embassy	2 A2
Bulgarian Embassy	3 A3
Café Astoria	4 A2
Canadian Embassy	5 A3
City Hospital	6 B3
Contact Café	(see 50)
German Embassy	7 A3
Greek Embassy	8 A2
Kultura Bookshop	9 B3
Main Post Office	10 B2
Neuromedica Clinic	11 B2
Stopanska Banka ATM	12 B3
Telephone Centre	(see 10)
The English Centre	(see 50)
Tourist Information Office	13 C2
Turkish Embassy	14 B1
World Press	15 B2

SIGHTS & ACTIVITIES (pp456–7)
Art Gallery	(see 16)
Čifte Amam	16 C2
Church of Sveti Spas	17 C2
City Museum	18 B3

SLEEPING (pp457–8)
Ferijal Hostel	27 C3
Feroturist Autocamp Park	28 A1
Hotel Ambasador	29 A2
Hotel Bristol	30 B3
Hotel Kanet	31 B2

EATING (p458)
Bit Pazar	32 C1
Dal Met Fu Restaurant	33 B3
El Toro	34 B2
Harmonija	35 D3
Kapan An	36 C2
Pivnica An	37 C2
Restoran Domini	(see 27)
St Patrick Irish Pub	38 B3
Tinex Supermarket	39 B3
Tinex Supermarket	40 B2

DRINKING (p458)
Bastion	41 B2
Colosseum	42 B3
Jukebox	43 A2
New Age Coffee & Tea House	44 A3

ENTERTAINMENT (p458)
Club MNT	45 C2
Colloseum, Cabrio and Element Clubs	46 A1
Kino Kultura	47 B3
Lady Blue	48 A2
Universal Hall	49 A2

SHOPPING (pp458–9)
Bunjakovec Shopping Centre	(see 4)
Gradski Trgovski Centar	50 B3

TRANSPORT (p459)
Budget Car Rentals	51 B3
Domestic Bus Station	52 B2
Eurofly	(see 50)
International Bus Station 1	53 B3
International Bus Station 2	54 C3
MAT Airline Offices	55 A2
Olympic Airways	56 B3

OTHER
Church of Sveta Dimitrija	57 C2
Concert Hall	58 B3
Macedonian National Theatre	(see 45)
Stadium	59 A1

STREET ADDRESSES

At the end of a number of addresses in this chapter, you'll notice the letters 'bb' instead of a street number. This shorthand, which stands for *bez broja* (without a number) is used by businesses or other nonresidential institutions, indicating that it's an official place without a street number.

ORIENTATION

Skopje's central zone is mostly a pedestrian area where you can stroll along the river and cross the Stone Bridge (Kamen Most) which divides the old and new towns. South of the river is the Ploštad Makedonija (the city's main square) and north is Čaršija (the city's ancient Turkish bazaar). The train station is a 15-minute walk southeast of the stone bridge, and the domestic bus station is just north of the bridge.

Maps

Detailed maps of Skopje are sold at the tourist information office. The best maps can be found at the **Kultura bookshop** (Ploštad Makedonija bb).

INFORMATION
Bookshops & Cultural Centres

The English Centre (☎ 3118 256; angliski-centar@mt .net.mk; Gradski Trgovski Centar; ⏲ 9am-5pm) Sells English-language books.

Internet Access

Café Astoria (Bunjakovec Centar; Bul Partizanski Odredi 27A; per hr 100MKD; ⏲ 9am-11pm) An atmospheric French style café with old computers. Scanning, faxing and printing services are available.

Contact Café (☎ 3296 365; 2nd fl, Gradski Trgovski Centar; per hr 120MKD; ⏲ 9am-10pm) This is the newest but most expensive place to check your email, with rather slow computers. It is however a smoke-free zone. Scanning, faxing and printing services are available.

Left Luggage

Domestic bus station left-luggage area (Kej 13 Noemvri; ⏲ 6am-9pm; per item 40MKD)
Train station left luggage office (☎ 3164 255; Blvd Jane Sandanski; per item 40MKD. ⏲ 24hr)

Medical Services

City hospital (☎ 3130 111; cnr ul 11 Oktomvri & Moše Pijade; ⏲ 24hr)

Neuromedica private clinic (☎ 3222 170; ul Partizanski 3-1, 4th fl; ⏲ 24hr)

Money

There are many private exchange offices scattered throughout the old and new towns where you can change your cash at a good rate.

Skopje has a number of ATMs, mainly in the city centre. There is one in the Bunjakovec Shopping Centre, two in the Gradski Trgovski Centar off Ploštad Makedonija, and another at the Stopanska Banka on ul Makedonija.

Post & Telephone

Main post office (☎ 3141 141; ul Orce Nikolov 1; ⏲ 7am-7.30pm Mon-Sat, 7.30am-2.30pm Sun) Located 75m northwest of Ploštad Makedonija, along the river.
Telephone centre (ul Orce Nikolov 1; ⏲ 24hr) Inside the main post office. You can also phone from kiosks (newsagents) with private telephones. The price of your call is displayed digitally as you speak.

Tourist Information & Travel Agencies

Eurofly (☎ 3136 619; fax 3136 320; 1st fl, Gradski Trgovski Centar) Of Skopje's abundance of travel agencies, the best and most practical for airline tickets is this modern travel agency, where ticket prices are listed boldly by the door in both euros and US dollars.
Tourist information office (☎ 3116 854; Kruševska; ⏲ 9am-7pm Mon-Fri & 9am-4pm Sat) This sad looking office, opposite the City Art Gallery, will unhappily be at your service. Some staff speak English. Theoretically it can arrange rooms in private homes starting at 1150MKD per person, but in practice it is not too helpful. Insist on a room near the centre of town.

SIGHTS

As you cross the **Kamen Most**, its arch will bring you right into the Old Town, or **Čaršija**, where you will come upon **Daud Paša Baths** (1466), once the largest Turkish bath in the Balkans, and now home to the **City Art Gallery** (☎ 3133 102; Kruševska 1A; admission 100MKD; ⏲ 9am-3pm Tue-Sun). The seven rooms housing mainly modern art are lit by the sun coming through the small star-shaped holes in the domed ceiling, and you can't help but imagine how great it must have been to bathe here a couple of hundred years ago.

Another beautiful old bath, now a contemporary art gallery, is **Čifte Amam** (admission 50MKD; ⏲ 9am-4.45pm Mon-Fri, Sat 9am-3pm, Sun 9am-

SKOPJE IN TWO DAYS

Catch the morning sun crossing the 15th-century **Kamen Most** (p456) to the heart of Skopje's old town. Step into the old Turkish baths, **Daud Paša Baths** and **Čifte Amam** (p456), now art galleries, and admire the domed ceilings curving above you. Wander around the Old Town, **Čaršija**, (p456) and lunch al fresco. Spend the afternoon visiting the **Church of Sveti Spas** (p457) and **Skopje's mosques** (p457). Eat a healthy dinner in **Harmonija** (p458), or tuck into a meaty dish at **Pivnica An** (p458).

On day two head for **Lake Matka** (p459) outside Skopje for hiking, climbing, or just plain relaxing by the smooth mirror of the lake.

1pm), north of Daud Paša Baths. The second largest bath in Skopje, this building gives you a taste of the original baths with one room left unplastered, its walls showing exposed brickwork, stone arches and the clay waterpipes that used to heat the rooms.

Step out and wander around Čaršija's small shops and tea houses, and go north along Samoilova for the magnificent **Church of Sveti Spas** (admission to church & tomb 100MKD; 8am-3pm Tue-Sun). The church was built below ground, since during Ottoman times it was illegal for a church to be taller than a mosque. It boasts an iconostasis 10m wide and 6m high, beautifully carved in the early 19th century by the master-craftsmen Makarije Frčkovski and the Filipovski brothers. The church courtyard leads to a room with the **Tomb and Museum of Goce Delčev**, leader of IMRO and the national hero, killed by the Turks in 1903. The latter is a somewhat less splendid experience than the church, however the ticket gives you access to both.

The 1492 **Mustafa Paša Mosque** (Samoilova bb), beyond the church, has an earthquake-cracked dome and a shady garden with a fountain. Climb up to the **Tvrdina Kale** ruins (city fort) across the street for panoramic views of Skopje from the 11th century Cyclopean wall. If you want more art, the **Museum of Contemporary Art** (3117 735; Samoilova bb; admission 100MKD; 9am-3pm Tue-Sun) is higher up the hill.

Back in Čaršija, beyond the mosque, is the white **Museum of Macedonia** (3116 044; Čurčiska

86; admission 100MKD; 9am-3pm Tue-Sun), which traces the region's civilisations over the centuries, but unfortunately only in Macedonian. Part of the museum is in **Kuršumli An** (1550), an impressive old caravanserai or inn, where traders would stop off and rest during Ottoman times. It was later used as a prison. The building now also houses a small art gallery in one of the cells.

On the other side of the city, in the new town, the sights are less obvious, but pay attention to the bizarre architecture of the **main post office building** (ul Orce Nikolov 1; 7am-7.30pm Mon-Sat, 7.30am-2.30pm Sun) by Kamen Most: a futuristic, insect-like structure, apparently an abstract take on church architecture. Further down check out the **City Museum** (3114 742; Mito Hadživasilev bb; admission free; 9am-3pm Tue-Sun), housed inside the old train station. Its **clock** is frozen at 5.17 on the morning of the great, tragic Skopje earthquake of 27 July 1963, which killed 1066 people and almost demolished the entire city. Walk around to the back of the old station and take a break at one of the small cafés that sit between old train carriages. On the wall behind them, a large socialist mural reads a message of moral support from Yugoslavia's President Tito to the shattered Skopjans after the earthquake.

SLEEPING

Prices are high in Skopje, so book early if you want one of the bargains.

Budget

Feroturist Autocamp Park (3228 246; fax 3162 677; camp site & 4 people 500MKD; Apr–mid-Oct) An urban camping option and just a 15-minute walk upstream from Kamen Most along the river's south bank. Bring plenty of mosquito repellent!

HI Ferijal Hostel (3114 849; fax 165 029; ul Prolet 25; members s/d incl breakfast 935/1280MKD; nonmembers s/d incl breakfast 1280/1590MKD; 24hr Apr–mid-Oct;) The best budget beds in town, near the train station and the centre, with clean, basic, individual rooms, air-conditioning and a cheerful youth hostel atmosphere.

Mid-Range & Top End

Pansion Brateks (3176 606, 070 243 232; ul Aco Karamanov 3; s/d 1920/3200MKD) This place feels a bit more up market with tidy, airy rooms, and it's often full, despite being a 20-minute walk from the centre. It's set in a classy neighbourhood at the foot of Mt Vodno.

Hotel Bristol (☎ 3237 502, fax 3166 556; ul Makedonija 15; s/d 2390/3680MKD) With mahogany-coloured wooden beds and white sheets, this place has an old-fashioned and elegant atmosphere, and a large airy restaurant downstairs.

Hotel Kanet (☎ 3238 353; Jordan Hadžikonstantinov Džinot 20; s/d 2500/3700MKD) Sitting right on the edge of the city park, this is a small wooden hotel, with comfortable rooms and intricate showers, TVs and telephones, and a buffet breakfast. You can hear frogs croaking in harmony in the park.

Hotel Ambasador (☎ 3215 510, fax 3121 383; ul Pirinska 36; s/d 2800/4340MKD) Pleasant, simple rooms with breakfast. On the top of the building, a 'Statue of Liberty' wields its torch. Located next to the Russian Embassy.

EATING

Restoran Domini (☎ 3115 519; ul Prolet 5; snacks 120MKD, mains 180MKD; ☼ 7.30am-11.30pm) Smart and well priced. Located in the basement of the Ferijal Hostel, this is an excellent budget choice.

Kapan An (Čaršija, behind Čifte Amam; meals 200MKD) Delicious *kebapci* with mouth-watering warm bread can be enjoyed al fresco in any of the restaurants in this shady cobblestone courtyard.

St Patrick Irish Pub (☎ 3220 431; Kej 13 Noemvri; mains 280MKD; ☼ 7.30am-midnight) is the place favoured by the ex-pat community, and resembles Irish pubs around the world. Sip your Guinness while you munch on Irish breakfasts from 7.30am onwards and meals such as beef in Guinness or Gaelic steak.

Dal Met Fu Restaurant (☎ 3112 482; Ploštad Makedonija; mains 280MKD; ☼ 7.30am-midnight) A popular glass-fronted restaurant with tables outside facing the main square, it serves good thin-base pizza and almost al-dente pasta.

Pivnica An (☎ 3212 111; Čaršija; mains 270-300MKD; 9am-midnight) Excellent traditional eating plus beer located in the old town, serving a wide range of Macedonian dishes and a relaxing atmosphere.

Harmonija (☎ 246 0985; Skopjanka Shopping Centre 27, Bulevar Jane Sandanski; mains 250MKD; ☼ 9am-11pm, closed Sunday) Located 500m southwest of the railway station, with a choice of fantastic vegetarian and macrobiotic meals served in a cosy atmosphere.

El Toro (☎ 322 1414; ul Pirinska 52; mains 100-300MKD; ☼ 9am-midnight) This Spanish tapas bar plays the dolorous sounds of the tango from its speakers and serves tapas and paella for two for 300MKD.

There are a number of self-catering options available:

Bit Pazar (btwn C Dimov & Bulevar K Misirkov; ☼ 7am-4pm) This open market, next to the Čaršija, is the best place for fruit, veg, spices, herbs and nuts, and has plenty of market hubbub – for those who want to cook their own grub.

Tinex Supermarket (ul Dame Gruev; also ul Makedonija 3; ☼ 8am-8pm) Both branches of this supermarket chain are well stocked.

DRINKING

There are many bars to choose from in Skopje, but these are a few favourites.

Bastion (☎ 322 3636; ul Pirinska 43; ☼ 9am-1am) A hip cocktail-and-beer crowd grooves to funky music in this trendy bar.

Jukebox (Orče Nikolov 99; ☼ 9am-1am) A buzzing place, it has jazz on Thursdays.

New Age Coffee and Tea House (☎ 3117 559; Kosta Šahov 9; ☼ 9am-midnight) Plush floor cushions indoors, chaise longues and peacocks in the garden, teas, beers or cocktails, the choice is yours in this bohemian hangout.

ENTERTAINMENT

Universal Hall (☎ 3224 158; Partizanski Odredi bb) Classical and other music performances, as well as Skopje's jazz festival, take place here in October every year.

Colloseum, **Cabrio** or **Element** (City Park; www .element.com.mk) in the city park are *the* places for summer outdoor clubbers and international DJs.

Club MNT (☎ 3220 767; Kej Dimitar Vlahov) Downstairs, below the Macedonian National Theatre, the crowd in this place gets grooving to disco music after 10pm.

Lady Blue (cnr Ivo Ribar Lola & Sveti Kliment Ohridski; ☼ 9pm-3am) Live jazz, blues and rock music spot with a varied crowd and a good atmosphere.

Kino Kultura (ul Makedonija; tickets 60-120MKD) Be entertained by some recent English-language movies. Tickets prices vary depending on the viewing time.

SHOPPING

The Čaršija is teaming with little shops that sell souvenirs such as copper coffee pots, rugs, or animal skins. The two shopping centres, **Gradski Trgovski Centar** (⏰ 9am-7pm) and **Bunjakovec Centar** (Bulevar Partizanski; ⏰ 9am-7pm), stock anything your heart may desire: from clothes, to music, to books. Some shops within the centres close for lunch, anywhere between 1pm and 3pm. You can spot a gem at the bric-a-brac market outside the Gradski Trgovski Centar where some old Yugoslav memorabilia is displayed.

GETTING THERE & AWAY
Air
A host of airlines serve Skopje's **Petrovac Airport** (☎ 02-3235 156), 21km east of the city. Some of them are: JAT Airlines (Serbia and Montenegro), Macedonian Airlines (MAT), Adria Airways, Croatia Airlines, Olympic Airways, Malév Hungarian Airlines, and Turkish Airlines. Swiss and Austrian Airlines offer flights from Skopje to a number of European destinations (for details of these, see p469).

It may be cheaper to fly into Thessaloniki in northern Greece; try to coordinate the flight times with the two daily trains that connect Thessaloniki with Skopje. Another good option is contacting the Skopje taxi driver **Sašo Trajkovski** (☎ 070-279 449; saso_taxi@yahoo.com) to pick you up in Thessaloniki and bring you to Skopje (see p469).

Bus
The slightly chaotic domestic **bus station** (☎ 3236 254) is on the northern side of the river close to the walls of the Tvrdina Kale. Buses to all domestic destinations as well as Kosovo depart from here.

There are two bus routes from Skopje to Lake Ohrid: the 167km route through Tetovo (300MKD, three hours) is much faster and more direct than the 261km route that goes via Veles and Bitola (four hours). Book a seat to Ohrid the day before if you're travelling in high season (May to August).

Skopje has two **international bus stations** (☎ 3166 254): one is next to the City Museum on Jasmin Mito Hadzivasilev, the other by the river on Kej 13 Noemvri. There doesn't appear to be any logic to which buses depart from which station.

Train
Frequent trains shoot out of Skopje's *Blade Runner*–style station. For details on international trains, see p470. Domestic rail des-

tinations include Bitola and Kičevo (in the west of the country), Veles (south of Skopje), Tabanovce (on the border with Serbia and Montenegro) and Gevgelija (on the Greek border north of Thessaloniki).

You will have to understand the Cyrillic alphabet to make any sense of timetables. The staff at the Information desk will be of limited use so come prepared with your phrasebook.

GETTING AROUND
To/From the Airport
There is no public transport to and from the airport. If you are flying to Skopje, try to arrange pick up through your hotel or hostel before you arrive, as you will otherwise be at the mercy of the airport taxi drivers who can charge anything between 1290MKD to 2200MKD. Getting to the airport from Skopje is a much more pleasant affair and will cost you around 660MKD. Do not get into taxis that don't have the official 'taxi' sign.

Bus
Inner-suburban city buses in Skopje cost 15MKD to 30MKD per trip, depending on what kind of bus it is and whether you buy your ticket on board or in advance; it is normally cheaper to buy your ticket in advance.

Car
Skopje is awash with car rental agencies, from the large ones (Hertz and Avis) to the smaller local companies. Rental prices generally start at around 2000MKD per day. Try **Budget Car Rental** (☎ 3290 222; Mito Hadzivasilev Jasmin bb; ⏰ 9am-5pm). The tourist office has a complete listing of car agencies in town.

Taxi
Skopje's **taxi system** (☎ 9177) is excellent, once you get beyond the taxis at the airport. All taxis have meters and they always turn them on without prompting. The first few kilometres are a flat 50MKD, and then it's 15MKD per kilometre.

LAKE MATKA ЕЗЕРО МАТКА
Only half an hour's drive away from busy Skopje, Lake Matka is a place of calm cool nature, where the steep canyon reflects in the green mirror of the lake and boats glide on its smooth surface. There is plenty to do for those who want action, with opportunities

for hiking and rock climbing, or you can go for a €10 boat ride and take a peek at the caves and their dark life.

The lake is artificial, created by the damming of the River Treška, and there are a number of restaurants along the dam, serving excellent fish and traditional Macedonian dishes. There are two interesting churches: the church of Sv Nikola, located just after the dam, across the bridge, and the church of Sv Andrej, further on. Next door is the mountaineering hut **Matka** (☎ 3052 655; per bed 500MKD) where you can sleep and hire guides and basic rock climbing gear.

To get to Lake Matka take bus No 60 (40 minutes, 50MKD), which leaves on the hour from Skopje's Bulevar Partizanski.

SOUTHERN MACEDONIA

OHRID ОХРИД

☎ 046 / pop 50,000

Ohrid is the most magnificent town in Macedonia, and the most popular town with visitors. Resting on the banks of the still waters of Lake Ohrid, the town has stunning Byzantine churches, small cobbled streets, art galleries, good budget accommodation and picturesque pebbly beaches to relax on. During the summer the town is packed with people and there are numerous festivals to entertain you. For quieter moments, the Galičica National Park is nearby, on the way to the marvellous monastery of

OHRID

0 ——— 500 m
0 ——— 0.3 miles

INFORMATION		
Asteroida Internet Cafe	1	C3
Cybercity	2	C3
Generalturist	3	C3
Hem Boi	4	C3
Ohridska Banka	5	C3
Post Office	6	C3
Telephone Office	7	C3
SIGHTS & ACTIVITIES	(pp461-2)	
Atanas Talevski Photographic		
Exhibition	8	B4
Barok	9	C4
Basilica Ruins	10	A3
Church of Sveta Sofija	11	B4
Church of Sveti Kliment	12	B3
Citadel	13	A3
Dom na Kultura	14	C4

Icon Gallery	(see 12)	
National Museum	15	B4
Plane Tree	16	C3
Popular Market	17	C2
Sv Jovan at Kaneo	18	A4
Sveta Bogorodica		
Bolnička Church	19	B4
Sveti Klement i Panteljmon		
Church	20	A4
Sveti Nikola Bolnički Church	21	C4
Upper Gate	22	B3
SLEEPING	(p462)	
Apartments Čekredi	23	D4
Hotel Riviera	24	D4
Lucija's	25	B4
Mimi Apartments	26	D4
Stefan Kanevče	27	A4

EATING	(pp462-3)	
Pizzeria Leonardo	28	B4
Restaurant Antiko	29	B4
Restaurant Dalga	30	B4
Restoran Neim	31	C3
Žito Leb	32	B4
DRINKING	(pp462-3)	
Jazz In	33	B4
TRANSPORT	(p463)	
Bus Station	34	C3
Queen-Rent-A-Car	35	D4
OTHER		
Roman Amphitheatre	36	B3
Tinex Supermarket	37	C3

Sveti Naum 20km south, towards the Albanian border.

Lake Ohrid, a natural tectonic lake shared with Albania, is one of the oldest in the world and at 294m is the deepest in the Balkans, and might remind you of the sea with its vastness and sometimes stormy behaviour.

Under Byzantium, Ohrid became the episcopal centre of Macedonia. The first Slavic university was founded here in 893 by Bishop (Saint) Kliment of Ohrid, a disciple of the inventors of the Cyrillic script, St Cyril and St Methodius. The revival of the archbishopric of Ohrid in 1958 and its independence from the Serbian Orthodox Church in 1967 were important steps on the road to modern nationhood.

Orientation

The Old Town of Ohrid is easy to get around on foot. The lake is to the south, and the picturesque Old Town rises from Sveti Kliment Ohridski street, the main pedestrian mall.

Information

INTERNET ACCESS

Asteroida (ul Dimitar Vlahov bb; per hr 60MKD) Internet access.

Cybercity (☎ 231 620; www.cybercity.com.mk; 3rd fl, ul Sveti Kliment Ohridski) Cheap overseas calls at 15MKD per minute can be made from here; also offers Internet access for 60MKD per hour.

LAUNDRY

Hem Boi (ul Goce Delčev 21) There are no self-service laundrettes in Ohrid, but you can dry clean your grubby gear here. Each item will cost around 100MKD.

MONEY

Ohridska Banka (ul Sveti Kliment Ohridski) Has an ATM, changes money and offers Visa advances, minus the commission.

POST & TELEPHONE

Post office (Bulevar Makedonski Prosvetiteli). You can also change money here.

Telephone centre (Bulevar Makedonski Prosvetiteli; ☼ 7am-8pm Mon-Sat, 9am-noon & 6-8pm Sun) Round the corner from the post office.

TOURIST INFORMATION & TRAVEL AGENCIES

There's no official tourist office, but travel agencies provide information and have assorted guided tours.

Generalturist (☎ 261 071, fax 260 415; ul Partizanska 6) The best travel agent in town.

Jana Poposka (☎ 263 875) To hire a personal guide try the voluble Jana who speaks good English and knows everything there is to know about Ohrid. She can usually be found at the church of Sveti Kliment.

Sights

Most of Ohrid's churches charge an entry fee of around 100MKD and if not, it is customary to leave some money at the icons. Most of this money goes towards preserving these historical sites.

Start your walk from the lower gate of the town wall and the two small 14th-century **churches**, of **Sveta Bogorodica Bolnička** and **Sveti Nikola Bolnički**. These two gems were originally hospital churches and boast delicate frescoes, and a sweet old granny called Slavica who'll show you around. A great example of 19th-century Macedonian architecture is the 1827 **National Museum** (☎ 267 173; Car Samoil 62; adult/student 100/50MKD; ☼ 10am-3pm Tue-Sun) on Car Samoil street. The museum collection is divided into the Robev Residence, which houses an archaeological display, and the Urania Residence with an ethnographic display. Both rooms make for an interesting hour of exploring Macedonia's history.

Further up Car Samoil is the grandiose 11th-century **Church of Sveta Sofija**, originally built as a cathedral. The frescoes are extremely well preserved thanks to having been whitewashed during the church's days as a mosque. An English-speaking guide is usually on hand.

Follow the signs for **Sv Jovan at Kaneo** through the winding streets and this amazing little 13th-century church will appear before you on the cliffs above the lake. As well as being one of the most popular churches in Ohrid, its stunning location has made it into the movies (see p453)!

Go up through the park towards the newly built **Sveti Klement i Pantelejmon**, standing next to the remains of Ohrid's oldest church of the same name. The foundations of the 5th-century basilica with their intricate mosaics are on display in front of the new church.

Continue towards the **Upper Gate** (Gorna Porta) to the gorgeous 13th-century **Church of Sveti Kliment** (admission 100MKD; ☼ 9am-5pm), patterned inside with vividly restored frescoes of biblical scenes. Opposite this church is an **icon gallery** (☼ 9am-3pm). The restored walls of the 10th-century **citadel** to the west offer splendid views.

A gnarled 900-year-old **plane tree**, which apparently used to house a café and a barber shop at different points of its long life, stands at the town's northern end. The medieval town wall isolates the Old Town from the surrounding valley.

Festivals & Events

The five-day Balkan Festival of Folk Dances and Songs, held at Ohrid in early July, draws folkloric groups from around the Balkans. The Ohrid Summer Festival, held from mid-July to mid-August, features classical concerts in the Church of Sveta Sofija, open-air theatre, and many other events. An international poetry festival, replete with food and drink in the streets, is held annually in nearby Struga on 25 and 26 August.

Ohrid hosts a swimming marathon each August, when swimmers race the 30km across Lake Ohrid from Sveti Naum to Ohrid.

Sleeping

BUDGET

Autocamp Gradište (☎ 285 945; camp site & 2 people 720MKD; ☺ May–mid-Sep) Located 17km south of Ohrid right on the lake, this is the nearest camping ground to Ohrid, and the best. It is a pleasant, grassy and shaded site with a long pebbly beach for swimmers.

Private rooms or apartments (per person 400-600MKD) Your best bet in Ohrid, private rooms or apartments can be organised either through Generalturist (see p461) or other local agencies. Rooms in the Old Town are more expensive.

Stefan Kanevče Rooms (☎ 070-212 352, 234 813; off ul Kočo Racin, Kaneo; per person €10) This spot is lakeside in Kaneo, the small settlement you can see west from the Church of Sv Jovan. Rooms in a 19th-century house with carved wooden ceilings, generous hospitality and Macedonian home cooking. Be warned that it is a bit of a hike from the Old Town.

Mimi Apartments (☎ 250 103; mimioh@mail.com .mk; ul Strašo Pinđur 2; r incl breakfast 800MKD) Friendly Mimi Apostolov owns eight comfortable, heated rooms, each of which have a fridge and satellite TV.

MID-RANGE & TOP END

Lucija's (☎ 265 608; Kosta Abraš 29; s/d €15/25) A fantastic place in the centre of the Old Town and near all the bars, its rooms are white, clean and spacious, balconies overlook the lake, and the patio is right on the water for a swim. Book early though, this place is popular.

Apartments Čekređi (☎ 261 733, 070 570 717; Kej Maršal Tito 27; d/tr 1500/2700MKD) These roomy, immaculate and spacious quarters close to the lake are good for a stay of a few days, as you can self-cater.

Hotel Riviera (☎ 268 735, fax 254 155; Kej Maršal Tito 4; s/d 1680/2640MKD) At this hotel, a step away from the centre, stuffed eagles and wooden sculptures greet you at the heavily ornamented reception. The rooms are very comfortable and there are three large apartments with lake views.

Hotel Lebed (☎ 250 004, fax 263 607; tani@mt.net .mk; Kej Maršal Tito bb; s/d 2170/3410MKD) You will have to walk about 1km east of town along the lake for some extra comfort and luxury in this small hotel. The rooms have relaxing wooden décor, phones, satellite TV, central heating and air-conditioning. Visa and MasterCard are accepted.

Eating & Drinking

Restaurants, quick eats, cafés and bars are dotted all around Ohrid.

Žito Leb (ul Kliment Ohridski bb; ☺ 9am-midnight) This small kiosk by the old plane tree is the best place for breakfast. Munch a fresh croissant or warm bread for 10MKD. Take away only.

Restoran Neim (☎ 254 504; Goce Delčev 71; ☺ 9am-midnight) Check out the local characters at this working man's hangout about 100m west of the old plane tree, and try some delicious *musaka* or *polneti piperki* (stuffed peppers).

Pizzeria Leonardo (☎ 260 359; Car Samoil 31; ☺ 9am-midnight) For a pizza and half a litre of draft wine at around 250MKD, this cosy little spot is the place to be.

Restaurant Dalga (☎ 31 948; Kosta Abraš bb) Here you can enjoy glorious lake views along with some Californian trout at 800MKD per kilo (the famous Ohrid Lake trout is now almost extinct – see p468).

Restaurant Antiko (☎ 265 523; Car Samoil 30; mains from 350MKD; ☺ 9am-midnight) This traditional place located in an old Ohrid house is one of the most popular restaurants in town, although it's rather pricey. Special warning: if you want to eat Macedonian specialities, you have to order them three hours in advance.

Popular Market (off Bulevar Turistička; ❤ 7am-4pm) Just north of the old plane tree, this place is great for picnic-minded travellers wanting to pick up supplies.

Jazz Inn (Kosta Abrašev 27; admission free; ❤ 10.30pm-1am) A vibrant, jazzy atmosphere, with live music on Thursdays and the weekend, this must be the most popular place in town.

Entertainment

Dom Na Kultura (Grigor Prličev; admission 50-100MKD) Ohrid's movie theatre, Dom Na Kultura faces the lakeside park. Cultural events are also held here.

Shopping

Pick up some interesting woodcarvings at **Barok** (☎ 263 151; barokohrid@yahoo.com; Car Samoil 24; ❤ 10am-2pm & 5-8pm), or some fine prints of photographs of rural Macedonia by photographer **Atanas Talevski** (☎ 254 059; Kosta Abraš bb; ❤ 9am-9pm). Small prints cost 200MKD and large ones 900MKD.

Getting There & Away

AIR

Only two airlines currently serve **Ohrid Airport** (☎ 262 503), which is 10km north of Ohrid. Adria Airways flies to Ljubljana on Wednesdays, Saturdays and Sundays. Odette Airways flies to Zürich on Saturdays.

BUS

No less than 10 buses a day run between Ohrid and Skopje (300MKD, three hours, 167km), via Kičevo. Another three go via Bitola. The first route is shorter, faster, more scenic and cheaper, so try to take it. During the summer rush, it pays to book a seat the day before.

There are nine buses a day travelling to Bitola (150MKD, 1¼ hours). Buses to Struga (14km) leave about every 15 minutes (5am to 9pm) from stand No 1 at the **bus station** (☎ 262 490; ul Dimitar Vlahov). Enter through the back doors and pay the conductor (30MKD).

Albania

To go to Albania, catch a bus or boat to Sveti Naum monastery, which is very near the border crossing. In summer there are six buses every day from Ohrid to Sveti Naum (80MKD, 29km), in winter, three daily. The bus continues on to the border post. From

Albanian customs it's 6km to Pogradec; taxis are waiting and should charge only US\$6 to US\$10 for the ride.

Bulgaria

There is one daily bus to Sofia from Ohrid (900MKD, 10 to 12 hours). It departs from Ohrid at 7am.

Greece

Ohrid has no direct transport links to Greece. Take a bus to Bitola and a taxi from there to the Greek border at Medžitlija/Niki (see p464).

Serbia & Montenegro

There are two buses each day at 5am and 3.30pm from Ohrid to Belgrade (1220MKD, 14 hours), via Bitola.

AROUND OHRID

Sveti Naum Свети Наум

The magnificent grounds of the Sveti Naum monastery, on the Albanian border 2km south of Ohrid, are a real treat. Standing just over the lake, the grounds are protected by peacocks and hide the source of Lake Ohrid's water. The beautiful 17th-century **Church of Sveti Naum** rises on a hill above the lake, surrounded by the monastery.

The original church of the Holy Archangels was built here in 900 by St Naum, and St Naum himself was buried here in 910. They say that you can still hear his heart beat if you put your ear on his tomb inside the chapel. The charming frescoes of the archangels inside the church are mostly 19th-century, though fragments of 16th- and 17th-century work remain. You can probably find an English speaker on hand to act as a guide. There's no need to pay the guide, but do leave some money by the icons. The monastery grounds also offer a view of the Albanian town of Pogradec across the lake. In the summer months you can take a half-hour boat trip from the monastery to the bubbling springs that feed Lake Ohrid (100MKD per person).

SLEEPING & EATING

Autocamp Sveti Naum (☎ 283 240; 2 people & small camp site 350MKD) If you are after a peaceful few days by the lake, you can stay at this family-oriented place. Located 2km north of the monastery, you can reach it on the Sveti Naum bus.

Sveti Naum Hotel (☎ 046 283 244; www.hotel -stnaum.com.mk; s/d incl breakfast 3360/4320MKD; 🔀) Standing at the heart of the monastery, this lovely hotel has magical views, excellent rooms with satellite TV, phone, central heating and air-conditioning. Book in advance during the popular summer months; prices drop at other times of the year. Visa and MasterCard accepted. The hotel restaurant serves food.

GETTING THERE & AWAY
Six buses a day run from Ohrid to Sveti Naum; it's 80MKD one way, payable on the bus. Buses generally return 40 minutes after they set out. The bus makes a stop going both ways at the Albanian border.

In summer you can also come by boat but it only leaves when a group of about five to eight people is present; ask about times at the wharf or at the travel agencies in town. The fare is about 150/200MKD one way/return.

BITOLA БИТОЛА
☎ 097 / pop 90,000
Bitola, the southernmost city of the former Yugoslavia and second largest in Macedonia, sits on a 660m-high plateau between mountains 16km north of the Greek border. As you enter, you will notice the two magnificent minarets of the 16th-century **Yeni Mosque** and **Yahdar-Kadi Mosque** piercing the sky opposite each other. Step in and take a look at these elegant stone buildings. Explore the city's colourful **old bazaar**, Stara Čaršija, which really gets buzzing on Tuesdays and Fridays, and relax in the cafés on the wide boulevards. Step into the **Church of Sv Dimitri**, a large lavish space with exquisite frescoes. It's probably best to visit Bitola as a day trip or a stopover between Skopje and Ohrid, as there are no private rooms; the one hotel, **Hotel Epinal** (☎ 224 777; Leninova bb; s/d €65/100), is dark and overpriced, and no left-luggage office is available.

The **Ilinden festival**, the most important event of the year, takes place on 2 August, when the Macedonians celebrate their uprising against the Ottomans with traditional food, music and general joy.

The **bus station** (☎ 231 420; ul Nikola Tesla) and the **train station** (☎ 237 110; ul Nikola Tesla) are adjacent to each other, about 1km south of the town centre. To get to the Greek

border, you must take a taxi from the bus station (350MKD to 450MKD) and then look for a taxi on the Greek side to the nearest town, Florina.

Heraclea Хераклеа
The main attraction of Bitola city is the magnificent **Heraclea ruins** (admission 100MKD, photos 500MKD; ⏰ 9am-3pm winter, 9am-5pm summer), beyond the old cemetery, 1km south of the bus and train stations. Founded in the 4th century BC by Philip II of Macedon, Heraclea was conquered by the Romans two centuries later and became an important stage on the Via Egnatia, the Roman road that connected ports on the Adriatic with Byzantium. From the 4th to 6th centuries AD it was an episcopal seat. Excavations of the site are continuing, but the Roman baths, portico and theatre are now visible. Other interesting attractions in Heraclea are the two early Christian basilicas and the episcopal palace, which contains some splendid mosaics.

Treskavec Monastery
Манастир Трескавец
This is the most magnificent – and perhaps the most remote – place in the country. Planted on the top of Mt Zlato 10km above the town of Prilep, you couldn't get a more breathtaking and dramatic setting. You will most certainly feel deliriously light-headed upon reaching the monastery when, after the two hour climb, you breathe the fresh air at the top. The valley stretches on all sides beneath you, and the thick rolling clouds move lightly above your head. The mountain itself is bare and the rock formations are like dinosaurs turned to stone mid-step, with a solitary tree grazed by the sweeping winds.

The monastery itself was rebuilt in the early 1990s after it was destroyed by a fire, and forms a sort of pentagon with a courtyard and church in the middle. Built on what was the ancient town of Kolobaise, which was inhabited from the 3rd century BC until the 7th century AD, you will be able to see the town's name inscribed into the stone cross base on the top of the church. The site also housed a temple to Apollo and Artemis in the 1st century BC.

Prepare to be amazed by some of the most colourful and intricate frescoes to be found in Macedonia at the 14th-century **Church of the Holy Mother of God** (Sveta Bogorodica), the monastery's spiritual heart. The incisions on the bare walls reveal yet more frescoes to be uncovered, like small windows into history. The church was built on the foundations of the original 6th century basilica and inside you can see some more Roman remains.

Take a look at the **old dining hall** to the right of the monastery entrance with its long stone tables and magnificent Roman water jugs and oil vats.

Inside the monastery you will be welcomed by the lovely Naumovski couple who will cook you dinner and let you sleep in the rooms for free; beds and blankets are provided. Leave some money at the icons; how much is up to you, but we recommend at least 200MKD per person.

To get to the monastery, you must first get to Prilep. There are frequent buses from Ohrid, Bitola and Skopje, and four trains from Skopje go every day (300MKD, three hours). From Prilep, there are two ways of getting to the monastery: one is by 4WD up a muddy mountain track. Ask for directions to the new town cemetery where you will have to watch out for a small sign for *Manastir Sveta Bogorodica, Treskavec*. Head straight up. The second option is on foot, and is far more rewarding, because you get to see the fantastic scenery around you and experience the priceless sight of the monastery appearing above you. Take a taxi to Dabnica village outside Prilep to the north and head for the cobbled track leading you up Mt Zlato. If you cannot see the cobbled track straight away, ask the driver to point you in the right direction. Go up the road, and after you reach the water fountain, continue on the straight path.

At the end of your mountain excursion, check out **Markovi Kuli** (Marko's Towers) on the hill above Prilep. King Marko, the last Macedonian king, was a brave warrior, and his courageous fighting against the Turks earned him the honour of having these awe-inspiring towers named after him. Archaeological findings show that the site dates back to the 3rd and 4th centuries BC, but most of the remains you will be able to see are from medieval times. This is another place from which to enjoy spectacular views.

WESTERN MACEDONIA

Western Macedonia has been called 'Little Switzerland' for its sharp and snow-capped mountain peaks, reflected in the smooth mirror of the clear lakes below, the lush nature, and most of all, the fantastic skiing opportunities. If you visit Macedonia in the winter time, this is the place to hit the slopes.

SV JOVAN BIGORSKI MONASTERY
СВЕТИ ЈОВАН БИГОРСКИ МАНАСТИР

This fully working monastery is one of the most popular with visitors in Macedonia. It was first established in 1020 on the spot where the icon of Sv Jovan (St John the Baptist) allegedly appeared, and has been rebuilt many times over the centuries after being burnt down or destroyed. The miraculous icon kept reappearing and the monastery kept being 'resurrected'. The present day structures date from the 18th and 19th centuries, and inside the church you can see what is supposedly the forearm of Sv Jovan himself. The church also holds one of the three iconostases and chairs carved by Makarije Frčkovski and the Filipovski brothers (see p456).

The monastery has **dormitories** (☎ 042 478 675; €4) where you can stay overnight, with self-catering facilities.

Set in the west of the country, the monastery is surrounded by some wonderful natural countryside, such as Lake Debar and sharp mountain edges. **Mavrovo National Park** is nearby, with opportunities for skiing, hunting, fishing, hiking and mountaineering.

To get to the monastery, take the Skopje–Ohrid bus going via Debar, and ask to be let off at the turning point for the Sv Jovan Bigorski Monastery *(manastir)*.

MACEDONIA DIRECTORY

ACCOMMODATION

Skopje's hotels are expensive but there are alternatives, such as camping grounds and private-room agencies. Skopje's convenient HI hostel is open throughout the year. Beds are also available at student dormitories in Skopje in summer. Prices in more expensive hotels are usually quoted in euros. The accommodation in Ohrid is generally good and affordable, with plenty of budget and mid-range options. Booking early is recommended for visits during the summer high season, Christmas (Orthodox, 7 January) and Easter (you can check the dates for Orthodox Easter at www.startinbusiness.co.uk/hols/easter.htm). Reviews in this chapter are ordered according to price.

ACTIVITIES

There is great skiing at Macedonia's top resort, Popova Šapka (1845m), on the southern slopes of Šar Planina west of Tetovo near the border with Kosovo. Mavrovo in western Macedonia comes a close second. Hiking is spectacular in any of the three national parks (Galičica and Pelister in the south, and Mavrovo) or at Lake Matka near Skopje, which offers climbing and sailing.

BOOKS

Lonely Planet's *Eastern Europe phrasebook* will help you with the language. Zoë Brân's *After Yugoslavia*, part of Lonely Planet's Journeys series, retraces the author's 1978 trip through the now much-changed former Yugoslavia. Brân travels through Croatia, Slovenia, Bosnia and Hercegovina, Serbia, and Montenegro in an attempt to make sense of what has happened since 1992.

A decent background book is *Who Are the Macedonians?* by Hugh Poulton, a political and cultural history. Rebecca West's *Black Lamb & Grey Falcon*, a between-the-wars Balkan travelogue, makes a brief mention of Macedonia. A recent study is *The New Macedonian Question* edited by James Pettifer – a collection of academic essays discussing this complex issue.

BUSINESS HOURS

Businesses tend to stay open late in Macedonia. Travellers will generally find them open from 8am to 8pm weekdays and 8am to 2pm on Saturday. Post offices open from 6.30am to 4pm and banks from 7am to 5pm, Monday to Friday.

CUSTOMS

Customs checks are generally cursory, though travellers with private cars may attract more attention at land borders. You may bring one litre of alcohol and 200 cigarettes in with you, and the maximum amount of currency that can be brought into the country without having to declare it is €10,000. You can take MKD freely back over the border with you, but there is not much point in doing so because it cannot be exchanged into any currency once outside of Macedonia.

DANGERS & ANNOYANCES

Macedonia is a safe country in general. However, travellers should be on the lookout for pickpockets in bus and train stations and exercise common sense in looking after their belongings.

DISABLED TRAVELLERS

Few public buildings or streets have facilities for wheelchairs, but some newer buildings and some of the most expensive hotels provide wheelchair ramps. There is no disabled access on public transport.

EMBASSIES & CONSULATES
Macedonian Embassies & Consulates

Macedonian embassies are found in the following countries:

Albania (☎ 042-330 36; fax 042-325 14; Rruga Lek Dukagjini, Vila 2, Tirana)

Australia (☎ 02-6249 8000; fax 02-6249 8088; Perpetual Bldg, Suite 2:05, 10 Rudd St Canberra ACT 2600)

Canada (☎ 613-234 3882; fax 613-233 1852; 130 Albert St, Suite 1006, Ottawa ON, K1P 5G4)

Turkey (☎ 012-446 9204; fax 012-446 9206; Filistin sokak 30-2/3, Gaziosman Paşa, Ankara)

UK (☎ 020-7499 5152; fax 020-499 2864; 19a Cavendish Square, London, W1M 9AD)

USA (☎ 202-337 3063; fax 020-337 3093; 3050 K Street NW, Washington DC, 20007)

Serbia and Montenegro (☎ 011-633 348; fax 011-182 287; Gospodar Jevremova 34, 11000 Belgrade)

Embassies & Consulates in Macedonia

The following countries have diplomatic representation in Skopje (area code ☎ 02):

Albania (☎ 2614 636; fax 2614 200; ul H T Karpoš 94a)

Australia (☎ 2361 114; fax 2361 834; ul Londonska 11b)

Bulgaria (☎ 3116 320; fax 3116 139; ul Zlatko Šnajder 3)

Canada (☎ 3125 228; fax 3122 681; ul Mitropolit Teodosie Gologanov 104)

Germany (☎ 3110 507; fax 3117 713; ul Veljko Vlahović 26)

Greece (☎ 3130 198; fax 3115 718; ul Borka Talevski 6)

Serbia and Montenegro (☎ 3129 298; fax 3129 427; Pitu Guli 8)

Turkey (☎ 3113 270; fax 3117 024; ul Slavej Planina bb)

UK (☎ 3116 772; fax 3117 005; ul Dimitri Čupovski 26)

USA (☎ 3116 180; fax 3117 103; Bulevar Ilindenska bb)

FESTIVALS & EVENTS

There are a good few festivals in Macedonia, especially in the summer time. Easter is a great time to be in Ohrid as the town is full of people and there are daily and midnight church services over the three festive days. July brings open-air evening concerts, opera and theatre to both Ohrid and Skopje. There is also a fun Folklore Festival in Ohrid in early July (see p462). The last weekend of August sees the International Swimming Marathon on Lake Ohrid, when the swimmers have to cross the 30km distance between Sveti Naum and Ohrid town.

One festival that all Macedonians rave about is the Galičnik village's wedding festival (in Mavrovo National Park), held on the second weekend in July. The entire village dresses up in traditional costume and takes part in a traditional wedding ceremony. It is so popular that couples must apply months in advance to get married here.

Skopje's autumn days are brightened up with the flickering screens of the international film festival and the warm sounds of Skopje Jazz Festival in October.

GAY & LESBIAN TRAVELLERS

Due to the macho culture of the Balkans, Macedonia does not generally endorse homosexuality, so it's best for visitors to maintain a low profile. Homosexuality was decriminalised in Macedonia in 1996.

HOLIDAYS

New Year 1 and 2 January
Orthodox Christmas 7 January
International Women's Day 8 March
Orthodox Easter Week March/April
Labour Day 1 May
Sts Cyril and Methodius Day 24 May
Ilinden or Day of the 1903 Rebellion 2 August
Republic Day 8 September
1941 Partisan Day 11 October

INTERNET RESOURCES

The website www.b-info.com/places/Mace donia/republic/ presents a good potpourri of data on the country. If you are interested in organised tours, check out www.gomace donia.com.

LANGUAGE

Macedonia's two official languages are Macedonian and Albanian. Macedonian, a South Slavic language, is spoken by the majority of the population. It is divided into two large groups, the western and eastern Macedonian dialects. The Macedonian literary language is based on the central dialects of Veles, Prilep and Bitola. Its script is Cyrillic, but you will see advertisements or place names in Latin script. There are certain grammatical similarities between Macedonian and Bulgarian, such as the omittance of cases, and speakers of Bulgarian, Serbian or Croatian should easily understand Macedonian. Russian speakers should also be able to get by without too much difficulty. For others, we recommend a good phrasebook, such as Lonely Planet's *Eastern Europe phrasebook*.

The Cyrillic alphabet is based on the one developed by two Thessaloniki brothers, St Cyril and St Methodius, in the 9th century. It was taught by their disciples at a monastery in Ohrid, from where it spread across the eastern Slavic world.

Despite the use of Latin script on road signs and some shop names, the Cyrillic alphabet is still predominant and street names are printed in Cyrillic script only, so it is a good idea to learn the Cyrillic alphabet before you travel to the country.

For a quick introduction to useful Macedonian words and phrases, see the Language chapter, p467.

MAPS

The best commercial map of the country is the 1:260,000 *Republic of Macedonia* map published by GiziMapis. It is only available in Macedonia. You can find it at Kultura Bookshop in central Skopje or in kiosks in Ohrid. *Baedeker's Greece* map also covers Macedonia.

The tourist office in Skopje has a free road- and tourist-map of the Republic of Macedonia.

MEDIA

The Macedonian media is large and varied, but often not entirely free of political bias. There are TV and radio stations, newspapers and news agencies in Macedonian, Albanian, Roma and Turkish languages, with the Macedonian language ones being predominant.

Newspapers & Magazines

English-language newspapers and magazines can only be found in Skopje. See that section for details. In Skopje, **World Press** (cnr ul Dame Gruev & Bul Partizanski Odredi) has quite a wide selection of foreign publications. You can find some English-language newspapers at the **St Patrick Irish Pub** (☎ 3220 431; Kej 13 Noemvri; mains 280MKD; ☽ 7.30am-midnight) in Skopje.

Radio
The BBC World Service is found on 9.41 MHz on the Short Wave, and the Voice of America on 107.5 FM.

TV
There is a choice of three state Macedonian TV stations and any number of private and satellite channels, including CBC, Eurosport and Euronews.

MONEY
Macedonian denar (MKD) notes come in denominations of 10, 50, 100, 500, 1000 and 5000, and there are coins of one, two and five denar. The denar is nonconvertible outside Macedonia. Restaurants, hotels and some shops will accept payment in euros (usually) and US dollars (sometimes); prices are often quoted in these currencies. Some prices in this chapter have been converted to denars from euros or US dollars, so the listed price may not be exact.

Small, private exchange offices throughout central Skopje and Ohrid exchange cash for a rate that is only slightly better than that which you can get at the banks, but banks cash travellers cheques as well. ATMs can be found in central Skopje and offer the most reliable exchange rate when withdrawing money.

Except for accommodation in Skopje, Macedonia is not an expensive country. If you stay in a private room in Skopje, you might keep costs to 1800MKD to 2100MKD a day; outside Skopje, frugal travellers may spend 1200MKD to 1500MKD per day.

POST
Mail services to and from Macedonia are efficient and reasonably fast, although sending money or valuables through normal post is not recommended as they may mysteriously disappear. Letters to the USA cost 38MKD, to Australia 40MKD and to Europe 35MKD. There are poste-restante services available at major post offices.

RESPONSIBLE TRAVEL
Ohrid Lake trout is almost extinct and in 2004 the government issued a seven-year ban on catching it. Despite this, many restaurants still offer it, thereby encouraging illegal trout fishing. Do try to resist ordering one and opt for Californian trout instead, which is just as tasty.

TELEPHONE & FAX
A long-distance call costs less at main post offices than in hotels. Drop the initial zero in the city codes when calling Macedonia from abroad. Buy phonecards in units of 100 (200MKD), 200 (300MKD), 500 (650MKD) or 1000 (1250MKD) from post offices. Some of the larger kiosks also sell the 100-unit cards. You can often make a cheap international phone call at Internet cafés for around 15MKD per minute for all countries.

Macedonia has a digital mobile phone network (MOBIMAK); numbers are preceded by ☎ 070. Your provider may have a global-roaming agreement with Macedonia's domestic network. Check before you leave home.

Fax services are available at the main post offices in Skopje and Ohrid.

EMERGENCY NUMBERS

- Ambulance ☎ 94
- Police ☎ 92
- Highway & roadside assistance ☎ 987

VISAS
At the time of writing citizens of EU countries don't need visas for Macedonia, but visas are required of most others. Australians need to get a visa in advance or on entry (US$25), while Canadians, South Africans and New Zealanders should get one in advance (US$12). US nationals are issued visas free of charge at their port of entry, but this may change frequently, so check with a Macedonian embassy before arrival.

WOMEN TRAVELLERS
Women travellers should feel no particular concern about travel in Macedonia. Other than possible cursory interest from men, travel is hassle-free and easy.

TRANSPORT IN MACEDONIA

GETTING THERE & AWAY

Air

Some airlines in Skopje (area code ☎ 02):

Adria Airways (code JP; ☎ 3117 009; www.adria.si)

Alitalia (code AZ; ☎ 3118 602; www.alitalia.it)

Croatia Airlines (code OU; ☎ 3115 858; www.croatia airlines.hr)

JAT (code JU; ☎ 3116 532; www.jat.com)

Macedonian Airlines (MAT) (code IN; ☎ 3116 333; www.mat.com.mk)

Malév Hungarian Airlines (code MA; ☎ 3111 214; www.malev.hu)

Olympic Airways (code OA; ☎ 3127 127; www.olympic airlines.com)

Turkish Airlines (code TK; ☎ 3117 214; www.turkish airlines.com)

Any of the innumerable travel agencies in Skopje or Ohrid can book flights with these airlines.

Land

Macedonia shares land borders with Greece, Albania, Bulgaria, and Serbia and Montenegro and one UN-monitored territory – Kosovo. Access to/from all neighbouring states is generally trouble-free and unrestricted. The Lake Ohrid crossings with Albania are no problem and you will spend up to half an hour while all the regularities are checked.

Visas are not necessary for travel to Kosovo, and it is quite easy to get there; the border crossing is just a 20-minute trip north from Skopje.

BUS

Skopje has two international bus stations: one is next to the City Museum (p456), the other by the river on Kej 13 Noemvri. Buses travel to Sofia (640MKD, six hours, three daily), Istanbul (1860MKD, 14 hours, three to four daily), Belgrade (800MKD, six hours, three daily), Frankfurt (6100MKD, 24 hours, weekly) and Zagreb (2560MKD, 15 hours, four per week). Buses also travel to Budapest, Vienna, and Sarajevo.

Buses between Skopje and Priština, the capital of Kosovo, are fairly frequent. To/from Albania you can travel from Tetovo

or Struga to Tirana by bus (six to seven hours, two daily), or walk across the border at Sveti Naum (see p463) or Kafa San.

CAR & MOTORCYCLE

There are several major highway border crossings into Macedonia from neighbouring countries. You will need a Green Card endorsed for Macedonia to bring a car into the country.

Albania

The crossings are Sveti Naum (29km south of Ohrid), Kafa San (12km southwest of Struga) and Blato (5km northwest of Debar).

Bulgaria

The main crossings are just east of Kriva Palanka (between Sofia and Skopje), and east of Delčevo (26km west of Blagoevgrad) and also Novo Selo (between Kulata and Strumica).

Greece

There are crossings at Gevgelija (between Skopje and Thessaloniki), Dojran (just east of Gevgelija) and Medžitlija (16km south of Bitola).

Kosovo

You can cross into Kosovo at Blace between Skopje and Uroševac and also at Jažince between Tetovo and Uroševac.

Serbia & Montenegro

Entry to Serbia and Montenegro is via Tabanovce (10km north of Kumanovo). Local trains go as far as Tabanovce.

Taxi

Taxis are a good way to get to Kosovo: 640MKD will get you to the border, where taxis are waiting on the other side to whisk you to Priština. Note that these taxis are more expensive and will probably cost €18 and up, depending on your negotiating skills.

One enterprising international taxi driver who offers transport to Thessaloniki (€120, up to four persons) and Sofia (€85, up to four persons) from Skopje or the Kosovo border is **Sašo Trajkovski** (☎ 070-279 449; saso_taxi@yahoo.com). The Thessaloniki service is a through-run, while the Sofia service involves a pre-arranged change of taxi at the border.

Train

There are a number of international trains leaving Skopje. There are two trains daily between Skopje and Belgrade via Niš (1209MKD, eight to nine hours). Sleepers are available. One train goes daily to Ljubljana in Slovenia (2690MKD, 12 hours) Two trains run daily between Skopje and Thessaloniki (700MKD, six hours) – one at 7.15am and the other at 5.18pm. Note that Thessaloniki in Macedonian is 'Solun'.

GETTING AROUND
Bicycle

Cycling around Macedonia is possible, if a little unsafe. It is pretty unusual, so car drivers may not be prepared for cyclists on the roads. The smaller roads are more or less suitable for cycling, if a little patchy.

Bus

Bus travel is well developed in Macedonia, with fairly frequent services from Skopje to Ohrid and Bitola. The domestic bus fleet is now getting rather old and creaky, but it is still serviceable. It is a good idea to book in advance when travelling to Ohrid in the busy summer season.

Car & Motorcycle

Skopje is awash with rental-car agencies, from the large ones (Hertz and Avis) to smaller local companies. The tourist office in Skopje has a complete listing. In Ohrid, **Queen-Rent-A-Car agency** (☎ 046 261 693/070 261 918; Partizanska bb; ☯ 9am-5pm Mon-Sat) rents small cars, starting at 200MKD per day. Unleaded and regular petrol is widely available, but is relatively expensive at 51MKD per litre.

Speed limits for cars and motorcycles are 120km/h on motorways, 80km/h on the open road and 50km/h to 60km/h in towns. Speeding fines start from around 1500MKD. It is compulsory to wear a seat belt, though you'll probably find that few people do.

The Macedonia-wide number for emergency highway assistance is ☎ 987.

Roads and highways are generally safe and the Macedonians are decent drivers, but always keep an eye for those wannabe formula one drivers.

Taxi

A quick way of getting around the country if the buses are not convenient is by taxi, especially if there are two or more of you to share the cost. A half-hour trip, from Skopje to Lake Matka for example, should cost around 350MKD.

Train

Macedonia has a limited network of domestic destinations. Possibly the only one of any real interest is the four-hour, three-times-daily service to Bitola from Skopje. Other destinations are: Kičevo in the west of the country; Veles, south of Skopje; Tabanovce on the border with Serbia and Montenegro; and Gevgelija on the Greek border, north of Thessaloniki. The most you'll pay for a domestic ticket is 370MKD for a return to Bitola.

Moldova

CONTENTS

Highlights	472	Business Hours	490
Itineraries	472	Customs	490
Climate & When To Go	472	Embassies & Consulates	491
History	472	Festivals & Events	491
People	475	Holidays	491
Arts	475	Money	491
Environment	476	Post	491
Food & Drink	476	Telephone	491
Chişinău	**476**	Visas	492
Orientation	477	**Transport**	**492**
Sights	477	Getting There & Away	492
Sleeping	480	Getting Around	493
Eating	480		
Drinking	481		
Entertainment	481		
Shopping	482		
Getting There & Away	482		
Getting Around	483		
Around Chişinău	483		
Transdniestr	**485**		
Tiraspol	486		
Bendery	488		
Gagauzia	**489**		
Comrat	489		
Moldova Directory	**490**		
Accommodation	490		

MOLDOVA

FAST FACTS

- **Area** 33,700 sq km
- **Capital** Chişinău
- **Currency** leu; €1 =15.48 lei; US$1 =12.37 lei; UK£1 = 22.30 lei; A$1 = 9.01 lei; ¥100 = 11.41 lei; NZ$1 = 8.48 lei
- **Famous for** wine, folk art
- **Key Phrases** *bună* (hello), *merci* (thank you), *cum vă numiţi?* (what's your name?)
- **Official Languages** Moldovan, Russian
- **Population** 4.43 million
- **Telephone Codes** country code ☎ 373; international access code ☎ 22
- **Visas** required for all EU, US, Canadian, Australian and New Zealand passport holders; see p492 for details

Moldova is not exactly what one would call a press darling. If there are any reports at all from this land-locked country, they highlight intense poverty, illegal organ trading, human trafficking, civil war and communism.

Such reports about this rarely visited country fail to mention the sunflower fields, enormous watermelons, bucolic pastoral lands, amazingly friendly people and rivers of delicious wine. They also miss the surreal beauty of remote monasteries cut into limestone cliffs, the warmth of villagers and the sheer vibrancy of urban pleasures in Chişinău, one of Europe's most party-bent capitals.

HIGHLIGHTS

- Stroll **Chişinău's** (p476) tree-studded avenues and experience its kick-ass nightlife
- See how 13th-century monks lived by visiting fantastic cave monasteries at **Orheiul Vechi** (p484)
- Visit the self-styled republic of **Transdniestr** (p485), a surreal, living museum of the Soviet Union
- Hike and canoe during the day and indulge in homemade wine in the evening in the **Lower Dniestr National Park** (p485)

ITINERARIES

- **One week** Arrive in Chişinău – spend a couple of days partying. Use Chişinău as your base, making a trip out to the cave monasteries at Orheiul Vechi. Hike and canoe in the Lower Dniestr National Park before returning home.
- **Two weeks** Do the above plus add on a few days travelling back in time in Transdniestr, the country that doesn't officially exist, then take an extended trip through the wine region around Chişinău before returning home.

CLIMATE & WHEN TO GO

Moldova has moderate winters and warm summers. Hikers and wine enthusiasts would do well to travel between May and September, when you have more guarantees that camping grounds and attractions will be open. As there is little tourism to Moldova there's no real low or high season.

HISTORY

Moldova today straddles two historic regions divided by the Nistru (Dniestr) River.

HOW MUCH?

- **Bottle of Cricova table wine** $1-3
- **Museum admission (adult)** $0.20-1
- **Short taxi ride** $2
- **Local bus ticket** $0.10
- **Internet** $0.25 per hr

LONELY PLANET INDEX

- **Litre of petrol** $0.50
- **Litre of bottled water** $0.35
- **Beer (Chişinău in a bar)** $0.45-1
- **Souvenir item** $3-5
- **Pizza slice from street kiosk** $0.50

Historic Romanian Bessarabia incorporated the region west of the Nistru, while tsarist Russia governed the territory east of the river (Transdniestr).

Bessarabia, part of the Romanian principality of Moldavia, was annexed in 1812 by the Russian empire. In 1918, after the October Revolution, Bessarabia declared its independence. Two months later the newly formed Democratic Moldavian Republic united with Romania. Russia never recognised this union.

Then in 1924 the Soviet Union created the Moldavian Autonomous Oblast on the eastern banks of the Nistru River, and incorporated Transdniestr into the Ukrainian Soviet Socialist Republic (SSR). A few months later the Soviet government

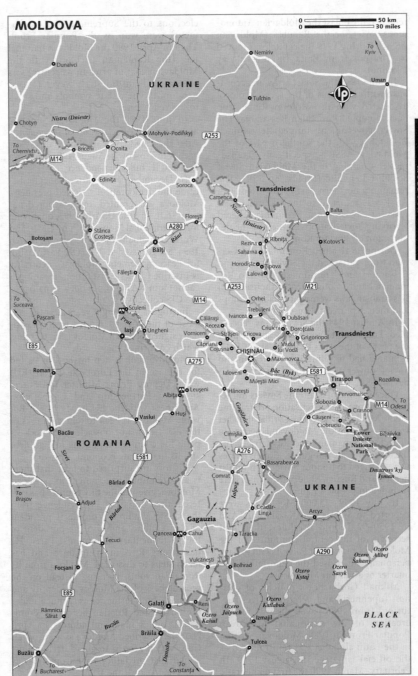

MOLDOVA

renamed the oblast the Moldavian Autonomous Soviet Socialist Republic (Moldavian ASSR). During 1929 the capital was moved to Tiraspol from Balta (in present-day Ukraine).

In June 1940 the Soviet army, in accordance with the terms of the secret protocol associated with the Molotov-Ribbentrop Pact, occupied Romanian Bessarabia. The Soviet government immediately joined Bessarabia with the southern part of the Moldavian ASSR – specifically, Transdniestr – naming it the Moldavian Soviet Socialist Republic (Moldavian SSR). The remaining northern part of the Moldavian ASSR was returned to the Ukrainian SSR (present-day Ukraine). Bessarabia suffered terrifying Sovietisation, marked by the deportation of 300,000 Romanians.

During 1941 allied Romanian and German troops attacked the Soviet Union, and Bessarabia and Transdniestr fell into Romanian hands. Consequently, thousands of Bessarabian Jews were sent to labour camps and then deported to Auschwitz.

In August 1944 the Soviet army reoccupied Transdniestr and Bessarabia. Under the terms of the Paris Peace Treaty of 1947, Romania had to relinquish the region and Soviet power was restored in the Moldavian SSR.

Once in control again the Soviets immediately enforced a Sovietisation programme on the Moldavian SSR. The Cyrillic alphabet was imposed on the Moldovan language (a dialect of Romanian) and Russian became the official state language. Street names were changed to honour Soviet communist heroes, and Russian-style patronymics were included in people's names.

In July 1949, 25,000 Moldovans were deported to Siberia and Kazakhstan. And in 1950–52 Leonid Brezhnev, then first secretary of the central committee of the Moldovan Communist Party, is said to have personally supervised the deportation of a quarter of a million Moldovans.

Mikhail Gorbachev's policies of *glasnost* (openness) and *perestroika* (restructuring) from 1986 paved the way for the creation of the nationalist Moldovan Popular Front in 1989. Moldovan written in the Latin alphabet was reintroduced as the official language in August 1989. In February–March 1990 the first democratic elections to the Supreme Soviet (parliament) were won by the Popular Front. Then in April 1990 the Moldovan national flag (the Romanian tricolour with the Moldavian coat of arms in its centre) was reinstated. Transdniestr, however, refused to adopt the new state symbols and stuck to the red banner.

In June 1990 the Moldovan Supreme Soviet passed a declaration of sovereignty. After the failed coup attempt against Gorbachev in Moscow in August 1991, Moldova declared its full independence.

In December 1991 Mircea Snegur became the democratically elected president. Moldova was granted 'most-favoured nation' status by the USA in 1992, qualifying for International Monetary Fund (IMF) and World Bank loans the same year. In March 1994 Snegur signed NATO's Partnership for Peace agreement. Moldova's neutrality is inscribed in its constitution, meaning it cannot join NATO and is not a signatory to the CIS collective security agreements.

In August 1999, eight years after the collapse of the Soviet Union, a treaty was finally signed between Moldova and Ukraine, which confirmed their borders.

Moldova took a step forward in its bid for a place in the European Union (EU) when Deputy Prime Minister Ion Sturza signed a Partnership and Cooperation Agreement with the EU in May 1999. But while Moldova is keen to join the ranks of the EU, two major obstacles still block its path: the country's mounting foreign debt and its inadequate economic growth.

Visitors are surprised to hear that there is a Communist government in power in Moldova, given all the tiny country has suffered after declaring independence from the USSR. Vladimir Voronin is president of the republic, and also the president of the parliamentary Communist Party. He has strong Russian sympathies and has taken steps to dissociate Moldova from its Romanian roots, focusing instead on the separateness of the Moldovan identity and language, both fashioned very much under the Soviet and Russian history of dominance. In his inaugural address in April 2001, he described Moldova as a European Cuba which needed to guard itself against 'imperialist predators' in Europe, just as Cuba had against the USA.

These officials have become highly unpopular. In 2002 several thousands took to the streets in Chişinău to protest a government plan to force school children to learn Russian. The government backed down but refused to step down, as the crowds were demanding. In November 2003 up to 50,000 took to the capital's streets in a peaceful protest demanding the government's resignation; they were incensed that Russian troops remain on Moldovan soil (in the breakaway region of Transdniestr) and about a Russian plan to change Moldova to a federation, giving self-rule to Transdniestr. Placards read: 'Down with Communists!' and 'We Want to Join NATO!'

In 2003 Russian troops started to honour their years-old agreement of pulling out of Transdniestr; by the end of the year, they had removed some 20,000 tons of weapons, ammunition and equipment – about half of all that had remained on the territory since the Communist era.

The government under Voronin has been both trying to buddy up to the EU and international bodies (they joined the WTO in 2001), as well as snuggling up to the Russian and Ukrainian governments. If the government survives until elections in 2004, a major change in government is expected.

PEOPLE

With 4.43 million inhabitants Moldova is the most densely populated region of the former Soviet Union. Moldovans make up 64.5% of the total population, Ukrainians 13.8%, Russians 13%, Gagauz 3.5%, Bulgarians 2%, Jews 1.5%, and other nationalities such as Belarusians, Poles and Roma 1.7%.

Most Gagauz and Bulgarians live in southern Moldova. In Transdniestr, Ukrainians and Russians total 53% of the region's population; Moldovans make up 40%. It's one of the least urbanised countries in Europe.

ARTS

There is a wealth of traditional folk art in Moldova, with carpet making, pottery, weaving and carving predominating.

Traditional dancing in Moldova is similar to the traditional dances of other Eastern European countries. Couples dance in a circle, a semicircle or a line to the sounds of bagpipes, flutes, panpipes and violins.

Two of Moldova's most prolific modern composers are Arkady Luxemburg and Evgeny Doga, who have both scored films and multimedia projects as well as written songs, concertos, suites and symphonies. Dimitrie Gagauz has for over three decades been the foremost composer of

---

NOT EXACTLY A NATIONAL SPORT

Did you know that Moldova is world famous for its underwater hockey teams? Well, OK, *infamous* then.

You wouldn't normally associate such a sport as underwater hockey with Moldova (come to think of it, there aren't any countries you'd associate it with, but that's another story...). However, in the 2000 Underwater Hockey Championships held in the world-renowned underwater-hockey metropolis of Hobart, in Tasmania, Australia, the Moldovan men's team puzzled referees and judges by not even knowing how to put their fins and flippers on properly. After being trounced by such stalwarts as Columbia 30-0 and Argentina 23-0, it came out that the entire team had filed for (and eventually received) refugee status with the Australian government.

It's a good thing for Moldovans that Canadians aren't known for their good memories or efficient bureaucracy. Two years later, after much hounding from a so-called Moldovan Underwater Hockey Federation based in Tiraspol (in probably the only time Transdniestran officials called themselves 'Moldovan'), the Canadian Embassy in Bucharest granted the women's team visas to participate in the world championships in Calgary.

There was much head-scratching as the Moldovan national anthem was played – and no team came out to play. But how could they? They were in Toronto, filing for refugee status. In this elaborate visa scam, each woman on the team (who no doubt wouldn't know what to do with an underwater puck even if it bit her) had paid organisers some $1200 – not bad for refugee status in Canada.

While this incident sadly spells out an uncertain future for the world of underwater hockey in Moldova, it does speak volumes about the creativity and persistence of Moldovans!

songs reflecting the folklore of the Turkic-influenced Gagauz population of southern Moldova.

The biggest name in Moldovan painting is Mihai Grecu (1916–98), who cofounded the National School of Painting and was also a poet and free love advocate. In sculpture, Anatol Coseac today produces some highly original woodworks.

ENVIRONMENT
Land

Moldova is tiny and landlocked. It's a flat country of gently rolling steppes, with a gradual sloping towards the Black Sea. With one of the highest percentages of arable land in the world, Moldova is blessed with rich soil. Fields of grains, fruits and sunflowers are characteristic of the countryside. Moldova counts some 16,500 species of animals (460 of which are vertebrates) as its citizens.

National Park

Moldova has one nascent national park: the Lower Dniestr National Park (Parcul Naţional Nistrul Inferior; p485) southeast of Chişinău. It hugs the Nistru River southwards to the border of Ukraine.

In addition to this, there are five scientific reserves (totalling 19,378 hectares) and 30 protected natural sites (covering 22,278 hectares). The reserves protect areas of bird migration, old beech and oak forests and important waterways. The Codru reserve, Moldova's oldest, boasts 924 plant species, 138 kinds of birds and 45 mammals; this is the most frequently visited reserve.

Environmental Issues

A great effort has been made by environmental groups to protect Moldova's wetland regions along the lower Prut and Nistru rivers.

Never heavily industrial, Moldova faces more issues of protection and conservation than pollution. The majority of its 3600 rivers and rivulets were drained, diverted or dammed, threatening ecosystems.

FOOD & DRINK

Hearty meals fit for an explorer are the name of the game here. No point in fussing about calories and arteries – food, as with life itself, is meant to be enjoyed to the full. It's easier to give in, and enjoy…

In Moldova, some Russian influences have seen that pickled fruits and vegetables are popular, as are Russian meals like *pelmeni* (similar to ravioli). A Turkic influence has arguably been strong in Moldova; in the south you may find the delicious Gagauz *sorpa*, a spicy ram soup.

There's no beating about the bush – vegetarians will find their meals limited. Locally grown fresh fruit and veg is always a bonus but expect to find few vegetarian choices. We've pointed them out when we've found them.

In Moldova, outside of Chişinău, where the choice of eateries is astounding, you'll be lucky to find a decent restaurant and will be stuck with hotel dining rooms, bars or cafeterias.

Moldova produces excellent wines and brandies. Red wines are called *negru* and *roşu*, white wine is *vin alb*, while *sec* means dry, *dulce* is sweet and *spumos* translates as sparkling.

CHIŞINĂU

☎ 22 / pop 709,900

This may be the capital of one of Europe's poorest countries, but you'd never know it walking its streets. In Chişinău ('kish-i-*now*' in Moldovan, 'kish-i-*nyov*' in Russian), Mercedes and Jaguars line up outside one fancy restaurant after another, and fashionably dressed youths strut down boutique-lined avenues. The jagged contrast between rich and poor certainly doesn't please the have-nots, but this vibrant, good-natured city is

---

CHIŞINĂU IN TWO DAYS

Forget any attempts at sightseeing. Spend both nights ensconced in Chişinău's legendary nightlife. Eat at the **Beer House** (p481), then sample their home-brew before moving on to cocktails at **Déja Vu** (p481). Dance the night away at **Soho** (p482).

Get a hearty breakfast at **Cactus Café** (p480). Wander through the **National History Museum** (p479) and **National Museum of Fine Arts** (p479) until recovered. Then do it all again until 6am at **Black Elephant** (p481).

so full of *joie de vivre* that it doesn't let it get in the way of what's most important here: having a good time.

First chronicled in 1420, Chişinău became a hotbed of anti-Semitism in the early 20th century; in 1903 the murder of 49 Jews sparked protests from Jewish communities worldwide, and in 1941 the notorious Chişinău pogrom was executed.

Chişinău was the headquarters of the USSR's southwestern military operations during Soviet rule. Between 1944 and 1990 the city was called Kishinev, its Russian name, which is still used by some of the few travel agencies abroad who actually know where it is.

ORIENTATION

Chişinău's street layout is a typically Soviet grid system of straight streets.

The train station is a five-minute walk from the centre on Aleea Gării. Exit the train station, turn right along Aleea Gării to Piaţa Negruzzi, then walk up the hill to Piaţa Libertăţii. From here the main street, B-dul Ştefan cel Mare, crosses the town from southeast to northwest. The city's main sights and parks radiate off this street.

INFORMATION

Bookshops

Cartea Academica (B-dul Ştefan cel Mare 148; 9am-6pm Mon-Sat)
Cartea Universală (; B-dul Ştefan cel Mare 54; 9.30am-8pm)

Cultural Centres

Alliance Française (234 510; Str Sfatul Ţării 18; 10am-6.30pm Tue-Sat) Has a well-equipped *media-thèque* and hosts regular cultural events.

Internet Access

Cave Net (247 467; Str Mitropolit Dosoftei 122; per hr $0.45; 24hr)
Central Telephone Office (B-dul Ştefan cel Mare 65; per hr $0.60; 24hr)

Medical Services

Contact the US embassy (p491) for a list of English-speaking doctors.
Felicia (223 725; B-dul Ştefan cel Mare 62; 24hr) Well-stocked pharmacy.
Hotel National (540 305; B-dul Ştefan cel Mare 4, 4th fl) The emergency suite on the 4th floor provides health care.

Money

There are ATMs all over the centre, in all the hotels and in shopping centres. Currency exchanges are concentrated around the bus and train stations and also along B-dul Ştefan cel Mare.
Eximbank (272 583; B-dul Ştefan cel Mare 6; 9am-5pm Mon-Fri) Can give you cash advances in foreign currency.
Victoriabank (233 065; Str 31 August 1989, 141; 9am-5pm Mon-Fri) Amex's representative in Moldova.

Post

Central post office (227 737; B-dul Ştefan cel Mare 134; 8am-7pm Mon-Sat, to 6pm Sun) There is also a post office on Aleea Gării (8am-8pm).

Telephone

Central telephone office (B-dul Ştefan cel Mare 65; 24hr) Book international calls inside the hall marked 'Convorbiri Telefonice Internaţionale'. Faxes and telegrams can also be sent from here.

Travel Agencies

There's no tourist information centre in Moldova, but there are plenty of agencies where you can get information. Most offer discounted rates in some hotels.
Moldovar Tur (270 488; B-dul Ştefan cel Mare 4; 9am-5pm Mon-Fri) The official state tourist agency can arrange Cricova and other vineyard tours. It can also find you chauffeured cars.
Soleil Tours (271 312; B-dul Negruzzi 5; 9am-6pm Mon-Fri) A very efficient organisation, it can book accommodation and transport tickets but is known for its multiday excursions into remote Moldova, taking in monasteries, places of interests and incorporating rural homestays.

SIGHTS

No one can accuse Chişinău of being overburdened with tourist sights. Lacking in 'must-sees', it's more a pleasant city to wander about in and discover as you go. As it was heavily bombed during WWII, little remains of its historic heart. Still, there are some great museums and parks, and it's fun to see how communist iconography merges with symbols of Moldovan nationalism.

A good place to begin is smack in the centre, where Chişinău's best-known parks diagonally oppose each other, forming two diamonds at the city's core. The highlights here are the Holy Gates (1841), more commonly known as Chişinău's own **Arc de Triomphe**. To its east sprawls **Parcul Catedralei**

MOLDOVA

MOLDOVA

CENTRAL CHIŞINĂU

INFORMATION		
Alliance Francaise	1	B4
American Embassy	2	A5
Antrec	3	A3
Cartea Academica	4	B4
Cartea Universală	5	D5
Cave Net	6	B3
Central Post Office	7	C4
Central Telephone Office	8	D6
Eximbank	9	D6
Felicia	10	D5
French Embassy	11	C5
German Embassy	12	B4
Hungarian Embassy	13	B3
Moldova Tur	(see 40)	
Municipal Clinical		
Emergency Hospital	14	A3
Post Office	15	F6

Romanian Consulate	16	B5
Romanian Embassy	17	C5
Russian Embassy	18	A3
Soleil Tours	19	E6
Turkish Embassy	20	B5
Ukrainian Embassy	21	B3
Victoriabank	22	A3

SIGHTS & ACTIVITIES	(pp477-80)	
Arc de Triomphe	23	C4
Archaeology & Ethnography		
Museum	24	B4
Chişinău History		
Museum	25	A5
Flower Market	26	C4
Government House	27	C4
National Ethnographic &		
Nature Museum	28	A4

National History Museum	29	B4
National Library	30	B4
National Museum		
of Fine Arts	31	B5
Orthodox Cathedral	32	C4
Parliament House	33	B3
Presidential Palace	34	B3
Pushkin Museum	35	C3
Statue of Ştefan cel Mare	36	B4

SLEEPING	(p480)	
Adresa	37	E6
Flowers	38	E6
Hotel Meridien	39	D5
Hotel National	40	E6
Hotel Turist	41	D3
Jolly Alon	42	B4
Mesogios	43	C6

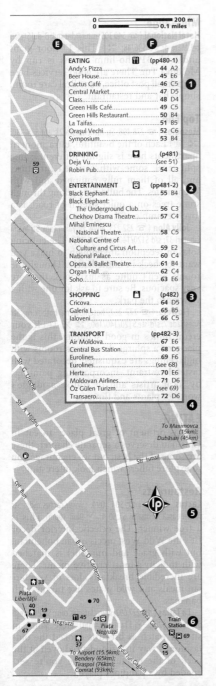

EATING 🍴 (pp480-1)
Andy's Pizza................................44 A2
Beer House..................................45 E6
Cactus Café.................................46 C5
Central Market.............................47 D5
Class...48 D4
Green Hills Café...........................49 C5
Green Hills Restaurant.................50 B4
La Taifas.....................................51 B5
Oraşul Vechi...............................52 C6
Symposium..................................53 B4

DRINKING 🍸 (p481)
Deja Vu..................................(see 51)
Robin Pub....................................54 C3

ENTERTAINMENT 🎭 (pp481-2)
Black Elephant.............................55 B4
Black Elephant:
    The Underground Club...............56 C3
Chekhov Drama Theatre...............57 C4
Mihai Eminescu
    National Theatre.......................58 C5
National Centre of
    Culture and Circus Art..............59 E2
National Palace............................60 C4
Opera & Ballet Theatre.................61 B4
Organ Hall...................................62 C4
Soho..63 E6

SHOPPING 🛍 (p482)
Cricova..64 D5
Galeria L......................................65 B5
Ialoveni.......................................66 C5

TRANSPORT (pp482-3)
Air Moldova.................................67 E6
Central Bus Station......................68 D5
Eurolines.....................................69 F6
Eurolines..................................(see 68)
Hertz...70 E6
Moldovan Airlines.........................71 D6
Öz Gülen Turizm........................(see 69)
Transaero.....................................72 D6

(Cathedral Park), dominated by the city's main **Orthodox Cathedral** with its lovely bell tower (1836). On the northwestern side of the park is a colourful 24-hour **flower market**.

Government House, where cabinet meets, is the gargantuan building opposite the Holy Gates. The parliament convenes in **Parliament House** (B-dul Ştefan cel Mare 123) further north. Opposite this is the **Presidential Palace**.

Grădina Publică Ştefan cel Mare şi Sfînt (Ştefan cel Mare Park) is the city's main strolling, cruising area. The park entrance is guarded by a **statue** (1928) of Ştefan himself; this medieval prince of Moldavia is the greatest symbol of Moldova's strong, brave past.

Museums

The very worthwhile **National History Museum** (☎ 242 194; muzeum@mac.md; Str 31 August 1989, 121A; admission $0.25; 🕙 9am-6pm Tue-Sat) is the grand-daddy of Chişinău's museums. There are archaeological artefacts from Orheiul Vechi, including Golden Horde coins, Soviet-era weaponry and a huge WWII diorama on the 1st floor where you can speak to a man who spent 12 years as a political prisoner at a worker's camp in desolate Vorkuta. A **statue** of Lupoaica Romei (the wolf of Rome) and the abandoned children Romulus and Remus stands in front of the museum. To Moldovans, this is a symbol of their Latin ancestry.

Opposite the **National Library** is the **National Museum of Fine Arts** (Muzeul de Arte Plastice; ☎ 241 730; Str 31 August 1989, 115; adult/child $0.60/0.30; 🕙 10am-6pm Tue-Sun), which has an interesting collection of contemporary European (mostly Romanian and Moldovan) art, folk art, icons and medieval knick-knacks.

The **Archaeology and Ethnography Museum** (☎ 238 307; Str Bănulescu Bodoni 35; admission $0.15; 🕙 10am-6pm Tue-Sat) displays reconstructions of traditional houses from Moldova's different regions and has a colourful exhibition of traditional hand-woven rugs, carpets and wall hangings.

The highlight of the **National Ethnographic and Nature Museum** (☎ 244 002; Str M Kogălniceanu 82; adult/child $1/0.50, English-language guided tour $5; 🕙 10am-6pm Tue-Sun) is a life-size reconstruction of a mammal skeleton which was discovered in the Rezine region in 1966. The museum has some pop art, lots of stuffed animals and exhibits covering the sciences of geology, botany and zoology.

The **Chişinău History Museum** (☎ 241 584; Str Mateevici 60A; admission $0.40; 🕙 10am-6pm Tue-Sun) surveys the city's history from its founding onwards, with archaeological exhibits and photographs; it's a treat mainly to visit the old water tower (1892) it's housed in.

Several blocks northeast of the central parks is the **Pushkin Museum** (☎ 292 685; Str Anton Pann 19; admission $0.40; 🕙 10am-6pm Tue-Sun), housed in a cottage where Russian poet Alexander Pushkin (1799–1837) spent an exiled three years between 1820 and 1823. It was here that he wrote *The Prisoner of the Caucasus* and other classics.

SLEEPING
Budget
Hotel Meridian (☎ 220 428; meridian@moldovacc.md; Str Tighina 42; dm $5-8, s/d $17/30, d with private shower $25, ste $50) This is for true budget-seekers or lovers of exotic locales; it faces the bus station so peaceful it's not, but surprisingly it's clean and pleasant, and staff are very accommodating. The staff will even arrange to pick you up from the train station ($5) or airport ($10 – three times less than what most agencies and hotels charge). All rooms except the dorm rooms have private toilets.

Motel Nord Vest (☎ 759 828; Calea Eşilor 30; s/d $20/25) This pleasant 100-bed motel is 4km northwest of the centre on the main Chişinău–Cojuşna highway. The motel has a tennis court, sauna and excellent restaurant and bar. Microbuses 135 and 136 as well as all buses to Cojuşna stop right in front.

Hotel Turist (☎ 220 637; B-dul Renaşterii 13; s $20-26, d $25, ste $40-130) For a cool blast of the Soviet past, try this friendly place: it overlooks a giant Soviet memorial to communist youth and sports a snazzy socialist mural on its façade. Rooms are comfortable, if slightly kitsch.

Adresa (☎ 544 392; adresa@mdl.net; B-dul Negruzzi 1; apt from $20; 🕙 24hr) This reliable agency offers great alternatives to hotels, renting out one- to three-room apartments throughout the city. It's also a great way to live as the locals do, using rusty elevators or climbing staircases somewhat less than sparkling. Still, they're all safe and clean. Adresa also handles visa registration.

Mid-Range
Hotel Naţional (☎ 540 305; mtur@dnt.md; B-dul Ştefan cel Mare 4; s/d $36/48; 🖳) This 17-floor giant and with 319 ho-hum rooms is run by Moldova Tur. There are good services here like a small post office, a medical care room, shops, bar and restaurant.

Top End
Mesogios (☎ 278 498; Str Armenească 23; apt $75-130; 🖳 🖳) Each of the beautiful, ultra-modern apartments here is slightly different, some split level, some with restored furniture, and all of them fully equipped and with kitchenettes. The building, peeking through some trees on a quiet stretch of road, is a lovely example of Art Nouveau.

Jolly Alon (☎ 232 233; www.jollyalon.com; Str Maria Cibotari 37; s/d $120/140, ste $145-195) The enticing sofas in reception are enough to make you want to check in immediately. Though the rooms aren't quite as luxurious, they are very spacious. Be sure to ask for one with a view onto the park.

Flowers (☎ 277 262; hotelflowers@hotbox.ru; Str Anestiade 7; s/d/ste $120/140/160; 🖳 🖳 🖳) If your credit limit's in good standing, this is the place for a splurge. Enormous rooms with high ceilings are exquisitely decorated with tasteful restraint, incorporating paintings by local artists and of course a jungle's worth of plants and flowers.

EATING
The assortment of great places to eat in Chişinău deserves a separate chapter; these are some of the best, but we encourage you to explore others which look interesting.

Restaurants
Cactus Café (☎ 504 094; www.cactus.md; Str Armenească 41; mains $1.50-4; 🕙 9am-10pm) This is a true winner. The eclectic interior décor (it's the Wild West meets urban bohemian, but with grace and humour) is matched with the city's most creative menu. There are incredible breakfasts, lots of vegetarian meals and wild plates like turkey with bananas.

La Taifas (☎ 227 692; www.lataifas.com; Str Bucureşti 67; mains $2-4; 🕙 11am-midnight) Here you can sit and watch as bread is cooked the old-fashioned way in a wood-fired oven at the back of the restaurant while you're serenaded by a panpipes player.

Green Hills Restaurant (☎ 220 451; Str 31 August 1989, 76; mains $2-4; ☼ 9am-midnight) What it saved on décor, it's passed on to you with the reasonably-priced, excellent food. There's a large, extremely pleasant terrace (where it sells a good selection of foreign-language newspapers!) that's perfect for a sit-down meal of a large selection of meat and vegetable dishes.

Oraşul Vechi (Old City; ☎ 225 063; Str Armenească 24; mains $2-7; ☼ noon-midnight) One of your best bets is this stylish folk restaurant, which doesn't overdo the folk thematic. The speciality is the fish.

Class (☎ 227 774; Str Vasile Alecsandri 121; mains $3-6; ☼ 11am-midnight) One of the country's rare Lebanese restaurants, Class doesn't disappoint with excellent starters, falafel and eggplant dishes. There are water-pipes ($2.50), plus Friday evenings there's exotic dancing and a $10 all-you-can-eat buffet.

Beer House (☎ 756 127; B-dul Negruzzi 6/2; mains $3-6; ☼ 11am-11pm) Of all Chişinău's hot dining places, you'll be returning to this brewery-cum-restaurant again and again – most likely for its four delicious home-brewed beers, but also for its excellent menu, which ranges from chicken wings and soups to rabbit and chicken grilled in cognac. Its relaxed ambience and impeccable service add to the charm.

Symposium (☎ 211 318; Str 31 August 1989, 78; mains $4-8; ☼ 11am-midnight) Though not as expensive as some top-class restaurants in town, this can be called one of the city's top dining experiences in terms of elegance and refinery. The French-style cuisine is succulent, with lamb dishes their speciality.

Cafés

When the sun shines, outdoor cafés sprout like mushrooms. There is a popular terrace outside the Opera & Ballet Theatre (p482). There are also some good outside cafés opposite the main entrance to the university on Str A Mateevici and in the opposite courtyard leading to Parcul Valea Morilor.

Green Hills Café (☎ 220 451; B-dul Ştefan cel Mare 77; ☼ 8.30am-10pm Mon-Sat, from 10am Sun) Though the meals are delicious here, most come here for a quick fix – delicious coffee, cocktails or beer, and of course to people-watch while sitting on the city's main drag.

Quick Eats

For the cheapest of cheap eats, there are some kiosks and small 'cafés' around the bus station and central market, where a dish of mystery meat or meat-filled pastries are less than $1. Most go there for beer and vodka shots.

Andy's Pizza (☎ 508 015; B-dul Ştefan cel Mare 169; mains $2-4; ☼ 10am-11pm) This popular chain has locations all around Chişinău, but this branch is a slick, almost techno-looking pizzeria, and is packed constantly. The thick and gooey pizzas, spaghetti and chicken wings keep clients happily purring.

Self-Catering

Since 1825 the **central market** (Piaţa Centrală; ☼ 7am-5pm) has been the place where Moldovans haggle over prices for fresh produce. It's well worth a visit for its choice of fresh food and lively ambience. It sprawls out around the central bus station on Str Bendery and Str Armeneasca.

DRINKING

Déja Vu (☎ 227 693; Str Bucureşti 67; ☼ 11am-2am) This is a true cocktail bar, where the menu of drinks on offer is tantalising and bartenders twirl glasses with aplomb. There's also a small dining hall serving meals, but most come here to lounge about being fabulous with multicoloured cocktails perched in their hands.

Robin Pub (Str Alexandru cel Bun 83; ☼ 11am-1am) A friendly local-pub feel reigns supreme in this relaxed, tastefully decorated hang-out, an ideal place to forget about the world for hours in a down-to-earth, unpretentious atmosphere.

ENTERTAINMENT

Posters listing 'what's on' are displayed on boards outside the city's various theatres.

Clubs

Chişinău rocks in all directions throughout the nights, but in some of the larger clubs be prepared to walk through metal detectors and deal with tough-guy posturing from goonish doormen.

Black Elephant: The Underground Club (☎ 234 715; Str 31 August 1989, 78a; ☼ 3pm-6am) A highlight of the club scene, this place mainly hosts jazz evenings, but something different goes on here every night. Film projections

MOLDOVA

(often jazz-related) and performances are also on the menu.

Soho (☎ 275 800; B-dul Negruzzi 2/4; ☯ 10pm-4am Tue-Sun) The best disco in town has lots of theme nights, special DJs and the occasional gay night. The crowd is mainly early 20s, though 'middle-aged customers are also welcome'.

Theatre, Opera & Ballet

The **Opera & Ballet Theatre** (☎ 244 163; B-dul Ştefan cel Mare 152; box office ☯ 10am-2pm & 5-7pm) is home to the esteemed national opera and ballet company.

Contemporary Romanian productions can be seen at the **Mihai Eminescu National Theatre** (☎ 221 177; B-dul Ştefan cel Mare 79; box office ☯ 10am-1pm & 3-6pm), founded in 1933, while plays in Russian are performed at the **Chekhov Drama Theatre** (Teatrul Dramatic A Cehov; ☎ 223 362; Str Pârcălab 75), situated where Chişinău's choral synagogue was until WWII.

Various cabarets, musicals and local theatre group productions take place at the **National Palace** (Palatul Naţional; ☎ 213 544; Str Puşkin 21; box office ☯ 11am-5pm).

Live Music

Black Elephant (p481) has nightly jazz music concerts. Classical concerts and organ recitals are held at the **Organ Hall** (Sala cu Orgă; ☎ 225 404; B-dul Ştefan cel Mare 79) next to the Mihai Eminescu National Theatre. Performances start at 6pm and tickets are sold at the box office in the Eminescu theatre.

Moldova's National Philharmonic is based at the **Philharmonic Concert Hall** (☎ 224 505; Str Mitropolit Varlaam 78).

Circus

Itching for the man on the flying trapeze? Head to the loftily titled **National Centre of Culture and Circus Art** (☎ 496 803; B-dul Renaşterii 33; box office ☯ 9am-6pm), across the river. Performances are held at 6.30pm Friday, and noon, 3pm and 6.30pm Saturday and Sunday. Bus No 27 from B-dul Ştefan cel Mare goes there.

Spectator Sports

Moldovans are big football fans and they have two stadiums to prove it. The main **Republic Stadium** (Stadionul Republican), south of the centre, has floodlighting. The main entrance is on Str Ismail with a smaller entrance at the southern end of Str Bucureşti. The entrance to the smaller **Dinamo Stadium** (Stadionul Dinamo) is north of the centre on the corner of Str Bucureşti and Str Lazo. Moldovans like football so much, in fact, there's an American football team called the Chişinău Barbarians, who hold occasional matches, in full gear.

SHOPPING

Cricova (☎ 222 775; B-dul Ştefan cel Mare 126; ☯ 10am-7pm Mon-Fri, to 6pm Sat, to 4pm Sun) The commercial outlet of the Cricova wine factory. It stocks many types of affordable wines and champagnes (only $2 to $5 each), plus the crystal glasses to drink them in.

Ialoveni (B-dul Ştefan cel Mare 128; ☯ 9am-6pm Mon-Fri, 10am-4pm Sat & Sun) This is the outlet for the Ialoveni sherry factory; staff will help you get loaded down with bottles of the good stuff.

Galeria L (☎ 221 975; Str Bucureşti 64; ☯ 10am-7pm Mon-Fri, to 5pm Sat) Holds temporary art exhibitions and sells small works of art and souvenirs crafted by local artists.

GETTING THERE & AWAY

Air

Moldova's only airport is in Chişinău, 14.5km southeast of the centre. It has only international flights.

There are two national airlines. **Moldavian Airlines** (www.mdv.md; Chişinău ☎ 549 339; B-dul Ştefan cel Mare 3; Airport ☎ 525 506) offers 12 weekly flights to Timişoara, and twice daily flights to Budapest, from where it has connections to other European destinations.

Air Moldova (www.airmoldova.md; Chişinău ☎ 546 464; B-dul Negruzzi 8; Airport ☎ 525 506) has direct flights to Amsterdam, Athens, Istanbul, Larnaca, Minsk, Moscow, Paris, Rome, St Petersburg, Sofia, Vienna and Yekaterinburg.

Transaero (www.transaero.md; Chişinău ☎ 542 454; B-dul Ştefan cel Mare 4; Airport ☎ 525 413) has three weekly flights to Amsterdam and Rome, two to Paris and Prague, one or two daily flights to Bucharest, Moscow and Istanbul, twice daily to Budapest, and one daily to Vienna.

Bus

Chişinău has two bus stations. Most buses within Moldova depart from the **central bus station** (Autogară Centrală; ☎ 542 185) on Str Mitropolit Varlaam. Tickets cannot be bought in advance.

MOLDOVA

Buses and microbuses go to Tiraspol and Bendery every 20 to 35 minutes from 6.30am to 6.30pm. Other services include 12 daily buses to Străşeni, and regular buses to Bălţi, Recea, Ediniţa and Briceni. There are buses every half-hour to Orhei. There are at least seven daily buses or microbuses to Bucharest ($14, 12 hours).

Bus services to/from Comrat, Hânceşti and other southern destinations use the less crowded **southwestern bus station** (Autogară Sud-vest; ☎ 723 983), 2km from the city centre on the corner of Şoseaua Hânceşti and Str Spicului. Daily local services include five buses to Comrat ($2.95) in Gagauzia and six to Hânceşti.

Eurolines (☎ 549 813, 271 476; www.eurolines.md) has offices at both the central bus station and the train station, plus regular routes to Italy, Spain and Germany (usually around $140 return) as well as to Moscow, St Petersburg and Minsk.

Buses to Turkey depart from the train station. **Öz Gülen Turizm** (☎ 273 748), also at the train station, runs a daily bus to Istanbul ($34, 6pm).

Train

The **train station** (☎ 252 737; Aleea Gării) has a 24-hour left luggage 100m north of the main entrance alongside the platform.

International routes include three daily trains to Moscow ($36, 27 to 33 hours), 11 to Odesa ($3, five hours), one each to St Petersburg ($42, 37 hours), Bucharest ($26, 14 hours) and Lviv ($7, eight hours) and two a week to Minsk ($29, 25 hours). To get to Budapest, you must change in Bucharest.

Within Moldova, both Odesa-bound and two of the Moscow-bound trains stop at Bendery ($1, two hours) and Tiraspol ($1.50, 2½ hours). There are 11 extra trains to Bendery and 25 to Tiraspol. There are five daily trains to Comrat and four to Ungheni.

GETTING AROUND
To/From the Airport

Bus No 65 departs every 30 minutes between 5am and 10pm from the central bus station to the airport. Microbus No 65 departs every 20 minutes from Str Ismail, near the corner of B-dul Ştefan cel Mare ($0.25).

Bus & Trolleybus

Bus No 45 and microbus No 45a run from the central bus station to the southwestern bus station. Bus No 1 goes from the train station to B-dul Ştefan cel Mare.

Trolleybus Nos 1, 4, 5, 8, 18 and 22 go to the train station from the city centre. Bus Nos 2, 10 and 16 go to the southwestern bus station. Tickets costing $0.15 for buses and $0.10 for trolleybuses are sold at kiosks or direct from the driver.

Most bus routes in town and to many outlying villages are served by nippy microbuses ($0.25 per trip, pay the driver). Route numbers, displayed on the front and side windows, are followed by the letter 'a' or 't'. Those with the letter 'a' follow the same route as the bus of the same number. Those with a letter 't' follow the trolleybus routes. Microbuses run regularly between 6am and midnight.

Car & Motorcycle

Hertz (☎ 274 097; www.hertz.md; Hotel Cosmos, Piaţa Negruzzi 2; ☿ 9am-7pm) A car with driver can be hired for $8 for four hours or $15 for eight hours (plus $0.15 per km), enough to see some sites around Chişinău. Also has a branch at the airport.

There is a 24-hour petrol station, Zimbru, northeast of the central bus station on the corner of Str Sfante Gheorghe and B-dul Avram Iancu.

Taxi

Drivers at official taxi stands often try to rip you off. Calling a **taxi** (☎ 746 565/705/706/707) is cheaper. The official rate is $0.25 per km.

AROUND CHIŞINĂU
Cricova

The grand duke of Moldovan wineries is **Cricova** (☎ 22-441 204; info@cricovawine.md; Str Ungureanu 1; ☿ 8am-4pm) – and it knows it.

Its underground wine kingdom, 15km north of Chişinău in the village if Cricova, is one of Europe's biggest. It boasts 120km of labyrinthine roadways, 60 of which are used for wine storage. These avenues are lined wall-to-wall with bottles. Up to 100m underground, the 'cellars' are kept at a temperature of between 12°C and 14°C, with humidity at 96% to 98% to best protect the 1.25 million bottles of rare and collectable wine plus the 30 million litres of wine the factory produces annually (during Soviet times, the output was two to three times this!). Tunnels have existed here since the 15th century, when limestone was dug out to help build Chişinău. They were converted into an underground wine emporium in the 1950s.

You must have private transport and advance reservations to get into Cricova. It's most easily done through travel agencies in Chişinău but you can call yourself and book a time. Your four-hour tour includes trips down streets with names like Str Cabernet, Str Pinot etc, wine tasting, a light meal and a few complimentary bottles ($27 per person).

Cojuşna

Cricova's competitors operate 12km northwest of Chişinău in the village of Cojuşna.

Cojuşna (☎ 22-744 820, 22-715 329; Str Lomtadze 4; 2-3hr tour per person $17; ☼ 8am-6pm Mon-Fri), founded in 1908, is geared for tourists and is therefore very flexible – it'll open the wine cellars and wine-tasting rooms for you at any hour of any day. The cellars comprise six 'alleys', each 100m long. The wine tasting comes with a full meal, served in an impressive and seductively cosy hall decorated with wooden furniture carved by a local 17-year-old boy and his father.

It is easy to organise your own tour of Cojuşna – you needn't pay exorbitant fees at Chişinău travel agencies – although Cojuşna will need advance warning if you require a tour in English. You can buy wines ($1 to $10 per bottle) from the Cojuşna shop in the complex.

Bus No 2 runs every 15 minutes from Str Vasile Alecsandri in Chişinău towards Cricova; get off at the Cojuşna stop. Ignore the turning on the left marked Cojuşna and walk or hitch the remaining 2km along the main road to the winery entrance, marked by a tall, totem pole–style pillar.

Orhei

☎ 235 / pop 37,500

The modern town of Orhei, not to be confused with Orheiul Vechi, is 45km north of Chişinău. Almost destroyed during WWII, Orhei is a depressed little town with little to offer tourists, but it might be worth a brief detour on the way to or from Orheiul Vechi.

On the main road to Chişinău, 1.5km from Orhei's southern border, lies the supposed **magnetic hill**. Nazis were reputed to have buried Jews alive here, and strange happenings are alleged to occur in the area. Motorists often park right in front of the nearby café, facing the main road, and slip their cars into neutral to see if it still advances, despite it going slightly uphill.

Daily buses depart every half-hour from Chişinău's central bus station to Orhei between 9am and 10pm ($1.20, two hours). All northbound buses from Chişinău stop in Orhei too, including daily buses to Bălţi, Ediniţa and Briceni. From Orhei there is one daily bus at 6am to Orheiul Vechi.

Orheiul Vechi

Ten kilometres southeast of Orhei lies Orheiul Vechi ('Old Orhei', marked on maps as the village of Trebujeni), arguably Moldova's most fantastic sight. It's certainly among its most haunting places.

The **Orheiul Vechi Monastery Complex** (Complexul Muzeistic Orheiul Vechi; ☎ 235-34 242; $0.40; ☼ 9am-5pm Tue-Sun), carved into a massive limestone cliff in this wild, rocky, remote spot, draws visitors from around the globe.

The **Cave Monastery** (Mănăstire în Peşteră), inside a cliff overlooking the gently meandering Răut River, was dug by Orthodox monks in the 13th century. It remained inhabited until the 18th century, and in 1996 a handful of monks returned to this secluded place of worship and are slowly restoring it. You can enter the cave via an entrance on the cliff's plateau.

Ştefan cel Mare built a fortress here in the 14th century but it was later destroyed by Tartars. In the 18th century the cave-church was taken over by villagers from neighbouring Butuceni. In 1905 they built a church above ground dedicated to the Ascension of St Mary. The church was shut down by the Soviets in 1944 and remained abandoned throughout the communist regime. Services resumed in 1996, though it still looks abandoned. Archaeologists have uncovered remnants of a defence wall surrounding the monastery complex from the 15th century.

On the main road to the complex you'll find the headquarters where you purchase your entrance tickets, and where you can also arrange guides and get general information. Shorts are forbidden and women must cover their heads while inside the monastery.

SLEEPING

Antrec-Moldova (☎ 22-237 823; antrec_ong@yahoo.com) Antrec, Romania's rural homestay network, is nascent in Moldova, and should be able to find you a place to stay near Orheiul Vechi for under $10 per person.

GETTING THERE & AWAY

Daily buses depart every half-hour from Chişinău's central bus station to Orhei ($1.20). From Orhei, a bus departs daily for Trebujeni at 6am. Ask to be dropped off by the signposted entrance to the complex. There is a daily afternoon bus (3pm) back to Orhei from Orheiul Vechi. A taxi from Orhei to Orheiul Vechi costs around $6.

Soroca

pop 39,600

Soroca is the Roma 'capital' of Moldova, but people come here to see the outstanding **Soroca fortress** (admission free). Part of a medieval chain of military fortresses built by Moldavian princes between the 14th and 16th centuries to defend Moldavia's boundaries, the fortress was founded by Ştefan cel Mare and rebuilt by his son, Petru Rareş, in 1543–45.

The fortress is administered by the **Soroca Museum of History and Ethnography** (☎ 230-22 264; Str Independentei 68; admission $0.60; 10am-6pm Tue-Sun). This well-designed museum is a real treat; its 25,000 exhibits cover archaeological finds, weapons and ethnographic displays. From Bălţi there are eight daily buses to Soroca; there are buses every half-hour between Bălţi and Chişinău ($2.65).

Lower Dniestr National Park

The Parcul Naţional Nistrul Inferior was set up in recent years by the nonprofit NGO **Biotica** (☎ 22-498 837; www.biotica-moldova.org). Comprising over 50,000 hectares of wetlands, forest and agricultural land, it encompasses some 40 sites of archaeological importance, observation points, many villages and some of Moldova's best vineyards (at Purcari and Tudora for example). Excursions and rural homestays are possible via Biotica. Canoeing, hiking, wine tasting and camping are all possible in this lovely area

Guesthouse **Meşter Faur** (☎ 242-35 259; Str Ştefan cel Mare 100) in the village of Cioburciu offers boat tours, visits to local village enterprises, wine tasting and relaxation galore.

TRANSDNIESTR

pop 633,600

The self-declared republic of Transdniestr (Pridnestrovskaya Moldavskaya Respublika, or PMR in Russian; population 633,600) is one of the world's last surviving bastions of communism. At least that's what most people say.

Transdniestr incorporates a narrow strip of land covering only 3567 sq km on the eastern bank of the Nistru River. It was the scene of a bloody civil war in the early 1990s when the area declared independence from Moldova. Travellers will be stunned by a region which is very much an independent state in all but name. It has its own currency, police force, army and borders, which are controlled by Transdniestran border guards. Western travellers are allowed to travel in the region. Russian is the predominant language. Transdniestrans boycott the Moldovan independence day and celebrate their own independence day on 2 September.

See http://geo.ya.com/travelimages/transdniestr.html for some excellent photos of the region, and www.cbpmr.net for the 'official' account of Transdniestr.

History

Igor Smirnov was elected president of Transdniestr in 1991 following the region's declaration of independence four months prior. Transdniestr insists it's an independent country and a sovereign state within Moldova. Most of the time, it pushes for the creation of a Moldovan federation, with proportionate representation between Moldova, Transdniestr and Gagauzia.

Neither Smirnov's presidency nor the Transdniestran parliament is recognised by the Moldovan – or any other – government. The Russian 14th army, headquartered in Tiraspol since 1956, covertly supplied Transdniestran rebels with weapons during the civil war. The continued presence of the

5000-strong Russian 'operational group' in Transdniestr today is seen by local Russian-speakers as a guarantee of their security.

The Ministry of State Security (MGB), a modern-day KGB, has sweeping powers, and has sponsored the creation of a youth wing, called the Young Guard, for 16- to 23-year-olds.

Alongside a number of agreements between Moldova and Transdniestr since 1991, there have been countless moves by both sides designed to antagonise or punish the other. In 2003 alone Smirnov, reacting to one of his demands being refused by Moldova, slapped exorbitant tariffs on all Moldovan imports, instantly halting trade over the 'border' and making life more difficult for ordinary people on both sides. In September 2003 Smirnov even severed phone connections between the two, so that calls could not be made between the regions.

Smirnov is becoming increasingly disliked and mistrusted by his 'electorate' and few people here believe that slogans and Lenin statues will better their lives in any way. Everyone knows that returning to the USSR is impossible.

Language

The official state languages in Transdniestr are Russian, Moldovan and Ukrainian. Students in schools and universities are taught in Russian, and the local government and most official institutions operate almost solely in Russian. All street signs are written in Russian, Moldovan in the Cyrillic alphabet, and sometimes Ukrainian.

Money

The only legal tender is the Transdniestran rouble (NH). Officially introduced in 1994, it quickly dissolved into an oblivion of zeros. To keep up with inflation, monetary reforms introduced in January 2001 slashed six zeros from the currency, with a new NH1 banknote worth one million roubles in old money. Not surprisingly, hard currency is desperately sought after by most taxi drivers, shopkeepers and market traders, who will gladly accept payment in US dollars.

Post

Transdniestran stamps featuring local hero General Suvorov can only be used for let-

ters sent within the Transdniestran republic and are not recognised anywhere else. For letters to Moldova, Romania and the West, you have to use Moldovan stamps (available here, but less conveniently than in Moldova).

Media

The predominantly Russian Transdniestran TV is broadcast in the republic between 9am and midnight. Transdniestran Radio is on air during the same hours.

The two local newspapers are in Russian. *The Transdniestra* is a purely nationalist affair advocating the virtues of an independent state; *N Pravda* is marginally more liberal.

TIRASPOL

☎ 284 / pop 194,000

Tiraspol (from Greek, meaning 'town on the Nistru' river), 70km east of Chişinău, would be the second-largest city in Moldova if only it weren't the capital of a nonexistent country. Instead, it's no doubt the world's largest open-air museum of Soviet-style communism, only one that's been plunged into capitalism for years. Thus, the have/have-not divide is glaring. The city was founded in 1792 following Russian domination of the region.

Orientation & Information

The train and bus stations are next to each other at the end of ul Lenina. Exit the train station and walk down ul Lenina, past Kirov Park, to ul 25 Oktober (the main street). Ul 25 Oktober, Tiraspol's backbone, is also its commercial strip, with most of the shops and restaurants.

Beltsy (ul 25 Oktober 74; ⊗ 9am-10pm) A well-stocked supermarket and department store which also has an exchange office.

Bunker (pereulok Naberezhnyi 1; per hr $0.40; ⊗ 9am-11pm) A modern Internet club.

Central telephone office (cnr uls 25 Oktober & Kommunisticheskaya; ⊗ 7am-8.45pm) You can buy phonecards ($2.15 or $7.75) to use in the modern pay telephones.

Post office (ul Lenina 17; ⊗ 7.30am-7pm Mon-Fri) Won't be of much use to you unless you want to send postcards to all your friends in Transdniestr (but if you do, be sure to bring your own postcards).

Prisbank (⊗ 8.30am-4.30pm Mon-Sat) Change money at this bank, next door to the central telephone office.

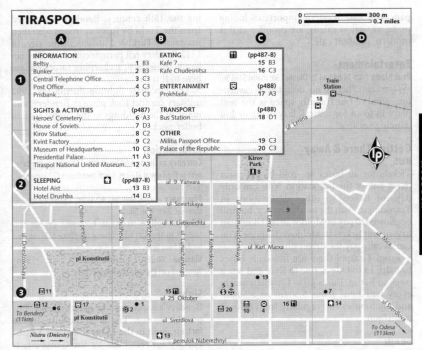

TIRASPOL

INFORMATION	
Beltsy	1 B3
Bunker	2 B3
Central Telephone Office	3 C3
Post Office	4 C3
Prisbank	5 C3

SIGHTS & ACTIVITIES	(p487)
Heroes' Cemetery	6 A3
House of Soviets	7 D3
Kirov Statue	8 C2
Kvint Factory	9 C2
Museum of Headquarters	10 C3
Presidential Palace	11 A3
Tiraspol National United Museum	12 A3

SLEEPING	(pp487-8)
Hotel Aist	13 B3
Hotel Drushba	14 D3

EATING	(pp487-8)
Kafe 7	15 B3
Kafe Chudesnitsa	16 C3

ENTERTAINMENT	(p488)
Prokhlada	17 A3

TRANSPORT	(p488)
Bus Station	18 D1

OTHER	
Militia Passport Office	19 C3
Palace of the Republic	20 C3

MOLDOVA

Sights

At the western end of ul 25 Oktober stands a Soviet armoured tank, from which the Transdniestran flag flies. Behind is the **Heroes' Cemetery** with its Tomb of the Unknown Soldier, flanked by an eternal flame in memory of those who died on 3 March 1992 during the first outbreak of fighting.

The **Tiraspol National United Museum** (ul 25 Oktober 42; admission $0.30; ☎ 9am-5pm Sun-Fri) is the closest the city has to a local history museum, with an exhibit focusing on poet Nikolai Dimitriovich Zelinskogo, who founded the first Soviet school of chemistry. Opposite is the **Presidential Palace**, from which Igor Smirnov rules his miniempire.

The **House of Soviets** (Dom Sovetov), towering over the eastern end of ul 25 Oktober, has Lenin's angry-looking bust peering out from its prime location. Inside is a **memorial** to those who died in the 1992 conflict. Close by is the military-themed **Museum of Headquarters** (ul Kommunisticheskaya 34; admission $0.30; ☎ 9am-5pm Mon-Sat).

The **Kvint factory** (☎ 37 333; www.kvint.com; ul Lenina 38) is one of Transdniestr's pride and joys – since 1897 it's been making some of Moldova's finest brandies.

Further north along ul Lenina, towards the bus and train stations, is **Kirov park**, with a **statue** of the Leningrad boss who was assassinated in 1934, conveniently sparking mass repressions throughout the USSR.

Sleeping & Eating

Hotel Drushba (☎ 34 266; ul 25 Oktober 116; r $9-32) There are several dozen categories of rooms on offer at this massive place that has seen better days. Some have hot water, TV, fridge, larger beds, private bath or shower.

Hotel Aist (☎ 37 174; pereulok Naberezhnyi 3; d $16-27) The grass in the cement cracks outside gives it a derelict feel, but this is a decent hotel. The more expensive rooms have luxuries such as hot water, private toilet and TV.

Kafe Chudesnitsa (ul 25 Oktober; mains $0.05-0.50; ☎ 8am-8pm) This one's a real blast – a true Soviet-style cafeteria with dirt-cheap meals which are bland but hit the spot fine.

Kafe 7 (☎ 32 311; ul 25 Oktober 77; mains $0.35-1.50; ☎ 9am-11pm) A great selection of tasty Russian fast food such as blini (stuffed pancakes) and Western imports including pizza, as well as salads, are on offer at this modern, pleasant café.

Entertainment

Prokhlada (☎ 34 642; ul 25 Oktober 50; mains $1-2.50; 🕙 4pm-6am) There's no doubt this cavernous, sombre but friendly space is the best place in town for a meal, lazy drink or hot dancing session.

Getting There & Away

BUS

Tickets for all buses are sold in the main ticket hall of the bus station. You can only pay for tickets to other destinations in Transdniestr with the local currency, but will be allowed to pay in Moldovan lei/Ukrainian hryvnia for tickets to Moldova/Ukraine. You can usually pay the driver directly also.

From Tiraspol there are five daily buses to Bălți, 13 to Odesa, one to Kyiv and one a week to Berlin. Buses go to Chişinău nearly every half hour from 5.50am to 8.50am, and microbuses run regularly from 6.30am to 6.10pm.

TRAIN

The train station is at the northern end of ul Lenina. Tickets for same-day departures are sold in the main train station ticket hall. Advance tickets (24 hours or more before departure) are sold in the ticket office on the 2nd floor.

Most eastbound trains from Chişinău to Ukraine and Russia stop in Tiraspol. Seven daily trains go to Chişinău ($0.90), three to Odesa ($2), two to Moscow and Minsk and one to St Petersburg.

BENDERY

☎ 282 / pop 133,000

Perhaps due to all the bloodshed in the city's history, Bendery (sometimes called Bender, and previously known as Tighina), on the western banks of the Nistru River, is a decidedly unpleasant town.

During the 16th century, Moldavian prince Ştefan cel Mare built a large defensive fortress here on the ruins of a fortified Roman camp. In 1538 the Ottoman sultan, Suleiman the Magnificent, conquered the fortress and transformed it into a Turkish *raia* (colony), renaming the city Bendery, meaning 'belonging to the Turks'. Dur-

ing the 18th century, Bendery was seized from the Turks by Russian troops who then massacred Turkish Muslims in the city. In 1812 Bendery fell permanently into Russian hands. Russian peacekeeping forces remain here to this day.

The bloodiest fighting during the 1992 military conflict took place in Bendery, and many of the buildings in the centre remain bullet-pocked.

Information

Currency exchange (ul Sovetskaya) Change money here, next to the Central Market. Local microbuses (70 kopeks) leave from here.

Pharmacy (cnr uls Suvorova & S Liazo; 🕙 8am-8pm Mon-Sat, 8am-4pm Sun)

Telephone office (cnr uls Liazo & Suvorova; 🕙 8am-6pm Mon-Fri, to 4pm Sat) International telephone calls can be booked from here.

Vlasana (☎ 29 477; ul Lenina 29; per hr $0.25; 🕙 9am-9pm) You can log onto the Internet here

Sights

Bendery's main sight is, paradoxically, impossible to see. The great Turkish **Tighina fortress**, built in the 1530s to replace a 12th-century fortress built by the Genovese, is now being used by the Transdniestran military as a training ground and is strictly off-limits. The best view of it is from the bridge going towards Tiraspol. At the entrance to the city, close to the famous **Bendery–Tiraspol bridge**, is a **memorial park** dedicated to local 1992 war victims. An eternal flame burns in front of an armoured **tank**, from which flies the Transdniestran flag. Haunting **memorials** to those shot dead during the civil war are evident throughout many of the main streets in the centre.

Sleeping & Eating

A three-tier pricing system is intact here, with prices for locals; Moldovans, Ukrainians and Belarusians; and all other foreigners.

Hotel Dniestr (☎ 29 478; ul Katachenka 10; s/d $9/23) Pricier doubles have hot water, TV and fridge. There's an adjacent restaurant and terrace café.

Café (cnr uls Kalinina & Lenina; mains $1-2; 🕙 9am-11pm) Located in the park across from the department store, this small restaurant has a popular, pleasant terrace where grilled-meat dishes are the favourite. It also doubles as a hang-out and bar.

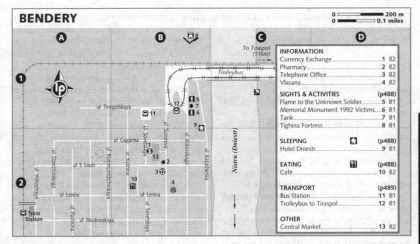

BENDERY

0 ————— 200 m
0 ————— 0.1 miles

To Tiraspol
(11km)

Trolleybus

Nistru (Dniestr)

ul Tiraspolskaya

ul Gagarina

ul Dzerzhinskogo

ul S Lazo

ul Voczanaya

ul Lenina

ul Moskovskaya

ul Pushkina

Train Station

ul Suvorova

ul Kotovskogo

ul Katuchenka

ul Lenina

ul Sovetskaya

INFORMATION	
Currency Exchange	1 B2
Pharmacy	2 B2
Telephone Office	3 B2
Vlasana	4 B2
SIGHTS & ACTIVITIES	(p488)
Flame to the Unknown Soldier	5 B1
Memorial Monument 1992 Victims	6 B1
Tank	7 B1
Tighina Fortress	8 B1
SLEEPING	(p488)
Hotel Dniestr	9 B1
EATING	(p488)
Café	10 B2
TRANSPORT	(p489)
Bus Station	11 B1
Trolleybus to Tiraspol	12 B1
OTHER	
Central Market	13 B2

MOLDOVA

Getting There & Away

The train station is at Privokzalnaya pl. There are at least 15 daily trains to Chişinău, including ones coming from Moscow and Odesa. There are buses and microbuses every half-hour or so to Chişinău, and two daily to Comrat.

Trolleybus No 19 for Tiraspol ($0.10) departs from the bus stop next to the main roundabout at the entrance to Bendery; microbuses also regularly make the 20-minute journey trip ($0.15). There are two daily buses to Odesa and one to Kyiv.

GAGAUZIA

pop 169,300

Gagauzia (Gagauz Yeri) is a self-governed republic covering 3000 sq km in southern Moldova. It has its own legislature, which is autonomous in regional affairs. On a national level, Gagauzia is represented by the assembly's elected *başkan* (head), who is a member of the Gagauz Halki political party and holds a safe seat in the Moldovan parliament.

Comrat is Gagauzia's capital. The republic is divided into three districts – Ceadăr-Linga, Comrat and Vulcăneşti. Wedged between these last two is the predominantly Bulgarian-populated district of Taraclia, which is not part of Gagauzia. Gagauz territory is further broken up by three Bulgarian villages in Ceadăr-Linga

and a predominantly Moldovan village in Comrat district, all of which are part of 'mainland' Moldova too.

The Gagauz are a Turkic-speaking, Christian ethnic minority whose Muslim antecedents fled the Russo-Turkish wars during the 18th century. They were permitted to settle in the region in exchange for their conversion to Christianity. The language is a dialect of Turkish, with vocabulary influenced by Russian Orthodoxy, as opposed to the Islamic influences that are inherent in Turkish. Unlike Moldovans, Gagauz lay no claim to any Latin roots or influences, but rather look to Turkey for cultural inspiration and heritage.

The republic has its own flag, police force, weekly journals, and university, partly funded by the Turkish government. Students are taught in Gagauzi, Moldovan and Russian – the official languages of the republic.

Gagauz autonomy was officially recognised by the Moldovan government in December 1994. Unlike the more militant separatists in Transdniestr, the Gagauz forfeited independence in preference for large-scale autonomy. Theirs is a predominantly agricultural region with little industry to sustain an independent economy.

COMRAT

☎ 298 / **pop 32,000**

Gagauzia's capital, 92km south of Chişinău, is no more than a dusty, provincial town. In 1990 it was the scene of clashes between

Gagauz nationalists and Moldovan armed forces, pre-empted by calls from local leaders for the Moldovan government to hold a referendum on the issue of Gagauz sovereignty.

Most street signs are in Russian; some older ones are in Gagauzi but in the Cyrillic script. Since 1989 Gagauzi has used the Latin alphabet.

From the bus station, walk south along the main street, Str Pobedy, past the market to pl Pobedy (Victory Sq). St John's Church stands on the western side of the square, behind which lies the central park. Pr Lenina runs parallel to Str Pobedy, west of the park.

Change money at the **Moldovan Agrobank** (Str Pobedy 52; ☾ 8am-2pm Mon-Fri). A small currency exchange is inside the entrance to the market. You can make international calls at the **post office** (Str Pobedy 55; ☾ 8am-6pm Mon-Fri, to 5pm Sat). Surf the web at **IATP** (☎ 25 875; Str Lenina 160; per hr $0.40; ☾ 9am-6pm Mon-Fri).

The regional **başkani** (assembly) is on pr Lenina. The Gagauzi and Moldovan flags fly from the roof.

Next to the assembly is the **Gagauz Culture House**, in front of which stands a statue of Lenin. West of pr Lenina at Str Galatsăna 17 is the **Gagauz University** (Komrat Devlet Üniversitesi), founded in 1990. Four faculties (national culture, agronomy, economics and law) serve 1500 students who learn in Russian and Gagauz. The main foreign languages taught are Romanian, English and Turkish.

On the eastern side of pl Pobedy is fairly modern **Hotel Aina** (☎ 22 572; Str Pobedy 127A; s/d $11/16). Its bar serves light meals, including delicious *şaşlik* and salads. The café/bar **Eugenia** (☎ 24 968; Str Pobedy 52; mains $1-3; ☾ 9am-midnight) isn't a bad place to grab a meal or hang out for a few drinks.

Getting There & Away

There are five daily return buses from Chişinău to Comrat ($2.95). From Comrat there are two buses daily via Bendery to Tiraspol, and one only as far as Bendery.

MOLDOVA DIRECTORY

ACCOMMODATION

Chişinău has a good range of hotels. Most towns have small hotels that have survived

from communist days. Basic singles or doubles with a shared bathroom cost €25 to €40 per room in Chişinău, but outside the capitals singles will usually be €15 to €25 and doubles €20 to €30.

You will be asked to briefly present your passport upon registration; they may keep it for several hours in order to register it.

Camping grounds *(popas turistic)* are practically nonexistent in Moldova. The good news is that wild camping is allowed anywhere unless otherwise prohibited.

In Moldova, the branch of the agro-tourism association **Antrec** (☎ 22-237 823; antrec_ong@yahoo.com; Str Serghei Lazo 13, Chişinău) is helpful, but their choices of places to stay is so far small – the idea of rural homestays in Moldova is in its infancy.

There are no hostels in Moldova.

BUSINESS HOURS

Banks can be expected to open from 9am to 3pm, with many closing for an hour around noon; most shops are open from 9am or 10am to 6pm or 7pm, some closing on Sundays; museums are usually open from 11am to 5pm, with most closing on Monday; post offices are open from 8am to 7pm Monday to Friday, until 4pm Saturday and closed Sunday; restaurants can be expected to stay open until at least 11pm nightly. Theatrical performances and concerts usually begin at 7pm.

CUSTOMS

Moldova has complicated customs procedures (Soviet legacies die slowly), but generally there should be little problem bringing whatever you like in and out of the country. See www.turism.md for the latest information on customs regulations.

There is no limit to the amount of foreign currency you can bring in or out of the country, but the amount must be declared upon entering on a customs declaration sheet you'll be given, and then again upon exiting the country; purportedly, this is to ensure you do not leave with more money than you arrived with. You might be asked to prove that you have at least $30 for each day of your stay.

You're allowed to cross the border either way with 1l of alcohol, 2l of beer and up to 200 cigarettes, though these rules are not strictly enforced. Visit the **customs office**

(☎ 22-569 460; Str Columna 65) in Chişinău for official permission to take antiques or large art pieces out of the country.

EMBASSIES & CONSULATES
Moldovan Embassies & Consulates
Moldova has embassies and consulates worldwide.

France (☎ 01 40 67 11 20; ambassade.moldavie@free.fr; 1 rue Sfax, Paris)

Germany (☎ 069-52 78 08; mongenmold@aol.com; Adelheidstrasse nr. 8, Frankfurt)

Romania (☎ 01-230 0474; moldova@customers.digiro.net; Aleea Alexandru 40, Bucharest) Consulate: (☎ 01-410 9827; B-dul Eroilor 8, Sector 5, Bucharest)

Russia (☎ 095-924 5353; moldebassy@online.ru; 18 Kuznetskii most, Moscow)

Turkey (☎ 312-446 5527; ambmold@superonline.com; Kaptanpasa Sok 49, Ankara)

Ukraine (☎ 044-290 7721; moldoukr@sovamua.com; ul Kutuzov 8, Kyiv)

USA (☎ 202-667 1130; embassyofmoldova@mcihispeed .net; 2101 S Street NW, Washington, DC)

Embassies & Consulates in Moldova
Countries with embassies or consulates in Chişinău include:

France (☎ 22-228 204; www.ambafrance.md; Str 31 August 1989, 101A)

Germany (☎ 22-234 607; www.ambasada-germana .org.md; Str Maria Cibotari 35)

Romania (☎ 22-228 126; ambrom@ch.moldpac.md; Str Bucureşti 66/1) Consulate: (☎ 22-237 622; Str Vlaicu Pircalab 39)

Russia (☎ 22-234 941; www.moldova.mid.ru; B-dul Ştefan cel Mare 153)

Turkey (☎ 22-242 608; tremb@moldova.md; Str V Cupcea 60)

UK (☎ 22-238 991; www.britishembassy.md; Str Bănulescu Bodoni 57/1)

Ukraine (☎ 22-582 124; www.mfa.gov.ua; Str V Lupu 17)

USA (☎ 22-233 772; www.usembassy.md; Str A Mateevici 103A)

FESTIVALS & EVENTS
Moldova is not a festival-heavy country, perhaps as its citizens find any excuse to party anytime throughout the year. Their major festival is the **Wine Festival** on the second Sunday in October (and for several wine-drenched days preceding and following it). The government has even instituted a visa-free regime for this period. Chişinău's **City Day** is 14 October.

HOLIDAYS
National holidays celebrated in Moldova include:

New Year's Day 1 January
Orthodox Christmas 7 January
International Women's Day 8 March
Orthodox Easter March/April/May
Victory (1945) Day 9 May
Independence Day 27 August
National Language Day 31 August

Transdniestrans boycott the Moldovan independence day and celebrate their own independence day on 2 September.

MONEY
Moldovan lei come in denominations of 1, 5, 10, 20, 50, 100, 200 and 500 lei. There are coins for 1, 5, 10, 25 and 50 bani (there are 100 bani in a leu).

Note that the breakaway Transdniestran republic has its own currency, which is useless anywhere else in the world (see p486).

It's easy to find ATMs in Chişinău, but not in other towns in Moldova. Eximbank will cash travellers cheques and give cash advances on major credit cards. It is almost impossible to use travellers cheques in stores or restaurants. While credit cards won't get you anywhere in rural areas, they are widely accepted in larger department stores, hotels and most restaurants in cities and towns. In Moldova, prices are often quoted in US dollars, and so that's what we've quoted costs in in this chapter.

POST
From Moldova, it costs $0.35 to send a postcard or letter under 20g to Western Europe, Australia and the USA.

DHL (www.dhl.com) is the most popular international courier service in the region. It has offices in Chişinău and Tiraspol. See the website for details.

TELEPHONE
Moldtelecom, the wonderfully named, state-run telephone company, sells pay cards which can be used to dial any number within Moldova only, for $2.25 or $3. These are sold at any telephone centre in the country. To make an international call using a prepaid card, you need to use a private company like Treitelecom. Their

MOLDOVA

cards are sold for from $3.75 to $35 at any Moldpressa newspaper stand (and can be used to make local calls too).

Mobile phone service in Moldova is provided by Chişinău-based Moldcell (run by Moldtelecom) and **Voxtel** (☎ 22-575 757; www .voxtel.md; Str Alba Iulia 75).

EMERGENCY SERVICES

- Fire ☎ 901
- Police ☎ 902
- Ambulance ☎ 903

VISAS

To obtain a visa, citizens of the EU, Canada, USA and Israel need only present their passports (valid for six months after the visa's expiration date) and one photo to the nearest Moldovan consulate. All others require either a tourist voucher from an accredited travel agency or an invitation from a company, organisation or individual (difficult to get). Tourist vouchers ensure that you have a hotel prebooked and prepaid. Payments to the consulates are usually in the form of a bank deposit at a specified bank.

Citizens of the EU, Japan, USA or Canada can buy visas on arrival at Chişinău airport or the three border points Sculeni (north of Iaşi), Leuşeni (main Bucharest–Chişinău border) and Cahul if arriving by bus or car from Romania. No invitation is required, but you may be asked to prove that you have at least $30 per day for each day you plan on being in the country. Citizens of countries normally requiring an invitation must present one at the border if buying a visa there.

However, in 2002 Moldova generously started instituting a visa-free regime for all foreigners wishing to partake in their Wine Festival (2nd Sunday in October). The visa can last for 10 days.

An HIV/AIDS test is required for foreigners intending to stay in Moldova longer than three months. Certificates proving HIV-negative status have to be in Russian and English.

See www.moldovavisa.com, or www.tu rism.md/eng/content/66 to check for the latest changes in the visa regime.

Costs & Registration

The price of a single/double-entry tourist visa valid for one month is US$60/75. Single/double-entry transit visas valid for 72 hours are $30/60. Special rates apply for tourist groups of more than 10 persons, and for children, the handicapped and the elderly.

Visas can be processed within a day at the **Moldovan consulate** (☎ 40-21-410 9827; B-dul Eroilor 8, Bucharest) in Romania. Applications must be made between 8.30am and 12.30pm weekdays. After paying for the visa at a specified bank in the city centre, you then collect your visa between 3pm and 4pm the same day.

Anyone staying longer than three days must have their visa registered by the local police. While this is an unfortunate Soviet holdover (and a good way of generating income), it's actually a simple process which is automatically done at hotels and apartment rental firms. If you need to do it yourself, call the **Office for Visas and Registration** (☎ 22-213 078) to find out where to register; you're liable for a fine on the way out if you fail to register.

TRANSPORT

GETTING THERE & AWAY

As a result of the Soviet legacy, travellers may experience some questioning or minor hassle on entering Moldova, but, thanks to the same legacy, any potential complication is easy to resolve on the spot – most often by offering a few dollars. Moldovan border guards are generally friendly and down-to-earth, although they may be curious about you as they see few foreign tourists.

Air

Moldova's only main airport is **Chişinău International** (☎ 22-526 060). **Voiaj Travel** (www .voiaj.md) in Chişinău publishes the latest airport schedules.

These airlines fly to and from Moldova:

Air Moldova (code 9U; ☎ 21-312 1258; www.airmoldova.md)
Austrian Airlines (code OS; ☎ 22-244 083; www .austrianair.com)
Moldavian Airlines (code 2M; www.mdv.md; Chişinău)
Tarom Romanian Air Transport (code RO; ☎ 0992 541 254; www.tarom.ro)
Transaero (code UN; ☎ 542 454; www.transaero.md)
Turkish Airlines (code TK; ☎ 22-527 078; www .turkishairlines.com)

Together, Air Moldova and Tarom operate daily flights between Chişinău and Bucharest, and Transaero also has flights on that route. Air Moldova also has daily flights to Timişoara.

Chişinău is connected with regular flights to and from Sofia, Minsk, Moscow, Budapest and Prague. Expect to pay about €200 to €350 for a return flight between Chişinău and any of these capitals.

While most of Moldova's international flights are eastward, Air Moldova has services to Vienna daily, four times a week to Rome, three times a week each to Athens and Amsterdam and twice a week to Paris.

Land

BUS

Moldova is well linked by bus lines to Central and Western Europe as well as Turkey. While not as comfortable as the train, buses tend to be faster, though not always cheaper.

Eurolines (www.eurolines.md) has a flurry of buses linking Moldova with Western Europe.

There's a daily bus between Chişinău and Istanbul in a modern coach, with air conditioning and refreshments.

Buses between Chişinău and Kyiv or Odesa run through Transdniestr and Tiraspol; even with a Moldovan visa, local authorities are likely to make you pay for an additional transit permit.

CAR & MOTORCYCLE

The Green Card (a routine extension of domestic motor insurance to cover most European countries) is valid in Moldova. Extra insurances can be bought at the borders.

TRAIN

From Chişinău, there are 11 daily trains to Odesa, one to Lviv and three to Moscow. Westbound, there are nightly trains to Romania and beyond.

There's an overnight service between Bucharest and Chişinău; at 12 hours, the journey is longer than taking a bus or microbus (the train heads north to Iaşi, then south again), but is more comfortable if you want to sleep.

GETTING AROUND

Bicycle

Moldova is flat as a board, making cycling an excellent way of getting around. That is, it would be if it weren't for the bad condition of most of the roads, and for the lack of infrastructure – outside of Chişinău, you'll have to rely on your own resources or sense of adventure (and trying to enlist help from friendly locals) if you run into mechanical trouble.

Bus & Microbus

Moldova has a good network of buses running to most towns and villages. Microbuses, which follow the same routes as the buses, are quicker and more reliable.

Car & Motorcycle

It is now possible for foreigners to hire and drive a car in Moldova. In Chişinău, travel agencies can arrange car rental (see p477).

Be wary, however, as the roads are in poor condition. EU driving licences are accepted here; otherwise, bring both your home country's driver's licence and the International Driver's Permit, which is recognised in Moldova.

MOLDOVA

DIVINE COMMUNICATION

When Mircea Cerari, the king of Moldova's Roma community, died at the age of 59 in July 1998, it was not his death but his entrance into the afterlife that raised eyebrows. Determined to keep in contact with loved ones from beyond the grave, the king had made arrangements to be buried with his computer, fax and mobile phone.

The lavish funeral, held in Soroca in northern Moldova two weeks after his death, was attended by some 15,000 Roma who had gathered from the far reaches of Europe to pay their respects. Also in attendance was Mircea Cerari's son Arthur, who has since inherited Moldova's Roma crown.

The king's impressive white marble grave contained not only his communication equipment but also a bar stocked with – what else? – vodka!

Arthur is also now the main representative for the **Cultural Society of Roma of Moldova** (☎ 22-229 975) in Chişinău.

The intercity speed limit is 90km and in built-up areas 60km; the legal blood alcohol limit is 0.03%. For road rescue, dial ☎ 901. The **Automobile Club Moldova** (ACM; ☎ 22-292 703; www.acm.md) can inform you of all regulations and offer emergency assistance (this is a members-only sevice).

Local Transport
In Moldova, buses cost about $0.10, trolley-buses $0.05 and city microbuses $0.20.

Taxi
In Moldova, there are official metered taxis, but following the handy Russian-style practice of waving a private car down for a 'ride' with someone who just happens to be going your way (for a fee!) is the more common way of getting lifts. With both, you'll often need to agree upon a price before driving off; a drive to anywhere inside Chişinău is unlikely to cost more than $3. The going rate is about $0.10 to $0.15 per km.

Poland

CONTENTS

Highlights	497	Great Masurian Lakes	561
Itineraries	497	**Poland Directory**	**564**
Climate & When To Go	497	Accommodation	564
History	497	Activities	565
People	499	Books	565
Religion	499	Business Hours	566
Arts	500	Dangers & Annoyances	566
Environment	500	Disabled Travellers	566
Food & Drink	501	Embassies & Consulates	566
Warsaw	**502**	Festivals & Events	567
History	502	Gay & Lesbian Travellers	567
Orientation	503	Holidays	567
Information	503	Internet Resources	567
Sights	504	Media	567
Sleeping	508	Money	568
Eating	509	Post	568
Drinking	**511**	Telephone	568
Entertainment	511	Visas	569
Shopping	511	**Transport in Poland**	**569**
Getting There & Away	512	Getting There & Away	569
Getting Around	513	Getting Around	570
Mazovia & Podlasie	**513**		
Łódź	514		
Białowieża National Park	514		
Małopolska	**515**		
Kraków	515		
Oświęcim	524		
Częstochowa	525		
Zakopane	526		
Tatra Mountains	529		
Dunajec Gorge	531		
Sanok	531		
Przemyśl	531		
Lublin	532		
Zamość	536		
Silesia	**538**		
Wrocław	538		
Sudeten Mountains	542		
Wielkopolska	**542**		
Poznań	542		
Pomerania	**547**		
Toruń	547		
Gdańsk	550		
Szczecin	558		
Warmia & Masuria	**559**		
Olsztyn	559		
Frombork	561		
Elbląg–Ostróda Canal	561		

POLAND

Stretching from the Baltic Sea to the Carpathian Mountains, Poland is a big country with a wide variety of landscapes and an ever-present sense of history. Centuries of war, foreign occupation and oppression failed to dampen the Poles' strong sense of nationhood, perhaps best exemplified by the ancient royal capital of Kraków, with its peerless castle, and the painstakingly restored Old Town in Warsaw, which had been bombed to dust and rubble by the end of WWII. Since the demise of communism, Poland has quickly modernised, reacquainting itself with capitalism, and its bustling cities, such as cosmopolitan Gdańsk and cultured Wrocław, are the antithesis of the old image of Eastern-Bloc greyness.

Poland's relatively undeveloped coastline, with its attractive, sandy beaches, and the rugged mountains of the south are sure to delight visitors, and there are plenty of off-the-beaten-track destinations to discover, from picturesque mountain villages seemingly lost in time to big towns where foreigners are still a rare sight.

Poland is still cheap by Western European standards, and represents excellent value for budget travellers. Prices are rising, though, a trend which is sure to continue apace now that Poland has joined the EU. On the upside, travelling here is easier than ever, and finally visa-free for many nationalities, making now the perfect time to visit.

POLAND

FAST FACTS

- **Area** 312, 685 sq km
- **Capital** Warsaw
- **Currency** złoty; €1=4.31zł; US$1=3.42zł; UK£1=6.22zł; A$1=2.52zł; ¥100=3.17zł; NZ$1=2.37zł
- **Famous for** Chopin, Joseph Conrad, Solidarity, Vodka
- **Key Phrases** *dzień dobry* (good morning /afternoon); *dziękuję* (thank you); *proszę* (please); *Gdje yest dworzec autobusowy /kolejowy?* (Where's the bus/train station?)
- **Official Language** Polish
- **Population** 39 million
- **Telephone Codes** country code ☎ 48; international access code ☎ 00
- **Visas** not required for EU citizens; US, Canadian, New Zealand and Australian citizens do not need visas for stays of less than 90 days.

HIGHLIGHTS

- Explore the rich history of Poland at Kraków's **Wawel Castle** (p517)
- Absorb the cosmopolitan atmosphere of **Gdańsk** (p550) and take a short trip to the seaside at **Sopot** (p556)
- Go hiking, skiing or just take in the spectacular views in the **Tatra Mountains** (p529)
- Take time some out and amble through Wrocław's charming **Botanic Gardens** (p540)
- Explore Warsaw's meticulously rebuilt **Old Town** (p504), visiting the grand Royal Palace and the amazing Old Town Square

ITINERARIES

- **One Week** Spend a couple of days exploring Warsaw with a tour round the Old Town and a visit to the Royal Castle, Warsaw Historical Museum and National Museum. On the third day, head to Kraków for a couple of days and then on to Zakopane for two days.
- **Two Weeks** Follow the above itinerary then on the eighth day go to Wrocław for two days. Head north and spend a day in Toruń before heading to Gdańsk and a relaxing couple of days at the seaside in Sopot.

CLIMATE & WHEN TO GO

Poland has a moderate continental climate with considerable maritime influence along the Baltic coast. As a result, the weather can be unpredictable. Summer is usually warm and sunny, with July the hottest month, but it's the season with the highest rainfall. Spring and autumn are pleasantly warm but can also be rainy. You can expect snow anywhere in Poland between December and March, lingering until April or even May in the mountains.

The tourist season runs roughly from May to September and peaks in July and August. Many Poles – and their children – go on holidays during these two months, so transport is crowded and accommodation is often limited. Most theatres and concert halls are also closed at this time.

The best time to visit Poland is either spring (late April to late June) or early autumn (September to mid-October). These periods are pleasantly warm and ideal for

HOW MUCH?

- **Night in a hostel** 40zł
- **Night in a mid-range double room** 150zł
- **Three-course restaurant meal for two** 90zł
- **Postcard** 2zł
- **Postage stamp** 2.10zł

LONELY PLANET INDEX

- **Litre of petrol** 3.50zł
- **Litre of water** 1.5zł
- **Beer** 4-5zł
- **Souvenir T-shirt** 30zł
- **Street snack (pierogi)** 8-10zł

general sightseeing and outdoor activities. Many cultural events still take place in both periods.

Mid-autumn to mid-spring is colder, darker and perhaps less attractive for most visitors. However, it's not a bad time to visit city sights and enjoy the cultural life. Except for skiing (from December to March), outdoor activities are less prominent in this period and many camping grounds and youth hostels are closed. See Climate Charts, p874, for more information.

HISTORY

During the early Middle Ages, Western Slavs moved into the flatlands between the Vistula and Odra Rivers, and became known as Polanians, or 'people of the plains'. In 966 Mieszko I, Duke of the Polanians, adopted Christianity and embarked on a campaign of conquest; by the time of his death in 992, the boundaries of the Polish state were roughly the same as today. Mieszko's son Bolesław Chrobry (Boleslaus the Brave) was crowned Poland's first king by a papal edict in 1025.

Poland's early success proved short-lived. German encroachment led to the relocation of the royal capital from Poznań to Kraków in 1038, and the rapaciousness of the nobles divided the realm. More trouble loomed in 1226 when the Prince of Mazovia invited a band of Germanic crusaders to help convert

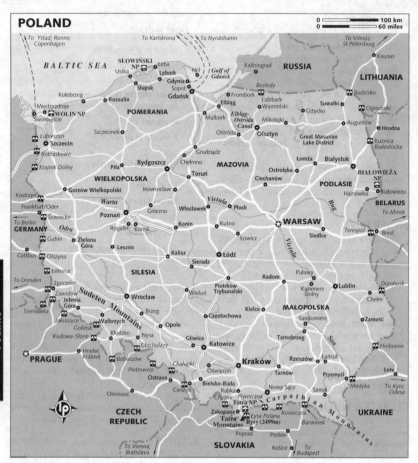

POLAND

the pagan tribes still living in the north. Subsequently, the Teutonic Knights quickly set up their own state along the Baltic coast, and the pagans and Poles were harshly dealt with. The south had its own problems to contend with as marauding Tatars overran Kraków twice in the mid-13th century.

The kingdom was finally reconstituted under Kazimierz III 'the Great' (1333–1370). Scores of new towns sprang up, while Kraków blossomed into one of Europe's leading cultural centres.

When the daughter of Kazimierz's nephew married the Grand Duke of Lithuania, Jagiełło, Poland and Lithuania were united, and came to form the largest state in Europe, stretching from the Baltic to the Black Sea.

During the 16th century, the enlightened King Zygmunt I ushered in the Renaissance, lavishly patronising the arts and sciences. Nicolaus Copernicus was busy revolutionising the field of astronomy and, in so doing, reordering the cosmos. In 1569 Poland and Lithuania formally merged into a single state, with Poland acting as senior partner, and both countries remained politically entwined until the late 18th century.

Throughout the 17th century, Poland was subject to Swedish and Russian invasions, and in 1773 Russia, Prussia and Austria carved up Polish territory between them in the First Partition; two more partitions followed, and in 1795 Poland disappeared completely from the map of Europe.

The Poles never surrendered their sense of nationhood, but they had to wait until the end of WWI and the subsequent break-up of the old imperial powers to see a sovereign Polish state restored. Very soon, however, Poland was again at war. Under the command of Marshal Jozef Piłsudski, Poland sought to reclaim its eastern territories from long-time nemesis Russia, now under the Bolsheviks. After two years of inconclusive fighting, the exhausted combatants agreed on a compromise, which returned Vilnius and Lviv to Poland.

Poland once again became a savage battleground between its more powerful neighbours, this time the Nazis and the Soviets, in WWII. On 1 September 1939, a Nazi blitzkrieg poured down on the Polish city of Gdańsk and Hitler was to use Poland as a headquarters and staging ground for the Nazi offensive against the Soviet Union. Six million Polish inhabitants died during WWII; the country's three million Jews were brutally annihilated in death camps. Poland's borders were redrawn yet again. The Soviet Union claimed the eastern territories and extended the western boundary at the expense of Germany. These border changes were accompanied by the forced resettlement of more than a million Poles, Germans and Ukrainians.

After WWII, Poland endured four decades of Soviet-dominated communist rule, punctuated by waves of protests, most notably the paralysing strikes of 1980–81, led by the Solidarity trade union. Finally, in open elections of 1989, the communists fell from power and in 1990 Solidarity leader Lech Wałęsa became Poland's first democratically elected president.

The postcommunist transition brought radical changes, which induced new social hardships and political crises. But within a decade Poland had built the foundations for a market economy, and reoriented its foreign relations towards the West. In March 1999, Poland was granted full NATO membership and joined the EU in May 2004, though only 20% of Polish voters turned out for the subsequent elections to the European parliament.

PEOPLE

Poland was for centuries a multinational country and home to large Jewish, German and Ukrainian communities. However, because of the ethnic cleansing and forced resettlements which followed WWII, Poland became an ethnically homogeneous country – about 98% of the population are now Poles. Poland's Jewish population once numbered more than three million but today it's between 5000 and 10,000.

Over 60% of the citizens live in towns and cities. Warsaw is by far the largest city, followed by Łódź, Kraków, Wrocław, Poznań and Gdańsk. Upper Silesia (around Katowice) is the most densely inhabited area while the northeastern border regions remain the least populated.

Between five and 10 million Poles live outside Poland. This émigré community, known as 'Polonia', is located mainly in the USA (particularly Chicago).

Poles are friendly and polite, but not overly formal. The way of life in large urban centres increasingly mimics Western styles and manners. In the countryside, however, a more conservative culture dominates, evidenced by traditional gender roles and strong family ties. Away from the big urban centres, foreigners, especially those with darker skins, may still attract stares, while open displays of affection between same-sex couples are likely to meet a hostile response. In both urban and rural settings, Poles are devoutly religious.

The Poles' sense of personal space may be a bit cosier than you are accustomed to – you may notice this trait when queuing for tickets or manoeuvring along city streets. When greeting each other, Polish men are passionate about shaking hands. Polish women, too, often shake hands with men, but the man should always wait for the woman to extend her hand first.

RELIGION

Over 80% of Poles are practising Roman Catholics. The Orthodox church exists along a narrow strip on the eastern frontier and its adherents constitute about 1% of the population.

The election of Karol Wojtyła, the archbishop of Kraków, as Pope John Paul II in 1978, and his triumphal visit to his homeland a year later, significantly enhanced the status of the church in Poland. The country is proud of its Polish Pope: his image is prominently displayed in public places and private homes throughout the country.

POLAND

The overthrow of communism was as much a victory for the Church as it was for democracy. The fine line between the Church and the state is often blurred in Poland. The Church today is a powerful lobby on social issues. Legislation has been passed that mandates Catholic religious instruction in public schools and 'Christian values' in broadcasting. Some Poles have recently grown wary of the Church's increasing influence in society and politics, but Poland remains one of Europe's most religious countries, and packed-out churches are not uncommon.

ARTS
Literature

Poland's rich literary tradition dates from the 15th century and its modern voice was shaped in the 19th century, during the period of foreign subjugation. Nationalist writers thrived, such as the poet Adam Mickiewicz (1798–1855) and Henryk Sienkiewicz (1846–1916), who won a Nobel prize in 1905 for *Quo Vadis?* This nationalist tradition was revived in the communist period when Czesław Miłosz was awarded a Nobel prize in 1980 for *The Captive Mind*.

At the turn of the 20th century, the avant-garde 'Young Poland' movement in art and literature developed in Kraków. The most notable representatives of this movement were the writer Stanisław Wyspiański (1869–1907), also famous for his stained-glass work; the playwright Stanisław Ignacy Witkiewicz (1885–1939), commonly known as Witkacy; and the Nobel laureate Władysław Reymont (1867–1925). In 1996, Wisława Szymborska (1923–) also received a Nobel prize for her ironic poetry.

Music

Unquestionably, Poland's most famous musician was Frédéric Chopin (1810–49), whose music displays the melancholy and nostalgia that became hallmarks of the Polish national style. Stanisław Moniuszko (1819–72) 'nationalised' 19th-century Italian opera music by introducing Polish folk songs and dances onto the stage. His *Halka* (1858), about a peasant girl abandoned by a young noble, is a staple of the national opera houses.

Visual Arts

Jan Matejko (1838–93) is Poland's best-known painter. His monumental historical paintings hang in galleries throughout the country. Wojciech Kossak (1857–1942) is another who documented Polish history; he is best remembered for the colossal painting *Panorama of Racławicka*, on display in Wrocław (p540).

Fashioning amber jewellery is popular in Poland. Amber is a fossil resin of vegetable origin that comes primarily from the Baltic region and appears in a variety of colours from pale yellow to reddish brown. The best places to buy are Gdańsk, Kraków and Warsaw.

Polish poster art has received international recognition; the best selection of poster galleries is in Warsaw and Kraków.

Cinema

Poland claims several world-renowned film directors. The most notable is Andrzej Wajda, who received an Honorary Award at the 1999 Academy Awards. Western audiences are probably more familiar with the work of Roman Polański, who directed critically acclaimed films such as *Rosemary's Baby* and *Chinatown*. In 2002 Polański released the incredibly moving film *The Pianist*, which was filmed in Poland and set in the Warsaw Ghetto of WWII. The film went on to win three Oscars and the Cannes Palme d'Or. The late Krzysztof Kieślowski is best known for the trilogy *Three Colours: Blue/White/Red*.

ENVIRONMENT
The Land

Bordered by seven states and one sea, Poland covers an area of 312,677 sq km: approximately as large as the UK and Ireland put together.

The northern edge of Poland meets the Baltic Sea. This broad, 524km-long coastline is spotted with sand dunes and seaside lakes. Also concentrated in the northeast are many postglacial lakes – more than any country in Europe except Finland.

The southern border is defined by the mountain ranges of the Sudetes and Carpathians. Poland's highest mountains are the rocky Tatras, a section of the Carpathian Range it shares with Slovakia. The highest peak of the Polish Tatras is Mt Rysy (2499m).

The area in between is a vast plain, sectioned by wide north-flowing rivers. Poland's longest river is the Vistula (Wisła), which winds 1047km from the Tatras to the Baltic.

Wildlife & National Parks

Forests cover about 28% of Poland and, admirably, up to 130 sq km of new forest is planted each year. Some 60% of the forests are pine trees, but the share of deciduous species, such as oak, beech and birch, is increasing.

Poland's fauna includes hare, red deer, wild boar and, less abundantly, elk, brown bear and wildcat. European bison, which once inhabited Europe in large numbers, were brought to the brink of extinction early in the 20th century and a few hundred now live in Białowieża National Park. The Great Masurian Lakes district attracts a vast array of bird life, such as storks and cormorants. The eagle, though rarely seen today, is Poland's national bird and appears on the Polish emblem.

Poland has 23 national parks, but they cover less than 1% of the country. No permit is necessary to visit these parks, but most have small admission fees. Camping in the parks is sometimes allowed, but only in specified sites. Poland also has a network of not-so-strictly-preserved areas called 'landscape parks'. About 105 of these parks, covering 6% of Poland, are scattered throughout the country.

FOOD & DRINK

The gastronomic scene in Poland has developed dramatically over recent years and most cities now have a wide range of dining options on offer, from the usual Western and home-grown fast-food outlets to gourmet restaurants serving top-quality Polish and international cuisine.

The cheapest place to eat is a milk bar *(bar mleczny)*, a no-frills, self-service cafeteria, popular with budget-conscious locals and backpackers alike. Though not as numerous as they once were, there are still plenty around, but quality does vary. The number of restaurants *(restauracja)* has ballooned in recent years, and in the big cities, at least, there is a wide range of cuisines on offer, although there will be less choice elsewhere. Meanwhile, there seems scarcely a town anywhere in the country that does not have at least a couple of pizzerias, which have become phenomenally popular with Poles.

Menus usually have several sections: soups *(zupy)*, main courses *(dania drugie)* and accompaniments *(dodatki)*. The price of the main course may not include a side dish – such as potatoes, French fries and salads – which you choose separately (and pay extra for) from the *dodatki* section. Also note that the price for some dishes (particularly fish and poultry) is often listed per 100g, so the price will depend on the total weight of the fish/meat.

Poles start their day with breakfast *(śniadanie)*, which is roughly similar to its Western counterpart. The most important and substantial meal of the day, *obiad*, is normally eaten between 2pm and 5pm. *Obiad* usually includes a hearty soup as well as a main course. The third meal is supper *(kolacja)*, which is often similar to breakfast.

Staples & Specialities

Polish cuisine has been influenced by various cultures, including Jewish, Ukrainian, Russian, Hungarian and German. Polish food is hearty and filling, abundant in potatoes and dumplings, and rich in meat.

Poland's most famous dishes are *bigos* (sauerkraut with a variety of meats), *pierogi* (ravioli-like dumplings stuffed with cottage cheese or minced meat or cabbage and wild mushrooms) and *barszcz* (red beetroot soup originating from Russian borscht).

Hearty soups such as *żurek* (sour soup with sausage and hard-boiled eggs) are a highlight of Polish cuisine. Main dishes are often made with pork, including *golonka* (boiled pig's knuckle served with horseradish) and *schab pieczony* (roast loin of pork seasoned with prunes and herbs). *Gołąbki* (cabbage leaves stuffed with minced beef and rice) is a tasty alternative.

Placki ziemniaczane (potato pancakes) and *naleśniki* (crepes) are popular snacks.

Drinks

Wódka (vodka) is the national drink, which the Poles claim was invented in their country. In Poland, vodka is usually drunk neat and comes in a number of flavours, including *myśliwska* (flavoured with juniper berries), *wiśniówka* (with cherries) and *jarzębiak* (with rowanberries). The most famous variety is *żubrówka* (bison vodka), flavoured with grass from the Białowieża Forest. Other notable spirits include *krupnik* (honey liqueur), *śliwowica* (plum brandy) and *goldwasser* (sweet liqueur containing flakes of gold leaf).

POLAND

Poles also appreciate the taste of *zimne piwo* (cold beer); the top brands, found everywhere, include Żywiec and Okocim, while regional brands are available in every city.

WARSAW

☎ 022 / pop 1.75 million

Warsaw, or Warszawa (vah-SHAH-vah) in Polish, is the political and economic heart of Poland, and the country's largest and most cosmopolitan city. Devastated during WWII (over half its population perished and 85% of its buildings were destroyed), Warsaw was largely rebuilt from scratch over the following decades; the Old Town

has been reconstructed and is an astounding monument to Polish national pride. There's also a wealth of less appealing Stalinist concrete, while recent years have witnessed a building-boom in the city centre.

Today, Warsaw's many museums and galleries, and the ever-increasing roll-call of good quality restaurants and bars, mean there's plenty to keep you occupied for several days, and the capital's position at the centre of Poland's transport network makes it an ideal base for exploring the surrounding countryside.

HISTORY

Warsaw began its life in the 14th century as a stronghold of the Mazovian dukes. When

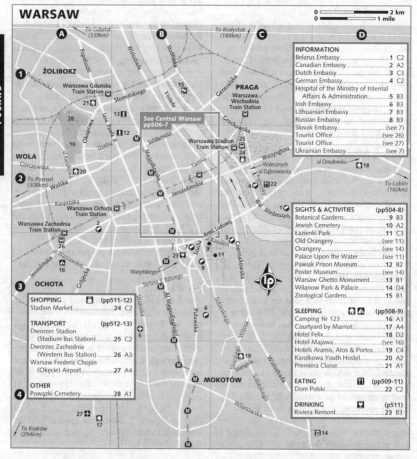

WARSAW

0 — 2 km
0 — 1 mile

INFORMATION
Belarus Embassy.....................................1 C2
Canadian Embassy.................................2 A2
Dutch Embassy......................................3 C3
German Embassy....................................4 C2
Hospital of the Ministry of Internal
Affairs & Administration.......................5 B3
Irish Embassy...6 B3
Lithuanian Embassy...............................7 B3
Russian Embassy....................................8 B3
Slovak Embassy..................................(see 7)
Tourist Office......................................(see 26)
Tourist Office......................................(see 27)
Ukrainian Embassy.............................(see 7)

SIGHTS & ACTIVITIES   (pp504-8)
Botanical Gardens..................................9 B3
Jewish Cemetery...................................10 A2
Łazienki Park...11 C3
Old Orangery....................................(see 11)
Orangery..(see 14)
Palace Upon the Water.....................(see 11)
Pawiak Prison Museum.........................12 B2
Poster Museum.................................(see 14)
Warsaw Ghetto Monument..................13 B1
Wilanów Park & Palace.........................14 D4
Zoological Gardens...............................15 B1

SLEEPING   (pp508-9)
Camping Nr 123....................................16 A3
Courtyard by Marriot............................17 A4
Hotel Felix..18 D2
Hotel Majawa...................................(see 16)
Hotels Aramis, Atos & Portos...............19 C4
Karolkowa Youth Hostel.......................20 A2
Premiera Classe.....................................21 A1

SHOPPING   🛍   (pp511-12)
Stadion Market.....................................24 C2

TRANSPORT   (pp512-13)
Dworzec Stadion
(Stadium Bus Station)........................25 C2
Dworzec Zachodnia
(Western Bus Station)........................26 A3
Warsaw Frederic Chopin
(Okęcie) Airport................................27 A4

OTHER
Powązki Cemetery................................28 A1

EATING   🍴   (pp509-11)
Dom Polski..22 C2

DRINKING   🍸   (p511)
Riviera Remont.....................................23 B3

Poland and Lithuania were unified in 1569, Warsaw's strategic central location came to the fore and the capital was transferred here from Kraków. Paradoxically, the 18th century – a period of catastrophic decline for the Polish state – witnessed Warsaw's greatest prosperity. A wealth of splendid churches, palaces and parks were built and cultural and artistic life flourished. The first constitution in Europe, however short-lived, was instituted in Warsaw in 1791.

The 19th century was a period of decay for Warsaw, which became a mere provincial town in the Russian empire. After WWI Warsaw was reinstated as the capital of a newly independent Poland and began to thrive once more.

ORIENTATION

The city is divided by the Vistula River into two very different parts. The western left-bank sector is much larger and features the city centre, including the Old Town, the historic nucleus of Warsaw. Almost all tourist attractions, as well as the lion's share of tourist facilities, are on this side of the river. The eastern right-bank part of Warsaw, the suburb of Praga, has no major sights and sees few tourists.

If arriving by train, Warszawa Centralna station is, as the name suggests, within walking distance of the city centre and main attractions. If you arrive by bus at Dworzec Centralny PKS station, hop on a train from the adjoining Warszawa Zachodnia station into the centre. From the Dworzec PKS Stadion, you can again catch a train to Warszawa Centralna from the Stadion train station.

INFORMATION
Bookshops
American Bookstore (Map pp506-7; ☎ 827 48 52; ul Nowy Świat 61) Offers a wide selection of Lonely Planet titles, English publications and maps.
EMPiK Megastore (Map pp506-7; ☎ 551 44 42; ul Marszałkowska 116/122) The largest array of foreign newspapers and magazines is in this shop, which has several other branches around town, including ul Nowy Świat 15/17.

Emergency
Ambulance ☎ 628 24 24
Police ☎ 826 24 24
Fire ☎ 844 00 71
Tourist Emergency ☎ 601 55 55

WARSAW IN TWO DAYS

Head for the **Old Town** (p504) via the '**Royal Way**' (p505) and tour the **Royal Castle** (p504). Have lunch at **Restauracja Przy Zamku** (p510) and drop by the **Warsaw Historical Museum** (p504) before heading south for a stroll through the **Saxon Gardens** (p505).

The next day, take a look round the **National Museum** (p505) in the morning, followed by lunch in one of the many eateries along ul Nowy Świat. Ride the lift to the top of the **Palace of Culture & Science** (p507) for breathtaking views, and in the evening, sip a cocktail at **Paparazzi** (p511) or enjoy a performance at **Teatr Wielki** (p511).

Internet Access
There are plenty of Internet cafés in Warsaw. Expect to pay around 4zł to 5zł per hour.
Casablanca (Map pp506-7; ☎ 828 14 47; ul Krakowskie Przedmieście 4/6; ☺ 9am-1am).
Internet Café (Map pp506-7; ☎ 826 60 62; ul Nowy Świat 18/20; ☺ 9am-11pm Mon-Fri, 10am-10pm Sat & Sun)
Verso Internet (Map pp506-7; ☎ 831 28 54; ul Freta 17; ☺ 8am-8pm Mon-Fri, 9am-5pm Sat, 10am-4pm Sun)

Several convenient but dingy **Internet cafés** are also located along the underground mezzanine level of the Warszawa Centralna train station.

Medical Services
For 24-hour medical information call ☎ 94 94. Some of the many pharmacies throughout the city stay open all night.
Apteka 21 (Map pp506-7; ☎ 825 69 86; Warszawa Centralna train station) An all-night pharmacy.
CM Medical Center (Map pp506-7; ☎ 458 70 00; 3rd fl, Marriott Hotel, Al Jerozolimskie 65/79) Offers specialist doctors, carries out laboratory tests and makes house calls.
Dental-Med (Map pp506-7; ☎ 629 59 38; ul Hoża 27) A central dentist's practice.
Hospital of the Ministry of Internal Affairs & Administration (Map p502; ☎ 602 15 78; ul Wołoska 137) A private hospital preferred by government officials and diplomats.

Money
Foreign-exchange offices, known as *kantors,* and ATMs are easy to find around the city centre. *Kantors* open 24 hours can be found at the Warszawa Centralna train station, and either side of the

POLAND

immigration counters at the airport, but exchange rates at these places are about 10% lower than in the city centre. Avoid changing money in the Old Town, where the rates are even lower. The following banks change major-brand travellers cheques, offer cash advances on Visa and MasterCard and have ATMs that take just about every known credit card.

American Express (Map pp506-7; Marriott Hotel, Al Jerozolimskie 65/79) Another place to cash major travellers cheques.

Bank Pekao (Map pp506-7: xxx ul Krakowskie Przedmieście) Bank Pekao has a dozen branches in the city, including one next to the Church of the Holy Cross.

PBK Bank (Map pp506-7; ground fl, Palace of Culture & Science Bldg)

PKO Bank (Map pp506-7; plac Bankowy 2).

Post

Main post office (Map pp506-7; ul Świętokrzyska 31/33; ⊙ 24hr) The most convenient place to send your letters and postcards is here.

Tourist Information

Official tourist organisation (☎ 9431; www.warsaw tour.pl) Has several branches, the most central being near the Royal Castle (Map pp506-7; ul Krakowskie Przedmieście 89; ⊙ 9am-8pm May-Sep, 9am-6pm Oct-Apr); airport arrivals hall (Map p502; ⊙ 8am-8pm May-Sep, 8am-6pm Oct-Apr); next to ticket office at Dworzec Zachodnia (Western Bus Station; Map p502; ⊙ 9am-5pm); main hall of Warszawa Centralna train station (Map pp506-7; ⊙ 8am-8pm May-Sep, 8am-6pm Oct-Apr).

Each branch provides free city maps and free booklets, such as the handy *Warsaw in Short* and *The Visitor*, sells maps of other Polish cities, and helps you book a hotel room. They also sell the **Warsaw Tourist Card**, which gives free or discounted access to most of the main museums, free public transport and discounts at some theatres, sports centres and restaurants. One- and three-day versions are available (45zł and 85zł respectively).

Free monthly tourist magazines worth seeking out include *Poland: What, Where, When; What's Up in Warsaw;* and *Welcome to Warsaw*. All are mines of information about cultural events and provide reviews of new restaurants, bars and nightclubs. They're available in the lobbies of most top-end hotels. The comprehensive monthly *Warsaw Insider* (8zł) and *Warsaw in Your Pocket* (5zł), are also useful.

Travel Agencies

Almatur (Map pp506-7; ☎ 826 26 39; dot@almatur.pl; ul Kopernika 23)

Mazurkas Travel (Map pp506-7; ☎ 629 18 78; www .mazurkas.com.pl; ul Nowogrodzka 24/26) Runs various coach tours of Warsaw, plus excursions to other cities.

Orbis Travel (Map pp506-7; ☎ 827 72 65; ul Bracka 16) Has branches all over Warsaw, as well as at the airport.

Our Roots (Map pp506-7; ☎ 620 05 56; ul Twarda 6) Warsaw's primary agency for anyone interested in tours about local Jewish heritage.

Trakt (Map pp506-7; ☎ 827 80 68; www.trakt.com.pl; ul Kredytowa 6) Guided tours of Warsaw and beyond in English and several other languages.

SIGHTS
Old Town   Map pp506-7

The main gateway to the Old Town is **Plac Zamkowy** (Castle Square). Amazingly, all of the 17th- and 18th-century buildings around this square were completely rebuilt from their foundations after WWII. The superb reconstruction earned the Old Town a place on Unesco's World Heritage List. In the centre of the square stands the **Monument to Sigismund III Vasa**, who moved the capital from Kraków to Warsaw.

The square is dominated by the massive **Royal Castle** (☎ 657 21 70; plac Zamkowy 4; adult/child 15/8zł, free Sun; ⊙ 10am-4pm Mon-Sat, 11am-4pm Sun). The castle was begun in the 13th century and grew as successive Polish kings added wings and redecorated the interior, but it was reduced to rubble in 1945, and was reconstructed between 1971 and 1984. The most interesting of the sumptuously decorated rooms is the Senators' Antechamber, where some 23 landscapes of 18th-century Warsaw by Bernardo Bellotto (Canaletto's nephew) are on show.

From the castle head down ul Świętojańska to the 15th-century Gothic **St John's Cathedral** (ul Świętojańska 8; admission crypt 1zł; ⊙ 10am-1pm & 3-5.30pm Mon-Sat), the oldest church in Warsaw. The small crypt houses the tombs of past pastors. This road continues to the magnificent **Rynek Starego Miasta** (Old Town Square).

Alongside this square is the **Warsaw Historical Museum** (☎ 635 16 25; Rynek Starego Miasta 42; adult/child 5/2.50zł, free Sun; ⊙ 11am-5.30pm Tue & Thu, 10am-3.30pm Wed & Fri, 10.30am-4.30pm Sat & Sun). At noon it shows an English-language film (included in the admission fee) that unforgettably depicts the wartime destruction of the city.

Nearby is the **Adam Mickiewicz Museum of Literature** (☎ 831 76 91; Rynek Starego Miasta 20; adult/child 5/4zł, free Sun; 🕙 10am-3pm Mon, Tue & Fri, 11am-6pm Wed & Thu, 11am-5pm Sun), which features manuscripts belonging to Poland's most revered literary figure, plus exhibits on other leading Polish writers.

Walk west for one block to the **Barbican**, part of a medieval wall that encircled Warsaw and was built on a bridge over a moat. To the north along ul Freta is the **Rynek Nowego Miasta** (New Town Square). On the way, the **Marie Skłodowska-Curie Museum** (☎ 631 80 92; ul Freta 16; adult/child 5/2zł; 🕙 10am-4pm Tue-Sat, 10am-2pm Sun) features modest displays about the great lady, who, along with husband Pierre, discovered radium and polonium, and laid the foundations for radiography, nuclear physics and cancer therapy.

Heading southwest, you'll find the **State Archaeological Museum** (☎ 831 15 37; ul Długa 52; adult/child 6/3zł, free Sun; 🕙 9am-4pm Mon-Thu, 11am-6pm Fri, 10am-4pm Sun), based in a 17th-century former arsenal. It houses some unremarkable bits and pieces excavated from all over Poland.

Royal Way (Szlak Królewski)

This 4km route links the Royal Castle with Łazienki Park (see p507) via ul Krakowskie Przedmieście, ul Nowy Świat and Al Ujazdowskie. If you want to save time and energy, jump on and off bus No 180, which stops at most places along this route and continues to Wilanów Park (see p507).

Just south of the Royal Castle is the 15th-century **St Anne's Church** (Map pp506-7; ul Krakowskie Przedmieście 68; 🕙 daylight hr), one of the most ornate churches in the city. You can climb the **tower** (Map pp506-7; admission 3.50zł; 🕙 10am-6pm Tue-Sun) for views of Plac Zamkowy and the castle. About 300m further south is the former **Carmelite Church** (Map pp506-7; ul Krakowskie Przedmieście 52/54; 🕙 daylight hr), also known as the Seminary Church. The nearby **Radziwiłł Palace** (Map pp506-7; not open to the public) is the official residence of the Polish president. Opposite, **Połocki Palace** (Map pp506-7; ☎ 421 01 25; ul Krakowskie Przedmieście 15/17; admission free; 🕙 10am-8pm) houses a contemporary art gallery.

To the west of the neoclassical Hotel Orbis Europejski are the **Saxon Gardens** (admission free; 🕙 24hr). At the entrance is the small but poignant **Tomb of the Unknown Soldier** (Map pp506-7), which occupies a fragment of an 18th-century royal palace destroyed in WWII. It's under permanent guard, and not open to the public. The ceremonial changing of the guard takes place here at noon on Sunday.

South of the tomb, the **Zachęta Contemporary Art Gallery** (Map pp506-7; ☎ 827 58 54; plac Małachowskiego 3; adult/child 10/7zł, free Thu; 🕙 noon-8pm Tue-Sun) stages exhibitions of contemporary painting, sculpture and photography. Some 200m further south is the **Ethnographic Museum** (Map pp506-7; ☎ 827 76 41; ul Kredytowa 1; adult/child 8/4zł; 🕙 9am-4pm Tue, Thu & Fri, 11am-6pm Wed, 10am-5pm Sat & Sun). This large building displays Polish folk costumes from across the country, plus regional arts and crafts.

Back along the Royal Way is the 17th-century **Church of the Holy Cross** (Map pp506-7; ul Krakowskie Przedmieście 3; 🕙 erratic). Chopin's heart is preserved in the second pillar on the left-hand side of the main nave. It was brought from Paris, where he died of tuberculosis aged only 39. If you want to know more, head along ul Tamka towards the river to the small **Chopin Museum** (Map pp506-7; ☎ 827 54 71; ul Okólnik 1; adult/child 8/4zł, free Wed; 🕙 10am-2pm Mon-Wed, Fri & Sat, noon-6pm Thu). On show, among other things, are the great man's last piano and a collection of his letters and hand-written musical scores.

Return to the Royal Way and head south along ul Nowy Świat to the roundabout at the junction of Al Jerozolimskie. On the way to the river is the enormous **National Museum** (Map pp506-7; ☎ 621 10 31; Al Jerozolimskie 3; museum adult/child 11/6zł, museum plus temporary exhibitions adult/child 15/8zł, museum only free Sat; 🕙 10am-4pm Tue, Wed & Fri-Sun, 10am-6pm Thu). It houses a varied and magnificent collection of Greek and Egyptian antiquities, Coptic frescoes, medieval woodcarvings and Polish paintings; look out for the surrealistic fantasies of Jacek Malczewski. Next door, and in the same massive complex, is the **Museum of the Polish Army** (Map pp506-7; ☎ 629 52 71; Al Jerozolimskie 3; admission grounds free, museum 6zł; 🕙 11am-5pm Wed-Sun May-Sep, 10am-4pm Wed-Sun Oct-Apr). The tanks, jet fighters, helicopters and guns in the grounds are worth a look, though the uniforms, weaponry and other militaria inside are probably only of specialist interest.

Go on south along Al Ujazdowskie and cross busy ul Armii Ludowej. Over the road is the cutting-edge **Center of Contemporary Art**

CENTRAL WARSAW

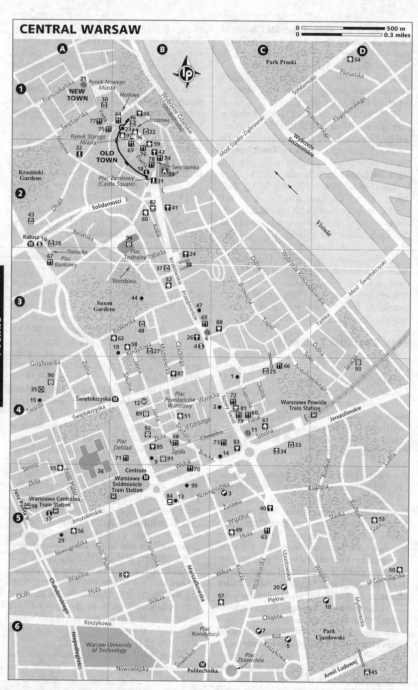

POLAND

0 — 500 m
0 — 0.3 miles

INFORMATION		
Almatur	**1**	C4
American Bookstore	**2**	C4
American Express	(see 56)	
Australian Embassy	**3**	C5
Bank Pekao	**4**	B3
British Embassy	**5**	C6
Casablanca	**6**	B3
CM Medical Centre	(see 56)	
Czech Embassy	**7**	C6
Dental-Med	**8**	B6
EMPiK Megastore	**9**	B4
French Embassy	**10**	D6
Internat Café	**11**	C4
Main Post Office	**12**	B4
Mazurkas Travel	**13**	B5
Orbis Travel	**14**	C4
Our Roots	**15**	A4
PBK Bank	(see 36)	
PKO Bank	**16**	A2
Tourist Office	**17**	A5
Tourist Office	**18**	B2
Trakt	**19**	B3
US Embassy	**20**	C6
Verso Internet	**21**	A1

SIGHTS & ACTIVITIES	(pp504-8)	
Adam Mickiewicz Museum of		
Literature	**22**	B1
Barbican	**23**	B1
Carmelite Church (Seminary Church)	**24**	B3
Center of Contemporary Art	(see 45)	
Centrum Sztuki Studio	(see 36)	
Chopin Museum	**25**	C4
Church of the Holy Cross	**26**	B3
Ethnographic Museum	**27**	B3
Jewish Historical Institute	**28**	A2
LOT Head Office	**29**	A5
Marie Skłodowska-Curie Museum	**30**	A1
Monument to Sigismund III Vasa	**31**	B2
Monument to the Warsaw Uprising	**32**	A2
Museum of the Polish Army	**33**	C4

National Museum	**34**	C4
Nozyk Synagogue	**35**	A4
Palace of Culture & Science	**36**	A5
Połocki Palace	**37**	B3
Radziwiłł Palace	**38**	B3
Royal Castle	**39**	B2
St Alexander's Church	**40**	C5
St Anne's Church	**41**	B2
St John's Cathedral	**42**	B2
State Archaeological Museum	**43**	A2
Tomb of the Unknown Soldier	**44**	B3
Ujazdów Castle	**45**	D6
Warsaw Historical Museum	**46**	B1
Warsaw University	**47**	B3
Zachęta Contemporary		
Art Gallery	**48**	B3

SLEEPING	⌂	(pp508-9)
City Apartments	**49**	C5
Dizzy Daisy	**50**	D5
Hotel Gromada Centrum	**51**	B4
Hotel Harenda	(see 88)	
Hotel Orbis Europejski	**52**	B3
Hotel Powiśle	**53**	D5
Hotel Praski	**54**	D1
Intercontinental Warszawa	**55**	A5
Marriott Hotel	**56**	A5
Nathan's Villa Hostel	**57**	C6
Oki Doki	**58**	B3
Old Town Apartments	**59**	B2
Old Town Apartments	**60**	B2
Smolna Youth Hostel No 2	**61**	C4
Sofitel Victoria	**62**	B3

EATING	🍴	(pp509-11)
Adler Bar & Restaurant	**63**	C5
Bar Mleczny Pod Barbakanem	**64**	B1
Bar Mleczny Uniwersytecki	**65**	B3
Bar Sałatkovy z Tukanem	**66**	C4
Bar Sałatkowy z Tukanem	**67**	A3
Bar Turecki	**68**	B4
Karczma Gessler	**69**	B2

London Steakhouse	**70**	B5
MarcPol Supermarket	**71**	B4
Melon	**72**	C4
Polska	**73**	C4
Puszkin	**74**	B2
Restauracja Barbakan	**75**	A1
Restauracja Bazyliszek	**76**	B2
Restauracja Pod Samsonem	**77**	A1
Restauracja Przy Zamku	**78**	B2
Restaurancja Wegetariańska	**79**	C4
Tam Tam	**80**	C4
Zgoda Grill Bar	(see 66)	
Zielony Świat	(see 79)	

DRINKING	🍷🍸	(p511)
Coffee Heaven	**81**	C4
Demmers Teahouse	**82**	B2
EMPiK Club	**83**	C4
Green Coffee	**84**	B5
Hybrydy	**85**	B4
Kokon	**86**	B1
Morgan's Irish Pub	(see 25)	
Paparazzi	**87**	B4
Pub Harenda	**88**	C3

ENTERTAINMENT	🎭	(p511)
Filharmonia Narodowa	**89**	B4
Jewish Theatre	**90**	A4
Kino Atlantic	**91**	B4
Kino Relax	**92**	B4
Teatr Ateneum	**93**	D4
Teatr Wielki	**94**	B2
ZASP Kasy Teatralne	**95**	B5

SHOPPING	🛍	(pp511-12)
Albert Supermarket	(see 9)	
Galeria 32	**96**	B1
Galeria Centrum	(see 9)	
Lapidarium	**97**	B1

TRANSPORT		(pp512-13)
Polski Express Bus Stop	**98**	A5

POLAND

(Map pp506-7; ☎ 628 12 72; Al Ujazdowskie 6; adult/child 10/5zł, free Thu; ☺ 11am-5pm Tue-Thu, Sat & Sun, 11am-9pm Fri). It's housed in the reconstructed **Ujazdów Castle**, built during the 1620s. Further down (towards the south) are the small **Botanical Gardens** (Map p502; ☎ 553 05 11; adult/child 4/2zł; ☺ 10am-7pm).

Łazienki Park
Map p502

This park (admission free; ☺ daylight hr) is large (74 hectares), shady and popular. It's best known for the 18th-century **Palace upon the Water** (☎ 625 79 44; adult/child 12/9zł; ☺ 9am-4pm Tue-Sun). It was the summer residence of Stanisław August Poniatowski, the last king of Poland, who was deposed by a Russian army and confederation of Polish magnates in 1792. The park was once a royal hunting ground attached to Ujazdów Castle.

The **Old Orangery** (☎ 621 82 12; admission by reservation only; English-language guides 80/150zł for 1/2hr tour) contains a gallery of sculpture and also an 18th-century theatre. Between noon and 4pm every Sunday in summer (May to September), piano recitals are held here among the rose gardens.

Wilanów Park
Map p502

This equally splendid **park** (ul Wisłostrada; admission free; ☺ 9.30am-dusk) is about 6km southeast of Łazienki Park. The centrepiece is the magnificent **Wilanów Palace** (☎ 842 07 95; adult/child 18/9zł, free Thu; ☺ 9.30am-2.30pm Wed-Mon). The palace was the summer residence of King Jan III Sobieski, who defeated the Turks at Vienna in 1683, thereby ending the Turkish threat to Central Europe. In summer, arrive early and be prepared to wait. The last tickets are sold two hours before closing time.

In the well-kept park behind the palace is the **Orangery** (adult/child 6/3zł, free Thu; ☺ 9.30am-2.30pm Wed-Mon), which houses an art gallery. The **Poster Museum** (☎ 842 26 06; adult/child 8/5zł, free Wed; ☺ 10am-3.30pm Tue-Sun), in the former royal stables, is one of the best places to see Poland's world-renowned poster art.

To reach Wilanów, take bus No 180 from anywhere along the Royal Way.

Palace of Culture & Science
Map pp506-7

This towering Stalinist eyesore (☎ 509 20 26; plac Defilad; ☺ 9am-8pm Mon-Fri, 9am-midnight Sat &

Sun) has a particularly sinister aspect at dusk, though its sheer size makes it a handy landmark if you get lost. The 'gift of friendship' from the Soviet Union to the Polish nation was built in the early 1950s and is still Poland's tallest (234m) building. It has a huge congress hall, three theatres and a cinema.

The **observation terrace** (admission 20zł; 9am-6pm) on the 30th floor is reached by an ear-popping lift ride, and provides a panoramic view. Note, though, that it can be mighty cold and windy way up there. Poles often joke that this is the best view of Warsaw because it's the only one that doesn't include the Palace of Culture & Science itself!

Jewish Heritage

The vast suburbs northwest of the Palace of Culture & Science were once predominantly inhabited by Warsaw's Jews. During WWII the Nazis established a Jewish ghetto in the area but razed it to the ground after crushing the Warsaw Ghetto Uprising in April 1943. This tragic event is immortalised by the **Monument to the Warsaw Uprising** (Map p506-7; cnr ul Długa & ul Miodowa).

The **Warsaw Ghetto Monument** (Map p502; cnr ul Anielewicza & ul Zamenhofa) also commemorates victims using pictorial plaques. The nearby **Pawiak Prison Museum** (Map p502; ☎ 831 13 17; ul Dzielna 24/26; admission free; 9am-5pm Wed, 9am-4pm Thu & Sat, 10am-5pm Fri, 10am-4pm Sun) occupies the former building used as a Gestapo prison during the Nazi occupation. Moving exhibits include letters and other personal items.

Arguably the most dramatic remnant of the Jewish legacy is the vast **Jewish Cemetery** (Map p502; ul Okopowa 49/51; admission free; 10am-4pm Mon-Thu, 9am-1pm Fri, 9am-4pm Sun). Founded in 1806, it still has over 100,000 gravestones and is the largest assemblage of its kind in Europe. Visitors must wear a head covering to enter the cemetery, which is accessible from the Old Town on tram No 22, 27 or 29.

The **Jewish Historical Institute** (Map pp506-7; ☎ 827 92 21; ul Tłomackie 3/5; adult/child 10/5zł; 9am-4pm Mon-Wed & Fri, 11am-6pm Thu) has permanent exhibits about the Warsaw Ghetto, as well as local Jewish artworks. Tucked away behind the **Jewish Theatre** is the neo-Romanesque **Nożyk Synagogue** (Map pp506-7; ☎ 620 43 24; ul Twarda 6; 3.50zł; 10am-8pm Sun-Thu, 10am-4pm Fri), Warsaw's only synagogue to survive WWII, now once more open for worship.

A walking tour of these – and around 20 other – Jewish sites is detailed (in English and with a map) in the free pamphlet, *Historical Sites of Jewish Warsaw*, available from the official tourist offices.

SLEEPING

Warsaw is the most expensive city in Poland for accommodation, and rates at many central hotels are often grossly inflated in comparison with other Polish cities. The number of upmarket hotels is rising, but there's also an increasing number of modern and reasonably priced hostels around town. You'll have to head further out to find economical hotels. The tourist offices will help.

Budget

Camping 123 (Map p502; ☎ 823 37 48; ul Warszawskiej 1920r 15/17; 10zł per tent;) Set in extensive grounds near the Dworzec Zachodnia bus station. Hotel rooms (45zł per person) are also available and there's a tennis court.

Karolkowa Youth Hostel (Map p502; ☎ 632 88 29; ssmnr6@ptsm.com.pl; ul Karolkowa 53a; dm from 30zł, s/d/tr from 80/90/150zł;) In the suburb of Wola and accessible by tram No 12 or 24 from the Warszawa Centralna train station. This well-established and friendly place has a wide range of hostel and hotel rooms on offer, and is a popular choice, though dorms have to be vacated between 11am and 5pm.

Smolna Youth Hostel No 2 (Map pp506-7; ☎ & fax 827 89 52; ul Smolna 30; dm 35zł, s/d 62/114zł) Very central and very popular; advance bookings are essential, especially in summer. Rooms are maintained to a high standard, but there's an 11pm curfew and a strict no-alcohol rule.

Nathan's Villa Hostel (Map pp506-7; ☎ 622 29 46; www.nathansvilla.com; ul Piękna 24/26; dm 45zł, s/d 120/140zł;) A very new, spotless hostel offering the same high standards as its sister establishment in Kraków. There's free laundry and no curfew.

Oki Doki (Map pp506-7; ☎ 826 51 12; www.okidoki.pl; plac Dąbrowskiego 3; dm 40zł, s/d 120/160zł) Another new, stylish place in a conveniently central location. Rooms are a decent size, and the décor is fresh and cheerful.

Dizzy Daisy (Map pp506-7; ☎ 0507 189 509; www .hostel.pl; ul Górnośląska 14; s/d/tr 120/140/180zł;) Offers simple, decent rooms (no dorms) in a renovated old building near the river. Kitchens are provided for the use of guests.

POLAND

Hotel Majawa (Map p502; ☎ 822 91 21; fax 823 37 48; ul Warszawskiej 1920r 15/17; d 109zł, bungalows from 84zł) Offers good value. The bungalows at this camping ground have shared bathrooms but are private and clean, while the hotel rooms are quiet, spotless and bright.

Mid-Range

Three near-identical one-star hotels under the same management as Hotel Felix (see below) on ul Mangalia offer good value (single/double 120/150zł at all three). To get there, catch bus No 118, 403, 503 or 513 along ul Sobieskiego. **Hotel Aramis** (Map p502; ☎ & fax 842 09 74; aramis@felix.com.pl; ul Mangalia 3b; P) is the largest and best set up. **Hotel Atos** (Map p502; ☎ & fax 841 43 95; atos@felix.com.pl; ul Mangalia 1; P) is smaller, but equally comfortable. **Hotel Portos** (Map p502; ☎ & fax 842 09 74; portos@felix .com.pl; ul Mangalia 3a; P) is of a similar standard; clean and simple.

Hotel Felix (Map p502; ☎ 610 21 82; www.felix.com .pl; ul Omulewska 24; d from 155zł; P) In an unexciting Soviet-style block, but spotlessly clean and good value. Rates decrease at weekends, in August and in winter, but breakfast is 20zł extra. Take tram No 9, 24 or 44 from the Warszawa Centralna train station.

Premiera Classe (Map p502; ☎ 624 08 00; ul Towarowa 2; s & d 159-169zł; ✕ P) The cheapest section of a very new complex of three hotels, offering a high standard of accommodation at a reasonable price, and just west of the city centre.

Hotel Praski (Map pp506-7; ☎ 818 49 89; www .praski.pl; Al Solidarności 61; s/d 160-240/180-270zł; P) On the other side of the river, but little more than 1km from the Old Town. The cheaper rooms have shared bathrooms, but this is still one of the best two-star places in the capital.

Hotel Powiśle (Map pp506-7; ☎ 621 03 41; www .hotelpowisle.ta.pl; ul Szara 10a; s/d 180/270zł; P) A quiet and friendly place, but a little out of the way of the better bars and restaurants. The rooms are large and feature new bathrooms.

Hotel Gromada Centrum (☎ 582 99 00; www .gromada.pl; plac Powstańców Warszawy 2; s 200-450zł, d 280-550zł; ✕ P) This is a huge, characterless place with comfy, decent-sized rooms, in a handy central location. The pricier 'modernised rooms' don't offer that much extra, and they can be noisy. Weekend rates are around 20% cheaper.

Old Town Apartments (Map pp506-7; ☎ 887 98 00; www.warsawshotel.com; Rynek Starego Miasta 12/14; studio/apt from €45/70) Offers spotless studios and one- and two-bedroom apartments in the Old Town. Weekly and monthly rates are available.

City Apartments (Map pp506-7; ☎ 825 39 12; www.hotelinwarsaw.pl; ul Nowowiejska 1/3; studio/apt from €60/85) Offers a similar service to Old Town Apartments, with discounts for longer stays.

Top End

Hotel Harenda (Map pp506-7; ☎ 826 00 71; www .hotelharenda.com.pl; ul Krakowskie Przedmieście 4/6; s/d 320/360zł, apt 500zł; ⊑ P) Boasts a pleasant location in the Old Town and an appealing ambience. The singles are remarkably small, but all the bathrooms are spotless.

Hotel Orbis Europejski (Map pp506-7; ☎ 826 50 51; europejski@orbis.pl; ul Krakowskie Przedmieście 13; s/ d €90/105, apt €200; ✕ P) This historic place is ideally placed near the Saxon Gardens and though rooms are a little old-fashioned and unremarkable, the location and sense of tradition are appealing.

Courtyard by Marriott (Map p502; ☎ 650 01 00; www.courtyard.com; ul Żwirki i Wigury 1; d/ste from €106/134; ⊑ ✕ P) Very conveniently located, just across the road from the airport, and provides the expected high level of comfort and service that's aimed squarely at the international business traveller. Breakfast is excellent, but a pricey 60zł extra.

Sofitel Victoria (Map pp506-7; ☎ 827 57 64; sof. victoria@orbis.pl; ul Królewska 11; d/ste from €195/400; ⊑ ⌕ ✕ P) A gigantic white monolith overlooking plac Piłsudskiego, offering all the five-star luxuries you could ask for, including a business centre and gym. Cheaper long-stay rates are available.

Intercontinental Warszawa (Map pp506-7; ☎ 328 88 88; www.warsaw-intercontinental.com; ul Emillii Plater 49; d/ste from €270/310; ⊑ ⌕ ✕ P) A stunning glass tower overlooking the Palace of Culture & Science, offering elegant, restful rooms and first-class service and facilities, including a fitness centre, three restaurants and a pool on the 44th floor.

EATING

Warsaw has undergone a gastronomic revolution in recent years, and everything from the cheapest snack bars to international-standard gourmet restaurants now clamours for business all around town. A good choice can be found along ul Nowy Świat and around.

POLAND

The free booklet *Warszawa Restaurants*, available from the official tourist offices, lists hundreds of restaurants serving every conceivable cuisine, while the English-language newspapers and magazines (see p504) provide reviews of what's currently in vogue.

Polish

The Old Town boasts some of Warsaw's best restaurants specialising in Polish cuisine, but prices are predictably high. Each is likely to offer a menu in English.

Zgoda Grill Bar (Map pp506-7; ☎ 827 99 34; ul Zgoda 4; mains 20-50zł; ☟ 10am-11pm) A bright, informal place serving up cheap and tasty Polish standards.

Polska (Map pp506-7; ☎ 826 38 77; ul Nowy Świat 21; mains from 25zł; ☟ noon-midnight) A popular spot serving up good-quality Polish cuisine, including game and the ubiquitous *pierogi*.

Dom Polski (Map p502; ☎ 616 24 32; ul Francuska 11; mains 30-90zł; ☟ noon-midnight) This is perennially popular with tour groups and out-of-towners looking for tasty food and reasonable prices. It's worth the pleasant walk over the bridge.

Restauracja Przy Zamku (Map pp506-7; ☎ 831 02 59; plac Zamkowy 15; mains from 35zł; ☟ 11am-midnight) An attractive, old-world kind of place with hunting trophies on the walls and attentive, white-aproned waiters. The top-notch Polish menu includes fish and game and a bewildering array of entrées – try the excellent hare pâté.

Restauracja Bazyliszek (Map pp506-7; ☎ 831 18 41; Rynek Starego Miasta 3/9; mains 38-75zł; ☟ noon-midnight) One of the longest-standing Polish restaurants in the capital and continuing to maintain high standards. It serves hearty, traditional fare (including lots of meaty game) in old-world surroundings.

Karczma Gessler (Map pp506-7; ☎ 831 44 27; Rynek Starego Miasta 21/21a; mains 50-100zł; ☟ 11am-midnight) Continues to be recommended by satisfied patrons. The food and decor in this romantic cellar are spectacular, though it's not cheap and vegetarians will not find much to satisfy their taste buds.

International
Map pp506-7

Restauracja Pod Samsonem (☎ 831 17 88; ul Freta 3/5; mains 15-50zł; ☟ 10am-11pm) Situated in the New Town, and frequented by locals looking for inexpensive and tasty meals with a Jewish flavour. It's always busy and you may have to wait for a table.

Restauracja Barbakan (☎ 831 45 20; ul Freta 1; mains 14-40zł; ☟ 10am-11pm) A huge menu of meat, fish and veggie dishes, and three-course set-menus starting at 22zł.

Tam Tam (☎ 828 26 22; ul Foksal 18; mains from 19zł; ☟ noon-midnight) Housed in a subterranean 'African-style' place with a varied menu, including pasta, goulash and kebabs, and a big list of teas and coffees. There's occasional live music in the evenings.

London Steakhouse (☎ 827 00 20; Al Jerozolimskie 42; mains 30-60zł; ☟ 11am-midnight) Offers up vaguely British-inspired dishes, alongside Polish standards. Steaks, naturally, dominate the menu, which also features fish and chips. Look out for the red phone box outside – and the mini-phone-box salt and pepper shakers.

Adler Bar & Restaurant (☎ 628 73 84; ul Mokotowska 69; mains 35-50zł; ☟ 8am-midnight Mon-Fri, 1pm-midnight Sat & Sun) A tiny oasis among the concrete jungle. Service is impeccable and a good variety of Polish and Bavarian *nouvelle cuisine* is on offer.

Puszkin (☎ 635 35 35; ul Świętojańska 2; mains 38-97zł; ☟ 10am-11pm) This is a new, upmarket Russian restaurant where waiters in Cossack outfits serve up traditional dishes such as caviar, sturgeon and wild boar in opulent surrounds.

Vegetarian
Map pp506-7

Melon (☎ 828 64 28; ul Nowy Świat 52; soups 8zł, mains 14-20zł; ☟ noon-8pm Mon-Sat) Cheap and delicious vegetarian food from a place tucked away in a courtyard. A few doors down, **Zielony Świat** (☎ 826 46 77; ul Nowy Świat 42; mains 10-25zł; ☟ 10am-9.30pm) is another enticing place for healthy, meat-free food.

Bar Sałatkowy z Tukanem (☎ 531 25 20; plac Bankowy 2; mains from 5zł; 10am-8pm Mon-Fri, 10am-4pm Sat & Sun) Has several outlets around the capital offering possibly the widest choice of salads in Poland.

Quick Eats
Map pp506-7

Bar Mleczny Pod Barbakanem (☎ 831 47 37; ul Mostowa 27/29; mains 8-12zł; ☟ 8am-5pm) Opposite the Barbican, this is a popular milk bar that has survived the fall of the Iron Curtain and continues to serve cheap, unpretentious food. Its position would be the envy of many upmarket eateries.

Bar Mleczny Uniwersytecki (☎ 826 07 93; ul Krakowskie Przedmieście 20; mains 8-12zł; ☼ 7am-8pm) Packed with students – probably there for the cheap prices rather than the food itself, which is basic.

Bar Turecki (☎ 826 44 93; ul Zgoda 3; mains 8-13zł) One of the best places to find cheap and filling Turkish food – seek out the tempting aroma wafting across the street.

Self-Catering   Map pp506-7

The most convenient places for groceries are the MarcPol Supermarket in front of the Palace of Culture & Science building, and the **Albert Supermarket** (ul Marszałkowska) close by under Galeria Centrum.

DRINKING   Map pp506-7

Warsaw is awash with all sorts of pubs and bars. The most charming, though inevitably most expensive, places for a drink are around Rynek Starego Miasta, in the Old Town. Coffee and tea bars are springing up all around town too.

Paparazzi (☎ 828 42 19; ul Mazowiecka 12; ☼ noon-1am Mon-Fri, 4pm-1am Sat & Sun) This is one of Warsaw's flashest venues, where you can sip a bewildering array of (pricey) cocktails under blown-up photos of Hollywood stars.

Morgan's Irish Pub (☎ 826 81 38; ul Okólnik 1; ☼ 9am-2am) This popular expat haunt, under the Chopin Museum, has a more down-to-earth atmosphere, offering live music (Thursday to Saturday, 7zł).

Pub Harenda (☎ 826 29 00; ul Krakowskie Przedmieście 4/6; ☼ 9am-3am) Located at the back of Hotel Harenda and often crowded. Live jazz music is performed here during the week and there's dance music on weekends.

If it's caffeine you're after, **Green Coffee** (☎ 629 83 73; ul Marszałkowska 84/92; ☼ 7am-11pm) and **Coffee Heaven** (☎ 828 20 57; ul Nowy Świat 46; ☼ 7.30am-10pm Mon-Thu, 7.30am-10.30pm Fri, 8am-10pm Sat & Sun) are comfy places to enjoy a cappuccino and a muffin. **Demmers Teahouse** (☎ 828 21 06; ul Krakowskie Przedmieście 61/63; ☼ 9am-9pm) has a staggering array of teas to try.

ENTERTAINMENT
Nightclubs

Riviera Remont (Map p502; ☎ 660 91 11; ul Waryńskiego 12; ☼ Jun-Sep) is a popular, cheap student club offering regular live music.

Kokon (Map pp506-7; ☎ 831 95 39; ul Brzozowa 37; admission 9zł; ☼ 4pm-3am) is a fashionable four-level gay club featuring '70s and '80s hits, 'gay house' music and a weekly drag show. **EMPiK Club** (Map pp506-7; ☎ 625 10 86; ul Nowy Świat 15/17; admission 7zł; ☼ 9am-2am Mon-Wed, 9am-5am Thu-Sat, 11am-midnight Sun) in the basement of the book and music store, gets lively, loud and crowded, with regular bands.

Hybrydy (☎ 822 30 03; ul Złota 7/9; ☼ 9pm-3am) has been going for some 45 years and is still cool! It features all sorts of live music most nights.

Theatre

Advance tickets for most events at most theatres can be bought at **ZASP Kasy Teatralne** (Map pp506-7; ☎ 621 93 83; Al Jerozolimskie 25; ☼ 11am-6pm Mon-Fri, 11am-2pm Sat) or at the **EMPiK Megastore** (Map pp506-7; ☎ 551 44 43; ul Marszałkowska 104/122). Otherwise, same-day tickets may be available at the box offices. Remember, most theatres close in July and August. **Teatr Ateneum** (Map pp506-7; ☎ 625 73 30; ul Jaracza 2) leans towards contemporary Polish-language productions. **Teatr Wielki** (Map pp506-7; ☎ 692 02 00; www.teatr wielki.pl; Grand Theatre; plac Teatralny 1; tickets 17-110zł) is the main venue for opera and ballet. **Filharmonia Narodowa** (Map pp506-7; ☎ 826 72 81; ul Jasna 5) holds regular classical music concerts.

In Łazienki Park (p507), piano recitals are held every Sunday from May to September and chamber concerts are staged there in summer at the Old Orangery.

If you're waiting for a flight, free jazz concerts take place at the airport at 3pm every other Thursday.

Cinemas   Map pp506-7

To fill in a rainy afternoon, or to avoid watching Polish TV in your hotel room, try catching a film at one of the 40 cinemas across the city. Two central options are **Kino Atlantic** (☎ 827 08 94; ul Chmielna 33) and **Kino Relax** (☎ 828 38 88; ul Złota 8). Tickets cost around 15zł. English-language films are usually subtitled rather than dubbed into Polish.

SHOPPING

An impressive display of Poland's relatively new free-market enthusiasm is the huge bazaar at the **Stadion Market** (Map p502; Al Jerozolimskie; ☼ dawn-around noon) in the suburb of Praga. It's busiest on weekends – beware of pickpockets.

POLAND

Galeria Centrum (Map pp506-7; ul Marszałowska 104/122) is a vast, modern shopping mall in the city centre, housing a branch of EMPiK, Western fashion outlets, cafés and a supermarket.

There are dozens of antique, arts and crafts shops around Rynek Starego Miasta. **Galeria 32** (Map pp506-7; ☎ 831 54 09; Rynek Starego Miasta 32; ☺ noon-6pm Tue-Sun) offers a fair selection of collectables, including 19th-century porcelain, Art Deco silver and modern Polish art and jewellery. **Lapidarium** (Map pp506-7; ☎ 635 68 28; ul Nowomiejska 15/17) houses a fascinating clutter of antiques and pricey jewellery.

GETTING THERE & AWAY
Air
The Warsaw Frédéric Chopin Airport is more commonly called Okęcie Airport, after the suburb, 10km southwest of the city centre, where it's based. This small airport has international arrivals downstairs and departures upstairs. Domestic arrivals and departures occupy a separate part of the same complex.

The useful tourist office is on the arrivals level of the international section. It sells city maps and can help find a place to stay. At the arrivals level, there are also a few ATMs that accept major international credit cards, and several *kantors*. Avoid the Orbis Travel office because of its astronomical fees and low exchange rates. There are also several car-rental companies, a left-luggage room and a newsagent where you can buy public transport tickets. Buses and taxis depart from this level.

Domestic and international flights on LOT can be booked at the **LOT** head office (☎ 9572; Al Jerozolimskie 65/79) in the Marriott Hotel complex or at any travel agency. Other airline offices are listed in the *Welcome to Warsaw* magazine, and on p569.

Bus
Warsaw has two major bus terminals for PKS buses.

Dworzec Zachodnia (Western Bus Station; Map p502; Al Jerozolimskie 144) handles all domestic buses heading south, north and west of the capital, including several daily to Częstochowa (25zł to 35zł), Gdańsk (47zł to 50zł), Kazimierz Dolny (22zł), Kraków (39zł), Olsztyn (32zł), Toruń (35zł), Wrocław (45zł) and Zakopane (53zł). This complex is southwest of the city centre and adjoins the Warszawa Zachodnia train station. Take the commuter train that leaves from Warszawa Śródmieście station.

Dworzec Stadion (Stadium Bus Station; Map p502; ul Sokola 1) adjoins the Warszawa Stadion train station. It is also easily accessible by commuter train from Warszawa Śródmieście. Dworzec Stadion handles some domestic buses to the east and southeast, including a few daily to Lublin (25zł), Białystok (23zł to 29zł) and Zamość (37zł), as well as Kazimierz Dolny.

Polski Express (☎ 844 55 55) operates coaches from the airport, but passengers can get on or off and buy tickets at the kiosk along Al Jana Pawła II, next to the Warszawa Centralna train station. Polski Express buses travel to Białystok (34zł, four daily); Częstochowa (50zł, two daily); Gdynia, via Gdańsk (72zł, two daily); Kraków (67zł, two daily); Lublin (34zł, eight daily); Szczecin (80zł, two daily); Toruń (48zł, 15 daily); and Wrocław (67zł, three daily).

International buses depart from and arrive at Dworzec Zachodnia or, occasionally, outside the Warszawa Centralna train station. Tickets for the international buses are available from the bus offices at Dworzec Zachodnia, from agencies at Warszawa Centralna or from any of the major travel agencies in the city, including Almatur.

Train
Warsaw has several train stations, but the one that most travellers will use almost exclusively is **Warszawa Centralna** (Warsaw Central; Al Jerozolimskie 54); it handles the overwhelming majority of domestic trains and all international services. Refer to the relevant town's Getting There & Away sections in this chapter for information about services to/from Warsaw.

Remember, Warszawa Centralna is not always where domestic and international trains start or finish, so make sure you get on or off the train at this station in the few minutes allotted. And watch your belongings closely at all times, because pickpocketing and theft are increasingly problems.

On the street level of the central station, the spacious main hall houses ticket counters, ATMs and snack bars, as well as a post office, newsagents and a tourist office. Along the underground mezzanine level leading to the tracks and platforms are a dozen *kantors* (one of which is open 24 hours), a **left-luggage office** (🕐 7am-9pm), lockers, eateries, several other places to buy tickets for local public transport, Internet cafés and bookshops.

Tickets for domestic and international trains are available from counters at the station (but allow at least an hour for possible queuing) or, in advance, from any major Orbis Travel office (p504). Tickets for immediate departures on domestic and international trains are also available from numerous, well-signed booths in the underpasses leading to Warszawa Centralna.

Some domestic trains also stop at Warszawa Śródmieście station, 300m east of Warszawa Centralna, and Warszawa Zachodnia, next to Dworzec Zachodnia bus station.

GETTING AROUND
To/From the Airport
The cheapest way of getting from the airport to the city centre (and vice versa) is on bus No 175. This bus leaves every 10 to 15 minutes for the Old Town, via ul Nowy Świat and the Warszawa Centralna train station. It operates daily from 5am to 11pm. If you arrive in the wee hours, night bus No 611 links the airport with Warszawa Centralna every 30 minutes.

The taxi fare between the airport and the city centre is about 25zł to 30zł. Make sure you take one of the official taxis with a name and telephone number on top and fares listed on the window; you can arrange this at one of the three official taxi counters on the arrivals level of the international section of the terminal. The 'Mafia' cabs still operate at the airport and charge astronomical rates.

Car Rental
There is little incentive to drive a rented car through Warsaw's horrendous traffic and confusing streets, and you're likely to get serious migraines looking for car parks anyway. But there are lots of good reasons to hire a car in Warsaw for jaunts around the countryside. Offices for major car-rental companies are listed in the local English-language newspapers and magazines, and include **Avis** (☎ 650 48 72; www.avis.pl), **Hertz** (☎ 650 28 96; www.hertz.com.pl) and **Payless Car Rental** (☎ 650 14 84; www.paylesscarental.pl). These agencies all have counters at Warsaw's Okęcie Airport. For more details about car rental see p571.

Public Transport
Users find Warsaw's public transport frequent, cheap and operates from 5am to 11pm daily. The fare (2.40zł) is a flat rate for a bus, tram, trolleybus or metro train travelling anywhere in the city, ie one 2.40zł fare is valid for one ride on one form of transport. Warsaw is the only place in Poland where ISIC cards get a public-transport discount (50%).

Tickets (valid on all forms of public transport) for 60/90 minutes cost 3.60/4.50zł, and passes (for all public transport) are available for one day (7.20zł), three days (12zł), one week (24zł) and one month (66zł). Buy tickets from kiosks (including those marked RUCH) before boarding and punch them in one of the small machines on board.

The 'sightseeing route' bus No 180, which links Powązki Cemetery with Wilanów Park, stops at most attractions listed in the Royal Way section earlier, as well as Łazienki Park, and travels via ul Krakowskie Przedmieście and ul Nowy Świat. Also useful is bus No 100, which runs on Saturdays and Sundays from Plac Zamkowy to Łazienki Park.

A metro line operates from the Ursynów suburb (Kabaty station) at the southern city limits to Ratusz (Town Hall), via the city centre (Centrum), but is of limited use to visitors. Local commuter trains head out to the suburbs from the Warszawa Śródieście station.

Taxi
Taxis are a quick and easy way to get around – as long as you use official taxis and drivers use their meters. Beware of 'Mafia' taxis parked in front of top-end hotels, at the airport, outside Warszawa Centralna train station and in the vicinity of most tourist sights.

MAZOVIA & PODLASIE

Mazovia only came to the fore when the capital was transferred to Warsaw in 1596. It has never been a fertile region, so there are few historic towns – the notable exception is Poland's second largest city, Łódź. To the east along the Belarus border is Podlasie, which literally means 'land close to the forest'. The highlight of the region is the magnificent Białowieża National Park.

ŁÓDŹ

☎ 042 / pop 840,000

Łódź (pronounced Woodge) is a lively, likeable city well off the usual tourist trail, with an attractive line in Art Nouveau architecture at its heart and plenty of parklands. It's an easy day trip from Warsaw.

Many of the attractions – and most of the banks, *kantors* and ATMs – are along, or just off, the main thoroughfare of ul Piotrkowska. You can't miss the bronze statues of local celebrities along this street, including pianist Arthur Rubenstein, seated at a baby grand. The helpful **tourist office** (☎ 638 59 55; www.uml.lodz.pl; al Kościuszki 88; ☯ 8.30am-4.30pm Mon-Fri, 9am-1pm Sat) is just off the southern tip of the main street and has plenty of free tourist brochures, including the handy *1-2-3 Days in Łódź*.

The **Historical Museum of Łódź** (☎ 654 03 23; ul Ogrodowa 15; adult/child 6/3zł, free Wed; ☯ 10am-4pm Tue & Thu, 2-6pm Wed, 10am-2pm Fri-Sun) is 200m northwest of plac Wolności, which is at the northern end of the main drag. Also worthwhile is the **Museum of Ethnography & Archaeology** (☎ 632 84 40; plac Wolności 14; adult/child 5/3zł, free Tue; ☯ 10am-5pm Tue, Thu & Fri, 9am-5pm Wed, 9am-4pm Sat, 10am-4pm Sun).

Herbst Palace (☎ 674 96 98; ul Przędalniana 72; adult/child 6/4zł; ☯ 10am-5pm Tue, noon-5pm Wed-Fri, noon-7pm Thu, 11am-4pm Sat & Sun) has been converted into an appealing museum. It's accessible by bus No 55 heading east from the cathedral at the southern end of ul Piotrkowska. The **Jewish Cemetery** (ul Bracka 40; admission 4zł; ☯ 9am-5pm Sun-Thu, 9am-3pm Fri Apr-Oct, 9am-3pm Sun-Fri Nov-Mar) is one of the largest in Europe. It's 3km northeast of the city centre and accessible by tram No 1 or 6 from near plac Wolności. Enter from ul Zmienna.

The tourist office can provide information about all kinds of accommodation. The **youth hostel** (☎ 630 66 80; www.youthhostel lodz.wp.pl; ul Legionów 27; dm from 30zł, s/d from 45/70zł) is one of the best in Poland, so book ahead. It's only 250m west of plac Wolności.

Hotel Urzędu Miasta (☎ 640 66 09; fax 640 66 45; ul Bojowników Getta Warszawskiego 9; s/d/tr 100/144/180zł) is good value and only 500m north of plac Wolności. The **Grand Hotel** (☎ 633 99 20; logrand@orbis.pl; ul Piotrkowska 72; s/d from 258/318zł) offers a touch of faded, if slightly overpriced, *fin de siècle* grandeur in the heart of town.

Esplanada (☎ 630 59 89; ul Piotrkowska 100; mains 35-50zł) is an excellent Belle Époque-style restaurant serving quality Polish cuisine, sometimes accompanied by live folk music.

LOT (☎ 633 48 15; ul Piotrkowska 122) flies to Warsaw four times a week and has a direct connection to Cologne. From the Łódź Kaliska train station, 1.2km southwest of central Łódź, trains go regularly to Wrocław, Poznań, Toruń and Gdańsk. For Warsaw (27.70zł) and Częstochowa, use the Łódź Fabryczna station, 400m east of the city centre. Buses go in all directions from the bus terminal, next to the Fabryczna train station.

BIAŁOWIEŻA NATIONAL PARK

☎ 085

Białowieża (Byah-wo-VYEH-zhah) is Poland's oldest national park and the only one registered by Unesco as a Biosphere Reserve *and* a World Heritage Site. The 5346 hectares protect the primeval forest, as well as 120 species of birds. Animal life includes elk, wild boar, wolf and, the uncontested king of the forest, the rare European bison (which was once thought to be extinct).

The ideal base is the charming village of Białowieża. The main road to Białowieża from Hajnówka leads to the southern end of Palace Park; alternatively, a slight detour around the park leads to the village's main street, ul Waszkiewicza. Along this street is a post office and Internet centre, but there's nowhere to change money. (The nearest *kantor* is in Hajnówka.)

You'll find the **PTTK office** (☎ 681 26 24; www .pttk.bialowieza.pl; ul Kolejowa 17; ☯ 8am-4pm) is at the southern end of Palace Park. Serious hikers should contact the **National Park Office** (☎ 681 23 06; www.bpn.com.pl; ☯ 9am-4pm) inside Palace Park. Most maps of the national park (especially the one published by PTOP) detail several enticing **hiking trails**.

Sights & Activities

A combined ticket (12zł) allows you entry to the museum, the bison reserve and the nature reserve. Alternatively, you can pay for each attraction separately.

The elegant **Palace Park** (admission free; ☯ daylight hr) is only accessible on foot, bicycle or horse-drawn cart across the bridge from the PTTK office. Over the river is the **Natural & Forestry Museum** (adult/child 10/5zł; ☯ 9am-4.30pm Apr-Sep, 9am-4pm Tue-Sun Oct-May), one of the best of its kind in the country, with displays on local flora and fauna and beekeeping.

The **European Bison Reserve** (☎ 681 23 98; adult/child 5/3zł; ☺ 9am-4pm) is a small park containing many of these mighty beasts, as well as wolves, strange horse-like tarpans and mammoth *żubrońs* (hybrids of bisons and cows). Entrance to the reserve is just north of the Hajnówka–Białowieża road, about 4.5km west of the PTTK office – look for the signs along the *żebra żubra* trail or follow the green or yellow marked trails.

The main attraction is the **Strict Nature Reserve** (admission 5zł; ☺ 9am-5pm), which starts about 1km north of the Palace Park. It can only be visited on a three-hour tour with a licensed guide along a 6km trail (180zł for English- or German-speaking guide). Licensed guides (in any language) can be arranged at the PTTK office or any travel agency in the village. Note that the reserve does close sometimes, due to inclement weather.

A more comfortable way to visit the nature reserve is by horse-drawn cart (with a guide), which costs 120zł (three hours) and holds four people. Otherwise, it may be possible (with permission from the PTTK office) to visit the reserve by bicycle (with a guide).

The PTTK office and **Zimorodek** (☎ 681 26 09; ul Waszkiewicza 2), opposite the post office, rent bikes.

Sleeping & Eating

There are plenty of homes along the road from Hajnówka offering private rooms for about 30/50zł for singles/doubles.

Paprotka Youth Hostel (☎ 681 25 60; www.hostel paprotka.com.pl; ul Waszkiewicza 6; dm 16zł, d 50zł) One of the best in the region. The rooms are light and spruce, bathrooms are clean and the kitchen is excellent.

Dom Turysty PTTK (☎ 681 26 24; dm from 22zł, d/tr from 50/96zł) Boasts a serene location inside the Palace Park. It has seen better days, but the position and rates are hard to beat. It has a **restaurant**.

Pension Gawra (☎ 681 28 04; fax 681 24 84; ul Poludniowa 2; d 60-100zł; **P**) This place is excellent value – it's a quiet, homely place with large rooms overlooking a typically pretty garden just off the main road from Hajnówka, about 400m southwest of Palace Park.

Pensjonacik Unikat (☎ 681 27 74; ul Waszkiewicza 39; d/tr from 90/150zł; **P**) Charmingly decorated (complete with bison hides on the wall) and good value. The restaurant offers traditional

food at reasonable prices and has a menu in both German and English.

Getting There & Away

From Warsaw, take the express train from Warszawa Centralna to Siedlce (1½ hours), wait for a connection on the slow train to Hajnówka (two hours), and then catch one of the nine daily buses to Białowieża (4.40zł, one hour).

Five buses a day travel from the Dworzec Stadion station in Warsaw to Białystok (23zł to 29zł, four hours), from where one bus goes to Białowieża (7.80zł, three hours) – but you may need to stay overnight in Białystok. Polski Express also runs four daily buses between Białystok and Warsaw (34zł, 3½ hours).

MAŁOPOLSKA

Małopolska (literally 'little Poland') encompasses the whole of southeastern Poland, from the Lublin Uplands in the north down to the Carpathian Mountains along the borders with Slovakia and Ukraine. The main draw is undoubtedly the former royal capital, Kraków, while the rugged beauty of the Tatra Mountains always attracts a steady stream of visitors.

KRAKÓW

☎ 012 / pop 770,000

Kraków is one of Poland's oldest, best-preserved and most cosmopolitan cities, dating back to the 7th century. Miraculously, the city survived WWII unscathed, and with its wealth of medieval churches, baroque architecture and the stunning Wawel Castle and Cathedral, it's also Poland's biggest tourist draw by far. The former Jewish district of Kazimierz, with its poignant, silent synagogues, is also a rewarding place to wander. Kraków boasts an excellent array of restaurants and bars, and while hotel prices may be above the national average, and tourist numbers overwhelming in the busy summer season, Kraków is an unmissable port of call on any Polish tour.

The city was founded by Prince Krak, who, according to legend, secured its prime location overlooking the Vistula River after outwitting the resident dragon.

Kraków flourished as the medieval capital of Poland, and the kings ruled from Wawel

Castle until 1596. Even after the capital was moved to Warsaw, Polish royalty continued to be crowned and buried at the Wawel Cathedral.

Information

BOOKSHOPS

EMPiK Megastore (Map pp518-19; ☎ 429 42 34; Rynek Główny 5; ⏰ 9am-8pm) Sells foreign newspapers and magazines, plus maps and a selection of English-language novels.

Jarden Jewish Bookshop (Map p520; ☎ 429 13 74; ul Szeroka 2) For publications related to Jewish issues, see this place, in Kazimierz.

Sklep Podróżnika (Map pp518-19; ☎ 429 14 85; ul Jagiellońska 6; ⏰ 11am-7pm Mon-Fri, 11am-3pm Sat) The widest selection of regional and city maps, as well as Lonely Planet titles, is in this place.

INTERNET ACCESS

Cyber Café U Luisa (Map pp518-19; ☎ 421 90 92; Rynek Główny 13; per hr 5zł; ⏰ 11am-11pm)

Klub Garinet (Map pp518-19; ☎ 423 22 33; ul Floriańska 18; per hr 5zł; ⏰ 10am-midnight)

MONEY

Kantors and ATMs can be found all over the city centre. It's worth noting, however, that most *kantors* close on Sunday and areas near Rynek Główny square and the main train station offer terrible exchange rates. There are also exchange facilities at the airport.

Bank Pekao (Map pp518-19; Rynek Główny 31) Cashes travellers cheques and also provides cash advances on MasterCard and Visa.

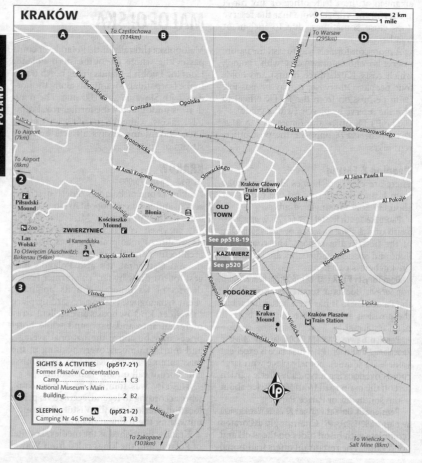

SIGHTS & ACTIVITIES (pp517-21)
Former Płaszów Concentration
Camp.....................................1 C3
National Museum's Main
Building................................2 B2

SLEEPING (pp521-2)
Camping Nr 46 Smok................3 A3

POST

Main post office (ul Westerplatte 20; ☺ 7.30am-8.30pm Mon-Fri, 8am-2pm Sat, 9am-11am Sun) The place to post your epistles.

TOURIST INFORMATION

The **Kraków Card** (www.krakowcard.com), available from tourist offices, gives free travel on public transport and free entry to many of the city's museums. Two- and three-day versions are available for 45zł and 65zł respectively.

Two free magazines, *Welcome to Craców & Małopolska* and *The Visitor: Kraków & Zakopane* are available at tourist offices and some travel agencies and upmarket hotels. The *Kraków in Your Pocket* booklet is also very useful.

Cultural Information Centre (Map pp518-19; ☎ 421 77 87; www.karnet.krakow2000.pl; ul Św Jana 2; ☺ 10am-6pm Mon-Fri, 11am-4pm Sat) The best place to get information about (and tickets for) the plethora of cultural events in the city.

Małopolska Tourism Information Centre (Map pp518-19; ☎ 421 77 06; www.mcit.pl; Rynek Główny 1/3; ☺ 9am-7pm Mon-Fri, 9am-4pm Sat & Sun Apr-Sep, 9am-5pm Mon-Fri, 9am-2pm Sat Oct-Mar) The main tourist office and ever busy.

Tourist office (Map pp518-19; ☎ 432 01 10; ul Szpitalna 25; ☺ 8am-8pm Mon-Fri, 9am-5pm Sat & Sun) Near the main train station, this place is smaller and less harried.

Tourist office (Map p520; ☎ 432 08 40; ul Józefa 7; closed for renovation at time of research) In Kazimierz and provides information about Jewish heritage in that area.

Sights & Activities

WAWEL HILL   Map pp518-19

South of the Old Town, **Wawel Hill** (admission grounds free; ☺ 6am-8pm May-Sep, 6am-5pm Oct-Apr) is Kraków's main draw for tourists. The hill is crowned with a castle and cathedral, both of which are iconic symbols of Poland.

There are several sections to the castle, each requiring a separate ticket, valid for a specific time. There's a limited daily quota of tickets for some parts, so arrive early if you want to see everything, or phone ahead to reserve. You will need a ticket even on 'free' days.

Inside the magnificent **Wawel Castle** (☎ 422 16 97), the largest and most popular sections are the **State Rooms** (adult/child 12/7zł; free Mon; ☺ 9.30am-noon Mon, 9.30am-4pm Tue & Fri, 9.30am-3pm Wed, Thu & Sat, 10am-3pm Sun) and the **Royal Private Apartments** (adult/child 15/12zł; ☺ 9.30am-4pm Tue & Fri, 9.30am-3pm Wed, Thu & Sat, 10am-3pm Sun). Entry

to the latter is only allowed on a guided tour (included in the admission fee). If you want a guide who speaks English, French or German contact the **guides office** (☎ 429 33 36) within the castle compound.

Dominating the hill is the 14th-century **Wawel Cathedral** (royal tombs & bell tower adult/child 8/4zł; ☺ 9am-3.45pm Mon-Sat, 12.15-3.45pm Sun). For four centuries it was the coronation and burial place of Polish royalty, as evidenced by the **Royal Tombs**, including that of King Kazimierz Wielki. The golden-domed **Sigismund Chapel** (1539), on the southern side of the cathedral, is considered to be the finest Renaissance construction in Poland, and the **bell tower** houses the country's largest bell (11 tonnes).

More ecclesiastical artefacts are displayed in the small **Cathedral Museum** (adult/child 5/2zł; ☺ 10am-3pm Tue-Sun).

Other attractions in the complex include the **Museum of Oriental Art** (adult/child 6/4zł; free Mon; ☺ 9.30am-noon Mon, 9.30am-4pm Tue & Fri, 9.30am-3pm Wed, Thu & Sat, 10am-3pm Sun); the **Treasury & Armoury** (adult/child 12/7zł; free Mon; ☺ 9.30am-noon Mon, 9.30am-4pm Tue & Fri, 9.30am-3pm Wed, Thu & Sat, 10am-3pm Sun); the **Lost Wawel** (adult/child 6/4zł; free Mon; ☺ 9.30am-noon Mon, 9.30am-4pm Tue & Fri, 9.30am-3pm Wed, Thu & Sat, 10am-3pm Sun), housing archaeological exhibits and the remains of the 10th-century Rotunda of Sts Felix and Adauctus; and the damp and atmospheric **Dragon's Cave** (admission 3zł; ☺ 10am-5pm Apr-Oct). Go here last, as the exit leads out of the Castle compound onto the river bank.

THE WAWEL CHAKRA

According to Hindu legend, the Lord Shiva once cast seven magic stones to seven parts of the Earth. One of these spots was Kraków, more specifically the northwestern corner of the Castle courtyard on Wawel Hill. The seven sites – including Delhi, Delphi, Rome, Jerusalem, Mecca and Velehrad – are held to be centres of great spiritual energy, and since the 1920s, when a Hindu traveller first expressed interest in the site, many more of his faith have come here to meditate, including the former Indian prime minister Nehru. More recently, dowsers, New Agers and others have come to try and tap into this mystical energy source. Whatever the truth of the matter, Wawel Hill is certainly a very special place.

KRAKÓW – OLD TOWN & WAWEL

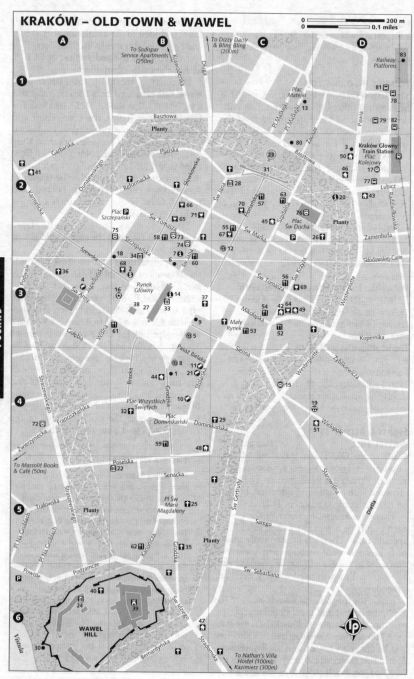

0   200 m
0   0.1 miles

To Sodispar
Service Apartments
(250m)

To Dizzy Daisy
& Bling Bling
(200m)

Railway
Platforms

Krawodecka

Długa

Plac
Matejki

Pl Matejki

Pl Mikołaj

Zacisze

Basztowa

Planty

Pawia

Garbarska

Pijarska

Basztowa

Kraków Główny
Train Station
Plac
Kolejowy

Dunajewskiego

Reformacka

Sławkowska

Św Jana

Floriańska

Lubicz

Radziwiłłowska

Plac
Szczepański

Św Tomasza

Planty

Zamenhofa

Karmelicka

Szewska

Szczepańska

Św Marka

Św Jana

Skłodowskiej-Curie

Podwale

Jagiellońska

Św Anny

Rynek
Główny

Św Tomasza

Św Krzyża

Weteranplatte

Kopernika

Gołębia

Wiślna

Mały
Rynek

Mikołajska

Zyblikiewicza

Bracka

Pasaż Bielaka

Sienna

Weteranplatte

Grodzka

Stolarska

Wielopole

Plac Wszystkich
Świętych

Plac
Dominikański

Dominikańska

Franciszkańska

Straszewskiego

Straszewskiego

Zwierzyniecka

To Massolit Books
& Café (50m)

Poselska

Senacka

Św Gertrudy

Starowiślna

Dietla

Pl Na Groblach

Pl Na Groblach

Tralowska

Planty

Pl Św
Marii
Magdaleny

Planty

Sarego

Kanonicza

Grodzka

Św Sebastiana

Powiśle

Podzamcze

Św Idziego

WAWEL
HILL

Stradomska

Bernardyńska

Vistula

To Nathan's Villa
Hostel (100m);
Kazimierz (300m)

POLAND

OLD TOWN   Map pp518-19

The magnificent **Rynek Główny** is the largest medieval town square in the whole of Europe (roughly 200m by 200m), dominated by the 16th-century Renaissance **Cloth Hall** (Sukiennice). On the ground floor is a large **souvenir market** and upstairs is the **Gallery of 19th-Century Polish Painting** (☎ 422 11 66; adult/child 5/2.50zł, free Sun; ☽ 10am-3pm Tue, Wed & Fri-Sun, 10am-5.30pm Thu), which includes several famous works by Jan Matejko.

The florid 14th-century **St Mary's Church** (Rynek Główny 4; adult/child 4/2zł; ☽ 11.30am-6pm Mon-Sat, 2-6pm Sun) fills the northeastern corner of the square. The huge main altarpiece by Wit Stwosz (Veit Stoss in German) of Nuremberg is the finest Gothic sculpture in Poland. Every hour a *hejnał* (bugle call) is played from the highest tower of the church. Today, it's a musical symbol of the city; the melody based on five notes was played in medieval times as a warning call. It breaks off abruptly to symbolise when, according to legend, the throat of a 13th-century trumpeter was pierced by a Tatar arrow.

West of the Cloth Hall is the 15th-century **Town Hall Tower** (☎ 422 99 22, ext 218; admission 4zł; ☽ 10am-4.30pm), which you can climb. The **Historical Museum of Kraków** (☎ 422 99 22; Rynek Główny 35; adult/child 4/2.50zł; ☽ 9am-3.30pm Tue, Wed & Fri, 11am-6pm Thu) has paintings, documents and oddments relating to the city.

From St Mary's Church, walk up (northeast) ul Floriańska to the 14th-century **Florian Gate**, the only survivor of the original eight gates. Behind the gate is the **Barbican** (adult/child 5/3zł; ☽ 10.30am-6pm Apr-Oct), a defensive bastion built in 1498. Nearby, the **Czartoryski Museum** (☎ 422 55 66; ul Św Jana 19; adult/child 7/4zł; ☽ 10am-3.30pm Tue-Thu, Sat & Sun, 10am-6pm Fri) features an impressive collection of European art, including Leonardo da Vinci's masterpiece *Lady with an Ermine*. Also on show are Turkish weapons and artefacts, including a campaign tent, recovered after the 1683 Battle of Vienna.

South of Rynek Główny, plac Wszystkich Świętych is dominated by two 13th-century monastic churches: the **Dominican Church** (ul Stolarska 12; admission free; ☽ 9am-6pm) to the east and the **Franciscan Church** (plac Wszystkich Świętych 5; admission free; ☽ 9am-5pm) to the west. The latter is noted for its stained-glass windows.

To the south, you'll find the **Archaeological Museum** (☎ 422 75 60; ul Poselska 3; adult/child 7/5zł; ☽ 9am-2pm Mon-Wed, 2-6pm Thu, 10am-2pm Fri & Sun), which has displays on local prehistory and, perhaps more engagingly, ancient Egyptian artefacts, including animal mummies and *ushabti* (little statues of servants placed in

POLAND

INFORMATION		
Almatur	1	B4
Bank Pekao	2	B3
Biuro Turystyki i Zakwaterowania		
Wawełtur	3	D2
British Embassy	4	A3
Centrum Internetowe	5	B3
Cracow Tours	6	B3
Cultural Information Centre	7	B3
Cyber Café U Luisa	8	B4
EMPiK Megastore	9	B3
French Consulate-General	10	B4
German Consulate-General	11	B4
Klub Garinet	12	C3
Księgarnia Językowa Bookshop	13	C1
Małopolska Tourism Information		
Centre	14	B3
Main Post Office	15	C4
Police Station	16	B3
Post & Telephone Office	17	D2
Sklep Podróżnika Bookshop	18	B3
Telephone Centre	19	D4
Tourist Office	20	D2
US Consulate	21	B4

SIGHTS & ACTIVITIES	(pp517-21)	
Archaeological Museum	22	B5
Barbican	23	C2
Cathedral Museum	24	A6
Church of SS Peter & Paul	25	B5
Church of the Holy Cross	26	D2
Cloth Hall	27	B3
Czartoryski Museum	28	C2
Dominican Church	29	C4
Dragon's Cave	30	A6

Florian Gate	31	C2
Franciscan Church	32	B4
Gallery of 19th-Century		
Polish Painting	33	B3
Historical Museum of Kraków	34	B3
St Andrew's Church	35	B5
St Anne's Church	36	A3
St Mary's Church	37	B3
Town Hall Tower	38	B3
Wawel Castle	39	B6
Wawel Cathedral	40	A6

SLEEPING	⌂	(pp521-2)
Hotel Alexander	41	A2
Hotel Amadeus	42	C3
Hotel Europejski	43	D2
Hotel Jan	44	B4
Hotel Pollera	45	C2
Hotel Polonia	46	D2
Hotel Royal	47	B6
Hotel Saski	(see 58)	
Hotel Wawel Tourist	48	B4
Hotel Wit Stwosz	49	C3
Jordan Tourist Information &		
Accommodation Center	50	D2
Wielopole Guest Rooms	51	D4

EATING	🍴	(pp522-3)
Bombaj Tandoori	52	C3
Casa della Pizza	53	C3
Green Way Bar Wegetariaski	54	C3
Gruzińskie Chaczapuri	55	C2
Ipanema	56	C3
Jama Michalika	57	C2
Metropolitan Restaurant	58	B2

Pod Aniołami	59	B4
Restauracja Chłopskie Jadło	60	B3
Restauracja Sphinx	61	B3
Smak Ukraiński	62	B5
Smaki Świata	63	C2

DRINKING	🍸	(p523)
Black Gallery	64	C3
Climatic Students' Club	65	B2
Equinox	66	B2
Indigo Jazz Club	67	C2
Klub Pasja	68	B3
Nic Nowego	69	C3
Piwnica Pod Złotą Pipą	70	C2
Pod Papugami	71	B2

ENTERTAINMENT	🎭	(pp523-4)
Filharmonia Krakówska	72	A4
Kino Apollo	73	C2
Kino Sztuka	74	B3
Stary Teatr	75	B2
Teatr im Słowackiego	76	C2

SHOPPING		
Souvenir Market	(see 27)	

TRANSPORT	(p524)	
Bus B to Airport	77	D2
Bus No 208 to Airport	78	D1
Bus Terminal	79	D1
LOT Office	80	C2
Minibuses to Wieliczka	81	D1
Private Buses to Zakopane	82	D1
Underground Passage to Buses to Oświecim		
(Auschwitz & Birkenau)	83	D1

the tomb to accompany the deceased into the afterlife). There's also a lovely garden planted with magnolia trees and roses.

Returning south along ul Grodzka is the early-17th-century Jesuit **Church of SS Peter & Paul** (ul Grodzka 64; dawn-dusk), the first baroque church built in Poland. The Romanesque 11th-century **St Andrew's Church** (ul Grodzka 56; 9am-6pm Mon-Fri) was the only building in Kraków to withstand the Tatars' attack of 1241.

KAZIMIERZ Map p520

Founded by King Kazimierz the Great in 1335, Kazimierz was, until the 1820s, an independent town with its own municipal charter and laws. In the 15th century, Jews were expelled from Kraków and forced to resettle in a small prescribed area in Kazimierz, separated by a wall from the larger Christian quarter. The Jewish quarter later became home to Jews fleeing persecution from all corners of Europe.

By the outbreak of WWII there were 65,000 Jews in Kraków (around 30% of the city's population), and most lived in Kazimierz. During the war the Nazis relocated Jews to a walled ghetto in Podgórze, just south of the Vistula River. They were exterminated in the nearby **Płaszów Concentration Camp**, as portrayed in Steven Spielberg's haunting film *Schindler's List*.

Kazimierz has two historically determined sectors. Its western Catholic quarter is dotted with churches. The 14th-century Gothic **St Catherine's Church** (ul Augustian 7; admission free; only during services) boasts a singularly imposing 17th-century gilded high altar, while the 14th-century **Corpus Christi Church** (ul Bożego Ciała 26; admission free; 9am-5pm Mon-Sat) is crammed with baroque fittings. The **Ethnographic Museum** (430 55 63; plac Wolnica 1; adult/child 4/3zł, free Sun; 10am-6pm Mon, 10am-3pm Wed-Fri, 10am-2pm Sat & Sun) in the Old Town Hall has a reasonably interesting collection of regional crafts and costumes.

The eastern Jewish quarter is dotted with synagogues, many of which miraculously survived the war. The most important is the 15th-century **Old Synagogue**, the oldest Jewish religious building in Poland. It now houses the **Jewish Museum** (422 09 62; ul Szeroka 24;

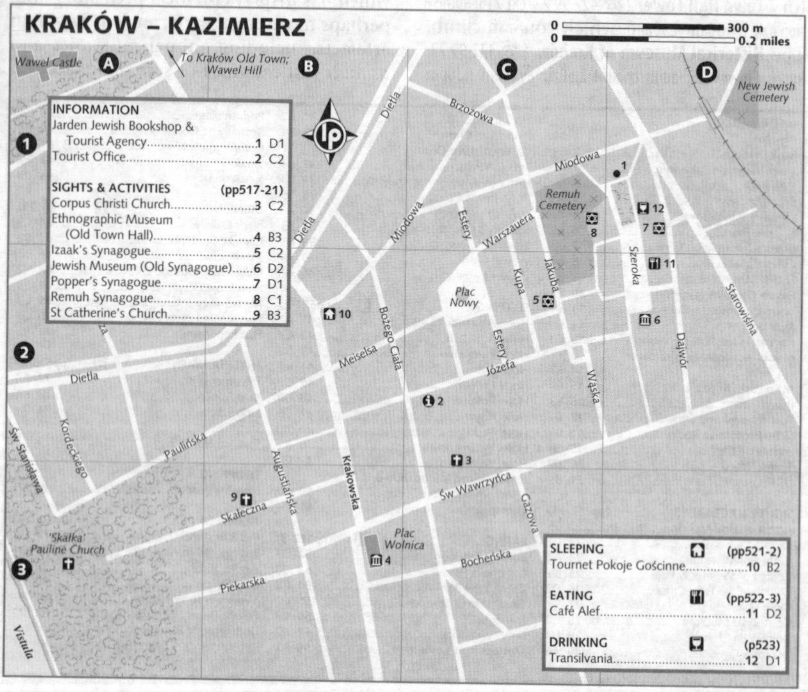
KRAKÓW – KAZIMIERZ
0 300 m
0 0.2 miles
Wawel Castle
To Kraków Old Town; Wawel Hill
New Jewish Cemetery
INFORMATION
Jarden Jewish Bookshop & Tourist Agency 1 D1
Tourist Office 2 C2
SIGHTS & ACTIVITIES (pp517-21)
Corpus Christi Church 3 C2
Ethnographic Museum (Old Town Hall) 4 B3
Izaak's Synagogue 5 C2
Jewish Museum (Old Synagogue) 6 D2
Popper's Synagogue 7 D1
Remuh Synagogue 8 C1
St Catherine's Church 9 B3
Dietla
Brzozowa
Miodowa
Remuh Cemetery
Estery
Warszauera
Szeroka
Starowiślna
Kupa
Jakuba
Plac Nowy
Bożego Ciała
Meiselsa
Józefa
Wąska
Dajwór
Kordeckiego
Św Stanisława
Paulińska
Augustiańska
Krakowska
Św Wawrzyńca
Gazowa
Skałeczna
'Skałka' Pauline Church
Plac Wolnica
Bocheńska
Piekarska
Vistula
SLEEPING (pp521-2)
Tournet Pokoje Gościnne 10 B2
EATING (pp522-3)
Café Alef 11 D2
DRINKING (p523)
Transilvania 12 D1

POLAND

admission 6zł; ⏰ 10am-2pm Mon, 10am-5pm Tue-Sun), with exhibitions on Jewish traditions.

A short walk north is the small 16th-century **Remuh Synagogue** (☎ 422 12 74; ul Szeroka 40; adult/child 5/2zł; ⏰ 9am-4pm Mon-Fri), the only one still used for religious services. Behind it, the **Remuh Cemetery** (admission free; ⏰ 9am-4pm Mon-Fri) boasts some extraordinary Renaissance gravestones. Nearby, the restored **Izaak's Synagogue** (☎ 430 55 77; ul Jakuba 25; admission 7zł; ⏰ 9am-7pm Sun-Fri) shows documentary films about life in the Jewish ghetto.

It's easy to take a self-guided walking tour around Kazimierz with the booklet *Jewish Kazimierz Short Guide*, available from the **Jarden Jewish Bookshop** (see p516).

WIELICZKA SALT MINE
Wieliczka (vyeh-LEECH-kah), 15km southeast of the city centre, is famous for the **Wieliczka Salt Mine** (☎ 278 73 02; www.kopalnia.pl; ul Daniłowicza 10; adult/child 34/20zł, 20% discount after 6pm & Nov-Feb; ⏰ 7.30am-7.30pm Apr-Oct, 8am-4pm Nov-Mar). Remarkably, this eerie world of pits and chambers is all hewn out by hand from solid salt, and every single element, from chandeliers to altarpieces, is made of salt. The mine is included on Unesco's World Heritage List.

The highlight of a mine visit is the richly ornamented **Chapel of the Blessed Kinga**, which is actually a church measuring 54m by 17m and is 12m high. Construction of this underground temple took more than 30 years (1895–1927), resulting in the removal of 20,000 tonnes of rock salt. The **museum** (admission 12zł) is on the 3rd floor of the mine.

The obligatory guided tour (included in the admission fee) through the mine takes about two hours (a 2km walk). Tours in English (July to August) operate at 10am, 11.30am, 12.30pm, 1.45pm, 3pm and 5pm (three daily in June and September); two tours a day (July and August) also run in German. If you're visiting independently, you must wait for a tour to start. Last admission to the mine is about three hours before closing time.

Minibuses to Wieliczka town depart every 10 minutes between 6am and 8pm from near the bus terminal in Kraków and drop passengers outside the salt mine (2zł). Trains between Kraków and Wieliczka leave every 45 minutes throughout the day (3.5zł), but the train station in Wieliczka is a fair walk from the mine.

Tours
The following companies operate tours of Kraków and surrounding areas:

Almatur (Map pp518-19; ☎ 422 09 02; ul Grodzka 2) All sorts of interesting outdoor activities in and around Kraków during summer.

Cracow Tours (Map pp518-19; ☎ 422 40 35; incoming@orbis.krakow.pl; Rynek Główny 41) Inside Orbis Travel, offering city tours and tours of Auschwitz and the salt mines.

Jarden Tourist Agency (Map p520; ☎ 421 71 66; www.jarden.pl; ul Szeroka 2; 2/3hr guided tour 35/45zł per person) The best agency for tours of Jewish heritage. Its showpiece – 'Retracing Schindler's List' – (two hours by car) costs 65zł per person. All tours require a minimum of three and must be arranged in advance. All tours are in English, but French- and German-speaking guides can be arranged.

Sleeping
Kraków is unquestionably Poland's major tourist destination, with prices to match, and while there's plenty of accommodation on offer, booking ahead in the busy summer months is recommended. Most hotels offer reduced rates at weekends and occasionally at less busy times of year.

Jordan Tourist Information & Accommodation Centre (Map pp518-19; ☎ 429 17 68; www.jordan.krakow.pl; ul Pawia 12; ⏰ 8am-6pm Mon-Fri, 9am-2pm Sat & Sun; s/d around 90/110zł) offers decent rooms around town.

BUDGET
Camping Nr 46 Smok (Map p516; ☎ 429 83 00; ul Kamedulska 18; per person/tent 15/19zł; **P**) It's small, quiet and pleasantly located 4km west of the Old Town. To get here from outside the Kraków Główny train station building, take tram No 2 to the end of the line in Zwierzyniec and change for any westbound bus (except No 100).

Dizzy Daisy (☎ 292 01 71; www.hostel.pl; ul Pędzichów 9; dm 35zł, d/tr 100/135zł; 🖳) A recently refurbished modern chain-hostel with great facilities, frequented by an international crowd of party people.

Nathan's Villa Hostel (Map pp518-19; ☎ 422 35 45; www.nathansvilla.com; ul Św Agnieszki 1; dm from 45zł; 🖳) The best hostel in town is conveniently located roughly halfway between the Old Town and Kazimierz. Comfy rooms, sparkling bathrooms, free laundry and a friendly atmosphere make this place a big hit with backpackers.

POLAND

Bling Bling (☎ 634 05 32; www.blingbling.pl; ul Pędzichów 7; dm 45zł) A couple of doors down from Dizzy Daisy, and offering a similarly shining standard of accommodation.

MID-RANGE

Tournet Pokoje Gościnne (Map p520; ☎ 292 00 88; www.accommodation.krakow.pl; ul Miodowa 7; s & d/tr from 100/220zł) This is a neat pension in Kazimierz, offering simple but comfortable and quiet rooms. The bathrooms are tiny, however.

Sodispar Service Apartments (Map pp518-19; ☎ 0602 247 438; www.sodispar.pl; ul Lubelska 12; apt 100-480zł) This business has several comfortable, modern apartments sleeping up to four people, north of the Old Town. There's a two-night minimum stay, and cheaper rates are available for longer stays. Rooms all have free Internet connections and computers can be rented for a small extra charge.

Wielopole Guest Rooms (Map pp518-19; ☎ 422 14 75; www.wielopole.pl; ul Wielopole 3; s/d from 150/225zł; ✗ P) This place has smart and simple modern rooms in a renovated block on the eastern edge of the Old Town, all with spotless bathrooms. Breakfast (served in your room) is extra. Great value.

Hotel Royal (Map pp518-19; ☎ 421 35 00; www.royal .com.pl; ul Św Gertrudy 26-29; s 160-210zł, d 220-300zł, tr 300-330zł, ste 360zł; P) This is an impressive Art Nouveau edifice and one of the surprisingly few places close to Wawel Hill. It's split into two sections: the higher-priced two-star rooms are cosy and far preferable to the fairly basic one-star rooms at the back.

Hotel Wawel Tourist (Map pp518-19; ☎ 424 13 00; www.wawel-tourist.com.pl; ul Poselska 22; s 190-270zł, d 280-360zł; ✗) Ideally located just off busy ul Grodzka, this is quite good value and the pricier, newly-renovated rooms are large and comfortable. It's far enough back from the main drag to avoid most of the noise.

Hotel Polonia (Map pp518-19; ☎ 422 12 33; www .hotel-polonia.com.pl; ul Basztowa 25; s/d 251/285zł, ste 450zł) Near the bus and train stations, this hotel is in a grand old building. The rooms are light and modern but many overlook the noisy main road.

Hotel Saski (Map pp518-19; ☎ 421 42 22; www .hotelsaski.com.pl; ul Sławkowska 3; s/d 260/330zł, ste 410zł; ✗) The Saski occupies an historic mansion just off Rynek Główny. The uniformed doorman, rattling old lift and ornate furnishings lend the place a certain glamour, though the rooms themselves are comparatively ordinary. Late-night noise from surrounding bars and cafés can be a problem. Breakfast, in the adjoining **Metropolitan Restaurant** is excellent.

TOP END

Hotel Jan (Map pp518-19; ☎ 430 19 92; www.hotel-jan .com.pl; ul Grodzka 11; s/d 275/360zł) This place is in a restored town house on a busy pedestrian street, just a stone's throw from the main square. Rooms are light and comfortable, though the grey marble-clad hallways are decidedly gloomy.

Hotel Alexander (Map pp518-19; ☎ 422 96 60; www.alexhotel.pl; ul Gabarska 18; s/d 280/360zł; ✗ P) The Alexander is a bright and very modern place, offering standard three-star comfort. It's on a shabby but quiet street just west of the Old Town.

Hotel Wit Stwosz (Map pp518-19; ☎ 429 60 26; www .wit-stwosz.com.pl; ul Mikołajska 28; s/d from 290/340zł) In a historic town house belonging to St Mary's church, and decorated in a suitably religious theme. It's comfortable, stylish and remarkably good value for a top-end hotel.

Hotel Pollera (Map pp518-19; ☎ 422 10 44; www .pollera.com.pl; ul Szpitalna 30; s/d 295/345zł; P) The Pollera is a classy place with large rooms crammed with elegant furniture. The singles are unexciting, but the doubles are far nicer. It's central and quiet.

Hotel Amadeus (☎ 429 60 70; www.hotel-amadeus.pl; ul Mikołajska 20; s/d US$160/170, ste US$240; ✗) Hotel Amadeus is one of Kraków's most upmarket hotels. Rooms are tastefully furnished but singles are rather small given the price. There's a sauna and fitness-centre, and a well-regarded restaurant.

Eating

By Polish standards, Kraków is a food paradise. The Old Town is tightly packed with gastronomic venues, serving a wide range of international cuisines. Cheaper takeaway fare can be found along ul Grodzka.

One local speciality is *obwarzanki*, a ring-shaped pretzel powdered with poppy seeds, and available from vendors dozing next to their pushcarts.

POLISH   Map pp518-19

Jama Michalika (☎ 422 15 61; ul Floriańska 45; mains 12-25zł; ⏰ 8am-10pm) A grand, slightly touristy, place with a very green interior and lots of puppets and theatrical etchings around the walls. The traditional Polish food is reasonable value but wait-staff seem very reluctant to show themselves.

Restauracja Chłopskie Jadło (☎ 429 51 57; ul Św Jana 3; mains 20-50zł; ☯ noon-midnight) Arranged as an old country inn and serving scrumptious Polish food from the 'Peasant's Kitchen'.

Pod Aniołami (☎ 421 39 99; ul Grodzka 35; mains 25-60zł; ☯ 1pm-midnight) The Pod offers high-quality typical Polish food in a pleasant cellar atmosphere, though it can get a little smoky.

INTERNATIONAL

Gruzińskie Chaczapuri (Map pp518-19; ☎ 604 508 380; cnr ul Floriańska & ul Św Marka; mains 8-20zł; ☯ 9am-midnight) This is a cheap and cheerful place serving up tasty Georgian dishes, with cheese pie being the speciality of the house. Grills, salads and steaks fill out the menu, and the wine's not bad either.

Bombaj Tandoori (Map pp518-19; ☎ 422 37 97; ul Mikołajska 11; mains 13-30zł; ☯ noon-11pm) The Bombaj Tandoori is the best curry house in Kraków, with friendly staff and a lengthy menu of Indian standards. The 13zł lunch specials are excellent value, while diners receive a 20% discount off their next evening meal.

Café Alef (Map p520; ☎ 421 38 70; ul Szeroka 17; mains 12-38zł; ☯ 9am-11pm) This is a quaint place in the heart of Kazimierz, and offers a wide array of Jewish-inspired dishes such as chicken *knedlach* and stuffed goose neck.

Ipanema (Map pp518-19; ☎ 422 53 23; ul Św Tomasza 28; mains from 15zł; ☯ noon-11pm) Ipanema is a laid-back Brazilian restaurant, brightly adorned with bananas and coffee-grinders, and featuring steaks, grills and a range of interesting 'Afro-Brazilian' dishes on the menu. Everything seems to come with a side-serving of good old Polish coleslaw, though.

Casa della Pizza (Map pp518-19; ☎ 421 64 98; Mały Rynek 2; mains 15-30zł; ☯ 11am-9pm) This amenable and unpretentious place is away from the bulk of the tourist traffic, with a long menu of pizzas and pasta.

Smak Ukraiński (Map pp518-19; ☎ 421 92 94; ul Kanonicza 15; mains 15-50zł; ☯ 11am-9pm) This Ukrainian restaurant presents authentic edibles in a cosy little cellar decorated with predictably folksy flair. Expect lots of dumplings, borscht and waiters in waistcoats.

Metropolitan Restaurant (Map pp518-19; ☎ 421 98 03; ul Sławkowska 3; mains 20-50zł; ☯ 7.30am-midnight) Attached to Hotel Saski, this place has photos of London plastering the walls and is a great place for breakfast. It also serves pasta, grills and steaks.

VEGETARIAN   Map pp518-19

Smaki Świata (☎ 428 27 70; ul Szpitalna 38; mains 10.50-16.80zł; ☯ 9am-9pm) Offers hearty, international vegetarian dishes, including moussaka and pasta, plus cheaper snacks and a big list of teas.

Green Way Bar Wegetariaski (☎ 431 10 27; ul Mikołajska 14; mains 8-11zł; ☯ 10am-10pm Mon-Sat, 11am-9pm Sun) The Green Way offers good value vegetarian fare such as veggie burgers, enchiladas and salads.

Drinking

There are more than 100 pubs and bars in the Old Town alone, many housed in ancient vaulted cellars, which get very smoky. Some of the best, and, inevitably, most expensive places to relax with a drink are scattered around Rynek Główny.

Pod Papugami (Map pp518-19; ☎ 422 82 99; ul Św Jana 18; ☯ 1pm-2am) This is a vaguely 'Irish' cellar pub decorated with old motorcycles and other assorted junk.

Transilvania (Map p520; ☎ 431 14 09; ul Szeroka 9; ☯ 10am-2am) The Transilvania is a convivial place in Kazimierz, with a rather more original vampire theme going on.

Nic Nowego (Map pp518-19; ☎ 421 61 88; ul Św Krzyża 15; ☯ 7am-3am Mon-Fri, 10am-3am Sat & Sun) This is another very popular, authentic Irish pub, which also serves food.

Piwnica Pod Złotą Pipą (Map pp518-19; ☎ 421 94 66; ul Floriańska 30; ☯ noon-midnight) Another inviting cellar bar. It's a more sedate place than the others, and better suited to conversation than listening to music.

For coffee, muffins and a leisurely browse through English-language books, try **Massolit Books & Café** (Map pp518-19; ☎ 432 41 50; ul Felicjanek 4; ☯ 10am-8pm Sun-Thu, 10am-10pm Sat & Sun).

Entertainment   Map pp518-19

The very comprehensive Polish/English-language booklet *Karnet* (3zł), published by the Cultural Information Centre (see p517), lists almost every event in the city.

NIGHTCLUBS

For foot-tapping jazz head to the **Indigo Jazz Club** (☎ 429 17 43; ul Floriańska 26), which often has top international acts performing.

Climatic Students' Club (☎ 421 17 71; ul Sławkowska 13-15; ☺ 5pm-late Tue-Sun) is a vast cellar club with techno and dance music attracting a young crowd at weekends.

Black Gallery (ul Mikołajska 24; ☺ noon-4am Mon-Sat, 2pm-2am Sun) is a sweaty, crowded underground pub-cum-nightclub that only gets going after midnight. It also has a more civilised courtyard. **Klub Pasja** (☎ 423 04 83; ul Szewska 5) occupies vast brick cellars. It is trendy, attractive and popular with foreigners.

THEATRE

The best-known venue, **Stary Teatr** (☎ 422 85 66; ul Jagiellońska 5), offers quality productions. **Teatr im Słowackiego** (☎ 422 45 75; plac Św Ducha 1), built in 1893, focuses on Polish classics and large productions. **Filharmonia Krakówska** (☎ 422 94 77; ul Zwierzyniecka 1) boasts one of the best orchestras in the country; concerts are usually held on Friday and Saturday.

CINEMAS

Two of the better and more convenient cinemas showing recent films are **Kino Apollo** (☎ 421 89 50; ul Św Tomasza 11a) and **Kino Sztuka** (☎ 421 41 99; cnr Św Tomasza & Św Jana). Tickets from 10zł. English-language films are generally shown in English with subtitles.

Getting There & Away

For information on travelling from Kraków to Zakopane, Częstochowa or Oświęcim (for Auschwitz), refer to the relevant Getting There & Away sections later.

AIR

The John Paul II International Airport is more often called the Balice Airport, after the suburb in which it's located about 15km west of the Old Town. LOT flies between Kraków and Warsaw several times a day, and offers direct flights from Kraków to Frankfurt, London, Paris and Rome.

In summer, LOT also flies directly from Chicago (April to September) and New York (June to September). In addition, Austrian Airlines flies directly between Kraków and Vienna several times a week. Bookings for all flights can be made at the **LOT office** (Map pp518-19; ☎ 422 42 15; ul Basztowa 15).

BUS

The main **bus terminal** (plac Kolejowy) is conveniently opposite the main train station build-

ing and only minutes on foot from the Old Town. However, trains are more frequent and faster so bus services are limited to the regional centres of minimal interest to travellers, as well as Lublin (22zł, three daily), Zamość (25zł, two daily), Warsaw (39zł, four daily), Wrocław (26zł, two daily) and Cieszyn (8.70zł, seven daily) on the Czech border.

Polski Express buses to Warsaw depart from a spot opposite the bus terminal.

TRAIN

The lovely old **Kraków Główny train station** (plac Dworcowy), on the northeastern outskirts of the Old Town, handles all international trains and almost all domestic rail services. (Note that the railway platforms are about 150m north of the station building.)

Each day from Kraków, ten trains head to Warsaw (37zł, 2¾ hours). Also every day from Kraków there are several trains to Wrocław (40.20zł, 3¾ hours), two to Poznań (56zł, six hours), two to Lublin (48zł, five hours) and four to Gdynia, via Gdańsk (78.20zł, 7¼ hours).

Advance tickets for international and domestic trains can be booked directly at the Kraków Główny station building or from **Cracow Tours** (p521).

OŚWIĘCIM

☎ 033 / pop 48,000

The name of Oświęcim (osh-FYEN-cheem), about 60km west of Kraków, may be unfamiliar to outsiders, but the German name, Auschwitz, is not. This was the scene of the most extensive experiment in genocide in the history of humankind.

The Auschwitz camp was established in April 1940 in the Polish army barracks next to Oświęcim. Originally intended to hold Polish political prisoners, the camp eventually developed into the largest centre for the extermination of European Jews. Towards this end, two additional camps were subsequently established: Birkenau (Brzezinka), or Auschwitz II, 3km west of Auschwitz; and Monowitz (Monowice), several kilometres west of Oświęcim. These death factories eliminated 1.5 to two million people – about 90% of whom were Jews.

Auschwitz

Auschwitz was only partially destroyed by the fleeing Nazis, so many of the original buildings remain as a bleak document of the camp's history. A dozen of the 30 surviving prison blocks house sections of the **State Museum Auschwitz-Birkenau** (☎ 844 81 00; admission free; ☿ 8am-7pm Jun-Aug, 8am-6pm May & Sep, 8am-5pm Apr & Oct, 8am-4pm Mar & Nov–mid-Dec, 8am-3pm mid-Dec–Feb).

About every half-hour, the cinema in the **Visitors' Centre** at the entrance to Auschwitz shows a 15-minute documentary film (admission 2zł) about the liberation of the camp by Soviet troops on 27 January 1945. It's shown in several different languages throughout the day; check the schedule at the information desk as soon as you arrive at the camp. The film is not recommended for children under 14 years old. The Visitors' Centre also has a cafeteria, *kantor* and left-luggage room, and several bookshops.

Some basic explanations in Polish, English and Hebrew are provided on-site, but you'll understand more if you buy the small *Auschwitz Birkenau Guide Book* (translated into about 15 languages) from the bookshops at the Visitors' Centre. English-language tours (25zł per person, 3½ hours) of Auschwitz and Birkenau leave at 11.30am daily, while another starts at 1pm if there's enough demand. Tours in German commence when a group of seven or eight can be found. But make sure that you receive your allotted time; some guides tell you to wander around Birkenau by yourself and to make your own way back to Auschwitz.

Birkenau

It was actually at **Birkenau** (admission free; ☿ 8am-7pm Jun-Aug, 8am-6pm May & Sep, 8am-5pm Apr & Oct, 8am-4pm Mar & Nov–mid-Dec, 8am-3pm mid-Dec–Feb), not Auschwitz, where the extermination of huge numbers of Jews took place. This vast (175 hectares), purpose-built and grimly efficient camp had over 300 prison barracks and four huge gas chambers complete with crematoria. Each gas chamber held 2000 people, and electric lifts raised the bodies to the ovens. The camp could hold 200,000 inmates at one time.

Although much of the camp was destroyed by retreating Nazis, the size of the place, fenced off with barbed wire stretching almost as far as the eye can see, provides some idea of the scale of this heinous crime. The viewing platform above the entrance provides further perspective. In some ways, Birkenau is even more shocking than Auschwitz and there are far fewer tourists.

Sleeping & Eating

For most visitors, Auschwitz and Birkenau is an easy day trip from Kraków.

The **cafeteria** in the Visitors' Centre is sufficient for a quick lunch.

Centrum Dialogu i Modlitwy (☎ 843 10 00; www .centrum-dialogu.oswiecim.pl; ul Kolbego 1; per camp site from €6, r per person from €20; ☐) is 700m southwest of Auschwitz. It's comfortable and quiet, and the price includes breakfast. Rooms with private bathroom cost slightly more, and full board is also offered.

Getting There & Away

From Kraków Główny station, 11 trains go to Oświęcim (19zł, 1½ hours) each day, though more depart from Kraków Płaszów station. Check the schedules the day before so you can plan your visit properly.

Far more convenient are the 12 buses (10zł, 1½ hours) per day to Oświęcim which depart from the small bus stop on ul Bosacka in Kraków; the stop is at the end of the underpass below the railway platforms. Get off at the final stop (outside the PKS bus maintenance building), 200m from the entrance to Auschwitz. The return bus timetable to Kraków is displayed at the Birkenau Visitors' Centre.

Every hour on the hour from 11am to 4pm (inclusive) between 15 April and 31 October buses shuttle passengers between the visitors' centres at Auschwitz and Birkenau. Otherwise, between both places follow the signs for an easy walk (3km) or take a taxi. Auschwitz is also linked to central Oświęcim and the town's train station by bus No 19 or any bus No 24 to 29 every 30 to 40 minutes.

Most travel agencies in Kraków offer organised tours of Auschwitz (including Birkenau). However, some tours do not provide private transport, so it's often easier (and far cheaper) to use the public transport system and join an official tour from the Visitors' Centre in Auschwitz.

CZĘSTOCHOWA

☎ 034 / pop 260,000

Częstochowa (chen-sto-HO-vah), 114km northwest of Kraków, is the spiritual heart of Poland. This likeable town owes its fame to the miraculous Black Madonna kept in

POLAND

the Jasna Góra monastery. The Paulites of Hungary founded the Jasna Góra monastery in 1382 and received the Black Madonna shortly thereafter. In 1430 the holy icon was stolen by the Hussites, who slashed the face of the Madonna. The wounds allegedly began to bleed, so the frightened thieves abandoned the icon and ran off. The monks who found the panel wanted to clean it, and a spring miraculously bubbled from the ground. The spring exists to this day, and St Barbara's Church was founded on the site. The picture was restored, but the scars on the face of the Virgin Mary were left as a reminder of the miracle.

Early in the 17th century the monastery was fortified, and it was one of the few places in the country to withstand the Swedish sieges of the 1650s. This miracle was again attributed to the Black Madonna. In 1717 the Black Madonna was crowned Queen of Poland.

From the train station, and adjacent bus terminal, turn right (north) up Al Wolności – along which there are several Internet cafés – to the main thoroughfare, Al Najświętszej Marii Panny (sensibly simplified to Al NMP). At the western end of this broad avenue is the monastery and at the eastern end is plac Daszyńskiego. Between both is the **tourist office** (☎ 368 22 60; Al NMP 65; ☻ 9am-5pm Mon-Fri, 9am-2pm Sat) and several banks and *kantors*.

Sights

The **Paulite Monastery on Jasna Góra** (admission free; ☻ dawn-dusk) retains the appearance of a hill-top fortress. Inside the grounds are three **museums** (donations welcome; ☻ all 9am-5pm): **The Arsenal**, with a variety of old weapons; the **600th-Anniversary Museum** (Muzeum Sześćsetlecia), which contains Lech Wałęsa's 1983 Nobel Peace Prize; and **The Treasury** (Skarbiec), featuring offerings presented by the faithful.

The **tower** (☻ 8am-4pm Apr-Nov) is the tallest (106m) historic church tower in Poland. The baroque church is beautifully decorated. The image of the Black Madonna on the high altar of the adjacent chapel is hard to see, so a copy is on display in the **Knights' Hall** (Sala Rycerska) in the monastery.

On weekends and holidays expect long queues for all three museums. The crowds in the chapel may be so thick that you're almost unable to enter, much less get near the icon.

In the Town Hall the **Częstochowa Museum** (☎ 324 32 75; plac Biegańskiego 45; admission 3zł; ☻ 8.30am-4pm Wed-Sat, 10am-4pm Sun) features an ethnographic collection and modern Polish paintings.

Festivals & Events

The major Marian feasts at Jasna Góra are 3 May, 16 July, 15 August (especially), 26 August, 8 September, 12 September and 8 December. On these days the monastery is packed with pilgrims.

Sleeping & Eating

The **youth hostel** (☎ 324 31 21; ul Jasnogórska 84/90; dm 20zł; ☻ July-Aug), two blocks north of the tourist office, has modest facilities.

Dom Pielgrzyma (☎ 324 70 11; ul Wyszyńskiego 1/31; dm from 20zł, s/d from 60/90zł) is a huge place behind the monastery. It offers numerous quiet and comfortable rooms, and is remarkably good value.

Plenty of **eateries** can be found near the Dom Pielgrzyma. Better restaurants are dotted along Al NMP, such as the classy **Restaurant Polonus** (☎ 801 33 18; Al NMP 75; mains from 15zł; ☻ 10am-midnight) near the path up to the monastery. **Bar Viking** (☎ 324 57 68; ul Nowowiejskiego 10; mains 10-28zł; ☻ 10am-10pm), about 200m south of the Częstochowa Museum, is cheap and cheerful.

Getting There & Away

Every day from the **bus terminal** (Al Wolności 45) three buses go to Kraków (9.60zł), three travel to Wrocław (17.50zł), one heads for Zakopane (16zł) and three speed off to Warsaw (25zł to 35zł).

From the impressive **train station** (Al Wolności 21), several trains a day go to Warsaw (53zł). There are also four to five daily trains to Gdynia, via Gdańsk, Łódź, Olsztyn and Zakopane; six to Kraków; and nine to Wrocław.

ZAKOPANE

☎ 018 / pop 30,000

Nestled at the foot of the Tatra Mountains, Zakopane is the most famous resort in Poland and the major winter-sports capital. Although essentially a base for skiing and hiking in the Tatras, Zakopane itself has an enjoyable, laid-back atmosphere, even if it is overbuilt, overpriced and commercialised.

In the late 19th century, Zakopane became popular with artists, many of whom came to settle and work here. The best known are the composer Karol Szymanowski and the writer and painter, Witkacy. The father of the latter, Stanisław Witkiewicz (1851–1915), was inspired by traditional local architecture and experimented with the so-called Zakopane style. Some buildings he designed still remain.

Information

INTERNET ACCESS

GraNet Internet Café (ul Krupówki 2) A convenient place to surf the Internet.

MONEY

Dozens of **kantors** can be found along the main streets. There are several banks along the pedestrian mall.

Bank Pekao (cnr ul Staszica & Al 3 Maja)

PKO Bank (ul Krupówki 19) Can handle your foreign exchange needs.

POST

Main post office (ul Krupówki) Along the main street and also houses the telephone centre.

TOURIST INFORMATION

Tourist Information Centre (☎ 201 22 11; ul Kościuszki 17; ☯ 8am-8pm) Helpful and knowledgeable English-speaking staff can arrange private rooms, inquire on your behalf about hotel vacancies, organise car rental and sell hiking and city maps. The centre can also arrange rafting trips down the Dunajec River (see p531) and guides for the Tatra Mountains.

TRAVEL AGENCIES

Centrum Przewodnictwa Tatrzańskiego (Tatra Guide Centre; ☎ 206 37 99; ul Chałubińskiego 42/44; ☯ 9am-3pm) Able to arrange English- and German-speaking mountain guides.

Księgarnia Górska (ul Zaruskiego 5) In the reception area of the Dom Turysty PTTK, this is by far the best place for regional hiking maps.

Orbis Travel (☎ 201 48 12; ul Krupówki 22) Offers the usual services, as well as accommodation in private homes.

Sights & Activities

The **Tatra Museum** (☎ 201 52 05; ul Krupówki 10; admission 4zł; ☯ 9am-4pm Tue-Sun) has exhibits about regional history, ethnography and geology, and plenty of displays about the flora and fauna of the Tatras. Head southwest on ul Kościeliska to **Villa Koliba** (ul Kościeliska 18), the first design (1892) by Witkiewicz in the Zakopane style. Predictably, it now

houses the **Museum of Zakopane Style** (☎ 201 36 02; admission 4zł; ☯ 9am-4pm Wed-Sun). About 350m southeast is **Villa Atma** (ul Kasprusie 19). Inside is **Szymanowksi Museum** (☎ 206 31 50; admission 2zł; ☯ 10am-4pm Tue-Sun), dedicated to the great musician who once lived there. There are piano recitals here in summer.

The **Tatra National Park Natural Museum** (☎ 201 41 92; ul Chałubińskiego 42a; admission 4zł; ☯ 9am-2pm Mon-Sat), near the Rondo en route to the national park, has some mildly interesting exhibits about the park's natural history.

A short walk northeast up the hill leads to **Villa Pod Jedlami** (ul Koziniec 1), another splendid house in the Zakopane style (the interior cannot be visited). Perhaps Witkiewicz's greatest achievement is the **Jaszczurówka Chapel**, about 1.5km further east along the road to Morskie Oko.

Mt Gubałówka (1120m) offers excellent views over the Tatras and is a favourite destination for tourists who don't feel like *too* much exercise. The **funicular** (one way/return 8/14zł) covers the 1388m-long route in less than five minutes and climbs 300m from the funicular station just north of ul Krupówki. It operates between 9am and 9pm from 1 May to 30 September, but at other times it only runs on weekends. An all-day pass for skiers costs 70zł; a one-day pass at other times for 10 rides costs 50zł.

Sleeping

Given the abundance of private rooms and decent hostels, few travellers actually stay in hotels. The tourist office usually knows of great bargains for guesthouses.

Most of the travel agencies in Zakopane can arrange **private rooms**, but in the peak season they may not want to offer you anything for less than three nights. Expect a double room (singles are rarely offered) to cost about 50zł in the peak season for anywhere in the town centre and about 40zł for somewhere a little further out.

Locals offering private rooms may also approach you at the bus or train stations; alternatively, just look out for the obvious signs posted in the front of private homes – *noclegi* and *pokoje* both mean 'rooms'. Another place to start looking and booking is at the tourist office.

Like all seasonal resorts, accommodation prices fluctuate considerably between the low season and high season (December to

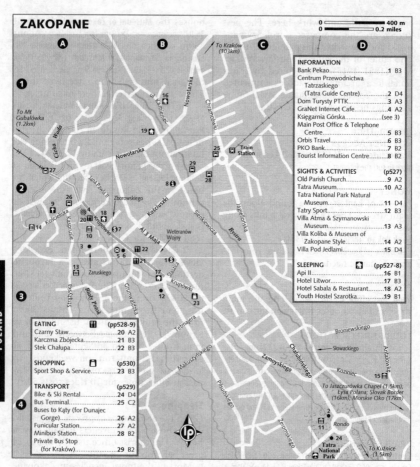

ZAKOPANE

0 | 400 m
0 | 0.2 miles

INFORMATION
Bank Pekao...1 B3
Centrum Przewodnictwa
 Tatrzaskiego
 (Tatra Guide Centre)................2 D4
Dom Turysty PTTK......................3 A3
GraNet Internet Cafe.................4 A2
Ksigegarnia Górska.....................(see 3)
Main Post Office & Telephone
 Centre.....................................5 B3
Orbis Travel.................................6 B3
PKO Bank.....................................7 B2
Tourist Information Centre.........8 B2

SIGHTS & ACTIVITIES (p527)
Old Parish Church......................9 A2
Tatra Museum...........................10 A2
Tatra National Park Natural
 Museum.................................11 D4
Tatry Sport...............................12 B3
Villa Atma & Szymanowski
 Museum.................................13 A3
Villa Koliba & Museum of
 Zakopane Style......................14 A2
Villa Pod Jedlami.....................15 D4

SLEEPING (pp527-8)
Api II..16 B1
Hotel Litwor.............................17 B3
Hotel Sabala & Restaurant.......18 A2
Youth Hostel Szarotka.............19 B1

EATING (pp528-9)
Czarny Staw..............................20 A2
Karczma Zbójecka.....................21 B3
Stek Chałupa.............................22 B3

SHOPPING (p530)
Sport Shop & Service.................23 B3

TRANSPORT (p529)
Bike & Ski Rental.......................24 D4
Bus Terminal.............................25 C2
Buses to Kąty (for Dunajec
 Gorge)...................................26 A2
Funicular Station.......................27 A2
Minibus Station.........................28 B2
Private Bus Stop
 (for Kraków)...........................29 B2

To Kraków (103km)

Train Station

To Mt Gubałówka (1.2km)

To Jaszczurówka Chapel (1.5km); Łysa Polana; Slovak Border (16km); Morskie Oko (17km)

Rondo

Tatra National Park

To Kuźnice (1.5km)

February and July to August). It is always wise to book accommodation in advance at these peak times, especially on weekends. Rates for the high seasons are listed below.

Youth Hostel Szarotka (☎ 201 36 18; ul Nowotarska 45; dm/d 35/50zł) This friendly and homely place gets packed (and untidy) in the high season, but rates are negotiable at other times. It's along a noisy road about a 10-minute walk from the town centre.

Api II (☎ 206 29 31; ul Kamieniec 13; d/tr 70/105zł; ☒) This is a central place offering good value for money, with big, well-maintained rooms.

Hotel Sabala (☎ 201 50 92; www.sabala.zakopane .pl; ul Krupówki 11; s/d from 195/260zł) Boasting a superb location overlooking the picturesque pedestrian thoroughfare and with cosy,

attic-style rooms. Half-board options are also available in the **restaurant**.

Hotel Litwor (☎ 201 27 39; www.litwor.pl; ul Krupówki 40; s/d €119/157; ☒ ℗ ☒) This sumptuous four-star place, with large, restful rooms, has all the usual top-end facilities. It also has an excellent **restaurant** serving traditional game dishes.

Eating

The main street, ul Krupówki, is lined with all sorts of eateries.

Karczma Zbójecka (☎ 201 38 56; ul Krupówki 28; mains 18-30zł; ☽ 11am-midnight) An attractive basement eatery with waiters dressed in traditional outfits and offering mouthwatering regional food, including fresh fish.

POLAND

Stek Chałupa (☎ 201 59 18; ul Krupówki 33; mains 15-25zł; ☽ noon-midnight) Stek Chałupa has a Wild West theme, so it specialises in meat dishes, although the salad bar is extensive.

Czarny Staw (☎ 201 38 56; ul Krupówki 2; mains 10-25zł; ☽ 10am-1am) Offers a tasty range of Polish dishes, including fish, and there's live music nightly.

Restaurant Sabała (☎ 201 50 92; ul Krupówki 11; mains 15-25zł; ☽ 11am-midnight) This lively, friendly place serves traditional local specialities, again with live music.

Getting There & Away

From the **bus terminal** (ul Chramcówki), fast PKS buses run to Kraków every 45 to 60 minutes (9zł, 2½ hours). Two private companies – Trans Frej and Szwagropol – also run comfortable buses (10zł) at the same frequency. These private buses leave from a stop along ul Kościuszki in Zakopane, and opposite the bus terminal in Kraków. At peak times (especially on weekends), buy your tickets for the private buses in advance from counters outside the departure points in Zakopane. Tickets are also available in Kraków for Trans Frej buses from **Biuro Turystyki i Zakwaterowania Waweltur** (Map pp518-19; ul Pawia 8) and for Szwagropol buses from **Jordan Tourist Information & Accommodation Centre** (Map pp518-19; ul Pawia 12).

From Zakopane, PKS buses also go twice daily to Lublin (45zł, six hours) Oświęcim and Warsaw (53zł, eight hours) and once to Przemyśl and Sanok. Two per week (daily in summer) also go to Budapest (nine hours) in Hungary. PKS buses – and minibuses from opposite the bus terminal – regularly travel to Lake Morskie Oko (right) and on to Polana Palenica. To cross into Slovakia, get off this bus/minibus at Łysa Polana, cross the border on foot and take another bus to Tatranská Lomnica in Slovakia.

From the **train station** (ul Chramcówki), trains for Kraków (46zł, 3½ hours) leave every two hours or so, but avoid the passenger train, which takes up to five hours. Between one and three trains a day go to Częstochowa, Gdynia via Gdańsk, Lublin, Łódź and Poznań, and five head to Warsaw.

TATRA MOUNTAINS
☎ 018

The Tatras, 100km south of Kraków, is the highest range of the Carpathian Mountains.

Roughly 60km long and about 15km wide, this mountain range stretches across the Polish-Slovak border. A quarter is in Poland and is now mostly part of the Tatra National Park (about 212 sq km). The Polish Tatras contain more than 20 peaks over 2000m, the highest of which is Mt Rysy (2499m).

Cable Car to Mt Kasprowy Wierch

Almost every Polish tourist has made the cable car trip (return 29zł; ☽ 7.30am-8pm summer, 7.30am-3.30pm winter) from Kuźnice (3km south of central Zakopane) to the summit of Mt Kasprowy Wierch (1985m). At the end of the trip, you can get off and stand with one foot in Poland and the other in Slovakia. The one-way journey takes 20 minutes and climbs 936m. The cable car normally shuts down for a few weeks in May, June and November, and won't operate if the snow and, particularly, the winds are dangerous.

The view from the top is spectacular (clouds permitting). Two chair lifts transport skiers to and from various slopes between December and April. A small **cafeteria** serves skiers and hikers alike. In the summer, many people return to Zakopane on foot down the Gąsienicowa Valley, and the most intrepid walk the ridges all the way across to Lake Morskie Oko via Pięciu Stawów, a strenuous hike taking a full day in good weather.

If you buy a return ticket, your trip back is automatically reserved for two hours after your departure, so buy a one-way ticket to the top (19zł) and another one down (10zł) if you want to stay longer. Mt Kasprowy Wierch is popular, so the lines for tickets are long; in summer, arrive early and expect to wait. PKS buses and minibuses to Kuźnice frequently leave from Zakopane.

Lake Morskie Oko

One of the most popular destinations in the Tatras is the emerald-green Lake Morskie Oko (Eye of the Sea), among the loveliest in the Tatras. The easiest way to reach the lake is by road from Zakopane. PKS buses and minibuses regularly depart from Zakopane for Polana Palenica (30 minutes), from where a road (9km) continues uphill to the lake. Cars, bikes and buses are not allowed up this road, so you'll have to walk, but it's not steep (allow about two hours

POLAND

one way). Alternatively, take a horse-drawn carriage (32/15zł uphill/downhill, but very negotiable) to within 2km of the lake. In winter, transport is by horse-drawn four-seater sledge, which is more expensive. The last minibus to Zakopane returns between 5pm and 6pm.

Hiking

If you're doing any hiking in the Tatras get a copy of the *Tatrzański Park Narodowy* map (1:25,000), which shows all hiking trails in the area. Better still, buy one or more of the 14 sheets of *Tatry Polskie* (available at Księgarnia Górska in Zakopane, p527). In July and August these trails can be overrun by tourists, so late spring and early autumn are the best times. Theoretically you can expect better weather in autumn (September to October), when rainfall is lower.

Like all alpine regions, the Tatras can be dangerous, particularly during the snowy time (November to May). Always use common sense and remember that the weather can be unpredictable. Bring proper hiking boots, warm clothing and waterproof rain gear – and be prepared to use occasional ropes and chains (provided along the trails) to get up and down some rocky slopes. Guides are not necessary because many of the trails are marked, but guides can be arranged in Zakopane (see p527 for details) for about 180zł per day.

There are several picturesque valleys south of Zakopane, including the **Dolina Strążyska**. You can continue from the Strążyska by the red trail up to **Mt Giewont** (1909m), 3½ hours from Zakopane, and then walk down the blue trail to Kuźnice in two hours.

Two long and beautiful forested valleys, the **Dolina Chochołowska** and the **Dolina Kościeliska**, are in the western part of the park, known as the Tatry Zachodnie (West Tatras). These valleys are also ideal for cycling. Both valleys are accessible by PKS buses and private minibuses from Zakopane.

The Tatry Wysokie (High Tatras) to the east offer quite different scenery: bare granite peaks and glacial lakes. One great way to get there is to take the cable car to **Mt Kasprowy Wierch** and then hike eastward along the red trail to Mt Świnica (2301m) and on to the Zawrat pass (2159m) – a tough three to four hours from Mt Kasprowy. From Zawrat, descend northwards to the Dolina

Gąsienicowa along the blue trail and then back to Zakopane.

Alternatively, head south (also along the blue trail) to the wonderful **Dolina Pięciu Stawów** (Five Lakes Valley), where there is a mountain refuge 1¼ hours from Zawrat. The blue trail heading west from the refuge passes **Lake Morskie Oko**, 1½ hours from the refuge.

Skiing

Zakopane boasts four major ski areas (and several smaller ones) with over 50 ski lifts. **Mt Kasprowy Wierch** and **Mt Gubałówka** offer the best conditions and most challenging slopes in the area, with the ski season extending until early May. Lift tickets cost 10zł for one ride. Alternatively, you can buy a 10-ride card (70zł), which allows you to skip the queues. Take the funicular or cable car and purchase your lift tickets on the mountain.

Ski equipment rental is available at all facilities except Mt Kasprowy Wierch. Otherwise, stop off on your way to Kuźnice at the **ski rental** place near the Rondo in Zakopane. Other places in Zakopane, such as **Tatry Sport** (ul Piłsudskiego 4) and **Sport Shop & Service** (ul Krupówki 52a), also rent ski gear.

Sleeping

Tourists are not allowed to take their own cars into the park; you must walk in, take the cable car or use an official vehicle owned by the park or a hotel/hostel.

Camping is also not allowed in the park, but eight PTTK mountain refuges/hostels provide simple accommodation. Most refuges are small and fill up fast; in midsummer and midwinter they're invariably packed beyond capacity. No one is ever turned away, however, though you may have to crash on the floor if all the beds are taken. Do not arrive too late, and bring along your own bed mat and sleeping bag. All refuges serve simple hot meals, but the kitchens and dining rooms close early (sometimes at 7pm).

The refuges listed here are open all year, but some may be temporarily closed for renovations or because of inclement weather. Check the current situation at the Dom Turysty PTTK in Zakopane or the regional **PTTK headquarters** (☎ 018-438 610) in Nowy Sącz.

The easiest refuge to reach from Zakopane is the large and decent **Kalatówki Hotel** (☎ 206 36 44; s/d/tr from 46/90/111zł), a 40-minute walk from the Kuźnice cable-car station. About 30 minutes beyond Kalatówki on the trail to Giewont is **Hala Kondratowa Hostel** (☎ 201 91 14; dm 20-22zł). It's in a great location and has a great atmosphere, but it is small.

Hikers wishing to traverse the park might begin at the **Roztoka Hostel** (☎ 207 74 42; dm 22-30zł), accessible by the bus/minibus to Morskie Oko. An early start from Zakopane, however, would allow you to visit Morskie Oko in the morning and stay at the **Morskie Oko Hostel** (☎ 207 76 09; dm from 35zł), or continue through to the **Dolina Pięciu Stawów Hostel** (☎ 207 76 07; dm from 25zł). This is the highest (1700m) and most scenically located refuge in the Polish Tatras.

DUNAJEC GORGE

An entertaining and leisurely way to explore the Pieniny Mountains is to go **rafting** on the Dunajec River, which winds its way along the Polish-Slovak border through a spectacular and deep gorge. Adrenalin junkies may be disappointed, however, because this isn't a white-water rafting experience. In recent years, the course of the river has changed so it now cuts through Slovakia for a few kilometres, but Polish and Slovak immigration officials don't wait on rafts to check passports.

The trip starts at the wharf (Przystan Flisacka) in Kąty, 46km northeast of Zakopane, and finishes at the spa town at Szczawnica. The 17km (2½ hours) raft trip operates between May and October, but only starts when there's a minimum of 10 passengers.

The gorge is an easy day trip from Zakopane. In summer, 10 PKS buses to Kąty leave from a spot along ul Kościeliska. Alternatively, catch a regular bus to Nowy Targ (30 minutes) from Zakopane and one of six daily buses (one hour) to Kąty. From Szczawnica, take the bus back to Zakopane or change at Nowy Targ. Each day, five buses also travel between Szczawnica and Kraków.

To avoid waiting around in Kąty for a raft to fill up, organise a trip at any travel agency in Zakopane or at the tourist office. The cost is around 35zł to 43zł per person, and includes transport, equipment and guides.

SANOK

☎ 013 / pop 40,000

Sanok is noted for its unique **Museum of Folk Architecture** (☎ 463 16 72; ul Rybickiego 3; admission 9zł; ❧ 8am-6pm May-Oct, 8am-4pm Nov-Apr), which features architecture from regional ethnic groups. Walk north from the town centre for 1.5km along ul Mickiewicza. The **Historical Museum** (☎ 464 13 66; ul Zamkowa 2; admission 10zł; ❧ 8am-10am Mon, 9am-5pm Tue & Wed, 9am-3pm Thu-Sun) is housed in a 16th-century castle and contains Poland's most impressive collection of Ruthenian icons.

Sanok is also an excellent base to explore surrounding villages, many of which have some lovely old churches. The best way to get around is along the marked **Icon Trail**. This **hiking** or **cycling** trail commences in Sanok and completes a 70km loop, passing by 10 village churches, as well as picturesque and pristine mountain countryside. More information and maps (in English) are available from the very helpful **PTTK office** (☎ 463 21 71; www.sanok.pl; ul 3 Maja 2; ❧ 8am-4pm Mon-Fri), near the main square, plac Św Michała. More brochures and information can be had at the tourist information desk inside **Orbis Travel** (☎ 463 28 59; ul Grzegorza 4; ❧ 8am-5pm Mon-Fri, 9am-1pm Sat). It can also arrange accommodation.

Convenient budget accommodation is available at **Hotel Pod Trzema Różami** (☎ & fax 463 09 22; ul Jagiellońska 13; s/d 75/95zł; **P**), about 200m south of the main square. Further south (about 400m) and up the scale is **Hotel Jagielloński** (☎ & fax 463 12 08; ul Jagiellońska 49; s/d/tr from 90/110/130zł; **P**), which has a very good **restaurant** (mains 16-32zł).

Karczma Jadło Karpackie (☎ 464 67 00; Rynek 12; mains 12-25zł; ❧ 9am-10pm) is an amenable, folksy bar and restaurant on the main square.

The **bus terminal** and adjacent **train station** are about 1km southeast of the main square. Four buses go daily to Przemyśl (5zł, one hour), and buses and fast trains go regularly to Kraków and Warsaw.

PRZEMYŚL

☎ 016 / pop 70,000

Perched on a hillside overlooking the San River and dominated by four mighty historic churches, Przemyśl (PSHEH-mishl) is a picturesque town with a sloping and well-preserved **Rynek** (town square). The **tourist office** (☎ 675 16 64; oitinform@wp.pl; ul Ratuszowa; ❧ 8am-4pm Mon-Fri, 9am-3pm Sat) is one block north of the Rynek. Check your emails at **Blue Net** (☎ 678 55 62; ul Słowackiego 14).

About 350m southwest of the Rynek are the ruins of a 14th-century **castle** (ul Zamkowa), built by Kazimierz Wielki. The **Regional Museum**

POLAND

(☎ 678 33 25; plac Czackiego 3; adult/child 4/2zł; ⊙ 10.30am-5.30pm Tue & Fri; 10am-2pm Wed, Thu, Sat & Sun) houses a splendid collection of Ruthenian icons, Austro-Hungarian militaria and a dry display of local archaeological finds. It's about 150m southeast of the Rynek.

More unusual displays are on show at the curious **Museum of Bells and Pipes** (☎ 678 96 66; ul Władycze 3; adult/child 4/2zł; ⊙ 10.30am-5.30pm Tue, Fri & Sat, 10am-2pm Wed & Thu, 11am-7pm Sun) in the old Clock Tower, where you can cast an eye over several floors worth of vintage bells, elaborately carved pipes and cigar cutters. Quite what the connection is though is unclear, especially as labelling is only in Polish. From the top of the tower, there's a great view of town.

Przemyśl has a wide selection of inexpensive accommodation, including the well-kept **Youth Hostel Matecznik** (☎ & fax 670 61 45; ul Lelewela 6; dm 16-20zł). It's about 3km northwest, across the river, from the Rynek or take one of the city buses. **Hotelik Pod Basztą** (☎ 670 82 68; ul Królowej Jadwigi 4; s/d from 39/89zł) is just below the castle. Rooms are a little old-fashioned, with shared bathrooms.

More comfort is available at **Hotel Pod Białym Orłem** (☎ 678 61 07; ul Sanocka 13; s/d 120/145zł), located around 1km west of the Old Town.

Restauracja M Tomaszewska (☎ 670 72 40; plac Konstytucji 3-go Maja 6; mains 12-45zł; ⊙ 9am-9pm), just north of the river, is an elegant and surprisingly inexpensive place serving good-quality Polish cuisine.

From Przemyśl, buses run to Lviv (95km) in Ukraine six times a day and regularly to all towns in southeastern Poland. Trains run regularly from Przemyśl to Lublin, Kraków and Warsaw and stop here on the way to/from Lviv. The bus terminal and adjacent train station in Przemyśl are about 1km northeast of the Rynek.

LUBLIN

☎ 081 / pop 360,000

For much of its history, Lublin was a strategically important border town – the Lublin Union, uniting Poland and Lithuania, was signed here in 1569, and it also experienced centuries of repeated invasions by numerous bellicose neighbours. Today, Lublin's small but well-preserved Old Town, with its elegant mix of Gothic, Renaissance and baroque architecture, is a pleasant place to wander.

Information

BOOKSHOPS

EMPiK Megastore (Galeria Centrum, 3rd fl, ul Krakowskie Przedmieście 16) Maps, books and international newspapers are available here.

INTERNET ACCESS

www.café (☎ 442 35 80; Rynek 9, 3rd fl; per hr 3zł; ⊙ 10am-10pm) In the heart of the Old Town.

MONEY

Bank Pekao (ul Królewska 1; ul Krakowskie Przedmieście 64) Changes travellers cheques and gives cash advances on Visa and MasterCard.

Plenty of ATMs can be found on ul Krakowskie Przedmieście, and several *kantors* along ul Peowiaków.

POST & TELEPHONE

Main post office (ul Krakowskie Przedmieście 50) Centrally placed, but the adjacent telephone centre is back from the main road.

TOURIST INFORMATION

LOIT Tourist Information Centre (☎ 532 44 12; www .lublin.pl; ul Jezuicka 1/3; ⊙ 10am-6pm Mon-Sat May-Sep, 9am-5pm Mon-Sat Oct-Apr) has helpful English-speaking staff, and lots of free brochures, including the city walking-route guides *Along the Multicultural Trail* and *Tourist Trail of Architectural Monuments*. It's also a good place to pick up maps of Lublin and other Polish and Ukrainian cities.

Sights

CASTLE

The imposing **castle**, which started life in the 14th century, stands on a hill northeast of the Old Town. What remains was actually rebuilt as a prison in the 1820s and remained as such until 1944. During the Nazi occupation, over 100,000 people passed through this prison before being deported to the death camps. Most of the edifice is now occupied by the **Lublin Museum** (☎ 532 50 01; www.zamek-lublin.pl; ul Zamkowa 9; adult/child 10/6zł; free Sat; ⊙ 9am-4pm Wed-Sat, 9am-5pm Sun). On show are paintings, silverware, porcelain, wood-carvings and weaponry, mostly labelled only in Polish. Check out the alleged 'devil's paw-print' on the 17th-century table in the foyer, linked to an intriguing local legend.

At the eastern end of the castle – but only accessible through the museum entrance – is the exquisite 14th-century **Chapel of the Holy Trinity** (adult/child with museum 10/6zł, without museum 6/4zł; ⊙ 9am-3.45pm Mon-Sat,

9am-4.45pm Sun). Its interior is entirely covered with polychrome Russo-Byzantine frescoes painted in 1418 – possibly the finest medieval wall paintings in Poland.

OLD TOWN

The compact historic quarter is centred on the **Rynek**, the irregularly shaped main square surrounding the neoclassical **Old Town Hall** (1781). The **Historical Museum of Lublin** (☎ 532 60 01; plac Łokietka 3; adult/child 3/1.50zł; ☼ 9am-4pm Wed-Sat, 9am-5pm Sun), with displays of documents and photos, is inside the 14th-century **Kraków Gate**, the only significant remnant of the medieval fortifications. At noon every day, a bugler comes from nowhere and plays a special tune from on top of the gate. (If you just love bugling, come here for the annual **National Bugle Contest** on 15 August.)

For an expansive **view** of the Old Town, climb to the top of the **Trinitarian Tower** (1819), which houses the **Religious Art Museum** (☎ 743 73 92; plac Kathedralny; adult/child 7/5zł; ☼ 10am-5pm Apr-Oct). Next to the tower is the 16th-century **cathedral** (plac Kathedralny; ☼ dawn-dusk) with impressive baroque frescoes. The painting of the Virgin Mary is said to have shed tears in 1945, so it's a source of pride and reverence for local believers.

MAJDANEK

About 4km southeast of the Old Town is the **State Museum of Majdanek** (☎ 744 19 55; admission free; ☼ 8am-6pm May-Sep, 8am-3pm Oct-Apr). It commemorates one of the largest death camps in Europe, where some 235,000 people, including over 100,000 Jews, were massacred. Barracks, guard towers and barbed wire fences remain as they were during WWII; even more chilling are the crematorium and gas chambers.

At the entrance to the site is a **Visitors' Centre,** where a short film (admission 2zł) can be seen. From the centre, the marked 'visiting route' (5km) passes the massive stone **Monument of Fight & Martyrdom** and finishes at the domed **mausoleum** holding the ashes of many victims.

Trolleybus No 156 from near the Bank Pekao along ul Królewska goes to the entrance of Majdanek.

Pick up the free *Heritage Trail of the Lublin Jews* pamphlet (in English) from the tourist office if you want to walk along the marked **Jewish Heritage Trail** around Lublin.

Sleeping
BUDGET

Camping Marina (☎ & fax 744 10 70; ul Krężnicka 6; per tent 8zł, cabin from 55zł; ☼ May-Sep) Lublin's only camping ground is serenely located on a lake about 8km south of the Old Town – take bus No 17, 20 or 21 from the train station to Stadion Sygnał and then catch bus No 25.

PTSM Youth Hostel (☎ & fax 533 06 28; ul Długosza 6; dm/tr 24/28zł) Modest but well run. It's 50m up a lane off ul Długosza and in the heart of the university district. Bed linen costs 6zł extra.

Wojewódzki Ośrodek Metodyczny (☎ 532 92 41; www.wodn.lublin.pl; ul Dominikańska 5; dm 45zł) This place has rooms with between two and five beds. It's good value and often busy, so book ahead. Look for the sign 'Wojewódzki Ośrodek Doskonalenia Nauczycieli' outside.

Hotel Piast (☎ 532 16 46; ul Pocztowa 2; s/d/tr 46/62/81zł) Opposite the train station, the Piast is ideal for a late-night arrival or early morning departure. However, it's a long way from anywhere else and in the rougher end of town.

MID-RANGE & TOP END

Motel PZM (☎ 533 42 32; ul Prusa 8; s/d from 120/160zł; P) The PZM is in an unexciting modern complex, but it's very handy for the bus station and represents good value.

Hotel Victoria (☎ 532 70 11; fax 532 90 26; ul Narutowicza 58/60; s/d from 190/290zł; ✕ P) Hotel Victoria is a gloomy concrete high-rise away from the centre, with small, pretty average rooms, though it's comfortable enough for a short stay.

Hotel Europa (☎ 535 03 03; www.hoteleuropa.pl; ul Krakowskie Przedmieście 29; s/d 290/380zł; ✕ P) Lublin's most central hotel offers smart, thoroughly modernised rooms in a restored 19th-century building on the city's main shopping street.

Hotel Mercure-Unia (☎ 533 72 12; www.orbis.pl; Al Racławickie 12; s/d from 320/380zł; ✕ P) The Mercure-Unia is big, central and convenient, and offers all modern conveniences, though it's lacking in atmosphere.

Grand Hotel Lublinianka (☎ 446 61 00; www.lublinianka.com; ul Krakowskie Przedmieście 56; s €65-117, d €75-140; ✕ P) Housed in a grandiose former bank, this is the swankiest place in town. The cheaper (3rd floor) rooms are rather small, but 'standard' rooms are spacious and have glitzy marble bathrooms. Facilities include free use of a sauna and Turkish

POLAND

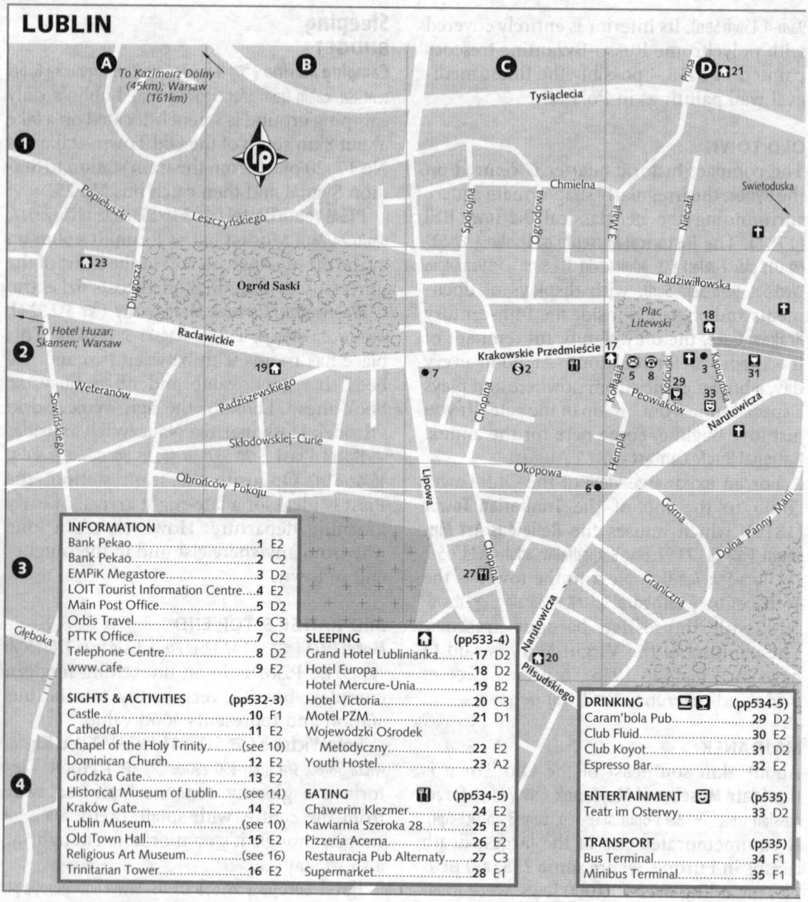
LUBLIN
To Kazimeirz Dolny (45km); Warsaw (161km)
Tysiąclecia
Prusa
Popiełuszki
Leszczyńskiego
Chmielna
Swietoduska
Spokojna
Ogrodowa
3 Maja
Niecała
Radziwiłłowska
Ogród Saski
Długosza
Plac Litewski
To Hotel Huzar; Skansen; Warsaw
Racławickie
Krakowskie Przedmieście
Weteranów
Radziszewskiego
Chopina
Kołłątaja
Kościuski
Kapucyńska
Peowiaków
Narutowicza
Sowińskiego
Skłodowskiej-Curie
Hempla
Okopowa
Obrońców Pokoju
Lipowa
Górna
Dolna Panny Marii
Graniczna
Głęboka
Piłsudskiego
INFORMATION
Bank Pekao 1 E2
Bank Pekao 2 C2
EMPiK Megastore 3 D2
LOIT Tourist Information Centre 4 E2
Main Post Office 5 D2
Orbis Travel 6 C3
PTTK Office 7 C2
Telephone Centre 8 D2
www.cafe 9 E2
SIGHTS & ACTIVITIES (pp532-3)
Castle 10 F1
Cathedral 11 E2
Chapel of the Holy Trinity (see 10)
Dominican Church 12 E2
Grodzka Gate 13 E2
Historical Museum of Lublin (see 14)
Kraków Gate 14 E2
Lublin Museum (see 10)
Old Town Hall 15 E2
Religious Art Museum (see 16)
Trinitarian Tower 16 E2
SLEEPING (pp533-4)
Grand Hotel Lublinianka 17 D2
Hotel Europa 18 D2
Hotel Mercure-Unia 19 B2
Hotel Victoria 20 C3
Motel PZM 21 D1
Wojewódzki Ośrodek Metodyczny 22 E2
Youth Hostel 23 A2
EATING (pp534-5)
Chawerim Klezmer 24 E2
Kawiarnia Szeroka 28 25 E2
Pizzeria Acerna 26 E2
Restauracja Pub Alternaty 27 C3
Supermarket 28 E1
DRINKING (pp534-5)
Caram'bola Pub 29 D2
Club Fluid 30 E2
Club Koyot 31 D2
Espresso Bar 32 E2
ENTERTAINMENT (p535)
Teatr im Osterwy 33 D2
TRANSPORT (p535)
Bus Terminal 34 F1
Minibus Terminal 35 F1

bath, and there's a good restaurant on-site. There's a 30% discount on weekends.

Eating & Drinking

Pizzeria Acerna (☎ 532 45 31, Rynek 2; pizzas from 11zł; 🕐 11am-10pm Mon-Thu & Sun, 11am-midnight Fri & Sat) The Acerna is a popular subterranean place on the main square and serves cheap pizzas and pasta.

Restauracja Pub Alternatywa (☎ 532 48 46; ul Chopina 11; mains 10-20zł; 🕐 11am-midnight Mon-Sat, 2pm-midnight Sun) This busy cellar pub offers regular live music and the ubiquitous pizzas.

Chawerim Klezmer (☎ 534 73 05; ul Złota 2; mains 12-19zł; 🕐 1-11pm Mon-Thu, 1pm-1am Fri & Sat, 1-10pm Sun) This is an intimate little place in a vaulted cellar off the main square, offering reasonably priced Polish and Jewish cuisine and a good wine list, including a number of Israeli wines. Be careful with the narrow steps down from the square though!

Kawiarnia Szeroka 28 (☎ 534 61 09; ul Grodzka 21; mains around 20zł; 🕐 11am-11pm) A charming, evocative place offering good Jewish and Polish cuisine and, of course, plenty of beer and vodka. There's a terrace at the back and regular live *klezmer* bands in the evenings (12zł extra).

Espresso Bar (☎ 534 49 43; Rynek 9; 🕐 noon-midnight) This is a cosy spot for a cappuccino or something stronger, and also serves snacks. Amazingly, not in a cellar.

Caram'bola Pub (☎ 534 63 80; ul Kościuszki 8; 🕐 11am-late) This pub is a pleasant place for a

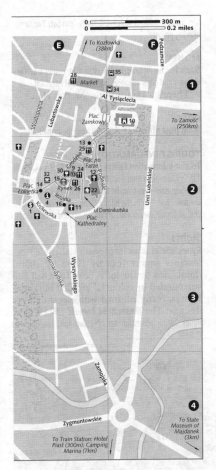

beer or two. Again, it also serves inexpensive bar food.

There is a supermarket located near the bus terminal.

Entertainment

The main venue for drama in Lublin is **Teatr im Osterwy** (☎ 532 42 44; ul Narutowicza 17), which features mostly classical plays with some emphasis on national drama. **Club Koyot** (☎ 743 67 35; ul Krakowskie Przedmieście 26; ✆ noon-late Mon-Fri, 5pm-late Sat & Sun), is hidden away in a little courtyard and features live music on most nights, while **Club Fluid** (☎ 607 689 383; ul Grodzka 1; ✆ noon-late) also plays host to various live acts; keep an eye out for posters around town.

Getting There & Away

The **bus terminal** (Al Tysiąclecia), opposite the castle, handles most of the traffic. At least one bus a day heads to Białystok (18.50zł), Kraków (25zł), Łódź (25zł), Olsztyn (50zł), Toruń (48zł) and Zakopane (33zł). Each day, six buses also go to Przemyśl (10.50zł), nine head to Zamość (10zł) and 12 to 15 travel to Warsaw (25zł, three hours). From the same terminal, Polski Express offers eight daily buses to Warsaw (34zł, three hours). Private minibuses head to various destinations, including Warsaw (25zł, 2½ hours, every half-hour), from bus stops north and west of the bus terminal.

The **Lublin Główny train station** (plac Dworcowy) is 1.2km south of the Old Town and accessible by trolleybus No 160. At least six trains go daily to Warsaw (47zł, 2½ hours) and two fast trains travel to Kraków (52zł, four hours). Tickets can be purchased at the station or from **Orbis Travel** (☎ 532 22 56; orbis .lublin@pbp.com.pl; ul Narutowicza 33a).

Around Lublin
KOZŁÓWKA

The hamlet of Kozłówka (koz-WOOF-kah), 38km north of Lublin, is famous for its sumptuous late-baroque **palace**, which now houses the **Museum of the Zamoyski Family** (☎ 852 83 00; www.muzeumzamoyskich.lublin.pl; adult/child 10/5zł; ✆ 10am-4pm Mon-Fri, 10am-5pm Sat & Sun Mar-Oct, 10am-3pm Nov-Dec). It features original furnishings, ceramic stoves and a large collection of paintings.

The palace is also noted for its **Socialist-Realist Art Gallery** (adult/child 4/2zł; ✆ 10am-4pm Mon-Fri, 10am-5pm Sat & Sun Mar-Oct, 10am-3pm Nov-Dec). It has an overwhelming number of portraits and statues of the revolutionary communist leaders, and also features many idealized proletarian scenes of farmers, factory workers and the like striving for socialism.

You can stay in the **palace rooms** and on an 'agrotourist' **farm** (☎ 852 83 00), but contact staff ahead about availability and current costs.

From Lublin, two buses head to Kozłówka each morning, usually on the way to Michów. Only a few buses return directly to Lublin in the afternoon, so check the timetable before visiting the museum. Alternatively, you can catch one of the frequent buses to/from Lubartów, which is regularly connected by bus and minibus to Lublin.

POLAND

ZAMOŚĆ

☎ 084 / pop 65,000

Zamość (ZAH-moshch) was founded in 1580 by Jan Zamoyski, chancellor and commander-in-chief of Renaissance Poland, who intended to create an impregnable barrier against Cossack and Tatar raids. During WWII, the Nazis renamed the town 'Himmlerstadt' and imported German colonists to create what Hitler had hoped would become an eastern bulwark for the Third Reich. The Polish inhabitants were expelled from the town and its environs, and most of the Jewish population was exterminated.

Fortunately, the tiny Old Town of Zamość escaped wartime destruction. The central square has been lovingly restored to its former splendour and the Old Town was added to Unesco's World Heritage List in 1992.

Information

INTERNET ACCESS

K@fejka Internetowa (☎ 639 29 32; Rynek Wielki10; per hr 3zł) The most central Internet café.
Library (cnr ul Zamenhofa & ul Bazyliańska; per hr 3zł;

☑ 8.30am-6.30pm Mon-Fri, 8.30am-3pm Sat) You can also log on here.

MONEY

Bank Pekao (ul Grodzka 2) Has an ATM, cashes travellers cheques and gives advances on Visa and MasterCard.

There's a kantor in the Market Hall.

POST

Main post office (ul Kościuszki) Near the cathedral.

TOURIST INFORMATION

Tourist Information Centre (☎ 639 22 93; Rynek Wielki 13; ☑ 8am-6pm Mon-Fri, 10am-4pm Sat, 10am-3pm Sun May-Sep, 8am-4pm Mon-Fri Oct-Apr) This helpful office is in the town hall. It sells the handy *Along the Streets of Zamość* (2zł), in English, French and German, and a good stock of maps.

Sights

Rynek Wielki is an impressive Italianate Renaissance square (exactly 100m by 100m) dominated by the lofty, pink **Town Hall** and surrounded by colourful arcaded burghers' houses, many adorned with elegant stucco designs. The **Museum of Zamość** (☎ 638 64 94; Rynek 24/26; admission 4zł; ☑ 9am-4pm Tue-Sun) is

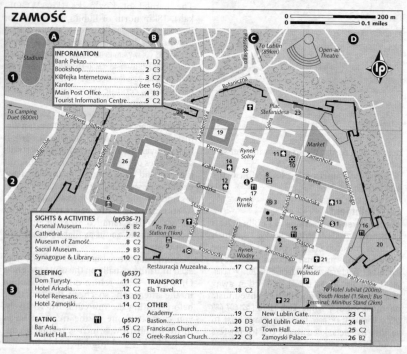

ZAMOŚĆ

0 ——————— 200 m
0 ——————— 0.1 miles

INFORMATION	
Bank Pekao	1 D2
Bookshop	2 C3
K@fejka Internetowa	3 C2
Kantor	(see 16)
Main Post Office	4 B3
Tourist Information Centre	5 C2

SIGHTS & ACTIVITIES	(pp536-7)
Arsenal Museum	6 B2
Cathedral	7 B2
Museum of Zamość	8 C2
Sacral Museum	9 B3
Synagogue & Library	10 C2

SLEEPING	(p537)
Dom Turysty	11 C2
Hotel Arkadia	12 C2
Hotel Renesans	13 D2
Hotel Zamojski	14 C2

EATING	(p537)
Bar Asia	15 C2
Market Hall	16 D2

Restauracja Muzealna	17 C2

TRANSPORT	
Ela Travel	18 C2

OTHER	
Academy	19 C2
Bastion	20 D3
Franciscan Church	21 D3
Greek-Russian Church	22 C3
New Lublin Gate	23 D2
Old Lublin Gate	24 B1
Town Hall	25 C2
Zamoyski Palace	26 B2

To Lublin (89km)
Open-air Theatre
Botaniczna
Plac Stefanidesa
Market
Rynek Solny
Pereca
Kollątaja
Grodzka
Rynek Wielki
Ormiańska
Staszica
To Train Station (1km)
Morando
Kościuszki
Rynek Wodny
Żeromskiego
Plac Wolności
Parlizantów
To Hotel Jubilat (200m); Youth Hostel (1.5km); Bus Terminal; Minibus Stand (2km)
To Camping Duet (600m)
Królowej Jadwigi
Podgroble
Zamkowa
Akademicka
Piłsudskiego
Sona
Zamenhofa
Łukasińskiego
Grecka
Bazyliańska
To Hotel Jubilat
Stadium
POLAND

based in two of the loveliest buildings on the Rynek and houses intriguing displays, including a scale model of the 16th-century town, paintings, folk costumes and archaeological finds.

Southwest of the square is the mighty 16th-century **cathedral** (ul Kolegiacka; ☽ dawn-dusk), which holds the tomb of Jan Zamoyski in the chapel to the right of the high altar. In the grounds, the **Sacral Museum** (admission 3zł; ☽ 10am-4pm Mon-Fri, 10am-1pm Sat & Sun May-Sep, 10am-1pm Sat & Sun only Oct-Apr) features various robes, paintings and sculptures.

Zamoyski Palace (closed to the public) lost much of its character when it was converted into a military hospital in the 1830s. Today it's used for government offices. Nearby, the **Arsenal Museum** (☎ 638 40 76; ul Zamkowa 2; adult/child 4/2.50zł; ☽ 9am-4pm Mon-Fri) holds a small and unremarkable collection of cannon, swords and firearms. To the north of the palace stretches a beautifully landscaped **park**.

Before WWII, Jews accounted for 45% of the town's population (of 12,000) and most lived in the area north and east of the palace. The most significant Jewish architectural relic is the Renaissance **synagogue** (cnr ul Zamenhofa & ul Bazyliańska), built in the early 17th century. It's now used as a public library, so you can go inside and see the faded murals, which are in need of some restoration.

On the eastern edge of the Old Town is the antiquated but bustling Hala Targowa, or **Market Hall**. Behind it is the best surviving **bastion** from the original wall that encircled Zamość.

Sleeping
BUDGET
Camping Duet (☎ 639 24 99; ul Królowej Jadwigi 14; s/d/tr 65/75/95zł; P ☒) About 1.5km west of the Old Town. It has neat bungalows, tennis courts, and a restaurant, sauna and Jacuzzi. Larger bungalows sleep up to six.

Youth Hostel (☎ 627 91 25; ul Zamoyskiego 4; dm 12-16zł; ☽ July & Aug) This hostel is in a school 1.5km east of the Old Town and not far from the bus terminal. It's pretty basic but functional, and very cheap.

Dom Turysty (☎ 639 26 39; ul Zamenhofa 11; s & d with shared bathrooms 45zł) This place has simple rooms, but it's in a very central location and the price is hard to beat.

MID-RANGE & TOP END
Prices at all the following include breakfast.

Hotel Jubilat (☎ 638 64 01; hoteljubilat@hoga.pl; ul Kardynała Wyszyńskiego 52; s/d 126/166zł; P) The Jubilat is a reasonable, if slightly drab, place to spend the night, right beside the bus station. It couldn't be handier for late arrivals or early departures, but it's a long way from anywhere else. Prices drop on weekends.

Hotel Renesans (☎ 639 20 01; hotelrenesans@hoga .pl; ul Grecka 6; s/d 128/183zł; P) Housed in an eye-wateringly ugly concrete box that certainly wasn't inspired by the Renaissance, though it's very central and rooms are comfortable enough, if you can ignore the brown-patterned carpets. The weekend rates are great value.

Hotel Arkadia (☎ 638 65 07; makben@wp.pl; Rynek Wielki 9; d/tr 150/180zł) With just six rooms, of which two overlook the main square, this is a grand old place with a lot of charm, but it has seen better days.

Hotel Zamojski (☎ 639 25 16; zamojski@orbis.pl; ul Kołłątaja 2/4/6; s/d 192/272zł; ☒ P) The Zamojski is the best place in town, set up in three connecting old houses leading off the square. The rooms are modern and tastefully furnished and there are two good on-site restaurants, open to nonguests, and a fitness centre. Weekend rates are less.

Eating
Bar Asia (☎ 639 23 04; ul Staszica 10; mains from 8zł; ☽ 8am-5pm Mon-Fri, 8am-3.30pm Sat) Bar Asia is a popular cafeteria-style place serving cheap and tasty Polish food.

Restauracja Muzealna (☎ 638 64 94; ul Ormianska 30; mains 10-25zł; ☽ noon-10pm Mon-Sat, 11am-9pm Sun) This restaurant is in an atmospheric cellar bedecked with murals, below the main square. It serves a better class of Polish cuisine, and has a well-stocked bar.

There are also a few cheap fast-food joints in the old Market Hall.

Getting There & Away
Buses are normally more convenient and quicker than trains. The **bus terminal** (ul Hrubieszowska) is 2km east of the Old Town and linked by frequent city buses. Daily, one or two fast buses go to Kraków (25zł), four or five to Warsaw (37zł, five hours) and nine to Lublin (10zł, two hours).

Far quicker, and surprisingly cheaper, are the minibuses that travel every 30 minutes

POLAND

between Lublin and Zamość (10zł, 1½ hours). They leave from the minibus stand across the road from the bus terminal in Zamość and from a disorganised corner northwest of the bus terminal in Lublin. Check the changeable timetable for departures to other destinations, including Warsaw and Kraków.

From the train station, about 1km southwest of the Old Town, several slow trains head to Lublin (about four hours) every day and three slow trains plod along to Warsaw (six hours). **Ela Travel** (☎ 638 57 75; ul Grodzka 18) sells international bus and air tickets.

SILESIA

Silesia in southwestern Poland includes Upper Silesia, the industrial heart of the country; Lower Silesia, a fertile farming region with a cultural and economic centre in Wrocław; and the Sudeten Mountains, a forested range that runs for over 250km along the Czech border. Silesia has spent much of its history under Austrian and Prussian rule, so the large Polish minority was often subject to Germanisation. Most of the region was reincorporated into Poland in the aftermath of WWII.

While visitors may not be attracted to the industrial wonders of Katowice and its vicinity, Wrocław is an historic and dignified city, and the Sudeten Mountains will lure hikers and nature lovers.

WROCŁAW

☎ 071 / pop 675,000

Wrocław (VROTS-wahf) was originally founded on the island of Ostrów Tumski on the Odra River. In the year 1000, Wrocław was chosen as one of the Piast dynasty's three bishoprics and it subsequently developed into a prosperous trading and cultural centre. The town passed to Bohemia in 1336, and, under the name of Breslau, was absorbed by Prussia in the 18th-century.

Wrocław returned to Poland in a sorry state; during the final phase of WWII, 70% of the city was destroyed. However, the old market square and many churches and other fine buildings have been beautifully restored and today Wrocław is a lively university town and cultural centre, and one of Poland's most attractive cities.

Information

BOOKSHOPS
EMPiK Megastore (Rynek 50) Offers the widest choice of foreign-language newspapers and magazines.
Księgarnia Podróżnika (ul Wita Stwosza 19/20). The best place for maps and guidebooks.

INTERNET ACCESS
Cyber & Tea Tavern (☎ 372 35 71; ul Kuźnicza 29; 10am-10pm) The place to check your emails.
W Sercu Miasta (Przejście Żelaźnicie; per hr 5zł) Down a laneway in the middle of the Rynek.

MONEY
Bank Pekao (ul Oławska 2) Offers the usual financial services.
There are *kantors* all over the city centre and a number in the bus and train stations. ATMs are also plentiful.

POST
Main post office (Rynek 28) Conveniently overlooks the main square.

TOURIST INFORMATION
Tourist information centre (☎ 344 11 11; www .wroclaw.pl; Rynek 14; 10am-7pm May-Sep, 10am-5pm Oct-Apr) Has several free brochures and maps.
Tourist information counter (☎ 369 54 97) In the Wrocław Główny train station.

Sights
The **Rynek** is Poland's second-largest old market square (after Kraków) and one of the largest (3.7 hectares) in Europe. The ornate **Town Hall** (built 1327–1504) on the southern side is certainly one of the most beautiful in Poland. Inside, the **Historical Museum** (☎ 347 16 90; adult/child 10/6zł; 10am-5pm Wed & Fri, 11am-5pm Thu & Sat, 10am-6pm Sun) has a few stately rooms on show, though it's disappointingly sparse given the price.

In the northwestern corner of the Rynek are two small houses called **Jaś i Małgosia** (ul Św Mikołaja; closed to public) linked by a baroque gate. Just behind them is the monumental 14th-century **St Elizabeth's Church** (ul Elżbiety 1; 9am-4pm Mon-Sat, 1-4pm Sun) with its 83m-high tower, which you can climb for city **views**. The southwestern corner of the Rynek spills into **Plac Solny** (Salt Square), once the site of the town's salt trade and now home to a 24hr flower market.

One block east of the Rynek is the Gothic **St Mary Magdalene's Church** (ul Łaciarska; admission free; 9am-4pm Mon-Sat) with a Romanesque

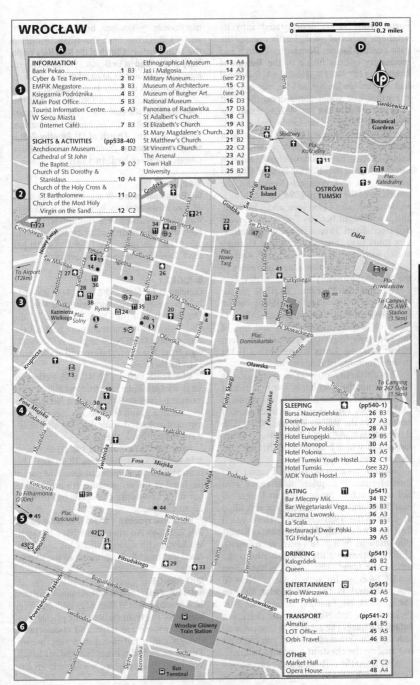

WROCŁAW

0	300 m
0	0.2 miles

INFORMATION
Bank Pekao....................................1 B3
Cyber & Tea Tavern.......................2 B2
EMPiK Megastore...........................3 B3
Księgarnia Podróżnika....................4 B3
Main Post Office............................5 B3
Tourist Information Centre..............6 A3
W Sercu Miasta
(Internet Café).............................7 B3

SIGHTS & ACTIVITIES (pp538–40)
Archdiocesan Museum....................8 D2
Cathedral of St John
the Baptist..................................9 D2
Church of Sts Dorothy &
Stanislaus................................10 A4
Church of the Holy Cross &
St Bartholomew......................11 D2
Church of the Most Holy
Virgin on the Sand..................12 C2

Ethnographical Museum................13 A4
Jaś i Małgosia..............................14 A3
Military Museum......................(see 23)
Museum of Architecture...............15 C3
Museum of Burgher Art...........(see 24)
National Museum.........................16 D3
Panorama of Racławicka...............17 D3
St Adalbert's Church....................18 C3
St Elizabeth's Church...................19 A3
St Mary Magdalene's Church.......20 B3
St Matthew's Church....................21 B2
St Vincent's Church.....................22 C2
The Arsenal.................................23 A2
Town Hall...................................24 B3
University...................................25 B2

SLEEPING 🛏 (pp540–1)
Bursa Nauczycielska.....................26 B3
Dorint..27 A3
Hotel Dwór Polski........................28 A3
Hotel Europejski..........................29 B5
Hotel Monopol............................30 A4
Hotel Polonia..............................31 A5
Hotel Tumski Youth Hostel...........32 C1
Hotel Tumski..........................(see 32)
MDK Youth Hostel......................33 B5

EATING 🍴 (p541)
Bar Mleczny Miś..........................34 B2
Bar Wegetariaski Vega..................35 B3
Karczma Lwowski.........................36 A3
La Scala.....................................37 B3
Restauracja Dwór Polski................38 A3
TGI Friday's................................39 A5

DRINKING 🍷 (p541)
Kalogródek.................................40 B2
Queen..41 C3

ENTERTAINMENT 🎭 (p541)
Kino Warszawa............................42 A5
Teatr Polski.................................43 A5

TRANSPORT (pp541–2)
Almatur.......................................44 B5
LOT Office..................................45 A5
Orbis Travel.................................46 B3

OTHER
Market Hall..................................47 C2
Opera House................................48 A4

POLAND

portal from 1280 incorporated into its southern external wall. Further east, the 15th-century former Bernardine church and monastery is now home to the **Museum of Architecture** (☎ 344 82 78; ul Bernardyńska 5; adult/child 4/3zł; ☯ 10am-4pm Tue, Wed, Sat & Sun, noon-6pm Thu).

Further east you'll come upon the giant **Panorama of Racławicka** (☎ 344 22 44; ul Purkyniego 11; adult/child 20/15zł; ☯ 9am-4pm Tue-Sun), a massive 360-degree painting of the 1794 Battle of Racławice, in which the Polish peasant army, led by Tadeusz Kościuszko, defeated Russian forces intent on partitioning Poland. Created by Jan Styka and Wojciech Kossak for the centenary of the battle in 1894, the painting is an overwhelming 114m long and 15m high, and was brought here by Polish immigrants displaced from Lviv after WWII. Obligatory tours (with English, French or German audio) run every 30 minutes (from 9.30am to 3.30pm). The ticket also allows free entry to the National Museum on the same day.

The **National Museum** (☎ 343 88 39; plac Powstańców Warszawy 5; adult/child 15/10zł, free Sat; ☯ 10am-4pm Wed-Sat, 10am-6pm Sun) contains exhibits of Silesian medieval art and one of the country's finest collections of modern Polish painting. Entry is free with a ticket to the Panorama of Racławicka.

The university quarter is north of the Rynek along the river bank. Further around is the **Arsenal**, the most significant remnant of the town's 15th-century fortifications. It now houses the **Military Museum** (☎ 344 15 71; ul Cieszyńskiego 9; adult/child 4/2zł, free Wed; ☯ 10am-4pm Tue-Sun), which features a predictable collection of old weapons.

North of the river is Ostrów Tumski (Cathedral Island), a quiet, picturesque area full of churches, though it's no longer an island (an arm of the Odra River was filled in during the 19th century). Here you'll find the Gothic **Cathedral of St John the Baptist** (plac Katedralny; ☯ 10am-6pm except during services). Uniquely, there's a lift to whisk you to the top of the **tower** (admission 4zł; ☯ 10am-5.30pm Mon-Sat, 2-4pm Sun) for superb views. Next to the cathedral is the **Archdiocesan Museum** (☎ 327 11 78; plac Katedralny 16; adult/child 2/1zł; ☯ 9am-3pm Tue-Sun). Nearby are the charming **Botanical Gardens** (☎ 322 51 40; ul Sienkiewicza 23; adult/child 5/3zł; ☯ 8am-6pm), where you can chill out among the chestnut trees and tulips.

West from the cathedral is the two-storey Gothic **Church of the Holy Cross & St Bartholomew**

(plac Kościelny; ☯ 9am-6pm), built between 1288 and 1350. Cross over the small bridge to the 14th-century **Church of the Most Holy Virgin Mary on the Sand** (ul Św Jadwigi; ☯ erratic) with its lofty Gothic vaults. Classical music concerts are often held in these two venues.

To the south of the Old Town are the **Ethnographical Museum** (☎ 344 33 13; ul Kazimierza Wielkiego 35; adult/child 4/3zł, free Sat; ☯ 10am-4pm Tue-Sun) and the **Church of Sts Dorothy & Stanislaus** (ul Świdnicka; ☯ dawn-dusk), a massive Gothic complex built in 1351.

Sleeping

Old Town Apartments (Map pp506-7; ☎ 022-887 98 00; www.warsawshotel.com; Rynek Starego Miasta 12/14, Warsaw) in Warsaw lets out modern, fully furnished one-bedroom apartments around Wrocław's main square (350zł to 420zł per day). Weekly rates are also available.

BUDGET

Camping Nr 267 Ślęza (☎ & fax 343 44 42; ul Na Grobli 16/18; per person/tent 14/3zł; d/tr bungalows 60/90zł; **P**) On the bank of the Odra, 2km east of the Old Town. No local transport goes all the way, so take tram No 4 to plac Wróblewskiego from the train station and walk about 1km further east.

MDK Youth Hostel (☎ 343 88 56; mdkkopernik .wp.pl; ul Kołątaja 20; dm from 16zł, d from 30zł) Not far from the train station, this is a basic place, located in a grand (but poorly sign-posted) mustard-coloured building. It's almost always full, so book ahead.

Hotel Tumski Youth Hostel (☎ 322 60 99; www .hotel-tumski.com.pl; Wyspa Słodowa 10; dm 30zł) This hostel is in a quiet, pleasant area, and part of the hotel of the same name. It's good value, but some rooms are cramped, and there's a 10pm curfew.

Bursa Nauczycielska (☎ 344 37 81; ul Kotlarska 42; s/d/q 50/90/104zł) Another rather basic but spotless hostel with shared bathrooms, ideally located just one block northeast of the Rynek.

MID-RANGE

Hotel Europejski (☎ 343 10 71; europejski@odratourist .pl; ul Piłsudskiego 88; s 99-188zł, d 129-198zł; ☒) Very handy for the train station. The pricier 'renovated' rooms are large and comfortable, though still a tad dated and very brown. The price includes breakfast and set lunch. Weekend discounts are available from Friday to Sunday.

Hotel Monopol (☎ 343 70 41; monopol@orbis.pl; ul Modrzejewskiej 2; s 115-170zł, d 150-240zł; ✗) Adolf Hitler was once a frequent visitor, and though it might not be up to tyrant standards these days, it's clean and does offer good value; discounted rates are available on weekends. It's beside the Opera House.

Hotel Polonia (☎ 343 10 21; polonia@odratourist.pl; ul Piłsudskiego 66; s 148-198zł, d 178-218zł; ✗) The sister hotel of the Europejski, and of a similar, rather dowdy standard, but rooms are perfectly clean and it's convenient. Weekend discounts are apply from Friday to Sunday.

Hotel Tumski (☎ 322 60 88; www.hotel-tumski .com.pl; Wyspa Słodowa 10; s/d 199/270zł, ste 480zł; ✗) This is a neat, recently refurbished hotel in a peaceful setting overlooking the river and offering reasonable value for money. It's ideal for exploring the lovely ecclesiastical quarter, and there's a good **restaurant** attached.

TOP END
Hotel Dwór Polski (☎ 372 34 15; www.dworpolski .wroclaw.pl; ul Kiełbaśnicza 2; s/d 240/290zł, ste 400zł; ✗ Ⓟ) Housed in a grand old 16th-century building just oozing charm and history, and set back from the road. Beds here are big and soft and bathrooms thoroughly modern, but the rest of the place could do with a makeover, including the minuscule breakfast room. Weekend rates are 25% less.

Dorint (☎ 358 83 00; www.dorint.com/wroclaw; ul Św Mikołaja 67; s/d from €103/108, ste from €152; ✗ Ⓟ) The ultimate in contemporary designer chic and housed in a great glassy structure just off the main square. Rooms are light and stylish, there's a top-class **restaurant**, and facilities include a sauna and fitness centre. Children up to 11 stay free and discounts are sometimes available. Breakfast costs €11 extra.

Eating
Bar Mleczny Wzorcowy (☎ 343 33 65; ul Piłsudskiego 66; mains 8-12zł; ⏱ 7am-7pm) This is a typical, old-style milk bar with a long menu (in Polish) and it's good for hearty, hot dishes at cheap prices.

Bar Mleczny Miś (☎ 343 49 63; ul Kuźnicza 45-47; mains 5-12zł; ⏱ 7am-6pm Mon-Fri, 8am-5pm Sat) In the university area, this bar is basic but popular with frugal university students.

Bar Wegetariański Vega (☎ 344 39 34; Rynek 1/2; mains 10-20zł; ⏱ 8am-7pm Mon-Fri, 8am-5pm Sat, 9am-5pm Sun) This is a cheap cafeteria in the centre of the Rynek, offering veggie dishes.

Karczma Lwowska (☎ 343 98 87; Rynek 4; mains 15-40zł; ⏱ 11am-midnight) Has a great spot on the main square, with outdoor seating in summer, and offers the usual meaty Polish standards. It's worth stopping by to try the beer, served in ceramic mugs.

TGI Friday's (☎ 342 56 01; ul Kościuszki 5; mains 16-40zł; ⏱ noon-11pm) An identikit branch of the international chain-restaurant, complete with rock 'n' roll décor and waitresses in daft hats, but the Tex-Mex food is reliable, and the cocktails extra-large.

Restauracja Dwór Polski (☎ 372 48 96; Rynek 5; mains 15-50zł; ⏱ 10am-midnight) The Dwór Polski is a classy place to sample good-quality Polish cuisine on the main square.

La Scala (☎ 372 53 94; Rynek 38; mains 25-60zł; ⏱ 10am-midnight) Offers authentic Italian food and particularly good deserts. Prices are high, but you're paying for the location.

Entertainment
Wrocław is an important cultural centre, so there's always something going on somewhere. Check out the (free and in English) bimonthly *Wrocław Cultural Guide* for details of what's on and where. It's available from the tourist offices and upmarket hotels.

Kalogródek (☎ 0501 778 346; ul Kuźnica 29; ⏱ 10am-midnight) A laid-back, ever-busy beer garden popular with local students and backpackers. The surrounding streets are packed with other cheap and friendly haunts.

Queen (☎ 343 55 29; ul Purkyniego 1; ⏱ noon-3am) This moody club housed in an old church is an OK place for a late-night drink. Occasional live music.

Teatr Polski (☎ 343 86 53; ul Zapolskiej 3) Wrocław's main theatrical venue, staging classic Polish and foreign drama.

Filharmonia (☎ 342 20 01; www.filharmonia.wroclaw .pl; ul Piłsudskiego 19) Hosts concerts of classical music, mostly Friday and Saturday nights.

Kino Warszawa (☎ 344 53 83; ul Piłsudskiego 64) Shows recent English-language films.

Getting There & Away
Orbis Travel (☎ 343 26 65; Rynek 29) and **Almatur** (☎ 344 47 28; ul Kościuszki 34) offer the usual services. If you're travelling to/from Wrocław on Friday, Saturday or Sunday, book your bus or train ticket as soon as possible, because thousands of itinerant university students travel to/from the city most weekends.

POLAND

AIR

Every day, LOT flies four to six times between Wrocław and Warsaw, once between Wrocław and Frankfurt-am-Main, and twice to Munich. Most days, SAS flies to Copenhagen, while Cirrus Airlines flies twice weekly to Paris. Tickets for all airlines can be bought at the **LOT office** (☎ 343 90 31; ul Piłsudskiego 36).

The airport is in Strachowice, about 12km west of the Old Town. Bus No 406 links the airport with Wrocław Główny train station and bus terminal, via the Rynek.

BUS

The **bus terminal** (ul Sucha 11) is just south of the main train station. Several PKS buses a day go to Warsaw (45zł, five hours), Poznań (22zł, 2½ hours), Częstochowa (20zł, three hours) and Białystok (60zł, seven hours). Polski Express also offers buses to Warsaw (67zł, 4½ hours, three daily). For most travel, however, the train is more convenient.

TRAIN

The **Wrocław Główny station** (ul Piłsudskiego 105) was built in 1856 and is a historical monument in itself. Every day, fast trains to Kraków depart every one or two hours (40.20zł, 3¾ hours), and several InterCity and express trains (65zł, six hours) go to Warsaw, usually via Łódź. Wrocław is also regularly linked by train to Poznań (19.30zł, 3½ hours), Częstochowa, Szczecin and Lublin.

SUDETEN MOUNTAINS

The Sudeten Mountains (Sudety) run for over 250km along the Czech–Polish border. The Sudetes feature dense forests, amazing rock formations and deposits of semiprecious stones, all of which can be explored along any of the extensive network of trails for **hiking** or **mountain biking**. The highest part of this old and eroded chain is Mt Śnieżka (1602m). Both the following towns offer the normal tourist facilities.

Szklarska Poręba in the northwestern end of the Sudetes offers superior facilities for **hiking** and **skiing**. It's at the base of Mt Szrenica (1362m), and the town centre is at the upper end along ul Jedności Narodowej. The small **tourist office** (☎ 075-717 24 49; szklarskaporeba.pl; ul Jedności Narodowej 3) has accommodation information and maps. Nearby, several trails begins at the intersection of ul Jedności Narodowej and ul Wielki Sikorskiego. The red

trail goes to Mt Szrenica (two hours) and offers a peek at Wodospad Kamieńczyka, a spectacular waterfall.

Karpacz to the southeast has a bit more to offer in terms of nightlife, though it attracts fewer serious mountaineers. It's loosely clustered along a 3km road winding through Łomnica Valley at the base of Mt Śnieżka. The **tourist office** (☎ 075-761 86 05; www.karpacz.pl; ul Konstytucji 3 Maja 25a) should be your first port of call. To reach the peak of Mt Śnieżka on foot, take one of the trails (three to four hours) from Hotel Biały Jar. Some of the trails pass by one of two splendid postglacial lakes, Mały Staw and Wielki Staw.

The bus is the fastest way of getting around the region. Every day from Szklarska Poręba, about four buses head to Wrocław and one slow train plods along to Warsaw. From Karpacz, get a bus to Jelenia Góra, where plenty of buses and trains go in all directions.

For the Czech Republic, take a bus from Szklarska Poręba to Jakuszyce, cross the border on foot to Harrachov (on the Czech side) and take another bus from there.

WIELKOPOLSKA

Wielkopolska (literally 'Great Poland') is often referred to as the Cradle of the Polish State, and is one of the most important cultural and historical regions of the country.

The main city, Poznań, is a major commercial centre, world renowned for its trade fairs, which have been held here since the 1920s. Poznań has plenty of museums and other attractions to make a visit worthwhile, and the surrounding countryside is popular with hikers and cyclists.

Despite the royal seat moving to Kraków in 1038, Wielkopolska remained Poland's most important province until the second partition in 1793, when it was annexed to Prussia. The region then passed back and forth between Polish and German hands several times, culminating in the liberation battles of 1945, which devastated the area.

POZNAŃ

☎ 061 / pop 610,000

Poznań is the historically rich capital of Wielkopolska, best known for its international trade fairs. It's strategic position between Berlin and Warsaw has ensured its importance for centuries, and today it's a busy city with a host of museums and an attractively restored Old Town. It's a cosmopolitan place, with a lively cultural scene, and as a major transport hub, it makes a good base to explore the region. In the 9th century AD the Polanian tribes built a wooden fort on the island of Ostrów Tumski, and from 968 to 1038 Poznań was the de facto capital of Poland. By the 15th century Poznań was already a trading centre and famous for its fairs. This commercial tradition was reinstituted in 1925, and today the fairs – held for a few days each month – dominate the economic and cultural life of the city.

Information
BOOKSHOPS
EMPiK Megastore (☎ 852 66 90; plac Wolności) Offers the largest choice of foreign magazines and newspapers.
Globtroter Turystyczna (ul Żydowska) Excellent for maps and Lonely Planet guidebooks.

INTERNET ACCESS
Internet Café Bajt (no phone; ul Zamkowa 5; per hr 3zł) Off the main square.

MONEY
Bank Pekao (ul Św Marcin 52/56; ul 23 Lutego) Probably the best place for travellers cheques and credit cards.

A few of the **kantors** in the city centre are shown on the map; there's also one in the bus terminal and another (open 24 hours) in the train station.

POST
Main post office (ul Kościuszki 77) West of the Old Town.

TOURIST INFORMATION
City Information Centre (☎ 851 96 45; ul Ratajczaka 44; ☽ 10am-7pm Mon-Fri, 10am-5pm Sat) Handles bookings for cultural events.
Tourist information centre (☎ 852 61 56; Stary Rynek 59; ☽ 9am-5pm Mon-Fri, 9am-2pm Sat) Helpful.

Sights
OLD TOWN
The Old Market Square, **Stary Rynek**, has been beautifully restored to its historic glory. The focal point is the Renaissance **Town Hall** (built 1550–60), with its decorative façade facing east. In accordance with a strange custom, every day at noon two metal goats high above the clock butt their

horns together 12 times. Inside the building, the **Poznań Historical Museum** (☎ 856 80 00; admission 5.50zł; ☽ 10am-4pm Mon & Tue, noon-6pm Wed, 10am-6pm Fri, 10am-3pm Sun) reveals the city's past through splendid period interiors.

The square also features the **Wielkopolska Military Museum** (☎ 852 67 39; Stary Rynek 9; adult/child 3.50/2.20zł; ☽ 10am-3pm Tue-Sun) and the unique **Museum of Musical Instruments** (☎ 852 08 57; Stary Rynek 45/47; admission 5.50zł, free Sat; ☽ 11am-5pm Tue-Sat, 11am-3pm Sun). The **Archaeological Museum** (☎ 852 82 51; ul Wodna 27; admission 3zł, free Sat; ☽ 10am-4pm Tue-Fri, 10am-6pm Sat, 10am-3pm Sun) contains displays on the prehistory of western Poland, as well as some Egyptian mummies.

The 17th-century **Franciscan Church** (ul Franciszkańska 2; ☽ 8am-8pm), one block west of the Rynek, has an ornate baroque interior, complete with wall paintings and rich stucco work. On a hill above the church is the **Museum of Applied Arts** (☎ 852 20 35; admission 3zł, free Sat; ☽ 10am-4pm Tue, Wed, Fri & Sat, 10am-3pm Sun), which has wide-ranging displays, including glassware, ceramics, silverware and clocks.

The nearby **National Museum: Paintings & Sculpture Gallery** (☎ 856 80 00; Al Marcinkowskiego 9; adult/child 10/6zł, free Sat; ☽ 10am-6pm Tue, 9am-5pm Wed, 10am-4pm Thu & Sun, 10am-5pm Fri & Sat) holds an excellent collection of mainly 19th- and 20th-century Polish paintings.

Two blocks south of Stary Rynek is the large, pink baroque **Parish Church of St Stanislaus** (ul Gołębia 1; ☽ erratic) with a three-naved interior with monumental altars built in the mid-17th century. A short stroll to the southeast is the **Wielkopolska Ethnographic Museum** (☎ 852 30 06; ul Grobla 25; admission 5.50zł, free Sat; ☽ 10am-4pm Tue, Wed, Fri & Sat, 10am-3pm Sun), which features a collection of woodcarving and traditional costumes of the area.

About 1.3km north of the Old Town is the 19th-century Prussian **Poznań Citadel**, where 20,000 German troops held out for a month in February 1945. The fortress was destroyed by artillery fire but a park was laid out on the site, which incorporates the **Poznań Army Museum** (☎ 820 45 03; Al Armii Poznań; admission 4zł, free Fri; ☽ 9am-4pm Tue, 10am-4pm Sun).

The massive 1956 strike by the city's industrial workers was the first major popular upheaval in communist Poland. The strike was cruelly crushed by tanks, leaving 76 dead and over 600 wounded. In a park in the new city centre, the moving **Monument to the Victims of June 1956** commemorates the event.

POLAND

POLAND

POZNAŃ

A **B** **C** **D**

INFORMATION
Bank Pekao..................................1 C4
Bank Pekao..................................2 E5
City Information Centre..............3 C4
EMPiK Megastore........................4 C4
Globtroter Turystyczna...............5 F5
Internet Cafe Bajt........................6 E5
Kantor..7 D5
Kantor..8 E6
Kantor..9 E5
Main Post Office.......................10 B4
Tourist Information Centre........11 E6

SIGHTS & ACTIVITIES (pp543-5)
Archaeological Museum............12 F6
Franciscan Church.....................13 E6
Monument to the Victims of
  June 1956................................14 B4
Museum of Applied Arts...........15 E5
Museum of Musical Instruments..16 F6
National Museum: Paintings &
  Sculpture Gallery....................17 D4
Parish Church of St Stanislaus...18 F6
Poznań Historical Museum....(see 20)
St Martin's Church....................19 D5
Town Hall.................................20 F6
Wielkopolska Ethnographic
  Museum..................................21 F5
Wielkopolska Military Museum..22 E6

SLEEPING (pp545-6)
Biuro Zakwaterowania Przemysław
  (Private Rooms).....................23 A6
Dizzy Daisy...............................24 C3
Dom Turysty.............................25 E5
Hotel Lech................................26 B4
Hotel Mercure Poznań..............27 A4
Hotel Royal...............................28 B4
Hotel Rzymski..........................29 D4

EATING (p546)
Bar Caritas...............................30 D4
Bar Pasibruzch.....................(see 31)
Bar Wegetariaski......................31 E6
Gruszecki..................................32 D5
Klio...33 F6
Pod Aniołem.............................34 E6
Restauracja Sphinx...................35 E6
Sioux..36 F5

DRINKING (p546)
Czarna Owca............................37 E6
Galaxy Klub..............................38 E5
Harry's Pub..........................(see 25)
Room 55...................................39 E5

ENTERTAINMENT (p546)
Filharmonia..............................40 B4
Teatr Wielki..............................41 B4

SHOPPING
Shopping Centre Pasaż.............42 D5

TRANSPORT (pp546-7)
Bus Terminal............................43 B6
LOT Office................................44 C5
Orbis Travel..............................45 D4

OTHER
Palace of Culture......................46 B4
Souvenir Stalls.........................47 F6
Weigh House.............................48 E6

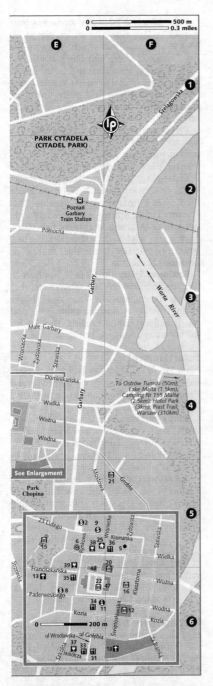

In **Park Wilsona**, less then 1km southwest of the train station, is the **Palm House** (☎ 865 89 07; ul Matejki 18; admission 5zł; 🕙 9am-5pm Tue-Sun). This huge greenhouse (built in 1910) contains 17,000 species of tropical and subtropical plants, including a remarkable collection of giant cacti and towering bamboo trees.

Ostrów Tumski is 1km east of the Old Town (take any eastbound tram from plac Wielkopolski). This river island is dominated by the monumental, double-towered **Poznań Cathedral** (ul Ostrów Tumski), originally built in 968 but rebuilt several times since. The Byzantine-style **Golden Chapel** (1841) and the **mausoleums** of Mieszko I and Boleslaus the Brave are behind the high altar. Opposite the cathedral is the 15th-century **Church of the Virgin Mary** (ul Panny Marii 1/3), possibly the purest Gothic building in the city.

Further out from Ostrów Tumski and about 2.5km east of the Old Town is **Lake Malta**. This 64-hectare artificial lake is a favourite weekend destination for Poles, and holds sailing regattas, outdoor concerts and other events in summer. The carnival atmosphere is enhanced by games, food and souvenir stands. To get to the lake hop on tram No 1, 4 or 8 from plac Wielkopolski.

Sleeping

During trade fairs, the rates of Poznań's hotels and private rooms tend to increase, often dramatically, and accommodation may be difficult to find. The hard part is knowing when a fair is actually taking place. The tourist office will help you find a room if you're having trouble; otherwise, it pays to book ahead. Prices given here are for non-fair periods.

BUDGET

Youth Hostel No 1 (☎ 866 40 40; ul Berwińskiego 2/4; dm 22zł) This is a 15-minute walk southwest of the train station along ul Głogowska and adjacent to Park Wilsona. It's a pretty basic 'no frills' option, but fills up fast with students and school groups.

Dizzy Daisy (☎ 506 075 306; www.hostel.pl; Al Niepodległości 26; dm 30zł, s/d 50/100zł; 🖳) Part of the nationwide chain, and one of the newest and most comfortable hostels in town, with free Internet, laundry and no curfew.

Dom Turysty (☎ & fax 852 88 93; Stary Rynek 91; dm 50zł, s/d/tr 150/250/300zł) Set in an 18th-century former mansion on the main square, this place is rather musty and old-fashioned, and rooms are far from palatial, but the location is unbeatable.

Biuro Zakwaterowania Przemysław (☎ 866 35 60; www.przemyslaw.com.pl; ul Głogowska 16; ☒ 8am-6pm Mon-Fri, 10am-2pm Sat; s/d from 40/60zł, apt from 120zł) Not far from the train station, and rates for weekends and stays of more than three nights are cheaper than the prices quoted above.

MID-RANGE & TOP END

Hotel Lech (☎ 853 01 51; www.hotel-lech.poznan.pl; ul Św Marcin 74; s/d 160/240zł) The Hotel Lech could do with some updating, but the bathrooms are modern and spotless, and it's good value on weekends, when prices drop.

Hotel Rzymski (☎ 852 81 21; www.rzymskihotel .com.pl; Al Marcinkowskiego 22; s/d 193/247zł) Offers the regular amenities of three-star comfort, and overlooks plac Wolności. While rooms are perfectly acceptable, they aren't quite as grand as the elegant façade suggests.

Hotel Royal (☎ 858 23 00; www.hotel-royal.com.pl; ul Św Marcin 71; s/d 290/370zł) This is a gorgeous place set back from the main road. Rooms have huge beds and sparkling bathrooms, while weekend prices come down by 35%.

Hotel Park (☎ 879 40 81; www.hotel-park.com.pl; ul Majakowskiego 77; s/d from 350/416; ☒ ℗) Hotel Park is a huge modern complex around 4km east of the Old Town, in a quiet setting overlooking Lake Malta. Again, weekend rates are great value.

Hotel Mercure Poznań (☎ 855 80 00; mer.poznan@ orbis.pl; ul Roosevelta 20; s/d from 548/596zł; ☒ ☐ ℗) In a gigantic modern place just off a very busy main road, this branch of the Mercure chain offers all the expected facilities for business travellers. It's handy for the train station and the fairgrounds, but a long slog from anywhere else.

Eating

Bar Caritas (☎ 852 51 30; plac Wolności 1; mains 8-15zł; ☒ 8am-7pm Mon-Fri, 10am-5pm Sat, noon-5pm Sun) You can point at what you want without resorting to your phrasebook at this cheap and convenient milk bar.

Sioux (☎ 851 62 86; Stary Rynek 93; mains 16-65zł; ☒ noon-11pm) As you'd expect, this is a 'Western'-themed place, complete with waiters dressed as cowboys. Bizarrely named dishes such as 'Bass Sam in search of his bowels' echo of joy in Rocky Mountains' (chicken and chips) are on the menu, along with lots of steaks, ribs, grills and enchiladas.

Pod Aniołem (☎ 852 98 54; ul Wrocławska 4; mains from 14zł; ☒ 11am-midnight Mon-Sat, 1pm-midnight Sun) This is a pleasant pub which serves up the usual range of cheap and filling Polish fare such as dumplings, salads and grilled meats.

Klio (☎ 855 75 52; ul Wrocławska 16; mains 18-65zł; ☒ 10am-midnight) Klio is a more upmarket place, with an unmissable organic façade, offering pasta, fish and steaks.

Bar Wegetariański (☎ 821 12 55; ul Wrocławska 21; mains from 5zł; ☒ 11am-8pm) This is a cheap vegetarian place in a cellar off the main road, offering the usual light, meat-free dishes.

Gruszecki (☎ 850 89 42; plac Wlosny Ludów 2; mains 10-40zł; ☒ 10am-9pm Mon-Sat, 10am-7pm Sun) Inside the Kupiec Poznański shopping centre, this is a small place serving a surprisingly wide range of dishes, including steaks, fish, pasta, fried snails and that perennial favourite, liver in raspberries. It also does more conventional breakfasts.

Restaurant Sphinx (☎ 852 80 25; Stary Rynek 77; mains 16-45zł; ☒ noon-late) The Sphinx is another branch of the ubiquitous kebab-and-cabbage chain, offering reasonable value grills and salads and a menu in English. The line for the takeaway counter is predictably long.

Entertainment

Room 55 (☎ 855 32 24; Stary Rynek 80/82; ☒ 9am-midnight Mon-Sat, noon-midnight Sun) One of several trendy places on the main square to enjoy a drink and something to eat.

Harry's Pub (☎ 852 61 69; Stary Rynek 91; ☒ 11am-late) Also on the main square. Harry's Pub, attached to Dom Turysty hotel, has an impressively long drinks menu, including 43 different whiskies. Also serves food.

Czarna Owca (☎ 853 07 92; ul Jaskółcza 13; ☒ noon-2am Mon-Fri, 5pm-2am Sat) Also called the 'Black Sheep', this is a popular club with nightly DJs playing a mix of R&B and hip-hop.

Galaxy Klub (☎ 851 60 22; Stary Rynek 85; ☒ 9pm-3am) A well-frequented place with a tacky sci-fi theme going on.

Teatr Wielki (☎ 852 82 91; ul Fredry 9) is the venue for opera and ballet, while **Filharmonia** (☎ 852 47 08; ul Św Marcin 81) offers classical concerts at least every Friday night.

Getting There & Away

LOT flies five times a day between Warsaw and Poznań. Also, LOT has flights from Poznań to Hanover and Düsseldorf most days; LOT and SAS fly daily to Copenhagen;

and Austrian Airlines goes regularly to Vienna. Tickets for all airlines are available from the **LOT office** (☎ 858 55 00; ul Piekary 6) or from **Orbis Travel** (☎ 853 20 52; Al Marcinkowskiego 21). The airport is in the western suburb of Ławica, 7km from the Old Town and accessible by bus No 59 or 78.

The **bus terminal** (ul Towarowa 17) is a 10-minute walk east of the train station. Bus services are relatively poor, but buses do travel from Poznań four or five times a day to Łódź, once a day to Toruń and three times a day to Wrocław, but the trains are better.

The busy **Poznań Główny train station** (ul Dworcowa 1) is well set up. Every day, it offers nine trains to Kraków (78zł, 6½ hours), a dozen to Szczecin (half of which continue to Świnoujście), to Gdańsk (60zł, five hours, seven daily), Toruń (30zł, 3½ hours, four daily) and Wrocław (19.30zł, 3½ hours, seven daily). About 15 trains a day also head to Warsaw (48zł, five hours), including several InterCity services (three hours).

POMERANIA

Pomerania (Pomorze) stretches along the Baltic coast from the German frontier to the lower Vistula Valley in the east. The region rests on two large urban pillars: Szczecin at its western end and Gdańsk to the east. Between them stretches the sandy coastline dotted with beach resorts. Further inland is a wide belt of rugged, forested lakeland sprinkled with medieval castles and towns, and the charming city of Toruń.

TORUŃ

☎ 056 / pop 208,000

Toruń is an historic city, characterised by narrow streets, burgher mansions and mighty Gothic churches. The compact Old Town was built on the slopes of the wide Vistula River and is one of the most appealing in central Poland. Toruń is famous as the birthplace of Nicolaus Copernicus, who spent his youth here and after whom the local university is named.

In 1233 the Teutonic Knights established an outpost in Toruń. Following the Thirteen Years' War (1454–66), the Teutonic Order and Poland signed a peace treaty here, which returned to Poland a large area of land stretching from Toruń to Gdańsk.

In the following centuries, Toruń suffered a fate similar to that of the surrounding region: Swedish invasions and Prussian domination until the early 20th century.

Fortunately, the city suffered little damage during WWII, so Toruń is the best-preserved Gothic town in Poland. The Old Town was added to Unesco's World Heritage List in 1997.

Information

BOOKSHOPS

EMPiK Megastore (☎ 622 48 95; ul Wielkie Garbary 18)

INTERNET ACCESS

Klub Internetowy Jeremi (☎ 663 51 00; Rynek Staromiejski 33; per hr 3zł)

MONEY

Bank Pekao (ul Wielkie Garbary 11)

PKO Bank (ul Szeroka) Offers the usual services.

ATMs can be found along ul Różana and ul Szeroka. A couple of handy **kantors** are shown on the map.

POST

Main post office (Rynek Staromiejski) Overlooks the main square.

TOURIST INFORMATION

Main tourist office (☎ 621 09 31; www.it.torun.pl; Rynek Staromiejski 25; ⏰ 9am-4pm Mon & Sat, 9am-6pm Tue-Fri, 9am-1pm Sun) Very helpful.

Tourist information counter (main train station)

The free, glossy *Toruń Tourist & Business Guide*, available from most decent hotels, advertises local eateries and nightclubs.

Sights

Most of Torun's museums are under central civic administration and can be contacted via one central phone number: ☎ 622 70 38.

Rynek Staromiejski is the focal point of the Old Town. The massive 14th-century **Old Town Hall** now shelters the **Regional Museum** (☎ 622 70 38; www.muzeum.torun.pl; Rynek Staromiejski 1; adult/child 7/5zł; ⏰ noon-6pm Tue & Thu, 10am-4pm Wed & Fri-Sun). On the ground floor, displays recall the town's guilds and there's an exhibition of medieval stained glass and religious paintings, while upstairs is a fine collection of 19th-and 20th-century Polish art. Climb the 40m-high **tower** (adult/child 6/4zł; ⏰ 10am-6pm Tue-Sun, May-Sep) for great views.

The richly decorated, 15th-century **Star House**, with its baroque façade and spiral

TORUŃ

INFORMATION
Bank Pekao...........................1 E3
EMPiK Megastore..................2 E3
Kantor..................................3 D3
Kantor..................................4 E3
Klub Internetowy Jeremi.......5 C3
Main Post Office...................6 C3
PKO Bank.............................7 D3
Tourist Office.......................8 C3

SIGHTS & ACTIVITIES (pp547-9)
Cathedral of SS John the Baptist
 & John the Evangelist...........9 D4
Church of the Holy Spirit.......10 C3
Eskens' House......................11 D4
Ethnographic Museum..........12 C1
Far Eastern Art Museum......(see 17)
Museum of Copernicus.........13 C4
Old Town Hall & Regional
 Museum...............................14 C3
St James' Church..................15 F2
St Mary's Church..................16 B3
Star House............................17 C3
Statue of Copernicus............18 C3
Teutonic Castle Ruins...........19 E3

SLEEPING (p549)
Hotel Gotyk.........................20 B3
Hotel Heban.........................21 E2
Hotel Petite Fleur.................22 B4
Hotel Pod Czarna Róza.........23 C4
Hotel Pod Orłem...................24 D3
Hotel Polonia.......................25 C2

EATING (pp549-50)
Bar Muzyczny Misz-Masz......26 F1
Gospoda Pod Modrym
 Fartuchem...........................27 E2
Pizzeria Verona....................28 C2
Restauracja Pod Arsenałem...29 D2

DRINKING (p550)
Piwnica Artystyczna Pod
 Aniołem..............................30 C3
Piwnica Ratusz.....................31 C3

wooden staircase, contains the **Far Eastern Art Museum** (☎ 622 70 38; Rynek Staromiejski 35; adult/child 5/3zł; ☷ 10am-4pm Tue-Sun).

Just off the northwestern corner of the square is the late-13th-century **St Mary's Church** (ul Panny Marii; ☷ dawn-dusk), a Gothic building with magnificent 15th-century stalls.

In 1473, Copernicus was born in the brick Gothic house that now contains the dry **Museum of Copernicus** (☎ 622 70 38; ul Kopernika 15/17; adult/child 7/5zł; ☷ 10am-4pm Tue, Thu & Sun, noon-6pm Wed, Fri & Sat May-Aug, 10am-4pm Tue-Sun Sep-Apr), with replicas of the great astronomer's instruments.

One block east of the museum is the **Cathedral of SS John the Baptist & John the Evangelist** (ul Żeglarska; adult/child 2/1zł; ☷ 9am-5.30pm Mon-Sat,

2-5.30pm Sun), founded in 1233 but not completed until over 200 years later. Its massive **tower** houses Poland's second-largest bell (after the Wawel Cathedral in Kraków).

Behind the church, the **Eskens' House** (☎ 622 70 38; ul Łazienna 16; adult/child 5/3zł; ☷ 10am-4pm Tue-Sun) is a disappointing affair displaying old photographs, a few swords and archaeological finds, only labelled in Polish. Further east are the ruins of the **Teutonic Castle** (☎ 622 70 39; ul Przedzamcze; admission 1zł; ☷ 9am-8pm), destroyed in 1454 by angry townsfolk protesting against the knights' oppressive regime.

In a park just north of the Old Town is the **Ethnographic Museum** (☎ 622 80 91; ul Wały Sikorskiego 19; adult/child 8/5zł; ☷ 9am-4pm Mon, Wed & Fri, 10am-6pm Tue, Thu, Sat & Sun Apr-Sep, 9am-4pm

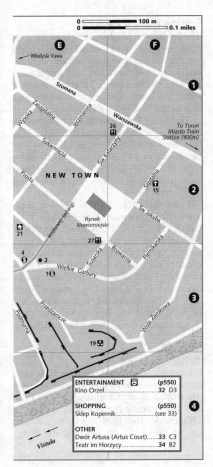

ENTERTAINMENT 🎭 (p550)
Kino Orzeł.................................32 D3

SHOPPING (p550)
Sklep Kopernik.....................(see 33)

OTHER
Dwór Artusa (Artus Court).....33 C3
Teatr im Horzycy......................34 B2

Tue-Sun Oct-Mar), showcasing traditional customs, costumes and weapons.

Sleeping

You'll find good budget and mid-range options in town, but no top-end hotels.

BUDGET

Camping Nr 33 Tramp (☎ & fax 654 71 87; ul Kujawska 14; camping per person/tent 6.50/10zł, d/tr/q 60/75/80zł; ☼ May-Sep) The cabins here are basic and it's alarmingly close to the train line. It's a five-minute walk west of the main train station.

Youth Hostel (☎ 659 61 84; ul Św Józefa 22/24; dm 13-19zł) Offers standard facilities 3.5km northwest of the centre. It's accessible on bus No 11 from the main train station and Old Town.

Schronisko Turystyczne Fort IV (☎ 655 82 36; www.fort.torun.pl; ul Chrobrego 86; dm 22zł) Atmospherically located in an old Prussian fort, with plain, barrack-like dorms. Although inconvenient for town, it's easy to reach on bus No 14 from the bus terminal and main train station.

MID-RANGE

Hotel Pod Orłem (☎ 622 50 24; www.hotel.torun.pl; ul Mostowa 17; s/d 110/140zł, apt 200zł; **P**) This hotel is great value, and although the rooms are smallish, have squeaky wooden floors, and some contain poky bathrooms, the service is good and it's central.

Hotel Polonia (☎ 657 18 00; www.polonia.torun.pl; plac Teatralny 5; s/d 130/160zł) The Polonia has smart, attractively furnished rooms in a restored 19th-century building a short walk from the main square. The hotel also has its own *kantor*.

Hotel Pod Czarna Róża (☎ 621 96 37; www.hotel czarnaroza.pl; ul Rabiańska 11; s/d 150/190zł) This hotel is extremely cosy. The rooms feature lovely antique-style furniture, and discounted weekend prices are especially good value.

Hotel Gotyk (☎ 658 40 00; www.hotel-gotyk.com.pl; ul Piekary 20; s/d 150/250zł) Housed in a fully modernised 14th-century building just off the main square. Rooms are very neat and all come with sparkling new bathrooms.

Hotel Petite Fleur (☎ 663 44 00; www.hotel-torun .com.pl; ul Piekary 25; s/d from 180/240zł) Just opposite the Gotyk, the Petite Fleur offers fresh, airy rooms in a recently renovated old town house, and has a French cellar **restaurant**. Weekend prices are 20% cheaper.

The **Hotel Heban** (☎ 652 15 55; www.hotel-heban .com.pl; ul Małe Garbary 7; s/d from 190/300zł; ☒) This is a stylish, upmarket hotel occupying an historic 17th-century building in a quiet street. It also has a good restaurant.

Eating

Bar Muzyczny Misz-Masz (☎ 652 23 24; ul Św Katarzyny 6; mains 5-10zł; ☼ 10am-9pm) This bar serves a huge range of cheap and filling fare, including dumplings, pasta, fish and chips and kebabs, plus lots of teas and stronger drinks.

Pizzeria Verona (☎ 622 04 80; ul Chełmińska 11; pizzas 6.50-27zł; ☼ 11am-late) The Verona offers a big menu of pizzas, plus a few pasta and salad options.

Gospoda Pod Modrym Fartuchem (☎ 622 26 26; Rynek Nowomiejski 8; mains from 14.50zł; ☼ 10am-10pm)

This is a very pleasant, folksy 15th-century pub on the New Town Square, serving the usual meat-and-cabbage Polish dishes at reasonable prices.

Restauracja Pod Arsenałem (☎ 658 34 40; ul Dominikańska 9; mains 15-60zł) This is a classier subterranean place serving excellent Polish cuisine, with dishes such as pheasant dumplings and roasts.

Toruń is famous for its gingerbread (*pierniki*), produced here since, well, forever. It comes in a variety of shapes, including figures of local hero Copernicus, and can be bought at **Sklep Kopernik** (☎ 622 88 32; Rynek Staromiejski 6) in Dwór Artusa.

Entertainment

Piwnica Artystyczna Pod Aniołem (☎ 622 70 39; Rynek Staromiejski 1), set in a splendid spacious cellar in the Old Town Hall, offers live music some nights. Other great places for a drink include **Gospoda Pod Modrym Fartuchem** (see p549) and **Piwnica Ratusz** (☎ 621 02 92; Rynek Staromiejski 1), which offers a few outdoor tables in the square and a huge cavernous area downstairs.

Teatr im Horzycy (☎ 622 50 21; plac Teatralny 1) is the main stage for theatre performances, while **Dwór Artusa** (☎ 655 49 29; Artus Court; Rynek Staromiejski 6) often presents classical music.

Kino Orzeł (☎ 622 45 31; ul Strumykowa 3; tickets 15zł) shows recent films. English-language movies are sometimes dubbed, sometimes subtitled; it's worth ringing ahead to check.

Getting There & Away

The **bus terminal** (ul Dąbrowskiego) is about a 10-minute walk north of the Old Town. It offers regular services to regional villages of minimal interest to travellers and surprisingly few long-distance buses. **Polski Express** (ul Mickiewicza) has hourly services to Warsaw (48zł, four hours) and two a day to Szczecin.

The main **Toruń Główny** train station (Al Podgórska) is on the opposite side of the Vistula River and linked to the Old Town by bus No 22 or 27. Some (but not all) trains stop and finish at the more convenient **Toruń Miasto** train station, about 500m east of the New Town.

From the Toruń Główny station, there are services to Poznań (30zł, 3½hours, three daily), Gdańsk (60zł, five hours, six daily), Kraków (55zł, 6½ hours, three daily), Łódź (seven daily), Olsztyn (nine daily), Szczecin (daily), Wrocław (45zł, 4½ hours, two daily) and Warsaw (58zł, four hours, five daily). Trains travelling between Toruń and Gdańsk often change at Bydgoszcz, and between Toruń and Kraków you may need to get another connection at Inowrocław.

GDAŃSK

☎ 058 / pop 475,000

Gdańsk was founded more than 1000 years ago, and was already a thriving trading centre when the Teutonic Knights seized it in 1308, and after joining the Hanseatic League in 1361, the city, then known as Danzig, became one of the wealthiest ports on the Baltic.

INFORMATION		
Almatur	1	C5
Bank Gdański	2	C5
Bank Gdański	3	A4
Bank Pekao	4	B4
EMPiK Megastore	5	A3
EMPiK	6	C5
Jazz 'n' Java	7	B5
Kantors	8	B5
Kantors	9	B4
Kantors	10	B4
Main Post Office	11	B5
Orbis Travel	12	C5
PTTK Office	13	C5
Rudy Kot	14	B4
Telephone Centre	15	B5

SIGHTS & ACTIVITIES	(pp552-3)	
Arsenal	16	B4
Artus Court Museum	17	C5
Central Maritime Museum	18	D4
Central Maritime Museum	19	D4
Church of SS Peter & Paul	20	B6
Church of the Holy Trinity	21	B6
Dom Uphagena	22	B5
Gdańsk Crane	(see 18)	
Gdańsk History Museum	23	C5

Golden Gate	24	B5
Golden House	25	C5
Great Mill	26	B3
Green Gate	27	C5
Monument to the Shipyard Workers	28	B1
National Museum	29	B6
Neptune's Fountain	30	C5
Roads to Freedom Exhibition (Solidarity Museum)	31	B1
St Bridget's Church	32	B3
St Catherine's Church	33	B3
St Mary's Church	34	C5
St Mary's Gate	(see 36)	
Sołdek Museum Ship	35	D4
State Archaeological Museum	36	D4
Upland Gate	37	A5

SLEEPING	🛏	(pp553-4)
Dom Aktora	38	C4
Dom Harcerza	39	B5
Hotel Hanza	40	D4
Mercure Hevelius Gdansk	41	B2
Targ Rybny	42	D3
Youth Hostel	43	B2

EATING	🍴	(pp554-5)
Bar Mleczny Neptun	44	C5

Grand Cafe Rotterdam	45	C5
Green Way	46	A4
Pod Łososiem	47	C4
Ratskeller Piwnica Rajców	48	C5
Restauracja Kubicki	49	D3
Złoty Kur	50	B5

DRINKING	🖵 🗖	(pp554-5)
Celtic Pub	51	B5
Jazz Club	52	C5
Maraska	53	B5

ENTERTAINMENT	🎭	(p555)
Teatr Wybrzeże	54	B4

SHOPPING		(p555)
Supermarket	(see 16)	

TRANSPORT		(pp555-6)
Bus Terminal	55	A3
Bus to Westerplatte	56	A3
Dock (for Excursion Boats)	57	C5
LOT Office	58	A5

OTHER		
Foregate	59	B5
St John's Gate	60	D4

POLAND

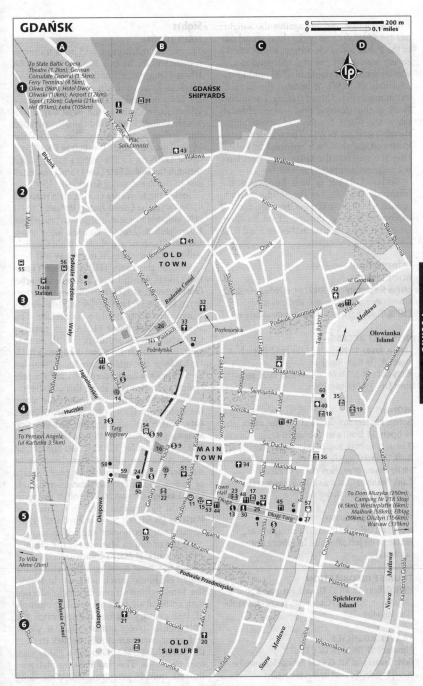

GDAŃSK

0 |======| 200 m
0 |======| 0.1 miles

To State Baltic Opera
Theatre (1.2km); German;
Consulate General (1.5km);
Ferry Terminal (4.5km);
Oliwa (9km); Hotel Dwór
Oliwski (10km); Airport (12km);
Sopot (12km); Gdynia (21km);
Hel (91km); Łeba (105km)

GDAŃSK
SHIPYARDS

Plac
Solidarności

**OLD
TOWN**

Train
Station

ul Grodska

Ołowianka
Island

Profesorska

**MAIN
TOWN**

To Pension Angela;
(ul Kartuska 3.5km)

Targ
Węglowy

Hucisko

Town Hall

To Dom Muzyka (250m);
Camping Nr 218 Stogi
(4.5km); Westerplatte (6km);
Malbork (58km); Elbląg
(59km); Olsztyn (156km);
Warsaw (339km)

Długi Targ

To Villa
Akme (2km)

Podwale Przedmiejskie

Spichlerze
Island

Św Trójcy

**OLD
SUBURB**

After a popular uprising against the Knights in 1454, Gdańsk came under the nominal rule of the Polish monarch, although it retained a strong measure of political independence. It was annexed by Prussia in 1793, and in the aftermath of WWI, it became the virtually autonomous Free City of Danzig. The importance of this strategic port was emphasised when the Nazis bombarded Westerplatte, thereby, starting WWII. The war devastated most of Gdańsk, which returned to Poland after the war, but the historic quarters have been almost completely rebuilt.

Today, Gdańsk is best known as the birthplace (in 1980) of the Solidarity trade union, which was the catalyst for the fall of communism in Europe. It's a bustling, cosmopolitan city that makes an ideal base for exploring the coast.

Information
BOOKSHOPS
EMPiK Megastore (☎ 301 72 44; ul Podwale Grodzkie 8) Across the road from the main train station.
EMPiK (Długi Targ) A smaller branch in the Main Town.

INTERNET ACCESS
Jazz 'n' Java (☎ 305 36 16; ul Tkacka 17/18; per hr about 5zł; ☺ 10am-10pm)
Rudy Kot (☎ 301 39 86; ul Garncarska 18/20; per hr about 5zł; ☺ 10am-midnight)

MONEY
Some **kantors** are located on the map; one is open 24 hours in the main train station. The city centre has plenty of ATMs.
Bank Gdański (Wały Jagiellońskie 14/16/Długi Targ 14/16) Also has other offices at central locations.
Bank Pekao (ul Garncarska 23) Will provide cash advances on Visa and MasterCard.

POST & TELEPHONE
Main Post Office (ul Długa 22). Next to the main entrance of the post office is the **Telephone Centre** (ul Długa 26).

TOURIST INFORMATION
PTTK Office (☎ 301 13 43; www.pttk-gdansk.pl; ul Długa 45; ☺ 9am-5pm) Conveniently placed opposite the Main Town Hall.

TRAVEL AGENCIES
Almatur (☎ 301 24 24; Długi Targ 11)
Orbis Travel (☎ 301 45 44; ul Podwale Staromiejskie 96/97) Provides the usual services to travellers.

Sights
MAIN TOWN
The richest architecture and most thorough restoration are in this historic quarter. Ul Długa (Long Street) and Długi Targ (Long Market) form its main thoroughfare, and are both now pedestrian streets. They are known collectively as the **Royal Way**, along which Polish kings traditionally paraded during their periodic visits. They entered the Main Town through the **Upland Gate** (built in the 1770s on a 15th-century gate), passed through the **Golden Gate** (1614) and proceeded east to the Renaissance **Green Gate** (1568).

Inside the towering Gothic **Main Town Hall** (ul Długa 47) is the **Gdańsk History Museum** (☎ 767 91 00; adult/child 9/5zł, adult/child incl Artus Court Museum & Dom Uphagena 12/6zł; ☺ 10am-4pm Tue-Sat, 11am-4pm Sun). On show are photos of old Gdańsk, and the damage caused during WWII.

Outside the Town Hall is **Neptune's Fountain** (1633), behind which stands the **Artus Court Museum** (☎ 767 91 00; ul Długi Targ 43/44; admission 5zł, free Wed; ☺ 10am-4pm Tue-Sat, 11am-4pm Sun), where merchants used to congregate. The adjacent **Golden House** (1618) has perhaps the richest façade in town. A little further west, the 18th-century **Dom Uphagena** (☎ 301 13 63; ul Długa; adult/child 6/3zł, free Sun; ☺ 10am-4pm Tue-Sat, 11am-4pm Sun) features ornate furniture typical of the houses along this old street.

Two blocks north of Green Gate along the waterfront is the 14th-century **St Mary's Gate**, which houses the **State Archaeological Museum** (☎ 301 50 31; ul Mariacka 25/26; adult/child 4/3zł; ☺ 9am-4pm Tue, Thu & Fri, 10am-5pm Wed, Sat & Sun). It features an inordinate number of diseased ancient human skulls, plus displays of amber, and offers **river views** from the adjacent **tower** (admission 2zł). Through this gate, the most picturesque street in Gdańsk – **ul Mariacka** (St Mary's St) – is lined with 17th-century burgher houses and amber shops.

At the end of ul Mariacka is the gigantic 14th-century **St Mary's Church** (adult/child 2/1zł; ☺ 8am-8pm, except during services), possibly the largest old brick church in the world. Inside, the 14m-high astronomical clock, adorned with zodiacal signs, is an amazing example of 15th-century craftsmanship; watch the little figures troop out at noon. If you're feeling fit, you can climb the 405 steps of the **tower** (adult/child 3/1.50zł) for a giddy view over the town. The tiny viewing platform, though, quickly gets crowded. West along ul Piwna (Beer St) is the Dutch Renaissance **Arsenal** (1609), now occupied by a market.

Further north along the waterfront is the 15th-century **Gdańsk Crane**, the largest of its kind in medieval Europe and capable of hoisting loads of up to 2000kg. It's now part of the **Central Maritime Museum** (☎ 301 86 11; ul Ołowianka 9-13; admission 6zł 1 section, 14zł all 4 sections; ☼ 10am-5pm Tue-Sun), but unless you can read the Polish-only labelling, you won't learn much. Far more user-friendly are the sections on the opposite bank of the river, offering a fascinating insight into Gdańsk's seafaring past, including the **Sołdek Museum Ship**, built here just after WWII.

OLD TOWN

Almost totally destroyed in 1945, the Old Town has never been completely rebuilt, apart from a handful of churches. The largest and most remarkable of these is **St Catherine's Church** (ul Wielkie Młyny; ☼ 8am-6pm Mon-Sat), Gdańsk's oldest church (begun in the 1220s). Opposite, the **Great Mill** (ul Wielkie Młyny) was built by the Teutonic Knights in around 1350. It used to produce 200 tonnes of flour per day and continued to operate until 1945. More recently, it has been converted into a modern shopping complex.

Right behind St Catherine's is **St Bridget's Church** (ul Profesorska 17; ☼ 10am-6pm Mon-Sat). Formerly Lech Wałęsa's place of worship, the church was a strong supporter of the shipyard workers and its priest often spoke about political issues during his sermons in the 1980s.

At the entrance to the Gdańsk Shipyards to the north stands the soaring **Monument to the Shipyard Workers** (plac Solidarności). It was erected in late 1980 in memory of 44 workers killed during the riots of December 1970. Down the street is the evocative **Roads to Freedom Exhibition** (☎ 308 42 80; ul Doki 1; adult/child 5/3zł, free Wed; ☼ 10am-4pm Tue-Sun), also known as the **Solidarity Museum**. Look out for the section of Berlin Wall outside.

OLD SUBURB

This section of Gdańsk was also reduced to rubble in 1945. Little of the former urban fabric has been reconstructed, except for the former Franciscan monastery that now houses the **National Museum** (☎ 301 70 61; ul Toruńska 1; adult/child 8/4zł; ☼ 9am-4pm Tue-Fri, 10am-4pm Sat & Sun). The museum is famous for its

Dutch and Flemish paintings, especially Hans Memling's 15th-century *Last Judgment*.

Adjoining the museum is the former Franciscan **Church of the Holy Trinity** (ul Św Trójcy; ☼ 10am-8pm Mon-Sat), which was built at the end of the 15th century.

OLIWA

About 9km northwest of the Main Town in the suburb of Oliwa is **Park Oliwski** (ul Cystersów). This lovely piece of greenery surrounds the soaring **Oliwa Cathedral** (☼ 8am-8pm), built in the 13th century with a Gothic façade and a long, narrow central nave. The famous baroque organ is used for recitals each hour between 10am and 3pm Monday to Saturday in June, July and August. Elsewhere in the park is the **Ethnographic Museum** (☎ 552 46 37; ul Cystersów 19; adult/child 6/3zł; ☼ 9am-4pm Tue-Fri, 10am-4pm Sat & Sun) in the Old Granary, and the **Modern Art Gallery** (☎ 552 12 71; adult/child 6/3zł; ☼ 9am-4pm Tue-Sun) in the former Abbots' Palace.

To reach the park, take the commuter train to the Gdańsk Oliwa station (2.80zł). From there, it's a 10-minute walk; head (west) up ul Poczty Gdańsk, turn right (north) along the highway and look for the signs (in English) to 'Ethnographic Museum' and 'Cathedral'.

WESTERPLATTE

When the German battleship *Schleswig-Holstein* began shelling the Polish naval post at Westerplatte at 4.45am on 1 September 1939, WWII had officially started. The 182-man Polish garrison held out against ferocious attacks for seven days before surrendering.

A park at Westerplatte, 7km north of the Main Town, now features a hilltop **memorial** (free; ☼ 24hr), a small **museum** (☎ 343 69 72; ul Sucharskiego 1; admission 2zł; ☼ 8am-7pm) and plenty of other **ruins** caused by the Nazi bombardment. The café at the bus stop serves light meals and drinks.

Bus No 106 (25 minutes) goes to the park every 15 minutes from a stop outside the main train station in Gdańsk. Alternatively, excursion boats (18/35zł one way/return) to and around Westerplatte leave from a dock near the Green Gate in Gdańsk between 1 April and 30 October.

Sleeping

If you're having trouble finding accommodation, the PTTK Office (opposite) is happy to ring around a few hotels and hostels (for no charge). Also you could consider staying in nearby Sopot (p556) or Gdynia (p556).

BUDGET

Camping Nr 218 Stogi (☎ 307 39 15; www.kemping
.gdansk.pl; ul Wydmy 9; per person/tent 10/10zł, cabins 40-
100zł; ☺ Apr-Oct; **P**) About 5.5km northeast of the Main Town, this camping ground is only 200m from the excellent beach in the seaside holiday centre of Stogi. Neat cabins sleep between two and five people and facilities include a volleyball court and children's playground. Take tram No 8 or 13 from the main train station in Gdańsk.

Youth Hostel (☎ & fax 301 23 13; ul Wałowa 21;
dm from 12zł, s/d from 25/50zł; ✖) This hostel is in a quiet, old building. It's often full, particularly in summer, so book ahead. Smoking and drinking are strictly forbidden and there's a midnight curfew.

Targ Rybny (☎ 301 56 27; www.gdanskhostel.com;
ul Grodzka 21; dm from 40zł, d/tr from 120/180zł; ☐)
The Targ Rybny is a very popular modern hostel in a great central location overlooking the quay. It's a little cramped, but clean and sociable, and there's bike rental and free Internet access.

Dom Harcerza (☎ 301 36 21; www.domharcerza.prv
.pl; ul Za Murami 2/10; d/tr from 96/106zł) The rooms are small but cosy, and the bathrooms are clean at this place, which offers the best value and location for any budget-priced hotel. It's popular (so get there early or book ahead) and it can get noisy when large groups are staying there.

MID-RANGE & TOP END

Pension Angela (☎ & fax 302 23 15; ul Beethowena 12;
s & d 100-200zł; **P**) This is a cosy, family-run pension offering comfortable rooms west of the centre. It's accessible by bus No 130 or 184 from the main train station.

Dom Muzyka (☎ 300 92 60; www.dom-muzyka.pl;
ul Łąkowa 1/2; s/d 120/180zł; ✖ **P**) With modern, spotless rooms inside the Music Academy, this place, about 300m east of the city centre is excellent value. There's no hotel sign anywhere; head for the door on the right end of the big yellow-brick building.

Dom Aktora (☎ 301 61 93; www.domaktora.pl; ul
Straganiarska 55/56; s/tw from 200/250zł, apt from 400zł)
The Dom Aktora is an historic and convenient place which is always popular, but it's a little drab and old-fashioned. Prices come down between October and May.

Hotel Hanza (☎ 305 34 27; www.hanza-hotel.com
.pl; ul Tokarska 6; s/d 565/595zł; ✖ **P**) The Hanza is attractively perched along the waterfront near the Gdańsk Crane. Rooms are spacious and modern, and some have enviable views. Prices between November and May are considerably cheaper.

Mercure Hevelius Gdańsk (☎ 321 00 00; mer
.hevelius@orbis.pl; ul Heweliusza 22; s/d from 360/420zł;
✖ ☐ **P**) Popular with international business travellers and offering an appropriately high and conservative standard of accommodation. Rooms on the higher floors have great views across town.

Hotel Dwór Oliwski (☎ 554 70 00; www.dwor
-oliwski.com.pl; ul Bytowska 4; s/d €105/126; ✖ ☘ **P**)
This is a charming 17th-century manor house set in peaceful grounds in the suburb of Oliwa, around 10km from the city-centre. It has its own spa and French restaurant.

Eating & Drinking

Bar Mleczny Neptun (☎ 301 49 88; ul Długa 33/34;
mains 5-10zł; ☺ 7.30am-6pm Mon-Fri, 9am-5pm Sat)
This joint is a cut above your run-of-the-mill milk bar.

Złoty Kur (☎ 301 61 63; ul Długa 4; mains 10-20zł;
☺ noon-7pm) Another cheap and cheerful place with plastic flowers on the tables and soups, salads and fuller meals such as chicken and chips on the menu.

Grand Café Rotterdam (☎ 305 45 80; Długi Targ
33/34; mains 12-20zł; ☺ 10am-2am) On the ground floor of the Dutch consulate, this café serves especially good savoury pancakes, plus other Dutch and Polish specialities. It's also a pleasant spot for an alfresco beer, and has a well-stocked cellar wine bar.

Green Way (☎ 301 41 21; ul Garncarska 4/6; mains
7-10zł; ☺ 10am-10pm) Always popular with local vegetarians for sandwiches, crepes and salads.

Restauracja Kubicki (☎ 301 00 50; ul Wartka 5; mains
20-50zł; ☺ noon-midnight) This is a decent mid-priced place to try Polish food, especially seafood. It claims to be one of the oldest places in Gdańsk (established 1918), and offers appropriately old-fashioned decor and service.

Pod Łososiem (☎ 301 76 52; ul Szeroka 52/54;
mains 40-100zł; ☺ noon-11pm) This is one of Gdańsk's oldest and most highly regarded restaurants, and is particularly famous for its salmon dishes. Red leather seats, brass chandeliers and a gathering of gas lamps fill out the sombre interior.

Ratskeller Piwinica Rajców (☎ 300 02 80; ul Długi Targ 44; mains 40-120zł; ⊘ 10am-midnight) The Ratskeller is an excellent cellar-restaurant where you can try some of the finest Polish cuisine to be had in Gdańsk. The wild boar comes recommended.

Celtic Pub (☎ 320 29 99; ul Lektykarska 3; ⊘ 5pm-1am Sun-Thu, 5pm-3am Fri & Sat) This pub is a popular and lively place, scattered with the usual pseudo-Irish junk.

Maraska (☎ 301 42 89; ul Długa 31/32; ⊘ 9am-9pm) The Maraska is a cosy teahouse with a big menu to choose from and deserts. You can also buy packets of tea to take away.

For self-catering, visit the **supermarket** inside the former Arsenal facing Targ Węglowy.

Entertainment

Jazz Club (☎ 301 54 33; Długi Targ 39/40; ⊘ 2pm-1am Sun-Thu, 2pm-4am Fri & Sat; admission 7zł) has live music on weekends, though not necessarily jazz.

State Baltic Opera Theatre (☎ 763 49 12; www .operabaltycka.pl; Al Zwycięstwa 15) is in the suburb of Wrzeszcz, not far from the train station at Gdańsk Politechnika.

Teatr Wybrzeże (☎ 301 70 21; Targ Węglowy 1), next to the Arsenal, is the main city theatre. Both Polish and foreign classics (all in Polish) are often part of the repertoire.

Getting There & Away

For information about international bus and train services to/from Gdańsk, and international ferry services to/from Gdańsk and Gdynia, see p570. For travel to surrounding places, see p569.

AIR

From Gdańsk, LOT has several daily flights to Warsaw and one or two a day to Frankfurt and Hamburg. SAS also flies daily to Copenhagen, and Air Polonia flies twice weekly to London. Tickets for all airlines, except the budget Air Polonia (www.airpolonia.com), can be bought at the **LOT office** (☎ 0801 300 952; ul Wały Jagiellońskie 2/4).

BOAT

Polferries uses the **ferry terminal** (ul Przemysłowa) in Nowy Port, about 5km north of the Main Town but only a short walk from the local commuter train station at Gdańsk Brzeżno. Orbis Travel and the PTTK Office in Gdańsk can provide information and sell tickets.

GOLDEN WATER

The origins of Gdańsk's oldest and most famous alcoholic tipple, **Goldwasser**, go back to at least the 16th century and are shrouded in legend. It is said that the god Neptune, greatly honoured by the locals' habit of tossing coins into the Neptune Fountain on Długi Targ, transformed the flowing water into potent alcohol. Pub landlords from all over town rushed to exploit this public bounty, and filled barrels full of the liquid to sell at their establishments. Only the landlord of Pod Łososiem (see opposite) abstained from this blatant theft, and a pleased Neptune rewarded him by turning all his regular vodka into glittering Goldwasser. Meanwhile, the thieving landlords found that their kegs were now filled only with plain water.

This sweet, strong liquor, flavoured with, amongst other things, angelica, rosewood and valerian, and containing thin flakes of real gold, is a great source of local pride, and is served all over town.

Between 1 May and 30 September, excursion boats leave regularly each day from the dock near the Green Gate in Gdańsk for Sopot (33/48zł one way/return) and Gdynia (38/56zł) – and you can even go to Hel (40/60zł)! From the same dock, boats also head out to Westerplatte (18/35zł) between 1 April and 30 October.

BUS

The **bus terminal** (ul 3 Maja 12) handles all domestic and international services. It's behind (west of) the main train station, and connected to ul Podwale Grodzkie by an underground passageway. Every day, there are buses to Olsztyn (19zł, four daily), Toruń (22zł, four daily), Warsaw (50zł, six hours, six daily) and one or two to Białystok and Świnoujście. Polski Express also offers daily buses to Warsaw from this bus terminal (72zł, two daily).

TRAIN

The city's main train station, **Gdańsk Główny** (ul Podwale Grodzkie 1), is conveniently located on the western outskirts of the Old Town. Most long-distance trains actually start or finish at Gdynia, so make sure you get on/off quickly at the Gdańsk Główny station.

POLAND

Each day about 18 trains head to Warsaw, including 10 express trains (66.20zł, 5½ hours) and five InterCity services (3½ hours). Also each day, there are trains to Olsztyn (35zł, three hours, six daily), Kraków (80zł, eight hours, 10 daily), Poznań (60zł, five hours, five daily), Toruń (36zł, three hours, seven daily) and Szczecin (60zł, 4½ hours, four daily). Trains also head to Białystok and Lublin once or twice a day.

Getting Around

The airport is in Rębiechowo, about 12km northwest of Gdańsk. It's accessible by bus No 110 from the Gdańsk Wrzeszcz local commuter train station or less frequently by Bus B from outside the Gdańsk Główny train station. Taxis will cost about 30zł one way.

The local commuter train, the SKM, runs every 15 minutes between 6am and 7.30pm, and less frequently thereafter, between Gdańsk Główny and Gdynia Główna stations, via Sopot and Gdańsk Oliwa stations. (Note: the line to Gdańsk Nowy Port, via Gdańsk Brzeźno, is a separate line that leaves less regularly from Gdańsk Główny.) Buy tickets at any station and validate them in the machines at the platform entrance.

Around Gdańsk

Gdańsk is part of the so-called Tri-City Area, which stretches 30km along the coast from Gdańsk to Gdynia and includes Sopot. Gdynia and Sopot are easy day trips from Gdańsk. Sopot, in particular, attracts large numbers of Polish holidaymakers, and has plenty of hotels, though there's little in the way of true budget options.

SOPOT

☎ 058 / pop 43,000

Sopot, 12km north of Gdańsk, has been one of Poland's most fashionable seaside resorts since the 19th century. It has an easy-going atmosphere and there are long stretches of sandy **beach**.

The **tourist office** (☎ 550 37 83; www.sopot.pl; ul Dworcowa 4; ☒ 8.30am-7.30pm Jun-Aug, 10am-6pm Sep-May) is about 50m from the main train station. From there, head down ul Bohaterów Monte Cassino, one of Poland's most attractive pedestrian streets, past the church to Poland's longest **pier** (515m). Signposted from along here is an Internet centre, **www.c@fe** (☎ 550 73 83; ul Chmielewskiego 5a; ☒ 8am-midnight).

Opposite Pension Wanda, **Museum Sopotu** (☎ 551 22 66; ul Poniatowskiego 8; adult/child 2/1zł; 10am-3pm Tue-Fri, 11am-4pm Sat & Sun) has displays recalling the town's 19th-century heyday.

Sleeping & Eating

There are no real budget options in Sopot, and prices increase during the busy summer season.

Hotel Eden (☎ 551 15 03; fax 550 26 37; ul Kordeckiego 4/6; s 80-170zł, d 130-240zł, tr 220-300zł) One of the less expensive places in town. It's a quiet, old-fashioned pension overlooking the town park one street from the beach. The cheaper rooms don't have private bathrooms.

Hotel Sopot (☎ 551 32 01; www.hotel-sopot.pl; ul Bitwy pod Płowcami 62; s/d/tr 154/198/253zł Jun-Sep) In a basic concrete block of a place, but nevertheless, rooms here are fresh and clean and it's just a brief stroll from the sea. It's cheaper outside the summer months.

Pension Wanda (☎ 550 30 38; fax 551 57 25; ul Poniatowskiego 7; s/d from 160/240zł, ste from 290zł) The Wanda is a homely place with a handy location (about 500m southeast of the pier) and some rooms with sea views.

Grand Hotel Orbis (☎ 551 00 41; rez.sogrand@orbis.pl; ul Powstańców Warszawy 12/14; s/d 330/410zł, apt 785zł; ☒ Ⓟ) The Orbis is an elegant old pile occupying a prime spot overlooking the beach. The fine **restaurant** offers marvellous views and impeccable service.

Bistros and **cafés** serving a wide range of cuisines sprout up in summer along the promenades. **Pasha's** (☎ 555 53 80; ul Bohaterów Monte Cassino 53/4; mains 9-30zł; ☒ 9am-11pm) is a decent Turkish restaurant and bar serving up kebabs and salads and has a huge drinks menu, though it's surrealistic 'melting' architecture is what sets this place apart; you really can't miss it.

Getting There & Away

From the **Sopot train station** (ul Dworcowa 7), local commuter trains run every 15 minutes to Gdańsk Główny (2.80zł, 15 minutes) and Gdynia Główna (1.20zł, 10 minutes) stations. Excursion boats leave several times a day (May to September) from the Sopot pier to Gdańsk, Gdynia and Hel.

GDYNIA

☎ 058 / pop 260,000

Gdynia, 9km north of Sopot, is the third part of the Tri-City Area. It has none of the history of Gdańsk, nor relaxed beach ambience of Sopot; it's just a busy, young city with an omnipresent port atmosphere.

From the main Gdynia Główna train station on plac Konstytucji – where there is a **tourist office** (☎ 628 54 66; it@gdynia.pl; ☼ 9am-5pm) – follow ul 10 Lutego east for about 1.5km to the pier. At the end of the pier is the **Oceanographic Museum & Aquarium** (☎ 621 70 21; adult/child 8.50/5zł; ☼ 10am-5pm Tue-Sun), which houses a vast array of sea creatures, both alive and embalmed.

A 20-minute walk uphill (follow the signs) from Teatr Muzyczny on plac Grunwaldzki (about 300m southwest of the start of the pier) leads to **Kamienna Góra**. This hill offers wonderful **views**.

Sleeping & Eating

Gdynia's accommodation options are limited, and it's probably best visited as a day trip. It does, though, have a vibrant bar and restaurant scene.

If you're looking for style you could try **Willa Lubicz** (☎ 668 47 40; www.willalubicz.pl; ul Orłowska 43; s/d 380/410zł; ✕), a quiet, upmarket place with a chic 1930s ambience at the southern end of town; Gdynia Orłowo is the nearest train station.

Cheaper rooms are available at **Hotel Antracyt** (☎ 620 12 39; ul Korzeniowskiego 19; www.antracyt .home.pl; s/d from 160/240zł; P), located on a hill with fine views over the sea.

There are plenty of basic **milk bars** in the city centre and several upmarket **fish restaurants** along the pier. **Bistro Kwadrans** (☎ 620 15 92; Skwer Kościuszki 20; mains 8-12zł; ☼ 9am-10pm), one block north of the median strip along ul 10 Lutego, is a great place for tasty Polish food.

Getting There & Away

Local commuter trains link **Gdynia Główna** station with Sopot and Gdańsk every 15 minutes (4zł, 25 minutes). From the same station, trains regularly go each day to Hel (in summer) and Lębork (for Łeba). From the small **bus terminal** outside this train station, minibuses also go to Hel and Łeba, and two buses run daily to Świnoujście.

Stena Line uses the **Terminal Promowy** (ul Kwiatkowskiego 60), about 5km northwest of Gdynia. Ask about the free shuttle central bus between Gdańsk and here, via Gdynia and Sopot, when you book your ticket, or take bus No 150 from outside the main train station.

Between May and September, excursion boats leave regularly throughout the day to Gdańsk, Sopot and Hel from a point halfway along the pier in Gdynia.

HEL

This old fishing village at the tip of the Hel Peninsula north of Gdańsk is now a popular beach resort. The pristine, windswept **beach** on the Baltic side stretches the length of the peninsula. On the other (southern) side the sea is popular for **windsurfing**; equipment can be rented at the villages of Władysławowo and Jastarnia. Hel is a popular day trip from Gdańsk and worth visiting – if only to say that you've been to Hel and back!

The **Fokarium** (☎ 675 08 36; ul Morska 2; admission 1zł; ☼ 8.30am-8pm), along the main road, is home to many endangered Baltic grey seals. The 15th-century **Gothic church** (ul Nadmorksi 2), along the esplanade near the Fokarium, houses the **Museum of Fishery** (☎ 675 05 52; admission 4zł; ☼ 10am-4pm).

The best places to stay are any of the numerous **private rooms** offered in local houses (mostly from May to September). Expect to pay about 80zł per double. **Captain Morgan** (☎ 675 00 91; www.captainmorgan.hel.org.pl; ul Wiejska 21; d/tr 100/130zł) offers plain, clean rooms and a good seafood restaurant.

To Hel, minibuses leave every hour or so from outside the main train station in Gdynia (10.70zł) and several slow trains depart from Gdańsk and Gdynia daily from May to September. Hel is also accessible by excursion boat from Gdańsk, Sopot and Gdynia.

ŁEBA

☎ 059 / pop 4100

Łeba (WEH-bah) is a sleepy fishing village that turns into a popular seaside resort between May and September. The wide sandy **beach** stretches in both directions and the water is reputedly the cleanest along the Polish coast – ideal if you're looking for a beach resort.

From the train station, and adjacent bus stop, head east along ul 11 Listopada as far as the main street, ul Kościuszko. Then turn left (north) and walk about 1.5km to the better eastern beach via the esplanade (ul Nadmorska); if in doubt, follow the signs to the beachside Hotel Neptune.

POLAND

The **tourist office** (☎ 866 25 65; 🕑 8am-4pm Mon-Fri May-Sep) is inside the train station. There are several **kantors** along ul 11 Listopada.

SŁOWIŃSKI NATIONAL PARK

This 186 sq km park begins just west of Łeba and stretches along the coast for 33km. It contains a diversity of habitats, including forests, lakes, bogs and beaches, but the main attraction is the huge number of massive (and shifting) **sand dunes** that create a desert landscape. The wildlife and birdlife is also remarkably rich.

From Łeba to the sand dunes, follow the signs from near the train station northwest along ul Turystyczna and take the road west to the park entrance in the hamlet of Rąbka. Minibuses ply this road in summer from Łeba; alternatively, it's a pleasant walk or bike ride (8km). No cars or buses are allowed beyond the park entrance.

Sleeping & Eating

Many houses offering **private rooms** open their doors all year, but finding a room during the summer tourist season can be tricky.

Camping Nr 41 Amber (☎ 866 24 72; www.ambre .leba.pl; ul Nadmorska 9a; per person/tent from 11/6zł; P) is a decent camping ground, but bring mosquito repellent if you don't want to be eaten alive.

Hotel Wodnik (☎ 866 13 66; www.wodnik.leba.pl; ul Nadmorska 10; s/d from 144/166zł; P 🐾) is one of several pensions along the esplanade on the eastern side of the beach.

There are plenty of decent **eateries** in the town centre and along ul Nadmorska.

Getting There & Away

The usual transit point is Lębork, 29km south of Łeba. To Lębork, slow trains run every hour or two from Gdańsk, via Gdynia, and there are buses every hour from Gdynia. In summer (June to August), two buses and two trains run directly between Gdynia and Łeba and one train a day travels to/from Warsaw (70zł, eight hours).

MALBORK

☎ 055 / pop 42,000

Malbork, 58km southeast of Gdańsk, is famed for **Malbork Castle** (☎ 647 08 00; adult/child 19.50/11.50zł; 🕑 10am-3pm Tue-Sun), the largest Gothic castle in Europe. It was built by the Teutonic Knights in 1276 and became

capital of the Grand Master of Teutonic Knights in 1309. It was badly damaged during WWII, but has been almost completely rebuilt since. It was placed on the Unesco World Heritage List in 1997.

The **Youth Hostel** (☎ 272 24 08; gimnazju@malbork .com; ul Żeromskiego 45; dm 20.50zł, d 41zł) is in a reasonable budget option in a local school about 500m south of the castle. Bed linen costs extra.

Hotel & Restaurant Zbyszko (☎ 272 26 40; www .hotel.malbork.pl; ul Kościuszki 43; s/d from 140/190zł; P) is a fairly drab but conveniently located place along the road to the castle. The unremarkable rooms are serviceable for a night.

Hotel & Restaurant Zamek (☎ 272 84 00; ul Starościńska 14; s/d 230/300zł; ✗ P) is inside a restored medieval building in the Lower Castle. The rooms are a bit old-fashioned, but the bathrooms are new.

The train and bus stations are about 1km southeast of the castle. As you leave the train station, turn right, cut across the highway, head down ul Kościuszki and follow the signs to the castle. Malbork is on the busy Gdańsk–Warsaw railway line, so it's an easy day trip from Gdańsk (7.80zł, 45 minutes). There are buses every hour to Malbork from Gdynia and five daily from Gdańsk. From Malbork, trains also regularly go to Toruń and Olsztyn.

SZCZECIN

☎ 091 / pop 425,000

Szczecin (SHCHEH-cheen) is the main urban centre and port in northwestern Poland. It has a colourful and stormy history, but sadly most remnants were destroyed during WWII. Therefore, Szczecin has none of the charm of Toruń or Poznań, but it's a worthwhile stopover if you're travelling to/from Germany.

The **tourist information office** (☎ 434 04 40; Al Niepodległości 1) is helpful but the **cultural & tourist information office** (☎ 489 16 30; 🕑 10am-6pm Mon-Sat) in the castle is better set up. The **post office** and most **kantors** and **Internet cafés** are along the main street, Al Niepodległości.

The city's major attraction is undoubtedly the huge and rather austere **Castle of the Pomeranian Princess** (ul Korsazy 34; admission free; 🕑 dawn-dusk), 500m northeast of the tourist office. Originally built in the mid-14th century, it was enlarged in 1577 and rebuilt after WWII. Inside the grounds, the **Castle**

Museum (☎ 434 73 91; admission 8zł; ☻ 10am-5pm Tue-Sun) features displays about the bizarre history of the castle.

A short walk down (south) from the castle is the 15th-century **Old Town Hall** (plac Rzepichy), which contains the **Museum of the City of Szczecin** (☎ 431 52 53; adult/child 6/3zł; ☻ 10am-6pm Tue, 9am-3.30pm Wed-Fri, 10am-4pm Sat & Sun). Nearby is the charmingly rebuilt 'old town' with cafés and bars. Three blocks northwest of the castle is the **National Museum** (☎ 431 52 36; ul Staromłyńska 27; adult/child 6/3zł; ☻ 10am-6pm Tue, Wed & Fri, 10am-4pm Thu, Sat & Sun).

Sleeping & Eating

Camping PTTK Marina (☎ & fax 460 11 65; ul Przestrzenna 23; per person/tent 10/7.50zł, s/d/tr cabins 42/70/100zł; ☻ May-Sep; P) On the shore of Lake Dąbie – get off at the Szczecin Dąbie train station and ask for directions (2km).

Youth Hostel PTSM (☎ 422 47 61; www.ptsm .home.pl; ul Monte Cassino 19a; dm 16-18zł, d 44zł; P) This hostel has clean, spacious rooms and is located 2km northwest of the tourist office. Bed linen costs 6zł extra.

Hotel Promorski (☎ 433 61 51; plac Brama Portowa 4; s/d with shared bathroom from 60/64zł) The Promorski is fairly basic but it is perfectly adequate. It's central (200m west of Al Niepodłegłości), but a little noisy.

Hotel Podzamcze (☎ 812 14 04; www.podzamcze .szczecin.pl; ul Sienna 1/3; s/d 170/195zł; P) This hotel is in a charming location near the Old Town Hall, with neat, well-maintained rooms. It's cheaper from Friday to Sunday.

One of the better restaurants in town is **Restauracja Stary Szczecin** (☎ 433 62 30; plac Batorego 2; mains 18-85zł; ☻ noon-late), which serves up a range of traditional Polish dishes in elegant surrounds.

Getting There & Away

LOT flies between Szczecin and Warsaw about seven times a day and most days to Copenhagen. Book at the **LOT office** (☎ 433 50 58; ul Wyzwolenia 17), about 200m up from the northern end of Al Niepodłegłości.

The **bus terminal** (plac Grodnicki) and the nearby **Szczecin Główny train station** (ul Kolumba) are 600m southeast of the tourist office. Two buses a day head for Gdynia, while Polski Express also runs buses to Warsaw (80zł, six hours, two daily). Express and fast trains travel regularly to Poznań (35zł, four hours), Gdańsk (30zł, 3½ hours) and Warsaw

(49zł, seven hours), and slow trains plod along every two hours to Świnoujście.

Advance tickets for trains and ferries are available from **Orbis Travel** (☎ 434 26 18; plac Zwycięstwa 1), about 200m west of the main post office.

WARMIA & MASURIA

Warmia and Masuria are in northeastern Poland, east of the lower Vistula Valley. Here the Scandinavian glacier left behind a typical postglacial landscape of some 3000 lakes, many linked by rivers and canals, enjoyed by yachties and canoeists. The winding shorelines are surrounded by hills and forests, making this picturesque lake district one of the most attractive areas in the country. There's little industry and therefore little pollution.

OLSZTYN

☎ 089 / pop 165,000

Olsztyn (OL-shtin) is a likeable transport hub with an attractive old town of cobblestone streets, art galleries, cafés, bars and restaurants. It's also the obvious base from where to explore the region, including the Great Masurian Lakes district (see p561).

Olsztyn's history has been a successive overlapping of Prussian and Polish influences. From 1466 to 1773 the town belonged to the kingdom of Poland. Nicolaus Copernicus, administrator of Warmia, commanded Olsztyn Castle from 1516 to 1520. With the first partition of Poland, Olsztyn became Prussian Allenstein and remained so until 1945. The city was badly damaged during WWII, but has been mostly rebuilt.

The **tourist office** (☎ 535 35 65; www.warmia .mazury.pl; ul Staromiejska 1; ☻ 9am-4pm Mon-Fri) is helpful. The few **kantors** around town are marked on the map; otherwise, try the **PKO Bank** (cnr ul 1 Maja & ul 11 Listopada).

For snail mail, go to the **main post office** (ul Pieniężnego); for cybermail, try the **Internet café** inside the telephone office (ul Pieniężnego) opposite. Books and maps are sold at **EMPiK** (ul 1 Maja).

Sights

The **High Gate** (or Upper Gate) is all that remains of the 14th-century city walls. A little further west, the 14th-century **Castle of**

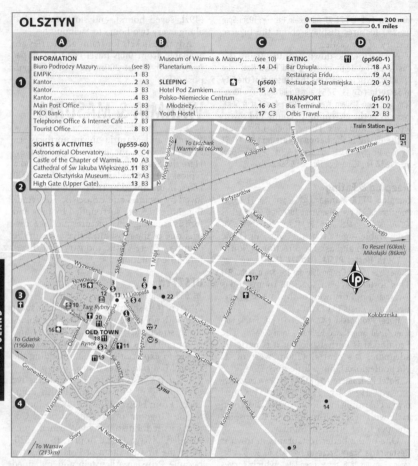

OLSZTYN

0 _____ 200 m
0 _____ 0.1 miles

INFORMATION
Biuro Podróóży Mazury...............(see 8)
EMPiK...**1** B3
Kantor.......................................**2** A3
Kantor.......................................**3** B3
Kantor.......................................**4** B3
Main Post Office.........................**5** B3
PKO Bank...................................**6** B3
Telephone Office & Internet Café...**7** B3
Tourist Office.............................**8** B3

SIGHTS & ACTIVITIES   (pp559-60)
Astronomical Observatory............**9** C4
Castle of the Chapter of Warmia....**10** A3
Cathedral of Św Jakuba Większego.**11** B3
Gazeta Olsztyńska Museum............**12** A3
High Gate (Upper Gate)...............**13** B3

Museum of Warmia & Mazury.......(see 10)
Planetarium...............................**14** D4

SLEEPING   (p560)
Hotel Pod Zamkiem......................**15** A3
Polsko-Niemieckie Centrum
  Młodzieży...............................**16** A3
Youth Hostel.............................**17** C3

EATING   (pp560-1)
Bar Dziupla................................**18** A3
Restauracja Eridu.........................**19** A4
Restauracja Staromiejska..............**20** A3

TRANSPORT   (p561)
Bus Terminal..............................**21** D2
Orbis Travel...............................**22** B3

the **Chapter of Warmia** (ul Zamkowa 2) contains the **Museum of Warmia & Mazury** (☎ 527 95 96; admission 6zł; ☯ 9am-5pm Tue-Sun May-Sep, 10am-4pm Tue-Sun Oct-Apr). It features plenty of exhibits about Copernicus, who made some astronomical observations here in the early 16th century, as well as some coins and art.

The **Rynek** (Market Square) was destroyed during WWII and rebuilt in a style only superficially reverting to the past. To the east, the red-brick Gothic **Cathedral of Św Jakuba Większego** (ul Długosza) dates from the 14th century. Its 60m tower was added in 1596.

Sleeping
Youth Hostel (☎ 527 66 50; fax 527 68 70; ul Kopernika 45; dm from 24zł) Conveniently between the Old

Town and the train station, this hostel is a well-run place and tidy.

Hotel Pod Zamkiem (☎ 535 12 87; http://hotel .olsztyn.com.pl; ul Nowowiejskiego 10; s/d 150/190zł; **P**) The best option in town is this cosy pension, with charming rooms in a convenient spot near the castle. Breakfast is excellent.

Polsko-Niemieckie Centrum Młodzieży (☎ 534 07 80; www.pncm.olsztyn.pl; ul Okopowa 25; s/d 160/180zł; **P**) This place is also ideally situated next to the castle. The rooms are very comfortable (some have views of the castle) and staff is friendly.

Eating
Bar Dziupla (☎ 527 50 83; Rynek 9/10; mains from 10zł; ☯ 9am-9pm) This is a small place renowned

among locals for its tasty Polish food, such as *pierogi*.

Restauracja Staromiejska (☎ 527 58 83; ul Stare Miasto 4/6; mains 20-25zł; 11am-10pm) The Staromiejska serves good quality Polish standards at reasonable prices.

Restauracja Eridu (☎ 534 94 67; ul Prosta 3/4; mains from 12zł; noon-11pm) The Eridu offers some inexpensive Middle Eastern choices.

Getting There & Away

Each day from the **bus terminal** (ul Partyzantów) buses travel to Białystok (four daily), Gdańsk (19zł, three hours, four daily) and Warsaw (32zł, five hours, 10 daily).

Also every day from the **Olsztyn Główny** train station (ul Partyzantów), trains go to Białystok (four daily), Warsaw (38zł, three daily), Gdańsk (35zł, eight daily), Poznań (two daily), Wrocław (two daily) and Toruń (six daily). **Orbis Travel** (☎ 527 44 55; Al Piłsudskiego) sells advance train tickets.

FROMBORK

☎ 055 / pop 2600

This small, sleepy town on the shore of the Vistula Lagoon was founded in the 13th century. A fortified ecclesiastical township was later erected on Cathedral Hill overlooking the lagoon. Frombork is most famous, however, as the place where Copernicus wrote his astounding *On the Revolutions of the Celestial Spheres*.

Cathedral Hill is now occupied by the extensive **Nicolaus Copernicus Museum** (☎ 243 72 18), with several sections requiring separate tickets. Most imposing is the red-brick Gothic **cathedral** (adult/child 3/2zł; 9.30am-5pm Mon-Sat), built in the 14th century. The nearby **Bishop's Palace** (adult/child 3/2zł; 9am-4.30pm Tue-Sun) has various exhibitions on local history, while the **Belfry** (adult/child 4/2zł; 9.30am-5pm) holds an example of **Foucault's Pendulum**.

Youth Hostel Copernicus (☎ 243 74 53; ul Elbląska 11; dm 18zł) also allows camping. It's 500m west of Cathedral Hill on the road to Elbląg.

Dom Familijny Rheticus (☎ 243 78 00; domfamilijny@gabo.pl; ul Kopernika 10; s/d 88/120zł;) is a small, quaint old place with cosy rooms and good facilities.

The bus and train stations are along the riverfront about 300m northwest of the castle. Frombork can be directly reached by bus from Elbląg (hourly), Gdańsk and Malbork.

ELBLĄG–OSTRÓDA CANAL

This 82km waterway between Elbląg and Ostróda is the longest navigable canal still used in Poland. Built between 1848 and 1876, it was used for transporting timber from the rich inland forests to the Baltic Sea. To resolve the 99.5m difference in water levels, the canal utilises an unusual system of five water-powered slipways so that boats are actually sometimes carried across dry land on rail-mounted trolleys.

Normally, **excursion boats** (mid-May–late-Sep) depart from both Elbląg and Ostróda daily at 8am (80zł, 11 hours), but actual departures depend on the number of available passengers. For information, call the **boat operators** (in Elbląg ☎ 055-232 43 07, in Ostróda ☎ 089-646 38 71; www.zegluga.com.pl).

In Elbląg, **Camping Nr 61** (☎ 055-232 43 07; www.camping-elblag.alpha.pl; ul Panieńska 14; per tent/cabin 12/60-80zł; May-Sep), right at the boat dock, is pleasant. **Hotel Młyn** (☎ 055-235 04 70; www.hotelmlyn.pl; ul Kościuszki 132; s/d from 220/280zł;   ), located in a picturesque old water mill, offers comfortable modern rooms. In Ostróda, try **Hotel Promenada** (☎ 642 81 00; ul Mickiewicza 3; s/d 140/190zł), 500m east of the bus and train stations.

Elbląg is easily accessible by train and bus from any of the cities of Gdańsk, Malbork, Frombork and Olsztyn. Ostróda is also regularly connected by train to Olsztyn and Toruń and by bus to Olsztyn and Elbląg.

GREAT MASURIAN LAKES

The Great Masurian Lakes district east of Olsztyn is a verdant land of rolling hills dotted with glacial lakes, peaceful farms and dense forests. The district has over 2000 lakes, the largest being **Lake Śniardwy** (110 sq km). About 200km of canals connect these lakes, so the area is a prime destination for yachties and canoeists, as well as those who prefer to hike, fish and mountain-bike.

The detailed *Wielkie Jeziora Mazurskie* map (1:100,000) is essential for anyone exploring the region by boat, canoe, bike, car or foot. The *Warmia i Mazury* map (1:300,000), published by Vicon and available at regional tourist offices, is perfect for anyone using private or public transport, and has explanations in English.

Getting Around

Yachties can sail the larger lakes all the way from Węgorzewo to Ruciane-Nida, while

POLAND

THE GREAT MASURIAN LAKES

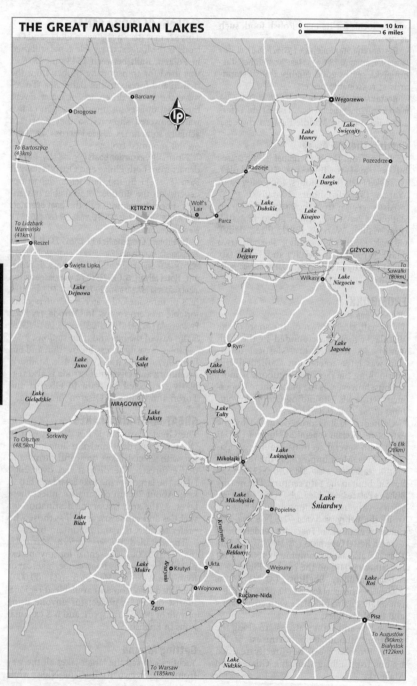

0 — 10 km
0 — 6 miles

Barciany

Drogosze

Węgorzewo

Lake Mamry

Lake Święcajty

To Bartoszyce (43km)

Radzieje

Pozezdrze

Lake Dargin

KĘTRZYN

Wolf's Lair

Parcz

Lake Dobskie

Lake Kisajno

To Lidzbark Warmiński (41km)

Reszel

Lake Dejguny

GIŻYCKO

Święta Lipka

Wilkasy

Lake Niegocin

To Suwałki (80km)

Lake Dejnowa

Ryn

Lake Juno

Lake Sałęt

Lake Ryńskie

Lake Jagodne

Lake Gielądzkie

MRĄGOWO

Lake Juksty

Lake Talty

To Olsztyn (48.5km)

Sorkwity

Mikołajki

Lake Łuknajno

To Ełk (28km)

Lake Śniardwy

Lake Mikołajskie

Popielno

Lake Białe

Krutynia

Lake Mokre

Krutyń

Ukta

Lake Beldany

Wejsuny

Lake Roś

Wojnowo

Zgon

Ruciane-Nida

Pisz

To Augustów (90km); Białystok (122km)

To Warsaw (185km)

Lake Nidzkie

POLAND

canoeists will perhaps prefer the more intimate surroundings along rivers and smaller lakes. The most popular kayak route takes about 10 days (106km) and follows rivers, canals and lakes from Sorkwity to Ruciane-Nida with places to stay and eat along the way. Brochures explaining this route are available at regional tourist offices. There's also an extensive network of trails – ideal for **hiking** and **mountain biking** – around the lakes.

Most travellers prefer to enjoy the lakes in comfort on the **excursion boats**. Boats run daily (May to September) between Giżycko and Ruciane-Nida, via Mikołajki; and daily (June to August) between Węgorzewo and Ruciane-Nida, via Giżycko and Mikołajki. In practice, however, services are more reliable from late June to late August. Schedules and fares are clearly posted at the lake ports.

Święta Lipka

This hamlet boasts an exquisite 17th-century **church** (☿ 7am-7pm), considered one of the purest examples of late-baroque architecture in Poland. One highlight of the interior is the lavishly decorated organ. The angels adorning the 5000 pipes play their instruments and dance to the music when the organ is sounded. This mechanism is demonstrated several times daily from May to September and recitals are held Friday nights from June to August.

Ask any of the regional tourist offices for a list of homes in Święta Lipka offering **private rooms**. There are several **eateries** and places to drink near the church.

Buses run to Kętrzyn every hour or so, but less often to Olsztyn.

Wolf's Lair

Hitler's wartime headquarters was at Gierłoż, 8km east of Kętrzyn, in **Wolf's Lair** (☎ 089-752 44 29; admission 7zł; ☿ 8am-dusk). Hitler arrived here on 26 June 1941 (four days after the invasion of the Soviet Union) and stayed until 20 November 1944, except for a few short trips to the outside world.

In July 1944 a group of pragmatic, high-ranking German officers tried to assassinate Hitler. The leader of the plot, Claus von Stauffenberg, arrived from Berlin on 20 July on the pretext of informing Hitler of the newly formed reserve army. As a frequent guest he had no problems entering the meeting with a bomb in his briefcase. He

placed his briefcase a few feet from Hitler and left to take a prearranged phone call. The explosion killed two staff members and wounded half a dozen others, but Hitler suffered only minor injuries. Stauffenberg and some 5000 people involved in the plot were subsequently executed.

On 24 January 1945, as the Red Army approached, the Germans blew up Wolfsschanze (as it was known in German), so most bunkers were destroyed. However, cement slabs – some 8.5m thick – and twisted metal remain, giving this hideous place an eerie feel.

A large map is posted at the entrance and the remaining bunkers are clearly labelled in English. Booklets allowing a self-guided walking tour are available in English and German at the kiosk in the car park.

Hotel Wilcze Gniazdo (☎ 089-752 44 29; fax 752 44 92; s/d 60/80zł) is fairly basic but adequate for one night. A **restaurant** is attached.

Catch one of several daily buses from Kętrzyn to Węgorzewo and get off at the entrance. Between May and September, bus No 1 from the train station in Kętrzyn also goes to the site.

Giżycko
☎ 087

Set on the northern shore of Lake Niegocin, Giżycko (ghee-ZHITS-ko) is the largest lakeside centre in the region. There are some significant ruins of the **Boyen Fortress** (admission free; ☿ 24hr), built by the Prussians between 1844 and 1855 to protect the border with Russia.

Near the main square (plac Grunwaldzki) are the **tourist information office** (☎ 428 52 65; www.gizycko.turystyka.pl; ul Warszawska 17; ☿ 9am-5pm) and **Bank Pekao** (ul Olsztyńska 17). There are some **kantors** in the town centre, including one at **Orbis Travel** (ul Dąbrowskiego 3), about 250m east of the main square.

Sailing boats are available from **Almatur** (☎ 428 33 88; ul Moniuszki 24), 700m west of the fortress, **Centrum Mazur** at Camping Nr 1 Zamek and **Orbis Travel**.

Hotel Wodnik rents out bicycles and kayaks, sell tickets for the excursion boats and arranges car rental.

SLEEPING & EATING

Just west of the canal, **Camping Nr 1 Zamek** (☎ 428 34 10; ul Moniuszki 1; per person/tent 15/10zł; ☿ May-end Sep; **P**) is simple but central. **Hotel**

POLAND

Zamek (☎ 428 24 19; d 130zł; **P**)) is part of the same complex and provides a decent standard of accommodation for the price.

The **Krasnal Youth Hostel** (☎ 428 22 24; www.ss mkrasnal.prv.pl; dm 15zł) is centrally located, near the lakefront, and offers the usual basic but clean facilities.

Hotel Wodnik (☎ 428 38 71; www.cmazur.pl; ul 3 Maja 2; s/d from 90/130zł; **P**)), just off the main square, offers probably the best standards. It's good value, and also has a good restaurant.

GETTING THERE & AWAY

From the train station, on the southern edge of town near the lake, around eight trains run daily to Kętrzyn and Olsztyn, and two head to Gdańsk.

From the adjacent bus terminal, buses travel regularly to Mikołajki, Kętrzyn and Olsztyn. Also, six buses daily head to Warsaw.

Mikołajki
☎ 087

Mikołajki (Mee-ko-WAHY-kee), 86km east of Olsztyn, is a picturesque little village and probably the best base for exploring the lakes. The **tourist office** (☎ 421 68 50; www .mikolajki.pl; plac Wolności 3) is in the town centre. There are several **kantors** nearby, but there is nowhere to change travellers cheques or get cash advances.

Sailing boats – and often **canoes** – can be hired from **Wioska Żeglarska** (☎ 421 60 40; ul Kowalska 3) at the waterfront, and also from the **Hotel Wałkuski** (☎ 421 64 70; ul 3 Maja 13a).

Lake Śniardwy and Lake Łuknajno are ideal for **cycling**. The tourist office can provide details and maps, and bikes can be rented from **Hotel Wałkuski** or **Pensjonat Mikołajki** (☎ 421 64 37; ul Kajki 18).

SLEEPING & EATING

Across the bridge, **Camping Nr 2 Wagabunda** (☎ 421 60 18; ul Leśna 2; per person/tent 15/12zł, cabins 80zł; Ⓨ May-Oct) is around 1km southwest of the town centre.

Several charming pensions and homes that offer **private rooms** are dotted all along ul Kajki, the main street leading around Lake Mikołajskie; another collection of pensions can be found along the roads to Ruciane-Nida and Ełk.

Pensonjat Złote Wrota (☎ 421 65 20; www.zlote wrota.mikolajki.pl; Stare Sady 3; s/d 90/160zł May-Aug; **P**)) is an attractive place overlooking Lake

Tałty, 4km north of town, which has its own beach and boat hire. It's cheaper from September to April.

Plenty of **eateries** spring up in summer along the waterfront and around the town square to cater for peak-season visitors.

GETTING THERE & AWAY

From the bus terminal, next to the train station on the southern edge of the town near the lake, four buses go to Olsztyn each morning (7zł, two hours). Otherwise, get a bus (hourly) to Mrągowo and change there for Olsztyn. Several buses also go daily to Giżycko (5zł, one hour) and two or three depart in summer for Warsaw.

From the sleepy train station, a few slow trains shuttle along daily to Olsztyn and Kętrzyn, and two fast trains head to Gdańsk and Białystok.

POLAND DIRECTORY

ACCOMMODATION
Camping

Poland has hundreds of camping grounds and many offer good-value cabins and bungalows. Theoretically, most are open from May to September, but some really only bother opening their gates between June and August.

Hostels

Youth hostels (*schroniska młodzieżowe*) in Poland are operated by Polskie Towarzystwo Schronisk Młodzieżowych (PTSM), a member of Hostelling International. Most only open in July and August, and are often very busy with school groups and Polish students; the year-round hostels are more reliable and have more facilities. Youth hostels are now open to all, members and non-members alike, with no age limit. Curfews are common, and many hostels are closed between 10am and 5pm.

An increasing number of privately operated hostels are springing up in the main cities, which are usually more geared towards international backpackers and offer more modern facilities than the old youth hostels, though prices are higher.

A dorm bed can cost anything from about 20zł to 45zł per person per night. Single/double rooms, if available, cost from about 50/70zł. In most major cities, a few student dorms open as hostels in summer.

Given the low prices, hostels are popular and often full. A particularly busy time is early May to mid-June, when the hostels are often crowded with groups of rowdy Polish school kids.

Mountain Refuges

PTTK runs a chain of mountain refuges (*schroniska górskie*) for trekkers. They are usually simple, but the price is right and the atmosphere is welcoming. They also serve cheap, hot meals. The more isolated refuges are obliged to accept everyone, regardless of how crowded they get. As a result, in the high season even a space on the floor can be hard to find. Refuges are normally open all year, but confirm with the nearest PTTK office before setting off.

Hotels

Most cities and towns offer a variety of old and new hotels ranging from the heart-sinkingly basic to full-on luxury. Rooms with a private bathroom can be considerably more expensive than those with shared facilities, sometimes twice as much. Hotel prices often vary according to the season and are usually posted at hotel reception desks. Top-end hotels sometimes quote prices in euros or US dollars. Discounted weekend rates are often available.

If possible, check the room before accepting. Don't be fooled by the hotel reception areas, which may look great in contrast to the rest of the establishment.

Two reliable companies can arrange accommodation (sometimes with substantial discounts) over the Internet through www.poland4u.com and www.hotelspoland.com.

Private Rooms & Apartments

Some cities and tourist-oriented towns have agencies – usually called a *biuro zakwaterowania* or *biuro kwater prywatnych* – which arrange accommodation in private homes. Rooms cost about 55/90zł for singles/doubles depending on the season, amenities provided and distance from the city centre. The most important factor to consider is location; if the home is in the suburbs, find out how far it is from reliable public transport.

During the high season, home owners also directly approach tourists. Prices are often lower (and open to bargaining), but you're more likely to be offered somewhere out in the sticks. Also, private homes in smaller resorts and villages often have signs outside their gates or doors offering a *pokoje* (room) or *noclegi* (lodging).

In Warsaw and Kraków a few agencies offer self-contained apartments. Discounts for longer stays can make them an affordable alternative to mid-range and top-end hotels.

ACTIVITIES

Hikers and long-distance trekkers can enjoy any of the thousands of kilometres of marked trails across the Tatra (p529) and Sudeten Mountains (p542), around Białowieża National Park (p514) and the Great Masurian Lakes district (p561), and at places near Poznań (p542) and Świnoujście. Trails are easy to follow and detailed maps are available at most larger bookshops.

Poland is fairly flat and ideal for cyclists. Bicycle routes along the banks of the Vistula River are popular in Warsaw (p502), Toruń (p547) and Kraków (p515). Many of the national parks – including Tatra (near Zakopane), Wolin (near Świnoujście) and Słowiński (near Łeba) – offer bicycle trails, as does the Great Masurian Lakes district. Bikes can be rented at most resort towns and larger cities. (Also see p570.)

Zakopane (p526) will delight skiers from December to March. Facilities tend to be significantly cheaper – though not as developed – as the ski resorts in Western Europe.

Throngs of yachties, canoeists and kayakers enjoy the network of waterways in the Great Masurian Lakes district every summer; boats are available for rent from all lakeside towns. Windsurfers can head to the windswept beaches of the Hel Peninsula (p556).

BOOKS

Lonely Planet's *Poland* is a more comprehensive guide to the country.

Jews in Poland by Iwo Cyprian Pogonowski provides a comprehensive record of half a millennium of Polish-Jewish relations in Poland.

God's Playground: A History of Poland by Norman Davies offers an in-depth analysis of Polish history. The condensed version, *The Heart of Europe: A Short History of Poland,* also by Davies, has greater emphasis on the 20th century. *The Polish Way: A Thousand-Year History of the Poles and their*

Culture by Adam Zamoyski is a superb cultural overview of Poland. It's crammed with maps and illustrations that bring the past 1000 years to life. *The Polish Revolution: Solidarity 1980–82* by Timothy Garton Ash is entertaining and thoroughly researched.

Łódz Ghetto Album is a unique and poignant collection of photographs, taken by the late Henryk Ross, of life in the Łódz Jewish ghetto just before WWII. It's a moving record of one of the bleakest episodes in Polish history, and a testimony to the human spirit of the ordinary men, women and children who lived, worked and played here.

BUSINESS HOURS

Most shops are open around 9am to 6pm Monday to Friday, and until about 2pm on Saturday. Supermarkets and larger stores often have longer opening hours. Banks in larger cities are open from about 8am to 5pm weekdays (sometimes until 2pm on Saturday), but have shorter hours in smaller towns. *Kantors* generally operate from 9am to 6pm on weekdays and until about 2pm on Saturday.

The opening hours of museums and other tourist attractions vary greatly. They tend to open any time between 9am and 11am and close some time from 3pm to 6pm. Most museums are open on weekends, but many close on Monday and also stay closed on the day following a public holiday.

DANGERS & ANNOYANCES

Poland is a relatively safe country, though crime has increased steadily since the fall of communism. Be particularly alert at any time around major train stations, such as Warszawa Centralna, which are favourite playgrounds for thieves and pickpockets. More worryingly, robberies have become increasingly common on night trains, especially on international routes. Try to share a compartment with other people if possible. Watch out too for bogus ticket-inspectors on public transport – ask to see ID if they try to fine you.

Theft from cars is becoming a plague, so keep your vehicle in a guarded car park whenever possible. Heavy drinking is common and drunks can be disturbing, though rarely dangerous. Smoking is common in all public places, especially on public transport and in bars and restaurants.

Poland is an ethnically homogeneous nation. Travellers who look racially different may attract some stares from locals, but this is more likely to be curiosity than anything hostile or ostensibly racist. Football (soccer) hooligans are not uncommon, so avoid travelling on public transport with them (especially if their team has lost!).

DISABLED TRAVELLERS

Poland is not well set up for people with disabilities, although there have been significant improvements over recent years. Wheelchair ramps are only available at some upmarket hotels and public transport will be a real challenge for anyone with mobility problems. Information (in Polish only) is available from **Intergracja** (☎ 022-635 13 30; www.intergracja.org).

EMBASSIES & CONSULATES
Polish Embassies & Consulates

Australia (☎ 02-6273 1208; 7 Turrana St, Yarralumla, ACT 2600) Consulate: Sydney (☎ 02-9363 9816; 10 Trelawny St, Woollhara, NSW 2025)

Canada (☎ 613-789 0468; 443 Daly Ave, Ottawa 2, Ontario K1N 6H3) Consulates: Toronto (☎ 416-252 5471; 2603 Lakeshore Blvd West), Vancouver (☎ 604-688 3530; 1177 West Hastings St, Suite 1600)

France (☎ 01 43 17 34 00; 1 rue de Talleyrand, 75007 Paris)

Germany (☎ 030-22 31 30; Lassenstrasse 19-21, 14193 Berlin) Consulate: Hamburg (☎ 040-611870; Gründgens-strasse 20)

Netherlands (☎ 070-799 01 00; Alexanderstraat 25, 2514 JM The Hague)

UK (☎ 0870-774 27 00; 47 Portland Pl, London W1B 1JH) Consulates: Edinburgh (☎ 0131-552 0301; 2 Kinnear Rd, EH3 5PE) Sheffield (☎ 0114- 276 6513; 4 Palmerston Rd, S10 2 TE)

USA (☎ 202-234 3800; 2640 16th St NW, Washington, DC 20009) Consulates: New York (☎ 212- 686 1541; 233 Madison Ave), Chicago (☎ 312-337 8166; 1530 North Lake Shore Dr), Los Angeles (☎ 310-442 8515; 12400 Wilshire Blvd)

Embassies & Consulates in Poland

All diplomatic missions listed are in Warsaw (area code ☎ 022) unless stated otherwise.

Australia (Map pp506-7; ☎ 521 34 44; www.australia.pl; ul Nowogrodzka 11)

Belarus (Map p502; ☎ 617 32 12; ul Ateńska 67)

Canada (Map p502; ☎ 584 31 31; www.canada.pl; ul Matejki 1/5)

Czech Republic (Map pp506-7; ☎ 628 72 21; warsaw@embassy.mzv.cz; ul Koszykowa 18)

France (Map pp506-7; ☎ 529 30 00; www.ambafrance
.org.pl; ul Puławska 17) Consulate-General: Kraków (Map
pp518-19; ☎ 012-424 53 00; ul Stolarska 15)
Germany (Map p502; ☎ 584 17 00; www.ambasadaniemiec
.pl; ul Dąbrowiecka 30) Consulate-General: Kraków (Map pp518-19;
☎ 012-424 30 00; ul Stolarska 7)
Ireland (Map p502; ☎ 849 66 33; www.irlandia.pl;
ul Humańska 10)
Lithuania (Map p502; ☎ 625 33 68; litwa.amb@waw
.pdi.net; Al Szucha 5)
Netherlands (Map p502; ☎ 559 12 00; fax 840 26 38;
ul Kawelerii 10)
Russia (Map p502; ☎ 621 34 53; ul Belwederska 49)
Slovakia (Map p502; ☎ 628 40 51; 6 Litewska St)
Ukraine (Map p502; ☎ 629 34 46; Al Szucha 7)
UK (Map pp506-7; ☎ 628 10 01; www.britishembassy.pl;
Al Róż 1) Consulate: Kraków (Map pp518-19; ☎ 012-421
70 30; ul Św Anny 9)
USA (Map pp506-7; ☎ 504 20 00; www.usinfo.pl; al
Ujazdowskie 29/31) Consulate: Kraków (☎ 012-424 51 00;
ul Stolarska 9)

FESTIVALS & EVENTS

Warsaw International Book Fair (May); Warsaw Summer
Jazz Days (late Jun/early Jul); Mozart Festival (Jun/Jul); Art
of the Street International Festival (Jul); Warsaw Autumn
Festival of Contemporary Music (Sep).
Kraków Organ Music Festival (Mar/Apr); Jewish Culture
Festival (Jun/Jul); International Festival of Street Theatre
(Jul); Summer Jazz Festival (Jul).
Seven days after Corpus Christi (a Thu in May or Jun), Kraków
has a colourful pageant headed by Lajkonik, a legendary
figure disguised as a Tatar riding a hobbyhorse.
Częstochowa The major Marian feasts at Jasna Góra
are 3 May, 16 July, 15 August (especially), 26 August, 8
September, 12 September and 8 December. On these days
the monastery is packed with pilgrims.
Wrocław Musica Polonica Nova Festival (Feb); Jazz on the
Odra International Festival (Mar or May); Wrocław Marathon
(Apr); Wratislavia Cantans Oratorio and Cantata Festival (Sep).
Poznań The largest trade fairs take place in January, June,
September and October. Smaller fairs occur through the
year. Cultural events include the St John's Fair (Jun) and
the Malta International Theatre Festival (late Jun).
Gdańsk The Dominican Fair (1st 2 weeks in Aug) is an annual
shopping fair dating back to 1260. Organ recitals are held at
the Oliwa Cathedral twice a week (mid-Jun–late-Aug) as part
of the International Organ Music Festival. St Mary's Church
is the stage for the International Organ, Choir & Chamber
Music Festival (every Fri in Jul and Aug). Also popular is the
International Street & Open-Air Theatre Festival (Jul).

GAY & LESBIAN TRAVELLERS

The Polish gay and lesbian scene is fairly
discreet; Warsaw and Kraków are the best

places to find bars, clubs and gay-friendly
accommodation. The free tourist brochure
The Visitor lists a few gay nightspots.

The best source of information in Warsaw
is the **Pride Society** (☎ 0504 299 065; pridesociety@yahoo
.com). Tourist offices in Warsaw may sporadically stock copies of *QC* (www.queercity.pl),
a gay listings magazine. Otherwise, check out
www.gej.net.

HOLIDAYS

Poland's official public holidays are:
New Year's Day 1 January
Easter Monday March or April
Labour Day 1 May
Constitution Day 3 May
Corpus Christi a Thursday in May or June
Assumption Day 15 August
All Saints' Day 1 November
Independence Day 11 November
Christmas 25 and 26 December

INTERNET RESOURCES

www.poland.pl – excellent place to start surfing
www.visit.pl – online accommodation booking service
www.insidepoland.com – current affairs and reasonable
links
www.polishworld.com – directories and travel bookings
www.polishvodka.com.pl – all you wanted to know
about the potent spirit
www.what-where-when.pl – online version of the
handy tourist magazine

MEDIA

The glossy, English-language *Poland Monthly*
and the *Warsaw Business Journal* are fairly
serious publications aimed at the business
community, while *Warsaw Insider* has more
general-interest features and useful listings
and reviews.

The excellent *Welcome to...* series of magazines covers Poznań, Wrocław, Kraków,
Gdańsk and Warsaw individually. *Poland:
What, Where, When* magazine covers Warsaw, Kraków and Gdańsk. These publications
are free.

Recent copies of newspapers and magazines from the UK, the USA, Germany and
France are readily available in the cities.
Look for them at EMPiK bookshops, which
are *everywhere*, and at newsstands in the
lobbies of upmarket hotels.

The state-run Polish Radio (Polskie
Radio) is the main broadcaster, while War-
saw-based Radio Zet and Kraków-based

POLAND

RFM are two nationwide private broadcasters. Plenty of other private competitors operate locally on FM.

Poland has several private TV channels, including PolSat, and two state-owned countrywide channels, but none of them provide any regular foreign-language programmes. Many programmes are so badly overdubbed – with one male voice covering all actors (including children and women) – that you can often still hear the original language. Most major hotels have access to European and US channels.

MONEY
ATMs
ATMs – called a *bankomat* – are a convenient way of obtaining local currency. ATMs, which accept many international credit cards, are now strategically located in the centre of all cities and most smaller towns. Banks without an ATM may provide cash advances over the counter on credit cards.

Currency
The official Polish currency is the złoty (zwo-ti), abbreviated to zł. (For reasons unclear, the currency is often abbreviated to PLN in English-language publications and documents.) The złoty is divided into 100 groszy, abbreviated to gr. Denominations of notes are 10, 20, 50, 100 and 200 zł (rare), and coins come in one, two five, 10, 20 and 50 gr, and one, two and five zł. Polish currency is convertible, so the black market for currency exchange has all but disappeared.

Changing Money
Private foreign-exchange offices – called *kantor* – are *everywhere;* in fact, there are often so many that we don't need to show them on our maps. *Kantors* require no paperwork and charge no commission. Exchange rates rarely vary, but rates at *kantors* in the midst of major tourist attractions, in top-end hotels and at airports are generally poor.

The most widely accepted currencies are the US dollar, the euro and the pound sterling (in that order). Foreign banknotes should be in perfect condition or *kantors* may refuse to accept them.

Travellers cheques are more secure than cash, but also less convenient. *Kantors* very rarely change travellers cheques. Not all banks do either and most charge 2% to 3%

commission. The best place to change travellers cheques are branches of Bank Pekao or PKO Bank. In remote regions, finding an open bank that cashes travellers cheques may be tricky, especially on weekends.

POST
Postal services are operated by Poczta Polska. Most cities have a dozen or more post offices, of which the Poczta Główna (main post office) has the widest range of services.

Letters and postcards sent by air from Poland take about one week to reach a European destination and up to two weeks if sent to anywhere else. The cost of sending a normal-sized letter (up to 20g) or a postcard to other European countries is 2.10zł, rising to 2.50zł for North America and 3.30zł for Australia.

TELEPHONE
Major telecommunications facilities in Poland are provided by Telekomunikacja Polska (TP), which usually has a telephone centre near or inside the main post office. Note that older public phones rarely work. All land-line numbers throughout Poland have seven digits.

To call Poland from abroad, dial the country code (☎ 48), then the two-digit area code (drop the initial '0' and don't use an operator code), and then the seven-digit local number. The Polish international access code for overseas calls from Poland is ☎ 00. If you need help, try the operators for local numbers (☎ 913), national numbers and codes (☎ 912) and international codes (☎ 908), but don't expect anyone to speak English.

Mobile Phones
The three mobile telephone providers are Idea, Era and Plus GSM. Mobile phones are extremely popular as a status symbol and a

---

EMERGENCY NUMBERS

- Pharmacy ☎ 911
- Fire ☎ 998
- Ambulance ☎ 999
- Police ☎ 997 – but call ☎ 112 from a mobile phone
- Roadside Assistance ☎ 981

more reliable alternative to the jammed land-lines and often unreliable public phones.

The website www.roaming.pl has plenty of information about using a mobile in Poland.

Phonecards

Most public telephones now use magnetic phonecards, which are available at post offices and kiosks. Phonecards are available in units of 15 (9zł), 30 (15zł) and 60 (24zł) – one unit represents one three-minute local call. The cards can be used for domestic and international calls.

VISAS

EU citizens do not need visas to visit Poland and can stay indefinitely. Citizens of the USA, Canada, Australia and New Zealand can stay in Poland for up to 90 days without a visa.

Other nationals should check with Polish embassies or consulates in their countries for current visa requirements.

TRANSPORT IN POLAND

GETTING THERE & AWAY

Air

The vast majority of international flights to Poland arrive at Warsaw's Okęcie Airport, while other important airports include Kraków Balice, Gdańsk and Wrocław. The national carrier, **LOT** (www.lot.com; LO; ☎ 048-95 72), flies to all major European cities, as well as almost everywhere in Germany. The budget airline, Air Polonia, only takes bookings via the Internet.

Other major airlines flying to Poland include:

Aeroflot (code SU; ☎ 048-628 25 57; www.aeroflot.com)
Air France (code AF; ☎ 048-556 64 00; www.airfrance.com)
Air Polonia (code APN; ☎ 048-332 08 01; www.airpolonia.com)
Alitalia (code AZ; ☎ 048-826 28 01; www.alitalia.it)
British Airways (code BA; ☎ 048-529 90 00; www.ba.com)
KLM (code KL; ☎ 048-862 70 00; www.klm.pl)
Lufthansa (code LH; ☎ 048-338 13 00; www.lufthansa.pl)
Malév (code MA; ☎ 048-697 74 72; www.malev.hu)
SAS Scandinavian Airlines (code SK; ☎ 048-850 05 00; www.scandanavian.net)

Land

BORDER CROSSINGS

Below is a list of major road border crossings that accept foreigners and are open 24 hours.

Belarus – south to north Terespol & Kuźnica Białostocka
Czech Republic – west to east Porajów, Zawidów, Jakuszyce, Lubawka, Kudowa-Słone, Boboszów, Głuchołazy, Pietrowice, Chałupki & Cieszyn
Germany – north to south Lubieszyn, Kołbaskowo, Krajnik Dolny, Osinów Dolny, Kostrzyn, Słubice, Świecko, Gubin, Olszyna, Łęknica, Zgorzelec & Sieniawka
Lithuania – east to west Ogrodniki & Budzisko
Slovakia – west to east Chyżne, Chochołów, Łysa Polana, Niedzica, Piwniczna, Konieczna & Barwinek
Ukraine – south to north Medyka, Hrebenne, Dorohusk & Zosin
Russia (Kaliningrad) – west to east Gronowo & Bezledy

If you're heading to Russia, be aware that you do need a Belarusian transit visa and you must obtain it in advance; see p80 for details.

BUS

International bus services throughout Western and Eastern Europe are offered by dozens of Polish and international companies. Prices for international buses are generally cheaper than for trains, but you will undoubtedly find it more comfortable, and probably quicker, to travel to/from Poland by train.

One of the major bus operators is Eurolines, a consortium of affiliated European bus companies including the Polish national bus company **PKS** (www.pekaesbus.com.pl).

PKS operates dozens of buses each week to all major cities in Germany, as well as to Copenhagen on Sunday, from the Dworzec Zachodnia (Western Bus Station) in Warsaw.

Three or four days every week (and daily during summer), **Eurolines** (☎ 032-351 20 20; www.eurolinespolska.pl) has services from London (Victoria) to Zamość, via Poznań, Łódź, Warsaw (Zachodnia) and Lublin; and from London to Kraków, via Wrocław and Częstochowa.

Three times a week, Eurolines goes from Paris to Białystok, via Poznań and Warsaw; from Paris to Kraków, via Wrocław and Częstochowa; and Paris to Gdynia, via Poznań, Toruń and Gdańsk.

Eurolines also offers regular services from major European cities, including from Stuttgart to Warsaw, Munich to Kraków via Wrocław, Prague to Warsaw via Kraków, from Rome to Gdańsk and from Madrid to Warsaw.

Heading east, Eurolines also runs links to Minsk, St Petersburg, Vilnius, Lviv and Riga; check the website for times and prices.

POLAND

CAR & MOTORCYCLE

To drive a car into Poland you will first need your driving licence from home – you can use this for six months after arrival in Poland, but then you'll have to apply for a local licence. Also required are vehicle registration papers and liability insurance ('green card'). If your insurance is not valid for Poland you must buy an additional policy at the border. The car registration number will be entered in your passport.

TRAIN

Every day, dozens of trains link Poland with every neighbouring country and beyond. International train travel is not cheap, however, especially for longer routes. To save money on train fares, look into the choice of special train tickets and rail passes – see p572. Domestic trains in Poland are significantly cheaper than international ones, so you'll save money if you buy a ticket to the first city you arrive at inside Poland and then take a local train. The official website www.wars.pl has information and you can also buy tickets for some services online.

Do note that some international trains to/from Poland have recently become notorious for theft. Some Poles are now too afraid to take any overnight train to/from Poland. Keep a grip on your bags, particularly on the Berlin–Warsaw, Prague–Warsaw and Prague–Kraków overnight trains, and on *any* train travelling to/from Gdańsk. Several readers have been gassed while in their compartments and have had everything stolen while they 'slept'. Always reinforce your carriage and, if possible, sleep in a compartment with others. First-class trains, in theory, should be safer.

Sea

Three companies operate passenger and car ferries all year:

Polferries (www.polferries.pl) Offers services between Gdańsk and Nynäshamn (18 hours) in Sweden every other day in summer (less frequently in the off season). It also has daily services from Świnoujście to Ystad (9½ hours) in Sweden, every Saturday to Rønne (six hours) in Denmark, and five days a week to Copenhagen (10½ to 11 hours).

Stena Line (www.stenaline.com) Operates between Gdynia and Karlskrona (11 hours) in Sweden.

Unity Line (www.unityline.pl) Runs ferries between Świnoujście and Ystad (eight hours).

Any travel agency in Scandinavia will sell tickets for these services. In Poland, inquire at any Orbis Travel office.

In summer, passenger boats ply the Baltic coast from Świnoujście to Ahlbeck, Heringsdorf, Bansin and Sassnitz in Germany.

GETTING AROUND
Air

The only domestic carrier, LOT, operates flights several times a day from Warsaw to Gdańsk, Kraków, Łódź, Poznań, Szczecin and Wrocław. So, flying between, for example, Kraków and Gdańsk means a connection in Warsaw and connections are not necessarily convenient.

Bicycle

Cycling is not great for getting around cities, but is often a perfect way to travel between villages. Major roads are busy but generally flat, while minor roads can be bumpy. If you get tired, or want to avoid the mountains in the south or travel a long distance in a short time, it's easy to place your bike in the special luggage compartment of a train. These compartments are at the front or rear of slow passenger trains, but rarely found on fast or express trains, and never on InterCity or EuroCity services. You'll need a special ticket for your bike from the railway luggage office.

Bus

Sometimes buses are convenient, especially on short routes and around the mountains in southern Poland. However, trains are almost always quicker and more comfortable for longer distances, and private minibuses are far quicker and more direct for short trips. If you can, avoid using buses altogether because they can be frustratingly slow and indirect.

Most buses are operated by the state bus company, PKS, which has bus terminals (*dworzec autobusowy PKS*) in all cities and towns. PKS provides two kinds of service: ordinary buses (marked in black on timetables), which cover mostly regional routes and stop anywhere and everywhere along the way; and fast buses (marked in red), which cover mainly long-distance routes and ignore minor stops.

Timetables are posted on boards either inside or outside PKS bus terminals. Always check any additional symbols next to the departure time of your bus; these symbols often indicate that the bus runs only on certain days or in certain seasons. Terminals in the larger cities normally have an information desk, but it's rarely staffed with anyone who speaks English.

The largest private bus operator is Polski Express, a joint venture with Eurolines National Express based in the UK. Polski Express operates several major long-distance routes to/from Warsaw (p512) and is faster, more comfortable and often cheaper than PKS buses. Polski Express buses normally arrive at/depart from or near the PKS bus terminals – exceptions are mentioned in the relevant Getting There & Away sections.

Tickets for PKS buses must be bought at the terminal. On long routes serviced by fast buses tickets can be bought up to 30 days in advance, but for short local routes tickets are only available on the same day. Tickets for Polski Express buses can be bought up to 14 days in advance at the terminals or stops where they arrive/depart.

COSTS
Bus travel in Poland is cheap, and the price of tickets is determined by the length, in kilometres, of the trip. Prices start at roughly 2zł for a journey of up to 5km and rise steadily thereafter. Minibuses charge set prices for journeys, and these are normally posted in the windows or on a timetable at the bus stop.

Car & Motorcycle
Poland's 220,000km of sealed roads are in an acceptable condition for leisurely driving. Plans to build a 2600km network of toll motorways stretching from the Baltic coast to the Czech border and from Germany to Ukraine are still in the pipeline.

FUEL & SPARE PARTS
Petrol is readily available at petrol stations, which have mushroomed throughout the country. These places sell several kinds and grades of petrol, including 94-octane leaded, 95-octane unleaded, 98-octane unleaded and diesel. Most petrol stations are open from 6am to 10pm (from 7am to 3pm Sunday), though some operate around the clock. Garages are similarly plentiful.

HIRE
Most of the major international car rental companies, like **Avis** (www.avis.pl), **Hertz** (www.hertz.pl) and **Europcar** (www.europcar.com.pl), are represented in larger cities and have smaller offices at the airports. The rates offered by these companies are not cheap: the prices are comparable to, or even higher than, full-price rental in Western Europe, and promotional discounts are not very often available.

The increasing number of local operators, such as **Payless Car Rental** (www.paylesscarrental.pl), provide a reliable and more affordable alternative. Some companies offer one-way rentals, but almost all will insist on keeping the car within Poland. And no agency will allow you to drive their precious vehicle into Russia, Ukraine or Belarus. There is nowhere in Poland to rent a motorcycle.

Rental agencies will need to see your passport, your local driving licence (which must be held for at least one year) and a credit card (for the deposit). You need to be at least 21 or 23 years of age to rent a car; sometimes 25 for a more expensive car.

It's usually cheaper to prebook a car in Poland from abroad rather than to front up at an agency inside Poland. It would be even cheaper to rent a car in Western Europe (eg Berlin or Geneva), and drive it into Poland, but few rental companies will allow this. If they do, special insurance is required.

ROAD RULES
The speed limit is 130km/h on motorways, 100km/h or 110km/h on two- or four-lane highways, 90km/h on other open roads and 60km/h in built-up areas (50km/h in Warsaw). If the background of the sign bearing the town's name is white you must reduce speed to 60km/h; if the background is green there's no need to reduce speed (unless road signs indicate otherwise). Radar-equipped police are very active, especially in villages with white signs. (Approaching cars often flash their lights in warning.)

Unless signs state otherwise, cars may park on pavements as long as a minimum 1.5m-wide walkway is left for pedestrians. Parking in the opposite direction to the flow of traffic is allowed. The permitted blood alcohol level is 0.02%, so it's best not to drink at all if you're driving.

Seat belts are compulsory for front seats, but the majority of Polish drivers think it's actually safer to drive *without* a belt! Motorbike helmets are also compulsory. Between 1 October and the end of February, all drivers must use their car (and motorbike) headlights during the day (and night!).

Train

Trains will be your main means of transport, especially for long distances. They are cheap, fairly reliable and rarely overcrowded (except for peak times in July and August). The Polish State Railways (PKP) operates more than 27,000km of railway lines and almost every place listed in this chapter (and many, many more) is accessible by train.

Express trains (*pociąg ekspresowy*) are a faster but more expensive way to travel, while fast trains (*pociąg pospieszny*) are a bit slower and maybe more crowded. Slow passenger trains (*pociąg osobowy*) stop at every tree at the side of the track and should be used only for short trips. Express and fast trains do not normally require seat reservations except at peak times; seats on passenger trains cannot be reserved.

InterCity trains operate on some major routes out of Warsaw, including Gdańsk, Kraków, Poznań and Szczecin. They only stop at major cities en route and are faster than express trains (averaging about 100km/h). These trains require seat reservations and a light meal is included in the fare.

Almost all trains carry two classes: 2nd class (*druga klasa*) and 1st class (*pierwsza klasa*), which is 50% more expensive. The carriages on long-distance trains are usually divided into compartments: 1st-class compartments have six seats and 2nd-class ones contain eight seats. There is often little difference in the standard between the two classes except that fewer people travel on 1st class so you'll always have more room.

In a couchette on an overnight train, compartments have four/six beds in 1st/2nd class. Sleepers have two/three people (1st/2nd class) in a compartment which is fitted with a washbasin, sheets and blankets. Most 2nd-class and all 1st-class carriages have nonsmoking compartments.

Train departures (*odjazdy*) are listed on a yellow board and arrivals (*przyjazdy*) on a white board. Ordinary trains are marked in black print, fast trains in red. An additional 'Ex' indicates an express train, and InterCity trains are identified by the letters 'IC'. The letter 'R' in a square indicates the train has compulsory seat reservation. The timetables clearly show the time of the train's arrival and departure and which platform (*peron*) it's using.

Timetable information is available on the PKP's official website www.pkp.pl, but it's in Polish.

Sleepers (*miejsca sypialne*) and couchettes (*kuszetki*) can be booked at special counters in larger train stations or from Orbis; advance reservations are advisable.

If a seat reservation is compulsory on your train, you will automatically be sold a reserved seat ticket (*miejscówka*). It's important to note that if you do not make a seat reservation, you can travel on *any* train (of the type requested, ie passenger, fast or express) to the destination indicated on your ticket and on the date specified.

Your ticket will list the class (*klasa*); the type of train (*poc*); the places the train is travelling from (*od*) and to (*do*); the major town or junction the train is travelling through (*prez*); and the total price (*cena*). If more than one place is listed under the heading *prez* (via), find out from the conductor *early* if you have to change trains at the junction listed or be in a specific carriage (the train may separate later).

If you get on a train without a ticket, you can buy one directly from the conductor for a small supplement – but do it right away. If the conductor finds you first, you'll be fined for travelling without a ticket. You can always upgrade from 2nd to 1st class for a small extra fee (about 5zł), plus the additional fare.

Romania

CONTENTS

Highlights	575	Mamaia	632
Itineraries	575	Eforie Nord	633
Climate & When to Go	575	Neptun-Olimp	634
History	575	Mangalia	634
People	578	**Danube Delta**	**635**
Religion	578	Tulcea	636
Arts	578	Tulcea to Sulina	638
Environment	579	**Romania Directory**	**638**
Food & Drink	579	Accommodation	638
Bucharest	**580**	Activities	638
Orientation	580	Business Hours	639
Information	580	Customs	639
Sights	582	Dangers & Annoyances	639
Sleeping	585	Embassies & Consulates	639
Eating	586	Festivals & Events	640
Drinking	587	Holidays	640
Entertainment	587	Legal Matters	640
Shopping	587	Money	640
Getting There & Away	588	Post	640
Getting Around	588	Telephone	641
Around Bucharest	589	Tourist Information	641
Wallachia	**590**	Visas	641
Curtea De Argeş	590	**Transport in Romania**	**641**
Transylvania	**591**	Getting There & Away	641
Sinaia	593	Getting Around	643
Braşov	595		
Bran & Râşnov	599		
Poiana Braşov	600		
Sighişoara	600		
Sibiu	602		
Făgăraş Mountains	606		
Cluj-Napoca	606		
Crişana & Banat	**610**		
Oradea	610		
Timişoara	613		
Maramureş	**616**		
Sighetu Marmaţiei	616		
Săpânţa	617		
Valea Izei	618		
Borşa	620		
Prislop Pass	620		
Moldavia	**620**		
Iaşi	620		
Southern Bucovina	**623**		
Suceava	624		
Bucovina Monasteries	627		
Northern Dobrogea	**628**		
Constanţa	629		

ROMANIA

Romania is among the last bastions of Europe's traditional heart and soul. Here, its pastoral heart beats on in unspoiled countryside. Isolated villages nestled in lush valleys carry on traditions long relegated to tourist attractions just a few hundred kilometres west: yes, gentle shepherds tend to their flock – only they'll be talking on their mobile phone as they do.

This 'final frontier' country may be a living museum to Europe's lost ways, but it's also defiantly modern and boldly strutting into the future. The nightlife in stylish Bucharest and Cluj-Napoca can hold its own against Western contemporaries.

And there's so much for travellers to bite into here: some of Europe's best skiing and hiking on dizzying mountaintops, the breathtaking landscape, friendly locals who offer swigs of delicious home-made wine, sun-drenched coastal resorts, picturesque castles (Romania isn't Dracula country for nothing) and painted monasteries, plus plush hotels and snazzy restaurants – all affordably priced.

ROMANIA

FAST FACTS

- **Area** 237, 500 sq km
- **Capital** Bucharest
- **Currency** leu: €1 = 41,590 lei; US$1 = 32,538 lei; UK£1 = 59,838 lei; A$1 = 24,219 lei; ¥100 = 30,492 lei; NZ$1 = 22,726 lei
- **Famous for** Dracula
- **Key Phrases** *bună* (hello), *da* (yes), *nu* (no), *unde este toaleta?* (where is the toilet?)
- **Official Language** Romanian
- **Population** 22.4 million
- **Telephone Codes** country code ☎ 40; international access code ☎ 00
- **Visas** Citizens of the EU, Canada and Japan visa-free for up to 90 days. US and many Eastern European citizens visa-free for 30 days. All others (including Australians and New Zealanders) require a visa; see p641

HIGHLIGHTS
- Ski, hike or swoon in delight at the mighty, majestic **Carpathian Mountains** (p591)
- See the monstrous Palace of Parliament, sip cocktails in a trendy bar or visit one of many great museums in **Bucharest** (p580)
- Go back in time, drink the local home-brew, dance by a camp fire and breathe in pure oxygen in the heart of rural Romania, **Maramureş** (p616)
- Sling back cheap, delicious beer in the bohemian paradise of medieval **Braşov** (p595)
- In tenacious **Timişoara** (p613), you can follow the heroic trail of the 1989 revolution

ITINERARIES
- **10 days** Explore Bucharest. Head to Sinaia and the Carpathians before going to Braşov, and the castles at Bran and Râşnov. Visit Sighişoara's citadel before heading back to Bucharest.
- **One month** Cover the whole country. Start off in Bucharest then head through Transylvania stopping at Sinaia and Braşov. From there you can get your neck down to Bran to Dracula's Castle. Head north to Sighişoara then on to Maramureş and spend a week chilling out. Explore charming Timişoara then head through the Roma territory of Wallachia back to Bucharest.

CLIMATE & WHEN TO GO
Romania is a year-round destination, and the best time to go depends on what you're most interested in doing there. There is much variation in its climate: the average annual temperature in the south is 11°C, 7°C in the north and only 2°C in the mountains. In the summer months, temperatures have risen to above 40°C in recent years in Bucharest and along the Black Sea Coast, while winter chills of below -35°C are not unknown in the Braşov depression. See Climate Charts p874.

HISTORY
Ancient Romania & Dracula
Ancient Romania was inhabited by Thracian tribes, more commonly known as Dacians. The Greeks established trading colonies along the Black Sea from the 7th century BC and the Romans conquered in AD 105–06. The slave-owning Romans brought with them their superior civilisation and the Latin language.

HOW MUCH?
- **Bottle of Mufatlar table wine** €1.50
- **Museum admission (adult)** €0.40 to €0.80
- **Local bus trip** €0.40
- **Short taxi ride** €3
- **Phonecard** €2.15

LONELY PLANET INDEX
- **Litre of petrol** €0.65
- **Litre of water** €0.40
- **Beer (in a Bucharest bar)** €0.50 to €0.90
- **Souvenir item** €3 to €6
- **Street snack (kebab)** €0.80

From the 10th century the Magyars (Hungarians) expanded into Transylvania and by the 13th century all of Transylvania was under the Hungarian crown.

The Romanian-speaking principalities of Wallachia and Moldavia offered strong resistance to the Ottomans' northern expansion in the 14th and 15th centuries. Mircea the Old, Vlad Ţepeş and Ştefan cel Mare (Steven the Great) were legendary figures in this struggle.

Vlad Ţepeş, ruling prince of Wallachia from 1456–62 and 1476–77, gained the name Ţepeş (Impaler) after his primary form of punishing his enemies – impaling. A wooden stake was carefully driven through the victim's backbone without touching any vital nerve, ensuring at least 48 hours of conscious suffering before death. He is perhaps more legendary as the inspiration for 19th-century novelist Bram Stoker's Count Dracula. (Vlad was called Dracula, meaning 'son of the dragon', after his father, Vlad Dracul, a knight of the Order of the Dragon.)

When the Turks conquered Hungary in the 16th century, Transylvania became a vassal of the Ottoman Empire. In 1600 the three Romanian states – Transylvania, Wallachia and Moldavia – were briefly united under Mihai Viteazul (Michael the Brave). In 1687 Transylvania fell under Habsburg rule.

ROMANIA

ROMANIA

Romania in WWI & WWII

In 1859 Alexandru Ioan Cuza was elected to the thrones of Moldavia and Wallachia, creating a national state, which in 1862 took the name Romania. The reformist Cuza was forced to abdicate in 1866 and his place was taken by the Prussian prince Karl of Hohenzollern, who took the name Carol I. Romania then declared independence from the Ottoman Empire in 1877 and, after the 1877–78 War of Independence, Dobrogea became part of Romania.

In 1916 Romania entered WWI on the side of the Triple Entente (Britain, France and Russia) with the objective of taking Transylvania – where 60% of the population was Romanian – from Austria-Hungary. The Central Powers (Germany and Austria-Hungary) occupied Wallachia. With the defeat of Austria-Hungary in 1918, the unification of Banat, Transylvania and Bucovina with Romania was finally achieved.

In the years leading to WWII, Romania, under foreign minister Nicolae Titulescu, sought security in a French alliance. On 30 August 1940 Romania was forced to cede northern Transylvania to Hungary by order of Nazi Germany and fascist Italy.

To defend the interests of the ruling classes, General Ion Antonescu forced King Carol II to abdicate in favour of his son Michael. Then Antonescu imposed a fascist dictatorship. June 1941 he joined Hitler's anti-Soviet war with gruesome results: 400,000 Romanian Jews and 36,000 Roma were murdered at Auschwitz and other camps.

On 23 August 1944 Romania suddenly changed sides, captured 53,159 German soldiers and declared war on Nazi Germany. By this act, Romania salvaged its independence and shortened the war.

Ceauşescu

After the war, the Soviet-engineered return of Transylvania enhanced the prestige of the left-wing parties, which won the parliamentary elections of November 1946. A year later the monarchy was abolished and the Romanian People's Republic was proclaimed.

Soviet troops withdrew in 1958 and after 1960 Romania adopted an independent foreign policy under two leaders, Gheorghe Gheorghiu-Dej (leader from 1952 to 1965) and his protégé Nicolae Ceauşescu (1965 to 1989).

Ceauşescu's domestic policy was chaotic and megalomaniac. In 1974 the post of president was created for him. He placed his wife Elena, son Nicu and three brothers in important political positions during the 1980s. Some of Ceauşescu's expensive follies were projects such as the Danube Canal from Agigea to Cernavo, the disruptive redevelopment of southern Bucharest in 1983–89, and the 'systemisation' of agriculture by the resettlement of rural villagers into concrete apartment blocks. (See The Dictator's Bright Ideas, p578.)

By the late 1980s the USA withdrew Romania's 'most favoured nation' trading status. Undaunted, Ceauşescu continued spending millions of dollars. In November 1987 workers rioted in Braşov and in the winter of 1988–89 the country suffered its worst food shortages in decades.

The spark that ignited Romania came on 15 December 1989, when Father Lászlo Tökés publicly condemned the dictator from his Hungarian church in Timişoara. Police attempts to arrest demonstrating parishioners failed and civil unrest quickly spread.

On 21 December in Bucharest, an address by Ceauşescu during a rally was cut short by anti-Ceauşescu demonstrators. They booed him, then retreated to the boulevard between Piaţa Universităţii and Piaţa Romană, only to be crushed hours later by police gunfire and armoured cars. The next morning thousands more demonstrators took to the streets, and a state of emergency was quickly announced. At midday Ceauşescu reappeared with his wife on the balcony of the Central Committee building to speak, only to be forced to flee by helicopter from the roof of the building. The couple were arrested in Târgovişte, taken to a military base and, on 25 December, executed by a firing squad.

The National Salvation Front (FSN) swiftly took control. In May 1990 it won the country's first democratic elections, placing Ion Iliescu at the helm as president and Petre Roman as prime minister. In Bucharest, student protests against this former communist ruler were ruthlessly squashed by 20,000 coal miners shipped in courtesy of Iliescu. Ironically, when the miners returned in September 1991, it was to force the resignation of Petre Roman whose free-market economic reforms, it was believed, had led to worsening living conditions.

Modern Romania

Romania's birth as a modern nation has been a difficult one. In December 1999 President Constantinescu dismissed Radul Vasile and replaced him with former National Bank of Romania governor Mugur Isărescu. But by mid-2000 Isărescu was fighting for his political life after the opposition accused him of mismanagement of the State Property Fund. This was followed in May 2000 by the collapse of the National Fund for Investment (NFI) which saw thousands of investors lose their savings.

Romania joined the Council of Europe in 1993. The EU started accession talks with Romania in March 2000; full EU membership is slated for 2007–10. In 2002 Romania was invited to join NATO. During the American war against Iraq in 2003, Romania was one of the first countries to guarantee access to airfields and allowed Americans to set up military bases on their soil.

PEOPLE

Romanians make up 89% of the population; Hungarians are the next largest ethnic group (6.6%), followed by Roma (2.5%), Ukrainians and Germans (each 0.3%). Russians and Turks each take up but 0.2%. Germans and Hungarians live almost exclusively in Transylvania, while Ukrainians and Russians live mainly near the Danube Delta, and Turks are found along the Black Sea Coast.

The government estimates that only 420,000 Roma live in Romania, although the community itself and the Budapest-based European Roma Rights Centre (http://errc .org) believes it to be at least 1.8 million, making it the largest such community in the world.

RELIGION

The majority of Romania's population (87%) is Eastern Orthodox Christian. The rest is split between Protestant (6.8%), Catholic (5.6%), Muslim (0.4%), plus there are some 39,000 Jehovah's Witnesses and 14,000 Jews. The Muslims mainly live in Northern Dobrogea, and the Protestants are mostly made up of Transylvanian Germans.

ARTS

Romania has a strong tradition of folk crafts, music and dance.

THE DICTATOR'S BRIGHT IDEAS

In the 1980s, in his attempts to eliminate foreign debt and look good in front of the world, Nicolae Ceaușescu exported Romania's food while his own people were forced to ration even staple goods (meat was all but unattainable by the mid-1980s) and instituted power cuts to save money. His opponents were at best harassed, at worst killed by experimental methods of torture. One method used by Ceaușescu on his political opponents, especially Hungarian nationalists, whom he despised, was known as Radu. Radu consisted of bombarding the body with low-level radiation and allowing cancer to settle. Many of those he had arrested eventually died of strange forms of cancer.

In March 1987 Ceaușescu embarked on a rural urbanisation programme that meant the destruction of 8000 villages (many in Transylvania) and the resettlement of the (mainly Hungarian) residents. After having bulldozed one-sixth of Bucharest to build his House of the People (p582), no-one doubted he'd proceed with his plans. Several dozen villages were razed, but thankfully the whole project went uncompleted.

Painting on glass and wood remains a popular folk art today. Considered to be of Byzantine origin, this traditional peasant art was widespread in Romania from the 17th century onwards. Superstition and strong religious beliefs surrounded these icons which were painted to protect a household from evil spirits. Well-known 19th-century icon painters include Dionisie Iuga.

The paintings of Nicolae Grigorescu (1838–1907) absorbed French impressionism and created canvasses alive with the colour of the Romanian peasantry. His work is popular with international collectors, and sells for up to US$50,000 each.

Romania's most famous sculptor is Constantin Brancusi (1876–1957), whose polished bronze and wood works are held at the Pompidou Centre in Paris, the Guggenheim, New York's MOMA, the Philadelphia Museum of Art, the Australian National Gallery in Canberra and in Romania at the Museum of Art in Craiova and Bucharest's National Art Museum (p584).

Modern literature emerged in the mid-19th century in the shape of romantic poet

Mihai Eminescu (1850–89), who captured the spirituality of the Romanian people in his work.

The Romanian classical music world is nearly synonymous with George Enescu (1881–1955), whose *Romanian Rhapsodies Nos 1 & 2* and opera *Odeipe* are considered classics.

ENVIRONMENT
The Land
Covering 237,500 sq km, oval-shaped Romania is made up of three main geographical regions, each with its particular features. The mighty Carpathian Mountains form the shape of a scythe swooping down into the country's centre from the Ukraine and curling up northwards.

West of this are large plateaus where villages and towns lie among the hills and valleys. East of the mountains are the low-lying plains (where most of the country's agricultural output comes from) which end at the Black Sea and Europe's second-largest delta region where the Danube spills into the sea.

Wildlife
Rural Romania has thriving animal populations, which include chamois, lynx, fox, deer, wolf, bear and badger. There are 33,792 species of animals here (707 of which are vertebrates; 55 of these are endangered) as well as 3700 species of plants (39 of which are endangered).

Birdlife in the Danube Delta (p635) is unmatched. It is a major migration hub for numerous bird species and home to 60% of the world's small pygmy cormorant population.

National Parks
Romania has over 500 protected areas, including 12 national parks, three biosphere reserves and one World Natural Heritage Site (the Danube Delta), totalling over 1.2 million hectares. Most of these are in the Carpathians.

Environmental Issues
It's a sad and distressing scenario that repeats itself throughout Romania: you'll be in the middle of nearly incomprehensible beauty when you suddenly stumble upon a dozen crushed beer cans or spot a pile of garbage floating in a creek.

For Non Government Organisations (NGOs) like **Pro Natura** (www.pronatura.ro) and the **Transylvania Ecological Club** (www.greenagenda.org), sensitising an apathetic public about how to diminish the impact of tourism on the environment are main priorities.

Romania, like all former Soviet satellite states, has the ongoing problem of cleaning up the pollution left by communist chemical plants.

FOOD & DRINK
Let's leave the debate as to whether or not something called Romanian cuisine actually exists and plunge, mouth open wide, into a world of tasty, hearty, simple food: Romanian cooking. Relying heavily upon pork (at least half their traditional meals feature this meat in some form) and staples like potatoes and cabbage, with liberal borrowings from the cultures which have traversed and occupied its land, Romanian cooking is not for those seeking to diet.

Mămăligă is a cornmeal mush boiled or fried and served at every meal. *Ciorbă* (soup) is the other mainstay of the Romanian diet. Favourites include *ciorbă de perişoare* (spicy soup with meatballs and vegetables) and *ciorbă de legume* (vegetable soup cooked with meat stock).

Other common dishes are *muşchi de vacă/porc/miel* (cutlet of beef/pork/lamb), *ficat* (liver), *piept de pui* (chicken breast) and *cabanos prajit* (fried sausages). Typical desserts include *plăcintă* (turnovers), *clătite* (crepes) and *cozonac* (a brioche).

Thanks to the Orthodox diet, you can always find some vegetarian dishes, unexciting and repetitious as they will come to be. If a plate of *mămăligă* does not turn you on, try *caşcaval pâine* (cheese covered in breadcrumbs and fried), *salată roşii* (tomato salad), *salată castraveţi* (cucumber salad) and *salată asortată* (mixed salad, usually just a mix of – guess what? – tomatoes and cucumbers). When you're really lucky, you'll find vegetable soup or stew, or a dish made from aubergine.

Among the best Romanian wines are Cotnari, Murfatlar, Odobeşti, Târnave and Valea Călugărească.

Ţuica is a once-filtered clear brandy made from fermented fruit (the tastiest and most popular is plum *ţuica*), usually 30 proof.

BUCHAREST

☎ 021 / pop 2 million

Forget Prague, forget Budapest –Bucharest (Bucureşti) is where explorers are heading. This is Eastern Europe's secret – but it's about to get out. It has a fascinating mix of architecture that maps Romania's chequered history. The ugly face of communism created by its bloody counterpart Nicolae Ceauşescu sits alongside the incredible beauty of Romania's elegant past and its Parisian pretensions. Down dingy side streets flanked by Soviet-style high-rises are exquisite 18th-century monasteries, pretty gardens and ornate Orthodox churches.

This city only threw off Ceauşescu's stranglehold less than two decades ago. Despite his crimes against architecture and the community (he bulldozed one-sixth of the city to build his vast House of the People, now called the Palace of Parliament, folly in the 1980s), his attempts to create a grandiose Stalinist capital failed. The memories of the city's struggle for freedom are everywhere – from bullet-marked buildings to candles lit in memory of those who perished. Yet this city has soul – and the fun is in finding it.

ORIENTATION

Bucharest's main train station, Gară de Nord, is a few kilometres northwest of Bucharest's centre. The station is connected by the metro

BUCHAREST IN TWO DAYS

Breathe in the morning air atop the **Arcul de Triumf** (p585) then saunter down elegant Şos Kiseleff to the **Village Museum** (p585). Lunch at **La Strada Terrace** (p586) inside the historic **Athénée Palace Hilton** (p584) off Piaţa Revoluţiei and see the balcony on the former **Central Committee of the Communist Party building** (p584) where Ceauşescu made his final speech. Head south down Calea Victoriei, Bucharest's bustling heart, to the **Palace of Parliament** (p582). Finish off with an evening stroll and a lakeside beer in **Cişmigiu Garden** (p584).

Discover Dracula's tomb on the second day by rowing across **Snagov Lake** (p589). Return via beautiful **Căldăruşani Monastery** (p589).

to Piaţa Victoriei on the northern side of the centre or to Piaţa Unirii on the southern side. Bus Nos 79, 86 and 133 will take you just north of the centre to Piaţa Romană. The main boulevard (and the north–south metro line) runs between Piaţa Victoriei, Piaţa Romană, Piaţa Universităţii and Piaţa Unirii, and changes its name three times.

INFORMATION
Cultural Centres

American Cultural Centre (Map p583; ☎ 210 1602; Str Jean Louis Calderon 7-9) Call for opening times.

British Council Library (Map p581; ☎ 210 0314; Calea Dorobanţilor 14; ☽ 10am-5pm Mon-Fri, 10am-noon Sat) English-language newspapers and Internet.

French Institute (Map p581; ☎ 210 0224; B-dul Dacia 77) Film screenings, has an excellent bistro as well as Internet.

Emergency

Main police station (Map p583; ☎ 311 2021; Calea Victoriei 17)

Internet Access

Internet cafés have sprung up like mushrooms, as they say in these parts. Rates vary from €0.30 to €1 per hour. Both Elvis Villa and Villa Helga hostels have free Internet for guests (see p585).

Brit C@fe (Map p581; ☎ 210 0314; Calea Dorobanţilor 14; ☽ 9.30am-9.30pm Mon-Fri, 10am-2pm Sat)

CNET (Map p583; ☎ 311 2682; Calea Victoriei 25; ☽ 9am-7pm Mon-Sat, 9am-1pm Sun)

Medical Services

Emergency Clinic Hospital (Map p581; ☎ 230 0106; Calea Floreasca 8; ☽ 24hr) Bucharest's 'showcase' hospital.

Pro-Dental Care (Map p583; ☎ 313 4781; Str Hristo Botev 7; ☽ 9am-6pm Mon-Fri)

Sensi-Blu B-dul Nicolae Bălescu (Map p583; ☎ 212 4923; B-dul Nicolae Bălescu 7); Calea Victoriei (Map p583; ☎ 315 3160; Calea Victoriei 12A) Excellent 24hr pharmacy chain.

Money

Currency exchanges are everywhere. Don't use the exchanges in the baggage claim hall of Otopeni Airport as they offer the worst rates in the city.

Alliance Exchange (Map p583; B-dul Nicolae Bălescu 30; ☽ 24hr)

IDM Exchange (Map p581; Gară de Nord; ☽ 5.50am-11.10pm)

ATMs are around every corner, including in Unirea Shopping Centre, inside the **Agenţie**

GREATER BUCHAREST

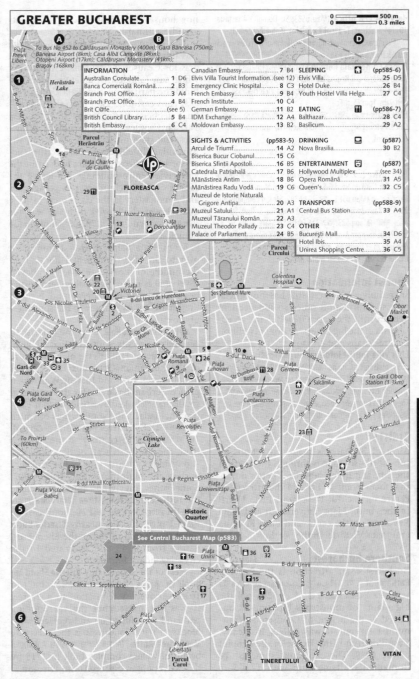

0 ————— 500 m
0 ————— 0.3 miles

Piaţa Presei Libere
To Bus No 452 to Căldăruşani Monastery (400m); Gară Băneasa (750m);
Băneasa Airport (8km); Casa Albă Campsite (8km);
Otopeni Airport (17km); Căldăruşani Monastery (41km);
Braşov (168km)

INFORMATION
Australian Consulate.................... 1 D6
Banca Comercială Română........... 2 B3
Branch Post Office....................... 3 A4
Branch Post Office....................... 4 B4
Brit C@fe...................................(see 5)
British Council Library.................. 5 B4
British Embassy............................ 6 C4
Canadian Embassy....................... 7 B4
Elvis Villa Tourist Information..(see 12)
Emergency Clinic Hospital........... 8 C3
French Embassy............................ 9 B3
French Institute.......................... 10 C4
German Embassy......................... 11 B2
IDM Exchange............................. 12 A4
Moldovan Embassy..................... 13 B2

SIGHTS & ACTIVITIES   (pp583-5)
Arcul de Triumf.......................... 14 A2
Biserica Bucur Ciobanul............. 15 C6
Biserica Sfinţii Apostoli.............. 16 B5
Catedrala Patriarhală................. 17 B6
Mănăstirea Antim....................... 18 B6
Mănăstirea Radu Vodă 19 C6
Muzeul de Istorie Naturală
    Grigore Antipa...................... 20 A3
Muzeul Satului........................... 21 A1
Muzeul Ţăranului Român............ 22 A3
Muzeul Theodor Pallady............. 23 C4
Palace of Parliament.................. 24 B5

SLEEPING   (pp585-6)
Elvis Villa.................................... 25 D5
Hotel Duke................................. 26 B4
Youth Hostel Villa Helga............. 27 C4

EATING   (pp586-7)
Balthazar.................................... 28 C4
Basilicum................................... 29 A2

DRINKING   (p587)
Nova Brasilia.............................. 30 B2

ENTERTAINMENT   (p587)
Hollywood Multiplex...............(see 34)
Opera Română........................... 31 A5
Queen's...................................... 32 C5

TRANSPORT   (pp588-9)
Central Bus Station..................... 33 A4

OTHER
Bucureşti Mall........................... 34 D6
Hotel Ibis................................... 35 A4
Unirea Shopping Centre............. 36 C5

ROMANIA

de Voiaj CFR office (Map p583; Str Domniţa Anastasia 10-14) and at Teatrul Excelsior (Calea Academei).

For cash transfer, travellers cheques and banking services:

Banca Comercială Română B-dul Regina Elisabeta (Map p583; B-dul Regina Elisabeta 5; ⊙ 9am-4pm Mon-Fri); Calea Victoriei (Map p583; Calea Victoriei 155; ⊙ 9am-1pm Mon-Fri)

HVB Bank (Map p583; ☎ 203 2222; www.hvb.ro; Calea Victoriei 88; ⊙ 9am-4pm Mon-Fri) Also shows art exhibitions.

Post

Post office (www.posta-romana.ro) Str Gării de Nord (Map p581; Str Gării de Nord 6-8; ⊙ 9am-5pm Mon-Fri); Str Ion Câmpineanu (Map p581; ☎ 212 6389; Str Ion Câmpineanu 21; ⊙ 7am-3pm Mon, Wed, Fri, 1-9pm Tue & Thu); Str Matei Millo (Map p583; ☎ 315 9030; Str Matei Millo 10; ⊙ 7.30am- 8pm Mon-Fri, 8am-2pm Sat) Collect post-restante mail from the central post office (Poştă Română Oficiul Bucureşti 1) on Str Matei Millo.

Tourist Information

Incredibly, Bucharest still has no official tourist information office so independent ventures fill the gap. Or pester the receptionists of the big hotels. The mighty Hilton has free maps and city tours.

Elvis Villa Tourist Information (Map p581; ☎ 312 1653; platform 2 Gară de Nord; ⊙ 7am-10pm) Friendly staff speak English, French, Italian and Japanese and organise city tours, Dracula tours and hand out free maps. They'll also book you a bed, a cab, an international bus or just point you in the right direction.

SIGHTS

Most of Bucharest's major attractions lie in a north–south axis through the heart of the city and inner suburbs. There's no actual focus point so life and the attractions centre on each of the plazas: Piaţa Unirii in the south, Piaţa Universităţii and Piaţa Revoluţiei in the centre and Piaţa Romană and Piaţa Victoriei in the north.

Southern Bucharest   Map p581

Bucharest's star attraction is the **Palace of Parliament** (☎ 311 3611; cic@camera.ro; Calea 13 Septembrie 1; adult/student €3/1.5; ⊙ 10am-4pm), the big mama of monstrous buildings. Conceived at the height of Ceauşescu's communist fervour it was called, ironically, Casa Poporului (the House of the People) before 1989. The enormous showcase of Romanian craftsmanship with 12 floors

now houses the chamber of deputies in its grandiose innards.

The urban wasteland that is **B-dul Unirii** was intended as the Champs Elysées–style axis for Ceauşescu's criminal civic project which saw him destroy an entire suburb to build the parliament and Piaţa Unirii.

It runs east for 3.2km from the square – built deliberately 6m longer than the real Parisian boulevard. Government ministries, the state prosecution office and the Romanian Intelligence Service (the successor to the Securitate) are housed in the vast civic centre buildings bordering the square. Some 26 churches, two synagogues and a monastery in the city's most historic quarter were bulldozed to make way for this project, and about 70,000 people made homeless.

From **Piaţa Unirii** metro station walk over to the large ornamental fountain in the middle of the square. The Dâmboviţa River snakes up to the northeastern corner before disappearing underground, beneath the square, on its journey to the southwest of the city.

Catedrala Patriahală (Patriarchal Cathedral; Str Dealul Mitropoliei) sits south of Piaţa Unirii, atop Patriarchy Hill. It's the majestic centre of the Romanian Orthodox faith. It was built between 1656 and 1658 by Wallachian prince Şerban Basarab. To the west is a small chapel, linked by a balcony to the Patriarchal Palace, the south wings of which date to 1932. Three beautifully carved, 16th- and 17th-century stone crosses flank the northern wall of the cathedral. Alongside is a belfry (1698) and a former parliament building dating from 1907. Some other surviving churches include the 16th-century **Mânăstirea Radu Vodă** (Prince Radu Monastery; Str Radu Vodă 24), southeast of Piaţa Unirii, and the nearby **Biserica Bucur Ciobanul** (Church of Bucur the Shepherd), dating from 1743 and dedicated to the city's legendary founder.

West of the square, tiny **Biserica Sfintii Apostoli** (St Apostles' Church; Str Apostoli 33a), built in 1636, survived systemisation to a degree. It was not moved but the surrounding parkland was ripped up and replaced with blocks of flats. Southwest is the surviving **Mânăstirea Antim** (Antim Monastery; Str Antim), a beautiful walled complex built in 1715 by the metropolitan bishop Antim Ivireanu.

Central Bucharest
Map p583

PIAŢA UNIVERSITĂŢII

Some of the fiercest fighting during the 1989 revolution took place here. Journalists watched tanks roll over Romanian freedom fighters and soldiers shoot into crowds of protestors from their viewpoint inside Hotel Inter-Continental. Scour the area and you'll find bullet marks in buildings and 10 stone crosses commemorating those killed. A black cross at B-dul Nicolae Bălescu 18 marks the spot where the first protestor, Mihai Gătlan, died at 5.30pm on 21 December 1989.

The **History & Art Museum** (☎ 315 6858; B-dul IC Brătianu 2; admission €0.50; ☒ 10am-6pm Tue-Sun) has costumes and artefacts from 19th- and 20th-

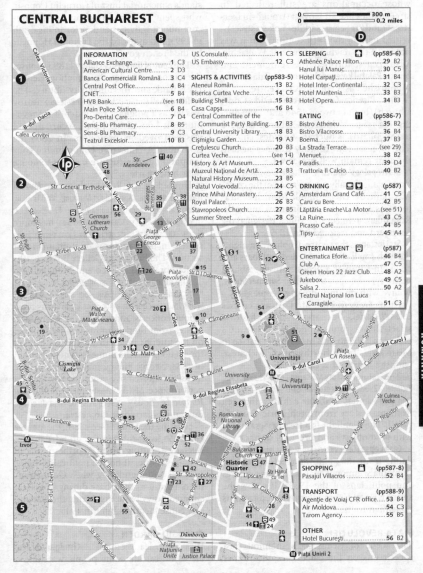

CENTRAL BUCHAREST

0 — 300 m
0 — 0.2 miles

INFORMATION
Alliance Exchange.....................1 C3
American Cultural Centre.........2 D3
Banca Commercială Română....3 C4
Central Post Office...................4 B4
CNET...5 B4
HVB Bank............................(see 18)
Main Police Station..................6 B4
Pro-Dental Care.......................7 D4
Sensi-Blu Pharmacy..................8 B5
Sensi-Blu Pharmacy..................9 C3
Teatrul Excelsior....................10 B3

US Consulate.........................11 C3
US Embassy............................12 C3

SIGHTS & ACTIVITIES   (pp583-5)
Ateneul Român......................13 B2
Biserica Curtea Veche............14 C5
Building Shell.........................15 B3
Casa Capşa............................16 B4
Central Committee of the
  Communist Party Building...17 B3
Central University Library.......18 B3
Cişmigiu Garden....................19 A3
Creţulescu Church..................20 B3
Curtea Veche.....................(see 14)
History & Art Museum............21 C4
Muzeul Naţional de Artă.........22 B3
Natural History Museum.........23 B5
Palatul Voievodal...................24 C5
Prince Mihai Monastery..........25 A5
Royal Palace..........................26 B3
Stavropoleos Church..............27 B5
Summer Street.......................28 C5

SLEEPING   (pp585-6)
Athénée Palace Hilton............29 B2
Hanul lui Manuc.....................30 C5
Hotel Carpaţi.........................31 B4
Hotel Inter-Continental..........32 C3
Hotel Muntenia......................33 B3
Hotel Opera...........................34 B3

EATING   (pp586-7)
Bistro Atheneu.......................35 B2
Bistro Vilacrosse....................36 B4
Boema...................................37 B3
La Strada Terrace...............(see 29)
Menuet..................................38 B2
Paradis..................................39 D4
Trattoria Il Calcio..................40 B2

DRINKING   (p587)
Amsterdam Grand Café..........41 C5
Caru cu Bere..........................42 B5
Lăptăria Enache\La Motor..(see 51)
La Ruine.................................43 C5
Picasso Café..........................44 B5
Tipsy.....................................45 A4

ENTERTAINMENT   (p587)
Cinematica Eforie...................46 B4
Club A...................................47 C5
Green Hours 22 Jazz Club......48 A2
Jukebox.................................49 C5
Salsa 2..................................50 A4
Teatrul Naţional Ion Luca
  Caragiale.............................51 C3

SHOPPING   (pp587-8)
Pasajul Villacros....................52 B4

TRANSPORT   (pp588-9)
Agenţie de Voiaj CFR office....53 B4
Air Moldova...........................54 C3
Tarom Agency........................55 B5

OTHER
Hotel Bucureşti......................56 B2

ROMANIA

century Bucharest. The document, issued by Vlad Ţepeş in 1459, in which the city was chronicled for the first time, is also here.

HISTORIC QUARTER & CALEA VICTORIEI

Bucharest's historic heart sprang up around the **Curtea Veche** (Old Princely Court) in the 15th century. Artisans and traders – whose occupations are still reflected in street names like Str Covaci (trough-makers street) and Str Şelari (saddle-makers street) – settled here in the 14th century, but it was not until the reigning prince of Wallachia, Vlad Ţepeş, fortified the settlement and built a **Palatul Voievodal** (Prince's Palace) that it flourished as a commercial centre.

The **Biserica Curtea Veche** (Old Court Church), built between 1546 and 1559 during the reign of Mircea Ciobanul (Mircea the Shepherd), is Bucharest's oldest church. The original 16th-century frescoes next to the altar remain well preserved.

Stavropoleos Church (Str Stavropoleos), whose street name literally means 'town of the cross', was built by Greek monk Ioanichie Stratonikeas in 1724 in late-Brâncoveanu style. Romanian architect Ion Mincu designed the courtyard and restored it in 1899.

Str Lipscani is the centre of bohemian nightlife with small streets crowded with bars and clubs. In summer a pedestrianised cobbled pathway, appropriately called **Summer Street**, is alive with music and party people.

At its western end, Str Lipscani crosses **Calea Victoriei**, Bucharest's most historic street. It was built under Brâncoveanu's orders in 1692 to link his summer palace in Mogoşoaia, 14km northwest of Bucharest, with the heart of his capital city.

The **Natural History Museum** (☎ 311 3356; Calea Victoriei 12; adult/student/child €1/0.50/0.30; ☉ 9am-5pm Wed-Sun) has 600,000 exhibits that tell Romania's story from prehistoric times to WWI. The highlight is a treasury crammed with gold objects and precious stones.

Casa Capşa (Calea Victoria 36) was a historic café dating from 1852 and the meeting place of Romania's eminent artists, literary figures and politicians of the 1930s. It's now the swanky Hotel Capşa – far removed from its bohemian roots.

PIAŢA REVOLUŢIEI

The scene of Ceauşescu's infamous last speech was on the balcony of the former

Central Committee of the Communist Party building on December 21 1989. Amid cries of 'Down with Ceauşescu' he briefly escaped in a helicopter from the roof. Meanwhile, the crowds were riddled with bullets, and many died.

Creţulescu Church (1722) stands just south of the square. The red-brick structure was damaged in the 1989 revolution. To the side stands a memorial bust of Corneliu Coposu, who spent 17 years in prison for his anticommunist activities and, prior to his death in 1995, was awarded the Légion d'Honneur by the French government.

The **Central University Library** (1895) houses the European Union Information Centre, HVB bank and the university library. The **building shell** (cnr Str Dobrescu & Str Boteanu) nearby was left as a poignant reminder of the revolution; it housed the hated Securitate and was destroyed by protestors. In 2003 the Romanian Architecture Union built a contemporary glass structure inside it to house their headquarters.

Housed in the Royal Palace, the **Muzeul Naţional de Artă** (National Art Museum; ☎ 313 3030; national.art@art.museum.ro; Calea Victoriei 49-53; adult €2, child & student €1; ☉ 10am-6pm Wed-Sun) has more than 700 icons, tapestries and carvings presented in the Treasures of Romanian Art section. The European Gallery boasts works by Rembrandt, El Greco and Breughel.

The **Ateneul Român** (Romanian Athenaeum; ☎ 315 8798; admission €1-5; ☉ 10am-4pm Mon, 2-10pm Tue, Wed & Fri, 2-4pm Thu, 10am-10pm Sat & Sun) hosts prestigious concerts and should not be missed. Scenes from Romanian history are featured on the interior fresco inside the Big Hall on the 1st floor and the dome is 41m high. Built in 1888, George Enescu made his debut here in 1898, followed five years later by the first performance of his masterpiece *Romanian Rhapsody*. Today it's home to the George Enescu Philharmonic Orchestra.

Housing the Hilton (see p586), the **Athénée Palace** (Str Episcopiei 1-3) is the grand dame of Bucharest. Sitting on the northern side of Piaţa Revoluţiei, it hosted political intrigue, scandals and high living when German officers used it as their base during WWII. It suffered heavy bombing during the war and was consequently rebuilt in 1945.

CIŞMIGIU GARDEN

West of Calea Victoriei is **Cişmigiu Garden**. Here you can do some people-watching –

the beloved pastime of Bucharestians. Get yourself settled on one of the green metal benches and indulge in some serious staring. Or, you can always be a 'flaunter' and give them something to look at!

Northern Bucharest
Map p581

The following sights are all on Sos Kiseleff.

On the northwestern side of Piaţa Vicotorei, at the start of Sos Kiseleff, is the interesting **Muzeul de Istorie Naturală Grigore Antipa** (Grigore Antipa Natural History Museum; ☎ 312 8826; Sos Kiseleff 1; adult/child €1/0.50; ⚅ 10am-5pm Tue-Sun). Children will love the live reptile displays and collections of shocked-looking stuffed mammals.

The **Muzeul Ţăranului Român** (Museum of the Romanian Peasant; ☎ 212 9661; Şos Kiseleff 3; adult/child €2/0.50; ⚅ 10am-6pm Tue-Sun) is the best in all Romania. Amazingly, inside you'll find the carcass of an 18th-century Transylvanian wooden church among other rural treasures. Downstairs is the must-see Communism Exhibition, which includes heart-rending accounts of those who objected to collectivisation.

North along tree-lined Şos Kiseleff is the **Arcul de Triumf** (Triumphal Arch). Based on Paris' namesake monument, it was a symbol of cultural ties prior to WWI. The 11m-tall arch, constructed from reinforced concrete and granite mined in Deva, was built between 1935 and 1936 to commemorate the reunification of Romania in 1918.

The **Muzeul Satului** (Village Museum; ☎ 212 9661; Şos Kiseleff 28-30; adult/child €1/0.50; ⚅ 9am-7pm Tue-Sun) is a shadow of its former self after fires wrecked many exhibits in 1997 and 2002. However, it's still worth an afternoon as there's a total of 50 complete homesteads, churches and windmills. Built in 1936, it is one of Europe's oldest open-air museums and a must for the children. Get here from the centre by taking bus No 131 or 331 from B-dul General Magheru or Piaţa Romană to the 'Muzeul Satului' stop.

Eastern Bucharest
Map p581

Muzeul Theodor Pallady (Theodor Pallady Museum; ☎ 211 4979; Str Spătarului 22; ⚅ 10am-6pm Wed-Sun) is housed inside the exquisite 18th-century Casa Melik, a former merchant's house. It contains the private art collection of the Raut family (part of the National Art Museum today).

SLEEPING

Aim for a room near the University or Piaţa Revoluţiei, which have some of the most characterful options. The cheapest – and grottiest – area is around Gară de Nord. There's a first-night tax of 3% on any room in Bucharest.

Budget

Casa Albă (☎ 230 5203; Aleea Privighetorilor 1-3; huts €12-15, camp sites €3-5; ⚅ mid-Apr–Oct) Pitch a tent or rent a two-bed wooden hut *(căsuţe)* in the well-maintained grounds. Take bus No 301 from Piaţa Romană to Şos Bucureşti-Ploieşti; get off at the stop after Băneasa Airport and head east along Aleea Privighetorilor to the Casa Albă complex. Bus No 783 to/from Otopeni Airport also stops here.

Elvis Villa (Map p581; ☎ 312 1653; www.elvisvilla.ro; Str Avram Iancu 5; dm €12) A backpacker favourite. Bucharest character Elvis (an Aussie) struts around his clean, funky hostel offering free washing, free Internet use and even free beer. He offers discounts for long-term stays. Take trolleybus 85 from Gară de Nord to Calea Moşilor. From Otopeni Airport, take the No 783 bus to Piaţa Universităţii then any trolleybus three stops east.

Youth Hostel Villa Helga (Map p581; ☎ 610 2214; Str Salcâmilor 2; dm incl breakfast €12) Centrally located, it offers peace and quiet in a friendly atmosphere with free laundry and Internet to guests. There are discounts for long-term stays. Take bus No 79 or 133 from Gară de Nord for six stops to Piaţa Gemeni or bus No 783 from Otopeni Airport to Piaţa Română, then walk or take bus No 79, 86, 133 or 126 two stops east to Piaţa Gemeni.

Hotel Muntenia (Map p583; ☎ 314 6010; muntenia@dial.kappa.ro; Str Academiei 19-21; s/d/tr €16/25/33) A fab ugly, cavernous hotel with large rooms and a faintly seedy air. Its great value and location make it a wise yet kitsch choice.

Hotel Carpaţi (Map p583; ☎ 315 0140; carpati@compace.ro; Str Matei Millo 16; s €11-16, d €29-40) A popular budget choice so book in advance. It's central with an excellent free breakfast, gleaming reception and clean rooms.

Hanul lui Manuc (Manuc's Inn; Map p583; ☎ 313 1415; hmanuc@rnc.ro; Str Franceză 62-64; s/d €20/35) An infamous hotel in one of Bucharest's oldest buildings. Originally a 19th-century merchants' inn (caravanserai), it has an equally colourful guest list from its past including prostitutes, criminals and rogues.

ROMANIA

Mid-Range

Hotel Duke (Map p581; ☎ 212 5344; office@hotelduke .ro; B-dul Dacia 33; s/d €100/130) A gorgeous little hotel in a lovely area. It's friendly and staff will pamper you and put chocolate on your pillow – it's that kind of place.

Hotel Opera (Map p583; ☎ 312 4857; Str Ion Brezoianu 37; s/d €125/143; 🔀 💻) It has benefited from a total refit and has a classical, though slightly overdone, music theme. It's in a central location and rooms are luxurious and have TV.

Top End

Hotel Inter-Continental (Map p583; ☎ 310 2020; marketing@interconti.com; B-dul Nicolae Bălcescu 2-4; s €294, d €320-420) It towers above Piaţa Universităţii, and was centre stage in the revolution. Inside it's a super-swanky 22-floor five-star wonder with a casino.

Athénée Palace Hilton (Map p583; ☎ 303 3777; hilton@hilton.ro; Str Episcopiei 1-3; s/d €310/340, tr €430-560) The queen of Bucharest's hotels. For glamour and style in sumptuous surroundings the Hilton surpasses them all. The fairy-light lit terrace (see La Strada Terrace p586) is the best in the city while the brassiere is *the* meeting point for expats, tourists and business travellers alike.

EATING
Restaurants

Bucharest is fast becoming a cosmopolitan city of international restaurants at prices to suit all budgets. Once the home of stodgy Eastern European delights, now there are restaurants to rival London with cuisines including Spanish, French, American and Lebanese. Most restaurants and cafés open from 8am or 9am and close at 11pm.

Paradis (Map p583; ☎ 315 2601; Str Hristo Botev 10; mains €5) Brilliant-value buffet lunch at this Lebanese joint. Aubergine stew, spicy rice and falafel for vegetarians while carnivores can tuck into lamb stew and mounds of flat bread. A budget gem.

Bistro Vilacrosse (Map p583; ☎ 315 4562; Pasajul Macca/Vilacrosse; mains €5-10) This place borrows its style heavily from Parisian side streets, with Edith Piaf warbling in the background, wood floors and gingham tablecloths. Settle into a seat and escape the city heat and crowds in this glass-domed passage while sipping fresh coffee and eating a mozzarella salad with (French!) fries, a warm baguette of your choice, or steak. Bizarrely a red English phone box is the entrance to the toilets!

Trattoria Il Calcio (Map p583; ☎ 0722 134 299; Str Mendeleev 14; mains €15) Drool over fabulous antipasto or snack on a lunch-time salad. This Italian in the heart of Piaţa Amzei is a popular choice.

Boema (Map p583; ☎ 313 3783; Str CA Rosetti 10; mains €15) Swathed in sheepskin rugs, handsewn tapestries and plumes of dried plants, this Romanian restaurant is a rustic treat in the city centre. The *borş* (soup) is excellent and the menu is flexible.

Menuet (Map p583; ☎ 312 0143; Str Nicolae Golescu 12; mains €15) Despite its heavy, old-style furnishings, Menuet dishes up excellent Romanian cuisine, including the crispiest, gooiest and tastiest *caşcaval pane* (fried cheese) around.

Basilicum (Map p581; ☎ 222 6779; Str Popa Savu 7; mains €20) A delightful rustic Italian with proper pasta dishes, mouthwatering salads such as avocado, smoked salmon and mango, and a candlelit back terrace. Just north of the centre. Very romantic.

Bistro Atheneu (Map p583; ☎ 313 4900; Str Episcopiei 3; mains €25) An old favourite. Its high-quality food and friendly, French-inspired atmosphere draws crowds, as does its serenading musicians who play most evenings.

La Strada Terrace (Map p583; ☎ 303 3777; Athénée Palace Hilton; mains €5-30) Hugely popular for a light vegetarian lunch of falafel in pitta bread or sophisticated night-time dining from an international menu on the leafy, beautifully lit terrace. An expat institution.

Balthazar (Map p581; ☎ 212 1460; Str Dumbrava Rosie 2; mains €30) Bucharest's best and hippest restaurant. A dreamy, creamy interior with subtle lighting lures in hungry food aficionados. The exquisite French/Thai fusion menu boasts delicate prawns dished in banana leaves, and a divine wine list. Indulge yourself on the fairy-light lit terrace with the city's A-list guests.

Cafés

Nova Brasilia (Map p581; ☎ 231 5540; Str Radu Beller 6) The city's queen of coffee. Choose from frothy cappuccinos, iced coffees and indulgent mochaccinos for €3. Divine cakes and pastries are also there to torment you.

Picasso Café (Map p583; ☎ 312 1576; Str Franceză 2-4) They may have overdone the art theme but it's a nice city haven for reading the paper and drinking coffee. There's a small selection of salads and cakes for €4.

DRINKING

Bucharest's budding bar scene is liveliest in the Lipscani area, which now has a dedicated pedestrianised road called Summer Street lined with trendy pubs and outside tables. Piaţa Universităţii is alive with revellers at the weekend, and hosts free outdoor pop concerts in summer. Other rocking venues include:

Amsterdam Grand Café (Map p583; ☎ 313 7580; Str Covaci 6; 🕙 10am-2am) Like being at home – yet much nicer, funkier and with good-looking bar staff and better cooking. Get there early and feast on massive portions of excellent food; the vegetable *fajitas* are particularly good, then enjoy the beer and eclectic crowds.

La Ruine (Map p583; ☎ 312 3943; Str Lipscani 88; 🕙 11am-6am) This outdoor, bamboo-clad bar is brilliantly set up in the space left by a demolished building, hence the name.

Tipsy (Map p583; B-dul Schitu Măgureanu 13; 🕙 3pm-4am) Funky little bar with hip crowd, good tunes, regular DJs and summer terrace. It also serves simple food.

Lăptăria Enache/La Motor (Map p583; B-dul Nicolae Bălcescu 2) Trendy joint on the 4th floor of the Ion Luca Caragiale National Theatre (with a rooftop bar another floor up). Lined with one long bar, a lively student crowd, huge metal sculptures and a new wooden seating area.

Caru cu Bere (Map p583; ☎ 313 7560; Str Stavropoleos 3-5) Bucharest's oldest beer hall (dating from 1875) and worth a visit for its lavish, Gothic-style décor if not for the average food (mains €15) and slow service. Roma bands play loudly most days from noon.

ENTERTAINMENT

Şapte Seri (Seven Evenings) is a free, weekly entertainment listings magazine. Plug into the local scene with cinema, theatre and opera programmes; details of the week's sporting events; and information on live gigs and concerts in Bucharest's bars and clubs.

Cinemas

Most films are shown in their original language with Romanian subtitles and cost around €1 to €3.

Hollywood Multiplex (Map p581; ☎ 327 7020; Bucureşti Mall, Calea Vitan 55-59) Bucharest's only multiscreen cinema.

Cinematica Eforie (Map p583; ☎ 313 0483; Str Eforie 2) Shows art-house and world films.

Gay & Lesbian Venues

Bucharest's fledgling gay scene remains stilted by lingering homophobic attitudes across both the city and country as a whole. But there is some action.

Queen's (Map p583; ☎ 0722 988 541; Str Juliu Barach 13; 🕙 noon-3am) The only 'real' gay venue in Bucharest. See www.bucharestonline.ro/enclubs.html for membership details.

Another option may be **Casablanca** (☎ 330 1206; Sala Polivalentă), a gay-friendly club.

Live Music

Green Hours 22 Jazz Club (Map p583; ☎ 314 5751; Calea Victoriei 120; 🕙 24hr) Hip cellar bar with live jazz, a weekend disco and even short theatre performances; the itinerary is posted inside. In summer hang out with the cool, bohemian crowd at the outside bar to the sound of smooth jazz.

Jukebox (Map p583; ☎ 314 8314; Str Sepcari 22; 🕙 8pm-3am Mon-Sat) Namesake band Jukebox gets this place jumping in the basement. It's heaving with fun-lovers at the weekend.

Show the locals how to boogie at:

Club A (Map p583; ☎ 315 6853, Str Blănari 14) Run by students, this club is a classic and beloved by all who go there. Indie pop/rock tunes play until 5am Friday and Saturday nights.

Salsa 2 (Map p583; ☎ 0723 412 267; Str Luterană 9; 🕙 3pm-6am) Bongos and steel drums make this a sexy, upbeat taste of Cuba.

Opera & Theatre

Opera Română (Opera House; Map p581; ☎ 314 6980; onr@kappa.ro; B-dul Mihail Kogălniceanu 70) Enjoy a full-scale opera for €1 to €4; the box office opens 10am to 1pm and 2pm to 7.30pm Tuesday to Sunday.

Teatrul Naţional Ion Luca Caragiale (Ion Luca Caragiale National Theatre; Map p583; ☎ 614 7171, 615 7446; B-dul Nicolae Bălcescu 2) The box office, found on the southern side of the building, opens 10am to 7pm.

SHOPPING

For beautifully made woven rugs, table runners, national Romanian costumes, ceramics and other local crafts, don't miss the excellent folk-art shop inside the **Muzeul Ţăranului Român** (Museum of the Romanian Peasant; ☎ 212 9661; Şos Kiseleff 3; 🕙 10am-6pm Tue-Sun).

ROMANIA

Interesting art galleries and antique shops are clustered in 'embassy land' around Str Jean Louis Calderon, and north of Hotel Bucureşti along Calea Victoriei. Don't miss **Pasajul Villacros** (Map p583; Calea Victoriei 16), a covered passage topped with an ornate yellow glass roof, which has some funky clothes and curiosities shops.

GETTING THERE & AWAY
Air
International flights use **Otopeni Airport** (☎ 201 4050, 204 1423; Şos Bucureşti-Ploieşti), 16km north of Bucharest on the road to Ploieşti. The airport has a new lower-level floor for internal flight arrivals and departures.

Arrivals use terminal A and departures leave from newer terminal B. The Otopeni Airport **information desk** (☎ 204 1000; www.otp -airport.ro) in terminal B is open 24 hours.

Romania's national airline, with its head office at Otopeni, is **Tarom** (Transporturile Aeriene Române; www.tarom.ro; ☎ 201 400, 201 1355, 204 1220). It also has an **agency** (Map p583; ☎ 337 0220; Splaiul Independentei 17) in central Bucharest. **Air Moldova** (Map p583; ☎ 312 1258; Str Batiştei 5) also serves Otopeni.

Băneasa Airport (☎ 232 0020; Şos Bucureşti-Ploieşti 40), 8km north of the centre, is used for internal flights and charter flights for package holidays. New domestic airline **Angel Airlines** (☎ 211 1701; ticketing@angelairlines.ro) operates flights from here.

Bus
Don't bother unless it's a short trip through the city. The state buses are poor, there's no distinct central bus station and they take ages.

The **central bus station** (Map p581; Calea Griviţei) – a few paltry stops rather than a station – is opposite Hotel Ibis. Services change regularly and it is wise to check the timetables stuck on the lampposts first. There is no ticket office; hop aboard the bus and buy a ticket from the driver.

A bus trip in the city costs a mere €0.20. Services nationally include to/from Tulcea, Braşov, Constanţa, Târgovişte and Ploieşti.

Hurray for maxitaxis, which are part bus, part taxi. These speedy little devils have rendered the stuffy, slow and dirty buses obsolete. They leave mostly when they're full but do have timetables. White maxitaxis leave from a spot in the centre of Piaţa Gară de

Nord. Services include to Braşov (€5, every 30 minutes, 6am to 7pm) and Craiova, (€5.50, every half-hour between 5.30am and 8pm).

Car & Motorcycle
Bucharest has some of Romania's worst potholes which, combined with the daredevil driving skills of most Romanians, makes for a hair-raising ride. Petrol costs approximately €0.75 a litre and diesel is €0.50 per litre. There are plenty of 24-hour petrol stations around the city which sell oil and accessories.

Parking a car in the centre, particularly off Piaţa Victoriei and Piaţa Universităţii, costs €0.30; look for the wardens in yellow-and-blue uniforms.

Train
Bucharest boasts a complex but comprehensive network which links the capital to the regions, the rest of Europe, and destinations to the East.

Gară de Nord (Map p581; ☎ 223 2060; Piaţa Gară de Nord 1) is the central station for national and international trains. It has two halls, one for 1st-class and international tickets, the other – much grottier and more crowded – is for 2nd-class tickets.

Tickets for local and national trains are only sold at the train station one or two hours before departure.

Some local trains to/from Cernica and Constanţa use **Gară Obor** (☎ 252 0204) station, east of the centre. Local trains to/from Snagov and a couple of seasonal *accelerat* (fast) trains to/from Mangalia on the Black Sea Coast and Cluj-Napoca sometimes use **Gară Băneasa** (☎ 223 2060; Şoseaua Bucureşti-Ploieşti), on the northern edge of town.

All advance tickets (up to 24 hours before departure) are bought from the **Agenţie de Voiaj CFR office** (Map p583; ☎ 313 2643; www.cfr.ro; Str Domnita Anastasia 10-14). A seat reservation is compulsory if you are travelling with an Inter-Rail pass. International tickets must be bought in advance.

Daily international trains include two to Sofia (€24), five to Budapest (€40) and one each to Belgrade (€20), Moscow (€55), Chişinău, Istanbul (€24) and Vienna.

GETTING AROUND
To/From the Airport
To get to Otopeni or Băneasa Airport take bus No 783 from the city centre, which de-

parts every 15 minutes between 5.37am and 11.23pm (every half-hour at weekends) from Piaţa Unirii and goes via Piaţa Victoriei.

Buy a ticket, valid for two trips, for €1 at any RATB (Régie Autonome de Transport de Bucureşti) bus-ticket booth near a bus stop. Once inside the bus remember to feed the ticket into the machine.

Băneasa is 20 minutes from the centre; get off at the 'aeroportul Băneasa' stop. Buses also link Băneasa with Piaţa Romană and Gară de Nord.

Otopeni is about 40 minutes from the city centre. The bus stops outside the departures hall (terminal B) then continues to arrivals (terminal A).

Taking a reputable taxi (see below) from the centre to Otopeni should cost no more than €5.

To get to the centre from Otopeni, catch bus No 783 from the stop in front of terminal A.

Gangs of private taxis have the monopoly at the airport and will try to charge you €25 to the centre. Avoid this rip-off by ringing a cab company who will race a driver to you and wait for it away from the arrivals hall.

Public Transport

For buses, trams and trolleybuses buy tickets (€0.20) at any RATB street kiosk, marked 'casa de bilete' or simply 'bilete'. Punch your ticket on board or risk a €10 on-the-spot fine.

Public transport runs from 5am to approximately 11pm (reduced service on Sunday). Buy a timetable (Ghidul Mijoacelor de Transport În Comun; €1) from ticket booths or check www.ratb.ro.

Bucharest's metro dates from 1979 and has four lines and 45 stations. Line M4 is brand new. Trains run every five to seven minutes during peak periods and about every 20 minutes off-peak between 5.30am and 11.30pm.

To use the metro buy a magnetic-strip ticket at the subterranean kiosks inside the main entrance to the metro station. Tickets valid for either two/10 journeys cost €0.20/1.50. A one-month unlimited travel ticket costs €4.50.

Taxi

Opt for a cab with a meter. Reputable companies include **CrisTaxi** (☎ 9461), **Meridian** (☎ 9444) and **Prof Taxi** (☎ 9422).

Always check the meter is on, as Bucharest is plagued by dodgy cab drivers, and stand your ground if they charge too much or try to avoid giving you change. But, the good news is, that at €0.20 per km they're an absolute bargain.

AROUND BUCHAREST
Căldăruşani Monastery

This idyllic monastery lies 6km southeast of Snagov. Be amazed at its incredible collection of icons painted by 16-year-old Nicolae Grigorescu in 1854 at the monastery's distinguished painting school. Eight exquisite icons line the walls of the former monks' dining hall, along with robes saturated in gold thread from the 19th century.

Today, 25 monks live in the beautiful white complex, which is open to visitors day or night. They also take in people who ask for hospitality, offering bed and board for a donation.

A state bus, No 452, leaves from the Press House in Bucharest at 7.30am and 5.30pm, returning to the city at 8.50am and 6.50pm. The journey takes one hour each way (€0.75) and goes straight to the monastery gates.

Snagov

The tomb of infamous tyrant Vlad Ţepeş lures visitors to this delightful spot – as much as the large lake and leisure complex. Devour the legend of Dracula by visiting the grave where his headless torso is said to lie, buried in the famous 16th-century **church and monastery** (admission €1) which is tucked away on an island in Snagov Lake.

A simple wooden church was built on the island in the 11th century by Mircea cel Bătrân. A monastery was added in the late 14th century during the reign of King Dan I (r 1383–86), and in 1453 the wooden church was replaced by a stone edifice which later sank in the lake. The present stone church, listed as a Unesco World Heritage site and under renovation for several years, dates from 1521. Some paintings date from 1563. The body of Vlad Ţepeş was reputedly buried below the dome, in front of the church's wooden iconostasis. However, when the grave was opened in 1931 it was reported to be empty. Nevertheless, there is mounting credibility given to the presence of a headless torso, evidence that the unfortunate owner was killed by the Turks.

ROMANIA

You can call upon the services of the burly Ana, who will row you there and back for €1.50 per person from the village of Silestru on the northern lakeshore – go to the end of the small wooden jetty at the foot of the radio mast and shout 'Ana'. To get to Silestru, go north along the E60 past the 'Snagav Sat 11km' turn-off and turn right in Ciolpani.

Get to Snagov by grabbing a maxi-taxi, which go every hour from the Piaţa Universităţii via Piaţa Romana, and the Press House in Bucharest (€1 each way).

Otherwise, there are five local trains that run between May and September to and from Gară de Nord and Snagov Plajă – a stop in the middle of oak forest – which is 10 minutes' walk from Complex Astoria.

Both Elvis Villa and Villa Helga hostels (p585) arrange informal guided tours to Snagov, and both charge €10 per person.

WALLACHIA

This flat region, in the south of Romania, has a tranquil charm all of its own which is waiting to be discovered. Some of Romania's most beautiful and peaceful monasteries lie on its northern edges, snuggled into the mountain seams. It is the heart of Roma culture; see flashing black eyes, horses and carts tearing through villages and strange Roma houses here. And the spectacular Transfăgărăşan highway – said to be one of the highest roads in Europe – cuts dramatically across the Făgăraş Mountains from its start point at Curtea de Argeş.

CURTEA DE ARGEŞ

☎ 0248 / 32,300

Curtea de Argeş was a princely seat in the 14th century and its church is considered to be the oldest monument preserved in its original form in Wallachia. The exquisite monastery (or Episcopal cathedral), sculpted from white stone, is unique for its chocolate-box architecture and the royal tombs it hides.

The historic town is a gateway to the Făgăraş Mountains.

Orientation

The train station, a 19th-century architectural monument, is 100m north of the bus station on Str Albeşti. The centre is a 10-minute walk along Str Albeşti then up the cobbled Str Castanilor and along Str Negru Vodă. Continue on until you reach a statue of Basarab I, from where all the major sights, camping ground and hotels (signposted) are a short walk.

Information

There is a **tourist office** (☎ 722 530; B-dul Basarabilor 27-29; ☾ 8am-4pm Mon-Fri, 10am-12.30pm Sat) within Hotel Posada.

Next to Hotel Posada is **Raiffeisen Bank** (B-dul Basarabilor; ☾ 8.30am-6.30pm Mon-Fri), where you can change money, cash travellers cheques or use the ATM.

The **post office** (B-dul Basarabilor 121; ☾ 7am-8pm Mon-Fri) and the telephone office are in the same building.

Sights

PRINCELY COURT

The ruins of the **Princely Court** (Curtea Domnească; ☾ 9am-5pm; admission €1), which originally comprised a church and palace, are in the city centre. The church was built in the 14th century by Basarab I, whose statue stands in the square outside the entrance to the court.

Basarab died in 1352. His burial place near the altar in the princely church at Curtea de Argeş was discovered in 1939. The princely court was rebuilt by Basarab's son, Nicolae Alexandru Basarab (r 1352–68), and completed by Vlaicu Vodă (r 1361–77). While little remains of the palace today, the 14th-century church (built on the ruins of a 13th-century church) is almost perfectly intact. The church is lovingly tended by a dedicated, French-speaking caretaker.

HISTORIC CENTRE

The **County Museum** (☎ 711 446; Str Negru Vodă 2; ☾ 9am-4pm Tue-Sun) charts the history of the region. Rising on a hill are the ruins of the 14th-century **Biserica Sân Nicoară** (Sân Nicoară Church).

CURTEA DE ARGEŞ MONASTERY

This fantastical **Episcopal cathedral** was built between 1514 and 1526 by Neagoe Basarab (r 1512–21) with marble and mosaic tiles from Constantinople. Legend has it that the wife of the master stonemason, Manole, was embedded in the church's walls, in accordance with a local custom obliging the mason to bury a loved one alive within the church to ensure the success of his work. The story goes that Manole told his workers that the first wife to bring their food the next day would be entombed. The workers went home and warned their women – and so it was Manole's wife who arrived first.

The current edifice dates from 1875 when French architect André Lecomte du Nouy was brought in to save the monastery, which was in near ruins, from demolition.

The white marble tombstones of Carol I (1839–1914) and his poet wife Elizabeth (1853–1916) lie on the right in the monastery's *pronaos* (entrance hall). On the left of the entrance are the tombstones of King Ferdinand I (1865–1927) and British-born Queen Marie (1875–1938) whose heart, upon her request, was put in a gold casket and buried in her favourite palace in Balcic in southern Dobrogea. Following the ceding of southern Dobrogea to Bulgaria in 1940, however, her heart was moved to a marble tomb in Bran. Neagoe Basarab and his wife are also buried in the *pronaos*.

In the park opposite lies the legendary **Manole's Well**. Legend has it that Manole tried – and failed – to fly from the monastery roof when his master, Neagoe, removed the scaffolding to prevent him building a more beautiful structure for anyone else. The natural spring marks his supposed landing pad.

Sleeping

Sân Nicoară (☎ 722 126; Str Plopis 34; d chalets €9, 6-bed apt €20) Located behind Sân Nicoară church, Sân Nicoară has six-bed apartments and wooden chalets with double beds. Turn right at the Basarab I statue along Str Sân Nicoară. The site is 100m up the hill on the right and has a terrace bar and small grocery kiosk.

Hotel Posada (☎ 721 451; posada@cyber.ro; B-dul Basarabilor 27-29; s €21-25, d €22-30) Try to get a front-facing room here to watch the sunset over the mountains. It offers both renovated and unrenovated rooms.

Hotel Confarg (☎ 728 020; Str Negru Vodă 5; s/d €21/33) A super-sleek and affordable option.

Eating & Drinking

Montana Pizzerie (B-dul Basarabilor; pizza €2) This place serves up fresh pizzas and beer. Most nights there is live music.

Restaurant Capra Neagră (☎ 721 619; Str Alexandru Lahovary; mains €3) Sit on the terrace here and enjoy its Romanian dishes.

Disco Ti Amo (B-dul Basarabilor; ☽ to 5am; admission €0.75) Pumps out big beats to red fairy lights until late/early.

Getting There & Away

There are six daily trains running to/from Piteşti; change at Piteşti for all train routes.

State buses run from the **bus station** (Str Albeşti) to/from Arefu, Câmpulung Muscel, Braşov and Bucharest (two daily). Check the station boards, as some buses travel only on weekdays and some only on weekends.

A daily maxitaxi to Bucharest via Piteşti leaves at 8am from outside Hotel Posada. Other maxitaxis go to/from Arefu and Piteşti from an unofficial **maxitaxi stop** (cnr Str Mai 1 & Str Lascăr Catargiu).

TRANSYLVANIA

Transylvania – the word alone conjures up images of haunted castles, werewolves and vampires. There's Gothic galore here to keep visitors happy even if they're likely to leave without bite marks on their necks. The 14th-century castles at Râşnov and Bran, for example, could be straight out of a Count Dracula movie. Yet its connections to a literary myth are but a small part of what makes Transylvania an enchanting – not to mention romantic and exciting – destination for travellers of all persuasions. Spectacular mountain ranges, whose sheer rock faces appear like gigantic walls, offer some of Romania's best hiking and skiing, not to mention pure eye candy that in Europe is matched only by Switzerland's mountain ranges.

The area is culturally vibrant thanks in part to Saxon and Hungarian communities living in towns their ancestors founded centuries ago. For medieval art and history buffs, Transylvania offers an unparalleled chance to experience an overlooked corner of the old Austro-Hungarian empire; it's a glimpse of what pre-Industrial Europe was like.

Transylvania forms the central region of Romania, bordered to the east, south and west by the Carpathian Mountains. Southeastern Transylvania is dominated by the Prahova Valley with Romania's leading ski resorts. The Făgăraş Mountains and a string of medieval Saxon cities are within easy reach. Just north and east of here is Romania's Hungarian enclave, known as Székely Land, the

TRANSYLVANIA

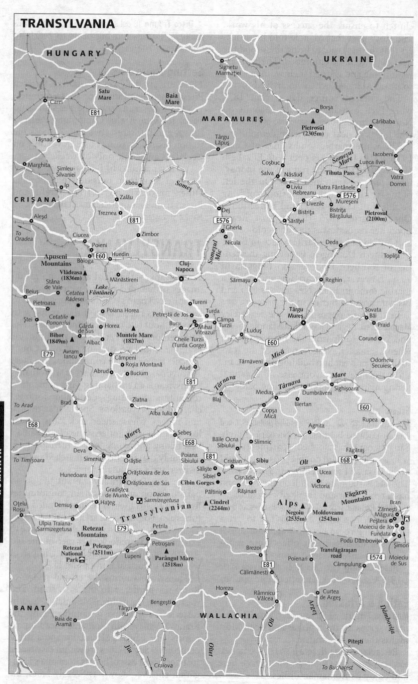

HUNGARY

UKRAINE

Sighetu
Marmaţiei

Carei

Satu
Mare

Baia
Mare

Borşa

Cârlibaba

E81

MARAMUREŞ

Pietrosul
(2305m)

Târgu
Lăpuş

Iacobeni

Tăşnad

Marghita

Şimleu-
Silvaniei

Ip

Coşbuc

Someşul
Mare

Lunca Ilvei

Vatra
Dornei

Salva

Năsăud

Tihuţa Pass

Jibou

Zalău

Someş

Liviu
Rebreanu

Piatra Fântânele

E576
Mureşeni

CRIŞANA

Treznea

Aleşd

E81

Zimbor

Dej

E576

Livezile

Bistriţa
Bârgăului

Pietrosul
(2100m)

To
Oradea

Ciucea

Poieni

Gherla

Sărăţel

Deda

Bologa

Huedin

Someşul
Mic

Nicula

Toplița

Apuseni
Mountains

E60

Cluj-
Napoca

Vlădeasa
(1836m)

Mănăstireni

Sărmaşu

Reghin

Stâna
de Vale

Cetatea
Rădesei

Lake
Fântânele

Beiuş

Pietroasa

Poiana Horea

Tureni

Turda

Câmpa
Turzii

Târgu
Mureş

Sovata
Băi

Ştei

Cetatile
Ponorului

Gârda
de Sus

Horea

Buru

Mihai
Viteazul

Luduş

Praid

Bihor
(1849m)

Albac

Muntele Mare
(1827m)

Cheile Turzii
(Turda Gorge)

E60

Corund

E79

Avram
Iancu

Câmpeni

Roşia Montană

Aiud

Târnăveni

Mică

Odorheiu
Secuiesc

Abrud

Bucium

Târnava

Mare

Sighişoara

Zlatna

Târnava

Mediaş

Dumbrăveni

To Arad

Brad

Alba Iulia

E81

Blaj

Biertan

E60

Rupea

E68

Mureş

Sebeş

Copşa
Mică

Agnita

Deva

E68

Băile Ocna
Sibiului

Făgăraş

To Timişoara

Simeria

Orăştie

Poiana
Sibiului

E81

Slimnic

Sibiu

Olt

E68

Hunedoara

Bucium

Orăştioara de Jos

Cristian

Ucea

Făgăraş
Mountains

Oţelu
Roşu

Densuş

Gradiştea
de Munte

Orăştioara de Sus

Dacian
Sarmizegetusa

Sălişte

Sibiel

Cibin Gorges

Cisnădie

Răşinari

Victoria

Bran

Ulpia Traiana-
Sarmizegetusa

Haţeg

Transylvanian

Pălţiniş

Cindrel
(2244m)

Alps

Negoiu
(2535m)

Moldoveanu
(2543m)

Zărneşti

Măgura

Peştera

Retezat
Mountains

E79

Petrila

Podu Dâmboviţei

Moieciu de Jos

Fundata

Retezat
National
Park

Peleaga
(2511m)

Petroşani

Parângul Mare
(2518m)

Lupeni

Brezoi

Transfăgărăşan
road

Simon

E574

Moieciu
de Sus

Poienari

Câmpulung

Călimăneşti

BANAT

Baia de
Aramă

Târgu
Jiu

Bengeşti

Horezu

WALLACHIA

Râmnicu
Vâlcea

Curtea
de Argeş

Argeş

Dâmboviţa

Jiu

To
Craiova

Olteţ

Olt

Piteşti

To Bucharest

ROMANIA

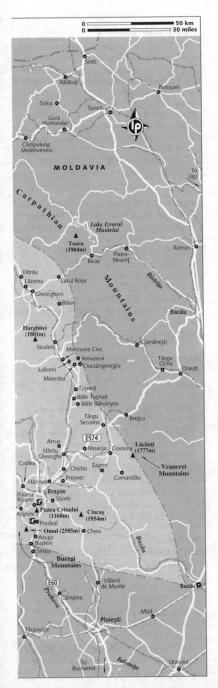

cradle of Magyar culture. The southwest of the region is home to a string of Dacian and Roman citadels, including the fantastic remains of the Roman capital Sarmizegetusa.

SINAIA

☎ 0244 / pop 14,240

It's not dubbed the Pearl of the Carpathians for nothing. Sinaia boasts not only Romania's hottest skiing, but also the country's most fabulous palace. Floating at an altitude of 800–930m in the narrow Prahova Valley and lying at the foot of the fir-clad Bucegi Mountains, Sinaia seems to have sprouted naturally from its wooded nest.

The resort is alleged to have gained its name from Romanian nobleman Mihai Cantacuzino who, following a pilgrimage he made to the biblical Mt Sinai in Israel in 1695, founded the Sinaia Monastery. It later developed into a major resort after King Carol I selected the area for his summer residence in 1870 and built what is today Romania's most beautiful palace.

For readers' convenience, this area has been included in Transylvania in this chapter, even though it is administratively part of Wallachia.

Orientation

The train station is directly below the centre of town. From the station climb up the stairway across the street to busy B-dul Carol I. Hotel Montana and the cable car are to the left; the monastery and palace are uphill to the right. Also to the right is the 1911 Edwardian-style casino, modelled after the famous one in Monte Carlo.

Information

Get onto the Net at **Internet Room** (Str Avram Iancu 1; per hr €0.50; ☀ 10am-10pm). It is in the Hotel International lobby.

If you run into problems in the mountains or need to check weather conditions, contact **Salvamont** (☎ 313 131; Primărie, B-dul Carol I). There's also one at Cota 2000 at the top of the chairlift.

The currency exchange inside the **Luxor Agenţie de Turism** (B-dul Carol I, 22; ☀ 8am-8pm) offers good rates. The **Banca Comercială Română** (B-dul Carol I; ☀ 8am-5.30pm Mon-Fri, 8.30am-12.30pm Sat), next to the *primărie* (town hall), cashes travellers cheques, gives cash advances on Visa/MasterCard and has an ATM.

ROMANIA

The central **post office** (☎ 311 591; ✆ 7am-8pm Mon-Fri, 8am-noon Sat) and **telephone office** (✆ 10am-6pm Mon-Fri, 10am-2pm Sat) are both at B-dul Carol I, 33.

Despite its tacky name, make **Dracula's Land** (☎ 311 441; mihneasutu@hotmail.com; B-dul Carol I, 14; ✆ 9am-6pm) your first stop in town. It's one of the country's most active, enthusiastic travel agencies and doubles as a tourist information bureau, happy to help with any kind of question even if unrelated to their own services which include booking accommodation (at a 25–40% discount) and arranging a wide array of hiking and ski tours.

Sights

From the train station walk up the stairway to town, turn left and make a quick right onto Str Octavian Goga, then curve left at the old *cazino*. There's a stairway here, at the top of which is **Mănăstirea Sinaia** (Sinaia Monastery), named after Mt Sinai. The large Orthodox church dates from 1846 and an older church (1695), with its original frescoes, is in the compound to the left. Beside the newer church is a small **Muzeul de Istorie** (history museum; adult/child €0.80/0.40 ✆ 10am-6pm).

Just past the monastery begins the road to **Peleş Castle** (☎ 310 918; compulsory tours adult/child €2.50/1.25; ✆ 11am-5pm Wed, 9am-5pm Thu-Sun), the former royal palace, dating from 1883. It is one of the country's finest castles, built in the German-Renaissance style for Prussian prince Carol I, first king of Romania (r 1866–1914). The queue can be long on weekends, but it's worth waiting as the interior rooms are magnificent. A few hundred metres uphill from the main palace is the smaller **Pelişor Palace** (☎ 312 184; compulsory tours adult/child €2/0.65; ✆ 11am-5pm Wed, 9am-5pm Thu-Sun) in mock-medieval style. Pelişor was built for Carol I's son, Ferdinand, and was decorated in the Art Nouveau style by Queen Marie. Tours for both are given between 9.15am and 3.15pm Wednesday to Sunday.

Behind the Hotel Palace in the central park, the small **Muzeul Rezervaţiei Bucegi** (Bucegi Nature Reserve Museum; ☎ 311 750; admission €0.40; ✆ 9am-7pm Tue-Sun, 9am-5pm Mon) features some of the natural wonders of the Bucegi Nature Reserve.

Activities

Sinaia is a great base for **hiking** in the Bucegi Mountains. Nonhikers should take the **cable**

BUCEGI MOUNTAINS

The Bucegi Mountains are Romania's best-kept secret, rivalling the Tatra Mountains of Slovakia and even the Alps for trekking. Getting lost is difficult, thanks to a network of marked trails, while *cabanas* (mountain cabins) are open year-round to shelter hikers and cross-country skiers. The only danger is the weather; winter is severe, waist-deep snow can linger to May and summer thunderstorms are common. If you sleep in *cabanas*, it's a good idea to bring extra food.

---

car (☎ 311 674; Str Telecabinei; return €2.40; open 8am-4pm Tue-Sun) from behind Hotel Montana to Cota 1400 (a station near Hotel Alpin) and continue on the cable car or ski lift up to Cota 2000 (near Cabana Mioriţa).

Sinaia's big attraction is **skiing**. It has 10 downhill tracts, three cross-country trails, three sleigh slopes and a bobsled slope. The **Snow ski school and gear shop** (☎ 311 198; Str Cuza Vodă 2a), at the foot of the cable-car station behind Hotel Montana, rents complete snowboard and ski equipment.

Sleeping

BUDGET

Cabana Brădet (☎ 315 491; bed €5) At 1300m, this has 28 beds in shared rooms.

Cabana Schiorilor (☎ 313 655; Str Drumul Cotei 7; d €22, 5-bed r €20) Pretty fancy as far as *cabanas* go, it has an on-site, elegant restaurant. It's easily walkable from the centre.

Hotel Furnica (☎ 311 851; Str Furnica 50; s/d €15/24) The building is so mightily impressive from the outside with its faux-Jacobean flourishes and grand courtyard, you can send a snapshot back home and everyone will think you came into fast money for having stayed here.

MID-RANGE

Hotel Economat (☎ 311 151; fax 311 150; Aleea Peleşului 2; s/d €20/24) Just a few minutes' walk from the Peleş Castle, the hotel also runs a series of other one- to three-star villas in the area and so can offer a wide range of accommodation starting from €10 per person. Though it's quite a hike up from the centre, it's one of the best bets in town.

Hotel Sinaia (☎ 311 551; fax 310 625; B-dul Carol I, 8; 2-star s/d €20/32, 3-star s/d €27/48) This looms forebodingly in all its concrete weightiness over the centre of town. In the 1960s this 242-room giant might have impressed; today it intimidates. Use of the fitness centre and pool costs extra.

Eating

There are numerous kebab and fast-food stands along B-dul Carol I and inside the Perla Bucegi shopping complex.

Pizzerie Carpaţi (☎ 310 680; B-dul Carol I, 39; mains €2-3; ⊗ 9am-11pm) Rely on this place for decent pizzas and traditional dishes.

Snow (☎ 311 198; Str Cuza Vodă; mains €2-4; ⊗ 8am-midnight) This is the kind of place you feel like moving into. Adjoining the ski shop and school of the same name, it offers one of the most pleasant dining experiences in the region, either on its airy double-decker terrace or in its bright yellow/green dining room. The menu is varied and inventive and the food mouthwatering: try their *cameleoni* pancake, a sinful combo of ham, sausage, mushrooms, cheese and an onion sauce (€2.40). Vegetarians will rejoice at having found a respite from cheese and potatoes, as many equally inventive dishes cater to them.

Ferdinand (☎ 0722 526 110; Str Furnica 63; mains €2.50-4; ⊗ 11am-midnight) One of the best bets in town, this has a high, arched ceiling topping a rustic dining room. Far enough from the busy centre to offer a relaxing setting for a few beers, it's also a good choice for a top-notch meal; chicken in raspberry wine sauce is their house speciality.

Getting There & Away

Sinaia is on the Bucharest–Braşov rail line, 126km from the former and 45km from the latter. All express trains stop here, and local trains to Buşteni (8km), Predeal (19km) and Braşov are frequent. Approaching Sinaia from the south, don't get off at the 'Halta Sinaia Sud', a small stop 2km south of Sinaia centre.

Buses run every 45 minutes between 6.20am and 10.45pm from the central bus stop on B-dul Carol I to Azuga and Buşteni. From here you can catch all maxitaxis linking Braşov with points south, such as Bucharest, Brăila and Constanţa.

BRAŞOV

☎ 0268 / pop 319,908

Dubbed the new Prague – Braşov (Brassó in Hungarian) is one of the most-visited cities in Romania – and for good reason. Piaţa Sfatului, the central square, is the finest in the country, and is lined with baroque façades and bohemian outdoor cafés. The ski resorts of Poiana Braşov and Sinaia, trails into the dramatic Bucegi Mountains and the castles of Bran and Râşnov are within easy reach.

A charming medieval town flanked by verdant hills on both sides, Braşov started out as a German mercantile colony named Kronstadt. At the border of three principalities, it became a major medieval trading centre. The Saxons built some ornate churches and town houses, protected by a massive wall that still remains.

Orientation

Str Republicii, Braşov's pedestrian-only promenade, is crowded with shops and cafés from Piaţa Sfatului to B-dul Eroilor and Parcul Central at its northern end. B-dul Eroilor also links two other main thoroughfares, Str Mureşenilor to its west and Str Nicolae Str Nicolae Bălcescu to its east.

The train station is 3km northeast of the city centre. Braşov has two main bus stations: Autogară 1, next to the train station, and Autogară 2, west of the train station.

Information

Bookshop **Librărie George Coşbuc** (☎ 444 395; Str Republicii 29; ⊗ 9am-5pm) has a selection of maps, souvenir photo books and some English-language texts.

For Internet check out **Blue Net Club** (☎ 0740 839 449; Str Michael Weiss 26; per hr €0.40; ⊗ 24hr). **Auro-farm** (☎ 443 560; Str Republicii 27; ⊗ 24hr) is a medical clinic and **EuroFarmacie** (☎ 411 248; Str Republicii 19; ⊗ 7.30am-9pm Mon-Fri, 8am-2pm Sat) is one of the best-stocked pharmacies in town.

There is a 24-hour exchange office inside the train station, and many others (along with numerous ATMs) along B-dul Eroilor, along Str Republicii and all throughout the centre. **Banca Comercială Română**, (Piaţa Sfatului 14; ⊗ 8.30am-5pm Mon-Fri, 8.30am-noon Sat) changes travellers cheques and gives cash advances on Visa/MasterCard.

The **central post office** (☎ 411 609; Str Iorga Nicolae 1; ⊗ 7am-8pm Mon-Fri, 8am-1pm Sat) is opposite the Heroes' Cemetery. The main **telephone centre** (B-dul Eroilor; ⊗ 7am-7pm) is between the Capitol and Aro Palace Hotels.

There are no tourist offices in Braşov so you have to rely on travel agencies and tour

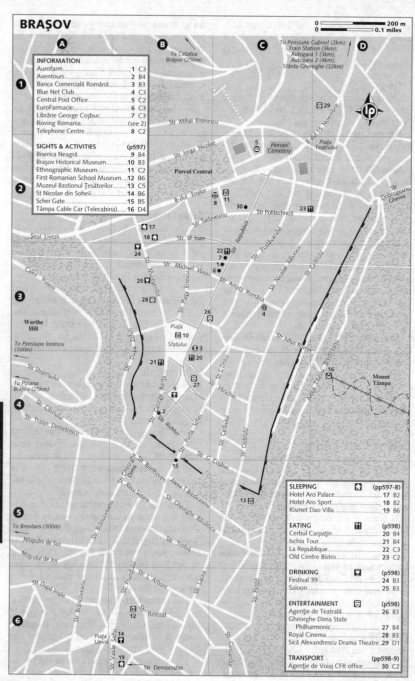

BRAŞOV

0 _____ 200 m
0 _____ 0.1 miles

INFORMATION
Aurofarm..1 C3
Aventours.....................................2 B4
Banca Comercială Română..........3 B3
Blue Net Club...............................4 C3
Central Post Office.......................5 C2
EuroFarmacie...............................6 C3
Librărie George Coşbuc...............7 C3
Roving Romania...................(see 2)
Telephone Centre........................8 C2

SIGHTS & ACTIVITIES   (p597)
Biserica Neagră............................9 B4
Braşov Historical Museum..........10 B3
Ethnographic Museum................11 C2
First Romanian School Museum...12 B6
Muzeul Bastionul Ţesătorilor.....13 C5
St Nicolae din Soheii..................14 B6
Schei Gate..................................15 B5
Tâmpa Cable Car (Telecabina).....16 D4

To Pensiune Gabriel (2km);
Train Station (3km);
Autogara 1 (3km);
Autogara 2 (4km);
Sfântu Gheorghe (32km)

To Cetatea
Braşov (250m)

Str Mihai Eminescu

Str Iorga Nicolae

Heroes'
Cemetery

Piaţa
Teatrului

B-dul 15 Noiembrie

Parcul Central

Str Dobrogeanu
Gherea

B-dul Eroilor

Str Politechnici

Str Sadoveanu

Str Republicii

Str Postăvarului

Str Nicolae Bălcescu

Str Castelului

Şirul Livezii

Str Sf Ioan

Calea Poienii

Str Michael Weiss

Str Piaţa Enescu

Str Mureşenilor

Str George Bariţa

Str Amata Română

Str Julius Romer

Warthe
Hill

To Pensiune Ionescu
(100m)

Piaţa
Sfatului

Str După Ziduri

To Poiana
Braşov (25km)

Str Stejerişului

Str Cibriului

Str Traian Demetrescu

Str George Bariţa

Str Porta Schei

Str Richter

Str C Drăcu

Str Hirscher

Str Cerbului

Str Castelului

Mount
Tâmpa

Alea Tiberiu Brediceanu

Str Beethoven

Str Gheorghe Dima

Alea T Brediceanu

Str G Coşbuc

Alea Săuna

Str Gheorghe Bălulescu

Str Băncoveanu

Str Trotuş

To Brextans (300m)

Nisipulni de Sus

Nisipulni de Jos

Str După Inişte

Str Băncoveanu

Str Prundului

Str L Arbore

Str Lăcea

Str Peţdi

Piaţa
Umirii

Str Vasile Saftu

Str Retezat

Str Curcanilor

Str Democratiei

SLEEPING   (pp597-8)
Hotel Aro Palace........................17 B2
Hotel Aro Sport.........................18 B2
Kismet Dao Villa.......................19 B6

EATING   (p598)
Cerbul Carpatin.........................20 B4
Ischia Tour................................21 B4
La Republique............................22 C3
Old Centre Bistro.......................23 C2

DRINKING   (p598)
Festival 39................................24 B3
Saloon.......................................25 B3

ENTERTAINMENT   (p598)
Agenţie de Teatrală...................26 B3
Gheorghe Dima State
    Philharmonic........................27 B4
Royal Cinema............................28 B3
Sică Alexandrescu Drama Theatre..29 D1

TRANSPORT   (pp598-9)
Agenţie de Voiaj CFR office.......30 C2

ROMANIA

operators, but luckily there are several good ones in town, including **Aventours** (☎ 0722 746 262; www.discoveromania.ro) and **Roving România** (☎ 0744 212 065; www.roving-romania.co.uk). These two share an office at Str Paul Richter 1 (☎ 472 718; no set office hours) and can provide indispensable information.

Sights

In the middle of Piaţa Sfatului is the Council House (1420), now the **Braşov Historical Museum** (☎ 472 363; adult/child €0.50/0.25; 🕙 10am-6pm Tue-Sun) in which the history of the Saxon guilds is recounted. The 58m Trumpeter's Tower above the building dates from 1582.

The Gothic **Biserica Neagră** (Black Church; 🕙 10am-5pm Mon-Sat, mass 10am Sun; adult/child €1/0.50), built between 1384 and 1477, looms just south of the square. The church's name comes from its appearance after a fire in 1689. As you walk around the building to the entrance, you'll see statues on the exterior of the apse. The originals are now inside and Turkish rugs (gifts from merchants who returned from shopping sprees in the southern Ottoman lands) hang from every balcony. Recitals are given on the 1839 organ at 6pm on Tuesday, Thursday and Saturday (€1.50) during July and August.

Go south a little to the neoclassical **Schei Gate** (1828), then walk 500m up Str Prundului to Piaţa Unirii. Through the gate the sober rows of Teutonic houses change to the small, simpler houses of the former Romanian settlement.

On Piaţa Unirii you'll find the black-spired 1595 **St Nicolae din Scheii** (St Nicholas' Cathedral; 🕙 6am-9pm). Beside the church is the 1495 **First Romanian School Museum** (☎ 443 879; adult/child €0.40/0.20; 🕙 9am-5pm Tue-Sun), which houses a collection of icons, paintings on glass and old manuscripts. The clock tower (1751) was financed by Elizabeth, empress of Russia.

Go back and turn right just before the Schei Gate to reach the 16th-century **Muzeul Bastionul Ţesătorilor** (Weavers' Bastion Museum; ☎ 472 368; adult/child €0.40/0.20; 🕙 10am-4pm Tue-Sun), slightly hidden above the sports field. This corner fort on the old city walls has a museum with a fascinating scale model of 17th-century Braşov, created in 1896.

Above the bastion is a pleasant promenade through the forest overlooking Braşov. Halfway along you'll come to the **Tâmpa cable car** (Telecabina Tâmpa; ☎ 443 732; adult/child return €0.80/0.40;

🕙 10am-6pm Tue-Fri, 10am-7pm Sat & Sun). The cable car rises from 640m to 960m and offers stunning views. You can hike to the top, following a series of zigzagging trails; it takes 45 minutes and is well worth the effort.

The art gallery that is inside the **Ethnographic Museum** (☎ 443 990; B-dul Eroilor 21; adult/child €0.40/0.20; 🕙 10am-6pm Tue-Sun), next to the Hotel Capitol, has a good Romanian collection on the upper floor.

Cetatea Braşov, a whitewashed fort on a hill overlooking Braşov, was built in 1580 to defend Kronstadt's Saxon merchants from marauding Turks. Today it houses an expensive restaurant.

Activities

Hire a helicopter for an aerial twirl of Braşov. Call **Brextrans** (☎ 443 666; Str Dealul Spirii 52). The downside? It's €400 an hour for up to eight people.

Braşov is a good base for biking, trekking, skiing and climbing in the Carpathians. **Suntours** (suntours_ro@hotmail.com) organises ski vacations.

Sleeping

Maria & Grig Bolea (☎ 311 962) This pair is hard to miss at the train station, even if you try; they meet almost every train. Maria is an institution unto herself in Braşov and she now has an international reputation. She places tourists in private homes (€10 per person), some of which can be winners, others not so great.

Hotel Aro Sport (☎ 442 840; Str Sfântu Ioan 3; s/d €9/12) Don't listen to what locals say about this hotel. It has a nasty reputation but is surprisingly pleasant for a bare-bones budget hotel. The shared washrooms are spotless and spacious, and rooms are tiny but quite decent.

Pensiune Ionescu (☎ 473 091; annabrasov@yahoo .com; Str Stejerişului 16; s/d €13/19) You feel like you're in the country here, in a lovely spot overlooking the city, though it's just a steep 10-minute walk up cobblestoned Str Cibinului from the Old Town. Each visitor gets a separate cabin in the sprawling garden.

Kismet Dao Villa (☎ 514 296; www.elvisvilla.com /brasov; Str Democratiei 2B; dm €10-11, d €26) This is one of the country's finest hostels: well organised, spotless, modern and well located (behind Piaţa Unirii). Dorm rooms have from five to nine beds. Take Bus No 4 from the train station to the last stop.

Pensiune Gabriel (☎ 0744 844 223; Str Toamnei 4, B11 Sc et1 ap1; per person €13) This comes recommended by a number of our readers. A 10-minute walk northeast of the centre, the place is clean and friendly and the owner super-helpful, often driving guests to Bran and other places.

Hotel Aro Palace (☎ 478 800; www.aro-palace.ro; Str Mureşenilor 12; s/d/ste €83/107/117) This is impressive mainly for its Art Deco façade facing Parcul Central. Plush rooms with cable TV, phone and fridge are nice if you don't mind the inflated price tag; credit cards are accepted.

Eating

La Republique (☎ 0744 351 668; Str Republicii 33; mains €0.50-3; ☼ 9am-midnight) That it's one of the most pleasant places on the pedestrian strip makes it worth a visit. That it's a creperie makes it all the more unique (both meat-filled and dessert crepes are delicious).

Old Centre Bistro (☎ 419 100; Str Nicolas Bălcescu 67; mains €2-3; ☼ 10am-midnight) While it isn't in the most appealing of locations, it serves up good cold platters and standard fast food.

Ischia Tour (☎ 478 693; Str George Bariţu 2; mains €2.50-4; ☼ 10am-midnight) Decorated to give the impression of being in an Italian village, this charming place has some Romanian dishes on their extensive menu, but you'd best go with their specialities like lasagne and fish dishes.

Cerbul Carpatin (Carpathian Stag; ☎ 443 981; Piaţa Sfatului 12; mains €3-6; ☼ 10am-midnight) Braşov's most famous restaurant is located in the 1545 Hirscher House. Romanian dishes are the highlight here, though the restaurant's interiors (a marble staircase, elegant wine cellar) get more raves than the food. Some nights there's live folk music.

Drinking

Festival 39 (☎ 478 664; Str Mureşenilor 23; ☼ 10am-1am) By far, this is the best bar in town for a relaxed drink. It manages to pull off both a lively and subdued atmosphere at the same time.

Saloon (☎ 477 317; Str Mureşenilor; ☼ 11am-2am) While its attempt to outdo the Wild West (can you say, 'more Catholic than the Pope'?) is mildly amusing, this is a great place to pull off your cowboy boots and relax. Rock and blues (and sometimes country) fills the air.

Entertainment

Tickets for theatrical and classical music and ballet performances can be purchased at the **Agenţie de Teatrală** (☎ 471 889; Str Republicii 4), just off Piaţa Sfatului.

Gheorghe Dima State Philharmonic (☎ 441 378; Str Apollania Hirscher 10) Has a good reputation and performs mainly between September and May.

Sică Alexandrescu Drama Theatre (☎ 418 850; Piaţa Teatrului 1) Has plays, recitals, and opera year-round.

Braşov has several cinemas, the most central of which is the **Royal** (☎ 419 965; Str Mureşenilor 7).

Getting There & Around
BUS

Most maxitaxis leave from **Autogara 1** (☎ 426 882), next to the train station. There are maxitaxis to Bucharest every half-hour from 6am to 7.30pm, plus hourly maxitaxis on a Târgu Mureş–Sighişoara–Braşov–Buşteni–Bucharest route. Two maxitaxis a day head to Bistriţa via Târgu Mureş, and two head to Constanţa via Slobozia. There are at least five maxitaxis to Făgăraş en route to Sibiu, and three a day to Galaţi and Braila. Regular bus services include one to Iaşi, Gheorgheni, Miercurea Ciuc, Piatra Neamţ, Târgu Neamţ, Târgu Mureş and Sfântu Gheorghe; and two to Târgovişte and Bacău.

Autogară 2 (☎ 426 332; Str Avram Iancu 114), west of the train station, has buses to Râşnov, Bran and Moieciu, marked 'Moieciu-Bran', every half-hour. Other major daily buses include one daily to Făgăraş Câmpulung and Curtea de Argeş, two to Piteşti and eleven to Zărneşti.

Bus No 4 runs from the train station and Autogară 1 into town. From Autogară 2, take bus No 12 or 22 from the 'Stadion Tineretului' stop on nearby Str Stadionului (turn right out of the station, walk to the end of the street) into the centre.

TRAIN

Advance tickets are sold at the **Agenţie de Voiaj CFR office** (☎ 470 696; Str Republicii 53; ☼ 8am-6pm Mon-Fri, 9am-1pm Sat). International tickets can also be purchased in advance from **Wasteels** (☎ 424 313; www.wasteelstravel.ro), in the main hall of the **train station** (☎ 410 233).

Braşov is well connected to Mangalia/ Constanţa (four per day), Sighişoara (€5, four per day), Cluj-Napoca (€8, four per day) and Oradea (one per day) by fast trains. Local trains to/from Sinaia run frequently. There are 10 trains to Sibiu (€5.50, 2½-3¾ hours) all stopping at Făgăraş (one hour). There are 18 trains to/from Bucharest (three to four hours), including the *Pannonia Expres* and the *Ister*, which go to Prague (10½ hours) and Budapest (11 hours) respectively and the Dacia which runs to Vienna (15 hours).

BRAN & RÂŞNOV
☎ 0268

No visit to Romania is complete without seeing **Bran Castle** (adult/child €1.60/0.50; ⏰ 9am-5.30pm Tue-Sun), dating from 1378. Though this fairy-tale castle is impressive in itself, don't be taken in by tales that Bran is Count Dracula's castle – it's unlikely the real Vlad Ţepeş ever set foot here. It was, however, a favourite summer retreat of Queen Marie in the 1920s.

Still, it's fun to run through the castle's 57 rooms. Your ticket also admits you to the **Muzeul Satului** (Village Museum) beside the entrance to the castle, with a collection of Transylvanian farm buildings, and the **Muzeul Vama Bran** (Vama Bran Museum) below the castle.

Râşnov offers the dual attraction of a convenient camping ground and the ruins of the 13th-century **Cetatea Râşnov** (Râşnov fortress; ☎ 230 255; adult/child €1.20/0.80 plus €0.25 parking; ⏰ 8am-5pm Tue-Sun).

Sleeping & Eating
Wild camping is not permitted around Bran Castle.

Antrec (☎ 236 884; Str Aureli Stoian 340; ⏰ 9am-8pm) arranges accommodation in private homes in and around Bran.

Cabana Bran Castel (☎ 236 404; dm €5) Just 600m from the castle, this place serves meals and it is open year-round. From the bus stop, turn right along Str Principală then right along Str Aureli Stoian (or cut across the park instead); continue for 50m and then turn left onto a narrow path by the side of the yellow-painted hospital. Cross the bridge over the stream and bear left up to the *cabana*.

Hanul Bran (☎ 236 556; Str Principală; d/tr €13/20) You get private shower and toilet (hot water not guaranteed) but in ratty surroundings whose grungy corridors even Count Dracula would have never darkened. It's just two blocks north of the castle.

Getting There & Away
Buses marked 'Bran-Moeciu' (€0.50, one hour) depart every half-hour from Braşov's Autogară 2. Return buses to Braşov leave Bran every half-hour between 5.30am and 7.30pm Monday to Friday and between 6.40am and 5.40pm Saturday and Sunday. All buses to Braşov stop at Râşnov and Cristian.

From Bran there are also 11 buses daily to Zărneşti (€0.30, 40 minutes).

SKIING AT POIANA BRAŞOV

Poiana Braşov has only two black slopes (though each is over 2km in length) but guarantees good intermediate skiing (maximum drop 755m) from December to mid-March. This resort is popular with snowboarders, and has the best-developed boarding and downhill-ski school in the country. There is little off-piste skiing here. The longest run is almost 4km long, easy but very scenic. Overall there are 12 runs, and the resort boasts three cable cars, one chairlift and eight drag lifts. Check out www.poiana-brasov.net for regular reports from skiers.

A gondola, stationed near Hotel Teleferic, takes you up to Cristianul Mare (1802m). Cable cars – one departing from next to the gondola station and the other from near Hotel Bradul – drop you off near Cabana Cristianul Mare (1690m; €3 return). Two of the more popular ski lifts are beyond the Hotel Poiana and are favoured by snowboarders for the slalom in the area.

A number of the hotels run ski schools, but the largest is run by the **Ana Group** (☎ 407 330). A six-day ski school, consisting of four hours' group tuition a day, costs €50/36 per adult/child (four-day course €24/17, five-day course €40/30). Private lessons are €12/20 for one/two adults an hour, and €8/14 for children. A three-day snowboarding course costs €24. Ski instructors speak English, German and French. Skis, poles, boots and snowboards can be hired through the ski school or at some hotels for about €10 a day.

ROMANIA

POIANA BRAŞOV

☎ 0268

Poiana Braşov (1030m), on the slopes of Postăvarul Massif in the southern Carpathians, is Romania's premier ski resort. Unlike its sister resort of Sinaia, 'Braşov's Clearing' offers few challenges for advanced skiers. But the beauty of this intermediate resort lies in its sheltered, forested location which guarantees good skiing between early December and mid-March.

Information

The local **Salvamont** (☎ 286 176; Cabana Cristianul Mare) will come to the rescue any time of the day in case of emergency.

There is no tourist information office in Poiana Braşov, but hotels compete in terms of the information and services they offer, so it pays to shop around. The best ski school in town is run by the **Ana Group** (☎ 407 330), which owns the Sport, Bradul and Poiana hotels.

Sleeping & Eating

Cabana Cristianul Mare (☎ 486 545; beds €5) At 1690m is this large wooden chalet with an attached restaurant overlooking the slopes. It is open throughout the year except for a few weeks in November.

Cabana Postăvarul (☎ 312 448; beds €5) At 1585m (15 minutes downhill), this one gets less tourists and so is a bit more relaxed.

Hotel Caraiman (☎ 262 208; Str Poiana Doamnei; s/d €17/22) This is a good mid-sized option, with 66 decent rooms. Mountain bikes are rented out here.

Hotel Alpin (☎ 262 380; www.hotelalpin.ro; Str Poiana Doamnei; s €37-46, d €49-75, ste €115; 🏊) You can't miss this hotel towering over its little hill, peeking through the trees at the lower town. It is a full-service centre, has a large pool, decent rooms and offers free ski rental.

Coliba Haiducilor (Outlaws' Hut; ☎ 262 137; Str Drumul Sulinarului; mains €2-5) This unbeatable place is at the southern end of the resort near the cable-car station. It is beautifully decorated in traditional rustic style, and a fire burns in the hearth wintertime while live folk bands play. There's even a mini 'museum' in which traditional weaving looms are displayed. The food is plentiful and wholesome.

Getting There & Away

From Braşov, bus No 20 (€0.50, every 30 minutes, 13km) from the Livada Poştei stop, at the western end of B-dul Eroilor, runs to Poiana Braşov.

SIGHIŞOARA

☎ 0265 / pop 36,180

Of all the dreamy spots throughout Transylvania that make you feel like you're floating through another time and space, Sighişoara's citadel wins the time-travel cake by a long shot. Sighişoara (Schässburg in German, Segesvár in Hungarian) has an enchantingly preserved medieval citadel as its core, and is surrounded by beautiful hilly countryside. It tends to seduce visitors' hearts more than any other city in Transylvania.

Sighişoara was also the birthplace of Vlad Ţepeş and therefore attracts hordes of Dracula tourists.

Orientation

Follow Str Gării south from the train station to the Soviet war memorial, where you turn left to the large St Treime Orthodox church. Cross the Târnava Mare River on the footbridge here and take Str Morii to the left, then keep going all the way up to Piaţa Hermann Oberth and the old town. Many of the facilities you'll want to use are found along Str 1 Decembrie 1918.

Information

There is Internet access at the **Burg Hostel** (Str Bastionului 4-6; per hr €0.40; ⏰ 7am-1am) and at **Internet Café** (☎ 771 269; Str Libertăţii 44; per hr €0.60; ⏰ 9am-11pm), directly across the train station.

There are numerous exchange offices lining the city's main street, Str 1 Decembrie 1918 and **Banca Comercială Română** (Str Justiţiei 12; ⏰ 8.30am-4pm Mon-Fri) offers banking services.

The **post office** (☎ 771 055; Str 1 Decembrie 1918, 17; ⏰ 7am-8pm Mon-Fri) and **telephone centre** (⏰ 7am-9pm Mon-Fri, 8am-8pm Sat) share the same building.

Sighişoara has no official tourist information office; instead **Steaua Agenţie de Turism** (☎ 772 499; fax 771 932; Str 1 Decembrie 1918, 12; ⏰ 9am-5pm Mon-Fri, 9am-1pm Sat) can sell city guides and maps, and arranges private accommodation.

Sights

All Sighişoara's sights are in the old town – the delightful medieval **citadel** – perched on a hillock and fortified with a 14th-century wall, to which 14 towers and five artillery

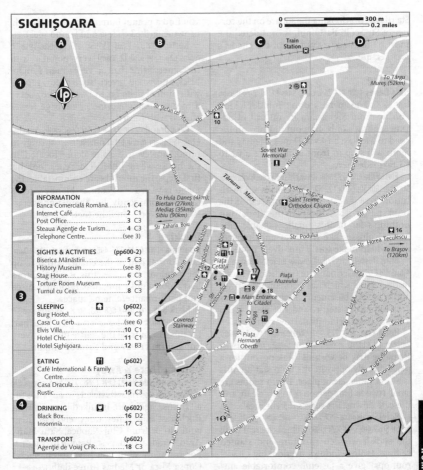

SIGHIŞOARA

INFORMATION	
Banca Comercială Română	1 C4
Internet Café	2 C1
Post Office	3 C3
Steaua Agenţie de Turism	4 C3
Telephone Centre	(see 3)

SIGHTS & ACTIVITIES	(pp600-2)
Biserica Mănăstirii	5 C3
History Museum	(see 8)
Stag House	6 C3
Torture Room Museum	7 C3
Turnul cu Ceas	8 C3

SLEEPING	(p602)
Burg Hostel	9 C3
Casa Cu Cerb	(see 6)
Elvis Villa	10 C1
Hotel Chic	11 C1
Hotel Sighişoara	12 B3

EATING	(p602)
Café International & Family Centre	13 C3
Casa Dracula	14 C3
Rustic	15 C3

DRINKING	(p602)
Black Box	16 D2
Insomnia	17 C3

TRANSPORT	(p602)
Agenţie de Voiaj CFR	18 C3

bastions were later added. Today the citadel, which is on the Unesco World Heritage list, retains just nine of its original towers and two of its bastions.

Entering the citadel, you pass under the massive **Turnul cu Ceas** (clock tower) – the 1648 clock still keeps time. The tower is now the **History Museum** (☎ 771 108; Piaţa Muzeului 1; adult/child €0.80/0.40; ☉ 10am-3pm Mon, 9am-6.30pm Tue-Fri, 9am-3.30pm Sat & Sun), with a scale model of the town and a superb view from the walkway on top. Under the tower on the left as you enter the citadel is the **Torture Room Museum** (€0.25; ☉ 10am-3pm Mon, 9am-6.30pm Tue-Fri, 9am-3.30pm Sat & Sun).

Immediately inside the citadel, on the northern side of the clock tower, is the 15th-century **Biserica Mănăstirii** (Church of the Dominican Monastery; ☉ 9am-7pm Mon-Sat, 10am-2pm Sun). The Gothic church became the Saxons' main Lutheran church in 1556. Classical, folk and baroque concerts are often held here.

Across Piaţa Muzeului is the house where Vlad (the Impaler) Ţepeş was born in 1431; it's now a restaurant, Casa Dracula (p602). Also known as Dracula because he was the son of Vlad Dracul (the Dragon), Vlad Ţepeş became a Wallachian prince who led Romanian resistance against Ottoman expansion in the 15th century.

The quiet, miniscule **Piaţa Cetăţii** is the heart of old Sighişoara. It was here that markets, craft fairs, public executions, impalings and witch trials were held. The 17th-century

Stag House, overlooking the square on the corner of Str Şcolli Bastionul, is considered the most representative example of the citadel's architecture.

Sleeping

Hula Daneş (☎ 774 754; camp sites €1.30, 2-/4-person huts €5/8) The owners don't mind picking you up from Sighişoara if you call in advance, but it's only 4km out of town on the road to Mediaş; buses to Daneş, Mediaş and Sibiu will stop in front of it, or it's a €2 to €3 taxi ride there.

Elvis Villa (☎ 772 546; www.elvisvilla.com/sighisoara; Str Libertăţii 10; bed €10; 💻) Practically an institution here. Located just 250m west of the train station, it's sadly not in the citadel, but nothing's far in this small, walkable city. Lots of plusses like free beer and Internet access help make this a fun, lively place.

Burg Hostel (☎ 778 489; www.ibz.ro; Str Bastionului 4-6; dm/d €7/24) German-run (ie efficient) hostel in the citadel which has a restaurant terrace and a smoky basement lounge bar. Rooms are simple but sterile, and the place has a vibrant, busy feel to its narrow corridors.

Hotel Chic (☎ 775 901; Str Libertăţii 44; dm with/without TV €13/10, d with/without private toilet €15/12) Its name may be wishful thinking, but for a place directly opposite the train station, this is a very quiet, clean place. Dorm rooms are small (two to four persons), toilets clean, and the café downstairs serves decent meals.

Hotel Sighişoara (☎ 771 000; hotelsighisoara@teleson .ro; Str Şcolii 4-6; s/d €40/45; 🍴) This is a great deal; the stylish wooden furniture and slanted ceilings (with windows overlooking citadel rooftops) give a tasteful, comfortable ambiance. Corridors under high arched ceilings lend a feel of pleasant roominess. Plus, there's an indoor pool!

Casa Cu Cerb (☎ 777 349; Str Şcolii 1; d €50) Of interest mainly to royalty fetishists; Prince Charles slept here on a visit in 2003. Otherwise, the rooms are elegant, yes, but cold and starchy; the overarching atmosphere is unfriendly and elitist.

Eating

Café International & Family Centre (☎ 777 844; Piaţa Cetăţii 8; mains €1-2) Right on the main square, this is a double-whammy oasis: to vegetarians (all the meals here – mainly quiches, soups and salads – are veggie) and homesick Americans (where else in Romania can you find a peanut butter and jam sandwich, brownie, grilled cheese and lemon pie?).

Rustic (☎ 0743 805 355; Str 1 Decembrie 1918, 7; mains €2-4; 🕑 9.30-12.30am) Very popular with foreigners, this has a very 'man's man' brick-and-wood tavern-style décor, replete with animal pelts on the walls. They serve a mean *sarmalute* (vine or cabbage leaves stuffed with meat).

Casa Dracula (☎ 771 596; Str Cositorarilor 5; mains €2-6; 🕑 10am-midnight) Tourist *trap* springs to mind; however, despite being located in the house where little Vlad Ţepeş took his first steps, the interiors are comfortable, the menu is varied – of course (bloody) steaks feature prominently, but there are vegetarian dishes too – and the food is good.

Drinking

Insomnia (☎ 0744 172 498; Str Turnului; 🕑 10am-2am) To the right of the citadel entrance up the outdoor staircase, this is Sighişoara's best club, a funky mix of bar, lounge, disco and performance/cinema space.

Black Box (☎ 0742 668 385; Str Horea Teleuscu 37; 🕑 10pm-4am Thu-Sat) For a grungier, local bar, try this one outside the centre that gets very popular on Friday and Saturday nights.

Getting There & Away

The **Agenţie de Voiaj CFR** (☎ 771 820; Str Goga 6A; 🕑 8am-4pm Mon-Fri) sells tickets in advance for all trains. Sighişoara is linked by train with Bucharest nine times a day, eight of them going to or from Cluj-Napoca, Satu Mare, Arad, Oradea, Budapest, Prague or Vienna. For trains to Sibiu you have to change at Copşa Mică or Mediaş (three daily).

The **bus station** (☎ 771 260) is next to the train station on Str Libertăţii. Daily bus or maxi-taxi services include between three and six to Sibiu and Bistriţa, eight to Târgu Mureş six to Apold, and hourly services (from 6.15am to 8.15pm) to Bucharest via Braşov.

SIBIU

☎ 0269 / pop 167,380

Enchanting Sibiu is just far enough off the beaten track to be spared the tourist tide that occasionally engulfs Braşov. Founded in the 12th century on the site of the former Roman village of Cibinium, Sibiu (Hermannstadt to the German Saxons, Nagyszében to Hungarians) has always been one of the leading cities of Transylvania. Destroyed by the Tatars in 1241, the town was later surrounded by strong walls that enabled the citizens to resist the Turks. Under the Habsburgs from 1703 to 1791 and again from 1849 to 1867, Sibiu served as the seat of the Austrian governors of Transylvania. Much remains from this colourful past, especially in the old town, which is one of the largest and best preserved in Romania. Sibiu is also a gateway to the spectacular Făgăraş Mountains.

Orientation

The adjacent bus and train stations are near the centre of town. Exit the station and stroll up Str General Magheru four blocks to Piaţa Mare, the historic centre.

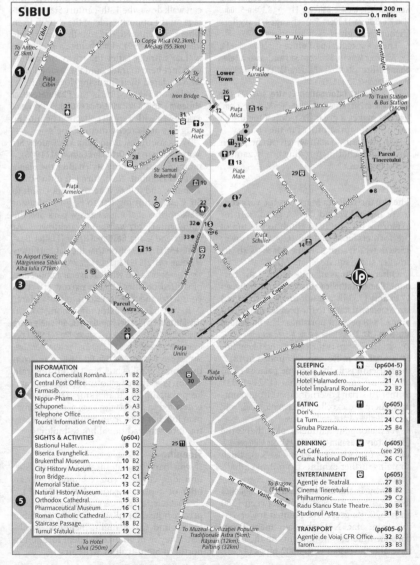

SIBIU

| 0 | 200 m |
| 0 | 0.1 miles |

INFORMATION	
Banca Comercială Română	1 B2
Central Post Office	2 B2
Farmasib	3 B3
Nippur-Pharm	4 C2
Schuponet	5 A3
Telephone Office	6 C3
Tourist Information Centre	7 C2

SIGHTS & ACTIVITIES	(p604)
Bastionul Haller	8 D2
Biserica Evanghelică	9 B2
Brukenthal Museum	10 B2
City History Museum	11 B2
Iron Bridge	12 C1
Memorial Statue	13 C2
Natural History Museum	14 C3
Orthodox Cathedral	15 B3
Pharmaceutical Museum	16 C1
Roman Catholic Cathedral	17 C2
Staircase Passage	18 B2
Turnul Sfatului	19 C2

SLEEPING	(pp604-5)
Hotel Bulevard	20 B3
Hotel Halamadero	21 A1
Hotel Împărarul Romanilor	22 B2

EATING	(p605)
Dori's	23 C2
La Turn	24 C2
Sinuba Pizzeria	25 B4

DRINKING	(p605)
Art Café	(see 29)
Crama National Domn'titi	26 C1

ENTERTAINMENT	(p605)
Agenţie de Teatrală	27 B3
Cinema Tineretului	28 B2
Philharmonic	29 C2
Radu Stancu State Theatre	30 B4
Studionul Astra	31 B1

TRANSPORT	(pp605-6)
Agenţie de Voiaj CFR Office	32 B3
Tarom	33 B3

ROMANIA

Information

For Internet go to **Schuponet** (☎ 0745 161 455; Str Dr I Lupas 21; per hr €0.40; ☺ 24hr).

Nippur-Pharm (Str Nicolae Bălcescu 5; ☺ 9am-7pm Mon-Fri, 9am-2pm Sat) and **Farmasib** (Str Nicolae Bălcescu 53; ☺ 7am-11pm Mon-Fri, 8am-10pm Sat & Sun) have medical supplies.

ATMs are located all over the centre as well as in most hotels. The **Banca Comercială Română** (Str Nicolae Bălcescu 11; ☺ 8.30am-5.30pm Mon-Fri, 8.30am-12.30pm Sat) changes travellers cheques and gives cash advances.

There's a **central post office** (Str Mitropoliei 14; ☺ 7am-8pm Mon-Fri, 8am-noon Sat) and also a **telephone office** (Str Nicolae Bălcescu 13; ☺ 7am-7.30pm Mon-Fri, noon-7.30pm Sat).

The **Tourist Information Centre** (☎ 211 110; www.sibiu.ro; Piaţa Mare 7; ☺ 9am-5pm Mon-Sat, 10am-1pm Sun) makes a great first stop. One of the few official tourist offices in the country, it has an ace, can-do staff which can help with anything, including puzzling out Byzantine bus schedules.

Sights

The expansive Piaţa Mare was the very centre of the old walled city. A good start for exploring the city is to climb to the top of the former **Turnul Sfatului** (Council Tower; 1588), which links Piaţa Mare with its smaller sister square, Piaţa Mică.

Other buildings of note include the baroque **Roman Catholic Cathedral**, built between 1726 and 1733 by a Jesuit order. In front is a large **memorial statue** to the people who fought in the 1848 peasant uprisings. The **Brukenthal Museum** (☎ 217 691; Piaţa Mare 4-5; adult/child €1/0.50; ☺ 9am-5pm Tue-Sun) is the oldest and likely finest art gallery in Romania. Founded in 1817, the museum is in the baroque palace (1785) of Baron Samuel Brukenthal (1721–1803), former Austrian governor. Apart from paintings, there are excellent archaeological, folk art and silverware collections.

West along Str Samuel Brukenthal is the **City History Museum** (☎ 218 143; Str Mitropoliei 2; adult/child €0.80/0.40; ☺ 10am-5pm Tue-Sun) which contains further exhibits from Brukenthal's palace.

Nearby is the Gothic **Biserica Evanghelică** (Evangelical church; Piaţa Huet), built between 1300 and 1520, its great five-pointed tower visible from afar. Note the four magnificent baroque funerary monuments on the upper nave and the organ with 6002 pipes (1772).

The tomb of Mihnea Vodă cel Rău (Prince Mihnea the Bad), son of Vlad Ţepeş, is in the closed-off section behind the organ. This prince (who ruled Wallachia from 1507 to 1510) was murdered in the church square after a service in March 1510. Don't miss the splendid fresco of the Crucifixion (1445) in the sanctuary.

To reach the lower town from here, you can walk down the 13th-century **Staircase Passage** on the opposite side of the church from where you entered, or cross the photogenic **Iron Bridge** (1859). The bridge's nickname is 'Liar's Bridge' after the tricky merchants who met here to trade, and the young lovers who declared their 'undying' love on it.

Also on Piaţa Mică is the **Pharmaceutical Museum** (☎ 218 191; adult/child €0.60/0.30; ☺ 10am-6pm Tue-Sun) with a small collection of antique drug jars and creepy medical tools.

Walk southwest from Piaţa Mică, along Str Mitropoliei to the **Orthodox Cathedral** (1906), a monumental building styled after the Hagia Sofia in Istanbul. Next, turn left onto Strada Tribunei and follow it across Piaţa Unirii to Str Cetăţii, turning left to begin a pleasant walk northeast along a narrow park and the 16th-century **city walls** and watchtowers. At the far end is the **Bastionul Haller** (Haller Bastion; 1551) and before that the **Natural History Museum** (☎ 218 191; Str Cetăţii 1; adult/child €0.80/0.40; ☺ 10am-5pm Tue-Sat) with an average collection of stuffed beasties. Take a narrow street on your left-hand side to return to Piaţa Mare.

If you have an extra afternoon, take in the **Muzeul Civilizaţiei Populare Tradiţionale Astra** (Museum of Traditional Folk Civilisation; ☎ 242 599; Calea Răşinarilor 14; adult/child €1.25/0.75; ☺ 10am-6pm Tue-Sun Jun-Sep, 9am-4pm Tue-Sun Oct-May), 5km from the centre. Trolleybus No 1 from the train station goes there (get off at the last stop and keep walking less than 1km). The museum is devoted to preserving all aspects of Romanian folk heritage, from musical and literary traditions to traditional house-building.

Sleeping

If you hang out at the bus or train station long enough, you're bound to get an offer of a private room. **Antrec** (☎ 220 179; sibiu@antrec.ro; Str D Bagdazar 6) arranges rooms in private houses in villages surrounding Sibiu for around €10 a night, including breakfast. They're in an inconvenient location in northern Sibiu (call or write first).

Hotel Halemadero (☎ 212 509; Str Măsarilor 10; d/tr €13/20) West of centre, this friendly, family-run hotel overlooks a pleasant garden and patio.

Hotel Bulevard (☎ 216 060; Piaţa Unirii 10; s/d/ste €24/27/45) This behemoth is well located in the centre, but dates from 1876 and for better or worse feels like it. There's a stalwart old-world grandeur to its exteriors and lobby, but in the stodgy rooms you feel boxed into the 1960s. It's wheelchair accessible.

Hotel Silva (☎ 442 141; fax 216 304; Aleea Eminescu 1; s/d €26/35) This chalet-style hotel overlooks the tennis courts in the tranquil, tree-filled Sub Arini Park. It's an easy walk southwest from the centre.

Hotel Împăratul Romanilor (Roman Emperor; ☎ 216 500; www.aurelius.compace.ro; Str Nicolae Bălcescu 2-4; s/d/ste €44/58/85) Founded in 1555 as a restaurant, this grand hotel is Sibiu's most luxurious.

Eating

Dori's (Piaţa Mică 14; ☼ 7am-5pm Mon-Fri, 8am-2pm Sat) Look no further in Sibiu for a cheap (ie a bit greasy but delicious) fill. The tiny patisserie serves freshly baked sesame-seed bread, meat rolls and yogurt. It's generally packed.

Sinuba Pizzeria (☎ 216 005; Calea Dumbrăvii 12; mains €1-3; ☼ 8am-11pm) Great fast food you can point to, including lasagne, *mămăligă* and the proverbial pizza, are served in a clean and always-packed hall which doubles as a friendly, boisterous hang-out.

La Turn (☎ 213 985; Piaţa Mare; mains €2-5; ☼ 11am-midnight) Its terrace right on the main square is always packed. The gruff service is made up for by an eye-catching menu including schnitzel stuffed with brains and numerous vegetarian choices. The relaxed décor is British pub meets American tavern. If you're with kids, its roominess makes it the most convenient place to bring them to.

Drinking

Crama National Domn'titi (☎ 218 238; Piaţa Mică 18; ☼ 7pm-1am) This is the city's main student hang-out. The spacious brick cellar bar boasts 10 kinds of beer, and plastic pizza slices for just €0.15!

Art Café (☎ 0722 265 992; Str Filarmonicii 2) A bohemian delight, this is located in a cosy cellar inside the state philharmonic building. Its walls are covered with graffiti and adorned with musical instruments, and there are regular exhibits of local art.

Entertainment

Cinema Tineretului (☎ 211 420; Str Alexandru Odobescu 4) The auditorium-cum-disco is filled with sofas and coffee tables, inviting you to sit back in comfort and relax over a beer while watching your favourite Hollywood hero in action.

Studionul Astra (☎ 218 195, extension 26; Piaţa Mică 11) This screens alternative art films; it also hosts the annual International Astra Film Festival in May.

Agenţie de Teatrală (☎ 217 575; Str Nicolae Bălcescu 17; ☼ 8am-8pm Mon-Fri, 9am-3pm Sat) Tickets for major events are sold here; check out the posters in the office.

Philharmonic (☎ 210 264; Str Filharmonicii 2) Founded in 1949, this has played a key role in maintaining Sibiu's prestige as a main cultural centre of Transylvania.

Radu Stancu State Theatre (☎ 413 114; B-dul Spitelor 2-4) Hosts the International Theatre Festival in June.

Getting There & Away

AIR

Sibiu Airport (☎ 229 235) is 5km west of the centre. **Tarom** (☎ 211 157; Str Nicolae Bălcescu 10; ☼ 8am-6pm Mon-Fri) runs a shuttle bus, leaving from its office one hour before flights depart. Trolleybus No 8 runs between the airport and the train station.

Tarom no longer operates flights to Bucharest, but you can hop on a Munich-bound plane five times weekly for as low as €255 return. **Carpatair** (☎ 229 161; www.carpatair.com), which has an office at the airport, has six weekly flights to Munich and three weekly to Stuttgart, via Timişoara.

BUS

The **bus station** (☎ 217 757) is opposite the train station. Daily bus and maxitaxi services include at least seven to Cluj-Napoca (€3.20, three hours), five to Târgu Mureş (€3, three hours), as well as to Timişoara, Bucharest, Alba Iulia, Braşov, Deva, Mangalia and Sighişoara.

Maxitaxis to Râsnari and Păltiniş (€1.15, 1¼ hours, three a day) leave from the roundabout in front of the train station, and buses to Cisnădie leave every half-hour from platform No 9.

ROMANIA

TRAIN

You can buy advance tickets at the **Agenţie de Voiaj CFR office** (☎ 216 441; Str Nicolae Bălcescu 6; ⏰ 7.30am-7.30pm Mon-Fri). The train station is at the eastern end of Str General Magheru, on Piaţa 1 Decembrie.

Sibiu lies at an awkward rail junction; getting here and away is best by bus and maxi-taxi. For Sighişoara, you have to change at Copşa Mică or Mediaş. For Alba Iulia, you will have to change at Vinţu de Jos. Cluj-Napoca is the most irksome to get to: there is one direct train a day (€5, four hours) leaving in the middle of the night; otherwise, you need to change at Copşa Mică or Vinţu de Jos.

Trolleybus No 1 connects the train station with the centre.

FĂGĂRAŞ MOUNTAINS
☎ 0268

The dramatic peaks of the Făgăraş Mountains cut a serrated line south of the main Braşov–Sibiu road and shelter dozens of glacial lakes. The famed Transfăgărăşan road cuts through the range from north to south.

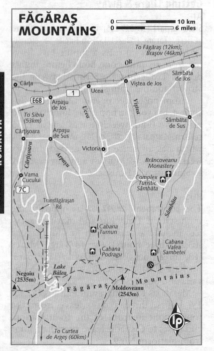

FĂGĂRAŞ MOUNTAINS

Despite its name, Făgăraş town (pop 43,900) is not the prime access point to the Făgăraş Massif. Most hikers pass straight through en route to neighbouring Victoria (pop 10,800), the main access point to hike south into the mountains (see boxed text, above).

CLUJ-NAPOCA
☎ 0264 / pop 331,990

In northern Transylvania, the university town of Cluj-Napoca and its residents have a sassy, savvy feel. Everyone here seems to walk with a strut, decked out in fashionable styles that may not have even made it to Bucharest. People are living in a hip, happening city, and they know it. While not as photogenic as other Transylvanian cities, there are trendy bars galore and cool places with cool people throughout the extended centre.

The history of Cluj-Napoca goes back to Dacian times. In AD 124, during the reign of Emperor Hadrian, Napoca attained municipal status and Emperor Marcus Aurelius elevated it to a colony. Documented references to the medieval town date back to 1183. German merchants arrived in the 12th century and, after the Tatar invasion of 1241, the medieval earthen walls of 'castrenses de Clus' were rebuilt in stone. From 1791 to 1848 and again after the union with

Hungary in 1867, Cluj-Napoca served as the capital of Transylvania.

In the mid-1970s the old Roman name of Napoca was added to the city's official title to emphasise its Daco-Roman origin, but almost everyone simply refers to the city as 'Cluj'.

Orientation

The *gară* (train station) is 1.5km north of the city centre. Walk left out of the station, buy a ticket at the red L&M kiosk across the street and catch tram No 101 or a trolleybus south down Str Horea. If you're on the trolleybus get off immediately after crossing the river; on tram No 101 go two stops, then walk south until you cross the river.

All major bus services arrive at and depart from Autogară 2, which is north of town.

Information

CULTURAL CENTRES

Resource Centre for the Roma Communities (☎ 420 480; Str Tebei 21; ⌚ 10am-7.30pm Mon-Thu, 10am-2pm Sat). An outgrowth of the Soros Open Foundation, it provides information on minorities in Romania, especially the Roma. It's west of the centre.

INTERNET ACCESS

Internet Café (B-dul 21 Decembrie 1989, 20; per hr €0.35; ⌚ 8am-2am)

Supernet (☎ 430 425; Str Iuliu Maniu 1; per hr €0.40; ⌚ 24hr) Supposedly open around the clock but often closes when staff feel like it.

MEDICAL SERVICES

Clematis (Piaţa Unirii 11; ⌚ 8am-10pm) A well-stocked and central pharmacy.

MONEY

Those sour-faced goons you see hanging around the western side of Piaţa Unirii are, well, goons in the outdated business of black-market moneychanging. Hence this area of the city centre is duly known by locals as 'Wall Street'. The city is full of ATMs and legitimate exchange offices.

Banca Comercială Română (☎ 591 227; Str Gheorghe Bariţiu 10-12; ⌚ 8am-3pm Mon-Fri) Gives cash advances and changes travellers cheques.

POST

Central post office (Str Regele Ferdinand 33; ⌚ 7am-8pm Mon-Fri, 8am-2pm Sat)

TELEPHONE

Telephone centre (Str Regele Ferdinand 33; ⌚ 7.30am-8pm Mon-Fri, 8am-1pm Sat) Shares the same building as the central post office.

TOURIST INFORMATION

See www.cjnet.ro for general information on the city, or try:

Pan Travel (☎ 420 516; www.pantravel.ro; Str Grozavescu 13) A top-notch outfit which can book accommodation, and car and mobile-phone rental, provide you with English- or French-speaking guides or prepare an à-la-carte tour circuit. It's west of the centre.

Youth Hostels România (YHR; ☎ 586 616; www.hihostels-romania.ro; Piaţa Lucian Blaga; ⌚ 9am-5pm Mon-Fri) Ideally located inside the imposing Casa de Culture a Studentilor (Student's Culture House), which lords over Piaţa Lucian Blaga, this office can make bookings for youth hostels throughout Romania.

Sights

CENTRAL CLUJ-NAPOCA

The vast 14th-century **St Michael's Church** dominates Piaţa Unirii. The neo-Gothic tower (1859) topping the Gothic hall church creates a great landmark. Flanking it to the south is a huge equestrian statue (1902) of the famous Hungarian king Matthias Corvinus (r 1458–90). On the eastern side of the square is the excellent **National Art Museum** (☎ 496 952; Piaţa Unirii 30; adult/child €0.80/0.40; ⌚ noon-7pm Wed-Sun), housed inside the baroque Banffy Palace (1791). Its 22 rooms are filled with paintings and artefacts including a 16th-century church altar.

To the west on Piaţa Muzeului is the interesting **National History Museum of Transylvania** (☎ 495 677; Str Constantin Daicoviciu 1; adult/child €0.50/0.25; ⌚ 10am-4pm Tue-Sun). This museum presents one of the most comprehensive accounts of Transylvanian history, with over 400,000 objects in its collection. Kids will love the mammoth tusks and ghoulish ancient human remains on the 1st floor.

There's also the **Muzeul Etnografic al Transilvaniei** (Ethnographic Museum; ☎ 592 344; Str Memorandumului 21; adult/child €0.80/0.40; ⌚ 9am-5pm Tue-Sun) with a fine collection of folk costumes and beautiful woven carpets.

OUTSIDE THE CENTRE

Cluj-Napoca's fragrant **Botanic Gardens** (☎ 597 604; Str Gheorghe Bilaşcu 42; adult/child €0.40/0.15; ⌚ 9am-8pm), from 1930, lie south of Piaţa Unirii. Covering 15 hectares, the

ROMANIA

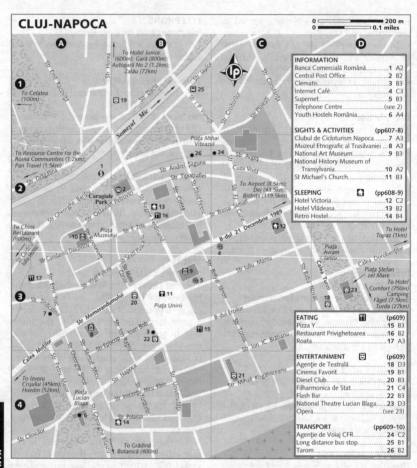

CLUJ-NAPOCA

INFORMATION	
Banca Comercială Română	1 A2
Central Post Office	2 B2
Clematis	3 B3
Internet Café	4 C3
Supernet	5 B3
Telephone Centre	(see 2)
Youth Hostels România	6 A4

SIGHTS & ACTIVITIES	(pp607-8)
Clubul de Cicloturism Napoca	7 A3
Muzeul Etnografic al Trasilvaniei	8 A3
National Art Museum	9 B3
National History Museum of Transylvania	10 A2
St Michael's Church	11 B3

SLEEPING	(pp608-9)
Hotel Victoria	12 C2
Hotel Vlădeasa	13 B2
Retro Hostel	14 B4

EATING	(p609)
Pizza Y	15 B3
Restaurant Privighetoarea	16 B2
Roata	17 A3

ENTERTAINMENT	(p609)
Agentie de Teatrală	18 D3
Cinema Favorit	19 B1
Diesel Club	20 B3
Filharmonica de Stat	21 C4
Flash Bar	22 B3
National Theatre Lucian Blaga	23 D3
Opera	(see 23)

TRANSPORT	(pp609-10)
Agentie de Voiaj CFR	24 C2
Long distance bus stop	25 B1
Tarom	26 B2

green lawns embrace greenhouses, a Japanese garden and a rose garden with some 600 different varieties.

For an overall view of Cluj-Napoca, climb up the steps behind Hotel Astoria to the **cetatea** (citadel; 1715), which sounds more impressive than it is.

Activities

Cluj is a major centre for **mountain biking**, **hiking** and **caving** enthusiasts. For details on the caves and hiking routes contact **Green Mountain Holidays** (☎ 257 142; www.greenmountainholidays.ro; Str Pincipală 305). Located in the village of Izvoru Crişului, 43km west of Cluj-Napoca on the road to Huedin, this is a terrific ecotourist organisation. Their website offers extremely

detailed information about the accommodation available (from €150 per week) and their hiking, caving, rock-climbing and horseback riding treks.

Clubul de Cicloturism Napoca (☎ 450 013; office@ccn.ro; Str Sindicatelor 3, Apt 8) These outdoors-lovers can help with all your two-wheeler questions.

Sleeping

Camping Făget (☎ 596 234; camp sites/2-person huts free/per person €2) You get what you pay for at this shabby camping ground 7km south of Cluj-Napoca. There's an on-site restaurant. Take bus No 35 from Piaţa Mihai Viteazul south down Calea Turzii to the end of the line. From here it is a marked 2km hike.

Retro Hostel (☎ 450 452; www.retro.ro; Str Potaissa 13; dm €10-13; ☐) Here you can buy maps and CD-ROMs, join fun tours of the surrounding areas, order a therapeutic massage and follow it with a bottle of *ţuica* from the front desk. Their tours are the least expensive and among the most comprehensive on offer in the city. Small but spotless rooms hold from three to eight people, and the atmosphere's always lively and super-friendly.

Hotel Vlădeasa (☎ 594 429; Str Regele Ferdinand 20; s/d/tr €17/24/32, with shared bathroom €14/21/27) OK, so it smells a tad musty but the place is clean and comfy, the rooms have grand, high ceilings and the motel-like entrance via a courtyard balcony is an exotic touch.

Hotel Junior (☎ 432 028; Str Câri Ferate 12; d €32, s/d with shared bathroom €16/24) It's on a busy, dusty street near the train station, but its rooms are simple and comfortable.

Hotel Comfort (☎ 598 410; Calea Turzii 48; s/d/ste €24/37/48; ☐) This is a modern, clean and friendly place. Beds are low, ceilings are high and soft pastels envelop you everywhere. It's south of the centre.

Hotel Victoria (☎ 597 963; B-dul 21 Decembrie 1989, 54-56; s/d/ste €35/43/51) This is a good deal with its elegant old-world exteriors, ultra-stylish, modern interiors and reliable service desk. There's also a pleasant terrace café.

Hotel Topaz (☎ 414 021; Str Septimiu Albini 10; s/d/ste €40/50/65) With bright colours splashed all over the place, this is a very pleasant hotel, with compact, nicely renovated modern rooms. It's about 1km east of the centre.

Eating

Pizza Y (☎ 0722 218 210; Piaţa Unirii 1; mains €1-3; ☒ 9am-midnight) In a courtyard just off the southern end of the square. It serves an amazing 34 types of pizza, and pastas and fresh salads.

Restaurant Privighetoarea (☎ 593 480; Str Regele Ferdinand 16; mains €1-3; ☒ 9am-7pm) This serves up hearty portions of meat, potatoes and more traditional soups, spicy meatballs and hot breaded cheese. The attached fast-food outlet to the left serves a variety of pizzas, salads and light snacks.

Roata (☎ 592 011; Str Alexandru Ciura 6A; mains €2-3.50; ☒ noon-midnight Tue-Sat, 1pm-midnight Sun & Mon) This is one of the city's highlights – period. The traditional Romanian dishes taste as good as home cooking here, and served as they are on a small terrace with moss-covered stones and

potted plants vying for space, you're likely to start feeling at home very quickly.

Chios Restaurant (☎ 596 395; mains €2-5; ☒ noon-1am) Right by the lakeside in Parcul Central (west of the centre) on the site of the former casino, this is popular more for its location and the adjoining terrace bar than for the food, which is decent but standard.

Entertainment

Şapte Seri (www.sapteseri.ro) is a free bi-weekly booklet listing all the latest goings-on (in Romanian). It's available in cafés, hotels and entertainment venues.

CINEMAS

Cinema Favorit (Str Horea 6) One of several cinemas in the centre.

BARS & CLUBS

Piaţa Unirii is the site of many watering holes, but clubs and bars are spread out throughout the centre, and in Cluj-Napoca, it pays to go exploring.

Diesel Bar (☎ 598 441; Piaţa Unirii 17) It tends to be the most happening disco come the weekend. It spins mainly pop-dance and retro hits in its cavernous space.

Flash Bar (☎ 599 020; Piaţa Unirii 10) It may not be as popular as Diesel Bar but it attracts a more stylish crowd who pose on the couches and by the beautifully lit bar.

THEATRE & CLASSICAL MUSIC

Organ recitals are held two or three times a week in St Michael's Church (see p607).

Tickets for the following three can be bought in advance from the **Agenţie de Teatrală** (☎ 595 363; Piaţa Ştefan cel Mare 14; ☒ 11am-5pm Tue-Fri).

National Theatre Lucian Blaga (☎ 591 799; Piaţa Ştefan cel Mare 24) Designed by the famous Viennese architects Fellner and Hellmer. Performances here are well attended.

Opera (☎ 597 175; Piaţa Ştefan cel Mare 24) In the same National Theatre Lucian Blaga building.

Filarmonica de Stat (State Philharmonic; ☎ 430 063; Str Mihail Kogălniceanu) Has classical concerts.

Getting There & Away

AIR

The airport is 8km east of the town centre.

Tarom (☎ 432 524; Piaţa Mihai Viteazul 11; ☒ 8am-7pm Mon-Fri, 9am-1pm Sat) has at least two daily direct flights to Bucharest (one way/return €99/110). They also have thrice weekly direct flights to Frankfurt and Vienna, and six weekly to Munich. **Carpatair** (☎ 416 016; cluj -napoca@carpatair.ro), based at the airport, runs flights to Italy.

BUS
From Autogară 2 (there is no No 1) one daily bus or maxitaxi goes to Braşov, two to Abrud, three to Zalău, four to each Dej, Piatra Neamţ, and Târgu Mureş, five to Baie Mare, and eight to Bistriţa. Ten weekly buses to Budapest and three weekly to Chişinău also leave from here. Other daily buses to Budapest leave from a parking lot 100m west of the train station.

TRAIN
Tickets for international trains have to be bought in advance at the **Agenţie de Voiaj CFR** (☎ 432 001; Piaţa Mihai Viteazul 20; ☉ 7am-7pm Mon-Fri).

Services include one daily to Iaşi (nine hours), Târgu Mureş (2¼ hours) and Sibiu (four hours), two daily to Mangalia (13 hours), three daily to Timişoara (seven hours), six daily to Bucharest (7½ hours), nine daily to Huedin (45 to 75 minutes) and 10 daily to Oradea (2¼ to 4½ hours). Two daily trains go to Budapest (five hours).

Around Cluj-Napoca
Thirty kilometres southeast of Cluj-Napoca is **Turda**, which was the seat of the Transylvanian diet (legislative assembly) in the mid-16th century. The reason to visit Turda is strictly practical – to hike or catch a bus to **Cheile Turzii** (Turda Gorge), a short but stunning break in the limestone mountains 9km southwest.

You can hike the gorge's length in under an hour, but you can camp for a night or two to explore the surrounding network of marked trails; the map outside the Cabana Cheile Turzii's restaurant details half a dozen different routes.

A good two-hour trek is to follow the red-cross trail through the gorge, then the steep red-dot trail up and over the peak before you return to the *cabana*.

It's also possible to go all the way from Turda Gorge to Cluj-Napoca along the vertical red-stripe trail via Deleni and Camp-

ing Făget (on the outskirts of Cluj). This 29km hike will take 10 to 12 hours.

SLEEPING & EATING
You can free camp in the grassy valley at the gorge's northern end.

Otherwise, try the noisy **Cabana Cheile Turzii** (camp sites/s/d €1.50/7/9) at the southern foot of the gorge. An on-site restaurant serves simple meals. To get there, buses to Corneşti or Câmpeni stop 2km west of Mihai Viteazul village, next to the signposted turn-off for Cheile Turzii (the gorge). From here it is a 5km hike along a gravel road to the *cabana*.

GETTING THERE & AWAY
From Cluj-Napoca's Piaţa Mihai Viteazul there are seven daily buses for Turda (€1, 40 minutes). From Turda there are buses to Corneşti and less frequent ones to Câmpeni, going via the Turda Gorge turn-off. Both depart from Piaţa Republicii in the centre of the town.

CRIŞANA & BANAT

Some of the country's best-kept secrets are here: the soaring Apuseni Mountains, deep caves, gorges, waterfalls and thermal waters alongside the exquisite, crumbling architecture of the Habsburg Empire. The areas of Crişana (north of the Mureş River) and Banat (to the south) have a spirited independence found nowhere else in Romania and a sense of regional identity, ethnic diversity and European influence. It was in Timişoara that the seeds of the 1989 revolution were sewn, a fact these charming, tenacious people are mightily proud of.

Crişana and Banat once merged imperceptibly into Vojvodina (now in Serbia and Montenegro) and Hungary's Great Plain. Until 1918 all three regions were governed jointly, and although Subotica (Serbia and Montenegro), Szeged (Hungary) and Timişoara now belong to three different countries, all three cities bear the unmistakable imprint of the Habsburgs.

ORADEA
☎ 0259 / pop 223,700
Elegant Oradea lies a few kilometres east of the Hungarian border, in the centre of the

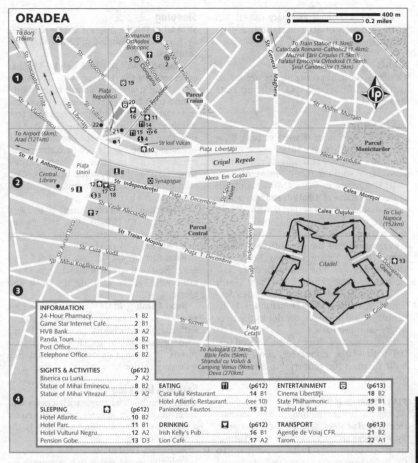

ORADEA

INFORMATION
24-Hour Pharmacy.....................1 B2
Game Star Internet Café............2 B1
HVB Bank...............................3 A2
Panda Tours...........................4 B2
Post Office.............................5 B1
Telephone Office......................6 B2

SIGHTS & ACTIVITIES (p612)
Biserica cu Lună......................7 A2
Statue of Mihai Eminescu...........8 B2
Statue of Mihai Viteazul............9 A2

SLEEPING (p612)
Hotel Atlantic.........................10 B2
Hotel Parc.............................11 B1
Hotel Vulturul Negru.................12 A2
Pension Gobe..........................13 D3

EATING (p612)
Casa Iulia Restaurant................14 B1
Hotel Atlantic Restaurant...........(see 10)
Paninoteca Faustos...................15 B2

DRINKING (p612)
Irish Kelly's Pub......................16 B1
Lion Café..............................17 A2

ENTERTAINMENT (p613)
Cinema Libertăţii.....................18 B2
State Philharmonic....................19 B1
Teatrul de Stat........................20 B1

TRANSPORT (p613)
Agenţie de Voiaj CFR.................21 B2
Tarom...................................22 A1

Crişana region, at the edge of the Carpathian Mountains.

Of all the cities of the Austro-Hungarian Empire, Oradea best retains its 19th-century romantic style. It was ceded to Romania in 1920 and has since taken on an air of faded grandeur but it is a lovely place to stop, whatever direction you're heading in.

Orientation

The train station is a couple of kilometres north of the centre; tram Nos 1 and 4 run south from Piaţa Bucureşti (outside the train station) to Piaţa Unirii, Oradea's main square. Tram No 4 also stops at the northern end of Calea Republicii, a five-minute walk south to the centre.

The main square north of the river is Piaţa Republicii (also called Piaţa Regele Ferdinand I).

Information

There's no official tourist information; instead try **Panda Tours** (☎ 477 222; Str Iosif Vulcan 6; 🕑 9am-7pm Mon-Fri, 9am-1pm Sat) which has English-speaking staff.

Cash transfer, ATMs and currency exchange facilities can be found at **HVB Bank** (☎ 406 700; Piaţa Unirii 24; 🕑 9am-4pm Mon-Fri).

There's a **post office** (☎ 136 420; Str Roman Ciorogariu 12; 🕑 7am-7.30pm Mon-Fri) and also a **telephone office** (Calea Republicii 5; 🕑 8am-8pm).

Check your email at **Game Star Internet Café** (Str Mihai Eminescu 4; per hr €0.50; 🕑 24hr).

There's a **24-hour pharmacy** (☎ 418 242) at the junction of Str Libertății and Piața Ferdinand.

Sights

Oradea's most imposing sights are on its two central squares, Piața Unirii and Piața Republicii.

PIAȚA UNIRII

The 1784 Orthodox **Biserica cu Lună** (Moon Church; Piața Unirii) has an unusual lunar mechanism on its tower that adjusts position in accordance with the moon's movement.

In the centre of Piața Unirii stands an equestrian **statue of Mihai Viteazul**, the prince of Wallachia (r 1593–1601), who is said to have rested in Oradea in 1600. East of this statue, overlooking the Crișul Repede River, you'll find the magnificent **Vulturul Negru** (Black Vulture; 1908) hotel and shopping centre. The mall with its fantastic stained-glass ceiling links Piața Unirii with Str Independenței and Str Vasile Alecsandri. A **statue of Mihai Eminescu**, the 19th-century Romantic poet, overlooks the river on its southern bank.

Further east of Piața Unirii is **Parcul Central**, with a large monument, and a citadel, built in the 13th century but since converted into government offices.

PIAȚA REPUBLICII & NORTH

Across the bridge the magnificent neoclassical **Teatrul de Stat** (State Theatre), designed by Viennese architects Fellner and Hellmer in 1900, dominates Piața Republicii. To its right begins the long, pedestrianised Calea Republicii, lined with bookshops and cafés.

Oradea's other worthy buildings are in a park a block southwest of the train station. Across the road is **Șirul Canonicilor** (Canon's Corridor), a series of archways that date back to the 18th century.

The **Catedrala Romano-Catolică** (Roman Catholic Cathedral; 1780) is the largest in Romania. The adjacent **Palatul Episcopia Ortodoxă** (Episcopal Palace; 1770), with 100 fresco-adorned rooms and 365 windows, was modelled after Belvedere Palace in Vienna. It houses the **Muzeul Țării Crișului** (Museum of the Land of the Criș Rivers; ☎ 412 725; B-dul Dacia 1-3; admission €1; 🕙 10am-5pm Tue-Sun), with history and art exhibits relevant to the region.

Sleeping

Strandul cu Voluti (cabins/camp sites per person €6/2; 🕙 May–mid-Sep) Camping in Băile 1 Mai, 9km southeast of Oradea.

Camping Venus (☎ 318 266; tents & 2-3 bed bungalows per person €10) This camping ground is 500m from Strandul cu Voluti. Take a southbound tram No 4 (black number) from the train station or an eastbound tram No 4 (red number) from Piața Unirii to the end of the line, then bus No 15 to the last stop.

Pension Gobe (☎ 414 845; Str Dobrogeanu Gherea 26; dm €12) A member of Youth Hostels România, it is the city's best budget option with three- to four-bed rooms, a small restaurant and a bar.

Hotel Vulturul Negru ('Black Vulture'; ☎ 449 259; Str Independenței 1; s/d/tr €5/10/22) Dark and slightly strange, this backpackers' institution is housed in a 1908 Art Nouveau building.

Hotel Parc (☎ 418 410; Calea Republicii 5-7; s/d €20/25) Best of the budget bunch. Ignore the crumbling façade – inside it's clean and gleaming white.

Hotel Atlantic (☎ 414 953; Str Iosif Vulcan 9; s/d €40/47) Rejoice! Classy contemporary rooms with marble bathrooms, Jacuzzis and your own private bar in its super-smart four rooms. It also has its own restaurant (see following section).

Eating & Drinking

Calea Republicii is lined with cheap and cheerful eateries and cafés. Oradeans enjoy a spot of evening strolling and this is the street to do it in.

Paninoteca Faustos (Str Republicii 3; mains €2) Watch the world go by while munching pizzas, salads and tiramisu.

Casa Iulia Restaurant (☎ 413 438; Calea Republicii 5; mains €7-10) Smart, minimalist joint with a trendy bar, and a massive outdoor terrace with live music on Thursday evening. Usual soups, salads and grilled dishes.

Hotel Atlantic Restaurant (☎ 414 953; Str Iosif Vulcan 9; mains €20) With an elegant interior, it has the best menu in town: hearty goulash, Mexican chicken, and speciality steak dishes. Sadly, there's little choice for vegetarians.

Most of Oradea's terrace cafés and restaurants double as bars in the evening.

Irish Kelly's Pub (☎ 413 419; Calea Republicii 2) Caters for a rowdy crowd in its outside terrace.

Lion Café (Str Independenței 1; 🕙 7am-1am) Trendy by day, packed by night.

Entertainment

Cinema Libertăţii (☎ 434 097; Str Independenţei 1) This highly atmospheric cinema in the Vulturul Negru building shows films in their original language with Romanian subtitles.

Tickets for performances at the **State Philharmonic** (Filarmonica de Stat; ☎ 430 853; Str Moscovei 5) can be purchased from its **ticket office** (☯ 10am-6pm Mon-Fri). The ticket office is inside the **Teatrul de Stat** (State Theatre; ☎ 130 885; Piaţa Ferdinand 4-6; ☯ 10am-11am, 5-7pm; tickets €3-12).

Getting There & Away

AIR

Tarom (☎ 131 918; Piaţa Ferdinand 2; ☯ 6.30am-8pm Mon-Fri, 10am-1pm Sat) has three flights a week to Baia Mare, daily flights to Bucharest and two weekly flights to Satu Mare from **Oradea Airport** (☎ 416 082; Calea Aradului km6). Note that Tarom accepts US dollars but not euros.

BUS

From Oradea **Autogară** (☎ 418 998; Str Râzboieni 81), south of the centre, there are daily services to Beiuş, Deva and Satu Mare. More than 20 maxitaxis run daily to and from Băile Felix.

A daily state bus runs to Budapest (€12, 10 hours) leaving from outside the train station. Purchase your ticket from the driver before departure.

Maxitaxis run daily to Budapest from outside the train station (€16 one way).

CAR & MOTORCYCLE

The border crossing into Hungary for motorists at Borş, 16km west of Oradea, is open 24 hours.

TRAIN

The **Agenţie de Voiaj CFR** (☎ 130 578; Calea Republicii 2; ☯ 7am-7pm Mon-Fri) sells advance tickets.

Daily fast trains from Oradea include three to Budapest (€28), two to Bucharest (€16), five to Băile Felix, three to Cluj-Napoca (€8), one to Braşov and three to Timişoara (€5).

TIMIŞOARA

☎ 0256 / pop 332,277

In the Banat region, tenacious Timişoara stunned the world as the birthplace of the 1989 revolution. Romania's fourth-largest city is known by residents as 'Primul Oraş Liber' (First Free Town). It was here that the Romanians' rebellious spirit flourished with the first anti-Ceauşescu protests, which prompted his fall from power. It's a city that's loved by residents and tourists alike, with a charming Mediterranean air, regal Habsburg buildings and thriving culture and sport.

Orientation

Confusingly, Timişoara-Nord (the northern train station) is west of the city centre. Walk east along B-dul Republicii to the Opera House and Piaţa Victoriei. To the north is Piaţa Libertăţii; Piaţa Unirii, the old town square, is two blocks further north. Timişoara's bus station is beside the Idsefin Market, three blocks from the train station. Take B-dul General Drăgălina south to the canal, cross the bridge and head west to the next bridge.

Information

INTERNET ACCESS

Internet Java (☎ 432 495; Str Pacha 6; per hr €0.75; ☯ 24hr) Inside the Java Coffee House.

MEDICAL SERVICES

Farmacie Remedia (B-dul Revoluţiei 1989; ☯ 7am-8pm Mon-Fri, 8am-3pm Sat)
Sensi Blu Pharmacy (☎ 406 153; Piaţa Victoriei 7; ☯ 8am-8pm Mon-Fri, 9am-8pm Sat & Sun)

MONEY

Cash travellers cheques, arrange transfers or access your decreasing funds at HVB Bank or Volksbank.
Cardinal Tourist Agency (B-dul Republicii 6; ☯ 8am-6pm Mon-Fri, 9am-1pm Sat) Has an ATM and currency exchange.
Hotel Continental (B-dul Revoluţiei 3; ☯ 8am-6pm Mon-Fri, 8am-1pm Sat) Has a currency exchange.
HVB Bank (☎ 306 800; Piaţa Victoriei 2; ☯ 9am-4pm Mon-Fri)
Volksbank (☎ 406 101; Str Piatra Craiului 2)

POST

Post office B-dul Revoluţiei (☎ 491 999; B-dul Revoluţiei 2; ☯ 8am-7pm Mon-Fri, 8am-noon Sat); Str Macieşilor (Str Macieşilor; ☯ 8am-7pm Mon-Fri) The central post office on B-dul Revoluţiei can get busy; if so, try the branch on Str Macieşilor.

TELEPHONE

Telephone office (B-dul Mihai Eminescu; ☯ 7am-9pm) Has fax facilities.

TOURIST INFORMATION

Information centre (☎ 437 973; Str Proclamatia de la Timişoara 1; ☯ 10am-8pm Tue-Sat, 10am-2pm Sun)

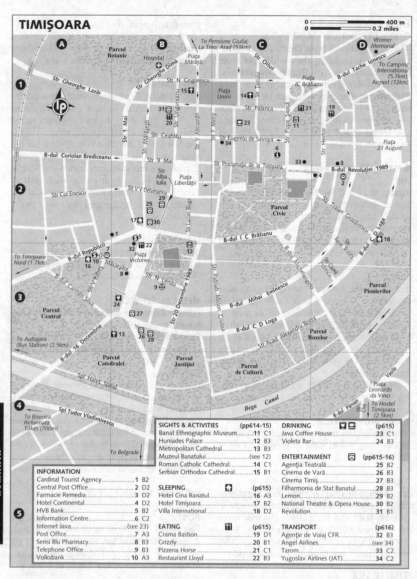

TIMIȘOARA

0 ——— 400 m
0 ——— 0.2 miles

INFORMATION	
Cardinal Tourist Agency	1 B2
Central Post Office	2 D2
Farmacie Remedia	3 D2
Hotel Continental	4 D2
HVB Bank	5 B2
Information Centre	6 C2
Internet Java	(see 23)
Post Office	7 A3
Sensi Blu Pharmacy	8 B3
Telephone Office	9 B3
Volksbank	10 A3

SIGHTS & ACTIVITIES	(pp614–15)
Banat Ethnographic Museum	11 C1
Huniades Palace	12 B3
Metropolitan Cathedral	13 B3
Muzeul Banatului	(see 12)
Roman Catholic Cathedral	14 C1
Serbian Orthodox Cathedral	15 B1

SLEEPING	(p615)
Hotel Cina Banatul	16 A3
Hotel Timișoara	17 B3
Villa International	18 D2

EATING	(p615)
Crama Bastion	19 D1
Grizzly	20 B1
Pizzeria Horse	21 C1
Restaurant Lloyd	22 B3

DRINKING	(p615)
Java Coffee House	23 C1
Violeta Bar	24 B3

ENTERTAINMENT	(pp615–16)
Agenție Teatrală	25 B2
Cinema de Vară	26 B3
Cinema Timiș	27 B3
Filharmonia de Stat Banatul	28 B3
Lemon	29 B2
National Theatre & Opera House	30 B2
Revolution	31 B1

TRANSPORT	(p616)
Agenție de Voiaj CFR	32 B3
Angel Airlines	(see 34)
Tarom	33 C2
Yugoslav Airlines (JAT)	34 C2

Timișoara boasts a brand-spanking new official information centre, where you can book canoe trips, wildlife tours or just hotels.

Sights

The centre of town is Piața Victoriei, a beautifully landscaped pedestrian mall lined with shops, cinemas and cafés, with the **National Theatre & Opera House** at its head. It was here that thousands of demonstrators gathered on 16 December 1989 (see p577), following the siege on Lászlo Tökés' house – and were promptly slaughtered. A memorial plaque on the front of the Opera House today reads: 'So you, who pass by this building, will dedicate a thought for free Romania.'

ROMANIA

Just east of the *piaţa* is the 15th-century Huniades Palace. It now houses the **Muzeul Banatului** (Banat History Museum; ☎ 491 339; Piaţa Huniade 1; admission €1; ☺ 10am-5pm), which is worth visiting. Note the column topped with the figures of Romulus and Remus, a gift from the city of Rome.

Towering over the mall's southwestern end is the 1946 Romanian Orthodox **Metropolitan Cathedral** with some unique electrical bells. Next to the cathedral is Parcul Central, and just south of it the Bega Canal runs along tree-lined banks.

The 1989 revolution began on 15 December 1989 at the **Biserica Reformată Tökés** (Tökés Reformed Church; ☎ 492 992; Str Timotei Cipariu 1), off B-dul 16 Decembrie just southeast of the centre, where Father Lászlo Tökés spoke out against the dictator.

Piaţa Libertăţii and the Primăria Veche (Old Town Hall; 1734) lie north. Piaţa Unirii is Timişoara's most picturesque square featuring a baroque 1754 **Roman Catholic Cathedral**, and the 1754 **Serbian Orthodox Cathedral**. **Banat Ethnographic Museum** (☎ 434 967; Str Ţarcului 1; admission €0.50; ☺ 10am-4pm Tue-Sun), housed in the oldest building in Timişoara, is the city's remaining 18th-century bastion.

Sleeping

Camping International (☎ 208 925; campinginternat ional@yahoo.com; Aleea Pădurea Verde 6; camp sites €2.50, 4-bed chalets with central heating €54) Nestled in the Green Wood forest on the opposite side of town from Timişoara-Nord train station. The main entrance of this excellent camping ground is on Calea Dorobanţilor. From the station catch trolleybus No 11 to the end of the line. The bus stops less than 50m from the camping ground. The site has a restaurant.

Hostel Timişoara (☎ 491 170; Str Arieş 19; dm €9) Large, super-modern building 2km from the centre. Take tram No 8 from the northern train station.

Hotel Cina Banatul (☎ 491 903; B-dul Republicii 3-5; s/d €25/30) The best-value pad with clean, ultramodern rooms and a good restaurant.

Pensiune Giulia (☎ 709 640; Str Etolia 3; s/d €24/30) Gorgeous *pension* north of the city centre with contemporary art on the walls and all the mod cons.

Hotel Timişoara (☎ 498 852, 295 278; Str 1 Mai 2; 2-star s/d €38/42, 3-star €42/52) Inside this soaring Soviet delight is a fabulously dated interior, grand comfort and a sauna and gym.

Villa International (☎ 499 339; B-dul CD Loga 48; s & d €60) Once used for the political elite, this relic of the Ceauşescu era is now a faded glory with a remarkable history.

Eating & Drinking

There are plenty of lovely terrace cafés lining Piaţ Unirii and Piaţa Victoriei where you can while away the time.

Pizzeria Horse (☎ 229 666; Str Popa Şapcă; mains €5) Slabs of mouth-watering pizza starting at €1 – bargain!

Grizzly (Str Ungureanu 7; mains €5) This cosy dark-wood bar with funky pink walls offers good choice for vegetarians with dishes such as spinach crepes, cauliflower soup and Serbian hotpot.

La Tino (☎ 226 455; Calea Aradului 14; mains €10) There's classy Italian food and scrummy pizzas at this place north of the city centre.

Crama Bastion (☎ 221 199; Str Hector 1; mains €15) Classic Romanian dishes vie with the wine list for attention in this traditional restaurant in 18th-century fortifications.

Restaurant Lloyd (☎ 294 949; Piaţa Victoriei 2; meals €30) Exquisite international/Romanian menu of shark, smoked salmon and a spit-roast joint; the cost is without wine.

Hang out with sociable locals at night in the terrace café-bars on Piaţa Victoriei, downing bottles of the local Timişoreana Pils beer for around €1 a bottle.

Violeta Bar (Piaţa Victoriei) At the southern end of the square, this bar is particularly popular.

At **Java Coffee House** (☎ 432 495; Str Pacha 6; ☺ 24hr) you can go online or just chill out with a frothy caffeine hit.

Entertainment

CINEMAS

Cinema Timis (☎ 491 290; Piaţa Victoriei 7) Movies are screened in their original language (tickets cost €1 to €3).

Cinema de Vara (B-dul CD Loga 2) Tickets at this brilliant outdoor cinema cost the same but it's far more fun!

NIGHTCLUBS

Be seen in these funky haunts:

Lemon (Str Alba Iulia 2; from ☺ 10pm) This club in the cellar of a piano bar has hip-hop and house DJs.

Revolution (Str Ungureanu 9) So trendy it hurts, this eclectic bar has techno/house DJs at weekends.

THEATRE & CLASSICAL MUSIC

Buy tickets (starting at €1) from **Agenția Teatrală** (☎ 499 908; ⏲ 10am-1pm, 5-7pm Tue-Sun) for performances at the following venues.

Filharmonia de Stat Banatul (State Philharmonic Theatre; ☎ 492 521; B-dul CD Loga 2) Classical concerts are held most evenings at this theatre. Tickets can also be bought at the box office inside the Philharmonic.

National Theatre & Opera House (Teatrul Național și Opera Română; ☎ 201 284; Str Mărășești 2) It is highly regarded.

Getting There & Away

AIR

The airport is 12km east of the centre. **Tarom** (☎ 490 150, 200 003; B-dul Revoluției 1989, 3–5; ⏲ 7am-7pm Mon-Fri, 7am-1pm Sat) has four daily flights to Bucharest (US$75 plus tax US$5; note Tarom does not accept euros) from Timișoara.

Angel Airlines (in Bucharest ☎ 021-211 1701; ticketing@angelairlines.ro; Str Eugeniu de Savoya 7) has three flights per week to Bucharest. At the same address **JAT** (Yugoslav Airlines; ☎ 495 747) runs daily international flights to Europe.

BUS

The small, shabby **Autogară** (☎ 493 471; B-dul Maniu Iuliu 54; ⏲ 6am-8pm Mon-Fri) has six platforms from where slow state buses run daily to Campeni, Arad, Sibiu and Rimincu Valcea, and one daily at 2pm to Budapest (2pm, €10). A weekly bus runs to Szeged in Hungary from *linea* 1 (platform 1). Inside the station is the **Murat office** (☎ 497 868) for buses to Istanbul. Maxitaxis run daily to Oradea, Arad, Deva and Campeni.

TRAIN

All major train services depart from **Gară Timișoara-Nord** (northern train station; ☎ 491 696; Str Gării 2). Purchase tickets in advance from the **Agenție de Voiaj CFR** (☎ 491 889; Piața Victoriei 2; ⏲ 8am-8pm Mon-Fri, 9am-7pm Mon-Fri for international tickets). Daily fast trains include eight to Bucharest (€16), one to Cluj-Napoca (€8), five to Băile Herculane (€6), one to Baia Mare via Arad (€9), three to Budapest (€38) and one to Belgrade (€14).

MARAMUREȘ

Travel no further. You've found what you were looking for. A place where rural medi-

eval life remains intact. Where peasants live off the land as their forefathers did, and generations before them. Where tiny villages, steeped in local customs and history, sit among rolling hills and dreamy landscapes. Imagine going back 100 years – welcome to Maramureș.

Idyllic, charming, harbouring memories of a forgotten time – there's simply too much to say about this world treasure. The last peasant culture in Europe is thriving here with hand-built ancient wooden churches, traditional music, colourful costumes and ancient festivals. Discovering this part of the world is a time-travel adventure. The region was effectively cut off from Transylvania by a fortress of mountains and has remained untouched by modern times. It escaped the collectivisation of the 1940s, systemisation of the '80s and the Westernisation of the '90s – and as such is living history.

SIGHETU MARMAȚIEI
☎ 0262 / pop 40,000

Sighetu Marmației practically touches the Ukrainian border as it's the northernmost town in Romania, lying on the confluence of the Tisa, Iza and Ronișoara Rivers.

Sighet (as it is known locally) is famed for its vibrant winter festival and its colourful peasant costumes. Its dusty streets bustle with markets, tucked beneath church domes of all denominations.

Information

Agro-Tur-Art (☎ 330 171; aramona@gmx.de) There's no official tourist office, but this is the region's best source of beds, books and information. In Vadu Izei (6km south), it's run by a friendly, dynamic team.

ATM (Piața Libertății 8) Outside Hotel Tisa.

Banca Română (Calea Ioan Mihaly de Apșa 24; ⏲ 9am-5pm Mon-Fri) ATM, and cash transfer and exchange facilities.

Millennium (Str Corneliu Coposu; per hr €0.20; ⏲ 10am-10pm Tue-Sat, noon-10pm Sun) Internet access.

MM Pangaea Proiect Turism (☎ 312 228; www.pangaeaturism.ro; Piața Libertății 15; ⏲ 9am-4pm Mon-Fri) Offers simple maps and group tours.

Post & telephone office (Str Ioan Mihaly de Apșa 39) Opposite the Maramureș Museum.

Sights

On Piața Libertății stands the **Hungarian Reformed Church**, built during the 15th century. Close by is the 16th-century **Roman Catholic Church**.

Nearby, the **Maramureş Museum** (Piaţa Libertăţii 15; admission €0.50; ☺ 10am-6pm Tue-Sun) displays colourful folk costumes, rugs and carnival masks.

Just off the square is Sighet's only remaining **synagogue** (Str Bessarabia 10). Before WWII there were eight synagogues serving a large Jewish community, which comprised 40% of the town's population.

The Jewish writer and 1986 Nobel Peace Prize winner, Elie Wiesel, who coined the term 'Holocaust' was born in (and later deported from) Sighet. His **house** is on the corner of Str Dragoş Vodă and Str Tudor Vladimirescu. Along Str Gheorghe Doja, there is a **monument** (Str Mureşan) to the victims of the Holocaust.

Visit traditional peasant houses from the Maramureş region at the open-air **Muzeul Satului** (Village Museum; ☎ 314 229; Str Dobăieş 40; adult/child €1/0.50; ☺ 10am-6pm Tue-Sun), southeast of Sighet's centre. Allow at least half a day to wander through the incredible constructions. Children love the wood dwellings, cobbled pathways and 'mini' villages. You can even stay overnight in tiny wooden cabins (€5.50).

Sleeping & Eating

Hotel Tisa (☎ 312 645; Piaţa Libertăţii 8; d/tr €24/36) Pleasant rooms slap-bang in the centre of Sighet. It has a passable restaurant serving traditional fodder.

Motel Buţi (☎ 311 035; Str Ştefan cel Mare 6; d/tr €25/40) Spotlessly clean but small rooms in a charming villa. Has a bar and pool table downstairs.

Getting There & Away

BUS

The **bus station** (Str Gării) is opposite the train station. There are several local buses daily to Baia Mare (€1.70, 65km), Satu Mare (€2, 122km), Borşa (€0.50), Budeşti (€0.50), Călineşti (€0.50), Vişeu de Sus (€1.20), and one bus daily to Bârsana, Botiza, Ieud and Mara.

TRAIN

Tickets are sold in advance at the **Agenţie de Voiaj CFR** (☎ 312 666; Piaţa Libertăţii 25; ☺ 7am-2pm Mon-Fri). There's one daily fast train to Timişoara (€14.50), Bucharest (€14.50, 12 hours), Cluj-Napoca (€9, six hours) and Arad (€13).

SĂPÂNŢA
☎ 0262

Săpânţa village has a unique place in the hearts of Romanians. It boasts the **'Merry Cemetery'**, famous for the colourfully painted wooden crosses that adorn the tombstones in the village's graveyard. Shown in art exhibitions across Europe, the crosses attract coachloads of visitors who marvel at the gentle humour and human warmth that created them.

Villagers seem utterly untouched by this fame. Life carries on as normal; the old women sit outside their cottages, colourful rugs are hung out on clotheslines and the odd horse and cart trundles past.

The village itself lies 12km northwest of Sighetu Marmaţiei, just 4km south of Ukraine. Find rooms at **Pensiunea Stan** (☎ 372

SIGHET PRISON

In May 1947 the Communist regime embarked on a reign of terror, slaughtering, imprisoning and torturing thousands of Romanians. While many leading prewar figures were sent to hard-labour camps, the regime's most feared intellectual opponents were interned in Sighet's maximum-security prison. Between 1948 and 1952, about 180 members of Romania's academic and government elite were imprisoned here.

Today four white marble plaques covering the barred windows of the prison list the 51 prisoners who died in the Sighet cells, notably the academic and head of the National Liberal Party (PNL), Constantin Brătianu; historian and leading member of the PNL, Gheorghe Brătianu; governor of the National Bank, Constantin Tătăranu; and Iuliu Maniu, president of the National Peasants' Party (PNŢ).

The prison, housed in the old courthouse, was closed in 1974. In 1989 it re-opened as the **Muzeu al Gândirii Arestate** (Museum of Arrested Thought; ☎ 314 224, 316 848; Str Corneliu Coposu 4; admission free; ☺ 9.30am-6.30pm, 9.30am-4.30pm 15 Oct-15 May). Photographs are displayed in the torture chambers and cells.

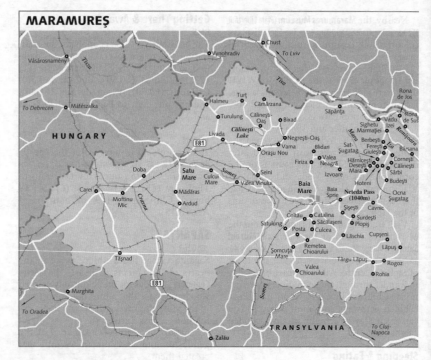

MARAMUREŞ

336; d €10), opposite the cemetery entrance, and **Pensiunea Ileana** (☎ 372 137; d €10), a green-tiled house to the right of Pensiunea Stan.

Camping Poieni (☎ 322 228; camp sites €1.50, cabins per person €3; ☯ 1 Jun-31 Aug), located 3km south of Săpânţa, and has an excellent trout restaurant.

A bus leaves for Săpânţa from Sighetu Marmaţiei every hour (8am to 2pm), returning at 4pm and 5pm.

VALEA IZEI
☎ 0262 / pop 3000

The Valea Izei (Izei Valley) follows the Iza River eastward from Sighetu Marmaţiei to Moisei. The valley is lined with small peasant villages that are renowned for their elaborately carved wooden gates and tall wooden churches.

Tourism is gradually developing in this region, providing visitors with the opportunity to sample traditional cuisine or try their hand at woodcarving, wool weaving and glass painting.

In mid-July, Vadu Izei, together with the neighbouring villages of Botiza and Ieud, hosts the **Maramuzical Festival**, a lively four-day international folk music festival. Guests stay in local homes or in tents.

Vadu Izei
Vadu Izei is at the confluence of the Iza and Mara Rivers, 6km south of Sighetu Marmaţiei.

Fundaţia OVR Agro-Tur-Art (☎ 330 171; www.va duizei.ovr.ro; house No 161) is an unrivalled source of local information and has rooms for rent in private homes (€13 to €17). **Nicolae Prisăcaru** (☎ 0721 046 730) or lovely **Ramona Ardelean** (☎ 0744 827 829) arrange excellent guided tours (in French or English, €12/20 per half/full day plus €0.25 per kilometre), as well as picnics, woodcarving or icon-painting workshops, and homestays.

Bârsana
From Vadu Izei continue southeast for 12km to Bârsana. Dating from 1326, the village acquired its first church in 1720 (its interior paintings were done by local artists). The Orthodox **Bârsana Monastery** is a popular pilgrimage spot in Maramureş. It was the

last Orthodox monastery to be built in the region before Serafim Petrovai, head of the Orthodox church in Maramureş, converted to Greco-Catholicism in 1711.

Maria Paşca (☎ 331 165; house No 377; bed/bed & full-board €10/17) has rooms to rent at her home.

Rozavlea

Continue south though Strâmtura to Rozavlea, first documented under the name of Gorzohaza in 1374. Its fine **church**, dedicated to the archangels Michael and Gabriel, was built between 1717 and 1720 in another village, then erected in Rozavlea on the site of an ancient church destroyed by the Tatars.

Botiza

From Rozavlea continue south for 3km to Şieu, then turn off for Botiza. Botiza's **old church**, built in 1694, is overshadowed by the large **new church** constructed in 1974 to serve the 500 or so devout Orthodox families.

Opération Villages Roumains (OVR) runs an efficient agrotourism scheme in Botiza. Bookings can be made with local representative **George Iurca** (☎ 334 110, 0722 942

140; botizavr@sintec.ro; house No 742; ☑ 8am-10pm). George also runs German-, French- and English-speaking tours of Maramureş (€10 to €15 per day) and Transylvania, rents out mountain bikes (€5 per day) and organises fishing trips.

Ieud

The oldest wooden church in Maramureş, dating from 1364, is in Ieud, 6km south of the main road from Şieu. Ieud was first documented in 1365. Its fabulous Orthodox '**Church on the Hill**' was built from fir wood and used to house the first document known to be written in Romanian (1391–92), in which the catechism and church laws pertaining to Ieud were coded. The church was restored in 1958 and in 1997.

Ieud's second **church**, Greco-Catholic, was built in 1717. It is unique to the region as it has no porch. At the southern end of the village it houses one of the largest collections of icons on glass found in Maramureş.

OVR runs a small agrotourism scheme in Ieud. You can make advance bookings through the office in Vadu Izei (p618) or go straight to local representatives **Chindis Dumitru** (☎ 336 100; bed €17), **Liviu Ilea** (☎ 336 039; house No 333) or **Vasile Rişco** (☎ 336 019; house No 705; half-/full-board €12/15).

Moisei

Moisei lies 7km northeast of Săcel, at the junction of route 17C and route 18. A small town at the foot of the Rodna Massif, Moisei is known for its traditional crafts and customs. It gained fame in 1944 when retreating Hungarian (Horthyst) troops gunned down 31 people before setting fire to the village.

In 1944, following the news that the front was approaching Moisei, villagers started to flee, including those forced-labour detachments stationed in the village. Occupying Hungarian forces organised a manhunt to track down the deserters. Thirty-one were captured and detained in a small camp in nearby Vişeu de Sus without food or water for three weeks. On 14 October 1944 Hungarian troops brought the 31 prisoners to a house in Moisei, locked them inside, then shot them through the windows – 29 were killed. Before abandoning the village, the troops set it on fire, leaving all 125 remaining families homeless.

ROMANIA

Only one house in Moisei survived the blaze: the one in which the prisoners were shot. Today it houses a small **museum** in tribute to those who died in the massacre. Opposite, on a hillock above the road and railway line, is a circular **monument** to the victims. The 12 upright columns symbolise sun and light. Each column is decorated with a traditional carnival mask, except for two that bear human faces based on the features of the two survivors.

The museum and monument are at the eastern end of the village. If the museum is locked, knock at the house next door and ask for the key.

BORŞA
☎ 0262

Ore has been mined at Borşa, 12km east of Moisei, since the mid-14th century. The area was colonised in 1777 by German miners from Slovakia; later, Bavarian-Austrian miners moved to Baia Borşa, 2km northeast of the town, to mine copper, lead and silver.

The **Complex Turistic Borşa**, a small ski resort and tourist complex 10km east of Borşa town, is a main entry point to the **Rodna Mountains**, part of which form the Pietrosul Rodnei Nature Reservation (5900 hectares). For useful information on the hiking trails leading into the massif talk to staff at the two-star **Hotel Cerbal** (☎ 344 199; Str Fântâna; s/d/tr incl breakfast €18/22/30).

In winter, you can ski down the 2030m-long ski run at the complex. There's a **ski lift** (Str Brădet 10; ☼ 7am-6pm), but ski hire is not available.

PRISLOP PASS

Famed for its remoteness, the Prislop Pass is the main route from Maramureş into Moldavia. Hikers can trek east from Borşa across the pass. From Moldavia you can head northeast to Câmpulung Moldovenesc and on to the monasteries of southern Bucovina; or south to the natural mineral waters of Vatra Dornei and through to the fantastic Bicaz Lake.

At 1416m a roadside monument marks the site of the last Tartar invasion prior to their final flight from the region in 1717. Nearby is the Hanul Prislop, site of the Hora de la Prislop, the major Maramureş festival, held yearly on the second Sunday in August.

MOLDAVIA

With its forest-clad hills and tranquil valleys, Moldavia rivals Transylvania when it comes to natural beauty, rich folklore and turbulent history. Yet the capital of Iaşi has enough urban pleasures to keep you on your toes or relaxing in chill-out lounges.

IAŞI
☎ 0232 / pop 348,700

Iaşi (pronounced yash) earns its love and respect slowly. Iaşi's past as Moldavia's capital has resulted in a city dotted with fabulous buildings, important monasteries and bust-lined streets and parks; yet in between are grey, oppressive concrete blocks.

Iaşi served as the national capital from 1859 until it was replaced by Bucharest in 1862. Iaşi has a great cultural tradition; the linden tree under which poet Mihai Eminescu meditated and the memorial houses of the city's most prolific writers remain powerful reminders of this city's literary past.

The streets of modern Iaşi bustle with student life, restaurants, bars and hot night spots.

Orientation

To reach Piaţa Unirii from Iaşi's Gară Centrală train station, walk northeast along Str Gării two blocks, then turn right onto Şos Arcu. From Piaţa Unirii, B-dul Ştefan cel Mare şi Sfânt runs southeast past the Mitropolia Moldovei (Moldavian Metropolitan Cathedral) to the Palatul Culturii (Palace of Culture).

Information
INTERNET ACCESS
Discovery (B-dul Ştefan cel Mare şi Sfânt 1; per hr €0.40; ☼ 8am-4am)
Take Net (Şos Arcu 1; per hr €0.40; ☼ 24hr)

MEDICAL SERVICES
Servicii Medicale Mobile (☎ 0722 376 370, 233 300) Offers 24-hour emergency service.
Sfântu Spiridon University Hospital (☎ 210 690; B-dul Independenţei 1) The city's largest, most central hospital.

MONEY
Banca Comercială Română (B-dul Ştefan cel Mare şi Sfânt 6; ☼ 8.30am-3pm Mon-Fri)

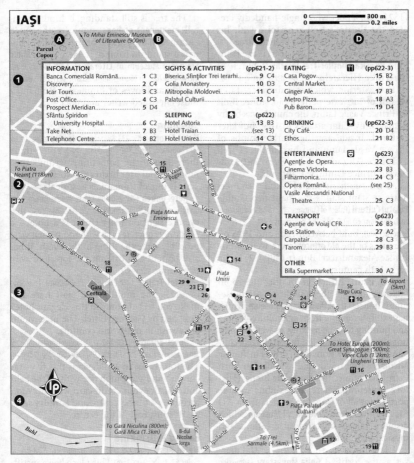

IAŞI

INFORMATION
Banca Comercială Română........... 1 C3
Discovery.. 2 C4
Icar Tours....................................... 3 C3
Post Office...................................... 4 C3
Prospect Meridian.......................... 5 D4
Sfântu Spiridon
University Hospital....................... 6 C2
Take Net... 7 B3
Telephone Centre........................... 8 B2

SIGHTS & ACTIVITIES (pp621-2)
Biserica Sfinţilor Trei Ierarhi........... 9 C4
Golia Monastery............................ 10 D3
Mitropolia Moldovei...................... 11 C4
Palatul Culturii.............................. 12 D4

SLEEPING (p622)
Hotel Astoria................................. 13 B3
Hotel Traian..............................(see 13)
Hotel Unirea................................. 14 C3

EATING (pp622-3)
Casa Pogov.................................... 15 B2
Central Market............................... 16 D4
Ginger Ale..................................... 17 B3
Metro Pizza................................... 18 A3
Pub Baron..................................... 19 D4

DRINKING (pp622-3)
City Café.. 20 D4
Ethos... 21 B2

ENTERTAINMENT (p623)
Agenţie de Opera........................... 22 C3
Cinema Victoria............................. 23 B3
Filharmonica.................................. 24 C3
Opera Română...........................(see 25)
Vasile Alecsandri National
Theatre.. 25 C3

TRANSPORT (p623)
Agenţie de Voiaj CFR..................... 26 B3
Bus Station.................................... 27 A2
Carpatair....................................... 28 C3
Tarom.. 29 B3

OTHER
Billa Supermarket.......................... 30 A2

POST
Post office (☎ 212 222; Str Cuza Vodă 10; ⏰ 7am-7pm Mon-Fri, 8am-noon Sat)

TELEPHONE
Telephone centre (Str Alexandru Lăpuşneanu; ⏰ 8am-8pm Mon-Fri, 8am-3pm Sat)

TOURIST INFORMATION
Iaşi has no official tourist office.

Icar Tours (☎ 216 319; www.icar.ro; B-dul Ştefan cel Mare şi Sfânt 8, basement; ⏰ 9am-6pm Mon-Fri) These are particularly helpful folk; they can help you rent the least expensive cars in town and book accommodation.

Prospect Meridan (☎ 211 060; Str Sfântu Lazar 24; ⏰ 9am-6pm Mon-Fri) Antrec agents arrange rural accommodation, city tours and trips to the Bucovina monasteries.

Sights
B-DUL ŞTEFAN CEL MARE ŞI SFÂNT & AROUND
Start your city tour on Piaţa Unirii, the main square, with a trip to the 13th floor of **Hotel Unirea** for a bird's-eye view of Iaşi.

Eastwards the tree-lined B-dul Ştefan cel Mare şi Sfânt leads to the **Mitropolia Moldovei** (Moldavian Metropolitan Cathedral; 1833–39) with a cavernous interior painted by Gheorghe Tattarescu. In mid-October thousands of pilgrims flock here to celebrate the day of St Paraschiva, the patron saint of the cathedral and of Moldavia.

Opposite is a park and at the northeastern end is the **National Theatre** (1894–96). In front of it is a statue of its founder Vasile Alecsandri

ROMANIA

(1821–90), a poet who single-handedly created the theatre's first repertoire with his Romanian adaptation of a French farce.

The boulevard's shining pearl is the fabulous **Biserica Sfinţilor Trei Ierarhi** (Church of the Three Hierarchs; 1637–39), unique for its rich exterior, which is embroidered in a wealth of intricate patterns in stone. Built by Prince Vasile Lupu, the church was badly damaged by Tatar attacks in 1650 but later restored. Inside are the marble tombs of Prince Vasile Lupu and his family, as well as Prince Alexandru Ioan Cuza and Moldavian prince Dimitrie Cantemir.

At the southern end of B-dul Ştefan cel Mare şi Sfânt stands the giant neo-Gothic **Palatul Culturii** (Palace of Culture; ☎ 218 383; adult/child each museum €0.60/0.30, all 4 museums €2/1; ☺ 10am-5pm Tue-Sun), built between 1906 and 1925 on the ruins of the **old princely court**, founded by Prince Alexandru cel Bun (r 1400–32) in the early 15th century.

The main attraction of the 365-room building today is the four first-class museums it houses: the **Ethnographic Museum**, which has exhibits ranging from agriculture, fishing and hunting to wine making, as well as traditional costumes and rugs; the **Art Museum** containing works by Romanian artists including Nicolae Grigorescu and Moldavian-born Petre Achiţemie; the **Muzeul de Istorie** (History Museum), where the exhibits include portraits of all of Romania's rulers from AD 81; and the **Science & Technical Museum** which displays various mechanical creations and musical instruments.

A few blocks north, past the central market, is the fortified **Golia Monastery** (admission free; Str Cuza Vodă), which was built in a late-Renaissance style. The monastery's walls and the 30m Golia tower at the entrance shelter a 17th-century church, noted for its vibrant Byzantine frescoes and intricately carved doorways.

PARCUL COPOU

To get to **Parcul Copou** (Copou Park; laid out between 1834 and 1848) catch the No 1 or 13 tram north from Piaţa Unirii. The park, which was established during the princely reign of Mihail Sturza, is famed as being a favourite haunt of poet Mihai Eminescu (1850–89). He allegedly wrote some of his best works beneath his favourite linden tree in this park.

The tree is still standing, behind a 13m-tall **monument of lions**, opposite the main entrance to the park. A bronze bust of Eminescu stands in front of it. Here is the **Mihai Eminescu Museum of Literature** (☎ 344 759; admission €0.20; ☺ 10am-5pm Tue-Sun), which recalls the life and loves of Eminescu, Romania's most cherished writer and poet.

Sleeping

Hotel Astoria (☎ 233 888; reservation@hotelastoria.ro; Str Lăpuşeanu 1; s/d/ste €18/26/35; ☒) You'd think there had to be something wrong: such modern, four-star luxury at two-star prices. This is one of Romania's best deals.

Hotel Unirea (☎ 240 404; office@hotelunirea.ro; Piaţa Unirii 5; s/d €26/30, unrenovated s/d €22/26) Yes, that eyesore right on Piaţa Unirii is a hotel – a 13-storey concrete blob with rooms that were probably quite the thing in the 1960s. It has a restaurant and café on the top floor with panoramic views.

Hotel Traian (☎ 266 666; Piaţa Unirii 1; s/d/ste €49/69/85) The multilingual staff here will make you feel at home in this elegant hotel, designed by Gustave Eiffel. The nice rooms are awash in old-world comfort.

Hotel Europa (☎ 242 000; www.hoteleuropa.ro; Str Anastasie Panu 26; s/d/ste €95/120/200; ☒ ☒ ▢) The top choice in Moldavia is this five-star chrome-and-glass high rise with all the bells and whistles your credit card will allow for, including a fitness centre and laundry service. It's just east of the centre.

Eating & Drinking

Metro Pizza (☎ 276 040; Str Străpungere Silvestru 8; mains €2-3; ☺ 9am-1am) This place has a justifiably good reputation among students for its great pizzas and the 50% discounts on some meals at weekends.

Pub Baron (☎ 206 076; Str Sfântu Lazăr 52; mains €2-4; ☺ 24hr) Cosy wooden interiors and a great eating option. They're heavy on fresh grills, cooked in brick ovens in the dining room, but there are many salads and fish dishes too.

Casa Pogov (☎ 243 006; Str Vasile Pogov 4; mains €2-4; ☺ 11am-midnight) Where to sit? In the insanely cosy (if damp) basement that used to house the famed Junimea wine cellar, the elegant main dining hall furnished with antiques or on the multi-tiered terrace looking out onto a quiet square? Iaşi's most pleasant restaurant also has vegetarian choices.

Ginger Ale (☎ 276 017; Str Săulescu 23; mains €2-5; ☯ 11am-1am) Advertised as an Irish-style pub/restaurant, this place feels more like an oversized, old-fashioned café with its antique furniture and cosy dining room. A great place for drinks or a full meal, this fun place also offers 20% to 50% discounts daily from noon to 4pm.

Trei Sarmale (☎ 237 255; Str Bucium 52; mains €2-5; ☯ 9am-2am) This traditional Romanian restaurant teeters on the edge of kitsch with it's folkier-than-thou décor, but the food is mouthwatering. Check before you head out there as it is often booked by tour groups. Take a €2 taxi or bus No 30 or 46 from Piaţa Mihai Eminescu and get off at the Bucium stop.

Ethos (Piaţa Mihai Eminescu; ☯ 9am-4am) Located inside the Student Cultural House, this is a fun pub to hang out for a beer or snack. There's usually a live rock band Thursday night.

City Café (Str Sfântu Lazăr 34; ☯ 11am-1am) This is where Iaşi's beautiful, moneyed people come for relaxed posing sessions. A high-tech, blue-lit, ultracool bar, it's known for its many cocktails.

The indoor **central market** (☯ 8am-4pm) is great for fresh fruit and vegetables. It has entrances on Str Costache Negri and Str Anastasie Panu.

Entertainment

Viper Club (Iulius Mall; ☯ 24hr, disco 11pm-4am) This entertainment emporium about a kilometre out of the centre features bowling alleys, billiards and video games, and turns itself into a House-music haven come night-time.

Cinema Victoria (☎ 312 502; Piaţa Uniiri 5) See your favourite Hollywood schlockbuster with Romanian subtitles here!

Filarmonica (Philharmonic; ☎ 212 509; Str Cuza Vodă 29; box office ☯ 10am-1pm & 5-7pm Mon-Fri) When the much-revered Iaşi State Philharmonic Orchestra is in town, its concerts are massively popular. Tickets cost from €2 with 50% student discounts.

Vasile Alecsandri National Theatre (☎ 316 778; Str Agatha Bârsescu 18) and the **Opera Română** (☎ 211 144) are located in the same impressive neobaroque building. For advance bookings go to the **Agenţia de Opera** (☎ 316 070; B-dul Ştefan cel Mare şi Sfânt 8; ☯ 9am-1pm & 3-5pm Mon-Fri). Tickets cost from €1.50, with 50% student discounts.

Getting There & Away

AIR

Tarom (☎ 267 768; Şos Arcu 3-5; ☯ 8am-6pm Mon-Fri, 8am-noon Sat) has 10 weekly flights to Bucharest (about €90). **Carpatair** (☎ 215 295; www .carpatair.com; Str Cuza Voda 2; ☯ 9am-5pm Mon-Fri) flies to Timişoara. **Angel Airlines** (☎ 270 457; ticketing@angelairlines.ro), whose office is at the airport, flies seven times weekly to Bucharest (Baneasa Airport; about €70) and three times weekly to Suceava (about €20).

BUS

The central **bus station** (☎ 214 720), off Şos Arcu, has four daily maxitaxis each to Târgu Neamţ (€1.60) and Suceava, eight to Bucharest, 18 to Bacau and almost 20 to Piatra Neamţ. Slower buses run to Vatra Dornei, Tulcea and Braşov.

Maxitaxis to Chişinău (€5) leave from outside the Billa supermarket three to four times daily while up to six daily (slower) buses to Chişinău depart from the bus station.

TRAIN

Nearly all trains arrive and depart from the Gară Centrală (also called Gară Mare and Gară du Nord) on Str Garii. Trains to Chişinău depart from the Gară Niculina (also called Gară International) on B-dul Nicolae Iorga about 800m south of the centre, and tickets for the trip must be bought from Gară Mică (the one with the sign saying 'Niculina' on it!), 500m south on Aleea Nicolina. The **Agenţie de Voiaj CFR** (☎ 247 673; Piaţa Unirii 10; ☯ 8am-8pm Mon-Fri) sells advance tickets.

There are five daily trains to Bucharest (€7, seven hours), and one service daily to each of Oradea, Galaţi, Timişoara and Mangalia.

SOUTHERN BUCOVINA

Southern Bucovina is a rural paradise as magical and deeply revered as Maramureş. Its painted churches are among the greatest artistic monuments of Europe – in 1993 they were collectively designated World Heritage sites by Unesco. Apart from religious art and fantastic churches, southern Bucovina is well worth visiting for its folklore, picturesque villages, bucolic scenery and colourful inhabitants, all as memorable as you'll find elsewhere in Romania.

ROMANIA

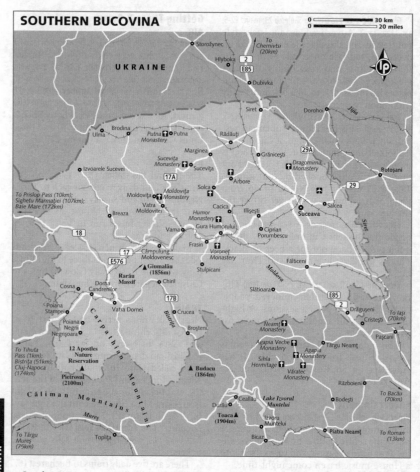

SOUTHERN BUCOVINA

Southern Bucovina embraces the north-western region of present-day Moldavia; northern Bucovina is in Ukraine.

SUCEAVA

☎ 0230 / pop 117,200

Suceava, the capital of Moldavia from 1388 to 1565, was a thriving commercial centre on the Lviv–Istanbul trading route. Today it's the seat of Suceava County and gateway to the painted churches of Bucovina.

Orientation

Piaţa 22 Decembrie is the centre of town. Suceava has two train stations, Suceava and Suceava Nord, both north of the city centre and easily reached by trolleybus.

From Suceava station, cross the street, buy a ticket at a kiosk and take trolleybus No 2 or 3 to the centre of town. From Suceava Nord take trolleybus No 5.

Information
INTERNET ACCESS

Assist (☎ 523 044; Piaţa 22 Decembrie; per hr €0.50; ☺ 9am-11pm)

Calculatore (☎ 524 795; Str Curtea Domnească 9; per hr €0.40; ☺ 10am-midnight)

MONEY

There are several ATMs on Piaţa 22 Decembrie and along Str Ştefan cel Mare.

Banca Comercială Română (Str Ştefan cel Mare 31; ☺ 8.30am-2pm Mon-Fri)

POST

Post office (☎ 512 222; Str Dimitrie Onciul; ⏲ 7am-7pm Mon-Fri, 8am-4pm Sat)

TELEPHONE

Telephone centre (cnr Str Nicolae Bălcescu & Str Firmu; ⏲ 7am-9pm Mon-Fri, 8am-4pm Sat)

TOURIST INFORMATION

There's no official tourist information centre but these may help:

Central Turism (☎ 523 024; central@suceava.iiruc.ro; Str Nicolae Bălcescu 2; ⏲ 8am-4pm Mon-Fri, 8am-1pm Sat) Inside Hotel Suceava, this small office can arrange day-long monastery tours with multilingual guides for about €60.

Ciprian Şlenku (☎ 0744 292 588; monasterytour@yahoo .com) This highly recommended private tour guide is a specialist in both religion and history and therefore a perfect person to visit the monasteries with. He's also a can-do kind of guy and arranges tours to suit your schedule.

Icar Tours (☎ 524 894; www.icar.ro; Str Ştefan cel Mare 24; ⏲ 9am-6pm Mon-Fri, 9am-1pm Sat) This helpful bunch specialises in monastery tours (€40 to €70 including car and driver; €15 extra for a guide) but they also arrange trips throughout the country, book air tickets and can arrange rural homestays in the villages near the monasteries.

Sights

The bulky **Casa de Cultură** (House of Culture) is at the western end of Piaţa 22 Decembrie, the city's main square. West of Piaţa 22 Decembrie is Hanul Domnesc, a 16th-century guesthouse that now houses an **Ethnographic Museum** (☎ 214 081; Str Ciprian Porumbescu 5; adult/

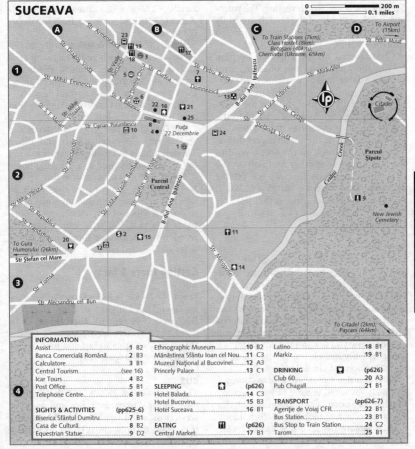

SUCEAVA

0 — 200 m
0 — 0.1 miles

INFORMATION	
Assist..1	B2
Banca Comercială Română.................2	B3
Calculatore......................................3	B1
Central Turism............................(see 16)	
Icar Tours..4	B2
Post Office.......................................5	B1
Telephone Centre.............................6	B1

SIGHTS & ACTIVITIES	(pp625-6)
Biserica Sfântul Dumitru....................7	B1
Casa de Cultură...............................8	B2
Equestrian Statue.............................9	D2

Ethnographic Museum.....................10	B2
Mănăstirea Sfântu Ioan cel Nou.......11	C3
Muzeul Naţional al Bucovinei...........12	A3
Princely Palace................................13	C1

SLEEPING	(p626)
Hotel Balada..................................14	C3
Hotel Bucovina...............................15	B1
Hotel Suceava................................16	B1

EATING	(p626)
Central Market................................17	B1

Latino..18	B1
Markiz..19	B1

DRINKING	(p626)
Club 60..20	A3
Pub Chagall....................................21	B1

TRANSPORT	(pp626-7)
Agenţie de Voiaj CFR.......................22	B1
Bus Station.....................................23	B1
Bus Stop to Train Station.................24	C2
Tarom..25	B1

ROMANIA

child €0.80/0.40; 9am-5pm Tue-Sun), with a good collection of folk costumes.

North of the bus stop along B-dul Ana Ipătescu lie the foundations of the 15th-century **Princely Palace**. To the west is **Biserica Sfântul Dumitru** (St Dimitru's church; 1535) built by Petru Rareş.

Return to Piața 22 Decembrie and follow Str Ştefan cel Mare south past Parcul Central (Central Park) to the informative **Muzeul Național al Bucovinei** (Bucovina History Museum; ☎ 216 439; Str Ştefan cel Mare 33; adult/child €0.80/0.40; 10am-6pm Tue-Sun). The presentation comes to an abrupt end at 1945 and old paintings now hang in rooms that formerly glorified the communist era.

The **Mănăstirea Sfântu Ioan cel Nou** (Monastery of St John the New; 1522), off Str Mitropoliei, is well worth visiting. The paintings on the outside of the church are badly faded, but they give you an idea of the painted churches that Bucovina is famous for.

Continue on Str Mitropoliei, keeping left on the main road out of town, until you see a large wooden gate marked 'Parcul Cetatii' on the left. Go through it and, when the path divides, follow the footpath with the park benches around to the left to the huge **equestrian statue** (1966) of the Moldavian leader, Ştefan cel Mare. Twenty metres back on the access road to the monument is another footpath on the left, which descends towards the **Cetatea de Scaun** (City of Residence; adult/child €0.25/0.15; 9am-6pm), a citadel fortress that held off Mehmed II, conqueror of Constantinople (Istanbul) in 1476.

Sleeping

Class Hostel (☎ 525 213; www.classhostel.home.ro; Str Aurel Vlaicu 195; per person €13) This hostel is on the edge of the city, but you'll feel as if you're in the country in this peaceful, spacious and ultra-modern two-floor house. Monica, your interminably good-natured host, can arrange monastery tours if you like, or show you around the city too. It's a super-friendly hostel, one of the country's best, 1km west of Gară de Nord.

Hotel Bucovina (☎ 217 048; B-dul Ana Ipătescu 5; s/d €16/21) Favoured among those searching for clues to Romania's communist past, this 11-storey concrete blob is a 1960s holdout.

Hotel Suceava (☎ 521 079; Str Bălcescu 2; s €17, d €24-32) This is your best bet in town for the

price. Smack in the city centre and featuring old-fashioned but perfectly comfortable rooms (the more expensive ones have been renovated somewhat), this a very pleasant place.

Hotel Balada (☎ 520 408; www.balada.ro; Str Mitropoliei 3; s/d/ste €50/60/95;) One of the top hotels in the region, this three-storey hotel offers elegance and comfort over pure luxury; rooms have everything you need but are simply furnished. It's on a lovely, quiet street.

Eating & Drinking

Latino (☎ 523 627; Str Curtea Domnească 9; mains €2-8; 11am-midnight) The classy, subdued décor is accentuated by impeccable service and a dazzlingly varied menu that runs the gamut from over 25 kinds of pizza (with real mozzarella!; €1.60 to €3), a dozen first-rate pasta dishes (€2.50) and steaming, fresh fish dishes (€3 to €8).

Markiz (☎ 520 219; Str Vasile Alecsandri 10; mains €1-3; 8am-11pm) On offer here are succulent meat and aubergine dishes, humus, salads and kebabs, all deliciously spiced (spices! imagine!); their pastry shop has sinful desserts.

The **central market** (cnr Str Petru Rareş & Str Avram Iancu) is close to the bus station.

Pub Chagall (☎ 0723 961 127; Str Ştefan cel Mare; 11am-1am) Cosy cellar pub and diner. Though it has a full menu of tasty meals (€1 to €3), it's mostly used as a drinking hole.

Club 60 (☎ 209 440; Str Ştefan cel Mare; 1pm-1am) Enter here at your own risk: you may never want to leave! Emanating some of the smoothest vibes of any club in the country is this vast, loft-style lounge/bar with wooden floors, antique furnishings, comfy sofas and billiard tables.

Getting There & Away

AIR

Tarom (☎ 214 686; Str Nicolae Bălcescu 2; 8.30am-5pm Mon-Fri) has a flight four times weekly to Bucharest (€99 return). **Angel Airlines** (in Bucharest ☎ 021-211 1701; ticketing@angelairlines.ro) has three weekly flights to Iaşi and four weekly to Bucharest (Baneasa Airport).

BUS

The **bus station** (☎ 216 089) is in the centre of town at Str Armenească. Bus and maxitaxi services include 13 daily to Gura Humorului (€1), eight to Botoşani (€1), six to Rădăuți (€1), five to Iaşi (€3) and Vatra Dornei

(€4.50), four to Bucharest (€8) and three to Târgu Neamţ (€2). Five daily buses go to Chernivtsi (Cernăuţi) in Ukraine (€4) and three a week to Chişinău in Moldova (€7).

TRAIN

The **Agenţie de Voiaj CFR** (☎ 214 335; Str Nicolae Bălcescu 8; ⊗ 7.30am-8pm Mon-Fri) sells advance tickets. Trains which originate or terminate in Suceava arrive/depart at Suceava Nord. Trains which transit Suceava arrive/depart from Suceava (Gară Burdujeni).

Train service includes nine to Gură Humorului (€1.50, 70 minutes), seven to Vatra Dornei (€5, 3¼ hours), three to Iaşi (€3, 2½ hours) and Timişoara (€13, 13½ hours) and one daily to Bucharest (€11, seven hours). To get to Moldoviţa, change at Vama.

BUCOVINA MONASTERIES

☎ 0230

Voroneţ

The *Last Judgment* fresco, which fills the entire western wall of the **Voroneţ Monastery** (adult/child €1/0.50; ⊗ 8am-8pm) is perhaps the most marvellous Bucovine fresco. At the top, angels roll up the signs of the zodiac to indicate the end of time. The middle fresco shows humanity being brought to judgment. On the left, St Paul escorts the believers, while on the right Moses brings forward the nonbelievers. Below is the *Resurrection*.

On the northern wall is *Genesis,* from Adam and Eve to Cain and Abel. The southern wall features a tree of Jesse (see p628 for details of the Suceviţa Jesse tree) with the genealogy of biblical personalities. In the vertical fresco to the left is the story of the martyrdom of St John of Suceava (who is buried in the Monastery of Sfântu Ioan cel Nou in Suceava). The vibrant, almost satiny blue pigment used throughout the frescoes is known worldwide as 'Voroneţ blue'.

In the narthex likes the tomb of Daniel the Hermit, the first abbot of Voroneţ Monastery. It was upon the worldly advice of Daniel, who told Ştefan cel Mare not to give up his battle against the Turks, that the Moldavian prince went on to win further victories against the Turks and then to build Voroneţ Monastery out of gratitude to God.

In 1785 the occupying Austrians forced Voroneţ's monks to abandon the monastery. Since 1991 the monastery has been inhabited by a small community of nuns.

SLEEPING & EATING

The town of Gura Humorlui is a perfect base to visit Voroneţ. Every second house takes in tourists. The usual rate per person per night in a so-called 'vila' is about €13. There's wild camping possible on the south bank of the Moldova River only 500m south of the bus station; follow the only path and cross the river.

Vila Simeria (☎ 230 746; Str Ana Ipătescu 19; d per person €13) Just 200m from the main post office in Gura Humorlui on a quiet side street is this modern, impeccably clean and pleasant two-storey villa.

Vila Ramona (☎ 232 133; Str Oborlui 6; s/d €14/20) A finely furnished home some 300m east of the bus and train station, this place also has a sauna.

Casa Elena (☎ 230 651; www.casaelena.ro; s/d €30/35) A 3.5km trip from Gura Humorlui on the northern edge of Voroneţ Monastery, this four-star option has 31 rooms in five different villas all in a large, luxurious complex.

GETTING THERE & AWAY

See p628 for bus and train services from Suceava to Gura Humorului. There are buses on weekdays from Gura Humorului to Voroneţ, departing at 7am, 12.30pm and 2.45pm. A lovely option is to walk the 4km along a narrow village road to Voroneţ. The route is clearly marked and it is impossible to get lost.

Humor

Of all the Bucovina monasteries, **Humor Monastery** (Mănăstirea Humorului; adult/child €0.40/0.20; ⊗ 8am-8pm) has the most impressive interior frescoes.

On the church's southern exterior wall (AD 1530) the 1453 siege of Constantinople is depicted, with the parable of the return of the prodigal son beside it. On the porch is the *Last Judgment* and, in the first chamber inside the church, scenes of martyrdom.

Aside from hitching a ride the 6km from Gura Humorlui, there are regular maxitaxis which depart next to the towering Best Western Hotel, at the start of the road towards the monastery.

Moldoviţa

Moldoviţa Monastery (adult/child €0.40/0.20; ⊗ 10am-6pm) is in the middle of a quaint village. It's a fortified enclosure with towers and brawny

ROMANIA

gates, and a magnificent painted church at its centre. The monastery has undergone careful restoration in recent years.

The fortifications here are actually more impressive than the frescoes. On the church's southern exterior wall is a depiction of the defence of Constantinople in AD 626 against Persians dressed as Turks, while on the porch is a representation of the *Last Judgment*, all on a background of blue. Inside the sanctuary, on a wall facing the original carved iconostasis, is a portrait of Prince Petru Rareş (Moldoviţa's founder) and his family offering the church to Christ. All these works date from 1537. In the monastery's small museum is Petru Rareş' original throne.

SLEEPING & EATING

See www.ruraltourism.ro for some great places to stay in Vama, a small village 14km south of Moldoviţa on the main Suceava–Vatra Dornei road.

Mărul de Aur (☎ 336 180; d & tr per person €7.50) Located between the train station and the monastery, this place has tired rooms. Downstairs is a restaurant serving basic meals and beer 24 hours. The complex also operates a **camping ground** (camp sites/cabins free/€3.50), 3km out of town on the road to Suceviţa.

Casa Alba (☎ 340 404; www.casa-alba.suceava.ro; Vama 5969; s/d/ste €39/46/64) You certainly won't feel a monastic asceticism in this lush, ultramodern and very comfortable villa. Follow the one road heading south 5km west of Frasin about 3km east of Vama.

GETTING THERE & AWAY

Moldoviţa Monastery is right above Vatra Moldoviţei's train station (be sure to get off at Vatra Moldoviţei, not Moldoviţa). From Suceava there are nine daily trains to Vama (1¼ hours), and from Vama three trains leave daily for Vatra Moldoviţei (35 minutes).

Suceviţa

Suceviţa (adult/child €0.40/0.20; ☒ 8am-8pm) is perhaps the largest and finest of the Bucovina monasteries.

The church inside the fortified quadrangular enclosure (built between 1582 and 1601) is almost completely covered in frescoes. As you enter you first see the *Virtuous Ladder* fresco covering most of the northern exterior wall, which depicts the 30 steps from hell to paradise. On the southern

exterior wall is a tree symbolising the continuity of the Old and New Testaments. The tree grows from the reclining figure of Jesse, who is flanked by a row of ancient philosophers. To the left is the Virgin as a Byzantine princess, with angels holding a red veil over her head. Mysteriously, the western wall remains blank. Legend has it that the artist fell off his scaffolding and died.

SLEEPING & EATING

It's worth spending a night here and doing a little hiking in the surrounding hills. Wild camping is possible in the field across the stream from the monastery, as well as along the road from Moldoviţa.

Pensiune Agroturistică (☎ 421 306; Suceviţa 478; per person €14) Just 700m from the monastery (signposted) is this delicious guesthouse surrounded by cherry and apple trees. All their food is organically grown on the premises and the price includes one full meal.

Popas Turistic Bucovina (☎ 417 000; camp sites/ huts/s/d €5/11/24/30) Located 3.5km south of Suceviţa on the road to Vatra Moldoviţei, this complex comprises two charming villas and an excellent Moldavian restaurant.

GETTING THERE & AWAY

Suceviţa is the most difficult monastery to reach on public transport. There are only two daily buses from Rădăuţi (six maxitaxis daily travel to Rădăuţi from Suceava; €1). Hitching or biking are your best bets.

NORTHERN DOBROGEA

Northern Dobrogea is a kingdom unto itself within Romania. Lacking what have become Romanian icons (mountains, wooden churches, Draculas), the land between the Danube River (Râul Dunarea) and the Black Sea (Marea Neagră) is enveloped in its own sweet mysteries. The 193.5km sea border gives it a *litoral* (coast) that's a magnet for beach bums, sun-worshippers and party animals. Yet those seeking waterfront seclusion, archaeological digs and swarms of exotic birds won't be disappointed either.

Many Romanians consider this region of the country the least typically 'Romanian'. Odd, as it is mainly here where Romania's much-vaunted ties with ancient Rome can be felt, thanks to a wealth of ancient treasure.

Statues, busts, sarcophagi and other archaeological finds are so numerous, you'll find them casually lying around in parks and squares, particularly in Constanţa and Mangalia. The region is likely considered 'other' partially as it's the country's most ethnically diverse. Sizeable Turkish, Tatar, Bulgarian, Ukrainian and Lippovani/Old Believer settlements add to the mix, giving the area a refreshing burst of multiculturalism.

CONSTANŢA
☎ 0241 / pop 337,200

If all port cities have an air of mystery, Constanţa's comes in blustery gusts. Romania's largest port evokes romantic notions of ancient seafarers, the Roman poet Ovid and even the classic legend of Jason and the Argonauts (they fled here from King Aietes). Constanţa's original name Tomis means 'cut to pieces', in reference to Jason's beloved Medea who cut up her brother Apsyrtus and threw the pieces into the sea near the present-day city.

The Romans renamed the city after emperor Constantine, who developed it in the 4th century AD. By the 8th century, the city had been destroyed by invading Avars. After it was taken by Romania in 1877, King Carol I turned it into an active port and seaside resort with a railway line to Bucharest.

Orientation
Constanţa's train station is about 2km west of the old town. To reach old Constanţa, exit the station, buy a ticket from the kiosk to the right and take trolleybus No 40, 41 or 43 down B-dul Ferdinand to Parcul Victoriei (Victoria Park) four stops from the station; or just walk along B-dul Ferdinand.

North of B-dul Ferdinand is Constanţa's business district. The area around Str Ştefan cel Mare is lined with shops and restaurants as well as theatres.

Information
Most hotels and travel agencies have exchange outlets, and there are numerous exchange offices, several of which are open around the clock, lining B-dul Tomis south of B-dul Ferdinand.

Banca Comerciala Româna (☎ 638 200; Str Traian 1 & Str Traian 68; 8.30am-5.30pm Mon-Fri, 8.30am-12.30pm Sat) Changes travellers cheques, gives unlimited cash advances on Visa/MasterCard and has an ATM.

Central post office (☎ 552 222; B-dul Tomis 79-81; 8.30am-8pm Mon-Fri, 8.30am-1pm Sat)
County Hospital (Spitalul Judetean; ☎ 662 222; B-dul Tomis 145) North of the centre.
Info Litoral Tourist Information Centre (☎ 555 000; www.infolitoral.ro; Str Traian 36, Scara C, Apt 31; 9am-5pm Mon-Fri) This is a highly recommended first stop – the friendly, well-informed staff will help answer any kind of question; enter from behind the building. They also sell maps and booklets.
Planet Games (☎ 552 377; cnr Str Ştefan cel Mare & Str Răscoala din 1907; per hr €0.50; 24hr)
Telephone office (B-dul Tomis 79-81; 8.30am-10pm) Shares the same building as the central post office.

Sights
Constanţa's most renowned attraction is the **History & Archaeological Museum** (☎ 618 763; Piaţa Ovidiu 12; adult/child €0.50/0.25; 9am-8pm Jun-Sep, 10am-6pm Tue-Sun Oct-May). There's something here for everyone. Kids will like the bones of a 2nd-century woman and the mammoth tusks.

The archaeological fragments of Roman Tomis spill over onto the surrounding square. Facing these is a glass museum, which shelters a gigantic 3rd-century **Roman mosaic** discovered in 1959. The **statue of Ovid**, erected on Piaţa Ovidiu in 1887, commemorates the Latin poet who was exiled to Constanţa in AD 8; rumour has it that he hated the place.

A block south is **Moscheia Mahmudiye** (Mahmudiye Mosque; Str Arhiepiscopiei), dating from 1910, with a 140-step minaret you can climb when the gate is unlocked. Two blocks further down the same street is an Orthodox **Catedrala** (1885). Along the promenade is the **Genoese lighthouse** (1860) and pier, with a fine view of old Constanţa.

Another museum in town worth checking out is the **Muzeul de Artă Populară** (Folk Art Museum; ☎ 616 133; B-dul Tomis 32; adult/child €0.40/0.20; 9am-8pm Jul & Aug, 10am-6pm Tue-Sun Sep-Jun), which has handicrafts and costumes. Further north along the boulevard is the **Art Museum** (☎ 617 012; B-dul Tomis 84; adult/child €0.50/0.25; 10am-6pm Tue-Sun), with mostly still-life and landscape paintings and sculptures. Contemporary exhibits are held in an adjoining art gallery. The **Muzeul Marinei Române** (Naval History Museum; ☎ 619 035; Str Traian 53; adult/child €0.80/0.40; 10am-6pm Tue-Sun Jun-Sep, 9am-5pm Tue-Sun Oct-May) is housed in the old Navy high school. The captions are in Romanian.

ROMANIA

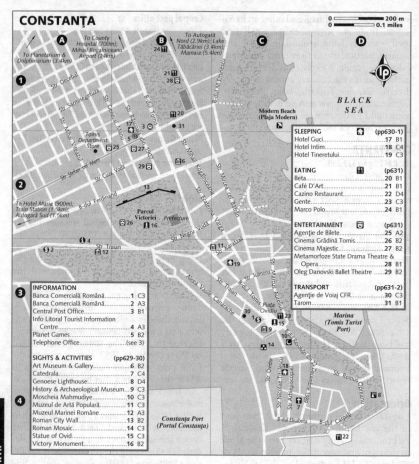

CONSTANŢA

To County Hospital (700m); Mihail Kogălniceanu Airport (24km)

To Planetarium & Dolphinarium (3.4km)

To Autogară Nord (2.9km); Lake Tăbăcăriei (3.4km); Mamaia (5.4km)

Str Decebal

Str Sarmisegetuza

Str General Manu

Str Mihai Viteazul

B-dul Tomis

B-dul M Eminescu

Modern Beach (Plaja Modern)

BLACK SEA

Tomis Department Store

Str Ştefan cel Mare

Str Cuza Vodă

Str General Manu 1907

Str Mihai Kogălniceanu

Str Mircea cel Bătrân

To Hotel Maria (900m); Train Station (1.5km); Autogară Sud (1.5km)

B-dul Ferdinand

Parcul Victoriei

Prefectura

Str Ecaterina Varga

Str Negru Vodă

Str Traian

Str Karatzali

Alcea Vasile Cănărache

Str Traian

Str Sulmona

Str Marcus Aurelius

Piaţa Ovidiu

Marina (Tomis Turist Port)

Str Ovidiu

Str Nicolae Titulescu

Str Arhiepiscopiei

Revoluţia din 22 Decembrie 1989

Str Remus Opreanu

B-dul Elisabeta

B-dul Carpaţi

Constanţa Port (Portul Constanţa)

INFORMATION
Banca Comercială Română	1 C3
Banca Comercială Română	2 A3
Central Post Office	3 B1
Info Litoral Tourist Information Centre	4 A3
Planet Games	5 B2
Telephone Office	(see 3)

SIGHTS & ACTIVITIES (pp629-30)
Art Museum & Gallery	6 B2
Catedrala	7 C4
Genoese Lighthouse	8 D4
History & Archaeological Museum	9 C3
Moscheia Mahmudiye	10 C3
Muzeul de Artă Populară	11 C3
Muzeul Marinei Române	12 A3
Roman City Wall	13 B2
Roman Mosaic	14 C3
Statue of Ovid	15 C3
Victory Monument	16 B2

SLEEPING ⓐ (pp630-1)
Hotel Guci	17 B1
Hotel Intim	18 C4
Hotel Tineretului	19 C3

EATING ⓘ (p631)
Beta	20 B1
Café D'Art	21 B1
Cazino Restaurant	22 D4
Gente	23 C3
Marco Polo	24 B1

ENTERTAINMENT ⓔ (p631)
Agenţie de Bilete	25 A2
Cinema Grădină Tomis	26 B2
Cinema Majestic	27 B2
Metamorfoze State Drama Theatre & Opera	28 B1
Oleg Danovski Ballet Theatre	29 B2

TRANSPORT (pp631-2)
Agenţie de Voiaj CFR	30 C3
Tarom	31 B1

0 ——— 200 m
0 ——— 0.1 miles

Near the city's main intersection, B-dul Ferdinand and B-dul Tomis, is Parcul Victoriei, which has remains of the 3rd-century **Roman city wall** and the 6th-century Butchers' tower, loads of Roman sculptures and the modern **Victory monument** (1968).

Heading north towards Mamaia, you pass Constanţa's **Planetarium & Dolphinarium** (☎ 831 553; B-dul Mamaia; adult/child €0.80/0.40; 8am-9pm Jun–mid-Sep, 8am-4pm mid-Sep–May), on the southeastern shores of Lake Tăbăcăriei.

Activities

You can sail on the **Condor** (☎ 0744 689 228; per person per hr for a group of 14 €4; around 9am May-Sep), moored at the Tomis Turist Port, at the east end of Str Remus Opreanu.

Delphi (☎ 0722 336 686) provides a flexible range of scuba-diving opportunities.

Sleeping

The nearest camping ground is north of Mamaia (see p632).

Hotel Tineretului (☎ 613 590; fax 611 290; B-dul Tomis 24; s/d €20/23) This five-storey two-star hotel has neat, clean rooms.

Hotel Intim (☎ 617 814; Str Nicolae Titulescu 9; s/d/ ste €23/29/35) On a quiet side street in the old town and once (in 1882) briefly home to the Romanian poet Mihai Eminescu, this hotel has a faded elegance – with bed covers and lampshades that would make granny smile – perfectly in keeping with the city. A great deal!

ROMANIA

Hotel Maria (☎ /fax 616 852; B-dul 1 Decembrie 1918; s/d €36/45; ✹) This more modern option, across from the park that faces the train station, has lots of glass, chrome and deep blue to soothe your sun-withered nerves. There's only 12 rooms, so it's cosy and quiet.

Hotel Guci (☎ /fax 695 500; Str Răscoala din 1907, 23; s/d/ste €60/67/85; ✕ ✹) Modern, moderately luxurious three-star hotel offering a Jacuzzi, laundry, massage and gym.

Eating

Café D'Art (☎ 612 133; B-dul Tomis 97; mains €1-3; ✹ 9am-1am) This is an intimate place snuggled up to the Drama Theatre. Especially popular as an evening drinking hole (cocktails are €2), it's also packed during the day by those seeking a good place to people-watch while enjoying a light meal.

Gente (☎ 709 383; Piaţa Ovidiu 7; mains €2-4; ✹ 10am-11pm) While technically a pizzeria, Gente's menu also has Romanian cuisine and a variety of salads. Their mussels in pesto sauce (€2.30) is a popular dish.

Beta (☎ 673 663; Str Ştefan cel Mare 6A; mains €2-4; ✹ 8am-1am) With a sprawling terrace and 100 different meals, from club sandwiches (€1.60) to Thai chicken (€3.40), from breakfast omelettes to special vegetarian and children's meals, this place won't disappoint.

Marco Polo (☎ 617 537; Str Mircea cel Bătrân 103; mains €2-5; ✹ 10am-1.30am) A splendid Italian restaurant where tables are separated from each other by plants, making you feel like you're in a private garden, only one with doting waiters! Portions are generous, the service kind and attentive. The pizza, pasta, meat, fish and veg dishes are delicious.

Cazino Restaurant (☎ 617 416; B-dul Elisabeta 2; mains €2-6; ✹ 11am-midnight) Only recommended for its large outdoor terrace overlooking the sea.

Entertainment

Cinema Majestic (☎ 664 411; Str Ştefan cel Mare 33) New foreign films are presented here.

Cinema Grădină Tomis (Parcul Victoriei) In summer, films are also screened at this outside cinema.

Tickets for the **Metamorfoze State Drama Theatre & Opera** (☎ 615 268; Str Mircea cel Bătrân 97) are sold at the **ticket office** (B-dul Tomis 97; ✹ 9am-6pm Mon-Fri, 9am-noon Sat, 5-6.50pm Sun). The theatre is also home to the **Filarmonica Marea Neagră** (Black Sea Philharmonic).

Tickets for all performances at the **Oleg Danovski Ballet Theatre** (☎ 519 045; Str Răscoala din 1907, 5) are sold at the **Agentie de Bilete** (☎ 664 076; Str Ştefan cel Mare 34; ✹ 10am-5pm).

Getting There & Away

AIR

In summer there are international flights from Athens and sometimes Istanbul to/from Constanţa's **Mihail Kogalniceanu Airport** (☎ 255 100), 25km from the centre.

Tarom (☎ 662 632; Str Ştefan cel Mare 15; ✹ 8am-6pm Mon-Fri, 8.30am-12.30pm Sat) has a once-weekly flight to Bucharest (one way adult/student €50/26).

BUS

Constanţa has two bus stations. From the **Autogară Sud** (southern bus station; ☎ 665 289; B-dul Ferdinand), next to the train station, buses to Istanbul (€25, 17½ hours) depart daily. Tickets are sold in advance from **Özlem Tur** (☎ 514 053) just outside the bus station. There are three maxitaxis daily to Braila (€4) and 10 daily to Galaţi (€4.80), each of which stop at the **Autogară Nord** (northern bus station; ☎ 641 379; Str Soveja 35) on the way. Maxitaxi No 23 to Mamaia also departs from here.

From Constanţa's northern bus station services include at least one daily maxitaxi to Chişinău (€9, nine hours) and Iaşi (€8, seven hours), and four to Histria (€1.25). Maxitaxis leave for Tulcea (€2.65, 2½ hours) every 30 minutes from 6am to 7.30pm.

If you're travelling south along the Black Sea Coast, buses are infinitely more convenient than trains. Exit Constanţa's train station, turn right and walk 50m to the long queue of maxitaxis, buses and private cars destined for Mangalia (€1, pay the driver).

TRAIN

Constanţa's train station is near the southern bus station at the west end of B-dul Ferdinand.

The **Agentie de Voiaj CFR** (☎ 617 930; Aleea Vasile Canarache 4; ✹ 7.30am-8.30pm Mon-Fri, 8am-1pm Sat) sells long-distance tickets only; for the local train service (down the coast) buy tickets at the train station.

There are 11 to 15 daily trains to Bucharest (€6.25, 2½ to 4½ hours). There are daily services to Suceava, Cluj-Napoca, Satu Mare, Galaţi, Timişoara and other destinations. As many as 19 trains a day head from Constanţa

ROMANIA

to Mangalia (€0.95, one to 1¼ hours). There are one to two daily trains to Chişinău in Moldova (€10, 12 hours). The Ovidius train to Budapest also runs overnight (€16, 17 hours) via Bucharest and Arad.

MAMAIA
☎ 0241

Mamaia is Romania's party central. It's a mere 8km strip of beach between the fresh-water Lake Mamaia (or Siutghiol) and the Black Sea, but it's Romania's most popular resort. It gloats over its golden sands, aqua park, restaurants, nightclubs and raucous atmosphere. There are over 60 hotels and tourist complexes squeezed together in a 100m strip along the shore.

Information

The **Agentia de Turism** (☎ 831 517; mamaia@gmb.ro; B-dul Mamaia; ⏱ 8am-9pm), on the highway side of Hotel Riviera, arranges car rental and accommodation.

Every hotel has a currency exchange, and ATMs are easy to find, but to change travellers cheques you have to go to Constanţa.

The **post office & telephone** (⏱ 8am-8pm Mon-Fri) is 200m south of the Cazino complex on the promenade.

Sights & Activities

Mamaia's number-one attraction is its wide, golden **beach** which stretches the length of the resort. The further north you go, the less crowded it becomes.

In summer, **boats** (☎ 252 494; return €3; every 30 min 9am-midnight) ferry tourists across Lake Mamaia to **Insula Ovidiu** (Ovidiu Island, where the poet's tomb is located) from the Tic-Tic wharf opposite the Statia Cazino bus station.

There's a huge **Aqua Park** (adult/child under 12/child under 3 €8/4/free; ⏱ 8am-10pm mid-May–mid-Sep).

Some 50m north of Hotel Bucuresti, by the banks of Lake Mamaia, is a **water-sports** school, offering waterskiing, yachting, windsurfing and rowing.

Sleeping

Centrul de Cazare Cazino (☎ 831 200, 555 555; ⏱ 10am-9pm mid-Jun–mid-Sep) Has lists of available accommodation.

Popas Hanul Piraţilor (☎ 831 454; camp sites/2-room huts €3/8) A camping ground 3km north of Mamaia's northern limit, this has shabby huts, but an on-site café and stretches of fine

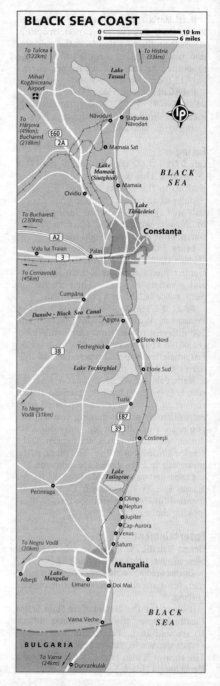

BLACK SEA COAST

sand nearby. Bus No 23 and maxitaxi 23E stop in front of it.

Hotel Dunărea (☎ 831 894; s/d €24/32) This is one of the resort's smaller hotels.

Hotel Perla (☎ 831 995; perlam@rdslink.ro; s/d/ste €45/48/69; 🛇 🖵) Lording over the resort's main entrance, this huge hotel is both a landmark and reliable service centre. It's a busy, efficiently run place, and fully wheelchair accessible.

Hotel Boulevard (☎ 831 533; fax 831 606; B-dul Mamaia 294; s/d €61/69) Modern and offering full services, it's also slightly out of the main drag (being just south of Mamaia proper) while just a 10- to 15-minute walk to the beach.

Eating

Almost every hotel has an adjoining restaurant and there are numerous fast-food stands and restaurants lining the boardwalk.

Orange Plazza (☎ 0722 500 577; mains €2-5; 🕑 10am-6am) Located in the northern part of the resort and a good bet. They change their eclectic international menu every three months. There's also an on-site pub and disco.

Getting There & Around

Tickets for trains departing Constanţa (see p631) can be bought in advance at the **Agentie de Voiaj CFR** (☎ 617 930) adjoining the post and telephone office on the promenade.

The quickest way to travel between Constanţa and Mamaia is by maxitaxi. Maxitaxis Nos 23, 23E and 301 depart regularly from Constanţa's train station, stopping at major hotels. Bus Nos 41 and 47 also take you from Constanţa to the northern end of Mamaia.

In summer a shuttle runs up and down Mamaia's 5km boardwalk.

If arriving in a non-Constanţa-registered vehicle, you are required to pay a €0.50 road tax at the roadblocked entrance to Mamaia.

EFORIE NORD
☎ 0241

Eforie Nord, 14km south of Constanţa, is the first large resort south of the city. Beaches are below 10m to 20m cliffs and are as crowded as in Mamaia.

Orientation

The train station is only a few minutes' walk from the post office and main street, B-dul Republicii. Exit the station and turn left; turn left again after Hotel Belvedere and then right onto B-dul Republicii.

Most hotels and restaurants are on Str Tudor Vladimirescu, which runs parallel to B-dul Republicii along the beach.

Information

There is a currency exchange in practically every hotel. The **telephone office** (☎ 7am-9pm Mon-Fri, 11am-7pm Sat & Sun) is inside the **central post office** (B-dul Republicii 11; 🕑 8am-8pm Mon-Fri, 8am-6pm Sat).

Sights & Activities

Tiny **Lake Belona**, just behind the southern end of the beach, is a popular bathing spot, as its water is warmer than the Black Sea.

Southwest of Eforie Nord is **Lake Techirghiol**, a former river mouth famous for its black sapropel mud, effective against rheumatism. The cold mud **public baths** (€1.05; 🕑 8am-8pm) are the only place in Romania where nudism is allowed (separate areas are designated for women and men). The lake is 2m below sea level, and its waters are four times saltier than the sea.

Sleeping & Eating

Camping Meduza (☎ 742 385; camp sites/d/2-bed huts €1.75/5.50/6.70) This cramped space is behind the Prahova Hotel at the northern end of town. Doubles are in a drab concrete building. The place is always noisy but it's close to the action and offers laundry service.

Hotel Decebal (☎ 742 977; s/d €20/27) A very pleasant, quiet hotel with a nice stone terrace. It's adjoining the train station.

Villa Horiana (☎ 741 388; Str Alexandru Cuza 13; s/d €35/55; 🛇) No doubt the best place to lay your party-weary head in Eforie Nord is here, in this converted bungalow. Some rooms have their own balcony and the home cooking by the super-friendly owners is reason enough to stay here.

Cofetăria Pescăruş (B-dul Republicii; mains €1-3; 🕑 11am-1am) Opposite the post office, this cafeteria-style joint is handy because you can point to the type of grease you want. It's good for a cheap fill-up and has live music from 9pm.

Nunta Zamfirei (☎ 741 651; Str Republicii; mains €2-6; 🕑 6pm-1am) This Romanian restaurant is famed for its folk song-and-dance shows. Walk north along B-dul Republicii and turn

ROMANIA

left onto the small track opposite the public thermal baths.

Getting There & Away

The **Agentie de Voiaj CFR** (☎ 617 930; B-dul Republicii 11) is inside the post office building.

All trains between Constanţa and Mangalia stop at Eforie Nord, but you're better off in a maxitaxi (€0.50).

NEPTUN-OLIMP

☎ 0241

Before the 1989 revolution, Neptun-Olimp was the exclusive tourist complex of Romania's Communist Party. Neptun-Olimp is in fact two resorts in one. Olimp, a huge complex of hotels facing the beach, is the party place. Neptun, 1km south, is separated from the Black Sea by two small lakes amid some lush greenery. Together they form a vast expanse of hotels and discos.

Neptun-Olimp is perhaps the nicest and most chic of the Romanian Black Sea resorts. The Info Litoral Tourist Information Centre in Constanţa (p629) can provide you with detailed information about these resorts, and they or any travel agency in Constanţa can help with hotel booking.

The resort complex offers a reasonable range of **activities**: tennis, windsurfing, jet-skiing, sailing, minigolf, billiards, bowling and discos.

Hotel Albert (☎ 731 514; hotelalbert@idilis.ro; d/ste €35/50) is one of the best bets along the coast, located smack in between Neptun and Olimp. It's slightly secluded from the bustle and tastefully mixes modernity with rustic décor.

Halta Neptun train station is within walking distance of the Neptun-Olimp hotels, midway between the two resorts. All trains travelling from Bucharest or Constanţa to Mangalia stop at Halta Neptun.

The **CFR office** (Str Plopilor) is inside Neptun's Hotel Apollo, northwest of Lake Neptun II.

Private maxitaxis run between the resort towns and Mangalia.

MANGALIA

☎ 0241 / pop 44,300

Formerly ancient Greek Callatis, Mangalia, founded in the 6th century BC, contains several minor archaeological sites. It is a quiet town, not a place for partying, and attracts many elderly European tour groups.

Orientation & Information

Mangalia's train station is 1km north of the centre. Turn right as you exit and follow Şos Constanţei (the main road) south. At the roundabout, turn left for Hotel Mangalia and the beach or go straight ahead for the pedestrianised section of Şos Constanţei and most facilities. Private and city buses stop in front of the train station.

There is a small tourist **information kiosk** (8.30am-4pm) outside the train station that gives out leaflets and can help with booking accommodation.

Most hotels have currency exchanges. One of the numerous **currency exchange offices** (Str Stefan cel Mare 16; 7.30am-10pm) is opposite the post office. Cash travellers cheques or get cash advances on Visa/MasterCard at the **Banca Comercială Română**, (Şos Constanţei 25; 8am-4pm Mon-Fri).

The **telephone office** (7am-10pm) and **post office** (7am-9pm Mon-Fri, 8am-4pm Sat, 11am-7pm Sun) is at Str Stefan cel Mare 14–15.

La Maxim (per hr €0.65; 24hr) is an Internet shack right on the beach, in front of Hotel Zenit.

Sights

The **Callatis Archaeological Museum** (☎ 753 580; Str Şoseaua Constanţei 26; 8am-8pm) has a good collection of Roman sculptures. Just past the high-rise building next to the museum are some remnants of a 4th-century **Roman-Byzantine necropolis**.

At the south side of Hotel Mangalia, along Str Izvor, are the ruins of a 6th-century **Palaeo-Christian basilica** and a **fountain** (Izvorul Hercules) dispensing sulphurous mineral water that, despite the smell, some people drink.

Cultural events take place in the **Casă de Cultură**, which has a large socialist mural on the façade. One block east of the post office is the Turkish **Moscheea Esmahan Sultan** (Sultan Esmahan Mosque; Str Oituz; admission €0.40; 9am-8pm). Built in 1525, it's surrounded by a lovely garden and well-kept cemetery.

From here, head east down Str Oituz to the beachfront where, in the basement of Hotel President, remains of the walls of the Callatis citadel dating from the 1st to 7th centuries are open in the **Muzeul Poarta Callatiana** (Callatiana Archaeological Reservation; 24hr).

Sleeping & Eating

Antrec (☎ 759 473; Str George Murnu 13, Block D, Apt 21; ☉ 24hr, calls only) They arrange rooms in private homes in Mangalia and other costal resorts from €13 a night.

Hotel Mangalia (☎ 752 052; mangalia.turism@radiotel .ro; Str Rozelor 35; s/d €26/40) A 1960s holdout, this is a popular choice. It's one of the few hotels on the coast with full wheelchair access; there are ramps onto the beach.

Hotel President (☎ 755 861; www.hpresident.com; Str Treilor 6; s/d/ste from €44/69/117) This is the top place to stay south of Constanța, a four-star luxury hotel with a fully-fledged business centre.

Hotel Zenit (☎ 751 645; Str Teilor 7), **Hotel Astra** (☎ 751 673; Str Teilor 9) and **Hotel Orion** (☎ 751 156; Str Teilor 11) are surprisingly pleasant three-star options on the promenade. All have singles/doubles with private bath for €26/31.

Cafe del Mar (☎ 0723 356 610; Str Treilor 4; mains €2-4; ☉ 24hr) You can't go wrong here. There's a great double-decker terrace, stylish interiors and one of the most varied, fanciful menus around – it's the only place on the coast to get US-style buffalo wings (€1.85) and potato skins (€1.70)! It's next to Hotel President.

Getting There & Away

BUS

Maxitaxis from Constanța stop at Mangalia's train station and in front of the post office, where all maxitaxis running up the coast to Olimp (every 20 minutes) and down to Vama Veche stop. Maxitaxis to Constanța (€1) run regularly from 5am to 11pm.

TRAIN

The **Agentie de Voiaj CFR** (☎ 752 818; Str Stefan cel Mare 14-15; ☉ 7.30am-8.30pm Mon-Sat, 8.30am-1.30pm Sun) adjoins the central post office.

Mangalia is at the end of the line from Constanța. From Constanța there are 19 trains daily in summer to Mangalia (€0.95, one to 1¼ hours), five of which are direct to/from Bucharest's Gară Obor (€7, 4½ hours). In summer there are also express trains to/from Iași, Sibiu, Suceava, Cluj-Napoca and Timișoara.

DANUBE DELTA

The mighty Danube River empties into the Black Sea just south of the Ukrainian border. At this point the Danube splits into

DELTA PERMITS

In principle, visitors need travel permits to travel in the delta. If on a group excursion of any kind, these are automatically handled by the operator. If you hire a local fisherman, ask to see his valid permit. The only time you'll need to buy one (€1) is if you go boating or foraging independently. The Information & Ecological Education Centre (p637) in Tulcea can issue these for you. If inspectors (and there are many of them) find you without one, you can be liable for a fine of up to €200. You need separate permits to fish or hunt.

three separate channels: the Chilia, Sulina and Sfântu Gheorghe arms, creating a 5800-sq-km wetland of marshes, floating reed islets and sandbars, providing sanctuary for 300 species of birds and 160 species of fish. Reed marshes cover 156,300 hectares, constituting one of the largest single expanses of reed beds existing in the world.

The Danube Delta (Delta Dunarii) is under the protection of the Administration of the Danube Delta Biosphere Reserve Authority (DDBRA), set up in response to the ecological disaster that befell the delta region during Ceaușescu's attempt to transform it into an agricultural region. Now there are 18 protected reserves (50,000 hectares) that are off limits to tourists or anglers, including the 500-year-old Lețea Forest and Europe's largest pelican colony. The Delta is also included in Unesco's World Heritage list.

The part of the delta most accessible to foreigners is the middle arm (Sulina), which cuts directly across from Tulcea to Crișan and Sulina (71km). Most river traffic uses the Sulina arm, including the ferries and touring boats from Tulcea.

It's also a bird-watcher's paradise with protected species such as the roller, white-tailed eagle, great white egret, mute and whooper swans, falcon and bee-eater.

Getting Around

Ibis Tours (p637) in Tulcea arranges bird-watching trips.

Be sure to take some food and water and lots of mosquito repellent on any expedition into the Delta. Warning: do not drink Danube water!

ROMANIA

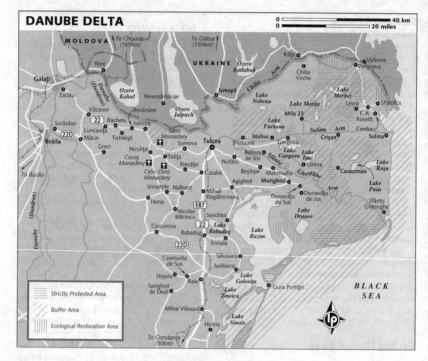

In the delta proper it's easy to hire rowing boats from fishermen. This is the only way to penetrate the delta's exotic backwaters.

FERRY

Navrom (☎ 0240-511553) operates passenger ferries year-round to towns and villages in the delta. It also runs its own tours on weekends. On Saturday, tours head to Sulina, leaving at 8am and returning at 8pm (€4.80); on Sunday at the same hours tours sail to Sfântu Gheorghe (€4.80). You get to see the landscape but there is little time for true exploring.

A regularly scheduled ferry for Sulina departs from Tulcea at 1.30pm Monday to Friday (€4, four hours). The Sfântu Gheorghe ferry departs from Tulcea at 1.30pm Monday, Wednesday, Thursday and Friday (€4, 5½ hours).

Ferries to Periprava from Tulcea depart at 1.30pm Monday, Tuesday, Wednesday and Friday (€5, four hours), stopping at Chilia Veche. Check timetables for return ferries.

Ferry tickets are sold at Tulcea's Navrom terminal from 11.30am to 1.30pm.

HYDROFOIL

Hydrofoils to Sulina (€5.25, 1½ hours) depart from Tulcea's AFDJ Galatia terminal, next to the floating ambulance, every day at 2pm. They stop in Maliuc (€1.80) and Crişan (€2.65) on the way. The return trip is at 7pm. Purchase tickets on board.

TULCEA

☎ 0240 / pop 94,750

Tulcea (tool-*cha*) is an important port and gateway to the Danube Delta paradise. It is usually passed through quickly en route to the delta, so most tourists miss its unassuming appeal. Despite visual reminders that Tulcea is mainly an industrial town, it has a lively energy and an allure of its own, with nightclubs and a sizeable Turkish population lending a multiethnic flavour.

It was settled by Dacians and Romans from the 7th to 1st centuries BC.

Tulcea hosts the annual International Folk Festival of Danubian Countries in August, where local songs, games and traditional activities are played out to a Danubian backdrop.

Orientation

Tulcea's bus and train stations, and the Navrom ferry terminal, are adjacent, overlooking the Danube at the western end of the riverfront promenade, which stretches east along the river to Hotel Delta. Lake Ciuperca is west of the stations. Inland two blocks, between Str Păcii and Str Babadag, is Piaţa Unirii, the centre of Tulcea.

Information

A floating **ambulance station** (staţia de ambulanţă; 24hr) is moored in front of the Culture House on the riverfront. Some of its crew speak also English. At the **Anason Pharmacy** (☎ 513 352; Str Babadag 8), there's an all-night dispenser.

All the hotels have currency exchanges. The **Banca Agricolă** (Str 9 Mai 4; 8am-3pm Mon-Fri), near the Delta Research Institute, cashes travellers cheques and gives cash advances.

To connect to the Internet, head to **Spatial Net** (Str Păcii 66; per hr €0.40; 24hr). The **post office** (☎ 512 869; Str Babadag 5; 7am-8pm Mon-Fri, 8am-noon Sat) and **telephone centre** (7am-8pm) share the same building.

The **Information & Ecological Education Centre** (☎ 519 214; www.deltaturism.ro; Str Portului 34A; 8am-6pm) is a representative of Antrec and run by the Danube Delta Biosphere Reserve. In a glass booth inside the building opposite the AFDJ hydrofoil terminal, it can book accommodation in homes, hotels and *pensiunes* (whole houses given over to tourists) and assist in making tours. It can also help you get fishing, hunting and travel permits.

Ibis Tours (☎ /fax 512 787; www.ibistours.net; Str Babadag 6, Apt 14) in Tulcea arranges wildlife and bird-watching tours in the delta and Dobrogea, led by professional ornithologists, from €30 a day.

Sights

As you stroll along the river you'll see the **Independence Monument** (1904) on Citadel Hill, at the far eastern end of town. You can reach this by following Str Gloriei from behind the Egreta Hotel to its end; the views are superb.

The **Natural History Museum & Aquarium** (☎ 515 866; Str Progresului 32) highlights the delta's fauna with lots of stuffed birds and a basement aquarium. The minaret of **Moscheia Azizie** (Azizie Mosque; 1863) is down Str Independenţei.

The **Folk Art & Ethnographic Museum** (☎ 516 204; Str 9 Mai, 4) has Turkish and Romanian traditional costumes, fishing nets, rugs and carpets. In front of the Greek Orthodox church is a **memorial** to the local victims of the 1989 revolution.

Sleeping

No camping is allowed within Tulcea's city limits. However, there are many areas where wild camping is permitted on the banks of the canal within a few kilometres of the city; ask at the Information & Ecological Education Centre for details.

Navitur House Boat (☎ 518 894; fax 518 953; d €10) The boat is not the cleanest and staff speak little English, but the tiny double cabins with shared bath (no hot water) are among the cheapest places to stay in town. It's moored opposite Hotel Delta.

Hotel Europolis (☎ 512 443; www.europolis.ro; Str Păcii 20; s/d €19/24;) Rejoice over the spacious rooms with huge bathrooms. For the same prices, you can stay at its Complexul Touristic Europolis, a resort-like hotel by Lake Câşla, 2km outside of Tulcea's city limits. Though favoured by groups, the site is lovely, in the thick of nature. Water-bikes and small boats can be rented and there are walking trails.

Hotel Delta (☎ 514 720; www.deltahotelro.com; Str Isaccei 2; s/d €35/47;) A city landmark, it boasts the most luxurious rooms around, some affording a nice view of the river. There's a restaurant and bar.

Atbad (☎ 514 114; www.atbad.ro; Str Babadag 11) The boatels Delta 2 and Delta 3 (three- and four-star respectively), run by Atbad, are worth considering. They dock about 100m north of Hotel Delta. The boatels go out on one-, two- or three-day excursions (about €50 per person, per day).

Eating & Drinking

Restaurant Select (☎ 510 301; Str Păcii 6; mains €2-4; 9am-midnight) Treat yourself to a top-notch meal here; the cuisine is excellent and prices extremely reasonable. From its varied menu, choose between fish, frog legs, pizza and the local speciality, *tochitura Dobrogeana* (pan-fried meat with spicy sauce).

Fast Food Trident (Str Babadag; mains €1-3; 11am-midnight) This is an excellent spot for cheesy pizzas and pasta. It's opposite the Diana Department Store.

ROMANIA

Carul cu Bere (Str Păcii 6; mains €1-3; 🕑 9am-midnight) Adjoins Restaurant Select and has a terrace; enjoy a beer and people-watch. A lively crowd usually heads here to pull back a few, but light meals are served too.

Getting There & Away

The **Agentie de Voiaj CFR** (☎ 511 360; Str Unirii 4; 🕑 9am-4pm Mon-Fri) is on the corner of Str Babadag. From the **train station** (☎ 513 706; Str Portului) there are only two, slow trains a day to Constanța (€3.65, five hours). There's one daily train to Bucharest (€7, six hours).

The **bus station** (☎ 513 304) adjoins the **Navrom ferry terminal** (Str Portului). As many as 15 buses and maxitaxis head to Bucharest (€7), at least nine to Galați (€2.25) and one a day each to Iași (€9) and Piatra Neamț (€9.75). Maxitaxis to Constanța (€4) leave every half-hour from 5.30am to 8pm. One bus a day heads to Istanbul (€34).

TULCEA TO SULINA

☎ 0240

The Sulina arm, the shortest channel of the Danube, stretches 63.7km from Tulcea to Sulina. The Navrom ferry's first stop is at **Partizani**, from where you can find a fisherman to row you to the three lakes to the north, Tataru, Lung and Mester. Next stop is **Maliuc**, where there is a hotel and camping ground for 80 people. North of Maliuc is **Lake Furtuna**, a snare for bird-watchers.

The ferry's next stop is the junction with Old Danube, 1km upstream from **Crişan**. There are several *pensiunes* in the village, all charging about €10 per person. Try **Pensiune Gheorghe Silviu** or **Pensiune Pocora** (both ☎ 511 279). There is also the DDBR's **Crişan Centre for Ecological Information & Education** (☎ 519 214; office@deltaturism.ro; 🕑 8am-4pm Tue-Sun), which features wildlife displays, a library and a video room. At the main Crişana ferry dock, ask about side trips to **Mila 23** or **Caraorman**.

You can camp on the beach at Sulina. As you get off the ferry, watch for people offering private rooms (around €10 per person).

A few hundred metres west along the riverfront from the Sulina Cinema is a small sign pointing to **Pensiune Astir** (☎ 543 379; s/d €10/20). The **Pensiune Delta Sulina** (☎ 0722 275 554; s/d €18/25) is a comfortable, three-star option.

For information on ferries and hydrofoils see p635 at the start of this Danube Delta section.

ROMANIA DIRECTORY

ACCOMMODATION

In this chapter, budget accommodation is under €20 per person, mid-range is from €20 to €70 for singles/doubles, and top-end choices cost €75 for a single room. Reviews in this chapter are ordered according to price. Accommodation is generally cheaper outside Bucharest. A particularly helpful website is www.rotravel.com.

Camping grounds in Romania are grubby and largely not recommended. They usually comprise *căsuțe* (wooden huts) which fit two to four people. The good news is that wild camping anywhere in Romania is legal unless otherwise prohibited.

Staying in a private home is the most down-to-earth type of accommodation for anyone wanting to get to the roots of Romanian home life. Check out agro-tourism (B&B in the countryside) on www.rural tourism.ro. Local travel agents can also usually help find a private home.

The largest agrotourism organisation in Romania is **Antrec** (National Association of Rural, Ecological & Cultural Tourism; www.antrec.iiruc.ro), which has branch offices or representatives in many regions.

Youth Hostels Romania (www.hihostels-romania.ro) is headquartered in Cluj-Napoca (p607).

In most mountain areas there's a network of *cabanas* (cabins or chalets) with restaurants and dormitories. Prices are much lower than those of hotels and no reservations are required, but arrive early if the *cabana* is in a popular location.

Romanian hotels are rated by a government star system, which should be used as a rough guide at best. Not much separates one- and two-star hotels. *Apă caldă* (hot water) is common but not a given. In rural towns, it can be restricted to a few hours in the morning and evening.

ACTIVITIES

While there are many beautiful and interesting sites to see in Romania, the diverse landscape lends itself so perfectly to active vacationing.

Ski and snowboard centres are fast becoming popular thanks to the Carpathian Mountains. Sinaia (p593) offers the best downhill skiing, Poiana Braşov (p600) is the best resort.

The Făgăraş Mountains (p606) are your best bet for longer distance ski treks.

The ski season runs from December to mid-March. You can hire gear for about €10 per day from all the major hotels in the resorts. Five- to seven-day ski courses usually cost €60 to €80/€40 to €60 for adults/children. Emergency rescue is provided by **Salvamont** (www.salvamont.org, in Romanian), a voluntary mountain rescue organisation with 21 stations countrywide.

The Carpathians also offer endless opportunities for hikers, the most popular areas being the Bucegi (p594) and Făgăraş (p606) ranges, south and west of Braşov.

Trails are generally well marked, and a system of *cabanas,* huts and hotels along the trails on the mountaintops and plateaus make even a several-day trek more than comfortable. A good source of guides can be found at www.alpineguide.ro.

Mountain biking has also taken off. The most active biking clubs are in Cluj-Napoca, Sibiu, and Oradea. Clubul de Cicloturism Napoca (p608) can offer the best advice for cycling in the region and organises summer tours. **Transylvania Adventure** (www.adventuretransylvania.com), located in Satu Mare, also offers good biking tours.

Romania is a country steeped in horse tradition. Throughout the Carpathians a network of trails leading to some of the country's most beautiful and remote areas can be explored on horseback. The best on offer is the **Ştefan cel Mare Equestrian Centre** (☎ 263-378 470; www.riding-holidays.ro) in the small village of Lunca Ilvei near Bistriţa in the heart of Dracula country.

Twitchers head to Europe's greatest wetlands, the Danube Delta (p635). Almost the entire world's population of red-breasted geese (up to 70,000) winter here, and in the summer, thousands of pygmy cormorants and white pelicans, along with birds from up to 300 other species, can be seen here.

BUSINESS HOURS
Banks can be expected to open from 9am to 3pm, with many closing for an hour around noon; most shops are open from 9am or 10am to 6pm or 7pm, some closing on Sundays; museums are usually open from 11am to 5pm, most closing on Monday; post offices are open from 8am to 7pm Monday to Friday, until 4pm Saturday and closed Sunday; restaurants can be expected to stay open until at least 11pm nightly. Theatrical performances and concerts usually begin at 7pm.

CUSTOMS
Officially, you're allowed to import hard currency up to a maximum of US$10,000. Valuable goods and foreign currency over US$1000 should be declared upon arrival. For foreigners, duty-free allowances are 4L of wine, 1L of spirits and 200 cigarettes.

DANGERS & ANNOYANCES
Bucharest is known for its prolific tourist scams but realise that most of the ways people try to take advantage of tourists is relatively harmless: a security guard at Bucharest's Gară de Nord train station might offer to help you decipher the train schedules – for a fee; or a ticket conductor on a bus might try to make you believe your ticket has been improperly punched – so you can pay the fine, straight into his pocket. Take steps not to be taken advantage of, but remember too the social backdrop of poverty and need (and sometimes greed). Stray dogs in Bucharest are more of an annoyance than a danger, but steer clear of bitches with puppies.

EMBASSIES & CONSULATES
Romanian Embassies & Consulates
Romanian embassies and consulates abroad include:

Australia (☎ 02-6286 2343; www.roembau.org; 4 Dalman Cres, O'Malley, ACT, Canberra)

Canada Montreal (☎ 514-876 1792; romcon@videotron.ca; 1111 St Urbain, Ste M01–04, Montreal); Ottawa (☎ 613-789 5345; www.cyberus.ca/~romania; 655 Rideau St, Ottawa, Ontario); Toronto (☎ 416-585 5802; cgrt@ca.inter.net; 111 Peter St, Ste 530, Toronto)

France (☎ 01 47 05 10 46; www.amb-roumanie.fr, in French; 5 rue de l'Exposition, Paris)

Germany (☎ 030-803 30 18; ro-amb.berlin@t-online.de; Matterhornstrasse 79, Berlin)

Ireland (☎ 031-269 2852; ambrom@eircom.net; 47 Ailesbury Rd, Ballsbridge, Dublin)

Moldova embassy (☎ 22-228 126; ambrom@ch.moldpac.md; Str Bucureşti 66/1, Chişinău); consulate (☎ 22-237 622; Str Vlaicu Parcalab 39, Chişinău) **UK** (☎ 020-7937 9666; www.roemb.co.uk; 4 Palace Green, Kensington Gardens, London)

USA Los Angeles (☎ 310-444 0043; 11766 Wilshire B-dul, Ste 1230, Los Angeles); New York (☎ 212-682 9120; www.romconsny.org; 200 East 38th St, New York); Washington DC (☎ 202-232 3694; www.roembus.org; 1607 23rd St NW, Washington DC)

ROMANIA

Embassies & Consulates in Romania

Unless stated otherwise, the following embassies are in Bucharest (city code ☎ 021):

Australia (Map p581; ☎ 021-320 9802; don.cairns@austrade.gov.au; B-dul Unirii 74)

Canada (Map p581; ☎ 021-307 5000; bucst-im@dfait-maeci.gc.ca; Str Nicolae Iorga 36)

France Bucharest (Map p581; ☎ 021-312 0217; www.ambafrance-ro.org, in French; Str Biserica Amzei 13-15); Bucharest (☎ 021-312 0991; Intrarea Cristian Tell 6)

Germany Bucharest (Map p581; ☎ 021-202 9853; Str Rabat 21); Sibiu (☎ 0269-211 133; Str Lucian Blaga 15-17, Sibiu); Timişoara (☎ 0256-220 796; Hotel Continental, B-dul Revoluţiei 1989 3, Timişoara) Consulates: Sibiu (☎ 0269-214 442; Str Hegel 3, Sibiu); Timişoara (☎ 0256-190 495; B-dul Republicii 6, Timişoara)

Ireland (☎ 021-211 3967; Str Vasile Lascăr 42-44)

Moldova Bucharest (Map p581; ☎ 021-230 0474; moldova@customers.dirigo.net; Aleea Alexandru 40); Bucharest (☎ 021-410 9827; B-dul Eroilor 8)

UK Bucharest (Map p581; ☎ 021-201 7200; www.britishembassy.gov.uk/romania; Str Jules Michelet 24); Constanţa (☎ 0241-638 282; B-dul Tomis 143A, Constanţa)

USA Bucharest (Map p583; ☎ 021-210 4042; www.usembassy.ro; Str Tudor Arghezi 7-9); Bucharest (Map p583; ☎ 021-210 4042; Str Nicolae Filipescu 26); Cluj-Napoca (☎ 0264-594 315; Str Universităţii 7-9, Cluj-Napoca)

FESTIVALS & EVENTS

Every part of Romania has some kind of festival going on throughout the year, from international film festivals to country get-togethers where shepherds meet and locals sell their wares. Our favourites are listed below and others are listed in the regional sections.

Juni Pageant (Apr) Braşov
Bucharest Carnival (late May–early Jun) Bucharest
Medieval Festival of the Arts (Jul) Sighişoara
International Folk Music & Dance Festival of Ethnic Minorities in Europe (Aug) Cluj-Napoca
Sâmbra Oilor (Sep) Bran
De la Colind la Stea (Dec) Braşov

HOLIDAYS

Public holidays in Romania are:
New Year 1 & 2 January
Catholic & Orthodox Easter Mondays In March/April
Labour Day 1 May
Romanian National Day 1 December
Christmas 25 & 26 December

LEGAL MATTERS

If you are arrested you can insist on seeing an embassy or consular officer straight away. It is not advisable to present your passport to people on the street unless you know for certain that they are authentic officials – cases of theft have been reported.

Romanians can legally drink, drive and vote (though not simultaneously!) at 18. The age of consent in Romania is 15.

MONEY

In Romania the only legal tender is the leu (plural: lei). But you'll see prices quoted in euros, consequently this chapter quotes prices in euros.

Romanian lei come in denominations of 2000, 10,000, 50,000, 100,000 and 500,000. There are (heavy) coins for one, five, 10, 20, 50, 100, 500 and 1000 lei.

In order to change money in Romania (exchange bureaus are easy to find in any city and town; in villages you'll be out of luck) you'll need to present your passport (supposedly so tax officials can better control the moneychangers). Some places will do it 'unofficially' without one. Dollars and euros are the easiest to exchange, though other major currencies like British pounds are widely accepted and at larger exchange bureaus, most major world currencies (and from neighbouring countries) can be changed.

ATMs giving 24-hour advances (Cirrus, Plus, Visa, MasterCard, Eurocard) are rife in Romanian cities and towns. You can only make withdrawals in lei; however, Banca Comercială Română will give you cash advances on your credit card in your home currency.

All branches of the Banca Comercială Română, among others, will cash travellers cheques. Credit cards won't get you anywhere in rural areas, but they are widely accepted in larger department stores, hotels and most restaurants in cities and towns.

POST

A postcard or letter under 20g to Europe from Romania costs €0.15 and takes seven to 10 days; to the rest of the world it costs €0.40 and takes 10 to 14 days. The postal system is reliable, if slow.

Poste-restante mail is held for one month (addressed c/o Poste Restante, Poştă Romana Oficiul Bucureşti 1, Str Matei Millo 10, RO-70700 Bucureşti, Romania) at Bucharest's central post office (p582).

EMERGENCY NUMBERS

Operators of emergency numbers are Romanian-speaking only.

- Police ☎ 955
- Fire ☎ 981
- Ambulance ☎ 961

TELEPHONE

Romania's international operator can be reached by dialling ☎ 971. Any European cell phone with roaming will work inside Romania.

Phonecards costing €2.15 or €4 can be bought at any telephone centre and at many newspaper kiosks. International calls can also be made with these.

TOURIST INFORMATION

Amazingly, Romania still has no national tourist office network, making information tough to track down. A handful of highly efficient, independently run tourist centres – such as the one in Sinaia – have sprung up in the past couple of years. Elsewhere, private travel agencies double as tourist offices, although their quality, usefulness and attitude varies dramatically.

In contrast to the disheartening lack of information locally, Romania runs a string of efficient tourist offices abroad, coordinated by Romania's **National Authority for Tourism** (☎ 021-410 1262; www.turism.ro; Str Apolodor 17, Bucharest).

VISAS

Your passport's validity must extend to at least six months beyond the date you enter the country in order to obtain a visa.

Citizens of Canada, Japan and all EU countries may travel visa-free for 90 days in Romania. US citizens and those from many Eastern European countries can travel visa-free for 30 days. All other foreign visitors (including Australians and New Zealanders) require a visa to enter. As visa requirements change frequently, check at the **Ministry of Foreign Affairs** (www.mae.ro) before departure.

Romania issues two types of visas to tourists: transit or single-entry. Transit visas (for those from countries other than the ones mentioned above) are for stays of

no longer than three days, and cannot be bought at the border.

To apply for a visa you need a passport, one recent passport photograph and the completed visa application form accompanied by the appropriate fee. Citizens of some countries (mainly African) need a formal invitation from a person or company in order to apply for a visa; see the above-mentioned website for details.

Regular single-entry visas (US$25) are valid for 60 days from the day you enter the country. Single-entry visas are usually issued within a week (depending on the consulate), but for an extra US$6 can be issued within 48 hours.

Transit visas can be either single-entry (US$15) – valid for three days and allowing you to enter Romania once – or double-entry (US$25), allowing you to enter the country twice and stay for three days each time.

Check your visa requirements for Serbia and Montenegro, Hungary, Bulgaria and Ukraine if you plan on crossing those borders. Contact the respective embassy in Bucharest for details. If you are taking the Bucharest–St Petersburg train you need Ukrainian and Belarusian transit visas on top of the Russian visa.

TRANSPORT IN ROMANIA

GETTING THERE & AWAY
Air

Tarom (Transporturile Aeriene Române; code RO; ☎ 21-337 2037; www.tarom.ro) is Romania's state airline. Nearly all international flights to Romania arrive at Bucharest's **Otopeni International Airport** (☎ 021-201 4050; www.otp-airport.ro).

The following are the major airlines flying into the country:

Aeroflot (code SU; ☎ 021-315 0314; www.aeroflot.org)

Air France (code AF; ☎ 021-312 0086; www.airfrance.com)

Air Moldova (code 9U; ☎ 021-312 1258; www.airmoldova.md)

Austrian Airlines (code OS; ☎ 021-312 0545; www.austrianair.com)

British Airways (code BA; ☎ 021-303 2222; www.british-airways.com)

ČSA (Czech Airlines; code OK; ☎ 021-315 3205; www.csa.cz)

KLM (code KL; ☎ 021-312 0149; www.klm.com)

LOT Polish Airlines (code LO; ☎ 021-212 8365; www.lot.com)

Lufthansa (code LH; ☎ 021-312 9559; www.lufthansa.com)

ROMANIA

Swiss International Air Lines (code LX; ☎ 021-312 0086; www.swiss.com)

Turkish Airlines (code TK; ☎ 021-311 2410; www.turkish airlines.com)

Air Moldova and Tarom together operate daily flights between Chişinău and Bucharest, and **Transaero** (www.transaero.md) also has flights on that route. Air Moldova also has daily flights to Timişoara.

Bucharest is connected with regular flights to and from Prague, Budapest, Warsaw, Sofia and Moscow. In addition, Tarom runs flights from Arad to Verona, from Timişoara to Milan, from Sibiu to Munich and Stuttgart, and from Cluj-Napoca to Vienna, Frankfurt and Munich. Tarom often has great specials; a 12-month return ticket to London is around €275.

Tarom operates regular flights between Bucharest and Istanbul that sometimes stop in Constanța from May to mid-September. Return fares are about €175. Turkish Airlines also flies this route.

Tarom has a flight at least once a week direct to/from New York. A sale price can be as low as US$500 return, but is usually around US$700.

From Australia, expect to pay around A$1500 return during low season and upwards of A$1900 during high season. Swissair, Lauda Air and Qantas all have some good fare deals. From New Zealand, count on around NZ$2399 for a return low-season fare from Auckland with either Swiss or Qantas.

Land

BORDER CROSSINGS

Expect long queues at checkpoints, particularly on weekends. Carry food and water for the wait. Don't try bribing a Romanian official and beware of unauthorised people charging dubious 'ecology', 'disinfectant' or other dodgy taxes at the border.

BUS

Romania is well linked by bus lines to central and Western Europe as well as Turkey. While not as comfortable as the train, buses usually tend to be faster, though not always cheaper.

Eurolines (www.eurolines.ro; www.eurolines.md) has a flurry of buses linking numerous cities in Romania with Western Europe. Buses to Germany cost €45 to €60 one way, and as far as Spain can cost €95 to €110. Many routes offer a 10% to 15% discount for those aged under 26 or over 60.

Eurolines and other private companies have many daily buses to Budapest from cities throughout Romania, including Bucharest, Arad, Braşov and Cluj-Napoca, with stops along the way.

Buses galore trundle the 804km between Bucharest and Istanbul in 14 to 16 hours. There are also some leaving from Constanța.

CAR & MOTORCYCLE

The best advice here is to make sure all your documents (personal ID, insurance, registration and visas, if required) are in order before crossing into Romania. The Green Card (a routine extension of domestic motor insurance to cover most European countries) is valid in Romania. Extra insurance can be bought at the borders.

See opposite for further information on road rules and car hire.

TRAIN

International train tickets are rarely sold at train stations, but rather at CFR (Romanian State Railways) offices in town (look for the Agenție de Voiaj CFR signs) or Wasteels offices. Tickets must be bought at least two hours prior to departure.

Those travelling on an Inter-Rail pass still need to make seat reservations (€2 to €3) on express trains within Romania. Even if you're not travelling with a rail pass, practically all international trains require a reservation (automatically included in tickets purchased in Romania). If you already have a ticket, you may be able to make reservations at the station an hour before departure, though it's preferable to do so at a CFR office at least one day in advance.

There's only one direct train service to Bucharest from Vienna (around €65 one way).

The Budapest–Bucharest train journey (873km) takes around 12 hours. To or from Arad it is a mere 28km to the Hungarian border town of Lököshaza, from where it is a further 225km (4½ hours) to Budapest. There are five daily trains between Bucharest and Budapest (around €40 one way). A one-way ticket from Arad or Oradea to Budapest costs around €30. It's also possible to pick up the Budapest-bound train from other Romanian cities including Constanţa, Braşov and Cluj-Napoca.

The train service between Romania and Bulgaria is slow and crowded but cheap. Between Sofia and Bucharest (11 hours) there are two daily trains, both of which stop in Ruse. Sleepers are only available on the overnight train; buy your ticket well in advance to guarantee yourself a bunk for the night.

The *Bosfor* overnight train travels from Bucharest to Istanbul (803km, 17 to 19 hours).

There's an overnight service between Bucharest and Chişinău. Between Romania and Ukraine, there is a daily Bucharest–Moscow train which goes via Kyiv. A second train, the Sofia–Moscow *Bulgaria Expres* takes a different route through western Ukraine to Chernivtsi (Cernăuţi in Romanian), and stops at Bucharest.

GETTING AROUND
Air
State-owned carrier **Tarom** (www.tarom.ro) is Romania's main carrier and in 2003 invested in new 747s and improved its already excellent on-board service. Smaller airlines like **Angel Airlines** (in Bucharest ☎ 021-211 1701; ticketing@angelairlines.ro) and **Carpatair** (www.carpatair .com) run domestic flights.

Bicycle
Cyclists are becoming a more frequent sight in Romania, particularly in Transylvania, Maramureş and Moldavia. It is possible to rent or buy bikes in most major towns, which also have bike-repair shops. Still, bringing as many spare parts with you as possible will save you time and headaches. Two good towns to get bikes from are Sibiu and Braşov in Transylvania.

Boat
Boat is the only way of getting around much of the Danube Delta. **Navrom** (☎ 0240-511 553) operates passenger ferries along the three main Danube channels from Tulcea. You can easily hire private motorboats, rowing boats and kayaks in Tulcea and all the Delta villages to explore the smaller waterways. Local fishermen and boatmen double as guides.

Bus
Regular buses travel to most corners of the country – slowly, clunkily, dustily, but surely. Endlessly better are the maxitaxis

(also referred to as microbuses or minibuses) which have blanketed the country in recent years. Timetables for regular buses posted in *autogară* (bus stations) are often incomplete or out of date, so always ask at the ticket window for details. Fares are cheap and calculated per kilometre: a 10km trip will cost €0.40, a 100km trip €2.40.

Maxitaxis are even more elusive creatures. Because routes are run by different private companies, which crop up all the time, there is no centralised system of information.

All this, of course, is contingent upon you actually knowing where buses and maxitaxis depart – in many cities, departure points can be not only at the bus station but at any nearby parking lot. In short, getting around by bus and maxitaxi is more than possible, it just takes a sense of adventure!

Car & Motorcycle
Don't drive in Romania unless your car is in good shape and has been serviced recently. Repair shops are common but, unless you're driving a Renault (the same as Romania's Dacia) or a Citroën (the basis of Romania's Oltcit model), parts are hard to come by. Most Romanian roads are best suited for 4WD vehicles that can take child-sized potholes in stride.

Romania has only a few short stretches of *autostrada* (motorway). Some *drum naţional* (major roads) have been resurfaced, but many remain in a poor (understatement!), potholed condition. *Drum judeţean* (secondary roads) can become dirt tracks, and *drum forestier* (mountain and forestry roads) can be impassable after heavy rain.

EC driving licences are accepted here; otherwise, bring both your home country's driving licence and the International Diver's Permit, which is recognised in Romania. There is a 0% blood-alcohol tolerance limit, seat belts are compulsory in the front and back (if fitted) seats, and children under 12 are forbidden to sit in the front seat. Speed limits are indicated, but are usually 90km/h on major roads, 100–110km/h on motorways, and 50km/h inside cities. Having a standard first aid kit is also compulsory.

Avis, Budget, Hertz and Europcar have offices in most cities and at Otopeni Airport in Bucharest. Consider renting a Dacia. Romania's national car might well be the butt of endless jokes but in the event of a breakdown you'll be glad you're not driving a Mercedes.

Local Transport

Buses, trams and trolleybuses provide transport within most towns and cities in Romania, although many are crowded. They usually run from about 5am to midnight, although services can get thin on the ground after 7pm in more remote areas. Purchase tickets at street kiosks marked *bilete* or *casă de bilete* before boarding, and validate them once aboard.

In many rural parts, the only vehicle that passes will be horse-powered. Horse and cart is the most popular form of transport in Romania. Many carts will stop and give you a ride, the driver expecting no more than a cigarette in payment.

Bucharest is the only city in Romania to boast a metro system.

Train

Rail has long been the most popular way of travelling around Romania. **Căile Ferate Române** (CFR; Romanian State Railways; www.cfr.ro) runs trains over 11,000km of track, providing service to most cities, towns and larger villages in the country. The *mersul trenurilor* (national train timetable) is published as a little red book each May and is sold for €2 from CFR offices. It's also available on their website, though it takes a degree in engineering to use it.

Sosire means 'arrivals' and *plecare* is 'departures'. On posted timetables, the number of the platform from which each train departs is listed under *linia*.

CLASSES & TYPES OF TRAINS

In Romania there are five different types of train, all of which travel at different speeds, offer varying levels of comfort and charge different fares for the same destination.

The cheapest trains are local personal trains. These trains are achingly slow. *Accelerat* trains are faster, hence a tad more expensive and less crowded. Seat reservations are obligatory and automatic when you buy your ticket. There's little difference between *rapid* and *expres* trains. Both travel at a fair speed and often have dining cars. Pricier Inter-City trains are the most comfortable but aren't faster than *expres* trains.

Vagon de dormit (sleepers) are available between Bucharest and Arad, Cluj-Napoca, Oradea, Timişoara, Tulcea and other points, and are a good way to cut accommodation expenses. First-class sleeping compartments generally have two berths, 2nd-class sleepers generally have four berths and 2nd-class couchettes have six berths. Book these in advance at a CFR office.

Fares listed in this chapter generally indicate one-way, 1st-class seats on *rapid* or *accelerat* trains. Fares for all Romanian trains comprise three parts: the basic fare, calculated on the kilometres you are travelling; a speed/comfort supplement; and a seat reservation (automatic on all but the personal trains).

Travelling 100km 1st class costs €2 on a personal train, €5 on a *rapid* or *expres* and €5.40 on an Inter-City train.

BUYING TICKETS

Tickets are sold in advance for all trains except local personal ones. Advance tickets are sold at an Agenţie de Voiaj CFR, a train-ticket office found in every city centre. When the ticket office is closed you have to buy your ticket immediately before departure at the station. Whenever possible, buy your ticket in advance. This saves time queuing at the train station and also guarantees you a seat.

Theoretically you can buy tickets at CFR offices up to two hours before departure. In reality many do not sell tickets for trains leaving the same day so try to buy your ticket at least the day before you intend to travel.

You can only buy tickets at train stations two hours – and in some cases just one hour – before departure. Get there early as queues can be horrendous. At major stations there are separate ticket lines for 1st and 2nd classes; you may opt for 1st class when you see how much shorter that line is. Your reservation ticket lists the code number of your train along with your assigned *vagon* (carriage) and *locul* (seat).

If you have an international ticket right through Romania, you're allowed to make stops along the route but you must purchase a reservation ticket each time you reboard an *accelerat* or *rapid* train. If the international ticket was issued in Romania, you must also pay the *expres* train supplement each time.

Russia Россия

CONTENTS

Highlights	647	**Russia Directory**	**691**
Itineraries	647	Accommodation	691
Climate & When to Go	647	Business Hours	691
History	647	Children	691
People	650	Courses	691
Sport	650	Customs	692
Religion	650	Dangers & Annoyances	692
Arts	650	Disabled Travellers	692
Environment	653	Embassies & Consulates	692
Food & Drink	653	Gay & Lesbian Travellers	693
Moscow	**654**	Holidays	693
History	654	Internet Resources	693
Orientation	655	Language	693
Information	655	Media	693
Dangers & Annoyances	658	Money	694
Sights	659	Post	694
Activities	663	Telephone	694
Sleeping	663	Travel Agencies	694
Eating	665	Visas	695
Drinking	666	Women Travellers	695
Entertainment	666	**Transport in Russia**	**695**
Shopping	667	Getting There & Away	695
Getting There & Away	667	Getting Around	696
Getting Around	668		
Around Moscow	668		
St Petersburg	**671**		
History	671		
Orientation	671		
Information	671		
Dangers & Annoyances	675		
Sights	675		
Activities	678		
Tours	679		
Festivals & Events	679		
Sleeping	679		
Eating	680		
Drinking	681		
Entertainment	681		
Shopping	682		
Getting Around	682		
Around St Petersburg	682		
Kaliningrad Region	**683**		
History	684		
People	685		
Environment	685		
Kaliningrad	685		
Svetlogorsk	690		
Kurshkaya Kosa	691		

Endlessly enigmatic, bureaucratic beyond belief and hopelessly romantic, Russia stands at the end of Eastern Europe, where it begins to slip away into Asia. Looming over the rest of Europe with its immense, inhuman size and dark, brutal history, Russia is an essential and fascinating destination for anyone wanting to see another side to the European continent in all its awkward, mysterious glory. Moscow and St Petersburg are two of Europe's biggest cities, yet are as dissimilar as it is possible to imagine. Stately, relaxed and oh-so-cultured, the former Russian capital of St Petersburg is quite simply one of the most beautiful cities in Europe, overflowing with 18th-century palaces and brightly painted Italianate mansions, divided by graceful canals. Brash, vulgar and stupendously hedonistic, Moscow is one of the most dynamic and fast-paced cities on earth, demanding your attention right now. While the Cold War still hangs in the air around the Kremlin and Red Square, elsewhere there's palpable excitement as the Las Vegas of the East continues its frantic pace of change.

Given the vast size of European Russia, this book only covers Moscow, St Petersburg and the Russian enclave of Kaliningrad, wedged between Poland and Lithuania on the Baltic Sea. Ignore what you may have heard about Russia in the past – come with an open mind and any trip here will be a hugely rewarding experience.

FAST FACTS

- **Area** 16,995,800 sq km
- **Capital** Moscow
- **Currency** rouble (R); €1 = R37; US$1 = R29; UK£1 = R53; A$1 = R21; ¥100 = R27; NZ$1 = R20
- **Famous for** vodka, communism, caviar, tATu
- **Key Phrases** privyet (hi), do svidaniya (goodbye), spasiba (thanks), izvinitye (excuse me), mozhno yesho stakanchik? (may I have another little glassful?)
- **Official Language** Russian
- **Population** 147 million
- **Telephone Codes** country code ☎ 7; international access code 8 (wait for second tone) 10
- **Visas** required by all and can be a real headache – begin preparing well in advance of your trip! See p695 for more

RUSSIA

HIGHLIGHTS

- Smell the power in the air at the Kremlin, nerve centre of the world's largest country, and see Lenin on daily display at fabulous **Red Square** (p659)
- One of Europe's most impressive piazzas, **Palace Square**, home to the **Winter Palace** and the **Hermitage** (p675), is unforgettable
- Experience a city that truly never sleeps during the **St Petersburg white nights** (p679) in late June
- Discard your inhibitions (and clothing) and get some 'nekkid' birch-twig whipping action in a Russian **banya** (p663) – it's a cultural experience, honest
- Explore Europe's second-highest sand dunes and scout for pieces of amber along the fabulous beaches in the fantastically remote **Kurshkaya Kosa** (p691) in Kaliningrad

HOW MUCH?

- Second-class overnight train between Moscow and St Petersburg R500–1300
- Standard taxi fare within a city centre R50–100
- Metro journey in Moscow R10
- Bootleg DVD R150
- George W Bush novelty nesting doll R500

LONELY PLANET INDEX

- Litre of petrol R15
- Litre of water R22
- Bottle of Baltika beer R25
- Souvenir T-shirt R200–300
- Street snack (blin) R30–50

ITINERARIES

- **Three Days in Moscow** Red Square and the Kremlin have to be your first stop, followed by the Pushkin Museum and Christ the Saviour's Church on the Moscow River. The next day go south of the river to the sublime Novodevichy Convent, then take the stunning metro to the Tretyakov Gallery and the All-Russia Exhibition. Check out Moscow's legendary nightlife in the evening. On day three, strike out and see one of the delightful Golden Ring towns.
- **Three days in St Petersburg** Wander up Nevsky Prospekt, see Palace Square, the mighty Neva River and the unforgettable Hermitage, where you can lose yourself for hours in the magnificent collection. Day two allows time for the historic St Peter & Paul Fortress, the Church on the Spilled Blood and the Alexander Nevsky Lavra. On day three, take one of the possible excursions out of the city and visit either Pushkin or Petrodvorets for a taste of how the tsars lived.
- **Three days in Kaliningrad** On the first day, you'll want to take in the main museums and cathedral, give some food to the animals in the Zoo, then wander through Amalienau and hit some restaurants and/or nightclubs. Day two should see you drive out to the coast for the sea air and views, preferably onto the Kurshkaya Kosa to climb some dunes and spend a peaceful night in nature. The next day you can visit Svetlogorsk on your way back to the city.

CLIMATE & WHEN TO GO

If Russia can be called a land of extremes, then its weather is no exception. The winters are extremely cold – temperatures regularly reach -10°C or even -20°C in both Moscow and St Petersburg – while summers are hot and humid. Spring and autumn are both notional concepts, each lasting about a month.

Despite its extremes of temperature, most times of year can be good for visiting Russia. The snow and ice make St Petersburg look quite magical, and Moscow surprisingly clean. If possible, avoid March and early April – the 'thaw' is the least pleasant time of year. The snow and ice melt, creating a ubiquitous brown sludge and general muddiness that makes walking about fairly unpleasant. The perfect times of year to visit are May, June and September. See p874 for more information on Russia's climate.

HISTORY

Russia has its cultural origins in Kyivan Rus, a kingdom located in what is today Ukraine and Belarus. From here the Slavs expanded into modern European Russia, converting to Christianity in the 9th and

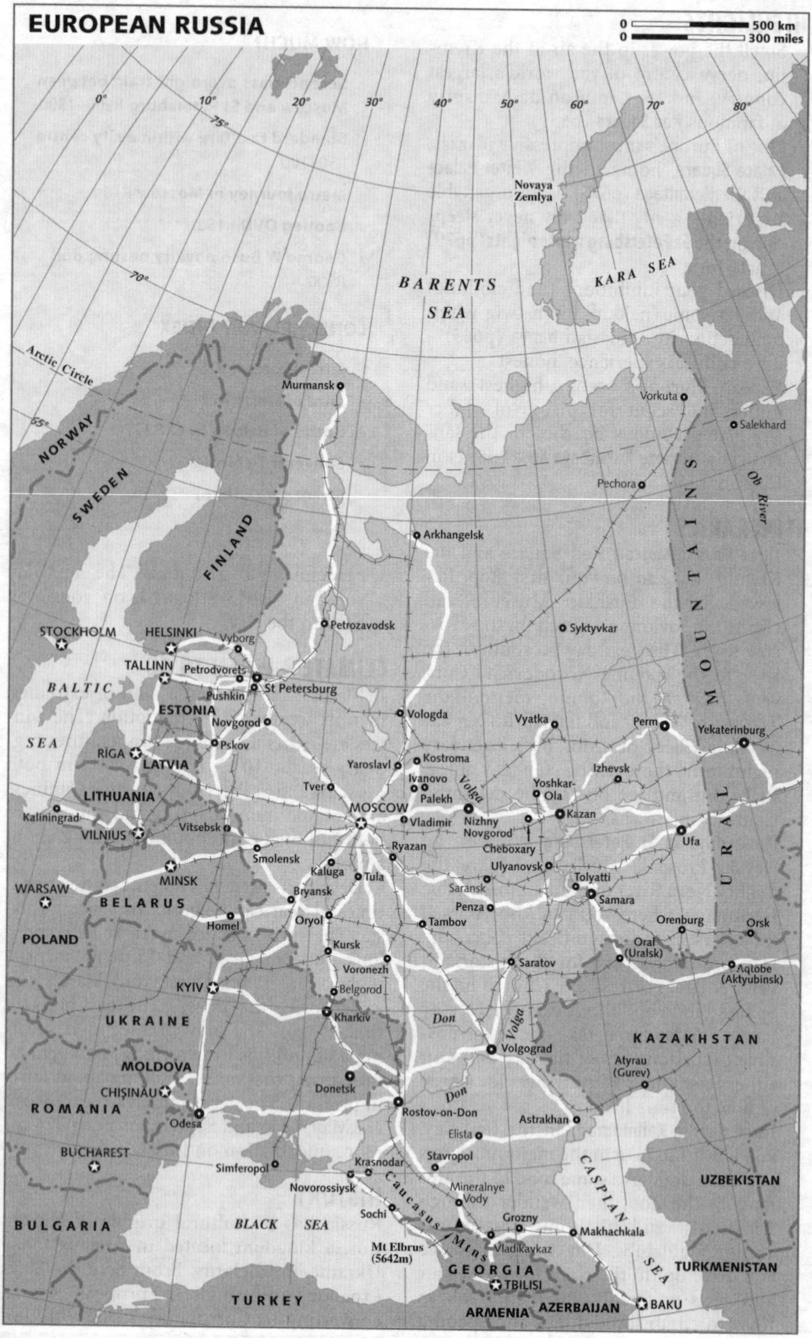
EUROPEAN RUSSIA
0 500 km
0 300 miles
0°
10°
20°
30°
40°
50°
60°
70°
80°
75°
70°
65°
Arctic Circle
Novaya Zemlya
BARENTS SEA
KARA SEA
NORWAY
SWEDEN
FINLAND
Murmansk
Vorkuta
Salekhard
Pechora
Ob River
URAL MOUNTAINS
Arkhangelsk
Petrozavodsk
Syktyvkar
STOCKHOLM
HELSINKI
Vyborg
TALLINN
Petrodvorets
St Petersburg
Pushkin
BALTIC SEA
ESTONIA
Novgorod
Vologda
Vyatka
Perm
Yekaterinburg
RĪGA
Pskov
LATVIA
Kostroma
Yaroslavl
Ivanovo
Palekh
Volga
Izhevsk
Yoshkar-Ola
Tver
LITHUANIA
Kaliningrad
VILNIUS
Vitsebsk
MOSCOW
Vladimir
Nizhny Novgorod
Kazan
Ufa
Cheboxary
Ryazan
Smolensk
MINSK
Kaluga
Tula
Ulyanovsk
Tolyatti
Saransk
WARSAW
BELARUS
Bryansk
Penza
Samara
Homel
Oryol
Tambov
Orenburg
Orsk
POLAND
Kursk
Oral (Uralsk)
Saratov
Aqtobe (Aktyubinsk)
Voronezh
KYIV
Belgorod
UKRAINE
Kharkiv
Don
Volga
Volgograd
KAZAKHSTAN
MOLDOVA
Donetsk
Atyrau (Gurev)
CHIŞINĂU
Don
ROMANIA
Odesa
Rostov-on-Don
Astrakhan
Elista
BUCHAREST
Stavropol
Simferopol
Krasnodar
CASPIAN SEA
UZBEKISTAN
Novorossiysk
Caucasus Mtns
Mineralnye Vody
Sochi
BULGARIA
BLACK SEA
Grozny
Makhachkala
Mt Elbrus (5642m)
Vladikavkaz
GEORGIA
TURKMENISTAN
TBILISI
TURKEY
ARMENIA
AZERBAIJAN
BAKU

RUSSIA

10th centuries. With conversion came the introduction of an alphabet, named Cyrillic after its creator, St Cyril, a Greek missionary. He used the Greek alphabet as a basis for the new one, explaining the presence of several Greek letters in Cyrillic to this day. The birth of the Russian state is usually identified with the founding of Novgorod in 862 AD, although until 1480 Russia was overrun by the Mongols.

The medieval period in Russia was a dark and brutal time, never more so than during the reign of Ivan the Terrible (r 1547–84), whose sobriquet was well-earned through his fantastically cruel punishments, such as boiling his enemies alive and, most famously, putting out the eyes of the architects who created his magnificent St Basil's Cathedral (p659) on Red Square.

Despite Ivan the Terrible's conquest of the Volga basin and obsession with reaching the Baltic (at that time controlled by the Lithuanians and Swedes), it was not until the Romanov dynasty (1613–1917) that Russia became the vast nation it is today – territorial expansion between the 17th and 19th centuries saw the country increase in size exponentially to include Siberia, the Arctic, the Far East, Central Asia and the Caucasus.

Peter the Great (r 1689–1725) can in many ways be seen as the father of the Russian state. It was he who dragged the country kicking and screaming out of the dark ages, setting up a Russian navy, educational centres and beginning the construction of a new capital – St Petersburg – in 1703. Russia's capital moved north from Peter's hated Moscow in 1712, and was to remain the capital until the Bolsheviks moved it back to Moscow over two centuries later.

Catherine the Great (r 1762–96), a provincial German princess with no legitimate claim to the throne, assumed power, having plotted to have her histrionic, pointless husband Peter III dispatched by palace guards. Catherine continued Peter the Great's progressive yet authoritarian policies to create a world power by the mid-18th century. Her 'enlightened despotism' saw the founding of the art collection that was to become the Hermitage, a huge expansion in the sciences and arts, a correspondence with Voltaire, and the strengthening of the nation. However,

it also saw her brutal suppression of a Cossack rebellion and intolerance for any institution that would threaten her authority.

The 19th century saw feverish capitalist development undermined by successively autocratic and backwards tsars. Alexander I (r 1801–25) was too preoccupied with Napoleon (who invaded Russia and torched Moscow in 1812, and was eventually beaten by the Russian winter), and despite Alexander II's (r 1855–81) brave freeing of the serfs in 1861, which paved the way to a modern capitalist economy, political reform was nowhere on the cards.

The revolutionary movement grew in the late 19th century, mainly in Switzerland, where many exiled radicals had based themselves. Nicholas II, the last tsar of Russia, ascended the throne in 1894, and was even weaker and more scared of change than his predecessors. It was his refusal to countenance serious reform that precipitated the 1917 revolution. What began as a liberal revolution was hijacked later the same year in a coup led by the Bolsheviks under Lenin, which resulted in the establishment of the world's first communist state.

Between 1917 and 1920 the Bolsheviks fought a bloody Civil War against the 'whites', who supported the monarchy. The tsar and his family were murdered in 1918 to deprive the whites of any figurehead, and eventually resistance to the communists trickled out.

By the time Lenin's died in 1924 – since when he has lain in state at his purpose-built mausoleum (p659) on Red Square – Russia had become the principal member of the Union of Soviet Socialist Republics, a communist superpower absorbing some 14 neighbouring states between 1922 and 1945. It was Stalin who, with incredibly single-minded brutality, dragged Russia into the 20th century. His forced industrialisation of the country involved the deaths of millions, but he got his results, making him an oddly ambivalent figure in Russia today. He saw Russia through the devastation of WWII, during which some 20 million Russians died, and by the time he himself died in 1953, the USSR had a full nuclear arsenal and half of Europe as satellite states.

After Stalin, Khrushchev (r 1957–64) began a cautious reform programme and denounced Stalin before being removed and replaced by Leonid Brezhnev, whose rule (1964–82) was marked by economic stagnation and growing internal dissent. Finally, Mikhail Gorbachev's period of reform, known as *perestroika,* began in 1985. Within six years, the USSR had collapsed alongside communism, and reformer Boris Yeltsin was elected the first ever president of Russia in 1991.

Yeltsin led Russia into a new world of cutthroat capitalism, which saw the creation of a new superclass of oligarchs – businessmen who made billions from buying once stateowned commodities and running them as private companies – while prices soared and incomes dropped in real terms for the vast majority of the population.

Since 2000, Russia has been led by Vladimir Putin, an ex-KGB officer who has steered a careful course between reform and centralisation, alarming the West with his control of the media and brutal clampdown on the independence movement in Chechnya. The Beslan school siege in September 2004 was the latest large-scale terrorist assault on Russia from Chechen separatists, whose activities have bedevilled Putin's presidency. Despite this, Putin remains an extremely popular president and Russia is in the grip of very healthy economic growth, even if this is not benefiting everybody.

PEOPLE

There's some truth to the local saying 'scratch a Russian and you'll find a Tatar'. Russia has absorbed people from a huge number of nationalities: from the Mongols, the Tatars, Siberian peoples, Ukrainians, Jews, Caucasians and other national minorities who have all been part of Russia for centuries. This means that while the vast majority of people you meet will describe themselves as Russian, ethnic homogeneity is not always that simple.

On a personal level, Russians have a reputation for being dour, depressed and unfriendly. In fact, most Russians are anything but, yet find constant smiling indicative of idiocy, and ridicule those who constantly display their happiness. Even though Russians can be unfriendly and even downright rude when you first meet them (especially those working behind glass windows of any kind), their warmth as soon as the ice is broken is quite astounding.

SPORT

Gone are the days of Cold War clashes at the Olympics (the US boycotted the 1980 Moscow Olympics, and the USSR in turn boycotted the Los Angeles Olympics in 1984), but despite this Russia remains a formidable sporting presence in the world arena: at the 2000 Sydney Olympics Russia came away with 32 gold medals, second only to the United States, although at Athens in 2004 Russia found itself squeezed into third place by China, winning a still hugely impressive 28 golds.

On the ground, football is the game that interests Russians most, although most people care more passionately about the English premier league than their own teams, especially since Russian billionaire Roman Abramovich bought London club Chelsea for himself in 2003.

RELIGION

The vast majority of Russians identify themselves as Orthodox Christians, although the proportion of those who actually practice their faith is small. The Russian Orthodox Church is led by Patriarch Alexei II, who has an increasingly visible role in Putin's Russia.

Religious freedom exists in Russia – St Petersburg boasts the world's most northerly Mosque and Buddhist Temple. There can be some residual chauvinism about Jews, although this is very rarely exhibited in anything other than the odd negative comment and some deeply entrenched stereotypes. There is certainly no reason for Jewish travellers to worry about coming to Russia.

ARTS

Blame it on the long winter nights, the constant struggle against authoritarianism or the long-debated qualities of the mysterious 'Russian soul', but Russia's artistic contribution to the world is nothing short of gobsmacking.

Literature

Russia's formal literary tradition began relatively late. It was set in motion in the early 19th century by playwright Griboyedov before reaching its zenith with the poetic genius of Alexander Pushkin (1799–1837), whose epic poem *Yevgeny Onegin* stands out as one of Russian literature's greatest achievements, an enormous, playful, philosophical poem from which any Russian can quote at least a few lines.

Pushkin's life was tragically cut short by a duel, and though his literary heir Mikhail Lermontov had the potential to equal or even surpass Pushkin's contribution – his novel *A Hero of Our Time* and his poetry spoke of incredible gifts – only a few years later Lermontov too was senselessly murdered in a duel in Southern Russia.

By the late 19th century, Russia was producing some of the world's great classics – Lev Tolstoy and Fyodor Dostoyevsky were the outstanding talents, two deeply different writers of unquestionable genius. Tolstoy brought the world enormous tapestries of Russian life such as *War and Peace* and *Anna Karenina*, while Dostoyevsky wrote dark and troubled philosophical novels such as *Crime and Punishment* and *The Brothers Karamazov*.

The early 20th century saw a continued literary flowering during what was widely known as the Silver Age, an enormously productive era of poetic creation, seeing movements as disparate as the acmeists, mystics and symbolists combine in unpredictable and often brilliant ways. This incredible literary ferment, which brought Blok, Akhmatova and Mandelstam worldwide fame, was dramatically curtailed by the revolution. Seismic changes in literature occurred in Russia post-1917. Despite an initial burst of creative energy – some of Russia's best writing, virtually unknown to audiences in the West, was written during the period between 1917 and 1925 – by the late 1920s, with Stalin's grip on power complete, all writers not spouting the party line were anathematised. Dissenting writers were either shot, took their own lives, fled or were silenced as Stalin revealed his 'socialist realism' model of writing, which brought novels with titles such as *Cement* and *How the Steel Was Tempered* to the toiling masses. Despite this, many writers kept on writing in secret, and novels such as Mikhail Bulgakov's *The Master and Margarita* and poems such as Anna Akhmatova's 'Requiem' survived Stalinism to become classics known the world over.

Despite Khrushchev allowing some literary debate to begin again (he allowed Solzhenitsyn's *A Day in the Life of Ivan Denisovich* to be published, a novella depicting life in one of Stalin's gulags), censorship continued until the mid-1980s when, thanks to Mikhail Gorbachev's policy of *glasnost* (openness), writers who had only been published through the illegal network of *samizdat* (the home printing presses) and were thus read only by the intelligentsia suddenly had millions of readers.

Since the end of the Soviet Union, Russian literature has developed quickly and embraced the postmodernism that was creatively proscribed by the Soviet authorities. Current literary big-hitters include Boris Akunin and Viktor Pelevin, both of whom are widely available in English.

Cinema & TV

Russia has produced some of the world's most famous film images – largely thanks to the father of the cinematic montage, Sergei Eisenstein, whose *Battleship Potemkin* (1925) and *Ivan the Terrible* (1944–46) are masterpieces and reference points for anyone serious about the history of film. Despite constant headaches with authority, Andrei Tarkovsky produced complex and iconoclastic films in the 1960s and 1970s; *The Mirror* and *Andrei Rublev* are generally considered to be his two greatest works.

In recent times Nikita Mikhailkov and Alexander Sokurov have established themselves as internationally renowned Russian directors. Mikhailkov took the best foreign film Oscar in 1994 for his *Burnt by the Sun*, and seemed to find a more sentimental and Hollywood-friendly style for his underwhelming *The Barber of Siberia* (1999), the biggest-budget Russian film ever made. Alexander Sokurov has made his name producing art-house historical dramas including *Taurus, Molokh* and 2002's astonishing *Russian Ark* – the only full-length film ever made using one long tracking shot. One final film that should not be missed under any circumstances is Andrei Zvyagintsev's stunning debut feature, *The Return* (2003), which scooped the Golden Lion at the Venice Film Festival.

Russian TV is not nearly as rich a feast. There are several channels available, although this varies across the country. The past few years have been characterised by a barely disguised attempt on the part of Putin's government to claw back the media control that the Kremlin had lost since *perestroika*. The takeover of once-trailblazing NTV, Russia's first professionally run TV station (and crucially, one critical of the Kremlin), has had a long-term effect on the vibrancy of the Russian media as a whole. In 2001 the Putin government effectively staged a takeover of the station on spurious legal grounds, leading to the mass resignation of NTV's journalists and editors. Since then NTV has been unable to re-establish the high standard of political journalism that was its trademark. There are currently no national TV channels independent of the Kremlin operating in Russia. Most channels run a dismal array of chat shows, old Soviet movies, chronic pop concerts and American straight-to-video movies clumsily dubbed into Russian with one voice.

Music

When ersatz lesbian teenyboppers Lena Katina and Julia Volkova – better known the world-over as tATu – reached number one in several countries with their 2003 smash hit *All the Things She Said*, Russian music suddenly meant something very different to the people of the world. tATu remain one of few Russian groups to be known beyond the former Soviet Union, although ginger matriarch Alla Pugacheva (a kind of Russian female version of Elton John complete with wardrobe) enjoys a cult following in some quarters.

More deservedly, Russia is of course famous for composers such as Tchaikovsky, Rimsky-Korsakov, Prokofiev and Shostakovich, and despite the enormous and almost universally horrific Russian pop music industry, music is taken extremely seriously in modern Russia. Indeed, on any night of the week in Moscow or St Petersburg there's likely to be a good choice of concerts, gigs, ballet and opera to choose from.

Architecture

Both Moscow and St Petersburg are treasure troves for anyone interested in architecture. Whether it be the dazzling Italianate style of old St Petersburg or the combination of medieval and monolithic in Moscow, neither is likely to disappoint.

Moscow's 20th-century heritage is somewhat under threat from the city government, which is tearing down some unique communist-era buildings at the aegis of populist mayor Yuri Luzhkov. While this may have meant ridding the city of the hugely ugly Intourist Hotel on Tverskaya ul, it has also meant the destruction of buildings such as the Hotel Moskva on Manezhnaya pl (built to two separate designs simultaneously, as Stalin had approved both and nobody dared ask which he actually wanted). Perhaps this wouldn't be so bad if it wasn't for the fact that Luzhkov's replacements have often been just as bad, in their own uniquely tasteless style. Zurab Tsereteli, Luzhkov's Albert Speer, is one of the worst offenders; among his contributions to the Moscow skyline is a statue of Peter the Great – one of the ugliest tributes to a national hero anywhere in the world.

In St Petersburg, the huge number of beautiful 18th- and 19th-century palaces and mansions needing renovation has outstripped the city's budget so entirely that in 2004 Governor Matvienko announced she would give the go-ahead to sell off many of these treasures to companies and individuals who have the resources to save them.

Königsberg (present-day Kaliningrad) was one of Prussia's finest cities and before its near-total destruction during WWII was one of Europe's architectural gems. What fine German buildings survived acted as a constant reminder to the populace of the area's non-Russianess. Collecting information about the city's architectural history became an act of dissent. After the collapse of the USSR, one of the first projects to get underway was to restore the fine Gothic Dom (cathedral) in the centre of what had become largely just another concrete-dominated Soviet city

Painting

Russian painting is fairly unknown in the West, the most celebrated artists being the avant-garde painters of the early 20th century such as Vasily Kandinsky and Kazimir Malevich. Most Russians will be surprised if you have heard of them and not the 'greats' of the 19th century such as Ilya Repin and the *peredvizhniki* (wanderers) – the generation of painters who rejected the strict formalism of the St Petersburg Academy.

Anyone visiting Russia will want to see the collection of foreign art held at the Hermitage (p675). The best galleries for Russian art are the Russian Museum (p676) in St Petersburg and the State Tretyakov Gallery (p662) in Moscow.

Theatre & Dance

Theatre is one of the more vibrant art forms in Russia today. Since Chekhov revolutionised Russian drama in the late 19th century, Russia has seen countless innovations, from Stanislavsky, who created method acting, to Meyerhold, the theatrical pioneer whom Stalin had arrested and murdered.

Among the most celebrated contemporary theatre directors today are St Petersburg-based Lev Dodin and Moscow-based Roman Vityuk. The world-famous Bolshoi (p666) and Mariinsky (Kirov) (p681) Theatres have worked hard to reinvent themselves since the end of the Soviet Union, and their performances are regularly seen around the world on lucrative tours.

ENVIRONMENT

While Russia as a country encompasses almost every conceivable type of landscape, European Russia around Moscow and St Petersburg is characterised by flatness. You can take the train from one city to the other and barely pass a hill or a valley.

Kaliningrad is strikingly different, with its half of the Curonian Spit, the Curonian Lagoon and the world's largest supply of amber (p683).

The disastrous environmental legacy of communism is enormous. As well as both Moscow and St Petersburg being polluted from traffic and heavy industry, the countryside is frequently blighted by factories and other industrial plants. Environmental consciousness remains relatively low, although things are slowly changing with the emergence of a small but vocal Russian environmental movement.

FOOD & DRINK

There's no denying it, Russian food is quite bland by most people's standards: spices are not widely used and dill is overwhelmingly the herb of choice, sprinkled onto almost everything. That said, you can eat extremely well in Russia – Caucasian food is popular throughout the country and is delicious. Moscow and St Petersburg both overflow with restaurants serving cuisine from all over the world.

While the variety is hardly as great in Kaliningrad and while world cuisine hasn't made much of a dent there, the choices in recent years have expanded such that dining out is a gastronomical pleasure.

Staples & Specialities

Russian soups are very good. Delicious *borsch* (beetroot soup), *solyanka* (a soup made from pickled vegetables) and *ukha* (fish soup) are always reliable. *Pelmeni*, are Russian ravioli – beef parcels wrapped in dough and served with sour cream *(smetana)* – and are the lowest common denominator in Russian cooking. Other more interesting possibilities are *zharkoye* (literally 'hot' – meat stew in a pot), blini, caviar, beef Stroganov, *goluptsy* (mincemeat wrapped in cabbage leaves) and fish specialities such as sturgeon, salmon and pikeperch.

Where to Eat & Drink

The *pelmennaya* is the archetypal workers café and serves *pelmeni* for pennies. Similar equivalents are the *cheburechnaya*, where *cheburekis* (meat filled Caucasian pasties) are sold, and *shaverma* bars, where various kebabs are sold. A *traktir* is a provincial inn, now making something of a comeback in the form of theme restaurants such as the ubiquitous Yolki-Palki chain.

Russian restaurants themselves tend to be quite formal, although there's an increasing number of relaxed diner-style eateries in evidence in Moscow and St Petersburg. Cafés, a Western import, have become extremely popular, although the *pivnoy bar*, or beer hall, is where most Russians prefer to drink. These relaxed, generally cheap and hearty Russian fare with live music of some description.

Vegetarians & Vegans

Russia can be tough for vegetarians, and near impossible for vegans. Vegetarians will find themselves eating blini with sour cream, mushrooms, cheese or savoury whey *(tvorog)*; mushroom julienne (mushrooms fried in garlic, cheese and cream); and visiting Georgian restaurants often. Vegans might be wishing they could go home.

Habits & Customs

Food etiquette is fairly straightforward. Symbolic of its importance in Russian culture, it's drinking that is full of unspoken rules. First of all, never drink vodka without *zakuski* (snacks) – you'll get drunk otherwise, whereas (according to any Russian) that will *never* happen if you consume pickled herring or gherkins with your vodka. Once a bottle (vodka or otherwise) has been finished, it's considered rude to put it back on the table – always put it on the floor instead. Don't talk during toasts, and always appear to drink to the toast (even if you dribble it down your chin or drink nothing at all). Men should always down a vodka shot in one. Women are let off this requirement, although being able to down a large shot will garner respect from all quarters.

MOSCOW MOCKBA

☎ 095 / pop 10 million

The biggest city in Europe, Moscow's sheer size is matched only by its brazen right-here-right-now hedonism, its lust for life, its shocking wealth and pitiful poverty. There are more billionaires living here than in any other city on earth, and judging by a walk almost anywhere in the centre, there's a similar surfeit of beggars. An ancient and brutal city whose architectural wealth encompasses everything from medieval churches to Stalin's fabulously Gothic Seven Sisters, Moscow is impressive, contradictory and immense fun. St Petersburg may once have been Russia's window on Europe, but Moscow is now its neon-lit showroom. Nowhere else in Russia today has more energy or creative fire. From the Kremlin to clubbing, it's all here for the taking.

HISTORY

While Moscow has been inhabited for over five millennia, it was mentioned for the first time in only 1147 by Prince Yury Dolgoruky, who to this day is acknowledged as the founder of the city by a huge equestrian statue of him on Tverskaya ul (p660). It was Yury who built wooden walls around the city and oversaw its rise as an economic centre. During the reign of the Mongol Horde in the 13th to 15th centuries, Moscow outstripped rivals Vladimir and Suzdal as the principal town of the Muscovy principality. Under Ivan the Great and Ivan the Terrible in the 16th century the city expanded

enormously, as Russia became a vast state absorbing Slav lands to the west, the Baltic, the Urals and the north. The Crimean Tatars sacked the city in 1571, burning much of it, which prompted the construction of stone walls around Kitay Gorod (p662) that can still be seen today. By the early 17th century, Moscow was the biggest city on earth.

The 18th century saw a huge decline for Moscow – Peter the Great moved the capital to his new northern city of St Petersburg in 1712 and fire, economic downturn and bubonic plague took their toll. Napoleon's onslaught on Moscow a century later was even more catastrophic – Muscovites burned most of the city rather than surrender to the French, although thankfully the Kremlin survived. Following Napoleon's retreat and eventual rout, Moscow regained its confidence and developed as Russia's economic powerhouse – becoming an industrial city full of factories, slums and revolutionaries by the end of the 19th century.

It was the Russian revolution that restored Moscow's prestige – the resulting Civil War forced Lenin, fearing St Petersburg's proximity to hostile foreign governments, to move the capital back to Moscow in 1918. As capital of the Union of Soviet Socialist Republics, Moscow became the nerve centre of a superpower. Under Stalin the Nazis were resisted (they came within 30km of the Kremlin), the vast and beautiful Moscow metro was built, countless churches including the now reconstructed Church of Christ the Saviour (p662) were demolished and vast, neo-Gothic architecture such as the Seven Sisters became the order of the day. Soviet Moscow's proudest moment came when it hosted the 1980 Olympic games – a last big fling for a declining nation that was soon to reform itself out of existence.

Moscow has seen no end of tumult since *perestroika* – the 1991 coup against Gorbachev, Yeltsin's attack on the parliament building in 1993, the terrible Ostankino TV Tower fire in August 2000 when the city's TV tower went up in a blazing inferno (becoming a metaphor for many despairing Muscovites of Russia's disintegrating infrastructure) and several large scale terrorist attacks, most famous of which is the Dubrovka Theatre Siege of October 2002 when Chechen terrorists took an entire theatre audience hostage, eventually culminating in a botched rescue attempt during which some 129 people were killed. Despite this, Moscow has reinforced its position as Russia's economic powerhouse and today it's a city looking far ahead into the future.

ORIENTATION

The medieval centre of the city, the Kremlin, is a triangle on the northern bank of the Moscow River. The modern city centre radiates around it, the main streets being Tverskaya ul and ul Novy Arbat.

INFORMATION
Bookshops

Anglia British Bookshop (Map pp656-8; ☎ 299 7766; www.anglophile.ru; Vorotnikovsky per 6; Ⓜ Mayakovskaya; ☜ 10am-7pm Mon-Fri, to 6pm Sat, 11am-5pm Sun) Has an excellent selection of books in English, including travel guides.

Moskovsky Dom Knigi (Map pp656-8; ☎ 290 4507; www.mdk-arbat.ru, in Russian; ul Novy Arbat 8; Ⓜ Arbatskaya; ☜ 10am-9pm Mon-Sat, to 8pm Sun) Moscow's main bookshop, excellent but crowded, where you can find books about pretty much anything, including a very decent selection of novels in English.

Internet Access

Internet Klub (Map pp656-8; ☎ 924 2140; www .iclub.ru; ul Kuznetsky Most 12; Ⓜ Kuznetsky Most; per hr R60; ☜ 9am-midnight) Nice and central.

NetCity (Map pp656-8; ☎ 969 2125; www.netcitycafé .ru, in Russian; Kamergersky per 6; per hr R60; ☜ 24hr) An excellent spot.

Phlegmatic Dog (Map pp656-8; ☎ 995 9545; www .phlegmaticdog.ru; Okhotny Ryad Mall, 2nd fl, Aleksandrovsky Garden entrance; Ⓜ Okhotny Ryad; ☜ 11am-1am Sun-Thu, noon-5am Fri & Sat) An 'Internet pub' where web access is free to anyone drinking.

Time Online (Map pp656-8; ☎ 363 0060; www.time online.ru/eng; Ⓜ Okhotny Ryad; per hr R60; ☜ 24hr) In the same mall as the Phlegmatic Dog.

Left Luggage

The many stations around Moscow all have left luggage services, known as *kamera khraneniya*. They will charge minimal rates of between R30 and R50 per 24 hours, although always check their opening times as even 24-hour ones can have 'technical breaks' of several hours.

Media

Moscow's huge expat population has created a large market for English-language publications. Most reliable is the daily *Moscow Times* (www.themoscowtimes.com), a professional and well-produced newspaper that is free and available everywhere. Its weekend edition is excellent for visitors and has comprehensive listings for all leisure activities.

The Exile (www.exile.ru) is a unique satirical bimonthly paper that has consistently outraged and offended since it began in the late 1990s. It's a great read, although not for the easily shocked.

The rest of the English-language press on offer is usually substandard and of little interest. For those who can read Russian, *Ne Spat!* and *Afisha* are the two best-known listings magazines and are available at any newsstand.

Medical Services

There are several expensive, foreign-run health services available in Moscow, including the **American Medical Centre** (Map pp656-8; ☎ 933 7700; fax 933 7701; Grokholsky per 1; Ⓜ Prospekt Mira; ☜ 24hr), which features an English-speaking **pharmacy** (Map pp656-8; ☜ 8am-8pm Mon-Fri, 9am-5pm Sat & Sun). The best Russian facility is **Botkin Hospital** (Map pp656-8; ☎ 945 0045; 2-y Botkinsky proezd 5; Ⓜ Dinamo; ☜ 24hr).

Money

ATMs and reliable money-changing facilities are located on every corner. Russian banks include Alfa Bank, Bank Moskvy and Sberbank; banks work full days (usually 8am to 7pm, Monday to Friday). Out of hours, most big hotels have a 24-hour bank or money-changing facility. **American Express** (☎ 933-6636; fax 9336635; ul Usacheva 33; Ⓜ Sportivnaya) can cash Amex travellers cheques.

Post

The convenient **Central Telegraph** (Map pp656-8; Tsentralny Telegraf; Tverskaya ul 7; Ⓜ Okhotny Ryad; postal counters ☜ 8am-10pm) offers post, telephone, fax and Internet services.

Telephone & Fax

Nearly all hotels have IDD from their rooms at exorbitant rates. It's far better to buy a phonecard and call from any pay phone around the city, or to go to the Central Telegraph (above) and use the booths there. You can also send faxes from here. The Moscow mobile phone market is huge, and

CENTRAL MOSCOW

A **B** **C** **D**

To Dinamo (2km);
STAR Travel (4km);
Rechnoy Vokzal (12km);
Sheremetevo 1 & 2
Airports (30km)

To Hostel
Sherstone (10km)

Novoslobodskaya Ⓜ

1

Hippodrome

5 ✚ Begovaya proezd

Belorusskaya Ⓜ Belorusskaya

78 Tverskaya
zastava pl

Belorussky Vokzal
(Belarus Station) Ⓜ

Myusskaya
pl

Aleksandra
Nevskogo
per

79 ●

Begovaya

2

Khodynskaya ul

ul Presnensky val

Sredny Tishinsky per

Bolshoy Tishinsky per

Tishinskaya pl

70 📮

Gashcka

Oruzheyny
per

Triumfalnaya pl 📮 52 Mayakovskaya Ⓜ
40 46 ● 2

14 ☕

ul Klimashkina

47 📮

59 📮

Pushkinskaya
Tverskaya Ⓜ

3

To Gorbushka
Market (3km)

Ulitsa 1905
Goda Ⓜ

Zvenigorodskoe sh

ul 1905 goda

Rastorguevsky per

Zoologichesky per

73 📮

29 📮

18 ⬆

Barrikadnaya Ⓜ

21 ☕

Krasnopresnenskaya Ⓜ
ul Zamorenova

Kudrinskaya
pl

50 📮

13 ☕

Bolshaya Nikitskaya ul

Malaya Bronnaya ul

34 ☕ 16 ☕

58 ☕

62 ☕
Sredny Kislovsky
per

9 ☕

4

Park
Krasnaya
Presnya

nab Tarasa Shevchenko

Moskva River

Kalininsky
most

ul Novy Arbat

ul Novy Arbat

Bolshoy 17 ☕
Devyatinsky per

11 ●

60 📮

Arbatskaya pl

ul Vozdvizhenka

Arbatskaya Ⓜ

57 📮

43 ⬆

15 ☕

Smolenskaya Ⓜ

Spasopeskovskaya pl

Karmanitsky per

53 📮

66 📮

ul Znamenka

81 ☕

5

Bolshaya Dorogomilovskaya ul

Borodinsky
most

Smolenskaya ul

1-y Nikoloshchepovsky per

Smolenskaya-
Sennaya pl

37 ⬆

3● 48

Denezhny per

30 ☕

Kropotkinskaya Ⓜ

Kievskaya Ⓜ

Kievsky Vokzal
(Kiev Station)

pl Kievskogo
Vokzala

Kievskaya

45 ⬆

Gagarinsky per

ul Prechistenka

24 ⬆

6

Berezhkovskaya nab

proezd Devichego Polya

To American Express; KLM;
Royal Dutch Airlines;
Novodevichy Convent (1.5km);
Spartak (1.7km)

Zubovskaya pl

82 ●

3 ☕

To Infinity Travel
(500m)

Park Kultury Ⓜ

Park Kultury Ⓜ

RUSSIA

0 — 300 m
0 — 0.2 miles

E
pl Kommuny

Frunze Central Army Park

F
84
71

To Riga Station (1.1km);
Tramp (4km);
All-Russia Exhibition
Centre (5km)

Prospekt Mira

G
To Travellers
Guest House
(1km)

Bezbozhny per

Moscow State
University
Botanic Garden

Grokholsky per

H

1

Yaroslavsky Vokzal
(Yaroslav Station)

Leningradsky
Vokzal
(Leningrad
Station)

86
83

Kalanchevskaya Station

To
Shchyolkovsky
Avtovokzal (10km)
Komsomolskaya

Komsomolskaya pl

39

Kazansky
Vokzal
(Kazan
Station)

2

Samotyechny per

ul Durova

Olimpsky prosp

Samotechnaya

Delegatskaya ul

ul Sadovaya-Samotechnaya

ul Sadovaya-Sukharevskaya

Sadovaya-Spasskaya ul

Bol Spasskaya ul

prosp Akademika Sakharova

Krasnye
Vorota

Lermontovskaya
pl

Park im
Baumana

Tsvetnoy
Bulvar

Tsvetnoy bul
Trubnaya ul

Hermitage
Gardens

Petrovsky bul

Chekhovskaya

Trubnaya pl

Rozhdestvensky bul

Turgenevskaya

Chistye
Prudy

prosp Akademika Sakharova

ul Myasnitskaya

Ogorodnaya
slobody per

Kharitonevsky per

Sadovaya-Chernogryazskaya ul

To
Zemlyanoy
val

3

Petrovskie linii ul

Zvonarsky
per

77
32

38

42
63
22
54

28

56
69
12

68

55
76

@ 10
Pushechnaya ul

25

Kuznetsky Most

Lubyanka

Bolshaya Lubyanka

Milyutinsky per

Myasnitskaya ul

Bolshoy Zlatoustinsky

Chistoprudny bul

35

Bolshoy Kharitonevsky per

Pokrovka

Kurskaya

Teatralnaya

Okhotny
Ryad

8

Teatralnaya
pl

44

Tretyakovsky proezd

Lubyanskaya pl

Lubyanka

33

65

61

Kursky Vokzal
(Kursk Station)

4

85

Pl Revolyutsii

26

4
72
67

Kitay-
Gorod

Maroseyka ul

Pokrovsky bul

ul Vorontsovo Pole

See Moscow Kremlin Map p661

Alexandrovsky
Garden

KITAY-GOROD

Red Square
(Krasnaya pl)

Kremlin

Borovitskaya

Biblioteka
im Lenina;
Borovitskaya

Manezhnaya

Mokhovaya

Vozdvizhenka

Rybny per

19

ul Ilyinka

Nikolsky per

ul Varvarka

20
31

27

41

64

51

ul Solyanka

Kitay-Gorod

Staraya pl

Novaya pl

Kitaygorodsky proezd

5

Bolshoy
Kamenny
most

Maly Kamenny
most

Volkhonka

Kremlevskaya nab
Sofiyskaya nab

Bolshoy
Moskvoretsky
most

Moskva
River

Rauzhskaya nab

Moskvoretskaya nab

Ustinsky pr

Bolshoy
Ustinsky
most

Bolshoy
Ustinsky
most

Kosmodemyanskaya nab

Serebryanicheskaya nab

Yauza
River

Bernikovskaya nab

Nikoloyamskaya ul

Yauzskaya ul

Zemlyanoy val

To Vernisazh
Market (6km)

Teterinsky per

5

pl Repina

Maly
Moskvoretsky
most

Chugunny
most

Vodootvodny

Ovchinnikovskaya nab

Canal

Pyatnitskaya ul

Verkhnyaya
Radishchevskaya ul

Taganskaya

To G&R Hostel
Asia (10km)

Goncharnaya

Novokuznetskaya

Tretyakovskaya

23

Klimentovsky per

Ordynka

ul Bolshaya

Sadovnicheskaya nab

Ozerkovskaya nab

Taganskaya pl

Taganskaya ul

Marksistskaya

Narodnaya

Bol Kamenshchiki

Taganskaya

6

To French
Embassy
(500m)

Polyanka

Bolshaya Yakimanka

To German
Embassy
(11.5km)

Bolshaya Ordynka

Pyatnitskaya ul

To Air France (1km);
Domodedovo
Airport (40km)

74

RUSSIA

INFORMATION
American Medical Centre...1 G1
Anglia British Bookshop...2 D2
Australian Embassy...3 C6
Belarusian Embassy...4 G4
Botkin Hospital...5 A1
Canadian Embassy...6 D5
Capital Tours...7 F4
Central Telegraph...8 E4
Dutch Embassy...9 D4
Internet Klub...10 F3
Moskovsky Dom Knigi...11 D4
NetCity...12 E3
New Zealand Embassy...13 C4
Pharmacy...(see 1)
Phlegmatic Dog...(see 75)
Polish Embassy...14 B2
Time Online...(see 75)
UK Embassy...15 B5
Ukrainian Embassy...16 D3
US Embassy...17 C4

SIGHTS & ACTIVITIES (pp659-63)
Alexander Pushkin Statue...18 D3
Central Committee Building...19 F4
Church of St Maxim the Blessed...20 F4
Entrance to Moscow Zoo...21 B3
Equestrian Statue of Yury Dolgoruky...22 E3
Gosudarstvennaya Tretyakovskaya galereya (State Tretyakov Gallery)...23 D6
Khram Khrista Spasitelya (Cathedral of Christ the Saviour)...24 D6
Lubyanka Building...25 F3
Monastery of the Epiphany...26 F4
Monastery of the Sign...27 F4
Moscow Mayor's Office...28 E3

Moscow Zoo...29 B3
Pushkin Fine Arts Museum...30 D5
St Barbara's Church...31 F5
Sandunovskiye Bani...32 F3

SLEEPING (p663)
Ararat Park Hyatt Moscow...33 F4
East-West Hotel...34 D3
Galina's Flat...35 H3
Golden Ring Hotel...36 B5
Hotel Arbat...37 C5
Hotel Budapest...38 E3
Hotel Leningradskaya...39 H2
Hotel Pekin...40 D2
Hotel Rossiya...41 F5
Hotel Tsentralnaya...42 E3
Hotel Ukraina...43 A5
Metropole Hotel...44 F4
Radisson SAS Slavyanskaya Hotel...45 B6

EATING (pp665-6)
City Grill...46 D2
Correa's...47 C2
Il Patio...48 C5
Jagannath...49 F3
Karetny Dvor...50 C4
Lyudi kak Lyudi...51 G4
Metropolis...52 D2
Moo-Moo...53 C5
Moskva-Roma...54 E3
Pelmeshka...55 E3
Prime...56 E3
Prime...57 D5
Sindibad's...58 D4
Starlite Diner...59 D2
Zhiguli...60 D4

DRINKING (p666)
Boar House...61 H4
Coffee Mania...62 D4
Gogol...63 E3
Kitaysky Lyotchik...64 G4
Proekt OGI...65 G4
Shokoladnitsa...66 C5

ENTERTAINMENT (pp666-7)
American House of Cinema...(see 45)
Art Garbage...67 G4
Bolshoi Theatre...68 E3
Chekhov Art Theatre...69 E3
Klub na Brestskoy...70 C2
Olimpiisky Sports Complex...71 F1
Propaganda...72 G4
Rossiya Concert Hall...(see 41)
Sixteen Tons...73 A3
Three Monkeys...74 G6

SHOPPING (p667)
Okhotny Ryad Shopping Mall...75 E4
TsUM...76 E3

TRANSPORT (p667)
Aeroflot...77 E3
Belarus Station...78 C1
British Airways...79 C2
Central Train Booking Office...80 G3
Delta Air Lines...81 D5
Finnair...82 C6
Leningrad Station...83 H1
Lufthansa Airlines...84 F1
Transaero Airlines...85 E4
Yaroslav Station...86 H1

most international phones with roaming will automatically switch over to a local network. It's perfectly feasible to buy a local SIM card if you are staying in town for any amount of time – just go to any of the hundreds of phone shops around the city.

Toilets

As a rule, the more you pay for a toilet, the worse it will be. Free toilets are normally available in museums, and there are nasty temporary toilets, which you pay for the honour of using, around metro stations. Free toilets in smart hotels, cafés and restaurants remain the best choice.

Tourist Information

An entrenched lack of interest in promoting tourism means that there is no tourist office in Moscow, but useful information can be obtained through travel agencies and at hostels.

Travel Agencies

Capital Tours (Map pp656-8; ☎ 232 2442; www.capital tours.ru; ul Ilyinka 4; Ⓜ Pl Revolyutsii) Offers both a city tour ($20, 11am and 2.30pm daily) and a Kremlin Cathedrals and Armoury tour ($37, 10.30am and 3pm Friday to

Wednesday) departing from their offices off Red Square. Both are highly recommended.

Infinity (☎ 234 6555; www.infinity.ru; Komsomolsky pr 13; Ⓜ Frunzenskaya) With an office in both south Moscow and St Petersburg, Infinity is well used to dealing with the needs of foreigners. The helpful English-speaking staff can make most travel arrangements.

STAR Travel (☎ 797 9555; www.startravel.ru; ul Baltiiskaya 9, 3rd fl; Ⓜ Sokol) The representative of STA Travel in Moscow, STAR can book student and young person's air and train tickets from their north Moscow office. Check their website for further offices in the city.

DANGERS & ANNOYANCES

Red Square repeatedly features in travellers' tales of harassment by police. This can often involve document checks where the officers in question find something wrong with your (perfectly above board) visa or registration. See p692 for tips on how to deal with this. Other scams in the area have involved hackneyed tricks such as someone dropping a wallet, and their accomplice pointing this out to you. You pick up and return the wallet to the man who dropped it, whereupon he miraculously finds lots of cash is missing and demands you pay him the cash back. Just don't get involved if you see someone drop his or her wallet.

SIGHTS

Red Square
Map p661

Palpably the centre of Moscow and even Russia as a whole, Red Square (Ⓜ Pl Revolyutsii) is a massively impressive sight that brings back the full force of the Cold War, despite the two decades that have passed since *perestroika*. Something of a misnomer for this grey and rectangular strip to the east side of the Kremlin, Red Square is surrounded by Lenin's Mausoleum to the west, the State History Museum to the north, GUM shopping centre to the east and fabulous St Basil's to the south. Begin your visit to Moscow by coming here – there's nothing else like it.

Entering Red Square through the Voskressensky Gates, you'll emerge with a superb view of the magnificently flamboyant **St Basil's Cathedral** (Sobor Vasilia Blazhennogo; ☎ 298 3304; admission R100; ⊗ 11am-5pm Wed-Mon). Ivan the Terrible was so keen to immortalise his victory over the Tatars at Kazan that he took the measure of blinding the architects after they completed the cathedral's dazzlingly bright onion domes in 1561 to ensure that nothing of comparable beauty could ever be built. Its design is the culmination of a wholly Russian style that had been developed through the building of wooden churches. The cathedral owes its name to the barefoot holy fool Vasily (Basil) the Blessed, who predicted Ivan's damnation (as yet unconfirmed) and added (correctly) that Ivan would murder his son. It's definitely worth going inside to see the stark medieval wall paintings.

Lenin's Mausoleum (Mavzoley V I Lenina; ☎ 923 5527; admission free; ⊗ 10am-1pm Tue-Thu, Sat & Sun) is global ground zero for nostalgic communists. Before joining the queue at the northwestern corner of Red Square, drop your camera at the **left-luggage office** (R60 per bag; ⊗ 9am-6.30pm) beneath Kutafya Tower, as you will not be allowed to take it with you. The hilariously sombre visit takes you into the very dark crypt under Red Square where Lenin lies swathed in red velvet. Any talking will provoke angry shushing from the soldiers who line the route. Bear in mind that Stalin had Lenin's brain removed in a rather fanciful attempt to study the 'pure communist' brain, leaving Vladimir Ilych looking decidedly green around the (probably wax) gills. Following the trip underground, you'll emerge beside the route along the Kremlin wall, where other

greats such as Stalin, Gagarin and Brezhnev are buried. Yeltsin-era plans to rebury Lenin in St Petersburg (where he apparently wished to spend eternity buried next to his mother) have faltered, and it appears that he isn't going anywhere in a hurry.

The **State History Museum** (Gosudarstvenny Istorichesky Muzey; ☎ 292 4019; www.shm.ru, in Russian; Red Sq; adult/student R150/75; ⊗ 10am-6pm Mon, Wed-Sat, 11am-7pm Sun) is the stunningly ornate red building at the northern end of the square. It has an enormous collection covering the whole of Russian history from the Stone Age on.

Finally, drop into **GUM** (⊗ 10am-10pm) to see the showpiece Soviet shopping centre turned designer mall for the new rich with its glass roof and centrepiece fountains.

The Kremlin
Map p661

The nerve centre of Russian politics, the ultimate goal of Cold War espionage, a symbol of power and intrigue recognised the world over – for most first-time visitors what's most unexpected about the Kremlin are the several huge cathedrals at its heart.

Kremlin simply means 'citadel' in Russian and any medieval Russian town had one. Moscow's is huge – in effect a walled city. The Kremlin (first built in the 1150s) grew with the importance of Moscow's princes and in the 1320s it became the headquarters of the Russian Orthodox Church, which shifted here from Vladimir. Between 1475 and 1516, Ivan the Great brought master builders from Pskov and Italy to supervise the construction of new walls and towers, three great cathedrals and more.

Before entering the **Kremlin** (☎ 203 0349; www.kreml.ru; adult/student R300/150, photography R50; ⊗ 10am-5pm Fri-Wed) deposit your bags at the **left-luggage office** (R60 per bag; ⊗ 9am-6.30pm), beneath the Kutafya Tower, just north of the main ticket office. The Kremlin ticket office, in the Aleksandrovsky Garden, closes at 4.30pm. The ticket covers admission to all buildings except the Armoury and Diamond Fund Exhibition (p660).

SOUTHWEST BUILDINGS

From the Kutafya Tower, which forms the main visitors' entrance, walk up the ramp and pass through the Kremlin walls beneath the **Troitskaya Bashnya** (Trinity Gate Tower). The lane to the right (south) passes the

17th-century **Poteshny Dvorets** (Poteshny Palace), where Stalin lived. The horribly out of place glass and concrete **Kremlyovksy Dvorets Syezdov** (Kremlin Palace of Congresses) houses a concert and ballet auditorium, where incongruously enough lots of Western pop stars play when they are in town.

ARMOURY & DIAMOND FUND

In the southwestern corner of the Kremlin, the **Armoury** (Oruzheynaya Palata; adult/student R350/175) is a numbingly opulent collection of treasures accumulated over centuries by the Russian State and Church. Your ticket will specify a time of entry. Highlights include the Fabergé eggs in room 2 and the reams of royal regalia in rooms 6 and 9.

If the Armoury hasn't sated your diamond lust, there are more in the separate **Vystavka Almaznogo Fonda** (Diamond Fund Exhibition; adult/student R350/175; ⓥ closed for lunch 1-2pm) in the same building.

SOBORNAYA PLOSHCHAD

On the northern side of Sobornaya pl is the 15th-century **Uspensky Sobor** (Assumption Cathedral), focal church of prerevolutionary Russia and the most impressive of the Kremlin ensemble. It's the burial place of the heads of the Russian Orthodox Church from the 1320s to 1700. The tombs are against the north, west and south walls.

The iconostasis dates from 1652, but its lowest level contains some older icons, including the *Virgin of Vladimir* (Vladimirskaya Bogomater), an early 15th-century Rublev School copy of Russia's most revered image. The 12th-century original, now in the Tretyakov Gallery, stood in the Assumption Cathedral from the 1480s to 1930. The oldest icon on display is the magnificent 12th-century red-clothed *St George,* brought here from Novgorod; it is positioned behind glass by the north wall.

The **Tserkov Rizopolozheniya** (Church of the Disposition of the Robe), opposite the Assumption Cathedral, was built between 1484 and 1485 and includes a delightful wooden sculpture exhibition and some lovely frescoes.

With its two golden domes rising above the eastern side of Sobornaya pl, the 16th-century **Kolokolnya Ivana Velikogo** (Ivan the Great Bell Tower) is the Kremlin's tallest structure. Beside the bell tower stands the

world's biggest bell, the **Tsar-kolokol** (Tsar Bell), a 202-tonne monster that cracked before it ever rang. North of the bell tower is the mammoth **Tsar-pushka** (Tsar Cannon), cast in 1586, but never shot.

Back on Sobornaya pl, the 1508 **Arkhangelsky Sobor** (Archangel Cathedral), at the square's southeastern corner, was for centuries the coronation, wedding and burial church of tsars. The tombs of all of Russia's rulers from the 1320s to the 1690s are here bar one (Boris Godunov, who was buried at Sergiev Posad).

Dating from 1489, the **Blagoveshchensky Sobor** (Annunciation Cathedral), at the southwest corner of Sobornaya pl, contains the celebrated icons of master painter Theophanes the Greek. He probably painted the six icons at the right-hand end of the diesis row, the biggest of the six tiers of the iconostasis. *Archangel Michael* (the third icon from the left on the diesis row) and the adjacent *St Peter* are ascribed to Russian master Andrei Rublev.

Around Red Square

Manezhnaya pl, at the northwestern end of Red Square, has transformed into the vast underground **Okhotny Ryad Shopping Mall** (Map pp656-8), worth a look just to shatter images of Russians queuing in the snow for bread. The former **Manezh Central Exhibition Hall** (Map p661), the long, low building on the southern side of the square, was home to some of Moscow's most popular art exhibitions until it was burnt to a shell in a mysterious fire in 2003. On the southwestern side of the square is the fine edifice of **Moscow State University** (Map p661), built in 1793. The 1930s Hotel Moskva, once fronting the northeastern side of the square, was being demolished at the time of writing, no doubt soon to be replaced by another of Mayor Luzhkov's idiosyncratic projects.

Teatralnaya pl opens out on both sides of Okhotny Ryad, 200m north from Manezhnaya pl. The northern half of the square is dominated by the **Bolshoi Theatre** (Map pp656-8), where Tchaikovsky's *Swan Lake* was premiered (unsuccessfully) in 1877. Look out too for the stunning Art Nouveau **Metropole Hotel**, one of Moscow's finest, on Teatralny proezd.

Moscow's main avenue, elegant **Tverskaya ul**, replete with fashionable shops and costly

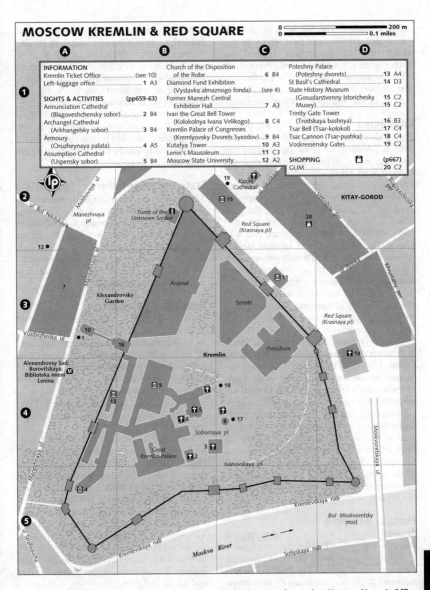

MOSCOW KREMLIN & RED SQUARE

0 ——————— 200 m
0 ——————— 0.1 miles

INFORMATION
Kremlin Ticket Office........................(see 10)
Left-luggage office.................................1 A3

SIGHTS & ACTIVITIES (pp659-63)
Annunciation Cathedral
(Blagoveshchensky sobor)............2 B4
Archangel Cathedral
(Arkhangelsky sobor)....................3 B4
Armoury
(Oruzheynaya palata)....................4 A5
Assumption Cathedral
(Uspensky sobor).............................5 B4

Church of the Disposition
of the Robe..6 B4
Diamond Fund Exhibition
(Vystavka almaznogo fonda)......(see 4)
Former Manezh Central
Exhibition Hall...................................7 A3
Ivan the Great Bell Tower
(Kolokolnya Ivana Velikogo).......8 C4
Kremlin Palace of Congresses
(Kremlyovsky Dvorets Syezdov)...9 B4
Kutafya Tower.....................................10 A3
Lenin's Mausoleum...........................11 C3
Moscow State University.................12 A2

Poteshny Palace
(Poteshny dvorets)....................13 A4
St Basil's Cathedral..........................14 D3
State History Museum
(Gosudarstvenny Istorichesky
Musey)..15 C2
Trinity Gate Tower
(Troitskaya bashnya)...................16 B3
Tsar Bell (Tsar-kolokol)..................17 C4
Tsar Cannon (Tsar-pushka) 18 C4
Voskressensky Gates........................19 C2

SHOPPING (p667)
GUM...20 C2

KITAY-GOROD

Kazan Cathedral
Red Square (Krasnaya pl)
Tomb of the Unknown Soldier
Manezhnaya pl
ul Bol' Nikitskaya
Mokhovaya ul
Arsenal
Alexandrovsky Garden
Senate
Red Square (Krasnaya pl)
Vozdvizhenka ul
Alexandrovsy Sad; Borovitskaya; Biblioteka imeni Lenina
Kremlin
Presidium
Manezhnaya ul
Soboronaya pl
Great Kremlin Palace
Ivanovskaya pl
Kremlevskaya nab
Bol Moskvoretsky most
Kremlevskaya nab
Moskva River
Sofiyskaya nab
ul Serafimovicha

cafés and restaurants, meanders uphill from Red Square and continues pretty much in a straight line all the way to St Petersburg. There's also the lovely pedestrianised side streets of **Kamergersky per** and **Stoleshnikov per** to walk down. Further up on Tverskaya ul there's the **equestrian statue of Yury Dolgoruky** (Map pp656-8), the founder of the city,

which now faces the **Moscow Mayor's Office** (Map pp656-8), where the Luzhkov administration concocts many of its hare-brained ideas.

Further up, on Pushkinskaya pl, there's the huge **Alexander Pushkin Statue**, a monument to Russia's national poet, behind which is the gaudy Rossiya cinema and

RUSSIA

casino complex. Another item of note on the square are Russia's first McDonald's, which saw lines stretching around the square when it opened in 1990. To this day it has the dubious honour of being the biggest McDonald's branch in the world, seating 700 burger munchers at any one time.

Kitay Gorod   Map p656–8

This 13th-century neighbourhood was the first in Moscow to grow up outside the Kremlin walls. While its name literally means China Town, do not expect anything Chinese – the name derives from an old Russian word meaning 'wattle', for the supports used for the walls that protected the suburb. This is the heart of medieval Moscow and parts of the suburb's walls are visible in places. The main places of interest are the collection of churches in the neighbourhood. Look out for the charming, brightly painted **Monastery of the Epiphany** opposite Ploshchad Revolyutsii Metro station and the small churches along ul Varvarka, incongruously surrounded by the massive Hotel Rossiya and general concrete sprawl. These are the 17th-century **Monastery of the Sign**, the **Church of St Maxim the Blessed** (1698) and **St Barbara's Church** (1795–1804). More recent history can be seen on Staraya pl, where the western side of the square is taken up with the **Central Committee Building**, once the most important decision-making organ of the communist party and thus the whole of the Soviet Union. Further up the hill, past Novaya pl, you'll see the huge and sinister **Lubyanka Building** crowning Lubyanka Hill. This was the headquarters of the dreaded KGB and remains today the nerve centre of its successor organisation, the Federal Security Bureau.

Pushkin Museum & Around   Map pp656–8

Moscow's premier foreign art museum is a short distance from the southwestern corner of the Kremlin. The **Pushkin Fine Arts Museum** (☎ 203 7412; ul Volkhonka 12; M Kropotkinskaya; adult/student R260/60, audio guide R200; ☯ 10am-6pm Tue-Sun) is famous for its impressionist and postimpressionist paintings, but also has a broad selection of European works from the Renaissance onward, mostly appropriated from private collections after the revolution. There are also interesting temporary exhibits on regular display.

Nearby is the gigantic **Khram Khrista Spasitelya** (Church of Christ the Saviour; ☎ 201 3847; M Kropotkinskaya; ☯ 10am-5pm), rebuilt at an estimated cost of US$360 million by Mayor Luzhkov on the site of the original cathedral, which was destroyed by Stalin, and replacing what was once the world's largest swimming pool. It's massively impressive with its vast golden dome, although the interior wouldn't look out of place in the equally gaudy Okhotny Ryad Shopping Mall.

State Tretyakov Gallery   Map pp656–8

The world's best collection of Russian icons is found in this **gallery** (Gosudarstvennaya Tretyakovskaya Galereya; ☎ 951 1362; www.tretyakov.ru; Lavrushinsky per 10; M Tretyakovskaya; adult/student R225/130, audio tour R120; ☯ 10am-6.30pm Tue-Sun), along with an outstanding collection of other prerevolutionary Russian art, particularly the 19th-century *peredvizhniki* (wanderers).

Novodevichy Convent

A cluster of sparkling domes behind turreted walls southeast of the centre on the Moscow River, **Novodevichy Monastyr** (Novodevichy Convent; ☎ 246 8526; M Sportivnaya; admission R30; ☯ 10am-5pm Wed-Mon) is resplendent with history and treasures. Founded in 1524 to celebrate the retaking of Smolensk from Lithuania, it gained notoriety as the place where Peter the Great imprisoned his half-sister Sofia for her part in the Streltsy Rebellion.

You enter the convent under the red-and-white Moscow-baroque **Transfiguration Gate-Church**. The oldest and dominant building in the grounds is the white **Smolensk Cathedral** (1524–25). **Sofia's tomb** lies among others in the south nave. The **bell tower** against the convent's east wall, completed in 1690, is generally regarded as Moscow's finest. The adjacent **Novodevichy Cemetery** contains the tombs of Khrushchev, Chekhov, Gogol, Mayakovsky, Stanislavsky, Prokofiev, Eisenstein, Raisa Gorbachev and other Russian and Soviet notables.

All-Russia Exhibition Centre

No other place in the country seems to sum up the rise and fall of the Soviet dream quite so well as the **Vserossiysky Vystavochny Tsentr** (All-Russia Exhibition Centre; VVTs; free admission; ☯ 24hr), 5km north of the city centre. The old initials by which it is still commonly known,

VDNKh, stand for Vystavka Dostizheniy Narodnogo Khozyaystva SSSR – USSR Economic Achievements Exhibition.

The centre was created in the 1950s and '60s to impress upon one and all the success of the Soviet economic system. Two kilometres long and 1km wide, it is composed of wide pedestrian avenues and grandiose pavilions, glorifying every aspect of socialist construction. The pavilions represent a huge variety of architectural styles, symbolic of the contributions from many diverse ethnic and artistic movements to the common goal. Here you'll find kitschy socialist realism, the most inspiring socialist optimism and – now – also the tackiest of capitalist consumerism. The centre was an early casualty when those in power finally admitted that the Soviet economy had become a disaster – funds were cut off by 1990. Today, the VVTs is a commercial centre, its pavilions given over to the sale of the very imported goods that were supposed to be inferior.

The soaring 100m titanium obelisk beside VDNKh metro is a monument to Soviet space flight. In its base is the **Muzey Kosmonavtiki** (Cosmonautics Museum; ☎ 283 7914; admission R30; ☽ 10am-7pm Tue-Sun), a series of displays from the glory days of the Soviet space programme. The long, dark room includes Yuri Gagarin's space suit and several capsules used during the 1960s and 1970s, as well as examples of the terminally unappetising space meals that the poor cosmonauts had to live on.

ACTIVITIES

Moscow has some of the swankiest *banyas* in the country, and it would be a shame to leave without trying one out. The most famous are the excellent **Sandunovskiye Bani** (☎ 925 4631; Neglinnaya ul 14; Ⓜ Tsvetnoy Bul; ☽ 8am-10pm), where you can enjoy a range of treats, from a communal bathing session for R500 to a private and extremely luxurious bathing chamber from R1000. There are *banyas* everywhere throughout the city – ask at your hotel if you need a local recommendation.

SLEEPING

Moscow is pricy, and nothing more so than its hotels. Bent on modernisation, the city has demolished the nasty but budget-friendly Intourist, Moskva and Minsk Hotels, and rumours are rife that Hotel Rossiya will be next. Unfortunately, there are few budget places opening to bridge the gap.

Budget

Galina's Flat (Map pp656-8; ☎ 921 6038; galinas .flat@mtu-net.ru; ul Chaplygina 8, flat 35; Ⓜ Chistiye Prudy; dm/s/d €8/15/21; ▯) A perennial favourite. Galina's central apartment functions as a home stay and is great value. There's Internet access and a kitchen that guests can use, as well as breakfast for an extra €2.

BANYA RITUAL

No experience is more Russian than the *banya*. Many Russians believe that it's the only true way to get clean, and for some it's the only place they ever wash. You can pay for a private (*lyuks*) *banya* if you are a mixed-sex group wanting to bathe together. For a more authentic experience, go to a communal *banya* – far cheaper and usually segregated.

You'll get sandals (*tapki*), and some sheets (*prostinya*) to cover yourself with. Before entering you should buy some snacks and drinks for your (equally important) breaks from the bathing ritual, and a bunch of birch twigs (*veniki*).

Once inside, you strip down, put your sheet around you and head for the dry sauna, where you get nice and hot before plunging into the steam bath (*parilka*). Here you get seriously sweaty and beat the toxins out of your skin with the birch twigs. Normally, people do their own legs and arms, and then lie down and allow their friends to whip their backs and stomachs. It's actually not that painful, unless your friend displays sadistic tendencies. Once you're sweating more than you thought possible and are covered in bits of twig and leaf, run out of the *parilka* and jump into the freezing plunge pool (alternatively, if you are in the countryside run out naked into the snow and roll around in it). After a break to drink beer or tea and snack while discussing world problems, repeat – several times over. Don't miss Moscow's superb Sandunovskiye Bani (p663) or St Petersburg's Krugliye Bani (p678), with its brilliant heated outdoor pool.

Hostel Sherstone (☎ 797 8075; www.sherstone.ru; Gostinichny proezd 8/1; Ⓜ Vladykino; dm/s/d €18/25/40) A branch of the G&R Hotel Asia with more than 100 beds, this hostel is a well-run and clean outfit, although rather far-flung in the north of the city.

G&R Hostel Asia (☎ 378 0001; www.hostels.ru; ul Zelenodolskaya 2/3; Ⓜ Ryzansky Pr; dm/s/d €25/35/40) Located in the old Soviet Hotel Asia, a good 10km southeast of the centre, this is nevertheless one of the best budget options in Moscow. Bathrooms are shared between two rooms, although en suite rooms are also available. Leave Ryazansky Pr metro from the end of the train and look for the tallest building around.

Tramp (☎ 551-2876; www.hostelling.ru; ul Selskoho zayistvennaya 17/2, Bldg 7; Ⓜ Botanichesky Sad; s/d €30/43) Located between the Botanic Gardens and the VVTs, Tramp is a great budget place, although it does not take people without advance reservations.

Travellers Guest House (TGH; ☎ 631 4059; www.tgh.ru; Bolshaya Pereyaslavskaya ul 50, 10th fl; Ⓜ Prospekt Mira; r €50, dm €19) The original Moscow hostel, the TGH is still the main hub for backpackers. Unfortunately it's not been touched since it opened in 1993, and is already looking rather shabby. Despite that, it's a safe and fun place to stay, a 10-minute walk from the metro.

Hotel Tsentralnaya (Map pp656-8; ☎ 229 8957; fax 292 1221; Tverskaya ul 10; Ⓜ Chekhovskaya; s €30, d €43-50) One of the city's best bargains – the Tsentralnaya is on Moscow's main street and offers great value. Rooms are very basic and Soviet, but clean and safe. All facilities are shared.

Hotel Leningradskaya (Map pp656-8; ☎ 975 1815; fax 975 1802; Kalanchevskaya ul 21/40; Ⓜ Komsomolskaya; s/d €50/80) This is smallest of the Seven Sisters buildings just off Station Sq, and therefore very well located for people arriving or leaving Moscow by train. Its rooms are nothing special, but good value all the same, and there's more than a little grand Soviet style in evidence here.

Mid-Range

Hotel Rossiya (Map pp656-8; ☎ 232 6046; fax 232 6248; ul Varvarka 6; Ⓜ Kitay Gorod; s/d €70/90) Few places cause more controversy than this humungous eyesore next to Red Square. While its rude staff, mediocre rooms and ugliness are indeed reasons to sneer, mid-level accommodation in Moscow is rarely this cheap or well located. May be demolished in the next few years by the city authorities.

Hotel Pekin (Map pp656-8; ☎ 209 2422; www.hotelpekin.ringnet.ru; Bolshaya Sadovaya ul 5/1; Ⓜ Mayakovskaya; r from €70-116) Built by Stalin in honour of Mao's newly communist China, the Pekin overlooks the Garden Ring and is in the cheaper end of mid-range accommodation in Moscow. Rooms are mediocre but large and the location excellent.

Hotel Arbat (Map pp656-8; ☎ 244 7628; fax 244 0093; Plotnikov per 12; Ⓜ Arbatskaya; s/d €110/130) On a side street off the Arbat, this hotel has a lovely courtyard. Its rooms are comfortable and well maintained.

Hotel Budapest (Map pp656-8; ☎ 923 2356; www.hotel-budapest.ru; Petrovskie linii 2/18; Ⓜ Teatralnaya; s/d €110/155) An unassuming hotel in a small central side street. Its rooms are stylishly decked out and the whole place has a rather elegant old-world feel to it.

East-West Hotel (Map pp656-8; ☎ 290 0404; www.eastwesthotel.ru; Tverskoy bul 4; Ⓜ Pushkinskaya; s/d €120/180) Quite unlike any other Moscow hotel, this old mansion has been done up in very Russian (read garish) décor and is gated from the street and thus very secure. The rooms are comfortable, although similarly located in interior-design purgatory.

Hotel Ukraina (Map pp656-8; ☎ 243 3030; fax 956 2078; Kutuzovsky pr 2/1; Ⓜ Kievskaya; s/d €140/160) The magnificent Stalinist façade of the Hotel Ukraina (it's one of the Seven Sisters) leaves you in no doubt that this was once one of the best hotels in the USSR. There are some stunning views over the river and the rooms are suitably grand, despite belonging very much to the past.

Top End

Radisson SAS Slavyanskaya Hotel (Map pp656-8; ☎ 941 8020; www.radissonsas.com; pl Evropy 2; Ⓜ Kievskaya; r €215-300, ste €260-1500; Ⓟ 🏊 🖳 🖳) Less a hotel than a self-contained city, the Radisson is a well-run, enormous complex of accommodation, restaurants, health club, shopping mall and even a cinema. There are often some very good offers available through their website.

Golden Ring Hotel (Map pp656-8; ☎ 725 0100; www.hotel-goldenring.ru; Smolenskaya ul 5; Ⓜ Smolenskaya; s/d €200/218, ste €660-1660; Ⓟ 🏊 🖳) An excellent Swiss-run business hotel. What it lacks in atmosphere it makes up for in views, service and location. The corner suites overlooking the Ministry of Foreign Affairs are excellent.

Ararat Park Hyatt Moscow (☎ 783 1234; www .moscow.park.hyatt.com; Neglinnaya ul 4; Ⓜ Teatralnaya; r €335, ste €400-1400; Ⓟ ⚡ 💻 🖥) Probably the best hotel in town, as reflected in its prohibitive prices. The stunning lobby sets the tone, and the 219 rooms do not disappoint. There are three restaurants and a superb health club too.

EATING

Like most things in Moscow, eating out can be a sumptuous but pricey experience. Check out ultra-cool Kamergersky per for a huge range of cafés and restaurants. For snacks on the run, there are plenty of street stands selling hot dogs, *chebureki* (Caucasian meat pasties) and blini around metro stations and on many central avenues.

Lyudi kak Lyudi (Map pp656-8; ☎ 921 1201; Solyansky tup 1/4; Ⓜ Kitay Gorod; mains R150; ⏰ 8am-11pm, to 6am at weekends) 'People are people' is a trendy and unpretentious café-restaurant popular with after-hours clubbers as well as young workers who swear by the excellent R110 business lunch.

Karetny Dvor (Map pp656-8; ☎ 291 6376; ul Povarskaya 52; Ⓜ Barrikadnaya; mains R200; ⏰ 24hr) Heavy security and lots of gangster jeeps parked outside may make you wary of entering this Georgian-Russian place – but don't let them. Once inside, you'll be well looked after and can enjoy rich, varied Georgian cooking at any hour of the day.

Il Patio (Map pp656-8; ☎ 290 5070; Smolenskaya ul 3; mains R200; ⏰ 11am-11pm) With over 15 outlets, this reliable Moscow chain changed its name from Patio Pizza to Il Patio recently. The pizzas are the same though – a big choice at reasonable prices.

Metropolis (☎ 299 7974; Sadovaya Triumfalnaya ul 4-10; Ⓜ Mayakovskaya; mains R250; ⏰ 10am-midnight) Vast, beautiful and seemingly having stolen many lighting fittings from the Moscow metro, Metropolis is a chic place to dine, with huge bay windows and an interesting modern Russian and European menu.

City Grill (Map pp656-8; ☎ 299 0953; www.city grill.ru in Russian; Sadovaya Triumfalnaya ul 2/30; Ⓜ Mayakovskaya; mains R350; ⏰ 11am-midnight) Beautifully refitted in dark wood and looking better than ever, this pioneering Moscow

institution is still one of the best places to eat modern European food in the Russian capital. Film buffs will be interested to know that a scene of the hit Russian movie 'Brother 2' was shot in the basement.

Sindibad's (Map pp656-8; ☎ 291 7115; Nikitsky bul 14; Ⓜ Arbatskaya; mains R350; ⏰ midday-11pm) Lebanese and Arabian cooking at its best – Sindibad's is hugely popular (booking advisable at weekends) with its unpretentious, delicious food, wooden interior and friendly staff. The big plate of mixed *mezze* (R350) is fantastic.

Correa's (Map pp656-8; ☎ 933 4684; Bolshaya Gruzinskaya ul 32; Ⓜ Barrikadnaya; mains R250-450; ⏰ 9ammidnight) A New York–style deli with a small restaurant, Correa's is universally known among the expat community as Isaac's, the name of its American chef. The sandwiches are wonderful, and the fresh supplies unrivalled. There's also a good breakfast menu and a delivery service available.

Starlite Diner (Map pp656-8; ☎ 290 9638; www .starlitediner.com; Bolshaya Sadovaya ul 16; mains R400; ⏰ 24hr) A well-deserved favourite – expats come to this surreal American diner for a taste of home. Food and service are great and the breakfasts are authentic and wonderfully calorific. There's now a second branch to the south by the Oktyabryskaya metro station.

Moskva-Roma (Map pp656-8; ☎ 229 5702; www .moscow-roma.ru, in Russian; Stoleshnikov per 12; Ⓜ Teatralnaya; mains R450; ⏰ 24hr) Funky and fun, Moskva-Roma combines a very high standard of modern Italian cooking with a happening atmosphere, having DJs most nights and some of the best staff in the city.

Cheap Eats

Prime (Map pp656-8; ☎ 737 5545; sandwiches R75-95; ⏰ 8.30am-11pm) Arbat (ul Arbat 9 Ⓜ Arbatskaya) Kamergersky per (Kamergersky per 5/7; Ⓜ Teatralnaya) Finally, a place to pick up a decent sandwich on the run. Prime is an unnerving copy of London's Prêt chain – but no complaints, as freshly cut sandwiches, salads and drinks are available in two central outlets.

Zhiguli (Map pp656-8; ☎ 291 4144; ul Novy Arbat 11; Ⓜ Arbatskaya; mains from R50; ⏰ noon-2am) Smart self-service canteen with a Brezhnevian theme. Good Russian food and low, low prices just off the Arbat.

Moo-Moo (Map pp656-8; ☎ 241 1364; ul Arbat 45/24; Ⓜ Smolenskaya; mains R100; ⏰ 10am-11pm)

RUSSIA

Always busy due to its large range of tasty and cheap Russian dishes, Moo-Moo is a self-service place. There's extra seating downstairs.

Pelmeshka (☎ 292 8392; ul Kuznetsky Most 4/3; Ⓜ Kuznetsky Most; mains R100; ⏰ 11am-midnight) Acid casualties should avoid looking at the giant psychedelic *pelmeshka* (Russian ravioli) that makes this Russian fast-food joint stand out on the street. However, once past it, you get a big choice of *pelmeni* and other Russian staples.

Jagannath (☎ 928 3580; ul Kuznetsky Most 11; Ⓜ Kuznetsky Most; mains R50-250; ⏰ 8am-11pm) A saviour for vegetarians, this excellent health food place with a strong Indian theme has both a self-service buffet and a sit-down restaurant. Food is superb, although arguably the lack of alcohol takes the concept of health food a little far.

DRINKING

Gravitate toward the Hermitage Garden (Ⓜ Pushkinskaya) or the Aleksandrovsky Garden (Ⓜ Okhotny Ryad) during the summer months for relaxed beer drinking amid the greenery. Other recommended bars include:

Boar House (Map pp656-8; ☎ 917 9986; Zemlyanoy val 26; Ⓜ Kurskaya; cover R60-100; ⏰ noon-6am) Run by the creator of the legendary Hungry Duck (once the wildest bar in Europe due to its famously hedonistic ladies night), the Boar House is busy throughout the week and attracts an expat crowd devoted to serious debauchery.

Gogol (Map pp656-8; ☎ 514 0944; Stoleshnikov per 11; Ⓜ Chekhovskaya; ⏰ 24hr) This is a brilliant, sprawling bar-cum-concert venue with a fantastic summer garden where groups often play in the evenings.

Kitaysky Lyotchik (☎ 924 5611; Lyublyansky proezd; Ⓜ Kitay Gorod; cover R150; ⏰ 10am-8am daily) The 'Chinese Pilot' is a long-standing favourite with the boho crowd, who come here for the live music and lack of aggressive door policy.

Proekt OGI (Map pp656-8; ☎ 229 5489; www .proektogi.ru, in Russian; Potapovsky per 8/12; Ⓜ Chistiye Prudy; cover R50-100) OGI is the acronym of a publishing house that diversified into bars and cafés and has become a phenomenon – the OGI bar/cafés (all with their own in house bookshop) can be found all over central Moscow.

Cafés

While it took off first in St Petersburg, the coffee culture in Moscow has grown into a huge industry, although it's almost impossible to find a place where the concept of takeaway coffee isn't totally alien – **Prime** (p665) is a rare exception. Of the huge choice, **Coffee Mania** (Map pp656-8; ☎ 229 3901; www.coffeemania.ru, in Russian; Bolshaya Nikitskaya ul 13; Ⓜ Arbatskaya), with its delicious food and cakes, is very highly recommended. Both chic **Shokoladnitsa** (Map pp656-8; ☎ 241 0620; www.shoko.ru, in Russian; ul Arbat 29; Ⓜ Arbatskaya) and **Coffee House** (www.coffee house.ru, in Russian; Tverskaya ul 6; Ⓜ Okhotny Ryad) serve great coffee. All three have branches scattered throughout the city.

ENTERTAINMENT
Theatre

When Chechen terrorists took an entire theatre audience hostage during a musical in Moscow in October 2002, the world looked on in horror as the siege ended in carnage, largely through the use of still undisclosed gases by the Russian military. Despite the horror of the Dubrovka Theatre siege, there's a varied and dynamic theatre scene in Moscow still.

Chekhov Art Theatre (Map pp656-8; ☎ 229 8760; www.mxat.ru, in Russian; Kamergersky per 3; Ⓜ Okhotny Ryad; tickets R100-500) The city's most famous dramatic venue is still known to most Muscavites as MKhAT, where, under Stanislavsky, method acting was born at the turn of the last century. There are sometimes performances in English here.

Bolshoi Theatre (Map pp656-8; www.bolshoi.ru; Teatralnaya pl 1; Ⓜ Teatralnaya; tickets R200-1500) A night at the Bolshoi is a treat – tickets are available online and through travel agencies at a premium, although the kiosks around the city *(teatralnaya kassa)* will often offer some good bargains. Be aware that foreigners are charged extra for tickets – if you buy one at the Russian price, you may be refused entry unless you stump up for a 400% mark up. Other notable theatres are the Maly and Lenkom Theatres. See *The Moscow Times* online (www.themoscowtimes.com) or its Friday edition for more details on other theatres and what's showing around town.

Nightclubs

Negotiating Moscow's legendarily lavish and hedonistic clubland is a challenge.

'Face control' (the Russian term for an unreasonable door policy administered by thugs) rules. *The Exile* (www.exile.ru) has an up-to-date, un-PC club guide. While many clubs disappear overnight, some enduringly popular venues include **Propaganda** (☎ 924 5732; Bol Zlatoustinksy per 7; Ⓜ Kitay Gorod; cover R50-200; ☽ midday-7am) and **Art Garbage** (☎ 928-8745; www.art-garbage.ru, in Russian; Starosadsky per 5/6; Ⓜ Kitay Gorod; cover free-R200; ☽ 9pm-6am).

Live Music

Moscow has a great variety of gigs and concerts, although don't expect to see Russian cult band *du jour* Leningrad soon – Mayor Luzhkov has banned them from performing in the city due to their swearing and nudity, an act of incredible philistinism even by his high standards. *The Moscow Times* weekend edition (or website) is a reliable source of information. Moscow is an increasingly popular stop-off on European tours for big international acts. The main venues are the Olimpiisky Sports Complex and the Rossiya Concert Hall. Some of the smaller venues are the **Sixteen Tons** (☎ 253 5300; www.16tons.ru; 1 Presnensky val; Ⓜ Ulitsa 1905 Goda; cover for gigs only R150-300; ☽ 6pm-late), **Klub na Brestskoy** (☎ 200 0936; 2-aya Brestkaya ul 6; ☽ midnight-late), which has its entrance on 1-aya Brestkaya ul, and Kitaysky Lyotchik (p666).

Gay & Lesbian Venues

Moscow is the centre of Russian gay life, and even if the gay population is barely visible, it's certainly a lot more socially acceptable than ever before in Russia to be queer. The best resource for checking the ever-changing club scene is www.gay.ru/english. The most fun and accessible gay venue is **Three Monkeys** (Map pp656-8; ☎ 951 1563; Sadovnicheskaya nab 71; Ⓜ Paveletskaya; cover free-R250; ☽ 9pm-9am), where the atmosphere is friendly. Check www.gay.ru/english for listings.

Cinemas

The **American House of Cinema** (☎ 941 8747; www.americanmovie.ru; pl Evropy 2; Ⓜ Kievskaya) in the Radisson SAS Slavyanskaya Hotel shows films in English (Russian translation is provided through headphones).

Sport

Football is definitely Moscow's main spectator sport. There are several teams in the city – the best known internationally are **Spartak** (☎ 201 1164; Luzhniki Stadium, Luzhnetskaya nab 24; Ⓜ Sportivnaya) and **Dinamo** (☎ 212 3132; Dinamo Stadium, Leningradsky pr 36; Ⓜ Dinamo). You can usually buy tickets on match days without much problem, either at the gate or from the theatre-ticket kiosks in most metro stations; prices start at R100.

SHOPPING

Stereotypes die hard, and none more than the Moscow bread queues of the late 1980s. However, shopping in Moscow is now reason enough alone for some to come here. The new wealth of Russia has created a class of monied Russians for whom nothing is too expensive or extravagant. If you have the cash, check out the designer boutiques of Tretyakovsky proezd, where Prada, Gucci and Armani jostle for your attention. Nearby Stoleshnikov per is also full of designer labels. **GUM** (Map p661; ☽ 10am-10pm) and **TsUM** (Map pp656-8; ☎ 292 1157; www.tsum.ru; ul Petrovka 2; Ⓜ Teatralnaya; ☽ 9am-9pm Mon-Sat, 11am-8pm Sun) are also great for big brand names.

Far more likely to appeal is the **Vernisazh Market** (☽ 7am-6pm Sat & Sun) at Izmailovsky Park – a huge collection of handicrafts, knick-knacks, souvenirs, clothing and art. Follow the crowds from Izmailovsky Park metro station on Saturdays and Sundays.

Although illegal in the West, pirated DVDs are available everywhere in Russia. In Moscow you'll see them on sale all over the place, usually in underpasses by metro stations and kiosks around the city. The famous electrical goods and pirate DVD market **Gorbushka** (☎ 730 0006; Barklaya ul 8; Ⓜ Bagrationovskaya; ☽ 10am-9pm) may be worth a visit if DVDs are your thing. It's a former TV factory that now houses an immense number of shops selling every conceivable type of technology at knock-down prices.

GETTING THERE & AWAY
Air

Of Moscow's five airports, the most-often used are Sheremetyevo to the north and Domodedovo to the south.

International airline offices in Moscow include:

Aeroflot (Map pp656-8; ☎ 753 5555; ul Petrovka 20/1; Ⓜ Teatralnaya)

Air France (☎ 937 3839; ul Korovy Val 7; Ⓜ Oktyabrskaya)

RUSSIA

British Airways (Map pp656-8; ☎ 363 2525; Business Centre Parus, ul 1-ya Tverskaya-Yamskaya 23; Ⓜ Belorusskaya)

Delta Air Lines (Map pp656-8; ☎ 937 9090; Gogolevsky bul 11; Ⓜ Kropotkinskaya)

Finnair (Map pp656-8; ☎ 933 0056; Kropotinsky per 7; Ⓜ Park Kultury)

KLM-Royal Dutch Airlines (☎ 258 3600; ul Usacheva 33/2; Ⓜ Sportivnaya)

Lufthansa Airlines (Map pp656-8; ☎ 737 6400; Renaissance Moscow Hotel, Olimpisky Prospekt 18; Ⓜ Prospekt Mira)

Transaero Airlines (Map pp656-8; ☎ 241 4800; Smolensky bul 3/4; Ⓜ Park Kultury)

Boat

The Moscow terminus for cruises to St Petersburg is 10km northeast of the centre at the **Severny Rechnoy Vokzal** (Northern River station; ☎ 459 7476; Leningradskoe shosse 51). Take the metro to Rechnoy Vokzal stop, then walk 15 minutes due west, passing under Leningradskoe shosse and through a nice park.

Bus

Buses run to a number of towns and cities within about 700km of Moscow, but they tend to be crowded. However, they are usually faster than the suburban (*prigorodny*) trains, and are convenient to some Golden Ring destinations (p668). To book a seat you have to go 15km east of the city to the long-distance bus station (Shchyolkovsky Avtovokzal) beside Shchyolkovskaya metro.

Train

Moscow is the heart of the Russian railway network, and internationally you can catch trains for destinations as far apart as Berlin and Beijing here.

Of the nine stations in Moscow, use **Leningradsky Vokzal** (Leningrad Station; Map pp656-8; Ⓜ Komsomolskaya) for trains to St Petersburg, Novgorod, Estonia and Finland; **Rizhsky vokzal** (Riga Station; Ⓜ Rizhskaya) for Latvia; **Belorussky vokzal** (Belarus Station; Ⓜ Belorusskaya) for Belarus, Lithuania, Kaliningrad, Poland, Germany and the Czech Republic; and **Yaroslavsky vokzal** (Yaroslavl Station; Ⓜ Komsomolskaya) for Siberia, Mongolia and China.

Besides the train stations proper, tickets are sold throughout the city at **Central Railway Agency ticket offices**, such as (Tsentralnoe Zheleznodorozhnoe Agentstvo; ☎ 262 2566; Maly Kharitonevsky per 6; ⏱ 8am-1pm & 2-7pm). Alternatively,

travel agencies and other ticket offices (*kassa zhelez!noy dorogi*) also sell tickets, sometimes for a small commission, but frankly it's worth it – it's much easier.

GETTING AROUND
To/From the Airports

From outside the ailing Sheremtyevo-2 terminal minibus Nos 48 and 49 and bus No 851 go to the nearest metro station, Rechnoy Vokzal. A taxi can be ordered from the official taxi office in the arrivals area and should cost between R650 to R800.

More and more flights come in to Domodedovo, including all British Airways flights. There is an express train service from Domodedovo to Paveletsky Vokzal in Central Moscow. The trains (R75, 40 minutes) run between the airport and city every hour on the hour between 8am and 10pm.

Metro

The magnificent Moscow metro is probably the best in the world. Over 150 stations in all parts of the city and a train every two minutes make it the best way to get around. The flat fare is R10 (30¢), although buying in bulk saves a lot of money (for example 10 rides cost R50).

Trolleybus, Tram and Bus

Short-term visitors are unlikely to use public transport beyond the metro. However, a comprehensive and dirt-cheap, although painfully slow, network of buses, trams and trolleybuses exists all over Moscow. In far-flung places it can be necessary to take one of these to get to the nearest metro station. If so, buy tickets on board.

Taxi

See the directory (p697) for information about hailing unofficial cabs in Russia. The standard rate for very short trips is R50, while longer ones will cost R100 to R150. Official taxis cost more. You can book through the central **Taxi Reservation Office** (☎ 927 0000; ⏱ 24 hr).

AROUND MOSCOW

Escaping Moscow is vital if you want to get some sense of how ordinary Russians live, given that the capital has as much in common with the provinces as Manhattan does with Kansas. The historic towns surrounding Moscow to the northeast (known as the Golden Ring due to their magnificent churches and medieval monasteries) are a great place to start. The most interesting and accessible towns, each of which preceded the present capital as the political and cultural heart of Russia, are Suzdal, Vladimir and Sergiev Posad. The towns' churches, monasteries, kremlins (citadels) and museums make a picturesque portfolio of early Russian art, architecture and history.

Suzdal Суздаль
☎ 09231 / pop 12,000

If you have the chance to visit only one of the Golden Ring towns, make it lovely Suzdal. Coming here from Moscow is a wonderful experience as you'll see a traditional Russian town overflowing with old monasteries, convents, churches and intricately decorated wooden cottages *(izbas)* dotted in green fields around the meandering Kamenka River. Green fields reach right into the centre and the whole town is architecturally protected. A greater contrast from Moscow is hard to imagine.

SIGHTS

At the eastern end of ul Kremlyovskaya, the 1.4km-long rampart of Suzdal's kremlin encloses the 13th-century **Rozhdestvensky Sobor** (Nativity of the Virgin Cathedral), the 1635 **bell tower** and the **Arkhiyereyskie Palati**

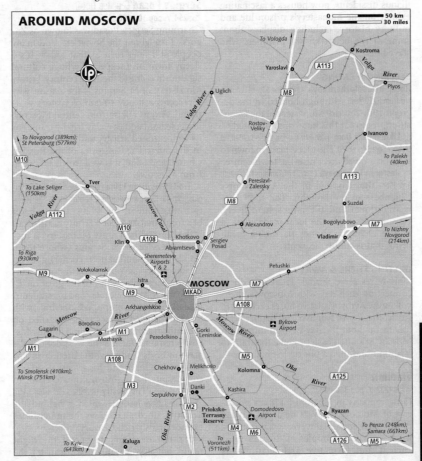

AROUND MOSCOW

0 ——— 50 km
0 ——— 30 miles

(Archbishop's Chambers). The latter houses the **Suzdal History Exhibition** (☎ 204 44; admission R30; ☺ 10am-5pm Wed-Mon). The exhibition includes the original 13th-century door from the cathedral, photos of its interior and a visit to the 18th-century **Krestovaya Palata** (Cross Hall).

Founded in the 14th century to protect the town's northern entrance, the **Spaso-Yevfimievsky Monastyr** (Saviour Monastery of St Euthymius; admission R150, photos R50; ☺ 10am-6pm Tue-Sun) is at the northern end of ul Lenina. Inside, standing before the seven-domed, 12th- and 13th-century **Cathedral of the Transfiguration of the Saviour**, a tall **bell tower** chimes a lovely 10-minute concert every hour. The old monastery **prison**, set up in 1764 for religious dissidents, now houses a fascinating exhibit on the monastery's prison life and military history, including displays about some of the better-known prisoners who stayed here.

SLEEPING & EATING

Hotel Rizopolozhenskaya (☎ 205 53; ul Lenina; s/d from R250/300) Although housed in the decrepit 19th-century Monastery of the Deposition, rooms at this hotel are renovated.

Likhoninsky Dom (☎ 219 01; fax 0922-327010; ul Slobodskaya 34; r R630) The nicest place in town to stay, on a quiet street near the town centre.

Restoran Trapeznaya (☎ 217 63; mains R100-200; ☺ 11am-11pm) Located in the Archbishop's Chambers in the kremlin. The food here is traditional and the atmosphere lively. Be sure to sample the local *medovukha*, a lightly alcoholic, honey-flavoured mead drink that is simply heavenly.

GETTING THERE & AWAY

Only buses serve Suzdal. There is a direct connection each day with Moscow's Shchyolkovsky Avtovokzal, two buses each day to Kostroma, five to Ivanovo, and regular services throughout the day to Vladimir. From Moscow it's often easier to take the train to Vladimir and then a bus on to Suzdal.

Vladimir Владимир

☎ 09222 / pop 360,000

Little remains in Vladimir, 178km northeast of Moscow, from its medieval heyday as Russia's capital. However, what does remain – several examples of Russia's most ancient and formative architecture – is worth pausing to see en route to or from the more charming town of Suzdal.

Begun in 1158, **Uspensky Sobor** (Assumption Cathedral; admission R30; ☺ about 1.30-5pm) is a white-stone version of Kyiv's brick Byzantine churches, and contains magnificent frescoes by Andrei Rublev and others. Nearby, the **Dmitrievsky Sobor** (Cathedral of St Dmitry), built from 1193 to 1197, is where the art of Vladimir-Suzdal stone carving reached its pinnacle.

From Moscow's Kursky Vokzal (Kursk station), there are numerous suburban trains and buses to Vladimir. There are also bus services to/from Moscow, Nizhny Novgorod, Kostroma, Ivanovo, Suzdal and Kazan.

Sergiev Posad Сергиев Посад

☎ 254 / pop 100,000

Charming Sergiev Posad was known as Zagorsk throughout the Soviet era, and many people still refer to it as that today. It's a sleepy town of unexpectedly huge cultural significance, due to the 15th-century Trinity Monastery of St Sergius – the reason why it receives a steady stream of visitors year-round. At just 60km from central Moscow, it's a pleasant and easy day trip by train. For its concentrated artistry and its unique role in the interrelated histories of the Russian Church and State, it is well worth a day trip from Moscow.

Troitse-Sergieva Lavra (Trinity Monastery of St Sergius; ☎ 45 356; admission free, photos R100; ☺ 10am-6pm) was built in the 1420s; the dark yet beautiful **Troitsky Sobor** (Trinity Cathedral) is the heart of the Trinity Monastery. A memorial service for St Sergius (whose tomb stands in the southeastern corner) goes on all day, every day. The icon-festooned interior is largely the work of the great medieval painter Andrei Rublev and his students. **Uspensky Sobor** (Assumption Cathedral), with its star-spangled domes, was modelled on the cathedral of the same name in the Moscow Kremlin. Outside the west door is the **grave** of Boris Godunov, the brother-in-law of Tsar Fyodor I and his eventual successor, despite having no legitimate claim to the throne. The **Vestry** (Riznitsa; admission R150; ☺ 10am-5.30pm Tue-Sun), which is behind the Trinity Cathedral, displays the monastery's extraordinarily rich treasury.

It's not necessary to spend the night really, but if you want to you can try the

Russky Dvorik (☎ 75 392; fax 75 391; ul Mitkina 14/2; s/d incl breakfast from US$50/70), which is a delightful small hotel a short walk east of the monastery. It also has a separate **restaurant** (☎ 45 114; ul Krasnoy Armii 134; meals R500), which does get overrun with the tour groups at lunch, but it's otherwise pleasant.

GETTING THERE & AWAY
From Moscow's Yaroslavsky Vokzal, buses and suburban trains (*elektrichki*) to Sergiev Posad leave every half hour or so, taking 75 to 90 minutes.

ST PETERSBURG
САНКТ ПЕТЕРБУРГ

☎ 812 pop / 5 million

Simply one of the most enchanting and impressive cities on earth, St Petersburg gives little indication that its incredible architectural wealth was originally built on a mosquito-infested swamp. Peter the Great, who wanted to create a modern capital for a country still stuck in the Dark Ages, founded St Petersburg on the shores of the Gulf of Finland in 1703. Since then it has grown to be Europe's fourth largest city and easily one of its most culturally significant. A 'window on Europe,' the city of Dostoyevsky and Shostakovich, cradle of the Russian Revolution – St Petersburg has more to offer the traveller than perhaps anywhere else in Russia.

HISTORY
St Petersburg was the brainchild of the young Peter the Great (1682–1725), who during his brutal childhood had come to hate Moscow and its plotting coteries of *boyars* (aristocrats). In 1703, at the mouth of the River Neva, Peter declared he would build a city, and with all the despotic powers at hand for a tsar, he soon had thousands of Swedish prisoners of war toiling in the toughest imaginable conditions to bring about his dream. St Petersburg became the capital of Russia in 1713 and the court, government and much of Russian economic life was transferred here from Moscow, prompting the city to grow with extreme speed. Much of the look of the city was determined by Empress Elizabeth, whose favourite architect, Bartolomeo Rastrelli, gave the city

the warm, extravagant Italian feel, which is still overwhelmingly evident in the city today. Catherine the Great refined and completed many of Elizabeth's projects, complementing the city's architectural ensemble with the introduction of neoclassicism.

Petrograd (as the city became in 1914, 'St Petersburg' being too Germanic) was the setting for the 1917 revolution that saw Nicholas II abdicate, and then the communist coup later the same year, after which Lenin led the socialist government from the Smolny Institute.

In 1918, in a significant blow to the city's future, Lenin moved the capital back to more easily defensible Moscow, where it remains today. In 1924, following Lenin's death, the city changed its name yet again to Leningrad.

Leningrad's darkest hour came during WWII, when the German advance on the city led to a siege lasting almost 900 days. During that time over one million people starved to death, a tragedy still fresh in the psyche of the city's citizens. Hitler's failure to take the city was however a huge dent to German morale.

After a 70-year experiment with communism, the city began a new era when it voted finally to change its name from Leningrad back to St Petersburg. With locally born-and-bred Vladimir Putin now running the country, the city has profited from central funding to restore many of its crumbling palaces. The city's 300th anniversary in 2003 set the tone for a new century of optimism and progress for Russia's graceful former capital.

ORIENTATION
St Petersburg is spread out across many different islands, some real and some created through the construction of canals. The central street is Nevsky Prospekt, which extends for some 4km from the Lavra Alexandera Nevskogo (Alexander Nevsky Monastery) to the Hermitage. The vast River Neva empties into the Gulf of Finland, filtered through a number of islands. The most significant of these are Vasilevsky and Petrogradsky Islands.

INFORMATION
Bookshops
The city's only English-language bookshop is the excellent **Anglia Books** (Map p677; ☎ 279-9294;

CENTRAL ST PETERSBURG

Petrovsky Park

A

MALAYA NEVA

To Krasnogo Kursanta ul
Bol Pushkarskaya ul

ul Krasnogo Kursanta
Ofitsersky per
Maly pr Kursanta

Zhdanovskaya nab

Sportivnaya
46

ul Blokhina

pr Dobrolyubova

Yubileyny Sports Palace

Tuchkov most

B

To Laima (800m)
Sytninskaya pl
Vvedenskaya ul
Monchegorskaya ul
Sezzhinskaya ul
per
Zverinskaya ul
ul Yablochkova
ul Blokhina

pr Dobrolyubova
Mytninskaya nab

KRONVERKSKY

RIVER

C

Gorkovskaya
Kronverksky pr

Alexandrovsky Park

Kronverksky proliv
Kronverkskaya nab

Peter & Paul Fortress
13
20
25

ZAYACHY

Troitsky most

D

To Pasadskiye Bani (50m)
To Troitsky Most (50m)
Kruglive Bani (5km)
Kamennoostrovsky pr
pr Korblyeva

Petrovskaya nab

nab Leytenantsa kanala

2

Maly pr
4-ya liniya
5-ya liniya
6-7 liniya
8-9 liniya

2-ya liniya
Tuchkov per
Sredny pr
Spezdovskaya ul
ul Repina
1-ya liniya
2-ya liniya 3-ya liniya
ul Repina

Vasileostrovskaya

nab Makarova

Vasilevsky

University Botanical Gardens

St Petersburg State University

Birzhevoy most

22
Birzhevaya pl

14
21
17
36
Birzhevoy proezd

Ermitazhny most

Dvortsovy most

Dvortsovaya nab
Millionnaya ul
38
4
35
nab r Moyki

Mars Field

Suvorovskaya pl

Dvortsovaya nab

See Nevsky Prospekt Map p677

Mikhailovsky Gardens

3

To VMF (750m)

Bolshoy pr
10-11 liniya
12-13 liniya
14-15 liniya
16-17 liniya
18-19 liniya

6-7 liniya
8-9 liniya

Universitetskaya nab
19

most Leytenanta Shmidta

BOLSHAYA NEVA

Angliyskaya nab
Galernaya ul

45

NEVA RIVER

pl Dekabristov
12
11
Admiralteysky proezd
Admiralteyskaya nab

Admiralteysky bul
ul Yakubovicha

Admiralty Gardens

23
30
1

Choynogo proezd

Nevsky pr

Admiralteysky proezd

Admiralteysky

Isaakievskaya pl

Moyka River

Nevsky pr

Gorokhovaya ul

Gostiny Dvor

Nevsky pr

4

Novoadmiralteysky

Admiralteysky canal
nab reki Moyki

Novaya Gollandiya

Kolomensky

Matisov

ul A Bloka

pr Maklina

Galernaya ul
pl Truda
Konnogvardeysky bul
Pochtamtskaya ul
3
Bolshaya Morskaya ul
Sinly most
River
Fonarny per
per Grivtsova

27
Potseluev most

Teatralnaya pl
44

Rimskogo-Korsakova

Nikolsky Gardens

Kazansky

nab kanala Griboedova

Kokushkin most

Sadovaya

Yusupov Gardens

Obukhovsky most

Sadovaya
Sennaya pl
Sadovaya

Semyonovsky most

Semyonovskaya pl

Spassky

Apraksin Torgovy per
Sadovaya ul

41

5

Pryazhki

ul Soyuza Pechatnikov
Vitebskaya ul
Pskovskaya ul
Lotsmanskaya ul
pr Maklina

ul Dekabristov

Pokrovsky

Griboedova Canal
Kanonerskaya ul
pl Turgeneva
ul Labutina
Sadovaya ul
28

nab kanala Griboedova
Rimskogo-Korsakova
Lermontovsky pr

Voznesensky pr

Fontanka River

nab reki Fontanki

Izmaylovsky Gardens

Polsky Gardens

Tehnologichesky Institut

Obukhovskaya pl
8
16

Vitebskaya pl

Vitebsk Station (Vitebsk Vokzal)

Pushkinskaya

Zvenigorodskaya ul
Marata ul

6

Staropeterhofsky pr

Rizhsky pr

Derptsky per
ul Tsiolkovskogo

Drovyanaya per

nab reki Fontanki

pr Moskvinoy
13 Krasnoarmeyskaya ul
8 Krasnoarmeyskaya ul
9 Krasnoarmeyskaya ul
10 Krasnoarmeyskaya ul
11 Krasnoarmeyskaya ul
12 Krasnoarmeyskaya ul

1 Krasnoarmeyskaya ul
2 Krasnoarmeyskaya ul
3 Krasnoarmeyskaya ul
4 Krasnoarmeyskaya ul
5 Krasnoarmeyskaya ul
6 Krasnoarmeyskaya ul
7 Krasnoarmeyskaya ul

Izmaylovsky pr

Moskovsky pr

ul Egorova

"Olimpia" Gardens
2

Kurlyandskaya ul

nab Obvodnogo kanala

nab Obvodnogo kanala

Malodetskoselsky pr

To Petrovsky College Student Hostel (1km)

Baltiyskaya

Baltiysky Vokzal (Baltic Station)

Varshavsky Vokzal (Warsaw Station)

Fruznenskaya

To Moskovskaya metro for buses to Pushkin & Pavlovsk (5.5km); Pulkovo Airport (17km)

RUSSIA

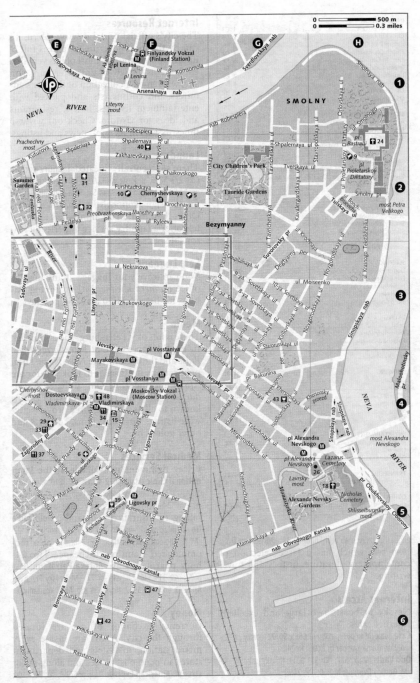

INFORMATION		
American Express	1	C3
Canadian Embassy	2	D6
Central Post Office	3	B4
French Consulate	4	D2
German Consulate	5	F2
International Clinic	6	E4
Laundry Service	7	E2
Poliklinika No 2	8	D5
UK Consulate	9	H2
US Consulate	10	F2

SIGHTS & ACTIVITIES	(pp675-9)	
Admiralty	11	C3
Bronze Horseman	12	C3
Cathedral of SS Peter & Paul	13	C1
Central Naval Museum (Old Stock Exchange)	14	C2
Dostoevsky Museum	15	F4
Kazachiye Bani	16	D5
Kunstkamera (Museum of Anthropology & Ethnography)	17	C2
Lavra Alexandra Nevskogo (Alexandr Nevsky Monastery)	18	H5
Menshikov Palace	19	B3
Peter & Paul Fortress	20	D1
Rostral Columns	21	C2
Rostral Columns	22	C2
St Isaac's Cathedral	23	C3
Smolny sobor (Smolny Cathedral)	24	H2
Start of Battlements walk	25	D1
Tikhvin Cemetery	26	H5
Yusupov Palace	27	B4

SLEEPING 🏠	(pp679-80)	
Domik v Kolomne	28	A5
Five Corners Hotel	29	E4
Hotel Astoria	30	C3
Hotel Neva	31	E2
Sleep Cheap	32	E2

EATING 🍴	(pp680-1)	
Imbir	33	E4
Kuznechny Market	34	E4
Pogreba Monakha	35	D2
Restoran	36	C2
Troitsky Most	37	E4

DRINKING 🍷	(p681)	
City Bar	38	D2
Griboedov	39	E5
JFC Jazz Club	40	F2
Manhattan	41	D4
Metro	42	E6
Moloko	43	G4

ENTERTAINMENT 🎭	(pp681-2)	
Mariinsky Theatre	44	B4
Ostrov	45	A4
Petrovsky Stadium	46	B1

TRANSPORT	(p682)	
Avtovokzal (Bus Station)	47	F6

OTHER		
Our Lady of Vladimir Church	48	E4

anglia@inbox.ru; nab reki Fontanki 38; Ⓜ Gostiny Dvor; 10am-7pm), which has a large selection of contemporary literature, history and travel writing.

Internet Access

Nevsky pr boasts two large and excellent Internet cafés:

Café Max (Map p677; ☎ 273 6655; 90/92 Nevsky pr; Ⓜ Mayakovskaya; per hr R60; ☾ 24hr)

Quo Vadis (Map p677; ☎ 311 8011; Nevsky pr 24; Ⓜ Gostiny Dvor; per hr R60; ☾ 24hr)

Internet Resources

The city's official portal is www.spb.ru; it's run by the local government and is full of information, although most of it is very dry. Far better is the www.saint-petersburg.com site, written by a collection of the city's admirers and enthusiasts and packed with entertainment listings, hotels, restaurants and ideas for visitors. Check out www.sp timesrussia.com for local news and listings.

Laundry

There's a centrally located **laundry service** (☎ 273 5806; ul Pestelya 17/25; Ⓜ Chernyshevskaya; per kg R22; ☾ 9am-8pm Mon-Sat, 9am-6pm Sun); look for the sign 'khimchistka i prachechnaya'. Other than that, many minihotels and hostels offer a laundry service at perfectly reasonable rates.

Left Luggage

You can leave your luggage at any luggage office (kamera khraneniya) of the big stations for between R30 and R50 per day.

Media

There is lots of St Petersburg–specific media. In English there's the *St Petersburg Times*, *Pulse* and the bottom-rate *Neva News*. Local publications in Russian to look out for are *Afisha* and the *Time Out*–affiliated *Kalendar*, as well as the far cheaper *Vash Dosug*, known to all as VD. All three provide citywide listings for clubs, films, concerts and other goings on.

Medical Services

Pricey treatment is available at the **International Clinic** (Map pp672-4; ☎ 320 3870; www.icspb .com; 19/21 ul Dostoevskogo; Ⓜ Ligovsky pr), which offers 24-hour emergency care and direct billing to insurance companies. **Poliklinika No 2** (Map pp672-4; ☎ 316 6272; Moskovsky pr 22; Ⓜ Technologichesky Institut; ☾ 24hr) is also recommended – and much cheaper. Two 24-hour pharmacies are **Apteka Petrofarm** (Map p677; ☎ 314 5401; Nevsky pr 22; Ⓜ Nevsky Pr) and **Apteka** (☎ 277 5962; Nevsky pr 83; Ⓜ Pl Vosstaniya).

Money

Currency exchange offices are located through the city. ATMs are inside every metro station, in hotels and department stores, in main post offices and along major streets. **American Express** (Map pp672-4; ☎ 326 4500;

fax 326 4501; ul Malaya Morskaya 23; ⊗ 9am-5pm Mon-Fri; Ⓜ Sadovaya/Nevsky Pr) only offers travel services: travellers cheques can be exchanged at most Russian banks (with commission, of course).

Post
The **central post office** (glavpochtamt; Map pp672-4; ☎ 312 8302; Pochtamtskaya ul 9; Ⓜ Sadovaya; ⊗ 9am-7.45pm Mon-Sat, 10am-5.45pm Sun) is open daily. You should come here to send large parcels abroad (small post offices will usually refuse to take them). You can also send telegrams from here.

Telephone & Fax
You can make international calls from most modern call boxes. Phonecards (*telefonaya karta*) can be bought in kiosks around town, as well as at metro station ticket offices. Call centres for placing long-distance calls can be found all over the place. One central one includes Nevsky pr 88.

Toilets
There are public toilets all over St Petersburg in varying states of cleanliness and repair. Convenient ones are located between the Kazan Cathedral and Kanal Griboyedova (R10). There are also toilets around most metro stations, although not those on Nevsky pr.

Tourist Information
Since 2000, St Petersburg has been home to Russia's one and only **tourist office** (☎ 310 2822; ⊗ 9am-5pm), a helpful kiosk on Palace Square next to the Hermitage where you can get information and buy guides in many languages.

Travel Agencies
Ost-West Kontaktservice (Map p677; ☎ 327 3416; www.ostwest.com; 105 Nevsky pr; Ⓜ Pl Vosstaniya) A reliable outfit, Ost-West charges $30 to register visas for those not staying in hotels.

Sindbad Travel International (Map p677; ☎ 327 8384; www.sindbad.ru, in Russian; 3-ya Sovetskaya ul 28; Ⓜ Pl Vosstaniya; ⊗ 9am-10pm Mon-Fri, 10am-5pm Sat-Sun) Based at the HI St Petersburg Hostel; can organise discounted travel.

DANGERS & ANNOYANCES
Never drink tap water in St Petersburg as it contains *Giardia lamblia*, a parasite that can cause horrific stomach cramps and nausea. Bottled water is available everywhere. If you must drink tap water, boil it for a good few minutes first.

The humidity and marshland location of St Petersburg makes it mosquito hell from May until October. Be prepared – bring repellent or the standard antimosquito tablets and socket plug. Alternatively you can buy these all over the city – ask for *sredstva protif kamarov*.

Human pests include the rising number of pickpockets on Nevsky pr in recent years. Be extra vigilant and look out particularly for the infamous gangs of children who work the street.

SIGHTS
The Historic Heart
Unquestionably your first stop should be the **Palace Square** (Dvortsovaya ploshchad), where the baroque/rococo **Winter Palace** (Zimny dvorets; Map p677) appears like a mirage under the archway at the start of Bolshaya Morskaya ul. Empress Elizabeth commissioned the palace from Bartolomeo Rastrelli in 1754. Along with a number of neighbouring buildings, some of the Winter Palace's 1057 rooms now house part of the astonishing **Hermitage** (Map p677; ☎ 311 3465; www.hermitagemuseum.org; mNevsky Pr; adult R300, students & children free, photo (no flash)/video ticket R100/350, audio guides R250; ⊗ 10.30am-6pm Tue-Sat, 10.30am-5pm Sun), which is one of the world's great art museums. Enter through the courtyard from Palace Square. To avoid queues in the summer months, you can book tickets online very easily. The collection is vast and can be overwhelming for a first-time visitor. Ask for an English map at the information desk in the ticket hall.

If your time is limited you should look out for the following highlights: the Jordan Staircase (directly ahead of you when you enter); room 100 (Ancient Egypt), rooms 178–97 (the State rooms for the apartments of the last imperial family); room 204 (the Pavilion Hall); rooms 228–38 (Italian Art, 16th to 18th centuries); room 271 (the Imperial family's cathedral); and concentrate most of your time on the fabulous 3rd floor, particularly rooms 333–50 for late-19th-century and early-20th-century European art, including a huge array of Matisse, Picasso, Monet, Van Gogh, Cézanne,

Gaugin, Pissaro, Rodin and Kandinsky. There are several cafés and shops within the museum, so you can easily spend a whole day there. Disabled access is now very good – call ☎ 110 9079 if you require any assistance.

Across the square from the winter palace is the fabulous **General Staff Building** (Map p677; adult/student R160/free; ⏲ 10.30am-6pm Tue-Sun), which also houses a museum and temporary exhibits, including French art of the 20th century and the former apartments of Prime Minister Count Nesselrohde – and in the middle of the square, the 47.5m **Alexander Column** commemorates the 1812 victory over Napoleon.

To the west across the road is the gilded spire of the **Admiralty** (Map pp672-4), which used to be the headquarters of the Russian navy. West of the Admiralty is **ploshchad Dekabristov** (Decembrists' Square; Map pp672-4), named after the Decembrists' Uprising of 14 December 1825.

Falconet's famous statue of Peter the Great, the **Bronze Horseman** (Map pp672-4), stands at the end of the square towards the river. Behind looms the splendid golden dome of **Isaakievsky Sobor** (St Isaac's Cathedral; Map pp672-4; ☎ 315 9732; Isaakievskaya pl; Ⓜ Sadovaya/ Nevksy Pr; admission to cathedral R250, to colonnade R100; ⏲ 11am-6pm Thu-Tue), built between 1818 and 1858. At this price think twice before going into the cathedral unless you like the ornate baroque style. The colonnade is far better value for money however, giving superb views over the city.

Nevsky Prospekt

The inner part of vast Nevsky pr runs from the Admiralty to Moskovsky Vokzal (Moscow Station) and is St Petersburg's main shopping thoroughfare. The most impressive sight along it is the great colonnaded arms of the **Kazansky Sobor** (Kazan Cathedral; Map p677; Kazanskaya pl 2; admission free; ⏲ 9am-6pm), built between 1801 and 1811.

At the end of Nevsky pr is the working **Lavra Alexandera Nevskogo** (Alexander Nevsky Monastery; Map pp672-4; ☎ 274 0409; Ⓜ pl Alexandra Nevskogo; adult/student R50/30; dawn-dusk, to 8pm in summer), where you'll find the **Tikhvin Cemetery** (admission R50; ⏲ 11am-dusk Fri-Wed), last resting place of some of Russia's most famous artistic figures, including Tchaikovsky and Dostoyevsky.

Between Nevsky & the Neva

A block north of Nevsky Pr metro station is lovely **ploshchad Iskusstv** (Arts Square), with a statue to national bard Alexander Pushkin at its centre. The yellow Mikhailovsky Palace, now the **Russian Museum** (Gosudarstvenny Russky muzey; Map p677; ☎ 311 1465; www.rusmuseum .ru; Ⓜ Nevsky Pr; adult/student R270/135; ⏲ 10am-5pm Wed-Mon), housing one of the country's finest collections of Russian art makes up the far side of the square. This is the perfect complement to the Hermitage, presenting a wonderful and easily navigable collection of Russian art throughout the ages in the palace's lovely halls. Behind it are the pleasant **Mikhailovsky Gardens**, which are popular year-round for walking and relaxing.

The polychromatic domes of the **Church on Spilled Blood** (Map p677; ☎ 315 1636; Konyushennaya pl; Ⓜ Gostiny Dvor; adult/student R250/125; ⏲ 11am-6pm Thu-Tue) are close by. Also known as the Church of the Resurrection of Christ, it was built from 1887 to 1907 on the spot where Alexander II had been assassinated in 1881. The interior is incredible and somewhat overwhelming – having been restored from Soviet times when the church was used as a potato warehouse.

The lovely **Letny Sad** (Summer Garden; Map pp672-4; admission R10; ⏲ 9am-10pm May-Oct, 10am-6pm Oct–mid-Apr, closed mid-Apr–late-Apr) is between the open space of Mars Field (Marsovo Pole) and the Fontanka River. Laid out for Peter the Great with fountains and pavilions along a geometrical plan, it's a great place in which to relax.

The greatest thing about the unmistakable Rastrelli-designed **Smolny Sobor** (Smolny Cathedral; Map pp672-4; ☎ 278 5596; pl Rastrelli; admission R100; ⏲ 11am-5pm Fri-Wed), 3km east of the Summer Garden, is the sweeping view from atop one of its 63m-high belfries.

South & West of Nevsky Prospekt
Map pp672–4

A short walk down the Moyka River from Isaakievskaya pl (St Issac's Sq) is the fascinating **Yusupov Palace** (☎ 314 9883; nab reki Moyki 94; Ⓜ Sadovaya; adult/student R300/250; ⏲ 11am-5pm). Notorious as the scene of Rasputin's grisly murder in 1916, the palace has some of the most magnificent interiors in the city. The entry price gets you a walkman which guides you through the palace in English giving a very interesting tour of the

NEVSKY PROSPEKT

0 _____ 200 m
0 _____ 0.1 miles

INFORMATION
Anglia Bookshop	1 D2
Apteka Petrofarm	2 B2
Apteka	3 E3
Australian Consulate	4 B1
Café Max	5 D2
Ost-West Contaktservice	6 F3
Quo Vadis	7 B2
Sindbad Travel International	(see 19)
Tourist kiosk	8 A1

SIGHTS & ACTIVITIES (pp675-9)
Alexander Column	9 A1
Church on Spilled Blood	10 B1
General Staff Building	11 A1
Hermitage	(see 15)
Kazan Cathedral	12 B2
Ploschad Iskusstv (Arts Square)	13 C1
Russian Museum	14 C1
Winter Palace	15 A1

SLEEPING (pp679-80)
Grand Hotel Europe	16 B2
Guesthouse	17 F2
Herzen University Hotel	18 B2
HI St Petersburg Hostel	19 F2
Kazanskaya 5	20 B2
Nevsky Inn	21 A2
Nord Hostel	22 A2
Oktyabrskaya	23 E3
Oktyabrsky Filial	24 E3
St Petersburg Puppet Hostel	25 D1

EATING (pp680-1)
Chaynaya Lozhka	26 F3
Chaynaya Lozhka	27 E2
Chaynaya Lozhka	28 C2
Oliva	29 A2
Tri	30 B2
Yolki Palki	31 D2
Zov Ilyicha	32 A3

DRINKING
Fish Fabrik	33 E3
Tsynik	34 A3

SHOPPING (p682)
Folk Crafts Shop	35 A2
Gostiny Dvor	36 C2
Grand Palace	37 D2
Passazh	38 C2

TRANSPORT (p681)
Central Train Booking Office	39 B2
Paromny Tsentr	40 E2

OTHER
Anichkov Palace	41 C2
Catherine the Great Statue	42 C2
Pushkin Theatre	43 C3
Radisson SAS	44 D2
Royal St Petersburg	(see 35)
Stroganov Palace	40 E2

RUSSIA

palace rooms, including the wonderful private theatre. You can also join a special **Rasputin tour** (adult/student/under 16 R300/250/150, 30 min, daily at 1.15 & 5.15pm) that takes you to parts of the palace not visited on the audiotour and traces the last hours of Rasputin's life.

Across the meandering Kanal Griboyedov is Sennaya pl, the heart of Dostoyevskyville. The author lived in several flats around here, and many of the locations turn up in *Crime and Punishment*. To find out more, head to the excellent **Dostoyevsky Museum** (☎ 164 6950; Kuznechny per 5/2; adult/student R60/30, audio tour in English R70; ⏲ 11am-5pm Tue-Sun), located in the house in which the writer died in 1881.

The Petrograd Side   Map pp672–4

The Petrograd Side refers to the cluster of delta islands between the Malaya Neva and Bolshaya Nevka channels. The principal attraction here is the **Peter & Paul Fortress** (Petropavlovskaya Krepost; ☎ 238 4550; Ⓜ Gorkovskaya; admission to grounds free, admission to all buildings adult/student R120/60; ⏲ 10am-5pm Thu-Mon, 10am-4pm Tue). Founded in 1703 as the original military fortress for the new city, it was mainly used as a political prison up to 1917: famous residents include Peter's own son Alexei, as well as Dostoyevsky, Gorky and Trotsky. At noon every day a cannon is fired from the **Naryshkin Bastion**, scaring the daylights out of tourists. It's fun to walk along the **battlements** (adult/student R50/30; ⏲ 10am-10pm). Most spectacular of all is the **St Peter & Paul Cathedral**, with its landmark needle-thin spire and magnificent baroque interior. All Russia's tsars since Peter the Great have been buried here. The latest addition was Nicholas II and his family, finally buried here by Yeltsin in 1998 – you'll find them in an anteroom to your right as you enter. Also look out for the famously ugly pinhead **statue** of Peter the Great in the centre of the fortress. The statue was created by Mikhail Shemyakin in 1990.

Vasilevsky Island   Map pp672–4

Peter the Great intended for this to become the centre of his new city and the buildings at the eastern end of the island are some of the oldest in the city. However, despite being the academic centre of the city, the lack of a bridge until the mid-19th century meant that development naturally focused on the other side of the Neva. There's plenty to be seen here though – the Strelka (Tongue of Land), beside the unusual red **Rostral Columns** (elaborate oil-fired navigation beacons, now only lit on special occasions), gives a magnificent view across the Neva and is a social hub during the summer months. The old Stock Exchange is now the grand **Central Naval Museum** (☎ 218 2502; Birzhevaya pl 4; Ⓜ Sportivnaya/Vasileostrovskaya; adult/student R90/30; ⏲ 11am-5.15pm Wed-Sun), a tribute to Russia's naval muscle.

On the University Embankment the pale blue and white building with the steeple is the **Kunstkamera** (Museum of Anthropology & Ethnography; ☎ 218 1412; Universitetskaya nab 3; adult/student R100/50; ⏲ 11am-4.45pm Tue-Sun); the entrance is around the corner on Tamozhyonny per. Founded by Peter himself in 1714, it contains his personal collection of 'curiosities' that were originally displayed to educate the populace. You'll see a ghoulish collection of babies in jars with a variety of physical defects.

The single most interesting place to visit on Vasilevsky Island is the **Menshikov Palace** (☎ 323 1112; Universitetskaya nab 15; adult/student R200/100; ⏲ 10.30am-4.30pm Tue-Sun). Now part of the Hermitage Museum, this 1712 palace was built for Peter the Great's close friend (and some say lover) Alexander Menshikov, the first governor of St Petersburg. The interiors are not much on the far later Yusupov Palace interiors, but are very revealing for anyone interested in the Petrine era. The very heavy, Dutch-influenced décor and furnishings were totally outmoded by the 19th century, but are very representative of the style of the times.

ACTIVITIES

There is plenty of opportunity to try out a Russian *banya* in St Petersburg. One of the most popular in town is **Krugliye Bani** (☎ 550 0958; ul Karbysheva 29A; Ⓜ Pl Muzhestva; ⏲ 8am-9pm Fri-Tue). There's also a fantastic open-air heated pool here that is great in the winter evenings. It's popular with expats on Wednesday. More central options include **Pasadskiye Bani** (☎ 233 5092; Malaya Pasadskaya ul 28/2; Ⓜ Gorkovskaya; ⏲ 8am-9pm Wed-Sun) and **Kazachiye Bany** (Map pp672-4; ☎ 112 5079; Bolshoy Kazachy per 11; Ⓜ Pushkinskaya; ⏲ 9am-9pm).

Swimming is also possible year-round, both inside and out. There are lots of pools in the city – try the **VMF** (☎ 322 4505; Sredny pr 87; Ⓜ Vasileostrovskaya; ☺ 7am-9pm) – a huge pool on Vasilevsky Island. However, for the quintessential Russian experience (or just to watch something quite spectacular during winter) head down to Zaychy Island (where the Peter & Paul Fortress is) and watch the famous ice swimmers, or 'walruses', who start the day with a bracing dip in the water, through a hole carved into the ice.

TOURS

It is quite hard to imagine a better deal than **Peter's Walking Tours** (www.peterswalk.com) run by Peter Kozyrev and his fantastic team of English-speaking guides. The tours leave from the HI St Petersburg Hostel (right) or Café Max (p674). Prices range from R320 to R480 per person for the various tours, which include a six-hour epic Siege of Leningrad Tour. Other walks include the Dostoyevsky and Communist Legacy Walks, as well as more standard city tours.

FESTIVALS & EVENTS

St Petersburg celebrates City Day on 27th May, which marks the founding of the city with mass festivities. The white nights (around the summer solstice in late June) are truly unique. The city comes alive and parties all night as the sun only barely sinks below the horizon, leaving the sky a magical grey-white throughout the night.

SLEEPING

As St Petersburg has a very definite 'season', room prices are at a premium between May and September. Outside this period, room prices decrease by between 10% and 30% on those quoted below.

Budget

Herzen University Hotel (Map p677; ☎ 314 7472; fax 314 7659; Kazanskaya ul 6; Ⓜ Nevsky Pr; s/d €16/40) A well-run hostel with a brilliant location, this place is used to foreigners. However, they don't register visas, so you'll need to register your visa elsewhere to stay here (they do not allow people with unregistered visas to spend more than three days here).

St Petersburg Puppet Hostel (Map p677; ☎ 272 5401; www.hostelling-russia.ru; ul Nekrasova 12; Ⓜ Mayakovskaya; dm/d €16/40) A great option – central, friendly and clean. Rates include breakfast and free tickets to the Puppet Theatre!

HI St Petersburg Hostel (☎ 329 8018; www.ryh.ru; 3-ya Sovetskaya ul 28; Ⓜ Pl Vosstaniya; dm/d €18/44) A 300m walk from Moscow station, this hostel is popular and prices include breakfast. Spotless dorms have three to six beds and there's one double; all are slightly cheaper in the winter and for holders of ISIC and HI cards.

Sleep Cheap (Map pp672–4; ☎ 115 1304; www .sleepcheap.spb.ru; Mokhovaya ul 18/32; Ⓜ Chernyshevskaya; dm €19) An excellently appointed small new hostel a 500m walk from Nevsky pr, Sleep Cheap has brand-new facilities and (like most hostels) plans to expand. Go through into the courtyard of No 18 and the hostel is on the left.

Nord Hostel (Map p677; ☎ 117 0342; www.nord hostel.com; Bolshaya Morskaya ul 10; Ⓜ Nevsky Pr; dm/d €24/48) This fantastic addition to the hostel scene has perhaps the most superb location, just metres from Palace Square. Book ahead, as its location and friendly management make it justly popular. Dorms have eight beds and are very clean. There's also one double room and there are plans to expand into a neighbouring apartment.

Mid-Range

Domik v Kolomne (Map pp672–4; ☎ 110 8351; www .colomna.nm.ru; nab Kanala Griboyedova 74a; s/d €50/60) Pushkin's family once rented rooms in this house, and the atmosphere of a large flat remains. Rooms have a homely Russian feel, there are private bathrooms and guests will be well looked after. Some rooms have lovely views over the canal.

Nevsky Inn (Map p677; ☎ 924 9805; www.nevskyinn .ru; Kirpichny per 2, flat 19; Ⓜ Nevksy Pr; s/d €60/75) Run by a joint British-Russian management, the Nevsky is one of the best in the city. Rooms are clean and comfortable and there's a modern kitchen that guests can use.

Guesthouse (Map pp672–4; ☎ 271 3089; www .ghspb.ru; Grechesky per 13; s/d €70/80) A fantastic place, despite its rather unimaginative name. Set behind the enormous Oktyabrsky Concert Hall, it's just a few minutes from Nevsky pr. Rooms are cosy and clean.

Hotel Neva (Map pp672–4; ☎ 278 5000; fax 273 2593; ul Chaikovskogo 17; Ⓜ Chernyshevskaya; s/d unmodernised €50/65, modernised €70/100) One of the city's oldest functioning hotels, the Neva opened its doors in 1913 and has a spectacular staircase to show for it. Unfortunately the rooms are not quite as grand, but they're still comfortable and clean. The location is good, a short walk from the Fontanka and the Neva.

Hotel Oktyabrskaya (Map p677; ☎ 277 6330; hotel@spb.cityline.ru; Ligovsky pr 10; Ⓜ Pl Vosstaniya; s/d €73/116) This enormous hotel around Ploshchad Vosstaniya has two buildings – the main one spans one side of the square and the smaller annexe, Oktyabrsky Filial, is to one side of Moscow Station. While it's enormous and impersonal, it's also well located and the rooms have all been renovated to high standards.

Five Corners Hotel (Map pp672-4; ☎ 380 8181; www.5ugol.ru; Zagorodny pr 13; Ⓜ Dostoyevskaya s/d/ste €130/150/200) This place is very stylish indeed. Its suites are some of the coolest in the city and overlook a trendy hub of streets a short walk from Nevsky pr. Staff are polite and efficient and expansion is on the cards.

Kazanskaya 5 (Map p677; ☎ 327 7466; www.kazansky5.com; Kazanskaya ul 5, 3rd fl; Ⓜ Nevsky Pr; s/d €110/125) Perfectly located and beautifully designed, Kazanskaya 5 attracts an in-the-know crowd of artists and musicians staying in the city. Stuffed full of antiques, the understated rooms nonetheless enjoy a thoroughly modern feel.

Top End

Hotel Astoria (Map pp672-4; ☎ 313-5757; www.rocofortehotels.com; 39 Bolshaya Morskaya ul; s/d €420/430, ste €745-2300; Ⓟ Ⓧ ⓠ) Given a new lease of life by the Rocco Forte group, which purchased this classic St Petersburg hotel in 1997, the Astoria is the only real rival to the Grand Hotel Europe as the best in town. Guests have included Lenin and George W Bush, and while rates are very steep, there's no doubting that this is a gorgeously designed five-star place.

Grand Hotel Europe (Map p677; ☎ 329 6000; www.grandhoteleurope.com; Mikhailovskaya ul 1/7; Ⓜ Nevsky Pr; s/d €350, ste €500-3200; Ⓟ Ⓧ ⓠ) Pricey, but spectacular, the Grand Hotel Europe endures as the best hotel in the city. Faultless location, gorgeous rooms and superb service, the executive suites with views over Arts Square may actually be worth the staggering price tag. Everyone has stayed here, from Isadora Duncan to Prince Charles.

EATING

Look out for blini (Russian pancakes) kiosks throughout the city. Their delicious blini are superb value (R20 to R30) and a great place to snack. As in Moscow, street food is sold around metro stations.

Yolki Palki (Map p677; ☎ 273 1594; Nevsky pr 88; Ⓜ Mayakovskaya; mains R100-200; ⏲ 11am-11pm) This Moscow chain now has an outlet on Nevsky pr – it's as kitsch as ever (you dine in a Russian forest attended by waiters in folk costume) but there's good Russian food served in a buffet style here.

Oliva (Map p677; ☎ 314 6563; www.tavernaoliva.ru, in Russian; Bolshaya Morskaya ul 31; Ⓜ Nevsky Pr; mains R150-300; ⏲ 10am-midnight) An authentic Greek addition to the St Petersburg dining scene, though there is nothing taverna-like about this cavernous place, subtly painted and decorated in an array of Greek styles. The menu is traditional and food is both excellent value and extremely good.

Imbir (Map pp672-4; ☎ 113-3215; Zagorodny pr 15; Ⓜ Vladimirskaya; mains R250-400; ⏲ 10am-midnight) Effortlessly cool, Imbir combines ornate tsarist décor with contemporary design to brilliant effect. With a great atmosphere, it's always full of a trendy local crowd, who come here for drinks and a very reasonably priced, mainly Russian menu.

Zov Ilyicha (Map p677; ☎ 117 8641; Kazanskaya ul 34; Ⓜ Sadovaya; mains R300-400; ⏲ 1pm-2am) 'Lenin's Mating Call' is the city's strangest restaurant. Worth a visit if you fancy a laugh and decent Russian food too. They show 'erotic films' in the dining area after 9pm, and the toilets have to be seen to be believed.

Restoran (Map pp672-4; ☎ 327 8979; Tamozhenny per 2; Ⓜ Vasileostrovskaya; mains R300-400; ⏲ noon-1am) Beautifully designed and lit, Restoran's prerevolutionary spelling of its name harks back to the days of Romanov splendour. The Russian cuisine is well realised and beautifully presented, although quality can sometimes be hit and miss.

Pogreba Monakha (Map pp672-4; ☎ 314 1353; Millionnaya ul 22; mains R450-600; ⏲ noon-midnight) For some well-realised Russian cooking, this 'Monk's Cellar' next to the Hermitage is atmospheric and serves very tasty food. Staff dressed as monks add to the candle-lit ambience.

Cheap Eats

Chaynaya Lozhka (Map p677; Nevsky pr 44 & 136, ul Vosstaniya 13; Ⓜ Pl Vosstaniya; mains R100; ⏲ 9am-10pm) This excellent chain serves delicious blini and offers a wide range of salads. The

DAN HERRICK

Medieval Soroca fortress (p485), Moldova

St Basil's Cathedral (p659) in Moscow, Russia

MARK NEWMAN

PAUL DAVID HELLANDER

Sv Jovan at Kaneo (p461), a tiny 13th-century church overlooking Lake Ohrid, Macedonia

Porcelains and historic paintings in the Russian Museum (p676), St Petersburg

STEVE KOKKER

KRZYSZTOF DYDYNSKI

The Baltic coast of Pomerania (p547) features sandy beaches, Poland

The 'new' medieval bridge of Prizren (p728), Kosovo, Serbia and Montenegro

PATRICK HOR

KRZYSZTOF DYDYNSKI

Jaszczurówka Chapel in Zakopane (p527), Poland

Gdańsk's reconstructed historic quarter, Main Town (p552), Poland

WAYNE WALTON

orange-clad staff members are extremely helpful and the fare is very cheap. Can get busy at lunchtime.

Tri (Map p677; ☎ 595 4183; Italyanskaya ul17; Ⓜ Gostiny Dvor; sandwiches R70; Ⓨ 24hr) A coffee, sandwich and oddly enough wine shop, Tri is good for a light lunch on the run.

Troitsky Most (☎ 232 6693; Kamenostrovsky Pr 9/2; Ⓜ Gorkovskaya; mains R100-200; & Map p677; ☎ 115 1998; Zagorodny Pr 38; Ⓜ Vladimirskaya) Superb vegetarian chain operating in four locations across the city. Their mushroom lasagne is legendary.

Of the city's food markets, **Kuznechny Market** (Map pp672-4; Kuznechny per 3; Ⓜ Vladimirskaya; Ⓨ 9am-9pm) should not be missed. The most colourful and pricey of the city's food halls, you can taste delicious fruit, honey and cheese here, although you'll inevitably be charmed into making some purchases.

DRINKING

City Bar (Map pp672-4; ☎ 314 1037; Millionnaya ul 10; Ⓜ Nevsky Pr; Ⓨ 10am-early) Run by the inimitable local celebrity Elaine, the City Bar has moved to smarter premises on millionaire's row, a short walk from the Hermitage. This is the hub of the expat community and it's full of foreigners most nights of the week.

Tsynik (Map p677; ☎ 312 9526; per Antonenko 4; Ⓨ 1pm-3am, to 7am Sat & Sun) Far more plugged in to the local scene is the grungy cool of Tsynik. Famous for its rowdy crowd and *grenki* (fried garlic black bread), this is the place to be seen misbehaving.

Fish Fabrik (Map p677; ☎ 164 4857; Ligovsky pr 53; Ⓜ Pl Vosstaniya; Ⓨ 3pm-6am) One of the city's longest-running boho joints, Fish Fabrik is a dive bar for drunken artists and student slackers. You'll inevitably end up playing table football with a stranger if you come.

Moloko (Map pp672-4; ☎ 274 9467; Perekupnoy per 2; Ⓜ Pl Alexandra Nevskogo; Ⓨ 7pm-midnight Tue-Sun) The quintessential slacker-boho concert venue, 'Milk' is a local institution. Very cheap, although it can be extremely crowded when there are gigs.

ENTERTAINMENT
Theatre

St Petersburg is arguably Russia's cultural capital and there is a huge range of theatre, ballet, opera and classical concerts to choose from. Check the *St Petersburg Times* on Fridays for listings. A visit to the **Mari-insky Theatre** (Map pp672-4; ☎ 326 4141; www.mariinsky.ru; Teatralnaya pl 1; Ⓜ Sennaya Pl) should not be missed.

Live Music

There's a lively rock scene in St Petersburg, home to classic Soviet rock groups such as Aquarium and Kino, and more recently rock stars–cum–performance artists Leningrad. There's always plenty going on. **Moloko** (Map pp672-4; ☎ 274 9467; www.molokoclub.ru, in Russian; Perekupnoy per 12; Ⓜ Pl Alexandra Nevskogo; cover R100), **Griboyedov** (Map pp672-4; ☎ 164 4355; www.Griboyedovclub.ru, in Russian; Voronezhskaya ul 2a; Ⓜ Ligovsky Pr; cover R100-200) and **Manhattan** (Map pp672-4; ☎ 113 1945; nab reki Fontanki 90; Ⓜ Pushkinskaya) are the best places to catch local groups doing gigs.

There's also a lively jazz scene. Try the **JFC Jazz Club** (Map pp672-4; ☎ 272 9850; www.jfc.sp.ru; 33 Shpalernaya ul; Ⓜ Chernyshevskaya; cover R50-200) and check out the *St Petersburg Times* for other jazz gigs.

Sport

The local soccer team Zenith provokes feverish passion in the hearts of young Petersburgers, and after a match there are always rowdy street scenes as mobs of blue-clad youth stream, drunk and excitable, from the stadium. You can usually buy tickets to see them play all over town (ask at any *teatralnaya kassa* in a metro station), and the season runs October to April. Their home ground is the **Petrovsky Stadium** (Map pp672-4; ☎ 119 5700; Petrovsky ostrov 2; Ⓜ Sportivnaya; admission R100).

Cinemas

The main cinemas in town line Nevsky pr. However, with very few exceptions foreign films (the vast majority of what is being shown) are dubbed into Russian, and so aren't great for non-Russian- speaking visitors. The *St Petersburg Times* usually lists films (if any) being shown in English.

Gay & Lesbian Venues

St Petersburg has three gay clubs and Russia's first lesbian club: check out www.xs.gay.ru for the latest city-specific information.

Nightclubs

Some of the best clubs include alternative Griboyedov (p681) classy **Ostrov** (Map pp672-4;

☎ 328 4649; nab Leitenanta Shmitd 37; M Vasileos-trovskaya) and student super-club **Metro** (Map pp672-4; ☎ 166 0204; www.metroclub.ru; Ligovsky pr 174; M Ligovsky pr).

SHOPPING

The enormous **Gostiny Dvor** (Map p677; ☎ 110 5200; Nevsky pr 35; M Gostiny Dvor; ☼ 10am-10pm) was one of the world's first shopping arcades, being built in the mid-18th century. You'll find almost everything here, and despite the 1st floor being increasingly devoted to designer outlets, the ground floor retains much of its Soviet-era charm.

Other smart shopping malls include the spanking-new **Grand Palace** (Map p677; ☎ 449 9411; Nevsky pr 44; M Gostiny Dvor; ☼ 11am-9pm) and the charming **Passazh** (Map p677; ☎ 311 7084; Nevsky pr 48; M Gostiny Dvor; ☼ 11am-9pm).

The best places for souvenir hunting include the souvenir market next to the Church on Spilled Blood, where you can find an endless array of *matryoshki* (Russian nesting dolls) and Soviet memorabilia. You should most definitely haggle. The **Folk Crafts Shop** (Stroganov Palace) is another good place for traditional Russian gifts.

GETTING AROUND
Metro

The metro (R8 flat fare) is best for covering large distances across the city. The four lines cross over in the city centre and go out to the suburbs. The most confusing aspect of the system is that all labelling is in Cyrillic. Listen out for the announcements of the station names, or ask locals who will usually go out of their way to help. A further confusion is that two stations sharing an exit will have different names. For example, Nevsky pr and Gostiny Dvor are in the same place, but as they are on different lines, they have different names.

Marshrutkas

Around the centre, *marshrutkas* (minibuses) are a quick alternative to the slow trolleybuses. Costs vary on each route, but the average fare is R14, and fares are displayed prominently inside each van. To stop a *marshrutka*, simply hold out your hand and it will stop. Jump in, sit down, pass the cash to the driver (a human chain operates if you are not seated nearby), and then call out '*ostanovityes pozhalusta!*' when you

want to get out and the driver will pull over. *Marshrutkas* are a very good way of getting to one end of Nevsky pr to another.

Taxi

Holding your arm out will cause non-official taxis to stop very quickly. The standard rate for a short distance (1km to 2km) is R50 and then R100 after that, although as a foreigner, expect to have the price raised – always agree on a price before getting into the car. To call an official cab, call ☎ 068. See p697 for more information about taxis in Russia.

AROUND ST PETERSBURG
Petrodvorets Петродворец

☎ 812

The most memorable of the tsarist palaces that stud the countryside around St Petersburg, **Petrodvorets** (☎ 427 9527; admission to grounds adult/student R120/60; ☼ 9am-9pm) has an imposing position 29km west of St Petersburg overlooking the Gulf of Finland. Despite its stunningly grand appearance, the **Grand Palace** (adult/student R250/125; ☼ 10am-6pm Tue-Sun) was in fact almost totally destroyed by the German advance into Russia during WWII – the restored interiors are still as opulent as those befitting any despotic emperor. In fact, the only room in the palace itself which survived the Nazi occupation was Peter's simple study.

In the summer months the most impressive sight is the centrepiece of the grounds, the magnificent (if thoroughly over-the-top) **Grand Cascade & Water Avenue**, a symphony of over 64 fountains and 37 bronze statues. This work of undoubted engineering genius extends from the palace all the way to the Gulf of Finland, and looks magnificent in an idiosyncratically look-how-rich-and-powerful-I-am imperialist manner.

Walking around the grounds is a treat, although in the summer bring some anti-mosquito spray or you may well be eaten alive in the woods.

Elsewhere in the large grounds are several other buildings of interest. Most significant is **Monplaisir**, Peter's two-floor villa, and the lovely **Marly Guesthouse**, which takes its name from Louis XIV's hunting lodge at Versailles and was a comfortable retreat for royals and their guests. It overlooks a small lake and with some wonderful interiors.

GETTING THERE & AWAY

In summer, the pricey Meteor hydrofoils (R350, 30 minutes) leave from outside the Hermitage museum every 20 to 30 minutes from 9.30am to at least 7pm. The trip is great, although don't leave it too late when returning as the crowds can be massive and you may have to wait for up to an hour to get on a boat.

Far cheaper is taking a suburban train (R16, 40 minutes, every 20 to 30 minutes); take any train terminating at Oranienbaum or Kalishe from the Baltic Station (**M** Balt-iiskaya) and alight at Novy Petrodvorets station. The station is still quite a walk (about 2km) from the palace, but buses run frequently from here.

Pushkin & Pavlovsk Пушкин & Павловск
☎ 812

More than anywhere the town of Pushkin is associated with Catherine the Great. A day trip here can be a challenge as it sometimes feels more crowded than St Petersburg itself, but it's also well worth the effort.

At Pushkin, 25km south of St Petersburg, you'll find **Tsarskoe Selo,** (www.tzar.ru) or the 'tsar's village', an estate created by Empresses Elizabeth and Catherine the Great between 1744 and 1796. The big drawcard here is the Rastrelli-designed, baroque **Catherine Palace** (**☎** 466 6669; adult/student R400/200; ⏱ 11am-5pm Wed-Mon), built between 1752 and 1756, but practically destroyed in WWII. The exterior and 20-odd rooms have been expertly restored; the gilt-adorned and mirrored Great Hall is particularly dazzling.

The most famous room in the Catherine Palace is the Amber Room – which was removed by the Nazis in 1941 and was believed to be the world's most valuable piece of missing art, valued at some $140m. The room was created by Rastrelli under Empress Elizabeth from priceless amber panels given to Peter the Great by Frederick I of Prussia in 1716. The panels sat alongside magnificent diamond mosaics and mirrors, creating a dazzling ensemble. The Amber Room took over a decade to restore and was reopened in 2003. The original was recently discovered to have been destroyed in Kaliningrad during the war (p685).

Just wandering around **Catherine Park** (adult/student R60/30; ⏱ 9am-5.30pm), which surrounds the palace, is a pleasure. In the outer section of the park is the **Great Pond**, fringed by an intriguing array of structures including a Chinese Pavilion, a purposely Ruined Tower and a Pyramid where Catherine the Great buried her dogs.

To escape the masses, head 4km further south to **Pavlovsk** (admission to grounds R50; ⏱ 9am-6pm), the park and palace designed by Charles Cameron between 1781 and 1786, and one of the most exquisite in Russia. Pavlovsk's **Great Palace** (**☎** 470 2155; adult/student R250/150; ⏱ 11am-5pm Sat-Thu), also partly restored after a trashing in WWII, has some delightful rooms, but it's the sprawling, peaceful park that's the real attraction.

GETTING THERE & AWAY

The most convenient way of getting to both Pushkin and Pavlovsk is to hop on one of the frequent *marshrutkas* (R20, 30 minutes) that leave from outside Moskovskaya metro station – not to be confused with Moskovsky vokzal – 8km south of the city centre; the *marshrutkas* stop within walking distance of Tsarskoe Selo and outside Pavlovsk. You can also take a train from the Vitebsk station's platform 1 to Detskoe Selo (Tsarskoe Selo's train station), and to Pavlovsk station for Pavlovsk (it's a 30-minute trip to either). Note that while there are several trains prior to 9am, there are far fewer later in the day.

KALININGRAD REGION
КАЛИНИНГРАДСКАЯ ОБЛАСТЬ

pop 946,700

If you think that travelling through Russia is already an adventure, wait until you get to Kaliningrad! Not only is it the country's newest and most westerly province (and one of its smallest), it also has a history that differs in all ways from that of the rest of Mother Russia, from which it's cut off by Lithuania and Belarus. It's now the only bit of Russia completely surrounded by EU-member states. Closer to Berlin, Stockholm and Warsaw than they are to Moscow, locals are in some ways more Western-oriented than their fellow Russians, but in other ways the enclave is behind the reforms of

RUSSIA

St Petersburg and Moscow and its politics a tad on the paranoid side.

Aside from the lively, leafy capital (leafy in the surviving bits of old Königsberg, that is; the rest is an aesthetic assembly of cracked concrete), this exciting region boasts moss-covered ruins of Prussian castles, the world's largest amber-producing mine, long stretches of pristine beach and some of Europe's highest sand dunes.

HISTORY

From the 13th century until 1945 the area was German, part of the core territory of the Teutonic Knights and their successors, the dukes and kings of Prussia. Its capital was the famous German city Königsberg, capital of East Prussia, where Prussian kings were crowned. Once one of Europe's most beautiful cities, Königsberg was a liberal and academically advanced Prussian outpost on the Baltic. Albertina University, founded in 1544 (whose most famous graduate was Immanuel Kant), helped ensure the city's position as a major educational and spiritual centre.

After WWI, East Prussia was separated from the rest of Germany when Poland regained statehood. Königsberg lost its dignity forever in a four-day series of intense air raids by the British RAF in August 1944 that destroyed most of the city. The three-month campaign by which the Red Army took it in 1945 was one of the fiercest of the war, with hundreds of thousands of casualties on both sides.

Russia's Baltic Fleet is headquartered at Baltiysk, and therefore the entire region was closed to Westerners until 1991. Despite a massive military downsizing since the 1990s, the area is still heavily militarised. The area has always been strategically important, and now is so again in light of NATO and EU expansion eastwards.

The enclave suffered through economically tragic times in the early 1990s. Things have much improved since then, and Kaliningrad is putting on a brave face vis-à-vis its increasing isolation from mainland Russia. Many locals are pinning their hopes and futures more on Europe than Mother Russia.

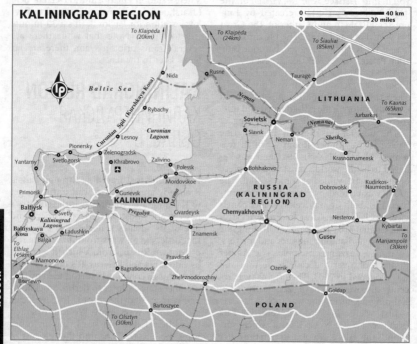

KALININGRAD REGION

PEOPLE

Kaliningrad's population is made up of almost 80% Russians, 10% Belarusians, 6% Ukrainians, and the rest Lithuanians and others.

ENVIRONMENT
The Land

The total territory of the Kaliningrad region is 15,100 sq km, extending a mere 205km east–west and 108km north–south. Its coastline stretches 147km, 100km of which is sandy beaches and 50km of which is made up of the Curonian Spit (Kurshkaya Kosa), shared with Lithuania. There are found Europe's second-highest sand dunes, which measure up to 60m in height. Much of the land is flat (some below sea level and protected by dykes), with elevations in the southeast rising to 231m.

Environmental Issues

Unesco placed the Curonian Spit on its list of World Heritage sites in 2000, securing the unique ecosystem's importance and its protection under international law. About the same time, Russian oil giant Lukoil announced it would build D6, a large series of oil rigs, just 22km from the spit's shores. In the event of a spill Lukoil can breathe easy: it only has responsibility to clean oil from the sea, not from the shore, where it will inevitably wash up. Kaliningrad-based environmental NGO Ecodefense cites several incidents of oil pollution near Kaliningrad since the early 1990s, which were downplayed by the authorities.

The EU has provided millions of euros to clean up environmental pollution in Kaliningrad, and institute waste-management and water-monitoring systems. There are 70 landfill sites in the region, none of acceptable operational standards.

KALININGRAD КАЛИНИНГРАД

☎ 22 (within the region)
☎ 0112 (from elsewhere) / pop 423,000

Photographs attest that, until 1945, Königsberg was one of Europe's gems – regal, vibrant, cultured. WWII, Soviet destruction of German-era constructions and misguided building projects have seen to it that today's Kaliningrad is not exactly eye candy. Yet this city's funkiness is a match for that of other comparably sized Russian cities – an almost surreal, *fin de siècle* attitude runs rampant here that injects vitality into all walks of life. As Kaliningrad, the city has never been this close to – and yet so far from – Europe, and the push and pull has created a giddy light-headedness.

There are lovely residential corners of the city that predate the war, a forest-like park and a few large ponds, which work as effective antidotes to all the concrete. A number of central areas have been given a recent and friendly face-lift.

History

Founded as a Teutonic order fort in 1255, Königsberg joined the Hanseatic League in 1340, and from 1457 to 1618 was the residence of the grand masters of the Teutonic order and their successors the dukes of Prussia. The first king of Prussia was crowned here in 1701. After WWII many of the surviving Germans were killed or sent to Siberia – the last 25,000 were deported to Germany in 1947–48, one of the most effective ethnic-cleansing campaigns in European history.

The city was renamed in 1946 after Mikhail Kalinin, one of Lenin's henchmen, who had conveniently died just as a new name for the city was needed. After the city opened up in 1991, many elderly Germans visited their *heimat* (homeland), often weeping upon seeing what it had become.

AMBER ROOM MYSTERY SOLVED

Kaliningrad was the centre of one of the 20th-century art world's greatest mysteries: the whereabouts of the spectacular amber room. A gift from Prussia's King Friedrich Wilhelm to Peter the Great in 1716, it was stolen wholesale from St Petersburg by the Nazis in 1941 and brought to Königsberg's castle. It then disappeared. For 60 years exhaustive searches in Kaliningrad and Germany turned up nothing.

In 2004 the mystery came to a crashing end when previously unseen archive papers proved that the room had been taken to Kaliningrad, but was destroyed in a fire while under Red Army occupation. The fire was never reported, to avoid Stalin's feared wrath, and the myth that the room was lost was perpetuated.

Kaliningrad'sstatus as a special economic zone hasn't helped the economy as much as was wished, but there are high hopes for its three coastal ports. At the time of writing, its 2005 City Day celebrations (first week-end in July) promised to be very robust as 'König' (the locals' nickname for their city) prepared to celebrate its 750th anniversary.

Orientation

Leninsky pr, a broad north–south avenue, is Kaliningrad's main artery, running over 3km from the bus and main train station, the Yuzhny Vokzal (South Station), to the suburban Severny Vokzal (North Station). Halfway it crosses the Pregolya River and passes the cathedral, the city's major land-mark. The city's real heart is further north, around the sprawling ploshchad Pobedy.

Information

INTERNET ACCESS

E-Type (☎ 44 72 42; Sovietsky pr 1; per hr R30; ☻ 9am-9pm Mon-Fri, 9am-7pm Sat)

Kiberda (☎ 51 18 30; Komsomolskaya ul 87; per hr R35; ☻ noon-midnight) Smoky, funky cellar Internet bar that also serves excellent meals.

MEDICAL SERVICES

Emergency Hospital (☎ 46 69 89; ul Alexander Nevskogo 90)

Formula Zdorovya (☎ 77 70 03; Leninsky pr 63-67; ☻ 24hr) Well-stocked pharmacy.

MONEY

There are exchange bureaus and ATMs at most hotels, alongside the State Techni-cal University and all along Leninsky pr. **Stroivestbank** (☎ 21 29 75; ul Gendelya 3a; ☻ 9am-5pm Mon-Fri) gives credit-card cash advances.

POST & TELEPHONE

Post office (☎ 56 33 21; ul Chernyakhovskogo 32; ☻ 9am-8pm Mon-Fri, 10am-3pm Sat) Opposite the central market, this is the most convenient branch, offering full services.

Telephone and fax centre (ul Teatralnaya 13/19; ☻ 24hr) You can order long-distance calls here and send faxes; self-dial long-distance calls can be made one block south at a second location.

TRAVEL AGENCIES

As there are no tourist information centres in Kaliningrad, travel agencies are the best source of advice.

Baltma Tours (☎ 21 18 80; www.baltmatours.com; pr Mira 49) This friendly, efficient, multilingual bunch can issue visa invitations, arrange accommodation and provide a surprising array of local excursions, including to Yantarny, home of the world's largest amber mine. The most exotic of their many guided tours is a fishing trip inside a local reserve – get your worms and shot glasses ready! Located just west of the Cosmonaut Monument, they are highly recommended.

Golden Orchid (☎ 53 85 53, 01145-21 098; www .enet.ru/~goldorch, in German & Russian; ul Frunze 6) It specialises in arranging trips to the military port city of Baltiysk (formerly Pillau), including permission, transport, guide and accommodation if desired. The agency isn't so user-friendly, but your persistence can result in an interesting expedition!

Sights

CATHEDRAL & AROUND

Ostrov Kanta (Kant's Island, previously Kneiphof) used to be the heart of Königs-berg. The great German remnant here is the red brick Gothic **cathedral** (Kafedralny Sobor; ☎ 27 25 83; adult/student R60/20; ☻ 9am-5pm). Founded in 1333, it was damaged during WWII and since 1992 has undergone full restoration. On the bottom floor are small Lutheran and Orthodox chapels, and up-stairs displays of old Königsberg and objects from archaeological digs. On the top floor is the creepy death mask of Immanuel Kant, whose rose marble **tomb** lies outside on the north side. The 18th-century philosopher was born, studied and died in Königsberg. A few metres away is a **memorial stone** marking the site of the original university.

West of the cathedral, along the Petra Velikogo embankment, is the **Oceanography Museum** (☎ 34 02 44; nab Petra Velikogo 1; each of its 3 sections adult/student R30/20; ☻ 10am-5pm Wed-Sun). Displays highlight Soviet sea and space exploration, and you can visit the B-413 sub-marine and see the skeleton of a 16.8m-long sperm whale. The fine blue Renaissance-style building just across the river to the south of the cathedral is the old **Stock Exchange** (Leninsky pr 83). Built in the 1870s, it's now the **Sailors' Culture Palace** (☎ 44 68 94; Leninsky pr 83), where local special-interest groups meet and occa-sional concerts and shows (Russian-language only) are held.

CATHEDRAL TO PLOSHCHAD POBEDY

Just north of the cathedral is **Tsentralnaya ploshchad** (Central Square), on which sits

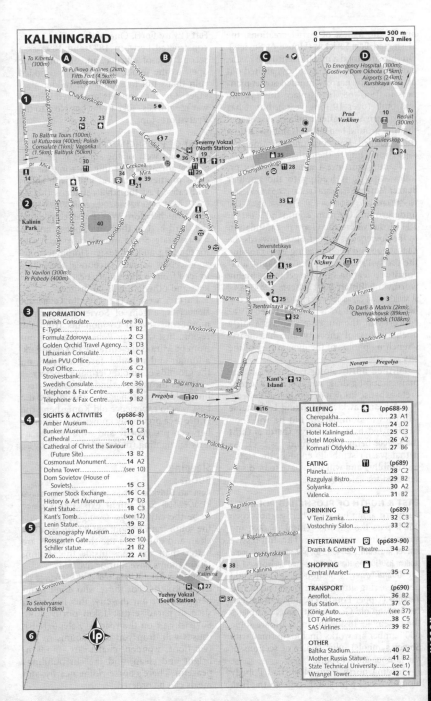

KALININGRAD

0 _____ 500 m
0 _____ 0.3 miles

INFORMATION
Danish Consulate...................(see 36)
E-Type.......................................**1** B2
Formula Zdorovya......................**2** C3
Golden Orchid Travel Agency...**3** D3
Lithuanian Consulate................**4** C1
Main PVU Office........................**5** B1
Post Office...............................**6** C2
Stroivestbank...........................**7** B1
Swedish Consulate................(see 36)
Telephone & Fax Centre............**8** B2
Telephone & Fax Centre............**9** B2

SIGHTS & ACTIVITIES (pp686-8)
Amber Museum........................**10** D1
Bunker Museum.......................**11** C3
Cathedral...............................**12** C4
Cathedral of Christ the Saviour
  (Future Site)..........................**13** B2
Cosmonaut Monument..............**14** A2
Dohna Tower.........................(see 10)
Dom Sovietov (House of
  Soviets)...............................**15** C3
Former Stock Exchange...........**16** C4
History & Art Museum..............**17** D3
Kant Statue............................**18** C3
Kant's Tomb..........................(see 12)
Lenin Statue...........................**19** B2
Oceanography Museum.............**20** B4
Rossgarten Gate.....................(see 10)
Schiller statue.........................**21** B2
Zoo.......................................**22** A1

SLEEPING (pp688-9)
Cherepakha.............................**23** A1
Dona Hotel..............................**24** D2
Hotel Kaliningrad.....................**25** C3
Hotel Moskva..........................**26** A2
Komnati Otdykha.....................**27** B6

EATING (p689)
Planeta..................................**28** C2
Razgulyai Bistro......................**29** B2
Solyanka................................**30** A2
Valencia.................................**31** B2

DRINKING (p689)
V Teni Zamka.........................**32** C3
Vostochniy Salon....................**33** C2

ENTERTAINMENT (pp689-90)
Drama & Comedy Theatre.........**34** B2

SHOPPING
Central Market........................**35** C2

TRANSPORT (p690)
Aeroflot.................................**36** B2
Bus Station.............................**37** C6
König Auto...........................(see 37)
LOT Airlines............................**38** C5
SAS Airlines............................**39** B2

OTHER
Baltika Stadium.......................**40** A2
Mother Russia Statue...............**41** B2
State Technical University.......(see 1)
Wrangel Tower........................**42** C1

RUSSIA

one of the ugliest of Soviet creations, the H-shaped **Dom Sovietov** (House of Soviets). On this site stood a magnificent 1255 castle, damaged during WWII but dynamited out of existence by narrow-minded Soviet planners in 1967–68. In its place this eyesore was built (over 10 long years), but it has never been used after builders discovered that the ground beneath it is hollow, with a (now flooded) four-level underground passage connecting to the cathedral. Duh.

Heading northwest along Leninsky pr, follow the signs leading to the popular **Bunker Museum** (Blindazh Lyasha; ☎ 53 65 93; Universitetskaya ul 2; admission R30; ☻ 10am-6pm), the underground German command post in 1945 from where the German capitulation to the Soviets was signed. Head towards the **Kant statue** and keep heading east, crossing the pretty Prud Nizhny (Lower Pond), a favourite recreation spot), to get to the highly worthwhile **History & Art Museum** (☎ 45 38 44; ul Klinicheskaya 21; adult/student R30/20; ☻ 10am-6pm Tue-Sun). Housed in a reconstructed 1912 concert hall, the museum displays a fairly open history of the city and has heart-wrenching photos of the dynamiting of the city's castle.

Further north along Leninsky pr, the main shopping drag, you'll come to a concrete expanse known as ploshchad Pobedy. A meek and awkward-looking **Lenin statue** still tries to dominate it, but he will soon be dwarfed by the massive **Church of Christ the Saviour** being built behind his back. As if that wasn't symbolic enough, the statue is crumbling and will soon have to be disassembled for safety reasons.

EAST & NORTH OF PLOSHCHAD POBEDY

Eastward along busy ul Chernyakhovskogo you'll pass the chaotic central market and some stylish restaurants. The impressive **Amber Museum** (☎ 46 15 63; pl Vasilievskogo 1; adult/student R50/30; ☻ 10am-5pm Tue-Sun) is housed in the **Dohna Tower**, a bastion of the city's old defensive ring sitting at the lower end of **Prud Verkhny** (Upper Pond). The adjacent **Rossgarten Gate**, an old German city gate, completes the ensemble. Inside the museum are some 6000 amber art works (including some wild Soviet symbols), plus copies of sections of the famous amber room.

Heading north from ploshchad Pobedy along Sovietsky pr you'll come to the **Fifth Fort** (Pyaty Fort). One of the city's 15 forts constructed between 1872 and 1892 as a second line of defence, and the only one open to the public, it's a heavily wooded ruin that's fun to explore for hidden passages. On the grounds are several Soviet war memorials. Take trolleybus No 1 to the Pyaty Fort stop.

WEST OF PLOSHCHAD POBEDY

Extending west of the square is pr Mira, a pleasant artery leading to some of the city's prettiest areas and lined with shops and cafés. Past the **Schiller statue** is the **zoo** (☎ 21 89 24; pr Mira 24; adult/student R40/20; ☻ 9am-8pm), which before WWII was considered the third best in the world, but is now in a sorry state. Some animals have been sold for funding, and, while signs forbid feeding, zoo keepers actually encourage the public to feed fruit to the hungry bears and monkeys and other animals on display.

Further west is the splendid **Cosmonaut Monument**, a gem of Soviet iconography honouring several cosmonauts from the region. Just where pr Pobedy branches out from pr Mira is the entrance to **Kalinin Park**, a funfair and splendid, forest-like park on the grounds of an old German cemetery.

Walks through the linden-scented, tree-lined old German neighbourhoods are the best way to experience old Königsberg: the entire area previously known as Amalienau between prs Pobedy and Mira is particularly enchanting (ul Kutuzova especially).

Sleeping
BUDGET
Komnati Otdykha (☎ 58 64 47; pl Kalinina; dm/s/d R150/280/560) You might expect this place to be the city's dregs, seeing as it's inside the south train station, but it's surprisingly clean and quiet, and the shared toilets are better than the ones inside the station! Dorm rooms have four or five beds.

Gostivoy Dom Okhota (☎ 22 69 94; Petrogo village; s/d R550/750) For those who don't mind being away from the city, this is a small slice of paradise just 15km north along Sovietsky pr on the road to Zelenogradsk (buses will drop you off). Rooms in this two-floor wooden chalet are modern, bright and clean, and the surroundings peaceful. There's horse-riding nearby, and meals can be ordered.

Hotel Moskva (☎ 27 20 89; pr Mira 19; s R1800, d R2000-2800, s/d with shared bath R450/600) There's one unrenovated floor left, and creaky floors, stern attendants and shared toilets, but huge rooms and a great location make this a great deal. The renovated rooms are great – bright, cheerful, spacious.

MID-RANGE & TOP END
Hotel Kaliningrad (☎ 46 94 40; www.hotel.kaliningrad .ru; Leninsky pr 81; s R1200-1900, d R1600-2800; ✕ ☼) Smack in the centre, this eight-storey hotel is convenient, but half the rooms face Dom Sovietov and incessant traffic, and the others face drab apartment blocks. Two floors have luxury rooms; the rest are merely average. Full services are on offer, however.

Cherepakha (☎ 55 75 00; Zoologicheski tupik 10; s/d R1800/2400, ste R3300-3900; ☼) Nestled up against a quiet corner of the zoo on a quiet, green street, this three-floor, elegant hotel of only 11 rooms has an intimate feel. Rooms are tasteful and spacious, and there's a garden for lounging – the perfect place to rest from the chaotic city centre!

Dona Hotel (☎ 35 16 50; http://dona.kaliningrad.ru; pl Vasilevskogo 2; s R1750, d R2800-4400; ☼) Definitely the region's funkiest hotel. Rooms here are small but cosy, and are ultra-modern in their pseudo–Philippe Starck design.

Eating
Eating out has become a pleasure in Kaliningrad over the last few years. The stiff formality of most eateries has given way to a more casual approach. In public places there's still a lot of tough-guy and pretty-girl posturing (even by Russian standards), but the eating-out scene is more relaxed and varied than ever. Cafés and restaurants are spread out across the city, and there is no real 'food strip', though Leninsky pr sports many small, hit-and-miss cafés.

Razgulyai Bistro (☎ 21 48 97; pl Pobedy 1; mains from R55; ☼ 10am-10pm) A dream come true: based on Riga's incredible Lido chain, there's a culinary splendour here with a huge selection of delicious meals to choose from, buffet-style, in a cosy, folksy interior. Try the fresh juice bar for a quick carrot- or kiwi-juice fix.

Solyanka (☎ 27 92 03; pr Mira 24; mains R50-70; ☼ 9am-11pm) Although there may be a doorman here, this is basically a cafeteria-style set-up (non-Russian speakers can point to

what they like) that serves tasty dishes at great prices.

Planeta (☎ 46 52 35; ul Chernyakhovskogo 26; mains R25-75, pizzas R50-165; ☼ noon-6am) This youth hang-out is an uneasy cross between mall food court, American diner and casino, but its creatively designed pizzas are great. Even cheaper grub is served cafeteria-style.

Serebryanie Rodniki (☎ 39 39 39; 13th KM Kaliningrad-Mamonovo road; mains R60-250; ☼ 11am-midnight Sun-Thu, 11am-3am Fri & Sat) For those who like a little bungee jumping before their meal, this is the place: a folk-styled restaurant with excellent food on the banks of a small lake above which people plunge some 40m. It makes a nice break from the city and is about a R200 cab ride from the centre.

Valencia (☎ 43 38 20; pl Pobedy 1; mains R150-400; ☼ 11am-midnight) Perhaps the city's top restaurant, due to its elegance, fine meals and extensive wine list. It has a parlour out front for afternoon-tea service or a cognac, and its wood-carved bar is the nicest in town. There are some vegetarian options.

Drinking
V Teni Zamka (Tsentralnaya pl, kiosk No 63; ☼ 11am-10pm) The city's tiniest café, in the so-called Kiosk Village, serves the best espresso, coffee cocktails and ice cream around.

Reduit (☎ 46 19 51; Litovsky Val 27; ☼ noon-midnight) There's lots of food on the menu, but the main reason to come here is the fresh beer, brewed on the premises – unfiltered is the best. There's a relaxed cellar, an excellent hangout. It's east of the Amber Museum.

Vostochniy Salon (☎ 9022 147 121; ul Proletarskaya 59a; ☼ 11am-9.30pm) Where Eastern kitsch meets New Age. The owners of this tiny water pipe and tea salon no doubt consulted junk shops and LaToya Jackson's website for décor tips, but it works – in its darkened folds you forget about all else and let the flavoured tobacco and green tea work their magic. Avoid the 'exotic' food on offer.

Entertainment
The commercial listings booklet *Kaliningrad – Putivoditel* (in Russian; R30), available at newspaper kiosks, and the bi-weekly events guide *Afishka* (in Russian; free), found in bars and clothes shops, are the best sources to see what's on around town. There's always heaps of detailed information at www .inyourpocket.com.

RUSSIA

Vagonka (☎ 55 66 77; Stanochnaya ul 12; ☽ 11pm-4am Fri & Sat) Kaliningrad's liveliest and most down-to-earth nightclub, this attracts a young, slightly alternative crowd for the excellent DJs and elaborate dance shows. Located west of Kalinin Park, it's not easy to find, so it's best to take a taxi there the first time.

Darfi & Matrix (☎ 45 77 77; Yaltinskaya ul 66; ☽ noon-2am) Darfi is a bowling and billiards emporium, lively and fun any time of the night or day; Matrix is a house-music club that has the hot young things sweating it out on weekends. Both places are east of Dom Sovietov.

Drama and Comedy Theatre (☎ 21 24 22; pr Mira 4) Plays, classical concerts and other events are regularly staged here in this 1927 building (reconstructed after WWII). Posters around town advertise them.

Getting There & Away

AIR
Kaliningrad's Khrabrovo **domestic** (☎ 45 94 26) and **international** (☎ 44 66 66) airports are 24km north of the city near the village of the same name. For international connections see p695. Within Russia, **Aeroflot** (☎ 51 64 55; pl Pobedy 4) has two to four daily flights to Moscow (R2700 one-way, two hours), and **Pulkovo Airlines** (☎ 32 56 18; Zelenaya ul 78/4), located northwest of the city centre, runs one to two daily flights to St Petersburg (R2400 one-way, 1½ hours).

BUS
The **bus station** (☎ 44 36 35) is on ploshchad Kalinina next to the southern train station. Buses depart from here to every corner of the region. Four daily buses go to Klaipёda (R115), and there are two daily buses each to Kaunas (R210) and Vilnius (R305). Daily buses go to Rīga (R315) and Tallinn (R570). There are two daily buses to Gdansk and Oltshyn, one daily to Warsaw, and four weekly to Berlin, Hamburg and Bremen. Buses to Poland and Germany are operated by **König Auto** (☎ 46 03 04).

CAR & MOTORCYCLE
From the south it is possible to enter Kaliningrad from Poland, although the lines at the Lithuanian borders of Kybartai and Nida are not as monstrous. Petrol is widely available. Kaliningrad city has some of the most potholed roads in Russia, and that's saying a lot – be warned!

TRAIN
There are two stations in the city: **Severny vokzal** (North station; ☎ 49 99 91) and the larger **Yuzhny vokzal** (South station; ☎ 49 26 75). All long-distance and many local trains go from Yuzhny vokzal, passing through but not always stopping at Severny vokzal.

There are at least four daily trains to Vilnius (R420 to R650, six hours), at least one daily to Moscow (R1100 to R1550, 23 hours), one daily to Berlin (R2150, 15 hours) and one every second day to both Kyiv (R1100, 25 hours) and St Petersburg (R1100, 25 hours).

Getting Around
Tickets (R7) for trams, trolleybuses, buses and minibuses are sold only by controllers on board. To get to the domestic airport, take bus No 128 from the bus station (R30). Taxis ask at least R400 for the ride from the airport, but it's cheaper going to the airport.

SVETLOGORSK СВЕТЛОГОРСК
☎ 253 (within the region)
☎ 01153 (from elsewhere) / pop 13,000
Hardly damaged by WWII bombing, Svetlogorsk (formerly Rauschen, founded in 1228), a pleasant, green coastal town 35km northwest of Kaliningrad, is a great place to see old Prussia – and get in some decent beach action. The narrow beach is backed by high, steep, sandy slopes, and the town is dotted with pretty wooden houses, which are the main reason visitors come here.

On Oktyabrskaya ul are the 25m **water tower** and the curious red-tile-domed Jugendstil (Art Nouveau) **bathhouse**. About 200m east of the main beach promenade is an impressive, colourful **sundial**, believed to be the largest in Europe.

The **Baltika** (☎ 214 45; ul Verestschagin 8; s R300-950, d R450-2400) hotel is mildly upscale and has several cheaper, unrenovated rooms with shared facilities; the nicer rooms are spacious, and some even have a Jacuzzi. Treat yourself! The small but warm and cosy **Stary Doktor** (☎ 213 62; ul Gagarina 12; s/d R1300/1850) hotel, in an old German home, also has one of the town's best restaurants and souvenir shops.

A Korean restaurant isn't quite what you'd expect to find here, but the dishes at **Kuksi** (☎ 362 69; ul Oktyabrskaya 3; mains from R70; ☺ noon-11pm) are very tasty. Nightclub and bar **Max** (☎ 220 40; ul Oktyabrskaya 36) is so popular that hordes of 20-somethings come here from Kaliningrad just to party for the evening.

Getting There & Away

Some 10 daily trains run between Kaliningrad and Svetlogorsk (¾ hour to 1¼ hours), but the over 20 buses and maxitaxis from the train station and northern train station are faster and more convenient. Svetlogorsk's bus station is 500m west of the train station, at the corner of ul Lenina and Kaliningradsky pr.

KURSHKAYA KOSA КУРШКАЯ КОСА

☎ 250 (within the region)
☎ 01150 (from elsewhere)

The Kurshkaya Kosa is the Russian half of the thin, 98km-long Curonian Spit, which divides the Curonian Lagoon from the Baltic Sea. The area is a Unesco World Heritage site. Its dramatic landscape – high sand dunes, pine forests, an exposed western coast and a calm lagoon – makes it one of Europe's natural highlights.

The **Kurshkaya Kosa National Park** (☎ 213 46; Lesnaya ul 7) is headquartered in Rybachy but runs a fascinating bird-ringing centre 7km north of Lesnoy, on the site of what was the world's first ornithological station. Some 25,000 visitors a year come to see some of the world's largest bird-trapping nets (one is 15m high, 30m wide and 70m long), which trap an average of 1000 birds a day for tagging.

A highly worthwhile, by-donation tour of the facilities here will show you how they catch and ring hundreds of birds before releasing them. There's also a museum at their headquarters in Rybachy. It is best to prearrange the tour.

The **Ecotourism Information Centre** (☎ 282 75; Tsentralnaya ul) in Lesnoy works in collaboration with the national park and organises excursions, transport and accommodation, and rents bicycles.

There are four buses a day from Kaliningrad (via Zelenogradsk) that take the road to Smiltyne in Lithuania at the northern tip of the peninsula.

RUSSIA DIRECTORY

ACCOMMODATION

Prices in this chapter are listed in budget order (from cheapest to most expensive). Budget accommodation is still hard to come by in Russia, and you are strongly recommended to book ahead during the summer months. During the white nights in St Petersburg in late June, booking early is essential.

Both Moscow and St Petersburg have a number of well-established and reliable (if underwhelming) youth hostels. They are significantly more expensive than in most countries (budget €25 per night). Hotels start from about €35, although these are mainly fairly shabby Intourist relics.

BUSINESS HOURS

Russians work from early in the morning until the mid-afternoon. Shops usually open between 9am and 11am and often stay open until 8pm or 9pm. Banks have more traditional opening hours – usually Monday to Friday 9am to 6pm. Bars and restaurants will often work later than their stated hours if the establishment is full. In fact, many simply say that they work *do poslednnogo klienta*, or until the last customer leaves.

CHILDREN

While Russia isn't an obvious place to take children, there's more than you might expect for them to get out of a visit. In St Petersburg the ghoulish freak show at the Museum of Anthropology & Ethnography (p678) is great fun for older kids, although younger ones may find its mutants rather upsetting. In Moscow, Gorky Park is the obvious choice, where there's always plenty to do. There's also the sprawling **Moscow Zoo** (Map pp656-8; ☎ 255 5375; www.zoo.ru; Bolshaya Gruzinskaya ul 1; Ⓜ Barrikadnaya; adult/under-18s R70/free; ☺ 10am-8pm Tue-Sun summer, to 5pm winter).

COURSES

Most people studying in Russia are there for the language, although cheap degrees and a high standard of scientific education make Russia very popular for students from Asia and Africa.

Organisations offering Russian language courses in Moscow and St Petersburg include the following:

RUSSIA

Lingua Service Worldwide (☎ 800 394 5327; www
.linguaserviceworldwide.com/russia.htm; 75 Prospect St,
Suite 4, Huntingdon, NY11743, USA)
Russia Language Study Centre (☎ 095 939 0980;
www.studyrussian.com; Moscow State University,
Leninskiye Gory; Ⓜ Universitet)
Russian Language Undergraduate Services
(☎ 01206 524399; www.rlus.co.uk; 2 Mercury Close,
Colchester, CO2 9RJ, UK)

CUSTOMS

Customs controls in Russia are relatively
relaxed these days. Searches beyond the
perfunctory are quite rare. Apart from the
usual restrictions, bringing in and out large
amounts of cash is limited, although the
amount at which you have to go through
the red channel changes frequently. At the
time of writing it was US$3000.

On entering Russia you will be given a
customs declaration *(deklaratsiya)*, which
you should fill out with a list of any currency you are carrying as well as any items
of worth. You should list mobile phones,
cameras and laptops to avoid any potential
problems on leaving Russia.

It's best if you can get your declaration
stamped on entry and then simply show
the same declaration when you exit Russia.
However, sometimes customs points are totally unmanned, so it's not always possible.
The system seems to be in total flux, with
officials usually very happy for you to fill
out exit declarations on leaving the country
if necessary.

DANGERS & ANNOYANCES

Despite the media fascination with gang-
land killings and the 'Russian mafia', travellers have nothing to fear on this score – the
increasingly respectable gangster classes are
not interested in such small fry. Travellers
need to be very careful of pickpockets,
though – most foreigners stand out a mile
in Russia and, while this is no problem in
itself, there's inevitably an increased chance
you'll be targeted. Also be careful of local
gangs that can surround and rob travellers
quite brazenly in broad daylight.

Bear in mind that, while things have improved slowly, many police officers and other
uniformed officials are on the take – some
of them are not much better than the people they are employed to protect the public
from. Never allow them to go through your

wallet or pockets, as you may find something
is missing later on. If you feel you are being
unfairly treated or the police try to make you
go somewhere with them, bring out a mobile
phone and threaten to call your embassy ('*ya
pozvonyu svoyu posolstvu*'). This threat will
usually be sufficient to make them leave you
alone. However, if they still want you to go
somewhere with them, it's best to call your
embassy immediately.

There's a nasty skinhead tradition of
attacking nonwhite people on Hitler's
birthday (20 April). This should not cause
undue concern to travellers, as targets are
nearly always unfortunate people from the
Caucasus, but nonwhite travellers should
be aware of this disgusting behaviour
despite the very small chance of anything
happening to them.

DISABLED TRAVELLERS

Disabled travellers are not well catered for
in Russia. There's a lack of access ramps and
lifts for wheelchairs. However, attitudes are
enlightened, and things are slowly changing. Major museums such as the Hermitage
and the Russian Museum all offer very good
disabled access.

EMBASSIES & CONSULATES
Russian Embassies & Consulates

Check www.russianembassy.net for more
listings of Russian embassies abroad.
Australia Embassy (☎ 02-6295 9033/9474; fax 6295 1847;
78 Canberra Ave, Griffith, ACT 2603) Consulate (☎ 02-9326
1188; fax 9327 5065; 7 Fullerton St, Woollahra, NSW 2025)
Canada Embassy (☎ 613-235 4341; fax 236 6342) visa
section (☎ 613-336 7220; fax 238 6158; 285 Charlotte St,
Ottawa, Ontario, KIN 8L5) Consulate (☎ 514-843 5901/5343;
fax 842 2012; 3685 Ave Du Musée, Montreal, Quebec, H3G 2EI)
Finland Embassy (☎ 09-66 14 49; fax 66 18 12;
Tehtaankatu 1B, FIN-00140 Helsinki)
Germany Embassy (☎ 030-220 2821, 226 6320;
fax 229 9397; Unter den Linden 63-65, 10117 Berlin)
Consulate (☎ 0228-312 085; fax 312 164; Waldstrasse 42,
53177 Bonn)
UK Embassy (☎ 020-7229 3628; fax 7727 8625;
13 Kensington Palace Gardens, London W8 4QX) Consular
section (☎ 020-7229 8027, visa information message
☎ 0891-171 271; fax 020-7229 3215; 5 Kensington
Palace Gardens, London W8 4QS)
USA Embassy (☎ 202-939 8907; fax 483 7579; 2641
Tunlaw Rd NW, Washington, DC 20007) Visa department
(☎ 202-939 8907; fax 939 8909; 1825 Phelps Place NW,
Washington, DC 20008)

Embassies in Moscow

Australia (Map pp656-8; ☎ 956 6070; fax 956 6170; Kropotkinsky per 2; Ⓜ Kropotkinskaya)
Belarus (Map pp656-8; ☎ 095-924 7031; fax 095-928 6633; Maroseyka ul 17/6, 101000 Moscow; Ⓜ Krasnye Vorota)
Canada (Map pp656-8; ☎ 105 6000; fax 105 6025; Starokonyushenny per 23; Ⓜ Kropotkinskaya)
France (☎ 937 1500; fax 937 1577; ul Bolshaya Yakimanka 45; Ⓜ Oktyabrskaya)
Germany (☎ 937 9500; fax 938 2354; ul Mosfilmovskaya 56) Consular section (☎ 936 2401; Leninsky pr 95A; Ⓜ Pr Verdanskogo/Noviye Chermushki)
Netherlands (Map pp656-8; ☎ 797 29 00; fax 797 2904; Kalashny per 6; Ⓜ Arbatskaya)
New Zealand (Map pp656-8; ☎ 956 3579; www .nzembassy.msk.ru; Povarskaya ul 44; Ⓜ Barrikadnaya)
Poland (Map pp656-8; ☎ 255 0017, visa section ☎ 254 36 21; ul Klimashkina 4; Ⓜ Ulitsa 1905 Goda)
UK (Map pp656-8; ☎ 956 7200; fax 956 7201; Smolenskaya nab 10; Ⓜ Smolenskaya)
Ukraine (☎ 095-229 1079; fax 095-924 8469; Leontevsky pereulok 18, Moscow; Ⓜ Pushkinskaya)
USA (Map pp656-8; ☎ 728 5000; fax 728 5090; Novinsky bul 19/23; Ⓜ Barrikadnaya)

Consulates in St Petersburg

Australia (Map p677; ☎ /fax 325 7333; Italyanskaya ul 1; Ⓜ Nevsky Pr)
Canada (Map pp672-4; ☎ 325 8448; fax 325 8393; Malodetskoselsky pr 32B; Ⓜ Tekhnologichesky Institut)
France (Map pp672-4; ☎ 312 1130; fax 311 7283; nab reki Moyki 15; Ⓜ Barrikadnaya)
Germany (Map pp672-4; ☎ 327 2400; fax 327 3117; Furshtadtskaya ul 39; Ⓜ Chernyshevskaya)
UK (Map pp672-4; ☎ 320 3200; fax 325 3111; pl Proletarskoy Diktatury 5; Ⓜ Chernyshevskaya)
USA (Map pp672-4; ☎ 275 1701; fax 110 7022; Furshtadtskaya ul 15; Ⓜ Chernyshevskaya)

Consulates in Kaliningrad

Lithuania (☎ 55 14 44; Proletarskaya ul 133)
Poland (☎ 55 04 19; Kashtanovaya alleya 51)
Sweden & Denmark (☎ 55 55 94; pl Pobedy 4)

GAY & LESBIAN TRAVELLERS

Homosexuality was legalised in Russia in the early 1990s but remains a divisive issue throughout the country. Young people have a fairly relaxed attitude towards both gay and lesbian relationships, especially in Moscow and St Petersburg – by far the most cosmopolitan cities in the country. But attempts in the Duma as recently as 2002 to ban homosexuality altogether reflect the strong conservative traditionalism of many older Russians who see homosexuality as some kind of Western import.

HOLIDAYS

The main public holidays are:
New Year's Day 1 January
Russian Orthodox Christmas Day 7 January
International Women's Day 8 March
International Labour Day/Spring Festival (1 & 2 May)
Victory (1945) Day (9 May)
Russian Independence Day (12 Jun)
Day of Reconciliation and Accord (the rebranded Revolution Day)(7 Nov)

Other days that are widely celebrated are Defenders of the Motherland Day (23 February), Easter Monday and Constitution Day (12 December). Much of Russia shuts down during the first half of May.

INTERNET RESOURCES

There is a huge amount of travel information about Russia on the Internet. The most up-to-date and accessible news sites are www.themoscowtimes.com and www .sptimesrussia.com.

One of the best general sites for visitors is www.waytorussia.net. This online information portal has an excellent website with up-to-the-minute visa and travel information, listings for bars and clubs, travel tips, and background on Russia and its culture.

For those planning railway trips in Russia and the former Soviet Union, www .poezda.net is an invaluable resource with a fully updated rail timetable uploaded to help you plan.

LANGUAGE

Russian is spoken – not to mention written – everywhere. Young people usually speak some broken English, but generally knowledge of foreign languages is very low. After English, French and German are the most commonly known languages.

Your trip to Russia will be hugely enhanced if you make an effort to learn the Cyrillic alphabet (see p926). Without it you'll find everything extremely hard work.

MEDIA

The Russian media has been the subject of an intense power struggle since the beginning of Putin's era in power. Seeking to

RUSSIA

claw back the control of the media lost since the end of communism, the Kremlin has been accused of illegally taking control of certain media groups that were critical of the government.

The most spectacular example of this was the takeover of national channel NTV by the Kremlin in 2001. While it's impossible to say that the media is centrally controlled in Russia, it's no overstatement to say that the scope of the free press is limited, often by self-censorship as much as by government intervention.

Magazines

There is a huge range of magazines on sale in Russia – many Western titles such as *Vogue* and *Elle* have their own Russian editions, and there is also plenty of home-grown talent. *Itogi* is the Russian equivalent to the *Economist* and has some very interesting news analysis pieces.

Newspapers

The tabloid is king in the new Russia, as pioneered by the weekly *Argumenti I Fakti* and also *Moskovsky Komsomolets,* the trashy, huge-selling daily that has defined post-communist Russia's fascination with the grubby celebrity classes of the Russian showbiz world. Far better for news and analysis are *Izvestia, Kommersant* and *Vedomsti* (affiliated with the *Financial Times* and *Wall Street Journal*). *The Moscow Times,* an English-language daily, has built its reputation on healthy scepticism of the Kremlin and pioneering investigative writing.

Radio

The Moscow station Ekho Moskvy (Echo of Moscow) is the only independent station in the country and has a huge following. Other Russian stations have a huge amount of advertising and are of negligible quality.

TV

The state-run ORT is the government mouthpiece and has been slowly raising broadcasting standards over the past decade to match NTV and RTR, its two main commercial rivals. A huge number of channels broadcast regionally as well. Other national channels include Kultura (the culture channel, showing high-brow documentaries, films and concerts) and the ultra-glossy MTV Russia,

which has been broadcasting in Russia since 1998, showing a mix of Russian and Western pop music.

MONEY

The currency in Russia is the rouble, which is made up of 100 kopeks. Notes come in denominations of 1000, 500, 100, 50 and 10 roubles; coins come in five-, two- and one-rouble and 50- and 10-kopek denominations. You can use all major credit and debit cards (including Cirrus and Maestro) in ATMs and in good restaurants and hotels. Travellers cheques are possible to exchange, although at a price. Euro or US dollar cash is the best to bring, and in general should be in pristine condition – crumpled or old notes are often refused. Most major currencies can be exchanged at change booths all over any town in Russia. Look for the sign *obmen valyut*. You may be asked for your passport. Businesses may quote prices in euros or US dollars; prices in this chapter conform to quotes of individual businesses.

POST

The Russian postal service gets an unfair rap. Postcards, letters and parcels sent abroad usually arrive within a couple of weeks, but there are occasional lapses. A postcard to anywhere in the world costs R10 and a letter R14.

TELEPHONE

The international code for Russia is ☎ 7. International access code from normal phones in Russia is ☎ 8, followed by 10 after the second tone, followed by the country code. From mobile phones, however, just dial +[country code] to place an international call.

EMERGENCY NUMBERS

- Fire ☎ 01
- Police ☎ 02
- Ambulance ☎ 03

TRAVEL AGENCIES

Independent travellers may need to use travel agents to secure visa invitations (see p695) and to book internal travel, as without Russian language skills this can sometimes be tricky to organise yourself if you want more than a simple train or plane ticket. The following can be recommended:

IMS Travel (☎ 7224 4678; www.imstravel.co.uk; 9 Mandeville Pl, London, W1U 3AU) The Russian Travel Centre at IMS Travel has a team of Russian-speaking specialists who can handle almost any travel requirements, including visa invitations, internal flights and transfers on the ground. The centre also has a handy courier service, so you can avoid waiting in line at the Russian embassy in London.

IntelService Center USA (☎ 1-800 339 2118; www .intelservice.ru; 1227 Monterey St, Pittsburgh, PA 15212) With offices in both the US and Moscow, the IntelService Center has plenty of experience in organising travel in Russia. As well as visa invitations, it can arrange discounted hotel rates and tours.

Travel Document Systems (☎ 1-800 874 5100; www .traveldocs.com; 925 15th St NW, Suite 300, Washington, D.C. 20005) The Washington-based TDS deals exclusively in visa documentation and can fax visa invitations anywhere in the world.

VISAS

Everyone needs a visa to visit Russia, and it might be your biggest single headache, so allow yourself at least a month before you travel to secure one. There are several types of visa, but most travellers will apply for a tourist visa, valid for 30 days from the date of entry. Your visa process has three stages – invitation, application and registration.

First of all you need an invitation. For a small fee (usually around €30) most hotels and hostels will issue an invitation (or 'visa support') to anyone staying with them. The invitation then allows you to apply for a visa at any Russian embassy. Costs can vary enormously, from $20 to $200 for same-day service, so try to plan as far ahead as possible. If you're not staying in a hotel or hostel you'll need to buy an invitation. This can be done through almost any travel agent. Some hostels will issue invitations for the equivalent cost of one night's accommodation with them.

On arrival you will need to fill out an immigration card – a long white form issued at passport control throughout the country. You surrender one half of the form immediately to the passport control, and keep the other for the duration of your stay, giving it up only when you exit Russia.

Finally, once you arrive in Russia you are – officially at least – obliged to register your visa within three working days. This can

nearly always be done by your hotel or hostel, but if you are not staying in one you will need to pay a travel agency (usually $30) to register it for you. Not registering your visa is a gamble – some travellers report leaving Russia unhindered without registration, but officially you are liable to large fines. It's best not to take chances.

Since February 2002 Russia has been running a trial scheme whereby tourists from Schengen countries and Britain, Switzerland and Japan who wish to visit St Petersburg and Moscow for less than 72 hours can get visas upon arrival. Travellers must apply at authorised tour operators in their home country 48 hours before departure. Check with your local Russian consulate for details. This form of visa allows little time in Russia and is only available through certain accredited agencies, so it's hard to get too enthusiastic about the scheme.

WOMEN TRAVELLERS

The most common problem faced by foreign women in Russia is sexual harassment. It can be quite common to be propositioned in public, especially if you are walking alone at night. Unpleasant as it may be, this is rarely dangerous and a simple *kak vam ne stydno* ('you should be ashamed of yourself') delivered in a suitably stern manner should send anyone on their way.

That said, Russian men are generally extremely polite, and will open doors, give up their seats and wherever possible help any female out to a far greater degree than their Western counterparts. Women are also very independent, and you won't attract attention by travelling alone as a female.

TRANSPORT IN RUSSIA

GETTING THERE & AWAY
Air

Moscow's two international airports are **Sheremetyevo Airport** (Map p669; ☎ 578 9101; www.sheremetyevo-airport.ru, in Russian) – fairly dire but the best connected in Russia, carrying flights from most major world cities – and the far better **Domodedovo Airport** (Map p669; ☎ 933 6666; www.domodedovo.ru), which recently lured high-profile airlines such as British Airways away from Sheremetyevo due to its modern facilities and enlightened approach to customer service. Between the two Moscow is connected to nearly all European capitals, New York, Washington, Los Angeles, Beijing, Tokyo, Hong Kong, Singapore and Delhi.

St Petersburg's recently renovated **Pulkovo-2 Airport** (☎ 104 3444; www.pulkovo.ru) is the city's international gateway. It's not nearly as well connected as Moscow but still has regular connections throughout Europe, including London, Paris, Frankfurt, Helsinki, Madrid, Rome, Prague and Vienna.

Kaliningrad's **Khrabrogo International Airport** (☎ 44 66 66) has six flights a week to/from Warsaw on LOT and one a week to/from Copenhagen on SAS.

The following list of carriers flying out of Russia has telephone numbers in Moscow/St Petersburg/Kaliningrad where applicable. Some airlines only have offices in Moscow and some only in Moscow and St Petersburg.

Aeroflot (code SU; ☎ 095 753 5555, 812 327 3872, 0112 51 64 55; www.aeroflot.com)

Air France (code AF; ☎ 095 937 3839, 812 325 8252; www.airfrance.com)

American Airlines (code AA; ☎ 095 234 4074; www.aa.com)

Austrian Airlines (code OS; ☎ 095 995 0995, 812 331 2005; www.aua.com)

British Airways (code BA; ☎ 095 363 2525, 812 380 0626; www.ba.com)

ČSA (Czech Airlines; code OK; ☎ 095 973 1847, 812 315 5259; www.czechairlines.com)

Delta Airlines (code DL; ☎ 095 937 9090, 812 117 5820; www.delta.com)

Finnair (code AY; ☎ 095 933 0056, 812 303 9898; www.finnair.com)

Germania Express (code ST; www.gexx.de) Web-based sales only.

Japan Airlines (code JL; ☎ 095 921 6448; www.jal.com)

KLM (code KL; ☎ 095 258 3600, 812 346 6868; www.klm.com)

LOT (code LO; ☎ 095 229 5771, 812 272 2982, 0112 34 27 07; www.lot.com)

Lufthansa (code LH; ☎ 095 737 6400, 812 320 1000; www.lufthansa.com)

Pulkovo Express (code FV; ☎ 095 299 1940, 812 303 9268, 0112 32 56 18; www.pulkovo-express.ru, in Russian)

SAS Scandinavian Airlines (code SK; ☎ 095 775 4747, 812 326 2600, 0112 43 49 43; www.scandinavian.net)

Siberia Airlines (code S7; www.s7.ru; Novosibirsk /Moscow/Irkutsk)

DEPARTURE TAX

There is no departure tax when leaving Russia.

Land
BORDER CROSSINGS

The Russian Federation has a huge number of border crossings, adjoining as it does some 13 countries. From Eastern Europe you are most likely to enter from Finland at Vyborg, Estonia at Narva, Latvia at Rēzekne, Belarus at Krasnoye or Ezjaryshcha and Ukraine at Chernihiv. You can enter Kaliningrad from Lithuania and Poland at any of five border posts. If you're going west to Europe through Belarus, note that you do need a transit visa and you must obtain it in advance; see p80 for details.

BUS

Given the distances involved, entering Russia by bus isn't always the most enjoyable or comfortable way to go. However, getting to St Petersburg from Helsinki (€34, eight hours) or the Baltics is very convenient, with daily overnight and daytime buses.

Sea

St Petersburg has regular ferries from Helsinki, Tallinn and Rostok (in Germany). They are a slow and not particularly cheap method of transport. Tickets can be bought at the sea port (Morskoy Vokzal) and through the **Paromny Tsentr** (Map p677; ☎ 279 6670; www.paromy.ru, in Russian; ul Vosstaniya 19; M Pl Vosstanitya), which sells tickets on all ferries. Prices for St Petersburg–Tallinn begin at €43 for an arm chair and at €65 for a bed in a four-berth cabin.

GETTING AROUND
Air

In a country of Russia's size, air is often the only reasonable way to get around. Flights link nearly every city in Russia to Moscow, and many to St Petersburg. When flying, reckon on paying two to three times the train fare for the same journey. Flights between Moscow and St Petersburg go every hour, and a seat costs €75 (one way). You can buy tickets at any *aviakassa* (air ticket office), at travel agents or directly from the airlines.

AIRLINES IN RUSSIA

Once the largest fleet in the world, Aeroflot has been broken up into many local franchises (often called 'babyflots'). Aeroflot still flies internationally alongside a number of private commercial airlines such as Transaero. Internally, planes are almost always Russian-made Tupolevs or Ilyushins. Despite looking rather rickety and old, their safety record should not be too much of a worry, although the safety records of airlines in Russia are worse than those of their European counterparts.

Bus

The cheapest way to get around Russia is by bus. The enormous size of the country makes it rather unappealing, but for short trips from major cities it can be faster than the train and have more regular connections. Some sample costs are R480 (Moscow–St Petersburg) and R145 (St Petersburg–Novgorod).

RESERVATIONS

There's almost no need to reserve a seat, and in most places it's impossible anyway. Just arrive a good 30 minutes to one hour before the departure is scheduled and buy a ticket.

The long-distance bus stations are at the following addresses:

Avtovokzal No. 2 (☎ 166 5777; nab Obvodnogo Kanala 36, St Petersburg; Ⓜ Ligovsky Pr)

Shchyolkovskaya Bus Station (☎ 468 0400; Shchyolkovskoye shosse 2, Moscow; Ⓜ Shchyolkovskaya)

Car & Motorcycle

It's perfectly possible to bring your own vehicle into Russia, but expect delays, bureaucracy and the attention of the roundly hated GAI, or traffic police, who take particular delight in stopping foreign cars for document checks.

To enter Russia with a vehicle you will need a valid international driving license, your passport, and the insurance and ownership documents for your car. Petrol (*benzin*) is no problem to find, although unleaded is still rare outside Moscow and St Petersburg. Avoid 76 petrol, and pay more for 95 or 98.

Driving in Russia is on the right, and traffic coming from the right has the right of way. Any amount of alcohol in your blood is likely to lead to complications if you are breathalysed. However, you have the right to demand a hospital blood test.

HIRE

Hiring a car is far preferable to bringing your own vehicle into Russia. As you don't really need a car to get around big cities, they are mainly of use when making trips out of town where public transport may not be so good. All the major agencies have offices in Moscow and St Petersburg. Check out www.hertz.com and www.avis.com.

Hitching & Unofficial Taxis

Hitching for free is something of an alien concept in Russia, but paying a small amount to be given a lift is a daily reality for millions. The system is so ingrained that drivers will often go to extraordinary lengths to get you to your destination. In cities you'll see people flagging down cars all the time; long-distance hitching is less common, but it's still quite acceptable if the price is right. Simply state your destination and ask '*skolko?*' (how much?). Obviously, use common sense: do not get into a car with more than one passenger and be especially careful if travelling alone at night.

Train

Russia is crisscrossed with an extensive train network. Suburban or short-distance trains are called *elektrichkas* and do not require advance booking – you can buy your ticket at the *prigorodny poezd kassa* (suburban train ticket offices) at train stations. Long-distance services need to be booked in advance.

CLASSES

First *(myagki)* class will get you a place in a two-person sleeping carriage, while 2nd *(kupeyny)* class will get you a place in a four-person car. *Platskartny* compartments, while cheaper, have open bunk accommodations and are not great for those who value privacy. *Obshchiy* (general) class simply has bench- or aeroplane-style seating.

COSTS

Train travel is pricier than bus travel, but it's still perfectly affordable and far more comfortable. Prices between Moscow and St Petersburg in 2nd class begin at R500, going up to R1500 for the fast day trains.

RUSSIA

RESERVATIONS

You are advised to reserve at least 24 hours in advance for any long-distance journey. It's quite a bureaucratic process, so make sure you bring your passport (or a photocopy), as without it you'll be unable to buy tickets. You can buy tickets for others if you bring their passports. The queues can be very long and move with interminable slowness. If you're in a hurry go to the service centres that exist in most big stations. Here you pay a R100 surcharge; thus, there are no queues. If you are in a real hurry most travel agents will organise the reservation and delivery of train tickets for a generous mark-up.

You can buy train tickets in all mainline train stations, and at the central reservation offices in both Moscow and St Petersburg.

Moscow Central Train Booking Office (Map pp656-8; ☎ 262 2566; Maly Kharitonevsky per 6; Ⓜ Chistiye Prudy)
St Petersburg Central Train Booking Office (Map p677; ☎ 162 3344; nab Kanala Griboyedova 24; Ⓜ Nevsky Pr)

Serbia & Montenegro

CONTENTS

Highlights   701
Itineraries   701
Climate & When to Go   701
History   701
People   703
Religion   704
Arts   704
Environment   704
Food & Drink   704
Serbia   **705**
Belgrade   705
Vojvodina   714
Southern Serbia   718
Kosovo   723
Montenegro   **728**
Podgorica   729
Coastal Montenegro   730
Northern Montenegro   735
Serbia & Montenegro
Directory   **737**
Accommodation   737
Activities   737
Books   737
Business Hours   737
Customs   737
Dangers & Annoyances   737
Discount Cards   737
Embassies & Consulates   737
Festivals & Events   738
Gay & Lesbian Travellers   738
Holidays   738
Internet Resources   738
Language   738
Maps   738
Money   739
Post   739
Telephone & Fax   739
Tourist Information   739
Tours   739
Visas   739
Women Travellers   740
Transport in Serbia
& Montenegro   **740**
Getting There & Away   740
Getting Around   741

Curious travellers are returning to Serbia and Montenegro now that the dust has settled on the past decade of isolation. They're finding a warm welcome, a richness of culture and range of glorious landscapes they probably didn't expect.

From the north the flat Hungarian plain of Vojvodina sweeps south to encompass the cosmopolitan city of Novi Sad and the green hills of Fruška Gora dotted with its monasteries and vineyards. The mighty citadel of Kalemegdan, fought over by Turks, Austrians and Serbs, stands defiant at the meeting of the country's two great rivers, the Sava and Danube. Sprawling behind is the metropolis of Belgrade, a gritty energetic European city that parties hard. Cultural buffs can revel in its history, architecture and museums, and foodies in its restaurants.

South, and rising hills give way to mountains, the ski slopes of Kopaonik and Zlatibor, and the nests of Serbian rebellion, Topola and Niš. Beyond the mountains lies the disputed vale of Kosovo, previously part of Serbia and a UN-NATO protectorate since June 1999. The UN still recognises Kosovo as part of Serbia until its future is decided.

To the southwest of Serbia stands once-independent Montenegro, where prince-bishops ruled from lofty Cetinje, a land of craggy mountains that crash down into the Adriatic leaving just enough space for a string of ancient seaside towns.

FAST FACTS

- **Area** 102,350 sq km
- **Capital** union and Serbian capital – Belgrade; Montenegrin – Podgorica
- **Currency** Serbia – dinar (DIN): €1 = 47DIN; US$1 = 56DIN; UK£1 = 107DIN; A$1 = 43DIN; ¥100 = 54DIN; NZ$1 = 47DIN; Kosovo and Montenegro – euro: US$1 = €0.78; UK£1 = €1.44; A$1 = €0.58; ¥100 = €0.73; NZ$1 = €0.55
- **Famous for** Monica Seles, basketball players
- **Key Phrases** Serbian *zdravo* (hello), *do viđenja* (goodbye), *hvala* (thanks); Kosovar Albanian *allo* (hello), *lamturmirë* (goodbye), *ju falem nderit* (thanks)
- **Official Language** Serbia and Montenegro – Serbian; Kosovo – Albanian
- **Population** 7.5 million excluding Kosovo (estimate 1.9 million)
- **Telephone Codes** country code ☎ 381; international access code ☎ 99
- **Visas** not required by most European, Australian, New Zealand, USA and Canadian citizens; see p739

HIGHLIGHTS

- In Belgrade, the mighty **Kalemegdan** Turkish citadel (see p707) dominates the Danube and Sava Rivers
- **Novi Sad** (p715) is a town with smart café-lined streets and the baroque Petrovaradin Citadel
- **Kotor** (p732) is a walled, labyrinthine old city sheltering inside southern Europe's biggest fjord
- **Durmitor National Park** (p736) is full of striking mountains sheltering pretty lakes and a canyon over a kilometre deep; there's plenty of winter and summer activities
- The former medieval capital of 'Old Serbia', **Prizren** (p728), is dominated by the old castle, and below it is Turkish-influenced architecture, riverside bars and cafés

ITINERARIES

- **One week** From Belgrade, visit Novi Sad and then move south to Kotor and Cetinje and maybe a dip in the sea at Budva.
- **Two to three weeks** The above plus Subotica, Niš, some glorious mountainscapes around Žabljak, and Ulcinj.

CLIMATE & WHEN TO GO

The north has a continental climate with cold winters and hot, humid summers. The coastal region has hot, dry summers and relatively cold winters with heavy snowfall inland.

The Montenegrin coast is at its best in May, June and September, but avoid July and August, when accommodation becomes quite scarce and expensive. The ski season is generally December to March, with January and February providing the best sport.

HISTORY

Celts supplanted the original inhabitants of the region, the Illyrians, from the 4th century BC; the Romans arrived in the 3rd century BC. In AD 395 Theodosius I divided the empire, with Serbia passing to the Byzantine Empire.

During the 6th century, Slavic tribes crossed the Danube and occupied much of the Balkan Peninsula. In 879 Saints Cyril and Methodius converted the Serbs to the Orthodox religion.

Serbian independence briefly flowered from 1217 with a 'Golden Age' during Stefan Dušan's reign (1346–55). After Stefan's death Serbia declined. At the pivotal Battle

> **HOW MUCH?**
>
> - **Short taxi ride** 150DIN/€2
> - **Internet access** 60-100DIN/€1 per hour
> - **Cup of coffee** 75DIN/€1
> - **Bottle of plum brandy** 500DIN/€7
> - **Postcard** 30DIN/€0.50
>
> **LONELY PLANET INDEX**
>
> - **Litre of petrol** Serbia 50DIN, Kosovo €0.80, Montenegro €0.88
> - **Litre of water** 70DIN/€1
> - **Half-litre of beer** 60DIN/€1
> - **Souvenir T-shirt** Serbia 600DIN
> - **Street snack (burek)** 30DIN/€0.50

of Kosovo in 1389 the Turks defeated Serbia, ushering in 500 years of Islamic rule. A revolt in 1815 led to de facto Serbian independence and complete independence in 1878.

On 28 June 1914 Austria-Hungary used the assassination of Archduke Ferdinand by a Bosnian Serb to invade Serbia, sparking WWI. After the war, Croatia, Slovenia, Bosnia and Hercegovina, Vojvodina, Serbia and its Kosovo province, Montenegro and Macedonia formed the Kingdom of Serbs, Croats and Slovenes under the king of Serbia. In 1929 the country became Yugoslavia.

In March 1941 Yugoslavia joined the fascist Tripartite Alliance. This sparked a military coup and an abrupt withdrawal from the Alliance. Germany replied by bombing Belgrade.

The Communist Party, under Josip Broz Tito, assisted in the liberation of the country and gained power in 1945. It abolished the monarchy and declared a federal republic. Serbia's size was reduced; Bosnia and Hercegovina, Montenegro and Macedonia were granted republic status but Kosovo and Vojvodina were denied it.

Tito broke with Stalin in 1948 and Yugoslavia became a nonaligned nation (ie belonging to neither of the post-WWII power blocs led by the USA and the USSR), albeit bolstered by Western aid. Growing regional inequalities pushed demands by Slovenia, Croatia and Kosovo for greater autonomy to counter Serbian expansionism.

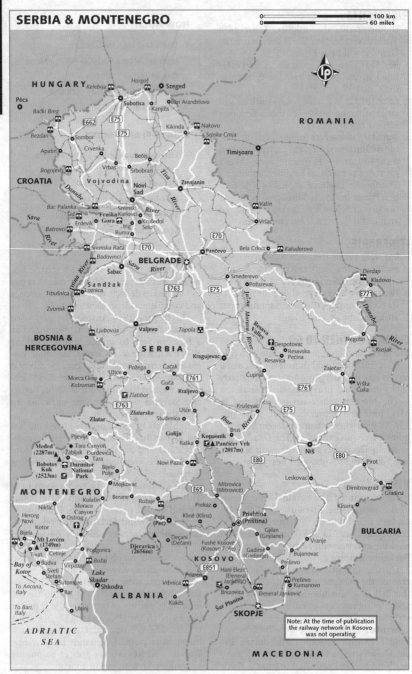

SERBIA & MONTENEGRO

| 0 | | 100 km |
| 0 | | 60 miles |

HUNGARY Kelebija
Horgoš
Szeged
Pécs
Bački Breg
Subotica
Ban Arandelovo
Kanjiža
ROMANIA
Bezdan
Sombor
Kikinda
Nakovo
Apatin
Crvenka
Srpska Crnja
Bogojevo
Bečej
Timişoara
CROATIA
Vrbas
Srbobran
Vojvodina
Zrenjanin
Novi
Sad
Tisa
River
Vatin
Bac Palanka
Sremski
Šid
Fruška
Karlovci
Vršac
Erdevik
Gora
Iriq
Kruśedol
Selo
Sava
Ruma
Batrovci
Sremska Rača
River
E70
Pančevo
Bela Crkva
Kaluderovo
Badovinci
BELGRADE
River
Šabac
Sava
River
Smederevo
Derdap
Sandžak
Požarevac
Kladovo
Trbušnica
Loznica
E763
E75
E771
Zvornik
Jušna Morava
Resava
Valley
Ljubovija
Valjevo
Topola
Despotovac
Negotin
Kusjak
BOSNIA &
Resavska
HERCEGOVINA
SERBIA
Resavica
Pećina
Kragujevac
Ćuprija
Zaječar
Užice
Požega
Čačak
E761
Vrška
Morca Gora
Guča
Ćuka
Kotroman
Zlatibor
Kraljevo
Kruševac
E763
Zlatarsko
Ušće
E75
E771
Zlatar
Studenica
Ibar
River
Golija
Brus
Pljevlja
Raška
Kopaonik
Pančićev Vrh
Niš
Međed
Tara Canyon
(2017m)
(2287m)
Žabljak
Durdevića
Novi Pazar
E80
E80
Bobotov
Tara
E65
Pirot
Kuk
Durmitor
Bijelo
(2523m)
National
Polje
Mitrovica
Leskovac
Park
(Mitrovicë)
Dimitrovgrad
MONTENEGRO
Mojkovac
Gradina
Berane
Rožaje
Prekaz
Kolašin
Prishtina
Klisura
Nikšić
Moraca
(Priština)
Canyon
Peja
Klinë (Klina)
Herceg
Ostrog
(Pec)
Gjilan
Novi
Kotor
(Gnjilane)
Vranje
BULGARIA
Bijela
Mt Lovćen
Dečani
Fushë Kosove
Bujanovac
Tivat
(1749m)
(Dečani)
(Kosovo Polje)
Gadimlje
Prševo
Podgorica
Djeravica
(Gadimljë)
Bay of
Budva
Božaj
(2656m)
Preševo
Kotor
Virpazar
KOSOVO
Hani Elezit
Kumanovo
Sveti
Lake
Prizren
E851
(Đeneral
Stefan
Skadar
Jankoviç)
Đeneral Janković
Sutomore
Shkodra
Vrbnica
To Ancona,
Brezovica
Italy
Bar
ALBANIA
Šar Planina
Ulcinj
Kukës
To Bari,
SKOPJE
Italy
ADRIATIC
Note: At the time of publication
SEA
the railway network in Kosovo
was not operating
MACEDONIA

By 1986 Serbian nationalists were espousing a Greater Serbia, a doctrine adopted by Slobodan Milošević, Communist Party leader in Serbia. This horrified the other republics, which managed to gain independence by 1992.

In April 1992 the remaining parties of Serbia and Montenegro formed the 'third' Yugoslav federation. The new constitution made no mention of 'autonomous provinces', infuriating Albanians in Kosovo, long brutally repressed by Serbia. Violence in Kosovo erupted in January 1998, largely provoked by the federal army and police.

The West provided a storm of protest plus an arms embargo. In March 1999 peace talks in Paris failed when Serbia rejected a US-brokered peace plan. In a reply to resistance in Kosovo, Serbian forces moved to empty the country of its Albanian population. Hundreds of thousands fled into Macedonia and Albania galvanised America and NATO into a 78-day bombing campaign. On 12 June 1999 Serbian forces withdrew from Kosovo.

In the September 2000 federal presidential elections the opposition, led by Vojislav Koštunica, declared victory, a claim denied by Milošević. Opposition supporters took over the streets, called a general strike and occupied parliament. Russia recognised Koštunica's presidency, removing Milošević's last support.

Koštunica restored ties with Europe, acknowledged Yugoslav atrocities in Kosovo and rejoined the UN. In April 2001 Milošević was arrested for misappropriating state funds and extradited to the international war crimes tribunal in the Netherlands.

In April 2002 a loose union of Serbia and Montenegro replaced Yugoslavia. The deal was brokered under heavy EU pressure seeking to prevent further regional violence. The union will be tested through a referendum in 2006.

In March 2003 Serbia's first democratically elected prime minister since WWII, Zoran Djindjic, was assassinated. He had been instrumental in handing over Milošević to the international war crimes tribunal and had been trying to clear out the criminal elements from politics and business. His alleged killers were crime bosses and Milošević-era paramilitary commanders.

MONEY MATTERS

During the 1990s economic sanctions and gross mishandling of the economy led to severe hyperinflation, the highest in European history. It became cheaper to use banknotes to paper walls than to buy the wallpaper. At one point a 500 billion dinar banknote was issued making every Serb an instant multimillionaire.

Many state industries were unable to pay their employees; they were paid in kind or issued worthless shares in the company. When a multinational bought up the local brewery in the small town of Apatin, the locals found their shares to be worth a fortune. Apatin is now one of the richest municipalities, per capita, in Serbia.

At the end of his term in January 2003 the Serbian president Milan Milutinovic surrendered to the Hague tribunal to plead not guilty to charges of crimes against humanity. Between 2003 and 2004 three attempts to elect a new president failed, due to low voter turnout. Parliamentary elections in December 2003 were inconclusive but saw the resurgence of nationalism, which is a worry to the rest of Europe. Power deals installed Koštunica as head of a centre-right coalition that relies on Milošević's Socialist Party. Finally, in June 2004, Serbia and Montenegro gained a new president in pro-European Boris Tadic.

PEOPLE

The last full census was in 1991. Only Serbia took a census in 2002, revealing a population of 7.5 million. Estimates for Montenegro are 651,000 and Kosovo 1.9 million.

These figures split into Serbs 62%, Albanians 17%, Montenegrins 5%, Hungarians 3% and other groups 13%.

Vojvodina is more multicultural with perhaps 28 ethnic groups and sizeable populations of Hungarians (25%), Ukrainians and Romanians.

There are large Slavic Muslim and Albanian minorities in Montenegro and southern Serbia; Belgrade has about 10,000 Muslims.

Serbs and Montenegrins have always seen eye-to-eye but in Kosovo the minority Serbs live in Kosovo Force (KFOR) protected ghettoes.

RELIGION

Religion and ethnicity broadly go together. About 65% of the population is Orthodox; Roman Catholics, who are Vojvodinan Hungarians, comprise 4%; and Albanian Kosovars and Slavic Muslims make up 19%.

ARTS
Literature

Bosnian-born, but a past Belgrade resident, Ivo Andrić was awarded a Nobel prize for his *Bridge over the Drina*. Other books worthy of the traveller's perusal are *In the Hold* by Vladimir Arsenijević, *Words Are Something Else* by David Albahari, *Petrija's Wreath* by Dragoslav Mihailović and *Fear and its Servant* by Mirjana Novaković.

Cinema & TV

The award-winning film *Underground,* by Sarajevo-born director Emir Kusturica, is worth seeing. Told in a chaotic, colourful style, the film deals with Yugoslav history. Bosnian director Danis Tanović's *No Man's Land* superbly deals with an encounter between a Serbian soldier and a Bosnian soldier stuck in a trench on their own during the Bosnian war.

Music

Serbia's vibrant dances are led by musicians using bagpipes, flutes and fiddles. Kosovar music bears the deep imprint of five centuries of Turkish rule with high-whine flutes carrying the tune above the beat of a goatskin drum.

Blehmuzika (brass music influenced by Turkish and Austrian military music) has become the national music of Serbia, with an annual festival at Guča in August.

Modern music covers anything from wild gypsy music to House, techno, blues, jazz, dub 'n' bass, or ethnic folk updated and crossed with techno producing a variant that many call turbofolk.

Serbia and Montenegro entered the Eurovision hall of fame by coming second in 2004 with a haunting love ballad that effectively blended Serbian and Turkish influences.

Architecture

Serbia and Montenegro displays the architecture of those who ruled the country. Towns in the south bear a Turkish imprint whereas the north has a dominance of 19th-century imperial Austro-Hungarian style. In Vojvodina, especially in Subotica, there are some magnificent buildings of the Hungarian Secessionist period.

Overlaying all are the post-WWII buildings bearing the modernist imprint of central planning and concrete.

Visual Arts

Artists in Serbia and Montenegro have been happy to follow European trends in art although there is a significant interest in icon painting. Galleries throughout the country present an eclectic range from landscapes and figurative art to abstract work.

ENVIRONMENT

Vojvodina is pancake-flat agricultural land, but south of the Danube the landscape rises through rolling green hills. These crest where the eastern outpost of the Dinaric Alps slices southeastwards across the country. Within these mountains is Kosovo, a lowland vale.

Djeravica (2656m) in western Kosovo is the highest mountain; Bobotov kuk (2523m) in the Durmitor Range is Montenegro's. Zlatibor and Kopaonik in Serbia, and Durmitor in Montenegro provide the winter snow playgrounds.

Montenegro's mountains are mainly limestone and carry the features of karst scenery, craggy grey-white outcrops, sparse vegetation and, beneath, caves. To the east the vast Lake Skadar, an important European bird sanctuary and pelican habitat, spans Montenegro and Albania.

Populations of lynx, wolf and brown bear keep away from humans and visitors are unlikely to come across them.

The major national parks of Serbia are Fruška Gora and Kopaonik, while those in Montenegro are Durmitor, Mt Lovcen and Lake Skadar. Unesco-recognised sites are Sopocani and Studenica monasteries in Serbia, and Kotor and Durmitor in Montenegro.

Sewage pollution of coastal waters, air pollution around Belgrade and rubbish dumping out in the countryside are the environmental issues the country has to face.

FOOD & DRINK
Staples & Specialities

The cheapest snack to be had is *burek,* a greasy pie made with *sir* (cheese), *meso* (meat), *krompiruša* (potato) or occasionally *pecurke* (mushrooms); with yogurt it makes a suitable breakfast filler. A filling midday meal can be made of soup or *čevapčiči* (grilled kebab of spiced minced meat).

Serbia is famous for its grilled meats, such as *čevapčiči*, *pljeskavica* (spicy hamburger) and *ražnjiči* (pork or veal kebabs). *Duveč* is grilled pork cutlets with spiced stewed peppers, courgettes and tomatoes on rice.

Other popular dishes are *musaka* (layers of aubergine, potato and minced meat), *sarma* (minced meat and rice-stuffed cabbage), *kapama* (stewed lamb, onions and spinach with yogurt) and *punjena tikvica* (courgettes stuffed with minced meat and rice).

Regional cuisines range from spicy Hungarian goulash in Vojvodina to Turkish kebab in Kosovo. In Montenegro, try *kajmak* (a salted cream turned to cheese).

Pivo (beer) is universally available. Nikšićko *pivo* (both light and dark), brewed at Nikšić in Montenegro, is terribly good. Many people distil their own *rakija* (brandy) out of plums and other fruit. Montenegrin red wine is a rich drop.

Currently popular in Belgrade is a bittersweet aperitif, Pelinkovac, made from grass and tasting just like medicine with a kick.

Coffee is usually served Turkish-style, 'black as hell, strong as death and sweet as love'. Superb espresso and cappuccino can be found but mostly in the north. If you want anything other than herbal teas (camomile or hibiscus) then ask for Indian tea.

Where to Eat & Drink

You won't go hungry in Serbia and Montenegro for want of eating places. Hole-in-the-wall counters, kiosks and bakeries offer *burek*, pizza, *čevapčiči* or sandwiches for those on the run. Plenty of small restaurants offer cheap, satisfying but limited menus in which meat dishes always dominate. Many can be found around the bus and train stations.

Hotel restaurants also figure in providing fine food. Resort areas have fewer restaurants, as the hotels capture their clients with half- and full-board accommodation. Vegetarian restaurants are a rarity but top-end restaurants will have several vegetarian dishes.

The distinction between café and bar is blurred. Cafés usually sell alcohol except

in Muslim areas; the more up-market ones add cocktails to their range.

Vegetarians & Vegans

Eating here can be a trial for vegetarians and almost impossible for vegans. There's always the ubiquitous vegetarian pizza. Satisfying salads are *Srpska salata* (Serbian salad) of raw peppers, onions and tomatoes, seasoned with oil, vinegar and maybe chilli, and *šopska salata*, consisting of chopped tomatoes, cucumber and onion, topped with grated soft white cheese. Also ask for *gibanica* (cheese pie), *zeljanica* (cheese pie with spinach) or *pasulj prebranac* (a dish of cooked and spiced beans). If you're happy with fish then there are plenty of fish restaurants.

Habits & Customs

People tend to skimp on breakfast and catch something on the way to work. Work hours are usually 7.30am to a 3.30pm finish that then becomes the time for lunch; this slides dinner back to 8, 9 or 10pm if eating out.

SERBIA СРБИЈА

Serbia *(Srbija)* consists of its more European northern province, Vojvodina, craggy and proud central Serbia, and the hapless province of Kosovo. Administered as a UN-NATO protectorate, Kosovo is a disputed land riven by different interpretations of history. For Serbs it is the cradle of their nationhood, for Kosovo Albanians it is their independent land.

BELGRADE БЕОГРАД
☎ 011 / pop 1.58 million
The lumpy hill flanked by the Sava and Danube Rivers was ideal for a fortified settlement. Trouble was that it attracted enemies and Belgrade was destroyed and rebuilt 40 times in its 2300-year history. Those fortifications, the massive Kalemegdan Citadel, changed by succeeding conquerors and defenders are now no more than fortified parkland.

Behind the citadel lies older Belgrade with a mishmash of architecture of the last two centuries. These buildings house comprehensive museums, fashion shops, cafés, bars and restaurants.

The rivers host strings of floating bars and clubs belting out music from traditional

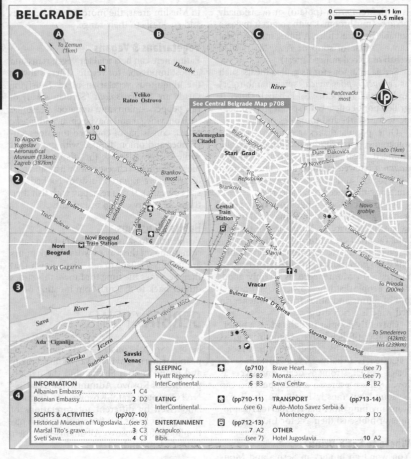

BELGRADE

0 — 1 km
0 — 0.5 miles

		(p710)	Brave Heart.....................................(see 7)
SLEEPING 🏠			Monza..(see 7)
Hyatt Regency.............................**5** B2			Sava Centar...................................**8** B2
InterContinental..........................**6** B3			
			TRANSPORT (pp713-14)
INFORMATION	**EATING** 🍴	(pp710-11)	Auto-Moto Savez Serbia &
Albanian Embassy.............................**1** C4	InterContinental..........................(see 6)		Montenegro..............................**9** D2
Bosnian Embassy..............................**2** D2			
	ENTERTAINMENT 🎭	(pp712-13)	**OTHER**
SIGHTS & ACTIVITIES (pp707-10)	Acapulco......................................**7** A2		Hotel Jugoslavia..........................**10** A2
Historical Museum of Yugoslavia....(see 3)	Bibis..(see 7)		
Maršal Tito's grave...........................**3** C3			
Sveti Sava...**4** C3			

Serbian folk to the latest in House and techno allowing Belgraders the joy of partying through the night.

Orientation

The central train station and two adjacent bus stations are on the southern side of the city centre. A couple of blocks northeast lies Terazije, the heart of modern Belgrade. Kneza Mihailova, Belgrade's lively pedestrian boulevard, runs northwest through the old town from Terazije to the Kalemegdan Citadel.

Information
BOOKSHOPS

Mamut (Map p708; ☎ 639 060; cnr Kneza Mihailova & Sremska; ⏰ 9am-10pm Mon-Sat, noon-10pm Sun) Big browse-around shop with many floors; it has books, magazines and newspapers in English as well as CDs, DVDs and gifts.

Plato Bookshop (Map p708; ☎ 625 834; 48 Kneza Mihailova; ⏰ 9am-midnight Mon-Sat, noon-midnight Sun) Stocks English literature, maps, books on Serbia and stationery.

INTERNET ACCESS

IPS (Map p708; ☎ 323 3344; off Makedonska 4; per hr 90DIN; ⏰ 24hr)

Plato Cyber Club (Map p708; ☎ 635 363; Vase Čarapiča 19; per hr 65DIN; ⏰ 24hr)

INTERNET RESOURCES

Belgrade City site (www.beograd.org.yu)
Tourist Organisation of Belgrade (www.belgrade tourism.org.yu)

LEFT LUGGAGE
Central train station (Map p708; Savski Trg 2; per piece per day 60DIN)

MEDICAL SERVICES
Boris Kidrič Hospital Diplomatic Section (Map p708; ☎ 643 839; Pasterova 1; ☼ 7am-7pm Mon-Fri)
Klinički Centar (Map p708; ☎ 361 8444; Miloša Porcerca Pasterova 2; ☼ 24hr) Medical clinics.
Prima 1 (Map p708; ☎ 361 0999; Nemanjina 2; ☼ 24hr) Pharmacy.

MONEY
More ATMs in central Belgrade than your bank balance can manage. Exchange offices, recognised by a large blue diamond sign, are widespread.
Atlas Bank (Map p708; ☎ 302 4000; Emilijana Joksimovića 4; ☼ 8am-5pm Mon-Fri, 8am-1pm Sat) Cashes travellers cheques.
Delta Banka (Map p708; ☎ 302 2624; Kneza Mihailova 30; ☼ 6.30am-10pm) ATM and cash travellers cheques.

POST
Central post office (Map p708; ☎ 633 492; Zmaj Jovina 17; ☼ 8am-7pm Mon-Sat)

TELEPHONE & FAX
Telephone centre (Map p708; ☎ 323 4484; Takovska 2; ☼ 7am-midnight Mon-Fri, 7am-10pm Sat & Sun) In the post office by Sveti Marko church.

TOURIST INFORMATION
Tourist Organisation of Belgrade (www.belgrade tourism.org.yu) Kneza Mihailova (Map p708; ☎ 629 992; Kneza Mihailova 18; ☼ 9am-8pm Mon-Fri, 9am-6pm Sat, 11am-5pm Sun); Terazije Underpass (Map p708; ☎ 635 622; fax 635 343; ☼ 9am-8pm Mon-Fri, 9am-4pm Sat) Cheery and friendly with useful brochures, city maps and a 'This month in Belgrade' events leaflet.

TRAVEL AGENCIES
Bas Turist (Map p708; ☎ 638 555; fax 784 859; BAS bus station) International buses.
KSR Beograd Tours (Map p708; ☎ 641 258; fax 687 447; Milovana Milovanovića 5; ☼ 6.30am-8pm) Train tickets at station prices without the crowds.
Lasta (Map p708; ☎ 641 251; fax 642 473; www.lasta.co.yu; Milovana Milovanovića 1; ☼ 7am-9pm) International buses.

Sights
KALEMEGDAN CITADEL   Map p708
Fortifications were started in Celtic times and extended down onto the flood plain during the Roman settlement of Singidunum.

BELGRADE IN TWO DAYS

Jump right in and catch tram No 2 anywhere on its circular route. Get off and roam **Kalemegdan Citadel** (p707), stroll through Kneza Mihailova taking in a coffee on **Trg Republike** (p712), take in the **National Museum** (p707) and the **Ethnographic Museum** (p709), and then dine out in **Skadarska** (p709).

Have a peek at the mighty Sveti Sava and Sveti Marko in **central Belgrade** (p709), catch a bus to **Zemun** (p714) for a late lunch, rest up and then go clubbing at **Andergraund** (p713) or **Oh! Cinema!** (p713).

Over the centuries the fortifications were attacked, destroyed and rebuilt as one conqueror removed another. The statistics for this piece of real estate, the key to power in the region, are staggering. Some 115 battles were fought over it and 44 times parts of it and the outer city were razed.

Subsequently much of what is seen today dates from the 18th century when the Austro-Hungarians and the Turks reconstructed the citadel three times.

The essence of the fortifications is the Upper Citadel accessed from outside by several massive gates and in places bridges (now wooden) over deep moats. The main entrance is the Stambol Gate built by the Turks around 1750.

Passing through this gate leads to the **Military Museum** (☎ 334 4408; Kalemegdan; admission 20DIN; ☼ 10am-5pm Tue-Sun), a large complex presenting a complete military history of former Yugoslavia. Proudly displayed are captured Kosovo Liberation Army (KLA) weapons and bits of a downed American stealth fighter. Outside are a number of bombs and missiles contributed from the air by NATO in 1999 and a line-up of old guns and tanks, some quite rare.

Most of the Upper Citadel is now parkland with little remaining of the old town. The massive walls are a favourite place for Belgraders to wander in good weather, to snatch an alfresco lunch during workdays, or for young couples to find a bit of romantic solitude.

STARI GRAD   Map p708
South of the citadel lies Stari Grad (Old Town) with a mishmash of architecture of

CENTRAL BELGRADE

0 — 500 m
0 — 0.3 miles

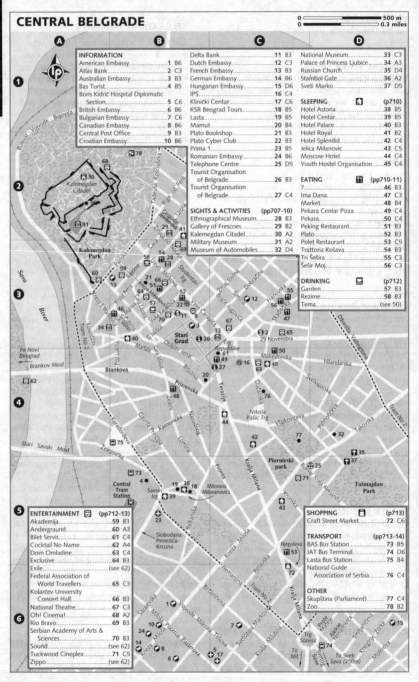

INFORMATION
American Embassy........................1 B6
Atlas Bank..................................2 C3
Australian Embassy......................3 B3
Bas Turist..................................4 B5
Boris Kidrič Hospital Diplomatic
Section.....................................5 C6
British Embassy...........................6 B6
Bulgarian Embassy......................7 C6
Canadian Embassy......................8 B6
Central Post Office......................9 B3
Croatian Embassy......................10 B6
Delta Bank...............................11 B3
Dutch Embassy..........................12 C3
French Embassy.........................13 B3
German Embassy........................14 B6
Hungarian Embassy....................15 D6
IPS..16 C4
Klinički Centar...........................17 C6
KSR Beograd Tours.....................18 B5
Lasta.......................................19 B5
Mamut....................................20 B4
Plato Bookshop.........................21 B3
Plato Cyber Club........................22 B3
Prima......................................23 B5
Romanian Embassy....................24 B6
Telephone Centre......................25 D5
Tourist Organisation
of Belgrade.............................26 B3
Tourist Organisation
of Belgrade.............................27 C4

SIGHTS & ACTIVITIES   (pp707-10)
Ethnographical Museum............28 B3
Gallery of Frescoes....................29 B2
Kalemegdan Citadel...................30 A2
Military Museum........................31 A2
Museum of Automobiles............32 D4

National Museum......................33 C3
Palace of Princess Ljubice..........34 A3
Russian Church.........................35 D4
Stambol Gate...........................36 A2
Sveti Marko..............................37 D5

SLEEPING   (p710)
Hotel Astoria............................38 B5
Hotel Centar.............................39 B5
Hotel Palace.............................40 B3
Hotel Royal...............................41 B2
Hotel Splendid..........................42 C4
Jelica Milanovic.........................43 C5
Moscow Hotel...........................44 C4
Youth Hostel Organisation.........45 C4

EATING   (pp710-11)
?...46 B3
Ima Dana.................................47 C3
Market....................................48 B4
Pekara Centar Pizza...................49 C4
Pekara.....................................50 C4
Peking Restaurant.....................51 B3
Plato..52 B3
Polet Restaurant.......................53 C5
Trattoria Košava........................54 B3
Tri Šešira..................................55 C3
Šešir Moj..................................56 C3

DRINKING   (p712)
Garden....................................57 B3
Rezime.....................................58 B3
Tema...................................(see 50)

ENTERTAINMENT   (pp712-13)
Akademija................................59 B3
Andergraund.............................60 A3
Bilet Servis...............................61 C4
Cocktail No Name......................62 A4
Dom Omladine..........................63 B3
Exclusive..............................(see 62)
Exile....................................(see 62)
Federal Association of
World Travellers.......................65 C3
Kolarčev University
Concert Hall............................66 B3
National Theatre.......................67 C3
Oh! Cinema!.............................68 A2
Rio Bravo.................................69 B3
Serbian Academy of Arts &
Sciences.................................70 B3
Sound..................................(see 62)
Tuckwood Cineplex....................71 C5
Zippo...................................(see 62)

SHOPPING   (p713)
Craft Street Market....................72 C6

TRANSPORT   (pp713-14)
BAS Bus Station.........................73 B5
JAT Bus Terminal.......................74 D6
Lasta Bus Station.......................75 B4
National Guide
Association of Serbia.................76 C4

OTHER
Skupština (Parliament)...............77 C4
Zoo..78 B2

the last two centuries starting from when Belgrade was grabbed from the declining Ottoman Empire and reenergized by the Habsburgs.

The lower two floors of prehistory and early Serbian art and culture at the **National Museum** (☎ 624 322; Trg Republike; admission 200DIN, free Sun; ☷ 10am-5pm Tue, Wed & Fri, noon-8pm Thu, 10am-2pm Sat & Sun) were closed for restoration at the time of research. The modern-art gallery on the 3rd floor displays just a fraction of a very large collection of national and European art, including work by Pablo Picasso and Claude Monet. Nadežeta Petrović (1873–1915), one of Serbia's first female artists, is well represented.

A few blocks away is the **Ethnographical Museum** (☎ 328 1888; Studentski Trg 13; admission 60DIN; ☷ 10am-5pm Tue-Sat, 10am-1pm Sun) with a comprehensive collection of Serbian costumes, folk art and items from everyday existence. There are detailed explanations in English.

Nearby is the **Gallery of Frescoes** (☎ 621 491; Cara Uroša 20; admission 50DIN; ☷ 10am-5pm Mon, Tue & Thu-Sat, 10am-2pm Sun) with full-size replicas (and some originals) of paintings from churches and monasteries. The replicas are exact down to reproducing scratches and wear.

The **Palace of Princess Ljubice** (☎ 638 264; Kneza Sime Markovića 8; admission 50DIN; ☷ 10am-5pm Tue-Fri, 10am-4pm Sat & Sun) is a Balkan-style palace (1831) built for the wife of Prince Miloš. What could be a memorable museum is at present just a formal arrangement of period furnishings: furniture, carpets and paintings. What's needed are all the trappings of a princely existence to bring it to life.

SKADARSKA Map p708

Often hailed as Belgrade's Montmartre, a bohemian hang-out of poets and artists in the early 1900s, Skadarska is a cobbled street known for its Balkan taverns, strolling musicians, cafés and art galleries. Activity blossoms in summer when inside and outside boundaries melt away and life flows onto the streets. Then musical, theatrical and cabaret performances enliven outdoor eating.

The restaurants rejoice in unusual names: Tri Šešira (Three Hats – once a hatmaking shop), Ima Dana (There Are Days), Dva Jelena (Two Deer) and Dva Bela Goluba (Two White Doves).

CENTRAL BELGRADE

Beside the telephone centre is **Sveti Marko** (Map p708; ☎ 323 1940; Bulevar Kralja Aleksandra 17), a solid Serbian Orthodox church, (massive pillars!), containing the grave of the Emperor Dušan (1308–55). Behind, and dwarfed, is the blue-domed **Russian Church** (Map p708) erected by refugees who fled the October Revolution.

Sveti Sava (Map p708; Svetog Save), billed as the biggest Orthodox church in the world, is a work in progress. The church is built on the reputed site where the Turks burnt the relics of St Sava, the youngest son of a 12th-century ruler, and founder of the independent Orthodox church.

Started in 1935, and interrupted by Hitler, communism and lack of cash, it's at the lock-up stage. Still, if the door's open for the builders, have a peek inside and feel puny under its massive dome.

The **Museum of Automobiles** (Map p708; ☎ 334 2625; Majke Jevrocime 30; admission 50DIN; ☷ 11am-7pm) is a compelling private collection of cars and motorcycles. Choice for our garage would be the '57 Cadillac convertible, only 25,000km and one careful owner – President Tito.

OUTER BELGRADE Map p706

Don't miss **Maršal Tito's grave** (Kuća Cveća or House of Flowers; ☎ 367 1485; Bulevar Mira; admission free; ☷ 9am-5pm Tue-Sun) with an interesting museum of gifts (embroidery, dubious-purpose smoking pipes, saddles and weapons) given by toadying comrades and fellow travellers. Check if the adjacent **Historical Museum of Yugoslavia** (☎ 367 1485; exhibitions ☷ 9am-2pm Tue-Sun) is open for one of its occasional exhibitions. Take trolleybus No 40 or 41.

At the airport, the exceptional **Yugoslav Aeronautical Museum** (☎ 670 992; Suracin; admission 300DIN; ☷ 9am-2pm Tue-Sun Nov-Apr, 9am-7pm Tue-Sun May-Oct) is engrossing if you're an aircraft buff. There are some rare planes here including a Hurricane, Spitfire and Messerschmitt from WWII and bits of that infamous American stealth fighter that air defences downed in 1999.

Ada Ciganlija, an island park in the Sava River, is Belgrade's summer retreat. Gentle choices are swimming in a lake (naturists 1km upstream), renting a bicycle or just strolling among the trees. Adrenaline junkies might fancy the bungy jumping or trying the water-ski tow. Plenty of places overlooking the lake sell restorative cold beers.

Tours

National Guide Association of Serbia (Map p708; ☎ 323 5910; www.utvs.org.yu; Dučanska 8, 5th fl; ◷ 9.30am-3pm Mon-Fri) Independent and licensed guides for city or country tours.

Romantika Steam-hauled train to Austro-Hungarian Sremski Karlovci. Contact KSR Beograd Tours (p707).

Tourist Organisation of Belgrade (www.belgrade tourism.org.yu) Kneza Mihailova (Map p708; ☎ 629 992; Kneza Mihailova 18; ◷ 9am-8pm Mon-Fri, 9am-6pm Sat, 11am-5pm Sun); Terazije Underpass (Map p708; ☎ 635 622; fax 635 343; ◷ 9am-8pm Mon-Fri, 9am-4pm Sat) Runs bus, boat and guided walking tours.

Festivals & Events

FEST film festival (Feb)
Beer festival (www.belgradebeerfest.com; Aug)
Jazz festival (Aug)
BITEF international theatre festival (Sep)
Classical music festival (Oct)

Sleeping

CITY CENTRE   **Map p708**
Budget

The **Youth Hostel organisation** (Ferijalni Savez Beograd; ☎ 324 8550; www.hostels.org.yu; Makedonska 22, 2nd fl; ◷ 9am-5pm) does deals with local hotels for discounts. You need HI membership (300DIN to join) or an international student card. They also book the **Jelica Milanovic** (☎ 323 1268; Krunska 8; per person from €7.50; ◷ Jul & Aug), which offers college accommodation during holiday time. No food is available.

    Hotel Royal (☎ 634 222; Kralja Petra 56; www .hotelroyal.co.yu; s/d from 910/1470DIN; 🖳) A very central and cheap hotel likely to become a travellers' legend. An always-open lobby bar is the matey hang-out of 'local businessmen', backpackers and early morning revellers. The action never stops. Rooms are basic and tidy, and the staff cheerful and friendly.

    Hotel Splendid (☎ 323 5444; www.splendid.co.yu; D Jovanovića 5; s/d from 1100/1560DIN) Tucked down a side street and sandwiched between its neighbours is a small comfy, easy-to-feel-at-home hotel with an obliging receptionist ready to answer the 'where is' questions.

    Hotel Astoria (☎ 264 5422; www.astoria.co.yu; Milovana Milovanovića 1a; s/d 1360/2260DIN, with shared bathroom 1060/1600DIN) A rattly old socialist hotel not yet a museum piece but still good

enough to make the mark. There's a conspiratorially cosy café/bar at the front of the hotel.

Similar is the **Hotel Centar** (☎ 264 4055; fax 657 838; Savski Trg 7; s/d 910/1380DIN; 🅿) next to the raunchy sex shop.

Mid-Range

Hotel Palace (☎ 185 585; Topličin Venac 23; s/d €55/80; 🖳) From the leather armchairs and the tinkling atrium waterfall in the lobby, this hotel shows what a bit of love and attention can do to a state hotel. The rooms are large and have the phones, TVs and bathroom bidets that you'd want for this tariff. Up on the top floor the Panorama restaurant reveals a city view.

    Moscow Hotel (Moskva; ☎ 268 6255; hotelmoskva@ absolutok.net; Balkanska; s €33-56, d from €102) A central hotel with character, although the 1906 Secessionist-period exterior suggests more. The cheaper single rooms make this an attractive stay and in case you forget which day it is the lift carpets are changed daily to remind you. The downstairs café/bar has huge windows looking onto Terazije; locals and visitors throng here to take coffee, gorge on some delicious cakes and watch their fellows through the glass.

OUTER BELGRADE   **Map p706**
Top End

Hyatt Regency (☎ 301 1234; www.belgrade.regency .hyatt.com; Milentija Popovića 5; s/d from €245/265) If you want to go overboard, this stately marble monument in Novi Beograd has all the mod cons and luxury shops you'll need, but will charge you heavily for the privilege.

Eating

Belgraders do well for restaurants, with many placed around the streets of Kneza Mihailova, 29 Novembra and Makedonska; off the latter is the famous street of Skadarska. There are also several floating restaurants on the Danube.

CITY CENTRE   **Map p708**
Budget

Belgraders do very well for fast food with kiosks and cafés offering *burek, čevapčići,* pastries and some inventive pizza. Those around Trg Republike are open 24 hours, as are most of the ones by the train and bus stations. You can fill up for under 100DIN.

Pekara Centar Pizza (Kolarčeva 10; pizza 40DIN; ❧ 24hr) With its bright and cheery interior open to the street Pekara Centar Pizza always has customers for its freshly made pizzas.

Another nearby **Pekara** (Makedonska 15; pizza 40DIN; ❧ 24hr) is an enticing bakery with *burek*, pastries and pizza.

Belgrade's main fruit and veg **market** (cnr Brankova Prizrenska & Narodnog Fronta; ❧ 6am-1pm) is a scrounging ground for DIY food; there are also many supermarkets around Belgrade.

Mid-Range

? (☎ 635 421; Kralja Petra 6; dishes 200-350DIN) The shortest restaurant name ever refers to a dispute between a previous owner and the Orthodox cathedral opposite. The then-name was something like the Cathedralside Tavern, which upset the abstemious clergy. The landlord changed the signboard to a '?' signalling his perplexity as to what the fuss was about. Inside is an original Balkans tavern with foot-polished floorboards, low wooden tables and equally low half-moon chairs. The menu reflects the national cuisine with an emphasis on chewy grills.

Plato (☎ 658 863; Akademski Plato 1; dishes 250-400DIN; ❧ 9am-2am Mon-Thu, 9am-3am Fri, 10am-3am Sat, noon-2am Sun) Plato (*plar-*to) is an eclectic mix of restaurant, café, bar and live music venue. It provides enjoyable food, mostly Italian, in a relaxed atmosphere where you can eat, drink or just listen to jazz or Cuban rhythms.

Polet Restaurant (Map p708; ☎ 323 2454; Kralja Milana 31; dishes 200-500DIN; ❧ 11am-11pm) Big, fat, shiny brass railings surrounding the upper mezzanine floor, and blue-and-white décor, and you feel as if you're out at sea. Eat low or eat high here; a tasty fish soup at 90DIN or scampi à la Parisienne at 1150DIN. The grilled calamari (390DIN) is chargrilled to perfection, misted with lemon, and succulent.

Peking Restaurant (☎ 181 931; Vuka Karadžića 2; dishes 300-400DIN; ❧ 11am-midnight Mon-Sat, 2pm-midnight Sun) A traditional Chinese-style restaurant with red flock wallpaper and red lanterns, but you won't find any Chinese staff here. It has 40 different cut-above-the-rest Chinese dishes to tempt you if you're hankering for a change, and even *kajmak* if you're not.

Trattoria Košava (☎ 627 344; Kralja Petra 6; dishes 400-600DIN; 9am-1am Mon-Fri, noon-1am Sat & Sun)

This Mediterranean-style Italian restaurant is light and airy with pretty pastel décor. Options are the downstairs café for a blow-in pizza snack, coffee and a give-me-more cherry strudel, or the restaurant upstairs for some serious eating.

Šešir Moj (My Hat; ☎ 322 8750; Skadarska 21; dishes 300-500DIN; ❧ 8am-late) An intimate little restaurant with alcove rooms and walls obscured with an art gallery of oils and pastels. A place for romantics, especially when members of a gypsy band swirl in playing their hauntingly passionate music. Go for the *punjena belavešanica*, which is a pork fillet stuffed with *kajmak*. Finish with Serbian coffee and a piece of *orasnica* (walnut cake) if you've any room left.

Also recommended in this street are **Ima Dana** (☎ 323 4422; Skadarska 38; dishes 250-350DIN; ❧ 11am-5pm & 7pm-1am) and **Tri Šešira** (Three Hats; ☎ 324 7501; Skadarska 29; dishes 300-460DIN; ❧ lunch & dinner) offering similar menus and entertainment.

OUTER BELGRADE

Priroda (☎ 411 890; Batutova 11; dishes 25-400DIN; ❧ 9am-9.30pm, food from 12.30pm) Give this restaurant owner a medal for battling against adversity: for providing a superb vegetarian restaurant in a land of human carnivores. Rediscover delicate flavours from vegetables and pulses that don't normally appear in traditional Serbian cuisine. The macrobiotic cake is a mouth stunner. Priroda is about 6km east of the central train station.

Dačo (☎ 278 1009; Patrisa Lumumbe 49; dishes 250-500DIN; ❧ 10.30am-midnight) A Serbian-themed restaurant with waiters in national dress that's causing gastronomic flutters among Belgraders and expats of all ages. Traditional music, fluttering trumpets and rousing voices accompany your meal and at the end you can buy Serbian mementos at a small shop. For authenticity the menu's in Cyrillic but English-speaking waiters will help you out. The entrées – *kajmak*, cheeses and *pršcuta* (prosciutto) and other cold meats and salad items – are served on wooden platters and are the restaurant's speciality.

Intercontinental (Map p706; ☎ 311 333; Vladimira Popovića, Novi Belgrade; buffet breakfast 650DIN; ❧ 7am-10pm) If you're fed up with iron-ration breakfasts, then whiz over here for a slap-up all-you-can-eat meal.

Drinking

CAFÉS

Belgrade has some top-class café/bars offering damn-good coffee straight from the bean, or something stronger in the way of beer, wine and spirits. Nearly all are open daily from early morning to midnight with a later start on Sundays. Most don't offer food.

Many pavements and pedestrian areas, like Trg Republike, sprout café terraces when the weather becomes warm enough for sitting outside.

Garden (Map p708; Vuka Karadžića 7a) Frothy cappuccinos come no better than from this slim narrow room off a Kneza Mihailova side street. There's a smooth laid-back atmosphere with a little background jazz.

Rezime (Map p708; ☎ 3284 276; Kralja Petra 41) The classy but non-elitist Rezime is on the ground floor of a magnificently ornate Art Nouveau building. Inside the décor matches the elegant exterior with polished wood, leather armchairs and waiters wearing bow ties. The owners are well into fashion – hence the fashion magazines for customers to browse through.

Tema (Map p708; ☎ 337 3859; Makedonska 11-13) Subtly lit modern bar that both young and old are welcome to linger in. It has a pleasant line in coffees with a spirit kick.

Entertainment

CONCERTS & THEATRE

The ticketing agency **Bilet Servis** (Map p708; ☎ 628 342; Trg Republike 5; ☷ 9am-8pm Mon-Fri, 9am-3pm Sat) sells tickets for concerts and theatre.

National Theatre (Map p708; ☎ 620 946; Trg Republike; box office ☷ 10am-2pm Tue-Sun) In winter there's opera at this elegant theatre.

Kolarčev University Concert Hall (Map p708; ☎ 630 550; Studentski Trg 5; box office ☷ 10am-noon & 6-8pm) Belgrade Philharmonia often perform at this concert hall.

Serbian Academy of Arts & Sciences (Map p708; ☎ 334 2400; Kneza Mihailova 35; concerts 6pm Mon & Thu) Hosts a number of free concerts and exhibitions; check its window for details.

Dom Omladine (Map p708; ☎ 324 8202; Makedonska 22) Has nonclassical music concerts, film festivals and multimedia events.

Sava Centar (Map p706; ☎ 213 9840; www.sava centar.com; Milentija Popovića 9, New Belgrade) Hosts major concerts.

For some free entertainment on a Sunday wander along to the outer part of the Kalemegdan citadel, where folk come to dance hand in hand the traditional way to pipe, accordion and drum.

CINEMAS

For the latest Hollywood blockbuster the **Tuckwood Cineplex** (Map p708; ☎ 323 6517; Kneza Miloša 7; tickets 150-280DIN) shows films in English or with English subtitles.

BARS & CLUBS

Party life revolves around the many barges and boats moored on the Sava and Danube Rivers. Clubs come and go or change their tunes. Many have regular bands at weekends or import the best DJs Europe has to offer.

Danube River Barges   **Map p706**

Adjacent to Hotel Jugoslavija, Novi Belgrade is a kilometre-long strip of some 20 barges. Bus Nos 15, 68, 603 and 701 from Trg Republike go to the Hotel Jugoslavija.

Brave Heart (Hrabo Scre; ☎ 851 1480; ☷ 10pm-4am) Heaves till dawn and appeals to the warrior clan with 'Hagar cartoon strip'-style chunky wood-slab furniture. A place to chill out with DJ music to midnight and then live music.

Bibis (☎ 319 2150; ☷ 10am-2am) A quiet place that's a useful starter to a night out; sit over a drink and chat about where to go later. It's popular in winter when other barges close.

Acapulco (☎ 784 760; ☷ noon-3am) Where young men who work out come to flaunt their money and female attachments. Mockingly referred to as sponsorship girls, they work on the basis of 'you look after me (plenty of gifts), and I'll look gorgeous beside you'. Music is fast and furious turbofolk.

Monza (☎ 319 0712; ☷ 10am-2am) More an afternoon place with a large outdoor terrace.

Sava River Barges   **Map p708**

On the western bank of the Sava River is another 1.5km strip of floating bars, restaurants and discos. Here you'll find **Cocktail No Name** playing pop and '80s music, **Zippo** for Serbian folk music, **Exile** pounding out techno and nearby **Sound** playing house and disco. Get there by walking over the Brankov Most or by tram No 7, 9 or 11. Most of these are only open in summer.

WITOLD SKRYPCZAK

Slovakia's largest castle, Spišský hrad (p775)

Hikers climbing ladders in Suchá Belá gorge,
Slovenský Raj National Park (p771), Slovakia
NEIL WILSON

DIANA MAYFIELD

Rural Transylvanian (p600) countryside, around Braşov, Romania

Palace of Parliament (p580), in Bucharest,
Romania
MICHAEL GEBICKI

Bled Castle overlooking the lake at Bled (p800), Slovenia

An overview of the Kyiv-Pechersk Lavra, or Caves Monastery (p833), and Dnipro River in Kyiv, Ukraine

Swallow's Nest perched above the Black Sea near Yalta (p860), Ukraine

City Bars & Clubs   Map p708

Exclusive (☎ 328 2288; Kneza Mihailova 41-45; 🕑 9am-2am Mon-Sat, noon-1am Sun) A basement beer joint, Belgrade's answer to a Munich beer hall. There's plenty of knees-up music for this lads' bar with big snacks – sausage, bread and chips (70DIN) – as a sound bedrock for serious drinking.

Rio Bravo (☎ 328 5050; Kralja Petra 54; 🕑 11am-2am Mon-Sat, 5pm-2am Sun) Hitch yer horse outside, mosey in and shoot down some hard liquor in this bar kitted out with redundant Western film sets.

Oh! Cinema! (☎ 328 4000; Kalemegdan Citadel; 9pm-5am) A rock-till-dawn bar on the eastern bulwarks of the citadel overlooking the Danube and zoo. Popular with the in-crowd but not with the insomniac tigers below.

Andergraund (Underground; ☎ 625 681; www.ander graund.com; Pariska 1a; 🕑 noon-midnight Sun-Thu, noon-2am Fri & Sat) Once an air-raid shelter and then a mushroom farm (still smells a bit that way), Andergraund is a warren of underground rooms where big-name DJs play, usually on Saturdays. On other days it's recorded music or the sports screen on the outside terrace. This is about the only nightclub with wheelchair access.

Federal Association of World Travellers (☎ 324 2303; 29 Novembra 7; 🕑 1pm-midnight Mon-Fri, 3pm-late Sat & Sun) A wonderfully eclectic bar hidden in a basement where you feel you've stumbled across someone's house party and been welcomed in. Just open the big black gate, follow the lights that suddenly come on and listen for the music, live every night.

Akademija (☎ 627 846; www.akademija.net, in Serbian; Rajićeva 10; 🕑 6pm-late) is also recommended for live music.

For a mix-and-match evening among the clubs the best place to wander is down Strahinića Bana, four blocks east of Studentski Trg.

Shopping

Not a place for tacky souvenirs – yet. Instead there's quite a bit of craftwork available. Visit the lace and knitted woollens sellers in Kalemegdan Park.

A **craft street market** (Map p708; cnr Kralja Milana & Njegoševa; 🕑 8am-5pm Mon-Sat) sells handcrafted jewellery items and original oil paintings.

Street sellers may offer you a set of 1990s currency from when unimaginable hyperinflation ruined Serbia. A 500 billion dinar note should be included; its only value now is the chance to boast billionaire status.

Getting There & Away
BUS
The country is well served by buses. Belgrade has two adjacent bus stations; **BAS** (Bus; Map p708; ☎ 636 299; Železnička 4) serves regional Serbia and some destinations in Montenegro, while **Lasta** (Map p708; ☎ 625 740; Železnička bb) deals with destinations around Belgrade.

Sample services are Subotica (440DIN, three hours), Niš (460DIN, three hours), Podgorica (940DIN, nine hours), Budva (1160DIN, 12 hours) and Novi Pazar (580DIN, three hours) for Kosovo.

International services to Western Europe are good with daily buses to destinations in Western Europe; see p741.

TRAIN
The **central train station** (Map p708; ☎ 629 400; Savski Trg 2) has a very helpful **information office** (☎ 361 8487; platform 1; 🕑 7am-7pm). There's also a **tourist office** (☎ 361 2732; 🕑 7am-9.30pm Mon-Sat, 10am-6pm Sun) for basic city information, an **exchange bureau** (🕑 6am-10pm) and **sales counter** (☎ /fax 265 8868; 🕑 9am-4pm Mon-Sat) for Eurail passes at the track end of the station.

Overnight trains run from Belgrade to Bar (1000DIN plus three-/six-berth couchette 1000/564DIN, 11½ hours). Frequent trains go to Novi Sad (185DIN, 1½ hours) and Subotica (350DIN, three hours).

For international trains see p741.

Getting Around
TO/FROM THE AIRPORT
Surcin airport is 18km west of Belgrade. The **JAT bus** (☎ 675 583; 120DIN; 🕑 5am-9pm hourly airport-town, 7am-8pm hourly town-airport) connects the airport with Trg Slavija and the central train station. Ignore the taxi sharks prowling in the airport; go outside and catch a cab to town for 450DIN to 600DIN.

CAR & MOTORCYCLE
Belgraders park on the pavements. It's even regulated, with three parking zones requiring tickets bought from a street kiosk.

PUBLIC TRANSPORT
Belgrade has trams and trolleybuses with limited routes, while buses ply all over the city, New Belgrade and the suburbs.

Tickets cost 12DIN from a street kiosk or 20DIN from the driver; make sure you validate the ticket in the machine on board.

Tram No 2 is useful for connecting Kalemegdan citadel with Trg Slavija, bus stations and the central train station.

TAXI

Belgrade's taxis are plentiful and most use meters. Flag fall is 25DIN and a 5km trip should cost around 150DIN. If the meter's not running then point it out to the driver.

Taxi sharks, usually in flash cars, prey around the airport, train and bus stations looking for a rich fare. Airport to city should be about 500DIN; at the stations move away from the entrance and pick up a cruising cab.

Have your hotel call you a taxi or phone **Maxis** (☎ 581 111) or **Plavi** (☎ 555 999).

Around Belgrade

ZEMUN ЗЕМУН

On the southern bank of the Danube, some 8km northwest of Central Belgrade, is the small town of Zemun. This was the most southerly point of the Austro-Hungarian empire when their opponents, the Turks, were in control of Belgrade. Visitors come for the fish restaurants, boating or just ambling alongside the Danube.

Catch bus No 83 from outside Belgrade's central train station and get off in the main street, Glavna, where the pedestrian-only Lenyinova street leads through a market down to the Danube. This older area of town has some once-resplendent 19th-century mansions standing proudly out from post-WWII concrete.

Above the market area narrow cobbled streets, remnants of the old village, lead uphill towards the **Gardoš**, a fortress with origins going back to the 9th century. All that remains are some 15th-century walls and more importantly the **Tower of Sibinjanin Janko,** built in 1896 to celebrate the millennial anniversary of the Hungarian state. A more useful reason was to keep an eye on the Turks.

Just back down the hill is the 1731 Orthodox **Nikolajevska Church** (Njegoševa St 43). Inside this high-vaulted church, gleaming out of the gloom, is an astoundingly beautiful iconostasis carved in the baroque style, gold plated on black and with rows of saints painted on golden backgrounds.

Zemun Museum (☎ 617 766; Glavna 9; admission 100DIN; ⏱ 9am-4pm Tue-Fri, 9am-3pm Sat & Sun) has a huge collection demonstrating the development of Serbian applied arts.

There are a host of fish restaurants along the riverside to choose from. In summer patrons flow out onto the terraces to drink the sunset down, listen to the music and belt out the old Serbian favourites once the *slivovitz* (plum brandy) has lubricated throats.

Aleksandar (☎ 199 462; Kej Oslobođenja 49; dishes 500DIN; ⏱ 9am-midnight) is a restaurant that revels in an expansive fish menu drawn from both sea and river. If you're here at lunch time and just want a filler, go for their fiery-red *riblja čorba* (a peppery fish soup) and a huge hunk of bread to mop up the remains.

SMEDEREVO СМЕДЕРЕВО

Some 46km southwest of Belgrade is the small town of Smederevo. This unremarkable town would be of little interest but for its imposing fortress guarding the southern bank of the Danube. A frequent bus service (130DIN, 1½ hours) from Belgrade's Lasta bus station makes this a pleasant day trip.

Smederevo Fortress (admission 10DIN; ⏱ daylight hrs) is a triangular fort with 25 towers and a water moat. An inner citadel overlooks the river. Built by despot Djuradj Brankovic, it served as his capital from 1428 to 1430. The fortifications were never really tested in battle with the only damage being wrought by time and the massive explosion of an ammunition train in WWII.

Smederevo Museum (admission 10DIN; ⏱ 10am-5pm Mon-Fri, 10am-3pm Sat & Sun) is a 'history of the town' museum with artefacts dating from Roman times and some interesting frescoes.

VOJVODINA ВОЈВОДИНА

North of the Danube, this flat fertile plain provides much of the food that fills the nation's larders. The hilly exception to this is the Fruška Gora National Park, an 80km-long upland island of rolling landscape, vineyards and some 14 monasteries. Novi Sad, capital of the region, revels in a similarity to Belgrade with a citadel, museums and a lively restaurant scene, while Subotica, influenced by nearby Hungary, has some architectural marvels to smarten up a provincial town.

Novi Sad Нови Сад

☎ 021 / pop 299,000

Novi Sad is Belgrade on Valium with much of what the capital has to offer but at a quieter pace. Some interesting cafés, bars, museums and pedestrian streets are attractions enough to merit a visit, even a day jaunt from Belgrade.

Dominating the town is the mighty Petrovaradin citadel built on a plug of volcanic rock.

ORIENTATION

The adjacent train and intercity bus stations lie at the northern end of Bulevar Oslobođenja. It's a 2.5km walk to the city centre or a bus ride (No 11A) to the city bus station. One block south is Zmaj Jovina leading into Trg Slobode, the heart of Novi Sad and dominated by the Catholic cathedral with chequered roof tiles. Leading off Zmaj Jovina is Dunavska, a small cobbled street, the cultural hub of Novi Sad with a mix of brand-name clothing shops, cafés, restaurants and antique shops.

Two road bridges lead over the Danube to the eastern bank and the old town. Stairs beside the large church lead up to Petrovaradin citadel.

In July the town hosts the vastly popular Exit festival (p715) and a jazz festival is held in November.

INFORMATION

Delta Bank (☎ 487 0000; Mihajla Pupina 4; ⏱ 8am-6pm Mon-Fri, 8am-1pm Sat) Cashes travellers cheques and has an all-cards ATM.

KSR Beograd Tours (☎ 27 455; fax 27 423; Svetozara Miletića 4; ⏱ 7am-7pm Mon-Fri, 7am-1pm Sat) Train tickets at train station prices.

Main post office and telephone centre (☎ 614 708; Narodnih Heroja 2; ⏱ 7am-7pm Mon-Sat, 8am-3pm Sun)

Tourist Information Centre (☎ 421 811; Mihajla Pupina 9; www.novisadtourism.org.yu; ⏱ 9am-8pm Mon-Fri, 9am-2pm Sat) On-the-button office with plenty of info.

Voyager (16 Strazilovska; per hr 60DIN; ⏱ 24hr) Internet.

SIGHTS

The **Petrovaradin Citadel**, a massive piece of work, often referred to as the 'Gibraltar of the Danube', was built between 1699 and 1780 and designed by the French architect Vauban.

There's a small **museum** (☎ 433 155; admission 70DIN; ⏱ 9am-5pm) and a **planetarium** (☎ 433 308; admission 40DIN; shows 7pm Thu, 5pm Sat & Sun) in the citadel. The chief pleasure is simply to walk the walls and enjoy the splendid view. Have a close look at the clock tower – the hour hand is the longer one so that the clock would be easy to read from the river.

The inner citadel stables in-house artist **studios** (⏱ 9am-5pm Mon-Sat); visitors are welcome and maybe over a coffee you'll find just that piece for back home.

Come July the citadel hosts the **Exit festival** (www.exitfest.org) with five or more stages shaking to the best in rock, hip-hop and techno presented by the finest in Europe. The event is hugely popular.

The main museum in Novi Sad is **Muzej Vojvodine** (☎ 420 566; Dunavska 35-37; admission 70DIN; ⏱ 9am-7pm Tue-Fri, 9am-2pm Sat & Sun), housed in two buildings. No 35 covers the history of Vojvodina from Palaeolithic times to the late 19th century; No 37 takes the story to 1945 with an emphasis on WWI and WWII. The collection is impressive in its thoroughness with the main explanatory panels in English.

SLEEPING

Brankovo Kolo (☎ /fax 528 263; www.hostelns.com; Episkopa Visariona 3; d/tr/q per person €8/7/6; ⏱ 1 Jul-25 Aug) Novi Sad's cheapie is student accommodation only available in summer.

Hotel Fontana (☎ 621 779; fax 621 779; Nikole Pašića 27; s/d 1500/2000DIN; P) A short haul from the local bus station and above a restaurant, the Fontana is a good find in a town stretched for cheap accommodation. The rooms are basic but clean and a geyser powers the hot water.

Hotel Vojvodina (☎ 622 122 vojvodina@visitnovisad .com; Trg Slobode 2; s/d 1800/2600DIN) An atmospheric old hotel looking over the central square of Novi Sad.

Zenit (☎ 621 444; www.hotelzenit.co.yu; Zmaj Jovina 8; 3500/4700DIN; P 🖳) A big glass frontage spotlights this brand-new up-market boutique hotel that's a favourite with foreigners visiting town. Rooms are well arranged, a little smaller than in the older hotels but provide a sort of homely warmth. The restaurant is for breakfast only. Internet use is 250DIN for 30 minutes.

EATING & DRINKING

Nesic (Pašiča 23; dishes 10-60DIN; ⏱ 8am-9pm) Worth a visit as much to buy a squidgy cake as to appreciate this 1950s cake shop that's still spick-and-span with red leatherette bench seats.

Atina (☎ 28 863; Njegoševa; dishes from 50DIN; ☺ 6am-10pm Mon-Sat, 9am-5pm Sun) Cheap, quick and something simple from the buffet; the stainless steel tables say that you're not going to linger long. If you wish to, then the restaurant section has waiter service and tablecloths.

Šecuan (☎ 528 020; Dunavska 16; dishes 300-400DIN; ☺ 9am-11pm Mon-Fri, 9am-1am Sat & Sun) Opened especially for 1981 when Novi Sad hosted the world table tennis championship. After wowing the Chinese team back then it still excels today.

Plava Frajle (☎ 613 675; Sutjeska 2; dishes 300-400DIN; ☺ 9am-midnight) A popular knees-up restaurant just southwest of the centre. On Thursdays and weekends traditional music bands play their hearts out, the clientele join in with gusto and the party rips on until dawn. A good taster of local food is the *paprika u pavlaci* (an appetiser of yellow peppers fermented in cream cheese). We never understood why chairs were fixed to the ceiling.

Kod Lipa (☎ 615 259; Svetozara Miletića 7; dishes from 290DIN; ☺ 10am-11pm) An 1880s restaurant where little has changed as the old photographs on the wall attest. Age and atmosphere plus traditional Vojvodinan food come together to make this a must-visit restaurant. Downstairs in the converted cellars vast wine barrels on their sides form secluded alcoves with seating within. The appetising aroma of mellow wine still lingers.

Red Cow (cnr Dunavska & Zmaj Jovina; ☺ 8am-1am) More Green Cow than Red given the paint job. The Cow is an Irish-lookalike pub with a warm, woody and beery atmosphere. Halt here for a refreshing Guinness, draught Nikšić or an evening out.

GETTING THERE & AWAY

Frequent trains link the **train station** (☎ 443 200; Bulevar Jaše Tomića 4) with Belgrade (185DIN, two hours) and Subotica (165DIN, 1½ hours).

Buses leave the **bus station** (☎ 442 021; Bulevar Jaše Tomića 6) frequently for Belgrade (250DIN, 1½ hours).

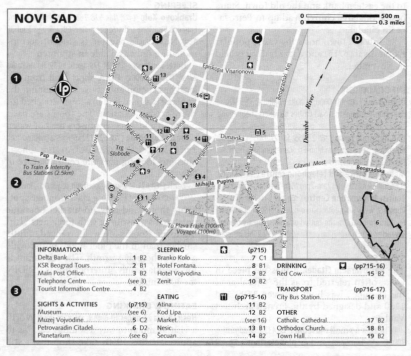

NOVI SAD

0 — 500 m
0 — 0.3 miles

INFORMATION	
Delta Bank	1 B2
KSR Beograd Tours	2 B1
Main Post Office	3 B2
Telephone Centre	(see 3)
Tourist Information Centre	4 B2

SIGHTS & ACTIVITIES	(p715)
Museum	(see 6)
Muzej Vojvodine	5 C2
Petrovaradin Citadel	6 D2
Planetarium	(see 6)

SLEEPING	(p715)
Branko Kolo	7 C1
Hotel Fontana	8 B1
Hotel Vojvodina	9 B2
Zenit	10 B2

EATING	(pp715-16)
Atina	11 B2
Kod Lipa	12 B2
Market	(see 16)
Nesic	13 B2
Šecuan	14 B2

DRINKING	(pp715-16)
Red Cow	15 B2

TRANSPORT	(pp716-17)
City Bus Station	16 B1

OTHER	
Catholic Cathedral	17 B2
Orthodox Church	18 B1
Town Hall	19 B2

AROUND NOVI SAD

Fruška Gora Фрушка Гора

A small island of rolling hills rising from the Vojvodina plain, Fruška Gora is given over to farming, vineyards and orchards. Thirty-five monasteries were built between the 15th and 18th centuries to protect Serbian culture and religion against the Turks to the south. Fifteen of those monasteries are preserved today, and Krušedol and Novo Hopovo are perhaps the best known and the most easily accessible.

Krušedol Monastery (nr Krušedol Selo) was built by Serbian ruler Đeorde Brankovic in the early 1500s. Like many monasteries in this area the church was severely damaged during one of the Turkish invasions and later rebuilt. Vivid frescoes, some original, leap out from the walls as a storyboard for biblical events.

Novo Hopovo (nr Irig) is one of the oldest monasteries (1576) in the region and influenced the design of later churches and suffered severe damage during WWII. Restoration of the frescoes revealed earlier work painted under the influence of Cretan masters who worked at Mt Athos Monastery in Greece. Many of the frescoes are incomplete but nevertheless they present powerful images.

Subotica Суботица

☎ 024 / pop 148,400

The tempter for visitors to Subotica is the Hungarian-style Art Nouveau architecture (1908–12), which adds a little magic to the relaxed atmosphere of this provincial town, and the lakeside resort at Palić. At 10km from the border, the town is a useful transit point to/from Szeged (Hungary); it's also worth a day trip from Belgrade.

ORIENTATION

Walk out of the train station and through the park to Đure Đrakovica. The left (southeast) leads to the bus station and on to Palić. On the right is the amazing Art Nouveau Modern Art Gallery. Also to the left, about 100m from the park, is a pedestrian street (Korzo) that leads down to the old heart of Subotica, Trg Republike and the town hall.

INFORMATION

Delta Bank (☎ 554 011; Cara Dušana; ☼ 8am-3pm Mon-Fri, 8am-noon Sat) All-cards ATM, cashes travellers cheques.

Exchange office (Train station; ☼ 7am-7pm Mon-Sat, 7am-noon & 3-7pm Sun)

IPS (☎ 551 004; Korzo 8; ☼ 9am-9pm Mon-Fri, 9am-3pm Sat) Some English titles plus books on Subotica.

Left-luggage office (Train station; per item 60DIN; ☼ 24hr)

Tourist Information Office (☎ 554 809; ticsu@yunord.net; Korzo 15; ☼ 8am-8pm Mon-Sat, 8am-noon Sun) Very helpful folk with maps, pamphlets and advice on what to see.

SIGHTS

The imposing Art Nouveau **town hall** (Trg Republike), built in 1910, contains an engaging **historical museum** (admission 50DIN; ☼ 9am-2pm Tue-Sat) displaying regional life and the skull of a mammoth. Check whether the exquisitely decorated council chambers are open. The dark varnished wood, green baize cloth and high-backed chairs give a succinct air of petty municipal power.

An equally exquisite piece of Art Nouveau architecture is the sinuously decorated **Modern Art Gallery** (☎ 553 725; Trg Lenina 5; ☼ 7am-1pm Mon, Wed & Fri, 7am-6pm Tue & Thu, 9am-noon Sat). One of the most beautiful buildings in Serbia, it's all swirling colourful lines employing ceramic tiles, mosaics and stained-glass windows.

SLEEPING & EATING

Student Centar (☎ 546 637; M V Tošinice 7) This is being developed by the Youth Hostel organisation to be Subotica's new youth hostel. It should be open by the time you read this but check with the Youth Hostel's website (www.hostels.org.yu) or the Tourist Information Office first.

Hotel Patria (☎ 554 500; www.patria-su.com, in Serbian; Đure Đakovica; s/d 1851/2902DIN) Cheeky prices considering that the average room's furnishings are dormitory-like but there are very few hotels in the area. In comparison the restaurant's quite best-behaviour posh.

Lipa (Đure Đakovića 13; burek 60DIN; ☼ 24hr) A bakery and *burek* shop that's a brekkie or late-night snack stop. A cheese-and-mushroom *burek* and yogurt is a cure-all for hunger or hangover.

Ravel (☎ 554 670; Nušićeva 2; 50-100DIN; ☼ 9am-10pm Mon-Sat, 11am-10pm Sun) With a beautifully decorated Art Nouveau interior, it just needs leather-gloved, top-hatted and walking-cane-bearing gentlemen with crinoline-dressed ladies on arm to complete the scenario. This café has the best in luscious cakes and some superb coffee.

Népkör (☎ 555 480; Žarka Zrenjanina 11; mains 250-350DIN; ☯ 8am-midnight Mon-Sat, 8am-4pm Sun) A chance to sample Hungarian cuisine so try their steaming goulash for 300DIN or *gombásztál* (mushroom and cheese dish) for 280DIN in this almost-flashy modern restaurant. On Sundays feed up with a buffet lunch for 400DIN.

GETTING THERE & AWAY
From the **train station** (☎ 555 606) there are two local trains to Szeged, Hungary (155DIN, 1¾ hours) and one international train. Trains to Belgrade (155DIN, 3½ hours) also call at Novi Sad.

For day trips to Subotica there's a handy train leaving Belgrade at 8.20am, arriving in Subotica at 11.28am; the return is 5.14pm arriving back in Belgrade at 8.15pm.

The **bus station** (☎ 555 566; Marksov Put) has regular services to Szeged (135DIN, 1½ hours), hourly buses to Novi Sad (300DIN, two hours) and Belgrade (400DIN, 3½ hours).

Palić Палић
Eight kilometres west of Subotica is the park resort of Palić edging onto a 5.5-sq-km lake. Activities include boating, swimming, fishing and sailing. Outside the park on the Subotica road is a string of shops, pizza joints and a supermarket. In mid-July Palić hosts an international film festival.

Bus No 6 from outside the Hotel Patria in Subotica goes to Palić (20 minutes, 35DIN); alternatively a taxi will cost 150DIN to 200DIN.

SOUTHERN SERBIA
Despotovac Деспотовац
☎ 035 / 25,500
This prosperous provincial town is towards the head of the Resava valley, an eastern offshoot of the Belgrade–Niš corridor. Rolling green valleys, small fields and copses of trees make this a fairly closed landscape with occasional glimpses of distant mountains.

Despotovac is a pleasant stopover on a casual wander south and there are two particular places of interest: Manasija Monastery and Resava Cave.

Grand Restaurant (☎ 611 552; bus station; dishes 200-300DIN; 6am-midnight Mon-Sat, 3pm-midnight Sun) is a surprisingly good restaurant that at first glance seems no more than a bus station café; the grilled local trout is a suitable choice.

There's another surprise in the good-value **Kruna Motel** (☎ 611 659; Rudnička bb; s/d 1050/1900DIN; ℗). The bedroom slippers are a fine extra touch. The hotel will organise transport to the cave and monastery for 1500DIN.

Belgrade buses leave four times a day (350DIN, three hours).

MANASIJA MONASTERY
From the outside this famous monastery, 2km north of the town, defies the concept of a monastery as a place of peace and spirituality. What confronts the visitor is a massive fortress, a solid block on the landscape.

This was built by a community in flight from the Turkish takeover of Kosovo with the church dating from the beginning of the 1400s. Despite looking such an impenetrable bulwark it was occupied several times by the Turks and consequently the remaining frescoes are only patchy. However, what's left is enough to startle the viewer with their vitality, colour and realism; it's as if the yet-to-come Italian renaissance visited here first.

RESAVA CAVE
Resavska Pećina (Resava Cave; ☎ 611 110; respec@ milnet.co.yu; adult/child 120/80DIN; ☯ 9am-5pm 1 Apr-1 Nov), up in the hills 20km beyond Despotovac, is a showcave (open to the ordinary public rather than just cavers) only discovered in 1962. Some 4km have been explored although less than 1km is open to the public. Tours take about 40 minutes through a variety of passages adorned with all manner of ancient formations.

There's no public transport to the cave from Despotovac so it'll cost about 1500DIN by taxi. Belgrade buses leave four times a day (350DIN, three hours).

Topola Топола
☎ 034 / 25,000
Many Serbs hold this small rural town sacred as it was from here that Karageorge Petrović pitched the Serbian insurrection against the Turks in 1804.

ORIENTATION & INFORMATION
The bus station is 10 minutes' walk north of the centre on the Belgrade road. From the Tourist Organisation office it's a five-

minute walk south to the museum and 15 to the Church of St George. There are no ATMs in town.

The **Tourist Organisation** (☎ 811 172; Kneginje Zorke 13; ☼ 8am-4pm Nov-Mar, 8am-7pm Apr-Oct) has some pieces in English on Karageorge plus a town map.

SIGHTS

The **museum** (Kralijice Marije; admission 100DIN; ☼ 9am-5pm) is one of the remnants of the fortified town built by Karageorge and from where he led his rebellion. The museum houses artefacts of that period plus personal effects. Within the entrance stands Karageorge's personal canon with one handle missing. This was removed by his grandson, King Petar I, to be made into his crown when he ascended to the Serbian throne in 1904.

The admission ticket also gives entry to the Church of St George and Petar House. Set in wooded parkland atop a hill, the **Church of St George** (Avenija Kralja Petra I; ☼ 8am-7pm Apr-Oct, 8am-4pm Nov-Mar) is a five-domed church built between 1904 and 1912 by King Petar I as a memorial to his grandfather, Karageorge. The marble interior is decorated with copies of the best Serbian medieval frescoes but executed in millions of mosaic pieces. Similar mosaics depict the medieval kings of Serbia holding the monasteries they founded. The southern tomb is Karageorge's while the other is King Petar's.

Just downhill from the Church of St George is a small house, **Petar House** (Avenija Kralja Petra I; ☼ 8am-7pm Apr-Oct, 8am-4pm Nov-Mar) used by workmen building the church. King Petar also stayed here on occasions when he came to inspect progress on the church. Today it houses temporary historical and art exhibitions.

SLEEPING & EATING

Hotel Oplenac (☎ 811 430; Avenija Kralja Petra I; s/d 1080/1760DIN) The only joint in town, Hotel Oplenac, like many state hotels, is waiting for a new owner, a refit and happier times. The barrack-like rooms are adequate but the staff could smile a bit more.

Breza (☎ 812 463; Krajiskih Brigada 25; dishes 120-250DIN; ☼ 8am-late) Five minutes' walk from the town centre, this rustic favourite with the locals has a no-nonsense, let's-get-down-to-lunch atmosphere. It's plain honest food and you can't go far wrong.

GETTING THERE & AWAY

Frequent buses travel to Belgrade (400DIN, three hours).

Niš Ниш

☎ 018 / pop 250,000

While some flit through on the way to Bulgaria, Macedonia or the south of the country, Niš has some significant attractions (one of which is exceptionally gruesome) that promise at least an interesting day's stay.

Niš was first settled in pre-Roman times and flourished during the time of local boy made good, Emperor Constantine (280–337 AD), whose extensive palace ruins lie 4km east of town.

Turkish rule lasted from 1386 until 1877 despite several Serb revolts. The Ćele Kula, a Turkish victory tower of Serbian skulls, is a grim pointer of their failure. The massive Tvrđava citadel is another remnant of their overlordship.

ORIENTATION

North of the Nišava River is the mighty Tvrđava Citadel, which shelters the adjacent market and the bus station. The train station is to the west on Dimitrija Tucovića; south of the river is the CBD.

The citadel hosts a blues, rock and pop festival in July and a jazz festival in October.

INFORMATION

Commercial Bank (Nikole Pašića 45) All-cards ATM.
KSR Beograd (☎ /fax 523 808; Trg Oslobođenja 9; ☼ 8am-4pm Mon-Fri, 9am-2pm Sat) Sells train tickets.
Post Office (Voždova Karađorđa 13a; ☼ 8am-8pm) There's also Internet access for 50DIN per hr.
Tourist Organisation of Niš (☎ 542 588; torg@ bankerinter.net; Voždova Karađorđa 7; ☼ 7.30am-7pm Mon-Fri, 9am-1pm Sat) Basic tourist literature; books domestic buses.

SIGHTS

To consolidate their hold on the region the Turks built the **Tvrđava** (Jadranska; ☼ 24hr) in 1396 on the site of a Roman fortress. Entrance is through the Stamboul Gate, a redoubtable double gate embedded in a substantial bastion. Within is a courtyard with souvenir shops and cafés.

The macabre **Ćele Kula** (Tower of Skulls; ☎ 322 228; Brače Tankosić bb; adult/child 40/30DIN; ⏰ 9am-4pm Mon-Sat, 10am-2pm Sun Nov-Apr, 8am-8pm May-Oct; Ⓟ) was erected by the Turks in 1809 as a ghoulish warning to would-be Serbian rebels. During 1809 a force under the duke of Resava trying to liberate Niš attacked a larger Turkish force. The Serbs suffered heavily and the duke desperately rushed the Turkish defences firing his pistol into their powder magazine. The resulting explosion reportedly wiped out 4,000 Serbs and 10,000 Turks but not enough to deny the Turks victory. The dead Serbs were beheaded, scalped and their skulls embedded in this squat tower. Only 58 skulls remain; the rest disappeared over time.

Mediana (☎ 550 433; Bulevar Cara Konstantina bb; admission museum adult/child 40/30DIN, site free; ⏰ 9am-4pm Tue-Sat 10am-2pm Sun), on the eastern outskirts of Niš, is what remains of a 4th-century Roman palace complex, possibly that of Constantine. Archaeological digging has revealed a palace, forum and an expansive grain-storage area with some sizeable, almost intact, pottery vessels.

SLEEPING & EATING

Hotel Ambassador (☎ /fax 541 800; Trg Oslobođenja bb; s/d/apt 2050/2560/4450DIN) Cheapest and slap-bang in the centre of town with very helpful staff. With its large noisy lobby and bar it seems that the world of Niš revolves through the doors. The rooms are quiet, have phones but no TV – you get that with the apartment. It's fine for a couple of days' stopover.

Haman (☎ 513 444; Tvrđava; dishes 200-400DIN; ⏰ 9am-midnight) Dinner in the bathroom, literally, as this restaurant is in a converted Turkish bath. The inner rooms make for intimate lunches in secluded alcoves lit by patterns of sunlight that come through the ceiling vents. Ordinary breakfasts and pizzas are available but there are also national dishes like *dimljena vešalica* (a roll of smoked pork stuffed with cream cheese and almonds).

Mama Pizza (☎ 45 044; Dušanova 43; dishes about 350DIN; ⏰ 9am-midnight) A restaurant decorated in Tuscan yellow, burnt umber and sienna, the colours of Italy all to accompany the pasta and pizza. Very popular venue with the 30-something crowd who come to munch, drink wine and listen to the smooth live music.

Also sharing the same turn-of-the-19th-century building, adorned with winsome cherubs, are two interesting café/bars.

Tramvaj (Tramway; ☎ 547 909; Pobode 20; ⏰ 8am-midnight) Take two Isle of Man trams and slice, build a servery out of one and install the seats from the other. Still, it's a rattling good cup of coffee and just the ticket after a slog around town.

Broz (☎ 064 979 9909; Pobode 20; ⏰ 10am-late) The basement is a cool retro homage to Josip Broz Tito, kitted out in very now shiny metal and red leatherette seats. A silver head of the big fella, hanging outside the 'girls', greets you as you slip down the stairs and throughout the club are photos of Broz sucking on a big Havana with his dealer, fellow socialist, Fidel Castro. Music is cool dub 'n' bass, and low enough for conversation, while drinks include a fine range of single malt whiskies.

GETTING THERE & AWAY

The **bus station** (Kneginje Ljubice) has frequent services to Belgrade (440DIN, three hours), Brus for Kopaonik (230DIN, 1½ hours), four daily to Novi Pazar (345DIN, four hours) and three to Užice for Zlatibor (455DIN, five hours).

Eight trains go to Belgrade (500DIN, 4½ hours) and two to Bar (1060DIN plus three-/six-berth couchette 680/317DIN, 11½ hours).

Kopaonik Копаоник

Serbia's prime ski area is based around the Pančićev Vrh peak (2017m) overlooking Kosovo. Ski runs totalling 44km range from nursery slopes to difficult, served by 22 lifts also linked to 20km of cross-country runs. Depending on the weather, the ski season here runs from the end of November to the end of March, or even early April.

ORIENTATION & INFORMATION

Commercial and Delta banks cash travellers cheques and have ATMs around the resort. The website www.kopaonik.net has some basic information and an area map.

There are several ski schools and equipment rental places, and daily and weekly lift passes are available.

ACTIVITIES

There's all the usual winter activities you'd expect – skiing and snowboarding plus snowmobiles. In summer there's hiking, horse riding and mountain biking.

SLEEPING & EATING
There are several large-scale hotels with restaurants, gym facilities, pizzerias, discos and shops. Expect to pay from 1300DIN to 3000DIN for a single and 2250DIN to 4000DIN per double depending on the time of year and whether you take bed and breakfast or full-board.

Possible accommodation options are the two-star **Hotel Jugobank** (☎ 036-71 040; Kopaonik) and **Hotel Junior** (☎ 037-825 051; fax 823 033; Brzeće), which is part of the Youth Hostel organisation. Inquiries can be made through the Youth Hostel organisation in Belgrade (see p710).

Balkan Holidays (www.balkanholidays.co.uk) is a British outfit that books ski holidays in Kopaonik. Their website has a topographical map showing the ski runs.

GETTING THERE & AWAY
In summer and winter seasons there are three daily buses from Belgrade and one from Niš.

Zlatibor Златибор
☎ 031 / pop 156,000
This large upland area in southwest Serbia is another ski resort but the season, December to February, is shorter than Kopaonik's due to lower altitude. In summer it draws more visitors for its mountain scenery and walking (marked routes).

ORIENTATION & INFORMATION
Zlatibor is a patchwork of small settlements centred on Tržni centar, a village of shops, eating and drinking places, a market and a bus stop.

Anitours (☎ /fax 841 855; www.anitours.co.yu; Tržni centar; ☽ 8am-6pm) Books accommodation and half-/one-day tours €10/20.

Gr@nd CyberCenter (Nasalji Sloboda; per hr 100DIN; ☽ 10am-2am) In the shopping complex near the Olimp hotel.

Komercijalna Bank (☎ 845 182; Tržni centar; ☽ 8am-8pm Mon-Fri, 9am-3pm Sat Jan, Feb, Jul & Aug, 8am-4pm Mon-Fri 8am-3pm Sat rest of year) Cashes travellers cheques and has an all-cards ATM.

M Tours (☎ 841 911; office@m-tours.co.yu; Tržni centar; ☽ 8am-6pm) Books accommodation and organises tours.

Tourist organisation (☎ 845 103; ☽ 8am-6pm Mar-Jun, 8am-10pm Jul-Feb) At the bus stop; provides tourist information, arranges private accommodation, sells bus tickets.

SIGHTS & ACTIVITIES
Zlatibor skiing is easy stuff with a ski pull although some harder runs are in preparation. There are ski schools and equipment-rental places in Tržni centar.

Other summer activities include visits to a museum village at Sirogojno, the Stopića cave at Rožanstvo, Uvac Monastery at Stublo and old wooden churches at Dobroselica, Jablanica and Kucani. It's also possible to visit the Mileševa Monastery, which houses the famous white angel fresco. Summer activities include paragliding, walking, horse riding and mountain biking

A day trip from Zlatibor can also incorporate the **Sargon 8 narrow gauge steam railway** (Morca Gora to Sargan Vitas; 2½hr trip 400DIN; ☽ Apr-Sep), famous for its figure of eight ascension of the mountains towards Bosnia and Hercegovina.

SLEEPING & EATING
Most visitors choose to stay in private rooms and apartments. There are two peak seasons: winter, January and February; summer, June to August. Typically apartments in season cost €25 to €75 for two to six people and €5 to €10 less out of season; full-board costs an extra €15. Cheaper rooms with shared bathrooms are available for €6 to €12 in season and €5 out of season.

The following hotels are open all year.

Olimp (☎ 842 555; fax 841 953; Naselje Sloboda bb; s/d/tr B&B from 1800/2800/6000DIN, s/d/tr half-board 2100/3400/6900DIN; P ☒) A modern hotel well decorated throughout with some striking works of art. All rooms have balconies; prices remain the same all year but reduce after three days' stay. The penthouse apartment at 2500DIN per person is suitable for six and has a vast acreage with three double bedrooms.

Hotel Jugopetrol (☎ 841 467; s/d/tr B&B from 2100/3600/4800DIN, s/d/tr half-board 2100/3600/5700DIN) The lengthy open foyer and reception suggests a hotel capable of dealing with coachloads at a time. The rooms are also large with TV, phone, a small balcony and a sweet on the pillow. Off the lobby is a glass conservatory selling naughty cakes. This hotel is about 200m southwest of Tržni centar.

There are more pizza and *čevapčići* joints, cafés and bars than you could visit in a month. The following are two 'good uns'.

Zlatni Bor restaurant (☎ 841 638; dishes from 250DIN; ✌ 7am-midnight) A hunger-stopping place for breakfast with a view over the lake. About 50m northeast of Tržni centar.

Zlatiborska Koliba (☎ 841 638; dishes 250-600DIN; ✌ 8am-midnght) Wooden ceilings, a big brick-arched bar, an open fireplace and good Serbian food chased by slugs of *rakija* make this a suitable place to recover from the exhaustion of skiing or hiking. In season there's live traditional music. The house speciality is *teleće grudi* (a stew of veal, potatoes, *kajmak* and vegetables in an earthenware pot cooked over an open fire).

SHOPPING
Apart from fruit and veg the market sells all manner of interesting things. For the nippy weather there's a range of brightly coloured chunky pullovers and gloves; for presents you could buy intricate lacework, a pair of *opanak* (traditional Serbian leather shoes) with the curly toes or *čutura* (wooden bottles) for holding your *rakija* stash.

On the food and drink front there's plenty of domestic *rakija*, honey, pickles, several varieties of *kajmak*, *pršuta* (smoked meats) and dried herbs for tea.

GETTING THERE & AROUND
Three daily express buses leave the **bus stand** (☎ 841 587) for Belgrade (400DIN, four hours), one bus daily heads to Niš (425DIN, four hours) and hourly ones go to Užice (65DIN, 45 minutes), the nearest railhead.

Minibuses ply the villages in season.

Novi Pazar Нови Пазар
☎ 020 / pop 86,000
Strange convoluted apartment blocks and the circular spaceship Hotel Vrbak, seemingly designed by an architect on psychedelics, mix in here with old Turkish houses and shops. The Turks were not ousted until 1912. This also is a gateway town for Kosovo, plus there are some worthwhile churches to visit.

ORIENTATION & INFORMATION
The Raška River runs through the town placing the old Turkish fortress, Turkish quarter and the mosque of Altun Alem on the southern side. Spanning the river is the peculiar Hotel Vrbak. Crossing the river is the street of 28 Novembar, which on the northern side has numerous cafés, bars and restaurants.

SIGHTS
Wandering the old town with its curious old shops can be an absorbing half day. Here old crafts like cobbling and tin smithing still exist alongside small cafés where old men sip strong coffee, play cards and sort the day out.

Sopoćani Monastery
King Uroš erected this **monastery**, 16km southwest of Novi Pazar, in the mid-13th century. It became the practice of medieval kings to endow monasteries to a saint who would intercede for them at the Day of Judgment – a sort of afterlife insurance. The monastery is a remarkable story of survival. Destroyed by the Turks at the end of the 17th century, it remained abandoned until restored in the 1920s. Much of the fresco work remains. It shows the definite influence of Romanesque art giving the figures a rhythm, plasticity and vibrancy that makes them actors in their own stories.

Petrova Crkva (Church of St Peter)
On a bluff on the Kraljevo road at the edge of town is a small stone **church**. It's the oldest in Serbia with parts dating from the 8th century. Surrounding it is an ancient cemetery. If locked ask at the nearest house for the keeper of the huge iron key.

Inside the rough masonry, a step-down baptismal well and feet-polished flagstones provide a tangible sense of the ancient. The 13th-century frescoes are incomplete due to damage.

Đurđevi Stupovi Monastery
Rising out of a copse 3km uphill from Petrova Crkva is the still-damaged monastery of **Đurđevi Stupovi** (Columns of St George), the oldest monastery in Serbia, dating from 1170. The story goes that St Simeon, then Stefan Nemanja, ruler of much of what is now southern Serbia, was captured by the Turks in 1172 and promised God that if he gained his freedom he would endow a monastery to St George. He was eventually released, and later in

life he abdicated in favour of his son and became the monk Simeon. St Simeon did indeed endow this monastery as promised, and was eventually buried here. The church was extensively damaged by the Turks in the same fit of destruction that befell Sopoćani. Repairs were done in the 1900s but undone in WWII when German troops removed stonework for their defences. Consequently only the western and northern sides of the church remain today.

SLEEPING & EATING

Hotel Vrbak (☎ 315 300; Maršala Tita bb; s/d from 1800/2500DIN) This spaceship suspended on cotton reel columns and berthed in the main square is the town's major hotel. The rooms have seen too many guests and the whole place needs a makeover but then you don't get many chances to stay in a strange place like this.

Hotel Kan (Cannes; ☎ /fax 315 300; Rifata Burdžovića 10; s/d/tr 1750/2625/3500DIN) This modern hotel, built in an Oriental style, has rather small-ish rooms compensated for by cable TV and minibar but it's clean and unfrayed. Say hi to the hamsters in reception.

Kafana Centar (☎ 27 799; 28 Novembar 21; dishes 150-170DIN; ☺ 7am-midnight) In a street of open cafés this traditional café, hiding behind lace curtains, is a favourite hang-out with the older generation of the town. The smiling matron welcomes foreigners incoherent in Serbian and can dish up a mighty helping of *čevapčići* and salad to be washed down with a local beer.

Hotel Tadz (☎ 311 904; Rifata Burdževića 79; dishes 150-350DIN; ☺ 7am-late; P) A restaurant in a new hotel with good food at reasonable street prices. The clientele look the well-heeled of the town who know a bargain. The *pstrmka* (trout) with a luscious garlic sauce is their *pièce de résistance*.

GETTING THERE & AWAY

Frequent buses go to Belgrade (432DIN, four hours), an overnight bus to Sarajevo (€13, seven hours) and four daily buses to Prishtina in Kosovo (330DIN, three hours).

KOSOVO

Kosovo seems a hidden vale surrounded by the mountains of Serbia, Montenegro and Albania. Often, while winter still blankets those countries in snow, Kosovo will be enjoying the first touches of spring.

Your government's travel advisory may have warned against travel to Kosovo. They are of necessity cautious and if you do decide to ignore their advice then it is safer to avoid areas of potential Serb/Kosovo Albanian tension such as Mitrovica and the boundary area with Serbia. Fortunately for visitors the sites of interest are outside these zones.

The ebb and flow of Islam and Orthodox Christianity has left Kosovo a legacy of several artistically beautiful buildings such as Gracanica Monastery near Prishtina, Decani Monastery near Peja and the Sinan Pasha Mosque in Prizren. These all escaped the violence of 1999 and 2004.

The countryside is pictorially attractive – wide-open plains in some places, rolling hills patch-worked with fields in others. Rearing up to the south, behind Peja in the southwest, are a set of tall mountains, often snow-clad, that include Djeravica (2656m), the tallest mountain in pre-1999 Serbia. Further east, nearer Macedonia, the mountains provide the ski slopes of Brezovica, closed as a result of the 2004 riots but expected to open again for the next season.

Serb influence in the province has ended to be replaced by an Albanian one and new buildings are no longer in the Yugoslav socialist style of concrete blocks. In Prishtina new monuments celebrate Albanian heroes while the displays in the museums of Prishtina and Prizren are exploring the province's Illyrian and Albanian past.

As Kosovo is a small province with an extensive bus network, it's perfectly reasonable to use Prishtina as a base and visit Peja and Prizren as day trips.

History

Following their defeat in 1389 by the Turks, the Serbs abandoned the region to the Albanians, descendants of the Illyrians, the original inhabitants.

Serbia regained control when the Turks departed in 1913. In the ensuing years 500,000 Albanians emigrated and Serbs were brought in to settle the vacated land. In WWII the territory was incorporated into Italian-controlled Albania and then liberated in October 1944 by Albanian partisans.

Tito wanted Albania united with Kosovo in the new Yugoslavia. It never happened. Three decades of pernicious neglect ensued until an autonomous province was created in 1974 and economic aid increased. However, little changed and the standard of living in Kosovo remained a quarter of the Yugoslav average. In 1981 demonstrations calling for full republic status were put down by the Serbian military; 300 died and 700 were imprisoned.

Trouble began anew in November 1988 with demonstrations against the sacking of local officials and President Azem Vllasi. Further unrest and strikes in February 1989 led to the suspension of Kosovo's autonomy and a state of emergency. Serious rioting followed with 24 Albanian Kosovars shot dead. In July 1990 Kosovo's autonomy was cancelled, broadcasts in Albanian ceased and the only Albanian-language newspaper was banned. Some 115,000 Albanians had their jobs taken by loyalist Serbs. Against Serbian opposition, a referendum with a 90% turnout produced a 98% vote for independence.

The Kosovo Liberation Army (KLA) was formed in 1996 out of frustrated attempts to negotiate autonomy. Using guerrilla tactics they began to fight the Serbs.

In March 1999, a US-backed plan to return Kosovo's autonomy was rejected by Serbia. Stepping up attacks on the KLA, Serbia moved to empty the province of its non-Serbian population. Nearly 850,000 Kosovo Albanians fled to Albania and Macedonia. Serbia ignored demands to desist and NATO unleashed a bombing campaign on 24 March 1999. On 2 June Milošević acquiesced to a UN settlement, Serbian forces withdrew and the Kosovo Force (KFOR) took over. Since June 1999 Kosovo has been administered as a UN-NATO protectorate.

Peace has not been easy. KFOR had to persuade the KLA to demilitarise and Serbian refugees to return home. Potential and real revenge attacks on the remaining Serbs made them isolated communities protected by KFOR.

The elections in November 2001 led to a coalition government with Ibrahim Rugova as the president of Kosovo. There was a gradual process to normalise relations with post-Milošević Serbia.

Kosovo slipped from the world's eye until March 2004, when three Kosovo Albanian children were allegedly chased into a river by Kosovo Serbs, and two drowned. This sparked a simmering discontent, mostly among youths, who attacked Serbian people, homes and churches. Nineteen people were killed, 600 homes burnt out and 29 monasteries and churches, many medieval, were destroyed. KFOR, which could have controlled much of the outrage, was disastrously slow to act.

Dangers & Annoyances

Various government travel advisories warn against visiting Kosovo. The events of March 2004 have shown that civil insurrection is but an incident away in which a foreign visitor may unwittingly get caught.

The country is thought to have been cleared of landmines but there is still unexploded ordnance about, so off the beaten track you will need KFOR (who are omnipresent) and local advice (try the police).

Getting There & Away

AIR

For air services see p740. Passengers with more than €10,000 have to complete a currency declaration form on arrival.

BUS

International

International bus services serve much of Europe; some sample fares from Prishtina are Skopje, Macedonia (€5.50, 1½ hours), Tirana, Albania (€20, 10 hours), Istanbul, Turkey (€30, 20 hours), and Sarajevo, Bosnia and Hercegovina (€30, 10 hours).

Montenegro

From Peja there's an overnight bus to Podgorica (€16, seven hours). Alternatively minibuses (€5) and taxis (€20) go to the Montenegrin town of Rožaje from outside the Peja bus station.

VISITING KOSOVO FIRST

Visitors coming into Kosovo first can then only legally enter Serbia via Macedonia, as there are no immigration facilities at the crossings between Kosovo and Serbia or Montenegro.

Serbia

Four daily buses connect Prishtina and Novi Pazar in Serbia (€5.50, three hours) with onward connections to Belgrade.

Getting Around

There is an excellent bus service linking all the main towns and villages. Buses operate very frequently between Prishtina, Prizren and Peja (€3 to €4, about two hours). There was a stab at resurrecting the railway but it ended after a short trial.

Prishtina

☎ 038 / pop 160,000

Prishtina is a bustling capital engorged with the activity and personnel of foreign agencies. Some postwar reconstruction has taken place but a lot has still to happen. Apart from the city and its activities there's not a lot to see and it's really a jumping-off point to the more interesting Peja and Prizren.

ORIENTATION

Bulevardi Nëna Terezë and Agim Ramadani run from the south and converge near the National Theatre in central Prishtina. The UN Interim Administration Mission in Kosovo (UNMIK) headquarters are off Nëna Terezë by the Grand Hotel and west of this is the Sports Complex shopping mall with restaurants and a supermarket. Bil Klinton (yes, him) runs southwest from Bulevardi Nëna Terezë passing the bus station, the airport (17km) and onto Peja.

INFORMATION

Barnatorja Pharmacy (☎ 224 245; Bulevardi Nëna Terezë; 🕒 7.30am-8pm Mon-Sat, 7.30am-8pm every 3rd Sun) Notice on window for other Sunday opening pharmacies.

Dukagjini (☎ 248 143; Bulevardi Nëna Terezë 20; 🕒 8am-8pm Mon-Sat) Sells novels and art books in English, and city maps.

Euro-s@-net (☎ 227 225; Luan Haradinaj; 🕒 9am-11pm Mon-Sat; per hr €1) Also phone calls worldwide for €0.30 per minute.

Humanitarian Community Information Centre (HCIC; ☎ 549 169; Luan Haradinaj 8; 🕒 8.30am-5pm Mon-Fri) Information on Kosovo as well as maps and books.

Newsstand (Luan Haradinaj; 🕒 9am-late) Foreign newspapers and magazines; latest papers arrive at 6pm. It's outside Monaco restaurant.

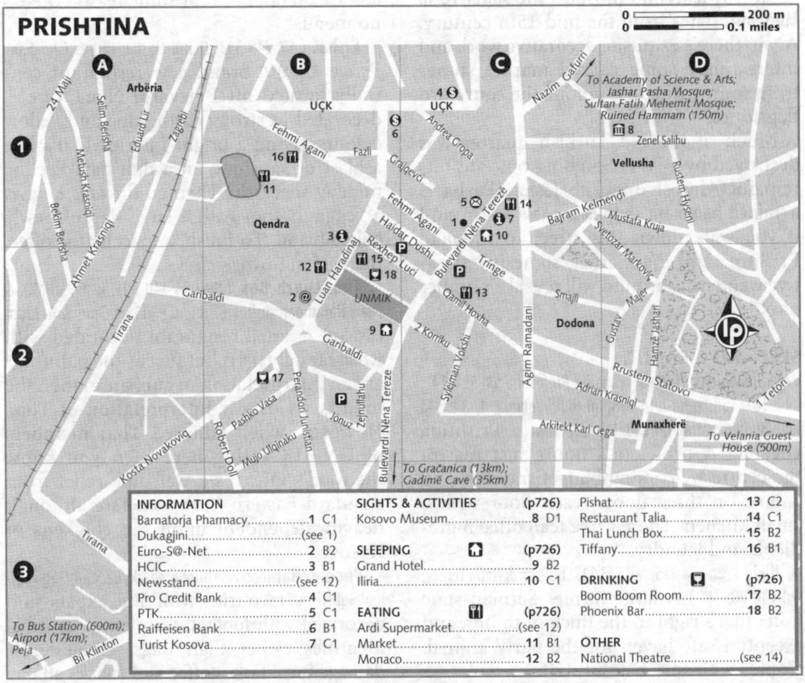
PRISHTINA
0 200 m
0 0.1 miles
Arbëria
Qendra
Vellusha
Dodona
Munaxherë
UÇK
UNMIK
24 Maji
Selim Berisha
Eduard Lir
Zagrebi
Metush Krasniqi
Bekim Berisha
Ahmet Krasniqi
Fehmi Agani
Fazli Grajqevci
Andrea Gropa
Nazim Gafurri
Zenel Salihu
Rustem Hyseni
Bajram Kelmendi
Mustafa Kruja
Svetozar Markoviç
Haidar Dushi
Rexhep Luci
Luan Haradinaj
Bulevardi Nëna Terezë
Tringe Smajli
Qamil Hoxha
Garibaldi
Tirana
2 Korriku
Sylejman Vokshi
Agim Ramadani
Gustav Majer
Hamzë Jashari
Rrustem Statovci
Adrian Krasniqi
Arkitekt Kari Gega
Pashko Vasa
Perandori Justinian
Zejnullahu
Jonuz
Robert Doll
Mujo Ulqinaku
Kosta Novakoviq
Bil Klinton
To Academy of Science & Arts; Jashar Pasha Mosque; Sultan Fatih Mehemit Mosque; Ruined Hammam (150m)
To Velania Guest House (500m)
To Gračanica (13km); Gadimë Cave (35km)
To Bus Station (600m); Airport (17km); Peja
INFORMATION
Barnatorja Pharmacy 1 C1
Dukagjini (see 1)
Euro-S@-Net 2 B2
HCIC 3 B1
Newsstand (see 12)
Pro Credit Bank 4 C1
PTK 5 C1
Raiffeisen Bank 6 B1
Turist Kosova 7 C1
SIGHTS & ACTIVITIES (p726)
Kosovo Museum 8 D1
SLEEPING (p726)
Grand Hotel 9 B2
Iliria 10 C1
EATING (p726)
Ardi Supermarket (see 12)
Market 11 B1
Monaco 12 B2
Pishat 13 C2
Restaurant Talia 14 C1
Thai Lunch Box 15 B2
Tiffany 16 B1
DRINKING (p726)
Boom Boom Room 17 B2
Phoenix Bar 18 B2
OTHER
National Theatre (see 14)

Post Telephone Kosova (PTK; ☎ 245 339; Bulevardi Nëna Terezë; ☯ 8am-9pm) Post and telephone.

Pro Credit Bank (☎ 240 248; Skënderbeu; ☯ 9am-4pm Mon-Fri) Cashes travellers cheques and has a MasterCard ATM.

Raiffeisen Bank (☎ 226 400; Migjeni 1; ☯ 8.30am-4.30pm Mon-Fri, 9am-noon Sat) Cashes travellers cheques and has a Visa card ATM.

Turist Kosova (☎ 223 815; Bulevardi Nëna Terezë 36; ☯ 8am-6pm Mon-Sat, 8am-noon Sun) Travel information, flights and international bus booking.

SIGHTS

Kosovo Museum (☎ 249 964; Marte e Driele; citizens/foreigners €1.50/5; ☯ 10.30am-7pm Tue-Sun) has a thoughtful and well-captioned exhibition on premedieval Kosovo.

Behind the museum is the **Jashar Pasha mosque**. Of note are the floral designs, the huge chandelier and the finely decorated mihrab (the niche showing the direction of Mecca, and the position of the person leading the congregation in prayer). Around the corner is a well-restored Balkan-style **house**, the home of the Academy of Science and Arts.

Nearby a second mosque, the **Sultan Fatih Mehemit**, dates from the mid-15th century. Again there's exquisite decorative work and interestingly some carved marble stones from some earlier use among the courtyard flagstones.

Much of the old Turkish quarter was destroyed by WWII bombing but odd bits remain. Almost opposite Jashar Pasha is a **ruined hammam** (bath house; Vasil Andori) and if you walk down this street to Xhemajl Prishtina and the market, some investigative wandering around will reveal a number of old houses.

SLEEPING & EATING

Velania Guest House (Pansion Profesor; ☎ 531 742, 044 167 455; besa-h4@hotmail.com; Velania 4, 34; s/d with shared bathroom €13/18) At last a Prishtina cheapie! A professor's house just east of the centre welcoming budget travellers; 10 rooms on three floors, each floor with a small kitchen. There's free tea/coffee ingredients and laundry.

Iliria (☎ 224 275; fax 548 117; Bulevardi Nëna Terezë; s/d €30/60; P) A large former Serbian state hotel that's right in the thick of things, and a central safe haven for the party animal. Comes with very helpful staff.

Grand Hotel (☎ 220 210; reception@grandhotel-pr.com; Bulevardi Nëna Terezë; s/d/tr €60/90/105; P) Prishtina's top-notch hotel with all the facilities you'd expect for the price but rated five stars, two too many in our opinion; it's a bit shabby round the edges. Booking is advisable as it's the hotel for the big shots when they come to town.

Cafés abound in the centre selling *burek* and hamburgers for €1 to €2; pasta and pizza cafés charge up to €2.50.

Restaurant Talia (☎ 244 715; behind National Theatre; dishes €3.50-5; ☯ 9am-midnight) Good pizza offered with Tabasco sauce to add heat if you feel like something spicy.

Monaco (☎ 227 490; Luan Haradinaj; pizza €3-6; ☯ 8am-late) Buy your newspaper from the vendor outside, sit down with a drink and mull over day-old news.

Tiffany (☎ 244 040; off Fehmi Agani; dishes from €6; ☯ 8am-11pm Mon-Sat, 6-11pm Sun) A crisp white linen, best-behaviour establishment where it's wise to come early to secure a table. This very popular restaurant is hidden down by the side of the Sports Stadium; a lack of signage doesn't help. Soups, grills and salads are on offer but for some reason there's no menu.

Pishat (☎ 245 333; Qamil Hoxha; dishes €2.5-5.00; ☯ 8am-11pm) A brand-new restaurant centrally located off Bulevardi Nëna Terezë, decorated in strong earth, blue and yellow colours giving a bright interior that's like a blast of sunshine on a dull day. Feeling midday snackish? Then go for *tavë e kuge*, a veggie hotpot with a large flap of newly baked bread. To finish, a macchiato coffee, the best in town.

Thai Lunch Box (☎ 044 140 791; btwn UNMIK & Luan Haradinaj; dishes €7-11; ☯ 11am-3pm & 6-11pm Mon-Sat) A small restaurant decorated with Kosovar cubist art but just as the paintings are an interpretation of cubism so then the food is a Kosovar interpretation of Thai. However, when you see Thai members of UNMIK eating here then you know the food's OK. It's a welcome relief from standard Eastern European fare although heavily dependent upon the chickens of Kosovo.

Phoenix Bar (opposite UNMIK; snacks €2.50-4; ☯ 7am-midnight) A favourite with the expats and decorated with football team strips as tribal identities rather than flags. Cholesterol-damage breakfasts, coffee and snacks all day plus booze are on offer. There's live music some weekends.

Boom Boom Room (Kosta Novakoviq; ⏰ 10am-late) Behind and west of UNMIK, this is a grungy big barn of a drinking joint with a considerable range of drinks and popular with the locals. There's live music on Wednesday nights when the room does go boom boom.

Ardi Supermarket (Luan Haradinaj; ⏰ 8am-8pm Mon-Sat) and the fruit and veg section of the **market** (off Fehmi Agani; ⏰ 8am-2pm Mon-Fri) can provide your DIY supplies.

GETTING THERE & AWAY
Air
For airlines operating from Prishtina **airport** (☎ 548 430) see p740. Unless included in your ticket departure tax is €15.

Bus
International and domestic services leave from the **bus station** (☎ 550 011; Mitrovicë-Prishtinë). For details see p741.

GETTING AROUND
Numbered minibuses roam the streets. Nos 1 and 2 go down Bil Klinton, from where it's a short walk back up Mitrovicë-Prishtinë to the bus station. The fare is €0.50.

The easiest way between town and the airport is by taxi. Try **Radio Taxi Victory** (☎ 550 889) or **Radio RGB** (☎ 515 515); the fare should be about €20.

AROUND PRISHTINA
Gračanica
Some 13km southeast of Prishtina is the superbly decorated Gracanica Monastery, built by the Serbian King Milutin in the early 14th century. It's in the shape of five-dome building on a cross-in-a-square plan typical of the best Byzantine architecture of the period. Most of the frescoes date from then and cover all the walls.

Entry is no problem once you've identified yourself to KFOR at the entrance. Catch one of the frequent buses to Gjilan which pass outside.

Gadimë Cave
Some 35km south of Prishtina, **Gadimë Cave** (Marble Cave; adult/child €2.50/0.50; ⏰ 9am-6pm), the only show cave in Kosovo, is definitely worth a plunge underground. It's renowned

for its helictites, thin stalactites growing at strange angles. There are several buses to Gadimë Cave from Prishtina or a taxi, wait and return, would cost €30.

Outer Kosovo
PEJA (PEĆ)
☎ 039
The nearness of Peja and Prizren to Prishtina means that you can avail yourself of the better sleeping and eating options in Prishtina and do day trips. While there are a number of eating places in Peja and Prizren, hotels are very few and overexpensive. Peja's attractions stand outside town, the medieval Patrijaršija Monastery and the Decani Monastery. Much work remains to be done restoring the old buildings in the market area but there's a superb picture-postcard backdrop of 2000m-plus mountains shearing straight up

Orientation & Information
The town revolves around the river and Shadrvan, a cobblestone plaza with a fountain in the middle. The **bus station** (☎ 31 152; Geromin de Rada) is on the Peja road, about 2km northwest from the centre.

The Prishtina road arrives from the northeast and ends by the Theranda Hotel by the river and the main bridge. Crossing the river just west of here is a 'new' medieval bridge built to replace the old one destroyed by floods in 1979.

After the Serbian departure in 1999 all Serbian names were removed. Unlike Prishtina and Prizren, Peja still hasn't renamed its streets so they remain nameless or are numbered. The Prishtina road runs into the northern part of town. Striking south, and into town, is the main road. The **bus station** (☎ 31 152) is at the intersection of these two routes.

Sights
Many of Peja's mosques and old buildings remain severely damaged but the colourful **bazaar** is the place to engage with the oriental atmosphere.

Two kilometres west of Peja is **Patrijaršija Monastery**, seat of the Serbian Orthodox Peć patriarchy. Although the monastery is open to visitors, KFOR at the gate may decide otherwise; if not you'll be rewarded with three mid-13th-century churches with glorious medieval frescoes.

Decani Monastery (1335) is 15km south and accessible by frequent local buses and a 2km walk. The monastery was the endowment of King, later Saint, Stefan, whose body is buried within the church. According to the monks it is still uncorrupted (not yet decayed), which is the hallmark of a saint.

PRIZREN
☎ 029

Although Prizren was the medieval capital of 'Old Serbia', the architectural influence is Turkish. The place seems like a party town as people throng the many bars and cafés along the river and in the plaza Shadrvan. The delight is wandering through small cobbled streets soaking up the history and atmosphere.

Unfortunately the Albanian Kosovar vandalism of March 2004 has added to the Serbian vandalism of 1999 and left an ugly scar of burnt-out houses up the hillside.

Orientation & Information
The town revolves around the river and Shadrvan, a cobblestone plaza with a fountain in the middle. The **bus station** (☎ 31 152; Geromin de Rada) is on the Peja road about 2km from the centre. Crossing the river just west of the main bridge is a 'new' medieval bridge built to replace the old one destroyed by floods in 1979.

A documentary film and photographic exhibition, Dokufest, happens in the first week of September.

Sights
A slow plod up from behind the Shadrvan brings you to the castle that's passed through Roman, Turkish, Serbian and KFOR army hands. The views are quite stupendous and if you're there when the imams call for prayers you'll hear a wave of chants sweep across the town.

The Orthodox churches were mostly destroyed in the March 2004 violence with little left except collapsed and burnt-out interiors.

The 1561 **Sinan Pasha Mosque** on the riverside dominates the centre and can be visited for its fine, decorated high-domed ceiling.

Near the Theranda Hotel, the newly restored **Gazi Mehmed Pasha Baths** (1563) have become an occasional exhibition space. The internal upper floor was destroyed during WWII; maybe it couldn't cope with being an Italian bordello.

Opposite the post office is a solitary **minaret-like tower** with the Star of David; it's believed to be the remnants of a synagogue.

Some 200m upriver from the Theranda Hotel is a small **museum complex** (☎ 44 487; adult/child €1/0.20; ☺ 10am-10pm Sun-Tue) celebrating the Albanian League of Prizren. This was an independence movement in Turkish times and the museum illustrates the League and historical Prizren.

BREZOVICA
This ski resort, 60km south of Prishtina, was seen as a bright spot in Kosovo's tourism future: Albanians working together with Serbs in a Serbian enclave to make a success of the resort. However, with the violence of March 2004 it was closed; it was also the end of the ski season. Hopefully it's a temporary closure.

Nine ski runs, served by seven chairlifts, lead down from 2500m; ski equipment and snowboards could be hired and lessons were available. Even if you're not a skier a trip up the ski lift was worth it to see the stunning snow scenery.

The **Molika Hotel** (☎ 290-70 452) with a restaurant, bars and cafés was the only hotel.

MONTENEGRO ЦРНА ГОРА

From an interior of alpine-type scenery with giddy-deep canyons, to a sparsely vegetated and highly folded limestone mountain range plummeting down to an azure Adriatic sea, this 13,812-sq-km republic has got the works.

North of Podgorica, both the railway and road run through the impressive Moraca Canyon, while 40km west of Mojkovac is the 1.3km-deep Tara Canyon. Other striking features include the winding Bay of Kotor (the largest fjord in southern Europe) and the vast, beautiful and ecologically significant Lake Skadar. Of historical interest are the old towns of Budva, Cetinje and the walled cities of Kotor and Herceg Novi.

Montenegro is a very popular holiday spot; the best times to visit are May, June and September. Visitors with time or transport can choose their accommodation from a range of 'sobe', 'Zimmer' or 'private room' signs all along the coast.

The railway connects Belgrade to Bar, where ferries sail to Italy. Frequent bus services (fares €2 to €4) link the coastal towns with Podgorica and Cetinje.

History

Only tiny Montenegro was able to keep its head above the Turkish tide that engulfed the Balkans for over four centuries from the 14th century onwards. From 1482 Montenegro was ruled from Cetinje by *vladike* (prince-bishops). With the defeat of the Turks in 1878, Montenegrin independence was assured and later recognised by the Congress of Berlin. Nicola I Petrovic, Montenegro's ruler, declared himself king in 1910 but was evicted by the Austrians in 1916. After the end of WWI Montenegro was incorporated into Serbia.

During WWII Montenegrins fought valiantly in Tito's partisan army and afterwards the region was rewarded with republic status within Yugoslavia.

The republic has been a stalwart of all Yugoslav federations and is now in a union with Serbia that may last no longer than the 2006 referendum.

PODGORICA ПОДГОРИЦА

☎ 081 / pop 170,000

Podgorica is a place to arrive in, do your errands, and sleep elsewhere. Accommodation is very expensive. It's far better to go south and stay at the cheaper private rooms and apartments on the coast.

Orientation

The **train station** (☎ 633 663) and **bus station** (☎ 620 430) are adjacent in the eastern part of the town. The commercial hub of the town centres around Slobode and intersecting with it is Hercegovačka, the shopping/café heart of the town.

Information

Atlas Bank (☎ 407 211; Stanka Dragojeviča 4; 8am-6pm Mon-Fri, 8am-12.30pm Sat) Cashes travellers cheques.
Crnogorska Komercijalna Bank (cnr Slobode & Novaka) MasterCard ATM.
Gorbis (☎ 230 624; Slobode 47; 8am-5pm) Tourist information, organises tours and books flights and ferries.
Internet cg (☎ 248 844; Vučedolska 13; per hr €1.50; 8am-8pm Mon-Fri, 9am-2pm Sat)

Meridian (☎ 234 944, 069 316 666; Cetinjski put; 8am-2pm & 6-8pm Mon-Fri, 8am-2pm Sat) Rents cars from €30 a day.

Sleeping & Eating

There are some cheap eating places around and in the bus station, and some pleasant cafés in Hercegovačka.

Europa (☎ 623 444; shole@cg.yu; Orahovačka 16; s/d €45/90) In a city of overexpensive hotels, this modern and well-equipped hotel near the train station is a weary traveller's best option if a night in Podgorica is a necessity.

Mimi Pekara (snacks €0.50-1.25; 6am-3am) Bustling around town might make you peckish enough for a *burek* or slice of pizza at this bakery that's open almost all hours.

Buda Bar (☎ 344 944; Stanka Dragojeviča 26; sandwiches €2.50; 8am-2am) A slinky ultramodern café/bar so laid-back that the meditative golden Buddha seems completely out of it. Equally reflective customers read their newspapers or stare into their espressos searching for the eternal truth. Come evening and the mood changes to a bustling chatty meeting place.

Getting There & Away

There are eight buses daily to Belgrade (€14, nine hours), one each at 9am and 3.30pm to Žabljak (€7.50, four hours), many to Rožaje, for Kosovo (€7, four hours), and four buses to Sarajevo (€12, nine hours).

You can fly to Belgrade for €43 or take the scenic train route (€15 plus €15/8 for a three-/six-berth sleeper on overnight trains, eight hours). There are frequent trains to Bar.

The regional airline **JAT** (☎ 244 248; fax 245 065; Ivana Milutinovica 20; 8am-7pm Mon-Fri, 8.30am-2pm Sat) runs an airport transfer bus (€4, 30 minutes) leaving from its office 1½ hours before every flight and returning following each arrival. **Montenegro Airlines** (☎ 224 406; www.montenegro-airlines.cg.yu; Slobode 23; 8.30am-7pm Mon-Fri, 8.30am-2pm Sat) flies to Frankfurt, Zürich and Budapest.

Around Podgorica

VIRPAZAR & LAKE SKADAR ВИРПАЗАР & СКАДАРСКО ЈЕЗЕРО

A causeway carries both road and rail traffic from Podgorica to Bar, passing over the western edge of the 44km-long Lake Skadar. The biggest lake in the Balkans, it is also one of the largest bird sanctuaries and remaining pelican habitats in Europe. Jutting westward from the causeway is the 400-year-old Turkish castle of Lesendro. Check with **Gorbis** (☎ 230 624; Slobode 47; ☻ 8am-5pm) in Podgorica about trips on the lake and water activities.

Alternatively, nose around Virpazar, where in summer there'll be sightseeing boats. You'll also find one of Montenegro's more interesting restaurants, the **Pelican** (☎ 081-711 011; Virpazar; dishes €6-8; ☻ 8am-midnight), exotically decorated with dried plants and herbs, old photographs and nautical ephemera. The service is top-notch and dessert is on the house. For starters try *dalmatinsko varvo* (a potato, onion and spinach pie) and follow that with a fish salad of perch, eel or trout – all fresh from the lake. Weekend evenings, May to September, there's live music. The Pelican also has accommodation (doubles with shared bathroom €20).

COASTAL MONTENEGRO

Bar Бар
☎ 085 / pop 37000

Backed by a precipitous coastal range, Bar, a modern city, is Serbia and Montenegro's only port and transport hub for the coast. Far more interesting is the thousand-year-old Stari Bar (Old Bar). Whether arriving from the north or by ferry from Italy, Bar will be most people's first stop in Coastal Montenegro.

ORIENTATION & INFORMATION
The ferry terminal in Bar is 300m from the town centre; the **bus station** (☎ 314 499) and adjacent **train station** (☎ 312 210) are about 2km southeast of the centre.

There are several ATMs around town.

Komercijalna Bank (☎ 311 827; Obala Kralja Nikole bb; ☻ 8am-4pm Mon-Fri, 8am-noon Sat) Cashes travellers cheques.

Montenegro Express (☎ /fax 312 589; Obala 13 Jula bb; ☻ 8am-8pm Mon-Sat Jul & Aug, 8am-2pm Mon-Sat Sep-Jun) Books accommodation along the coast and organises tours.

Tourist Information Centar (☎ 311 633; Obala 13 Jula bb; ☻ 7am-2pm Mon-Fri Sep-Jun, 7am-8pm Jul & Aug) Limited tourist information.

SIGHTS
The impressive **Stari Bar** (admission €1; ☻ 9am-5pm Apr-Oct) lies some 4km northeast of the modern town, off the Ulcinj road. Nearly all the 240 buildings lie in ruin, a result of Montenegrin shelling when they captured the town from the Turks back in 1878. The origins go back much further, to pre-Roman times; a few buildings have been put back together and visitors can wander around the old streets.

SLEEPING & EATING
Putnik Gold (☎ 311 588; putnikgold@cg.yu; Obala 13 Jula bb; ☻ 8am-3pm Mon-Sat) Books accommodation along the coast. Private rooms without breakfast start at €9, B&B apartments from €12, half-board apartments from €17 and hotels from €30 to €100.

Montenegro Express (☎ /fax 312 589; Obala 13 Jula bb; private rooms €7-20, hotels €30-100; ☻ 8am-8pm Mon-Sat Jul & Aug, 8am-2pm Mon-Sat Sep-Jun) Another agency with similar deals.

Places to eat are limited with drinks-only cafés and bars outnumbering restaurants.

Pizeria Bell (Vladimira Rolovića bb; pizza €3, pasta €4-5; ☻ 7am-11pm) A small cosy pizza/pasta joint that's open year-round with juicy portions and efficient service.

Primorka Supermarket (☎ 312 619; Vladimira Rolovića bb; ☻ 8am-8pm) Sells all you need for a feed-yourself holiday.

GETTING THERE & AWAY
Four daily trains link Bar and Belgrade (€15 plus €15/8 for a three-/six-berth sleeper, nine hours).

Boats to Italy
Barska Plovidba (☎ 312 336; mlinesagency@cg.yu; Obala 13 Jula bb; ☻ 8am-10pm) is the agent for Montenegro Lines, which sails several times a week to Bari (Italy). For times and prices check www.montenegrolines.net.

Mecur (☎ 313 617; www.mercuradriatica.com, in Serbian; Obala 13 Jula bb; ☻ 8am-8pm Mon-Fri, 9am-2pm Sat) Books Adriatica ferries to Ancona (Italy). A Thursday service leaves at 5.30pm and arrives at 9.30am, and costs from €51/61/82 for passage only/deck seat/cabin bed.

Ulcinj Улцињ
☎ 085 / 24,000

The town of Ulcinj heads a series of fine beaches from Mala Plaža (Small Beach) below the old town to Velika Plaža (Great Beach), a famous 12km-long beach stretching eastwards towards Albania. In July and

August Ulcinj bulges with tens of thousands of holidaymakers. The Stari Grad (Old Town) is a maze of private houses intermingled with expensive restaurants exploiting the view.

Ulcinj gained notoriety as a North African pirate base and slave market between 1571 and 1878. The Turks ruled here for over 300 years, and today the town shelters many Muslim Albanians.

ORIENTATION & INFORMATION

The **bus station** (☎ 413 225) is on the edge of town. Travel into town by turning right onto 26 Novembar at the first major junction. Mala Plaža and Stari Grad are 3km below at the end of 26 Novembar. Just up from Mala Plaža is a small market area.

Velika Plaža begins about 5km southeast of the town (take the Ada bus or a minibus in season).

Euromarket Bank (☎ 422 370; 26 Novembar bb; ☼ 8.30am-3pm Mon-Fri, 8.30am-12.30pm Sat) Cashes travellers cheques, Visa ATM.

Integral Caffe (☎ 401 144; 26 Novembar bb; per hr €2.50; ☼ 9am-2pm) Internet, up an alley opposite the mosque.

SIGHTS

The ancient ramparts of old Ulcinj (Stari Grad) overlook the sea, but most of the buildings inside were shattered by earthquakes in 1979 and later reconstructed. The **museum** (☎ 421 419; Stari Grad; admission €1; ☼ 8am-2pm Mon-Fri) containing Montenegrin and Turkish artefacts is by the upper gate. You can walk among the houses and along the wall for the view.

SLEEPING

Real Estate Tourist Agency (☎ 421 612; 26 Novembar bb; ☼ 8am-9pm) Accommodation is available in private rooms (from €10, no meals), in hotels (doubles from €16, half-board) and two-/three-/four-person apartments (€27/36/43, half-board). The agency also runs tours.

Tomi camping ground (☼ May-Sep) A camping ground under the trees located east of Milena and adjacent to Velika Plaža.

HTP Velika Plaža (☎ 413 145; www.velikaplaza .cg.yu; Ada road) Further towards Ada this holiday camp has a variety of accommodation from €19 to €23 per person or €35 to €100 for an apartment, full-board.

Albatros (☎ 423 266; s/d from €22.10/34; 🏊) A pleasant rambling holiday hotel, 1km up the hill from Mala Plaža, where guests have access to a sauna, fitness room and swimming pool.

Dvori Balšiča and the adjacent **Palata Vene-cija** (☎ /fax 421 457; leart@cg.yu; Stari Grad; 2-/4-/6-person apt low season from €22/32/75, Jul & Aug €39/59/82) Steal of the Adriatic: spacious two-room apartments with kitchenette and views out over the Old City walls to the lapping sea. The stone terrace outside has waiter service for those sundowner drinks as you laze back and consider yourself 'king of the castle', as indeed the previous owners were. Breakfast/half-board/full-board is €3/8/10.

EATING & DRINKING

On the seafront is a string of restaurants specialising in seafood.

Bella Vista (☎ 067 315 266; 26 Novembar bb; dishes €4-8; ☼ 7am-late) Suitable for an early breakfast or late-night drink; the owners also have accommodation (half-board from €25).

Bazar (☎ 421 639; 26 Novembar bb; dishes €5-8; ☼ 8am-late) An upstairs restaurant that's an ideal idling place when the streets are heaving with summer tourists below. Gloat in comfort as you enjoy a plate of fried *lignje na žaru* (calamari), which is the restaurant's speciality.

Marinero (☎ 423 009; Mala Plaža; dishes €5-9; ☼ 7am-late) The owner was once a ship's cook and ships cooks don't last long unless they're good. Often seafaring mates gather here, speaking three or four languages, so for a coffee or *rakija* you'll get the history of the town and tales of the sea. Come here for a slap-up seafood meal.

Gallo Nero (☎ 315 245; 26 Novembar bb; dishes €5-12; ☼ 10am-late) For the best pizza or remarkable pasta matched by amiable service. You can come here for a snack or a full-blown meal.

Rock (26 Novembar bb; ☼ 8am-late) A wannabe Irish pub. Guinness is an occasional visitor but there are still enough alternatives to cool the heat of summer. You can listen to live music on the weekend.

GETTING THERE & AWAY

Many minibuses ply the road to Ada (and Velika Plaža) from the market place for €1.50 in season.

Budva Будва

☎ 086 / pop 11,700

Budva is the hub of the Montenegrin holiday coast. Fine beaches punctuate the coastline all the way from Budva to Sveti Stefan. Backing them is a large strip of hotels, cafés and shops that open for the July and August holiday rush.

In June the town hosts a national music festival and a summer festival in July and August.

ORIENTATION & INFORMATION

The **bus station** (☎ 456 000; Ivana Milutinovića) is about 1km from the Stari Grad (Old Town). The road called Mediteranska leads into Budva, ending at the harbour and Stari Grad.

Crnogorska Komercijalna Bank (☎ 451 075; Mediteranska 7; ☺ 8am-1pm Mon-Fri Sep-Jun, 8am-7.30pm Mon-Sat Jul & Aug) MasterCard ATM, cashes travellers cheques

Euromarket Bank (☎ 455 106; Mediteranska 4; ☺ 8.30am-2.30pm Mon-Fri, 8.30am-12.30pm Sat) Visa ATM, cashes travellers cheques.

JAT (☎ 41 641; Mediteranska 2; ☺ 8am-4pm Mon-Fri, 8am-1pm Sat) Airline office.

SIGHTS

Budva's big tourist-puller is Stari Grad, its old **walled town**. Levelled by two earthquakes in 1979, it has since been completely rebuilt as a tourist attraction with small boutique shops, restaurants, cafés and bars. It's so picturesque it seems almost contrived.

Recently renovated, the **Budva Museum** (☎ 457 994; Petra I Petrovića, Stari Grad; adult/child €1.50/0.50; ☺ 9am-7pm Mon-Fri, 11am-5pm Sat & Sun) now shows off its exhibits on three floors against a gleaming cream interior. Artefacts cover the everyday from pre-Roman to the late 1700s. The interesting feature is a dugout on the ground floor revealing the original street below.

Budva's main beach is pebbly and average. **Mogren Beach** is better: follow the coastal path southwards for 500m from the Grand Hotel Avala.

About 5km southeast of Budva is the former island fishing village of **Sveti Stefan**, now linked to the mainland. It is now a luxury hotel complex. Admission to the hotel complex is not really worth the €5 fee, so settle for the long-range picture-postcard view instead.

SLEEPING & EATING

Two options for camping are **Autocamp Avala** (☎ 451 205; ☺ Jun-Sep) at Boreti, 2km on the road to Bar and **Budva Autocamp** (tent & 2 people €4), contact JAMB.

JAMB travel (☎ 452 992; www.jamb-travel.com; Mediteranska 23; r €5.90-13.50, 2-/5-person apt €16/80, half-board/full-board €9/13; ☺ 8am-3pm Mon-Fri Nov-May, 8am-8pm Jun-Oct) Books accommodation and organises day tours around Montenegro.

Hotel Mogren (☎ 451 780; fax 452 041; Mediteranska 1; s/d €40/60 Sep-Jun, €55/84 Jul & Aug, half-board €6) The handiest best-value hotel is the elderly, privatised Mogren just outside the northern gate of Stari Grad. Rooms have been recently painted in the stock blue and white Mediterranean colours while the furniture has that student accommodation look. Generally, the best rooms are those with a view.

Budva has no shortage of expensive bars and restaurants in Stari Grad or along the harbourside.

Bus station café (Ivana Milutinovića; dishes €2-3; ☺ 7am-9pm). The best cheap eats in town in a choose-and-point cafeteria.

Restaurant Jadran (☎ 451 028; Slovenska Obala 10; dishes €5-10; ☺ 8am-late) When you want to feel special you come and dine at the Jadran, which is considered Budva's best restaurant. You can eat high with lobster at €60 a kg or eat low with a substantial soup or *čevapčići* for €2, the choice is your wallet's. Mussels Jadran are a justifiable excuse to enjoy a scintillating emulsion of oil, lemon and garlic mopped up with wads of bread and washed down with a chilled Montenegrin white wine.

Donna kod Nikole (☎ 451 531; Budva Marina; dishes €5-8; ☺ 8am-late) Another recommended harbourside restaurant for more seafood dishes.

Lazo i Milan (☎ 451 468; 13 Jul bb; dishes €4-8; ☺ 9am-11pm) Pasta dishes just like mama makes them except this mama is a burly Montenegrin chef who can cook up a storm of gastronomic delight with his sauces.

MB Ice Club (☎ 452 552; Starogradski square; treats €3-6; ☺ 9am-2am) Cool down with ice creams or cocktails to silky Cuban rhythms.

Kotor Котор

☎ 082 / pop 22,500

Picturesque Kotor with its walled town nestled at the head of southern Europe's deepest fjord has Montenegro's most dramatic setting. Stari Grad (Old Town) lies under the lee of a tall cliff while brooding mountains protect the whole bay. Cobbled laneways form a labyrinth connecting small squares with ancient churches and former aristocratic mansions.

ORIENTATION

The western flank of the funnel-shaped Stari Grad lies against Kotor Bay. An 18th-century gateway off Jadranski Put, which runs along the waterside, leads into the city, where Kotor's places of interest lie. The **bus station** (☎ 325 809) is 1km away on the Budva road.

INFORMATION

Euromarket Bank (☎ 323 946; Trg Octobarske Revolucije; ☯ 8am-8pm Mon-Fri, 8am-4pm Sat, until 8pm Sat Jun-Sep) Cashes travellers cheques, has a Visa ATM.

IDK Computers (☎ 301 046; Stari Grad; per hr €2; ☯ 2pm-midnight summer, 5pm-midnight rest of year)

Information booth (☎ 325 950; western gateway; ☯ 9am-1pm & 5-8pm Mon-Sat) Information on the town and private accommodation.

Opportunity Bank (Trg Octobarske Revolucije) MasterCard ATM.

SIGHTS

The fun is simply wandering this atmospheric town popping into the old churches, dawdling for coffee at the pavement cafés and people-watching. Energetic? Then slog up the steep winding steps to the old fortifications on the mountainside above Kotor. You'll be rewarded with stunning views of Kotor fjord (Kotorski Zaliv).

If you have transport then travel to Cetinje via the string of hairpin bends over the mountains. The views are marvellous. Alternatively, drive around the fjord and see all the little stone harbours protecting small boats against the chopping waves.

Once a Mediterranean naval power, Kotor has a proud maritime history and the **Maritime Museum** (☎ 325 646; Stari Grad; admission €1; ☯ 9am-5pm Mon-Fri, 9am-noon Sat) covers much of it over its three storeys of displays. A leaflet in English is available.

St Tryphon Cathedral was originally built in the 11th century but earthquakes have forced subsequent reconstructions. The interior is a masterpiece of Romanesque-Gothic architecture with slender columns

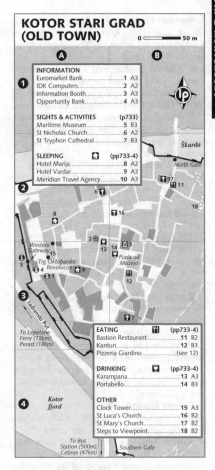

thrusting upwards to support a series of vaulted roofs. A reliquary chapel holds some of the remains of St Tryphon, the patron saint of Kotor, plus a portion of the Holy Cross.

Breathe in the smell of incense and beeswax in the plain and unadorned 1909 Orthodox **St Nicholas Church**. The silence, the iconostasis with its silver panels in bas relief, the dark wood against bare grey walls and the filtered rays of light through the upper dome create an eerie atmosphere.

SLEEPING & EATING

The **information booth** (☎ 325 950; Jadranski Put; ☯ 9am-1pm & 5-8pm Mon-Sat) has some information on private accommodation.

Meridian Travel Agency (☎ 322 968; travel@cg .yu; r €8-15, apt €30-55, s €25-44, d €41-63; ☯ 9am-2pm & 6-7pm Mon-Fri, 9am-2pm Sat) This ever-helpful agency in a small lane behind the clock tower books private and hotel accommodation in and around the city.

Hotel Vardar (☎ 325 084; Trg Octobarske Revolucije; s/d from €25/41) Overlooking the clock tower, the Vardar is the best value central hotel with large rooms. The large windows of those at the front give a stalls-view of the activity in the square.

Hotel Marija (☎ 325 062; fax 325 073; Stari Grad; s/d €45/65; ☒) A boutique hotel that's panelled everywhere in oak providing an elegant interior to match the baroque exterior. You should feel well looked after here, as former customer Austrian Emperor Franz Joseph might have testified.

The lanes house several bakeries. Munch on *burek,* pizza slices and, for an afternoon break, cherry-filled strudel, a speciality of the region.

Kantun (☎ 325 757; Pjaća od muzejo; dishes €3-6; ☯ 9am-midnight) Ignore the background techno music and this wood-beam hut with a bare stone interior could be out in the countryside and not serving up traditional Montenegrin fare in the middle of Kotor. Things to sample here are the Njegoša cheeses and the *roštiljska kobasica* (homemade sausages).

Pizzeria Giardino (☎ 323 324; Pjaća od muzejo; pizza €4-5; ☯ 9am-late) A neighbour to the Kantun and recommended for the pizza.

Bastion Restaurant (☎ 322 116; dishes €6-9; ☯ 10am-late) By St Mary's church, Bastion Restaurant is more favoured as a lunchtime venue in which case it's best to go early. Any slight indecision in ordering and the waiter will wheel in a platter of fish to tempt you and if those don't say 'eat me' there's an expansive menu with veg options to choose from. The seafood salad starter is recommended.

Kotor's cafés and bars, quiet places by day, turn werewolf on weekend nights when they throb to techno and other rhythms. Try the **Portabello** (Pjaća od muzejo; ☯ 9am-1am) or **Karampana** (☎ 051 451; ☯ 9am-late), tucked away down an unnamed side alley.

GETTING THERE & AWAY
If you are driving, the shortest way to Herceg Novi is via the ferry at Lepetane (€3.50

per car, every half hour). Otherwise, it's a 43km drive around the bay, compared with 27km via the ferry.

AROUND KOTOR
Perast is a small waterside village about 18km from Kotor. The interest here is the small island in the fjord called **Lady of the Rock**. What is remarkable is that this is an artificial island created by the locals over 550 years by taking and dropping stones on the site every 22 July. An underwater rock helped the work start and a later sinking of 87 captured ships loaded with rocks made creating the island a little easier.

St. Nicholas, in the village, is an unfinished church with a small **museum** (admission €0.50; ☯ 9am-5pm) with a collection of vestments, icons and copies of Italian religious art.

Between mid-May and mid-October boats regularly ply between the island and Perast for €1 return; just ask on the waterfront. An hourly minibus service connects with Kotor for €1.

Cetinje Цетиње
☎ 086 / pop 20,000
Nestled in a green vale surrounded by rough, grey mountains, Cetinje is an unusual mix of former capital and village where buildings range from one-storey cottages to palaces.

Much of old Cetinje still remains from when princes ruled and European ambassadors fêted the social scene from their stately mansions. Several of those buildings are now museums while Cetinje Monastery, also with a significant museum, remains the town's spiritual home.

Further afield is some astounding scenery: the panoramic view of Lake Skadar from Pavlova Strana; the old bridge at Rijeka Crnojevića; or the plummeting road down to Kotor.

Given the reliable bus service and lack of accommodation Cetinje is perhaps best tackled as a day trip from Kotor, Budva or Podgorica. It's also possible to visit as a day trip from Herceg Novi or Bar.

ORIENTATION & INFORMATION
A short walk from the bus stand leads to Balšica Pazar, the main square, with a big wall map to help you get oriented.

There are no banks here for exchanging your money, so be prepared.

SIGHTS
Museums

The most imposing building is the former parliament, now the **National Museum of Montenegro** (☎ 231 477; Novice Cerovića; admission €5; ⊗ 9am-5pm). The ticket also covers entry to the Art Gallery (housed in the same building), the Biljarda Hall and the State Museum.

The Art Gallery celebrates 19th- and 20th-century Montenegrin and regional art. The prime exhibit is the precious 5th-century Icon of Phillarmos, Madonna and Child. The History exhibits showcase Montenegro from 60,000 BC to the present day. On display are many old books, some copies of frescoes, 44 captured Turkish flags and the coat (three bullet holes in the back) of Duke Danlo, last *vladike*, who was killed in Kotor in 1860.

Opposite the National Museum, the **Biljarda Hall** (Billiard Hall; ☎ 231 050; ⊗ 9am-5pm Apr-Oct, 9am-3pm Mon-Fri Nov-Mar) was the 1832 residence of *vladike* Njegoš and is now a museum dedicated to him. The hall housed the nation's first billiard table, hence the name, and possesses a fascinating scale relief map of Montenegro created by the Austrians in 1917.

The **State Museum** (☎ 230 555; King Nikola Sq; ⊗ 9am-5pm Apr-Oct, 9am-5pm Mon-Fri Nov-Mar) was the former residence (built 1871) of Nicola Petrović I, last king of Montenegro. Although looted during WWII, sufficient furnishings, many stern portraits and period weapons remain to give a picture of the times.

Cetinje Monastery

Founded in 1484, and rebuilt in 1785, **Cetinje Monastery** (☎ 231 021; ⊗ 8am-7pm May-Oct) chapel has for the curious, or devout, a portion of the true Cross and some of the mummified right hand of St John the Baptist. Important as the hand that baptised Christ it's set in a bejewelled casket with a little glass window. With one finger in Istanbul and another in Sienna some imagination is needed to conjure it as a hand.

The monastery **museum**, only open to groups or according to your persuasive abilities, contains a copy of the 1494 *Oktoih* (Book of the Eight Voices), one of the oldest collections of liturgical songs in a Slavic language. There's also a collection of portraits, vestments, ancient hand-written texts and gifts from Russian churches.

Scenery

Some 7km along the road to Podgorica road a turning leads another 7km to Rijeka Crnojevića. This is the tail end of Lake Skadar and spanning part of it is a most unusual oldish four-arch pedestrian bridge that descends to a path through the lake. Late afternoon, golden sunlight, a mirror reflection in the water – just magic.

Another 5km on the bridge road is Pavlova Strana with a bird's-eye view of a sweeping double-back bend that the lake takes around a mountain spur. In the distance under a two-humped mountain the town of Virpazar shines above the lake.

Twenty kilometres from Cetinje is **Mt Lovćen** (1749m), the 'Black Mountain' that gave Montenegro its Italian name (*monte* is 'mountain', *negro* 'black'). Take a taxi and then climb 461 steps to the summit and the mausoleum of Petar II Petrovic Njegoš, revered poet and ruler. From the top are sweeping views of the Bay of Kotor, mountains, coast and, on a clear morning, Italy.

Herceg Novi Херцег Нови
☎ 088 / pop 30,000

Herceg Novi is another pretty walled town, a day trip from Kotor or Budva. It's also the nearest town to the Croatian border. The **bus station** (☎ 21 225) is on the main highway. The 2.15pm 'Dubrovnik' bus actually only goes to the border, needing a half-kilometre walk (hope you're not loaded with luggage) to a bus waiting at a café on the Croatia side.

The travel agency **Gorbis** (☎ 26 085; Njegoševa 64; r €5-8, s/d €25/36; ⊗ 8am-7pm) books accommodation, transfers to Dubrovnik and flight and ferry tickets. **Crnogorska Komercijalna Bank** (☎ 322 666; Trg Nikole Đurkovića; ⊗ 7am-8pm Mon-Sat) cashes travellers cheques and has a MasterCard ATM, while **Euromarket Bank** (☎ 323 523; by Njegoševa 12; ⊗ 8.30am-3pm Mon-Fri, 8.30am-12.30pm Sat) cashes travellers cheques and has a Visa ATM.

There are frequent bus services to the nearby towns of Kotor (€2.50, 1½ hours) and Budva (€3, 1¾ hours).

NORTHERN MONTENEGRO
Ostrog Острог

Some 20km south of Nikšić is the **monastery of Ostrog**, precipitously resting on a cliff face

900m above the Zeta valley floor. A long windy road off the Podgorica–Nikšić road eventually makes it to a lower car park, from where pilgrims then plod another 3km uphill to the monastery. Nonpilgrims or the pure of heart can drive to the upper car park.

The monastery was built out of two caves in 1665 when Archbishop Vasilije Jovanovic fled from the Turks in Bosnia. Vasilije is still there, or least his bones are, and are credited with curing the most serious of illnesses.

Durmitor National Park Дурмитор
☎ 089 / pop 4900

Magnificent scenery ratchets up to the awesome in this national park where ice has carved out a dramatic mountain landscape. Some 18 lakes dot the Durmitor Range with the largest, **Crno jezero** (Black Lake), walkable from Žabljak. Dominating all is the rounded mass of Međed (2287m) rearing up behind the lake and flanked by other peaks, including Bobotov Kuk (2523m).

The 1.3km-deep **Tara Canyon** that slits open the earth's crust for 80km is best seen from a rock promontory at Curevac, a €10 taxi ride away from Žabljak.

In winter (December to March) Durmitor is Montenegro's ski resort; in summer (June to September) it's a popular place for hiking, rafting and many other activities. Be prepared though, as the weather is very changeable, even in summer.

ORIENTATION & INFORMATION
Žabljak town centre is where the Nikšić road meets the Đurđevica Tara bridge road. Here there's a **tourist information centre** (☎ 61 659; town centre; ☽ 8am-8pm Dec-Mar, 8am-3pm Apr-Nov), with maps and fine picture books, a taxi stand and a bus stop. The **bus station** (☎ 61 318), on the Nikšić road, is at the southern end of town.

SLEEPING & EATING
Autocamp Ivan-do is just a fenced-off field, without facilities, uphill from the national park office.

Sveti Đorđije (☎ /fax 61 367; tasaint@cg.yu; Njegoševa bb; s/d €10/16, 2-/3-/4-person apt €26/30/39, B&B/half-board €3/9; ☽ 8am-8pm) This agency has its finger on private accommodation.

Hotel Jezera (☎ 61 103; fax 61 579; Njegoševa bb; s/ d/tr B&B €22/36/48, half-board €25/40/54; **P**) A large hotel catering to big parties of skiers and summer tourists with large rooms and a pleasant restaurant and aperitif bar.

Planinka (☎ 61 344; s/d B&B €20/36, half-board €25/46; **P**) Offers much the same as the Jezera.

All the hotels have restaurants open to nonresidents.

National Restaurant (☎ 261 337; Božidara Žugića 8; dishes €3-8; ☽ 8am-late) A pearl of a place! Small, but not crowded; a happy restaurant offering the best food around: broths and hot appetisers with slugs of domestic brandy to defeat the winter chill or grilled trout and salad in summer.

Restaurant Durmitor (☎ 637 316; Božidara Žugića bb; dishes €4-8; ☽ 7am-11pm) 'Don't hesitate to tell us if you have a complaint', says the menu, which shows a (justifiable) confidence in their food The food is special home-cooking in what is just a small wooden hut seating 20 bodies – should be warm in winter.

ACTIVITIES
In winter there's skiing, snowboarding, or having fun with a dog-drawn team. In summer there's rafting trips through the steeply forested Tara Gorge and over countless foaming rapids. There's also horse riding, hiking, cycling, mountaineering and paragliding.

Ski Centar Durmitor (☎ 61 144; www.durmitorcg .com/ski_centar.php; ☽ 8am-6pm Mon-Sat), in the Hotel Žabljak adjacent to the tourist information centre, arranges ski passes (€6.15/35.79 per day/week), ski lessons (€3.07/17.90 for one/seven lessons) and also equipment rental (€3.07/17.90 per day/week).

Rafting is a group activity but individuals can join by prior arrangement. **Sveti Đorđije** (☎ /fax 61 367; tasaint@cg.yu; Njegoševa bb; ☽ 8am-8pm) is a fount of information (English spoken) and offers two-/three-day trips for €200/250 per person including transfers, accommodation and food. An inclusive one-day trip costs €80.

Sveti Đorđije also organises summer day tours typically for six to eight people (individuals may join) at €30 each to the **Piva Monastery**, near the Bosnian border, which has remarkable frescoes.

The **Durmitor National Park office** (☎ 61 474; fax 61 346; ☽ 7am-2pm Mon-Fri), by Hotel Durmitor, has park maps and runs rafting trips for €150 for a group of 10, horse-riding tours (half/whole day €25/50) led by an English-speaking guide, and walking tours.

GETTING THERE & AWAY

There's one bus daily to Belgrade (€18, 10 hours, departs 4.30pm), several to Nikšić (€3.50, two hours) and four to Podgorica (€6, 3½ hours).

SERBIA & MONTENEGRO DIRECTORY

ACCOMMODATION

The availability of hostel accommodation has declined but contact the Youth Hostel organisation (p710) for current hotel deals. Belgrade hotels are reasonably priced for a capital city, Montenegrin hotels outside the coast and Žabljak are iniquitously expensive, and in Kosovo accommodation is scarce and pricey.

The cheapest option is private rooms (along the coast, seldom inland and not in Belgrade) organised through travel agencies. The Montenegrin coast has some summer camping grounds. 'Wild' camping would be possible outside national parks, but not in Kosovo due to the odd chance of an undiscovered mine. An overnight bus or train will always save you a night's accommodation.

The quoted accommodation prices in Montenegro are for the high season. Unless otherwise mentioned the tariff includes breakfast and rooms have private bathrooms. Places are listed in our Sleeping sections in order of ascending price.

ACTIVITIES

Serbia's main ski resorts are Zlatibor (p721) and Kopaonik (p720), while Montenegro's is Durmitor (p736). Kosovo's resort is at Brezovica (p728). The ski season is from December to March; the resorts are also popular for hiking in summer. For whitewater rafting the Tara River in Montenegro's Durmitor National Park is the most important river in the country.

BOOKS

Rebecca West's 1941 *Black Lamb & Grey Falcon* is a classic piece of travel writing but now extremely dated. Consider *The Serbs: History, Myth and the Destruction of Yugoslavia* by Tim Judah and *Balkan Babel* by Sabrina Ramet, an engaging look

at Yugoslavia from Tito to Milošević. Specifically for Kosovo read *Kosovo: A Short History* by Noel Malcolm.

BUSINESS HOURS

Banks keep long hours, often 7am to 7pm weekdays and 7am to noon Saturday. On weekdays many shops open at 7am, close noon to 4pm but reopen to 8pm. Department stores, supermarkets and some restaurants and bars are open all day. Most government offices close on Saturday; although shops stay open until 2pm many other businesses close at 3pm.

CUSTOMS

If you're bringing in more than €2000 then you have to complete a currency declaration form on arrival and show it on departure. In practice it's ignored but the reality is that if customs officials wanted to play by the rules they could confiscate your money. Play it safe and declare.

DANGERS & ANNOYANCES

Travel nearly everywhere is safe but your government travel advisories will warn against travel to Kosovo. Avoid southeastern Serbia, where Serb-Albanian tension remains. Kosovo is thought to have been cleared of landmines but there is still unexploded ordnance about, so if you are off the beaten track you will need KFOR (who are omnipresent) and local advice (try the police).

Many people are chain-smokers and give the same consideration to nonsmokers as lift farters do to their fellow passengers.

It's fine to discuss politics if you're also willing to listen.

Check with the police before photographing any official building they're guarding.

DISCOUNT CARDS

The EURO<26 discount card (www.euro26 .org.yu) can provide holders with discounts on rail travel, air travel with JAT and Montenegro Airlines, and some selected hotels.

EMBASSIES & CONSULATES
Serbian & Montenegrin Embassies & Consulates

Albania (☎ 042-23 042, 042-232-091; ambatira@icc-al .org; Skender Beg Building 8/3-II, Tirana)

Australia (☎ 02-6290 2630; yuembau@ozemail.com.au; 4 Bulwarra Close, O'Malley, ACT 2606)

Bosnia and Hercegovina (☎ 033-260 090; yugoamba@bih.net.ba; Obala Marka Dizdara 3a, Sarajevo 71000)

Bulgaria (☎ 02-946 16 35, 946 10 59; ambasada-scg-sofija@infotel.bg; Veliko Târnovo 3, Sofia 1504)

Canada (☎ 613-233 6289; www.embscg.ca/consular.html; 17 Blackburn Ave, Ottawa, Ontario, K1A 8A2)

Croatia (☎ 01-457 90 6; ambasada@ambasada-srj.hr; Pantovcak 245, Zagreb)

France (☎ 01 40 72 24 24; ambasadapariz@wanadoo.fr; 54 rue Faisanderie, 75116 Paris)

Germany (☎ 030-895 77 00; info@botschaft-smg.de; Taubert Strasse 18, Berlin D-14193)

Hungary (☎ 1-322 9838; ambjubp@mail.datanet.hu; Dozsa Gyorgy ut 92/b, Budapest H-1068)

Netherlands (☎ 070-363 23 97; yuambanl@bart.nl; Groot Hertoginnelaan 30, The Hague 2517 EG)

Romania (☎ 021-211 98 71; ambiug@ines.ro; Calea Dorobantilor 34, Bucharest)

UK (☎ 0207-235 9049; www.yugoslavembassy.org.uk; 28 Belgrave Sq, London, SW1X 8QB)

USA (☎ 202-332 0333; www.yuembusa.org; 2134 Kalorama Rd NW, Washington, DC, 20008)

Embassies & Consulates in Serbia & Montenegro

The following countries have representation in Belgrade:

Albania (Map p706; ☎ 306 6642; Bulevar Mira 25A)

Australia (Map p708; ☎ 330 3400; Čika Ljubina 13)

Bosnia and Hercegovina (Map p706; ☎ 329 1277; Milana Tankosića 8)

Bulgaria (Map p708; ☎ 361 3980; Birčaninova 26)

Canada (Map p708; ☎ 306 3000; Kneza Miloša 75)

Croatia (Map p708; ☎ 361 0535; Kneza Miloša 62)

France (Map p708; ☎ 302 3500; Pariska 11)

Germany (Map p708; ☎ 306 4300; Kneza Miloša 74-6)

Hungary (Map p708; ☎ 244 0472; Krunska 72)

Netherlands (Map p708; ☎ 361 8327; Kneza Miloša 70)

UK (Map p708; ☎ 264 5055; Resavska 46)

USA (Map p708; ☎ 361 9344; Kneza Miloša 50)

FESTIVALS & EVENTS

There's plenty of variety for all tastes. Pop, techno and electronic aficionados from all over Europe flock to Novi Sad's **Exit festival** in July, while those who like beer with their rock will want to sink a few at Belgrade's August **Beer festival**.

On a different note there's the famous festival of brass band music at Guča near Čačak in the last week of August each year. For those who want to hear something different and tap directly into an exhibition of Serbian pride and culture, this is the festival to attend.

GAY & LESBIAN TRAVELLERS

Homosexuality has been legal in Yugoslavia since 1932 (the age of consent for male-male sex is 18 in Serbia but 14 in Montenegro, female-female sex is 14 in both), but significant homophobia has meant that gay and lesbian events and meeting places are very underground. For more information check www.gay-serbia.com.

HOLIDAYS

Public holidays in Serbia and Montenegro include:

New Year 1 January
Orthodox Christmas 7 January
Nation Day 27 April
International Labour Days 1 and 2 May
Victory Day 9 May
Republic Day 29 Nov

Additionally Montenegro has Uprising Day (13 July).

Orthodox churches celebrate Easter between one and five weeks later than other churches.

In Kosovo, 28 November is Flag Day and Easter Monday is a public holiday.

INTERNET RESOURCES

Fruška Gora (www.fruskagora-natl-park.co.yu)
Montenegro Tourist Organisation (www.visit-monte negro.cg.yu)
Serbian Government (www.srbija.sr.gov.yu)
Serbian Tourist Organisation (www.serbia-tourism.org)

LANGUAGE

Serbian is the common language Serbia and Montenegro but only Albanian is spoken in Kosovo. Many people know some English and German.

Hungarians in Vojvodina use the Latin alphabet, Montenegrins and Serbs use both Latin and Cyrillic. See the language section (p912) for useful phrases and the Cyrillic alphabet.

MAPS

The Freytag & Berndt map *Yugoslavia, Slovenia, Croatia* covers the former republics of Yugoslavia. The *Savezna Republika Jugoslavija Autokarta* map shows the new borders and has some maps of towns too. *Plan Grada Beograd* is a detailed Belgrade city map. The latter two are available free from the Tourist Organisation of Belgrade (see p707). M@gic M@p's *Crna Gora* is good for navigating around Montenegro and International Travel Maps' *Kosovo* is a decent topographical map.

MONEY

Montenegro and Kosovo use the euro; Serbia retains the dinar although some hotels may want payment in euros. Some international train journeys may require part payment in dinar and part in euros. **Western Union** (www.westernunion.com) transfers can be made at most banks and major post offices. ATMs accepting Visa, MasterCard and their variants are widespread in major towns. MasterCard, Visa and Diners Club are widely accepted by businesses too. The euro is the favoured hard currency. Many exchange offices in Serbia will readily change these and other hard currencies into dinars and back again when you leave. Look for their large blue diamond signs hanging outside. Some Belgrade banks are installing 24-hour machines for changing foreign notes. A large number of banks cash hard currency travellers cheques, the euro is preferable.

POST

Parcels should be taken unsealed to the main post office for inspection. Allow time to check the post office's repacking and complete the transaction.

You can receive mail, addressed poste restante, in all towns for a small charge.

TELEPHONE & FAX

Fax

Faxes can be sent from post offices or any large hotel. In Serbia they charge 172/236/236DIN to fax per page to Europe/Australia/North America; from Kosovo €2.10/3/3. Faxes can be sent from post offices but take a photocopy as they keep the original.

Phonecards

Phonecards don't give enough time for an international call so use telephone centres at post offices.

Telephone

Press the *i* button on public phones in Serbia and Montenegro for dialling commands in English.

Serbia to Europe/Australia/North America costs 42/76/76DIN a minute.

Montenegro to Europe/Australia/North America costs €0.90/1.64/1.64 per minute

Kosovo to Europe/Australia/North America costs €0.65/1.42/1.42 per minute.

Some premises do not have landline telephones but can be contacted through mobile phones. These numbers usually start with a 06 or 04.

EMERGENCY NUMBERS

- Ambulance ☎ 94
- Fire service ☎ 93
- Motoring assistance in Belgrade ☎ 987
- Motoring assistance outside Belgrade ☎ 011 9800
- Police ☎ 92

TOURIST INFORMATION

Serbia's getting it together with their tourist offices and top marks to Belgrade, Novi Sad and Subotica. They have plenty of maps and brochures to hand out and their English-speaking staff are a fountain of useful information. Montenegro's facilities, given the tourist potential, are woeful with little literature available and offices only open for short periods of time outside the tourist season. The best bet are the travel agencies mentioned in the Montenegro section. Kosovo has a tourist office in Prishtina but its non-English-speaking staff are of little assistance and have no literature. The better bet is the travel agencies, but even their knowledge is limited.

TOURS

Ace Cycling and Mountaineering Center (☎ /fax 018-27 287; www.ace-adventurecentre.com; B. Krsmanovica 51/8 Niš) organises guided cycling and walking tours in Serbia.

VISAS

Tourist visas for less than 90 days are not required for citizens of many European countries, Australia, New Zealand, Canada and the USA. The website of the Ministry of Foreign Affairs (www.mfa.gov.yu) has details.

If you're not staying at a hotel or in a private home then you have to register with the police within 24 hours of arrival and subsequently on changing address.

WOMEN TRAVELLERS

Other than a cursory interest shown by men towards solo women travellers, travelling is hassle-free and easy. In Muslim areas a few women wear a headscarf but most young women adopt Western fashions.

Dress more conservatively than usual in Muslim areas of Kosovo.

TRANSPORT IN SERBIA & MONTENEGRO

GETTING THERE & AWAY
Air

Serbia and Montenegro is well served by regional airlines that pick up at intercontinental hubs. Travellers from Australasia can fly to Dubai and pick up a JAT flight to Belgrade or fly with Lufthansa via Frankfurt or Austrian Air via Vienna. Travellers from North America would pick up regional connecting flights in London or Frankfurt. As of yet none of the European discount airlines fly to or near Belgrade.

Belgrade's **Surcin Airport** (☎ 601 424, 601 431; www.airport-belgrade.co.yu) handles the majority of international flights. Office telephone numbers are in Belgrade (area code ☎ 011).

Aeroflot (code SU; ☎ 3235 814; www.aeroflot.com)

Air France (code AF; ☎ 638 378; www.airfrance.com)

Air India (code AI; ☎ 133 551; www.airindia.com)

Alitalia (code AZ; ☎ 3245 344; www.alitalia.com)

Austrian Airlines (code OS; ☎ 3248 077; www.aua.com)

Balkan (code LZ; ☎ 322 4230; www.balkan.com/menu2.htm)

British Airways (code BA; ☎ 3281 303; www.british airways.com)

ČSA (Czech Airlines; code OK; ☎ 3614 592; www.csa.cz)

Emirates (code EK; ☎ 624 435; www.ekgroup.com)

JAT (code JU; ☎ 3024 077; www.jat.com)

KLM (code KL; ☎ 3282 747; www.klm.com)

LOT Polish Airlines (code LOT; ☎ 3248 892; www.lot.com)

Lufthansa (code LH; ☎ 3224 975; www.lufthansa.com)

Macedonian Airlines (MAT; code IN; ☎ 187 123; www.mat.com.mk)

Malév (Hungarian Airlines; code MA; ☎ 626 377; www.malev.hu)

Montenegro Airlines (code YM; ☎ 262 1122; www.montenegro-airlines.com)

Olympic Airways (code OA; ☎ 3226 800; www.olympic-airways.gr)

Royal Jordanian (code RJ; ☎ 645 555; www.rja.com.jo)

Swiss International Air Lines (code LX; ☎ 3030 140; www.swiss.com)

Turkish Airlines (code TK; ☎ 3232 561; www.turkish airlines.com)

AIRLINES SERVING PODGORICA & TIVAT IN MONTENEGRO

Charter and other airlines fly into **Podgorica** (☎ 081-242912) and **Tivat** (☎ 082-671894) airports in Montenegro. Office telephone numbers are in Podgorica (area code ☎ 081).

Adria Airlines (code JP; ☎ 310 000; www.adria-airways.com)

JAT (code JU; ☎ 230 027; www.jat.com)

Malév (Hungarian Airlines; code MA; www.malev.hu)

Montenegro Airlines (code YM; ☎ 224 406; www.montenegro-airlines.cg.yu)

AIRLINES SERVING PRISHTINA IN KOSOVO

Kosovo's airport is at **Prishtina** (☎ 548 430). Office telephone numbers are in Prishtina (area code ☎ 038).

Adria Airways (code JP; ☎ 548 437; www.adria-airways.com)

Austrian Airlines (code OS; ☎ 548 661; www.aua.com)

British Airways (code BA; ☎ 548 661; www.britishair ways.com)

Kosova Airlines (code KOS; ☎ 249 158; www.kosova airlines.com)

Malév (Hungarian Airlines; code MA; ☎ 535 535; www.malev.hu)

Turkish Airlines (code TK; ☎ 502 052; www.turkishair lines.com)

DEPARTURE TAX

Departure tax for domestic/international flights is 500/1000DIN, although this may be covered in the price of your ticket.

Land
BICYCLE

No problems bringing a bicycle but remember it's a hilly country. There are not many cyclists so road-users are not cycle savvy.

BORDER CROSSINGS

You can easily enter Serbia or Montenegro by land from any of their neighbours. Decent maps of the region such as the Freytag & Berndt map (see p]) and the National

Tourist Organisation of Serbia brochure *In Serbia by Car* show borders.

Crossing from Montenegro to Croatia by bus involves a change of buses at the border.

Kosovo can be entered from Serbia via Novi Pazar, Montenegro via Rožaje, and from Macedonia and Albania; see the boxed text (p724).

BUS
There's a well-developed bus service to Western Europe and Turkey. Contact any of the travel agencies mentioned in this chapter. Sample routes from Belgrade are Malmo in Sweden (€103, 34 hours, Friday), Munich (€55, 17 hours, daily), Paris (€97, 28 hours, Monday, Tuesday, Thursday and Friday) and Zurich (€87, 23 hours, Saturday).

CAR & MOTORCYCLE
Drivers need an International Driving Permit and vehicles need Green Card insurance, otherwise insurance (from €80 a month) must be bought at the border. See also p741.

TRAIN
All international rail connections out of Serbia originate in Belgrade with most calling at Novi Sad and Subotica heading north and west, and at Niš going east. Montenegro and Kosovo have no international connections. Curiously, tickets for international trains have to be paid for in euros, but sleeper supplements have to be paid for in DIN. Sample services from Belgrade are:

Destination	Frequency	Duration	Cost	Sleeper
Bucharest	daily	14hr	€27	680DIN
Budapest	daily	7hr	€37	980DIN
Istanbul	daily	26hr	€44	360*DIN
Ljubljana	daily	10hr	€28	810DIN
Moscow	daily	50hr	€125	1520DIN
Munich	daily	17hr	€87	870DIN
Sofia	daily	11hr	€12	360DIN
Thessaloniki	daily	16hr	€30	680DIN
Vienna	daily	11hr	€65	980DIN
Zagreb	daily	7hr	€18	870DIN

* to Thessaloniki only

Sea
A ferry service operates between Bar and Italy (see p730).

GETTING AROUND
Air
AIRLINES IN SERBIA & MONTENEGRO
JAT and Montenegro Airlines fly daily between Belgrade and Podgorica or Tivat. For their Belgrade and Podgorica details see p740.

Bicycle
Cyclists are rare on the country's roads, even in the cities, and there are no special provisions. For cycling tours see (p739).

Bus
The bus service is extensive and reliable and covers all of Serbia and Montenegro and Kosovo. Buses are rarely full and there's usually a row available for everyone; luggage carried below is charged at 50DIN/€0.50 per piece.

RESERVATIONS
Reservations are really only worth considering for international buses, at holiday times and on long-distance journeys with infrequent services.

Car & Motorcycle
Independent travel by car or motorcycle is an ideal way to gad about and discover the country.

Traffic police are everywhere so drive carefully and stick to speed limits: 120km/h on motorways, 100km/h on dual carriageways, 80km/h on main roads, and 60km/h in urban areas.

AUTOMOBILE ASSOCIATIONS
The **Auto-Moto Savez Serbia and Montenegro** (Serbia and Montenegro Automotive Association; Map p706; ☎ 011 9800; www.amsj.co.yu; Ruzveltova 18, Belgrade) web page has details on road conditions, tolls, insurance and petrol prices.

DRIVING LICENCE
You'll need an International Driving Permit available from your home country motoring organisation.

FUEL & SPARE PARTS
Filling up is no problem in any medium-sized town but don't leave it until the last drop as there are few late-night petrol stations. Spare parts for major brands (check with your dealer before you travel) will be

SERBIA & MONTENEGRO

no problem in the cities and mechanics are available everywhere for simple repairs.

HIRE

There are plenty of hire companies; **VIP** (☎ 690 107), **Hertz** (☎ 600 634) and **Europcar** (☎ 601 555) all have offices at Belgrade airport. The typical cost of small-car hire in Serbia is €45 a day.

Car hire is cheaper in Montenegro with a small car costing from €30 a day from **Meridian Rent a Car** (☎ 081-234 944; 069 316 66) in Podgorica, Budva and Bar.

ROAD RULES

Serbia and Montenegro has right-hand drive, seat belts must be worn and the drink-driving limit is .05.

Hitching

Locals occasionally hitch and if you decide to do so exercise much caution and present yourself where a vehicle can easily and safely stop.

Train

Jugoslovenske Železnice (JŽ; www.yurail.co.yu, in Serbian) provides adequate railway services from Belgrade serving Novi Sad, Subotica and the highly scenic line down to Bar; the website gives timetable details. Trains are slower than buses due to lack of infrastructure investment.

Different classes of train travel require different tickets, so when you buy, state the service you'll use.

No trains run in Kosovo at present.

Slovakia

Highlights	745
Itineraries	745
Climate & When to Go	745
History	745
People	747
Sport	747
Religion	747
Arts	747
Environment	748
Food & Drink	748
Bratislava	**749**
History	749
Orientation	751
Information	751
Sights & Activities	752
Festivals & Events	754
Sleeping	755
Eating	755
Drinking	756
Entertainment	756
Shopping	757
Getting There & Away	757
Getting Around	757
Around Bratislava	758
West Slovakia	**758**
Trenčín	758
Central Slovakia	**760**
Žilina	760
Malá Fatra National Park	761
East Slovakia	**763**
Vysoké Tatry	763
Poprad	768
Kežmarok	769
Dunajec Gorge	770
Slovenský Raj	771
Levoča	772
Spišské Podhradie	775
Bardejov	775
Košice	777
Slovakia Directory	**781**
Accommodation	781
Activities	781
Business Hours	781
Dangers & Annoyances	781
Disabled Travellers	781
Embassies & Consulates	782
Festivals & Events	782
Holidays	782
Internet Resources	782
Money	782
Post	782
Telephone	783
Tourist Information	783
Visas	783
Transport in Slovakia	**783**
Getting There & Away	783
Getting Around	783

Whimsical folk music and rickety horse-drawn carts, snow-clad summits and Stalinist sky-scraping suburbs, the clichéd images of this quiet corner of Middle Europe have long placed Slovakia in an incongruous hinterland between Soviet Moscow and the rural idyll of picture-book fairy tale.

And at the beginning of the 21st century, Slovakia's personality appears to be splitting still further. Joining the EU club in May 2004, and with a calorific slice of boom-time economic pie now within grasp, Bratislava, at least, is emerging from its frumpy, communist-era chrysalis to take on the trappings of a booming free market. Cappuccino bars and fast cars are just the tip of the iceberg.

Slovakia remains a nation of two halves. While the free market beams some Slovakians into a world of fickle fashion and status symbols, many others, most notably the Roma, continue to live a life that has remained unchanged for decades, keeping alive the vibrant folk traditions that might otherwise have vanished.

And therein lies Slovakia's appeal. Beyond the highlife and nightlife of the big cities, this is a country of towering mountains and thick forests, a land where history is lived, rather than just remembered.

FAST FACTS

- **Area** 49,035 sq km
- **Capital** Bratislava
- **Currency** Koruna (Sk); €1 = 40Sk; US$1 = 31Sk; UK£1 = 58Sk; A$1 = 23Sk; ¥100 = 29Sk; NZ$1 = 22Sk
- **Famous for** ice hockey, hiking, folk culture, Roma
- **Key Phrases** Ahoj (hello), Dovidenia (Goodbye), D'akujem (Thank you), Nevyzním sa tu (I'm lost)
- **Official Language** Slovak
- **Population** 5.4 million
- **Telephone Codes** country code ☎ + 421; international access code ☎ 00
- **Visas** Citizens of the EU, US, Canada, Australia, New Zealand and Japan can enter Slovakia without a visa. South Africans must arrange a visa before they leave home. See the Slovakia Directory (p783) for more details.

HIGHLIGHTS

- Conquer the looming peaks and photogenic valleys of the magnificent **Vysoké Tatry (High Tatra)** (p763)
- Sip a coffee in the old town, before going wild at an ice hockey game in vibrant **Bratislava** (p749)
- Amble through **Levoča** (p772), a sleepy step back into old Slovakia
- From picturesque **Devín Castle** (p758) to ghostly **Spišský hrad** (p775), delve into Slovakia's grandiose Stone Age and explore some of the region's finest forts
- Hightail it off the map and lose yourself in the stunning landscapes of the **Slovenský raj** (p771)

ITINERARIES

- **One week** Explore the historic squares and bustling bars of Bratislava, before heading east through Trenčín and up into the mighty Vysoké Tatry. Spend a couple of days hiking, before coming down in sleepy Levoča and enjoying a final fling in Košice.
- **Two weeks** Bolt on a couple of days among the stunning vistas of Malá Fatra and the Slovenský raj, get off the beaten track in beautiful Bardejov and soak up the history surrounding Spišské Podhradie.

CLIMATE & WHEN TO GO

With hot summers and icy winters, Slovakia's climate fluctuates between extremes, with spring and autumn offering a mixed bag of sun and drizzle.

Locals take their holidays in July and August, when the mountain areas like the Tatras and Malá Fatra are at their most crowded, but cities like Bratislava have lower hotel prices and cheap student dorm beds available. The accommodation options in the mountain resorts are cheapest from May to June and again from September to October, and these are generally the best times to visit.

HISTORY

In many ways, Slovakia started the 21st century full of confidence. After centuries in the closet, it now has its name on the registers of many of the world's major clubs, joining NATO in March 2004 and the European Union two months later.

It has been a long journey. First occupied by Slavic tribes in the hazy days of

---

HOW MUCH?

- **Night in hostel** 300Sk
- **Double room in pension** 1000Sk
- **Day's ski hire** 300Sk
- **Pair of hiking boots** 1800Sk
- **Postcard** 6Sk

LONELY PLANET INDEX

- **Litre of petrol** 37Sk
- **Litre of bottled water** 40Sk
- **A beer** 30Sk
- **Souvenir T-shirt** 250Sk
- **Street snack – hot dog** 20Sk

---

the 5th century, Slovakia was soon caught up in centuries of European power play. In the early 16th century, the Hungarians moved their capital to Bratislava and instigated a policy of 'Magyarisation' (Hungarian assimilation). To counter this, Slovak intellectuals cultivated ties with the Czechs and after WWI, took their nation into the united Czechoslovakia.

But Slovaks wearied of Czech political domination and the day before Hitler's troops invaded Czech territory in March 1939, a fascist puppet state was set up as a German ally. It was not, however, a populist move and in August 1944 Slovak partisans instigated the Slovak National Uprising (*Slovenské Národné Povstanie,* or SNP), a source of ongoing national pride.

After the communist takeover in 1948, power was again centralised in Prague and resistance was ruthlessly eliminated.

In 1989, however, the Velvet Revolution brought down the curtains on the communist regime. The 1992 elections brought to power the nationalist Movement for a Democratic Slovakia (HZDS), headed by Vladimír Mečiar. In July the Slovak parliament voted to declare sovereignty, and the federation dissolved peacefully on 1 January 1993.

Mečiar's reign, however, was characterised by antidemocratic laws and discrimination, with as many as 4000 civil servants being fired for 'liberal' views. The international community quickly turned on the regime and with their nation fast becoming a

SLOVAKIA

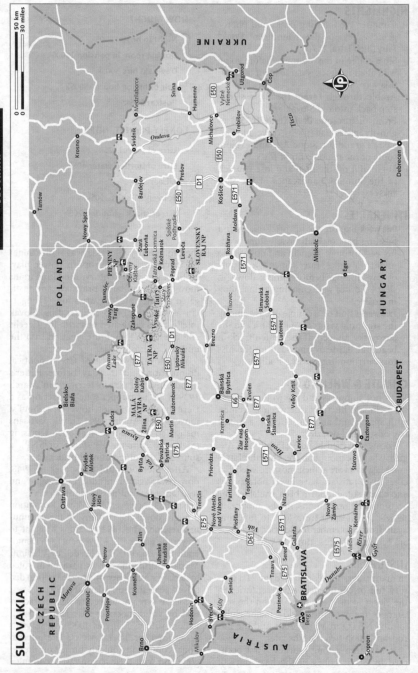

European pariah, so too did the Slovak people, ousting Mečiar in the 1998 elections.

Reforms have brought Slovakia back into the international fold. But opinion remains starkly divided and two weeks before the country took its place at the EU table, a former Mečiar lackey, Ivan Gasparovic, was elected president. Gasparovic has since distanced himself from Mečiar, but the political future of the country still hangs in the balance and the plight of Slovakia's Roma minority is a source of ongoing concern.

PEOPLE

Religious, conservative and proud, many Slovakians have a strong sense of identity and a seemingly insatiable appetite for folk culture. True to the stereotypes, some may find older Slovakians standoffish on first meeting, but the country is fast shedding its reputation for surliness and most Slovaks are hospitable.

For many Slovaks, weekends are best spent in the great outdoors, soaking up the country's fabulous scenery. Wherever you go, you will doubtless run into a backpack-toting Slovak wandering idly through the wilderness.

Slovakia's population of 5,395,000 is 86% Slovak, 10% Hungarian and 1% Czech. There are also as many as 400,000 Roma in Slovakia and, despite EU accession, many still exist as second-class citizens, with living standards and rates of employment well below the national average.

SPORT

Three things dominate Slovakian sport: ice hockey, ice hockey and ice hockey. Wander into any bar during puck-pushing season (September to April) and 12 large men and an ice rink will never be far from the TV screen. And it is no surprise that the Slovaks indulge their obsession so passionately. The national team scooped second place in the 2000 world championship, stole the title in 2002 and brought home bronze in 2003.

Football fills the summer months, and while the Slovaks have yet to attain the dizzy heights the Czechs sometimes aspire to, their club game is a reliable source of red-blooded terrace bravado. SK Slovan Bratislava is the nation's most successful team – just be careful where you sport their colours.

Check out www.sportslovakia.sk for a roll call of Slovakia's sporting achievements.

RELIGION

Slovakia's first Christian church was founded in Nitra in AD 833 and things have been on the up ever since. Today, 84.1% of the population consider themselves religiously affiliated. Roman Catholics form the majority, but Evangelicals are also numerous; East Slovakia has many Greek Catholics and Orthodox believers.

ARTS

Thankfully, 21st-century Slovakia is as passionate about folk culture as it ever was. Some city dwellers may have been put off by the clichéd image of the Communist-era 'happy peasant', but get out into the countryside and traditional arts are an integral part of community life, pervading everything from music to architecture.

Architecture & Visual Arts

Slovakia has more than its fair share of grandiose artistic and architectural icons. Magnificent religious frescoes decorate the Church of St James in Levoča (p772) and the Cathedral of St Elizabeth in Košice (p779), while the brutal architecture of the communist epoch, as evocative as it is ugly, still holds sway over many of Slovakia's towns and cities. Historic towns like Levoča are also peppered with beautifully restored Renaissance buildings.

Cinema

Slovak cinema first made its mark as part of the Czechoslovak New Wave of the 1960s, with classic films like *Smrt si rika Engelchen* (Death Calls Itself Engelchen; 1963) directed by Ján Kádar and *Obchod na korze* (The Shop on the Main Street; 1965) by Elmar Klos. The Czechoslovak film industry stagnated after the 1968 Soviet invasion, and lack of funding has meant that little serious movie-making has been done since 1993. Recently, Martin Sulík has been one of Slovakia's most promising new directors, winning an Oscar nomination for *Všetko, čo mám rád* (Everything I Like, 1992), and receiving international acclaim for *Záhrada* (The Garden; 1995) and *Krajinka* (The Landscape; 2000).

Music

Traditional Slovak folk instruments include the *fujara* (a 2m-long flute), the *gajdy* (bagpipes) and the *konkovka* (a strident shepherd's flute). Folk songs helped preserve the Slovak language during Hungarian rule, and in East Slovakia ancient musical folk traditions are an integral part of village life.

In classical music, the 19th-century works of Ján L Bela and the symphonies of Alexander Moyzes receive world recognition. Slovakia's contemporary music scene is small, but vibrant. Names to look out for on the rock and pop scene include No Name, Peha and Jana Kirschner.

ENVIRONMENT
The Land

Slovakia sits in the heart of Europe, straddling the northwestern end of the Carpathian Mountains. This hilly 49,035 sq km country forms a clear physical barrier between the plains of Poland and Hungary. Almost 80% of Slovakia is more than 750m above sea level, and forests, mainly beech and spruce, cover 40% of the country.

Southwestern Slovakia is a fertile lowland stretching from the foothills of the Carpathians down to the Danube River, which forms the border with Hungary from Bratislava to Štúrovo.

Central Slovakia is dominated by the Vysoké Tatry (High Tatra) mountains along the Polish border, Gerlachovský štít (2654m), the highest peak in the Carpathians, and the forested ridges of the Nízke Tatry, the Malá Fatra and the Veľká Fatra. South are the limestone ridges and caves of Slovenský raj and Slovenský kras. The longest river, the Váh, rises in the Tatras and flows 390km west and south to join the Danube at Komárno.

Wildlife & National Parks

Slovakia's national parks contain bears, marmots, wolves, lynxes, chamois, mink and otters. Deer, pheasants, partridges, ducks, wild geese, storks, eagles, grouse and other birds of prey can be seen across the country.

National parks and protected areas make up 20% of Slovakia. The parks surrounding the Vysoké Tatry, Slovenský raj and Malá Fatra regions should not be missed.

Environmental Issues

Slovakia is a mixed bag in environmental terms. No doubt due to most Slovaks' penchant for all things outdoorsy, large swathes of the countryside are passionately protected, offering up some of the most pristine landscapes in Eastern Europe. On the other hand, the country also seems to have more than its fair share of grimy, industrial cityscapes and big centres such as Bratislava and Košice do suffer from air pollution.

The Gabčíkovo hydroelectric project, on the Danube west of Komárno, has long been an environmental hot potato. Although it produces enough power to cover the needs of every home in Slovakia, some believe it exacerbated the damage caused by the 2002 floods and many fear it might do so again.

For more information on Slovakia's environment, check out the Slovak Environmental Agency's website at www.sazp.sk.

Responsible Travel

Tens of thousands of hikers pass through Slovakia's parks and protected areas every year – try to do your bit to keep them pristine. Wherever possible, carry out your rubbish, avoid using detergents or toothpaste in or near watercourses, stick to established trails (this helps prevent erosion), cook on a kerosene stove rather than an open fire and do not engage in or encourage – by purchasing goods made from endangered species – hunting.

FOOD & DRINK
Staples & Specialities

The Slovak for menu is *jedálny lístok*. The main categories are *predjedlá* (starters), *polievky* (soups), *hotová jedlá* (ready-to-serve dishes), *jedlá na objednávku* (dishes prepared as they are ordered), *mäsité jedlá* (meat dishes), *ryby* (fish), *zelenina* (vegetables), *šaláty* (salads), *ovoce* (fruit), *zákusok* (dessert) and *nápoje* (drinks). Anything that comes with *knedle* (dumplings) will be a hearty meal.

Soups include *cesnaková polievka* (garlic soup), a treat that is not to be missed. Slovakia's traditional dish is *bryndžové halušky* (dumplings baked with sheep's-milk cheese and bits of bacon).

Meat dishes come with potatoes – either boiled, fried or as chips. Goulash or *segedín* (also known as *koložárska kapusta* – a beef goulash with sauerkraut in cream sauce) comes with *knedle*. *Kapor* (carp) or *pstruh* (trout) can be crumbed and fried or baked.

Ovocné knedle or *guľky* (fruit dumplings), with whole fruit inside, come with cottage cheese or crushed poppy seeds, as well as melted butter.

Drinks

Slovak wine is good and cheap. Well-known brands include Tokaj from southern Slovakia, and Kláštorné (a red) and Venušíno čáro (a white), both from the Modra region north of Bratislava.

Slovak *pivo* (beer) is as good as the Czech stuff – try Zlatý Bažant from Hurbanovo or Martiner from Martin.

Coffee is sometimes served Turkish-style (*turecká káva*) with sludgy grounds in the cup. For ordinary black/white coffee order *espresso/espresso s mliekom*. Tea (*čaj*) can be enjoyed in a tearoom (*čajovná*).

Where to Eat & Drink

The staple eateries are the self-service restaurants called *jedáleň* or *bistro,* which sometimes have tasty dishes like barbecued chicken or hot German-style sausage. Train station buffets and busy beer halls are also popular. If the place is crowded with locals, is noisy and looks chaotic, chances are it will have great lunch specials at low prices.

Lunches are generally bigger and cheaper than dinners. Dinner is usually eaten early, between 6pm and 7pm. Don't expect to be served at any restaurant if you arrive within half an hour of closing time.

Cafés (*kaviáreň* or *cukráreň*) offer cakes, puddings and coffee as good as anything you'll find in neighbouring Austria at a fraction of the price.

Slowly but surely, all manner of world cuisine is finding a foothold in Slovakia. Most of the new openings, representing everything from Fusion to French, are in Bratislava, but most towns now at least offer a pizzeria and a Chinese takeaway.

Vegetarians & Vegans

Vegetarians are catered for at a small but increasing number of restaurants and health-food shops, although in small towns you might be restricted to salads and *vysmážaný syr* (deep-fried cheese). Note that many of the innocent-looking vegetable-based soups may use a ham or beef stock, and dishes advertised as vegetarian (*bezmasa*) may actually contain meat!

Habits & Customs

It is not compulsory to tip. If you were happy with the service, feel free to round up the bill to the next 5Sk (or to the next 10Sk if the bill is over 100Sk).

BRATISLAVA

☎ 02 / pop 442,288

Slovakia has had a roller coaster ride through history and the capital still rings with the echoes of the highs and lows. Bratislava's small old town harks back to the stately days of imperial grandeur, gigantic suburban housing projects stand like tombstones to the faceless days of communist-era oppression and the centre fizzes with the eurochic trimmings that have come in the wake of EU accession and a growing sense of economic confidence.

First impressions, however, are likely to be rather more one-dimensional. On a rainy day, new arrivals are confronted with a grey, imposing city, where functionality is the buzzword and where Slovakia's vibrant, traditional culture appears to be on the back foot.

But that is not the whole picture. Focused on the city's meagre, but beautiful, historic centre, Bratislava is a youthful city, bursting with big ideas and fresh optimism. Bars and restaurants are popping up across town and the city plays host to most of the country's best museums and galleries. In fact, for travellers tired of ogling the sights of Budapest and Prague, down-to-earth Bratislava, roughly halfway between the two and largely devoid of tourists, offers an ideal (and cheapish) reality check.

HISTORY

Founded in AD 907, Bratislava was already a large city in the 12th century. Commerce developed in the 14th and 15th centuries, and in 1467 the Hungarian Renaissance monarch Matthias Corvinus founded a university here, the Academia Istropolitana. The city became Hungary's capital in 1541, after the Turks captured Buda, and remained so from 1563 to 1830. In St Martin's Cathedral 11 Hungarian kings and seven queens were crowned. Bratislava flourished during the reign of Maria Teresa of Austria (1740–80), when some imposing

BRATISLAVA

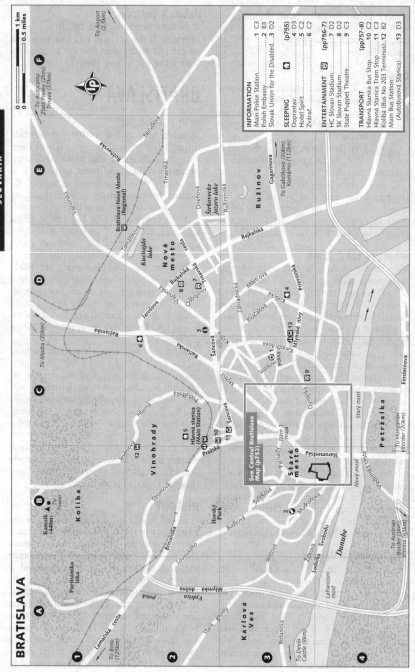

SLOVAKIA

See Central Bratislava Map (p752)

INFORMATION
Main Police Station.................1 C3
Polish Embassy......................2 B3
Slovak Union for the Disabled......3 D2

SLEEPING (p755)
Dopravstav............................4 D3
Hotel Spirit..........................5 C2
Zvárač................................6 C2

ENTERTAINMENT (pp756-7)
HC Slovan Stadium....................7 D2
SK Slovan Stadium....................8 D2
State Puppet Theatre.................9 C3

TRANSPORT (pp757-8)
Hlavná Stanica Bus Stop.............10 C2
Hlavná Stanica Tram Stop............11 C3
Koliba (Bus No 203 Terminus)........12 B2
Main Bus Station
(Autobusová Stanica)..............13 D3

baroque palaces were built. In 1918 the city was included in the newly formed Republic of Czechoslovakia, in 1969 it became the state capital of a federal Slovak Republic, and in 1993 it was named the capital of an independent Slovakia.

ORIENTATION

Hviezdoslavovo nám is a convenient reference point, with the old town to the north, the Danube to the south, the Slovak National Theatre to the east and Bratislava Castle situated to the west.

Bratislava's main train station, Hlavná stanica, is located several kilometres north of the centre. Tram No 1 runs from the station to nám L Štúra, just south of Hviezdoslavovo nám. For the sake of convenience, námesti has been shortened to nám throughout this chapter.

The main bus station (autobusová stanica) is on Mlynské nivy, a little over 1km east of the old town. Bus No 210 shuttles between the bus station and the main train station.

INFORMATION
Bookshops

Interpress (Map pp752-3; Sedlárska 2; www.interpress.sk; ❧ 7am-10pm Mon-Fri, 9am-10pm Sat, 10am-10pm Sun) For an excellent range of foreign newspapers and magazines.

Svet Knihy (Map pp752-3; ☎ 54 64 88 37; Obchodná 4; ❧ 9am-7pm Mon-Fri, to 5pm Sat) Has English-language titles on the 1st floor.

Cultural Centres

British Council (Map pp752-3; ☎ 54 43 10 74; www .britishcouncil.sk; Panská 17; ❧ 1-5pm Mon-Fri)

Emergency

Main police station (Polícia; Map p750; ☎ 0961-01 11 11; Sasinkova 23)

Internet Access

Internet Centrum (Map pp752-3; ☎ 0905-95 72 07; cnr Michalská & Sedlárska; per min 2Sk; ❧ 9am-midnight) Has discounted rates (per min 1Sk) from 9am to 10am and 9pm to midnight.

Megalnet (Map pp752-3; ☎ 54 43 55 67; Klariská 4; per min 1Sk; ❧ 9am-10pm Mon-Fri, from 2pm Sat & Sun)

Left Luggage

Left-luggage office (Map p750; main bus station; ❧ 5.30am-10pm Mon-Fri, with 2 30-min breaks, 6am-6pm Sat & Sun)

> ### BRATISLAVA IN TWO DAYS
>
> Start by soaking up the morning views from the ramparts of **Bratislava Castle** (p752), before wandering through the **Historical Museum** (p752), exploring the **Museum of Jewish Culture** (p753) and taking a lazy lunch at **Modrá hviezda** (p756). Spend the afternoon strolling through the **old town** (p752) before catching an **ice hockey game** (p756) come nightfall. The following day, head out of town to **Devín Castle** (p758), before making a beeline back into Bratislava in time for an opera at the **Slovak National Theatre** (p757).

Left-luggage office (Map p750; main train station; ❧ 6.30am-11pm)

Medical Services

24-hour Pharmacy (Map pp752-3; ☎ 54 43 29 52; nám SNP 20)

Poliklinika (Map pp752-3; ☎ 52 96 24 61; Bezručova 8) Offers a wide range of medical services.

Money

There are banks with ATMs and exchange facilities across town, including an **exchange office** (❧ 7.30am-6pm) and ATM at the main train station near the Bratislava Culture & Information Service desk.

Agentura Alex (Map pp752-3; ☎ 54 41 40 20; Kuzmányho 8; ❧ 8.30am-5pm Mon-Fri) The local Amex agent.

Istrobanka (Map pp752-3; cnr Laurinská & Rybárska; ❧ 8.30am-4.30pm Mon-Fri)

Post

Main post office (Map pp752-3; nám SNP 34; ❧ 7am-8pm Mon-Fri, to 2pm Sat) Mail addressed c/o poste restante, 81000 Bratislava 1, can be collected at window No 6. To mail a parcel, go to the office marked 'podaj a výdaj balíkov', through the next entrance, at nám SNP 35.

Tourist Information

Bratislava Culture & Information Centre (Map pp752-3; ☎ 54 43 37 15; www.bratislava.sk; Klobučnícka 2; ❧ 8.30am-7pm Mon-Fri, 10am-5pm Sat & Sun Jun-Sep, 8.30am-6pm Mon-Fri, 9am-2pm Sat Oct-May) The main tourist office.

Bratislava Culture & Information Service (Map pp752-3; ☎ 52 49 59 06; Hlavná stanica; ❧ 7.30am-7pm Mon-Fri, 7.30am-2.30pm Sat & Sun Jun-Sep,

8am-6pm Mon-Fri, 9am-2pm Sat Oct–May) A smaller outlet at the main train station.

Travel Agencies

Tatratour (Map pp752-3; ☎ 52 92 78 88; www .tatratour.sk, in Slovak; Mickiewiczova 2; ☒ 8am-6pm Mon-Fri) Books international air, bus and train tickets, accommodation and tours.

SIGHTS & ACTIVITIES

Perched on a hill overlooking the old town, boxy **Bratislava Castle** (Map pp752-3; Bratislavský hrad; admission free; ☒ 9am-8pm Apr-Sep, to 6pm Oct-Mar) is typically (for Bratislava) unostentatious. From the 1st to the 5th centuries, it was a frontier post of the Roman Empire and has been rebuilt several times since the 9th century; it was the seat of Hungarian royalty until it burnt down in 1811. It now offers sweeping views from its ramparts and houses the interesting **Historical Museum** (Historické Múzeum; Map pp752-3; ☎ 59 34 16 26; adult/concession 60/30Sk; ☒ 9am-5pm Tue-Sun), which incorporates the inevitable ice hockey hall of fame, as well as a plethora of fine art, furniture and historical exhibits. Music junkies should then head to the quirky **Museum of Folk Music** (Hudobné Múzeum; ☎ 54 41 33 49; adult/concession 20/10Sk; ☒ 9am-5pm Tue-Sun), at the north end of the castle complex.

The **Slovak National Parliament** meets in the modern complex that overlooks the river just beyond the castle.

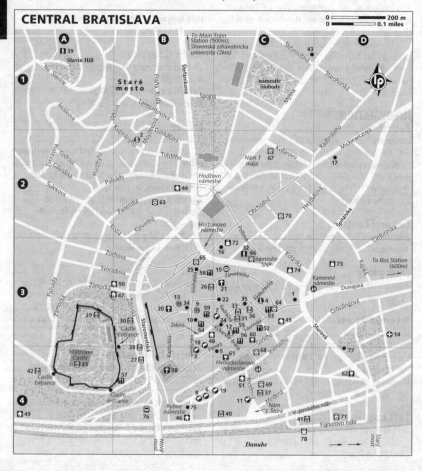

CENTRAL BRATISLAVA

Running along the base of the castle, Židovská houses more excellent museums, including the **Museum of Arts & Crafts** (Expozícia Umeleckých Remesiel; Map pp752-3; ☎ 54 41 27 84; Beblavého 1; adult/concession 50/20Sk; 🕙 10am-5pm Tue-Sun), the **Museum of Jewish Culture** (Múzeum Židovskej Kultúry; Map pp752-3; ☎ 54 41 85 07; Židovská 17; adult/concession 50/20Sk; 🕙 11am-5pm Sun-Fri), providing a fascinating insight into one of the city's smaller communities, and the vital (for the time-conscious) **Museum of Clocks** (Expozícia Historických Hodín; Map pp752-3; ☎ 54 41 19 40; Židovská 1; adult/concession 50/20Sk; 🕙 10am-5pm Tue-Sun).

Back in town, on the riverfront, the **Slovak National Gallery** (Slovenská Národná Galéria; Map pp752-3; ☎ 54 43 20 81; Rázusovo nábrežie 2; adult/concession 80/40Sk; 🕙 10am-5.30pm Tue-Sun) incorporates an 18th-century palace into its unusual 'Stalinist chic' design. It houses the nation's eclectic art collection and is well worth a visit.

The nearby **Slovak National Museum** (Slovenské Národné Múzeum; Map pp752-3; ☎ 59 34 91 22; Vajanského nábrežie 2; adult/concession 20/10Sk, free last Sun of month; 🕙 9am-5pm Tue-Sun) is a bit dowdy, but remains Slovakia's natural history showcase and features plenty of dusty exhibits.

Backtrack slightly to nám L Štúra where you'll find the neobaroque 1914 **Reduta Palace** (see p757), which is now Bratislava's main concert hall. Go north up Mostová

to the recently renovated Hviezdoslavovo nám, a broad, tree-lined space dominated by the flamboyant 1886 **Slovak National Theatre** (Map pp752-3; see p757) on the right, with **Ganymede's Fountain** (1888) in front.

Bustling, narrow Rybárska brána runs through the old town to Hlavné nám; at the centre is **Roland's Fountain** (1572). To one side is the **old town hall** (1421), now the **Municipal Museum** (Mestské Múzeum v Bratislave; Map pp752-3; ☎ 59 21 30; Hlavné nám; adult/concession 50/20Sk; 🕙 10am-5pm Tue-Fri, 11am-6pm Sat & Sun), with gory torture chambers in the cellar and an extensive historical collection housed in finely decorated rooms. You enter the museum from the picturesque inner courtyard, where concerts are held in summer.

Leave the courtyard through the east gate and you'll be on the square in front of the **Primate's Palace** (Primaciálny Palác; Map pp752-3; adult/concession 40/20Sk; 🕙 10am-5pm Tue-Sun). Enter to see the Hall of Mirrors where Napoleon and the Austrian emperor Franz I signed a peace treaty in 1805. In the municipal gallery on the 2nd floor are rare English tapestries (1632). St George's Fountain stands in the courtyard. On Saturday, the palace echoes with the coy giggles of newly married couples, but it's still open to visitors.

Return through the old town hall courtyard and turn left into Radničná, where

INFORMATION	
24-Hour Pharmacy	1 C3
Agentura Alex	2 B2
Austrian Embassy	3 B4
Bratislava Culture & Information Centre	4 C3
British Council	5 C4
Czech Embassy	6 B4
French Embassy	7 C3
German Embassy	8 B4
Internet Centrum	9 B3
Interpress	10 B3
Irish Embassy	11 C4
Istrobanka	12 C3
Megalnet	13 B3
Polikinika	14 D3
Post Office	15 C3
Svet Knihy	16 C3
Tatratour	17 D2
UK Embassy	18 B3
US Embassy	19 C4
SIGHTS & ACTIVITIES	(pp752-4)
Church of the Clarissine Order	20 B3
Franciscan Church of the Annunciation	21 C3
Františkánske námestie	22 C3
Historical Museum	23 A4
Hlavné námestie	24 C3
Michael's Tower	25 B3
Mirbach Palace	26 C3
Municipal Museum	(see 33)
Museum of Arts & Crafts	27 B4
Museum of Clocks	28 B4

Museum of Folk Music	29 A3
Museum of Jewish Culture	30 B3
Museum of Viticulture	31 C3
Námestie SNP & Monument	32 C3
Old Town Hall	33 C3
Palace of the Royal Chamber (University Library)	34 B3
Primaciálne námestie	35 C3
Primate's Palace	36 C3
Reduta Palace	37 C4
St Martin's Cathedral	38 B4
Slavín War Memorial	39 A1
Slovak National Gallery	40 C4
Slovak National Museum	41 C4
Slovak National Parliament	42 A4
Slovak Radio	43 C1
SLEEPING	(p755)
Downtown Backpackers	44 B2
Gremium Penzión	45 C3
Hotel Danube	46 B4
Hotel Ibis	47 B3
Hotel Perugia	48 B3
Penzión Caribic	49 A4
Penzión Chez David	50 B3
Radisson Carlton Hotel	51 C4
EATING	(pp755-6)
Divesta diétna jedálen	52 B3
Exit	53 C3
Hacienda Mexicana	54 B3
Kaffee Mayer	55 C3
London Café	(see 5)
Mezzo Mezzo	56 C3

Modrá Hviezda	57 B4
Prašná Bašta	58 B3
Tempus Fugit	59 B3
DRINKING	(p756)
People's Lounge	60 B3
Slang Pub	61 C4
The Dubliner	(see 54)
Trafená Hus	62 D4
ENTERTAINMENT	(pp756-7)
Apollon Club	63 B2
Café Štúdio Club	64 C3
Hlbočina	65 B3
Kino Hviezda	66 C3
Nová Scéna	67 C2
Slovak National Theatre & Booking Office	68 C4
Slovenská Filharmonia Ticket Office	69 C4
Spider Club	70 C2
Spojka	71 D4
SHOPPING	(p757)
Folk Folk	72 C3
Tesco Department Store	73 D3
Uľuv	74 C3
TRANSPORT	(pp757-8)
Altadis	(see 78)
Austrian Airlines	75 B4
Avis	(see 46)
Bus to Devín Castle	76 B4
ČSA	77 D4
Hydrofoil Terminal	78 C4

enthusiastic tipplers will find solace in the **Museum of Viticulture** (Expozícia Vinohradníctva a Vinárstva; Map pp752-3; ☎ 59 20 51 41; Radničná 1; adult/concession 30/20Sk; ☯ 10am-5pm Mon-Fri, 11am-6pm Sat & Sun May-Sep, 9.30am-4.30pm Tue-Sun Oct-Apr) in the Apponyi Palace (1762). You can buy a museum guidebook in English.

Next, head north on Františkánske nám to the 13th-century **Franciscan Church of the Annunciation** (Kostol Zvestovania-Františkáni; Map pp752-3; admission free). The original Gothic chapel, with the skeleton of a saint enclosed in glass, is accessible through a door on the left near the front. Opposite this church is the **Mirbach Palace** (Mirbachov Palác; Františkánske nám 11; Map pp752-3; ☎ 54 43 15 56; adult/concession 60/30Sk; ☯ 11am-6pm Tue-Sun), built in 1770, which is a beautiful rococo building that now houses a good collection of art.

From the palace continue along narrow Zámočnícka to **Michael's Tower** (Michalská Veža; adult/concession 40/20Sk; ☯ 10am-5pm Tue-Fri, 11am-6pm Sat & Sun May-Sep, 9.30am-4.30pm Tue-Sun Oct-Apr), with a collection of antique arms and a great view from the top.

Stroll south down Michalská to the **Palace of the Royal Chamber** (Map pp752-3; Michalská 1), built in 1756. Now the university library, this building was once the seat of the Hungarian parliament. In 1848 serfdom was abolished here.

Take the passage west through the palace to the Gothic **Church of the Clarissine Order** (Kostol Klarisiek; Map pp752-3), which has a pentagonal tower supported by buttresses. Continue west on Farská, then turn left into Kapitulská and go straight ahead to the Gothic coronation church, the 14th-century **St Martin's Cathedral** (Dóm sv Martina; Map pp752-3; admission free; ☯ 10am-4.45pm Mon-Sat, 2-4.45pm Sun). Despite the cathedral's relatively modest interior, nine Hungarian Hapsburg kings and eight queens were crowned here between 1563 and 1830.

The busy motorway in front of St Martin's follows the moat of the former city walls. Construction of this route and the adjacent bridge was controversial, as several of the city's historic structures had to be pulled down and vibrations from the traffic have structurally weakened the cathedral.

As you return from the Bratislava Castle, take a stroll across the Danube on one of the pedestrian walkways on the sweeping **Nový most** (New Bridge), built in 1972. On the far side you can take a stroll along the river.

On a quirkier note, visitors to Bratislava are unlikely to miss the three photogenic, life-size bronze statues dubbed **The Peeper**, **The Frenchman** and **The Photographer**. The Frenchman leans on a park bench on Hlavné nám, The Photographer guards a corner on Laurinská and The Peeper leers out from a manhole on Panská.

Communist Bratislava

The focal point of nám SNP is the **Monument to the Slovak National Uprising** and its heroes. The monument drew huge crowds in the run-up to the fall of communism in November 1989 and was a popular staging post for nationalists prior to the Velvet Divorce from the Czech Republic.

From here, head north to Hodžovo nám and along Mýtna to the corner with Štefanovičova, where the chunky **Slovak Radio** (Map pp752-3; Slovenský rozhlas) building, like an upside-down stepped pyramid, sits among the housing estates.

On Slavín Hill, northwest of the old town, the **Slavín War Memorial** (Map p750) honours the 6847 Soviet soldiers who died in the battle for Bratislava in 1945. There's a good view of modern Bratislava from the surrounding gardens, especially of the prefabricated suburb of Petržalka to the south.

Hiking

To get out of the city and up into the forested Little Carpathian Mountains, take bus No 203 northeast from Hodžovo nám to the end of the line at Koliba, then walk up the road for about 20 minutes to the **TV tower** on Kamzík hill (440m). There is a viewing platform and a restaurant.

Maps posted at the tower outline the many hiking possibilities in the area, including a 6km walk that goes down the Vydrica Valley to Partisan Meadow. Continue down the road to Vojenská hospital from where bus No 212 runs back to Hodžovo nám.

FESTIVALS & EVENTS

Bratislava's best events are arts related. Must-sees include the **Bratislava Music Festival** (Bratislavské hudobné slávnosti; ☎ 54 43 45 46), which runs from late September to mid-October, and the **Cultural Summer Festival** (Kultúrne leto; ☎ 54 41 30 63), when a smorgasbord of arts events bring razzmatazz to the old town between June and September.

SLEEPING

The Bratislava Culture & Information Service (p751) can assist in finding accommodation in private rooms (from 400Sk per person), student dormitories (usually open during summer only, from 200Sk per person), pensions (from about 1200Sk a double) and hotels. Reservations are recommended year-round.

Budget

Autocamp Zlaté Piesky (Map p750; ☎ 44 25 73 73; kempi@netax.sk; Senecká Cesta 2; per person/tent 60/60Sk, d 250Sk; ☺ May-Sep; ℗) This lakeside resort 7km northeast of Bratislava has water sports, a camping ground and chalets. Tram No 2 from the train station terminates here.

Downtown Backpackers (Map pp752-3; ☎ 54 64 11 91; www.backpackers.sk; Panenská 31; dm 500Sk, d with shared bathroom 800Sk) Bratislava's only tailor-made backpackers' den has oodles of cosy charm, with womb-red décor and plenty of trendy exposed brickwork. There's always plenty of action in the snug communal area and some of the upstairs doubles have balconies. Take bus No 81, 91 or 93 two stops from the train station.

Less expensive, but rather less charming, are the student-oriented hostels listed below. You may be lucky if you call ahead, but most only take guests during the summer months.

Zvárač (Map p750; ☎ 49 24 66 00; ubyt@cert.vuz.sk; Pionierska 17; s/d with shared bathroom 600/850Sk) It's clean, friendly and (generally) quiet, but this place is functional, rather than fabulous. Take tram No 3 from the train station or bus No 50 from the bus station.

Other recommendations:

Doprastav (Map p750; ☎ 55 57 43 13; Košická 52; s/d with shared bathroom 456/798Sk) Open all year.

Slovenská zdravotnícka univerzita (☎ 59 37 01 11; Limbová 12; s/d with shared bathroom 380/760Sk) For no-frills, student-style sleeps.

Mid-Range

Gremium Penzión (Map pp752-3; ☎ 54 13 10 26; fax 54 43 06 53; Gorkého 11; s/d 920/1350Sk) With five comfortable rooms above a buzzing eatery/sports bar, this has a lively atmosphere and rocks with cheers and tears during the weekend ice hockey matches, which are shown on giant TV screens.

Hotel Spirit (Map p750; ☎ 54 77 75 61; www.hotelspirit .sk, in Slovak; Vančurova 1; s/d 990/1430Sk; ☐) Avant-

garde décor rules the roost in this angular, colourful place. It is right next to the train station, but the rooms are a tad spartan.

Penzión Caribic (Map pp752-3; ☎ 54 41 83 34; caribics@stonline.sk; Žižkova 1/A; s/d 990/1980Sk) Recent refurbishments have brought a touch of class to the peaceful, modern rooms in this little pension.

Penzión Chez David (☎ 54 41 38 24; recepcia@ chezdavid.sk; Zámocká 13; s/d €44/63; ℗) The boxy, cyan-blue exterior of this 'Jewish Style' pension is a little functional, but there's a friendly atmosphere and the rooms are comfy. There's a €10 discount on doubles at the weekend.

Hotel Ibis (Map pp752-3; ☎ 59 29 20 20; www.ibis -bratislava.sk; Zámocká 38; r €64; ✖ ℗) Sparkling new, and with prefabricated styling, this spotless, simple place is a good bet for those who place reliable standards over quirky charm. There's a 15% discount at weekends and they have two disabled-friendly rooms.

Top End

Hotel Perugia (Map pp752-3; ☎ 54 43 18 18; www .perugia.sk; Zelená 5; s/d incl breakfast 4280/5080Sk; ✖) This four-star place, in the heart of the old town, makes a few concessions to boutique-style comfort and charges accordingly. Unfortunately, modern trimmings and muzak detract slightly from the charm of the old-world, townhouse architecture.

Radisson Carlton (Map pp752-3; ☎ 59 39 05 00; www .radissonsas.com; Hviezdoslavovo nám; r €190; ✖ ✖ ℗) Bratislava's showcase hotel has a prime location, oodles of facilities (including a fitness centre and sauna), and an unblemished international reputation.

Hotel Danube (Map pp752-3; ☎ 59 34 08 33; www .hoteldanube.com; Rybné nám 1; s/d incl breakfast €177/199; ✖ ✖ ℗ ☎) A big hit with business types, this riverside number jostles with the Radisson Carlton for pole position in the prime hotel stakes.

EATING
Restaurants

There are dozens of jazzy, if slightly pricey, eateries in the old town and a wide selection of cheaper, student-oriented bars/eateries along Obchodná.

Divesta diétna jedáleň (Map pp752-3; Laurinská 8; mains 58-68Sk; ☺ 11am-3pm Mon-Fri) The big queues speak volumes about the excellent-value veggie tucker at this central buffet.

Modrá hviezda (Map pp752-3; ☎ 54 43 27 47; Beblavého 14; mains 80-150Sk; 🕙 11.30am-11pm Mon-Sat) On the way up to the castle – follow the mouthwatering smells – this cosy place features Slovak music, plenty of exposed timber and a vibrant atmosphere.

Prašná Bašta (Map pp752-3; ☎ 54 43 49 57; Zámočnícka 11; mains 100-185Sk; 🕙 11am-11pm) This dark, atmospheric hideaway oozes old Bratislava charm and whips up a range of hearty, filling fare.

Hacienda Mexicana (Map pp752-3; ☎ 0904-55 68 86; Sedlárska 6; mains 100-200Sk; 🕙 9am-3am) Harley Davidson memorabilia, saloon-style décor and fiery-hot *fajitas* set the scene in this bustling bar/eatery. It could be the setting for an *El Mariachi*-style shoot-out.

Mezzo Mezzo (Map pp752-3; ☎ 54 43 43 93; Rybárska 9; mains 100-400Sk; 🕙 noon-10pm) This classy, bijou little number oozes slick sophistication and offers an upmarket and reasonably innovative selection of dishes from foie gras to red mullet. It may be a little too posh a little too soon though, as it can get really quite quiet during the week.

Tempus Fugit (Map pp752-3; ☎ 54 41 43 57; Sedlárska 5; mains 300-900Sk; 🕙 noon-10pm) Arguably central Bratislava's classiest eatery, this stylish place offers a highbrow gourmet experience, with plenty of fireworks on the French-style menu and tasteful soft furnishings and flickering candlelight providing the atmosphere.

Cafés

The streets of central Bratislava have been taken over by countless cafés in the last few years.

Exit (Map pp752-3; ☎ 54 43 20 87; Laurinská 11; snacks 30-90Sk; 🕙 10am-10pm) This artsy and perennially cosy hideaway plays groovy tunes and is decorated with a starburst of dangling bric-a-brac.

London Café (Map pp752-3; ☎ 54 43 17 93; Panská 17; snacks 30-90Sk; 🕙 9am-9pm Mon-Fri, to 6pm Sat) This is a cheaper, English-speaking coffee house in the British Council's courtyard.

Kaffee Mayer (Map pp752-3; ☎ 54 43 17 41; Hlavné nám 4; snacks 50-100Sk; 🕙 9am-1am) Classy coffee and an effete, sedate atmosphere prevail at this central option.

Self-Catering

Tesco (Kamenné nám; 🕙 8am-10pm Mon-Fri, to 7pm Sat & Sun) In the heart of town, this is a well-stocked supermarket and department store.

DRINKING

The Dubliner (Map pp752-3; ☎ 54 41 07 06; Sedlárska 6; 🕙 11am-3am Mon-Sat, to 1am Sun) This snug Irish bar flies the green flag for Bratislava, with log fires, draught Guinness and lashings of late night *craic*.

People's Lounge (Map pp752-3; ☎ 54 64 07 77; Gorkého 1; 🕙 11am-1am Mon-Sat, to midnight Sun) At the trendy end of the spectrum, this minimalist, halogen-lit venue draws Bratislava's beautiful set like moths to a candle. Expect a flick of holier-than-thou snobbery.

Slang Pub (Map pp752-3; ☎ 0908-79 80 61; Hviezdoslavovo nám 23; 🕙 11am-1am Mon-Sat, to midnight Sun) Big-screen MTV and a lively, young crowd bring this basement place plenty of character. They also do huge plates of scrumptious snacks.

Trafená Hus (Map pp752-3 ☎ 52 92 54 73; Šafarikovo nám 7; 🕙 7am-midnight Mon-Fri, from 10am Sat & Sun) With delicious snacks, cold beers and bountiful crowds, this popular place offers everything a bar should. Popular with a down-to-earth, youthful crowd, it's also a good place to hook up with the local set.

ENTERTAINMENT
Nightclubs

Spojka (Map pp752-3; ☎ 52 73 33 76; Prešernova 4; admission 100Sk) For trance, drum'n'bass and more progressive dance sounds head to this perennially popular nightspot.

Hlbočina (Map pp752-3; Kapucínska; admission 120Sk) This weekend favourite offers more dance music and a ground floor chill-out space.

Cinema

Films (110Sk) are generally shown in the original language, with Slovak subtitles. You can catch a fair selection of the latest blockbusters at **Kino Hviezda** (Map pp752-3; ☎ 54 43 50 49; nám 1 mája 11).

Gay & Lesbian Venues

The gay scene is limited, but there are a couple of options worth noting.

Apollon Club (Map pp752-3; Panenská 24) Stays open until 5am at the weekend.

Spider Club (Map pp752-3; ☎ 0903-75 80 96; Jedlíkova 9) A little rougher round the edges.

Sport

HC Slovan (Map p750; ☎ 44 45 65 00; Odbojárov 3) Bratislava's hallowed ice hockey team plays at a stadium northeast of the old town.

Theatre & Live Music

Opera and ballet are performed at the **Slovak National Theatre** (Slovenské Národné Divadlo; Map pp752-3; Hviezdoslavovo nám). Book tickets at the **booking office** (pokladňa; Map pp752-3; ☎ 54 43 37 64; www.snd.sk; cnr Jesenského & Komenského; ☉ 8am-5.30pm Mon-Fri, 9am-1pm Sat) behind the theatre.

The **Slovenská filharmónia** (Map pp752-3; cnr nám L Štúra & Medená) is based in the Reduta Palace. The **ticket office** (☎ 54 43 33 51; filharmonia@filharmonia.sk; ☉ 1-7pm Mon, Tue, Thu & Fri, 8am-2pm Wed) is inside the building.

Nová scéna (Map pp752-3; ☎ 52 92 11 39; www.nova-scena.sk, in Slovak; Kollárovo nám 20) presents operettas, musicals and drama (the latter in Slovak). The ticket office is open 12.30pm to 7pm weekdays and an hour before performances (by which time they're usually sold out).

State Puppet Theatre (Štátne Bábkové divadlo; Map p750; ☎ 52 63 47 40; Dunajská 36) puts on puppet shows for kids, usually at 9am or 10am and sometimes again at 1.30pm or 2.30pm.

Café Štúdio Club (Map pp752-3; ☎ 54 43 17 96; cnr Laurinská & Nedbalova; ☉ 10am-midnight Mon-Fri, from 2pm Sat & Sun) hosts live music, specialising in jazz, blues and folksy numbers.

SHOPPING

For folk handicrafts head to **Úľuv** (Map pp752-3; ☎ 52 92 38 02; nám SNP 12; ☉ 9am-4pm Mon-Fri, to noon Sat) or **Folk Folk** (Map pp752-3; ☎ 54 43 42 92; Obchodná 10; ☉ 9am-4pm Mon-Fri, to noon Sat).

GETTING THERE & AWAY
Air

No-frills **Sky Europe Airlines** (☎ 02-48 50 11 11; www.skyeurope.com; Ivanská cesta 26, Bratislava) offers budget online fares to Amsterdam, Barcelona, London, Paris and Split from €25 one way.

Austrian Airlines (Map pp752-3; ☎ 54 41 16 10; www.austrian.sk; Rybné nám 1; ☉ 9am-5pm Mon-Fri) flies daily to Paris (4755Sk return), London (4602Sk return) and Brussels (4739Sk return, except Saturday).

ČSA (Map pp752-3; ☎ 52 96 13 25; Štúrova 13; ☉ 9am-5pm Mon-Fri) has four flights daily to Prague (3462Sk return).

For a full list of carriers serving Bratislava see p783.

Boat

Boats to Vienna (€22 one way) and Budapest (€68 one way) leave daily from the **hydrofoil terminal** (Map pp752-3; Fajnorovo nábrežie 2) between April and September. Tickets can

be bought from **Altadis** (Map pp752-3; ☎ 52 96 35 18; www.lod.sk; ☉ 9am-5pm Mon-Fri, to noon Sat), inside the terminal.

Bus

At Bratislava's **main bus station** (Map p750; SAD information line ☎ 55 56 73 49; www.sad-kds.sk, in Slovak; Mlynské nivy), east of the city centre, you buy your ticket from the ticket windows.

National buses leaving Bratislava daily include nine to Košice (512Sk, seven hours), seven to Bardejov (560Sk, nine hours), six to Žilina (260Sk, 3½ hours) and 14 to Poprad (428Sk, six hours). For all times and prices, visit www.vlaky.sk.

Eurolines (international information ☎ 55 57 13 12; reservations ☎ 55 56 73 49; www.eurolines.sk) buses run from Bratislava's main bus station to destinations across Europe. Destinations, with one-way fares, include: Vienna (210Sk, 1½ hours, daily), Prague (410Sk, 4½ hours, daily), Paris (3500Sk, 20 hours, four weekly), London (3800Sk, 22 hours, five weekly), Venice (1700Sk, 12 hours, Friday), Hamburg (2500Sk, 18½ hours, Thursday and Friday) and Györ, in Hungary (240Sk, 2½ hours, Wednesday).

Train

Five express trains a day between Budapest (520Sk, 2¾ hours) and Prague (700Sk, 4½ hours) – via Brno (250Sk, 1½ hours) – call at Bratislava. There are frequent trains from Bratislava to Košice (590Sk, six hours), via Žilina (242Sk, 2¾ hours) and Poprad (384Sk, 4¾ hours).

There are two trains daily to Warsaw (1400Sk, 7¾ hours), one to Moscow (2100Sk, 33 hours) and seven to Vienna (376Sk, 1¼ hours).

Train times and prices can be found at www.zsr.sk or www.vlaky.sk.

GETTING AROUND
To/From the Airport

Bratislava's airport (Letisko MR Štefánika) is 7km northeast of the city centre. Bus No 61 links the airport with the main train station (16Sk, 20 minutes), or get there by taxi (approximately 350Sk) – make sure they use the meter.

Bus & Tram

Dopravný podnik Bratislava (DPB; ☎ 59 50 59 50; www.dpb.sk) offers an extensive tram network complemented by bus and trolleybus. You can buy tickets (14/16/20Sk for 10/30/60 minutes) at DPB offices and from machines at main tram and bus stops; validate the ticket in the little red machines when you board.

Tourist tickets (turistické cestovné lístky) for one/two/three/seven days (80/150/185/275Sk) are sold at DPB offices and train and bus stations.

Car
Avis (Map pp752-3; ☎ 53 41 61 11; www.avis.sk; Rybné nám 1) has a desk in the Hotel Danube, but prices are high at from 1200Sk per day.

Cheaper, local companies offer older cars from 699Sk per day – most deliver to your hotel. Try **Favorit** (☎ 44 88 41 52) or **Auto Danubius** (☎ 44 37 25 02).

Taxi
Bratislava's taxis have meters – make sure they use them. Call **BP** (☎ 16 333), or **VIP** (☎ 16 000).

AROUND BRATISLAVA
From the 1st to the 5th centuries AD, **Devín Castle** (☎ 65 73 01 05; Muranská; adult/concession 40/10Sk; ☽ 10am-5pm Tue-Fri, to 6pm Sat & Sun May-Oct) was a frontier post of the Roman Empire. During the 9th century the castle was a major stronghold of the Great Moravian Empire. The castle withstood the Turks but was blown up in 1809 by the French. Today it is regarded as a symbol of the Slovaks, who have maintained their identity despite a millennium of foreign rule. The Gothic ruins contain an exhibit of artefacts found on site. Austria is just across the river.

Getting There & Away
Catch bus No 29 (two per hour) from the bus stop beneath the Nový most (New Bridge) in Bratislava to the castle, which is on a hill 9km from the city, where the Morava and Danube Rivers meet. Stay on the bus to the end of the line and walk back to the castle.

WEST SLOVAKIA

Most travellers hightail it through West Slovakia en route between Bratislava and the Vysoké Tatry, but this pretty lowland region offers plenty to reward the slower-moving traveller, not least the historic town of Trenčín, with its magnificent castle.

TRENČÍN
☎ 032 / pop 57,000
Roman legionnaires were the first foreign visitors to take a fancy to the site of modern day Trenčín, establishing a military post, Laugaricio, here in the 2nd century AD. A rock inscription in the town still recalls the 2nd Legion's victory over the Germanic Kvad tribes, but 21st-century Trenčín is better known for a more recent fortress. The mighty castle that now stands watch over the pretty market square was first noted in a Viennese chronicle of 1069 and despite countless renovations remains Trenčín's undisputed drawcard, forming the ideal centrepiece of a town peppered with Renaissance buildings and cut through with a distinctly sedate pace of living.

Orientation & Information
From the adjacent bus and train stations walk west through the city park and underneath the highway to the Hotel Tatra, where a street bears left uphill to Mierové nám, the main square.

EMERGENCY
Police station (☎ 159) It's in the same building as the AiCES information centre.

INTERNET ACCESS
Internet Klub Modra Linka (www.modralinka.sk; ☽ 10am-10pm; per min 1Sk) Next to the information centre.

MONEY
ČSOB (Vajanského 3; ☽ 7.30am-5pm Mon-Thu, to 4pm Fri) Has an ATM and change facilities.

POST
Main post office (Mierové nám 21; ☽ 7.30am-7pm Mon-Fri, to 11am Sat) The telephone centre is in here too.

TOURIST INFORMATION
AiCES information centre (☎ 161 86; www.trencin.sk; Štúrovo nám 10; ☽ 8am-6pm Mon-Fri, 8am-1pm Sat May-Sep, 8am-5pm Mon-Fri Oct-Apr) The helpful, well-informed staff here can also help find accommodation.

Sights
Trenčín Castle (Trenčiansky Hrad; ☎ 743 56 57; adult/concession 100/50Sk; ☽ 9.15am-5.45pm May-Oct, to

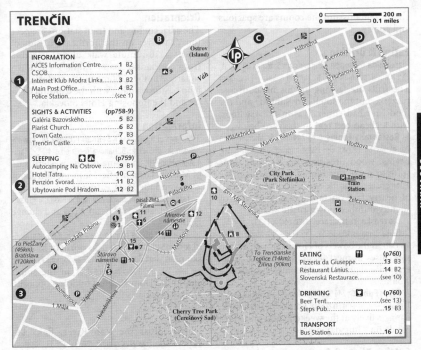

TRENČÍN

INFORMATION	
AiCES Information Centre.........**1** B2	
ČSOB...................................**2** A3	
Internet Klub Modra Linka......**3** B2	
Main Post Office....................**4** B2	
Police Station.........................(see 1)	
SIGHTS & ACTIVITIES	(pp758-9)
Galéria Bazovského..................**5** B2	
Piarist Church.........................**6** B2	
Town Gate..............................**7** B3	
Trenčín Castle..........................**8** C2	
SLEEPING	(p759)
Autocamping Na Ostrove.........**9** B1	
Hotel Tatra.............................**10** C2	
Penzión Svorad.......................**11** B2	
Ubytovanie Pod Hradom..........**12** B2	
EATING	(p760)
Pizzeria da Giuseppe................**13** B3	
Restaurant Lánius....................**14** B2	
Slovenská Restaurace...............(see 10)	
DRINKING	(p760)
Beer Tent................................(see 13)	
Steps Pub................................**15** B3	
TRANSPORT	
Bus Station..............................**16** D2	

SLOVAKIA

4.45pm Nov-Apr), astride a rocky crag above the main square with sweeping views of the Váh plain, is unmissable. The highlight of the tour (in Slovak) are the vertiginous vistas from the tower. The so-called Well of Love on the first terrace is 70m deep. At night, the castle is lit with green and purple fairy lights and in summer, nightly, two-hour **Medieval Days shows** (adult/concession 80/40Sk) include sword fighting, ghosts, fun and frolics.

At the western end of Mierové nám are the baroque **Piarist Church** (Piaristický kostol) and the 16th-century **town gate** (Mestská brána), which contains a clock that plays old-fashioned tunes on the hour. The **Galéria Bazovského** (☎ 743 68 58; Palackého 27; adult/concession 20/10Sk; ☷ 9am-5pm Tue-Sun), in a restored 19th-century palace, houses a collection of works by local painter Miloš Bazovský (1899–1968).

The famous **Roman inscription** of AD 179 is on the cliff behind the Hotel Tatra and can only be seen through a viewing window on the hotel's staircase – ask at reception for permission to see it. The translation reads: 'To the victory of the emperor and the army which, numbering 855 soldiers, resided at Laugaricio. By order of Maximianus, legate of the 2nd auxiliary legion'.

Sleeping

Autocamping na Ostrove (☎ 743 40 13; autocamping .tn@mail.pvt.sk; 130Sk per person; ☷ mid-May–mid-Sep; Ⓟ) On an island in the Váh River, opposite the sports stadium near the city centre, this decent camping ground also has cabins (200Sk per person).

Penzión Svorad (☎ 743 03 22; svorad@host.sk; Palackého 4; s/d 450/800Sk; ✗) There is a whiff of Colditz about this pension in the grammar school building, but the staff can squeeze out a smile and it is a good budget option. It is all nonsmoking.

Ubytovanie Pod Hradom (☎ 744 25 07; www .podhradom.sk, in Slovak; Matúša Čaka 23; r 1400Sk) On a winding wee street en route to the castle, this pretty little spot has a distinctly personal feel, with a prime location and a sprinkling of fairy-tale charm.

Hotel Tatra (☎ 650 61 11; www.hotel-tatra.sk; gen MR Štefánika 2; s/d incl breakfast 3590/4690Sk; Ⓟ ✗) The town's most chi-chi option is a little frumpy, but a fair bit of Art Nouveau charm remains and the rooms are spacious and comfy.

Eating & Drinking

Pizzeria da Giuseppe (Štúrovo nám 5; mains 60-110Sk; ⏰ 10am-11pm Mon-Thu, to 1am Fri & Sat, 1-11pm Sun) The frills are lacking at this no-nonsense pizzeria, but the smells are sublime and the food isn't bad either. It's on the 1st floor, with a cheap **beer tent** in the yard below.

Restaurant Lánius (☎ 744 19 78; Mierové nám 20; mains 80-180Sk; ⏰ 10am-midnight) Creaking beams, wood fires and low lighting conspire to make this one of the town's more authentic options, with a decent spread of hearty fare on tap and a good deal of slightly dumbed-down rustic charm.

Slovenská restaurace (☎ 650 61 11; gen MR Štefánika 2; mains 100-180Sk; ⏰ 11am-2am Mon-Fri, from 6pm Sat) In the bowels of Hotel Tatra, this place specialises in meat feasts, waistcoated waiters and – slightly less welcome – wandering violinists.

Steps Pub (☎ 744 62 52; Sládkovičova 4; ⏰ 10.30am-1am Sun-Thu, to 4am Fri & Sat) This cosy Irish-style bar gets lively at the weekend and hosts jazz bands on Thursday nights.

Getting There & Away

Trains from Bratislava (162Sk, 1¾ hours) to Košice via Žilina stop here. There are six buses a day to Bratislava (142Sk, two hours), Žilina (106Sk, 1½ hours) and Košice (375Sk, five hours).

CENTRAL SLOVAKIA

Central Slovakia is a region of landscapes and few are more spectacular than the peaks and forests of the Malá Fatra (Little Fatra) mountain range, a pocket of natural beauty that is both painfully pretty and uniquely Slovakian.

ŽILINA

☎ 041 / pop 85,500

Founded back in the 13th century, Žilina left an indelible mark as a major transport hub. Few tourists pass through on the railways these days though, making Žilina a distinctly Slovakian city with few tacky tourist trappings and an attractive main square to explore. It is the major jumping-off point for those heading into the Malá Fatra mountains.

Orientation

The adjacent bus and train stations are near the Váh River on the northeastern side of town, a 10-minute walk along Národná from Mariánské nám, Žilina's old town square. Another 200m south of Mariánské nám is Štúrova nám, with the Cultural Centre and the imposing Hotel Slovakia.

Information

The travel agency **CK Selinan** (☎ 562 14 78; www .selinan.sk, in Slovak; Burianova medzierka 4; ⏰ 8am-4.30pm Mon-Fri), in a lane off the western side of Mariánské nám, offers information about Žilina and the Malá Fatra area.

Tatra Banka (cnr Mariánské nám & Farská; ⏰ 8am-6pm Mon-Fri, to noon Sat) has an ATM and change facility.

The **post office** (Sladkovičova 1; ⏰ 8am-5pm Mon-Fri, to noon Sat) is three blocks north of Mariánské nám. **Net Bar** (☎ 0903-32 84 75; Veľká Okružná; per min 1Sk; ⏰ 10am-midnight) is in the south end of the Dom Kultúry building opposite Hotel Slovakia.

Sights

North across the Váh River, flaky **Budatín Castle** (Budatín zámok; ☎ 562 00 33; Topoľová 1; adult/concession 30/15Sk; ⏰ 8am-4pm Tue-Sun) houses the **Považské Museum**, featuring a collection of naive figures sculpted from metal and wire. Other than that, you're left with a stroll through the town's pleasant old town and its main square, Mariánské námestie.

Sleeping

CK Selinan (above) can help with private rooms from 300Sk per person.

Penzión Majovey (☎ 562 41 52; fax 562 52 39; Jána Milca 3; s/d 700/1300Sk) There are few fireworks in the city's accommodation scene and this is no exception. The rooms are well dusted though, and the receptionists offer a higher smile quota than most.

Penzión GMK Centrum (☎ 562 21 36; www.gmk .sk; Mariánské nám 3; s/d 800/1300Sk) This so-so option has smallish rooms, and is tucked away in an upstairs passage off the square.

Hotel Slovakia (☎ 562 32 65; hotelslovakiamanager@ bb.telecom.sk; Štúrová nám 2; s/d incl breakfast 1100/1600Sk; ℗) This Stalinist-style hulk offers a tad more flash than the town's other outfits, with stacks of decent rooms and a pretentious cocktail bar.

Eating & Drinking

Campari Pizza (Zaymusova 4; mains 75-120Sk; ☷ 11am-9pm Mon-Fri) On the north side of Štúrova nám, this has a nice back terrace where you can wash down pseudo-pizza with cheap red wine.

Pizzeria da Giuseppe (Štúrovo nám 5; mains 60-110Sk; ☷ 10am-11pm Mon-Thu, to 1am Fri & Sat, 1-11pm Sun) You'll find the frills lacking at this no-nonsense pizzeria, but the smells are sublime and the food isn't bad either. It's on the 1st floor, with a cheap **beer tent** in the yard below.

Boston (☎ 0905-48 12 14; Mariánské 24; ☷ 9am-midnight Sun-Thu, to 2am Fri & Sat) Jazz rules the roost at this lively venue.

Getting There & Away

Žilina is on the main railway line from Bratislava to Košice. Regular express trains head to Trenčín (104Sk, one hour), Bratislava (242Sk, 2¾ hours), Poprad (180Sk, two hours) and Košice (286Sk, three hours).

MALÁ FATRA NATIONAL PARK

☎ 041

A knot of jagged peaks, topped with eerie, sentinel-like formations, the Malá Fatra National Park (Národný park Malá Fatra) incorporates a chocolate-box-pretty, 200 sq km swathe of the Malá Fatra (Little Fatra) mountain range and offers plentiful skiing and hiking. At the heart of the park is the Vrátna dolina, a beautiful mountain valley with forested slopes on all sides.

There are plenty of places to stay and eat, but accommodation is tight during winter and midsummer. The valley is an easy day trip from Žilina. The mountains are accessible by road, trail and chairlift for anyone with the urge to enjoy their beauty.

Information

Združenie Turizmu Terchová (☎ 599 31 00; www.terchovaregion.sk; Hurbanova 4, Terchová; ☷ 9am-5pm Mon-Fri, 10am-5pm Sat, 10am-2pm Sun), in Terchová, has information and Internet access (100Sk per hour). **Slovenská Sporiteľňa** (Hurbanova 4; ☷ 8am-noon, 12.30-3.30pm Mon-Fri), next door, has an ATM and change facilities.

About 1km up the Štefanová road is the **Mountain Rescue Service** (Horská služba; ☎ 569 52 32), an excellent source of trail information.

If you plan to hike, you should get the VKÚ's 1:50,000 *Malá Fatra – Vrátna* map (sheet No 110).

Sights & Activities

The road enters the Vrátna dolina just south of Terchová, where it runs through the **Tiesňavy Gorge** with rocky crags on both sides. One rock resembles a person praying (turn and look back after you've passed through the gorge).

A **ski lift** (☎ 569 56 42; www.vratna.sk, in Slovak; 160Sk return) runs from **Starý Dvor**, opposite the Reštaurácia Starý Majer, to **Grúň** (989m), from where colour-coded trails wind their way over the surrounding peaks. From here, a short, yellow-marked trail scales

---

SLOVAKIA'S ROBIN HOOD

There are many Robin Hood characters in the annals of Slovakian history, but Juraj Jánošík is far and away the most famous.

Jánošík, the focus of untold folk songs and stories, is a mixture of fact and fiction. Born into a peasant family in 1688 in Terchová, he joined up with Ferenc Rákóczi II in 1703 to fight the Habsburgs. When the rebellion was crushed in 1711, he headed for Kežmarok. While away his mother died and his father was beaten to death by their landlord for taking time off to bury her. Jánošík then took to the hills and spent the next two years robbing from the rich and giving to the poor, although some say he didn't make much of a distinction about who he stole from.

In 1713 he was captured in a local pub; legend has it that the landlord betrayed him and as he went to escape he slipped on some peas an old lady had thrown on the floor. He was sentenced to an excruciating death – hung on a hook by the ribs in the town of Liptovský Mikuláš. Even the location of his execution is in dispute; some say it was the town's main square, others 1.5km west near the prison where he was tortured or about 2km east of the square in what is now a residential area.

If you want to know more about the man, just ask any Slovakian; they'll surely be able to spin a few yarns about his superhuman feats.

SLOVAKIA

MALÁ FATRA NATIONAL PARK

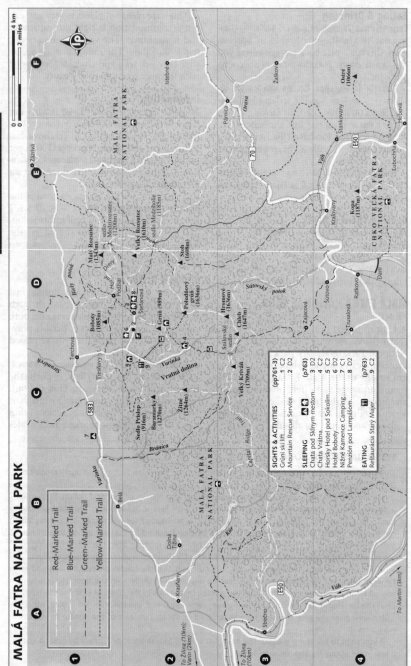

SLOVAKIA

Legend:
- Red-Marked Trail
- Blue-Marked Trail
- Green-Marked Trail
- Yellow-Marked Trail

SIGHTS & ACTIVITIES	(pp761–3)
Grúň ski lift	1 C2
Mountain Rescue Service	2 D2

SLEEPING	(p763)
Chata pod Sklným mestom	3 D2
Chata Vrátna	4 C2
Horský Hotel pod Sokolím	5 C2
Hotel Boboty	6 D2
Nižné Kamence Camping	7 C1
Penzión pod Lampášom	8 D2

EATING	(p763)
Reštaurácia Starý Majer	9 C2

Map labels visible: Zázrivá, Istebné, Orava, Párnica, Žaškov, Ostré (1066m), Stankovany, Váh, K라ľovany, Ľubochňa, Hrboltová, Kopa (1187m), CHKO VEĽKÁ FATRA NATIONAL PARK, Dam, Ratkovo, Šútovo, Zázrivá, Biely potok, Malý Rozsutec (1343m), sedlo Medzirozsutec (1200m), Veľký Rozsutec (1610m), sedlo Medziholie (1185m), Stoh (1608m), Podžiar, Štefanová, Grúň (989m), Poludňový grúň (1636m), Hromové (1636m), Chleb (1647m), Snilovské sedlo, Šútovský potok, Zajacová, Trusalová, Sútovská, Boboty (1085m), Diery, Tiesňavy, Terchová, Stráník, Štúrovo, Varinka, Vrátna dolina, Varínka, Sedlo Príslop (916m), Baranlarky (1270m), Žitné (1264m), Veľký Kríváň (1709m), Capital Ridge Trail, Brānica, Belá, Dolná Tižina, Krasňany, MALÁ FATRA NATIONAL PARK, Kúr, Váh, Strečno, E50, To Žilina (10km); Varín (2km), To Žilina (10km), To Žilina (10km), To Martin (3km)

Scale: 0 — 4 km / 0 — 2 miles

Poludňový grúň (1636m), where a red-marked trail continues on over **Hromové** (1636m) and **Chleb** (1647m) to **Snilovské sedlo** headed south, or over **Stoh** (1608m) to **sedlo Medziholie** (1185m), beneath the summit of **Velký Rozsutec** (1610m), headed northeast.

From Medziholie it's easy to descend via a green trail to **Štefanová**, a picturesque village of log houses. You can do the hike from Snilovské sedlo to Štefanová via sedlo Medziholie in about four hours.

SKIING
The Vrátna dolina offers some good, cheap skiing and there are plenty of tows and lifts. A day/week pass costs 680/3100Sk for adults, 470/1990Sk for children. Check in at Združenie Turizmu Terchová (p761).

Sleeping & Eating
No camping is allowed in the Vrátna dolina. The nearest **camping grounds** are at Nižné Kamence, 3.5km west of Terchová, and at Varín, another 11km towards Žilina.

There are lots of **private rooms** in Terchová from 250Sk per person – ask at the Združenie Turizmu Terchová office.

Chata Vrátna (☎ 569 57 39; www.vratna.sk, in Slovak; dm 180Sk, d with shared bathroom 500Sk; **P**) At the far end of the Vrátna dolina, this timber, chalet-style outfit fills up with muddy hikers and fragrant wood smoke smells. If you are allergic to large groups of giggling children, be aware that it often caters to school groups.

Horsky Hotel pod Sokolím (☎ 569 53 26; s/d 595/969Sk; **P**) Overlooking the chairlift and Reštaurácia Starý Majer, this offers photogenic views, a pleasant bar area and a hulking big St Bernard dog.

Reštaurácia Starý Majer (☎ 569 54 19; mains 60-200Sk; ✆ 10am-9pm) The crowds flock here for platefuls of hearty Slovak tucker. It is decorated with the usual rustic bric-a-brac, from cartwheels to horseshoes.

ŠTEFANOVÁ
There are a clutch of decent places to stay in the little hamlet of Štefanová.

Penzión pod Lampášom (☎ 569 53 92; s/d 350/700Sk; **P**) A few minutes' walk up the green trail, this homey, alpine-style place features wooden trimmings galore and a pleasant, snug atmosphere.

Chata pod Sklnym mestom (☎ 569 53 63; www .slovak-holiday.sk; s/d 250/500Sk; **P**) A little closer to the centre of the hamlet, this is a bit less atmospheric, but boasts a few more creature comforts, including a basketball court and a sauna. Prices almost double during high season.

Hotel Boboty (☎ 569 52 28; www.vratna.sk, in Slovak; s/d 800/1000Sk; **P** ☎) Boboty's unsympathetic concrete architecture is rather incongruous, but the views from the skyscraping dining room windows are magnificent. It is functional, but has a good array of facilities. It's a five-minute walk up from the bus stop near Štefanová.

Getting There & Around
Buses link Žilina with Terchová (38Sk, 45 minutes) and Chata Vrátna (50Sk, one hour) at least every two hours.

You can hire bicycles in Terchová – ask at the information centre for details.

EAST SLOVAKIA

East Slovakia is one of the most attractive touring areas in Central Europe. In one compact region, you can enjoy superb hiking in the Vysoké Tatry mountains, rafting on the Dunajec River, historic towns such as Levoča and Bardejov, the great medieval castle at Spišské Podhradie and city life in Košice. Getting around is easy, with frequent trains and buses to all these sights, plus easy access to Poland and Hungary. In spite of all these attractions, the region still feels somewhat off the beaten track.

VYSOKÉ TATRY (HIGH TATRAS)
☎ 052
The roof of Slovakia, the Vysoké Tatry (High Tatra) mountains tower over most of Central Europe, culminating in the vertiginous 2654m peak of Gerlachovský štít, the loftiest summit in the entire Carpathian range. The massif measures just 25km across, but in terms of natural beauty, the peaks are truly monumental, offering the kind of photo opportunities that will get you fantasising about a career in *National Geographic*. Pristine snowfields, ultramarine mountain lakes, crashing waterfalls – as well as the slightly less welcome crowds – come as standard.

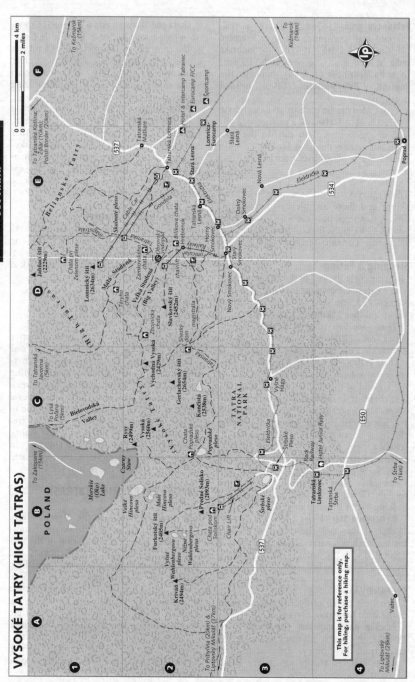

VYSOKÉ TATRY (HIGH TATRAS)

This map is for reference only.
For hiking, purchase a hiking map.

Since 1949, most of the Slovak part of this jagged range has been included in the Tatra National Park (Tanap), the first national park to be created in the former Czechoslovakia and complementing a similar park in Poland. A 600km network of hiking trails reaches all the alpine valleys and many peaks. The red-marked Tatranská magistrála trail follows the southern slopes of the Vysoké Tatry for 65km through a variety of striking landscapes. Other routes are also colour-coded and easy to follow. Park regulations require you to keep to the marked trails and to refrain from picking flowers.

Climate & When to Go

When planning your trip, keep in mind that the higher trails are closed from November to mid-June, to protect the delicate environment. There's snow by November (on the highest passes as early as September), and many snowfields linger until May or even June. Beware of sudden thunderstorms, especially on ridges and peaks where there's no protection. Always wear hiking boots and carry warm clothing. Remember that the assistance of the Mountain Rescue Service is not free. July and August are the warmest (and most crowded) months, while August and September are the best for high-altitude hiking. Hotel prices are lowest from April to mid-June.

For the latest weather and tramping advice contact the **Mountain Rescue Service** (Horská Záchranná Služba; ☎ 18 300; www.hzs.sk, in Slovak).

Orientation

Starý Smokovec, an early 20th-century resort that is well connected to the rest of the country by road and rail, makes a pleasant base camp. Small electric trains trundle frequently between here and Štrbské Pleso, Tatranská Lomnica and Poprad, where they connect up with the national railway system. Buses also run frequently between the resorts. Cable cars, chairlifts and a funicular railway carry you up the slopes to hiking trails that soon lead you away from the throng. During winter, skiers flock to the area. All three main train stations have left-luggage offices.

MAPS

Our Vysoké Tatry map is intended for initial orientation only. Buy a proper VKÚ 1:25,000

(sheet No 2) or 1:50,000 *Vysoké Tatry* (sheet No 113) hiking map when you arrive – both cost 112Sk. Good maps are usually available at hotels, shops and newsstands inside the park. When buying your map, make sure you get a green one with summer hiking trails and not a blue one with winter ski routes.

Information

MONEY

Slovenská Sporiteľňa (Česta Slobody 25, Starý Smokovec; ☼ 8am-noon & 12.30-3.30pm Mon-Fri) Has an ATM and change facilities on the main road through Starý Smokovec.

POST

Post office (☼ 7.30am-noon & 1-4pm Mon-Fri, 8am-10am Sat) Near Starý Smokovec train station.

TOURIST INFORMATION

AiCES Tatra information centre (☎ 442 34 40; www.tatry.sk; ☼ 8am-8pm Mon-Fri, to 1pm Sat) In the Dom služieb shopping centre, northwest of Starý Smokovec train station – oodles of information.

AiCES branch (☎ 446 81 18; www.tatry.sk; ☼ 10am-6pm Mon-Fri, 9am-1pm Sat) On the main road through Tatranská Lomnica.

Also check out the website maintained by the **Tatra National Park** (www.tanap.sk) – it is packed with useful information on accommodation, mountain guides, equipment rental and trail conditions.

TRAVEL AGENCIES

Satur (☎ 442 24 97; www.satur.sk; ☼ 8am-4pm Mon-Fri) Just above the train station at Starý Smokovec, this provides accommodation, transport and activities advice.

Sights & Activities

ABOVE STARÝ SMOKOVEC

From Starý Smokovec take a **funicular railway** (Tatranské Lanové Dráhy; ☎ 446 76 18; one way/return 90/130Sk; ☼ 7.30am-7pm), built in 1908, takes you up to **Hrebienok** (1280m), a ski resort with a view into the Veľká Studená (Big Valley). Alternatively, it takes an hour to walk up to Hrebienok on a yellow trail.

A good option for the reasonably fit is to take the green path from Hrebienok, past the Bilíkova *chata* (chalet) to **Obrovsky vodopad** (waterfalls). From there, make the four- to five-hour climb up the **Veľká Studená** valley along the blue trail to the **Zbojnícka chata**, where you can get a bed and a hot meal. The next day, you can make the ascent of **Východná Vysoká** (2429m), offering some great views of **Gerlachovský štít**.

Alternatively, follow the red trail from Hrebienok to **Zamkovského chata**, where a green trail leads into the **Malá Studená** valley. Four hours will see you at **Téryho chata**, which is beside a lake at 2010m.

A tough, two-day trek from Hrebienok goes up the valley of the Veľká Studená to **Zbojnícka chata**, over a 2373m pass and down the long Bielovodská Valley to **Tatranská Javorina**, where buses make the run back to Starý Smokovec.

ŠTRBSKÉ PLESO

From the modern ski resort of Štrbské Pleso with its glacial lake (1346m), take the red-marked Magistrála trail for about an hour up to **Popradské pleso**, an idyllic lake at 1494m. The Magistrála runs along the south shore of Štrbské pleso lake – just head uphill from the train station to find it. From Popradské pleso the Magistrála zigzags steeply up the mountainside then traverses east towards **Sliezský dom** and **Hrebienok** (four hours).

Another option is to hike up the blue trail from Popradské pleso to **Velké Hincovo pleso** (1946m), biggest and deepest of the park's tarns.

There is also a year-round **chair lift** (one way/return 130/190Sk) to **Soilsko**, from where it's a one-hour walk north along a red trail to the 2093m summit of **Predné Solisko**.

TATRANSKÁ LOMNICA

An extremely popular **cable car** (Kabínková Lanová Draha) links Tatranská Lomnica with the bustling lake and winter sports area of **Skalnaté pleso** (1751m; one way/return 220/320Sk; ⊙ 8.30am-7pm Jul-Aug, to 4pm Sep-Jun). From there, another cable car goes on to the precipitous 2634m summit of **Lomnický štít** (380Sk return; ⊙ 8.30am-7pm Jul-Aug, to 3.30pm Sep-Jun). Queues are huge during peak season, so get there early.

Alternatively, you can yomp it up to Skalnaté (2½ hours), where there is also an ordinary **chairlift** (adult/child 150/90Sk; ⊙ 8.30am-5.30pm Jul-Aug, 8.30am-4.30pm Sep-Jun) running up to **Lomnické sedlo**, a 2190m saddle below the summit – pack warm clothing.

The **Tatra National Park Museum** (Múzeum Tatranského Národného Parku; ☎ 446 79 51; adult/concession 30/10Sk; ⊙ 8am-noon & 1-5pm Mon-Fri, 8am-3pm Sat & Sun), a few hundred metres from the bus station, has a ho-hum natural history exhibit.

MOUNTAIN CLIMBING

You can reach the summit of **Slavkovský štít** (2452m) via the blue trail from Starý Smokovec (seven to eight hours return). **Rysy** (2499m), right on the Polish border, is a nine-hour return trip from Štrbské pleso (via Popradské pleso and chata pod Rysmi). You can do these routes on your own, but to scale the peaks without marked hiking trails (Gerlachovský štít included) you must hire a mountain guide. Members of recognised climbing clubs are exempt from this requirement.

Right in front of Satur in Starý Smokovec, the **Mountain Guides Society Office** (☎ 442 20 66; www.tatraguide.sk; ⊙ 10am-6pm Mon-Fri, noon-6pm Sat & Sun Jun-Sep, 10am-6pm Mon-Fri Oct-May) offers advice, as well as guides for hikes, climbing excursions and mountain bike tours (from 2000Sk).

SKIING & SNOWBOARDING

Štrbské Pleso, Starý Smokovec and Tatranská Lomnica all have lifts offering fairly average downhill skiing and snowboarding, as well as good cross-country skiing trails. Štrbské Pleso and Starý Smokovec are much better suited to beginners and intermediates, while Tatranská Lomnica is more suitable for intermediates and experts.

You can hire skis (299Sk per day) and mountain bikes (299Sk per day) from **Tatrasport** (☎ 442 52 41; www.tatry.net/tatrasport; ⊙ 8am-noon & 1-6pm), in Starý Smokovec.

Sleeping
CAMPING

No wild camping is permitted within Tatra National Park.

There are three camping grounds 2km from Tatranská Lomnica (near Tatranská Lomnica-Eurocamp train station on the line to Studený potok).

Eurocamp FICC (☎ 446 77 41; www.eurocamp-ficc .sk; per person/tent 90/120Sk; ⊙ year-round; P ☺) Five minutes' stroll from the train station, Eurocamp has restaurants (which include the good folkloric Koliba Restaurant), bars, shops, a supermarket, a swimming pool, tennis, sauna, disco, hot water and row upon row of parked caravans. They also have two-, three- and four-bed bungalows (1000/1500/1700Sk).

An eight-minute walk south of Eurocamp is the less expensive, and rather less

attractive, **Športcamp** (☎ 446 72 88; per person/
tent 90/90Sk; ☺ Jun-Sep; **P**). A 10-minute walk
north of Eurocamp, towards Tatranská
Lomnica, is the **Hotel & Intercamp Tatranec**
(☎ 446 70 92; www.tanap.sk/tatranec.html; per person/
tent 100/90Sk; **P**), where you can also pick
up two-bed, A-frame bungalows (1000Sk)
throughout the year.

CHATY

Up on the hiking trails are mountain chalets
(*chaty*), but given their limited capacity and
the popularity of the area, they may all be
full in midsummer. Many of the chalets close
for maintenance in November and May. Although food is available at the chalets, you
should bring some of your own supplies. A
stay in a *chata* is one of the best mountain
experiences the Tatras have to offer.

Satur (p765) in Starý Smokovec can reserve beds at most chalets. High-season
prices are 300Sk to 500Sk per person.

The following are the main chalets on the
upper trails, from west to east:

Chata pod Soliskom (☎ 0905-65 20 36; 1800m)
Small, busy chalet above Štrbské Pleso.
Chata Popradské pleso (☎ 449 21 77; 1500m) Large,
hotel-like *chata* with restaurant.
Sliezský dom (☎ 442 52 61; 1670m) Large mountain
hotel with restaurant and cafeteria.
Zbojnícka chata (☎ 0903-63 80 00; 1960m) Alpine
bunks and restaurant.
Téryho chata (☎ 442 52 45; 2015m) Alpine bunks and
restaurant.
Zamkovského chata (☎ 442 26 36; 1475m) Alpine
bunks and restaurant.
Chata pri Zelenom plese (☎ 446 74 20; 1540m)
Dorm accommodation and restaurant.
Bilíkova chata (☎ 442 24 39; 1220m) Attractive
wooden chalet with double rooms.

PRIVATE ROOMS

Satur can help out with private rooms (250Sk
to 500Sk per person) and apartments. You
can also check out the website for the **Tatra
National Park** (www.tanap.sk/homes.html).

HOTELS

In the high seasons (mid-December to February and mid-June to September), hotel
prices almost double compared with the
low seasons (March to mid-June and October to mid-December). Most prices quoted
in this section are *averages*.

The Satur office (p765) in Starý Smokovec can help you to find a room in all categories, from budget to deluxe. They do not
always know about last-minute cancella-
tions in hotels though, so if they can't direct
you to any accommodation, then tramp
around to see what you can find.

Starý Smokovec & Around
Hotel Sport (☎ 442 23 61; fax 442 27 19; s/d 310/550Sk;
P) On the eastern edge of Starý Smokovec,
this is cheap, but more than a little tatty.

Hotel Smokovec (☎ 442 51 91; www.hotels
mokovec.sk; r 1000Sk; **P** ☻) Smelling of fresh
varnish, this newly renovated place mixes
plenty of mountain charm, with slick service and all the mod cons. It is immediately
above Starý Smokovec train station.

Pension Vesna (☎ 442 27 74; vesna@sinet.sk; r per
person from 500Sk; **P**) Daubed in sparkling,
washing powder-white paint, this immaculate place offers spotless apartments and
excellent service – they even organise 'fireplace parties'. It is behind the large sanatorium, below Nový Smokovec train station.

Villa Dr Szontagh (☎ 442 20 61; szontagh@isternet
.sk; s/d 1500/1700Sk; **P**) Back in Nový Smokovec, this homey place is named after the
town's physician founding-father and harks
back to halcyon Victorian days with its alpine-style, wooden architecture.

Grand Hotel (☎ 442 21 54; www.grandhotel.sk;
s/d incl breakfast 1800/3100Sk; **P** ☒ ☻) Stately
and sophisticated, the Grand takes a step
back towards the old school, a place where
high-status hikers are pampered with plush
rooms and plentiful creature comforts. It is
just off the main road through town, across
from the train station.

Tatranská Lomnica
Penzión Bělín (☎ 446 77 78; www.belin.sk; s/d with
shared bathroom 260/520Sk; **P**) This tumbling,
hostel-style place is a wee bit flaky, but
warm welcomes come as standard and the
price is right. By the time you leave, you'll
probably know everyone in the joint.

Penzión Encian (☎ 446 75 20; penzion.encian@sinet
.sk; s/d 450/900Sk; **P**) All dressed up like a
Christmas tree, with fairy lights and decorative pine branches aplenty, this pretty
place has lashings of charm, a convenient
setting and effortlessly steals the village's
top bed accolade. It's on the main road
through town.

Grandhotel Praha (☎ 446 79 41; www.grandhotel praha.sk; s/d incl breakfast 2100/3000Sk; P ⊠) Indisputably grand, but more than a little frumpy, this once opulent place is now uncannily reminiscent of *The Shining* set. That said, there's still more than a little grace left in its once hallowed corridors and if you have cash to spend, this is the place to do it.

Štrbské Pleso

Hotel Panoráma (☎ 449 21 11; www.hotelpanorama.sk, in Slovak; s/d 830/1400Sk; P) Beamed from a whole different universe of architectural taste, this bizarre pyramid is one of Slovakia's more dramatic eyesores. The rooms are good though, and the view is much nicer looking out. It's above Štrbské Pleso train station.

You'll find some cheaper options down the hill in Tatranská Štrba, including **Hotel Junior Rysy** (☎ 448 48 45; hotel.rysy@ke.telecom.sk; s/d 700/900Sk; P).

Eating & Drinking

Most of the hotels and chalets (see p766) have their own restaurants. The self-service restaurant at **Hotel Smokovec** (mains 80-150Sk) is particularly pleasant, with outdoor seating for summer, alfresco dining. The dining room at **Hotel Grand** (mains 200-350Sk) is the poshest option in Starý Smokovec, and is the ideal treat if you've spent the last week hiking on a diet of bread, cheese and glucose bars.

There are **supermarkets** (*potraviny*) in Starý Smokovec, Tatranská Lomnica and Štrbské Pleso.

Cukráreň Tatra (snacks 30-100Sk; ⏰ 9am-7pm) Also on Starý Smokovec's main thoroughfare, this no-frills café is a cheap and cheerful spot for a restorative hot one and a sticky bun.

Restaurant Koliba (☎ 442 22 04; mains 100-150Sk; ⏰ 11am-10pm) This cosy little bolthole flies the flag for traditional Slovak food – bring on those carbs! It's just southwest of Starý Smokovec train station.

Tatry Pub (☎ 442 24 48; mains 60-160Sk; ⏰ 1-11pm Mon-Thu, 1am-midnight Fri-Sun) This Starý Smokovec institution is the official watering hole of the Mountain Guide Club. Expect hearty food, plenty of beer and lots of mountain-man machismo. It is on the main street, by the car park.

Zbojnícka Koliba (mains 90-160Sk; ⏰ 11am-10pm) Leather-faced fiddlers wander the tables at this distinctly Slovak eatery, while growling stomachs are filled to bursting with rich,

local food. It is in Tatranská Lomnica, just off the road to Grandhotel Praha.

Getting There & Away

BUS

Daily, early morning buses link Bratislava with Starý Smokovec (428Sk, 6½ hours) and Tatranská Lomnica (435Sk, seven hours).

From Starý Smokovec, there are five buses a day to Lysá Poľana (53Sk, one hour), six to Levoča (53Sk, one hour), four to Žilina (188Sk, 3¼ hours) and one to Trenčín (296Sk, five hours).

TRAIN

To reach Vysoké Tatry, catch one of the express trains running between Prague, Bratislava and Košice, and change at Poprad (see opposite for details). There are frequent narrow-gauge electric trains between Poprad and Starý Smokovec (see Getting Around below).

WALKING INTO POLAND

For anyone interested in walking into Poland, there's a highway border crossing at Lysá Poľana near Tatranská Javorina, 30km from Tatranská Lomnica, via Ždiar, by bus (40Sk, 45 minutes).

Also ask Satur (p765) about its excursion buses to Zakopane and Kraków.

Getting Around

Electric trains (*električka*) run from Poprad to Starý Smokovec (16Sk, 30 minutes) and Štrbské Pleso (26Sk, one hour) every hour, and from Starý Smokovec to Tatranská Lomnica (11Sk, 15 minutes) every 30 to 60 minutes. A three-/seven-day ticket on the *električka* costs 119/229Sk.

A rack-railway connects Tatranská Štrba (on the main Žilina–Poprad railway line) with Štrbské Pleso (28Sk, 15 minutes).

Local buses run between the resorts every 20 minutes and tend to be quicker than the train – they have fewer stops though.

You can hire **mountain bikes** from Tatrasport in Starý Smokovec (see p766).

POPRAD

☎ 052 / pop 53,000

Poprad is a modern industrial city with little to interest visitors. However, it is an important transportation hub and a handy gateway to the Vysoké Tatry and Slovenský raj.

The **Poprad Information Agency** (PIA; ☎ 772 17 00; www.poprad.sk; nám Sv Egídia 114; ☺ 8am-6pm Mon-Fri, 9am-noon Sat Jul-Aug, 8.30am-5pm Mon-Fri, 9am-noon Sat Sep-Jun) covers the whole Tatry region and has an excellent accommodation booking service. You can check your email at **Sinet** (nám Sv Egídia 28; per hr 40Sk; ☺ 9am-9pm Mon-Sat, from 1pm Sun).

The **Tatra Museum** (Podtatranské Múzeum; ☎ 772 19 24; Vajanského 4; adult/concession 20/10Sk; ☺ 8am-3.30pm Tue-Sun) is just west of the PIA and features enough natural history exhibits to fill a rainy half-hour.

Charm is not the buzzword at the giant **Hotel Poprad** (☎ 787 08 11; www.hotel-poprad.sk; Partizánska 677/18; s/d incl breakfast 1500/2900Sk; **P**), but the modern rooms are clean and many have views of the high peaks beyond.

The village of Spišská Sobota, 2km northeast of the centre, is now a Poprad suburb and has some excellent, homey options. Recommendations include **Apropo** (☎ 776 90 23; ppas@stonline.sk; Sobotské nám 1743/38; s/d 500/900Sk), which has bright, spacious rooms and some great views, and **Sabato** (☎ 776 95 80; www.sabato.sk; Sobotské nám 1730/6; r €45), which is small and cosy with antiques and charm a-plenty.

Some may find the medieval theme of **Mystery Pub** (☎ 772 29 52; nám Sv Egídia 3643; mains 100-150Sk; ☺ 11am-10pm) a little naff, but this Slovak restaurant, right in the middle of the square, whips up some grand grub and has a pleasant terrace on the 1st floor.

At the busy Italian joint **Pizzeria da Pippo** (nám SV Egídia 2; mains 100-130Sk; ☺ 11am-10pm Sun-Thu, to midnight Fri & Sat), big pizzas steal the show.

Getting There & Away

Express trains are the easiest way to get in and out of Poprad and run to Bratislava (384Sk, 4¼ hours), Žilina (155Sk, two hours) and Košice (138Sk, 1½ hours) every couple of hours. Electric trains climb 13km to Starý Smokovec, the main Vysoké Tatry resort (see opposite), every hour or so.

There are buses to destinations across Slovakia from the bus station next to the train station, including Bratislava (355Sk, four hours) and Košice (130Sk, two hours).

KEŽMAROK

☎ 052 / pop 21,100
You would expect any town overshadowed by the giant, broody peaks of the Vysoké Tatry to develop a fierce sense of identity –

and so it is with Kežmarok. Ever since it was colonised by Germans back in the 13th century, Kežmarok has been treading a subtly different path from the rest of the country – the residents even declared themselves an independent republic in 1918. Independence, however, was short-lived – it was swiftly incorporated into the new Czechoslovakia – and these days quiet Kežmarok is a sleepy place, sporadically brought to life by a busload of passing tourists. There's not much reason to linger, but you can happily fill an afternoon wandering through the three fine churches and the town's castle.

If you can make it to Kežmarok on the second weekend in July, don't miss the **Festival of European Folk Crafts**, Slovakia's biggest crafts fair, with plenty of eating, drinking, music and traditional handiwork.

Orientation & Information

The bus and train stations are side by side, northwest of the old town, just across the Poprad River.

There's an extremely useful **Tourist Information Office** (☎ 452 40 47; www.kezmarok.net; Hlavné nám 46; ☺ 8.30am-noon & 1-5pm Mon-Fri, 9am-2pm Sat year-round, 9am-2pm Sun Jun-Sep) on the main square, offering plenty of information on the whole region.

Sights

The **New Evangelical Church** (Nový Evanjelický Kostol; cnr Toporcerova & Hviezdoslavovo; ☺ 9am-noon & 2-5pm May-Sep), built in 1894, is a huge red and green pseudo-Moorish structure housing the mausoleum of Imre Thököly, who fought with Ferenc Rákóczi against the Habsburg takeover of Hungary. Next door, the **Wooden Articulated Church** (Drevený Kostol; ☺ 9am-noon & 2-5pm May-Sep) was built in 1717 without a single iron nail and has an amazing cross-shaped interior of carved and painted wood. The 30Sk ticket covers entry to both churches.

North of Hlavné nám is the 15th-century Gothic **Basilica of the Holy Cross** (Bazilika SV Kríža; nám Požárnikov; 10Sk; ☺ 9am-5pm Mon-Fri Jun-Sep), with its beautifully carved wooden altars, supposedly crafted by students of Master Pavol of Levoča.

Kežmarok Castle (☎ 452 26 18; adult/concession 60/30Sk; ☺ 9am-noon & 1-4pm Tue-Sun May-Sep, 8am-noon & 1-3pm Mon-Fri Oct-Apr) dates back to the 15th century, and now houses a museum featuring history, archaeology and period-furniture exhibits.

Sleeping & Eating

Kúpalisko Camping (☎ 452 34 79; per person/tent 75/75Sk; ☺ Jun-Aug; ℗) This pleasant camping ground features a spa and can be found in the little village of Vrbov, 7km south of Kežmarok.

Penzión Hidalgo (☎ 452 42 58; www.hidalgo.szm .sk; Starý trh 65; d 790Sk; ℗) This sparkling little place near the castle has blooming window boxes and cheery staff. It is a bit sparse, but spotless all the same.

Club Hotel (☎ 452 40 51; hotelclub@sinet.sk; Dr Alexandra 24; s/d 1200/1700Sk; ℗) This cosy hotel has lashings of once-upon-a-time charm, decent rooms and an excellent restaurant with a breezy terrace. Dr Alexandra runs north from the southwestern corner of Hlavné nám.

Pizza Palermo (☎ 452 38 21; Dr Alexandra; mains 80-120Sk; ☺ noon-10pm) Mediterranean, terracotta styling adds authenticity to this bustling little Italian place. The pizzas are spot on, there are plenty of giant pepper-grinders on show and there's a pleasant suntrap for summer eating out back.

Getting There & Away

Buses are faster and more plentiful than trains – they run hourly to/from Poprad (22Sk, 30 minutes), and there are eight daily to/from Starý Smokovec (30Sk, 40 minutes). From Monday to Friday, there are three buses a day (only one Saturday and Sunday) to Červený Kláštor (55Sk, 1½ hours).

DUNAJEC GORGE

☎ 052

The Pieniny National Park (21 sq km), created in 1967, combines with a similar park in Poland to protect the 9km Dunajec Gorge between the Slovak village of Červený Kláštor and Szczawnica, Poland. Pieniny means 'foam' in Slovak, a name that evokes the torrent of water bubbling between the impressive 500m-tall cliffs that form the maws of the gorge. Those wishing to explore the gorge in detail should pick up VKÚ's 1:25,000 *Pieninský Národný Park* map (sheet No 7).

At the mouth of the gorge is a fortified 14th-century **Carthusian monastery** (☎ 482 29 55; adult/concession 50/25Sk; ☺ 9am-5pm May-Oct), now used as a park administrative centre and museum with a good collection of statuary and old prints of the area. Two kilometres west of the monastery is an **information centre** (☎ 482 21 22; www.pieniny.sk; ☺ 9am-5pm May-Oct).

From May to October, **river trips** (adult/child 250/100Sk) on wooden rafts (*pltě*) depart from two locations at Červený Kláštor: opposite the monastery, and 1km upriver west of the village. A raft will set out only when enough passengers appear. When business is slow you may have to wait. Don't expect whitewater rafting – the Dunajec is a rather sedate experience.

From the downriver terminus you can hike back to the monastery in a little over an hour. The rafting operation on the Polish side is larger and better organised (see Dunajec Gorge in the Poland chapter for details), and the Slovak raft trip is much shorter than the Polish one.

Even if you don't go rafting, it's still worth hiking along the riverside trail through the gorge.

Sleeping

Across a small stream from the monastery is a **camping ground** (per person/tent 35/45Sk; ☺ mid-Jun–mid-Sep; ℗) – no bungalows are available.

For private rooms, try **CK Pieniny Klub** (☎ 439 73 03; www.sl.sinet.sk/pieniny; per person from 230Sk) in Lesnica.

There are several pensions in Červený Kláštor plus the above-average **Hotel Pltník** (☎ 482 25 25; pltnik@szm.sk; s/d 300/600Sk; ℗), which has a restaurant, but is often booked out in summer.

One kilometre up the road to Veľký Lipník from the monastery is **Hotel Dunajec** (☎ 439 71 05; s/d 600/1200Sk; ℗). It quickly fills up with tour groups, but has a **camping ground** (per person/tent 50/50Sk) and rents out mountain bikes for 350Sk per day.

Close to Lesnica, which is just 2km east of Cerveny Klastor, near the downstream end of the rafting trip, is the inexpensive **Pieniny chata** (☎ 439 75 30; s/d 240/480Sk). It is cheap, cheerful and ideal for those on a budget.

Getting There & Away

Buses run between Červený Kláštor and Poprad (83Sk, two hours), and to Košice (152Sk, 3½ hours) via Stara Ľubovňa.

Seven kilometres west of the monastery, at Spišská Stara Ves, there is a border crossing into Poland.

SLOVENSKÝ RAJ

☎ 053

Raj by name, paradise by nature, the **Slovak Paradise National Park** (Národní Park Slovenský Raj; www.slovenskyraj.sk) contains some of East Slovakia's great, unspoilt beauty spots, combining a dazzling roll call of waterfalls, thick forests and rolling hill tops, with an excellent array of flora and fauna. Whether it's hiking in the balmy summer months, or cross-country skiing when the park vanishes under a blanket of snow, the Slovenský Raj is a paradise for the passionately outdoorsy.

Orientation & Information

The nearest town is **Spišská Nová Ves**, 23km southeast of Poprad. The main trailheads on the northern edge of the national park are at Čingov, 5km west of Spišská Nová Ves, and Podlesok, 1km southwest of Hrabušice.

MONEY

Slovenská sporiteľňa (nám MR Štefánika; ✆ 9am-4pm Mon-Fri) You can cash travellers cheques or use the 24-hour ATM here.

POST

Main post office (nám MR Štefánika 7; ✆ 7am-7pm Mon-Fri, 7am-11am Sat) The telephone centre is also here.

TOURIST INFORMATION

AiCES information centre (☎ 442 82 92; www .slovenskyraj.sk; Letná 49; ✆ 8am-5pm Mon-Fri, 9.30am-1.30pm Sat Jun-Sep, 8am-4.30pm Mon-Fri Oct-May) In Spišská Nová Ves, this place can help with accommodation and national park information. You can buy VKÚ's 1:25,000 Slovenský raj hiking map (sheet No 4) here.

Sights & Activities

For comprehensive trail information, visit the **Mountain Rescue Service** (Horská Služba; ☎ 449 11 82; ✆ 8am-6pm), in Čingov.

From Čingov a blue trail leads up the **Hornád River gorge**, passing below **Tomášovský výhľad**, to **Letanovský mlyn**. The trail up the river is narrow and there are several ladders and ramps where hikers can only pass one by one. During peak periods hikers are allowed to travel only in an upstream direction from Čingov, returning over Tomášovský výhľad.

One kilometre beyond Letanovský mlyn, a green trail leaves the river and climbs sharply up to **Kláštorisko**, where there's a **restaurant** (☎ 449 33 07; chalets per person 250Sk; ✆ year-round), with chalet (chaty) accommodation. To stay here in midsummer, you should call ahead to check availability. From Kláštorisko you can follow another blue trail back down the ridge towards Čingov. You'll need around six hours to do the entire circuit, lunch at Kláštorisko included.

From Podlesok, an excellent day's hike heads up the **Suchá Belá gorge** (with several steep ladders), then east to Kláštorisko on a yellow then red trail. From here, take the blue trail down to the Hornád River, then follow the river gorge upstream to return to Podlesok. Allow six to seven hours.

The **Dobšinská Ice Cave** (Dobšinská Ľadová Jaskyňa; ☎ 788 14 70; adult/concession 120/60Sk; ✆ 9am-4pm Tue-Sun Jun-Aug, 9.30am-2pm Tue-Sun May & Sep), west of Stratená, is coated in ice and the Grand Hall (Veľká Sieň) features an array of dazzling formations. Tours leave every hour or so.

Sleeping

Autocamping Ýurkovec (☎ 429 71 05; fax 429 71 06; per person/tent 60/60Sk, 2-bed bungalow 720Sk; P) About 20 minutes' walk west from Čingov bus stop, this spot has camping and cabins.

Autocamp Podlesok (☎ 429 91 65; slovrajbela@ stonline.sk; per person/tent 60/60Sk; P) Pitch a tent or take a two-bed bungalow (750Sk) at this place, which is a 2km walk from Hrabušice.

Hotel Trio (☎ 429 98 36; www.hoteltrio.sk, in Slovak; s/d 390/780Sk; P) This hotel is a spotless, chalet-style place with helpful owners, a welcoming air and a starburst of flowers in the grounds. If it's fully booked, nearby **Hotel Čingov** (☎ 443 36 63; www.hotelcingov.sk; r 960Sk; P) is a little more battered, but has a sauna for post-hike recuperation. Better, refurbished rooms cost 1250Sk. Both hotels are just east of Čingov, en route to Spišska Nová Ves.

Getting There & Away

Spišska Nová Ves is the main access point for the Slovenský Raj region. Regular buses link the town with Levoča (17Sk, 20 minutes) and there are also hourly trains to/ from Levoča (17Sk, 15 minutes) and regular services to/from Žilina (200Sk, 2¼ hours) and Košice (104Sk, one hour).

From Spišska Nová Ves, buses run to the trailheads of Čingov (8Sk, 15 minutes, nine

SPIŠSKÁ NOVÁ VES & SLOVENSKÝ RAJ

daily Monday to Friday, once daily Saturday and Sunday) and Dedinky (60Sk, 1½ hours, three buses Monday to Friday).

LEVOČA

☎ 053 / pop 13,000

Few towns evoke images of the old Slovakia as readily as historic Levoča. Largely untouched by modern development, the walled old town is apparently cut off from the 21st century and life goes on around the main square's stunning Renaissance buildings at a distinctly measured pace.

In the 13th century the king of Hungary invited Saxon Germans to colonise the Spiš region on the eastern borderlands of his kingdom, as a protection against Tatar incursions and to develop mining. Levoča was one of the towns founded at this time.

The town is an easy stop on the way from Poprad to Košice.

Orientation & Information

The train and bus stations are 1km south of town. The most convenient bus stop is nám Štefana Kluberta, outside the Košice Gate.

INTERNET ACCESS

Levonet Internet Café (nám Majstra Pavla 38; per min 1.5Sk; ⏰ 10am-10pm) At the southern end of the square.

MONEY

Slovenská sporiteľňa (nám Majstra Pavla 56; ⏰ 8am-3pm Mon, Tue, Thu & Fri, to 4pm Wed) Changes travellers cheques and has an ATM.

POST

Post office (nám Majstra Pavla 42; ⏰ 8am-noon & 1-5pm Mon-Fri, 8-10.30am Sat) The telephone centre is in here too.

TOURIST INFORMATION

AiCES information centre (☎ 451 37 63; www .levoca.sk; nám Majstra Pavla 58; ⏰ 9am-5pm Mon-Sat, 10am-2pm Sun May-Oct, 9am-4.30pm Mon-Fri Nov-Apr) At the top of the square.

Sights

Nám Majstra Pavla, Levoča's central square, is choc-a-bloc with superb Gothic and Renaissance buildings. The 15th-century **Church of St James** (chrám sv Jakuba; ☎ 442 45 00; adult/concession 50/30Sk; ⏰ tours 8.30, 9.30, 10.30 & 11.30am,

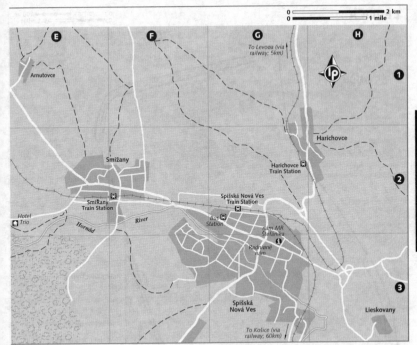

1, 2, 3 & 4pm Tue-Sat) contains a towering Gothic altar (1517) by Majster Pavol (Master Paul) of Levoča, one of the largest and finest of its kind in Europe. The Madonna on this altar appears on the 100Sk banknote. Buy tickets in the **Municipal Weights House** (☺ as church) opposite the north door.

Next to St James' is the Gothic **town hall**, enlivened by Renaissance arcades and murals of the civic virtues. Today it houses the **Spiš Museum** (Spišske Múzeum; ☎ 451 24 49; adult/concession 30/15Sk; ☺ 9am-5pm), but the medieval rooms are more interesting than the exhibits they contain. Beside the town hall is a 16th-century **cage of shame**, where prisoners were once exhibited, to the delight of sadistic locals.

There's also a good **crafts museum** (Výtvarná Kultúra na Spiši; nám Majstra Pavla; adult/concession 30/15Sk; ☺ 9am-5pm), housed in a beautiful, 15th-century house on the main square. While you're there have a peek in the courtyard of No 43; its Renaissance architecture is well worth a look.

There are plenty of photogenic old artisans' houses on the main square. The **Thur-zov dom** (1532) at No 7, which now houses the State Archives, sports a fine orange wash and frescoes galore. At No 20 you'll find the **Majster Pavol Museum**, with icons that were painted by Majster Pavol of Levoča – it was closed at the time of writing, but will reopen in 2005.

On a hill 2km north of town is the large neo-Gothic **Church of Mariánska hora**, where the largest Catholic pilgrimage in Slovakia takes place in early July.

During winter, you can take to the pistes at the new **ski centre** (☎ 451 37 63; http://suz.levoca.sk), 5km north of town. All-day ski passes cost 350Sk.

Sleeping

AiCES can book accommodation, including **private rooms** from 250Sk per person. You can camp at **Levočská Dolina Autocamp** (☎ 451 27 05; per person 80Sk; ☺ mid-Jun–Aug; ℗), 5km northwest of the centre.

Hotel Faix (☎ 451 11 11; Probstnerova cesta 22; s/d 250/500Sk) Glamorous it is not, but this no-frills place is within easy reach of the train station and old town, and the beds

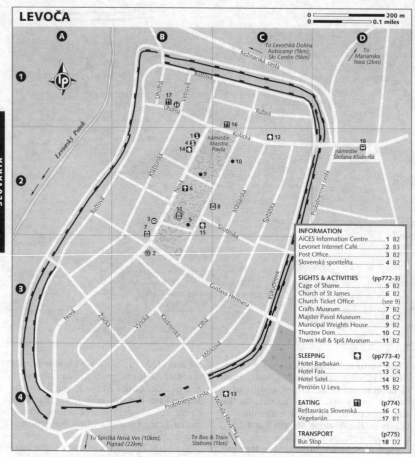

LEVOČA

INFORMATION
AiCES Information Centre	1 B2
Levonet Internet Café	2 B3
Post Office	3 B2
Slovenská sporiteľňa	4 B2

SIGHTS & ACTIVITIES (pp772–3)
Cage of Shame	5 B2
Church of St James	6 B2
Church Ticket Office	(see 9)
Crafts Museum	7 B2
Majster Pavol Museum	8 C2
Municipal Weights House	9 B2
Thurzov Dom	10 C2
Town Hall & Spiš Museum	11 B2

SLEEPING (pp773–4)
Hotel Barbakan	12 C2
Hotel Faix	13 C4
Hotel Satel	14 B2
Penzión U Leva	15 B2

EATING (p774)
Reštaurácia Slovenská	16 C1
Vegetarián	17 B1

TRANSPORT (p775)
Bus Stop	18 D2

are cheap. Most of the rooms have shared bathrooms.

Hotel Barbakan (☎ 451 43 10; recepcia.hot@barbakan.sk; Košická 15; s/d incl breakfast 1150/1450Sk) Carrying a decent dose of old Levoča charm right into the cosy bedrooms, this atmospheric place is well worth checking out, if just for its creaking floorboards and upmarket restaurant.

Penzión U Leva (☎ 450 23 11; www.uleva.szm.sk; nám Majstra Pavla 24; s/d 1100/1900Sk; P) You can smell the fresh paint in this sparkling new place. Accommodation is in self-contained apartments, with kitchenettes and satellite TV, and tip-top standards are on the house.

Hotel Satel (☎ 451 29 43; www.satel-slovakia.sk; nám Majstra Pavla 55; s/d incl breakfast 1850/2500Sk; P)

This grandiose place is really quite swish, with rooms around an enclosed, monastic-style courtyard, plenty of (artificial) flowers and immaculate rooms. It also has a sauna and spa.

Eating
Vegetarián (☎ 451 45 76; Uholná 137; mains 30–70Sk; ☼ 10am-3.15pm Mon-Fri) Wholesome smells and a no-fuss menu make this basic veggie haunt a hit with locals. It is off the northwest corner of the main square.

Reštaurácia Slovenská (☎ 451 23 29; nám Majstra Pavla 62; mains 60–140Sk; ☼ 10am-10pm) Slovak meat feasts, a homely atmosphere and an extremely affordable menu make this a top tip for hungry travellers.

Getting There & Away

Hourly trains run to Spišská Nová Ves (17Sk, 15 minutes), on the main Bratislava to Košice line. Bus travel is more practical, as there are frequent services to Poprad (38Sk, 30 minutes) and Spišské Podhradie (22Sk, 20 minutes) and eight daily to Košice (120Sk, two hours). All buses stop at nám Štefana Kluberta and some local buses also stop at the train station.

SPIŠSKÉ PODHRADIE
☎ 053

Spišské Podhradie is a dusty, bedraggled little town, but sits between two of East Slovakia's hottest tourist trail tickets: Spišský hrad (Spiš castle) and Spišská Kapitula.

Sights

If you're arriving by bus from Levoča, ask the driver to drop you at **Spišská Kapitula**, on a ridge 1km west of Spišské Podhradie. This 13th-century ecclesiastical settlement is completely encircled by a 16th-century wall and the single street running between the two medieval gates is peppered with picturesque Gothic houses.

At the upper end is the magnificent **St Martin's Cathedral** (adult/concession 20/10Sk; 11.15am-2.45pm), built in 1273, with twin Romanesque towers and a Gothic sanctuary. Inside are three folding Gothic altars (1499) and, near the door, a Romanesque white lion. On either side of the cathedral are the **seminary** and the Renaissance **bishop's palace** (1652). Buy tickets from the nearby **information office** (☎ 0907-38 84 11; as cathedral), where you can also pick up a guide.

Crowning a ridge on the far side of Spišské Podhradie is ghostly **Spišský hrad** (☎ 454 13 36; adult/concession 60/30Sk; 8.30am-5.15pm May-Oct, by appointment Nov-Apr), the largest castle in Slovakia. In 1993 it was added to Unesco's World Heritage list. The castle is directly above the train station, 1km south of Spišské Podhradie's bus stop. Cross at the tracks near the station and follow the yellow markers up to the castle. The first gate is always locked, so carry on to the second one higher up. (If you're driving or cycling, the access road is off the Prešov highway east of town).

The castle was founded in 1209 – the defenders of Spišský are said to have repulsed the Tatars in 1241 – and reconstructed in the

15th century. Until 1710 the Spiš region was administered from here. Although the castle burnt down in 1780, the ruins and the site are still spectacular. The highest castle enclosure contains a round Gothic tower, a cistern, a chapel and a rectangular Romanesque palace perched over the abyss. Weapons and instruments of torture are exhibited in the dungeon (explanations in Slovak only).

Sleeping

Penzión Podzámok (☎ 454 17 55; www.penzion podzamok.sk; Podzámková 28; s/d with shared bathroom 250/500Sk) This cosy, basic place is the best option in town. To get there, turn left after the bridge, just south of Mariánské nám.

Kolping House (☎ 450 21 11; www.hotelkolping.sk; s/d 1100/1600Sk; P) This romantic little outfit makes an excellent treat. It drips old world charm and is actually inside the walls of Spišská Kapitula.

Getting There & Away

A railway line connects Spišské Podhradie to Spišské Vlachy (12Sk, 15 minutes), a station on the main line from Poprad to Košice. Relatively frequent buses run to Levoča (22Sk, 20 minutes) and Poprad (55Sk, 50 minutes).

BARDEJOV
☎ 054 / pop 32,500

The construction work never seems to stop in the pretty, historic town of Bardejov. Which is no bad thing. Peppered with dreamy, Gothic-Renaissance houses and surrounded by the moats and bastions of the old defensive walls, this market town is being enthusiastically preserved, creating one of the region's treasures – it earned Unesco World Heritage status in 2000. There's not a whole lot to do but waddle around the sloping central square full of local beer, but Bardejov makes a pleasant stop for those after some peace and quiet.

The town hosts several festivals, one of the liveliest being The Market (jarmork), when, at the end of August, Radničné nám turns into a maze of stalls, with lots of food, drink and good times included.

History

Bardejov received its royal charter in 1376, and grew rich on trade between Poland and Russia. After an abortive 17th-century

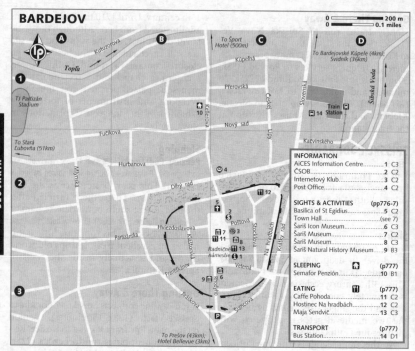

BARDEJOV

INFORMATION	
AiCES Information Centre	1 C3
ČSOB	2 C2
Internetový Klub	3 C2
Post Office	4 C2

SIGHTS & ACTIVITIES	(pp776-7)
Basilica of St Egídius	5 C2
Town Hall	(see 7)
Šariš Icon Museum	6 C3
Šariš Museum	7 C3
Šariš Museum	8 C3
Šariš Natural History Museum	9 B3

SLEEPING	(p777)
Semafor Penzión	10 B1

EATING	(p777)
Caffe Pohoda	11 C2
Hostinec Na hradbách	12 C2
Maja Sendvič	13 C3

TRANSPORT	(p777)
Bus Station	14 D1

revolt against the Habsburgs, Bardejov's fortunes declined, but the medieval town survived. In late 1944 heavy fighting took place at the Dukla Pass on the Polish border, 54km northeast of Bardejov on the road to Rzeszów (preserved WWII Soviet tanks can be seen from the road).

Orientation

The bus and train station is a five-minute walk northeast from Radničné nám, the main square in Bardejov.

Information

INTERNET ACCESS

Internetový Klub (☎ 0903-18 04 17; 2nd fl, Radničné nám 12; ☽ 10am-10pm Mon-Fri, from 2pm Sat & Sun; per 30 min 21Sk)

MONEY

ČSOB (Radničné nám 7; ☽ 8am-5pm Mon-Thu, to 4pm Fri) Has an ATM and change facilities.

POST

Main post office (Dlhý rad 14; ☽ 7am-6pm Mon-Fri, 7.30-10.30am Sat) Also houses the telephone centre.

TOURIST INFORMATION

AiCES information centre (☎ 472 62 73; spirit@spirit -travel.sk; Radničné nám 21; ☽ 9am-4.30pm Mon-Fri) Can assist with accommodation and guided tours – helpful.

Sights

The interior of the 14th-century **Basilica of St Egídius** (Bazilika Sv Egídia; adult/concession 25/15Sk, tower 40/20Sk; ☽ 10am-3pm Mon-Fri, to 2pm Sat, 11.30am-2pm Sun) is packed with Gothic marvels, with no less than 11 tall altarpieces, built from 1460 to 1510, all with their own original paintings and sculptures.

There are also four branches of the **Šariš Museum** (☎ 472 49 66; adult/concession 40/20Sk; ☽ 8am-noon & 12.30-4pm Tue-Sun) on and around the main square. The first, housing altarpieces and a historical collection, is in the **old town hall** (1509), which takes pride of place in the middle of the square. This magnificent structure was the first Renaissance building in Slovakia. Two more museums face one another on Rhodyho, at the southern end of the square: one has an excellent natural history exhibit, the other a dazzling collection of icons. A fourth branch, at Radničné nám 13, has temporary art exhibits.

Sleeping

There's not a lot to choose from. The **AiCES** can arrange private rooms from 300Sk per person.

Semafor Penzión (☎ 0905-83 09 84; semafor@stonline .sk; cnr Kellerova & BS Timravy; s/d 700/900Sk; **P**) The large, bright rooms are the main selling point of this newly renovated pension. The helpful owners come a close second and there's a communal kitchen for guests.

Hotel Bellevue (☎ 472 84 04; fax 472 84 09; Mihalov; s/d 1800/2200Sk; **P**) As flash as Bardejov's meagre hotel selection allows, this slightly swanky place sits on a hill top 3km southwest of the centre; take bus No 8 westbound from Dlhý rad.

Eating

Again, there is not much choice.

Maja Sendvič (☎ 091-94 10 64; Radničné nám 15; ☺ 8am-9pm Mon-Thu, 8am-11pm Fri, 3-11pm Sat, 3-8pm Sun) This fly-by sandwich shop has cornered Bardejov's fast-food market, selling huge baguettes for around 30Sk.

Hostinec Na hradbách (Stöcklova 16; mains 60-120Sk; ☺ 10am-10pm Mon-Fri, 11am-3pm Sat & Sun) Frothy moustaches and meaty fare rule the day at this no-frills, Slovakian beer hall.

Caffe Pohoda (Radničné nám 39; mains 80-180Sk; ☺ 10am-10pm) At the other end of the spectrum, this basement café opts for contemporary décor and scented candles. There's a reasonable range of coffees and light meals on offer, but the basement setting gets quite claustrophobic.

Getting There & Away

There are frequent buses from Bardejov to Košice (53Sk, one hour). If you want to go to the Vysoké Tatry, there are hourly buses for Poprad (128Sk, 2½ hours); there are also two buses daily direct to Starý Smokovec (152Sk, three hours), three to Bratislava (572Sk, nine hours) and six to Žilina (308Sk, five hours).

KOŠICE

☎ 055 / pop 236,500

Steel manufacturing forms Košice's economic backbone, but Slovakia's second city has a heart of gold, with a beautifully restored old town square rivalling anything in Bratislava, and a vibrant, youthful buzz. Stalinist tower blocks today jostle for hegemony over the city's historic monuments, but East Slovakia's urban hub retains a strong sense of identity and offers a fascinating insight into the country's wilder half.

History

The Transylvanian prince Ferenc Rákóczi II had his headquarters at Košice during the Hungarian War of Independence against the Habsburgs (1703–11). The town became part of Czechoslovakia in 1918 but was again occupied by Hungary between 1938 and 1945. From 21 February to 21 April 1945, Košice served as the capital of the liberated Czechoslovakia. On 5 April 1945 the Košice Government Program – which made communist dictatorship in Czechoslovakia a virtual certainty – was announced here.

Orientation

The adjacent bus and train stations are just east of the old town. A five-minute walk along Mlynská will bring you into Hlavná (Main Street), which broadens to accommodate the squares of Hlavné nám and nám Slobody.

Information

BOOKSHOPS

BP Press (Hlavná 102; ☺ 7am-8pm Mon-Fri, 8am-8pm Sat, 10am-8pm Sun) A good range of foreign magazines and newspapers.

Marsab (☎ 625 67 03; Hlavná 41; ☺ 8am-6pm Mon-Fri, 9am-1pm Sat) Sells hiking maps, town plans and a small selection of English-language titles.

EMERGENCY

Police station (☎ 159; cnr Štúrova & Fejova) Just south of the centre.

INTERNET ACCESS

Internet Café (☎ 622 11 87; Hlavná 27; per hr 35Sk; ☺ 9am-10pm) In the East Slovak Gallery.

Municipal information centre (☎ 625 88 88; Hlavná 59; per hr 30Sk; ☺ 9am-6pm Mon-Fri, 9am-1pm Sat)

MEDICAL SERVICES

Hospital (Fakultná nemocnica L Pasteura; ☎ 615 31 11; Rastislavova 45)

MONEY

ČSOB (Hlavná 23; ☺ 8am-5pm Mon-Thu, to 4pm Fri) Has an ATM and change facilities.

KOŠICE

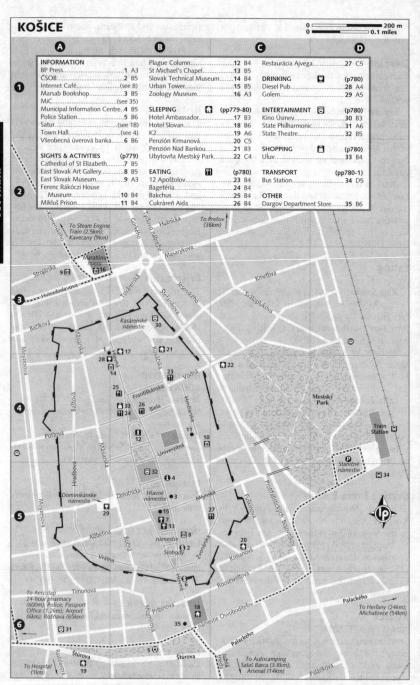

0 ———— 200 m
0 ———— 0.1 miles

A

INFORMATION
BP Press.............................1 A3
ČSOB...............................2 B5
Internet Café.................(see 8)
Marsab Bookshop...............3 B5
MiC.............................(see 35)
Municipal Information Centre..4 B5
Police Station....................5 B6
Satur............................(see 18)
Town Hall.....................(see 4)
Všeobecná úverová banka....6 B6

SIGHTS & ACTIVITIES   (p779)
Cathedral of St Elizabeth.......7 B4
East Slovak Art Gallery..........8 B5
East Slovak Museum.............9 A3
Ferenc Rákóczi House
   Museum........................10 B4
Mikluš Prison....................11 B4

B

Plague Column...................12 B4
St Michael's Chapel..............13 B5
Slovak Technical Museum......14 B4
Urban Tower.....................15 B5
Zoology Museum................16 A3

SLEEPING   (pp779–80)
Hotel Ambassador...............17 B3
Hotel Slovan....................18 B6
K2...............................19 A6
Penzión Krmanová..............20 C5
Penzión Nad Bankou...........21 B3
Ubytovňa Mestský Park........22 C4

EATING   (p780)
12 Apoštolov....................23 B4
Bagetéria........................24 B4
Bakchus.........................25 B4
Cukráreň Aida...................26 B4

C

Restaurácia Ajvega.............27 C5

DRINKING   (p780)
Diesel Pub.......................28 A4
Golem...........................29 A5

ENTERTAINMENT   (p780)
Kino Úsmev.....................30 B3
State Philharmonic..............31 A6
State Theatre....................32 B5

SHOPPING   (p780)
Úľuv.............................33 B4

TRANSPORT   (pp780–1)
Bus Station......................34 D5

OTHER
Dargov Department Store.......35 B6

EAST SLOVAKIA •• Košice **779**

Všeobecná úverová banka (Hlavná 8; ⏰ 8am-5pm Mon-Thu, until 4pm Fri)

POST
Main post office (Poštová 18; ⏰ 7am-7pm Mon-Fri, 7am-2pm Sat)

TOURIST INFORMATION
MiC (☎ 16 168; www.mickosice.sk; ⏰ 8am-5pm Mon-Fri, 9am-1pm Sat) A small information bureau in the Dargov department store, opposite Hotel Slovan.
Municipal information centre (☎ 625 88 88; www .kosice.sk/icmk, in Slovak; Hlavná 59; ⏰ 9am-6pm Mon-Fri, 9am-1pm Sat) A larger enterprise in the town hall, with maps and accommodation information.

TRAVEL AGENCIES
Satur (☎ 622 31 23; www.satur.sk; Hlavná 1; ⏰ 9am-5pm Mon-Fri) Next to Hotel Slovan. Sells international bus, plane and train tickets.

Sights
Košice's magnificent 1345 **Cathedral of St Elizabeth** (Dóm sv Alžbety; ☎ 0908-66 70 93; guided tours adult/concession 35/20Sk, crypt & tower 30/15Sk; ⏰ 9.30am-4.30pm Mon-Fri, 9am-1.30pm Sat, cathedral nave ⏰ 8am-8pm), Europe's easternmost Gothic cathedral, dominates the old town square and is the sight most likely to grace your Košice postcard home. In a crypt on the left side of the nave is the tomb of Duke Ferenc Rákóczi, who was exiled to Turkey after the failed 18th-century Hungarian revolt against Austria. On the south side of the cathedral is the 14th-century **St Michael's Chapel** (closed for renovations), and to the north is the **Urban Tower** (closed to the public).

Art lovers should poke their nose into the nearby **East Slovak Art Gallery** (Východoslovenská galéria; ☎ 622 11 87; Hlavná 27; adult/concession 20/10Sk; ⏰ 10am-6pm Tue-Fri, 1-5.30pm Sat, 2-5.30pm Sun), housed in a building that dates from 1779 and from which the 1945 Košice Government Program was proclaimed.

Most of Košice's other historic sites are located north along Hlavná. In the centre of the square is the ornate 1899 **State Theatre** (see p780), with a kitsch musical fountain in front. Facing it at Hlavná 59, is the former **town hall** (1780), and north of the theatre is a large baroque **plague column** (1723).

Further north is the **Slovak Technical Museum** (Slovenské Technické Múzeum; ☎ 622 40 35; Hlavná 88; adult/concession 20/10Sk; ⏰ 8am-5pm Tue-Fri, 9am-2pm Sat, noon-5pm Sun), which is full of examples of old technology that technophiles will find interesting.

The **East Slovak Museum** (Východoslovenské Múzeum; ☎ 622 03 09; Hviezdoslavovo 3; adult/concession 30/10Sk; ⏰ 9am-5pm Tue-Sat, 9am-1pm Sun), at the northern end of Hlavná, is dedicated to regional culture, history and archaeology. Don't miss the Košice Gold Treasure in the basement, a hoard of 2920 gold coins dating from the 15th to 18th centuries and discovered by chance in 1935.

In the park behind the museum building is an old wooden church and across the square is the so-so **Zoology Museum** (adult/concession 30/10Sk; ⏰ 9am-5pm Tue-Sat, to 1pm Sun).

Walk back along Hlavná towards the State Theatre and turn left on narrow Univerzitná to **Mikluš Prison** (Miklušova Važnici; ☎ 622 28 56; Pri Mikluševej Važnici; adult/concession 30/10Sk; ⏰ 9am-5pm, to 1pm Sun). This pair of 16th-century houses once served as a prison equipped with medieval torture chambers and cells. The nearby **Ferenc Rákóczi House Museum** (Hrnčiarska 7; adult/concession 30/10Sk; ⏰ 9am-5pm Tue-Sat, to 1pm Sun) is housed in the Executioner's Bastion, a section of the town's 15th-century defensive walls. Rákóczi was exiled to Turkey after Hungary's failed 18th-century rebellion against Austria. The highlight here is the replica of his house. Tickets for both museums are bought here.

Sleeping
BUDGET
The Municipal information centre (above) can help with private rooms from 300Sk per person.

Autocamping Salaš Barca (☎ 623 33 97; Alejová 24; per person 70Sk) There's not a whole lot here, but this place, south of the city, remains the best bet for Košice's campers. Call ahead for directions.

Ubytovňa Mestský Park (☎ 633 39 04; fax 671 07 66; Mestský Park 13; s/d with shared bathroom 220/440Sk) In the town park, east of the centre, this no-frills hostel is a little rougher and a little cheaper.

K2 (☎ 625 59 48; Štúrova 32; s/d with shared bathroom 330/660Sk) This reasonably central sports complex is the city's cheap sleeps champion, with chirpy staff and a restaurant, fitness centre and sauna.

MID-RANGE & TOP END
Penzión Nad Bankou (☎ 683 82 21; vaskoj@isternet .sk; Kováčska 63; s/d 900/1200Sk; P) White-washed walls and pine furniture dominate

this simple, airy place. The clean rooms are poky, but comfortable, and there's a small restaurant below.

Penzión Krmanová (☎ 623 05 65; krmanova@elvs .sk; Krmanová 14; s/d 1350/1850Sk) This pretty pension is central, cheerful and charming, offering big modern rooms and chirpy staff.

Hotel Ambassador (☎ 720 37 20; www.abba.sk; Hlavná 101; s/d incl breakfast 2190/2800Sk) Košice's most intimate, upmarket option has plenty of boutique charm and a bustling outdoor café, which attracts town's elegant espresso set like wasps to a soda.

Hotel Slovan (☎ 622 73 78; www.hotelslovan.sk; Hlavná 1; s/d with breakfast 2840/3400Sk; P 🐶) Home for visiting business and government types, Košice's showcase hotel is sadly haunted by an enduring, communist-era gloom.

Eating & Drinking

Cukráreň Aida (cnr Hlavná 81; snacks 30-100Sk; 🕑 8am-10pm) Despite the pigeon pooh-spattered awnings, this is one of Košice's most popular cafés and is famed for its heavenly ice cream. You can also get cheap baguette sandwiches at nearby **Bagetéria** (Hlavná 74).

Bakchus (☎ 622 18 14; Hlavná 80; mains 55-90Sk; 🕑 10am-11pm) Right on the main square, this bustling place has a cosy pub out back, a hipper restaurant up front and a beer terrace for raucous summer tipples in between. Hearty Slovakian food is the staple.

Reštaurácia Ajvega (Orlia 10; mains 90-135Sk; 🕑 10am-10pm) Mountains of vegetarian and Mexican food steal the show here.

12 Apoštolov (☎ 729 51 05; Kováčska 51; mains 100-200Sk; 🕑 10.30am-11pm Sat-Tue, to midnight Wed-Fri) If the Last Supper had been hosted in Košice, this would have been the venue – at least that's the look the owners are going for. With classic décor, ever-so-religious pew seating and plenty of atmosphere, this is a top place to sample mountains of East Slovakia's speciality fare.

Diesel Pub (☎ 622 21 86; Hlavná 92; 🕑 noon-midnight Mon-Thu, to 1am Fri-Sun) Down an alley full of 'music clubs', this Celtic-inspired haunt promises oodles of good cheer and rivers of (slightly overpriced) booze.

Golem (☎ 728 91 01; Dominikánske nám; 🕑 noon-midnight) This hideaway pub and eatery moonlights as one of Slovakia's finest microbreweries. If you want to indulge in the idiosyncrasies of Slovak beer, this is an excellent place to start.

Entertainment

A flick through free monthly publication *Kam do Mesta* is the best way to get to the bottom of the whats, wheres and whens of Košice's entertainment scene.

CINEMAS

Kino Usmev (☎ 622 12 22; Kasárenské nám 1) Shows the latest Hollywood flicks.

THEATRE & LIVE MUSIC

The renovated **State Theatre** (Štá Divadlo Košice; ☎ 622 12 31; www.sdke.sk; Hlavná 58; box office 🕑 9am-5.30pm Mon-Fri, 10am-1pm Sat) stages regular performances.

The **State Philharmonic** (Štátna Filharmónia Košice; ☎ 622 45 14; Moyzesova 66) is the city's principal orchestra and performs across town.

Shopping

Úľuv (Hlavná 76; 🕑 9am-5pm Mon-Fri, to noon Sat) has a good selection of local handicrafts.

Getting There & Away

BUS

Several buses run daily to Levoča (120Sk, two hours), Poprad (130Sk, two hours) and Bratislava (512Sk, seven hours). Buses also travel to Uzhhorod, Ukraine (140Sk, 2½ hours) three times daily, to Nowy Targ, Poland (180Sk, four hours) every Thursday and Saturday, and to Krosno, Poland (170Sk, 3½ hours) every Wednesday, Friday and Saturday.

There's a bus from Košice to Miskolc (120Sk, two hours), in Hungary, on Monday, Thursday, Friday and Saturday.

For further times and prices, check www .vlaky.sk.

CAR

You will find **Hertz** (☎ 729 28 41) and **Avis** (☎ 632 58 63) desks at the airport. Call ahead if you want a car delivered to your hotel.

TRAIN

Regular domestic trains run to Poprad (138Sk, 1½ hours), Žilina (286Sk, three hours), Trenčín (375Sk, five hours) and Bratislava (590Sk, six hours).

A sleeper train leaves Košice every morning for Kyiv (Kiev), in the Ukraine (1600Sk, 22½ hours). Overnight trains also run to Prague (1200Sk, 11 hours) and Brno (830Sk, nine hours), in the Czech Republic.

Three daily trains run to Kraków, Poland (930Sk, 6½ hours) and four travel to Miskolc, Hungary (330Sk, two hours), with three of these carrying on to Budapest (900Sk, four hours).

For further times and prices visit www.zsr.sk or www.vlaky.sk.

Getting Around
Bus and tram tickets are available for 12Sk from tobacconists, newsstands and public transport kiosks. Visit www.kosice.sk or call ☎ 622 59 25 for information.

SLOVAKIA DIRECTORY

ACCOMMODATION
Prices fluctuate according to season, with high season running from May to September, plus the Christmas/New Year and Easter holidays. We quote *average* prices. Reviews in this chapter are ordered according to price.

If you want to check options before you leave, www.travelguide.sk and www.ubytujsa.sk are useful.

Camping
Most grounds open from May to September and are often accessible on public transport. Most have a snack bar and small cabins that are cheaper than a hotel. Camping wild in national parks is prohibited.

Hostels
There are very few backpacker-style hostels in Slovakia, but there's no shortage of cheap places to sleep. The Hostelling International (HI) handbook lists an impressive network of student-style hostels, but they're mostly open in July and August only. Apply for your HI card before you leave home, as it will net you discounts of up to 25%. Satur and tourist information offices usually have information on hostels.

Turistické ubytovňy (tourist hostels) that provide very basic and cheap dormitory accommodation are not connected to the HI network. You can ask about them at information offices.

Private Rooms, Pensions & Hotels
Private rooms (look for signs reading '*privát*' or '*zimmer frei*') are usually available in tourist areas (from 250Sk per person). Tourist information offices can book them.

Many small pensions offer more personalised service and cheaper rates than hotels.

Hotels in Bratislava are considerably more expensive than in the rest of the country. Two-star rooms are typically 800/1200Sk per single/double.

ACTIVITIES
Slovakia is one of Eastern Europe's best areas for hiking: see the Malá Fatra (p761) and Vysoké Tatry (p763) sections for details). There is also excellent rock climbing and mountaineering in the Vysoké Tatry. Contact the **Mountain Guides Society Office** (☎ 052-442 20 60/6; www.tatraguide.sk), in Starý Smokovec, for more information.

Slovakia, especially in the east, also offers some of the best cycling terrain in Central Europe. Mountain biking in the Vysoké Tatry is excellent. **Tatrasport** (☎ 052-442 52 41; www.tatry.net/tatrasport) has a branch in Starý Smokovec and rents mountain bikes for 299Sk a day.

The country has some of Europe's cheapest ski resorts, but the skiable areas are small. The season runs from December to April in the Vysoké Tatry and Malá Fatra. Ski hire starts at 299Sk per day.

BUSINESS HOURS
On weekdays, shops open around 8am or 9am and close at 5pm or 6pm. Many small shops, particularly those in country areas, close for lunch between noon and 2pm, and almost everything closes on Saturday afternoon and all day Sunday.

Most museums and castles are closed on Monday and the day following a public holiday. Many tourist attractions are closed from November to March and open on weekends only in April and October. Major museums stay open all year.

DANGERS & ANNOYANCES
Crime is low compared with the West. Some taxi drivers and waiters have been known to overcharge foreigners. Robberies on international trains have been increasing.

DISABLED TRAVELLERS
Slovakia is behind many EU countries in terms of facilities for the disabled. For more information contact the **Slovak Union for the**

Disabled (Slovenský zväz telesne postihnutých; Map p750; ☎ 02-50 22 87 08; Trnavské mýto 1, Bratislava).

EMBASSIES & CONSULATES
Slovak Embassies & Consulates
For a comprehensive list, check www.foreign.gov.sk.

Australia (☎ 02-6290 1516; 47 Culgoa Circuit, O'Malley, Canberra, ACT 2606)

Austria (☎ 01-318 905 5200; Armbrustergasse 24, 1-1190 Wien)

Canada (☎ 613-749 4442; 50 Rideau Terrace, Ottawa, Ontario K1M 2A1)

Czech Republic (☎ 233 113 051; Pod Hradbami 1, 160 00 Praha 6)

France (☎ 01-44 14 56 00; 125 rue de Ranelagh, 75016 Paris)

Germany (☎ 030-889 2620; Pariser Strasse 44, Berlin 107 07)

Hungary (☎ 01-460 9010; Stefania ut 22-24, H-1143 Budapest XIV)

Ireland (☎ 01-660 0012; 20 Clyde Rd, Ballsbridge, Dublin 4)

UK (☎ 020-7313 6470; 25 Kensington Palace Gardens, London W8 4QY)

USA (☎ 202-237 1054; 3523 International Court NW, Washington, DC 20008)

Embassies & Consulates in Slovakia
Australia and New Zealand do not have embassies in Slovakia; the nearest are in Vienna and Berlin respectively. The following are all in Bratislava (area code ☎ 02).

Austria (Map pp752-3; ☎ 54 43 29 85; Ventúrska 10)

Czech Republic (Map pp752-3; ☎ 59 20 33 01; Hviezdoslavovo nám 8)

France (Map pp752-3; ☎ 59 34 71 11; Hlavné nám 7)

Germany (Map pp752-3; ☎ 54 41 96 40; Hviezdoslavovo nám 10)

Ireland (Map pp752-3; ☎ 54 43 57 15; Carlton Savoy Bldg, Mostová 2)

Poland (Map p750; ☎ 54 43 27 44; Zelená 6)

UK (Map pp752-3; ☎ 59 98 20 00; Panská 16)

USA (Map pp752-3; ☎ 54 43 08 61; Hviezdoslavovo nám 4)

FESTIVALS & EVENTS
During late June or early July folk dancers from all over Slovakia meet at the Východná Folklore Festival, 32km west of Poprad. There are folk festivals in June in Červený Kláštor and Kežmarok, and in many other towns from June to August. The two-week Bratislava Music Festival is held in late September to early October, and the Bratislava Jazz Days weekend is in late October.

The **Slovak Tourist Board's website** (www.slovakiatourism.sk) is a useful resource when festival planning.

HOLIDAYS
New Year's & Independence Day 1 January
Three Kings Day 6 January
Good Friday & Easter Monday March/April
Labour Day 1 May
Cyril & Methodius Day 5 July
SNP Day 29 August
Constitution Day 1 September
Our Lady of Sorrows Day 15 September
All Saints' Day 1 November
Christmas 24 to 26 December

INTERNET RESOURCES
The **Slovakia Document Store** (http://slovakia.eunet.sk) contains links to a wealth of information on Slovakia. The **Slovak Tourism Board's website** (www.slovakiatourism.sk) is also worthwhile. See www.adc.sk/english/slovakia/for a blow-by-blow account of Slovakia's history.

MONEY
Slovakia's currency is the Slovak crown, or Slovenská koruna (Sk), containing 100 *halier* (hellers). There are coins of 10, 20 and 50 hellers, and one, two, five and 10 crowns (Sk). Banknotes come in denominations of 20, 50, 100, 200, 500, 1000 and 5000 crowns.

The easiest place to change cash and travellers cheques is at a branch of the Všeobecná úver-ová banka (VÚB; General Credit Bank), Slovenská sporiteľňa (Slovak Savings Bank) or the Investičná banka (Investment Bank), where you'll be charged a standard 1% commission.

Credit cards are widely accepted. Some of the larger branches of major banks give cash advances on credit cards. ATMs *(bankomat)* are widespread.

If you camp or stay in hostels, eat in local pubs and take local transport, expect to spend €18 to €25 a day. Double this amount if you are looking to bed down in pensions and dine in smarter eateries. Some businesses quote prices in euros; prices in this chapter conform to quotes of individual businesses.

POST
Poste-restante mail can be sent to major post offices in larger cities and will be kept for one month; when you collect your mail, take your passport for identification.

TELEPHONE
Phone Codes

Slovakia's country code is ☎ 421 – when dialling from abroad drop the initial 0 of the area code.

To dial internationally from inside Slovakia, dial ☎ 00, the country code and the number. Phonecards are the easiest, and cheapest, way to phone home.

Phonecards

Telecards (www.telecard.sk), available in most newsagents, come in denominations of 200Sk and 400Sk and can be used from any phone.

TOURIST INFORMATION

There is an extensive network of **municipal information centres** (Mestské informačné centrum; ☎ 16 186) belonging to the Association of Information Centres of Slovakia (AiCES). The staff speak English, can organise sightseeing tours and guides, and can assist with accommodation. Branches of Satur can also help with accommodation.

VISAS

Slovakia joined the EU in May 2004 and citizens of other EU countries can now enter the country indefinitely without a visa. Australian, New Zealand, Canadian and Japanese citizens can enter visa-free for up to 90 days, US citizens for stays of up to 30 days. At time of writing, South Africans did need a visa (€33). If you do require a visa, it *must* be bought in advance – they are *not* issued on arrival.

TRANSPORT IN SLOVAKIA

GETTING THERE & AWAY
Air

Bratislava's **MR Štefánika Airport** (code BTS; ☎ 02-48 57 33 53; www.airportbratislava.sk) receives a limited number of flights from the following carriers:

Aeroflot (☎ 02-43 33 75 81; www.aeroflot.com; MR Štefánika Airport)
Air Slovakia (☎ 02-43 42 76 68; www.airslovakia.sk; MR Štefánika Airport)
Austrian Airlines (Map pp752-3; ☎ 54 41 16 10; www.austrian.sk; Rybné nám 1, Bratislava)
ČSA (Czech Airlines; Map pp752-3; ☎ 02-52 96 13 25; Sturova 13, Bratislava)
SkyEurope Airlines (☎ 02-48 50 11 11; www.skyeurope.com; Ivanská cesta 26, Bratislava)
Slovak Airlines (☎ 02-48 57 51 70; www.slovakairlines.sk; MR Štefánika Airport)

Vienna's **Schwechat Airport** (code VIE; ☎ 0043-1-70 070; www.viennaairport.com) is just 60km from Bratislava, and is served by a vast range of international flights.

Land
BUS

Eurolines (☎ 02-55 57 13 12; www.eurolines.sk) offers an extremely comprehensive service linking Bratislava with the rest of Eastern Europe (see p757 for details). You can even get to London (3800Sk one way) in about 24 hours.

CAR & MOTORCYCLE

All foreign driving licences with photo ID are valid in Slovakia. As well as your vehicle's registration papers, you need a 'green card', which shows you are covered by at least third-party liability insurance. Your vehicle must display a nationality sticker and carry a first-aid kit and warning triangle.

TRAIN

Bratislava is linked by train to destinations across Eastern Europe, including Budapest (520Sk, 2¾ hours), Prague (700Sk, 4½ hours) and Moscow (2100Sk, 33 hours) – see p757 and p780 for details of some of the direct services.

River

An interesting and unusual way to enter or leave Slovakia is on the hydrofoils that ply the Danube, linking Bratislava with Vienna and Budapest daily from April to September (see p757 for details).

GETTING AROUND
Bicycle

Roads are often narrow and potholed; in towns, cobblestones and tram tracks can be a dangerous mix. Theft is a problem, so a lock is a must. You can hire bikes, especially in popular biking areas like the Vysoké Tatry. The cost of transporting a bicycle by rail is usually 10% of the train ticket.

Bus

Intercity buses, operated by **Slovenská autobusová doprava** (SAD; ☎ 02-55 56 73 49; www .sad-kds.sk), are a little less comfortable than the train, but equally good value. One-way bus tickets cost around 110Sk per 100km.

When trying to decipher bus schedules beware of departure times bearing footnotes you don't completely understand. It is helpful to know that *premáva* means 'it operates' and *nepremáva* means 'it doesn't operate'.

For times and prices, check www.vlaky.sk.

Car & Motorcycle

DRIVING LICENCE

You can drive in Slovakia using your own licence.

HIRE

Avis has offices in Bratislava and Košice, but there are also much cheaper local hire car companies (see p758 for details).

ROAD RULES

In order to use Slovakia's motorways (denoted by green signs) all vehicles must have a motorway sticker *(nálepka)*, which should be displayed in the windscreen. You can buy stickers at border crossings, petrol stations or Satur offices (100Sk for 15 days, 600Sk for a year, for vehicles up to 1.5 tonnes).

Parking restrictions are Draconian and eagerly enforced – always buy a ticket.

Local Transport

City buses and trams operate from around 4.30am to 11.30pm daily. Tickets are sold at public transport offices, from ticket machines and newsstands and must be validated once you're aboard.

Train

Slovak Republic Railways (Železnice Slovenskej republiky or ŽSR; www.zsr.sk) provides a cheap and efficient service – charges run at approximately 120Sk per 100km. Most of the places covered in this chapter are on or near the main railway line between Bratislava and Košice. For times and prices, check www.vlaky.sk.

Slovenia

CONTENTS

Highlights	787	Festivals & Events	819
Itineraries	787	Gay & Lesbian Travellers	819
Climate & When to Go	787	Holidays	819
History	787	Internet Access	820
People	789	Internet Resources	820
Religion	789	Language	820
Arts	789	Money	820
Environment	790	Post	820
Food & Drink	790	Telephone	820
Ljubljana	**790**	Toilets	820
History	790	Tourist Information	820
Orientation	791	Visas	820
Information	791	Women Travellers	821
Sights	794	**Transport in Slovenia**	**821**
Tours	795	Getting There & Away	821
Sleeping	795	Getting Around	822
Eating	796		
Drinking	798		
Entertainment	798		
Getting There & Away	799		
Getting Around	799		
Julian Alps	**800**		
Kranj	800		
Bled	800		
Bohinj	803		
Kranjska Gora	804		
Upper Soča Valley	805		
Novo Gorica/Gorizia	806		
Karst & Coast	**806**		
Postojna	806		
Škocjan Caves & Divača	807		
Lipica	807		
Koper	808		
Izola	810		
Piran	810		
Portorož	813		
Sečovlje	814		
Eastern Slovenia	**814**		
Kamnik	814		
Celje	814		
Rogaška Slatina	815		
Maribor	815		
Ptuj	817		
Slovenia Directory	**817**		
Accommodation	817		
Activities	818		
Business Hours	818		
Embassies & Consulates	819		

Few countries pack in as many delights per sq km as loveable little Slovenia (Slovenija). Imagine: a patchwork of emerald alpine meadows crisscrossed by idyllically quiet yet well-paved rural lanes; picture-book villages crowned with baroque churches, reminiscent of unspoilt Austria; soaring grey peaks fringed with forests and wild valleys, offering affordable adrenaline rushes for extreme-sports fanatics; lowland hills covered with vines and riddled with breathtaking caves. The short, developed coastline has no real beaches, but there's a trio of quaint old Venetian ports. From the most perfect of these, Piran, you can scuba dive to WWII wrecks. Many Slovenian towns have picturesque Habsburg cores: Ljubljana's is a 'mini-Prague', with stylishly atmospheric street cafés and impressive galleries. The capital also has a small but superbly idiosyncratic counterculture centre at Metelkova.

Safe, clean and not yet overrun by Austrian caravanners, Slovenia isn't the cheapest place in Eastern Europe, but it's fabulously good value. Locals are welcoming, multilingual and broad-minded – just don't show them the title of this book. Slovenes are genuinely perplexed that anyone would consider their country as part of 'Eastern' Europe: emotionally, spiritually and geographically, Slovenia is right at the heart of the continent.

SLOVENIA

FAST FACTS

- **Area** 20,256 sq km
- **Capital** Ljubljana
- **Currency** tolar (SIT); €1 = 239SIT; US$1 = 188SIT; UK£1 = 345SIT; A$1 = 140SIT; ¥100 = 176SIT; NZ$1 = 131SIT
- **Famous for** mountain sports, Lipizzaner horses, plonky Ljutomer Riesling
- **Key Phrases** *živijo* (hello), *dober dan* (informal hello), *nasvidenje* (goodbye), *hvala* (thanks), *oprostite* (sorry)
- **Official Language** Slovene; English, Italian and German are widely understood
- **Population** 2 million
- **Telephone Codes** country code ☎ 386; international access code ☎ 00; ☎ toll free 080
- **Visas** not required for most; see p820

HIGHLIGHTS

- The romantic Venetian mini-city of **Piran** (p810)
- Fairy-tale lakeland scenes around **Bled** (p800) and **Bohinj** (p803)
- Dramatic mountain scenery at **Bovec** (p805), glimpsed as you slither down waterfalls or jump off mountains
- Graffiti art and unpredictable entertainment in the daunting but inspirational venues of **Metelkova** (p799), lovely Ljubljana's alter ego
- The dizzying underground gorge within the **Škocjan Caves** (p807)

ITINERARIES

- **Three days** Enjoy a long weekend sampling the great cafés and nightlife of Ljubljana, and perhaps an excursion to Kamnik.
- **One week** Fly for peanuts to Trieste (Italy), cross into Slovenia at Novo Gorica and take the train up the valley of the vivid-blue Soca, then unwind in Bohinj or romantic Bled beside idyllic mountain lakes. Spend a couple of days in Ljubljana, then loop south to picturesque Piran via the magnificent Škocjan Caves. A bus from Koper takes you back to Trieste (although they are rare at weekends).
- **Two weeks** As above, adding some extreme sports in Bovec or plenty of hiking around Bohinj.

CLIMATE & WHEN TO GO

The ski season lasts from December to March, though avalanche risks may keep the Vršič Pass (p804) closed until May. Lake Bled freezes over in winter, but the short coastline has a contrastingly mild, typically Mediterranean climate. April is often wet, but this means accommodation is cheaper and the vivid blossom-dappled forests are at their scenic best. May and June are warmer, but during these months hotel prices start to rise, peaking in August, when rooms can be hard to find at any price. Nonetheless, midsummer is the only time of year that cheap student hostels are open. Moving into autumn, warm September days are calm and ideal for hiking and climbing, while October can be damp.

HISTORY

Slovenes claim they invented democracy. By AD 611 their Slavic forebears had founded

the Duchy of Carantania based around Klagenfurt (now in Austria). Ruling dukes were elected by landowners and invested with power before the ordinary citizens. This model was noted by French political theorist Bodin, whose work was a key reference for Thomas Jefferson when writing the American Declaration of Independence. Carantania, later called Carinthia, was fought over by Franks and Magyars and later divided up among the Austro-Germanic nobles and bishops, who protected themselves within ever-multiplying castles. By 1335 Carantania and all present-day Slovenia, except for the Venetian-controlled coastal towns, were dominated by the Habsburgs.

Indeed Austria ruled on until 1918 apart from a brief but important interlude when Napoleonic France claimed the area among its 'Illyrian Provinces' (1809–13). Napoleon dealt the tourist industry a blow by demolishing many castles. However, he proved a popular conqueror, as his relatively liberal Illyrian regime de-Germanised the education system. Slovene was taught in schools for the first time in generations, leading to a blossoming of national consciousness. In tribute, Ljubljana still has a French Revolution Square (Trg francoske revolucije) today, although it was actually named more than a century after the event.

SLOVENIA

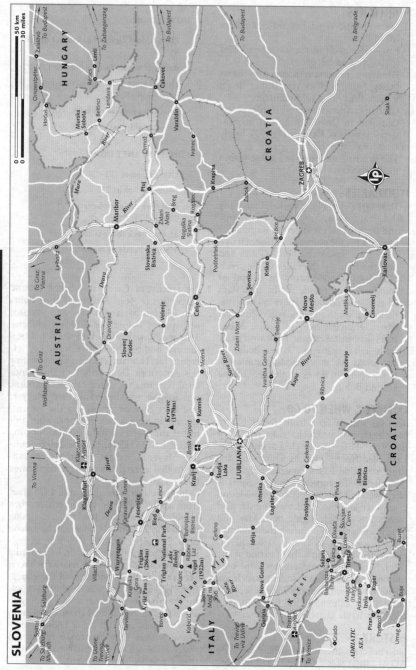

SLOVENIA

WWI fighting was particularly savage along Slovenia's Soča valley (the 'Isonzo Front'), which was occupied by Italy then dramatically retaken by German-led Austrian forces. Many fighters' tunnels are still visible around Kobarid (p805). WWI ended with the collapse of Austria-Hungary, which handed western Slovenia to Italy as postwar reparations. Northern Carinthia (including the towns of Villach and Klagenfurt) voted to stay with Austria in a 1920 plebiscite, which most Slovenes still believe was fixed. What little was left of Slovenia joined fellow southern (*yugo*) Slavs in forming the Kingdom of Serbs, Croats and Slovenes, later Yugoslavia.

Nazi occupation in WWII was courageously resisted by Slovenian partisans, who ended the war by regaining Italian-held areas from Piran to Bovec. However, Trst (Trieste), including most of divided Gorica/Gorizia, became a politically nebulous occupied zone, somewhat like Berlin. Key parts of this 'Free Territory' eventually ended up as part of Italy, although incredibly, the territory's divided political status was only finally confirmed as permanent in 1975.

Slovenia was the economic powerhouse of Tito's postwar Yugoslavia. By the 1980s the federation was becoming increasingly Serb-dominated and Slovenes, who already felt taken for granted economically, feared losing their political autonomy. After free elections and careful planning, which contrasted markedly with Croatia's haste, Slovenia broke away from Yugoslavia on 25 June 1991. A 10-day war followed; it might have been much worse, but Milošević's rump Yugoslavia swiftly signed a truce and concentrated on bashing Croatia instead. Slovenia was admitted to the UN in May 1992 and rapidly proved itself a model of economic common sense.

When Slovenia joined the EU on 1 May 2004, the rainy skies and half-hearted celebrations mirrored wide-spread public ambivalence. Already wealthy, relatively self-sufficient and deeply democratic (with referenda ad nauseam), most Slovenes saw joining as an inevitable duty, but one with few obvious benefits. Slovenia will be a net contributor to the EU, and sponsoring a number of poorer countries, from Portugal to Poland, is not the most exciting idea for a nation that escaped a similar situation within Yugoslavia just 13 years before.

PEOPLE

The population is relatively homogeneous. Almost 90% is ethnic Slovene, with the remainder being Croat, Serbian and Bosnian minorities and small, long-term enclaves of Italians and Hungarians. Some reports estimate that 130,000 long-term residents were controversially 'erased', losing all passport rights, when they failed to register after independence.

Slovenes are ethnically Slavic, typically multilingual, friendly without being pushy, and miraculously manage to combine a Germanic work ethic with an easy-going, Mediterranean *joie de vivre*.

RELIGION

Constitutionally, Slovenes are left free to choose (and not obliged to publicly declare) their religion. A 2003 survey estimated that 67.9% consider themselves at least nominally Catholic, 26% atheist or agnostic, 2.3% Orthodox Christian and 1.2% Muslim. Although Sundays remain 'holy' (ie shops close), many locals prefer to use their uncluttered weekends to find spirituality through mountain sports rather than by churchbound worship.

ARTS

Far and away Slovenia's best-loved writer is romantic poet France Prešeren (1800–49), whose statue commands old-Ljubljana's central square (p794). Prešeren's patriotic yet humanistic verse was a driving force in raising Slovene national consciousness. Fittingly a stanza of his poem *Zdravljica* (The Toast) is now the national anthem. It calls for neighbourliness and an end to war, a very marked contrast to the enemy-confounding sentiment of Britain's anthem. Visit www.preseren.net/ang for English translations of this and other works by Prešeren.

Many of Ljubljana's most characteristic features, including its idiosyncratic recurring pyramid motifs, were added by celebrated Slovene architect Jože Plečnik (1872–1957), who cut his professional teeth working on Prague's Hradčany Castle.

Slovenia has some excellent modern and contemporary artists including Rudi Skočir, whose Klimt-with-muscles style reflects a taste for Viennese Art Nouveau that continues to permeate day-to-day Slovenian interior design.

The long-running, controversial, contemporary art collective Neue Slowenische Kunst (NSK) embraces politically informed painting and physical theatre. It also spawned the internationally known industrial-music group Laibach (www.laibach.nsk.si). Slovenia's vibrant music scene embraces rave (notably in Izola, p810), techno, jazz, punk, thrash-metal and *chanson* (eg Vita Mavrič). There's also a folk music revival: listen out for Katice and Ljoba Jenče (http://users.volja.net/folkslo/people.htm). In mid-August Radovljica, near Bled, holds an important festival of ancient music (http://festival-radovljica.amis.net).

Damjan Kozole's 2004 film *Spare Parts* was successful Europe-wide, but don't take the depressing Krško of the movie to be representative of otherwise delightful Slovenia.

ENVIRONMENT

Slovenia is amazingly green. It is home to some 2900 plant species, and in April patches of the widespread, variegated forests burst gloriously into blossom. Triglav National Park (p800) is particularly rich in indigenous mountain flowers. Living deep in the Karst caves, the endemic 'living fossils' *Proteus anguinus* are cute, blind, salamanders that can survive for years without eating; see some while at Postojna (p806).

FOOD & DRINK

It's relatively hard to find archetypal Slovene foods like *žlikrofi* (potato-filled ravioli) in *bakalca* (lamb sauce), *mlinci* (corn-pasta sheets in gravy) and *ajdovi žganci* (buckwheat groats). Inns (*gostilna* or *gostišče*) or restaurants (*restavracija*) more frequently serve pizzas, *rižota* (risotto), *klobasa* (sausage), *zrezek* (cutlet/steak), *golaž* (goulash) and *paprikaš* (stew). Fish (*riba*) meals are sometimes priced by the *dag* (0.01kg). Trout (*postrv*) generally costs half the price of other fish, though grilled squid (*lignji na žaru*) doused in garlic butter is a ubiquitous bargain at 1200SIT to 1500SIT per plate.

Also common are Balkan favourites *cevapčiči* (ground-meat 'fingers'), *pleskavica* (big burger-style patties) and *raznjiči* (shish kebabs). Add 350SIT to 500SIT for the *krompir* (potatoes). Certain better restaurants ask 100SIT to 300SIT for bread/cover charge, and at some of the cheapest it is customary to share tables with other customers when things get busy.

You can snack cheaply on takeaway pizza slices or slabs of *burek* (300SIT to 450SIT), a lasagne-esque pasta layered with cheese, meat or apple. Alternatives include *štruklji* (cheese dumplings) and *palačinke* (sweet or savoury pancakes).

Some restaurants have bargain-value *dnevno kosilo* four-course lunch menus, including *juha* (soup) and *solata* (salad), for 1000SIT to 1600SIT. This can be less than the price of a cheap main course, and usually one option will be vegetarian.

Tap water is safe to drink. Distinctively Slovenian wines (*vino*) include hearty red *Teran* made from *Refošk* grapes and the light-red *Cviček* with a plummy sourness. Slovenes are justly proud of their top vintages. However cheaper bar-standard 'open-wines' (90SIT to 200SIT per 0.1l glass) are often pure gut-rot. Some fascinating *suho* (dry) whites are made from sweet grapes like Tokaj and Muskat but *sladko* and *polsladko* (sweet/semisweet) wines can be very sugary indeed.

Beer (*piva*), whether *svetlo* (lager) or *temno* (dark), is best on draught (*točeno*).

There are dozens of hard-hitting *žganje* fruit liquors including *češnovec* (from cherries), *sadjevec* (apples), *brinjevec* (juniper), *hruška* (pears) and *slivovka* (plums). *Na zdravje!* (Cheers!).

LJUBLJANA

☎ 01 / pop 269,800

Inspiring Ljubljana (pronounced 'Loob-li-yana') has a small but charming old core, a vibrant street-café culture, a buzzing student community and an alternative-lifestyle centre at Metelkova. Viewed from Ljubljana Castle, the less exciting skirt of concrete suburbs is overshadowed by a magnificent alpine horizon, which seems to be almost leaping distance from the ramparts. Although the city may lack big-name attractions, the great galleries, atmospheric bars and varied, accessible nightlife make it tempting to while away weeks here.

HISTORY

If the city really was founded by the Golden Fleece–stealing Argonauts, they left no proof of their sojourn. All that survives of the later Roman city of Emona is a ragged wall on Mirje ul, which was wrecked by the Huns and rebuilt by Slavs. The city took its present form (as 'Laibach') under the Austrian Habsburgs, but it gained regional prominence in 1809, when it became the capital of Napoleon's short-lived Illyrian Provinces. Some fine Art-Nouveau buildings filled up the holes left by an 1895 earthquake, and fortunately most later 20th-century development was relegated to the suburbs. The brutal, concrete Trg Republike is a marked exception.

ORIENTATION

Prešernov trg is the heart of Ljubljana's delightful, if relatively small, old-city area, which follows the north and west flanks of castle hill on both sides of the Ljubljanica River. Walk 10 minutes north up Miklošičeva cesta to the bus and train stations.

Despite being called 'Ljubljana Aerodrome', the airport is actually at Brnik near Kranj, some 23km north of Ljubljana.

Maps

Excellent free maps, some of which show the complete bus network, are available from the various tourist information offices. Even better are Kod-&-Kam maps, which cost from 1620SIT and are sold at bookshops and tourist information centres (TICs).

INFORMATION
Bookshops

Geonavtik (www.geonavtik.com, in Slovene; Kongresni trg 1; 8.30am-8.30pm Mon-Fri, 8.30am-3pm Sat) Stocks Lonely Planet guides.

Kod-&-Kam (Trg francoske revolucije 7; 9am-7pm Mon-Fri, 8am-1pm Sat) Map specialist.

Internet Access

Web connection is available at many hostels and hotels, plus the following:

Kotiček (Bus station; per 10min 100SIT; 7am-8.30pm)

Napotnice.com (Trg Ajdovščina 1; per 15min 200SIT; 8am-11pm) Small café in the City Center minimall above the Pelican Pub.

Xplorer (Petkovškovo nab 23; per 5min 110SIT, per hr 800SIT; 10am-10pm Mon-Fri, noon-10pm Sat & Sun) Good connection, plus discounts of 20% before noon, and 10% for students.

Laundry

Washing machines are available, even to nonguests, at the **Celicia Hostel** (430 1890;

LJUBLJANA IN TWO DAYS

Start at **Ljubljana Castle** (p794) to get your visual and historical bearings. After a traditional Slovene lunch at **Sokol** (p796), explore the old town, café-hopping as you go. Midweek nights party at **Jazz Club Gajo** (p799) or **K4** (p798), and on weekends try **Bachus** (p799), **Global** (p798), or venture into **Metelkova** (p799).

Next day stroll through **Park Tivoli** to the **Museum of Contemporary History** (p795), check out some of the area's **art galleries** (p795), and then return to dine in the old town. Alternatively, do the 2pm **Celicia Hostel tour** (p795), then hop on the 4.15pm train for a four-hour sunset excursion to **Kamnik** (p814).

---

www.souhostel.com; Metelkova 8) for 1200SIT per load, including powder.

Left Luggage

Bus station (320SIT; 5am-8.30pm)

Train station (400SIT or €2; 24hr) Coin lockers on platform No 1.

Medical Services

Klinični Center (232 3060; Bohoričeva ul 9; 24hr) Emergency clinic.

Zdravstveni Dom Center (472 3700; Metelkova ul 9; 7.30am-7pm) Nonemergency doctors.

Money

There are ATMs at every turn, including in both the train and bus stations, where you'll also find **currency exchange booths** (6am-10pm). Dozens of banks have ATMs and change money:

Gorenska Banka (Dalmatinova ul 4; 9am-11.30am & 2-5pm Mon-Fri, 8am-11am Sat) Pseudo Art-Nouveau furnishings make amends for the travesty of this bank's façade, which mars the architectural splendour of Miklošičev Park. Exchanges travellers cheques.

Ljubljanska Banka (Mestni trg 16; 8am-noon & 2.30-4.30pm) Handily central ATM.

Post

Post office (Slovenska cesta 32; 7am-8pm Mon-Fri, 7am-1pm Sat) Holds poste restante mail for 30 days.

Tourist Information

All three TICs have great free maps, themed brochures, tips and events listings.

LJUBLJANA

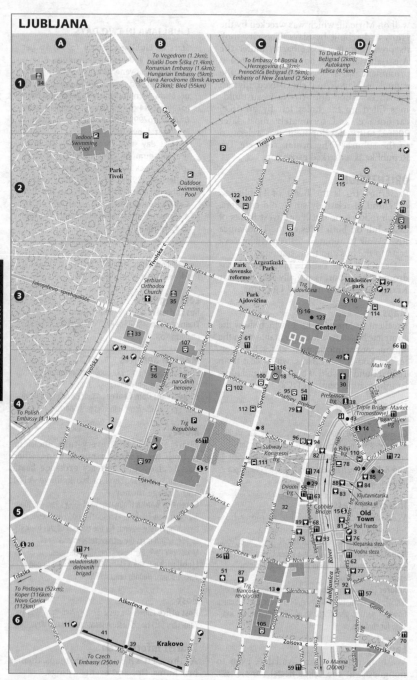

To Vegedrom (1.2km);
Dijaški Dom Šiška (1.4km);
Romanian Embassy (1.6km);
Hungarian Embassy (5km);
Ljubljana Aerodrome (Brnik Airport)
(23km); Bled (55km)

To Embassy of Bosnia &
Herzegovina (1.3km);
Prenočišča Bežigrad (1.5km);
Embassy of New Zealand (2.5km)

To Dijaški Dom
Bežigrad (2km);
Autokamp
Ježica (4.5km)

Park
Tivoli

Indoor
Swimming
Pool

Outdoor
Swimming
Pool

Jakopičevo sprehajališče

Serbian
Orthodox
Church

Park
slovenske
reforme

Argentinski
Park

Park
Ajdovščina

Miklošičev
park

Center

Trg
narodnih
herojev

Trg
Republike

Presērnov
trg

Triple Bridge Market
(Tromostovje)

To Polish
Embassy (1.1km)

Subway
Kongresni
trg

Dvorni
trg

Cobbler
Bridge

Old
Town

Pod Tranto

Klepanska steza

Vodna steza

To Postojna (52km);
Koper (116km);
Novo Gorica
(112km)

Trg
mladinskih
delovnih
brigad

Trg
francoske
revolucije

Krakovo

To Czech
Embassy (250m)

To Manna
(200m)

Ljubljanica River

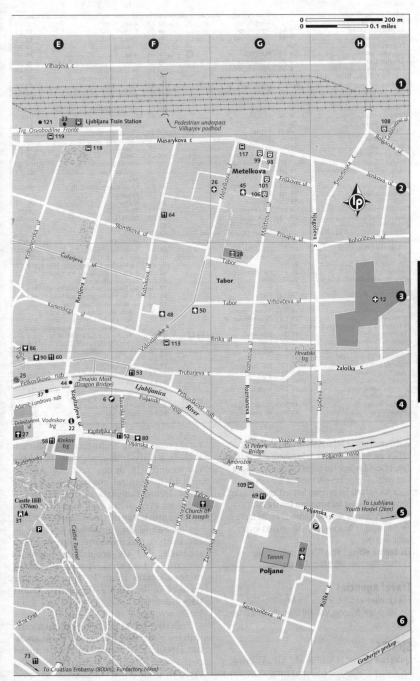

INFORMATION		
Australian Consulate	1	B4
Austrian Embassy	2	B4
Belgian Embassy	(see 1)	
Bulgarian Embassy	3	D5
Canadian Consulate	4	D2
Cankarjev Dom Ticket Office	5	B5
Currency Exchange Booth	(see 119)	
Currency Exchange Booth	(see 23)	
Dutch Embassy	6	E4
French Embassy	7	B6
Geonavtik Bookshop	8	C4
German Embassy	9	B4
Gorenska Banka	10	D3
Irish Embassy	(see 6)	
Italian Embassy	11	A6
Klinični Center	12	H3
Kod & Kam Bookshop	13	C6
Kotiček	(see 119)	
Ljubljana Tourist Information Centre	14	D4
Ljubljanska Banka	15	D5
Napotnice.com	16	C3
Norwegian Embassy	17	D3
Post Office	18	C4
Russian Embassy	19	B3
Slovak Embassy	20	A5
South African Consulate	21	D2
STIC (Slovenian Tourist Information Centre)	22	E4
TIC Branch Office	23	E1
UK Embassy	(see 1)	
US Embassy	24	B4
Xplorer	25	E4
Zdravstveni Dom Medical Center	26	G2

SIGHTS & ACTIVITIES	(pp794-5)	
Cathedral of St Nicholas	27	E4
Ethnographic Museum	28	G3
Filharmonija	29	D5
Franciscan Church of the Annunciation	30	D4
Ljubljana Castle	31	E5
Ljubljana University	32	C5
Modern Art Museum	33	B3
Museum of Contemporary History	34	A1
National Gallery	35	B3
National Museum	36	B4
Plečnik Collonade	37	E4
Prešeren Statue	38	D4
Pyramid Gateway	39	B6
Robba Fountain	40	D5
Roman Walls	41	A6

Town Hall	42	D5
Triple Bridge (Tromostovje)	43	D4
Zmajsji Most (Dragon Bridge)	44	E4

SLEEPING	(pp795-6)	
Celica Hostel Metelkova 8	45	G2
Celica Youth Hostel	(see 45)	
Cityhotel Turist	46	D3
Dijaška Dom Ivana Cankarja	47	G5
Dijaški Dom Tabor	48	F3
Grand Union Hotel	49	D4
Park Hotel	50	F3
Pri Mraku	51	C6

EATING	(pp796-8)	
Alamut Orient House	52	F4
Čerin Pizzeria	53	F4
Cantina Mexicana	54	C4
Delikatesen Ljubljana Dvor	55	C5
Foculus Pizzeria	56	C5
Gostilna Pri Pavli	57	D6
Gostilna Vodnikov Hram	58	E4
Harambaša	59	C6
Hot Horse	60	E4
Joe Pena's	61	C3
Julija	62	D5
Ljubljanski Dvor	63	D5
Market Tabor mini-market	64	F2
Maximarket Supermarket	65	B4
Napoli Pizzeria	66	C4
Nobel Burek	67	D2
Oriental Café	(see 45)	
Paninoteka	68	D5
Pinki	69	G5
Piri Sv Florijanu	70	D6
Puccini	71	A5
Sokol	72	D4
Taverna Tatjana	73	E6
Živila mini-market	74	D5

DRINKING	(p798)	
BiKoFe	75	C5
Čajna Hiša	76	D5
Café Antico	77	D6
CN7 Patisserie	78	D5
Cutty Sark	79	C4
Fabrika	80	F4
Fraga Gallery-bar	81	D5
Makalonca	82	D4
Maček	83	D5
Minimal	84	D5

Movia Vinoteka	85	D5
Patrick's	86	E3
Petit Café	87	C6
Pr'skelet	88	D5
Roza	89	C5
Salon	90	E4
Sir William's	91	D3
Slaščičarna Privodnjaku	92	D6
Zlata Ladjica	93	D5
Zvezda	94	D4

ENTERTAINMENT	(pp798-9)	
As	95	C4
Bacchus	96	C4
Cankarjev Dom	97	B5
Club Tiffany	98	G2
Gala Hala	99	G2
Global	100	C4
Gromka	101	G2
Jazz Club Gajo	102	C4
K4	103	C2
Kinoteka & Marilyn Caffe	104	D2
Križanke	105	C6
MariČo	106	C4
Monokel Club	(see 98)	
Opera House	107	B3
Orto Bar	108	H1

TRANSPORT	(pp799-800)	
Bicycle Rental Kiosk	(see 83)	
Bus No 13 to Ljubljana Youth Hostel	109	G5
Bus No 13 to Ljubljana Youth Hostel	110	D4
Bus No 13 to Ljubljana Youth Hostel	111	C5
Bus No 3 to Funfactory	112	C4
Bus No 5 to Ljubljana Youth Hostel	113	F3
Bus No 5 to Ljubljana Youth Hostel	114	D3
Bus No 6 & 8 to Dijaški Dom Bežigrad/Autokamp Ježice and No 14 to Prenočišča Bežigrad	115	D2
Bus No 6 to Dijaški Dom Bežigrad/Autokamp Ježice and No 14 to Prenočišča Bežigrad	116	C4
Bus No 9 to Ljubljana Youth Hostel	117	G2
Bus No 9 to Ljubljana Youth Hostel	118	E2
Bus Station	119	E2
Buses towards Vegedrom and Dijaška Dom Šiška	120	C2
Hertz Car Rental	121	E1
Hotel Lev (Bicycle Rental)	122	C2
STA Ljubljana	123	D3
Tourist Tram	(see 38)	

Ljubljana Tourist Information Centre (TIC; ☎ 306 1215; www.ljubljana-tourism.si; Stritarjeva ul 2; ☺ 8am-7pm, to 9pm Jun-Sep) This centre's three-day Ljubljana Card (3000SIT) gives free city transport and various discounts, but only big museum fans will recoup the cost.

Slovenian Tourist Information Centre (STIC; ☎ 306 4575; www.slovenia-tourism.si; Krekov trg 10; ☺ 8am-7pm, to 9pm Jun-Sep) Internet and bicycle rental available.

TIC branch office (☎ 433 9475; train station; ☺ 8am-10pm Jun-Sep, 10am-7pm Oct-May)

Travel Agencies

STA Ljubljana (☎ 439 1690; Trg Ajdovščina Mall; ☺ 10am-1pm & 2-5pm Mon-Fri) Offers discount airfares for students.

SIGHTS

Ljubljana Castle (Ljubljanski Grad) crowns an abrupt, wooded hill that forms the city's focal point. It's an architectural mishmash including early-16th-century walls, a 1489 chapel and a 1970s concrete café. Admission to the central courtyard and some north-facing ramparts is free. However, there are even better 360° views from the 19th-century **tower** (adult/student 790/490SIT; ☺ 10am-6pm Tue-Sun), and visits include an excellent 'virtual museum'. Don your 3-D spectacles and 'fly' around the Ljubljana of various historical epochs. Reaching the castle takes about 15 minutes, either on foot or by taking the hourly **tourist tram** (adult/child 550/350SIT; ☺ 9am-9pm) from Prešernov trg.

Prešernov trg is Ljubljana's central square, with the pink **Franciscan Church of the Annunciation** (1660) and a **statue** (1905) of national poet France Prešeren. Furtively observing Prešeren from a fake window on Wolfova

ul is a bust of his unrequited love (and poetic inspiration), Julija Primic (Primicova).
Wander north of the square to admire the
fine **Art-Nouveau buildings** of Miklošičeva cesta,
including the still-grand **Grand Hotel Union
Executive** (☎ 308 1270; www.gh-union.si; Miklošičeva
cesta 1). Built in 1905, the hotel was comman-
deered during WWI for use as the command
centre for the Soča/Isonzo-front campaign.
Today it retains many elements of *Jugendt-
stil* style, including the 'Blue' meeting room,
the Unionska Klet cellar-restaurant, and a
sweeping interior stone stairway with splendid original brass lantern stands.

South of Prešernov trg you cross the small
but much celebrated **Triple Bridge** (Tromostovje). The original 1842 span had two side
bridges added in 1931 by Ljubljana's super-
star architect Jože Plečnik, who also plonked
the curious **Pyramid Gateway** on top of the
city's minimal **Roman Walls** (Mirje ul). A baroque
Robba Fountain stands before the Gothic **Town
Hall** (1718) in Mestni trg, which leads south
into **Stari trg** and **Gornji trg**. These squares
wind picturesquely around the castle bluff –
delightfully sprinkled with cafés, they are arguably Ljubljana's greatest overall attraction.

East of the Triple Bridge, the 1708 **Cathedral of St Nicholas** (☉ 8am-noon & 3-7pm) is filled
with a riot of splendid frescoes (partly hidden during ongoing renovation at the time
of research). To get inside, heave open what
appear to be super-heavy bronze sculptures,
but which, on closer inspection, turn out
to be the doors. Behind the cathedral is a
lively **market** (☉ closed Sun) selling all kinds of
stuff, a Plečnik **colonnade** and the 1901 **Zma-
jski Most**, a bridge guarded by cute verdigris
dragons which have become city mascots.

The grand if rather pompous main build-
ing of **Ljubljana University** (Kongresni trg 12) was
formerly the regional parliament (1902).
The more restrained **Filharmonija** (Kongresni trg
10) dates from an 1898 reconstruction, despite the prominent 1701 plaque. It's home
to the Slovenian Philharmonic Orchestra.

Of several major galleries and museums
west of Slovenska cesta, the best are the
impressive **National Gallery** (☎ 241 5434; www
.ng-slo.si; Prešernova cesta 24; adult/student 800/600SIT;
Sat afternoon free; ☉ 10am-6pm Tue-Sun), the vibrant, inspiring but outwardly drab 1940s
Modern Art Museum (☎ 251 4106; www.mg-lj.si; Cankarjeva cesta 15; adult/student 1000/700SIT; ☉ 10am-6pm
Tue-Sat, 10am-1pm Sun), and the quiet **Museum**

of Contemporary History (☎ 300 9610; www.muzej
-nz.si; Park Tivoli; adult/student 500/300SIT; ☉ 10am-6pm
Tue-Sat) with its imaginative look at 20th-
century Slovenia, via the milk carton. The
latter museum also plunges you unexpectedly into a WWI trench.

The **National Museum** (☎ 241 4404; www.narmuz
-lj.si; Muzejska ul 1; adult/student 1000/700SIT; ☉ 10am-6pm
Fri-Wed, 10am-8pm Thu) occupies an elegant 1888
building. It has a rich archaeological collection, but at the time of writing only temporary exhibitions and the natural history
section were accessible, while the main galleries were closed for long-term renovation.

Metelkova, an ex-army garrison taken over
by squatters after independence, is now a
somewhat daunting, free-living commune –
a miniature version of Copenhagen's Chris-
tiania. To really 'feel' Metelkova (which is
around 500m east of the train station), visit
after midnight (p799). Even if you're staying
there, a tour of Metelkova's ultra-hip **Celicia
Hostel** (free; ☉ 2pm) is intriguing, especially on
Tuesday and Wednesday when you usually
get to meet one of the architects.

The **Ethnographic Museum** (☎ 432 5403; www
.etno-muzej.si; Metelkova ul 2) has a very extensive
collection, but was being totally rebuilt on
the southern edge of Metelkova at the time
of research. Some temporary exhibitions
may be operating.

TOURS

Guided **city tours** (adult/student 1550/800SIT) start
from in front of the **Town Hall** (Mestni trg 1). At
the time of writing, departures in English
were 6pm (May to September) and 10am
(October to April), but times vary year by
year; check with the TIC.

SLEEPING

Ljubljana is not overendowed with accommodation choices. The selection following
includes all of the central budget and mid-
range options. The TICs have comprehensive
details of other hotels further out in the suburbs, of similarly inconvenient private rooms
and of the four other central top-end hotels,
all of which charge over €140 for a double.

Budget

Autokamp Ježica (☎ 568 3913; camp sites per person
Jun-Aug/off-season 2262/1892SIT; ☉) This attractively tree-shaded camping ground is 4.5km
north of the stations, but easily reached on

bus No 8 (to terminus) or the more frequent No 6 (stop Ježica).

Ljubljana Youth Hostel (BIT Center Hotel; ☎ 548 0055; www.bit-center.net; Litijska 57; dm/s/tr 2990/6790/9590SIT, breakfast 800SIT; **P**) Stylish new IYHA bunk-dorms and functionally modern en suite rooms are attached to the large BIT sports centre 3km east of the centre. Take Bus No 5, 9 or 13 to the Emona bus stop, walk 250m further east, turn north onto Pesarska cesta, then immediately right through an expansive car park.

Celicia Hostel (☎ 430 1890; www.souhostel.com; Metelkova 8; dm/s/d 3500/7000/9500SIT; ☐) This stylishly revamped former prison has designer 'cells', complete with original bars, and a packed-full, popular dorm. Room 116 has a round bed. Check-in starts at 3pm but advance bookings (advisable) are usually only held till 5pm. Discounts (5%) come with Ljubljana Cards, TIC 'Byways' tokens or VIP Backpackers (available at www.backpackers.com.au), but not IYHA, membership. Surcharges include 500SIT for one-night stays, another 500SIT for being unfashionably over 35 years old. Free Internet for guests.

SEASONAL HOSTELS

Several fairly spartan student hostels with shared bathrooms only accept travellers during midsummer. Breakfast is not included. The most central are **Dijaški Dom Tabor** (☎ 234 8840; ssljddta1s@guest.arnes.si; beds €17-20; ✆ Jul-Aug), entered from Kotnikova ul, and **Dijaški Dom Ivana Cankarja** (☎ 474 8600; dd.lj-ic@guest.arnes.si; Poljanska cesta 26B; s/d/tr 3960/6520/8580SIT; ✆ Jul) with 10% student discounts. Ignore the misleading sign on the door of Poljanska cesta 26: the actual entrance is from the west side of block B. The correct doorway faces onto a tennis court.

North of the centre are the less convenient **Dijaški Dom Bežigrad** (☎ 534 2867; dd.lj-bezigrad@guest.arnes.si; Kardeljeva pl 28; bus No 6; dm from €12; ✆ Jul-Aug), and **Dijaški Dom Šiška** (☎ 500 7804; www.ddsiska.com; Aljaževa ul 32; dm adult/student €11/9; ✆ Jun-Aug) near pointy-towered Sv Frančišek Church (Verovškova ul). Take Bus No 1, 3, 15 or 16 west-bound to the Stara Cerkev stop, walk 500m due north on Aljaževa, and the hostel is on your right.

Mid-Range

Prenočišča Bežigrad (☎ 231 1559; www.prenocisca-bezigrad.com; Podmilščakova ul 51; bus No 14; s/d/tr

without breakfast 7000/10,000/13,000SIT) Bright, well-equipped new rooms off hospital-style corridors are good value, despite the road noise and semi-industrial location.

Park Hotel (☎ 433 1306; www.hotelpark.si; Tabor 9; s €45-49, d €58-63; **P**) In a handily central if rather uninviting area, this tower-block hotel is central Ljubljana's best-value mid-range choice. Pleasant, well-renovated standard rooms are bright and unpretentiously well equipped. Cheaper rooms have en suite toilet but share showers.

Pri Mraku (☎ 433 4049; www.daj-dam.si/ang/Mrak/mrakmain.htm; Rimska cesta 4; s €56.50-70, d €69-100) Above a well-respected but misleadingly dowdy looking restaurant of the same name, this hotel offers inviting rooms with all the creature comforts: great value for such an ideal location. Higher-priced rooms have air-con.

Cityhotel Turist (City Hotel, Hotel Turist; ☎ 432 9130; www.hotelturist.si; Dalmatinova ul 15; s €57-95, d €110-120; ▓) When they offer you a 'small' room here, they're not joking. This functionally business-like property has recently had a much-needed modernisation, but the only compelling attraction remains its position. The nearby Park Hotel is less polished but better value.

Top End

Grand Hotel Union Executive (☎ 308 1270; www.gh-union.si; Miklošičeva cesta 1; s €136-165, d €145-175, ste €300-360; ▓) Although not the capital's most expensive hotel, the Union is nonetheless its star address, thanks to the great 1905 architecture and perfect position. For all the Art-Nouveau flourishes, including brilliant brass lantern stands on sweeping stone stairways, be sure to choose the executive section. The slightly cheaper business section is a comfortable but entirely functional later addition.

EATING

The old town has plenty of appealing restaurants, though the choice of restaurants isn't quite as overwhelming as that of cafés. For cheaper options try Poljanska cesta or the dull but functional snack bars around the stations.

Restaurants

Sokol (☎ 439 6855; www.gostilna-sokol.com, in Slovene; Ciril Metodov trg 18; mains 900-2500SIT; ✆ 6am-11pm) In this old vaulted house, traditional

Slovene food is served on heavy tables by costumed waiters, who stop just short of Disneyesque self-parody. Pizzas and vegetarian options are available if sausage and groats don't appeal. Even if you think you'd hate blood pudding, the country feast platter may pleasantly surprise you.

Harambaša (☎ 041-675 155; Vrtna ul 8; mains 850-1000SIT; ✷ 10am-10pm Mon-Fri, noon-10pm Sat, noon-6pm Sun) Here you'll find Bosnian cuisine served at low tables in a charming modern cottage atmosphere with quiet Balkan music.

Alamut Orient House (☎ 031-545 595; Poljanska cesta 7; mains 850-1500SIT; ✷ 8am-10pm Mon-Sat) Persian rugs and Lurish swords decorate this cosy little Iranian restaurant, whose 1400SIT lunch menus are popular with intellectuals and vegetarians. Subtle herbs and yogurt are used to masterful effect in the 1200SIT *polnjen malancan* (stuffed aubergine).

Gostilna Vodnikov Hram (Vodnikov trg 2; mains 1000-1700SIT; ✷ food to 4pm Mon-Sat) Vegetarian and meaty lunch specials are a bargain at from 780SIT to 1100SIT in this inviting vaulted pub.

Puccini (☎ 426 9136; Trg mladiniskih delovnih brigad; mains 1040-1720SIT; ✷ 11am-10pm Mon-Sat, noon-5pm Sun) Great pastas and salad bar star at this old house with sepia photos and curious door-ceilings.

Julija (☎ 425 6463; Stari trg 9; mains 1300-1400SIT; ✷ 8am-10pm, café to midnight) At Julija, risottos and pastas are served outside or in a pseudo-Delft tiled backroom behind a café decorated with 1920s prints.

Vegedrom (☎ 519 3901; Vodnikova 35; mains 1300-2000SIT; ✷ 9am-10pm Mon-Fri, noon-10pm Sat) This very appealing if pricey vegan restaurant is sadly inconvenient to reach. Follow the signs for the M Hotel up Celovška cesta, turn west and walk to the end of Na Jami (bus No 7 stops here) and it's to your left. The Dijaški Dom Šiška is walking distance (800m) to the northeast.

Gostilna Pri Pavli (☎ 425 9275; Stari trg 1; pizzas from 900SIT, mains 1200-2400SIT; ✷ 6am-11pm) This attractive, country-style inn serves Slovene food that's unspectacular, but surprisingly affordable for such a perfect location. Service is homely and the atmosphere calmly sedate.

Manna (☎ 283 5294; www.kulinarika-manna.com; Eippova 1A; mains 2800-3500SIT; ✷ noon-midnight Mon-Sat) Plush red interiors with Klimt prints and a tempting Viennese bar area make this the most stylishly upmarket of several

eateries and pubs along an attractive tree-shaded stretch of canal, a short walk south of the city centre. Try the rocket dumplings with scampi and saffron (1500SIT).

Pri Sv Florijanu (☎ 351 2214; Gornji trg 20; mains 2600-3700SIT; ✷ noon-11pm) This top-rate restaurant, housed in an old building with a stylishly modern interior, is famed for its creative nouveau-Slovene cuisine. Come before 4pm and you can choose three-course vegetarian, fish or meat menus for just 1890SIT. Venture downstairs (open from 6pm) and you are atmospherically transported to North Africa for Moroccan food or a puff on a water pipe.

Taverna Tatjana (☎ 421 0087; Gornji trg 38; fish per kg 6000-20,000SIT, garnish extra 600SIT; ✷ 5pm-midnight) Looking like an olde-worlde wooden-beamed cottage pub, this is actually a rather exclusive fish restaurant with a tiny, brilliant two-seat bar for your apéritif. As you leave, the view from the doorway is one of Ljubljana's most picturesque.

Joe Pena's (☎ 251 0868; Cankarjeva 6; mains 1800-2800SIT; ✷ 10am-1am Mon-Sat, noon-midnight Sun) Lazily whirring ceiling fans, earth-tone walls and wooden floors create plenty of atmosphere at Joe Pena's, Ljubljana's best, mood-lit Mexican restaurant.

Cantina Mexicana (☎ 426 9325; Knafljev prehod; ✷ 11am-late) This luridly colourful Mexican place has a fabulous terrace equipped with sofas and lanterns; perfect for a preprandial margarita.

Pre-eminent pizzerias include riverfront **Ljubljanski Dvor** (☎ 251 6555; Dvorni trg 1; pizzas from 850SIT; ✷ 10am-midnight Mon-Sat, 1-11pm Sun), warmly vaulted **Foculus** (☎ 251 5643; www.foculus .com; Gregorčičeva ul 3; ✷ 10am-11.30pm Mon-Fri, noon-11.30pm Sat & Sun), good-value **Napoli** (☎ 231 2949; Prečna ul 7) and trusty **Čerin** (☎ 232 0990; Trubarjeva 52; ✷ 10am-11pm Mon-Fri, noon-11pm Sat & Sun), which has bargain 980SIT lunch menus before 3pm. Otherwise pizzas range from 1200SIT to 1800SIT almost anywhere.

Quick Eats

Delikatesen Ljubljana Dvor (Gosposka ul; ✷ 9am-midnight Mon-Sat; pizza slices 250-350SIT) Locals queue for huge, bargain pizza slices, salads and sold-by-weight braised veggies to take away or stand-and-eat.

Nobel Burek (Miklošičeva cesta 30; burek 450SIT; ✷ 24hr) This place serves up Slovenian-style fast food.

SLOVENIA

Paninoteka (Jurčičev trg; sandwiches 450-650SIT; ✆ 8am-1am Mon-Sat, 9am-11pm Sun) Healthy sandwich creations on olive ciabatta are sold here to take away or to eat outside on a lovely little square with castle views.

Hot Horse (Trubarjeva cesta 31; snacks 350-800SIT; ✆ 8am-midnight Mon-Sat, noon-midnight Sun; burgers 400-700SIT) Fill up with giant 'horseburgers' and vegeburgers or pop next door for sandwiches.

Pinki (☎ 544 1111; Poljanska cesta 22; mains 700-800SIT; ✆ 6.30am-10pm Mon-Sat) Serving lasagnes, tortillas and pizzas, this cheap and cheerful student-oriented diner also does a 240SIT coffee-and-doughnut breakfast.

Self-Catering

Handy minimarkets **Živila** (Kongresni trg 9; ✆ 7am-9pm) and **Market Tabor** (Kotnikova ul 12; ✆ 7.30am-10pm) open even on Sundays.

DRINKING

Few cities have central Ljubljana's concentration of fabulously inviting cafés and bars, many with outdoor seating. Unless noted, those listed below open daily till late and charge from 160SIT to 200SIT for an espresso, 300SIT to 350SIT for small beers, and 900SIT to 1000SIT for cocktails. Just choose the ambience that appeals.

Movia Vinoteka (☎ 425 5448; Mestni trg 2; ✆ noon-midnight Mon-Sat) If you've been disappointed by mediocre Slovenian vintages, this atmospheric 1820 wine bar beside the Town Hall is the place to taste the really good ones. Sip slowly, however, as the 0.07l measures barely wet the bottom of the giant globe glasses. And at 600SIT to 3500SIT a pop, you'll need a few before you're tipsy.

BiKoFe (Gosposka 7) This spot has a soft, jazzy, mellow vibe, attracting both a straight and gay clientele.

Pr'skelet (Ključavničarska 5; ✆ 10am-1am) Skeletons here enjoy all-day two-for-one cocktails in an amusing Rocky Horror–style basement.

Makalonca (Hribarjevo nab) An unpretentious, cult bar on a glassed-in jetty, Makalonca is at the bottom of some easy-to-miss steps.

Salon (Trubarjeva cesta 23) This dazzling designer-kitsch cocktail bar features gold ceilings and leopard-skin couches.

Petit Café (Trg francoske revolucije 4) The wonderful Petit Café magically transports you to Montmartre.

Fabrika (Poljanska cesta 9; cocktails from 500SIT) For something much less polished try the bars of traffic-blighted Poljanska cesta, including Fabrika, a joyously grungy club-bar popular with students.

Oriental Café (Metelkova 8) Many backpackers are so enchanted by the Celicia Hostel's Oriental Café they forget to explore next-door Metelkova (p799).

For *Clockwork Orange* designer cool try **Fraga Gallery-Bar** (Mestni trg 15), audacious, white-on-white **Minimal** (Mestni trg 4; small beers 450SIT) or the less exclusive cake-café **Zvezda** (Kongresni trg).

If it had longer opening hours, **Gostilna Vodnikov Hram** (Vodnikov trg 2; ✆ 8am-8pm Mon-Sat) would knock the spots off Anglo-Irish pubs like **Patrick's** (Prečna ul 6), **Sir William's** (Tavčarjeva 8a; ✆ closed Sun) or the ever-popular **Cutty Sark** (Knafljev prehod).

Quaint 'olde'-style places include **Café Antico** (Stari trg), wood-panelled **Roza** (Židovska 6) and patisserie cafés like **Čajna Hisa** (Stari trg 3; ✆ 9am-11pm Mon-Sat) and **Slaščičarna Privodnjaku** (Stari trg 30).

Riverside classics:

Maček (Cankarjevo nab 19; ✆ happy hr 4-7pm)

Zlata Ladjica (Jurčičev trg) Has DJs at weekends.

CN7 Patisserie (Cankarjevo nab 7; coffee 200SIT, beers from 350SIT; ✆ 8am-1pm) CN7's willow-whipped stools offer arguably the best-positioned riverbank perch.

ENTERTAINMENT

Where to? In *Ljubljana* and *Ljubljana Calling* (www.ljubljana-calling.com) list cultural events, sports and nightlife options. Glossy *Ljubljana Life* (www.ljubljanalife.com) has some refreshingly frank reviews. All are free from TICs, hotels and some restaurants.

Nightclubs & Live Music

Global (☎ 426 9020; Tomšičeva ul 2; admission before midnight free, after midnight 1000SIT) After 11pm, Thursday to Saturday, this retro cocktail bar with Ljubljana's best city views becomes a popular dance venue. Take the bouncer-guarded elevator on Slovenska cesta to the top.

K4 (www.klubk4.org, in Slovene; Kersnikova ul 4; ✆ 10pm-4am) Two stark dance-floors beneath the student organisation Roza Klub (p819) – enter from rear – feature rave-electronic music Friday and Saturday (1000SIT to 1500SIT), with other styles of music weeknights, and a popular gay-and-lesbian night on Sundays (500SIT after 11pm).

Bachus (☎ 241 8244; www.bachus-center.com, in Slovene; Kongresni trg; ☺ vary) This well-designed, smart and trendy bar-restaurant complex holds weekend discos.

As (☎ 425 8822; www.gostilnaas.si, in Slovene; Knafljev prehod; ☺ 9am-3am) Thursday to Saturday DJs transform this candle-lit basement bar, hidden beneath this incongruously upmarket restaurant, into a pumping, crowd-pulling nightclub.

Jazz Club Gajo (☎ 425 3206; www.jazzclubgajo.com; Beethovnova ul 8; admission free; ☺ 11am-2am Mon-Fri, 7pm-midnight Sat & Sun, closed mid-Jul–mid-Aug) For Monday night student jams, midweek concerts or just a convivial drink, the Gajo is always inviting.

Orto Bar (☎ 232 1674; Grabloviceva ul 1; ☺ 8pm-4am) Popular for late-night drinking and dancing with occasional live music, the Orto has red padded walls, whirring steel propeller fans and a taste for Joy Division. It's just five minutes' walk from Metelkova.

Funfactory (☎ 428 9690; www.discoteka-funfactory .com; Jurckova cesta 224; bus No 3 to the end; ☺ 9pm-dawn Thu-Sat) Strangely, Ljubljana's biggest club is hidden in a shopping centre opposite the Leclerc Hypermarket in the far southeast suburbs. By the time the club closes buses should be running again.

Metelkova (www.metelkova.org) In this two-courtyard block, half a dozen wonderfully idiosyncratic venues hide behind mostly unmarked doors, coming to life after midnight Thursday to Saturday. You might well feel uncomfortable amid the street-art, graffiti and shadow-lurking youth gangs, but this is all part of Metelkova's unique atmosphere. Entering from Masarykova cesta, to the right is **Gala Hala** (www.ljudmila.org/kapa/program, in Slovene) with live bands and club nights. Easy to miss in the first building to the left are Club Tiffany (a gay café-club) and Monokel Club (for lesbians). Beyond the first courtyard, well-hidden Gromka (folk, improv, possibly anything) is beneath the body-less heads. Close by, a purloined blue-arrow road sign marks marvellously idiosyncratic Marico (psycho-blues). Cover charges and midweek openings are rare but erratic for all Metelkova venues.

Theatre & Classical Music

Cankarjev Dom (www.cd-cc.si, in Slovene; Trg Republike) is a complex of around a dozen venues offering a remarkable smorgasbord of performance arts. Its **ticket office** (☎ 241 7100;

☺ 10am-2pm & 4.30-8pm Mon-Fri, 10am-1pm Sat, & 1hr before performances) lurks within the basement floor of Maximarket Mall. Also check for classical concerts at the attractive **Filharmonija** (☎ 241 0800; Kongresni trg) and for ballets at the neo-Renaissance 1882 **Opera House** (☎ 425 4840; Zupanciceva ul). **Krizanke** (☎ 252 6544; Trg francoske revolucije) stages part of the **Ljubljana Summer Festival** (www.festival-lj.si) in what was originally a 13th-century monastic complex.

Cinema

Kinoteka (www.kinoteka.si, in Slovene; Milosiceva cesta 28; admission 1400SIT) offers the most imaginative programme, including rare, old and cult movies, in an Art-Deco mansion. If the linguistic challenges of following a Slovene soundtrack are getting you down, slope off for a drink in the attached, atmospheric, movie-themed **Marilyn Caffe** (big beers 380SIT).

GETTING THERE & AWAY

The shed-like **bus station** (Avtobusna postaja; ☎ 234 4600; www.ap-ljubljana.si; Trg Osvobodilne Fronte; ☺ 5.30am-9pm) has bilingual info-phones, and its timetable is very useful once you get the hang of it – nominate your destination first. Hourly weekday buses serve Bohinj (1940SIT, two hours) via Bled (1400SIT, 1¼ hours). Most buses to Piran (2670SIT, three hours, up to eight daily) go via Koper (2460SIT, 2½ hours, up to ten daily) and Postojna (1320SIT, 1¼ hours, 20 daily). Most Maribor buses (2760SIT, three hours, seven daily) leave in the afternoon. All services are much less frequent at weekends.

Ljubljana **train station** (☎ 291 3332; Trg Osvobodilne Fronte) has up to 19 daily services to Maribor (1660SIT to 2790SIT, 1¾ to 2¾ hours). There are four buses daily to Koper (2½ hours), costing 1980SIT at 9.30am and 4.45pm, or 1660SIT at 8.50am and 3.25pm on an IC (InterCity) train. Alternatively take the Sezana-bound train (6am) and change (rapidly – you've got six minutes!) at Divaca (1¾ hours). For international services see p822.

GETTING AROUND

The cheapest way to **Ljubljana Aerodrome** (www.ap-ljubljana.si) is by city bus from bus station lane No 28 (740SIT, 45 minutes). These run hourly, from 5.10am to 8.10pm Monday to Friday, but only seven times daily at weekends. Another seven Marun/

Adria coaches (1000SIT, 30 minutes) run daily. Big hotels offer an airport shuttle for 2500SIT per person or 8800SIT per shuttle, if there are few passengers.

The heavily pedestrianised city centre's one-way system makes driving confusing. Street parking is feasible, though not always easy in the museum area and near Metelkova. Once you've found a space it's generally most efficient to walk.

Ljubljana has excellent city buses, most lines operating every 10 to 20 minutes from 3.15am to midnight. However, the central area is perfectly walkable, so buses are really only necessary if you're staying out of town. Buy tokens in advance (180SIT) from newsstands, or pay 250SIT once aboard. Ljubljana Cards (3000SIT for 72 hours; p794) give you free city-bus travel.

In summer you can rent bicycles at the train station, at **Hotel Lev** (Vošnjakova ul 1; per day 3000SIT), and at a kiosk near **Maček Café** (Cankarjevo nab 19). Free hire is also available from STIC (p794).

JULIAN ALPS

Dramatic rocky mountain spires straddle the Italian border. Within Slovenia these Julian Alps (named for Caesar) climax at tri-peaked Mt Triglav (2864m), the country's highest summit. Along with neighbouring mountains, forests, and breathtakingly beautiful valleys, the area forms the Triglav National Park. At weekends, half of Ljubljana's population decamps here to ski, cycle, fish, climb or hike. There are adventure sports to suit every level of insanity, many based in Bovec (p805), and few places in Europe offer better rafting, paragliding or canyoning at such affordable prices.

KRANJ
☎ 04 / pop 37,000

Backed by a threatening battalion of mountains, Kranj's old core looks most picturesque when seen from across the Sava River, looking to the northeast. This is a view you'll enjoy briefly from the right-hand windows of buses headed from Ljubljana to Bled/Kranjska Gora, between gaps in the light-industrial foreground.

The frequent weekday buses between Kranj and 'Ljubljana Aerodrome' (in Brnik)

make it possible to head straight from the plane to the Julian Alps without diverting to Ljubljana. While awaiting your Bled- or Kranjska Gora–bound bus, consider poking around the mildly appealing Kranj old town. It starts near the Art-Nouveau **former post office** (Maistrov trg), a 500m walk south from the bus station past the over-priced **Hotel Creina** (☎ 202 4550; www.hotel-creina.si; Koroška cesta; s/d/tr 11,500/16,000/20,400SIT). Most places of interest are along just three south-bound pedestrianised streets – Prešernova, Britov and Tomišičeva ulicas – two of which bring you to the impressive **Sv Kancijan Church**, with its frescoes and ossuary. As far south again, the old town dead-ends near the **Serbian Orthodox church** with a 16th-century **defence tower**. Colourfully stylish, student-oriented **Cukrama** (Britov 73; beers 400SIT; ⊗ 11am-late) is a great place for a drink, and boasts a gas-heated balcony overlooking an abyss.

From Kranj it's a relatively easy 10km excursion to **Škofja Loka**, which has one of Slovenia's most beautiful town squares (Mestni trg) and a fine **castle** (Loski Grad; 13 Grajski pot) containing a decent **ethnographical museum** (☎ 517 04 00; adult/child 500/400SIT; ⊗ 9am-6pm Tue-Sun Apr-Oct, 9am-5pm Sat & Sun Nov-Mar). Buses run approximately hourly from Kranj (490SIT, 25 minutes).

BLED
☎ 04 / pop 5467

Genteel, millennium-old Bled is the gateway to the mountains. Its attraction is an absolutely idyllic setting on a 2km-long subalpine lake with a castle crag and romantic island placed exactly where you'd want them. It's a scene that seems designed for some god of tourism, not for the 13th century Bishops of Brixen. Bled town is not architecturally memorable, but it's small, convenient and a delightful base from which to simply stroll and gaze. Beware: in midsummer the beauty is diluted a little by the ever-expanding crowds and prices.

Information
Kompas (Bled Shopping Centre; ⊗ 9am-7pm) Sells maps, rents bicycles, offers tours and changes money.
SKB Banka (Bled Shopping Centre; ⊗ 9-11.30am & 2-5pm Mon-Fri) One of several banks with an ATM.
Tourist Office (TIC; ☎ 574 1122; www.bled.si; ⊗ 9am-7pm Mon-Sat, 11am-4pm Sun, later in summer) On the lakefront near the Park Hotel.

SLOVENIA

Union 99 (www.union-bled.com; Ljubljanska cesta 9; per 15min 270SIT; 🕗 8am-midnight) An appealing upstairs café-bar with an Internet connection.

Sights

On its own romantically tiny island (Blejski Otok) the baroque **Church of the Assumption** (🕗 8am-dusk, variable in winter) is Bled's photogenic trademark. Getting there by piloted 'gondola' (*plenta*, €10 per person, 1½ hours return) is the archetypal tourist experience. Gondola prices are standard from any jetty, and you'll stay on the island long enough to ring the 'lucky' bell. Ordinary row-yourself boats cost 3000SIT per hour.

Topping a sheer 100m-cliff, **Bled Castle** (🕿 574 1230; Blejski Grad; adult/student 1000/600SIT; 🕗 9am-8pm May-Sep, 9am-6pm Oct-Apr) is the perfect backdrop to lake views, notably those from Mlino, on the lake's southern bank. One of many access footpaths leads up from beside Bledec Hostel. Admission includes a historical **museum** section and the fabulous views. After official closing time you can get those views for free by having a meal or sunset beer at the superbly situated terrace of the **Castle Restaurant** (Restavracija Blejski Grad; 🕿 574 1607; mains 2000-3200SIT, beers 450SIT; 🕗 9am-10pm).

Hidden away in its own lakeside park beyond Mlino is **Vila Bled** (🕿 579 1500; www.vila-bled.com; Cesta Svobode 26). This is now a Relais & Chateaux hotel, but it started life as Tito's summer retreat. Its basic design is somewhat forbiddingly 1950s, but there

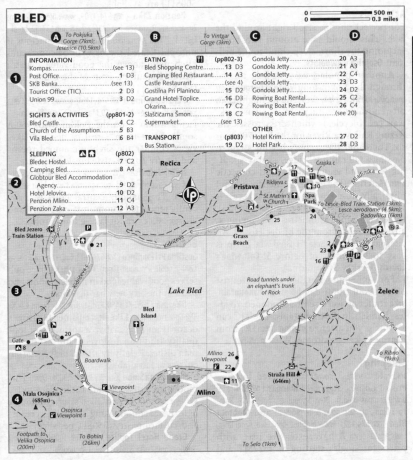

are some brilliant communist murals and a delightful outside terrace between arches of a colonnade. It's well worth the price of a drink to look around.

About 7km southeast of Bled, the town of **Radovljica** appears to be an amorphous, modern sprawl. However, it has a particularly delightful old town square where there's a restored, painted **manor house**, an interesting **gallery** and the fascinating **bee-keeping museum** (Čebelarski Muzej; ☎ 532 0520; www.muzeji-radovljica.si; Linhartov trg; adult/student 400/300SIT; ☺ 10am-1pm & 3-6pm Tue-Sun May-Oct, closed in winter except some weekends & Wed). The square starts 300m southwest of Radovljica bus station (via Gorenjska cesta), or just 150m north up narrow Kolovorska ul from the train station.

Activities

For perfect photos, stroll right around the lake. This should take around two hours including the short, steep climb to the brilliant **Osojnica viewpoints**.

Another popular, easy **walk** is to and through the 1.6km-long **Vintgar Gorge** (adult/child 500/300SIT; ☺ May-Oct). The highlight is an oft-renovated, century-old wooden walkway (no bicycles) which crisscrosses the fizzing Radovna River for the first 700m or so. Thereafter the scenery becomes tamer, passing a tall railway bridge, a spray-spouting weir, and ending at the anti-climactic **Sum Waterfall**. The gorge is officially but not physically closed in winter. Easiest access is via the appealing Gostilna Vintgar (an inn), three well-signed kilometres away on quiet, attractive roads from the Bledec Hostel. An alternative path back to Bled via Zasip is easy to lose track of before **St Catherine's Church** (Cerkev Sv Katarina).

For something tougher ask the tourist office about multi-day **hikes** and **mountain-bike** routes between semi-abandoned, roadless hamlets in the mountains. The TIC can also help you arrange **gliding** (from €30) from nearby Lesce aerodrome. What a view!

Sleeping

Private rooms (*sobe*) are offered by dozens of homes. Agencies **Kompas** (☎ 574 1515; www.kompas-bled.si; Bled Shopping Centre; ☺ 8am-7pm Mon-Sat, 8am-noon & 4-7pm Sun) and **Globtour Bled** (☎ 574 1821; www.globtour-bled.com; Hotel Krim, Ljubljanska cesta 7) have extensive lists, with prices for singles starting at 4322SIT and

moving up. Prices per night drop for stays of three nights or more.

Camping Bled (☎ 575 2000; www.camping.bled.si; adult/child low season 1580/1110SIT, Jun & Sep 2080/1460SIT, Jul–25 Aug 2320/1625SIT; ☺ Apr–mid-Oct) This well-kept, popular site fills a rural valley behind a waterside restaurant at the western end of the lake. It rents mountain bikes (per day 2300SIT) and can arrange ballooning, rafting, parachuting and more.

Bledec Hostel (☎ 574 5250; Grajska cesta 17; dm/d low season €17/42, high season €19/46, IYHA discount €2; 🖳) Outwardly a typical *penzion*, this well-organised youth hostel has new four-bed dorms with attached bathrooms. It's quiet yet very central. Laundry (per load 1500SIT) and Internet (per half-hour 500SIT) are available.

Penzion Zaka (☎ 574 1709; www.bled-zaka.com; Županiičeva 9; s/d Sep-Jun €28/42, Jul & Aug €33/52, breakfast €3) This *penzion* offers seven spacious if unsophisticated rooms with balconies and kitchenette above the good-value Regatni Center restaurant. Four of the rooms have lake views.

Penzion Mlino (☎ 574 1404; www.mlino.si; Cesta Svobode 45; s/d Nov-Apr €32/50, May-Oct €37/60) The lake-facing Mlino is on the Bohinj road, 900m southwest of town. Great castle- and lake-views counter the slightly cramped rooms and *Fawlty Towers*–style breakfast service.

Hotel Jelovica (☎ 579 6000; www.hotel-jelovica.si; Cesta Svobode 8; s/d low season €39/54, high season €49/74) This handily central hotel is a decently renovated communist-era resort, and charges €5 extra for lake-glimpse rooms.

Eating

Gostilna Pri Planincu (☎ 574 1613; Grajska cesta 8; mains 1200-2000SIT; ☺ noon-10pm) This 1903 village pub serves good-value food in its back rooms and pizza in the airy new bar upstairs.

Okarina (☎ 574 1458; Riklijeva cesta 9; mains €7-20; ☺ 6pm-midnight) Like its cuisine, Okarina's décor is an imaginative assortment of top-quality traditional Slovene and exotic Indian dishes. Relatively affordable vegetarian curries are available.

Slaščičarna Šmon (Grajska 3; ☎ 7.30am-9pm) This renowned patisserie-café is the place to try *krema snežna rezina*, Bled's scrumptiously light if anaemic-looking speciality, cream-and-custard pastry (350SIT per slice).

Grand Hotel Toplice (☎ 579 1000; www.hotel-toplice.com; Cesta Svobode 12; cappuccino 500SIT, beers

850SIT) If you're prepared to dress up a little and are not daunted by the hovering bow-tied waiters, venture into the hushed, hallowed lounge bar of Bled's most exclusive hotel. Sitting in the magnificent bay window, lapped outside by lake waters, easily justifies the 750SIT for a succulent slice of cake. Perhaps the low Edward VII settees where you're sitting were previously warmed by bottoms as famous as Prince Charles' or Madeleine Albright's. En route to the toilets notice the photos of other such celebrity guests in the corridor.

Stock up on supplies at the supermarkets on Prešernova cesta or in **Bled shopping centre** (Ljubljanska cesta 4). The latter also has several decent café-bars.

Getting There & Around

Hourly buses to Bohinj (from 7.20am) and Ljubljana (1400SIT, 1½ hours) use the helpfully central bus station. Buses to Radovljica via Lesce-Bled station (300SIT, 15 minutes) run every 30 minutes. Bled has no central train station. Trains for Most na Soči and Nova Gorica use sweet little Bled Jezero station, which is 2km west of central Bled – handy for the camping ground and Pension Zaka but nothing else. Trains for Austria (up to eight daily) and Ljubljana (1050SIT, 55 minutes, frequent) use Lesce-Bled station, 4km to the east of town. However if you're off to Ljubljana it's much nicer (if marginally less convenient) to wait for your train in attractive Radovljica.

In summer, pint-sized 'tourist-trains' (adult/child 550/350SIT) trundle around the lakeside every 40 minutes, passing *penzions* Mlino and Zaka.

BOHINJ
☎ 04

Bohinj is not a town but a delightful valley of quaint meadowland villages culminating at magnificent Lake Bohinj. The mirrored waters are hemmed by high mountains that rise almost vertically from the walking trail along the lake's 3km-long northern shore.

The minuscule main tourist hub is **Ribčev Laz**, at the lake's east end. Its five-shop commercial centre contains a supermarket, pizzeria, post office (with ATM) and the obliging **tourist office** (☎ 574 6010; www.bohinj .si; ☙ 8am-6pm Mon-Sat, 9am-3pm Sun mid-Sep–Jun, 8am-8pm daily summer), which changes money,

sells fishing licences (from €20 per day) and can help with accommodation, including mountain-hikers' huts. **Alpinsport** (☎ 572 3486; www.alpinsport.si; ☙ closed Apr) rents kayaks, canoes, bicycles and skis from a kiosk near the stone bridge, across which is the **Church of St John the Baptist** (☙ very rarely) containing celebrated 15th-century frescoes.

For brochure-worthy photos of Lake Bohinj climb 25 minutes up Peč Hill from Stara Fužina village, 1.5km further north. Stara Fužina also has an appealing little **Alpine Dairy Museum** (Planšarski Musej; adult/child 400/300SIT; ☙ 10am-noon & 4-6pm Tue-Sun, 11am-7pm Tue-Sun midsummer). Along with similarly attractive villages **Studor** and **Češnica**, it makes a delightful but easy bike ride from Ribčev Laz. The route is dotted with specially fine *kozolci* and *toplarji*, Slovenia's unique single and double hayracks.

Summer tourist boats (single 1300SIT to 1500SIT, return 1600SIT to 1900SIT, 15 minutes, seven or eight per day) from Ribčev Laz terminate in Ukanc (aka Zlatorog) at the lake's far west end. Just 300m from the jetty a cable car (single/return 1400/2000SIT, half hourly from 9am to 6pm, or 8am to 8pm midsummer) whisks you up a vertical kilometre to 1540m; from here, ski lifts or hiking paths, according to season, continue up **Mt Vogel** for astonishing views.

Bohinjska Bistrica (population 3080), Bohinj's biggest village, is 6km east of the Ribčev Laz and useful mainly for its train station.

Sleeping

Private rooms (s €13-19, d €22-32), mainly in outlying villages, are available through the tourist office. Nightly rates are cheaper for three-day stays.

Autokamp Zlatorog (☎ 572 3482; camp sites per person 1500-2200SIT; ☙ May-Sep) A pine-shaded caravan site, with camping spots too, right beside the Ukanc jetty.

Penzion Rožic (☎ 572 3393; www.penzion-rozic .com; per person without breakfast 3954-4654SIT; 🖳) This unpretentious chalet-style guesthouse and restaurant is cheaper than most Ribčev Laz hotels. It's just 100m east of the tourist office, behind a bike-rental kiosk.

Ski Hotel Vogel (s/d low season 7150/12,900SIT, in summer 9600/17,500SIT) With a stupendous position at the top of the Mt Vogel cable car, this is one of five Bohinj hotels run by **Alpinum** (☎ 577 8000; www.alpinum.net).

SLOVENIA

Hotel Jezero (☎ 572 9100; hotel.jezero@cc-line.si; s/d from €51/68) This relatively comfortable place is the closest hotel to the lake, right by the stone bridge in Ribčev Laz. Rooms with a balcony cost slightly more.

Getting There & Around

Buses run hourly (except Sundays) from Ukanc to Ljubljana via Ribčev Laz (400SIT), Bohinjska Bistrica and Bled, with six extra buses daily between Bohinjska Bistrica and Ukanc. Buses to Ukanc will be marked to 'Bohinj Zlatorog'. From Bohinjska Bistrica, passenger trains to Novo Gorica (1010SIT, 1½ hours, eight daily weekdays, less on weekends), plus six daily Avtovlak trains to Most na Soči (910SIT including bicycle, 50 minutes), use a long tunnel that offers the only direct option for reaching the Soča Valley. Avtovlak trains carry cars for 2600SIT.

KRANJSKA GORA

☎ 04 / pop 2000

As ski resorts go, compact little Kranjska Gora is relatively cute and sits right beside the ski lifts to Slovenia's best-regarded pistes. There are world record–setting ski jumps 4km west at Planica. Several places, including **Skipass Travel** (www.skipasstravel.si, in Slovene), rent skis, poles and boots for 5300SIT per set. One-day lift passes cost 4900/4300SIT per adult/student.

The in-your-face mountain valleys also beckon summer climbers, hikers and anglers alike. For cyclists and motorists there's the awesome drama of the Vršič Pass.

Borovška cesta, 300m south of the bus station, is the old heart of the village, with an endearing **museum** (Borovška 61), an attractive **church** and a few wooden-roofed old

houses. At its newer western end it passes the helpful **tourist office** (☎ 588 1768; www .kranjska-gora.si; Tičarjeva 2; ☽ variable), a bank with ATM and money exchange, a couple of supermarkets and the post office.

Sleeping & Eating

Accommodation pricing is very complex, peaking December to February, at Mardi Gras and in midsummer. April is the cheapest season, though many hotels close for repairs at this time. **Private rooms** (s/d from €18/25) and mountain huts can be arranged with help from the tourist office.

Youth Hostel Nika (Penzion Portentov Dom; ☎ 588 1436; Čičare 2; dm 2000-3000SIT; ☽ 8am-11pm) Somewhat institutional dorm-rooms are available in this large black-and-lilac house 800m northeast of the centre, some 200m beyond the Šanghai Chinese restaurant.

Hotel Kotnik (☎ 588 1564; kotnik@siol.net; Borovška 75; d €56-74) In the old centre, this appealing, very well appointed hotel has 'turrets', red-tiled roofs, and flowers in the window boxes. It's painted in unmissable bright yellow. There's a cosy little lounge, a well-reputed restaurant and a good pizzeria attached.

Gostilna Pri Martinu (☎ 582 0300; Borovška 61; mains 1100-2100SIT, d €46-52; ☽ 10am-10pm, bar 10am-11pm) This atmospheric tavern-restaurant serves up giant portions and offers four vegetarian options. It's *ajdova kaša* (buckwheat with fresh mushrooms in garlic-cream sauce) is superb. It also has rooms.

Getting There & Away

Buses run hourly to Ljubljana via Jesenice (change for Bled or Villach), and direct to Bled at 9.15am and 1.10pm, weekdays only. In July and August there's a service to

---

HIKING MT TRIGLAV

The Julian Alps offer some of Europe's finest hiking. In summer around 165 mountain huts (*planinska koča* or *planinski dom*) operate, none more than five hours' walk from the next. These huts get very crowded, especially at weekends, when it seems that half of Ljubljana leaves the city to climb Mt Triglav or explore the splendid surrounding valleys – so booking ahead is wise. If the weather turns bad, however, you shouldn't be refused refuge.

At 4800SIT per person in a private room or up to 3000SIT in a dorm, the huts aren't cheap, but as they serve meals you can travel light. Not too light, however. Sturdy boots and warm clothes are indispensable, even in midsummer. Trails are generally well marked with a white-centred red circle, but you can still get lost and it's very unwise to trek alone – take a friend.

TICs in Bled, Bohinj, Kranjska Gora and Bovec all have plenty of hiking information, sell great maps in a variety of useful scales, and can help you book huts in their respective regions.

Bovec (1530SIT, 1¾ hours, five daily) via the spectacular Vršič Pass. A taxi direct to Villach (in Austria) costs from €30 to €35 when the ultra-steep Wurzenpass is open; it's often closed in winter after snow.

UPPER SOČA VALLEY

☎ 05

The bluer-than-blue water of the Soča River changes tone with the seasons, but is always surreally vivid. It has carved out one of the loveliest valleys in the Julian Alps.

Bovec

pop 1610

For alpine drama, the views are best around Bovec, above which towers Mt Kanin, Slovenia's highest ski area. Although Bovec itself is no great beauty, it makes an ideal base for hiking, biking or climbing into the marvellous valley beyond and is nationally famous for extreme sports.

The compact village square (Trg Golobarskih Žrtev) has everything you need. There are cafés, a hotel, a very helpful **tourist office** (☎ 384 1919; www.bovec.si; ☺ vary) and several adrenaline-rush adventure-sports companies: **Planet Sport** (☎ 040-639 433; www .drustvo-planet.si), **Sportmix** (☎ 389 6160; www.sport mix.traftbovec.si), **Top Rafting** (☎ 041-620 636; www .top.si) and experienced, well-organised **Soča Rafting** (☎ 389 6200; www.SocaRafting.si).

Activities include:

Guided canyoning 7900-8700SIT for two hours at Sušec.

Hydrospeed Like riding down a river on a boogie board; 6700-7400SIT for 8km.

White-water rafting Around 4700SIT for 8km, 7600SIT for 20km, April to October.

Kayaking Guided 10km paddle from 6500SIT per person, two-day training courses from €55.

Caving From €25 per person with guide.

Save 10% to 15% with student cards, the TIC's 'Byways' booklet, or by simply avoiding midsummer and weekends. **Avantura** (☎ 041-718 317; www.bovec.net/avantura.html) offers awesome tandem-jump **paragliding** (22,000SIT): in winter when the ski lifts operate you jump off the top of Mt Kanin!

Chalet-villages throughout the valley have private-room accommodation from €12 per person (plus various supplements). There is an extensive list of contacts at www.bovec .net, and **Avrigo Tour agency** (☎ 386 6022; avrigotours .bovec@avrigo.si; Trg Golobarskih Žrtev 47; ☺ 8.30-11.30am

& 3.30-7pm Mon-Sat, 9am-noon & 3-5pm Sun) can help, but finding anything at all in August can be tough. The central **Alp Hotel** (☎ 388 6370; www .bovec.net/hotelalp; Trg Golobarskih Žrtev 48; s €36.80-39.80, d €57.20-63.20, s/d Aug €45.80/75.20) is smart and good value. Camping facilities are better in Kobarid, but camping ground **Polovnik** (☎ 041-641 898; camp sites from 1431SIT, showers 120SIT) is handily central.

Kobarid

pop 1240

Nearby **Kobarid** village (Caporetto in Italian) is quainter than Bovec, though the woodland scenery is somewhat tamer. On its main square is extreme-sports agency, **XPoint** (☎ 388 5308; www.xpoint.si; ☺ vary), Internet-equipped **Bar Cinca Marinca** (Trg Svobode 10; per half-hr 250SIT; ☺ 8am-11pm) and renowned **Restaurant Kotlar** (www.kotlar-sp.si; mains 1500-3000SIT; ☺ noon-11pm Thu-Mon). The tourist office is within Kobarid's **museum** (adult/student 800/600SIT; ☺ 9am-6pm), which is otherwise devoted mainly to the region's WWI battles. These killed over 200,000 people and formed the backdrop to Ernest Hemingway's *Farewell to Arms*. The daring Austro-German breakthrough at Kobarid in October 1917 invented Blitzkrieg. Remnant WWI troop emplacements as well as Roman and 6th-century archaeological sites can be seen on an easy-to-follow, half-day hiking loop to the impressive **Slap Kozjak** (waterfalls).

Close to Kobarid's central church, **Apartmaji-Sobe Ivančič** (☎ 389 1007; apartma-ra@siol .net; Gregorčičeva 6C; s €18-30, d €30-50) is a popular central homestay. It's neat and clean, with bathrooms shared between pairs of cheaper rooms.

Lazar Kamp (☎ 388 5333; www.lazar-sp.si; per person €6.50-9; ☺ Apr-Oct) is perched idyllically above the Soča River, 1.7km southeast of Kobarid, halfway to Slap Kozjak. Probably Slovenia's finest camping ground, the multilingual owners are conscientious and hospitable. Their wild west–style saloon-café serves delicious *palačinka* crepes. Go on, try the 'bear's blood'!

Getting There & Away

Public transport in the area is poor. Weekday buses from Bovec via Kobarid run five times daily to Novo Gorica (1670SIT, two hours) and thrice to Ljubljana (3030SIT, 3¾ hours), passing Most na Soči train station (for Bled and Bohinj). In July and August only, six daily buses cross the spectacular Vršič Pass to Kranjska Gora; from here hourly buses continue to Ljubljana.

NOVO GORICA/GORIZIA

Novo Gorica, a green but unexciting casino- and border-town, was torn from Italian-held old Gorizia after WWII. Today the two towns lie side-by-side on each side of the border. Novo Gorica is useful mainly as a money-saving public transport route between Italy's budget airline–served western cities of Trieste and Treviso and Slovenia's Julian Alps. Part of the mini-'Berlin Wall' dividing the cities was pulled down to great fanfare in 2004, leaving the anomalous Piazza Transalpina straddling the border right behind Novo Gorica station. At the piazza there's no fence and (usually) no guards, so in reality there's rarely anything to physically stop you wandering across to the Italian side, where the frequent Italian bus No 1 will pick you up and conveniently whisk you to Gorizia station. Bizarrely, however, this is NOT a legal border crossing, and it won't be until Slovenia joins the Schengen Convention. Meanwhile EU (plus Icelandic, Norwegian and Swiss) citizens may use a less direct shuttle bus (www.atpgorizia.it, 230SIT or €1, 25 minutes, almost hourly) between the two train stations, or cross on foot at the **Gabrielle border crossing** (🕒 8am-8pm Mon-Sat; no banks). Gabrielle is a two-minute stroll south of Novo Gorica train station, or 10 minutes southwest from the bus station: head straight down Erjavčeva ul which becomes Via San Gabriele in Italy. Continue five minutes to the five-way junction Piazza Medaglie d'Oro to pick up southbound Italian bus No 1 for Gorizia station.

Other nationalities can't use the Gabrielle crossing. Instead they are expected to use the 24-hour Rožna Dolina–Cassa Rosa crossing (where there are banks with ATMs). That's reached by half-hourly buses (any number) from Novo Gorica bus station, or by walking 20 minutes south from the train station: follow the railway line through the cycletunnel, immediately thereafter cross the tracks on a footbridge and continue along ul Pinka Tomažiča and Pot na Pristavo. From Cassa Rosa take Italian bus No 8 northbound along its convoluted route, which loops back to Gorizia bus/train stations.

There are banks with ATMs at Rožna Dolina and Novo Gorica bus station but not at Gabrielle, nor at the train station, which nonetheless does accept euros for tickets (at some 10% below market rates).

Novo Gorica's only inexpensive accommodation is **Prenočišče Pertout** (☎ 303 2194; s/d €23/35), a well-marked house just 50m east then north from the Rožna Dolina border crossing. It's surprisingly peaceful and comfortable.

Buses travel between Novo Gorica and Ljubljana (2280SIT, 2½ hours) approximately hourly via Postojna and five times daily to Bovec via Kobarid.

Trains run to Bohinjski Bistrica (1010SIT, 1½ hours) and Bled or via Sežana and Divača to Postojna and Ljubljana.

KARST & COAST

Slovenia's 45km sliver of coastline has no beach worthy of the name, although that hasn't stopped Portorož becoming a major resort. The coast's real appeal lies in its charming old Venetian ports: Koper, Izola and picture-perfect Piran. En route from Ljubljana you'll cross Karst (Kras), Slovenia's west-central region, which is synonymous with eccentrically eroded limestone landscapes and riddled with magnificent caves. Slovenia's two most famous caves – theme park–style Postojna and quietly awesome Škocjan – couldn't be more different.

POSTOJNA

☎ 05 / pop 8500

Slovenia's foremost tourist attraction, **Postojna Cave** (☎ 700 0100; www.postojnska-jama.si; adult/student/child 3290/2190/1990SIT) is a very obvious 2km stroll northwest of unremarkable Postojna town. Inside, impressive stalagmites and stalactites stretch almost endlessly in all directions, as do the chattering crowds who shuffle past them. A visit involves a 1.7km walk, with some gradients but no steps. It culminates in a quick encounter with a cute, endemic *Proteus anguinus* 'human-fish'. The very jolly highlight which both starts and finishes the tour is chugging between the limestone formations on an underground train. Dress warmly or rent a coat (700SIT): even on blistering summer days it's only 8°C to 10°C inside the cave, the train seats may be wet, and there's some wind chill on the open carriages.

Entry times are fixed. At a minimum there will be departures at 10am and 2pm daily plus at noon and 4pm on weekends. Frequency rises steadily towards summer, becoming hourly (from 9am to 6pm) between June and October.

Close to the cave and much cheaper using a combined ticket is a **Speliobiological Station** (adult/student 1000/700SIT; ☺ hourly 'shows' 10am-3pm, in summer 9am-6pm). This gives a video introduction to underground zoology, then lets you into a small, semidark cave to peep at some of the shy creatures you've just learnt about. Don't expect tigers; most are so minuscule you can hardly see them. Non biologists may find more interest in the 19th-century cave graffiti.

Idyllic **Predjama** village is 9km northwest of Postojna. It consists of half a dozen houses, a rural inn, a mock-medieval jousting course and a remarkable **castle** (☎ 700 0100; adult/student 900/600SIT; ☺ 10am-4pm Sep-May, 9am-7pm Jun-Aug) which appears to grow out of a yawning cave. The partly furnished interior boasts costumed wax mannequins, one of which dangles from the dripping rock-roofed torture chamber. Beneath are stalactite-adorned **caves** (1000SIT, cave-castle combination ticket adult/student 1690/1100SIT), which lack Postojna's crowds, but also much of its grandeur.

Sleeping & Eating

Dozens of Postojna houses rent **rooms** (s/d from 4500/7500SIT). Central **Kompas** (☎ 726 4281; info@kompas-postojna.si; Titov trg; ☺ 8am-6pm Mon-Fri, 9am-3pm Sat) or the cave-side **tourist office** (www.postojna.si; ☺ 10am-4pm, 9am-6pm May-Oct) can help.

Hotel Kras (☎ 726 4071; Titov trg; s/d/tr €33/47/66) This unlovely and somewhat tatty concrete box–style hotel is right on the central square, 200m stroll north of the bus station.

Gostilna Požar (☎ 751 5252; tw 7600SIT ☺ closed Wed) Facing the cave-mouth castle in Predjama, this brilliantly situated inn has simple rooms with shared bathrooms, and is above the village restaurant.

Getting There & Away

Buses from Ljubljana to Koper, Piran or Novo Gorica all stop in Postojna (1¼ hours). The train is less useful as the station is 1km east of town near the bypass, ie 3km from the caves. At the time of writing there were plans for a

summer-only tourist shuttle between Postojna Caves and Predjama. Otherwise, five local buses run on schooldays only (390SIT) from Postojna bus station to Bukovje village. That's just 1.3km short of Predjama, a delightful, well-signposted walk.

ŠKOCJAN CAVES & DIVAČA
☎ 05

The perky church tower of a tiny, red-roofed hamlet pokes jauntily through fluffy forests. Just beneath, the limestone earth cracks like broken egg shells, releasing the turbulent Reka River from the immense **Škocjan Caves** (www.park-skocjanske-jame.si; adult/student 2000/1300SIT). Harder to reach and much less commercialised than Postojna, these caves have been declared a Unesco World Heritage site. With relatively few stalactites, the attraction here is the sheer depth of the awesome underground chasm, which you cross by a dizzying little footbridge. To see this you must join a shepherded two-hour walking tour, involving hundreds of steps and ending with a rickety funicular ride. Year-round departures are assured at 10am and 1pm daily plus 3pm Sundays. June to September they leave additionally at 11.30am, 2pm, 3pm, 4pm and 5pm daily. Unlike Postojna the caves warm up somewhat in summer so there's no need for unseasonable coats.

The nearest town with accommodation is Divača, 4km to the northwest. Here the modest **Gostilna Risnik** (☎ 763 0008; Kraška 24; s/tw 3500/6000SIT) is 200m northeast of the train station above a smoky bar. The quieter, better **Gostilna Malovec** (☎ 763 1225; Kraška 30a; s/d €20/40) is 300m beyond. Both have restaurants.

Ljubljana-to-Koper buses and trains both stop at **Divača** half an hour after Postojna. Kindly staff at the train station often give visitors a photocopied route map for walking to the caves. Alternatively, stay on the bus a couple of minutes longer and get dropped off at a signposted junction just 1.6km from the caves. Timetables rarely mesh with cave-visit times, but you can make pleasant short hikes around the cave's visitor centre, where there's a bar and restaurant for those conserving their energy.

LIPICA
☎ 05 / pop 130

Since the 18th century, **Lipica** has been breeding snow-white Lipizzaner horses for the world-famous Imperial Spanish Riding School in Vienna. The village is basically just a hotel complex and the **Stud Farm** (☎ 739 1580; www.lipica.org; tours per adult/student from 1400/700SIT) which offers equestrian fans a variety of rides, lessons and tours (safest bets at 1pm, 2pm and 3pm). For comprehensive timetables and prices check the website carefully. The **Hotel Maestoso** (www.lipica.org; s/tw low season €61/80, mid-season €70/92, high season €79/102) has excellently appointed modern rooms looking over the golf course–like landscape. For cheaper options drive 3km west to Basovizza in Italy.

Divača to Lipica is only 10km but there's no viable public transport. With your own wheels stop halfway there in the village of **Lokev**, where the intriguing 1485 **Tabor tower**

houses a cheap bar and a little **armaments museum** (☎ 707 0107; ⏰ 10am-noon Wed-Fri, 9am-noon & 2-6pm Sat & Sun), just off (and easily visible from) the main Divača–Lipica road.

KOPER

☎ 05 / pop 24,000

As you swing around it on the motorway, Koper appears to be a sprawling, industrial town dominated by container-port cranes. Yet its central core is delightfully quiet, quaint and much less touristy than nearby Piran. Also, being a working city, its accommodation is not quite as stretched as Piran's in summer.

Koper grew rich as a key Venetian salt trading port. Known then as Capodistria,

KOPER

0 ——————— 300 m
0 ——————— 0.2 miles

INFORMATION	
Banka Koper.......................1 B2
Ilirika.............................2 A3
Libris.............................3 B3
Maki Currency Exchange Bureau..4 A3
Net Bar...........................5 D3
Pina..............................6 A2
Post Office.......................7 B2
Tourist Information Centre........8 B3

SIGHTS & ACTIVITIES	(p809)
Cathedral of St Lazarus..........9 B2
Da Ponte Fountain................10 B4
Fontico...........................11 C3

| Koper Regional Museum.........12 B2 |
| Loggia...........................13 B2 |
| Medieval Houses..................14 A2 |
| Muda Gate........................15 B4 |
| Praetorian Palace.............(see 8) |
| St Jacobs........................16 C3 |
| Salt Warehouse...................17 A3 |
| Stone Pillar.....................18 A3 |
| Tower............................19 B3 |

SLEEPING	(p809)
Dijaški Dom Koper................20 C2
Hotel Koper......................21 A3
Hotel Vodišek....................22 C4

| Kompas...........................23 A3 |
| Vila Milka.......................24 D2 |

EATING	(p810)
Delfi............................25 A3
Istrska Klet.....................26 B3
Skipper..........................27 A2
Slaščičarna Kroštola............28 A2

DRINKING	(p810)
Skica............................29 B3

TRANSPORT	(p810)
Boat to Piran....................30 A3

Koper Bay

it was capital of Istria under the 15th- and 16th-century Venetian Republic. At that time it was an island commanding a U-shaped bay of saline ponds, something hard to imagine now, given the centuries of land reclamation that have joined it very firmly to the mainland.

Orientation

The joint bus and train station (bicycle hire available) is 1.4km southeast of central Titov trg. To walk into town, just head towards the cathedral's Moroccan-style bell tower; alternatively, take Bus No 1, 2 or 3 to the Muda Gate. Pristaniška ul and Vojkovo nab mark what was once the southern coast of the medieval island.

Information

Banka Koper (Kidričeva ul 14; ☿ 8.30am-noon & 3-5pm Mon-Fri, 8.30am-noon Sat) Changes money.

Libris (Prešernov trg 9; www.libris.si, in Slovene; ☿ 8am-7pm Mon-Fri, 9am-1pm Sat) Bookshop with postcards.

Maki Currency Exchange Bureau (Pristaniška ul; ☿ 7.30am-7.30pm Mon-Fri, 7.30am-1pm Sat) Compare rates with Ilirika across the road.

Net Bar (Vojkovo nab 33; beers 330SIT; ☿ 6am-11pm Mon-Fri, 8am-11pm Sat, noon-11pm Sun) Twenty minutes free Internet access when you buy a drink.

Pina (Kidričeva 43; Internet per min adult/student 15/5SIT; ☿ 9am-8pm)

Tourist Information Centre (☎ /fax 627 3791; tic@koper.si; Praetorian Palace, Titov trg 3; ☿ 9am-5pm Mon-Fri, 9am-1pm Sat Jun-Sep, 9am-9pm Mon-Sat, 9am-noon Sun Jul & Aug) The TIC's useful tourist map includes potted histories of key buildings.

Sights

As in Piran, the greatest attraction of Koper is purposeless wandering. You change centuries abruptly passing through the 1516 **Muda Gate**. Continue north past the 1666 **Da Ponte Fountain** (Prešernov trg) and up Čevljarska ul, the petite commercial artery, to reach Titov trg. This fine central square is dominated by the 1480 **tower** attached to the part-Gothic, part-Renaissance **Cathedral of St Lazarus**. The renovated 15th-century **Praetorian Palace** (Titov trg 3; admission free) contains the city hall and an old pharmacy which is now a museum, as well as the tourist office. Opposite, the splendid 1463 **loggia** is now an elegant yet affordable **café** (☎ 627 4171; wine per glass from 200SIT; ☿ 7am-10pm), with several better wines by the glass.

Several more fine façades face **Trg Brolo**, a wide, peacefully Mediterranean square. One such is the shield-dotted **Fontico** that started life as a 1392 grain warehouse. Beside this, with a small, simple campanile, is the 14th-century stone **Church of St Jacobs** (Martinčev trg).

The **Koper Regional Museum** (Kidričeva ul 19; adult/student 350/250SIT; ☿ 8am-3pm Mon-Fri, 8am-1pm Sat) is within the Belgramoni-Tacco mansion and features an Italianate sculpture garden. Weekday evenings from June to August it's also open 6pm to 8pm. Kidričeva ul also has a few appealing **medieval houses** with beamed overhangs. It leads west into Carpacciov trg, the former fish market with a 15th-century **salt warehouse**, a 1571 **stone pillar**, a pub and a couple of street cafés.

Sleeping

Dijaški Dom Koper (☎ 627 3252; www.d-dom.kp.edus.si; Cankarjeva ul 5; dm 3500SIT; ☿ Jul-Aug) In July and August this brilliantly central student dorm becomes a hostel.

Vila Milka (☎ 040-835 155; Brkinska ul 6; per person €15) Multilingual Diorje Ivovanovic's eccentric homestay is a cult backpacker bolt hole on the eastern edge of the old town. The price and welcome are more attractive than the cramped rooms, clunky bathrooms and steep stairways. Don't expect much privacy.

Capris Time (☎ 631 1555; www.capristime-sp.si; s/d Sep-Jun from 4290/7150SIT, Jul & Aug from 5000/8580SIT; ☿ 8am-4pm Mon-Fri) This station-based agency arranges private rooms with discounts for three-day stays. Similarly priced rooms are offered by **Kompas** (☎ 627 1581; Pristaniška ul 17; ☿ 8am-7pm Mon-Fri, 8am-1pm Sat).

Motel Port (☎ 639 3260; Ankaranska 7; s/d/tr 5162/9124/13,686SIT) Hidden on the top floor of a Mondrianesque shopping centre, this brand new place has excellent en suite rooms. However, its position beside the truck terminal results in a deep traffic rumble and the mainly male, lorry-driver clientele may discourage single women. Air-con costs 1000SIT extra.

Hotel Vodišek (☎ 639 3668; Kolodvorska cesta 2; s/d early-Sep–mid-Jul €37.80/58.70, mid-Jul–early-Sep €45/75; P ☒) Halfway to the bus and train stations, this somewhat anonymous new hotel has clean, no-nonsense motel-style rooms.

Hotel Koper (☎ 610 0500; www.terme-catez.si; Pristaniška ul 3; s/d 13,100/23,800SIT, d with air-con 26,200SIT; ☒) This very smartly renovated business hotel is Koper's most central.

Eating & Drinking

Delfi (Pristaniška ul; snacks 190-400SIT; ⏰ 10am-10pm) Good-value *burek* and pizza slices that you can eat on a fairly pleasant terrace. There are other bars and eateries in adjoining units.

Istrska Klet (Župančičeva ul 39; mains 900-1200SIT; ⏰ 7am-9pm) Squeeze together with fellow diners at the two communal tables of this characterful old wine cellar–restaurant. Meals are authentic and accompanied by typical, inexpensive Teran wine from the cask.

Skipper (☎ 626 1810; Kopališko nab 3; mains 1290-3500SIT; ⏰ 9am-10pm) In the sunshine, the marina-view terrace of this otherwise rather characterless, upstairs restaurant is *the* place to eat fresh fish (7500SIT per kg).

Slaščičarna Krǒštola (ice-cream cones 160SIT; ⏰ 8am-9pm) Perched on Koper's pitifully small pebble beach, the Krǒštola is the best positioned of several alluring ice-cream parlour cafés.

Skica (big beers 330SIT; ⏰ 7.30am-midnight Mon-Sat, noon-11pm Sun) This rough-edged, thoroughly local bar has a little photo-gallery and a taste for blues music, and serves screwdrivers made with freshly squeezed oranges. Squint and you'll see Janis Joplin.

Getting There & Away

Buses run to Piran (590SIT, ½ hour) frequently on weekdays from 5am to 10.15pm, and every 40 minutes at weekends. Up to 10 buses daily run to Ljubljana (2460SIT, two to 2½ hours), though the train is more comfortable with IC services (1980SIT, 2¼ hours) at 5.55am and 2.55pm, and local services (1660SIT, 2½ hours) at 10.05am and 7.13pm. Boats to Piran leave from the Marina up to four times daily in summer.

Buses to Trieste (610SIT/€3, one hour, Monday to Saturday) run nine times daily, usually winding along the coast via Ankaran and Muggia. Destinations in Croatia include Rijeka (2000SIT, 10.10am Monday to Friday), Rovinj (3.55pm daily June to September), Pula (2700SIT, 2pm) via Poreč (1700SIT) plus up to three to Poreč only, notably at 7.30am Monday to Friday. There are summer ferries to Zadar, Croatia (see p202).

IZOLA

☎ 05 / pop 11,000

Overshadowed by much nicer Piran and swamped by vacationing local children, Izola is bypassed by most foreign visitors. However it does have a minor Venetian charm, a few narrow old alleys, and some nice waterfront bars and restaurants. The school of catering's seasonal hostel **Dijaški Dom Izola** (☎ 662 1740; Prekomorskih Brigad ul 7; dm from 3500SIT; ⏰ Jul & Aug) offers about the cheapest beds you'll find within striking distance of Piran. Out in Izola's industrial suburbs, **Ambasada Gavioli** (☎ 641 8212; www.ambasada-gavioli.com; Industrija cesta; ⏰ Sat & party nights from midnight) is Slovenia's top rave club, featuring a procession of international star DJs.

Regular Koper–Piran bendy-buses drive via Izola, and there's a catamaran service to Venice.

PIRAN

☎ 05 / pop 4400

Little Piran (Pirano in Italian) is as picturesque a port as you can imagine, especially when viewed at sunset from the saw-toothed 16th-century walls that guard its hilly western flank. In summer the town gets pretty overrun by tourists, but in April or October it's hard not to fall in love with the winding Venetian-Gothic alleyways and tempting fish restaurants. The name derives from *pyr* (Greek for fire), referring to the Punta lighthouse at the tip of the town's peninsula. Since misty antiquity, this lighthouse has helped ships reach the great salt-port at Koper.

Orientation

Buses from everywhere except Portorož arrive at the bus station, just 300m stroll along the harbourside Cankarjevo nab from central Tartinijev trg. Be warned that a car is an encumbrance not a help in Piran. Vehicles are stopped at a tollgate 200m south of the bus station where the sensible choice is to use the huge Fornače car park (180SIT per hour, 1800SIT per day). You could take a ticket and drive on in to the centre (first hour free, then 600SIT per hour) but old Piran is so small, parking is so limited and its alleyways so narrow (mostly footpaths) that you're likely to regret it.

Information

Banka Koper (Tartinijev trg; ⏰ 8.30am-noon & 3-5pm Mon-Fri, 8.30am-noon Sat) Money exchange and ATM.

Library (Tartinijev trg; membership 500SIT; ⏰ 10am-6pm Mon-Fri, 8am-1pm Sat) Housed in the attractive old courthouse building, the library has one rather slow Internet computer for members. Connection is better in Portorož (p813).

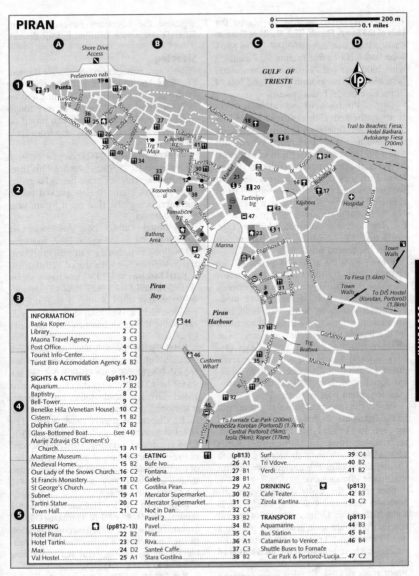

PIRAN

0 — 200 m
0 — 0.1 miles

INFORMATION	
Banka Koper	1 C2
Library	2 C2
Maona Travel Agency	3 C3
Post Office	4 C3
Tourist Info-Center	5 C2
Turist Biro Accomodation Agency	6 B2

SIGHTS & ACTIVITIES	(pp811-12)
Aquarium	7 B2
Baptistry	8 C2
Bell-Tower	9 C2
Beneške Hiša (Venetian House)	10 C2
Cistern	11 B2
Dolphin Gate	12 B2
Glass-Bottomed Boat	(see 44)
Marije Zdravja (St Clement's) Church	13 A1
Maritime Museum	14 C3
Medieval Homes	15 B2
Our Lady of the Snows Church	16 C2
St Francis Monastery	17 D2
St George's Church	18 C1
Subnet	19 A1
Tartini Statue	20 C2
Town Hall	21 C2

SLEEPING	(pp812-13)
Hotel Piran	22 B2
Hotel Tartini	23 C2
Max	24 D2
Val Hostel	25 A1

EATING	(p813)
Bufe Ivo	26 A1
Fontana	27 B1
Galeb	28 B1
Gostilna Piran	29 A2
Mercator Supermarket	30 B2
Mercator Supermarket	31 C3
Noč in Dan	32 C4
Pavel 2	33 B2
Pavel	34 B2
Pirat	35 C4
Riva	36 A1
Santeé Caffe	37 C3
Stara Gostilna	38 B2

Surf	39 C4
Tri Vdove	40 B2
Verdi	41 B2

DRINKING	(p813)
Cafe Teater	42 B3
Zizola Kantina	43 C2

TRANSPORT	(p813)
Aquamarine	44 B3
Bus Station	45 B4
Catamaran to Venice	46 B4
Shuttle Buses to Fornače Car Park & Portorož-Lucija	47 C2

SLOVENIA

Tourist Information Center (☎ 673 0220; www.piran .si; Town Hall, Tartinijev trg; ⏰ 10am-5pm Tue-Fri, 10am-2pm Sat & Sun Oct-May, 9am-1.30pm & 3-9pm daily Jun-Sep) Has maps, accommodation listings and excursion ideas.

Sights & Activities
Piran is dominated by **St George's Church** (Adamičeva ul 2; ⏰ temporarily closed for renovation)

whose soaring 1609 **bell tower** was clearly modelled on the San Marco Campanile in Venice. The 1650 octagonal **baptistry** (*krstilnica*) has imaginatively recycled a 2nd-century Roman sarcophagus for use as its font. **St Francis Monastery** (ul Bolniška 20), just west of Tartinijev trg, has a delightful cloister and while you're passing, notice the superb

15th-century arch painting in nearby **Our Lady of the Snows Church**. The **Maritime Museum** (Cankarjevo nab 3; adult/student 600/500SIT; 9am-noon & 3-6pm Tue-Sun) is in a fine marina-side mansion with 2000-year-old Roman amphorae (jars) beneath the glass ground floor, and lots of impressive model boats upstairs.

One of Piran's most eye-catching structures is the red 15th-century **Beneške Hiša** (Venetian House; Tartinijev trg 4), with its tracery windows and stone lion relief. When built this would have surveyed Piran's inner port; however, the inner port was filled in 1894 to form Tartinijev trg. The square was named for violinist and composer Giuseppe Tartini (1692–1770) who was born at what's now No 7. His **statue** stands in the square's middle. The square is dominated by the large, porticoed 19th-century **Town Hall** which houses the tourist office.

Piran's greatest appeal is probably the chance to wander idly through the narrow alleys as they burrow and weave between antique houses. Behind the market, **medieval homes** (Obzidna trg) have been built into an ancient defensive wall that's punctured by the **Dolphin Gate** (Dolfinova Vrata). The anachronistically named Trg 1 Maja (1st May Sq) may sound like a socialist parade ground but in fact it's one of Piran's cutest squares, with a 19th-century, statue-guarded **cistern** pool in the middle.

Punta, the historical 'nose' of Piran, still has a **lighthouse**, but today's is small and modern. Just behind it, however, the round, serrated-top tower of 18th-century **Marije Zdravja Church** (alternatively referred to as St Clement's) evokes the ancient *pyr* beacon that made Piran's name.

Back near the centre, there's a mini-**Aquarium** (Kidričevo nab 4; 500SIT; closed 16 Oct–24 Mar) which shows living examples of several species that might soon grace your plate in a nearby restaurant. Try to spot them in a more natural environment from the **glass-bottomed boat** (641 8301; www.slo-istra.com/aquamarine; 2500SIT, 45 min, 2 to 4 times daily) that swings around the peninsula to Strunjan and back, but don't expect Red Sea–style corals. In fact the most unusual underwater sight hereabouts is the wreck of a WWII seaplane in Portorož bay. To see that you'll need to go scuba diving. **Subnet** (041-590 746; www.sub-net.si; Prešernovo nab 24), a well-equipped dive shop offering PADI open-water courses from 35,000SIT, can organise the necessary boat dives from 7000SIT per person (minimum four divers).

Sleeping

Piran's accommodation options are limited. For loads more choice but less style, try Portorož, 2km to 7km away. Finding a room in both Piran and Portorož is very tough indeed in midsummer, when you might do better to visit Piran as a day trip from Izola or Koper.

Autokamp Fiesa (674 6230; camp sites per person low/high season 1577/1877SIT; Apr-Oct) This insecure handkerchief of grass behind a grotty caravan park is nonetheless packed full in summer, being just 1km from Piran, near Hotel Barbara.

Val Hostel (673 2555; yhostel.val@siol.net; Gregorčičeva ul 38A; dm IYHA member €18-20, nonmember €23-24) Book well ahead for this superbly central hostel-*penzion* with shared bathrooms.

Hotel Barbara (617 9000; hotel.barbarafiesa@rlv .si; s 8500-11,100SIT, d 13,000-18,200SIT;) This good-value holiday hotel is one of two at Fiesa pebble-beach, a 1km-long shore-front walk east along the north coast from St George's Church.

Hotel Tartini (671 1666; www.hotel-tartini -piran.com; Tartinijev trg 15; s/tw/d Oct-Mar except New Year €37-49/62/82, mid-season €45-63/76/104, high season €57-78/94/130) Right on the central square, Hotel Tartini's façade looks misleadingly traditional, yet the interior attempts a dramatic display of trendy modernism. The effect is impressive and the prize €230 to €346 apartment amazing. However, several of the ordinary rooms already have touches of peeling paint and some 'balconies' are so minuscule they barely exist. Add up to €12 for rooms with views.

Hotel Piran (676 2100; www.hoteli-piran.si; Stjenkova ul 1; s €47-69, d €57-88, air-con extra €10;) Smart, business-standard accommodation in the town centre's ugliest building. Double rooms with wonderful sea views cost €16 to €20 extra.

Max (041-692 928; ul IX Korpusa 26; www.max hotel-piran.com; s/d without breakfast €55/60) Piran's most romantic accommodation has only six rooms, each named rather than numbered. Upper floors look out towards the church tower.

Private rooms are available through **Maona travel agency** (673 4519; www.maona.si; Cankarjevo nab 7; 9am-7pm Mon-Sat, 10am-2pm some Sun) for prices upwards of €26. Prices go up in the high season, and come down for stays of three or more nights. **Turist Biro** (☎ 673 2509; www.turistbiro-ag.si; Tomažičev trg) lists similarly priced rooms but asks a €14 reservation fee.

Eating & Drinking

One of Piran's attractions is its plethora of fish restaurants, though don't expect any bargains. Virtually all charge around 1300SIT to 1500SIT for a plate of grilled squid, from 8000SIT per kg for fish and 400SIT to 500SIT for potatoes. Almost all open from 11am to 10pm or later in summer.

Riva (Prešernovo nab; pizza 1100-1500SIT) Menus often include other Western dishes as at Riva, where the richly gooey seafood pizza is deliciously laced with garlic.

Galeb (Pusterla ul 5; ⏰ 11am-3pm & 6-11.30pm Wed-Mon) Some visitors prefer Galeb's 'family atmosphere', but the lack of décor doesn't make it any cheaper.

Santeé Caffe (Cankarjevo nab; ⏰ 7am-midnight; sandwiches 300-500SIT) This café has sandwiches, salads and walls painted in colours as vivid as its excellent ice creams.

Pavel 2 (Prešernovo nab) is marginally the suavest of the main sea-facing row of restaurants that includes the essentially similar Gostilna Piran, Bife Ivo, Pavel and Tri Vdove.

Inland you might prefer the characterful atmosphere of **Stara Gostilna** (Savurdrijska ul 2), the cistern-facing setting of **Fontana** (Trg 1 Maja), or smart little **Verdi** (Verdijeva ul), which on summer days spills out onto the nearby square of Savudrijska ul.

Multimenu dining is marginally cheaper at **Pirat** (Cankarjevo nab) and **Surf** (Grudnova ul) towards the bus station. The latter has outdoor tables shaded by a rare little patch of greenery, and medium pizzas from 800SIT. The **Hotel Piran** (Stjenkova ul 1) restaurant does 1000SIT lunch deals. Hop on the No 1 shuttle bus to Portorož–Lucija for Mexican or Chinese food.

Piran has two **Mercator supermarkets**, but minimart **Noč in Dan** (Cankarjevo nab; ⏰ 6am-midnight) opens longer.

Behind the Aquarium, atmospheric but expensive **Cafe Teater** (Kidričevo nab) is Piran's top pub and has a lively terrace. **Zizola Kantina** (Tartinijev trg; ⏰ 9am-midnight) is an appealing nautically themed bar, with tables right on the main square.

Getting There & Away

From the bus station buses run every 20 to 40 minutes to Koper (590SIT) via Izola, five per day head to Trieste (1200SIT, 1¾ hours, Monday to Saturday) and up to eight to Ljubljana (2670SIT, 2½ to three hours) via Divača and Postojna.

From Tartinijev trg, minibuses shuttle to Portorož-Lucija (No 1, 220SIT) and Portorož via Strunjan (No 3). There's also a free shuttle to the car park, but it's generally more comfortable and often quicker to walk. **Aquamarine** (☎ 641 8301) run summer ferries to Koper (one way/return 1400/1900SIT) up to four times daily via Izola. Piran and Izola despatch catamarans to Venice at least once a week.

PORTOROŽ

☎ 05 / pop 13,000

In a long arc of woodland-backed bay, Slovenia's big hotel-resort town of Portorož (Portorose) is not unpleasant, but it's not much of an attraction either. The only beaches are pay-to-enter handkerchiefs of imported sand; if you want seaside fun you'd be better off continuing on to Croatia. Nonetheless, its vast assortment of accommodation makes Portorož a useful fall back if everything's full in nearby Piran. Greater Portorož stretches in a 5km-long arc, technically consisting of four subdistricts. From west (Piran side) to east these are Bernardin, Korotan, Portorož Centre and Lucija, though there's no noticeable boundaries between these districts. All are linked by the 5km-long curve of Obala, the main avenue and nearest road to the shore.

Full accommodation listings are available at the **tourist information office** (☎ 674 0231; www.portoroz.si; Obala 16; ⏰ 10am-5pm Sep-Jun, 9am-1.30pm & 3-9.30pm Jul-Aug) or from Piran TIC (p810). Handily close to Piran, the unusually upmarket, summer-only hostel **Prenočišča Korotan** (☎ 674 5400; www.prenocisca -korotan.vsk-sdp.si; Obala 11, Korotan; ⏰ Jul & Aug; 🖳) has en suite rooms and its Internet computers are open to nonguests year-round. The cheaper, more basic **DIŠ Hostel** (Dijaški in Študentski Dom Portorož; ☎ 674 6340; Sočna Pot 20; dm from 3500SIT; ⏰ Jul & Aug) is also in Korotan: walk 400m up the hill from the satanic-looking old salt warehouses at Obala 10, or from Piran follow Rozmanova ul and descend from Belokriška cesta.

There are dozens of decent pizzerias all along Obala. In Lucija is the very atmospheric Mexican taverna **Papa Chico** (☎ 677 9310; Obala 26; mains 950-2100SIT, lunch menu 1350SIT; ⏰ 11am-midnight). Behind in the same block is the elegant Chinese restaurant **Kitajski Zid** (☎ 677 5084; Obala 26; mains incl rice 1250-2500SIT; ⏰ noon-11pm).

Every 20 minutes shuttle bus No 1 from Piran trundles right along Obala to Lucija, passing the Prenočišča Korotan. From Bernardin and Korotan you could even walk into Piran in around 45 minutes, though the roads are unpleasantly busy.

SEČOVLJE
☎ 05 / pop 200

About 7km southeast of Portorož, in no-man's-land between the Slovenian and Croatian borders, is the fascinating **Sečovlje Salt-making Museum** (☎ 671 0040; adult/student 600/500SIT; ⏰ 9am-6pm Apr-May & Sep-Oct, 9am-8pm Jun-Aug). In one restored house there's an interesting little exhibition of salt-makers' equipment and lifestyles. Poignantly, many of the antique-looking photos were taken a mere 45 years ago.

However 'museum' is a misleading term, as the main attraction is the eerily desolate landscape sparsely dotted with abandoned old salt-diggers' homes amid a paddy-like patchwork of saltpans. Salt production here, at Koper and at Strunjan (between Piran and Izola) was once the region's economic *raison d'être*. What may look like simple square evaporation ponds are in fact the fruit of exceedingly complex engineering. Working entirely on wind and tidal power, these were the ultimate examples of ecoenergy efficiency. Don't stand in the mud or you'll destroy a painstakingly cultivated 'skin' of protective algae which keeps the salt white. The dedicated staff laboriously maintain the delicate pools and still produce salt, which you can buy in souvenir burlap minisacks.

If you don't have your own vehicle or bicycle, the only practical way to visit Sečovlje is a 9.30am boat ride from Piran (2600SIT return including admission). The main problem with this is that you're locked into a whole-day excursion, since boats don't usually return to pick you up until 4pm. Realistically an hour or so would be ample to get the idea.

EASTERN SLOVENIA

The rolling vineyard hills of eastern Slovenia are attractive but much less dramatic than the Julian Alps. If you're taking a bus from Ljubljana to Zagreb (Croatia), look left immediately after leaving Novo Mesto bus station (you'll stop briefly at the station) for picturesque views of Novo Mesto's old-town core rising directly across the Krka River. Travelling by car it would be nicer to drive via charming Kamnik then cross-country via chocolate-box villages like Motnik, big but pleasant Celje and the tiny but elegant spavillage Rogaška Slatina (p815).

If you're heading by train to Vienna via Graz (Austria) it saves money to stop in lively Maribor (p815); international tickets are very expensive per km, so doing as much travelling as possible on domestic trains saves cash. While there, consider visiting postcard-perfect Ptuj (p817).

KAMNIK
☎ 02 / pop 11,500

Magnificent views from the central ruins of Kamnik's **old castle** *(stari grad)* make for awesome photos, thanks to the perfect conjugation of red-tiled roofs, church towers and a dramatically close horizon of jostling snow-streaked peaks. Otherwise the town's charm is focused around its mostly pedestrianised main street, the very attractive Šutna ul/Glavny trg, along which are several appealing **galleries** and cafés. As this is all just two minutes' walk west of the bus station, Kamnik makes an easy half-day excursion from Ljubljana, 23km south.

Buses from Ljubljana (550SIT, 45 minutes) run almost every 30 minutes on weekdays. If you take the hourly train (430SIT, 45 minutes, hourly to 8.15pm), hop off at derelict-looking Kamnik Mesto, one stop after the main Kamnik station. The old castle is barely 100m east.

CELJE
☎ 03 / pop 40,000

While probably not worth a special detour, Celje has a long history, Roman remains and many elements of charm. A quick stopover is easy: all Ljubljana–Maribor trains stop here. Walk west out of the train station along grand, pedestrianised Krekov trg, which becomes Prešernova ul at the halfway bend. After 700m you'll reach the imposing **Narodni Dom**, in the side of which is the **tourist information office** (Prešernova ul; ☿ 8am-4pm Mon-Fri), handy for maps and inspiration. A short dog-leg south and east from here is an arcaded palace containing the interesting **Pokrajinski Museum** (www2.arnes.si/~pokmuzce/index1.htm, in Slovene; Muzejski trg; admission 800SIT; ☿ 10am-6pm Tue-Sun). Far and away its greatest attraction is a truly magnificent 17th-century trompe l'oeil ceiling, the Celjski strop (Celje Ceiling), 'discovered' in 1926.

West of the museum, attractive, time-warp Glavni trg has some pleasant terrace cafés and a **plague pillar**. Swerve round **St Daniel's Church** (Slomškov trg) and south down Savinjska ul to a fine riverside **viewpoint** (Savinjsko nab). You'll spot **St Cecilia's Church** (Maistrova ul) directly across the water, up a curious covered stairway. Harder to make out to its west is a reconstructed 2nd-century **Temple of Hercules**. Very obvious on a hill top high above to the southeast is the impressive if awkward-to-reach **Celje Castle**. From the viewpoint, walk five minutes northeast to return to the train station, passing medieval water- and defence-towers that incorporate recycled Roman stone blocks.

Trains to Ljubljana (1210SIT, 1½ hours) depart up to 28 times daily.

ROGAŠKA SLATINA

Slovenia's oldest health retreat defies easy description. It's simultaneously grand yet rural, stylish yet ugly, bustling yet tranquil. For locals, the overwhelming attraction is magnesium-rich Donat-Mg spring water which is sold expensively in bottles throughout Slovenia, but can be drunk direct from the spring here. Well almost. Don't imagine a limpid forest pool – someone's built a multistorey 1970s glass monstrosity on top of the **spring** (admission 300SIT). However, this eyesore is in a beautifully manicured park and in front of it, facing the lawns of Zdravilški trg, the Grand Hotel looks something like a golden-yellow Buckingham Palace and has a vast chandeliered ballroom to match. At the other (southern) end of Zdravilški trg is the **tourist office** (tic.rogaska@siol.net; ☿ 9am-4pm Mon-Fri, 9am-noon Sat), bus station, and the Escheresque **Hotel Slovenija**, with columns supporting nothing in particular. There are plenty more hotels (see www.terme-rogaska.si), all aimed

at cure seekers who spend a week or so mooching about in dressing gowns, sipping the miracle waters – hot, cold, fizzy or flat – from curious tall, narrow glasses.

Of course, the pure air and simple living are probably as healthy as the sip-sipping. This then casts the brilliant 1904 Art-Nouveau tavern **Tempel** (☿ 8am-1am Mon-Thu, 8am-3am Fri & Sat) in the devil's role of temptress. Water or beer? Choose both – a half litre of Donat-Mg supposedly prevents even the most well-earned hangover after a night on the tiles. You'll find Tempel in a park just off Kidrčeva ul (the main Celje road), where it bypasses the southern end of Zdravilška trg by a hundred metres or so.

Rogaška Slatina's also famous for colourful glassware, notably displayed in the Hotel Donat, on the way to its in-house casino.

The tourist office may be able to arrange private accommodation; the cheapest hotel is the **Slovenija** (☎ 811 5000; hotel.slovenija@siol.net; d from €74). Standard rooms are somewhat dingy, much better renovated ones cost €84 and a three-day cure starts at 22,500SIT.

The only convenient public transport access is from Celje; buses (600SIT, 40 minutes) run up to twice hourly on weekdays. Rogatec-bound trains (410SIT, 50 minutes, five daily) stop 300m south of Rogaška Slatina bus station.

MARIBOR

☎ 02 / pop 116,000

Slovenia's light-industrial second city has no unmissable 'sights', but oozes with charm thanks to its delightful, patchily grand old town. Pedestrianised central streets buzz with cafés and student life and in late June and early July the old, riverside 'Lent' district hosts a major arts festival. From the train station and nearby bus station, follow Partizanska cesta as it curls some 700m westwards to reach Grajski trg, where the nicest area of town begins with a somewhat dishevelled castle museum and Orel Hotel.

Information

You'll find ATMs all over town and in the bus and train stations.

KIT/Kibla (☎ 252 4440; Glavny trg 14; per 30min 150SIT; ☿ 9am-10pm Mon-Fri, 9am-2pm Sat) Central, fast and modern Internet access.

Kreditna Banka Maribor (46 Partizanska cesta; ☿ 8am-1pm & 2-5pm Mon-Fri) Changes travellers cheques.

Post office (Slomškov Trg; ☼ 8am-7pm Mon-Fri, 8am-1pm Sat) This architectural masterpiece is painted goose-dropping green and draped with statues. Like other branches at Partizanska cesta 54 and Partizanska cesta 1, it changes money.

Tourist Information Centre (TIC; ☎ 234 6611; www .maribor.si; Partinzanska cesta 47; ☼ 9am-6pm Mon-Fri, 9am-1pm Sat) Helpful, especially for motorists seeking *vinska cestas* (wine routes). The office is handily opposite the train station.

Sights

Two café-packed blocks southwest of Grajski trg, the **cathedral** (Slomškov trg) sits in an oasis of fountain-cooled calm. Follow little Poštna ul south from here into photogenic but traffic-divided **Glavny trg**. A block further south down alleys Mesarski or Splavarski Prehod is the Drava River's north bank. Here you'll find **Stara Trta** (Vojašniška 8), the world's oldest living grapevine, which has been trained along an old riverfront house. It has been a source of famous Maribor wine for over 400 years.

The pleasantly semirural Pod-Pohorje district is 6km south of the city centre. Much of Maribor's accommodation clusters here, near the foot of a **cable car** (www. pohorje.org) that whisks summer hikers and winter skiers alike up the lushly forested dumpling called **Pohorje**.

Sleeping

Dijaški Dom 26 Junij (☎ 480 1710; Zeleznikova ul 12; bus No 3; dm 2700SIT; ☼ Jul & Aug) This typical student dormitory/summer hostel is 2km west of the town centre.

Uni Hotel (☎ 250 6700; uni.hotel@termemb.si; Gosposka ul; beds 4360SIT) This fantastically central new hostel is only open to IYHA members and membership cards are not sold here. Check-in and reservations (highly advisable) are via the much better-known **Orel Hotel** (☎ 250 6700; www.termemb.si; Glavni trg; s/d Sep-Jun €63/89, Jul & Aug €74/104) in the block behind (east).

Gostilna Pohorka (☎ 614 0110; ul Begara 2; bus No 6; s/d 5000/7000SIT) Among some dozen guesthouses in Pod-Pohorje, the best deal is the Podhorka. Here are four unpretentious but fully equipped rooms above an appealingly peaceful terraced restaurant. It's right at the forest's edge, 900m west of the cable car via Villa Merano, but a shorter walk by the woodland footpath.

Gostišče Janez (☎ 420 4404; Pri Janezu; Ciril Metodova ul 4; bus No 4; s/d 7200/10,200SIT) Rooms are fair value in this inn above a Bavarian-look local pub, but the location on a rather bleak highway intersection 2km southwest of the centre leaves much to be desired.

Hotel Tabor (☎ 421 6410; ul Heroja Zidanška 18; bus No 6; s/d 7900/12,500SIT; Ⓟ) About 20 minutes walk southwest of Glavny trg (via Gorkega ul), this is the most central of several no-frills motel-style places dotted about the suburbs. All of these have parking, and similar price ranges, and most tend to put functional cleanliness over charm; ask at the TIC for details.

Eating

Gostilna Pri Stari Trti (☎ 250 0035; Splavarski Prehod 5; meals 960SIT; ☼ 10am-7pm Mon-Fri) Incredible value four-item meals are available in this appealingly beamed pub-restaurant, entered through a giant barrel just behind the world's oldest grapevine.

Takos (☎ 252 7150; Mesarski Prehod; mains 1200-2100SIT, cocktails 600SIT; ☼ 11am-late Mon-Sat, 11am-5pm Sun) This atmospheric Mexican restaurant becomes Maribor's top night-spot after the 11pm happy hour on Fridays and Saturdays.

Studio Caffe (Poštna ul; coffee 200SIT; ☼ 8am-10pm Mon-Sat, noon-10pm Sun) This is just one of many fine terraced cafés found in the alleys north of Glavny trg, with many more between here and the Orel Hotel.

There's a **Mercator supermarket** (☼ 7am-8pm Mon-Fri, 7am-6pm Sat, 8am-11am Sun) at the bus station, and cheap *burek* stands outside the train station.

Getting There & Away

Buses run to Ljubljana (2580SIT to 2760SIT depending on routing, up to 10 daily), Ptuj (790SIT, two per hour Monday to Friday, 11 on Saturday, five on Sunday), Rogaška Slatina (6.18am, 7.18am and 12.43pm Monday to Friday) and to various German cities including Munich (€37). The 7.30am bus to Graz (Austria) costs 1700SIT.

Up to 18 direct trains daily link Maribor to Ljubljana (1660SIT, 2¾ hours normal, 1980SIT, 2¼ hours IC, or 2790SIT, 1¾ hours ICS express). International destinations include Zagreb (3331SIT, 2¾ hours, two daily), and Vienna (8636SIT, four hours, two daily) via Graz (2665SIT, 1¼ hours).

Getting Around

Maribor's bus system is extensive. Single rides cost 240SIT if you pay on board. Purchased ahead, a return ticket costs 330SIT. Most useful routes start at the train station, including the No 6 to Pod-Pohorje, which terminates at the cable car.

PTUJ

☎ 02 / pop 19,100

Rising gently above a wide, almost flat valley, the compact old town of Ptuj (Roman Poetovio) forms a symphony of red-tile roofs viewed most photogenically from across the Drava River. It culminates in a well-proportioned castle containing the fine **Regional Museum** (www.pok-muzej-ptuj.si/english/ptgrad.htm; adult/child 600/300SIT; ⏰ 9am-5pm, later in summer). For 10 days around Mardi Gras (usually in February) international crowds arrive to spot the shaggy Kurent straw men at Slovenia's foremost carnival. The **tourist office** (☎ 779 6011; www.ptuj-tourism.si; Slovenski trg 3; ⏰ 8am-5pm Mon-Fri, 8am-noon Sat) faces a **medieval tower** in the old centre. To reach it walk south from the bus and train stations, turn west passing the Hotel Poetovio (which stocks free maps), the classic **Haloze Wine Cellars** (☎ 787 9810; tour-tastings 1500-1800SIT; ⏰ by appointment) and the street cafés of Lacova ul, Mestni trg and Morkova ul.

West of the centre along grand Prešernov ul, the 18th-century **Mala Grad** (Small Castle; Prešernova ul 33-35) now houses a library with Internet connection.

Sleeping & Eating

Terme Ptuj (☎ 782 7211; www.terme-ptuj.si; camp sites Jun-Aug/off-peak 2620/2420SIT; ⏰ 20 Apr-10 Oct, check-in 5-8pm) This small, starkly unshaded camping ground is attached to a spa/swimming pool complex on the Drava's south bank, 1.4km from the old town via a footbridge.

Krapša Guesthouse (☎ 787 7570; rozalija_k@hotmail.com; Maistrova ul 19; s/d/tr 4000/8000/12,000SIT) All but two rooms of this utterly delightful homestay are bright, brand new and en suite. It's set quietly between cherry trees at the dead-end of a 900m (as yet) unpaved track that starts west of castle hill. There are no single or short-stay supplements and the friendly hosts are as effervescent as their home-made wines.

Hotel Poetovio (☎ 779 8201; memorija@volja.net; Vinarska trg 5; s/d/apt 6680/9360/11,540SIT) This hotel's slightly worn peach-walled rooms off gloomy corridors are comfortable for the price if somewhat noisy. A small casino is attached.

Garni Hotel Mitra (☎ 787 7455; www.hotelptuj .com; Prešernova ul 6; s/d/apt 9000/13,500/17,000SIT) This superbly central hotel has a colourful antique façade, but rooms have somewhat less panache than the artistic stairways would suggest.

Ribič (☎ 771 4671; Dravska ul 9; set meals 2200-3600SIT; ⏰ 10am-11pm) This old house with a great riverside terrace is the ideal spot to splurge on a fish dinner. The cheapest option is trout with courgettes at 1590SIT.

There's an **open-air market** (Novi trg; ⏰ 7am-3pm) for self-caterers.

Getting There & Away

Buses to Maribor (790SIT, 40 minutes) run at least hourly on weekdays but are very infrequent on Sundays. There are only five buses per week to Rogaška Slatina but if you're driving there's a delightful country road via Breg and Rogatec. The latter has a sweet little open-air museum of rural architecture. Two daily trains from Ljubljana (2½ hours) stop en route to Budapest (six hours) departing Ptuj at 9.44am, or 4.16pm (IC).

SLOVENIA DIRECTORY

ACCOMMODATION

Accommodation listings in this guide have been ordered by pricing from cheapest to most expensive (ie budget to top end).

Slovenia's small but growing handful of youth hostels includes Ljubljana's unbelievably trendy Celicia. However, many other hostels are moonlighting college dormitories which only accept travellers in July and August. Thank goodness they do open then: in midsummer almost all other accommodation substantially raises prices and it can be hard to find a room at any price. Unless stated hostel rooms share bathrooms. A hostel bed typically costs from €12 to €20.

Guesthouses (penzion, gostišče, or prenočišča) are often cosy and better value than full-blown hotels, some of which are ugly if well-renovated Communist-era Frankensteins. Nonetheless it can be difficult to find a double room for under €50. Beware that locally listed rates are usually quoted per person assuming double occupancy. The 150SIT to 200SIT per person tourist tax and a hefty single-occupancy supplement often lurk in the footnotes. This book quotes the total you'll pay. Unless otherwise indicated, room rates include en suite toilet, shower with towels and soap, and a ham and cheese breakfast.

Tourist information offices can help you access extensive networks of private rooms, apartments and tourist farms or can recommend private agencies who will. Such accommodation can appear misleadingly cheap if you carelessly overlook the 30% to 50% surcharge levied on one- or two-night stays (this book incorporates them). Also beware that many such properties are in outlying villages with minimal public transport, and that the cheapest one-star category rooms with shared bathroom are actually very rare, so you'll often pay well above the quoted minimum. Depending on the season you might save a little money by going directly to any house with a sign reading *sobe* (rooms).

Camping grounds generally charge per person, whether you're camping or caravanning. Rates usually include hot showers. Almost all sites close November to April. Camping 'rough' is illegal, and this is enforced, especially around Bled.

ACTIVITIES

Slovenia is a very well-organised outdoor-activities paradise.

Extreme sports

Several areas specialise in adrenaline-rush activities, the greatest range being available at Bovec (see p805), famous for white-water rafting, hydro-speed, kayaking, and especially for canyoning – ie slithering down gullies and waterfalls in a neoprene wetsuit with the very important aid of a well-trained guide. Bovec is also a great place for paragliding; in winter you ascend Mt Kanin via ski lifts and then jump off. Gliding costs are remarkably reasonable from Lesce near Bled (p802). Scuba diving from Piran (p810) is also good value.

Hiking

Hiking is extremely popular, with much of the capital's population heading for Triglav National Park at weekends. There are around 7000km of marked paths, and in summer 165 mountain huts offer comfortable trailside refuge (see box p804). Several shorter treks are helpfully outlined in the Sunflower Guide *Slovenia* (www.sunflowerbooks.co.uk), which has excellent map-text correlation.

Skiing

Skiing is a Slovenian passion, with slopes particularly crowded at New Year and early in February. Maribor's **Pohorje** (www.pohorje .org) is a popular choice (p816). Although relatively low (1347m) it's easily accessible, with very varied downhill pistes and relatively short lift queues. Enjoyable Pohorje **torch parties** (☎ 041-775 175; mopa@siol.net; 3700SIT plus ski lift) are organised, where party goers ascend the slope at night with a glass of bubbly, ski with flaming torches to a barbecue, and hope that the shots of blueberry hooch don't stop them from skiing back again.

Kranjska Gora (1600m; p804) has some challenging runs, and the world record for ski-jumping was set at nearby Planica. Above Lake Bohinj (p803), Vogel (up to 1840m) is particularly scenic, as is Kanin (2300m), above Bovec (p805); Kanin has snow as late as May. Cerkno (1291m, www.cerkno.si, in Slovene) is popular with snowboarders. Being relatively close to Ljubljana, Krvavec (1970m), northeast of Kranj, can have particularly long lift queues. See www.sloveniatourism.si /skiing for much more information.

Other

The Soča River near Kobarid and the Sava in Bohinj are great for **fly-fishing** (season Apr-Oct). **Licences** (per day €45, catch-&-release €30) are sold at TICs and hotels. Bohinj lake-fishing licences are cheaper (€22, March to September).

Mountain bikes are available for rent at Bovec, Bled and Bohinj travel agencies. However the rental 'season' is usually limited to May through to October.

In late October there's a Ljubljana marathon (http://maraton.slo-timing.com/).

Spa cures (www.terme-giz.si) are very popular. Most towns have a spa complex and hotels often offer free or bargain-rate entry to their guests. The most celebrated spa resort is Rogaška Slatina (p815).

BUSINESS HOURS

Virtually all businesses post their opening times (*delovni čas*) on the door. Many shops close Saturday afternoons. Sundays are still 'holy'; although a handful of grocery stores open, including some branches of the ubiquitous Mercator chain, on Sunday most shopping areas are as lively as Chernobyl. Museums often close on Monday. Banks often take lengthy lunch breaks and some open Saturday mornings.

Restaurants typically open until at least 10pm, bars until midnight, though they may have longer hours at the weekend and shorter on Sunday.

The closer winter approaches the earlier many attractions close and the fewer visits they allow. This leads to intricately complex tables of opening times that are beyond the scope of this book to reproduce in detail. Fortunately, most attractions have websites and leaflets displaying complete schedules in their full glory.

EMBASSIES & CONSULATES
Slovenian Embassies & Consulates
Slovenian representations abroad are fully listed on www.gov.si/mzz/eng and include:

Australia (☎ 02-2624 34830; vca@mzz-dkp.gov.si; lv 6, St George's Bldg, 60 Marcus Clarke St, Canberra ACT 2601)

Austria (☎ 01-586 13 09; Nibelungengasse 13, Vienna; 🕘 9am-11am Mon-Fri)

Belgium (☎ 02-646 90 99; Ave Louise 179, Brussels)

Bosnia and Hercegovina (☎ 033-271 250; Bentbasa 7, Sarajevo)

Canada (☎ 613-565 5781; 150 Metcalfe St, Suite 2101, Ottawa)

Croatia (☎ 01-63 11 000; Savska cesta 41, Zagreb; 🕘 9am-noon Mon-Fri)

Czech Republic (☎ 02-33 08 12 11; Pod Hradbami 15, Prague; 🕘 9am-noon Mon, Wed, Fri)

France (☎ 01 44 96 50 71; 28 rue Bois-le-Vent, Paris)

Germany (☎ 030-206 1450; Hausvogteiplatz 3-4, Berlin)

Hungary (☎ 01-438 5600; Cseppkő ut 68, Budapest; 🕘 9am-noon Mon-Fri)

Ireland (☎ 01-670 5240; Morrison Chambers, 32 Nassau St, Dublin)

Netherlands (☎ 070-310 86 90; Anna Paulownastraat 11, Den Haag)

New Zealand (☎ 04-567 0027; PO Box 30247, Eastern Hutt Rd, Pormare, Lower Hutt, Wellington)

UK (☎ 020-7222 5400; 10 Little College St, London SW1; 🕘 9am-2pm Mon-Fri)

US (☎ 202-667 5363; 1525 New Hampshire Ave NW, Washington DC)

Embassies & Consulates in Slovenia
Among the embassies and consulates in Ljubljana (☎ 01) are:

Australia (☎ 425 4252; Trg Republike 3/XII)
Belgium (☎ 200 6010; Trg Republike 3/XII)
Bosnia and Hercegovina (☎ 432 4042; Kolarjeva 26)
Canada (☎ 430 3570; Miklošičeva cesta 19)
Croatia (☎ 425 6220; Gruberjevo nab 6)
France (☎ 479 0400; Barjanska 1)
Germany (☎ 479 0300; Prešernova cesta 27)
Hungary (☎ 512 1882; ul Konrada Babnika 5)
Ireland (☎ 300 8970; Poljanski nasip 6)
Netherlands (☎ 420 1461; Poljanski nasip 6)
New Zealand (☎ 580 3055; ul Verovškova 57)
Romania (☎ 505 8294; Podlimbarskega 43)
South Africa (☎ 200 6300; Pražakova ul 4)
UK (☎ 200 3910; Trg Republike XII)
USA (☎ 200 5500; Prešernova cesta 31)

FESTIVALS & EVENTS
Shaggy Kurent straw men make Ptuj carnival the place to be at Mardi Gras, though the Julian Alpine villages have several lesser-known equivalents. On 30 April villages hold bonfires and 'tree-raising' nights. Maribor's 'Lent' street-theatre festival is not pre-Easter but the last week of June; check with the **Maribor TIC** (☎ 234 6611; www.maribor.si; Partinzanska cesta 47; 🕘 9am-6pm Mon-Fri, 9am-1pm Sat) for details. Throughout the summer there are dozens of musical and cultural events, notably in Ljubljana, Piran and Koper. For lots more information consult www.slovenia-tourism.si.

GAY & LESBIAN TRAVELLERS
The typical Slovene personality, rather like the Dutch, is quietly conservative but deeply self-confident, remarkably broad-minded and particularly tolerant. **Roza Klub** (☎ 01-430 4740; Kersnikova ul 4, Ljubljana) is composed from gay and lesbian branches of the ŠKUC (Student Cultural Centre).

The **GALfon** (☎ 01-432 4089; 🕘 7-10pm) is a hotline and source of general information for gays and lesbians. The websites of **Slovenian Queer Resources Directory** (www.ljudmila.org/siqrd) and **Out In Slovenia** (www.outinslovenija.com) are both extensive and partially in English.

HOLIDAYS
New Year (1 & 2 Jan) For a week hotel prices go mad especially in ski resorts.
Prešren Day of Culture (8 Feb)
Mardi Gras (usually Feb) Not a national holiday but a big event, especially in Ptuj.
Easter Monday (Mar/Apr)
Insurrection Day (27 Apr) Commemorates the insurrection against WWII Nazi occupation.

Labour Days (1 & 2 May) Villagers light bonfires on the night of 30 April, and indulge in 'tree raising', a local semi-sport where competitors take a tree trunk and have to raise it vertically.

National Day (25 Jun)

Assumption (15 Aug) Around this date virtually all accommodation will be booked solid.

Reformation Day (31 Oct)

All Saints' Day (1 Nov)

Christmas (25 Dec)

Independence Day (26 Dec)

INTERNET ACCESS

There is Internet access in most towns but so-called cyber-cafés rarely have more than one or two terminals. In some places you may have to resort to the local library, school or university. Note: Slovene keyboards are neither qwerty nor azerty but qwertz, reversing the y and z keys, but otherwise following the Anglophone norm.

INTERNET RESOURCES

Website www.slovenia-tourism.si is tremendously useful. Most Slovenian towns have very good websites often accessed by typing www.townname.si or www.townname-tourism.si. Specially good are www.ljubljana-tourism.si and www.maribor-tourism.si. For a particularly interesting series of Slovenian links try www.prah.net/slovenia, www.niagara.com/~jezovnik, or www.matkurja.com/eng.

LANGUAGE

Closely related to Croatian and Serbian, Slovene *(Slovensko)* sounds like Russian soaked in wine and honey. It's written in the Latin alphabet with the notable pronunciations c=ts, č=ch, š=sh, ž=zh and j=y, though a 'j' is effectively silent on the end of a word. On toilets M (Moški) indicates men, and Ž (Ženske) women. Slovene for 'no smoking' may raise a giggle if you speak Slovak, in which language the same phrase means 'no farting'. Virtually everyone in Slovenia speaks at least one other language; restaurant menus and ATMs are commonly in Slovene, Italian, German and English. See the language chapter (p929) for key phrases and words.

MONEY

Until 2007 Slovenia's legal currency will remain the tolar (SIT) but euros are already very widely accepted. Exchanging cash is simple at banks, major post offices, travel agencies and *menjalnica* (exchange bureaus). Prices listed in this chapter are in euros or tolar, depending on which currency was quoted by the business reviewed. Travellers cheques are less convenient. Major credit and debit cards are accepted almost everywhere and ATMs are astonishingly ubiquitous. Slovenian and Italian prices are similar, and you'll find Slovenia considerably more expensive than Hungary or the Czech Republic.

POST

An international airmail stamp costs 107SIT. Poste restante is free: address it to and pick it up at Slovenska cesta 32, 1101 Ljubljana.

TELEPHONE

Public telephones require a phonecard *(telefonska kartica)*, available at post offices and most newsstands. The cheapest card (700SIT, 25-unit) gives about four-minutes' calling time to other European countries. Most locals have a mobile phone. Some businesses quote only a mobile number, identifiable by codes 030, 031, 040 and 041.

EMERGENCY NUMBERS

- Police ☎ 113
- Fire brigade or ambulance ☎ 112
- AMZS automobile assistance information ☎ 530 5300
- Road emergency or towing ☎ 1987

TOILETS

Toilets are generally free in restaurants but occasionally incur a 50SIT charge at bus stations.

TOURIST INFORMATION

The super-helpful **Slovenian Tourist Board** (www.slovenia-tourism.si) has dozens of information centres (TICs) in Slovenia and branches in nine cities abroad; see the website for details. Request its free *Guide to Slovenia's Byways,* which contains tokens for 5% to 15% savings on various hotels, activities and sights, including the Škocjan Caves.

VISAS

Passport holders from Australia, Canada, Iceland, Israel, Japan, Norway, New Zealand,

Switzerland, the USA and EU countries can stay 90 days without visas. South Koreans get 15 days. Most other citizens, including South Africans, must apply for a visa (multiple entry €35) at a Slovenian embassy or consulate before arriving in Slovenia. Note that there is no consulate in South Africa. You'll need travel insurance, passport photocopies and hotel bookings plus one photo. Same-day processing is possible in Zagreb (Croatia) but elsewhere it takes from three working days (London) to a week (Budapest).

EU and Swiss citizens can enter using a national identity card for 30-day stays.

WOMEN TRAVELLERS

Crime is low and harassment rare, but in emergencies contact the **women's crisis helpline** (☎ 080 1155). Normally someone online will speak English.

TRANSPORT IN SLOVENIA

GETTING THERE & AWAY
Air

Slovenia's only international airport is **Brnik** (code LJU; www.lju-airport.si) near Kranj, some 23km north of Ljubljana. From here the national carrier, Adria Airways, serves up to 20 European destinations depending on the season, and operates code-share flights for Lufthansa and Air France. Adria flights can be remarkably good value, but as yet easyJet is the only low-cost carrier to fly direct to Slovenia. Adria connections include two to five per day from Frankfurt, three daily from Munich, one or two daily from Paris CDG, daily from Istanbul, London Gatwick and Zurich, five weekly from Amsterdam, twice weekly from Manchester, and useful connections to Prishtina (Kosovo), Ohrid (Macedonia) and Tirana (Albania). Flight frequency drops in winter.

AIRLINES FLYING TO & FROM SLOVENIA
Adria Airways (code JP; ☎ 01-239 1010; www.adria -airways.com)
Austrian Airlines (code OS; ☎ 01-239 1900; www.aua .com/at/eng/) Daily to Vienna.
ČSA (Czech Airlines; code OK; ☎ 04-206 1750; www.csa.cz) Flights to Prague.
EasyJet (code EZY; ☎ 04-206 1677; www.easyjet.com) Low-cost flights to London Stansted and Berlin Shönefeld.
JAT (code JU; ☎ 01-231 4340; www.jat.com) Daily to Belgrade.

Malév (Hungarian Airlines; code MA; ☎ 04-206 1676; www.malev.hu) Daily to Budapest.

Before you book your flight, look closely at a map. There are four alternative airports just beyond Slovenia's borders, all offering low-cost flights to and from London Stansted on **Ryanair** (www.ryanair.com), plus a variety of other destinations.

Trieste Airport (www.aeroporto.fvg.it) may be in Italy but it's much closer to Koper, Piran and the Soča Valley than Brnik. From the airport terminal there are direct if infrequent buses (€2.20, 15 minutes) to the border town Gorizia/Novo Gorica.

Treviso Airport (www.trevisoairport.it), often misdescribed as Venice-Treviso, is also handy for western Slovenia. Bus No 6 (€0.80 if prepaid), from outside the terminal, goes to Treviso Centrale; from here trains (€6.90, two hours) whisk you to Gorizia. That's quicker and cheaper than from Ljubljana. Low-cost flights from Treviso include **BasiqAir** (www.basiqair.com) to Amsterdam, **Carpatair** (www.carpatair.com) to Timişoara (Romania) and **Ryanair** (www.ryanair.com) to London Stansted, Charleroi (Belgium), Girona (Spanish Catalonia), and Hahn (Germany, near Mainz).

Graz Airport (www.flughafen-graz.at) in Austria is handily positioned for Maribor. Low-cost flights include **Welcome Air** (www.welcomeair.at) to Innsbruck, Hanover and Gothenburg.

Klagenfurt Airport (www.klagenfurt-airport.com), also in Austria, is a possible arrival point for Kranjska Gora and Bled. There are cheap connections on **Ryanair** (www.ryanair.com) to Rome and London Stansted or on **Happag Lloyd Express** (www.hlx.com) to Hanover, Stuttgart, Berlin and Cologne-Bonn.

Land
BUS

International bus destinations from Ljubljana include Frankfurt (18,400SIT, 12 hours, 7.30pm daily) via Munich (8300SIT, 6¾ hours), Sarajevo (8250SIT, 10 hours, 7.15pm Monday, Wednesday and Friday), Split (6550SIT, 10½ hours, 7.40pm daily) via Rijeka (2280SIT, 2½ hours), and Zagreb (3070SIT, three hours, 2.30am, 7.30am and 8.40am) via attractive Novo Mesto.

There are regular, if very slow, Koper–Trieste buses, plus one direct Ljubljana–Trieste service (2360SIT, 6.25am Monday to Saturday).

TRAIN

Daily Ljubljana–Vienna trains (12,979SIT, 6¼ hours) via Graz (6761SIT) are expensive. Save money by going first to Maribor (1380SIT): buy a Maribor–Graz ticket (2665SIT, 1¼ hours, six daily) then continue on domestic tickets from Graz to Vienna (€13.50, 2¾ hours). Similar savings apply via Jesenice and Villach and/or Klagenfurt.

Three trains daily depart Ljubljana for Munich (from 15,199SIT, 6¾ hours). The 11.30pm departure has sleeping carriages available.

Ljubljana–Trieste–Venice trains (7945SIT) depart at 2.50am or 10.30am. It's vastly cheaper to go first to Novo Gorica (1570SIT), walk to Gorizia then take an Italian train to Venice (€7.90, 2¼ hours); see p806 for details.

For Zagreb (Croatia) there are two direct trains daily from both Maribor (3331SIT, 2¾ hours) and Ljubljana (2739SIT, 2½ hours). Several trains serve Rijeka (Croatian coast) from Ljubljana (2665SIT, 2½ hours) via Postojna. Ljubljana–Budapest trains (three daily) go via Ptuj and Hodoš (14,854SIT, 8¾ hours) or via Maribor and Graz (17,124SIT, 9½ hours, 2am). The 9.05pm train to Thessaloniki (Greece, 19,912SIT, 25 hours) goes via Belgrade (9450SIT, nine hours).

Seat reservations, often compulsory, cost 800SIT extra.

Sea

From Venice, **Venezia Lines** (call Atlas Express agency ☎ 05-6745 6772; www.venezialines.com) catamarans sail to Piran (one way/return €42/65, 2¼ hours, mid-April to late September). The **Prince of Venice** (Kompas; ☎ 05-617 8000; portoroz@kompas.si) catamaran from nearby Izola also serves Venice (10,800SIT to 14,000SIT, 2¼ hours, March to October). Both operate between once and four times a week, generally returning the same evening. The **Marina** (jadroagent-zadar@zd .htnet.hr) sails weekly from Koper to Zadar in Croatia (5500SIT, 14 hours, mid-June to early September).

GETTING AROUND

Trains are usually cheaper but less frequent than buses. Beware: frequency on both drops off very significantly on weekends and in school holidays.

Bus

Especially for Friday afternoon travel it's worth booking longer-distance buses ahead. Many buses charge 360SIT per bag for luggage. The online bus timetable www.ap -ljubljana.si/ is extensive but does not cover routes that avoid Ljubljana. Enter the destination first, then the departure point.

Car & Bicycle

Renting a car is recommended, and can even save you money as you can access cheaper out-of-centre hotels and farm or village homestays. Daily rates usually start at €45 including unlimited mileage, collision-damage waiver and theft protection. However, **Hertz** (☎ 01-234 4646; www.hertz.si), beside Ljubljana bus station, currently offers a tiny Smart at €22, and some Ljubljana hostels advertise Skoda Favorits from €19. Unleaded 95-octane petrol (*bencin*) costs only 193SIT to 196SIT per litre. Keep sidelights on even in daylight.

Bicycles are available for hire at a few stations, TICs, agencies and hotels. You'll find mountain bikes easiest to rent in Bled and Bovec, and in Bovec sports agencies also rent motor scooters.

Hitching

Hitchhiking is fairly common and perfectly legal, except on motorways and a few major highways. Even young women hitch in Slovenia, but it's never totally safe and Lonely Planet doesn't recommend it.

Train

Slovenske Železnice (Slovenian Railways; ☎ 01-291 3332; www.slo-zeleznice.si; ☻ 5am-10pm) has a useful online timetable that's in Slovene but easy to use. Buy tickets before boarding or you'll incur a 200SIT supplement. Be aware that IC (InterCity) trains include a 320SIT surcharge on top of standard quoted fares.

A useful and very scenic rail line from Bled Jezero station via Bohinjska Bistrica (Bohinj) cuts under roadless mountains to Most na Soči (for Kobarid), then down the Soča Valley to Nova Gorica. Cars are carried through the tunnel section on special Avtovlak trains.

Ukraine
Україна

CONTENTS

Highlights	824	Information	852
Itineraries	824	Sights	852
Climate & When to Go	824	Sleeping	853
History	824	Eating & Drinking	854
People	828	Getting There & Away	854
Religion	828	Getting Around	855
Arts	829	**Crimea**	**855**
Environment	829	Simferopol	856
Food & Drink	830	Bakhchysaray	858
Kyiv	**830**	Yalta	858
Orientation	830	Sevastopol	861
Information	831	**Ukraine Directory**	**862**
Sights	833	Accommodation	862
Festival & Events	835	Activities	862
Sleeping	835	Books	862
Eating	836	Business Hours	862
Drinking	837	Embassies & Consulates	862
Entertainment	837	Festivals & Events	863
Shopping	837	Holidays	863
Getting There & Away	837	Insurance	863
Getting Around	838	Internet Resources	863
Western Ukraine	**838**	Language	863
Lviv	839	Money	863
Uzhhorod	844	Post	864
Ivano-Frankivsk	845	Telephone & Fax	864
Carpathian National Natural Park	847	Visas	864
Chernivtsi	848	**Transport in Ukraine**	**865**
Kamyanets-Podilsky	850	Getting There & Away	865
Odesa	**851**	Getting Around	867

UKRAINE

FAST FACTS

- **Area** 603,700 sq km
- **Capital** Kyiv
- **Currency** hryvnia (hry); €1 = 6.79hry; US$1 = 5.32hry; UK£ = 9.78hry; A$1 = 3.97hry; ¥100 = 4.98hry; NZ$1 =3.70hry
- **Famous for** great gymnasts, Chornobyl, chicken Kiev, host of Eurovision 2005
- **Official Language** Ukrainian
- **Population** 48 million
- **Telephone codes** country code ☎ 38; international access code ☎ 8+ 10
- **Visa** required for all, complex to obtain; see p883

With a name that means 'borderlands,' it's no surprise that Ukraine has a long history of invasions and occupations, or that it has struggled for its own identity and independence since the beginning of its civilisation. But that struggle has ended, and now Ukrainians are facing an exciting time as they tackle the task of figuring out who they are and what they want to become.

Kyiv, the cradle of Eastern Slavic civilization, was once a model Soviet city but now the energetic, frenetic city is as cosmopolitan as many Western European capitals. The heart of Ukrainian nationalism lies in the west, particularly in Lviv. There, the fragrant laid-back cafés, meandering cobblestone alleys and Gothic churches blackened with time conspire to maintain the steady pulse of a city that always seems to be just waking from a peaceful slumber. Once you head southward, towards Odesa and Crimea, you'll run smack bang into gorgeous natural landscapes and charming resort towns, with seaside palaces that are both picturesque and memorable.

HIGHLIGHTS

- Survey a litter of historic churches and cathedrals and feed off the contagious energy of **Kyiv** (p830), a capital in the process of reinvention
- Retreat to lonely alleys packed with smudgy, centuries-old buildings, then wake up to modernity with an espresso or tap-beer in **Lviv** (p839)
- From Simferopol take the longest trolleybus ride in the world along a winding road, flanked with cliff-faced mountains, to the cerulean, horseshoe coast of **Yalta** (p858)
- Walk across a bridge over a deep gorge dotted with fluffy trees and homes to the dramatic vistas and castle of **Kamyanets-Podilsky** (p850), an historic town on an 'island' of rock

ITINERARIES

- **One week** Split your time evenly between Kyiv and Lviv.
- **Two weeks** Spend a leisurely week each in Kyiv and Lviv, or follow the one-week plan and then head down to Crimea for a week of breathing fresh sea air, making Yalta your base.

CLIMATE & WHEN TO GO

Inland Ukraine enjoys a relatively moderate continental climate. The hottest month, July, averages 23°C, while the coldest, January, is literally freezing. Along the coast, Yalta and Odesa enjoy a marginally subtropical climate and are much milder in winter. See Climate Charts p874.

Near Odesa and in Crimea, tourism is at its peak from June to August (reserve accommodation in advance). Boat trips along the Dnipro River and Black Sea coast only operate from May to September. If you're visiting any city in Ukraine around the May 1 holidays, make travel and accommodation reservations well in advance.

All in all, mid-April to early June is the best time to visit the country.

HISTORY
Early History & Kyivan Rus

The land that is now Ukraine was populated as far back as 6000 years ago by an agricultural civilization called the Trypillians. They grew wheat and raised livestock, and lived in long, rectangular log cabins.

Possibly because of its rich, fertile earth (called chernozem), Ukraine has long been a hot spot for invasions. From the 2nd to the 9th centuries AD, Ukraine was yanked back and forth among the Ostrogoths (a Germanic people from northern Poland), the Huns, and Khazars (nomadic Turkic and Iranian tribes).

In 882 Oleh of Novgorod, of the Varyagi (a Scandinavian civilization), declared himself ruler of Kyiv. The city prospered and grew into a large, unified Varyagi (or Rus) state that during its peak stretched between the Volga River, the Danube River and Baltic Sea. Internecine wars were a weakness over the coming centuries, and power often changed hands – sometimes even going to outsiders such as the Khazars or Turkic Pechnegs – but not for long. During the 10th and 11th centuries, Kyivan Rus was at its peak – and was the most powerful state in Europe.

In 988 Prince Volodymyr visited Constantinople, accepted Christianity and converted his subjects, thereby founding the Russian and Ukrainian Orthodox Church. By the 11th and 12th centuries, the Varyagi state began to splinter into 10 rival princedoms. When prince of Suzdal Andriy Bogolyubov sacked Kyiv in 1169, followed by the Mongols 70 years later, the end of the Varyagi era was complete.

The regions of present-day western, central and northern Ukraine later united under Prince Roman Mstyslavych, who gained control of Kyiv in 1203. There was a period of relative prosperity under his dynamic son King Danylo and grandson Lev. During this time, much of eastern and southern Ukraine came under the control of the Volga-based Golden Horde. Its empire was emasculated, however, in the 14th century by the Black Death, as well as by the growing military strength of Russian, Polish and Lithuanian rulers.

Cossacks & Russian Control

By the turn of the 15th century, the uncontrolled steppe in southern Ukraine began to attract runaway serfs, criminals, Orthodox refugees and other outcasts from Poland and Lithuania. Along with a few semi-independent Tatars, the inhabitants formed self-governing militaristic communities and became known as *kazaki* (Cossacks), from the Turkic word meaning 'outlaw, adventurer or free person'. Ukrainian Cossacks eventually developed the self-ruling Cossack Hetmanate, which to some degree reasserted the concept of Ukrainian self-determination.

In 1648 Hetman Bogdan Khmelnytsky (aided by Tatar cavalry) overcame the Polish rulers at the battle of Pyliavtsi. He was forced to engage in a formal but controversial military alliance with Muscovy in

---

HOW MUCH?

- Kyiv metro ride 50 kopecks
- Bottle of Medoff vodka 25hry
- Cup of brewed coffee 7hry
- Ticket to opera in Kyiv 20hry
- Ticket to football game at Dynamo stadium in Kyiv 15hry

LONELY PLANET INDEX

- Litre of petrol 3.10hry
- Litre of bottled water 2hry
- Half litre Chernihivsky beer 4hry
- High-quality matryoshka (stacking doll) 50hry
- Street snack (Kyivska perepichka – meat roll) 4hry

1654, but in 1660 a war broke out between Poland and Russia over control of Ukraine. This ended with treaties that granted control over Kyiv and northern Ukraine to Russia and territory to the west of the Dnipro River to the Poles.

During the course of the 18th century Russia expanded into southern Ukraine and also gained most of Western Ukraine from Poland, except for the far west, which went to the Habsburg Empire. Perpetual occupation fuelled Ukrainian nationalism, which was born in Kyiv during the 1840s and inspired by the prolific writer and poet Taras Shevchenko.

The 20th Century

Following WWI and the collapse of tsarist power, Ukraine had a chance – but failed – to gain independence. Civil war broke out and exploded into anarchy: six different armies vied for power and Kyiv changed hands five times within a year. Eventually Ukraine was again divided between Poland, Romania, Czechoslovakia and Russia. The Russian part became a founding member of the USSR in 1922, but Stalin looked upon Ukraine as a laboratory for testing Soviet restructuring, while stamping out 'harmful' nationalism. Consequently, in 1932–33 he engineered a famine that killed millions of Ukrainians.

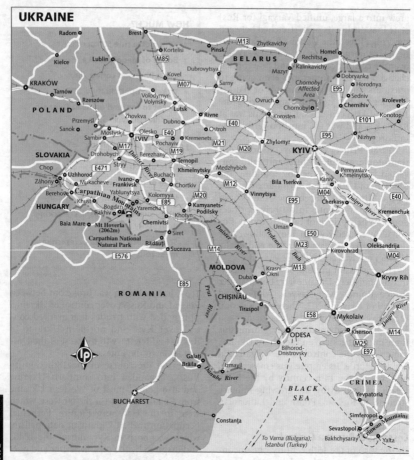

The Soviet Red Army rolled into Polish Ukraine in September 1939. The Germans attacked in 1941 and by the end of the year controlled virtually all of Ukraine. Kharkiv and Kyiv were retaken by the Red Army, however, two years later. An estimated six million Ukrainians died in the war, which left most of the country's cities in ruin. After WWII the USSR kept the territory it had taken from Poland in 1939.

The focus of the glasnost-era opposition to Soviet rule developed from the Church in Western Ukraine and the disastrous explosion of a nuclear reactor at Chornobyl in 1986 (see p829. Discontent about the latter was exacerbated by the slow government response and subsequent cover-up. Anti-Soviet riots started in 1988 in Lviv. In July 1990 the Ukrainian parliament did issue a sovereignty declaration, but this was too little for the growing independence movement. In October a wave of protests in Kyiv forced the resignation of the old-guard Prime Minister.

Independence

Shortly after a failed Soviet coup in August 1991, the Verkhovna Rada (Supreme Council) of Ukraine adopted a declaration of independence.

Inevitably, factions arose within the new government. Growing dissatisfaction forced the government to resign in September 1992, but difficulties still plagued the second gov-

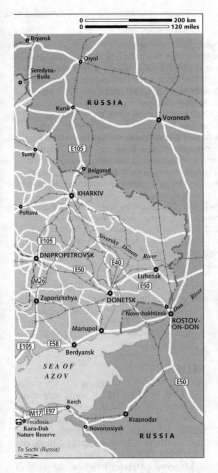

mentary elections, the Ukrainian Communist Party again stormed to victory.

Despite Ukraine witnessing its first positive growth in GDP since independence, the fragile economy failed to weather the financial storm that ripped across Russia in 1998. Consumer power in Ukraine plummeted as the *hryvnia*, in September alone, took a 51% tumble in value.

Presidential elections in October 1999 saw the incorrigible President Kuchma re-elected. International observers believed that the parliamentary elections held in March 2002 were fairer than before, but still far from perfect. However, tampering with elections may be only one of Kuchma's crimes. Former Prime Minister Pavel Lazarenko, now in a California prison awaiting trial for money-laundering charges, claims the president knew the whole time what his then-prime minister was doing. In 2000, one year after journalist Georgy Gongadze pressed the president on his knowledge of his Prime Minister's crimes, his headless

ernment. Disagreements and tensions with Russia and the West escalated, while sky-rocketing hyperinflation, fuel shortages and plummeting consumer power caused further widespread dissatisfaction. Paradoxically, the 1994 presidential elections saw the rise of the re-established Ukrainian Communist Party.

Relative economic stability was achieved during the mid-1990s under pro-Russian reformer Leonid Kuchma, when inflation fell from an inconceivable 10,000% in 1993 to 10% in 1997. The *hryvnia*, Ukraine's new currency, was introduced in 1996 and a process of privatisation kick-started the economy. Despite all this, living conditions declined and the government couldn't pay its workers. After the March 1998 parlia-

---

LOSE OR DIE

During WWII, when Kyiv was occupied by Nazi Germany, the members of the talented Dynamo soccer team were challenged to a public match with a team of German soldiers. The Ukrainians formed a team called Start, and despite physical weakness brought on by the occupation, they started off ahead. At half-time German officers came into the locker room and commanded them to let up. Nevertheless, Start continued to play hard, and before the game finished the referee blew the whistle and called it off (with a score of 4–1).

The Germans reshuffled their players, and Start was offered another chance to lose. Instead they won. Next, Start was matched with a Hungarian team – and won again. Finally, the enraged Germans challenged Start to a match against their finest, undefeated team, Flakelf. When the 'ubermensh' of Flakelf lost, the Nazis gave up – and proceeded to arrest most of the Start players. They were executed at Babyn Yar (p835). There is a monument to them at Dynamo Stadium in Kyiv, and their story inspired the movie *Victory*, starring Sylvester Stallone and Pele.

UKRAINE

ORTHODOXY & VISITING CHURCHES

Christianity was founded by the apostles of Christ themselves, and for a thousand years after the Crucifixion there was only one Christian religion, with five patriarchs (in Jerusalem, Constantinople, Alexandria, Antioch and Rome). Then, during the Great Schism of 1054, the Roman patriarch thought there should be only one ruler (him), and so the Roman church broke from the rest and created the papacy and Catholicism. At that point, Orthodoxy – which claims to have an unbroken apostolic lineage – began to develop in Russia.

Orthodoxy is in many ways separate from Catholicism and other Christian religions. For example, you'll notice that Orthodox believers (vyer-oo-yoo-shee) cross themselves in the opposite (up, down, right, left) way from other Christians. But not just the rituals are different – the whole atmosphere of the church and its ceremonies is deeply mystical and even mysterious. Stepping inside a Russian Orthodox Church for the first time is a spellbinding and sensual experience. In the dim light you're surrounded by the beauty of icons, mystical echoes and candle-lit devotion. You see a long-bearded, black-clad priest chanting and swinging a censer in the echoey shadows, and the relaxing, alluring fragrance of incense fills your nostrils.

Before entering, know that there are some restrictions that should be taken seriously. Women must have their hair covered with a scarf of some kind, and must wear a below-the-knee skirt (pack a scarf and a pull-over or wraparound skirt to put over your pants if you don't want to wear a skirt all day). Men may not wear shorts. The arms of both sexes should be covered (no tank tops). Do not put your hands in your pockets (it's considered disrespectful).

---

body was found in a ditch. He is one of many journalists to have died or disappeared under mysterious circumstances.

Looking Forward

As we went to press, presidential elections were scheduled for October 2004. Kuchma will not be running. Of the possibilities, opposition leader and former prime minister under Kuchma, Viktor Yushchenko (Our Ukraine party), ranks highest in popularity, but isn't well liked by the highly influential oligarchic powers. But even if he's no longer president, Kuchma has other ways of running the government. He has been focussing on constitutional amendments that would curtail the potency of the presidency, switching the powers instead to the parliament, where he has plenty of allies and puppets. In December 2003, for example, a draft bill was passed that would allow the parliament to elect the president, as opposed to the people of Ukraine. That was voted on again in February 2004, and lost, but there may still be time for Kuchma to work his dirty tricks before election time.

PEOPLE

Ukraine's population of 48,000,000 has been steadily declining since independence. About 66% live in urban areas like Kyiv, Kharkiv, Dnipropetrovsk, Odesa and Donetsk. Some 78% are Ukrainian and another 17% are ethnic Russians. The remainder includes Belarusians, Moldovans, Bulgarians, Poles, Hungarians, Romanians, Tatars and Jews. Almost all of the country's Tatar population (about 250,000) lives in Crimea (see p855).

RELIGION

Almost 97% of Ukrainians are Christian, and most of those follow some sort of orthodoxy. (See also boxed text above).

Orthodoxy in Ukraine has a complex history of its own, but basically, central and southern Ukraine mostly follow the Ukrainian Orthodox Church (UOC; with a Moscow patriarch), while the rest of the country follows the Ukrainian Autocephalous Orthodox Church (UAOC; with a Kyiv patriarch). To make matters more confusing, the UOC split in 1992, with a breakaway new church called the Ukrainian Orthodox Church of Kyiv and All-Ukraine, which recognises the Kyiv patriarch.

But wait, there's more. The Uniate Church, which is also referred to as the Ukrainian-Greek Catholic Church, follows Orthodox worship and ritual but recognises the Roman pope as its leader. Uniate priests are the only Catholic priests in the world allowed to marry.

There are some small Jewish minorities in all cities, while Muslim communities, primarily Tatars, live in Crimea.

ARTS

Many Ukrainians believe that to understand their heritage you must appreciate the significance of Taras Shevchenko, who was punished by exile in 1847 for his satirical poems about Russian oppression. Arguably the most talented and prolific Ukrainian writer of the early 20th century was Ivan Franko (p839), whose scholarly and moving works shed light on the issues plaguing Ukrainian society. He was, of course, imprisoned by the Russians. Lesia Ukrainka, a wealthy young woman whose frail health kept her indoors writing moody poetry, could be considered the Emily Dickinson of Ukraine.

In the cinema world, Aleksandr Dovzhenko's 1930 silent film *Earth* is considered by some critics to be one of the most significant films of all time. The most notable contemporary Ukrainian director (although she was born in a part of Romania that's now in Moldova) is Kira Muratova. Her absurdist, cruel style and fascination with the repulsive have earned her films much critical acclaim, if not a huge fan base.

The art of creating *pysanky*, or brightly coloured, detailed eggshells, is uniquely Ukrainian. During Easter you will be able to find some for sale (great souvenirs but hard to pack safely), and there are year-round wooden-egg samples for purchase.

ENVIRONMENT

The largest country wholly within Europe, Ukraine has a topography consisting almost completely of steppe; gently rolling, partially wooded plains, bisected by the Dnipro River. The only serious mountains are the Carpathians, in the west, and the Crimeans, in the south. A central belt of fertile, thick,

---

CHORNOBYL

And the third angel sounded, and there fell a great star from heaven, burning as it were a lamp, and it fell up on the third part of the rivers, and upon the fountains of waters; And the name of the star is called Wormwood: and the third part of the waters became wormwood; and many men died of the waters, because they were made bitter.

From Revelations 8:10-11

Chornobyl means 'wormwood'.

On 26 April 1986 reactor No 4 at Chornobyl nuclear power station, 100km north of Kyiv, exploded and nearly nine tonnes of radioactive material (90 times as powerful as the Hiroshima bomb) spewed into the sky. An estimated 4.9 million people in northern Ukraine, southern Belarus and southwestern Russia were affected. Some people – especially the elderly, who cannot conceive of the dangers of this invisible stuff called radiation – have refused to leave, and even live off the small gardens they've planted by their homes. Undoubtedly the most tragically affected were the young and unborn children. For more information about the situation and how to help, visit www.childrenofchornobyl.org, and watch the Oscar-winning documentary *Chernobyl Heart*.

Western monitors now conclude that radioactivity levels at Chornobyl are negligible, so organised tours of the site and surrounding 'ghost' villages have started to pop up. But visiting Chornobyl should not be a frivolous undertaking. Firstly, although the half-life of the thyroid-attacking iodine isotopes is long past, the dangerous plutonium ones will not decompose for another 20,000 or so years. (Although tour agencies may claim they won't go to plutonium-affected areas, it's hard to imagine how an explosion of radioactive particles could be contained into certain zones). Secondly, the cement 'sarcophagus' that was built over the still-burning reactor is crumbling and unstable. Before jumping into a decision to take extreme tourism to the subatomic level, do your own research and make an informed decision.

If you do decide to go, interrogate your tour agency beforehand. You should be provided with some sort of protective gear (if only overalls and boots) and a Geiger counter. The standard price for a six-hour visit is about €160, which includes transportation from Kyiv. One established organisation can be reached at uims@yandex.ru. Make arrangements well in advance, as you will need to obtain special official permission to visit. Because of the anniversary of the tragedy, late April is the busiest time of year.

If you opt to play it safe and eschew Chornobyl itself, do pay a visit to the riveting Chornobyl Museum (p835) in Kyiv.

UKRAINE

humus-rich soil in Ukraine spawned the term chernozem (meaning 'black earth') and is what gave the country the nickname 'the breadbasket of Europe'.

Visitors don't come for rare-wildlife watching, but there is a good amount of diversity including elk, deer, wild boars, brown bears, and wolves. Lost of geese and ducks, and small furry mammals such as rabbits and muskrats, can be seen from trains. Ukrainians take great pride in their trees and flowers; even children know the different names of the species (and they'll probably be surprised if you don't know the English-language equivalent). Ukraine has a few national parks, the most significant of which is the Carpathian National Natural Park (p847).

In addition to the destructive Soviet industrialisation of the countryside, Ukraine still suffers from the effects of Chornobyl (Chernobyl in Russian), the worst nuclear accident in history (see p829).

The Green Party is the political wing of the organisation Zeleny Svit (Green World). Although small, it is a crucial voice in raising issues and encouraging politicians to protect the environment.

FOOD & DRINK

In addition to the rampant breads, sautéed mushrooms, pickled or smoked fishes and 'salads' (usually mayonnaise-laden cheese, meat and a couple of veggies) also found in Russia and Belarus, there are a few uniquely Ukrainian dishes.

Some tasty tradition dishes are *varenyky* (traditional dumplings made with rolled dough), *borshch* (based on a beet and meat broth) and *holubtsi* (cabbage rolls stuffed with seasoned rice, meat or buckwheat). Chicken Kiev (*kotleta po-Kyivsky*), the internationally known chunk of deep-fried boneless chicken stuffed with butter, is disappointingly hard to find in Ukraine – or is sometimes bizarrely covered in ketchup and mayo. And beware of *salo* (slices of pig fat) – it can look like cheese.

Crimea produces excellent wines, and champagne from around Odesa is surprisingly palatable. The most popular Ukrainian beers are Slavutych, Chernihivsky and Obolon. Sold on practically every street corner in Kyiv during summer is *kvas* (a sweet sort of beer made from fermented meal or bread). It tastes vaguely of gingerbread. Try it from a store-bought bottle if you have hygiene concerns (which you probably should).

Vegetarians can have a hard time, but it's very possible to get by. In this chapter, we've made a particular effort to seek out places where people can indulge themselves while remaining meat-free. Here's how to say 'I am a vegetarian (male/female)': 'ya vyeh-gyeh-tah-ree-AHN-yets/-ka'.

Smoking is allowed in most restaurants; in fact, nonsmoking sections in restaurants are rare. For tips on social etiquette, see the boxed text (p66).

KYIV КИЇВ

☎ 044 / pop 2.6 million

Slavophiles, look no further – this is where it all began. This ancient city, believed to be at least 1500 years old, was the hub of the culture, language and religion now associated with this part of the world. Nowadays, it's a cosmopolitan centre where even the short-term visitor can pick up the vibrant pulse of a city in the process of reinvention. Situated along the Dnipro River, Kyiv (Kiev in Russian) is less overwhelming and more laid-back than Moscow and St Petersburg, and there is plenty to see and do while planning your assault on the rest of Ukraine.

Kyiv is the cradle of Slavic civilisation – and this cradle rocks.

ORIENTATION

Both the modern and the historic centres are on the west side of the Dnipro River. The Old Town (Upper Town, Verkhni Gorod) is concentrated around the north end of vulitsa Volodymyrska, near St Sophia Cathedral.

Kyiv's main commercial promenade is vulitsa Khreshchatyk, which heads north towards maydan Nezalezhnosti, the main square. On weekends vulitsa Khreshchatyk is closed to traffic, and *kyivlany* (Kyivans) flood the street, giving the area an atmosphere of mild chaos. To cross Khreshchatyk (and other wide, busy Ukrainian streets), you often must go through an underground passage (called a pe-re-*khod*). During the Soviet era, these *perekhodi* were commonly populated with kiosks and black-marketeers, but now, many have been turned into Western-style shopping malls – a perfect example of the capitalism that is now raging in Kyiv.

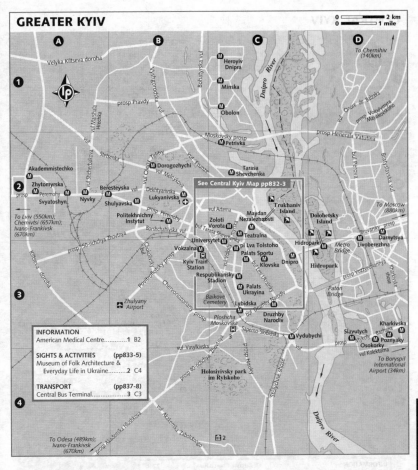

GREATER KYIV

0 _____ 2 km
0 _____ 1 mile

To Chernihiv (140km)

Heroyiv Dnipra

Minska

Obolon

Velyka Kiltseva doroha

prosp Pravdy

Vyshgorodska vul

Bohatyrska vul

Dnipro River

Moskovsky prosp

Petrivka

prosp Henerala Vatutina

bul Perova

Bratyslavska vul

To Moscow (880km)

Darnytsya

Livoberezhna

Metro Bridge

Hidropark

Akademmistechko

Zhytomyrska

prosp Peremohy

Svyatoshyn

Beresteyska vul

Nyvky

Shulyavska

Politekhnichny Instytut

Borshchahlvska vul

Dorogozhychi

vul Melnykova

Dekhtyarivska vul

Lukyanivska

Tarasa Shevchenka

Zoloti Vorota

Maydan Nezalezhnosti

Trukhaniv Island

Dolobetsky Island

Teatralna

Universytet

Vokzalna

Kyiv Train Station

Respublikansky Stadion

Baikove Cemetery

pl Lva Tolstoho

Palats Sportu

Klovska

Palats Ukrayina

Lybidska

Dnipro

Klvska

Hidropark

Hidropark

Paton Bridge

prosp Vozziednannya

Kharkivska

Slavutych

Poznyaky

Osokorky

vul Kolektorna

To Boryspil International Airport (34km)

Ploshcha Moskovska

Saperno-Slobidska

Vydubychi

Zhulyany Airport

See Central Kyiv Map pp832-3

vul Artema

bul Tarasa Shevchenka

Druzhby Narodiv

vul Vasylkivska

vul 40-richchya Zhovtnya

Holosiyivsky park im Rylskoho

prosp Nauky

Stolychne shose

Dnipro River

To Odesa (489km); Ivano-Frankivsk (670km)

prosp Akademika Hlushkova

vul Akademika Zabolotnoho

To Lviv (550km); Chernivtsi (657km); Ivano-Frankivsk (670km)

Chervonoarmiyska prosp

INFORMATION
American Medical Centre............1 B2

SIGHTS & ACTIVITIES (pp833-5)
Museum of Folk Architecture &
Everyday Life in Ukraine..........2 C4

TRANSPORT (pp837-8)
Central Bus Terminal................3 C3

UKRAINE

The area north of the Old Town from around St Andrew's Church to Kontraktova ploshcha is Podil (Lower Town), the historic merchants' quarter and river port.

Across the river, on the sort of seedy east (left) bank, are a cluster of islands hugged by beaches and parkland. Beyond that lie grey housing blocks.

INFORMATION

In addition to the places listed here, Internet access is available at the post office until 9pm. If you go a little deeper into maydan Nezalezhnosti, towards the McDonald's, on the left is a 24-hour Internet centre. Access in Kyiv generally costs 10hry per hour.

American Medical Centre (Map p831; ☎ 490 76 00; www.amcenters.com; vulitsa Berdychivsta 1; Ⓜ Lukyanivska) Near metro Lukianivska; handles routine and emergency medical and dental. Staff speak English.

Baboon Book Coffee Shop (Map pp832-3; ☎ 235 59 80; vulitsa Bohdana Khmelnytskoho 39; Ⓜ Universitet; ☼ 9am-2am) A bookstore-restaurant (mains 12hry to 36hry) that has maps and a clued-up English-language selection.

Central post office (Map pp832-3; ☎ 065; vulitsa Khreshchatyk 22; Ⓜ Khreshchatyk; ☼ 8am-9pm Mon-Fri, 8am-7pm Sat)

Naukova Dumka (Map pp832-3; ☎ 228 06 96; vulitsa Grushevskogo 4; Ⓜ Maydan Nezalezhnosti; ☼ 10am-6pm Mon-Fri) Has a good selection of topographical maps.

Telephone office (Map pp832-3; next to the post office; Ⓜ Khreshchatyk; ☼ 24hr)

CENTRAL KYIV

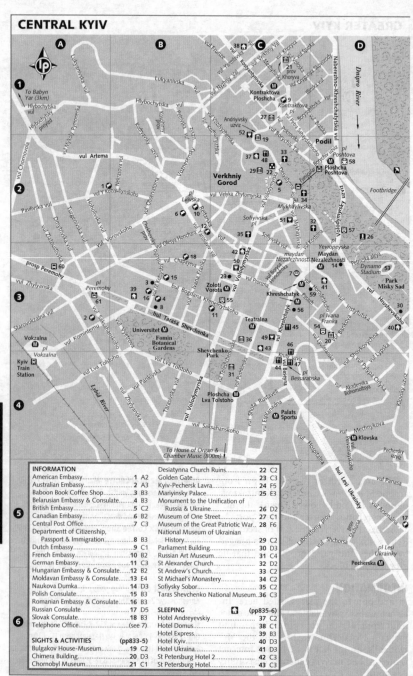

INFORMATION
American Embassy	1 A2
Australian Embassy	2 A3
Baboon Book Coffee Shop	3 B3
Belarusian Embassy & Consulate	4 B3
British Embassy	5 C2
Canadian Embassy	6 B2
Central Post Office	7 C3
Departmentt of Citizenship, Passport & Immigration	8 B3
Dutch Embassy	9 C1
French Embassy	10 B2
German Embassy	11 C3
Hungarian Embassy & Consulate	12 B2
Moldavan Embassy & Consulate	13 E4
Naukova Dumka	14 D3
Polish Consulate	15 B3
Romanian Embassy & Consulate	16 B3
Russian Consulate	17 D5
Slovak Consulate	18 B3
Telephone Office	(see 7)

SIGHTS & ACTIVITIES (pp833-5)
Bulgakov House-Museum	19 C2
Chimera Building	20 D3
Chornobyl Museum	21 C1
Desiatynna Church Ruins	22 C2
Golden Gate	23 C3
Kyiv-Pechersk Lavra	24 F5
Mariyinsky Palace	25 E3
Monument to the Unification of Russia & Ukraine	26 D2
Museum of One Street	27 C1
Museum of the Great Patriotic War	28 F6
National Museum of Ukrainian History	29 C2
Parliament Building	30 D3
Russian Art Museum	31 C4
St Alexander Church	32 D2
St Andrew's Church	33 C2
St Michael's Monastery	34 C2
Sofiysky Sobor	35 C2
Taras Shevchenko National Museum	36 C3

SLEEPING (pp835-6)
Hotel Andreyevskiy	37 C2
Hotel Domus	38 C1
Hotel Express	39 B3
Hotel Kyiv	40 D3
Hotel Ukraina	41 D3
St Petersburg Hotel 2	42 C3
St Petersburg Hotel	43 C3

UKRAINE

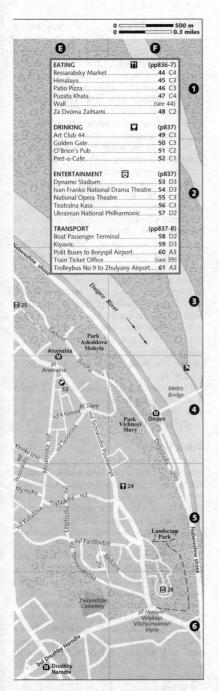

EATING	🍴	(pp836-7)
Bessarabsky Market	44	C4
Himalaya	45	C3
Patio Pizza	46	C3
Puzata Khata	47	C4
Wall	(see 44)	
Za Dvoma Zaitsami	48	C2

DRINKING	🍸	(p837)
Art Club 44	49	C3
Golden Gate	50	C3
O'Brien's Pub	51	C2
Pret-a-Cafe	52	C1

ENTERTAINMENT	🎭	(p837)
Dynamo Stadium	53	D3
Ivan Franko National Drama Theatre	54	D3
National Opera Theatre	55	C3
Teatralna Kasa	56	C3
Ukrainian National Philharmonic	57	D2

TRANSPORT		(pp837-8)
Boat Passenger Terminal	58	D2
Kiyavia	59	D3
Polit Buses to Boryspil Airport	60	A3
Train Ticket Office	(see 39)	
Trolleybus No 9 to Zhulyany Airport	61	A3

SIGHTS

Caves Monastery

Commonly known in English as the Caves Monastery, the **Kyiv-Pechersk Lavra** (Map pp832-3; ☎ 290 30 71; vulitsa Sichnevoho Povstannya; admission 10hry; ⏰ 8am-late evening) deserves at least a half-day of your visit. It is the single most fascinating and extensive tourist site in the city and a highlight of Ukraine. Rolling across 28 hectares of wooded slopes above the Dnipro, the complex is the spiritual heart of the Ukrainian people.

The monastery was the first in Kyivan Rus and was founded by monks Antony and Feodosiy in 1051 – just before Christianity splintered into different factions during the Great Schism of 1054 (see Orthodoxy & Visiting Churches, p828). The monks worshipped here, living in caves they dug out themselves. When they died, their bodies were placed in their caves, and because of the stable cool temperature and humid atmosphere, the monks' corpses are naturally preserved to this day (as you can see for yourself). The fact that the monks' bodies did not decompose confirmed the convictions of believers that they were true holy men.

The main entrance is through the striking **Trinity Gate Church**, a well-preserved piece of early-12th-century architecture. Just north is the small, late-17th-century **St Nicholas' Church**. Further along is the unmistakable **Dormition Cathedral** and its 97m-high **Great Belfry** (1731–44), which

UKRAINE

has wonderful views. Directly south is the **Refectory Church of Sts Anthony & Feodosiy**, which sports the monastery's most famous gold-striped dome. Other highlights include the fascinating **Museum of Microcaricature**, the **Historical Treasures Museum** and the 17th-century **All Saints' Church**. The **Nearer Caves** are a few minutes' walk southeast of the cathedral and through the southern gate. Inside the caves, dozens of niches contain open, glass-topped coffins with mummified monks' bodies. Women have to cover their head with a scarf, and men are obliged to remove their hats. Wearing shorts and T-shirts, and using a video/still camera, are also forbidden.

Sunday is definitely the busiest day. The museums and churches inside the preserve have extra admission fees (3hry to 6hry each) and are open daily from about 10am to 5pm. The **excursion bureau** (☎ 291 31 71) is on the left just past the main entrance of the monastery complex. Three-hour guided tours in just about every conceivable language cost 200hry per group (including admission fees), but need to be prebooked. Unofficial guides lingering inside the complex offer two-hour tours in English for about 50hry per small group.

St Sophia Cathedral Complex

St Sophia's Cathedral (Sofiysky Sobor; Map pp832-3; ☎ 228 61 52; Sofiyivska ploshcha; Ⓜ Maydan Nezalezhnosti; adult/child 11/4hry; bell tower 3hry; ⏲ 10am-5.30pm Fri-Tue & 10am-4.30pm Wed, grounds ⏲ 8.30am-8pm) is the city's oldest standing church. Built from 1017 to 1031 and named after Hagia Sofia (Holy Wisdom) Cathedral in Istanbul, its Byzantine plan and decoration announced the new religious and political authority of Kyiv. The cathedral was also a centre of learning and culture, housing the first school and library in Kyivan Rus. The 13-cupola cathedral emanates history – especially from the interior, where there are mosaics and frescoes dating back to the beginning of the 11th century, when the cathedral was built. The complex was included on Unesco's World Heritage List in 1990, but the massive amount of new construction near St Sophia's has threatened its Unesco status. At the time of research, city planners and Unesco were in talks to try to work out a solution.

Andriyivsky Uzviz

Your visit – and your souvenir shopping – wouldn't be complete without a walk along steep, cobblestoned Andriyivsky uzviz (Andrew's Descent), one of the oldest and definitely the quaintest street in town. It's lined with tables where people sell crafts and gifts both desirable and bizarre. Avoid the incline by taking the **funicular** (Ⓜ Poshtova Ploshcha; admission 50 kopeks; ⏲ 6.30am-11pm) to the top of the hill, where you'll find the marvellous **St Michael's Monastery**, with its seven-cupola cathedral; inside the reconstructed, three-tiered bell tower is a small **museum** (admission 5hry; ⏲ 10am-4pm Wed-Sun) dedicated to the reconstruction of the monastery. Further down the street is the gorgeous baroque **St Andrew's Church** (admission 4hry), built in 1754 in St Petersburg (as was Mariyinsky Palace, below). Across from St Andrew's, up a small flight of stairs and on the ground before the National Museum of Ukrainian History (below) are the **Desyatynna Church ruins**. Prince Volodymyr (p824) ordered it built in 989 and used 10% of his income for it, hence the name (*desyatyn* means 'one-tenth'). The church came to an end in 1240, when it collapsed under the weight of the people who took refuge on its roof during a Tatar siege.

From here, take souvenir stall-lined Andriyivsky uzviz down the hill to start your descent into the realm of *matryoshkas* (stacking dolls).

Other Sights

Originally erected in 1037 but reconstructed in 1982, the **Golden Gate** (Zolotoi Vorota; Map pp832-3; vulitsa Volodymyrska 40A; Ⓜ Zolotoi Vorota) was the original entrance into Old Kyiv. It was closed for repairs during research, but it still requires a visit to at least glimpse it from the street (notice the chapel at the top).

The 19th-century **St Alexander Church** (Map pp832-3; vulitsa Kostolna 17) is recognisable by its large central dome and twin bell towers. Continue southeast along vulitsa Grushevskogo to the **Parliament Building** (Map pp832-3; closed to the public) and the adjacent baroque, 18th-century **Mariyinsky Palace** (Map pp832-3). It's surrounded by a lovely park with good city views, but entrance to the palace is not allowed – it's reserved for diplomatic meetings.

The very Gaudí-like **Chimera Building** (Map pp832-3; vulitsa Bankovaya 10; M Khreshchatyk), with its demonic-looking animals and gargoyles, is probably the weirdest building in the city. It was constructed at the beginning of the 20th century by architect Vladislav Gorodetski, a pretty crazed genius, who made it his home.

Views during the funicular ride are obstructed by trees, so go to the metal-rainbow **Monument to the Unification of Russia & Ukraine** (Map pp832-3; M Maydan Nezalezhnosti) for excellent vistas of the city along the Dnipro; there's also a good viewpoint at Mariyinsky Palace (above).

Just outside of metro Dorohozhychi, in a quiet park where young lovers lie in the sun and kiss, is **Babyn Yar**, the location of a WWII execution site and mass grave used by Nazis. Over 100,000 *kyivlany* – mostly Jews – were murdered here from 1941-43. The monument here is ugly and not representative – its vibe is more like sexy than suffering. And actually, the monument is in the wrong spot. A small marble monument nearby marks the actual place of execution. See also Lose or Die (p827).

Museums

The following is a list of museums, ranked by an approximation of interest and popularity. Know that little is posted in English.

Chornobyl Museum (Map pp832-3; ☎ 470 54 22; provulok Khoryva; M Kontraktova Ploshcha; admission 5hry; ⏲ 10am-6pm Mon-Sat, closed last Mon of month) This extremely artistic and moving display is a must-see. In case you're wondering, the signs above the stairs represent the 'ghost' cities in the area of the disaster.

Bulgakov House-Museum (Map pp832-3; ☎ 416 31 88; Andriyivsky uzviz 13; M Kontraktova Ploshcha; admission 3hry; ⏲ 10am-5pm Thu-Tue) The beloved author of *The Master & Margarita* lived here in the early 20th century, and his home has been turned into a museum. During the May 1 holidays, the place is booked up with tour groups.

Museum of the Great Patriotic War (Map pp832-3; ☎ 295 94 52; vulitsa Sichnevoho Povstannya 44; admission 4hry; ⏲ 10am-4pm Tue-Sun) Triumphant displays of Soviet heroism. Visible from miles around is 'Rodina Mat', or 'Defence of the Motherland Monument' – a 62m-high titanium statue of a valiant woman with shield and sword.

Museum of Folk Architecture & Everyday Life in Ukraine (Map p831; ☎ 266 55 42; vulitsa Chervonoznamenna; admission 5hry; ⏲ 10am-4pm Thu-Tue) Numerous 17th- to 20th-century wooden cottages, churches, farmsteads and windmills. Take *marshrutka* (minibus) No 24 from the Lybidska metro station; the entrance is hard to miss. A taxi will cost about 40hry one way.

Russian Art Museum (Map pp832-3; ☎ 224 62 18; vulitsa Tereshchenkivska 9; M Ploshcha Lva Tolstoho; admission 7hry; ⏲ 10am-6pm Fri-Sun, 11am-6pm Mon & Tue, closed last Mon of month) One of the largest collections of Russian artwork in the world.

Taras Shevchenko National Museum (Map pp832-3; ☎ 234 25 56; bulvar Tarasa Shevchenka 12; M Teatralna; adult/child 3/1; ⏲ 10am-5pm Tue-Sun, closed last Thu of month) Over 4000 items related to this revered and multitalented 19th-century Ukrainian poet-cum-artist (see p839).

Museum of One Street (Map pp832-3; ☎ 416 03 98; Andriyivsky uzviz 2B; M Kontraktova Ploshcha; admission 5hry; ⏲ noon-6pm Tue-Sun) Engagingly recaptures some of Andriyivsky uzviz's turn-of-the-20th-century history.

National Museum of Ukrainian History (Map pp832-3; ☎ 228 29 24; vulitsa Volodymyrska 2; adult/child 10/5hry; ⏲ 10am-5pm Thu-Tue) Houses about 600,000 exhibits of archaeological and recent historical interest.

FESTIVALS & EVENTS

Kyiv will host the 2005 Eurovision song context (see p863).

On the last weekend of May, the capital celebrates **Kyiv Days** with fireworks, folk festivals and a big beauty contest.

In October, Kyiv holds both its **International Music Festival** and its **International Film Festival**.

SLEEPING

If you're staying in Kyiv for more than a few days, it's certainly worth booking an apartment. **Rostick Gavrilov** (gavrilov@iptelecom .net.ua) can set you up with a cheap, central one (starting from US$15 per night). More expensive hotels can be booked through **Hotel Service** (www.hotel.kiev.ua) or one of the agencies listed in the *Kyiv Post* and *Kyiv Business Directory*.

Budget

Hotel Andreyevskiy (Map pp832-3; ☎ 416 22 56; vulitsa Vozdvizhenskaya 60; s 180-408hry; d 300-408 hry)

UKRAINE

Con: all hallways dark and spooky; some bathrooms dank and stinky. Pro: right off cute-as-a-button Andriyivsky uzviz; rooms far brighter than halls. There is only one cheap single, but the five cheap doubles are good value. Its semisuite (588hry) could fit four backpackers.

Other options are **St Petersburg Hotel** (Map pp832-3; ☎ 229 73 64; s-peter@i.kiev.ua; bulvar Tarasa Shevchenka 4; Ⓜ Treatralna; s 129-343hry, d 182-572hry, tr 213hry) and its illiterate buck-toothed stepsister, **St Petersburg Hotel 2** (Map pp832-3; ☎ 229 59 43; s-peter@i.kiev.ua vulitsa Volodymyrska 36; Ⓜ Zolotoi Vorota; s/d/tr/q 73-127/206-314/150/172hry), which is depressing and only for the desperately low on funds.

Mid-Range

Hotel Express (Map pp832-3; ☎ 239 89 95; bulvar Tarasa Shevchenka 8/40; Ⓜ Universitet; s/d from 195/275hry, ste 1055-1355hry; Ⓟ ⊠ 🖳) Conveniently within walking distance to the train station, and even more conveniently sharing the same building as the train ticket office, is Hotel Express, with a wide range of rooms. Billiards, sauna, hot tub and gym are all onsite. The young staff seem a little inexperienced, but that should work itself out soon.

Hotel Ukraina (Map pp832-3; ☎ 229 03 47; www .ukraine-hotel.kiev.ua; vulitsa Instytutska 4; Ⓜ Maydan Nezalezhnosti; s 210-460, d330-850hry, 6th-fl s/d/ste 530/580/600-1450hry; Ⓟ) Nothing can beat the location of Hotel Ukraina. Perched high on a hill above maydan Nezalezhnosti, in one of the less stodgy-looking Soviet buildings, this hotel has a lot to offer. The sixth-floor has been Westernised and is therefore pricier, but great deals can be had on the other floors. Sauna rental is 300hry.

Hotel Kyiv (Map pp832-3; ☎ 253 30 90; www.htl .kiev.ua; vulitsa Grushevskogo 26; Ⓜ Arsenalna; s 340-400hry, d/t 440/480hry; Ⓟ 🖳) The singles here are pricey, but since the doubles and triples aren't that much more, they are a pretty good deal. The hotel is in a Soviet structure, but rooms are tidy – even a little quaint – and it's right by Mariyinsky Palace. Parking is free, but breakfast is 70hry.

Top End

Hotel Domus (Map pp832-3; ☎ 462 51 20; www .domus-hotel.kiev.ua; vulitsa Yaroslavska 19; Ⓜ Kontraktova Ploshcha; s/d US$140/190, ste US$220-430; ⊠ 🖳) This small, cosy hotel has a slightly romantic atmosphere, with nice touches like a doorman, modern lift, hypoallergenic beds, hair dryers and a filtered water system. Breakfast is US10 extra. One drawback is that there are no tubs, only showers. The Ukrainian-Italian restaurant here has a decent reputation.

EATING

Eating is a great thing in Kyiv. There's a large selection of cuisines and price ranges, so you can get almost anything you want. This is a small list, but you'll easily find more extensive listings in free English-language booklets, kept at pricier hotels and in restaurants; or buy a copy of the extremely thorough *Kyiv Business Directory*, which is published quarterly and for sale outside the Central Post Office (p831).

In addition to what's listed here, don't forget that Baboon Book Coffee Shop (p831) has good food – including Western breakfasts.

Bessarabsky Market (Map pp832-3; Bessarabska ploshcha; Ⓜ Treatralna; ⊙ 9am-5pm) A beautiful, historic indoor market with lots of produce.

Puzata Khata (Map pp832-3; ☎ 246 72 45; Baseyna vulitsa 1/2; Ⓜ Treatralna; mains 10-15hry; ⊙ 8am-11pm) Costumed girls ladle out fresh old-fashioned Ukrainian goodness in this popular cafeteria-style eatery. It's quite a scene and an even better deal. The desserts here are delicious too. Enough is on offer that vegetarians can be satisfied. It's hard not to gorge yourself here, which is why the name translates as 'The Hut of the Big Belly.'

Wall (Map pp832-3; ☎ 235 80 45; Bessarabsky ploshcha 2; Ⓜ Treatralna; mains 7-25hry; ⊙ 9am-midnight) It's easy to miss this little place on the back side of the Bessarabsky Market. But if you're looking for a small pub atmosphere and a mean morning omelette – this is the place. Look for the little red sign over the door, which leads downstairs.

Himalaya (Map pp832-3; ☎ 462 04 37; vulitsa Khreshchatyk 23; Ⓜ Treatralna; mains 25-52hry; ⊙ 11.30am-11.30pm) Indian food apparently hasn't caught on with *kyivlany* but the place is good, moderately elegant and has vegetarian food. The curries and samosas are tasty, but the spinach sauce is not. During the week, the set lunch (noon to 3.30pm) is only 40hry.

Patio Pizza (Map pp832-3; ☎ 246 43 27; Bessarabska ploshcha 5A; Ⓜ Treatralna; mains 15-64hry, salad bar

35hry; noon-10pm) It's a big chain, but there are reasons for its success. It also happens to be next to another chain restaurant that needs no advertisement. This particular Patio Pizza happens to have a pleasant, two-storey dining area. Service is good, the food is tasty and the menu is large (plus there's a real salad bar). You can also create your own pizzas and pastas with your favourite ingredients.

Za Dvoma Zaitsami (Map pp832-3; ☎ 229 79 72; Andriyivsky uzviz 34; mains 45-130hry; 11am-11pm) Here's a precious little restaurant for a precious little street. The décor represents early 20th-century Kyiv, and the food, which is very good, focuses on rabbit. (The name means 'Going after Two Rabbits'.) It's dimly lit and romantic.

DRINKING

Pret-a-Cafe (Map pp832-3; ☎ 416 12 97; Andriyivsky uzviz 10a; Kontraktova Ploshcha; 8am-11pm) This stylish café makes a welcome respite from souvenir shopping on the *uzviz*. The coffee is good, but the pastries and chocolates are better.

Art Club 44 (Map pp832-3; ☎ 229 41 37; vulitsa Khreshchatyk 44; Treatralna; 10am-2am) It feels like a speakeasy in here, and is decorated with musical instruments. To find it, go through the arch and then through the door by the red sign, then through the door that's (finally) signed Art Club 44.

Golden Gate (Map pp832-3; ☎ 235 51 88; vulitsa Volodymyrska 40/2; Zolotoi Vorota; 11am-1am) This is also not easy to find (it's sort of behind the casino on the corner). But it's worth the effort: voted best breakfast in town for its weekend eggs Benedict, and the Georgian president came here in 2004 and had a grand old time. Lots of good tap beers (including Guinness), billiards and darts make this the 'third home' of many expats.

O'Brien's Pub (Map pp832-3; ☎ 229 15 84; vulitsa Mykhailivska 17A; Maydan Nezalezhnosti; 8am-2am) It's no longer the favourite pub in Kyiv but it will always be the first. Irish food and all other good things an Irish pub need are right here waiting to be adored.

ENTERTAINMENT

Nightlife in Kyiv involves casinos, loud expensive nightclubs laced with plenty of prostitutes, and strip clubs, which are well marketed and need no review here. If you're looking for something a little more refined, you're also in luck – there's plenty on offer, and you won't have to blow your budget. Tickets to most performances can be purchased in advance at a театральна каса (*teatralna kasa*; ticket office) on vulitsa Khreshchatyk, including **Teatralna Kasa** (Map pp832-3; vulitsa Khreshchatyk 21; Khreshchatyk); they are easily recognisable by the schedules posted all around the window. Same-day tickets can be purchased at the venue.

National Opera Theatre (Map pp832-3; ☎ 229 11 69; vulitsa Volodymyrska 50; Zolotoi Vorota) A performance at this lavish opera house is a grandiose affair.

Ivan Franko National Drama Theatre (Map pp832-3; ploshcha Ivana Franka 3; Khreshchatyk) Not far from the Chimera Building, this theatre's performances are highly respected.

Ukrainian National Philharmonic (Map pp832-3; ☎ 228 16 97; Volodymyrska uzviz 2; Maydan Nezalezhnosti) Housed in a beautiful white building. Inside is a phenomenal organ.

House of Organ & Chamber Music (☎ 268 31 86; vulitsa Chervonoarmiyska 77) Classical concerts are held in the cool Gothic St Nicholas' Church.

Dynamo Stadium (Map pp832-3; ☎ 229 02 09; vulitsa Grushevskogo 3; Maydan Nezalezhnosti) This is Ukraine's most beloved stadium, named for Ukraine's most beloved team (see p827).

SHOPPING

Without a doubt, the place to shop for souvenirs is along the cobblestoned Andriyivsky uzviz (p834).

Western-style malls and shopping centres are quickly becoming ubiquitous in the centre of town, even though the number of people who can shop there hasn't quite justified the sheer quantity of them. They're easily spotted by their sleek façades in the centre – and underground crosswalks have been turned into modern shopping centres too (you'll probably have to walk through one from time to time in order to cross the street).

GETTING THERE & AWAY
Air

The **Boryspil International Airport** (☎ 296 76 09; www.airport-borispol.kiev.ua) is a good 35km, or 45 minutes, from central Kyiv. All international flights use this airport.

All domestic flights and some flights to other Commonwealth of Independent States (CIS) countries arrive and leave from **Zhulyany Airport** (Map p831; ☎ 242 23 08; www.air port.kiev.ua, in Ukrainian); it's conveniently close to the centre (about 8km away).

Boat

All long-distance trips along the Dnipro River (p867) start and finish at the **Boat Passenger Terminal** (Map pp832-3; ☎ 416 12 68; Poshtova ploshcha; Ⓜ Poshtova ploshcha).

Bus

Almost all long-distance buses – including the privately owned **Autolux** (www.autolux.com .ua) – use the **Central Bus Terminal** (Map p831; ☎ 265 57 74; ploshcha Moskovska 3; Ⓜ Lybidska). To get there, take any minibus, bus or trolley-bus, or walk (20 minutes) south from the Lybidska metro station; if in doubt, look for the 'golden arches'.

From Kyiv, buses go to Odesa (36-57hry, 10 hours, 10 daily), Simferopol (100hry, 16 hours, four daily), Lviv (45hry, 10 hours, seven daily), Kamyanets-Podilsky (36hry, 12 hours, three daily), Ivano-Frankivsk (30hry, nine hours, four daily) and Chernivtsi (44hry, 10 hours, one daily).

Train

The modern **Kyiv Train Station** (Map pp832-3; ☎ 23 11 11; www.uz.gov.ua, not in English) is located right next to the Vokzalna metro station; it's easy to navigate because of the English-language signs. You'll need your passport for purchase (windows No 40 and 41 are for foreigners and international trains). The **Train Ticket Office** (Map pp832-3; ☎ 050; bulvar Tarasa Shevchenka 38/40; Ⓨ 8am-8pm), next to the Hotel Express, is less hectic for advance ticket purchase.

Options include second (*kupeyny*) class or the cheaper *platskartny* compartments. For more information see p866.

Train destinations from Kyiv include services to Chop, near Uzhhorod, (*kupeyny/platskartny* 56/37hry, 19 hours, four daily), Ivano-Frankivsk (51/29hry 19 hours, one to two daily), Kamyanets-Podilsky (31/21hry, 11 hours, one daily), Lviv (36/32hry, 11 hours, five to six daily), Sevastopol (52/39hry, 17 hours, two daily) and Simferopol (48/30hry, 17 hours, one to two daily).

GETTING AROUND
To/From the Airport

Every 30 minutes from 5am to 11pm, **Polit** (☎ 296 73 67) buses run to and from the Boryspil International Airport (10hry, 45 to 60 minutes). They leave from a stop beside the LukOil petrol station on prospekt Peremohi. A taxi will set you back about 100hry.

To Zhulyany Airport, take trolleybus No 9 (40 minutes) from ploshcha Peremohi. Buses to town leave from the front of the airport.

Public Transport

Crowded buses, trams and trolleybuses shuttle around Kyiv between 5.30am and midnight every day. Tickets (50 kopeks) are available at street kiosks or directly from the driver or conductor. Many routes are also serviced by *marshrutkas*.

The metro is the quickest and most direct form of public transport, so you'll spend less time standing with your face under someone else's armpit. However, stations are poorly marked in any language, so keep a metro map handy.

Taxi

The uncommon yellow **taxis** (☎ 058) with chequered black-and-white stripes down their sides have meters and charge about 1hry per kilometre. Otherwise, flag down an unofficial taxi or private car on the street, but don't pay more than 10hry for a short trip within the city centre.

WESTERN UKRAINE

There's no place more Ukrainian than Western Ukraine, the hot bed of the country's nationalist movement. Although Russian (and sometimes even Polish and English) is understood, most people here prefer to speak Ukrainian, and you'll find more monuments and references to nationalists here than anywhere else in the country.

Under Polish and Habsburg rule, Western Ukraine was allowed more liberty than the rest of the country, which came under Russian rule earlier on. Furthermore, it eluded being pinned under the Soviet iron thumb until WWII, which surprisingly left much of the region intact, including many elaborate historic buildings. As a result of all of these things, Western Ukraine in many ways feels like a nation of its own.

See Don't Let This Happen to You (p867) before you take any train trip between Western Ukraine and Odesa.

LVIV ЛЬВІВ

☎ 0322 / pop 685,800

Lviv (Lvov in Russian), the largest city in Western Ukraine, is a gem. Because it escaped bombing during WWII, the city is packed with original defensive walls, towers, churches and spires dating from as far back as the 14th century. The Old Town, which was included on Unesco's World Heritage List in 1998, is easily one of the major highlights of a visit to Ukraine.

Information

Bank Nadra (☎ 97 11 56; vulitsa Kopernika 4; ☒ 9.30am-1pm & 2-5.30pm Mon-Fri, 10am-3pm Sat)

Internet Klub (☎ 72 27 38; vulitsa Dudaeva 12; per hr 4hry; ☒ 24hr) Has about a dozen computers with a relatively speedy connection, as well as cheap international calls.

Khuru Books (☎ 72 25 50; ploshcha Mitskevycha; ☒ 10am-6pm Mon-Fri, 10am-3pm Sat) Weirdly compartmentalised, with separate sections having separate entrances. At least one section has local maps and guides; another section has some novels in English.

Main post office (☎ 065; vulitsa Slovatskoho; ☒ 9am-5pm Mon-Fri, 8am-2pm Sat)

Tourist Information Centre (☎ 97 57 67; www .tourism.lviv.ua; vulitsa Pidvalna 3; ☒ 10am-1pm & 2-6pm Mon-Fri) Free maps and brochures and English-speaking staff can make recommendations, answer your questions and arrange city tours or day trips.

Sights

In addition to doing the walking tour (p841) and checking out some museums, make a point to visit the **Lychakiv Cemetery** (vulitsa Mechinikova; admission 3hry; ☒ 9am-5pm Mon-Fri), and bring a camera – it's one of the loveliest cemeteries in Eastern Europe. If you get on Tram No 7 at the stop on vulitsa Pidvalna, it arrives right in front of the cemetery five stops later (if you get confused, ask for the *klad*-bee-sheh). Ivan Franko (p829 and above) is buried here.

There are loads of museums in town, the **National Museum** (☎ 74 22 80; prospekt Svabody 20; admission 11hry; ☒ 10am-6pm Sat-Thu) features 15th- to 19th-century icons and works by Ukrainian artists.

UKRAINIAN FREEDOM FIGHTERS

Following are some Ukrainians who have died fighting for Ukrainian freedom.

- **Taras Shevchenko** (1814-61) – born a serf, he found a benefactor who took him to St Petersburg, where he was educated in the arts. He became a master painter and wonderful Ukrainian-language poet. His popularity, nationalism and anti-tsarism turned out to be a bad combination, and he was shipped off to Siberia for 10 years, leading to a premature death.

- **Ivan Franko** (1857-1916) – a talented and extraordinarily prolific writer (poems, stories, plays, social commentary...). He was arrested in 1877, 1880 and 1889 for various antiestablishment charges, but managed to die a normal death in 1916. He is buried in Lviv's Lychakiv Cemetery (left).

- **Stepan Bandera** (1909-59) – controversial leader of the Organisation of Ukrainian Nationalism. He was assassinated in Munich by a KGB agent, who later came clean about the whole thing when trying to defect before the construction of the Berlin Wall – he also admitted that his reward for the assassination was a new camera. Bandera's name inspires much emotion: he was a charismatic leader whose name was muddied by accusations of complicity with Nazi Germany. To this day, people from Western Ukraine are sometimes snidely referred to as 'Banderistas.'

Journalist Georgy Gongadze's (p827) murder is technically unsolved, but he may well have died because of his efforts in the fight of a corruption-free Ukraine.

There are two branches of the **Museum of Ethnography & Historic Artefacts** (☎ 72 70 12; ploshcha Rynok 10 & prospekt Svabody 15; admission 2hry; ☒ 10am-5.30pm Wed-Sun). Both buildings hold exhibits on farm culture and village life. English-language books are available here

The **Lviv History Museum** (☎ 72 06 71; ploshcha Rynok 4/6 & 24; admission per Bldg 1hry; ☒ 10am-5pm Thu-Tue) contains over 250,000 items about the history of Lviv and Western Ukraine.

UKRAINE

LVIV

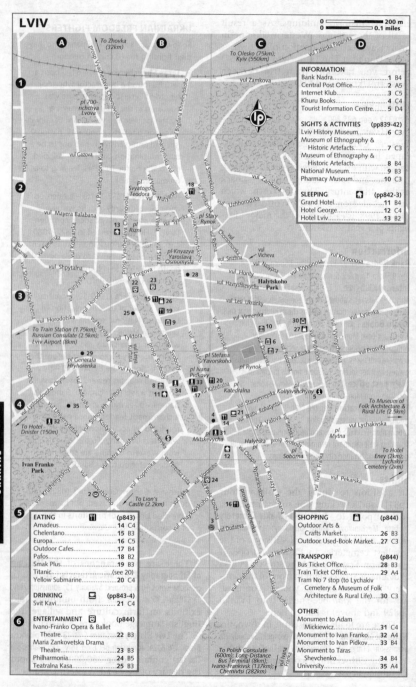

0 — 200 m
0 — 0.1 miles

INFORMATION
Bank Nadra........................1 B4
Central Post Office.............2 A5
Internet Klub...................3 C5
Khuru Books.....................4 C4
Tourist Information Centre......5 D4

SIGHTS & ACTIVITIES (pp839-42)
Lviv History Museum.............6 C3
Museum of Ethnography &
  Historic Artefacts............7 C3
Museum of Ethnography &
  Historic Artefacts............8 B4
National Museum.................9 B3
Pharmacy Museum................10 C3

SLEEPING (pp842-3)
Grand Hotel....................11 B4
Hotel George...................12 C4
Hotel Lviv.....................13 B2

EATING (p843)
Amadeus........................14 C4
Chelentano.....................15 B3
Europa.........................16 C5
Outdoor Cafes..................17 B4
Pafos..........................18 B2
Smak Plus......................19 B3
Titanic.................(see 20)
Yellow Submarine...............20 C4

DRINKING (pp843-4)
Svit Kavi......................21 C4

ENTERTAINMENT (p844)
Ivano-Franko Opera & Ballet
  Theatre......................22 B3
Maria Zankovetska Drama
  Theatre......................23 B3
Philharmonia...................24 B5
Teatralna Kasa.................25 B3

SHOPPING (p844)
Outdoor Arts &
  Crafts Market................26 B3
Outdoor Used-Book Market.......27 C3

TRANSPORT (p844)
Bus Ticket Office..............28 B3
Train Ticket Office............29 A4
Tram No 7 stop (to Lychakiv
  Cemetery & Museum of Folk
  Architecture & Rural Life)...30 C3

OTHER
Monument to Adam
  Mickiewicz...................31 C4
Monument to Ivan Franko........32 A4
Monument to Ivan Pidkov........33 B4
Monument to Taras
  Shevchenko...................34 B4
University.....................35 A4

UKRAINE

The **Pharmacy Museum** (☎ 72 20 41; vulitsa Drukarska 2; admission 1hry; 🕑 10am-5pm Mon-Fri & 10am-4pm Sat & Sun) is in the back of a functioning pharmacy (pay the pharmacists to open it up for you, and walk into a world of containers, drawers and other gadgets for herbs and tinctures and salves). Ask for a sample of 'iron wine'.

The **Museum of Folk Architecture & Rural Life** (☎ 71 80 17; vulitsa Chernecha Hora 1; adult/child 1.50/0.75hry; 🕑 11am-5pm Tue-Sun) is a bit of a trek from the centre but is well worth the journey. You can spend several hours wandering around the large park here, which holds over 100 old wooden homes and churches. To get here, take Tram No 7 from the stop on vulitsa Pidvalna, get off four stops later, cross the street you're on, walk ahead in the direction the tram was going for about 100m, then turn left on vulitsa Krupyrska (Крупярьска), where you'll see a wooden sign for the museum. Walk up for about 500m, then go up a short flight of stairs. Turn right and follow the road to the museum, on the left.

Walking Tour

There are more religious buildings in Lviv than you could possibly believe until you see it for yourself, and since the city has changed hands so many times over the years, the influences in architecture are extremely diverse.

The tour, of around 5km, starts at ploshcha Rynok (Market Square), which was the hub of political and commercial life during the Middle Ages. The town hall, which takes up the majority of space in the square, was originally built in the 14th century, but it was rebuilt several times since then, most recently in 1851. From the southwest corner of the square, walk south to ploshcha Katedralna, where you can't miss the **Roman Catholic Cathedral** (1). It took more than 100 years to build it (1370–1480) and therefore a few different styles (Gothic, Renaissance, baroque) are apparent. At the southeastern corner of the cathedral is the 1617 **Boyim Chapel** (2), the burial chapel of a wealthy Hungarian merchant family. Its west entrance façade is covered in magnificent carvings. Two family portraits are on the exterior eastern wall.

Head back toward ploshcha Rynok, and go a block north of it on vulitsa Krakivska,

turning right on vulitsa Virmenska, and on the left you'll see the 1363 **Armenian Cathedral** (3). Head back to vulitsa Krakivska and continue a bit north to the corner of vulitsa Krakivska and vulitsa Lesi Ukrainky, where you'll find the late-17th-century, twin-bell towered **Transfiguration Church** (4); the first church in the city to revert to Ukrainian Catholic after independence. Turn east onto vulitsa Lesi Ukrainky and walk for about 200m, then turn right on vulitsa Drukarska. Turn left onto vulitsa Virnenska, then right onto vulitsa Fedorova. Almost immediately on your left is a square, where you'll see the **Dominican Church & Monastery** (5), distinguished by its large dome and its rococo, baroque and classical features. Just

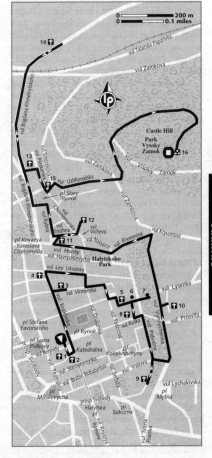

a bit further east is the arched façade of the **Royal Arsenal (6)**. Built between 1639 and 1646, it once held weapons to be used in wars against the Turks; it now holds the city's archives. Cross vulitsa Pidvalna and head toward the 16th-century **Gunpowder Tower (7)**. In wartime, weapons were stored inside; in peacetime, it was filled with grain and other goods. Over the last four centuries the bottom 2m of the tower have slowly become covered in soil.

Head back across vulitsa Pidvalna, turning south at the Royal Arsenal, to one of the most memorable moments of the tour. To your right, you'll find the **Assumption Church & Three Saints Chapel (8)**. The church (1591–1629) is easily distinguished by the 65m-high, triple-tiered Kornyakt Bell Tower (1572–78). The Three Saints Chapel (1578–91) is nestled beneath the tower and built into the north side of the church, in a wonderful little courtyard. Together, the two structures are considered to be the historic centre of the city.

Continue south on vulitsa Pidvalna for about 200m to the 17th-century **Bernadine Church & Monastery (9)**. Go back the way you came on vulitsa Pidvalna, turning right on vulitsa Valova and then left on vulitsa Vynnychenka. Head north about 200m to the 1644 **St Mary Carmelite Monastery (10)**. Some fragments of its original defensive walls can still be seen. Walk back to vulitsa Vynnychenka, and continue north about 300m to vulitsa Kryvonosa, where you'll turn left. Continue west on this street, which turns into vulitsa Honty, for about 400m. On your right, up a small set of steps, is the tiny 18th-century stone church, the **Church of Maria Snizhna (11)**. After the church, turn right onto vulitsa Snizhna, pass vulitsa Rybna, and on your left, through a cast-iron gate, is the **Nunnery of the Benedictines (12)**. Note the detailed, crown-like stone carving at the top of the tower. Return to the corner of vulitsa Rybna and head north on that street, through ploshcha Stary Rynok (Old Market Square), then up vulitsa Bohdana Khmelnytskoho to the green-domed **St Nicholas Church (13)**. Dating from the 13th century and remodelled in the 16th century, its Old Rus Quarter is an excellent example of early Byzantine architecture.

Continue north, and when you reach the railroad tracks go through the underground passageway then continue north for about 100m to the **Church of Good Friday (14)**. It was originally built in the 13th century, but was reconstructed in the mid-17th century. If you can get inside, there is a beautiful 17th-century iconostasis.

Go back the way you came, under the tracks. Make a left just past St Nicholas Church, then a right onto vulitsa Pylnykarska. When you get to ploshcha Stary Rynok, make a left, and you'll see the humble little brick-and-stone church of **St John the Baptist (15)**, originally built in 1260.

Take vulitsa Uzhhorodska, the road just south of the church, for about 200m, cross vulitsa Zamkova and then veer left up a road that leads to the **High Castle (16)**. At the top of the hill (the wind can be strong), you'll have an all-inclusive view of what you've seen up close – although you may have to squint through some trees.

Now's a perfect time to take a break over a cup of coffee and a pastry in one of Lviv's popular cafés (opposite).

Festivals & Events

Lviv's city celebrations are at the first weekend of May. Also in May, Lviv holds **Virtuozi**, an international music festival. In July, Lviv holds the annual **Halba Beer Festival**; contact the Tourist Information Centre for details.

Sleeping

Hotel Lviv (☎ 72 86 51; prospekt Vyacheslava Chornovola 7; s 100-120hry, d 140-240hry, s with shared bathroom 40hry, d with shared bathroom 80hry) Hotel Lviv does the job for *kopek*-pinchers, but the building is ugly and the staff is nonexistent. It's only worthwhile if your budget won't stretch to the George.

Hotel George (☎ 72 59 52; www.georgehotel.ukrbiz.net; ploshcha Mitskevycha 1; s 283-411hry, d 316-415hry, s with shared bathroom 105-121hry, d with shared bathroom 109-124hry) Housed in an elegant, if worn, 100-year-old building, the George offers good value for the rooms with shared bathroom (which are kept pretty clean). Breakfast is 20hry more and includes a hot dish. Rooms are huge and staff are friendly, professional and speak some English.

Lion's Castle (Zamok Leva; ☎ 35 11 00; www.lionscastle.com; vulitsa Hlinki 7; d incl breakfast US$40-100; P) Housed in a pretty, castle-like stone building in a leafy suburb a 2.5km walk southwest of the centre. Management claims to have had guests the likes of Gorbachev. The cheaper rooms in the basement have showers but share a communal toilet; dearer rooms feature elegant bathrooms.

Hotel Dnister (☎ 97 43 17; www.dnister.lviv.ua; vulitsa Mateika 6; d incl breakfast 270-610hry, ste incl breakfast 820hry; P ✗ ⌨) The Dnister is a totally decent deal for a higher-end hotel, especially if you're travelling in twos and can split the cost. The service is very good (staff speak English), and the facilities are quite modern. Its location is the best part – just southeast of the centre and right near the pretty Ivan Franko Park and the university, which is gorgeous. The suites and highest priced doubles have air-conditioning and the breakfast has been raved about.

Hotel Eney (☎ 76 87 99; www.eney.lviv.ua; vulitsa Shimzeriv 2; d €70-80, ste €90-120, apt €190; P ✗) Little Eney is a private, villa-style place just by the Lychakiv Cemetery and a pleasant 30-minute walk to the centre (although tram No 7 will take you there as well). It's very suitable for business groups or parties who want some privacy and special attention, but it could be good for a romantic couple, too. Rooms are simple and tidy, in a Scandinavian way. On the premises are a sauna, billiards, a bar, restaurant, security and English-speaking staff.

Grand Hotel (☎ 72 49 42; www.ghgroup.com.ua; prospekt Svabody 13; s 530-590hry, d 670-835hry, ste 840-1540hry; P ✗ ⌨) It's award-winning and posh, but seems overpriced when you see the teeny rooms and meet the rather overproud staff. Still, all the niceties (champagne in the room, satellite TV, fancy restaurant, piano bar, gym access) are included. Like the George, the location is as central as it gets, and the interior of the 1892 building is truly lush with a gorgeous wooden staircase, a sturdy Western-style lift, shiny marble floors and interesting local art on the walls.

Eating

In addition to these listings, there are several good outdoor cafés on the east side of prospekt Svabody – although they are sort of tourist magnets and can be a little overpriced.

Smak Plus (☎ 72 89 50; prospekt Svabody 22; mains 1-7hry; ☸ 10am-11.30pm) At Smak, you'll find simple Ukrainian food in a fast-food, cafeteria-style setting, with salads, meats, beer and booze.

Chelentano (☎ 74 11 35; prospekt Svabody 24; mains 1-8hry; ☸ 10am-11pm) This popular pizza chain almost has the pizza-pub thing down pat. A good selection of salads and pastas are available too.

Pafos (☎ 97 15 67; vulitsa Pilnikarska 5; mains 3-20hry; ☸ 11am-11pm) It's not often you find a Cypriot restaurant – here's your chance. It's small, with an outdoor terrace right near St Nicholas and St John the Baptist Churches.

Titanic (☎ 97 55 21; vulitsa Teatralna 6; mains 3-25hry; ☸ 11am-11pm) 'Once…more…you open the door' – in several different variations – can be heard here, along with a good mix of decent Russian, Ukrainian and Belarusian rock. Staff are 'decked' out in sailor gear and the décor of the bar-like upstairs has a kitschy maritime bent. Downstairs is slightly less casual and has a more interesting, and slightly more expensive, menu (schnitzel, steaks) than the upstairs with its *pelmeni* (dumplings), chicken, salads.

Yellow Submarine (☎ 97 55 21; vulitsa Teatralna 4; mains 8-22hry; ☸ 11am-11pm) Beatlemaniacs look no further. Fab Four memorabilia abounds at this cosy little restaurant, which focuses on fondue but also has steaks and typical Ukrainian dishes. There are two beers on tap, a mural of the sub itself, and a wall that is designed to look like part of a sub.

Europa (☎ 72 58 62; prospekt Shevchenka 14; mains 12-25hry; ☸ 8am-11pm Mon-Fri, 10am-11pm Sat & Sun) Small, cosy and relatively quiet, Europa is a good place for a filling meal. Only the TV is a drawback to the ambience. The Ukrainian *borshch* is tasty and the menu has some imaginative offerings such as halibut with shrimp in champagne sauce.

Amadeus (☎ 97 80 22; ploshcha Katedralna 7; mains 30-177hry; ☸ 11am-11pm) This small, bistro-like restaurant is perfect for romance, with meals like risotto or fondue for two. There's no TV; the music is lilting and at a mild volume. The housemade espresso is perfect for a postmeal pick-up.

Drinking

Lviv is known for and proud of its many cafés, where they serve actual coffee (not the Nescafé served in lieu of the real stuff in most former Soviet Union countries). The old part of town has numerous such cafés – you can literally follow your nose to them. One option is crowded little **Svit Kavi** (vulitsa

Staroyevreyska; ⊙ 9am-10pm), which is tucked behind the Roman Catholic Cathedral.

There are plenty of little bars to discover in town too, and most restaurants have good beer on tap. The numerous summertime sidewalk cafés along the east side of prospekt Svabody are a great place to sit under an umbrella and sip on a Ukrainian tap beer.

Entertainment

For a perfect evening, enjoy a drink at one of the cafés and a performance at the beautiful **Ivano-Franko Opera & Ballet Theatre** (☎ 72 85 62; prospekt Svobody 28), the **Philharmonia** (☎ 74 10 86; vulitsa Chaykovskoho 7). If you speak Ukrainian, see a play at the well-respected **Maria Zankovetska Drama Theatre** (☎ 72 07 62; vulitsa Lesi Ukrainky 1).

Tickets to any performance are affordable (5hry to 100hry) and are sold onsite or at the **teatralna kasa** (prospekt Svobody 37).

Shopping

Souvenirs of all sorts – as well as interesting odds and ends – are sold at the **Outdoor Arts & Crafts Market** (⊙ morning-sunset) off of prospekt Svabody. The Museum of Ethnography & Historic Artefacts (p839) has good-quality crafts for sale. If you're into old books, there's a quirky outdoor used-book market by the Royal Arsenal.

Getting There & Away

AIR

The **Lviv airport** (☎ 69 21 12) is at the end of vulitsa Lyubinska, which veers left off the southwest-heading vulitsa Horodotska. It's about 8km from the main part of town.

BUS

Lviv has eight bus terminals, but only one is of use to most travellers – the **long-distance bus terminal** (☎ 63 24 73; vulitsa Stryiska 189), about 8km south of the city centre. From the same terminal, privately run **Autolux** (www.autolux.com.ua) also operates nice, modern buses regularly to Kyiv and other cities; see the website for details.

Advance tickets for public buses to Ivano-Frankivsk (11hry, three hours, hourly) and Kyiv (52hry, nine hours, three daily), as well as to Riga, for Brest, Warsaw and Prague (see p865), are sold at the **bus ticket office** (vulitsa Teatralna 26; ⊙ 9am-2pm & 3-6pm); it's

easy to walk past the place, which is also a CD shop – look for the каса sign.

TRAIN

The **train station** (☎ 35 33 60; ploshcha Dvirtseva) is 1.75km west of the city centre. Advance tickets are more easily obtained from the less irritated staff at the **train ticket office** (☎ 748 20 68; vulitsa Hnatyuka 20; ⊙ 8am-8pm Mon-Fri, 8am-6pm Sat & Sun); have your passport (or a copy of it) ready.

From Lviv, there are several daily trains to Kyiv (kupeyny/platskartny 53/32hry, 10 hours) and daily trains to Odesa (55/35hry, 12 hours) and Simferopol (75/50hry, 25 hours), as well as three platskartny-only trains daily to Ivano-Frankivsk (25hry, 2½ hours).

Getting Around

Trams and trolleybuses cost 45 kopeks per ride. Buy tickets onboard.

The airport is accessible by trolleybus No 9 from the university building on vulitsa Universytetska. Tram No 1 or 9, or marshrutka No 66, 67 or 68 (80 kopeks) link the train station with prospekt Svobody and ploshcha Rynok, while trolleybus No 5 connects ploshcha Rynok with the long-distance bus terminal.

UZHHOROD УЖГОРОД

☎ 03122 (5-digit Nos), 0312 (6-digit Nos) / pop 110,000

This pretty little town is the southern gateway to the Ukrainian section of the Carpathian Mountains. It's an ideal staging post for anyone travelling to/from Slovakia or Hungary, but probably too far off the beaten track for other travellers.

Information

Banks, exchange offices and ATMs are easy to find in the central part of town. For Internet access, try **Planeta I-Net** (naberezhnaya Nezalezhnosti 1; per hr 3hry; ⊙ 24hr), which is run by a bunch of rowdy boys. The connection is slow, and you don't get your change back if you're online for less time than you planned.

Sights

The 15th-century **Uzhhorod Castle** (vulitsa Kapitulna; adult/child 3hry/50 kopeks, grounds only 1hry; ⊙ 9am-5pm Tue-Sun) is on an obvious hill about 400m northeast of the main square.

It features the Art Gallery & Museum of Local Lore. Across the way from the castle is the enchanting, open-air **Museum of Folk Architecture & Rural Life** (adult/child 2hry/50 kopeks; 🕙 10am-5pm Wed-Mon).

Downhill from the castle is the twin-towered, 1640 **cathedral** (vulitsa Kapitulna) and the **Art Museum** (ploshcha Zhupanatska 3; adult/child 3hry/50 kopeks; 🕙 10am-5pm Tue-Sun), which is about 500m northwest of the main square.

For a 50hry return-trip taxi ride, you can visit the nearby **Nivitsky Zamok** (Bride-to-Be Castle), the ruins of an old castle where villagers used to hide women during enemy attacks. Views from the castle are beautiful.

Sleeping & Eating

Hotel Svitanok (☎ 34 309; fax 35 268; vulitsa Koshytska 30; s/d with shared bathroom 41/82hry) Simple, dorm-style rooms here have balconies and pleasant views of a stream and hillside. Staff are friendly and helpful and there's an attached restaurant. Further up the hill, in the area known as 'Millionnaire's Row', you'll see a couple of elite-only hotels and the newly, dubiously built homes of the newly, dubiously built rich, who drive their BMWs like maniacs – be careful when walking.

Hotel Zakarpatye (☎ 97 510; ploshcha 50-Letya SSSR 5; s/d/ste 90/120/205; 🅿 🖳) It's another Soviet monstrosity – but the rooms are funky in a fun, 60s way and the hallways are, oddly enough, pleasantly fragrant. Many rooms have a balcony and some sport some cool retro floor lamps. Staff are congenial and speak some English. However, the location isn't so easy on the eyes.

Kaktus Kafe (☎ 32 515; vulitsa Korzo 7; 🕙 10am-midnight) Probably the most popular hangout in town, this smoky, noisy joint is full of beer and coffee drinkers. The theme is decidedly Wild West.

Delfin (☎ 3 50 93; Kyivskaya naberezhnaya 2; mains 15-60hry, 🕙 11am-11pm) Locals consider this one of the better restaurants in town. European and Ukrainian dishes are served.

Getting There & Away
BUS

Twice-daily buses go from the **bus terminal** (prospekt Svobody) to Chernivtsi (31hry, 10 to 12 hours), Ivano-Frankivsk (23hry, 10 hours) and Lviv (20hry, four hours). You can also get very cheap, uncomfortable buses to Slovakia and Hungary here (see p865).

TRAIN

The Uzhhorod train station was under construction at the time of research, so although you can take a train to the city, you don't stop at an actual station. You hop down to the ground and hobble across the rocks and dirt and tracks to the makeshift interim station building, where there are no services and little information. Luckily, the bus terminal is only about 200m away, and there you'll find left-luggage and transport (taxis, buses and *marshrutkas*) into town. All departures (and train ticket purchases) are currently being done in Chop, so even if you arrive in Uzhhorod, to leave you'll first have to go to Chop, which is luckily very easy. Every 15 minutes or so from 7am to 10pm, a *marshrutka* to Chop leaves from in front of the bus terminal (2hry, 45 minutes).

Once a day, trains from Chop go to Chernivtsi (*kupeyny/platskartny* 29/20hry, 14 hours), Ivano-Frankivsk (25/17hry, 11 hours) and Simferopol (85hry, 26 hours, *kupe* only). Thrice-daily trains go to Kyiv (60/40hry, 19 hours) and Lviv (25/16hry, eight hours).

Call ☎ 051 for a taxi. A taxi ride within Uzhhorod will set you back 5 or 6 hry.

IVANO-FRANKIVSK ІВАНО-ФРАНКІВСЬК
☎ 03422 (5-digit Nos), 0342 (6-digit Nos) / pop 215,000

Named for nationalistic writer Ivan Franko, the city of Ivano-Frankivsk is the traditional cultural and economic capital of the Carpathian region. It boasts numerous parks, squares and churches, and is one of the more appealing cities in Western Ukraine. Ivano-Frankivsk has fewer historic attractions than Lviv, but reconstruction has been booming and the city is enthusiastically Westernising.

Information

Currency exchanges, ATMs, and Western Unions are common at banks and are easily found along the pedestrian zone of vulitsa Nezalezhnosti.

Central post office (☎ 23 10 41; vulitsa Sichovych Striltsiv 13A) The telephone office is across the square, next to the Internet Centre.

Bukinist (☎ 2 38 28; vulitsa Nezalezhnosti 19; 🕙 10am-6pm Mon-Fri & 10am-2pm Sat) Friendly staff and local maps. There are two bookstores under the white columns here; Bukinist is the smaller one, with the far-right corner entrance.

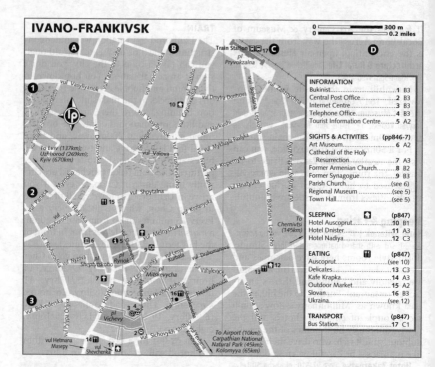

IVANO-FRANKIVSK

0 — 300 m
0 — 0.2 miles

INFORMATION
Bukinist	1 B3
Central Post Office	2 B3
Internet Centre	3 B3
Telephone Office	4 B3
Tourist Information Centre	5 A2

SIGHTS & ACTIVITIES (pp846-7)
Art Museum	6 A2
Cathedral of the Holy Resurrection	7 A3
Former Armenian Church	8 B2
Former Synagogue	9 B3
Parish Church	(see 6)
Regional Museum	(see 5)
Town Hall	(see 5)

SLEEPING (p847)
Hotel Auscoprut	10 B1
Hotel Dnister	11 A3
Hotel Nadiya	12 C3

EATING (p847)
Auscoprut	(see 10)
Delicates	13 C3
Kafe Krapka	14 A3
Outdoor Market	15 A2
Slovan	16 B3
Ukraina	(see 12)

TRANSPORT (p847)
Bus Station	17 C1

Internet Centre (☎ 55 25 80; vulitsa Nezalezhnosti 5; per hr 4-5hry; ☼ 24hr)

Nadia Tours (☎ 53 70 42; nadia@utel.net.ua; vulitsa Nezalezhnosti 40) In Hotel Nadiya; does Carpathian tours.

Tourist Information Centre (ploshcha Rynok 4; ☼ 10am-6pm Mon-Fri) In the Town Hall; lots of pamphlets but most are about other cities in the region. It's still new though and will probably be improving as the city continues renovate.

Sights
MUSEUMS

Don't miss the **Art Museum** (☎ 3 00 39; ploshcha Sheptytsky 8; adult/child 2hry/50 kopeks; ☼ 10am-6pm Wed-Sun). Housed in the 1672–1703 Parish Church (aka the Church of the Blessed Virgin Mary), this peaceful museum displays fascinating 16th- to 18th-century icons, sculptures, antiquarian books and etchings, many with English-language display cards. The focus is on religious art, and the church's interior is worth a visit in itself. Piano concerts are sometimes held here.

Ploshcha Rynok is dominated by the **Town Hall** (built in 1695 but totally redone in 1929–32 in a boring constructivist style with some

Art Deco elements), which houses the two-storey **Regional Museum** (☎ 2 23 26; ploshcha Rynok 4A; adult/child 60/40 kopeks; ☼ 10am-5pm Tue-Sun), covering a broad range of exhibits. The 1st floor is the most interesting and focuses on local archaeology. (Also look for the beautiful old faded *pysanky*). The 2nd floor has some tacky temporary exhibits but is worth the stairs for the mysterious futuristic machine and really old manual-start (crank-it-up!) car. There's also a depressing natural history exhibit with some sad-looking taxidermy victims and a little 19th-century furniture.

CHURCHES

Diagonal from the Art Museum/Parish Church is the active baroque **Cathedral of the Holy Resurrection** (ploshcha Sheptytsky 22), a Ukrainian Greek Catholic church. If you happen to be around during Catholic Easter, you'll probably see an orange-neon Христос Воскрес! (Christ has Risen!) sign inside – which looks pretty out of place with the beautiful iconography that surrounds it. Built from 1753 to 1763, the church was restored in 1885, 1995 and 2004.

East of the square is the 1742–62 **former Armenian Church** (vulitsa Virmenska 6) with its attractive baroque façade and rounded bell towers.

Sleeping

Hotel Dnister (☎ 2 35 33; vulitsa Sichovykh Striltsiv 12; d 120hry, s/d with shared bathroom 53/66hry) Dnister has decent staff but depressing rooms, and the shared bathrooms could use a little scrubbing. There is no hot water at night, and even when there is hot water you'll have to let it run for about 10 minutes before it starts to warm up.

Hotel Nadiya (☎ 5 37 75; www.nadia.if.ua; vulitsa Nezalezhnosti 40; s 100hry, d 170-330hry, ste 210-350hry) The grand white marble lobby might make you think the rooms cost a fortune here, but it's not the case. Formerly a more Soviet-style place called Hotel Ukraina, Nadiya is getting a makeover from the ground up – but so far only the ground really shows it. The rooms are relatively nice and good value but don't match the expectations the lobby gives. The cheapest rooms are on par with the Dnister's but have a private bathroom. Prices may rise as remodelling continues. Nadia Tours here arranges tours of the Carpathians.

Hotel Auscoprut (☎ 2 34 01; auscoprut@inf.ukrpack .net; vulitsa Gryunvaldska 7/9; s 160-320hry, d 220-400hry, ste 450-550hry; P ⊠) Auscoprut is an Austrian–Ukrainian joint venture housed in a small beautiful 1912 baroque building with stained glass. Staff are professional and speak English, and the lift is modern, although the stairs are a prettier way to get up and down. Suites have air-conditioning and all prices include a buffet breakfast in the hotel restaurant, which has wonderful food (see below).

Eating

In addition to what's listed here, there are several pizzerias and cafés along the pedestrian zone of vulitsa Nezalezhnosti.

Kafe Krapka (☎ 2 54 09; vulitsa Sichovykh Striltsiv 10; mains 5-13hry; ⊗ 11am-11pm) Sitting quietly around the corner from the Hotel Dnister, popular Krapka is interesting in that it offers a small nonsmoking section. Staff work pretty hard and the food is very decent – but steer clear of the chicken Kiev, which is foul (smothered in mayo and ketchup).

Slovan (☎ 2 25 94; vulitsa Shashevycha 4; mains 8-29hry; ⊗ 11am-midnight) With yummy pizzas and bold dishes such as Tijuana chicken (11.50hry) and stewed rabbit in wine sauce (8hry), Slovan is the clear favourite in town. Save room for the locally famous sundaes (4hry to 8hry). Staff are more eager to please than most. The décor borders on tasteful and in spring and summer there's outdoor seating in a pedestrian area – great for people-watching.

Auscoprut (☎ 2 34 01; vulitsa Gryunvaldska 7/9; mains 4-14hry; ⊗ 8am-11pm) Here's a hotel restaurant that deserves a visit even if you're not a staying at the Auscoprut. Try the *satsivi* (a delicious Georgian dish of chicken breast in a creamy nut sauce; 8hry).

Ukraina (☎ 5 37 75; vulitsa Nezalezhnosti 40; mains 4-15hry; ⊗ 7am-midnight) This somewhat formal restaurant attached to the Hotel Nadiya has a menu with listings in English and German and a small but interesting choice of mains, such as pork with dried apricots and bananas (18.50hry).

The outdoor market in the huge square between vulitsas Halytska and Shpytalna is a good place for fresh fruit to snack on.

Getting There & Away

From the **airport** (☎ 59 83 48), 10km south of the city centre, there are daily flights to Kyiv (260hry) from June to October. Bus Nos 21, 24 and 65 (60 kopecks, 30 minutes) leave every 15 minutes from the train station and go to the airport.

The train station and bus station are conveniently right next to each other, on ploshcha Privozksalna.

Buses from Ivano-Frankivsk go to Chernivtsi (12hry, 3½ hours, thrice daily), Kyiv (37hry to 44hry, 12 hours, twice daily), Lviv (12hry, 3½ hours, 12 daily) and Uzhhorod (24hry, 9 hours, twice daily). On Sundays, there are buses to Odesa (59hry, 16 hours).

Trains to Chernivtsi (*kupeyny/platskartny* 18/12hry, 3½ hours, two daily) leave superearly in the morning. There are daily trains to Kyiv (42/28hry, 14 hours) and Simferopol (80hry, 33 hours, *kupe* only) and twice-daily trains to Lviv (20/14hry, 3½ to seven hours). On odd dates, there are daily trains to Odesa (43/28hry, 21 hours) and Uzhhorod (24/16hry, 11 hours).

CARPATHIAN NATIONAL NATURAL PARK

About 45km south of Ivano-Frankivsk lies Carpathian National Natural Park (CNNP),

UKRAINE

Ukraine's largest (503 sq km). The park protects wolves, brown bears, lynx, bison and deer. Hutsuls, a people descended from a nomadic horde, still live in the park, and the country's highest peak, Mt Hoverla (2062m), is here as well.

Visits to the park can be arranged in Ivano-Frankivsk and other towns in Western Ukraine, but direct access is most easily obtained from the towns of Yaremcha and Rakhiv.

The primary downhill skiing area is in Yablunitsiya, a pretty village 30km south of Yaremcha. Equipment can be hired in Yaremcha and Rakhiv. Downhill and cross-country skiing is also possible around Bogdan (1500m), 20km east of Rakhiv.

During summer the park is transformed into a busy hiking area. Some of the trails are marked, but most are impossible to follow without the help of a local guide. The few available hiking maps are also not 100% accurate and paradoxically they actually feature few hiking trails.

The useful **CNNP office** (☎ 03434-22 817; cnpp@jar.if.ua; vulitsa Stussa 6) in Yaremcha can arrange guides for around 100hry per day. The CNNP office also provides information and maps, organises tours and arranges accommodation in private homes (about 25hry per person).

Wild camping is allowed in the park. Contact the CNNP office about the hiking cabins that are around the park, but bring your own food and bedding. Also, **Green Rural Tourism** (www.tourism-carpathian.com.ua) arranges homestays and B&Bs near the park, and **Lviv Ecotour** (www.lvivecotour.com) specialises in activity-oriented trips to the Carpathians.

Exploring the park by public transport can be very time-consuming so unless you have a car, organise a tour with Hotel Auscoprut or Hotel Nadiya in Ivano-Frankivsk (see p845).

A taxi from Ivano-Frankivsk to Yaremche will cost about 84hry.

CHERNIVTSI ЧЕРНІВЦІ

☎ 03722 (5-digit Nos), 0372 (6-digit Nos) / pop 240,000

In addition to once being part of the Habsburg Empire and also falling within Romania, Chernivtsi was once the chief city of Bucovina (Beech Tree Land), the northernmost part of old Moldavia (now Moldova). The mixed

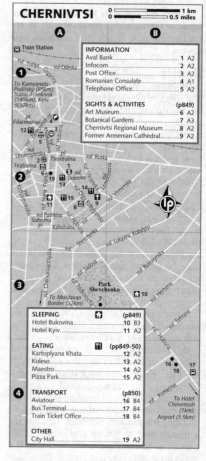

history of this charming, hilly town has resulted in a wide variety of architectural styles, from Byzantine to baroque, along its many cobblestone streets. Before WWII the city had large Jewish, Armenian and German minorities. Today it has a more southern and relaxed feel than many Ukrainian cities.

Information

There are several currency exchanges and ATMs around town.

Aval Bank (vulitsa Olgi Kolbilyanskoi 3; ☒ 8am-7pm Mon-Fri & 10am-6pm Sat) Has a currency exchange, ATM and Western Union.

InfoCom (☎ 55 27 39; vulitsa Universytetska 1; per hr 5-6hry; ☒ 8am-7pm Mon-Fri, 10am-6pm Sat) Behind a cast-iron gate; four slow but sure computers and pleasant staff.

Post office (vulitsa Khudyakova) The telephone office is next door.

Sights

Chernivtsi is not spilling over with attractions; the main thing to do is just walk around and explore it. A stroll along vulitsa Olha Kobylyanska is particularly pleasant, or you can visit Park Kalinina, where there are **botanical gardens**.

The **Chernivtsi Regional Museum** (☎ 25 062; vulitsa Olgy Kobylyanskoyi 28; adult/child 1hry/50 kopeks; ☑ 9am-4.30pm Tue-Sun) focuses on local history: books, photos and some paintings as well. Once you enter from the street, go up the stairs on the right. The **Art Museum** (☎ 26 071; ploshcha Tsentralna 10; adult/child 1hry/50 kopeks; ☑ 9am-4.30pm Tue-Sun) has a solid collection of well-done historic portraits, some moody etchings and very good temporary exhibits of local artists.

The **former Armenian Cathedral** (vulitsa Ukrainska 30; admission free; ☑ 8am-5pm Mon-Sat), built in 1869–75, houses an organ and concert hall. Its design is based on ancient Armenian architecture featuring beautiful masonry detailing.

Sleeping

Hotel Kyiv (☎ 22 483; vulitsa Holovna 46; s with hot water 53hry, d with hot water 90-114hry, s without hot water 40-48hry, d without hot water 80hry) Its location – right in the centre – is the only thing going for it. But its location is also a drawback – it's right on a busy street (bring earplugs). Rooms are typically rundown for a budget hotel in Ukraine, and it's the type of place where a plumber will decide to start banging on the pipes in the next room at 11pm.

Hotel Bukovina (☎ /fax 58 56 25; vulitsa Holovna 141; s 70hry, d 91-106hry, tr 108hry, ste 125-300hry; **P**) New management took this big mustard-yellow bull by the horns and broke in. In front of the hotel is a green garden with gazebos and little huts, as well as a pond with a garden gnome or two. The rooms are a very good deal, and many of them have spacious balconies. There's lots of stained glass and staff is upbeat and cheerful, as is the brightly painted bar (the Pink Rhinoceros). On the ground floor is a Ukrainian folk-themed restaurant, with servers in traditional costume. The director is apparently friends with Alla Pugachova (the Russian pop diva). To get here, take trolleybus

No 3 from the centre, the train station or the bus station.

Hotel Cheremosh (☎ 47 500; fax 41 314; vulitsa Komarova 13A; s 106-186hry, d 134-266hry, ste 342-498hry, s & d with shared bathroom 70hry; **P**) This place is such a haul from the centre that you should stay here only if you are really desperate for a few niceties. The rooms are a bit better than Bukovina's, and there are more facilities, which sort of make up for the distant locale and the huge imposing Sovietness of the exterior (the vast lobby feels like a train terminal). Staff do aim to please and like to give out pamphlets, including one that features a photo of a shirtless man chugging a can of beer in the hotel's hot tub – very appealing. Trolleybus No 6 goes to the centre but there are almost always taxis out front too.

Eating

In addition to what's in this section, keep in mind that all listed hotels have restaurants.

Pizza Park (☎ 274 85; vulitsa Holovna 77; mains 1-6hry; ☑ 10am-2.45pm & 4-10pm) The surly staff and typically strange pizzas (toppings include corn, potatoes, ketchup and mayonnaise) draw in the crowds at this fast-food restaurant. Decent, cheap *pelmeni* and the other Ukrainian food on the menu may be the better bet here.

Kartoplyana Khata (☎ 51 24 00; vulitsa Zankovetskoi 11; mains 3-6hry; ☑ 10am-11pm) The name – which is deceiving – means 'potato hut'. But this is no Ukrainian village restaurant. It's got a Wild West, cowboys-and-Indians décor, southwestern food and Gypsy Kings music. Bold attempts at burritos are actually tasty, if totally inauthentic (plus they serve it in a DIY, fajita-style way – and assembly instructions are supplied at each table). Other treats include chilli con carne and (thin) milkshakes. It's a cheerful, fast-food sort of place.

Koleso (☎ 23 700; vulitsa Olgy Kobylyanskoyi 6; mains 9-20hry; ☑ noon-11pm) If you're not staying at Bukovina, which has its own themed restaurant, try this laid-back, cavern-like restaurant, which also has costumed servers and tasty Ukrainian cuisine. Seat yourself at one of the wooden picnic tables and order some *varenyky* and a beer on tap.

Maestro (☎ 28 147; vulitsa Ukrainska 30; mains 13-25hry; ☑ noon-11pm) The great location –

right next to the former Armenian Cathedral – only adds to the plusses of this upscale banquet-style restaurant with a musical theme. Ukrainian food with unique, creative twists is served. Stop by or call ahead, as much of Maestro's business comes from weddings or other large parties who rent out the whole place. There's also live music and outdoor seating when the weather is fair.

Getting There & Around

The airport is 3.5km from the centre. **Aviatour** (☎ 40 332; vulitsa Holovna 128; ⏰ 9am-1pm & 2-6pm), near the bus terminal, is your best bet for getting air tickets.

Trolleybus No 3 takes you to/from the **bus terminal** (vulitsa Holovna 219). From Chernivtsi, there are thrice-daily buses to Ivano-Frankivsk (12hry, four hours) and Kamyanets-Podilsky (10hry, 12 hours), a twice-daily bus to Odesa (56hry, 10 hours) and daily buses to Kyiv (40hry, 12 hours), Simferopol (84hry, 11 hours) and Yalta (95hry, seven hours).

To get to/from the **train station** (☎ vulitsa Yuri Gagarina 38), take trolleybus No 3. The train ticket office, next to Aviatour, sells advance tickets.

There are one to three daily trains to Kyiv (*kupeyny/platskartny* 45/29hry, 16 hours) and daily trains to Ivano-Frankivsk (19/10hry, three hours), Lviv (25/17hry, 11 hours), Odesa (53/34hry, 19 hours) and Simferopol (92hry, 37 hours, *kupe* only).

Trolleybuses cost 40 kopeks and buses cost 45 kopeks (pay on board). A taxi from the train station or bus station to the centre should cost about 5hry and they are easy to find.

KAMYANETS-PODILSKY
КАМ'ЯНЕЦЬ-ПОДІЛЬСЬКИЙ
☎ 03849 / pop 95,000

Kamyanets-Podilsky, which is 85km northeast of Chernivtsi, has stood since at least the 11th century on a sheer-walled rock 'island'. The combination of historic architecture and dramatic landscape makes this town one of the highlights of Ukraine.

The main settlers of the old town were Ukrainians, Poles, Armenians and Jews. Each traditionally occupied a different quarter. In the town's heyday, during the interwar period, there were five Roman

Catholic churches, 18 Orthodox churches and a Jewish community of 23,500 served by 31 prayer houses. Only 13 churches survived WWII.

Information

The fortified Old Town is accessible by two bridges. The western bridge takes you to the castle and the eastern bridge heads to the 'New Town'. The road (partially called vulitsa Starobulvarna) between the two bridges passes ploshcha Virmenskyi (the old town square).

In the Old Town, **Aval Bank** (vulitsa Starobulvarna 10) can handle most financial transactions. In the New Town, at the northeast corner of vulitsa Soborna and vulitsa Lesi Ukrainky (diagonal from Hotel Ukraina) is a bank with an outdoor, 24-hour ATM. The **post office** (vulitsa Soborna 9), in the New Town, also has a telephone office.

Sights

The walk across the bridge to the Old Town is probably one of the best parts of visiting Kamyanets-Podilsky. Once you're there, the main sight is the old **castle** (vulitsa Zamkova; admission 3hry; ⏰ 9am-6pm), which was originally built of wood in the 10th century but reconstructed of stone some 500 years later. On the north side of the courtyard is the worthwhile **Ethnographic Museum** (admission 2.50hry; ⏰ 9am-5pm).

The faded salmon-coloured **Dominican Monastery & Church** (ploshcha Virmenskyi) features a tall bell tower. It was founded in the 14th century but was expanded in baroque style in the 18th century. In a park just to the north is the 14th-century **Town Hall**, currently under reconstruction.

Another 500m further the north is the 16th-century **Cathedral of SS Peter & Paul** (vulitsa Tatarska). About two minutes' walk further north is the 16th-century **Porokhovi Gate** and the seven-storey, stone **Kushnir Tower**.

Sleeping & Eating

There are no hotels in the Old Town, but those listed here are each within a 10-minute walk of it.

Hotel Ukraina (☎ 32 300; vulitsa Lesi Ukrainky 32; d 100-180hry, tr 198hry, s with shared bathroom 25-33hry, d with shared bathroom 44-99hry) It feels lonely inside this hotel, and reception seems surprised to see anyone walking through the door. It's fair value though, with a cosier feel than the others and an attempt at cheer in décor. There is no lift or restaurant.

Hotel Smotrich (☎ 30 392; vulitsa Soborna 4; s/d/tr 50-70/60-80/90hry, d without hot water 40hry; **P**) In the same space as Arnika (next), Smotrich is a lesser choice for a similar price. Staff are professional, but the spartan, clean rooms offer no personality – although some rooms have pretty views.

Hotel Arnika (☎ 31 817; arnika@kp.rel.com.ua; vulitsa Soborna 4; s/ste 55/200hry, d 75-90hry; **P**) It's as if a marketing experiment is being done in this cement-clod building, home to two hotels. Cheerful (bright pink) paint on the hallways, renovated bathrooms and young, cordial staff make it hard to imagine why anyone wouldn't spend the few extra *hryvnia* for it. The tastefully decorated suite is actually a very good deal. Tours of the Old Town can be arranged here too.

Fort-Post Kafe (☎ 25 366; vulitsa Vali; mains 4-13hry; ☽ 10am-midnight) This is one of the only restaurants in town not attached to a hotel. It's in the old town, right next to a cool stone tower (called the Black Tower), which is seen on the left as you cross the bridge from New to Old Town. The décor is tasteful in a banquet-hall sort of way, but there's a big-screen TV playing music videos loudly. Food is typical Ukrainian cuisine, and is tasty.

Getting There & Away

There are many more buses than trains that go to/from town. There are dozens of buses a day to Chernivtsi (10hry, 2½ hours), and several to Kyiv (35hry, 12 hours). One or two buses a day go to Ivano-Frankivsk (16hry, five hours) and Odesa (51hry, 13 hours), and one goes to Sevastopol (90hry,

22 hours). The **bus terminal** (vulitsa Koriatovychiv) is 500m east of the new town, and about 1km from the bridge that leads into the Old Town. A taxi ride within the town costs 4hry to 6hry.

The only direct trains from Kamyanets-Podilsky are to Kyiv (*kupeyny/platskartny* 31/21hry, 11 hours, one daily) and Odesa (33/23hry, 10 hours, even dates), but you can connect to other cities from there.

The train station is 1.3km north of the bus terminal. A taxi into town should be about 6hry, or you can take bus No 1 into the New or Old Town.

ODESA ОДЕСА

☎ 0482 (6-digit Nos), 048 (7-digit Nos) / pop 1.01 million

Throughout history, Odesa (Odessa in Russian) has been a city unique to Ukraine. Because of its location, the city has always been the country's gateway to the Black Sea and therefore a crossroads of cultures, languages and trade.

Odesa manages to juggle two elements that are seemingly mutually exclusive: it's a hectic industrial city with polluted seas, but it's also and a popular holiday centre where people flock to laze on beaches and stroll through leafy streets lined with ornate, pretty architecture.

Like their city, the inhabitants also manage to combine two incongruous elements: reputedly being both hilariously funny and somewhat arrogant.

Odesa has a proud heritage that is separate from the rest of Ukraine. Russian is by far the predominant language here.

ODESA'S CINEMATIC CLAIM TO FAME

Fame was showered upon the Potemkin Steps (p852) by Russian film director Sergei Eisenstein (1898–1948), who used them to shoot a massacre scene in his legendary 1925 film *Battleship Potemkin*. The B&W epic told the tale of mutiny aboard the battleship *Potemkin Tavrichesky*, sparked off by meagre, maggot-ridden food rations. As local Odesans run down the steps towards the ship in support of the sailors' uprising, they are fired on by Tsarist troops. Blood spills down the steps, and a runaway pram, baby inside, methodically bounces down; a brilliant trick that induces strong feelings of tension, suspense and impotence in the viewer.

The film was considered too provocative by the authorities and banned. It was not screened in Europe until 1954. In Britain it became the second-longest-running ban in cinema history. Meanwhile, the film's most spellbinding scene (that of the runaway pram) has been 'borrowed' numerous times, including in Brian de Palma's *The Untouchables* (1987).

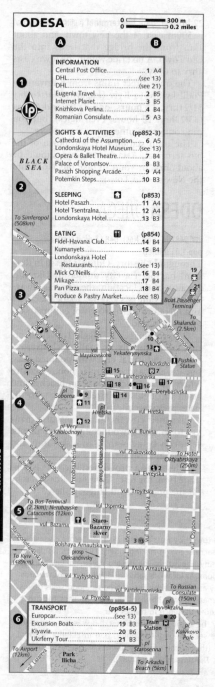

ODESA

| 0 | 300 m |
| 0 | 0.2 miles |

INFORMATION
Central Post Office	1 A4
DHL	(see 13)
DHL	(see 21)
Eugenia Travel	2 B5
Internet Planet	3 B5
Knizhkova Perlina	4 B4
Romanian Consulate	5 A3

SIGHTS & ACTIVITIES (pp852-3)
Cathedral of the Assumption	6 A5
Londonskaya Hotel Museum	(see 13)
Opera & Ballet Theatre	7 B4
Palace of Vorontsov	8 B3
Pasazh Shopping Arcade	9 B4
Potemkin Steps	10 B3

SLEEPING (p853)
Hotel Pasazh	11 A4
Hotel Tsentralna	12 A4
Londonskaya Hotel	13 B3

EATING (p854)
Fidel-Havana Club	14 B4
Kumanyets	15 B4
Londonskaya Hotel Restaurants	(see 13)
Mick O'Neills	16 B4
Mikage	17 B4
Pan Pizza	18 B4
Produce & Pastry Market	(see 18)

TRANSPORT (pp854-5)
Europcar	(see 13)
Excursion Boats	19 B3
Kiyavia	20 B6
Ukrferry Tour	21 B3

INFORMATION

Note that it's best to entirely disregard the street signs posted on poles on corners – they are usually twisted to point the wrong way. Banks with ATMs and Western Union offices are all over the place and easy to spot.

Central post office (☎ 26 64 67; vulitsa Sadovaya 10)

DHL boat terminal (vulitsa Primorskaya 6, 3rd fl; 🕙 10am-5pm Mon-Fri); Londonskaya Hotel (Primorsky bulvar 11; 🕙 24hr) The Londonskaya Hotel also has a travel agency.

Eugenia Travel (☎ 22 03 31; www.eugeniatravel.com; vulitsa Rishelievskaya 23; 🕙 9am-6pm) Long established and very knowledgeable, the staff at Eugenia can arrange city tours, boat trips along the Black Sea coast or to/from Istanbul, and pretty much anything else Odesa-related.

Internet Planet (☎ 724 21 77; vulitsa Richelievskaya 58; per hr 6hry; 🕙 24hr) Hip and air-conditioned, with a snack bar, cheap phones and photo exhibits. Staffed by older gamers.

Knizhnaya Perlina (☎ 35 84 04; vulitsa Deribasovskaya 14; 🕙 10am-10pm) Informed selection of English-language titles and helpful staff. Some maps are here, too.

SIGHTS

Everyone gravitates toward **Prymorsky bulvar**, where they're greeted by a typical Odesan combination of the lovely and the loathsome. The beauty lies in the early-19th-century buildings, the shady promenade, the strip of park tumbling towards the sea – and the sweep of the **Potemkin Steps** (see Odesa's Cinematic Claim to Fame, p851). These 192 waterfront steps (1837–41) spill down the hillside from a statue of the Duke de Richelieu to the Black Sea; they are best viewed from the bottom, where they seem higher than they are, thanks to a gradual narrowing from bottom (21m wide) to top (13m wide). A jarringly functional note is struck by what lies at the foot of the steps: no vista of sparkling waters, or chapel as in the film, but truck-infested vulitsa Primorskaya and the clanking noises of the passenger port.

At the northwestern end of Prymorsky bulvar is the 1826 **Palace of Vorontsov** (not open to the public), the residence of a former governor. The terrace behind the palace offers brilliant views over the port. There is a footbridge to the left, supposedly built at the request of a communist official to make it easier for his mother to visit him, which leads to a park and the pleasing pedestrian extension of the promenade.

On vulitsa Lanzheronovskaya, facing down vulitsa Rishielevskaya, sits the elaborate **Opera & Ballet Theatre**. It was designed in the 1880s by Viennese architects Ferdinand Fellner and Hermann Helmer in the Habsburg baroque style that was popular at the time, with a number of Italian Renaissance features thrown in to liven up the ensemble.

A block south is Odesa's main commercial street, vulitsa Derybasivska (mostly pedestrian), named after a Frenchman, De Ribas, who led the capture of Odesa from the Turks in 1789. Two pleasant tree-filled parks lie at its western end.

The **Pasazh Shopping Arcade** (vulitsa Preobrazhenskaya) is an ornate, dusty shopping mall built in 1897–98 with rows of baroque sculptures. The impressive, blue-and-white **Cathedral of the Assumption** (vulitsa Preobrazhenskaya 70) is six blocks south.

The Londonskaya Hotel (right) is gorgeous (worth a look around no matter what) and has a small, 3rd-floor **Londonskaya Hotel Museum** (admission free; ✆ 24hr) showing photographs and memorabilia of famous people who have stayed there over the years. Guests have included the likes of the poet Vladimir Mayakovsky, acting guru Konstantin Stanislavsky, playwright Anton Chekhov, musician and poet Vladimir Vysotsky and contemporary film director Nikita Mikhalkov – and even Aleksandr Pushkin himself. The exhibit is in a large

---

DANGERS & ANNOYANCES

If you decide to visit in summer, know that it's going to be hard to just show up and get a hotel room, although stays in a private home are always possible (see Sleeping, below). Also keep in mind that Odesa has a reputation for muggings and pickpockets. Women travellers should exercise extra caution at night.

---

hallway on the 3rd floor, so it's technically open 24 hours, but you should go during daylight hours to be able to see clearly.

On April Fool's Day (1 April), Odesa celebrates **Humourina**, a street carnival centred around comedy.

SLEEPING

During summer it's pretty easy to arrange a private room in the home of one of the older ladies hanging around the train station. Expect to pay 45hry to 60hry per person per day including meals, and try in advance to figure out the location and proximity to public transport.

From June to August it's highly recommended that you book hotels in advance.

Hotel Pasazh (✆ 22 48 49; fax 22 41 50; vulitsa Preobrazhenskaya 34; s/d with cold water 39-86/82-84hry, with hot water 46-87/120-186hry) In the centre, this is one of two rundown budget hotels with surly staff and sporadic hot water.

Hotel Tsentralna (✆ 26 84 06; fax 26 86 89; vulitsa Preobrazhenskaya 40; s/d 108/162hry) Slightly better than Hotel Pasazh.

Hotel Oktyabrskaya (✆ 28 06 66; vulitsa Kanatna 35; d US$60-70) This small, mid-range hotel has a sort of bed-and-breakfast feel and pleasant rooms. It's good value considering how central it is (about 250m east of the centre).

Londonskaya Hotel (✆ 225 53 25; hotel@londred .com; Primorsky bulvar 11; s 540-1080hry, d 702-1242hry, ste 1080-1620hry; P ☒ ☒) Since 1824 the gorgeous Londonskaya has had its doors open to the rich and famous. Staff are courteous and highly trained to please; the rooms have all the niceties: hairdryers, bidets, robes and satellite TV. A sauna and small gym is onsite, and a delicious breakfast is included. Wine tastings are often held in the evenings. For information on the hotel museum see opposite.

THE AUTHOR'S CHOICE

If you want the best kind of Odesa experience, stay at one of the beaches. It does take some time to get to the centre, but the relative peace and friendlier service makes it worthwhile. In particular, **Shalanda** (✆ 742 07 30, 8-067-729 09 17; Lanzheron Beach; d US$40-70; ☒) is an unbeatable small hotel with lovely staff and delicious food. There are only a few rooms (call ahead June to August), all of them meeting and exceeding Western standards and all facing the sea with big bay windows. Hot water around the clock, fluffy big beach and bath towels, and super comfy beds make you never want to leave. Taxis will know the beach, but may not know the hotel; call Anatoli (p855) if you have doubts about being able to find it.

UKRAINE

THE CATACOMBS OF ODESA

The limestone below Odesa is riddled with more than 1000km of catacombs (so some buildings in the city are literally sinking). They weren't used as cemeteries, but were formed by Cossacks and other residents who mined the land for the limestone, which was used to build the city. The resulting network of tunnels turned out to be a great place for smugglers, revolutionaries and fugitives throughout history.

One network of tunnels in Nerubayske, 12km northwest of Odesa, sheltered a group of partisans during WWII. This event is explained at the **Museum of Partisan Glory** (admission 6hry; ☾ 9am-4pm), which includes a fascinating, flashlight tour of the catacombs, with exhibits showing what life was like for the underground fighters who hid and lived here when they weren't derailing Nazi trains or otherwise thwarting the fascists.

You can just show up in Nerubayske in a taxi (80hry return trip), but you may have to rustle up staff to open the doors if they're not expecting you, and tours will be in Russian only. It would be better to arrange a visit in advance through a tour agency such as Eugenia Travel (p852). Keep in mind that it will be dark and close in the catacombs (claustrophobes beware), as well as chilly – no matter how warm the day is.

Each year at least one person wanders into a catacomb entrance they discover around Odesa and never comes out. Don't be one of them. Stick to the tour.

EATING & DRINKING

Behind Pan Pizza (below) is a great indoor **produce and pastry market** (☾ 9am-7pm); you'd be wise to stock up there before a train journey. The Hotel Londonskaya has a couple of great restaurants that are surprisingly affordable.

Pan Pizza (☎ 37 71 54; vulitsa Deribasovskaya 22; pizza 25-45hry; pasta 8-20hry; ☾ 9.30am-11.30pm) On the pedestrian part of vulitsa Deribasovskaya, this popular bright-yellow chain has fast good pizzas and is often packed.

Kumanyets (☎ 37 69 46; vulitsa Havana 7; mains 8-45hry; ☾ 11am-midnight) This is a full-on Ukrainian-themed restaurant with down-home country dishes. Friendly staff wear kitschy costumes with nary a tic of irony.

Mick O'Neills (☎ 26 84 37; vulitsa Deribasovskaya 13; mains 14-88hry; ☾ 24hr) Two storeys of wooden railings and all the trappings of pub décor (paper money from all over the world, billiards, pinball machines) set the scene for this restaurant and hangout. The large menu has burgers and an all-day breakfast and Guinness is on tap.

Fidel-Havana Club (☎ 22 71 16; vulitsa Deribasovskaya 23; mains 7-100hry; ☾ 9am-2am) Surprisingly not too smoky considering all the smoking that's going on in here, this club-restaurant is populated with the beautiful and cool people in town, as well as some tourists. The extensive menu (available in English) has everything from sandwiches to tiger shrimp. There's a full bar and live Cuban music some evenings.

Mikage (☎ 34 97 68; vulitsa Lanzheronovskaya 9; meals US$20-50; ☾ 11am-midnight) Across from the Opera & Ballet Theatre, Mikage has delectable sushi and excellent service in a traditional Japanese setting. It's super-pricey, but if you come just for *miso* and a couple of pieces of *nigiri*, you could walk out for under US$10.

GETTING THERE & AWAY

See 'Don't Let This Happen to You' p867 before you take any train trip between Odesa and Western Ukraine.

The airport, 12km southwest of the city centre, is accessible by bus No 129 from the train station, where there is a **Kiyavia** (☎ 27 62 59) air-ticket office.

The **bus terminal** (vulitsa Kolontaevskaya 58) is 3km southwest of the city centre. Once or twice a day, buses leave from Odesa for Chernivtsi (53hry, 15 hours), Sevastopol (48hry, 14 hours), Simferopol (43hry, 12 hours) and Yalta (48hry, 15 hours), and there are a dozen or more buses to Kyiv (37hry to 60hry, eight hours). From the same terminal, **Autolux** (www.autolux.com.ua) runs fast private buses to Kyiv and other cities.

During summer boats regularly leave the **boat passenger terminal** (vulitsa Primorskaya) for both long-distance and excursion boat trips around the Black Sea and up the Dnipro

River; contact Eugenia Travel (p852) or go to www.ukrferry.com for details.

In-city rental cars can be arranged through **Europcar** (☎ 777 40 11; ua@europcar.relc .com; Primorsky bulvar 11; ☯ 9am-5pm Mon-Fri, 10am-2pm Sat) in the Hotel Londonskaya. For rates and details, see www.europcar.ua.

The **train station** (ploshcha Pryvokzalna) is a big busy place. Tickets for future dates or with non-CIS destinations must be bought at the Сервисний Центр (Service Centre; ☯ 7am-9.30pm), inside the station. To find it from the main entrance, go right and walk to the end, turn left past the pharmacy and look for the signed double doors. Once you're there, go to **window 5** (☯ 8am-7pm) for non-CIS destinations. All other windows can help with tickets for future dates.

Twice daily, trains from Odesa head to Kyiv (kupeyny/platskartny 44/27hry, 11 hours). Daily trains from Odesa go to Chop/ Uzhhorod (56hry, 20 hours, kupe only), Lviv (50/35hry, 12 hours) and Simferopol (42/27hry, 13 hours). On odd dates, there are daily trains to Chernivtsi (49/36hry, 19 hours) and Kamyanets-Podilsky (29hry, 16 hours, platskartny only); on even dates there are daily trains to Ivano-Frankivsk (53/39hry, 21 hours).

GETTING AROUND

Along with those in Crimea, Odesa taxis are some of the most expensive in the country. For an in-town ride, you'll pay about 5hry; to get to/from the centre from the

train station it costs around 10hry; from the airport you'll pay US$15-30. Instead, you could take bus No 129 (1.50hry) which runs regularly between the train station and the airport. **Elit-Taxi** (☎ 37 10 30) is reliable, or you can call **Anatoli** (☎ 8-067-762 30 90, dispatcher ☎ 37 10 30), who is a driver for Elit-Taxi. He's reliable, speaks a little English and can take you to the catacombs. He looks like a Ukrainian Roy Scheider and is charming.

CRIMEA КРИМ

Crimea has a hot-potato sort of history. Geographically, it formed a land bridge merging East and West, and thus it was fought over for centuries by the Greeks, Khazars, Tatars and Genoese before the Russians had the last say in 1783.

The blunder-strewn, stalemated Crimean War of 1854–56 was a classic clash of imperial ambitions. Much to the chagrin of its rival empires, Russia wanted to take over the faltering Turkish Empire, and when Tsar Nicholas I sent troops into the Ottoman provinces of Moldavia and Wallachia (ostensibly to protect the Christians there), the British and French assembled in Varna (now in Bulgaria) to protect Istanbul. Both sides lost about 250,000 soldiers in the war, many from bad medical care – to which British nurse Florence Nightingale drew attention.

The peninsula became a chic leisure spot in the 1860s, when Russia's imperial family

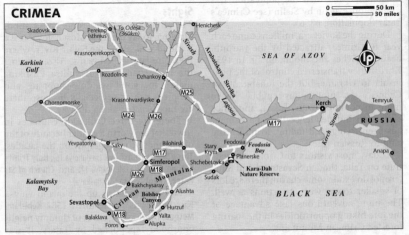

CRIMEA'S TATAR POPULATION

On 18 May 1944 Stalin accused the Crimea's Tatars of collaborating with the Nazis, and deported the entire Muslim population to Central Asia and Siberia. The Tatar language was banned and all traces of the culture were obliterated. Crimea was repopulated with Ukrainians, Russians, Bulgarians and Germans. It is estimated that more than 46% percent of the Tatars died during deportation.

Since the late 1980s, about 260,000 Tatars have returned to their lost homeland and have been trying to re-establish themselves and their culture. It hasn't been easy. Few speak their Turkic mother tongue and many still live in poor, slumlike conditions with no water or electricity. However, the Ukrainian government has started giving money to the cause of the returning deportees, and conditions are improving. You will probably see new Tatar homes being constructed in the foothills.

---

built a summer pad at the Livadia estate on the outskirts of Yalta (the same palace later used for the post-WWII Yalta Conference of Churchill, Stalin and Roosevelt).

During the civil war that followed the Russian Revolution (p647), Crimea was one of the last 'white' bastions. The Germans occupied the peninsula for three years during WWII and Crimea lost nearly half its inhabitants, and then the population was drained once again by Stalin (see Crimea's Tatar Population, p856).

During the Soviet era, millions came each year to Crimea, attracted by the warmth, beauty, beaches and mountain air. In 1954 Khrushchev transferred control of the peninsula to Ukraine, but the inhabitants of Crimea – an autonomous republic – have more in common with Russia, and since Ukrainian independence their parliament has been trying, and failing, to return the land to Russian rule.

Today, most visitors to Crimea concentrate on Yalta, though Sevastopol and Simferopol do exude some charm; there are lots of smaller towns with attractions as well. The more adventurous take advantage of the rare hiking opportunities in the soaring forested Crimean Mountains.

Private rooms in family homes are a popular option around Crimea during summer. Look out for older ladies – especially at train stations – with signs around their necks reading кімнати (*kimnaty*, Ukrainian) or комнаты (*komnaty*, Russian), both of which mean 'rooms'. Before deciding, however, always check the exact location and proximity to public transport. The cost ranges from 45hry to 80hry per person per night.

SIMFEROPOL СІМФЕРОПОЛЬ

☎ 0652 / pop 337,600

If you're heading to Crimea, you're probably going to stop for a bit in Simferopol, the capital of the Autonomous Republic of Crimea and the regional transport hub. The city isn't a huge attraction in itself, but you can definitely spend a few hours there by strolling along its pedestrian avenues.

Information

Bukva Books (☎ 27 31 53; vulitsa Sevastopolskaya 6) Offers a good selection of English-language classics and contemporary pulp fiction.

Central post office (☎ 27 22 55; vulitsa Rozy Lyuxemburg 1) Also has an ATM, telephone office and Internet centre, all with 24-hour access.

Internet Cafe (☎ 27 33 77; vulitsa Pavlenko 20; per hr 3-4hry; ☽ 24hr) Has a dozen computers, young gaming boys and a rarity – webcams (perhaps for those pining-away future brides).

Ukrosoubank (☎ 51 02 55; prospekt Kirova 36) Has a 24hour ATM and a Western Union.

Sights

The attractions of Simferopol aren't mindblowing, to say the least. Most enjoyable is a tranquil walk along the Salhir River, where there are landscaped paths. Also, strolling the pedestrian zone of vulitsa Pushkina makes for good window-shopping and people-watching, especially because there are nice benches along the way.

There are three Orthodox churches in town that are worth a gander because of the ornate mosaic iconography on the façades: **Three Saints Church** (vulitsa Hoholya 16), **Holy Trinity Cathedral** (vulitsa Odessakaya 12) and **Church of Sts Peter & Paul** (vulitsa Oktyabrskaya).

East of the centre, up the quaint vulitsa Kurchatova, is the restored 1502 **Kebi-Jami Mosque**, overlooking a sort of slummy neighbourhood repopulated by Tatars. It was

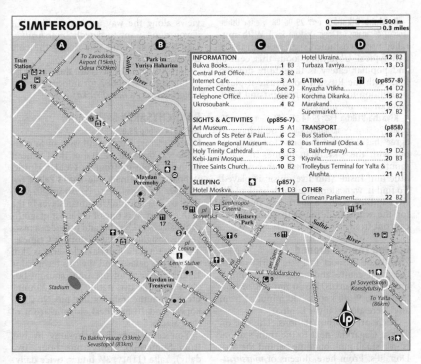

SIMFEROPOL

0 — 500 m
0 — 0.3 miles

INFORMATION	
Bukva Books	1 B3
Central Post Office	2 B2
Internet Cafe	3 A1
Internet Centre	(see 2)
Telephone Office	(see 2)
Ukrosoubank	4 B2

SIGHTS & ACTIVITIES	(pp856-7)
Art Museum	5 A1
Church of Sts Peter & Paul	6 C2
Crimean Regional Museum	7 B2
Holy Trinity Cathedral	8 C3
Kebi-Jami Mosque	9 C3
Three Saints Church	10 B2

SLEEPING	(p857)
Hotel Moskva	11 D3

Hotel Ukraina	12 B2
Turbaza Tavriya	13 D3

EATING	(pp857-8)
Knyazha Vtikha	14 D2
Korchma Dikanka	15 B2
Marakand	16 C2
Supermarket	17 B2

TRANSPORT	(p858)
Bus Station	18 A1
Bus Terminal (Odesa & Bakhchysaray)	19 D2
Kiyavia	20 B3
Trolleybus Terminal for Yalta & Alushta	21 A1

OTHER	
Crimean Parliament	22 B2

reconstructed in the 17th century and is the oldest building in the city.

The town's **Crimean Regional Museum** (vulitsa Hoholya 14; admission 6hry; ☉ 9am-5pm Wed-Mon) features plenty of maps, tombstones and weaponry. In a grand yellow building, the **Art Museum** (☎ 25 05 34; vulitsa Libknekhta 35; admission 1hry; ☉ 10am-4pm Tue-Sun) has temporary exhibits in the one-storey building on the corner. The adjacent two-storey building has the permanent exhibition, which includes paintings in a variety of styles and subject matters. The 2nd floor is more staid, with historic portraits and a couple of icons.

Sleeping

Hotel Moskva (☎ 23 75 20; fax 23 97 95; vulitsa Kyivskaya 2; s 57-142hry, d 97-207hry, ste 284-364hry; **P**) Curmudgeonly staff sit at reception in this stiff Soviet-style block building, just waiting to be difficult. Moskva is a massive, former government-run place with acceptable rooms (price includes breakfast) and the restaurant actually has wonderful bar and wait staff.

Turbaza Tavriya (☎ 23 20 24; vulitsa Bespalova 21; s 60-150hry, d 100-300hry; **P**) This tranquil, hill-side place is a bit far from the centre, but if you can't stay at the Hotel Ukraina, it beats nearby Hotel Moskva by a long shot. Staff are friendly and the surroundings are peaceful. It's sometimes booked with groups.

Hotel Ukraina (☎ 51 01 65; jscukrcomp@crimea.ua; vulitsa Rozy Lyuxemburg 7; s 152-222hry, d 181-244hry, tr 246 hry, ste 190-400hry) A complete renovation has made this central hotel a good deal. Rooms have fresh carpet and new furniture and appliances, and some rooms have balconies. The entrance is set back from the street, behind the pinkish building.

Eating

There's a Western-style **supermarket** (cnr vulitsas Pushkina & Karla Marxa) for all you self-caterers out there.

Marakand (☎ 52 46 98; vulitsa Vorovskoho 17; mains 1-6hry; ☉ 8am-11pm Mon-Sat) Don't miss this lively Central Asian restaurant, where you can get *plov* (meat and rice) and *shashlik* (shish kebab) grilled over an open fire before your eyes. The local Muslim community hangs out here, drinking tea and chewing over debates.

UKRAINE

Korchma Dikanka (☎ 29 06 08; vulitsa Ushin-skoho 2/46; mains 6-13hry; ☺ 9am-5pm) With mu-ralled walls, costumed staff, wooden tables and typical Ukrainian food, this central and popular eatery is thankfully not too loud with the Russian pop music it plays. In addition to *varenyky*, *pelmeni* and *blini*, you can sample *holubtsi*.

Kiyazha Vtikha (☎ 29 14 89; vulitsa Turgeneva 35; mains 17-35hry; ☺ noon-midnight) You'll have to agree that this wins the prize for going all-out with the Ukrainian theme. In warm months you can dine outside in your own little hut. Inside, fun live music is played. To find it, walk along the north bank of the river until it makes a sharp left, then look for the white building with shutters and cars out front.

Getting There & Around

Zavodskoe Airport is 15km northwest of the town centre and accessible by mini-buses *(marshrutkas)* No 50 and 115, or trol-leybus No 9 (40 kopeks, 30 minutes) from anywhere along bulvar Lenina.

There are two bus stations. The one on vulitsa Gagarina, next to the train station, is in a small pink building behind the Mc-Donald's. From here, dozens of *marshrut-kas* leave for destinations around Crimea (except Bakhchysaray) including two to Yalta (9.05hry, two hours) and to Sevas-topol (9.50hry, two hours).

The bus terminal on vulitsa Kyivskaya, by Hotel Moskva, has regular buses, micro-buses and 'lux' buses to Odesa (37hry to 57hry, 12 hours, one daily) and Bakhchy-saray (5hry, one hour, five daily), as well as to other destinations around Crimea, including Sevastopol (9hry to 10hry, two hours, 12 daily).

Most trains to/from Simferopol are very busy, especially June to August, so book your tickets as early as possible. To Kyiv, (*kupeyny/platskartny* 75/42hry, 15 hours) there are three or four daily, and once per day, trains leave for Lviv (75/49hry, 26 hours) and Odesa (38/26hry, 15 hours).

From 5am to 8pm, the world's longest – and slowest! – trolleybus ride leaves from the **trolleybus terminal** (vulitsa Gagarina), near the train station, for Yalta (6.12hry, 2½ hours, every 20 minutes), stopping in Alushta. It's not the most time-efficient method of transport, but it's definitely a novelty. The views along the way are spectacular, but if you don't want to dawdle, *marshrutkas* take the same route and zip by the cute trolleys.

Marshrutkas and taxis are the way to go in this town. See p682 for information on flagging down a *marshrutka*.

BAKHCHYSARAY БАХЧИСАРАЙ
☎ 06554 / pop 28,000

Bakhchysaray, 33km southwest of Simfer-opol, was once the capital of the Crimean khanate, a spin-off from the Golden Horde. It boasts the remarkable **Khan's Palace** (vu-litsa Lenina 129; admission 6hry; ☺ 9am-5pm Thu-Mon). Built by Russian and Ukrainian slaves in the 16th century, it is one of the most magnifi-cent palaces in Ukraine and provides a mar-vellous insight into the history of Crimea.

The train station in Bakhchysaray is 3km west of the palace, and the bus terminal is 1.5km northeast of the train station; bus No 4 links the two stations (2hry, 20 min-utes). From the train station, bus No 2 (80 kopeks and 10 minutes) stops in front of the palace.

You can get to Bakhchysaray by bus from Simferopol (5hry, one hour, five daily), Yalta (11hry, 3½ hours, twice daily) and Sevastopol (5hry to 8hry, one hour, 22 daily).

YALTA ЯЛТА
☎ 0654 / pop 83,000

Yalta is overwhelmingly *the* major attrac-tion in Crimea for Ukrainian and Russian tourists. Coming into the town – possible only by road through the craggy Crimean Mountains to the sparkling Black Sea – is no doubt most one of the spectacular trips in the country, and the resort town can have a very relaxing, laid-back atmosphere, with lazy waterfront strollers and night-time fireworks for no particular reason. That said, you may want to avoid the summer, when the place can get impossibly crowded (the beaches aren't all that anyway).

Information

Aval Bank (ploshcha Lenina) Booth No 14 of the post office; handles Western Union and cash advances.
Central post office (☎ 31 20 73; ploshcha Lenina 1)
Internet Centre (vulitsa Ekaterninskaya 3; per hr 4-5hry; ☺ 24hr) A dozen computers run by bratty post-teen gamers.

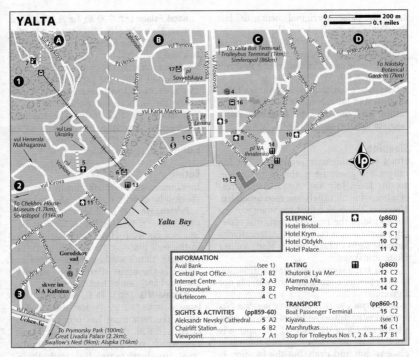

YALTA

0 — 200 m
0 — 0.1 miles

To Yalta Bus Terminal;
Trolleybus Terminal (1km);
Simferopol (86km)

To Nikitsky
Botanical
Gardens (7km)

To Chekhov House-
Museum (1.7km);
Sevastopol (116km)

Yalta Bay

Gorodskoy
sad

skver im
N A Kalinina

Uchan-Su

To Prymorsky Park (100m);
Great Livadia Palace (2.2km);
Swallow's Nest (9km); Alupka (16km)

SLEEPING	🛏	(p860)
Hotel Bristol.................................8	C2
Hotel Krym...................................9	C1
Hotel Otdykh...............................10	C2
Hotel Palace................................11	A2

INFORMATION		
Aval Bank...............................(see 1)
Central Post Office........................1	B2
Internet Centre.............................2	A3
Ukrosoubank................................3	B2
Ukrtelecom..................................4	C1

EATING	🍴	(p860)
Khutorok Lya Mer.......................12	C2
Mamma Mia................................13	B2
Pelmennaya................................14	C2

SIGHTS & ACTIVITIES	(p859-60)
Aleksandr Nevsky Cathedral.....5	A2
Chairlift Station............................6	B2
Viewpoint....................................7	A1

TRANSPORT		(pp860-1)
Boat Passenger Terminal............15	C2
Kiyavia...................................(see 1)
Marshrutkas................................16	C1
Stop for Trolleybus Nos 1, 2 & 3...17	B1

Ukrosoubank (naberezhnaya imeni Lenina 5) Western Union and outdoor 24-hour ATM.

Ukrtelecom (vulitsa Moskovskaya 9; per hr 4-5hry; 🕐 24hr) Internet and phone calls.

Sights

IN-TOWN SIGHTS

The **promenade**, naberezhnaya imeni Lenina, stretches past numerous piers, palm trees, (pebble) beaches, snack bars, gardens and souvenir stalls as far as Prymorsky Park. Vulitsas Kyivskaya and Moskovskaya combine to form a major thoroughfare that's a little hectic but nonetheless interesting to stroll along.

From vulitsa Kirova look for the path to the **chairlift station** (return trip 10hry; 🕐 10am-5pm Apr-Sep). Buy your ticket, step into a dented bucket, and you're off, swinging above dilapidated rooftops to a bizarre pseudo-Greek temple and **viewpoint**. Near the bottom chairlift station, the 1903 **Aleksandr Nevsky Cathedral** (vulitsa Sadovaya 2) is a beautiful example of neo-Byzantine architecture. The architect was Nikolai Krasnov, who designed many palaces on Crimea's southern coast.

Anton Chekhov wrote *The Cherry Orchard* and the *Three Sisters* in what is now the **Chekhov House-Museum** (☎ 39 49 47; vulitsa Kirova 12; adult/child 5/2.50hry; 🕐 10am-5pm Wed-Sun). If you take Trolleybus No 1 from ploshcha Sovietskaya it's a couple of blocks uphill (north) of the sixth stop. It will still be a little hard to find; you can ask passersby for the mu-*zyey che*-kho-va. Tours (in Russian) are included in the price, and the grounds are lovely.

NEARBY SIGHTS

See p861 for information on getting to these places from Yalta.

If the grounds of the Chekhov Museum got you in the mood for more flowers and pretty pathways, head to the 1000-hectare **Nikitsky Botanical Gardens** (☎ 33 55 30; adult/child 6/3hry; 🕐 8am-6pm).

In February 1945 Stalin, Roosevelt and Churchill held their Yalta Conference in the **Great Livadia Palace** (☎ 31 55 81; admission 6hry; 🕐 10am-5pm Thu-Tue), 3km southwest of central Yalta. It features photos and memorabilia about this historic event, and displays

UKRAINE

about the palace's original owner, the last Russian emperor, Nicholas II.

Possibly the most internationally famous landmark on the peninsula is the magnificent cliff-side castle known as the **Swallow's Nest** (admission 8hry; ☉ 8am-6pm Tue-Sun).

The palace-park complex at Alupka 16km southwest of Yalta, boasts a stunning coastal setting and the majestic **Alupkinsky Palace** (admission 10hry; ☉ 10am-5pm Tue-Thu, Sat & Sun).

Sleeping

Hotel prices fluctuate seasonally, but full ranges are given here; the higher prices are for June, July and August, when reservations for all hotels are recommended. However, this is also the time when women hang around the main bus terminal offering private rooms (see p855). Alternatively, look for signs outside homes along vulitsa Ekaterininskaya.

Many hotel rooms have air-conditioning in their pricier rooms, but hot water is not a given.

Hotel Krym (☎ 27 17 01; director@hotelkrim.yalta .crimea.ua; vulitsa Moskovskaya 1/6; s 20-50hry, d 50-90hry, tr 45-120, q 60-160, ste 110-300hry; 🗱) Reception is not the least bit welcoming, and the whole place is dim and drab, but the location is central, and boy is it cheap. The cheaper rooms for each category have a shared bathroom, and the priciest doubles and triples have air-conditioning.

Hotel Otdich (☎ 35 30 67; otdyh@yalita.com; vulitsa Drazhynskoho 14; d incl breakfast 75-325hry; 🗱) Once a 19th-century brothel for visiting government dignitaries, Hotel Otdich is now a quiet *pension* along a quiet residential street – the oldest street in town. On Sunday you can hear the peals of church bells. The English-speaking staff are superhelpful and outgoing, and rooms are bright. The on-site restaurant has tasty food and hookahs even. If that doesn't sell you, the hotel has a private stretch of beach and lends towels to its residents.

Hotel Bristol (☎ 27 16 03; www.hotel-bristol .ua; vulitsa Ruzvelta 10; s 92-691hry, d 219-747hry, apt 556-1180hry; P 🗱 🗶) Formerly called Hotel Yuzhnaya, Bristol is a fancy place opposite the boat passenger terminal. The rooms are thoroughly renovated and great value, and breakfast is included in the rates (which are completely complex – see the website for the exact schematics).

Hotel Palace (☎ 32 43 80; fax 23 04 92; vulitsa Chekhova 8; s incl breakfast 225-495hry, d incl breakfast 352-520hry; 🗱) The building is vaguely palatial, and a fair deal too (the cheapest rooms here are nicer than the equivalent at Bristol. There's no lift, but the pretty marble staircase is decorated with interesting Crimean art on the walls to make the time pass as you trudge up and down. The spacious rooms often have large balconies (great for watching fireworks) with sea views, and the bathrooms are remodelled.

Eating

In summer, naberezhnaya imeni Lenina is chock-a-block with open-air cafés and bars.

Pelmennaya (☎ 32 39 32; vulitsa Sverdlova 8; mains 5-7hry; ☉ 8am-11pm Mon-Fri, 10am-7pm Sat & Sun) Not far from Hotel Otdich, this hole-in-the-wall place is great for a quick hot bite with Yalta's working class. *Pelmeni* of course is the main offering, but *varenyky* and *blini* and can be had here too.

Mamma Mia (☎ 31 60 61; naberezhnaya imeni Lenina 15; mains 18-27hry; ☉ 10am-midnight) This cellar-like restaurant has pop music that doesn't fit with the yummy thin-crust pizzas, which you can cover with another crust for 3hry more. But wait, there's more: spaghetti, ravioli and risotto too, as well as meats and fish. You can watch the puffy-hatted pizzaman bake your pie in the red-hot oven while you debate whether the place's mascot is really Mamma or actually Uncle Guido in drag.

Khutorok Lya Mer (☎ 27 18 15; vulitsa Sverdlova 9; mains 22-89hry; ☉ 11am-2am) This place is decked out like a wooden ship, but the menu (available in English) strangely features more meat than fish, such as the daring bull's balls with horseradish (48hry). There's an eclectic wine list with Crimean, Georgian and Aussie selections.

Getting There & Away

Kiyavia (☎ 32 59 43; ploshcha Lenina) is in booth No 13 of the post office.

There are no trains or flights to Yalta.

Trolleybuses to Simferopol (p858) start/finish at the **trolleybus terminal** (vulitsa Moskovskaya), opposite the Yalta bus terminal, a five-minute ride on trolleybus No 1, 2 or 3 along vulitsa Moskovskaya/Kyivskaya from central Yalta. From here, buses go to Crimean cities including Bakhchysaray (11hry, 3½ hours, twice daily), Sevastopol (8hry to 10hry, two hours, half-hourly) and Simferopol (7hry to 9hry, two hours, four hourly) as well as Odesa (47hry, 14½ hours, once daily) and Chisinau in Moldova (see p865).

For details on ferries from Yalta to international locations, see p866.

Getting Around

A trolleybus ride is 40 kopeks. Taxis are relatively expensive (a short ride in town will probably cost 7hry to 10hry), and drivers are less eager for your business (hard to bargain). They hang out around hotels and busy intersections, or you can call ☎ 058.

In front of Ukrtelecom, there is a station for *marshrutkas* that go to various local sights and cities. In-town trips cost about 1hry to 3hry per ride. Trips to sights around Yalta are a little more. Marshrutka No 27 goes to Alupka (27hry), and Swallow's Nest (27hry), No 34 goes to Nikitsky Gardens (34hry), and No 5 goes to Livadia (5hry).

SEVASTOPOL СЕВАСТОПОЛЬ

☎ 0692 / pop 328,600

As a major Russian naval port, Sevastopol was devastated in the Crimean War and WWII, and was closed to tourists until 1996. It is probably a bit more charming than Simferopol, but unless you're very interested in the tumultuous history of the Black Sea Fleet, there's not much reason to show up.

Information

Kiosks sell city maps.

Central post office (☎ 54 48 81; vulitsa Bolshaya Morskaya 21; ☾ 9am-7pm Mon-Fri, 9am-2pm Sat) Internet centre (per hr 2h-3hry) inside.

Kiyavia (☎ 54 28 29; vulitsa Lenina 13; ☾ 9am-2pm & 3-7pm Mon-Fri) Has a Western Union and Aval Bank.

Telephone office (☾ 9am-10pm) Next door to the post office.

Sights

The most major sight in town is the **Panorama** (☎ 57 97 38; Istorichesky bulvar; admission 6hry; ☾ 9.30am-5.30pm Tue-Sun), a massive work of art commemorating the defence of Sevastopol in the Crimean War. The **Black Sea Fleet Museum** (☎ 54 22 80; vulitsa Lenina 11; admission 10hry; ☾ 10am-5pm Wed-Sun, closed last Fri of month) provides colourful displays about the controversial Russian fleet. If you've got kids in tow, try the **dolphinarium** (☎ 55 99 55; naberezhnaya Kornilova 2; admission 18hry; ☾ 10am-4.30pm Tue-Sun). Rumour has it that the dolphins were used for military purposes when the city was closed. Now, between performances, they are involved in therapy for sick or stuttering children. Next to the dolphinarium is the **aquarium** (☎ 54 38 92; adult/child 6/3hry; ☾ 10am-7pm).

Noteworthy churches include **St Vladimir's Cathedral** and the gorgeous **Intercession Cathedral**.

Sleeping & Eating

June to August, hotel prices can be triple what's listed here.

Hotel Sevastopol (☎ 46 64 00; fax 46 64 09; prospekt Nakhimova 8; s 73-130hry, d 116-250hry, ste 280-480hry, s/d/tr with shared bathroom 30-40/55-65/72-84hry) In a palatial, historic (no lift) building, Hotel Sevastopol has surly reception but sweet floor staff. The rooms are typically tawny in hue and down in the mouth, but the bathrooms can be surprisingly more uplifting.

Hotel Ukraina (☎ 54 21 27; fax 54 53 78; vulitsa Hoholya 2; s 122-250hry, d 187-323hry) Ukraina is definitely a step above the Sevastopol, with a stylish lobby and sitting area, more pleasant staff, and slightly better rooms.

For fish meals and harbour views, try any of the cafés and restaurants along the waterfront between the park and Lunacharskoho Theatre. In the peaceful park surrounding the Panorama are several other decent eateries.

Getting There & Around

The bus station and train station are within visible walking distance of each other. Any minibus or trolleybus from the bus or train stations will take you to ploshcha Suvorova, a major central square.

Regular buses, microbuses and 'lux' buses leave from the **bus terminal** (vulitsa Vokzalnaya). From Sevastopol, make sure that you avoid any bus going to Simferopol (8hry to 12hry, two hours, 32 daily) that takes the very laborious detour via Yalta (9hry to 12hry, two hours, 20 daily). To Bakhchysaray (5hry to 8hry, one hour), there are 22 buses every day, and there is one bus a day each to Chernivtsi (92hry, 24 hours) and Odesa (44hry, 13 hours).

UKRAINE

There are not many direct trains from the Sevastopol **train station** (vulitsa Portovaya), except to Kyiv (*kupeyny/platskartny* 60/40hry, 17 hours, twice daily) and international trains to Moscow, St Petersburg and Minsk (see p865), but you can transfer in Simferopol (p858) to other destinations.

UKRAINE DIRECTORY

ACCOMMODATION
Organised camping grounds are rare anywhere in Ukraine and are usually at least 10km from the city centre. See p847 for information on camping in the Carpathians. Book in advance if you'll be in the country during the May 1 holidays.

There aren't any hostels in Ukraine, but some may be developing in the near future. Check the Lonely Planet Thorn Tree (http://thorntree.lonelyplanet.com) or www.brama.com for updates.

Most budget hotels are unsightly Soviet monstrosities built in the '60s and '70s. Rooms are often well-worn with outdated furniture, but are reasonably comfortable and cheap. Many hotels have cheaper rooms with a shared bathroom – bring your own towel, soap and toilet paper. Readers have reported foot fungus to be a problem in the country, so wear flip flops (thongs) in shared showers. Hot water can be an issue at budget hotels, especially in Odesa.

Mid-range hotels or more expensive rooms in budget hotels may have more polite staff and remodelled, Western-style bathrooms, but the rest of the rooms will probably not be too different from a budget hotel's. Top end hotels usually meet most Western standards of service and aesthetics. Reviews in this chapter are ordered according to price.

ACTIVITIES
Hiking opportunities are richest in the Carpathian National Natural Park (p847) and around Crimea (p855). Before arrival, try to buy the *Hiking Guide to Poland & Ukraine*, by Tim Burford, which describes different hikes around Ukraine. Available in Kyiv are the detailed Topograficheskaya Karta series of maps, though hiking trails are poorly marked on the maps or not at all.

The virtually untouched slopes of the Carpathians (p847) are also popular with skiers between November and March.

See **Lviv Ecotours** (www.lvivecotour.com) for package hiking, mountain-biking, skiing and other trips in the Carpathians.

BOOKS
Ukraine-related fiction titles that make for great train reads are *Everything Is Illuminated*, by Jonathan Safran Foer, and *Death and the Penguin*, by Andrey Kurkov. Probably the best read of history books is *Borderland – A Journey through the History of Ukraine*, by Anna Reid.

BUSINESS HOURS
Official working hours are 9am (or 10am) to 5pm (or 6pm) Monday to Friday, with an hour-long break anywhere between noon and 2pm. Shops often open until about 8pm on weekdays and all day Saturday. Most restaurants tend to open from 10am until 11pm or midnight; bars stay open later.

EMBASSIES & CONSULATES
Ukrainian Embassies & Consulates
Australia (☎ 02-6230 5789; fax 02-6230 7298; Level 12, George Centre, 60 Marcus Clarke St, Canberra)
Belarus (☎ 017-283 19 80; fax 017-283 19 90; vulitsa Staravilenska 51, Minsk)
Canada (☎ 613-230 2961; fax 613-230 2400; 310 Somerset St West, Ottawa)
France (☎ 01 43 06 07 37; fax 01 43 06 02 94; 21 ave de Saxe, Paris)
Germany (☎ 030-288 871 16; fax 030-288 871 63; Albrechtstrasse 26, Berlin)
Hungary (☎ 1-422 4120; fax 1-220 9873; 77 Stefania St; Magyarorszag, Budapest)
Ireland (☎ 01 668 8601, 01 668 518916; ukrembassy@eircom.net; Eglin Rd Ballsbridge Dublin 4)
Netherlands (☎ 070-362 60 95; fax 070-361 55 65; 26 Groot Hertoginnelaan, The Hague)
Poland (☎ 022-622 4797; fax 022-629 8103; 7 Aleja Szucha, Warsaw)
Romania (☎ 01-201 69 86; fax 01-211 69 49; Calea Dorobantilor nr 16, Bucharest)
Russia (☎ 095-229 1079; fax 095-924 8469; Leontevsky pereulok 18, Moscow)
Slovakia (☎ 02-5920 2811; fax 02-5441 2651; Radvanska 35, Bratislava)
UK (☎ 020-7727 6312; fax 020-7792 1708; 60 Holland Park, London)
USA (☎ 202-333 0606; fax 202-333 0817; 3350 M St NW, Washington, DC)

Embassies & Consulates in Ukraine

The following are in Kyiv (☎ 044) unless otherwise noted.

Australia (Map pp832-3; ☎ /fax 235 75 86; vulitsa Kominternu 18/137; Ⓜ Vokzalna)

Belarus (Map pp832-3; ☎ 537 52 03; ukraine@belembassy.org; vulitsa Mykhayla Kotsyubynskoho 3; Ⓜ Universitet)

Canada (Map pp832-3; ☎ 464 11 44; www.kyiv.gc.ca; vulitsa Yaroslaviv val 31)

France (Map pp832-3; ☎ 228 73 69; www.ambafrance .kiev.ua; vulitsa Reitarska 39)

Germany (Map pp832-3; ☎ 247 68 00; www.german -embassy.kiev.ua, in German; vulitsa Bohdana Khmelnytskoho 25; Ⓜ Zolotoi Vorota)

Hungary (Map pp832-3; ☎ 238 63 81; hungary@kiev .farlep.net; vulitsa Reitarska 33; Ⓜ Zolotoi Vorota)

Moldova (Map pp832-3; ☎ 290 77 21; moldoukr@ sovamua.com; vulitsa Sichnevoho Povstannya 6 Ⓜ Arsenalna)

Netherlands (Map pp832-3; ☎ 490 82 00; nlambkie@ ukrpack.net; Kontraktova ploshcha 7; Ⓜ Kontraktova Ploshcha)

Poland Kyiv (Map pp832-3; ☎ 234 92 36; consulate@ svitonline.com; vulitsa Bohdana Khmelnytskoho; Ⓜ Zolotoi Vorota); Lviv (☎ 76 05 44; fax 76 09 74; vulitsa Ivana Franka 110)

Romania Kyiv (Map pp832-3; ☎ 234 52 61; romania@iptelecom.net.ua; vulitsa Mykhayla Kotsyubynskoho 8; Ⓜ Universitet); Odesa (☎ 0842 23 62 98; fax 222 09 28; konsulro@tm.odessa.ua; vulitsa Pastyora); Chernivtsi (☎ 0372 54 09 00; fax 54 09 10; konsulro@infocom.cv.ua; vulitsa Holovna 14)

Russia Kyiv (Map pp832-3; ☎ 296 45 04; embrus@ public.icyb.kiev.ua; vulitsa Kutuzova 8; Ⓜ Pecherska); Odesa (☎ 22 22 32, 54 29 25; gencon.rf.od@farlep.net; vulitsa Kanatanaya 83); Lviv (☎ 69 20 36; fax 69 20 33; onsrus@lviv.gu.net; vulitsa Patona 7a)

Slovakia (Map pp832-3; ☎ 234 06 06; slovak@kiev.ua; vulitsa Chapayeva 4; Ⓜ Zolotoi Vorota)

UK (Map pp832-3; ☎ 490 36 00; www.britemb-ukraine .net; vulitsa Desyatynna 9)

USA (Map pp832-3; ☎ 490 00 00; www.usemb.kiev.ua; vulitsa Y Kotsyubynskoho 10;)

FESTIVALS & EVENTS

Kyiv will host the 2005 Eurovision song contest. The city of Kyiv is budgeting about 60 million hryvnia to upgrade hotels, so options may be more palatable by then.

International Labour Day (1 May) is always a big deal no matter where you are in the former Soviet Union; bigger cities have fireworks, concerts and other performances. On 24 August, **Independence Day**, each city in Ukraine hosts a festival and parade.

HOLIDAYS

New Year's Day 1 January
Ukrainian Orthodox Christmas 7 January
International Women's Day 8 March
Taras Shevchenko Day 9 March
Labour Day 1-2 May
Victory Day 9 May
Constitution Day 28 June
Ukrainian Independence Day 24 August
Catholic Christmas 25 December

INSURANCE

Sometimes foreign travellers are asked to prove they have valid medical insurance when entering the country, and not all insurances are deemed acceptable. Unfortunately, the rules are not clear on what's accepted and what's not. However, if they don't like your insurance, they will say you must by a Ukrainian policy, which is usually pretty cheap (about US$0.50 a day).

INTERNET RESOURCES

You may wish to access one of the following websites before or during your travels:
www.brama.com Great travel bulletin board.
www.greentour.com.ua Recreation and home-stay opportunities in rural areas.
www.travel-2-ukraine.com Tours and visa support.
www.tryukraine.com Information on a work-study program, among other things.

LANGUAGE

Ukrainian was adopted as the sole official language at independence. However, apart from the west, many Ukrainians (especially in the south), prefer to speak Russian. A hybrid of the two languages, called Surzhyk, is spoken in Kyiv and other major cities. In the Carpathians, some people living outside of city centres speak a Ukrainian dialect that is influenced by Polish, Slovak and Russian; they usually understand Russian well, but it may be difficult to understand their Russian.

MONEY

The *hryvnia* is divided into 100 units, each called a *kopek*. In addition to the new one-*hryvnia* coins, *kopek* coins come in denominations of one, two, five, 10, 25 and 50 *kopeks*, while there are one, two, five, 10, 20, 50, 100 and 200 *hryvnia* notes.

The only things you can legally pay for in foreign currency (usually US dollars)

UKRAINE

are international flights and foreign visas. Although many hotels give prices in US dollars or euros, you will still be paying in *hryvnia*.

ATMs and foreign-exchange offices (euros and US dollars only) are easily found even in small cities in Ukraine, and Western Union seems to have a desk in most banks. Exchanging money on the black market is unnecessary and illegal. Avoid bringing traveller's cheques – they're hard to change.

POST

Normal-sized letters or postcards cost 3hry to anywhere outside Ukraine by 'ordinary mail' or 3.50hry for 'express' service. Domestic services take three days to a week; international takes a week to 10 days. There are offices of DHL and FedEx in many cities.

TELEPHONE & FAX

You may be able to reach an English-speaking operator by dialling ☎ 8, waiting for the tone, and then dialling ☎ 191. Often, they won't speak English but will at least be able to understand you a bit.

When dialling Ukraine from abroad, dial the country code (☎ 38), the area code and then the relevant number. To call overseas from Ukraine, dial ☎ 810, followed by the country code, area code and number. You can reach an AT&T operator by dialling ☎ 8-10-011 and an MCI operator by dialling ☎ 8-10-013.

For interstate calls within Ukraine, dial ☎ 8, the area code and then the appropriate number – there should always be a 10-digit combination. If a telephone number has seven digits, use the first two digits of the area code, but if the telephone number has five/six digits use the first four/three digits of the area code.

Every city and large town has a telephone centre (many open 24 hours), usually near the central post office. To make interstate or international calls, pay in advance at the counter inside the telephone centre (you will get change for unused time). Avoid using public phone booths, which require specific phonecards and are a hassle.

Your GSM mobile phone will probably work in Ukraine, but contact your own operator to make sure. Ukrainian mobile phone companies include **Kyivstar** (www.kyivstar.net) and UMC. Rentals can be arranged in Kyiv. Mobile phone numbers, which sometimes cannot be dialled from hotel rooms, start with an '8' and are followed by a three-digit code that starts with a '0' before the actually phone number begins. If you are dialling a Ukrainian cell phone number from outside the country, omit the '8'.

Faxes can be sent and received from any major post office for the cost of the equivalent telephone call.

EMERGENCY NUMBERS

- Ambulance ☎ 03
- Fire ☎ 01
- Police ☎ 02

VISAS

With the exception of citizens of the CIS and few other countries, all visitors need a visa (US$40 to US$100). Always get your visa in advance and disregard anything you read that tells you that you can get any kind of visa (including transit) upon arrival.

Visas are not difficult to obtain, but visa regulations are in disarray. The requirements seem to vary not only from consulate to consulate, but even from visa application to visa application within a single consulate. To save time and money, contact your consulate before applying to find out what it requires.

The technical truth is that private, business and transit visas do not require 'visa support' (an invitation from a hotel or tourist agency, or proof of prebooked accommodation for at least the first night), but the visa that applies to most visitors – the tourist visa – does require it. However, many readers (including the author) have recently received a tourist visa without having to first obtain visa support.

People whose consulate requires an invitation for tourist visas have reported that they have had no trouble if they just apply for a private visa instead, making up a place they'll be staying on the form. If your consulate for whatever reason does request visa support, you can get one from online agencies (US$30 to US$50); search under 'ukraine tourist visa'. Transit visas are required (a Russian visa doesn't cut it), *are not* issued on arrival (get yours in advance) and cannot be extended.

For more information, look at the following websites:

www.ukremb.com

www.usemb.kiev.ua

http://thorntree.lonelyplanet.com Eastern Europe branch

www.brama.com Travel bulletin board for Ukraine.

Visa Extensions

Tourist visas can be extended for a maximum of two months at the **Department of Citizenship, Passport & Immigration** (Map pp832-3; ☎ 044-224 90 51; bulvar Tarasa Shevchenka 34, Kyiv; Ⓜ Universitet; ☉ 9am-5pm Mon-Fri). The cost of the extension is about 10hry (US$2) per day. If you have applied for a tourist visa through a Ukrainian-based travel agency it should arrange the extension (for an extra fee of about US$30). Tourist visas are valid for six months.

TRANSPORT IN UKRAINE

GETTING THERE & AWAY
Air

Departure tax is included in the cost of all flights whether the ticket is bought inside or outside the country.

All international flights use Kyiv's **Boryspil International Airport** (☎ 044-296 76 09; www.airport-borispol.kiev.ua). Ukraine's international airline carriers are **AeroSvit** (☎ 044-490 34 90; www.aerosvit.com) and **Ukraine International Airlines** (☎ 044-461 50 50; www.ukraine-international.com).

The following are the main international airlines with offices in Kyiv (area code ☎ 044). Complete airline information can be found in the quarterly *Kyiv Business Directory* (sold outside Kyiv's Central Post Office).

Aeroflot (code SU; ☎ 245 42 39; www.aeroflot.com)

Air Baltic (code BT; ☎ 238 26 49; www.airbaltic.com)

Air France (code AF; ☎ 464 10 10; www.airfrance.com)

Austrian Airlines (code OS; ☎ 244 35 40; www.austrianair.com)

British Airways (code BA; ☎ 490 60 60; www.british-airways.com)

ČSA (Czech Airlines; code OK; ☎ 246 56 27; www.csa.cz)

Delta Airlines (code DL; ☎ 246 56 56; www.delta.com)

El Al (code LY; ☎ 230 69 93; www.elal.co.il)

Estonian Air (code OV; ☎ 220 05 20; www.estonian-air.ee)

Finnair (code AY; ☎ 247 57 77; www.finnair.com)

KLM (code KL; ☎ 490 24 90; www.klm.com)

LOT Polish Airlines (code LO; ☎ 246 56 20; www.lot.com)

Lufthansa (code LH; ☎ 490 38 00; www.lufthansa.com)

Malév (Hungarian Airlines; code MA; ☎ 490 73 42; www.malev.hu)

Siberia Airlines (code S7; ☎ 247 57 90; www.s7.ru) Cheapest flight to/from Moscow.

Transaero (code UN; ☎ 490 65 65; http://eagle.transaero.ru/english/)

Turkish Airlines (code TK; ☎ 490 59 33; www.turkishairlines.com)

Within Eastern Europe there are daily flights to/from Kyiv and Budapest (US$312 round trip, three daily, two hours), Moscow ($160 round trip, at least two daily, 1½ hours), Prague and Warsaw ($350, daily, 1½ hours). Sofia flights are twice a week, and Tallinn flights are thrice weekly. Flights to/from Riga happen daily except Saturday. Simferopol is connected with Tallinn, Sofia, Moscow and St Petersburg.

Also, there are direct flights between Lviv and Warsaw ($220 round trip, 1½ hours, at least one weekly), and AeroSvit connects Odesa with Budapest ($310, 1½ hours, one to five weekly) and Warsaw ($300, two hours, five weekly).

Land
BUS

Buses are far slower, less frequent and less comfortable than the trains for long-distance travel. From the Kyiv central bus station there are buses to Chisinau (48hry, 13 hours, two daily) and Moscow (75hry, 21 hours, one daily).

From Lviv, there are daily buses to Brest (20hry, 19 hours) and Warsaw (88hry, 10 hours) and twice-weekly buses to Riga (233hry, 18 hours).

From Uzhhorod, there are one or two daily buses to the Slovak cities of Košice (26.50hry, three hours) and Michalovce (12.50hry, two hours), and to the Hungarian city of Nyiregyhaza (25.50hry, three hours).

From Ivano-Frankivsk, you can get to the Polish cities of Lublin (60hry, 10 hours, Sunday to Friday) and Warsaw (94hry, 14 hours, one to three daily) and to Prague (220hry, 24 hours, one to two daily).

From Chernivtsi, there are daily buses to Brest (56hry, 15 hours).

UKRAINE

From Odesa, there are ten daily buses to Chisinau (20hry, seven hours) and thrice-weekly buses to Prague (320hry, 32 hours, Tuesday, Friday and Sunday).

From Yalta, there is one bus a day to Chisinau (86hry, 19 hours).

CAR & MOTORCYCLE

At the border, foreigners must sign a document saying they will be exiting the country with the car by a given date (no more than two months later). You'll also require appropriate vehicle insurance, which can be purchased at the border, but since border guards have been known to sell useless policies, try to get it in advance. See (opposite) for more information.

TRAIN

See the boxed text Train-riding Etiquette (p82) for tips on how to mix with fellow passengers.

Classes

Second (kupeyny) class will get you a place in a four-person car. Platskartny compartments, while cheaper, have open bunk accommodations. They are not great for those who value privacy but are good for socialising with locals.

Costs

The following trains leave from Kyiv:

Destination	Cost (k/p)	Duration	Frequency
Belgrade	671hry/-	34hr	1 daily
Brest	103/66hry	15hr	odd dates
Chişinău	99/65hry	17hr	3 daily
Kraków	388hry/-	16hr	3 weekly
Minsk	102/64hry	12hr	1-2 daily
Moscow	134/86hry	15hr	13-15 daily
Prague	567hry/-	35hr	1 daily
Sofia	420hry/-	16hr	1 daily
St Petersburg	175/113hry	26hr	1 daily
Warsaw	313hry/-	18hr	1 daily
Zagreb	810hry/-	31hr	each Thu

From Lviv, there are daily trains to Brest (kupeyny/platskartny 62/39hry, 11 hours), Moscow (205/135hry, 25 hours), Prague (390hry, 24 hours, kupe only) and St Petersburg (205/135hry, 31 hours) and three daily to Warsaw (210hry, 11 hours, kupe only).

From Chop, near Uzhhorod, there are daily trains to Moscow (260/160hry, 24 hours), Budapest (229hry, four hours, sitting only) and Bratislava (280hry, 12 hours, kupe only) and three a week to Zagreb (451hry, 15 hours, Monday, Thursday and Saturday, kupe only).

From Ivano-Frankivsk, there are daily trains to Moscow (205/131hry, 15 hours). On odd dates, there are trains to Minsk (101/65hry, 26 hours). Four times a week, there are trains to St Petersburg (220/141hry, 42 hours). On even dates, there are trains to Brest (88/57hry, 16 hours).

From Chernivtsi, there are trains to Brest (97/63hry, 19 hours) and St Petersburg (229/147hry, 45 hours) on even dates. Trains bound for Moscow (190/125hry, 35 hours) leave twice daily, and there are daily trains to Sofia (287hry, 24 hours, kupe only).

From little ol' Kamyanets-Podilsky, trains leave daily to Brest (46hry, 15 hours).

Odesa has several foreign-bound trains. Two per day leave for Chisinau (14.50hry, five hours, sitting only). There is least one train a day to Moscow (220/135hry, 26 hours) and St Petersburg (250/150hry, 12 hours). On even dates, there are trains to Warsaw (380hry, 25 hours, kupe only), and twice a week there are trains to Minsk (170/109hry, 23 hours, Tuesday and Saturday).

From Simferopol, there are twice-daily trains to Moscow (213/148hry, 25 hours) and daily trains to St Petersburg (247/175hry, 32 hours). On even dates, there are trains to Minsk (192/123hry, 34 hours).

From Sevastopol, there are daily trains to Moscow (213/137hry, 29 hours) and St Petersburg (289/185hry, 34 hours). On even dates, trains leave for Minsk (192/127hry, 31 hours).

Sea

Between May and September, boats cruise to Varna (Bulgaria), Istanbul and Sochi (Russia) from Odesa, Sevastopol and Yalta. Information about, and tickets for, all boats around the Black Sea from Ukraine are available from Eugenia Travel (p852).

Orthodox Cruises (www.cruise.ru) offers a variety of cruises along the Dnipro River and into the Black Sea, with stops in Russia, Ukraine and Romania.

The **boat passenger terminal** (☎ 32 30 64; fax 32 30 64; vulitsa Ruzvelta) in Yalta is severely underused and underadvertised, but has cruises to/from Istanbul (one way/return US$95/170-255). Also, there are eight-day cruises from Yalta that stop in Odesa, Sochi (Russia), Batumi (Georgia) and Istanbul (US$399 to US$1950). However, since this is so poorly marketed, the boats sometimes don't fill enough and can be cancelled. It's best to check at the terminal, or try Eugenia Travel (p852) in Odesa.

GETTING AROUND
Air
Schedules can be confusing, so you may want to consider booking your tickets with a reputable travel agency. In Kyiv, there are several offices of **Kiyavia** (Map pp832-3; ☎ 056 or 490 49 49; www.kiyavia.com; vulitsa Horodetskoho 4; Ⓜ Khreshchatyk). Tickets within the CIS can be booked by email through Kiyavia but must be picked up in person. Departure taxes are included in the cost of the ticket.

Domestic flights run between Kyiv, Lviv, Odesa, Chernivtsi, Simferopol and Ivano-Frankivsk. In Kyiv, virtually all domestic flights arrive at and depart from **Zhulyany Airport** (Map p831; ☎ 242 23 08; www.airport.kiev .ua, in Ukrainian) For the most part, tickets for domestic flights can only be bought in the country. In winter, flights on smaller planes (such as Yak-40s and An-24s) are sometimes delayed or cancelled.

Lviv Airlines (☎ 0322-69 21 12; www.avia.lviv.ua) is one of the major Ukrainian airlines, along with AeroSvit and Ukraine International Airlines, who also fly internationally.

Bus
Travelling around the country by train is often far quicker and more comfortable than by bus, so long-distance bus routes are gradually disappearing throughout Ukraine. Most public buses are decrepit, but a few private bus companies, such as **Autolux** (www.autolux.com.ua), offer comfortable services between points in Crimea, Kyiv, Odesa and Lviv. Schedules and price information are available on the website.

Larger cities often have several *avtovok-zal* (bus terminals) but only one normally handles long-distance routes of interest to travellers. Tickets can be bought one or two days in advance at the major bus terminal

and sometimes at separate ticket offices in the city centres.

Boat
Passenger boats cruise along the Black Sea coast during summer; contact Eugenia Travel (p852) for details of these cruises, and for Dnipro River trips.

Car & Motorcycle
To drive a private or rented vehicle to and around Ukraine you'll need an International Driving Permit/Licence and acceptable insurance. Ukraine participates in the Green Card System (p898), so procure one in advance, as border guards have been known to sell useless policies.

In theory, cars should be driven on the right. Speed limits are normally 60km/h in towns, 90km/h on major roads and 130km/h on highways. It's illegal to drive if you have drunk *anything* beforehand, and drivers and front-seat passengers must wear seat belts (although the latter is commonly flouted).

Carry your registration, insurance and all other documents at all times. Traffic cops cannot issue on-the-spot fines; they can only write you a ticket. Many drivers find they can avoid a ticket by keeping a spare 10hry or so tucked into their documents.

Major international car rental companies, such as Avis, Europcar and Hertz, have offices at the airports in Kyiv and Odesa. You may need special permission from the rental

---

DON'T LET THIS HAPPEN TO YOU

When travelling by train between Western Ukraine and Odesa, be very warned. Some of those trains travel through Moldova, for which you need a visa if you don't want to be tossed off the train at the border (probably at night).

The person selling you your ticket won't just offer up a warning. If you don't speak Ukrainian, ask 'Ts-*ey po*-yizd id-*e cher*-ez Mol-do-*vu*?' (Does this train go through Moldova?) or point to this: Цей поїзд іде через Молдову?

Although the train between Kyiv and Chernivtsi briefly crosses into Moldova, Moldovan immigration officials don't seem perturbed if you can prove that you're going back into Ukraine.

UKRAINE

company to drive outside the Kyiv or Odesa areas. You can also rent a car with a driver through larger hotels and better travel agencies in Kyiv, Lviv, Ivano-Frankivsk, Yalta and Odesa. For day trips, haggle with a taxi driver, but pay no more than 30hry per hour or about 1hry per kilometre.

Parking has apparently just been an afterthought for city planners. Only now are proper parking lots and garages starting to be built. Many drivers just park on sidewalks; this is sometimes controlled (paid, or fined).

Local Transport

Cheap but crowded trolleybuses, trams and buses operate in all cities and major towns. Tickets can be bought on board and *must* be punched to be validated – look for others doing this to see how.

One form of transport (both city- and nation-wide) that doesn't exist in western Europe is the shared *marshrutka*. These quick but cramped minibuses are used throughout Ukraine as a form of both intercity and city transport.

The fare for any given *marshrutka* is displayed prominently in each bus. To stop a *marshrutka*, simply hold out your hand

and it will stop. Jump in, sit down, pass cash to the driver (a human chain operates if you are not sat nearby) and then call out '*ostanovityes pozhalusta!*' when you want to get out and the driver will pull over.

Trams and trolleys are another phenomenon of the former Soviet Union. They are cheaper but slower than buses and *marshrutkas*. For buses, trams and trolleys, you can pay on board.

Although it's often possible to hire an official taxi in larger towns, private taxis are a popular and surprisingly safe alternative, but it's too difficult to do this if you don't speak Ukrainian or Russian. You can flag down a taxi (private or public) like a *marshrutka*. Negotiate a price before you get in, and never get into a car if there's already a passenger.

Train

Train travel is normally frequent, cheap and efficient. An overnight train is an economical way to get around, and most services are timed to depart at dusk and arrive in the morning (after dawn). For information on train classes and terminology, see p866.

If you will be travelling during the May 1 holidays, book tickets in advance.

Regional Directory

CONTENTS

Accommodation	869
Activities	871
Business Hours	873
Children	873
Climate Charts	873
Courses	873
Customs	873
Dangers & Annoyances	875
Disabled Travellers	876
Discount Cards	876
DVD & Video Systems	877
Electricity	877
Embassies & Consulates	878
Gay & Lesbian Travellers	878
Holidays	878
Insurance	878
Internet Access	878
Maps	879
Money	879
Photography & Video	880
Post	881
Solo Travellers	881
Telephone	881
Time	882
Tourist Information	882
Visas & Documents	883
Women Travellers	884
Work	885

The regional directory gives general overviews of conditions and information that apply to the whole of Eastern Europe. Given the vast size of the region, this has meant some generalisation, so for specifics on any given topic, see the relevant directory for the country you require information on.

ACCOMMODATION

As a rule, for each accommodation listing we have used the currency you are most likely to be quoted a price in. This means that for some hotels we give hotel prices in local currency, others are listed in euros or US dollars.

In Eastern Europe, as in the rest of Europe, the cheapest places to find a place to rest your head are camping grounds, followed by hostels and student accommodation. Guesthouses, pensions, private rooms and cheap hotels are also good value. Self-catering flats in the city and cottages in the countryside are worth considering if you're in a group, especially if you plan to stay put for a while.

See the directory sections in the individual country chapters for an overview of local accommodation options. During peak holiday periods, accommodation can be hard to find and, unless you're camping, it's advisable to book ahead where possible. Even some camping grounds can fill up, particularly popular ones near large towns and cities.

Hostels and cheap hotels in popular tourist destinations, such as Prague, Budapest and Kraków, fill up very quickly – especially the well-run ones in desirable or central neighbourhoods. It's a good idea to make reservations as many weeks ahead as possible – at least for the first night or two. A two- or three-minute international phone call to book a bed or room is a more sensible use of time than wasting your first day in a city searching for a place to stay.

If you arrive in a country by air, there is often an accommodation-booking desk at the airport, although it rarely covers the lower strata of hotels. Tourist offices often have extensive accommodation lists, and the more helpful ones will go out of their way to find you something suitable. In most countries the fee for this service is very low, and if the accommodation market is tight, it can save you a lot of running around.

The accommodation options in each city or town are listed according to price range. Starting with budget options, then mid-range and top end, we try to include a balanced representation of what's available in each place. Of course, in some cities there's a lack of budget accommodation and too many top end places to list, or vice versa. Where possible though, we try to keep these as balanced as we can. Within these subsections, the accommodation options are listed in ascending price order, with camping first.

REGIONAL DIRECTORY

Camping

The cheapest way to go is camping, and there are many camping grounds throughout the region. Many are large sites intended mainly for motorists, though they're often easily accessible by public transport and there's almost always space for backpackers with tents. Many camping grounds in Eastern Europe rent small on-site cabins, bungalows or caravans for double or triple the regular camping fee. In the most popular resorts all the bungalows will probably be full in July and August. Some countries, including Albania and Belarus, have yet to develop any camping grounds at all.

The standard of camping grounds in the rest of Eastern Europe varies from country to country. They're unreliable in Romania, crowded in Hungary (especially on Lake Balaton) and Slovenia, and variable in the Czech Republic, Poland, Slovakia and Bulgaria. Croatia's coast has nudist camping grounds galore (signposted 'FKK', the German acronym for 'naturist'); they're excellent places to stay because of their secluded locations – if you don't mind baring it all.

Camping grounds may be open from April to October, May to September, or perhaps only June to August, depending on the category of the facility, the location and demand. A few private camping grounds are open year-round. In Eastern Europe you are sometimes allowed to build a campfire (ask first). Camping in the wild is usually illegal; ask local people about the situation before you pitch your tent on a beach or in an open field.

Farmhouses

'Village tourism', which means staying at a farmhouse, is highly developed in Estonia, Latvia, Lithuania and Slovenia, and popular in Hungary. In the Baltic countries and Slovenia it's like staying in a private room or pension, except that the participating farms are in picturesque rural areas and may offer nearby activities such as horse riding, kayaking, skiing and cycling. It's highly recommended.

Guesthouses & Pensions

Small private pensions are now very common in parts of Eastern Europe. Priced somewhere between hotels and private rooms, pensions typically have less than a dozen rooms and sometimes a small restaurant or bar on the premises. You'll get much more personal service at a pension than you would at a hotel at the expense of a wee bit of privacy. If you arrive at night or on a weekend when the travel agencies assigning private rooms are closed, pensions can be a lifesaver. Call ahead to check prices and ask about reservations – someone will usually speak some halting English, German or Russian.

Homestays & Private Rooms

Homestays are often the best and most authentic way to see daily life in Eastern Europe. It's perfectly legal to stay with someone in a private home (although in countries such as Russia, where visa registration is necessary, you'll have to pay a travel agency to register your visa with a hotel). Staying with Eastern European friends will be a wonderful experience, thanks to the full hospitality the region is justly famous for. Make sure you bring some small gifts for your hosts – it's a deeply ingrained cultural tradition throughout the region.

In most Eastern European countries, travel agencies can arrange accommodation in private rooms in local homes. In Hungary you can get a private room almost anywhere, but in the other countries only the main tourist centres have them. Some 1st-class rooms are like mini-apartments, with cooking facilities and private bathrooms for the sole use of guests. Prices are low but there's often a 30% to 50% surcharge if you stay less than three nights. In Hungary, the Czech Republic and Croatia, higher taxation has made such a deal less attractive than before, but it's still good value and cheaper than a hotel.

People will frequently approach you at train or bus stations in Eastern Europe offering a private room or a hostel bed. This can be good or bad – it's impossible to generalise. Just make sure it's not in some cardboard-quality housing project in the outer suburbs and that you negotiate a clear price. Obviously, if you are staying with strangers like this, you shouldn't leave your valuables behind when you go out; certainly don't leave your money, credit cards or passport.

You don't have to go through an agency or an intermediary on the street for a private room. Any house, cottage or farmhouse with *zimmer frei, sobe* or *szoba kiadó* displayed outside is advertising the availability of private rooms (these examples are in German, Slovene and Hungarian); just knock on the door and ask if any are available.

Hostels

Hostels offer the cheapest (secure) roof over your head in Eastern Europe, and you don't have to be a youngster to take advantage of them. Most hostels are part of the national Youth Hostel Association (YHA), which is affiliated with the Hostelling International (HI) umbrella organisation.

Hostels affiliated with HI can be found in most Eastern European countries. A hostel card is seldom required, though you sometimes get a small discount if you have one. If you don't have a valid HI membership card, you can buy one at some hostels.

To join the HI, you can ask at any hostel or contact your local or national hostelling office. There's a very useful website at www .iyhf.org, with links to most HI sites.

At a hostel, you get a bed for the night plus use of communal facilities, often including a kitchen where you can prepare your own meals. You may be required to have a sleeping sheet – simply using your sleeping bag is often not allowed. If you don't have a sleeping sheet, you can sometimes hire one for a small fee.

Hostels vary widely in their character and quality. The hostels in Poland tend to be extremely basic but they're inexpensive and friendly. In the Czech Republic and Slovakia many hostels are actually fairly luxurious 'junior' hotels with double rooms, often fully occupied by groups. Many Hungarian hostels outside Budapest are student dormitories open to travellers for six or seven weeks in summer only. In Budapest and Prague a number of privately run hostels now operate year-round and are serious party venues. The hostels in Bulgaria are in cities, resort and mountain areas.

There are many available hostel guides with listings, including the bible, HI's *Europe*. Many hostels accept reservations by phone, fax or email, but not always during peak periods (though they might hold a bed for you for a couple of hours if you call from the train or bus station). You can also book hostels through national hostel offices.

Hotels

At the bottom of the bracket, cheap hotels may be no more expensive than private rooms or guesthouses, while at the other extreme they extend to five-star hotels with price tags to match. Categorisation varies from country to country and the hotels recommended in this book accommodate every budget. We have endeavoured, where possible, to provide a combination of budget, mid-range and top-end accommodation in each city or town. Where the full gauntlet of price ranges isn't available, we simply make a note of what is.

Single rooms can be hard to find in Eastern Europe, where you are generally charged by the room and not by the number of people in it; many local people still refuse to believe that anyone would actually take to the road alone. The cheapest rooms sometimes have a washbasin but no bathroom, which means you'll have to go down the corridor to use the toilet and shower. Breakfast may be included in the price of a room or be extra – and mandatory.

University Accommodation

Some universities rent out space in student halls in July and August. This is quite popular in the Baltic countries, Croatia, the Czech Republic, Hungary, Macedonia, Poland, Russia, Slovakia and Slovenia. Accommodation will sometimes be in single rooms (but is more commonly in doubles or triples), and cooking facilities may be available. Inquire at the college or university, at student information services or at local tourist offices.

ACTIVITIES
Canoeing & Kayaking

Those travelling with folding kayaks will want to launch them on the waterways surrounding Poland's Great Masurian Lakes district, on the Danube, Rába and Tisza Rivers in Hungary, the Soča River in Slovenia, the Vltava River in the Czech Republic and Latvia's Gauja and Salaca Rivers and its Latgale lakes region. Special kayaking and canoeing tours are offered in these countries, as well as in Croatia.

Cycling

Along with hiking, cycling is the best way to really get close to the scenery and the people, keeping you fit in the process. It's also a good way to get around many cities and towns and to see remote corners of a country you wouldn't ordinarily get to.

The hills and mountains of Eastern Europe can be heavy going, but this is offset by the abundance of things to see. Physical fitness is *not* a major prerequisite for cycling on the plains of eastern Hungary (they're flatter than pancakes!) but the persistent wind might slow you down. Popular holiday cycling areas in Eastern Europe include the Danube Bend in Hungary, most of eastern Slovakia, the Karst region of Slovenia, and the Curonian Spit and Palanga in western Lithuania. The valleys of Maramureş in northern Romania are a great place for a cycling tour. Most airlines will allow you to put a bicycle in the hold for a surprisingly small fee. Alternatively, this book lists possible places where you can hire one.

See Bicycle in the Transport in Eastern Europe section (p896) for more information on bicycle touring, and the individual country chapters and destination sections for rental outfits as well as routes and tips on places to go.

Hiking

There's excellent hiking in Eastern Europe, with well-marked trails through forests, mountains and national parks. Public transport will often take you to the trailheads; chalets or mountain huts in Poland, Bulgaria, Slovakia, Romania and Slovenia offer dormitory accommodation and basic meals. In this book we include information about hiking in the High Tatra Mountains of Poland and Slovakia, the Malá Fatra of Slovakia, the Bucegi and Făgăraş Ranges in Romania's Carpathian Mountains, the Rila Mountains of Bulgaria, the Julian Alps of Slovenia and the spectacular Crimean mountain range of Ukraine, but there are many other hiking areas that are less well known, including the Bieszczady in Poland, Risnjak and Paklenica National Parks in Croatia and the Zemplén Hills in Hungary. The best months for hiking are from June to September, especially late August and early September when the summer crowds will have disappeared.

Horse Riding

Though horse riding is possible throughout Eastern Europe, the sport is best organised – and cheapest – in Hungary, whose people, it is said, 'were created by God to sit on horseback'. The best centres are on the Great Plain, though you'll also find riding schools in Transdanubia and northern Hungary. Horse riding is also very popular (and affordable) in the Baltic countries, Czech Republic, Poland and Slovenia.

Sailing

Eastern Europe's most famous yachting area is the passage between the long rugged islands off Croatia's Dalmatian coast. Yacht tours and rentals are available, although this is certainly not for anyone on a budget. If your means are more limited, the Great Masurian Lakes of northeastern Poland are a better choice, as small groups can rent sailing boats by the day for very reasonable rates. Hungary's Lake Balaton is also popular among sailing enthusiasts.

Skiing

Eastern Europe's premier skiing areas are the High Tatra Mountains of Slovakia and Poland; the Carpathians near Braşov in Romania and Yablunytsia in Ukraine; Borovets in the Rila Mountains near Sofia; Pamporovo in the Rodopi Mountains in Bulgaria and Slovenia's Julian Alps. The skiing season generally lasts from early December to late March, though at higher altitudes it may extend an extra month either way. Snow conditions can vary greatly from year to year and region to region, but January and February tend to be the best (and busiest) months. Snowboarding is especially popular in Slovakia, as is cross-country skiing in the Czech Republic and Ukraine.

Thermal Baths & Saunas

There are hundreds of thermal baths in Eastern Europe open to the public. The most affordable are in the Czech Republic, Hungary and Slovenia, as well as along the Black Sea in Romania. Among the best are the thermal lake at Hévíz, the Turkish baths of Budapest and the spa town of Harkány in Hungary; the *fin-de-siécle* spas of Karlovy Vary (Karlsbad) and Mariánské Lázně (Marienbad) in the Czech Republic; and the spas at Rogaška Slatina in Slovenia.

The Baltic countries are famous for the proliferation of saunas – both the traditional 'smoke' variety and the clean and smokeless modern sauna. A good example of the latter is in Hotel Olümpia in Tallinn, while the traditionalist will find many opportunities to take in an old-style sauna in Lithuania. Another must for lovers of heat and sweat is the traditional Russian *banya* where you can be beaten into cleanliness with birch twigs!

White-Water Rafting

This exciting activity is possible in summer on two of Eastern Europe's most scenic rivers: the Tara River in Montenegro and the Soča River in Slovenia. Rafting on the Dunajec River along the border of Poland and Slovakia is fun, but it's not a whitewater experience.

BUSINESS HOURS

Eastern Europe tends to have similar working patterns to Western Europe and North America. Saturdays and Sundays are usually days off, although only banks and offices are shut – most shops, restaurants and cafés are open everyday of the week.

Banks are usually open from 9am to 5pm Monday to Friday, often with an hour or two off for lunch. During the hot summer months, some enterprises will shut for two or three hours in the early afternoon, reopening at 3pm or 4pm and working into the evening when it's cooler. See the directory of whichever country you are in for more specific detail.

CHILDREN

Successful travel with young children requires planning and effort. Don't try to overdo things; even for adults, packing too much into the time available can cause problems. And make sure the activities include the kids as well – balance that morning at Budapest's Museum of Fine Arts with a performance at the Puppet Theatre.

Include children in the trip planning; if they've helped to work out where you will be going, they will be much more interested when they get there. In Eastern Europe most car-rental firms have children's safety seats for hire at a small cost, but it is essential that you book them in advance. The same goes for high chairs and cots (cribs);

they're standard in many restaurants and hotels but numbers are limited. The choice of baby food, infant formulas, soy and cow's milk, disposable nappies (diapers) and the like can be as great in the supermarkets of many Eastern European countries as it is back home, but the opening hours may be quite different to what you are used to. Don't get caught out on the weekend.

CLIMATE CHARTS

The weather in Eastern Europe can be fairly extreme at times, but never enough to prevent travel. It's a fascinating place to visit any time of year – even during the icy winter (and that's particularly icy in the Baltic countries, Russia and Ukraine) the cities take on a magical frosty charm. July and August can be uncomfortably hot in the cities and throughout the Balkans, but this is the time when the alpine areas such as the High Tatras, the Carpathians and the Rila Mountains are best to visit, not to mention the beaches. All in all, May, June and September are the best times to visit from a climatic point of view, as nowhere will be too warm or too cool.

COURSES

Apart from learning new physical skills by doing something like a ski course in Slovenia or horse riding in Hungary, you can enrich your mind with a variety of structured courses in Eastern Europe, on anything from language to alternative medicine. Language courses are often available to foreigners through universities or private schools, and are justifiably popular, as the best way to learn a language is in the country where it's spoken.

In general, the best sources of information are the cultural institutes maintained by many European countries around the world; failing that, you could try national tourist offices or embassies. Student exchange organisations, student travel agencies, and organisations such as Hostelling International (HI) can also put you on the right track.

CUSTOMS

While there's no problem with bringing in and taking out personal effects, be aware that antiques, books printed before 1945, crystal glass, gemstones, lottery tickets,

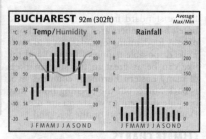

BUCHAREST 92m (302ft)

Average Max/Min

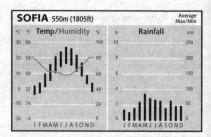

SOFIA 550m (1805ft)

Average Max/Min

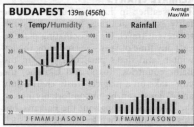

BUDAPEST 139m (456ft)

Average Max/Min

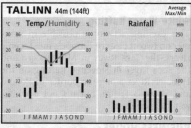

TALLINN 44m (144ft)

Average Max/Min

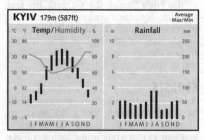

KYIV 179m (587ft)

Average Max/Min

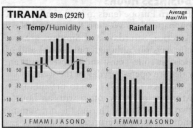

TIRANA 89m (292ft)

Average Max/Min

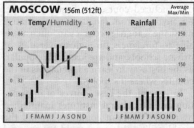

MOSCOW 156m (512ft)

Average Max/Min

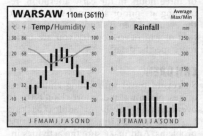

WARSAW 110m (361ft)

Average Max/Min

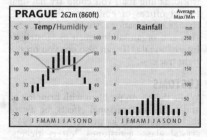

PRAGUE 262m (860ft)

Average Max/Min

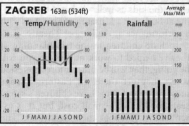

ZAGREB 163m (534ft)

Average Max/Min

philatelic materials, precious metals (gold, silver, platinum), securities and valuable works of art may still have to be declared in writing or even accompanied by a 'museum certificate' (available from the place of purchase) in many Eastern European countries. There may also be restrictions on the import/export of local currency, although the amounts allowed these days are actually quite large.

Throughout most of Eastern Europe, the usual allowances for tobacco (eg 200 to 250 cigarettes, but a lung-busting 1000 cigarettes in Belarus), alcohol (2L of wine, 1L of spirits) and perfume (50g) apply to duty-free goods purchased at airports or on ferries. Customs checks are pretty cursory and you probably won't even have to open your bags, but don't be lulled into a false sense of security.

DANGERS & ANNOYANCES

Eastern Europe is as safe – or unsafe – as any other part of the developed world. If you can handle yourself in the big cities of Western Europe, North America or Australia, you'll have little trouble dealing with the less pleasant sides of Eastern Europe. Look purposeful, keep alert and you'll be OK.

Whatever you do, don't leave friends and relatives worrying about how to get in touch with you in case of emergency. Work out a list of places where they can contact you or, best of all, email or phone home now and then.

Some locals will regale you with tales of how dangerous their city is and recount various cases of muggings, break-ins, kidnappings etc. Mostly they're comparing the present situation with that under communism when the crime rate was almost zero or, more usually, went unreported in the press. Bosnia and Kosovo have a unique form of danger – land mines. It's the only time Lonely Planet will ever advise you *not* to venture off the beaten track.

Low-level corruption is disappearing fast as the back-scratching system so common during the communist regimes claims its rightful place in the dustbin of history, so do *not* pay bribes to persons in official positions, such as police, border guards, train conductors, ticket inspectors etc. If corrupt cops want to hold you up because some obscure stamp is missing from your

documentation or on some other pretext, just let them and consider the experience an integral part of your trip. Threatening to call your embassy is always a good move; if the situation is brought to the attention of the officer's superiors, they will, unsurprisingly, get in trouble.

Don't worry at all if you're taken to the police station for questioning as you'll have a unique opportunity to observe the quality of justice in that country from the inside, and more senior officers will eventually let you go (assuming, of course, you haven't committed a real crime). If you do have to pay a fine or supplementary charge, insist on a proper receipt before turning over any money; this is now law in Hungary, for example, where traffic police were once notorious for demanding (and getting) 'gifts' from motorists guilty of some alleged infraction. In all of this, try to maintain your cool, as any threats from you will only make matters worse.

Drugs

Always treat drugs with a great deal of caution. There are a lot of drugs available in the region, but that doesn't mean they are legal. The continual fighting in the former Serbia and Montenegro in the 1990s forced drug traders to seek alternative routes from Asia to Western Europe, sometimes crossing through Hungary, Slovakia, the Czech Republic and Poland. Now EU members, these countries do not look lightly upon drug abuse.

Scams

A word of warning about credit cards: fraudulent shopkeepers have been known to make several charge-slip imprints with your credit card when you're not looking and then simply copy your signature from the authorised slip. There have also been reports of these unscrupulous people making quick and very high-tech duplicates of credit or debit card information with a machine. If your card leaves your possession for longer than you think necessary, consider cancelling it.

Now that most Eastern European currencies have reached (or are approaching) convertibility, the days of getting five times the official rate for cash on the streets of Warsaw and Bucharest are well and truly over. Essentially there is no longer a black market in most countries of this region; anyone who approaches you offering such a deal (an uncommon occurrence these days) is your average, garden-variety thief.

Theft

Theft is definitely a problem in Eastern Europe, and the threat comes from both local thieves and fellow travellers. The most important things to guard are your passport, other documents, tickets and money – in that order. It's always best to carry these next to your skin or in a sturdy leather pouch on your belt. Train-station lockers or luggage-storage counters are useful to store your luggage (but not valuables) while you get your bearings in a new town. Be very suspicious of people who offer to help you operate your locker. Carry your own padlock for hostel lockers.

You can lessen the risks further by being wary of snatch thieves. Cameras or shoulder bags are great for these people, who sometimes operate from motorcycles or scooters and slash the strap before you have a chance to react. A small daypack is better, but watch your rear. Be very careful at cafés and bars; loop the strap around your leg while seated. While it makes pickpocketing harder, carrying a backpack on your front will both let everyone know you are a tourist (and one who thinks everyone is a thief) as well as make you look like a prize idiot. Far better is to keep all valuables in inside pockets and only have things you could stand to lose in easily accessible pockets.

Pickpockets are most active in dense crowds, especially in busy train stations and on public transport during peak hours. A common ploy in the Budapest and Prague metros has been for a group of well-dressed young people to surround you, chattering away while one of the group zips through your pockets or purse.

Be careful even in hotels; don't leave valuables lying around in your room.

Parked cars containing luggage or other bags are prime targets for petty criminals in most cities, and cars with foreign number plates and/or rental agency stickers attract particular attention. While driving in cities, beware of snatch thieves when you pull up at the lights – keep doors locked and windows rolled up high.

In case of theft or loss, always report the incident to the police and ask for a statement. Otherwise your travel-insurance company won't pay up.

Violence

Though it's unlikely that travellers will encounter any violence while in Eastern Europe, skinheads and neo-Nazis have singled out the resident Roma, blacks and Asians as scapegoats for their own problems, while foreigners have been attacked in Hungary and the Czech Republic. Avoid especially run-down areas in cities and *never* fight back. These people can be extremely dangerous. Russian neo-Nazis have developed a charming tradition of seeking out fights with nonwhite people on Hitler's birthday (20 April). People of non-European origin should exercise caution if they are in Moscow or St Petersburg on this date.

DISABLED TRAVELLERS

Eastern Europe can be very unpredictable when it comes to facilities for the disabled. The golden rule is never to expect much and you won't be disappointed, which is not exactly encouraging. Most major museums and sites have disabled access, although there are still exceptions. However, hotels outside the top bracket and public transport are still universally poor, however, and it's fair to say that access for the disabled has not been a priority in the region's past decade of rapid reform.

If you have a physical disability, get in touch with your national support organisation (preferably the travel officer if there is one) and ask about the countries you plan to visit. They often have complete libraries devoted to travel, with useful things like access guides, and they can put you in touch with travel agencies who specialise in tours for the disabled. The **Royal Association for Disability & Rehabilitation** (RADAR; UK ☎ 020-7250 3222, fax 7250 0212; www.radar.org.uk; 12 City Forum, 250 City Rd, London EC1V 8AF) is a very helpful association with a number of publications for the disabled on sale.

DISCOUNT CARDS
Camping Card International

The Camping Card International (CCI) is a camping ground ID valid for a year that can be used instead of a passport when checking in to camping grounds and includes third-party insurance. As a result, many camping grounds will offer a small discount (usually 5% to 10%) if you have one. CCIs are issued by automobile associations, camping federations and, sometimes, on the spot at camping grounds. The CCI is also useful as it can sometimes serve as a guarantee, so that you don't have to leave your passport at reception.

Hostel Cards

A hostelling card is useful – if not mandatory – for staying at hostels. Most hostels in Eastern Europe don't require that you be a hostelling association member, but they sometimes charge less if you have a card. Some hostels will issue one on the spot or after a few days' stay, though this might cost a bit more than getting it at home.

International Student, Youth & Teacher Cards

An International Student Identity Card (ISIC), a plastic ID-style card with your photograph, provides discounts on many forms of transport (including airlines and local transport), cheap or free admission to museums and sights, and inexpensive meals in some student cafeterias and restaurants. If you're under 26 but not a student, you are eligible to apply for an International Youth Travel Card (IYTC, formerly GO25), issued by the Federation of International Youth Travel Organisations, or the Euro26 card (the latter card may not be recognised in Albania, Moldova, Romania, and Serbia and Montenegro). Both go under different names in different countries and give much the same discounts and benefits as an ISIC. An International Teacher Identity Card (ITIC) identifies the holder as an instructor and offers similar deals. All these cards are issued by student unions, hostelling organisations or youth-oriented travel agencies.

Senior Cards

Many attractions offer reduced-price admission for people over 60 or 65 (sometimes as low as 55 for women). Make sure you bring proof of age. For a fee of around €20, European residents aged 60 and over can get a Railplus Card as an add-on to their national rail senior pass. It entitles the holder to train-fare reductions of around 25%.

In your home country, a lower age may already entitle you to all sorts of interesting travel packages and discounts (on car hire, for instance) through organisations and travel agents that cater for senior travellers. Start hunting at your local senior citizens' advice bureau. European residents over 60 are eligible for the Railplus Card.

DVD & VIDEO SYSTEMS

DVDs are sold throughout Eastern Europe, and the further east you go, the less likely they are to be licensed. This can result in great bargains for those don't mind buying pirated copies, but you should also realise that unlicensed DVDs are illegal in most countries, although you're unlikely to be caught bringing a few cheap DVDs home. In general, DVDs sold in Eastern Europe will be Region 2 DVDs, which mean that unless you have a multiregion DVD player, they will not play in North America (Region 1) or anywhere where Region 2 is not the norm. Even if a film has had its title and cover translated into a local language, if the original was English (and often even if it wasn't) there will be the option to watch the DVD in English.

If you want to record or buy video tapes to play back home, you won't get the picture if the image registration systems are different. Like Australia and most of the rest of Europe, Eastern Europe usually uses PAL (but sometimes the French SECAM system so check on your arrival), which is incompatible with the North American and Japanese NTSC system.

ELECTRICITY

Eastern European countries run on 220V, 50Hz AC; check the voltage and cycle (usually 50Hz) used on your appliances. Most appliances set up for 220V will quite happily handle 240V without modification (and vice versa); the same goes for 110V and 125V combinations. It's preferable to adjust your appliance to the exact voltage if you can (some modern battery chargers and radios will do this automatically). Don't mix 110/125V with 220/240V without a transformer, which will be built in if the appliance can, in fact, be adjusted.

Several countries outside Europe (the USA and Canada, for instance) have 60Hz AC, which will affect the speed of electric motors even after the voltage has been adjusted, so CD and tape players (where motor speed is all-important) will be useless. But appliances such as electric razors, hair dryers, irons and radios will work fine.

Plugs in Eastern Europen are the standard round two-pin variety, sometimes called the 'europlug'. If your plugs are of a different design, you'll need an adapter.

EMBASSIES & CONSULATES
See the individual country chapters for the addresses of embassies and consulates both in Eastern Europe and in your home country.

It's important to realise what your embassy can and cannot do to help if you get into trouble while abroad. Generally speaking, it won't be much help in emergencies if the trouble you're in is remotely your own fault. Remember that you are bound by the laws of the country you are visiting.

In genuine emergencies you might get some assistance, but only if other channels have been exhausted. For example, if you need to get home urgently, a free ticket back is exceedingly unlikely – the embassy would expect you to have insurance. If you have all your money and documents stolen, it might assist with getting a new passport, but a loan for onward travel is almost always out of the question.

GAY & LESBIAN TRAVELLERS
Eastern Europe has an unpredictable reaction to homosexuality in all its forms. For the first time, it is now 100% legal in all countries covered by this book. This, however, does not mean a great deal on street level; in fact in some countries such as Romania open displays of homosexuality are banned. Whether or not this is the case where you are travelling, public displays of affection are still best avoided.

Most capital cities have lively, if small, gay scenes, usually centred around one or two bars and clubs. Exceptions to this rule are Tirana, Skopje, Sarajevo and Chişinău where there is nothing gay- or lesbian-specific. Outside large population centres, gay and lesbian life is almost nonexistent.

Good resources for gay travellers include websites such as www.gaydar.com and www.gay.com. Listings are given wherever possible in the individual country sections.

HOLIDAYS
Eastern Europe's school calendar is nothing unusual – children get the summer months off (usually July and August) as well as breaks for Easter and Christmas. Even in countries with a large Muslim population such as Bosnia and Hercegovina and Albania, these dates are generally followed: a hangover from communist times. See the relevant country's directory for details of local public holidays and festivals.

INSURANCE
A travel insurance policy to cover theft, loss and medical problems is a good idea. The policies written by STA Travel and other student travel organisations are usually good value. Some policies offer lower and higher medical expense options; the higher ones are chiefly for countries like the USA that have extremely expensive medical costs. There is a wide variety of policies available, so check the fine print.

Some insurance policies will specifically exclude 'dangerous activities', which can include scuba diving, motorcycling and even trekking. Some even exclude entire countries (eg Bosnia and Hercegovina or Serbia and Montenegro).

You may prefer a policy that pays doctors or hospitals directly rather than you having to pay on the spot and claim later. If you have to claim later make sure you keep all documentation. Some policies ask you to call back (reverse charges) to a centre in your home country where an immediate assessment of your problem is made. Check that the policy covers ambulances and an emergency flight home. For more information on health insurance, see p904.

For details on car insurance, see right.

INTERNET ACCESS
With the exception of rural areas, almost any decent sized town in Eastern Europe has Internet access. Connections may be slow, Internet 'cafés' may not serve coffee or any other drinks, and sometimes you'll be limited to a monitor in a dark, smelly room full of teenage boys playing war games – but one way or another you'll never be far from your email account, even in less developed nations such as Albania or Moldova. Indeed, in some more developed cities, Internet cafés can be a social hub

and a great way of meeting locals as well as travellers. Make sure you have a web-based email account so you can pick up email on the road without your own laptop.

If you're travelling with a notebook or hand-held computer, be aware that your modem may not work once you leave your home country. The safest option is to buy a reputable 'global' modem before you leave home, or buy a local PC-card modem if you're spending an extended time in any one country. For more information on travelling with a portable computer, see www.teleadapt.com.

See Photography & Video for information on digital cameras, p880.

MAPS

Bringing a good regional map will make things a great deal easier if you are planning a long trip taking in more than a couple of countries. There's a huge range available but we recommend *Eastern Europe,* produced by Latvian publishers Jana Seta and *Eastern Europe* from Freytag & Berndt.

In general, buying city maps in advance is unnecessary, as nearly all large towns produce them locally for a fraction of the price you'll pay at home. However, maps of Eastern European capitals and other major towns are widely available from travel bookshops if you want a particularly detailed map in advance.

MONEY

Things have simplified in Eastern Europe these days, with no real worries about 'soft' and 'hard' currencies. The main problem you'll face is constant currency changes as you flit between the crown, zloty, rouble, lei, lev, lek, dinar and various other national currencies. There is no longer any particular desire for 'hard' currency (long gone are the days where hoteliers would slash the rates if you payed in US dollars) and the convertibility of almost all Eastern European currencies makes them stable and reliable ways to carry cash.

The accession of half of the region to the EU has raised the issue of euro introduction. While this is inevitable in the long run, it's unlikely to be much before the end of the decade. In the meantime regional governments are busy getting their economic houses in order.

ATMs & Credit Cards

The hassle of trying to change travellers cheques at the weekend and rip-off *bureaux de change* is a thing of the past in most parts of Eastern Europe, with the arrival of ATMs that accept most credit and cash cards from the Balkans to the Baltic. Until recently, Tirana was still without a reliable network of ATMs, but they have begun to pop up here too, and before you know it they'll be everywhere. All other countries have plenty of ATMs, and not only in the capital city.

As purchase tools, credit cards are still not as commonly used as in Western Europe but they're gaining ground: especially Amex, Visa and MasterCard. You'll be able to use them at upmarket restaurants, shops, hotels, car-rental firms, travel agencies and many petrol stations.

Cash or debit cards, which you use at home to withdraw money directly from your bank account or savings account, can be used throughout Eastern Europe at those ATMs linked to international networks like Cirrus and Maestro. The major advantage of using ATMs is that you don't pay commission charges to exchange money and the exchange rate is usually at a better interbank rate than that offered for travellers cheques or cash exchanges. Bear in mind that if you use a credit card for purchases, exchange rates may have changed by the time your bill is processed, which can work out to your advantage or disadvantage.

Charge cards like Amex, and to a lesser extent Diners Club, have offices in most countries and they can generally replace a lost card within 24 hours. That's because they treat you as a customer of the company rather than of the bank that issued the card. Their major drawback is that they're not widely accepted off the beaten track. Charge cards may also be hooked up to some ATM networks. Credit and credit/debit cards like Visa and MasterCard are more widely accepted because they tend to charge merchants lower commissions.

If you choose to rely on plastic, go for two different cards – this allows one to be used as backup in the case of loss, or more commonly, because a certain bank will take one credit card and not another for no discernable reason. Better still is a combination of credit card and travellers cheques so you have something to fall back on if an

ATM swallows your card or the banks in the area won't accept it (a not uncommon and always inexplicable occurrence). There are also a couple of tricky scams involving credit cards; see p875.

Cash

This is, of course, the easiest way to carry money, but remember that if you lose it, that's it. The two most favoured currencies throughout Eastern Europe are the euro and the US dollar. However, it is however, perfectly easy to exchange virtually any other major world currency in big cities, but you are inevitably at the mercy of the exchange office and their rates. Far better is to change your money into euro or US dollars before you leave home and you'll have no problems whatsoever.

Moneychangers

Shop around, never stop at the first place you see, and if you happen to be in a tourist area you can rest assured you'll be offered crappy rates everywhere. So don't bother shopping around, just leave for a less-touristed neighbourhood. Examples are around the Charles Bridge in Prague or the Old Town Square in Kraków.

Tipping

Throughout Eastern Europe you tip by rounding up restaurant bills and taxi fares to the next whole figure as you're paying. In some countries restaurants will already have added a service charge to your bill, so you needn't round it up much (if at all). A tip of 10% is quite sufficient if you feel you have been well attended. The waiters in any place catering mostly to foreign tourists will usually expect such a tip. If you're dissatisfied with the food or service at a restaurant, or feel you have been overcharged, you can convey the message by paying the exact amount without a gratuity included. If 'rounding up' means you're only giving honest waiters a couple of cents, add a few more coins to keep them happy.

Travellers Cheques

The main idea of using travellers cheques rather than cash is the protection they offer from theft, though they have lost their once enormous popularity as more and more travellers – including those on tight budgets – withdraw cash through ATMs as they go along.

Banks usually charge from 1% to 2% commission to change travellers cheques (up to 5% in Bulgaria, Estonia, Latvia, Lithuania and Romania). Their opening hours are sometimes limited. In the individual chapters, we recommend the most efficient banks of each country.

The privately owned exchange offices in Albania, Bulgaria, Poland, Romania and Slovenia change cash at excellent rates without commission. Not only are their rates sometimes higher than those offered by the banks for travellers cheques but they stay open much longer hours, occasionally even 24 hours. However, do take care in Belarus, the Czech Republic, Estonia, Hungary, Latvia, Lithuania, Moldova, Slovakia and Ukraine, as some big moneychangers take exorbitant commissions unless you cash a small fortune with them. Before signing a travellers cheque or handing over any cash always check the commission and rate.

Amex and Thomas Cook representatives cash their own travellers cheques without commission, but both give poor rates of exchange. If you're changing more than US$20, you're usually better off going to a bank and paying the standard 1% to 2% commission to change there.

Western Union

If all goes horribly wrong – your money, travellers cheques and credit cards are all stolen – don't despair. While it's a terrible (and highly unusual) situation, as long as you know the phone number of a friend or relative back home, they will be able to wire money to you anywhere in Eastern Europe via Western Union. We don't bother listing WU representatives in this guide, as there are literally thousands of them. Just look for the distinctive yellow and black sign, and if you're somewhere remote, ask the person sending you the money to ask WU for the nearest office to you. The sender will be given a code that they then communicate to you and you take to the nearest office, along with your passport, to receive your cash.

PHOTOGRAPHY & VIDEO

Film and camera equipment is available everywhere in Eastern Europe, but shops in the larger places have a wider choice.

Avoid buying film at tourist sites in Europe, such as the Castle District in Budapest or by Charles Bridge in Prague. It may have been stored badly or reached its sell-by date. It certainly will be more expensive than in normal photography shops.

Eastern Europe was once notorious for its photographic restrictions – taking shots of anything 'strategic' such as bridges or train stations was strictly forbidden. These days local officials are much less paranoid, but you need to use common sense when it comes to this issue; photographing military installations, for example, is never a good idea. More importantly, have the courtesy to ask permission before taking close-up photos of people.

In most countries, it is easy to obtain video cartridges in large towns and cities, but make sure you buy the correct format. It is usually worth buying at least a few cartridges duty-free at the start of your trip.

Be aware that museums often demand that you buy permission to photograph or video their displays. Do this when you buy your tickets, if you think you will, as you'll have to retrace your steps if you don't – no laughing matter in the Hermitage.

Anyone using a digital camera should check that you have enough memory to store your snaps – two 128 MB cards will probably be enough. If you do run out of memory space your best bet is to burn your photos onto a CD. Increasing numbers of processing labs now offer this service.

To download your pics at an Internet café you'll need a USB cable and a card reader. Some places provide a USB on request but be warned that many of the bigger chain cafés don't let you plug your gear into their computers, meaning that it's back to plan A – the CD.

POST

Details of post offices are given in the information sections of each city or town in the individual country chapters, and postage costs given in the country directory. Both efficiency and cost vary enormously. There seem to be no set rules, but EU-accession countries are likely to be faster, more reliable and more expensive than the non-EU states. Don't send anything back home from Russia, Ukraine, Belarus or Moldova unless you can deal with its possible loss.

Poste restante (having letters sent to you care of local post offices) is unreliable, not to mention an increasingly unnecessary communication method in the 21st century. If you desperately need something posted to you, do your research – find a friend of a friend who could receive the mail at their address, or ask nicely at a hotel you plan to stay at. You can also have mail sent to you at Amex offices as long as you have an Amex card or are carrying its travellers cheques. When you buy Amex cheques, ask for a booklet listing all its office addresses worldwide. Amex will forward mail for a small fee, but what it won't do is accept parcels, registered letters, notices for registered letters, answer telephone inquiries about mail or hold mail longer than 30 days.

To send a parcel from Eastern Europe you usually have to take it unwrapped to a main post office. Parcels weighing over 2kg often must be taken to a special customs post office. They will usually wrap the parcels for you. They may ask to see your passport and note the number on the form. If you don't have a return address within the country put your name care of any large tourist hotel to satisfy them.

SOLO TRAVELLERS

Travelling alone is a unique experience. There are a huge number of advantages – you do exactly what you want to do, see what you want to see and are more likely to meet locals and socialise with people you'd otherwise never speak to. However, it can also be lonely and less fun when things get frustrating or don't work out. Backpacking and hostel culture is very adapted to people travelling alone, however, and hostels are great places to meet others. Indeed, you may find you'll spend a few days here and there with others you've met in hostels and who are heading in your direction, or keen to share the cost of a day trip or two. The best advice for solo travellers therefore is to head for your nearest hostel if you feel like some company. Most big cities in Eastern Europe have expat bars (usually the ubiquitous Irish pubs) if you are missing a slice of ersatz-home.

TELEPHONE

Telephone service has improved throughout the region in a very short time. Cities

REGIONAL DIRECTORY

throughout the region have a huge number of call centres – increasingly the domain of entrepreneurs who offer discounted rates, although there are also the state-run call centres, which are often in the same building as the main post office. Here you can often make your call from one of the booths inside an enclosed area, paying the cashier as you leave. Public telephones are almost always found at post offices. Local telephone cards, available from post offices, telephone centres, newsstands or retail outlets, are popular everywhere in the region. In fact, in many countries they have become the norm.

There's a wide range of local and international phonecards. For local calls you're usually better off with a local phonecard.

To call abroad you simply dial the international access code for the country you are calling from (most commonly ☎ 00 in Eastern Europe, but ☎ 8/wait for tone/10 in Russia, Belarus, Moldova and Ukraine).

To make a domestic call to another city in the same country in Eastern Europe dial the area code with the initial zero and the number. Area codes for individual cities and regions are provided in the country chapters.

Mobile Phones

Like being in some horribly saccharine mobile phone commercial, today you'll see farmers travelling by horse and cart chatting on their mobiles in rural Romania, while old grannies selling sunflower seeds on a quiet St Petersburg side street write text messages to their grandchildren. The expansion of mobile phones has been nothing short of breathtaking in the region and this can be great for travellers too. If you plan to spend more than a week or so in one country, seriously consider buying a SIM card to slip into your phone (check before you leave with your provider at home that your handset has not been blocked). SIM cards can cost as little as €10 and can be topped up with cards available at supermarkets and any mobile phone dealers. Alternatively, if you have roaming, your phone will usually switch automatically over to a local network. This can be expensive if you use the phone a great deal, but can be very useful for ad hoc use on the road.

Phone Codes

Every country's international dialling code and international access code is given in the Fast Facts section at the beginning of each chapter. Every town has its local code within the country listed directly underneath its chapter heading.

TIME

Eastern Europe spans three time zones. Greenwich Mean Time (GMT) is five hours ahead of New York, eight hours ahead of Los Angeles and 10 hours behind Sydney. Thus, at noon in New York, it's 6pm in Warsaw, 7pm in Minsk and 8pm in Moscow.

Central European Time (GMT+1 hour) Albania, Bosnia and Hercegovina, Croatia, Czech Republic, Hungary, Macedonia, Poland, Serbia and Montenegro, Slovakia and Slovenia.

Eastern European Time (GMT+2 hours) Belarus, Bulgaria, Estonia, Kaliningrad, Latvia, Lithuania, Moldova, Romania and Ukraine.

Moscow Time (GMT+3 hours) Moscow and St Petersburg.

All countries employ daylight savings. Clocks are put forward an hour usually on the last Sunday in March. They are set back one hour on the last Sunday in September.

TOURIST INFORMATION

The provision of tourist information varies enormously. While countries that have successfully realised their potential as holiday destinations have developed a network of excellent Tourist Information Centres (TICs), there are still many countries that take little or no interest in the economic benefits tourism can bring. Among the best prepared are Slovenia, Croatia, the Czech Republic, Hungary, Poland and Bulgaria, many of which have tourist offices abroad as well as throughout the country. Countries in the latter category are (unsurprisingly) Ukraine, Belarus and Moldova. Russia is similarly badly organised, although a lone tourist information office has existed in St Petersburg since 2000 doing very little. However, it's a start and things look set to improve. The Baltic countries, Montenegro, Albania and Macedonia fall in a middle category of places actively trying to encourage tourism, but whose efforts remain rather obscure at the moment. See individual country entries for details of TICs locally.

VISAS & DOCUMENTS
Copies

The hassles created by losing your passport can be considerably reduced if you have a record of its number and issue date or, even better, photocopies of the relevant data pages. A photocopy of your birth certificate can also be useful.

Also note the serial numbers of your travellers cheques (cross them off as they're cash them) and take photocopies of your credit cards, air ticket and any other travel documents. Keep all this emergency material separate from your passport, cheques and cash, and leave extra copies with someone you can rely on at home. Add some

emergency money (eg €50 to €100 in cash) to this separate stash as well. If you do lose your passport, notify the police immediately to get a statement, and contact your nearest consulate.

Passport

Your most important travel document is your passport, which should remain valid until well after you return home. If it's just about to expire, renew it before you travel. Some countries insist your passport remain valid for a specified period (usually three months) beyond the expected date of your departure from that country. In practice, this is rarely checked.

SPONTANEITY VS PLANNING AHEAD

Visa regulations vary throughout Eastern Europe; for some countries you won't need a visa at all, while for other obtaining a visa is a trial of skill, patience and preplanning. This table outlines visa requirements and availablily for the region as at the time of writing; see individual country chapters for more detail. Be aware, however, that visa regulations can and do change, so you should always check with the individual embassies or a reputable travel agency before travelling.

	Visa on arrival	EU citizens	US citizens	Canadian citizens	Australian citizens	NZ citizens
Albania	Yes*	Yes	Yes	Yes	Yes	Yes
Belarus	No**	Yes	Yes	Yes	Yes	Yes
Bosnia & Hercegovina	Not needed	No	No	No	No	No
Bulgaria	Not needed	No	No	No	No	No
Croatia	Not needed	No	No	No	No	No
Czech Republic	Not needed	No	No	No	No	No
Estonia	Not needed	No	No	No	No	No
Hungary	Not needed	No	No	No	No	No
Latvia	Not needed	No	No	No	No	No
Lithuania	Not needed	No	No	No	No	No
Macedonia	Varies	No	Yes	Yes	Yes	Yes
Moldova	Varies	No	Yes	Yes	Yes	Yes
Poland	Not needed	No	No	No	No	No
Romania	No	No	No	No	Yes	Yes
Russia	No**	Yes	Yes	Yes	Yes	Yes
Serbia & Montenegro	Not needed	No	No	No	No	No
Slovakia	Not needed	No	No	No	No	No
Slovenia	Not needed	No	No	No	No	No
Ukraine	No	Yes	Yes	Yes	Yes	Yes

* Tourist visa (€10) available only on arrival.

** Technically there are situations in which visas can be issued on arrival, but the complexities and restrictions make this unrecommended.

Once you start travelling, carry your passport (or a copy of it) at all times and guard it carefully (see Copies, p883, for advice about carrying copies of your passport and other important documents). Camping grounds and hotels sometimes insist that you hand over your passport for the duration of your stay, which is very inconvenient, but a driving licence or Camping Card International (CCI) usually solves the problem.

Visas

A visa is a stamp in your passport or a separate piece of paper permitting you to enter the country in question and stay for a specified period of time. Often you can get the visa at the border or at the airport on arrival, but not always, especially if you're travelling by train or bus and the procedure is likely to hold up others. Check first with the embassies or consulates of the countries you plan to visit; otherwise you could find yourself stranded at the border. With a valid passport and visa (if required) you'll be able to visit most Eastern European countries for up to three (and sometimes even six) months, provided you have some sort of onward or return ticket and/or 'sufficient means of support'.

In line with the Schengen Agreement, there are no longer passport controls at the borders between most EU countries, but procedures between EU and non-EU countries can still be fairly thorough. For those who do require visas, it's important to remember that these will have a 'use-by' date, and you'll be refused entry after that period has elapsed.

Consulates sometimes issue visas on the spot, although some levy a 50% to 100% surcharge for 'express service'. If there's a choice between getting a visa in advance and on the border, go for the former option if you have the time. They're often cheaper in your home country and this can save bureaucratic procedure.

Decide in advance if you want a tourist or transit visa. Transit visas, usually valid for just 48 or 72 hours, are often cheaper and issued faster, but it's usually not possible to extend a transit visa or change it to a tourist visa.

The visa form may instruct you to report to police within 48 hours of arrival. If you're staying at a hotel or other official accommodation (camping ground, hostel, private room arranged by a travel agency etc), this will be taken care of for you by the travel agency, hotel or camping ground. If you're staying with friends, relatives or in a private room arranged on the street or at the train station, you're supposed to register with the police yourself. During the communist days these regulations were strictly enforced, but things are pretty casual in most countries nowadays. However, consult the visa section in the relevant country's directory for full information.

WOMEN TRAVELLERS

Frustrating though it is, women travellers continue to face more challenging situations when travelling than men do. If you are a woman traveller, especially a solo woman, you may find it helpful to understand the status of local women to better understand the responses you elicit from locals. Hopes of travelling inconspicuously, spending time alone and absorbing the surroundings are often thwarted by men who assume a lone woman desires company, or who seemingly find it impossible to avert their penetrating gaze. Bear in mind that most of this behaviour is harmless, more often than not. Don't let it deter you! Hopefully the more women that travel, whether alone, in pairs, or in groups, the less unwanted attention lone female travellers in the region will attract

Despite feminism's grip on many European countries, women remain underrepresented in positions of power, in both governmental and corporate spheres. Despite the exciting progress to elevate the status of women in recent years, women's leadership at the upper levels of institutions still leaves a lot to be desired. In many areas, you may notice the glut of women in low-paid, menial jobs. As is the case worldwide, women remain over-represented among the illiterate and unemployed.

In Muslim countries, where conservative conceptions of the largely house-bound role of women still tend to prevail, women travelling alone or with other women will certainly be of interest or curiosity to both local men and women. Unmarried men rarely have contact with women outside their family unit, which is why many men in, for example, Albania and Bosnia and Hercegovina, may afford travelling women so much attention. In such areas, women travelling with a male companion will often experience the opposite, and may need to pinch themselves as a reminder that yes, they actually exist.

WORK

With unemployment still a problem throughout the region, Eastern European countries aren't keen on handing out jobs to foreigners. The paperwork involved in arranging a work permit can be almost impossible, especially for temporary work.

That doesn't prevent enterprising travellers from topping up their funds occasionally, and they don't always have to do this illegally. If you do find a temporary job in Eastern Europe, though, the pay is likely to be abysmally low. Do it for the experience – not to earn your fortune – and you won't be disappointed. Teaching English is the easiest way to make some extra cash, but the market is saturated in places like Prague and Budapest. You'll probably be much more successful in less popular places like Sofia and Bucharest.

If you play an instrument or have other artistic talents, you could try working the streets. As every Peruvian pipe player (and his fifth cousin) *still* knows, busking is fairly common in major Eastern European cities like Prague, Budapest and Ljubljana. Some countries may require municipal permits for this sort of thing. Talk to other street artists before you start.

There are several references and websites that publicise specific positions across Eastern Europe. Transitions Abroad publishes *Work Abroad: The Complete Guide to Finding a Job Overseas* and the *Alternative Travel Directory: The Complete Guide*

to Work, Study and Travel Overseas as well as a colour magazine, *Transitions Abroad*. Its website lists paid positions and volunteer and service programmes. **Action Without Borders** (www.idealist.org) and **GoAbroad.com** (www.goabroad.com) list hundreds of jobs and volunteer opportunities.

Work Your Way Around the World by Susan Griffith gives good, practical advice on a wide range of issues. The publisher, **Vacation Work** (www.vacationwork.co.uk), has many other useful titles, including *The Directory of Summer Jobs Abroad,* edited by David Woodworth. *Working Holidays* by Ben Jupp (Central Bureau for Educational Visits & Exchanges in the UK), is another good source, as is *Now Hiring! Jobs in Eastern Europe* by Clarke Canfield (Perpetual Press).

Volunteer Work

Organising a volunteer work placement is a great way to gain a deeper insight into local culture. If you're staying with a family, or working alongside local colleagues, you'll probably learn much more about life here than you would if you were travelling through the country.

In some instances volunteers are paid a living allowance, sometimes they work for their keep and other programmes require the volunteer to pay.

There are several websites that can help you search for volunteer work opportunities in Eastern Europe. As well as the websites mentioned earlier, try **WorkingAbroad** (www.workingabroad.com) – it's a good resource for researching possibilities and applying for positions. The **Coordinating Committee for International Voluntary Service** (www.unesco.org/ccivs) is an umbrella organisation with over 140 member organisations worldwide. It's useful if you want to find out about your country's national volunteer placement agency.

Transport in Eastern Europe

CONTENTS

Getting There & Away	**886**
Entry Requirements	886
Air	887
Land	893
Sea	895
Getting Around	**896**
Air	896
Bicycle	896
Bus	897
Car & Motorcycle	897
Hitching	899
Local Transport	900
Tours	900
Train	901

THINGS CHANGE

The information in this chapter is particularly vulnerable to change. Check directly with the airline or a travel agent to make sure you understand how a fare (and ticket you may buy) works and be aware of the security requirements for international travel. Shop carefully. The details given in this chapter should be regarded as pointers and are not a substitute for your own careful, up-to-date research.

GETTING THERE & AWAY

Eastern Europe is very well connected by air to Western Europe, and to a lesser extent to North America and parts of the Middle East. From other parts of the world the region is far less easily reached, but things have been improving slowly and steadily over the past few years. With severe competition between long-haul airlines and the advent of so many no-frills carriers in both Europe and the USA, there are plenty of cheap tickets available to a variety of gateway cities. Most people arriving from outside Europe will still probably end up travelling through Western Europe, simply because the best fares and most frequent connections go through a number of Western European gateway cities.

Some travellers choose alternatively and get there by train – a far more exciting and atmospheric way to enter Eastern Europe than flying. Particularly thrilling of course is to approach Eastern Europe from Asia on the mythic trans-Siberian, trans-Mongolian or trans-Manchurian express trains. Not as pumped full of kudos perhaps, but still fun (not to mention cheaper and quicker), is taking the train from Western Europe over the psychological boundary between East and West that still exists, despite EU enlargement.

There are many ferry services operating in the Baltic Sea linking Scandinavia and Germany with countries such as Poland, Lithuania, Latvia and Estonia. Other routes cross the Adriatic from Italy to Slovenia and Croatia, or cross the Black Sea from Turkey. This is a truly old-world way to travel, and lots of fun for that.

Of course, bus, bicycle and car are also popular ways to enter the region – and whichever method you choose you'll find some helpful, practical information in the relevant sections in this chapter.

ENTRY REQUIREMENTS

All countries obviously require travellers to have a valid passport, preferably with a good window between the time of departure and the document's expiration date. Increasingly, EU travellers from countries that issue national identity cards use these to travel within the EU, although it's impossible to use these as the sole travel documents outside the EU.

Visas are another thing to consider. Countries may require some nationalities to buy a document that allows entry to the country between certain dates. Visas are sometimes free, sometimes available at the border for a price, and sometimes only available in advance and with not inconsiderable bureaucratic wrangling. Wherever you are going, be clear on the visa requirements and plan getting them in advance to save yourself headaches. See the Directory for each country for visa information.

AIR

Moscow is Eastern Europe's single best-connected city, but cheap air travel has yet to catch on there. Indeed, the commercial air hubs of Eastern Europe are increasingly the central European capitals – Prague, Budapest and Warsaw, all of which now enjoy regular bargain fares as the subject of some competition between airlines, as well as the growing market in the region for so-called 'no frills' or budget airlines.

Airports & Airlines

Eastern Europe is covered in international airports. The biggest in the region is Moscow's Sheremetyevo airport, the hub of transport behemoth (and butt of many a joke) Aeroflot and its many subdivisions.

Other significant regional airlines are ČSA (Czech Airlines), whose hub is in Prague's Ruzyně airport, Malév (Hungarian Airlines), based in Budapest and LOT Polish Airlines in Warsaw.

AIRLINES SERVING EASTERN EUROPE

Ada Air (code ZY; www.adaair.com; Tirana)
Adria Airways (code JP; www.adria-airways.com; Ljubljana)
Aer Lingus (code EI; www.aerlingus.com; Dublin)
Aeroflot (code SU; www.aeroflot.com; Moscow)
Aerosvit (code VV; www.aerosvit.ua; Kyiv)
Air Baltic (code BT; www.airbaltic.com; Rīga)
Air Berlin (code AB; www.airberlin.com; Berlin)
Air Canada (code AC; www.aircanada.ca; Toronto/Montreal)
Air France (code AF; www.airfrance.com; Paris)
Air India (code AI; www.airindia.com; Delhi)
Air Malta (code KM; www.airmalta.com; Valetta)
Air Moldova (code 9U; www.airmoldova.md; Chişinău)
Air Polonia (code APN; www.airpolonia.com; Warsaw)
Air Slovakia (code GM; www.airslovakia.sk; Bratislava)
Albanian Airlines (code LV; www.flyalbanian.com; Tirana)
Alitalia (code AZ; www.alitalia.com; Rome)
American Airlines (code AA; www.aa.com; Dallas/Chicago/New York)
ANA (All Nippon Airways; code NH; www.fly-ana.com; Tokyo)
Austrian Airlines (code OS; www.aua.com; Vienna)
Balkan (code LZ; www.balkan.com/menu2.htm; Belgrade)

Belavia (code B2; www.belavia.by; Minsk)
British Airways (code BA; www.ba.com; London Heathrow)
Bulgaria Air (code FB; www.air.bg; Sofia)
Cathay Pacific (code CX; www.cathaypacific.com; Hong Kong)
Croatia Airlines (code OU; www.croatiaairlines.hr; Zagreb)
ČSA (Czech Airlines; code OK; www.czech-airlines.com; Prague)
Delta Airlines (code DL; www.delta.com; Atlanta)
EasyJet (code EZY; www.easyjet.com; London Luton)
El Al (code LY; www.elal.co.il; Tel Aviv)
Emirates (code EK; www.ekgroup.com; Dubai)
Estonian Air (code OV; www.estonian-air.ee; Tallinn)
Finnair (code AY; www.finnair.com; Helsinki)
Germania Express (www.gexx.de; Düsseldorf/Berlin/Munich)
Hemus Air (code DU; www.hemusair.bg; Sofia)
Iberia (code IB; www.iberia.com; Madrid)
Japan Airlines (code JL; www.jal.com; Tokyo)
JAT (code JU; www.jat.com; Belgrade)
KLM (code KL; www.klm.com; Amsterdam)
Kosova Airlines (code KOS; www.kosovaairlines.com, in Albanian; Prishtina)
Lithuanian Airlines (code TE; www.lal.lt; Vilnius)
LOT Polish Airlines (code LO; www.lot.com; Warsaw)
Lufthansa (code LH; www.lufthansa.com; Frankfurt)
Macedonian Airlines (MAT; code IN; www.mat.com.mk; Skopje)
Malév (Hungarian Airlines; code MA; www.malev.com; Budapest)
Moldavian Airlines (code 2M; www.mdv.md; Chişinău)
Montenegro Airlines (code YM; www.montenegro-airlines.com; Podgorica)
Olympic Airways (code OA; www.olympicairlines.com; Athens)
Pulkovo (code FV; www.pulkovo-express.ru; St Petersburg)
Royal Jordanian (code RJ; www.rja.com.jo; Amman)
Ryanair (code FR; www.ryanair.com; Dublin/London)
SAS Scandinavian Airlines (code SK; www.scandinavian.net; Copenhagen)
Siberia Airlines (code S7; www.s7.ru; Novosibirsk/Moscow/Irkutsk)
SkyEurope Airlines (code NE; www.skyeurope.com; Warsaw/Vienna-Bratislava/Budapest)
Slovak Airlines (code 6Q; www.slovakairlines.sk; Bratislava)
SN Brussels Airlines (code SN; www.flysn.com; Brussels)
Swiss International Air Lines (code LX; www.swiss.com; Zürich)
Tarom Romanian Air Transport (code RO; www.tarom.ro; Bucharest)
Thai International Airways (code TG; www.thaiairways.com; Bangkok)

Transaero (code UN; www.transaero.ru; Moscow)
Turkish Airlines (code TK; www.turkishairlines.com; Istanbul)
Ukraine International Airlines (code PS; www.ukraine-international.com; Kyiv)

Air Routes

ALBANIA

Albania is fairly poorly served by international flights. Those that do come go to Tirana's Mother Teresa airport, the country's only international gateway. The two Albanian airlines, Ada Air and Albanian Airlines connect Tirana to Bari, Bologna and Rome in Italy, Athens and Thessaloniki in Greece and also Frankfurt and Istanbul. Other major carriers to Albania include Austrian Airlines from Vienna, Lufthansa from Frankfurt and Munich, Olympic Airways from Athens and Turkish Airlines from Istanbul.

BELARUS

Belarus has good links with its former Soviet neighbours, particularly with Moscow. National carrier Belavia links Minsk to Amsterdam, Frankfurt, London, Paris, Rome, Stockholm and Zürich.

BOSNIA & HERCEGOVINA

It's served by a few European airlines such as Austrian Airlines, Lufthansa and Adria Airways, who pick up at intercontinental hubs such as Frankfurt, London and Vienna. No discount airlines fly into Bosnia and Hercegovina yet, but cheap flights to Dubrovnik in Croatia and a bus trip into the country could be a possibility.

BULGARIA

Bulgaria's main international hub is at Sofia, but there are also a huge number of (mainly chartered) international flights to Varna and Burgas, the gateways for the popular Black Sea resorts. Sofia is connected to Amsterdam, Berlin, Frankfurt, Lisbon, London, Milan, Paris and Rome by a number of carriers including national airline Bulgaria Air and also British Airways and Lufthansa.

CROATIA

Zagreb is connected to most European capitals as well as Frankfurt, Munich, Istanbul and Damascus. Elsewhere in the country there are these scheduled flights: Dubrovnik has direct flights to Glasgow, London, Manchester and Vienna; Split has direct flights to London, Manchester and Rome; Rijeka has direct flights to London; and Pula has a direct flight to Manchester.

CZECH REPUBLIC

As the major gateway city to the region, Prague has a huge number of international flights, as well as lots of bargain no-frills airlines connecting to it. Prague's Ruzyně airport has links to all Western European capitals, Cairo, Dubai, Kuwait, Mexico City, New York and Tel Aviv.

ESTONIA

Estonia enjoys plenty of European connections, including regular direct flights between Tallinn and Amsterdam, Berlin, Copenhagen, London, Munich, Paris and Stockholm.

TRAVELLING TO EASTERN EUROPE ON THE CHEAP

If saving money is more important than saving time, then consider a cheap flight to Western Europe, then travelling on overland by bus, train or boat. It can work out very reasonably if you fly from London, Amsterdam or Paris on to Eastern Germany, Austria, Italy, Greece or Finland. From those destinations, you can take a boat (Helsinki is linked to Tallinn and St Petersburg by ferry, lots of Italian ports have ferries to Slovenia, Croatia, Montenegro and Albania, and there are ferries from Corfu to Albania as well), a bus (see p893 for a huge range of connections into the region) or a train (a similarly massive number of routes exist – see p894).

For cheap flights to the edge of, or perhaps into, Eastern Europe check with budget airlines such as **Ryanair** (www.ryanair.com), **EasyJet** (www.easyjet.com), **Air Berlin** (www.airberlin.com), **Germania Express** (www.gexx.de), **Air Polonia** (www.airpolonia.com) and **SkyEurope Airlines** (www.skyeurope.com) for their cheapest deals. The latter two are unique as they fly all their flights into Eastern Europe proper; Sky Europe have three hubs at Vienna-Bratislava Airport, Budapest and Warsaw, and Air Polonia fly out of Warsaw and several other Polish cities.

HUNGARY

Big international carriers fly in and out of Budapest's Ferihegy 2, with main destinations including the UK, mainland Western Europe, the USA, Canada. Malév is the Hungarian national airline. Low-cost airlines such as SkyEurope and Air Berlin use the older Ferihegy 1 Airport, a few kilometres down the road. Alternatively, Vienna's Schwechart airport is only about three hours from Budapest by bus or train and often has less expensive international airfares as it handles more traffic.

LATVIA

Rīga Airport is serviced by direct flights from Amsterdam, Berlin, Brussels, Copenhagen, Frankfurt, Helsinki, London and Stockholm. National carrier Air Baltic does cheap no-frills deals with flights to Amsterdam, Berlin, Cologne, Dublin, Hamburg, London and Manchester among others.

LITHUANIA

Vilnius Airport is served by direct flights from Amsterdam, Berlin, Brussels, Copenhagen, Frankfurt, Helsinki, London and Stockholm. Low-cost Latvian carrier Air Baltic has cheap flights direct from Vilnius to Berlin, Cologne, Copenhagen, Dublin, Hamburg, Helsinki, Oslo and Vienna.

MACEDONIA

Still poorly served by international routes, Macedonia has one international airport, Skopje, which has direct connections with Lufthansa to/from Frankfurt and on Turkish Airlines to/from Istanbul. Swiss and Austrian Airlines offer flights from Skopje to a number of European destinations.

MOLDOVA

Moldova's only international airport is the originally named Chişinău International. Air Moldova is the national carrier. While most of Moldova's international flights are within Eastern Europe, Air Moldova has a daily service to Vienna, as well as flying four times a week to Rome, three times a week to Amsterdam and Athens and twice a week to Paris.

POLAND

Warsaw is the major destination for most foreign airlines, though Katowice, Kraków, Gdańsk, Poznań, Slupsk and Wrocław have flights to several European cities, although timetables seem to be very changeable. National carrier LOT and all major European carriers fly to Warsaw. Air Polonia is a budget, Internet-booking-only airline that flies to a large range of Western European cities from all over Poland and is probably the cheapest way to get here. It connects Warsaw to Athens, Brussels, Frankfurt, London, Madrid, Milan, Paris, Rome and Venice. Apart from Europe LOT connects Warsaw directly to Beirut, New York, Tel Aviv and Toronto.

ROMANIA

Tarom is Romania's state airline. Nearly all international flights to Romania arrive at Bucharest's Otopeni International Airport. Bucharest is well linked with all the major European capitals. In addition, Tarom runs flights from Arad to Verona, from Timişoara to Milan, from Sibiu to Munich and Stuttgart, and from Cluj-Napoca to Frankfurt, Munich and Vienna. Tarom operates regular flights to Istanbul that sometimes stop in Constanţa, May to mid-September. Turkish Airlines also flies this route. Tarom has a flight at least once a week direct to/from New York.

RUSSIA

Moscow is far and away the largest air hub in Eastern Europe, although no-frills airlines have largely ignored it as a destination. One exception is Germania Express, which flies to Moscow daily from several airports in Germany for very reasonable fares. Both Moscow and St Petersburg have great links throughout Europe – with flights from all major European cities including Berlin, Frankfurt, London, Madrid, Paris and Rome.

From outside Europe, Moscow is connected to all the capitals of the former Soviet Union as well to Bangkok, Beijing, Beirut, Damascus, Dubai, Hanoi, Hong Kong, Mumbai, Seoul, Tehran, Tokyo and Ulan Bator in Asia and the Middle East; Havana, Los Angeles, New York, San Francisco, Seattle, Toronto and Washington in the Americas and with Cairo and Luanda in Africa.

Kaliningrad is connected once a week to Copenhagen by SAS.

THE KOSOVO PUZZLE

While Kosovo is still legally part of Serbia, it is administered separately by the UN and has no immigration facilities at its boundary with the rest of Serbia or Montenegro. This means that for travellers who arrive in Kosovo without going through Serbia or Montenegro first, it's necessary to enter Montenegro through Albania, or Serbia via Macedonia – you can't cross directly from Kosovo in to Serbia or Montenegro proper. Bear this in mind when crossing through the Balkans, as it could force you to take a diversion.

SERBIA & MONTENEGRO

The growing number of connections from Belgrade (the main international airport) throughout Europe includes Amsterdam, Athens, Copenhagen, Düsseldorf, Frankfurt, London, Milan, Munich, Paris, Rome and Zürich. There are also flights to Cairo. The city is well served by regional airlines that pick up at intercontinental hubs, so travellers from Australia and New Zealand can fly to Dubai and pick up a JAT flight to Belgrade or fly with Lufthansa via Frankfurt or Austrian Air via Vienna. Travellers from North America are most likely to pick up connecting flights in London or Frankfurt. As of yet none of the European discount airlines fly to or near Belgrade.

SLOVAKIA

The national carrier is Air Slovakia, a small airline than nonetheless has mainly non-European international routes including Amritsar, Beirut, Kuwait and Tel Aviv. Within Europe, Air Slovakia links Bratislava to Birmingham and Larnaca. No-frills SkyEurope Airlines offers budget online fares to Amsterdam, Barcelona, London, Paris and Split from €25 one way. Austrian Airlines flies daily between Bratislava and Brussels, London and Paris.

SLOVENIA

For a little country, Slovenia's Brnik airport is surprisingly well connected throughout Europe, notably on Adria Airways, which serves Amsterdam, Brussels, Copenhagen, Dublin, Frankfurt, Istanbul, London, Manchester, Munich, Vienna and Zürich direct.

EasyJet has low-cost flights from London Stansted. Several other low-cost carriers serve a selection of nearby airports just across the Italian and Austrian borders.

UKRAINE

Foreign airlines flying into Kyiv include KLM, British Airways, Finnair, Lufthansa, Turkish Airlines, Air France and Austrian Airlines, all connecting Kyiv to their hubs. There were no direct flights to/from North America at the time of writing, but there was talk of introducing a direct flight on Aerosvit to New York and Toronto. Other international direct flights include Bangkok, Beijing and Delhi.

Tickets

Traditionally there has never been much to gain by buying tickets directly from an airline – discounted tickets were released to selected travel agencies and specialist discount agencies, and these were usually the cheapest deals going. While this is still the case for long-haul flights, shorter European routes are now routinely sold at decent prices by the airlines themselves. If dealing with the expanding number of no-frills carriers, this is often the only way to purchase tickets. Unlike the full-service airlines, no-frills carriers often make one-way tickets available at around half the return fare, meaning that it is easy to put together an open-jaw ticket (flying to one place but leaving from another). Crossing the whole of Eastern Europe is a lot more fun if you know you don't have to retrace your steps.

It's often easiest and cheapest to book airline tickets online. Even scheduled flights on commercial airlines can be profitably booked online through a number of websites; see p891. Shop around but always make sure that the price you are quoted includes the relevant taxes, as these can make the difference between a good price and a great price.

You may find the cheapest flights are advertised by obscure agencies. Most such firms are honest and solvent, but there are some fly-by-night outfits operating. Paying by credit card generally offers protection, as most card issuers provide refunds if you can prove you didn't get what you paid for. Similar protection can be obtained by buying a ticket from a bonded agency, such as one covered by the Air Travel Organisers' Licensing (ATOL) scheme in the UK. Agencies that accept only cash should hand over the tickets straight away and not tell you to 'come back tomorrow'. After you've made a booking or paid your deposit, call the airline and confirm that the booking was made. It's generally not advisable to send money (even cheques) through the post unless the agency is very well established – some travellers have reported being ripped off by fly-by-night mail-order ticket agencies.

If you purchase a ticket and later decide you want to make changes to your route or even get a refund, you need to contact the original travel agency. Airlines issue refunds only to the purchaser of a ticket – usually the travel agency who bought the ticket on your behalf. Many travellers change their routes halfway through their trip, so think carefully before you buy a ticket that is not easily refunded or changed. Don't bother buying half-used tickets from other travellers, no matter how low the price. You won't be able to board the flight unless the name on the ticket matches that on your passport.

You may decide to pay more than the rock-bottom fare by opting for the safety of one of the better-known travel agencies. Firms such as STA Travel, which has offices worldwide, are long-standing companies that generally offer good prices to most destinations.

Round-the-World (RTW) tickets are a useful option for long-haul travellers. Usually tickets are valid for between 90 days and a year. Make sure you understand what restrictions apply – there'll be a limit to how many stops (or kilometres) you are permitted, and you won't be able to backtrack.

Africa

Coming from Africa, there are connections to Prague and Moscow from Cairo as well as a regular link between Moscow and Luanda. Many chartered airlines fly between North Africa (mainly Morocco and Tunisia) and Eastern Europe too. However, flying via Western Europe on a busy route may prove to be far cheaper.

Nairobi and Johannesburg are probably the best places in East and Southern Africa to buy cheap tickets to Europe. One of the best agencies in Nairobi is **Flight Centre** (☎ 02-210 024; 2nd fl, Lakhamshi House, Biashara St).

In Johannesburg **STA Travel** (☎ 011-447 5414; rosebank@statravel.co.za; Rosebank Mall, 50 Bath Ave, Rosebank) and also **Rennies Travel** (☎ 011-833 1441; www.renniestravel.co.za; Unitas Bldg, 42 Marshall St) are recommended. Several West African countries, such as Gambia, Burkina Faso and especially Morocco offer cheap charter flights to France, from where you can travel on to Eastern Europe.

Asia

All the major hubs in Asia are linked with Moscow. There are also useful connections between Kyiv and Beijing, Bangkok and Delhi. Amritsar in India is linked to Slovakia on Air Slovakia. However, the cheapest option will often be a low-cost flight to Western Europe from one of the discount-airfare capitals of Asia: Hong Kong, Singapore and Bangkok.

In Singapore **STA Travel** (☎ 6737 7188; www.statravel.com.sg; 400 Orchard Rd, 07-02 Orchard Towers) has competitive fares. In Hong Kong try **STA Travel** (☎ 2736 1618; Suite 1703, 17/F, Tower One, Silvercord Centre, 30 Canton Rd, Kowloon) or **Phoenix Services** (☎ 2722 7378; room B, 6th fl, Milton mansion, 96 Nathan Rd, Tsimshatsui).

In India, cheap tickets can be bought from the bucket shops around Connaught Pl in Delhi. Check with other travellers about which is the most trustworthy.

Australia & New Zealand

There are no direct flights to Eastern Europe from Australia and New Zealand. The best option will nearly always be flying to Western Europe and connecting to your destination from there, although some Asian and Middle Eastern gateways such

---

ONLINE TICKETS

Some recommended air-ticket websites include those listed below. They usually levy a booking fee on any flights bought, but even if you don't buy through them, their software can be very useful for checking that the flight prices offered to you by other travel agents are the best ones available.

www.ebookers.com
www.opodo.com
www.flybudget.com
www.itasoftware.com
www.statravel.com

as Bangkok, Dubai and Hong Kong may also offer good deals. The cheapest fares to Europe are routed through Asia.

STA Travel (☎ 1300 733 035; www.statravel.com.au) and **Flight Centre** (☎ 133 133; www.flightcentre.com.au) are major dealers in the airfare game in Australia. Saturday's travel sections in the *Sydney Morning Herald* and Melbourne's *Age* have many ads offering cheap fares to Europe. With Australia's large and organised ethnic populations, it pays to check special deals in the ethnic press, too.

Thai Airways International, Malaysia Airlines, Qantas and Singapore Airlines all fly to Europe and have frequent promotional fares. Flights from Perth are usually a couple of hundred dollars cheaper than from east-coast cities. **Passport Travel** (☎ 03-9867-3888; www.travelcentre.com.au) in Melbourne are recognised Russian specialists and will be able to suggest some of the best routes and find good fares.

In New Zealand **STA Travel** (☎ 0508 782 872; www.statravel.co.nz) and **Flight Centre** (☎ 0800 243 544; www.flightcentre.co.nz) are two of the most popular travel agencies in New Zealand. Also check the *New Zealand Herald* for ads.

North America

The flight options across the north Atlantic, the world's busiest long-haul air corridor, are bewildering. In the USA, The *New York Times*, *LA Times*, *Chicago Tribune* and *San Francisco Chronicle* all have weekly travel sections in which you will find any number of budget travel agencies' advertisements. **Priceline** (www.priceline.com) is a 'name-your-price' auction service on the Web.

STA Travel (☎ 800 781 4040; www.statravel.com) has offices in all major cities in the USA and Canada, or check its website for your preliminary planning. You should be able to fly between New York and Europe (although not necessarily to an Eastern European city) very cheaply, especially outside of the high season. Direct flights include ČSA to Prague, Delta to Moscow and Malév to Budapest.

Travel CUTS (☎ 800 667 2887; www.travelcuts.com) has offices in all major Canadian cities. You might also scan the travel agencies' ads in the *Globe & Mail, Toronto Star* and *Vancouver Province*. From Toronto or Montreal, return flights to London are generally the cheapest option, from where

you can travel on to Eastern Europe on a budget airline.

South & Central America

Direct flight between South America and Eastern Europe are few and far between, although ČSA flies from Mexico City via New York to Prague and Aeroflot has regular flights to and from Havana. The most likely option is connecting in Western Europe (usually London, Lisbon, Madrid or Paris) to a second flight into Eastern Europe.

UK & Ireland

If you're looking for a cheap way to or from Eastern Europe, London is Europe's major centre for discounted fares. However, if you are connecting in London, remember that some 'London' airports are a huge distance from the city – you need to check before giving yourself just a couple of hours in transit, which is certainly insufficient to get you between Heathrow and Stansted, or Gatwick and Luton, for example.

For destinations in or close to Eastern Europe, some of the best deals are offered discount airlines such as EasyJet, Ryanair and SkyEurope Airlines. You can often find airfares from London that either match or beat surface alternatives in terms of cost – however, beware of the taxes, which can be very high here.

Plenty of budget travel agents advertise in the travel sections of weekend newspapers and also in the entertainment listings magazine *Time Out* and the **TNT Magazine** (www.tntmagazine.com).

STA Travel (☎ 0870 1600 599; www.statravel.co.uk; 86 Old Brompton Rd, London SW7) has 65 branches throughout the UK and sells tickets to all travellers but caters especially to young people and students.

Other recommended travel agents are: **Trailfinders** (☎ 020-7937 1234; www.trailfinders.co.uk; 215 Kensington High St, London W8), with branch offices in Manchester, Glasgow and several other British cities; **Bridge the World** (☎ 0870 814 4400; www.b-t-w.co.uk; 45-47 Chalk Farm Rd, London, NW1); and also **Flightbookers** (☎ 0870 814 0000; www.ebookers.com; 34-42 Woburn Pl, London WC1).

Charter flights can be a cheaper alternative to scheduled flights, especially for those who do not qualify for under-26 and student discounts. See your travel agency for possibilities.

Western Europe

Although London is the travel discount capital of Europe, there are several other cities in the region where you'll find a wide range of good deals, namely Amsterdam, Frankfurt, Munich and Paris. Budget airlines have totally revolutionised European air transport in the past few years. See the boxed text on p888 for information about no-frills services to the region and nearby. Nearly all budget airlines are best booked online, where you'll get an electronic ticket and will avoid paying the standard booking fee you'll be liable for if you book over the phone.

STA Travel (www.statravel.co.uk) has offices throughout Europe where cheap tickets can be purchased and STA-issued tickets can be altered (usually for a small fee); check on the website for contact details. **Nouvelles Frontières** (www.nouvelles-frontieres.fr) also has branches throughout the world.

France has a network of student travel agencies that supply discount tickets to travellers of all ages. **OTU Voyages** (☎ 0820 817 817; www.otu.fr) and **Voyageurs du Monde** (☎ 01 42 86 17 20; www.vdm.com) have branches throughout the country and offer some of the best services and deals. **CTS Viaggi** (☎ 06 441111; www.cts.it) is a student and youth specialist in Italy; in Spain agencies include **Usit Unlimited** (☎ 902 32 52 75; www.unlimited.es) and **Barcelo Viajes** (☎ 902 11 62 26; www.barceloviajes .es, in Spanish).

LAND
Border Crossings

With the advent of the EU, border crossing in the region has never been simpler. Even candidate members, Bulgaria and Romania, have cleaned up their acts, with polite and efficient staff checking you on entry and exit and levels of harassment falling hugely over recent years.

The region can be entered from all sides with no problem at all. Some of the major routes are from Germany and Austria into the Czech Republic, into Bulgaria from Turkey or Greece, into Slovenia from Italy and Austria and into Russia from Finland.

The only time real complications crossing borders are likely to arise is when crossing between Kosovo and Serbia and Montenegro (p890) and when crossing between Russia and Belarus (p902)

For details of overland transport into individual countries refer to the Transport sections in the country chapters.

Bus

Major gateway cities to the region by bus include Budapest, Prague, Warsaw and Ljubljana, among others.

ALBANIA

Buses to Thessaloniki (€35, 10 hours) go daily from Tirana, and three times a week to Athens (€50, 24 hours).

BULGARIA

From Sofia there are bus services to Greece and Turkey: Athens (€45, 12 to 13 hours, one or two daily), Thessaloniki (€20, six to seven hours, two to six daily) and Istanbul (€10, eight to 10 hours, nine daily).

CZECH REPUBLIC

Prague's main international bus station is ÚAN Praha Florenc. From Prague there are buses to and from Amsterdam (€65, 15 hours), Frankfurt (€40, 8½ hours), London (€60, 20 hours), Geneva (€70, 15 hours), Paris (€68, 15 hours), Salzburg (€28, 7½ hours) and Vienna (€18, five hours).

HUNGARY

Buses run from Budapest to Vienna (€21, 3½ hours, four daily), Frankfurt (€85, 15 hours, four weekly) via Munich (€68, nine hours), Paris (€109, 22 hours, four weekly), London (€128, 26 hours, daily) and, finally, Rome (€93, 15 hours, six weekly) via Florence (€74, 11 hours).

LATVIA & LITHUANIA

Daily international buses run from Vilnius to Amsterdam (€100), Brussels (€107), London (€144, two daily), Rome (€130), Stockholm (€55) and Vienna (€87).

Rīga is also part of the European international bus circuit. Daily services include buses to Amsterdam (€90), Berlin (€67), Hamburg (€76), Karlshamn (€26), Kristianstad (€26), London (€117), Oslo (€38), and Paris (€105).

MACEDONIA

Buses go to Istanbul from Skopje three or four times a day (€30, 14 hours), and to Frankfurt once a week (€98, 24 hours).

POLAND

From Warsaw there are daily buses to and from Amsterdam (€67.50, 20½ hours), Cologne (€47, 20 hours), London (€96, 27 hours), Paris (€67, 25 hours), Rome (€89, 27 hours) and Vienna (€29, 15 hours).

RUSSIA

There are several buses a day between the Finnish capital, Helsinki, and St Petersburg (€34, eight hours).

SLOVAKIA

Bratislava is well connected by bus to Europe. One-way fares include: Hamburg (€62, 18½ hours, twice weekly), London (€94, 22 hours, five weekly), Paris (€87, 20 hours, four weekly), Venice (€42, 12 hours, once weekly) and Vienna (€5, 1½ hours, daily).

SLOVENIA

To Ljubljana buses arrive from various German cities including Frankfurt (€77, 12 hours, daily) via Munich (€35, seven hours). Buses bound for Zagreb from several German cities drop off passengers in Maribor (eg Munich €37). Monday to Saturday there are roughly hourly buses from Koper to Trieste in Italy (€3, one hour) plus one direct Ljubljana–Trieste service (€10) at 6.25am. A 7.30am bus runs from Maribor to Graz, Austria (€7, 1¼ hours).

Car & Motorcycle

Travelling by car or motorcycle gives you an immense amount of freedom and is generally worry-free in Eastern Europe. Travelling by car between EU states is no problem at all, but trickier to non-EU members. Some insurance packages (especially those covering rental cars) do not include all European countries; for example hiring a car in Italy and driving it to Croatia will cause problems unless you have the correct insurance stamp (ask the agency to insure you for wherever you plan to travel). Due to high theft levels and terrible roads, Albania remains something of a no-go area for many, although the roads have been improving steadily and criminality declining slowly. Russia, Belarus and Ukraine still remain tediously difficult places to drive into – border controls can take a long time and bribes are often the order of the day.

Hitching

See the section under Hitching in Getting Around, p899.

Train

There are numerous routes into Eastern Europe by train, most of these from Western Europe. The big railway hubs in Eastern Europe are Prague, Budapest, Bucharest, Belgrade and Moscow. Albania is unique in Eastern Europe, having no international train services at all.

AUSTRIA

Services from Vienna include Budapest (€26, 3½ hours, five daily), Prague (€29, 4½ hours), Belgrade (€65, 11 hours, daily), Bucharest (€65), as well as Ljubljana (€52, 6¼ hours, daily) via Graz (€27).

From Salzburg there are also services such as that to Prague (€37, eight hours).

FINLAND

From Finland there are two daily connections between Helsinki and St Petersburg (€54, six hours) and one nightly train to Moscow (€85, 16 hours). From here you can connect throughout the region, although there are no direct trains to elsewhere in Eastern Europe from Finland.

GERMANY

Germany is a great for connecting by train to Eastern Europe. The numerous routes include Berlin to Prague (€44, five hours), Frankfurt to Prague (€61, 7½ hours), Munich to Budapest (€90, 7½ hours, two daily), Munich to Ljubljana (€60, 6¾ hours), Munich to Belgrade (€87, 17 hours, daily).

GREECE

Services to Eastern Europe include the daily service from Athens to Sofia (€32, 16½ hours), one daily service from Thessaloniki to Belgrade (€30, 16 hours) and two daily trains between Skopje and Thessaloniki (€11, six hours).

ITALY

Northern Italy is well connected to the Central European capitals. Routes include Venice to Budapest (€101, 16 hours, one overnight train daily), Venice to Prague and Venice to Ljubljana (€32, four hours) via Trieste.

TURKEY

One of the main routes into Eastern Europe is the Istanbul–Sofia train (€18, 14½ hours, daily), the overnight Istanbul–Bucharest train (€40, 17 to 19 hours) and the daily Belgrade train (€44, 26 hours).

ELSEWHERE

There are also connections from Switzerland and France. For example: Zürich to Budapest (€102, 12½ hours, one overnight train daily).

From Asia, there are of course the trans-Siberian, trans-Manchurian and trans-Mongolian express trains, which connect Moscow to the Russian far east, Ulan Bator (Mongolia) and Beijing. Central Asian cities such as Tashkent, Almaty and Dushanbe are also regularly connected by long distance trains to and from Moscow. Moscow is so well connected to the rest of the region that travelling on from here is easy.

SEA

More and more travellers arrive in Eastern Europe by water these days. Italy, Finland, Germany, Greece and Turkey all offer regular ferries to various ports on the Mediterranean, Black and Baltic Seas. All the following prices are for a seat only – cabins send the price soaring very quickly.

GEORGIA

The Georgian ports of Batumi and Poti have regular connections to Ilycheyevsk in Ukraine and Sochi in Russia.

GERMANY

Every three to four days, the **Silja Line's** (in Tallinn ☎ 611 6661; www.silja.fi) Finnjet connects Rostok (Germany) with Tallinn (€96, 25 hours), going on to St Petersburg (€117, a further 11 hours from Tallinn).

GREECE

A daily ferry and hydrofoil service plies the 27km between the Greek island of Corfu and the sleepy southern Albanian town of Saranda (€14 one way). Call **Finikas Lines** (in Corfu ☎ 30-9-4485 3228) for schedules.

ITALY

This is one of the most popular ways to get to the Balkans. Catching cheap flights to Ancona, Venice or Bari and then taking the ferry can often work out cheaper than a direct flight to Tirana or Split. Regular boats from several companies connect Italy with Croatia, Slovenia, Montenegro and Albania.

Jadrolinija (www.jadrolinija.hr; Rijeka ☎ 51-211 444; fax 211 485; Riva 16; Ancona ☎ 071-20 71 465; Bari ☎ 080-52 75 439), Croatia's national boat line, runs car ferries from Ancona to Split (€44, 10 hours) and Zadar (€41, seven hours), and also a route from Bari to Dubrovnik (€49, eight hours).

SEM (www.sem-marina.hr; Split ☎ 21-338 292; fax 21-338 291; Gat Sv Duje; Ancona ☎ 071-20 40 90) connects Ancona with Zadar and Split, continuing on to Stari Grad (Hvar).

SNAV (www.snav.com; Ancona ☎ 071-20 76 116; Naples ☎ 081-76 12 348; Split ☎ 21 322 252) has a fast car ferry that links Pescara and Ancona with Split (€73, 4½ hours) and Pescara with Hvar (€80, 3½ hours), as well as a passenger boat that connects Civitanova and Ancona with Zadar (€70, 3¼ hours).

La Rivera (www.lariverabus.it, in Italian; Rome ☎ 06-509 16 061; Naples ☎ 081-76 45 808) offers a combination bus-and-boat trip two or three times a week from May to October, departing from Rome and Naples to Korčula (€117, 9¼ hours) and Dubrovnik (€139, 12½ hours).

Adriatica di Navigazione (www.adriatica.it; Venice ☎ 041-781 611; Ancona ☎ 071-20 74 334) operates ferry services to Durrës from Bari (€60, 8½ hours) daily and from Ancona (€85, 19 hours) four times a week, leaving Albania and Italy at 10pm and docking at the other end at 7am. Cars cost €90/100 respectively; bicycles are carried free. It also connects Ancona and Split and runs between Trieste and Rovinj (€15.49, 3½ hours).

In Trieste, **Agemar** (☎ 39-40-363 222; info@agemar.it) car ferry *Expresso (Grecia)* runs each Tuesday and Saturday at 1pm to Durrës from Trieste (and returns on Wednesday and Sunday at 7pm). The trip on deck costs €35/45 in low/high season.

Venezia Lines (☎ 041-52 22 568; www.venezialines .com; Santa Croce 518/A, Venice 30135) runs a weekly boat from Venice to Pula (€45, three hours) and other Istrian coastal towns (€42, 2¼ hours, mid-April to late September). The **Prince of Venice** (Kompas; ☎ 05-617 8000; portoroz@kompas.si) catamaran from Venice also serves Izola (€45 to €60, 2½ hours, March to October). It operates between once and four times a week, generally returning the same evening. Though fun, it's much cheaper to take the Venice–Trieste train in conjunction with a Trieste–Koper–Izola–Piran bus.

Montenegro Lines (in Bari ☎ 578 98 11; www.montenegrolines.net) sails from Bari to Bar three times a week (€44, 10 hours) and once a week from Ancona to Bar (€77, 16 hours).

SCANDINAVIA

Even in the cold winter months, ferries plough the Gulf of Finland connecting Helsinki with Tallinn and St Petersburg, as well as the wide open Baltic, linking Gdańsk and Gdynia with Sweden and Denmark.

Since 2004 **Tallink** (in Helsinki ☎ 09 228 311; www.tallink.fi) has had a Helsinki–St Petersburg route (€55, 17 hours). The drag is that it sails via Tallinn on the outbound route, although from St Petersburg, the journey is direct. Boats leave Helsinki every other day at 4pm, arriving the same evening in Tallinn and then docking in St Petersburg at 9am the next day.

Viking Line (in Helsinki ☎ 09 123 577; www.vikingline.fi) sails its luxury *Rosella* daily in both directions between Helsinki and Tallinn (€21, three hours).

Polferries (www.polferries.pl) offers services between Gdańsk and Nynäshamn (18 hours) in Sweden every other day in summer (less frequently in the off season). It also has daily services from Świnoujście to Ystad (9½ hours) in Sweden, every Saturday to Rønne (six hours) in Denmark, and five days a week to Copenhagen (11 hours).

Stena Line (www.stenaline.com) operates between Gdynia and Karlskrona (11 hours) in Sweden.

TURKEY

From Istanbul, there's a weekly boat to Yalta and another to Sevastopol, as well as irregular connections up the Black Sea coast of Bulgaria and Romania to Varna and Constanţa.

GETTING AROUND

AIR

The major Eastern European cities are connected by a schedule of regular flights but, unless you are in a big hurry, taking the train

is always a cheaper and more interesting option. The major regional air hubs are Moscow, Prague and Budapest.

Many countries offer domestic flights, although, again, unless you are in a particular rush, there's no need to take these. Russia is the exception – flying from either Moscow or St Petersburg to Kaliningrad saves you the trouble of getting a double-entry Russian visa (by boat or land, you are given an exit stamp, thus invalidating your single-entry visa).

Airlines in Eastern Europe

For a full list of airlines operating in Eastern Europe see p887.

BICYCLE

A tour of Eastern Europe by bike may seem a daunting prospect but help is at hand. The **Cyclists' Touring Club** (CTC; ☎ 0870 873 0060; www.ctc.org.uk; Cotterell House, 69 Meadrow, Godalming, Surrey GU7 3HS) is based in the UK and offers its members an information service on all matters associated with cycling (including maps, cycling conditions, itineraries and detailed routes). If the club is not able to answer your questions the chances are someone will know someone who can.

The key to a successful bike trip is to travel light. What you carry should be largely determined by your destination and type of trip. Even for the shortest and most basic trip it's worth carrying the tools necessary for repairing a puncture. You might want to consider packing spare brake and gear cables, spanners, Allen keys, spare spokes and strong adhesive tape. Before you set off, ensure that you are competent at carrying out basic repairs. There's no point in loading up with equipment that you haven't got a clue how to use. Always check over your bike thoroughly each morning and again at night when the day's touring is over. Take a good lock and always use it when you leave your bike unattended.

The wearing of helmets is not compulsory but is certainly advised.

A seasoned cyclist can average about 80km a day but this depends on the terrain and how much weight is being carried. Don't overdo it – there's no point burning yourself out during the initial stages.

One major drawback to cycling in Eastern Europe is the disgusting exhaust put out by Eastern European vehicles, especially buses and trucks. You'll often find yourself gasping in a cloud of blue or black smoke as these vehicles lumber along quiet country roads.

Rental

Except for in a few of the more visited regions, it can be difficult to hire bikes in most of Eastern Europe. The best hunting grounds are often camping grounds and resort hotels in season. See the country chapters for more details.

Purchase

For major cycle tours, it's best to have a bike you're familiar with, so consider bringing your own (see the following section) rather than buying on arrival. If you can't be bothered with the hassle then there are places to buy in Eastern Europe (shops selling new and second-hand bicycles or you can check local papers for private vendors), but you'll need a specialist bicycle shop for a machine capable of withstanding touring. CTC can provide members with a leaflet on purchasing.

Transporting a Bicycle

If you want to bring your own bicycle to Europe, you should be able to take it on the plane. You can either take it apart and pack all the pieces in a bike bag or box, or simply wheel it to the check-in desk, where it should be treated as a piece of check-in luggage. You may have to remove the pedals and turn the handlebars sideways so that it takes up less space in the aircraft's hold; check all this with the airline well in advance, preferably before you pay for your ticket. If your bicycle and other luggage exceed your weight allowance, ask about alternatives or you may find yourself being charged a fortune for excess baggage.

Within Europe, bikes can usually be transported as luggage subject to a fairly small supplementary fee. If it's possible, book your tickets in advance.

BUS

Buses are a viable alternative to the rail network in most Eastern European countries. Generally they tend to complement the rail system rather than duplicate it, though in some countries – notably Hungary, the Czech Republic and Slovakia – you'll almost always have a choice.

In general, buses are slightly more expensive and slower than trains; in Russia, Poland, Hungary, the Czech Republic and Slovakia they cost about the same. Buses tend to be best for shorter hops such as getting around cities and reaching remote rural villages. They are often the only option in mountainous regions. The ticketing system varies in each country, but advance reservations are rarely necessary. It's always safest to buy your ticket in advance at the station, but on long-distance buses you usually just pay upon boarding.

See also the individual country chapters for more details about long-distance buses.

CAR & MOTORCYCLE

Travelling with your own vehicle allows increased flexibility and the option to get off the beaten track. Cars can be inconvenient in city centres when you have to negotiate strange one-way systems or find somewhere to park in a confusing concrete jungle. Also, theft from vehicles is a problem in many parts of the region.

Driving Licence & Documentation

Proof of ownership of a private vehicle should always be carried (a Vehicle Registration Document for British-registered cars) when touring Europe. An EU driving licence is acceptable for driving throughout most of Eastern Europe as are North American and Australian ones. But to be on the safe side – or if you have any other type of licence – you should obtain an International Driving Permit (IDP) from your motoring organisation. You'll need a certified Russian translation for driving in Russia; so find a translation agency that can notarise their translation for you. Always check which type of licence is required in your chosen destination before departure.

Fuel & Spare Parts

The problems associated with finding the right kind of petrol (or petrol of any kind without special coupons) are all but over in Eastern Europe. Fuel prices still vary considerably from country to country and may bear little relation to the general cost of living; relatively affluent Slovenia, for example, has very cheap fuel while the opposite is true in inexpensive Hungary. Savings can be made if you fill up in the right place. Russia is the cheapest – then Romania, which has prices half those of neighbouring Hungary. Motoring organisations such as the **RAC** (in UK ☎ 0800 550 055; www.rac .co.uk) can give more details.

Unleaded petrol of 95 or 98 octane is now widely available throughout Eastern Europe, though maybe not at the odd station on back roads, or outside main cities in Russia. To be on the safe side in Russia, bring a 20L can to carry an extra supply, especially if your car is fitted with a catalytic converter, as this expensive component can be ruined by leaded fuel. Unleaded fuel is usually slightly cheaper than super (premium grade). Look for the pump with green markings and the word *Bleifrei*, German for 'unleaded'. Diesel is usually significantly cheaper in Eastern Europe.

Good quality petrol is easy to find in the Baltics, but stations seem to be placed somewhat erratically. Several may be within a few kilometres of each other and then there may not be any for incredibly long stretches. Make sure you fill up your tank wherever possible – especially if you are travelling off the main highways.

Hire

Hiring a car is now a relatively straight forward procedure. The big international firms will give you reliable service and a good standard of vehicle. Prebooked rates are generally lower than walk-in rates at rental offices, but either way you'll pay about 20% to 40% more than in Western Europe. However, renting from small local companies is nearly always cheaper.

You should be able to make advance reservations online. Check out the following websites:

Avis www.avis.com
Budget www.budget.com
Europcar www.europcar.com
Hertz www.hertz.com

If you're coming from North America, Australia or New Zealand, ask your airline if it has any special deals for rental cars in Europe, or check the ads in the weekend travel sections of major newspapers. You can often find very competitive deals.

Although local companies not connected with any chain will usually offer lower prices than the multinationals, when comparing rates beware of printed tariffs intended only for local residents, which may be lower than the prices foreigners are charged. If in doubt, ask. The big chain companies sometimes offer the flexibility of allowing you to pick up the vehicle from one place and drop it off at another at no additional charge.

Insurance

Third-party motor insurance is compulsory throughout Europe. For non-EU countries make sure you check the requirements with your insurer. For further advice and more information contact the **Association of British Insurers** (☎ 020-7600 3333; www.abi.org.uk).

In general you should get your insurer to issue a Green Card (which may cost extra), an internationally recognised proof of insurance, and check that it lists all the countries you intend to visit. You'll need this in the event of an accident outside the country where the vehicle is insured. The European Accident Statement (known as the 'Constat Amiable' in France) is available from your insurance company and is copied so that each party at an accident can record information for insurance purposes. The Association of British Insurers has more details. Never sign accident statements you cannot understand or read – insist on a translation and sign that only if it's acceptable.

If the Green Card doesn't list one of the countries you're visiting and your insurer cannot (or will not) add it, you will have to take out separate third-party cover at the border of the country in question. This will probably be the case for Bulgaria and almost certainly for Russia. Note that the Green Card is also not accepted in the Baltic countries and you should allow extra time at borders to purchase insurance. Delays can sometimes last several hours.

Taking out a European breakdown assistance policy, such as the Five Star Service with **AA** (in UK ☎ 0870 550 0600) or the Eurocover Motoring Assistance with **RAC** (in UK ☎ 0800 550 055; www.rac.co.uk), is a good investment. Non-Europeans might find it cheaper to arrange for international coverage with their own national motoring organisation before leaving home. Ask your motoring organisation for details about free and reciprocal services offered by affiliated organisations around Europe.

Every vehicle travelling across an international border should display a sticker that shows the country of registration. It's compulsory to carry a warning triangle almost everywhere in Europe, which must be displayed in the event of a breakdown. Recommended accessories are a first-aid kit (this is compulsory in Croatia, Slovenia and Serbia and Montenegro), a spare bulb kit and a fire extinguisher (compulsory in Bulgaria). Contact the RAC or the AA for more information.

Road Rules

Motoring organisations are able to supply their members with country-by-country information on motoring regulations, or they may produce motoring guidebooks for general sale. The RAC provides comprehensive destination-specific notes with a summary of national road rules and regulations.

According to statistics, driving in Eastern Europe is much more dangerous than in Western Europe. Driving at night can be particularly hazardous in rural areas as the roads are often narrow and winding, and you may encounter horse-drawn vehicles, cyclists, pedestrians and domestic animals. In the event of an accident you're supposed to notify the police and file an insurance claim. If your car has significant body damage from a previous accident, point this out to customs upon arrival and have it noted somewhere, as damaged vehicles may only be allowed to leave the country with police permission.

Standard international road signs are used throughout all of Eastern Europe. You drive on the right-hand side of the road throughout the region and overtake on the left. Keep right except when overtaking, and use your indicators for any change of lane and when pulling away from the kerb. You're not allowed to overtake more than one car at a time, whether they are moving or stationary.

Speed limits are posted, and are generally 110km/h or 120km/h on motorways (freeways), 100km/h on highways, 80km/h on secondary and tertiary roads and 50km/h or 60km/h in built-up areas. Motorcycles are usually limited to 90km/h on motorways, and vehicles with trailers to 80km/h.

In towns you may only sound the horn to avoid an accident.

Everywhere in Eastern Europe the use of seat belts is mandatory and motorcyclists (and their passengers) must wear a helmet. In most countries, children under 12 and intoxicated passengers are not allowed in the front seat. Driving after drinking *any* alcohol is a serious offence – most Eastern European countries have a 0% blood-alcohol concentration (BAC) limit (0.02% in Poland).

Throughout Eastern Europe, when two roads of equal importance intersect, the vehicle coming from the right has right of way unless signs indicate otherwise. In many countries this rule also applies to cyclists, so take care. On roundabouts (traffic circles) vehicles already in the roundabout have the right of way. Public transport vehicles pulling out from a stop also have right of way. Stay out of lanes marked 'bus' except when you're making a right-hand turn. Pedestrians have right of way at marked crossings and whenever you're making a turn. In Europe it's prohibited to turn right against a red light even after coming to a stop.

It's usually illegal to stop or park at the top of slopes, in front of pedestrian crossings, at bus or tram stops, on bridges or at level crossings. You must use a red reflector warning triangle when parking on a highway (in an emergency). If you don't use the triangle and another vehicle hits you from behind, you will be held responsible.

Beware of trams (streetcars) as these have priority at crossroads and when they are turning right (provided they signal the turn). Don't pass a tram that is stopping to let off passengers until everyone is out and the tram doors have closed again (unless, of course, there's a safety island). Never pass a tram on the left or stop within 1m of tram tracks. A police officer who sees you blocking a tram route by waiting to turn left will flag you over. Traffic police administer fines on the spot (always ask for a receipt).

HITCHING

Hitching is never entirely safe in *any* country, and we don't recommend it. Travellers who decide to hitch should understand that they are taking a small but potentially serious risk. People who do choose to hitch will be safer if they travel in pairs and let someone know where they plan to go.

Also, as long as public transport remains cheap in Eastern Europe, hitchhiking is more for the adventure than the transport. In Russia, Albania, Romania and occasionally times Poland, drivers expect riders to pay the equivalent of a bus fare. In Romania traffic is light, motorists are probably not going far, and almost everywhere you'll face small vehicles overloaded with passengers. If you want to give it a try, though, make yourself a small, clearly written cardboard destination sign, remembering to use the local name for the town or city ('Praha' not 'Prague', or 'Warszawa' not 'Warsaw'). Don't try to hitch from the city centres; city buses will usually take you to the edge of town. Hitchhiking on a motorway (freeway) is usually prohibited; you must stand near an entrance ramp. If you look like a Westerner your chances of getting a ride might improve.

Women will find hitchhiking safer than in Western Europe, but the standard precautions should be taken: never accept a ride with two or more men, don't let your pack be put in the boot (trunk), only sit next to a door you can open, ask drivers where they are going before you say where you're going etc. Don't hesitate to refuse a ride if you feel at all uncomfortable, and insist on being let out at the first sign of trouble. Best of all, try to find a travelling companion (although three people will have a very hard time getting a lift).

Travellers considering hitching as a way of getting around Eastern Europe may find the following websites useful. For general facts, destination-based information and rideshare options visit www.bugeurope .com. The useful www.hitchhikers.org connects hitchhikers and drivers worldwide.

LOCAL TRANSPORT

Public transport in Eastern Europe has been developed to a far greater extent than in Western Europe. There are excellent metro networks in Moscow, St Petersburg, Warsaw, Prague, Kyiv, Minsk, Budapest and Bucharest. It is a great way to cover distances for a small flat fare.

One form of transport (both city- and nation-wide) that doesn't exist in Western Europe is the shared minibus (*marshrutka* in the former Soviet Union, *furgon* in the Balkans). These quick but cramped minibuses are used throughout Eastern Europe as a

form of both intercity and city transport. St Petersburg would cease to function without them, and it's also the most likely way you'll travel between mountain towns in Albania.

Trolleybuses are another phenomenon of the one-time Soviet block. Despite their slowness, they are very environmentally friendly (being powered by electricity and having no emissions in the city) and can be found throughout the former Soviet Union, including the world's longest trolleybus route (see p858) running between Simferopol and Yalta in Ukraine.

Trams are popular throughout Eastern Europe and vary hugely in their speed and modernity. Those in Russia are borderline antiques that seem to derail on a daily basis, while Prague's fleet of sleek trams have everything from electronic destination displayers to pickpockets.

TOURS

A package tour is worth considering only if your time is very limited or you have a special interest such as skiing, canoeing, sailing, horse riding, cycling or spa treatments. Cruises on the Danube River are available but they're very expensive. Most tour prices are for double occupancy, which means singles have to share a double room with a stranger of the same sex or pay a supplement to have the room to themselves.

New Millennium Holidays (☎ 0870 240 3217; www.newmillennium-holidays.com; Icon House, 209 Yardley Rd, Birmingham B27 6LZ) runs inexpensive bus or air tours all year from the UK to Central and Eastern Europe, including Russia. Packages vary from 10 to 17 days, some combining two or three countries, with half-board or B&B accommodation. Another British company highly experienced in booking travel to Eastern Europe is **Regent Holidays** (☎ 0117-921 1711, fax 0117-925 4866; www.regent -holidays.co.uk; 15 John St, Bristol BS1 2HR). Check out the website. There's also **Exodus** (☎ 0870 240 5550; www.exodus.co.uk) and **Exploreworldwide** (☎ 01252-760000; www.exploreworldwide.com).

For tours of the Baltic region, including weekend city breaks, activity holidays and cycling tours, **Baltic Holidays** (☎ 0161-286 0830; www.balticholidays.com; 30 Cartwright Rd, Manchester M21 9EY) is an option. It also arranges independent travel.

In Australia you can obtain a detailed brochure outlining dozens of upmarket tours (including to Russia) from the **Eastern Europe Travel Bureau** (☎ 02-9262 1144; www.eetbtravel.com; Level 5, 75 King St, Sydney, NSW 2000). Less upmarket and good value is **Intrepid Travel** (☎ 1300 360 887; www.intrepidtravel.com).

Young revellers can party on Europe-wide bus tours. **Contiki** (in London ☎ 020-8290 6422; www.contiki.com) and **Top Deck** (in Adelaide ☎ 08-8232 7222; www.topdecktravel.com) offer either camping or hotel-based bus tours for the 18-to-35 age group. The duration of Contiki's tours that include Eastern Europe or Russia are 22 to 46 days.

For people aged over 50, **Saga Holidays** (UK ☎ 0800 300 500; www.sagaholidays.com; Saga Bldg, Middelburg Sq, Folkestone, Kent CT20 1AZ; USA ☎ 617-262 2262; 222 Berkeley St, Boston, MA 02116) offers holidays ranging from cheap coach tours to luxury cruises (and has cheap travel insurance).

National tourist offices in most countries offer trips to points of interest. These may range from one-hour city tours to excursions of several days' duration into regional areas. They are often more expensive than going it alone, but are sometimes worth it if you are pressed for time. A short city tour will give you a quick overview of the place and can be a good way to begin your visit.

TRAIN

Trains are the most atmospheric, comfortable and fun way to make long overland journeys in Eastern Europe. All major cities are on the rail network, and it's perfectly feasible for train travel to be your only form of intercity transport. Overnight trains also have the benefit of saving you a night's accommodation. It's a great way to meet locals – and it's not unusual to be invited to stay for a night or two with people who shared your couchette.

When you'll be travelling overnight (nearly always the case when going between countries) you'll get a bed reservation included in the price of your ticket, although you may have to pay a few euros extra for the bedding once on board. Each wagon is administered by a steward or stewardess who will look after your ticket and – crucially, if you arrive during the small hours – who will make sure that you get off at the correct stop. Each wagon has a toilet and washbasin at either end, although their state of cleanliness can vary massively. Be aware that toilets may be closed while the train is at a station.

If you plan to travel extensively by train, it might be worth getting hold of the *Thomas Cook European Timetable*, which gives a complete listing of train schedules and indicates where supplements apply or where reservations are necessary. It is updated monthly and is available from **Thomas Cook** (www.thomascook.com) outlets in the UK, and from **Forsyth Travel Library** (☎ 800-367 7984; www.forsyth.com) in the USA. In Australia, look for it in a Thomas Cook outlet or one of the bigger bookstores, which can order in copies if they don't have any in stock. If you intend to stick to one or a handful of countries it might be worthwhile getting hold of the national timetable(s) published by the state railway(s). A particularly useful online resource for timetables in Eastern Europe is the DeutcheBahn website at www.bahn.de, in German. Train fares and schedules in US and Canadian dollars for the most popular routes in Europe, including information on rail and youth passes, can be found on www.raileurope.com. For fares in UK pounds go to www.raileurope.co.uk.

Classes

Throughout Eastern Europe there exists a similar system of classes on trains as there is in Western Europe. Short trips, or longer ones that don't involve sleeping on the train, are usually seated like a normal train – benches (on suburban trains) or aeroplane-style seats (on smarter intercity services).

There are generally three classes of sleeping accommodation on trains – each country has a different name for them, but for the sake of simplicity, we'll call them 3rd, 2nd and 1st class.

Third-class accommodation is not available everywhere, but it's the cheapest way to sleep, although you may feel your privacy has been slightly invaded. The accommodation consists of six berths in each compartment (in the former Soviet Union this is called *platzkart*; there are no compartments as such, just one open carriage with beds everywhere).

Second class (known as *kupeyny* in the former Soviet Union) has four berths in a closed compartment. If there are a couple of you, you will share your accommodation with two strangers. However, if there are three of you, you'll often not be joined by anyone.

First class, or *myagky* (soft) class in the former Soviet Union, is a treat, although you are paying for space rather than décor or unsurly service in most countries. Here you'll find two berths in a compartment, usually adorned with plastic flowers to remind you what you've paid for.

Costs

While it's reasonable, train travel is pricier than bus travel in some countries. First-class tickets are double the price of 2nd-class tickets, which are in turn approximately twice the price of 3rd-class tickets.

Reservations

It is always advisable to buy a ticket in advance. Seat reservations are also advisable but only necessary if the timetable specifies one is required. Out of season, reservations can be made pretty much up to an hour before departure, but never count on this. On busy routes and during the summer, always try to reserve a seat several days in advance. For peace of mind, you may prefer to book tickets via travel agencies before you leave home, although this will be more expensive than booking on arrival in Central Europe. You can book most routes in the region from any main station in Central Europe.

Safety

Be aware that trains, while generally extremely safe, can attract petty criminals. Carry your valuables on your person at all times – don't even go to the bathroom without taking your cash, wallet and passport. If you are sharing a compartment with others,

you'll have to decide whether or not you trust them. If there's any doubt, be very cautious about leaving the compartment. At night, make sure your door is locked from the inside. If you have a compartment to yourself, you can ask the steward/ess to lock it while you go to the dining car or go for a wander outside when the train is stopped. However, be aware that most criminals strike when they can easily disembark the train, and – in a tiny minority of cases – the stewards have been complicit.

In the former Soviet Union, the openplan 3rd-class accommodation is by far the most vulnerable to thieves.

Train Passes

Not all countries in Eastern Europe are covered by rail passes, but the passes do include a number of destinations and so can be worthwhile if you are concentrating your travels around the region. They may also be useful for getting to or from neighbouring countries. Of the countries covered in this book, Eurail passes are valid only in Hungary; check out the excellent summary of available passes and their pros and cons at www.seat61.com/Railpass.htm.

INTERRAIL

These passes are available to European residents of more than six months' standing (passport identification is required). Terms and conditions vary slightly from country to country, but when travelling in the country where you bought the pass, there is only a discount of about 50% on normal fares. The InterRail pass is split into zones.

CROSSING INTO RUSSIA: WARNING

Travellers have reported problems with entering Russia from Ukraine and Belarus. As there is often no border control (particularly between Belarus and Russia) and Ukrainians and Belarusians entering Russia don't need to have their passports stamped, travellers don't get a migration card when entering, or their passports aren't stamped on entry. Without a stamp in your passport showing you've entered Russia, hotels won't register your visa. And when leaving you again face problems for not having a migration card. Some travel agencies recommend that you fly into Russia from Belarus and Ukraine instead of taking the train, until this gets sorted out.

In addition to problems with train travel, flying to Moscow's Domodedovo airport from Minsk can be problematic as you don't go through customs. There is no problem flying between Ukraine and Russia.

If you do not receive a migration card when entering Russia, contact your embassy immediately upon arrival to find out how to get one. If you do not receive an entry stamp, go to the local OVIR (Visa and Registration) office in Russia and bring a full supply of patience.

Zone D is the Czech Republic, Slovakia, Poland, Hungary and Croatia; G includes Slovenia; and H is Bulgaria, Romania, Serbia and Montenegro and Macedonia.

The normal InterRail pass is for people under 26, though travellers over 26 can get the InterRail 26+ version. The price for any single zone is UK£159/223 for those aged under 26/26 and over for 16 days of travel. Two-zone passes are valid for 22 days and cost UK£215/303, and the all-zone Global Pass is UK£295/415 for one month of travel.

EURODOMINO

There is a Eurodomino pass for each of the countries covered by the InterRail pass, and they are probably only worth considering if you're concentrating on a particular region. Adults (travelling 1st or 2nd class) and people aged under 26 can opt for three- to eight-days' travel within one month.

EUROPEAN EAST PASS

The European East Pass can be purchased by anyone not permanently resident in Europe (including the UK). The pass is valid for travel in Austria, Hungary, Czech Republic, Slovakia and Poland, with benefits such as discounted Danube river trips with DDSG Blue Danube.

This pass is sold in North America, Australia and the UK. In the USA, **Rail Europe** (☎ 800 257 2887; www.raileurope.com) charges US$226/160 for five days of 1st/2nd-class travel within one month; extra rail days (maximum five) cost US$26/19 each.

The European East Pass can also be bought via **RailChoice** (☎ 0870 165 7300; www.railchoice.co.uk), which charges UK£121 (2nd class) for five days plus approximately an extra UK£15 per extra day of validity. Note that Eurodomino passes are only for people who've been resident in Europe for six months or more, so this option is for nonresidents.

NATIONAL RAIL PASSES

If you're intending to travel extensively within either Bulgaria, Czech Republic, Hungary or Romania, you might be interested in their national rail passes. You'll probably need to travel extensively to recoup your money but they will save you the time and hassle of buying individual tickets that don't require reservations. You need to plan ahead if you intend to take this option, as some passes can only be purchased prior to arrival in the country concerned. Some national flexipasses, near-equivalents to the Eurodomino passes mentioned above, are only available to non-Europeans. See www.raileurope.com for details.

TRANSPORT IN EASTERN EUROPE

Health

CONTENTS

Before You Go	**904**
Insurance	904
Recommended Vaccinations	904
Internet Resources	904
Further Reading	904
In Transit	**905**
Deep Vein Thrombosis (DVT)	905
Jet Lag & Motion Sickness	905
In Eastern Europe	**905**
Availability & Cost of Health Care	905
Infectious Diseases	905
Traveller's Diarrhoea	906
Environmental Hazards	906
Travelling with Children	906
Women's Health	907
Sexual Health	907

Travel health depends on your predeparture preparations, your daily health care while travelling and how you handle any medical problem that does develop. Eastern Europe is generally an exceptionally safe place to visit from a medical point of view, with no tropical diseases and an extensive, if basic, healthcare system throughout the region.

BEFORE YOU GO

Prevention is the key to staying healthy while abroad. A little preplanning, particularly for pre-existing illnesses, will save trouble later: see your dentist before a long trip, carry spare contact lenses or glasses, and take your optical prescription with you. Bring medications in their original, clearly labelled, containers, along with a signed and dated letter from your physician describing your medical conditions and medications, including generic names. If carrying syringes or needles, be sure to have a physician's letter documenting their medical necessity.

INSURANCE

If you're an EU citizen, an E111 form, available from health centres or UK post offices,

covers you for most medical care. E111 will not cover you for nonemergencies or emergency repatriation home. Others should find out if there is a reciprocal arrangement for free medical care between their country and the country visited. If you do need health insurance, strongly consider a policy that covers you for the worst possible scenario, such as an accident requiring an emergency flight home. Find out if your insurance plan will make payments directly to providers or reimburse you later for overseas health expenditures. The former option is generally preferable, as it doesn't require you to pay out of pocket in a foreign country.

RECOMMENDED VACCINATIONS

The WHO recommends that all travellers should be covered for diphtheria, tetanus, measles, mumps, rubella and polio, regardless of their destination. Since most vaccines don't produce immunity until at least two weeks after they're given, visit a physician at least six weeks before departure.

INTERNET RESOURCES

The WHO's publication *International Travel and Health* is revised annually and is available on line at www.who.int/ith/. Some other useful websites include www.mdtravelhealth .com (travel health recommendations for every country, updated daily), www.fitfor travel.scot.nhs.uk (general travel advice for the layperson), www.ageconcern.org.uk (advice on travel for the elderly) and www.mariestopes .org.uk (information on women's health and contraception).

TRAVEL HEALTH WEB SITES

It's usually a good idea to consult your government's travel health website before departure, if one is available:
Australia www.dfat.gov.au/travel/
Canada www.travelhealth.gc.ca
UK www.doh.gov.uk/traveladvice/
US www.cdc.gov/travel/

FURTHER READING

'Health Advice for Travellers' (currently called the 'T6' leaflet) is an annually updated

departure as some vaccines are not suitable for children less than one year old.

In hot, moist climates any wound or break in the skin is likely to let in infection. The area should be cleaned and kept dry.

Remember to avoid contaminated food and water. If your child has vomiting or diarrhoea, lost fluid and salts must be replaced. It may be helpful to take rehydration powders for reconstituting with boiled water.

Children should be encouraged to avoid and mistrust any dogs or other mammals because of the risk of rabies and other diseases. Any bite, scratch or lick from a warm blooded, furry animal should immediately be thoroughly cleaned. If there is any possibility that the animal is infected with rabies, immediate medical assistance should be sought.

WOMEN'S HEALTH

Emotional stress, exhaustion and travelling through different time zones can all contribute to an upset in the menstrual pattern. If using oral contraceptives, remember some antibiotics, diarrhoea and vomiting can stop the pill from working and lead to the risk of pregnancy – remember to take condoms with you just in case. Time zones, gastrointestinal upsets and antibiotics do not affect injectable contraception.

Travelling during pregnancy is usually possible but there are important things to consider. Always seek a medical check-up before planning your trip. The most risky times for travel are during the first 12 weeks of pregnancy and after 30 weeks. Antenatal facilities vary greatly between countries and

you should think carefully before travelling to a country with poor medical facilities or where there are major cultural and language differences from home.

Illness during pregnancy can be more severe so take special care to avoid contaminated food and water and insect and animal bites. A general rule is to only use vaccines, like other medications, if the risk of infection is substantial. Remember that the baby could be at serious risk if you were to contract infections such as typhoid or hepatitis. Some vaccines are best avoided (eg those that contain live organisms). However there is very little evidence that damage has been caused to an unborn child when vaccines have been given to a woman very early in pregnancy before the pregnancy was suspected.

Take written records of the pregnancy with you. Ensure your insurance policy covers pregnancy delivery and postnatal care, but remember insurance policies are only as good as the facilities available. Always consult your doctor before you travel.

SEXUAL HEALTH

Emergency contraception is most effective if taken within 24 hours after unprotected sex. The International Planned Parent Federation (www.ippf.org) can advise about the availability of contraception in different countries.

When buying condoms, look for a European CE mark, which means they have been rigorously tested, and then keep them in a cool dry place or they may crack and perish. Safe condoms are available throughout the region.

HEALTH

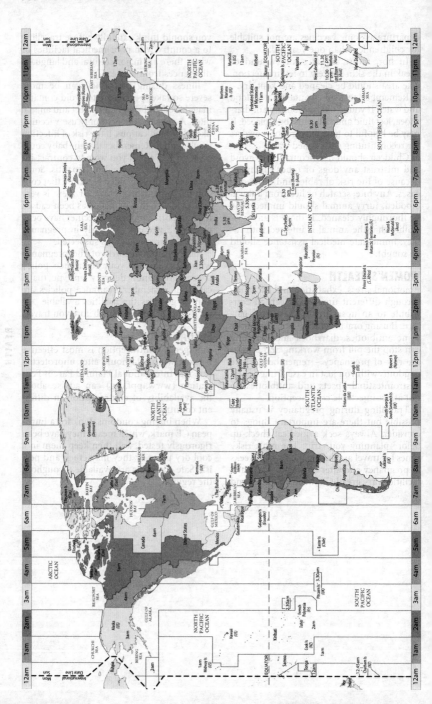

Language

CONTENTS

Albanian	909
Bulgarian	910
Croatian & Serbian	912
Czech	914
Estonian	915
Hungarian	916
Latvian	918
Lithuanian	919
Macedonian	920
Polish	922
Romanian	924
Russian	925
Slovak	928
Slovene	929

This language guide offers basic vocabulary to help you get around Eastern Europe. For more extensive coverage of the languages included in this guide, pick up a copy of Lonely Planet's *Eastern Europe Phrasebook* or *Baltic Phrasebook*.

Some of the languages in this chapter use polite and informal modes of address (indicated by the abbreviations 'pol' and 'inf' respectively). Use the polite form when addressing older people, officials or service staff.

ALBANIAN

PRONUNCIATION

Written Albanian is phonetically consistent and pronunciation shouldn't pose too many problems for English speakers. Each vowel in a diphthong is pronounced and the **rr** is trilled. However, Albanian possesses certain letters that are present in English but rendered differently. These include:

ë	often silent; at the beginning of a word it's like the 'a' in 'ago'
c	as the 'ts' in 'bits'
ç	as the 'ch' in 'church'
dh	as the 'th' in 'this'
gj	as the 'gy' in 'hogyard'
j	as the 'y' in 'yellow'
q	between 'ch' and 'ky', similar to the 'cu' in 'cure'
th	as in 'thistle'
x	as the 'dz' in 'adze'
xh	as the 'j' in 'jewel'

ACCOMMODATION

hotel	hotel
camping ground	kamp pushimi
Do you have any rooms available?	A keni ndonjë dhomë të lirë?
a single room	një dhomë më një krevat
a double room	një dhomë më dy krevat
How much is it per night/person?	Sa kushton për një natë/njeri?
Does it include breakfast?	A e përfshin edhe mëngjesin?

CONVERSATION & ESSENTIALS

Hello.	Tungjatjeta/Allo.
Goodbye.	Lamtumirë.
	Mirupafshim. (inf)
Yes.	Po.
No.	Jo.
Please.	Ju lutem.
Thank you.	Ju falem nderit.
That's fine.	Është e mirë.
You're welcome.	S'ka përse.
Excuse me.	Me falni. (to get past)
	Më vjen keq. (before a request)

EMERGENCIES – ALBANIAN

Help!	Ndihmë!
Call a doctor!	Thirrni doktorin!
Call the police!	Thirrni policinë!
Go away!	Zhduku!/Largohuni!
I'm lost.	Kam humbur rrugë.

I'm sorry.	Më falni, ju lutem.
Do you speak English?	A flisni anglisht?
How much is it?	Sa kushton?
What's your name?	Si quheni ju lutem?
My name is ...	Unë quhem .../Mua më quajnë ..

SHOPPING & SERVICES

a bank	një bankë
chemist/pharmacy	farmaci
the ... embassy	... ambasadën
the market	pazarin
newsagency	agjensia e lajmeve
the post office	postën
the telephone centre	centralin telefonik
the tourist office	zyrën e informimeve turistike
What time does it open/close?	Në ç'ore hapet/mbyllet?

TIME, DAYS & NUMBERS

What time is it?	Sa është ora?
today	sot
tomorrow	nesër
yesterday	dje
in the morning	në mëngjes
in the afternoon	pas dreke
Monday	e hënë
Tuesday	e martë
Wednesday	e mërkurë
Thursday	e ënjte
Friday	e premte
Saturday	e shtunë
Sunday	e diel
1	një
2	dy
3	tre
4	katër
5	pesë
6	gjashtë
7	shtatë
8	tetë
9	nëntë
10	dhjetë
100	njëqind
1000	njëmijë

TRANSPORT

What time does the ... leave/arrive?	Në ç'orë niset/arrin ...?
boat	barka/lundra
bus	autobusi
tram	tramvaji
train	treni
I'd like ...	Dëshiroj ...
a one-way ticket	një biletë vajtje
a return ticket	një biletë kthimi
(1st/2nd) class	klas (i parë/i dytë)
timetable	orar
bus stop	stacion autobusi

Directions

Where is ...?	Ku është ...?
Go straight ahead.	Shko drejt.
Turn left.	Kthehu majtas.
Turn right.	Kthehu djathtas.
near/far	afër/larg

SIGNS – ALBANIAN	
Hyrje	Entrance
Dalje	Exit
Informim	Information
Hapur	Open
Mbyllur	Closed
E Ndaluar	Prohibited
Policia	Police
Stacioni I Policisë	Police Station
Nevojtorja	Toilets
Burra	Men
Gra	Women

BULGARIAN

Bulgarian uses the Cyrillic alphabet and it's definitely worth famiairising yourself with it (see p926).

ACCOMMODATION

camping ground
къмпингуване   *kâmpinguvane*

guesthouse
пансион   *pansion*

hotel
хотел   *khotel*

private room
стоя в частна квартира   *stoya v chastna kvartira*

youth hostel
общежитие   *obshtezhitie*

single room
единична стая   *edinichna staya*

double room
двойна стая   *dvoyna staya*

Do you have any rooms available?
Имате ли свободни стаи?
imateh li svobodni stai?

How much is it?
Колко струва?
kolko struva?

Is breakfast included?
Закуската включена ли е?
zakuskata vklyuchena li e?

CONVERSATION & ESSENTIALS

Hello.
Здравейте.   *zdraveyte*
Hi.
Здрасти. (inf)   *zdrasti*
Goodbye.
Довиждане.   *dovizhdane*
Чао. (inf)   *chao*
Yes.
Да.   *da*
No.
Не.   *ne*
Please.
Моля.   *molya*
Thank you.
Благодаря.   *blagodarya*
Мерси. (inf)   *mersi*
I'm sorry.
Съжалявам.   *sázhalyavam*
Excuse me.
Извинете ме.   *izvinete me*
I don't understand.
Аз не разбирам.   *az ne razbiram*
What's it called?
Как се казва това?   *kak se kazva tova?*
How much is it?
Колко струва?   *kolko struva?*

EMERGENCIES – BULGARIAN

Help!
Помош!   *pomosh!*
Call a doctor!
Повикайте лекар!   *povikayte lekar!*
Call the police!
Повикайте полиция!   *povikayte politsiya!*
Go away!
Махайте се!   *mahayte se!*
I'm lost.
Загубих се.   *zagubih se*

SHOPPING & SERVICES

the bank
банката   *bankata*
the church
църквата   *tsárkvata*
the hospital
болницата   *bolnitsata*
the market
пазара   *pazara*
the museum
музея   *muzeya*
the post office
пощата   *poshtata*

the tourist office
бюрото за туристи-   *byuroto za turisticheska*
ческа информация   *informatsiya*

TIME, DAYS & NUMBERS

What time is it?
Колко е часът?   *kolko e chasát?*

today	днес	*dnes*
tonight	довечера	*dovechera*
tomorrow	утре	*utre*
yesterday	вчера	*vchera*
in the morning	сутринта	*sutrinta*
in the evening	вечерта	*vecherta*

Monday	понеделник	*ponedelnik*
Tuesday	вторник	*vtornik*
Wednesday	сряда	*sryada*
Thursday	четвъртък	*chetvârták*
Friday	петък	*peták*
Saturday	събота	*sábota*
Sunday	неделя	*nedelya*

0	нула	*nula*
1	едно	*edno*
2	две	*dve*
3	три	*tri*
4	четири	*chetiri*
5	пет	*pet*
6	шест	*shest*
7	седем	*sedem*
8	осем	*osem*
9	девет	*devet*
10	десет	*deset*
20	двайсет	*dvayset*
100	сто	*sto*
1000	хиляда	*hilyada*

TRANSPORT

What time does the ... leave/arrive?
В колко часа заминава/пристига ...?
v kolko chasa zaminava/pristiga ...?
city bus
градският автобус   *gradskiyat avtobus*
intercity bus
междуградският   *mezhdugradskiyat*
автобус   *avtobus*
plane
самолетът   *samolehtát*
train
влакът   *vlakát*
tram
трамваят   *tramvayat*

SIGNS – BULGARIAN	
Вход	Entrance
Изход	Exit
Информация	Information
Отворено	Open
Затворено	Closed
Забранено	Prohibited
Полицейско Управление	Police Station
Тоалетни	Toilets
Мъже	Men
Жени	Women

arrival	пристигане	*pristigane*
departure	заминаване	*zaminavane*
timetable	разписание	*razpisanie*

Where is the bus stop?
Къде е автобусната спирка?
kâde e avtobusnata spirka?

Where is the train station?
Къде е железопътната гара?
kâde e zhelezopâtnata gara?

Where is the left-luggage office?
Къде е гардеробът?
kâde e garderobât?

Please show me on the map.
Моля покажете ми на картата.
molya pokazhete mi na kartata

Directions

straight ahead	направо	*napravo*
left/right	ляво/дясно	*lyavo/dyasno*

CROATIAN & SERBIAN

PRONUNCIATION

The writing systems of Croatian and Serbian are phonetically consistent: every letter is pronounced and its sound will not vary from word to word. With regard to the position of stress, only one rule can be given: the last syllable of a word is never stressed. In most cases the accent falls on the first vowel in the word.

Serbian uses the Cyrillic alphabet so it's worth familiarising yourself with it (see p926). Croatian uses a Roman alphabet and many letters are pronounced as in English – the following are some specific pronunciations.

c	as the 'ts' in 'cats'
ć	as the 'tch' sound in 'future'
č	as the 'ch' in 'chop'
đ	as the 'dy' sound in 'verdure'
dž	as the 'j' in 'just'
j	as the 'y' in 'young'
lj	as the 'lli' in 'million'
nj	as the 'ny' in 'canyon'
š	as the 'sh' in 'hush'
ž	as the 's' in 'pleasure'

The principal difference between Serbian and Croatian is in the pronunciation of the vowel 'e' in certain words. A long 'e' in Serbian becomes 'ije' in Croatian, eg *reka/rijeka* (river), and a short 'e' in Serbian becomes 'je' in Croatian, eg *pesma*, *pjesma* (song). Sometimes, however, the vowel 'e' is the same in both languages, as in *selo* (village). This chapter uses Croatian pronunciation for both languages. There are a number of variations in vocabulary between the two languages. In the following phrase list these are indicated by 'C/S' for Croatian/Serbian.

ACCOMMODATION

hotel
hotel   хотел
guesthouse
privatno prenoćište   приватно пренођиште
youth hostel
omladinsko prenoćište   омладинско пренођиште
camping ground
kamping   кампинг

Do you have any rooms available?
Imate li slobodne sobe?
Имате ли слободне собе?

How much is it per night/per person?
Koliko košta za jednu noć/po osobi?
Колико кошта за једну ноћ/по особи?

Does it include breakfast?
Da li je u cijenu uključen i doručak?
Да ли је у цену укључен и доручак?

I'd like ...
Želim ...   Желим ...
a single room
sobu sa jednim krevetom   собу са једним креветом
a double room
sobu sa duplim krevetom   собу са дуплим креветом

CONVERSATION & ESSENTIALS

Hello.
Zdravo.   Здраво.
Goodbye.
Dovidenja.   Довиђења.
Yes.
Da.   Да.

No.
Ne. / Не.
Please.
Molim. / Молим.
Thank you.
Hvala. / Хвала.
That's fine/You're welcome.
U redu je/ / У реду је/
Nema na čemu. / Нема на чему.
Excuse me.
Pardon. / Пардон.
Sorry.
Oprostite. / Опростите.
Do you speak English?
Govorite li engleski? / Говорите ли енглески?
What's your name?
Kako se zovete? / Како се зове?
My name is ...
Zovem se ... / Зовем се ...

SHOPPING & SERVICES
I'm looking for ...
Tražim ...
Тражим ...
  a bank
  banku / банку
  the ... embassy
  ... ambasadu / ... амбасаду
  the market
  pijacu / пијацу
  the post office
  poštu / пошту
  the telephone centre
  telefonsku centralu / телефонску централу
  the tourist office
  turistički biro / туристички биро

How much is it ...?
Koliko košta ...? / Колико кошта ...?

TIME, DAYS & NUMBERS
What time is it?	*Koliko je sati?*	Колико је сати?
today	*danas*	данас
tomorrow	*sutra*	сутра
yesterday	*jučer*	јуче
in the morning	*ujutro*	ујутро
in the afternoon	*popodne*	поподне

Monday	*ponedeljak*	понедељак
Tuesday	*utorak*	уторак
Wednesday	*srijeda*	среда
Thursday	*četvrtak*	четвртак
Friday	*petak*	петак
Saturday	*subota*	субота
Sunday	*nedjelja*	недеља

1	један	*jedan*
2	два	*dva*
3	три	*tri*
4	четири	*četiri*
5	пет	*pet*
6	шест	*šest*
7	седам	*sedam*
8	осам	*osam*
9	девет	*devet*
10	десет	*deset*
100	сто	*sto*
1000	хиљада	*hiljada* (S)/ *tisuću* (C)

TRANSPORT
What time does the ... leave/arrive?
Kada ... polazi/dolazi?
Када ... полази/долази?
  boat
  brod / брод
  city bus
  gradski autobus / градски аутобус
  intercity bus
  međugradski autobus / међуградски аутобус
  train
  vlak (C)/voz (S) / воз
  tram
  tramvaj / трамвај

one-way ticket
kartu u jednom pravcu / карту у једном правцу
return ticket
povratnu kartu / повратну карту
1st class
prvu klasu / прву класу
2nd class
drugu klasu / другу класу

SIGNS – CROATIAN & SERBIAN

Ulaz/Izlaz	Entrance/Exit
Улаз/Излаз	
Otvoreno/Zatvoreno	Open/Closed
Отворено/Затворено	
Informacije	Information
Информације	
Policija	Police
Полиција	
Stanica Policije	Police Station
Станица Полиције	
Zabranjeno	Prohibited
Забрањено	
Toaleti/WC	Toilets
Тоалети/WC	

Where is the bus/tram stop?
   Gdje je autobuska/tramvajska postaja?
   Где је аутобуска/трамвајска станица?
Can you show me (on the map)?
   Možete li mi pokazati (na karti)?
   Можете ли ми показати (на карти)?

Directions

Go straight ahead.
   Idite pravo naprijed.   Идите право напред.
Turn left.
   Skrenite lijevo   Скрените лево
Turn right.
   Skrenite desno.   Скрените десно.
near
   blizu   близу
far
   daleko   далеко

CZECH

PRONUNCIATION

Many Czech letters are pronounced as per their English counterparts. An accent lengthens a vowel and the stress is always on the first syllable. Words are pronounced as written, so if you follow the guidelines below you should have no trouble being understood. When consulting indexes on Czech maps, be aware that **ch** comes after **h**.

c	as the 'ts' in 'bits'
č	as the 'ch' in 'church'
ch	as in Scottish *loch*
ď	as the 'd' in 'duty'
ě	as the 'ye' in 'yet'
j	as the 'y' in 'you'
ň	as the 'ni' in 'onion'
ř	as the sound 'rzh'
š	as the 'sh' in 'ship'
ť	as the 'te' in 'stew'
ž	as the 's' in 'pleasure'

ACCOMMODATION

hotel	*hotel*
guesthouse	*penzión*
youth hostel	*ubytovna*
camping ground	*kemping*
private room	*privát*
single room	*jednolůžkový pokoj*
double room	*dvoulůžkový pokoj*
Do you have any rooms available?	*Máte volné pokoje?*
Does it include breakfast?	*Je v tom zahrnuta snídane?*

CONVERSATION & ESSENTIALS

Hello/Good day.	*Dobrý den.* (pol)
Hi.	*Ahoj.* (inf)
Goodbye.	*Na shledanou.*
Yes.	*Ano.*
No.	*Ne.*
Please.	*Prosím.*
Thank you.	*Dekuji.*
That's fine/You're welcome.	*Není zač/Prosím.*
Sorry.	*Promiňte.*
I don't understand.	*Nerozumím.*
What's it called?	*Jak se to jmenuje?*

EMERGENCIES – CZECH

Help!	*Pomoc!*
Call a doctor/ ambulance/police!	*Zavolejte doktora/ sanitku/policii!*
Go away!	*Běžte pryč!*
I'm lost.	*Zabloudil jsem.* (m)
	Zabloudila jsem. (f)

SHOPPING & SERVICES

How much is it?	*Kolik to stojí?*
the bank	*banka*
the chemist	*lékárna*
the church	*kostel*
the market	*trh*
the museum	*muzeum*

the post office	pošta
the tourist office	turistické informační centrum (středisko)
travel agency	cestovní kancelář

TIME, DAYS & NUMBERS

What time is it?	Kolik je hodin?
today	dnes
tonight	dnes večer
tomorrow	zítra
yesterday	včera
in the morning	ráno
in the evening	večer

Monday	pondělí
Tuesday	úterý
Wednesday	středa
Thursday	čtvrtek
Friday	pátek
Saturday	sobota
Sunday	neděle

1	jeden
2	dva
3	tři
4	čtyři
5	pět
6	šest
7	sedm
8	osm
9	devět
10	deset
100	sto
1000	tisíc

SIGNS – CZECH

Vchod	Entrance
Východ	Exit
Informace	Information
Otevřeno	Open
Zavřeno	Closed
Zakázáno	Prohibited
Policie	Police Station
Telefon	Telephone
Záchody/WC/ Toalety	Toilets

TRANSPORT

What time does the ... leave/arrive?	Kdy odjíždí/přijíždí ...?
boat	loď
city bus	městský autobus
intercity bus	meziměstský autobus

| train | vlak |
| tram | tramvaj |

arrival	příjezdy
departure	odjezdy
timetable	jízdní řád
Where is the bus stop?	Kde je autobusová zastávka?
Where is the station?	Kde je nádraží?
Where is the left-luggage office?	Kde je úschovna zavazadel?
Please show me on the map.	Prosím, ukažte mi to na mapě.

Directions

Where is it?	Kde je to?
left	vlevo
right	vpravo
straight ahead	rovně

ESTONIAN

ALPHABET & PRONUNCIATION

The letters of the Estonian alphabet are: **a b d e f g h i j k l m n o p r s š z ž t u v õ ä ö ü**.

a	as the 'u' in 'cut'
b	similar to English 'p'
g	similar to English 'k'
j	as the 'y' in 'yes'
š	as 'sh'
ž	as the 's' in 'pleasure'
õ	somewhere between the 'e' in 'bed' and the 'u' in 'fur'
ä	as the 'a' in 'cat'
ö	as the 'u' in 'fur' but with rounded lips
ü	as a short 'you'
ai	as the 'ai' in 'aisle'
ei	as in 'vein'
oo	as the 'a' in 'water'
uu	as the 'oo' in 'boot'
öö	as the 'u' in 'fur'

CONVERSATION & ESSENTIALS

Hello.	Tere.
Goodbye.	Head aega/Nägemiseni.
Yes.	Jah.
No.	Ei.
Excuse me.	Vabandage.
Please.	Palun.
Thank you.	Tänan/Aitäh. (inf)
Do you speak English?	Kas te räägite inglise keelt?

EMERGENCIES – ESTONIAN

Help!	*Appi!*
I'm ill.	*Ma olen haige.*
I'm lost.	*Ma olen eksinud.*
Go away!	*Minge ära!*
Call ...!	*Kutsuge ...!*
a doctor	*arst*
an ambulance	*kiirabi*
the police	*politsei*

SHOPPING & SERVICES

bank	*pank*
chemist	*apteek*
currency exchange	*valuutavahetus*
market	*turg*
toilet	*tualett*
Where?	*Kus?*
How much?	*Kui palju?*

TIME, DAYS & NUMBERS

today	*täna*
tomorrow	*homme*
yesterday	*eile*
Monday	*esmaspäev*
Tuesday	*teisipäev*
Wednesday	*kolmapäev*
Thursday	*neljapäev*
Friday	*reede*
Saturday	*laupäev*
Sunday	*pühapäev*
1	*üks*
2	*kaks*
3	*kolm*
4	*neli*
5	*viis*
6	*kuus*
7	*seitse*
8	*kaheksa*
9	*üheksa*
10	*kümme*
100	*sada*
1000	*tuhat*

TRANSPORT

airport	*lennujaam*
bus station	*bussijaam*
port	*sadam*
stop (eg bus stop)	*peatus*

train station	*raudteejaam*
bus	*buss*
taxi	*takso*
train	*rong*
tram	*tramm*
trolleybus	*trollibuss*

SIGNS – ESTONIAN

Sissepääs	Entrance
Väljapääs	Exit
Avatud/Lahti	Open
Suletud/Kinni	Closed
Mitte Suitsetada	No Smoking
WC	Public Toilet
Meestele	Women
Naistele	Men

---

ticket	*pilet*
ticket office	*piletikassa/kassa*
soft class/deluxe	*luksus*
sleeping carriage	*magamisvagun*
compartment (class)	*kupee*

HUNGARIAN

PRONUNCIATION

The pronunciation of Hungarian consonants can be simplified by pronouncing them more or less as in English; the exceptions are listed below. Double consonants **ll**, **tt** and **dd** aren't pronounced as one letter as in English but lengthened so you can almost hear them as separate letters. Also, **cs**, **zs**, **gy** and **sz** (consonant clusters) are separate letters in Hungarian and appear that way in telephone books and other alphabetical listings. For example, the word *cukor* (sugar) appears in the dictionary before *csak* (only).

c	as the 'ts' in 'hats'
cs	as the 'ch' in 'church'
gy	as the 'j' in 'jury'
j	as the 'y' in 'yes'
ly	as the 'y' in 'yes'
ny	as the 'ni' in 'onion'
r	like a slightly trilled Scottish 'r'
s	as the 'sh' in 'ship'
sz	as the 's' in 'set'
ty	as the 'tu' in British English 'tube'
w	as 'v' (found in foreign words only)
zs	as the 's' in 'pleasure'

Vowels are a bit trickier, and the semantic difference between **a**, **e** or **o** with and without an accent mark is great. For example, *hát* means 'back' while *hat* means 'six'.

a	as the 'o' in hot
á	as in 'father'
e	short, as in 'set'
é	as the 'e' in 'they' with no 'y' sound
i	as in 'hit' but shorter
í	as the 'i' in 'police'
o	as in 'open'
ó	a longer version of **o** above
ö	as the 'u' in 'burst' without the 'r' sound
ő	a longer version of **ö** above
u	as in 'pull'
ú	as the 'ue' in 'blue'
ü	similar to the 'u' in 'flute'; purse your lips tightly and say 'ee'
ű	a longer, breathier version of **ü** above

EMERGENCIES – HUNGARIAN

Help!	*Segítség!*
Call a doctor!	*Hívjon egy orvost!*
Call an ambulance!	*Hívja a mentőket!*
Call the police!	*Hívja a rendőrséget!*
Go away!	*Menjen el!*
I'm lost.	*Eltévedtem.*

ACCOMMODATION

hotel	*szálloda*
guesthouse	*fogadót*
youth hostel	*ifjúsági szálló*
camping ground	*kemping*
private room	*fizetővendég szoba*
Do you have rooms available?	*Van szabad szobájuk?*
How much is it per night/person?	*Mennyibe kerül éjszakánként/ személyenként?*
Does it include breakfast?	*Az ár tartalmazza a reggelit?*
single/double room	*egyágyas/kétágyas szoba*

CONVERSATION & ESSENTIALS

Hello.	*Szia/Szervusz.* (inf/pol)
Good afternoon/day.	*Jó napot kívánok.* (pol)
See you later.	*Viszontlátásra.*
Goodbye.	*Szia/Szervusz.* (inf/pol)
Yes.	*Igen.*
No.	*Nem.*
Please.	*Kérem.*

Thank you.	*Köszönöm.*
Sorry.	*Sajnálom.*
Excuse me.	*Bocsánat.* (to get past) *Elnézést.* (to get attention)
What's your name?	*Hogy hívják?* (pol)/ *Mi a neved?* (inf)
My name is ...	*A nevem ...*
I don't understand.	*Nem értem.*
Do you speak English?	*Beszél angolul?*
What's it called?	*Hogy hívják?*

SHOPPING & SERVICES

Where is ...?	*Hol van ...?*
a bank	*bank*
a chemist	*gyógyszertár*
the market	*a piac*
the museum	*a múzeum*
the post office	*a posta*
a tourist office	*idegenforgalmi iroda*
How much is it?	*Mennyibe kerül?*
What time does it open?	*Mikor nyit ki?*
What time does it close?	*Mikor zár be?*

TIME, DAYS & NUMBERS

What time is it?	*Hány óra?*
today	*ma*
tonight	*ma este*
tomorrow	*holnap*
yesterday	*tegnap*
in the morning	*reggel*
in the evening	*este*
Monday	*hétfő*
Tuesday	*kedd*
Wednesday	*szerda*
Thursday	*csütörtök*
Friday	*péntek*
Saturday	*szombat*
Sunday	*vasárnap*
1	*egy*
2	*kettő*
3	*három*
4	*négy*
5	*öt*
6	*hat*
7	*hét*
8	*nyolc*
9	*kilenc*
10	*tíz*
100	*száz*
1000	*ezer*

SIGNS – HUNGARIAN

Bejárat	Entrance
Kijárat	Exit
Információ	Information
Nyitva	Open
Zárva	Closed
Tilos	Prohibited
Rendőrőr-	Police Station
Kapitányság	
Toalett/WC	Toilets
Férfiak	Men
Nők	Women

TRANSPORT

What time does	Mikor indul/érkezik a ...?
the ... leave/arrive?	
boat/ferry	hajó/komp
city bus	helyi autóbusz
intercity bus	távolsági autóbusz
plane	repülőgép
train	vonat
tram	villamos
arrival	érkezés
departure	indulás
timetable	menetrend
Where is ...?	Hol van ...?
the bus stop	az autóbuszmegálló
the station	a pályaudvar
the left-luggage	a csomagmegőrző
office	
Please show me on	Kérem, mutassa meg a térképen.
the map.	

Directions

(Turn) left.	(Forduljon) balra.
(Turn) right.	(Forduljon) jobbra.
(Go) straight ahead.	(Menyen) egyenesen elore.
near/far	közel/messze

LATVIAN

ALPHABET & PRONUNCIATION

The letters of the Latvian alphabet are: **a b c č d e f g ģ (Ģ) h i j k ķ l ļ m n ņ o p r s š t u v z ž**.

c	as the 'ts' in 'bits'
č	as the 'ch' in 'church'
ģ	as the 'j' in 'jet'
j	as the 'y' in 'yes'

ķ	as the 'tu' in 'tune'
ļ	as the 'lli' in 'billiards'
ņ	as the 'ni' in 'onion'
o	as the 'a' in 'water'
š	as the 'sh' in 'ship'
ž	as the 's' in 'pleasure'
ai	as in 'aisle'
ei	as in 'vein'
ie	as in 'pier'
ā	as the 'a' in 'barn'
ē	as the 'e' in 'where'
ī	as the 'i' in 'marine'
ū	as the 'oo' in 'boot'

CONVERSATION & ESSENTIALS

Hello.	Labdien/Sveiki.
Goodbye.	Uz redzēšanos/Atā.
Yes.	Jā.
No.	Nē.
Excuse me.	Atvainojiet.
Please.	Lūdzu.
Thank you.	Paldies.
Do you speak English?	Vai jūs runājat angliski?

EMERGENCIES – LATVIAN

Help!	Palīgā!
I'm ill.	Es esmu slims/slima. (m/f)
I'm lost.	Es esmu apmaldījies/ apmaldījusies. (m/f)
Go away!	Ejiet projam!
Call ...!	Izsauciet ...!
a doctor	ārstu
an ambulance	ātro palīdzību
the police	policiju

SHOPPING & SERVICES

bank	banka
chemist	aptieka
currency exchange	valūtas maiņa
hotel	viesnīca
market	tirgus
post office	pasts
toilet	tualete
Where?	Kur?
How much?	Cik?

TIME, DAYS & NUMBERS

today	šodien
yesterday	vakar
tomorrow	rīt

SIGNS – LATVIAN

Ieeja	Entrance
Izeja	Exit
Informācija	Information
Atvērts	Open
Slēgts	Closed
Smēķēt Aizliegts	No Smoking
Policijas Iecirknis	Police Station
Maksas Tualetes	Public Toilets
Sieviešu	Women
Vīriešu	Men

Sunday	svētdiena
Monday	pirmdiena
Tuesday	otrdiena
Wednesday	trešdiena
Thursday	ceturtdiena
Friday	piektdiena
Saturday	sestdiena

0	nulle
1	viens
2	divi
3	tris
4	četri
5	pieci
6	seši
7	septiņi
8	astoņi
9	deviņi
10	desmit
11	vienpadsmit
12	divpadsmit
100	simts
1000	tūkstots

TRANSPORT

airport	lidosta
train station	dzelzceļa stacija
train	vilciens
bus station	autoosta
bus	autobuss
port	osta
taxi	taksometrs
tram	tramvajs
stop (eg bus stop)	pietura
departure time	atiešanas laiks
arrival time	pienākšanas laiks
ticket	biļete
ticket office	kase

LITHUANIAN

ALPHABET & PRONUNCIATION

The letters of the Lithuanian alphabet are:
a b c č d e f g h i/y j k l m n o p r s š t u v z ž. In some circumstances the **i** and **y** are interchangeable.

c	as 'ts'
č	as 'ch'
y	between the 'i' in 'tin' and the 'ee' in 'feet'
j	as the 'y' in 'yes'
š	as 'sh'
ž	as the 's' in 'pleasure'
ei	as the 'ai' in 'pain'
ie	as the 'ye' in 'yet'
ui	as the 'wi' in 'win'

Accent marks above and below vowels (eg **ā**, **ė** and **į**) all have the general effect of lengthening the vowel:

ā	as the 'a' in 'father'
ę	as the 'e' in 'there'
į	as the 'ee' in 'feet'
ų	as the 'oo' in 'boot'
ū	as the 'oo' in 'boot'
ė	as the 'e' in 'they'

EMERGENCIES – LITHUANIAN

Help!	Gelėbkite!
I'm ill.	Aš sergu.
I'm lost.	Aš paklydęs/paklydusi. (m/f)
Go away!	Eik šalin!
Call ...!	Iššaukite ...!
a doctor	gydytoją
an ambulance	greitąją
the police	policiją

CONVERSATION & ESSENTIALS

Hello.	Labas/Sveikas.
Goodbye.	Sudie/Viso gero.
Yes.	Taip.
No.	Ne.
Excuse me.	Atsiprašau.
Please.	Prašau.
Thank you.	Ačiū.
Do you speak English?	Ar kalbate angliškai?

LANGUAGE

SHOPPING & SERVICES

bank	bankas
chemist	vaistinė
currency exchange	valiutos keitykla
hotel	viešbutis
market	turgus
post office	paštas
toilet	tualetas
Where?	Kur?
How much?	Kiek?

TIMES, DAYS & NUMBERS

today	šiandien
tomorrow	rytoj
yesterday	vakar
Monday	pirmadienis
Tuesday	antradienis
Wednesday	trečiadienis
Thursday	ketvirtadienis
Friday	penktadienis
Saturday	šeštadienis
Sunday	sekmadienis
1	vienas
2	du
3	trys
4	keturi
5	penki
6	šeši
7	septyni
8	aštuoni
9	devyni
10	dešimt
100	šimtas
1000	tūkstantis

TRANSPORT

airport	oro uostas
bus station	autobusų stotis
port	uostas
train station	geležinkelio stotis
stop (eg bus stop)	stotelė
bus	autobusas
taxi	taksi
train	traukinys
tram	tramvajus
departure time	išvykimo laikas
arrival time	atvykimo laikas
ticket	bilietas
ticket office	kasa

MACEDONIAN

There are 31 letters in the Macedonian Cyrillic alphabet and it's well worth familiarising yourself with it (see p926).

ACCOMMODATION

hotel
хотел — *hotel*
guesthouse
приватно сметување — *privatno smetuvanje*
youth hostel
младинско — *mladinsko*
  преноќиште — *prenočište*
camping ground
кампинг — *kamping*

Do you have any rooms available?
Дали имате слободни соби?
Dali imate slobodni sobi?
How much is it per night/per person?
Која е цената по ноќ/по особа?
Koja e cenata po noč/po osoba?
Does it include breakfast?
Дали е вклучен појадок?
Dali e vključen pojadok?
a single room
соба со еден кревет
soba so eden krevet
a double room
соба со брачен кревет
soba so bračen krevet
for one/two nights
за една/два вечери
za edna/dva večeri

CONVERSATION & ESSENTIALS

Hello.
Здраво. — *Zdravo.*
Goodbye.
Приатно. — *Priatno.*
Yes.
Да. — *Da.*
No.
Не. — *Ne.*

Excuse me.
  Извинете.   *Izvinete.*
Please.
  Молам.   *Molam.*
Thank you.
  Благодарам.   *Blagodaram.*
You're welcome.
  Нема зошто/   *Nema zošto/*
  Мило ми е.   *Milo mi e.*
Sorry.
  Опростете ве молам.   *Oprostete ve molam.*
Do you speak English?
  Зборувате ли   *Zboruvate li*
  англиски?   *angliski?*
What's your name?
  Како се викате?   *Kako se vikate?*
My name is ...
  Јас се викам ...   *Jas se vikam ...*

SHOPPING & SERVICES
bank
  банка   *banka*
chemist/pharmacy
  аптека   *apteka*
the embassy
  амбасадата   *ambasadata*
my hotel
  мојот хотел   *mojot hotel*
the market
  пазарот   *pazarot*
newsagents
  киоск за весници   *kiosk za vesnici*
the post office
  поштата   *poštata*
stationers
  книжарница   *knižarnica*
the telephone centre
  телефонската   *telefonskata*
  централа   *centrala*
the tourist office
  туристичкото биро   *turističkoto biro*

How much is it?
  Колку чини тоа?
  Kolku čini toa?
What time does it open/close?
  Кога се отвора/затвора?
  Koga se otvora/zatvora?

TIME, DAYS & NUMBERS
What time is it?
  Колку е часот?   *Kolku e časot?*

today   денес   *denes*
tomorrow   утре   *utre*

yesterday	вчера	*včera*
morning	утро	*utro*
afternoon	попладне	*popladne*
Monday	понеделник	*ponedelnik*
Tuesday	вторник	*vtornik*
Wednesday	среда	*sreda*
Thursday	четврток	*četvrtok*
Friday	петок	*petok*
Saturday	сабота	*sabota*
Sunday	недела	*nedela*
0	нула	*nula*
1	еден	*eden*
2	два	*dva*
3	три	*tri*
4	четири	*četiri*
5	пет	*pet*
6	шест	*šest*
7	седум	*sedum*
8	осум	*osum*
9	девет	*devet*
10	десет	*deset*
100	сто	*sto*
1000	илада	*ilada*

EMERGENCIES – MACEDONIAN
Help!
  Помош!   *Pomoš!*
Call a doctor!
  Повикајте лекар!   *Povikajte lekar!*
Call the police!
  Викнете полиција!   *Viknete policija!*
Go away!
  Одете си!   *Odete si!*
I'm lost.
  Јас загинав.   *Jas zaginav.*

TRANSPORT
What time does the next ... leave/arrive?
  Кога доаѓа/заминува идниот ...?
  Koga doagja/zaminuva idniot ...?
boat
  брод   *brod*
city bus
  автобус градски   *avtobus gradski*
intercity bus
  автобус меѓуградски   *avtobus megjugradski*
train
  воз   *voz*
tram
  трамвај   *tramvaj*

LANGUAGE

SIGNS – MACEDONIAN

Влез	Entrance
Излез	Exit
Отворено	Open
Затворено	Closed
Информации	Information
Полиција	Police
Полициска Станица	Police Station
Забането	Prohibited
Клозети	Toilets
Машки	Men
Женски	Women

I'd like ...
Сакам ...
Sakam ...

  a one-way ticket
  билет во еден правец *bilet vo eden pravec*
  a return ticket
  повратен билет *povraten bilet*
  1st class
  прва класа *prva klasa*
  2nd class
  втора класа *vtora klasa*

timetable
возен ред *vozen red*
bus stop
автобуска станица *avtobuska stanica*
train station
железничка станица *zheleznička stanica*

I'd like to hire a car/bicycle.
Сакам да изнајмам кола/точак.
Sakam da iznajmam kola/točak.

Directions
Where is ...?
Каде је ...? *Kade je ...?*
Go straight ahead.
Одете право напред. *Odete pravo napred.*
Turn left/right.
Свртете лево/десно. *Svrtete levo/desno.*
near/far
блиску/далеку *blisku/daleku*

POLISH

PRONUNCIATION
Written Polish is phonetically consistent, which means that the pronunciation of letters or clusters of letters doesn't vary from

word to word. The stress almost always falls on the second-last syllable.

Vowels
a	as the 'u' in 'cut'
e	as in 'ten'
i	similar to the 'ee' in 'feet' but shorter
o	as in 'lot'
u	a bit shorter than the 'oo' in 'book'
y	similar to the 'i' in 'bit'

There are three vowels unique to Polish:

ą	a nasal vowel sound like the French *un*, similar to 'own' in 'sown'
ę	also nasalised, like the French *un*, but pronounced as 'e' in 'ten' when word-final
ó	similar to Polish **u**

Consonants
In Polish, the consonants **b, d, f, k, l, m, n, p, t, v** and **z** are pronounced more or less as they are in English. The following consonants and clusters of consonants sound very different to their English counterparts:

c	as the 'ts' in 'its'
ch	similar to the 'ch' in the Scottish *loch*
cz	as the 'ch' in 'church'
ć	much softer than Polish **c** (as 'tsi' before vowels)
dz	similar to the 'ds' in 'suds' but shorter
dź	as **dz** but softer (as 'dzi' before vowels)
dż	as the 'j' in 'jam'
g	as in 'get'
h	as **ch**
j	as the 'y' in 'yet'
ł	as the 'w' in 'wine'
ń	as the 'ny' in 'canyon' (as 'nee' before vowels)
r	always trilled
rz	as the 's' in 'pleasure'
s	as in 'set'
sz	as the 'sh' in 'show'
ś	as **s** but softer (as 'si' before vowels)
w	as the 'v' in 'van'
ź	softer version of **z** (as 'zi' before vowels)
ż	as **rz**

EMERGENCIES – POLISH

Help!	Pomocy!/Ratunku!
Call a doctor!	Proszę wezwać lekarza!
Call the police!	Proszę wezwać policję!
I'm lost.	Zgubiłem się. (m)/
	Zgubiłam się. (f)

ACCOMMODATION

hotel	hotel
youth hostel	schronisko młodzieżowe
camping ground	kemping
Do you have any rooms available?	Czy są wolne pokoje?
Does it include breakfast?	Czy śniadanie jest wliczone?
single room	pokój jednoosobowy
double room	pokój dwuosobowy
private room	kwatera prywatna

CONVERSATION & ESSENTIALS

Hello.	Cześć. (inf)
Hello/Good morning.	Dzień dobry.
Goodbye.	Do widzenia.
Yes/No.	Tak/Nie.
Please.	Proszę.
Thank you.	Dziękuję.
Excuse me/Sorry.	Przepraszam.
I don't understand.	Nie rozumiem.
What's it called?	Jak to się nazywa?

SHOPPING & SERVICES

the bank	bank
the chemist	apteka
the church	kościół
the city centre	centrum miasta
the market	targ/bazar
the museum	muzeum
the post office	poczta
the tourist office	informacja turystyczna
How much is it?	Ile to kosztuje?
What time does it open/close?	O której otwierają/zamykają?

TIME, DAYS & NUMBERS

What time is it?	Która jest godzina?
today	dzisiaj
tonight	dzisiaj wieczorem
tomorrow	jutro
yesterday	wczoraj

in the morning	rano
in the evening	wieczorem
Monday	poniedziałek
Tuesday	wtorek
Wednesday	środa
Thursday	czwartek
Friday	piątek
Saturday	sobota
Sunday	niedziela
1	jeden
2	dwa
3	trzy
4	cztery
5	pięć
6	sześć
7	siedem
8	osiem
9	dziewięć
10	dziesięć
20	dwadzieścia
100	sto
1000	tysiąc

SIGNS – POLISH

Wejście	Entrance
Wyjście	Exit
Informacja	Information
Otwarte	Open
Zamknięte	Closed
Wzbroniony	Prohibited
Posterunek Policji	Police Station
Toalety	Toilets
Panowie	Men
Panie	Women

TRANSPORT

What time does the ... leave/arrive?	O której godzinie przychodzi/odchodzi ...?
plane	samolot
boat	statek
bus	autobus
train	pociąg
tram	tramwaj
arrival	przyjazd
departure	odjazd
timetable	rozkład jazdy
Where is the bus stop?	Gdzie jest przystanek autobusowy?
Where is the station?	Gdzie jest stacja kolejowa?

LANGUAGE

Where is the left-luggage office?	Gdzie jest przechowalnia bagażu?
Please show me on the map.	Proszę pokazać mi to na mapie.

Directions

straight ahead	prosto
left	lewo
right	prawo

ROMANIAN

PRONUNCIATION

Until the mid-19th century, Romanian was written in the Cyrillic alphabet. Today Romanian employs 28 Latin letters, some of which bear accents. At the beginning of a word, **e** and **i** are pronounced 'ye' and 'yi', while at the end of a word **i** is almost silent. At the end of a word **ii** is pronounced 'ee'. The stress is usually on the second last syllable.

ă	as the 'a' in 'ago'
î	as the 'i' in 'river'
c	as 'k', except before **e** and **i**, when it's as the 'ch' in 'chip'
ch	always as the 'k' in 'king'
g	as in 'go', except before **e** and **i**, when it's as in 'gentle'
gh	always as the 'g' in 'get'
ş	as 'sh'
ţ	as the 'tz' in 'tzar'

ACCOMMODATION

hotel	hotel
guesthouse	casa de oaspeţi
youth hostel	camin studentesc
camping ground	camping
private room	cameră particulară
single room	o cameră pentru o persoană
double room	o cameră pentru două persoane
Do you have any rooms available?	Aveţi camere libere?
How much is it?	Cît costă?
Does it include breakfast?	Include micul dejun?

CONVERSATION & ESSENTIALS

Hello.	Bună.
Goodbye.	La revedere.
Yes.	Da.
No.	Nu.

EMERGENCIES – ROMANIAN	
Help!	Ajutor!
Call a doctor!	Chemaţi un doctor!
Call the police!	Chemaţi poliţia!
Go away!	Du-te!/Pleacă!
I'm lost.	Sînt pierdut.

Please.	Vă rog.
Thank you.	Mulţumesc.
Sorry.	Iertaţi-mă.
Excuse me.	Scuzaţi-mă.
I don't understand.	Nu înţeleg.
What's it called?	Cum se cheamă?

SHOPPING & SERVICES

How much is it?	Cît costă?
the bank	banca
the chemist	farmacistul
the city centre	centrum oraşului
the ... embassy	ambasada ...
the market	piaţa
the museum	muzeu
the post office	poşta
the tourist office	birou de informatii turistice

TIME, DAYS & NUMBERS

What time is it?	Ce oră este?
today	azi
tonight	deseară
tomorrow	mîine
yesterday	ieri
in the morning	dimineaţa
in the evening	seară

Monday	luni
Tuesday	marţi
Wednesday	miercuri
Thursday	joi
Friday	vineri
Saturday	sîmbătă
Sunday	duminică

1	unu
2	doi
3	trei
4	patru
5	cinci
6	şase
7	şapte
8	opt
9	nouă
10	zece
100	o sută
1000	o mie

TRANSPORT

What time does	*La ce oră*
the ... leave/arrive?	*pleacă/soseşte ...?*
boat	*vaporul*
bus	*autobusul*
train	*trenul*
tram	*tramvaiul*
plane	*avionul*
arrival	*sosire*
departure	*plecare*
timetable	*mersul/orar*

Where is the bus stop?	*Unde este staţia de autobuz?*
Where is the station?	*Unde este gară?*
Where is the left-	*Unde este biroul pentru*
luggage office?	*bagaje de mînă?*
Please show me	*Vă rog arătaţi-mi pe hartă.*
on the map.	

SIGNS – ROMANIAN

Intrare	Entrance
Ieşire	Exit
Informaţii	Information
Deschis	Open
Închis	Closed
Nu Intraţi	No Entry
Staţie de Poliţie	Police Station
Toaleta	Toilets

Directions

straight ahead	*drept înainte*
left	*stînga*
right	*dreapta*

RUSSIAN

THE CYRILLIC ALPHABET

The Russian Cyrillic alphabet, with Roman-letter equivalents and common pronunciations, is shown on the chart on p926.

PRONUNCIATION

The sounds of **а**, **о**, **е** and **я** are 'weaker' when the stress in the word does not fall on them, eg in вода (*voda*, water) the stress falls on the second syllable, so it's pronounced 'va-DA'. The vowel **й** only follows other vowels in so-called diphthongs, eg **ой** 'oy', **ей** 'ey/yey'. Russians usually print **ё** without the dots, a source of confusion in pronunciation.

The 'voiced' consonants **б**, **в**, **г**, **д**, **ж** and **з** are not voiced at the end of words or before voiceless consonants. For example, хлеб (bread) is pronounced 'khlyep'. The **г** in the common adjective endings '-ero' and '-oro' is pronounced 'v'.

ACCOMMODATION

hotel	гостиница	*gastinitsa*
room	номер	*nomer*
breakfast	завтрак	*zaftrak*

How much is a room?
Сколько стоит номер? *skol'ka stoit nomer?*

CONVERSATION & ESSENTIALS

Hello.
Здравствуйте. *zdrastvuyte*
Good morning.
Доброе утро. *dobraye utra*
Good afternoon.
Добрый день. *dobryy den'*
Good evening.
Добрый вечер. *dobryy vecher*
Goodbye.
До свидания. *da svidaniya*
Bye!
Пока! (inf) *paka!*
How are you?
Как дела? *kak dila?*
Yes.
Да. *dat*
No.
Нет. *net*
Please.
Пожалуйста. *pazhalsta*
Thank you (very much).
(Большое) спасибо. *(bal'shoye) spasiba*
Pardon me.
Простите/Пожалуйста. *prastite/pazhalsta*
No problem/Never mind.
Ничего. *nichevo* (literally, 'nothing')
Do you speak English?
Вы говорите *vy gavarite*
по-английски? *pa angliyski?*
What's your name?
Как вас зовут? *kak vas zavut?*
My name is ...
Меня зовут ... *minya zavut ...*

SHOPPING & SERVICES

How much is it?
Сколько стоит? *skol'ka stoit?*

THE CYRILLIC ALPHABET

CYRILLIC	ROMAN	PRONUNCIATION
А а	a	as in 'father'; also as in 'ago' when unstressed in Russian
Б б	b	as in 'but'
В в	v	as in 'van'
Г г	g	as in 'go'
Ѓ ѓ	gj	as the 'gu' in 'legume' (Macedonian only)
Д д	d	as the 'd' in 'dog'
Е е	ye	as in 'yet' when stressed; as in 'year' when unstressed (Russian)
	e	as in 'bet' (Bulgarian); as in 'there' (Macedonian)
Ё ё	yo	as in 'yore' (Russian only)
Ж ж	zh	as the 's' in 'measure'
З з	z	as in 'zoo'
Ѕ ѕ	zj	as the 'ds' in 'suds' (Macedonian only)
И и	i	as the 'ee' in 'meet'
Й й	y	as in 'boy'
Ј ј	j	as the 'y' in 'young' (Macedonian only)
К к	k	as in 'kind'
Ќ ќ	kj	as the 'cu' in 'cure' (Macedonian only)
Л л	l	as in 'lamp'
Љ љ	lj	as the 'lli' in 'million' (Macedonian only)
М м	m	as in 'mat'
Н н	n	as in 'not'
Њ њ	nj	as the 'ny' in 'canyon' (Macedonian only)

CYRILLIC	ROMAN	PRONUNCIATION
О о	o	as the 'a' in 'water' when stressed; as the 'a' in 'ago' when un-stressed (Russian); as in 'hot' (Bulgarian & Macedonian)
П п	p	as in 'pick'
Р р	r	as in 'rub' (but rolled)
С с	s	as in 'sing'
Т т	t	as in 'ten'
У у	u	as in 'rule'
Ф ф	f	as in 'fan'
Х х	kh	as the 'ch' in 'Bach' (Russian)
	h	as in 'hot' (Macedonian)
Ц ц	ts	as in 'bits'
Џ џ	dz	as the 'j' in 'judge' (Macedonian only)
Ч ч	ch	as in 'chat'
Ш ш	sh	as in 'shop'
Щ щ	shch	as 'shch' in 'fresh chips' (Russian)
	sht	as the '-shed' in pushed (Bulgarian)
Ъ ъ	â	as the 'a' in 'ago' (Bulgarian only)
ъ		'hard' sign (Russian only)
Ы ы	y	as the 'i' in 'ill' (Russian only)
ь		'soft' sign (Russian only)
Э э	e	as in 'end' (Russian only)
Ю ю	yu	as the word 'you'
Я я	ya	as in 'yard'

bank
банк · *bank*

market
рынок · *rynak*

pharmacy
аптека · *apteka*

post office
почтам · *pochta*

telephone booth
телефонная будка · *tilifonnaya budka*

open
открыто · *otkryta*

closed
закрыто · *zakryta*

TIME, DATE & NUMBERS

What time is it?
Который час? · *katoryy chas?*

today
сегодня · *sivodnya*

yesterday
вчера · *vchira*

tomorrow
завтра · *zaftra*

am/in the morning
утра · *utra*

pm/in the afternoon
дня · *dnya*

in the evening
вечера · *vechira*

EMERGENCIES – RUSSIAN

Help!

| На помощь!/ | na pomashch'!/ |
| Помогите! | pamagite! |

I'm sick.

| Я болен./Я больна. | ya bolen (m)/ya bal'na (f) |

I need a doctor.

| Мне нужен врач. | mne nuzhin vrach |

hospital

| больница | bal'nitsa |

police

| милиция | militsiya |

I'm lost.

| Я заблудился. | ya zabludilsya (m) |
| Я заблудилась. | ya zabludilas' (f) |

0	ноль	nol'
1	один	adin
2	два	dva
3	три	tri
4	четыре	chityri
5	пять	pyat'
6	шесть	shest'
7	семь	sem'
8	восемь	vosim'
9	девять	devit'
10	десять	desit'
11	одиннадцать	adinatsat'
100	сто	sto
1000	тысяча	tysyacha

TRANSPORT

What time does the ... leave?

В котором часу прибывает ...?
f katoram chasu pribyvaet ...?

What time does the ... arrive?

В котором часу отправляется ...?
f katoram chasu atpravlyaetsa ...?

bus

| автобус | aftobus |

fixed-route minibus

| маршрутное такси | marshrutnaye taksi |

steamship

| пароход | parakhot |

train

| поезд | poyezt |

tram

| трамвай | tramvay |

trolleybus

| троллейбус | traleybus |

pier/quay

| причал/пристань | prichal/pristan' |

UKRAINIAN

Because of Ukraine's history of domination by outside powers, the language was often considered inferior or subservient to the dominant languages of the time – Russian in the east, Polish in the west. Today, the Ukrainian language is slowly being revived, and in 1990 it was adopted as the official language. Russian is understood everywhere by everyone, so although it may be diplomatic and polite to speak Ukrainian (especially in the west), you'll have no problem being understood if you speak Russian.

Alphabet & Pronunciation

Around 70% of the Ukrainian language is identical or similar to Russian and Belarusian. The Cyrillic alphabet chart on p926 covers the majority of letters used in the Ukrainian alphabet. Ukrainian has three additional letters not found in Russian, **і**, **ї**, and **є**, all of which are neutral vowel sounds (the Russian letter **o** is often replaced by a Ukrainian **і**). The Ukrainian **г** usually has a soft 'h' sound. The Ukrainian alphabet doesn't include the Russian letters **ё**, **ы** and **э**, and has no hard sign, **ъ**, although it does include the soft sign, **ь**. These differences between the two languages are sometimes quite simple in practice: for example, the town of Chernigov in Russian is Chernihiv in Ukrainian. Overall, Ukrainian is softer sounding and less guttural than Russian.

The -**я** *(-ya)* ending for nouns and names in Russian (especially in street names) is dropped in Ukrainian, and the letter **и** is transliterated as *y* in Ukrainian, whereas in Russian it's transliterated as *i*, eg a street named *Deribasovskaya* in Russian would be *Derybasivska* in Ukrainian.

train station

железно дорожный (ж. д.) вокзал
zhilezna darozhnyy vagzal

stop (bus/trolleybus/tram)

остановка
astanofka

one-way ticket

| билет в один конец | bilet v adin kanets |

return ticket

| билет в оба конца | bilet v oba kantsa |

SIGNS – RUSSIAN	
Вход	Entrance
Выход	Exit
Открыто	Open
Закрыто	Closed
Справки	Information
Касса	Ticket Office
Больница	Hospital
Милиция	Police
Туалет	Toilets
Мужской (M)	Men
Женский (Ж)	Women

two tickets
два билета · *dva bilety*

soft or 1st-class (compartment)
мягкий · *myahkiy*

hard or 2nd-class (compartment)
купейный · *kupeyny*

reserved-place or 3rd-class (carriage)
плацкартный · *platskartny*

Directions

Where is ...?
Где ...? · *gde ...?*

to/on the left
налево · *naleva*

to/on the right
направо · *naprava*

straight on
прямо · *pryama*

SLOVAK

PRONUNCIATION

In Slovak words of three syllables or less the stress falls on the first syllable. Longer words generally also have a secondary accent on the third or fifth syllable. There are thirteen vowels (**a**, **á**, **ä**, **e**, **é**, **i**, **í**, **o**, **ó**, **u**, **ú**, **y**, **ý**), three semi-vowels (**l**, **ľ**, **r**) and five diphthongs (**ia**, **ie**, **iu**, **ou**, **ô**). Letters and diphthongs that may be unfamiliar to native English speakers include the following:

c	as the 'ts' in 'its'
č	as the 'ch' in 'church'
dz	as the 'ds' in 'suds'
dž	as the 'j' in 'judge'
ia	as the 'yo' in 'yonder'
ie	as the 'ye' in 'yes'
iu	as the word 'you'
j	as the 'y' in 'yet'
ň	as the 'ni' in 'onion'
ô	as the 'wo' in 'won't'
ou	as the 'ow' in 'know'
š	as the 'sh' in 'show'
y	as the 'i' in 'machine'
ž	as the 'z' in 'azure'

ACCOMMODATION

hotel	*hotel*
guesthouse	*penzion*
youth hostel	*mládežnícka ubytovňa*
camping ground	*kemping*
private room	*privat*
single room	*jednolôžková izba*
double room	*dvojlôžková izba*

Do you have any rooms available?	*Máte voľné izby?*
How much is it?	*Koľko to stojí?*
Is breakfast included?	*Sú raňajky zahrnuté v cene?*

CONVERSATION & ESSENTIALS

Hello.	*Ahoj.*
Goodbye.	*Dovidenia.*
Yes.	*Áno.*
No.	*Nie.*
Please.	*Prosím.*
Thank you.	*Ďakujem.*
Excuse me.	*Prepáčte mi.*
I'm sorry.	*Ospravedlňujem sa.*
I don't understand.	*Nerozumiem.*
What's it called?	*Ako sa do volá?*

EMERGENCIES – SLOVAK	
Help!	*Pomoc!*
Call a doctor!	*Zavolajte doktora/lekára!*
Call an ambulance!	*Zavolajte záchranku!*
Call the police!	*Zavolajte políciu!*
Go away!	*Chod preč!* (sg)/ *Chodte preč!* (pl)
I'm lost.	*Nevyznám sa tu.*

SHOPPING & SERVICES

How much is it?	*Koľko to stojí?*
the bank	*banka*
the chemist	*lekárnik*
the church	*kostol*
the city centre	*stred (centrum) mesta*
the market	*trh*

the museum	múzeum
the post office	pošta
the telephone centre	telefónnu centrálu
the tourist office	turistické informačné centrum

TIME, DAYS & NUMBERS

What time is it?	Koľko je hodín?
today	dnes
tonight	dnes večer
tomorrow	zajtra
yesterday	včera
in the morning	ráno
in the evening	večer

Monday	pondelok
Tuesday	utorok
Wednesday	streda
Thursday	štvrtok
Friday	piatok
Saturday	sobota
Sunday	nedeľa

1	jeden
2	dva
3	tri
4	štyri
5	päť
6	šesť
7	sedem
8	osem
9	deväť
10	desať
100	sto
1000	tisíc

TRANSPORT

What time does the ... leave/arrive?	Kedy odchádza/prichádza ...?
boat	loč
city bus	mestský autobus
intercity bus	medzimestský autobus
plane	lietadlo
train	vlak
tram	električka

arrival	príchod
departure	odchod
timetable	cestovný poriadok

Where's the bus stop?	Kde je autobusová zastávka?
Where's the station?	Kde je vlaková stanica?
Where's the left-luggage office?	Kde je úschovňa batožín?
Please show me on the map.	Prosím, ukážte mi to na mape.

SIGNS – SLOVAK	
Vchod	Entrance
Východ	Exit
Informácie	Information
Otvorené	Open
Zatvorené	Closed
Zakázané	Prohibited
Polícia	Police Station
Telefón	Telephone
Záchody/WC/Toalety	Toilets

Directions
left	vľavo
right	vpravo
straight ahead	rovno

SLOVENE

PRONUNCIATION

Slovene pronunciation isn't difficult. The alphabet consists of 25 letters, most of which are very similar to English. It doesn't have the letters 'q', 'w', 'x' and 'y', but you will find ê, é, ó, ò, č, š and ž. Each letter represents only one sound, with very few exceptions. The letters l and v are both pronounced like the English 'w' when they occur at the end of syllables and before vowels. Though words like *trn* (thorn) look unpronounceable, most Slovenes (depending on dialect) add a short vowel like an 'a' or the German 'ö' in front of the 'r' to give a Scot's pronunciation of 'tern' or 'tarn'. Here is a list of letters specific to Slovene:

c	as the 'ts' in 'its'
č	as the 'ch' in 'church'
ê	as the 'a' in 'apple'
e	as the 'a' in 'ago' (when unstressed)
é	as the 'ay' in 'day'
j	as the 'y' in 'yellow'
ó	as the 'o' in 'more'
ò	as the 'o' in 'soft'
r	a rolled 'r' sound
š	as the 'sh' in 'ship'
u	as the 'oo' in 'good'
ž	as the 's' in 'treasure'

ACCOMMODATION
hotel	hotel
guesthouse	gostišče
camping ground	kamping

Do you have a ...?	Ali imate prosto ...?
bed	posteljo
cheap room	poceni sobo
single room	enoposteljno sobo
double room	dvoposteljno sobo

How much is it ...?	Koliko stane ...?
per night/person	za eno noč/osebo
for one/two nights	za eno noč/za dve noči

Is breakfast included? Ali je zajtrk vključen?

CONVERSATION & ESSENTIALS

Hello.	Pozdravljeni. (pol)
	Zdravo/Živivo. (inf)
Good day.	Dober dan!
Goodbye.	Nasvidenje!
Yes.	Da/Ja. (inf)
No.	Ne.
Please.	Prosim.
Thank you (very much).	Hvala (lepa).
You're welcome.	Prosim/Ni za kaj!
Excuse me.	Oprostite.
What's your name?	Kako vam je ime?
My name is ...	Jaz sem ...
Where are you from?	Od kod ste?
I'm from ...	Sem iz ...

EMERGENCIES – SLOVENE

Help!	Na pomoč!
Call a doctor!	Pokličite zdravnika!
Call the police!	Pokličite policijo!
Go away!	Pojdite stran!

SHOPPING & SERVICES

Where is the/a ...?	Kje je ...?
bank/exchange	banka/menjalnica
embassy	konzulat/ambasada
post office	pošta
telephone centre	telefonska centrala
tourist office	turistični informacijski urad

TIME, DAYS & NUMBERS

today	danes
tonight	nocoj
tomorrow	jutri
in the morning	zjutraj
in the evening	zvečer

Monday	ponedeljek
Tuesday	torek
Wednesday	sreda

SIGNS – SLOVENE

Vhod	Entrance
Izhod	Exit
Informacije	Information
Odprto	Open
Zaprto	Closed
Prepovedano	Prohibited
Stranišče	Toilets

Thursday	četrtek
Friday	petek
Saturday	sobota
Sunday	nedelja

1	ena
2	dve
3	tri
4	štiri
5	pet
6	šest
7	sedem
8	osem
9	devet
10	deset
100	sto
1000	tisoč

TRANSPORT

What time does ... the leave/arrive?	Kdaj odpelje/pripelje ...?
boat/ferry	ladja/trajekt
bus	avtobus
train	vlak

timetable	spored
train station	železniška postaja
bus station	avtobusno postajališče
one-way (ticket)	enosmerna (vozovnica)
return (ticket)	povratna (vozovnica)

Can you show me on the map?	A mi lahko pokažete na mapi?

Also available from Lonely Planet:
Eastern Europe Phrasebook

Behind the Scenes

THIS BOOK

Many people have helped to create this 8th edition of *Eastern Europe*. *Eastern Europe* is part of Lonely Planet's Europe series, which includes *Western Europe*, *Mediterranean Europe*, *Central Europe*, *Scandinavian Europe* and *Europe on a Shoestring*. Lonely Planet also publishes phrasebooks to these regions.

THANKS From the Authors

Tom Masters Thanks to Imogen Franks for entrusting this book to me, to Fiona Christie for her constant hard work and all the production team in Melbourne for their huge input. In Moscow, most of all thanks to Clem, Cecil and Malinka for letting me stay with them, Alex Tampokopolous for great company and the inimitable Dima Makarov for comic value. In St Petersburg huge thanks to Simon Patterson, Marc de Mauny, Dmitry Dzhafarov, Misha Krasanov, Galina Stolyarova, Rosemary Masters and Gillian Argyle for all their good company and support. Thanks also to all the authors who worked so hard on the new edition of this book, especially those who made such an effort to help me with my endless questions.

Lisa Dunford A big thanks goes to all my cousins in Hungary. Whether in Budapest, Tokaj or Balaton, you helped me feel at home, and you fed me way, way too much! I appreciate all the suggestions I received from other Lonely Planet readers along the way, including Ken Tippette on history, Fábián Zsuzsi on hiking, Paul Laszlo, Vági Kati, and Chris Lacey on nightlife, and the guy from Mexico City that I accosted reading *Eastern Europe 7* on the metro, on the Castle Hill itinerary – sorry I didn't get your name. Also, Anna Cserei, you're a great teacher, and Billy, without you, I couldn't be doing what I love. Thanks go to Lonely Planet for a fabulous experience as always: Imogen Franks started the ball rolling with style, Fiona Christie was a pleasure to work with as editor, Tom Masters kept us all together as coordinating author, Cinzia Cavallaro and Imogen Bannister who did a such a thorough job in the copy-editing process, and the cartography team – without their terrific maps the readers and I would be lost.

Mark Elliot So many Slovenians were so incredibly helpful that it is generally unfair to single out individuals, though I must especially thank Nika Kozjak for her patience, comments, suggestions and feedback. Endless thanks to Dani Systermans and 'the Kids', whose advice and constant help were and remain an inspiration.

Patrick Horton Authors are always indebted to the folk on the ground with the local knowledge. Accordingly I'd like to send a big thanks to the following: in Serbia Dejan Veselinov of the Tourist Organisation of Belgrade, Lilana Cerovic of the Serbia and Montenegro Tourist Organisation and the helpful staff of the Novi Sad, Subotica and Topola tourist information offices who provided the building blocks of local knowledge. Thanks to Jotsa Tipold and colleague, Milan, who sped me around central Serbia and with Zorica Velj-kovic revealed Novi Sad's secrets. As always a big *hvala* to Miroslav Maric, who is my touchstone in Belgrade. In Kosovo it's *falem nderit* to fellow photographer Naim Shala for his help and comradeship. In Bosnia and Hercegovina big thanks to the Sarajevo Tourist Information Centre for their quickfire responses to my many questions. Similarly I'd like to thank the tourist organisations in Bihać and Mostar and Fortuna Travel and Sead Kustric in Mostar. Lastly many thanks to Sunny and Sead in Sarajevo, and Gaye Facer, who took me to some interesting clubs.

Steve Kokker Thanks Misha and Albert at Baltma tours in Kaliningrad, as well as Rodion, Sasha and Andrei for all their help and for the fun times. Thanks to the customs officers in Sovetsk for a unique experience. Also to Dmitry Podcovyrin at Komsomolskaya Pravda. In Estonia, thanks to Henri Kaasik-Aaslav.

Vesna Maric A million thanks go to Rafael (¡gracias amor!), because of whom I enjoyed every single moment of the journey and who was such a help. Great big thank yous to Gabriel for his grammar fascism, patience and kindness; also to Tom for being a friend and answering all my boring questions and to Imogen Franks for taking me on. Big thanks to Balina for showing us her country and taking care, and to Blerina and Andi for being so kind. More thanks to Beni Andoni in Tirana, and Koli and his scary driving. Special thanks to Ines, Gianfranco and Annalisa for all their care in Bari. My eternal thanks to my mama.

Jeanne Oliver Innumerable people in Croatia went out of their way to make my stay enjoyable and my work smoother. Among them were Andrea Petrov of the National Tourist Board, Mark van Bloeman and the Begovićs in Dubrovnik, Tomislav Vukusić in Opatija and Radenko Sloković in Pazin. At home, I'd like to thank David and Ginna Zoellner for looking after Raymond and John and Cédric Enée for their love and support during the course of this project.

Robert Reid Big thanks go to George Kamen and Hristo Georgiev the Bulgarian tutor for helping me prepare for my trip from New York City, and to Lonely Planet UK's Imogen Franks and Fiona Christie for sending me in the first place. Also to Charlotte Orr and Imogen Bannister for editing the thing. Scores of folks went out of their way to help me get info. Notable thanks goes to Assen Davidov in Sofia (for introducing me to his Roma friends and much more), former Prime Minister Philip Dimitrov for getting me Dunkin' Donuts coffee, Stefan of Veliko for bringing me along to the all-night birthday party in the forest, Emil Svetan of Vidin (and family) for putting me up when the Belogradchik bus didn't show, Maria Tutundjian of Plovdiv for the canal walk, Tony Paskov for last-second info, all the Peace Corps folks (Dave Elmstrom, Jennifer Nikolaeff, Nellie Goddard), Dobrich TV for putting me on the airways of northeastern Bulgaria and countless folks like the Shumen bus-station clerk for showing me photos of her family as the line stacked up behind me.

Matt Warren Big thanks go out to Sammy and Matt for all the late nights and long mornings and to the people of Slovakia for all the good cheer and warm welcomes along the way. Thanks also to The Dubliner for the Guinness and the tourist board for pointing me in the right direction whenever I lost my way.

Wendy Taylor A huge thanks to my friends in Minsk: Robert Heuer, Goran Subotic, Ilija 'Ika' Todorovic, Tatsiana Aliakseyeva and last, but far from least, Inna Bukshtynovich – St Inna is henceforth deemed the patron saint of travel guidebook writers. Also, Nickolay G Takounov and Eugene V Makarenko at Belintourist in Minsk have great taste in music and were extremely helpful. In Ukraine, the Lviv Tourist Board (especially Diana!), the Carpathian Tourist Board and Eugenia Travel supplied me with lots of facts, and in Kyiv, Rostick Gavrilov of Come2Ukraine.com set me up with everything I needed. So much preparatory information came from Lonely Planet author Steve Kokker, and Justin

Marler helped with information about Orthodoxy. My research never could have been written up in Dushanbe without the hospitality and generosity of Garth Willis, Gulshan Toshbekova and especially my good friends Brian Vitunic and Alexis Menten, who were indispensable: they gave me a bed and a dial-up connection and plied me with cosmopolitans on the *tapchan*. Matthew Wood, my dearest friend and partner, provided those indispensable, ineffable intangibles that make it all worthwhile.

Richard Watkins Many thanks are due to Aneta at the Warsaw tourist office for guiding me around her city and whose insider knowledge of the Polish capital was invaluable. A big thank you also goes to the helpful and professional staff at tourist offices in Łódź, Lublin, Wrocław, Premyśl, Sanok and Toruń. I would also like to thank Jan Piotrowski, Gosia Graczyk and staff at the Polish Embassy in London for their kind assistance with my research.

Neil Wilson *Mockrat děkuji* to tourist office staff around the Czech Republic, and to Richard Nebeský and Tomaš Harabís for their insights into Czech society. And as always, a big thank you to Carol for helping with the restaurants and shops in Prague.

CREDITS

Eastern Europe 8 was commissioned and developed in Lonely Planet's UK office by Imogen Franks and Fiona Christie with assistance from Tom Masters. The book was coordinated by Imogen Bannister (editorial) and Valentina Kremenchutskaya (cartography). Sarah Bailey, Andrea Baster, Charlotte Orr, Cinzia Cavallaro, Emma Koch, Katie Lynch, Sally O'Brien, Sarah Hassall, Linda Suttie and Michelle Coxall assisted with editing and proofing. Barbara Benson, Country Cartographics, Daniel Fennessy, Jenny Jones, Kim McDonald, Adrian Persoglia, Amanda Sierp and Lyndell Stringer assisted with cartography. Pablo Gastar and Adam Bextream laid the book out, Yvonne Bischofberger designed the colour content, Pepi Bluck designed the cover and Yukiyoshi Kamimura produced the cover artwork. Wayne Murphy produced the back-cover map. Vicki Beale, Kaitlin Beckett, Laura Jane, Evan Jones, Michael Ruff and Wibowo Rusli assisted with layout. Huw Fowles, Rachel Imeson, Craig Kilburn, Kate McLeod, Adriana Mammarella and Kate McDonald assisted with layout checking. Quentin Frayne prepared the Language chapter, and Kate McLeod and Imogen Bannister prepared the index. The health chapter was adapted from material written by Dr Caroline Evans, a GP specialising in travel medicine. Overseeing production were Ray Thomson (Project Manager), Bruce Evans (Managing Editor) and Mark Griffiths (Managing Cartographer). The series was designed by James Hardy, with mapping development by Paul Piaia.

THANKS from Lonely Planet

Many thanks to the travellers who used the last edition and wrote to us with helpful hints, useful advice and interesting anecdotes:

A E Adams, Madhu Anhes, Suttipong Aramkun, Hilmir Ásgeirsson **B** Peter Baker, Peter Baloh, Jonathan Baum, Miriam Baxter, Huub Bellemakers, Andy Bennett, Ronald Bensema, Christopher Bentley, Edo Berger, Jim Berry, Ron Blair, Simone Bleumink, Bojan Boric, Ravter Bostjan, Jason Brown, Malcolm & Joan Brown, Dr John D Brunton, Peter Bugarski, Chris Burin, John T Burke, Janelle Burrows **C** Helen M Campbell, Morag Casey, Tony Chamberlain, Cass Chan, Seni Choueri, Nick Cleary, Yoav Cohen, Merle Cooke **D** Feri Daca, Jennie Dalling, Matthew D'Arcy, Huw Davies, Bruce Davis, Sylvain De Crecy, Katrijn De Ronde, Matthias Dekan, Jodi Dennis, Janet Denye, Rachel Derrico, CA Donkin, David Doughan, Nelson Duarte, Euan Duncan, Phil Dunn, Jon Durham **E** Moray Easdale, Michael J Eatroff **F** Susannah Farnworth, Alexandre & Nicole Fauchere, Janet Fearnley, Dr Med Lars Floter, Pernille & Kennet Foh, Philip Francis, Heather Fraser, Addie Fryeweaver **G** Natasha George, Dr Giuseppe Gianolio, Jim Gilchrist, Brad Gledhill, Tim Goddard, Sam Golledge, Denise Gomez, Vid Gorjan, Pete Gray, Piero Grimalda, Caroline Grogan, Ignacio Morejon Guerrero, Raoul Gunning, Olena Guseva, Heather Gutkowski, Rafal Guzewicz **H** Michael Haberland, Alex Hall, Geoff Hall, Joshua Hartshorne, Terje Hensrud, Frank Hettler, Louise Hope, Kathryn Horn, Henri Hovine, Kevan Hubberd, Denis Hughes, Gareth Hughes, Marcin Hunderuk **I** Hiroshi Ikeda, Claudia Immisch, Vanessa Inall **J** Jurian Jansen, Martin Jennings, Jimmy Johnson, Jimmy & Anja Johnson, Alan Jones **K** Minte Kamphuis, Dushan Karageorgevitch, Kapka Kassabova, James Kirk, Ciaran Kissane, Ruth Kitching, Andrew Knight, Mark Koltun, Berit Kreuze, Agata Krynicka, David Kvapil **L** Chris & Jolene Laing, Kam Lam, Ruud Lampf, Griet Langbeen, Milan Lazarevic, Martin Leahy, Jonathan Legg, Una Lemeshonok, Aaron Lester, Clare Lester, Angelika Lichnerova, Karin Lindsten, Espen Loken, Dennis Long, Maricarmen Lopez Estecha, J Lowet **M** Vladimir Macarov, Stephen Mak, William Malone, Arthur Markham, James Marks, Richard McBride, Carol McGillivray, Dr JS McLintock, Loic Meuley, Alan Millward, Don Munro, Allison Murray **N** Dhruv Narain, Ellen Nemhauser, Bryce Newman, Emma Newton, Mic Nov **O** Jutta Loiuse Oechler, Franziska Ohnsorge, Lucy Openshaw, Chris Owen **P** Erlandas Paplauskis, Don Parris, Mario Pavesi, Stjepan Perkovic, Lea Ann Pestotnik, Pavla Peterova, Charles Philpott, Carl Pickerill, Mirjana Plazonic, Jacek Pliszka, Aleksandar Popovic, **R** Kent Raju, Rachel Reeson, Jason Rico, Jan Rieger, Noami Rinat, Achalavira Rose, Sergiu Rudeanu, Jack Rush **S** Constantin Salagor, Annelie Scheider, Larry Schwarz, Aneta Singh, Ernie Soh, Damian Spellman, Karla A Spinks, Maarten Stam, Timo Stewart, Ethan Stone **T** Julie Tabor, Niels Ten Oever, Eleanor Thom, Nicholas Thompson, Bruce Thomson, Paul Tiebosch, Bobby Tim, Alessio Tixi, Lucy Tovchikh, Rokas Tracevskis, Wojciech Tyszlewicz, **V** Dessislav Valkanov, Judith Vasey, B Verbaan, Daan Vervoort, Else Von Schopp, Robert Vrlak, Vladimir Vucinic, Masha Vukanovic **W** Terry Walker, Deborah Wallace, EJ Walsh, Henk Wardenaar, Michael Wegner, Peter Weller, Philipp Wendtland, Robert Whistance, Chad Williams, Hywel Williams, John Williams, Isobel Wilson, Michael Wodzicki, Joseph and Elaine Wojtowicz, Frankas Wurft **Z** Natalie Zara, Taleh Ziyadov, K Zoglin, Evan Zoldan

ACKNOWLEDGMENTS

Many thanks to the following for the use of their content:

Map data contained in colour highlights map & globe on back cover – Mountain High Maps® © 1993 Digital Wisdom, Inc

BEHIND THE SCENES

Index

ABBREVIATIONS

Al	Albania
Be	Belarus
B&H	Bosnia & Hercegovina
Bu	Bulgaria
Cr	Croatia
Cz	Czech Republic
E	Estonia
H	Hungary
La	Latvia
Li	Lithuania
Mk	Macedonia
Md	Moldova
P	Poland
Ro	Romania
Ru	Russia
S&M	Serbia & Montenegro
Sk	Slovakia
Slo	Slovenia
U	Ukraine

A

accommodation 869-71, *see also individual countries & cities*
activities 871-3, *see also individual activities*
Adršpach-Teplice Rocks 279-80, **360-1**
Aegna 313
air travel 887-93, 896
to/from Eastern Europe 887-93
within Eastern Europe 896
Albania 27-60, **29**
    accommodation 53
    activities 53-4
    arts 33
    beaches 47-9
    books 33, 54
    border crossings 57-8
    dangers 54
    drinking 35
    embassies 55
    emergencies 57
    environment 34
    food 35
    highlights 28
    history 30

000 Map pages
000 Location of colour photographs

itineraries 28
    language 55, 909-10
    money 56
    postal services 56-7
    telephone services 57
    tourist information 57
    travel to/from 57-9
    travel within 59-60
    visas 57
Albena 164
Amber Room 683, 685
ancient ruins
    Apollonia (Al) 45-6
    Butrint (Al) 49-50
    Diocletian's Palace (Cr) 207-8
    Heraclea (Mk) 464
    Mediana (S&M) 720
    Solin (Cr) 210-11
    Theatre of Ancient Philippopolis (Bu) 135
    Tsarevets Fortress (Bu) 147-8
Angla 325-6
Apollonia 45-6
Apparition Hill (B & H) 104
Apuseni Mountains 610
Arbanasi 150
art galleries, *see* museums & galleries
ATMs 879-80
Aukštaitija National Park 434-5
Auschwitz 524-5
Austerlitz 284

B

Babyn Yar 835
Bachkovo Monastery 140
Bakhchysaray 858
Balatonfüred 367-8, **367**
Balchik 164-5
Banat 610-16
Banja Luka 106-8, **107**
Bansko 133-4, 328-9
banyas 663, 678
Bar 730
Bardejov 775-7, **776**
Bârsana 618-19
Baška 201-2
beaches
    Albania 47-9
    Bulgaria 154-65
    Croatia 201, 202-23, 328-9
    Estonia 313, 327, 332
    Latvia 408-13
    Lithuania 442, 443
    Poland 556, 557, 558, **680-1**
    Romania 628-35
    Russia 690
    Serbia & Montenegro 730-5
    Ukraine 853, 859

Belarus 61-82, **63**
    accommodation 78
    arts 65
    border crossings 902
    drinking 66
    embassies 78-9
    emergencies 80
    environment 65
    festivals 79
    food 66
    highlights 62
    history 63-4
    itineraries 62
    language 79
    money 79
    postal services 80
    telephone services 80
    travel to/from 81-2
    travel within 82
    visas 80-1
Belavezhskaja Pushcha National Park 65
Belgrade 705-14, **706, 708**
    accommodation 710
    attractions 707-10
    drinking 712
    entertainment 712-13
    festivals 710
    food 710-11
    information 706-7
    shopping 713
    travel to/from 713
    travel within 713-14
Belogradchik 165-6
Bendery 488-9, **489**
Berat 46, 328-9
Białowieża National Park 514-15
bicycle travel, *see* cycling
Bihać 108-10
bird-watching
    Albania 53
    Hungary 387
    Latvia 414
    Lithuania 445
    Romania 639
Birkenau 525
Bishop's Castle 325, 360-1
Bitola 464-5
Bjelašnica 99
Blagoevgrad 131
Bled 800-3, **801**, 712-13
Bohemia 265-80
Bohemian Switzerland National Park 267
Bohinj 803-4
Bolshoi Theatre 660, 666
books 10-11, *see also individual countries*
border crossings 890, 893, 902, *see also individual countries*

Borovets 132-3
Borşa 620
Bosnia & Hercegovina 83-114, **86, 87**
  accommodation 110
  activities 110
  arts 88-9
  border crossings 113
  civil war 87-8, 90, 99-103
  dangers 98, 109, 111
  drinking 89
  embassies 111
  emergencies 112
  environment 89
  food 89
  highlights 84
  history 85-8
  itineraries 85
  language 112
  money 112
  postal services 112
  telephone services 112
  tourist information 112
  travel to/from 113-14
  travel within 103, 114
  visas 112-13
Botiza 619
Bovec 805
Boyana 129
Bran 599
Braşov 595-9, **596**
Bratislava 749-58, **750, 752**
  accommodation 755
  attractions 752-4
  drinking 756
  entertainment 756-7
  festivals 754
  food 755-6
  information 751-2
  shopping 757
  travel to/from 757
  travel within 757-8
Brest 74-6, **75**, 328-9
Brezovica 728
Brijuni Islands 197
breweries & wineries
  Budweiser Budvar Brewery (Cz) 275
  Cojuşna (Md) 484
  Cricova (Md) 483-4
  Jaaremaa (E) 325
  Magyar Borok Háza (H) 346
  Mitko Manolev Winery (Bu) 132
  Moravian wine country (Cz) 287
  National Wine Salon (Cz) 287
  Pilsner Urquell Brewery (Cz) 272
  Szépasszony völgy (H) 382-3
  Tokaj (H) 385-7
Brno 280-5, **281**
Bucegi Mountains 594
Bucharest 580-90, **581, 583**
  accommodation 585-6
  attractions 582
  drinking 587
  entertainment 587

food 586-7
  information 580-2
  shopping 587-8
  travel to/from 588
  travel within 588-589
Budapest 339-55, **340-1, 343, 344, 6**
  accommodation 348-50
  attractions 346-8
  dangers 345-6
  drinking 352
  entertainment 352-3
  food 350-2
  information 342-5
  shopping 353
  travel to/from 354
  travel within 354-5
Budva 732
Budweiser Budvar Brewery 275
Bükk Nezmeti Park 385
Bulgaria 115-72, **118**
  accommodation 166-7
  activities 167
  arts 120
  beaches 154-65
  books 167
  border crossings 171
  dangers 168
  drinking 120-1
  embassies 168
  emergencies 170
  environment 120
  festivals 168
  food 120-1
  highlights 117
  history 117-19
  itineraries 117
  language 119, 169, 910-12
  money 169
  postal services 170
  telephone services 170
  tourist information 170
  travel to/from 170-1
  travel within 158, 171-2
  visas 170
Burgas 154-6, **155**
bus travel
  to/from Eastern Europe 893-4
  within Eastern Europe 897
business hours 873
Butrint 49-50

C
Căldăruşani Monastery 589
Capuchin Monastery (Cz) 282
Carpathian National Natural Park 847-8
car travel 894, 897-9
castles & palaces
  Bishop's Castle (E) 325, **360-1**
  Bled Castle (Slo) 801, **712-13**
  Bran Castle (Ro) 599
  Catherine Palace (Ru) 683
  Český Krumlov Castle (Cz) 276-8
  Esterházy Kasthély (H) 365

Festetics Kastély (H) 370-1
  Hluboká nad Vltavou (Cz) 276
  Karlštejn Castle (Cz) 262
  Khan's Palace (U) 858
  Konopiště Chateau (Cz) 262-3
  Lublin Castle (P) 532
  Malbork Castle (P) 558
  Pavlovsk (Ru) 683
  Peleş Castle (Ro) 594
  Petrodvorets (Ru) 682-3
  Prague Castle (Cz) 248-50, **249**
  Royal Castle (P) 504
  Spišský hrad (Sk) 775, **712-13**
  Swallow's Nest (U) 860, **712-13**
  Trakai (Li) 434, **360-1**
  Visegrád (H) 357-8
  Wallenstein Palace (Cz) 251
  Water Chateau (Cz) 286
  Wawel Castle (P) 517
  Winter Palace (Ru) 675, 7
  Yusupov Palace (Ru) 676-8
catacombs, Odesa 854
cathedrals, see churches & cathedrals
Catherine Palace 683
Caves Monastery (U) 833, **712-13**
caving
  Bulgaria 167
  Czech Republic 285
  Latvia 410-11
  Romania 608
  Serbia & Montenegro 718, 727
  Slovakia 771
  Slovenia 805, 806, 807
Celje 814-15
cell phones 882
Central Balkans National Park 146
Cēsis 411-12
České Budějovice 274-6, **274**
Český Krumlov 276-9, **277**
Cetinje 734-5
Charles Bridge 251
Chekhov Art Theatre 666
Chernivtsi 848-50, **848**
Chernobyl, see Chornobyl
children, travel with 873, 906
Chişinău 476-85, **478-9**
  accommodation 480
  attractions 477-80
  drinking 481
  entertainment 481-2
  food 480-1
  information 477
  shopping 482
  travel agencies 477
  travel to/from 482-3
  travel within 483
Chornobyl 65, 826, 829
churches & cathedrals
  Boyana Church (Bu) 129
  Catedrala Patriahală (Ro) 582
  Church of the Assumption (Slo) 801
  Church on Spilled Blood (Ru) 676
  Dome Cathedral (La) 402

churches & cathedrals *continued*
  Esztergom Bazilika (H) 359
  etiquette 828
  Euphrasian Basilica (Cr) 191
  Farny Cathedral (Be) 77
  Khram Khrista Spasitelya (Ru) 662
  Petrova Crkva (S&M) 722
  Sanctuary of Our Lady of Loreta
    (Cz) 250
  St Basil's Cathedral (Ru) 659, 680-1
  St Mary's Church (P) 519
  St Nicholas Church (Cz) 251
  St Peter & Paul Cathedral (Ru) 678
  St Sophia's Cathedral (U) 834
  St Vitus Cathedral (Cz) 249-50
  Sv Jovan at Kaneo (Mk) 461, 680-1
  Uspensky Sobor (Ru) 660
cinema 13, 25-6
climate 9, 873-4
climbing
  Bulgaria 167
  Czech Republic 279-80
  Slovakia 766, 781
Cluj-Napoca 606-10, **608**
Cojuşna 484
Comrat 489-90
Constanţa 629-32, **630**
consulates 878, *see also individual
  countries*
corruption 875
costs 9-10, 30, 62
courses 873
credit cards 879-80
Cricova 483-4
Crimea 855-62, **855**
Crişan 638
Crişana 610-16
Crno jezero 736
Croatia 173-232, **175**
  accommodation 223-4
  activities 224
  arts 179
  beaches 201, 202-23
  books 224-5
  civil war 177
  dangers 225
  drinking 180-1
  embassies 225-6
  emergencies 227
  environment 179-80
  festivals 226
  food 180-1
  highlights 174
  history 175-8
  itineraries 174-5
  language 912-14
  money 226-7
  postal services 227

  telephone services 227
  tourist information 227
  travel to/from 228-230
  travel within 230-2, **210**
  visas 228
Curonian Spit 691
Curtea de Argeş 590-3
customs regulations 873-5
cycling 872, 896-7
  Bulgaria 167
  Czech Republic 288
  Estonia 326
  Lithuania 445
  Poland 565
  Romania 639
  Slovakia 781
  Slovenia 818
Cyrillic alphabet 926
Czech Republic 233-94, **235**
  accommodation 287
  activities 288
  arts 239
  books 239
  border crossings 292
  dangers 288
  drinking 240
  embassies 289
  emergencies 290
  environment 240
  festivals 289
  food 240
  highlights 234
  history 236
  itineraries 236
  language 914-15
  money 290
  postal services 290
  telephone services 290
  tourist information 291
  travel to/from 291
  travel within 292
  visas 291
Częstochowa 525-6

D
Dalmatia 202-23, **210**
Danès River 440
dangers 875-6
Danube Delta 635-8, **636**
Danube River 355-60, 635
Dayton Agreement 87-8, 178
Despotovac 718
Dhërmi 48
Diocletian's Palace 207-8
disabled travellers 876
discount cards 876-7
Dracula, *see* Vlad Ţepeş
drinking, *see individual countries & cities*
driving licence 897
drugs 875
Druskininkai 435
Dryanovo Monastery 150
Drymades 48

Dubrovnik 217-23, **218-19**, **221**, 6
  accommodation 220-1
  attractions 219
  drinking 222
  entertainment 222
  festivals 220
  food 221-2
  information 218-9
  travel to/from 222-3
Dudutki 73
Dunajec Gorge 531, 770-1
Durmitor National Park 736-7
Durrës 42-4, **43**
DVDs 877

E
Eforie Nord 633-4
Eger 382-5, **383**
Elbląg-Ostróda Canal 561
electricity 877-8
embassies 878, *see also individual
  countries*
Esterházy Kasthély 365
Estonia 295-330, **297**
  accommodation 326
  activities 326-27
  arts 299-301
  beaches 313, 327, 332, 328-9
  drinking 302
  embassies 327
  emergencies 328
  environment 301-2
  festivals 327
  food 302
  highlights 297
  history 297-9
  itineraries 297
  language 328, 915-16
  money 328
  postal services 328
  telephone services 328
  travel to/from 329
  travel within 330
  visas 328-9
Esztergom 358-61, **359**
Etâr 150
European Bison Reserve 515
extreme sports 805

F
Făgăraş Mountains 606, **606**
festivals 13-14, 567
  Exit festival (S&M) 14, 715
  Festival of European Folk Crafts
    (Slo) 769
  Jaanipäev (Estonia) 14, 327
  Prague Spring (Cz) 13, 253
  Sziget Festival (H) 14, 389
  White Nights (Ru) 13, 679
fortresses
  Brest Fortress (Be) 74-5, 328-9
  Egri Vár (H) 383
  Kalemegdan Citadel 707

Kaleto Fortress (Bu) 166
Peter & Paul Fortress (Ru) 678
Petrovaradin Citadel (S&M) 715
Rozafa Fortress (Al) 52
Shumen Fortress (Bu) 151
Smederevo Fortress (S&M) 714
Soroca fortress 485, **680-1**
Tighina fortress (Md) 488
Tsarevets Fortress (Bu) 147-8
Vyšehrad (Cz) 252
Frombork 561
Fruška Gora 717

G
Gadimë Cave 727
Gagauzia 489-90
Gauja National Park (La) 411
gay & lesbian travellers 878
Gdańsk 550-8, **551**, **680-1**
Gdynia 556-7
Giżycko 563-4
Gjirokastra 50
Golden Ring 669-71
Golden Sands 164
Goldwasser 555
Gorizia 806
Gračanica 727
Great Masurian Lakes 561-4, **562**
Gulf of Kvarner 197-202
Gyógytó 371
Győr 361-4, **362**

H
Haanja Nature Park 320
Harkány 376
health 904-7
Hel 557
Heraclea 464
Herceg Novi 735
Hermitage 675, **7**
Hévíz 371
Hiiumaa 324-5
hiking 872
    Bosnia & Hercegovina 110
    Bulgaria 130, 134, 167
    Croatia 200, 224
    Czech Republic 279-80, 288
    Hungary 387
    Latvia 414
    Lithuania 445
    Macedonia 466
    Poland 530, 542, 563, 565
    Romania 594, 606, 608, 610, 639
    Slovakia 754, 765, 766, 781
    Slovenia 802, 804, 818
    Ukraine 862
Hill of Crosses 439-40
Himara 48
hitchhiking 894, 899-900
Hluboká nad Vltavou 276
holidays 878
horse riding 872
    Hungary 387
    Romania 639

Hrodna 76-8, **77**
Humor 627
Hungary 331-94, **334**
    accommodation 387
    activities 387
    arts 336-7
    books 337, 388
    border crossing 392
    drinking 338-9
    embassies 389
    emergencies 390
    environment 337-8
    festivals 389
    folk music 336-7
    food 338-9
    highlights 332
    history 333-6
    itineraries 332-3
    language 389-90, 916-18
    money 390
    postal services 390
    telephone services 390
    tourist information 391
    travel to/from 391-3
    travel within 393-4
    visas 391
Hvar 212-14, **328-9**

I
Iaşi 620-4, **621**
Ieud 619
Independent Republic of Užupis 428
insurance 878, 904
Internet access 878-9
Internet resources 11
Ionian Coast 48, **6**
Istria 190-7
itineraries 15-20, *see also individual
    countries*
    author's favourite trip 21
Ivano-Frankivsk 845-7, **846**
Ivanovo Rock Monastery 154
Izola 810

J
Jaanipäev 14, 327
Jahorina 98-9
Julian Alps 800-6, **7**
Juodkrantė 444
Jūrmala 408-9

K
Kaali 325-6
Kadriorg 307
Kalemegdan Citadel 707
Kaleto Fortress 166
Kaliakra Cape 165
Kaliningrad, city 685-90, **687**
    accommodation 688-9
    attractions 686-8
    drinking 689
    entertainment 689-90
    food 689

    information 686
    travel agencies 686
    travel to/from 690
    travel within 690
Kaliningrad, region 683-91, **684**
    history 684
Kamnik 814
Kamyanets-Podilsky 850-1
Karlovo 143-4
Karlovy Vary 267-71, **269**
Karlštejn 262
Karst Coast 806-14
Kaunas 435-9, **436-7**
kayaking, *see* watersports
Kazanlâk 144
Kazimierz 520-1
Kecskemét 376-9, **377**
Keszthely 369-72, **370**
Kežmarok 769-70
Khatyn 74
Kihnu Island 323
Kiskunsági National Park 379
Klaipėda 440-3, **441**
Kobarid 805-6
Konopiště 262-3
Kopaonik 720-1
Koper 808-10, **808**
Koprivshtitsa 142-3, **142**
Korça 50-1
Korčula 214-16
Košice 777-81, **778**
Kosovo 723-29
    civil war 703
    dangers 724
    history 723-4
    travel to/from 724
Kotel 145
Kotor 732-4, **733**
Kotor fjord 733, **8**
Kozłówka 535
Kraków 515-24, **516**, **518**, **520**, **7**
    accommodation 521-2
    attractions 517
    drinking 523
    entertainment 523-4
    food 522-3
    information 516
    travel to/from 524
Kranj 800
Kranjska Gora 804-5
Kremlin, the 659-60
Krk 201-2
Kruja 44-5
Kuldīga 412-13
Kuressaare 325-6
Kurshkaya Kosa 691
Kutná Hora 263-5, **263**
Kyiv 830-8, **831**, **832-3**
    accommodation 835-6
    attractions 833-5
    drinking 837
    entertainment 837

Kyiv *continued*
    food 836-7
    information 831
    shopping 837
    travel to/from 837-8
    travel within 838
Kyiv-Pechersk Lavra 833, **712-13**

L
Lahemaa National Park 314-15
Lake Balaton 366-72
Lake Furtuna 638
Lake Matka 459-60
Lake Morskie Oko 529-30
Lake Ohrid 460-3
Lake Skadar 729-30
Lake Śniardwy 561
land mines 85
languages 909-30, *see also individual*
    countries
Latvia 395-418, **397**
    accommodation 413-14
    activities 414
    arts 398
    beaches 408-13
    books 414
    children, travel with 414
    drinking 398-9
    embassies 414-15
    emergencies 416
    environment 398
    festivals 415
    food 398-9
    highlights 396
    history 397-8
    itineraries 396
    language 415, 918-19
    money 415-16
    postal services 416
    telephone services 416
    tourist information 416
    travel to/from 416-17
    travel within 417-18
    visas 416
Łazienki Park 507
Łeba 557-8
Lednice 287
Lednice-Valtice Cultural Landscape 287
Lenin's Mausoleum 659
lesbian travellers, *see* gay & lesbian
    travellers
Levoča 772-5, **774**
Lezha 53
Liepāja 413
Lipica 807-8
literature, *see* books
Lithuania 419-48, **421**
    accommodation 444-5
    activities 445

arts 422-3
beaches 442, 443
drinking 423-4
embassies 445-6
emergencies 446
environment 423
festivals 446
food 423-4
highlights 420
history 421-2
itineraries 421
language 919-20
money 446
postal services 446
telephone services 446
tourist information 446-7
travel to/from 447
travel within 447-8
Litoměřice 265-6
Ljubljana 790-800, **792-3**
    accommodation 795-6
    bookshops 791
    drinking 798
    entertainment 798-9
    food 796-8
    information 791-4
    travel agencies 794
    travel to/from 799
    travel within 799-800
Llogaraja Pass 48
Łódź 514
Loket 271
Lower Dniestr National Park 485
Lublin 532-5, **534-5**
Lviv 839-844, **840**, 8

M
Macedonia 449-70, **451**
    accommodation 465-6
    activities 466
    arts 453-4
    books 466
    dangers 466
    drinking 454-5
    embassies 466
    emergencies 468
    environment 454
    festivals 467
    food 454-5
    highlights 450
    history 451-3
    independence 452
    itineraries 450
    language 467, 920-2
    money 468
    postal services 468
    telephone services 468
    travel to/from 469-70
    travel within 470
    visas 468
Madara 152
Malá Fatra National Park 761-3, **762**

Malbork 558
Maliuc 638
Małopolska 515-38
Mamaia 632-3
Manasija Monastery 718
Mangalia 634-6
maps 879
Maramureş 616-20, **618-19**
Maribor 815-17
Masuria 559-64
Mazovia 513-15
Međugorje 103-5
Melnik 132
Mikołajki 564
Mikulov 287
Minsk 66-74, **68**
    accommodation 69-70
    attractions 67-9
    drinking 71
    entertainment 71
    food 70-1
    information 66
    shopping 71-2
    travel to/from 72
    travel within 72-3
    walking tour 67
Mir 73
Mljet Island 216-17
mobile phones 882
Moisei 619-20
Moldavia 620-3
Moldova 471-4, **473**
    accommodation 490
    arts 475-6
    drinking 476
    embassies 491
    emergencies 492
    environment 476
    festivals 491
    food 476
    highlights 472
    history 472-5
    independence 474
    itineraries 472
    money 491
    postal services 491
    telephone services 491-2
    travel to/from 492-3
    travel within 493-4
    visas 492
Moldoviţa 627-8
monasteries
    Bachkovo Monastery (Bu) 140
    Căldăruşani Monastery (Ro) 589
    Capuchin Monastery (Cz) 282
    Cave Monastery (Md) 484
    Caves Monastery (U) 833, **712-13**
    Cetinje Monastery (S&M) 735
    Curtea de Argeş Monastery (Ro)
        590-1
    Dryanovo Monastery (Bu) 150

Đurđevi Stupovi Monastery (S&M) 722-3
Gračanica (S&M) 727
Humor (Ro) 627
Ivanovo Rock Monastery (Bu) 154
Kyiv-Pechersk Lavra (U) 833, **712-13**
Lavra Alexandera Nevskogo (Ru) 676
Manasija Monastery (S&M) 718
Moldoviţa (Ro) 627-8
Novodevichy Monastyr (Ru) 662
Orheiul Vechi Monastery Complex (Md) 484
Ostrog (S&M) 735-6
Pannonhalma Abbey (H) 361-3
Rila Monastery (Bu) 130-1, **328-9**
Rozhen Monastery (Bu) 132
Sergiev Posad (Ru) 670-1
Sopoćani Monastery (S&M) 722
Suceviţa (Ro) 628
Sveti Naum (Mk) 463-4
Sv Jovan Bigorski Monastery (Mk) 465
Treskavec Monastery (Mk) 464-6
Troyan Monastery (Bu) 146
Voronet (Ro) 627
money 9-10, 879-80 *see also individual countries*
    discount cards 876-7
Montenegro, *see* Serbia & Montenegro
Moravia 280-7
Moravian Karst 285
Moravský Krumlov 285
Moscow 654-71, **656-7**, **661**, **669**
    accommodation 663-5
    attractions 659-63
    dangers 658
    drinking 666
    entertainment 666-7
    food 665-6
    history 654-5
    information 655-8
    shopping 667
    travel to/from 667-8
    travel within 668
mosques
    Et'hem Bey Mosque (Al) 38
    Many-Coloured Mosque (B&H) 106
    Mecset Templom (H) 373
Mostar 99-103, **100**
motorcycle travel 894, 897-9
Mt Dajti National Park 45
Mt Kasprowy Wierch 529
Mt Križevac 104
Mt Lovćen 735
Mt Triglav 804
museums & galleries
    Aquincumi Múzeum (H) 347
    Chornobyl Museum (U) 835
    Hermitage (Ru) 675, 7
    Mendel Museum (Cz) 283
    Mucha Museum (Cz) 252
    Municipal House (Cz) 251
    Museum of Genocide Victims (Li) 429

Museum of the Great Patriotic War (Be) 69
Museum of the Occupation of Latvia (La) 403-4
Museum Vasil Levski (Bu) 143
Muzeul Ţăranului Român (Ro) 585
Pushkin Fine Arts Museum (Ru) 662
Rumšiškės Open Air Museum (Li) 438
Russian Museum (Ru) 676, **680-1**
State Museum of Majdanek (P) 533
State Tretyakov Gallery (Ru) 662

N
Naissaar 313
Narva 315
national parks & nature reserves 180
    Adršpach-Teplice Rocks (Cz) 279-80, **360-1**
    Aukštaitija National Park (Li) 434-5
    Belavezhskaja Pushcha National Park (Be) 65
    Białowieża National Park (P) 514-15
    Bohemian Switzerland National Park (Cz) 267
    Brijuni National Park (Cr) 197
    Bükk Nezmeti Park (H) 385
    Carpathian National Natural Park (U) 847-8
    Central Balkans National Park (Bu) 146
    Durmitor National Park (S&M) 736-7
    European Bison Reserve (P) 515
    Gauja National Park (La) 411
    Haanja Nature Park (E) 320
    Kaliakra Nature Reserve (Bu) 165
    Kiskunsági National Park (H) 379
    Kurshkaya Kosa National Park (Ru) 691
    Lahemaa National Park (E) 314-15
    Llogaraja Pass (National Park) (Al) 48
    Lower Dniestr National Park (Md) 485
    Malá Fatra National Park (Sk) 761-3, **762**
    Mljet National Park (Cr) 216
    Mt Dajti National Park (Al) 45
    Pieniny National Park (Sk) 770
    Plitvice Lakes National Park (Cr) 205, **328-9**
    Rusenski Lom Nature Park (Bu) 154
    Slovenský Raj (Sk) 771-2, **772-3**, **712-13**
    Słowiński National Park (P) 558
    Soomaa National Park (E) 324
    Tatra National Park (Sk) 765
Nemunas Delta 444
Neptun-Olimp 634
Neringa 443-4
Nesebâr 159-60, **160**
Nida 443-4
Ninth Fort 438
Niš 719-20
Nistru (Dniestr) River 472

Njasvizh 73-4
Northern Dobrogea 628-35
Novi Pazar 722-3
Novi Sad 715-17, **716**
Novo Gorica 806
Novodevichy Monastyr 662

O
Odesa 851-5, **852**
Ohrid 460-3, **460**
Oliwa 553
Olsztyn 559-61, **560**
Opatija 200-1
Oradea 610-13, **611**
Orebić 216
Orhei 484
Orheiul Vechi 484-485
Ostrog 735-6
Oświęcim 524-5
Otepää 319

P
Palace of Parliament 582, **712-13**
palaces, *see* castles & palaces
Palanga 443
Palić 718
Pamporovo 140
Paneriai (Ponar) 433
Pannonhalma Abbey 361-3
Pärnu 320-3, **321**
Partizani 638
passports 883-4, 886, *see also* visas
Pavlovsk 683
Pécs 372-6, **374**
Peja 727-8
Peleş Castle 594
Perast 734
Peter & Paul Fortress 678
Petrodvorets 682-3
Petrova Crkva 722
photography 880-1
Pieniny National Park 770
Pilsner Urquell Brewery 272
Piran 810-13, **811**
Pirin Mountains 130-4
planning 9-14
    discount cards 876-7
Pleven 145-6
Plitvice Lakes National Park 205, **328-9**
Plovdiv 134-40, **136**
Plovdiv Mountains 134-41
Plzeň 271-3, **273**
Podgorica 729-30
Podlasie 513-15
Poiana Braşov 599, 600
Poland 495-572, **498**
    accommodation 564-5
    activities 565
    arts 500
    beaches 556, 557, 558, **680-1**
    books 500, 565
    border crossings 569
    dangers 566

Poland *continued*
  drinking 501-2
  embassies 566
  emergencies 568
  environment 500-1
  food 501-2
  highlights 497
  history 497-9
  itineraries 497
  language 922-4
  money 568
  postal services 568
  telephone services 568-9
  travel to/from 568
  travel within 570-2
  visas 569
Poprad 768-9
Poreč 191-2
Portorož 813-14
postal services 881, *see also individual countries*
Postojna 806-7
Potemkin Steps 851, 852
Poznań 542-7, **544-5**
Prague 241-65, **242-3**, **246-7**, 7, 360-1
  accommodation 253-5
  attractions 248-52
  dangers 245-8
  drinking 256-7
  entertainment 257-9
  festivals 253
  food 255-6
  information 244-5
  shopping 259-20
  travel to/from 260
  travel within 260-2
Pomerania 547-59
Prague Castle 248-50, **249**
Pravčická Brána 267
Primorski Park 161
Primorsko 158
Princely Court 590
Prishtina 725-27, **725**
Prislop Pass 620
Prizren 728, 680-1
Przemyśl 531-2
Ptuj 817
Pühajärv 319
Pula 195-8, **195**
Punkva Caves 285
Pushkin 683
Pushkin Fine Arts Museum 662

R
rafting, *see* watersports
Râşnov 599
Red Square 659
Republika Srpska 87-8

Resavska Pećina 718
responsible travel 14
Ribčev Laz 803
Riga 399-409, **400-1**, 360-1
  accommodation 404-5
  attractions 402-4
  dangers 402
  drinking 407
  entertainment 407
  food 405-6
  information 399-402
  travel to/from 407
  travel within 407-8
Rijeka 198-200, **198**
Rila Monastery 130-1, 328-9
Rila Mountains 130-4
road rules 899
Rodopi Mountains 134-41
Rogaška Slatina 815
Romania 573-644, **576**, **632**
  accommodation 638
  activities 638-9
  arts 578
  beaches 628-35
  border crossings 642
  dangers 639
  drinking 579
  embassies 639-40
  emergencies 641
  environment 579
  festivals 640
  food 579
  highlights 575
  history 575
  itineraries 575
  language 924-5
  money 640
  postal services 640
  telephone services 641
  tourist information 641
  travel to/from 641-3
  travel within 643-4
  visas 641
Rovinj 192-5
Rozavlea 619
Rozhen Monastery 132
Ruhnu Island 323
Ruse 152-3
Rusenski Lom Nature Park 154
Russia 645-98, **648**
  accommodation 691
  arts 650-3
  beaches 690
  books 650-1
  border crossings 696, 902
  dangers 692
  drinking 653-4
  embassies 692-3
  emergencies 694
  environment 653
  food 653-4
  history 647-50

  itineraries 647
  language 693, 925-8
  money 694
  postal services 694
  telephone services 694
  travel agencies 694-5
  travel to/from 695-6
  travel within 696-8
  visas 695

S
Saaremaa 325-6
sailing, *see* watersports
St Basil's Cathedral 659, 680-1
St Peter & Paul Cathedral 678
St Petersburg 671-83, **672-3**, **677**
  accommodation 679-80
  attractions 675-8
  dangers 675
  drinking 681
  entertainment 681-2
  festivals 679
  food 680-1
  history 671
  information 674-5
  shopping 682
  travel agencies 675
  travel within 682
St Sophia's Cathedral 834
St Vitus Cathedral 249-50
Salaspils 409
Sandanski 131-2
Sanok 531
Săpânța 617-18
Sarajevo 90-9, **91-3**
  accommodation 95
  attractions 92-4
  drinking 97
  entertainment 97
  festivals 95
  food 95-7
  information 91-2
  shopping 97
  travel to/from 97-8
  travel within 98
Saranda 48-50
saunas 872, *see also* banyas, spas
  Estonia 327
  Lithuania 445
Sava River 800
scams 875-6
sea travel 895-6
Sečovlje 814
Sedlec Ossuary 264
Serbia & Montenegro 699-42, **702**
  accommodation 737
  activities 737
  arts 704
  beaches 730-5
  books 704
  border crossings 724, 740-1, 890
  civil war 703, 724

dangers 723-9, 737
drinking 704-5
embassies 737-8
emergencies 739
environment 704
festivals 738
food 704-5
highlights 701
history 701-3
itineraries 701
language 738, 912-14
money 739
postal services 739
telephone services 739
tourist information 739
travel to/from 740-1
travel within 741-2
visas 739-0
Sergiev Posad 670-1
Setumaa 320
Sevastopol 861-2
Shipka Pass 151
Shiroka Lâka 141
Shkodra 51-3
Shumen 151-2
Šiauliai 439-40
Sibiu 602-6, **603**
Sighetu Marmaţiei 616-17
Sighişoara 600-2, **601**
Sigulda 410-11, **411**
Simferopol 856-8, **857**
Sinaia 593-5
skiing 872
    Bosnia & Hercegovina 98-9, 110
    Bulgaria 130, 132-3, 140, 167
    Estonia 327
    Latvia 414
    Macedonia 466
    Poland 526-9, 530, 542, 565
    Romania 594, 599, 600, 638-9
    Serbia & Montenegro 720-2, 728,
        736, 737
    Slovakia 761, 766, 781
    Slovenia 804-5, 816, 818
    Ukraine 848, 862
Škocjan Caves 807
Skopje 454-60, **455**
    accommodation 457-8
    attractions 456-7
    drinking 458
    entertainment 458
    food 458
    information 456
    shopping 458-9
    travel to/from 459
    travel within 459
Slânchev Bryag 160
Slavkov u Brna 284
Sliven 144-5
Slovakia 743-84, **746**
    accommodation 781
    activities 781
    arts 747-8

dangers 781
drinking 748-9
embassies 782
emergencies 783
environment 748
festivals 782
food 748-9
highlights 745
history 745-7
itineraries 745
language 928-9
money 782
postal services 782
telephone services 783
tourist information 783
travel to/from 783
travel within 783-4
visas 783
Slovak Paradise National Park 771-2,
    772-3
Slovenia 785-822, **788**
    accommodation 817-18
    activities 818
    arts 789-90
    border crossing 806
    drinking 790
    embassies 819
    emergency numbers 820
    environment 790
    festivals 819
    food 790
    highlights 787
    history 787-9
    itineraries 787
    language 820, 929-30
    money 820
    postal services 820
    telephone services 820
    tourist information 820
    travel to/from 821-2
    travel within 822
    visas 820-1
Slovenský Raj 771-2, **772-3**, 712-13
Słowiński National Park 558
Smederevo 714-15
Smiltynė 442
Smolyan 140-1
Snagov 589-90
snowboarding, see skiing
Soča River 805
Sofia 121-30, **122**
    accommodation 125-6
    attractions 124-5
    drinking 127
    entertainment 127
    food 126-7
    information 123-4
    shopping 127
    travel to/from 127-9
    travel within 129
Solin 210-11, **211**
Soomaa National Park 324
Sopoćani Monastery 722

Sopot 556
Sopron 364-7, **364**
Soroca 485
Sõrve Peninsula 325-6
Southern Bucovina 623-8, **624**
Sozopol 156-8, **157**
spas 387, 388, 872
    Castle Spa (Cz) 270
    Gellért Fürdő (H) 346
    Harkány (H) 376
    Hévíz (H) 371
    Druskininkai (Li) 435
    Széchenyi Fürdő (H) 347, 360-1
Spišské Podhradie 775
Spišský hrad 775, 712-13
Split 205-10, **206, 207**
Stara Planina 141
Štefanová 763
Štrbské Pleso 766
Subotica 717-18
Suceava 624-7, **625**
Suceviţa 628
Sudeten Mountains 542
Šumava 279
Sunny Beach (Bu) 160
Suur Munamägi 320
Suzdal 669-70
Sveti Konstantin 164
Sveti Naum 463-4
Svetlogorsk 690-1
Sv Jovan at Kaneo 461, 680-1
Sv Jovan Bigorski Monastery 465
Swallow's Nest 860, 712-13
Święta Lipka 563
synagogues
    Great Synagogue 272
    Nagy Zsinagóga 347
Szczecin 558-9
Szeged 379-82, **380**
Szentendre 355-7, **356**
Sziget Festival 14, 389
Szilvásvárad 385

T
Tallinn 302-14, **304**
    accommodation 308-9
    attractions 305-8
    drinking 311
    entertainment 311-12
    food 309-11
    information 303-5
    shopping 312
    travel to/from 312-13
    travel within 314
Tara Canyon 736
Tartu 315-19, **316**
Tatars 856
Tatranská Lomnica 766
Tatra Mountains 526, 529-31, 767-8
Tatra National Park 765
Telč 285-7, **286**
telephone services 881-2, see
    also individual countries

Teplice Rock Town 279-80
Terezín 265
theft 876
thermal baths, *see* spas
Tihany 368-9
time 882
Timișoara 613-16, **614**
tipping 880
Tirana 36-46, **37**
    accommodation 39-40
    attractions 38
    dangers 38
    entertainment 41
    food 40-1
    information 36-8
    shopping 41
    travel to/from 41-2
    travel within 42
    walking tour 39
Tiraspol 486-8, **487**
Tokaj 385-7
Topola 718-19
Toruń 547-50, **548-9**
tourist information 882, *see also individual countries*
tours 900-1
train travel 894-5, 901-3
    classes 901-2
    rail passes 902-3
    safety 902
    to/from Eastern Europe 894-5
    within Eastern Europe 901-3
Trakai 433-4, 360-1
Transdniestr 485-9
Transylvania 591-610, **592-3**, 712-13
travellers cheques 880
Travnik 105-06
Trenčín 758-60, **759**
Trigrad 141
Trogir 212
Troyan 146
truffles 194
Tryavna 150-1
Tulcea 636-8
Turda 610

U
Ukraine 823-68, **826-7**
    accommodation 862
    activities 862
    arts 829
    beaches 853, 859
    books 862
    border crossings 902
    drinking 830
    embassies 862
    emergencies 864
    environment 829-30
    festivals 863

food 830
highlights 824
history 824-8
independence 826
itineraries 824
language 863, 927
money 863-4
postal services 864
telephone services 864
travel to/from 865-7
travel within 867-8
visas 864-5, 867
Ulcinj 730-1
Uzhhorod 844-5

V
vaccinations 904
Vadu Izei 618
Valea Izei 618-20
Valmiera 412
Valtice 287
Varna 160-4, **162-3**
Veliki Preslav 152
Veliko Târnovo 146-9, **147**, 8
Venta River 412
Ventas Rumba 412
Ventspils 413
video 877, 880-1
Vidin 165
Viljandi 323-4
Vilnius 424-34, **426**
    accommodation 430-1
    attractions 425-30
    drinking 432
    entertainment 432
    food 431-2
    information 424-5
    shopping 432
    travel to/from 432
    travel within 433
Vintgar Gorge 802
Virpazar 729-30
visas 883-4, *see also individual countries*, passports
Visegrád 357-8
Vitosha 129-30
Vladimir 670
Vlad Țepeș 575, 589, 600
Vlora 47
Vojvodina 714-18
volunteering 885
Voronet 627
Vyšehrad 252
Vysoké Tatry 763-8, **764**, 8

W
Wallachia 590-1
Wallenstein Palace 251
Warmia 559-64
Warsaw 502-13, **502**, **506**
    accommodation 508-9
    attractions 504-8
    drinking 511
    entertainment 511

food 509-11
information 503
shopping 511-12
travel to/from 512
travel within 513
Warsaw Ghetto 508
war memorials
    Babyn Yar (U) 835
    Brest Fortress (Be) 74-5, 328-9
    Freedom Monument (Bu) 151
    Khatyn (Be) 74
    Ninth Fort (Li) 438
    Salaspils (La) 409
    Slavín War Memorial (Sk) 754
    State Museum of Majdanek (P) 533
    Terezín (Cz) 265
    Westerplatte (P) 553
water 906
Water Chateau 286
watersports 871, 872, 873
    Bosnia & Hercegovnia 110
    Czech Republic 224
    Latvia 414
    Lithuania 445
    Poland 545
    Serbia & Montenegro 737
    Slovenia 818
Wawel Castle 517
websites 11
Westerplatte 553
White Nights 13, 679
Wieliczka Salt Mine 521
Wilanów Park 507
wineries, *see* breweries & wineries
Winter Palace 675, 7
Wolf's Lair 563
women travellers 884-5, 907
work 885
World Heritage sites 12
Wrocław 538-42, **539**

Y
Yalta 858-61, **859**

Z
Zadar 202-5, **203**
Zagreb 181-90, **182-3**
    accommodation 186-7
    attractions 185-6
    drinking 188
    entertainment 188-9
    festivals 186
    food 187-8
    information 184-5
    shopping 189
    travel to/from 189-90
    travel within 190
Zakopane 526-9, **528**, 680-1
Zamość 536, **536**
Zemgale 409
Zemun 714
Žilina 760-1
Zlatibor 721-2
Zlatni Pysâtsi 164

000 Map pages
000 Location of colour photographs